Immigration Law and Practice in the United Kingdom

Ninth edition

Volume 2

General Editors

Ian A Macdonald QC
Garden Court Chambers

Ronan Toal
Garden Court Chambers

and a team of specialist Contributing Editors

LexisNexis®

Members of the LexisNexis Group worldwide

United Kingdom	LexisNexis, a Division of Reed Elsevier (UK) Ltd, Lexis House, 30 Farringdon Street, London EC4A 4HH, and London House, 20-22 East London Street, Edinburgh EH7 4BQ
Australia	Reed International Books Australia Pty Ltd trading as LexisNexis, Chatswood, New South Wales
Austria	LexisNexis Verlag ARD Orac GmbH & Co KG, Vienna
Benelux	LexisNexis Benelux, Amsterdam
Canada	LexisNexis Canada, Markham, Ontario
China	LexisNexis China, Beijing and Shanghai
France	LexisNexis SA, Paris
Germany	LexisNexis GmbH, Dusseldorf
Hong Kong	LexisNexis Hong Kong, Hong Kong
India	LexisNexis India, New Delhi
Italy	Giuffrè Editore, Milan
Japan	LexisNexis Japan, Tokyo
Malaysia	Malayan Law Journal Sdn Bhd, Kuala Lumpur
New Zealand	LexisNexis New Zealand Ltd, Wellington
Singapore	LexisNexis Singapore, Singapore
South Africa	LexisNexis, Durban
USA	LexisNexis, Dayton, Ohio

First edition 1983, Second edition 1987, Third edition 1991, Fourth edition 1995, Fifth edition 2001, Sixth edition 2005, Seventh edition 2008, Eighth edition 2010, Ninth edition 2014

© Reed Elsevier (UK) Ltd 2014

Published by LexisNexis

ISBN 978-1-4057-9941-6

9 781405 799416

ISBN 978-1-4057-9942-3

9 781405 799423

ISBN for this volume: 978 1 4057 9941 6

ISBN for the set: 978 1 4057 9942 3

Printed and bound by CPI Group (UK) Ltd, Croydon, CR0 4YY

Contributors

General Editors

Ian A Macdonald QC
Garden Court Chambers

Ronan Toal
Garden Court Chambers

Contributors

Navtej Ahluwalia
Garden Court Chambers

Ali Bandegani
Garden Court Chambers

Adrian Berry
Garden Court Chambers

Michelle Brewer
Garden Court Chambers

Rebecca Chapman
Garden Court Chambers

Kathryn Cronin
Garden Court Chambers

Jared Ficklin
Garden Court North Chambers

Helen Foot
Garden Court Chambers

Hannah Graves
Solicitor at Fisher Jones Greenwood

v

Contributors

Alex Grigg
Garden Court Chambers

Raza Halim
Garden Court Chambers

Stephanie Harrison QC
Garden Court Chambers

Alison Harvey
Immigration Law Practitioners' Association

Louise Hooper
Garden Court Chambers

Bijan Hoshi
Garden Court Chambers

Vijay Jagadesham
Garden Court North Chambers

David Jones
Garden Court Chambers

Peter Jorro
Garden Court Chambers

Patrick Lewis
Garden Court Chambers

Shu Shin Luh
Garden Court Chambers

Lucy Mair
Garden Court North Chambers

Joseph Markus
Garden Court North Chambers

Maria Moodie
Garden Court Chambers

Sonali Naik
Garden Court Chambers

Greg O'Ceallaigh
Garden Court Chambers

Rory O'Ryan

Garden Court North Chambers

Bryony Poynor

Garden Court Chambers

Desmond Rutledge

Garden Court Chambers

Sadat Sayeed

Garden Court Chambers

Abigail Smith

Garden Court Chambers

Kerry Smith

Garden Court North Chambers

Mark Symes

Garden Court Chambers

Rajeev Thacker

Garden Court Chambers

Anthony Vaughan

Garden Court Chambers

Camille Warren

Garden Court North Chambers

Amanda Weston

Garden Court Chambers

Jo Wilding

Garden Court Chambers

Natalie Wilkins

Garden Court North Chambers

Colin Yeo

Garden Court Chambers

Preface

This has been one of the most trying editions to produce, mostly because of the amount of new material since the last edition, but also because there has been such a radical reshaping of some of the fundamental parts of immigration law.

Let us start with removals and appeals. The Immigration Appeals Act 1969 was passed in response to the report of the Wilson Committee on Immigration Appeals, set up in 1966 and chaired by Sir Roy Wilson QC.[1] The report had been commissioned to provide Commonwealth citizens (but not aliens) with appeals against exclusion, removal and other decisions affecting immigrants. In January 1973 the right of appeal was extended to aliens as well as Commonwealth citizens and included an appeal against deportation. Paragraph 85 got to the heart of the matter, stating that the right of appeal is to provide 'a sense of protection against oppression and injustice, and . . . reassurance against fears of arbitrary action on the part of the Immigration Service' and to ensure a more consistent and rational decision-making process.

Other judicial voices have also made it clear that 'The right of access to justice . . . is a fundamental and constitutional principle of a legal system'[2] and 'a right of access to a tribunal or other adjudicative mechanism established by the state is just as important and fundamental as a right of access to the ordinary courts'.[3] Two important features of a Tribunal appeal are that (a) it is suspensive, meaning that the possibility of removal is suspended until the appeal process is exhausted, and (b) it allows there to be a reconsideration by the Tribunal of the facts by calling witnesses to give live evidence and to produce fresh documentary evidence within certain limits set out in the immigration laws. A Tribunal appeal is, therefore, quite different and more far reaching than judicial review.

Over the years there has been an expansion of appeal rights,[4] coupled with legal aid and assistance to appellants. However, since 2002 there has been a slow whittling down of appeal rights and their suspensive effect by successive governments. This has culminated in the radical changes proposed by the Immigration Act 2014 and being put into effect by successive commencement orders. These involve a root and branch change to the power of removal and to the appellate system, as we have known and used it for so many years. The changes are not only far reaching but also mark a set back to one of the fundamental and constitutional principles of our legal system.

The timing of the commencement orders with the transitional provisions contained in them has meant that we have felt obliged to delay the publication of Volume 1 so that we could properly revise some of our chapters in the light of these developments.

Immigration law is such a moving tapestry of change that it is in fact very difficult not to be already out of date on or soon after our publication date on at least one topic. But we felt that the changes to the powers of removal and to the ambit of appeal rights are of such importance that we needed to be as up to date as possible. Thus the delay in publishing Volume 1 until early 2015.

As well as changing removal powers and rights of appeal, the Immigration Act 2014 accelerates the process of drawing ever more state and non-state actors into the apparatus of immigration control. The effect is to create a society that is suspicious of and hostile to people perceived to be migrants, an aim recently and chillingly articulated by the government when it explained its refusal to support operations to rescue drowning migrants from the Mediterranean on the basis that to do so would encourage others.[5] Now landlords, banks, health practitioners, and driving licensors are turned into quasi-immigration officers because they are required by the Act to regulate access to their property and services according to the immigration status of their would-be tenants, customers, patients and licensees. The danger is the Act will further the creation of a class of outlaws and promote widespread discrimination by these new regulators who, out of fear of being penalised for providing assistance to outlaws, will refuse their services to those who look like or talk like migrants or have foreign names. The Act also adds to the information gathering and information sharing powers of the state.

Other notable changes since the publication of the last Supplement have been the changes to the availability of legal aid in immigration cases for both Tribunal appeals, such as they now are, and to judicial review. We now have over 50 immigration specialist barristers in Garden Court and Garden Court North. All but two of the contributors to this edition are from these two chambers. Many spend a large chunk of their time speaking at training conferences and passing their knowledge and experience to other practitioners. Many also take part with other practitioners in ILPA training sessions. All this effort to try and keep practitioners abreast of the law is of diminished value if our learning and experience cannot be brought to the benefit of immigration clients because they no longer have access to justice in the absence of available legal aid.

Legal aid is not a topic that we have dealt with in previous editions other than in passing. In this edition we have covered legal aid in a separate section of Chapter 1, prepared by Alison Harvey the Legal Director of the Immigration Law Practitioners' Association.

Although the new family and 'private life' rules were first introduced as long ago as July 2012, they are dealt with for the first time in this edition of the book together with the increasingly important list of relevant cases. But we still have to live with the dreadful lettering/numbering of the paragraphs in Appendix FM (thankfully not followed in Appendix FM S-E). We have it on good authority that the lady in the Home Office who drafted the rules makes no admission whatsoever that she had anything to do with the lettering/numbering. But whoever was responsible, it is one more example of an ongoing process of making immigration law impossibly complex and impenetrable.

Article 8 of the European Convention on Human Rights so far as it applies to immigration and asylum now appears to have two or possibly three sets of identities – first of all there are the Immigration Rules, first introduced in July 2012 and repeatedly altered thereafter. Then there is the Immigration Act 2014 and last but not least the autonomous meaning applicable to all signatory countries to the Convention and referred to in section 6 of the Human Rights Act 1998. It would appear that these identities sometimes cross paths; they sometimes coincide; and they sometimes run in separate but parallel paths. The Courts have been trying to make sense of it all since the 2012 rule changes. Now the Immigration Act 2014 has added its own statutory interpretation. It is all very confusing. We try to give guidance in the chapters of this edition.

We have included a new Chapter on human trafficking. It is a subject that has attracted increasing attention from international, European and domestic legislators, courts and policy makers as well as from UN bodies and international and national NGOs. This is having an impact on the legal framework for controlling immigration as well as on the protective obligations that the UK has towards migrants who may have been trafficked and may still be being trafficked.

A number of changes have been made to the Chapter numbers. The former Chapters 3 and 4 are now contained in one Chapter 3. This means that ex Chapters 5-9 become 4-8; ex Chapter 9A (students) becomes Chapter 9. Chapters 10, 11 and 12 remain the same, the new chapter on trafficking comes in as Chapter 13. So all the following chapters cease to be Chapters 13-21 and become Chapters 14-22.

We would like to thank Alison Harvey of ILPA and all the other contributors who are listed after this Preface, and who have given up so much of their time to do either bits of chapters or in some cases to supervise the editing of whole chapters. We would also like to thank Tania Poscotis for co-ordinating the whole process in chambers and who liaised with our publishers. We would also like to thank Brigid and Cameron Baillie and Amarjit Ahluwalia and William Toal for their support and forbearance during the whole process of writing and editing.

The law in Volume 2 is stated as at 1 November 2014.

Ian Macdonald QC
Ronan Toal
5 December 2014

---

[1] 1967 Cmnd 3387

[2] R (on the application of Anufrijeva) v Secretary of State for the Home Department [2003] UKHL 36, [2004] 1 AC 604, per Lord Steyn at para 26.

[3] R (Asifa Saleem) v Secretary of State for the Home Department [2000] EWCA Civ 186, [2000] 4 All ER 814, per Hale LJ

[4] Such as the suspensive right of appeal for nearly all asylum seekers under the Asylum and Immigration Appeals Act 1993, the setting up of SIAC under the Special Immigration Appeals Commission Act 1997, and the right to argue human rights breaches under section 6 of the Human Rights Act 1998, when it came into force in 2000.

[5] Baroness Anelay, Minister of State, Foreign Office, House of Lords Hansard, 15.10.2014 WA 41

Contents

Contents

Contents

Contents

Contents

Appendix 1

UK IMMIGRATION STATUTES

Contents

IMMIGRATION ACT 1971

1971 c 77

An Act to amend and replace the present immigration laws, to make certain related changes in the citizenship law and enable help to be given to those wishing to return abroad, and for purposes connected therewith

[28 October 1971]

Modification

In relation to the extension of this Act, with modifications, to the Isle of Man, see the Immigration (Isle of Man) Order 2008, SI 2008/680.

This Act is modified, in its application to the Channel Tunnel, by the Channel Tunnel (International Arrangements) Order 1993, SI 1993/1813

This Act is modified, in relation to its application to frontier controls between the United Kingdom, France and Belgium, by the Channel Tunnel (Miscellaneous Provisions) Order 1994, SI 1994/1405

PART I
REGULATION OF ENTRY INTO AND STAY IN UNITED KINGDOM

1 1 General principles

(1)   All those who are in this Act expressed to have the right of abode in the United Kingdom shall be free to live in, and to come and go into and from, the United Kingdom without let or hindrance except such as may be required under and in accordance with this Act to enable their right to be established or as may be otherwise lawfully imposed on any person.

(2)   Those not having that right may live, work and settle in the United Kingdom by permission and subject to such regulation and control of their entry into, stay in and departure from the United Kingdom as is imposed by this Act; and indefinite leave to enter or remain in the United Kingdom shall, by virtue of this provision be treated as having been given under this Act to those in the United Kingdom at its coming into force, if they are then settled there (and not exempt under this Act from the provisions relating to leave to enter or remain).

(3)   Arrival in and departure from the United Kingdom on a local journey from or to any of the Islands (that is to say, the Channel Islands and Isle of Man) or the Republic of Ireland shall not be subject to control under this Act, nor shall a person require leave to enter the United Kingdom on so arriving, except in so far as any of those places is for any purpose excluded from this subsection under the powers conferred by this Act; and in this Act the United Kingdom and those places, or such of them as are not so excluded, are collectively referred to as "the common travel area".

(4)   The rules laid down by the Secretary of State as to the practice to be followed in the administration of this Act for regulating the entry into and stay in the United Kingdom of persons not having the right of abode shall include provision for admitting (in such cases and subject to such restrictions as may be provided by the rules, and subject or not to conditions as to length of stay or otherwise) persons coming for the purpose of taking employment, or for purposes of study, or as visitors, or as dependants of persons lawfully in or entering the United Kingdom.

(5)   . . .

Amendment

Sub-s (5): repealed by the Immigration Act 1988, s 1.

[2   Statement of right of abode in United Kingdom

(1)   A person is under this Act to have the right of abode in the United Kingdom if—

    (a)   he is a British citizen; or

    (b)   he is a Commonwealth citizen who—

        (i)   immediately before the commencement of the British Nationality Act 1981 was a Commonwealth citizen having the right of abode in the United Kingdom by virtue of section 2(1)(d) or section 2(2) of this Act as then in force; and

        (ii)   has not ceased to be a Commonwealth citizen in the meanwhile.

(2)   In relation to Commonwealth citizens who have the right of abode in the United Kingdom by virtue of subsection (1)(b) above, this Act, except this section and [section 5(2)], shall apply as if they were British citizens; and in this Act (except as aforesaid) "British citizen" shall be construed accordingly.]

Amendment

Substituted by the British Nationality Act 1981, s 39(2).

Sub-s (2): words in square brackets substituted by the Immigration Act 1988, s 3(3).

[2A   Deprivation of right of abode

(1)   The Secretary of State may by order remove from a specified person a right of abode in the United Kingdom which he has under section 2(1)(b).

(2) The Secretary of State may make an order under subsection (1) in respect of a person only if the Secretary of State thinks that it would be conducive to the public good for the person to be excluded or removed from the United Kingdom.

(3) An order under subsection (1) may be revoked by order of the Secretary of State.

(4) While an order under subsection (1) has effect in relation to a person—

    (a)   section 2(2) shall not apply to him, and

    (b)   any certificate of entitlement granted to him shall have no effect.]

Amendment

    Inserted by the Immigration, Asylum and Nationality Act 2006, s 57(1).

3 General provisions for regulation and control

(1) Except as otherwise provided by or under this Act, where a person is not [a British citizen]—

    (a)   he shall not enter the United Kingdom unless given leave to do so in accordance with [the provisions of, or made under,] this Act;

    (b)   he may be given leave to enter the United Kingdom (or, when already there, leave to remain in the United Kingdom) either for a limited or for an indefinite period;

    [(c)   if he is given limited leave to enter or remain in the United Kingdom, it may be given subject to all or any of the following conditions, namely—

        (i)   a condition restricting his employment or occupation in the United Kingdom;

        [(ia)   a condition restricting his studies in the United Kingdom;]

        (ii)   a condition requiring him to maintain and accommodate himself, and any dependants of his, without recourse to public funds; . . .

        (iii)   a condition requiring him to register with the police;

        [(iv)   a condition requiring him to report to an immigration officer or the Secretary of State; and

        (v)   a condition about residence].]

(2) The Secretary of State shall from time to time (and as soon as may be) lay before Parliament statements of the rules, or of any changes in the rules, laid down by him as to the practice to be followed in the administration of this Act for regulating the entry into and stay in the United Kingdom of persons required by this Act to have leave to enter, including any rules as to the period for which leave is to be given and the conditions to be attached in different circumstances; and section 1(4) above shall not be taken to require uniform provision to be made by the rules as regards admission of persons for a purpose or in a capacity specified in section 1(4) (and in particular, for this as well as other purposes of this Act, account may be taken of citizenship or nationality).

If a statement laid before either House of Parliament under this subsection is disapproved by a resolution of that House passed within the period of forty days beginning with the date of laying (and exclusive of any period during which Parliament is dissolved or prorogued or during which both Houses are adjourned for more than four days), then the Secretary of State shall as soon as may be make such changes or further changes in the rules as appear to him to be required in the circumstances, so that the statement of those changes be laid before Parliament at latest by the end of the period of forty days beginning with the date of the resolution (but exclusive as aforesaid).

(3) In the case of a limited leave to enter or remain in the United Kingdom,—

    (a)   a person's leave may be varied, whether by restricting, enlarging or removing the limit on its duration, or by adding, varying or revoking conditions, but if the limit on its duration is removed, any conditions attached to the leave shall cease to apply; and

3

(b)   the limitation on and any conditions attached to a person's leave [(whether imposed originally or on a variation) shall], if not superseded, apply also to any subsequent leave he may obtain after an absence from the United Kingdom within the period limited for the duration of the earlier leave.

(4)   A person's leave to enter or remain in the United Kingdom shall lapse on his going to a country or territory outside the common travel area (whether or not he lands there), unless within the period for which he had leave he returns to the United Kingdom in circumstances in which he is not required to obtain leave to enter; but, if he does so return, his previous leave (and any limitation on it or conditions attached to it) shall continue to apply.

[(5)   A person who is not a British citizen is liable to deportation from the United Kingdom if—

(a)   the Secretary of State deems his deportation to be conducive to the public good; or

(b)   another person to whose family he belongs is or has been ordered to be deported.]

(6)   Without prejudice to the operation of subsection (5) above, a person who is not [a British citizen] shall also be liable to deportation from the United Kingdom if, after he has attained the age of seventeen, he is convicted of an offence for which he is punishable with imprisonment and on his conviction is recommended for deportation by a court empowered by this Act to do so.

(7)   Where it appears to Her Majesty proper so to do by reason of restrictions or conditions imposed on [British citizens, [British overseas territories citizens] or British Overseas citizens] when leaving or seeking to leave any country or the territory subject to the government of any country, Her Majesty may by Order in Council make provision for prohibiting persons who are nationals or citizens of that country and are not [British citizens] from embarking in the United Kingdom, or from doing so elsewhere than at a port of exit, or for imposing restrictions or conditions on them when embarking or about to embark in the United Kingdom; and Her Majesty may also make provision by Order in Council to enable those who are not [British citizens] to be, in such cases as may be prescribed by the Order, prohibited in the interests of safety from so embarking on a ship or aircraft specified or indicated in the prohibition.

Any Order in Council under this subsection shall be subject to annulment in pursuance of a resolution of either House of Parliament.

(8)   When any question arises under this Act whether or not a person is [a British citizen], or is entitled to any exemption under this Act, it shall lie on the person asserting it to prove that he is.

[(9)   A person seeking to enter the United Kingdom and claiming to have the right of abode there shall prove it by means of—

(a)   a United Kingdom passport describing him as a British citizen,

(b)   a United Kingdom passport describing him as a British subject with the right of abode in the United Kingdom, [or]

(c)   . . .

(d)   . . .

(e)   a certificate of entitlement.]

Amendment

Sub-s (1): words in first pair of square brackets substituted by the British Nationality Act 1981, s 39(6), Sch 4, paras 2, 4.

Sub-s (1): in para (a) words in square brackets inserted by the Immigration and Asylum Act 1999, s 169(1), Sch 14, paras 43, 44(1).

Sub-s (1): para (c)(ia) inserted by the Borders, Citizenship and Immigration Act 2009, s 50(1).

Sub-s (1): word omitted from para (c)(ii) repealed and para (c)(iv), (v) inserted, by the UK Borders Act 2007, ss 16, 58, Schedule.

(c)   the leave expires without the application for variation having been decided.

(2)   The leave is extended by virtue of this section during any period when—

    (a)   the application for variation is neither decided nor withdrawn,

    (b)   an appeal under section 82(1) of the Nationality, Asylum and Immigration Act 2002 could be brought[, while the appellant is in the United Kingdom] against the decision on the application for variation (ignoring any possibility of an appeal out of time with permission), . . .

    (c)   an appeal under that section against that decision[, brought while the appellant is in the United Kingdom,] is pending (within the meaning of section 104 of that Act)[; or

    [(d)   an administrative review of the decision on the application for variation—

        (i)   could be sought, or

        (ii)   is pending.]

(3)   Leave extended by virtue of this section shall lapse if the applicant leaves the United Kingdom.

(4)   A person may not make an application for variation of his leave to enter or remain in the United Kingdom while that leave is extended by virtue of this section.

(5)   But subsection (4) does not prevent the variation of the application mentioned in subsection (1)(a).

[(6)   The Secretary of State may make regulations determining when an application is decided for the purposes of this section; and the regulations—

    (a)   may make provision by reference to receipt of a notice,

    (b)   may provide for a notice to be treated as having been received in specified circumstances,

    (c)   may make different provision for different purposes or circumstances,

    (d)   shall be made by statutory instrument, and

    (e)   shall be subject to annulment in pursuance of a resolution of either House of Parliament.]

[(7)   In this section—

"administrative review" means a review conducted under the immigration rules; the question of whether an administrative review is pending is to be determined in accordance with the immigration rules.]

Amendment

Substituted (for this section as inserted by the Immigration and Asylum Act 1999, s 3) by the Nationality, Immigration and Asylum Act 2002, s 118.

Sub-s (2): in para (b) words ", while the appellant is in the United Kingdom" in square brackets inserted by the Immigration, Asylum and Nationality Act 2006, s 11(1), (2).

Sub-s (2): word "or" omitted from para (b) repealed by the Immigration Act 2014, s 73, Sch 9, Pt 4, paras 20, 21(1), (2)(a), as from 20 October 2014 (see SI 2014/2771, art 2), subject to savings in SI 2014/2771, arts 9–11.

Sub-s (2): in para (c) words ", brought while the appellant is in the United Kingdom," in square brackets inserted by the Immigration, Asylum and Nationality Act 2006, s 11(1), (3).

Sub-s (2): para (d) inserted together with word preceding it, by the Immigration Act 2014, s 73, Sch 9, Pt 4, paras 20, 21(1), (2)(b), as from 20 October 2014 (see SI 2014/2771, art 2), subject to savings in SI 2014/2771, arts 9–11.

Sub-s (6): substituted by the Immigration, Asylum and Nationality Act 2006, s 11(1), (4).

Sub-s (7): added by the Immigration Act 2014, s 73, Sch 9, Pt 4, paras 20, 21(1), (3), as from 20 October 2014 (see SI 2014/2771, art 2), subject to savings in SI 2014/2771, arts 9–11.

Subordinate Legislation

Immigration (Continuation of Leave) (Notices) Regulations 2006, SI 2006/2170.

[3D Continuation of leave following revocation]

[(1) This section applies if a person's leave to enter or remain in the United Kingdom—

    (a)   is varied with the result that he has no leave to enter or remain in the United Kingdom, or

    (b)   is revoked.

(2)   The person's leave is extended by virtue of this section during any period when—

    (a)   an appeal under section 82(1) of the Nationality, Immigration and Asylum Act 2002 could be brought, while the person is in the United Kingdom, against the variation or revocation (ignoring any possibility of an appeal out of time with permission), . . .

    (b)   an appeal under that section against the variation or revocation, brought while the appellant is in the United Kingdom, is pending (within the meaning of section 104 of that Act)[; or

    (c)   an administrative review of the variation or revocation—

        (i)   could be sought, or

        (ii)   is pending.]

(3)   A person's leave as extended by virtue of this section shall lapse if he leaves the United Kingdom.

(4)   A person may not make an application for variation of his leave to enter or remain in the United Kingdom while that leave is extended by virtue of this section.

[(5)   In this section—

    "administrative review" means a review conducted under the immigration rules; the question of whether an administrative review is pending is to be determined in accordance with the immigration rules.]]

Amendment

   Inserted by the Immigration, Asylum and Nationality Act 2006, s 11(5).

   Sub-s (2): word "or" omitted from para (a) repealed by the Immigration Act 2014, s 73, Sch 9, Pt 4, paras 20, 22(1), (2)(a), as from 20 October 2014 (see SI 2014/2771, art 2), subject to savings in SI 2014/2771, arts 9–11.

   Sub-s (2): para (c) inserted together with word preceding it, by the Immigration Act 2014, s 73, Sch 9, Pt 4, paras 20, 22(1), (2)(b), as from 20 October 2014 (see SI 2014/2771, art 2), subject to savings in SI 2014/2771, arts 9–11.

   Sub-s (5): inserted by the Immigration Act 2014, s 73, Sch 9, Pt 4, paras 20, 22(1), (3), as from 20 October 2014 (see SI 2014/2771, art 2), subject to savings in SI 2014/2771, arts 9–11.

4 Administration of control

(1)   The power under this Act to give or refuse leave to enter the United Kingdom shall be exercised by immigration officers, and the power to give leave to remain in the United Kingdom, or to vary any leave under section 3(3)(a) (whether as regards duration or conditions), shall be exercised by the Secretary of State; and, unless otherwise [allowed by or under] this Act, those powers should be exercised by notice in writing given to the person affected, except that the powers under section 3(3)(a) may be exercised generally in respect of any class of persons by order made by statutory instrument.

(2)   The provisions of Schedule 2 to this Act shall have effect with respect to—

    (a)   the appointment and powers of immigration officers and medical inspectors for purposes of this Act;

    (b)   the examination of persons arriving in or leaving the United Kingdom by ship or aircraft [. . .], and the special powers exercisable in the case of those who arrive as, or with a view to becoming, members of the crews of ships and aircraft; and

    (c)   the exercise by immigration officers of their powers in relation to entry into the United Kingdom, and the removal from the United Kingdom of persons refused leave to enter or entering or remaining unlawfully; and

(d)   the detention of persons pending examination or pending removal from the United Kingdom;

and for other purposes supplementary to the foregoing provisions of this Act.

(3) The Secretary of State may by regulations made by statutory instrument, which shall be subject to annulment in pursuance of a resolution of either House of Parliament, make provision as to the effect of a condition under this Act requiring a person to register with the police; and the regulations may include provision—

(a)   as to the officers of police by whom registers are to be maintained, and as to the form and content of the registers;

(b)   as to the place and manner in which anyone is to register and as to the documents and information to be furnished by him, whether on registration or on any change of circumstances;

(c)   as to the issue of certificates of registration and as to the payment of fees for certificates of registration;

and the regulations may require anyone who is for the time being subject to such a condition to produce a certificate of registration to such persons and in such circumstances as may be prescribed by the regulations.

(4) The Secretary of State may by order made by statutory instrument, which shall be subject to annulment in pursuance of a resolution of either House of Parliament, make such provision as appears to him to be expedient in connection with this Act for records to be made and kept of persons staying at hotels and other premises where lodging or sleeping accommodation is provided, and for persons (whether [British citizens] or not) who stay at any such premises to supply the necessary information.

Amendment

Sub-s (1): words in square brackets substituted by the Immigration and Asylum Act 1999, s 169(1), Sch 14, paras 43, 45.

Sub-s (2): words omitted, originally inserted by SI 1990/2227, art 3, Sch 1, Part I, para 1, and repealed by SI 1993/1813, art 9, Sch 6, Part I.

Sub-s (4): words in square brackets substituted by the British Nationality Act, s 39(6), Sch 4, para 2.

Subordinate Legislation

Immigration (Revocation of Employment Restrictions) Order 1972, SI 1972/1647; Immigration (Hotel Records) Order 1972, SI 1972/1689; Immigration (Registration with Police) Regulations 1972, SI 1972/1758; Immigration (Variation of Leave) Order 1976, SI 1976/1572; Immigration (Registration with Police) (Amendment) (No 2) Regulations 1982, SI 1982/1024; Immigration (Hotel Records) (Amendment) Order 1982, SI 1982/1025; Immigration (Variation of Leave) (Amendment) Order 1989, SI 1989/1005; Immigration (Registration with Police) (Amendment) Regulations 1990, SI 1990/400; Immigration (Variation of Leave) (Revocation) Order 1991, SI 1991/980; Immigration (Variation of Leave) (No 2) Order 1991, SI 1991/1083; Immigration (Variation of Leave) (Amendment) Order 1993, SI 1993/1657; Immigration (Registration with Police) (Amendment) Regulations 1995, SI 1995/2928; Immigration (Variation of Leave) (Amendment) Order 2000, SI 2000/2445.

5 Procedure for, and further provisions as to, deportation

(1) Where a person is under section 3(5) or (6) above liable to deportation, then subject to the following provisions of this Act the Secretary of State may make a deportation order against him, that is to say an order requiring him to leave and prohibiting him from entering the United Kingdom; and a deportation order against a person shall invalidate any leave to enter or remain in the United Kingdom given him before the order is made or while it is in force.

(2) A deportation order against a person may at any time be revoked by a further order of the Secretary of State, and shall cease to have effect if he becomes [a British citizen].

(3) A deportation order shall not be made against a person as belonging to the family of another person if more than eight weeks have elapsed since the other person left the United Kingdom after the making of the deportation order against him; and a

deportation order made against a person on that ground shall cease to have effect if he ceases to belong to the family of the other person, or if the deportation order made against the other person ceases to have effect.

(4) For purposes of deportation the following shall be those who are regarded as belonging to another person's family—

(a)   where that other person is a man, his wife [or civil partner,] and his or her children under the age of eighteen; and

[(b)   where that other person is a woman, her husband [or civil partner,] and her or his children under the age of eighteen;]

and for purposes of this subsection an adopted child, whether legally adopted or not, may be treated as the child of the adopter and, if legally adopted, shall be regarded as the child only of the adopter; an illegitimate child (subject to the foregoing rule as to adoptions) shall be regarded as the child of the mother; and "wife" includes each of two or more wives.

(5) The provisions of Schedule 3 to this Act shall have effect with respect to the removal from the United Kingdom of persons against whom deportation orders are in force and with respect to the detention or control of persons in connection with deportation.

(6) Where a person is liable to deportation under section [3(5)] or (6) above but, without a deportation order being made against him, leaves the United Kingdom to live permanently abroad, the Secretary of State may make payments of such amounts as he may determine to meet that person's expenses in so leaving the United Kingdom, including travelling expenses for members of his family or household.

Amendment

Sub-s (2): words in square brackets substituted by the British Nationality Act 1981, s 39(6), Sch 4, para 2.

Sub-s (4): in para (a) words "or civil partner," in square brackets inserted by the Civil Partnership Act 2004, s 261(1), Sch 27, para 37(a).

Sub-s (4): para (b) substituted by the Asylum and Immigration Act 1996, s 12(1), Sch 2, para 2.

Sub-s (4): in para (b) words "or civil partner," in square brackets inserted by the Civil Partnership Act 2004, s 261(1), Sch 27, para 37(b).

Sub-s (6): reference in square brackets substituted by the Immigration Act 1988, s 10, Schedule, para 2.

Subordinate Legislation

Pensions Increase (Speakers' Pensions) Regulations 1972, SI 1972/1653.

Pensions Increase (Parliamentary Pensions) Regulations 1972, SI 1972/1655.

Pensions (Increase) Act 1971 (Modification) (Teachers) Regulations 1972, SI 1972/1676.

Increase of Pensions (Teachers' Family Benefits) Regulations 1972, SI 1972/1905.

6 Recommendations by court for deportation

(1) Where under section 3(6) above a person convicted of an offence is liable to deportation on the recommendation of a court, he may be recommended for deportation by any court having power to sentence him for the offence unless the court commits him to be sentenced or further dealt with for that offence by another court:

Provided that in Scotland the power to recommend a person for deportation shall be exercisable only by the sheriff or the High Court of Justiciary, and shall not be exercisable by the latter on an appeal unless the appeal is against a conviction on indictment or against a sentence upon such a conviction.

(2) A court shall not recommend a person for deportation unless he has been given not less than seven days notice in writing stating that a person is not liable to deportation if he is [a British citizen], describing the persons who are [British citizens] and stating (so far as material) the effect of section 3(8) above and section 7 below; but the powers of adjournment conferred by [section 10(3) of the Magistrates' Courts Act 1980], [section 179 or 380 of the Criminal Procedure (Scotland) Act 1975] or any corresponding enactment for the time being in force in Northern Ireland shall include

power to adjourn, after convicting an offender, for the purpose of enabling a notice to be given to him under this subsection or, if a notice was so given to him less than seven days previously, for the purpose of enabling the necessary seven days to elapse.

(3)   For purposes of section 3(6) above—

  (a)   a person shall be deemed to have attained the age of seventeen at the time of his conviction if, on consideration of any available evidence, he appears to have done so to the court making or considering a recommendation for deportation; and

  (b)   the question whether an offence is one for which a person is punishable with imprisonment shall be determined without regard to any enactment restricting the imprisonment of young offenders or [persons who have not previously been sentenced to imprisonment];

and for purposes of deportation a person who on being charged with an offence is found to have committed it shall, notwithstanding any enactment to the contrary and notwithstanding that the court does not proceed to conviction, be regarded as a person convicted of the offence, and references to conviction shall be construed accordingly.

(4)   Notwithstanding any rule of practice restricting the matters which ought to be taken into account in dealing with an offender who is sentenced to imprisonment, a recommendation for deportation may be made in respect of an offender who is sentenced to imprisonment for life.

(5)   Where a court recommends or purports to recommend a person for deportation, the validity of the recommendation shall not be called in question except on an appeal against the recommendation or against the conviction on which it is made; but—

  (a)   . . . the recommendation shall be treated as a sentence for the purpose of any enactment providing an appeal against sentence; . . .

  (b)   . . .

(6)   A deportation order shall not be made on the recommendation of a court so long as an appeal or further appeal is pending against the recommendation or against the conviction on which it was made; and for this purpose an appeal or further appeal shall be treated as pending (where one is competent but has not been brought) until the expiration of the time for bringing that appeal or, in Scotland, until the expiration of twenty-eight days from the date of the recommendation.

(7)   For the purpose of giving effect to any of the provisions of this section in its application to Scotland, the High Court of Justiciary shall have power to make rules by act of adjournal.

Amendment

Sub-s (2): first and second words in square brackets substituted by the British Nationality Act 1981, s 39(6), Sch 4, para 2; third words in square brackets substituted by the Magistrates' Courts Act 1980, s 154, Sch 7, para 105; final words in square brackets substituted by the Criminal Procedure (Scotland) Act 1975, s 461(1), Sch 9, para 47.

Sub-s (3): words in square brackets substituted by the Criminal Justice Act 1972, s 64(1), Sch 5, and the Criminal Justice Act 1982, s 77, Sch 15.

Sub-s (5): words omitted repealed by the Criminal Justice (Scotland) Act 1980, s 83(3), Sch 8, and the Criminal Justice Act 1982, ss 77, 78, Sch 15, para 15, Sch 16.

7 Exemption from deportation for certain existing residents

(1)   Notwithstanding anything in section 3(5) or (6) above but subject to the provisions of this section, a Commonwealth citizen or citizen of the Republic of Ireland who was such a citizen at the coming into force of this Act and was then ordinarily resident in the United Kingdom—

  (a)   . . .

  [(b)   shall not be liable to deportation under section 3(5) if at the time of the Secretary of State's decision he had for the last five years been ordinarily resident in the United Kingdom and Islands;] and

(c)   shall not on conviction of an offence be recommended for deportation under section 3(6) if at the time of the conviction he had for the last five years been ordinarily resident in the United Kingdom and Islands.

(2)   A person who has at any time become ordinarily resident in the United Kingdom or in any of the Islands shall not be treated for the purposes of this section as having ceased to be so by reason only of his having remained there in breach of the immigration laws.

(3)   The "last five years" before the material time under subsection (1)(b) or (c) above is to be taken as a period amounting in total to five years exclusive of any time during which the person claiming exemption under this section was undergoing imprisonment or detention by virtue of a sentence passed for an offence on a conviction in the United Kingdom and Islands, and the period for which he was imprisoned or detained by virtue of the sentence amounted to six months or more.

(4)   For purposes of subsection (3) above—

(a)   "sentence" includes any order made on conviction of an offence; and

(b)   two or more sentences for consecutive (or partly consecutive) terms shall be treated as a single sentence; and

(c)   a person shall be deemed to be detained by virtue of a sentence—

(i)   at any time when he is liable to imprisonment or detention by virtue of the sentence, but is unlawfully at large; and

(ii)   (unless the sentence is passed after the material time) during any period of custody by which under any relevant enactment the term to be served under the sentence is reduced.

In paragraph (c)(ii) above "relevant enactment" means [section 240[, 240ZA or 240A] of the Criminal Justice Act 2003] (or, before that section operated, section 17(2) of the Criminal Justice Administration Act 1962) and any similar enactment which is for the time being or has (before or after the passing of this Act) been in force in any part of the United Kingdom and Islands.

(5)   Nothing in this section shall be taken to exclude the operation of section 3(8) above in relation to an exemption under this section.

Amendment

Sub-s (1): para (a) repealed by the Nationality, Immigration and Asylum Act 2002, ss 75(1), (2), 161, Sch 9.

Sub-s (1): para (b) substituted by the Nationality, Immigration and Asylum Act 2002, s 75(1), (3).

Sub-s (4): words "section 240 of the Criminal Justice Act 2003" in square brackets substituted by the Criminal Justice Act 2003, s 304, Sch 32, Pt 1, para 16.

Sub-s (4): words ", 240ZA or 240A" in square brackets inserted by the Legal Aid, Sentencing and Punishment of Offenders Act 2012, s 110(13), Sch 13, Pt 2, para 7. Date in force: 3 December 2012: see SI 2012/2906, art 2(d), (k).

8 Exceptions for seamen, aircrews and other special cases

(1)   Where a person arrives at a place in the United Kingdom as a member of the crew of a ship or aircraft under an engagement requiring him to leave on that ship as a member of the crew, or to leave within seven days on that or another aircraft as a member of its crew, then unless either—

(a)   there is in force a deportation order made against him; or

(b)   he has at any time been refused leave to enter the United Kingdom and has not since then been given leave to enter or remain in the United Kingdom; or

(c)   an immigration officer requires him to submit to examination in accordance with Schedule 2 to this Act;

he may without leave enter the United Kingdom at that place and remain until the departure of the ship or aircraft on which he is required by his engagement to leave.

(b) references to embarking in the United Kingdom do not apply to embarking for a local journey to a place in the United Kingdom or elsewhere in the common travel area.

(3) Except in so far as the context otherwise requires, references in this Act to arriving in the United Kingdom by ship shall extend to arrival by any floating structure, and "disembark" shall be construed accordingly; but the provisions of this Act specially relating to members of the crew of a ship shall not by virtue of this provision apply in relation to any floating structure not being a ship.

(4) For purposes of this Act "common travel area" has the meaning given by section 1(3), and a journey is, in relation to the common travel area, a local journey if but only if it begins and ends in the common travel area and is not made by a ship or aircraft which—

    (a) in the case of a journey to a place in the United Kingdom, began its voyage from, or has during its voyage called at, a place not in the common travel area; or

    (b) in the case of a journey from a place in the United Kingdom, is due to end its voyage in, or call in the course of its voyage at, a place not in the common travel area.

(5) A person who enters the United Kingdom lawfully by virtue of section 8(1) above, and seeks to remain beyond the time limited by section 8(1), shall be treated for purposes of this Act as seeking to enter the United Kingdom.

Amendment

Sub-s (1): words "or by Part III of the Immigration and Asylum Act 1999" in square brackets inserted by the Immigration and Asylum Act 1999, s 169(1), Sch 14, paras 43, 48, as from a day to be appointed.

Sub-s (1): words "or section 62 of the Nationality, Immigration and Asylum Act 2002" in square brackets inserted by the Nationality, Immigration and Asylum Act 2002, s 62(8).

Sub-s (1): words "or by section 68 of the Nationality, Immigration and Asylum Act 2002" in square brackets inserted by SI 2003/1016, art 3, Schedule, para 1.

Sub-s (1A): inserted by SI 1990/2227, art 3, Sch 1, Part I, para 3; repealed by SI 1993/1813, art 9, Sch 6.

12–23

(Repealed by the Immigration and Asylum Act 1999, s 169(1), (3), Sch 14, paras 43, 49, Sch 16.)

PART II
APPEALS

PART III
CRIMINAL PROCEEDINGS

24 Illegal entry and similar offences

(1) A person who is not [a British citizen] shall be guilty of an offence punishable on summary conviction with a fine of not more than [[level 5] on the standard scale] or with imprisonment for not more than six months, or with both, in any of the following cases:—

    (a) if contrary to this Act he knowingly enters the United Kingdom in breach of a deportation order or without leave;

    [(aa) . . .]

    (b) if, having only a limited leave to enter or remain in the United Kingdom, he knowingly either—

        (i) remains beyond the time limited by the leave; or

        (ii) fails to observe a condition of the leave;

(c) if, having lawfully entered the United Kingdom without leave by virtue of section 8(1) above, he remains without leave beyond the time allowed by section 8(1);

(d) if, without reasonable excuse, he fails to comply with any requirement imposed on him under Schedule 2 to this Act to report to a medical officer of health, or to attend, or submit to a test or examination, as required by such an officer;

(e) if, without reasonable excuse, he fails to observe any restriction imposed on him under Schedule 2 or 3 to this Act as to residence, as to his employment or occupation or as to reporting to the police[, to an immigration officer or to the Secretary of State];

(f) if he disembarks in the United Kingdom from a ship or aircraft after being placed on board under Schedule 2 or 3 to this Act with a view to his removal from the United Kingdom;

(g) if he embarks in contravention of a restriction imposed by or under an Order in Council under section 3(7) of this Act.

[(1A) A person commits an offence under subsection (1)(b)(i) above on the day when he first knows that the time limited by his leave has expired and continues to commit it throughout any period during which he is in the United Kingdom thereafter; but a person shall not be prosecuted under that provision more than once in respect of the same limited leave.]

(2) ...

(3) The extended time limit for prosecutions which is provided for by section 28 below shall apply to offences under [subsection (1)(a) and (c)] above.

(4) In proceedings for an offence against subsection (1)(a) above of entering the United Kingdom without leave,—

(a) any stamp purporting to have been imprinted on a passport or other travel document by an immigration officer on a particular date for the purpose of giving leave shall be presumed to have been duly so imprinted, unless the contrary is proved;

(b) proof that a person had leave to enter the United Kingdom shall lie on the defence if, but only if, he is shown to have entered within six months before the date when the proceedings were commenced.

Amendment

Sub-s (1): words "a British citizen" in square brackets substituted by the British Nationality Act 1981, s 39(6), Sch 4, para 2.

Sub-s (1): words "level 5" in square brackets substituted by the Asylum and Immigration Act 1996, s 6.

Sub-s (1): words in square brackets ending with the words "standard scale" substituted by virtue of the Criminal Justice Act 1982, ss 37, 38, 46.

Sub-s (1): para (aa) (as originally inserted by the Asylum and Immigration Act 1996, s 4) repealed by the Immigration and Asylum Act 1999, s 169(1), (3), Sch 14, paras 43, 50, Sch 16.

Sub-s (1): in para (e) words "as to his employment or occupation" in square brackets inserted by the Immigration Act 1988, s 10, Schedule, para 10(3), (4).

Sub-s (1): in para (e) words ", to an immigration officer or to the Secretary of State" in square brackets substituted by the Nationality, Immigration and Asylum Act 2002, s 62(9).

Sub-s (1A): inserted by the Immigration Act 1988, s 6(1), except in relation to a person whose leave expired before 10 July 1988.

Sub-s (2): repealed by the Immigration and Asylum Act 1999, s 169(1), (3), Sch 14, paras 43, 50, Sch 16.

Sub-s (3): words in square brackets substituted by the Immigration Act 1988, s 6(2), except in relation to a person whose leave expired before 10 July 1988.

[24A Deception]

[(1) A person who is not a British citizen is guilty of an offence if, by means which include deception by him—

    (i)   until he is acquitted, the charge against him is dismissed or the proceedings are discontinued; or

    (ii) if he has been convicted, until the court decides whether or not to order forfeiture of the ship, aircraft or vehicle.

(2) A ship, aircraft or vehicle is a relevant ship, aircraft or vehicle, in relation to an arrested person, if it is one which the officer or constable concerned has reasonable grounds for believing could, on conviction of the arrested person for the offence for which he was arrested, be the subject of an order for forfeiture made under [section 25C].

[(3) A person (other than the arrested person) may apply to the court for the release of a ship, aircraft or vehicle on the grounds that—

    (a) he owns the ship, aircraft or vehicle,

    (b) he was, immediately before the detention of the ship, aircraft or vehicle, in possession of it under a hire-purchase agreement, or

    (c) he is a charterer of the ship or aircraft.]

(4) The court to which an application is made under subsection (3) may, on such security or surety being tendered as it considers satisfactory, release the ship, aircraft or vehicle on condition that it is made available to the court if—

    (a) the arrested person is convicted; and

    (b) an order for its forfeiture is made under [section 25C].

(5) In the application to Scotland of subsection (1), for paragraphs (a) and (b) substitute—

"(a) until a decision is taken as to whether or not to institute criminal proceedings against the arrested person for that offence; or

(b) if criminal proceedings have been instituted against the arrested person—

    (i)   until he is acquitted or, under section 65 or 147 of the Criminal Procedure (Scotland) Act 1995, discharged or liberated or the trial diet is deserted simpliciter;

    (ii) if he has been convicted, until the court decides whether or not to order forfeiture of the ship, aircraft or vehicle,

and for the purposes of this subsection, criminal proceedings are instituted against a person at whichever is the earliest of his first appearance before the sheriff on petition, or the service on him of an indictment or complaint."

(6) "Court" means—

    (a) in England and Wales—

        [(ia) if the arrested person has not been charged, or he has been charged but proceedings for the offence have not begun to be heard, a magistrates' court;]

        (iii) if he has been charged and proceedings for the offence are being heard, the court hearing the proceedings;

    (b) in Scotland, the sheriff; and

    (c) in Northern Ireland—

        (i)   if the arrested person has not been charged, the magistrates' court for the county court division in which he was arrested;

        (ii) if he has been charged but proceedings for the offence have not begun to be heard, the magistrates' court for the county court division in which he was charged;

        (iii) if he has been charged and proceedings for the offence are being heard, the court hearing the proceedings.

(7) . . .

(8) "Senior officer" means an immigration officer not below the rank of chief immigration officer.]

Appendix 1 — UK Immigration Statutes

Amendment

Inserted by the Immigration and Asylum Act 1999, s 38(2), (4).

Section heading: renumbered and substituted by the Nationality, Immigration and Asylum Act 2002, s 144(1), (2).

Sub-s (1): words "section 25, 25A or 25B" in square brackets substituted by the Nationality, Immigration and Asylum Act 2002, s 144(1), (2)(a).

Sub-s (2): words "section 25C" in square brackets substituted by the Nationality, Immigration and Asylum Act 2002, s 144(1), (2)(b).

Sub-s (3): substituted by the Nationality, Immigration and Asylum Act 2002, s 144(1), (2)(c).

Sub-s (4): in para (b) words "section 25C" in square brackets substituted by the Nationality, Immigration and Asylum Act 2002, s 144(1), (2)(b).

Sub-s (6): para (a)(ia) substituted, for paras (a)(i), (ii) as originally enacted, by the Courts Act 2003, s 109(1), Sch 8, para 147.

Sub-s (7): repealed by the Nationality, Immigration and Asylum Act 2002, ss 144(1), (2)(d), 161, Sch 9.

26 General offences in connection with administration of Act

(1) A person shall be guilty of an offence punishable on summary conviction with a fine of not more than [[level 5] on the standard scale] or with imprisonment for not more than six months, or with both, in any of the following cases—

(a) if, without reasonable excuse, he refuses or fails to submit to examination under Schedule 2 to this Act;

(b) if, without reasonable excuse, he refuses or fails to furnish or produce any information in his possession, or any documents in his possession or control, which he is on an examination under that Schedule required to furnish or produce;

(c) if on any such examination or otherwise he makes or causes to be made to an immigration officer or other person lawfully acting in the execution of [a relevant enactment] a return, statement or representation which he knows to be false or does not believe to be true;

(d) if, without lawful authority, he alters any [certificate of entitlement], entry clearance, work permit or other document issued or made under or for the purposes of this Act, or uses for the purposes of this Act, or has in his possession for such use, any passport, [certificate of entitlement], entry clearance, work permit or other document which he knows or has reasonable cause to believe to be false;

(e) if, without reasonable excuse, he fails to complete and produce a landing or embarkation card in accordance with any order under Schedule 2 to this Act;

(f) if, without reasonable excuse, he fails to comply with any requirement or regulations under section 4(3) or of an order under section 4(4) above;

(g) if, without reasonable excuse, he obstructs an immigration officer or other person lawfully acting in the execution of this Act.

(2) The extended time limit for prosecutions which is provided for by section 28 below shall apply to offences under subsection (1)(c) and (d) above.

[(3) "Relevant enactment" means—

(a) this Act;

(b) the Immigration Act 1988;

(c) the Asylum and Immigration Appeals Act 1993 (apart from section 4 or 5); . . .

(d) the Immigration and Asylum Act 1999 (apart from Part VI)[; or

(e) the Nationality, Immigration and Asylum Act 2002 (apart from Part 5)].]

Amendment

Sub-s (1): words ending with "standard scale" in square brackets substituted by virtue of the Criminal Justice Act 1982, ss 37, 38, 46.

Sub-s (1): words "level 5" in square brackets substituted by the Asylum and Immigration Act 1996, s 6.

Sub-s (1): in para (c) words "a relevant enactment" in square brackets substituted by the Immigration and Asylum Act 1999, s 30(1), (2).

Sub-s (1): in para (d) words "certificate of entitlement" in square brackets, in both places they occur, substituted by the British Nationality Act 1981, s 39(6), Sch 4, para 3(1).

Sub-s (3): inserted by the Immigration and Asylum Act 1999, s 30(1), (3).

Sub-s (3): in para (c) word omitted repealed by the Nationality, Immigration and Asylum Act 2002, ss 151(a), 161, Sch 9.

Sub-s (3): para (e) and word "; or" immediately preceding it inserted by the Nationality, Immigration and Asylum Act 2002, s 151(b).

[26A Registration card]

[(1) In this section "registration card" means a document which—

(a) carries information about a person (whether or not wholly or partly electronically), and

[(b) is issued by the Secretary of State to the person wholly or partly in connection with—

(i) a claim for asylum (whether or not made by that person), or

(ii) a claim for support under section 4 of the Immigration and Asylum Act 1999 (whether or not made by that person)].

(2) In subsection (1) "claim for asylum" has the meaning given by section 18 of the Nationality, Immigration and Asylum Act 2002.

(3) A person commits an offence if he—

(a) makes a false registration card,

(b) alters a registration card with intent to deceive or to enable another to deceive,

(c) has a false or altered registration card in his possession without reasonable excuse,

(d) uses or attempts to use a false registration card for a purpose for which a registration card is issued,

(e) uses or attempts to use an altered registration card with intent to deceive,

(f) makes an article designed to be used in making a false registration card,

(g) makes an article designed to be used in altering a registration card with intent to deceive or to enable another to deceive, or

(h) has an article within paragraph (f) or (g) in his possession without reasonable excuse.

(4) In subsection (3) "false registration card" means a document which is designed to appear to be a registration card.

(5) A person who is guilty of an offence under subsection (3)\(a), (b), (d), (e), (f) or (g) shall be liable—

(a) on conviction on indictment, to imprisonment for a term not exceeding ten years, to a fine or to both, or

(b) on summary conviction, to imprisonment for a term not exceeding six months, to a fine not exceeding the statutory maximum or to both.

(6) A person who is guilty of an offence under subsection (3)\(c) or (h) shall be liable—

(a) on conviction on indictment, to imprisonment for a term not exceeding two years, to a fine or to both, or

(b) on summary conviction, to imprisonment for a term not exceeding six months, to a fine not exceeding the statutory maximum or to both.

(7) The Secretary of State may by order—

(a) amend the definition of "registration card" in subsection (1);

(b) make consequential amendment of this section.

(8) An order under subsection (7)—

(a) must be made by statutory instrument, and

(b) may not be made unless a draft has been laid before and approved by resolution of each House of Parliament.]

Amendment

Inserted by the Nationality, Immigration and Asylum Act 2002, s 148.

Sub-s (1): para (b) substituted by SI 2008/1693, art 2.

Subordinate Legislation

Immigration (Registration Card) Order 2008, SI 2008/1693.

[26B Possession of immigration stamp]

[(1) A person commits an offence if he has an immigration stamp in his possession without reasonable excuse.

(2) A person commits an offence if he has a replica immigration stamp in his possession without reasonable excuse.

(3) In this section—

(a) "immigration stamp" means a device which is designed for the purpose of stamping documents in the exercise of an immigration function,

(b) "replica immigration stamp" means a device which is designed for the purpose of stamping a document so that it appears to have been stamped in the exercise of an immigration function, and

(c) "immigration function" means a function of an immigration officer or the Secretary of State under the Immigration Acts.

(4) A person who is guilty of an offence under this section shall be liable—

(a) on conviction on indictment, to imprisonment for a term not exceeding two years, to a fine or to both, or

(b) on summary conviction, to imprisonment for a term not exceeding six months, to a fine not exceeding the statutory maximum or to both.]

Amendment

Inserted by the Nationality, Immigration and Asylum Act 2002, s 149.

27 Offences by persons connected with ships or aircraft or with ports

A person shall be guilty of an offence punishable on summary conviction with a fine of not more than [[level 5] on the standard scale] or with imprisonment for not more than six months, or with both, in any of the following cases—

(a) if, being the captain of a ship or aircraft,—

(i) he knowingly permits a person to disembark in the United Kingdom when required under Schedule 2 or 3 to this Act to prevent it, or fails without reasonable excuse to take any steps he is required by or under Schedule 2 to take in connection with the disembarkation or examination of passengers or for furnishing a passenger list or particulars of members of the crew; or

(ii) he fails, without reasonable excuse, to comply with any directions given him under Schedule 2 or 3 [or under the Immigration and Asylum Act 1999] with respect to the removal of a person from the United Kingdom;

(b) if, as owner or agent of a ship or aircraft,—

(i) he arranges, or is knowingly concerned in any arrangements, for the ship or aircraft to call at a port other than a port of entry contrary to any provision of Schedule 2 to this Act; or

(ii) he fails, without reasonable excuse, to take any steps required by an order under Schedule 2 for the supply to passengers of landing or embarkation cards; or

(iii) he fails, without reasonable excuse, to make arrangements for [or in connection with] the removal of a person from the United Kingdom when required to do so by directions given under Schedule 2 or 3 to this Act [or under the Immigration and Asylum Act 1999; or

[(iiia) he fails, without reasonable excuse, to comply with a direction under paragraph 5B of Schedule 2; or]

(iv) he fails, without reasonable excuse, to comply with [[any other requirement] imposed by or under Schedule 2]];

(c) if, . . . as a person concerned in the management of a port, he fails, without reasonable excuse, to take any steps required by Schedule 2 in relation to the embarkation or disembarkation of passengers where a control area is designated;

[(ca) if as a person concerned in the management of a port he fails, without reasonable excuse, to comply with a direction under paragraph 5B of Schedule 2.]

[(d) . . .].

Amendment

In para (a)(ii) words "or under the Immigration and Asylum Act 1999" in square brackets inserted by the Immigration and Asylum Act 1999, s 169(1), Sch 14, paras 43, 52(1), (2).

In para (b)(iii) words "or in connection with" in square brackets inserted by the Immigration and Asylum Act 1999, s 169(1), Sch 14, paras 43, 52(1), (3)(a).

In para (b)(iii) words "or under the Immigration and Asylum Act 1999; or" in square brackets and para (b)(iv) inserted by the Immigration and Asylum Act 1999, s 169(1), Sch 14, paras 43, 52(1), (3)(b).

Para (b)(iiia) inserted by the Immigration Act 2014, s 67, Sch 8, para 7(1), (2)(a), as from 28 July 2014: see SI 2014/1820.

In para (b)(iv) words in outer square brackets substituted by the Immigration, Asylum and Nationality Act 2006, s 31(4)(a).

In para (b)(iv) words in inner square brackets substituted by the Immigration Act 2014, s 67, Sch 8, para 7(1), (2)(b), as from 28 July 2014: see SI 2014/1820.

In para (c) words omitted repealed by the Immigration, Asylum and Nationality Act 2006, ss 31(4)(b), 61, Sch 3.

Para (ca) inserted by the Immigration Act 2014, s 67, Sch 8, para 7(1), (3), as from 28 July 2014: see SI 2014/1820.

Para (d) inserted by SI 1990/2227, art 3, Sch 1, Pt I, para 4; repealed by SI 1993/1813, art 9, Sch 6.

28 Proceedings

(1) Where the offence is one to which, under section 24. . . or 26 above, an extended time limit for prosecutions is to apply, then—

(a) an information relating to the offence may in England and Wales be tried by a magistrates' court if it is laid within six months after the commission of the offence, or if it is laid within three years after the commission of the offence and not more than two months after the date certified by [an officer of police above the rank of chief superintendent] to be the date on which evidence sufficient to justify proceedings came to the notice of an officer of [the police force to which he belongs]; and

(b) summary proceedings for the offence may in Scotland be commenced within six months after the commission of the offence, or within three years after the commission of the offence and not more than two months after the date on which evidence sufficient in the opinion of the Lord Advocate to justify proceedings came to his knowledge; and

(c) a complaint charging the commission of the offence may in Northern Ireland be heard and determined by a magistrates' court if it is made within six months after the commission of the offence, or if it is made within three years after the commission of the offence and not more than two months after the date on which a warrant to apprehend or to cite the accused is granted, if such warrant is executed without undue delay; and a certificate of the Lord Advocate as to the date on which such evidence as is mentioned in subsection (1)(b) came to his knowledge shall be conclusive evidence.

(2) For purposes of subsection (1)(b) above proceedings shall be deemed to be commenced on the date on which a warrant to apprehend or to cite the accused is granted, if such warrant is executed without undue delay; and a certificate of the Lord Advocate as to the date on which such evidence as is mentioned in subsection (1)(b) came to his knowledge shall be conclusive evidence.

(3) For the purposes of the trial of a person for an offence under this Part of this Act, the offence shall be deemed to have been committed either at the place at which it actually was committed or at any place at which he may be.

(4) Any powers exercisable under this Act in the case of any person may be exercised notwithstanding that proceedings for an offence under this Part of this Act have been taken against him.

Amendment

Sub-s (1): references omitted repealed by the Nationality, Immigration and Asylum Act 2002, ss 156(1), 161, Sch 9.

Sub-s (1): in para (a) words in square brackets substituted by the Immigration Act 1988, s 10, Schedule, para 4.

[28A Arrest without warrant]

[(1) [An] immigration officer may arrest without warrant a person—

   (a)   who has committed or attempted to commit an offence under section 24 or 24A; or

   (b)   whom he has reasonable grounds for suspecting has committed or attempted to commit such an offence.

(2) But subsection (1) does not apply in relation to an offence under section 24(1)(d).

(3) An immigration officer may arrest without warrant a person—

   (a)   who has committed an offence under [section 25, 25A or 25B]; or

   (b)   whom he has reasonable grounds for suspecting has committed that offence.

(4) ...

(5) An immigration officer may arrest without warrant a person ("the suspect") who, or whom he has reasonable grounds for suspecting—

   (a)   has committed or attempted to commit an offence under section 26(1)(g);

    or

   (b)   is committing or attempting to commit that offence.

(6) The power conferred by subsection (5) is exercisable only if either the first or the second condition is satisfied.

(7) The first condition is that it appears to the officer that service of a summons (or, in Scotland, a copy complaint) is impracticable or inappropriate because—

   (a)   he does not know, and cannot readily discover, the suspect's name;

   (b)   he has reasonable grounds for doubting whether a name given by the suspect as his name is his real name;

   (c)   the suspect has failed to give him a satisfactory address for service; or

   (d)   he has reasonable grounds for doubting whether an address given by the suspect is a satisfactory address for service.

(8) The second condition is that the officer has reasonable grounds for believing that arrest is necessary to prevent the suspect—

   (a)   causing physical injury to himself or another person;

   (b)   suffering physical injury; or

   (c)   causing loss of or damage to property.

(9) For the purposes of subsection (7), an address is a satisfactory address for service if it appears to the officer—

(a) that the suspect will be at that address for a sufficiently long period for it to be possible to serve him with a summons (or copy complaint); or

(b) that some other person specified by the suspect will accept service of a summons (or copy complaint) for the suspect at that address.

[(9A) [An] immigration officer may arrest without warrant a person—

(a) who has committed an offence under section 26A or 26B; or

(b) whom he has reasonable grounds for suspecting has committed an offence under section 26A or 26B.]

(10) In relation to the exercise of the powers conferred by subsections (3)(b) . . . and (5), it is immaterial that no offence has been committed.

(11) In Scotland the powers conferred by subsections (3) . . . and (5) may also be exercised by a constable.]

Amendment

Inserted by the Immigration and Asylum Act 1999, s 128.

Sub-s (1): word "An" in square brackets substituted in relation to England, Wales and Scotland by the Serious Organised Crime and Police Act 2005, s 111, Sch 7, Pt 4, para 53 and in relation to Northern Ireland by SI 2007/288, art 15(4), Sch 1, para 16.

Sub-s (3): in para (a) words "section 25, 25A or 25B" in square brackets substituted by the Nationality, Immigration and Asylum Act 2002, s 144(1), (3)(a).

Sub-s (4): repealed by the Nationality, Immigration and Asylum Act 2002, ss 144(1), (3)(b), 161, Sch 9.

Sub-s (9A): inserted by the Nationality, Immigration and Asylum Act 2002, s 150(1).

Sub-s (9A): word "An" in square brackets substituted in relation to England, Wales and Scotland by the Serious Organised Crime and Police Act 2005, s 111, Sch 7, Pt 4, para 53 and in relation to Northern Ireland by SI 2007/288, art 15(4), Sch 1, para 16.

Sub-s (10): reference omitted repealed by the Nationality, Immigration and Asylum Act 2002, ss 144(1), (3)(c), 161, Sch 9.

Sub-s (11): reference omitted repealed by the Nationality, Immigration and Asylum Act 2002, ss 144(1), (3)(d), 161, Sch 9.

[28AA Arrest with warrant]

[(1) This section applies if on an application by an immigration officer a justice of the peace is satisfied that there are reasonable grounds for suspecting that a person has committed an offence under—

(a) section 24(1)(d), or

[(b) section 21(1) of the Immigration, Asylum and Nationality Act 2006].

(2) The justice of the peace may grant a warrant authorising any immigration officer to arrest the person.

(3) In the application of this section to Scotland a reference to a justice of the peace shall be treated as a reference to the sheriff or a justice of the peace.]

Amendment

Inserted by the Nationality, Immigration and Asylum Act 2002, s 152.

Sub-s (1): para (b) substituted by the UK Borders Act 2007, s 27.

[28B Search and arrest by warrant]

[(1) Subsection (2) applies if a justice of the peace is, by written information on oath, satisfied that there are reasonable grounds for suspecting that a person ("the suspect") who is liable to be arrested for a relevant offence is to be found on any premises.

(2) The justice may grant a warrant authorising any immigration officer or constable to enter, if need be by force, the premises named in the warrant for the purpose of searching for and arresting the suspect.

(3) Subsection (4) applies if in Scotland the sheriff or a justice of the peace is by evidence on oath satisfied as mentioned in subsection (1).

(4) The sheriff or justice may grant a warrant authorising any immigration officer or constable to enter, if need be by force, the premises named in the warrant for the purpose of searching for and arresting the suspect.

(5) "Relevant offence" means an offence under section 24(1)(a), (b), (c), (d), (e) or (f)[, 24A][, 26A or 26B].]

Amendment

Inserted by the Immigration and Asylum Act 1999, s 129.

Sub-s (5): reference to ", 24A" in square brackets substituted by the Nationality, Immigration and Asylum Act 2002, s 144(1), (4).

Sub-s (5): words ", 26A or 26B" in square brackets inserted by the Nationality, Immigration and Asylum Act 2002, s 150(2).

[28C Search and arrest without warrant]

[(1) An immigration officer may enter and search any premises for the purpose of arresting a person for an offence under [section 25, 25A or 25B].

(2) The power may be exercised—

    (a) only to the extent that it is reasonably required for that purpose; and

    (b) only if the officer has reasonable grounds for believing that the person whom he is seeking is on the premises.

(3) In relation to premises consisting of two or more separate dwellings, the power is limited to entering and searching—

    (a) any parts of the premises which the occupiers of any dwelling comprised in the premises use in common with the occupiers of any such other dwelling; and

    (b) any such dwelling in which the officer has reasonable grounds for believing that the person whom he is seeking may be.

(4) The power may be exercised only if the officer produces identification showing that he is an immigration officer (whether or not he is asked to do so).]

Amendment

Inserted by the Immigration and Asylum Act 1999, s 130.

Sub-s (1): words "section 25, 25A or 25B" in square brackets substituted by the Nationality, Immigration and Asylum Act 2002, s 144(1), (5).

[28CA Business premises: entry to arrest]

[(1) A constable or immigration officer may enter and search any business premises for the purpose of arresting a person—

    (a) for an offence under section 24,

    (b) for an offence under section 24A, or

    (c) under paragraph 17 of Schedule 2.

(2) The power under subsection (1) may be exercised only—

    (a) to the extent that it is reasonably required for a purpose specified in subsection (1),

    (b) if the constable or immigration officer has reasonable grounds for believing that the person whom he is seeking is on the premises,

    (c) with the authority of the Secretary of State (in the case of an immigration officer) or a Chief Superintendent (in the case of a constable), and

    (d) if the constable or immigration officer produces identification showing his status.

(3) Authority for the purposes of subsection (2)(c)—

    (a) may be given on behalf of the Secretary of State only by a civil servant of the rank of at least Assistant Director, and

    (b) shall expire at the end of the period of seven days beginning with the day on which it is given.

(4) Subsection (2)(d) applies—

   (a) whether or not a constable or immigration officer is asked to produce identification, but

   (b) only where premises are occupied.

(5) Subsection (6) applies where a constable or immigration officer—

   (a) enters premises in reliance on this section, and

   (b) detains a person on the premises.

(6) A detainee custody officer may enter the premises for the purpose of carrying out a search.

(7) In subsection (6)—

"detainee custody officer" means a person in respect of whom a certificate of authorisation is in force under section 154 of the Immigration and Asylum Act 1999 (c 33) (detained persons: escort and custody), and

"search" means a search under paragraph 2(1)(a) of Schedule 13 to that Act (escort arrangements: power to search detained person).]

Amendment

Inserted by the Nationality, Immigration and Asylum Act 2002, s 153(1).

[28D Entry and search of premises]

[(1) If, on an application made by an immigration officer, a justice of the peace is satisfied that there are reasonable grounds for believing that—

   (a) a relevant offence has been committed,

   (b) there is material on premises specified in the application which is likely to be of substantial value (whether by itself or together with other material) to the investigation of the offence,

   (c) the material is likely to be relevant evidence,

   (d) the material does not consist of or include items subject to legal privilege, excluded material or special procedure material, and

   (e) any of the conditions specified in subsection (2) applies,

he may issue a warrant authorising an immigration officer to enter and search the premises.

(2) The conditions are that—

   (a) it is not practicable to communicate with any person entitled to grant entry to the premises;

   (b) it is practicable to communicate with a person entitled to grant entry to the premises but it is not practicable to communicate with any person entitled to grant access to the evidence;

   (c) entry to the premises will not be granted unless a warrant is produced;

   (d) the purpose of a search may be frustrated or seriously prejudiced unless an immigration officer arriving at the premises can secure immediate entry to them.

(3) An immigration officer may seize and retain anything for which a search has been authorised under subsection (1).

(4) "Relevant offence" means an offence under section 24(1)(a), (b), (c), (d), (e) or (f), [24A, 25, 25A, 25B][, 26A or 26B].

(5) In relation to England and Wales, expressions which are given a meaning by the Police and Criminal Evidence Act 1984 have the same meaning when used in this section.

(6) In relation to Northern Ireland, expressions which are given a meaning by the Police and Criminal Evidence (Northern Ireland) Order 1989 have the same meaning when used in this section

(7) In the application of subsection (1) to Scotland—

   (a) read the reference to a justice of the peace as a reference to the sheriff or a justice of the peace; and

Appendix 1 — UK Immigration Statutes

    (b)   in paragraph (b), omit the reference to excluded material and special procedure material.]

Amendment

Inserted by the Immigration and Asylum Act 1999, s 131.

Sub-s (4): reference to "24A, 25, 25A or 25B" in square brackets substituted by the Nationality, Immigration and Asylum Act 2002, s 144(1), (6).

Sub-s (4): words ", 26A or 26B" in square brackets inserted by the Nationality, Immigration and Asylum Act 2002, s 150(3).

[28E Entry and search of premises following arrest]

[[(1) This section applies if a person is arrested for an offence under this Part at a place other than a police station.

(2) An immigration officer may enter and search any premises—

    (a)   in which the person was when arrested, or

    (b)   in which he was immediately before he was arrested,

for evidence relating to the offence for which the arrest was made ("relevant evidence").

(3) The power may be exercised—

    (a)   only if the officer has reasonable grounds for believing that there is relevant evidence on the premises; and

    (b)   only to the extent that it is reasonably required for the purpose of discovering relevant evidence.

(4) In relation to premises consisting of two or more separate dwellings, the power is limited to entering and searching—

    (a)   any dwelling in which the arrest took place or in which the arrested person was immediately before his arrest; and

    (b)   any parts of the premises which the occupier of any such dwelling uses in common with the occupiers of any other dwellings comprised in the premises.

(5) An officer searching premises under subsection (2) may seize and retain anything he finds which he has reasonable grounds for believing is relevant evidence.

(6) Subsection (5) does not apply to items which the officer has reasonable grounds for believing are items subject to legal privilege.]

Amendment

Inserted by the Immigration and Asylum Act 1999, s 132(1).

[28F *Entry and search of premises following arrest under section 25(1)* [Entry and search of premises following arrest under section 25, 25A or 25B]]

[(1) An immigration officer may enter and search any premises occupied or controlled by a person arrested for an offence under [section 25, 25A, 25B].

(2) The power may be exercised—

    (a)   only if the officer has reasonable grounds for suspecting that there is relevant evidence on the premises;

    (b)   only to the extent that it is reasonably required for the purpose of discovering relevant evidence; and

    (c)   subject to subsection (3), only if a senior officer has authorised it in writing.

(3) The power may be exercised—

    (a)   before taking the arrested person to a place where he is to be detained; and

    (b)   without obtaining an authorisation under subsection (2)(c),

if the presence of that person at a place other than one where he is to be detained is necessary for the effective investigation of the offence.

(4) An officer who has relied on subsection (3) must inform a senior officer as soon as is practicable.

(5) The officer authorising a search, or who is informed of one under subsection (4), must make a record in writing of—

(a) the grounds for the search; and

(b) the nature of the evidence that was sought.

(6) An officer searching premises under this section may seize and retain anything he finds which he has reasonable grounds for suspecting is relevant evidence.

(7) "Relevant evidence" means evidence, other than items subject to legal privilege, that relates to the offence in question.

(8) "Senior officer" means an immigration officer not below the rank of chief immigration officer.]

Amendment

Inserted by the Immigration and Asylum Act 1999, s 133.

Section heading; words "Entry and search of premises following arrest under section 25(1)" in italics repealed and subsequent words in square brackets substituted by the Nationality, Immigration and Asylum Act 2002, s 144(1), (7), as from a day to be appointed.

Sub-s (1): words "section 25, 25A, 25B" in square brackets substituted by the Nationality, Immigration and Asylum Act 2002, s 144(1), (7).

[28FA Search for personnel records: warrant unnecessary]

[(1) This section applies where—

(a) a person has been arrested for an offence under section 24(1) or 24A(1),

(b) a person has been arrested under paragraph 17 of Schedule 2,

(c) a constable or immigration officer reasonably believes that a person is liable to arrest for an offence under section 24(1) or 24A(1), or

(d) a constable or immigration officer reasonably believes that a person is liable to arrest under paragraph 17 of Schedule 2.

(2) A constable or immigration officer may search business premises where the arrest was made or where the person liable to arrest is if the constable or immigration officer reasonably believes—

(a) that a person has committed an immigration employment offence in relation to the person arrested or liable to arrest, and

(b) that employee records, other than items subject to legal privilege, will be found on the premises and will be of substantial value (whether on their own or together with other material) in the investigation of the immigration employment offence.

(3) A constable or officer searching premises under subsection (2) may seize and retain employee records, other than items subject to legal privilege, which he reasonably suspects will be of substantial value (whether on their own or together with other material) in the investigation of—

(a) an immigration employment offence, or

(b) an offence under section 105 or 106 of the Immigration and Asylum Act 1999 (c 33) (support for asylum-seeker: fraud).

(4) The power under subsection (2) may be exercised only—

(a) to the extent that it is reasonably required for the purpose of discovering employee records other than items subject to legal privilege,

(b) if the constable or immigration officer produces identification showing his status, and

(c) if the constable or immigration officer reasonably believes that at least one of the conditions in subsection (5) applies.

(5) Those conditions are—

(a) that it is not practicable to communicate with a person entitled to grant access to the records,

(b) that permission to search has been refused,

(c) that permission to search would be refused if requested, and

(d) that the purpose of a search may be frustrated or seriously prejudiced if it is not carried out in reliance on subsection (2).

(6) Subsection (4)(b) applies—

(a) whether or not a constable or immigration officer is asked to produce identification, but

(b) only where premises are occupied.

(7) In this section "immigration employment offence" means [an offence under section 21 of the Immigration, Asylum and Nationality Act 2006] (employment).]

Amendment

Inserted by the Nationality, Immigration and Asylum Act 2002, s 154.

Sub-s (7): words "an offence under section 21 of the Immigration, Asylum and Nationality Act 2006" in square brackets substituted by the UK Borders Act 2007, s 28.

[28FB Search for personnel records: with warrant]

[(1) This section applies where on an application made by an immigration officer in respect of business premises a justice of the peace is satisfied that there are reasonable grounds for believing—

(a) that an employer has provided inaccurate or incomplete information under section 134 of the Nationality, Immigration and Asylum Act 2002 (compulsory disclosure by employer),

(b) that employee records, other than items subject to legal privilege, will be found on the premises and will enable deduction of some or all of the information which the employer was required to provide, and

(c) that at least one of the conditions in subsection (2) is satisfied.

(2) Those conditions are—

(a) that it is not practicable to communicate with a person entitled to grant access to the premises,

(b) that it is not practicable to communicate with a person entitled to grant access to the records,

(c) that entry to the premises or access to the records will not be granted unless a warrant is produced, and

(d) that the purpose of a search may be frustrated or seriously prejudiced unless an immigration officer arriving at the premises can secure immediate entry.

(3) The justice of the peace may issue a warrant authorising an immigration officer to enter and search the premises.

(4) Subsection (7)(a) of section 28D shall have effect for the purposes of this section as it has effect for the purposes of that section.

(5) An immigration officer searching premises under a warrant issued under this section may seize and retain employee records, other than items subject to legal privilege, which he reasonably suspects will be of substantial value (whether on their own or together with other material) in the investigation of—

(a) an offence under section 137 of the Nationality, Immigration and Asylum Act 2002 (disclosure of information: offences) in respect of a requirement under section 134 of that Act, or

(b) an offence under section 105 or 106 of the Immigration and Asylum Act 1999 (c 33) (support for asylum-seeker: fraud).]

Amendment

Inserted by the Nationality, Immigration and Asylum Act 2002, s 154.

[28G Searching arrested persons]

[(1) This section applies if a person is arrested for an offence under this Part at a place other than a police station.

(2) An immigration officer may search the arrested person if he has reasonable grounds for believing that the arrested person may present a danger to himself or others.

(3) The officer may search the arrested person for—

  (a) anything which he might use to assist his escape from lawful custody; or

  (b) anything which might be evidence relating to the offence for which he has been arrested.

(4) The power conferred by subsection (3) may be exercised—

  (a) only if the officer has reasonable grounds for believing that the arrested person may have concealed on him anything of a kind mentioned in that subsection; and

  (b) only to the extent that it is reasonably required for the purpose of discovering any such thing.

(5) A power conferred by this section to search a person is not to be read as authorising an officer to require a person to remove any of his clothing in public other than an outer coat, jacket or glove; but it does authorise the search of a person's mouth.

(6) An officer searching a person under subsection (2) may seize and retain anything he finds, if he has reasonable grounds for believing that that person might use it to cause physical injury to himself or to another person.

(7) An officer searching a person under subsection (3) may seize and retain anything he finds, if he has reasonable grounds for believing—

  (a) that that person might use it to assist his escape from lawful custody; or

  (b) that it is evidence which relates to the offence in question.

(8) Subsection (7)(b) does not apply to an item subject to legal privilege.]

Amendment

Inserted by the Immigration and Asylum Act 1999, s 134(1).

[28H Searching persons in police custody]

[(1) This section applies if a person—

  (a) has been arrested for an offence under this Part; and

  (b) is in custody at a police station or in police detention at a place other than a police station.

(2) An immigration officer may, at any time, search the arrested person in order to see whether he has with him anything—

  (a) which he might use to—

    (i) cause physical injury to himself or others;

    (ii) damage property;

    (iii) interfere with evidence; or

    (iv) assist his escape; or

  (b) which the officer has reasonable grounds for believing is evidence relating to the offence in question.

(3) The power may be exercised only to the extent that the custody officer concerned considers it to be necessary for the purpose of discovering anything of a kind mentioned in subsection (2).

(4) An officer searching a person under this section may seize anything he finds, if he has reasonable grounds for believing that—

  (a) that person might use it for one or more of the purposes mentioned in subsection (2)(a); or

  (b) it is evidence relating to the offence in question.

(5) Anything seized under subsection (4)(a) may be retained by the police.

(6) Anything seized under subsection (4)(b) may be retained by an immigration officer.

(7) The person from whom something is seized must be told the reason for the seizure unless he is—

(a) violent or appears likely to become violent; or

(b) incapable of understanding what is said to him.

(8) An intimate search may not be conducted under this section.

(9) The person carrying out a search under this section must be of the same sex as the person searched.

(10) "Custody officer"—

(a) in relation to England and Wales, has the same meaning as in the Police and Criminal Evidence Act 1984;

(b) in relation to Scotland, means the officer in charge of a police station; and

(c) in relation to Northern Ireland, has the same meaning as in the Police and Criminal Evidence (Northern Ireland) Order 1989.

(11) "Intimate search"—

(a) in relation to England and Wales, has the meaning given by section 65 of the Act of 1984;

(b) in relation to Scotland, means a search which consists of the physical examination of a person's body orifices other than the mouth; and

(c) in relation to Northern Ireland, has the same meaning as in the 1989 Order.

(12) "Police detention"—

(a) in relation to England and Wales, has the meaning given by section 118(2) of the 1984 Act; and

(b) in relation to Northern Ireland, has the meaning given by Article 2 of the 1989 Order.

(13) In relation to Scotland, a person is in police detention if—

(a) he has been taken to a police station after being arrested for an offence; or

(b) he is arrested at a police station after attending voluntarily at the station, accompanying a constable to it or being detained under section 14 of the Criminal Procedure (Scotland) Act 1995,

and is detained there or is detained elsewhere in the charge of a constable, but is not in police detention if he is in court after being charged.]

Amendment

Inserted by the Immigration and Asylum Act 1999, s 135(1).

[28I Seized material: access and copying]

[(1) If a person showing himself—

(a) to be the occupier of the premises on which seized material was seized, or

(b) to have had custody or control of the material immediately before it was seized,

asks the immigration officer who seized the material for a record of what he seized, the officer must provide the record to that person within a reasonable time.

(2) If a relevant person asks an immigration officer for permission to be granted access to seized material, the officer must arrange for him to have access to the material under the supervision—

(a) in the case of seized material within subsection (8)(a), of an immigration officer;

(b) in the case of seized material within subsection (8)(b), of a constable.

(3) An immigration officer may photograph or copy, or have photographed or copied, seized material.

(4) If a relevant person asks an immigration officer for a photograph or copy of seized material, the officer must arrange for—

  (a) that person to have access to the material for the purpose of photographing or copying it under the supervision—

    (i) in the case of seized material within subsection (8)\a), of an immigration officer;

    (ii) in the case of seized material within subsection (8)\(b), of a constable; or

  (b) the material to be photographed or copied.

(5) A photograph or copy made under subsection (4)\(b) must be supplied within a reasonable time.

(6) There is no duty under this section to arrange for access to, or the supply of a photograph or copy of, any material if there are reasonable grounds for believing that to do so would prejudice—

  (a) the exercise of any functions in connection with which the material was seized; or

  (b) an investigation which is being conducted under this Act, or any criminal proceedings which may be brought as a result.

(7) "Relevant person" means—

  (a) a person who had custody or control of seized material immediately before it was seized, or

  (b) someone acting on behalf of such a person.

(8) "Seized material" means anything—

  (a) seized and retained by an immigration officer, or

  (b) seized by an immigration officer and retained by the police,

under this Part.]

Amendment

Inserted by the Immigration and Asylum Act 1999, s 136(1).

[28J Search warrants: safeguards]

[(1) The entry or search of premises under a warrant is unlawful unless it complies with this section and section 28K.

(2) If an immigration officer applies for a warrant, he must—

  (a) state the ground on which he makes the application and the provision of this Act under which the warrant would be issued;

  (b) specify the premises which it is desired to enter and search; and

  (c) identify, so far as is practicable, the persons or articles to be sought.

(3) In Northern Ireland, an application for a warrant is to be made by a complaint in writing and substantiated on oath.

(4) Otherwise, an application for a warrant is to be made ex parte and supported by an information in writing or, in Scotland, evidence on oath.

(5) The officer must answer on oath any question that the justice of the peace or sheriff hearing the application asks him.

(6) A warrant shall authorise an entry on one occasion only.

(7) A warrant must specify—

  (a) the name of the person applying for it;

  (b) the date on which it is issued;

  (c) the premises to be searched; and

  (d) the provision of this Act under which it is issued.

(8) A warrant must identify, so far as is practicable, the persons or articles to be sought.

(9) Two copies of a warrant must be made.

(10) The copies must be clearly certified as copies.

(11) "Warrant" means a warrant to enter and search premises issued to an immigration officer under this Part or under paragraph 17(2) [or 25A(6A)] of Schedule 2.]

Amendment

Inserted by the Immigration and Asylum Act 1999, s 137.

Sub-s (11): words in square brackets inserted by the Immigration Act 2014, s 4, Sch 1, para 4, as from 28 July 2014: see SI 2014/1820.

[28K Execution of warrants]

[[(1) A warrant may be executed by any immigration officer.

(2) A warrant may authorise persons to accompany the officer executing it.

(3) Entry and search under a warrant must be—

(a) within one month from the date of its issue; and

(b) at a reasonable hour, unless it appears to the officer executing it that the purpose of a search might be frustrated.

(4) If the occupier of premises which are to be entered and searched is present at the time when an immigration officer seeks to execute a warrant, the officer must—

(a) identify himself to the occupier and produce identification showing that he is an immigration officer;

(b) show the occupier the warrant; and

(c) supply him with a copy of it.]

(5) If—

(a) the occupier is not present, but

(b) some other person who appears to the officer to be in charge of the premises is present,

subsection (4) has effect as if each reference to the occupier were a reference to that other person.

(6) If there is no person present who appears to the officer to be in charge of the premises, the officer must leave a copy of the warrant in a prominent place on the premises.

(7) A search under a warrant may only be a search to the extent required for the purpose for which the warrant was issued.

(8) An officer executing a warrant must make an endorsement on it stating—

(a) whether the persons or articles sought were found; and

(b) whether any articles, other than articles which were sought, were seized.

(9) A warrant which has been executed, or has not been executed within the time authorised for its execution, must be returned—

[(a) if issued by a justice of the peace in England and Wales, to the designated officer for the local justice area in which the justice was acting when he issued the warrant;]

(b) if issued by a justice of the peace in Northern Ireland, to the clerk of petty sessions for the petty sessions district in which the premises are situated;

(c) if issued by a justice of the peace in Scotland, to the clerk of the district court for the commission area for which the justice of the peace was appointed;

(d) if issued by the sheriff, to the sheriff clerk.

(10) A warrant returned under subsection (9)(a) must be retained for 12 months by the [designated officer].

(11) A warrant issued under subsection (9)(b) or (c) must be retained for 12 months by the clerk.

(12) A warrant returned under subsection (9)(d) must be retained for 12 months by the sheriff clerk.

(13) If during that 12 month period the occupier of the premises to which it relates asks to inspect it, he must be allowed to do so.

(14) "Warrant" means a warrant to enter and search premises issued to an immigration officer under this Part or under paragraph 17(2) [or 25A(6A)] of Schedule 2.]

Amendment

Inserted by the Immigration and Asylum Act 1999, s 138; for transitional provisions see Sch 15, para 4(b) thereto.

Sub-s (9): para (a) substituted by the Courts Act 2003, s 109(1), Sch 8, para 148(1), (2).

Sub-s (10): words "designated officer" in square brackets substituted by the Courts Act 2003, s 109(1), Sch 8, para 148(1), (3).

Sub-s (14): words in square brackets inserted by the Immigration Act 2014, s 4, Sch 1, para 4, as from 28 July 2014: see SI 2014/1820.

[28L Interpretation of Part III]

[[(1)] In this Part, "premises" and "items subject to legal privilege" have the same meaning—

(a) in relation to England and Wales, as in the Police and Criminal Evidence Act 1984;

(b) in relation to Northern Ireland, as in the Police and Criminal Evidence (Northern Ireland) Order 1989"; and

(c) in relation to Scotland, as in section [412 of the Proceeds of Crime Act 2002].

[(2) In this Part "business premises" means premises (or any part of premises) not used as a dwelling.

(3) In this Part "employee records" means records which show an employee's—

(a) name,

(b) date of birth,

(c) address,

(d) length of service,

(e) rate of pay, or

(f) nationality or citizenship.

(4) The Secretary of State may by order amend section 28CA(3)(a) to reflect a change in nomenclature.

(5) An order under subsection (4)—

(a) must be made by statutory instrument, and

(b) shall be subject to annulment in pursuance of a resolution of either House of Parliament.]]

Amendment

Inserted by the Immigration and Asylum Act 1999, s 139(1).

Sub-s (1): numbered as such by the Nationality, Immigration and Asylum Act 2002, s 155.

Sub-s (1): in para (c) words "412 of the Proceeds of Crime Act 2002" in square brackets substituted by the Proceeds of Crime Act 2002, s 456, Sch 11, paras 1, 6.

Sub-ss (2)–(5): inserted by the Nationality, Immigration and Asylum Act 2002, s 155.

PART IV
SUPPLEMENTARY

29, 30

(S 29 repealed by the Nationality, Immigration and Asylum Act 2002, ss 58(5)(a), 161, Sch 9; s 30 repealed by the British Nationality Act 1981, s 52(8), Sch 9, and the Mental Health

31 Expenses

There shall be defrayed out of moneys provided by Parliament any expenses incurred [by the Lord Chancellor under Schedule 5 to this Act or] by a Secretary of State under or by virtue of this Act—

(a)   by way of administrative expenses . . . ; or

(b)   in connection with the removal of any person from the United Kingdom under Schedule 2 or 3 to this Act or the departure with him of his dependants, or his or their maintenance pending departure; or

(c)   . . .

(d)   . . .

Amendment

Words in first pair of square brackets inserted by SI 1987/465, art 3(4).]

In para (a) words omitted repealed by the British Nationality Act 1981, s 52(8), Sch 9.

Para (c) repealed by SI 1987/465, art 3(4).

Para (d) repealed by the Nationality, Immigration and Asylum Act 2002, ss 58(5)(b), 161, Sch 9.

31A

(Inserted by the Immigration and Asylum Act 1999, s 165 and repealed by the Immigration, Asylum and Nationality Act 2006, ss 50(3)(a), 61, Sch 3.)

32 General provisions as to Orders in Council, etc

(1)   Any power conferred by Part 1 of this Act to make an Order in Council or order (other than a deportation order) or to give any directions includes power to revoke or vary the Order in Council, order or directions.

(2)   Any document purporting to be an order, notice or direction made or given by the Secretary of State for the purposes of [the Immigration Acts] and to be signed by him or on his behalf, and any document purporting to be a certificate of the Secretary of State so given and to be signed by him [or on his behalf], shall be received in evidence, and shall, until the contrary is proved, be deemed to be made or issued by him.

(3)   Prima facie evidence of any such order, notice, direction or certificate as aforesaid may, in any legal proceedings or [other proceedings under the Immigration Acts], be given by the production of a document bearing a certificate purporting to be signed by or on behalf of the Secretary of State and stating that the document is a true copy of the order, notice, direction or certificate.

(4)   Where an order under section 8(2) above applies to persons specified in a schedule to the order, or any directions of the Secretary of State given for the purposes of [the Immigration Acts] apply to persons specified in a schedule to the directions, prima facie evidence of the provisions of the order or directions other than the prima facie evidence of the provisions of the order or directions other than the schedule and of any entry contained in the schedule may, in any legal proceedings or [other proceedings under the Immigration Acts], be given by the production of a document purporting to be signed by or on behalf of the Secretary of State and stating that the document is a true copy of the said provisions and of the relevant entry.

[(5)   . . .]

Amendment

Sub-s (2): words "the Immigration Acts" in square brackets substituted by the Immigration and Asylum Act 1999, s 169(1), Sch 14, paras 43, 54(1), (2)(a); for the application of this amendment see para 54(6) thereto.

Sub-s (2): words "or on his behalf" in square brackets inserted by the Immigration and Asylum Act 1999, s 169(1), Sch 14, paras 43, 54(1), (2)(b).

Sub-s (3): words "other proceedings under the Immigration Acts" in square brackets substituted by the Immigration and Asylum Act 1999, s 169(1), Sch 14, paras 43, 54(1), (3).

Sub-s (4): words "the Immigration Acts" and "other proceedings under the Immigration Acts" in square brackets substituted by the Immigration and Asylum Act 1999, s 169(1), Sch 14, paras 43, 54(1), (4).

Sub-s (5): inserted by the Immigration and Asylum Act 1999, s 169(1), Sch 14, paras 43, 54(1), (5).

Sub-s (5): repealed by the Immigration, Asylum and Nationality Act 2006, ss 61, 64(3)(a), Sch 3.

33 Interpretation

(1) For purposes of this Act, except in so far as the context otherwise requires—

"aircraft" includes hovercraft, "airport" includes hoverport and "port" includes airport;

"captain" means master (of a ship) or commander (of an aircraft);

["certificate of entitlement" means a certificate under section 10 of the Nationality, Immigration and Asylum Act 2002 that a person has the right of abode in the United Kingdom;]

["Convention adoption" has the same meaning as in the Adoption Act 1976 and the [the Adoption and Children (Scotland) Act 2007] [or in the Adoption and Children Act 2002];]

[. . .]

"crew", in relation to a ship or aircraft, means all persons actually employed in the working or service of the ship or aircraft, including the captain, and "member of the crew" shall be construed accordingly;

["entrant" means a person entering or seeking to enter the United Kingdom and "illegal entrant" means a person—

(a) unlawfully entering or seeking to enter in breach of a deportation order or of the immigration laws, or

(b) entering or seeking to enter by means which include deception by another person,

and includes also a person who has entered as mentioned in paragraph (a) or (b) above;]

"entry clearance" means a visa, entry certificate or other document which, in accordance with the immigration rules, is to be taken as evidence [or the requisite evidence] of a person's eligibility, though not [a British citizen], for entry into the United Kingdom (but does not include a work permit);

"immigration laws" means this Act and any law for purposes similar to this Act which is for the time being or has (before or after the passing of this Act) been in force in any part of the United Kingdom and Islands;

"immigration rules" means the rules for the time being laid down as mentioned in section 3(2) above;

"the Islands" means the Channel Islands and the Isle of Man, and "the United Kingdom and Islands" means the United Kingdom and the Islands taken together;

"legally adopted" means adopted in pursuance of an order made by any court in the United Kingdom and Islands[, under a Convention adoption] or by any adoption specified as an overseas adoption by order of the Secretary of State under [section 87 of the Adoption and Children Act 2002] [or by regulations made by the Scottish Ministers under section 67(1) of the Adoption and Children (Scotland) Act 2007];

"limited leave" and "indefinite leave" mean respectively leave under this Act to enter or remain in the United Kingdom which is, and one which is not, limited as to duration;

"settled" shall be construed in accordance [with subsection (2A) below];

"ship" includes every description of vessel used in navigation;

[. . .]

["United Kingdom passport" means a current passport issued by the Government of the United Kingdom, or by the Lieutenant-Governor of any of the Islands or by the Government of any territory which is for the time being a [British overseas territory] within the meaning of the British Nationality Act 1981;]

"work permit" means a permit indicating, in accordance with the immigration rules, that a person named in it is eligible, though not [a British citizen], for entry into the United Kingdom for the purpose of taking employment.

[(1A)   A reference to being an owner of a vehicle, ship or aircraft includes a reference to being any of a number of persons who jointly own it.]

(2)   It is hereby declared that, except as otherwise provided in this Act, a person is not to be treated for the purposes of any provision of this Act as ordinarily resident in the United Kingdom or in any of the Islands at a time when he is there in breach of the immigration laws.

[(2A)   Subject to section 8(5) above, references to a person being settled in the United Kingdom are references to his being ordinarily resident there without being subject under the immigration laws to any restriction on the period for which he may remain.]

(3)   The ports of entry for purposes of this Act, and the ports of exit for purposes of any Order in Council under section 3(7) above, shall be such ports as may from time to time be designated for the purpose by order of the Secretary of State made by statutory instrument.

[(4)   For the purposes of this Act, the question of whether an appeal is pending shall be determined [in accordance with section 104 of the Nationality, Immigration and Asylum Act 2002 (pending appeals)].]

(5)   This Act shall not be taken to supersede or impair any power exercisable by Her Majesty in relation to aliens by virtue of Her prerogative.

Amendment

Sub-s (1): definition "certificate of entitlement" substituted by the Nationality, Immigration and Asylum Act 2002, s 10(5)(b).

Sub-s (1): definition "Convention adoption" inserted by the Adoption (Intercountry Aspects) Act 1999, s 15(1), Sch 2, para 2(a).

Sub-s (1): in definition "Convention adoption" words "the Adoption and Children (Scotland) Act 2007" in square brackets substituted by SI 2011/1740, art 2, Sch 1, Pt 1, para 1(a). Date in force: 15 July 2011: see SI 2011/1740, art 1(2).

Sub-s (1): in the definition "Convention adoption" words "or in the Adoption and Children Act 2002" in square brackets inserted by the Adoption and Children Act 2002, s 139(1), Sch 3, para 15(a).

Sub-s (1): in definition "legally adopted" words ", under a Convention adoption" in square brackets inserted by the Adoption (Intercountry Aspects) Act 1999, s 15(1), Sch 2, para 2(b).

Sub-s (1): in definition "legally adopted" words "section 87 of the Adoption and Children Act 2002" in square brackets substituted by the Adoption and Children Act 2002, s 139(1), Sch 3, para 15(b).

Sub-s (1): in definition "legally adopted" words from "or by regulations" to "Adoption and Children (Scotland) Act 2007" in square brackets inserted by SI 2011/1740, art 2, Sch 1, Pt 1, para 1(b).

Date in force: 15 July 2011: see SI 2011/1740, art 1(2).

Sub-s (1): in definition "United Kingdom passport" words "British overseas territory" in square brackets substituted by virtue of the British Overseas Territories Act 2002, s 1(2).

Sub-s (1A): inserted by the Nationality, Immigration and Asylum Act 2002, s 144(1), (8).

Sub-s (2A): inserted by the British Nationality Act 1981, s 39(6), Sch 4, para 7.

Sub-s (4): substituted by the Immigration and Asylum Act 1999, s 169(1), Sch 14, paras 43, 55.

Sub-s (4): words "or section 7 of the Special Immigration Appeals Commission Act 1997" in square brackets inserted by the Special Immigration Appeals Commission Act 1997, s 7/4).

Sub-s (4): words "in accordance with section 104 of the Nationality, Immigration and Asylum Act 2002 (pending appeals)" in square brackets substituted by the Nationality, Immigration and Asylum Act 2002, s 114(3), Sch 7, para 1.

Subordinate Legislation

Immigration (Ports of Entry) Order 1987, SI 1987/177.

34 Repeal, transitional and temporary

(1) Subject to the following provisions of this section, the enactments mentioned in Schedule 6 to this Act are hereby repealed, as from the coming into force of this Act, to the extent mentioned in column 3 of the Schedule; and—

   (a) this Act, as from its coming into force, shall apply in relation to entrants or others arriving in the United Kingdom at whatever date before or after it comes into force; and

   (b) after this Act comes into force anything done under or for the purposes of the former immigration laws shall have effect, in so far as any corresponding action could be taken under or for the purposes of this Act, as if done by way of action so taken, and in relation to anything so done this Act shall apply accordingly.

(2) Without prejudice to the generality of subsection (1)(a) and (b) above, a person refused leave to land by virtue of the Aliens Restriction Act 1914 shall be treated as having been refused leave to enter under this Act, and a person given leave to land by virtue of that Act shall be treated as having been given leave to enter under this Act; and similarly with the Commonwealth Immigrants Acts 1962 and 1968.

(3) A person treated in accordance with subsection (2) above as having leave to enter the United Kingdom—

   (a) shall be treated as having an indefinite leave, if he is not at the coming into force of this Act subject to a condition limiting his stay in the United Kingdom; and

   (b) shall be treated, if he is then subject to such a condition, as having a limited leave of such duration, and subject to such conditions (capable of being attached to leave under this Act), as correspond to the conditions to which he is then subject, but not to conditions not capable of being so attached.

This subsection shall have effect in relation to any restriction or requirement imposed by Order in Council under the Aliens Restriction Act 1914 as if it had been imposed by way of a landing condition.

(4) Notwithstanding anything in the foregoing provisions of this Act, the former immigration laws shall continue to apply, and this Act shall not apply,—

   (a) in relation to the making of deportation orders and matters connected therewith in any case where a decision to make the order has been notified to the person concerned before the coming into force of this Act;

   (b) in relation to removal from the United Kingdom and matters connected therewith (including detention pending removal or pending the giving of directions for removal) in any case where a person is to be removed in pursuance of a decision taken before the coming into force of this Act or in pursuance of a deportation order to the making of which paragraph (a) above applies;

   (c) in relation to appeals against any decision taken or other thing done under the former immigration laws, whether taken or done before the coming into force of this Act or by virtue of this subsection.

(5) Subsection (1) above shall not be taken as empowering a court on appeal to recommend for deportation a person whom the court below could not recommend for deportation, or as affecting any right of appeal in respect of a recommendation for deportation made before this Act comes into force, or as enabling a notice given before

this Act comes into force and not complying with section 6(2) to take the place of the notice required by section 6(2) to be given before a person is recommended for deportation.

(6) ...

Amendment

Sub-s (6): repealed by the Statute Law (Repeals) Act 1993.

35 Commencement, and interim provisions

(1) Except as otherwise provided by this Act, Parts I to III of this Act shall come into force on such day as the Secretary of State may appoint by order made by statutory instrument; and references to the coming into force of this Act shall be construed as references to the beginning of the day so appointed.

(2) Section 25 above, except section 25(2), and section 28 in its application to offences under section 25(1) shall come into force at the end of one month beginning with the date this Act is passed.

(3)–(5) ...

Amendment

Sub-ss (3)–(5): repealed by the Statute Law (Repeals) Act 1986.

Subordinate Legislation

Immigration Act 1971 (Commencement) Order 1972, SI 1972/1514.

36 Power to extend to Islands

Her Majesty may by Order in Council direct that any of the provisions of this Act shall extend, with such exceptions, adaptations and modifications, if any, as may be specified in the Order, to any of the Islands; and any Order in Council under this subsection may be varied or revoked by a further Order in Council.

Subordinate Legislation

Criminal Justice Act 1982 (Isle of Man) Order 1983, SI 1983/1898.
Immigration (Guernsey) Order 1993, SI 1993/1796.
Immigration (Jersey) Order 1993, SI 1993/1797.
Immigration and Asylum Act 1999 (Jersey) Order 2003, SI 2003/1252.
Immigration (Isle of Man) Order 2008, SI 2008/680.
Immigration (Isle of Man) (Amendment) Order 2011, SI 2011/1408.
Immigration and Asylum (Jersey) Order 2012, SI 2012/2593.

37 Short title and extent

(1) This Act may be cited as the Immigration Act 1971.

(2) It is hereby declared that this Act extends to Northern Ireland, and (without prejudice to any provision of Schedule 1 to this Act as to the extent of that Schedule) where an enactment repealed by this Act extends outside the United Kingdom, the repeal shall be of like extent.

SCHEDULE 1

(Repealed by the British Nationality Act 1981, s 52(8), Sch 9.)

SCHEDULE 2

ADMINISTRATIVE PROVISIONS AS TO CONTROL ON ENTRY ETC

Section 4

PART I

GENERAL PROVISIONS

Immigration officers and medical inspectors

1

(1) Immigration officers for the purposes of this Act shall be appointed by the Secretary of State, and he may arrange with the Commissioners of Customs and Excise for the employment of officers of customs and excise as immigration officers under this Act.

(2) Medical inspectors for the purposes of this Act may be appointed by the Secretary of State or, in Northern Ireland, by the Minister of Health and Social Services or other appropriate Minister of the Government of Northern Ireland in pursuance of arrangements made between that Minister and the Secretary of State, and shall be fully qualified medical practitioners.

[(2A) The Secretary of State may direct that his function of appointing medical inspectors under sub-paragraph (2) is also to be exercisable by such persons specified in the direction who exercise functions relating to health in England or Wales.]

(3) In the exercise of their functions under this Act immigration officers shall act in accordance with such instructions (not inconsistent with the immigration rules) as may be given them by the Secretary of State, and medical inspectors shall act in accordance with such instructions as may be given them by the Secretary of State or, in Northern Ireland, as may be given in pursuance of the arrangements mentioned in sub-paragraph (2) above by the Minister making appointments of medical inspectors in Northern Ireland.

(4) An immigration officer or medical inspector may board any ship [or aircraft] for the purpose of exercising his functions under this Act.

(5) An immigration officer, for the purpose of satisfying himself whether there are persons he may wish to examine under paragraph 2 below, may search any ship [or aircraft] and anything on board it, or any vehicle taken off a ship or aircraft in which it has been brought to the United Kingdom.

Examination by immigration officers, and medical examination

2

(1) An immigration officer may examine any persons who have arrived in the United Kingdom by ship [or aircraft] (including transit passengers, members of the crew and others not seeking to enter the United Kingdom) for the purpose of determining—

(a) whether any of them is or is not [a British citizen]; and

(b) whether, if he is not, he may or may not enter the United Kingdom without leave; and

[(c) whether, if he may not—

(i)   he has been given leave which is still in force,

(ii) he should be given leave and for what period or on what conditions (if any), or

(iii) he should be refused leave].

(2) Any such person, if he is seeking to enter the United Kingdom, may be examined also by a medical inspector or by any qualified person carrying out a test or examination required by a medical inspector.

(3) A person, on being examined under this paragraph by an immigration officer or medical inspector, may be required in writing by him to submit to further examination; but a requirement under this sub-paragraph shall not prevent a person who arrives as a transit passenger, or as a member of the crew of a ship or aircraft, or for the purpose of joining a ship or aircraft as a member of the crew, from leaving by his intended ship or aircraft.

[*Examination of persons who arrive with continuing leave*

2A

(1) This paragraph applies to a person who has arrived in the United Kingdom with leave to enter which is in force but which was given to him before his arrival.

(2) He may be examined by an immigration officer for the purpose of establishing—

   (a) whether there has been such a change in the circumstances of his case, since that leave was given, that it should be cancelled;

   (b) whether that leave was obtained as a result of false information given by him or his failure to disclose material facts; or

   (c) whether there are medical grounds on which that leave should be cancelled.

[(2A) Where the person's leave to enter derives, by virtue of section 3A(3), from an entry clearance, he may also be examined by an immigration officer for the purpose of establishing whether the leave should be cancelled on the grounds that the person's purpose in arriving in the United Kingdom is different from the purpose specified in the entry clearance.]

(3) He may also be examined by an immigration officer for the purpose of determining whether it would be conducive to the public good for that leave to be cancelled.

(4) He may also be examined by a medical inspector or by any qualified person carrying out a test or examination required by a medical inspector.

(5) A person examined under this paragraph may be required by the officer or inspector to submit to further examination.

(6) A requirement under sub-paragraph (5) does not prevent a person who arrives—

   (a) as a transit passenger,

   (b) as a member of the crew of a ship or aircraft, or

   (c) for the purpose of joining a ship or aircraft as a member of the crew,

from leaving by his intended ship or aircraft.

(7) An immigration officer examining a person under this paragraph may by notice suspend his leave to enter until the examination is completed.

(8) An immigration officer may, on the completion of any examination of a person under this paragraph, cancel his leave to enter.

(9) Cancellation of a person's leave under sub-paragraph (8) is to be treated for the purposes of this Act and [Part 5 of the Nationality, Immigration and Asylum Act 2002 [appeals in respect of protection and human rights claims]]] as if he had been refused leave to enter at a time when he had a current entry clearance.

(10) A requirement imposed under sub-paragraph (5) and a notice given under sub-paragraph (7) must be in writing.]

3

(1) An immigration officer [or designated person] may examine any person who is embarking or seeking to embark in the United Kingdom . . . for the purpose of determining whether he is [a British citizen] [and, if he is not a British citizen, for the purpose of establishing—

   (a) his identity;

   (b) whether he entered the United Kingdom lawfully;

(c) whether he has complied with any conditions of leave to enter or remain in the United Kingdom;

(d) whether his return to the United Kingdom is prohibited or restricted.

[(1A) If a person is examined under sub-paragraph (1) (whether by an immigration officer or designated person), an immigration officer may require the person, by notice in writing, to submit to further examination by the immigration officer for a purpose specified in that sub-paragraph.]]

(2) So long as any Order in Council is in force under section 3(7) of this Act, an immigration officer may examine any person who is embarking or seeking to embark in the United Kingdom [. . .] for the purpose of determining—

(a) whether any of the provisions of the Order apply to him; and

(b) whether, if so, any power conferred by the Order should be exercised in relation to him and in what way.

Information and documents

4

(1) It shall be the duty of any person examined under paragraph 2[, 2A] or 3 above to furnish to the person carrying out the examination all such information in his possession as that person may require for the purpose of [that or any other person's functions] under that paragraph.

(2) A person on his examination under paragraph 2[, 2A] or 3 above by an immigration officer[, or on his examination under paragraph 3 above by a designated person, shall, if so required by an immigration officer or designated person]—

(a) produce either a valid passport with photograph or some other document satisfactorily establishing his identity and nationality or citizenship; and

(b) declare whether or not he is carrying or conveying[, or has carried or conveyed,] documents of any relevant description specified by [the immigration officer or designated person], and produce any documents of that description which he is carrying or conveying.

In paragraph (b), "relevant description" means any description appearing to [the immigration officer or designated person] to be relevant for the purposes of the examination.

[(2A) . . .]

(3) Where under sub-paragraph (2)(b) above a person has been required to declare whether or not he is carrying or conveying[, or has carried or conveyed,] documents of any description—

[(a) he and any baggage or vehicle belonging to him or under his control; and

(b) any ship, aircraft or vehicle in which he arrived in the United Kingdom,]

may be searched with a view to ascertaining whether he is doing [or, as the case may be, has done] so by the [an immigration officer or a person acting under the directions of an immigration officer]:

Provided that no woman or girl shall be searched except by a woman.

[(4) Where a passport or other document is [produced to or found by an immigration officer] in accordance with this paragraph], the immigration officer] may examine it and detain it—

(a) for the purpose of examining it, for a period not exceeding 7 days;

(b) for any purpose, until the person to whom the document relates is given leave to enter the United Kingdom or is about to depart or be removed following refusal of leave or until it is decided that the person does not require leave to enter;

(c) after a time described in paragraph (b), while the immigration officer thinks that the document may be required in connection with proceedings in respect of an appeal under the Immigration Acts or in respect of an offence.

[(4A) Where a passport or other document is produced to a designated person in accordance with this paragraph, the designated person—

(a) may examine it and detain it; and

(b) must deliver any detained passport or document to an immigration officer as soon as reasonably practicable.

(4B) If a passport or document is delivered to an immigration officer in accordance with sub-paragraph (4A)(b), sub-paragraph (4) applies as if the immigration officer had detained the document (and, accordingly, the immigration officer may continue to detain it in accordance with sub-paragraph (4)(a), (b) or (c)).]

(5) For the purpose of ascertaining that a passport or other document produced or found in accordance with this paragraph relates to a person examined under paragraph 2, 2A or 3 above, the person carrying out the examination, or any immigration officer or designated person,] may require the person being examined to provide [biometric] information (whether or not by submitting to a process by means of which information is obtained or recorded) . . . .]

[(6) Biometric information" has the meaning given by section 15 of the UK Borders Act 2007.]

[(7) A person ("P") who is under 16 may not be required to provide biometric information under sub-paragraph (5) unless—

(a) the decision to require P to provide the information has been confirmed by a chief immigration officer, and

(b) the information is provided in the presence of a person of full age who is—

(i) P's parent or guardian, or

(ii) a person who for the time being takes responsibility for P.

(8) The person mentioned in sub-paragraph (7)(b)(ii) may not be—

(a) a person who is entitled to require the provision of information under sub-paragraph (5) (an "authorised person"), or

(b) an officer of the Secretary of State who is not such a person.

(9) Sub-paragraph (7) does not prevent an authorised person requiring the provision of biometric information by a person the authorised person reasonably believes to be 16 or over.]

5

The Secretary of State may by order made by statutory instrument make provision for [requiring—

(a) passengers] disembarking or embarking in the United Kingdom, or any class of such passengers, to produce to an immigration officer, if so required, landing or embarkation [cards, and

(b) passengers embarking in the United Kingdom, or any class of such passengers, to produce to a designated person, if so required, embarkation cards,

in such form] as the Secretary of State may direct, and for requiring the owners or agents of ships and aircraft to supply such cards to those passengers.

[*Designated persons*

5A

(1) In this Schedule "designated person" means a person designated by the Secretary of State for the purposes of this Schedule.

(2) A designation under this paragraph is subject to such limitations as may be specified in the designation.

(3) A limitation under sub-paragraph (2) may, in particular, relate to the functions that are exercisable by virtue of the designation (and, accordingly, the exercise of functions under this Schedule by a designated person is subject to any such limitations specified in the person's designation).

(4) A designation under this paragraph—

    (a) may be permanent or for a specified period,

    (b) may (in either case) be withdrawn, and

    (c) may be varied.

(5) The power to designate, or to withdraw or vary a designation, is exercised by the Secretary of State giving notice to the person in question.

(6) The Secretary of State may designate a person under this paragraph only if the Secretary of State is satisfied that the person—

    (a) is capable of effectively carrying out the functions that are exercisable by virtue of the designation,

    (b) has received adequate training in respect of the exercise of those functions, and

    (c) is otherwise a suitable person to exercise those functions.]

[Directions to carriers and operators of ports etc

5B

(1) The Secretary of State may direct—

    (a) an owner or agent of a ship or aircraft, or

    (b) a person concerned in the management of a port,

to make arrangements for designated persons to exercise a specified function, or a function of a specified description, in relation to persons of a specified description.

(2) A direction under this paragraph must specify—

    (a) the port where, and

    (b) the date (or dates) and time (or times) when,

a function is to be exercised under the arrangements.

(3) A direction under this paragraph must be in writing.

(4) A direction under this paragraph may specify a description of persons by reference, in particular, to—

    (a) the destination to which persons are travelling;

    (b) the route by which persons are travelling;

    (c) the date and time when the persons are travelling.

(5) In this paragraph—

    "function" means a function under this Schedule;

    "specified" means specified in a direction under this paragraph.]

Notice of leave to enter or of refusal of leave

6

(1) Subject to sub-paragraph (3) below, where a person examined by an immigration officer under paragraph 2 above is to be given a limited leave to enter the United Kingdom or is to be refused leave, the notice giving or refusing leave shall be given not later than [twenty-four hours] after the conclusion of his examination (including any further examination) in pursuance of that paragraph; and if notice giving or refusing leave is not given him before the end of those [twenty-four hours], he shall (if not [a British citizen]) be deemed to have been given [leave to enter the United Kingdom for a period of six months subject to a condition prohibiting his taking employment] and the immigration officer shall as soon as may be give him written notice of that leave.

(2) Where on a person's examination under paragraph 2 above he is given notice of leave to enter the United Kingdom, then at any time before the end of [twenty-four hours] from the conclusion of the examination he may be given a further notice in writing by an immigration officer cancelling the earlier notice and refusing him leave to enter.

(3) Where in accordance with this paragraph a person is given notice refusing him leave to enter the United Kingdom, that notice may at any time be cancelled by notice in writing given by an immigration officer; and where a person is given a notice of cancellation under this sub-paragraph, [and the immigration officer does not at the same time give him indefinite or limited leave to enter [or require him to submit to further examination], he shall be deemed to have been given leave to enter for a period of six months subject to a condition prohibiting his taking employment and the immigration officer shall as soon as may be give him written notice of that leave.]

(4) Where an entrant is a member of a party in charge of a person appearing to the immigration officer to be a responsible person, any notice to be given in relation to that entrant in accordance with this paragraph shall be duly given if delivered to the person in charge of the party.

[Power to require medical examination after entry]

7

(1) This paragraph applies if an immigration officer examining a person under paragraph 2 decides—

(a) that he may be given leave to enter the United Kingdom; but

(b) that a further medical test or examination may be required in the interests of public health.

(2) This paragraph also applies if an immigration officer examining a person under paragraph 2A decides—

(a) that his leave to enter the United Kingdom should not be cancelled; but

(b) that a further medical test or examination may be required in the interests of public health.

(3) The immigration officer may give the person concerned notice in writing requiring him—

(a) to report his arrival to such medical officer of health as may be specified in the notice; and

(b) to attend at such place and time and submit to such test or examination (if any), as that medical officer of health may require.

(4) In reaching a decision under paragraph (b) of sub-paragraph (1) or (2), the immigration officer must act on the advice of—

(a) a medical inspector; or

(b) if no medical inspector is available, a fully qualified medical practitioner.]

Removal of persons refused leave to enter and illegal entrants

8

(1) Where a person arriving in the United Kingdom is refused leave to enter, an immigration officer may, subject to sub-paragraph (2) below—

(a) give the captain of the ship or aircraft in which he arrives directions requiring the captain to remove him from the United Kingdom in that ship or aircraft; or

(b) give the owners or agents of that ship or aircraft directions requiring them to remove him from the United Kingdom in any ship or aircraft specified or indicated in the directions, being a ship or aircraft of which they are the owners or agents; or

(c) give those owners or agents [. . .] directions requiring them to make arrangements for his removal from the United Kingdom in any ship or aircraft specified or indicated in the direction to a country or territory so specified being either—

    (i) a country of which he is a national or citizen; or

    (ii) a country or territory in which he has obtained a passport or other document of identity; or

    (iii) a country or territory in which he embarked for the United Kingdom; or

    (iv) a country or territory to which there is reason to believe that he will be admitted.

(2) No directions shall be given under this paragraph in respect of anyone after the expiration of two months beginning with the date on which he was refused leave to enter the United Kingdom [(ignoring any period during which an appeal by him under the Immigration Acts is pending)] [except that directions may be given under sub-paragraph (1)(b) or (c) after the end of that period if the immigration officer has within that period given written notice to the owners or agents in question of his intention to give directions to them in respect of that person].

9

[(1)] Where an illegal entrant is not given leave to enter or remain in the United Kingdom, an immigration officer may give any such directions in respect of him as in a case within paragraph 8 above are authorised by paragraph 8(1).

[(2) Any leave to enter the United Kingdom which is obtained by deception shall be disregarded for the purposes of this paragraph.]

10

(1) Where it appears to the Secretary of State either—

    (a) that directions might be given in respect of a person under paragraph 8 or 9 above, but that it is not practicable for them to be given or that, if given, they would be ineffective; or

    (b) that directions might have been given in respect of a person under paragraph 8 above [but that the requirements of paragraph 8(2) have not been complied with];

then the Secretary of State may give to the owners or agents of any ship or aircraft any such directions in respect of that person as are authorised by paragraph 8(1)(c).

(2) Where the Secretary of State may give directions for a person's removal in accordance with sub-paragraph (1) above, he may instead give directions for his removal in accordance with arrangements to be made by the Secretary of State to any country or territory to which he could be removed under sub-paragraph (1).

(3) The costs of complying with any directions given under this paragraph shall be defrayed by the Secretary of State.

[10A

Where directions are given in respect of a person under any of paragraphs 8 to 10 above, directions to the same effect may be given under that paragraph in respect of a member of the person's family.]

11

A person in respect of whom directions are given under any of paragraphs 8 to 10 above may be placed, under the authority of an immigration officer [or the Secretary of State], on board any ship or aircraft in which he is to be removed in accordance with the directions.

Seamen and aircrews

12

(1) If, on a person's examination by an immigration officer under paragraph 2 above, the immigration officer is satisfied that he has come to the United Kingdom for the purpose of joining a ship or aircraft as a member of the crew, then the immigration officer may limit the duration of any leave he gives that person to enter the United Kingdom by requiring him to leave the United Kingdom in a ship or aircraft specified or indicated by the notice giving leave.

(2) Where a person (not being [a British citizen]) arrives in the United Kingdom for the purpose of joining a ship or aircraft as a member of a crew and, having been given leave to enter as mentioned in sub-paragraph (1) above, remains beyond the time limited by that leave, or is reasonably suspected by an immigration officer of intending to do so, an immigration officer may—

(a) give the captain of that ship or aircraft directions requiring the captain to remove him from the United Kingdom in that ship or aircraft; or

(b) give the owners or agents of that ship or aircraft directions requiring them to remove him from the United Kingdom in any ship or aircraft specified or indicated in the directions, being a ship or aircraft of which they are the owners or agents; or

(c) give those owners or agents directions requiring them to make arrangements for his removal from the United Kingdom in any ship or aircraft specified or indicated in the directions to a country or territory so specified, being either—

(i) a country of which he is a national or citizen; or

(ii) a country or territory in which he has obtained a passport or other document of identity; or

(iii) a country or territory in which he embarked for the United Kingdom; or

(iv) a country or territory where he was engaged as a member of the crew of the ship or aircraft which he arrived in the United Kingdom to join; or

(v) a country or territory to which there is reason to believe that he will be admitted.

13

(1) Where a person being a member of the crew of a ship or aircraft is examined by an immigration officer under paragraph 2 above, the immigration officer may limit the duration of any leave he gives that person to enter the United Kingdom—

(a) in the manner authorised by paragraph 12(1) above; or

(b) if that person is to be allowed to enter the United Kingdom in order to receive hospital treatment, by requiring him, on completion of that treatment, to leave the United Kingdom in accordance with arrangements to be made for his repatriation; or

(c) by requiring him to leave the United Kingdom within a specified period in accordance with arrangements to be made for his repatriation.

(2) Where a person (not being [a British citizen]) arrives in the United Kingdom as a member of the crew of a ship or aircraft, and either—

(A) having lawfully entered the United Kingdom without leave by virtue of section 8(1) of this Act, he remains without leave beyond the time allowed by section 8(1), or is reasonably suspected by an immigration officer of intending to do so; or

(B) having been given leave limited as mentioned in sub-paragraph (1) above, he remains beyond the time limited by that leave, or is reasonably suspected by an immigration officer of intending to do so;

an immigration officer may—

(a) give the captain of the ship or aircraft in which he arrived directions requiring the captain to remove him from the United Kingdom in that ship or aircraft; or

(b) give the owners or agents of that ship or aircraft directions requiring them to remove him from the United Kingdom, being a ship or aircraft specified or indicated in the directions, being a ship or aircraft of which they are the owners or agents; or

(c) give those owners or agents directions requiring them to make arrangements for his removal from the United Kingdom in any ship or aircraft specified or indicated in the directions to a country or territory so specified, being either—

(i) a country of which he is a national or citizen; or

(ii) a country or territory in which he has obtained a passport or other document of identity; or

(iii) a country in which he embarked for the United Kingdom; or

(iv) a country or territory in which he was engaged as a member of the crew of the ship or aircraft in which he arrived in the United Kingdom; or

(v) a country or territory to which there is reason to believe that he will be admitted.

14

(1) Where it appears to the Secretary of State that directions might be given in respect of a person under paragraph 12 or 13 above, but that it is not practicable for them to be given or that, if given, they would be ineffective, then the Secretary of State may give to the owners or agents of any ship or aircraft any such directions in respect of that person as are authorised by paragraph 12(2)(c) or 13(2)(c).

(2) Where the Secretary of State may give directions for a person's removal in accordance with sub-paragraph (1) above, he may instead give directions for his removal in accordance with arrangements to be made by the Secretary of State to any country or territory to which he could be removed under sub-paragraph (1).

(3) The costs of complying with any directions given under this paragraph shall be defrayed by the Secretary of State.

15

A person in respect of whom directions are given under any of paragraphs 12 to 14 above may be placed, under the authority of an immigration officer, on board any ship or aircraft in which he is to be removed in accordance with the directions.

Detention of persons liable to examination or removal

16

(1) A person who may be required to submit to examination under paragraph 2 above may be detained under the authority of an immigration officer pending his examination and pending a decision to give or refuse him leave to enter.

[(1A) A person whose leave to enter has been suspended under paragraph 2A may be detained under the authority of an immigration officer pending—

(a) completion of his examination under that paragraph; and

(b) a decision on whether to cancel his leave to enter.]

[(1B) A person who has been required to submit to further examination under paragraph 3(1A) may be detained under the authority of an immigration officer, for a period not exceeding 12 hours, pending the completion of the examination.]

[(2) If there are reasonable grounds for suspecting that a person is someone in respect of whom directions may be given under any of paragraphs [8 to 10A] or 12 to 14, that person may be detained under the authority of an immigration officer pending—

(a)   a decision whether or not to give such directions;

(b)   his removal in pursuance of such directions.]

[(2A)   But the detention of an unaccompanied child under sub-paragraph (2) is subject to paragraph 18B.]

(3)   A person on board a ship or aircraft may, under the authority of an immigration officer, be removed from the ship or aircraft under this paragraph; but if an immigration officer so requires the captain of a ship or aircraft shall prevent from disembarking in the United Kingdom any person who has arrived in the United Kingdom in the ship or aircraft and been refused leave to enter, and the captain may for that purpose detain him in custody on board the ship or aircraft.

(4)   The captain of a ship or aircraft, if so required by an immigration officer, shall prevent from disembarking in the United Kingdom or before the directions for his removal have been fulfilled any person placed on board the ship or aircraft under paragraph 11 or 15 above, and the captain may for that purpose detain him in custody on board the ship or aircraft.

[(4A)   . . .]

17

(1)   A person liable to be detained under paragraph 16 above may be arrested without warrant by a constable or by an immigration officer.

(2)   If—

(a)   a justice of the peace is by written information on oath satisfied that there is reasonable ground for suspecting that a person liable to be arrested under this paragraph is to be found on any premises; or

(b)   in Scotland, a sheriff, or a . . . justice of the peace, having jurisdiction in the place where the premises are situated is by evidence on oath so satisfied;

he may grant a warrant [authorising any immigration officer or constable to enter,] [if need be by reasonable force], the premises named in the warrant for the purposes of searching for and arresting that person.

[(3)   Sub-paragraph (4) applies where an immigration officer or constable—

(a)   enters premises in reliance on a warrant under sub-paragraph (2), and

(b)   detains a person on the premises.

(4)   A detainee custody officer may enter the premises, if need be by reasonable force, for the purpose of carrying out a search.

(5)   In sub-paragraph (4)—

"detainee custody officer" means a person in respect of whom a certificate of authorisation is in force under section 154 of the Immigration and Asylum Act 1999 (c 33) (detained persons: escort and custody), and

"search" means a search under paragraph 2(1)(a) of Schedule 13 to that Act (escort arrangements: power to search detained person).]

18

(1)   Persons may be detained under paragraph 16 above in such places as the Secretary of State may direct (when not detained in accordance with paragraph 16 on board a ship or aircraft).

[(1A)   But the detention of an unaccompanied child under paragraph 16(2) is subject to paragraph 18B.]

(2)   Where a person is detained [or liable to be detained] under paragraph 16, any immigration officer, constable or prison officer, or any other person authorised by the Secretary of State, may take all such steps as may be reasonably necessary for photographing, measuring or otherwise identifying him.

[(2A) The power conferred by sub-paragraph (2) includes power to take [biometric information (within the meaning given by section 15 of the UK Borders Act 2007)].]

[(2B) Paragraph 4(7) to (9) applies to sub-paragraph (2) as it applies to paragraph 4(5).]

(3) Any person detained under paragraph 16 may be taken in the custody of a constable, [an immigration officer, or] any person acting under the authority of an immigration officer, to and from any place where his attendance is required for the purpose of ascertaining his citizenship or nationality or of making arrangements for his admission to a country or territory other than the United Kingdom, or where he is required to be for any other purpose connected with the operation of this Act.

(4) A person shall be deemed to be in legal custody at any time when he is detained under paragraph 16 or is being removed in pursuance of sub-paragraph (3) above.

[18A

(1) An immigration officer or constable may search a person ("P") who is detained under paragraph 16 for anything which P might use—

(a) to cause physical injury to P or others, or

(b) to assist P's escape from legal custody.

(2) The power to search P—

(a) unless sub-paragraph (3) applies, does not include power to require P to remove any clothing other than an outer coat, jacket or glove, but

(b) includes power to require P to open P's mouth.

(3) This sub-paragraph applies if an immigration officer or constable has reasonable grounds to believe that there is concealed on P anything which P might use as mentioned in sub-paragraph (1).

(4) The power to search P may be exercised only to the extent reasonably required for the purpose of discovering anything which P might use as mentioned in sub-paragraph (1).

(5) An intimate search (as defined in section 28H(11)) may not be conducted under this paragraph.

(6) An immigration officer or constable may seize and retain anything found on a search of P if the officer or constable has reasonable grounds to believe P might use it as mentioned in sub-paragraph (1).

(7) Nothing seized under sub-paragraph (6) may be retained when P is released from detention under paragraph 16.]

[18B

(1) Where a person detained under paragraph 16(2) is an unaccompanied child, the only place where the child may be detained is a short-term holding facility, except where—

(a) the child is being transferred to or from a short-term holding facility, or

(b) sub-paragraph (3) of paragraph 18 applies.

(2) An unaccompanied child may be detained under paragraph 16(2) in a short-term holding facility for a maximum period of 24 hours, and only for so long as the following two conditions are met.

(3) The first condition is that—

(a) directions are in force that require the child to be removed from the short-term holding facility within the relevant 24 hour period, or

(b) a decision on whether or not to give directions is likely to result in such directions.

(4) The second condition is that the immigration officer under whose authority the child is being detained reasonably believes that the child will be removed from the short-term holding facility within the relevant 24 hour period in accordance with those directions.

(5) An unaccompanied child detained under paragraph 16(2) who has been removed from a short-term holding facility and detained elsewhere may be detained again in a short-term holding facility but only if, and for as long as, the relevant 24 hour period has not ended.

(6) An unaccompanied child who has been released following detention under paragraph 16(2) may be detained again in a short-term holding facility in accordance with this paragraph.

(7) In this paragraph—

"relevant 24 hour period", in relation to the detention of a child in a short-term holding facility, means the period of 24 hours starting when the child was detained (or, in a case falling within sub-paragraph (5), first detained) in a short-term holding facility;

"short-term holding facility" has the same meaning as in Part 8 of the Immigration and Asylum Act 1999;

"unaccompanied child" means a person—

   (a) who is under the age of 18, and

   (b) who is not accompanied (whilst in detention) by his or her parent or another individual who has care of him or her.]

19

(1) Where a person is refused leave to enter the United Kingdom and directions are given in respect of him under paragraph 8 or 10 above, then subject to the provisions of this paragraph the owners or agents of the ship or aircraft in which he arrived [...] shall be liable to pay the Secretary of State on demand any expenses incurred by the latter in respect of the custody, accommodation or maintenance of that person [for any period (not exceeding 14 days)] after his arrival while he was detained or liable to be detained under paragraph 16 above.

(2) Sub-paragraph (1) above shall not apply to expenses in respect of a person who, when he arrived in the United Kingdom, held a [current work permit; and for this purpose a document purporting to be a [certificate of entitlement] or a current entry clearance or was the person named in a [certificate of entitlement], entry clearance or work permit is to be regarded as being one unless its falsity is reasonably apparent.

(3) If, before the directions for a person's removal under paragraph 8 or 10 above have been carried out, he is given leave to enter the United Kingdom, or if he is afterwards given that leave in consequence of the determination in his favour of an appeal under this Act (being an appeal against a refusal of leave to enter by virtue of an which the directions were given), or it is determined on an appeal under this Act that he does not require leave to enter (being an appeal occasioned by such a refusal), no sum shall be demanded under sub-paragraph (1) above for expenses incurred in respect of that person and any sum already demanded and paid shall be refunded.

(4) Sub-paragraph (1) above shall not have effect in relation to directions which, in consequence of an appeal under this Act, have ceased to have effect or are for the time being of no effect; and the expenses to which that sub-paragraph applies include expenses in conveying the person in question to and from the place where he is detained or accommodated unless the journey is made for the purpose of attending an appeal by him under this Act.

20

(1) Subject to the provisions of this paragraph, in either of the following cases, that is to say,—

   (a) where directions are given in respect of an illegal entrant under paragraph 9 or 10 above; and

   (b) where a person has lawfully entered the United Kingdom without leave by virtue of section 8(1) of this Act, but directions are given in respect of him under paragraph 13(2)(A) above or, in a case within paragraph 13(2)(A), under paragraph 14;

the owners or agents of the ship or aircraft in which he arrived in the United Kingdom [. . .] shall be liable to pay the Secretary of State on demand any expenses incurred by the latter in respect of the custody, accommodation or maintenance of that person [for any period (not exceeding 14 days)] after his arrival while he was detained or liable to be detained under paragraph 16 above.

[(1A) Sub-paragraph (1) above shall not apply to expenses in respect of an illegal entrant if he obtained leave to enter by deception and the leave has not been cancelled under paragraph 6(2) above.]

(2) If, before the directions for a person's removal from the United Kingdom have been carried out, he is given leave to remain in the United Kingdom, no sum shall be demanded under sub-paragraph (1) above for expenses incurred in respect of that person and any sum already demanded and paid shall be refunded.

(3) Sub-paragraph (1) above shall not have effect in relation to directions which, in consequence of an appeal under this Act, are for the time being of no effect; and the expenses to which that sub-paragraph applies include expenses in conveying the person in question to and from the place where he is detained or accommodated unless the journey is made for the purpose of attending an appeal by him under this Act.

Temporary admission or release of persons liable to detention

21

(1) A person liable to detention or detained under paragraph 16[(1), (1A) or (2)] above may, under the written authority of an immigration officer, be temporarily admitted to the United Kingdom without being detained or be released from detention; but this shall not prejudice a later exercise of the power to detain him.

(2) So long as a person is at large in the United Kingdom by virtue of this paragraph, he shall be subject to such restrictions as to residence[, as to his employment or occupation] and as to reporting to the police or an immigration officer as may from time to time be notified to him in writing by an immigration officer.

[(2A) The provisions that may be included in restrictions as to residence imposed under sub-paragraph (2) include provisions of such a description as may be prescribed by regulations made by the Secretary of State.

(2B) The regulations may, among other things, provide for the inclusion of provisions—

    (a)   prohibiting residence in one or more particular areas;

    (b)   requiring the person concerned to reside in accommodation provided under section 4 of the Immigration and Asylum Act 1999 and prohibiting him from being absent from that accommodation except in accordance with the restrictions imposed on him.

(2C) The regulations may provide that a particular description of provision may be imposed only for prescribed purposes.

(2D) The power to make regulations conferred by this paragraph is exercisable by statutory instrument and includes a power to make different provision for different cases.

(2E) But no regulations under this paragraph are to be made unless a draft of the regulations has been laid before Parliament and approved by a resolution of each House.]

[(3) Sub-paragraph (4) below applies where a person who is at large in the United Kingdom by virtue of this paragraph is subject to a restriction as to reporting to an immigration officer with a view to the conclusion of his examination under paragraph 2 [or 2A] above.

(4) If the person fails at any time to comply with that restriction—

    (a)   an immigration officer may direct that the person's examination . . . shall be treated as concluded at that time; but

(b)   nothing in paragraph 6 above shall require the notice giving or refusing him leave to enter the United Kingdom to be given within twenty-four hours after that time.]

22

[(1)   The following, namely—

(a)   a person detained under paragraph 16(1) above pending examination;

[(aa)   a person detained under paragraph 16(1A) above pending completion of his examination or a decision on whether to cancel his leave to enter;] and

(b)   a person detained under paragraph 16(2) above pending the giving of directions,

may be released on bail in accordance with this paragraph.

(1A)   An immigration officer not below the rank of chief immigration officer or [the First-tier Tribunal] may release a person so detained on his entering into a recognizance or, in Scotland, bail bond conditioned for his appearance before an immigration officer at a time and place named in the recognizance or bail bond or at such other time and place as may in the meantime be notified to him in writing by an immigration officer.

(1B)   Sub-paragraph (1)(a) above shall not apply unless seven days have elapsed since the date of the person's arrival in the United Kingdom.]

(2)   The conditions of a recognizance or bail bond taken under this paragraph may include conditions appearing to the [immigration officer or [the First-tier Tribunal]] to be likely to result in the appearance of the person bailed at the required time and place; and any recognizance shall be with or without sureties as the [immigration officer or [the First-tier Tribunal]] may determine.

(3)   In any case in which an [immigration officer or [the First-tier Tribunal]] has power under this paragraph to release a person on bail, the [officer or [the First-tier Tribunal]] may, instead of taking the bail, fix the amount and conditions of the bail (including the amount in which any sureties are to be bound) with a view to its being taken subsequently by any such person as may be specified by [the First-tier Tribunal]; and on the recognizance or bail bond being so taken the person to be bailed shall be released.

[(4)   A person must not be released on bail in accordance with this paragraph without the consent of the Secretary of State if—

(a)   directions for the removal of the person from the United Kingdom are for the time being in force, and

(b)   the directions require the person to be removed from the United Kingdom within the period of 14 days starting with the date of the decision on whether the person should be released on bail.]

23

(1)   Where a recognizance entered into under paragraph 22 above appears to [the First-tier Tribunal] to be forfeited, [the First-tier Tribunal] may by order declare it to be forfeited and adjudge the persons bound thereby, whether as principal or sureties, or any of them, to pay the sum in which they are respectively bound or such part of it, if any, as [the First-tier Tribunal] thinks fit; and an order under this sub-paragraph shall specify a magistrates' court or, in Northern Ireland court of summary jurisdiction, and—

(a)   the recognizance shall be treated for the purposes of collection, enforcement and remission of the sum forfeited as having been forfeited by the court so specified; and

(b)   [the First-tier Tribunal] shall, as soon as practicable, give particulars of the recognizance to the [proper officer] of that court.

[(1A)   In sub-paragraph (1) "proper officer" means—

(a) in relation to a magistrates' court in England and Wales, the [designated officer] for the court; and

(b) in relation to a court of summary jurisdiction in Northern Ireland, the clerk of the court.]

(2) Where a person released on bail under paragraph 22 above as it applies in Scotland fails to comply with the terms of his bail bond, [the First-tier Tribunal] may declare the bail to be forfeited, and any bail so forfeited shall be transmitted by [the First-tier Tribunal] to the sheriff court having jurisdiction in the area where the proceedings took place, and shall be treated as having been forfeited by that court.

(3) Any sum the payment of which is enforceable by a magistrates' court in England and Wales by virtue of this paragraph shall be treated for the [purposes of section 38 of the Courts Act 2003 (application of receipts of designated officers) as being] due under a recognizance forfeited by such a court . . .

(4) Any sum the payment of which is enforceable by virtue of this paragraph by a court of summary jurisdiction in Northern Ireland shall, for the purposes of section 20(5) of the Administration of Justice Act (Northern Ireland) 1954, be treated as a forfeited recognizance.

24

(1) An immigration officer or constable may arrest without warrant a person who has been released by virtue of paragraph 22 above—

(a) if he has reasonable grounds for believing that that person is likely to break the condition of his recognizance or bail bond that he will appear at the time and place required or to break any other condition of it, or has reasonable grounds to suspect that that person is breaking or has broken any such other condition; or

(b) if, a recognizance with sureties having been taken, he is notified in writing by any sureties of the surety's belief that that person is likely to break the first-mentioned condition, and of the surety's wish for that reason to be relieved of his obligation as a surety;

and paragraph 17(2) above shall apply for the arrest of a person under this paragraph as it applies for the arrest of a person under paragraph 17.

(2) A person arrested under this paragraph—

(a) if not required by a condition on which he was released to appear before an immigration officer within twenty-four hours after the time of his arrest, shall as soon as practicable be brought before [the First-tier Tribunal] or, if that is not practicable within those twenty-four hours, before [in England and Wales, a justice of the peace, in Northern Ireland,] a justice of the peace acting for the petty sessions area in which he is arrested or, in Scotland, the sheriff; and

(b) if required by such a condition to appear within those twenty-four hours before an immigration officer, shall be brought before that officer.

(3) [Where a person is brought before [the First-tier Tribunal], a justice of the peace or the sheriff by virtue of sub-paragraph (2)](a), the Tribunal, justice of the peace or sheriff]—

(a) if of the opinion that that person has broken or is likely to break any condition on which he was released, may either—

(i) direct that he be detained under the authority of the person by whom he was arrested; or

(ii) release him, on his original recognizance or on a new recognizance, with or without sureties, or, in Scotland, on his original bail or on new bail; and

(b) if not of that opinion, shall release him on his original recognizance or bail.

[25

[(1)] Tribunal Procedure Rules [must] make provision with respect to applications to the First-tier Tribunal under paragraphs 22 to 24 and matters arising out of such applications.

[(2) Tribunal Procedure Rules must secure that, where the First-tier Tribunal has decided not to release a person on bail under paragraph 22, the Tribunal is required to dismiss without a hearing any further application by the person for release on bail (whether under paragraph 22 or otherwise) that is made during the period of 28 days starting with the date of the Tribunal's decision, unless the person demonstrates to the Tribunal that there has been a material change in circumstances.]]

[Entry and search of premises]

25A

(1)   This paragraph applies if—

   (a)   a person is arrested under this Schedule; or

   (b)   a person who was arrested [other than under this Schedule] is detained by an immigration officer under this Schedule.

(2)   An immigration officer may enter and search any premises—

   (a)   occupied or controlled by the arrested person, or

   (b)   in which that person was when he was arrested, or immediately before he was arrested,

for relevant documents.

(3)   The power may be exercised—

   (a)   only if the officer has reasonable grounds for believing that there are relevant documents on the premises;

   (b)   only to the extent that it is reasonably required for the purpose of discovering relevant documents; and

   (c)   subject to sub-paragraph (4), only if a senior officer has authorised its exercise in writing.

(4)   An immigration officer may conduct a search under sub-paragraph (2)—

   (a)   before taking the arrested person to a place where he is to be detained; and

   (b)   without obtaining an authorisation under sub-paragraph (3)(c),

if the presence of that person at a place other than one where he is to be detained is necessary to make an effective search for any relevant documents.

(5)   An officer who has conducted a search under sub-paragraph (4) must inform a senior officer as soon as is practicable.

(6)   The officer authorising a search, or who is informed of one under sub-paragraph (5), must make a record in writing of—

   (a)   the grounds for the search; and

   (b)   the nature of the documents that were sought.

[(6A)   If, on an application made by an immigration officer, a justice of the peace is satisfied that—

   (a)   there are reasonable grounds for believing that relevant documents may be found on premises not within sub-paragraph (2) which are specified in the application, and

   (b)   any of the conditions in sub-paragraph (6B) is met,

the justice of the peace may issue a warrant authorising an immigration officer to enter and search the premises.

(6B)   The conditions are that—

   (a)   it is not practicable to communicate with any person entitled to grant entry to the premises;

(b) it is practicable to communicate with a person entitled to grant entry to the premises but it is not practicable to communicate with any person entitled to grant access to the relevant documents;

(c) entry to the premises will not be granted unless a warrant is produced;

(d) the purpose of a search may be frustrated or seriously prejudiced unless an immigration officer arriving at the premises can secure immediate entry.

(6C) In the application of sub-paragraph (6A) to Scotland, references to a justice of the peace are to be treated as references to the sheriff or a justice of the peace.]

(7) An officer searching premises under [this paragraph]—

(a) may seize . . . any documents which he finds which he has reasonable grounds for believing are relevant documents; . . .

(b) . . .

(8) But sub-paragraph (7)(a) does not apply to documents which the officer has reasonable grounds for believing are items subject to legal privilege.

[(8A) An immigration officer may retain a document seized under sub-paragraph (7) while the officer has reasonable grounds for believing that—

(a) the arrested person may be liable to removal from the United Kingdom in accordance with a provision of the Immigration Acts, and

(b) retention of the document may facilitate the person's removal.]

(9) "Relevant documents" means any documents which might—

(a) establish the arrested person's identity, nationality or citizenship; or

(b) indicate the place from which he has travelled to the United Kingdom or to which he is proposing to go.

(10) "Senior officer" means an immigration officer not below the rank of chief immigration officer.]

[Searching persons arrested by immigration officers

25B

(1) This paragraph applies if a person is arrested under this Schedule.

(2) An immigration officer may search the arrested person if he has reasonable grounds for believing that the arrested person may present a danger to himself or others.

(3) The officer may search the arrested person for—

(a) anything which he might use to assist his escape from lawful custody; or

(b) any document which might—

(i) establish his identity, nationality or citizenship; or

(ii) indicate the place from which he has travelled to the United Kingdom or to which he is proposing to go.

(4) The power conferred by sub-paragraph (3) may be exercised—

(a) only if the officer has reasonable grounds for believing that the arrested person may have concealed on him anything of a kind mentioned in that sub-paragraph; and

(b) only to the extent that it is reasonably required for the purpose of discovering any such thing.

(5) A power conferred by this paragraph to search a person is not to be read as authorising an officer to require a person to remove any of his clothing in public other than an outer coat, jacket or glove; but it does authorise the search of a person's mouth.

(6) An officer searching a person under sub-paragraph (2) may seize and retain anything he finds, if he has reasonable grounds for believing that the person searched might use it to cause physical injury to himself or to another person.

(7) An officer searching a person under sub-paragraph (3)(a) may seize and retain anything he finds, if he has reasonable grounds for believing that he might use it to assist his escape from lawful custody.

(8) An officer searching a person under sub-paragraph (3)(b) may seize and retain anything he finds, other than an item subject to legal privilege, if he has reasonable grounds for believing that it might be a document falling within that sub-paragraph.

(9) Nothing seized under sub-paragraph (6) or (7) may be retained when the person from whom it was seized—

   (a) is no longer in custody, or

   (b) is in the custody of a court but has been released on bail.]

[Searching persons in police custody]

25C

(1) This paragraph applies if a person—

   (a) has been arrested under this Schedule; and

   (b) is in custody at a police station.

(2) An immigration officer may, at any time, search the arrested person in order to ascertain whether he has with him—

   (a) anything which he might use to—

      (i) cause physical injury to himself or others;

      (ii) damage property;

      (iii) interfere with evidence; or

      (iv) assist his escape; or

   (b) any document which might—

      (i) establish his identity, nationality or citizenship; or

      (ii) indicate the place from which he has travelled to the United Kingdom or to which he is proposing to go.

(3) The power may be exercised only to the extent that the officer considers it to be necessary for the purpose of discovering anything of a kind mentioned in sub-paragraph (2).

(4) An officer searching a person under this paragraph may seize and retain anything he finds, if he has reasonable grounds for believing that—

   (a) that person might use it for one or more of the purposes mentioned in sub-paragraph (2)(a); or

   (b) it might be a document falling within sub-paragraph (2)(b).

(5) But the officer may not retain anything seized under sub-paragraph (2)(a)—

   (a) for longer than is necessary in view of the purpose for which the search was carried out; or

   (b) when the person from whom it was seized is no longer in custody or is in the custody of a court but has been released on bail.

(6) The person from whom something is seized must be told the reason for the seizure unless he is—

   (a) violent or appears likely to become violent; or

   (b) incapable of understanding what is said to him.

(7) An intimate search may not be conducted under this paragraph.

(8) The person carrying out a search under this paragraph must be of the same sex as the person searched.

(9) "Intimate search" has the same meaning as in section 28H(11).]

[Access and copying]

25D

(1) If a person showing himself—

    (a) to be the occupier of the premises on which seized material was seized, or

    (b) to have had custody or control of the material immediately before it was seized,

asks the immigration officer who seized the material for a record of what he seized, the officer must provide the record to that person within a reasonable time.

(2) If a relevant person asks an immigration officer for permission to be granted access to seized material, the officer must arrange for that person to have access to the material under the supervision of an immigration officer.

(3) An immigration officer may photograph or copy, or have photographed or copied, seized material.

(4) If a relevant person asks an immigration officer for a photograph or copy of seized material, the officer must arrange for—

    (a) that person to have access to the material under the supervision of an immigration officer for the purpose of photographing or copying it; or

    (b) the material to be photographed or copied.

(5) A photograph or copy made under sub-paragraph (4)(b) must be supplied within a reasonable time.

(6) There is no duty under this paragraph to arrange for access to, or the supply of a photograph or copy of, any material if there are reasonable grounds for believing that to do so would prejudice—

    (a) the exercise of any functions in connection with which the material was seized; or

    (b) an investigation which is being conducted under this Act, or any criminal proceedings which may be brought as a result.

(7) "Relevant person" means—

    (a) a person who had custody or control of seized material immediately before it was seized, or

    (b) someone acting on behalf of such a person.

(8) "Seized material" means anything which has been seized and retained under this Schedule.]

[**25E**

Section 28L applies for the purposes of this Schedule as it applies for the purposes of Part III.]

Supplementary duties of those connected with ships or aircraft or with ports

26

(1) The owners or agents of a ship or aircraft employed to carry passengers for reward shall not, without the approval of the Secretary of State, arrange for the ship or aircraft to call at a port in the United Kingdom other than a port of entry for the purpose of disembarking passengers, if any of the passengers on board may not enter the United Kingdom without leave . . ., or for the purpose of embarking passengers unless the owners or agents have reasonable cause to believe all of them to be [British citizens].

[(1A) Sub-paragraph (1) does not apply in such circumstances, if any, as the Secretary of State may by order prescribe.]

(2) The Secretary of State may from time to time give written notice to the owners or agents of any ships or aircraft designating control areas for the embarkation or disembarkation of passengers in any port in the United Kingdom and specifying the

27

(1) The captain of a ship or aircraft arriving in the United Kingdom—

  (a) shall take such steps as may be necessary to secure that persons on board do not disembark there unless either they have been examined by an immigration officer, or they disembark in accordance with arrangements approved by an immigration officer, or they are members of the crew who may lawfully enter the United Kingdom without leave by virtue of section 8(1) of this Act; and

  (b) where the examination of persons on board is to be carried out on the ship or aircraft, shall take such steps as may be necessary to secure that those to be examined are presented for the purpose in an orderly manner.

[(2) The Secretary of State may by order require, or enable an immigration officer to require, a responsible person in respect of a ship or aircraft to supply—

  (a) a passenger list showing the names and nationality or citizenship of passengers arriving or leaving on board the ship or aircraft;

  (b) particulars of members of the crew of the ship or aircraft.

(3) An order under sub-paragraph (2) may relate—

  (a) to all ships or aircraft arriving or expected to arrive in the United Kingdom;

  (b) to all ships or aircraft leaving or expected to leave the United Kingdom;

  (c) to ships or aircraft arriving or expected to arrive in the United Kingdom from or by way of a specified country;

  (d) to ships or aircraft leaving or expected to leave the United Kingdom to travel to or by way of a specified country;

  (e) to specified ships or specified aircraft.

(4) For the purposes of sub-paragraph (2) the following are responsible persons in respect of a ship or aircraft—

  (a) the owner or agent, and

  (b) the captain.

(5) An order under sub-paragraph (2)—

  (a) may specify the time at which or period during which information is to be provided,

  (b) may specify the form and manner in which information is to be provided,

  (c) shall be made by statutory instrument, and

  (d) shall be subject to annulment in pursuance of a resolution of either House of Parliament.]

[27A

. . .]

conditions and restrictions (if any) to be observed in any control area; and where by notice given to any owners or agents a control area is for the time being designated for the embarkation or disembarkation of passengers at any port, the owners or agents shall take all reasonable steps to secure that, in the case of their ships or aircraft, passengers do not embark or disembark, as the case may be, at the port outside the control area and that any conditions or restrictions notified to them are observed.

(3) The Secretary of State may also from time to time give to any persons concerned with the management of a port in the United Kingdom written notice designating control areas in the port and specifying conditions or restrictions to be observed in any control area; and any such person shall take all reasonable steps to secure that any conditions or restrictions as notified to him are observed.

[(3A) The power conferred by sub-paragraph (1A) is exercisable by statutory instrument; and any such instrument shall be subject to annulment by a resolution of either House of Parliament.]

[Passenger information [or service information]

27B

(1) This paragraph applies to ships or aircraft—

   (a) which have arrived, or are expected to arrive, in the United Kingdom; or

   (b) which have left, or are expected to leave, the United Kingdom.

(2) If an immigration officer asks the owner or agent ("the carrier") of a ship or aircraft for passenger information [or service information], the carrier must provide that information to the officer.

(3) The officer may ask for passenger information [or service information] relating to—

   (a) a particular ship or particular aircraft of the carrier;

   (b) particular ships or aircraft (however described) of the carrier; or

   (c) all of the carrier's ships or aircraft.

(4) The officer may ask for—

   (a) all passenger information [or service information] in relation to the ship or aircraft concerned; or

   (b) particular passenger information [or service information] in relation to that ship or aircraft.

[(4A) The officer may ask the carrier to provide a copy of all or part of a document that relates to a passenger and contains passenger information [or service information].]

(5) A request under sub-paragraph (2)—

   (a) must be in writing;

   (b) must state the date on which it ceases to have effect; and

   (c) continues in force until that date, unless withdrawn earlier by written notice by an immigration officer.

(6) The date may not be later than six months after the request is made.

(7) The fact that a request under sub-paragraph (2) has ceased to have effect as a result of sub-paragraph (5) does not prevent the request from being renewed.

(8) The information must be provided—

   (a) in such form and manner as the Secretary of State may direct; and

   (b) at such time as may be stated in the request.

(9) "Passenger information" means such information relating to the passengers carried, or expected to be carried, by the ship or aircraft as may be specified.

[(9A) "Service information" means such information relating to the voyage or flight undertaken by the ship or aircraft as may be specified.]

(10) "Specified" means specified in an order made by statutory instrument by the Secretary of State.

(11) Such an instrument shall be subject to annulment in pursuance of a resolution of either House of Parliament.]

[Notification of non-EEA arrivals

27C

(1) If a senior officer, or an immigration officer authorised by a senior officer, gives written notice to the owner or agent ("the carrier") of a ship or aircraft, the carrier must inform a relevant officer of the expected arrival in the United Kingdom of any ship or aircraft—

   (a) of which he is the owner or agent; and

   (b) which he expects to carry a person who is not an EEA national.

(2) The notice may relate to—

   (a) a particular ship or particular aircraft of the carrier;

(b)   particular ships or aircraft (however described) of the carrier; or

(c)   all of the carrier's ships or aircraft.

(3)   The notice—

(a)   must state the date on which it ceases to have effect; and

(b)   continues in force until that date, unless withdrawn earlier by written notice given by a senior officer.

(4)   The date may not be later than six months after the notice is given.

(5)   The fact that a notice under sub-paragraph (1) has ceased to have effect as a result of sub-paragraph (3) does not prevent the notice from being renewed.

(6)   The information must be provided—

(a)   in such form and manner as the notice may require; and

(b)   before the ship or aircraft concerned departs for the United Kingdom.

(7)   If a ship or aircraft travelling to the United Kingdom stops at one or more places before arriving in the United Kingdom, it is to be treated as departing for the United Kingdom when it leaves the last of those places.

(8)   "Senior officer" means an immigration officer not below the rank of chief immigration officer.

(9)   "Relevant officer" means—

(a)   the officer who gave the notice under sub-paragraph (1); or

(b)   any immigration officer at the port at which the ship or aircraft concerned is expected to arrive.

(10)   "EEA national" means a national of a State which is a Contracting Party to the Agreement on the European Economic Area signed at Oporto on 2nd May 1992 as it has effect for the time being.]

Amendment

Para 1: sub-para (2A) inserted by the Health Protection Agency Act 2004, s 11(1), Sch 3, para 3.

Para 1: in sub-paras (4), (5) words in square brackets substituted by SI 1993/1813, art 8, Sch 5, Pt I, para 1(a).

Para 2: in sub-para (1)(a) words in square brackets substituted by the British Nationality Act 1981, s 39(6), Sch 4, para 2 and SI 1993/1813, art 8, Sch 5, Pt I, para 1(b).

Para 2: sub-para (1)(c) substituted by the Immigration and Asylum Act 1999, s 169(1), Sch 14, paras 43, 56.

Para 2A: inserted by the Immigration and Asylum Act 1999, s 169(1), Sch 14, paras 43, 57.

Para 2A: sub-para (2A) inserted by the Asylum and Immigration (Treatment of Claimants, etc) Act 2004, s 18.

Para 2A: in sub-para (9) words in outer pair of square brackets substituted by the Nationality, Immigration and Asylum Act 2002, s 114(3), Sch 7, para 2.

Para 2A: in sub-para (9) words in inner pair of square brackets substituted (for original words "(immigration and asylum appeals)" by the Immigration Act 2014, s 73, Sch 9, Pt 4, paras 20, 23, as from 20 October 2014 (see SI 2014/2771, art 2), subject to savings in SI 2014/2771, arts 9–11.

Para 3: in sub-para (1) words omitted inserted by SI 1990/2227, art 3, Sch 1, Pt I, para 8 and repealed by SI 1993/1813, art 9, Sch 6, Pt I.

Para 3: in sub-para (1) words "a British citizen" in square brackets substituted by the British Nationality Act 1981, s 39(6), Sch 4, para 2.

Para 3: in sub-para (1) words "or designated person" inserted by the Immigration Act 2014, s 67, Sch 8, paras 1, 2(1), (2), as from 28 July 2014: see SI 2014/1820.

Para 3: in sub-para (1) words from "and, if he" to "prohibited or restricted." in square brackets and sub-para (1A) substituted by the Immigration, Asylum and Nationality Act 2006, s 42(1), (2).

Para 3: in sub-para (1A) inserted by the Immigration Act 2014, s 67, Sch 8, paras 1, 2(1), (3), as from 28 July 2014: see SI 2014/1820.

Para 4: in sub-para (1) reference to ", 2A" in square brackets inserted by the Immigration and Asylum Act 1999, s 169(1), Sch 14, paras 43, 58; words in square brackets in sub-para (1) substituted by the Immigration Act 2014, s 67, Sch 8, paras 1, 3(1), (2), as from 28 July 2014: see SI 2014/1820.

Para 4: in sub-para (2) reference to ", 2A" in square brackets inserted by the Immigration and Asylum Act 1999, s 169(1), Sch 14, paras 43, 58.

Para 4: in sub-para (2)(b) words " or has carried or conveyed," in square brackets inserted by the Asylum and Immigration Act 1996, s 12(1), Sch 2, para 5(1); other words in square brackets in sub-para (2) substituted by the Immigration Act 2014, s 67, Sch 8, paras 1, 3(1), (3), as from 28 July 2014: see SI 2014/1820.

Para 4: sub-para (2A) inserted by the Immigration Act 1988, s 10, Schedule, paras 6, 10 and repealed by the Immigration, Asylum and Nationality Act 2006, ss 27(2), 61, Sch 3.

Para 4: in sub-para (3) words "or has carried or conveyed" in square brackets inserted by the Asylum and Immigration Act 1996, s 12(1), Sch 2, para 5(2)(a).

Para 4: sub-para (3)(a), (b) substituted by the Asylum and Immigration Act 1996, s 12(1), Sch 2, para 5(2)(b).

Para 4: in sub-para (3) words "or, as the case may be, has done" in square brackets inserted by the Asylum and Immigration Act 1996, s 12(1), Sch 2, para 5(2)(c).

Para 4: in sub-para (3) words beginning "an immigration officer" in square brackets substituted by the Immigration Act 2014, s 67, Sch 8, paras 1, 3(1), (4), as from 28 July 2014: see SI 2014/1820.

Para 4: sub-paras (4), (5) substituted, for sub-para (4) as originally enacted, by the Immigration, Asylum and Nationality Act 2006, s 27(1).

Para 4: in sub-para (4) words in square brackets substituted by the Immigration Act 2014, s 67, Sch 8, paras 1, 3(1), (5), as from 28 July 2014: see SI 2014/1820.

Para 4: sub-paras (4A), (4B) inserted by the Immigration Act 2014, s 67, Sch 8, paras 1, 3(1), (6), as from 28 July 2014: see SI 2014/1820.

Para 4: in sub-para (5) first words in square brackets inserted by the Immigration Act 2014, s 67, Sch 8, paras 1, 3(1), (7), as from 28 July 2014: see SI 2014/1820.

Para 4: in sub-para (5) second word in square brackets inserted and words omitted repealed by the Immigration Act 2014, s 12, Sch 2, para 1(1), (2), as from 28 July 2014: see SI 2014/1820.

Para 4: in sub-para (6) inserted by the Immigration Act 2014, s 12, Sch 2, para 1(1), (3), as from 28 July 2014: see SI 2014/1820.

Para 4: sub-paras (7)–(9) inserted by the Immigration Act 2014, s 13(1), (2), as from 28 July 2014: see SI 2014/1820.

Para 5: words in square brackets substituted by the Immigration Act 2014, s 67, Sch 8, paras 1, 4, as from 28 July 2014: see SI 2014/1820.

Para 5A: inserted by the Immigration Act 2014, s 67, Sch 8, paras 1, 5, as from 28 July 2014: see SI 2014/1820.

Para 5B: inserted by the Immigration Act 2014, s 67, Sch 8, paras 1, 6, as from 28 July 2014: see SI 2014/1820.

Para 6: in sub-para (1) words "twenty-four hours" in both places they occur in square brackets substituted by the Immigration Act 1988, s 10, Schedule, paras 7, 8.

Para 6: in sub-para (1) words "a British citizen" in square brackets substituted by the British Nationality Act 1981, s 39, Sch 4, para 2.

Para 6: in sub-para (1) words from "leave to enter" to "his taking employment" in square brackets substituted by the Immigration Act 1988, s 10, Schedule, paras 7, 8.

Para 6: in sub-para (2) words "twenty-four hours" in square brackets substituted by the Immigration Act 1988, s 10, Schedule, paras 7, 8.

Para 6: in sub-para (3) words from "and the immigration officer" to "of that leave" in square brackets substituted by the Immigration Act 1988, s 10, Schedule, paras 7, 8.

Para 6: in sub-para (3) words "or require him to submit to further examination" in square brackets inserted by the Nationality, Immigration and Asylum Act 2002, s 119.

Para 7: substituted by the Immigration and Asylum Act 1999, s 169(1), Sch 14, paras 43, 59.

Para 8: words omitted from sub-para (1), originally inserted by SI 1990/2227, art 3, Sch 1, Part I, para 9, repealed by SI 1993/1813, art 9, Sch 6, Part I.

Para 8: in sub-para (2) words "(ignoring any period during which an appeal by him under the Immigration Acts is pending)" in square brackets inserted by the Nationality, Immigration and Asylum Act 2002, s 114(3), Sch 7, para 4.

Para 8: in sub-para (2) words in square brackets inserted by the Immigration Act 1988, s 10, Schedule, para 9.

Appendix 1 — UK Immigration Statutes

Para 9: sub-para (1) numbered as such, and sub-para (2) inserted, by the Asylum and Immigration Act 1996, s 12(1), Sch 2, para 6.

Para 10: words in square brackets in sub-para (1) substituted by the Immigration Act 1988, s 10, Schedule, para 9.

Para 10A: inserted by the Nationality, Immigration and Asylum Act 2002, s 73(1).

Para 11: words in square brackets inserted by the Immigration and Asylum Act 2002, s 73, Sch 9, para 1, as from 20 October 2014: see SI 2014/2771.

Paras 12, 13: words "a British citizen" in square brackets substituted by the British Nationality Act 1981, s 39(6), Sch 4, para 2.

Para 16: sub-para (1A) inserted by the Immigration and Asylum Act 1999, s 169(1), Sch 14, paras 43, 60.

Para 16: sub-para (1B) inserted by the Immigration, Asylum and Nationality Act 2006, s 42(1), (3).

Para 16: sub-para (2) substituted by the Immigration and Asylum Act 1999, s 140(1).

Para 16: in sub-para (2) words "8 to 10A" in square brackets substituted by the Nationality, Immigration and Asylum Act 2002, s 73(5).

Para 16: sub-para (2A) inserted by the Immigration Act 2014, s 5(1), (2), as from 28 July 2014: see SI 2014/1820.

Para 16: sub-para (4A) inserted by SI 1990/2227, art 3, Sch 1, Part I, para 10, repealed by SI 1993/1813, art 9, Sch 6, Part I.

Para 17: first words omitted apply to Scotland only, repealed in part by the Asylum and Immigration Act 1996, ss 12(1), (3), Sch 2, para 7, Sch 4.

Para 17: in sub-para (2)(b) words omitted repealed by the Asylum and Immigration Act 1996, s 12(3), Sch 4.

Para 17: in sub-para (2) words in square brackets beginning with the words "authorising any" substituted by the Immigration and Asylum Act 1999, s 140(2).

Para 17: in sub-para (2) words "if need be by reasonable force" in square brackets substituted by the Nationality, Immigration and Asylum Act 2002, s 63.

Para 17: sub-paras (3)–(5) inserted by the Nationality, Immigration and Asylum Act 2002, s 64.

Para 18: sub-para (1A) inserted by the Immigration Act 2014, s 5(1), (3), as from 28 July 2014: see SI 2014/1820.

Para 18: in sub-para (2) words in square brackets inserted by the Immigration Act 2014, s 9, as from 28 July 2014: see SI 2014/1820.

Para 18: sub-para (2B) inserted by the Immigration Act 2014, s 13(1), (3), as from 28 July 2014: see SI 2014/1820.

Para 18: sub-para (2A) inserted by the Immigration and Asylum Act 1999, s 169(1), Sch 14, paras 43, 61.

Para 18: in sub-para (2A) words in square brackets substituted by the Immigration Act 2014, s 12, Sch 2, para 1(1), (4), as from 28 July 2014: see SI 2014/1820.

Para 18: words in square brackets in sub-para (3) substituted by the Immigration Act 2014, s 4, Sch 1, para 1, as from 28 July 2014: see SI 2014/1820.

Para 18A: inserted by the Immigration Act 2014, s 4, Sch 1, para 2(1), as from 28 July 2014: see SI 2014/1820.

Para 18B: inserted by the Immigration Act 2014, s 5(1), (4), as from 28 July 2014: see SI 2014/1820.

Para 19: words omitted from sub-para (1) inserted by SI 1990/2227, Sch 1, Part I, para 11, repealed by SI 1993/1813, art 9, Sch 6, Part I.

Para 19: words in square brackets in sub-para (1) substituted by the Asylum and Immigration Act 1996, s 12(1), Sch 2, para 8.

Para 19: words in square brackets in sub-para (2) substituted by the British Nationality Act 1981, s 39(6), Sch 4, para 3(1).

Para 20: words omitted from sub-para (1) inserted by SI 1990/2227, Sch 1, Part I, para 12, repealed by SI 1993/1813, art 9, Sch 6, Part I.

Para 20: words in square brackets in sub-para (1) substituted by the Asylum and Immigration Act 1996, s 12(1), Sch 2, para 9(1).

Para 20: sub-para (1A) inserted by the Asylum and Immigration Act 1996, s 12(1), Sch 2, para 9(2).

Para 21: in sub-para (1) words "(1), (1A) or (2)" in square brackets inserted by the Immigration, Asylum and Nationality Act 2006, s 42(1), (4).

Para 21: in sub-para (2) words in square brackets inserted by the Immigration Act 1988, s 10, Schedule, paras 6, 10.

Para 21: sub-paras (2A)–(2E) inserted by the Immigration and Asylum Act 1999, s 169(1), Sch 14, paras 43, 62(1), (2).

Para 21: sub-paras (3), (4) inserted by the Asylum and Immigration Act 1996, s 12(1), Sch 2, para 10.

Para 21: in sub-para (3) words "or 2A" in square brackets inserted by the Immigration and Asylum Act 1999, s 169(1), Sch 14, paras 43, 62(1), (3).

Para 21: in sub-para (4)(a) words omitted repealed by the Immigration and Asylum Act 1999, s 169(1), (3), Sch 14, paras 43, 62(1), (4), Sch 16.

Para 22: sub-paras (1), (1A), (1B) substituted, for sub-para (1) as originally enacted, by the Asylum and Immigration Act 1996, s 12(1), Sch 2, para 11(1).

Para 22: sub-para (1)(aa) inserted by the Immigration and Asylum Act 1999, s 169(1), Sch 14, paras 43, 63.

Para 22: in sub-para (1A) words "the First-tier Tribunal" in square brackets substituted by SI 2010/21, art 5(1), Sch 1, paras 1, 2.

Para 22: in sub-paras (2), (3) words in square brackets beginning with the words "officer" and "immigration officer or" substituted by the Asylum and Immigration Act 1996, s 12(1), Sch 2, para 11(2).

Para 22: in sub-paras (2), (3) words "the First-tier Tribunal" in square brackets in each place they occur substituted by SI 2010/21, art 5(1), Sch 1, paras 1, 2.

Para 22: sub-para (4) inserted by the Immigration Act 2014, s 7(1), (2), as from 28 July 2014: see SI 2014/1820.

Para 23: in sub-paras (2), (3) words "the First-tier Tribunal" in square brackets in each place they occur substituted by SI 2010/21, art 5(1), Sch 1, paras 1, 2.

Para 23: in sub-para (1) words "the First-tier Tribunal" in square brackets in each place they occur substituted by SI 2010/21, art 5(1), Sch 1, paras 1, 2.

Para 23: in sub-para (1)(b) words "proper officer" in square brackets substituted by the Access to Justice Act 1999, s 90(1), Sch 13, para 70(1), (2).

Para 23: sub-para (1A) inserted by the Access to Justice Act 1999, s 90(1), Sch 13, para 70(1), (3).

Para 23: in sub-para (1A)(a) words "designated officer" in square brackets substituted by the Courts Act 2003, s 109(1), Sch 8, para 149(1), (2).

Para 23: in sub-para (2) words "the First-tier Tribunal" in square brackets in each place they occur substituted by SI 2010/21, art 5(1), Sch 1, paras 1, 2.

Para 23: in sub-para (3) words "purposes of section 38 of the Courts Act 2003 (application of receipts of designated officers) as being" in square brackets substituted by the Courts Act 2003, s 109(1), Sch 8, para 149(1), (3).

Para 23: in sub-para (3) words from "Where a person" to "or sheriff" in square brackets substituted by the Asylum and Immigration (Treatment of Claimants, etc) Act 2004, s 26(7), Sch 2, Pt 1, para 1(1), (3).

Para 23: in sub-para (3) words omitted repealed by the Criminal Justice Act 1972, ss 64(2), 66(7), Sch 6, Pt II.

Para 24: in sub-para (2)(a) words "the First-tier Tribunal" in square brackets substituted by SI 2010/21, art 5(1), Sch 1, paras 1, 2.

Para 24: in sub-para (2)(a) words "in England and Wales, a justice of the peace, in Northern Ireland," in square brackets inserted by the Courts Act 2003, s 109(1), Sch 8, para 149(1), (4).

Para 24: in sub-para (3) words from "Where a person" to "or sheriff" in square brackets substituted by the Asylum and Immigration (Treatment of Claimants, etc) Act 2004, s 26(7), Sch 2, Pt 1, para 1(1), (3).

Para 24: in sub-para (3) words "the First-tier Tribunal" in square brackets substituted by SI 2010/21, art 5(1), Sch 1, paras 1, 2.

Para 25: substituted by SI 2010/21, art 5(1), Sch 1, paras 1, 3.

Para 25: sub-para (1) numbered as such, word "must" in square brackets substituted and sub-para (2) added by the Immigration Act 2014, s 7(1), (3), as from 20 October 2014: see SI 2014/2771.

Para 25A: inserted by the Immigration and Asylum Act 1999, s 132(2).

Para 25A: words in square brackets in sub-para (1)(b) substituted by the Immigration Act 2014, s 4, Sch 1, para 3(1), (2), as from 28 July 2014: see SI 2014/1820.

Para 25A: sub-paras (6A)–(6C) inserted by the Immigration Act 2014, s 4, Sch 1, para 3(1), (3), as from 28 July 2014: see SI 2014/1820.

Para 25A: words in square brackets in sub-para (7) substituted and words omitted repealed, by the Immigration Act 2014, s 4, Sch 1, para 3(1), (4), as from 28 July 2014: see SI 2014/1820.

Para 25A: sub-para (8A) inserted by the Immigration Act 2014, s 4, Sch 1, para 3(1), (5), as from 28 July 2014: see SI 2014/1820.

Para 25B: inserted by the Immigration and Asylum Act 1999, s 134(2).

Para 25C: inserted by the Immigration and Asylum Act 1999, s 135(2).

Para 25D: inserted by the Immigration and Asylum Act 1999, s 136(2).

Para 25E: inserted by the Immigration and Asylum Act 1999, s 139(2).

Para 26: in sub-para (1) words omitted repealed by the Immigration and Asylum Act 1999, s 169(1), (3), Sch 14, paras 43, 64(1), (2), Sch 16.

Para 26: in sub-para (1) words "British citizens" in square brackets substituted by the British Nationality Act 1981, s 39(6), Sch 4, para 2.

Para 26: sub-para (1A) inserted by the Immigration and Asylum Act 1999, s 169(1), Sch 14, paras 43, 64(1), (3).

Para 26: sub-para (3A) inserted by the Immigration and Asylum Act 1999, s 169(1), Sch 14, paras 43, 64(1), (4).

Para 27: sub-paras (2)–(5) substituted, for sub-para (2) as originally enacted, by the Immigration, Asylum and Nationality Act 2006, s 31(1), (2).

Para 27A: inserted by SI 1990/2227, art 3, Sch 1, Part I, para 13; repealed by SI 1993/1813, art 9, Sch 6, Part I.

Para 27B: inserted by the Immigration and Asylum Act 1999, s 18.

Para 27B: heading: words "or service information" in square brackets inserted by the Immigration, Asylum and Nationality Act 2006, s 31(1), (3)(a).

Para 27B: in sub-paras (2)–(4), (4A) words "or service information" in square brackets in each place they occur inserted by the Immigration, Asylum and Nationality Act 2006, s 31(1), (3)(a).

Para 27B: sub-para (4A) inserted by the Asylum and Immigration (Treatment of Claimants, etc) Act 2004, s 16, as from a day to be appointed.

Para 27B: sub-para (9A) inserted by the Immigration, Asylum and Nationality Act 2006, s 31(1), (3)(b).

Para 27C: inserted by the Immigration and Asylum Act 1999, s 19.

See Further

See further, in relation to the application of paras 2, 4, 7, 16 above, with modifications, in respect of a person who claims a right of admission to the United Kingdom under the Immigration (European Economic Area) Regulations 2006, SI 2006/1003, reg 11: the Immigration (European Economic Area) Regulations 2006, SI 2006/1003, reg 22.

See further, in relation to the extension of paras 27, 27B above, with modifications, to Guernsey: the Immigration, Asylum and Nationality Act 2006, s 31(2), (3) (as modified by SI 2011/2444, art 4, Sch 1).

Subordinate Legislation

Immigration (Landing and Embarkation Cards) Order 1975, SI 1975/65.

Immigration and Police (Passenger, Crew and Service Information) Order 2008, SI 2008/5.

. . .

PART II
EFFECT OF APPEALS

Grant of bail pending appeal

28

. . .

29

(1) Where a person (in the following provisions of this Schedule referred to as "an appellant") has an appeal pending under [Part 5 of the Nationality, Immigration and

Asylum Act 2002] and is for the time being detained under Part I of this Schedule, he may be released on bail in accordance with this paragraph [(and paragraph 22 does not apply)].

(2) An immigration officer not below the rank of chief immigration officer or a police officer not below the rank of inspector may release an appellant on his entering into a recognizance or, in Scotland, bail bond conditioned for his appearance before [the First-tier Tribunal] at a time and place named in the recognizance or bail bond.

(3) [The First-tier Tribunal] may release an appellant on his entering into a recognizance or, in Scotland, bail bond conditioned for his appearance before [the Tribunal], or the [Immigration Appeal Tribunal] at a time and place named in the recognizance or bail bond; . . .

(4) . . .

(5) The conditions of a recognizance or bail bond taken under this paragraph may include conditions appearing to the person fixing the bail to be likely to result in the appearance of the appellant at the time and place named; and any recognizance shall be with or without sureties as that person may determine.

(6) In any case in which [the First-tier Tribunal] has power or is required by this paragraph to release an appellant on bail, [the Tribunal] may, instead of taking the bail, fix the amount and conditions of the bail (including the amount in which any sureties are to be bound) with a view to its being taken subsequently by any such person as may be specified by [the Tribunal]; and on the recognizance or bail bond so taken the appellant shall be released.

Restrictions on grant of bail

30 (1) An appellant shall not be released under paragraph 29 above without the consent of the Secretary of State if—

(a) directions for the removal of the appellant from the United Kingdom are for the time being in force, [and

(b) the directions require the person to be removed from the United Kingdom within the period of 14 days starting with the date of the decision on whether the person should be released on bail.]

(2) Notwithstanding paragraph 29(3) or (4) above, [the Tribunal] shall not be obliged to release an appellant unless the appellant enters into a proper recognizance, with sufficient and satisfactory sureties if required, or in Scotland sufficient and satisfactory bail is found if so required; and [the Tribunal] shall not be obliged to release an appellant if it appears to [the Tribunal]—

(a) that the appellant, having on any previous occasion been released on bail (whether under paragraph 24 or under any other provision), has failed to comply with the conditions of any recognizance or bail bond entered into by him on that occasion;

(b) that the appellant is likely to commit an offence unless he is retained in detention;

(c) that the release of the appellant is likely to cause danger to public health;

(d) that the appellant is suffering from mental disorder and that his continued detention is necessary in his own interests or for the protection of any other person; or

(e) that the appellant is under the age of seventeen, that arrangements ought to be made for his care in the event of his release and that no satisfactory arrangements for that purpose have been made.

Forfeiture of recognizances

31

(1) Where under paragraph 29 above (as it applies in England and Wales or in Northern Ireland) a recognizance is entered into conditioned for the appearance of an appellant before [the Tribunal], and it appears to [the Tribunal], to be forfeited, [the Tribunal] may by order declare it to be forfeited and adjudge the persons bound thereby, whether as principal or sureties, or any of them, to pay the sum in which they are respectively bound or such part of it, if any, as [the Tribunal] thinks fit.

(2) An order under this paragraph shall, for the purposes of this sub-paragraph, specify a magistrates' court or, in Northern Ireland, court of summary jurisdiction; and the recognizance shall be treated for the purposes of collection, enforcement and remission of the sum forfeited as having been forfeited by the court so specified.

(3) Where [the Tribunal] makes an order under this paragraph [the Tribunal] shall, as soon as practicable, give particulars of the recognizance to the [proper officer] of the court specified in the order in pursuance of sub-paragraph (2) above.

[(3A) In sub-paragraph (3) "proper officer" means—

(a) in relation to a magistrates' court in England and Wales, the [designated officer] for the court; and

(b) in relation to a court of summary jurisdiction in Northern Ireland, the clerk of the court.]

(4) Any sum the payment of which is enforceable by a magistrates' court in England or Wales by virtue of this paragraph shall be treated for the [purposes of section 38 of the Courts Act 2003 (application of receipts of designated officers) as being] due under a recognizance forfeited by such a court . . .

(5) Any sum the payment of which is enforceable by virtue of this paragraph by a court of summary jurisdiction in Northern Ireland shall, for the purposes of section 20(5) of the Administration of Justice Act (Northern Ireland) 1954, be treated as a forfeited recognizance.

32

Where under paragraph 29 above (as it applies in Scotland) a person released on bail fails to comply with the terms of a bail bond conditioned for his appearance before [the Tribunal], [the Tribunal] may declare the bail to be forfeited, and any bail so forfeited shall be transmitted by [the Tribunal] to the sheriff court having jurisdiction in the area where the proceedings took place, and shall be treated as having been forfeited by that court.

Arrest of appellants released on bail

33

(1) An immigration officer or constable may arrest without warrant a person who has been released by virtue of this Part of this Schedule—

(a) if he has reasonable grounds for believing that that person is likely to break the condition of his recognizance or bail bond that he will appear at the time and place required or to break any other condition of it, or has reasonable ground to suspect that that person is breaking or has broken any such other condition; or

(b) if, a recognizance with sureties having been taken, he is notified in writing by any surety of the surety's belief that that person is likely to break the first-mentioned condition, and of the surety's wish for that reason to be relieved of his obligations as a surety;

and paragraph 17(2) above shall apply for the arrest of a person under this paragraph as it applies for the arrest of a person under paragraph 17.

(2) A person arrested under this paragraph—

(a) if not required by a condition on which he was released to appear before [the Tribunal] within twenty-four hours after the time of his arrest, shall as soon as practicable be brought [before the Tribunal] or, if that is not practicable within those twenty-four hours, before [in England and Wales, a justice of the peace, in Northern Ireland,] a justice of the peace acting for the petty sessions area in which he is arrested or, in Scotland, the sheriff; and

(b) if required by such a condition to appear within those twenty-four hours [before the Tribunal], shall be brought [before it].

(3) [Where a person is brought before [the First-tier Tribunal], a justice of the peace or the sheriff by virtue of sub-paragraph (2)(a), the Tribunal, justice of the peace or sheriff]—

(a) if of the opinion that that person has broken or is likely to break any condition on which he was released, may either—

(i) direct that he be detained under the authority of the person by whom he was arrested; or

(ii) release him on his original recognizance or on a new recognizance, with or without sureties, or, in Scotland, on his original bail or on new bail; and

(b) if not of that opinion, shall release him on his original recognizance or bail.

[33A

(1) Tribunal Procedure Rules must make provision with respect to applications to the First-tier Tribunal under paragraphs 29 to 33 and matters arising out of such applications.

(2) Tribunal Procedure Rules must secure that, where the First-tier Tribunal has decided not to release a person on bail under paragraph 29, the Tribunal is required to dismiss without a hearing any further application by the person for release on bail (whether under paragraph 29 or otherwise) that is made during the period of 28 days starting with the date of the Tribunal's decision, unless the person demonstrates to the Tribunal that there has been a material change in circumstances.]

[Grant of bail pending removal

34

(1) Paragraph 22 above shall apply in relation to a person—

(a) directions for whose removal from the United Kingdom are for the time being in force; and

(b) who is for the time being detained under Part I of this Schedule,

as it applies in relation to a person detained under paragraph 16(1) above pending examination[, detained under paragraph 16(1A) above pending completion of his examination or a decision on whether to cancel his leave to enter] or detained under paragraph 16(2) above pending the giving of directions.

(2) Paragraphs 23 to 25 above shall apply as if any reference to paragraph 22 above included a reference to that paragraph as it applies by virtue of this paragraph.]

Amendment

Para 28: repealed by the Immigration and Asylum Act 1999, s 169(1), (3), Sch 14, paras 43, 65, Sch 16.

Para 29: in sub-para (1) words "Part 5 of the Nationality, Immigration and Asylum Act 2002" in square brackets substituted by the Nationality, Immigration and Asylum Act 2002, s 114(3), Sch 7, para 6(a).

Para 29: in sub-para (1) words "(and paragraph 22 does not apply)" inserted by the Immigration Act 2014, s 7(1), (4), as from 20 October 2014: see SI 2014/2771.

Para 29: in sub-para (2) words "the First-tier Tribunal" in square brackets substituted by SI 2010/21, art 5(1), Sch 1, paras 1, 2.

Para 29: in sub-para (3) words "the Tribunal" in square brackets substituted by the Asylum and Immigration (Treatment of Claimants, etc) Act 2004, s 26(7), Sch 2, Pt 1, para 1(1), (4)(b)(ii).

Para 29: in sub-para (3) words "Immigration Appeal Tribunal" in square brackets substituted by the Nationality, Immigration and Asylum Act 2002, s 114(3), Sch 7, para 6(b).

Para 29: in sub-para (3) words "The First-tier Tribunal" in square brackets substituted by SI 2010/21, art 5(1), Sch 1, paras 1, 2.

Para 29: sub-para (4) repealed by the Asylum and Immigration (Treatment of Claimants, etc) Act 2004, ss 26(7), 47, Sch 2, Pt 1, para 1(1), (4)(c), Sch 4.

Para 29: in sub-para (6) words "the First-tier Tribunal" in square brackets substituted by SI 2010/21, art 5(1), Sch 1, paras 1, 2.

Para 29: in sub-para (6) words "the Tribunal" in square brackets substituted by the Asylum and Immigration (Treatment of Claimants, etc) Act 2004, s 26(7), Sch 2, Pt 1, para 1(1), (4)(d)(ii).

Para 30: words in square brackets in sub-para (1) substituted by the Immigration Act 2014, s 7(1), (5), as from 28 July 2014: see SI 2014/1820.

Para 30: in sub-para (2) words "the Tribunal" in square brackets in the first and second places they occur substituted by the Asylum and Immigration (Treatment of Claimants, etc) Act 2004, s 26(7), Sch 2, Pt 1, para 1(1), (5)(a); for transitional provisions see s 26(7), Sch 2, Pt 2 thereto.

Para 30: in sub-para (2) words "the Tribunal" in square brackets in the final place they occur substituted by the Asylum and Immigration (Treatment of Claimants, etc) Act 2004, s 26(7), Sch 2, Pt 1, para 1(1), (5)(c); for transitional provisions see s 26(7), Sch 2, Pt 2 thereto.

Para 31: words "the Tribunal" in square brackets in first and fifth places they occur substituted by the Asylum and Immigration (Treatment of Claimants, etc) Act 2004, s 26(7), Sch 2, Pt 1, para 1(1), (5)(b); for transitional provisions see s 26(7), Sch 2, Pt 2 thereto.

Para 31: in sub-para (1) words "the Tribunal" in square brackets in the second place they occur substituted by the Asylum and Immigration (Treatment of Claimants, etc) Act 2004, s 26(7), Sch 2, Pt 1, para 1(1), (5)(c); for transitional provisions see s 26(7), Sch 2, Pt 2 thereto.

Para 31: words "the Tribunal" in square brackets in the third, fourth and final places they occur substituted by the Asylum and Immigration (Treatment of Claimants, etc) Act 2004, s 26(7), Sch 2, Pt 1, para 1(1), (5)(d); for transitional provisions see s 26(7), Sch 2, Pt 2 thereto.

Para 31: in sub-para (3) words "proper officer" in square brackets substituted by the Access to Justice Act 1999, s 90(1), Sch 13, para 70(1), (4).

Para 31: sub-para (3A) inserted by the Access to Justice Act 1999, s 90(1), Sch 13, para 70(1), (5).

Para 31: in sub-para (3A)(a) words "designated officer" in square brackets substituted by the Courts Act 2003, s 109(1), Sch 8, para 149(1), (2).

Para 31: in sub-para (4) words "purposes of section 38 of the Courts Act 2003 (application of receipts of designated officers) as being" in square brackets substituted by the Courts Act 2003, s 109(1), Sch 8, para 149(1), (3).

Para 32: words "the Tribunal" in square brackets in the second place they occur substituted by the Asylum and Immigration (Treatment of Claimants, etc) Act 2004, s 26(7), Sch 2, Pt 1, para 1(1), (5)(d); for transitional provisions see s 26(7), Sch 2, Pt 2 thereto.

Para 31: in sub-para (4) words omitted repealed by the Criminal Justice Act 1972, s 64(2), Sch 6, Pt II.

Para 32: words "the Tribunal" in square brackets in the first place they occur substituted by the Asylum and Immigration (Treatment of Claimants, etc) Act 2004, s 26(7), Sch 2, Pt 1, para 1(1), (5)(b); for transitional provisions see s 26(7), Sch 2, Pt 2 thereto.

Para 32: words "the Tribunal" in square brackets in the final place they occur substituted by the Asylum and Immigration (Treatment of Claimants, etc) Act 2004, s 26(7), Sch 2, Pt 1, para 1(1), (5)(e); for transitional provisions see s 26(7), Sch 2, Pt 2 thereto.

Para 33: in sub-para (2)(a) words "the Tribunal" in square brackets substituted by the Asylum and Immigration (Treatment of Claimants, etc) Act 2004, s 26(7), Sch 2, Pt 1, para 1(1), (5)(f); for transitional provisions see s 26(7), Sch 2, Pt 2 thereto.

Para 33: in sub-para (2)(a) words "before the Tribunal" in square brackets substituted by the Asylum and Immigration (Treatment of Claimants, etc) Act 2004, s 26(7), Sch 2, Pt 1, para 1(1), (6)(a); for transitional provisions see s 26(7), Sch 2, Pt 2 thereto.

Para 33: in sub-para (2)(a) words "in England and Wales, a justice of the peace, in Northern Ireland," in square brackets inserted by the Courts Act 2003, s 109(1), Sch 8, para 149(1), (4).

Para 33: in sub-para (2)(b) words "before the Tribunal" in square brackets substituted by the Asylum and Immigration (Treatment of Claimants, etc) Act 2004, s 26(7), Sch 2, Pt 1, para 1(1), (5)(g); for transitional provisions see s 26(7), Sch 2, Pt 2 thereto.

Para 33: in sub-para (2)(b) words "before it" in square brackets substituted by the Asylum and Immigration (Treatment of Claimants, etc) Act 2004, s 26(7), Sch 2, Pt 1, para 1(1), (6)(b); for transitional provisions see s 26(7), Sch 2, Pt 2 thereto.

Para 33: in sub-para (3) words from "Where a person" to "peace or sherriff" in square brackets substituted by the Asylum and Immigration (Treatment of Claimants, etc) Act 2004, s 26(7), Sch 2, Pt 1, para 1(1), (6)(c); for transitional provisions see s 26(7), Sch 2, Pt 2 thereto.

Para 33: in sub-para (3) words "the First-tier Tribunal" in square brackets substituted by SI 2010/21, art 5(1), Sch 1, paras 1, 2.

Para 33A: inserted by the Immigration Act 2014, s 7(1), (6), as from 20 October 2014: see SI 2014/2771.

Para 34: inserted by the Asylum and Immigration Act 1996, s 12(1), Sch 12, para 12.

Para 34: in para (1) words from ", detained under" to "leave to enter" in square brackets inserted by the Immigration and Asylum Act 1999, s 169(1), Sch 14, paras 43, 67.

Modification

Paras 29–33 modified, in relation to a person detained on certain grounds relating to national security, by the Special Immigration Appeals Commission Act 1997, Sch 3, paras 4–8.

See Further

See further, in relation to the disapplication of para 29(1) above (as amended), where an appeal is made under Pt II hereof: the Nationality, Immigration and Asylum Act 2002 (Commencement No 4) Order 2003, SI 2003/754, art 3, Sch 2, para 2(10)(b)(i) and the Immigration (Isle of Man) Order 2008, SI 2008/680, arts 4, 5, Sch 2, paras 1, 2(10)(b)(i).

SCHEDULE 3

SUPPLEMENTARY PROVISIONS AS TO DEPORTATIONS

Section 5

Removal of persons liable to deportation

1

(1) Where a deportation order is in force against any person, the Secretary of State may give directions for his removal to a country or territory specified in the directions being either—

    (a)   a country of which he is a national or citizen; or

    (b)   a country or territory to which there is reason to believe that he will be admitted.

(2) The directions under sub-paragraph (1) above may be either—

    (a)   directions given to the captain of a ship or aircraft about to leave the United Kingdom requiring him to remove the person in question in that ship or aircraft; or

    (b)   directions given to the owners or agents of any ship or aircraft requiring them to make arrangements for his removal in a ship or aircraft specified or indicated in the directions; or

    (c)   directions for his removal in accordance with arrangements to be made by the Secretary of State.

(3) In relation to directions given under this paragraph, paragraphs 11 and 16(4) of Schedule 2 to this Act shall apply, with the substitution of references of references to the Secretary of State for references to an immigration officer, as they apply in relation to directions for removal given under paragraph 8 of that Schedule.

(4) The Secretary of State, if he thinks fit, may apply in or towards payment of the expenses of or incidental to the voyage from the United Kingdom of a person against whom a deportation order is in force, or the maintenance until departure of such a person and his dependants, if any, any money belonging to that person; and except so far as they are paid as aforesaid, those expenses shall be defrayed by the Secretary of State.

Detention or control pending deportation

2

(1) Where a recommendation for deportation made by a court is in force in respect of any person, [and that person is not detained in pursuance of the sentence or order of any court], he shall, unless the court by which the recommendation is made otherwise directs, [or a direction is given under sub-paragraph (1A) below,] be detained pending the making of a deportation order in pursuance of the recommendation, unless the Secretary of State directs him to be released pending further consideration of his case [or he is released on bail].

[(1A) Where—

    (a)   a recommendation for deportation made by a court on conviction of a person is in force in respect of him; and

    (b)   he appeals against his conviction or against that recommendation,

the powers that the court determining the appeal may exercise include power to direct him to be released without setting aside the recommendation.]

(2) Where notice has been given to a person in accordance with regulations under [section 105 of the Nationality, Immigration and Asylum Act 2002 (notice of decision)] of a decision to make a deportation order against him, [and he is not detained in pursuance of the sentence or order of a court], he may be detained under the authority of the Secretary of State pending the making of the deportation order.

(3) Where a deportation order is in force against any person, he may be detained under the authority of the Secretary of State pending his removal or departure from the United Kingdom (and if already detained by virtue of sub-paragraph (1) or (2) above when the order is made, shall continue to be detained unless [he is released on bail or] the Secretary of State directs otherwise).

(4) In relation to detention under sub-paragraph (2) or (3) above, paragraphs 17[to 18A and 25A to 25E] of Schedule 2 to this Act shall apply as they apply in relation to detention under paragraph 16 of that Schedule[; and for that purpose the reference in paragraph 17(1) to a person liable to detention includes a reference to a person who would be liable to detention upon receipt of a notice which is ready to be given to him].

[(4A) Paragraphs 22 to 25 of Schedule 2 to this Act apply in relation to a person detained under sub-paragraph (1), (2) or (3) as they apply in relation to a person detained under paragraph 16 of that Schedule.]

[(5) A person to whom this sub-paragraph applies shall be subject to such restrictions as to residence[, as to his employment or occupation] and as to reporting to the police [or an immigration officer] as may from time to time be notified to him in writing by the Secretary of State.]

[(6) The persons to whom sub-paragraph (5) above applies are—

    (a)   a person liable to be detained under sub-paragraph (1) above, while by virtue of a direction of the Secretary of State he is not so detained; and

    (b)   a person liable to be detained under sub-paragraph (2) or (3) above, while he is not so detained.]

[3

So far as they relate to an appeal under section 82(1) of the Nationality, Immigration and Asylum Act 2002 against a decision [that relates to a deportation order], paragraphs 29 to [33A] of Schedule 2 to this Act shall apply for the purposes of this Schedule as if the reference in paragraph 29(1) to Part I of that Schedule were a reference to this Schedule.]

[Powers of courts pending deportation

4

Where the release of a person recommended for deportation is directed by a court, he shall be subject to such restrictions as to residence[, as to his employment or occupation] and as to reporting to the police as the court may direct.

5

(1) On an application made—

    (a) by or on behalf of a person recommended for deportation whose release was so directed; or

    (b) by a constable; or

    (c) by an immigration order,

the appropriate court shall have the powers specified in sub-paragraph (2) below.

(2) The powers mentioned in sub-paragraph (1) above are—

    (a) if the person to whom the application relates is not subject to any such restrictions imposed by a court as are mentioned in paragraph 4 above, to order that he shall be subject to any such restrictions as the court may direct; and

    (b) if he is subject to such restrictions imposed by a court by virtue of that paragraph or this paragraph—

        (i) to direct that any of them shall be varied or shall cease to have effect; or

        (ii) to give further directions as to his residence and reporting.

6

(1) In this Schedule "the appropriate court" means except in a case to which sub-paragraph (2) below applies, the court which directed release.

(2) This sub-paragraph applies where the court which directed release was—

    (a) the Crown Court;

    (b) the Court of Appeal;

    (c) the High Court of Justiciary;

    (d) the Crown Court in Northern Ireland; or

    (e) the Court of Appeal in Northern Ireland.

[(2A) Where the Crown Court directed release, the appropriate court is that court or a magistrates' court.]

(3) Where . . . the Crown Court in Northern Ireland directed release, the appropriate court is—

    (a) the court that directed release; or

    (b) a magistrates' court acting for the . . . county court division where the person to whom the application relates resides.

(4) Where the Court of Appeal or the Court of Appeal in Northern Ireland gave the direction, the appropriate court is the Crown Court or the Crown Court in Northern Ireland, as the case may be.

(5) Where the High Court of Justiciary directed release, the appropriate court is—

Appendix 1 — UK Immigration Statutes

(a)   that court; or

(b)   in a case where release was directed by a court on appeal, the court from which the appeal was made.

7   —(1) A constable or immigration officer may arrest without warrant any person who is subject to restrictions imposed by a court under this Schedule and who at the time of the arrest is in the relevant part of the United Kingdom—

(a)   if he has reasonable grounds to suspect that that person is contravening or has contravened any of those restrictions; or

(b)   if he has reasonable grounds for believing that that person is likely to contravene any of them.

(2) In sub-paragraph (1) above "the relevant part of the United Kingdom" means—

(a)   England and Wales, in a case where a court with jurisdiction in England or Wales imposed the restrictions;

(b)   Scotland, in a case where a court with jurisdiction in Scotland imposed them; and

(c)   Northern Ireland, in a case where a court in Northern Ireland imposed them.

8   —(1) A person arrested in [England or Wales in pursuance of paragraph 7 above shall be brought as soon as practicable and in any event within twenty-four hours after his arrest before a justice of the peace in England or Wales, and a person arrested in] Northern Ireland in pursuance of paragraph 7 above shall be brought as soon as practicable and in any event within 24 hours after his arrest before a justice of the peace for the petty sessions . . . district in which he was arrested.

(2) In reckoning for the purposes of this paragraph any period of 24 hours, no account shall be taken of Christmas Day, Good Friday or any Sunday.

9   —(1) A person arrested in Scotland in pursuance of paragraph 7 above shall wherever practicable be brought before the appropriate court not later than in the course of the first day after his arrest, such day not being a Saturday, a Sunday or a court holiday prescribed for that court under section 10 of the Bail etc (Scotland) Act 1980.

(2) Nothing in this paragraph shall prevent a person arrested in Scotland being brought before a court on a Saturday, a Sunday or such a court holiday as is mentioned in sub-paragraph (1) above where the court is, in pursuance of section 10 of the said Act of 1980, sitting on such day for the disposal of criminal business.

10   Any justice of the peace or court before whom a person is brought by virtue of paragraph 8 or 9 above—

(a)   if of the opinion that that person is contravening, has contravened or is likely to contravene any restriction imposed on him by a court under this Schedule, may direct—

    (i)   that he be detained; or

    (ii)   that he be released subject to such restrictions as to his residence and reporting to the police as the court may direct; and

(b)   if not of that opinion, shall release him without altering the restrictions as to his residence and his reporting to the police.]

Amendment

Para 2: in sub-para (1) words "and that person is not detained in pursuance of the sentence or order of any court" in square brackets substituted by the Asylum and Immigration (Treatment of Claimants, etc) Act 2004, s 34(1).

Para 2: in sub-para (1) words "or a direction is given under sub-paragraph (1A) below" in square brackets substituted by the Criminal Justice Act 1982, s 64, Sch 10.

Para 2: in sub-para (1) words "or he is released on bail" in square brackets inserted by the Immigration and Asylum Act 1999, s 54(1), (2).

Para 2: sub-paras (1A), (6) inserted by the Criminal Justice Act 1982, s 64, Sch 10.

Para 2: in sub-para (2) words "section 105 of the Nationality, Immigration and Asylum Act 2002" in square brackets substituted by the Nationality, Immigration and Asylum Act 2002, s 114(3), Sch 7, para 7.

Para 2: in sub-para (2) words "and he is not detained in pursuance of the sentence or order of a court" in square brackets substituted by the Asylum and Immigration (Treatment of Claimants, etc) Act 2004, s 34(2).

Para 2: in sub-para (3) words "he is released on bail or" in square brackets inserted by the Immigration and Asylum Act 1999, s 54(1), (3).

Para 2: in sub-para (4) words in first outer square brackets substituted by the Immigration and Asylum Act 1999, s 169(1), Sch 14, paras 43, 68.

Para 2: in sub-para (4) words in second inner square brackets substituted by the Immigration Act 2014, s 4, Sch 1, para 2(2), as from 28 July 2014: see SI 2014/1820.

Para 2: in sub-para (4) words in final square brackets inserted by the Immigration, Asylum and Nationality Act 2006, s 53.

Para 2: sub-para (4A) inserted by the Immigration and Asylum Act 1999, s 54(1), (4).

Para 2: sub-para (5) substituted by the Criminal Justice Act 1982, s 64, Sch 10.

Para 2: in sub-para (5) words in first pair of square brackets inserted by the Immigration Act 1988, s 10, Schedule; words in second pair of square brackets inserted by the Asylum and Immigration Act 1996, s 12(1), Sch 2, para 13.

Para 3: substituted by the Nationality, Immigration and Asylum Act 2002, s 114(3), Sch 7, para 8.

Para 3: reference to "33A" in square brackets substituted by the Immigration Act 2014, s 73, Sch 9, para 9, as from 28 July 2014: see SI 2014/1820.

Para 3: words "that relates to a deportation order" in square brackets substituted by the Immigration Act 2014, s 73, Sch 9, Pt 4, paras 20, 24, as from 20 October 2014 (see SI 2014/2771, art 2), subject to savings in SI 2014/2771, arts 9–11.

Para 4–10: inserted by the Criminal Justice Act 1982, s 64, Sch 10, para 2.

Para 4: words in square brackets inserted by the Immigration Act 1988, s 10, Schedule, para 10.

Para 6: sub-para (2A) inserted by the Courts Act 2003, s 109(1), Sch 8, para 150(1), (2).

Para 6: in sub-para (3) words omitted repealed by the Courts Act 2003, s 109(1), (3), Sch 8, para 150(1), (3), Sch 10.

Para 6: in sub-para (3)(b) words omitted repealed by the Courts Act 2003, s 109(1), (3), Sch 8, para 150(1), (3), Sch 10.

Para 8: in sub-para (1) words from "England or Wales" to "person arrested in" in square brackets substituted by the Courts Act 2003, s 109(1), Sch 8, para 150(1), (4)(a).

Para 8: in sub-para (1) words omitted repealed by the Courts Act 2003, s 150(1), (3), Sch 8, para 150(1), (4)(b), Sch 10.

SCHEDULE 4

INTEGRATION WITH UNITED KINGDOM LAW OF IMMIGRATION LAW OF ISLANDS

Section 9

Leave to enter

1

(1) Where under the immigration laws of any of the Islands a person is or has been given leave to enter or remain in the island, or is or has been refused leave, this Act shall have effect in relation to him, if he is not [a British citizen], as if the leave were leave (of like duration) given under this Act to enter or remain the United Kingdom, or, as the case may be, as if he had under this Act been refused leave to enter the United Kingdom.

(2)   Where under the immigration laws of any of the Islands a person has a limited leave to enter or remain in the Island subject to any such conditions as are authorised in the United Kingdom by section 3(1) of this Act (being conditions imposed by notice given to him, whether the notice of leave or a subsequent notice), then on his coming to the United Kingdom this Act shall apply, if he is not [a British citizen], as if those conditions related to his stay in the United Kingdom and had been imposed by notice under this Act.

(3)   Without prejudice to the generality of sub-paragraphs (1) and (2) above, anything having effect in the United Kingdom by virtue of either of those sub-paragraphs may in relation to the United Kingdom be varied or revoked under this Act in like manner, and subject to the like appeal (if any), as if it had originated under this Act as mentioned in that sub-paragraph.

(4)   Where anything having effect in the United Kingdom by virtue of sub-paragraph (1) or (2) above ceases to have effect or is altered in effect as mentioned in sub-paragraph (3) or otherwise by anything done under this Act, sub-paragraph (1) or (2) shall not thereafter apply to it or, as the case may be, shall apply to it as so altered in effect.

(5)   Nothing in this paragraph shall be taken as conferring on a person a right of appeal under this Act against any decision or action taken in any of the Islands.

2

Notwithstanding section 3(4) of this Act, leave given to a person under this Act to enter or remain in the United Kingdom shall not continue to apply on his return to the United Kingdom after an absence if he has during that absence entered any of the Islands in circumstances in which he is required under the immigration laws of that island to obtain leave to enter.

Deportation

[3

(1)   This Act has effect in relation to a person who is subject to an Islands deportation order as if the order were a deportation order made against him under this Act.

(2)   Sub-paragraph (1) does not apply if the person concerned is—

    (a)   a British citizen;

    (b)   an EEA national;

    (c)   a member of the family of an EEA national; or

    (d)   a member of the family of a British citizen who is neither such a citizen nor an EEA national.

(3)   The Secretary of State does not, as a result of sub-paragraph (1), have power to revoke an Islands deportation order.

(4)   In any particular case, the Secretary of State may direct that paragraph (b), (c) or (d) of sub-paragraph (2) is not to apply in relation to the Islands deportation order.

(5)   Nothing in this paragraph makes it unlawful for a person in respect of whom an Islands deportation order is in force in any of the Islands to enter the United Kingdom on his way from that island to a place outside the United Kingdom.

(6)   "Islands deportation order" means an order made under the immigration laws of any of the Islands under which a person is, or has been, ordered to leave the island and forbidden to return.

(7)   Subsections (10) and (12) to (14) of section 80 of the Immigration and Asylum Act 1999 apply for the purposes of this section as they apply for the purposes of that section.]

Illegal entrants

4

Notwithstanding anything in section 1(3) of this Act, it shall not be lawful for a person who is not [a British citizen] to enter the United Kingdom from any of the Islands where his presence was unlawful under the immigration laws of that island, unless he is given leave to enter.

Amendment

Para 1: in sub-paras (1), (2) words in square brackets substituted by the British Nationality Act 1981, s 39(6), Sch 4, para 2.

Para 3: substituted by the Immigration and Asylum Act 1999, s 169(1), Sch 14, paras 43, 70.

Para 4: words in square brackets substituted by the British Nationality Act 1981, s 39(6), Sch 4, para 2.

SCHEDULES 5, 6

(Sch 5 repealed by the Immigration and Asylum Act 1999, s 169(3), Sch 16; Sch 6 contains repeals.)

IMMIGRATION ACT 1988

1988 c 14

An Act to make further provision for the regulation of immigration into the United Kingdom; and for connected purposes

[10 May 1988]

Modification

In relation to the extension of this Act, with modifications, to the Isle of Man, see the Immigration (Isle of Man) Order 2008, SI 2008/680.

1

(This section repeals the Immigration Act 1971, s 1(5).)

2 Restriction on exercise of right of abode in cases of polygamy

(1) This section applies to any woman who—

(a) has the right of abode in the United Kingdom under section 2(1)(b) of the principal Act as, or as having been, the wife of a man ("the husband")—

(i) to whom she is or was polygamously married; and

(ii) who is or was such a citizen of the United Kingdom and Colonies, Commonwealth citizen or British subject as is mentioned in section 2(2)(a) or (b) of that Act as in force immediately before the commencement of the British Nationality Act 1981; and

(b) has not before the coming into force of this section and since her marriage to the husband been in the United Kingdom.

(2) A woman to whom this section applies shall not be entitled to enter the United Kingdom in the exercise of the right of abode mentioned in subsection (1)(a) above or to be granted a certificate of entitlement in respect of that right if there is another woman living (whether or not one to whom this section applies) who is the wife or widow of the husband and who—

   (a)   is, or at any time since her marriage to the husband has been, in the United Kingdom; or

   (b)   has been granted a certificate of entitlement in respect of the right of abode mentioned in subsection (1)(a) above or an entry clearance to enter the United Kingdom as the wife of the husband.

(3)   So long as a woman is precluded by subsection (2) above from entering the United Kingdom in the exercise of her right of abode or being granted a certificate of entitlement in respect of that right the principal Act shall apply to her as it applies to a person not having a right of abode.

(4)   Subsection (2) above shall not preclude a woman from re-entering the United Kingdom if since her marriage to the husband she has at any time previously been in the United Kingdom and there was at that time no such other woman living as is mentioned in that subsection.

(5)   Where a woman claims that this section does not apply to her because she had been in the United Kingdom before the coming into force of this section and since her marriage to the husband it shall be for her to prove that fact.

(6)   For the purposes of this section a marriage may be polygamous although at its inception neither party has any spouse additional to the other.

(7)   For the purposes of subsections (1)(b), (2)(a), (4) and (5) above there shall be disregarded presence in the United Kingdom as a visitor or an illegal entrant and presence in circumstances in which a person is deemed by section 11(1) of the principal Act not to have entered the United Kingdom.

(8)   In subsection (2)(b) above the reference to a certificate of entitlement includes a reference to a certificate treated as such a certificate by virtue of section 39(8) of the British Nationality Act 1981.

(9)   No application by a woman for a certificate of entitlement in respect of such a right of abode as is mentioned in subsection (1)(a) above or for an entry clearance shall be granted if another application for such a certificate or clearance is pending and that application is made by a woman as the wife or widow of the same husband.

(10)   For the purposes of subsection (9) above an application shall be regarded as pending so long as it and any appeal proceedings relating to it have not been finally determined.

3–5

   (*Section 3 amends the Immigration Act 1971, ss 2, 3, 13, and the British Nationality Act 1981, s 39; s 4 amends the Immigration Act 1971, s 8; s 5 repealed by the Immigration and Asylum Act 1999, s 169(1), (3), Sch 14, paras 83, 84, Sch 16.*)

6 Knowingly overstaying limited leave

(1), (2) . . .

(3)   These amendments do not apply in relation to a person whose leave has expired before the coming into force of this section.

Amendment

Sub-ss (1), (2): amend the Immigration Act 1971, s 24.

7 Persons exercising Community rights and nationals of member States

(1)   A person shall not under the principal Act require leave to enter or remain in the United Kingdom in any case in which he is entitled to do so by virtue of an enforceable [EU] right or of any provision made under section 2(2) of the European Communities Act 1972.

(2)   The Secretary of State may by order made by statutory instrument give leave to enter the United Kingdom for a limited period to any class of persons who are nationals of member States but who are not entitled to enter the United Kingdom as

mentioned in subsection (1) above; and any such order may give leave subject to such conditions as may be imposed by the order.

(3) References in the principal Act to limited leave shall include references to leave given by an order under subsection (2) above and a person having leave by virtue of such an order shall be treated as having been given that leave by a notice given to him by an immigration officer within the period specified in paragraph 6(1) of Schedule 2 to that Act.

Amendment

Sub-s (1): reference to "EU" in square brackets substituted by SI 2011/1043, art 6(1)(f).

8 Examination of passengers prior to arrival

(1) This section applies to a person who arrives in the United Kingdom with a passport or other travel document bearing a stamp which—

    (a) has been placed there by an immigration officer before that person's departure on his journey to the United Kingdom or in the course of that journey; and

    (b) states that the person may enter the United Kingdom either for an indefinite or a limited period and, if for a limited period, subject to specified conditions.

(2) A person to whom this section applies shall for the purposes of the principal Act be deemed to have been given on arrival in the United Kingdom indefinite or, as the case may be, limited leave in terms corresponding to those of the stamp.

(3) A person who is deemed to have leave by virtue of this section shall be treated as having been given it by a notice given to him by an immigration officer within the period specified in paragraph 6(1) of Schedule 2 to the principal Act.

(4) A person deemed to have leave by virtue of this section shall not on his arrival in the United Kingdom be subject to examination under paragraph 2 of Schedule 2 to the principal Act but may be examined by an immigration officer for the purpose of establishing that he is such a person.

(5) The leave which a person is deemed to have by virtue of this section may, at any time before the end of the period of twenty-four hours from his arrival at the port at which he seeks to enter the United Kingdom or, if he has been examined under subsection (4) above, from the conclusion of that examination, be cancelled by an immigration officer by giving him a notice in writing refusing him leave to enter.

(6) Sub-paragraphs (3) and (4) of paragraph 6 of Schedule 2 to the principal Act shall have effect as if any notice under subsection (5) above were a notice under that paragraph.

(7) References in this section to a person's arrival in the United Kingdom are to the first occasion on which he arrives after the time when the stamp in question was placed in his passport or travel document, being an occasion not later than seven days after that time.

[(8) . . .]

Amendment

Repealed by the Immigration and Asylum Act 1999, s 169(1), (3), Sch 14, paras 83, 85, Sch 16 (as from a day to be appointed: see the Immigration and Asylum Act 1999, s 170(4)).

Sub-s (8): inserted by SI 1990/2227, art 3, Sch 1, Part II and repealed by SI 1993/1813, art 9, Sch 6, Part I.

9

(Repealed by the Immigration and Asylum Act 1999, s 169(1), (3), Sch 14, paras 83, 86, Sch 16.)

10 Miscellaneous minor amendments

The principal Act shall have effect with the amendments specified in the Schedule to this Act.

11 Expenses and receipts

(1) There shall be paid out of money provided by Parliament any expenses incurred by the Secretary of State in consequence of this Act.

(2) Any sums received by the Secretary of State by virtue of this Act shall be paid into the Consolidated Fund.

12 Short title, interpretation, commencement and extent

(1) This Act may be cited as the Immigration Act 1988.

(2) In this Act "the principal Act" means the Immigration Act 1971 and any expression which is also used in that Act has the same meaning as in that Act.

(3) Except as provided in subsection (4) below this Act shall come into force at the end of the period of two months beginning with the day on which it is passed.

(4) Sections 1, 2, 3, 4, 5 and 7(1) and paragraph 1 of the Schedule shall come into force on such day as may be appointed by the Secretary of State by an order made by statutory instrument; and such an order may appoint different days for different provisions and contain such transitional provisions and savings as the Secretary of State thinks necessary or expedient in connection with any provision brought into force.

(5) This Act extends to Northern Ireland and section 36 of the principal Act (power to extend any of its provisions to the Channel Islands or the Isle of Man) shall apply also to the provisions of this Act.

Subordinate Legislation

Immigration Act 1988 (Commencement No 1) Order 1988, SI 1988/1133; Immigration Act 1988 (Commencement No 2) Order 1991, SI 1991/1001; Immigration (Jersey) Order 1993, SI 1993/1797.

1–6

...

Section 10

SCHEDULE

MINOR AMENDMENTS

7

(1) ...

(2) This amendment does not apply in relation to any person whose examination under paragraph 2 began before the coming into force of this paragraph.

Time-limit for giving, refusing or cancelling leave to enter

8

(1), (2) ...

(3) The amendment in sub-paragraph (1) above does not apply in relation to any person in whose case the time-limit in paragraph 6(1) of Schedule 2 has expired before the coming into force of this paragraph; and the amendment in sub-paragraph (2) above does not apply in relation to a person given a notice of cancellation under paragraph 6(3) of Schedule 2 before the coming into force of this paragraph.

Leave in default of notice giving or refusing leave or cancelling refusal

Time-limit for removal directions

9

(1)–(3) . . .

(4) These amendments do not apply in relation to any person refused leave to enter the United Kingdom before the coming into force of this paragraph.

Restriction on work in case of persons temporarily admitted etc

10

(1)–(3) . . .

(4) These amendments apply in relation to persons granted temporary admission or released from detention under paragraph 21 of Schedule 2, becoming liable to detention under paragraph 2(2) or (3) of Schedule 3, or directed to be released as mentioned in paragraph 4 of that Schedule, as the case may be, before as well as after the coming into force of this paragraph.

Amendment

Paras 1, 2, 4. 5: amend the Immigration Act 1971, ss 3(3)(b), 5(6), 28(1)(a), 33(1).
Paras 3, 6: spent.
Para 7: sub-para (1) amends the Immigration Act 1971, Sch 2, para 6(1), (2).
Para 8: sub-paras (1), (2) amend the Immigration Act 1971, Sch 2, para 6(1), (3).
Para 9: sub-paras (1)–(3) amend the Immigration Act 1971, Sch 2, paras 8(2), 10(1)(b), 28(4).
Para 10: sub-paras (1)–(3) amend the Immigration Act 1971, s 24(1)(e), Sch 2, para 21(2), Sch 3, paras 2(5), 4.

ASYLUM AND IMMIGRATION APPEALS ACT 1993

1993 c 23

An Act to make provision about persons who claim asylum in the United Kingdom and their dependants; to amend the law with respect to certain rights of appeal under the Immigration Act 1971; and to extend the provisions of the Immigration (Carriers' Liability) Act 1987 to transit passengers   [1 July 1993]

Introductory

1 Interpretation

In this Act—

"the 1971 Act" means the Immigration Act 1971;

"claim for asylum" means a claim made by a person (whether before or after the coming into force of this section) that it would be contrary to the United Kingdom's obligations under the Convention for him to be removed from, or required to leave, the United Kingdom; and

"the Convention" means the Convention relating to the Status of Refugees done at Geneva on 28th July 1951 and the Protocol to that Convention.

2 Primacy of Convention

Nothing in the immigration rules (within the meaning of the 1971 Act) shall lay down any practice which would be contrary to the Convention.

Appendix 1 — UK Immigration Statutes

3

(Repealed by the Immigration and Asylum Act 1999, s 169(1), (3), Sch 14, paras 99, 100, Sch 16.)

4, 5

(Repealed, in relation to England and Wales, by the Housing Act 1996, s 227, Sch 19, Part VIII. Repealed, in relation to Scotland and Northern Ireland, by the Immigration and Asylum Act 1999, ss 120(6), 121(3), 169(1), (3), Sch 14, paras 99, 101, Sch 16.)

6–9

(Repealed by the Immigration and Asylum Act 1999, s 169(1), (3), Sch 14, paras 99, 102–104, Sch 16.)

9A

(Inserted by the Asylum and Immigration Act 1996, s 12(2), Sch 3, para 3. Repealed by the Asylum and Immigration (Treatment of Claimants, etc) Act 2004, ss 26(7), 47, Sch 2, Pt 1, para 9, Sch 4.)

10–12

(Repealed by the Immigration and Asylum Act 1999, s 169(1), (3), Sch 14, paras 99, 104, 107, Sch 16.)

Supplementary

13 Financial provision

(1) There shall be paid out of money provided by Parliament—

    (a) any expenditure incurred by the Secretary of State under this Act; and

    (b) any increase attributable to this Act in the sums payable out of such money under any other enactment.

(2) Any sums received by the Secretary of State by virtue of this Act shall be paid into the Consolidated Fund.

14 Commencement

(1) Sections 4 to 11 above (and section 1 above so far as it relates to those sections) shall not come into force until such day as the Secretary of State may by order appoint, and different days may be appointed for different provisions or for different purposes.

(2) An order under subsection (1) above—

    (a) shall be made by statutory instrument; and

    (b) may contain such transitional and supplemental provisions as the Secretary of State thinks necessary or expedient.

(3) Without prejudice to the generality of subsections (1) and (2) above, with respect to any provision of section 4 above an order under subsection (1) above may appoint different days in relation to different descriptions of asylum-seekers and dependants of asylum-seekers; and any such descriptions may be framed by reference to nationality,

citizenship, origin or other connection with any particular country or territory, but not by reference to race, colour or religion.

Subordinate Legislation

Asylum and Immigration Appeals Act 1993 (Commencement and Transitional Provisions) Order 1993, SI 1993/1655.

15 Extent

(1) Her Majesty may by Order in Council direct that any of the provisions of this Act shall extend, with such modifications as appear to Her Majesty to be appropriate, to any of the Channel Islands or the Isle of Man.

(2) This Act extends to Northern Ireland.

16 Short title

This Act may be cited as the Asylum and Immigration Appeals Act 1993.

SCHEDULES 1, 2

(Repealed by the Immigration and Asylum Act 1999, s 169(1), (3), Sch 14, paras 99, 101, 104, Sch 16.)

ASYLUM AND IMMIGRATION ACT 1996

1996 c 49

An Act to amend and supplement the Immigration Act 1971 and the Asylum and Immigration Appeals Act 1993; to make further provision with respect to persons subject to immigration control and the employment of such persons; and for connected purposes

[24 July 1996]

1–11

(Ss 1–3 repealed by the Immigration and Asylum Act 1999, s 169(3), Sch 16; ss 4–6 amend the Immigration Act 1971, ss 24–27; ss 7, 9–11 repealed by the Immigration and Asylum Act 1999, s 169(1), (3), Sch 14, paras 108–112, Sch 16; s 8 repealed by the Immigration, Asylum and Nationality Act 2006, ss 26, 61, Sch 3; s 8A inserted by the Immigration and Asylum Act 1999, s 22 and repealed by the Immigration, Asylum and Nationality Act 2006, ss 26, 61, Sch 3.)

Miscellaneous and supplemental

12 Other amendments and repeals

(1) Schedule 2 to this Act (which contains amendments of the 1971 Act and a related amendment of the Immigration Act 1988) shall have effect.

(2) Schedule 3 to this Act (which contains amendments of the 1993 Act) shall have effect.

(3) The enactments specified in Schedule 4 to this Act are hereby repealed to the extent specified in the third column of that Schedule.

13 Short title, interpretation, commencement and extent

(1) This Act may be cited as the Asylum and Immigration Act 1996.

(2) In this Act—

"the 1971 Act" means the Immigration Act 1971;

"the 1993 Act" means the Asylum and Immigration Appeals Act 1993;

"person subject to immigration control" means a person who under the 1971 Act requires leave to enter or remain in the United Kingdom (whether or not such leave has been given).

(3)   This Act, except section 11 and Schedule 1, shall come into force on such day as the Secretary of State may by order made by statutory instrument appoint, and different days may be appointed for different purposes.

(4)   An order under subsection (3) above may make such transitional and supplemental provision as the Secretary of State thinks necessary or expedient.

(5)   Her Majesty may by Order in Council direct that any of the provisions of this Act shall extend, with such modifications as appear to Her Majesty to be appropriate, to any of the Channel Islands or the Isle of Man.

(6)   This Act extends to Northern Ireland.

Subordinate Legislation

Asylum and Immigration Act 1996 (Commencement No 1) Order 1996, SI 1996/2053; Asylum and Immigration Act 1996 (Commencement No 2) Order 1996, SI 1996/2127; Asylum and Immigration Act 1996 (Commencement No 3 and Transitional Provisions) Order 1996, SI 1996/2970; Asylum and Immigration Act 1996 (Jersey) Order 1998, SI 1998/1070; Asylum and Immigration Act 1996 (Guernsey) Order 1998, SI 1998/1264; Immigration (Isle of Man) Order 2008, SI 2008/680.; Immigration (Isle of Man) (Amendment) Order 2011, SI 2011/1408; Immigration and Asylum (Jersey) Order 2012, SI 2012/2593.

(Sch 1 repealed by the Immigration and Asylum Act 1999, s 169(1), (3), Sch 14, paras 108, 113; Schs 2–4 contain amendments and repeals which, in so far as relevant to this work, have been incorporated in this work.)

SPECIAL IMMIGRATION APPEALS COMMISSION ACT 1997

1997 c 68

An Act to establish the Special Immigration Appeals Commission; to make provision with respect to its jurisdiction; and for connected purposes.

[17 December 1997]

1 Establishment of the Commission

(1)   There shall be a commission, known as the Special Immigration Appeals Commission, for the purpose of exercising the jurisdiction conferred by this Act.

(2)   Schedule 1 to this Act shall have effect in relation to the Commission.

[(3)   The Commission shall be a superior court of record.

(4)   A decision of the Commission shall be questioned in legal proceedings only in accordance with—

    (a)   section 7, . . .

    (b)   . . .]

Amendment

Sub-ss (3), (4): inserted by the Anti-terrorism, Crime and Security Act 2001, s 35.

Sub-s (4): para (b) and word omitted immediately preceding it repealed by the Prevention of Terrorism Act 2005, s 16(2)(b).

[2 Jurisdiction: appeals

(1) A person may appeal to the Special Immigration Appeals Commission against a decision if—

    (a)   he would be able to appeal against the decision under section 82(1)[, 83(2) or 83A(2)] of the Nationality, Immigration and Asylum Act 2002 but for a certificate of the Secretary of State under section 97 of that Act (national security, &c), or

    (b)   an appeal against the decision under section 82(1)[, 83(2) or 83A(2)] of that Act lapsed under section 99 of that Act by virtue of a certificate of the Secretary of State under section 97 of that Act.

(2) The following provisions shall apply, with any necessary modifications, in relation to an appeal against an immigration decision under this section as they apply in relation to an appeal under section 82(1) of the Nationality, Immigration and Asylum Act 2002—

    (a)   section 3C [or 3D] of the Immigration Act 1971 (c 77) [continuation of leave],

    (b)   section 78 of the Nationality, Immigration and Asylum Act 2002 (no removal while appeal pending),

    (c)   section 79 of that Act (deportation order: appeal),

    [(ca)   section 78A of that Act (restriction on removal of children and their parents),]

    (d)   *section 82(3) of that Act (variation or revocation of leave to enter or remain: appeal),*

    (e)   section 84 of that Act (grounds of appeal),

    (f)   section 85 of that Act (matters to be considered),

    (g)   section 86 of that Act (determination of appeal),

    (h)   *section 87 of that Act (successful appeal: direction),*

    (i)   section 96 of that Act (earlier right of appeal),

    (j)   section 104 of that Act (pending appeal),

    (k)   section 105 of that Act (notice of immigration decision), and

    (l)   *section 110 of that Act (grants).*

(3) *The following provisions shall apply, with any necessary modifications, in relation to [an appeal against a decision other than an immigration decision] under this section as they apply in relation to an appeal under section 83(2) [or 83A(2)] of the Nationality, Immigration and Asylum Act 2002—*

    (a)   section 85(4) of that Act (matters to be considered),

    (b)   *section 86 of that Act (determination of appeal),*

    (c)   *section 87 of that Act (successful appeal: direction), and*

    (d)   *section 110 of that Act (grants).*

(4) *An appeal against the rejection of a claim for asylum under this section shall be treated as abandoned if the appellant leaves the United Kingdom.*

(5) A person may bring or continue an appeal against an immigration decision under this section while he is in the United Kingdom only if he would be able to bring or continue the appeal while he was in the United Kingdom if it were an appeal under section 82(1) of that Act.

(6) *In this section "immigration decision" has the meaning given by section 82(2) of the Nationality, Immigration and Asylum Act 2002.]*

Amendment

Substituted by the Nationality, Immigration and Asylum Act 2002, s 114(3), Sch 7, para 20.

Appendix 1 — UK Immigration Statutes

Sub-s (1): in paras (a), (b) words in square brackets and italics substituted by the Immigration, Asylum and Nationality Act 2006, s 14, Sch 1, para 14(a) and repealed by the Immigration Act 2014, s 73, Sch 9, Pt 4, para 26(1), (2)(a), (b), as from a day to be appointed.

Sub-s (2): in para (a) words in first pair of square brackets inserted and words in second pair of square brackets substituted by the Immigration, Asylum and Nationality Act 2006, s 14, Sch 1, para 14(b).

Sub-s (2): para (ca) inserted by the Immigration Act 2014, s 73, Sch 9, para 2, as from 28 July 2014: see SI 2014/1820.

Sub-s (2): paras (d), (h), (l) repealed by the Immigration Act 2014, s 73, Sch 9, Pt 4, para 26(1), (2)(c), as from a day to be appointed.

Sub-s (3): words in first pair of square brackets substituted and words in second pair of square brackets inserted by the Immigration, Asylum and Nationality Act 2006, s 14, Sch 1, para 14(c).

Sub-s (3): repealed by the Immigration Act 2014, s 73, Sch 9, Pt 4, para 26(1), (2)(d), as from a day to be appointed.

Sub-s (4): repealed by the Immigration Act 2014, s 73, Sch 9, Pt 4, para 26(1), (2)(d), as from a day to be appointed.

Sub-s (5): words in italics repealed by the Immigration Act 2014, s 73, Sch 9, Pt 4, para 26(1), (2)(e), as from a day to be appointed.

Sub-s (6): repealed by the Immigration Act 2014, s 73, Sch 9, Pt 4, para 26(1), (2)(d), as from a day to be appointed.

[2A]

(Inserted by the Immigration and Asylum Act 1999, s 169(1), Sch 14, paras 118, 121. Repealed by the Nationality, Immigration and Asylum Act 2002, ss 114(3), 161, Sch 7, para 21, Sch 9.)

[2B]

A person may appeal to the Special Immigration Appeals Commission against a decision to make an order under section 40 of the British Nationality Act 1981 (c 61) (deprivation of citizenship) if he is not entitled to appeal under section 40A(1) of that Act because of a certificate under section 40A(2) [*(and section 40A(3)(a) shall have effect in relation to appeals under this section)*].]

Amendment

Inserted by the Nationality, Immigration and Asylum Act 2002, s 4(2).

[2C Jurisdiction: review of certain exclusion decisions

(1) Subsection (2) applies in relation to any direction about the exclusion of a non-EEA national from the United Kingdom which—

(a) is made by the Secretary of State wholly or partly on the ground that the exclusion from the United Kingdom of the non-EEA national is conducive to the public good,

(b) is not subject to a right of appeal, and

(c) is certified by the Secretary of State as a direction that was made wholly or partly in reliance on information which, in the opinion of the Secretary of State, should not be made public—

(i) in the interests of national security,

(ii) in the interests of the relationship between the United Kingdom and another country, or

(iii) otherwise in the public interest.

(2) The non-EEA national to whom the direction relates may apply to the Special Immigration Appeals Commission to set aside the direction.

(3) In determining whether the direction should be set aside, the Commission must apply the principles which would be applied in judicial review proceedings.

(4) If the Commission decides that the direction should be set aside, it may make any such order, or give any such relief, as may be made or given in judicial review proceedings.

(5) In this section—

"non-EEA national" means any person who is not a national of an EEA state, and references in this section to the Secretary of State are to the Secretary of State acting in person.]

Amendment

Inserted by the Justice and Security Act 2013, s 15, as from 25 June 2013: see SI 2013/1482, art 2; for transitional provisions see arts 3, 4 thereof.

[2D Jurisdiction: review of certain naturalisation and citizenship decisions

(1) Subsection (2) applies in relation to any decision of the Secretary of State which—

(a) is either—

(i) a refusal to issue a certificate of naturalisation under section 6 of the British Nationality Act 1981 to an applicant under that section, or

(ii) a refusal to grant an application of the kind mentioned in section 41A of that Act (applications to register an adult or young person as a British citizen etc), and

(b) is certified by the Secretary of State as a decision that was made wholly or partly in reliance on information which, in the opinion of the Secretary of State, should not be made public—

(i) in the interests of national security,

(ii) in the interests of the relationship between the United Kingdom and another country, or

(iii) otherwise in the public interest.

(2) The applicant to whom the decision relates may apply to the Special Immigration Appeals Commission to set aside the decision.

(3) In determining whether the decision should be set aside, the Commission must apply the principles which would be applied in judicial review proceedings.

(f4) If the Commission decides that the decision should be set aside, it may make any such order, or give any such relief, as may be made or given in judicial review proceedings.]

Amendment

Inserted by the Justice and Security Act 2013, s 15, as from 25 June 2013: see SI 2013/1482, art 2; for transitional provisions see arts 3, 4 thereof.

[2E Jurisdiction: review of certain deportation decisions

(1) Subsection (2) applies in relation to a relevant deportation decision which has been certified under section 97 or 97A(1) of the Nationality, Immigration and Asylum Act 2002 (certification on grounds of national security etc).

(2) The person to whom the decision relates may apply to the Special Immigration Appeals Commission to set aside the decision.

(3) In determining whether the decision should be set aside, the Commission must apply the principles which would be applied in judicial review proceedings.

(4) If the Commission decides that the decision should be set aside, it may make any such order, or give any such relief, as may be made or given in judicial review proceedings.

(5) In this section, "relevant deportation decision" means a decision of the Secretary of State about the deportation of a person from the United Kingdom, if and to the extent that—

    (a) the decision is not subject to a right of appeal, or

    (b) the decision (being subject to a right of appeal) gives rise to issues which may not be raised on such an appeal.]

Amendment

Inserted by the Immigration Act 2014, s 18, as from a day to be appointed.

3 Jurisdiction: bail

(1) In the case of a person to whom subsection (2) below applies, the provisions of Schedule 2 to the Immigration Act 1971 specified in Schedule 3 to this Act shall have effect with the modifications set out there.

(2) This subsection applies to a person who is detained under the Immigration Act 1971 [or the Nationality, Immigration and Asylum Act 2002] if—

    (a) the Secretary of State certifies that his detention is necessary in the interests of national security,

    (b) he is detained following a decision to refuse him leave to enter the United Kingdom on the ground that his exclusion is in the interests of national security, or

    (c) he is detained following a decision to make a deportation order against him on the ground that his deportation is in the interests of national security.

Amendment

Sub-s (2): words in square brackets inserted by SI 2003/1016, art 3, Schedule, para 10.

4

(Repealed by the Nationality, Immigration and Asylum Act 2002, ss 114(3), 161 Sch 7, para 22, Sch 9.)

5 Procedure in relation to jurisdiction under sections 2 and 3

(1) The Lord Chancellor may make rules—

    (a) for regulating the exercise of the rights of appeal conferred by section 2 [. . .] [or 2B] above,

    (b) for prescribing the practice and procedure to be followed on or in connection with appeals under [section 2 . . . [or 2B] above], including the mode and burden of proof and admissibility of evidence on such appeals, and

    (c) for other matters preliminary or incidental to or arising out of such appeals, including proof of the decisions of the Special Immigration Appeals Commission.

(2) Rules under this section shall provide that an appellant has the right to be legally represented in any proceedings before the Commission on an appeal under section 2 [. . .] [or 2B] above, subject to any power conferred on the Commission by such rules.

[(2A) Rules under this section may, in particular, do anything which may be done by [Tribunal Procedure Rules].]

(3) Rules under this section may, in particular—

    (a) make provision enabling proceedings before the Commission to take place without the appellant being given full particulars of the reasons for the decision which is the subject of the appeal,

Special Immigration Appeals Commission Act 1997

(b) make provision enabling the Commission to hold proceedings in the absence of any person, including the appellant and any legal representative appointed by him,

(c) make provision about the functions in proceedings before the Commission of persons appointed under section 6 below, and

(d) make provision enabling the Commission to give the appellant a summary of any evidence taken in his absence.

(4) Rules under this section may also include provision—

(a) enabling any functions of the Commission which relate to matters preliminary or incidental to an appeal, or which are conferred by Part II of Schedule 2 to the Immigration Act 1971, to be performed by a single member of the Commission, or

(b) conferring on the Commission such ancillary powers as the Lord Chancellor thinks necessary for the purposes of the exercise of its functions.

(5) The power to make rules under this section shall include power to make rules with respect to applications to the Commission under paragraphs 22 to 24 of Schedule 2 to the Immigration Act 1971 and matters arising out of such applications.

[(5A) Rules under this section must secure that, where the Commission has decided not to release a person on bail under paragraph 22 or 29 of Schedule 2 to the Immigration Act 1971, the Commission is required to dismiss any further application by the person for release on bail that is made during the period of 28 days starting with the date of the Commission's decision, unless there has been a material change in circumstances.]

(6) In making rules under this section, the Lord Chancellor shall have regard, in particular, to—

(a) the need to secure that decisions which are the subject of appeals are properly reviewed, and

(b) the need to secure that information is not disclosed contrary to the public interest.

(7) . . .

(8) The power to make rules under this section shall be exercisable by statutory instrument.

(9) No rules shall be made under this section unless a draft of them has been laid before and approved by resolution of each House of Parliament.

Amendment

Sub-s (1): in para (a) words omitted inserted by the Race Relations (Amendment) Act 2000, s 9(1), Sch 2, para 28(a) and repealed by the Nationality, Immigration and Asylum Act 2002, ss 114(3), 161, Sch 7, para 23(a), Sch 9.

Sub-s (1): in para (a) words "or 2B" in square brackets inserted by the Nationality, Immigration and Asylum Act 2002, s 4(3).

Sub-s (1): in para (b) words in square brackets beginning with the words "section 2" substituted by the Race Relations (Amendment) Act 2000, s 9(1), Sch 2, para 28(b).

Sub-s (1): in para (b) words omitted repealed and words "or 2B" in square brackets inserted by the Nationality, Immigration and Asylum Act 2002, ss 4(3), 114(3), 161, Sch 7, para 23(a), Sch 9.

Sub-s (2): words omitted inserted by the Race Relations (Amendment) Act 2000, s 9(1), Sch 2, para 28(c); words omitted repealed and words "or 2B" in square brackets inserted by the Nationality, Immigration and Asylum Act 2002, ss 4(3), 114(3), 161, Sch 7, para 23(a), Sch 9.

Sub-s (2A): inserted by the Nationality, Immigration and Asylum Act 2002, s 114(3), Sch 7, para 23(b).

Sub-s (2A): words "Tribunal Procedure Rules" in square brackets substituted by SI 2010/21, art 5(1), Sch 1, paras 14, 15, as from 15 February 2010: see SI 2010/21, art 1; for transitional provisions and savings see art 5(4), Sch 4, paras 14–18, 21 thereto.

Sub-s (5A): inserted by the Immigration Act 2014, s 73, Sch 9, para 10(1), (2), as from 20 October 2014 (see SI 2014/2771, art 2), subject to savings in SI 2014/2771, arts 9–11.

Sub-s (7): repealed by the Regulation of Investigatory Powers Act 2000, s 82(2), Sch 5.

Subordinate Legislation

Special Immigration Appeals Commission (Procedure) Rules 2003, SI 2003/1034; Special Immigration Appeals Commission (Procedure) (Amendment) Rules 2007, SI 2007/1285; Special Immigration Appeals Commission (Procedure) (Amendment No 2) Rules 2007, SI 2007/3370; Special Immigration Appeals Commission (Procedure) (Amendment) Rules 2013, SI 2013/2995.

6 Appointment of person to represent the appellant's interests

(1) The relevant law officer may appoint a person to represent the interests of an appellant in any proceedings before the Special Immigration Appeals Commission from which the appellant and any legal representative of his are excluded.

(2) For the purposes of subsection (1) above, the relevant law officer is—

(a) in relation to proceedings before the Commission in England and Wales, the Attorney General,

(b) in relation to proceedings before the Commission in Scotland, the Lord Advocate, and

(c) in relation to proceedings before the Commission in Northern Ireland, the *Attorney General for Northern Ireland* [Advocate General for Northern Ireland].

(3) A person appointed under subsection (1) above—

(a) if appointed for the purposes of proceedings in England and Wales, shall have a general qualification for the purposes of section 71 of the Courts and Legal Services Act 1990,

(b) if appointed for the purposes of proceedings in Scotland, shall be—

(i) an advocate, or

(ii) a solicitor who has by virtue of section 25A of the Solicitors (Scotland) Act 1980 rights of audience in the Court of Session and the High Court of Justiciary, and

(c) if appointed for the purposes of proceedings in Northern Ireland, shall be a member of the Bar of Northern Ireland.

(4) A person appointed under subsection (1) above shall not be responsible to the person whose interests he is appointed to represent.

Amendment

Sub-s (2): in para (c) words "Attorney General for Northern Ireland" in italics repealed and subsequent words in square brackets substituted by the Counter-Terrorism Act 2008, s 91(1), (2), as from a day to be appointed.

[6A Procedure in relation to jurisdiction under sections 2C [to 2E]

(1) Sections 5 and 6 apply in relation to reviews under section 2C[, 2D or 2E] as they apply in relation to appeals under section 2 or 2B.

(2) Accordingly—

(a) references to appeals are to be read as references to reviews (and references to appeals under section 2 or 2B are to be read as references to reviews under section 2C[, 2D or 2E]), and

(b) references to an appellant are to be read as references to an applicant under section 2C(2)[, 2D(2) or (as the case may be) 2E(2)].]

Amendment

Inserted by the Justice and Security Act 2013, s 19(1), Sch 2, Pt 2, para 9(1), (2), as from 25 June 2013: see SI 2013/1482, art 2; for transitional provisions see arts 3, 4 thereof.

Section headings: words in square brackets substituted (for original words "and 2D") by the Immigration Act 2014, s 73, Sch 9, Pt 4, para 26(1), (4)(a), as from 20 October 2014 (see SI 2014/2771, art 2), subject to savings in SI 2014/2771, arts 9–11.

Sub-s (1): words in square brackets substituted (for original words "or 2D") by the Immigration Act 2014, s 73, Sch 9, Pt 4, para 26(1), (4)(b), as from 20 October 2014 (see SI 2014/2771, art 2), subject to savings in SI 2014/2771, arts 9–11.

Sub-s (2): words in square brackets in paras (a), (b) substituted (for original words "or 2D" and "or (as the case may be) 2D(2)" respectively) by the Immigration Act 2014, s 73, Sch 9, Pt 4, para 26(1), (4)(c), as from 20 October 2014 (see SI 2014/2771, art 2), subject to savings in SI 2014/2771, arts 9–11.

7 Appeals from the Commission

(1) Where the Special Immigration Appeals Commission has made a final determination of an appeal, any party to the appeal may bring a further appeal to the appropriate appeal court on any question of law material to that determination.

[(1A) Where the Commission has made a final determination of a review under section 2C or 2D, any party to the review may bring an appeal against that determination to the appropriate appeal court.]

(2) An appeal under this section may be brought only with the leave of the Commission or, if such leave is refused, with the leave of the appropriate appeal court.

(3) In this section "the appropriate appeal court" means—

    (a)   in relation to a determination made by the Commission in England and Wales, the Court of Appeal,

    (b)   in relation to a determination made by the Commission in Scotland, the Court of Session, and

    (c)   in relation to a determination made by the Commission in Northern Ireland, the Court of Appeal in Northern Ireland.

(4) . . . . . .

Amendment

Sub-s (1A): inserted by the Justice and Security Act 2013, s 19(1), Sch 2, Pt 2, para 9(1), (3), as from 25 June 2013: see SI 2013/1482, art 2; for transitional provisions see arts 3, 4 thereof.

Sub-s (1A): for the words in italics there are substituted the words ", 2D or 2E" by the Immigration Act 2014, s 73, Sch 9, Pt 4, para 26(1), (5), as from a day to be appointed.

Sub-s (4): repealed by the Immigration and Asylum Act 1999, s 169(1), (3), Sch 14, paras 118, 123, Sch 16.

[7A]

(Inserted by the Immigration and Asylum Act 1999, s 169(1), Sch 14, paras 118, 124. Repealed by the Nationality, Immigration and Asylum Act 2002, ss 114(3), 161, Sch 7, para 24, Sch 9.)

8 Procedure on applications to the Commission for leave to appeal

(1) The Lord Chancellor may make rules regulating, and prescribing the procedure to be followed on, applications to the Special Immigration Appeals Commission for leave to appeal under section 7 above.

(2) Rules under this section may include provision enabling an application for leave to appeal to be heard by a single member of the Commission.

(3) The power to make rules under this section shall be exercisable by statutory instrument.

(4) No rules shall be made under this section unless a draft of them has been laid before and approved by resolution of each House of Parliament.

Subordinate Legislation

Special Immigration Appeals Commission (Procedure) (Amendment) Rules 2007, SI 2007/1285; Special Immigration Appeals Commission (Procedure) (Amendment No 2) Rules

2007, SI 2007/3370; Special Immigration Appeals Commission (Procedure) (Amendment) Rules 2013, SI 2013/2995.

9 Short title, commencement and extent

(1) This Act may be cited as the Special Immigration Appeals Commission Act 1997.

(2) This Act, except for this section, shall come into force on such day as the Secretary of State may by order made by statutory instrument appoint; and different days may be so appointed for different purposes.

(3) Her Majesty may by Order in Council direct that any of the provisions of this Act shall extend, with such modifications as appear to Her Majesty to be appropriate, to any of the Channel Islands or the Isle of Man.

(4) This Act extends to Northern Ireland.

Subordinate Legislation

Special Immigration Appeals Commission Act 1997 (Commencement No 1) Order 1998, SI 1998/1336 and Special Immigration Appeals Commission Act 1997 (Commencement No 2) Order 1998, SI 1998/1892 (both made under sub-s (2)).

Section 1

SCHEDULE 1
THE COMMISSION

Members

1

(1) The Special Immigration Appeals Commission shall consist of such number of members appointed by the Lord Chancellor as he may determine.

(2) A member of the Commission shall hold and vacate office in accordance with the terms of his appointment and shall, on ceasing to hold office, be eligible for re-appointment.

(3) A member of the Commission may resign his office at any time by notice in writing to the Lord Chancellor.

Chairman

2

The Lord Chancellor shall appoint one of the members of the Commission to be its chairman.

Payments to members

3

(1) The Lord Chancellor may pay to the members of the Commission such remuneration and allowances as he may determine.

(2) The Lord Chancellor may, if he thinks fit in the case of any member of the Commission pay such pension, allowance or gratuity to or in respect of the member, or such sums towards the provision of such pension, allowance or gratuity, as he may determine.

(3) If a person ceases to be a member of the Commission and it appears to the Lord Chancellor that there are special circumstances which make it right that the person should receive compensation, he may pay to that person a sum of such amount as he may determine.

Proceedings

4

The Commission shall sit at such times and in such places as the Lord Chancellor may direct and may sit in two or more divisions.

5

The Commission shall be deemed to be duly constituted if it consists of three members of whom—

(a) at least one holds or has held high judicial office (within the meaning of [Part 3 of the Constitutional Reform Act 2005) or is or has been a member of the Judicial Committee of the Privy Council], and

[(b) at least one is or has been [a judge of the First-tier Tribunal, or of the Upper Tribunal, who is assigned to a chamber with responsibility for immigration and asylum matters]].

6

The chairman or, in his absence, such other member of the Commission as he may nominate, shall preside at sittings of the Commission and report its decisions.

Staff

7

The Lord Chancellor may appoint such officers and servants for the Commission as he thinks fit.

Expenses

8

The Lord Chancellor shall defray the remuneration of persons appointed under paragraph 7 above and such expenses of the Commission as he thinks fit.

Amendment

Para 5: in sub-para (a) words from "Part 3 of" to "the Privy Council" in square brackets substituted by the Constitutional Reform Act 2005, s 145, Sch 17, Pt 2, para 28.

Para 5: sub-para (b) substituted by the Asylum and Immigration (Treatment of Claimants, etc) Act 2004, s 26(7), Sch 2, Pt 1, paras 10, 12.

Para 5: in sub-para (b) words from "a judge of" to "and asylum matters" in square brackets substituted by SI 2010/21, art 5(1), Sch 1, paras 14, 16, as from 15 February 2010: see SI 2010/21, art 1; for transitional provisions and savings see art 5(4), Sch 4, paras 14–18, 21 thereto.

SCHEDULE 2

(Repealed by the Nationality, Immigration and Asylum Act 2002, ss 114(3), 161, Sch 7, para 26, Sch 9.)

SCHEDULE 3

BAIL: MODIFICATIONS OF SCHEDULE 2 TO THE IMMIGRATION ACT 1971

Section 3

1

(1) Paragraph 22 shall be amended as follows.

(2) In sub-paragraph (1A), for the words from the beginning to ["Tribunal"] there shall be substituted "The Special Immigration Appeals Commission .

Appendix 1 — UK Immigration Statutes

(3) In sub-paragraph (2)—

    (a) for the words "immigration officer or [[the First-tier Tribunal]]" there shall be substituted "Special Immigration Appeals Commission", and

    (b) for the words "officer or [[the First-tier Tribunal]]" there shall be substituted "Commission".

(4) In sub-paragraph (3)—

    (a) for "an immigration officer or [[the First-tier Tribunal]]" there shall be substituted "the Special Immigration Appeals Commission", and

    (b) for "officer or [[the First-tier Tribunal]]", in both places, there shall be substituted "Commission".

2

(1) Paragraph 23 shall be amended as follows.

(2) In sub-paragraph (1)—

    (a) for [["the First-tier Tribunal]"] there shall be substituted "the Special Immigration Appeals Commission", and

    (b) for [["the First-tier Tribunal]"], in each place, there shall be substituted "the Commission".

(3) In sub-paragraph (2)—

    (a) for [["the First-tier Tribunal]"] there shall be substituted "the Special Immigration Appeals Commission", and

    (b) for [["the First-tier Tribunal]"] there shall be substituted "the Commission".

3

(1) Paragraph 24 shall be amended as follows.

(2) For sub-paragraph (2), there shall be substituted—

    "(2) A person arrested under this paragraph shall be brought before the Special Immigration Appeals Commission within twenty-four hours."

(3) In sub-paragraph (3), for the words from the beginning to "above" there shall be substituted "Where a person is brought before the Special Immigration Appeals Commission by virtue of sub-paragraph (2) above, the Commission—"

4

(1) Paragraph 29 shall be amended as follows.

[(1A) In sub-paragraph (1) after "2002" there shall be inserted "or section 2 of the Special Immigration Appeals Commission Act 1997 or a review pending under section 2E of that Act.]

(2) For sub-paragraphs (2) to (4) there shall be substituted—

    "(2) The Special Immigration Appeals Commission may release an appellant on his entering into a recognizance or, in Scotland, bail bond conditioned for his appearance before the Commission at a time and place named in the recognizance or bail bond."

(3) For sub-paragraph (6) there shall be substituted—

    "(6) In any case in which the Special Immigration Appeals Commission has power to release an appellant on bail, the Commission may, instead of taking the bail, fix the amount and conditions of the bail (including the amount in which any sureties are to be bound) with a view to its being taken subsequently by any such person as may be specified by the Commission; and on the recognizance or bail bond being so taken the appellant shall be released."

5

Paragraph 30(2) shall be omitted.

6

(1) Paragraph 31 shall be amended as follows.

(2) In sub-paragraph (1)—

    (a)   for ["the Tribunal"] there shall be substituted "the Special Immigration Appeals Commission",

    (b)   for ["the Tribunal"] there shall be substituted "the Commission", and

    (c)   for ["the Tribunal"], in both places, there shall be substituted "the Commission".

(3) In sub-paragraph (3)—

    (a)   for ["the Tribunal"] there shall be substituted "the Special Immigration Appeals Commission", and

    (b)   for ["the Tribunal"] there shall be substituted "it".

7

Paragraph 32 shall be amended as follows—

    (a)   for ["the Tribunal"] there shall be substituted "the Special Immigration Appeals Commission",

    (b)   for ["the Tribunal"] there shall be substituted "the Commission", and

    (c)   for ["the Tribunal"] there shall be substituted "the Commission".

8

(1) Paragraph 33 shall be amended as follows.

(2) For sub-paragraph (2), there shall be substituted—

"(2) A person arrested under this paragraph shall be brought before the Special Immigration Appeals Commission within twenty-four hours."

(3) In sub-paragraph (3), for the words from the beginning to "above" there shall be substituted "Where a person is brought before the Special Immigration Appeals Commission by virtue of sub-paragraph (2) above, the Commission—".

Amendment

Para 1: in sub-para (2) word ' "Tribunal" ' in square brackets substituted by the Asylum and Immigration (Treatment of Claimants, etc) Act 2004, s 26(7), Sch 2, Pt 1, paras 10, 13(1), (2).

Para 1: in sub-paras (3), (4), words "the First-tier Tribunal" in square brackets substituted by SI 2010/21, art 5(1), Sch 1, paras 14, 17, as from 15 February 2010: see SI 2010/21, art 1; for transitional provisions and savings see art 5(4), Sch 4, paras 14–18, 21 thereto.

Para 2: in sub-paras (2), (3), words "the First-tier Tribunal" in square brackets substituted by SI 2010/21, art 5(1), Sch 1, paras 14, 17, as from 15 February 2010: see SI 2010/21, art 1; for transitional provisions and savings see art 5(4), Sch 4, paras 14–18, 21 thereto.

Para 4: sub-para (1A) inserted by the Immigration Act 2014, s 73, Sch 9, para 10(1), (3), as from 28 July 2014: see SI 2014/1820.

Para 6: in sub-paras (2), (3), words "the Tribunal" in square brackets in each place substituted by the Asylum and Immigration (Treatment of Claimants, etc) Act 2004, s 26(7), Sch 2, Pt 1, paras 10, 13(1), (10)–(14).

Para 7: words ' "the Tribunal" ' in square brackets in each place substituted by the Asylum and Immigration (Treatment of Claimants, etc) Act 2004, s 26(7), Sch 2, Pt 1, paras 10, 13(1), (15)–(17).

IMMIGRATION AND ASYLUM ACT 1999

1999 c 33

An Act to make provision about immigration and asylum; to make provision about procedures in connection with marriage on superintendent registrar's certificate; and for connected purposes.

[11 November 1999]

Modification

In relation to the extension of this Act, with modifications, to the Isle of Man, see the Immigration (Isle of Man) Order 2008, SI 2008/680.

PART I

IMMIGRATION: GENERAL

Leave to enter, or remain in, the United Kingdom

1–3

(Ss 1–3 insert the Immigration Act 1971, ss 3A–3C.)

4 [Accommodation]

[(1)] The Secretary of State may provide, or arrange for the provision of, facilities for the accommodation of persons—

(a) temporarily admitted to the United Kingdom under paragraph 21 of Schedule 2 to the 1971 Act;

(b) released from detention under that paragraph; or

(c) released on bail from detention under any provision of the Immigration Acts.

[(2)] The Secretary of State may provide, or arrange for the provision of, facilities for the accommodation of a person if—

(a) he was (but is no longer) an asylum-seeker, and

(b) his claim for asylum was rejected.

(3) The Secretary of State may provide, or arrange for the provision of, facilities for the accommodation of a dependant of a person for whom facilities may be provided under subsection (2).

(4) The following expressions have the same meaning in this section as in Part VI of this Act (as defined in section 94)—

(a) asylum-seeker,

(b) claim for asylum, and

(c) dependant.]

[(5)] The Secretary of State may make regulations specifying criteria to be used in determining—

(a) whether or not to provide accommodation, or arrange for the provision of accommodation, for a person under this section;

(b) whether or not to continue to provide accommodation, or arrange for the provision of accommodation, for a person under this section.

(6) The regulations may, in particular—

(a) provide for the continuation of the provision of accommodation for a person to be conditional upon his performance of or participation in community activities in accordance with arrangements made by the Secretary of State;

(b) provide for the continuation of the provision of accommodation to be subject to other conditions;

(c) provide for the provision of accommodation (or the continuation of the provision of accommodation) to be a matter for the Secretary of State's discretion to a specified extent or in a specified class of case.

(7) For the purposes of subsection (6)(a)—

(a) "community activities" means activities that appear to the Secretary of State to be beneficial to the public or a section of the public, and

(b) the Secretary of State may, in particular—

(i) appoint one person to supervise or manage the performance of or participation in activities by another person;

(ii) enter into a contract (with a local authority or any other person) for the provision of services by way of making arrangements for community activities in accordance with this section;

(iii) pay, or arrange for the payment of, allowances to a person performing or participating in community activities in accordance with arrangements under this section.

(8) Regulations by virtue of subsection (6)(a) may, in particular, provide for a condition requiring the performance of or participation in community activities to apply to a person only if the Secretary of State has made arrangements for community activities in an area that includes the place where accommodation is provided for the person.

(9) A local authority or other person may undertake to manage or participate in arrangements for community activities in accordance with this section.]

[(10) The Secretary of State may make regulations permitting a person who is provided with accommodation under this section to be supplied also with services or facilities of a specified kind.

(11) Regulations under subsection (10)—

(a) may, in particular, permit a person to be supplied with a voucher which may be exchanged for goods or services,

(b) may not permit a person to be supplied with money,

(c) may restrict the extent or value of services or facilities to be provided, and

(d) may confer a discretion.]

Amendment

Section heading: substituted by the Nationality, Immigration and Asylum Act 2002, s 49(2). Sub-s (1): numbered as such by the Nationality, Immigration and Asylum Act 2002, s 49(2). Sub-ss (2)–(4): inserted by the Nationality, Immigration and Asylum Act 2002, s 49(1). Sub-ss (5)–(9): inserted by the Asylum and Immigration (Treatment of Claimants, etc) Act 2004, s 10(1), (6). Sub-ss (10), (11): inserted by the Immigration, Asylum and Nationality Act 2006, s 43(7).

Subordinate Legislation

Immigration and Asylum (Provision of Accommodation to Failed Asylum-Seekers) Regulations 2005, SI 2005/930; Immigration and Asylum (Provision of Services or Facilities) Regulations 2007, SI 2007/3627.

5–8

(*S 5 repealed by the Immigration, Asylum and Nationality Act 2006, ss 52(7), 61, Sch 2, para 3, Sch 3; s 6 amends the Immigration Act 1971, s 8; ss 7, 8 insert ss 8A, 8B of that Act.*)

9 Treatment of certain overstayers

(1) During the regularisation period overstayers may apply, in the prescribed manner, for leave to remain in the United Kingdom.

(2) The regularisation period begins on the day prescribed for the purposes of this subsection and is not to be less than three months.

(3) The regularisation period ends—

(a) on the day prescribed for the purposes of this subsection; or

(b) if later, on the day before that on which section 65 comes into force.

(4) Section 10 and paragraph 12 of Schedule 15 come into force on the day after that on which the regularisation period ends.

(5) The Secretary of State must publicise the effect of this section in the way appearing to him to be best calculated to bring it to the attention of those affected.

(6) "Overstayer" means a person who, having only limited leave to enter or remain in the United Kingdom, remains beyond the time limited by the leave.

Subordinate Legislation

Immigration (Regularisation Period for Overstayers) Regulations 2000, SI 2000/265.

[10 Removal of persons unlawfully in the United Kingdom

(1) A person may be removed from the United Kingdom under the authority of the Secretary of State or an immigration officer if the person requires leave to enter or remain in the United Kingdom but does not have it.

(2) Where a person ("P") is liable to be or has been removed from the United Kingdom under subsection (1), a member of P's family who meets the following three conditions may also be removed from the United Kingdom under the authority of the Secretary of State or an immigration officer, provided that the Secretary of State or immigration officer has given the family member written notice of the intention to remove him or her.

(3) The first condition is that the family member is—

(a) P's partner,

(b) P's child, or a child living in the same household as P in circumstances where P has care of the child,

(c) in a case where P is a child, P's parent, or

(d) an adult dependent relative of P.

(4) The second condition is that—

(a) in a case where the family member has leave to enter or remain in the United Kingdom, that leave was granted on the basis of his or her family life with P;

(b) in a case where the family member does not have leave to enter or remain in the United Kingdom, in the opinion of the Secretary of State or immigration officer the family member—

(i) would not, on making an application for such leave, be granted leave in his or her own right, but

(ii) would be granted leave on the basis of his or her family life with P, if P had leave to enter or remain.

(5) The third condition is that the family member is neither a British citizen, nor is he or she entitled to enter or remain in the United Kingdom by virtue of an enforceable EU right or of any provision made under section 2(2) of the European Communities Act 1972.

(6) A notice given to a family member under subsection (2) invalidates any leave to enter or remain in the United Kingdom previously given to the family member.

(7) For the purposes of removing a person from the United Kingdom under subsection (1) or (2), the Secretary of State or an immigration officer may give any such direction for the removal of the person as may be given under paragraphs 8 to 10 of Schedule 2 to the 1971 Act.

(8) But subsection (7) does not apply where a deportation order is in force against a person (and any directions for such a person's removal must be given under Schedule 3 to the 1971 Act).

(9) The following paragraphs of Schedule 2 to the 1971 Act apply in relation to directions under subsection (7) (and the persons subject to those directions) as they apply in relation to directions under paragraphs 8 to 10 of Schedule 2 (and the persons subject to those directions)—

  (a) paragraph 11 (placing of person on board ship or aircraft);

  (b) paragraph 16(2) to (4) (detention of person where reasonable grounds for suspecting removal directions may be given or pending removal in pursuance of directions);

  (c) paragraph 17 (arrest of person liable to be detained and search of premises for person liable to arrest);

  (d) paragraph 18 (supplementary provisions on detention);

  (e) paragraph 18A (search of detained person);

  (f) paragraph 18B (detention of unaccompanied children);

  (g) paragraphs 19 and 20 (payment of expenses of custody etc);

  (h) paragraph 21 (temporary admission to UK of person liable to detention);

  (i) paragraphs 22 to 25 (bail);

  (j) paragraphs 25A to 25E (searches etc).

(10) The Secretary of State may by regulations make further provision about—

  (a) the time period during which a family member may be removed under subsection (2);

  (b) the service of a notice under subsection (2).

(11) In this section "child" means a person who is under the age of 18.]

Amendment

Substituted by the Immigration Act 2014, s 1, as from 20 October 2014 (see SI 2014/2771, art 2), subject to savings in SI 2014/2771, arts 9–11. Prior to this substitution, s 10 and the notes relating to it read as follows:

"10 Removal of certain persons unlawfully in the United Kingdom

(1) A person who is not a British citizen may be removed from the United Kingdom, in accordance with directions given by an immigration officer, if—

  (a) having only a limited leave to enter or remain, he does not observe a condition attached to the leave or remains beyond the time limited by the leave;

  [(b) he uses deception in seeking (whether successfully or not) leave to remain;] or

  [(ba) his indefinite leave to enter or remain has been revoked under section 76(3) of the Nationality, Immigration and Asylum Act 2002 (person ceasing to be refugee);]

  (c) directions . . . have been given for the removal, under this section, of a person . . . to whose family he belongs.

(2) Directions may not be given under subsection (1)(a) if the person concerned has made an application for leave to remain in accordance with regulations made under section 9.

[(3) Directions for the removal of a person may not be given under subsection (1)(c) unless the Secretary of State has given the person written notice of the intention to remove him.

(4) A notice under subsection (3) may not be given if—

  (a) the person whose removal under subsection (1)(a) or (b) is the cause of the proposed directions under subsection (1)(c) has left the United Kingdom, and

  (b) more than eight weeks have elapsed since that person's departure.

(5) If a notice under subsection (3) is sent by first class post to a person's last known address, that subsection shall be taken to be satisfied at the end of the second day after the day of posting.

(5A) Directions for the removal of a person, under subsection (1)(c) cease to have effect if he ceases to belong to the family of the person whose removal under subsection (1)(a) or (b) is the cause of the directions under subsection (1)(c).]

(6) Directions under this section—

(a)   may be given only to persons falling within a prescribed class;

(b)   may impose any requirements of a prescribed kind.

(7) In relation to any such directions, paragraphs 10, 11, 16 to 18, 21 and 22 to 24 of Schedule 2 to the 1971 Act (administrative provisions as to control of entry), apply as they apply in relation to directions given under paragraph 8 of that Schedule.

[(8) When a person is notified that a decision has been made to remove him in accordance with this section, the notification invalidates any leave to enter or remain in the United Kingdom previously given to him.]

(9) The costs of complying with a direction given under this section (so far as reasonably incurred) must be met by the Secretary of State.

[(10) A person shall not be liable to removal from the United Kingdom under this section at a time when section 7(1)(b) of the Immigration Act 1971 (Commonwealth and Irish citizens ordinarily resident in United Kingdom) would prevent a decision to deport him.]

Amendment

Sub-s (1): para (b) substituted by the Nationality, Immigration and Asylum Act 2002, s 74.
Sub-s (1): para (ba) inserted by the Nationality, Immigration and Asylum Act 2002, s 76(7).
Sub-s (1): in para (c) words omitted repealed by the Nationality, Immigration and Asylum Act 2002, ss 73(2), (3), 161, Sch 9.
Sub-ss (3)–(5), (5A): substituted, for sub-ss (3)–(5) as originally enacted, by the Nationality, Immigration and Asylum Act 2002, s 73(2), (4).
Sub-s (8): substituted by the Immigration, Asylum and Nationality Act 2006, s 48.
Sub-s (10): inserted by the Nationality, Immigration and Asylum Act 2002, s 75(4).

Subordinate Legislation

Immigration (Removal Directions) Regulations 2000, SI 2000/2243.".

11, 12

(Repealed by the Asylum and Immigration (Treatment of Claimants, etc) Act 2004, ss 33(2), 47, Sch 4.)

13 Proof of identity of persons to be removed or deported

(1) This section applies if a person—

    (a)   is to be removed from the United Kingdom to a country of which he is a national or citizen; but

    (b)   does not have a valid passport or other document establishing his identity and nationality or citizenship and permitting him to travel.

(2) If the country to which the person is to be removed indicates that he will not be admitted to it unless identification data relating to him are provided by the Secretary of State, he may provide them with such data.

(3) In providing identification data, the Secretary of State must not disclose whether the person concerned has made a claim for asylum.

(4) For the purposes of paragraph 4(1) of Schedule 4 to the Data Protection Act 1998, the provision under this section of identification data is a transfer of personal data which is necessary for reasons of substantial public interest.

(5) "Identification data" means—

    (a)   fingerprints taken under section 141; or

    (b)   data collected in accordance with regulations made under section 144.

(6) "Removed" means removed as a result of directions given under section 10 or under Schedule 2 or 3 to the 1971 Act.

14 Escorts for persons removed from the United Kingdom under directions

(1) Directions for, or requiring arrangements to be made for, the removal of a person from the United Kingdom may include or be amended to include provision for the person who is to be removed to be accompanied by an escort consisting of one or more persons specified in the directions.

(2) The Secretary of State may by regulations make further provision supplementing subsection (1).

(3) The regulations may, in particular, include provision—

  (a) requiring the person to whom the directions are given to provide for the return of the escort to the United Kingdom;

  (b) requiring him to bear such costs in connection with the escort (including, in particular, remuneration) as may be prescribed;

  (c) as to the cases in which the Secretary of State is to bear those costs;

  (d) prescribing the kinds of expenditure which are to count in calculating the costs incurred in connection with escorts.

15

(Repealed by the Nationality, Immigration and Asylum Act 2002, ss 77(5), 161, Sch 9.)

Provision of financial security

16 Security on grant of entry clearance

(1) In such circumstances as may be specified, the Secretary of State may require security to be given, with respect to a person applying for entry clearance, before clearance is given.

(2) In such circumstances as may be specified—

  (a) the Secretary of State may accept security with respect to a person who is applying for entry clearance but for whom security is not required; and

  (b) in determining whether to give clearance, account may be taken of any security so provided.

(3) "Security" means—

  (a) the deposit of a sum of money by the applicant, his agent or any other person, or

  (b) the provision by the applicant, his agent or any other person of a financial guarantee of a specified kind,

with a view to securing that the applicant will, if given leave to enter the United Kingdom for a limited period, leave the United Kingdom at the end of that period.

(4) Immigration rules must make provision as to the circumstances in which a security provided under this section—

  (a) is to be repaid, released or otherwise cancelled; or

  (b) is to be forfeited or otherwise realised by the Secretary of State.

(5) No security provided under this section may be forfeited or otherwise realised unless the person providing it has been given an opportunity, in accordance with immigration rules, to make representations to the Secretary of State.

(6) Immigration rules may, in particular—

  (a) fix the maximum amount that may be required, or accepted, by way of security provided under this section;

  (b) specify the form and manner in which such a security is to be given or may be accepted;

  (c) make provision, where such a security has been forfeited or otherwise realised, for the person providing it to be reimbursed in such circumstances as may be specified;

  (d) make different provision for different cases or descriptions of case.

(7) "Specified" means specified by immigration rules.

(8) Any security forfeited or otherwise realised by the Secretary of State under this section must be paid into the Consolidated Fund.

17 Provision of further security on extension of leave

(1) This section applies if security has been provided under section 16(1) or (2) with respect to a person who, having entered the United Kingdom (with leave to do so), applies—

   (a) to extend his leave to enter the United Kingdom; or

   (b) for leave to remain in the United Kingdom for a limited period.

(2) The Secretary of State may refuse the application if security of such kind as the Secretary of State considers appropriate is not provided, or continued, with respect to the applicant.

(3) Immigration rules must make provision as to the circumstances in which a security provided under this section—

   (a) is to be repaid, released or otherwise cancelled; or

   (b) is to be forfeited or otherwise realised.

(4) No security provided under this section may be forfeited or otherwise realised unless the person providing it has been given an opportunity, in accordance with immigration rules, to make representations to the Secretary of State.

(5) Subsection (7) of section 16 applies in relation to this section as it applies in relation to that section.

(6) Any security forfeited or otherwise realised by the Secretary of State under this section must be paid into the Consolidated Fund.

Commencement

To be appointed: see s 170(4).

18, 19

Information

(Amend the Immigration Act 1971, Sch 2.)

---

20 Supply of information to Secretary of State

(1) This section applies to information held by—

   (a) a chief officer of police;

   [(b) the [National Crime Agency];]

   (d) . . .

   (e) a person with whom the Secretary of State has made a contract or other arrangements under section 95 or 98 or a sub-contractor of such a person; or

   (f) any specified person, for purposes specified in relation to that person.

[(1A) This section also applies to a document or article which—

   (a) comes into the possession of a person listed in subsection (1) or someone acting on his behalf, or

   (b) is discovered by a person listed in subsection (1) or someone acting on his behalf.]

(2) The information[, document or article] may be supplied to the Secretary of State for use for immigration purposes.

[(2A) The Secretary of State may—

   (a) retain for immigration purposes a document or article supplied to him under subsection (2), and

   (b) dispose of a document or article supplied to him under subsection (2) in such manner as he thinks appropriate (and the reference to use in subsection (2) includes a reference to disposal).]

(3) "Immigration purposes" means any of the following—

   (a) the administration of immigration control under the Immigration Acts;

   (b) the prevention, detection, investigation or prosecution of criminal offences under those Acts;

   (c) the imposition of penalties or charges under Part II;

   (d) the provision of support for asylum-seekers and their dependants under Part VI;

   (e) such other purposes as may be specified.

(4) "Chief officer of police" means—

   (a) the chief officer of police for a police area in England and Wales;

   [(b) the chief constable of the Police Service of Scotland;]

   (c) the [Chief Constable of the Police Service of Northern Ireland].

(5) "Specified" means specified in an order made by the Secretary of State.

(6) This section does not limit the circumstances in which information[, documents or articles] may be supplied apart from this section.

Amendment

Sub-s (1): para (b) substituted, for paras (b), (c) as originally enacted, by the Serious Organised Crime and Police Act 2005, s 59, Sch 4, paras 122, 123.

Sub-s (1): in para (b) words "National Crime Agency" in square brackets substituted by the Crime and Courts Act 2013, s 15(3), Sch 8, Pt 2, paras 64, 65, as from 7 October 2013: see SI 2013/1682, art 3(u), (v).

Sub-s (1): para (d) repealed by the UK Borders Act 2007, ss 40(6)(a), 58, Schedule.

Sub-s (1A): inserted by the Nationality, Immigration and Asylum Act 2002, s 132(1), (2).

Sub-s (2): words in square brackets inserted by the Nationality, Immigration and Asylum Act 2002, s 132(1), (3).

Sub-s (2A): inserted by the Nationality, Immigration and Asylum Act 2002, s 132(1), (4).

Sub-s (4): para (b) substituted by SI 2013/602, art 26, Sch 2, Pt 1, para 31, as from 1 April 2013: see SI 2013/602, art 1(2); for transitional provisions and savings see art 27, Sch 3 thereto.

Sub-s (4): in para (c) words in square brackets substituted by the Police (Northern Ireland) Act 2000, s 78(2)(a).

Sub-s (6): words in square brackets inserted by the Nationality, Immigration and Asylum Act 2002, s 132(1), (5).

Subordinate Legislation

Immigration (Supply of Information to the Secretary of State for Immigration Purposes) Order 2008, SI 2008/2077.

21 Supply of information by Secretary of State

(1) This section applies to information held by the Secretary of State in connection with the exercise of functions under any of the Immigration Acts.

(2) The information may be supplied to—

   (a) a chief officer of police, for use for police purposes;

   [(b) the National Crime Agency, for use in connection with the discharge of any function of that Agency;]

   (d) the Commissioners of Customs and Excise, or a person providing services to them, for use for customs purposes; or

   (e) any specified person, for use for purposes specified in relation to that person.

(3) "Police purposes" means any of the following—

   (a) the prevention, detection, investigation or prosecution of criminal offences;

   (b) safeguarding national security;

   (c) such other purposes as may be specified.

[(4) ...]

(6) "Customs purposes" means any of the Commissioners' functions in relation to—

(a) the prevention, detection, investigation or prosecution of criminal offences;

(b) the prevention, detection or investigation of conduct in respect of which penalties which are not criminal penalties are provided for by or under any enactment;

(c) the assessment or determination of penalties which are not criminal penalties;

(d) checking the accuracy of information relating to, or provided for purposes connected with, any matter under the care and management of the Commissioners or any assigned matter (as defined by section 1(1) of the Customs and Excise Management Act 1979);

(e) amending or supplementing any such information (where appropriate);

(f) legal or other proceedings relating to anything mentioned in paragraphs (a) to (e);

(g) safeguarding national security; and

(h) such other purposes as may be specified.

(7) "Chief officer of police" and "specified" have the same meaning as in section 20.

(8) This section does not limit the circumstances in which information may be supplied apart from this section.

Amendment

Sub-s (2): para (b) substituted by the Crime and Courts Act 2013, s 15(3), Sch 8, Pt 2, paras 64, 66(1), (2), 7 October 2013: see SI 2013/1682, art 3(u), (v).

Sub-s (4): substituted, for sub-ss (4), (5) as originally enacted, by the Serious Organised Crime and Police Act 2005, s 59, Sch 4, paras 122, 124(1), (3) and repealed by the Crime and Courts Act 2013, s 15(3), Sch 8, Pt 2, paras 64, 66(1), (3), as from 7 October 2013: see SI 2013/1682, art 3(u), (v).

22

(Inserts the Asylum and Immigration Act 1996, s 8A.)

Monitoring entry clearance

23 Monitoring refusals of entry clearance

[(1) *The Secretary of State must appoint a person to monitor, in such manner as the Secretary of State may determine, refusals of entry clearance in cases where, as a result of section 88A of the Nationality, Immigration and Asylum Act 2002 (c 41) (entry clearance: non-family visitors and students), an appeal under section 82(1) of that Act may be brought only) on the grounds referred to in section 84(1)(b) and (c) of that Act (racial discrimination and human rights).]*

(2) *But the Secretary of State may not appoint a member of his staff.]*

(3) *The monitor must make an annual report on the discharge of his functions to the Secretary of State.*

(4) *The Secretary of State must lay a copy of any report made to him under subsection (3) before each House of Parliament.*

(5) *The Secretary of State may pay to the monitor such fees and allowances as he may determine.*

Amendment

Repealed by the Immigration Act 2014, s 73, Sch 9, Pt 4, paras 27, 28, as from 20 October 2014 (see SI 2014/2771, art 2), subject to savings in SI 2014/2771, arts 9–11.

Sub-s (1): substituted by the Immigration, Asylum and Nationality Act 2006, s 4(2).

Reporting suspicious marriages

24 Duty to report suspicious marriages

(1) Subsection (3) applies if—

(a) a superintendent registrar to whom a notice of marriage has been given under section 27 of the Marriage Act 1949,

[(aa) a superintendent registrar; or registrar of births, deaths and marriages, who receives information in advance of a person giving such a notice,]

(b) any other person who, under section 28(2) of that Act, has attested a declaration accompanying such a notice,

(c) a district registrar to whom a marriage notice or an approved certificate has been submitted under section 3 of the Marriage (Scotland) Act 1977,

. . . .

[(ca) a district registrar who receives information in advance of a person submitting such a notice or certificate,]

(d) a registrar or deputy registrar to whom notice has been given under section 13 of the Marriages (Ireland) Act 1844 or section 4 of the Marriage Law (Ireland) Amendment Act 1863, [or

(da) a registrar or deputy registrar who receives information in advance of a person giving such a notice,]

has reasonable grounds for suspecting that the marriage will be a sham marriage.

(2) Subsection (3) also applies if—

(a) a marriage is solemnized in the presence of a registrar of marriages or, in relation to Scotland, an authorised registrar (within the meaning of the Act of 1977); and

(b) before, during or immediately after solemnization of the marriage, the registrar has reasonable grounds for suspecting that the marriage will be, or is, a sham marriage.

(3) The person concerned must report his suspicion to the Secretary of State without delay and in such form and manner as may be prescribed by regulations.

(4) The regulations are to be made—

(a) in relation to England and Wales, by the Registrar General for England and Wales with the approval of [the Secretary of State];

(b) in relation to Scotland, by the Secretary of State after consulting the Registrar General of Births, Deaths and Marriages for Scotland;

(c) in relation to Northern Ireland, by the Secretary of State after consulting the Registrar General in Northern Ireland.

(5) "Sham marriage" means a marriage (whether or not void)—

(a) entered into between a person ("A") who is neither a British citizen nor a national of an EEA State other than the United Kingdom and another person (whether or not such a citizen or such a national); and

(b) entered into by A for the purpose of avoiding the effect of one or more provisions of United Kingdom immigration law or the immigration rules.

Amendment

Sub-s (1): paras (aa), (ca), (da) inserted and word omitted from para (c) repealed by the Immigration Act 2014, s 56(1), (2), as from 14 July 2014.

Sub-s (4): in para (a) words in square brackets substituted by SI 2008/678, arts 3(1), 5, Sch 1, para 11(a), Sch 2, para 11(a).

Subordinate Legislation

Reporting of Suspicious Marriages and Registration of Marriages (Miscellaneous Amendments) Regulations 2000, SI 2000/3164; Reporting of Suspicious Marriages (Northern Ireland) Regulations 2000, SI 2000/3233.

[24A Duty to report suspicious civil partnerships

(1) Subsection (3) applies if—

(a) a registration authority to whom a notice of proposed civil partnership has been given under section 8 of the Civil Partnership Act 2004,

[(aa) a registration authority that receives information in advance of a person giving such a notice,]

(b) any person who, under section 8 of the 2004 Act, has attested a declaration accompanying such a notice,

(c) a district registrar to whom a notice of proposed civil partnership has been given under section 88 of the 2004 Act, ...

[(ca) a district registrar who receives information in advance of a person giving such a notice,]

(d) a registrar to whom a civil partnership notice has been given under section 139 of the 2004 Act, [or

(da) a registrar who receives information in advance of a person giving such a notice,]

has reasonable grounds for suspecting that the civil partnership will be a sham civil partnership.

(2) Subsection (3) also applies if—

(a) two people register as civil partners of each other under Part 2, 3 or 4 of the 2004 Act in the presence of the registrar, and

(b) before, during or immediately after they do so, the registrar has reasonable grounds for suspecting that the civil partnership will be, or is, a sham civil partnership.

(3) The person concerned must report his suspicion to the Secretary of State without delay and in such form and manner as may be prescribed by regulations.

(4) The regulations are to be made—

(a) in relation to England and Wales, by the Registrar General for England and Wales with the approval of [the Secretary of State];

(b) in relation to Scotland, by the Secretary of State after consulting the Registrar General of Births, Deaths and Marriages for Scotland;

(c) in relation to Northern Ireland, by the Secretary of State after consulting the Registrar General in Northern Ireland.

(5) "Sham civil partnership" means a civil partnership (whether or not void)—

(a) formed between a person ("A") who is neither a British citizen nor a national of an EEA State other than the United Kingdom and another person (whether or not such a citizen or such a national), and

(b) formed by A for the purpose of avoiding the effect of one or more provisions of United Kingdom immigration law or the immigration rules.

(6) "The registrar" means—

(a) in relation to England and Wales, the civil partnership registrar acting under Part 2 of the 2004 Act;

(b) in relation to Scotland, the authorised registrar acting under Part 3 of the 2004 Act;

(c) in relation to Northern Ireland, the registrar acting under Part 4 of the 2004 Act.]

Amendment

Inserted by the Civil Partnership Act 2004, s 261(1), Sch 27, para 162.

Sub-s (1): paras (aa), (ca), (da) inserted and word omitted from para (c) repealed by the Immigration Act 2014, s 56(1), (3), as from 14 July 2014.

Sub-s (4): in para (a) words in square brackets substituted by SI 2008/678, arts 3(1), 5, Sch 1, para 11(b), Sch 2, para 11(b).

Subordinate Legislation

Reporting of Suspicious Civil Partnerships Regulations 2005, SI 2005/3174.

Immigration control: facilities and charges

25 Provision of facilities for immigration control at ports

(1) The person responsible for the management of a control port ("the manager") must provide the Secretary of State free of charge with such facilities at the port as the Secretary of State may direct as being reasonably necessary for, or in connection with, the operation of immigration control there.

(2) Before giving such a direction, the Secretary of State must consult such persons likely to be affected by it as he considers appropriate.

(3) If the Secretary of State gives such a direction, he must send a copy of it to the person appearing to him to be the manager.

(4) If the manager persistently fails to comply with the direction (or part of it), the Secretary of State may—

   (a) in the case of a control port which is not a port of entry, revoke any approval in relation to the port given under paragraph 26(1) of Schedule 2 to the 1971 Act;

   (b) in the case of a control port which is a port of entry, by order revoke its designation as a port of entry.

(5) A direction under this section is enforceable, on the application of the Secretary of State—

   (a) by injunction granted [in England and Wales by the county court or in Northern Ireland] by a county court; or

   (b) in Scotland, by an order under section 45 of the Court of Session Act 1988.

(6) "Control port" means a port in which a control area is designated under paragraph 26(3) of Schedule 2 to the 1971 Act.

(7) "Facilities" means accommodation, facilities, equipment and services of a class or description specified in an order made by the Secretary of State.

Amendment

Sub-s (5): in para (a) words in square brackets inserted by the Crime and Courts Act 2013, s 17(5), Sch 9, Pt 3, para 90(a), as from 22 April 2014.

Subordinate Legislation

Immigration Control (Provision of Facilities at Ports) Order 2003, SI 2003/612.

26 Charges: immigration control

(1) The Secretary of State may, at the request of any person and in consideration of such charges as he may determine, make arrangements—

   (a) for the provision at any control port of immigration officers or facilities in addition to those (if any) needed to provide a basic service at the port;

   (b) for the provision of immigration officers or facilities for dealing with passengers of a particular description or in particular circumstances.

(2) "Control port" has the same meaning as in section 25.

(3) "Facilities" includes equipment.

(4) "Basic service" has such meaning as may be prescribed.

Subordinate Legislation

Immigration Control (Charges) (Basic Service) Regulations 2003, SI 2003/1502.

(Repealed by the Immigration, Asylum and Nationality Act 2006, ss 52(7), 61, Sch 2, para 3, Sch 3, as from 2 April 2007; see SI 2007/1109, arts 4, 5, Schedule.)

28–30

(S 28 inserts the Immigration Act 1971, s 24A; ss 29, 30 amend ss 25, 26 of that Act.)

Offences

31 Defences based on Article 31(1) of the Refugee Convention

(1) It is a defence for a refugee charged with an offence to which this section applies to show that, having come to the United Kingdom directly from a country where his life or freedom was threatened (within the meaning of the Refugee Convention), he—

   (a) presented himself to the authorities in the United Kingdom without delay;

   (b) showed good cause for his illegal entry or presence; and

   (c) made a claim for asylum as soon as was reasonably practicable after his arrival in the United Kingdom.

(2) If, in coming from the country where his life or freedom was threatened, the refugee stopped in another country outside the United Kingdom, subsection (1) applies only if he shows that he could not reasonably have expected to be given protection under the Refugee Convention in that other country.

(3) In England and Wales and Northern Ireland the offences to which this section applies are any offence, and any attempt to commit an offence, under—

   (a) Part 1 of the Forgery and Counterfeiting Act 1981 (forgery and connected offences);

   [(aa) section 4 or 6 of the Identity Documents Act 2010;]

   (b) section 24A of the 1971 Act (deception); or

   (c) section 26(1)(d) of the 1971 Act (falsification of documents).

(4) In Scotland, the offences to which this section applies are those—

   (a) of fraud,

   (b) of uttering a forged document,

   [(ba) under section 4 or 6 of the Identity Documents Act 2010,]

   (c) under section 24A of the 1971 Act (deception), or

   (d) under section 26(1)(d) of the 1971 Act (falsification of documents),

and any attempt to commit any of those offences.

(5) A refugee who has made a claim for asylum is not entitled to the defence provided by subsection (1) in relation to any offence committed by him after making that claim.

(6) "Refugee" has the same meaning as it has for the purposes of the Refugee Convention.

(7) If the Secretary of State has refused to grant a claim for asylum made by a person who claims that he has a defence under subsection (1), that person is to be taken not to be a refugee unless he shows that he is.

(8) A person who—

   (a) was convicted in England and Wales or Northern Ireland of an offence to which this section applies before the commencement of this section, but

   (b) at no time during the proceedings for that offence argued that he had a defence based on Article 31(1),

may apply to the Criminal Cases Review Commission with a view to his case being referred to the Court of Appeal by the Commission on the ground that he would have had a defence under this section had it been in force at the material time.

(9) A person who—

(a) was convicted in Scotland of an offence to which this section applies before the commencement of this section, but

(b) at no time during the proceedings for that offence argued that he had a defence based on Article 31(1),

may apply to the Scottish Criminal Cases Review Commission with a view to his case being referred to the High Court of Justiciary by the Commission on the ground that he would have had a defence under this section had it been in force at the material time.

(10) The Secretary of State may by order amend—

(a) subsection (3), or

(b) subsection (4),

by adding offences to those for the time being listed there.

(11) Before making an order under subsection (10)(b), the Secretary of State must consult the Scottish Ministers.

Amendment

Sub-s (3): para (aa) inserted by the Identity Cards Act 2006, s 30(2)(a) and substituted by the Identity Documents Act 2010, s 12, Schedule, para 10(1), (2), as from 21 January 2011.

Sub-s (4): para (ba) inserted by the Identity Cards Act 2006, s 30(2)(b) and substituted by the Identity Documents Act 2010, s 12, Schedule, para 10(1), (3), as from 21 January 2011.

PART II
CARRIERS' LIABILITY

Clandestine entrants

32 Penalty for carrying clandestine entrants

(1) A person is a clandestine entrant if—

(a) he arrives in the United Kingdom concealed in a vehicle, ship or aircraft,

[(aa) he arrives in the United Kingdom concealed in a rail freight wagon,]

(b) he passes, or attempts to pass, through immigration control concealed in a vehicle, or

(c) he arrives in the United Kingdom on a ship or aircraft, having embarked—

(i) concealed in a vehicle; and

(ii) at a time when the ship or aircraft was outside the United Kingdom,

and claims, or indicates that he intends to seek, asylum in the United Kingdom or evades, or attempts to evade, immigration control.

(2) *The person (or persons) responsible for a clandestine entrant is (or are together) liable to—*

(a) *a penalty of the prescribed amount in respect of the clandestine entrant; and*

(b) *an additional penalty of that amount in respect of each person who was concealed with the clandestine entrant in the same transporter.*

[(2) The Secretary of State may require a person who is responsible for a clandestine entrant to pay—

(a) a penalty in respect of the clandestine entrant;

(b) a penalty in respect of any person who was concealed with the clandestine entrant in the same transporter.

(2A) In imposing a penalty under subsection (2) the Secretary of State—

Appendix 1 — UK Immigration Statutes

    (a) must specify an amount which does not exceed the maximum prescribed for the purpose of this paragraph,

    (b) may, in respect of a clandestine entrant or a concealed person, impose separate penalties on more than one of the persons responsible for the clandestine entrant, and

    (c) may not impose penalties in respect of a clandestine entrant or a concealed person which amount in aggregate to more than the maximum prescribed for the purpose of this paragraph.]

[(3) A penalty imposed under this section must be paid to the Secretary of State before the end of the prescribed period.

(4) *Payment of the full amount of a penalty by one or more of the persons responsible for the clandestine entrant discharges the liability of each of the persons responsible for that entrant.*

[(4) Where a penalty is imposed under subsection (2) on the driver of a vehicle who is an employee of the vehicle's owner or hirer—

    (a) the employee and the employer shall be jointly and severally liable for the penalty imposed on the driver (irrespective of whether a penalty is also imposed on the employer), and

    (b) a provision of this Part about notification, objection or appeal shall have effect as if the penalty imposed on the driver were also imposed on the employer (irrespective of whether a penalty is also imposed on the employer in his capacity as the owner or hirer of the vehicle).

(4A) In the case of a detached trailer, subsection (4) shall have effect as if a reference to the driver were a reference to the operator.]

(5) In the case of a clandestine entrant to whom subsection (1)(a) applies, each of the following is a responsible person—

    (a) if the transporter is a ship or aircraft, the owner or [and] captain;

    (b) if it is a vehicle (but not a detached trailer), the owner, hirer or [and] driver of the vehicle;

    (c) if it is a detached trailer, the owner, hirer or [and] operator of the trailer.

[(5A) In the case of a clandestine entrant to whom subsection (1)(aa) applies, the responsible person is—

    (a) where the entrant arrived concealed in a freight train, the train operator who, at the train's last scheduled stop before arrival in the United Kingdom, was responsible for certifying it as fit to travel to the United Kingdom, or

    (b) where the entrant arrived concealed in a freight shuttle wagon, the operator of the shuttle-train of which the wagon formed part.]

(6) In the case of a clandestine entrant to whom subsection (1)(b) or (c) applies, each of the following is a responsible person—

    (a) if the transporter is a detached trailer, the owner, hirer or [and] operator of the trailer;

    (b) if it is not, the owner, hirer or [and] driver of the vehicle.

[(6A) Where a person falls within the definition of responsible person in more than one capacity, a separate penalty may be imposed on him under subsection (2) in respect of each capacity.]

(7) Subject to any defence provided by section 34, it is immaterial whether a responsible person knew or suspected—

    (a) that the clandestine entrant was concealed in the transporter; or

    (b) that there were one or more other persons concealed with the clandestine entrant in the same transporter.

(8) Subsection (9) applies if a transporter ("the carried transporter") is itself being carried in or on another transporter.

(9) If a person is concealed in the carried transporter, the question whether any other person is concealed with that person in the same transporter is to be determined by reference to the carried transporter and not by reference to the transporter in or on which it is carried.

(10) "Immigration control" means United Kingdom immigration control and includes any United Kingdom immigration control operated in a prescribed control zone outside the United Kingdom.

Amendment

Sub-s (1): para (aa) inserted by the Nationality, Immigration and Asylum Act 2002, s 125, Sch 8, paras 1, 2(1), (2). Date in force (for the purpose of enabling the Secretary of State to exercise the power to make subordinate legislation under ss 32(2A), 35(5), (7), (9), (12), (13), 37(5B), (7) and 40A(4), (6) hereof) 8 December 2002 (except in relation to a penalty notice issued to a person before that date): see SI 2002/2811, arts 2, 4, Schedule. Date in force (for the purposes of clandestine entrants who pass, or attempt to pass, through immigration control concealed in a vehicle) 11 May 2012: see SI 2012/1263, art 2. Date in force (for remaining purposes) to be appointed.

Sub-s (2): substituted, by subsequent sub-ss (2), (2A), by the Nationality, Immigration and Asylum Act 2002, s 125, Sch 8, paras 1, 2(1), (3), as from the dates noted above.

Sub-s (4): substituted, by subsequent sub-ss (4), (4A), by the Nationality, Immigration and Asylum Act 2002, s 125, Sch 8, paras 1, 2(1), (4), as from the dates noted above, as from the dates noted above.

Sub-s (5): in para (a) word "or" in italics repealed and subsequent word in square brackets substituted by the Nationality, Immigration and Asylum Act 2002, s 125, Sch 8, paras 1, 2(1), (5)(a), as from the dates noted above.

Sub-s (5): in paras (b), (c) word "or" in italics repealed and subsequent word in square brackets substituted by the Nationality, Immigration and Asylum Act 2002, s 125, Sch 8, paras 1, 2(1), (5)(b), as from the dates noted above.

Sub-s (5A): inserted by the Nationality, Immigration and Asylum Act 2002, s 125, Sch 8, paras 1, 2(1), (6).

Sub-s (6): in paras (a), (b) word "or" in italics repealed and subsequent words in square brackets substituted by the Nationality, Immigration and Asylum Act 2002, s 125, Sch 8, paras 1, 2(1), (7), as from the dates noted above.

Sub-s (6A): inserted by the Nationality, Immigration and Asylum Act 2002, s 125, Sch 8, paras 1, 2(1), (8), as from the dates noted above.

Subordinate Legislation

Carriers' Liability Regulations 2002, SI 2002/2817; Carriers' Liability (Amendment) Regulations 2004, SI 2004/244.

[32A Level of penalty: code of practice

(1) The Secretary of State shall issue a code of practice specifying matters to be considered in determining the amount of a penalty under section 32.

(2) The Secretary of State shall have regard to the code (in addition to any other matters he thinks relevant)—

(a) when imposing a penalty under section 32, and

(b) when considering a notice of objection under section 35(4).

(3) Before issuing the code the Secretary of State shall lay a draft before Parliament.

(4) After laying the draft code before Parliament the Secretary of State may bring the code into operation by order.

(5) The Secretary of State may from time to time revise the whole or any part of the code and issue the code as revised.

(6) Subsections (3) and (4) also apply to a revision or proposed revision of the code.]

Amendment

Inserted by the Nationality, Immigration and Asylum Act 2002, s 125, Sch 8, paras 1, 3.

Date in force (for the purpose of enabling the Secretary of State to exercise the power under sub-ss (1), (3) and (4) above to lay a draft code of practice before Parliament and bring the code of practice into force): 14 November 2002 (except in relation to a penalty notice issued to a person before that date): see SI 2002/2811, arts 2, 4, Schedule.

Date in force (for the purposes of clandestine entrants who arrive in the United Kingdom concealed in a vehicle or a rail freight wagon): 8 December 2002 (except in relation to a penalty notice issued to a person before that date): see SI 2002/2811, arts 2, 4, Schedule.

Date in force (for the purposes of clandestine entrants who pass, or attempt to pass, through immigration control concealed in a vehicle): 11 May 2012: see SI 2012/1263, art 2.

Date in force (for remaining purposes): to be appointed.

Subordinate Legislation

Carriers' Liability (Clandestine Entrants) (Level of Penalty: Revised Code of Practice) Order 2004, SI 2004/251.

33 *Code of practice* [Prevention of clandestine entrants: code of practice]

(1) The Secretary of State must issue a code of practice to be followed by any person operating a system for preventing the carriage of clandestine entrants.

(2) Before issuing the code, the Secretary of State must—

    (a)   consult such persons as he considers appropriate; and

    (b)   lay a draft before *both Houses of* Parliament.

(3) The requirement of subsection (2)(a) may be satisfied by consultation before the passing of this Act.

(4) After laying the draft code before Parliament, the Secretary of State may bring the code into operation by an order.

(5) The Secretary of State may from time to time revise the whole or any part of the code and issue the code as revised.

(6) Subsections (2) and (4) also apply to any revision, or proposed revision, of the code.

Amendment

Section heading: substituted by the Nationality, Immigration and Asylum Act 2002, s 125, Sch 8, paras 1, 4.

Date in force (for the purposes of clandestine entrants who arrive in the United Kingdom concealed in a vehicle or a rail freight wagon): 8 December 2002 (except in relation to a penalty notice issued to a person before that date): see SI 2002/2811, arts 2, 4, Schedule. Date in force (for the purposes of clandestine entrants who pass, or attempt to pass, through immigration control concealed in a vehicle): 11 May 2012: see SI 2012/1263, art 2. Date in force (for remaining purposes): to be appointed: see the Nationality, Immigration and Asylum Act 2002, s 162(1).

Sub-s (2): in para (b) words "both Houses of" in italics repealed by the Nationality, Immigration and Asylum Act 2002, ss 125, 161, Sch 8, paras 1, 5, Sch 9, as from the dates noted above.

See Further

See further, in relation to certain codes of practice which have effect by virtue of this section and s 39 hereof: the Nationality, Immigration and Asylum Act 2002, Sch 8, para 17.

Subordinate Legislation

Carriers' Liability (Clandestine Entrants) (Code of Practice for Rail Freight) Order 2001, SI 2001/312; Carriers' Liability (Clandestine Entrants) (Code of Practice for Freight Shuttle Wagons) Order 2001, SI 2001/3233; Carriers' Liability (Clandestine Entrants) (Revised Code of Practice for Vehicles) Order 2004, SI 2004/250.

34 Defences to claim that penalty is due under section 32

(1) *This section applies if it is alleged that a person ("the carrier") is liable to a penalty under section 32.*

[(1) A person ("the carrier") shall not be liable to the imposition of a penalty under section 32(2) if he has a defence under this section.]

(2) It is a defence for the carrier to show that he, or an employee of his who was directly responsible for allowing the clandestine entrant to be concealed, was acting under duress.

(3) It is also a defence for the carrier to show that—

   (a) he did not know, and had no reasonable grounds for suspecting, that a clandestine entrant was, or might be, concealed in the transporter;

   (b) an effective system for preventing the carriage of clandestine entrants was in operation in relation to the transporter; and

   (c) *that* on the occasion in question the person or persons responsible for operating that system did so properly.

[(3A) It is also a defence for the carrier to show that—

   (a) he knew or suspected that a clandestine entrant was or might be concealed in a rail freight wagon, having boarded after the wagon began its journey to the United Kingdom;

   (b) he could not stop the train or shuttle-train of which the wagon formed part without endangering safety;

   (c) an effective system for preventing the carriage of clandestine entrants was in operation in relation to the train or shuttle-train; and

   (d) on the occasion in question the person or persons responsible for operating the system did so properly.]

(4) In determining, for the purposes of this section, whether a particular system is effective, regard is to be had to the code of practice issued by the Secretary of State under section 33.

(5) *If there are two or more persons responsible for a clandestine entrant, the fact that one or more of them has a defence under subsection (3) does not affect the liability of the others.*

(6) *But if a person responsible for a clandestine entrant has a defence under subsection (2), the liability of any other person responsible for that entrant is discharged.*

[(6) Where a person has a defence under subsection (2) in respect of a clandestine entrant, every other responsible person in respect of the clandestine entrant is also entitled to the benefit of the defence.]

Amendment

Sub-s (1): substituted by the Nationality, Immigration and Asylum Act 2002, s 125, Sch 8, paras 1, 6(1), (2). Date in force (for the purposes of clandestine entrants who arrive in the United Kingdom concealed in a vehicle or a rail freight wagon): 8 December 2002 (except in relation to a penalty notice issued to a person before that date): see SI 2002/2811, arts 2, 4, Schedule. Date in force (for the purposes of clandestine entrants who pass, or attempt to pass, through immigration control concealed in a vehicle): 11 May 2012: see SI 2012/1263, art 2. Date in force (for remaining purposes): to be appointed.

Sub-s (3): in para (c) word "that" in italics repealed by the Nationality, Immigration and Asylum Act 2002, ss 125, 161, Sch 8, paras 1, 6(1), (3), Sch 9, as from the dates noted above.

Sub-s (3A): inserted by the Nationality, Immigration and Asylum Act 2002, s 125, Sch 8, paras 1, 6(1), (4), as from the dates noted above.

Sub-s (5): repealed by the Nationality, Immigration and Asylum Act 2002, ss 125, 161, Sch 8, paras 1, 6(1), (5), Sch 9, as from the dates noted above.

Sub-s (6): substituted by the Nationality, Immigration and Asylum Act 2002, s 125, Sch 8, paras 1, 6(1), (6), as from the dates noted above.

35 Procedure

(1) If the Secretary of State decides that a person ("P") is liable to one or more penalties under section 32, he must notify P of his decision.

(2) A notice under subsection (1) (a "penalty notice") must—

   (a) state the Secretary of State's reasons for deciding that P is liable to the penalty (or penalties);

   (b) state the amount of the penalty (or penalties) to which P is liable;

   (c) specify the date before which, and the manner in which, the penalty (or penalties) must be paid; and

(d)   include an explanation of the steps—

      (i)   that P *must* [may] take if he objects to the penalty;

      (ii)   that the Secretary of State may take under this Part to recover any unpaid penalty.

(3)   *Subsection (4) applies if more than one person is responsible for a clandestine entrant.*

(4)   If a penalty notice is served on one of the responsible persons, the Secretary of State is to be taken to have served the required penalty notice on each of them.

(5)   The Secretary of State must nevertheless take reasonable steps, while the penalty remains unpaid, to secure that the penalty notice is actually served on each of those responsible persons.

(6)   *If a person on whom a penalty notice is served, or who is treated as having had a penalty notice served on him, alleges that he is not liable for one or more, or all, of the penalties specified in the penalty notice, he may give written notice of his allegation to the Secretary of State.*

(7)   *Notice under subsection (6) ("a notice of objection") must—*

      (a)   give reasons for the allegation; and

      (b)   be given before the end of such period as may be prescribed.

(8)   If a notice of objection is given before the end of the prescribed period, the Secretary of State must consider it and determine whether or not any penalty to which it relates is payable.

[(3)   Subsection (4) applies where a person to whom a penalty notice is issued objects on the ground that—

      (a)   he is not liable to the imposition of a penalty, or

      (b)   the amount of the penalty is too high.

(4)   The person may give a notice of objection to the Secretary of State.

(5)   A notice of objection must—

      (a)   be in writing,

      (b)   give the objector's reasons, and

      (c)   be given before the end of such period as may be prescribed.

(6)   Where the Secretary of State receives a notice of objection to a penalty in accordance with this section he shall consider it and—

      (a)   cancel the penalty,

      (b)   reduce the penalty,

      (c)   increase the penalty, or

      (d)   determine to take no action under paragraphs (a) to (c).

(7)   Where the Secretary of State considers a notice of objection under subsection (6) he shall—

      (a)   inform the objector of his decision before the end of such period as may be prescribed or such longer period as he may agree with the objector,

      (b)   if he increases the penalty, issue a new penalty notice under subsection (1), and

      (c)   if he reduces the penalty, notify the objector of the reduced amount.]

(9)   The Secretary of State may by regulations provide, in relation to detached trailers, for a penalty notice which is *served* [issued] in such manner as may be prescribed to have effect as a penalty notice properly *served on* [issued to] the responsible person or persons concerned under this section.

(10)   Any sum payable to the Secretary of State as a penalty under section 32 may be recovered by the Secretary of State as a debt due to him.

[(11)   In proceedings for enforcement of a penalty under subsection (10) no question may be raised as to—

      (a)   liability to the imposition of the penalty, or

      (b)   its amount.

(12) A document which is to be issued to or served on a person outside the United Kingdom for the purpose of subsection (1) or (7) or in the course of proceedings under subsection (10) may be issued or served—

    (a) in person,

    (b) by post,

    (c) by facsimile transmission, or

    (d) in another prescribed manner.

(13) The Secretary of State may by regulations provide that a document issued or served in a manner listed in subsection (12) in accordance with the regulations is to be taken to have been received at a time specified by or determined in accordance with the regulations.]

Amendment

Sub-s (2): in para (d)(i) word "must" in italics repealed and subsequent word in square brackets substituted by the Nationality, Immigration and Asylum Act 2002, s 125, Sch 8, paras 1, 7(1), (2). Date in force (for the purposes of clandestine entrants who arrive in the United Kingdom concealed in a vehicle or a rail freight wagon): 8 December 2002 (except in relation to a penalty notice issued to a person before that date); see SI 2002/2811, arts 2, 4, Schedule. Date in force (for the purposes of clandestine entrants who pass, or attempt to pass, through immigration control concealed in a vehicle): 11 May 2012: see SI 2012/1263, art 2. Date in force (for remaining purposes): to be appointed.

Sub-ss (3)–(8): substituted, by subsequent sub-ss (3)–(7), by the Nationality, Immigration and Asylum Act 2002, s 125, Sch 8, paras 1, 7(1), (3), as from the dates noted above.

Sub-s (9): word "served" in italics repealed and subsequent word in square brackets substituted by the Nationality, Immigration and Asylum Act 2002, s 125, Sch 8, paras 1, 7(1), (4)(a), as from the dates noted above.

Sub-s (9): words "served on" in italics repealed and subsequent words in square brackets substituted by the Nationality, Immigration and Asylum Act 2002, s 125, Sch 8, paras 1, 7(1), (4)(b), as from the dates noted above.

Sub-ss (11)–(13): inserted by the Nationality, Immigration and Asylum Act 2002, s 125, Sch 8, paras 1, 7(1), (5), as from the dates noted above

Subordinate Legislation

Carriers' Liability Regulations 2002, SI 2002/2817.

[35A Appeal]

[(1) A person may appeal to the court against a penalty imposed on him under section 32 on the ground that—

    (a) he is not liable to the imposition of a penalty, or

    (b) the amount of the penalty is too high.

(2) On an appeal under this section the court may—

    (a) allow the appeal and cancel the penalty,

    (b) allow the appeal and reduce the penalty, or

    (c) dismiss the appeal.

(3) An appeal under this section shall be a re-hearing of the Secretary of State's decision to impose a penalty and shall be determined having regard to—

    (a) any code of practice under section 32A which has effect at the time of the appeal,

    (b) the code of practice under section 33 which had effect at the time of the events to which the penalty relates, and

    (c) any other matters which the court thinks relevant (which may include matters of which the Secretary of State was unaware).

(4) Subsection (3) has effect despite any provision of Civil Procedure Rules.

(5) An appeal may be brought by a person under this section against a penalty whether or not—

    (a) he has given notice of objection under section 35(4);

    (b) the penalty has been increased or reduced under section 35(6).]

Amendment

Inserted by the Nationality, Immigration and Asylum Act 2002, s 125, Sch 8, paras 1, 8. Date in force (for the purposes of clandestine entrants who arrive in the United Kingdom concealed in a vehicle or a rail freight wagon): 8 December 2002 (except in relation to a penalty notice issued to a person before that date): see SI 2002/2811, arts 2, 4, Schedule. Date in force (for the purposes of clandestine entrants who pass, or attempt to pass, through immigration control concealed in a vehicle): 11 May 2012: see SI 2012/1263, art 2. Date in force (for remaining purposes): to be appointed.

36 Power to detain vehicles etc in connection with penalties under section 32

(1) If a penalty notice has been *given* [issued] under section 35, a senior officer may detain any relevant—

(a) vehicle,

(b) small ship, . . . ,

(c) small aircraft, [or

(d) rail freight wagon,]

until all penalties to which the notice relates, and any expenses reasonably incurred by the Secretary of State in connection with the detention, have been paid.

(2) That power—

(a) may be exercised only if, in the opinion of the senior officer concerned, there is a significant risk that the penalty (or one or more of the penalties) will not be paid before the end of the prescribed period if the transporter is not detained; and

(b) may not be exercised if alternative security which the Secretary of State considers is satisfactory, has been given.

[(2A) A vehicle may be detained under subsection (1) only if—

(a) the driver of the vehicle is an employee of its owner or hirer,

(b) the driver of the vehicle is its owner or hirer, or

(c) a penalty notice is issued to the owner or hirer of the vehicle.

(2B) A senior officer may detain a relevant vehicle, small ship, small aircraft or rail freight wagon pending—

(a) a decision whether to issue a penalty notice,

(b) the issue of a penalty notice, or

(c) a decision whether to detain under subsection (1).

(2C) That power may not be exercised in any case—

(a) for longer than is necessary in the circumstances of the case, or

(b) after the expiry of the period of 24 hours beginning with the conclusion of the first search of the vehicle, ship, aircraft or wagon by an immigration officer after it arrived in the United Kingdom.]

(3) If a transporter is detained under this section, the owner, consignor or any other person who has an interest in any freight or other thing carried in or on the transporter may remove it, or arrange for it to be removed, at such time and in such way as is reasonable.

(4) The detention of a transporter under this section is lawful even though it is subsequently established that the penalty notice on which the detention was based was ill-founded in respect of all or any of the penalties to which it related.

(5) But subsection (4) does not apply if the Secretary of State was acting unreasonably in issuing the penalty notice.

Amendment

Sub-s (1): word "given" in italics repealed and subsequent word in square brackets substituted by the Nationality, Immigration and Asylum Act 2002, s 125, Sch 8, paras 1, 9(1), (2)(a). Date in force (for the purposes of clandestine entrants who arrive in the United Kingdom concealed in a vehicle or a rail freight wagon): 8 December 2002 (except in relation to a penalty notice issued to a person before that date): see SI 2002/2811, arts 2, 4, Schedule. Date in force (for the purposes of clandestine entrants who pass, or attempt to pass, through immigration control concealed in a vehicle): 11 May 2012: see SI 2012/1263, art 2. Date in force (for remaining purposes): to be appointed.

Sub-s (1): in para (b) word omitted repealed by the Nationality, Immigration and Asylum Act 2002, ss 125, 161, Sch 8, paras 1, 9(1), (2)(b), Sch 9.

Sub-s (1): para (d) and word "or" immediately preceding it inserted by the Nationality, Immigration and Asylum Act 2002, s 125, Sch 8, paras 1, 9(1), (2)(c).

Sub-ss (2A)–(2C): inserted by the Nationality, Immigration and Asylum Act 2002, s 125, Sch 8, paras 1, 9(1), (3), as from the dates noted above.

Subordinate Legislation

Carriers' Liability Regulations 2002, SI 2002/2817.

[36A Detention in default of payment]

[(1) This section applies where a person to whom a penalty notice has been issued under section 35 fails to pay the penalty before the date specified in accordance with section 35(2)(c).

(2) The Secretary of State may make arrangements for the detention of any vehicle, small ship, aircraft or rail freight wagon which the person to whom the penalty notice was issued uses in the course of a business.

(3) A vehicle, ship, aircraft or wagon may be detained under subsection (2) whether or not the person to whom the penalty notice was issued owns it.

(4) But a vehicle may be detained under subsection (2) only if the person to whom the penalty notice was issued—

(a)   is the owner or hirer of the vehicle, or

(b)   was an employee of the owner or hirer of the vehicle when the penalty notice was issued.

(5) The power under subsection (2) may not be exercised while an appeal against the penalty under section 35A is pending or could be brought (ignoring the possibility of an appeal out of time with permission).

(6) The Secretary of State shall arrange for the release of a vehicle, ship, aircraft or wagon detained under this section if the person to whom the penalty notice was issued pays—

(a)   the penalty, and

(b)   expenses reasonably incurred in connection with the detention.]

Amendment

Inserted by the Nationality, Immigration and Asylum Act 2002, s 125, Sch 8, paras 1, 10. Date in force (for the purposes of clandestine entrants who arrive in the United Kingdom concealed in a vehicle or a rail freight wagon): 8 December 2002 (except in relation to a penalty notice issued to a person before that date): see SI 2002/2811, arts 2, 4, Schedule. Date in force (for the purposes of clandestine entrants who pass, or attempt to pass, through immigration control concealed in a vehicle): 11 May 2012: see SI 2012/1263, art 2. Date in force (for remaining purposes): to be appointed.

37 Effect of detention

(1) This section applies if a transporter is detained under *section 36* [section 36(1)].

(2) The person to whom the penalty notice was addressed, or the owner or any other person *claiming an interest in the transporter,* [whose interests may be affected by detention of the transporter,] may apply to the court for the transporter to be released.

(3) The court may release the transporter if it considers that—

(a)   satisfactory security has been tendered in place of the transporter for the payment of the penalty alleged to be due and connected expenses;

(b)   there is no significant risk that the penalty (or one or more of the penalties) and any connected expenses will not be paid; or

(c)   there is a significant doubt as to whether the penalty is payable *and the applicant has a compelling need to have the transporter released.*

[(3A) The court may also release the transporter on the application of the owner of the transporter under subsection (2) if—

  (a)   a penalty notice was not issued to the owner or an employee of his, and

  (b)   the court considers it right to release the transporter.

(3B) In determining whether to release a transporter under subsection (3A) the court shall consider—

  (a)   the extent of any hardship caused by detention,

  (b)   the extent (if any) to which the owner is responsible for the matters in respect of which the penalty notice was issued, and

  (c)   any other matter which appears to the court to be relevant (whether specific to the circumstances of the case or of a general nature).

(4)   If the court has not ordered the release of the transporter, the Secretary of State may sell it if the penalty in question and connected expenses are not paid before the end of the period of 84 days beginning with the date on which the detention began.

(5)   "Connected expenses" means expenses reasonably incurred by the Secretary of State in connection with the detention.

[(5A) The power of sale under subsection (4) may be exercised only when no appeal against the imposition of the penalty is pending or can be brought (ignoring the possibility of an appeal out of time with permission).

(5B) The power of sale under subsection (4) shall lapse if not exercised within a prescribed period.]

(6)   Schedule 1 applies to the sale of transporters under this section.

[(7) This section applies to a transporter detained under section 36A as it applies to a transporter detained under section 36(1); but for that purpose—

  (a)   the court may release the transporter only if the court considers that the detention was unlawful or under subsection (3A) (and subsection (3) shall not apply), and

  (b)   the reference in subsection (4) to the period of 84 days shall be taken as a reference to a period prescribed for the purpose of this paragraph.]

Amendment

Sub-s (1): words "section 36" in italics repealed and subsequent words in square brackets substituted by the Nationality, Immigration and Asylum Act 2002, s 125, Sch 8, paras 1, 11(1), (2). Date in force (for the purposes of clandestine entrants who arrive in the United Kingdom concealed in a vehicle or a rail freight wagon): 8 December 2002 (except in relation to a penalty notice issued to a person before that date): see SI 2002/2811, arts 2, 4, Schedule. Date in force (for the purposes of clandestine entrants who pass, or attempt to pass, through immigration control concealed in a vehicle): 11 May 2012: see SI 2012/1263, art 2. Date in force (for remaining purposes): to be appointed.

Sub-s (2): words "claiming an interest in the transporter," in italics repealed and subsequent words in square brackets substituted by the Nationality, Immigration and Asylum Act 2002, s 125, Sch 8, paras 1, 11(1), (3), as from the dates noted above.

Sub-s (3): in para (c) words "and the applicant has a compelling need to have the transporter released" in italics repealed by the Nationality, Immigration and Asylum Act 2002, ss 125, 161, Sch 8, paras 1, 11(1), (4), Sch 9, as from the dates noted above.

Sub-ss (3A), (3B): inserted by the Nationality, Immigration and Asylum Act 2002, s 125, Sch 8, paras 1, 11(1), (5), as from the dates noted above.

Sub-ss (5A), (5B): inserted by the Nationality, Immigration and Asylum Act 2002, s 125, Sch 8, paras 1, 11(1), (6), as from the dates noted above.

Sub-s (7): inserted by the Nationality, Immigration and Asylum Act 2002, s 125, Sch 8, paras 1, 11(1), (7), as from the dates noted above.

Subordinate Legislation

Carriers' Liability Regulations 2002, SI 2002/2817.

(S 38 amends the Immigration Act 1971, s 25 and inserts s 25A of that Act; s 39 repealed with savings by the Nationality, Immigration and Asylum Act 2002, ss 125, 161, Sch 8, paras 1, 12, Sch 9, as from 8 December 2002.)

Passengers without proper documents

[40 Charge in respect of passenger without proper documents]

[(1)   This section applies if an individual requiring leave to enter the United Kingdom arrives in the United Kingdom by ship or aircraft and, on being required to do so by an immigration officer, fails to produce—

(a)   an immigration document which is in force and which satisfactorily establishes his identity and his nationality or citizenship, and

(b)   if the individual requires a visa, a visa of the required kind.

(2)   The Secretary of State may charge the owner of the ship or aircraft, in respect of the individual, the sum of £2,000.

(3)   The charge shall be payable to the Secretary of State on demand.

(4)   No charge shall be payable in respect of any individual who is shown by the owner to have produced the required document or documents to the owner or his employee or agent when embarking on the ship or aircraft for the voyage or flight to the United Kingdom.

(5)   For the purpose of subsection (4) an owner shall be entitled to regard a document as—

(a)   being what it purports to be unless its falsity is reasonably apparent, and

(b)   relating to the individual producing it unless it is reasonably apparent that it does not relate to him.

(6)   For the purposes of this section an individual requires a visa if—

(a)   under the immigration rules he requires a visa for entry into the United Kingdom, or

(b)   as a result of section 41 he requires a visa for passing through the United Kingdom.

(7)   The Secretary of State may by order amend this section for the purpose of applying it in relation to an individual who—

(a)   requires leave to enter the United Kingdom, and

(b)   arrives in the United Kingdom by train.

(8)   An order under subsection (7) may provide for the application of this section—

(a)   except in cases of a specified kind;

(b)   subject to a specified defence.

(9)   In this section "immigration document" means—

(a)   a passport, and

(b)   a document which relates to a national of a country other than the United Kingdom and which is designed to serve the same purpose as a passport.

(10)   The Secretary of State may by order substitute a sum for the sum in subsection (2).]

Amendment

Substituted, together with ss 40A, 40B for this section as originally enacted, by the Nationality, Immigration and Asylum Act 2002, s 125, Sch 8, paras 1, 13.

[40A Notification and objection]

[(1)   If the Secretary of State decides to charge a person under section 40, the Secretary of State must notify the person of his decision.

(2) A notice under subsection (1) (a "charge notice") must—

   (a) state the Secretary of State's reasons for deciding to charge the person,

   (b) state the amount of the charge,

   (c) specify the date before which, and the manner in which, the charge must be paid,

   (d) include an explanation of the steps that the person may take if he objects to the charge, and

   (e) include an explanation of the steps that the Secretary of State may take under this Part to recover any unpaid charge.

(3) Where a person on whom a charge notice is served objects to the imposition of the charge on him, he may give a notice of objection to the Secretary of State.

(4) A notice of objection must—

   (a) be in writing,

   (b) give the objector's reasons, and

   (c) be given before the end of such period as may be prescribed.

(5) Where the Secretary of State receives a notice of objection to a charge in accordance with this section, he shall—

   (a) consider it, and

   (b) determine whether or not to cancel the charge.

(6) Where the Secretary of State considers a notice of objection, he shall inform the objector of his decision before the end of—

   (a) such period as may be prescribed, or

   (b) such longer period as he may agree with the objector.

(7) Any sum payable to the Secretary of State as a charge under section 40 may be recovered by the Secretary of State as a debt due to him.

(8) In proceedings for enforcement of a charge under subsection (7) no question may be raised as to the validity of the charge.

(9) Subsections (12) and (13) of section 35 shall have effect for the purpose of this section as they have effect for the purpose of section 35(1), (7) and (10).]

Amendment

Substituted, together with ss 40, 40B for s 40 as originally enacted, by the Nationality, Immigration and Asylum Act 2002, s 125, Sch 8, paras 1, 13.

Subordinate Legislation

Carriers' Liability Regulations 2002, SI 2002/2817.

[40B Appeal]

[(1) A person may appeal to the court against a decision to charge him under section 40.

(2) On an appeal under this section the court may—

   (a) allow the appeal and cancel the charge, or

   (b) dismiss the appeal.

(3) An appeal under this section—

   (a) shall be a re-hearing of the Secretary of State's decision to impose a charge, and

   (b) may be determined having regard to matters of which the Secretary of State was unaware.

(4) Subsection (3)(a) has effect despite any provision of Civil Procedure Rules.

(5) An appeal may be brought by a person under this section against a decision to charge him whether or not he has given notice of objection under section 40A(3).]

Amendment

Substituted, together with ss 40, 40A for s 40 as originally enacted, by the Nationality, Immigration and Asylum Act 2002, s 125, Sch 8, paras 1, 13.

41 Visas for transit passengers

(1) The Secretary of State may by order require transit passengers to hold a transit visa.

(2) "Transit passengers" means persons of any description specified in the order who on arrival in the United Kingdom pass through to another country without entering the United Kingdom; and "transit visa" means a visa for that purpose.

(3) The order—

(a) may specify a description of persons by reference to nationality, citizenship, origin or other connection with any particular country but not by reference to race, colour or religion;

(b) may not provide for the requirement imposed by the order to apply to any person who under the 1971 Act has the right of abode in the United Kingdom;

(c) may provide for any category of persons of a description specified in the order to be exempt from the requirement imposed by the order;

(d) may make provision about the method of application for visas required by the order.

Subordinate Legislation

Immigration (Passenger Transit Visa) Order 2014, SI 2014/2702.

42

(Repealed by the Nationality, Immigration and Asylum Act 2002, ss 125, 161, Sch 8, paras 1, 14, Sch 9.)

Interpretation

43 Interpretation of Part II

[(1)] In this Part—

"aircraft" includes hovercraft;

"captain" means the master of a ship or commander of an aircraft;

"concealed" includes being concealed in any freight, stores or other thing carried in or on the vehicle, ship[, aircraft or rail freight wagon] concerned;

. . .

"detached trailer" means a trailer, semi-trailer, caravan or any other thing which is designed or adapted for towing by a vehicle but which has been detached for transport—

(a) in or on the vehicle concerned; or

(b) in the ship or aircraft concerned (whether separately or in or on a vehicle);

"equipment", in relation to an aircraft, includes—

(a) any certificate of registration, maintenance or airworthiness of the aircraft;

(b) any log book relating to the use of the aircraft; and

(c) any similar document;

["freight shuttle wagon" means a wagon which—

(a) forms part of a shuttle-train, and

(b) is designed to carry commercial goods vehicles;

"freight train" means any train other than—

(a) a train engaged on a service for the carriage of passengers, or

(b) a shuttle-train;]

Appendix 1 — UK Immigration Statutes

"hirer", in relation to a vehicle, means any person who has hired the vehicle from another person;

"operating weight", in relation to an aircraft, means the maximum total weight of the aircraft and its contents at which the aircraft may take off anywhere in the world, in the most favourable circumstances, in accordance with the certificate of airworthiness in force in respect of the aircraft;

"owner" includes—

   (a)   in relation to a ship or aircraft, the agent or operator of the ship or aircraft; . . .

   (b)   . . . and

["rail freight wagon" means]

in relation to a transporter which is the subject of a hire-purchase agreement, includes the person in possession of it under that agreement;

"penalty notice" has the meaning given in section 35(2);

   (a)   any rolling stock, other than a locomotive, which forms part of a freight train, or

   (b)   a freight shuttle wagon,

and for the purpose of this definition, "rolling stock" and "locomotive" have the meanings given by section 83 of the Railways Act 1993 (c 43);]

"senior officer" means an immigration officer not below the rank of chief immigration officer;

"ship" includes every description of vessel used in navigation;

["shuttle-train" has the meaning given by section 1(9) of the Channel Tunnel Act 1987 (c 53);]

"small aircraft" means an aircraft which has an operating weight of less than 5,700 kilogrammes;

"small ship" means a ship which has a gross tonnage of less than 500 tonnes;

"train" means a train which—

   (a)   is engaged on an international service as defined by section 13(6) of the Channel Tunnel Act 1987; but

   (b)   is not a shuttle train as defined by section 1(9) of that Act;

"train operator", in relation to a person arriving in the United Kingdom on a train, means the operator of trains who embarked that person on that train for the journey to the United Kingdom;

"transporter" means a vehicle, ship[, aircraft or rail freight wagon] together with—

   (a)   its equipment; and

   (b)   any stores for use in connection with its operation;

"vehicle" includes a trailer, semi-trailer, caravan or other thing which is designed or adapted to be towed by another vehicle.

[(2)   A reference in this Part to "the court" is a reference—

   (a)   in England and Wales, to [the county court],

   (b)   in Scotland, to the sheriff, and

   (c)   in Northern Ireland, to a county court.

(3)   But—

   (a)   a county court [in Northern Ireland, or the county court in England and Wales,] may transfer proceedings under this Part to the High Court, and

   (b)   the sheriff may transfer proceedings under this Part to the Court of Session.]

Amendment

Sub-s (1): numbered as such by the Nationality, Immigration and Asylum Act 2002, s 125, Sch 8, paras 1, 15.

Sub-s (1): in definition "concealed" words ", aircraft or rail freight wagon" in square brackets substituted by the Nationality, Immigration and Asylum Act 2002, s 125, Sch 8, paras 1, 15(a).

Sub-s (1): definition "court" (omitted) repealed by the Nationality, Immigration and Asylum Act 2002, s 125, Sch 8, paras 1, 15(b).

Sub-s (1): definitions "freight shuttle wagon" and "freight train" inserted by the Nationality, Immigration and Asylum Act 2002, s 125, Sch 8, paras 1, 15(c).

Sub-s (1): in definition "owner" para (b) and word omitted immediately preceding it repealed by the Nationality, Immigration and Asylum Act 2002, ss 125, 161, Sch 8, paras 1, 15(d), Sch 9.

Sub-s (1): definition "rail freight wagon" substituted by the Nationality, Immigration and Asylum Act 2002, s 125, Sch 8, paras 1, 15(e).

Sub-s (1): definition "shuttle-train" inserted by the Nationality, Immigration and Asylum Act 2002, s 125, Sch 8, paras 1, 15(f).

Sub-s (1): in definition "transporter" words ", aircraft or rail freight wagon" in square brackets substituted by the Nationality, Immigration and Asylum Act 2002, s 125, Sch 8, paras 1, 15(g).

Sub-ss (2), (3): inserted by the Nationality, Immigration and Asylum Act 2002, s 124, Sch 8, paras 1, 15(h).

Sub-s (2): in para (a) words in square brackets substituted by the Crime and Courts Act 2013, s 17(5), Sch 9, Pt 3, para 52(1)(b), (2), as from 22 April 2014: see SI 2014/954.

Sub-s (3): in para (a) words in square brackets inserted by the Crime and Courts Act 2013, s 17(5), Sch 9, Pt 3, para 90(b), as from 22 April 2014: see SI 2014/954.

44–52

(Repealed by the Nationality, Immigration and Asylum Act 2002, ss 68(6)(a), 161, Sch 9.)

PART III
BAIL

Bail hearings under other enactments

53 Applications for bail in immigration cases

(1) The Secretary of State may by regulations make new provision in relation to applications for bail by persons detained under the 1971 Act [or under section 62 of the Nationality, Immigration and Asylum Act 2002].

(2) The regulations may confer a right to be released on bail in prescribed circumstances.

(3) The regulations may, in particular, make provision—

 (a) creating or transferring jurisdiction to hear an application for bail by a person detained under the 1971 Act [or under section 62 of the Nationality, Immigration and Asylum Act 2002];

 (b) as to the places in which such an application may be held;

 (c) as to the procedure to be followed on, or in connection with, such an application;

 (d) as to circumstances in which, and conditions (including financial conditions) on which, an applicant may be released on bail;

 (e) amending or repealing any enactment so far as it relates to such an application.

(4) The regulations must include provision for securing that an application for bail made by a person who has brought an appeal under any provision of [the Nationality, Immigration and Asylum Act 2002] or the Special Immigration Appeals Commission Act 1997 is heard by the appellate authority hearing that appeal.

(5) . . .

(6) Regulations under this section require the approval of the Lord Chancellor.

[(6A) In so far as regulations under this section relate to England and Wales, the Lord Chancellor must consult the Lord Chief Justice of England and Wales before giving his approval.

(6B) In so far as regulations under this section relate to Northern Ireland, the Lord Chancellor must consult the Lord Chief Justice of Northern Ireland [and the Department of Justice in Northern Ireland] before giving his approval.]

(7) In so far as regulations under this section relate to the sheriff or the Court of Session, the Lord Chancellor must obtain the consent of the Scottish Ministers before giving his approval.

[(8) The Lord Chief Justice of England and Wales may nominate a judicial office holder (as defined in section 109(4) of the Constitutional Reform Act 2005) to exercise his functions under this section.

(9) The Lord Chief Justice of Northern Ireland may nominate any of the following to exercise his functions under this section—

(a) the holder of one of the offices listed in Schedule 1 to the Justice (Northern Ireland) Act 2002;

(b) a Lord Justice of Appeal (as defined in section 88 of that Act).]

Amendment

Sub-s (1): words "or under section 62 of the Nationality, Immigration and Asylum Act 2002" in square brackets inserted by the Nationality, Immigration and Asylum Act 2002, s 62(13)(a). Sub-s (3): in para (a) words "or under section 62 of the Nationality, Immigration and Asylum Act 2002" in square brackets inserted by the Nationality, Immigration and Asylum Act 2002, s 62(13)(b).

Sub-s (4): words "the Nationality, Immigration and Asylum Act 2002" in square brackets substituted by the Nationality, Immigration and Asylum Act 2002, s 114(3), Sch 7, para 28. Sub-s (5): repealed by the Nationality, Immigration and Asylum Act 2002, ss 68(6)(b), 161, Sch 9.

Sub-ss (6A), (6B): inserted by the Constitutional Reform Act 2005, s 15(1), Sch 4, Pt 1, paras 283, 284(1), (2).

Sub-s (6B): words "and the Department of Justice in Northern Ireland" in square brackets inserted by SI 2012/2595, art 9(1), (2). Date in force: 18 October 2012: see SI 2012/2595, art 1(2); for transitional provisions see arts 24–28 thereof.

Sub-ss (8), (9): inserted by the Constitutional Reform Act 2005, s 15(1), Sch 4, Pt 1, paras 283, 284(1), (3).

54, 55

(*S 54 amends the Immigration Act 1971, Sch 3; s 55 repealed by the Nationality, Immigration and Asylum Act 2002, ss 68(6)(c), 161, Sch 9*)

56–81

(*Repealed by the Nationality, Immigration and Asylum Act 2002, ss 114(1), (2), 161, Sch 9*)

PART IV

PART V
IMMIGRATION ADVISERS AND IMMIGRATION SERVICE PROVIDERS

Interpretation

82 Interpretation of Part V

(1) In this Part—

"claim for asylum" means a claim that it would be contrary to the United Kingdom's obligations under—

    (a)   the Refugee Convention, or

    (b)   Article 3 of the Human Rights Convention,

for the claimant to be removed from, or required to leave, the United Kingdom;

"the Commissioner" means the Immigration Services Commissioner;

"the complaints scheme" means the scheme established under paragraph 5(1) of Schedule 5;

"designated judge" has the same meaning as in section 119(1) of the Courts and Legal Services Act 1990;

"designated professional body" has the meaning given by section 86;

["designated qualifying regulator" has the meaning given by section 86A;]

"immigration advice" means advice which—

       relates to a particular individual;

    (a)   relates to a particular individual;

    (b)   is given in connection with one or more relevant matters;

    (c)   is given by a person who knows that he is giving it in relation to a particular individual and in connection with one or more relevant matters; and

    (d)   is not given in connection with representing an individual before a court in criminal proceedings or matters ancillary to criminal proceedings;

"immigration services" means the making of representations on behalf of a particular individual—

    (a)   in civil proceedings before a court, tribunal or adjudicator in the United Kingdom, or

    (b)   in correspondence with a Minister of the Crown or government department,

in connection with one or more relevant matters;

"Minister of the Crown" has the same meaning as in the Ministers of the Crown Act 1975;

"qualified person" means a person who is qualified for the purposes of section 84;

"registered person" means a person who is registered with the Commissioner under section 85;

"relevant matters" means any of the following—

    (a)   a claim for asylum;

    (b)   an application for, or for the variation of, entry clearance or leave to enter or remain in the United Kingdom;

    [(ba) an application for an immigration employment document;]

    (c)   unlawful entry into the United Kingdom;

    (d)   nationality and citizenship under the law of the United Kingdom;

    (e)   citizenship of the European Union;

    (f)   admission to Member States under [EU] law;

    (g)   residence in a Member State in accordance with rights conferred by or under Community law;

    (h)   removal or deportation from the United Kingdom;

    (i)   an application for bail under the Immigration Acts or under the Special Immigration Appeals Commission Act 1997;

    (j)   an appeal against, or an application for judicial review in relation to, any decision taken in connection with a matter referred to in paragraphs (a) to (i); . . . .]

. . . . .

(2) In this Part, references to the provision of immigration advice or immigration services are to the provision of such advice or services by a person—

(a) in the United Kingdom (regardless of whether the persons to whom they are provided are in the United Kingdom or elsewhere); and

(b) in the course of a business carried on (whether or not for profit) by him or by another person.

[(3) In the definition of "relevant matters" in subsection (1) "immigration employment document" means—

(a) a work permit (within the meaning of section 33(1) of the Immigration Act 1971 (interpretation)), and

(b) any other document which relates to employment and is issued for a purpose of immigration rules or in connection with leave to enter or remain in the United Kingdom.]

Amendment

Sub-s (1): definition "designated qualifying regulator" inserted by the Legal Services Act 2007, s 186, Sch 18, Pt 2, paras 9, 10. Date in force: 1 April 2011: see SI 2011/720, art 2(c).

Sub-s (1): in definition "relevant matters" para (ba) inserted by the Nationality, Immigration and Asylum Act 2002, s 123(1), (2).

Sub-s (1): in definition "relevant matters" in para (f) reference to "EU" in square brackets substituted by SI 2011/1043, art 6(2)(a). Date in force: 22 April 2011: see SI 2011/1043, art 2; for transitional savings see art 3(3) thereof.

Sub-s (1): in definition "relevant matters" in para (i) word omitted repealed by SI 2010/22, art 5(1), Sch 2, paras 32, 33.

Sub-s (1): definition "the Tribunal" (omitted) repealed by SI 2010/22, art 5(1), Sch 2, paras 32, 33.

Sub-s (3): inserted by the Nationality, Immigration and Asylum Act 2002, s 123(1), (3).

The Immigration Services Commissioner

83 The Commissioner

(1) There is to be an Immigration Services Commissioner (referred to in this Part as "the Commissioner").

(2) The Commissioner is to be appointed by the Secretary of State after consulting the Lord Chancellor[, the Department of Justice in Northern Ireland] and the Scottish Ministers.

(3) It is to be the general duty of the Commissioner to promote good practice by those who provide immigration advice or immigration services.

(4) In addition to any other functions conferred on him by this Part, the Commissioner is to have the regulatory functions set out in Part I of Schedule 5.

(5) The Commissioner must exercise his functions so as to secure, so far as is reasonably practicable, that those who provide immigration advice or immigration services—

(a) are fit and competent to do so;

(b) act in the best interests of their clients;

(c) do not knowingly mislead any court, tribunal or adjudicator in the United Kingdom;

(d) do not seek to abuse any procedure operating in the United Kingdom in connection with immigration or asylum (including any appellate or other judicial procedure);

(e) do not advise any person to do something which would amount to such an abuse.

(6) The Commissioner—

(a) must arrange for the publication, in such form and manner and to such extent as he considers appropriate, of information about his functions and about matters falling within the scope of his functions; and

(b) may give advice about his functions and about such matters.

[(6A) The duties imposed on the Commissioner by subsections (3) and (5) apply in relation to persons within section 84(2)(ba) only to the extent that those duties have effect in relation to the Commissioner's functions under section 92 or 92A.]

(7) Part II of Schedule 5 makes further provision with respect to the Commissioner.

Amendment

Sub-s (2): words ", the Department of Justice in Northern Ireland" in square brackets inserted by SI 2012/2595, art 9(1), (3), as from 18 October 2012: see SI 2012/2595, art 1(2); for transitional provisions see arts 24–28 thereof.

Sub-s (6A): inserted by the Legal Services Act 2007, s 186, Sch 18, Pt 2, paras 9, 11, as from 1 April 2011: see SI 2011/720, art 2(c).

The general prohibition

84 Provision of immigration services

(1) No person may provide immigration advice or immigration services unless he is a qualified person.

[(2) A person is a qualified person if he is—
  (a) a registered person,
  (b) authorised by a designated professional body to practise as a member of the profession whose members the body regulates,
  [(ba) a person authorised to provide immigration advice or immigration services by a designated qualifying regulator,]
  (c) the equivalent in an EEA State of—
    (i) a registered person, or
    (ii) a person within paragraph (b) [or (ba)],
  (d) a person permitted, by virtue of exemption from a prohibition, to provide in an EEA State advice or services equivalent to immigration advice or services, or
  (e) acting on behalf of, and under the supervision of, a person within any of paragraphs (a) to (d) (whether or not under a contract of employment).

(3) Subsection (2)(a) and (e) are subject to any limitation on the effect of a person's registration imposed under paragraph 2(2) of Schedule 6.]

[(3A) A person's entitlement to provide immigration advice or immigration services by virtue of subsection (2)(ba)—
  (a) is subject to any limitation on that person's authorisation imposed by the regulatory arrangements of the designated qualifying regulator in question, and
  (b) does not extend to the provision of such advice or services by the person other than in England and Wales (regardless of whether the persons to whom they are provided are in England and Wales or elsewhere).

(3B) In subsection (3A) "regulatory arrangements" has the same meaning as in the Legal Services Act 2007 (see section 21 of that Act).]

(4) Subsection (1) does not apply to a person who—
  (a) is certified by the Commissioner as exempt ("an exempt person");
  (b) is employed by an exempt person;
  (c) works under the supervision of an exempt person or an employee of an exempt person; or
  (d) who falls within a category of person specified in an order made by the Secretary of State for the purposes of this subsection.

(5) A certificate under subsection (4)(a) may relate only to a specified description of immigration advice or immigration services.

(6) Subsection (1) does not apply to a person—
  (a) holding an office under the Crown, when acting in that capacity;

(b) employed by, or for the purposes of, a government department, when acting in that capacity;

(c) acting under the control of a government department; or

(d) otherwise exercising functions on behalf of the Crown.

(7) An exemption given under subsection (4) may be withdrawn by the Commissioner.

Amendment

Sub-ss (2), (3): substituted by the Asylum and Immigration (Treatment of Claimants, etc) Act 2004, s 37(1).

Sub-s (2): para (ba) inserted by the Legal Services Act 2007, s 186, Sch 18, Pt 2, paras 9, 12(1), (2)(a). Date in force: 1 April 2011: see SI 2011/720, art 2(c).

Sub-s (2): in para (c)(ii) words "or (ba)" in square brackets inserted by the Legal Services Act 2007, s 186, Sch 18, Pt 2, paras 9, 12(1), (2)(b). Date in force: 1 April 2011: see SI 2011/720, art 2(c).

Sub-ss (3A), (3B): inserted by the Legal Services Act 2007, s 186, Sch 18, Pt 2, paras 9, 12(1), (3). Date in force: 1 April 2011: see SI 2011/720, art 2(c).

Subordinate Legislation

Immigration and Asylum Act 1999 (Part V Exemption: Educational Institutions and Health Sector Bodies) Order 2001, SI 2001/1403; Immigration and Asylum Act 1999 (Part V Exemption: Relevant Employers) Order 2003, SI 2003/3214; Immigration and Asylum Act 1999 (Part V Exemption: Licensed Sponsors Tiers 2 and 4) Order 2009, SI 2009/506.

85 Registration exemption by the Commissioner

(1) The Commissioner must prepare and maintain a register for and the purposes of section 84(2)(a) . . . .

(2) The Commissioner must keep a record of the persons to whom he has issued a certificate of exemption under section 84(4)(a).

(3) Schedule 6 makes further provision with respect to registration.

Amendment

Sub-s (1): words omitted repealed by the Asylum and Immigration (Treatment of Claimants, etc) Act 2004, ss 37(2), 47, Sch 4.

86 Designated professional bodies

(1) "Designated professional body" means—

(a) . . .

(b) The Law Society of Scotland;

(c) The Law Society of Northern Ireland;

(d) . . .

(e) . . .

(f) The Faculty of Advocates; or

(g) The General Council of the Bar of Northern Ireland.

[(2) The Secretary of State may by order remove a body from the list in subsection (1) if he considers that the body—

(a) has failed to provide effective regulation of its members in their provision of immigration advice or immigration services, or

(b) has failed to comply with a request of the Commissioner for the provision of information (whether general or in relation to a particular case or matter).]

(3) If a designated professional body asks the Secretary of State to amend subsection (1) so as to remove its name, the Secretary of State may by order do so.

(4) If the Secretary of State is proposing to act under subsection (2) he must, before doing so—

(a) consult the Commissioner;

(b) . . . .

(c) consult the [Scottish Legal Complaints Commission], if the proposed order would affect a designated professional body in Scotland;

(d) consult the lay observers appointed under Article 42 of the Solicitors (Northern Ireland) Order 1976, if the proposed order would affect a designated professional body in Northern Ireland;

(e) notify the body concerned of his proposal and give it a reasonable period within which to make representations; and

(f) consider any representations so made.

(5) An order under subsection (2) requires the approval of—

(a) the [Department of Justice in Northern Ireland], if it affects a designated professional body in . . . Northern Ireland;

(b) the Scottish Ministers, if it affects a designated professional body in Scotland.

[(6) Before deciding whether or not to give its approval under subsection (5)(a), the Department of Justice in Northern Ireland must consult the Lord Chief Justice of Northern Ireland.]

(7) Before deciding whether or not to give their approval under subsection (5)(b), the Scottish Ministers must consult the Lord President of the Court of Session.

(8) If the Secretary of State considers that a body [(other than a body in England and Wales)] which—

(a) is concerned (whether wholly or in part) with regulating the legal profession, or a branch of it, in an EEA State,

(b) is not a designated professional body, and

(c) is capable of providing effective regulation of its members in their provision of immigration advice or immigration services,

ought to be designated, he may by order amend subsection (1) to include the name of that body.

(9) The Commissioner must—

(a) keep under review the list of designated professional bodies set out in subsection (1); and

[(b) report to the Secretary of State if the Commissioner considers that a designated professional body—

(i) is failing to provide effective regulation of its members in their provision of immigration advice or immigration services, or

(ii) has failed to comply with a request of the Commissioner for the provision of information (whether general or in relation to a particular case or matter)].

[(9A) A designated professional body shall comply with a request of the Commissioner for the provision of information (whether general or in relation to a specified case or matter).]

(10) For the purpose of meeting the costs incurred by the Commissioner in discharging his functions under this Part, each designated professional body must pay to the Commissioner, in each year and on such date as may be specified, such fee as may be specified.

(11) Any unpaid fee for which a designated professional body is liable under subsection (10) may be recovered from that body as a debt due to the Commissioner.

(12) "Specified" means specified by an order made by the Secretary of State.

Amendment

Sub-s (1): para (a) repealed by the Legal Services Act 2007, ss 186, 210, Sch 18, Pt 2, paras 9, 13(1), (2), Sch 23.

Sub-s (1): para (d) repealed by the Legal Services Act 2007, ss 186, 210, Sch 18, Pt 2, paras 9, 13(1), (2), Sch 23.

Sub-s (1): para (e) repealed by the Legal Services Act 2007, ss 186, 210, Sch 18, Pt 2, paras 9, 13(1), (2), Sch 23.

Sub-s (2): substituted by the Asylum and Immigration (Treatment of Claimants, etc) Act 2004, s 41(1), (2).

Sub-s (4): para (b) repealed by the Legal Services Act 2007, ss 186, 210, Sch 18, Pt 2, paras 9, 13(1), (2), Sch 23.

Sub-s (4): in para (c) words "Scottish Legal Complaints Commission" in square brackets substituted by the Legal Services Act 2007, s 196(2)(a).

Sub-s (5): in para (a) words "Department of Justice in Northern Ireland" in square brackets substituted by SI 2012/2595, art 9(1), (4)(a). Date in force: 18 October 2012: see SI 2012/2595, art 1(2); for transitional provisions see arts 24–28 thereof.

Sub-s (5): in para (a) words omitted repealed by the Legal Services Act 2007, ss 186, 210, Sch 18, Pt 2, paras 9, 13(1), (3), Sch 23.

Sub-s (6): substituted by SI 2012/2595, art 9(1), (4)(b). Date in force: 18 October 2012: see SI 2012/2595, art 1(2); for transitional provisions see arts 24–28 thereof.

Sub-s (8): words "other than a body in England and Wales)" in square brackets inserted by the Legal Services Act 2007, s 186, Sch 18, Pt 2, paras 9, 13(1), (5). Date in force: 1 April 2011: see SI 2011/720, art 2(c).

Sub-s (9): para (b) substituted by the Asylum and Immigration (Treatment of Claimants, etc) Act 2004, s 41(1), (3).

Sub-s (9A): inserted by the Asylum and Immigration (Treatment of Claimants, etc) Act 2004, s 41(1), (4).

[86A Designated qualifying regulators

(1) "Designated qualifying regulator" means a body which is a qualifying regulator and is listed in subsection (2).

(2) The listed bodies are—

    (a)   the Law Society;

    (b)   the Institute of Legal Executives;

    (c)   the General Council of the Bar.

(3) The Secretary of State may by order remove a body from the list in subsection (2) if the Secretary of State considers that the body has failed to provide effective regulation of relevant authorised persons in their provision of immigration advice or immigration services.

(4) If a designated qualifying regulator asks the Secretary of State to amend subsection (2) so as to remove its name, the Secretary of State may by order do so.

(5) Where, at a time when a body is listed in subsection (2), the body ceases to be a qualifying regulator by virtue of paragraph 8(1)(a) of Schedule 18 to the Legal Services Act 2007 (loss of approved regulator status), the Secretary of State must, by order, remove it from the list.

(6) If the Secretary of State considers that a body which—

    (a)   is a qualifying regulator,

    (b)   is not a designated qualifying regulator, and

    (c)   is capable of providing effective regulation of relevant authorised persons in their provision of immigration advice or immigration services,

ought to be designated, the Secretary of State may, by order, amend the list in subsection (2) to include the name of that body.

(7) If the Secretary of State is proposing to act under subsection (3) or (6), the Secretary of State must, before doing so, consult the Commissioner.

(8) If the Secretary of State is proposing to act under subsection (3), the Secretary of State must, before doing so, also—

    (a)   notify the body concerned of the proposal and give it a reasonable period within which to make representations, and

    (b)   consider any representations duly made.

(9) An order under subsection (3), or (6) requires the approval of the Lord Chancellor.

(10) If the Legal Services Board considers that a designated qualifying regulator is failing to provide effective regulation of relevant authorised persons in their provision of immigration advice or immigration services, the Legal Services Board must make a report to this effect to—

    (a)   the Secretary of State, and

    (b)   the Lord Chancellor.

(11) In this section—

"qualifying regulator" means a body which is a qualifying regulator for the purposes of this Part of this Act by virtue of Part 1 of Schedule 18 to the Legal Services Act 2007 (approved regulators approved by the Legal Services Board in relation to immigration matters);

"relevant authorised persons", in relation to a designated qualifying regulator, means persons who are authorised by the designated qualifying regulator to provide immigration advice or immigration services.]

Amendment

Inserted by the Legal Services Act 2007, s 186, Sch 18, Pt 2, paras 9, 14, as from 1 April 2011: see SI 2011/720, art 2(c).

[*Appeals to the First-tier Tribunal*]

Amendment

Cross-heading: substituted by SI 2010/22, art 5(1), Sch 2, paras 32, 34.

[87 Appeals to the First-tier Tribunal]

(1) …

(2) Any person aggrieved by a relevant decision of the Commissioner may appeal to the [First-tier Tribunal] against the decision.

(3) "Relevant decision" means a decision—

    (a)   to refuse an application for registration made under paragraph 1 of Schedule 6;

    (b)   to withdraw an exemption given under section 84(4)(a);

    (c)   under paragraph 2(2) of that Schedule to register with limited effect;

    (d)   to refuse an application for continued registration made under paragraph 3 of that Schedule;

    (e)   to vary a registration on an application under paragraph 3 of that Schedule;

    [(ea) to vary a registration under paragraph 3A of that Schedule;] or

    (f)   …

[(3A) A relevant decision of the Commissioner is not to have effect while the period within which an appeal may be brought against the decision is running.

(3B) In the case of an appeal under this section, Tribunal Procedure Rules may include provision permitting the First-tier Tribunal to direct that while the appeal is being dealt with—

    (a)   no effect is to be given to the decision appealed against; or

    (b)   only such limited effect is to be given to it as may be specified in the direction.

(3C) If provision is made in Tribunal Procedure Rules by virtue of subsection (3B), the rules must also include provision requiring the First-tier Tribunal to consider applications by the Commissioner for the cancellation or variation of directions given by virtue of that subsection.]

[(4) For a further function of the First-tier Tribunal under this Part, see paragraph 9(1)(e) of Schedule 5 (disciplinary charges laid by the Commissioner).]

(5) …

Amendment

Section heading: substituted by SI 2010/22, art 5(1), Sch 2, paras 32, 35(a).

Sub-s (1): repealed by SI 2010/22, art 5(1), Sch 2, paras 32, 35(b).

Sub-s (2): words "First-tier Tribunal" in square brackets substituted by SI 2010/22, art 5(1), Sch 2, paras 32, 35(c).

Sub-s (3): para (ea) inserted by the Nationality, Immigration and Asylum Act 2002, s 140(3).

Sub-s (3): para (f) repealed by the Asylum and Immigration (Treatment of Claimants, etc) Act 2004, ss 40, 47, Sch 4.

Sub-ss (3A)–(3C): inserted by SI 2010/22, art 5(1), Sch 2, paras 32, 35(d).

Sub-s (4): substituted by SI 2010/22, art 5(1), Sch 2, paras 32, 35(e).

Sub-s (5): repealed by SI 2010/22, art 5(1), Sch 2, paras 32, 35(b).

88 Appeal upheld by the [First-tier Tribunal]

(1) This section applies if the [First-tier Tribunal] allows an appeal under section 87.

(2) If the [First-tier Tribunal] considers it appropriate, it may direct the Commissioner—

   (a) to register the applicant or to continue the applicant's registration;

   (b) to make or vary the applicant's registration so as to have limited effect in any of the ways mentioned in paragraph 2(2) of Schedule 6;

   (c) to restore an exemption granted under section 84(4)(a); or

   (d) to quash a decision recorded under paragraph 9(1)(a) of Schedule 5 and the record of that decision.

Amendment

Words "First-tier Tribunal" in square brackets substituted by SI 2010/22, art 5(1), Sch 2, paras 32, 36.

89 Disciplinary charge upheld by the [First-tier Tribunal]

(1) This section applies if the [First-tier Tribunal] upholds a disciplinary charge laid by the Commissioner under paragraph 9(1)(e) of Schedule 5 against a person ("the person charged").

[(2) If the person charged is a registered person or acts on behalf of a registered person, the [First-tier Tribunal] may—

   (a) direct the Commissioner to record the charge and the [First-tier Tribunal's] decision for consideration in connection with the registered person's next application for continued registration;

   (b) direct the registered person to apply for continued registration as soon as is reasonably practicable.]

(4) If the person charged is certified by the Commissioner as exempt under section 84(4)(a), the [First-tier Tribunal] may direct the Commissioner to consider whether to withdraw his exemption.

(5) If the person charged is found to have charged unreasonable fees for immigration advice or immigration services, the [First-tier Tribunal] may direct him to repay to the clients concerned such portion of those fees as it may determine.

(6) The [First-tier Tribunal] may direct the person charged to pay a penalty to the Commissioner of such sum as it considers appropriate.

(7) A direction given by the [First-tier Tribunal] under subsection (5) (or under subsection (6)) may be enforced by the clients concerned (or by the Commissioner)—

   (a) as if it were an order of a county court [in Northern Ireland or the county court in England and Wales]; or

   (b) in Scotland, as if it were an extract registered decree arbitral bearing a warrant for execution issued by the sheriff court of any sheriffdom in Scotland.

(8) The [First-tier Tribunal] may direct that the person charged or any person [acting on his behalf or] under his supervision is to be—

   (a) subject to such restrictions on the provision of immigration advice or immigration services as the [First-tier Tribunal] considers appropriate;

   (b) suspended from providing immigration advice or immigration services for such period as the [First-tier Tribunal] may determine; or

   (c) prohibited from providing immigration advice or immigration services indefinitely.

(9) The Commissioner must keep a record of the persons against whom there is in force a direction given by the [First-tier Tribunal] under subsection (8).

Amendment

Words "First-tier Tribunal" in each place in square brackets substituted by SI 2010/22, art 5(1), Sch 2, paras 32, 37.

Sub-s (2): substituted, for sub-ss (2), (3) as originally enacted, by the Asylum and Immigration (Treatment of Claimants, etc) Act 2004, s 37(3)(a).

Sub-s (7): in para (a) words "in Northern Ireland or the county court in England and Wales" in square brackets inserted by the Crime and Courts Act 2013, s 17(5), Sch 9, Pt 3, para 90(c), as from 22 April 2014: see SI 2014/954, art 2(c).

Sub-s (8): words "acting on his behalf or" in square brackets substituted by the Asylum and Immigration (Treatment of Claimants, etc) Act 2004, s 37(3)(b).

90 Orders by disciplinary bodies

(1) A disciplinary body may make an order directing that a person subject to its jurisdiction is to be—

   (a) subject to such restrictions on the provision of immigration advice or immigration services as the body considers appropriate;

   (b) suspended from providing immigration advice or immigration services for such period as the body may determine; or

   (c) prohibited from providing immigration advice or immigration services indefinitely.

(2) "Disciplinary body" means any body—

   [(a) appearing to the Secretary of State to be established for the purpose of hearing disciplinary charges against—

     (i) members of a designated professional body, or

     (ii) persons regulated by designated qualifying regulators; and]

   (b) specified in an order made by the Secretary of State.

(3) The Secretary of State must consult the designated professional body [or designated qualifying regulator] concerned before making an order under subsection (2)(b).

(4) For the purposes of this section, a person is subject to the jurisdiction of a disciplinary body if he is an authorised person or [is acting on behalf of] an authorised person.

(5) "Authorised person" means[—

   (a)] a person who is authorised by the designated professional body concerned to practise as a member of the profession whose members are regulated by that body], or

   (b) a person who is authorised by the designated qualifying regulator concerned to provide immigration advice or immigration services].

Amendment

Sub-s (2): para (a) substituted by the Legal Services Act 2007, s 186, Sch 18, Pt 2, paras 9, 15(1), (2). Date in force: 1 April 2011: see SI 2011/720, art 2(c).

Sub-s (3): words "or designated qualifying regulator" in square brackets inserted by the Legal Services Act 2007, s 186, Sch 18, Pt 2, paras 9, 15(1), (3). Date in force: 1 April 2011: see SI 2011/720, art 2(c).

Sub-s (4): words "is acting on behalf of" in square brackets substituted by the Asylum and Immigration (Treatment of Claimants, etc) Act 2004, s 37(4).

Sub-s (5): para (a) numbered as such and "—" immediately preceding it inserted by the Legal Services Act 2007, s 186, Sch 18, Pt 2, paras 9, 15(1), (4)(a). Date in force: 1 April 2011: see SI 2011/720, art 2(c).

Sub-s (5): para (b) and word ", or" immediately preceding it inserted by the Legal Services Act 2007, s 186, Sch 18, Pt 2, paras 9, 15(1), (4)(b). Date in force: 1 April 2011: see SI 2011/720, art 2(c).

Enforcement

91 Offences

(1) A person who provides immigration advice or immigration services in contravention of section 84 or of a restraining order is guilty of an offence and liable—

   (a) on summary conviction, to imprisonment for a term not exceeding six months or to a fine not exceeding the statutory maximum, or to both; or

   (b) on conviction on indictment, to imprisonment for a term not exceeding two years or to a fine, or to both.

(2) "Restraining order" means—

   (a) a direction given by the [First-tier Tribunal] under section 89(8) or paragraph 9(3) of Schedule 5; or

   (b) an order made by a disciplinary body under section 90(1).

(3) If an offence under this section committed by a body corporate is proved—

   (a) to have been committed with the consent or connivance of an officer, or

   (b) to be attributable to neglect on his part,

the officer as well as the body corporate is guilty of the offence and liable to be proceeded against and punished accordingly.

(4) "Officer", in relation to a body corporate, means a director, manager, secretary or other similar officer of the body, or a person purporting to act in such a capacity.

(5) If the affairs of a body corporate are managed by its members, subsection (3) applies in relation to the acts and defaults of a member in connection with his functions of management as if he were a director of the body corporate.

(6) If an offence under this section committed by a partnership in Scotland is proved—

   (a) to have been committed with the consent or connivance of a partner, or

   (b) to be attributable to neglect on his part,

the partner as well as the partnership is guilty of the offence and liable to be proceeded against and punished accordingly.

(7) "Partner" includes a person purporting to act as a partner.

Amendment

Sub-s (2): in para (a) words "First-tier Tribunal" in square brackets substituted by SI 2010/22, art 5(1), Sch 2, paras 32, 38.

92 Enforcement

(1) If it appears to the Commissioner that a person—

   (a) is providing immigration advice or immigration services in contravention of section 84 or of a restraining order, and

   (b) is likely to continue to do so unless restrained,

the Commissioner may apply to a county court [in Northern Ireland or the county court in England and Wales] for an injunction, or to the sheriff for an interdict, restraining him from doing so.

(2) If the court is satisfied that the application is well-founded, it may grant the injunction or interdict in the terms applied for or in more limited terms.

(3) "Restraining order" has the meaning given by section 91.

Amendment

Sub-s (1): words in square brackets inserted by the Crime and Courts Act 2013, s 17(5), Sch 9, Pt 3, para 90(c), as from 22 April 2014: see SI 2014/954.

[92A Investigation of offence: power of entry]

[(1) On an application made by the Commissioner a justice of the peace may issue a warrant authorising the Commissioner to enter and search premises.

(2) A justice of the peace may issue a warrant in respect of premises only if satisfied that there are reasonable grounds for believing that—

(a) an offence under section 91 has been committed,

(b) there is material on the premises which is likely to be of substantial value (whether by itself or together with other material) to the investigation of the offence, and

(c) any of the conditions specified in subsection (3) is satisfied.

(3) Those conditions are—

(a) that it is not practicable to communicate with a person entitled to grant entry to the premises,

(b) that it is not practicable to communicate with a person entitled to grant access to the evidence,

(c) that entry to the premises will be prevented unless a warrant is produced, and

(d) that the purpose of a search may be frustrated or seriously prejudiced unless the Commissioner can secure immediate entry on arrival at the premises.

(4) The Commissioner may seize and retain anything for which a search is authorised under this section.

(5) A person commits an offence if without reasonable excuse he obstructs the Commissioner in the exercise of a power by virtue of this section.

(6) A person guilty of an offence under subsection (5) shall be liable on summary conviction to—

(a) imprisonment for a term not exceeding six months,

(b) a fine not exceeding level 5 on the standard scale, or

(c) both.

(7) In this section—

(a) a reference to the Commissioner includes a reference to a member of his staff authorised in writing by him,

(b) a reference to premises includes a reference to premises used wholly or partly as a dwelling, and

(c) a reference to material—

(i) includes material subject to legal privilege within the meaning of the Police and Criminal Evidence Act 1984 (c 60),

(ii) does not include excluded material or special procedure material within the meaning of that Act, and

(iii) includes material whether or not it would be admissible in evidence at a trial.

(8) In the application of this section to Scotland—

(a) a reference to a justice of the peace shall be taken as a reference to the sheriff,

(b) for sub-paragraph (i) of subsection (7)(c) there is substituted—

"(i) includes material comprising items subject to legal privilege (as defined by section 412 of the Proceeds of Crime Act 2002 (c 29))," and

(c) sub-paragraph (ii) of subsection (7)(c) shall be ignored.

(9) In the application of this section to Northern Ireland the reference to the Police and Criminal Evidence Act 1984 shall be taken as a reference to the Police and Criminal Evidence (Northern Ireland) Order 1989 (SI 1989/1341 (NI 12)).]

Amendment

Inserted by the Asylum and Immigration (Treatment of Claimants, etc) Act 2004, s 38(1).

[92B Advertising]

[(1) A person commits an offence if—

    (a) he offers to provide immigration advice or immigration services, and

    (b) provision by him of the advice or services would constitute an offence under section 91.

(2) For the purpose of subsection (1) a person offers to provide advice or services if he—

    (a) makes an offer to a particular person or class of person,

    (b) makes arrangements for an advertisement in which he offers to provide advice or services, or

    (c) makes arrangements for an advertisement in which he is described or presented as competent to provide advice or services.

(3) A person guilty of an offence under this section shall be liable on summary conviction to a fine not exceeding level 4 on the standard scale.

(4) Subsections (3) to (7) of section 91 shall have effect for the purposes of this section as they have effect for the purposes of that section.

(5) An information relating to an offence under this section may in England and Wales be tried by a magistrates' court if—

    (a) it is laid within the period of six months beginning with the date (or first date) on which the offence is alleged to have been committed, or

    (b) it is laid—

        (i) within the period of two years beginning with that date, and

        (ii) within the period of six months beginning with a date certified by the Immigration Services Commissioner as the date on which the commission of the offence came to his notice.

(6) In Scotland, proceedings for an offence under this section may be commenced—

    (a) at any time within the period of six months beginning with the date (or first date) on which the offence is alleged to have been committed, or

    (b) at any time within both—

        (i) the period of two years beginning with that date, and

        (ii) the period of six months beginning with a date specified, in a certificate signed by or on behalf of the procurator fiscal, as the date on which evidence sufficient in his opinion to warrant such proceedings came to his knowledge,

and any such certificate purporting to be so signed shall be deemed so signed unless the contrary is proved and be conclusive as to the facts stated in it.

(7) Subsection (3) of section 136 of the Criminal Procedure (Scotland) Act 1995 (c 46) (date on which proceedings are deemed commenced) has effect for the purposes of subsection (6) as it has effect for the purposes of that section.

(8) A complaint charging the commission of an offence under this section may in Northern Ireland be heard and determined by a magistrates' court if—

    (a) it is made within the period of six months beginning with the date (or first date) on which the offence is alleged to have been committed, or

    (b) it is made—

        (i) within the period of two years beginning with that date, and

(ii)   within the period of six months beginning with a date certified by the Immigration Services Commissioner as the date on which the commission of the offence came to his notice.]

Amendment

Inserted by the Asylum and Immigration (Treatment of Claimants, etc) Act 2004, s 39.

Miscellaneous

93 Information

(1) No enactment or rule of law prohibiting or restricting the disclosure of information prevents a person from—

(a)   giving the Commissioner information which is necessary for the discharge of his functions; or

(b)   giving the [First-tier Tribunal] information which is necessary for the discharge of its functions.

(2) No relevant person may at any time disclose information which—

(a)   has been obtained by, or given to, the Commissioner under or for purposes of this Act,

(b)   relates to an identified or identifiable individual or business, and

(c)   is not at that time, and has not previously been, available to the public from other sources,

unless the disclosure is made with lawful authority.

(3) For the purposes of subsection (2), a disclosure is made with lawful authority only if, and to the extent that—

(a)   it is made with the consent of the individual or of the person for the time being carrying on the business;

(b)   it is made for the purposes of, and is necessary for, the discharge of any of the Commissioner's functions under this Act or any [EU] obligation of the Commissioner;

(c)   it is made for the purposes of any civil or criminal proceedings arising under or by virtue of this Part, or otherwise; or

(d)   having regard to the rights and freedoms or legitimate interests of any person, the disclosure is necessary in the public interest.

(4) A person who knowingly or recklessly discloses information in contravention of subsection (2) is guilty of an offence and liable—

(a)   on summary conviction, to a fine not exceeding the statutory maximum; or

(b)   on conviction on indictment, to a fine.

(5) "Relevant person" means a person who is or has been—

(a)   the Commissioner;

(b)   a member of the Commissioner's staff; or

(c)   an agent of the Commissioner.

Amendment

Sub-s (1): in para (b) words "First-tier Tribunal" in square brackets substituted by SI 2010/22, art 5(1), Sch 2, paras 32, 39.

Sub-s (3): in para (b) reference to "EU" in square brackets substituted by SI 2011/1043, art 6(1)(e). Date in force: 22 April 2011: see SI 2011/1043, art 2; for transitional savings see art 3(3) thereof.

PART VI
SUPPORT FOR ASYLUM-SEEKERS

Interpretation

94 Interpretation of Part VI

(1) In this Part—

"..."

["asylum-seeker" means a person—

(a) who is at least 18 years old,

(b) who is in the United Kingdom,

(c) who has made a claim for asylum at a place designated by the Secretary of State,

(d) whose claim has been recorded by the Secretary of State, and

(e) whose claim has not been determined;]

"asylum-seeker" means a person who is not under 18 and has made a claim for asylum which has been recorded by the Secretary of State but which has not been determined;

"claim for asylum" means a claim that it would be contrary to the United Kingdom's obligations under the Refugee Convention, or under Article 3 of the Human Rights Convention, for the claimant to be removed from, or required to leave, the United Kingdom;

"the Department" means the Department of Health and Social Services for Northern Ireland;

"dependant", in relation to an asylum-seeker or a supported person, means a person in the United Kingdom who—

(a) is his spouse;

(b) is a child of his, or of his spouse, who is under 18 and dependent on him; or

(c) falls within such additional category, if any, as may be prescribed;

["dependant" in relation to an asylum-seeker or a supported person means a person who—

(a) is in the United Kingdom, and

(b) is within a prescribed class;]

"the Executive" means the Northern Ireland Housing Executive;

"housing accommodation" includes flats, lodging houses and hostels;

"local authority" means—

(a) in England and Wales, a county council, a county borough council, a district council, a London borough council, the Common Council of the City of London or the Council of the Isles of Scilly;

(b) in Scotland, a council constituted under section 2 of the Local Government etc (Scotland) Act 1994;

["Northern Ireland authority" has the meaning given by section 110(9);]

"supported person" means—

(a) an asylum-seeker, or

(b) a dependant of an asylum-seeker,

who has applied for support and for whom support is provided under section 95.

(2) References in this Part to support provided under section 95 include references to support which is provided under arrangements made by the Secretary of State under that section.

(3) For the purposes of this Part, a claim for asylum is determined at the end of such period beginning—

    (a)   on the day on which the Secretary of State notifies the claimant of his decision on the claim, or

    (b)   if the claimant has appealed against the Secretary of State's decision, on the day on which the appeal is disposed of,

as may be prescribed.

[(3) A claim for asylum shall be treated as determined for the purposes of subsection (1) at the end of such period as may be prescribed beginning with—

    (a)   the date on which the Secretary of State notifies the claimant of his decision on the claim, or

    (b)   if the claimant appeals against the Secretary of State's decision, the date on which the appeal is disposed of.

(3A) A person shall continue to be treated as an asylum-seeker despite paragraph (e) of the definition of "asylum-seeker" in subsection (1) while—

    (a)   his household includes a dependant child who is under 18, and

    (b)   he does not have leave to enter or remain in the United Kingdom.]

(4) An appeal is disposed of when it is no longer pending for the purposes of the Immigration Acts or the Special Immigration Appeals Commission Act 1997.

(5) If an asylum-seeker's household includes a child who is under 18 and a dependant of his, he is to be treated (for the purposes of this Part) as continuing to be an asylum-seeker while—

    (a)   the child is under 18; and

    (b)   he and the child remain in the United Kingdom.

(6) Subsection (5) does not apply if, on or after the determination of his claim for asylum, the asylum-seeker is granted leave to enter or remain in the United Kingdom (whether or not as a result of that claim).

(7) For the purposes of this Part, the Secretary of State may inquire into, and decide, the age of any person.

(8) A notice under subsection (3) must be given in writing.

(9) If such a notice is sent by the Secretary of State by first class post, addressed—

    (a)   to the asylum-seeker's representative, or

    (b)   to the asylum-seeker's last known address,

it is to be taken to have been received by the asylum-seeker on the second day after the day on which it was posted.

Amendment

Sub-s (1): definition "adjudicator" (omitted) repealed by SI 2008/2833, art 9(1), Sch 3, paras 179, 180.

Sub-s (1): definition "asylum-seeker" substituted by the Nationality, Immigration and Asylum Act 2002, s 44(1), (2), as from a day to be appointed.

Sub-s (1): definition "dependant" substituted by the Nationality, Immigration and Asylum Act 2002, s 44(1), (3), as from a day to be appointed.

Sub-s (1): definition "Northern Ireland authority" inserted by the Nationality, Immigration and Asylum Act 2002, s 60(2).

Sub-s (3): substituted, by subsequent sub-ss (3), (3A), by the Nationality, Immigration and Asylum Act 2002, s 44(1), (4), as from a day to be appointed.

Sub-ss (5), (6): repealed by the Nationality, Immigration and Asylum Act 2002, ss 44(1), (5), 161, Sch 9, as from a day to be appointed.

Subordinate Legislation

Asylum Support (Interim Provisions) Regulations 1999, SI 1999/3056; Asylum Support Regulations 2000, SI 2000/704.

Provision of support

95 Persons for whom support may be provided

(1) The Secretary of State may provide, or arrange for the provision of, support for—

    (a)   asylum-seekers, or

    (b)   dependants of asylum-seekers,

who appear to the Secretary of State to be destitute or to be likely to become destitute within such period as may be prescribed.

(2) In prescribed circumstances, a person who would otherwise fall within subsection (1) is excluded.

(3) For the purposes of this section, a person is destitute if—

    (a)   he does not have adequate accommodation or any means of obtaining it (whether or not his other essential living needs are met); or

    (b)   he has adequate accommodation or the means of obtaining it, but cannot meet his other essential living needs.

(4) If a person has dependants, subsection (3) is to be read as if the references to him were references to him and his dependants taken together.

(5) In determining, for the purposes of this section, whether a person's accommodation is adequate, the Secretary of State—

    (a)   must have regard to such matters as may be prescribed for the purposes of this paragraph; but

    (b)   may not have regard to such matters as may be prescribed for the purposes of this paragraph or to any of the matters mentioned in subsection (6).

(6) Those matters are—

    (a)   the fact that the person concerned has no enforceable right to occupy the accommodation;

    (b)   the fact that he shares the accommodation, or any part of the accommodation, with one or more other persons;

    (c)   the fact that the accommodation is temporary;

    (d)   the location of the accommodation.

(7) In determining, for the purposes of this section, whether a person's other essential living needs are met, the Secretary of State—

    (a)   must have regard to such matters as may be prescribed for the purposes of this paragraph; but

    (b)   may not have regard to such matters as may be prescribed for the purposes of this paragraph.

(8) The Secretary of State may by regulations provide that items or expenses of such a description as may be prescribed are, or are not, to be treated as being an essential living need of a person for the purposes of this Part.

[(2) Where a person has dependants, he and his dependants are destitute for the purpose of this section if they do not have and cannot obtain both—

    (a)   adequate accommodation, and

    (b)   food and other essential items.

(3) Where a person does not have dependants, he is destitute for the purpose of this section if he does not have and cannot obtain both—

    (a)   adequate accommodation, and

    (b)   food and other essential items.

(4) In determining whether accommodation is adequate for the purposes of subsection (2) or (3) the Secretary of State must have regard to any matter prescribed for the purposes of this subsection.

(5) In determining whether accommodation is adequate for the purposes of subsection (2) or (3) the Secretary of State may not have regard to—

Immigration and Asylum Act 1999

(a) whether a person has an enforceable right to occupy accommodation,

(b) whether a person shares all or part of accommodation,

(c) whether accommodation is temporary or permanent,

(d) the location of accommodation, or

(e) any other matter prescribed for the purposes of this subsection.

(6) The Secretary of State may by regulations specify items which are or are not to be treated as essential items for the purposes of subsections (2) and (3).

(7) The Secretary of State may by regulations—

(a) provide that a person is not to be treated as destitute for the purposes of this Part in specified circumstances;

(b) enable or require the Secretary of State in deciding whether a person is destitute to have regard to income which he or a dependant of his might reasonably be expected to have;

(c) enable or require the Secretary of State in deciding whether a person is destitute to have regard to support which is or might reasonably be expected to be available to the person or a dependant of his;

(d) enable or require the Secretary of State in deciding whether a person is destitute to have regard to assets of a prescribed kind which he or a dependant of his has or might reasonably be expected to have;

(e) make provision as to the valuation of assets.]

(9) Support may be provided subject to conditions.

[(9A) A condition imposed under subsection (9) may, in particular, relate to—

(a) any matter relating to the use of the support provided, or

(b) compliance with a restriction imposed under paragraph 21 of Schedule 2 to the 1971 Act (temporary admission or release from detention) or paragraph 2 or 5 of Schedule 3 to that Act (restriction pending deportation).]

(10) The conditions must be set out in writing.

(11) A copy of the conditions must be given to the supported person.

(12) Schedule 8 gives the Secretary of State power to make regulations supplementing this section.

(13) Schedule 9 makes temporary provision for support in the period before the coming into force of this section.

Amendment

Sub-ss (2)–(8): substituted, by subsequent sub-ss (2)–(7), by the Nationality, Immigration and Asylum Act 2002, s 44(1), (6), as from a day to be appointed.

Sub-s (9A): inserted by the Nationality, Immigration and Asylum Act 2002, s 50(1).

96 Ways in which support may be provided

(1) Support may be provided under section 95—

(a) by providing accommodation appearing to the Secretary of State to be adequate for the needs of the supported person and his dependants (if any);

(b) *by providing what appear to the Secretary of State to be essential living needs of the supported person and his dependants (if any);*

[(b) by providing the supported person and his dependants (if any) with food and other essential items;]

(c) to enable the supported person (if he is the asylum-seeker) to meet what appear to the Secretary of State to be expenses (other than legal expenses or other expenses of a prescribed description) incurred in connection with his claim for asylum;

(d) to enable the asylum-seeker and his dependants to attend bail proceedings in connection with his detention under any provision of the Immigration Acts; or

145

(e) to enable the asylum-seeker and his dependants to attend bail proceedings in connection with the detention of a dependant of his under any such provision.

(2) If the Secretary of State considers that the circumstances of a particular case are exceptional, he may provide support under section 95 in such other ways as he considers necessary to enable the supported person and his dependants (if any) to be supported.

(3) ...

(4) ...

(5) ...

(6) ...

Amendment

Sub-s (1): para (b) substituted by the Nationality, Immigration and Asylum Act 2002, s 45(1), as from a day to be appointed.

Sub-s (3): repealed by SI 2002/782, art 2.

Sub-ss (4)–(6): repealed by the Nationality, Immigration and Asylum Act 2002, ss 61(a), 161, Sch 9.

97 Supplemental

(1) When exercising his power under section 95 to provide accommodation, the Secretary of State must have regard to—

(a) the fact that the accommodation is to be temporary pending determination of the asylum-seeker's claim;

(b) the desirability, in general, of providing accommodation in areas in which there is a ready supply of accommodation; and

(c) such other matters (if any) as may be prescribed.

(2) But he may not have regard to—

(a) any preference that the supported person or his dependants (if any) may have as to the locality in which the accommodation is to be provided; or

(b) such other matters (if any) as may be prescribed.

(3) The Secretary of State may by order repeal all or any of the following—

(a) subsection (1)(a);

(b) subsection (1)(b);

(c) subsection (2)(a).

(4) When exercising his power under section 95 to provide *essential living needs* [food and other essential items], the Secretary of State—

(a) must have regard to such matters as may be prescribed for the purposes of this paragraph; but

(b) may not have regard to such other matters as may be prescribed for the purposes of this paragraph.

(5) In addition, when exercising his power under section 95 to provide *essential living needs* [food and other essential items], the Secretary of State may limit the overall amount of the expenditure which he incurs in connection with a particular supported person—

[(za) to such portion of the maximum amount of an award of universal credit under section 8(1) of the Welfare Reform Act 2012, or]

(a) *to such portion of the income support applicable amount provided under section 124 of the Social Security Contributions and Benefits Act 1992,* or

[(a) to such portion of the applicable amount in respect of an income-based jobseeker's allowance provided under section 4 of the Jobseekers Act 1995, or]

(b) to such portion of any components [or elements] of that amount, as he considers appropriate having regard to the temporary nature of the support that he is providing.

(6) For the purposes of subsection (5), any support of a kind falling within section 96(1)(c) is to be treated as if it were the provision of essential *living needs* [items].

(7) In determining how to provide, or arrange for the provision of, support under section 95, the Secretary of State may disregard any preference which the supported person or his dependants (if any) may have as to the way in which the support is to be given.

Amendment

Sub-s (4): words "essential living needs" in italics repealed and subsequent words in square brackets substituted by the Nationality, Immigration and Asylum Act 2002, s 45(2)(a), as from a day to be appointed.

Sub-s (5): words "essential living needs" in italics repealed and subsequent words in square brackets substituted by the Nationality, Immigration and Asylum Act 2002, s 45(2)(b), as from a day to be appointed.

Sub-s (5): para (za) inserted by the Welfare Reform Act 2012, s 31, Sch 2, paras 52, 53(a). Date in force: 29 April 2013: see SI 2013/983, art 3(1)(b)(i).

Sub-s (5): para (a) substituted by the Welfare Reform Act 2009, s 9(3)(a), Sch 2, para 8; for further provision in relation to this amendment see s 9(1), (2), (4)–(10) thereof, as from a day to be appointed.

Sub-s (5): para (a) repealed by the Welfare Reform Act 2012, s 147, Sch 14, Pt 1, as from a day to be appointed.

Sub-s (5): para (b) words "or elements" in square brackets inserted by the Welfare Reform Act 2012, s 31, Sch 2, paras 52, 53(b). Date in force: 29 April 2013: see SI 2013/983, art 3(1)(b)(i).

Sub-s (6): words "living needs" in italics repealed and subsequent word in square brackets substituted by the Nationality, Immigration and Asylum Act 2002, s 45(2)(c), as from a day to be appointed.

Subordinate Legislation

Asylum Support Regulations 2000, SI 2000/704.

98 Temporary support

(1) The Secretary of State may provide, or arrange for the provision of, support for—

   (a)   asylum-seekers, or

   (b)   dependants of asylum-seekers,

who it appears to the Secretary of State may be destitute.

(2) Support may be provided under this section only until the Secretary of State is able to determine whether support may be provided under section 95.

(3) Subsections (2) to (11) of section 95 apply for the purposes of this section as they apply for the purposes of that section.

Support and assistance by local authorities etc

99 Provision of support by local authorities

(1) A local authority [or Northern Ireland authority] may provide support for [persons] in accordance with arrangements made by the Secretary of State under section [4,] 95 [or 98].

[(2) Support may be provided by an authority in accordance with arrangements made with the authority or with another person.

(3) Support may be provided by an authority in accordance with arrangements made under section 95 only in one or more of the ways mentioned in section 96(1) and (2).]

(4) [An authority] may incur reasonable expenditure in connection with the preparation of proposals for entering into arrangements under section [4,] 95 [or 98].

(5) The powers conferred on [an authority] by this section include power to—

   (a)   provide services outside their area;

(b)   provide services jointly with one or more [other bodies];

(c)   form a company for the purpose of providing services;

(d)   tender for contracts (whether alone or with any other person).

Amendment

Sub-s (1): words "or Northern Ireland authority" in square brackets inserted by the Nationality, Immigration and Asylum Act 2002, s 56(1), (2)(a).

Sub-s (1): word "persons" in square brackets substituted by the Immigration, Asylum and Nationality Act 2006, s 43(1)(a).

Sub-s (1): reference to "4," in square brackets inserted by the Immigration, Asylum and Nationality Act 2006, s 43(1)(b).

Sub-s (1): words "or 98" in square brackets inserted by the Nationality, Immigration and Asylum Act 2002, s 56(1), (2)(b).

Sub-ss (2), (3): substituted by the Nationality, Immigration and Asylum Act 2002, s 56(1), (3).

Sub-s (4): words "An authority" in square brackets substituted by the Nationality, Immigration and Asylum Act 2002, s 56(1), (4)(a).

Sub-s (4): reference to "4," in square brackets inserted by the Immigration, Asylum and Nationality Act 2006, s 43(2).

Sub-s (4): words "or 98" in square brackets inserted by the Nationality, Immigration and Asylum Act 2002, s 56(1), (4)(b).

Sub-s (5): words "an authority" in square brackets substituted by the Nationality, Immigration and Asylum Act 2002, s 56(1), (5)(a).

Sub-s (5): in para (b) words "other bodies" in square brackets substituted by the Nationality, Immigration and Asylum Act 2002, s 56(1), (5)(b).

100 Local authority and other assistance for Secretary of State

(1)   This section applies if the Secretary of State asks—

   (a)   a local authority,

   [(aa) a private registered provider of social housing,]

   (b)   a registered social landlord,

   (c)   a registered housing association in Scotland or Northern Ireland, or

   (d)   the Executive,

to assist him to exercise his power under section 95 to provide accommodation.

(2)   The person to whom the request is made must co-operate in giving the Secretary of State such assistance in the exercise of that power as is reasonable in the circumstances.

(3)   Subsection (2) does not require [a private registered provider of social housing or] a registered social landlord to act beyond its powers.

(4)   A local authority must supply to the Secretary of State such information about their housing accommodation (whether or not occupied) as he may from time to time request.

(5)   The information must be provided in such form and manner as the Secretary of State may direct.

(6)   "Registered social landlord" has the same meaning as in Part I of the Housing Act 1996.

(7)   "Registered housing association" has the same meaning—

   (a)   in relation to Scotland, as in the Housing Associations Act 1985; and

   (b)   in relation to Northern Ireland, as in Part II of the Housing (Northern Ireland) Order 1992.

Amendment

Sub-s (1): para (aa) inserted by SI 2010/866, art 5, Sch 2, para 118(1), (2).

Sub-s (3): words "a private registered provider of social housing or" in square brackets inserted by SI 2010/866, art 5, Sch 2, para 118(1), (3).

101 Reception zones

Amendment

(1)   The Secretary of State may by order designate as reception zones—

(a) areas in England and Wales consisting of the areas of one or more local authorities;

(b) areas in Scotland consisting of the areas of one or more local authorities;

(c) Northern Ireland.

(2) Subsection (3) applies if the Secretary of State considers that—

(a) a local authority whose area is within a reception zone has suitable housing accommodation within that zone; or

(b) the Executive has suitable housing accommodation.

(3) The Secretary of State may direct the local authority or the Executive to make available such of the accommodation as may be specified in the direction for a period so specified—

(a) to him for the purpose of providing support under section 95; or

(b) to a person with whom the Secretary of State has made arrangements under section 95.

(4) A period specified in a direction under subsection (3)—

(a) begins on a date so specified; and

(b) must not exceed five years.

(5) A direction under subsection (3) is enforceable, on an application made on behalf of the Secretary of State, by injunction or in Scotland an order under section 45(b) of the Court of Session Act 1988.

(6) The Secretary of State's power to give a direction under subsection (3) in respect of a particular reception zone must be exercised by reference to criteria specified for the purposes of this subsection in the order designating that zone.

(7) The Secretary of State may not give a direction under subsection (3) in respect of a local authority in Scotland unless the Scottish Ministers have confirmed to him that the criteria specified in the designation order concerned are in their opinion met in relation to that authority.

(8) Housing accommodation is suitable for the purposes of subsection (2) if it—

(a) is unoccupied;

(b) would be likely to remain unoccupied for the foreseeable future if not made available; and

(c) is appropriate for the accommodation of persons supported under this Part or capable of being made so with minor work.

(9) If housing accommodation for which a direction under this section is, for the time being, in force—

(a) is not appropriate for the accommodation of persons supported under this Part, but

(b) is capable of being made so with minor work,

the direction may require the body to whom it is given to secure that that work is done without delay.

(10) The Secretary of State must make regulations with respect to the general management of any housing accommodation for which a direction under subsection (3) is, for the time being, in force.

(11) Regulations under subsection (10) must include provision—

(a) as to the method to be used in determining the amount of rent or other charges to be payable in relation to the accommodation;

(b) as to the times at which payments of rent or other charges are to be made;

(c) as to the responsibility for maintenance of, and repairs to, the accommodation;

(d) enabling the accommodation to be inspected, in such circumstances as may be prescribed, by the body to which the direction was given;

(e) with respect to the condition in which the accommodation is to be returned when the direction ceases to have effect.

(12) Regulations under subsection (10) may, in particular, include provision—

  (a) for the cost, or part of the cost, of minor work required by a direction under this section to be met by the Secretary of State in prescribed circumstances;

  (b) as to the maximum amount of expenditure which a body may be required to incur as a result of a direction under this section.

(13) The Secretary of State must by regulations make provision ("the dispute resolution procedure") for resolving disputes arising in connection with the operation of any regulations made under subsection (10).

(14) Regulations under subsection (13) must include provision—

  (a) requiring a dispute to be resolved in accordance with the dispute resolution procedure;

  (b) requiring the parties to a dispute to comply with obligations imposed on them by the procedure; and

  (c) for the decision of the person resolving a dispute in accordance with the procedure to be final and binding on the parties.

(15) Before—

  (a) designating a reception zone in Great Britain,

  (b) determining the criteria to be included in the order designating the zone, or

  (c) making regulations under subsection (13),

the Secretary of State must consult such local authorities, local authority associations and other persons as he thinks appropriate.

(16) Before—

  (a) designating Northern Ireland as a reception zone, or

  (b) determining the criteria to be included in the order designating Northern Ireland,

the Secretary of State must consult the Executive and such other persons as he thinks appropriate.

(17) Before making regulations under subsection (10) which extend only to Northern Ireland, the Secretary of State must consult the Executive and such other persons as he thinks appropriate.

(18) Before making any other regulations under subsection (10), the Secretary of State must consult—

  (a) such local authorities, local authority associations and other persons as he thinks appropriate; and

  (b) if the regulations extend to Northern Ireland, the Executive.

102

Appeals

103 Appeals [103 Appeals: general]

(1) If, on an application for support under section 95, the Secretary of State decides that the applicant does not qualify for support under that section, the applicant may appeal to [the First-tier Tribunal].

(2) If the Secretary of State decides to stop providing support for a person under section 95 before that support would otherwise have come to an end, that person may appeal to [the First-tier Tribunal].

(Repealed by SI 2008/2833, art 9(1), Sch 3, paras 179, 181.)

[[(2A) *If the Secretary of State decides not to provide accommodation for a person under section 4, or not to continue to provide accommodation for a person under section 4, the person may appeal to [the First-tier Tribunal].*]

(3) *On an appeal under this section, the [First-tier Tribunal] may—*

    (a)   *require the Secretary of State to reconsider the matter;*

    (b)   *substitute [its] decision for the decision appealed against; or*

    (c)   *dismiss the appeal.*

(4) *. . .*

(5) *The decision of the [First-tier Tribunal] is final.*

(6) *If an appeal is dismissed, no further application by the appellant for support under [section 4 or 95] is to be entertained unless the Secretary of State is satisfied that there has been a material change in the circumstances.*

(7) *The Secretary of State may by regulations provide for decisions as to where support provided under [section 4 or 95] is to be provided to be appealable to [the First-tier Tribunal] under this Part.*

(8) *Regulations under subsection (7) may provide for any provision of this section to have effect, in relation to an appeal brought by virtue of the regulations, subject to such modifications as may be prescribed.*

(9) *The Secretary of State may pay any reasonable travelling expenses incurred by an appellant in connection with attendance at any place for the purposes of an appeal under this section.*

[[(1) This section applies where a person has applied for support under all or any of the following provisions—

    (a)   section 4,

    (b)   section 95, and

    (c)   section 17 of the Nationality, Immigration and Asylum Act 2002.]

<u>(2)</u> <u>The person may appeal to [the First-tier Tribunal] against a decision that the person is not qualified to receive the support for which he has applied.</u>

<u>(3)</u> <u>The person may also appeal to [the First-tier Tribunal] against a decision to stop providing support under a provision mentioned in subsection (1).</u>

<u>(4)</u> <u>But subsection (3) does not apply—</u>

    <u>(a)</u>   <u>to a decision to stop providing support under one of the provisions mentioned in subsection (1) if it is to be replaced immediately by support under [another of those provisions], or</u>

    <u>(b)</u>   <u>to a decision taken on the ground that the person is no longer an asylum-seeker or the dependant of an asylum-seeker.</u>

<u>(5)</u> <u>On an appeal under this section [the First-tier Tribunal] may—</u>

    <u>(a)</u>   <u>require the Secretary of State to reconsider a matter;</u>

    <u>(b)</u>   <u>substitute [its] decision for the decision against which the appeal is brought;</u>

    <u>(c)</u>   <u>dismiss the appeal.</u>

<u>(6)</u> <u>. . .</u>

<u>(7)</u> <u>If an appeal under this section is dismissed the Secretary of State shall not consider any further application by the appellant for support under a provision mentioned in [subsection (1)] unless the Secretary of State thinks there has been a material change in circumstances.</u>

<u>(8)</u> <u>An appeal under this section may not be brought or continued by a person who is outside the United Kingdom.</u>]

Amendment

Substituted, together with ss 103A, 103B for this section as originally enacted, by the Nationality, Immigration and Asylum Act 2002, s 53, as from a day to be appointed.

Sub-s (1): words "the First-tier Tribunal" in square brackets substituted by SI 2008/2833, art 9(1), Sch 3, paras 179, 182(a).

Appendix 1 — UK Immigration Statutes

Sub-s (2): words "the First-tier Tribunal" in square brackets substituted by SI 2008/2833, art 9(1), Sch 3, paras 179, 182(a).

Sub-s (2A): inserted by the Asylum and Immigration (Treatment of Claimants, etc) Act 2004, s 10(3)(a), (6).

Sub-s (2A): words "the First-tier Tribunal" in square brackets substituted by SI 2008/2833, art 9(1), Sch 3, paras 179, 182(a).

Sub-s (3): words "First-tier Tribunal" in square brackets substituted by SI 2008/2833, art 9(1), Sch 3, paras 179, 182(b).

Sub-s (3): in para (b) word "its" in square brackets substituted by SI 2008/2833, art 9(1), Sch 3, paras 179, 182(c).

Sub-ss (6), (7): words "section 4 or 95" in square brackets substituted by the Asylum and Immigration (Treatment of Claimants, etc) Act 2004, s 10(4)(a);

Sub-s (4): repealed by SI 2008/2833, art 9(1), Sch 3, paras 179, 182(d).

Sub-s (5): words "First-tier Tribunal" in square brackets substituted by SI 2008/2833, art 9(1), Sch 3, paras 179, 182(b).

Sub-s (7): words "the First-tier Tribunal" in square brackets substituted by SI 2008/2833, art 9(1), Sch 3, paras 179, 182(a).

Sub-s (1) (as substituted by the Nationality, Immigration and Asylum Act 2002, s 53): substituted by the Asylum and Immigration (Treatment of Claimants, etc) Act 2004, s 10(4)(a);
(6).

Sub-s (2) (as substituted by the Nationality, Immigration and Asylum Act 2002, s 53): words "the First-tier Tribunal" in square brackets substituted by SI 2008/2833, art 9(1), Sch 3, paras 179, 183(i).

Sub-s (3) (as substituted by the Nationality, Immigration and Asylum Act 2002, s 53): words "the First-tier Tribunal" in square brackets substituted by SI 2008/2833, art 9(1), Sch 3, paras 179, 183(i).

Sub-s (4) (as substituted by the Nationality, Immigration and Asylum Act 2002, s 53): in para (a) words "another of those provisions" in square brackets substituted by SI 2008/2833, art 9(1), Sch 3, Immigration (Treatment of Claimants, etc) Act 2004, s 10(b), (6).

Sub-s (5) (as substituted by the Nationality, Immigration and Asylum Act 2002, s 53): words "the First-tier Tribunal" in square brackets substituted by SI 2008/2833, art 9(1), Sch 3, paras 179, 183(i).

Sub-s (5) (as substituted by the Nationality, Immigration and Asylum Act 2002, s 53): in para (b) word "its" in square brackets substituted by SI 2008/2833, art 9(1), Sch 3, paras 179, 183(ii).

Sub-s (6) (as substituted by the Nationality, Immigration and Asylum Act 2002, s 53): repealed by SI 2008/2833, art 9(1), Sch 3, paras 179, 183(iii).

Sub-s (7) (as substituted by the Nationality, Immigration and Asylum Act 2002, s 53): words "subsection (1)" in square brackets substituted by the Asylum and Immigration (Treatment of Claimants, etc) Act 2004, s 10(5), (6).

103A Appeals: location of support under [section 4 or 95]]

[(1) The Secretary of State may by regulations provide for a decision as to where support provided under [section 4 or 95] is to be provided to be appealable to [the First-tier Tribunal] under this Part.

(2) Regulations under this section may provide for a provision of section 103 to have effect in relation to an appeal under the regulations with specified modifications.]

Amendment

Substituted, together with ss 103, 103B for s 103 as originally enacted, by the Nationality, Immigration and Asylum Act 2002, s 53, as from a day to be appointed.

Section heading: words "section 4 or 95" in square brackets substituted by the Asylum and Immigration (Treatment of Claimants, etc) Act 2004, s 10(5), (6).

Sub-s (1): words "section 4 or 95" in square brackets substituted by the Asylum and Immigration (Treatment of Claimants, etc) Act 2004, s 10(5), (6).

Sub-s (1): words "the First-tier Tribunal" in square brackets substituted by SI 2008/2833, art 9(1), Sch 3, paras 179, 184.

103B Appeals: travelling expenses]

[The Secretary of State may pay reasonable travelling expenses incurred by an appellant in connection with attendance for the purposes of an appeal under or by virtue of section 103 or 103A.]

Amendment

Substituted, together with ss 103, 103A for s 103 as originally enacted, by the Nationality, Immigration and Asylum Act 2002, s 53, as from a day to be appointed.

104

(Repealed by SI 2008/2833, art 9(1), Sch 3, paras 179, 185.)

Offences

105 False representations

(1) A person is guilty of an offence if, with a view to obtaining support for himself or any other person under any provision made by or under this Part, he—

(a) makes a statement or representation which he knows is false in a material particular;

(b) produces or gives to a person exercising functions under this Part, or knowingly causes or allows to be produced or given to such a person, any document or information which he knows is false in a material particular;

(c) fails, without reasonable excuse, to notify a change of circumstances when required to do so in accordance with any provision made by or under this Part; or

(d) without reasonable excuse, knowingly causes another person to fail to notify a change of circumstances which that other person was required to notify in accordance with any provision made by or under this Part.

(2) A person guilty of an offence under this section is liable on summary conviction to imprisonment for a term not exceeding *three months* [51 weeks] or to a fine not exceeding level 5 on the standard scale, or to both.

Amendment

Sub-s (2): words "three months" in italics repealed and subsequent words in square brackets substituted by the Criminal Justice Act 2003, s 280(2), (3), Sch 26, para 53(1), (2), as from a day to be appointed.

106 Dishonest representations

(1) A person is guilty of an offence if, with a view to obtaining any benefit or other payment or advantage under this Part for himself or any other person, he dishonestly—

(a) makes a statement or representation which is false in a material particular;

(b) produces or gives to a person exercising functions under this Part, or causes or allows to be produced or given to such a person, any document or information which is false in a material particular;

(c) fails to notify a change of circumstances when required to do so in accordance with any provision made by or under this Part; or

(d) causes another person to fail to notify a change of circumstances which that other person was required to notify in accordance with any provision made by or under this Part.

(2) A person guilty of an offence under this section is liable—

(a) on summary conviction, to imprisonment for a term not exceeding six months or to a fine not exceeding the statutory maximum, or to both; or

(b) on conviction on indictment, to imprisonment for a term not exceeding seven years or to a fine, or to both.

(3) In the application of this section to Scotland, in subsection (1) for "dishonestly" substitute "knowingly".

107 Delay or obstruction

(1) A person is guilty of an offence if, without reasonable excuse, he—

(a) intentionally delays or obstructs a person exercising functions conferred by or under this Part; or

(b) refuses or neglects to answer a question, give any information or produce a document when required to do so in accordance with any provision made by or under this Part.

(2) A person guilty of an offence under subsection (1) is liable on summary conviction to a fine not exceeding level 3 on the standard scale.

108 Failure of sponsor to maintain

(1) A person is guilty of an offence if, during any period in respect of which he has given a written undertaking in pursuance of the immigration rules to be responsible for the maintenance and accommodation of another person—

(a) he persistently refuses or neglects, without reasonable excuse, to maintain that person in accordance with the undertaking; and

(b) in consequence of his refusal or neglect, support under any provision made by or under this Part is provided for or in respect of that person.

(2) A person guilty of an offence under this section is liable on summary conviction to imprisonment for a term not exceeding *3 months* [51 weeks] or to a fine not exceeding level 4 on the standard scale, or to both.

(3) For the purposes of this section, a person is not to be taken to have refused or neglected to maintain another person by reason only of anything done or omitted in furtherance of a trade dispute.

Amendment

Sub-s (2): words "3 months" in italics repealed and subsequent words in square brackets substituted by the Criminal Justice Act 2003, s 280(2), (3), Sch 26, para 53(1), (3), as from a day to be appointed.

109 Supplemental

(1) If an offence under section 105, 106, 107 or 108 committed by a body corporate is proved—

(a) to have been committed with the consent or connivance of an officer, or

(b) to be attributable to neglect on his part,

the officer as well as the body corporate is guilty of the offence and liable to be proceeded against and punished accordingly.

(2) "Officer", in relation to a body corporate, means a director, manager, secretary or other similar officer of the body, or a person purporting to act in such a capacity.

(3) If the affairs of a body corporate are managed by its members, subsection (1) applies in relation to the acts and defaults of a member in connection with his functions of management as if he were a director of the body corporate.

(4) If an offence under section 105, 106, 107 or 108 committed by a partnership in Scotland is proved—

(a) to have been committed with the consent or connivance of a partner, or

(b) to be attributable to neglect on his part,

the partner as well as the partnership is guilty of the offence and liable to be proceeded against and punished accordingly.

(5) "Partner" includes a person purporting to act as a partner.

[109A Arrest

An immigration officer may arrest without warrant a person whom the immigration officer reasonably suspects has committed an offence under section 105 or 106.]

Amendment

Inserted by the UK Borders Act 2007, s 18.

[109B Entry, search and seizure

(1) An offence under section 105 or 106 shall be treated as—

    (a) a relevant offence for the purposes of sections 28B and 28D of the Immigration Act 1971, and

    (b) an offence under Part 3 of that Act (criminal proceedings) for the purposes of sections 28(4), 28E, 28G and 28H (search after arrest, &c.) of that Act.

(2) The following provisions of the Immigration Act 1971 (c 77) shall have effect in connection with an offence under section 105 or 106 of this Act as they have effect in connection with an offence under that Act—

    (a) section 28I (seized material: access and copying),

    (b) section 28J (search warrants: safeguards),

    (c) section 28K (execution of warrants), and

    (d) section 28L(1) (interpretation).]

Amendment

Inserted by the UK Borders Act 2007, s 18.

Expenditure

110 Payments to local authorities

(1) The Secretary of State may from time to time pay to any local authority or Northern Ireland authority such sums as he considers appropriate in respect of expenditure incurred, or to be incurred, by the authority in connection with—

    (a) persons who are, or have been, asylum-seekers; and

    (b) their dependants.

(2) The Secretary of State may from time to time pay to any—

    (a) local authority,

    (b) local authority association, or

    (c) Northern Ireland authority,

such sums as he considers appropriate in respect of services provided by the authority or association in connection with the discharge of functions under this Part.

(3) The Secretary of State may make payments to any local authority towards the discharge of any liability of supported persons or their dependants in respect of council tax payable to that authority.

(4) The Secretary of State must pay to a body to which a direction under section 101(3) is given such sums as he considers the reasonable costs to that body of complying with the direction.

(5) The Secretary of State must pay to a directed body sums determined to be payable in relation to accommodation made available by that body under section 101(3)(a).

(6) The Secretary of State may pay to a directed body sums determined to be payable in relation to accommodation made available by that body under section 101(3)(b).

(7) In subsections (5) and (6)—

"determined" means determined in accordance with regulations made by virtue of subsection (11)(a) of section 101, and

"directed body" means a body to which a direction under subsection (3) of section 101 is given.

(8) Payments under subsection (1), (2) or (3) may be made on such terms, and subject to such conditions, as the Secretary of State may determine.

(9) "Northern Ireland authority" means—

(a) the Executive; or

(b) a Health and Social Services Board established under Article 16 of the Health and Personal Social Services (Northern Ireland) Order 1972[; or

(c) a Health and Social Services trust established under the Health and Personal Social Services (Northern Ireland) Order 1991 (SI 1991/194 (NI 1)].

Amendment

Sub-s (9): para (c) and word "; or" immediately preceding it inserted by the Nationality, Immigration and Asylum Act 2002, s 60(1).

111 Grants to voluntary organisations

(1) The Secretary of State may make grants of such amounts as he thinks appropriate to voluntary organisations in connection with—

(a) the provision by them of support (of whatever nature) to persons who are, or have been, asylum-seekers and to their dependants; and

(b) connected matters.

(2) Grants may be made on such terms, and subject to such conditions, as the Secretary of State may determine.

112 Recovery of expenditure on support: misrepresentation etc

(1) This section applies if, on an application made by the Secretary of State, the court determines that—

(a) a person ("A") has misrepresented or failed to disclose a material fact (whether fraudulently or otherwise); and

(b) as a consequence of the misrepresentation or failure, support has been provided under section 95 or 98 (whether or not to A).

(2) If the support was provided by the Secretary of State, the court may order A to pay to the Secretary of State an amount representing the monetary value of the support which would not have been provided but for A's misrepresentation or failure.

(3) If the support was provided by another person ("B") in accordance with arrangements made with the Secretary of State under section 95 or 98, the court may order A to pay to the Secretary of State an amount representing the payment to B which would not have been made but for A's misrepresentation or failure.

(4) "Court" means a county court [in Northern Ireland or the county court in England and Wales] or, in Scotland, the sheriff.

Amendment

Sub-s (4): words in square brackets inserted by the Crime and Courts Act 2013, s 17(5), Sch 9, Pt 3, para 90(c), as from 22 April 2014: see SI 2014/954.

113 Recovery of expenditure on support from sponsor

(1) This section applies if—

(a) a person ("the sponsor") has given a written undertaking in pursuance of the immigration rules to be responsible for the maintenance and accommodation of another person; and

(b) during any period in relation to which the undertaking applies, support under section 95 is provided to or in respect of that other person.

(2) The Secretary of State may make a complaint against the sponsor to a magistrates' court for an order under this section.

(3) The court—

(a) must have regard to all the circumstances (and in particular to the sponsor's income); and

(b) may order him to pay to the Secretary of State such sum (weekly or otherwise) as it considers appropriate.

(4) But such a sum is not to include any amount attributable otherwise than to support provided under section 95.

(5) In determining—

(a) whether to order any payments to be made in respect of support provided under section 95 for any period before the complaint was made, or

(b) the amount of any such payments,

the court must disregard any amount by which the sponsor's current income exceeds his income during that period.

(6) An order under this section is enforceable as a magistrates' court maintenance order within the meaning of section 150(1) of the Magistrates' Courts Act 1980.

(7) In the application of this section to Scotland—

(a) omit subsection (6);

(b) for references to a complaint substitute references to an application; and

(c) for references to a magistrates' court substitute references to the sheriff.

(8) In the application of this section to Northern Ireland, for references to a magistrates' court substitute references to a court of summary jurisdiction and for subsection (6) substitute—

"(6) An order under this section is an order to which Article 98(11) of the Magistrates' Courts (Northern Ireland) Order 1981 applies."

114 Overpayments

(1) Subsection (2) applies if, as a result of an error on the part of the Secretary of State, support has been provided to a person under section 95 or 98.

(2) The Secretary of State may recover from a person who is, or has been, a supported person an amount representing the monetary value of support provided to him as a result of the error.

(3) An amount recoverable under subsection (2) may be recovered as if it were a debt due to the Secretary of State.

(4) The Secretary of State may by regulations make provision for other methods of recovery, including deductions from support provided under section 95.

Subordinate Legislation
Asylum Support Regulations 2000, SI 2000/704.

Exclusions

115 Exclusion from benefits

(1) No person is entitled [to universal credit under Part 1 of the Welfare Reform Act 2012 or] *to income-based jobseeker's allowance under the Jobseekers Act 1995* [or to state pension credit under the State Pension Credit Act 2002] [*or to income-related allowance under Part 1 of the Welfare Reform Act 2007 (employment and support allowance*] [*or to personal independence payment*] or to—

(a) attendance allowance,

(b) severe disablement allowance,

(c) [carer's allowance],

(d) *disability living allowance,*

(e) *income support,*

(f) . . .

(g) . . .

(h) a social fund payment,

[(ha) health in pregnancy grant,] [or]

(i) child benefit,

   (j)   *housing benefit, or*

   (k)   *council tax benefit,*

under the Social Security Contributions and Benefits Act 1992 while he is a person to whom this section applies.

(2) No person in Northern Ireland is entitled to [state pension credit under the State Pension Credit Act (Northern Ireland) 2002, or to]—

   (a)   income-based jobseeker's allowance under the Jobseekers (Northern Ireland) Order 1995, or

   (b)   [disability living allowance or] any of the benefits mentioned in paragraphs *(a) to (i)* [(a) to (i)] of subsection (1),

under the Social Security Contributions and Benefits (Northern Ireland) Act 1992 while he is a person to whom this section applies.

(3) This section applies to a person subject to immigration control unless he falls within such category or description, or satisfies such conditions, as may be prescribed.

(4) Regulations under subsection (3) may provide for a person to be treated for prescribed purposes only as not being a person to whom this section applies.

(5) In relation to [health in pregnancy grant or] [child benefit], "prescribed" means prescribed by regulations made by the Treasury,

(6) In relation to the matters mentioned in subsection (2) (except so far as it relates to [health in pregnancy grant or] [child benefit]), "prescribed" means prescribed by regulations made by the Department.

(7) Section 175(3) to (5) of the Social Security Contributions and Benefits Act 1992 (supplemental powers in relation to regulations) applies to regulations made by the Secretary of State or the Treasury under subsection (3) as it applies to regulations made under that Act.

(8) Sections 133(2), 171(2) and 172(4) of the Social Security Contributions and Benefits (Northern Ireland) Act 1992 apply to regulations made by the Department under subsection (3) as they apply to regulations made by the Department under that Act.

(9) "A person subject to immigration control" means a person who is not a national of an EEA State and who—

   (a)   requires leave to enter or remain in the United Kingdom but does not have it;

   (b)   has leave to enter or remain in the United Kingdom which is subject to a condition that he does not have recourse to public funds;

   (c)   has leave to enter or remain in the United Kingdom given as a result of a maintenance undertaking; or

   (d)   has leave to enter or remain in the United Kingdom only as a result of paragraph 17 of Schedule 4.

(10) "Maintenance undertaking", in relation to any person, means a written undertaking given by another person in pursuance of the immigration rules to be responsible for that person's maintenance and accommodation.'

Amendment

Sub-s (1): words "to universal credit under Part 1 of the Welfare Reform Act 2012 or" in square brackets inserted by the Welfare Reform Act 2012, s 31, Sch 2, paras 52, 54. Date in force: 29 April 2013: see SI 2013/983, art 3(1)(b)(i).

Sub-s (1): words "to income-based jobseeker's allowance under the Jobseekers Act 1995 or" in italics repealed by the Welfare Reform Act 2012, s 147, Sch 14, Pt 1, as from a day to be appointed.

Sub-s (1): words "or to state pension credit under the State Pension Credit Act 2002" in square brackets inserted by the State Pension Credit Act 2002, s 4(2).

Sub-s (1): words from "or to income-related" to "and support allowance)" in square brackets inserted by the Welfare Reform Act 2007, s 28(1), Sch 3, para 19.

Sub-s (1): words from "or to income-related" to "and support allowance)" in italics repealed by the Welfare Reform Act 2012, s 147, Sch 14, Pt 1, as from a day to be appointed.

Sub-s (1): words "or to personal independence payment" in square brackets inserted by the Welfare Reform Act 2012, s 91, Sch 9, paras 37, 44(a). Date in force (in relation to personal independence payment for certain purposes): 10 June 2013: see SI 2013/358, art 7(1), (2)(k), Sch 3. Date in force (for remaining purposes): 10 June 2013: see SI 2013/1250, art 2.

Sub-s (1): in para (c) words "carer's allowance" in square brackets substituted by SI 2002/1457, art 2, Schedule, paras 1, 3(c).

Sub-s (1): para (d) repealed by the Welfare Reform Act 2012, s 147, Sch 14, Pt 9 as from a day to be appointed.

Sub-s (1): para (e) repealed by the Welfare Reform Act 2009, ss 9(3)(b), 58(1), Sch 7, Pt 1; for further provision in relation to this repeal see s 9(1), (2), (4)–(10) thereof, as from a day to be appointed.

Sub-s (1): para (e) repealed by the Welfare Reform Act 2012, s 147, Sch 14, Pt 1, as from a day to be appointed.

Sub-s (1): paras (f), (g) repealed by the Tax Credits Act 2002, s 60, Sch 6.

Sub-s (1): para (ha) inserted by the Health and Social Care Act 2008, s 138(2).

Sub-s (1): in para (ha) word "or" in square brackets inserted by the Welfare Reform Act 2012, s 33(3), Sch 3, para 9(a), as from a day to be appointed.

Sub-s (1): paras (j), (k) repealed by the Welfare Reform Act 2012, s 147, Sch 14, Pt 1, as from a day to be appointed.

Sub-s (2): words "state pension credit under the State Pension Credit Act (Northern Ireland) 2002, or to" in square brackets inserted by the State Pension Credit Act (Northern Ireland) 2002, s 4(2).

Sub-s (2): in para (b) words "disability living allowance or" in square brackets inserted by the Welfare Reform Act 2012, s 91, Sch 9, paras 37, 44(b). Date in force (in relation to personal independence payment for certain purposes): 8 April 2013: see SI 2013/358, art 7(1), (2)(k), Sch 3. Date in force (for remaining purposes): 10 June 2013: see SI 2013/1250, art 2.

Sub-s (2): in para (b) words "(a) to (j)" in italics repealed and subsequent words in square brackets substituted by the Welfare Reform Act 2012, s 33(3), Sch 3, para 9(b), as from a day to be appointed.

Sub-s (5): words "health in pregnancy grant or" in square brackets inserted by the Health and Social Care Act 2008, s 138(3).

Sub-s (5): words "child benefit" in square brackets substituted by the Tax Credits Act 2002, s 51, Sch 4, paras 20, 21.

Sub-s (6): words "health in pregnancy grant or" in square brackets inserted by the Health and Social Care Act 2008, s 138(3).

Sub-s (6): words "child benefit" in square brackets substituted by the Tax Credits Act 2002, s 51, Sch 4, paras 20, 21.

Subordinate Legislation

Social Security (Immigration and Asylum) Consequential Amendments Regulations 2000, SI 2000/636; Social Security Amendment (Carer's Allowance) Regulations 2002, SI 2002/2497; State Pension Credit (Transitional and Miscellaneous Provisions) Amendment Regulations 2003, SI 2003/2274; Immigration (Eligibility for Assistance) (Scotland and Northern Ireland) (Revocation) Regulations 2005, SI 2005/2412; Health in Pregnancy Grant (Entitlement and Amount) Regulations 2008, SI 2008/3108.

116

(S 116 amends the National Assistance Act 1948, s 21; s 117 amends the Health Services and Public Health Act 1968, s 45, repeals the Housing Act 1996, s 186 and amends s 187 thereof.)

118 Housing authority accommodation

(1) Each housing authority must secure that, so far as practicable, a tenancy of, or licence to occupy, housing accommodation provided under the accommodation provisions is not granted to a person subject to immigration control unless—

(a) he is of a class specified in an order made by the Secretary of State; or

(b) the tenancy of, or licence to occupy, such accommodation is granted in accordance with arrangements made under section [4, 95 or 98].

(2) "Housing authority" means—

(a) in relation to England and Wales, a local housing authority within the meaning of the Housing Act 1985;

(b) in relation to Scotland, a local authority within the meaning of the Housing (Scotland) Act 1987; and

(c) in relation to Northern Ireland, the Executive.

(3) "Accommodation provisions" means—

(a) in relation to England and Wales, Part II of the Housing Act 1985;

(b) in relation to Scotland, Part I of the Housing (Scotland) Act 1987;

(c) in relation to Northern Ireland, Part II of the Housing (Northern Ireland) Order 1981.

(4) "Licence to occupy", in relation to Scotland, means a permission or right to occupy.

(5) "Tenancy", in relation to England and Wales, has the same meaning as in the Housing Act 1985.

(6) "Person subject to immigration control" means a person who under the 1971 Act requires leave to enter or remain in the United Kingdom (whether or not such leave has been given).

(7) This section does not apply in relation to any allocation of housing to which Part VI of the Housing Act 1996 (allocation of housing accommodation) applies.

Amendment

Sub-s (1): in para (b) words "4, 95 or 98" in square brackets substituted by the Immigration, Asylum and Nationality Act 2006, s 43(3).

Subordinate Legislation

Persons subject to Immigration Control (Housing Authority Accommodation and Homelessness) Order 2000, SI 2000/706.

Persons Subject to Immigration Control (Housing Authority Accommodation) (Wales) Order 2000, SI 2000/1036.

Persons Subject to Immigration Control (Housing Authority Accommodation and Homelessness) (Amendment) Order 2006, SI 2006/2521.

Persons subject to Immigration Control (Housing Authority Accommodation and Homelessness) (Amendment) Order 2008, SI 2008/1768.

119 Homelessness: Scotland and Northern Ireland

(1) A person subject to immigration control—

(a) is not eligible for accommodation or assistance under the homelessness provisions, and

(b) is to be disregarded in determining for the purposes of those provisions, whether [a person falling within subsection (1A)]—

(i) is homeless or is threatened with homelessness, or

(ii) has a priority need for accommodation,

unless he is of a class specified in an order made by the Secretary of State.

[(1A) A person falls within this subsection if the person—

(a) falls within a class specified in an order under subsection (1); but

(b) is not a national of an EEA State or Switzerland.]

(2) An order under subsection (1) may not be made so as to include in a specified class any person to whom section 115 applies.

(3) "The homelessness provisions" means—

(a) in relation to Scotland, Part II of the Housing (Scotland) Act 1987; and

(b) in relation to Northern Ireland, Part II of the Housing (Northern Ireland) Order 1988.

(4) "Person subject to immigration control" has the same meaning as in section 118.

Amendment

Sub-s (1): in para (b) words "a person falling within subsection (1A)" in square brackets substituted by the Housing and Regeneration Act 2008, s 314, Sch 15, Pt 2, para 22(1), (2).

Sub-s (1A): inserted by the Housing and Regeneration Act 2008, s 314, Sch 15, Pt 2, para 22(1), (3).

Subordinate Legislation

Persons subject to Immigration Control (Housing Authority Accommodation and Homelessness) Order 2000, SI 2000/706.

Persons Subject to Immigration Control (Housing Authority Accommodation and Homelessness) (Amendment) Order 2006, SI 2006/2521.

Persons subject to Immigration Control (Housing Authority Accommodation and Homelessness) (Amendment) Order 2008, SI 2008/1768.

120, 121

(Contain amendments which, in so far as relevant to this work, have been incorporated at the appropriate place.)

122 Support for children [122 Family with children]

(1) In this section "eligible person" means a person who appears to the Secretary of State to be a person for whom support may be provided under section 95.

(2) Subsections (3) and (4) apply if an application for support under section 95 has been made by an eligible person whose household includes a dependant under the age of 18 ("the child").

(3) If it appears to the Secretary of State that adequate accommodation is not being provided for the child, he must exercise his powers under section 95 by offering, and if his offer is accepted by providing or arranging for the provision of, adequate accommodation for the child as part of the eligible person's household.

(4) If it appears to the Secretary of State that essential living needs of the child are not being met, he must exercise his powers under section 95 by offering, and if his offer is accepted by providing or arranging for the provision of, essential living needs for the child as part of the eligible person's household.

(5) No local authority may provide assistance under any of the child welfare provisions in respect of a dependant under the age of 18, or any member of his family, at any time when—

    (a)   the Secretary of State is complying with this section in relation to him; or

    (b)   there are reasonable grounds for believing that—

        (i)   the person concerned is a person for whom support may be provided under section 95; and

        (ii)   the Secretary of State would be required to comply with this section if that person had made an application under section 95.

(6) "Assistance" means the provision of accommodation or of any essential living needs.

(7) "The child welfare provisions" means—

    (a)   section 17 of the Children Act 1989 (local authority support for children and their families);

    (b)   section 22 of the Children (Scotland) Act 1995 (equivalent provision for Scotland); and

    (c)   Article 18 of the Children (Northern Ireland) Order 1995 (equivalent provision for Northern Ireland).

(8) Subsection (9) applies if accommodation provided in the discharge of the duty imposed by subsection (3) has been withdrawn.

(9) Only the relevant authority may provide assistance under any of the child welfare provisions in respect of the child concerned.

(10) *"Relevant authority"* means—

(a) in relation to Northern Ireland, the authority within whose area the withdrawn accommodation was provided;

(b) in any other case, the local authority within whose area the withdrawn accommodation was provided.

(11) *In such circumstances as may be prescribed, subsection (5) does not apply.*

[(1) This section applies where a person ("the asylum-seeker") applies for support under section 95 of this Act or section 17 of the Nationality, Immigration and Asylum Act 2002 (accommodation centres) if—

(a) the Secretary of State thinks that the asylum-seeker is eligible for support under either or both of those sections, and

(b) the asylum-seeker's household includes a dependant child who is under 18.

(2) The Secretary of State must offer the provision of support for the child, as part of the asylum-seeker's household, under one of the sections mentioned in subsection (1).

(3) A local authority (or, in Northern Ireland, an authority) may not provide assistance for a child if—

(a) the Secretary of State is providing support for the child in accordance with an offer under subsection (2),

(b) an offer by the Secretary of State under subsection (2) remains open in respect of the child, or

(c) the Secretary of State has agreed that he would make an offer in respect of the child under subsection (2) if an application were made as described in subsection (1).

(4) In subsection (3) "assistance" means assistance under—

(a) section 17 of the Children Act 1989 (c 41) (local authority support),

(b) section 22 of the Children (Scotland) Act 1995 (c 36) (similar provision for Scotland), or

(c) Article 18 of the Children (Northern Ireland) Order 1995 (SI 1995/755 (NI 2)) (similar provision for Northern Ireland).

(5) The Secretary of State may by order disapply subsection (3) in specified circumstances.

(6) Where subsection (3) ceases to apply to a child because the Secretary of State stops providing support, no local authority may provide assistance for the child except the authority for the area within which the support was provided.]

Amendment

Substituted by the Nationality, Immigration and Asylum Act 2002, s 47, as from a day to be appointed.

Subordinate Legislation

Immigration (Eligibility for Assistance) (Scotland and Northern Ireland) (Revocation) Regulations 2005, SI 2005/2412.

123

124 Secretary of State to be corporation sole for purposes Part VI

(1) For the purpose of exercising his functions under this Part, the Secretary of State is a corporation sole.

(Repealed by the Asylum and Immigration (Treatment of Claimants, etc) Act 2004, ss 12(1), 47, Sch 4.)

(2) Any instrument in connection with the acquisition, management or of disposal of property, real or personal, heritable or moveable, by the Secretary of State under this Part may be executed on his behalf by a person authorised by him for that purpose.

(3) Any instrument purporting to have been so executed on behalf of the Secretary of State is to be treated, until the contrary is proved, to have been so executed on his behalf.

125 Entry of premises

(1) This section applies in relation to premises in which accommodation has been provided under section 95 or 98 for a supported person.

(2) If, on an application made by a person authorised in writing by the Secretary of State, a justice of the peace is satisfied that there is reason to believe that—

    (a) the supported person or any dependants of his for whom the accommodation is provided is not resident in it,

    (b) the accommodation is being used for any purpose other than the accommodation of the asylum-seeker or any dependant of his, or

    (c) any person other than the supported person and his dependants (if any) is residing in the accommodation,

he may grant a warrant to enter the premises to the person making the application.

(3) A warrant granted under subsection (2) may be executed—

    (a) at any reasonable time;

    (b) using reasonable force.

(4) In the application of subsection (2) to Scotland, read the reference to a justice of the peace as a reference to the sheriff or a justice of the peace.

126 Information from property owners

(1) The power conferred by this section is to be exercised with a view to obtaining information about premises in which accommodation is or has been provided for supported persons.

(2) The Secretary of State may require any person appearing to him—

    (a) to have any interest in, or

    (b) to be involved in any way in the management or control of,

such premises, or any building which includes such premises, to provide him with such information with respect to the premises and the persons occupying them as he may specify.

(3) A person who is required to provide information under this section must do so in accordance with such requirements as may be prescribed.

(4) Information provided to the Secretary of State under this section may be used by him only in the exercise of his functions under this Part.

127 Requirement to supply information about redirection of post

(1) The Secretary of State may require any person conveying postal packets to supply redirection information to the Secretary of State—

    (a) for use in the prevention, detection, investigation or prosecution of criminal offences under this Part;

    (b) for use in checking the accuracy of information relating to support provided under this Part; or

    (c) for any other purpose relating to the provision of support to asylum-seekers.

(2) The information must be supplied in such manner and form, and in accordance with such requirements, as may be prescribed.

(3) The Secretary of State must make payments of such amount as he considers reasonable in respect of the supply of information under this section.

(4) "Postal packet" has the same meaning as in the [Postal Services Act 2000].

(5) "Redirection information" means information relating to arrangements made with any person conveying postal packets for the delivery of postal packets to addresses other than those indicated by senders on the packets.

Amendment

Sub-s (4): words "Postal Services Act 2000" in square brackets substituted by SI 2001/1149, art 3(1), Sch 1, para 124.

128–140

PART VII

POWER TO ARREST, SEARCH AND FINGERPRINT

Fingerprinting

(*Insert the Immigration Act 1971, ss 28A–28L and amend Sch 2 thereto.*)

141 Fingerprinting

(1) Fingerprints may be taken by an authorised person from a person to whom this section applies.

(2) Fingerprints may be taken under this section only during the relevant period.

(3) Fingerprints may not be taken under this section from a person under the age of sixteen ("the child") except in the presence of a person of full age who is—

(a) the child's parent or guardian; or

(b) a person who for the time being takes responsibility for the child.

(4) The person mentioned in subsection (3)(b) may not be—

(a) an officer of the Secretary of State who is not an authorised person;

(b) an authorised person.

(5) "Authorised person" means—

(a) a constable;

(b) an immigration officer;

(c) a prison officer;

(d) an officer of the Secretary of State authorised for the purpose; or

(e) a person who is employed by a contractor in connection with the discharge of the contractor's duties under a [removal centre] contract.

(6) In subsection (5)(e) "contractor" and "[removal centre] contract" have the same meaning as in Part VIII.

(7) This section applies to—

(a) any person ("A") who, on being required to do so by an immigration officer on his arrival in the United Kingdom, fails to produce a valid passport with photograph or some other document satisfactorily establishing his identity and nationality or citizenship;

(b) any person ("B") who has been refused leave to enter the United Kingdom but has been temporarily admitted under paragraph 21 of Schedule 2 to the 1971 Act if an immigration officer reasonably suspects that B might break any condition imposed on him relating to residence or as to reporting to the police or an immigration officer;

[(c) any person ("C") in respect of whom the Secretary of State has decided—

(i) to make a deportation order, or

(ii) that section 32(5) of the UK Borders Act 2007 (automatic deportation of foreign criminals) applies;

(ca) any person ("CA") who requires leave to enter or remain in the United Kingdom but does not have it;]

(d) any person ("D") who has been [detained under paragraph 16 of Schedule 2 to the 1971 Act or arrested under paragraph 17 of that Schedule];

(e) any person ("E") who has made a claim for asylum;

(f) any person ("F") who is a dependant of any of those persons[, other than a dependant of a person who falls within [paragraph (c)(ii)]].

(8) "The relevant period" begins—

(a) for A, on his failure to produce the passport or other document;

(b) for B, on the decision to admit him temporarily;

[(c) for C, when he is notified of the decision mentioned in subsection (7)(c);]

(ca) for CA, when he becomes a person to whom this section applies;]

(d) for D, on his [detention or arrest];

(e) for E, on the making of his claim for asylum; and

(f) for F, at the same time as for the person whose dependant he is.

(9) "The relevant period" ends on the earliest of the following—

(a) the grant of leave to enter or remain in the United Kingdom;

(b) for A, B, C[, CA] or D, his removal or deportation from the United Kingdom;

[(c) for C—

 (i) the time when the [decision mentioned in subsection (7)(c)] ceases to have effect, whether as a result of an appeal or otherwise, or

 (ii) if a deportation order has been made against him, its revocation or its otherwise ceasing to have effect;]

[(ca) for CA, when he no longer requires leave to enter or remain in the United Kingdom;]

(d) for D, his release if he is no longer liable to be detained under paragraph 16 of Schedule 2 to the 1971 Act;

(e) for E, the final determination or abandonment of his claim for asylum; and

(f) for F, at the same time as for the person whose dependant he is.

(10) No fingerprints may be taken from A if the immigration officer considers that A has a reasonable excuse for the failure concerned.

(11) No fingerprints may be taken from B unless the decision to take them has been confirmed by a chief immigration officer.

(12) An authorised person may not take fingerprints from a person under the age of sixteen unless his decision to take them has been confirmed—

(a) if he is a constable, by a person designated for the purpose by the chief constable of his police force;

(b) if he is a person mentioned in subsection (5)(b) or (e), by a chief immigration officer;

(c) if he is a prison officer, by a person designated for the purpose by the governor of the prison;

(d) if he is an officer of the Secretary of State, by a person designated for the purpose by the Secretary of State.

(13) Neither subsection (3) nor subsection (12) prevents an authorised person from taking fingerprints if he reasonably believes that the person from whom they are to be taken is aged sixteen or over.

(14) For the purposes of subsection (7)(f), a person is a dependant of another person if—

(a) he is that person's spouse or child under the age of eighteen; and

(b) he does not have a right of abode in the United Kingdom or indefinite leave to enter or remain in the United Kingdom.

(15) "Claim for asylum" has the same meaning as in Part VI.

[(16) "Relevant immigration decision" means[—

(a)] a decision of the kind mentioned in section 82(2)(g), (h), (i), (i) or (k) of the Nationality, Immigration and Asylum Act 2002 (c 41)[, or

(b)] a decision that section 32(5) of the UK Borders Act 2007 applies (whether made before, or on or after, the day appointed for the commencement of section 51 of the Borders, Citizenship and Immigration Act 2009 which inserted this paragraph)].]

[(17) Section 157(1) applies to this section (in so far as it relates to removal centres by virtue of subsection (5)(e)) as it applies to Part VIII.]

Amendment

Sub-s (5): in para (e) words "removal centre" in square brackets substituted by the Nationality, Immigration and Asylum Act 2002, s 66(2)(a), (3)(n).

Sub-s (6): words "removal centre" in square brackets substituted by the Nationality, Immigration and Asylum Act 2002, s 66(2)(a), (3)(n).

Sub-s (7): paras (c), (ca) substituted for original para (c) by the Immigration Act 2014, s 73, Sch 9, Pt 4, paras 27, 29(1), (2)(a), as from 20 October 2014 (see SI 2014/2771, art 2), subject to savings in SI 2014/2771, arts 9–11. Para (c) previously read as follows:
"(c)   any person ("C") in respect of whom a relevant immigration decision has been made;"

Sub-s (7): in para (d) words from "detained under paragraph 16" to "of that Schedule" in square brackets substituted by the Immigration, Asylum and Nationality Act 2006, s 28(1), (2).

Sub-s (7): in para (f) words in outer square brackets inserted by the Borders, Citizenship and Immigration Act 2009, s 51(1), (2), and words in inner square brackets substituted (for original words "paragraph (c) by reason of a relevant immigration decision within subsection (16)(b) having been made in respect of that person" by the Immigration Act 2014, s 73, Sch 9, Pt 4, paras 27, 29(1), (2)(b), as from 20 October 2014 (see SI 2014/2771, art 2), subject to savings in SI 2014/2771, arts 9–11.

Sub-s (8): paras (c), (ca) substituted for original para (c) by the Immigration Act 2014, s 73, Sch 9, Pt 4, paras 27, 29(1), (3), as from 20 October 2014 (see SI 2014/2771, art 2), subject to savings in SI 2014/2771, arts 9–11. Para (c) originally read as follows:
"(c)   for C, on the service on him of notice of the relevant immigration decision by virtue of section 105 of the Nationality, Immigration and Asylum Act 2002
(c 41);."

Sub-s (8): in para (d) words "detention or arrest" in square brackets substituted by the Immigration, Asylum and Nationality Act 2006, s 28(1), (3).

Sub-s (9): para (c) substituted by the Asylum and Immigration (Treatment of Claimants, etc) Act 2004, s 15(1), (4).

Sub-s (9): reference in square brackets in para (b) inserted, words in square brackets in para (c) substituted (for original words "relevant immigration decision" and para (ca) inserted by the Immigration Act 2014, s 73, Sch 9, Pt 4, paras 27, 29(1), (4), as from 20 October 2014 (see SI 2014/2771, art 2), subject to savings in SI 2014/2771, arts 9–11.

Sub-s (16): inserted by the Asylum and Immigration (Treatment of Claimants, etc) Act 2004, s 15(1), (5) and repealed by the Immigration Act 2014, s 73, Sch 9, Pt 4, paras 27, 29(1), (5), as from 20 October 2014 (see SI 2014/2771, art 2), subject to savings in SI 2014/2771, arts 9–11.

Sub-s (17): inserted by the Immigration, Asylum and Nationality Act 2006, s 28(1), (4).

142 Attendance for fingerprinting

(1)   The Secretary of State may, by notice in writing, require a person to whom section 141 applies to attend at a specified place for fingerprinting.

[(2)   In the case of a notice given to a person of a kind specified in section 141(7)(a) to (d) or (f) (in so far as it applies to a dependant of a person of a kind specified in section 141(7)(a) to (d)), the notice—

(a)   must require him to attend during a specified period of at least seven days beginning with a day not less than seven days after the date given in the notice as its date of issue, and

(b)   may require him to attend at a specified time of day or during specified hours.

(2A) In the case of a notice given to a person of a kind specified in section 141(7)(e) or (f) (in so far as it applies to a dependant of a person of a kind specified in section 141(7)(e)), the notice—

(a) may require him to attend during a specified period beginning with a day not less than three days after the date given in the notice as its date of issue,

(b) may require him to attend on a specified day not less than three days after the date given in the notice as its date of issue, and

(c) may require him to attend at a specified time of day or during specified hours.]

(3) A constable or immigration officer may arrest without warrant a person who has failed to comply with a requirement imposed on him under this section (unless the requirement has ceased to have effect).

(4) Before a person arrested under subsection (3) is released—

(a) he may be removed to a place where his fingerprints may conveniently be taken; and

(b) his fingerprints may be taken (whether or not he is so removed).

(5) A requirement imposed under subsection (1) ceases to have effect at the end of the relevant period (as defined by section 141).

Amendment

Sub-ss (2), (2A): substituted, for sub-s (2) as originally enacted, by the Immigration, Asylum and Nationality Act 2006, s 29.

143 Destruction of fingerprints

(1) If they have not already been destroyed, fingerprints must be destroyed before the end of the specified period beginning with the day on which they were taken.

(2) If a person from whom fingerprints were taken proves that he is—

(a) a British citizen, or

(b) a Commonwealth citizen who has a right of abode in the United Kingdom as a result of section 2(1)(b) of the 1971 Act,

the fingerprints must be destroyed as soon as reasonably practicable.

(3) . . .

(4) . . .

(5) . . .

(6) . . .

(7) . . .

(8) . . .

(9) Fingerprints taken from F [[(within the meaning of section 141(7))] must be destroyed when fingerprints taken from the person whose dependant he is have to be destroyed.

(10) The obligation to destroy fingerprints under this section applies also to copies of fingerprints.

(11) The Secretary of State must take all reasonably practicable steps to secure—

(a) that data which are held in electronic form and which relate to fingerprints which have to be destroyed as a result of this section are destroyed or erased; or

(b) that access to such data is blocked.

(12) The person to whom the data relate is entitled, on request, to a certificate issued by the Secretary of State to the effect that he has taken the steps required by subsection (11).

(13) A certificate under subsection (12) must be issued within three months of the date of the request for it.

(14) . . .

(15) "Specified period" means—

    (a) such period as the Secretary of State may specify by order;

    (b) if no period is so specified, ten years.

Amendment

Sub-ss (3)–(8): repealed by the Anti-terrorism, Crime and Security Act 2001, ss 36(1)(a), (2), 125, Sch 8, Pt 3.

Sub-s (9): words "(within the meaning of section 141(7))" in square brackets inserted by the Anti-terrorism, Crime and Security Act 2001, s 36(1)(b), (2).

Sub-s (14): repealed by the Anti-terrorism, Crime and Security Act 2001, ss 36(1)(c), (2), 125, Sch 8, Pt 3.

144 Other methods of collecting data about physical characteristics

[(1)] The Secretary of State may make regulations containing provisions equivalent to sections 141, 142 and 143 in relation to such other methods of collecting [biometric information] as may be prescribed.

[(2) Biometric information" has the meaning given by section 15 of the UK Borders Act 2007.]

Amendment

Sub-s (1): numbered as such by the Nationality, Immigration and Asylum Act 2002, s 128(1).

Sub-s (1): words in square brackets substituted by the Immigration Act 2014, s 12, Sch 2, para 2(1), (2), as from 28 July 2014: see SI 2014/1820.

Sub-s (2): inserted by the Nationality, Immigration and Asylum Act 2002, s 128(1) and substituted by the Immigration Act 2014, s 12, Sch 2, para 2(1), (3), as from 28 July 2014: see SI 2014/1820.

[144A Use and retention of fingerprints etc

(1) Section 8 of the UK Borders Act 2007 (power to make regulations about use and retention of biometric information) applies to—

    (a) fingerprints taken by virtue of section 141, and

    (b) biometric information taken by virtue of regulations under section 144,

as it applies to biometric information provided in accordance with regulations under section 5(1) of that Act.

(2) Regulations made by virtue of subsection (1)(a) must require fingerprints taken from a person ("F") by virtue of section 141(7)(f) to be destroyed when fingerprints taken from the person whose dependant F is are destroyed.

(3) Regulations made by virtue of subsection (1)(b) must make equivalent provision in relation to biometric information taken by virtue of any provision of regulations under section 144 which is equivalent to section 141(7)(f).]

Amendment

Inserted by the Immigration Act 2014, s 14(2), as from 28 July 2014: see SI 2014/1820.

Codes of practice

145 Codes of practice

(1) An immigration officer exercising any specified power to—

    (a) arrest, question, search or take fingerprints from a person,

    (b) enter and search premises, or

    (c) seize property found on persons or premises,

must have regard to such provisions of a code as may be specified.

(2) Subsection (1) also applies to an authorised person exercising the power to take fingerprints conferred by section 141.

[(2A) A person exercising a power under regulations made by virtue of section 144 must have regard to such provisions of a code as may be specified.]

(3) Any specified provision of a code may have effect for the purposes of this section subject to such modifications as may be specified.

(4) "Specified" means specified in a direction given by the Secretary of State.

(5) "Authorised person" has the same meaning as in section 141.

(6) "Code" means—

(a) in relation to England and Wales, any code of practice for the time being in force under the Police and Criminal Evidence Act 1984;

(b) in relation to Northern Ireland, any code of practice for the time being in force under the Police and Criminal Evidence (Northern Ireland) Order 1989.

(7) This section does not apply to any person exercising powers in Scotland.

Amendment

Sub-s (2A): inserted by the Nationality, Immigration and Asylum Act 2002, s 128(2).

Use of force

146 Use of force

(1) An immigration officer exercising any power conferred on him by [the Immigration Acts] may, if necessary, use reasonable force.

[(2) A person exercising a power under any of the following may if necessary use reasonable force—

(a) section 28CA, 28FA or 28FB of the 1971 Act (business premises: entry to arrest or search),

(b) section 141 or 142 of this Act, and

(c) regulations under section 144 of this Act.]

Amendment

Sub-s (1): words in square brackets substituted by the Immigration Act 2014, s 4, Sch 1, para 5, as from 28 July 2014: see SI 2014/1820.

Sub-s (2): substituted by the Nationality, Immigration and Asylum Act 2002, s 153(2).

PART VIII

[REMOVAL CENTRES] AND DETAINED PERSONS

Amendment

Part heading: words "Removal Centres" in square brackets substituted by virtue of the Nationality, Immigration and Asylum Act 2002, s 66(2)(b).

Interpretation

147 Interpretation of Part VIII

In this Part—

"certificate of authorisation" means a certificate issued by the Secretary of State under section 154;

"certified prisoner custody officer" means a prisoner custody officer certified under section 89 of the Criminal Justice Act 1991, or section 114 of the Criminal Justice and Public Order Act 1994, to perform custodial duties;

"contract monitor" means a person appointed by the Secretary of State under section 149(4);

"contracted out [removal centre]" means a [removal centre] in relation to which a [removal centre] contract is in force;

"contractor", in relation to a [removal centre] which is being run in accordance with a [removal centre] contract, means the person who has contracted to run it;

"custodial functions" means custodial functions at a [removal centre];

["detained children" means detained persons who are under the age of 18;]

"detained persons" means persons detained or required to be detained under the 1971 Act [or under section 62 of the Nationality, Immigration and Asylum Act 2002 (detention by Secretary of State)];

"detainee custody officer" means a person in respect of whom a certificate of authorisation is in force;

...

"removal centre] contract" means a contract entered into by the Secretary of State under section 149;

"removal centre] rules" means rules made by the Secretary of State under section 153;

"directly managed [removal centre]" means a [removal centre] which is not a contracted out [removal centre];

"escort arrangements" means arrangements made by the Secretary of State under section 156;

"escort functions" means functions under escort arrangements;

"escort monitor" means a person appointed under paragraph 1 of Schedule 13;

[" pre-departure accommodation" means a place used solely for the detention of detained children and their families for a period of—

(a)   not more than 72 hours, or

(b)   not more than seven days in cases where the longer period of detention is authorised personally by a Minister of the Crown (within the meaning of the Ministers of the Crown Act 1975);]

"prisoner custody officer"—

(a)   in relation to England and Wales, has the same meaning as in the Criminal Justice Act 1991;

(b)   in relation to Scotland, has the meaning given in section 114(1) of the Criminal Justice and Public Order Act 1994,

(c)   in relation to Northern Ireland, has the meaning given in section 122(1) of that Act of 1994;

["removal centre" means a place which is used solely for the detention of detained persons but which is not a short-term holding facility, [pre-departure accommodation,] a prison or part of a prison;]

"short-term holding facility" means a place used[—

(a)   solely for the detention of detained persons for a period of not more than seven days or for such other period as may be prescribed[, or

(b)   for the detention of—

(i)   detained persons for a period of not more than seven days or for such other period as may be prescribed, and

(ii)   persons other than detained persons for any period].

[but which is not pre-departure accommodation.]

Amendment

In definition "contracted out removal centre", words "removal centre" in square brackets in each place they occur substituted by the Nationality, Immigration and Asylum Act 2002, s 66(2)(a), (3)(a).

In definition "contractor" words "removal centre" in square brackets in both places they occur substituted by the Nationality, Immigration and Asylum Act 2002, s 66(2)(a), (3)(a).

In definition "custodial functions" words "removal centre" in square brackets substituted by the Nationality, Immigration and Asylum Act 2002, s 66(2)(a), (3)(a).

Definitions "detained children" and "pre-departure accommodation" inserted and words in square brackets in definition "removal centre" and "short-term holding facility" inserted by the Immigration Act 2014, s 6(1), (2), as from 28 July 2014: see SI 2014/1820.

In definition "detained person" words "or under section 62 of the Nationality, Immigration and Asylum Act 2002 (detention by Secretary of State)" in square brackets inserted by the Nationality, Immigration and Asylum Act 2002, s 62(14).

Definition "detention centre" (omitted) repealed by the Nationality, Immigration and Asylum Act 2002, ss 66(1)/a), 161, Sch 9.

In definition "removal centre contract" words "removal centre" in square brackets substituted by the Nationality, Immigration and Asylum Act 2002, s 66(2)(a), (3)(a).

In definition "removal centre rules" words "removal centre" in square brackets substituted by the Nationality, Immigration and Asylum Act 2002, s 66(2)(a), (3)(a).

In definition "directly managed removal centre" words "removal centre" in square brackets in each place they occur substituted by the Nationality, Immigration and Asylum Act 2002, s 66(2)(a), (3)(a).

Definition "removal centre" inserted by the Nationality, Immigration and Asylum Act 2002, s 66(1)(b).

In definition "short-term holding facility" para (a) designated as such by the Borders, Citizenship and Immigration Act 2009, s 25(a).

In definition "short-term holding facility" para (b) and word ", or" immediately preceding it inserted by the Borders, Citizenship and Immigration Act 2009, s 25(b).

[Removal centres]

Amendment

Cross-heading: substituted by virtue of the Nationality, Immigration and Asylum Act 2002, s 66(2)(b).

148 Management of [removal centres]

(1) A manager must be appointed for every [removal centre].

(2) In the case of a contracted out [removal centre], the person appointed as manager must be a detainee custody officer whose appointment is approved by the Secretary of State.

(3) The manager of a [removal centre] is to have such functions as are conferred on him by [removal centre] rules.

(4) The manager of a contracted out [removal centre] may not—

(a) enquire into a disciplinary charge laid against a detained person;

(b) conduct the hearing of such a charge; or

(c) make, remit or mitigate an award in respect of such a charge.

(5) The manager of a contracted out [removal centre] may not, except in cases of urgency, order—

(a) the removal of a detained person from association with other detained persons;

(b) the temporary confinement of a detained person in special accommodation; or

(c) the application to a detained person of any other special control or restraint (other than handcuffs).

Amendment

Section heading: words "removal centres" in square brackets substituted by the Nationality, Immigration and Asylum Act 2002, s 66(2)(b), (3)(b).

Sub-ss (1)–(5): words "removal centre" in square brackets substituted by the Nationality, Immigration and Asylum Act 2002, s 66(2)(a), (3)(b).

Subordinate Legislation

Detention Centre Rules 2001, SI 2001/238.

149 Contracting out of certain [removal centres]

(1) The Secretary of State may enter into a contract with another person for the provision or running (or the provision and running) by him, or (if the contract so

Appendix 1 — UK Immigration Statutes

provides) for the running by sub-contractors of his, of any [removal centre] or part of a [removal centre].

(2) While a [removal centre] contract for the running of a [removal centre] or part of a [removal centre] is in force—

    (a) the [removal centre] or part is to be run subject to and in accordance with the provisions of or made under this Part; and

    (b) in the case of a part, that part and the remaining part are to be treated for the purposes of those provisions as if they were separate [removal centres].

(3) If the Secretary of State grants a lease or tenancy of land for the purposes of a [removal centre] contract, none of the following enactments applies to the lease or tenancy—

    (a) Part II of the Landlord and Tenant Act 1954 (security of tenure);

    (b) section 146 of the Law of Property Act 1925 (restrictions on and relief against forfeiture);

    (c) section 19(1), (2) and (3) of the Landlord and Tenant Act 1927 and the Landlord and Tenant Act 1988 (covenants not to assign etc);

    (d) the Agricultural Holdings Act 1986;

    (e) sections 4 to 7 of the Law Reform (Miscellaneous Provisions) (Scotland) Act 1985 (irritancy clauses);

    (f) the Agricultural Holdings (Scotland) Act 1991 [and the Agricultural Holdings (Scotland) Act 2003 (asp 11)];

    (g) section 14 of the Conveyancing Act 1881;

    (h) the Conveyancing and Law of Property Act 1892;

    (i) the Business Tenancies (Northern Ireland) Order 1996.

(4) The Secretary of State must appoint a contract monitor for every contracted out [removal centre].

(5) A person may be appointed as the contract monitor for more than one [removal centre].

(6) The contract monitor is to have—

    (a) such functions as may be conferred on him by [removal centre] rules;

    (b) the status of a Crown servant.

(7) The contract monitor must—

    (a) keep under review, and report to the Secretary of State on, the running of a [removal centre] for which he is appointed; and

    (b) investigate, and report to the Secretary of State on, any allegations made against any person performing custodial functions at that centre.

(8) The contractor, and any sub-contractor of his, must do all that he reasonably can (whether by giving directions to the officers of the [removal centre] or otherwise) to facilitate the exercise by the contract monitor of his functions.

(9) "Lease or tenancy" includes an underlease, sublease or sub-tenancy.

(10) In relation to a [removal centre] contract entered into by the Secretary of State before the commencement of this section, this section is to be treated as having been in force at that time.

Amendment

Section heading: words "removal centres" in square brackets substituted by the Nationality, Immigration and Asylum Act 2002, s 66(2)(b), (3)(c).

Sub-s (1): words "removal centre" in square brackets in both places they occur substituted by the Nationality, Immigration and Asylum Act 2002, s 66(2)(a), (3)(c).

Sub-s (2): words "removal centre" and "removal centres" in square brackets in each place they occur substituted by the Nationality, Immigration and Asylum Act 2002, s 66(2), (3)(c).

Sub-s (3): words "removal centre" in square brackets substituted by the Nationality, Immigration and Asylum Act 2002, s 66(2)(a), (3)(c).

Sub-s (3): in para (f) words "and the Agricultural Holdings (Scotland) Act 2003 (asp 11)" in square brackets inserted by the Agricultural Holdings (Scotland) Act 2003, s 94, Schedule, para 52.

Sub-s (4): words "removal centre" in square brackets substituted by the Nationality, Immigration and Asylum Act 2002, s 66(2)(a), (3)(c).

Sub-s (5): words "removal centre" in square brackets substituted by the Nationality, Immigration and Asylum Act 2002, s 66(2)(a), (3)(c).

Sub-s (6): in para (a) words "removal centre" in square brackets substituted by the Nationality, Immigration and Asylum Act 2002, s 66(2)(a), (3)(c).

Sub-s (7): in para (a) words "removal centre" in square brackets substituted by the Nationality, Immigration and Asylum Act 2002, s 66(2)(a), (3)(c).

Sub-s (8): words "removal centre" in square brackets substituted by the Nationality, Immigration and Asylum Act 2002, s 66(2)(a), (3)(c).

Sub-s (10): words "removal centre" in square brackets substituted by the Nationality, Immigration and Asylum Act 2002, s 66(2)(a), (3)(c).

Subordinate Legislation

Detention Centre Rules 2001, SI 2001/238.

150 Contracted out functions at directly managed [removal centres]

(1) The Secretary of State may enter into a contract with another person—

   (a) for functions at, or connected with, a directly managed [removal centre] to be performed by detainee custody officers provided by that person; or

   (b) for such functions to be performed by certified prisoner custody officers who are provided by that person.

(2) For the purposes of this section "[removal centre]" includes a short-term holding facility.

Amendment

Section heading: words "removal centres" in square brackets substituted by the Nationality, Immigration and Asylum Act 2002, s 66(2)(b), (3)(c).

Sub-s (1): in para (a) words "removal centre" in square brackets substituted by the Nationality, Immigration and Asylum Act 2002, s 66(2)(a), (3)(c).

Sub-s (2): words "removal centre" in square brackets substituted by the Nationality, Immigration and Asylum Act 2002, s 66(2)(a), (3)(c).

151 Intervention by Secretary of State

(1) The Secretary of State may exercise the powers conferred by this section if it appears to him that—

   (a) the manager of a contracted out [removal centre] has lost, or is likely to lose, effective control of the centre or of any part of it; or

   (b) it is necessary to do so in the interests of preserving the safety of any person, or of preventing serious damage to any property.

(2) The Secretary of State may appoint a person (to be known as the Controller) to act as manager of the [removal centre] for the period—

   (a) beginning with the time specified in the appointment; and

   (b) ending with the time specified in the notice of termination under subsection (5).

(3) During that period—

   (a) all the functions which would otherwise be exercisable by the manager or the contract monitor are to be exercisable by the Controller;

   (b) the contractor and any sub-contractor of his must do all that he reasonably can to facilitate the exercise by the Controller of his functions; and

   (c) the staff of the [removal centre] must comply with any directions given by the Controller in the exercise of his functions.

(4) The Controller is to have the status of a Crown servant.

(5). If the Secretary of State is satisfied that a Controller is no longer needed for a particular [removal centre], he must (by giving notice to the Controller) terminate his appointment at a time specified in the notice.

(6) As soon as practicable after making an appointment under this section, the Secretary of State must give notice of the appointment to those entitled to notice.

(7) As soon as practicable after terminating an appointment under this section, the Secretary of State must give a copy of the notice of termination to those entitled to notice.

(8) Those entitled to notice are the contractor, the manager, the contract monitor and the Controller.

Amendment

Sub-s (1): in para (a) words "removal centre" in square brackets substituted by the Nationality, Immigration and Asylum Act 2002, s 66(2)(a), (3)(d).

Sub-s (2): words "removal centre" in square brackets substituted by the Nationality, Immigration and Asylum Act 2002, s 66(2)(a), (3)(d).

Sub-s (3): in para (c) words "removal centre" in square brackets substituted by the Nationality, Immigration and Asylum Act 2002, s 66(2)(a), (3)(d).

Sub-s (5): words "removal centre" in square brackets substituted by the Nationality, Immigration and Asylum Act 2002, s 66(2)(a), (3)(d).

152 Visiting Committees and inspections

(1) The Secretary of State must appoint a committee (to be known as the Visiting Committee) for each [removal centre].

(2) The functions of the Visiting Committee for a [removal centre] are to be such as may be prescribed by the [removal centre] rules.

(3) Those rules must include provision—

(a) as to the making of visits to the centre by members of the Visiting Committee;

(b) for the hearing of complaints made by persons detained in the centre;

(c) requiring the making of reports by the Visiting Committee to the Secretary of State.

(4) Every member of the Visiting Committee for a [removal centre] may at any time enter the centre and have free access to every part of it and to every person detained there.

(5) In section 5A of the Prison Act 1952 (which deals with the appointment and functions of Her Majesty's Chief Inspector of Prisons), after subsection (5), insert—

"(5A) Subsections (2) to (5) apply to [removal centres] (as defined by section 147 of the Immigration and Asylum Act 1999 and including any in Scotland) and persons detained in such [removal centres] as they apply to prisons and prisoners."

Amendment

Sub-s (1): words "removal centre" in square brackets substituted by the Nationality, Immigration and Asylum Act 2002, s 66(2)(a), (3)(e).

Sub-s (2): words "removal centre" in square brackets in both places they occur substituted by the Nationality, Immigration and Asylum Act 2002, s 66(2)(a), (3)(e).

Sub-s (4): words "removal centre" in square brackets substituted by the Nationality, Immigration and Asylum Act 2002, s 66(2)(a), (3)(e).

Sub-s (5): in the Prison Act 1952, s 5A (as set out) words "removal centres" in square brackets in both places they occur substituted by the Nationality, Immigration and Asylum Act 2002, s 66(2)(b), (3)(e).

Subordinate Legislation

Detention Centre Rules 2001, SI 2001/238.

153 [Removal centre] rules

(1) The Secretary of State must make rules for the regulation and management of [removal centres].

(2) [Removal centre] rules may, among other things, make provision with respect to the safety, care, activities, discipline and control of detained persons.

Amendment

Section heading: words "Removal centre" in square brackets substituted by the Nationality, Immigration and Asylum Act 2002, s 66(2)(a), (3)(f).

Sub-s (1): words "removal centres" in square brackets substituted by the Nationality, Immigration and Asylum Act 2002, s 66(2)(b), (3)(f).

Sub-s (2): words "Removal centre" in square brackets substituted by the Nationality, Immigration and Asylum Act 2002, s 66(2)(a), (3)(f).

Subordinate Legislation

Detention Centre Rules 2001, SI 2001/238.

[153A Detained persons: national minimum wage]

[A detained person does not qualify for the national minimum wage in respect of work which he does in pursuance of removal centre rules.]

Amendment

Inserted by the Immigration, Asylum and Nationality Act 2006, s 59(1), as from 31 August 2006: see SI 2006/2226, art 3, Sch 1.

Custody and movement of detained persons

154 Detainee custody officers

(1) On an application made to him under this section, the Secretary of State may certify that the applicant—

   (a)   is authorised to perform escort functions; or

   (b)   is authorised to perform both escort functions and custodial functions.

(2) The Secretary of State may not issue a certificate of authorisation unless he is satisfied that the applicant—

   (a)   is a fit and proper person to perform the functions to be authorised; and

   (b)   has received training to such standard as the Secretary of State considers appropriate for the performance of those functions.

(3) A certificate of authorisation continues in force until such date, or the occurrence of such event, as may be specified in the certificate but may be suspended or revoked under paragraph 7 of Schedule 11.

(4) A certificate which authorises the performance of both escort functions and custodial functions may specify one date or event for one of those functions and a different date or event for the other.

[(5) The Secretary of State may confer functions of detainee custody officers on prison officers or prisoner custody officers.]

(6) A prison officer acting under arrangements made under subsection (5) has all the powers, authority, protection and privileges of a constable.

(7) Schedule 11 makes further provision about detainee custody officers.

Amendment

Sub-s (5): substituted by the Nationality, Immigration and Asylum Act 2002, s 65(1).

155 Custodial functions and discipline etc at [removal centres]

(1) Custodial functions may be discharged at a [removal centre] only by—

   (a)   a detainee custody officer authorised, in accordance with section 154(1), to perform such functions; or

(b)   a prison officer, or a certified prisoner custody officer, exercising functions in relation to the [removal centre]—

    (i)   in accordance with arrangements made under section 154(5); or

    (ii)   as a result of a contract entered into under section 150(1)(b).

(2)   Schedule 12 makes provision with respect to discipline and other matters at [removal centres] and short-term holding facilities [and in pre-departure accommodation].

Amendment

Section heading: words "removal centres" in square brackets substituted by the Nationality, Immigration and Asylum Act 2002, s 66(2)(b), (3)(g).

Sub-s (1): words "removal centre" in square brackets in both places they occur substituted by the Nationality, Immigration and Asylum Act 2002, s 66(2)(a), (3)(g).

Sub-s (2): words "removal centres" in square brackets substituted by the Nationality, Immigration and Asylum Act 2002, s 66(2)(b), (3)(g).

Sub-s (2): words "and in pre-departure accommodation" inserted by the Immigration Act 2014, s 6(1), (3), as from 28 July 2014: see SI 2014/1820.

156 Arrangements for the provision of escorts and custody

(1)   The Secretary of State may make arrangements for—

(a)   the delivery of detained persons to premises in which they may lawfully be detained;

(b)   the delivery of persons from any such premises for the purposes of their removal from the United Kingdom in accordance with directions given under the 1971 Act or this Act;

(c)   the custody of detained persons who are temporarily outside such premises;

(d)   the custody of detained persons held on the premises of any court.

(2)   Escort arrangements may provide for functions under the arrangements to be performed, in such cases as may be determined by or under the arrangements, by detainee custody officers.

(3)   "Court" includes—

    [(a)   the First-tier Tribunal;

    (b)   the Upper Tribunal; and]

    (c)   the Commission.

(4)   Escort arrangements may include entering into contracts with other persons for the provision by them of—

(a)   detainee custody officers; or

(b)   prisoner custody officers who are certified under section 89 of the Criminal Justice Act 1991, or section 114 or 122 of the Criminal Justice and Public Order Act 1994, to perform escort functions.

(5)   Schedule 13 makes further provision about escort arrangements.

(6)   A person responsible for performing a function of a kind mentioned in subsection (1), in accordance with a transfer direction, complies with the direction if he does all that he reasonably can to secure that the function is performed by a person acting in accordance with escort arrangements.

(7)   "Transfer direction" means—

    [(a)]   a transfer direction given under—

        [(i)]   section 48 of the Mental Health Act 1983 . . . (removal to hospital of, among others, persons detained under the 1971 Act); or

        [(ii)]   in Northern Ireland, article 54 of the Mental Health (Northern Ireland) Order 1986 (provision corresponding to section 48 of the 1983 Act); [or

    (b)   a transfer for treatment direction given under section 136 of the Mental Health (Care and Treatment) (Scotland) Act 2003 as applied by article 13 of the Mental Health (Care and Treatment) (Scotland) Act 2003 (Consequential Provisions) Order 2005].

Sub-s (3): paras (a), (b) substituted, for para (a), by SI 2010/21, art 5(1), Sch 1, para 19.

Sub-s (7): para (a) numbered as such by SI 2005/2078, art 15, Sch 1, para 5(a).

Sub-s (7): para (a)(i), (ii) numbered as such by SI 2005/2078, art 15, Sch 1, para 5(b).

Sub-s (7): in para (a)(i) words omitted repealed by SI 2005/2078, art 15, Sch 1, para 5(c).

Sub-s (7): para (b) inserted by SI 2005/2078, art 15, Sch 1, para 5(d).

157 Short-term holding facilities

(1) The Secretary of State may by regulations extend any provision made by or under this Part in relation to [removal centres] (other than one mentioned in subsection (2)) to short-term holding facilities.

(2) Subsection (1) does not apply to section 150.

(3) The Secretary of State may make rules for the regulation and management of short-term holding facilities.

Amendment

Sub-s (1): words "removal centres" in square brackets substituted by the Nationality, Immigration and Asylum Act 2002, s 66(2)(b), (3)(h).

Subordinate Legislation

Immigration (Short-term Holding Facilities) Regulations 2002, SI 2002/2538.

[157A Pre-departure accommodation

(1) The following provisions of this Part apply to pre-departure accommodation as they apply to removal centres—

(a) section 149 (contracting out of certain removal centres);

(b) section 150 (contracting out functions at directly managed removal centres);

(c) section 151 (intervention by Secretary of State).

(2) In the application of those provisions to pre-departure accommodation—

(a) references to a removal centre contract are to be read as a contract made under section 149(1) for the provision or running of pre-departure accommodation;

(b) references to a contracted out removal centre are to be read as references to pre-departure accommodation in relation to which a contract under section 149(1) is in force;

(c) references to a directly managed removal centre are to be read as references to pre-departure accommodation in relation to which there is no contract under section 149(1) in force;

(d) references to removal centre rules are to be read as references to rules made under subsection (4).

(3) The Secretary of State may by regulations extend to pre-departure accommodation any other provision made by or under this Part in relation to removal centres.

(4) The Secretary of State may make rules for the regulation and management of pre-departure accommodation.]

Amendment

Inserted by the Immigration Act 2014, s 6(1), (4), as from 28 July 2014: see SI 2014/1820.

Miscellaneous

158 Wrongful disclosure of information

(1) A person who is or has been employed (whether as a detainee custody officer, prisoner custody officer or otherwise)—

(a) in accordance with escort arrangements,

(b) at a contracted out [removal centre], or

(c) to perform contracted out functions at a directly managed [removal centre],

is guilty of an offence if he discloses, otherwise than in the course of his duty or as authorised by the Secretary of State, any information which he acquired in the course of his employment and which relates to a particular detained person.

(2) A person guilty of such an offence is liable—

  (a) on conviction on indictment, to imprisonment for a term not exceeding two years or to a fine or to both;

  (b) on summary conviction, to imprisonment for a term not exceeding six months or to a fine not exceeding the statutory maximum or to both.

(3) "Contracted out functions" means functions which, as the result of a contract entered into under section 150, fall to be performed by detainee custody officers or certified prisoner custody officers.

Amendment

Sub-s (1): in paras (b), (c) words "removal centre" in square brackets substituted by the Nationality, Immigration and Asylum Act 2002, s 66(2)(a), (3)(i).

159 Power of constable to act outside his jurisdiction

(1) For the purpose of taking a person to or from a [removal centre] under the order of any authority competent to give the order, a constable may act outside the area of his jurisdiction.

(2) When acting under this section, the constable concerned retains all the powers, authority, protection and privileges of his office.

Amendment

Sub-s (1): words "removal centre" in square brackets substituted by the Nationality, Immigration and Asylum Act 2002, s 66(2)(a), (3)(i).

160–163

PART IX
REGISTRAR'S CERTIFICATES: PROCEDURE

(*Amend the Marriage Act 1949, ss 26, 27, 31, repeal s 32 of that Act and insert ss 28A, 31A thereof.*)

164, 165

PART X
MISCELLANEOUS AND SUPPLEMENTAL

(*S 164 amends the Prosecution of Offences Act 1985, s 3; s 165 inserts the Immigration Act 1971, s 31A.*)

166 Regulations and orders

(1) Any power to make rules, regulations or orders conferred by this Act is exercisable by statutory instrument.

(2) But subsection (1) does not apply in relation to [orders made under section 90(1),] rules made under paragraph 1 of Schedule 5 or immigration rules.

(3) Any statutory instrument made as a result of subsection (1) may—

  (a) contain such incidental, supplemental, consequential and transitional provision as the person making it considers appropriate;

    (b) make different provision for different cases or descriptions of case; and

    (c) make different provision for different areas.

(4) No order is to be made under—

    (a) section 20,

    (b) section 21,

    (c) section 31(10),

    (d) section 86(2),

    [(da) section 86A(3),]

    (e) . . .

    (f) section 97(3),

    (g) section 143(15), or

    (h) paragraph 4 of Schedule 5,

unless a draft of the order has been laid before Parliament and approved by a resolution of each House.

(5) No regulations are to be made under—

    [(za) section 4(5),]

    (a) section 9,

    (b) section 46(8),

    (c) section 53, or

    (d) section 144,

unless a draft of the regulations has been laid before Parliament and approved by a resolution of each House.

(6) Any statutory instrument made under this Act, apart from one made—

    (a) under any of the provisions mentioned in subsection (4) or (5), or

    (b) under section 24(3)[, 24A(3)] or 170(4) or (7),

shall be subject to annulment by a resolution of either House of Parliament.

Amendment

Sub-s (2): words "orders made under section 90(1)," in square brackets inserted by the Asylum and Immigration (Treatment of Claimants, etc) Act 2004, s 41(5).

Sub-s (4): para (da) inserted by the Legal Services Act 2007, s 186, Sch 18, Pt 2, paras 9, 16. Date in force: 1 April 2011: see SI 2011/720, art 2(c).

Sub-s (4): para (e) repealed by the Nationality, Immigration and Asylum Act 2002, ss 61(b), 161, Sch 9.

Sub-s (5): para (za) inserted by the Asylum and Immigration (Treatment of Claimants, etc) Act 2004, s 10(2), (6).

Sub-s (6): in para (b) reference to ", 24A(3)" in square brackets inserted by the Civil Partnership Act 2004, s 261(1), Sch 27, para 163.

167 Interpretation

(1) In this Act—

"the 1971 Act" means the Immigration Act 1971;

"adjudicator" (except in Part VI) means an adjudicator appointed under section 57;

"Chief Adjudicator" means the person appointed as Chief Adjudicator under section 57(2);

"claim for asylum" (except in Parts V and VI and section 141) means a claim that it would be contrary to the United Kingdom's obligations under the Refugee Convention for the claimant to be removed from, or required to leave, the United Kingdom;

"the Commission" means the Special Immigration Appeals Commission;

"country" includes any territory;

"EEA State" means a State which is a Contracting Party to the Agreement on the European Economic Area signed at Oporto on 2nd May 1992 as it has effect for the time being;

"the Human Rights Convention" means the Convention for the Protection of Human Rights and Fundamental Freedoms, agreed by the Council of Europe at Rome on 4th November 1950 as it has effect for the time being in relation to the United Kingdom;

. . .

(2) The following expressions have the same meaning as in the 1971 Act—

"certificate of entitlement";

"entry clearance";

"illegal entrant";

"immigration officer";

"immigration rules";

"port";

"United Kingdom passport";

"work permit".

Amendment

Sub-s (1): definition "the Immigration Acts" (omitted) repealed by the Immigration, Asylum and Nationality Act 2006, ss 61, 64(3)(b), Sch 3.

168 Expenditure and receipts

(1) There is to be paid out of money provided by Parliament—

(a) any expenditure incurred by the Secretary of State or the Lord Chancellor in consequence of this Act; and

(b) any increase attributable to this Act in the sums so payable by virtue of any other Act.

(2) Sums received by the Secretary of State under section 5, 32, 40, 112 or 113 or by the Lord Chancellor under section 48(4) or 49(4) must be paid into the Consolidated Fund.

169 Minor and consequential amendments, transitional provisions and repeals

(1) Schedule 14 makes minor and consequential amendments.

(2) Schedule 15 contains transitional provisions and savings.

(3) The enactments set out in Schedule 16 are repealed.

170 Short title, commencement and extent

(1) This Act may be cited as the Immigration and Asylum Act 1999.

(2) Subsections (1) and (2) of section 115 come into force on the day on which the first regulations made under Schedule 8 come into force.

(3) The following provisions come into force on the passing of this Act—

(a) section 4;

(b) section 9;

(c) section 15;

(d) section 27;

(e) section 31;

(f) section 94;

(g) section 95(13);

(h) section 99(4) and (5);

(i) sections 105 to 109;
(j) section 110(1), (2) and (8) (so far as relating to subsections (1) and (2));
(k) section 111;
(l) section 124;
(m) section 140;
(n) section 145;
(o) section 146(1);
(p) sections 166 to 168;
(q) this section;
(r) Schedule 9;
(s) paragraphs 62(2), 73, 78, 79, 81, 82, 87, 88 and 102 of Schedule 14; paragraphs 2 and 13 of Schedule 15.
(t)

(4) The other provisions of this Act, except section 10 and paragraph 12 of Schedule 15 (which come into force in accordance with section 9), come into force on such day as the Secretary of State may by order appoint.

(5) Different days may be appointed for different purposes.

(6) This Act extends to Northern Ireland.

(7) Her Majesty may by Order in Council direct that any of the provisions of this Act are to extend, with such modifications (if any) as appear to Her Majesty to be appropriate, to any of the Channel Islands or the Isle of Man.

Subordinate Legislation

Immigration and Asylum Act 1999 (Commencement No 1) Order 1999, SI 1999/3190; Immigration and Asylum Act 1999 (Commencement No 2 and Transitional Provisions) Order 2000, SI 2000/168; Immigration and Asylum Act 1999 (Commencement No 3) Order 2000, SI 2000/464; Immigration and Asylum Act 1999 (Commencement No 4) Order 2000, SI 2000/1282; Immigration and Asylum Act 1999 (Commencement No 5 and Transitional Provisions) Order 2000, SI 2000/1985; Immigration and Asylum Act 1999 (Commencement No 9) Order 2001, SI 2001/239; Immigration and Asylum Act 1999 (Commencement No 10) Order 2001, SI 2001/1394; Immigration and Asylum Act 1999 (Commencement No 11) Order 2002, SI 2002/2815; Immigration and Asylum Act 1999 (Commencement No 12) Order 2003, SI 2003/2; Immigration and Asylum Act 1999 (Commencement No 13) Order 2003, SI 2003/758; Immigration and Asylum Act 1999 (Jersey) Order 2003, SI 2003/1252; Immigration and Asylum Act 1999 (Commencement No 14) Order 2003, SI 2003/1469; Immigration and Asylum Act 1999 (Commencement No 15) Order 2003, SI 2003/1862; Immigration and Asylum Act 1999 (Guernsey) Order 2003, SI 2003/2900; Immigration and Asylum Act 1999 (Commencement No 16) Order 2004, SI 2004/2997; Immigration (Isle of Man) Order 2008, SI 2008/680; Immigration (Guernsey) Order 2011, SI 2011/2444; Immigration (Jersey) Order 2012, SI 2012/1763.

SCHEDULE 1
SALE OF TRANSPORTERS

Sections 37(6) and 42(8)

Leave of court required

1
(1) The sale of a transporter requires the leave of the court.
(2) The court is not to give its leave except on proof—
(a) that the penalty or *charge* is or was due;
(b) that the person liable to pay it or any connected expenses has failed to do so; and
(c) that the transporter which the Secretary of State seeks leave to sell is liable to sale.

Notice of proposed sale

2

Before applying for leave to sell a transporter, the Secretary of State must take such steps as may be prescribed—

(a) for bringing the proposed sale to the notice of persons whose interests may be affected by a decision of the court to grant leave; and

(b) for affording to any such person an opportunity of becoming a party to the proceedings if the Secretary of State applies for leave.

[2A

Where the owner of a transporter is a party to an application for leave to sell it, in determining whether to give leave the court shall consider—

(a) the extent of any hardship likely to be caused by sale,

(b) the extent (if any) to which the owner is responsible for the matters in respect of which the penalty notice was issued, and

(c) any other matter which appears to the court to be relevant (whether specific to the circumstances of the case or of a general nature).]

Duty to obtain best price

3

If leave for sale is given, the Secretary of State must secure that the transporter is sold for the best price that can reasonably be obtained.

Effect of failure to comply with paragraph 2 or 3

4

Failure to comply with any requirement of paragraph 2 or 3 in respect of any sale—

(a) is actionable against the Secretary of State at the suit of any person suffering loss in consequence of the sale; but

(b) after the sale has taken place, does not affect its validity.

Application of proceeds of sale

5

(1) Any proceeds of sale arising from a sale under section 37 or 42 must be applied—

(a) in making prescribed payments; and

(b) in accordance with such provision as to priority of payments as may be prescribed.

(2) The regulations may, in particular, provide for proceeds of sale to be applied in payment—

(a) of customs or excise duty,

(b) of value added tax,

(c) of expenses incurred by the Secretary of State,

(d) of any penalty or charge which the court has found to be due,

(e) in the case of the sale of an aircraft, of charges due as a result of regulations made under section 73 of the Civil Aviation Act 1982,

(f) of any surplus to or among the person or persons whose interests in the transporter have been divested as a result of the sale,

but not necessarily in that order of priority.

Amendment

Para 1: in sub-para (2)(a) words "or charge" in italics repealed by the Nationality, Immigration and Asylum Act 2002, ss 125, 161, Sch 8, paras 1, 16(1), (2), Sch 9.

Date in force (for the purposes of clandestine entrants who arrive in the United Kingdom concealed in a vehicle or a rail freight wagon): 8 December 2002 (except in relation to a penalty notice issued to a person before that date): see SI 2002/2811, arts 2, 4, Schedule.

Date in force (for remaining purposes): to be appointed: see the Nationality, Immigration and Asylum Act 2002, s 162(1).

Para 2A: inserted by the Nationality, Immigration and Asylum Act 2002, s 125, Sch 8, paras 1, 16(1), (3).

Date in force (for the purposes of clandestine entrants who arrive in the United Kingdom concealed in a vehicle or a rail freight wagon): 8 December 2002 (except in relation to a penalty notice issued to a person before that date): see SI 2002/2811, arts 2, 4, Schedule.

Date in force (for the purposes of clandestine entrants who pass, or attempt to pass, through immigration control concealed in a vehicle): 11 May 2012: see SI 2012/1263, art 2.

Date in force (for remaining purposes): to be appointed: see the Nationality, Immigration and Asylum Act 2002, s 162(1).

Para 5: in sub-para (1) words "or 42" in italics repealed by the Nationality, Immigration and Asylum Act 2002, ss 125, 161 Sch 8, paras 1, 16(1), (4), Sch 9.

Date in force (for the purposes of clandestine entrants who arrive in the United Kingdom concealed in a vehicle or a rail freight wagon): 8 December 2002 (except in relation to a penalty notice issued to a person before that date): see SI 2002/2811, arts 2, 4, Schedule.

Date in force (for remaining purposes): to be appointed: see the Nationality, Immigration and Asylum Act 2002, s 162(1).

Para 5: in sub-para (2)(d) words "or charge" in italics repealed by the Nationality, Immigration and Asylum Act 2002, ss 125, 161, Sch 8, paras 1, 16(1), (5), Sch 9.

Date in force (for the purposes of clandestine entrants who arrive in the United Kingdom concealed in a vehicle or a rail freight wagon): 8 December 2002 (except in relation to a penalty notice issued to a person before that date): see SI 2002/2811, arts 2, 4, Schedule.

Date in force (for remaining purposes): to be appointed: see the Nationality, Immigration and Asylum Act 2002, s 162(1).

Subordinate Legislation

Carriers' Liability Regulations 2002, SI 2002/2817.

SCHEDULES 2–4

(Repealed by the Nationality, Immigration and Asylum Act 2002, ss 114(1), (2), 161, Sch 9; for transitional provisions see Sch 6 thereto.)

SCHEDULE 5

THE IMMIGRATION SERVICES COMMISSIONER

Section 83

PART I

REGULATORY FUNCTIONS

The Commissioner's rules

1

(1) The Commissioner may make rules regulating any aspect of the professional practice, conduct or discipline of—

    (a)   registered persons, and

    [(b)   those acting on behalf of registered persons,]

in connection with the provision of immigration advice or immigration services.

(2) Before making or altering any rules, the Commissioner must consult such persons appearing to him to represent the views of persons engaged in the provision of immigration advice or immigration services as he considers appropriate.

(3) In determining whether a registered person is competent or otherwise fit to provide immigration advice or immigration services, the Commissioner may take into account any breach of the rules by—

(a) that person; and

[(b) any person acting on behalf of that person].

(4) The rules may, among other things, make provision requiring the keeping of accounts or the obtaining of indemnity insurance.

2

(1) The Commissioner's rules must be made or altered by an instrument in writing.

(2) Such an instrument must specify that it is made under this Schedule.

(3) Immediately after such an instrument is made, it must be printed and made available to the public.

(4) The Commissioner may charge a reasonable fee for providing a person with a copy of the instrument.

(5) A person is not to be taken to have contravened a rule made by the Commissioner if he shows that at the time of the alleged contravention the instrument containing the rule had not been made available in accordance with this paragraph.

(6) The production of a printed copy of an instrument purporting to be made by the Commissioner on which is endorsed a certificate signed by an officer of the Commissioner authorised by him for that purpose and stating—

(a) that the instrument was made by the Commissioner,

(b) that the copy is a true copy of the instrument, and

(c) that on a specified date the instrument was made available to the public in accordance with this paragraph,

is evidence (or in Scotland sufficient evidence) of the facts stated in the certificate.

(7) A certificate purporting to be signed as mentioned in sub-paragraph (6) is to be treated as having been properly signed unless the contrary is shown.

(8) A person who wishes in any legal proceedings to rely on an instrument containing the Commissioner's rules may require him to endorse a copy of the instrument with a certificate of the kind mentioned in sub-paragraph (6).

Code of Standards

3

(1) The Commissioner must prepare and issue a code setting standards of conduct which those to whom the code applies are expected to meet.

(2) The code is to be known as the Code of Standards but is referred to in this Schedule as "the Code".

(3) The Code is to apply to any person providing immigration advice or immigration services other than—

(a) a person who is authorised by a designated professional body to practise as a member of the profession whose members are regulated by that body;

[(aa) a person who is authorised by a designated qualifying regulator to provide immigration advice or immigration services;]

[(b) a person who is acting on behalf of a person who is within paragraph (a) [or (aa)];]

(c) a person mentioned in section 84(6).

(4) It is the duty of any person to whom the Code applies to comply with its provisions in providing immigration advice or immigration services.

(5) If the Commissioner alters the Code, he must re-issue it.

(6) Before issuing the Code or altering it, the Commissioner must consult—

(a) each of the designated professional bodies;

[(aa) each of the designated qualifying regulators;]

(b) . . .

(c) the Lord President of the Court of Session;

(d) the Lord Chief Justice of Northern Ireland; and

(e) such other persons appearing to him to represent the views of persons engaged in the provision of immigration advice or immigration services as he considers appropriate.

(7) The Commissioner must publish the Code in such form and manner as the Secretary of State may direct.

Extension of scope of the Code

4

(1) The Secretary of State may by order provide for the provisions of the Code, or such provisions of the Code as may be specified by the order, to apply to—

(a) persons authorised by any designated professional body to practise as a member of the profession whose members are regulated by that body; and

[(b) persons acting on behalf of persons who are within paragraph (a)].

(2) If the Secretary of State is proposing to act under sub-paragraph (1) he must, before doing so, consult—

(a) the Commissioner;

(b) . . .

(c) the [Scottish Legal Complaints Commission], if the proposed order would affect a designated professional body in Scotland;

(d) the lay observers appointed under Article 42 of the Solicitors (Northern Ireland) Order 1976, if the proposed order would affect a designated professional body in Northern Ireland.

(3) An order under sub-paragraph (1) requires the approval of—

(a) the [Department of Justice in Northern Ireland], if it affects a designated professional body in . . . Northern Ireland;

(b) the Scottish Ministers, if it affects a designated professional body in Scotland.

[(4) Before deciding whether or not to give its approval under sub-paragraph (3)(a), the Department of Justice in Northern Ireland must consult the Lord Chief Justice of Northern Ireland.]

(5) Before deciding whether or not to give their approval under sub-paragraph (3)(b), the Scottish Ministers must consult the Lord President of the Court of Session.

[Inspections]

4A

The Commissioner may carry out inspections of the activities and businesses of registered persons.]

Investigation of complaints

5

(1) The Commissioner must establish a scheme ("the complaints scheme") for the investigation by him of relevant complaints made to him in accordance with the provisions of the scheme.

(2) Before establishing the scheme or altering it, the Commissioner must consult—

(a) each of the designated professional bodies; and

(b) such other persons appearing to him to represent the views of persons engaged in the provision of immigration advice or immigration services as he considers appropriate.

(3) A complaint is a relevant complaint if it relates to—

(a) the competence or fitness of a person to provide immigration advice or immigration services,

(b) the competence or fitness of a person [acting on behalf of] a person providing immigration advice or immigration services,

(c) an alleged breach of the Code,

(d) an alleged breach of one or more of the Commissioner's rules by a person to whom they apply, or

[(e) an alleged breach of a rule of a relevant regulatory body,]

[but not if the complaint is excluded by sub-paragraph (3A)].

[(3A) A complaint is excluded if—

(a) it relates to a person who is excluded from the application of subsection (1) of section 84 by subsection (6) of that section, or

(b) it relates to a person within section 84(2)[(ba).]

(4) The Commissioner may, on his own initiative, investigate any matter which he would have power to investigate on a complaint made under the complaints scheme.

(5) In investigating any such matter on his own initiative, the Commissioner must proceed as if his investigation were being conducted in response to a complaint made under the scheme.

6

(1) The complaints scheme must provide for a person who is the subject of an investigation under the scheme to be given a reasonable opportunity to make representations to the Commissioner.

(2) Any person who is the subject of an investigation under the scheme must—

(a) take such steps as are reasonably required to assist the Commissioner in his investigation; and

(b) comply with any reasonable requirement imposed on him by the Commissioner.

(3) If a person fails to comply with sub-paragraph (2)(a) or with a requirement imposed under sub-paragraph (2)(b) the Commissioner may—

(a) in the case of a registered person, cancel his registration;

(b) in the case of a person certified by the Commissioner as exempt under section 84(4)(a), withdraw his exemption; or

[(c) in any other case, refer the matter to any relevant regulatory body].

Power to enter premises

7

(1) This paragraph applies if—

(a) the Commissioner is investigating a complaint under the complaints scheme;

(b) the complaint falls within paragraph 5(3)(a), (b)[, (c)] or (d); and

(c) there are reasonable grounds for believing that particular premises are being used in connection with the provision of immigration advice or immigration services by a [registered or exempt person].

[(1A) This paragraph also applies if the Commissioner is investigating a matter under paragraph 5(5) and—

    (a) the matter is of a kind described in paragraph 5(3)(a), (b)[, (c)] or (d) (for which purpose a reference to an allegation shall be treated as a reference to a suspicion of the Commissioner), and

    (b) there are reasonable grounds for believing that particular premises are being used in connection with the provision of immigration advice or immigration services by a [registered or exempt person].]

(2) The Commissioner, or a member of his staff authorised in writing by him, may enter the premises at reasonable hours.

(3) Sub-paragraph (2) does not apply to premises to the extent to which they constitute a private residence.

(4) A person exercising the power given by sub-paragraph (2) ("the investigating officer") may—

    (a) take with him such equipment as appears to him to be necessary;

    (b) require any person on the premises—

        (i) to produce any document which he considers relates to any matter relevant to the investigation; and

        (ii) if the document is produced, to provide an explanation of it;

    (c) require any person to state, to the best of his knowledge and belief, where any such document is to be found;

    (d) take copies of, or extracts from, any document which is produced;

    (e) require any information which is held in a computer and is accessible from the premises and which the investigating officer considers relates to any matter relevant to the investigation, to be produced in a form—

        (i) in which it can be taken away; and

        (ii) in which it is visible and legible.

(5) Instead of exercising the power under sub-paragraph (2), the Commissioner may require such person as he may determine ("his agent") to make a report on the provision of immigration advice or immigration services from the premises.

(6) If the Commissioner so determines, his agent may exercise the power conferred by sub-paragraph (2) as if he were a member of the Commissioner's staff appropriately authorised.

(7) If a registered person fails without reasonable excuse to allow access under sub-paragraph (2) or (6) to any premises under his occupation or control, the Commissioner may cancel his registration.

(8) The Commissioner may also cancel the registration of a registered person who—

    (a) without reasonable excuse fails to comply with a requirement imposed on him under sub-paragraph (4);

    (b) intentionally delays or obstructs any person exercising functions under this paragraph; or

    (c) fails to take reasonable steps to prevent an employee of his from obstructing any person exercising such functions.

[(9) Sub-paragraphs (7) and (8) shall apply to an exempt person as they apply to a registered person, but with a reference to cancellation of registration being treated as a reference to withdrawal of exemption.

[(10) In this paragraph "exempt person" means a person certified by the Commissioner as exempt under section 84(4)(a).]

Appendix 1 — UK Immigration Statutes

Determination of complaints

8

(1) On determining a complaint under the complaints scheme, the Commissioner must give his decision in a written statement.

(2) The statement must include the Commissioner's reasons for his decision.

(3) A copy of the statement must be given by the Commissioner to—

    (a)   the person who made the complaint; and

    (b)   the person who is the subject of the complaint.

9

(1) On determining a complaint under the complaints scheme, the Commissioner may—

    (a)   if the person to whom the complaint relates is a registered person [or is acting on behalf of] a registered person, record the complaint and the decision on it for consideration when that registered person next applies for his registration to be continued;

    (b)   if the person to whom the complaint relates is a registered person [or is acting on behalf of] a registered person and the Commissioner considers the matter sufficiently serious to require immediate action, require that registered person to apply for continued registration without delay;

    [(c) refer the complaint and his decision on it to a relevant regulatory body;]

    (d)   if the person to whom the complaint relates is certified by the Commissioner as exempt under section 84(4)(a) or is employed by, or working under the supervision of, such a person, consider whether to withdraw that person's exemption;

    (e)   lay before the [First-tier Tribunal] a disciplinary charge against a relevant person.

(2) Sub-paragraph (3) applies if—

    (a)   the [First-tier Tribunal] is considering a disciplinary charge against a relevant person; and

    (b)   the Commissioner asks it to exercise its powers under that sub-paragraph.

(3) The [First-tier Tribunal] may give directions (which are to have effect while it is dealing with the charge)—

    [(a) imposing restrictions on the provision of immigration advice or immigration services by the relevant person or by a person acting on his behalf or under his supervision;

    (b)   prohibiting the provision of immigration advice or immigration services by the relevant person or a person acting on his behalf or under his supervision].

(4) "Relevant person" means a person providing immigration advice or immigration services who is—

    (a)   a registered person;

    [(b) a person acting on behalf of a registered person;]

    (e)   a person certified by the Commissioner as exempt under section 84(4)(a);

    (f)   a person to whom section 84(4)(d) applies; or

    (g)   a person employed by, or working under the supervision of, a person to whom paragraph (e) or (f) applies.

Complaints referred to designated professional bodies

10

(1) This paragraph applies if the Commissioner refers a complaint to a designated professional body under paragraph 9(1)(c).

(2) The Commissioner may give directions setting a timetable to be followed by the designated professional body—

    (a)   in considering the complaint; and

    (b)   if appropriate, in taking disciplinary proceedings in connection with the complaint.

(3) In making his annual report to the Secretary of State under paragraph 21, the Commissioner must take into account any failure of a designated professional body to comply (whether wholly or in part) with directions given to it under this paragraph.

(4) Sub-paragraph (5) applies if the Commissioner or the Secretary of State considers that a designated professional body has persistently failed to comply with directions given to it under this paragraph.

(5) The Commissioner must take the failure into account in determining whether to make a report under section 86(9)(b) and the Secretary of State must take it into account in determining whether to make an order under section 86(2).

Amendment

Para 1: sub-para (1)(b) substituted by the Asylum and Immigration (Treatment of Claimants, etc) Act 2004, s 37(5)(a).

Para 1: sub-para (3)(b) substituted by the Asylum and Immigration (Treatment of Claimants, etc) Act 2004, s 37(5)(b).

Para 3: sub-para (3)(aa) inserted by the Legal Services Act 2007, s 186, Sch 18, Pt 2, paras 9, 17(1), (2)(a). Date in force: 1 April 2011: see SI 2011/720, art 2(c).

Para 3: sub-para (3)(b) substituted by the Asylum and Immigration (Treatment of Claimants, etc) Act 2004, s 37(5)(c).

Para 3: in sub-para (3)(b) words "or (aa)" in square brackets inserted by the Legal Services Act 2007, s 186, Sch 18, Pt 2, paras 9, 17(1), (2)(b). Date in force: 1 April 2011: see SI 2011/720, art 2(c).

Para 3: sub-para (6)(aa) inserted by the Legal Services Act 2007, s 186, Sch 18, Pt 2, paras 9, 17(1), (2)(c). Date in force: 1 April 2011: see SI 2011/720, art 2(c).

Para 3: sub-para (6)(b) repealed by the Legal Services Act 2007, ss 186, 210, Sch 18, Pt 2, paras 9, 17(1), (2)(d), Sch 23.

Para 4: sub-para (1)(b) substituted by the Asylum and Immigration (Treatment of Claimants, etc) Act 2004, s 37(5)(d).

Para 4: sub-para (2)(b) repealed by the Legal Services Act 2007, ss 186, 210, Sch 18, Pt 2, paras 9, 17(1), (3)(a), Sch 23.

Para 4: in sub para (2)(c) words "Scottish Legal Complaints Commission" in square brackets substituted by the Legal Services Act 2007, s 196(2)(b).

Para 4: in sub-para (3)(a) words "Department of Justice in Northern Ireland" in square brackets substituted by SI 2012/2595, art 9(1), (5)(a). Date in force: 18 October 2012: see SI 2012/2595, art 1(2); for transitional provisions see arts 24–28 thereof.

Para 4: in sub-para (3)(a) words omitted repealed by the Legal Services Act 2007, ss 186, 210, Sch 18, Pt 2, paras 9, 17(1), (3)(b), Sch 23.

Para 4: sub-para (4) substituted by SI 2012/2595, art 9(1), (5)(b). Date in force: 18 October 2012: see SI 2012/2595, art 1(2); for transitional provisions see arts 24–28 thereof.

Para 4A: inserted by the Immigration Act 2014, s 63, Sch 7, paras 1, 6, as from 28 July 2014: see SI 2014/1820.

Para 5: in sub-para (3)(b) words "acting on behalf of" in square brackets substituted by the Asylum and Immigration (Treatment of Claimants, etc) Act 2004, s 37(5)(e).

Para 5: sub-para (3)(e) substituted by the Asylum and Immigration (Treatment of Claimants, etc) Act 2004, s 37(5)(f).

Para 5: in sub-para (3) words "but not if the complaint is excluded by sub-paragraph (3A)" in square brackets substituted by the Legal Services Act 2007, s 186, Sch 18, Pt 2, paras 9, 17(1), (4)(a). Date in force: 1 April 2011: see SI 2011/720, art 2(c).

Para 5: sub-para (3A) inserted by the Legal Services Act 2007, s 186, Sch 18, Pt 2, paras 9, 17(1), (4)(b). Date in force: 1 April 2011: see SI 2011/720, art 2(c).

Para 6: sub-para (3)(c) substituted by the Asylum and Immigration (Treatment of Claimants, etc) Act 2004, s 37(5)(g).

Para 7: in sub-para (1)(b) reference to ", (c)" in square brackets inserted by the Asylum and Immigration (Treatment of Claimants, etc) Act 2004, s 38(2)(a).

Para 7: in sub-para (1)(c) words "registered or exempt person" in square brackets substituted by the Asylum and Immigration (Treatment of Claimants, etc) Act 2004, s 38(2)(b).

Para 7: sub-para (1A) inserted by the Nationality, Immigration and Asylum Act 2002, s 140(1).

Para 7: in sub-para (1A)(a) reference to ", (c)" in square brackets inserted by the Asylum and Immigration (Treatment of Claimants, etc) Act 2004, s 38(2)(c).

Para 7: in sub-para (1A)(b) words "registered or exempt person" in square brackets substituted by the Asylum and Immigration (Treatment of Claimants, etc) Act 2004, s 38(2)(d).

Para 7: sub-paras (9), (10) inserted by the Asylum and Immigration (Treatment of Claimants, etc) Act 2004, s 38(2)(e).

Para 9: in sub-paras (1)(a), (b) words "or is acting on behalf of" in square brackets substituted by the Asylum and Immigration (Treatment of Claimants, etc) Act 2004, s 37(5)(h).

Para 9: sub-para (1)(c) substituted by the Asylum and Immigration (Treatment of Claimants, etc) Act 2004, s 37(5)(i).

Para 9: in sub-para (1)(e) words "First-tier Tribunal" in square brackets substituted by SI 2010/22, art 5(1), Sch 2, paras 32, 40.

Para 9: in sub-para (2)(a) words "First-tier Tribunal" in square brackets substituted by SI 2010/22, art 5(1), Sch 2, paras 32, 40.

Para 9: in sub-para (3) words "First-tier Tribunal" in square brackets substituted by SI 2010/22, art 5(1), Sch 2, paras 32, 40.

Para 9: sub-paras (3)(a), (b) substituted by the Asylum and Immigration (Treatment of Claimants, etc) Act 2004, s 37(5)(j).

Para 9: sub-para (4)(d) substituted, for sub-para (4)(b)–(d) as originally enacted, by the Asylum and Immigration (Treatment of Claimants, etc) Act 2004, s 37(5)(k).

PART II
COMMISSIONER'S STATUS, REMUNERATION AND STAFF ETC

Status

11

(1) The Commissioner is to be a corporation sole.

(2) The Commissioner and the members of the Commissioner's staff are not to be regarded as the servants or agents of the Crown or as having any status, privilege or immunity of the Crown.

Period of office

12

(1) The Commissioner—

  (a) is to hold office for a term of five years; but

  (b) may resign at any time by notice in writing given to the Secretary of State.

(2) The Secretary of State may dismiss the Commissioner—

  (a) on the ground of incapacity or misconduct; or

  (b) if he is satisfied—

    (i) that he has been convicted of a criminal offence; or

    (ii) that a bankruptcy order has been made against him, or his estate has been sequestrated, or he has made a composition or arrangement with, or granted a trust deed for, his creditors.

(3) The Commissioner is eligible for re-appointment when his term of office ends.

Terms and conditions of appointment

13

Subject to the provisions of this Schedule, the Commissioner is to hold office on such terms and conditions as the Secretary of State may determine.

Remuneration, expenses and pensions

14

(1) There is to be paid to the Commissioner such remuneration and expenses as the Secretary of State may determine.

(2) The Secretary of State may pay, or provide for the payment of, such pensions, allowances or gratuities to or in respect of the Commissioner as he may determine.

Compensation

15

If a person ceases to be the Commissioner, otherwise than when his term of office ends, and it appears to the Secretary of State that there are special circumstances which make it right for him to receive compensation, the Secretary of State may make a payment to him of such amount as the Secretary of State may determine.

Deputy Commissioner

16

(1) The Secretary of State must appoint a person to act as Deputy Commissioner.

(2) During any vacancy in the office of Commissioner, or at any time when he is unable to discharge his functions, the Deputy Commissioner may act in his place.

(3) Paragraphs 11(2) and 12 to 15 apply to the Deputy Commissioner as they apply to the Commissioner.

Staff

17

(1) Subject to obtaining the approval of the Secretary of State as to numbers and terms and conditions of service, the Commissioner may appoint such staff as he considers appropriate.

(2) Subject to obtaining the approval of the Secretary of State, the Commissioner may pay, or provide for the payment of, such pensions, allowances or gratuities (including by way of compensation for loss of office or employment) to or in respect of his staff as he considers appropriate.

(3) Any functions of the Commissioner may, to the extent authorised by him, be performed by the Deputy Commissioner or any of his staff.

(4) The Employers' Liability (Compulsory Insurance) Act 1969 is not to require insurance to be effected by the Commissioner.

Expenditure

18

The Secretary of State may pay to the Commissioner—

(a) any expenses incurred or to be incurred by the Commissioner in respect of his staff; and

(b) with the approval of the Treasury, such other sums for enabling the Commissioner to perform his functions as the Secretary of State thinks fit.

Receipts

19

(1) Subject to any general or specific directions given to him by the Secretary of State, sums received by the Commissioner in the exercise of his functions must be paid to the Secretary of State.

(2) Sums received by the Secretary of State under this paragraph must be paid into the Consolidated Fund.

(3) The approval of the Treasury is required for any direction given under this paragraph.

Accounts and records

20

(1) The Commissioner must—

    (a) keep proper accounts and proper records in relation to his accounts;

    (b) prepare a statement of accounts for each financial year; and

    (c) send copies of the statement to the Secretary of State and to the Comptroller and Auditor General on or before the specified date.

(2) The statement of accounts must be in such form as the Secretary of State may, with the approval of the Treasury, direct.

(3) The Comptroller and Auditor General must—

    (a) examine, certify and report on each statement received by him under this paragraph; and

    (b) lay copies of each statement and of his report before each House of Parliament.

(4) "Financial year" means the period of 12 months beginning with 1st April.

(5) "Specified date" means—

    (a) 31st August next following the end of the year to which the statement relates; or

    (b) such earlier date after the end of that year as the Treasury may direct.

Annual report

21

(1) The Commissioner must, as soon as is practicable after the end of each financial year, report to the Secretary of State on the performance of his functions in that year.

[(2) The report must, in particular, set out the Commissioner's opinion as to the extent to which each designated professional body has—

    (a) provided effective regulation of its members in their provision of immigration advice or immigration services, and

    (b) complied with requests of the Commissioner for the provision of information.]

(3) The Secretary of State must lay a copy of the report before each House of Parliament.

(4) "Financial year" has the same meaning as in paragraph 20.

Proof of instruments

22

A document purporting to be an instrument issued by the Commissioner and to be signed by or on behalf of the Commissioner is to be received in evidence and treated as such an instrument unless the contrary is shown.

23–25

. . .

Amendment

Para 21: sub-para (2) substituted by the Asylum and Immigration (Treatment of Claimants, etc) Act 2004, s 41(6).

Paras 23–25: amend legislation outside the scope of this work.

SCHEDULE 6
REGISTRATION

Section 85(3)

Applications for registration

1

(1) An application for registration under section 84(2)(a) . . . must—

   (a) be made to the Commissioner in such form and manner, and

   (b) be accompanied by such information and supporting evidence,

as the Commissioner may from time to time determine.

(2) When considering an application for registration, the Commissioner may require the applicant to provide him with such further information or supporting evidence as the Commissioner may reasonably require.

Registration

2

(1) If the Commissioner considers that an applicant for registration is competent and otherwise fit to provide immigration advice and immigration services, he must register the applicant.

(2) Registration may be made so as to have effect—

   (a) only in relation to a specified field of advice or services;

   (b) only in relation to the provision of advice or services to a specified category of person;

   (c) only in relation to the provision of advice or services to a member of a specified category of person; or

   (d) only in specified circumstances.

Review of qualifications

3

(1) At such intervals as the Commissioner may determine, each registered person must submit an application for his registration to be continued.

(2) Different intervals may be fixed by the Commissioner in relation to different registered persons or descriptions of registered person.

(3) An application for continued registration must—

   (a) be made to the Commissioner in such form and manner, and

   (b) be accompanied by such information and supporting evidence, as the Commissioner may from time to time determine.

(4) When considering an application for continued registration, the Commissioner may require the applicant to provide him with such further information or supporting evidence as the Commissioner may reasonably require.

(5) If the Commissioner considers that an applicant for continued registration is no longer competent or is otherwise unfit to provide immigration advice or immigration services, he must cancel the applicant's registration.

(6) Otherwise, the Commissioner must continue the applicant's registration but may, in doing so, vary the registration—

    (a)   so as to make it have limited effect in any of the ways mentioned in paragraph 2(2); or

    (b)   so as to make it have full effect.

(7) If a registered person fails, without reasonable excuse—

    (a)   to make an application for continued registration as required by sub-paragraph (1) or by a direction given by the [First-tier Tribunal] under [section 89(2)(b)], or

    (b)   to provide further information or evidence under sub-paragraph (4),

the Commissioner may cancel the person's registration as from such date as he may determine.

3A

[Variation of registration

The Commissioner may vary a person's registration—

    (a)   so as to make it have limited effect in any of the ways mentioned in paragraph 2(2); or

    (b)   so as to make it have full effect.]

Disqualification of certain persons

4

A person convicted of an offence under section 25 or 26(1)(d) or (g) of the 1971 Act is disqualified for registration of persons on the register.

Fees

5

(1) The Secretary of State may by order specify fees for the registration or continued registration of persons on the register.

(2) No application under paragraph 1 or 3 is to be entertained by the Commissioner unless it is accompanied by the specified fee.

Open registers

6

(1) The register must be made available for inspection by members of the public in a legible form at reasonable hours.

(2) A copy of the register or of any entry in the register must be provided—

    (a)   on payment of a reasonable fee;

    (b)   in written or electronic form; and

    (c)   in a legible form.

(3) Sub-paragraphs (1) and (2) also apply to—

(a)   the record kept by the Commissioner of the persons to whom he has issued a certificate of exemption under section 84(4)(a); and

(b)   the record kept by the Commissioner of the persons against whom there is in force a direction given by the [First-tier Tribunal] under section 89(8).

Amendment

Para 1: in sub-para (1) words omitted repealed by the Asylum and Immigration (Treatment of Claimants, etc) Act 2004, ss 37(6)(a), 47, Sch 4.

Para 3: in sub-para (7)(a) words "First-tier Tribunal" in square brackets substituted by SI 2010/22, art 5(1), Sch 2, paras 32, 41.

Para 3: in sub-para (7)(a) words "section 89(2)(b)" in square brackets substituted by the Asylum and Immigration (Treatment of Claimants, etc) Act 2004, s 37(6)(b).

Para 3A: inserted by the Nationality, Immigration and Asylum Act 2002, s 140(2).

Para 6: in sub-para (3)(b) words "First-tier Tribunal" in square brackets substituted by SI 2010/22, art 5(1), Sch 2, paras 32, 41.

Subordinate Legislation

Immigration Services Commissioner (Application Fee) Order 2011, SI 2011/1366.

SCHEDULE 7

(Repealed by SI 2010/22, art 5(1), Sch 2, paras 32, 42.)

SCHEDULE 8

PROVISION OF SUPPORT: REGULATIONS

Section 95(12)

General regulation-making power

1

The Secretary of State may by regulations make such further provision with respect to the powers conferred on him by section 95 as he considers appropriate.

Determining whether a person is destitute

2

(1) The regulations may provide, in connection with determining whether a person is destitute, for the Secretary of State to take into account, except in such circumstances (if any) as may be prescribed—

(a)   income which the person concerned, or any dependant of his, has or might reasonably be expected to have, and

(b)   support which is, or assets of a prescribed kind which are, or might reasonably be expected to be, available to him or to any dependant of his, otherwise than by way of support provided under section 95.

(2) The regulations may provide that in such circumstances (if any) as may be prescribed, a person is not to be treated as destitute for the purposes of section 95.

Prescribed levels of support

3

The regulations may make provision—

    (a)   as to the circumstances in which the Secretary of State may, as a general rule, be expected to provide support in accordance with prescribed levels or of a prescribed kind;

    (b)   as to the circumstances in which the Secretary of State may, as a general rule, be expected to provide support otherwise than in accordance with the prescribed levels.

Provision of items and services

4

The regulations may make provision for prescribed items or services to be provided or made available to persons receiving support under section 95 for such purposes and in such circumstances as may be prescribed.

Support and assets to be taken into account

5

The regulations may make provision requiring the Secretary of State, except in such circumstances (if any) as may be prescribed, to take into account, when deciding the level or kind of support to be provided—

    (a)   income which the person concerned, or any dependant of his, has or might reasonably be expected to have, and

    (b)   support which is, or assets of a prescribed kind which are, or might reasonably be expected to be, available to him or to any dependant of his, otherwise than by way of support provided under section 95.

Valuation of assets

6

The regulations may make provision as to the valuation of assets.

Breach of conditions

7

The regulations may make provision for the Secretary of State to take into account, when deciding—

    (a)   whether to provide, or to continue to provide, support under section 95, or

    (b)   the level or kind of support to be provided,

the extent to which any condition on which support is being, or has previously been, provided has been complied with.

Suspension or discontinuation of support

8

    (1)   The regulations may make provision for the suspension or discontinuance of support under section 95 in prescribed circumstances (including circumstances in which the Secretary of State would otherwise be under a duty to provide support).

    (2)   The circumstances which may be prescribed include the cessation of residence—

        (a)   in accommodation provided under section 95; or

        (b)   at an address notified to the Secretary of State in accordance with the regulations.

Notice to quit

9

(1) The regulations may provide that if—

(a) as a result of support provided under section 95, a person has a tenancy or a licence to occupy accommodation,

(b) one or more of the conditions mentioned in sub-paragraph (2) are satisfied, and

(c) he is given such notice to quit as may be prescribed by the regulations,

his tenancy or licence is to be treated as ending with the period specified in that notice, regardless of when it could otherwise be brought to an end.

(2) The conditions are that—

(a) the support provided under section 95 is suspended or discontinued as a result of any provision of a kind mentioned in paragraph 8;

(b) the relevant claim for asylum has been determined;

(c) the supported person has ceased to be destitute;

(d) he is to be moved to other accommodation.

Contributions to support

10

The regulations may make provision requiring a supported person to make payments to the Secretary of State, in prescribed circumstances, by way of contributions to the cost of the provision of that support.

Recovery of sums by Secretary of State

11

(1) The regulations may provide for the recovery by the Secretary of State of sums representing the whole or part of the monetary value of support provided to a person under section 95 where it appears to the Secretary of State—

(a) that that person had, at the time when he applied for support, assets of any kind in the United Kingdom or elsewhere which were not capable of being realised; but

(b) that those assets have subsequently become, and remain, capable of being realised.

(2) An amount recoverable under regulations made by virtue of sub-paragraph (1) may be recovered—

(a) as if it were a debt due to the Secretary of State; or

(b) by such other method of recovery, including by deduction from support provided under section 95 as may be prescribed.

Procedure

12

The regulations may make provision with respect to procedural requirements including, in particular, provision as to—

(a) the procedure to be followed in making an application for support;

(b) the information which must be provided by the applicant;

(c) the circumstances in which an application may not be entertained [(which may, in particular, provide for an application not to be entertained where the Secretary of State is not satisfied that the information provided is complete or accurate or that the applicant is co-operating with enquiries under paragraph (d)];

(d) the making of further enquiries by the Secretary of State;

(e) the circumstances in which, and person by whom, a change of circumstances of a prescribed description must be notified to the Secretary of State.

Amendment

Paras 2, 6: repealed by the Nationality, Immigration and Asylum Act 2002, ss 45(3), 161, Sch 9, as from a day to be appointed.

Para 12: in sub-para (c) words from "(which may, in" to "under paragraph (d))" in square brackets inserted by the Nationality, Immigration and Asylum Act 2002, s 57.

Subordinate Legislation

Asylum Support Regulations 2000, SI 2000/704.

SCHEDULE 9

ASYLUM SUPPORT: INTERIM PROVISIONS

Section 95(13)

1

(1) The Secretary of State may by regulations make provision requiring prescribed local authorities or local authorities falling within a prescribed description of authority to provide support, during the interim period, to eligible persons.

(2) "Eligible persons" means—

(a) asylum-seekers, or

(b) their dependants,

who appear to be destitute or to be likely to become destitute within such period as may be prescribed.

(3) For the purposes of sub-paragraph (1), in Northern Ireland, a Health and Social Services Board established under Article 16 of the Health and Personal Social Services (Northern Ireland) Order 1972 is to be treated as a local authority.

2

(1) The regulations must provide for the question whether a person is an eligible person to be determined by the local authority concerned.

(2) The regulations may make provision for support to be provided, before the determination of that question, to a person making a claim for support under the regulations by the Secretary of State or such local authority as may be prescribed.

(3) "The local authority concerned" has such meaning as may be prescribed.

3

Subsections (3) to (8) of section 95 [Subsections (2) to (6) of section 95] apply for the purposes of the regulations as they apply for the purposes of that section, but for the references in *subsections (5) and (7)* [subsections (4) and (5)] to the Secretary of State substitute references to the local authority concerned.

4

The regulations may prescribe circumstances in which support for an eligible person—

(a) must be provided;

(b) must or may be refused; or

(c) must or may be suspended or discontinued.

5

The regulations may provide that support—

(a) is to be provided in prescribed ways;

(b) is not to be provided in prescribed ways.

6

The regulations may include provision—

(a) as to the level of support that is to be provided;

(b) for support to be provided subject to conditions;

(c) requiring any such conditions to be set out in writing;

(d) requiring a copy of any such conditions to be given to such person as may be prescribed.

[6A

The regulations may, in particular, require support to be provided subject to a condition of compliance with any restriction imposed under paragraph 21 of Schedule 2 to the 1971 Act (temporary admission or release from detention) or paragraph 2 or 5 of Schedule 3 to that Act (restriction pending deportation).]

7

The regulations may make provision that, in providing support, a local authority—

(a) are to have regard to such matters as may be prescribed;

(b) are not to have regard to such matters as may be prescribed.

8

The regulations may include provision—

(a) prescribing particular areas, or descriptions of area, (which may include a locality within their own area) in which a local authority may not place asylum-seekers while providing support for them;

(b) prescribing circumstances in which a particular area, or description of area, (which may include a locality within their own area) is to be one in which a local authority may not place asylum-seekers while providing support for them;

(c) as to the circumstances (if any) in which any such provision is not to apply.

9

(1) The regulations may make provision for the referral by one local authority to another of a claim for support made under the regulations if the local authority to whom the claim is made consider that it is not manifestly unfounded but—

(a) they are providing support for a number of asylum-seekers equal to, or greater than, the maximum number of asylum-seekers applicable to them; or

(b) they are providing support for a number of eligible persons equal to, or greater than, the maximum number of eligible persons applicable to them.

(2) For the purposes of any provision made as a result of sub-paragraph (1), the regulations may make provision for the determination by the Secretary of State of—

(a) the applicable maximum number of asylum-seekers;

(b) the applicable maximum number of eligible persons.

(3) The regulations may make provision for any such determination to be made—

(a) for local authorities generally;

(b) for prescribed descriptions of local authority; or

(c) for particular local authorities.

(4) The regulations may provide that a referral may not be made—

(a) to a prescribed local authority;

(b) to local authorities of a prescribed description; or

(c) in prescribed circumstances.

(5)   The regulations may make provision for the payment by a local authority of any reasonable travel or subsistence expenses incurred as a result of a referral made by them.

(6)   The regulations may make provision for the transfer of a claim for support, or responsibility for providing support, under the regulations from one local authority to another on such terms as may be agreed between them.

(7)   In exercising any power under the regulations to refer or transfer, a local authority must have regard to such guidance as may be issued by the Secretary of State with respect to the exercise of the power.

10

(1)   The regulations may make provision for the referral of claims for support made to the Secretary of State to prescribed local authorities or local authorities of a prescribed description.

(2)   The regulations may make provision for the payment by the Secretary of State of any reasonable travel or subsistence expenses incurred as a result of a referral made by him as a result of provision made by virtue of sub-paragraph (1).

11

The regulations may make provision requiring prescribed local authorities or other prescribed bodies to give reasonable assistance to local authorities providing support under the regulations.

12

The regulations may make provision for the procedure for making and determining claims for support.

13

The regulations may make provision for an asylum-seeker or a dependant of an asylum-seeker who has received, or is receiving, any prescribed description of support from a local authority to be taken to have been accepted for support under the regulations by a prescribed local authority.

14

A person entitled to support under the regulations is not entitled to any prescribed description of support, except to such extent (if any) as may be prescribed.

15

"The interim period" means the period—

(a)   beginning on such day as may be prescribed for the purposes of this paragraph; and

(b)   ending on such day as may be so prescribed.

Amendment

Para 3: words "Subsections (3) to (8) of section 95" in italics repealed and subsequent words in square brackets substituted by the Nationality, Immigration and Asylum Act 2002, s 45(4)(a), as from a day to be appointed.

Para 3: words "subsections (5) and (7)" in italics repealed and subsequent words in square brackets substituted by the Nationality, Immigration and Asylum Act 2002, s 45(4)(b), as from a day to be appointed.

Para 6A: inserted by the Nationality, Immigration and Asylum Act 2002, s 50(2).

Subordinate Legislation

Asylum Support (Interim Provisions) Regulations 1999, SI 1999/3056.

SCHEDULE 10

(*Repealed by SI 2008/2833, art 9(1), Sch 3, paras 179, 186.*)

SCHEDULE 11

DETAINEE CUSTODY OFFICERS

Section 154(7)

Obtaining certificates of authorisation by false pretences

1

A person who, for the purpose of obtaining a certificate of authorisation for himself or for any other person—

   (a)   makes a statement which he knows to be false in a material particular, or

   (b)   recklessly makes a statement which is false in a material particular,

is guilty of an offence and liable on summary conviction to a fine not exceeding level 4 on the standard scale.

Powers and duties of detainee custody officers

2

(1) A detainee custody officer exercising custodial functions has power—

   (a)   to search (in accordance with rules made by the Secretary of State) any detained person in relation to whom the officer is exercising custodial functions; and

   (b)   to search any other person who is in, or is seeking to enter, any place where any such detained person is or is to be held, and any article in the possession of such a person.

(2) The power conferred by sub-paragraph (1)(b) does not authorise requiring a person to remove any of his clothing other than an outer coat, jacket or glove.

(3) As respects a detained person in relation to whom he is exercising custodial functions, it is the duty of a detainee custody officer—

   (a)   to prevent that person's escape from lawful custody;

   (b)   to prevent, or detect and report on, the commission or attempted commission by him of other unlawful acts;

   (c)   to ensure good order and discipline on his part; and

   (d)   to attend to his wellbeing.

(4) The powers conferred by sub-paragraph (1), and the powers arising by virtue of sub-paragraph (3), include power to use reasonable force where necessary.

Short-term holding facilities [and pre-departure accommodation]

3

(1) A detainee custody officer may perform functions of a custodial nature at a short-term holding facility [or in pre-departure accommodation] (whether or not he is authorised to perform custodial functions at a [removal centre]).

(2) When doing so, he is to have the same powers and duties in relation to the facility [or accommodation] and persons detained there as he would have if the facility [or accommodation] were a [removal centre].

Assaulting a detainee custody officer

4

A person who assaults a detainee custody officer who is—

   (a)   acting in accordance with escort arrangements,

   (b)   performing custodial functions, or

(c)   performing functions of a custodial nature at a short-term holding facility [or in pre-departure accommodation],

is guilty of an offence and liable on summary conviction to a fine not exceeding level 5 on the standard scale or to imprisonment for a term not exceeding six months or to both.

Obstructing detainee custody officers

5

A person who resists or wilfully obstructs a detainee custody officer who is—

(a)   acting in accordance with escort arrangements,

(b)   performing custodial functions, or

(c)   performing functions of a custodial nature at a short-term holding facility [or in pre-departure accommodation],

is guilty of an offence and liable on summary conviction to a fine not exceeding level 3 on the standard scale.

Uniforms and badges

6

For the purposes of paragraphs 4 and 5, a detainee custody officer is not to be regarded as acting in accordance with escort arrangements or custodial functions, he may revoke that officer's certificate so far as it authorises the performance of those functions.

(2)   If it appears to the escort monitor that a detainee custody officer is not a fit and proper person to perform escort functions, he may—

(a)   refer the matter to the Secretary of State; or

(b)   in such circumstances as may be prescribed, suspend the officer's certificate pending a decision by the Secretary of State as to whether to revoke it.

Suspension and revocation of certificates of authorisation

7

(1)   If it appears to the Secretary of State that a detainee custody officer is not a fit and proper person to perform escort functions or custodial functions, he may revoke that officer's certificate so far as it authorises the performance of those functions.

(2)   If it appears to the contract monitor for the [removal centre] concerned that a detainee custody officer is not a fit and proper person to perform custodial functions, he may—

(a)   refer the matter to the Secretary of State; or

(b)   in such circumstances as may be prescribed, suspend the officer's certificate pending a decision by the Secretary of State as to whether to revoke it.

[*Prison officers and prisoner custody officers*]

8

A reference in this Schedule to a detainee custody officer includes a reference to a prison officer or prisoner custody officer exercising custodial functions.]

Amendment

Para 3: words in square brackets in the heading inserted by the Immigration Act 2014, s 73, Sch 9, para 12(1), (2)(a), as from 28 July 2014: see SI 2014/1820.

Para 3: in sub-paras (1), (2) words "or in pre-departure accommodation" and "or accommodation" in square brackets inserted by the Immigration Act 2014, s 73, Sch 9, para 12(1), (2)(b), as from 28 July 2014: see SI 2014/1820

Para 3: in sub-paras (1), (2) words "removal centre" in square brackets substituted by the Nationality, Immigration and Asylum Act 2002, s 66(2)(a), (3)(k).

Para 4: words in square brackets in sub-para (c) inserted by the Immigration Act 2014, s 73, Sch 9, para 12(1), (2)(c), as from 28 July 2014: see SI 2014/1820

Para 5: words in square brackets in sub-para (c) inserted by the Immigration Act 2014, s 73, Sch 9, para 12(1), (2)(d), as from 28 July 2014: see SI 2014/1820

Para 7: in sub-para (3) words "removal centre" in square brackets substituted by the Nationality, Immigration and Asylum Act 2002, s 66(2)(a), (3)(k).

Para 8: inserted by the Nationality, Immigration and Asylum Act 2002, s 65(2).

Subordinate Legislation

Immigration (Suspension of Detainee Custody Officer Certificate) Regulations 2001, SI 2001/241; Detention Centre Rules 2001, SI 2001/238.

SCHEDULE 12

DISCIPLINE ETC AT [REMOVAL CENTRES]

Amendment

Schedule heading: words "Removal Centres" in square brackets substituted by the Nationality, Immigration and Asylum Act 2002, s 66(2)(b), (3)(l). Section 155(2)

Measuring and photographing detained persons

1

(1) [Removal centre] rules may (among other things) provide for detained persons to be measured and photographed.

(2) The rules may, in particular, prescribe—

    (a) the time or times at which detained persons are to be measured and photographed;

    (b) the manner and dress in which they are to be measured and photographed; and

    (c) the numbers of copies of measurements or photographs that are to be made and the persons to whom they are to be sent.

Testing for drugs or alcohol

2

(1) If an authorisation is in force, a detainee custody officer may, at the centre to which the authorisation applies and in accordance with [removal centre] rules, require a detained person who is confined in the centre to provide a sample for the purpose of ascertaining—

    (a) whether he has a drug in his body; or

    (b) whether he has alcohol in his body.

(2) The sample required may be one or more of the following—

    (a) a sample of urine;

    (b) a sample of breath;

    (c) a sample of a specified description.

(3) Sub-paragraph (2)(c)—

    (a) applies only if the authorisation so provides; and

    (b) does not authorise the taking of an intimate sample.

(4) "Authorisation" means an authorisation given by the Secretary of State for the purposes of this paragraph in respect of a particular [removal centre].

(5) "Drug" means a drug which is a controlled drug for the purposes of the Misuse of Drugs Act 1971.

(6) "Specified" means specified in the authorisation.

(7) "Intimate sample"—

(a) in relation to England and Wales, has the same meaning as in Part V of the Police and Criminal Evidence Act 1984;

(b) in relation to Scotland, means—

(i) a sample of blood, semen or any other tissue fluid, urine or pubic hair;

(ii) a dental impression;

(iii) a swab taken from a person's body orifice other than the mouth; and

(c) in relation to Northern Ireland, has the same meaning as in Part VI of the Police and Criminal Evidence (Northern Ireland) Order 1989.

Medical examinations

3

(1) This paragraph applies if—

(a) an authorisation is in force for a [removal centre]; and

(b) there are reasonable grounds for believing that a person detained in the centre is suffering from a disease which is specified in an order in force under sub-paragraph (7).

(2) A detainee custody officer may require the detained person to submit to a medical examination at the centre.

(3) The medical examination must be conducted in accordance with [removal centre] rules.

(4) A detained person who fails, without reasonable excuse, to submit to a medical examination required under this paragraph is guilty of an offence.

(5) A person guilty of an offence under sub-paragraph (4) is liable on summary conviction to imprisonment for a term not exceeding six months or to a fine not exceeding level 5 on the standard scale.

(6) "Authorisation" means an authorisation given by the manager of the [removal centre] for the purpose of this paragraph.

(7) The Secretary of State may by order specify any disease which he considers might, if a person detained in a [removal centre] were to suffer from it, endanger the health of others there.

Assisting detained persons to escape

4

(1) A person who aids any detained person in escaping or attempting to escape from a [removal centre], a short-term holding facility or pre-departure accommodation is guilty of an offence.

(2) A person who, with intent to facilitate the escape of any detained person from a [removal centre], a short-term holding facility or pre-departure accommodation]—

(a) conveys any thing into the centre], facility or accommodation] or to a detained person,

(b) sends any thing (by post or otherwise) into the centre], facility or accommodation] or to a person detained there,

(c) places any thing anywhere outside the centre], facility or accommodation] with a view to its coming into the possession of a person detained there, is guilty of an offence.

(3) A person guilty of an offence under this section is liable—

(a) on summary conviction, to imprisonment for a term not exceeding six months or to a fine not exceeding the statutory maximum or to both; or

(b) on conviction on indictment, to imprisonment for a term not exceeding two years or to a fine or to both.

Alcohol

5

(1) A person who, contrary to [removal centre] rules, brings or attempts to bring any alcohol into a [removal centre], or to a detained person, is guilty of an offence.

(2) A person who places alcohol anywhere outside a [removal centre], intending that it should come into the possession of a detained person there, is guilty of an offence.

(3) A detainee custody officer or any other person on the staff of a [removal centre] who, contrary to [removal centre] rules, allows alcohol to be sold or used in the centre is guilty of an offence.

(4) A person guilty of an offence under this paragraph is liable on summary conviction to imprisonment for a term not exceeding six months or to a fine not exceeding level 3 on the standard scale or to both.

(5) "Alcohol" means any spirituous or fermented liquor.

Introduction of other articles

6

(1) A person who—

(a) conveys or attempts to convey any thing into or out of a [removal centre] or to a detained person, contrary to [removal centre] rules, and

(b) is not as a result guilty of an offence under paragraph 4 or 5,

is guilty of an offence under this paragraph.

(2) A person who—

(a) places any thing anywhere outside a [removal centre], intending it to come into the possession of a detained person, and

(b) is not as a result guilty of an offence under paragraph 4 or 5,

is guilty of an offence under this paragraph.

(3) A person guilty of an offence under this paragraph is liable on summary conviction to a fine not exceeding level 3 on the standard scale.

Notice of penalties

7

(1) In the case of a contracted out [removal centre], the contractor must cause a notice setting out the penalty to which a person committing an offence under paragraph 4, 5 or 6 is liable to be fixed outside the centre in a conspicuous place.

(2) In the case of any other [removal centre], the Secretary of State must cause such a notice to be fixed outside the centre in a conspicuous place.

8

(1) In the case of a contracted out short-term holding facility [or contracted out pre-departure accommodation], the contractor must cause a notice setting out the penalty to which a person committing an offence under paragraph 4 is liable to be fixed outside the facility in a conspicuous place.

Appendix 1 — UK Immigration Statutes

(2) In the case of any other short-term holding facility [or pre-departure accommodation], the Secretary of State must cause such a notice to be fixed outside the facility in a conspicuous place.

[Prison officers and prisoner custody officers]

9

A reference in this Schedule to a detainee custody officer includes a reference to a prison officer or prisoner custody officer exercising custodial functions.]

Amendment

Para 1: in sub-para (1) words "Removal centre" in square brackets substituted by the Nationality, Immigration and Asylum Act 2002, s 66(2)(a), (3)(l).

Para 2: in sub-paras (1), (4) words "removal centre" in square brackets substituted by the Nationality, Immigration and Asylum Act 2002, s 66(2)(a), (3)(l).

Para 3: in sub-paras (1)(a), (3), (6), (7) words "removal centre" in square brackets substituted by the Nationality, Immigration and Asylum Act 2002, s 66(2)(a), (3)(l).

Para 4: in sub-paras (1), (2) words "removal centre" in square brackets substituted by the Nationality, Immigration and Asylum Act 2002, s 66(2)(a), (3)(l).

Para 4: all other words in square brackets substituted by the Immigration Act 2014, s 73, Sch 9, para 12(1), (3)(a), as from 28 July 2014: see SI 2014/1820

Para 5: in sub-paras (1)–(3) words "removal centre" in square brackets substituted by the Nationality, Immigration and Asylum Act 2002, s 66(2)(a), (3)(l).

Para 6: in sub-paras (1)(a), (2)(a) words "removal centre" in square brackets in each place they occur substituted by the Nationality, Immigration and Asylum Act 2002, s 66(2)(a), (3)(l).

Para 7: in sub-paras (1), (2) words "removal centre" in square brackets in each place they occur substituted by the Nationality, Immigration and Asylum Act 2002, s 66(2)(a), (3)(l).

Para 8: words in square brackets substituted by the Immigration Act 2014, s 73, Sch 9, para 12(1), (3)(b), as from 28 July 2014: see SI 2014/1820

Para 9: inserted by the Nationality, Immigration and Asylum Act 2002, s 65(3).

Subordinate Legislation

Detention Centre (Specified Diseases) Order 2001, SI 2001/240; Detention Centre Rules 2001, SI 2001/238.

SCHEDULE 13
ESCORT ARRANGEMENTS

Section 156(5)

Monitoring of escort arrangements

1

(1) Escort arrangements must include provision for the appointment of a Crown servant as escort monitor.

(2) The escort monitor must—

    (a) keep the escort arrangements under review and report on them to the Secretary of State as required in accordance with the arrangements;

    (b) from time to time inspect the conditions in which detained persons are transported or held in accordance with the escort arrangements;

    (c) make recommendations to the Secretary of State, with a view to improving those conditions, whenever he considers it appropriate to do so;

    (d) investigate, and report to the Secretary of State on, any allegation made against a detainee custody officer or prisoner custody officer in respect of any act done, or failure to act, when carrying out functions under the arrangements;

(3) Paragraph (d) of sub-paragraph (2) does not apply in relation to—

(a) detainee custody officers employed as part of the Secretary of State's staff; or

(b) an act or omission of a prisoner custody officer so far as it falls to be investigated by a prisoner escort monitor under section 81 of the Criminal Justice Act 1991 or under section 103 or 119 of the Criminal Justice and Public Order Act 1994.

Powers and duties of detainee custody officers

2

(1) A detainee custody officer acting in accordance with escort arrangements has power—

(a) to search (in accordance with rules made by the Secretary of State) any detained person for whose delivery or custody the officer is responsible in accordance with the arrangements; and

(b) to search any other person who is in, or is seeking to enter, any place where any such detained person is or is to be held, and any article in the possession of such a person.

(2) The power conferred by sub-paragraph (1)(b) does not authorise requiring a person to remove any of his clothing other than an outer coat, jacket or glove.

(3) As respects a detained person for whose delivery or custody he is responsible in accordance with escort arrangements, it is the duty of a detainee custody officer—

(a) to prevent that person's escape from lawful custody;

(b) to prevent, or detect and report on, the commission or attempted commission by him of other unlawful acts;

(c) to ensure good order and discipline on his part; and

(d) to attend to his wellbeing.

(4) The Secretary of State may make rules with respect to the performance by detainee custody officers of their duty under sub-paragraph (3)(d).

(5) The powers conferred by sub-paragraph (1), and the powers arising by virtue of sub-paragraph (3), include power to use reasonable force where necessary.

Breaches of discipline

3

(1) Sub-paragraph (2) applies if a detained person for whose delivery or custody a person ("A") has been responsible in accordance with escort arrangements is delivered to a [removal centre].

(2) The detained person is to be treated, for the purposes of such [removal centre] rules as relate to disciplinary offences, as if he had been in the custody of the director of the [removal centre] at all times while A was so responsible.

(3) Sub-paragraph (4) applies if a detained person for whose delivery or custody a person ("B") has been responsible in accordance with escort arrangements is delivered to a prison.

(4) The detained person is to be treated, for the purposes of such prison rules as relate to disciplinary offences, as if he had been in the custody of the governor or controller of the prison at all times while B was so responsible.

(5) "Director" means—

(a) in the case of a contracted out [removal centre], the person appointed by the Secretary of State in relation to the centre under section 149 or such other person as the Secretary of State may appoint for the purposes of this paragraph;

(b) in the case of any other [removal centre], the manager of the [removal centre].

(6) This paragraph does not authorise the punishment of a detained person under [removal centre] rules or prison rules in respect of any act or omission of his for which he has already been punished by a court.

(7) "Prison rules" means—

(a) rules made under section 47 of the Prison Act 1952;

(b) rules made under section 19 of the Prisons (Scotland) Act 1989;

(c) rules made under section 13 of the Prison Act (Northern Ireland) 1953.

Amendment

Para 3: in sub-paras (1), (2), (5)(a), (b), (6) words "removal centre" in square brackets in each place they occur substituted by the Nationality, Immigration and Asylum Act 2002, s 66(2)(a), (3)(m).

Subordinate Legislation

Detention Centre Rules 2001, SI 2001/238.

SCHEDULE 14

(Sch 14 contains amendments which, in so far as relevant to this work, have been incorporated at the appropriate place.)

Section 169(2)

SCHEDULE 15

TRANSITIONAL PROVISIONS AND SAVINGS

Leave to enter or remain

1

(1) An order made under section 3A of the 1971 Act may make provision with respect to leave given before the commencement of section 1.

(2) An order made under section 3B of the 1971 Act may make provision with respect to leave given before the commencement of section 2.

Section 2 of the Asylum and Immigration Act 1996

2

(1) This paragraph applies in relation to any time before the commencement of the repeal by this Act of section 2 of the Asylum and Immigration Act 1996.

(2) That section has effect, and is to be deemed always to have had effect, as if the reference to section 6 of the Asylum and Immigration Appeals Act 1993 were a reference to section 15, and any certificate issued under that section is to be read accordingly.

Adjudicators and the Tribunal

3

(1) Each existing member of the Tribunal is to continue as a member of the Tribunal as if he had been duly appointed by the Lord Chancellor under Schedule 2.

(2) Each existing adjudicator is to continue as an adjudicator as if he had been duly appointed by the Lord Chancellor under Schedule 3.

(3) The terms and conditions for a person to whom sub-paragraph (1) or (2) applies remain those on which he held office immediately before the appropriate date.

(4) The provisions of Schedule 7 to the Judicial Pensions and Retirement Act 1993 (transitional provisions for retirement dates), so far as applicable in relation to an

existing member or adjudicator immediately before the appropriate date, continue to have effect.

(5) The repeal by this Act of Schedule 5 to the 1971 Act (provisions with respect to adjudicators and the Tribunal) does not affect any entitlement which an existing member or adjudicator had immediately before the appropriate date as a result of a determination made under paragraph 3(1)(b) or 9(1)(b) of that Schedule.

(6) "The appropriate date" means—

(a) in relation to existing members of the Tribunal, the date on which section 56 comes into force; and

(b) in relation to existing adjudicators, the date on which section 57 comes into force.

(7) "Existing member" means a person who is a member of the Tribunal immediately before the appropriate date.

(8) "Existing adjudicator" means a person who is an adjudicator immediately before the appropriate date.

References to justices' chief executive

4

At any time before the coming into force of section 90 of the Access to Justice Act 1999—

(a) the reference in section 48(3)(b) to the justices' chief executive appointed by the magistrates' court committee whose area includes the petty sessions area for which the specified court acts is to be read as a reference to the clerk of that court; and

(b) the reference in section 28K(9)(a) and (10) of the 1971 Act (inserted by section 138) to the justices' chief executive appointed by the magistrates' court committee whose area includes the petty sessions area for which the justice acts is to be read as a reference to the clerk to the justices for the petty sessions area for which the justice acts.

Duties under National Assistance Act 1948

5

Section 116 has effect, in relation to any time before section 115 is brought into force, as if section 115 came into force on the passing of this Act.

Duties under Health Services and Public Health Act 1968

6

Section 117(1) has effect, in relation to any time before section 115 is brought into force, as if section 115 came into force on the passing of this Act.

Duties under Social Work (Scotland) Act 1968

7

Subsections (1) to (3) of section 120 have effect, in relation to any time before section 115 is brought into force, as if section 115 came into force on the passing of this Act.

Duties under Health and Personal Social Services (Northern Ireland) Order 1972

8

Subsections (1) and (2) of section 121 have effect, in relation to any time before section 115 is brought into force, as if section 115 came into force on the passing of this Act.

Duties under National Health Service Act 1977

9

Section 117(2) has effect, in relation to any time before section 115 is brought into force, as if section 115 came into force on the passing of this Act.

10

...

Appeals relating to deportation orders

11

Section 15 of the 1971 Act, section 5 of the Immigration Act 1988 and the Immigration (Restricted Right of Appeal against Deportation) (Exemption) Order 1993 are to continue to have effect in relation to any person on whom the Secretary of State has, before the commencement of the repeal of those sections, served a notice of his decision to make a deportation order.

12

(1) Sub-paragraph (2) applies if, on the coming into force of section 10, sections 15 of the 1971 Act and 5 of the Immigration Act 1988 have been repealed by this Act.

(2) Those sections are to continue to have effect in relation to any person—

  (a) who applied during the regularisation period fixed by section 9, in accordance with the regulations made under that section, for leave to remain in the United Kingdom, and

  (b) on whom the Secretary of State has since served a notice of his decision to make a deportation order.

Assistance under Part VII of the Housing Act 1996

13

(1) The Secretary of State may by order provide for any provision of Part VII of the Housing Act 1996 (homelessness) to have effect in relation to section 185(2) persons, during the interim period, with such modifications as may be specified in the order.

(2) An order under this paragraph may, in particular, include provision—

  (a) for the referral of section 185(2) persons by one local housing authority to another by agreement between the authorities;

  (b) as to the suitability of accommodation for such persons;

  (c) as to out-of-area placements of such persons.

(3) "Interim period" means the period beginning with the passing of this Act and ending on the coming into force of the repeal of section 186 of the Act of 1996 (asylum-seekers and their dependants) by this Act (as to which see section 117(5)).

(4) "Local housing authority" has the same meaning as in the Act of 1996.

(5) "Section 185(2) person" means a person who—

(a) is eligible for housing assistance under Part VII of the Act of 1996 as a result of regulations made under section 185(2) of that Act; and

(b) is not made ineligible by section 186 (or any other provision) of that Act,

(6) The fact that an order may be made under this paragraph only in respect of the interim period does not prevent it from containing provisions of a kind authorised under section 166(3)(a) which are to have continuing effect after the end of that period.

Provision of support

14

(1) The Secretary of State may, by directions given to a local authority to whom Schedule 9 applies, require the authority to treat the interim period fixed for the purposes of that Schedule as coming to an end—

(a) for specified purposes,

(b) in relation to a specified area or locality, or

(c) in relation to persons of a specified description,

on such earlier day as may be specified.

(2) The Secretary of State may, by directions given to an authority to whom an amended provision applies, provide for specified descriptions of person to be treated—

(a) for specified purposes, or

(b) in relation to a specified area or locality,

as being persons to whom section 115 applies during such period as may be specified.

(3) Directions given under this paragraph may—

(a) make such consequential, supplemental or transitional provision as the Secretary of State considers appropriate; and

(b) make different provision for different cases or descriptions of case.

(4) "Specified" means specified in the directions.

(5) "Amended provision" means any provision amended by—

(a) section 116;

(b) section 117(1) or (2);

(c) section 120; or

(d) section 121.

Amendment

Para 10: repealed by the Mental Health (Care and Treatment) (Scotland) Act 2003, s 331(2), Sch 5, Pt 1.

Subordinate Legislation

Homelessness (Asylum-Seekers) (Interim Period) (England) Order 1999, SI 1999/3126.

SCHEDULE 16

(Sch 16 contains repeals which, in so far as relevant to this work, have been incorporated at the appropriate place.)

NATIONALITY, IMMIGRATION AND ASYLUM ACT 2002

2002 c 41

An Act to make provision about nationality, immigration and asylum; to create offences in connection with international traffic in prostitution; to make provision about international projects connected with migration; and for connected purposes.

[7 November 2002]

See further: as to the extension of this Act with modifications to the Isle of Man, the Immigration (Isle of Man) Order 2008, SI 2008/680.

PART 1
NATIONALITY

1, 2

(Amend the British Nationality Act 1981.)

3 Citizenship ceremony, oath and pledge

Schedule 1 (which makes provision about citizenship ceremonies, oaths and pledges) shall have effect.

4–9

(Ss 4, 5, 7–9 amend the British Nationality Act 1981, the British Nationality (Hong Kong) Act 1990 and the Special Immigration Appeals Commission Act 1997.; s 6 repealed by the Equality Act 2010, s 211(2), Sch 27, Pt 1A and SI 2011/1060, art 4(a).)

10 Right of abode: certificate of entitlement

(1) The Secretary of State may by regulations make provision for the issue to a person of a certificate that he has the right of abode in the United Kingdom.

(2) The regulations may, in particular—

  (a) specify to whom an application must be made;

  (b) specify the place (which may be outside the United Kingdom) to which an application must be sent;

  (c) provide that an application must be [accompanied by specified information];

  (d) provide that an application must be accompanied by specified documents;

  (e) . . .

  (f) specify the consequences of failure to comply with a requirement under any of paragraphs [(a) to (d)] above;

  (g) provide for a certificate to cease to have effect after a period of time specified in or determined in accordance with the regulations;

  (h) make provision about the revocation of a certificate.

(3) The regulations may—

  (a) make provision which applies generally or only in specified cases or circumstances;

  (b) make different provision for different purposes;

  (c) include consequential, incidental or transitional provision.

(4) The regulations—

(a) must be made by statutory instrument, and

(b) shall be subject to annulment in pursuance of a resolution of either House of Parliament.

(5) The Immigration Act 1971 (c 77) shall be amended as follows—

   (a) in section 3(9)(b) (proof of entitlement to right of abode) the words "issued by or on behalf of the Government of the United Kingdom certifying that he has such a right of abode" shall cease to have effect, and

   (b) in section 33(1) for the definition of "certificate of entitlement" substitute—

"certificate of entitlement" means a certificate under section 10 of the Nationality, Immigration and Asylum Act 2002 that a person has the right of abode in the United Kingdom;".

(6) Regulations under this section may, in particular, include provision saving, with or without modification, the effect of a certificate which—

   (a) is issued before the regulations come into force, and

   (b) is a certificate of entitlement for the purposes of sections 3(9) and 33(1) of the Immigration Act 1971 as those sections have effect before the commencement of subsection (5) above.

Amendment

Sub-s (2): in para (c) words "accompanied by specified information" in square brackets substituted by the Immigration, Asylum and Nationality Act 2006, s 50(5).

Sub-s (2): para (e) repealed by the Immigration, Asylum and Nationality Act 2006, ss 52(7), 61, Sch 2, para 4(a), Sch 3.

Sub-s (2): in para (f) words "(a) to (d)" in square brackets substituted by the Immigration, Asylum and Nationality Act 2006, s 52(7), Sch 2, para 4(b).

Subordinate Legislation

Immigration (Certificate of Entitlement to Right of Abode in the United Kingdom) Regulations 2006, SI 2006/3145; Immigration (Certificate of Entitlement to Right of Abode in the United Kingdom) (Amendment) Regulations 2011, SI 2011/2682.

11–13

(S 11 *repealed by the Borders, Citizenship and Immigration Act 2009, ss 48(2), 56, Schedule, Pt 2; ss 12, 13 amend the British Nationality Act 1981.*)

14 Hong Kong

A person may not be registered as a British overseas territories citizen under a provision of the British Nationality Act 1981 (c 61) by virtue of a connection with Hong Kong.

15 Repeal of spent provisions

Schedule 2 (which repeals spent provisions) shall have effect.

PART 2

ACCOMMODATION CENTRES

Establishment

16 Establishment of centres

(1) The Secretary of State may arrange for the provision of premises for the accommodation of persons in accordance with this Part.

(2) A set of premises provided under this section is referred to in this Act as an "accommodation centre".

(3) The Secretary of State may arrange for—

   (a) the provision of facilities at or near an accommodation centre for sittings of adjudicators appointed for the purpose of Part 5 in accordance with a determination . . . under paragraph 2 of Schedule 4;

   (b) the provision of facilities at an accommodation centre for the taking of steps in connection with the determination of claims for asylum (within the meaning of section 18(3)).

Amendment

Sub-s (3): in para (a) words omitted repealed by the Constitutional Reform Act 2005, s 146, Sch 18, Pt 2.

Use of centres

17 Support for destitute asylum-seeker

(1) The Secretary of State may arrange for the provision of accommodation for a person in an accommodation centre if—

   (a) the person is an asylum-seeker or the dependant of an asylum-seeker, and

   (b) the Secretary of State thinks that the person is destitute or is likely to become destitute within a prescribed period.

(2) The Secretary of State may make regulations about procedure to be followed in respect of the provision of accommodation under this section.

(3) The regulations may, in particular, make provision—

   (a) specifying procedure to be followed in applying for accommodation in an accommodation centre;

   (b) providing for an application to be combined with an application under or in respect of another enactment;

   (c) requiring an applicant to provide information;

   (d) specifying circumstances in which an application may not be considered (which provision may, in particular, provide for an application not to be considered where the Secretary of State is not satisfied that the information provided is complete or accurate or that the applicant is co-operating with enquiries under paragraph (e));

   (e) about the making of enquiries by the Secretary of State;

   (f) requiring a person to notify the Secretary of State of a change in circumstances.

(4) Sections 18 to 20 define the following expressions for the purpose of this Part—

   (a) asylum-seeker,

   (b) dependant, and

   (c) destitute.

Commencement

To be appointed: see s 162(1).

18 Asylum-seeker: definition

(1) For the purposes of this Part a person is an "asylum-seeker" if—

   (a) he is at least 18 years old,

   (b) he is in the United Kingdom,

   (c) a claim for asylum has been made by him at a place designated by the Secretary of State,

   (d) the Secretary of State has recorded the claim, and

   (e) the claim has not been determined.

(2) A person shall continue to be treated as an asylum-seeker despite subsection (1)(e) while—

   (a) his household includes a dependent child who is under 18, and

(b) he does not have leave to enter or remain in the United Kingdom.

(3) A claim for asylum is a claim by a person that to remove him from or require him to leave the United Kingdom would be contrary to the United Kingdom's obligations under—

   (a) the Convention relating to the Status of Refugees done at Geneva on 28th July 1951 and its Protocol, or

   (b) Article 3 of the Convention for the Protection of Human Rights and Fundamental Freedoms agreed by the Council of Europe at Rome on 4th November 1950.

Commencement

To be appointed: see s 162(1).

19 Destitution: definition

(1) Where a person has dependants, he and his dependants are destitute for the purpose of this Part if they do not have and cannot obtain both—

   (a) adequate accommodation, and

   (b) food and other essential items.

(2) Where a person does not have dependants, he is destitute for the purpose of this Part if he does not have and cannot obtain both—

   (a) adequate accommodation, and

   (b) food and other essential items.

(3) In determining whether accommodation is adequate for the purposes of subsection (1) or (2) the Secretary of State must have regard to any matter prescribed for the purposes of this subsection.

(4) In determining whether accommodation is adequate for the purposes of subsection (1) or (2) the Secretary of State may not have regard to—

   (a) whether a person has an enforceable right to occupy accommodation,

   (b) whether a person shares all or part of accommodation,

   (c) whether accommodation is temporary or permanent,

   (d) the location of accommodation, or

   (e) any other matter prescribed for the purposes of this subsection.

(5) The Secretary of State may by regulations specify items which are or are not to be treated as essential items for the purposes of subsections (1) and (2).

(6) The Secretary of State may by regulations—

   (a) provide that a person is not to be treated as destitute for the purposes of this Part in specified circumstances;

   (b) enable or require the Secretary of State in deciding whether a person is destitute to have regard to income which he or a dependant of his might reasonably be expected to have;

   (c) enable or require the Secretary of State in deciding whether a person is destitute to have regard to support which is or might reasonably be expected to be available to the person or a dependant of his;

   (d) enable or require the Secretary of State in deciding whether a person is destitute to have regard to assets of a prescribed kind which he or a dependant of his has or might reasonably be expected to have;

   (e) make provision as to the valuation of assets.

Commencement

To be appointed: see s 162(1).

20 Dependant: definition

For the purposes of this Part a person is a "dependant" of an asylum-seeker if (and only if) that person—

   (a) is in the United Kingdom, and

(b) ... is within a prescribed class.

Commencement

To be appointed: see s 162(1).

21 Sections 17 to 20: supplementary

(1) This section applies for the purposes of sections 17 to 20.

(2) The Secretary of State may inquire into and decide a person's age.

(3) A claim for asylum shall be treated as determined at the end of such period as may be prescribed beginning with—

    (a) the date on which the Secretary of State notifies the claimant of his decision on the claim, or

    (b) if the claimant appeals against the Secretary of State's decision, the date on which the appeal is disposed of.

(4) A notice under subsection (3)(a)—

    (a) must be in writing, and

    (b) if sent by first class post to the claimant's last known address or to the claimant's representative, shall be treated as being received by the claimant on the second day after the day of posting.

(5) An appeal is disposed of when it is no longer pending for the purpose of—

    (a) Part 5 of this Act, or

    (b) the Special Immigration Appeals Commission Act 1997 (c 68).

Commencement

To be appointed: see s 162(1).

22 Immigration and Asylum Act 1999, s 95

The Secretary of State may provide support under section 95 of the Immigration and Asylum Act 1999 (c 33) (destitute asylum-seeker) by arranging for the provision of accommodation in an accommodation centre.

Commencement

To be appointed: see s 162(1).

23 Person subject to United Kingdom entrance control

(1) A residence restriction may include a requirement to reside at an accommodation centre.

(2) In subsection (1) "residence restriction" means a restriction imposed under—

    (a) paragraph 21 of Schedule 2 to the Immigration Act 1971 (c 77) (temporary admission or release from detention), or

    (b) paragraph 2(5) of Schedule 3 to that Act (control pending deportation).

(3) Where a person is required to reside in an accommodation centre by virtue of subsection (1) the Secretary of State must arrange for the provision of accommodation for the person in an accommodation centre.

(4) But if the person is required to leave an accommodation centre by virtue of section 26 or 30 he shall be treated as having broken the residence restriction referred to in subsection (1).

(5) The Secretary of State may provide support under section 4 of the Immigration and Asylum Act 1999 (persons subject to entrance control) (including that section as amended by section 49 of this Act) by arranging for the provision of accommodation in an accommodation centre.

Commencement

To be appointed: see s 162(1).

24 Provisional assistance

(1) If the Secretary of State thinks that a person may be eligible for the provision of accommodation in an accommodation centre under section 17, he may arrange for the provision for the person, pending a decision about eligibility, of—

  (a) accommodation in an accommodation centre, or

  (b) other support or assistance (of any kind).

(2) Section 99 of the Immigration and Asylum Act 1999 (c 33) (provision of support by local authority) shall have effect in relation to the provision of support for persons under subsection (1) above as it has effect in relation to the provision of support for asylum-seekers under sections 95 and 98 of that Act.

Commencement

  To be appointed: see s 162(1).

25 Length of stay

(1) The Secretary of State may not arrange for the provision of accommodation for a person in an accommodation centre if he has been a resident of an accommodation centre for a continuous period of six months.

(2) But—

  (a) subsection (1) may be disapplied in respect of a person, generally or to a specified extent, by agreement between the Secretary of State and the person, and

  (b) if the Secretary of State thinks it appropriate in relation to a person because of the circumstances of his case, the Secretary of State may direct that subsection (1) shall have effect in relation to the person as if the period specified in that subsection were the period of nine months.

(3) Section 51 is subject to this section.

(4) The Secretary of State may by order amend subsection (1) or (2)(b) so as to substitute a shorter period for a period specified.

Commencement

  To be appointed: see s 162(1).

26 Withdrawal of support

(1) The Secretary of State may stop providing support for a person under section 17 or 24 if—

  (a) the Secretary of State suspects that the person or a dependant of his has committed an offence by virtue of section 35, or

  (b) the person or a dependant of his has failed to comply with directions of the Secretary of State as to the time or manner of travel to accommodation provided under section 17 or 24.

(2) The Secretary of State may by regulations specify other circumstances in which he may stop providing support for a person under section 17 or 24.

(3) In determining whether or not to provide a person with support or assistance under section 17 or 24 of this Act or section 4, 95 or 98 of the Immigration and Asylum Act 1999 (asylum-seeker) the Secretary of State may take into account the fact that—

  (a) he has withdrawn support from the person by virtue of this section or section 30(4) or (5), or

  (b) circumstances exist which would have enabled the Secretary of State to withdraw support from the person by virtue of this section had he been receiving support.

(4) This section is without prejudice to section 103 of the Immigration and Asylum Act 1999 (c 33) (appeal against refusal to support).

Commencement

  To be appointed: see s 162(1).

27 Resident of centre

A reference in this Part to a resident of an accommodation centre is a reference to a person for whom accommodation in the centre is provided—

(a) under section 17,

(b) by virtue of section 22,

(c) by virtue of section 23, or

(d) under section 24.

Commencement

To be appointed: see s 162(1).

28 Manager of centre

A reference in this Part to the manager of an accommodation centre is a reference to a person who agrees with the Secretary of State to be wholly or partly responsible for the management of the centre.

Commencement

To be appointed: see s 162(1).

29 Facilities

(1) The Secretary of State may arrange for the following to be provided to a resident of an accommodation centre—

(a) food and other essential items;

(b) money;

(c) assistance with transport for the purpose of proceedings under the Immigration Acts or in connection with a claim for asylum;

(d) transport to and from the centre;

(e) assistance with expenses incurred in connection with carrying out voluntary work or other activities;

(f) education and training;

(g) facilities relating to health;

(h) facilities for religious observance;

(i) anything which the Secretary of State thinks ought to be provided for the purpose of providing a resident with proper occupation and for the purpose of maintaining good order;

(j) anything which the Secretary of State thinks ought to be provided for a person because of his exceptional circumstances.

(2) The Secretary of State may make regulations specifying the amount or maximum amount of money to be provided under subsection (1)(b).

(3) The Secretary of State may arrange for the provision of facilities in an accommodation centre for the use of a person in providing legal advice to a resident of the centre.

(4) The Secretary of State shall take reasonable steps to ensure that a resident of an accommodation centre has an opportunity to obtain legal advice before any appointment made by an immigration officer or an official of the Secretary of State for the purpose of obtaining information from the resident to be used in determining his claim for asylum.

(5) The Secretary of State may by order amend subsection (1) so as to add a reference to facilities which may be provided.

Commencement

To be appointed: see s 162(1).

30 Conditions of residence

(1) The Secretary of State may make regulations about conditions to be observed by residents of an accommodation centre.

(2) Regulations under subsection (1) may, in particular, enable a condition to be imposed in accordance with the regulations by—

  (a) the Secretary of State, or

  (b) the manager of an accommodation centre.

(3) A condition imposed by virtue of this section may, in particular—

  (a) require a person not to be absent from the centre during specified hours without the permission of the Secretary of State or the manager;

  (b) require a person to report to an immigration officer or the Secretary of State.

(4) If a resident of an accommodation centre breaches a condition imposed by virtue of this section, the Secretary of State may—

  (a) require the resident and any dependant of his to leave the centre;

  (b) authorise the manager of the centre to require the resident and any dependant of his to leave the centre.

(5) If a dependant of a resident of an accommodation centre breaches a condition imposed by virtue of this section, the Secretary of State may—

  (a) require the resident and any dependant of his to leave the centre;

  (b) authorise the manager of the centre to require the resident and any dependant of his to leave the centre.

(6) Regulations under this section must include provision for ensuring that a person subject to a condition is notified of the condition in writing.

(7) A condition imposed by virtue of this section is in addition to any restriction imposed under paragraph 21 of Schedule 2 to the Immigration Act 1971 (c. 77) (control of entry to United Kingdom) or under paragraph 2(5) of Schedule 3 to that Act (control pending deportation).

(8) A reference in this Part to a condition of residence is a reference to a condition imposed by virtue of this section.

Commencement

To be appointed: see s 162(1).

31 Financial contribution by resident

(1) A condition of residence may, in particular, require a resident of an accommodation centre to make payments to—

  (a) the Secretary of State, or

  (b) the manager of the centre.

(2) The Secretary of State may make regulations enabling him to recover sums representing the whole or part of the value of accommodation and other facilities provided to a resident of an accommodation centre if—

  (a) accommodation is provided for the resident in response to an application by him for support,

  (b) when the application was made the applicant had assets which were not capable of being realised, and

  (c) the assets have become realisable.

(3) In subsection (2) "assets" includes assets outside the United Kingdom.

(4) An amount recoverable by virtue of regulations made under subsection (2) may be recovered—

  (a) as a debt due to the Secretary of State;

  (b) by another prescribed method (which may include the imposition or variation of a residence condition).

Commencement

To be appointed: see s 162(1).

32 Tenure

(1) A resident of an accommodation centre shall not be treated as acquiring a tenancy of or other interest in any part of the centre (whether by virtue of an agreement between the resident and another person or otherwise).

(2) Subsection (3) applies where—

    (a) the Secretary of State decides to stop arranging for the provision of accommodation in an accommodation centre for a resident of the centre, or

    (b) a resident of an accommodation centre is required to leave the centre in accordance with section 30.

(3) Where this subsection applies—

    (a) the Secretary of State or the manager of the centre may recover possession of the premises occupied by the resident, and

    (b) the right under paragraph (a) shall be enforceable in accordance with procedure prescribed by regulations made by the Secretary of State.

(4) Any licence which a resident of an accommodation centre has to occupy premises in the centre shall be an excluded licence for the purposes of the Protection from Eviction Act 1977 (c 43).

(5) . . .

(6) . . .

(7) In this section a reference to an accommodation centre includes a reference to premises in which accommodation is provided under section 24(1)(b).

Commencement

To be appointed: see s 162(1).

Amendment

Sub-ss (5), (6) amend legislation outside the scope of this work.

33 Advisory Groups

(1) The Secretary of State shall appoint a group (to be known as an Accommodation Centre Advisory Group) for each accommodation centre.

(2) The Secretary of State may by regulations—

    (a) confer functions on Advisory Groups;

    (b) make provision about the constitution and proceedings of Advisory Groups.

(3) Regulations under subsection (2)(a) must, in particular, provide for members of an accommodation centre's Advisory Group—

    (a) to visit the centre;

    (b) to hear complaints made by residents of the centre;

    (c) to report to the Secretary of State.

(4) The manager of an accommodation centre must permit a member of the centre's Advisory Group on request—

    (a) to visit the centre at any time;

    (b) to visit any resident of the centre at any time, provided that the resident consents.

(5) A member of an Advisory Group shall hold and vacate office in accordance with the terms of his appointment (which may include provision about retirement, resignation or dismissal).

(6) The Secretary of State may—

    (a) defray expenses of members of an Advisory Group;

    (b) make facilities available to members of an Advisory Group.

Commencement

To be appointed: see s 162(1).

34

(Repealed by the UK Borders Act 2007, ss 54(b), 58, Schedule.)

35 Ancillary provisions

(1) The following provisions of the Immigration and Asylum Act 1999 (c 33) shall apply for the purposes of this Part as they apply for the purposes of Part VI of that Act (support for asylum-seeker)—

(a) section 105 (false representation),

(b) section 106 (dishonest representation),

(c) section 107 (delay or obstruction),

(d) section 108 (failure of sponsor to maintain),

(e) section 109 (offence committed by body),

(f) section 112 (recovery of expenditure),

(g) section 113 (recovery of expenditure from sponsor),

(h) section 124 (corporation sole), and

(i) section 127 (redirection of post).

(2) In the application of section 112 a reference to something done under section 95 or 98 of that Act shall be treated as a reference to something done under section 17 or 24 of this Act.

(3) In the application of section 113 a reference to section 95 of that Act shall be treated as a reference to section 17 of this Act.

Commencement

Sub-s (1)(h): Royal Assent: 7 November 2002: see s 162(2)(g). Sub-ss (1)(a)–(g), (i), (2), (3): To be appointed: see s 162(1).

36 Education: general

(1) For the purposes of section 13 of the Education Act 1996 (c 56) (general responsibility of [local authority]) a resident of an accommodation centre shall not be treated as part of the population of a [local authority's] area.

(2) A child who is a resident of an accommodation centre may not be admitted to a maintained school or a maintained nursery (subject to section 37).

(3) But subsection (2) does not prevent a child's admission to a school which is—

(a) a community special school or a foundation special school, and

(b) named in a statement in respect of the child under section 324 of the Education Act 1996 (c 56) (special educational needs).

(4) In subsections (2) and (3)—

(a) "maintained school" means a maintained school within the meaning of section 20(7) of the School Standards and Framework Act 1998 (c 31) (definition), and

(b) "maintained nursery" means a facility for nursery education, within the meaning of section 117 of that Act, provided by a [local authority].

(5) The following shall not apply in relation to a child who is a resident of an accommodation centre (subject to section 37)—

(a) section 86(1) and (2) of the School Standards and Framework Act 1998 (parental preference),

(b) section 94 of that Act (appeal),

(c) section 19 of the Education Act 1996 (education out of school),

(d) section 316(2) and (3) of that Act (child with special educational needs to be educated in mainstream school), and

(e) paragraphs 3 and 8 of Schedule 27 to that Act (special education needs: making of statement: parental preference),.

(6) The power of the [First-tier Tribunal or the Special Educational Needs Tribunal for Wales] under section 326(3) of the Education Act 1996 (appeal against content of statement) is subject to subsection (2) above.

(7) A person exercising a function under this Act or the Education Act 1996 shall (subject to section 37) secure that a child who is a resident of an accommodation centre and who has special educational needs shall be educated by way of facilities provided under section 29(1)(f) of this Act unless that is incompatible with—

(a) his receiving the special educational provision which his learning difficulty calls for,

(b) the provision of efficient education for other children who are residents of the centre, or

(c) the efficient use of resources.

(8) A person may rely on subsection (7)(b) only where there is no action—

(a) which could reasonably be taken by that person or by another person who exercises functions, or could exercise functions, in respect of the accommodation centre concerned, and

(b) as a result of which subsection (7)(b) would not apply.

(9) An accommodation centre is not a school within the meaning of section 4 of the Education Act 1996 (definition); but—

(a) [Part 1 of the Education Act 2005 (school inspections)] shall apply to educational facilities provided at an accommodation centre as if the centre were a school (for which purpose a reference to the appropriate authority shall be taken as a reference to the person (or persons) responsible for the provision of education at the accommodation centre),

(b) section 329A of the Education Act 1996 (review or assessment of educational needs at request of responsible body) shall have effect as if—

(i) an accommodation centre were a relevant school for the purposes of that section,

(ii) a child for whom education is provided at an accommodation centre under section 29(1)(f) were a registered pupil at the centre, and

(iii) a reference in section 329A to the responsible body in relation to an accommodation centre were a reference to any person providing education at the centre under section 29(1)(f), and

(c) section 140 of the Learning and Skills Act 2000 (c 21) (learning difficulties: assessment of post-16 needs) shall have effect as if an accommodation centre were a school.

(10) Subsections (1), (2) and (5) shall not apply in relation to an accommodation centre if education is not provided for children who are residents of the centre under section 29(1)(f).

(11) An expression used in this section and in the Education Act 1996 (c 56) shall have the same meaning in this section as in that Act.

Commencement

To be appointed: see s 162(1).

Amendment

Sub-s (1): words "local authority" and "local authority's" in square brackets substituted by SI 2010/1158, art 5(1), Sch 2, Pt 2, para 51(1),(2)(a).

Sub-s (4): in para (b) words "local authority" in square brackets substituted by SI 2010/1158, art 5(1), Sch 2, Pt 2, para 51(1),(2)(b).

Sub-s (6): words "the Special Educational Needs Tribunal for Wales" in square brackets substituted by SI 2008/2833, art 9(1), Sch 3, para 197.

Sub-s (9): in para (a) words "Part 1 of the Education Act 2005 (school inspections)" in square brackets substituted by the Education Act 2005, s 61, Sch 9, para 30.

37 Education: special cases

(1)   This section applies to a child if a person who provides education to residents of an accommodation centre recommends in writing to the [local authority] for the area in which the centre is that this section should apply to the child on the grounds that his special circumstances call for provision that can only or best be arranged by the authority.

(2)   A [local authority] may—

    (a)   arrange for the provision of education for a child to whom this section applies;

    (b)   disapply a provision of section 36 in respect of a child to whom this section applies.

(3)   In determining whether to exercise a power under subsection (2) in respect of a child a [local authority] shall have regard to any relevant guidance issued by the Secretary of State.

(4)   The governing body of a maintained school shall comply with a requirement of the [local authority] to admit to the school a child to whom this section applies.

(5)   Subsection (4) shall not apply where compliance with a requirement would prejudice measures taken for the purpose of complying with a duty arising under section 1(6) of the School Standards and Framework Act 1998 (c 31) (limit on infant class size).

(6)   A [local authority] may not impose a requirement under subsection (4) in respect of a school unless the authority has consulted the school in accordance with regulations made by the Secretary of State.

(7)   In the case of a maintained school for which the [local authority] are the admission authority, the authority may not arrange for the admission of a child to whom this section applies unless the authority has notified the school in accordance with regulations made by the Secretary of State.

(8)   In this section—

    (a)   "maintained school" means a maintained school within the meaning of section 20(7) of the School Standards and Framework Act 1998 (definition), and

    (b)   an expression which is also used in the Education Act 1996 (c 56) shall have the same meaning as it has in that Act.

Commencement

To be appointed: see s 162(1).

Amendment

Sub-ss (1)–(4): words "local authority" in square brackets substituted by SI 2010/1158, art 5(1), Sch 2, Pt 2, para 51(1), (3).

Sub-ss (6), (7): words "local authority" in square brackets substituted by SI 2010/1158, art 5(1), Sch 2, Pt 2, para 51(1), (3).

38 Local authority

(1)   A local authority may in accordance with arrangements made by the Secretary of State—

    (a)   assist in arranging for the provision of an accommodation centre;

    (b)   make premises available for an accommodation centre;

    (c)   provide services in connection with an accommodation centre.

(2)   In particular, a local authority may—

    (a)   incur reasonable expenditure;

(b) provide services outside its area;

(c) provide services jointly with another body;

(d) form a company;

(e) tender for or enter into a contract;

(f) do anything (including anything listed in paragraphs (a) to (e)) for a preparatory purpose.

(3) In this section "local authority" means—

(a) a local authority within the meaning of section 94 of the Immigration and Asylum Act 1999 (c 33), and

(b) a Northern Ireland authority within the meaning of section 110 of that Act and an Education and Library Board established under Article 3 of the Education and Libraries (Northern Ireland) Order 1986 (SI 1986/594 (NI 3)).

39 "Prescribed": orders and regulations

(1) In this Part "prescribed" means prescribed by the Secretary of State by order or regulations.

(2) An order or regulations under this Part may—

(a) make provision which applies generally or only in specified cases or circumstances (which may be determined wholly or partly by reference to location);

(b) make different provision for different cases or circumstances;

(c) include consequential, transitional or incidental provision.

(3) An order or regulations under this Part must be made by statutory instrument.

(4) An order or regulations under any of the following provisions of this Part shall be subject to annulment in pursuance of a resolution of either House of Parliament—

(a) section 17,

(b) section 19,

(c) section 20,

(d) section 21,

(e) section 26,

(f) section 29,

(g) section 31,

(h) section 32,

(i) section 33,

(j) section 37,

(k) section 40, and

(l) section 41.

(5) An order under section 25 or regulations under section 30 may not be made unless a draft has been laid before and approved by resolution of each House of Parliament.

Commencement

To be appointed: see s 162(1).

40 Scotland

(1) The Secretary of State may not make arrangements under section 16 for the provision of premises in Scotland unless he has consulted the Scottish Ministers.

(2) The Secretary of State may by order make provision in relation to the education of residents of accommodation centres in Scotland.

(3) An order under subsection (2) may, in particular—

(a) apply, disapply or modify the effect of an enactment (which may include a provision made by or under an Act of the Scottish Parliament);

(b) make provision having an effect similar to the effect of a provision of section 36 or 37.

Commencement

Sub-s (1): Royal Assent: 7 November 2002: see s 162(2)(j). Sub-ss (2), (3): To be appointed: see s 162(1).

41 Northern Ireland

(1) The Secretary of State may not make arrangements under section 16 for the provision of premises in Northern Ireland unless he has consulted the First Minister and the deputy First Minister.

(2) The Secretary of State may by order make provision in relation to the education of residents of accommodation centres in Northern Ireland.

(3) An order under subsection (2) may, in particular—

(a) apply, disapply or modify the effect of an enactment (which may include a provision made by or under Northern Ireland legislation);

(b) make provision having an effect similar to the effect of a provision of section 36 or 37.

Commencement

Sub-s (1): Royal Assent: 7 November 2002: see s 162(2)(j). Sub-ss (2), (3): To be appointed: see s 162(1).

42 Wales

The Secretary of State may not make arrangements under section 16 for the provision of premises in Wales unless he has consulted the National Assembly for Wales.

PART 3
OTHER SUPPORT AND ASSISTANCE

43 Asylum-seeker: form of support

(1) The Secretary of State may make an order restricting the application of section 96(1)(b) of the Immigration and Asylum Act 1999 (c 33) (support for asylum-seeker: essential living needs)—

(a) in all circumstances, to cases in which support is being provided under section 96(1)(a) (accommodation), or

(b) in specified circumstances only, to cases in which support is being provided under section 96(1)(a).

(2) An order under subsection (1)(b) may, in particular, make provision by reference to—

(a) location;

(b) the date of an application.

(3) An order under subsection (1) may include transitional provision.

(4) An order under subsection (1)—

(a) must be made by statutory instrument, and

(b) may not be made unless a draft has been laid before and approved by resolution of each House of Parliament.

44–50

(Amend the Immigration and Asylum Act 1999 and other legislation outside the scope of this work.)

51 Choice of form of support

(1)   The Secretary of State may refuse to provide support for a person under a provision specified in subsection (2) on the grounds that an offer has been made to the person of support under another provision specified in that subsection.

(2)   The provisions are—

   (a)   sections 17 and 24 of this Act,

   (b)   section 4 of the Immigration and Asylum Act 1999 (accommodation for person temporarily admitted or released from detention), and

   (c)   sections 95 and 98 of that Act (support for destitute asylum-seeker).

(3)   In deciding under which of the provisions listed in subsection (2) to offer support to a person the Secretary of State may—

   (a)   have regard to administrative or other matters which do not concern the person's personal circumstances;

   (b)   regard one of those matters as conclusive;

   (c)   apply different criteria to different persons for administrative reasons (which may include the importance of testing the operation of a particular provision).

Commencement

To be appointed: see s 162(1).

52, 53

(S 52 repealed by the Asylum and Immigration (Treatment of Claimants, etc) Act 2004, s 47, Sch 4; s 53 amends the Immigration and Asylum Act 1999 .)

54 Withholding and withdrawal of support

Schedule 3 (which makes provision for support to be withheld or withdrawn in certain circumstances) shall have effect.

Subordinate Legislation

Withholding and Withdrawal of Support (Travel Assistance and Temporary Accommodation) Regulations 2002, SI 2002/3078.

55 Late claim for asylum: refusal of support

(1)   The Secretary of State may not provide or arrange for the provision of support to a person under a provision mentioned in subsection (2) if—

   (a)   the person makes a claim for asylum which is recorded by the Secretary of State, and

   (b)   the Secretary of State is not satisfied that the claim was made as soon as reasonably practicable after the person's arrival in the United Kingdom.

(2)   The provisions are—

   (a)   sections 4, 95 and 98 of the Immigration and Asylum Act 1999 (c 33) (support for asylum-seeker, &c), and

   (b)   sections 17 and 24 of this Act (accommodation centre).

(3)   An authority may not provide or arrange for the provision of support to a person under a provision mentioned in subsection (4) if—

   (a)   the person has made a claim for asylum, and

   (b)   the Secretary of State is not satisfied that the claim was made as soon as reasonably practicable after the person's arrival in the United Kingdom.

(4)   The provisions are—

   (a)   section 29(1)(b) of the Housing (Scotland) Act 1987 (c 26) (accommodation pending review),

   (b)   section 188(3) or 204(4) of the Housing Act 1996 (c 52) (accommodation pending review or appeal), . . .

(c) section 2 of the Local Government Act 2000 (c 22) (promotion of well-being)[, and

(d) section 1 of the Localism Act 2011 (local authority's general power of competence)].

(5) This section shall not prevent—

(a) the exercise of a power by the Secretary of State to the extent necessary for the purpose of avoiding a breach of a person's Convention rights (within the meaning of the Human Rights Act 1998 (c 42)),

(b) the provision of support under section 95 of the Immigration and Asylum Act 1999 (c 33) or section 17 of this Act in accordance with section 122 of that Act (children), or

(c) the provision of support under section 98 of the Immigration and Asylum Act 1999 or section 24 of this Act (provisional support) to a person under the age of 18 and the household of which he forms part.

(6) An authority which proposes to provide or arrange for the provision of support to a person under a provision mentioned in subsection (4)—

(a) must inform the Secretary of State if the authority believes that the person has made a claim for asylum,

(b) must act in accordance with any guidance issued by the Secretary of State to determine whether subsection (3) applies, and

(c) shall not be prohibited from providing or arranging for the provision of support if the authority has complied with paragraph (a) and (b) and concluded that subsection (3) does not apply.

(7) The Secretary of State may by order—

(a) add, remove or amend an entry in the list in subsection (4);

(b) provide for subsection (3) not to have effect in specified cases or circumstances.

(8) An order under subsection (7)—

(a) may include transitional, consequential or incidental provision,

(b) must be made by statutory instrument, and

(c) may not be made unless a draft has been laid before and approved by resolution of each House of Parliament.

(9) For the purposes of this section "claim for asylum" has the same meaning as in section 18.

(10) A decision of the Secretary of State that this section prevents him from providing or arranging for the provision of support to a person is not a decision that the person does not qualify for support for the purpose of section 103 of the Immigration and Asylum Act 1999 (appeals).

(11) This section does not prevent a person's compliance with a residence restriction imposed in reliance on section 70 (induction).

56, 57

(Amend the Immigration and Asylum Act 1999, s 99 and Sch 8.)

Amendment

Sub-s (4): in para (b) word omitted repealed by SI 2012/961, art 2, Sch 1, paras 2, 3(a). Date in force: 28 March 2012: see SI 2012/961, art 1(2).

Sub-s (4): para (d) and word ", and" immediately preceding it inserted by SI 2012/961, art 2, Sch 1, paras 2, 3(b). Date in force: 28 March 2012: see SI 2012/961, art 1(2).

58 Voluntary departure from United Kingdom

(1) A person is a "voluntary leaver" for the purposes of this section if—

(a) he is not a British citizen or an EEA national,

(b) he leaves the United Kingdom for a place where he hopes to take up permanent residence (his "new place of residence"), and

(c) the Secretary of State thinks that it is in the person's interest to leave the United Kingdom and that the person wishes to leave.

(2) The Secretary of State may make arrangements to—

(a) assist voluntary leavers;

(b) assist individuals to decide whether to become voluntary leavers.

(3) The Secretary of State may, in particular, make payments (whether to voluntary leavers or to organisations providing services for them) which relate to—

(a) travelling and other expenses incurred by or on behalf of a voluntary leaver, or a member of his family or household, in leaving the United Kingdom;

(b) expenses incurred by or on behalf of a voluntary leaver, or a member of his family or household, on or shortly after arrival in his new place of residence;

(c) the provision of services designed to assist a voluntary leaver, or a member of his family or household, to settle in his new place of residence;

(d) expenses in connection with a journey undertaken by a person (with or without his family or household) to prepare for, or to assess the possibility of, his becoming a voluntary leaver.

(4) In subsection (1)(a) "EEA national" means a national of a State which is a contracting party to the Agreement on the European Economic Area signed at Oporto on 2nd May 1992 (as it has effect from time to time).

(5) The following provisions of the Immigration Act 1971 (c 77) shall cease to have effect—

(a) section 29 (contributions to expenses of persons returning abroad), and

(b) section 31(d) (expenses).

59 International projects

(1) The Secretary of State may participate in a project which is designed to—

(a) reduce migration,

(b) assist or ensure the return of migrants,

(c) facilitate co-operation between States in matters relating to migration,

(d) conduct or consider research about migration, or

(e) arrange or assist the settlement of migrants (whether in the United Kingdom or elsewhere).

(2) In particular, the Secretary of State may—

(a) provide financial support to an international organisation which arranges or participates in a project of a kind described in subsection (1);

(b) provide financial support to an organisation in the United Kingdom or another country which arranges or participates in a project of that kind;

(c) provide or arrange for the provision of financial or other assistance to a migrant who participates in a project of that kind;

(d) participate in financial or other arrangements which are agreed between Her Majesty's Government and the government of one or more other countries and which are or form part of a project of that kind.

(3) In this section—

(a) "migrant" means a person who leaves the country where he lives hoping to settle in another country (whether or not he is a refugee within the meaning of any international Convention), and

(b) "migration" shall be construed accordingly.

(4) Subsection (1) does not—

(a) confer a power to remove a person from the United Kingdom, or

(b) affect a person's right to enter or remain in the United Kingdom.

(Amends the Immigration and Asylum Act 1999, ss 94, 110.)

---

61 Repeal of spent provisions

The following provisions of the Immigration and Asylum Act 1999 shall cease to have effect—

(a) section 96(4) to (6) (which relate to a provision about support for asylum-seekers which has been repealed by order), and

(b) section 166(4)(e) (order under section 96(5): procedure).

PART 4
DETENTION AND REMOVAL

Detention

62 Detention by Secretary of State

(1) A person may be detained under the authority of the Secretary of State pending—

 (a) a decision by the Secretary of State whether to give directions in respect of the person under [section 10 of the Immigration and Asylum Act 1999 (removal of persons unlawfully in the United Kingdom) or] paragraph 10, 10A or 14 of Schedule 2 to the Immigration Act 1971 (c 77) (control of entry: removal), or

 (b) removal of the person from the United Kingdom in pursuance of directions given by the Secretary of State under any of those [provisions].

(2) Where the Secretary of State is empowered under section 3A of [the Immigration Act 1971] (powers of Secretary of State) to examine a person or to give or refuse a person leave to enter the United Kingdom, the person may be detained under the authority of the Secretary of State pending—

 (a) the person's examination by the Secretary of State,

 (b) the Secretary of State's decision to give or refuse the person leave to enter,

 (c) a decision by the Secretary of State whether to give directions in respect of the person under paragraph 8 or 9 of Schedule 2 to that Act (removal), or

 (d) removal of the person in pursuance of directions given by the Secretary of State under either of those paragraphs.

(3) A provision of Schedule 2 to that Act about a person who is detained or liable to detention under that Schedule shall apply to a person who is detained or liable to detention under this section: and for that purpose—

 (a) a reference to paragraph 16 of that Schedule shall be taken to include a reference to this section,

 [(aa) a reference in paragraph 18B of that Schedule shall be read as a reference to the Secretary of State,]

 (b) a reference in paragraph 21 of that Schedule to an immigration officer shall be taken to include a reference to the Secretary of State, and

 (c) a reference to detention under that Schedule or under a provision or Part of that Schedule shall be taken to include a reference to detention under this section.

(4) In the case of a restriction imposed under paragraph 21 of that Schedule by virtue of this section—

   (a) a restriction imposed by an immigration officer may be varied by the Secretary of State, and

   (b) a restriction imposed by the Secretary of State may be varied by an immigration officer.

(5) *In subsection (1) the reference to paragraph 10 of that Schedule includes a reference to that paragraph as applied by virtue of section 10 of the Immigration and Asylum Act 1999 (c 33) (persons unlawfully in United Kingdom: removal).*

(6) *Subsection (5) is without prejudice to the generality of section 159.*

(7) A power under this section which is exercisable pending a decision of a particular kind by the Secretary of State is exercisable where the Secretary of State has reasonable grounds to suspect that he may make a decision of that kind.

(8)–(16) . . .

Amendment

Sub-s (1): words in square brackets in para (a) inserted and word in square brackets in para (b) substituted (for original word "paragraphs") by the Immigration Act 2014, s 73, Sch 9, Pt 1, para 3(1), (2)(a), as from 20 October 2014 (see SI 2014/2771, arts 9–11

Sub-s (2): words in square brackets substituted (for original words "that Act") by the Immigration Act 2014, s 73, Sch 9, Pt 1, para 3(1), (2)(b), as from 20 October 2014 (see SI 2014/2771, art 2), subject to savings in SI 2014/2771, arts 9–11

Sub-s (3): para (aa) inserted by the Immigration Act 2014, s 73, Sch 9, para 13, as from 28 July 2014: see SI 2014/1820.

Sub-ss (5), (6): repealed by the Immigration Act 2014, s 73, Sch 9, Pt 1, para 3(1), (2)(c), as from 20 October 2014 (see SI 2014/2771, art 2), subject to savings in SI 2014/2771, arts 9–11

Sub-ss (8)–(14): contain amendments to legislation which, in so far as relevant to this work, have been incorporated at the appropriate place.

Sub-ss (15), (16): repealed by the Prevention of Terrorism Act 2005, s 16(2)(c).

63–66

(Contain amendments to legislation which, in so far as relevant to this work, have been incorporated at the appropriate place.)

67 Construction of reference to person liable to detention

(1) This section applies to the construction of a provision which—

   (a) does not confer power to detain a person, but

   (b) refers (in any terms) to a person who is liable to detention under a provision of the Immigration Acts.

(2) The reference shall be taken to include a person if the only reason why he cannot be detained under the provision is that—

   (a) he cannot presently be removed from the United Kingdom, because of a legal impediment connected with the United Kingdom's obligations under an international agreement,

   (b) practical difficulties are impeding or delaying the making of arrangements for his removal from the United Kingdom, or

   (c) practical difficulties, or demands on administrative resources, are impeding or delaying the taking of a decision in respect of him.

(3) This section shall be treated as always having had effect.

Temporary release

68 Bail

(1) This section applies in a case where an immigration officer not below the rank of chief immigration officer has sole or shared power to release a person on bail in accordance with—

(a) a provision of Schedule 2 to the Immigration Act 1971 (c 77) (control of entry) (including a provision of that Schedule applied by a provision of that Act or by another enactment), or

(b) section 9A of the Asylum and Immigration Appeals Act 1993 (c 23) (pending appeal from Immigration Appeal Tribunal).

(2) In respect of an application for release on bail which is instituted after the expiry of the period of eight days beginning with the day on which detention commences, the power to release on bail—

(a) shall be exercisable by the Secretary of State (as well as by any person with whom the immigration officer's power is shared under the provision referred to in subsection (1)), and

(b) shall not be exercisable by an immigration officer (except where he acts on behalf of the Secretary of State).

(3) In relation to the exercise by the Secretary of State of a power to release a person on bail by virtue of subsection (2), a reference to an immigration officer shall be construed as a reference to the Secretary of State.

(4) The Secretary of State may by order amend or replace subsection (2) so as to make different provision for the circumstances in which the power to release on bail may be exercised by the Secretary of State and not by an immigration officer.

(5) An order under subsection (4)—

(a) may include consequential or transitional provision,

(b) must be made by statutory instrument, and

(c) may not be made unless a draft has been laid before and approved by resolution of each House of Parliament.

(6) The following provisions of Part III of the Immigration and Asylum Act 1999 (c 33) (Bail) shall cease to have effect—

(a) sections 44 to 52 (routine bail hearings),

(b) section 53(5) (bail under regulations to match bail under Part III), and

(c) section 55 (grants to advisory organisations).

69 Reporting restriction: travel expenses

(1) The Secretary of State may make a payment to a person in respect of travelling expenses which the person has incurred or will incur for the purpose of complying with a reporting restriction.

(2) In subsection (1) "reporting restriction" means a restriction which—

(a) requires a person to report to the police, an immigration officer or the Secretary of State, and

(b) is imposed under a provision listed in subsection (3).

(3) Those provisions are—

(a) paragraph 21 of Schedule 2 to the Immigration Act 1971 (c 77) (temporary admission or release from detention),

(b) paragraph 29 of that Schedule (bail), and

(c) paragraph 2 or 5 of Schedule 3 to that Act (pending deportation).

70 Induction

(1) A residence restriction may be imposed on an asylum-seeker or a dependant of an asylum-seeker without regard to his personal circumstances if—

   (a) it requires him to reside at a specified location for a period not exceeding 14 days, and

   (b) the person imposing the residence restriction believes that a programme of induction will be made available to the asylum-seeker at or near the specified location.

(2) In subsection (1) "residence restriction" means a restriction imposed under—

   (a) paragraph 21 of Schedule 2 to the Immigration Act 1971 (temporary admission or release from detention), or

   (b) paragraph 2(5) of Schedule 3 to that Act (control pending deportation).

(3) In this section—

"asylum-seeker" has the meaning given by section 18 of this Act but disregarding section 18(1)(a),

"dependant of an asylum-seeker" means a person who appears to the Secretary of State to be making a claim or application in respect of residence in the United Kingdom by virtue of being a dependant of an asylum-seeker, and

"programme of induction" means education about the nature of the asylum process.

(4) Regulations under subsection (3)—

   (a) may make different provision for different circumstances,

   (b) must be made by statutory instrument, and

   (c) shall be subject to annulment in pursuance of a resolution of either House of Parliament.

(5) Subsection (6) applies where the Secretary of State arranges for the provision of a programme of induction (whether or not he also provides other facilities to persons attending the programme and whether or not all the persons attending the programme are subject to residence restrictions).

(6) A local authority may arrange for or participate in the provision of the programme or other facilities.

(7) In particular, a local authority may—

   (a) incur reasonable expenditure;

   (b) provide services outside its area;

   (c) provide services jointly with another body;

   (d) form a company;

   (e) tender for or enter into a contract;

   (f) do anything (including anything listed in paragraphs (a) to (e)) for a preparatory purpose.

(8) In this section "local authority" means—

   (a) a local authority within the meaning of section 94 of the Immigration and Asylum Act 1999 (c 33), and

   (b) a Northern Ireland authority within the meaning of section 110 of that Act.

71 Asylum-seeker: residence, &c restriction

(1) This section applies to—

   (a) a person who makes a claim for asylum at a time when he has leave to enter or remain in the United Kingdom, and

   (b) a dependant of a person within paragraph (a).

(2) The Secretary of State or an immigration officer may impose on a person to whom this section applies any restriction which may be imposed under paragraph 21 of Schedule 2 to the Immigration Act 1971 (c 77) (control of entry: residence, reporting and occupation restrictions) on a person liable to detention under paragraph 16 of that Schedule.

(3) Where a restriction is imposed on a person under subsection (2)—

(a)   the restriction shall be treated for all purposes as a restriction imposed under paragraph 21 of that Schedule, and

(b)   if the person fails to comply with the restriction he shall be liable to detention under paragraph 16 of that Schedule.

(4)   A restriction imposed on a person under this section shall cease to have effect if he ceases to be an asylum-seeker or the dependant of an asylum-seeker.

(5)   In this section—

"asylum-seeker" has the same meaning as in section 70,

"claim for asylum" has the same meaning as in section 18, and

"dependant" means a person who appears to the Secretary of State to be making a claim or application in respect of residence in the United Kingdom by virtue of being a dependant of another person.

(6)   Regulations under subsection (5)—

(a)   may make different provision for different circumstances,

(b)   must be made by statutory instrument, and

(c)   shall be subject to annulment in pursuance of a resolution of either House of Parliament.

Removal

72 Serious criminal

(1)   This section applies for the purpose of the construction and application of Article 33(2) of the Refugee Convention (exclusion from protection).

(2)   A person shall be presumed to have been convicted by a final judgment of a particularly serious crime and to constitute a danger to the community of the United Kingdom if he is—

(a)   convicted in the United Kingdom of an offence, and

(b)   sentenced to a period of imprisonment of at least two years.

(3)   A person shall be presumed to have been convicted by a final judgment of a particularly serious crime and to constitute a danger to the community of the United Kingdom if—

(a)   he is convicted outside the United Kingdom of an offence,

(b)   he is sentenced to a period of imprisonment of at least two years, and

(c)   he could have been sentenced to a period of imprisonment of at least two years had his conviction been a conviction in the United Kingdom of a similar offence.

(4)   A person shall be presumed to have been convicted by a final judgment of a particularly serious crime and to constitute a danger to the community of the United Kingdom if—

(a)   he is convicted of an offence specified by order of the Secretary of State, or

(b)   he is convicted outside the United Kingdom of an offence and the Secretary of State certifies that in his opinion the offence is similar to an offence specified by order under paragraph (a).

(5)   An order under subsection (4)—

(a)   must be made by statutory instrument, and

(b)   shall be subject to annulment in pursuance of a resolution of either House of Parliament.

(6)   A presumption under subsection (2), (3) or (4) that a person constitutes a danger to the community is rebuttable by that person.

(7)   A presumption under subsection (2), (3) or (4) does not apply while an appeal against conviction or sentence—

(a)   is pending, or

    (b)   could be brought (disregarding the possibility of appeal out of time with leave).

(8) Section 34(1) of the Anti-terrorism, Crime and Security Act 2001 (c 24) (no need to consider gravity of fear or threat of persecution) applies for the purpose of considering whether a presumption mentioned in subsection (6) has been rebutted as it applies for the purpose of considering whether Article 33(2) of the Refugee Convention applies.

(9) Subsection (10) applies where—

    (a)   a person appeals under section 82 . . . of this Act or under section 2 of the Special Immigration Appeals Commission Act 1997 (c 68) wholly or partly on the ground [mentioned in section 84(1)(a) or (3)(a) of this Act (breach of the United Kingdom's obligations under the Refugee Convention), and]

    (b)   the Secretary of State issues a certificate that presumptions under subsection (2), (3) or (4) apply to the person (subject to rebuttal).

(10) The . . . Tribunal or Commission hearing the appeal—

    (a)   must begin substantive deliberation on the appeal by considering the certificate, and

    (b)   if in agreement that presumptions under subsection (2), (3) or (4) apply (having given the appellant an opportunity for rebuttal) must dismiss the appeal in so far as it relies on the ground specified in subsection (9)(a).

[(10A) Subsection (10) also applies in relation to the Upper Tribunal when it acts under section 12(2)(b)(ii) of the Tribunals, Courts and Enforcement Act 2007.]

(11) For the purposes of this section—

    (a)   "the Refugee Convention" means the Convention relating to the Status of Refugees done at Geneva on 28th July 1951 and its Protocol, and

    (b)   a reference to a person who is sentenced to a period of imprisonment of at least two years—

        (i)   does not include a reference to a person who receives a suspended sentence (*unless at least two years of the sentence are not suspended*) [(unless a court subsequently orders that the sentence or any part of it is to take effect)],

        [(ia)   does not include a reference to a person who is sentenced to a period of imprisonment of at least two years only by virtue of being sentenced to consecutive sentences which amount in aggregate to more than two years,]

        (ii)   includes a reference to a person who is sentenced to detention, or ordered or directed to be detained, in an institution other than a prison (including, in particular, a hospital or an institution for young offenders), and

        (iii)   includes a reference to a person who is sentenced to imprisonment or detention, or ordered or directed to be detained, for an indeterminate period (provided that it may last for two years).

Amendment

Sub-s (9): in para (a) figure ", 83A" (omitted) repealed and words in square brackets substituted (for original words "that to remove him from or to require him to leave the United Kingdom would breach the United Kingdom's obligations under the Refugee Convention, and") by the Immigration Act 2014, s 73, Sch 9, Pt 4, paras 30, 31, as from 20 October 2014 (see SI 2014/2771, art 2), subject to savings in SI 2014/2771, arts 9–11.

Sub-s (10): word omitted repealed by the Asylum and Immigration (Treatment of Claimants, etc) Act 2004, ss 26(7), 47, Sch 2, Pt 1, paras 16, 17, Sch 4.

Sub-s (10A): inserted by SI 2010/21, art 5(1), Sch 1, paras 20, 21.

Sub-s (11): in para (b)(i) words "(unless at least two years of the sentence are not suspended)" in italics repealed and subsequent words in square brackets substituted by the UK Borders Act 2007, s 39(1), (2), as from a day to be appointed.

Sub-s (11): sub-para (ia) inserted by the UK Borders Act 2007, s 39(1), (3), as from a day to be appointed.

Subordinate Legislation

Nationality, Immigration and Asylum Act 2002 (Specification of Particularly Serious Crimes) Order 2004, SI 2004/1910.

73–75

(Contain amendments to legislation which, in so far as unrepealed and relevant to this work, have been incorporated at the appropriate place.)

76 Revocation of leave to enter or remain

(1) The Secretary of State may revoke a person's indefinite leave to enter or remain in the United Kingdom if the person—

    (a) is liable to deportation, but

    (b) cannot be deported for legal reasons.

(2) The Secretary of State may revoke a person's indefinite leave to enter or remain in the United Kingdom if—

    (a) the leave was obtained by deception,

    (b) *the person would be liable to removal because of the deception, but*

    (c) *the person cannot be removed for legal or practical reasons.*

(3) The Secretary of State may revoke a person's indefinite leave to enter or remain in the United Kingdom if the person, or someone of whom he is a dependant, ceases to be a refugee as a result of—

    (a) voluntarily availing himself of the protection of his country of nationality,

    (b) voluntarily re-acquiring a lost nationality,

    (c) acquiring the nationality of a country other than the United Kingdom and availing himself of its protection, or

    (d) voluntarily establishing himself in a country in respect of which he was a refugee.

(4) In this section—

"indefinite leave" has the meaning given by section 33(1) of the Immigration Act 1971 (c 77) (interpretation),

"liable to deportation" has the meaning given by section 3(5) and (6) of that Act (deportation),

"refugee" has the meaning given by the Convention relating to the Status of Refugees done at Geneva on 28th July 1951 and its Protocol, and

"removed" means removed from the United Kingdom under—

    (a) paragraph 9 or 10 of Schedule 2 to the Immigration Act 1971

        (control of entry: directions for removal), or

    (b) section 10(1)(b) of the Immigration and Asylum Act 1999 (c 33)

        (removal of persons unlawfully in United Kingdom: deception).

(5) A power under subsection (1) or (2) to revoke leave may be exercised—

    (a) in respect of leave granted before this section comes into force;

    (b) in reliance on anything done before this section comes into force.

(6) A power under subsection (3) to revoke leave may be exercised—

    (a) in respect of leave granted before this section comes into force, but

    (b) only in reliance on action taken after this section comes into force.

(7) . . .

Amendment

Sub-s (2): paras (b), (c) repealed by the Immigration Act 2014, s 73, Sch 9, Pt 1, para 3(1), (3)(a), as from 20 October 2014 (see SI 2014/2771, art 2), subject to savings in SI 2014/2771, arts 9–11

Sub-s (4): definition "removed" (omitted) repealed by the Immigration Act 2014, s 73, Sch 9, Pt 1, para 3(1), (3)(b), as from 20 October 2014 (see SI 2014/2771, art 2), subject to savings in SI 2014/2771, arts 9–11

Sub-s (7): amended the Immigration and Asylum Act 1999, s 10) repealed by the Immigration Act 2014, s 73, Sch 9, Pt 1, para 7, as from 20 October 2014 (see SI 2014/2771, art 2), subject to savings in SI 2014/2771, arts 9–11

77 No removal while claim for asylum pending

(1) While a person's claim for asylum is pending he may not be—

(a) removed from the United Kingdom in accordance with a provision of the Immigration Acts, or

(b) required to leave the United Kingdom in accordance with a provision of the Immigration Acts.

(2) In this section—

(a) "claim for asylum" means a claim by a person that it would be contrary to the United Kingdom's obligations under the Refugee Convention to remove him from or require him to leave the United Kingdom, and

(b) a person's claim is pending until he is given notice of the Secretary of State's decision on it.

(3) In subsection (2) "the Refugee Convention" means the Convention relating to the Status of Refugees done at Geneva on 28th July 1951 and its Protocol.

(4) Nothing in this section shall prevent any of the following while a claim for asylum is pending—

(a) the giving of a direction for the claimant's removal from the United Kingdom,

(b) the making of a deportation order in respect of the claimant, or

(c) the taking of any other interim or preparatory action.

(5) Section 15 of the Immigration and Asylum Act 1999 (c 33) (protection from removal or deportation) shall cease to have effect.

78 No removal while appeal pending

(1) While a person's appeal under section 82(1) is pending he may not be—

(a) removed from the United Kingdom in accordance with a provision of the Immigration Acts, or

(b) required to leave the United Kingdom in accordance with a provision of the Immigration Acts.

(2) In this section "pending" has the meaning given by section 104.

(3) Nothing in this section shall prevent any of the following while an appeal is pending—

(a) the giving of a direction for the appellant's removal from the United Kingdom,

(b) the making of a deportation order in respect of the appellant (subject to section 79), or

(c) the taking of any other interim or preparatory action.

(4) This section applies only to an appeal brought while the appellant is in the United Kingdom in accordance with section 92.

[78A Restriction on removal of children and their parents etc

(1) This section applies in a case where—

(a) a child is to be removed from or required to leave the United Kingdom, and

(b) an individual who—

    (i) is a parent of the child or has care of the child, and

    (ii) is living in a household in the United Kingdom with the child,

is also to be removed from or required to leave the United Kingdom (a "relevant parent or carer").

(2) During the period of 28 days beginning with the day on which the relevant appeal rights are exhausted—

    (a) the child may not be removed from or required to leave the United Kingdom; and

    (b) a relevant parent or carer may not be removed from or required to leave the United Kingdom if, as a result, no relevant parent or carer would remain in the United Kingdom.

(3) The relevant appeal rights are exhausted at the time when—

    (a) neither the child, nor any relevant parent or carer, could bring an appeal under section 82 (ignoring any possibility of an appeal out of time with permission), and

    (b) no appeal brought by the child, or by any relevant parent or carer, is pending within the meaning of section 104.

(4) Nothing in this section prevents any of the following during the period of 28 days mentioned in subsection (2)—

    (a) the giving of a direction for the removal of a person from the United Kingdom,

    (b) the making of a deportation order in respect of a person, or

    (c) the taking of any other interim or preparatory action.

(5) In this section—

"child" means a person who is aged under 18;

references to a person being removed from or required to leave the United Kingdom are to the person being removed or required to leave in accordance with a provision of the Immigration Acts.]

Amendment

Inserted by the Immigration Act 2014, s 2, as from 28 July 2014: see SI 2014/1820.

79 Deportation order: appeal

(1) A deportation order may not be made in respect of a person while an appeal under section 82(1) [that may be brought or continued from within the United Kingdom relating to] the decision to make the order—

    (a) could be brought (ignoring any possibility of an appeal out of time with permission), or

    (b) is pending.

(2) In this section "pending" has the meaning given by section 104.

[(3) This section does not apply to a deportation order which states that it is made in accordance with section 32(5) of the UK Borders Act 2007.

(4) But a deportation order made in reliance on subsection (3) does not invalidate leave to enter or remain, in accordance with section 5(1) of the Immigration Act 1971, if and for so long as section 78 above applies.]

Amendment

Sub-s (1): words in square brackets substituted (for original word "against") by the Immigration Act 2014, s 73, Sch 9, Pt 4, paras 30, 32, as from 20 October 2014 (see SI 2014/2771, art 2), subject to savings in SI 2014/2771, arts 9–11.

Sub-ss (3), (4): inserted by the UK Borders Act 2007, s 35(1), (2). Date in force (for certain purposes): 1 August 2008: see SI 2008/1818, art 2(a), Schedule. Date in force (for remaining purposes): to be appointed: see the UK Borders Act 2007, s 59(2).

80

(Repealed by the Asylum and Immigration (Treatment of Claimants, etc) Act 2004, ss 33(3)(a), 47, Sch 4.)

PART 5

[APPEALS IN RESPECT OF PROTECTION AND HUMAN RIGHTS CLAIMS]

Amendment

Part heading substituted (for original words "Immigration and Asylum Appeals") by the Immigration Act 2014, s 73, Sch 9, Pt 4, paras 30, 33, as from 20 October 2014 (see SI 2014/2771, art 2), subject to savings in SI 2014/2771, arts 9–11.

[Appeal to Tribunal]

[81 Meaning of "the Tribunal"

In this Part "the Tribunal" means the First-tier Tribunal.]

Amendment

Substituted by SI 2010/21, art 5(1), Sch 1, paras 20, 22.

[82 Right of appeal to the Tribunal

(1) A person ("P") may appeal to the Tribunal where—

   (a)   the Secretary of State has decided to refuse a protection claim made by P,

   (b)   the Secretary of State has decided to refuse a human rights claim made by P, or

   (c)   the Secretary of State has decided to revoke P's protection status.

(2) For the purposes of this Part—

   (a)   a "protection claim" is a claim made by a person ("P") that removal of P from the United Kingdom—

      (i)   would breach the United Kingdom's obligations under the Refugee Convention, or

      (ii)   would breach the United Kingdom's obligations in relation to persons eligible for a grant of humanitarian protection;

   (b)   P's protection claim is refused if the Secretary of State makes one or more of the following decisions—

      (i)   that removal of P from the United Kingdom would not breach the United Kingdom's obligations under the Refugee Convention;

      (ii)   that removal of P from the United Kingdom would not breach the United Kingdom's obligations in relation to persons eligible for a grant of humanitarian protection;

   (c)   a person has "protection status" if the person has been granted leave to enter or remain in the United Kingdom as a refugee or as a person eligible for a grant of humanitarian protection;

   (d)   "humanitarian protection" is to be construed in accordance with the immigration rules;

   (e)   "refugee" has the same meaning as in the Refugee Convention.

(3) The right of appeal under subsection (1) is subject to the exceptions and limitations specified in this Part.]

Amendment

Substituted by the Immigration Act 2014, s 15(1), (2), as from 20 October 2014 (see SI 2014/2771, art 2), subject to savings in SI 2014/2771, arts 9–11. Prior to this substitution, s 82 and the notes relating to it, read as follows:

"82 Right of appeal: general

(1) Where an immigration decision is made in respect of a person he may appeal [to the Tribunal].

(2) In this Part "immigration decision" means—

(a) refusal of leave to enter the United Kingdom,

(b) refusal of entry clearance,

(c) refusal of a certificate of entitlement under section 10 of this Act,

(d) refusal to vary a person's leave to enter or remain in the United Kingdom if the result of the refusal is that the person has no leave to enter or remain,

(e) variation of a person's leave to enter or remain in the United Kingdom if when the variation takes effect the person has no leave to enter or remain,

(f) revocation under section 76 of this Act of indefinite leave to enter or remain in the United Kingdom,

(g) a decision that a person is to be removed from the United Kingdom by way of directions under section 10(1)(a), (b), (ba) or (c)] of the Immigration and Asylum Act 1999 (c 33) (removal of person unlawfully in United Kingdom),

(h) a decision that an illegal entrant is to be removed from the United Kingdom by way of directions under paragraphs 8 to 10 of Schedule 2 to the Immigration Act 1971 (c 77) (control of entry: removal),

[(ha) a decision that a person is to be removed from the United Kingdom by way of directions under section 47 of the Immigration, Asylum and Nationality Act 2006 (removal: persons with statutorily extended leave),]

(i) a decision that a person is to be removed from the United Kingdom by way of directions given by virtue of paragraph 10A of that Schedule (family),

[(ia) a decision that a person is to be removed from the United Kingdom by way of directions under paragraph 12(2) of Schedule 2 to the Immigration Act 1971 (c 77) (seamen and aircrews),]

[(ib) a decision to make an order under section 2A of that Act (deprivation of right of abode),]

(j) a decision to make a deportation order under section 5(1) of that Act, and

(k) refusal to revoke a deportation order under section 5(2) of that Act.

(3) . . .

[(3A) Subsection (2)(j) does not apply to a decision to make a deportation order which states that it is made in accordance with section 32(5) of the UK Borders Act 2007; but—

(a) a decision that section 32(5) applies is an immigration decision for the purposes of this Part, and

(b) a reference in this Part to an appeal against an automatic deportation order is a reference to an appeal against a decision of the Secretary of State that section 32(5) applies.]

(4) The right of appeal under subsection (1) is subject to the exceptions and limitations specified in this Part.

Amendment

Sub-s (1): words "to the Tribunal" in square brackets substituted by the Asylum and Immigration (Treatment of Claimants, etc) Act 2004, s 26(2).

Sub-s (2): in para (g) words "section 10(1)(a), (b), (ba) or (c)" in square brackets substituted by the Immigration, Asylum and Nationality Act 2006, s 2.

Sub-s (2): para (ha) inserted by the Immigration, Asylum and Nationality Act 2006, s 47(6).

Sub-s (2): para (ia) inserted by the Asylum and Immigration (Treatment of Claimants, etc) Act 2004, s 31.

Sub-s (2): para (ib) inserted by the Immigration, Asylum and Nationality Act 2006, s 57(2).

Sub-s (3): repealed by the Immigration, Asylum and Nationality Act 2006, ss 11(6), 61, Sch 3.

Sub-s (3A): inserted by the UK Borders Act 2007, s 35(1), (3).".

83 Appeal: asylum claim

(1) *This section applies where a person has made an asylum claim and—*

(a) *his claim has been rejected by the Secretary of State, but*

(b) he has been granted leave to enter or remain in the United Kingdom for a period exceeding one year (or for periods exceeding one year in aggregate).

(2) The person may appeal [to the Tribunal] against the rejection of his asylum claim.

Amendment

Repealed by the Immigration Act 2014, s 15(1), (3), as from 20 October 2014 (see SI 2014/2771, art 2), subject to savings in SI 2014/2771, arts 9–11.

Sub-s (2): words "to the Tribunal" in square brackets substituted by the Asylum and Immigration (Treatment of Claimants, etc) Act 2004, s 26(3).

[**83A Appeal: variation of limited leave**]

[(1) This section applies where—

(a) a person has made an asylum claim,

(b) he was granted limited leave to enter or remain in the United Kingdom as a refugee within the meaning of the Refugee Convention,

(c) a decision is made that he is not a refugee, and

(d) following the decision specified in paragraph (c) he has limited leave to enter or remain in the United Kingdom otherwise than as a refugee.

(2) The person may appeal to the Tribunal against the decision to curtail or to refuse to extend his limited leave.]

Amendment

Inserted by the Immigration, Asylum and Nationality Act 2006, s 1.

Repealed by the Immigration Act 2014, s 15(1), (3), as from 20 October 2014 (see SI 2014/2771, art 2), subject to savings in SI 2014/2771, arts 9–11.

[**84 Grounds of appeal**]

(1) An appeal under section 82(1)(a) (refusal of protection claim) must be brought on one or more of the following grounds—

(a) that removal of the appellant from the United Kingdom would breach the United Kingdom's obligations under the Refugee Convention;

(b) that removal of the appellant from the United Kingdom would breach the United Kingdom's obligations in relation to persons eligible for a grant of humanitarian protection;

(c) that removal of the appellant from the United Kingdom would be unlawful under section 6 of the Human Rights Act 1998 (public authority not to act contrary to Human Rights Convention).

(2) An appeal under section 82(1)(b) (refusal of human rights claim) must be brought on the ground that the decision is unlawful under section 6 of the Human Rights Act 1998.

(3) An appeal under section 82(1)(c) (revocation of protection status) must be brought on one or more of the following grounds—

(a) that the decision to revoke the appellant's protection status breaches the United Kingdom's obligations under the Refugee Convention;

(b) that the decision to revoke the appellant's protection status breaches the United Kingdom's obligations in relation to persons eligible for a grant of humanitarian protection.]

Amendment

Substituted by the Immigration Act 2014, s 15(1), (4), as from 20 October 2014 (see SI 2014/2771, art 2), subject to savings in SI 2014/2771, arts 9–11. Prior to this substitution, s 84 and the notes relating to it, read as follows:

"84 Grounds of appeal

(1) An appeal under section 82(1) against an immigration decision must be brought on one or more of the following grounds—

(a) that the decision is not in accordance with immigration rules;

(b) that the decision is unlawful by virtue of . . . [Article 20A of the Race Relations (Northern Ireland) Order 1997] [or by virtue of section 29 of the Equality Act 2010 (discrimination in the exercise of public functions etc) so far as relating to race as defined by section 9(1) of that Act];

(c) that the decision is unlawful under section 6 of the Human Rights Act 1998 (c 42) (public authority not to act contrary to Human Rights Convention) as being incompatible with the appellant's Convention rights;

(d) that the appellant is an EEA national or a member of the family of an EEA national and the decision breaches the appellant's rights under the [EU] Treaties in respect of entry to or residence in the United Kingdom;

(e) that the decision is otherwise not in accordance with the law;

(f) that the person taking the decision should have exercised differently a discretion conferred by immigration rules;

(g) that removal of the appellant from the United Kingdom in consequence of the immigration decision would breach the United Kingdom's obligations under the Refugee Convention or would be unlawful under section 6 of the Human Rights Act 1998 as being incompatible with the appellant's Convention rights.

(2) In subsection (1)(d) "EEA national" means a national of a State which is a contracting party to the Agreement on the European Economic Area signed at Oporto on 2nd May 1992 (as it has effect from time to time).

(3) An appeal under section 83 must be brought on the grounds that removal of the appellant from the United Kingdom would breach the United Kingdom's obligations under the Refugee Convention.

[(4) An appeal under section 83A must be brought on the grounds that removal of the appellant from the United Kingdom would breach the United Kingdom's obligations under the Refugee Convention.]

Amendment

Sub-s (1): in para (b) words omitted repealed by SI 2011/1060, art 4(b). Date in force: 4 April 2011: see SI 2011/1060, art 1(2).

Sub-s (1): in para (b) words "or Article 20A of the Race Relations (Northern Ireland) Order 1997" in square brackets inserted by the Race Relations Order (Amendment) Regulations (Northern Ireland) 2003, SR 2003/341, art 60.

Sub-s (1): in para (b) words from "or by virtue" to "of that Act" in square brackets inserted by the Crime and Courts Act 2013, s 51(1). Date in force: 8 May 2013: see SI 2013/1042, art 2(i).

Sub-s (1): in para (d) reference to "EU" in square brackets substituted by SI 2011/1043, art 6(1)(a). Date in force: 22 April 2011: see SI 2011/1043, art 2; for transitional savings see art 3(3) thereof.

Sub-s (4): inserted by the Immigration, Asylum and Nationality Act 2006, s 3.".

85 Matters to be considered

(1) An appeal under section 82(1) against a decision shall be treated by [the Tribunal] as including an appeal against any decision in respect of which the appellant has a right of appeal under section 82(1).

(2) If an appellant under section 82(1) makes a statement under section 120, [the Tribunal] shall consider any matter raised in the statement which constitutes a ground of appeal of a kind listed in section [84] against the decision appealed against.

(3) Subsection (2) applies to a statement made under section 120 whether the statement was made before or after the appeal was commenced.

(4) On an appeal under section 82(1) . . . against a decision [the Tribunal] may consider . . . any matter which [it] thinks relevant to the substance of the decision, including . . . a matter arising after the date of the decision.

[(5) But the Tribunal must not consider a new matter unless the Secretary of State has given the Tribunal consent to do so.

(6) A matter is a "new matter" if—

(a) it constitutes a ground of appeal of a kind listed in section 84, and

(b) the Secretary of State has not previously considered the matter in the context of—

(i) the decision mentioned in section 82(1), or

(ii) a statement made by the appellant under section 120.]

Amendment

Sub-s (1): words "the Tribunal" square brackets substituted by the Asylum and Immigration (Treatment of Claimants, etc) Act 2004, s 26(7), Sch 2, Pt 1, paras 16, 18(1)(b), (2)(a); for transitional provisions see s 26(7), Sch 2, Pt 2 thereto.

Sub-s (2): words "the Tribunal" in square brackets substituted by the Asylum and Immigration (Treatment of Claimants, etc) Act 2004, s 26(7), Sch 2, Pt 1, paras 16, 18(1)(b), (2)(a); for transitional provisions see s 26(7), Sch 2, Pt 2 thereto.

Sub-s (2): reference to "84" in square brackets substituted (for original reference to "84(1)" by the Immigration Act 2014, s 73, Sch 9, Pt 4, paras 16, 18(1)(c), (2)(a); as from 20 October 2014 (see SI 2014/2771, art 2), subject to savings in SI 2014/2771, arts 9–11.

Sub-s (4): words "the Tribunal" in square brackets substituted by the Asylum and Immigration (Treatment of Claimants, etc) Act 2004, s 26(7), Sch 2, Pt 1, paras 16, 18(1)(b), (2)(a); for transitional provisions see s 26(7), Sch 2, Pt 2 thereto.

Sub-s (4): word "it" in square brackets substituted by the Asylum and Immigration (Treatment of Claimants, etc) Act 2004, s 26(7), Sch 2, Pt 2 thereto.

Sub-s (4): words "the Tribunal" in square brackets substituted by the Asylum and Immigration (Treatment of Claimants, etc) Act 2004, s 26(7), Sch 2, Pt 1, paras 16, 18(1)(c), (2)(a); for transitional provisions see s 26(7), Sch 2, Pt 2 thereto.

Sub-s (4): words ", 83(2) or 83A(2)" (omitted) repealed by the Immigration Act 2014, s 73, Sch 9, Pt 4, paras 30, 34(b), as from 20 October 2014 (see SI 2014/2771, arts 9–11.

Sub-ss (5), (6) substituted for sub-s (5) (as previously substituted by the UK Borders Act 2007, s 19(1)) by the Immigration Act 2014, s 15(1), (5), as from 20 October 2014 (see SI 2014/2771, art 2), subject to savings in SI 2014/2771, arts 9–11. Sub-s (5) previously read as follows:

"(5) But subsection (4) is subject to the exceptions in section 85A.]".

[85A Matters to be considered: new evidence; exceptions]

[(1) This section sets out the exceptions mentioned in section 85(5).

(2) Exception 1 is that in relation to an appeal under section 82(1) against an immigration decision of a kind specified in section 82(2)(b) or (c) the Tribunal may consider only the circumstances appertaining at the time of the decision.

(3) Exception 2 applies to an appeal under section 82(1) if—

(a) the appeal is against an immigration decision of a kind specified in section 82(2)(a) or (d),

(b) the immigration decision concerned an application of a kind identified in immigration rules as requiring to be considered under a "Points Based System", and

(c) the appeal relies wholly or partly on grounds specified in section 84(1)(a), (e) or (f).

(4) Where Exception 2 applies the Tribunal may consider evidence adduced by the appellant only if it—

(a) was submitted in support of, and at the time of making, the application to which the immigration decision related,

(b) relates to the appeal in so far as it relies on grounds other than those specified in subsection (3)(c),

(c) is adduced to prove that a document is genuine or valid, or

(d) is adduced in connection with the Secretary of State's reliance on a discretion under immigration rules, or compliance with a requirement of immigration rules, to refuse an application on grounds not related to the acquisition of "points" under the "Points Based System".

[(5) Tribunal Procedure Rules may make provision, for the purposes of subsection (4)(a), about the circumstances in which evidence is to be treated, or not treated, as submitted in support of, and at the time of making, an application.]]

Amendment

Inserted by the UK Borders Act 2007, s 19(2). Date in force: 23 May 2011: see SI 2011/1293, art 2; for transitional provisions see art 3 thereof.

Sub-s (5): inserted by SI 2010/21, art 5(1), Sch 1, paras 20, 23. Date in force: 15 February 2010: see SI 2010/21, art 1; for transitional provisions and savings see art 5(4), Sch 4, paras 14–18, 21 thereto.

Repealed by the Immigration Act 2014, s 73, Sch 9, Pt 4, paras 30, 35, as from 20 October 2014 (see SI 2014/2771, art 2), subject to savings in SI 2014/2771, arts 9–11.

86 Determination of appeal

(1) This section applies on an appeal under section 82(1) . . . .

(2) [The Tribunal] must determine—

    (a) any matter raised as a ground of appeal . . . , and

    (b) any matter which section 85 requires [it] to consider.

(3) [The Tribunal] must allow the appeal in so far as [it] thinks that—

    (a) a decision against which the appeal is brought or is treated as being brought was not in accordance with the law (including immigration rules), or

    (b) a discretion exercised in making a decision against which the appeal is brought or is treated as being brought should have been exercised differently.

(4) For the purposes of subsection (3) a decision that a person should be removed from the United Kingdom under a provision shall not be regarded as unlawful if it could have been lawfully made by reference to removal under another provision.

(5) In so far as subsection (3) does not apply, [the Tribunal] shall dismiss the appeal.

(6) Refusal to depart from or to authorise departure from immigration rules is not the exercise of a discretion for the purposes of subsection (3)(b).

Amendment

Sub-s (1): words ", 83 or 83A" omitted repealed by the Immigration Act 2014, s 73, Sch 9, Pt 4, paras 30, 36(a), as from 20 October 2014 (see SI 2014/2771, art 2), subject to savings in SI 2014/2771, arts 9–11.

Sub-s (2): words "The Tribunal" in square brackets substituted by the Asylum and Immigration (Treatment of Claimants, etc) Act 2004, s 26(7), Sch 2, Pt 1, paras 16, 18(1)(b), (2)(b); for transitional provisions see s 26(7), Sch 2, Pt 2 thereto.

Sub-s (2): words "(whether or not by virtue of section 85(1))" omitted from para (a) repealed by the Immigration Act 2014, s 73, Sch 9, Pt 4, paras 30, 36(a), as from 20 October 2014 (see SI 2014/2771, art 2), subject to savings in SI 2014/2771, arts 9–11.

Sub-s (2): in para (b) word "it" in square brackets substituted by the Asylum and Immigration (Treatment of Claimants, etc) Act 2004, s 26(7), Sch 2, Pt 1, paras 16, 18(1)(d), (2)(b); for transitional provisions see s 26(7), Sch 2, Pt 2 thereto.

Sub-s (3): words "The Tribunal" in square brackets substituted by the Asylum and Immigration (Treatment of Claimants, etc) Act 2004, s 26(7), Sch 2, Pt 1, paras 16, 18(1)(b), (2)(b); for transitional provisions see s 26(7), Sch 2, Pt 2 thereto.

Sub-s (3): word "it" in square brackets substituted by the Asylum and Immigration (Treatment of Claimants, etc) Act 2004, s 26(7), Sch 2, Pt 1, paras 16, 18(1)(c), (2)(b); for transitional provisions see s 26(7), Sch 2, Pt 2 thereto.

Sub-s (5): words "the Tribunal" in square brackets substituted by the Asylum and Immigration (Treatment of Claimants, etc) Act 2004, s 26(7), Sch 2, Pt 1, paras 16, 18(1)(b), (2)(b); for transitional provisions see s 26(7), Sch 2, Pt 2 thereto.

Sub-ss (3)–(6): repealed by the Immigration Act 2014, s 73, Sch 9, Pt 4, paras 30, 36(c), as from 20 October 2014 (see SI 2014/2771, art 2), subject to savings in SI 2014/2771, arts 9–11.

87 *Successful appeal: direction*

(1) If [the Tribunal] allows an appeal under section 82[, 83 or 83A] [it] may give a direction for the purpose of giving effect to [its] decision.

(2) A person responsible for making an immigration decision shall act in accordance with any relevant direction under subsection (1).

[(3) But a direction under this section shall not have effect while—

   (a)   an application for permission to appeal under section 11 or 13 of the Tribunals, Courts and Enforcement Act 2007 could be made or is awaiting determination,

   (b)   permission to appeal to the Upper Tribunal or a court under either of those sections has been granted and the appeal is awaiting determination,

      or

   (c)   an appeal has been remitted under section 12 or 14 of that Act and is awaiting determination.]

(4)   A direction under subsection (1) shall be treated [as part of the Tribunal's decision on the appeal for the purposes of section [11 of the Tribunals, Courts and Enforcement Act 2007]].

Amendment

Repealed by the Immigration Act 2014, s 73, Sch 9, Pt 4, paras 30, 37, as from 20 October 2014 (see SI 2014/2771, art 2), subject to savings in SI 2014/2771, arts 9–11.

Sub-s (1): words "the Tribunal" in square brackets substituted by the Asylum and Immigration (Treatment of Claimants, etc) Act 2004, s 26(7), Sch 2, Pt 1, paras 16, 18(1)(a), (2)(c); for transitional provisions see s 26(7), Sch 2, Pt 2 thereto.

Sub-s (1): words ", 83 or 83A" in square brackets substituted by the Immigration, Asylum and Nationality Act 2006, s 14, Sch 1, paras 1, 5.

Sub-s (1): word "it" in square brackets substituted by the Asylum and Immigration (Treatment of Claimants, etc) Act 2004, s 26(7), Sch 2, Pt 1, paras 16, 18(1)(c), (2)(c); for transitional provisions see s 26(7), Sch 2, Pt 2 thereto.

Sub-s (1): word "its" in square brackets substituted by the Asylum and Immigration (Treatment of Claimants, etc) Act 2004, s 26(7), Sch 2, Pt 1, paras 16, 18(1)(e), (2)(c); for transitional provisions see s 26(7), Sch 2, Pt 2 thereto.

Sub-s (3): substituted by SI 2010/21, art 5(1), paras 20, 24(a). Date in force: 15 February 2010: see SI 2010/21, art 1; for transitional provisions and savings see art 5(4), Sch 4, paras 2–19, 21 thereto.

Sub-s (4): repealed by the Asylum and Immigration (Treatment of Claimants, etc) Act 2004, s 47, Sch 4. Date in force: to be appointed: see the Asylum and Immigration (Treatment of Claimants, etc) Act 2004, s 48(3)–(6).

Sub-s (4): words in square brackets beginning with the words "as part of" substituted by the Asylum and Immigration (Treatment of Claimants, etc) Act 2004, s 26(7), Sch 2, Pt 1, paras 16, 19(b); for transitional provisions see s 26(7), Sch 2, Pt 2 thereto.

Sub-s (4): words "11 of the Tribunals, Courts and Enforcement Act 2007" in square brackets substituted by SI 2010/21, art 5(1), Sch 1, paras 20, 24(b).

Exceptions and limitations

88 Ineligibility

(1)   This section applies to an immigration decision of a kind referred to in section 82(2)(a), (b), (d) or (e).

(2)   A person may not appeal under section 82(1) against an immigration decision which is taken on the grounds that he or a person of whom he is a dependant—

   (a)   does not satisfy a requirement as to age, nationality or citizenship specified in immigration rules,

   (b)   does not have an immigration document of a particular kind (or any immigration document),

   [(ba)   has failed to supply a medical report or a medical certificate in accordance with a requirement of immigration rules,]

   (c)   is seeking to be in the United Kingdom for a period greater than that permitted in his case by immigration rules, or

   (d)   is seeking to enter or remain in the United Kingdom for a purpose other than one for which entry or remaining is permitted in accordance with immigration rules.

(3) In subsection (2)(b) "immigration document" means—

(a) entry clearance,

(b) a passport,

(c) a work permit or other immigration employment document within the meaning of section 122, and

(d) a document which relates to a national of a country other than the United Kingdom and which is designed to serve the same purpose as a passport.

(4) Subsection (2) does not prevent the bringing of an appeal on any or all of the grounds referred to in section 84(1)(b), (c) and (g).

Amendment

Repealed by the Immigration Act 2014, s 73, Sch 9, Pt 4, paras 30, 37, as from 20 October 2014 (see SI 2014/2771, art 2), subject to savings in SI 2014/2771, arts 9–11.

Sub-s (2): para (ba) inserted by the Immigration, Asylum and Nationality Act 2006, s 5.

[88A Entry clearance]

[(1) A person may not appeal under section 82(1) against refusal of an application for entry clearance unless the application was made for the purpose of—

(a) . . .

(b) entering as the dependant of a person in circumstances prescribed by regulations for the purpose of this subsection.

(2) Regulations under subsection (1) may, in particular—

(a) . . .

(b) provide for the determination of whether one person is dependent on another;

(c) make provision by reference to the [circumstances of the applicant or of the person] on whom he depends, or of both (and the regulations may, in particular, include provision by reference to—

(i) whether or not a person is lawfully settled in the United Kingdom within such meaning as the regulations may assign;

(ii) the duration of two individuals' residence together);

(d) make provision by reference to an applicant's purpose in entering as a dependant;

(e) make provision by reference to immigration rules;

(f) confer a discretion.

(3) Subsection (1)—

(a) does not prevent the bringing of an appeal on either or both of the grounds referred to in section 84(1)(b) and (c), and

(b) is without prejudice to the effect of section 88 in relation to an appeal under section 82(1) against refusal of entry clearance.]]

Amendment

Inserted by the Asylum and Immigration (Treatment of Claimants, etc) Act 2004, s 29(1). Substituted, together with ss 90, 91, by new s 88A, by the Immigration, Asylum and Nationality Act 2006, s 4(1); for effect see s 4(3) thereof. Date in force (for certain purposes): 1 April 2008: see SI 2008/310, art 3(a). Date in force (for remaining purposes): to be appointed: see the Immigration, Asylum and Nationality Act 2006, s 62(1).

Repealed by the Immigration Act 2014, s 73, Sch 9, Pt 4, paras 30, 37, as from 20 October 2014 (see SI 2014/2771, art 2), subject to savings in SI 2014/2771, arts 9–11.

Sub-s (1): para (a) repealed by the Crime and Courts Act 2013, s 52(1), (3). Date in force: 25 June 2013: see SI 2013/1042, art 4(a); for transitional and saving provision see art 5 thereof.

Sub-s (2): para (a) repealed by the Crime and Courts Act 2013, s 52(1), (4).Date in force: 25 June 2013: see SI 2013/1042, art 4(a); for transitional and saving provision see art 5 thereof.

Sub-s (2): in para (c) words "circumstances of the applicant or of the person" in square brackets substituted by the Crime and Courts Act 2013, s 52(1), (5). Date in force: 25 June 2013: see SI 2013/1042, art 4(a); for transitional and saving provision see art 5 thereof.

Subordinate Legislation

Immigration Appeals (Family Visitor) Regulations 2012, SI 2012/1532.

[89 Refusal of leave to enter]

[(1) A person may not appeal under section 82(1) against refusal of leave to enter the United Kingdom unless—

   (a)   on his arrival in the United Kingdom he had entry clearance, and

   (b)   the purpose of entry specified in the entry clearance is the same as that specified in his application for leave to enter.

(2) Subsection (1) does not prevent the bringing of an appeal on any or all of the grounds referred to in section 84(1)(b), (c) and (g).]

Amendment

Substituted by the Immigration, Asylum and Nationality Act 2006, s 6.

Repealed by the Immigration Act 2014, s 73, Sch 9, Pt 4, paras 30, 37, as from 20 October 2014 (see SI 2014/2771, art 2), subject to savings in SI 2014/2771, arts 9–11.

90 Non-family visitor

(1) A person who applies for entry clearance for the purpose of entering the United Kingdom as a visitor may appeal under section 82(1) against refusal of entry clearance only if the application was made for the purpose of visiting a member of the applicant's family.

(2) In subsection (1) the reference to a member of the applicant's family shall be construed in accordance with regulations.

(3) Regulations under subsection (2) may, in particular, make provision wholly or partly by reference to the duration of two individuals' residence together.

(4) Subsection (1) does not prevent the bringing of an appeal on either or both of the grounds referred to in section 84(1)(b) and (c).

Amendment

Repealed by the Immigration Act 2014, s 73, Sch 9, Pt 4, paras 30, 37, as from 20 October 2014 (see SI 2014/2771, art 2), subject to savings in SI 2014/2771, arts 9–11.

Substituted, together with ss 88A, 91, by new s 88A, by the Immigration, Asylum and Nationality Act 2006, s 4(1); for effect see s 4(3) thereof.

Date in force (for certain purposes): 1 April 2008: see SI 2008/310, art 3(a); for savings see SI 2012/1531, art 3.

Date in force (for remaining purposes): to be appointed: see the Immigration, Asylum and Nationality Act 2006, s 62(1) and SI 2008/310, art 4.

91 Student

(1) A person may not appeal under section 82(1) against refusal of entry clearance if he seeks it—

   (a)   in order to follow a course of study for which he has been accepted and which will not last more than six months,

   (b)   in order to study but without having been accepted for a course, or

   (c)   as the dependant of a person seeking entry clearance for a purpose described in paragraph (a) or (b).

(2) Subsection (1) does not prevent the bringing of an appeal on either or both of the grounds referred to in section 84(1)(b) and (c).

Amendment

Repealed by the Immigration Act 2014, s 73, Sch 9, Pt 4, paras 30, 37, as from 20 October 2014 (see SI 2014/2771, art 2), subject to savings in SI 2014/2771, arts 9–11.

Substituted, together with ss 88A, 90, by new s 88A, by the Immigration, Asylum and Nationality Act 2006, s 4(1); for effect see s 4(3) thereof.

Date in force (for certain purposes): 1 April 2008: see SI 2008/310, art 3(a).

Date in force (for remaining purposes): to be appointed: see the Immigration, Asylum and Nationality Act 2006, s 62(1) and SI 2008/310, art 4.

[92 Place from which an appeal may be brought or continued

(1) This section applies to determine the place from which an appeal under section 82(1) may be brought or continued.

(2) In the case of an appeal under section 82(1)(a) (protection claim appeal), the appeal must be brought from outside the United Kingdom if—

(a) the claim to which the appeal relates has been certified under section 94(1) or (7) (claim clearly unfounded or removal to safe third country), or

(b) paragraph 5(3)(a), 10(3), 15(3) or 19(b) of Schedule 3 to the Asylum and Immigration (Treatment of Claimants, etc) Act 2004 (removal of asylum seeker to safe third country) applies.

Otherwise, the appeal must be brought from within the United Kingdom.

(3) In the case of an appeal under section 82(1)(b) (human rights claim appeal) where the claim to which the appeal relates was made while the appellant was in the United Kingdom, the appeal must be brought from outside the United Kingdom if—

(a) the claim to which the appeal relates has been certified under section 94(1) or (7) (claim clearly unfounded or removal to safe third country) or section 94B (certification of human rights claims made by persons liable to deportation), or

(b) paragraph 5(3)(b) or (4), 10(4), 15(4) or 19(c) of Schedule 3 to the Asylum and Immigration (Treatment of Claimants, etc) Act 2004 (removal of asylum seeker to safe third country) applies.

Otherwise, the appeal must be brought from within the United Kingdom.

(4) In the case of an appeal under section 82(1)(b) (human rights claim appeal) where the claim to which the appeal relates was made while the appellant was outside the United Kingdom, the appeal must be brought from outside the United Kingdom.

(5) In the case of an appeal under section 82(1)(c) (revocation of protection status)—

(a) the appeal must be brought from within the United Kingdom if the decision to which the appeal relates was made while the appellant was in the United Kingdom;

(b) the appeal must be brought from outside the United Kingdom if the decision to which the appeal relates was made while the appellant was outside the United Kingdom.

Otherwise, the appeal must be brought from within the United Kingdom.

(6) If, after an appeal under section 82(1)(a) or (b) has been brought from within the United Kingdom, the Secretary of State certifies the claim to which the appeal relates under section 94(1) or (7) or section 94B, the appeal must be continued from outside the United Kingdom.

(7) Where a person brings or continues an appeal under section 82(1)(a) (refusal of protection claim) from outside the United Kingdom, for the purposes of considering whether the grounds of appeal are satisfied, the appeal is to be treated as if the person were not outside the United Kingdom.

(8) Where an appellant brings an appeal from within the United Kingdom but leaves the United Kingdom before the appeal is finally determined, the appeal is to be treated as abandoned unless the claim to which the appeal relates has been certified under section 94(1) or (7) or section 94B.]

Amendment

Substituted by the Immigration Act 2014, s 17(1), (2), as from 20 October 2014 (see SI 2014/2771, art 2), subject to savings in SI 2014/2771, arts 9–11, 15. Prior to this substitution, s 92 and the notes relating to it read as follows:

"92 Appeal from within United Kingdom: general

(1)   A person may not appeal under section 82(1) while he is in the United Kingdom unless his appeal is of a kind to which this section applies.

(2)   This section applies to an appeal against an immigration decision of a kind specified in section 82(2)(c), (d), (e), (f)[, (ha)] and (j).

[(2A)   So far as it relates to an immigration decision of a kind specified in section 82(2)(e), subsection (2) is subject to section 97B.]

[(3)   This section also applies to an appeal against refusal of leave to enter the United Kingdom if—

(a)   at the time of the refusal the appellant is in the United Kingdom, and

(b)   on his arrival in the United Kingdom the appellant had entry clearance.

(3A)   But this section does not apply by virtue of subsection (3) if subsection (3B) or (3C) applies to the refusal of leave to enter.

(3B)   This subsection applies to a refusal of leave to enter which is a deemed refusal under paragraph 2A(9) of Schedule 2 to the Immigration Act 1971 (c 77) resulting from cancellation of leave to enter by an immigration officer—

(a)   under paragraph 2A(8) of that Schedule, and

(b)   on the grounds specified in paragraph 2A(2A) of that Schedule.

(3C)   This subsection applies to a refusal of leave to enter for which specifies that the grounds for refusal are that the leave is sought for a purpose other than that specified in the entry clearance.

(3D)   This section also applies to an appeal against refusal of leave to enter the United Kingdom if at the time of the refusal the appellant—

(a)   is in the United Kingdom,

(b)   has a work permit, and

(c)   is any of the following (within the meaning of the British Nationality Act 1981 (c 61))—

(i)   a British overseas territories citizen,

(ii)   a British Overseas citizen,

(iii)   a British National (Overseas),

(iv)   a British protected person, or

(v)   a British subject.]

(4)   This section also applies to an appeal against an immigration decision if the appellant—

(a)   has made an asylum claim, or a human rights claim, while in the United Kingdom, or

(b)   is an EEA national or a member of the family of an EEA national and makes a claim to the Secretary of State that the decision breaches the appellant's rights under the [EU] Treaties in respect of entry to or residence in the United Kingdom.

Amendment

Sub-s (2): reference to ", (ha)" in square brackets inserted by the Immigration, Asylum and Nationality Act 2006, s 47(7).

Sub-s (2A): inserted by the Crime and Courts Act 2013, s 53(1), (2). Date in force: 25 June 2013: see SI 2013/1042, art 4(b).

Sub-ss (3), (3A)–(3D): substituted, for sub-s (3) as originally enacted, by the Asylum and Immigration (Treatment of Claimants, etc) Act 2004, s 28.

Sub-s (4): in para (b) reference to "EU" in square brackets substituted by SI 2011/1043, art 6(1)(a). Date in force: 22 April 2011: see SI 2011/1043, art 2; for transitional savings see art 3(3) thereof.".

93

(Repealed by the Asylum and Immigration (Treatment of Claimants, etc) Act 2004, ss 33(3)(b), 47, Sch 4.)

94 Appeal from within United Kingdom: unfounded human rights or [protection] claim

[(1)   The Secretary of State may certify a protection claim or human rights claim as clearly unfounded.]

(3)   If the Secretary of State is satisfied that [a] claimant is entitled to reside in a State listed in subsection (4) he shall certify the claim under [subsection (1)] unless satisfied that it is not clearly unfounded.

(4) Those States are—

(a) . . . . . .
(b) . . . . . .
(c) . . . . . .
(d) . . . . . .
(e) . . . . . .
(f) . . . . . .
(g) . . . . . .
(h) . . . . . .
(i) . . . . . .
(j) the Republic of Albania,
[(k) . . . . . .
(l) . . . . . .
(m) Jamaica,
(n) Macedonia,
(o) the Republic of Moldova, . . .
(p) . . .], . . .
[(q) . . .
(r) Bolivia,
(s) Brazil,
(t) Ecuador,
(u) South Africa, and
(v) Ukraine],
(w) India],
(x) Mongolia,
[(y) Ghana (in respect of men),
(z) Nigeria (in respect of men)],
(aa) Bosnia-Herzegovina,
(bb) Gambia (in respect of men),
(cc) Kenya (in respect of men),
(dd) Liberia (in respect of men),
(ee) Malawi (in respect of men),
(ff) Mali (in respect of men),
(gg) Mauritius,
(hh) Montenegro,
(ii) Peru,
(jj) Serbia,
(kk) Sierra Leone (in respect of men)],
(ll) Kosovo,
[(mm) South Korea].

(5) The Secretary of State may by order add a State, or part of a State, to the list in subsection (4) if satisfied that—

(a) there is in general in that State or part no serious risk of persecution of persons entitled to reside in that State or part, and

(b) removal to that State or part of persons entitled to reside there will not in general contravene the United Kingdom's obligations under the Human Rights Convention.

[(5A) If the Secretary of State is satisfied that the statements in subsection (5) (a) and (b) are true of a State or part of a State in relation to a description of person, an order under subsection (5) may add the State or part to the list in subsection (4) in respect of that description of person.

(5B) Where a State or part of a State is added to the list in subsection (4) in respect of a description of person, subsection (3) shall have effect in relation to a claimant only if the Secretary of State is satisfied that he is within that description (as well as being satisfied that he is entitled to reside in the State or part).

(5C) A description for the purposes of subsection (5A) may refer to—

  (a) gender,

  (b) language,

  (c) race,

  (d) religion,

  (e) nationality,

  (f) membership of a social or other group,

  (g) political opinion, or

  (h) any other attribute or circumstance that the Secretary of State thinks appropriate.]

[(5D) In deciding whether the statements in subsection (5) (a) and (b) are true of a State or part of a State, the Secretary of State—

  (a) shall have regard to all the circumstances of the State or part (including its laws and how they are applied), and

  (b) shall have regard to information from any appropriate source (including other member States and international organisations).]

[(6) The Secretary of State may by order amend the list in subsection (4) so as to omit a State or part added under subsection (5); and the omission may be—

  (a) general, or

  (b) effected so that the State or part remains listed in respect of a description of person.]

[(6A) Subsection (3) shall not apply in relation to [a] claimant who—

  (a) is the subject of a certificate under section 2 or 70 of the Extradition Act 2003 (c 41),

  (b) is in custody pursuant to arrest under section 5 of that Act,

  (c) is the subject of a provisional warrant under section 73 of that Act,

  (d) is the subject of an authority to proceed under section 7 of the Extradition Act 1989 (c 33) or an order under paragraph 4(2) of Schedule 1 to that Act, or

  (e) is the subject of a provisional warrant under section 8 of that Act or of a warrant under paragraph 5(1)(b) of Schedule 1 to that Act.]

(7) [The Secretary of State may certify a protection claim or human rights claim made by a person if]—

  (a) it is proposed to remove the person to a country of which he is not a national or citizen, and

  (b) there is no reason to believe that the person's rights under the Human Rights Convention will be breached in that country.

(8) In determining whether a person in relation to whom a certificate has been issued under subsection (7) may be removed from the United Kingdom, the country specified in the certificate is to be regarded as—

  (a) a place where a person's life and liberty is not threatened by reason of his race, religion, nationality, membership of a particular social group, or political opinion, and

  (b) a place from which a person will not be sent to another country otherwise than in accordance with the Refugee Convention [or with the United Kingdom's obligations in relation to persons eligible for a grant of humanitarian protection].

(9) *Where a person in relation to whom a certificate is issued under this section subsequently brings an appeal under section 82(1) while outside the United Kingdom, the appeal shall be considered as if he had not been removed from the United Kingdom.*

Amendment

Section heading: word in square brackets substituted (for original word "asylum") by the Immigration Act 2014, s 73, Sch 9, Pt 4, paras 30, 38(1), (2), as from 20 October 2014 (see SI 2014/2771, art 2), subject to savings in SI 2014/2771, arts 9–11.

Sub-s (1): substituted for original sub-ss (1), (2) (and sub-s (1A) as inserted by the Asylum and Immigration (Treatment of Claimants, etc) Act 2004, s 27(1), (2)) by the Immigration Act 2014, s 73, Sch 9, Pt 4, paras 30, 38(1), (3), as from 20 October 2014 (see SI 2014/2771, art 2), subject to savings in SI 2014/2771, arts 9–11. Sub-ss (1), (1A), (2) previously read as follows:

"(1) This section applies to an appeal under section 82(1) where the appellant has made an asylum claim or a human rights claim (or both).

[(1A) A person may not bring an appeal against an immigration decision of a kind specified in section 82(2)(c), (d)[, (e) or (ha)] in reliance on section 92(2) if the Secretary of State certifies that the claim or claims mentioned in subsection (1) above is or are clearly unfounded.]

(2) A person may not bring an appeal to which this section applies [in reliance on section 92(4)(a)] if the Secretary of State certifies that the claim or claims mentioned in subsection (1) is or are clearly unfounded.".

Sub-s (3): words in square brackets substituted (for original words "an asylum claimant or human rights" and "subsection (2)" respectively) by the Immigration Act 2014, s 73, Sch 9, Pt 4, paras 30, 38(1), (4), as from 20 October 2014 (see SI 2014/2771, art 2), subject to savings in SI 2014/2771, arts 9–11.

Sub-s (4): paras (a)–(i) repealed by the Asylum and Immigration (Treatment of Claimants, etc) Act 2004, ss 27(1), (4), 47, Sch 4.

Sub-s (4): paras (k)–(q) inserted by SI 2003/970, art 3.

Sub-s (4): paras (l) repealed by SI 2006/3215, art 2.

Sub-s (4): para (m) repealed by SI 2007/2221, art 3.

Sub-s (4): in para (p) word omitted repealed by virtue of SI 2003/1919, art 2.

Sub-s (4): para (q) repealed by SI 2006/3215, art 2.

Sub-s (4): paras (r)–(x) inserted by SI 2003/1919, art 2.

Sub-s (4): para (r) repealed by SI 2005/1016, art 2.

Sub-s (4): para (v) repealed by SI 2006/3275, art 2.

Sub-s (4): para (y) inserted by SI 2005/330, art 2.

Sub-s (4): paras (z), (aa), (bb) inserted by SI 2005/3306, art 2.

Sub-s (4): paras (cc)–(mm) inserted by SI 2007/2221, art 2.

Sub-s (4): paras (nn), (oo) inserted by SI 2010/561, art 3.

Sub-ss (5A)–(5C): inserted by the Asylum and Immigration (Treatment of Claimants, etc) Act 2004, s 27(1), (5).

Sub-s (5D): inserted by SI 2007/3187, reg 3.

Sub-s (6): substituted by the Asylum and Immigration (Treatment of Claimants, etc) Act 2004, s 27(1), (6).

Sub-s (6A): inserted by the Asylum and Immigration (Treatment of Claimants, etc) Act 2004, s 27(1), (7).

Sub-s (6A): word in square brackets substituted (for original words "an asylum claimant or human rights") by the Immigration Act 2014, s 73, Sch 9, Pt 4, paras 30, 38(1), (5), as from 20 October 2014 (see SI 2014/2771, art 2), subject to savings in SI 2014/2771, arts 9–11.

Sub-s (7): words in square brackets substituted (for original words "A person may not bring an appeal to which this section applies in reliance on section 92(4) if the Secretary of State certifies that", by the Immigration Act 2014, s 73, Sch 9, Pt 4, paras 30, 38(1), (6), as from 20 October 2014 (see SI 2014/2771, art 2), subject to savings in SI 2014/2771, arts 9–11.

Sub-s (8): word in square brackets in para (b) inserted by the Immigration Act 2014, s 73, Sch 9, Pt 4, paras 30, 38(1), (7), as from 20 October 2014 (see SI 2014/2771, art 2), subject to savings in SI 2014/2771, arts 9–11.

Sub-s (9): repealed by the Immigration Act 2014, s 73, Sch 9, Pt 4, paras 30, 38(1), (8), as from 20 October 2014 (see SI 2014/2771, art 2), subject to savings in SI 2014/2771, arts 9–11.

Subordinate Legislation

Asylum (Designated States) Order 2003, SI 2003/970; Asylum (Designated States) (No 2) Order 2003, SI 2003/1919; Asylum (Designated States) Order 2005, SI 2005/330, Asylum (Designated States) (Amendment) Order 2005, SI 2005/1016; Asylum (Designated States) (No 2) Order 2005, SI 2005/3306; Asylum (Designated States) (Amendment) (No 2) Order 2006, SI 2006/3275; Asylum (Designated States) (Amendment) (No 2) Order 2006, SI 2006/3215; Asylum (Designated States) Order 2007, SI 2007/2221; Asylum (Designated States) Order 2010, SI 2010/561.

[94A European Common List of Safe Countries of Origin

(1) The Secretary of State shall by order prescribe a list of States to be known as the 'European Common List of Safe Countries of Origin''.

(2) Subsections (3) and (4) apply where a person makes [a protection claim] or a human rights claim (or both) and that person is—

    (a)   a national of a State which is listed in the European Common List of Safe Countries of Origin, or

    (b)   a Stateless person who was formerly habitually resident in such a State.

(3) The Secretary of State shall consider the claim or claims mentioned in subsection (2) to be unfounded unless satisfied that there are serious grounds for considering that the State in question is not safe in the particular circumstances of the person mentioned in that subsection.

(4) The Secretary of State shall also certify the claim or claims mentioned in subsection (2) under section [94(1)] unless satisfied that the claim or claims is or are not clearly unfounded.

(5) An order under subsection (1)—

    (a)   may be made only if the Secretary of State thinks it necessary for the purpose of complying with the United Kingdom's obligations under [EU] law,

    (b)   may include transitional, consequential or incidental provision,

    (c)   shall be made by statutory instrument, and

    (d)   shall be subject to annulment in pursuance of a resolution of either House of Parliament.]

Amendment

Inserted by SI 2007/3187, reg 4.

Sub-s (2): words in square brackets substituted (for original words "an asylum claim") by the Immigration Act 2014, s 73, Sch 9, Pt 4, paras 30, 39(a), as from 20 October 2014 (see SI 2014/2771, art 2), subject to savings in SI 2014/2771, arts 9–11.

Sub-s (4): reference in square brackets substituted (for original reference to "94(2)") by the Immigration Act 2014, s 73, Sch 9, Pt 4, paras 30, 39(b), as from 20 October 2014 (see SI 2014/2771, art 2), subject to savings in SI 2014/2771, arts 9–11.

Sub-s (5): in para (a) reference to "EU" in square brackets substituted by SI 2011/1043, art 6(2)(a). Date in force: 22 April 2011: see SI 2011/1043, art 2; for transitional savings see art 3(3) thereof.

[94B Appeal from within the United Kingdom: certification of human rights claims made by persons liable to deportation

(1) This section applies where a human rights claim has been made by a person ("P") who is liable to deportation under—

    (a)   section 3(5)(a) of the Immigration Act 1971 (Secretary of State deeming deportation conducive to public good), or

    (b)   section 3(6) of that Act (court recommending deportation following conviction).

(2) The Secretary of State may certify the claim if the Secretary of State considers that, despite the appeals process not having been begun or not having been exhausted, removal of P to the country or territory to which P is proposed to be removed, pending

the outcome of an appeal in relation to P's claim, would not be unlawful under section 6 of the Human Rights Act 1998 (public authority not to act contrary to Human Rights Convention).

(3) The grounds upon which the Secretary of State may certify a claim under subsection (2) include (in particular) that P would not, before the appeals process is exhausted, face a real risk of serious irreversible harm if removed to the country or territory to which P is proposed to be removed.]

Amendment

Inserted by the Immigration Act 2014, s 17(1), (3), as from 28 July 2014: see SI 2014/1820..

95 Appeal from outside United Kingdom: removal

A person who is outside the United Kingdom may not appeal under section 82(1) on the ground specified in section 84(1)(g) (except in a case to which section 94(9) applies).

Amendment

Repealed by the Immigration Act 2014, s 73, Sch 9, Pt 4, paras 30, 40, as from 20 October 2014 (see SI 2014/2771, art 2), subject to savings in SI 2014/2771, arts 9–11.

96 Earlier right of appeal

[(1) [A person may not bring an appeal under section 82 against a decision ("the new decision")] if the Secretary of State or an immigration officer certifies—

   (a) that the person was notified of a right of appeal under that section against another . . . decision ("the old decision") (whether or not an appeal was brought and whether or not any appeal brought has been determined),

   (b) that the claim or application to which the new decision relates relies on a [ground] that could have been raised in an appeal against the old decision, and

   (c) that, in the opinion of the Secretary of State or the immigration officer, there is no satisfactory reason for that [ground] not having been raised in an appeal against the old decision.

[(2) A person may not bring an appeal under section 82 if the Secretary of State or an immigration officer certifies—

   (a) that the person has received a notice under section 120(2),

   (b) that the appeal relies on a ground that should have been, but has not been, raised in a statement made under section 120(2) or (5), and

   (c) that, in the opinion of the Secretary of State or the immigration officer, there is no satisfactory reason for that ground not having been raised in a statement under section 120(2) or (5).]

(4) In subsection (1) "notified" means notified in accordance with regulations under section 105.

(5) [Subsections (1) and (2) apply to prevent] a person's right of appeal whether or not he has been outside the United Kingdom since an earlier right of appeal arose or since a requirement under section 120 was imposed.

(6) In this section a reference to an appeal under section 82(1) includes a reference to an appeal under section 2 of the Special Immigration Appeals Commission Act 1997 (c 68) which is or could be brought by reference to an appeal under section 82(1).

[(7) A certificate under subsection (1) or (2) shall have no effect in relation to an appeal instituted before the certificate is issued.]

Amendment

Sub-s (1): words in first pair of square brackets substituted (for original words "An appeal under section 82(1) against an immigration decision ("the new decision") in respect of a person may not be brought)", word "immigration"; omitted repealed and word in square brackets in paras (b), (c) substituted (for original word "matter") by the Immigration Act 2014, s 73, Sch 9, Pt 4, paras 30, 41(1), (2), as from 20 October 2014 (see SI 2014/2771, art 2), subject to savings in SI 2014/2771, arts 9–11.

Sub-ss (1), (2): substituted, for sub-ss (1)–(3) as originally enacted, by the Asylum and Immigration (Treatment of Claimants, etc) Act 2004, s 30(1), (2).

Sub-s (2): further substituted by the Immigration Act 2014, s 73, Sch 9, Pt 4, paras 30, 41(1), (3), as from 20 October 2014 (see SI 2014/2771, art 2), subject to savings in SI 2014/2771, arts 9–11, and prior to substitution by the 2014 Act, read as follows:

"(2) An appeal under section 82(1) against an immigration decision ("the new decision") in respect of a person may not be brought if the Secretary of State or an immigration officer certifies—

(a)   that the person received a notice under section 120 by virtue of an application other than that to which the new decision relates or by virtue of a decision other than the new decision,

(b)   that the new decision relates to an application or claim which relies on a matter that should have been, but has not been, raised in a statement made in response to that notice, and

(c)   that, in the opinion of the Secretary of State or the immigration officer, there is no satisfactory reason for that matter not having been raised in a statement made in response to that notice."

Sub-s (5): words "Subsections (1) and (2) apply to prevent" in square brackets substituted by the Asylum and Immigration (Treatment of Claimants, etc) Act 2004, s 30(1), (3).

Sub-s (7): inserted by the Asylum and Immigration (Treatment of Claimants, etc) Act 2004, s 30(1), (4).

97 National security, &c

(1)   An appeal under section 82(1) . . . against a decision in respect of a person may not be brought or continued if the Secretary of State certifies that the decision is or was taken—

(a)   by the Secretary of State wholly or partly on a ground listed in subsection (2), or

(b)   in accordance with a direction of the Secretary of State which identifies the person to whom the decision relates and which is given wholly or partly on a ground listed in subsection (2).

(2)   The grounds mentioned in subsection (1) are that the person's exclusion or removal from the United Kingdom is—

(a)   in the interests of national security, or

(b)   in the interests of the relationship between the United Kingdom and another country.

(3)   An appeal under section 82(1) . . . against a decision may not be brought or continued if the Secretary of State certifies that the decision is or was taken wholly or partly in reliance on information which in his opinion should not be made public—

(a)   in the interests of national security,

(b)   in the interests of the relationship between the United Kingdom and another country, or

(c)   otherwise in the public interest.

(4)   In subsections (1)(a) and (b) and (3) a reference to the Secretary of State is to the Secretary of State acting in person.

Amendment

Sub-s (1): words ", 83(2) or 83A(2)" (omitted) repealed by the Immigration Act 2014, s 73, Sch 9, Pt 4, paras 30, 42(a), as from 20 October 2014 (see SI 2014/2771, art 2), subject to savings in SI 2014/2771, arts 9–11.

Sub-s (3): words ", 83(2) or 83A(2)" (omitted) repealed by the Immigration Act 2014, s 73, Sch 9, Pt 4, paras 30, 42(b), as from 20 October 2014 (see SI 2014/2771, art 2), subject to savings in SI 2014/2771, arts 9–11.

[97A National security: deportation]

[(1) This section applies where the Secretary of State certifies that the decision to make a deportation order in respect of a person was taken on the grounds that his removal from the United Kingdom would be in the interests of national security.

[(1A) This section also applies where the Secretary of State certifies, in the case of a person in respect of whom a deportation order has been made which states that it is made in accordance with section 32(5) of the UK Borders Act 2007, that the person's removal from the United Kingdom would be in the interests of national security.]

(2) Where this section applies—

  (a) section 79 shall not apply,

  (b) the Secretary of State shall be taken to have certified the decision to make the deportation order under section 97, and

  [(c) section 2(5) of the Special Immigration Appeals Commission Act 1997 (whether appeals brought against decisions certified under section 97 may be brought from within the United Kingdom) does not apply, but see instead the following provisions of this section].

[(2A) The person while in the United Kingdom may not bring or continue an appeal under section 2 of the Special Immigration Appeals Commission Act 1997—

  (a) against the decision to make the deportation order, or

  (b) against any refusal to revoke the deportation order,

unless the person has made a human rights claim while in the United Kingdom.

(2B) Subsection (2A) does not allow the person while in the United Kingdom to bring or continue an appeal if the Secretary of State certifies that removal of the person—

  (a) to the country or territory to which the person is proposed to be removed, and

  (b) despite the appeals process not having been begun or not having been exhausted,

would not [be unlawful under section 6 of the Human Rights Act 1998 (public authority not to act contrary to Human Rights Convention)].

(2C) The grounds upon which a certificate may be given under subsection (2B) include (in particular)—

  (a) that the person would not, before the appeals process is exhausted, face a real risk of serious irreversible harm if removed to the country or territory to which the person is proposed to be removed;

  (b) that the whole or part of any human rights claim made by the person is clearly unfounded.

(2D) Subsection (2A) does not allow the person while in the United Kingdom to bring an appeal on a non-human-rights ground, or to continue an appeal so far as brought on non-human-rights grounds, if the Secretary of State certifies that removal of the person—

  (a) to the country or territory to which the person is proposed to be removed, and

  (b) despite the appeals process, so far as relating to appeal on non-human-rights grounds, not having been begun or not having been exhausted,

would not breach the United Kingdom's obligations under the Human Rights Convention.

(2E) In subsection (2D) "non-human-rights ground" means any ground other than the ground that removal of the person from the United Kingdom in consequence of the decision to make the deportation order would be unlawful under section 6 of the Human Rights Act 1998 as being incompatible with a person's Convention rights.

(2F) If a certificate in respect of a person is given under subsection (2B), the person may apply to the Special Immigration Appeals Commission to set aside the certificate.

(2G) If a person makes an application under subsection (2F) then the Commission, in determining whether the certificate should be set aside, must apply the principles that would be applied in judicial review proceedings.

(2H) The Commission's determination of a review under subsection (2F) is final.

(2J) The Commission may direct that a person who has made and not withdrawn an application under subsection (2F) is not to be removed from the United Kingdom at a time when the review has not been finally determined by the Commission.

(2K) Sections 5 and 6 of the Special Immigration Appeals Commission Act 1997 apply in relation to reviews under subsection (2F) (and to applicants for such reviews) as they apply in relation to appeals under section 2 or 2B of that Act (and to persons bringing such appeals).

(2L) Any exercise of power to make rules under section 5 of that Act in relation to reviews under subsection (2F) is to be with a view to securing that proceedings on such reviews are handled expeditiously.]

(3) *A person in respect of whom a certificate is issued under subsection [(2D)] may appeal to the Special Immigration Appeals Commission against the issue of the certificate; and for that purpose the Special Immigration Appeals Commission Act 1997 shall apply as to an appeal against an immigration decision to which section 92 of this Act applies.*

(4) The Secretary of State may repeal this section by order.]

Amendment

Inserted by the Immigration, Asylum and Nationality Act 2006, s 7(1).

Sub-s (1A): inserted by the Crime and Courts Act 2013, s 54(1), (2). Date in force: 25 June 2013: see SI 2013/1042, art 4(c).

Sub-s (2): para (c) substituted by the Crime and Courts Act 2013, s 54(1), (3). Date in force: 25 June 2013: see SI 2013/1042, art 4(c).

Sub-ss (2A)–(2L): inserted by the Crime and Courts Act 2013, s 54(1), (4). Date in force: 25 June 2013: see SI 2013/1042, art 4(c).

Sub-s (2B): words in square brackets substituted (for original words "breach the United Kingdom's obligations under the Human Rights Convention") by the Immigration Act 2014, s 73, Sch 9, Pt 4, paras 30, 43(a), as from 20 October 2014 (see SI 2014/2771, art 2), subject to savings in SI 2014/2771, arts 9–11.

Sub-ss (2D), (2E), (3): repealed by the Immigration Act 2014, s 73, Sch 9, Pt 4, paras 30, 43(b), as from 20 October 2014 (see SI 2014/2771, art 2), subject to savings in SI 2014/2771, arts 9–11.

Sub-s (3): reference to "(2D)" in square brackets substituted by the Crime and Courts Act 2013, s 54(1), (5). Date in force: 25 June 2013: see SI 2013/1042, art 4(c).

See Further

See further, in relation to the application of this section, with modifications, in relation to an appeal against an EEA decision where the Secretary of State has certified under the Immigration (European Economic Area) Regulations 2006, SI 2006/1003, reg 28(2) or (4) that the EEA decision was taken in the interests of national security: the Immigration (European Economic Area) Regulations 2006, SI 2006/1003, reg 28A (as inserted by SI 2013/3032, reg 4, Sch 1, para 24).

[97B Variation of leave on grounds of public good: rights of appeal]

[(1) This section applies to an immigration decision of a kind referred to in section 82(2)(e) if the Secretary of State, acting in person, certifies that the decision is or was taken wholly or partly on the ground that it is no longer conducive to the public good for the person to have leave to enter or remain in the United Kingdom.

(2) If the person concerned is outside the United Kingdom when the immigration decision is taken, an appeal under section 82(1) against that decision may be brought only from outside the United Kingdom.

(3) Accordingly, the person concerned may not enter the United Kingdom for the purposes of an appeal against that decision and the person's appeal against that decision is not one of a kind to which section 92 applies.]

Amendment

Inserted by the Crime and Courts Act 2013, s 53(1), (3). Date in force: 25 June 2013: see SI 2013/1042, art 4(b). Repealed by the Immigration Act 2014, s 73, Sch 9, Pt 4, paras 30, 44, as from 20 October 2014 (see SI 2014/2771, art 2), subject to savings in SI 2014/2771, arts 9–11.

98 Other grounds of public good

(1) This section applies to an immigration decision of a kind referred to in section 82(2)(a) or (b).

(2) An appeal under section 82(1) against an immigration decision may not be brought or continued if the Secretary of State certifies that the decision is or was taken—

   (a) by the Secretary of State wholly or partly on the ground that the exclusion or removal from the United Kingdom of the person to whom the decision relates is conducive to the public good, or

   (b) in accordance with a direction of the Secretary of State which identifies the person to whom the decision relates and which is given wholly or partly on that ground.

(3) In subsection (2)(a) and (b) a reference to the Secretary of State is to the Secretary of State acting in person.

(4) Subsection (2) does not prevent the bringing of an appeal on either or both of the grounds referred to in section 84(1)(b) and (c).

(5) Subsection (2) does not prevent the bringing of an appeal against an immigration decision of the kind referred to in section 82(2)(a) on the grounds referred to in section 84(1)(g).

Amendment

Repealed by the Immigration Act 2014, s 73, Sch 9, Pt 4, paras 30, 45, as from 20 October 2014 (see SI 2014/2771, art 2), subject to savings in SI 2014/2771, arts 9–11.

99 [Section 97]: appeal in progress

(1) This section applies where a certificate is issued under section . . . 97 . . . in respect of a pending appeal.

(2) The appeal shall lapse.

Amendment

Section heading: words in square brackets substituted (for original words "Sections 97 and 98") by the Immigration Act 2014, s 73, Sch 9, Pt 4, paras 30, 46(a), as from 20 October 2014 (see SI 2014/2771, art 2), subject to savings in SI 2014/2771, arts 9–11.

Sub-s (1): words omitted repealed by the Crime and Courts Act 2013, s 51(2)(a), as from 8 May 2013: see SI 2013/1042, art 2(i) and words "or 98" (omitted) repealed by the Immigration Act 2014, s 73, Sch 9, Pt 4, paras 30, 46(b), as from 20 October 2014 (see SI 2014/2771, art 2), subject to savings in SI 2014/2771, arts 9–11.

100–103

(Repealed by the Asylum and Immigration (Treatment of Claimants, etc) Act 2004, ss 26(5)(a), 47, Sch 4; for transitional provisions see s 26(7), Sch 2, Pt 2 thereto.)

103A–103E

(Inserted by the Asylum and Immigration (Treatment of Claimants, etc) Act 2004, s 26(6), and repealed by SI 2010/21, art 5(1), Sch 1, paras 20, 25.)

104 Pending appeal

(1) An appeal under section 82(1) is pending during the period—

   (a)   beginning when it is instituted, and

   (b)   ending when it is finally determined, withdrawn or abandoned (or when it lapses under section 99).

[(2) An appeal under section 82(1) is not finally determined for the purpose of subsection (1)(b) while—

   (a)   an application for permission to appeal under section 11 or 13 of the Tribunals, Courts and Enforcement Act 2007 could be made or is awaiting determination,

   (b)   permission to appeal under either of those sections has been granted and the appeal is awaiting determination, or

   (c)   an appeal has been remitted under section 12 or 14 of that Act and is awaiting determination.]

(3)   . . .

[(4)   An appeal under section 82(1) brought by a person while he is in the United Kingdom shall be treated as abandoned if the appellant leaves the United Kingdom.

(4A)   An appeal under section 82(1) brought by a person while he is in the United Kingdom shall be treated as abandoned if the appellant is granted leave to enter or remain in the United Kingdom (subject to [subsection (4B)]).

(4B)   Subsection (4A) shall not apply to an appeal in so far as it is brought on [a ground specified in section 84(1)(a) or (b) or 84(3) (asylum or humanitarian protection)] where the appellant—

   (a)   is granted leave to enter or remain in the United Kingdom for a period exceeding 12 months, and

   (b)   gives notice, in accordance with [Tribunal Procedure Rules], that he wishes to pursue the appeal in so far as it is brought on that ground.

(4C)   Subsection (4A) shall not apply to an appeal in so far as it is brought on the ground specified in section 84(1)(b) where the appellant gives notice, in accordance with [Tribunal Procedure Rules], that he wishes to pursue the appeal in so far as it is brought on that ground.]

(5)   An appeal under section 82(2)(a), (c), (d), (e) or (f) shall be treated as finally determined if a deportation order is made against the appellant.

Amendment

Sub-s (2): substituted by SI 2010/21, Sch 1, paras 20, 26(a).

Sub-s (3): repealed by the Asylum and Immigration (Treatment of Claimants, etc) Act 2004, ss 26(7), 47, Sch 2, Pt 1, paras 16, 20(b), Sch 4.

Sub-ss (4), (4A)–(4C): substituted, for sub-s (4) as originally enacted, by the Immigration, Asylum and Nationality Act 2006, s 9.

Sub-s (4): repealed by the Immigration Act 2014, s 73, Sch 9, Pt 4, paras 30, 47(1), (2), as from 20 October 2014 (see SI 2014/2771, art 2), subject to savings in SI 2014/2771, arts 9–11.

Sub-s (4A): words in square brackets substituted (for original words "subsections (4B) and (4C)" by the Immigration Act 2014, s 73, Sch 9, Pt 4, paras 30, 47(1), (3), as from 20 October 2014 (see SI 2014/2771, art 2), subject to savings in SI 2014/2771, arts 9–11.

Sub-s (4B): first words in square brackets substituted (for original words "the ground relating to the Refugee Convention specified in section 84(1)(g)") and para (a) repealed by the

Immigration Act 2014, s 73, Sch 9, Pt 4, paras 30, 47(1), (4), as from 20 October 2014 (see SI 2014/2771, art 2), subject to savings in SI 2014/2771, arts 9–11.

Sub-s (4B): in para (b) words "Tribunal Procedure Rules" in square brackets substituted by SI 2010/21, art 5(1), Sch 1, paras 20, 26(b).

Sub-s (4C): repealed by the Immigration Act 2014, s 73, Sch 9, Pt 4, paras 30, 47(1), (5), as from 20 October 2014 (see SI 2014/2771, art 2), subject to savings in SI 2014/2771, arts 9–11.

Sub-s (5): repealed by the Immigration Act 2014, s 73, Sch 9, Pt 4, paras 30, 47(1), (5), as from 20 October 2014 (see SI 2014/2771, art 2), subject to savings in SI 2014/2771, arts 9–11.

105 Notice of immigration decision

(1) The Secretary of State may make regulations requiring a person to be given written notice where an [appealable] decision is taken in respect of him.

(2) The regulations may, in particular, provide that a notice under subsection (1) of [an appealable decision] must state—

    (a)   that there is a right of appeal under [section 82], and

    (b)   how and when that right may be exercised.

(3) The regulations may make provision (which may include presumptions) about service.

[(4) In this section "appealable decision" means a decision mentioned in section 82(1).]

Amendment

Sub-s (1): word in square brackets substituted (for original word "immigration") by the Immigration Act 2014, s 73, Sch 9, Pt 4, paras 30, 48(1), (2), as from 20 October 2014 (see SI 2014/2771, art 2), subject to savings in SI 2014/2771, arts 9–11.

Sub-s (2): words in first and second pairs of square brackets substituted (for original words "a decision against which the person is entitled to appeal under section 82(1)" and "section 82" respectively) by the Immigration Act 2014, s 73, Sch 9, Pt 4, paras 30, 48(1), (3), as from 20 October 2014 (see SI 2014/2771, art 2), subject to savings in SI 2014/2771, arts 9–11.

Sub-s (4): added by the Immigration Act 2014, s 73, Sch 9, Pt 4, paras 30, 48(1), (4), as from 20 October 2014 (see SI 2014/2771, art 2), subject to savings in SI 2014/2771, arts 9–11.

Subordinate Legislation

Immigration (Notices) Regulations 2003, SI 2003/658.
Immigration (Notices) (Amendment) Regulations 2006, SI 2006/2168.
Immigration (Notices) (Amendment) Regulations 2008, SI 2008/684.
Immigration (Notices) (Amendment) (No 2) Regulations 2008, SI 2008/1819.
Immigration (Notices) (Amendment) Regulations 2013, SI 2013/793.

106 Rules

(1) . . . .

[(1A) . . . .]

(2) . . .

[(3) In the case of an appeal under section 82 . . . or by virtue of section 109, Tribunal Procedure Rules may enable the Tribunal to certify that the appeal had no merit (and shall make provision for the consequences of the issue of a certificate).]

(4) A person commits an offence if without reasonable excuse he fails to comply with a requirement imposed in accordance with [Tribunal Procedure Rules in connection with proceedings under section 82 . . . or by virtue of section 109] to attend before . . . the Tribunal—

    (a)   to give evidence, or

    (b)   to produce a document.

(5) A person who is guilty of an offence under subsection (4) shall be liable on summary conviction to a fine not exceeding level 3 on the standard scale.

Amendment

Sub-ss (1), (1A), (2): repealed by SI 2010/21, art 5(1), Sch 1, paras 20, 27(a).

Sub-s (1A): inserted by the Asylum and Immigration (Treatment of Claimants, etc) Act 2004, s 26(7), Sch 2, Pt 1, paras 16, 21(c); for transitional provisions see s 26(7), Sch 2, Pt 2 thereto.

Sub-s (3): substituted by SI 2010/21, art 5(1), Sch 1, paras 20, 27(b).

Sub-s (3): words ", 83 or 83A" (omitted) repealed by the Immigration Act 2014, s 73, Sch 9, Pt 4, paras 30, 49(a), as from 20 October 2014 (see SI 2014/2771, art 2), subject to savings in SI 2014/2771, arts 9–11.

Sub-s (4): words from "Tribunal Procedure Rules" to " of section 109" in square brackets substituted by SI 2010/21, art 5(1), Sch 1, paras 20, 27(c).

Sub-s (4): words ", 83 or 83A" (omitted in the first place) repealed by the Immigration Act 2014, s 73, Sch 9, Pt 4, paras 30, 49(b), as from 20 October 2014 (see SI 2014/2771, art 2), subject to savings in SI 2014/2771, arts 9–11.

Sub-s (4): second words omitted repealed by the Asylum and Immigration (Treatment of Claimants, etc) Act 2004, ss 26(7), 47, Sch 2, Pt 1, paras 16, 21(t), Sch 4.

107 Practice directions

(1) . . .

[(1A) . . .]

(2) . . .

[(3) In the case of proceedings under section 82 . . ., or by virtue of section 109, or proceedings in the Upper Tribunal arising out of such proceedings, practice directions under section 23 of the Tribunals, Courts and Enforcement Act 2007—

(a)   may require the Tribunal to treat a specified decision of the Tribunal or Upper Tribunal as authoritative in respect of a particular matter; and

(b)   may require the Upper Tribunal to treat a specified decision of the Tribunal or Upper Tribunal as authoritative in respect of a particular matter.]

[(3A) In subsection (3) the reference to a decision of the Tribunal includes—

(a)   a decision of the Asylum and Immigration Tribunal, and

(b)   a decision of the Immigration Appeal Tribunal.]

[(4) . . .

(5) . . .

(6) . . .

(7) . . .]

Amendment

Sub-s (1): repealed by SI 2010/21, art 5(1), Sch 1, paras 20, 28(a).

Sub-s (1A): inserted by the Tribunals, Courts and Enforcement Act 2007, s 48(1), Sch 8, para 54(1), (2) and repealed by SI 2010/21, art 5(1), Sch 1, paras 20, 28(a).

Sub-s (2): repealed by the Asylum and Immigration (Treatment of Claimants, etc) Act 2004, ss 26(7), 47, Sch 2, Pt 1, paras 16, 22(1)(b), Sch 4.

Sub-s (3): substituted by SI 2010/21, art 5(1), Sch 1, paras 20, 28(b).

Sub-s (3): words ", 83 or 83A" (omitted) repealed by the Immigration Act 2014, s 73, Sch 9, Pt 4, paras 30, 50, as from 20 October 2014 (see SI 2014/2771, art 2), subject to savings in SI 2014/2771, arts 9–11.

Sub-s (3A): inserted by SI 2010/21, art 5(1), Sch 1, paras 20, 28(c).

Sub-ss (4)–(7): inserted by the Tribunals, Courts and Enforcement Act 2007, s 48(1), Sch 8, para 54(1), (3) and repealed by SI 2010/21, art 5(1), Sch 1, paras 20, 28(a).

108 Forged document: proceedings in private

(1) This section applies where it is alleged—

(a)   that a document relied on by a party to an appeal under section 82 . . . is a forgery, and

(b)   that disclosure to that party of a matter relating to the detection of the forgery would be contrary to the public interest.

(2) [The Tribunal]—

(a)   must investigate the allegation in private, and

(b)   may proceed in private so far as necessary to prevent disclosure of the matter referred to in subsection (1)(b).

Amendment

Sub-s (1): words ", 83 or 83A" (omitted) repealed by the Immigration Act 2014, s 73, Sch 9, Pt 4, paras 30, 51, as from 20 October 2014 (see SI 2014/2771, art 2), subject to savings in SI 2014/2771, arts 9–11.

Sub-s (2): words "The Tribunal" in square brackets substituted by the Asylum and Immigration (Treatment of Claimants, etc) Act 2004, s 26(7), Sch 2, Pt 1, paras 16, 23(b); for transitional provisions see s 26(7), Sch 2, Pt 2 thereto.

General

109 European Union and European Economic Area

(1) Regulations may provide for, or make provision about, an appeal against an immigration decision taken in respect of a person who has or claims to have a right under any of the [EU] Treaties.

(2) The regulations may—

     (a)   apply a provision of this Act or the Special Immigration Appeals Commission Act 1997 (c 68) with or without modification;

     (b)   make provision similar to a provision made by or under this Act or that Act;

     (c)   disapply or modify the effect of a provision of this Act or that Act.

(3) In subsection (1) "immigration decision" means a decision about—

     (a)   a person's entitlement to enter or remain in the United Kingdom, or

     (b)   removal of a person from the United Kingdom.

Amendment

Sub-s (1): reference to "EU" in square brackets substituted by SI 2011/1043, art 6(1)(a). Date in force: 22 April 2011: see SI 2011/1043, art 2; for transitional savings see art 3(3) thereof.

Subordinate Legislation

Immigration (European Economic Area) Regulations 2006, SI 2006/1003.

110, 111

(S 110 repealed by the Immigration, Asylum and Nationality Act 2006, ss 10, 61, Sch 3; s 111 repealed by the UK Borders Act 2007, ss 54(c), 58, Schedule..)

112 Regulations, &c

(1) Regulations under this Part shall be made by the Secretary of State.

(2) Regulations . . . under this Part . . . —

     (a)   must be made by statutory instrument, and

     (b)   shall be subject to annulment in pursuance of a resolution of either House of Parliament.

(3) Regulations . . . under this Part—

     (a)   may make provision which applies generally or only in a specified case or in specified circumstances,

     (b)   may make different provision for different cases or circumstances,

     (c)   may include consequential, transitional or incidental provision, and

     (d)   may include savings.

[(3A)   An order under section 88A—

     (a)   must be made by statutory instrument,

     (b)   may not be made unless a draft has been laid before and approved by resolution of each House of Parliament, and

     (c)   *may include transitional provision.]*

(4)   An order under section 94(5) . . . —

     (a)   must be made by statutory instrument,

     (b)   may not be made unless a draft has been laid before and approved by resolution of each House of Parliament, and

     (c)   may include transitional provision.

(5)   An order under section 94(6) . . . —

     (a)   must be made by statutory instrument,

     (b)   shall be subject to annulment in pursuance of a resolution of either House of Parliament, and

     (c)   may include transitional provision.

[(5A)   If an instrument makes provision under section 94(5) and 94(6)—

     (a)   subsection (4)(b) above shall apply, and

     (b)   subsection (5)(b) above shall not apply.]

[(5B)   An order under section 97A(4)—

     (a)   must be made by statutory instrument,

     (b)   shall be subject to annulment in pursuance of a resolution of either House of Parliament, and

     (c)   may include transitional provision.]

[(6)   . . .]

[(7)   . . .]

Amendment

Sub-s (2): words omitted repealed by SI 2010/21, art 5(1), Sch 1, paras 20, 29(a).

Sub-s (3): words omitted repealed by SI 2010/21, art 5(1), Sch 1, paras 20, 29(b).

Sub-s (3A): inserted by the Asylum and Immigration (Treatment of Claimants, etc) Act 2004, s 29(2) and repealed by the Immigration Act 2014, s 73, Sch 9, Pt 4, paras 30, 52(a), as from 20 October 2014 (see SI 2014/2771, art 2), subject to savings in SI 2014/2771, arts 9–11.

Sub-s (4): words "or 115(8)" omitted repealed by the Immigration Act 2014, s 73, Sch 9, Pt 4, paras 52(b), as from 20 October 2014 (see SI 2014/2771, art 2), subject to savings in SI 2014/2771, arts 9–11.

Sub-s (5): words "or 115(9)" omitted repealed by the Immigration Act 2014, s 73, Sch 9, Pt 4, paras 52(c), as from 20 October 2014 (see SI 2014/2771, art 2), subject to savings in SI 2014/2771, arts 9–11.

Sub-s (5B): inserted by the Immigration, Asylum and Nationality Act 2006, s 7(2).

Sub-ss (6), (7): substituted, for sub-s (6) as originally enacted, by the Asylum and Immigration (Treatment of Claimants, etc) Act 2004, s 26(7), Sch 2, Pt 1, paras 16, 24(1), (3) and repealed by SI 2010/21, art 5(1), Sch 1, paras 20, 29(c).

113 Interpretation

(1)   In this Part, unless a contrary intention appears—

"asylum claim" means a claim made by a person to the Secretary of State at a place designated by the Secretary of State that to remove the person from or require him to leave the United Kingdom would breach the United Kingdom's obligations under the Refugee Convention,

"entry clearance" has the meaning given by section 33(1) of the Immigration Act 1971 (c 77) (interpretation),

"human rights claim" means a claim made by a person to the Secretary of State at a place designated by the Secretary of State that to remove the person from or require him to leave the United Kingdom [or to refuse him entry into the United Kingdom] would be unlawful under section 6 of the Human Rights Act 1998 (c 42) (public authority not to act contrary to Convention) . . . , "the Human Rights Convention" has the same meaning as "the Convention" in the Human Rights Act 1998 and "Convention rights" shall be construed in accordance with section 1 of that Act,

["humanitarian protection" has the meaning given in section 82(2);]

"*illegal entrant*" *has the meaning given by section 33(1) of the Immigration Act 1971,*

"immigration rules" means rules under section 1(4) of [the Immigration Act 1971] (general immigration rules),

"*prescribed*" *means prescribed by regulations,*

["protection claim" has the meaning given in section 82(2)]

["protection status" has the meaning given in section 82(2)]

"the Refugee Convention" means the Convention relating to the Status of Refugees done at Geneva on 28th July 1951 and its Protocol,

"*visitor*" *means a visitor in accordance with immigration rules, and*

"*work permit*" *has the meaning given by section 33(1) of the Immigration Act 1971 (c 77) (interpretation).*

(2) *A reference to varying leave to enter or remain in the United Kingdom does not include a reference to adding, varying or revoking a condition of leave.*

Amendment

Sub-s (1): in definition "human rights claim" words in square brackets inserted and words "as being incompatible with his Convention rights" (omitted) repealed by the Immigration Act 2014, s 73, Sch 9, Pt 4, paras 30, 53(1), (2)(a), as from 20 October 2014 (see SI 2014/2771, art 2), subject to savings in SI 2014/2771, arts 9–11.

Sub-s (1): definitions "humanitarian protection", "protection claim" and "protection status" inserted by the Immigration Act 2014, s 73, Sch 9, Pt 4, paras 30, 53(1), (2)(b), as from 20 October 2014 (see SI 2014/2771, art 2), subject to savings in SI 2014/2771, arts 9–11.

Sub-s (1): definitions "entry clearance", "illegal entrant", "prescribed", "visitor" and "work permit" (omitted) repealed by the Immigration Act 2014, s 73, Sch 9, Pt 4, paras 30, 53(1), (2)(c), as from 20 October 2014 (see SI 2014/2771, art 2), subject to savings in SI 2014/2771, arts 9–11.

Sub-s (1): in definition "immigration rules" words in square brackets substituted (for original words "that Act") by the Immigration Act 2014, s 73, Sch 9, Pt 4, paras 30, 53(1), (2)(d), as from 20 October 2014 (see SI 2014/2771, art 2), subject to savings in SI 2014/2771, arts 9–11.

Sub-s (2): repealed by the Immigration Act 2014, s 73, Sch 9, Pt 4, paras 30, 53(1), (3), as from 20 October 2014 (see SI 2014/2771, art 2), subject to savings in SI 2014/2771, arts 9–11.

114 Repeal

(1) Part IV of the Immigration and Asylum Act 1999 (c 33) (appeals) shall cease to have effect.

(2) Schedule 6 (which makes transitional provision in connection with the repeal of Part IV of that Act and its replacement by this Part) shall have effect.

(3) Schedule 7 (consequential amendments) shall have effect.

115 Appeal from within United Kingdom: unfounded human rights or asylum claim: transitional provision

(1) A person may not bring an appeal under section 65 or 69 of the Immigration and Asylum Act 1999 (human rights and asylum) while in the United Kingdom if—

(a) the Secretary of State certifies that the appeal relates to a human rights claim or an asylum claim which is clearly unfounded, and

(b) the person does not have another right of appeal while in the United Kingdom under Part IV of that Act.

(2) A person while in the United Kingdom may not bring an appeal under section 69 of that Act, or raise a question which relates to the Human Rights Convention under section 77 of that Act, if the Secretary of State certifies that—

(a) it is proposed to remove the person to a country of which he is not a national or citizen, and

(b)   there is no reason to believe that the person's rights under the Human Rights Convention will be breached in that country;

(3) A person while in the United Kingdom may not bring an appeal under section 65 of that Act (human rights) if the Secretary of State certifies that—

(a)   it is proposed to remove the person to a country of which he is not a national or citizen, and

(b)   there is no reason to believe that the person's rights under the Human Rights Convention will be breached in that country.

(4) In determining whether a person in relation to whom a certificate has been issued under subsection (2) or (3) may be removed from the United Kingdom, the country specified in the certificate is to be regarded as—

(a)   a place where a person's life and liberty is not threatened by reason of his race, religion, nationality, membership of a particular social group, or political opinion, and

(b)   a place from which a person will not be sent to another country otherwise than in accordance with the Refugee Convention.

(5) Where a person in relation to whom a certificate is issued under this section subsequently brings an appeal or raises a question under section 65, 69 or 77 of that Act while outside the United Kingdom, the appeal or question shall be considered as if he had not been removed from the United Kingdom.

(6) If the Secretary of State is satisfied that a person who makes a human rights claim or an asylum claim is entitled to reside in a State listed in subsection (7), he shall issue a certificate under subsection (1) unless satisfied that the claim is not clearly unfounded.

(7) Those States are—

(a)   the Republic of Cyprus,
(b)   the Czech Republic,
(c)   the Republic of Estonia,
(d)   the Republic of Hungary,
(e)   the Republic of Latvia,
(f)   the Republic of Lithuania,
(g)   the Republic of Malta,
(h)   the Republic of Poland,
(i)   the Slovak Republic,
(j)   the Republic of Slovenia,
[(k)   the Republic of Albania,
(l)   Bulgaria,
(m)   Serbia and Montenegro,
(n)   Jamaica,
(o)   Macedonia,
(p)   the Republic of Moldova, and
(q)   Romania].

(8) The Secretary of State may by order add a State, or part of a State, to the list in subsection (7) if satisfied that—

(a)   there is in general in that State or part no serious risk of persecution of persons entitled to reside in that State or part, and

(b)   removal to that State or part of persons entitled to reside there will not in general contravene the United Kingdom's obligations under the Human Rights Convention.

(9) The Secretary of State may by order remove from the list in subsection (7) a State or part added under subsection (8).

(10) In this section "asylum claim" and "human rights claim" have the meanings given by section 113 but—

   (a)   a reference to a claim in that section shall be treated as including a reference to an allegation, and

   (b)   a reference in that section to making a claim at a place designated by the Secretary of State shall be ignored.

Amendment

Repealed by the Immigration Act 2014, s 73, Sch 9, Pt 4, paras 30, 54, as from 20 October 2014 (see SI 2014/2771, art 2); subject to savings in SI 2014/2771, arts 9–11.

Sub-s (7): paras (k)–(q) inserted by SI 2003/970, art 4.

Subordinate Legislation

Asylum (Designated States) Order 2003, SI 2003/970.

116, 117

(S 116 repealed by the Legal Aid, Sentencing and Punishment of Offenders Act 2012, s 39(1), Sch 5, Pt 2. Date in force: 1 April 2013: see SI 2013/453, art 3(a), (b); for savings and transitional provisions see SI 2013/534, regs 6(1), 7, 8; s 117 amends legislation outside the scope of this work.)

[PART 5A
ARTICLE 8 OF THE ECHR: PUBLIC INTEREST CONSIDERATIONS

117A Application of this Part

(1) This Part applies where a court or tribunal is required to determine whether a decision made under the Immigration Acts—

   (a)   breaches a person's right to respect for private and family life under Article 8, and

   (b)   as a result would be unlawful under section 6 of the Human Rights Act 1998.

(2) In considering the public interest question, the court or tribunal must (in particular) have regard—

   (a)   in all cases, to the considerations listed in section 117B, and

   (b)   in cases concerning the deportation of foreign criminals, to the considerations listed in section 117C.

(3) In subsection (2), "the public interest question" means the question of whether an interference with a person's right to respect for private and family life is justified under Article 8(2).]

Amendment

Part 5A (ss 117A–117D) inserted by the Immigration Act 2014, s 19, as from 28 July 2014: see SI 2014/1820.

[117B Article 8: public interest considerations applicable in all cases

(1) The maintenance of effective immigration controls is in the public interest.

(2) It is in the public interest, and in particular in the interests of the economic well-being of the United Kingdom, that persons who seek to enter or remain in the United Kingdom are able to speak English, because persons who can speak English—

   (a)   are less of a burden on taxpayers, and

   (b)   are better able to integrate into society.

(3) It is in the public interest, and in particular in the interests of the economic well-being of the United Kingdom, that persons who seek to enter or remain in the United Kingdom are financially independent, because such persons—

   (a)   are not a burden on taxpayers, and

   (b)   are better able to integrate into society.

(4) Little weight should be given to—

(a)   a private life, or

(b)   a relationship formed with a qualifying partner,

that is established by a person at a time when the person is in the United Kingdom unlawfully.

(5)   Little weight should be given to a private life established by a person at a time when the person's immigration status is precarious.

(6)   In the case of a person who is not liable to deportation, the public interest does not require the person's removal where—

(a)   the person has a genuine and subsisting parental relationship with a qualifying child, and

(b)   it would not be reasonable to expect the child to leave the United Kingdom.]

Amendment

Part 5A (ss 117A–117D) inserted by the immigration Act 2014, s 19, as from 28 July 2014: see SI 2014/1820.

[117C Article 8: additional considerations in cases involving foreign criminals

(1)   The deportation of foreign criminals is in the public interest.

(2)   The more serious the offence committed by a foreign criminal, the greater is the public interest in deportation of the criminal.

(3)   In the case of a foreign criminal ("C") who has not been sentenced to a period of imprisonment of four years or more, the public interest requires C's deportation unless Exception 1 or Exception 2 applies.

(4)   Exception 1 applies where—

(a)   C has been lawfully resident in the United Kingdom for most of C's life,

(b)   C is socially and culturally integrated in the United Kingdom, and

(c)   there would be very significant obstacles to C's integration into the country to which C is proposed to be deported.

(5)   Exception 2 applies where C has a genuine and subsisting relationship with a qualifying partner, or a genuine and subsisting parental relationship with a qualifying child, and the effect of C's deportation on the partner or child would be unduly harsh.

(6)   In the case of a foreign criminal who has been sentenced to a period of imprisonment of at least four years, the public interest requires deportation unless there are very compelling circumstances, over and above those described in Exceptions 1 and 2.

(7)   The considerations in subsections (1) to (6) are to be taken into account where a court or tribunal is considering a decision to deport a foreign criminal only to the extent that the reason for the decision was the offence or offences for which the criminal has been convicted.]

Amendment

Part 5A (ss 117A–117D) inserted by the immigration Act 2014, s 19, as from 28 July 2014: see SI 2014/1820.

[117D Interpretation of this Part

(1)   In this Part—

"Article 8" means Article 8 of the European Convention on Human Rights;

"qualifying child" means a person who is under the age of 18 and who—

(a)   is a British citizen, or

(b)   has lived in the United Kingdom for a continuous period of seven years or more;

"qualifying partner" means a partner who—

(a)   is a British citizen, or

(b)   who is settled in the United Kingdom (within the meaning of the Immigration Act 1971—see section 33(2A) of that Act);

(2) In this Part, "foreign criminal" means a person—

  (a) who is not a British citizen,

  (b) who has been convicted in the United Kingdom of an offence, and

  (c) who—

    (i) has been sentenced to a period of imprisonment of at least 12 months,

    (ii) has been convicted of an offence that has caused serious harm, or

    (iii) is a persistent offender.

(3) For the purposes of subsection (2)(b), a person subject to an order under—

  (a) section 5 of the Criminal Procedure (Insanity) Act 1964 (insanity etc),

  (b) section 57 of the Criminal Procedure (Scotland) Act 1995 (insanity etc), or

  (c) Article 50A of the Mental Health (Northern Ireland) Order 1986 (insanity etc),

has not been convicted of an offence.

(4) In this Part, references to a person who has been sentenced to a period of imprisonment of a certain length of time—

  (a) do not include a person who has received a suspended sentence (unless a court subsequently orders that the sentence or any part of it (of whatever length) is to take effect);

  (b) do not include a person who has been sentenced to a period of imprisonment of that length of time only by virtue of being sentenced to consecutive sentences amounting in aggregate to that length of time;

  (c) include a person who is sentenced to detention, or ordered or directed to be detained, in an institution other than a prison (including, in particular, a hospital or an institution for young offenders) for that length of time; and

  (d) include a person who is sentenced to imprisonment or detention, or ordered or directed to be detained, for an indeterminate period, provided that it may last for at least that length of time.

(5) If any question arises for the purposes of this Part as to whether a person is a British citizen, it is for the person asserting that fact to prove it.]

Amendment

Part 5A (ss 117A–117D) inserted by the Immigration Act 2014, s 19, as from 28 July 2014: see SI 2014/1820.

PART 6
IMMIGRATION PROCEDURE

Applications

118, 119

_____

(*Substitute the Immigration Act 1971, s 3C and amend Sch 2 thereto.*)

[120 Requirement to state additional grounds for application etc

(1) Subsection (2) applies to a person ("P") if—

  (a) P has made a protection claim or a human rights claim,

  (b) P has made an application to enter or remain in the United Kingdom, or

  (c) a decision to deport or remove P has been or may be taken.

(2) The Secretary of State or an immigration officer may serve a notice on P requiring P to provide a statement setting out—

    (a)   P's reasons for wishing to enter or remain in the United Kingdom,

    (b)   any grounds on which P should be permitted to enter or remain in the United Kingdom, and

    (c)   any grounds on which P should not be removed from or required to leave the United Kingdom.

(3)   A statement under subsection (2) need not repeat reasons or grounds set out in—

    (a)   P's protection or human rights claim,

    (b)   the application mentioned in subsection (1)(b), or

    (c)   an application to which the decision mentioned in subsection (1)(c) relates.

(4)   Subsection (5) applies to a person ("P") if P has previously been served with a notice under subsection (2) and—

    (a)   P requires leave to enter or remain in the United Kingdom but does not have it, or

    (b)   P has leave to enter or remain in the United Kingdom only by virtue of section 3C or 3D of the Immigration Act 1971 (continuation of leave pending decision or appeal).

(5)   Where P's circumstances have changed since the Secretary of State or an immigration officer was last made aware of them (whether in the application or claim mentioned in subsection (1) or in a statement under subsection (2) or this subsection) so that P has—

    (a)   additional reasons for wishing to enter or remain in the United Kingdom,

    (b)   additional grounds on which P should be permitted to enter or remain in the United Kingdom, or

    (c)   additional grounds on which P should not be removed from or required to leave the United Kingdom,

P must, as soon as reasonably practicable, provide a supplementary statement to the Secretary of State or an immigration officer setting out the new circumstances and the additional reasons or grounds.

(6)   In this section—

"human rights claim" and "protection claim" have the same meanings as in Part 5;

references to "grounds" are to grounds on which an appeal under Part 5 may be brought (see section 84).]

Amendment

Substituted by the Immigration Act 2014, s 73, Sch 9, Pt 4, paras 30, 55, as from 20 October 2014 (see SI 2014/2771, art 2), subject to savings in SI 2014/2771, arts 9–11. Prior to this substitution, s 120 read as follows:

"120 Requirement to state additional grounds for application

(1)   This section applies to a person if—

    (a)   he has made an application to enter or remain in the United Kingdom, or

    (b)   an immigration decision within the meaning of section 82 has been taken or may be taken in respect of him.

(2)   The Secretary of State or an immigration officer may by notice in writing require the person to state—

    (a)   his reasons for wishing to enter or remain in the United Kingdom,

    (b)   any grounds on which he should be permitted to enter or remain in the United Kingdom, and

    (c)   any grounds on which he should not be removed from or required to leave the United Kingdom.

(3)   A statement under subsection (2) need not repeat reasons or grounds set out in—

    (a)   the application mentioned in subsection (1)(a), or

    (b)   an application to which the immigration decision mentioned in subsection (1)(b) relates.".

(S 121 amends the Immigration Act 1971, s 31A; s 122 repealed by the Immigration, Asylum and Nationality Act 2006, ss 52(7), 61, Sch 2, para 5, Sch 3; s 123 amends the Immigration and Asylum Act 1999, s 82.)

Authority-to-carry scheme

121 Authority to carry

(1) The Secretary of State may authorise him to require a person (a "carrier") to pay a penalty if the carrier brings a passenger to the United Kingdom and—

    (a) the carrier was required by an authority-to-carry scheme to seek authority under the scheme to carry the passenger, and

    (b) the carrier did not seek authority before the journey to the United Kingdom did not seek authority before the scheme.

(2) An "authority-to-carry scheme" is a scheme operated by the Secretary of State which requires carriers to seek authority to bring passengers to the United Kingdom.

(3) An authority-to-carry scheme must specify—

    (a) the class of carrier to which it applies (which may be defined by reference to a method of transport or otherwise), and

    (b) the class of passenger to which applies (which may be defined by reference to nationality, the possession of specified documents or otherwise).

(4) The Secretary of State may operate different authority-to-carry schemes for different purposes.

(5) Where the Secretary of State makes regulations under subsection (1) he must—

    (a) identify in the regulations the authority-to-carry scheme to which they refer, and

    (b) lay the authority-to-carry scheme before Parliament.

(6) Regulations under subsection (1) may, in particular—

    (a) apply or make provision similar to a provision of sections 40 to 43 of and Schedule 1 to the Immigration and Asylum Act 1999 (c 33) (charge for passenger without document);

    (b) do anything which may be done under a provision of any of those sections;

    (c) amend any of those sections.

(7) Regulations by virtue of subsection (6)(a) may, in particular—

    (a) apply a provision with modification;

    (b) apply a provision which confers power to make legislation.

(8) The grant or refusal of authority under an authority-to-carry scheme shall not be taken to determine whether a person is entitled or permitted to enter the United Kingdom.

(9) Regulations under this section—

    (a) must be made by statutory instrument, and

    (b) may not be made unless a draft has been laid before and approved by resolution of each House of Parliament.

Commencement

18 July 2012: see SI 2012/1887, art 2.

Subordinate Legislation

Nationality, Immigration and Asylum Act 2002 (Authority to Carry) Regulations 2012, SI 2012/1894.

Evasion of procedure

125 Carriers' liability

Schedule 8 (which amends Part II of the Immigration and Asylum Act 1999 (carriers' liability)) shall have effect.

Provision of information by traveller

126 Physical data: compulsory provision

(1) The Secretary of State may by regulations—

(a) require an immigration application to be accompanied [specified [biometric information];

(b) enable an authorised person to require an individual who makes an immigration application to provide [biometric information];

(c) enable an authorised person to require an entr to provide [biometric information].

(2) In subsection (1) "immigration application" me an application for—

(a) entry clearance,

(b) leave to enter or remain in the United Kingdom, or

(c) variation of leave to enter or remain in the United Kingdom.

[(d) a transit visa (within the meaning of section 41 of the Immigration and Asylum Act 1999), or

(e) a document issued evidence that a person who is not a national of an EEA state or Switzerland is entitled to enter or remain in the United Kingdom by virtue of an enforceable EU right or of any provision made under section 2(2) of the European Communities Act 1972.]

(3) Regulations under subsection (1) may not—

(a) impose a requirement in respect of a person to whom section 141 of the Immigration and Asylum Act 1999 (c 33) (fingerprinting) applies, during the relevant period within the meaning of that section, or

(b) enable a requirement to be imposed in respect of a person to whom that section applies, during the relevant period within the meaning of that section.

(4) Regulations under subsection (1) may, in particular—

(a) require, or enable an authorised person to require, the provision of [biometric] information in a specified form;

(b) require an individual to submit, or enable an authorised person to require an individual to submit, to a specified process by means of which [biometric] information is obtained or recorded;

(c) make provision about the effect of failure to provide [biometric] information or to submit to a process (which may, in particular, include provision for an application to be disregarded or dismissed if a requirement is not satisfied);

(d) confer a function (which may include the exercise of a discretion) on an authorised person;

(e) require an authorised person to have regard to a code (with or without modification);

(f) require an authorised person to have regard to such provisions of a code (with or without modification) as may be specified by direction of the Secretary of State;

[(fa) provide for biometric information to be recorded on any document issued as a result of the application in relation to which the information was provided;]

(g)   make provision about the use and retention of information provided (which may include provision permitting the use of information for specified purposes which do not relate to immigration);

(h)   make provision which applies generally or only in specified cases or circumstances;

(i)   make different provision for different cases or circumstances.

(5)   Regulations under subsection (1) must—

(a)   include provision about the destruction of information obtained or recorded by virtue of the regulations,

(b)   require the destruction of information at the end of the period of ten years beginning with the day on which it is obtained or recorded in a case for which destruction at the end of another period is not required by or in accordance with the regulations, and

(c)   include provision similar to section 143(2) and (10) to (13) of the Immigration and Asylum Act 1999 (c 33) (fingerprints: destruction of copies and electronic data).

(6)   In so far as regulations under subsection (1) require an individual under the age of 16 to submit to a process, the regulations must make provision similar to section 141(3) to (5) and (13) of the Immigration and Asylum Act 1999 (fingerprints: children).

(7)   In so far as regulations under subsection (1) enable an authorised person to require an individual under the age of 16 to submit to a process, the regulations must make provision similar to section 141(3) to (5), (12) and (13) of that Act (fingerprints: children).

(8)   Regulations under subsection (1)—

(a)   must be made by statutory instrument, and

(b)   shall not be made unless a draft of the regulations has been laid before and approved by resolution of each House of Parliament.

[(8A)   Section 8 of the UK Borders Act 2007 (power to make regulations about use and retention of biometric information) applies to biometric information provided in accordance with regulations under subsection (1) as it applies to biometric information provided in accordance with regulations under section 5(1) of that Act.]

(9)   In this section—

"authorised person" has the meaning given by section 141(5) of the Immigration and Asylum Act 1999 (authority to take fingerprints),

["biometric information" has the meaning given by section 15 of the UK Borders Act 2007,]

"code" has the meaning given by section 145(6) of that Act (code of practice),

["document" includes a card or sticker and any other method of recording information (whether in writing or by the use of electronic or other technology or by a combination of methods),]

"entrant" has the meaning given by section 33(1) of the Immigration Act 1971 (c 77) (interpretation),

"entry clearance" has the meaning given by section 33(1) of that Act . . . .

Amendment

Sub-s (1): words in square brackets substituted by the Immigration Act 2014, s 12, Sch 2, para 3(1), (2), as from 28 July 2014: see SI 2014/1820.

Sub-s (2): paras (d), (e) inserted by the Immigration Act 2014, s 8(1), (2), as from 28 July 2014: see SI 2014/1820.

Sub-s (3): words in square brackets inserted by the Immigration Act 2014, s 12, Sch 2, para 3(1), (3), as from 28 July 2014: see SI 2014/1820.

Sub-s (4): para (fa) inserted by the Immigration Act 2014, s 8(1), (3), as from 28 July 2014: see SI 2014/1820.

Sub-s (8A): inserted by the Immigration Act 2014, s 14(3), as from 28 July 2014: see SI 2014/1820.

Sub-s (9): definition "biometric information" inserted and definition "external physical characteristics" (omitted), repealed, together with word preceding it, by the Immigration Act 2014, s 12, Sch 2, para 3(1), (4), (5), as from 28 July 2014: see SI 2014/1820.

Sub-s (9): definition "document" inserted by the Immigration Act 2014, s 8(1), (4), as from 28 July 2014: see SI 2014/1820.

Subordinate Legislation

Immigration (Provision of Physical Data) Regulations 2006, SI 2006/1743; Immigration (Provision of Physical Data) (Amendment) Regulations 2011, SI 2011/1779.

127 Physical data: voluntary provision

(1) The Secretary of State may operate a scheme under which an individual may supply, or submit to the collection or recording of, [biometric information] to be used (wholly or partly) in connection with entry to the United Kingdom.

(2) In particular, the Secretary of State may—

   (a) require an authorised person to use [biometric] information supplied under a scheme;

   (b) make provision about the collection, use and retention of [biometric] information supplied under a scheme (which may include provision requiring an authorised person to have regard to a code);

   (c) charge for participation in a scheme.

(3) In this section the following expressions have the same meaning as in section 126—

   (a) "authorised person",

   [(aa) biometric information", and]

   (b) "code" ...

   (c) ...

128

(*Amends the Immigration and Asylum Act 1999, ss 144, 145.*)

Disclosure of information by public authority

129 Local authority

(1) The Secretary of State may require a local authority to supply information for the purpose of establishing where a person is if the Secretary of State reasonably suspects that—

   (a) the person has committed an offence under section 24(1)(a), (b), (c), (e) or (f), 24A(1) or 26(1)(c) or (d) of the Immigration Act 1971 (c 77) (illegal entry, deception, &c), and

   (b) the person is or has been resident in the local authority's area.

(2) A local authority shall comply with a requirement under this section.

(3) In the application of this section to England and Wales "local authority" means—

   (a) a county council,

Amendment

Sub-s (1): words in square brackets substituted by the Immigration Act 2014, s 12, Sch 2, para 4(1), (2), as from 28 July 2014: see SI 2014/1820.

Sub-s (2): words in square brackets inserted by the Immigration Act 2014, s 12, Sch 2, para 4(1), (3), as from 28 July 2014: see SI 2014/1820.

Sub-s (3): para (aa) inserted and words omitted repealed by the Immigration Act 2014, s 12, Sch 2, para 4(1), (4), as from 28 July 2014: see SI 2014/1820.

[(iia) Healthcare Improvement Scotland established under section 10A of the 1978 Act,] [or]

[(iii) . . .]

(d) in relation to Northern Ireland—

(i) a Health and Social Services Board established under the Health and Personal Social Services (Northern Ireland) Order 1972 (SI 1972/1265 (NI 14)),

(ii) a Health and Social Services trust established under the Health and Personal Social Services (Northern Ireland) Order 1991 (SI 1991/194 (NI 1)), . . .

[(iia) the Regional Agency for Public Health and Social Well-being established under section 12 of the Health and Social Care (Reform) Act (Northern Ireland) 2009, or]

(iii) the Department of Health, Social Services and Public Safety. . .

[(iv) . . .].

Amendment

Sub-s (4): para (a)(ai) inserted by the Health and Social Care Act 2012, s 56(4), Sch 7, paras 12(1), (2)(a). Date in force: 1 April 2013: see SI 2013/160, art 2; for transitional provisions and savings see arts 5–8 thereof.

Sub-s (4): para (a)(i) repealed by the Health and Social Care Act 2012, s 55(2), Sch 5, para 107(a). Date in force: 1 April 2013: see SI 2013/160, art 2; for transitional provisions and savings see arts 5–7, 10, Schedule thereto.

Sub-s (4): para (a)(ia)–(ic) inserted by the Health and Social Care Act 2012, s 55(2), Sch 5, para 107(b). Date in force: 1 April 2013: see SI 2013/160, art 2; for transitional provisions and savings see arts 5–7, 10, Schedule thereto.

Sub-s (4): in para (a)(ii) words from "section 25 of" to "National Health Service (Wales) Act 2006" in square brackets substituted by the National Health Service (Consequential Provisions) Act 2006, s 2, Sch 1, paras 227, 228(b).

Sub-s (4): in para (a)(ii) words "section 25 of the National Health Service Act 2006 or" in italics repealed by the Health and Social Care Act 2012, s 179(6), Sch 14, Pt 2, para 83. Date in force: to be appointed: see the Health and Social Care Act 2012, s 306(4).

Sub-s (4): para (a)(iia) inserted by the Health and Social Care (Community Health and Standards) Act 2003, s 34, Sch 4, paras 127, 128.

Sub-s (4): para (a)(iii) repealed by the Health and Social Care Act 2012, s 55(2), Sch 5, para 107(c). Date in force: 1 April 2013: see SI 2013/160, art 2; for transitional provisions and savings see arts 5–7, 10, Schedule thereto.

Sub-s (4): in para (a)(iii) word "or" in square brackets inserted by the Health and Social Care (Community Health and Standards) Act 2003, s 190(2), Sch 13, para 12(a).

Sub-s (4): in para (a)(iv) words from "section 28 of" to "National Health Service (Wales) Act 2006" in square brackets substituted by the National Health Service (Consequential Provisions) Act 2006, s 2, Sch 1, paras 227, 228(d).

Sub-s (4): para (a)(v) and word omitted immediately preceding it repealed by the Health and Social Care (Community Health and Standards) Act 2003, ss 190(2), 196, Sch 13, para 12(a), Sch 14, Pt 7.

Sub-s (4): para (a)(vi) and word omitted immediately preceding it inserted by the Health Protection Agency Act 2004, s 11(1), Sch 3, para 17(1), (2).

Sub-s (4): para (a)(vi) and word omitted immediately preceding it repealed by the Health and Social Care Act 2012, s 56(4), Sch 7, para 12(1), (2)(b).

Sub-s (4): para (b)(i) substituted by the National Health Service (Consequential Provisions) Act 2006, s 2, Sch 1, paras 227, 228(e).

Sub-s (4): in para (b)(i) word "or" in square brackets inserted by the Health and Social Care Act 2012, s 56(4), Sch 7, para 12(1), (3)(a). Date in force: 1 April 2013: see SI 2013/160, art 2; for transitional provisions and savings see arts 5–8 thereof.

Sub-s (4): in para (b)(ii) words from "section 25 of" to "National Health Service (Wales) Act 2006" in square brackets substituted by the National Health Service (Consequential Provisions) Act 2006, s 2, Sch 1, paras 227, 228(f).

Sub-s (4): in para (b)(ii) words "section 25 of the National Health Service Act 2006 or" in italics repealed by the Health and Social Care Act 2012, s 179(6), Sch 14, Pt 2, para 83.

Date in force: to be appointed: see the Health and Social Care Act 2012, s 306(4).

Sub-s (4): para (b)(iii) and word omitted immediately preceding it repealed by the Health and Social Care (Community Health and Standards) Act 2003, ss 190(2), 196, Sch 13, para 12(b), Sch 14, Pt 7.

Sub-s (4): para (b)(iv) and word omitted immediately preceding it inserted by the Health Protection Agency Act 2004, s 11(1), Sch 3, para 17(1), (3).

Sub-s (4): para (b)(iv) and word omitted immediately preceding it repealed by the Health and Social Care Act 2012, s 56(4), Sch 7, paras 12(1), (3)(b). Date in force: 1 April 2013: see SI 2013/160, art 2; for transitional provisions and savings see arts 5–8 thereof.

Sub-s (4): para (c)(ai) inserted by the Health and Social Care Act 2012, s 56(4), Sch 7, para 12(1), (4)(a). Date in force: 1 April 2013: see SI 2013/160, art 2; for transitional provisions and savings see arts 5–8 thereof.

Sub-s (4): in para (c)(i) word omitted repealed by the Health Protection Agency Act 2004, s 11(1), (2), Sch 3, para 17(1), (4)(a), Sch 4.

Sub-s (4): para (c)(iia) inserted by SI 2011/2581, art 2, Sch 2, Pt 1, para 5. Date in force: 28 October 2011: see SI 2011/2581, art 1(2)(b).

Sub-s (4): in para (c)(iia) word "or" in square brackets inserted by the Health and Social Care Act 2012, s 56(4), Sch 7, para 12(1), (4)(b). Date in force: 1 April 2013: see SI 2013/160, art 2; for transitional provisions and savings see arts 5–8 thereof.

Sub-s (4): para (c)(iii) inserted by the Health Protection Agency Act 2004, s 11(1), Sch 3, para 17(1), (4)(b).

Sub-s (4): para (c)(iii) repealed by the Health and Social Care Act 2012, s 56(4), Sch 7, para 12(1), (4)(c). Date in force: 1 April 2013: see SI 2013/160, art 2; for transitional provisions and savings see arts 5–8 thereof.

Sub-s (4): in para (d)(ii) word omitted repealed by the Health Protection Agency Act 2004, s 11(1), (2), Sch 3, para 17(1), (5)(a), Sch 4.

Sub-s (4): para (d)(iia) inserted by the Health and Social Care Act 2012, s 56(4), Sch 7, para 12(1), (5)(a). Date in force: 1 April 2013: see SI 2013/160, art 2; for transitional provisions and savings see arts 5–8 thereof.

Sub-s (4): para (d)(iv) and word omitted immediately preceding it repealed by the Health and Social Care Act 2012, s 56(4), Sch 7, paras 12(1), (5)(b). Date in force: 1 April 2013: see SI 2013/160, art 2; for transitional provisions and savings see arts 5–8 thereof.

Sub-s (4): para (d)(iv) and word "or" immediately preceding it inserted by the Health Protection Agency Act 2004, s 11(1), Sch 3, para 17(1), (5)(b).

Disclosure of information by private person

134 Employer

(1) The Secretary of State may require an employer to supply information about an employee whom the Secretary of State reasonably suspects of having committed an offence under—

    (a)   section 24(1)(a), (b), (c), (e) or (f), 24A(1) or 26(1)(c) or (d) of the Immigration Act 1971 (c 77) (illegal entry, deception, &c),

    (b)   section 105(1)(a), (b) or (c) of the Immigration and Asylum Act 1999 (c 33) (support for asylum-seeker: fraud), or

    (c)   section 106(1)(a), (b) or (c) of that Act (support for asylum-seeker: fraud).

(2) The power under subsection (1) may be exercised to require information about an employee only if the information—

    (a)   is required for the purpose of establishing where the employee is, or

    (b)   relates to the employee's earnings or to the history of his employment.

(3) In this section a reference to an employer or employee—

    (a)   includes a reference to a former employer or employee, and

    (b)   shall be construed in accordance with section 8(8) of the Asylum and Immigration Act 1996 (c 49) (restrictions on employment).

(4) Where—

(a) a business (the "employment agency") arranges for one person (the "worker") to provide services to another (the "client"), and

(b) the worker is not employed by the employment agency or the client,

this section shall apply as if the employment agency were the worker's employer while he provides services to the client.

135 Financial institution

(1) The Secretary of State may require a financial institution to supply information about a person if the Secretary of State reasonably suspects that—

(a) the person has committed an offence under section 105(1)(a), (b) or (c) or 106(1)(a), (b) or (c) of the Immigration and Asylum Act 1999 (c 33) (support for asylum-seeker: fraud),

(b) the information is relevant to the offence, and

(c) the institution has the information.

(2) In this section "financial institution" means—

(a) a person who has permission under [Part 4A] of the Financial Services and Markets Act 2000 (c 8) to accept deposits, and

(b) a building society (within the meaning given by the Building Societies Act 1986 (c 53)).

Amendment

Sub-s (2): in para (a) words "Part 4A" in square brackets substituted by the Financial Services Act 2012, s 114(1), Sch 18, Pt 2, para 96.

Date in force: 1 April 2013: see SI 2013/423, art 3, Schedule.

136 Notice

(1) A requirement to provide information under section 134 or 135 must be imposed by notice in writing specifying—

(a) the information,

(b) the manner in which it is to be provided, and

(c) the period of time within which it is to be provided.

(2) A period of time specified in a notice under subsection (1)(c)—

(a) must begin with the date of receipt of the notice, and

(b) must not be less than ten working days.

(3) A person on whom a notice is served under subsection (1) must provide the Secretary of State with the information specified in the notice.

(4) Information provided under subsection (3) must be provided—

(a) in the manner specified under subsection (1)(b), and

(b) within the time specified under subsection (1)(c).

(5) In this section "working day" means a day which is not—

(a) Saturday,

(b) Sunday,

(c) Christmas Day,

(d) Good Friday, or

(e) a day which is a bank holiday under the Banking and Financial Dealings Act 1971 (c 80) in any part of the United Kingdom.

137 Disclosure of information: offences

(1) A person commits an offence if without reasonable excuse he fails to comply with section 136(3).

(2) A person who is guilty of an offence under subsection (1) shall be liable on summary conviction to—

(a) imprisonment for a term not exceeding *three months* [51 weeks],

(b) a fine not exceeding level 5 on the standard scale, or

(c) both.

Amendment

Sub-s (2): in para (a) words "3 months" in italics repealed and subsequent words in square brackets substituted by the Criminal Justice Act 2003, s 280(2), (3), Sch 26, para 58, as from a day to be appointed.

138 Offence by body

(1) Subsection (2) applies where an offence under section 137 is committed by a body corporate and it is proved that the offence—

   (a)   was committed with the consent or connivance of an officer of the body,

      or

   (b)   was attributable to neglect on the part of an officer of the body.

(2) The officer, as well as the body, shall be guilty of the offence.

(3) In this section a reference to an officer of a body corporate includes a reference to—

   (a)   a director, manager or secretary,

   (b)   a person purporting to act as a director, manager or secretary, and

   (c)   if the affairs of the body are managed by its members, a member.

(4) Where an offence under section 137 is committed by a partnership (other than a limited partnership), each partner shall be guilty of the offence.

(5) Subsection (1) shall have effect in relation to a limited partnership as if—

   (a)   a reference to a body corporate were a reference to a limited partnership, and

   (b)   a reference to an officer of the body were a reference to a partner.

139 Privilege against self-incrimination

(1) Information provided by a person pursuant to a requirement under section 134 or 135 shall not be admissible in evidence in criminal proceedings against that person.

(2) This section shall not apply to proceedings for an offence under section 137.

140

(*Amends the Immigration and Asylum Act 1999, s 87, Schs 5, 6.*)

Immigration services

Immigration control

141 EEA ports: juxtaposed controls

(1) The Secretary of State may by order make provision for the purpose of giving effect to an international agreement which concerns immigration control at an EEA port (whether or not it also concerns other aspects of frontier control at the port).

(2) An order under this section may make any provision which appears to the Secretary of State—

   (a)   likely to facilitate implementation of the international agreement (including those aspects of the agreement which relate to frontier control other than immigration control), or

   (b)   appropriate as a consequence of provision made for the purpose of facilitating implementation of the agreement.

(3) In particular, an order under this section may—

   (a)   provide for a law of England and Wales to have effect, with or without modification, in relation to a person in a specified area or anything done in a specified area;

(b) provide for a law of England and Wales not to have effect in relation to a person in a specified area or anything done in a specified area;

(c) provide for a law of England and Wales to be modified in its effect in relation to a person in a specified area or anything done in a specified area;

(d) disapply or modify an enactment in relation to a person who has undergone a process in a specified area;

(e) disapply or modify an enactment otherwise than under paragraph (b), (c) or (d);

(f) make provision conferring a function (which may include—

    (i) provision conferring a discretionary function;

    (ii) provision conferring a function on a servant or agent of the government of a State other than the United Kingdom);

(g) create or extend the application of an offence;

(h) impose or permit the imposition of a penalty;

(i) require the payment of, or enable a person to require the payment of, a charge or fee;

(j) make provision about enforcement (which may include—

    (i) provision conferring a power of arrest, detention or removal from or to any place;

    (ii) provision for the purpose of enforcing the law of a State other than the United Kingdom);

(k) confer jurisdiction on a court or tribunal;

(l) confer immunity or provide for indemnity;

(m) make provision about compensation;

(n) impose a requirement, or enable a requirement to be imposed, for a person to co-operate with or to provide facilities for the use of another person who is performing a function under the order or under the international agreement (which may include a requirement to provide facilities without charge);

(o) make provision about the disclosure of information.

(4) An order under this section may—

(a) make provision which applies generally or only in specified circumstances;

(b) make different provision for different circumstances;

(c) amend an enactment.

(5) An order under this section—

(a) must be made by statutory instrument,

(b) may not be made unless the Secretary of State has consulted with such persons as appear to him to be appropriate, and

(c) may not be made unless a draft has been laid before and approved by resolution of each House of Parliament.

(6) In this section—

"EEA port" means a port in an EEA State from which passengers are commonly carried by sea to or from the United Kingdom,

"EEA State" means a State which is a contracting party to the Agreement on the European Economic Area signed at Oporto on 2nd May 1992 (as it has effect from time to time),

"frontier control" means the enforcement of law which relates to, or in so far as it relates to, the movement of persons or goods into or out of the United Kingdom or another State,

"immigration control" means arrangements made in connection with the movement of persons into or out of the United Kingdom or another State, "international agreement" means an agreement made between Her Majesty's Government and the government of another State, and "specified area" means an area (whether of the United Kingdom or of another State) specified in an international agreement.

Subordinate Legislation

Nationality, Immigration and Asylum Act 2002 (Juxtaposed Controls) Order 2003, SI 2003/2818.

Nationality, Immigration and Asylum Act 2002 (Juxtaposed Controls) (Amendment) Order 2006, SI 2006/2908.

Nationality, Immigration and Asylum Act 2002 (Juxtaposed Controls) (Amendment) Order 2011, SI 2011/1786.

142

(Repealed by the UK Borders Act 2007, ss 54(d), 58, Schedule.)

143–156

PART 7
OFFENCES

(Ss 143, 144, 147–156 amend the Immigration Act 1971 and the Asylum and Immigration Act 1996; ss 145, 146 repealed by the Sexual Offences Act 2003; ss 139, 140, Sch 6, para 48, Sch 7.)

PART 8
GENERAL

157 Consequential and incidental provision

(1) The Secretary of State may by order make consequential or incidental provision in connection with a provision of this Act.

(2) An order under this section may, in particular—

    (a)   amend an enactment;

    (b)   modify the effect of an enactment.

(3) An order under this section must be made by statutory instrument.

(4) An order under this section which amends an enactment shall not be made unless a draft has been laid before and approved by resolution of each House of Parliament.

(5) Any other order under this section shall be subject to annulment pursuant to a resolution of either House of Parliament.

Subordinate Legislation

Nationality, Immigration and Asylum Act 2002 (Consequential and Incidental Provisions) Order 2003, SI 2003/1016.

158

(Repealed by the Immigration, Asylum and Nationality Act 2006, ss 61, 64(3)(c), Sch 3.)

159 Applied provision

(1) Subsection (2) applies where this Act amends or refers to a provision which is applied by, under or for purposes of—

    (a)   another provision of the Act which contains the provision, or

    (b)   another Act.

(2) The amendment or reference shall have effect in relation to the provision as applied.

(3) Where this Act applies a provision of another Act, a reference to that provision in any enactment includes a reference to the provision as applied by this Act.

160 Money

(1) Expenditure of the Secretary of State or the Lord Chancellor in connection with a provision of this Act shall be paid out of money provided by Parliament.

(2) An increase attributable to this Act in the amount payable out of money provided by Parliament under another enactment shall be paid out of money provided by Parliament.

(3) A sum received by the Secretary of State or the Lord Chancellor in connection with a provision of this Act shall be paid into the Consolidated Fund.

161 Repeals

The provisions listed in Schedule 9 are hereby repealed to the extent specified.

162 Commencement

(1) Subject to subsections (2) to (5), the preceding provisions of this Act shall come into force in accordance with provision made by the Secretary of State by order.

(2) The following provisions shall come into force on the passing of this Act—

   (a) section 6,

   (b) section 7,

   (c) section 10(1) to (4) and (6),

   (d) section 11,

   (e) section 15 (and Schedule 2),

   (f) section 16,

   (g) section 35(1)(h),

   (h) section 38,

   (i) section 40(1),

   (j) section 41(1),

   (k) section 42,

   (l) section 43,

   (m) section 48,

   (n) section 49,

   (o) section 50,

   (p) section 56,

   (q) section 58,

   (r) section 59,

   (s) section 61,

   (t) section 67,

   (u) section 69,

   (v) section 70,

   (w) section 115 and paragraph 29 of Schedule 7 (and the relevant entry in Schedule 9),

   (x) section 157, and

   (y) section 160.

(3) Section 5 shall have effect in relation to—

   (a) an application made after the passing of this Act, and

   (b) an application made, but not determined, before the passing of this Act.

(4) Section 8 shall have effect in relation to—

   (a) an application made on or after a date appointed by the Secretary of State by order, and

    (b)   an application made, but not determined, before that date.

(5)   Section 9 shall have effect in relation to a child born on or after a date appointed by the Secretary of State by order.

(6)   An order under subsection (1) may—

    (a)   make provision generally or for a specified purpose only (which may include the purpose of the application of a provision to or in relation to a particular place or area);

    (b)   make different provision for different purposes;

    (c)   include transitional provision;

    (d)   include savings;

    (e)   include consequential provision;

    (f)   include incidental provision.

(7)   An order under this section must be made by statutory instrument.

Subordinate Legislation

Nationality, Immigration and Asylum Act 2002 (Commencement No 1) Order 2002, SI 2002/2811; Nationality, Immigration and Asylum Act 2002 (Commencement No 2) Order 2003, SI 2003/1; Nationality, Immigration and Asylum Act 2002 (Commencement No 3) Order 2003, SI 2003/249; Nationality, Immigration and Asylum Act 2002 (Commencement No 4) Order 2003, SI 2003/754; Nationality, Immigration and Asylum Act 2002 (Commencement No 4) (Amendment of Transitional Provisions) Order 2003, SI 2003/1040; Nationality, Immigration and Asylum Act 2002 (Commencement No 4) (Amendment) (No 2) Order 2003, SI 2003/1339; Nationality, Immigration and Asylum Act 2002 (Commencement No 5) Order 2003, SI 2003/1747; Nationality, Immigration and Asylum Act 2002 (Commencement No 4) (Amendment) (No 3) Order 2003, SI 2003/2993; Nationality, Immigration and Asylum Act 2002 (Commencement No 6) Order 2003, SI 2003/3156; Nationality, Immigration and Asylum Act 2002 (Commencement No 7) Order 2004, SI 2004/1201; Nationality, Immigration and Asylum Act 2002 (Commencement No 8) Order 2004, SI 2004/1707; Nationality, Immigration and Asylum Act 2002 (Commencement No 9) Order 2004, SI 2004/2998; Nationality, Immigration and Asylum Act 2002 (Commencement No 10) Order 2005, SI 2005/2782; Nationality, Immigration and Asylum Act 2002 (Commencement No 11) Order 2006, SI 2006/1498; Nationality, Immigration and Asylum Act 2002 (Commencement No 12) Order 2006, SI 2006/3144; Nationality, Immigration and Asylum Act 2002 (Commencement No 13) Order 2012, SI 2012/1263; Nationality, Immigration and Asylum Act 2002 (Commencement No 14) Order 2012, SI 2012/1887.

163 Extent

(1)   A provision of this Act which amends or repeals a provision of another Act or inserts a provision into another Act has the same extent as the provision amended or repealed or as the Act into which the insertion is made (ignoring, in any case, extent by virtue of an Order in Council).

(2)   Sections 145 and 146 extend only to—

    (a)   England and Wales, and

    (b)   Northern Ireland.

(3)   A provision of this Act to which neither subsection (1) nor subsection (2) applies extends to—

    (a)   England and Wales,

    (b)   Scotland, and

    (c)   Northern Ireland.

(4)   Her Majesty may by Order in Council direct that a provision of this Act is to extend, with or without modification or adaptation, to—

    (a)   any of the Channel Islands;

    (b)   the Isle of Man.

(5)   Subsection (4) does not apply in relation to the extension to a place of a provision which extends there by virtue of subsection (1).

Nationality, Immigration and Asylum Act 2002

Subordinate Legislation

Immigration (Isle of Man) Order 2008, SI 2008/680; Immigration (Isle of Man) (Amendment) Order 2011, SI 2011/1408.

164 Short title

This Act may be cited as the Nationality, Immigration and Asylum Act 2002.

SCHEDULES 1, 2

(Amend the British Nationality Act 1981.)

SCHEDULE 3

WITHHOLDING AND WITHDRAWAL OF SUPPORT

Section 54

Ineligibility for support

1

(1) A person to whom this paragraph applies shall not be eligible for support or assistance under—

    (a) section 21 or 29 of the National Assistance Act 1948 (c 29) (local authority: accommodation and welfare),

    (b) section 45 of the Health Services and Public Health Act 1968 (c 46) (local authority: welfare of elderly),

    (c) section 12 or 13A of the Social Work (Scotland) Act 1968 (c 49) (social welfare services),

    (d) Article 7 or 15 of the Health and Personal Social Services (Northern Ireland) Order 1972 (SI 1972/1265 (NI 14)) (prevention of illness, social welfare, &c),

    [(e) section 254 of, and Schedule 20 to, the National Health Service Act 2006, or section 192 of, and Schedule 15 to, the National Health Service (Wales) Act 2006 (social services),]

    (f) section 29(1)(b) of the Housing (Scotland) Act 1987 (c 26) (interim duty to accommodate in case of apparent priority need where review of a local authority decision has been requested),

    (g) section 17, 23C, [23CA,] 24A or 24B of the Children Act 1989 (c 41) (welfare and other powers which can be exercised in relation to adults),

    (h) Article 18, 35 or 36 of the Children (Northern Ireland) Order 1995 (SI 1995/755 (NI 2)) (welfare and other powers which can be exercised in relation to adults),

    (i) sections 22, 29 and 30 of the Children (Scotland) Act 1995 (c 36) (provisions analogous to those mentioned in paragraph (g)),

    (j) section 188(3) or 204(4) of the Housing Act 1996 (c 52) (accommodation pending review or appeal),

    (k) section 2 of the Local Government Act 2000 (c 22) (promotion of well-being),

    [(ka) section 1 of the Localism Act 2011 (local authority's general power of competence),]

    (l) a provision of the Immigration and Asylum Act 1999 (c 33), or

    (m) a provision of this Act.

(2) A power or duty under a provision referred to in sub-paragraph (1) may not be exercised or performed in respect of a person to whom this paragraph applies (whether

or not the person has previously been in receipt of support or assistance under the provision).

(3) An approval or directions given under or in relation to a provision referred to in sub-paragraph (1) shall be taken to be subject to sub-paragraph (2).

2

(1) Paragraph 1 does not prevent the provision of support or assistance—

    (a) to a British citizen, or

    (b) to a child, or

    (c) under or by virtue of regulations made under paragraph 8, 9 or 10 below, or

    (d) in a case in respect of which, and to the extent to which, regulations made by the Secretary of State disapply paragraph 1, or

    (e) in circumstances in respect of which, and to the extent to which, regulations made by the Secretary of State disapply paragraph 1.

(2) Regulations under sub-paragraph (1)(d) may confer a discretion on the Secretary of State.

(3) Regulations under sub-paragraph (1)(e) may, in particular, disapply paragraph 1 to the provision of support or assistance by a local authority to a person where the authority—

    (a) has taken steps in accordance with guidance issued by the Secretary of State to determine whether paragraph 1 would (but for the regulations) apply to the person, and

    (b) has concluded on the basis of those steps that there is no reason to believe that paragraph 1 would apply.

(4) Regulations under sub-paragraph (1)(d) or (e) may confer a discretion on an authority.

(5) A local authority which is considering whether to give support or assistance to a person under a provision listed in paragraph 1(1) shall act in accordance with any relevant guidance issued by the Secretary of State under sub-paragraph (3)(a).

(6) A reference in this Schedule to a person to whom paragraph 1 applies includes a reference to a person in respect of whom that paragraph is disapplied to a limited extent by regulations under sub-paragraph (1)(d) or (e), except in a case for which the regulations provide otherwise.

3

Paragraph 1 does not prevent the exercise of a power or the performance of a duty if, and to the extent that, its exercise or performance is necessary for the purpose of avoiding a breach of—

    (a) a person's Convention rights, or

    (b) a person's rights under the [EU] Treaties.

First class of ineligible person: refugee status abroad

4

(1) Paragraph 1 applies to a person if he—

    (a) has refugee status abroad, or

    (b) is the dependant of a person who is in the United Kingdom and who has refugee status abroad.

(2) For the purposes of this paragraph a person has refugee status abroad if—

    (a) he does not have the nationality of an EEA State, and

(b) the government of an EEA State other than the United Kingdom has determined that he is entitled to protection as a refugee under the Refugee Convention.

Second class of ineligible person: citizen of other EEA State

5

Paragraph 1 applies to a person if he—

(a) has the nationality of an EEA State other than the United Kingdom, or

(b) is the dependant of a person who has the nationality of an EEA State other than the United Kingdom.

Third class of ineligible person: failed asylum-seeker

6

(1) Paragraph 1 applies to a person if—

(a) he was (but is no longer) an asylum-seeker, and

(b) he fails to cooperate with removal directions issued in respect of him.

(2) Paragraph 1 also applies to a dependant of a person to whom that paragraph applies by virtue of sub-paragraph (1).

Fourth class of ineligible person: person unlawfully in United Kingdom

7

Paragraph 1 applies to a person if—

(a) he is in the United Kingdom in breach of the immigration laws within the meaning of [section 50A of the British Nationality Act 1981], and

(b) he is not an asylum-seeker.

[*Fifth class of ineligible person: failed asylum-seeker with family*

7A

(1) Paragraph 1 applies to a person if—

(a) he—

(i) is treated as an asylum-seeker for the purposes of Part VI of the Immigration and Asylum Act 1999 (c 33) (support) by virtue only of section 94(3A) (failed asylum-seeker with dependent child), or

(ii) is treated as an asylum-seeker for the purposes of Part 2 of this Act by virtue only of section 18(2),

(b) the Secretary of State has certified that in his opinion the person has failed without reasonable excuse to take reasonable steps—

(i) to leave the United Kingdom voluntarily, or

(ii) to place himself in a position in which he is able to leave the United Kingdom voluntarily,

(c) the person has received a copy of the Secretary of State's certificate, and

(d) the period of 14 days, beginning with the date on which the person receives the copy of the certificate, has elapsed.

(2) Paragraph 1 also applies to a dependant of a person to whom that paragraph applies by virtue of sub-paragraph (1).

(3) For the purpose of sub-paragraph (1)(d) if the Secretary of State sends a copy of a certificate by first class post to a person's last known address, the person shall be treated as receiving the copy on the second day after the day on which it was posted.

(4) The Secretary of State may by regulations vary the period specified in sub-paragraph (1)(d).]

Travel assistance

8

The Secretary of State may make regulations providing for arrangements to be made for the accommodation of a person to whom paragraph 1 applies pending the implementation of arrangements made by virtue of paragraph 8.

Temporary accommodation

9

(1) The Secretary of State may make regulations providing for arrangements to be made for the accommodation of a person to whom paragraph 1 applies by virtue of paragraph 4 or 5 to leave the United Kingdom.

(2) Arrangements for a person by virtue of this paragraph—

(a) may be made only if the person has with him a dependent child, and

(b) may include arrangements for a dependent child.

10

(1) The Secretary of State may make regulations providing for arrangements to be made for the accommodation of a person if—

(a) paragraph 1 applies to him by virtue of paragraph 7, and

(b) he has not failed to cooperate with removal directions issued in respect of him.

(2) Arrangements for a person by virtue of this paragraph—

(a) may be made only if the person has with him a dependent child, and

(b) may include arrangements for a dependent child.

Assistance and accommodation: general

11

Regulations under paragraph 8, 9 or 10 may—

(a) provide for the making of arrangements under a provision referred to in paragraph 1(1) or otherwise;

(b) confer a function (which may include the exercise of a discretion) on the Secretary of State, a local authority or another person;

(c) provide that arrangements must be made in a specified manner or in accordance with specified principles;

(d) provide that arrangements may not be made in a specified manner;

(e) require a local authority or another person to have regard to guidance issued by the Secretary of State in making arrangements;

(f) require a local authority or another person to comply with a direction of the Secretary of State in making arrangements.

12

(1) Regulations may, in particular, provide that if a person refuses an offer of arrangements under paragraph 8 or fails to implement or cooperate with arrangements made for him under that paragraph—

(a) new arrangements may be made for him under paragraph 8, but

(b) new arrangements may not be made for him under paragraph 9.

(2) Regulations by virtue of this paragraph may include exceptions in the case of a person who—

(a) has a reason of a kind specified in the regulations for failing to implement or cooperate with arrangements made under paragraph 8, and

(b) satisfies any requirements of the regulations for proof of the reason.

Offences

13 (1) A person who leaves the United Kingdom in accordance with arrangements made under paragraph 8 commits an offence if he—

(a) returns to the United Kingdom, and

(b) requests that arrangements be made for him by virtue of paragraph 8, 9 or 10.

(2) A person commits an offence if he—

(a) requests that arrangements be made for him by virtue of paragraph 8, 9 or 10, and

(b) fails to mention a previous request by him for the making of arrangements under any of those paragraphs.

(3) A person who is guilty of an offence under this paragraph shall be liable on summary conviction to imprisonment for a term not exceeding six months.

Information

14 (1) If it appears to a local authority that paragraph 1 applies or may apply to a person in the authority's area by virtue of [paragraph 6, 7 or 7A], the authority must inform the Secretary of State.

(2) A local authority shall act in accordance with any relevant guidance issued by the Secretary of State for the purpose of determining whether paragraph 1 applies or may apply to a person in the authority's area by virtue of [paragraph 6, 7 or 7A].

Power to amend Schedule

15 The Secretary of State may by order amend this Schedule so as—

(a) to provide for paragraph 1 to apply or not to apply to a class of person;

(b) to add or remove a provision to or from the list in paragraph 1(1);

(c) to add, amend or remove a limitation or exception to paragraph 1.

Orders and regulations

16 (1) An order or regulations under this Schedule must be made by statutory instrument.

(2) An order or regulations under this Schedule may—

(a) make provision which applies generally or only in specified cases or circumstances or only for specified purposes;

(b) make different provision for different cases, circumstances or purposes;

(c) make transitional provision;

(d) make consequential provision (which may include provision amending a provision made by or under this or another Act),

(3) An order under this Schedule, regulations under paragraph 2(1)(d) or (e) or other regulations which include consequential provision amending an enactment shall not be

made unless a draft has been laid before and approved by resolution of each House of Parliament.

(4) Regulations under this Schedule to which sub-paragraph (3) does not apply shall be subject to annulment in pursuance of a resolution of either House of Parliament.

Interpretation

17

(1) In this Schedule—

"asylum-seeker" means a person—

   (a) who is at least 18 years old,

   (b) who has made a claim for asylum (within the meaning of section 18(3)), and

   (c) whose claim has been recorded by the Secretary of State but not determined,

"Convention rights" has the same meaning as in the Human Rights Act 1998 (c 42),

"child" means a person under the age of eighteen,

"dependant" and "dependent" shall have such meanings as may be prescribed by regulations made by the Secretary of State,

"EEA State" means a State which is a contracting party to the Agreement on the European Economic Area signed at Oporto on 2nd May 1992 (as it has effect from time to time),

"local authority"—

   (a) in relation to England and Wales, has the same meaning as in section 129(3),

   (b) in relation to Scotland, has the same meaning as in section 129(4), and

   (c) in relation to Northern Ireland, means a health service body within the meaning of section 133(4)(d) and the Northern Ireland Housing Executive (for which purpose a reference to the authority's area shall be taken as a reference to Northern Ireland),

"the Refugee Convention" means the Convention relating to the status of Refugees done at Geneva on 28th July 1951 and its Protocol, and

"removal directions" means directions under Schedule 2 to the Immigration Act 1971 (c 77) (control of entry, &c), under Schedule 3 to that Act (deportation) or under section 10 of the Immigration and Asylum Act 1999 (c 33) (removal of person unlawfully in United Kingdom).

(2) For the purpose of the definition of "asylum-seeker" in sub-paragraph (1) a claim is determined if—

   (a) the Secretary of State has notified the claimant of his decision,

   (b) no appeal against the decision can be brought (disregarding the possibility of an appeal out of time with permission), and

   (c) any appeal which has already been brought has been disposed of.

(3) For the purpose of sub-paragraph (2)(c) an appeal is disposed of when it is no longer pending for the purpose of—

   (a) Part 5 of this Act, or

   (b) the Special Immigration Appeals Commission Act 1997 (c 68).

(4) The giving of directions in respect of a person under a provision of the Immigration Acts is not the provision of assistance to him for the purposes of this Schedule.

Amendment

Para 1: sub-para (1)(e) substituted by the National Health Service (Consequential Provisions) Act 2006, s 2, Sch 1, paras 227, 229.

Para 1: in sub-para (1)(g) reference to "23CA," in square brackets inserted by the Children and Young Persons Act 2008, s 22(6). Date in force (in relation to England): 1 April 2011: see SI 2010/2981, art 4(g). Date in force (in relation to Wales): 19 June 2012: see SI 2012/1553, art 2(a).

Para 1: sub-para (1)(ka) inserted by SI 2012/961, art 2, Sch 1, paras 2, 4. Date in force: 28 March 2012: see SI 2012/961, art 1(2).

Para 3: in sub-para (b) reference to "EU" in square brackets substituted by SI 2011/1043, art 6(1)(a). Date in force: 22 April 2011: see SI 2011/1043, art 2; for transitional savings see art 3(3) thereof.

Para 7: in sub-para (a) words "section 50A of the British Nationality Act 1981" in square brackets substituted by the Borders, Citizenship and Immigration Act 2009, s 48(6).

Para 7A: inserted by the Asylum and Immigration (Treatment of Claimants, etc) Act 2004, s 9(1).

Para 14: words "paragraph 6, 7 or 7A" in square brackets in both places they occur substituted by the Asylum and Immigration (Treatment of Claimants, etc) Act 2004, s 9(2).

Subordinate Legislation

Withholding and Withdrawal of Support (Travel Assistance and Temporary Accommodation) Regulations 2002, SI 2002/3078.

SCHEDULES 4, 5

(Sch 4 repealed by SI 2010/21, art 5(1), Sch 1, paras 20, 30; Sch 5 repealed by the Asylum and Immigration (Treatment of Claimants, etc) Act 2004, ss 26(5)(b), 47, Sch 4; for transitional provisions see s 26(7), Sch 2, Pt 2 thereto.)

SCHEDULE 6

IMMIGRATION AND ASYLUM APPEALS: TRANSITIONAL PROVISIONS

Section 114

"Commencement"

1

In this Schedule "commencement" means the coming into force of Part 5 of this Act.

Adjudicator

2

Where a person is an adjudicator under section 57 of the Immigration and Asylum Act 1999 (c 33) immediately before commencement his appointment shall have effect after commencement as if made under section 81 of this Act.

Tribunal

3

(1) Where a person is a member of the Immigration Appeal Tribunal immediately before commencement his appointment shall have effect after commencement as if made under Schedule 5.

(2) Where a person is a member of staff of the Immigration Appeal Tribunal immediately before commencement his appointment shall have effect after commencement as if made under Schedule 5.

4

In the application of section 96—

(a) a reference to an appeal or right of appeal under a provision of this Act includes a reference to an appeal or right of appeal under the Immigration and Asylum Act 1999,

(b) a reference to a requirement imposed under this Act includes a reference to a requirement of a similar nature imposed under that Act,

(c) a reference to a statement made in pursuance of a requirement imposed under a provision of this Act includes a reference to anything done in compliance with a requirement of a similar nature under that Act, and

(d) a reference to notification by virtue of this Act includes a reference to notification by virtue of any other enactment.

Saving

5

(1) This Schedule is without prejudice to the power to include transitional provision in an order under section 162.

(2) An order under that section may, in particular, provide for a reference to a provision of Part 5 of this Act to be treated as being or including a reference (with or without modification) to a provision of the Immigration and Asylum Act 1999 (c 33).

SCHEDULES 7–9

(Contain amendments and repeals which, in so far as relevant to this work, have been incorporated at the appropriate place.)

ASYLUM AND IMMIGRATION (TREATMENT OF CLAIMANTS, ETC) ACT 2004

2004 c 19

An Act to make provision about asylum and immigration.

[22 July 2004]

Modification

In relation to the extension of this Act, with modifications, to the Isle of Man, see the Immigration (Isle of Man) Order 2008, SI 2008/680.

1

Offences

(Amends the Immigration Act 1971, s 25.)

2 Entering United Kingdom without passport, &c

(1) A person commits an offence if at a leave or asylum interview he does not have with him an immigration document which—

(a) is in force, and

(b) satisfactorily establishes his identity and nationality or citizenship.

(2) A person commits an offence if at a leave or asylum interview he does not have with him, in respect of any dependent child with whom he claims to be travelling or living, an immigration document which—

(a) is in force, and

(b) satisfactorily establishes the child's identity and nationality or citizenship.

(3) But a person does not commit an offence under subsection (1) or (2) if—

(a) the interview referred to in that subsection takes place after the person has entered the United Kingdom, and

(b) within the period of three days beginning with the date of the interview the person provides to an immigration officer or to the Secretary of State a document of the kind referred to in that subsection.

(4) It is a defence for a person charged with an offence under subsection (1)—

(a) to prove that he is an EEA national,

(b) to prove that he is a member of the family of an EEA national and that he is exercising a right under the [EU] Treaties in respect of entry to or residence in the United Kingdom,

(c) to prove that he has a reasonable excuse for not being in possession of a document of the kind specified in subsection (1),

(d) to produce a false immigration document and to prove that he used that document as an immigration document for all purposes in connection with his journey to the United Kingdom, or

(e) to prove that he travelled to the United Kingdom without, at any stage since he set out on the journey, having possession of an immigration document.

(5) It is a defence for a person charged with an offence under subsection (2) in respect of a child—

(a) to prove that the child is an EEA national,

(b) to prove that the child is a member of the family of an EEA national and that the child is exercising a right under the [EU] Treaties in respect of entry to or residence in the United Kingdom,

(c) to prove that the person has a reasonable excuse for not being in possession of a document of the kind specified in subsection (2),

(d) to produce a false immigration document and to prove that it was used as an immigration document for all purposes in connection with the child's journey to the United Kingdom, or

(e) to prove that he travelled to the United Kingdom with the child without, at any stage since he set out on the journey, having possession of an immigration document in respect of the child.

(6) Where the charge for an offence under subsection (1) or (2) relates to an interview which takes place after the defendant has entered the United Kingdom—

(a) subsections (4)(c) and (5)(c) shall not apply, but

(b) it is a defence for the defendant to prove that he has a reasonable excuse for not providing a document in accordance with subsection (3).

(7) For the purposes of subsections (4) to (6)—

(a) the fact that a document was deliberately destroyed or disposed of is not a reasonable excuse for not being in possession of it or for not providing it in accordance with subsection (3), unless it is shown that the destruction or disposal was—

(i) for a reasonable cause, or

(ii) beyond the control of the person charged with the offence, and

(b) in paragraph (a)(i) "reasonable cause" does not include the purpose of—

(8) A person shall be presumed for the purposes of this section not to have a document with him if he fails to produce it to an immigration officer or official of the Secretary of State on request.

(9) A person guilty of an offence under this section shall be liable—

    (a) on conviction on indictment, to imprisonment for a term not exceeding two years, to a fine or to both, or

    (b) on summary conviction, to imprisonment for a term not exceeding twelve months, to a fine not exceeding the statutory maximum or to both.

(10) If [an] immigration officer reasonably suspects that a person has committed an offence under this section he may arrest the person without warrant.

(11) An offence under this section shall be treated as—

    (a) a relevant offence for the purposes of sections 28B and 28D of the Immigration Act 1971 (c 77) (search, entry and arrest), and

    (b) an offence under Part III of that Act (criminal proceedings) for the purposes of sections 28(4), 28E, 28G and 28H (search after arrest, &c) of that Act.

(12) In this section—

"EEA national" means a national of a State which is a contracting party to the Agreement on the European Economic Area signed at Oporto on 2nd May 1992 (as it has effect from time to time),

"immigration document" means—

    (a) a passport, and

    (b) a document which relates to a national of a State other than the United Kingdom and which is designed to serve the same purpose as a passport, and

"leave or asylum interview" means an interview with an immigration officer or an official of the Secretary of State at which a person—

    (a) seeks leave to enter or remain in the United Kingdom, or

    (b) claims that to remove him from or require him to leave the United Kingdom would breach the United Kingdom's obligations under the Refugee Convention or would be unlawful under section 6 of the Human Rights Act 1998 (c 42) as being incompatible with his Convention rights.

(13) For the purposes of this section—

    (a) a document which purports to be, or is designed to look like, an immigration document, is a false immigration document, and

    (b) an immigration document is a false immigration document if and in so far as it is used—

        (i) outside the period for which it is expressed to be valid,

        (ii) contrary to provision for its use made by the person issuing it, or

        (iii) by or in respect of a person other than the person to or for whom it was issued.

(14) Section 11 of the Immigration Act 1971 (c 77) shall have effect for the purpose of the construction of a reference in this section to entering the United Kingdom.

(15) In so far as this section extends to England and Wales, subsection (9)(b) shall, until the commencement of section 154 of the Criminal Justice Act 2003 (c 44)

    (i) delaying the handling or resolution of a claim or application or the taking of a decision,

    (ii) increasing the chances of success of a claim or application, or

    (iii) complying with instructions or advice given by a person who offers advice about, or facilitates, immigration into the United Kingdom, unless in the circumstances of the case it is unreasonable to expect non-compliance with the instructions or advice.

(increased limit on magistrates' power of imprisonment), have effect as if the reference to twelve months were a reference to six months.

(16) In so far as this section extends to Scotland, subsection (9)(b) shall have effect as if the reference to twelve months were a reference to six months.

(17) In so far as this section extends to Northern Ireland, subsection (9)(b) shall have effect as if the reference to twelve months were a reference to six months.

Amendment

Sub-s (4): in para (b) reference to "EU" in square brackets substituted by SI 2011/1043, art 6(1)(a). Date in force: 22 April 2011: see SI 2011/1043, art 2; for transitional savings see art 3(3) thereof.

Sub-s (5): in para (b) reference to "EU" in square brackets substituted by SI 2011/1043, art 6(1)(a). Date in force: 22 April 2011: see SI 2011/1043, art 2; for transitional savings see art 3(3) thereof.

Sub-s (10): word "an" in square brackets substituted in relation to England, Wales and Scotland by the Serious Organised Crime and Police Act 2005, s 111, Sch 7, Pt 4, para 63(a) and in relation to Northern Ireland by SI 2007/288, art 15(4), Sch 1, para 39(1).

3

(Repealed by the Identity Cards Act 2006, s 44(2), Sch 2.)

4 Trafficking people for exploitation

[(1A) A person ("A") commits an offence if A intentionally arranges or facilitates—

  (a) the arrival in, or entry into, the United Kingdom or another country of another person ("B"),

  (b) the travel of B within the United Kingdom or another country, or

  (c) the departure of B from the United Kingdom or another country,

with a view to the exploitation of B.

(1B) For the purposes of subsection (1A)(a) and (c) A's arranging or facilitating is with a view to the exploitation of B if (and only if)—

  (a) A intends to exploit B, after B's arrival, entry or (as the case may be) departure but in any part of the world, or

  (b) A believes that another person is likely to exploit B, after B's arrival, entry or (as the case may be) departure but in any part of the world.

(1C) For the purposes of subsection (1A)(b) A's arranging or facilitating is with a view to the exploitation of B if (and only if)—

  (a) A intends to exploit B, during or after the journey and in any part of the world, or

  (b) A believes that another person is likely to exploit B, during or after the journey and in any part of the world.]

[(3A) A person to whom section 5(2) applies commits an offence if—

  (a) in relation to an individual (the "passenger"), he arranges or facilitates—

    (i) the arrival in or the entry into a country other than the United Kingdom of the passenger,

    (ii) travel by the passenger within a country other than the United Kingdom,

    (iii) the departure of the passenger from a country other than the United Kingdom, and

  (b) he—

    (i) intends to exploit the passenger, or

    (ii) believes that another person is likely to exploit the passenger,

(wherever the exploitation is to occur).]

(4) For the purposes of this section a person is exploited if (and only if)—

293

(a) he is the victim of behaviour that contravenes Article 4 of the Human Rights Convention (slavery and forced labour),

(b) he is encouraged, required or expected to do anything

[(i)] as a result of which he or another person would commit an offence *under the Human Organ Transplants Act 1989 (c 31)* [Part 1 of the Human Tissue (Scotland) Act 2006 (asp 4)] *or* [under section 32 or 33 of the Human Tissue Act 2004] [as it has effect in the law of England and Wales], [or]

[(ii)] which, were it done in England and Wales, would constitute an offence within sub-paragraph (i),]

[(ba)] he is encouraged, required or expected to do anything in connection with the removal of any part of a human body—

(i) as a result of which he or another person would commit an offence under the law of Scotland [(other than an offence mentioned in paragraph (b)(i)), or

(ii) which, were it done in Scotland, would constitute an offence,]

(c) he is subjected to force, threats or deception designed to induce him—

(i) to provide services of any kind,

(ii) to provide another person with benefits of any kind, or

(iii) to enable another person to acquire benefits of any kind, or

(d) a person uses or attempts to use him for any purpose within sub-paragraph (i), (ii) or (iii) of paragraph (c), having chosen him for that purpose on the grounds that—

(i) he is mentally or physically ill or disabled, he is young or he has a family relationship with a person, and

(ii) a person without the illness, disability, youth or family relationship would be likely to refuse to be used for that purpose].

[(4A) A person who is a UK national commits an offence under this section regardless of—

(a) where the arranging or facilitating takes place, or

(b) which country is the country of arrival, entry, travel or (as the case may be) departure.

(4B) A person who is not a UK national commits an offence under this section if—

(a) any part of the arranging or facilitating takes place in the United Kingdom, or

(b) the United Kingdom is the country of arrival, entry, travel or (as the case may be) departure.]

(5) A person guilty of an offence under this section shall be liable—

(a) on conviction on indictment, to imprisonment for a term not exceeding 14 years, to a fine or to both, or

(b) on summary conviction, to imprisonment for a term not exceeding twelve months, to a fine not exceeding the statutory maximum or to both.

Amendment

Sub-ss (1A)–(1C) substituted for original sub-ss (1)–(3), by subsequent, in relation to England and Wales, by the Protection of Freedoms Act 2012, s 110(1), (2).

Date in force: 6 April 2013: see SI 2013/470, art 2(b); for transitional provisions see arts 3(a), 4, 6–8 thereof.

Sub-s (3A): inserted by the Criminal Justice and Licensing (Scotland) Act 2010, s 46(2)(c).

Date in force: 28 March 2011 (with effect in relation to offences committed on or after that date): see SSI 2011/178, art 2, Schedule.

Sub-s (4): para (b)(i) numbered as such in relation to England and Wales by the Protection of Freedoms Act 2012, s 110(1), (3)(b) and in relation to Scotland by the Criminal Justice and Licensing (Scotland) Act 2010, s 46(2)(d)(i).

Date in force (in relation to Scotland): 28 March 2011 (with effect in relation to offences committed on or after that date): see SSI 2011/178, art 2, Schedule.

Date in force (in relation to England and Wales): 6 April 2013: see SSI 2013/470, art 2(b); for transitional provisions see arts 3(a), 4, 6–8 thereof.

Sub-s (4): in para (b)(i) words "under the Human Organ Transplants Act 1989 (c 31) or" in italics repealed, in relation to England and Wales, by the Protection of Freedoms Act 2012, ss 110(1), (3)(a)(i), 115(2), Sch 10, Pt 9.

Date in force: 6 April 2013: see SI 2013/470, art 2(b), (e), (f); for transitional provisions see arts 3(a), 4, 6–8 thereof.

Sub-s (4): in para (b)(i) words "the Human Organ Transplants Act 1989 (c 31)" in italics repealed and subsequent words in square brackets substituted, in relation to Scotland, by SSI 2008/259, art 2.

Sub-s (4): in para (b)(i) words "under section 32 or 33 of the Human Tissue Act 2004" in square brackets substituted by the Human Tissue Act 2004, s 56, Sch 6, para 7.

Sub-s (4): in para (b)(i) words "as it has effect in the law of England and Wales" in square brackets inserted, in relation to England and Wales, by the Protection of Freedoms Act 2012, s 110(1), (3)(a)(ii).

Date in force: 6 April 2013: see SI 2013/470, art 2(b); for transitional provisions see arts 3(a), 4, 6–8 thereof.

Sub-s (4): para (b)(ii) and word "or" immediately preceding it inserted in relation to England and Wales by the Protection of Freedoms Act 2012, s 110(1), (3)(c); a corresponding amendment has been made in relation to Scotland by the Criminal Justice and Licensing (Scotland) Act 2010, s 46(2)(d)(ii).

Date in force (in relation to Scotland): 28 March 2011 (with effect in relation to offences committed on or after that date): see SSI 2011/178, art 2, Schedule. Date in force (in relation to England and Wales): 6 April 2013: see SI 2013/470, art 2(b); for transitional provisions see arts 3(a), 4, 6–8 thereof.

Sub-s (4): para (ba) inserted by the Criminal Justice and Licensing (Scotland) Act 2010, s 46(2)(d)(iii).

Date in force: 28 March 2011 (with effect in relation to offences committed on or after that date): see SSI 2011/178, art 2, Schedule.

Sub-s (4): para (d) substituted, in relation to England, Wales and Northern Ireland, by the Borders, Citizenship and Immigration Act 2009, s 54 and, in relation to Scotland, by the Criminal Justice and Licensing (Scotland) Act 2010, s 46(2)(d)(iv).

Date in force (in relation to England, Wales and Northern Ireland): 10 November 2009: see SI 2009/2731, art 3(b). Date in force (in relation to Scotland): 28 March 2011 (with effect in relation to offences committed on or after that date): see SSI 2011/178, art 2, Schedule.

Sub-ss (4A), (4B): inserted, in relation to England and Wales, by the Protection of Freedoms Act 2012, s 110(1), (4).

Date in force: 6 April 2013: see SI 2013/470, art 2(b); for transitional provisions see arts 3(a), 4, 6–8 thereof.

5

(1) . . .

[(2A) A person may be prosecuted, tried and punished for any offence to which section 4 applies—

    (a)   in any sheriff court district in which the person is apprehended or is in custody, or

    (b)   in such sheriff court district as the Lord Advocate may determine,

as if the offence had been committed in that district (and the offence is, for all purposes incidental to or consequential on the trial or punishment, to be deemed to have been committed in that district).

(2B) In subsection (2A), "sheriff court district" is to be construed in accordance with section 307(1) of the Criminal Procedure (Scotland) Act 1995 (c 46) (interpretation).]

(3) [In section 4—

"country" includes any territory or other part of the world,] "the Human Rights Convention" means the Convention for the Protection of Human Rights and Fundamental Freedoms agreed by the Council of Europe at Rome on 4th November 1950,

["UK national" means—

    (a) a British citizen,

    (b) a person who is a British subject by virtue of Part 4 of the British Nationality Act 1981 and who has the right of abode in the United Kingdom, or

    (c) a person who is a British overseas territories citizen by virtue of a connection with Gibraltar].

(4) Sections 25C and 25D of the Immigration Act 1971 (c 77) (forfeiture or detention of vehicle) shall apply in relation to an offence under section 4 of this Act as they apply in relation to an offence under section 25 of that Act.

(5)–(10) . . .

(11) . . . subsection (5)(b) shall, until the commencement of section 154 of the Criminal Justice Act 2003 (c. 44) (increased limit on magistrates' power of imprisonment), have effect as if the reference to twelve months were a reference to six months.

(12) . . .

(13) . . .

Amendment

Sub-s (1): repealed by the Protection of Freedoms Act 2012, ss 110(1),(5), 115(2), Sch 10, Pt 9. Date in force: 6 April 2013: see SI 2013/470, art 2(b), (e), (f); for transitional provisions see arts 3(a), 4, 6–8 thereof.

Sub-ss (2A), (2B): inserted by the Criminal Justice and Licensing (Scotland) Act 2010, s 46(3)(c). Date in force: 28 March 2011 (with effect in relation to offences committed on or after that date): see SSI 2011/178, art 2, Schedule.

Sub-s (3): words in first pair of square brackets substituted, in relation to England and Wales, by the Protection of Freedoms Act 2012, s 110(1), (6)(a), (b). Date in force: 6 April 2013: see SI 2013/470, art 2(b); for transitional provisions see arts 3(a), 4, 6–8 thereof.

Sub-s (3): definition "UK national" inserted, in relation to England and Wales, by the Protection of Freedoms Act 2012, s 110(1), (6)(c). Date in force: 6 April 2013: see SI 2013/470, art 2(b); for transitional provisions see arts 3(a), 4, 6–8 thereof.

Sub-ss (5)–(10): amend the Immigration Act 1971 and other legislation outside the scope of this work.

Sub-s (11): words omitted repealed, in relation to England and Wales, by the Protection of Freedoms Act 2012, s 115(1), (2), Sch 9, Pt 10, para 141(1), (2)(a), Sch 10, Pt 9. Date in force: 6 April 2013: see SI 2013/470, art 2(c), (d).

Sub-ss (12), (13): repealed, in relation to England and Wales, by the Protection of Freedoms Act 2012, s 115(1), (2), Sch 9, Pt 10, para 141(1), (2)(b), Sch 10, Pt 9. Date in force: 6 April 2013: see SI 2013/470, art 2(c), (d).

6, 7

6, 7 . . .

(S 6 amends the Asylum and Immigration Act 1996, s 8; s 7 amends legislation outside the scope of this work.)

Treatment of claimants

8 Claimant's credibility

(1) In determining whether to believe a statement made by or on behalf of a person who makes an asylum claim or a human rights claim, a deciding authority shall take account, as damaging the claimant's credibility, of any behaviour to which this section applies.

(2) This section applies to any behaviour by the claimant that the deciding authority thinks—

   (a) is designed or likely to conceal information,

   (b) is designed or likely to mislead, or

   (c) is designed or likely to obstruct or delay the handling or resolution of the claim or the taking of a decision in relation to the claimant.

(3) Without prejudice to the generality of subsection (2) the following kinds of behaviour shall be treated as designed or likely to conceal information or to mislead—

   (a) failure without reasonable explanation to produce a passport on request to an immigration officer or to the Secretary of State,

   (b) the production of a document which is not a valid passport as if it were,

   (c) the destruction, alteration or disposal, in each case without reasonable explanation, of a passport,

   (d) the destruction, alteration or disposal, in each case without reasonable explanation, of a ticket or other document connected with travel, and

   (e) failure without reasonable explanation to answer a question asked by a deciding authority.

(4) This section also applies to failure by the claimant to take advantage of a reasonable opportunity to make an asylum claim or human rights claim while in a safe country.

(5) This section also applies to failure by the claimant to make an asylum claim or human rights claim before being notified of an immigration decision, unless the claim relies wholly on matters arising after the notification.

(6) This section also applies to failure by the claimant to make an asylum claim or human rights claim before being arrested under an immigration provision, unless—

   (a) he had no reasonable opportunity to make the claim before the arrest, or

   (b) the claim relies wholly on matters arising after the arrest.

(7) In this section—

"asylum claim" has the meaning given by section 113(1) of the Nationality, Immigration and Asylum Act 2002 (c 41) (subject to subsection (9) below),

"deciding authority" means—

   (a) an immigration officer,

   (b) the Secretary of State,

   (c) [the First-tier Tribunal], or

   (d) the Special Immigration Appeals Commission,

"human rights claim" has the meaning given by section 113(1) of the Nationality, Immigration and Asylum Act 2002 (subject to subsection (9) below),

"immigration decision" means—

   (a) refusal of leave to enter the United Kingdom,

   (b) refusal to vary a person's leave to enter or remain in the United Kingdom,

   (c) grant of leave to enter or remain in the United Kingdom,

   (d) a decision that a person is to be removed from the United Kingdom by way of directions under section 10 . . . of the Immigration and Asylum Act 1999 (c 33) (removal of persons unlawfully in United Kingdom),

   (e) a decision that a person is to be removed from the United Kingdom by way of directions under paragraphs 8 to 12 of Schedule 2 to the Immigration Act 1971 (c 77) (control of entry: removal),

   (f) a decision to make a deportation order under section 5(1) of that Act, and

(g) a decision to take action in relation to a person in connection with extradition from the United Kingdom,

"immigration provision" means—

(a) sections 28A, 28AA, 28B, 28C and 28CA of the Immigration Act 1971 (immigration offences: enforcement),

(b) paragraph 17 of Schedule 2 to that Act (control of entry),

(c) section 14 of this Act, and

(d) a provision of the Extradition Act 1989 (c 33) or 2003 (c 41),

"notified" means notified in such manner as may be specified by regulations made by the Secretary of State,

"passport" includes a document which relates to a national of a country other than the United Kingdom and which is designed to serve the same purpose as a passport, and

"safe country" means a country to which Part 2 of Schedule 3 applies.

(8) A passport produced by or on behalf of a person is valid for the purposes of subsection (3)(b) if it—

(a) relates to the person by whom or on whose behalf it is produced,

(b) has not been altered otherwise than by or with the permission of the authority who issued it, and

(c) was not obtained by deception.

(9) In subsection (4) a reference to an asylum claim or human rights claim shall be treated as including a reference to a claim of entitlement to remain in a country other than the United Kingdom made by reference to the rights that a person invokes in making an asylum claim or a human rights claim in the United Kingdom.

[(9A) In paragraph (c) of the definition of a "deciding authority" in subsection (7) the reference to the First-tier Tribunal includes a reference to the Upper Tribunal when acting under section 12(2)(b)(ii) of the Tribunals, Courts and Enforcement Act 2007.]

(10) Regulations under subsection (7) specifying a manner of notification may, in particular—

(a) apply, or refer to regulations under section 105 of the Nationality, Immigration and Asylum Act 2002 (c 41) (notice of immigration decisions);

(b) make provision similar to provision that is or could be made by regulations under that section;

(c) modify a provision of regulations under that section in its effect for the purpose of regulations under this section;

(d) provide for notice to be treated as received at a specified time if sent to a specified class of place in a specified manner.

(11) Regulations under subsection (7) specifying a manner of notification—

(a) may make incidental, consequential or transitional provision,

(b) shall be made by statutory instrument, and

(c) shall be subject to annulment in pursuance of a resolution of either House of Parliament.

(12) This section shall not prevent a deciding authority from determining not to believe a statement on the grounds of behaviour to which this section does not apply.

(13) . . .

Amendment

Sub-s (7): in definition "deciding authority" in para (c) words "the First-tier Tribunal" in square brackets substituted by SI 2010/21, art 5(1), Sch 1, paras 31, 32(a).

Date in force: 15 February 2010: see SI 2010/21, art 1; for transitional provisions and savings see art 5(4), Sch 4, paras 14–18, 21 thereto.

Sub-s (7): words "(1)(a), (b), (ba) or (c)" omitted from para (d) of the definition "immigration decision" repealed by the Immigration Act 2014, s 73, Sch 9, Pt 1, para 4, as from 20 October 2014 (see SI 2014/2771, art 2), subject to savings in SI 2014/2771, arts 9–11

Sub-s (9A): inserted by SI 2010/21, Sch 1, paras 31, 32(b).

Date in force: 15 February 2010: see SI 2010/21, art 1; for transitional provisions and savings see art 5(4), Sch 4, paras 14–18, 21 thereto.

Sub-s (13): repealed by SI 2010/21, art 5(1), Sch 1, paras 31, 32(c).

Date in force: 15 February 2010: see SI 2010/21, art 1; for transitional provisions and savings see art 5(4), Sch 4, paras 14–18, 21 thereto.

Subordinate Legislation

Immigration (Claimant's Credibility) Regulations 2004, SI 2004/3263.

9 Failed asylum seekers: withdrawal of support

(1) . . .

(2) . . .

(3) No appeal may be brought under section 103 of the Immigration and Asylum Act 1999 (asylum support appeal) against a decision—

(a) that by virtue of a provision of Schedule 3 to the Nationality, Immigration and Asylum Act 2002 (c 41) other than paragraph 7A a person is not qualified to receive support, or

(b) on the grounds of the application of a provision of that Schedule other than paragraph 7A, to stop providing support to a person.

(4) On an appeal under section 103 of the Immigration and Asylum Act 1999 (c 33) against a decision made by virtue of paragraph 7A of Schedule 3 to the Nationality, Immigration and Asylum Act 2002 the [First-tier Tribunal] may, in particular—

(a) annul a certificate of the Secretary of State issued for the purposes of that paragraph;

(b) require the Secretary of State to reconsider the matters certified.

(5) An order under section 48 providing for this section to come into force may, in particular, provide for this section to have effect with specified modifications before the coming into force of a provision of the Nationality, Immigration and Asylum Act 2002.

Amendment

Sub-ss (1), (2): amend the Nationality, Immigration and Asylum Act 2002, Sch 3.

Sub-s (4): words "First-tier Tribunal" in square brackets substituted by SI 2008/2833, art 9(1), Sch 3, para 203.

Subordinate Legislation

Asylum and Immigration (Treatment of Claimants, etc) Act 2004 (Commencement No 2) Order 2004, SI 2004/2999.

10–12

(Contain amendments which, in so far as relevant to this work, have been incorporated at the appropriate place.)

[13 Integration loans for refugees and others]

(1) The Secretary of State may make regulations enabling him to make loans[—

(a) to refugees, and

(b) to such other classes of person, or to persons other than refugees in such circumstances, as the regulations may prescribe].

(2) A person is a refugee for the purpose of subsection (1) if the Secretary of State has—

(a) recorded him as a refugee within the meaning of the Convention relating to the Status of Refugees done at Geneva on 28 July 1951, and

(b) [granted him leave to enter or remain] in the United Kingdom (within the meaning of section 33(1) of the Immigration Act 1971 (c 77)).

Appendix 1 — UK Immigration Statutes

(3) Regulations under subsection (1)—

(a) shall specify matters which the Secretary of State shall, in addition to other matters appearing to him to be relevant, take into account in determining whether or not to make a loan (and those matters may, in particular, relate to—

   (i) a person's income or assets,

   (ii) a person's likely ability to repay a loan, or

   (iii) the length of time since a person was recorded as a refugee [or since some other event]]),

(b) shall enable the Secretary of State to specify (and vary from time to time) a minimum and a maximum amount of a loan,

(c) shall prevent a person from receiving a loan if—

   (i) he is under the age of 18,

   (ii) he is insolvent, within a meaning given by the regulations, or

   (iii) he has received a loan under the regulations,

(d) shall make provision about repayment of a loan (and may, in particular, make provision—

   (i) about interest;

   (ii) for repayment by deduction from a social security benefit or similar payment due to the person to whom the loan is made),

(e) shall enable the Secretary of State to attach conditions to a loan (which may include conditions about the use of the loan),

(f) shall make provision about—

   (i) the making of an application for a loan, and

   (ii) the information, which may include information about the intended use of a loan, to be provided in or with an application,

(g) may make provision about steps to be taken by the Secretary of State in establishing an applicant's likely ability to repay a loan,

(h) may make provision for a loan to be made jointly to more than one [person], and

(i) may confer a discretion on the Secretary of State.

(4) Regulations under this section—

(a) shall be made by statutory instrument, and

(b) may not be made unless a draft has been laid before and approved by resolution of each House of Parliament.

Amendment

Section heading: substituted by the Immigration, Asylum and Nationality Act 2006, s 45(1), (6).

Sub-s (1): paras (a), (b) substituted by the Immigration, Asylum and Nationality Act 2006, s 45(1), (2).

Sub-s (2): in para (b) words "granted him leave to enter or remain" in square brackets substituted by the Immigration, Asylum and Nationality Act 2006, s 45(1), (3).

Sub-s (3): in para (a)(iii) words "or since some other event]" in square brackets inserted by the Immigration, Asylum and Nationality Act 2006, s 45(1), (4).

Sub-s (3): in para (h) word "person" in square brackets substituted by the Immigration, Asylum and Nationality Act 2006, s 45(1), (5).

Subordinate Legislation

Integration Loans for Refugees and Others Regulations 2007, SI 2007/1598.

Enforcement powers

14 Immigration officer: power of arrest

(1) Where an immigration officer in the course of exercising a function under the Immigration Acts forms a reasonable suspicion that a person has committed or attempted to commit an offence listed in subsection (2), he may arrest the person without warrant.

(2) Those offences are—

(a) the offence of conspiracy at common law (in relation to conspiracy to defraud),

(b) at common law in Scotland, any of the following offences—

    (i) fraud,

    (ii) conspiracy to defraud,

    (iii) uttering and fraud,

    (iv) bigamy,

    (v) theft, and

    (vi) reset,

(c) an offence under section 57 of the Offences against the Person Act 1861 (c 100) (bigamy),

(d) an offence under section 3 or 4 of the Perjury Act 1911 (c 6) (false statements),

(e) an offence under section 7 of that Act (aiding, abetting &c.) if it relates to an offence under section 3 or 4 of that Act,

(f) an offence under section 53 of the Registration of Births, Deaths and Marriages (Scotland) Act 1965 (c 49) (knowingly giving false information to district registrar, &c),

(g) an offence under any of the following provisions of the Theft Act 1968 (c 60)—

    (i) section 1 (theft),

    (ii) . . . ,

    (iii) . . . ,

    (iv) section 17 (false accounting), and

    (v) section 22 (handling stolen goods),

(h) an offence under section 1, . . ., 17 or 21 of the Theft Act (Northern Ireland) 1969 (c 16) (NI),

[(ha) an offence under either of the following provisions of the Fraud Act 2006—

    (i) section 1 (fraud);

    (ii) section 11 (obtaining services dishonestly),]

(i) . . . ,

(j) . . . ,

(k) an offence under Article 8 or 9 of the Perjury (Northern Ireland) Order 1979 (SI 1979/1714 (NI 19)),

(l) an offence under Article 12 of that Order if it relates to an offence under Article 8 or 9 of that Order,

(m) an offence under any of the following provisions of the Forgery and Counterfeiting Act 1981 (c 45)—

    (i) section 1 (forgery),

    (ii) section 2 (copying false instrument),

    (iii) section 3 (using false instrument),

    (iv) section 4 (using copy of false instrument), and

    (v) section 5(1) and (3) (false documents),

(n)   an offence under any of sections 57 to [59A] of the Sexual Offences Act 2003 (c 42) (trafficking for sexual exploitation),

(o)   an offence under section 22 of the Criminal Justice (Scotland) Act 2003 (asp 7) (trafficking in prostitution), . . .,

(p)   an offence under section 4 of this Act,

[(q)   an offence under any of sections 4 to 6 of the Identity Documents Act 2010].

(3)   The following provisions of the Immigration Act 1971 (c 77) shall have effect for the purpose of making, or in connection with, an arrest under this section as they have effect for the purpose of making, or in connection with, arrests for offences under that Act—

(a)   section 28C (entry and search before arrest),

(b)   sections 28E and 28F (entry and search after arrest),

(c)   sections 28G and 28H (search of arrested person), and

(d)   section 28I (seized material).

(4)   In section 19D(5)(a) of the Race Relations Act 1976 (c 74) (permitted discrimination)—

(a)   for "within the meaning of section 158 of the Nationality, Immigration and Asylum Act 2002" substitute "(within the meaning of section 44 of the Asylum and Immigration (Treatment of Claimants, etc) Act 2004)", and

(b)   at the end add ", and excluding section 14 of the Asylum and Immigration (Treatment of Claimants, etc) Act 2004".

Amendment

3.

Sub-s (2): para (g)(ii), (iii) repealed by the Fraud Act 2006, s 14(1), (3), Sch 1, para 35(1), Sch 2.

Sub-s (2): in para (h) reference omitted repealed by the Fraud Act 2006, s 14(1), (3), Sch 1, para 35(1), Sch 3.

Sub-s (2): para (ha) inserted by the Fraud Act 2006, s 14(1), Sch 1, para 35(2).

Sub-s (2): paras (i), (j) repealed by the Fraud Act 2006, s 14(1), (3), Sch 1, para 35(1), Sch 3.

Sub-s (2): in para (n) reference to "59A" in square brackets substituted by the Protection of Freedoms Act 2012, s 115(1), Sch 9, Pt 10, para 141(1), (3).

Date in force: 6 April 2013: see SI 2013/470, art 2(c), (d).

Sub-s (2): in para (o) word omitted repealed by the Identity Cards Act 2006, s 44(2), Sch 2.

Sub-s (2): para (q) (as inserted by the Identity Cards Act 2006, s 30(3)) substituted by the Identity Documents Act 2010, s 12, Schedule, para 18.

Date in force: 21 January 2011: see the Identity Documents Act 2010, s 14(2).

15, 16

(Amend the Immigration Act 1971, Sch 2 and the Immigration and Asylum Act 1999, s 141.)

---

17 Retention of documents

Where a document comes into the possession of the Secretary of State or an immigration officer in the course of the exercise of an immigration function, the Secretary of State or an immigration officer may retain the document while he suspects that—

(a)   a person to whom the document relates may be liable to removal from the United Kingdom in accordance with a provision of the Immigration Acts, and

(b)   retention of the document may facilitate the removal.

Asylum and Immigration (Treatment of Claimants, etc) Act 2004

(*Amends the Immigration Act 1971, Sch 2.*)

Procedure for marriage

19 England and Wales

(1) This section applies to a marriage—

   (a) which is to be solemnised on the authority of certificates issued by a superintendent registrar under Part III of the Marriage Act 1949 (c 76), and

   (b) a party to which is subject to immigration control.

(2) In relation to a marriage to which this section applies, the notices under section 27 of the Marriage Act 1949—

   (a) shall be given to the superintendent registrar of a registration district specified for the purpose of this paragraph by regulations made by the Secretary of State,

   (b) shall be delivered to the superintendent registrar in person by the two parties to the marriage,

   (c) may be given only if each party to the marriage has been resident in a registration district for the period of seven days immediately before the giving of his or her notice (but the district need not be that in which the notice is given and the parties need not have resided in the same district), and

   (d) shall state, in relation to each party, the registration district by reference to which paragraph (c) is satisfied.

(3) . . .

(4) For the purposes of this section—

   (a) a person is subject to immigration control if—

      (i) he is not an EEA national, and

      (ii) under the Immigration Act 1971 (c 77) he requires leave to enter or remain in the United Kingdom (whether or not leave has been given),

   (b) "EEA national" means a national of a State which is a contracting party to the Agreement on the European Economic Area signed at Oporto on 2nd May 1992 (as it has effect from time to time),

   (c) . . .

   (d) . . .

Amendment

Sub-s (3): repealed by SI 2011/1158, art 2(1)(a).
Date in force: 9 May 2011: see SI 2011/1158, art 1(1).
Sub-s (4): paras (c), (d) repealed by SI 2011/1158, art 2(1)(b).
Date in force: 9 May 2011: see SI 2011/1158, art 1(1).

Subordinate Legislation

Immigration (Procedure for Marriage) Regulations 2011, SI 2011/2678.
Immigration (Procedure for Marriage) (Amendment) Regulations 2013, SI 2013/226.

20 England and Wales: supplemental

(1) The Marriage Act 1949 (c 76) shall have effect in relation to a marriage to which section 19 applies—

   (a) subject to that section, and

   (b) with any necessary consequential modification.

(2) In particular—

  (a) section 28(1)(b) of that Act (declaration: residence) shall have effect as if it required a declaration that—

    (i) the notice of marriage is given in compliance with section 19(2) above, ..., and

    (ii) ... and

  (b) section 48 of that Act (proof of certain matters not essential to validity of marriage) shall have effect as if the list of matters in section 48(1)(a) to (e) included compliance with section 19 above.

(3) [Regulations under section 19(2)(a)—]

  (a) may make transitional provision,

  (b) shall be made by statutory instrument, and

  (c) shall be subject to annulment in pursuance of a resolution of either House of Parliament.

(4) Before making regulations under section 19(2)(a) the Secretary of State shall consult the Registrar General.

(5) An expression used in section 19 or this section and in Part III of the Marriage Act 1949 (c 76) has the same meaning in section 19 or this section as in that Part.

(6) ...

Amendment

Sub-s (2): para (a)(ii) and word omitted immediately preceding it repealed by SI 2011/1158, art 2(1)(c).

Date in force: 9 May 2011: see SI 2011/1158, art 1(1).

Sub-s (3): words "Regulations under section 19(2)(a)—" in square brackets substituted by SI 2011/1158, art 2(2).

Date in force: 9 May 2011: see SI 2011/1158, art 1(1).

Sub-s (6): repealed by the Legislative and Regulatory Reform Act 2006, s 30(1), Schedule.

21 Scotland

(1) This section applies to a marriage—

  (a) which is intended to be solemnised in Scotland, and

  (b) a party to which is subject to immigration control.

(2) In relation to a marriage to which this section applies, notice under section 3 of the Marriage (Scotland) Act 1977 (c 15)—

  (a) may be submitted to the district registrar of a registration district prescribed for the purposes of this section, and

  (b) may not be submitted to the district registrar of any other registration district.

(3) ...

(4) Where the district registrar to whom notice is submitted by virtue of subsection (2) (here the "notified registrar") is not the district registrar for the registration district in which the marriage is to be solemnised (here the "second registrar")—

  (a) the notified registrar shall ... send the notices and any fee, certificate or declaration [submitted in pursuance of section 3 of the Marriage (Scotland) Act 1977 (c 15) in relation to the marriage], to the second registrar, and

  (b) the second registrar shall be treated as having received the notices from the parties to the marriage on the dates on which the notified registrar received them.

(5) Subsection (4) of section 19 applies for the purposes of this section as it applies for the purposes of that section. ...

Amendment

Sub-s (3): repealed by SI 2011/1158, art 2(1)(d).

Date in force: 9 May 2011: see SI 2011/1158, art 1(1).

Sub-s (4): in para (a) words omitted repealed by SI 2011/1158, art 2(1)(e).

Date in force: 9 May 2011: see SI 2011/1158, art 1(1).

Sub-s (4): in para (a) words from "submitted in pursuance" to "to the marriage" in square brackets substituted by the Local Electoral Administration and Registration Services (Scotland) Act 2006, s 59(4).

Sub-s (5): words omitted repealed by SI 2011/1158, art 2(1)(f).

Date in force: 9 May 2011: see SI 2011/1158, art 1(1).

Subordinate Legislation

Immigration (Procedure for Marriage) Regulations 2011, SI 2011/2678.

22 Scotland: supplemental

(1) The Marriage (Scotland) Act 1977 shall have effect in relation to a marriage to which section 21 applies—

   (a) subject to that section, and

   (b) with any necessary consequential modification.

(2) In subsection (2)(a) of that section "prescribed" means prescribed by regulations made by the Secretary of State after consultation with the Registrar General for Scotland; and other expressions used in subsections (1) to (4) of that section and in the Marriage (Scotland) Act 1977 have the same meaning in those subsections as in that Act.

(3) Regulations made by of the Secretary of State under subsection (2)(a) . . . . of that section—

   (a) may make transitional provision,

   (b) shall be made by statutory instrument, and

   (c) shall be subject to annulment in pursuance of a resolution of either House of Parliament.

Amendment

Sub-s (3): words omitted repealed by SI 2011/1158, art 2(1)(g).

Date in force: 9 May 2011: see SI 2011/1158, art 1(1).

23 Northern Ireland

(1) This section applies to a marriage—

   (a) which is intended to be solemnised in Northern Ireland, and

   (b) a party to which is subject to immigration control.

(2) In relation to a marriage to which this section applies, the marriage notices—

   (a) shall be given only to a prescribed registrar, and

   (b) shall, in prescribed cases, be given by both parties together in person at a prescribed register office.

(3) . . .

(4) . . . If the prescribed registrar is not the registrar for the purposes of Article 4 of that Order, the prescribed registrar shall send him the marriage notices and he shall be treated as having received them from the parties to the marriage on the dates on which the prescribed registrar received them.

(5) . . .

(6) For the purposes of this section—

   (a) a person is subject to immigration control if—

      (i) he is not an EEA national, and

      (ii) under the Immigration Act 1971 (c 77) he requires leave to enter or remain in the United Kingdom (whether or not leave has been given),

   (b) "EEA national" means a national of a State which is a contracting party to the Agreement on the European Economic Area signed at Oporto on 2nd May 1992 (as it has effect from time to time),

   (c) . . .

(d) ...

Amendment

Sub-s (3): repealed by SI 2011/1158, art 2(1)(h).

Date in force: 9 May 2011: see SI 2011/1158, art 1(1).

Sub-s (4): words omitted repealed by SI 2011/1158, art 2(1)(i).

Date in force: 9 May 2011: see SI 2011/1158, art 1(1).

Sub-s (5): repealed by SI 2011/1158, art 2(1)(i).

Date in force: 9 May 2011: see SI 2011/1158, art 1(1).

Sub-s (6): paras (c), (d) repealed by SI 2011/1158, art 2(1)(k).

Date in force: 9 May 2011: see SI 2011/1158, art 1(1).

Subordinate Legislation

Immigration (Procedure for Marriage) Regulations 2011, SI 2011/2678.

24 Northern Ireland: supplemental

(1) The Marriage (Northern Ireland) Order 2003 (SI 2003/413 (NI 3)) shall have effect in relation to a marriage to which section 23 applies—

    (a) subject to section 23, and

    (b) with any necessary consequential modification.

(2) In section 23 "prescribed" means prescribed for the purposes of that section by regulations made by the Secretary of State after consulting the Registrar General for Northern Ireland and other expressions used in that section or this section and the Marriage (Northern Ireland) Order 2003 have the same meaning in section 23 or this section as in that Order.

(3) Section 18(3) of the Interpretation Act (Northern Ireland) 1954 (c 33 (NI)) (provisions as to holders of offices) shall apply to section 23 as if that section were an enactment within the meaning of that Act.

(4) Regulations of the Secretary of State under section 23—

    (a) may make transitional provision,

    (b) shall be made by statutory instrument, and

    (c) shall be subject to annulment in pursuance of a resolution of either House of Parliament.

25–32

Removal and detention

33 Removing asylum seeker to safe country

(1) Schedule 3 (which concerns the removal of persons claiming asylum to countries known to protect refugees and to respect human rights) shall have effect.

(2) Sections 11 and 12 of the Immigration and Asylum Act 1999 (c 33) (removal of asylum claimant to country under standing or other arrangements) shall cease to have effect.

(3) The following provisions of the Nationality, Immigration and Asylum Act 2002 (c 41) shall cease to have effect—

    (a) section 80 (new section 11 of 1999 Act), and

    (b) section 93 (appeal from within United Kingdom: "third country" removal).

(S 25 repealed by the Immigration, Asylum and Nationality Act 2006, ss 50(3)(b), 61, Sch 3; ss 26–31 contain amendments which have been incorporated at the appropriate place in this work; s 32 repealed by the Prevention of Terrorism Act 2005, s 16(2)(d).)

(Amends the Immigration Act 1971, Sch 3.)

35 Deportation or removal: cooperation

(1) The Secretary of State may require a person to take specified action if the Secretary of State thinks that—

    (a) the action will or may enable a travel document to be obtained by or for the person, and

    (b) possession of the travel document will facilitate the person's deportation or removal from the United Kingdom.

(2) In particular, the Secretary of State may require a person to—

    (a) provide information or documents to the Secretary of State or to any other person;

    (b) obtain information or documents;

    [(c) provide biometric information (within the meaning of section 15 of the UK Borders Act 2007), or submit to a process by means of which such information is obtained or recorded;]

    (d) make, or consent to or cooperate with the making of, an application to a person acting for the government of a State other than the United Kingdom;

    (e) cooperate with a process designed to enable determination of an application;

    (f) complete a form accurately and completely;

    (g) attend an interview and answer questions accurately and completely;

    (h) make an appointment.

(3) A person commits an offence if he fails without reasonable excuse to comply with a requirement of the Secretary of State under subsection (1).

(4) A person guilty of an offence under subsection (3) shall be liable—

    (a) on conviction on indictment, to imprisonment for a term not exceeding two years, to a fine or to both, or

    (b) on summary conviction, to imprisonment for a term not exceeding twelve months, to a fine not exceeding the statutory maximum or to both.

(5) If [an] immigration officer reasonably suspects that a person has committed an offence under subsection (3) he may arrest the person without warrant.

(6) An offence under subsection (3) shall be treated as—

    (a) a relevant offence for the purposes of sections 28B and 28D of the Immigration Act 1971 (c 77) (search, entry and arrest), and

    (b) an offence under Part III of that Act (criminal proceedings) for the purposes of sections 28(4), 28E, 28G and 28H (search after arrest, &c) of that Act.

(7) In subsection (1)—

"travel document" means a passport or other document which is issued by or for Her Majesty's Government or the government of another State and which enables or facilitates travel from the United Kingdom to another State, and

"removal from the United Kingdom" means removal under—

    (a) Schedule 2 to the Immigration Act 1971 (control on entry) (including a provision of that Schedule as applied by another provision of the Immigration Acts),

    (b) section 10 of the Immigration and Asylum Act 1999 (c 33) (removal of person unlawfully in United Kingdom), or

    (c) Schedule 3 to this Act.

(8) While sections 11 and 12 of the Immigration and Asylum Act 1999 continue to have effect, the reference in subsection (7)(c) above to Schedule 3 to this Act shall be treated as including a reference to those sections.

(9) In so far as subsection (3) extends to England and Wales, subsection (4)(b) shall, until the commencement of section 154 of the Criminal Justice Act 2003 (c 44) (increased limit on magistrates' power of imprisonment), have effect as if the reference to twelve months were a reference to six months.

(10) In so far as subsection (3) extends to Scotland, subsection (4)(b) shall have effect as if the reference to twelve months were a reference to six months.

(11) In so far as subsection (3) extends to Northern Ireland, subsection (4)(b) shall have effect as if the reference to twelve months were a reference to six months.

Amendment

Sub-s (2): para (c) substituted by the Immigration Act 2014, s 12, Sch 2, para 5, as from 28 July 2014: see SI 2014/1820.

Sub-s (5): word "an" in square brackets substituted in relation to England, Wales and Scotland by the Serious Organised Crime and Police Act 2005, s 111, Sch 7, Pt 4, para 63(b) and in relation to Northern Ireland by SI 2007/288, art 15(4), Sch 1, para 39(2).

36 Electronic monitoring

(1) In this section—

(a) "residence restriction" means a restriction as to residence imposed under—

    (i) paragraph 21 of Schedule 2 to the Immigration Act 1971 (c 77) (control on entry) (including that paragraph as applied by another provision of the Immigration Acts), or

    (ii) Schedule 3 to that Act (deportation),

(b) "reporting restriction" means a requirement to report to a specified person imposed under any of those provisions,

(c) "employment restriction" means a restriction as to employment or occupation imposed under any of those provisions, and

(d) "immigration bail" means—

    (i) release under a provision of the Immigration Acts on entry into a recognizance or bail bond,

    (ii) bail granted in accordance with a provision of the Immigration Acts by a court, a justice of the peace, the sheriff, [the First-tier Tribunal], the Secretary of State or an immigration officer (but not by a police officer), and

    (iii) bail granted by the Special Immigration Appeals Commission.

(2) Where a residence restriction is imposed on an adult—

(a) he may be required to cooperate with electronic monitoring, and

(b) failure to comply with a requirement under paragraph (a) shall be treated for all purposes of the Immigration Acts as failure to observe the residence restriction.

(3) Where a reporting restriction could be imposed on an adult—

(a) he may instead be required to cooperate with electronic monitoring, and

(b) the requirement shall be treated for all purposes of the Immigration Acts as a reporting restriction.

(4) Immigration bail may be granted to an adult subject to a requirement that he cooperate with electronic monitoring; and the requirement may (but need not) be imposed as a condition of a recognizance or bail bond.

(5) In this section a reference to requiring an adult to cooperate with electronic monitoring is a reference to requiring him to cooperate with such arrangements as the person imposing the requirement may specify for detecting and recording by electronic means the location of the adult, or his presence in or absence from a location—

    (a) at specified times,

    (b) during specified periods of time, or

    (c) throughout the currency of the arrangements.

(6) In particular, arrangements for the electronic monitoring of an adult—

    (a) may require him to wear a device;

    (b) may require him to make specified use of a device;

    (c) may prohibit him from causing or permitting damage of or interference with a device;

    (d) may prohibit him from taking or permitting action that would or might prevent the effective operation of a device;

    (e) may require him to communicate in a specified manner and at specified times or during specified periods of time;

    (f) may involve the performance of functions by persons other than the person imposing the requirement to cooperate with electronic monitoring (and those functions may relate to any aspect or condition of a residence restriction, of a reporting restriction, of an employment restriction, of a requirement under this section or of immigration bail).

(7) In this section "adult" means an individual who is at least 18 years old.

(8) The Secretary of State—

    (a) may make rules about arrangements for electronic monitoring for the purposes of this section, and

    (b) when he thinks that satisfactory arrangements for electronic monitoring are available in respect of an area, shall notify persons likely to be in a position to exercise power under this section in respect of the area.

(9) Rules under subsection (8)(a) may, in particular, require that arrangements for electronic monitoring impose on a person of a specified description responsibility for specified aspects of the operation of the arrangements.

(10) A requirement to cooperate with electronic monitoring—

    (a) shall comply with rules under subsection (8)(a), and

    (b) may not be imposed in respect of an adult who is or is expected to be in an area unless the person imposing the requirement has received a notification from the Secretary of State under subsection (8)(b) in respect of that area.

(11) Rules under subsection (8)(a)—

    (a) may include incidental, consequential or transitional provision,

    (b) may make provision generally or only in relation to specified cases, circumstances or areas,

    (c) shall be made by statutory instrument, and

    (d) shall be subject to annulment in pursuance of a resolution of either House of Parliament.

(12) . . .

Amendment

Sub-s (1): in para (d)(ii) words "the First-tier Tribunal" in square brackets substituted by SI 2010/21, art 5(1), Sch 1, paras 31, 33(a).

Date in force: 15 February 2010: see SI 2010/21, art 1; for transitional provisions and savings see art 5(4), Sch 4, paras 14–18, 21 thereto.

Sub-s (12): repealed by SI 2010/21, art 5(1), Sch 1, paras 31, 33(b). Date in force: 15 February 2010: see SI 2010/21, art 1; for transitional provisions and savings see art 5(4), Sch 4, paras 14–18, 21 thereto.

42 Amount of fees

(1) . . .

(2) . . .

[(2A) . . .]

(3) An Order in Council under section 1 of the Consular Fees Act 1980 (c 23) (fees) which prescribes a fee in relation to an application for the issue of a certificate under section 10 of the Nationality, Immigration and Asylum Act 2002 (right of abode: certificate of entitlement) may prescribe an amount which is intended to—

    (a)   exceed the administrative costs of determining the application, and

    (b)   reflect benefits that in the opinion of Her Majesty in Council are likely to accrue to the applicant if the application is successful.

[(3A)   The amount of a fee under section 1 of the Consular Fees Act 1980 in respect of a matter specified in subsection (3B) may be set so as to reflect costs referable to the exercise of any function in respect of which the Secretary of State has made an order under section 68 of the Immigration Act 2014.

(3B)   The matters are—

    (a)   the determination of applications for entry clearances (within the meaning given by section 33(1) of the Immigration Act 1971),

    (b)   the determination of applications for transit visas under section 41 of the Immigration and Asylum Act 1999, or

    (c)   the determination of applications for certificates of entitlement to the right of abode in the United Kingdom under section 10 of the Nationality, Immigration and Asylum Act 2002.]

(4)   Where an instrument prescribes a fee in reliance on this section it may include provision for the refund, where an application is unsuccessful or a process is not completed, of that part of the fee which is intended to reflect the matters specified in subsection . . . (3)(b).

(5)   Provision included by virtue of subsection (4)—

    (a)   may determine, or provide for the determination of, the amount to be refunded;

    (b)   may confer a discretion on the Secretary of State or another person (whether in relation to determining the amount of a refund or in relation to determining whether a refund should be made).

(6)   An instrument may not be made in reliance on this section unless the Secretary of State has consulted with such persons as appear to him to be appropriate.

(7)   An instrument may not be made in reliance on this section unless a draft has been laid before and approved by resolution of each House of Parliament . . .

(8)   This section is without prejudice to the power to make an order under section 102 of the Finance (No 2) Act 1987 (c 51) (government fees and charges) in relation to a power under a provision specified in this section.

Amendment

Sub-ss (1), (2): repealed by the Immigration Act 2014, s 73, Sch 9, Pt 11, para 73(1), (2), as from 15 December 2014: see SI 2014/2771.

Sub-s (2A): inserted by the UK Borders Act 2007, s 20(1), (3) and repealed by the Immigration Act 2014, s 73, Sch 9, Pt 11, para 73(1), (2), as from 15 December 2014: see SI 2014/2771.

Sub-ss (3A), (3B): substituted for sub-s (3A) (as inserted by the UK Borders Act 2007, s 20(1), (4)) by the Immigration Act 2014, s 73, Sch 9, Pt 11, para 73(1), (3), as from 15 December 2014: see SI 2014/2771.

Sub-s (4): words omitted repealed by the Immigration Act 2014, s 73, Sch 9, Pt 11, para 73(1), (4), as from 15 December 2014: see SI 2014/2771.

Sub-s (7): words omitted repealed by the Immigration Act 2014, s 73, Sch 9, Pt 11, para 73(1), (5), as from 15 December 2014: see SI 2014/2771.

General

44

(*Repealed by the Immigration, Asylum and Nationality Act 2006, ss 61, 64(3)(d), Sch 3.*)

45 Interpretation: immigration officer

In this Act "immigration officer" means a person appointed by the Secretary of State as an immigration officer under paragraph 1 of Schedule 2 to the Immigration Act 1971.

46 Money

There shall be paid out of money provided by Parliament—

(a) any expenditure incurred by a Minister of the Crown in connection with this Act, and

(b) any increase attributable to this Act in the sums payable under any other enactment out of money provided by Parliament.

47 Repeals

The enactments listed in Schedule 4 are hereby repealed to the extent specified.

48 Commencement

(1) Sections 2, 32(2) and 35 shall come into force at the end of the period of two months beginning with the date on which this Act is passed.

(2) Section 32(1) shall have effect in relation to determinations of the Special Immigration Appeals Commission made after the end of the period of two months beginning with the date on which this Act is passed.

(3) The other preceding provisions of this Act shall come into force in accordance with provision made—

(a) in the case of section 26 or Schedule 1 or 2, by order of the Lord Chancellor,

(b) in the case of sections 4 and 5 in so far as they extend to Scotland, by order of the Scottish Ministers, and

(c) in any other case, by order of the Secretary of State.

(4) An order under subsection (3)—

(a) may make transitional or incidental provision,

(b) may make different provision for different purposes, and

(c) shall be made by statutory instrument.

(5) Transitional provision under subsection (4)(a) in relation to the commencement of section 26 may, in particular, make provision in relation to proceedings which, immediately before commencement—

(a) are awaiting determination by an adjudicator appointed, or treated as if appointed, under section 81 of the Nationality, Immigration and Asylum Act 2002 (c 41),

(b) are awaiting determination by the Immigration Appeal Tribunal,

(c) having been determined by an adjudicator could be brought before the Immigration Appeal Tribunal,

(d) are awaiting the determination of a further appeal brought in accordance with section 103 of that Act,

(e) having been determined by the Immigration Appeal Tribunal could be brought before another court by way of further appeal under that section,

(f) are or could be made the subject of an application under section 101 of that Act (review of decision on permission to appeal to Tribunal), or

Appendix 1 — UK Immigration Statutes

(g) are or could be made the subject of another kind of application to the High Court or the Court of Session.

(6) Provision made under subsection (5) may, in particular—

(a) provide for the institution or continuance of an appeal of a kind not generally available after the commencement of section 26,

(b) provide for the termination of proceedings, or

(c) make any other provision that the Lord Chancellor thinks appropriate.

Subordinate Legislation

Asylum and Immigration (Treatment of Claimants etc) Act 2004 (Commencement) (Scotland) Order 2004, SSI 2004/494.

Asylum and Immigration (Treatment of Claimants, etc) Act 2004 (Commencement No 1) Order 2004, SI 2004/2523.

Asylum and Immigration (Treatment of Claimants, etc) Act 2004 (Commencement No 2) Order 2004, SI 2004/2999.

Asylum and Immigration (Treatment of Claimants, etc) Act 2004 (Commencement No 3) Order 2004, SI 2004/3398.

Asylum and Immigration (Treatment of Claimants, etc) Act 2004 (Commencement No 4) Order 2005, SI 2005/372.

Asylum and Immigration (Treatment of Claimants, etc) Act 2004 (Commencement No 5 and Transitional Provisions) Order 2005, SI 2005/565.

Asylum and Immigration (Treatment of Claimants, etc) Act 2004 (Commencement No 6) Order 2006, SI 2006/1517.

Asylum and Immigration (Treatment of Claimants, etc) Act 2004 (Commencement No 1) (Northern Ireland) Order 2007, SI 2007/845.

Asylum and Immigration (Treatment of Claimants, etc) Act 2004 (Commencement No 7 and Transitional Provisions) Order 2007, SI 2007/1602.

49 Extent

(1) This Act extends (subject to subsection (2)) to—

(a) England and Wales,

(b) Scotland, and

(c) Northern Ireland.

(2) An amendment effected by this Act has the same extent as the enactment, or as the relevant part of the enactment, amended (ignoring extent by virtue of an Order in Council).

(3) Her Majesty may by Order in Council direct that a provision of this Act is to extend, with or without modification or adaptation, to—

(a) any of the Channel Islands;

(b) the Isle of Man.

Subordinate Legislation

Immigration (Isle of Man) Order 2008, SI 2008/680.

Immigration (Isle of Man) (Amendment) Order 2011, SI 2011/1408.

50 Short title

This Act may be cited as the Asylum and Immigration (Treatment of Claimants, etc) Act 2004.

SCHEDULE 1

(Repealed by SI 2010/21, art 5(3), Sch 3. Date in force: 15 February 2010: see SI 2010/21, art 1; for transitional provisions and savings see art 5(4), Sch 4, paras 14–18, 21 thereto.)

Section 26

SCHEDULE 2

(Part 1 contains amendments which have been incorporated at the appropriate place in this work.)

PART 2

TRANSITIONAL PROVISION

26

In this Part "commencement" means the coming into force of section 26.

27

A person who immediately before commencement is, or is to be treated as, an adjudicator appointed under section 81 of the Nationality, Immigration and Asylum Act 2002 (c 41) (appeals) (as it has effect before commencement) shall be treated as having been appointed as a member of the Asylum and Immigration Tribunal under paragraph 1 of Schedule 4 to that Act (as it has effect after commencement) immediately after commencement.

28

Where immediately before commencement a person is a member of the Immigration Appeal Tribunal—

(a) he shall be treated as having been appointed as a member of the Asylum and Immigration Tribunal under paragraph 1 of Schedule 4 to that Act immediately after commencement, and

(b) if he was a legally qualified member of the Immigration Appeal Tribunal (within the meaning of Schedule 5 to that Act) he shall be treated as having been appointed as a legally qualified member of the Asylum and Immigration Tribunal.

29

A person who immediately before commencement is a member of staff of adjudicators appointed or treated as appointed under section 81 of the Nationality, Immigration and Asylum Act 2002 (c 41) or of the Immigration Appeal Tribunal shall be treated as having been appointed as a member of the staff of the Asylum and Immigration Tribunal under paragraph 9 of Schedule 4 to the Nationality, Immigration and Asylum Act 2002 immediately after commencement.

30

. . .

Amendment

Para 30: repealed by SI 2010/21, art 5(3), Sch 3.

Date in force: 15 February 2010: see SI 2010/21, art 1; for transitional provisions and savings see art 5(4), Sch 4, paras 14–18, 21 thereto.

Subordinate Legislation

Civil Procedure (Amendment) Rules 2005, SI 2005/352.

SCHEDULE 3

Section 33

REMOVAL OF ASYLUM SEEKER TO SAFE COUNTRY

PART 1

INTRODUCTORY

1

(1) In this Schedule—

"asylum claim" means a claim by a person that to remove him from or require him to leave the United Kingdom would breach the United Kingdom's obligations under the Refugee Convention,

"Convention rights" means the rights identified as Convention rights by section 1 of the Human Rights Act 1998 (c 42) (whether or not in relation to a State that is a party to the Convention),

"human rights claim" means a claim by a person that to remove him from or require him to leave the United Kingdom would be unlawful under section 6 of the Human Rights Act 1998 (public authority not to act contrary to Convention) as being incompatible with his Convention rights,

"immigration appeal" means an appeal under section 82(1) of the Nationality, Immigration and Asylum Act 2002 (c 41) (appeal against immigration decision), and

"the Refugee Convention" means the Convention relating to the Status of Refugees done at Geneva on 28th July 1951 and its Protocol.

(2) In this Schedule a reference to anything being done in accordance with the Refugee Convention is a reference to the thing being done in accordance with the principles of the Convention, whether or not by a signatory to it.

[(3) Section 92 of the Nationality, Immigration and Asylum Act 2002 makes further provision about the place from which an appeal relating to an asylum or human rights claim may be brought or continued.]

Amendment

Para 1: sub-para (3) added by the Immigration Act 2014, s 73, Sch 9, Pt 4, para 56(1), (2), as from 20 October 2014 (see SI 2014/2771, art 2), subject to savings in SI 2014/2771, arts 9–11.

PART 2

FIRST LIST OF SAFE COUNTRIES (REFUGEE CONVENTION AND HUMAN RIGHTS (1))

2

This Part applies to—

    (a)   Austria,

    (b)   Belgium,

    [(ba) Bulgaria,]

    (c)   Republic of Cyprus,

    (d)   Czech Republic,

    (e)   Denmark,

    (f)   Estonia,

    (g)   Finland,

    (h)   France,

    (i)   Germany,

    (j)   Greece,

    (k)   Hungary,

    (l)   Iceland,

    (m) Ireland,

(n) Italy,
(o) Latvia,
(p) Lithuania,
(q) Luxembourg,
(r) Malta,
(s) Netherlands,
(t) Norway,
(u) Poland,
(v) Portugal,
[(va) Romania,]
(w) Slovak Republic,
(x) Slovenia,
(y) Spain, . . .
(z) Sweden,
[(z1) Switzerland].

3

(1) This paragraph applies for the purposes of the determination by any person, tribunal or court whether a person who has made an asylum claim or a human rights claim may be removed—

    (a) from the United Kingdom, and

    (b) to a State of which he is not a national or citizen.

(2) A State to which this Part applies shall be treated, in so far as relevant to the question mentioned in sub-paragraph (1), as a place—

    (a) where a person's life and liberty are not threatened by reason of his race, religion, nationality, membership of a particular social group or political opinion,

    (b) from which a person will not be sent to another State in contravention of his Convention rights, and

    (c) from which a person will not be sent to another State otherwise than in accordance with the Refugee Convention.

4

Section 77 of the Nationality, Immigration and Asylum Act 2002 (c 41) (no removal while claim for asylum pending) shall not prevent a person who has made a claim for asylum from being removed—

    (a) from the United Kingdom, and

    (b) to a State to which this Part applies;

provided that the Secretary of State certifies that in his opinion the person is not a national or citizen of the State.

5

(1) This paragraph applies where the Secretary of State certifies that—

    (a) it is proposed to remove a person to a State to which this Part applies, and

    (b) in the Secretary of State's opinion the person is not a national or citizen of the State.

(2) *The person may not bring an immigration appeal by virtue of section 92(2) or (3) of that Act (appeal from within United Kingdom: general).*

(3) The person may not bring an immigration appeal [from within the United Kingdom] in reliance on—

    (a) an asylum claim which asserts that to remove the person to a specified State to which this Part applies would breach the United Kingdom's obligations under the Refugee Convention, or

(b)   a human rights claim in so far as it asserts that to remove the person to a specified State to which this Part applies would be unlawful under section 6 of the Human Rights Act 1998 because of the possibility of removal from that State to another State.

(4)   The person may not bring an immigration appeal [from within the United Kingdom] in reliance on a human rights claim to which this sub-paragraph applies if the Secretary of State certifies that the claim is clearly unfounded; and the Secretary of State shall certify a human rights claim to which this sub-paragraph applies unless satisfied that the claim is not clearly unfounded.

(5)   Sub-paragraph (4) applies to a human rights claim if, or in so far as, it asserts a matter other than that specified in sub-paragraph (3)(b).

6

A person who is outside the United Kingdom may not bring an immigration appeal on any ground that is inconsistent with treating a State to which this Part applies as a place—

(a)   where a person's life and liberty are not threatened by reason of his race, religion, nationality, membership of a particular social group or political opinion,

(b)   from which a person will not be sent to another State in contravention of his Convention rights, and

(c)   from which a person will not be sent to another State otherwise than in accordance with the Refugee Convention.

Amendment

Para 2: sub-para (ba) inserted by SI 2006/3393, art 2(1), (2).

Para 2: sub-para (va) inserted by SI 2006/3393, art 2(1), (3).

Para 2: in sub-para (y) word omitted repealed by SI 2010/2802, art 2(a).

Para 2: sub-para (z1) inserted by SI 2010/2802, art 2(b).

Para 5: sub-para (2) repealed and words in square brackets in sub-paras (3), (4) substituted (for original words "by virtue of section 92(4)(a) of that Act (appeal from within United Kingdom: asylum or human rights)" and "by virtue of section 92(4)(a) of that Act" respectively) by the Immigration Act 2014, s 73, Sch 9, Pt 4, para 56(1), (3), as from 20 October 2014 (see SI 2014/2771, art 2), subject to savings in SI 2014/2771, arts 9–11.

PART 3
SECOND LIST OF SAFE COUNTRIES (REFUGEE CONVENTION AND HUMAN RIGHTS (2)

7

(1)   This Part applies to such States as the Secretary of State may by order specify.

(2)   An order under this paragraph—

(a)   shall be made by statutory instrument, and

(b)   shall not be made unless a draft has been laid before and approved by resolution of each House of Parliament.

8

(1)   This paragraph applies for the purposes of the determination by any person, tribunal or court whether a person who has made an asylum claim may be removed—

(a)   from the United Kingdom, and

(b)   to a State of which he is not a national or citizen.

(2)   A State to which this Part applies shall be treated, in so far as relevant to the question mentioned in sub-paragraph (1), as a place—

(a)   where a person's life and liberty are not threatened by reason of his race, religion, nationality, membership of a particular social group or political opinion, and

(b) from which a person will not be sent to another State otherwise than in accordance with the Refugee Convention.

9

Section 77 of the Nationality, Immigration and Asylum Act 2002 (c 41) (no removal while claim for asylum pending) shall not prevent a person who has made a claim for asylum from being removed—

(a) from the United Kingdom, and

(b) to a State to which this Part applies;

provided that the Secretary of State certifies that in his opinion the person is not a national or citizen of the State.

10

(1) This paragraph applies where the Secretary of State certifies that—

(a) it is proposed to remove a person to a State to which this Part applies, and

(b) in the Secretary of State's opinion the person is not a national or citizen of the State.

(2) *The person may not bring an immigration appeal by virtue of section 92(2) or (3) of that Act (appeal from within United Kingdom: general).*

(3) The person may not bring an immigration appeal [from within the United Kingdom] in reliance on an asylum claim which asserts that to remove the person to a specified State to which this Part applies would breach the United Kingdom's obligations under the Refugee Convention.

(4) The person may not bring an immigration appeal [from within the United Kingdom] in reliance on a human rights claim if the Secretary of State certifies that the claim is clearly unfounded; and the Secretary of State shall certify a human rights claim where this paragraph applies unless satisfied that the claim is not clearly unfounded.

11

A person who is outside the United Kingdom may not bring an immigration appeal on any ground that is inconsistent with treating a State to which this Part applies as a place—

(a) where a person's life and liberty are not threatened by reason of his race, religion, nationality, membership of a particular social group or political opinion, and

(b) from which a person will not be sent to another State otherwise than in accordance with the Refugee Convention.

Amendment

Para 10: sub-para (2) repealed and words in square brackets in sub-paras (3), (4) substituted (for original words "by virtue of section 92(4)(a) of that Act (appeal from within United Kingdom: asylum or human rights)" and "by virtue of section 92(4)(a) of that Act" respectively) by the Immigration Act 2014, s 73, Sch 9, Pt 4, para 56(1), (4), as from 20 October 2014 (see SI 2014/2771, art 2), subject to savings in SI 2014/2771, arts 9–11.

PART 4

THIRD LIST OF SAFE COUNTRIES (REFUGEE CONVENTION ONLY)

12

(1) This Part applies to such States as the Secretary of State may by order specify.

(2) An order under this paragraph—

(a) shall be made by statutory instrument, and

(b) shall not be made unless a draft has been laid before and approved by resolution of each House of Parliament.

13

(1) This paragraph applies for the purposes of the determination by any person, tribunal or court whether a person who has made an asylum claim may be removed—

    (a)   from the United Kingdom, and

    (b)   to a State of which he is not a national or citizen.

(2) A State to which this Part applies shall be treated, in so far as relevant to the question mentioned in sub-paragraph (1), as a place—

    (a)   where a person's life and liberty are not threatened by reason of his race, religion, nationality, membership of a particular social group or political opinion, and

    (b)   from which a person will not be sent to another State otherwise than in accordance with the Refugee Convention.

14

Section 77 of the Nationality, Immigration and Asylum Act 2002 (c 41) (no removal while claim for asylum pending) shall not prevent a person who has made a claim for asylum from being removed—

    (a)   from the United Kingdom, and

    (b)   to a State to which this Part applies;

provided that the Secretary of State certifies that in his opinion the person is not a national or citizen of the State.

15

(1) This paragraph applies where the Secretary of State certifies that—

    (a)   it is proposed to remove a person to a State to which this Part applies, and

    (b)   in the Secretary of State's opinion the person is not a national or citizen of the State.

(2) *The person may not bring an immigration appeal by virtue of section 92(2) or (3) of that Act (appeal from within United Kingdom: general).*

(3) The person may not bring an immigration appeal [from within the United Kingdom] in reliance on an asylum claim which asserts that to remove the person to a specified State to which this Part applies would breach the United Kingdom's obligations under the Refugee Convention.

(4) The person may not bring an immigration appeal [from within the United Kingdom] in reliance on a human rights claim if the Secretary of State certifies that the claim is clearly unfounded.

16

A person who is outside the United Kingdom may not bring an immigration appeal on any ground that is inconsistent with treating a State to which this Part applies as a place—

    (a)   where a person's life and liberty are not threatened by reason of his race, religion, nationality, membership of a particular social group or political opinion, and

    (b)   from which a person will not be sent to another State otherwise than in accordance with the Refugee Convention.

Amendment

Para 15: sub-para (2) repealed and words in square brackets in sub-paras (3), (4) substituted (for original words "by virtue of section 92(4)(a) of that Act (appeal from within United Kingdom: asylum or human rights)" and "by virtue of section 92(4)(a) of that Act" respectively) by the Immigration Act 2014, s 73, Sch 9, Pt 4, para 56(1), (5), as from 20 October 2014 (see SI 2014/2771, art 2), subject to savings in SI 2014/2771, arts 9–11.

PART 5

COUNTRIES CERTIFIED AS SAFE FOR INDIVIDUALS

17 This Part applies to a person who has made an asylum claim if the Secretary of State certifies that—

(a) it is proposed to remove the person to a specified State,

(b) in the Secretary of State's opinion the person is not a national or citizen of the specified State, and

(c) in the Secretary of State's opinion the specified State is a place—

   (i) where the person's life and liberty will not be threatened by reason of his race, religion, nationality, membership of a particular social group or political opinion, and

   (ii) from which the person will not be sent to another State otherwise than in accordance with the Refugee Convention.

18 Where this Part applies to a person section 77 of the Nationality, Immigration and Asylum Act 2002 (c 41) (no removal while claim for asylum pending) shall not prevent his removal to the State specified under paragraph 17.

19 Where this Part applies to a person—

(a) he may not bring an immigration appeal by virtue of section 92(2) or (3) of that Act (appeal from within United Kingdom: general),

(b) he may not bring an immigration appeal [from within the United Kingdom] in reliance on an asylum claim which asserts that to remove the person to the State specified under paragraph 17 would breach the United Kingdom's obligations under the Refugee Convention,

(c) he may not bring an immigration appeal [from within the United Kingdom] in reliance on a human rights claim if the Secretary of State certifies that the claim is clearly unfounded, and

(d) he may not while outside the United Kingdom bring an immigration appeal on any ground that is inconsistent with the opinion certified under paragraph 17(c).

Amendment

Para 19: sub-para (a) repealed and words in square brackets in sub-paras (b), (c) substituted (for original words "by virtue of section 92(4)(a) of that Act (appeal from within United Kingdom: asylum or human rights)" and "by virtue of section 92(4)(a) of that Act" respectively) by the Immigration Act 2014, s 73, Sch 9, Pt 4, para 56(1), (6), as from 20 October 2014 (see SI 2014/2771, art 2), subject to savings in SI 2014/2771, arts 9–11.

PART 6

AMENDMENT OF LISTS

20 (1) The Secretary of State may by order add a State to the list specified in paragraph 2.

(2) The Secretary of State may by order—

(a) add a State to a list specified under paragraph 7 or 12, or

(b) remove a State from a list specified under paragraph 7 or 12.

21 (1) An order under paragraph 20(1) or (2)(a)—

(a) shall be made by statutory instrument,

(b) shall not be made unless a draft has been laid before and approved by resolution of each House of Parliament, and

(c) may include transitional provision.

(2) An order under paragraph 20(2)(b)—

(a) shall be made by statutory instrument,

(b) shall be subject to annulment in pursuance of a resolution of either House of Parliament, and

(c) may include transitional provision.

SCHEDULE 4

(Contains repeals which, in so far as relevant to this work, been incorporated at the appropriate place.)

Subordinate Legislation

Asylum (First List of Safe Countries) (Amendment) Order 2006, SI 2006/3393.

Asylum (First List of Safe Countries) (Amendment) Order 2010, SI 2010/2713.

IMMIGRATION, ASYLUM AND NATIONALITY ACT 2006

2006 c 13

An Act to make provision about immigration, asylum and nationality; and for connected purposes.

[30 March 2006]

Appeals

1–13

(Ss 1–13 (in so far as unrepealed) contain amendments which, in so far as relevant to this work, have been incorporated at the appropriate place.)

( )

Employment

14 Consequential amendments

Schedule 1 (which makes amendments consequential on the preceding provisions of this Act) shall have effect.

15 Penalty

(1) It is contrary to this section to employ an adult subject to immigration control if—

(a) he has not been granted leave to enter or remain in the United Kingdom, or

(b) his leave to enter or remain in the United Kingdom—

(i) is invalid,

(ii) has ceased to have effect (whether by reason of curtailment, revocation, cancellation, passage of time or otherwise), or

    (iii)   is subject to a condition preventing him from accepting the employment.

(2) The Secretary of State may give an employer who acts contrary to this section a notice requiring him to pay a penalty of a specified amount not exceeding the prescribed maximum.

(3) An employer is excused from paying a penalty if he shows that he complied with any prescribed requirements in relation to the employment.

(4) But the excuse in subsection (3) shall not apply to an employer who knew, at any time during the period of the employment, that it was contrary to this section.

(5) The Secretary of State may give a penalty notice without having established whether subsection (3) applies.

(6) A penalty notice must—

  (a) state why the Secretary of State thinks the employer is liable to the penalty,

  (b) state the amount of the penalty,

  (c) specify a date, at least 28 days after the date specified in the notice as the date on which it is given, before which the penalty must be paid,

  (d) specify how the penalty must be paid,

  (e) explain how the employer may object to the penalty [or make an appeal against it], and

  (f) explain how the Secretary of State may enforce the penalty.

(7) An order prescribing requirements for the purposes of subsection (3) may, in particular—

  (a) require the production to an employer of a document of a specified description;

  (b) require the production to an employer of one document of each of a number of specified descriptions;

  (c) require an employer to take specified steps to verify, retain, copy or record the content of a document produced to him in accordance with the order;

  (d) require action to be taken before employment begins;

  (e) require action to be taken at specified intervals or on specified occasions during the course of employment.

Amendment

Sub-s (6): words in square brackets in para (e) inserted by the Immigration Act 2014, s 73, Sch 9, para 61, as from 28 July 2014: see SI 2014/1820

Subordinate Legislation

Immigration (Restrictions on Employment) Order 2007, SI 2007/3290; Immigration (Employment of Adults Subject to Immigration Control) (Maximum Penalty) Order 2008, SI 2008/132; Immigration (Restrictions on Employment) (Amendment) Order 2009, SI 2009/2908; Immigration (Restrictions on Employment) (Codes of Practice and Amendment) Order 2014, SI 2014/1183.

16 Objection

(1) This section applies where an employer to whom a penalty notice is given objects on the ground that—

  (a) he is not liable to the imposition of a penalty,

  (b) he is excused payment by virtue of section 15(3), or

  (c) the amount of the penalty is too high.

(2) The employer may give a notice of objection to the Secretary of State.

(3) A notice of objection must—

  (a) be in writing,

  (b) give the objector's reasons,

(c) be given in the prescribed manner, and

(d) be given before the end of the prescribed period.

(4) Where the Secretary of State receives a notice of objection to a penalty he shall consider it and—

(a) cancel the penalty,

(b) reduce the penalty,

(c) increase the penalty, or

(d) determine to take no action.

(5) Where the Secretary of State considers a notice of objection he shall—

(a) have regard to the code of practice under section 19 (in so far as the objection relates to the amount of the penalty),

(b) inform the objector of his decision before the end of the prescribed period or such longer period as he may agree with the objector,

(c) if he increases the penalty, issue a new penalty notice under section 15, and

(d) if he reduces the penalty, notify the objector of the reduced amount.

Subordinate Legislation

Immigration (Restrictions on Employment) Order 2007, SI 2007/3290.

17 Appeal

(1) An employer to whom a penalty notice is given may appeal to the court on the ground that—

(a) he is not liable to the imposition of a penalty,

(b) he is excused payment by virtue of section 15(3), or

(c) the amount of the penalty is too high.

(2) The court may—

(a) allow the appeal and cancel the penalty,

(b) allow the appeal and reduce the penalty, or

(c) dismiss the appeal.

(3) An appeal shall be a re-hearing of the Secretary of State's decision to impose a penalty and shall be determined having regard to—

(a) the code of practice under section 19 that has effect at the time of the appeal (in so far as the appeal relates to the amount of the penalty), and

(b) any other matters which the court thinks relevant (which may include matters of which the Secretary of State was unaware);

and this subsection has effect despite any provision of rules of court.

[(4A) An appeal may be brought only if the employer has given a notice of objection under section 16 and the Secretary of State—

(a) has determined the objection by issuing to the employer the penalty notice (as a result of increasing the penalty under section 16(4)(c)),

(b) has determined the objection by—

(i) reducing the penalty under section 16(4)(b), or

(ii) taking no action under section 16(4)(d), or

(c) has not informed the employer of a decision before the end of the period that applies for the purposes of section 16(5)(b).

(4B) An appeal must be brought within the period of 28 days beginning with the relevant date.

(4C) Where the appeal is brought under subsection (4A)(a), the relevant date is the date specified in the penalty notice issued in accordance with section 16(5)(c) as the date on which it is given.

(4D) Where the appeal is brought under subsection (4A)(b), the relevant date is the date specified in the notice informing the employer of the decision for the purposes of section 16(5)(b) as the date on which it is given.

(4E) Where the appeal is brought under subsection (4A)(c), the relevant date is the date on which the period that applies for the purposes of section 16(5)(b) ends.]

(6) In this section "the court" means—

(a) where the employer has his principal place of business in England and Wales, [the county court],

(b) where the employer has his principal place of business in Scotland, the sheriff, and

(c) where the employer has his principal place of business in Northern Ireland, a county court.

Amendment

Sub-ss (4A)–(4E): substituted for original sub-ss (4), (5), by the Immigration Act 2014, s 44, as from 28 July 2014: see SI 2014/1820.

Sub-s (6): in para (a) words in square brackets substituted by the Crime and Courts Act 2013, s 17(5), Sch 9, Pt 3, para 52(1)(b), (2). Date in force 22 April 2014: see SI 2014/954, art 2(a), (c);

18 Enforcement

[(1) This section applies where a sum is payable to the Secretary of State as a penalty under section 15.

(1A) In England and Wales the penalty is recoverable as if it were payable under an order of the county court.

(1B) In Scotland, the penalty may be enforced in the same manner as an extract registered decree arbitral bearing a warrant for execution issued by the sheriff court of any sheriffdom in Scotland.

(1C) In Northern Ireland the penalty is recoverable as if it were payable under an order of a county court in Northern Ireland.

(1D) Where action is taken under this section for the recovery of a sum payable as a penalty under section 15, the penalty is—

(a) in relation to England and Wales, to be treated for the purposes of section 98 of the Courts Act 2003 (register of judgments and orders etc) as if it were a judgment entered in the county court;

(b) in relation to Northern Ireland, to be treated for the purposes of Article 116 of the Judgments Enforcement (Northern Ireland) Order 1981 (SI 1981/226 (N.I. 6)) (register of judgments) as if it were a judgment in respect of which an application has been accepted under Article 22 or 23(1) of that Order.]

(3) Money paid to the Secretary of State by way of penalty shall be paid into the Consolidated Fund.

Amendment

Sub-ss (1)–(1D): substituted for original sub-ss (1), (2), by the Immigration Act 2014, s 45, as from 28 July 2014: see SI 2014/1820.

19 Code of practice

(1) The Secretary of State shall issue a code of practice specifying factors to be considered by him in determining the amount of a penalty imposed under section 15.

(2) The code—

(a) shall not be issued unless a draft has been laid before Parliament, and

(b) shall come into force in accordance with provision made by order of the Secretary of State.

(3) The Secretary of State shall from time to time review the code and may revise and re-issue it following a review; and a reference in this section to the code includes a reference to the code as revised.

Subordinate Legislation

Immigration (Restrictions on Employment) Order 2007, SI 2007/3290; Immigration (Restrictions on Employment) (Codes of Practice and Amendment) Order 2014, SI 2014/1183.

20 Orders

(1) An order of the Secretary of State under section 15, 16 or 19—

   (a) may make provision which applies generally or only in specified circumstances,

   (b) may make different provision for different circumstances,

   (c) may include transitional or incidental provision, and

   (d) shall be made by statutory instrument.

(2) An order under section 15(2) may not be made unless a draft has been laid before and approved by resolution of each House of Parliament.

(3) Any other order shall be subject to annulment in pursuance of a resolution of either House of Parliament.

21 Offence

(1) A person commits an offence if he employs another ("the employee") knowing that the employee is an adult subject to immigration control and that—

   (a) he has not been granted leave to enter or remain in the United Kingdom, or

   (b) his leave to enter or remain in the United Kingdom—

      (i) is invalid,

      (ii) has ceased to have effect (whether by reason of curtailment, revocation, cancellation, passage of time or otherwise), or

      (iii) is subject to a condition preventing him from accepting the employment.

(2) A person guilty of an offence under this section is liable—

   (a) on conviction on indictment—

      (i) to imprisonment for a term not exceeding two years,

      (ii) to a fine, or

      (iii) to both, or

   (b) on summary conviction—

      (i) to imprisonment for a term not exceeding 12 months in England and Wales or 6 months in Scotland or Northern Ireland,

      (ii) to a fine not exceeding the statutory maximum, or

      (iii) to both.

(3) An offence under this section shall be treated as—

   (a) a relevant offence for the purpose of sections 28B and 28D of the Immigration Act 1971 (c 77) (search, entry and arrest), and

   (b) an offence under Part III of that Act (criminal proceedings) for the purposes of sections 28E, 28G and 28H (search after arrest).

(4) In relation to a conviction occurring before the commencement of section 154(1) of the Criminal Justice Act 2003 (c 44) (general limit on magistrates' powers to imprison) the reference to 12 months in subsection (2)(b)(i) shall be taken as a reference to 6 months.

22 Offence: bodies corporate, &c

(1) For the purposes of section 21(1) a body (whether corporate or not) shall be treated as knowing a fact about an employee if a person who has responsibility within the body for an aspect of the employment knows the fact.

(2) If an offence under section 21(1) is committed by a body corporate with the consent or connivance of an officer of the body, the officer, as well as the body, shall be treated as having committed the offence.

(3) In subsection (2) a reference to an officer of a body includes a reference to—

   (a) a director, manager or secretary,

   (b) a person purporting to act as a director, manager or secretary, and

   (c) if the affairs of the body are managed by its members, a member.

    (c)   "reserved matters" has the same meaning as in the Scotland Act 1998 (c 46)[, and

    (d)   "ship" includes—

        (i)   every description of vessel used in navigation, and

        (ii)   hovercraft].

(6)   A requirement imposed under subsection (2)—

    (a)   must be in writing,

    (b)   may apply generally or only to one or more specified ships or aircraft,

    (c)   must specify a period, not exceeding six months and beginning with the date on which it is imposed, during which it has effect,

    (d)   must state—

        (i)   the information required, and

        (ii)   the date or time by which it is to be provided.

(7)   The Secretary of State may make an order specifying a kind of information under subsection (5)(a) only if satisfied that the nature of the information is such that there are likely to be circumstances in which it can be required under subsection (2) without breaching Convention rights (within the meaning of the Human Rights Act 1998 (c 42)).

(8)   An order under subsection (5)(a)—

    (a)   may apply generally or only to specified cases or circumstances,

    (b)   may make different provision for different cases or circumstances,

    (c)   may specify the form and manner in which information is to be provided,

    (d)   shall be made by statutory instrument, and

    (e)   shall be subject to annulment in pursuance of a resolution of either House of Parliament.

Amendment

Sub-s (1): paras (a), (b) substituted by the Police and Justice Act 2006, s 14(1), (2), as from a day to be appointed.

Sub-s (5): in para (b) word "and" in italics repealed by the Police and Justice Act 2006, s 52, Sch 15, Pt 2, as from a day to be appointed.

Sub-s (5): para (d) and word ", and" immediately preceding it inserted by the Police and Justice Act 2006, s 14(1), (3), as from a day to be appointed.

See Further

See further, in relation to the application of this section, with modifications, for the purposes of the Channel Tunnel (International Arrangements) Order 1993, SI 1993/1813: the Channel Tunnel (International Arrangements) Order 1993, SI 1993/1813, art 7(1), Sch 4, para 3A(a) (as inserted by SI 2007/3579, art 2(1), (4)).

See further, in relation to the extension of this section, with modifications, to Guernsey: the Immigration (Guernsey) Order 2011, SI 2011/2444, art 4, Sch 1.

See further, in relation to the extension of this section, with modifications, to Jersey: the Immigration (Jersey) Order 2012, SI 2012/1763, art 2, Sch 1.

Subordinate Legislation

Immigration and Police (Passenger, Crew and Service Information) Order 2008, SI 2008/5.

33 Freight information: police powers

(1)   This section applies to ships, aircraft and vehicles which are—

    (a)   arriving, or expected to arrive, in the United Kingdom, or

    (b)   leaving, or expected to leave, the United Kingdom.

(2)   If a constable of the rank of superintendent or above requires a person specified in subsection (3) to provide freight information he shall comply with the requirement.

(3)   The persons referred to in subsection (2) are—

    (a)   in the case of a ship or aircraft, the owner or agent,

    (b)   in the case of a vehicle, the owner or hirer, and

(c)   in any case, persons responsible for the import or export of the freight into or from the United Kingdom.

(4)   A constable may impose a requirement under subsection (2) only if he thinks it necessary—

    (a)   in the case of a constable in England, Wales or Northern Ireland, for police purposes, or

    (b)   in the case of a constable in Scotland, for police purposes which are or relate to reserved matters.

(5)   In this section—

    (a)   "freight information" means information which is of a kind specified by order of the Secretary of State and which relates to freight carried,

    (b)   "police purposes" has the meaning given by section 21(3) of the Immigration and Asylum Act 1999 (c 33) (disclosure by Secretary of State), *and*

    (c)   "reserved matters" has the same meaning as in the Scotland Act 1998 (c 46)[, and

    (d)   "ship" includes—

        (i)   every description of vessel used in navigation, and

        (ii)   hovercraft].

(6)   A requirement imposed under subsection (2)—

    (a)   must be in writing,

    (b)   may apply generally or only to one or more specified ships, aircraft or vehicles,

    (c)   must specify a period, not exceeding six months and beginning with the date on which it is imposed, during which it has effect, and

    (d)   must state—

        (i)   the information required, and

        (ii)   the date or time by which it is to be provided.

(7)   The Secretary of State may make an order specifying a kind of information under subsection (5)(a) only if satisfied that the nature of the information is such that there are likely to be circumstances in which it can be required under subsection (2) without breaching Convention rights (within the meaning of the Human Rights Act 1998 (c 42)).

(8)   An order under subsection (5)(a)—

    (a)   may apply generally or only to specified cases or circumstances,

    (b)   may make different provision for different cases or circumstances,

    (c)   may specify the form and manner in which the information is to be provided,

    (d)   shall be made by statutory instrument, and

    (e)   shall be subject to annulment in pursuance of a resolution of either House of Parliament.

Amendment

Sub-s (5): in para (b) word "and" in italics repealed by the Police and Justice Act 2006, s 52, Sch 15, Pt 2, as from a day to be appointed.

Sub-s (5): para (d) and word ", and" immediately preceding it inserted by the Police and Justice Act 2006, s 14(1), (3), as from a day to be appointed.

34 Offence

(1)   A person commits an offence if without reasonable excuse he fails to comply with a requirement imposed under section 32(2) or (3) or 33(2).

(2)   But—

    (a)   a person who fails without reasonable excuse to comply with a requirement imposed under section 32(2) or 33(2) by a constable in England and Wales or Northern Ireland otherwise than in relation to a reserved matter (within the meaning of the Scotland Act 1998 (c 46)) shall not be treated as having committed the offence in Scotland (but has committed the offence in England and Wales or Northern Ireland), and

(b) a person who fails without reasonable excuse to comply with a requirement which is imposed under section 32(3) for the purpose of complying with a requirement to which paragraph (a) applies—

　　(i) shall not be treated as having committed the offence in Scotland, but

　　(ii) shall be treated as having committed the offence in England and Wales or Northern Ireland.

(3) A person who is guilty of an offence under subsection (1) shall be liable on summary conviction to—

(a) imprisonment for a term not exceeding 51 weeks in England and Wales or 6 months in Scotland or Northern Ireland,

(b) a fine not exceeding level 4 on the standard scale, or

(c) both.

(4) In relation to a conviction occurring before the commencement of section 281(5) of the Criminal Justice Act 2003 (c 44) (51 week maximum term of sentences) the reference to 51 weeks in subsection (2)(a) shall be taken as a reference to three months.

See Further

See further, in relation to the application of this section, with modifications, for the purposes of the Channel Tunnel (International Arrangements) Order 1993, SI 1993/1813: the Channel Tunnel (International Arrangements) Order 1993, SI 1993/1813, art 7(1), Sch 4, para 3A(b) (as inserted by SI 2007/3579, art 2(1), (4)).

See further, in relation to the extension of this section, with modifications, to Guernsey: the Immigration (Guernsey) Order 2011, SI 2011/2444, art 4, Sch 1.

See further, in relation to the extension of this section, with modifications, to Jersey: the Immigration (Jersey) Order 2012, SI 2012/1763, art 2, Sch 1.

35

(Amends the Customs and Excise Management Act 1979, s 35.)

---

36 Duty to share information

(1) This section applies to—

[(a) designated customs officials,

(aa) immigration officers,

(ab) the Secretary of State in so far as the Secretary of State has general customs functions,

(ac) the Secretary of State in so far as the Secretary of State has functions relating to immigration, asylum or nationality,

(ad) the Director of Border Revenue and any person exercising functions of the Director,]

(b) a chief officer of police, and

(c) Her Majesty's Revenue and Customs.

(2) The persons specified in subsection (1) shall share information to which subsection (4) applies and which is obtained or held by them in the course of their functions to the extent that the information is likely to be of use for—

(a) immigration purposes,

(b) police purposes, or

(c) Revenue and Customs purposes.

(3) But a chief officer of police in Scotland shall share information under subsection (2) only to the extent that it is likely to be of use for—

>   (a)   immigration purposes,
>   (b)   police purposes, in so far as they are or relate to reserved matters within the meaning of the Scotland Act 1998, or
>   (c)   Revenue and Customs purposes other than the prosecution of crime.

(4)   This subsection applies to information which—
>   (a)   is obtained or held in the exercise of a power specified by the Secretary of State and the Treasury jointly by order and relates to—
>   (i)   passengers on a ship or aircraft,
>   (ii)   crew of a ship or aircraft,
>   (iii)   freight on a ship or aircraft, or
>   (iv)   flights or voyages, or
>   (b)   relates to such other matters in respect of travel or freight as the Secretary of State and the Treasury may jointly specify by order.

(5)   The Secretary of State and the Treasury may make an order under subsection (4) which has the effect of requiring information to be shared only if satisfied that—
>   (a)   the sharing is likely to be of use for—
>   (i)   immigration purposes,
>   (ii)   police purposes, or
>   (iii)   Revenue and Customs purposes, and
>   (b)   the nature of the information is such that there are likely to be circumstances in which it can be shared under subsection (2) without breaching Convention rights (within the meaning of the Human Rights Act 1998 (c 42)).

(6)   Information shared in accordance with subsection (2)—
>   (a)   shall be made available to each of the persons [or descriptions of persons] specified in subsection (1), and
>   (b)   may be used for immigration purposes, police purposes or Revenue and Customs purposes (regardless of its source).

(7)   An order under subsection (4) may not specify—
>   (a)   a power of Her Majesty's Revenue and Customs if or in so far as it relates to a matter to which section 7 of the Commissioners for Revenue and Customs Act 2005 (c 11) (former Inland Revenue matters) applies, or
>   (b)   a matter to which that section applies.

(8)   An order under subsection (4)—
>   (a)   shall be made by statutory instrument, and
>   (b)   may not be made unless a draft has been laid before and approved by resolution of each House of Parliament.

(9)   In this section—
"chief officer of police" means—
>   (a)   in England and Wales, the chief officer of police for a police area specified in section 1 of the Police Act 1996 (c 16),
>   (b)   in Scotland, the chief constable of [the Police Service of Scotland], and
>   (c)   in Northern Ireland, the chief constable of the Police Service of Northern Ireland,
["designated customs official" and "general customs function" have the meanings given by Part 1 of the Borders, Citizenship and Immigration Act 2009,]
"immigration purposes" has the meaning given by section 20(3) of the Immigration and Asylum Act 1999 (c 33) (disclosure to Secretary of State),
"police purposes" has the meaning given by section 21(3) of that Act (disclosure by Secretary of State), *and*
"Revenue and Customs purposes" means those functions of Her Majesty's Revenue and Customs specified in section 21(6) of that Act[, and

"ship" includes—
> (a) every description of vessel used in navigation, and
> (b) hovercraft].

(10) This section has effect despite any restriction on the purposes for which information may be disclosed or used.

Amendment

Sub-s (1): paras (a), (aa)–(ad) substituted, for para (a) as originally enacted, by the Borders, Citizenship and Immigration Act 2009, s 21(1).

Sub-s (6): in para (a) words "or descriptions of persons" in square brackets inserted by the Borders, Citizenship and Immigration Act 2009, s 21(2).

Sub-s (9): in definition "chief officer of police" in para (b) words "the Police Service of Scotland" in square brackets substituted by SI 2013/602, art 26, Sch 2, Pt 1, para 50(1), (2). Date in force: 1 April 2013: see SI 2013/602, art 1(2); for transitional provisions and savings see art 27, Sch 3 thereto.

Sub-s (9): definition "designated customs official" and "general customs function" inserted by the Borders, Citizenship and Immigration Act 2009, s 21(3).

Sub-s (9): in definition "police purposes" word "and" in italics repealed by the Police and Justice Act 2006, s 52, Sch 15, Pt 2, as from a day to be appointed.

Sub-s (9): definition "ship" and word ", and" immediately preceding it inserted by the Police and Justice Act 2006, s 14(1), (4), as from a day to be appointed.

See Further

See further, in relation to the application of this section, with modifications, for the purposes of the Channel Tunnel (International Arrangements) Order 1993, SI 1993/1813: the Channel Tunnel (International Arrangements) Order 1993, SI 1993/1813, art 7(1), Sch 4, para 3A(c) (as inserted by SI 2007/3579, art 2(1), (4)).

Subordinate Legislation

Immigration, Asylum and Nationality Act 2006 (Duty to Share Information and Disclosure of Information for Security Purposes) Order 2008, SI 2008/539.

37 Information sharing: code of practice

(1) The Secretary of State and the Treasury shall jointly issue one or more codes of practice about—
> (a) the use of information shared in accordance with section 36(2), and
> (b) the extent to which, or form or manner in which, shared information is to be made available in accordance with section 36(6).

(2) A code—
> (a) shall not be issued unless a draft has been laid before Parliament, and
> (b) shall come into force in accordance with provision made by order of the Secretary of State and the Treasury jointly.

(3) The Secretary of State and the Treasury shall jointly from time to time review a code and may revise and re-issue it following a review; and subsection (2) shall apply to a revised code.

(4) An order under subsection (2)—
> (a) shall be made by statutory instrument, and
> (b) shall be subject to annulment in pursuance of a resolution of either House of Parliament.

See Further

See further, in relation to the application of this section, with modifications, for the purposes of the Channel Tunnel (International Arrangements) Order 1993, SI 1993/1813: the Channel Tunnel (International Arrangements) Order 1993, SI 1993/1813, art 7(1), Sch 4, para 3A(d) (as inserted by SI 2007/3579, art 2(1), (4)).

Subordinate Legislation

Immigration, Asylum and Nationality Act 2006 (Data Sharing Code of Practice) (Revocation) Order 2007, SI 2007/3447; Immigration, Asylum and Nationality Act 2006 (Data Sharing Code of Practice) Order 2008, SI 2008/8.

(Repealed by the Counter-Terrorism Act 2008, ss 20(4), 99, Sch 1, para 4, Sch 9, Pt 2. .)

39 Disclosure to law enforcement agencies

(1) A chief officer of police may disclose information obtained in accordance with section 32 or 33 to—

    (a)   the States of Jersey police force;

    (b)   the salaried police force of the Island of Guernsey;

    (c)   the Isle of Man constabulary;

    (d)   any other foreign law enforcement agency.

(2) In subsection (1) "foreign law enforcement agency" means a person outside the United Kingdom with functions similar to functions of—

    (a)   a police force in the United Kingdom, or

    (b)   the [National Crime Agency].

(3) In subsection (1) "chief officer of police" means—

    (a)   in England and Wales, the chief officer of police for a police area specified in section 1 of the Police Act 1996,

    (b)   in Scotland, the chief constable of [the Police Service of Scotland], and

    (c)   in Northern Ireland, the chief constable of the Police Service of Northern Ireland.

Amendment

Sub-s (2): in para (b) words "National Crime Agency" in square brackets substituted by the Crime and Courts Act 2013, s 15(3), Sch 8, Pt 3, para 186. Date in force: 7 October 2013: see SI 2013/1682, art 3(u), (v).

Sub-s (3): in para (b) words "the Police Service of Scotland" in square brackets substituted by SI 2013/602, art 26, Sch 2, Pt 1, para 50(1), (3). Date in force: 1 April 2013: see SI 2013/602, art 1(2); for transitional provisions and savings see art 27, Sch 3 thereto.

See Further

See further, in relation to the application of this section, with modifications, for the purposes of the Channel Tunnel (International Arrangements) Order 1993, SI 1993/1813: the Channel Tunnel (International Arrangements) Order 1993, SI 1993/1813, art 7(1), Sch 4, para 3A(f) (as inserted by SI 2007/3579, art 2(1), (4)).

See further, in relation to the extension of this section, with modifications, to Guernsey: the Immigration (Guernsey) Order 2011, SI 2011/2444, art 4, Sch 1.

See further, in relation to the extension of this section, with modifications, to Jersey: the Immigration (Jersey) Order 2012, SI 2012/1763, art 2, Sch 1.

40 Searches: contracting out

(1) An authorised person may, in accordance with arrangements made under this section, search a searchable ship, aircraft, vehicle or other thing for the purpose of satisfying himself whether there are individuals whom an immigration officer might wish to examine under paragraph 2 of Schedule 2 to the Immigration Act 1971 (c 77) (control of entry: administrative provisions).

(2) For the purposes of subsection (1)—

    (a)   "authorised" means authorised for the purpose of this section by the Secretary of State, and

    (b)   a ship, aircraft, vehicle or other thing is "searchable" if an immigration officer could search it under paragraph 1(5) of that Schedule.

(3) The Secretary of State may authorise a specified class of constable for the purpose of this section.

(4) The Secretary of State may, with the consent of the Commissioners for Her Majesty's Revenue and Customs, authorise a specified class of officers of Revenue and Customs for the purpose of this section.

(5)   The Secretary of State may authorise a person other than a constable or officer of Revenue and Customs for the purpose of this section only if—

(a)   the person applies to be authorised, and

(b)   the Secretary of State thinks that the person is—

(i)   fit and proper for the purpose, and

(ii)   suitably trained.

(6)   The Secretary of State—

(a)   may make arrangements for the exercise by authorised constables of the powers under subsection (1),

(b)   may make arrangements with the Commissioners for Her Majesty's Revenue and Customs for the exercise by authorised officers of Revenue and Customs of the powers under subsection (1), and

(c)   may make arrangements with one or more persons for the exercise by authorised persons other than constables and officers of Revenue and Customs of the power under subsection (1).

(7)   Where in the course of a search under this section an authorised person discovers an individual whom he thinks an immigration officer might wish to examine under paragraph 2 of that Schedule, the authorised person may—

(a)   search the individual for the purpose of discovering whether he has with him anything of a kind that might be used—

(i)   by him to cause physical harm to himself or another,

(ii)   by him to assist his escape from detention, or

(iii)   to establish information about his identity, nationality or citizenship or about his journey;

(b)   retain, and as soon as is reasonably practicable deliver to an immigration officer, anything of a kind described in paragraph (a) found on a search under that paragraph;

(c)   detain the individual, for a period which is as short as is reasonably necessary and which does not exceed three hours, pending the arrival of an immigration officer to whom the individual is to be delivered;

(d)   take the individual, as speedily as is reasonably practicable, to a place for the purpose of delivering him to an immigration officer there;

(e)   use reasonable force for the purpose of doing anything under paragraphs (a) to (d).

(8)   Despite the generality of subsection (7)—

(a)   an individual searched under that subsection may not be required to remove clothing other than an outer coat, a jacket or a glove (but he may be required to open his mouth), and

(b)   an item may not be retained under subsection (7)(b) if it is subject to legal privilege—

(i)   in relation to a search carried out in England and Wales, within the meaning of the Police and Criminal Evidence Act 1984 (c 60),

(ii)   in relation to a search carried out in Scotland, within the meaning of section 412 of the Proceeds of Crime Act 2002 (c 29), and

(iii)   in relation to a search carried out in Northern Ireland, within the meaning of the Police and Criminal Evidence (Northern Ireland) Order 1989 (SI 1989/1341 (NI 12)).

41 Section 40: supplemental

(1)   Arrangements under section 40(6)(c) must include provision for the appointment of a Crown servant to—

(a)   monitor the exercise of powers under that section by authorised persons (other than constables or officers of Revenue and Customs),

    (b)   inspect from time to time the way in which the powers are being exercised by authorised persons (other than constables or officers of Revenue and Customs), and

    (c)   investigate and report to the Secretary of State about any allegation made against an authorised person (other than a constable or officer of Revenue and Customs) in respect of anything done or not done in the purported exercise of a power under that section.

(2)   The authorisation for the purpose of section 40 of a constable or officer of Revenue and Customs or of a class of constable or officer of Revenue and Customs—

    (a)   may be revoked, and

    (b)   shall have effect, unless revoked, for such period as shall be specified (whether by reference to dates or otherwise) in the authorisation.

(3)   The authorisation of a person other than a constable or officer of Revenue and Customs for the purpose of section 40—

    (a)   may be subject to conditions,

    (b)   may be suspended or revoked by the Secretary of State by notice in writing to the authorised person, and

    (c)   shall have effect, unless suspended or revoked, for such period as shall be specified (whether by reference to dates or otherwise) in the authorisation.

(4)   A class may be specified for the purposes of section 40(3) or (4) by reference to—

    (a)   named individuals,

    (b)   the functions being exercised by a person,

    (c)   the location or circumstances in which a person is exercising functions, or

    (d)   any other matter.

(5)   An individual or article delivered to an immigration officer under section 40 shall be treated as if discovered by the immigration officer on a search under Schedule 2 to the Immigration Act 1971 (c 77).

(6)   A person commits an offence if he—

    (a)   absconds from detention under section 40(7)(c),

    (b)   absconds while being taken to a place under section 40(7)(d) or having been taken to a place in accordance with that paragraph but before being delivered to an immigration officer,

    (c)   obstructs an authorised person in the exercise of a power under section 40, or

    (d)   assaults an authorised person who is exercising a power under section 40.

(7)   But a person does not commit an offence under subsection (6) by doing or failing to do anything in respect of an authorised person who is not readily identifiable—

    (a)   as a constable or officer of Revenue and Customs, or

    (b)   as an authorised person (whether by means of a uniform or badge or otherwise).

(8)   A person guilty of an offence under subsection (6) shall be liable on summary conviction to—

    (a)   imprisonment for a term not exceeding 51 weeks, in the case of a conviction in England and Wales, or six months, in the case of a conviction in Scotland or Northern Ireland,

    (b)   a fine not exceeding level 5 on the standard scale, or

    (c)   both.

(9)   In relation to a conviction occurring before the commencement of section 281(5) of the Criminal Justice Act 2003 (c 44) (51 week maximum term of sentences) the reference in subsection (8)(a) to 51 weeks shall be treated as a reference to six months.

See Further

See further, in relation to the application of this section, for the purpose of enabling immigration officers to exercise immigration control in a Control Zone in France: the Nationality, Immigration and Asylum Act 2002 (Juxtaposed Controls) Order 2003, SI 2003/2818, art 11(1)(g) (as inserted by SI 2006/2908, art 2(a)).

42

(Contains amendments which, in so far as relevant to this work, have been incorporated at the appropriate place.)

Claimants and applicants

43

(Contains amendments which, in so far as relevant to this work, have been incorporated at the appropriate place.)

44 Failed asylum-seekers: withdrawal of support

(1) The Secretary of State may by order provide for paragraph 7A of Schedule 3 to the Nationality, Immigration and Asylum Act 2002 (c 41) (failed asylum-seeker with family: withdrawal of support) to cease to have effect.

(2) An order under subsection (1) shall also provide for the following to cease to have effect—

    (a) section 9(1), (2) and (4) of the Asylum and Immigration (Treatment of Claimants, etc) Act 2004 (c 19) (which insert paragraph 7A of Schedule 3 and make consequential provision), and

    (b) in section 9(3)(a) and (b) of that Act, the words "other than paragraph 7A."

(3) An order under subsection (1)—

    (a) may include transitional provision,

    (b) shall be made by statutory instrument, and

    (c) shall be subject to annulment in pursuance of a resolution of either House of Parliament.

Commencement

To be appointed: see s 62(1).

45, 46

(S 45 amends the Asylum and Immigration (Treatment of Claimants, etc) Act 2004, s 13; s 46 amends the Prison Acts 1952.)

47 Removal: persons with statutorily extended leave

[(1) *Where the Secretary of State gives written notice of a pre-removal decision to the person affected, the Secretary of State may—*

    (a) *in the document containing that notice,*

    (b) *in a document enclosed in the same envelope as that document,*

    (c) *otherwise on the occasion when that notice is given to the person, or*

    (d) *at any time after that occasion but before an appeal against the pre-removal decision is brought under section 82(1) of the Nationality, Immigration and Asylum Act 2002,* also give the person written notice that the person is to be removed from the United Kingdom under this section in accordance with directions given by an immigration officer if and when the person's leave to enter or remain in the United Kingdom expires.

(1A) In subsection (1) "pre-removal decision" means—

(a) a decision on an application—

(i) for variation of limited leave to enter or remain in the United Kingdom, and

(ii) made before the leave expires,

(b) a decision to revoke a person's leave to enter or remain in the United Kingdom, or

(c) a decision to vary a person's leave to enter or remain in the United Kingdom where the variation will result in the person having no leave to enter or remain in the United Kingdom.]

(2) Directions under this section may impose any requirements of a kind prescribed for the purpose of section 10 of the Immigration and Asylum Act 1999 (c 33) (removal of persons unlawfully in United Kingdom).

(3) In relation to directions under this section, paragraphs 10, 11, 16 to 18, 21 and 22 to 24 of Schedule 2 to the Immigration Act 1971 (administrative provisions as to control of entry) apply as they apply in relation to directions under paragraph 8 of that Schedule.

(4) The costs of complying with a direction given under this section (so far as reasonably incurred) must be met by the Secretary of State.

(5) A person shall not be liable to removal from the United Kingdom under this section at a time when section 7(1)(b) of the Immigration Act 1971 (Commonwealth and Irish citizens ordinarily resident in United Kingdom) would prevent a decision to deport him.

(6) In section 82(2) of the Nationality, Immigration and Asylum Act 2002 (c 41) (right of appeal: general) after paragraph (h) insert—

"(ha) a decision that a person is to be removed from the United Kingdom by way of directions under section 47 of the Immigration, Asylum and Nationality Act 2006 (removal: persons with statutorily extended leave),".

(7) In section 92(2) of that Act (appeal from within United Kingdom) after " (f)" insert ", (ha)".

(8) In section 94(1A) of that Act (appeal from within United Kingdom: unfounded claim) for "or (e)" substitute "(e) or (ha)".

Amendment

Repealed by the Immigration Act 2014, s 73, Sch 9, Pt 1, paras 5, 7, as from 20 October 2014 (see SI 2014/2771, art 2), subject to savings in SI 2014/2771, arts 9–11;

Sub-ss (1), (1A): substituted, for sub-s (1) as originally enacted, by the Crime and Courts Act 2013, s 51(3). Date in force: 8 May 2013: see SI 2013/1042, art 2(i).

48 Removal: cancellation of leave

For section 10(8) of 9 (c 33) (removal directions: cancellation of leave to enter or remain in UK) substitute—

"(8) When a person is notified that a decision has been made to remove him in accordance with this section, the notification invalidates any leave to enter or remain in the United Kingdom previously given to him."

NOTES

Initial Commencement

To be appointed

To be appointed: see s 62(1).

Appointment

Appointment: 16 June 2006: see SI 2006/1497, art 3, Schedule.

See Further

See further, the extension of this section to the Isle of Man: the Immigration (Isle of Man)
Order 2008, SI 2008/680, art 20(1), (2)(l).

48, 49

(*S 48 amends the Immigration and Asylum Act 1999, s 10; s 49 inserts the British Nationality Act
1981, s 44A.*)

50 Procedure

(1)   Rules under section 3 of the Immigration Act 1971 (c 77)—

    (a)   may require a specified procedure to be followed in making or pursuing
an application or claim (whether or not under those rules or any other
enactment),

    (b)   may, in particular, require the use of a specified form and the submission
of specified information or documents,

    (c)   may make provision about the manner in which a fee is to be paid, and

    (d)   may make provision for the consequences of failure to comply with a
requirement under paragraph (a), (b) or (c).

(2)   In respect of any application or claim in connection with immigration (whether
or not under the rules referred to in subsection (1) or any other enactment) the
Secretary of State—

    (a)   may require the use of a specified form,

    (b)   may require the submission of specified information or documents, and

    (c)   may direct the manner in which a fee is to be paid;

and the rules referred to in subsection (1) may provide for the consequences of failure
to comply with a requirement under paragraph (a), (b) or (c).

(3)   The following shall cease to have effect—

    (a)   section 31A of the Immigration Act 1971 (procedure for applications),
and

    (b)   section 25 of the Asylum and Immigration (Treatment of Claimants etc)
Act 2004 (c 19) (marriage: application for permission).

(4)   At the end of section 41(1) of the British Nationality Act 1981 (procedure) add—

    "(j)   as to the consequences of failure to comply with provision made
under any of paragraphs (a) to (i)."

(5)   In section 10(2)(c) of the Nationality, Immigration and Asylum Act 2002 (c 41)
(right of abode: certificate of entitlement: procedure) for "made in a specified form;"
substitute "accompanied by specified information;".

(6)   Paragraph 2(3) of Schedule 23 to the Civil Partnership Act 2004 (c 33)
(immigration: procedure) shall cease to have effect.

See Further

See further, with modifications, the extension of this section to the Isle of Man: the Immigration
(Isle of Man) Order 2008, SI 2008/680, arts 20(1), (2)(m), 21, Sch 9, para 5, Sch 10, Pt 7.

(Repealed by the Immigration Act 2014, s 73, Sch 9, Pt 11, para 74, as from 15 December 2014: see SI 2014/2771.)

52 Fees: supplemental

(1)   A fee imposed under section 51 may relate to a thing whether or not it is done wholly or partly outside the United Kingdom; but that section is without prejudice to—

    (a)   section 1 of the Consular Fees Act 1980 (c 23), and

    (b)   any other power to charge a fee.

(2)   Section 51 is without prejudice to the application of section 102 of the Finance (No 2) Act 1987 (c 51) (government fees and charges); and an order made under that section in respect of a power repealed by Schedule 2 to this Act shall have effect as if it related to the powers under section 51 above in so far as they relate to the same matters as the repealed power.

(3)   An order or regulations under section 51—

    (a)   may make provision generally or only in respect of specified cases or circumstances,

    (b)   may make different provision for different cases or circumstances,

    (c)   may include incidental, consequential or transitional provision, and

    (d)   shall be made by statutory instrument.

(4)   An order under section 51—

    (a)   may be made only with the consent of the Treasury, and

    (b)   may be made only if a draft has been laid before and approved by resolution of each House of Parliament.

(5)   Regulations under section 51—

    (a)   may be made only with the consent of the Treasury, and

    (b)   shall be subject to annulment in pursuance of a resolution of either House of Parliament.

(6)   A reference in section 51 to anything in connection with immigration or nationality includes a reference to anything in connection with an enactment (including an enactment of a jurisdiction outside the United Kingdom) that relates wholly or partly to immigration or nationality.

(7)   Schedule 2 (consequential amendments) shall have effect.

See Further

See further, with modifications, the extension of this section to the Isle of Man: the Immigration (Isle of Man) Order 2008, SI 2008/680, arts 20(1), (2)(o), (p), 21, Sch 9, para 7, Sch 10, Pt 7.

Subordinate Legislation

Immigration and Nationality (Cost Recovery Fees) Regulations 2014, SI 2014/581; Immigration and Nationality (Fees) Regulations 2014, SI 2014/922.

Miscellaneous

53

(Amends the Immigration Act 1971, Sch 3.)

54 Refugee Convention: construction

(1)   In the construction and application of Article 1(F)(c) of the Refugee Convention the reference to acts contrary to the purposes and principles of the United Nations shall be taken as including, in particular—

(a)   acts of committing, preparing or instigating terrorism (whether or not the acts amount to an actual or inchoate offence), and

(b)   acts of encouraging or inducing others to commit, prepare or instigate terrorism (whether or not the acts amount to an actual or inchoate offence).

(2)   In this section—

"the Refugee Convention" means the Convention relating to the Status of Refugees done at Geneva on 28th July 1951, and

"terrorism" has the meaning given by section 1 of the Terrorism Act 2000 (c 11).

See Further

See further, with modifications, the extension of this section to the Isle of Man: the Immigration (Isle of Man) Order 2008, SI 2008/680, arts 20(1), (2)(s), 21, Sch 9, para 8, Sch 10, Pt 7.

55 Refugee Convention: certification

(1)   This section applies to an asylum appeal where the Secretary of State issues a certificate that the appellant is not entitled to the protection of Article 33(1) of the Refugee Convention because—

(a)   Article 1(F) applies to him (whether or not he would otherwise be entitled to protection), or

(b)   Article 33(2) applies to him on grounds of national security (whether or not he would otherwise be entitled to protection).

(2)   In this section—

(a)   "asylum appeal" means an appeal—

(i)   which is brought under section 82 . . . of the Nationality, Immigration and Asylum Act 2002 (c 41) or section 2 of the Special Immigration Appeals Commission Act 1997 (c 68), and

[(ii)   which is brought on the ground mentioned in section 84(1)(a) or (3)(a) of that Act (breach of United Kingdom's obligations under the Refugee Convention);]

(b)   "the Refugee Convention" means the Convention relating to the Status of Refugees done at Geneva on 28th July 1951.

(3)   The [First-tier Tribunal] or the Special Immigration Appeals Commission must begin substantive deliberations on the asylum appeal by considering the statements in the Secretary of State's certificate.

(4)   If the Tribunal or Commission agrees with those statements it must dismiss such part of the asylum appeal as amounts to an asylum claim (before considering any other aspect of the case).

(5)   Section 72(10)(a) of the Nationality, Immigration and Asylum Act 2002 (serious criminal: Tribunal or Commission to begin by considering certificate) shall have effect subject to subsection (3) above.

[(5A)   Subsections (3) and (4) also apply in relation to the Upper Tribunal when it acts under section 12(2)(b)(ii) of the Tribunals, Courts and Enforcement Act 2007.]

(6)   Section 33 of the Anti-terrorism, Crime and Security Act 2001 (c 24) (certificate of non-application of Refugee Convention) shall cease to have effect.

Amendment

Sub-s (2): in para (a) words omitted repealed and words in square brackets substituted by the Immigration Act 2014, s 73, Sch 9, Pt 4, para 57(1), (4), as from 20 October 2014 (see SI 2014/2771, art 2), subject to savings in SI 2014/2771, arts 9–11. Para (a) previously read as follows:

" "asylum appeal" means an appeal—

which is brought under section 82, 83 or 101 of the Nationality, Immigration and Asylum Act 2002 (c 41) or section 2 of the Special Immigration Appeals Commission Act 1997 (c 68), and

in which the appellant claims that to remove him from or require him to leave the United Kingdom would be contrary to the United Kingdom's obligations under the Refugee Convention, and".

Sub-s (3): words "First-tier Tribunal" in square brackets substituted by SI 2010/21, art 5(1), Sch 1, para 35(a).

Sub-s (5A): inserted by SI 2010/21, art 5(1), Sch 1, para 35(b).

56–59

(*S 56 amends the British Nationality Act 1981, ss 40, 40A, 108; s 57 inserts the Immigration Act 1971, s 2A and amends the Nationality, Immigration and Asylum Act 2002, s 82; s 58 repealed by the Borders, Citizenship and Immigration Act 2009, s 56, Schedule, Pt 2. Date in force: 13 January 2010: see SI 2009/2731, art 4(i), (j); s 59 inserts the Immigration and Asylum Act 1999, s 153A and the National Minimum Wage Act 1998, s 45B.*)

General

60 Money

There shall be paid out of money provided by Parliament—
  (a)   any expenditure of the Secretary of State in connection with this Act, and
  (b)   any increase attributable to this Act in sums payable under another enactment out of money provided by Parliament.

61 Repeals

Schedule 3 (repeals) shall have effect.

62 Commencement

(1)   The preceding provisions of this Act shall come into force in accordance with provision made by order of the Secretary of State.
(2)   An order under subsection (1)—
  (a)   may make provision generally or only for specified purposes,
  (b)   may make different provision for different purposes,
  (c)   may include transitional or incidental provision or savings, and
  (d)   shall be made by statutory instrument.

Subordinate Legislation

Immigration, Asylum and Nationality Act 2006 (Commencement No 1) Order 2006, SI 2006/1497; Immigration, Asylum and Nationality Act 2006 (Commencement No 2) Order 2006, SI 2006/2226; Immigration, Asylum and Nationality Act 2006 (Commencement No 3) Order 2006, SI 2006/2838; Immigration, Asylum and Nationality Act 2006 (Commencement No 4) Order 2007, SI 2007/182; Immigration, Asylum and Nationality Act 2006 (Commencement No 5) Order 2007, SI 2007/467; Immigration, Asylum and Nationality Act 2006 (Commencement No 6) Order 2007, SI 2007/1109; Immigration, Asylum and Nationality Act 2006 (Commencement No 7) Order 2007, SI 2007/3138; Immigration, Asylum and Nationality Act 2006 (Commencement No 7) (Amendment) Order 2007, SI 2007/3580; Immigration, Asylum and Nationality Act 2006 (Commencement No 8 and Transitional and Saving Provisions) Order 2008, SI 2008/310; Immigration, Asylum and Nationality Act 2006 (Commencement No 8 and Transitional and Saving Provisions) (Amendment) Order 2012, SI 2012/1531.

63 Extent

(1)   This Act extends to—
  (a)   England and Wales,
  (b)   Scotland, and

    (c)   Northern Ireland.

(2) But—

    (a)   an amendment by this Act of another Act has the same extent as that Act or as the relevant part of that Act (ignoring extent by virtue of an Order in Council), and

    (b)   a provision of this Act shall, so far as it relates to nationality, have the same extent as the British Nationality Act 1981 (c 61) (disregarding excepted provisions under section 53(7) of that Act).

(3) Her Majesty may by Order in Council direct that a provision of this Act is to extend, with or without modification or adaptation, to—

    (a)   any of the Channel Islands;

    (b)   the Isle of Man.

[(3A) In subsection (3), the reference to this Act includes—

    (a)   a reference to this Act as it has effect with the amendments and repeals made in it by the Police and Justice Act 2006, and

    (b)   a reference to this Act as it has effect without those amendments and repeals.]

(4) Subsection (3) does not apply in relation to the extension to a place of a provision which extends there by virtue of subsection (2)(b).

Amendment

Sub-s (3A): inserted by the Police and Justice Act 2006, s 54(7).

Subordinate Legislation

Immigration (Isle of Man) Order 2008, SI 2008/680; Immigration (Isle of Man) (Amendment) Order 2011, SI 2011/1408; Immigration (Guernsey) Order 2011, SI 2011/2444; Immigration (Jersey) Order 2012, SI 2012/1763.

64 Citation

(1) This Act may be cited as the Immigration, Asylum and Nationality Act 2006.

(2) . . .

(3) The following shall cease to have effect—

    (a)   section 32(5) of the Immigration Act 1971 ("the Immigration Acts"),

    (b)   in section 167(1) of the Immigration and Asylum Act 1999, the definition of "the Immigration Acts",

    (c)   section 158 of the Nationality, Immigration and Asylum Act 2002 ("the Immigration Acts"), and

    (d)   section 44 of the Asylum and Immigration (Treatment of Claimants, etc) Act 2004 ("the Immigration Acts").

(4) . . .

Amendment

Sub-s (2): repealed by the UK Borders Act 2007, ss 58, 61(3), Schedule.

Sub-s (4): outside the scope of this work.

See Further

See further, with modifications, the extension of this section to the Isle of Man: the Immigration (Isle of Man) Order 2008, SI 2008/680, arts 20(1), (2)(u), 21, Sch 9, para 9, Sch 10, Pt 7.

SCHEDULES 1–3

(Schs 1–3 contain amendments and repeals which, in so far as relevant to this work, have been incorporated at the appropriate place.)

UK BORDERS ACT 2007

2007 c 30

An Act to make provision about immigration and asylum; and for connected purposes.

[30 October 2007]

Detention at ports

1 Designated immigration officers

(1)   The Secretary of State may designate immigration officers for the purposes of section 2.

(2)   The Secretary of State may designate only officers who the Secretary of State thinks are—

    (a)   fit and proper for the purpose, and

    (b)   suitably trained.

(3)   A designation—

    (a)   may be permanent or for a specified period, and

    (b)   may (in either case) be revoked.

2 Detention

(1)   A designated immigration officer at a port in England, Wales or Northern Ireland may detain an individual if the immigration officer thinks that the individual—

    (a)   may be liable to arrest by a constable under section 24(1), (2) or (3) of the Police and Criminal Evidence Act 1984 (c 60) or Article 26(1), (2) or (3) of the Police and Criminal Evidence (Northern Ireland) Order 1989 (SI 1989/1341 (NI 12)), or

    (b)   is subject to a warrant for arrest.

[(1A)   A designated immigration officer at a port in Scotland may detain an individual if the immigration officer thinks that the individual is subject to a warrant for arrest.]

(2)   A designated immigration officer who detains an individual—

    (a)   must arrange for a constable to attend as soon as is reasonably practicable,

    (b)   may search the individual for, and retain, anything that might be used to assist escape or to cause physical injury to the individual or another person,

    (c)   must retain anything found on a search which the immigration officer thinks may be evidence of the commission of an offence, and

    (d)   must, when the constable arrives, deliver to the constable the individual and anything retained on a search.

(3)   An individual may not be detained under this section for longer than three hours.

(4)   A designated immigration officer may use reasonable force for the purpose of exercising a power under this section.

(5)   Where an individual whom a designated immigration officer has detained or attempted to detain under this section leaves the port, a designated immigration officer may—

    (a)   pursue the individual, and

    (b)   return the individual to the port.

(6)   Detention under this section shall be treated as detention under the Immigration Act 1971 (c 77) for the purposes of Part 8 of the Immigration and Asylum Act 1999 (c 33) (detained persons).

Amendment

Sub-s (1A): inserted by the Borders, Citizenship and Immigration Act 2009, s 52(1), as from 27 October 2014: see SI 2014/2634.

3 Enforcement

(1) An offence is committed by a person who—

  (a) absconds from detention under section 2,

  (b) assaults an immigration officer exercising a power under section 2, or

  (c) obstructs an immigration officer in the exercise of a power under section 2.

(2) A person guilty of an offence under subsection (1)(a) or (b) shall be liable on summary conviction to—

  (a) imprisonment for a term not exceeding 51 weeks,

  (b) a fine not exceeding level 5 on the standard scale, or

  (c) both.

(3) A person guilty of an offence under subsection (1)(c) shall be liable on summary conviction to—

  (a) imprisonment for a term not exceeding 51 weeks,

  (b) a fine not exceeding level 3 on the standard scale, or

  (c) both.

(4) In the application of this section to Northern Ireland—

  (a) the reference in subsection (2)(a) to 51 weeks shall be treated as a reference to six months, and

  (b) the reference in subsection (3)(a) to 51 weeks shall be treated as a reference to one month.

[(4A) In the application of this section to Scotland, the references in subsections (2)(a) and (3)(a) to 51 weeks shall be treated as references to 12 months.]

(5) In relation to an offence committed before the commencement of section 281(5) of the Criminal Justice Act 2003 (c 44) (51 week maximum term of sentences)—

  (a) the reference in subsection (2)(a) to 51 weeks shall be treated as a reference to six months, and

  (b) the reference in subsection (3)(a) to 51 weeks shall be treated as a reference to one month.

Amendment

Sub-s (4A): inserted by the Borders, Citizenship and Immigration Act 2009, s 52(2), as from 27 October 2014: see SI 2014/2634.

4 Interpretation: "port"

(1) In section 2 "port" includes an airport and a hoverport.

(2) A place shall be treated for the purposes of that section as a port in relation to an individual if a designated immigration officer believes that the individual—

  (a) has gone there for the purpose of embarking on a ship or aircraft, or

  (b) has arrived there on disembarking from a ship or aircraft.

Biometric registration

5 Registration regulations

(1) The Secretary of State may make regulations—

  (a) requiring a person subject to immigration control to apply for the issue of a document recording biometric information (a "biometric immigration document");

  (b) requiring a biometric immigration document to be used—

    (i) for specified immigration purposes,

    (ii) in connection with specified immigration procedures, or

(iii)   in specified circumstances, where a question arises about a person's status in relation to nationality or immigration;

(c)   requiring a person who produces a biometric immigration document by virtue of paragraph (b) to provide information for comparison with information provided in connection with the application for the document.

(2)   Regulations under subsection (1)(a) may, in particular—

(a)   apply generally or only to a specified class of persons subject to immigration control (for example, persons making or seeking to make a specified kind of application for immigration purposes);

(b)   specify the period within which an application for a biometric immigration document must be made;

(c)   make provision about the issue of biometric immigration documents;

(d)   make provision about the content of biometric immigration documents (which may include non-biometric information);

(e)   make provision permitting a biometric immigration document to be combined with another document;

(f)   make provision for biometric immigration documents to begin to have effect, and cease to have effect, in accordance with the regulations;

(g)   require a person who acquires a biometric immigration document, without the consent of the person to whom it relates or of the Secretary of State, to surrender it to the Secretary of State as soon as is reasonably practicable;

(h)   permit the Secretary of State to require the surrender of a biometric immigration document in other specified circumstances;

(i)   permit the Secretary of State on issuing a biometric immigration document to require the surrender of other documents connected with immigration or nationality.

(3)   Regulations under subsection (1)(a) may permit the Secretary of State to cancel a biometric immigration document—

(a)   if the Secretary of State thinks that information provided in connection with the document was or has become false, misleading or incomplete,

(b)   if the Secretary of State thinks that the document has been lost or stolen,

(c)   if the Secretary of State thinks that the document (including any information recorded in it) has been altered, damaged or destroyed (whether deliberately or not),

(d)   if the Secretary of State thinks that an attempt has been made (whether successfully or not) to copy the document or to do anything to enable it to be copied,

(e)   if the Secretary of State thinks that a person has failed to surrender the document in accordance with subsection (2)(g) or (h),

(f)   if the Secretary of State thinks that the document should be re-issued (whether because the information recorded in it requires alteration or for any other reason),

(g)   if the Secretary of State thinks that the holder is to be given leave to enter or remain in the United Kingdom,

(h)   if the Secretary of State thinks that the holder's leave to enter or remain in the United Kingdom is to be varied, cancelled or invalidated or to lapse,

(i)   if the Secretary of State thinks that the holder has died,

(j)   if the Secretary of State thinks that the holder has been removed from the United Kingdom (whether by deportation or otherwise),

(k)   if the Secretary of State thinks that the holder has left the United Kingdom without retaining leave to enter or remain, and

(l)   in such other circumstances as the regulations may specify.

(4)   Regulations under subsection (1)(a) may require notification to be given to the Secretary of State by the holder of a biometric immigration document—

(a)   who knows or suspects that the document has been lost or stolen,

(b)   who knows or suspects that the document has been altered or damaged (whether deliberately or not),

(c)   who knows or suspects that information provided in connection with the document was or has become false, misleading or incomplete,

(d)   who was given leave to enter or remain in the United Kingdom in accordance with a provision of rules under section 3 of the Immigration Act 1971 (c 77) (immigration rules) and knows or suspects that owing to a change of the holder's circumstances the holder would no longer qualify for leave under that provision, or

(e)   in such other circumstances as the regulations may specify.

(5)   Regulations under subsection (1)(a) may require a person applying for the issue of a biometric immigration document to provide information (which may include biographical or other non-biometric information) to be recorded in it or retained by the Secretary of State; and, in particular, the regulations may—

(a)   require, or permit an authorised person to require, the provision of information in a specified form;

(b)   require an individual to submit, or permit an authorised person to require an individual to submit, to a specified process by means of which biometric information is obtained or recorded;

(c)   confer a function (which may include the exercise of a discretion) on an authorised person;

(d)   permit the Secretary of State, instead of requiring the provision of information, to use or retain information which is (for whatever reason) already in the Secretary of State's possession.

(6)   Regulations under subsection (1)(b) may, in particular, require the production or other use of a biometric immigration document that is combined with another document . . .

(7)   Regulations under subsection (1)(b) may not make provision the effect of which would be to require a person to carry a biometric immigration document at all times.

(8)   Regulations under subsection (1)(c) may, in particular, make provision of a kind specified in subsection (5)(a) or (b).

(9)   Rules under section 3 of the Immigration Act 1971 (c 77) may require a person applying for the issue of a biometric immigration document to provide non-biometric information to be recorded in it or retained by the Secretary of State.

(10)   Subsections (5) to (9) are without prejudice to the generality of section 50 of the Immigration, Asylum and Nationality Act 2006 (c 13) (procedure).

Amendment

Sub-s (6): words omitted repealed by the Identity Documents Act 2010, s 12, Schedule, para 19, as from 21 January 2011.

Subordinate Legislation

Immigration (Biometric Registration) Regulations 2008, SI 2008/3048; Immigration (Biometric Registration) (Amendment) Regulations 2009, SI 2009/819; Immigration (Biometric Registration) (Amendment No 2) Regulations 2009, SI 2009/3321; Immigration (Biometric Registration) (Amendment) Regulations 2010, SI 2010/2958; Immigration (Biometric Registration) (Amendment) Regulations 2012, SI 2012/594.

6 Regulations: supplemental

(1)   This section applies to regulations under section 5(1).

(2)   Regulations amending or replacing earlier regulations may require a person who holds a biometric immigration document issued under the earlier regulations to apply under the new regulations.

(3)   In so far as regulations require an individual under the age of 16 to submit to a process for the recording of biometric information, or permit an authorised person to require an individual under the age of 16 to submit to a process of that kind, the regulations must make provision similar to section 141(3) to (5) and (13) of the Immigration and Asylum Act 1999 (c 33) (fingerprints: children).

(4)   Rules under section 3 of the Immigration Act 1971 (immigration rules) may make provision by reference to compliance or non-compliance with regulations.

(5)   Information in the Secretary of State's possession which is used or retained in accordance with regulations under section 5(5)(d) shall be treated, for the purpose of requirements about treatment and destruction, as having been provided in accordance with the regulations at the time at which it is used or retained in accordance with them.

(6)   Regulations—

    (a)   may make provision having effect generally or only in specified cases or circumstances,

    (b)   may make different provision for different cases or circumstances,

    (c)   may include incidental, consequential or transitional provision,

    (d)   shall be made by statutory instrument, and

    (e)   may not be made unless a draft has been laid before and approved by resolution of each House of Parliament.

Subordinate Legislation

Immigration (Biometric Registration) Regulations 2008, SI 2008/3048; Immigration (Biometric Registration) (Amendment No 2) Regulations 2009, SI 2009/3321; Immigration (Biometric Registration) (Amendment) Regulations 2010, SI 2010/2958; Immigration (Biometric Registration) (Amendment) Regulations 2012, SI 2012/594.

7 Effect of non-compliance

(1)   Regulations under section 5(1) must include provision about the effect of failure to comply with a requirement of the regulations.

(2)   In particular, the regulations may—

    (a)   require or permit an application for a biometric immigration document to be refused;

    (b)   require or permit an application or claim in connection with immigration to be disregarded or refused;

    (c)   require or permit the cancellation or variation of leave to enter or remain in the United Kingdom;

    (d)   require the Secretary of State to consider giving a notice under section 9;

    (e)   provide for the consequence of a failure to be at the discretion of the Secretary of State.

[(2A)   If the regulations require a biometric immigration document to be used in connection with an application or claim, they may require or permit the application or claim to be disregarded or refused if that requirement is not complied with.]

(3)   The regulations may also permit the Secretary of State to designate an adult as the person responsible for ensuring that a child complies with requirements of the regulations; and for that purpose—

    (a)   "adult" means an individual who has attained the age of 18,

    (b)   "child" means an individual who has not attained the age of 18, and

    (c)   sections 9 to 13 shall apply (with any necessary modifications) to a designated adult's failure to ensure compliance by a child with a requirement of regulations as they apply to a person's own failure to comply with a requirement.

Amendment

Sub-s (2A): inserted by the Immigration Act 2014, s 11, as from 28 July 2014: see SI 2014/1820, art 3(j).

Subordinate Legislation

Immigration (Biometric Registration) Regulations 2008, SI 2008/3048; Immigration (Biometric Registration) (Amendment) Regulations 2012, SI 2012/594.

[8 Use and retention of biometric information

(1) The Secretary of State must by regulations make provision about the use and retention by the Secretary of State of biometric information provided in accordance with regulations under section 5(1).

(2) The regulations must provide that biometric information may be retained only if the Secretary of State thinks that it is necessary to retain it for use in connection with—

    (a)   the exercise of a function by virtue of the Immigration Acts, or

    (b)   the exercise of a function in relation to nationality.

(3) The regulations may include provision permitting biometric information retained by virtue of subsection (2) also to be used—

    (a)   in connection with the prevention, investigation or prosecution of an offence,

    (b)   for a purpose which appears to the Secretary of State to be required in order to protect national security,

    (c)   in connection with identifying persons who have died, or are suffering from illness or injury,

    (d)   for the purpose of ascertaining whether a person has acted unlawfully, or has obtained or sought anything to which the person is not legally entitled, and

    (e)   for such other purposes (whether in accordance with functions under an enactment or otherwise) as the regulations may specify.

(4) The regulations must include provision about the destruction of biometric information.

(5) In particular the regulations must require the Secretary of State to take all reasonable steps to ensure that biometric information is destroyed if the Secretary of State—

    (a)   no longer thinks that it is necessary to retain the information for use as mentioned in subsection (2), or

    (b)   is satisfied that the person to whom the information relates is a British citizen, or a Commonwealth citizen who has a right of abode in the United Kingdom as a result of section 2(1)(b) of the Immigration Act 1971.

(6) The regulations must also—

    (a)   require that any requirement to destroy biometric information by virtue of the regulations also applies to copies of the information, and

    (b)   require the Secretary of State to take all reasonable steps to ensure—

        (i)   that data held in electronic form which relates to biometric information which has to be destroyed by virtue of the regulations is destroyed or erased, or

        (ii)   that access to such data is blocked.

(7) But a requirement to destroy biometric information or data is not to apply if and in so far as the information or data is retained in accordance with and for the purposes of another power.

(8) The regulations must include provision—

    (a)   entitling a person whose biometric information has to be destroyed by virtue of the regulations, on request, to a certificate issued by the Secretary of State to the effect that the Secretary of State has taken the steps required by virtue of subsection (6)(b), and

(b)   requiring such a certificate to be issued within the period of 3 months beginning with the date on which the request for it is received by the Secretary of State.

(9) Section 6(6) applies to regulations under this section as it applies to regulations under section 5(1).]

Amendment

Substituted by the Immigration Act 2014, s 14(1), as from 28 July 2014: see SI 2014/1820, art 3(m).

9 Penalty

(1) The Secretary of State may by notice require a person to pay a penalty for failing to comply with a requirement of regulations under section 5(1).

(2) The notice must—

(a)   specify the amount of the penalty,

(b)   specify a date before which the penalty must be paid to the Secretary of State,

(c)   specify methods by which the penalty may be paid,

(d)   explain the grounds on which the Secretary of State thinks the person has failed to comply with a requirement of the regulations, and

(e)   explain the effect of sections 10 to 12.

(3) The amount specified under subsection (2)(a) may not exceed £1,000.

(4) The date specified under subsection (2)(b) must be not less than 14 days after the date on which the notice is given.

(5) A person who has been given a notice under subsection (1) for failing to comply with regulations may be given further notices in the case of continued failure; but a person may not be given a new notice—

(a)   during the time available for objection or appeal against an earlier notice, or

(b)   while an objection or appeal against an earlier notice has been instituted and is neither withdrawn nor determined.

(6) The Secretary of State may by order amend subsection (3) to reflect a change in the value of money.

10 Penalty: objection

(1) A person (P) who is given a penalty notice under section 9(1) may by notice to the Secretary of State object on the grounds—

(a)   that P has not failed to comply with a requirement of regulations under section 5(1),

(b)   that it is unreasonable to require P to pay a penalty, or

(c)   that the amount of the penalty is excessive.

(2) A notice of objection must—

(a)   specify the grounds of objection and P's reasons,

(b)   comply with any prescribed requirements as to form and content, and

(c)   be given within the prescribed period.

(3) The Secretary of State shall consider a notice of objection and—

(a)   cancel the penalty notice,

(b)   reduce the penalty by varying the penalty notice,

(c)   increase the penalty by issuing a new penalty notice, or

(d)   confirm the penalty notice.

(4) The Secretary of State shall act under subsection (3) and notify P—

(a)   in accordance with any prescribed requirements, and

(b)   within the prescribed period or such longer period as the Secretary of State and P may agree.

Subordinate Legislation
Immigration (Biometric Registration) (Objection to Civil Penalty) Order 2008, SI 2008/2830.

11 Penalty: appeal

(1) A person (P) who is given a penalty notice under section 9(1) may appeal to—

    (a)   [the county court in England and Wales or a county court in] Northern Ireland, or

    (b)   the sheriff, in Scotland.

(2) An appeal may be brought on the grounds—

    (a)   that P has not failed to comply with a requirement of regulations under section 5(1),

    (b)   that it is unreasonable to require P to pay a penalty, or

    (c)   that the amount of the penalty is excessive.

(3) The court or sheriff may—

    (a)   cancel the penalty notice,

    (b)   reduce the penalty by varying the penalty notice,

    (c)   increase the penalty by varying the penalty notice (whether because the court or sheriff thinks the original amount insufficient or because the court or sheriff thinks that the appeal should not have been brought), or

    (d)   confirm the penalty notice.

(4) An appeal may be brought—

    (a)   whether or not P has given a notice of objection, and

    (b)   irrespective of the Secretary of State's decision on any notice of objection.

(5) The court or sheriff may consider matters of which the Secretary of State was not and could not have been aware before giving the penalty notice.

(6) Rules of court may make provision about the timing of an appeal under this section.

Amendment
Sub-s (1): in para (a) words in square brackets substituted by the Crime and Courts Act 2013, s 17(5), Sch 9, Pt 3, para 138, as from 22 April 2014: see SI 2014/954, art 2(c).

Subordinate Legislation
Act of Sederunt (Sheriff Court Rules) (Miscellaneous Amendments) (No 2) 2008, SSI 2008/365 (made under sub-s (6)).

12 Penalty: enforcement

(1) Where a penalty has not been paid before the date specified in the penalty notice in accordance with section 9(2)(b), it may be recovered as a debt due to the Secretary of State.

(2) Where a notice of objection is given in respect of a penalty notice, the Secretary of State may not take steps to enforce the penalty notice before—

    (a)   deciding what to do in response to the notice of objection, and

    (b)   informing the objector.

(3) The Secretary of State may not take steps to enforce a penalty notice while an appeal under section 11—

    (a)   could be brought (disregarding any possibility of an appeal out of time with permission), or

    (b)   has been brought and has not been determined or abandoned.

(4) In proceedings for the recovery of a penalty no question may be raised as to the matters specified in sections 10 and 11 as grounds for objection or appeal.

(5) Money received by the Secretary of State in respect of a penalty shall be paid into the Consolidated Fund.

13 Penalty: code of practice

(1)   The Secretary of State shall issue a code of practice setting out the matters to be considered in determining—

    (a)   whether to give a penalty notice under section 9(1), and

    (b)   the amount of a penalty.

(2)   The code may, in particular, require the Secretary of State to consider any decision taken by virtue of section 7.

(3)   A court or the sheriff shall, when considering an appeal under section 11, have regard to the code.

(4)   The Secretary of State may revise and re-issue the code.

(5)   Before issuing or re-issuing the code the Secretary of State must—

    (a)   publish proposals,

    (b)   consult members of the public, and

    (c)   lay a draft before Parliament.

(6)   The code (or re-issued code) shall come into force at the prescribed time.

Subordinate Legislation

Immigration (Biometric Registration) (Civil Penalty Code of Practice) Order 2008, SI 2008/3049.

14 Penalty: prescribed matters

(1)   In sections 10 to 13 "prescribed" means prescribed by the Secretary of State by order.

(2)   An order under subsection (1) or under section 9(6)—

    (a)   may make provision generally or only for specified purposes,

    (b)   may make different provision for different purposes,

    (c)   shall be made by statutory instrument, and

    (d)   shall be subject to annulment in pursuance of a resolution of either House of Parliament.

(3)   But the first order under section 13(6) shall not be made unless a draft has been laid before and approved by resolution of each House of Parliament (and shall not be subject to annulment).

Subordinate Legislation

Immigration (Biometric Registration) (Civil Penalty Code of Practice) Order 2008, SI 2008/3049.

15 Interpretation

(1)   For the purposes of section 5—

    (a)   "person subject to immigration control" means a person who under the Immigration Act 1971 (c 77) requires leave to enter or remain in the United Kingdom (whether or not such leave has been given),

    (b)   . . .

    (c)   . . .

    (d)   "document" includes a card or sticker and any other method of recording information (whether in writing or by the use of electronic or other technology or by a combination of methods),

    (e)   "authorised person" has the meaning given by section 141(5) of the Immigration and Asylum Act 1999 (c 33) (authority to take fingerprints),

    (f)   "immigration" includes asylum, and

    (g)   regulations permitting something to be done by the Secretary of State may (but need not) permit it to be done only where the Secretary of State is of a specified opinion.

[(1A)   For the purposes of section 5 "biometric information" means—

(a)   information about a person's external physical characteristics (including in particular fingerprints and features of the iris), and

(b)   any other information about a person's physical characteristics specified in an order made by the Secretary of State.

(1B)   An order under subsection (1A)(b)—

(a)   may specify only information that can be obtained or recorded by an external examination of a person;

(b)   must not specify information about a person's DNA.

(1C)   Section 6(6) applies to an order under subsection (1A)(b) as it applies to regulations under section 5(1).]

(2)   An application for a biometric immigration document is an application in connection with immigration for the purposes of—

(a)   section 50(1) and (2) of the Immigration, Asylum and Nationality Act 2006 (c 13) (procedure), and

[(b)   section 68 of the Immigration Act 2014 (fees);]

and in the application of either of those sections to an application for a biometric immigration document, the prescribed consequences of non-compliance may include any of the consequences specified in section 7(2) above.

Amendment

Sub-s (1): paras (b), (c) repealed by the Immigration Act 2014, s 12(1), (2), as from 28 July 2014: see SI 2014/1820, art 3(k).

Sub-ss (1A)–(1C): inserted by the Immigration Act 2014, s 12(1), (3), as from 28 July 2014: see SI 2014/1820, art 3(k).

Sub-s (2): para (b) substituted by the Immigration Act 2014, s 73, Sch 9, Pt 11, para 75, as from 15 December 2014: see SI 2014/2771.

Subordinate Legislation

Immigration (Biometric Registration) Regulations 2008, SI 2008/3048.

Treatment of claimants

16

(Amends the Immigration Act 1971, s 3.)

17 Support for failed asylum-seekers

(1)   This section applies for the purposes of—

(a)   Part 6 (and section 4) of the Immigration and Asylum Act 1999 (support and accommodation for asylum-seekers),

(b)   Part 2 of the Nationality, Immigration and Asylum Act 2002 (c 41) (accommodation centres), and

(c)   Schedule 3 to that Act (withholding and withdrawal of support).

(2)   A person (A-S) remains (or again becomes) an asylum-seeker, despite the fact that the claim for asylum made by A-S has been determined, during any period when—

(a)   A-S can bring an in-country appeal . . . under section 82 of the 2002 Act or section 2 of the Special Immigration Appeals Commission Act 1997 (c 68), or

(b)   an in-country appeal, brought by A-S under either of those sections . . . , is pending (within the meaning of section 104 of the 2002 Act).

(3)   For the purposes of subsection (2)—

(a)   "in-country" appeal means an appeal brought while the appellant is in the United Kingdom, and

(b) the possibility of an appeal out of time with permission shall be ignored.

(4) For the purposes of the provisions mentioned in subsection (1)(a) and (b), a person's status as an asylum-seeker by virtue of subsection (2)(b) continues for a prescribed period after the appeal ceases to be pending.

(5) In subsection (4) "prescribed" means prescribed by regulations made by the Secretary of State; and the regulations—

    (a) may contain incidental or transitional provision,

    (b) may make different provision for different classes of case,

    (c) shall be made by statutory instrument, and

    (d) shall be subject to annulment in pursuance of a resolution of either House of Parliament.

(6) This section shall be treated as always having had effect.

Amendment

Sub-s (2): words "against an immigration decision" omitted in both places, repealed by the Immigration Act 2014, s 73, Sch 9, Pt 4, para 58, as from 20 October 2014 (see SI 2014/2771, art 2), subject to savings in SI 2014/2771, arts 9–11.

Subordinate Legislation

Asylum Support (Prescribed Period following Appeal) Regulations 2007, SI 2007/3102.

18–21

(*S 18 inserts the Immigration and Asylum Act 1999, ss 109A, 109B; ss 19, 20 contained amendments only and are repealed by the Immigration Act 2014, s 73, Sch 9, Pt 4, para 60, Pt 11, para 76(a); s 21 repealed by the Borders, Citizenship and Immigration Act 2009, ss 55(8), 56, Schedule, Pt 4, as from 2 November 2009: see SI 2009/2731, art 2.*)

Enforcement

22 Assaulting an immigration officer: offence

(1) A person who assaults an immigration officer commits an offence.

(2) A person guilty of an offence under this section shall be liable on summary conviction to—

    (a) imprisonment for a period not exceeding 51 weeks,

    (b) a fine not exceeding level 5 on the standard scale, or

    (c) both.

(3) In the application of this section to Northern Ireland the reference in subsection (2)(a) to 51 weeks shall be treated as a reference to 6 months.

(4) In the application of this section to Scotland the reference in subsection (2)(a) to 51 weeks shall be treated as a reference to 12 months.

(5) In relation to an offence committed before the commencement of section 281(5) of the Criminal Justice Act 2003 (c 44) (51 week maximum term of sentences) the reference in subsection (2)(a) to 51 weeks shall be treated as a reference to 6 months.

23 Assaulting an immigration officer: powers of arrest, &c

(1) An immigration officer may arrest a person without warrant if the officer reasonably suspects that the person has committed or is about to commit an offence under section 22.

(2) An offence under section 22 shall be treated as—

    (a) a relevant offence for the purposes of sections 28B and 28D of the Immigration Act 1971 (c 77) (search, entry and arrest), and

    (b) an offence under Part 3 of that Act (criminal proceedings) for the purposes of sections 28(4), 28E, 28G and 28H (search after arrest, &c.) of that Act.

(3) The following provisions of the Immigration Act 1971 shall have effect in connection with an offence under section 22 of this Act as they have effect in connection with an offence under that Act—

    (a)   section 28I (seized material: access and copying),

    (b)   section 28J (search warrants: safeguards),

    (c)   section 28K (execution of warrants), and

    (d)   section 28L(1) (interpretation).

24 Seizure of cash

(1) Chapter 3 of Part 5 of the Proceeds of Crime Act 2002 (c 29) (recovery of cash) shall apply in relation to an immigration officer as it applies in relation to a constable.

(2) For that purpose—

    [(a)   unlawful conduct", in or in relation to section 289, means conduct which—

        (i)   relates to the entitlement of one or more persons who are not nationals of the United Kingdom to enter, transit across, or be in, the United Kingdom (including conduct which relates to conditions or other controls on any such entitlement), or

        (ii)   is undertaken for the purposes of, or otherwise in relation to, a relevant nationality enactment,

and (in either case) constitutes an offence,]

    (c)   "senior officer" in *section 290* [sections 290 and 297A] means an official of the Secretary of State who is a civil servant [at or above the grade which is designated by the Secretary of State as being equivalent to the rank of police inspector],

    (d)   in section 292 the words "(in relation to England and Wales . . .)" shall be disregarded,

    (e)   [sections 293 and 293A] shall not apply,

    (f)   an application for an order under section 295(2) must be made—

        (i)   in relation to England and Wales or Northern Ireland, by an immigration officer, and

        (ii)   in relation to Scotland, by the Scottish Ministers in connection with their functions under section 298 or by a procurator fiscal,

    (g)   an application for forfeiture under section 298 must be made—

        (i)   in relation to England and Wales or Northern Ireland, by an immigration officer, and

        (ii)   in relation to Scotland, by the Scottish Ministers, and

    (h)   any compensation under section 302 shall be paid by the Secretary of State.

[(2A) In subsection (2)(a)(ii) "relevant nationality enactment" means any enactment in—

    (a)   the British Nationality Act 1981,

    (b)   the Hong Kong Act 1985,

    (c)   the Hong Kong (War Wives and Widows) Act 1996,

    (d)   the British Nationality (Hong Kong) Act 1997,

    (e)   the British Overseas Territories Act 2002, or

    (f)   an instrument made under any of those Acts.]

(3) The Secretary of State may by order amend subsection (2)(c) to reflect a change in nomenclature; and an order—

    (a)   shall be made by statutory instrument, and

    (b)   shall be subject to annulment in pursuance of a resolution of either House of Parliament.

Amendment

Sub-s (2): para (a) substituted for original paras (a), (b), by the Crime and Courts Act 2013, s 55(6)(a), as from 25 June 2013: see SI 2013/1042, art 4(g).

Sub-s (2): in para (c) words "section 290" in italics repealed and subsequent words in square brackets substituted by the Policing and Crime Act 2009, s 112(1), Sch 7, Pt 7, para 113, as from a day to be appointed.

Sub-s (2): in para (c) words in second pair of square brackets substituted by the Crime and Courts Act 2013, s 55(14), Sch 21, Pt 1, para 39, as from 25 June 2013: see SI 2013/1042, art 4(l).

Sub-s (2): in para (d) words omitted repealed by SI 2012/2595, art 16(1), (2), as from 18 October 2012: see SI 2012/2595, art 1(2); for transitional provisions see arts 24–28 thereof.

Sub-s (2): in para (e) words in square brackets substituted by SI 2012/2595, art 16(1), (3), as from 18 October 2012: see SI 2012/2595, art 1(2); for transitional provisions see arts 24–28 thereof.

Sub-s (2A): inserted by the Crime and Courts Act 2013, s 55(6)(b), as from 25 June 2013: see SI 2013/1042, art 4(g).

25 Forfeiture of detained property

(1) A court making a forfeiture order about property may order that the property be taken into the possession of the Secretary of State (and not of the police).

(2) An order may be made under subsection (1) only if the court thinks that the offence in connection with which the order is made—

    (a)   related to immigration or asylum, or

    (b)   was committed for a purpose connected with immigration or asylum.

(3) In subsection (1) "forfeiture order" means an order under—

    (a)   section 143 of the Powers of Criminal Courts (Sentencing) Act 2000 (c 6), or

    (b)   Article 11 of the Criminal Justice (Northern Ireland) Order 1994 (SI 1994/2795 (NI 15)).

26 Disposal of property

(1) In this section "property" means property which—

    (a)   has come into the possession of an immigration officer, or

    (b)   has come into the possession of the Secretary of State in the course of, or in connection with, a function under the Immigration Acts.

(2) A magistrates' court may, on the application of the Secretary of State or a claimant of property—

    (a)   order the delivery of property to the person appearing to the court to be its owner, or

    (b)   if its owner cannot be ascertained, make any other order about property.

(3) An order shall not affect the right of any person to take legal proceedings for the recovery of the property, provided that the proceedings are instituted within the period of six months beginning with the date of the order.

(4) An order may be made in respect of property forfeited under section 25, or under section 25C of the Immigration Act 1971 (c 77) (vehicles, &c.), only if—

    (a)   the application under subsection (2) above is made within the period of six months beginning with the date of the forfeiture order, and

    (b)   the applicant (if not the Secretary of State) satisfies the court—

        (i)   that the applicant did not consent to the offender's possession of the property, or

        (ii)   that the applicant did not know and had no reason to suspect that the property was likely to be used, or was intended to be used, in connection with an offence.

(5) The Secretary of State may make regulations for the disposal of property—

    (a)   where the owner has not been ascertained,

    (b)   where an order under subsection (2) cannot be made because of subsection (4)(a), or

    (c)   where a court has declined to make an order under subsection (2) on the grounds that the court is not satisfied of the matters specified in subsection (4)(b).

(6)   The regulations may make provision that is the same as or similar to provision that may be made by regulations under section 2 of the Police (Property) Act 1897 (c 30) (or any similar enactment applying in relation to Scotland or Northern Ireland); and the regulations—

    (a)   may apply, with or without modifications, regulations under that Act,

    (b)   may, in particular, provide for property to vest in the Secretary of State,

    (c)   may make provision about the timing of disposal (which, in particular, may differ from provision made by or under the Police (Property) Act 1897),

    (d)   shall have effect only in so far as not inconsistent with an order of a court (whether or not under subsection (2) above),

    (e)   shall be made by statutory instrument, and

    (f)   shall be subject to annulment in pursuance of a resolution of either House of Parliament.

(7)   For the purposes of subsection (1) it is immaterial whether property is acquired as a result of forfeiture or seizure or in any other way.

(8)   In the application of this section to Scotland a reference to a magistrates' court is a reference to the sheriff.

Subordinate Legislation

Immigration (Disposal of Property) Regulations 2008, SI 2008/786.

27–31

(Ss 27–30 amend the Immigration Act 1971, ss 25, 25A, 25B, 28AA, 28FA; s 31 repealed, in relation to England and Wales, by the Protection of Freedoms Act 2012, s 115(2), Sch 10, Pt 9, as from 6 April 2013: see SI 2013/470, art 2(e), (f).)

Deportation of criminals

32 Automatic deportation

(1)   In this section "foreign criminal" means a person—

    (a)   who is not a British citizen,

    (b)   who is convicted in the United Kingdom of an offence, and

    (c)   to whom Condition 1 or 2 applies.

(2)   Condition 1 is that the person is sentenced to a period of imprisonment of at least 12 months.

(3)   Condition 2 is that—

    (a)   the offence is specified by order of the Secretary of State under section 72(4)(a) of the Nationality, Immigration and Asylum Act 2002 (c 41) (serious criminal), and

    (b)   the person is sentenced to a period of imprisonment.

(4)   For the purpose of section 3(5)(a) of the Immigration Act 1971 (c 77), the deportation of a foreign criminal is conducive to the public good.

(5)   The Secretary of State must make a deportation order in respect of a foreign criminal (subject to section 33).

(6)   The Secretary of State may not revoke a deportation order made in accordance with subsection (5) unless—

(a)   he thinks that an exception under section 33 applies,

(b)   the application for revocation is made while the foreign criminal is outside the United Kingdom, or

(c)   section 34(4) applies.

(7) Subsection (5) does not create a private right of action in respect of consequences of non-compliance by the Secretary of State.

33 Exceptions

(1) Section 32(4) and (5)—

(a)   do not apply where an exception in this section applies (subject to subsection (7) below), and

(b)   are subject to sections 7 and 8 of the Immigration Act 1971 (Commonwealth citizens, Irish citizens, crew and other exemptions).

(2) Exception 1 is where removal of the foreign criminal in pursuance of the deportation order would breach—

(a)   a person's Convention rights, or

(b)   the United Kingdom's obligations under the Refugee Convention.

(3) Exception 2 is where the Secretary of State thinks that the foreign criminal was under the age of 18 on the date of conviction.

(4) Exception 3 is where the removal of the foreign criminal from the United Kingdom in pursuance of a deportation order would breach rights of the foreign criminal under the [EU] treaties.

(5) Exception 4 is where the foreign criminal—

(a)   is the subject of a certificate under section 2 or 70 of the Extradition Act 2003 (c 41),

(b)   is in custody pursuant to arrest under section 5 of that Act,

(c)   is the subject of a provisional warrant under section 73 of that Act,

(d)   is the subject of an authority to proceed under section 7 of the Extradition Act 1989 (c 33) or an order under paragraph 4(2) of Schedule 1 to that Act, or

(e)   is the subject of a provisional warrant under section 8 of that Act or of a warrant under paragraph 5(1)(b) of Schedule 1 to that Act.

(6) Exception 5 is where any of the following has effect in respect of the foreign criminal—

(a)   a hospital order or guardianship order under section 37 of the Mental Health Act 1983 (c 20),

(b)   a hospital direction under section 45A of that Act,

(c)   a transfer direction under section 47 of that Act,

(d)   a compulsion order under section 57A of the Criminal Procedure (Scotland) Act 1995 (c 46),

(e)   a guardianship order under section 58 of that Act,

(f)   a hospital direction under section 59A of that Act,

(g)   a transfer for treatment direction under section 136 of the Mental Health (Care and Treatment) (Scotland) Act 2003 (asp 13), or

(h)   an order or direction under a provision which corresponds to a provision specified in paragraphs (a) to (g) and which has effect in relation to Northern Ireland.

[(6A) Exception 6 is where the Secretary of State thinks that the application of section 32(4) and (5) would contravene the United Kingdom's obligations under the Council of Europe Convention on Action against Trafficking in Human Beings (done at Warsaw on 16th May 2005).]

(7) The application of an exception—

(a)   does not prevent the making of a deportation order;

(b)   results in it being assumed neither that deportation of the person concerned is conducive to the public good nor that it is not conducive to the public good;

but section 32(4) applies despite the application of Exception 1 or 4.

Amendment

Sub-s (4): reference to "EU" in square brackets substituted by SI 2011/1043, art 6(1)(a), as from 22 April 2011: see SI 2011/1043, art 2; for transitional savings see art 3(3) thereof.

Sub-s (6A): inserted by the Criminal Justice and Immigration Act 2008, s 146, as from 1 April 2009.

34 Timing

(1) Section 32(5) requires a deportation order to be made at a time chosen by the Secretary of State.

(2) A deportation order may not be made under section 32(5) while an appeal or further appeal against the conviction or sentence by reference to which the order is to be made—

(a)   has been instituted and neither withdrawn nor determined, or

(b)   could be brought.

(3) For the purpose of subsection (2)(b)—

(a)   the possibility of an appeal out of time with permission shall be disregarded, and

(b)   a person who has informed the Secretary of State in writing that the person does not intend to appeal shall be treated as being no longer able to appeal.

(4) The Secretary of State may withdraw a decision that section 32(5) applies, or revoke a deportation order made in accordance with section 32(5), for the purpose of—

(a)   taking action under the Immigration Acts or rules made under section 3 of the Immigration Act 1971 (c 77) (immigration rules), and

(b)   subsequently taking a new decision that section 32(5) applies and making a deportation order in accordance with section 32(5).

35

(Amends the Nationality, Immigration and Asylum Act 2002, ss 79, 82.)

36 Detention

(1) A person who has served a period of imprisonment may be detained under the authority of the Secretary of State—

(a)   while the Secretary of State considers whether section 32(5) applies, and

(b)   where the Secretary of State thinks that section 32(5) applies, pending the making of the deportation order.

(2) Where a deportation order is made in accordance with section 32(5) the Secretary of State shall exercise the power of detention under paragraph 2(3) of Schedule 3 to the Immigration Act 1971 (c 77) (detention pending removal) unless in the circumstances the Secretary of State thinks it inappropriate.

(3) A court determining an appeal against conviction or sentence may direct release from detention under subsection (1) or (2).

(4) Provisions of the Immigration Act 1971 which apply to detention under paragraph 2(3) of Schedule 3 to that Act shall apply to detention under subsection (1) (including provisions about bail).

(5) Paragraph 2(5) of Schedule 3 to that Act (residence, occupation and reporting restrictions) applies to a person who is liable to be detained under subsection (1).

37 Family

(1)   Where a deportation order against a foreign criminal states that it is made in accordance with section 32(5) ("the automatic deportation order") this section shall have effect in place of the words from "A deportation order" to "after the making of the deportation order against him" in section 5(3) of the Immigration Act 1971 (period during which family members may also be deported).

(2)   A deportation order may not be made against a person as belonging to the family of the foreign criminal after the end of the relevant period of 8 weeks.

(3)   In the case of a foreign criminal who has not appealed in respect of the automatic deportation order, the relevant period begins when an appeal can no longer be brought (ignoring any possibility of an appeal out of time with permission).

(4)   In the case of a foreign criminal who has appealed in respect of the automatic deportation order, the relevant period begins when the appeal is no longer pending (within the meaning of section 104 of the Nationality, Immigration and Asylum Act 2002 (c 41)).

38 Interpretation

(1)   In section 32(2) the reference to a person who is sentenced to a period of imprisonment of at least 12 months—

  (a)   does not include a reference to a person who receives a suspended sentence (unless a court subsequently orders that the sentence or any part of it (of whatever length) is to take effect),

  (b)   does not include a reference to a person who is sentenced to a period of imprisonment of at least 12 months only by virtue of being sentenced to consecutive sentences amounting in aggregate to more than 12 months,

  (c)   includes a reference to a person who is sentenced to detention, or ordered or directed to be detained, in an institution other than a prison (including, in particular, a hospital or an institution for young offenders) for at least 12 months, and

  (d)   includes a reference to a person who is sentenced to imprisonment or detention, or ordered or directed to be detained, for an indeterminate period (provided that it may last for 12 months).

(2)   In section 32(3)(b) the reference to a person who is sentenced to a period of imprisonment—

  (a)   does not include a reference to a person who receives a suspended sentence (unless a court subsequently orders that the sentence or any part of it is to take effect), and

  (b)   includes a reference to a person who is sentenced to detention, or ordered or directed to be detained, in an institution other than a prison (including, in particular, a hospital or an institution for young offenders).

(3)   For the purposes of section 32 a person subject to an order under section 5 of the Criminal Procedure (Insanity) Act 1964 (c 84) (insanity, &c.) has not been convicted of an offence.

(4)   In sections 32 and 33—

  (a)   "British citizen" has the same meaning as in section 3(5) of the Immigration Act 1971 (c 77) (and section 3(8) (burden of proof) shall apply),

  (b)   "Convention rights" has the same meaning as in the Human Rights Act 1998 (c 42),

  (c)   "deportation order" means an order under section 5, and by virtue of section 3(5), of the Immigration Act 1971, and

  (d)   "the Refugee Convention" means the Convention relating to the Status of Refugees done at Geneva on 28th July 1951 and its Protocol.

(*Amends the Nationality, Immigration and Asylum Act 2002, s 72.*)

Information

40 Supply of Revenue and Customs information

(1) Her Majesty's Revenue and Customs (HMRC) and [the Crown Prosecution Service (the CPS)] may each supply the Secretary of State with information for use for the purpose of—

(a) administering immigration control under the Immigration Acts;

(b) preventing, detecting, investigating or prosecuting offences under those Acts;

(c) determining whether to impose, or imposing, penalties or charges under Part 2 of the Immigration and Asylum Act 1999 (c 33) (carriers' liability);

(d) determining whether to impose, or imposing, penalties under section 15 of the Immigration, Asylum and Nationality Act 2006 (c 13) (restrictions on employment);

(e) providing facilities, or arranging for the provision of facilities, for the accommodation of persons under section 4 of the Immigration and Asylum Act 1999;

(f) providing support for asylum-seekers and their dependants under Part 6 of that Act;

(g) determining whether an applicant for naturalisation under the British Nationality Act 1981 (c 61) is of good character;

[(h) determining whether, for the purposes of an application referred to in section 41A of the British Nationality Act 1981, the person for whose registration the application is made is of good character;

(ha) determining whether, for the purposes of an application under section 1 of the Hong Kong (War Wives and Widows) Act 1996, the woman for whose registration the application is made is of good character;

(hb) determining whether, for the purposes of an application under section 1 of the British Nationality (Hong Kong) Act 1997 for the registration of an adult or young person within the meaning of subsection (5A) of that section, the person is of good character;]

(i) determining whether to make an order in respect of a person under section 40 of the British Nationality Act 1981 (deprivation of citizenship);

(j) doing anything else in connection with the exercise of immigration and nationality functions.

(2) This section applies to a document or article which comes into the possession of, or is discovered by, HMRC or [the CPS], or a person acting on behalf of HMRC or [the CPS], as it applies to information.

(3) The Secretary of State—

(a) may retain for a purpose within subsection (1) a document or article supplied by virtue of subsection (2);

(b) may dispose of a document or article supplied by virtue of subsection (2).

(4) In subsection (1) "immigration and nationality functions" means functions exercisable by virtue of—

(a) the Immigration Acts,

(b) the British Nationality Act 1981 (c 61),

(c) the Hong Kong Act 1985 (c 15),

     (d)   the Hong Kong (War Wives and Widows) Act 1996 (c 41), or

     (e)   the British Nationality (Hong Kong) Act 1997 (c 20).

[(4A)   Subsections (1) and (2) are subject to subsection (4B).

(4B)   In relation to the CPS, this section applies to—

     (a)   information held by the CPS in connection with a Revenue and Customs function of the Director of Public Prosecutions;

     (b)   a document or article which comes into the possession of, or is discovered by, the CPS, or a person acting on behalf of the CPS, in the exercise of a Revenue and Customs function of the Director of Public Prosecutions.

(4C)   In subsection (4B) "Revenue and Customs function of the Director of Public Prosecutions" means—

     (a)   a function of the Director of Public Prosecutions under section 3(2)(ab), (bb) or (ee) of the Prosecution of Offences Act 1985, or

     (b)   a function of the Director of Public Prosecutions under the Proceeds of Crime Act 2002 that relates to a function of the Commissioners for Her Majesty's Revenue and Customs or an officer of Revenue and Customs.]

(5)   A power conferred by this section on HMRC or [the CPS] may be exercised on behalf of HMRC or [the CPS] by a person who is authorised (generally or specifically) for the purpose.

[(5A)   Nothing in this section affects any power to supply information apart from this section.]

(6)   The following provisions (which relate to the supply of information to the Secretary of State) shall cease to have effect—

     (a)   section 20(1)(d) of the Immigration and Asylum Act 1999 (c 33),

     (b)   section 130 of the Nationality, Immigration and Asylum Act 2002 (c 41), and

     (c)   paragraphs 17 and 20 of Schedule 2 to the Commissioners for Revenue and Customs Act 2005 (c 11).

Amendment

    Sub-s (1): words in first pair of square brackets substituted by SI 2014/834, reg 3(3), Sch 2, paras 54, 55(1), (2). Date in force: 27 March 2014: see SI 2014/834, art 1.

    Sub-s (1): paras (h), (ha), (hb) substituted, for original para (h), by the Borders, Citizenship and Immigration Act 2009, s 47(5), as from 13 January 2010: see SI 2009/2731, art 4(f).

    Sub-s (2): words in square brackets substituted by SI 2014/834, reg 3(3), Sch 2, paras 54, 55(1), (3). Date in force: 27 March 2014: see SI 2014/834, art 1.

    Sub-ss (4A)–(4C): inserted by SI 2014/834, reg 3(3), Sch 2, paras 54, 55(1), (4). Date in force: 27 March 2014: see SI 2014/834, art 1.

    Sub-s (5): words in square brackets substituted by SI 2014/834, reg 3(3), Sch 2, paras 54, 55(1), (5). Date in force: 27 March 2014: see SI 2014/834, art 1.

    Sub-s (5A): inserted by SI 2014/834, reg 3(3), Sch 2, paras 54, 55(1), (6). Date in force: 27 March 2014: see SI 2014/834, art 1.

41 Confidentiality

(1)   A person to whom relevant information is supplied (whether before or after the commencement of this section) may not disclose that information.

(2)   Information is relevant information if it is supplied by or on behalf of HMRC or [the CPS] under—

     (a)   section 20 of the Immigration and Asylum Act 1999,

     (b)   section 130 of the Nationality, Immigration and Asylum Act 2002,

     (c)   section 36 of the Immigration, Asylum and Nationality Act 2006 (c 13) (except in so far as that section relates to information supplied to a chief officer of police), or

     (d)   section 40 of this Act.

(3)   But subsection (1) does not apply to a disclosure—

(a) which is made for a purpose within section 40(1),

(b) which is made for the purposes of civil proceedings (whether or not within the United Kingdom) relating to an immigration or nationality matter,

(c) which is made for the purposes of a criminal investigation or criminal proceedings (whether or not within the United Kingdom) relating to an immigration or nationality matter,

(d) which is made in pursuance of an order of a court,

(e) which is made with the consent (which may be general or specific) of HMRC or [the CPS], depending on by whom or on whose behalf the information was supplied, or

(f) which is made with the consent of each person to whom the information relates.

(4) Subsection (1) is subject to any other enactment permitting disclosure.

(5) The reference in subsection (1) to a person to whom relevant information is supplied includes a reference to a person who is or was acting on behalf of that person.

(6) The reference in subsection (2) to information supplied under section 40 of this Act includes a reference to documents or articles supplied by virtue of subsection (2) of that section.

(7) In subsection (3) "immigration or nationality matter" means a matter in respect of which the Secretary of State has immigration and nationality functions (within the meaning given in section 40(4)).

(8) In subsection (4) "enactment" does not include—

(a) an Act of the Scottish Parliament,

(b) an Act of the Northern Ireland Assembly, or

(c) an instrument made under an Act within paragraph (a) or (b).

Amendment

Sub-s (2): words in square brackets substituted by SI 2014/834, reg 3(3), Sch 2, paras 54, 56. Date in force: 27 March 2014: see SI 2014/834, art 1.

Sub-s (3): words in square brackets in para (e) substituted by SI 2014/834, reg 3(3), Sch 2, paras 54, 56. Date in force: 27 March 2014: see SI 2014/834, art 1.

[41A Supply of information to UK Border Agency

(1) HMRC and [the CPS] may each supply a person to whom this section applies with information for use for the purpose of the customs functions exercisable by that person.

(2) This section applies to—

(a) a designated customs official,

(b) the Secretary of State by whom general customs functions are exercisable,

(c) the Director of Border Revenue, and

(d) a person acting on behalf of a person mentioned in paragraphs (a) to (c).

(3) This section applies to a document or article which comes into the possession of, or is discovered by, HMRC or [the CPS], or a person acting on behalf of HMRC or [the CPS], as it applies to information.

(4) A person to whom this section applies—

(a) may retain for a purpose within subsection (1) a document or article supplied by virtue of subsection (3);

(b) may dispose of a document or article supplied by virtue of subsection (3).

[(4A) Subsections (1) and (3) are subject to subsection (4B).

(4B) In relation to the CPS, this section applies to—

(a) information held by the CPS in connection with a Revenue and Customs function of the Director of Public Prosecutions;

   (b)   a document or article which comes into the possession of, or is discovered
          by, the CPS, or a person acting on behalf of the CPS, in the exercise of a
          Revenue and Customs function of the Director of Public Prosecutions.
(4C)   In this section "Revenue and Customs function of the Director of Public
Prosecutions" has the meaning given by section 40(4C).]
(5)   A power conferred by this section on HMRC or [the CPS] may be exercised on
behalf of HMRC or [the CPS] by a person who is authorised (generally or specifically)
for the purpose.
(6)   In this section and section 41B "customs function" and "general customs
function" have the meanings given by Part 1 of the Borders, Citizenship and
Immigration Act 2009.]
[(7)   Nothing in this section affects any power to supply information apart from this
section.]]

Amendment

Inserted by the Borders, Citizenship and Immigration Act 2009, s 20(1).
Sub-s (1): words in square brackets substituted by SI 2014/834, reg 3(3), Sch 2, paras 54,
57(1), (2). Date in force: 27 March 2014: see SI 2014/834, art 1.
Sub-s (3): words in square brackets substituted by SI 2014/834, reg 3(3), Sch 2, paras 54,
57(1), (3). Date in force: 27 March 2014: see SI 2014/834, art 1.
Sub-ss (4A)–(4C): inserted by SI 2014/834, reg 3(3), Sch 2, paras 54, 57(1), (4). Date in force:
27 March 2014: see SI 2014/834, art 1.
Sub-s (5): words in square brackets substituted by SI 2014/834, reg 3(3), Sch 2, paras 54,
57(1), (5). Date in force: 27 March 2014: see SI 2014/834, art 1.
Sub-s (7): inserted by SI 2014/834, reg 3(3), Sch 2, paras 54, 57(1), (6). Date in force:
27 March 2014: see SI 2014/834, art 1.

[41B   UK Border Agency: onward disclosure

(1)   A person to whom information is supplied under section 41A may not disclose
that information.
(2)   But subsection (1) does not apply to a disclosure—
   (a)   which is made for the purpose of a customs function, where the
          disclosure does not contravene any restriction imposed by
          the Commissioners for Her Majesty's Revenue and Customs;
   (b)   which is made for the purposes of civil proceedings (whether or not
          within the United Kingdom) relating to a customs function;
   (c)   which is made for the purpose of a criminal investigation or criminal
          proceedings (whether or not within the United Kingdom);
   (d)   which is made in pursuance of an order of a court;
   (e)   which is made with the consent (which may be general or specific) of
          HMRC or [the CPS], depending on by whom or on whose behalf the
          information was supplied;
   (f)   which is made with the consent of each person to whom the information
          relates.
(3)   Subsection (1) is subject to any other enactment permitting disclosure.
(4)   The reference in subsection (1) to information supplied under section 41A
includes a reference to documents or articles supplied by virtue of subsection (3) of
that section.
(5)   The reference in that subsection to a person to whom information is supplied
includes a reference to a person who is or was acting on behalf of that person.
(6)   In subsection (3) "enactment" does not include—
   (a)   an Act of the Scottish Parliament,
   (b)   an Act of the Northern Ireland Assembly, or
   (c)   an instrument made under an Act within paragraph (a) or (b).]

Amendment

Inserted by the Borders, Citizenship and Immigration Act 2009, s 20(1).

Sub-s (2): words in square brackets in para (e) substituted by SI 2014/834, reg 3(3), Sch 2, paras 54, 58. Date in force: 27 March 2014: see SI 2014/834, art 1.

42 Wrongful disclosure

(1) An offence is committed by a person who contravenes section 41 [or 41B] by disclosing information relating to a person whose identity—

    (a)   is specified in the disclosure, or

    (b)   can be deduced from it.

(2) Subsection (1) does not apply to the disclosure of information about internal administrative arrangements of HMRC or [the CPS] (whether relating to Commissioners, officers, members of [the CPS] or others).

(3) It is a defence for a person (P) charged with an offence under this section of disclosing information to prove that P reasonably believed—

    (a)   that the disclosure was lawful, or

    (b)   that the information had already and lawfully been made available to the public.

(4) A person guilty of an offence under this section shall be liable—

    (a)   on conviction on indictment, to imprisonment for a term not exceeding two years, to a fine or to both, or

    (b)   on summary conviction, to imprisonment for a term not exceeding 12 months, to a fine not exceeding the statutory maximum or to both.

(5) The reference in subsection (4)(b) to 12 months shall be treated as a reference to six months—

    (a)   in the application of this section to Northern Ireland;

    (b)   in the application of this section to England and Wales, in relation to an offence under this section committed before the commencement of section 282 of the Criminal Justice Act 2003 (c 44) (imprisonment on summary conviction for certain offences in England and Wales);

    (c)   in the application of this section to Scotland, until the commencement of section 45(1) of the Criminal Proceedings etc (Reform) (Scotland) Act 2007 (asp 6) (corresponding provision in Scotland).

(6) A prosecution for an offence under this section may be instituted—

    (a)   in England and Wales, only with the consent of the Director of Public Prosecutions;

    (b)   in Northern Ireland, only with the consent of the Director of Public Prosecutions for Northern Ireland.

Amendment

Sub-s (1): words "or 41B" in square brackets inserted by the Borders, Citizenship and Immigration Act 2009, s 20(2).

Sub-s (2): words in square brackets substituted by SI 2014/834, reg 3(3), Sch 2, paras 54, 59. Date in force: 27 March 2014: see SI 2014/834, art 1.

43

(*Amends the Nationality, Immigration and Asylum Act 2002, s 131.*)

44 Search for evidence of nationality

(1) This section applies where an individual has been arrested on suspicion of the commission of an offence and an immigration officer or a constable suspects—

    (a)   that the individual may not be a British citizen, and

    (b)   that nationality documents relating to the individual may be found on—

        (i)   premises occupied or controlled by the individual,

        (ii)   premises on which the individual was arrested, or

        (iii)   premises on which the individual was, immediately before being arrested.

(2) The immigration officer or constable may enter and search the premises for the purpose of finding those documents.

(3) The power of search may be exercised only with the written authority of a senior officer; and for that purpose—

    (a)   "senior officer" means—

        (i)   in relation to an immigration officer, an immigration officer of at least the rank of chief immigration officer, and

        (ii)   in relation to a constable, a constable of at least the rank of inspector, and

    (b)   a senior officer who gives authority must arrange for a written record to be made of—

        (i)   the grounds for the suspicions in reliance on which the power of search is to be exercised, and

        (ii)   the nature of the documents sought.

(4) The power of search may not be exercised where the individual has been released without being charged with an offence.

(5) In relation to an individual "nationality document" means a document showing—

    (a)   the individual's identity, nationality or citizenship,

    (b)   the place from which the individual travelled to the United Kingdom, or

    (c)   a place to which the individual is proposing to go from the United Kingdom.

45 Search for evidence of nationality: other premises

(1) This section applies where an individual—

    (a)   has been arrested on suspicion of the commission of an offence, and

    (b)   has not been released without being charged with an offence.

(2) If, on an application made by an immigration officer or a constable, a justice of the peace is satisfied that there are reasonable grounds for believing that—

    (a)   the individual may not be a British citizen,

    (b)   nationality documents relating to the individual may be found on premises specified in the application,

    (c)   the documents would not be exempt from seizure under section 46(2), and

    (d)   any of the conditions in subsection (3) below applies,

the justice of the peace may issue a warrant authorising an immigration officer or constable to enter and search the premises.

(3) The conditions are that—

    (a)   it is not practicable to communicate with any person entitled to grant entry to the premises;

    (b)   it is practicable to communicate with a person entitled to grant entry to the premises but it is not practicable to communicate with any person entitled to grant access to the nationality documents;

    (c)   entry to the premises will not be granted unless a warrant is produced;

    (d)   the purpose of a search may be frustrated or seriously prejudiced unless an immigration officer or constable arriving at the premises can secure immediate entry.

(4) Sections 28J and 28K of the Immigration Act 1971 (c 77) (warrants: application and execution) apply, with any necessary modifications, to warrants under this section.

(5) In the application of this section to Scotland a reference to a justice of the peace shall be treated as a reference to the sheriff or a justice of the peace.

46 Seizure of nationality documents

(1) An immigration officer or constable searching premises under section 44 or 45 may seize a document which the officer or constable thinks is a nationality document in relation to the arrested individual.

(2) Subsection (1) does not apply to a document which—

    (a)   in relation to England and Wales or Northern Ireland, is subject to legal professional privilege, or

    (b)   in relation to Scotland, is an item subject to legal privilege within the meaning of section 412 of the Proceeds of Crime Act 2002 (c 29).

(3) An immigration officer or constable may retain a document seized under subsection (1) while the officer or constable suspects that—

    (a)   the individual to whom the document relates may be liable to removal from the United Kingdom in accordance with a provision of the Immigration Acts, and

    (b)   retention of the document may facilitate the individual's removal.

(4) Section 28I of the Immigration Act 1971 (c 77) (seized material: access and copying) shall have effect in relation to a document seized and retained by an immigration officer.

(5) Section 21 of the Police and Criminal Evidence Act 1984 (c 60) or Article 23 of the Police and Criminal Evidence (Northern Ireland) Order 1989 (SI 1989/1341 (NI 12)) (seized material: access and copying) shall have effect in relation to a document seized and retained by a constable in England and Wales or Northern Ireland.

47

_____

(*Amends the Police Reform Act 2002, Sch 4.*)

_____

Border and Immigration Inspectorate

48 Establishment

(1) The Secretary of State shall appoint a person as Chief Inspector of [the UK Border Agency].

[(1A) The Chief Inspector shall monitor and report on the efficiency and effectiveness of the performance of functions by the following—

    (a)   designated customs officials, and officials of the Secretary of State exercising customs functions;

    (b)   immigration officers, and officials of the Secretary of State exercising functions relating to immigration, asylum or nationality;

    (c)   the Secretary of State in so far as the Secretary of State has general customs functions;

    (d)   the Secretary of State in so far as the Secretary of State has functions relating to immigration, asylum or nationality;

    (e)   the Director of Border Revenue and any person exercising functions of the Director.

(1B) The Chief Inspector shall monitor and report on the efficiency and effectiveness of the services provided by a person acting pursuant to arrangements relating to the discharge of a function within subsection (1A).]

(2) . . . in particular, the Chief Inspector shall consider and make recommendations about—

(a)   consistency of approach [among the persons listed in subsections (1A) and (1B) (the "listed persons")],

(b)   the practice and performance of [the listed persons] compared to other persons doing similar things,

(c)   practice and procedure in making decisions,

(d)   the treatment of claimants and applicants,

(e)   certification under section 94 of the Nationality, Immigration and Asylum Act 2002 (c 41) (unfounded claim),

(f)   compliance with law about discrimination in the exercise of functions, including reliance on [paragraph 17 of Schedule 3 to the Equality Act 2010] (exception for immigration functions),

(g)   practice and procedure in relation to the exercise of enforcement powers (including powers of arrest, entry, search and seizure),

[(ga)   practice and procedure in relation to the prevention, detection and investigation of offences,

(gb)   practice and procedure in relation to the conduct of criminal proceedings,

(gc)   whether customs functions have been appropriately exercised by the Secretary of State and the Director of Border Revenue,]

(h)   the provision of information,

(i)   the handling of complaints, and

(j)   the content of information about conditions in countries outside the United Kingdom which the Secretary of State compiles and makes available, for purposes connected with immigration and asylum, to immigration officers and other officials.

[(2A)   Unless directed to do so by the Secretary of State, the Chief Inspector shall not monitor and report on the exercise by the listed persons of—

(a)   functions at removal centres and short term holding facilities [and in pre-departure accommodation], and under escort arrangements, in so far as Her Majesty's Chief Inspector of Prisons has functions under section 5A of the Prison Act 1952 in relation to such functions, and

(b)   functions at detention facilities, in so far as Her Majesty's Inspectors of Constabulary, the Scottish inspectors or the Northern Ireland inspectors have functions by virtue of section 29 of the Borders, Citizenship and Immigration Act 2009 in relation to such functions.]

(3)   . . .

[(3A)   In this section "customs function", "designated customs official" and "general customs function" have the meanings given by Part 1 of the Borders, Citizenship and Immigration Act 2009.]

(4)   The Chief Inspector shall not aim to investigate individual cases (although this subsection does not prevent the Chief Inspector from considering or drawing conclusions about an individual case for the purpose of, or in the context of, considering a general issue).

Amendment

Sub-s (1): words in square brackets substituted by the Borders, Citizenship and Immigration Act 2009, s 28(1) (for further effect see s 28(10) thereof).

Sub-ss (1A), (1B): inserted by the Borders, Citizenship and Immigration Act 2009, s 28(2) .

Sub-s (2): words omitted repealed by the Borders, Citizenship and Immigration Act 2009, ss 28(3)(a), 56, Schedule, Pt 1.

Sub-s (2): words in square brackets in paras (a), (b) substituted by the Borders, Citizenship and Immigration Act 2009, s 28(3)(b), (c).

Sub-s (2): in para (f) words in square brackets substituted by the Equality Act 2010, s 211(1), Sch 26, Pt 1, para 96 (as inserted by SI 2010/2279, arts 2, 12, Sch 1, para 6).

Sub-s (2): paras (ga)–(gc) inserted by the Borders, Citizenship and Immigration Act 2009, s 28(3)(d).

Sub-s (2A): inserted by the Borders, Citizenship and Immigration Act 2009, s 28(4).

Sub-s (2A): words in square brackets in para (a) inserted by the Immigration Act 2014, s 73, Sch 9, para 16, as from 28 July 2014: see SI 2014/1820.

Sub-s (3): repealed by the Borders, Citizenship and Immigration Act 2009, ss 28(5), 56, Schedule, Pt 1.

Sub-s (3A): inserted by the Borders, Citizenship and Immigration Act 2009, s 28(6).

49 Chief Inspector: supplemental

(1) The Secretary of State shall pay remuneration and allowances to the Chief Inspector.

(2) The Secretary of State—

    (a) shall before the beginning of each financial year specify a maximum sum which the Chief Inspector may spend on functions for that year,

    (b) may permit that to be exceeded for a specified purpose, and

    (c) shall defray the Chief Inspector's expenditure for each financial year subject to paragraphs (a) and (b).

(3) The Chief Inspector shall hold and vacate office in accordance with terms of appointment (which may include provision about retirement, resignation or dismissal).

(4) The Chief Inspector may appoint staff.

(5) A person who is employed by or in any of the following may not be appointed as Chief Inspector—

    (a) a government department,

    (b) the Scottish Administration,

    (c) the National Assembly for Wales, and

    (d) a department in Northern Ireland.

50 Reports

(1) The Chief Inspector shall report in writing to the Secretary of State—

    (a) once each calendar year, in relation to the performance of the functions under section 48 generally, and

    (b) at other times as requested by the Secretary of State in relation to specified matters.

(2) The Secretary of State shall lay before Parliament a copy of any report received under subsection (1).

(3) But a copy may omit material if the Secretary of State thinks that its publication—

    (a) is undesirable for reasons of national security, or

    (b) might jeopardise an individual's safety.

51 Plans

(1) The Chief Inspector shall prepare plans describing the objectives and terms of reference of proposed inspections.

(2) Plans shall be prepared—

    (a) at prescribed times and in respect of prescribed periods, and

    (b) at such other times, and in respect of such other periods, as the Chief Inspector thinks appropriate.

(3) A plan must—

    (a) be in the prescribed form, and

    (b) contain the prescribed information.

(4) In preparing a plan the Chief Inspector shall consult—

    (a) the Secretary of State, and

    (b) prescribed persons.

(5) As soon as is reasonably practicable after preparing a plan the Chief Inspector shall send a copy to—

(a)   the Secretary of State, and

(b)   each prescribed person.

(6)   The Chief Inspector and a prescribed person may by agreement disapply a requirement—

(a)   to consult the person, or

(b)   to send a copy of a plan to the person.

(7)   Nothing in this section prevents the Chief Inspector from doing anything not mentioned in a plan.

52 Relationship with other bodies: general

(1)   The Chief Inspector shall cooperate with prescribed persons in so far as the Chief Inspector thinks it consistent with the efficient and effective performance of the functions under section 48.

(2)   The Chief Inspector may act jointly with prescribed persons where the Chief Inspector thinks it in the interests of the efficient and effective performance of the functions under section 48.

(3)   The Chief Inspector may assist a prescribed person.

(4)   The Chief Inspector may delegate a specified aspect of the functions under section 48 to a prescribed person.

Subordinate Legislation

UK Borders Act 2007 (Border and Immigration Inspectorate) (Joint Working etc) Order 2012, SI 2012/2876.

53 Relationship with other bodies: non-interference notices

(1)   Subsection (2) applies if the Chief Inspector believes that—

(a)   a prescribed person proposes to inspect any aspect of the work of [a person listed in section 48(1A) or (1B)], and

(b)   the inspection may impose an unreasonable burden on [such a person].

(2)   The Chief Inspector may give the prescribed person a notice prohibiting a specified inspection.

(3)   The prescribed person shall comply with the notice, unless the Secretary of State cancels it on the grounds that the inspection would not impose an unreasonable burden on [a person listed in section 48(1A) or (1B)].

(4)   A notice must—

(a)   be in the prescribed form, and

(b)   contain the prescribed information.

(5)   The Secretary of State may by order make provision about—

(a)   the timing of notices;

(b)   the publication of notices;

(c)   the revision or withdrawal of notices.

Amendment

Sub-s (1): in paras (a), (b) words in square brackets substituted by the Borders, Citizenship and Immigration Act 2009, s 28(7).

Sub-s (3): words in square brackets substituted by the Borders, Citizenship and Immigration Act 2009, s 28(8).

54 Abolition of other bodies

The following shall cease to have effect—

(a)   section 19E of the Race Relations Act 1976 (c 74) (monitor of immigration exception),

(b)   section 34 of the Nationality, Immigration and Asylum Act 2002 (c 41) (Monitor of Accommodation Centres),

(c)   section 111 of that Act (monitor of certification of claims as unfounded), and

(d)   section 142 of that Act (Advisory Panel on Country Information).

55 Prescribed matters

(1) In sections 48 to 53 "prescribed" means prescribed by order of the Secretary of State.

(2) An order under any of those sections—

    (a)   may make provision generally or only for specified purposes,

    (b)   may make different provision for different purposes, and

    (c)   may include incidental or transitional provision.

(3) An order under any of those sections prescribing a person may specify—

    (a)   one or more persons, or

    (b)   a class of person.

(4) An order under any of those sections—

    (a)   shall be made by statutory instrument, and

    (b)   shall be subject to annulment in pursuance of a resolution of either House of Parliament.

56 Senior President of Tribunals

(1)   . . .

(2) In exercising the function under section 43 of the Tribunals, Courts and Enforcement Act 2007 (c 15) the Senior President of Tribunals shall have regard to—

    (a)   the functions of the Chief Inspector of [the UK Border Agency], and

    (b)   in particular, the Secretary of State's power to request the Chief Inspector to report about specified matters.

Amendment

Sub-s (1): repealed by SI 2010/21, art 5(3), Sch 3; for transitional provisions and savings see art 5(4), Sch 4, paras 14–18, 21 thereto.

Sub-s (2): in para (a) words "the UK Border Agency" in square brackets substituted by the Borders, Citizenship and Immigration Act 2009, s 28(9).

General

[56A No rehabilitation for certain immigration or nationality purposes

(1) Section 4(1), (2) and (3) of the Rehabilitation of Offenders Act 1974 (effect of rehabilitation) do not apply—

    (a)   in relation to any proceedings in respect of a relevant immigration decision or a relevant nationality decision, or

    (b)   otherwise for the purposes of, or in connection with, any such decision.

(2) In this section—

"immigration officer" means a person appointed by the Secretary of State as an immigration officer under paragraph 1 of Schedule 2 to the Immigration Act 1971,

"relevant immigration decision" means any decision, or proposed decision, of the Secretary of State or an immigration officer under or by virtue of the Immigration Acts, or rules made under section 3 of the Immigration Act 1971 (immigration rules), in relation to the entitlement of a person to enter or remain in the United Kingdom (including, in particular, the removal of a person from the United Kingdom, whether by deportation or otherwise),

"relevant nationality decision" means any decision, or proposed decision, of the Secretary of State under or by virtue of—

    (a)   the British Nationality Act 1981,

    (b)   the British Nationality (Hong Kong) Act 1990, or

    (c)   the Hong Kong (War Wives and Widows) Act 1996,

in relation to the good character of a person.

(3) The references in subsection (2) to the Immigration Acts and to the Acts listed in the definition of "relevant nationality decision" include references to any provision made under section 2(2) of the European Communities Act 1972, or of EU law, which relates to the subject matter of the Act concerned.]

Amendment

Inserted by the Legal Aid, Sentencing and Punishment of Offenders Act 2012, s 140; for transitional provisions see s 141(7)–(9) thereof, as from 1 October 2012: see SI 2012/2412, arts 2(e), (f), 3.

57 Money

The following shall be paid out of money provided by Parliament—

    (a)   any expenditure of a Minister of the Crown in consequence of this Act, and

    (b)   any increase attributable to this Act in sums payable out of money provided by Parliament under another enactment.

Commencement

To be appointed.

58 Repeals

The enactments listed in the Schedule are repealed to the extent specified.

59 Commencement

(1) Section 17 comes into force on the day on which this Act is passed.

(2) The other preceding provisions of this Act shall come into force in accordance with provision made by the Secretary of State by order.

(3) An order—

    (a)   may make provision generally or only for specified purposes,

    (b)   may make different provision for different purposes, and

    (c)   may include incidental, consequential or transitional provision.

(4) In particular, transitional provision—

    (a)   in the case of an order commencing section 16, may permit the adding of a condition to leave given before the passing of this Act;

    (b)   in the case of an order commencing section 25, may permit an order to be made in proceedings instituted before the passing of this Act;

    (c)   in the case of an order commencing section 26, may permit an order or regulations to have effect in relation to property which came into the possession of an immigration officer or the Secretary of State before the passing of this Act;

    (d)   in the case of an order commencing section 32—

        (i)   may provide for the section to apply to persons convicted before the passing of this Act who are in custody at the time of commencement or whose sentences are suspended at the time of commencement;

        (ii)   may modify the application of the section in relation to those persons so as to disapply, or apply only to a specified extent, Condition 2.

(5) An order shall be made by statutory instrument.

Subordinate Legislation

UK Borders Act 2007 (Commencement No 1 and Transitional Provisions) Order 2008, SI 2008/99; UK Borders Act 2007 (Commencement No 2 and Transitional Provisions) Order 2008, SI 2008/309; UK Borders Act 2007 (Commencement No 3 and Transitional Provisions) Order 2008, SI 2008/1818; UK Borders Act 2007 (Commencement No 4) Order 2008, SI 2008/2822; UK Borders Act 2007 (Commencement No 5) Order 2008, SI 2008/3136; UK Borders Act 2007 (Commencement No 6) Order 2010, SI 2010/606; UK Borders Act 2007 (Commencement No 7 and Transitional Provisions) Order 2011, SI 2011/1293.

60 Extent

(1)   Sections . . . 25 and 31(1) and (2) extend to—

    (a)   England and Wales, and

    (b)   Northern Ireland.

(2)   Other provisions of this Act extend (subject to subsection (3)) to—

    (a)   England and Wales,

    (b)   Scotland, and

    (c)   Northern Ireland.

(3)   A provision of this Act which amends another Act shall (subject to subsection (1)) have the same extent as the relevant part of the amended Act (ignoring extent by virtue of an Order in Council).

(4)   Her Majesty may by Order in Council direct that a provision of this Act is to extend, with or without modification or adaptation, to—

    (a)   any of the Channel Islands;

    (b)   the Isle of Man.

Amendment

Sub-s (1): words omitted repealed by the Borders, Citizenship and Immigration Act 2009, ss 52(3), 56, Schedule, Pt 3, as from 27 October 2014: see SI 2014/2634.

61 Citation

(1)   This Act may be cited as the UK Borders Act 2007.

(2)   A reference (in any enactment, including one passed or made before this Act) to "the Immigration Acts" is to—

    (a)   the Immigration Act 1971 (c 77),

    (b)   the Immigration Act 1988 (c 14),

    (c)   the Asylum and Immigration Appeals Act 1993 (c 23),

    (d)   the Asylum and Immigration Act 1996 (c 49),

    (e)   the Immigration and Asylum Act 1999 (c 33),

    (f)   the Nationality, Immigration and Asylum Act 2002 (c 41),

    (g)   the Asylum and Immigration (Treatment of Claimants, etc) Act 2004 (c 19),

    (h)   the Immigration, Asylum and Nationality Act 2006 (c 13), . . .

    (i)   this Act[; and

    (j)   the Immigration Act 2014.]

(3)   Section 64(2) of the Immigration, Asylum and Nationality Act 2006 (meaning of "Immigration Acts") shall cease to have effect.

(4)   . . .

Amendment

Sub-s (2): word omitted from para (h) repealed and para (j) inserted together with word preceding it, by the Immigration Act 2014, s 73(5), as from 14 May 2014.

Sub-s (4): amends the Interpretation Act 1978, Sch 1.

SCHEDULE

(The Schedule contains repeals which have been incorporated at the appropriate place in the work.)

CRIMINAL JUSTICE AND IMMIGRATION ACT 2008

2008 c 4

An Act to make further provision about criminal justice (including provision about the police) and dealing with offenders and defaulters; to make further provision about the management of offenders; to amend the criminal law; to make further provision for combatting crime and disorder; to make provision about the mutual recognition of financial penalties; to amend the Repatriation of Prisoners Act 1984; to make provision for a new immigration status in certain cases involving criminality; to make provision about the automatic deportation of criminals under the UK Borders Act 2007; to amend section 127 of the Criminal Justice and Public Order Act 1994 and to confer power to suspend the operation of that section; and for connected purposes.

[8 May 2008]

PART 10
SPECIAL IMMIGRATION STATUS

130 Designation

(1)   The Secretary of State may designate a person who satisfies Condition 1 or 2 (subject to subsections (4) and (5)).

(2)   Condition 1 is that the person—

    (a)   is a foreign criminal within the meaning of section 131, and

    (b)   is liable to deportation, but cannot be removed from the United Kingdom because of section 6 of the Human Rights Act 1998 (c 42) (public authority not to act contrary to Convention).

(3)   Condition 2 is that the person is a member of the family of a person who satisfies Condition 1

(4)   A person who has the right of abode in the United Kingdom may not be designated.

(5)   The Secretary of State may not designate a person if the Secretary of State thinks that an effect of designation would breach—

    (a)   the United Kingdom's obligations under the Refugee Convention, or

    (b)   the person's rights under the [EU] treaties.

Commencement

To be appointed: see s 153(7).

Amendment

Sub-s (5): in para (b) reference to "EU" in square brackets substituted by SI 2011/1043, art 6(1)(a). Date in force: 22 April 2011: see SI 2011/1043, art 2; for transitional savings see art 3(3) thereof.

131 "Foreign criminal"

(1)   For the purposes of section 130 "foreign criminal" means a person who—

    (a)   is not a British citizen, and

    (b)   satisfies any of the following Conditions.

(2)   Condition 1 is that section 72(2)(a) and (b) or (3)(a) to (c) of the Nationality, Immigration and Asylum Act 2002 (c 41) applies to the person (Article 33(2) of the Refugee Convention: imprisonment for at least two years).

(3)   Condition 2 is that—

    (a)   section 72(4)(a) or (b) of that Act applies to the person (person convicted of specified offence), and

(b)   the person has been sentenced to a period of imprisonment.

(4)   Condition 3 is that Article 1F of the Refugee Convention applies to the person (exclusions for criminals etc).

(5)   Section 72(6) of that Act (rebuttal of presumption under section 72(2) to (4)) has no effect in relation to Condition 1 or 2.

(6)   Section 72(7) of that Act (non-application pending appeal) has no effect in relation to Condition 1 or 2.

Commencement

To be appointed: see s 153(7).

132 Effect of designation

(1)   A designated person does not have leave to enter or remain in the United Kingdom.

(2)   For the purposes of a provision of the Immigration Acts and any other enactment which concerns or refers to immigration or nationality (including any provision which applies or refers to a provision of the Immigration Acts or any other enactment about immigration or nationality) a designated person—

(a)   is a person subject to immigration control,

(b)   is not to be treated as an asylum-seeker or a former asylum-seeker, and

(c)   is not in the United Kingdom in breach of the immigration laws.

(3)   Despite subsection (2)(c), time spent in the United Kingdom as a designated person may not be relied on by a person for the purpose of an enactment about nationality.

(4)   A designated person—

(a)   shall not be deemed to have been given leave in accordance with paragraph 6 of Schedule 2 to the Immigration Act 1971 (c 77) (notice of leave or refusal), and

(b)   may not be granted temporary admission to the United Kingdom under paragraph 21 of that Schedule.

(5)   Sections 134 and 135 make provision about support for designated persons and their dependants.

Commencement

To be appointed: see s 153(7).

133 Conditions

(1)   The Secretary of State or an immigration officer may by notice in writing impose a condition on a designated person.

(2)   A condition may relate to—

(a)   residence,

(b)   employment or occupation, or

(c)   reporting to the police, the Secretary of State or an immigration officer.

(3)   Section 36 of the Asylum and Immigration (Treatment of Claimants, etc) Act 2004 (c 19) (electronic monitoring) shall apply in relation to conditions imposed under this section as it applies to restrictions imposed under paragraph 21 of Schedule 2 to the Immigration Act 1971 (with a reference to the Immigration Acts being treated as including a reference to this section).

(4)   Section 69 of the Nationality, Immigration and Asylum Act 2002 (c 41) (reporting restrictions: travel expenses) shall apply in relation to conditions imposed under subsection (2)(c) above as it applies to restrictions imposed under paragraph 21 of Schedule 2 to the Immigration Act 1971.

(5)   A person who without reasonable excuse fails to comply with a condition imposed under this section commits an offence.

(6)   A person who is guilty of an offence under subsection (5) shall be liable on summary conviction to—

    (a)   a fine not exceeding level 5 on the standard scale,

    (b)   imprisonment for a period not exceeding 51 weeks, or

    (c)   both.

(7) A provision of the Immigration Act 1971 (c 77) which applies in relation to an offence under any provision of section 24(1) of that Act (illegal entry etc) shall also apply in relation to the offence under subsection (5) above.

(8) In the application of this section to Scotland or Northern Ireland the reference in subsection (6)(b) to 51 weeks shall be treated as a reference to six months.

Commencement

  To be appointed: see s 153(7).

134 Support

(1) Part VI of the Immigration and Asylum Act 1999 (c 33) (support for asylum-seekers) shall apply in relation to designated persons and their dependants as it applies in relation to asylum-seekers and their dependants.

(2) But the following provisions of that Part shall not apply—

    (a)   section 96 (kinds of support),

    (b)   section 97(1)(b) (desirability of providing accommodation in well-supplied area),

    (c)   section 100 (duty to co-operate in providing accommodation),

    (d)   section 101 (reception zones),

    (e)   section 108 (failure of sponsor to maintain),

    (f)   section 111 (grants to voluntary organisations), and

    (g)   section 113 (recovery of expenditure from sponsor).

(3) Support may be provided under section 95 of the 1999 Act as applied by this section—

    (a)   by providing accommodation appearing to the Secretary of State to be adequate for a person's needs;

    (b)   by providing what appear to the Secretary of State to be essential living needs;

    (c)   in other ways which the Secretary of State thinks necessary to reflect exceptional circumstances of a particular case.

(4) Support by virtue of subsection (3) may not be provided wholly or mainly by way of cash unless the Secretary of State thinks it appropriate because of exceptional circumstances.

(5) Section 4 of the 1999 Act (accommodation) shall not apply in relation to designated persons.

(6) . . .

Commencement

  To be appointed: see s 153(7).

Amendment

  Sub-s (6): repealed by the Housing and Regeneration Act 2008, ss 314, 321(1), Sch 15, Pt 3, paras 23, 24, Sch 16.

135 Support: supplemental

(1) A reference in an enactment to Part VI of the 1999 Act or to a provision of that Part includes a reference to that Part or provision as applied by section 134 above; and for that purpose—

    (a)   a reference to section 96 shall be treated as including a reference to section 134(3) above,

    (b)   a reference to a provision of section 96 shall be treated as including a reference to the corresponding provision of section 134(3), and

(c) a reference to asylum-seekers shall be treated as including a reference to designated persons.

(2) A provision of Part VI of the 1999 Act which requires or permits the Secretary of State to have regard to the temporary nature of support shall be treated, in the application of Part VI by virtue of section 134 above, as requiring the Secretary of State to have regard to the nature and circumstances of support by virtue of that section.

(3) . . .

(4) Any . . . instrument under Part VI of the 1999 Act—

    (a) may make provision in respect of that Part as it applies by virtue of section 134 above, as it applies otherwise than by virtue of that section, or both, and

    (b) may make different provision for that Part as it applies by virtue of section 134 above and as it applies otherwise than by virtue of that section.

(5) In the application of paragraph 9 of Schedule 8 to the 1999 Act (regulations: notice to quit accommodation) the reference in paragraph (2)(b) to the determination of a claim for asylum shall be treated as a reference to ceasing to be a designated person.

(6) The Secretary of State may by order repeal, modify or disapply (to any extent) section 134(4).

(7) . . .

Commencement

    To be appointed: see s 153(7).

Amendment

    Sub-s (3): repealed by SI 2009/1307, art 5(1), (2), Sch 1, para 288(a).

    Sub-s (4): word omitted repealed by SI 2009/1307, art 5(1), (2), Sch 1, para 288(b).

    Sub-s (7): repealed by the Housing and Regeneration Act 2008, ss 314, 321(1), Sch 15, Pt 3, paras 23, 25, Sch 16.

136 End of designation

(1) Designation lapses if the designated person—

    (a) is granted leave to enter or remain in the United Kingdom,

    (b) is notified by the Secretary of State or an immigration officer of a right of residence in the United Kingdom by virtue of the [EU] treaties,

    (c) leaves the United Kingdom, or

    (d) is made the subject of a deportation order under section 5 of the Immigration Act 1971 (c 77).

(2) After designation lapses support may not be provided by virtue of section 134, subject to the following exceptions.

(3) Exception 1 is that, if designation lapses under subsection (1)(a) or (b), support may be provided in respect of a period which—

    (a) begins when the designation lapses, and

    (b) ends on a date determined in accordance with an order of the Secretary of State.

(4) Exception 2 is that, if designation lapses under subsection (1)(d), support may be provided in respect of—

    (a) any period during which an appeal against the deportation order may be brought (ignoring any possibility of an appeal out of time with permission),

    (b) any period during which an appeal against the deportation order is pending, and

    (c) after an appeal ceases to be pending, such period as the Secretary of State may specify by order.

Commencement

To be appointed: see s 153(7).

Amendment

Sub-s (1): in para (b) reference to "EU" in square brackets substituted by SI 2011/1043, art 6(1)(a). Date in force: 22 April 2011: see SI 2011/1043, art 2; for transitional savings see art 3(3) thereof.

137 Interpretation: general

(1) This section applies to sections 130 to 136.

(2) A reference to a designated person is a reference to a person designated under section 130.

(3) "Family" shall be construed in accordance with section 5(4) of the Immigration Act 1971 (c 77) (deportation: definition of "family").

(4) "Right of abode in the United Kingdom" has the meaning given by section 2 of that Act.

(5) "The Refugee Convention" means the Convention relating to the Status of Refugees done at Geneva on 28th July 1951 and its Protocol.

(6) "Period of imprisonment" shall be construed in accordance with section 72(11)(b)(i) and (ii) of the Nationality, Immigration and Asylum Act 2002 (c 41).

(7) A voucher is not cash.

(8) A reference to a pending appeal has the meaning given by section 104(1) of that Act.

(9) A reference in an enactment to the Immigration Acts includes a reference to sections 130 to 136.

Commencement

To be appointed: see s 153(7).

BORDERS, CITIZENSHIP AND IMMIGRATION ACT 2009

2009 c 11

An Act to provide for customs functions to be exercisable by the Secretary of State, the Director of Border Revenue and officials designated by them; to make provision about the use and disclosure of customs information; to make provision for and in connection with the exercise of customs functions and functions relating to immigration, asylum or nationality; to make provision about citizenship and other nationality matters; to make further provision about immigration and asylum; and for connected purposes.

[21 July 2009]

PART 1
BORDER FUNCTIONS

General customs functions of the Secretary of State

1 General customs functions of the Secretary of State

(1) The functions of the Commissioners for Her Majesty's Revenue and Customs that are exercisable in relation to general customs matters are exercisable by the Secretary of State concurrently with the Commissioners.

(2)   For the purposes of this Part, a "general customs matter" is a matter in relation to which the Commissioners, or officers of Revenue and Customs, have functions, other than—

- (a)   a matter listed in Schedule 1 to the Commissioners for Revenue and Customs Act 2005 (c 11),
- (b)   any tax, duty or levy not mentioned in that Schedule,
- (c)   a matter in respect of which functions were transferred to the Commissioners from the Paymaster General under the Transfer of Functions (Office of Her Majesty's Paymaster General) Order 2006 (SI 2006/607),
- (d)   the subject matter of Directive 2005/60/EC on the prevention of the use of the financial system for the purpose of money laundering and terrorist financing (as amended from time to time), and
- (e)   the subject matter of Regulation (EC) No 1781/2006 on information on the payer accompanying transfers of funds (as amended from time to time).

(3)   If a function is exercisable by the Commissioners—

- (a)   in relation to a general customs matter, and
- (b)   in relation to any other matter,

the function is exercisable by the Secretary of State in relation to the general customs matter only.

(4)   So far as is appropriate for the purposes of or in connection with this section, references to the Commissioners for Her Majesty's Revenue and Customs, or to Her Majesty's Revenue and Customs, in an enactment, instrument or document to which this section applies are to be construed as including a reference to the Secretary of State.

(5)   References in this section (other than in subsection (8))—

- (a)   to functions of the Commissioners are to functions conferred by an enactment to which this section applies;
- (b)   to functions of officers of Revenue and Customs are to functions conferred by an enactment to which section 3 (designation of general customs officials) applies.

(6)   This section applies to—

- (a)   an enactment passed or made before the end of the session in which this Act is passed,
- [(aa)   sections 98 and 99 of the Energy Act 2013 (HMRC functions in relation to Office for Nuclear Regulation etc),] and
- (b)   an instrument or document issued before the passing of this Act.

(7)   This includes—

- (a)   section 5(2)(b) of the Commissioners for Revenue and Customs Act 2005 (c 11) (Commissioners' initial functions),
- (b)   section 9 of that Act (ancillary powers),
- (c)   section 25A(2) of that Act (certificates of debt),
- (d)   section 31 of that Act (obstruction), and
- (e)   section 33 of that Act (power of arrest) other than in its application to an offence under section 30 of that Act (impersonation),

but does not include any other enactment contained in that Act.

(8)   In this Part "general customs function" means—

- (a)   a function that is exercisable—
  - (i)   by the Secretary of State by virtue of this section, or
  - (ii)   by general customs officials by virtue of section 3,

(b) a function that is conferred on general customs officials or the Secretary of State by or by virtue of any of sections 22 to 24 (investigations and detention), or

(c) a function under [EU] law that is exercisable by the Secretary of State or general customs officials in relation to a matter—

   (i) in relation to which functions under [EU] law are exercisable by the Commissioners or officers of Revenue and Customs, and

   (ii) that is not listed in paragraphs (a) to (e) of subsection (2).

Amendment

Sub-s (6): para (aa) inserted by the Energy Act 2013, s 116(1), Sch 12, Pt 5, para 101(1), (2), as from 1 April 2014: see SI 2014/251, art 4(1).

Sub-s (8): in para (c) reference to "EU" in square brackets in both places it occurs substituted by SI 2011/1043, art 6(2)(a), as from 22 April 2011: see SI 2011/1043, art 2; for transitional savings see art 3(3) thereof.

2 Power of Secretary of State to modify functions

(1) The Secretary of State may by order—

(a) amend section 1(2) (matters that are general customs matters) so as to add, modify or remove a matter;

(b) amend that section so as to exclude its application in relation to a function of the Commissioners for Her Majesty's Revenue and Customs or to modify or remove a reference to a function previously so excluded;

(c) make provision for that section to apply in relation to a function conferred on the Commissioners by an enactment passed or made after the end of the session in which this Act is passed;

(d) modify any enactment (including an enactment passed or made after the passing of this Act) in consequence of provision made under any of paragraphs (a) to (c);

(e) make provision for a function of the Secretary of State or general customs officials to be treated, or not to be treated, as a general customs function.

(2) The power under subsection (1)(a) may not be exercised to add any of the following to section 1(2)—

(a) a matter listed in Schedule 1 to the Commissioners for Revenue and Customs Act 2005 (c 11),

(b) value added tax,

(c) a customs revenue matter (as to which, see section 7), or

(d) a matter listed at section 7(2)(e).

(3) The Secretary of State must consult the Treasury before exercising the power under this section.

General customs officials

3 Designation of general customs officials

(1) The Secretary of State by whom general customs functions are exercisable may designate—

(a) an immigration officer, or

(b) any other official in that Secretary of State's department,

as a general customs official.

(2) A general customs official—

(a) has, in relation to a general customs matter, the same functions as an officer of Revenue and Customs would have, and

(b) may exercise the functions conferred on the Secretary of State by section 1 (general customs functions of the Secretary of State).

(3) This does not prevent the exercise of the Secretary of State's functions by any other official of the Secretary of State.

(4) If a function within subsection (2) is exercisable—

    (a) in relation to a general customs matter, and

    (b) in relation to any other matter,

the function is exercisable by a general customs official in relation to the general customs matter only.

(5) So far as is appropriate for the purposes of or in connection with this section, references to an officer of Revenue and Customs, or to Her Majesty's Revenue and Customs, in an enactment, instrument or document to which this section applies are to be construed as including a reference to a general customs official.

(6) References in this section to functions of an officer of Revenue and Customs are to functions conferred by an enactment to which this section applies.

(7) This section applies to—

    (a) an enactment passed or made, or an instrument or document issued, before this Act is passed, and

    (b) subject to express provision to the contrary, an enactment passed or made, or an instrument or document issued, after this Act is passed.

(8) This includes—

    (a) section 2(4) of the Commissioners for Revenue and Customs Act 2005 (c 11) (continuation of anything begun by one officer by another),

    (b) section 6 of that Act (officers' initial functions),

    (c) section 25(1) and (5) of that Act (conduct of civil proceedings in a magistrates' court or in the sheriff court),

    (d) section 25A(1) of that Act (certificates of debt),

    (e) section 31 of that Act (obstruction),

    (f) section 32 of that Act (assault), and

    (g) section 33 of that Act (power of arrest) other than in its application to an offence under section 30 of that Act (impersonation),

but does not otherwise include any enactment contained in that Act.

(9) This section has effect subject to—

    (a) any limitation specified in the official's designation under section 4 (supplementary provisions about designation), and

    (b) any designation of the official under section 11 (designation of customs revenue officials).

4 Designation: supplementary

(1) A designation under section 3 is subject to such limitations as may be specified in the designation.

(2) A limitation specified under subsection (1) may, in particular, relate to—

    (a) the functions that are exercisable by virtue of the designation, or

    (b) the purposes for which those functions are exercisable.

(3) A designation under section 3—

    (a) may be permanent or for a specified period,

    (b) may (in either case) be withdrawn, and

    (c) may be varied.

(4) The power to designate, or to withdraw or vary a designation, is exercised by the Secretary of State giving notice to the official in question.

(5) The Secretary of State may designate an official under section 3 only if the Secretary of State is satisfied that the official—

    (a) is capable of effectively carrying out the functions that are exercisable by virtue of the designation,

(b)   has received adequate training in respect of the exercise of those functions, and

(c)   is otherwise a suitable person to exercise those functions.

5 Directions by the Secretary of State

A general customs official must comply with the directions of the Secretary of State in the exercise of general customs functions.

The Director of Border Revenue

6 The Director of Border Revenue

(1)   The Secretary of State must designate an official in the department of the Secretary of State by whom general customs functions are exercisable as the Director of Border Revenue.

(2)   Before making a designation under this section, the Secretary of State must obtain the consent of the Treasury to the designation.

7 Customs revenue functions of the Director

(1)   The functions of the Commissioners for Her Majesty's Revenue and Customs that are exercisable in relation to customs revenue matters are exercisable by the Director of Border Revenue concurrently with the Commissioners.

(2)   For the purposes of this Part, each of the following is a "customs revenue matter"—

    (a)   agricultural levies (within the meaning given by section 6(8) of the European Communities Act 1972 (c 68));

    (b)   anti-dumping duty (within the meaning of Council Regulation (EC) No 384/96, as amended from time to time);

    (c)   countervailing duty (within the meaning of Council Regulation (EC) No 2026/97, as amended from time to time);

    (d)   customs duties;

    (e)   duties of excise other than—

        (i)   . . . .

        (ii)   bingo duty,

        (iii)   gaming duty,

        (iv)   general betting duty,

        (v)   lottery duty,

        (vi)   pool betting duty, . . .

        (vii)   remote gaming duty, [and

        (viii)   machine games duty];

    (f)   value added tax so far as relating to the export of goods from, or the import of goods into, the United Kingdom.

(3)   Subsection (1) does not apply to—

    (a)   any function of making, by statutory instrument, any regulations, rules or an order;

    (b)   any function of issuing notices, directions or conditions that relate to value added tax and that apply generally to any person falling within their terms.

(4)   If a function is exercisable by the Commissioners—

    (a)   in relation to a customs revenue matter, and

    (b)   in relation to any other matter,

the function is exercisable by the Director in relation to the customs revenue matter only.

(5)   So far as is appropriate for the purposes of or in connection with this section, references to the Commissioners for Her Majesty's Revenue and Customs, or to Her

the function is exercisable by a customs revenue official in relation to the customs revenue matter only.

(4)   So far as is appropriate for the purposes of or in connection with this section, references to an officer of Revenue and Customs, or to Her Majesty's Revenue and Customs, in an enactment, instrument or document to which this section applies are to be construed as including a reference to a customs revenue official.

(5)   References in this section to functions of an officer of Revenue and Customs are to functions conferred by an enactment to which this section applies.

(6)   This section applies to—

    (a)   an enactment passed or made, or an instrument or document issued, before this Act is passed, and

    (b)   subject to express provision to the contrary, an enactment passed or made, or an instrument or document issued, after this Act is passed.

(7)   This includes—

    (a)   section 2(4) of the Commissioners for Revenue and Customs Act 2005 (c 11) (continuation of anything begun by one officer by another),

    (b)   section 6 of that Act (officers' initial functions),

    (c)   section 25(1), (1A) and (5) of that Act (conduct of civil proceedings),

    (d)   section 25A(1) of that Act (certificates of debt),

    (e)   section 26 of that Act (rewards),

    (f)   section 31 of that Act (obstruction),

    (g)   section 32 of that Act (assault), and

    (h)   section 33 of that Act (power of arrest) other than in its application to an offence under section 30 of that Act (impersonation),

but does not otherwise include any enactment contained in that Act.

(8)   This section has effect subject to—

    (a)   any limitation specified in the official's designation under section 12 (supplementary provisions about designation), and

    (b)   any designation of the official under section 3 (designation of general customs officials).

12 Designation: supplementary

(1)   A designation under section 11 is subject to such limitations as may be specified in the designation.

(2)   A limitation specified under subsection (1) may, in particular, relate to—

    (a)   the functions that are exercisable by virtue of the designation, or

    (b)   the purposes for which those functions are exercisable.

(3)   A designation under section 11—

    (a)   may be permanent or for a specified period,

    (b)   may (in either case) be withdrawn, and

    (c)   may be varied.

(4)   The power to designate, or to withdraw or vary a designation, is exercised by the Director of Border Revenue giving notice to the official in question.

(5)   The Director may designate an official under section 11 only if the Director is satisfied that the official—

    (a)   is capable of effectively carrying out the functions that are exercisable by virtue of the designation,

    (b)   has received adequate training in respect of the exercise of those functions, and

    (c)   is otherwise a suitable person to exercise those functions.

13 Directions by the Director

A customs revenue official must comply with the directions of the Director of Border Revenue in the exercise of customs revenue functions.

14 Use and disclosure of customs information

(1)   A person to whom this section applies may—

    (a)   use customs information acquired by that person in connection with a function exercisable by that person for the purpose of any other function exercisable by that person, and

    (b)   disclose customs information to any other person to whom this section applies for the purpose of a function exercisable by that person.

(2)   The persons to whom this section applies are—

    (a)   a designated customs official,

    (b)   an immigration officer,

    (c)   the Secretary of State by whom general customs functions are exercisable,

    (d)   any other Minister of the Crown in the department of that Secretary of State,

    (e)   the Director of Border Revenue, and

    (f)   a person acting on behalf of a person mentioned in paragraphs (a) to (e).

(3)   This section is subject to any provision that restricts or prohibits the use or disclosure of information and that is contained in—

    (a)   this Part,

    (b)   any other enactment, or

    (c)   an international or other agreement to which the United Kingdom or Her Majesty's Government is party.

(4)   In subsection (3) the reference to an enactment does not include an enactment contained in, or in an instrument made under—

    (a)   an Act of the Scottish Parliament,

    (b)   a Measure or Act of the National Assembly for Wales, or

    (c)   Northern Ireland legislation.

(5)   This section is without prejudice to—

    (a)   the use by a person to whom it applies of information other than customs information;

    (b)   the disclosure by or to a person to whom it applies of information other than customs information.

(6)   In this Part—

"customs function" means a general customs function or a customs revenue function;

"customs information" means information acquired or capable of being acquired as a result of the exercise of a customs function;

"customs revenue information" means information acquired or capable of being acquired as a result of the exercise of a customs revenue function;

"designated customs official" means a general customs official or a customs revenue official.

(7)   It is immaterial for the purposes of subsection (6)—

    (a)   whether the information was acquired or is capable of being acquired by the person by whom it is held or another person;

    (b)   whether the information was also acquired or is also capable of being acquired in the exercise of any other function.

15 Prohibition on disclosure of personal customs information

(1)   A person who is or was a relevant official, the Secretary of State by whom general customs functions are exercisable or another Minister of the Crown in that Secretary of State's department may not disclose personal customs information to a person who is not—

    (a)   a relevant official, or

    (b)   a Minister of the Crown in that department.

(2)   A person who is or was a relevant official may not disclose personal customs revenue information to a Minister of the Crown.

(3)   In this Part "relevant official" means—

    (a)   a designated customs official,

    (b)   an immigration officer,

    (c)   the Director of Border Revenue, or

    (d)   a person acting on behalf of—

        (i)   the Secretary of State by whom general customs functions are exercisable, or

        (ii)   a person mentioned in paragraphs (a) to (c).

(4)   In this Part—

"personal customs information" means customs information relating to a person that—

    (a)   identifies that person, or

    (b)   enables that person to be identified (either by itself or in combination with other information);

"personal customs revenue information" means customs revenue information relating to a person that—

    (a)   identifies that person, or

    (b)   enables that person to be identified (either by itself or in combination with other information).

(5)   A person—

    (a)   does not breach subsection (1) by disclosing information the person knows was acquired otherwise than as the result of the exercise of a customs function;

    (b)   does not breach subsection (2) by disclosing information the person knows was acquired otherwise than as the result of the exercise of a customs revenue function.

(6)   Subsections (1) and (2) are also subject to—

    (a)   section 16 (exceptions to the prohibition in this section), and

    (b)   any enactment (other than an enactment contained in this Part) permitting disclosure, where the disclosure in question does not contravene any restriction imposed by the Commissioners for Her Majesty's Revenue and Customs on the disclosure of customs revenue information.

(7)   This section does not apply to information supplied by or on behalf of Her Majesty's Revenue and Customs [or to information supplied by or on behalf of the Crown Prosecution Service under section 40 or 41A of the UK Borders Act 2007].

This is without prejudice to any other restriction on the disclosure of such information.

(8)   In subsection (6) the reference to an enactment does not include an enactment contained in, or in an instrument made under—

    (a)   an Act of the Scottish Parliament,

    (b)   a Measure or Act of the National Assembly for Wales, or

    (c)   Northern Ireland legislation.

Amendment

  Sub-s (7): words in square brackets substituted by SI 2014/834, reg 3(3), Sch 2, paras 65, 66. Date in force: 27 March 2014: see SI 2014/834, art 1.

16 Exceptions to section 15 prohibition

(1)   A person does not breach section 15(1) or (2) by making a disclosure—

    (a)   to which any of subsections (3) to (8) applies, and

(b)   which, in the case of a disclosure of customs revenue information, does not contravene any restriction imposed by the Commissioners for Her Majesty's Revenue and Customs.

(2) Subsection (1)(b) does not apply if the person making the disclosure knows that the information was acquired otherwise than as the result of the exercise of a customs revenue function.

(3) This subsection applies to a disclosure which is made for the purposes of—

(a)   a customs function,

(b)   a function relating to immigration, asylum or nationality,

(c)   a function relating to national security, or

(d)   a function relating to the prevention or detection of crime.

(4) This subsection applies to a disclosure which is made to a person exercising public functions (whether or not within the United Kingdom) for the purposes of any of those functions.

(5) This subsection applies to a disclosure which—

(a)   is made for the purposes of civil proceedings (whether or not within the United Kingdom) relating to a function within subsection (3),

(b)   is made for the purposes of a criminal investigation or criminal proceedings (whether or not within the United Kingdom), or

(c)   is made in pursuance of an order of a court.

(6) This subsection applies to a disclosure which is made with the consent of each person to whom the information relates.

(7) This subsection applies to a disclosure which is made in order to comply with an obligation of the United Kingdom, or Her Majesty's Government, under an international or other agreement.

(8) This subsection applies to a disclosure—

(a)   to a person specified in regulations made jointly by the Treasury and the Secretary of State, or

(b)   of a kind specified in such regulations.

17 Prohibition on further disclosure

(1) A person to whom information is disclosed in reliance on section 16 or this section may not disclose that information without the consent of a relevant official (which may be general or specific).

(2) A person does not breach subsection (1) by making a disclosure—

(a)   to which any of subsections (3) to (8) of section 16 applies, and

(b)   which, in the case of a disclosure of customs revenue information, does not contravene any restriction imposed by the Commissioners for Her Majesty's Revenue and Customs.

(3) Subsection (2)(b) does not apply if the person making the disclosure knows that the information was acquired otherwise than as the result of the exercise of a customs revenue function.

(4) This section is also subject to any other enactment permitting disclosure.

(5) In subsection (4) the reference to an enactment does not include an enactment contained in, or in an instrument made under—

(a)   an Act of the Scottish Parliament,

(b)   a Measure or Act of the National Assembly for Wales, or

(c)   Northern Ireland legislation.

18 Offence of wrongful disclosure

(1) A person commits an offence if the person breaches section 15(1) or (2) or 17(1).

(2) It is a defence for a person charged with an offence under this section to prove that the person reasonably believed—

(a)   that the disclosure was lawful, or

    (b)   that the information had already and lawfully been made available to the public.

(3)   A prosecution for an offence under this section—

    (a)   may be brought in England and Wales only with the consent of the Director of Public Prosecutions . . . ;

    (b)   may be brought in Northern Ireland only with the consent of the Director of Public Prosecutions for Northern Ireland.

(4)   This section is without prejudice to the pursuit of any remedy or the taking of any action in relation to a breach of section 15(1) or (2) or 17(1) (whether or not this section applies to the breach).

(5)   A person guilty of an offence under this section is liable—

    (a)   on conviction on indictment to imprisonment for a term not exceeding 2 years, or to a fine, or to both;

    (b)   on summary conviction—

        (i)   in England and Wales, to imprisonment for a term not exceeding 12 months, or to a fine not exceeding the statutory maximum, or to both;

        (ii)   in Scotland, to imprisonment for a term not exceeding 12 months, or to a fine not exceeding the statutory maximum, or to both;

        (iii)   in Northern Ireland, to imprisonment for a term not exceeding 6 months, or to a fine not exceeding the statutory maximum, or to both.

(6)   In relation to an offence under this section committed before the commencement of section 282 of the Criminal Justice Act 2003 (c 44) (increase in maximum sentence on summary conviction of offence triable either way), the reference in subsection (5)(b)(i) to 12 months has effect as if it were a reference to 6 months.

Amendment

Sub-s (3): words omitted from para (a) repealed by SI 2014/834, reg 3(3), Sch 2, paras 65, 67. Date in force: 27 March 2014: see SI 2014/834, art 1.

19 Application of statutory provisions

(1)   Nothing in sections 14 to 17 authorises the making of a disclosure which—

    (a)   contravenes the Data Protection Act 1998 (c 29), or

    (b)   is prohibited by Part 1 of the Regulation of Investigatory Powers Act 2000 (c 23).

(2)   Information whose disclosure is prohibited by section 15(1) or (2) or 17(1) is exempt information by virtue of section 44(1)(a) of the Freedom of Information Act 2000 (c 36).

(3)   Sections 15(6), 16 and 17(2) and (4) are to be disregarded in determining for the purposes of subsection (2) whether the disclosure of personal customs information is prohibited by section 15(1) or (2) or 17(1).

(4)   In section 23 of the Commissioners for Revenue and Customs Act 2005 (c 11) (freedom of information), after subsection (1) insert—

    "(1A)   Subsections (2) and (3) of section 18 are to be disregarded in determining for the purposes of subsection (1) of this section whether the disclosure of revenue and customs information relating to a person is prohibited by subsection (1) of that section."

20, 21

(S 20 inserts the UK Borders Act 2007, ss 41A, 41B and amends s 42 of that Act; s 21 amends the Immigration, Asylum and Nationality Act 2006, s 36.)

Investigations and detention

22 Application of the PACE orders

(1) Subject as follows, the PACE orders—

    (a) apply to criminal investigations conducted by designated customs officials and relating to a general customs matter or customs revenue matter as they apply to relevant investigations conducted by officers of Revenue and Customs, and

    (b) apply to persons detained by designated customs officials as they apply to persons detained by officers of Revenue and Customs.

(2) Each of the following is a PACE order for the purposes of this section—

    (a) . . .

    (b) the Police and Criminal Evidence (Application to Revenue and Customs) Order (Northern Ireland) 2007 (SR 2007/464).

(3) In the application of the PACE orders by virtue of this section—

    (a) subject to the following provisions of this subsection, references in those orders to an officer of Revenue and Customs are to be read as references to a designated customs official;

    (b) references in those orders to the Commissioners are to be read as references to—

        (i) the Secretary of State in relation to general customs matters, or

        (ii) the Director of Border Revenue in relation to customs revenue matters;

    (c) references in those orders to Her Majesty's Revenue and Customs or to Revenue and Customs are to be read as references to—

        (i) the Secretary of State in so far as the Secretary of State has general customs functions,

        (ii) the Director of Border Revenue, and

        (iii) designated customs officials;

    (d) references in those orders to an office of Revenue and Customs are to be read as references to an office of the UK Border Agency;

    (e) references in those orders to a designated office of Revenue and Customs are to be read as references to a designated office of the UK Border Agency;

    (f) references in those orders to a relevant indictable offence are to be read as references to an indictable offence that relates to a general customs matter or a customs revenue matter;

    (g) references in those orders to a relevant investigation are to be read as references to a criminal investigation conducted by a designated customs official that relates to a general customs matter or a customs revenue matter;

    (h) references in those orders to a person being in Revenue and Customs detention are to be read as references to a person being in UK Border Agency detention;

    (i) references in those orders to an officer of Revenue and Customs of at least the grade of officer are to be read as references to a designated customs official of at least the grade of immigration officer or executive officer;

    (j) references in those orders to an officer of Revenue and Customs of at least the grade of higher officer are to be read as references to a designated customs official of at least the grade of chief immigration officer or higher executive officer;

    (k)   references in those orders to an officer of Revenue and Customs of at least the grade of senior officer are to be read as references to a designated customs official of at least the grade of immigration inspector or senior executive officer;

    (l)   any other references in those orders to an officer of Revenue and Customs occupying a specified post or grade are to be read as references to the Secretary of State.

(4)   For the purposes of this section—

    (a)   a person is in UK Border Agency detention if—

        (i)   the person has been taken to an office of the UK Border Agency after being arrested for an offence, or

        (ii)   the person is arrested at an office of the UK Border Agency after attending voluntarily at the office or accompanying a designated customs official to it,

and is detained there or is detained elsewhere in the charge of a designated customs official, and

    (b)   "office of the UK Border Agency" means premises wholly or partly occupied by designated customs officials.

(5)   This section does not apply to the following provisions of the PACE orders—

    (a)–(d) . . .

    (e)   in article 2(1) of the Police and Criminal Evidence (Application to Revenue and Customs) Order (Northern Ireland) 2007 (SR 2007/464), the definitions of "the Commissioners", "office of Revenue and Customs", "relevant indictable offence" and "relevant investigation";

    (f)   article 2(2) of that order (Revenue and Customs detention);

    (g)   article 7 of that order (restriction on other powers to apply for production of documents);

    (h)   article 15 of that order (authorisation).

(6)   A person may be transferred—

    (a)   between UK Border Agency detention and Revenue and Customs detention;

    (b)   between Revenue and Customs detention and UK Border Agency detention;

    (c)   between UK Border Agency detention and police detention;

    (d)   between police detention and UK Border Agency detention.

[(6A)   Subsection (6) has effect only in relation to Northern Ireland.]

(7)   The references to police detention in subsection (6)—

    (a)   . . .

    (b)   in relation to Northern Ireland, are to be construed in accordance with the Police and Criminal Evidence (Northern Ireland) Order 1989 (SI 1989/1341 (NI 12)).

(8)   Expressions used in this section that are defined in a PACE order have the same meaning as in that PACE order.

(9)   This section does not affect the generality of sections 1(4), 3(5), 7(5) and 11(4) (construction of statutory Etc references to the Commissioners for Her Majesty's Revenue and Customs, officers of Revenue and Customs and Her Majesty's Revenue and Customs).

Amendment

Sub-s (2): para (a) repealed by SI 2013/1542, art 32(1), (2), as from 25 June 2013.

Sub-s (5): paras (a)–(d) repealed by SI 2013/1542, art 32(1), (3), as from 25 June 2013.

Sub-s (6A): inserted by SI 2013/1542, art 32(1), (4), as from 25 June 2013.

Sub-s (7): para (a) repealed by SI 2013/1542, art 32(1), (5), as from 25 June 2013.

23 Investigations and detention: England and Wales and Northern Ireland

(1) The Secretary of State may by order provide for any provision of an enactment listed in subsection (2) that relates to investigations of offences conducted by police officers or to persons detained by the police to apply, subject to such modifications as the order may specify, in relation to—

    (a)   investigations conducted by designated customs officials,

    (b)   persons detained by designated customs officials,

    (c)   investigations conducted by immigration officers, or

    (d)   persons detained by immigration officers.

(2) Those enactments are—

    (a)   the Police and Criminal Evidence Act 1984 (c 60), and

    (b)   the Police and Criminal Evidence (Northern Ireland) Order 1989 (SI 1989/1341 (NI 12)).

(3) An order under this section may make, in relation to designated customs officials, immigration officers, the Secretary of State or the Director of Border Revenue, provision similar to that which may be made in relation to officers of Revenue and Customs or the Commissioners for Her Majesty's Revenue and Customs under—

    (a)   section 114 of the Police and Criminal Evidence Act 1984, or

    (b)   article 85 of the Police and Criminal Evidence (Northern Ireland) Order 1989.

(4) If an order under this section provides that a function may be exercised only by a person acting with the authority of the Secretary of State or the Director of Border Revenue, a certificate of the Secretary of State or (as the case may be) the Director that the person had authority to exercise the function is conclusive evidence of that fact.

(5) An order under this section may amend or repeal section 22 (application of the PACE orders).

Subordinate Legislation

Police and Criminal Evidence Act 1984 (Application to immigration officers and designated customs officials in England and Wales) Order 2013, SI 2013/1542.

24, 25

(S 24 inserts the Criminal Law (Consolidation) (Scotland) Act 1995, s 26C; s 25 amends the Immigration and Asylum Act 1999, s 147.)

Transfer of property etc

26 Transfer schemes

(1) The Commissioners for Her Majesty's Revenue and Customs may make one or more schemes for the transfer of specified property, rights or liabilities or property, rights or liabilities of a specified description between—

    (a)   the Commissioners or officers of Revenue and Customs, and

    (b)   the Secretary of State, the Director of Border Revenue or designated customs officials.

(2) A scheme under subsection (1) may, in particular—

    (a)   create interests or rights, or impose liabilities, in relation to property, rights or liabilities transferred by virtue of the scheme or retained by a transferor;

    (b)   apportion property, rights or liabilities between a transferor and a transferee.

(3) A scheme under subsection (1) may—

> (a) provide for anything done by or in relation to a transferor in connection with anything transferred to have effect as if done by or in relation to a transferee;
>
> (b) permit anything (including any legal proceedings) relating to anything transferred by the scheme which is in the process of being done by or in relation to a transferor when the transfer takes effect to be continued by or in relation to a transferee;
>
> (c) provide for references to a transferor in an agreement (whether written or not), instrument or other document relating to anything transferred by the scheme to be treated as references to a transferee;
>
> (d) include other incidental, supplementary, consequential, transitional or transitory provision or savings.

(4) A scheme under subsection (1) may provide for a transfer of property, rights or liabilities—

> (a) whether or not they would otherwise be capable of being transferred,
>
> (b) without any instrument or other formality being required, and
>
> (c) irrespective of any requirement for consent that would otherwise apply.

(5) The Commissioners may make one or more schemes providing for—

> (a) any specified thing or anything of a specified description done by or in relation to the Commissioners or an officer of Revenue and Customs in connection with a relevant function to have effect as if done by or in relation to the Secretary of State, the Director or a designated customs official;
>
> (b) any specified thing or anything of a specified description (including any legal proceedings) relating to a relevant function done by or in relation to the Commissioners or an officer of Revenue and Customs to be continued by or in relation to the Secretary of State, the Director or a designated customs official.

(6) A scheme under this section—

> (a) comes into force in accordance with its terms;
>
> (b) may be amended or revoked.

(7) In this section—

"relevant function" means a function which before the passing of this Act was exercisable by the Commissioners or officers of Revenue and Customs (whether or not it remains so exercisable) and that—

> (a) is conferred by or by virtue of this Part on the Secretary of State, the Director or a designated customs official, or
>
> (b) is a function under [EU] law that is exercisable by the Secretary of State, the Director or a designated customs official;

"specified" means specified in the scheme.

Amendment

Sub-s (7): in definition "relevant function" in para (b) reference to "EU" in square brackets substituted by SI 2011/1043, art 6(2)(a), as from 22 April 2011: see SI 2011/1043, art 2; for transitional savings see art 3(3) thereof.

27 Facilities and services

(1) Her Majesty's Revenue and Customs may make facilities and services available to any person by whom functions relating to immigration, asylum or nationality, or customs functions, are exercisable for the purposes of the exercise of any of those functions.

(2) A person by whom functions relating to immigration, asylum or nationality, or customs functions, are exercisable may make facilities and services available to Her Majesty's Revenue and Customs for the purposes of the exercise of a function of Her Majesty's Revenue and Customs.

Inspection and oversight

28 Inspections by the Chief Inspector of the UK Border Agency

(1)–(9) . . .

(10) The person holding the office of the Chief Inspector of the Border and Immigration Agency immediately before the day on which this section comes into force is to be treated, on and after that day, as if appointed as the Chief Inspector of the UK Border Agency under section 48(1) of the UK Borders Act 2007 (c 30).

Amendment
  Sub-ss (1)–(9) amend the UK Borders Act 2007, ss 48, 53, 56.

29 Inspections by Her Majesty's Inspectors of Constabulary etc

(1) The Secretary of State may make regulations conferring functions on Her Majesty's Inspectors of Constabulary, the Scottish inspectors or the Northern Ireland inspectors in relation to—

  (a) designated customs officials, and officials of the Secretary of State exercising customs functions;

  (b) immigration officers, and officials of the Secretary of State exercising functions relating to immigration, asylum or nationality;

  (c) the Secretary of State in so far as the Secretary of State has general customs functions;

  (d) the Secretary of State in so far as the Secretary of State has functions relating to immigration, asylum or nationality;

  (e) the Director of Border Revenue and any person exercising functions of the Director;

  (f) persons providing services pursuant to arrangements relating to the discharge of a function of a person mentioned in paragraphs (a) to (e).

(2) Regulations under subsection (1) may—

  (a) in relation to Her Majesty's Inspectors of Constabulary, apply (with or without modification) or make provision similar to any provision of sections 54 to 56 of the Police Act 1996 (c 16) (inspection);

  (b) in relation to the Scottish inspectors, apply (with or without modification) or make provision similar to any provision of [Chapter 11 of Part 1 of the Police and Fire Reform (Scotland) Act 2012 (Her Majesty's inspectors of constabulary)];

  (c) in relation to the Northern Ireland inspectors, apply (without or without modification) or make provision similar to any provision of section 41 or 42 of the Police (Northern Ireland) Act 1998 (c 32) (inspection).

(3) Regulations under subsection (1)—

  (a) may enable a Minister of the Crown to require an inspection to be carried out;

  (b) must provide for a report of an inspection to be made and, subject to any exceptions required or permitted by the regulations, published;

  (c) must provide for an annual report by Her Majesty's Inspectors of Constabulary;

  (d) may make provision for payment to or in respect of Her Majesty's Inspectors of Constabulary, the Scottish inspectors or the Northern Ireland inspectors.

(4) An inspection carried out by virtue of this section may not address a matter of a kind which the Comptroller and Auditor General may examine under section 6 of the National Audit Act 1983 (c 44).

(5) An inspection carried out by virtue of this section must be carried out jointly by Her Majesty's Inspectors of Constabulary and the Scottish inspectors—

  (a) if it is carried out wholly in Scotland, or

(b)   in a case where it is carried out partly in Scotland, to the extent that it is carried out there.

(6) In this section—

(a)   "the Scottish inspectors" means the inspectors of constabulary appointed under [section 71(2) of the Police and Fire Reform (Scotland) Act 2012];

(b)   "the Northern Ireland inspectors" means the inspectors of constabulary appointed under section 41(1) of the Police (Northern Ireland) Act 1998.

Amendment

Sub-s (2): in para (b) words in square brackets substituted by SI 2013/602, art 26, Sch 2, Pt 1, para 61(a), as from 1 April 2013.

Sub-s (6): in para (a) words in square brackets substituted by SI 2013/602, art 26, Sch 2, Pt 1, para 61(b), as from 1 April 2013.

Subordinate Legislation

Customs (Inspections by Her Majesty's Inspectors of Constabulary and the Scottish Inspectors) Regulations 2012, SI 2012/2840; Customs (Inspections by Her Majesty's Inspectors of Constabulary and the Scottish Inspectors) (Amendment) Regulations 2014, SI 2014/907.

30

(Amends the Police and Justice Act 2006, s 41.)

Other provisions

31

(Repealed by SI 2014/834, reg 3(3), Sch 2, paras 65, 68. Date in force: 27 March 2014: see SI 2014/834, art 1.)

32 Payment of revenue to the Commissioners

(1) The Director of Border Revenue must pay money received by way of revenue or security for revenue in the exercise of the Director's customs revenue functions to the Commissioners for Her Majesty's Revenue and Customs.

(2) The Secretary of State must pay money received by way of revenue in the exercise of the Secretary of State's general customs functions to the Commissioners.

(3) A payment under subsection (1) or (2) must be made—

(a)   at such times and in such manner as the Treasury directs, and

(b)   after deduction of payments in connection with drawback and repayments.

(4) If the Commissioners think that the funds available to the Director or the Secretary of State may be insufficient to make a payment in connection with drawback or a repayment, the Commissioners may—

(a)   pay money to the Director or the Secretary of State (as the case may be) to enable the payment or repayment to be made, or

(b)   make the payment or repayment on behalf of the Director or the Secretary of State (as the case may be).

(5) Subsection (4) applies whether or not the reason for a deficiency is or may be that an amount has been paid or retained on the basis of an estimate that has proved or may prove to be inaccurate.

(6) A payment by the Commissioners under that subsection is to be treated for the purposes of the Commissioners for Revenue and Customs Act 2005 (c 11) as a disbursement of a kind specified in section 44(3) of that Act.

(7) In this section—

"repayments" includes—

> (a) payments in respect of actual or deemed credits relating to any tax, duty or levy, and
>
> (b) payments of interest (or repayment supplement) on—
>> (i) repayments, or
>> (ii) payments treated as repayments;

"revenue" means—

> (a) taxes, duties and levies,
>
> (b) the proceeds of forfeitures made and penalties imposed under the customs and excise Acts (within the meaning of section 1 of the Customs and Excise Management Act 1979 (c 2)),
>
> (c) a sum paid, or the proceeds of sale, under paragraph 16 of Schedule 3 to that Act, and
>
> (d) the proceeds of penalties imposed in accordance with Regulation (EC) No 1889/2005 on controls of cash entering or leaving the [European Union] (including penalties imposed under that Regulation as amended from time to time);

"security for revenue" means any sum paid as security for a tax or duty.

Amendment

Sub-s (7): in definition "revenue" in para (d) words "European Union" in square brackets substituted by SI 2011/1043, art 4(1), as from 22 April 2011: see SI 2011/1043, art 2; for transitional savings see art 3(3) thereof.

33 Power to require payment into the Consolidated Fund

(1) The Treasury may by order make provision for—

> (a) requiring the payment of sums received by the Secretary of State or the Director in the exercise of their functions into the Consolidated Fund;
>
> (b) permitting the deduction of disbursements before such payments are made;
>
> (c) requiring the Secretary of State or the Director to provide accounts of the receipt and disposal of revenue;
>
> (d) permitting the Treasury to make payments to the Secretary of State or the Director out of the Consolidated Fund to enable them to make disbursements.

(2) An order under this section may amend or repeal section 32 (payment of revenue to the Commissioners).

34

(*This section ceased to have effect on the coming into force of s 55 of this Act (ie 2 November 2009: see SI 2009/2731, art 2(a)), by virtue of sub-s (6) hereof.*)

Supplementary

35 Power to modify enactments

(1) The Secretary of State may by order provide for an enactment (or a description of enactments) to apply in relation to—

> (a) relevant persons, or
>
> (b) the exercise of functions by relevant persons,

with such modifications as the Secretary of State considers necessary or expedient.

(2) In this section—

> (a) "relevant persons" means—

(i)   the Secretary of State by whom general customs functions are exercisable,

(ii)   the Director of Border Revenue, and

(iii) designated customs officials, immigration officers and officials in the department of that Secretary of State, and

(b)   a reference to relevant persons includes a reference to any description of relevant persons.

(3) An order under this section may, in particular, include provision for or in connection with—

(a)   extending to relevant persons an exemption or protection afforded by an enactment to any other description of persons;

(b)   providing for the disclosure of information to, or the doing of other things in relation to, relevant persons.

(4) The Secretary of State must consult the Commissioners for Her Majesty's Revenue and Customs before making an order under this section that—

(a)   makes provision in relation to a general customs matter or a customs revenue matter, or

(b)   makes provision in relation to the exercise of a customs function.

36 Power to make supplementary etc provision

(1) The Secretary of State may by order make—

(a)   such incidental, supplementary or consequential provision, or

(b)   such transitional or transitory provision or savings,

as the Secretary of State considers appropriate for the general purposes, or any particular purpose, of this Part, or in consequence of, or for giving full effect to, any provision made by or under this Part.

(2) An order under subsection (1) may amend, repeal, revoke or otherwise modify any enactment (including this Act).

(3) The power to make an order under subsection (1) includes power to repeal or revoke an enactment which is spent.

(4) Nothing in this Part affects the generality of the power conferred by this section.

37 Subordinate legislation

(1) Orders and regulations under this Part must be made by statutory instrument.

(2) An order or regulations under this Part may—

(a)   include incidental, supplementary and consequential provision;

(b)   make transitional or transitory provision or savings;

(c)   make different provision for different cases or circumstances.

(3) A statutory instrument containing an order or regulations to which subsection (4) applies may not be made unless a draft of the instrument has been laid before, and approved by a resolution of, each House of Parliament.

(4) This subsection applies to—

(a)   an order under section 2 (power of Secretary of State to modify functions);

(b)   an order under section 8 (power of Treasury to modify Director's functions);

(c)   regulations under section 16(8) (power to permit disclosure);

(d)   an order under section 23 (application of provisions about investigations and detention: England and Wales and Northern Ireland);

(e)   an order under section 35 (power to modify enactments);

(f)   an order under section 36 (power to make supplementary etc provision) that amends or repeals primary legislation.

(5) A statutory instrument containing only—

(a)   regulations under section 29 (inspections by Her Majesty's Inspectors of Constabulary etc), or

(b)   an order under section 36 that does not amend or repeal primary legislation,

is subject to annulment in pursuance of a resolution of either House of Parliament.

(6)   A statutory instrument containing an order under section 33 (power to require payment into the Consolidated Fund) is subject to annulment in pursuance of a resolution of the House of Commons.

(7)   In this section "primary legislation" means—

(a)   an Act of Parliament,

(b)   an Act of the Scottish Parliament,

(c)   a Measure or Act of the National Assembly for Wales, or

(d)   Northern Ireland legislation.

(8)   . . .

Amendment

Sub-s (8): repealed by SI 2014/834, reg 3(3), Sch 2, paras 65, 69. Date in force: 27 March 2014: see SI 2014/834, art 1.

38 Interpretation

In this Part—

"[EU] law" means—

(a)   all the rights, powers, liabilities, obligations and restrictions from time to time created or arising by or under the [EU] Treaties, and

(b)   all the remedies and procedures from time to time provided for by or under the [EU] Treaties,

as in accordance with the [EU] Treaties are without further enactment to be given legal effect or used in the United Kingdom;

"customs function" has the meaning given by section 14(6);

"customs information" has the meaning given by section 14(6);

"customs revenue function" has the meaning given by section 7(9);

"customs revenue information" has the meaning given by section 14(6);

"customs revenue matter" has the meaning given by section 7(2);

"customs revenue official" means a customs revenue official designated under section 11(1);

"designated customs official" has the meaning given by section 14(6);

"enactment" includes—

(a)   an enactment contained in subordinate legislation within the meaning of the Interpretation Act 1978 (c 30);

(b)   an enactment contained in, or in an instrument made under, an Act of the Scottish Parliament;

(c)   an enactment contained in, or in instrument made under, Northern Ireland legislation;

(d)   an enactment contained in, or in an instrument made under, a Measure or Act of the National Assembly for Wales;

"function" means any power or duty (including a power or duty that is ancillary to another power or duty);

"general customs function" has the meaning given by section 1(8);

"general customs matter" has the meaning given by section 1(2);

"general customs official" means a general customs official designated under section 3(1);

"personal customs information" has the meaning given by section 15(4);

"personal customs revenue information" has the meaning given by section 15(4);

"relevant official" has the meaning given by section 15(3).

Amendment

References to "EU" in square brackets in each place they appear, substituted by SI 2011/1043, art 6(1)(a), (2)(a), as from 22 April 2011: see SI 2011/1043, art 2; for transitional savings see art 3(3) thereof.

PART 2
CITIZENSHIP

39–47

(Ss 39–45 amend the British Nationality Act 1981, ss 1, 3, 4B, 4C, 6, 41, Sch 1; s 46 inserts s 4D of that Act; s 47 inserts the British Nationality Act 1981, s 41A and amends the Hong Kong (War Wives and Widows) Act 1996, s 1, the British Nationality (Hong Kong) Act 1997, s 1, the Nationality, Immigration and Asylum Act 2002, s 131 and the UK Borders Act 2007, s 40.)

Interpretation etc

48 Meaning of references to being in breach of immigration laws

(1) . . .

(2) Section 11 of the Nationality, Immigration and Asylum Act 2002 (c 41) ("the 2002 Act") (unlawful presence in the United Kingdom) ceases to have effect.

(3) Notwithstanding its repeal, section 11 of the 2002 Act is to continue to have effect for the purpose of determining on or after the relevant day—

    (a)   whether a person born before the relevant day is a British citizen under section 1(1) of the British Nationality Act 1981 (c 61),

    (b)   whether, on an application under section 1(3) or 4(2) of that Act made but not determined before the relevant day, a person is entitled to be registered as a British citizen,

    (c)   whether, on an application under section 6(1) or (2) of that Act made but not determined before the relevant day, the applicant fulfils the requirements of Schedule 1 for naturalisation as a British citizen under section 6(1) or (2) of that Act, or

    (d)   whether, in relation to an application under section 1(3) or 6(1) or (2) of that Act made on or after the relevant day, a person was in the United Kingdom "in breach of the immigration laws" at a time before 7 November 2002 (the date of commencement of section 11 of the 2002 Act).

(4) Where section 11 of the 2002 Act continues to have effect by virtue of paragraph (d) of subsection (3) for the purpose of determining on or after the relevant day the matter mentioned in that paragraph, section 50A of the British Nationality Act 1981 is not to apply for the purpose of determining that matter.

(5) The relevant day for the purposes of subsection (3) is the day appointed for the commencement of this section.

(6) In paragraph 7(a) of Schedule 3 to the 2002 Act (definition of persons unlawfully in the UK who are ineligible for support), for "section 11" substitute "section 50A of the British Nationality Act 1981".

Amendment

Sub-s (1): inserts the British Nationality Act 1981, s 50A.

49

(Amends the British Nationality Act 1981, s 50 and Sch 1.)

PART 3
IMMIGRATION

50–52

(S 50 amends the Immigration Act 1971, s 3; s 51 amends the Immigration and Asylum Act 1999, s 141; s 52 amends the UK Borders Act 2007, ss 2, 3, 60.)

PART 4
MISCELLANEOUS AND GENERAL

53, 54

(S 53 repealed by the Crime and Courts Act 2013, s 22(4), as from 1 November 2013 (see SI 2013/2200, art 5); s 54 amends the Asylum and Immigration (Treatment of Claimants, etc) Act 2004, s 4.)

Children

[54A Independent Family Returns Panel

(1) The Independent Family Returns Panel is established.

(2) The Secretary of State must consult the Independent Family Returns Panel—

    (a) in each family returns case, on how best to safeguard and promote the welfare of the children of the family, and

    (b) in each case where the Secretary of State proposes to detain a family in pre-departure accommodation, on the suitability of so doing, having particular regard to the need to safeguard and promote the welfare of the children of the family.

(3) A family returns case is a case where—

    (a) a child who is living in the United Kingdom is to be removed from or required to leave the United Kingdom, and

    (b) an individual who—

        (i) is a parent of the child or has care of the child, and

        (ii) is living in a household in the United Kingdom with the child,

    is also to be removed from or required to leave the United Kingdom.

(4) The Secretary of State may by regulations make provision about—

    (a) additional functions of the Independent Family Returns Panel,

    (b) its status and constitution,

    (c) the appointment of its members,

    (d) the payment of remuneration and allowances to its members, and

    (e) any other matters in connection with its establishment and operation.

(5) Regulations under this section must be made by statutory instrument.

(6) An instrument containing regulations under this section is subject to annulment in pursuance of a resolution of either House of Parliament.

(7) In this section—

    "child" means a person who is under the age of 18;

    "pre-departure accommodation" has the same meaning as in Part 8 of the Immigration and Asylum Act 1999;

    references to a person being removed from or required to leave the United Kingdom are to the person being removed or required to leave in accordance with a provision of the Immigration Acts.]

Amendment
Inserted by the Immigration Act 2014, s 3, as from 28 July 2014.

55 Duty regarding the welfare of children

(1)   The Secretary of State must make arrangements for ensuring that—

(a)   the functions mentioned in subsection (2) are discharged having regard to the need to safeguard and promote the welfare of children who are in the United Kingdom, and

(b)   any services provided by another person pursuant to arrangements which are made by the Secretary of State and relate to the discharge of a function mentioned in subsection (2) are provided having regard to that need.

(2)   The functions referred to in subsection (1) are—

(a)   any function of the Secretary of State in relation to immigration, asylum or nationality;

(b)   any function conferred by or by virtue of the Immigration Acts on an immigration officer;

(c)   any general customs function of the Secretary of State;

(d)   any customs function conferred on a designated customs official.

(3)   A person exercising any of those functions must, in exercising the function, have regard to any guidance given to the person by the Secretary of State for the purpose of subsection (1).

(4)   The Director of Border Revenue must make arrangements for ensuring that—

(a)   the Director's functions are discharged having regard to the need to safeguard and promote the welfare of children who are in the United Kingdom, and

(b)   any services provided by another person pursuant to arrangements made by the Director in the discharge of such a function are provided having regard to that need.

(5)   A person exercising a function of the Director of Border Revenue must, in exercising the function, have regard to any guidance given to the person by the Secretary of State for the purpose of subsection (4).

(6)   In this section—

"children" means persons who are under the age of 18;

"customs function", "designated customs official" and "general customs function" have the meanings given by Part 1.

(7)   A reference in an enactment (other than this Act) to the Immigration Acts includes a reference to this section.

(8)   Section 21 of the UK Borders Act 2007 (c 30) (children) ceases to have effect.

General

56 Repeals
The Schedule contains repeals.

57 Extent

(1)   Subject to the following provisions of this section, this Act extends to—

(a)   England and Wales,

(b)   Scotland, and

(c)   Northern Ireland.

(2)   Sections 22 (application of the PACE orders) and 23 (investigations and detention: England and Wales and Northern Ireland) extend to England and Wales and Northern Ireland only.

(3)   An amendment, modification or repeal by this Act has the same extent as the enactment or relevant part of the enactment to which it relates (ignoring extent by virtue of an Order in Council under any of the Immigration Acts).

(4)   Subsection (3) does not apply to—

(a)   the amendments made by section 52 (detention at ports in Scotland);

(b)   the amendment made by section 54 (trafficking people for exploitation), which extends to England and Wales and Northern Ireland only.

(5)   Her Majesty may by Order in Council provide for any of the provisions of this Act, other than any provision of Part 1 (border functions) or section 53 (transfer of certain immigration judicial review applications), to extend, with or without modifications, to any of the Channel Islands or the Isle of Man.

(6)   Subsection (5) does not apply in relation to the extension to a place of a provision which extends there by virtue of subsection (3).

58 Commencement

(1)   Part 1 (border functions) comes into force on the day this Act is passed.

(2)   The provisions of Part 2 (citizenship) come into force on such day as the Secretary of State may by order appoint.

(3)   In Part 3 (immigration)—

(a)   section 50 (restriction on studies) comes into force on the day this Act is passed;

(b)   sections 51 (fingerprinting of foreign criminals) and 52 (detention at ports in Scotland) come into force on such day as the Secretary of State may by order appoint.

(4)   In this Part—

(a)   section 53 (transfer of certain immigration judicial review applications) comes into force on such day as the Lord Chancellor may by order appoint;

(b)   sections 54 (trafficking people for exploitation) and 55 (duty regarding the welfare of children) come into force on such day as the Secretary of State may by order appoint.

(5)   Any repeal in the Schedule (and section 56 so far as relating to the repeal) comes into force in the same way as the provisions of this Act to which the repeal relates.

(6)   The other provisions of this Part come into force on the day this Act is passed.

(7)   An order under this section must be made by statutory instrument.

(8)   An order under this section—

(a)   may appoint different days for different purposes;

(b)   may include transitional or incidental provision or savings.

(9)   An order commencing sections 39 to 41 (acquisition of British citizenship by naturalisation) must include provision that the amendments made by those sections do not have effect in relation to an application for naturalisation as a British citizen if—

(a)   the date of the application is before the date on which those sections come into force in accordance with the order ("the date of commencement"), or

(b)   the date of the application is before the end of the period of 24 months beginning with the date of commencement and the application is made by a person who falls within subsection (10) or (11).

(10)   A person falls within this subsection if on the date of commencement the person has indefinite leave to remain in the United Kingdom.

(11)   A person falls within this subsection if the person is given indefinite leave to remain in the United Kingdom on an application—

(a)   the date of which is before the date of commencement, and

(b)   which is decided after the date of commencement.

(b)   paragraph 16(2) to (4) (detention of person where reasonable grounds for suspecting removal directions may be given or pending removal in pursuance of directions);

(c)   paragraph 17 (arrest of person liable to be detained and search of premises for person liable to arrest);

(d)   paragraph 18 (supplementary provisions on detention);

(e)   paragraph 18A (search of detained person);

(f)   paragraph 18B (detention of unaccompanied children);

(g)   paragraphs 19 and 20 (payment of expenses of custody etc);

(h)   paragraph 21 (temporary admission to UK of person liable to detention);

(i)   paragraphs 22 to 25 (bail);

(j)   paragraphs 25A to 25E (searches etc).

(10)   The Secretary of State may by regulations make further provision about—

(a)   the time period during which a family member may be removed under subsection (2);

(b)   the service of a notice under subsection (2).

(11)   In this section "child" means a person who is under the age of 18."

2 Restriction on removal of children and their parents etc

After section 78 of the Nationality, Immigration and Asylum Act 2002, insert—

"78A Restriction on removal of children and their parents etc

(1)   This section applies in a case where—

(a)   a child is to be removed from or required to leave the United Kingdom, and

(b)   an individual who—

(i)   is a parent of the child or has care of the child, and

(ii)   is living in a household in the United Kingdom with the child, is also to be removed from or required to leave the United Kingdom (a "relevant parent or carer").

(2)   During the period of 28 days beginning with the day on which the relevant appeal rights are exhausted—

(a)   the child may not be removed from or required to leave the United Kingdom; and

(b)   a relevant parent or carer may not be removed from or required to leave the United Kingdom if, as a result, no relevant parent or carer would remain in the United Kingdom.

(3)   The relevant appeal rights are exhausted at the time when—

(a)   neither the child, nor any relevant parent or carer, could bring an appeal under section 82 (ignoring any possibility of an appeal out of time with permission), and

(b)   no appeal brought by the child, or by any relevant parent or carer, is pending within the meaning of section 104.

(4)   Nothing in this section prevents any of the following during the period of 28 days mentioned in subsection (2)—

(a)   the giving of a direction for the removal of a person from the United Kingdom,

(b)   the making of a deportation order in respect of a person, or

(c)   the taking of any other interim or preparatory action.

(5)   In this section—

"child" means a person who is aged under 18;

references to a person being removed from or required to leave the United Kingdom are to the person being removed or required to leave in accordance with a provision of the Immigration Acts."

3 Independent Family Returns Panel

Before section 55 of the Borders, Citizenship and Immigration Act 2009, insert—

"54A Independent Family Returns Panel

(1) The Independent Family Returns Panel is established.

(2) The Secretary of State must consult the Independent Family Returns Panel—

    (a) in each family returns case, on how best to safeguard and promote the welfare of the children of the family, and

    (b) in each case where the Secretary of State proposes to detain a family in pre-departure accommodation, on the suitability of so doing, having particular regard to the need to safeguard and promote the welfare of the children of the family.

(3) A family returns case is a case where—

    (a) a child who is living in the United Kingdom is to be removed from or required to leave the United Kingdom, and

    (b) an individual who—

        (i)   is a parent of the child or has care of the child, and

        (ii) is living in a household in the United Kingdom with the child,

is also to be removed from or required to leave the United Kingdom.

(4) The Secretary of State may by regulations make provision about—

    (a) additional functions of the Independent Family Returns Panel,

    (b) its status and constitution,

    (c) the appointment of its members,

    (d) the payment of remuneration and allowances to its members, and

    (e) any other matters in connection with its establishment and operation.

(5) Regulations under this section must be made by statutory instrument.

(6) An instrument containing regulations under this section is subject to annulment in pursuance of a resolution of either House of Parliament.

(7) In this section—

"child" means a person who is under the age of 18;

"pre-departure accommodation" has the same meaning as in Part 8 of the Immigration and Asylum Act 1999;

references to a person being removed from or required to leave the United Kingdom are to the person being removed or required to leave in accordance with a provision of the Immigration Acts."

Powers of immigration officers

4 Enforcement powers

Schedule 1 (enforcement powers) has effect.

Detention and bail

5 Restrictions on detention of unaccompanied children

(1) Schedule 2 to the Immigration Act 1971 (administrative provisions as to control on entry etc) is amended as follows.

(2) In paragraph 16, after paragraph (2) insert—

"(2A)   But the detention of an unaccompanied child under sub-paragraph (2) is subject to paragraph 18B."

(3)   In paragraph 18, after sub-paragraph (1) insert—

"(1A)   But the detention of an unaccompanied child under paragraph 16(2) is subject to paragraph 18B."

(4)   After paragraph 18A (as inserted by paragraph 2 of Schedule 1) insert—

"**18B**

(1)   Where a person detained under paragraph 16(2) is an unaccompanied child, the only place where the child may be detained is a short-term holding facility, except where—

(a)   the child is being transferred to or from a short-term holding facility, or

(b)   sub-paragraph (3) of paragraph 18 applies.

(2)   An unaccompanied child may be detained under paragraph 16(2) in a short-term holding facility for a maximum period of 24 hours, and only for so long as the following two conditions are met.

(3)   The first condition is that—

(a)   directions are in force that require the child to be removed from the short-term holding facility within the relevant 24 hour period, or

(b)   a decision on whether or not to give directions is likely to result in such directions.

(4)   The second condition is that the immigration officer under whose authority the child is being detained reasonably believes that the child will be removed from the short-term holding facility within the relevant 24 hour period in accordance with those directions.

(5)   An unaccompanied child detained under paragraph 16(2) who has been removed from a short-term holding facility and detained elsewhere may be detained again in a short-term holding facility but only if, and for as long as, the relevant 24 hour period has not ended.

(6)   An unaccompanied child who has been released following detention under paragraph 16(2) may be detained again in a short-term holding facility in accordance with this paragraph.

(7)   In this paragraph—

"relevant 24 hour period", in relation to the detention of a child in a short-term holding facility, means the period of 24 hours starting when the child was detained (or, in a case falling within sub-paragraph (5), first detained) in a short-term holding facility;

"short-term holding facility" has the same meaning as in Part 8 of the Immigration and Asylum Act 1999;

"unaccompanied child" means a person—

(a)   who is under the age of 18, and

(b)   who is not accompanied (whilst in detention) by his or her parent or another individual who has care of him or her."

6 Pre-departure accommodation for families

(1)   Part 8 of the Immigration and Asylum Act 1999 (removal centres and detained persons) is amended as follows.

(2)   In section 147 (interpretation)—

(a)   after the definition of "custodial functions" insert—

""detained children" means detained persons who are under the age of 18;";

(b)   after the definition of "escort monitor" insert—

""pre-departure accommodation" means a place used solely for the detention of detained children and their families for a period of—

    (a)   not more than 72 hours, or

    (b)   not more than seven days in cases where the longer period of detention is authorised personally by a Minister of the Crown (within the meaning of the Ministers of the Crown Act 1975);";

(c)   in the definition of "removal centre", after "facility," insert "pre-departure accommodation,";

(d)   in the definition of "short-term holding facility", at the end insert—
"but which is not pre-departure accommodation."

(3)   In section 155 (custodial functions and discipline), in subsection (2), at the end insert "and in pre-departure accommodation".

(4)   After section 157 insert—

"157A Pre-departure accommodation

(1)   The following provisions of this Part apply to pre-departure accommodation as they apply to removal centres—

    (a)   section 149 (contracting out of certain removal centres);

    (b)   section 150 (contracting out functions at directly managed removal centres);

    (c)   section 151 (intervention by Secretary of State).

(2)   In the application of those provisions to pre-departure accommodation—

    (a)   references to a removal centre contract are to be read as a contract made under section 149(1) for the provision or running of pre-departure accommodation;

    (b)   references to a contracted out removal centre are to be read as references to pre-departure accommodation in relation to which a contract under section 149(1) is in force;

    (c)   references to a directly managed removal centre are to be read as references to pre-departure accommodation in relation to which there is no contract under section 149(1) in force;

    (d)   references to removal centre rules are to be read as references to rules made under subsection (4).

(3)   The Secretary of State may by regulations extend to pre-departure accommodation any other provision made by or under this Part in relation to removal centres.

(4)   The Secretary of State may make rules for the regulation and management of pre-departure accommodation."

7 Immigration bail: repeat applications and effect of removal directions

(1)   Schedule 2 to the Immigration Act 1971 (administrative provisions as to control on entry etc) is amended as follows.

(2)   In paragraph 22 (bail) at the end insert—

"(4)   A person must not be released on bail in accordance with this paragraph without the consent of the Secretary of State if—

    (a)   directions for the removal of the person from the United Kingdom are for the time being in force, and

    (b)   the directions require the person to be removed from the United Kingdom within the period of 14 days starting with the date of the decision on whether the person should be released on bail."

(3)   In paragraph 25—

    (a)   the existing paragraph is re-numbered as sub-paragraph (1);

    (b)   in that sub-paragraph, for "may" substitute "must";

(c)   after that sub-paragraph insert—

"(2)   Tribunal Procedure Rules must secure that, where the First-tier Tribunal has decided not to release a person on bail under paragraph 22, the Tribunal is required to dismiss without a hearing any further application by the person for release on bail (whether under paragraph 22 or otherwise) that is made during the period of 28 days starting with the date of the Tribunal's decision, unless the person demonstrates to the Tribunal that there has been a material change in circumstances."

(4)   In paragraph 29 (grant of bail pending appeal), in sub-paragraph (1), at the end insert "(and paragraph 22 does not apply)".

(5)   In paragraph 30 (restrictions on grant of bail pending appeal), in sub-paragraph (1)—

    (a)   after "if" insert "—(a)";

    (b)   for "or the power to give such directions is for the time being exercisable" substitute

       "and

       (b)   the directions require the person to be removed from the United Kingdom within the period of 14 days starting with the date of the decision on whether the person should be released on bail."

(6)   After paragraph 33, insert—

"33A

(1)   Tribunal Procedure Rules must make provision with respect to applications to the First-tier Tribunal under paragraphs 29 to 33 and matters arising out of such applications.

(2)   Tribunal Procedure Rules must secure that, where the First-tier Tribunal has decided not to release a person on bail under paragraph 29, the Tribunal is required to dismiss without a hearing any further application by the person for release on bail (whether under paragraph 29 or otherwise) that is made during the period of 28 days starting with the date of the Tribunal's decision, unless the person demonstrates to the Tribunal that there has been a material change in circumstances."

Biometrics

8 Provision of biometric information with immigration applications

(1)   Section 126 of the Nationality, Immigration and Asylum Act 2002 (power to require provision of physical data with certain immigration applications) is amended as follows.

(2)   In subsection (2), after paragraph (c) insert—

    "(d)   a transit visa (within the meaning of section 41 of the Immigration and Asylum Act 1999), or

    (e)   a document issued as evidence that a person who is not a national of an EEA state or Switzerland is entitled to enter or remain in the United Kingdom by virtue of an enforceable EU right or of any provision made under section 2(2) of the European Communities Act 1972."

(3)   In subsection (4), after paragraph (f) insert—

    "(fa)   provide for biometric information to be recorded on any document issued as a result of the application in relation to which the information was provided;".

(4)   In subsection (9), after the definition of "code" insert—

> ""document" includes a card or sticker and any other method of recording information (whether in writing or by the use of electronic or other technology or by a combination of methods),".

9 Identifying persons liable to detention

In paragraph 18(2) of Schedule 2 to the Immigration Act 1971 (power to take steps for identifying persons detained under paragraph 16 of that Schedule) after "detained" insert "or liable to be detained".

10 Provision of biometric information with citizenship applications

(1) Section 41 of the British Nationality Act 1981 (regulations for giving effect to the Act) is amended as follows.

(2) In subsection (1), after paragraph (b) insert—

> "(bza) requiring an application for registration or naturalisation of a person as a British citizen to be accompanied by biometric information, or enabling an authorised person to require an individual to whom such an application relates to provide biometric information;".

(3) After subsection (1) insert—

> "(1ZA) In subsection (1)(bza) "authorised person" and "biometric information" have the same meaning as in section 126 of the Nationality, Immigration and Asylum Act 2002.
>
> (1ZB) Section 126(4) to (7) of that Act applies to regulations under subsection (1)(bza) as it applies to regulations under section 126(1) of that Act.
>
> (1ZC) Section 8 of the UK Borders Act 2007 (power to make regulations about use and retention of biometric information) applies to biometric information provided in accordance with regulations under subsection (1)(bza) as it applies to biometric information provided in accordance with regulations under section 5(1) of that Act.
>
> (1ZD) But (despite section 8(5)(b) of that Act) regulations made by virtue of subsection (1ZC) may provide for photographs of a person who is registered or naturalised as a British citizen to be retained until the person is issued with a United Kingdom passport describing the person as a British citizen."

(4) In subsection (8)(b) for "(1)(bc)" substitute "(1)(bza), (bc)".

11 Biometric immigration documents

After section 7(2) of the UK Borders Act 2007 (effect of failure to comply with regulations about biometric immigration documents) insert—

> "(2A) If the regulations require a biometric immigration document to be used in connection with an application or claim, they may require or permit the application or claim to be disregarded or refused if that requirement is not complied with."

12 Meaning of "biometric information"

(1) Section 15 of the UK Borders Act 2007 (biometric immigration documents: interpretation) is amended as follows.

(2) In subsection (1), omit paragraphs (b) and (c).

(3) After subsection (1) insert—

> "(1A) For the purposes of section 5 "biometric information" means—
>
> (a) information about a person's external physical characteristics (including in particular fingerprints and features of the iris), and
>
> (b) any other information about a person's physical characteristics specified in an order made by the Secretary of State.
>
> (1B) An order under subsection (1A)(b)—

(a) may specify only information that can be obtained or recorded by an external examination of a person;

(b) must not specify information about a person's DNA.

(1C) Section 6(6) applies to an order under subsection (1A)(b) as it applies to regulations under section 5(1)."

(4) Schedule 2 (which amends other enactments) has effect.

13 Safeguards for children

(1) Schedule 2 to the Immigration Act 1971 (entry control) is amended as follows.

(2) In paragraph 4 (power to take biometric information on examination), after sub-paragraph (6) (as inserted by paragraph 1(3) of Schedule 2) insert—

"(7) A person ("P") who is under 16 may not be required to provide biometric information under sub-paragraph (5) unless—

(a) the decision to require P to provide the information has been confirmed by a chief immigration officer, and

(b) the information is provided in the presence of a person of full age who is—

(i) P's parent or guardian, or

(ii) a person who for the time being takes responsibility for P.

(8) The person mentioned in sub-paragraph (7)(b)(ii) may not be—

(a) a person who is entitled to require the provision of information under sub-paragraph (5) (an "authorised person"), or

(b) an officer of the Secretary of State who is not such a person.

(9) Sub-paragraph (7) does not prevent an authorised person requiring the provision of biometric information by a person the authorised person reasonably believes to be 16 or over."

(3) In paragraph 18 (power to take biometric information from detained persons), after sub-paragraph (2A) insert—

"(2B) Paragraph 4(7) to (9) applies to sub-paragraph (2) as it applies to paragraph 4(5)."

14 Use and retention of biometric information

(1) For section 8 of the UK Borders Act 2007 substitute—

"8 Use and retention of biometric information

(1) The Secretary of State must by regulations make provision about the use and retention by the Secretary of State of biometric information provided in accordance with regulations under section 5(1).

(2) The regulations must provide that biometric information may be retained only if the Secretary of State thinks that it is necessary to retain it for use in connection with—

(a) the exercise of a function by virtue of the Immigration Acts, or

(b) the exercise of a function in relation to nationality.

(3) The regulations may include provision permitting biometric information retained by virtue of subsection (2) also to be used—

(a) in connection with the prevention, investigation or prosecution of an offence,

(b) for a purpose which appears to the Secretary of State to be required in order to protect national security,

(c) in connection with identifying persons who have died, or are suffering from illness or injury,

(d) for the purpose of ascertaining whether a person has acted unlawfully, or has obtained or sought anything to which the person is not legally entitled, and

(e)   for such other purposes (whether in accordance with functions under an enactment or otherwise) as the regulations may specify.

(4)   The regulations must include provision about the destruction of biometric information.

(5)   In particular the regulations must require the Secretary of State to take all reasonable steps to ensure that biometric information is destroyed if the Secretary of State—

    (a)   no longer thinks that it is necessary to retain the information for use as mentioned in subsection (2), or

    (b)   is satisfied that the person to whom the information relates is a British citizen, or a Commonwealth citizen who has a right of abode in the United Kingdom as a result of section 2(1)(b) of the Immigration Act 1971.

(6)   The regulations must also—

    (a)   require that any requirement to destroy biometric information by virtue of the regulations also applies to copies of the information, and

    (b)   require the Secretary of State to take all reasonable steps to ensure—

        (i)   that data held in electronic form which relates to biometric information which has to be destroyed by virtue of the regulations is destroyed or erased, or

        (ii)   that access to such data is blocked.

(7)   But a requirement to destroy biometric information or data is not to apply if and in so far as the information or data is retained in accordance with and for the purposes of another power.

(8)   The regulations must include provision—

    (a)   entitling a person whose biometric information has to be destroyed by virtue of the regulations, on request, to a certificate issued by the Secretary of State to the effect that the Secretary of State has taken the steps required by virtue of subsection (6)(b), and

    (b)   requiring such a certificate to be issued within the period of 3 months beginning with the date on which the request for it is received by the Secretary of State.

(9)   Section 6(6) applies to regulations under this section as it applies to regulations under section 5(1)."

(2)   In the Immigration and Asylum Act 1999, after section 144 insert—

"144A Use and retention of fingerprints etc

(1)   Section 8 of the UK Borders Act 2007 (power to make regulations about use and retention of biometric information) applies to—

    (a)   fingerprints taken by virtue of section 141, and

    (b)   biometric information taken by virtue of regulations under section 144,

as it applies to biometric information provided in accordance with regulations under section 5(1) of that Act.

(2)   Regulations made by virtue of subsection (1)(a) must require fingerprints taken from a person ("F") by virtue of section 141(7)(f) to be destroyed when fingerprints taken from the person whose dependant F is are destroyed.

(3)   Regulations made by virtue of subsection (1)(b) must make equivalent provision in relation to biometric information taken by virtue of any provision of regulations under section 144 which is equivalent to section 141(7)(f)."

(3)   In section 126 of the Nationality, Immigration and Asylum Act 2002 (power to require provision of physical data with certain immigration applications), after subsection (8) insert—

"(8A) Section 8 of the UK Borders Act 2007 (power to make regulations about use and retention of biometric information) applies to biometric information provided in accordance with regulations under subsection (1) as it applies to biometric information provided in accordance with regulations under section 5(1) of that Act."

PART 2
APPEALS ETC

15 Right of appeal to First-tier Tribunal

(1) Part 5 of the Nationality, Immigration and Asylum Act 2002 (immigration and asylum appeals) is amended as follows.

(2) For section 82 substitute—

"82 Right of appeal to the Tribunal

(1) A person ("P") may appeal to the Tribunal where—

    (a) the Secretary of State has decided to refuse a protection claim made by P,

    (b) the Secretary of State has decided to refuse a human rights claim made by P, or

    (c) the Secretary of State has decided to revoke P's protection status.

(2) For the purposes of this Part—

    (a) a "protection claim" is a claim made by a person ("P") that removal of P from the United Kingdom—

        (i) would breach the United Kingdom's obligations under the Refugee Convention, or

        (ii) would breach the United Kingdom's obligations in relation to persons eligible for a grant of humanitarian protection;

    (b) P's protection claim is refused if the Secretary of State makes one or more of the following decisions—

        (i) that removal of P from the United Kingdom would not breach the United Kingdom's obligations under the Refugee Convention;

        (ii) that removal of P from the United Kingdom would not breach the United Kingdom's obligations in relation to persons eligible for a grant of humanitarian protection;

    (c) a person has "protection status" if the person has been granted leave to enter or remain in the United Kingdom as a refugee or as a person eligible for a grant of humanitarian protection;

    (d) "humanitarian protection" is to be construed in accordance with the immigration rules;

    (e) "refugee" has the same meaning as in the Refugee Convention.

(3) The right of appeal under subsection (1) is subject to the exceptions and limitations specified in this Part."

(3) Sections 83 and 83A (appeal rights in respect of asylum claims) are repealed.

(4) For section 84 substitute—

"84 Grounds of appeal

(1) An appeal under section 82(1)(a) (refusal of protection claim) must be brought on one or more of the following grounds—

    (a) that removal of the appellant from the United Kingdom would breach the United Kingdom's obligations under the Refugee Convention;

    (b)   that removal of the appellant from the United Kingdom would breach the United Kingdom's obligations in relation to persons eligible for a grant of humanitarian protection;

    (c)   that removal of the appellant from the United Kingdom would be unlawful under section 6 of the Human Rights Act 1998 (public authority not to act contrary to Human Rights Convention).

(2)   An appeal under section 82(1)(b) (refusal of human rights claim) must be brought on the ground that the decision is unlawful under section 6 of the Human Rights Act 1998.

(3)   An appeal under section 82(1)(c) (revocation of protection status) must be brought on one or more of the following grounds—

    (a)   that the decision to revoke the appellant's protection status breaches the United Kingdom's obligations under the Refugee Convention;

    (b)   that the decision to revoke the appellant's protection status breaches the United Kingdom's obligations in relation to persons eligible for a grant of humanitarian protection."

(5)   In section 85 (matters to be considered), for subsection (5) substitute—

"(5)   But the Tribunal must not consider a new matter unless the Secretary of State has given the Tribunal consent to do so.

(6)   A matter is a "new matter" if—

    (a)   it constitutes a ground of appeal of a kind listed in section 84, and

    (b)   the Secretary of State has not previously considered the matter in the context of—

        (i)   the decision mentioned in section 82(1), or

        (ii)   a statement made by the appellant under section 120."

16 Report by Chief Inspector on administrative review

(1)   Before the end of the period of 12 months beginning on the day on which section 15 comes into force, the Secretary of State must commission from the Chief Inspector a report that addresses the following matters—

    (a)   the effectiveness of administrative review in identifying case working errors;

    (b)   the effectiveness of administrative review in correcting case working errors;

    (c)   the independence of persons conducting administrative review (in terms of their separation from the original decision-maker).

(2)   On completion of the report, the Chief Inspector must send it to the Secretary of State.

(3)   The Secretary of State must lay before Parliament a copy of the report received under subsection (2).

(4)   In this section—

"administrative review" means review conducted under the immigration rules;

"case working error" has the meaning given in the immigration rules;

the "Chief Inspector" means the Chief Inspector established under section 48 of the UK Borders Act 2007;

"immigration rules" has the same meaning as in the Immigration Act 1971.

17 Place from which appeal may be brought or continued

(1)   Part 5 of the Nationality, Immigration and Asylum Act 2002 (immigration and asylum appeals) is amended as follows.

(2)   For section 92 substitute—

"92 Place from which an appeal may be brought or continued

(1)   This section applies to determine the place from which an appeal under section 82(1) may be brought or continued.

(2)   In the case of an appeal under section 82(1)(a) (protection claim appeal), the appeal must be brought from outside the United Kingdom if—

> (a)   the claim to which the appeal relates has been certified under section 94(1) or (7) (claim clearly unfounded or removal to safe third country), or
>
> (b)   paragraph 5(3)(a), 10(3), 15(3) or 19(b) of Schedule 3 to the Asylum and Immigration (Treatment of Claimants, etc) Act 2004 (removal of asylum seeker to safe third country) applies.

Otherwise, the appeal must be brought from within the United Kingdom.

(3)   In the case of an appeal under section 82(1)(b) (human rights claim appeal) where the claim to which the appeal relates was made while the appellant was in the United Kingdom, the appeal must be brought from outside the United Kingdom if—

> (a)   the claim to which the appeal relates has been certified under section 94(1) or (7) (claim clearly unfounded or removal to safe third country) or section 94B (certification of human rights claims made by persons liable to deportation), or
>
> (b)   paragraph 5(3)(b) or (4), 10(4), 15(4) or 19(c) of Schedule 3 to the Asylum and Immigration (Treatment of Claimants, etc) Act 2004 (removal of asylum seeker to safe third country) applies.

Otherwise, the appeal must be brought from within the United Kingdom.

(4)   In the case of an appeal under section 82(1)(b) (human rights claim appeal) where the claim to which the appeal relates was made while the appellant was outside the United Kingdom, the appeal must be brought from outside the United Kingdom.

(5)   In the case of an appeal under section 82(1)(c) (revocation of protection status)—

> (a)   the appeal must be brought from within the United Kingdom if the decision to which the appeal relates was made while the appellant was in the United Kingdom;
>
> (b)   the appeal must be brought from outside the United Kingdom if the decision to which the appeal relates was made while the appellant was outside the United Kingdom.

(6)   If, after an appeal under section 82(1)(a) or (b) has been brought from within the United Kingdom, the Secretary of State certifies the claim to which the appeal relates under section 94(1) or (7) or section 94B, the appeal must be continued from outside the United Kingdom.

(7)   Where a person brings or continues an appeal under section 82(1)(a) (refusal of protection claim) from outside the United Kingdom, for the purposes of considering whether the grounds of appeal are satisfied, the appeal is to be treated as if the person were not outside the United Kingdom.

(8)   Where an appellant brings an appeal from within the United Kingdom but leaves the United Kingdom before the appeal is finally determined, the appeal is to be treated as abandoned unless the claim to which the appeal relates has been certified under section 94(1) or (7) or section 94B."

(3)   After section 94A, insert—

"94B Appeal from within the United Kingdom: certification of human rights claims made by persons liable to deportation

(1)   This section applies where a human rights claim has been made by a person ("P") who is liable to deportation under—

(a)   section 3(5)(a) of the Immigration Act 1971 (Secretary of State deeming deportation conducive to public good), or

(b)   section 3(6) of that Act (court recommending deportation following conviction).

(2)   The Secretary of State may certify the claim if the Secretary of State considers that, despite the appeals process not having been begun or not having been exhausted, removal of P to the country or territory to which P is proposed to be removed, pending the outcome of an appeal in relation to P's claim, would not be unlawful under section 6 of the Human Rights Act 1998 (public authority not to act contrary to Human Rights Convention).

(3)   The grounds upon which the Secretary of State may certify a claim under subsection (2) include (in particular) that P would not, before the appeals process is exhausted, face a real risk of serious irreversible harm if removed to the country or territory to which P is proposed to be removed."

18 Review of certain deportation decisions by Special Immigration Appeals Commission

In the Special Immigration Appeals Commission Act 1997, after section 2D insert—

"2E Jurisdiction: review of certain deportation decisions

(1)   Subsection (2) applies in relation to a relevant deportation decision which has been certified under section 97 or 97A(1) of the Nationality, Immigration and Asylum Act 2002 (certification on grounds of national security etc).

(2)   The person to whom the decision relates may apply to the Special Immigration Appeals Commission to set aside the decision.

(3)   In determining whether the decision should be set aside, the Commission must apply the principles which would be applied in judicial review proceedings.

(4)   If the Commission decides that the decision should be set aside, it may make any such order, or give any such relief, as may be made or given in judicial review proceedings.

(5)   In this section "relevant deportation decision" means a decision of the Secretary of State about the deportation of a person from the United Kingdom, if and to the extent that—

(a)   the decision is not subject to a right of appeal, or

(b)   the decision (being subject to a right of appeal) gives rise to issues which may not be raised on such an appeal."

19 Article 8 of the ECHR: public interest considerations

After Part 5 of the Nationality, Immigration and Asylum Act 2002 insert—

"PART 5A
ARTICLE 8 OF THE ECHR: PUBLIC INTEREST CONSIDERATIONS

117A Application of this Part

(1)   This Part applies where a court or tribunal is required to determine whether a decision made under the Immigration Acts—

(a)   breaches a person's right to respect for private and family life under Article 8, and

(b)   as a result would be unlawful under section 6 of the Human Rights Act 1998.

(2)   In considering the public interest question, the court or tribunal must (in particular) have regard—

(a)   in all cases, to the considerations listed in section 117B, and

(b)   in cases concerning the deportation of foreign criminals, to the considerations listed in section 117C.

(3) In subsection (2), "the public interest question" means the question of whether an interference with a person's right to respect for private and family life is justified under Article 8(2).

117B Article 8: public interest considerations applicable in all cases

(1) The maintenance of effective immigration controls is in the public interest.

(2) It is in the public interest, and in particular in the interests of the economic well-being of the United Kingdom, that persons who seek to enter or remain in the United Kingdom are able to speak English, because persons who can speak English—

    (a)   are less of a burden on taxpayers, and

    (b)   are better able to integrate into society.

(3) It is in the public interest, and in particular in the interests of the economic well-being of the United Kingdom, that persons who seek to enter or remain in the United Kingdom are financially independent, because such persons—

    (a)   are not a burden on taxpayers, and

    (b)   are better able to integrate into society.

(4) Little weight should be given to—

    (a)   a private life, or

    (b)   a relationship formed with a qualifying partner,

that is established by a person at a time when the person is in the United Kingdom unlawfully.

(5) Little weight should be given to a private life established by a person at a time when the person's immigration status is precarious.

(6) In the case of a person who is not liable to deportation, the public interest does not require the person's removal where—

    (a)   the person has a genuine and subsisting parental relationship with a qualifying child, and

    (b)   it would not be reasonable to expect the child to leave the United Kingdom.

117C Article 8: additional considerations in cases involving foreign criminals

(1) The deportation of foreign criminals is in the public interest.

(2) The more serious the offence committed by a foreign criminal, the greater is the public interest in deportation of the criminal.

(3) In the case of a foreign criminal ("C") who has not been sentenced to a period of imprisonment of four years or more, the public interest requires C's deportation unless Exception 1 or Exception 2 applies.

(4) Exception 1 applies where—

    (a)   C has been lawfully resident in the United Kingdom for most of C's life,

    (b)   C is socially and culturally integrated in the United Kingdom, and

    (c)   there would be very significant obstacles to C's integration into the country to which C is proposed to be deported.

(5) Exception 2 applies where C has a genuine and subsisting relationship with a qualifying partner, or a genuine and subsisting parental relationship with a qualifying child, and the effect of C's deportation on the partner or child would be unduly harsh.

(6) In the case of a foreign criminal who has been sentenced to a period of imprisonment of at least four years, the public interest requires deportation unless there are very compelling circumstances, over and above those described in Exceptions 1 and 2.

(7) The considerations in subsections (1) to (6) are to be taken into account where a court or tribunal is considering a decision to deport a foreign criminal

only to the extent that the reason for the decision was the offence or offences for which the criminal has been convicted.

117D Interpretation of this Part

(1)   In this Part—

"Article 8" means Article 8 of the European Convention on Human Rights;

"qualifying child" means a person who is under the age of 18 and who—

    (a)   is a British citizen, or

    (b)   has lived in the United Kingdom for a continuous period of seven years or more;

"qualifying partner" means a partner who—

    (a)   is a British citizen, or

    (b)   who is settled in the United Kingdom (within the meaning of the Immigration Act 1971—see section 33(2A) of that Act).

(2)   In this Part, "foreign criminal" means a person—

    (a)   who is not a British citizen,

    (b)   who has been convicted in the United Kingdom of an offence, and

    (c)   who—

        (i)   has been sentenced to a period of imprisonment of at least 12 months,

        (ii)   has been convicted of an offence that has caused serious harm, or

        (iii) is a persistent offender.

(3)   For the purposes of subsection (2)(b), a person subject to an order under—

    (a)   section 5 of the Criminal Procedure (Insanity) Act 1964 (insanity etc),

    (b)   section 57 of the Criminal Procedure (Scotland) Act 1995 (insanity etc), or

    (c)   Article 50A of the Mental Health (Northern Ireland) Order 1986 (insanity etc),

has not been convicted of an offence.

(4)   In this Part, references to a person who has been sentenced to a period of imprisonment of a certain length of time—

    (a)   do not include a person who has received a suspended sentence (unless a court subsequently orders that the sentence or any part of it (of whatever length) is to take effect);

    (b)   do not include a person who has been sentenced to a period of imprisonment of that length of time only by virtue of being sentenced to consecutive sentences amounting in aggregate to that length of time;

    (c)   include a person who is sentenced to detention, or ordered or directed to be detained, in an institution other than a prison (including, in particular, a hospital or an institution for young offenders) for that length of time; and

    (d)   include a person who is sentenced to imprisonment or detention, or ordered or directed to be detained, for an indeterminate period, provided that it may last for at least that length of time.

(5)   If any question arises for the purposes of this Part as to whether a person is a British citizen, it is for the person asserting that fact to prove it."

PART 3
ACCESS TO SERVICES ETC

CHAPTER 1

RESIDENTIAL TENANCIES
Key interpretation

20 Residential tenancy agreement

(1) This section applies for the purposes of this Chapter.

(2) "Residential tenancy agreement" means a tenancy which—

    (a)   grants a right of occupation of premises for residential use,

    (b)   provides for payment of rent (whether or not a market rent), and

    (c)   is not an excluded agreement.

(3) In subsection (2), "tenancy" includes—

    (a)   any lease, licence, sub-lease or sub-tenancy, and

    (b)   an agreement for any of those things,

and in this Chapter references to "landlord" and "tenant", and references to premises being "leased", are to be read accordingly.

(4) For the purposes of subsection (2)(a), an agreement grants a right of occupation of premises "for residential use" if, under the agreement, one or more adults have the right to occupy the premises as their only or main residence (whether or not the premises may also be used for other purposes).

(5) In subsection (2)(b) "rent" includes any sum paid in the nature of rent.

(6) In subsection (2)(c) "excluded agreement" means any agreement of a description for the time being specified in Schedule 3.

(7) The Secretary of State may by order amend Schedule 3 so as to—

    (a)   add a new description of excluded agreement,

    (b)   remove any description, or

    (c)   amend any description.

21 Persons disqualified by immigration status or with limited right to rent

(1) For the purposes of this Chapter, a person ("P") is disqualified as a result of their immigration status from occupying premises under a residential tenancy agreement if—

    (a)   P is not a relevant national, and

    (b)   P does not have a right to rent in relation to the premises.

(2) P does not have a "right to rent" in relation to premises if—

    (a)   P requires leave to enter or remain in the United Kingdom but does not have it, or

    (b)   P's leave to enter or remain in the United Kingdom is subject to a condition preventing P from occupying the premises.

(3) But P is to be treated as having a right to rent in relation to premises (in spite of subsection (2)) if the Secretary of State has granted P permission for the purposes of this Chapter to occupy premises under a residential tenancy agreement.

(4) References in this Chapter to a person with a "limited right to rent" are references to—

    (a)   a person who has been granted leave to enter or remain in the United Kingdom for a limited period, or

    (b)   a person who—

        (i)   is not a relevant national, and

        (ii)   is entitled to enter or remain in the United Kingdom by virtue of an enforceable EU right or of any provision made under section 2(2) of the European Communities Act 1972.

(5)   In this section "relevant national" means—
- (a)   a British citizen,
- (b)   a national of an EEA State other than the United Kingdom, or
- (c)   a national of Switzerland.

Penalty notices

22 Persons disqualified by immigration status not to be leased premises

(1)   A landlord must not authorise an adult to occupy premises under a residential tenancy agreement if the adult is disqualified as a result of their immigration status.

(2)   A landlord is to be taken to "authorise" an adult to occupy premises in the circumstances mentioned in subsection (1) if (and only if) there is a contravention of this section.

(3)   There is a contravention of this section in either of the following cases.

(4)   The first case is where a residential tenancy agreement is entered into that, at the time of entry, grants a right to occupy premises to—
- (a)   a tenant who is disqualified as a result of their immigration status,
- (b)   another adult named in the agreement who is disqualified as a result of their immigration status, or
- (c)   another adult not named in the agreement who is disqualified as a result of their immigration status (subject to subsection (6)).

(5)   The second case is where—
- (a)   a residential tenancy agreement is entered into that grants a right to occupy premises on an adult with a limited right to rent,
- (b)   the adult later becomes a person disqualified as a result of their immigration status, and
- (c)   the adult continues to occupy the premises after becoming disqualified.

(6)   There is a contravention as a result of subsection (4)(c) only if—
- (a)   reasonable enquiries were not made of the tenant before entering into the agreement as to the relevant occupiers, or
- (b)   reasonable enquiries were so made and it was, or should have been, apparent from the enquiries that the adult in question was likely to be a relevant occupier.

(7)   Any term of a residential tenancy agreement that prohibits occupation of premises by a person disqualified by their immigration status is to be ignored for the purposes of determining whether there has been a contravention of this section if—
- (a)   the landlord knew when entering into the agreement that the term would be breached, or
- (b)   the prescribed requirements were not complied with before entering into the agreement.

(8)   It does not matter for the purposes of this section whether or not—
- (a)   a right of occupation is exercisable on entering into an agreement or from a later date;
- (b)   a right of occupation is granted unconditionally or on satisfaction of a condition.

(9)   A contravention of this section does not affect the validity or enforceability of any provision of a residential tenancy agreement by virtue of any rule of law relating to the validity or enforceability of contracts in circumstances involving illegality.

(10)   In this Chapter—

"post-grant contravention" means a contravention in the second case mentioned in subsection (5);

"pre-grant contravention" means a contravention in the first case mentioned in subsection (4);

"relevant occupier", in relation to a residential tenancy agreement, means any adult who occupies premises under the agreement (whether or not named in the agreement).

23 Penalty notices: landlords

(1) If there is a contravention of section 22, the Secretary of State may give the responsible landlord a notice requiring the payment of a penalty.

(2) The amount of the penalty is such an amount as the Secretary of State considers appropriate, but the amount must not exceed £3,000.

(3) "Responsible landlord" means—

    (a)   in relation to a pre-grant contravention, the landlord who entered into the residential tenancy agreement;

    (b)   in relation to a post-grant contravention, the person who is the landlord under the agreement at the time of the contravention.

(4) But if there is a superior landlord in relation to the residential tenancy agreement who is responsible for the purposes of this section, the "responsible landlord" means that superior landlord (and references to the landlord in the following provisions of this Chapter are to be read accordingly).

(5) A superior landlord is "responsible for the purposes of this section" if arrangements in writing have been made in relation to the residential tenancy agreement between the landlord and the superior landlord under which the superior landlord accepts responsibility for—

    (a)   contraventions of section 22 generally, or

    (b)   contraventions of a particular description and the contravention in question is of that description.

(6) The Secretary of State may by order amend the amount for the time being specified in subsection (2).

24 Excuses available to landlords

(1) This section applies where a landlord is given a notice under section 23 requiring payment of a penalty.

(2) Where the notice is given for a pre-grant contravention, the landlord is excused from paying the penalty if the landlord shows that—

    (a)   the prescribed requirements were complied with before the residential tenancy agreement was entered into, or

    (b)   a person acting as the landlord's agent is responsible for the contravention (see section 25(2)).

(3) The prescribed requirements may be complied with for the purposes of subsection (2)(a) at any time before the residential tenancy agreement is entered into.

(4) But where compliance with the prescribed requirements discloses that a relevant occupier is a person with a limited right to rent, the landlord is excused under subsection (2)(a) only if the requirements are complied with in relation to that occupier within such period as may be prescribed.

(5) The excuse under subsection (2)(a) or (b) is not available if the landlord knew that entering into the agreement would contravene section 22.

(6) Where the notice is given for a post-grant contravention, the landlord is excused from paying the penalty if any of the following applies—

    (a)   the landlord has notified the Secretary of State of the contravention as soon as reasonably practicable;

    (b)   a person acting as the landlord's agent is responsible for the contravention;

    (c)   the eligibility period in relation to the limited right occupier whose occupation caused the contravention has not expired.

(7)   For the purposes of subsection (6)(a), the landlord is to be taken to have notified the Secretary of State of the contravention "as soon as reasonably practicable" if the landlord—

    (a)   complied with the prescribed requirements in relation to each limited right occupier at the end of the eligibility period, and

    (b)   notified the Secretary of State of the contravention without delay on it first becoming apparent that the contravention had occurred.

(8)   Notification under subsection (6)(a) must be in the prescribed form and manner.

(9)   In this Chapter "limited right occupier", in relation to a residential tenancy agreement, means a relevant occupier who had a limited right to rent at the time when the occupier was first granted a right to occupy the premises under the agreement.

Subordinate Legislation

Immigration (Residential Accommodation) (Prescribed Requirements and Codes of Practice) Order 2014, SI 2014/2874.

25 Penalty notices: agents

(1)   Subsection (3) applies where—

    (a)   a landlord contravenes section 22, and

    (b)   a person acting as the landlord's agent ("the agent") is responsible for the contravention.

(2)   For the purposes of this Chapter, an agent is responsible for a landlord's contravention of section 22 if (and only if)—

    (a)   the agent acts in the course of a business, and

    (b)   under arrangements made with the landlord in writing, the agent was under an obligation for the purposes of this Chapter to comply with the prescribed requirements on behalf of the landlord.

(3)   The Secretary of State may give the agent a notice requiring the agent to pay a penalty.

(4)   The amount of the penalty is such an amount as the Secretary of State considers appropriate, but the amount must not exceed £3,000.

(5)   The Secretary of State may by order amend the amount for the time being specified in subsection (4).

26 Excuses available to agents

(1)   This section applies where an agent is given a notice under section 25 requiring payment of a penalty.

(2)   Where the notice is given for a pre-grant contravention, the agent is excused from paying the penalty if the agent shows that the prescribed requirements were complied with before the residential tenancy agreement was entered into.

(3)   The prescribed requirements may be complied with for the purposes of subsection (2) at any time before the residential tenancy agreement is entered into.

(4)   But where compliance with the prescribed requirements discloses that a relevant occupier is a person with a limited right to rent, the agent is excused under subsection (2) only if the requirements are complied with in relation to that occupier within such period as may be prescribed.

(5)   The excuse under subsection (2) is not available if the agent—

    (a)   knew that the landlord would contravene section 22 by entering into the agreement,

    (b)   had sufficient opportunity to notify the landlord of that fact before the landlord entered into the agreement, but

    (c)   did not do so.

(6)   Where the notice is given for a post-grant contravention, the agent is excused from paying the penalty if either of the following applies—

(a) notify the recipient of the decision (including the amount of any increased or reduced penalty) before the end of the prescribed period or such longer period as the Secretary of State may agree with the recipient, and

(b) if the penalty is increased, issue a new penalty notice under section 23 or (as the case may be) section 25.

Subordinate Legislation

Immigration (Residential Accommodation) (Prescribed Requirements and Codes of Practice) Order 2014, SI 2014/2874.

30 Appeals

(1) The recipient may appeal to the court on the ground that—

(a) the recipient is not liable to the imposition of a penalty,

(b) the recipient is excused payment as a result of section 24 or 26, or

(c) the amount of the penalty is too high.

(2) The court may—

(a) allow the appeal and cancel the penalty,

(b) allow the appeal and reduce the penalty, or

(c) dismiss the appeal.

(3) An appeal is to be a re-hearing of the Secretary of State's decision to impose a penalty and is to be determined having regard to—

(a) the code of practice under section 32 that has effect at the time of the appeal, and

(b) any other matters which the court thinks relevant (which may include matters of which the Secretary of State was unaware).

(4) Subsection (3) has effect despite any provisions of rules of court.

(5) An appeal may be brought only if the recipient has given a notice of objection under section 29 and the Secretary of State—

(a) has determined the objection by issuing to the recipient the penalty notice (as a result of increasing the penalty under section 29(5)(c)),

(b) has determined the objection by—

(i) reducing the penalty under section 29(5)(b), or

(ii) taking no action under section 29(5)(d), or

(c) has not informed the recipient of a decision before the end of the period that applies for the purposes of section 29(6)(a).

(6) An appeal must be brought within the period of 28 days beginning with the relevant date.

(7) Where the appeal is brought under subsection (5)(a), the relevant date is the date specified in the penalty notice issued in accordance with section 29(6)(b) as the date on which it is given.

(8) Where the appeal is brought under subsection (5)(b), the relevant date is the date specified in the notice informing the recipient of the decision for the purposes of section 29(6)(a) as the date on which it is given.

(9) Where the appeal is brought under subsection (5)(c), the relevant date is the date on which the period that applies for the purposes of section 29(6)(a) ends.

(10) In this section "the court" means—

(a) the county court, if the appeal relates to a residential tenancy agreement in relation to premises in England and Wales;

(b) the sheriff, if the appeal relates to a residential tenancy agreement in relation to premises in Scotland;

(c) a county court in Northern Ireland, if the appeal relates to a residential tenancy agreement in relation to premises in Northern Ireland.

31 Enforcement

(1)   This section applies where a sum is payable to the Secretary of State as a penalty under this Chapter.

(2)   In England and Wales the penalty is recoverable as if it were payable under an order of the county court in England and Wales.

(3)   In Scotland the penalty may be enforced in the same manner as an extract registered decree arbitral bearing a warrant for execution issued by the sheriff court of any sheriffdom in Scotland.

(4)   In Northern Ireland the penalty is recoverable as if it were payable under an order of a county court in Northern Ireland.

(5)   Where action is taken under this section for the recovery of a sum payable as a penalty under this Chapter, the penalty is—

    (a)   in relation to England and Wales, to be treated for the purposes of section 98 of the Courts Act 2003 (register of judgments and orders etc) as if it were a judgment entered in the county court;

    (b)   in relation to Northern Ireland, to be treated for the purposes of Article 116 of the Judgments Enforcement (Northern Ireland) Order 1981 (SI 1981/226 (N.I. 6)) (register of judgments) as if it were a judgment in respect of which an application has been accepted under Article 22 or 23(1) of that Order.

(6)   Money paid to the Secretary of State by way of a penalty must be paid into the Consolidated Fund.

Codes of practice

32 General matters

(1)   The Secretary of State must issue a code of practice for the purposes of this Chapter.

(2)   The code must specify factors that the Secretary of State will consider when determining the amount of a penalty imposed under this Chapter.

(3)   The code may contain guidance about—

    (a)   factors that the Secretary of State will consider when determining whether—

        (i)   a residential tenancy agreement grants a right of occupation of premises for residential use, or

        (ii)   a person is occupying premises as an only or main residence;

    (b)   the reasonable enquiries that a landlord should make to determine the identity of relevant occupiers in relation to a residential tenancy agreement (so far as they are not named in the agreement);

    (c)   any other matters in connection with this Chapter that the Secretary of State considers appropriate.

(4)   Guidance under subsection (3)(a) may in particular relate to the treatment for the purposes of this Chapter of arrangements that are made in connection with holiday lettings or lettings for purposes connected with business travel.

(5)   The Secretary of State must from time to time review the code and may revise and re-issue it following a review.

(6)   The code (or revised code)—

    (a)   may not be issued unless a draft has been laid before Parliament, and

    (b)   comes into force in accordance with provision made by order of the Secretary of State.

Subordinate Legislation

Immigration (Residential Accommodation) (Prescribed Requirements and Codes of Practice) Order 2014, SI 2014/2874.

33 Discrimination

(1) The Secretary of State must issue a code of practice specifying what a landlord or agent should or should not do to ensure that, while avoiding liability to pay a penalty under this Chapter, the landlord or agent also avoids contravening—

  (a)   the Equality Act 2010, so far as relating to race, or

  (b)   the Race Relations (Northern Ireland) Order 1997 (SI 1997/869 (N.I. 6)).

(2) The Secretary of State must from time to time review the code and may revise and re-issue it following a review.

(3) Before issuing the code (or a revised code) the Secretary of State must consult—

  (a)   the Commission for Equality and Human Rights,

  (b)   the Equality Commission for Northern Ireland, and

  (c)   such persons representing the interests of landlords and tenants as the Secretary of State considers appropriate.

(4) After consulting under subsection (3) the Secretary of State must—

  (a)   publish a draft code, and

  (b)   consider any representations made about the published draft.

(5) The code (or revised code)—

  (a)   may not be issued unless a draft has been laid before Parliament (prepared after considering representations under subsection (4)(b) and with or without modifications to reflect the representations), and

  (b)   comes into force in accordance with provision made by order of the Secretary of State.

(6) A breach of the code—

  (a)   does not make a person liable to civil or criminal proceedings, but

  (b)   may be taken into account by a court or tribunal.

Subordinate Legislation

Immigration (Residential Accommodation) (Prescribed Requirements and Codes of Practice) Order 2014, SI 2014/2874.

General

34 Orders

(1) An order prescribing requirements for the purposes of this Chapter may, in particular, require a landlord or agent to—

  (a)   obtain a document of a prescribed description from relevant occupiers before or during the course of a residential tenancy agreement;

  (b)   obtain one document of each of a number of prescribed descriptions from relevant occupiers before or during the course of a residential tenancy agreement;

  (c)   take steps to verify, retain, copy or record the content of a document obtained in accordance with the order;

  (d)   take such other steps before or during the course of a residential tenancy agreement as the order may specify.

(2) If the draft of an instrument containing an order under or in connection with this Chapter would, apart from this subsection, be a hybrid instrument for the purposes of the standing orders of either House of Parliament, it is to proceed in that House as if it were not a hybrid instrument.

Subordinate Legislation

Immigration (Residential Accommodation) (Prescribed Requirements and Codes of Practice) Order 2014, SI 2014/2874.

35 Transitional provision

(1) This Chapter does not apply in relation to a residential tenancy agreement entered into before the commencement day.

(2) This Chapter does not apply in relation to a residential tenancy agreement entered into on or after the commencement day ("the renewed agreement") if—

    (a)   another residential tenancy agreement was entered into before the commencement day between the same parties ("the original agreement"), and

    (b)   the tenant has always had a right of occupation of the premises leased under the renewed agreement since entering into the original agreement.

(3) In this section "the commencement day" means such day as the Secretary of State may by order appoint; and different days may be appointed for different purposes or areas.

36 Crown application

This Chapter binds the Crown, except where the Crown is the responsible landlord for the purposes of section 23.

37 Interpretation

(1) In this Chapter—

    "adult" means a person who has attained the age of 18;

    "agreement" includes an agreement in any form (whether or not in writing);

    "eligibility period", in relation to a limited right occupier, is to be read in accordance with section 27;

    "limited right occupier" has the meaning given in section 24(9);

    "occupy" means occupy as an only or main residence;

    "penalty notice" means a penalty notice given under this Chapter;

    "person with a limited right to rent" has the meaning given in section 21(4);

    "post-grant contravention" has the meaning given in section 22(10);

    "pre-grant contravention" has the meaning given in section 22(10);

    "premises" includes land, buildings, moveable structures, vehicles and vessels;

    "prescribed" means prescribed in an order made by the Secretary of State;

    "recipient" means the recipient of a penalty notice;

    "relevant occupier" has the meaning given in section 22(10);

    "residential tenancy agreement" has the meaning given in section 20(2).

(2) For the purposes of this Chapter a residential tenancy agreement grants a person a right to occupy premises if—

    (a)   the agreement expressly grants that person the right (whether or not by naming the person), or

    (b)   the person is permitted to occupy the premises by virtue of an express grant given to another person,

and references to a person occupying premises under an agreement are to be read accordingly.

(3) A reference in this Chapter to the "prescribed requirements", in connection with compliance with the requirements at a particular time, is a reference only to such of the requirements as are capable of being complied with at that time.

(4) Where two or more persons jointly constitute the landlord in relation to a residential tenancy agreement—

    (a)   the references to the landlord in—

        (i)   section 22(7)(a),

        (ii)   section 24(5), (6)(a) and (7), and

        (iii)   section 26(6)(a) and (7)(b),

    are to be taken as references to any of those persons;

(b)   any other references to the landlord in this Chapter are to be taken as references to all of those persons.

(5)   Where two or more persons jointly constitute the agent in relation to a residential tenancy agreement—

(a)   the references to the agent in section 26(5), (6)(a) and (7) are to be taken as references to any of those persons;

(b)   any other references to the agent in this Chapter are to be taken as references to all of those persons.

(6)   The Secretary of State may by order prescribe cases in which—

(a)   a residential tenancy agreement is, or is not, to be treated as being entered into for the purposes of this Chapter;

(b)   a person is, or is not, to be treated as occupying premises as an only or main residence for the purposes of this Chapter.

(7)   An order under subsection (6) prescribing a case may modify the application of this Chapter in relation to that case.

(8)   The cases mentioned in subsection (6)(a) include, in particular, cases where—

(a)   an option to renew an agreement is exercised;

(b)   rights of occupation under an agreement are varied;

(c)   an agreement is assigned (whether by the landlord or the tenant);

(d)   a periodic tenancy arises at the end of a fixed term;

(e)   an agreement grants a right of occupation on satisfaction of a condition;

(f)   there is a change in the persons in occupation of the premises leased under an agreement or in the circumstances of any such person.

Subordinate Legislation

Immigration (Residential Accommodation) (Prescribed Requirements and Codes of Practice) Order 2014, SI 2014/2874.

CHAPTER 2

OTHER SERVICES ETC
National Health Service

38 Immigration health charge

(1)   The Secretary of State may by order provide for a charge to be imposed on—

(a)   persons who apply for immigration permission, or

(b)   any description of such persons.

(2)   "Immigration permission" means—

(a)   leave to enter or remain in the United Kingdom for a limited period,

(b)   entry clearance which, by virtue of provision made under section 3A(3) of the Immigration Act 1971, has effect as leave to enter the United Kingdom for a limited period, or

(c)   any other entry clearance which may be taken as evidence of a person's eligibility for entry into the United Kingdom for a limited period.

(3)   An order under this section may in particular—

(a)   impose a separate charge on a person in respect of each application made by that person;

(b)   specify the amount of any charge (and different amounts may be specified for different purposes);

(c)   make provision about when or how a charge may or must be paid to the Secretary of State;

(d)   make provision about the consequences of a person failing to pay a charge (including provision for the person's application to be refused);

(e)   provide for exemptions from a charge;

    (f)   provide for the reduction, waiver or refund of part or all of a charge (whether by conferring a discretion or otherwise).

(4)   In specifying the amount of a charge under subsection (3)(b) the Secretary of State must (among other matters) have regard to the range of health services that are likely to be available free of charge to persons who have been given immigration permission.

(5)   Sums paid by virtue of an order under this section must—

    (a)   be paid into the Consolidated Fund, or

    (b)   be applied in such other way as the order may specify.

(6)   In this section—

"entry clearance" has the meaning given by section 33(1) of the Immigration Act 1971;

"health services" means services provided as part of the health service in England, Wales, Scotland and Northern Ireland;

and the references to applying for leave to enter or remain for a limited period include references to applying for a variation of leave to enter or remain which would result in leave to enter or remain for a limited period.

39 Related provision: charges for health services

(1)   A reference in the NHS charging provisions to persons not ordinarily resident in Great Britain or persons not ordinarily resident in Northern Ireland includes (without prejudice to the generality of that reference) a reference to—

    (a)   persons who require leave to enter or remain in the United Kingdom but do not have it, and

    (b)   persons who have leave to enter or remain in the United Kingdom for a limited period.

(2)   The "NHS charging provisions" are—

    (a)   section 175 of the National Health Service Act 2006 (charges in respect of persons not ordinarily resident in Great Britain);

    (b)   section 124 of the National Health Service (Wales) Act 2006 (charges in respect of persons not ordinarily resident in Great Britain);

    (c)   section 98 of the National Health Service (Scotland) Act 1978 (charges in respect of persons not ordinarily resident in Great Britain);

    (d)   Article 42 of the Health and Personal Social Services (Northern Ireland) Order 1972 (SI 1972/1265 (N.I. 14)) (provision of services to persons not ordinarily resident in Northern Ireland).

Bank accounts

40 Prohibition on opening current accounts for disqualified persons

(1)   A bank or building society (B) must not open a current account for a person (P) who is within subsection (2) unless—

    (a)   B has carried out a status check which indicates that P is not a disqualified person, or

    (b)   at the time when the account is opened B is unable, because of circumstances that cannot reasonably be regarded as within its control, to carry out a status check in relation to P.

(2)   A person is within this subsection if he or she—

    (a)   is in the United Kingdom, and

    (b)   requires leave to enter or remain in the United Kingdom but does not have it.

(3)   For the purposes of this section—

    (a)   carrying out a "status check" in relation to P means checking with a specified anti-fraud organisation or a specified data-matching authority whether, according to information supplied to that organisation or authority by the Secretary of State, P is a disqualified person;

(b) a "disqualified person" is a person within subsection (2) for whom the Secretary of State considers that a current account should not be opened by a bank or building society;

(c) opening an account for P includes—

(i) opening a joint account for P and others;

(ii) opening an account in relation to which P is a signatory or is identified as a beneficiary;

(iii) adding P as an account holder or as a signatory or identified beneficiary in relation to an account.

(4) In subsection (3)(a)—

"anti-fraud organisation" has the same meaning as in section 68 of the Serious Crime Act 2007;

"data-matching authority" means a person or body conducting data matching exercises, within the meaning of Schedule 9 to the Local Audit and Accountability Act 2014, under or by virtue of that or any other Act;

"specified" means specified by an order made by the Secretary of State for the purposes of this section.

(5) Subsection (1)(b) does not apply where—

(a) a bank or building society is required to pay a reasonable fee for carrying out status checks, and

(b) its inability to carry out a status check is due to its failure to pay the fee.

(6) A bank or building society that refuses to open a current account for someone on the ground that he or she is a disqualified person must tell the person, if it may lawfully do so, that that is the reason for its refusal.

Subordinate Legislation

Immigration Act 2014 (Specified Anti-fraud Organisation) Order 2014, SI 2014/1798.

41 Regulation by Financial Conduct Authority

(1) The Treasury may make regulations to enable the Financial Conduct Authority to make arrangements for monitoring and enforcing compliance with the prohibition imposed on banks and building societies by section 40.

(2) The regulations may (in particular)—

(a) provide for the Financial Conduct Authority to be given free access to the information to which banks and building societies are given access when carrying out status checks under section 40;

(b) apply, or make provision corresponding to, any of the provisions of the Financial Services and Markets Act 2000, including in particular those mentioned in subsection (3), with or without modification.

(3) The provisions are—

(a) provisions about investigations, including powers of entry and search and criminal offences;

(b) provisions for the grant of an injunction (or, in Scotland, an interdict) in relation to a contravention or anticipated contravention;

(c) provisions giving the Financial Conduct Authority powers to impose disciplinary measures (including financial penalties) or to give directions;

(d) provisions giving a Minister of the Crown (within the meaning of the Ministers of the Crown Act 1975) or the Financial Conduct Authority powers to make subordinate legislation;

(e) provisions for the Financial Conduct Authority to charge fees.

42 "Bank" and "building society"

(1) In sections 40 and 41 "bank" means an authorised deposit-taker that has its head office or a branch in the United Kingdom.

This is subject to subsection (4).

(2) In subsection (1) "authorised deposit-taker" means—

   (a)   a person who under Part 4A of the Financial Services and Markets Act 2000 has permission to accept deposits;

   (b)   an EEA firm of the kind mentioned in paragraph 5(b) of Schedule 3 to that Act that has permission under paragraph 15 of that Schedule (as a result of qualifying for authorisation under paragraph 12(1) of that Schedule) to accept deposits.

(3) A reference in subsection (2) to a person or firm with permission to accept deposits does not include a person or firm with permission to do so only for the purposes of, or in the course of, an activity other than accepting deposits.

(4) "Bank" does not include—

   (a)   a building society;

   (b)   a person who is specified, or is within a class of persons specified, by an order under section 38 of the Financial Services and Markets Act 2000 (exemption orders);

   (c)   a credit union within the meaning given by section 31(1) of the Credit Unions Act 1979 or by Article 2(2) of the Credit Unions (Northern Ireland) Order 1985;

   (d)   a friendly society within the meaning given by section 116 of the Friendly Societies Act 1992.

(5) In sections 40 and 41, and in subsection (4), "building society" means a building society incorporated (or deemed to be incorporated) under the Building Societies Act 1986.

43 Power to amend

(1) The Treasury may by order amend any of sections 40 to 42 so as—

   (a)   to alter the categories of financial institution to which those sections apply;

   (b)   to alter the categories of account to which the prohibition in section 40(1) applies;

   (c)   to include provision defining a category of account specified in that section;

   (d)   to provide for the prohibition in section 40(1) not to apply in the case of an account to be operated (or an account that is operated) by or for a person or body of a specified description.

(2) An order under subsection (1) may amend a section so that it provides for a matter to be specified in a further order to be made by the Treasury.

(3) In subsection (1) "account" includes a financial product by means of which a payment may be made.

Work

44 Appeals against penalty notices

In section 17 of the Immigration, Asylum and Nationality Act 2006 (appeal), for subsections (4) and (5) substitute—

   "(4A)   An appeal may be brought only if the employer has given a notice of objection under section 16 and the Secretary of State—

   (a)   has determined the objection by issuing to the employer the penalty notice (as a result of increasing the penalty under section 16(4)(c)),

   (b)   has determined the objection by—

(i)   reducing the penalty under section 16(4)(b), or

(ii)   taking no action under section 16(4)(d), or

(c)   has not informed the employer of a decision before the end of the period that applies for the purposes of section 16(5)(b).

(4B)   An appeal must be brought within the period of 28 days beginning with the relevant date.

(4C)   Where the appeal is brought under subsection (4A)(a), the relevant date is the date specified in the penalty notice issued in accordance with section 16(5)(c) as the date on which it is given.

(4D)   Where the appeal is brought under subsection (4A)(b), the relevant date is the date specified in the notice informing the employer of the decision for the purposes of section 16(5)(b) as the date on which it is given.

(4E)   Where the appeal is brought under subsection (4A)(c), the relevant date is the date on which the period that applies for the purposes of section 16(5)(b) ends."

45 Recovery of sums payable under penalty notices

In section 18 of the Immigration, Asylum and Nationality Act 2006 (enforcement), for subsections (1) and (2) substitute—

"(1)   This section applies where a sum is payable to the Secretary of State as a penalty under section 15.

(1A)   In England and Wales the penalty is recoverable as if it were payable under an order of the county court.

(1B)   In Scotland, the penalty may be enforced in the same manner as an extract registered decree arbitral bearing a warrant for execution issued by the sheriff court of any sheriffdom in Scotland.

(1C)   In Northern Ireland the penalty is recoverable as if it were payable under an order of a county court in Northern Ireland.

(1D)   Where action is taken under this section for the recovery of a sum payable as a penalty under section 15, the penalty is—

(a)   in relation to England and Wales, to be treated for the purposes of section 98 of the Courts Act 2003 (register of judgments and orders etc) as if it were a judgment entered in the county court;

(b)   in relation to Northern Ireland, to be treated for the purposes of Article 116 of the Judgments Enforcement (Northern Ireland) Order 1981 (SI 1981/226 (N.I. 6)) (register of judgments) as if it were a judgment in respect of which an application has been accepted under Article 22 or 23(1) of that Order."

Driving licences

46 Grant of driving licences: residence requirement

(1)   In section 97 of the Road Traffic Act 1988 (grant of licences), in the opening words of subsection (1), after "who" insert "meets the relevant residence requirement (see section 97A) and".

(2)   After that section insert—

"97A Residence requirement

(1)   For the purposes of an application under section 97, a person meets the relevant residence requirement if, on the date the application is made—

(a)   in the case of an application that is made by virtue of section 89(1)(ea) (application by holder of Community licence), the applicant is lawfully resident in the United Kingdom and—

(i)   is also normally resident in the United Kingdom, or

> > (ii) has been attending a course of study in the United Kingdom during the period of six months ending on that date;
> (b) in the case of an application that is made by virtue of section 89(1)(f) (application by holder of exchangeable licence), the applicant is normally and lawfully resident in Great Britain but has not been so resident for more than the prescribed period;
> (c) in the case of an application that is made by virtue of section 97(2) (application for provisional licence), the applicant is lawfully resident in Great Britain and the Secretary of State is satisfied that the applicant will remain so for not less than 185 days; and
> (d) in any other case, the applicant is normally and lawfully resident in Great Britain.

(2) For the purposes of subsection (1) a person is not lawfully resident in Great Britain or the United Kingdom if the person requires leave to enter or remain in the United Kingdom but does not have it."

(3) In Article 13 of the Road Traffic (Northern Ireland) Order 1981 (SI 1981/154 (NI 1)) (grant of licences), in the opening words of paragraph (1), after "who" insert "meets the relevant residence requirement (see Article 13A) and".

(4) After that Article insert—

"13A Residence requirement

(1) For the purposes of an application under Article 13, a person meets the relevant residence requirement if, on the date the application is made—

> (a) in the case of an application that is made by virtue of Article 5(1)(ea) (application by holder of Community licence), the applicant is lawfully resident in the United Kingdom and—
> > (i) is also normally resident in the United Kingdom, or
> > (ii) has been attending a course of study in the United Kingdom during the period of six months ending on that date;
> (b) in the case of an application that is made by virtue of Article 5(1)(f) (application by holder of exchangeable licence), the applicant is normally and lawfully resident in Northern Ireland but has not been so resident for more than the prescribed period;
> (c) in the case of an application that is made by virtue of Article 13(2) (application for provisional licence), the applicant is lawfully resident in Northern Ireland and the Department is satisfied that the applicant will remain so for not less than 185 days; and
> (d) in any other case, the applicant is normally and lawfully resident in Northern Ireland.

(2) For the purposes of paragraph (1) a person is not lawfully resident in Northern Ireland or the United Kingdom if the person requires leave to enter or remain in the United Kingdom but does not have it."

47 Revocation of driving licences on grounds of immigration status

(1) In section 99 of the Road Traffic Act 1988 (duration of licences)—

> (a) after subsection (3) insert—

"(3ZA) Where it appears to the Secretary of State that a licence holder is not lawfully resident in the United Kingdom, the Secretary of State may serve notice in writing on that person revoking the licence and requiring the person to surrender the licence and its counterpart forthwith to the Secretary of State, and it is the duty of that person to comply with the requirement.

(3ZB) For the purposes of subsection (3ZA) a person is not lawfully resident in the United Kingdom if the person requires leave to enter or remain in the United Kingdom but does not have it.";

> (b) in subsection (5), after "(3)" insert ", (3ZA)";

50 Conduct of investigation

(1) An investigation must be conducted in accordance with any regulations made by the Secretary of State for this purpose.

(2) In conducting an investigation, regard must also be had to any guidance published by the Secretary of State for this purpose.

(3) A relevant party must comply with a requirement specified in regulations made under section 51(4) if—

    (a)   the section 48 notice given to the relevant party states that he or she must do so, or

    (b)   the Secretary of State subsequently notifies the relevant party (orally or in writing) that he or she must do so;

and the relevant party must comply with that requirement in the manner stated in the section 48 notice or in the Secretary of State's notification (if such a manner is stated there).

(4) As part of an investigation, the Secretary of State must decide whether or not each of the relevant parties has complied with the investigation (the "compliance question").

(5) The compliance question must be decided in accordance with any regulations made by the Secretary of State for this purpose.

(6) In deciding the compliance question, regard must also be had to any guidance published by the Secretary of State for this purpose.

(7) Within the 70 day period, the Secretary of State must—

    (a)   decide the compliance question; and

    (b)   give notice of that decision to the persons to whom the Secretary of State gave the section 48 notice relating to the proposed marriage or civil partnership.

(8) If the Secretary of State's decision is that one or both of the relevant parties have not complied with the investigation, the notice under subsection (7) must include a statement of the Secretary of State's reasons for reaching that decision.

(9) Regulations made under this section may, in particular, make provision about—

    (a)   the circumstances in which a relevant party is to be taken to have failed to comply with a relevant requirement;

    (b)   the consequences of a relevant party's failure to comply with a relevant requirement.

(10) The provision that may be made under subsection (9)(b) includes provision for the compliance question to be decided (in whole or in part) by reference to a relevant party's compliance or non-compliance with one or more relevant requirements.

(11) In this section—

    "70 day period" means the period of 70 days beginning with the day on which the relevant statutory period begins;

    "investigation" means an investigation, conducted following a decision by the Secretary of State under section 48, whether a proposed marriage or civil partnership is a sham;

    "relevant party" means a person who is a party to a proposed marriage or civil partnership that is the subject of an investigation;

    "relevant requirement" means any requirement imposed by law, including a requirement imposed by or in accordance with—

        (a)   subsection (3);

        (b)   section 27E, 28B or 28C of the Marriage Act 1949;

        (c)   regulations under section 28D of that Act;

        (d)   section 8A, or any of sections 9 to 9B, of the Civil Partnership Act 2004.

51 Investigations: supplementary

(1)   A section 48 notice which states that the Secretary of State has decided to investigate whether a proposed marriage or civil partnership is a sham must include—

- (a)   notice that the compliance question must be decided within the period of 70 days mentioned in section 50(7);
- (b)   notice of the date on which that period will end;
- (c)   notice that a relevant party may be required to comply with one or more requirements imposed by the Secretary of State subsequently in accordance with section 50(3); and
- (d)   prescribed information about the investigation.

(2)   The section 48 notice may also include such other information as the Secretary of State considers appropriate.

(3)   For the purposes of subsection (1)(d) "prescribed information" means information prescribed by the Secretary of State by regulations; and the information that may be prescribed includes information about—

- (a)   the conduct of the investigation;
- (b)   requirements with which the relevant parties must comply in relation to the investigation;
- (c)   the consequence of a failure to comply with those or any other requirements;
- (d)   the possible outcomes of the investigation;
- (e)   the consequences of those outcomes.

(4)   The Secretary of State may, by regulations, specify requirements relating to the conduct of investigations which may be imposed on a relevant party by the section 48 notice or by the Secretary of State subsequently in accordance with section 50(3).

(5)   Regulations made under subsection (4) may, in particular, specify any of the following requirements—

- (a)   a requirement to make contact with a particular person or description of persons in a particular way (including by telephoning a particular number) within a particular time period;
- (b)   a requirement to be present at a particular place at a particular time;
- (c)   a requirement to be visited at home;
- (d)   a requirement to be interviewed;
- (e)   a requirement to provide information (whether orally or in writing);
- (f)   a requirement to provide photographs;
- (g)   a requirement to provide evidence.

(6)   The provisions of this Part, and any investigation or other steps taken under those provisions (including the decision of the compliance question), do not limit the powers of the Secretary of State in relation to marriages or civil partnerships that are, or are suspected to be, a sham (including any powers to investigate such marriages or civil partnerships).

(7)   In this section "investigation", "relevant party" and "compliance question" have the same meanings as in section 50.

Referral

52 Referral of proposed marriages and civil partnerships in England and Wales

Schedule 4 (referral of proposed marriages and civil partnerships in England and Wales) has effect.

Scotland and Northern Ireland

53 Extension of scheme to Scotland and Northern Ireland

(1) The Secretary of State may, by order, make such provision as the Secretary of State considers appropriate for extending the referral and investigation scheme to any of the following—

    (a)   proposed marriages under the law of Scotland;

    (b)   proposed civil partnerships under the law of Scotland;

    (c)   proposed marriages under the law of Northern Ireland;

    (d)   proposed civil partnerships under the law of Northern Ireland.

(2) An order under this section may—

    (a)   make provision having a similar effect to the provision made by section 58, Schedule 4, or Parts 1, 2 and 4 of Schedule 6;

    (b)   confer functions on any person;

    (c)   amend, repeal or revoke any enactment (including an enactment contained in this Act).

(3) The power under subsection (2)(b) to confer functions includes power to impose a duty of referral on persons exercising functions in Scotland or Northern Ireland in relation to marriage or civil partnership.

(4) But an order under this section may not impose that or any other duty, or otherwise confer functions, on—

    (a)   the Scottish Ministers,

    (b)   the First Minister and deputy First Minister in Northern Ireland,

    (c)   a Northern Ireland Minister, or

    (d)   a Northern Ireland department.

(5) In this section—

"duty of referral" means a duty to refer a proposed marriage or proposed civil partnership to the Secretary of State in a case where—

    (a)   one of the parties is not an exempt person, or

    (b)   both of the parties are not exempt persons;

"enactment" includes—

    (a)   an enactment contained in subordinate legislation within the meaning of the Interpretation Act 1978;

    (b)   an enactment contained in, or in an instrument made under, an Act of the Scottish Parliament;

    (c)   an enactment contained in, or in an instrument made under, Northern Ireland legislation;

"referral and investigation scheme" means the provision made by sections 48 to 51.

54 Supplementary provision

(1) This section applies if the referral and investigation scheme is extended by an order under section 53 (an "extension order").

(2) The Secretary of State may make administrative regulations in connection with the application of the scheme—

    (a)   to proposed marriages or civil partnerships under the law of Scotland (insofar as the scheme is extended to them), and

    (b)   to proposed marriages or civil partnerships under the law of Northern Ireland (insofar as the scheme is extended to them).

(3) For that purpose "administrative regulations" means regulations of any kind set out in Schedule 5 (sham marriage and civil partnership: administrative regulations).

(4) The Secretary of State may by order make provision about—

    (a)   the information that must or may be given, or

(b)   the matters in respect of which evidence must or may be given,

in relation to proposed marriages or civil partnerships under the law of Scotland or Northern Ireland in cases where one or both of the parties is not a relevant national.

(5) An order under subsection (4) may amend, repeal or revoke any enactment (including an enactment contained in this Act or in provision made by an extension order or an order under subsection (4)).

(6) If an extension order makes provision ("information disclosure provision") having similar effect to the provision made by paragraph 2 of Schedule 6 about the disclosure of information for immigration purposes, the Secretary of State may by order specify other immigration purposes (in addition to those specified in provision made by an extension order or in any provision made under this subsection) for which information may be disclosed under the information disclosure provision.

(7)   The Secretary of State must consult—

    (a)   the Registrar General for Scotland before making administrative regulations, or an order under subsection (4), in relation to proposed marriages or civil partnerships under the law of Scotland;

    (b)   the Registrar General for Northern Ireland before making administrative regulations, or an order under subsection (4), in relation to proposed marriages or civil partnerships under the law of Northern Ireland.

(8)   Expressions used in this section or Schedule 5 that are also used in section 53 have the same meanings in this section or Schedule 5 as in section 53.

CHAPTER 2

Sham Marriage And Civil Partnership

55 Meaning of "sham marriage" and "sham civil partnership"

(1) The Immigration and Asylum Act 1999 is amended in accordance with this section.

(2) In section 24 (duty to report suspicious marriages), for subsection (5) substitute—

   "(5)   A marriage (whether or not it is void) is a "sham marriage" if—

    (a)   either, or both, of the parties to the marriage is not a relevant national,

    (b)   there is no genuine relationship between the parties to the marriage, and

    (c)   either, or both, of the parties to the marriage enter into the marriage for one or more of these purposes—

       (i)   avoiding the effect of one or more provisions of United Kingdom immigration law or the immigration rules;

       (ii)   enabling a party to the marriage to obtain a right conferred by that law or those rules to reside in the United Kingdom.

 (6)   In subsection (5)—

   "relevant national" means—

    (a)   a British citizen,

    (b)   a national of an EEA State other than the United Kingdom, or

    (c)   a national of Switzerland;

   "United Kingdom immigration law" includes any subordinate legislation concerning the right of relevant nationals to move between and reside in member States.".

(3) In section 24A (duty to report suspicious civil partnerships), for subsection (5) substitute—

   "(5)   A civil partnership (whether or not it is void) is a "sham civil partnership" if—

(a) either, or both, of the parties to the civil partnership is not a relevant national,

(b) there is no genuine relationship between the parties to the civil partnership, and

(c) either, or both, of the parties to the civil partnership enter into the civil partnership for one or more of these purposes—

(i) avoiding the effect of one or more provisions of United Kingdom immigration law or the immigration rules;

(ii) enabling a party to the civil partnership to obtain a right conferred by that law or those rules to reside in the United Kingdom.

(5A) In subsection (5)—

"relevant national" means—

(a) a British citizen,

(b) a national of an EEA State other than the United Kingdom, or

(c) a national of Switzerland;

"United Kingdom immigration law" includes any subordinate legislation concerning the right of relevant nationals to move between and reside in member States.".

56 Duty to report suspicious marriages and civil partnerships

(1) The Immigration and Asylum Act 1999 is amended in accordance with this section.

(2) In section 24 (duty to report suspicious marriages), in subsection (1)—

(a) after paragraph (a) insert—

"(aa) a superintendent registrar, or registrar of births, deaths and marriages, who receives information in advance of a person giving such a notice,";

(b) at the end of paragraph (c), omit "or";

(c) after paragraph (c) insert—

"(ca) a district registrar who receives information in advance of a person submitting such a notice or certificate,";

(d) after paragraph (d) insert

"or

(da) a registrar or deputy registrar who receives information in advance of a person giving such a notice,".

(3) In section 24A (duty to report suspicious civil partnerships), in subsection (1)—

(a) after paragraph (a) insert—

"(aa) a registration authority that receives information in advance of a person giving such a notice,";

(b) at the end of paragraph (c), omit "or";

(c) after paragraph (c) insert—

"(ca) a district registrar who receives information in advance of a person giving such a notice,";

(d) after paragraph (d) insert

"or

(da) a registrar who receives information in advance of a person giving such a notice,".

CHAPTER 3

OTHER PROVISIONS

Persons not relevant nationals etc: marriage on superintendent registrar's certificates

57 Solemnization of marriage according to rites of Church of England

(1)   The Marriage Act 1949 is amended in accordance with this section.

(2)   In section 5 (methods of authorising marriages)—

(a)   at the beginning insert—

"(1)

(b)   in the words after paragraph (d), for "except that paragraph (a)" substitute—

"(2)   Subsection (1)(a)";

(c)   at the end insert—

"(3)   In a case where one or both of the persons whose marriage is to be solemnized is not a relevant national—

(a)   subsection (1)(a) shall not apply unless the banns are published in accordance with section 14 (whether or not the banns are also published otherwise);

(b)   subsection (1)(c) shall not apply.".

(3)   In section 8 (notice to clergy before publication of banns)—

(a)   at the beginning insert—

"(1)

(b)   for "delivered to him a notice" substitute

"delivered to him—

(a)   a notice";

(c)   at the end insert

", and

(b)   specified evidence that both of the persons are relevant nationals.

(2)   In this section "specified evidence" means evidence that is in accordance with regulations made under section 28G.".

(4)   In section 16 (provisions as to common licences), before subsection (2) insert—

"(1C)   A common licence shall not be granted unless the persons to be married deliver to the person granting the licence specified evidence that both of the persons are relevant nationals.

(1D)   For that purpose "specified evidence" means evidence that is in accordance with regulations made under section 28G.".

58 Requirement as to giving of notice of marriage or civil partnership

(1)   Section 19 of the Asylum and Immigration (Treatment of Claimants, etc) Act 2004 (procedure for marriage in England and Wales) is amended in accordance with subsections (2) and (3).

(2)   For subsection (1) substitute—

"(1)   This section applies to a marriage that is to be solemnised on the authority of certificates issued by a superintendent registrar under Part 3 of the Marriage Act 1949 (the "1949 Act") unless each party to the marriage falls within exception A or exception B.

(1A)   A party to the marriage falls within exception A if the person is a relevant national.

(1B)   A party to the marriage falls within exception B if—

(a)   the person is exempt from immigration control, and

(b)   the notice of marriage is accompanied by the specified evidence required by section 28C(2) of the 1949 Act that the person is exempt from immigration control.".

(3)   For subsection (4) substitute—

"(4)   In this section—

(a)   a reference to a person being a relevant national, or being exempt from immigration control, has the same meaning as in section 49 of the Immigration Act 2014;

(b)   "notice of marriage" means a notice of marriage given under section 27 of the 1949 Act.".

(4)   Schedule 23 to the Civil Partnership Act 2004 (immigration control and formation of civil partnerships) is amended in accordance with subsections (5) to (9).

(5)   Before paragraph 1 insert—

"A1

(1)   Part 2 of this Schedule applies to a civil partnership that is to be formed in England and Wales by signing a civil partnership schedule unless each party to the civil partnership falls within exception A or exception B.

(2)   A party to the civil partnership falls within exception A if the person is a relevant national.

(3)   A party to the civil partnership falls within exception B if—

(a)   the person is exempt from immigration control, and

(b)   the notice of civil partnership is accompanied by the specified evidence required by section 9A(2) that the person is exempt from immigration control.

(4)   In this paragraph, a reference to a person being a relevant national, or being exempt from immigration control, has the same meaning as in section 49 of the Immigration Act 2014.".

(6)   For paragraph 1(1) substitute—

"1

(1A)   Part 3 of this Schedule applies if—

(a)   two people wish to register in Scotland as civil partners of each other, and

(b)   one of them is subject to immigration control.

(1B)   Part 4 of this Schedule applies if—

(a)   two people wish to register in Northern Ireland as civil partners of each other, and

(b)   one of them is subject to immigration control.".

(7)   For paragraph 3 substitute—

"3

This Part of this Schedule applies as mentioned in paragraph A1.".

(8)   For paragraph 8 substitute—

"8

This Part of this Schedule applies as mentioned in paragraph 1(1A).".

(9)   For paragraph 12 substitute—

"12

This Part of this Schedule applies as mentioned in paragraph 1(1B).".

Information

59 Information

Schedule 6 (information) has effect.

Miscellaneous

60 Regulations about evidence

(1) The Secretary of State may make regulations about evidence relevant to the determination of any of the following questions for a purpose of this Part—

(a)   whether a person is a relevant national;

(b)   whether a person has the appropriate immigration status;

(c)   whether a person has a relevant visa.

(2) The regulations may, in particular, make provision about—

(a)   the kind of evidence which is to be supplied;

(b)   the form in which evidence is to be supplied;

(c)   the manner in which evidence is to be supplied;

(d)   the period within which evidence is to be supplied;

(e)   the supply of further evidence;

(f)   the sufficiency of evidence supplied;

(g)   the consequences of failing to supply sufficient evidence in accordance with the regulations (including provision to secure that, in such a case, a particular decision is made or is to be treated as having been made);

(h)   the retention or copying of evidence supplied.

(3) The Secretary of State must consult the Registrar General before making regulations under this section.

(4) In this section "evidence" includes a photograph or other image.

61 Notices

(1) The Secretary of State may, by regulations, make provision about the giving of—

(a)   notices under any provision of this Part;

(b)   notices relating to the referral of proposed marriages under section 28H of the Marriage Act 1949 which are given under any provision of that Act;

(c)   notices relating to the referral of proposed civil partnerships under section 12A of the Civil Partnership Act 2004 which are given under any provision of that Act.

(2) The regulations may, in particular, make provision that a notice given in accordance with the regulations is to be presumed to have been received by the person to whom it is given.

(3) The Secretary of State must consult the Registrar General before making regulations under this section.

62 Interpretation of this Part

(1) These expressions have the meanings given—

"exempt person" has the meaning given in section 49;

"registrar" means a registrar of births, deaths and marriages;

"Registrar General" means the Registrar General for England and Wales;

"registration authority" has the same meaning as in the Civil Partnership Act 2004 (see section 28 of that Act);

"relevant national" means—

(a)   a British citizen,

(b)   a national of an EEA State other than the United Kingdom, or

(c)   a national of Switzerland;

"relevant statutory period" means—

(a)   in relation to a proposed marriage, the period—

(i)   beginning the day after notice of the proposed marriage is entered in the marriage book in accordance with Part 3 of the Marriage Act 1949, or is entered in an approved electronic form by virtue of section 27(4A) of that Act, and

(ii)   ending at the end of the period of 28 days beginning with that day;

(b)   in relation to a proposed civil partnership, the period—

(i)   beginning the day after notice of the proposed civil partnership is recorded in the register in accordance with Chapter 1 of Part 2 of the Civil Partnership Act 2004, and

(ii)   ending at the end of the period of 28 days beginning with that day;

"section 48 notice" means a notice given under section 48(7) or (8);

"superintendent registrar" means a superintendent registrar of births, deaths and marriages.

(2)   A reference to a person being a party to a proposed marriage or civil partnership is a reference to a person who would be a party to the marriage or civil partnership if it took place as proposed.

(3)   A reference to a proposed marriage or civil partnership being a sham is a reference to a marriage or civil partnership which would (if it took place as proposed) be a sham marriage or sham civil partnership (within the meaning of the Immigration and Asylum Act 1999—see section 24 or 24A of that Act).

(4)   For provision about the interpretation of the following expressions, see section 49—

(a)   the appropriate immigration status;

(b)   a relevant visa.

(5)   This section, and the provision mentioned in subsection (4), apply for the purposes of this Part.

PART 5
OVERSIGHT

Office of the Immigration Services Commissioner

63 Immigration advisers and immigration service providers
Schedule 7 (immigration advisers and immigration service providers) has effect.

Police Ombudsman for Northern Ireland

64 Police Ombudsman for Northern Ireland
After section 60ZA of the Police (Northern Ireland) Act 1998 insert—

"60ZB Immigration and customs enforcement functions

(1)   The Ombudsman and the Secretary of State may enter into an agreement to establish, in relation to the exercise of specified enforcement functions by relevant officials, procedures which correspond to or are similar to any of those established by virtue of this Part.

(2)   Where no such procedures are in force in relation to a particular kind of relevant official, the Secretary of State may by order establish such procedures in relation to the exercise of specified enforcement functions by that kind of relevant official.

(3)　"Relevant officials" means—

(a)　immigration officers and other officials of the Secretary of State exercising functions relating to immigration or asylum;

(b)　designated customs officials, and officials of the Secretary of State, exercising customs functions (within the meaning of Part 1 of the Borders, Citizenship and Immigration Act 2009);

(c)　the Director of Border Revenue exercising customs revenue functions (within the meaning of that Part of that Act), and persons exercising such functions of the Director;

(d)　persons providing services pursuant to arrangements relating to the discharge of a function within paragraph (a), (b), or (c).

(4)　"Enforcement functions" includes, in particular—

(a)　powers of entry,

(b)　powers to search persons or property,

(c)　powers to seize or detain property,

(d)　powers to arrest persons,

(e)　powers to detain persons, and

(f)　powers to examine persons or otherwise to obtain information (including powers to take fingerprints or to acquire other personal data).

(5)　"Specified" means specified in an agreement under subsection (1) or an order under subsection (2).

(6)　"Immigration officer" means a person appointed under paragraph 1(1) of Schedule 2 to the Immigration Act 1971.

60ZC Section 60ZB: supplementary

(1)　An agreement under section 60ZB may at any time be varied or terminated—

(a)　by the Secretary of State, or

(b)　by the Ombudsman, with the consent of the Secretary of State.

(2)　Before making an order under section 60ZB the Secretary of State must consult the Ombudsman and such persons as the Secretary of State thinks appropriate.

(3)　An agreement or order under section 60ZB may provide for payment by the Secretary of State to or in respect of the Ombudsman.

(4)　An agreement or order under section 60ZB must relate only to the exercise of enforcement functions—

(a)　wholly in Northern Ireland, or

(b)　partly in Northern Ireland and partly in another part of the United Kingdom.

(5)　An agreement or order under section 60ZB must relate only to the exercise of enforcement functions on or after the day on which the agreement or order is made.

(6)　An agreement or order under section 60ZB must not provide for procedures in relation to so much of any complaint or matter as relates to functions conferred by or under Part 8 of the Immigration and Asylum Act 1999 (detained persons & removal centres etc)."

PART 6
MISCELLANEOUS

Citizenship

65 Persons unable to acquire citizenship: natural father not married to mother
After section 4D of the British Nationality Act 1981 insert—

"4E The general conditions
For the purposes of sections 4F to 4I, a person ("P") meets the general conditions
if—

(a)   P was born before 1 July 2006;

(b)   at the time of P's birth, P's mother—

(i)   was not married, or

(ii)   was married to a person other than P's natural father;

(c)   no person is treated as the father of P under section 28 of the
Human Fertilisation and Embryology Act 1990; and

(d)   P has never been a British citizen.

4F Person unable to be registered under other provisions of this Act
(1)   A person ("P") is entitled to be registered as a British citizen on an
application made under this section if—

(a)   P meets the general conditions; and

(b)   P would be entitled to be registered as a British citizen under—

(i)   section 1(3),

(ii)   section 3(2),

(iii)   section 3(5),

(iv)   paragraph 4 of Schedule 2, or

(v)   paragraph 5 of Schedule 2,

had P's mother been married to P's natural father at the time of P's birth.
(2)   In the following provisions of this section "relevant registration provision"
means the provision under which P would be entitled to be registered as a British
citizen (as mentioned in subsection (1)(b)).
(3)   If the relevant registration provision is section 3(2), a person who is
registered as a British citizen under this section is a British citizen by descent.
(4)   If the relevant registration provision is section 3(5), the Secretary of State
may, in the special circumstances of the particular case, waive the need for any or
all of the parental consents to be given.
(5)   For that purpose, the "parental consents" are—

(a)   the consent of P's natural father, and

(b)   the consent of P's mother,

insofar as they would be required by section 3(5)(c) (as read with section 3(6)(b)),
had P's mother been married to P's natural father at the time of P's birth.

4G Person unable to become citizen automatically after commencement
(1)   A person ("P") is entitled to be registered as a British citizen on an
application made under this section if—

(a)   P meets the general conditions; and

(b)   at any time in the period after commencement, P would have
automatically become a British citizen at birth by the operation of
any provision of this Act or the British Nationality (Falkland
Islands) Act 1983, had P's mother been married to P's natural father
at the time of P's birth.

(2)   A person who is registered as a British citizen under this section is a British citizen by descent if the British citizenship which the person would have acquired at birth (as mentioned in subsection (1)(b)) would (by virtue of section 14) have been British citizenship by descent.

(3)   If P is under the age of 18, no application may be made unless the consent of P's natural father and mother to the registration has been signified in the prescribed manner.

(4)   But if P's natural father or mother has died on or before the date of the application, the reference in subsection (3) to P's natural father and mother is to be read as a reference to either of them.

(5)   The Secretary of State may, in the special circumstances of a particular case, waive the need for any or all of the consents required by subsection (3) (as read with subsection (4)) to be given.

(6)   The reference in this section to the period after commencement does not include the time of commencement (and, accordingly, this section does not apply to any case in which a person was unable to become a British citizen at commencement).

4H Citizen of UK and colonies unable to become citizen at commencement

(1)   A person ("P") is entitled to be registered as a British citizen on an application made under this section if—

- (a)   P meets the general conditions;
- (b)   P was a citizen of the United Kingdom and Colonies immediately before commencement; and
- (c)   P would have automatically become a British citizen at commencement, by the operation of any provision of this Act, had P's mother been married to P's natural father at the time of P's birth.

(2)   A person who is registered as a British citizen under this section is a British citizen by descent if the British citizenship which the person would have acquired at commencement (as mentioned in subsection (1)(c)) would (by virtue of section 14) have been British citizenship by descent.

4I Other person unable to become citizen at commencement

(1)   A person ("P") is entitled to be registered as a British citizen on an application made under this section if—

- (a)   P meets the general conditions;
- (b)   P is either—
  - (i)   an eligible former British national, or
  - (ii)   an eligible non-British national; and
- (c)   had P's mother been married to P's natural father at the time of P's birth, P—
  - (i)   would have been a citizen of the United Kingdom and Colonies immediately before commencement, and
  - (ii)   would have automatically become a British citizen at commencement by the operation of any provision of this Act.

(2)   P is an "eligible former British national" if P was not a citizen of the United Kingdom and Colonies immediately before commencement and either—

- (a)   P ceased to be a British subject or a citizen of the United Kingdom and Colonies by virtue of the commencement of any independence legislation, but would not have done so had P's mother been married to P's natural father at the time of P's birth, or
- (b)   P was a British subject who did not automatically become a citizen of the United Kingdom and Colonies at commencement of the

British Nationality Act 1948 by the operation of any provision of it, but would have done so had P's mother been married to P's natural father at the time of P's birth.

(3) P is an "eligible non-British national" if—

    (a)   P was never a British subject or citizen of the United Kingdom and Colonies; and

    (b)   had P's mother been married to P's natural father at the time of P's birth, P would have automatically become a British subject or citizen of the United Kingdom and Colonies—

        (i)   at birth, or

        (ii)   by virtue of paragraph 3 of Schedule 3 to the British Nationality Act 1948 (child of male British subject to become citizen of the United Kingdom and Colonies if the father becomes such a citizen).

(4) A person who is registered as a British citizen under this section is a British citizen by descent if the British citizenship which the person would have acquired at commencement (as mentioned in subsection (1)(c)(ii)) would (by virtue of section 14) have been British citizenship by descent.

(5) In determining for the purposes of subsection (1)(c)(i) whether P would have been a citizen of the United Kingdom and Colonies immediately before commencement, it must be assumed that P would not have—

    (a)   renounced or been deprived of any notional British nationality, or

    (b)   lost any notional British nationality by virtue of P acquiring the nationality of a country or territory outside the United Kingdom.

(6) A "notional British nationality" is—

    (a)   in a case where P is an eligible former British national, any status as a British subject or a citizen of the United Kingdom and Colonies which P would have held at any time after P's nationality loss (had that loss not occurred and had P's mother had been married to P's natural father at the time of P's birth);

    (b)   in a case where P is an eligible non-British national—

        (i)   P's status as a British subject or citizen of the United Kingdom and Colonies mentioned in subsection (3)(b), and

        (ii)   any other status as a British subject or citizen of the United Kingdom and Colonies which P would have held at any time afterwards (had P's mother been married to P's natural father at the time of P's birth).

(7) In this section—

"British subject" has any meaning which it had for the purposes of the British Nationality and Status of Aliens Act 1914;

"independence legislation" means an Act of Parliament or any subordinate legislation (within the meaning of the Interpretation Act 1978) forming part of the law in the United Kingdom (whenever passed or made, and whether or not still in force)—

    (a)   providing for a country or territory to become independent from the United Kingdom, or

    (b)   dealing with nationality, or any other ancillary matters, in connection with a country or territory becoming independent from the United Kingdom;

"P's nationality loss" means P's—

    (a)   ceasing to be a British subject or citizen of the United Kingdom and Colonies (as mentioned in subsection (2)(a)), or

    (b)   not becoming a citizen of the United Kingdom and Colonies (as mentioned in subsection (2)(b)).

4J Sections 4E to 4I: supplementary provision

(1) In sections 4E to 4I and this section, a person's "natural father" is a person who satisfies the requirements as to proof of paternity that are prescribed in regulations under section 50(9B).

(2) The power under section 50(9B) to make different provision for different circumstances includes power to make provision for the purposes of any provision of sections 4E to 4I which is different from other provision made under section 50(9B).

(3) The following provisions apply for the purposes of sections 4E to 4I.

(4) A reference to a person automatically becoming a British citizen, or a citizen of the United Kingdom and Colonies, is a reference to the person becoming such a citizen without the need for—

> (a) the person to be registered as such a citizen by the Secretary of State or any other minister of the Crown;
>
> (b) the birth of the person to be registered by a diplomatic or consular representative of the United Kingdom; or
>
> (c) the person to be naturalised as such a citizen.

(5) If the mother of a person could not actually have been married to the person's natural father at the time of the person's birth (for whatever reason), that fact does not prevent an assumption being made that the couple were married at the time of the birth."

66 Deprivation if conduct seriously prejudicial to vital interests of the UK

(1) In section 40 of the British Nationality Act 1981 (deprivation of citizenship), after subsection (4) insert—

"(4A) But that does not prevent the Secretary of State from making an order under subsection (2) to deprive a person of a citizenship status if—

> (a) the citizenship status results from the person's naturalisation,
>
> (b) the Secretary of State is satisfied that the deprivation is conducive to the public good because the person, while having that citizenship status, has conducted him or herself in a manner which is seriously prejudicial to the vital interests of the United Kingdom, any of the Islands, or any British overseas territory, and
>
> (c) the Secretary of State has reasonable grounds for believing that the person is able, under the law of a country or territory outside the United Kingdom, to become a national of such a country or territory."

(2) In deciding whether to make an order under subsection (2) of section 40 of the British Nationality Act 1981 in a case which falls within subsection (4A) of that Act, the Secretary of State may take account of the manner in which a person conducted him or herself before this section came into force.

(3) After section 40A of the British Nationality Act 1981 insert—

"40B Review of power under section 40(4A)

(1) The Secretary of State must arrange for a review of the operation of the relevant deprivation power to be carried out in relation to each of the following periods—

> (a) the initial one year period;
>
> (b) each subsequent three year period.

(2) The "relevant deprivation power" is the power to make orders under section 40(2) to deprive persons of a citizenship status in the circumstances set out in section 40(4A).

(3) A review must be completed as soon as practicable after the end of the period to which the review relates.

(4)   As soon as practicable after a person has carried out a review in relation to a particular period, the person must—

    (a)   produce a report of the outcome of the review, and

    (b)   send a copy of the report to the Secretary of State.

(5)   The Secretary of State must lay before each House of Parliament a copy of each report sent under subsection (4)(b).

(6)   The Secretary of State may, after consultation with the person who produced the report, exclude a part of the report from the copy laid before Parliament if the Secretary of State is of the opinion that it would be contrary to the public interest or prejudicial to national security for that part of the report to be made public.

(7)   The Secretary of State may—

    (a)   make such payments as the Secretary of State thinks appropriate in connection with the carrying out of a review, and

    (b)   make such other arrangements as the Secretary of State thinks appropriate in connection with the carrying out of a review (including arrangements for the provision of staff, other resources and facilities).

(8)   In this section—

"initial one year period" means the period of one year beginning with the day when section 40(4A) comes into force;

"subsequent three year period" means a period of three years beginning with the first day after the most recent of—

    (a)   the initial one year period, or

    (b)   the most recent subsequent three year period."

Embarkation checks

67 Embarkation checks

Schedule 8 (embarkation checks) has effect.

Fees

68 Fees

(1)   The Secretary of State may provide, in accordance with this section, for fees to be charged in respect of the exercise of functions in connection with immigration or nationality.

(2)   The functions in respect of which fees are to be charged are to be specified by the Secretary of State by order ("a fees order").

(3)   A fees order—

    (a)   must specify how the fee in respect of the exercise of each specified function is to be calculated, and

    (b)   may not provide for a fee to be charged in respect of the exercise of a function otherwise than in connection with an application or claim, or on request.

(4)   For any specified fee, a fees order must provide for it to comprise one or more amounts each of which is—

    (a)   a fixed amount, or

    (b)   an amount calculated by reference to an hourly rate or other factor.

(5)   Where a fees order provides for a fee (or part of a fee) to be a fixed amount, it—

    (a)   must specify a maximum amount for the fee (or part), and

    (b)   may specify a minimum amount.

(6) Where a fees order provides for a fee (or part of a fee) to be calculated as mentioned in subsection (4)(b), it—

    (a)   must specify—

        (i)   how the fee (or part) is to be calculated, and

        (ii)   a maximum rate or other factor, and

    (b)   may specify a minimum rate or other factor.

(7) For any specified fee, the following are to be set by the Secretary of State by regulations ("fees regulations")—

    (a)   if the fee (or any part of it) is to be a fixed amount, that amount;

    (b)   if the fee (or any part of it) is to be calculated as mentioned in subsection (4)(b), the hourly rate or other factor by reference to which it (or that part) is to be calculated.

(8) An amount, or rate or other factor, set by fees regulations for a fee in respect of the exercise of a specified function—

    (a)   must not—

        (i)   exceed the maximum specified for that amount, or rate or other factor;

        (ii)   be less than the minimum, if any, so specified;

    (b)   subject to that, may be intended to exceed, or result in a fee which exceeds, the costs of exercising the function.

(9) In setting the amount of any fee, or rate or other factor, in fees regulations, the Secretary of State may have regard only to—

    (a)   the costs of exercising the function;

    (b)   benefits that the Secretary of State thinks are likely to accrue to any person in connection with the exercise of the function;

    (c)   the costs of exercising any other function in connection with immigration or nationality;

    (d)   the promotion of economic growth;

    (e)   fees charged by or on behalf of governments of other countries in respect of comparable functions;

    (f)   any international agreement.

This is subject to section 69(5).

(10) In respect of any fee provided for under this section, fees regulations may—

    (a)   provide for exceptions;

    (b)   provide for the reduction, waiver or refund of part or all of a fee (whether by conferring a discretion or otherwise);

    (c)   make provision about—

        (i)   the consequences of failure to pay a fee;

        (ii)   enforcement;

        (iii)   when a fee may or must be paid.

(11) Any provision that may be made by fees regulations by virtue of subsection (10) may be included instead in a fees order (and any provision so included may be amended or revoked by fees regulations).

(12) In this section and sections 69 and 70—

    "costs" includes—

        (a)   the costs of the Secretary of State, and

        (b)   the costs of any other person (whether or not funded from public money);

    "fees order" has the meaning given by subsection (2);

    "fees regulations" has the meaning given by subsection (7);

    "function" includes a power or a duty;

"function in connection with immigration or nationality" includes a function in connection with an enactment (including an enactment of a jurisdiction outside the United Kingdom) that relates wholly or partly to immigration or nationality;

"specified" means specified in a fees order.

(13) Any reference in this section or section 70 to the exercise of a function includes a reference to its exercise in particular circumstances, including its exercise—

    (a)   at particular times or in a particular place;

    (b)   under particular arrangements;

    (c)   otherwise in particular ways,

and, for this purpose, "arrangements" includes arrangements for the convenience of applicants, claimants or persons making requests for the exercise of a function.

69 Fees orders and fees regulations: supplemental

(1) A fees order or fees regulations may be made only with the consent of the Treasury.

(2) A fee under section 68 may relate to something done outside the United Kingdom.

(3) Fees payable by virtue of section 68 may be recovered as a debt due to the Secretary of State.

(4) Fees paid to the Secretary of State by virtue of section 68 must—

    (a)   be paid into the Consolidated Fund, or

    (b)   be applied in such other way as the relevant order may specify.

(5) Section 68 is without prejudice to—

    (a)   section 1 of the Consular Fees Act 1980 (fees for consular acts etc);

    (b)   section 102 of the Finance (No 2) Act 1987 (government fees and charges), or

    (c)   any other power to charge a fee.

70 Power to charge fees for attendance services in particular cases

(1) This section applies where a person exercises a function in connection with immigration or nationality in respect of which a fee is chargeable by virtue of a fees order (a "chargeable function") in a particular case and—

    (a)   in doing so attends at a place outside the United Kingdom, and time, agreed with a person ("the client"), and

    (b)   does so at the request of the client.

It is immaterial whether or not the client is a person in respect of whom the chargeable function is exercised.

(2) In this section "attendance service" means the service described in subsection (1) except so far as it consists of the exercise of a chargeable function.

(3) The following are to be disregarded in determining whether a fee is chargeable in respect of a function by virtue of a fees order—

    (a)   any exception provided for by a fees order or fees regulations;

    (b)   any power so provided to waive or refund a fee.

(4) The person exercising the chargeable function may charge the client such fee for the purposes of recovering the costs of providing the attendance service as the person may determine.

(5) Fees paid to the Secretary of State by virtue of this section must be paid into the Consolidated Fund.

(6) A fee payable by virtue of this section may be recovered as a debt due to the Secretary of State.

(7) This section is without prejudice to—

    (a)   section 68;

    (b)   section 1 of the Consular Fees Act 1980 (fees for consular acts etc);

(c)   section 102 of the Finance (No 2) Act 1987 (government fees and charges), or

(d)   any other power to charge a fee.

Welfare of children

71 Duty regarding the welfare of children

For the avoidance of doubt, this Act does not limit any duty imposed on the Secretary of State or any other person by section 55 of the Borders, Citizenship and Immigration Act 2009 (duty regarding the welfare of children).

PART 7
FINAL PROVISIONS

72 Financial provision

The following are to be paid out of money provided by Parliament—

(a)   expenditure incurred under or by virtue of this Act by the Secretary of State, and

(b)   any increase attributable to this Act in the sums payable under any other Act out of money so provided.

73 Transitional and consequential provision

(1)   The Secretary of State may, by order, make such transitional, transitory or saving provision as the Secretary of State considers appropriate in connection with the coming into force of any provision of this Act.

(2)   The Secretary of State may, by order, make such provision as the Secretary of State considers appropriate in consequence of this Act.

(3)   The provision that may be made by an order under subsection (2) includes provision amending, repealing or revoking any enactment.

(4)   "Enactment" includes—

(a)   an enactment contained in subordinate legislation within the meaning of the Interpretation Act 1978;

(b)   an enactment contained in, or in an instrument made under, an Act of the Scottish Parliament;

(c)   an enactment contained in, or in an instrument made under, a Measure or Act of the National Assembly for Wales;

(d)   an enactment contained in, or in an instrument made under, Northern Ireland legislation.

(5)   In section 61(2) of the UK Borders Act 2007 (definition of "the Immigration Acts")—

(a)   at the end of paragraph (h), omit "and";

(b)   at the end of paragraph (i) insert ", and

(j)   the Immigration Act 2014.".

(6)   Schedule 9 (transitional and consequential provision) has effect.

74 Orders and regulations

(1)   Any power of the Secretary of State or Treasury to make an order or regulations under this Act is exercisable by statutory instrument.

(2)   A statutory instrument containing any of the following orders or regulations may not be made unless a draft of the instrument has been laid before each House of Parliament and approved by a resolution of each House of Parliament—

(a)   an order under section 20(7), 23(6) or 25(5);

(b)   an order under section 38;

(c)   regulations under section 41;

(d)   an order under section 43, or under a section amended by such an order;

(e)   the first regulations under section 50(1);

(f)   the first regulations under section 50(5);

(g)   the first regulations under section 51(3);

(h)   the first regulations under section 51(4);

(i)   an order under section 53 or 54(4) or (6);

(j)   a fees order (within the meaning of section 68);

(k)   an order under section 73(2) which amends or repeals primary legislation;

(l)   an order under paragraph 2(3)(e) of Schedule 6.

(3)   "Primary legislation" means any of the following—

(a)   a public general Act;

(b)   an Act of the Scottish Parliament;

(c)   a Measure or Act of the National Assembly for Wales;

(d)   Northern Ireland legislation.

(4)   A statutory instrument containing any other order or regulations made by the Secretary of State or Treasury under this Act is subject to annulment in pursuance of a resolution of either House of Parliament.

(5)   But subsection (4) does not apply to a statutory instrument containing an order under any of sections 35(3), 73(1) and 75(3) (subject to subsection (7)).

(6)   Subsection (7) applies if an order under section 75(3) is made which—

(a)   brings into force a provision of Chapter 1 of Part 3,

(b)   brings that provision into force only in relation to a particular area or areas within England and Wales, Scotland or Northern Ireland, and

(c)   is the first order to be made bringing into force a provision of that Chapter only in relation to an area or areas within England and Wales, Scotland or Northern Ireland.

(7)   A statutory instrument containing any subsequent order under section 75(3) (after the order mentioned in subsection (6)) that brings into force a provision of Chapter 1 of Part 3 for anywhere other than the area or areas mentioned in paragraph (b) of that subsection is subject to annulment in pursuance of a resolution of either House of Parliament.

(8)   An order or regulations made by the Secretary of State or Treasury under this Act may—

(a)   make different provision for different purposes or areas,

(b)   make provision which applies generally or only for particular purposes or areas,

(c)   make transitional, transitory or saving provision, or

(d)   make incidental, supplementary or consequential provision.

75 Commencement

(1)   This Part, other than section 73(6) and Schedule 9, comes into force on the day on which this Act is passed.

(2)   Section 56, section 59 and Schedule 6, and section 62 come into force at the end of the period of two months beginning with the day on which this Act is passed.

(3)   Subject to subsections (1) and (2), this Act comes into force on such day as the Secretary of State may by order appoint; and different days may be appointed for different purposes or areas.

76 Extent

(1)   This Act extends to England and Wales, Scotland and Northern Ireland.

(2)   Subsection (1) is subject to subsection (3).

(3)   Section 59 and Schedule 6 extend to England and Wales only.

(4)   Subsections (1) to (3) do not apply to an amendment, repeal or revocation made by this Act.

(5)   An amendment, repeal or revocation made by this Act has the same extent as the provision amended, repealed or revoked (ignoring extent by virtue of an Order in Council).

(6)   Her Majesty may by Order in Council provide for any of the provisions of this Act to extend, with or without modifications, to any of the Channel Islands or the Isle of Man.

(7)   Subsection (6) does not apply in relation to the extension to a place of a provision which extends there by virtue of subsection (5).

77 Short title

This Act may be cited as the Immigration Act 2014.

Section 4

Power to escort detained persons

1

In Schedule 2 to the Immigration Act 1971, in paragraph 18(3) (power to escort detained persons) for the first "or of" substitute "an immigration officer, or".

Power to search detained persons

2

(1)   In Schedule 2 to the Immigration Act 1971, after paragraph 18 insert—

"**18A**

(1)   An immigration officer or constable may search a person ("P") who is detained under paragraph 16 for anything which P might use—

(a)   to cause physical injury to P or others, or

(b)   to assist P's escape from legal custody.

(2)   The power to search P—

(a)   unless sub-paragraph (3) applies, does not include power to require P to remove any clothing other than an outer coat, jacket or glove, but

(b)   includes power to require P to open P's mouth.

(3)   This sub-paragraph applies if an immigration officer or constable has reasonable grounds to believe that there is concealed on P anything which P might use as mentioned in sub-paragraph (1).

(4)   The power to search P may be exercised only to the extent reasonably required for the purpose of discovering anything which P might use as mentioned in sub-paragraph (1).

(5)   An intimate search (as defined in section 28H(11)) may not be conducted under this paragraph.

(6)   An immigration officer or constable may seize and retain anything found on a search of P if the officer or constable has reasonable grounds to believe P might use it as mentioned in sub-paragraph (1).

(7)   Nothing seized under sub-paragraph (6) may be retained when P is released from detention under paragraph 16."

(2)   In paragraph 2(4) of Schedule 3 to the Immigration Act 1971 (which applies certain provisions of Schedule 2 to that Act), for ", 18" substitute "to 18A".

(3)   In section 10(7) of the Immigration and Asylum Act 1999 (which applies certain provisions of Schedule 2 to the Immigration Act 1971), for "18" substitute "18A".

(4) In section 47(3) of the Immigration, Asylum and Nationality Act 2006 (which applies certain provisions of Schedule 2 to the Immigration Act 1971), for "18" substitute "18A".

(5) In regulation 22(2) of the Immigration (European Economic Area) Regulations 2006 (SI 2006/1003) (which applies certain provisions of Schedule 2 to the Immigration Act 1971), for "18" substitute "18A".

Entry and search of premises

3

(1) Paragraph 25A of Schedule 2 to the Immigration Act 1971 (power to enter premises and search for documents following arrest) is amended as follows.

(2) In sub-paragraph (1)(b) for "by a constable (other than under this Schedule)" substitute "other than under this Schedule".

(3) After sub-paragraph (6) insert—

"(6A)   If, on an application made by an immigration officer, a justice of the peace is satisfied that—

  (a)   there are reasonable grounds for believing that relevant documents may be found on premises not within sub-paragraph (2) which are specified in the application, and

  (b)   any of the conditions in sub-paragraph (6B) is met,

the justice of the peace may issue a warrant authorising an immigration officer to enter and search the premises.

(6B)   The conditions are that—

  (a)   it is not practicable to communicate with any person entitled to grant entry to the premises;

  (b)   it is practicable to communicate with a person entitled to grant entry to the premises but it is not practicable to communicate with any person entitled to grant access to the relevant documents;

  (c)   entry to the premises will not be granted unless a warrant is produced;

  (d)   the purpose of a search may be frustrated or seriously prejudiced unless an immigration officer arriving at the premises can secure immediate entry.

(6C)   In the application of sub-paragraph (6A) to Scotland, references to a justice of the peace are to be treated as references to the sheriff or a justice of the peace."

(4)   In sub-paragraph (7)—

  (a)   for "sub-paragraph (2)" substitute "this paragraph";

  (b)   in paragraph (a) omit "and retain";

  (c)   omit paragraph (b) and the "but" before it.

(5)   After sub-paragraph (8) insert—

"(8A)   An immigration officer may retain a document seized under sub-paragraph (7) while the officer has reasonable grounds for believing that—

  (a)   the arrested person may be liable to removal from the United Kingdom in accordance with a provision of the Immigration Acts, and

  (b)   retention of the document may facilitate the person's removal."

4

In sections 28J(11) and 28K(14) of the Immigration Act 1971 (warrants - safeguards and execution) after "paragraph 17(2)" insert "or 25A(6A)".

General power to use reasonable force

5

In section 146(1) of the Immigration and Asylum Act 1999 (power of immigration officer to use reasonable force when exercising powers under certain enactments) for "the 1971 Act or this Act" substitute "the Immigration Acts".

Section 12

Immigration Act 1971 (c 77)

1

(1) Schedule 2 to the Immigration Act 1971 (entry control) is amended as follows.

(2) In paragraph 4(5)—

　　(a)　　after "provide" insert "biometric";

　　(b)　　omit from "about his external physical characteristics" to the end.

(3) After paragraph 4(5) insert—

　　"(6) Biometric information" has the meaning given by section 15 of the UK Borders Act 2007."

(4) In paragraph 18(2A), for "fingerprints" substitute "biometric information (within the meaning given by section 15 of the UK Borders Act 2007)".

Immigration and Asylum Act 1999 (c 33)

2

(1) Section 144 of the Immigration and Asylum Act 1999 (provision for collecting physical data other than fingerprints) is amended as follows.

(2) In subsection (1), for "data about external physical characteristics" substitute "biometric information".

(3) For subsection (2) substitute—

　　"(2) Biometric information" has the meaning given by section 15 of the UK Borders Act 2007."

Nationality, Immigration and Asylum Act 2002 (c 41)

3

(1) Section 126 of the Nationality, Immigration and Asylum Act 2002 (power to require provision of physical data with certain immigration applications) is amended as follows.

(2) In subsection (1)—

　　(a)　　in paragraph (a), for "information about external physical characteristics of the applicant" substitute "biometric information";

　　(b)　　in paragraphs (b) and (c), for "information about his external physical characteristics" substitute "biometric information".

(3) In subsection (4)(a), (b) and (c), before "information" insert "biometric".

(4) In subsection (9), after the definition of "authorised person" insert—

　　　　""biometric information" has the meaning given by section 15 of the UK Borders Act 2007,".

(5) In that subsection, omit the definition of "external physical characteristics" (and the "and" before it).

4

(1) Section 127 of that Act (voluntary provision of physical data) is amended as follows.

(2)   In subsection (1), for "information about his external physical characteristics" substitute "biometric information".

(3)   In subsection (2)(a) and (b), before "information" insert "biometric".

(4)   In subsection (3)—

(a)   after paragraph (a) insert—

"(aa)   biometric information", and";

(b)   omit the "and" at the end of paragraph (b);

(c)   omit paragraph (c).

Asylum and Immigration (Treatment of Claimants, etc) Act 2004 (c 19)

5

In section 35(2) of the Asylum and Immigration (Treatment of Claimants, etc) Act 2004 (imposition of requirements to facilitate deportation or removal), for paragraph (c) substitute—

"(c)   provide biometric information (within the meaning of section 15 of the UK Borders Act 2007), or submit to a process by means of which such information is obtained or recorded;".

Section 20

Social housing

1

(1)   An agreement that grants a right of occupation in social housing.

(2)   "Social housing" means accommodation provided to a person by virtue of a relevant provision.

(3)   "Relevant provision" means a provision of—

(a)   in relation to England and Wales—

(i)   Part 2 of the Housing Act 1985, or

(ii)   Part 6 or 7 of the Housing Act 1996;

(b)   in relation to Scotland, Part 1 or 2 of the Housing (Scotland) Act 1987;

(c)   in relation to Northern Ireland—

(i)   Chapter 4 of Part 2 of the Housing (Northern Ireland) Order 1981 (SI 1981/156 (N.I. 3)), or

(ii)   Part 2 of the Housing (Northern Ireland) Order 1988 (SI 1988/1990 (N.I. 23)).

(4)   Accommodation provided to a person by virtue of a relevant provision includes accommodation provided in pursuance of arrangements made under any such provision.

2

(1)   This paragraph applies for the purposes of paragraph 1.

(2)   An allocation of housing accommodation by a local housing authority in England to a person who is already—

(a)   a secure or introductory tenant, or

(b)   an assured tenant of housing accommodation held by a private registered provider of social housing or a registered social landlord,

is to be treated as an allocation of housing accommodation by virtue of Part 6 of the Housing Act 1996 (and accordingly section 159(4A) of that Act is to be ignored).

(3)   An allocation of housing accommodation that falls within a case specified in, or prescribed under, section 160 of the Housing Act 1996 (cases where provisions about allocation under Part 6 of that Act do not apply) is to be treated as an allocation of

housing accommodation by virtue of Part 6 of that Act (and accordingly that section is to be ignored).

(4)   An allocation of housing accommodation by virtue of Part 1 of the Housing (Scotland) Act 1987 is to be treated as provided by virtue of a relevant provision only if it is provided by a local authority within the meaning of that Act (or in pursuance of arrangements made under or for the purposes of that Part with a local authority).

(5)   Accommodation provided to a person in Northern Ireland by a registered housing association is to be treated as provided to the person by virtue of a relevant provision.

(6)   Terms used in sub-paragraphs (2) and (3) have the same meanings as in Part 6 of the Housing Act 1996.

(7)   In sub-paragraph (5) "registered housing association" means a housing association, within the meaning of Part 2 of the Housing (Northern Ireland) Order 1992 (SI 1992/1725 (N.I. 15)), that is registered in the register of housing associations maintained under Article 14 of that Order.

Care homes

3

(1)   An agreement that grants a right of occupation in a care home.

(2)   "Care home" means—

   (a)   in relation to England and Wales, an establishment that is a care home for the purposes of the Care Standards Act 2000;

   (b)   in relation to Scotland, accommodation that is provided as a care home service within the meaning of Part 5 of the Public Services Reform (Scotland) Act 2010;

   (c)   in relation to Northern Ireland, an establishment that is a residential care home, or a nursing home, for the purposes of the Health and Personal Social Services (Quality, Improvement and Regulation) (Northern Ireland) Order 2003 (SI 2003/431 (N.I. 9)).

Hospitals and hospices

4

(1)   An agreement that grants a right of occupation of accommodation in a hospital or hospice.

(2)   "Hospital"—

   (a)   in relation to England, has the meaning given in section 275 of the National Health Service Act 2006;

   (b)   in relation to Wales, has the meaning given in section 206 of the National Health Service (Wales) Act 2006;

   (c)   in relation to Scotland, has the meaning given in section 108 of the National Health Service (Scotland) Act 1978;

   (d)   in relation to Northern Ireland, has the meaning given in Article 2(2) of the Health and Personal Social Services (Northern Ireland) Order 1972 (SI 1972/1265 (N.I. 14)).

(3)   "Hospice" means an establishment other than a hospital whose primary function is the provision of palliative care to persons resident there who are suffering from a progressive disease in its final stages.

Other accommodation relating to healthcare provision

5

(1)   An agreement—

(a)   under which accommodation is provided to a person as a result of a duty imposed on a relevant NHS body by an enactment, and

(b)   which is not excluded by another provision of this Schedule.

(2) "Relevant NHS body" means—

    (a)   in relation to England—

        (i)   a clinical commissioning group, or

        (ii)   the National Health Service Commissioning Board;

    (b)   in relation to Wales, a local health board;

    (c)   in relation to Scotland, a health board constituted by order made under section 2 of the National Health Service (Scotland) Act 1978;

    (d)   in relation to Northern Ireland, a Health and Social Services trust.

Hostels and refuges

6

(1) An agreement that grants a right of occupation of accommodation in a hostel or refuge.

(2) "Hostel" means a building which satisfies the following two conditions.

(3) The first condition is that the building is used for providing to persons generally, or to a class of persons—

    (a)   residential accommodation otherwise than in separate and self-contained premises, and

    (b)   board or facilities for the preparation of food adequate to the needs of those persons (or both).

(4) The second condition is that any of the following applies in relation to the building—

    (a)   it is managed by a registered housing association;

    (b)   it is not operated on a commercial basis and its costs of operation are provided wholly or in part by a government department or agency, or by a local authority;

    (c)   it is managed by a voluntary organisation or charity.

(5) "Refuge" means a building which satisfies the second condition in sub-paragraph (4) and is used wholly or mainly for providing accommodation to persons who have been subject to any incident, or pattern of incidents, of—

    (a)   controlling, coercive or threatening behaviour,

    (b)   physical violence,

    (c)   abuse of any other description (whether physical or mental in nature), or

    (d)   threats of any such violence or abuse.

(6) In this paragraph—

    "government department" includes—

        (a)   any part of the Scottish Administration;

        (b)   a Northern Ireland department;

        (c)   the Welsh Assembly Government;

        (d)   any body or authority exercising statutory functions on behalf of the Crown;

    "registered housing association" means—

        (a)   a private registered provider of social housing;

        (b)   a registered social landlord within the meaning of Part 1 of the Housing Act 1996 or section 165 of the Housing (Scotland) Act 2010;

        (c)   a housing association which is registered in a register maintained under Article 14 of the Housing (Northern Ireland) Order 1992 (SI 1992/1725 (N.I. 15));

"voluntary organisation" means a body, other than a public or local authority, whose activities are not carried on for profit.

Accommodation from or involving local authorities

7

(1)   An agreement—

    (a)   under which accommodation is provided to a person as a result of a duty or relevant power that is imposed or conferred on a local authority by an enactment (whether or not provided by the local authority), and

    (b)   which is not excluded by another provision of this Schedule.

(2)   "Relevant power" means a power that is exercised for, or in connection with, a purpose of providing accommodation to a person who is homeless or is threatened with homelessness.

(3)   In sub-paragraph (2) the reference to a person who is homeless or is threatened with homelessness is to be read in accordance with—

    (a)   in relation to England and Wales, section 175 of the Housing Act 1996;

    (b)   in relation to Scotland, section 24 of the Housing (Scotland) Act 1987;

    (c)   in relation to Northern Ireland, Article 3 of the Housing (Northern Ireland) Order 1988 (SI 1988/1990 (N.I. 23)).

Accommodation provided by virtue of immigration provisions

8

An agreement granting a right of occupation of accommodation that is provided to an individual by virtue of any of the following provisions of the Immigration and Asylum Act 1999—

    (a)   section 4 (provision of accommodation to persons granted temporary admission etc);

    (b)   section 95 (provision of support to asylum seekers etc);

    (c)   section 98 (provision of temporary support to asylum seekers etc).

Mobile homes

9

An agreement to which the Mobile Homes Act 1983 applies.

Tied accommodation

10

(1)   An agreement that grants a right of occupation of tied accommodation.

(2)   "Tied accommodation" means accommodation that is provided—

    (a)   by an employer to an employee in connection with a contract of employment, or

    (b)   by a body providing training in a trade, profession or vocation to an individual in connection with that training.

(3)   In this paragraph "employer" and "employee" have the same meanings as in the Employment Rights Act 1996 (see section 230 of that Act).

Student accommodation

11

(1)   An agreement that grants a right of occupation in a building which—

4

After section 27D insert—

"27E Additional information if party not relevant national

(1)   This section applies to notice of marriage given to a superintendent registrar in accordance with section 27 if one, or each, of the parties to the proposed marriage is not a relevant national.

(2)   But this section does not apply if section 39A applies to the proposed marriage.

(3)   For each party to the proposed marriage who is not a relevant national, the notice must include whichever of statements A, B or C is applicable to that person.

(4)   Statement A is a statement that the person has the appropriate immigration status.

(5)   Statement B is a statement that the person holds a relevant visa in respect of the proposed marriage.

(6)   Statement C is a statement that the person neither—

    (a)   has the appropriate immigration status, nor

    (b)   holds a relevant visa in respect of the proposed marriage.

(7)   If the notice contains the statement referred to in the first column of an entry in this table, the notice must be accompanied by the information and photographs referred to in the second column of that entry (insofar as that entry is applicable to the parties to the proposed marriage)—

If the notice includes this statement...	...the notice must be accompanied by...
Statement A (in respect of one or both of the parties to the proposed marriage)	For each party in respect of whom statement A is made, details of the particular immigration status which that party has
Statement B (in respect of one or both of the parties to the proposed marriage)	1 For each party, a specified photograph of that party
	2 For each party in respect of whom statement B is made, details of the relevant visa which that party has
Statement C (in respect of one or both of the parties to the proposed marriage)	1 For each party, a specified photograph of that party
	2 For each party, the usual address of that party
	3 For each party whose usual address is outside the United Kingdom, an address in the United Kingdom at which that party can be contacted by post
	4 For each party who has previously used any name or names other than the person's name stated in the notice in accordance with section 27(3), a statement of the other name or names
	5 For each party who currently uses, or has previously used, an alias or aliases, a statement of the alias or aliases

(8)   If the notice contains more than one of statements A, B and C, subsection (7) must be complied with in relation to each of those statements; but where the notice contains statements B and C, subsection (7) does not require the notice to be accompanied by more than one specified photograph of each party.

(9) If the notice includes statement C for a party to the proposed marriage—

    (a)   the notice may be accompanied by a statement ("statement D") of that person's immigration position in the United Kingdom;

    (b)   if the notice is accompanied by statement D for a party to the proposed marriage, the person may provide the superintendent registrar with details of his or her immigration position in the United Kingdom; and

    (c)   if any such details are provided, the superintendent registrar must record them.

(10) In this section—

    (a)   a reference—

        (i)   to a person having the appropriate immigration status, or

        (ii)   to a person holding a relevant visa,

has the same meaning as in section 49 of the Immigration Act 2014;

    (b)   a reference to the particular immigration status which a person has is a reference to the immigration status set out in any of paragraphs (a) to (c) of section 49(2) of that Act which the person has;

    (c)   a reference to a person's immigration position in the United Kingdom includes a reference to the person's not being entitled to be in the United Kingdom.

(11) In this section "specified photograph" means a photograph that is in accordance with regulations made under section 28G (and for this purpose "photograph" includes other kinds of images).".

5

In section 28 (declaration to accompany notice of marriage), in subsection (1), after paragraph (c) insert—

        "(d)   that he or she believes all of the information stated in the notice, and all information and evidence supplied with the notice, is true.".

6

(1) Section 28A (power to require evidence) is amended in accordance with this paragraph.

(2) For the title substitute "**Power to require evidence of consent to marriages of same sex couples**".

(3) Omit subsection (1).

(4) In subsection (2), for the words before "may" substitute "A requirement under subsection (1A)".

(5) Omit subsection (3).

7

After section 28A insert—

"28B Provision of evidence

(1) A notice of marriage under section 27 must, in relation to each of the parties to the marriage, be accompanied by specified evidence of the following matters—

    (a)   the person's name and surname;

    (b)   the person's date of birth;

    (c)   the person's place of residence;

    (d)   the person's nationality.

(2) A person giving a notice of marriage under section 27 must provide the superintendent registrar to whom the notice is given with specified evidence—

(a)   as to whether the person has previously been married or formed a civil partnership; and

(b)   if so, as to the ending of the marriage or civil partnership.

(3)   In this section "specified evidence" means evidence that is in accordance with regulations made under section 28G.

28C Additional evidence if party not relevant national

(1)   This section applies to notice of marriage given to a superintendent registrar in accordance with section 27 if one, or each, of the parties to the proposed marriage is not a relevant national.

(2)   If the notice includes statement A (referred to in section 27E(4)), and accordingly is accompanied by details of the particular immigration status which a party to the proposed marriage has, the notice must be accompanied by specified evidence of that status.

(3)   If the notice includes statement B (referred to in section 27E(5)), the notice must be accompanied by specified evidence of the holding of the relevant visa by the party to the proposed marriage.

(4)   If, in accordance with section 27E(7), the notice is accompanied by the usual address of a party to the proposed marriage, the notice must also be accompanied by specified evidence that it is that party's usual address.

(5)   If the notice includes statement D (referred to in section 27E(9)), the notice may be accompanied by evidence of the person's immigration position in the United Kingdom.

(6)   If subsection (2) or (3) applies to the notice, and the notice is not accompanied by the specified evidence required by that subsection, the notice must be accompanied by—

(a)   photographs and addresses of the kinds referred to in paragraphs 1 and 2 in the relevant entry in section 27E(7);

(b)   as respects the usual address of each party that is provided in accordance with paragraph (a), specified evidence that the address provided is that party's usual address; and

(c)   addresses, names and aliases of the kinds referred to in paragraphs 3 to 5 in the relevant entry in section 27E(7) (insofar as those paragraphs are applicable to the parties to the proposed marriage).

(7)   In this section—

"relevant entry in section 27E(7)" means the second column of the last entry in the table in section 27E(7);

"specified evidence" means evidence that is in accordance with regulations made under section 28G.

28D Change of usual address or UK contact address

(1)   The Secretary of State may, by regulations, make provision about the giving to the Secretary of State of—

(a)   notice of a person's usual address, if the person's notified usual address changes;

(b)   notice of a UK contact address, if the person's notified usual address is not in the United Kingdom;

(c)   notice of a person's UK contact address, if the person's notified UK contact address changes;

(d)   evidence of any address notified in accordance with regulations under paragraph (a), (b) or (c).

(2)   The provision that may be made in regulations under this section includes—

(a)   provision imposing a requirement on a person;

(b)   provision about the rejection of information or evidence which there are reasonable grounds to suspect to be false.

(3)   Regulations under subsection (1)(d) may, in particular, make any provision of the kind that may be made under section 28G(3).

(4)   Regulations under this section are to be made by statutory instrument; and a statutory instrument containing such regulations is subject to annulment in pursuance of a resolution of either House of Parliament.

(5)   In this section—

"notified UK contact address" means an address in the United Kingdom, at which a person can be contacted by post, that has been notified in accordance with—

(a)   section 27E(7) or 28C(6), or

(b)   regulations under this section;

"notified usual address" means the usual address of a person that has been notified in accordance with—

(a)   section 27E(7) or 28C(6), or

(b)   regulations under this section.

28E Rejection of false information or evidence

(1)   A superintendent registrar may reject—

(a)   any information or photograph provided under section 27, 27E or 28C, or

(b)   any evidence provided under section 28A, 28B or 28C,

if (in particular) the superintendent registrar has reasonable grounds for suspecting that the information, photograph or evidence is false.

(2)   If the superintendent registrar rejects any information, photograph or evidence, the superintendent registrar may proceed under this Act as if the rejected information, photograph or evidence had not been provided.

(3)   This section does not limit the powers of superintendent registrars to reject anything provided under any other enactment.

28F Amendment of notice and evidence provisions

(1)   The Secretary of State may by order—

(a)   amend section 27, 27E or 28C so as to vary the information that must or may be given in cases where that section applies;

(b)   amend section 28B or 28C so as to vary the matters in respect of which evidence must or may be given in cases where that section applies;

(c)   make such provision (including provision amending section 27ZA, 28D or 28G or any other enactment) as the Secretary of State considers appropriate in consequence of provision made under paragraph (a) or (b).

(2)   The Secretary of State must consult the Registrar General before making an order under this section.

(3)   An order under this section is to be made by statutory instrument; and no statutory instrument containing such an order may be made unless a draft of it has been laid before, and approved by resolution of, each House of Parliament.

28G Specified evidence

(1)   The Registrar General may make regulations about the evidence that is required to be given for the purposes of section 8, 16 or 28B.

(2)   The Secretary of State may make regulations about the evidence that is required to be given for the purposes of section 28C.

(3)   Regulations under this section may, in particular, make provision about—

(a)   the kind of evidence which is to be supplied;

(b)   the form in which evidence is to be supplied;

> (c)   the manner in which evidence is to be supplied;
>
> (d)   the period within which evidence is to be supplied;
>
> (e)   the supply of further evidence;
>
> (f)   the sufficiency of evidence supplied;
>
> (g)   the consequences of failing to supply sufficient evidence in accordance with the regulations (including provision to secure that, in such a case, a particular decision is made or is to be treated as having been made);
>
> (h)   the retention or copying of evidence supplied.

(4)   In this section "evidence" includes a photograph or other image.

(5)   The Secretary of State must consult the Registrar General before making regulations under this section.

(6)   The Registrar General must obtain the approval of the Secretary of State before making regulations under this section.

(7)   Regulations under this section are to be made by statutory instrument.

(8)   A statutory instrument containing regulations under this section made by the Secretary of State is subject to annulment in pursuance of a resolution of either House of Parliament.".

Referral to Secretary of State

8

After section 28G insert—

"28H Referral of proposed marriage to Secretary of State

(1)   On every occasion when notice of marriage is given under section 27, a superintendent registrar must decide whether or not each of the parties to the proposed marriage is an exempt person.

(2)   But this section does not apply if section 39A applies to the proposed marriage.

(3)   In making a decision under subsection (1) about a party to a proposed marriage, a superintendent registrar may rely on any advice given in relation to that decision by the Secretary of State.

(4)   In a case where—

> (a)   section 27E applies to the notice of marriage, and
>
> (b)   specified evidence required by section 28C(2) or (3) in relation to a party to the proposed marriage is not produced in accordance with that section,

the superintendent registrar must decide that that party to the proposed marriage is not an exempt person.

(5)   If the superintendent registrar decides that either of the parties is not an exempt person, or that both of the parties are not exempt persons, the superintendent registrar must—

> (a)   refer the proposed marriage to the Secretary of State;
>
> (b)   notify the parties to the proposed marriage that the proposed marriage must be referred to the Secretary of State;
>
> (c)   give the parties to the proposed marriage prescribed information about—
>
> > (i)   the effects of the referral;
> >
> > (ii)   the requirement under regulations under section 28D to notify the Secretary of State of changes of address.

(6)   The superintendent registrar must act in accordance with regulations when complying with the duty in subsection (5)(a) to refer a proposed marriage to the Secretary of State.

(7)   Regulations may, in particular, make provision about—

    (a)   the form, manner or timing of the referral of a proposed marriage;

    (b)   information, photographs or evidence—or copies of any of those things—to be included with the referral of a proposed marriage.

(8)   Regulations are to be made by statutory instrument; and a statutory instrument containing regulations is subject to annulment in pursuance of a resolution of either House of Parliament.

(9)   If the superintendent registrar refers the proposed marriage to the Secretary of State, this Act has effect in relation to the proposed marriage subject to the modifications in Schedule 3A.

(10)   In this section—

    (a)   a reference to a person being an exempt person has the same meaning as in section 49 of the Immigration Act 2014;

    (b)   "prescribed information" means information prescribed in regulations;

    (c)   "regulations" means regulations made by the Secretary of State after consulting the Registrar General.".

9

Before Schedule 4 insert—

Introduction

1

(1)   These are the modifications subject to which this Act has effect if the superintendent registrar refers a proposed marriage to the Secretary of State.

(2)   In this Schedule—

    "2014 Act" means the Immigration Act 2014;

    "referred marriage" means the proposed marriage referred to the Secretary of State.

No certificate to be issued until decision about investigation etc

2

(1)   The duty under section 31(2) to issue a certificate in respect of the referred marriage does not apply unless and until one of the following events occurs.

(2)   Event 1 occurs if—

    (a)   the Secretary of State gives the superintendent registrar the section 48 notice, and

    (b)   that notice is of a decision not to investigate whether the referred marriage is a sham.

(3)   Event 2 occurs if—

    (a)   the relevant statutory period ends, and

    (b)   the Secretary of State has not given the superintendent registrar the section 48 notice.

(4)   Event 3 occurs if—

    (a)   the Secretary of State gives the superintendent registrar the section 48 notice,

    (b)   that notice is of a decision to investigate whether the referred marriage is a sham,

    (c)   the Secretary of State gives the superintendent registrar the section 50 notice, and

    (d)   that notice is of a decision that both of the parties to the referred marriage have complied with the investigation.

(5) Event 4 occurs if—

    (a)   the 70 day period ends, and

    (b)   the Secretary of State has not given the superintendent registrar the section 50 notice.

(6) Event 5 occurs if the Secretary of State gives the superintendent registrar notice that the duty under section 31(2) is applicable.

(7) The Secretary of State may give a notice for that purpose only if—

    (a)   the Secretary of State has given the superintendent registrar the section 48 notice,

    (b)   that notice is of a decision to investigate whether the referred marriage is a sham,

    (c)   the Secretary of State has given the superintendent registrar the section 50 notice, and

    (d)   that notice is of a decision that one or both of the parties to the referred marriage have not complied with the investigation.

(8) This paragraph applies in addition to any other requirements applicable to the issue of the certificate.

(9) This paragraph is subject to paragraph 4.

(10) In this paragraph—

    "70 day period" has the same meaning as in section 50 of the 2014 Act;

    "relevant statutory period" has the same meaning as in section 48 of the 2014 Act;

    "section 48 notice" means notice under section 48(7) of the 2014 Act;

    "section 50 notice" means notice under section 50(7) of the 2014 Act.

Marriage to be investigated: extension of waiting period to 70 days

3

(1) The modifications in this paragraph have effect if the Secretary of State gives the superintendent registrar notice under section 48(7) of the 2014 Act of a decision to investigate whether the referred marriage is a sham.

(2) Section 31(2): the reference to the said period of 28 days has effect as a reference to the relevant 70 day period.

(3) Section 31(4A)(a): the reference to the period of 28 days has effect as a reference to the relevant 70 day period.

(4) Section 31(5A) and (5C): the reference to the 28 day period has effect as a reference to the relevant 70 day period.

(5) Section 31(5B) does not apply.

(6) Section 75(3)(a): the reference to 28 days has effect as a reference to 70 days (and the reference in section 31(5C) to 28 days has effect accordingly).

(7) In this paragraph "relevant 70 day period" means the period—

    (a)   beginning the day after notice of the proposed marriage is entered in the marriage book in accordance with Part 3 of the Marriage Act 1949, or is entered in an approved electronic form by virtue of section 27(4A) of that Act, and

    (b)   ending at the end of the period of 70 days beginning with that day.

Effect of reducing statutory period

4

(1) This paragraph applies if—

    (a)   the Secretary of State gives notice under section 31(5EB) of the grant of an application made under section 31(5A) (reduction of statutory period) in relation to the referred marriage, and

    (b)   that notice is given at a time when the duty under section 31(2) to issue a certificate in respect of the referred marriage has not arisen in accordance with paragraph 2.

(2) The duty under subsection 31(2) to issue a certificate in respect of the referred marriage arises on the giving of the notice, subject to any other requirements applicable to the issue of the certificate being met.

(3) But the requirements of paragraph 2 are not applicable in such a case.

(4) The Secretary of State is not prevented from deciding to conduct, conducting, or continuing, an investigation if a certificate in respect of the referred marriage is issued as mentioned in sub-paragraph (2).

(5) But in such a case, nothing in the 2014 Act requires the Secretary of State to decide whether to conduct, to conduct, or to continue, an investigation.

(6) In this paragraph "investigation" means an investigation, conducted following a decision by the Secretary of State under section 48 of the 2014 Act, whether a proposed marriage is a sham.".

Notice period

10

(1) Section 31 (marriage under certificate without licence) is amended in accordance with this paragraph.

(2) In section 31—

    (a)   for "15 successive days" (in each place) substitute "28 successive days";

    (b)   for "15 days" (in each place) substitute "28 days";

    (c)   for "15 day period" (in each place) substitute "28 day period".

(3) After subsection (5E) insert—

"(5EA) If a proposed marriage is referred to the Secretary of State under section 28H—

    (a)   any application under subsection (5A) is to be made to the Secretary of State; and

    (b)   the power conferred by subsection (5A) is exercisable by the Secretary of State;

and the reference to the Registrar General in subsection (5C) accordingly has effect as a reference to the Secretary of State.

(5EB) If the Secretary of State grants an application made under subsection (5A), the Secretary of State must give notice of the grant of the application to the applicant and to the superintendent registrar to whom notice of the marriage was given.

(5EC) Regulations under subsection (5D) do not apply to applications made to the Secretary of State in accordance with subsection (5EA).

(5ED) The Secretary of State may by regulations make provision with respect to the making, and granting, of applications made in accordance with subsection (5EA).

(5EE) The Secretary of State must consult the Registrar General before making regulations under subsection (5ED).".

(4) In subsection (5H), after "(5D)" insert "or (5ED)".

Marriage referred to Secretary of State: issue of certificates

11

(1) In section 31 (marriage under certificate without licence), at the end insert—
"(7)   This section has effect subject to section 31ZA.".

(2) After section 31 insert—

"31ZA Notice of marriage: false information or evidence

(1) A superintendent registrar may refuse to issue a certificate under section 31(2) in a case where—

(a)   notice of marriage has been given under section 27, and

(b)   a superintendent registrar has reasonable grounds for suspecting that a relevant decision was made incorrectly because of the provision of false information or evidence.

(2) If the superintendent registrar refuses to issue the certificate, the parties to the proposed marriage are to be taken not to have given notice under section 27; but that does not prevent criminal proceedings from being brought against either party, or any other person, in relation to the giving of the notice.

(3) This section does not limit the powers of superintendent registrars to refuse to issue certificates under section 31 in respect of marriages.

(4) In this section—

"evidence" includes a photograph or other image;

"exempt person" has the same meaning as in section 28H;

"relevant decision" means a decision of a superintendent registrar that a party to a proposed marriage is an exempt person.".

(3) In section 31A (appeal on refusal under section 31(2)(a))—

(a)   in the title, at the end insert "or 31ZA";

(b)   in subsection (1), after "31(2)(a)" insert "or 31ZA";

(c)   after subsection (2) insert—

"(2A)   In a case where—

(a)   in reliance on section 31ZA, a superintendent registrar refuses to issue a certificate, and

(b)   on an appeal against the refusal, the Registrar General directs that a certificate be issued,

section 31ZA(2) is of no effect—and is to be taken to have never had any effect—in relation to the parties' giving of notice under section 27.";

(d)   after subsection (3) insert—

"(3A)   If—

(a)   relying on section 31ZA, a superintendent registrar refuses to issue a certificate, and

(b)   on an appeal against the refusal, the Registrar General declares the appeal to have been frivolous,

the person making the appeal is liable for the costs of the proceedings before the Registrar General.";

(e)   in subsection (4)—

(i)   for "such costs and damages" substitute "costs and damages in accordance with subsection (3) or (3A)";

(ii)   at the end insert "(in the case of subsection (3)) or evidence that the Registrar General has declared the appeal to have been frivolous (in the case of subsection (3A))".

Certificates

12

(1) Section 35 (marriage in registration district in which neither party resides) is amended in accordance with sub-paragraphs (2) and (3).

(2) After subsection (3) insert—

"(3A)   In a case where one or both of the persons to be married ("the couple") are not relevant nationals, a superintendent registrar may issue a certificate for the solemnization of a marriage in a qualifying church or chapel, notwithstanding that it is not within a registration district in which either of the couple resides.

(3B)   In subsection (3A) "qualifying church or chapel" means a church or chapel which is not the usual place of worship of the couple but in which it would be possible—

    (a)   (if section 5(3)(a) were disregarded) for the marriage of the couple to be solemnized in accordance with section 5(1)(a) (marriage after publication of banns), or

    (b)   (if section 5(3)(b) were disregarded) for the marriage of the couple to be solemnized in accordance with section 5(1)(c) (marriage on authority of common licence).".

(3) After subsection (5) insert—

"(6)   Where a marriage is intended to be solemnized on the authority of certificates of a superintendent registrar issued under subsection (3A), each notice of marriage given to the superintendent registrar and each certificate issued by the superintendent registrar shall state, in addition to the description of the church or chapel in which the marriage is to be solemnized, that it would be possible for the marriage of the couple to be solemnized in that church or chapel after the publication of banns or on the authority of a common licence (if section 5(3) were disregarded).".

(4) Omit section 38.

One party resident in Scotland

13

In section 37 (one party resident in Scotland), in subsection (1)(b), for the words from "with" to "Act" (in the first place) substitute "with section 27 and the other provisions of this Act".

Proof of certain matters not necessary to validity of marriages

14

In section 48 (proof of certain matters not necessary to validity of marriages), in subsection (1)—

    (a)   omit the word "or" at the end of paragraph (e) (inserted by paragraph 14(c) of Schedule 7 to the Marriage (Same Sex Couples) Act 2013);

    (b)   at the end of paragraph (ea) (inserted by that provision of the Marriage (Same Sex Couples) Act 2013) insert

"or

    (eb)   that, in the case of a marriage to which Schedule 3A applied, any of the events listed in paragraph 2(2) to (6) of that Schedule occurred.".

Regulations etc

15

In section 74 (regulations), after subsection (2) insert—

"(3) Any order or regulations made under this Act may make different provision for different cases.".

Offences

16

In section 75 (offences relating to solemnization of marriages), in subsection (3)(a), for "15 days" substitute "28 days".

Relevant nationals

17

In section 78 (interpretation of the 1949 Act), in subsection (1), after the definition of "registration district" insert—

""relevant national" means—

    (a) a British citizen,

    (b) a national of an EEA State other than the United Kingdom, or

    (c) a national of Switzerland;".

PART 2
CIVIL PARTNERSHIP

Introduction

18

The Civil Partnership Act 2004 is amended in accordance with this Part of this Schedule.

Supply of additional information and evidence

19

(1) Section 8 (notice of proposed civil partnership and declaration) is amended in accordance with this paragraph.

(2) In subsection (4), after paragraph (b) insert—

"(c) that the proposed civil partner believes all of the information stated in the notice, and all information and evidence supplied with the notice, is true.".

(3) After subsection (5) insert—

"(5A) Subsection (5) is subject to section 9F.".

20

After section 8 insert—

"8A Additional information if party not relevant national

(1) This section applies to notice of proposed civil partnership given to a registration authority in accordance with section 8 if one, or each, of the parties to the proposed civil partnership is not a relevant national.

(2) But this section does not apply if Schedule 3 applies to the proposed civil partnership.

(3)   For each party to the proposed civil partnership who is not a relevant national, the notice must include whichever of statements A, B or C is applicable to that person.

(4)   Statement A is a statement that the person has the appropriate immigration status.

(5)   Statement B is a statement that the person holds a relevant visa in respect of the proposed civil partnership.

(6)   Statement C is a statement that the person neither—

      (a)   has the appropriate immigration status, nor

      (b)   holds a relevant visa in respect of the proposed civil partnership.

(7)   If the notice contains the statement referred to in the first column of an entry in this table, the notice must be accompanied by the information and photographs referred to in the second column of that entry (insofar as that entry is applicable to the parties to the proposed civil partnership)—

If the notice includes this statement...	...the notice must be accompanied by...
Statement A (in respect of one or both of the parties to the proposed civil partnership)	For each party in respect of whom statement A is made, details of the particular immigration status which that party has
Statement B (in respect of one or both of the parties to the proposed civil partnership)	1 For each party, a specified photograph of that party
	2 For each party in respect of whom statement B is made, details of the relevant visa which that party has
Statement C (in respect of one or both of the parties to the proposed civil partnership)	1 For each party, a specified photograph of that party
	2 For each party, the usual address of that party
	3 For each party whose usual address is outside the United Kingdom, an address in the United Kingdom at which that party can be contacted by post
	4 For each party who has previously used any name or names other than the person's name stated in the notice of proposed civil partnership in accordance with regulations under section 8(2), a statement of the other name or names
	5 For each party who currently uses, or has previously used, an alias or aliases, a statement of the alias or aliases

(8)   If the notice contains more than one of statements A, B and C, subsection (7) must be complied with in relation to each of those statements; but where the notice contains statements B and C, subsection (7) does not require the notice to be accompanied by more than one specified photograph of each party.

(9)   If the notice includes statement C for a party to the proposed civil partnership—

      (a)   the notice may be accompanied by a statement ("statement D") of that person's immigration position in the United Kingdom;

      (b)   if the notice is accompanied by statement D for a party to the proposed civil partnership, the person may provide the registration authority with details of his or her immigration position in the United Kingdom; and

(c) if any such details are provided, the registration authority must record them.

(10) In this section—

  (a) a reference—

    (i) to a person having the appropriate immigration status, or

    (ii) to a person holding a relevant visa,

has the same meaning as in section 49 of the Immigration Act 2014;

  (b) a reference to the particular immigration status which a person has is a reference to the immigration status set out in any of paragraphs (a) to (c) of section 49(2) of that Act which the person has;

  (c) a reference to a person's immigration position in the United Kingdom includes a reference to the person's not being entitled to be in the United Kingdom.

(11) In this section "specified photograph" means a photograph that is in accordance with regulations made under section 9E (and for this purpose "photograph" includes other kinds of images).".

21

For section 9 substitute—

"9 Evidence

(1) A notice of proposed civil partnership under section 8 must, in relation to each of the parties to the civil partnership, be accompanied by specified evidence of the following matters—

  (a) the person's name and surname;

  (b) the person's date of birth;

  (c) the person's place of residence;

  (d) the person's nationality.

(2) A person giving a notice of proposed civil partnership under section 8 must provide the registration authority to which the notice is given with specified evidence—

  (a) as to whether the person has previously formed a civil partnership or been married; and

  (b) if so, as to the ending of the civil partnership or marriage.

(3) In this section "specified evidence" means evidence that is in accordance with regulations made under section 9E.

9A Additional evidence if party not relevant national

(1) This section applies to notice of proposed civil partnership given to a registration authority in accordance with section 8 if one, or each, of the parties to the proposed civil partnership is not a relevant national.

(2) If the notice includes statement A (referred to in section 8A(4)), and accordingly is accompanied by details of the particular immigration status which a party to the proposed civil partnership has, the notice must be accompanied by specified evidence of that status.

(3) If the notice includes statement B (referred to in section 8A(5)), the notice must be accompanied by specified evidence of the holding of the relevant visa by the party to the proposed civil partnership.

(4) If, in accordance with section 8A(7), the notice is accompanied by the usual address of a party to the proposed civil partnership, the notice must also be accompanied by specified evidence that it is that party's usual address.

(5) If the notice includes statement D (referred to in section 8A(9)), the notice may be accompanied by evidence of the person's immigration position in the United Kingdom.

(6)   If subsection (2) or (3) applies to the notice, and the notice is not accompanied by the specified evidence required by that subsection, the notice must be accompanied by—

    (a)   photographs and addresses of the kinds referred to in paragraphs 1 and 2 in the relevant entry in section 8A(7);

    (b)   as respects the usual address of each party that is provided in accordance with paragraph (a), specified evidence that the address provided is that party's usual address; and

    (c)   addresses, names and aliases of the kinds referred to in paragraphs 3 to 5 in the relevant entry in section 8A(7) (insofar as those paragraphs are applicable to the parties to the proposed civil partnership).

(7)   In this section—

    "relevant entry in section 8A(7)" means the second column of the last entry in the table in section 8A(7);

    "specified evidence" means evidence that is in accordance with regulations made under section 9E.

9B Change of usual address or UK contact address

(1)   The Secretary of State may, by regulations, make provision about the giving to the Secretary of State of—

    (a)   notice of a person's usual address, if the person's notified usual address changes;

    (b)   notice of a UK contact address, if the person's notified usual address is not in the United Kingdom;

    (c)   notice of a person's UK contact address, if the person's notified UK contact address changes;

    (d)   evidence of any address notified in accordance with regulations under paragraph (a), (b) or (c).

(2)   The provision that may be made in regulations under this section includes—

    (a)   provision imposing a requirement on a person;

    (b)   provision about the rejection of information or evidence which there are reasonable grounds to suspect to be false.

(3)   Regulations under subsection (1)(d) may, in particular, make any provision of the kind that may be made under section 9E(3).

(4)   In this section—

    "notified UK contact address" means an address in the United Kingdom, at which a person can be contacted by post, that has been notified in accordance with—

        (a)   section 8A(7) or 9A(6), or

        (b)   regulations under this section;

    "notified usual address" means the usual address of a person that has been notified in accordance with—

        (a)   section 8A(7) or 9A(6), or

        (b)   regulations under this section.

9C Rejection of false information or evidence

(1)   A registration authority may reject—

    (a)   any information or photograph provided under section 8, 8A or 9A, or

    (b)   any evidence provided under section 9 or 9A,

if (in particular) the registration authority has reasonable grounds for suspecting that the information, photograph or evidence is false.

(2) If the registration authority rejects any information, photograph or evidence, the registration authority may proceed under this Act as if the rejected information, photograph or evidence had not been provided.

(3) This section does not limit the powers of registration authorities to reject anything provided under any other enactment.

9D Amendment of notice and evidence provisions

(1) The Secretary of State may by order—

    (a) amend section 8A or 9A so as to vary the information that must or may be given in cases where that section applies;

    (b) amend section 9 or 9A so as to vary the matters in respect of which specified evidence must or may be given in cases where that section applies;

    (c) make such provision (including provision amending section 9B or 9E or any other enactment) as the Secretary of State considers appropriate in consequence of provision made under paragraph (a) or (b).

(2) The Secretary of State must consult the Registrar General before making an order under this section.

9E Specified evidence

(1) The Registrar General may make regulations about the evidence that is required to be given for the purposes of section 9.

(2) The Secretary of State may make regulations about the evidence that is required to be given for the purposes of section 9A.

(3) Regulations under this section may, in particular, make provision about—

    (a) the kind of evidence which is to be supplied;

    (b) the form in which evidence is to be supplied;

    (c) the manner in which evidence is to be supplied;

    (d) the period within which evidence is to be supplied;

    (e) the supply of further evidence;

    (f) the sufficiency of evidence supplied;

    (g) the consequences of failing to supply sufficient evidence in accordance with the regulations (including provision to secure that, in such a case, a particular decision is made or is to be treated as having been made);

    (h) the retention or copying of evidence supplied.

(4) In this section "evidence" includes a photograph or other image.

(5) The Registrar General must obtain the approval of the Secretary of State before making regulations under this section.

(6) The Secretary of State must consult the Registrar General before making regulations under this section.

9F Recording of information in the register: compliance with requirements

The registration authority must not enter in the register the information relating to a proposed civil partnership mentioned in section 8(5) in a case where any of the requirements imposed by or under any of the following provisions of this Act is applicable but is not complied with—

    section 8A(3) to (7);

    section 8A(8);

    section 9(1);

    section 9A(4) or (6);

    section 18(3);

    section 19(3);

paragraph 5(1) of Schedule 1;

paragraph 4 of Schedule 23.".

Notice period

22

In section 11 (meaning of "the waiting period"), for "15" substitute "28".

23

(1) Section 12 (power to shorten the waiting period) is amended in accordance with this paragraph.

(2) In subsection (1), for "15" substitute "28".

(3) After subsection (3) insert—

"(4) If a proposed civil partnership is referred to the Secretary of State under section 12A—

(a) any application under subsection (1) is to be made to the Secretary of State; and

(b) the power conferred by subsection (1) is exercisable by the Secretary of State.

(5) If the Secretary of State grants an application made under subsection (1), the Secretary of State must give notice of the grant of the application to—

(a) the applicant,

(b) the registration authority to which notice of the proposed civil partnership was given, and

(c) if different, the registration authority responsible for issuing the civil partnership schedule under section 14(1) in relation to the proposed civil partnership.

(6) Regulations under subsection (2) do not apply to applications made to the Secretary of State in accordance with subsection (4).

(7) The Secretary of State may by regulations make provision with respect to the making, and granting, of applications made in accordance with subsection (4).

(8) The Secretary of State must consult the Registrar General before making regulations under subsection (7).".

Referral to Secretary of State

24

After section 12 insert—

"12A Referral of proposed civil partnership to Secretary of State

(1) On every occasion when notice of proposed civil partnership is given under section 8, the registration authority must decide whether or not each of the parties to the proposed civil partnership is an exempt person.

(2) But this section does not apply if Schedule 3 applies to the proposed civil partnership.

(3) In making a decision under subsection (1) about a party to a proposed civil partnership, a registration authority may rely on any advice given in relation to that decision by the Secretary of State.

(4) In a case where—

(a) section 8A applies to the notice of proposed civil partnership, and

(b) specified evidence required by section 9A(2) or (3) in relation to a party to the proposed civil partnership is not produced in accordance with that section, the registration authority must decide that that party to the proposed civil partnership is not an exempt person.

(5) If the registration authority decides that either of the parties is not an exempt person, or that both of the parties are not exempt persons, the registration authority must—

> (a) refer the proposed civil partnership to the Secretary of State;
>
> (b) notify the parties to the proposed civil partnership that the proposed civil partnership must be referred to the Secretary of State;
>
> (c) give the parties to the proposed civil partnership prescribed information about—
>
>> (i) the effects of the referral;
>>
>> (ii) the requirement under regulations under section 9B to notify the Secretary of State of changes of address.

(6) The registration authority must act in accordance with regulations when complying with the duty in subsection (5)(a) to refer a proposed civil partnership to the Secretary of State.

(7) Regulations may, in particular, make provision about—

> (a) the form, manner or timing of the referral of a proposed civil partnership;
>
> (b) information, photographs or evidence—or copies of any of those things—to be included with the referral of a proposed civil partnership.

(8) If the registration authority refers the proposed civil partnership to the Secretary of State, this Act has effect in relation to the proposed civil partnership subject to the modifications in Schedule 3A.

(9) In this section—

> (a) a reference to a person being an exempt person has the same meaning as in section 49 of the Immigration Act 2014;
>
> (b) "prescribed information" means information prescribed in regulations;
>
> (c) "regulations" means regulations made by the Secretary of State after consulting the Registrar General.".

25

After Schedule 3 insert—

Introduction

1

(1) These are the modifications subject to which this Act has effect if the registration authority refers a proposed civil partnership to the Secretary of State.

(2) In this Schedule—

> "2014 Act" means the Immigration Act 2014;
>
> "referred civil partnership" means the proposed civil partnership referred to the Secretary of State.

No civil partnership schedule to be issued until decision about investigation etc

2

(1) The duty under section 14(1) to issue a civil partnership schedule in respect of the referred civil partnership does not apply unless and until one of the following events occurs.

(2) Event 1 occurs if—

>   (a)   the Secretary of State gives the registration authority or authorities the section 48 notice, and
>
>   (b)   that notice is of a decision not to investigate whether the referred civil partnership is a sham.

(3)   Event 2 occurs if—

>   (a)   the relevant statutory period ends, and
>
>   (b)   the Secretary of State has not given the registration authority or authorities the section 48 notice.

(4)   Event 3 occurs if—

>   (a)   the Secretary of State gives the registration authority or authorities the section 48 notice,
>
>   (b)   that notice is of a decision to investigate whether the referred civil partnership is a sham,
>
>   (c)   the Secretary of State gives the registration authority or authorities the section 50 notice, and
>
>   (d)   that notice is of a decision that both of the parties to the referred civil partnership have complied with the investigation.

(5)   Event 4 occurs if—

>   (a)   the 70 day period ends, and
>
>   (b)   the Secretary of State has not given the registration authority or authorities the section 50 notice.

(6)   Event 5 occurs if the Secretary of State gives the registration authority or authorities notice that the duty under section 14(1) is applicable.

(7)   The Secretary of State may give a notice for that purpose only if—

>   (a)   the Secretary of State has given the registration authority or authorities the section 48 notice,
>
>   (b)   that notice is of a decision to investigate whether the referred civil partnership is a sham,
>
>   (c)   the Secretary of State has given the registration authority or authorities the section 50 notice, and
>
>   (d)   that notice is of a decision that one or both of the parties to the referred civil partnership have not complied with the investigation.

(8)   This paragraph applies in addition to any other requirements applicable to the issue of the civil partnership schedule.

(9)   This paragraph is subject to paragraph 4.

(10)   In this paragraph—

> "70 day period" has the same meaning as in section 50 of the 2014 Act;
>
> "relevant statutory period" has the same meaning as in section 48 of the 2014 Act;
>
> "section 48 notice" means notice under section 48(8) of the 2014 Act;
>
> "section 50 notice" means notice under section 50(7) of the 2014 Act.

Civil partnership to be investigated: extension of waiting period to 70 days

3

(1)   The modifications in this paragraph have effect if the Secretary of State gives the registration authority notice under section 48(8) of the 2014 Act of a decision to investigate whether the referred civil partnership is a sham.

(2)   Section 11(b): the reference to the period of 28 days has effect as a reference to the relevant 70 day period.

(3)   But, for the purposes of section 10, the waiting period is not extended by sub-paragraph (2).

(4)   In this paragraph "relevant 70 day period" means the period—

(a)   beginning the day after notice of the proposed civil partnership is recorded in the register in accordance with section 8(5), and

(b)   ending at the end of the period of 70 days beginning with that day.

Effect of shortening waiting period

4

(1)   This paragraph applies if—

(a)   the Secretary of State gives notice under section 12(5) of the grant of an application made under section 12(1) (power to shorten the waiting period) in relation to the referred civil partnership, and

(b)   that notice is given at a time when the duty under section 14(1) to issue a civil partnership schedule in respect of the referred civil partnership has not arisen in accordance with paragraph 2.

(2)   The duty under section 14(1) to issue a civil partnership schedule in respect of the referred civil partnership arises on the giving of the notice under section 12(5), subject to any other requirements applicable to the issue of the schedule being met.

(3)   But the requirements of paragraph 2 are not applicable in such a case.

(4)   The Secretary of State is not prevented from deciding to conduct, conducting, or continuing, an investigation if a schedule in respect of the referred civil partnership is issued as mentioned in sub-paragraph (2).

(5)   But in such a case, nothing in the 2014 Act requires the Secretary of State to decide whether to conduct, or to continue, an investigation.

(6)   In this paragraph "investigation" means an investigation, conducted following a decision by the Secretary of State under section 48 of the 2014 Act, whether a proposed civil partnership is a sham.".

Civil partnership referred to Secretary of State: issue of civil partnership schedule

26

(1)   In section 14 (issue of civil partnership schedule), at the end insert—

   "(6)   This section has effect subject to section 14A.".

(2)   After section 14 insert—

"14A Notice of proposed civil partnership: false information or evidence

(1)   A registration authority may refuse to issue a civil partnership schedule under section 14(1) in a case where—

(a)   notice of a proposed civil partnership has been given under section 8, and

(b)   a registration authority has reasonable grounds for suspecting that a relevant decision was made incorrectly because of the provision of false information or evidence.

(2)   If a registration authority refuses to issue the schedule, the parties to the proposed civil partnership are to be taken not to have given notice under section 8; but that does not prevent criminal proceedings from being brought against either party, or any other person, in relation to the giving of the notice.

(3)   This section does not limit the powers of registration authorities to refuse to issue civil partnership schedules.

(4)   In this section—

   "evidence" includes a photograph or other image;

   "exempt person" has the same meaning as in section 12A;

   "relevant decision" means a decision of a registration authority that a party to the proposed civil partnership is an exempt person.".

(3)   In section 15 (appeal against refusal to issue civil partnership schedule)—
    (a)   in subsection (1)(b), after "14(3)" insert "or 14A";
    (b)   after subsection (2) insert—
"(3)   In a case where—
        (a)   in reliance on section 14A, a registration authority refuses to issue a civil partnership schedule, and
        (b)   on an appeal against the refusal, the Registrar General directs that a civil partnership schedule be issued,
section 14A(2) is of no effect—and is to be taken to have never had any effect—in relation to the parties' giving of notice under section 8.".
(4)   In section 16 (frivolous objections and representations: liability for costs etc)—
    (a)   in the title, after "**representations**" insert "**and appeals**";
    (b)   after subsection (3) insert—
"(3A)   If—
        (a)   in reliance on section 14A, a registration authority refuses to issue a civil partnership schedule, and
        (b)   on an appeal against the refusal, the Registrar General declares that the appeal is frivolous,
the person making the appeal is liable for the costs of the proceedings before the Registrar General.";
    (c)   in subsection (4), for "such costs and damages" substitute "costs and damages in accordance with subsection (3) or (3A)".

Relevant nationals

27

After section 30 insert—

"**30A Relevant nationals**
In this Chapter "relevant national" means—
        (a)   a British citizen,
        (b)   a national of an EEA State other than the United Kingdom, or
        (c)   a national of Switzerland.".

Regulations and orders

28

(1)   Section 36 (regulations and orders) is amended in accordance with this paragraph.
(2)   In subsection (3), after "6A" insert "9B, 9E(2), 12(7) or 12A".
(3)   In subsection (5), after "6A" insert "9B, 9E(2) or 12A".
(4)   In subsection (6), after "section" insert "9D or".

Proof of certain matters not necessary to validity of civil partnership

29

In section 52 (proof of certain matters not necessary to validity of civil partnership), in subsection (1)—
    (a)   omit the word "or" at the end of paragraph (a);
    (b)   at the end of paragraph (aa) insert
        "or

(ab) that, in the case of a civil partnership to which Schedule 3A applied, any of the events listed in paragraph 2(2) to (6) of that Schedule occurred.".

Section 54

Introduction

1

(1) This Schedule sets out the kinds of regulations which may be made by the Secretary of State under section 54(2).

(2) In this Schedule—

"extension order" has the meaning given in section 54(1);

"proposed Scottish or Northern Ireland marriage or civil partnership" means a proposed marriage or civil partnership under the law of Scotland or Northern Ireland.

Notices

2

(1) The Secretary of State may make regulations which make provision about the giving of relevant notices.

(2) Regulations under this paragraph may, in particular, provide that a relevant notice given in accordance with the regulations is to be presumed to have been received by the person to whom it is given.

(3) In this paragraph "relevant notice" means—

(a) a notice, under any provision of the referral and investigation scheme, which relates to a proposed Scottish or Northern Ireland marriage or civil partnership, and

(b) any other notice relating to the referral of a proposed Scottish or Northern Ireland marriage or civil partnership to the Secretary of State for the purposes of the referral and investigation scheme,

(whether or not the notice falls to be given by virtue of provision made by an extension order).

Evidence

3

(1) The Secretary of State may make regulations about the supply of evidence in accordance with a relevant evidence provision.

(2) Regulations under this paragraph may, in particular, make provision about—

(a) the kind of evidence which is to be supplied;

(b) the form in which evidence is to be supplied;

(c) the manner in which evidence is to be supplied;

(d) the period within which evidence is to be supplied;

(e) the supply of further evidence;

(f) the sufficiency of evidence supplied;

(g) the consequences of failing to supply sufficient evidence in accordance with the regulations (including provision to secure that, in such a case, a particular decision is made or is to be treated as having been made);

(h) the retention or copying of evidence supplied.

(3) In this paragraph—

"evidence" includes a photograph or other image;

"relevant evidence provision" means provision (whether or not made by an extension order) about the supply of evidence in relation to a proposed Scottish or Northern Ireland marriage or civil partnership in a case where one or both of the parties is not a relevant national.

Change of address

4

(1)   The Secretary of State may, by regulations, make provision about the giving to the Secretary of State of—

  (a)   notice of a relevant person's usual address, if the person's notified usual address changes;

  (b)   notice of a relevant person's UK contact address, if the person's notified usual address is not in the United Kingdom;

  (c)   notice of a relevant person's UK contact address, if the person's notified UK contact address changes;

  (d)   evidence of any address notified in accordance with regulations under paragraph (a), (b) or (c).

(2)   Regulations under this paragraph may, in particular, make—

  (a)   provision imposing a requirement on a person;

  (b)   provision about the rejection of information or evidence which there are reasonable grounds to suspect to be false.

(3)   Regulations under sub-paragraph (1)(d) may, in particular, make any provision of the kind that may be made under paragraph 3(2).

(4)   In this paragraph—

"notified", in relation to an address of a relevant person, means notified (whether to the Secretary of State or another person) in connection with the proposed Scottish or Northern Ireland marriage or civil partnership (including any such address notified in accordance with provision made by an extension order or regulations made under this paragraph);

"relevant person" means a person who is a party to a proposed Scottish or Northern Ireland marriage or civil partnership in a case where that person or the other party is not a relevant national (or both of them are not relevant nationals);

"UK contact address" means an address in the United Kingdom at which a person can be contacted by post.

Referral

5

(1)   The Secretary of State may make regulations requiring a person to act in accordance with the regulations when complying with a duty of referral.

(2)   The regulations may, in particular, make provision about—

  (a)   the form, manner or timing of the referral;

  (b)   information, photographs or evidence—or copies of any of those things—to be included with the referral.

(3)   The Secretary of State may make regulations requiring a person who refers a proposed marriage or civil partnership in accordance with a duty of referral to give the parties to the proposed marriage information prescribed in the regulations about—

  (a)   the effects of the referral;

  (b)   any requirements under regulations under paragraph 4 to notify the Secretary of State of changes of address.

(4)   In this paragraph—

"duty of referral" means a duty (whether or not contained in provision made by an extension order) to refer a proposed Scottish or Northern Ireland marriage or civil partnership to the Secretary of State for the purposes of the referral and investigation scheme;

"referral" means the referral of a proposed Scottish or Northern Ireland marriage or civil partnership under a duty of referral.

Applications for shortening of waiting period

6

(1) The Secretary of State may make regulations about the making, and granting, of applications for the shortening of a waiting period in cases where a proposed Scottish or Northern Ireland marriage or civil partnership is referred to the Secretary of State in accordance with a duty of referral.

(2) Regulations may be made under this paragraph—
  (a) whether the application falls to be made by virtue of provision made by an extension order or otherwise;
  (b) whether the application falls to be made to the Secretary of State or another person.

(3) In this paragraph—
"duty of referral" has the same meaning as in paragraph 5;
"waiting period", in relation to a proposed Scottish or Northern Ireland marriage or civil partnership, means a period during which it is not possible for the marriage to be solemnized or civil partnership to be formed (but which falls after notice of the proposed marriage or civil partnership has been given for the purposes of enabling it to be solemnized or formed in due course).

Section 59

PART 1

DISCLOSURE OF INFORMATION ETC WHERE PROPOSED MARRIAGE OR CIVIL PARTNERSHIP REFERRED TO SECRETARY OF STATE

1

(1) This paragraph applies if—
  (a) a superintendent registrar refers a proposed marriage to the Secretary of State under section 28H of the Marriage Act 1949, or
  (b) a registration authority refers a proposed civil partnership to the Secretary of State under section 12A of the Civil Partnership Act 2004.

(2) The Secretary of State may—
  (a) disclose relevant information to a registration official, or
  (b) supply a document containing relevant information to a registration official.

(3) In this paragraph "relevant information" means any of the following information—
  (a) the fact that the proposed marriage or civil partnership has been referred to the Secretary of State;
  (b) the names of the parties to the proposed marriage or civil partnership;
  (c) in the case of a proposed marriage—
    (i) any information included with the referral in accordance with regulations under section 28H of the Marriage Act 1949;
    (ii) any address of a party to the proposed marriage notified to the Secretary of State in accordance with such regulations or regulations under section 28D of the Marriage Act 1949;
  (d) in the case of a proposed civil partnership—

        (i)   any information included with the referral in accordance with regulations under section 12A of the Civil Partnership Act 2004;

        (ii)   any address of a party to the proposed civil partnership notified to the Secretary of State in accordance with such regulations or regulations under section 9B of the Civil Partnership Act 2004;

  (e)   details of any immigration enforcement action taken by the Secretary of State in respect of a party to the proposed marriage or civil partnership (including any action taken after solemnization of the marriage or formation of the civil partnership);

  (f)   details of any immigration decision taken wholly or partly by reference to the marriage or civil partnership (whether while it was proposed or after it was solemnized or formed).

PART 2
DISCLOSURE OF INFORMATION ETC FOR IMMIGRATION PURPOSES ETC

Disclosures by registration officials

2

(1) A registration official may—

  (a)   disclose any information held by the registration official, or

  (b)   supply any document held by the registration official,

to the Secretary of State, or to another registration official, for use for either of the following purposes.

(2) Those purposes are—

  (a)   immigration purposes;

  (b)   purposes connected with the exercise of functions relating to—

        (i)   the referral of proposed marriages to the Secretary of State under section 28H of the Marriage Act 1949, or

        (ii)   the referral of proposed civil partnerships to the Secretary of State under section 12A of the Civil Partnership Act 2004.

(3) In this paragraph "immigration purposes" means—

  (a)   the administration of immigration control under the Immigration Acts;

  (b)   the prevention, detection, investigation or prosecution of criminal offences relating to immigration;

  (c)   the imposition of penalties or charges under Part 3 of the Immigration and Asylum Act 1999;

  (d)   the provision of support for asylum-seekers and their dependants under Part 6 of that Act;

  (e)   such other purposes as may be specified by the Secretary of State by order.

3

A registration official may disclose to another registration official—

  (a)   the fact that a suspicion about a marriage or civil partnership has been reported to the Secretary of State under section 24 or 24A of the Immigration and Asylum Act 1999, and

  (b)   the content of any such report,

(whether or not the suspicion was reported by the registration official making the disclosure).

Disclosures by the Secretary of State

4

(1)   The Secretary of State may—

    (a)   disclose any information held by the Secretary of State, or

    (b)   supply any document held by the Secretary of State,

to a registration official for use for verification purposes.

(2)   In this paragraph "verification purposes" means—

    (a)   assisting in the verification of information provided to a relevant official by a person giving—

        (i)   notice of marriage under section 27 of the Marriage Act 1949, or

        (ii)   notice under section 8 of the Civil Partnership Act 2004;

    (b)   assisting in the verification of the immigration status of a person who contacts a relevant official in connection with the exercise of a function by a registration official;

    (c)   assisting in the verification of whether a person who contacts a relevant official in connection with the exercise of a function by a registration official—

        (i)   is suspected of involvement in crime relating to immigration, or

        (ii)   has been convicted of an offence relating to immigration.

(3)   In this paragraph "relevant official" means—

    (a)   a registration official, or

    (b)   any other person employed to assist the exercise of functions by registration officials.

PART 3
DISCLOSURE OF INFORMATION ETC FOR PREVENTION OF CRIME ETC

5

(1)   A registration official may—

    (a)   disclose any information held by the registration official, or

    (b)   supply any document held by the registration official,

to an eligible person, or to another registration official in England and Wales, for use for crime-fighting purposes.

(2)   Information is disclosed, or a document is supplied, for use for crime-fighting purposes if condition A and condition B are met.

(3)   Condition A is met if the registration official disclosing the information or supplying the document has reasonable grounds for suspecting that a criminal offence has been, is being, or is going to be committed.

(4)   Condition B is met if the registration official discloses the information or supplies the document for use for one or both of these purposes—

    (a)   assisting in the verification of information supplied to that or any other registration official;

    (b)   assisting in the prevention, detection, investigation or prosecution of a criminal offence.

(5)   In this section "eligible person" means—

    (a)   the Secretary of State;

    (b)   the Commissioners for Her Majesty's Revenue and Customs;

    (c)   a member of a police force operating in England and Wales or any part of it;

    (d)   a county council, a district council or a county borough council;

    (e)   the Greater London Authority, a London borough council or the Common Council of the City of London.

PART 4
GENERAL PROVISIONS

Limitations on powers

6

This Schedule does not authorise—

    (a)   a disclosure, in contravention of any provisions of the Data Protection Act 1998, of personal data which are not exempt from those provisions, or

    (b)   a disclosure which is prohibited by Part 1 of the Regulation of Investigatory Powers Act 2000.

No breach of confidentiality etc

7

A disclosure of information which is authorised by this Schedule does not breach—

    (a)   an obligation of confidence owed by the person making the disclosure, or

    (b)   any other restriction on the disclosure of information (however imposed).

Retention, copying and disposal of documents

8

A person to whom a document is supplied under any provision of this Schedule may—

    (a)   retain the document;

    (b)   copy the document;

    (c)   dispose of the document in such manner as the person thinks appropriate.

Saving for existing powers

9

This Schedule does not limit any other power under which—

    (a)   information may be disclosed, or

    (b)   documents may be supplied.

Meaning of "registration official"

10

A "registration official" is any of the following—

    (a)   the Registrar General;

    (b)   a superintendent registrar;

    (c)   a registrar;

    (d)   a registration authority or a person exercising the functions of a registration authority;

    (e)   a civil partnership registrar (within the meaning of Chapter 1 of Part 2 of the Civil Partnership Act 2004—see section 29 of that Act).

Section 63

Introductory

1

Part 5 of the Immigration and Asylum Act 1999 (which makes provision for the regulation of immigration advisers and immigration service providers) is amended in accordance with this Schedule.

Removal of Commissioner's power of exemption from registration

2

(1)   In section 84(4) (persons exempt from prohibition on provision of immigration advice and services by unqualified persons)—

    (a)   omit paragraphs (a), (b) and (c) (and the word "or" which follows paragraph (c));

    (b)   in paragraph (d) omit "who".

(2)   Omit the following provisions—

    (a)   section 84(5) and (7);

    (b)   section 85(2);

    (c)   section 87(3)(b);

    (d)   section 88(2)(c);

    (e)   section 89(4);

    (f)   paragraph 6(3)(b) and 9(1)(d) of Schedule 5;

    (g)   paragraph 6(3)(a) of Schedule 6.

Waiver of fees for registration

3

(1)   Paragraph 5 of Schedule 6 (fees for registration) is amended as follows.

(2)   In sub-paragraph (1)—

    (a)   after "order" insert "(a)";

    (b)   at the end insert—

        "(b)   make provision for, and in connection with, requiring or authorising the Commissioner to waive all or part of the specified fee in particular cases."

(3)   In sub-paragraph (2) at the end insert "(but this is subject to any waiver in accordance with provision under sub-paragraph (1)(b))".

Cancellation of registration by Commissioner

4

(1)   In section 87(3) (decisions of Commissioner which may be appealed to First-tier Tribunal) after paragraph (ea) insert—

        "(eb)   to cancel a registration under paragraph 4A(e) of that Schedule."

(2)   In paragraph 9 of Schedule 5 (powers of Commissioner on determining a complaint)—

    (a)   omit sub-paragraph (1)(b);

    (b)   after sub-paragraph (1A) (inserted by paragraph 7(4) of this Schedule) insert—

"(1B)   Sub-paragraph (1)(a) is subject to paragraph 4A(e) of Schedule 6 (duty of Commissioner to cancel registration of a person who is no longer competent or is otherwise unfit)."

(3) In paragraph 3 of Schedule 6 (applications for continued registration)—
    (a)   omit sub-paragraph (5);
    (b)   in sub-paragraph (6) for "Otherwise," substitute "Unless the Commissioner is required by paragraph 4A to cancel the applicant's registration";
    (c)   in sub-paragraph (7)(a) omit "or by a direction given by the First-tier Tribunal under section 89(2)(b)".

(4) In Schedule 6 (registration) after paragraph 4 insert—

"Further provision for the cancellation of registration

4A

The Commissioner must cancel a person's registration if—
    (a)   the person asks for it to be cancelled;
    (b)   the person dies (in a case where the person is an individual) or is dissolved or wound up (in any other case);
    (c)   the person is convicted of an offence under section 25 or 26(1)(d) or (g) of the 1971 Act;
    (d)   under section 89(2A)(b) the First-tier Tribunal directs the Commissioner to cancel the person's registration; or
    (e)   the Commissioner considers that the person is no longer competent or is otherwise unfit to provide immigration advice or immigration services."

Suspension of registration

5

(1) In section 84(3) (limitations on effect of registration)—
    (a)   after "subject to" insert "(a)";
    (b)   at the end insert—
        "(b) paragraph 4B(5) of that Schedule (effect of suspension of registration)."

(2) In section 87(4) (further functions of First-tier Tribunal)—
    (a)   for "a further function" substitute "further functions";
    (b)   at the end insert "and paragraph 4B of Schedule 6 (suspension of registration by First-tier Tribunal)".

(3) After paragraph 4A of Schedule 6 (inserted by paragraph 4(4) of this Schedule) insert—

"Suspension of registration

4B

(1) The First-tier Tribunal may, on an application made to it by the Commissioner, suspend a person's registration if the person is for the time being charged with—
    (a)   an offence involving dishonesty or deception;
    (b)   an indictable offence; or
    (c)   an offence under section 25 or 26(1)(d) or (g) of the 1971 Act.

(2) The suspension of the person's registration ceases to have effect if one of these occurs—
    (a)   the person is acquitted of the offence;
    (b)   the charge is withdrawn;
    (c)   proceedings in respect of the charge are discontinued;

(d)   an order is made for the charge to lie on the file, or in relation to Scotland, the diet is deserted p*ro loco et tempore.*

(3)   If the person is convicted of an offence under section 25 or 26(1)(d) or (g) of the 1971 Act, the suspension of the person's registration continues to have effect until the Commissioner cancels the person's registration (as required by paragraph 4A(c)).

(4)   If the person is convicted of any other offence within sub-paragraph (1)—

(a)   the Commissioner must as soon as reasonably practicable consider whether the person is no longer competent or is otherwise unfit to provide immigration advice or immigration services (so that the person's registration must be cancelled under paragraph 4A(e));

(b)   the suspension of the person's registration continues to have effect until the Commissioner either cancels the person's registration, or decides that the person is competent and otherwise fit to provide immigration advice and immigration services.

(5)   A person whose registration is suspended is not to be treated as a registered person for the purposes of section 84 (but is to be treated as a registered person for the purposes of the other provisions of this Part).

(6)   Where a person's registration is suspended the Commissioner must as soon as reasonably practicable record the suspension in the register.

(7)   Where a suspension ceases to have effect (and the person's registration is not cancelled) the Commissioner must as soon as reasonably practicable remove the record of the suspension from the register."

Inspections

6

After paragraph 4 of Schedule 5 insert—

"Inspections

4A

The Commissioner may carry out inspections of the activities and businesses of registered persons."

Complaints and investigations

7

(1)   For section 89(2) (powers of Tribunal on hearing charge against registered person) substitute—

"(2)   Subsections (2A) and (2B) apply if the person charged was, at the time to which the charge relates, a registered person or a person acting on behalf of a registered person.

(2A)   If the registered person mentioned in subsection (2) is still registered, the First-tier Tribunal may direct the Commissioner—

(a)   to record the charge and the First-tier Tribunal's decision on it for consideration in connection with that person's next application for continued registration;

(b)   to cancel that person's registration.

(2B)   If the registered person mentioned in subsection (2) is no longer registered, the First-tier Tribunal may direct the Commissioner to record the charge and the First-tier Tribunal's decision on it for consideration in connection with any application by that person for registration."

(2) In paragraph 5(3) of Schedule 5 (complaints which may be investigated by Commissioner)—

(a) before paragraph (a) insert—

"(za) the competence or fitness to provide immigration advice or immigration services of a person who, at the time to which the complaint relates, was a registered person,";

(b) in paragraph (a) for "a person" substitute "any other person";

(c) after paragraph (a) insert—

"(aa) the competence or fitness of a person who, at the time to which the complaint relates, was acting on behalf of a registered person,";

(d) in paragraph (b) for the first "a person" substitute "any other person";

(e) in paragraph (d) for "a person to whom they apply" substitute "a person who, at the time to which the complaint relates, was a registered person or a person acting on behalf of a registered person".

(3) For paragraph 9(1)(a) of that Schedule (Commissioner's powers on determining a complaint) substitute—

"(a) if the person to whom the complaint relates was at the time to which the complaint relates—

(i) a registered person, or

(ii) a person acting on behalf of a registered person,

record the complaint and the decision on it to be considered in connection with the next relevant application;".

(4) After paragraph 9(1) insert—

"(1A) In sub-paragraph (1)(a) "relevant application" means—

(a) if the registered person referred to in that sub-paragraph is still registered, an application by that person for continued registration, and

(b) otherwise, an application by that person for registration."

(5) For paragraph 9(4) substitute—

"(4) Relevant person" means—

(a) a person who, at the time to which the charge relates, was providing immigration advice or immigration services and was—

(i) a registered person, or

(ii) a person acting on behalf of a registered person;

(b) a person providing immigration advice or immigration services who is—

(i) a person to whom section 84(4)(d) applies, or

(ii) a person employed by, or working under the supervision of, such a person."

Power of entry and inspection

8

(1) Omit paragraph 7 of Schedule 5 (and the cross-heading before it).

(2) After paragraph 10 of that Schedule insert—

"Power of entry and inspection

10A

(1) On an application made by the Commissioner a justice of the peace (or in Scotland, the sheriff) may issue a warrant authorising the Commissioner to enter premises.

(2)   A justice of the peace or sheriff may issue a warrant in respect of premises if satisfied that there are reasonable grounds for believing that—

    (a)   the premises are being used, or have been used, in connection with the provision of immigration advice or immigration services by a registered person,

    (b)   entry to the premises is reasonably required for the exercise of any of the Commissioner's functions, and

    (c)   entry to the premises may be prevented or delayed unless a warrant is produced.

(3)   The Commissioner may enter premises by virtue of this paragraph only at a reasonable hour.

(4)   Where the Commissioner enters premises by virtue of this paragraph the Commissioner may—

    (a)   take onto the premises any equipment that appears to the Commissioner to be necessary;

    (b)   require any person on the premises to produce any relevant document and, if the document is produced, to provide any explanation of it;

    (c)   require any person on the premises to state, to the best of the person's knowledge and belief, where any relevant document is to be found;

    (d)   take copies of, or extracts from, any relevant document on the premises which is produced;

    (e)   require any relevant information which is held in a computer and is accessible from the premises to be produced in a form—

        (i)   in which it can be taken away; and

        (ii)   in which it is visible and legible.

(5)   For the purposes of sub-paragraph (4), a document or information is "relevant" if the document or information relates to any matter connected with the provision of immigration advice or immigration services.

(6)   The powers conferred on the Commissioner by sub-paragraphs (1) to (5) may also be exercised by—

    (a)   a member of the Commissioner's staff authorised by the Commissioner in writing, and

    (b)   if the Commissioner so determines, a person appointed by the Commissioner to make a report on the provision of immigration advice or immigration services from the premises in question.

(7)   If a registered person fails without reasonable excuse to allow access under this paragraph to any premises under the person's occupation or control, the Commissioner may cancel the person's registration.

(8)   The Commissioner may also cancel the registration of a registered person who—

    (a)   without reasonable excuse fails to comply with a requirement imposed under sub-paragraph (4);

    (b)   intentionally delays or obstructs any person exercising functions under this paragraph; or

    (c)   fails to take reasonable steps to prevent an employee of the registered person from obstructing any person exercising such functions.

(9)   In this paragraph "premises" includes premises used wholly or partly as a dwelling."

PART 1
FUNCTIONS EXERCISABLE BY DESIGNATED PERSONS

Introduction

1

Schedule 2 to the Immigration Act 1971 (administrative provisions as to control on entry etc) is amended in accordance with this Part of this Schedule.

Examinations by designated person

2

(1) Paragraph 3 is amended as follows.

(2) In sub-paragraph (1), after "immigration officer" insert "or designated person".

(3) For sub-paragraph (1A) substitute—

"(1A) If a person is examined under sub-paragraph (1) (whether by an immigration officer or designated person), an immigration officer may require the person, by notice in writing, to submit to further examination by the immigration officer for a purpose specified in that sub-paragraph.".

Information and documents

3

(1) Paragraph 4 is amended as follows.

(2) In sub-paragraph (1), for "his functions" substitute "that or any other person's functions".

(3) In sub-paragraph (2)—

    (a) for "shall, if so required by the immigration officer" substitute ", or on his examination under paragraph 3 above by a designated person, shall, if so required by an immigration officer or designated person";

    (b) in paragraph (b), for "the immigration officer" substitute "the immigration officer or designated person";

    (c) in the words after paragraph (b), for "the immigration officer" substitute "the immigration officer or designated person".

(4) In sub-paragraph (3), for the words from "the immigration officer" to the second "officer" substitute "an immigration officer or a person acting under the directions of an immigration officer".

(5) In sub-paragraph (4), in the words before paragraph (a)—

    (a) for "produced or found" substitute "produced to or found by an immigration officer";

    (b) for "an immigration officer" substitute ", the immigration officer".

(6) After sub-paragraph (4) insert—

"(4A) Where a passport or other document is produced to a designated person in accordance with this paragraph, the designated person—

    (a) may examine it and detain it; and

    (b) must deliver any detained passport or document to an immigration officer as soon as reasonably practicable.

(4B) If a passport or document is delivered to an immigration officer in accordance with sub-paragraph (4A)(b), sub-paragraph (4) applies as if the immigration officer had detained the document (and, accordingly, the immigration officer may continue to detain it in accordance with sub-paragraph (4)(a), (b) or (c)).".

(7)   In sub-paragraph (5), after "examination" insert ", or any immigration officer or designated person,".

Embarkation cards

4

(1)   Paragraph 5 is amended in accordance with sub-paragraphs (2) and (3).

(2)   For "requiring passengers" substitute

"requiring—

>   (a)   passengers".

(3)   For "cards in such form" substitute

>   "cards, and
>
>   (b)   passengers embarking in the United Kingdom, or any class of such passengers, to produce to a designated person, if so required, embarkation cards,

in such form".

Designations

5

After paragraph 5 insert—

"Designated persons

5A

(1)   In this Schedule "designated person" means a person designated by the Secretary of State for the purposes of this Schedule.

(2)   A designation under this paragraph is subject to such limitations as may be specified in the designation.

(3)   A limitation under sub-paragraph (2) may, in particular, relate to the functions that are exercisable by virtue of the designation (and, accordingly, the exercise of functions under this Schedule by a designated person is subject to any such limitations specified in the person's designation).

(4)   A designation under this paragraph—

>   (a)   may be permanent or for a specified period,
>
>   (b)   may (in either case) be withdrawn, and
>
>   (c)   may be varied.

(5)   The power to designate, or to withdraw or vary a designation, is exercised by the Secretary of State giving notice to the person in question.

(6)   The Secretary of State may designate a person under this paragraph only if the Secretary of State is satisfied that the person—

>   (a)   is capable of effectively carrying out the functions that are exercisable by virtue of the designation,
>
>   (b)   has received adequate training in respect of the exercise of those functions, and
>
>   (c)   is otherwise a suitable person to exercise those functions.".

Directions to carriers and operators of ports

6

After paragraph 5A (inserted by paragraph 5 above) insert—

"*Directions to carriers and operators of ports etc*"

5B

(1) The Secretary of State may direct—

   (a)   an owner or agent of a ship or aircraft, or

   (b)   a person concerned in the management of a port,

to make arrangements for designated persons to exercise a specified function, or a function of a specified description, in relation to persons of a specified description.

(2) A direction under this paragraph must specify—

   (a)   the port where, and

   (b)   the date (or dates) and time (or times) when,

a function is to be exercised under the arrangements.

(3) A direction under this paragraph must be in writing.

(4) A direction under this paragraph may specify a description of persons by reference, in particular, to—

   (a)   the destination to which persons are travelling;

   (b)   the route by which persons are travelling;

   (c)   the date and time when the persons are travelling.

(5) In this paragraph—

   "function" means a function under this Schedule;

   "specified" means specified in a direction under this paragraph.".

PART 2
OTHER PROVISION

Offences

7

(1) Section 27 of the Immigration Act 1971 (offences by persons connected with ships or aircraft or with ports) is amended as follows.

(2) In paragraph (b)—

   (a)   after sub-paragraph (iii) insert—

      "(iiia) he fails, without reasonable excuse, to comply with a direction under paragraph 5B of Schedule 2; or";

   (b)   in sub-paragraph (iv) for "a requirement" substitute "any other requirement".

(3) After paragraph (c) insert—

      "(ca) if as a person concerned in the management of a port he fails, without reasonable excuse, to comply with a direction under paragraph 5B of Schedule 2.".

Section 73

PART 1
PROVISION RELATING TO REMOVAL

Immigration Act 1971 (c 77)

1

In Schedule 2 to the Immigration Act 1971 (administrative provisions as to control on entry etc), in paragraph 11, after "immigration officer" insert "or the Secretary of State".

2

In section 2 of the Special Immigration Appeals Commission Act 1997 (jurisdiction: appeals), in subsection (2), after paragraph (c) insert—

> "(ca) section 78A of that Act (restriction on removal of children and their parents),".

Nationality, Immigration and Asylum Act 2002 (c 41)

3

(1) The Nationality, Immigration and Asylum Act 2002 is amended as follows.

(2) In section 62 (detention by Secretary of State)—

    (a) in subsection (1)—

        (i) in paragraph (a), after "under" insert "section 10 of the Immigration and Asylum Act 1999 (removal of persons unlawfully in the United Kingdom) or";

        (ii) in paragraph (b), for "paragraphs" substitute "provisions";

    (b) in subsection (2), for "that Act" substitute "the Immigration Act 1971";

    (c) omit subsections (5) and (6).

(3) In section 76 (revocation of leave to enter or remain)—

    (a) in subsection (2), omit paragraphs (b) and (c);

    (b) in subsection (4), omit the definition of "removed".

Asylum and Immigration (Treatment of Claimants, etc) Act 2004 (c 19)

4

In section 8(7) of the Asylum and Immigration (Treatment of Claimants, etc) Act 2004 (claimant's credibility; definitions), in paragraph (d) of the definition of "immigration decision", omit "(1)(a), (b), (ba) or (c)".

Immigration, Asylum and Nationality Act 2006 (c 13)

5

In the Immigration, Asylum and Nationality Act 2006, section 47 (removal of persons with statutorily extended leave) is repealed.

Legal Aid, Sentencing and Punishment of Offenders Act 2012 (c 10)

6

In Schedule 1 to the Legal Aid, Sentencing and Punishment of Offenders Act 2012 (civil legal services), in paragraph 19(10), in the definition of "removal directions", omit paragraph (e).

Consequential repeals

7

The provisions shown in the table below are repealed in consequence of the amendments made by section 1 and this Part of this Schedule.

Title	Extent of repeal
Nationality, Immigration and Asylum Act 2002	Section 73(2) to (4).
	Section 74.
	Section 75(4).
	Section 76(7).
Immigration, Asylum and Nationality Act 2006	Section 48.
Crime and Courts Act 2013	Section 51(3).
Immigration Act 2014	In Schedule 1, paragraph 2(3) and (4).

PART 2
PROVISION RELATING TO DETENTION AND BAIL

Prison Act 1952 (c 52)

8

(1)   Section 5A of the Prison Act 1952 (appointment and functions of Her Majesty's Chief Inspector of Prisons) is amended as follows.

(2)   In subsection (5A)—

    (a)   omit "and" at the end of paragraph (b);

    (b)   after paragraph (b) insert—

        "(ba) in relation to pre-departure accommodation within the meaning of that section, and".

(3)   In subsection (5B)—

    (a)   in paragraph (a), after "facilities" insert ", accommodation";

    (b)   in paragraph (b)(i), after "facilities" insert ", pre-departure accommodation".

Immigration Act 1971 (c 77)

9

In Schedule 3 to the Immigration Act 1971 (supplementary provisions as to deportation), in paragraph 3, for "33" substitute "33A".

Special Immigration Appeals Commission Act 1997 (c 68)

10

(1)   The Special Immigration Appeals Commission Act 1997 is amended as follows.

(2)   In section 5 (procedure in relation to SIAC's jurisdiction on appeals and bail), after subsection (5) insert—

    "(5A)   Rules under this section must secure that, where the Commission has decided not to release a person on bail under paragraph 22 or 29 of Schedule 2 to the Immigration Act 1971, the Commission is required to dismiss any further application by the person for release on bail that is made during the period of 28 days starting with the date of the Commission's decision, unless there has been a material change in circumstances."

(3)   In Schedule 3 (bail: modifications of Schedule 2 to the Immigration Act 1971), in paragraph 4, after sub-paragraph (1) insert—

"(1A)   In sub-paragraph (1) after "2002" there shall be inserted "or section 2 of the Special Immigration Appeals Commission Act 1997 or a review pending under section 2E of that Act."

Northern Ireland Act 1998 (c 47)

11

In section 69C of the Northern Ireland Act 1998 (investigations: places of detention), in subsection (3)(g), for "or short-term holding facility" substitute ", a short-term holding facility or pre-departure accommodation".

Immigration and Asylum Act 1999 (c 33)

12

(1)   The Immigration and Asylum Act 1999 is amended as follows.

(2)   In Schedule 11 (detainee custody officers)—

    (a)   in the heading above paragraph 3, at the end insert "and pre-departure accommodation";

    (b)   in paragraph 3—

        (i)   in sub-paragraph (1), after "facility" insert "or in pre-departure accommodation";

        (ii)   in sub-paragraph (2), after "facility" (in both places) insert "or accommodation";

    (c)   in paragraph 4(c), after "facility" insert "or in pre-departure accommodation";

    (d)   in paragraph 5(c), after "facility" insert "or in pre-departure accommodation".

(3)   In Schedule 12 (discipline etc at removal centres)—

    (a)   in paragraph 4 (assisting detained persons to escape)—

        (i)   in sub-paragraph (1), for "or short-term holding facility" substitute ", a short-term holding facility or pre-departure accommodation";

        (ii)   in the opening words of sub-paragraph (2), for "or short-term holding facility" substitute ", a short-term holding facility or pre-departure accommodation";

        (iii)   in sub-paragraph (2)(a), for "or facility" substitute ", facility or accommodation";

        (iv)   in sub-paragraph (2)(b), for "or facility" substitute ", facility or accommodation";

        (v)   in sub-paragraph (2)(c), for "or facility" substitute ", facility or accommodation";

    (b)   in paragraph 8 (notice of penalties)—

        (i)   in sub-paragraph (1), after "facility" insert "or contracted out pre-departure accommodation";

        (ii)   in sub-paragraph (2), after "facility" insert "or pre-departure accommodation".

Nationality, Immigration and Asylum Act 2002 (c 41)

13

In section 62 of the Nationality, Immigration and Asylum Act 2002 (detention by Secretary of State), in subsection (3), after paragraph (a) insert—

"(aa) a reference in paragraph 18B of that Schedule to an immigration officer shall be read as a reference to the Secretary of State,".

Safeguarding Vulnerable Groups Act 2006 (c 47)

14

In section 59 of the Safeguarding Vulnerable Groups Act 2006 (vulnerable adults), in subsection (7)(d), after "facility" insert "or in pre-departure accommodation".

Corporate Manslaughter and Corporate Homicide Act 2007 (c 19)

15

In section 2 of the Corporate Manslaughter and Corporate Homicide Act 2007 (meaning of "relevant duty of care")—

(a) in subsection (2)(b), for "or short-term holding facility" substitute ", a short-term holding facility or in pre-departure accommodation";

(b) in subsection (7), for "and "short-term holding facility"" substitute ", "short-term holding facility" and "pre-departure accommodation"".

UK Borders Act 2007 (c 30)

16

In section 48 of the UK Borders Act 2007 (establishment of border and immigration inspectorate), in subsection (2A)(a), after "facilities" insert "and in pre-departure accommodation".

PART 3
PROVISION RELATING TO BIOMETRICS

Immigration and Asylum Act 1999 (c 33)

17

(1) The Immigration and Asylum Act 1999 is amended as follows.

(2) Section 143 (destruction of fingerprints) is repealed.

(3) In section 144(1) (power to make provision about other biometric information) for ", 142 and 143" substitute "and 142".

(4) Omit section 166(4)(g) (Parliamentary procedure for orders under section 143).

Anti-terrorism, Crime and Security Act 2001 (c 24)

18

Section 36 of the Anti-terrorism, Crime and Security Act 2001 (which amends section 143 of the Immigration and Asylum Act 1999) is repealed.

Nationality, Immigration and Asylum Act 2002 (c 41)

19

In section 126 of the Nationality, Immigration and Asylum Act 2002 (power to require provision of physical data with certain immigration applications) omit—

(a) the "or" at the end of subsection (2)(b),

(b) subsection (4)(g), and

(c) subsection (5).

PART 4
PROVISION RELATING TO APPEALS

Immigration Act 1971 (c 77)

20

The Immigration Act 1971 is amended as follows.

21

(1) Section 3C (continuation of leave pending variation decision) is amended as follows.

(2) In subsection (2)—

    (a)   omit the "or" at the end of paragraph (b);

    (b)   after paragraph (c) insert

        ", or

    (d)   an administrative review of the decision on the application for variation—

        (i)   could be sought, or

        (ii)   is pending."

(3) After subsection (6) insert—

    "(7)   In this section—

    "administrative review" means a review conducted under the immigration rules;

    the question of whether an administrative review is pending is to be determined in accordance with the immigration rules."

22

(1) Section 3D (continuation of leave following revocation) is amended as follows.

(2) In subsection (2)—

    (a)   omit the "or" at the end of paragraph (a);

    (b)   after paragraph (b) insert,

        "or

    (c)   an administrative review of the variation or revocation—

        (i)   could be sought, or

        (ii)   is pending."

(3) After subsection (4) insert—

    "(5)   In this section—

    "administrative review" means a review conducted under the immigration rules;

    the question of whether an administrative review is pending is to be determined in accordance with the immigration rules."

23

In Schedule 2 (administrative provisions as to control on entry etc), in paragraph 2A(9), for "(immigration and asylum appeals)" substitute "(appeals in respect of protection and human rights claims)".

24

In Schedule 3 (supplementary provisions as to deportation), in paragraph 3, for the words from "of the kind" to "order)" substitute "that relates to a deportation order".

British Nationality Act 1981 (c 61)

25

In section 40A of the British Nationality Act 1981 (deprivation of citizenship: appeal), in subsection (3)—

(a)   omit ", 83 or 83A";

(b)   omit paragraph (a).

Special Immigration Appeals Commission Act 1997 (c 68)

26

(1)   The Special Immigration Appeals Commission Act 1997 is amended as follows.

(2)   In section 2 (jurisdiction: appeals)—

(a)   in subsection (1)(a), omit ", 83(2) or 83A(2)";

(b)   in subsection (1)(b), omit ", 83(2) or 83A(2)";

(c)   in subsection (2), omit paragraphs (d), (h) and (l);

(d)   omit subsections (3) and (4);

(e)   in subsection (5), omit "against an immigration decision";

(f)   omit subsection (6).

(3)   In section 2B (appeal to SIAC against deprivation of citizenship), omit the words from "(and" to the end.

(4)   In section 6A (procedure in relation to review jurisdiction)—

(a)   in the heading, for "and 2D" substitute "to 2E";

(b)   in subsection (1), for "or 2D" substitute ", 2D or 2E";

(c)   in subsection (2)—

(i)   in paragraph (a), for "or 2D" substitute ", 2D or 2E";

(ii)   in paragraph (b), for "or (as the case may be) 2D(2)" substitute ", 2D(2) or (as the case may be) 2E(2)".

(5)   In section 7 (appeals from the Commission), in subsection (1A), for "or 2D" substitute ", 2D or 2E".

Immigration and Asylum Act 1999 (c 33)

27

The Immigration and Asylum Act 1999 is amended as follows.

28

Section 23 (monitoring refusals of entry clearance) is repealed.

29

(1)   Section 141 (fingerprinting) is amended as follows.

(2)   In subsection (7)—

(a)   for paragraph (c) substitute—

"(c)   any person ("C") in respect of whom the Secretary of State has decided—

(i)   to make a deportation order, or

(ii)   that section 32(5) of the UK Borders Act 2007 (automatic deportation of foreign criminals) applies;

(ca)   any person ("CA") who requires leave to enter or remain in the United Kingdom but does not have it;";

(b)   in paragraph (f), for the words from "paragraph (c)" to the end substitute "paragraph (c)(ii)".

(3)   In subsection (8), for paragraph (c) substitute—

"(c)   for C, when he is notified of the decision mentioned in subsection (7)(c);

(ca)   for CA, when he becomes a person to whom this section applies;".

(4)   In subsection (9)—

(a)   in paragraph (b), after "C" insert ", CA";

(b)   in paragraph (c)(i) for "relevant immigration decision" substitute "decision mentioned in subsection (7)(c)";

(c)   after paragraph (c) insert—

"(ca)   for CA, when he no longer requires leave to enter or remain in the United Kingdom;".

(5)   Omit subsection (16).

Nationality, Immigration and Asylum Act 2002 (c 41)

30

The Nationality, Immigration and Asylum Act 2002 is amended as follows.

31

In section 72 (serious criminal), in subsection (9)(a)—

(a)   omit ", 83, 83A or 101";

(b)   for the words from "that to remove him" to the end substitute "mentioned in section 84(1)(a) or (3)(a) of this Act (breach of the United Kingdom's obligations under the Refugee Convention), and".

32

In section 79 (deportation order: appeal), in subsection (1) for "against" substitute "that may be brought or continued from within the United Kingdom relating to".

33

For the heading to Part 5, substitute "Appeals in respect of Protection and Human Rights Claims".

34

In section 85 (matters to be considered)—

(a)   in subsection (2), for "84(1)" substitute "84";

(b)   in subsection (4)—

(i)   omit ", 83(2) or 83A(2)";

(ii)   omit "evidence about";

(iii)   omit "evidence which concerns".

35

Section 85A (matters to be considered: new evidence: exceptions) is repealed.

36

In section 86 (determination of appeal)—

(a)   in subsection (1), omit ", 83 or 83A";

(b)   in subsection (2), omit "(whether or not by virtue of section 85(1))";

(c)   omit subsections (3) to (6).

37

Sections 87 to 91 are repealed.

38

(1)   Section 94 (appeal from within the United Kingdom) is amended as follows.

(2)   In the heading, for "asylum" substitute "protection".

(3)   For subsections (1) to (2) substitute—

"(1) The Secretary of State may certify a protection claim or human rights claim as clearly unfounded."

(4) In subsection (3)—

    (a)   for "an asylum claimant or human rights" substitute "a";

    (b)   for "subsection (2)" substitute "subsection (1)".

(5) In subsection (6A) for "an asylum claimant or human rights" substitute "a".

(6) In subsection (7), for the words from the beginning to "certifies that" substitute "The Secretary of State may certify a protection claim or human rights claim made by a person if".

(7) In subsection (8)(b), at the end insert "or with the United Kingdom's obligations in relation to persons eligible for a grant of humanitarian protection".

(8) Omit subsection (9).

39

In section 94A (European Common List of Safe Countries of Origin)—

    (a)   in subsection (2), for "an asylum claim" substitute "a protection claim";

    (b)   in subsection (4) for "94(2)" substitute "94(1)".

40

Section 95 (appeal from outside the United Kingdom: removal) is repealed.

41

(1) Section 96 (earlier right of appeal) is amended as follows.

(2) In subsection (1)—

    (a)   in the opening words, for the words from the beginning to "brought" substitute "A person may not bring an appeal under section 82 against a decision ("the new decision")";

    (b)   in paragraph (a), omit "immigration";

    (c)   in paragraph (b) for "matter" substitute "ground";

    (d)   in paragraph (c) for "matter" substitute "ground".

(3) For subsection (2) substitute—

"(2) A person may not bring an appeal under section 82 if the Secretary of State or an immigration officer certifies—

    (a)   that the person has received a notice under section 120(2),

    (b)   that the appeal relies on a ground that should have been, but has not been, raised in a statement made under section 120(2) or (5), and

    (c)   that, in the opinion of the Secretary of State or the immigration officer, there is no satisfactory reason for that ground not having been raised in a statement under section 120(2) or (5)."

42

In section 97 (national security etc)—

    (a)   in subsection (1), omit ", 83(2) or 83A(2)";

    (b)   in subsection (3), omit ", 83(2) or 83A(2)".

43

In section 97A (national security: deportation)—

    (a)   in subsection (2B), for the words from "breach" to the end substitute "be unlawful under section 6 of the Human Rights Act 1998 (public authority not to act contrary to Human Rights Convention)";

    (b)   omit subsections (2D), (2E) and (3).

44

Section 97B (variation of leave on grounds of public good: rights of appeal) is repealed.

45

Section 98 (other grounds of public good) is repealed.

46

In section 99—

- (a) in the heading, for "Sections 97 and 98" substitute "Section 97";
- (b) in subsection (1), omit "or 98".

47

(1) Section 104 (pending appeal) is amended as follows.

(2) Omit subsection (4).

(3) In subsection (4A), for "subsections (4B) and (4C)" substitute "subsection (4B)".

(4) In subsection (4B)—

- (a) for "the ground relating to the Refugee Convention specified in section 84(1)(g)" substitute "a ground specified in section 84(1)(a) or (b) or 84(3) (asylum or humanitarian protection)";
- (b) omit paragraph (a) (and the "and" immediately following it).

(5) Omit subsections (4C) and (5).

48

(1) Section 105 (notice of immigration decision) is amended as follows.

(2) In subsection (1), for "immigration" substitute "appealable".

(3) In subsection (2)—

- (a) in the opening words, for "a decision against which the person is entitled to appeal under section 82(1)" substitute "an appealable decision";
- (b) in paragraph (a) for "that section" substitute "section 82".

(4) At the end insert—

"(4) In this section "appealable decision" means a decision mentioned in section 82(1)."

49

In section 106 (rules)—

- (a) in subsection (3), omit ", 83 or 83A";
- (b) in subsection (4), omit ", 83 or 83A".

50

In section 107 (practice directions), in subsection (3), omit ", 83 or 83A".

51

In section 108 (forged documents: proceedings in private), in subsection (1)(a), omit ", 83 or 83A".

52

In section 112 (regulations etc)—

- (a) omit subsection (3A);
- (b) in subsection (4), omit "or 115(8)";
- (c) in subsection (5), omit "or 115(9)".

53

(1) Section 113 (interpretation) is amended as follows.

(2) In subsection (1)—

- (a) in the definition of "human rights claim"—
  - (i) after "Kingdom" insert "or to refuse him entry into the United Kingdom";
  - (ii) omit "as being incompatible with his Convention rights";
- (b) at the appropriate places insert—

""humanitarian protection" has the meaning given in section 82(2);"

""protection claim" has the meaning given in section 82(2)";

""protection status" has the meaning given in section 82(2)";

(c)   omit the definitions of "entry clearance", "illegal entrant", "prescribed", "visitor" and "work permit";

(d)   in the definition of "immigration rules", for "that Act" substitute "the Immigration Act 1971".

(3)   Omit subsection (2).

54

Section 115 (appeal from within United Kingdom: unfounded human rights or asylum claim: transitional provision) is repealed.

55

For section 120 (requirement to state additional grounds for application) substitute—

"120 Requirement to state additional grounds for application etc

(1)   Subsection (2) applies to a person ("P") if—

(a)   P has made a protection claim or a human rights claim,

(b)   P has made an application to enter or remain in the United Kingdom, or

(c)   a decision to deport or remove P has been or may be taken.

(2)   The Secretary of State or an immigration officer may serve a notice on P requiring P to provide a statement setting out—

(a)   P's reasons for wishing to enter or remain in the United Kingdom,

(b)   any grounds on which P should be permitted to enter or remain in the United Kingdom, and

(c)   any grounds on which P should not be removed from or required to leave the United Kingdom.

(3)   A statement under subsection (2) need not repeat reasons or grounds set out in—

(a)   P's protection or human rights claim,

(b)   the application mentioned in subsection (1)(b), or

(c)   an application to which the decision mentioned in subsection (1)(c) relates.

(4)   Subsection (5) applies to a person ("P") if P has previously been served with a notice under subsection (2) and—

(a)   P requires leave to enter or remain in the United Kingdom but does not have it, or

(b)   P has leave to enter or remain in the United Kingdom only by virtue of section 3C or 3D of the Immigration Act 1971 (continuation of leave pending decision or appeal).

(5)   Where P's circumstances have changed since the Secretary of State or an immigration officer was last made aware of them (whether in the application or claim mentioned in subsection (1) or in a statement under subsection (2) or this subsection) so that P has—

(a)   additional reasons for wishing to enter or remain in the United Kingdom,

(b)   additional grounds on which P should be permitted to enter or remain in the United Kingdom, or

(c)   additional grounds on which P should not be removed from or required to leave the United Kingdom,

P must, as soon as reasonably practicable, provide a supplementary statement to the Secretary of State or an immigration officer setting out the new circumstances and the additional reasons or grounds.

(6)   In this section—

"human rights claim" and "protection claim" have the same meanings as in Part 5;

references to "grounds" are to grounds on which an appeal under Part 5 may be brought (see section 84)."

Asylum and Immigration (Treatment of Claimants, etc) Act 2004 (c 19)

56

(1)   Schedule 3 to the Asylum and Immigration (Treatment of Claimants, etc) Act 2004 (removal of asylum seeker to safe third country) is amended as follows.

(2)   In paragraph 1, at the end insert—

"(3)   Section 92 of the Nationality, Immigration and Asylum Act 2002 makes further provision about the place from which an appeal relating to an asylum or human rights claim may be brought or continued."

(3)   In paragraph 5—

(a)   omit sub-paragraph (2);

(b)   in sub-paragraph (3), for the words from "by virtue of" to "rights)" substitute "from within the United Kingdom";

(c)   in sub-paragraph (4), for "by virtue of section 92(4)(a) of that Act" substitute "from within the United Kingdom".

(4)   In paragraph 10—

(a)   omit sub-paragraph (2);

(b)   in sub-paragraph (3), for the words from "by virtue of" to "rights)" substitute "from within the United Kingdom";

(c)   in sub-paragraph (4), for "by virtue of section 92(4)(a) of that Act" substitute "from within the United Kingdom".

(5)   In paragraph 15—

(a)   omit sub-paragraph (2);

(b)   in sub-paragraph (3), for the words from "by virtue of" to "rights)" substitute "from within the United Kingdom";

(c)   in sub-paragraph (4), for "by virtue of section 92(4)(a) of that Act" substitute "from within the United Kingdom".

(6)   In paragraph 19—

(a)   omit paragraph (a);

(b)   in paragraph (b), for the words from "by virtue of" to "rights)" substitute "from within the United Kingdom";

(c)   in paragraph (c), for "by virtue of section 92(4)(a) of that Act" substitute "from within the United Kingdom".

Immigration, Asylum and Nationality Act 2006 (c 13)

57

(1)   The Immigration, Asylum and Nationality Act 2006 is amended as follows.

(2)   In section 12(3) (new definition of human rights claims), in paragraph (a) of the definition of "human rights claim"—

(a)   after "Kingdom" insert "or to refuse him entry into the United Kingdom";

(b)   omit "as being incompatible with his Convention rights".

(3)   Section 13 (appeal from within the United Kingdom: certification of unfounded claim) is repealed.

(4)   In section 55 (Refugee Convention: certification), in subsection (2)(a)—

(a)   in sub-paragraph (i), omit ", 83 or 101";

(b)   for sub-paragraph (ii) substitute—

"(ii)   which is brought on the ground mentioned in section 84(1)(a) or (3)(a) of that Act (breach of United Kingdom's obligations under the Refugee Convention);".

(5) In Schedule 1 (consequential amendments) paragraph 11 (amendment to section 112(5) of the 2002 Act) is repealed.

UK Borders Act 2007 (c 30)

58

In section 17 of the UK Borders Act 2007 (support for failed asylum-seekers), in subsection (2)—

(a)   in paragraph (a), omit "against an immigration decision";

(b)   in paragraph (b), omit "against an immigration decision".

Equality Act 2010 (c 15)

59

In section 115 of the Equality Act 2010 (immigration cases), in subsection (8) after "2D" insert "and 2E".

Consequential repeals

60

The provisions shown in the table below are repealed in consequence of the amendments made by sections 15 to 18 and this Part of this Schedule.

Title	Extent of repeal
Nationality, Immigration and Asylum Act 2002	In Schedule 7, paragraph 27.
Asylum and Immigration (Treatment of Claimants, etc) Act 2004	Section 15(2), (3) and (5).
	Section 26(2) and (3).
	Section 27(2) and (3).
	Sections 28 and 29.
	Section 31.
	In Schedule 2, paragraphs 18(2)(c) and 19
Immigration, Asylum and Nationality Act 2006	Sections 1 to 6.
	Section 11(6).
	Section 47(6) to (8).
	Section 57(2).
	In Schedule 1, paragraphs 2 to 6, 10, 11, 13, 14(a) and (c).
UK Borders Act 2007	Section 19.
	Section 35(3).
Borders, Citizenship and Immigration Act 2009	Section 51(3).
Crime and Courts Act 2013	Section 51(1).
	Sections 52 and 53.

PART 5
PROVISION RELATING TO EMPLOYMENT

Immigration, Asylum and Nationality Act 2006 (c 13)

61

In section 15 of the Immigration, Asylum and Nationality Act 2006 (penalty), in subsection (6)(e), after "penalty" insert "or make an appeal against it".

PART 6
PROVISION RELATING TO DRIVING LICENCES

Road Traffic (Northern Ireland) Order 1981 (SI 1981/154 (N.I. 1))

62

In Article 5 of the Road Traffic (Northern Ireland) Order 1981 (tests of competence to drive)—
    (a)   in paragraph (1), omit "meets the relevant residence requirement and";
    (b)   omit paragraph (1A);
    (c)   in paragraph (4)(aa) for "normally resident in Northern Ireland or the United Kingdom" insert "normally and lawfully resident in Northern Ireland or the United Kingdom (within the meaning of Article 13A)".

Road Traffic Act 1988 (c 52)

63

In section 89 of the Road Traffic Act 1988 (tests of competence to drive)—
    (a)   in subsection (1), omit "meets the relevant residence requirement and";
    (b)   omit subsection (1A);
    (c)   in subsection (4)(aa) for "normally resident in Great Britain or the United Kingdom" substituted "normally and lawfully resident in Great Britain or the United Kingdom (within the meaning of section 97A)".

Road Safety Act 2006 (c 49)

64

In Schedule 3 to the Road Safety Act 2006 (endorsement: all drivers), in paragraph 9—
    (a)   after sub-paragraph (3) insert—
    "(3A)   In subsection (3ZA), omit "and its counterpart".";
    (b)   in sub-paragraph (6A)(b), at the end insert "in both places".

Road Traffic (Northern Ireland) Order 2007 (SI 2007/916 (NI 10))

65

In Schedule 5 to the Road Traffic (Northern Ireland) Order 2007 (endorsement: all drivers: consequential amendments), in paragraph 6, after sub-paragraph (a) insert—
    "(aa) in paragraph (5ZA), omit "and its counterpart"."

PART 7
PROVISION RELATING TO MARRIAGE AND CIVIL PARTNERSHIP

Transitional provision

66

The provisions of sections 48 to 51, and the amendments made by Schedule 4, apply only to proposed marriages and civil partnerships in respect of which notice under section 27 of the Marriage Act 1949 or under section 8 of the Civil Partnership Act 2004 is given after the day on which the provisions and amendments come into force.

PART 8
PROVISION RELATING TO IMMIGRATION ADVISERS AND IMMIGRATION SERVICE PROVIDERS

Transitional provision

67

(1)   On the day on which paragraph 2 of Schedule 7 comes into force the Immigration Services Commissioner must register in the register maintained under section 85(1) of the Immigration and Asylum Act 1999 each person who, immediately before that day, was an exempt person (within the meaning given by section 84(4)(a) of that Act).

(2)   The registration of a person by reason of sub-paragraph (1) may be made so as to have effect only in relation to a specified field of advice or services.

68

(1)   In the provisions listed in sub-paragraph (2)—

    (a)   references to a person who, at the time to which a charge or (as the case may be) a complaint relates, was a registered person do not include a person who ceased to be a registered person before the day on which paragraph 7 of Schedule 7 comes into force;

    (b)   references to a person who, at the time to which a charge or (as the case may be) a complaint relates, was acting on behalf of a registered person do not include—

        (i)   a person who ceased to act on behalf of a registered person before that day;

        (ii)   a person who was acting on behalf of a person who ceased to be a registered person before that day.

(2)   The provisions are—

    (a)   section 89(2) to (2B) of the Immigration and Asylum Act 1999;

    (b)   paragraph 5(3)(za), (aa) and (d) of Schedule 5 to that Act;

    (c)   paragraph 9(1)(a), (1A) and (4)(a) of Schedule 5 to that Act.

69

(1)   The provisions listed in paragraph 68(2) (apart from paragraph 5(3)(d) of Schedule 5 to the Immigration and Asylum Act 1999) apply in relation to a person who—

    (a)   was an exempt person immediately before the day on which paragraph 2 of Schedule 7 comes into force, and

    (b)   became a registered person on that day by virtue of paragraph 67(1),

as if, while the person was an exempt person, the person had been a registered person.

(2)   In paragraph 10A(2)(a) of Schedule 5 to the Immigration and Asylum Act 1999, the reference to premises which have been used in connection with the provision of immigration advice or immigration services by a registered person includes premises which have been so used by an exempt person.

(3) In this paragraph "exempt person" has the meaning given by section 84(4)(a) of the Immigration and Asylum Act 1999.

PART 9
PROVISION RELATING TO PERSONS UNABLE TO ACQUIRE NATIONALITY BECAUSE NATURAL FATHER NOT MARRIED TO MOTHER

British Nationality Act 1981

70

(1) The British Nationality Act 1981 is amended as follows.

(2) In section 14 (meaning of "British citizen "by descent""), in subsection (1), after paragraph (d) insert—

> "(da) the person is a British citizen by descent by virtue of section 4F(3), 4G(2), 4H(2) or 4I(4); or".

(3) In section 41A (registration: requirement to be of good character), in subsection (1), after "4D," insert "4F, 4G, 4H, 4I".

British Nationality (General) Regulations 2003

71

(1) In regulation 14 of the British Nationality (General) Regulations 2003—

> (a) after "4D(3)" insert "or 4G(3)";
>
> (b) after "section 4D" insert "or 4G".

(2) The provision inserted into regulation 14 by this paragraph may be amended or revoked by the exercise of the powers conferred by section 41 of the British Nationality Act 1981 as if that provision had been inserted by those powers.

PART 10
PROVISION RELATING TO EMBARKATION CHECKS

Transitional provision

72

(1) Any order or direction under paragraph 5 of Schedule 2 to the Immigration Act 1971 that has effect immediately before commencement has, after commencement, the same effect in relation to the production of embarkation cards to designated persons as it has in relation to the production of such cards to immigration officers.

(2) This paragraph is subject to the exercise, after commencement, of the powers under paragraph 5 of Schedule 2 to the Immigration Act 1971.

(3) In this paragraph "commencement" means the day when the amendments made by Part 1 of Schedule 8 come into force.

PART 11
PROVISION RELATING TO FEES

Asylum and Immigration (Treatment of Claimants, etc) Act 2004 (c 19)

73

(1) Section 42 of the Asylum and Immigration (Treatment of Claimants, etc) Act 2004 (amount of fees) is amended as follows.

(2) Omit subsections (1) to (2A).

(3) For subsection (3A) substitute—

"(3A)   The amount of a fee under section 1 of the Consular Fees Act 1980 in respect of a matter specified in subsection (3B) may be set so as to reflect costs referable to the exercise of any function in respect of which the Secretary of State has made an order under section 68 of the Immigration Act 2014.

(3B)   The matters are—

(a)   the determination of applications for entry clearances (within the meaning given by section 33(1) of the Immigration Act 1971),

(b)   the determination of applications for transit visas under section 41 of the Immigration and Asylum Act 1999, or

(c)   the determination of applications for certificates of entitlement to the right of abode in the United Kingdom under section 10 of the Nationality, Immigration and Asylum Act 2002."

(4)   In subsection (4) omit "(1)(b) or".

(5)   In subsection (7) omit from "(and any provision" to the end.

Immigration, Asylum and Nationality Act 2006 (c 13)

74

Sections 51 and 52 of the Immigration, Asylum and Nationality Act 2006 (fees) are repealed.

UK Borders Act 2007 (c 30)

75

For section 15(2)(b) of the UK Borders Act 2007 (application of certain provisions to applications for biometric immigration documents) substitute—

"(b)   section 68 of the Immigration Act 2014 (fees);".

Consequential repeals

76

The following provisions are repealed in consequence of the amendments made by this Part of this Schedule—

(a)   paragraph 6 of Schedule 2 to the Immigration, Asylum and Nationality Act 2006;

(b)   section 20 of the UK Borders Act 2007.

Appendix 2

OTHER RELEVANT STATUTES

Contents

NATIONAL ASSISTANCE ACT 1948

1948 c 29

An Act to terminate the existing poor law and to provide in lieu thereof for the assistance of persons in need by the National Assistance Board and by local authorities; to make further provision for the welfare of disabled, sick, aged and other persons and for regulating homes for disabled and aged persons and charities for disabled persons; to amend the law relating to non-contributory old age pensions; to make provision as to the burial or cremation of deceased persons; and for purposes connected with the matters aforesaid

[13 May 1948]

PART III
LOCAL AUTHORITY SERVICES

Provision of Accommodation

21 Duty of local authorities to provide accommodation

(1)   [Subject to and in accordance with the provisions of this Part of this Act, a local authority may with the approval of the Secretary of State, and to such extent as he may direct shall, make arrangements for providing]—

    (a)   residential accommodation for persons [aged eighteen or over] who by reason of age, [illness, disability] or any other circumstances are in need of care and attention which is not otherwise available to them; [and

    (aa)   residential accommodation for expectant and nursing mothers who are in need of care and attention which is not otherwise available to them.]

    (b)   . . .

[(1A)   A person to whom section 115 of the Immigration and Asylum Act 1999 (exclusion from benefits) applies may not be provided with residential accommodation under subsection (1)(a) if his need for care and attention has arisen solely—

    (a)   because he is destitute; or

    (b)   because of the physical effects, or anticipated physical effects, of his being destitute.

(1B)   Subsections (3) and (5) to (8) of section 95 of the Immigration and Asylum Act 1999, and paragraph 2 of Schedule 8 to that Act, apply for the purposes of subsection (1A) as they apply for the purposes of that section, but for the references in subsections (5) and (7) of that section and in that paragraph to the Secretary of State substitute references to a local authority.

[(1B)   Section 95(2) to (7) of that Act shall apply for the purposes of subsection (1A) above; and for that purpose a reference to the Secretary of State in section 95(4) or (5) shall be treated as a reference to a local authority.]]

(2)   In [making any such arrangements] a local authority shall have regard to the welfare of all persons for whom accommodation is provided, and in particular to the need for providing accommodation of different descriptions suited to different descriptions of such persons as are mentioned in the last foregoing subsection.

[(2A)   In determining for the purposes of paragraph (a) or (aa) of subsection (1) of this section whether care and attention are otherwise available to a person, a local authority shall disregard so much of the person's resources as may be specified in, or determined in accordance with, regulations made by the Secretary of State for the purposes of this subsection.

(2B)   In subsection (2A) of this section the reference to a person's resources is a reference to his resources within the meaning of regulations made for the purposes of that subsection.]

(3)   . . .

(4)   [Subject to the provisions of section 26 of this Act] accommodation provided by a local authority in the exercise of their [functions under this section] shall be provided in premises managed by the authority or, to such extent as may be [determined in accordance with the arrangements] under this section, in such premises managed by another local authority as may be agreed between the two authorities and on such terms, including terms as to the reimbursement of expenditure incurred by the said other authority, as may be so agreed.

(5)   References in this Act to accommodation provided under this Part thereof shall be construed as references to accommodation provided in accordance with this and the five next following sections, and as including references to board and other services, amenities and requisites provided in connection with the accommodation except where in the opinion of the authority managing the premises their provision is unnecessary.

(6) References in this Act to a local authority providing accommodation shall be construed, in any case where a local authority agree with another local authority for the provision of accommodation in premises managed by the said other authority, as references to the first-mentioned local authority.

(7) Without prejudice to the generality of the foregoing provisions of this section, a local authority may—

  (a)   provide, in such cases as they may consider appropriate, for the conveyance of persons to and from premises in which accommodation is provided for them under this Part of the Act;

  [(b) make arrangements for the provision on the premises in which accommodation is being provided of such other services as appear to the authority to be required.]

. . .

(8) . . . nothing in this section shall authorise or require a local authority to make any provision authorised or required to be made (whether by that or by any other authority) by or under any enactment not contained in this Part of this Act [or authorised or required to be provided under [the National Health Service Act 2006 or the National Health Service (Wales) Act 2006]].

Amendment

Repealed in relation to Scotland by the Social Work (Scotland) Act 1968, s 95(2), Sch 9, Pt I.

Sub-s (1): first words in square brackets substituted by the Local Government Act 1972, s 195, Sch 23, para 2; second words in square brackets inserted by the Children Act 1989, s 108(5), Sch 13, para 11(1); third words in square brackets substituted, and final words in square brackets inserted, by the National Health Service and Community Care Act 1990, s 42(1); para (b) repealed by the Housing (Homeless Persons) Act 1977, s 20(4), Schedule.

Sub-ss (1A), (1B): inserted by the Immigration and Asylum Act 1999, s 116; for transitional provisions see Sch 15, para 5 thereto.

Sub-s (1B): substituted by the Nationality, Immigration and Asylum Act 2002, s 45(5). Date in force: to be appointed: see the Nationality, Immigration and Asylum Act 2002, s 162(1).

Sub-s (2): words "making any such arrangements" in square brackets substituted by the Local Government Act 1972, s 195, Sch 23, para 2.

Sub-ss (2A), (2B) (as inserted by the Community Care (Residential Accommodation) Act 1998, s 1): substituted by the Health and Social Care Act 2001, s 53.

Sub-s (3): repealed by the Local Government Act 1972, ss 195, 272, Sch 23, para 2, Sch 30.

Sub-s (4): first words in square brackets inserted by the National Health Service and Community Care Act 1990, s 66(1), Sch 9, para 5(1); other words in square brackets substituted by the Local Government Act 1972, s 195, Sch 23, para 2.

Sub-s (7): para (b) substituted, for paras (b), (c) as originally enacted, by the National Health Service and Community Care Act 1990, s 66(1), Sch 9, para 5(2); words omitted repealed by the National Health Service Reorganisation Act 1973, s 58, Sch 5.

Sub-s (8): words omitted repealed by the National Health Service and Community Care Act 1990, s 66(2), Sch 10.

Sub-s (8): words in square brackets beginning with the words "or authorised or" inserted by the National Health Service and Community Care Act 1990, s 66(1), Sch 9, para 5(3).

Sub-s (8): words "the National Health Service Act 2006 or the National Health Service (Wales) Act 2006" in square brackets substituted by the National Health Service (Consequential Provisions) Act 2006, s 2, Sch 1, paras 5, 6.

Transfer of Functions

Functions of a Minister of the Crown, so far as exercisable in relation to Wales, transferred to the National Assembly for Wales, by the National Assembly for Wales (Transfer of Functions) Order 1999, SI 1999/672, art 2, Sch 1.

Subordinate Legislation

National Assistance (Residential Accommodation) (Disregarding of Resources) (England) Regulations 2001, SI 2001/3067; National Assistance (Residential Accommodation) (Disregarding of Resources) (Wales) Regulations 2003, SI 2003/969.

Welfare Services

29 Welfare arrangements for blind, deaf, dumb and crippled persons, etc

(1)   A local authority [may, with the approval of the Secretary of State, and to such extent as he may direct in relation to persons ordinarily resident in the area of the local authority shall] make arrangements for promoting the welfare of persons to whom this section applies, that is to say persons [aged eighteen or over] who are blind, deaf or dumb [or who suffer from mental disorder of any description], and other persons [aged eighteen or over] who are substantially and permanently handicapped by illness, injury, or congenital deformity or such other disabilities as may be prescribed by the Minister.

(2), (3)   . . .

(4)   Without prejudice to the generality of the provisions of subsection (1) of this section, arrangements may be made thereunder—

  (a)   for informing persons to whom arrangements under that subsection relate of the services available for them thereunder;

  (b)   for giving such persons instruction in their own homes or elsewhere in methods of overcoming the effects of their disabilities;

  (c)   for providing workshops where such persons may be engaged (whether under a contract of service or otherwise) in suitable work, and hostels where persons engaged in the workshops, and other persons to whom arrangements under subsection (1) of this section relate and for whom work or training is being provided in pursuance of the Disabled Persons (Employment) Act 1944 [or the Employment and Training Act 1973] may live;

  (d)   for providing persons to whom arrangements under subsection (1) of this section relate with suitable work (whether under a contract of service or otherwise) in their own homes or elsewhere;

  (e)   for helping such persons in disposing of the produce of their work;

  (f)   for providing such persons with recreational facilities in their own homes or elsewhere;

  (g)   for compiling and maintaining classified registers of the persons to whom arrangements under subsection (1) of this section relate.

[(4A)   Where accommodation in a hostel is provided under paragraph (c) of subsection (4) of this section—

  (a)   if the hostel is managed by a local authority, section 22 of this Act shall apply as it applies where accommodation is provided under section 21;

  (b)   if the accommodation is provided in a hostel managed by a person other than a local authority under arrangements made with that person, subsections (2) to (4A) of section 26 of this Act shall apply as they apply where accommodation is provided under arrangements made by virtue of that section; and

  (c)   [section 32 shall apply as it applies] where accommodation is provided under sections 21 to 26;

and in this subsection references to "accommodation" include references to board and other services, amenities and requisites provided in connection with the accommodation, except where in the opinion of the authority managing the premises or, in the case mentioned in paragraph (b) above, the authority making the arrangements their provision is unnecessary.]

(5)   . . .

(6)   Nothing in the foregoing provisions of this section shall authorise or require—

  (a)   the payment of money to persons to whom this section applies, other than persons for whom work is provided under arrangements made by virtue of paragraph (c) or paragraph (d) of subsection (4) of this section or who are engaged in work which they are enabled to perform in consequence of anything done in pursuance of arrangements made under this section; or

(b) the provision of any accommodation or services required to be provided under [the National Health Service Act 2006 or the National Health Service (Wales) Act 2006] . . .

(7) A person engaged in work in a workshop provided under paragraph (c) of subsection (4) of this section, or a person in receipt of a superannuation allowance granted on his retirement from engagement in any such workshop, shall be deemed for the purposes of this Act to continue to be ordinarily resident in the area in which he was ordinarily resident immediately before he [was accepted for work in that workshop; and for the purposes of this subsection a course of training in such a workshop shall be deemed to be work in that workshop].

Amendment

Repealed in relation to Scotland by the Social Work (Scotland) Act 1968, s 95(2), Sch 9, Part I.

Sub-s (1): first words in square brackets substituted by the Local Government Act 1972, s 195, Sch 23, para 2; second and final words in square brackets inserted by the Children Act 1989, s 108(5), (6), Sch 13, para 11(2), Sch 14, para 1; third words in square brackets substituted by the Mental Health (Scotland) Act 1960, ss 113(1), 114, Sch 4.

Sub-ss (2), (3): repealed by the Local Government Act 1972, ss 195, 272(1), Sch 23, para 2, Sch 30.

Sub-s (4): words in square brackets inserted by the Employment and Training Act 1973, s 14(1), Sch 3, para 3.

Sub-s (4A): inserted by the National Health Service and Community Care Act 1990, s 44(7).

Sub-s (4A): in para (c) words "section 32 shall apply it applies" in square brackets substituted by the Health and Social Care Act 2008, s 147(2).

Sub-s (5): repealed by the Health and Social Services and Social Security Adjudications Act 1983, s 30, Sch 10, Part I.

Sub-s (6): words in square brackets substituted by the National Health Service Act 1977, s 129, Sch 15, para 6; words omitted repealed by the Social Work (Scotland) Act 1968, s 95(2), Sch 9, Part I. Para (b) words "the National Health Service Act 2006 or the National Health Service (Wales) Act 2006" in square brackets substituted by the National Health Service (Consequential Provisions) Act 2006, s 2, Sch 1, paras 5, 8.

Sub-s (7): words in square brackets substituted retrospectively by the National Assistance (Amendment) Act 1959, s 1(2).

Transfer of Functions

Functions of the Minister of Health transferred to the Secretary of State for Health by virtue of the Secretary of State for Social Services Order 1968, SI 1968/1699, and the Transfer of Functions (Health and Social Services) Order 1988, SI 1988/1843.

Functions under this section, so far as exercisable in relation to Wales, transferred to the National Assembly for Wales, by the National Assembly for Wales (Transfer of Functions) Order 1999, SI 1999/672, art 2, Sch 1.

EUROPEAN COMMUNITIES ACT 1972

1972 c 68

An Act to make provision in connection with the enlargement of the European Communities to include the United Kingdom, together with (for certain purposes) the Channel Islands, the Isle of Man and Gibraltar

[17 October 1972]

PART I
GENERAL PROVISIONS

2 General implementation of Treaties

(1)   All such rights, powers, liabilities, obligations and restrictions from time to time created or arising by or under the Treaties, and all such remedies and procedures from time to time provided for by or under the Treaties, as in accordance with the Treaties are without further enactment to be given legal effect or used in the United Kingdom shall be recognised and available in law, and be enforced, allowed and followed accordingly; and the expression ["enforceable EU right"] and similar expressions shall be read as referring to one to which this subsection applies.

(2)   Subject to Schedule 2 to this Act, at any time after its passing Her Majesty may by Order in Council, and any designated Minister or department may [by order, rules, regulations or scheme], make provision—

(a)   for the purpose of implementing any [EU obligation] of the United Kingdom, or enabling any such obligation to be implemented, or of enabling any rights enjoyed or to be enjoyed by the United Kingdom under or by virtue of the Treaties to be exercised; or

(b)   for the purpose of dealing with matters arising out of or related to any such obligation or rights or the coming into force, or the operation from time to time, of subsection (1) above;

and in the exercise of any statutory power or duty, including any power to give directions or to legislate by means of orders, rules, regulations or other subordinate instrument, the person entrusted with the power or duty may have regard to the [objects of the EU] and to any such obligation or rights as aforesaid.

In this subsection "designated Minister or department" means such Minister of the Crown or government department as may from time to time be designated by Order in Council in relation to any matter or for any purpose, but subject to such restrictions or conditions (if any) as may be specified by the Order in Council.

(3)   There shall be charged on and issued out of the Consolidated Fund or, if so determined by the Treasury, the National Loans Fund the amounts required to meet any [EU obligation] to make payments to [the EU or a member State], or any [EU obligation] in respect of contributions to the capital or reserves of the European Investment Bank or in respect of loans to the Bank, or to redeem any notes or obligations issued or created in respect of any such [EU obligation]; and, except as otherwise provided by or under any enactment,—

(a)   any other expenses incurred under or by virtue of the Treaties or this Act by any Minister of the Crown or government department may be paid out of moneys provided by Parliament; and

(b)   any sums received under or by virtue of the Treaties or this Act by any Minister of the Crown or government department, save for such sums as may be required for disbursements permitted by any other enactment, shall be paid into the Consolidated Fund or, if so determined by the Treasury, the National Loans Fund.

(4)   The provision that may be made under subsection (2) above includes, subject to Schedule 2 to this Act, any such provision (of any such extent) as might be made by Act of Parliament, and any enactment passed or to be passed, other than one contained in this Part of this Act, shall be construed and have effect subject to the foregoing provisions of this section; but, except as may be provided by any Act passed after this Act, Schedule 2 shall have effect in connection with the powers conferred by this and the following sections of this Act to make Orders in Council [or orders, rules, regulations or schemes].

(5)   . . . and the references in that subsection to a Minister of the Crown or government department and to a statutory power or duty shall include a Minister or

department of the Government of Northern Ireland and a power or duty arising under or by virtue of an Act of the Parliament of Northern Ireland.

(6) A law passed by the legislature of any of the Channel Islands or of the Isle of Man, or a colonial law (within the meaning of the Colonial Laws Validity Act 1865) passed or made for Gibraltar, if expressed to be passed or made in the implementation of the Treaties and of the obligations of the United Kingdom thereunder, shall not be void or inoperative by reason of any inconsistency with or repugnancy to an Act of Parliament, passed or to be passed, that extends to the Island or Gibraltar or any provision having the force and effect of an Act there (but not including this section), nor by reason of its having some operation outside the Island or Gibraltar; and any such Act or provision that extends to the Island or Gibraltar shall be construed and have effect subject to the provisions of any such law.

AMENDMENT

Sub-s (1): words ""enforceable EU right"" in square brackets substituted by the European Union (Amendment) Act 2008, s 3(3), Schedule, Pt 1.

Sub-s (2): words "by order, rules, regulations or scheme" in square brackets substituted by the Legislative and Regulatory Reform Act 2006, s 27(1)(a).

Sub-s (2): in para (a) words "EU obligation" in square brackets substituted by the European Union (Amendment) Act 2008, s 3(3), Schedule, Pt 1.

Sub-s (2): words "objects of the EU" in square brackets substituted by the European Union (Amendment) Act 2008, s 3(3), Schedule, Pt 1.

Sub-s (3): words "EU obligation" in square brackets in each place they occur substituted by the European Union (Amendment) Act 2008, s 3(3), Schedule, Pt 1.

Sub-s (3): words "the EU or a member State" in square brackets substituted by the European Union (Amendment) Act 2008, s 3(3), Schedule, Pt 1.

Sub-s (4): words "or orders, rules, regulations or schemes" in square brackets substituted by the Legislative and Regulatory Reform Act 2006, s 27(1)(b).

Sub-s (5): words omitted repealed by the Northern Ireland Constitution Act 1973, s 41(1), Sch 6, Part I.

SCHEDULE 2

PROVISIONS AS TO SUBORDINATE LEGISLATION

Section 2

1

(1) The powers conferred by section 2(2) of this Act to make provision for the purposes mentioned in section 2(2)(a) and (b) shall not include power—

    (a)   to make any provision imposing or increasing taxation; or

    (b)   to make any provision taking effect from a date earlier than that of the making of the instrument containing the provision; or

    (c)   to confer any power to legislate by means of orders, rules, regulations or other subordinate instrument, other than rules of procedure for any court or tribunal; or

    (d)   to create any new criminal offence punishable with imprisonment for more than two years or punishable on summary conviction with imprisonment for more than *three months* [the prescribed term] or with a fine of more than [level 5 on the standard scale] (if not calculated on a daily basis) or with a fine of more than [£100 a day].

(2) Sub-paragraph (1)(c) above shall not be taken to preclude the modification of a power to legislate conferred otherwise than under section 2(2), or the extension of any such power to purposes of the like nature as those for which it was conferred; and a power to give directions as to matters of administration is not to be regarded as a power to legislate within the meaning of sub-paragraph (1)(c).

[(3) In sub-paragraph (1)(d), "the prescribed term" means—

(a)   in relation to England and Wales, where the offence is a summary offence, 51 weeks;

(b)   in relation to England and Wales, where the offence is triable either way, twelve months;

(c)   in relation to Scotland and Northern Ireland, three months.]

[1A

(1)   Where—

(a)   subordinate legislation makes provision for a purpose mentioned in section 2(2) of this Act,

(b)   the legislation contains a reference to a [EU instrument] or any provision of a [EU instrument], and

(c)   it appears to the person making the legislation that it is necessary or expedient for the reference to be construed as a reference to that instrument or that provision as amended from time to time,

the subordinate legislation may make express provision to that effect.

(2)   In this paragraph "subordinate legislation" means any Order in Council, order, rules, regulations, scheme, warrant, byelaws or other instrument made after the coming into force of this paragraph under any Act, Act of the Scottish Parliament[, Measure or Act of the National Assembly for Wales] or Northern Ireland legislation passed or made before or after the coming into force of this paragraph.]

2

(1)   Subject to paragraph 3 below, where a provision contained in any section of this Act confers power to make [any order, rules, regulations or scheme] (otherwise than by modification or extension of an existing power), the power shall be exercisable by statutory instrument.

(2)   Any statutory instrument containing an Order in Council or [any order, rules, regulations or scheme] made in the exercise of a power so conferred, if made without a draft having been approved by resolution of each House of Parliament, shall be subject to annulment in pursuance of a resolution of either House.

[2A

(1)   This paragraph applies where, pursuant to paragraph 2(2) above, a draft of a statutory instrument containing provision made in exercise of the power conferred by section 2(2) of this Act is laid before Parliament for approval by resolution of each House of Parliament and—

(a)   the instrument also contains provision made in exercise of a power conferred by any other enactment; and

(b)   apart from this paragraph, any of the conditions in sub-paragraph (2) below applies in relation to the instrument so far as containing that provision.

(2)   The conditions referred to in sub-paragraph (1)(b) above are that—

(a)   the instrument, so far as containing the provision referred to in sub-paragraph (1)(a) above, is by virtue of any enactment subject to annulment in pursuance of a resolution of either House of Parliament;

(b)   the instrument so far as containing that provision is by virtue of any enactment required to be laid before Parliament after being made and to be approved by resolution of each House of Parliament in order to come into or remain in force;

(c)   in a case not falling within paragraph (a) or (b) above, the instrument so far as containing that provision is by virtue of any enactment required to be laid before Parliament after being made;

(d)   the instrument or a draft of the instrument so far as containing that provision is not by virtue of any enactment required at any time to be laid before Parliament.

(3) Where this paragraph applies in relation to the draft of a statutory instrument—

(a) the instrument, so far as containing the provision referred to in sub-paragraph (1)(a) above, may not be made unless the draft is approved by a resolution of each House of Parliament;

(b) in a case where the condition in sub-paragraph (2)(a) above is satisfied, the instrument so far as containing that provision is not subject to annulment in pursuance of a resolution of either House of Parliament;

(c) in a case where the condition in sub-paragraph (2)(b) above is satisfied, the instrument is not required to be laid before Parliament after being made (and accordingly any requirement that the instrument be approved by each House of Parliament in order for it to come into or remain in force does not apply); and

(d) in a case where the condition in sub-paragraph (2)(c) above is satisfied, the instrument so far as containing that provision is not required to be laid before Parliament after being made.

(4) In this paragraph, references to an enactment are to an enactment passed or made before or after the coming into force of this paragraph.

2B

(1) This paragraph applies where, pursuant to paragraph 2(2) above, a statutory instrument containing provision made in exercise of the power conferred by section 2(2) of this Act is laid before Parliament under section 5 of the Statutory Instruments Act 1946 (instruments subject to annulment) and—

(a) the instrument also contains provision made in exercise of a power conferred by any other enactment; and

(b) apart from this paragraph, either of the conditions in sub-paragraph (2) below applies in relation to the instrument so far as containing that provision.

(2) The conditions referred to in sub-paragraph (1)(b) above are that—

(a) the instrument so far as containing the provision referred to in sub-paragraph (1)(a) above is by virtue of any enactment required to be laid before Parliament after being made but—

(i) is not subject to annulment in pursuance of a resolution of either House of Parliament; and

(ii) is not by virtue of any enactment required to be approved by resolution of each House of Parliament in order to come into or remain in force;

(b) the instrument or a draft of the instrument so far as containing that provision is not by virtue of any enactment required at any time to be laid before Parliament.

(3) Where this paragraph applies in relation to a statutory instrument, the instrument, so far as containing the provision referred to in sub-paragraph (1)(a) above, is subject to annulment in pursuance of a resolution of either House of Parliament.

(4) In this paragraph, references to an enactment are to an enactment passed or made before or after the coming into force of this paragraph.

2C

Paragraphs 2A and 2B above apply to a Scottish statutory instrument containing provision made in the exercise of the power conferred by section 2(2) of this Act (and a draft of any such instrument) as they apply to any other statutory instrument containing such provision (or, as the case may be, any draft of such an instrument), but subject to the following modifications—

(a) references to Parliament and to each or either House of Parliament are to be read as references to the Scottish Parliament;

(b)   references to an enactment include an enactment comprised in, or in an instrument made under, an Act of the Scottish Parliament; and

(c)   the reference in paragraph 2B(1) to section 5 of the Statutory Instruments Act 1946 is to be read as a reference to [section 28 of the Interpretation and Legislative Reform (Scotland) Act 2010 (asp 10)].]

3

Nothing in paragraph 2 above shall apply to any Order in Council made by the Governor of Northern Ireland or to any [any order, rules, regulations or scheme] made by a Minister or department of the Government of Northern Ireland; but where a provision contained in any section of this Act confers power to make such an Order in Council or [any order, rules, regulations or scheme], then any Order in Council or [any order, rules, regulations or scheme] made in the exercise of that power, if made without a draft having been approved by resolution of each House of the Parliament of Northern Ireland, shall be subject to negative resolution within the meaning of section 41(6) of the Interpretation Act (Northern Ireland) 1954 as if the Order or [any order, rules, regulations or scheme] were a statutory instrument within the meaning of that Act.

[4

(1)   The power to make orders under section 5(1) or (2) of this Act shall be exercisable in accordance with the following provisions of this paragraph.

(2)   The power to make such orders shall be exercisable by statutory instrument and includes power to amend or revoke any such order made in the exercise of that power.

(3)   Any statutory instrument containing any such order shall be subject to annulment in pursuance of a resolution of the House of Commons except in a case falling within sub-paragraph (4) below.

(4)   Subject to sub-paragraph (6) below, where an order imposes or increases any customs duty, or restricts any relief from customs duty under the said section 5, the statutory instrument containing the order shall be laid before the House of Commons after being made and, unless the order is approved by that House before the end of the period of 28 days beginning with the day on which it was made, it shall cease to have effect at the end of that period, but without prejudice to anything previously done under the order or to the making of a new order.

In reckoning the said period of 28 days no account shall be taken of any time during which Parliament is dissolved or prorogued or during which the House of Commons is adjourned for more than 4 days.

(5)   Where an order has the effect of altering the rate of duty on any goods in such a way that the new rate is not directly comparable with the old, it shall not be treated for the purposes of sub-paragraph (4) above as increasing the duty on those goods if it declares the opinion of the Treasury to be that, in the circumstances existing at the date of the order, the alteration is not calculated to raise the general level of duty on the goods.

(6)   Sub-paragraph (4) above does not apply in the case of an instrument containing an order which states that it does not impose or increase any customs duty or restrict any relief from customs duty otherwise than in pursuance of a [EU obligation].

5

As soon as may be after the end of each financial year the Secretary of State shall lay before each House of Parliament a report on the exercise during that year of the powers conferred by section 5(1) and (2) of this Act with respect to the imposition of customs duties and the allowance of exemptions and reliefs from duties so imposed (including the power to amend or revoke orders imposing customs duties or providing for any exemption or relief from duties so imposed).]

Amendment

Para 1: in sub-para (1)(d) words "three months" in italics repealed and subsequent words in square brackets substituted by the Criminal Justice Act 2003, s 283, Sch 27, para 3(1), (2), as from a day to be appointed.

Para 1: in sub-para (1)(d) first-mentioned maximum fine increased and converted to a level on the standard scale by the Criminal Justice Act 1982, ss 37, 40, 46.

Para 1: in sub-para (1)(d) words "£100 a day" in square brackets substituted by the Criminal Law Act 1977, ss 32(3), 65(10).

Para 1: sub-para (3) inserted by the Criminal Justice Act 2003, s 283, Sch 27, para 3(1), (3), as from a day to be appointed.

Para 1A: inserted by the Legislative and Regulatory Reform Act 2006, s 28.

Para 1A: in sub-para (1)(b) words "EU instrument" in square brackets in both places they occur substituted by the European Union (Amendment) Act 2008, s 3(3), Schedule, Pt 1.

Para 1A: in sub-para (2) words ", Measure or Act of the National Assembly for Wales" in square brackets inserted by SI 2007/1388, art 3, Sch 1, para 1.

Para 2: in sub-para (1) words "any order, rules, regulations or scheme" in square brackets substituted by the Legislative and Regulatory Reform Act 2006, s 27(2)(a).

Para 2: in sub-para (2) words "any order, rules, regulations or scheme" in square brackets substituted by the Legislative and Regulatory Reform Act 2006, s 27(2)(a).

Paras 2A–2C: inserted by the Legislative and Regulatory Reform Act 2006, s 29.

Para 2C: in sub-para (c) words "section 28 of the Interpretation and Legislative Reform (Scotland) Act 2010 (asp 10)" in square brackets substituted by SSI 2011/396, art 11.

Para 3: words "any order, rules, regulations or scheme" in square brackets in each place they occur substituted by the Legislative and Regulatory Reform Act 2006, s 27(2)(b).

Paras 4, 5: inserted by the Customs and Excise Duties (General Reliefs) Act 1979, s 19(1), Sch 2, para 5.

Para 4: in sub-para (6) words "EU obligation" in square brackets substituted by the European Union (Amendment) Act 2008, s 3(3), Schedule, Pt 1.

CUSTOMS AND EXCISE MANAGEMENT ACT 1979

1979 c 2

An Act to consolidate the enactments relating to the collection and management of the revenues of customs and excise and in some cases to other matters in relation to which the Commissioners of Customs and Excise for the time being perform functions, with amendments to give effect to recommendations of the Law Commission and the Scottish Law Commission

[22 March 1979]

PART XII
GENERAL AND MISCELLANEOUS

General powers, etc

[157A General information powers in relation to persons entering or leaving the United Kingdom

(1) The proper officer of Revenue and Customs may require any person entering or leaving the United Kingdom—

    (a)   to produce the person's passport or travel documents for examination, or

    (b)   to answer any questions put by the proper officer of Revenue and Customs about the person's journey.

(2) In subsection (1) "passport" means—

(a)   a United Kingdom passport (within the meaning of the Immigration Act 1971),

(b)   a passport issued by or on behalf of the authorities of a country or territory outside the United Kingdom, or by or on behalf of an international organisation, or

(c)   a document that can be used (in some or all circumstances) instead of a passport.

(3)   Subsections (1) and (2) apply in relation to a transit air passenger arriving at the passenger's final destination in the United Kingdom as they apply in relation to a person entering the United Kingdom.

(4)   For the purposes of subsection (3) a transit air passenger is a person—

(a)   who has arrived by air in the United Kingdom; and

(b)   whose journey is continued or resumed by air to a destination in the United Kingdom which is not the place where the person is regarded for the purposes of this section as entering the United Kingdom;

and the passenger's final destination is the destination of the continued or resumed journey.]

Amendment

Inserted by the Policing and Crime Act 2009, s 98(1), as from 25 January 2010: see SI 2010/52, art 2.

CONSULAR FEES ACT 1980

1980 c 23

An Act to re-enact with amendments so much of the Consular Salaries and Fees Act 1891 as relates to consular fees together with certain enactments amending that Act

[1 May 1980]

1 Fees for doing consular and similar acts

(1)   Her Majesty may, by Order in Council, prescribe the fees to be levied by persons authorised by the Secretary of State to exercise consular functions, or functions in the United Kingdom which correspond with consular functions, for doing anything in the exercise of such functions.

(2)   "Consular functions" means any of the functions described in Article 5 of the Vienna Convention on Consular Relations set out in Schedule 1 to the Consular Relations Act 1968 but subsection (1) above applies in relation to persons who are not as well as in relation to persons who are consular officers.

(3)   All fees prescribed under subsection (1) above shall be levied, accounted for and applied, and may be remitted, in accordance with regulations made by the Secretary of State by statutory instrument with the approval of the Treasury.

(4)   Copies of or extracts from the table of fees so prescribed shall be exhibited in every office where such fees are levied.

[(4A)   In prescribing a fee under subsection (1) for the doing of a particular thing, Her Majesty in Council may take into account—

(a)   the expenses that will be or have been incurred in doing that thing, both in the circumstances in relation to which the fee is prescribed and in other circumstances;

(b)   the expenses that will be or have been incurred in doing such other things in the exercise of functions mentioned in that subsection as She thinks fit; and

(c)   such differences between different persons in relation to whom things may be or have been done as She thinks fit.

(4B)   The power of Her Majesty in Council under subsection (1) to prescribe fees and the power of the Secretary of State under subsection (3) to make regulations each includes power—

(a)   to make different provision for different cases;

(b)   to make provision subject to such exemptions and exceptions as the person exercising the power thinks fit; and

(c)   to make such incidental, supplemental, consequential and transitional provision as that person thinks fit.

(4C)   References in this section to expenses that will be incurred for any purpose include references to expenses that Her Majesty in Council considers are likely to be incurred for that purpose over such period as She thinks appropriate, including expenses that will only be incurred after the commencement of a particular enactment.]

(5)   . . .

Amendment

Sub-ss (4A)–(4C): inserted by the Identity Cards Act 2006, s 36; continued in force and set out as amended by the Identity Documents Act 2010, ss 1(3), 12, Schedule, para 2. Date in force: 21 January 2011: see the Identity Documents Act 2010, s 14(2).

Sub-s (5): repeals the Consular Salaries and Fees Act 1891, the Fees (Increase) Act 1923, s 8, the Consular Relations Act 1968, s 13(4) and amends the Foreign Marriage Act 1892, s 20 and the Marriage with Foreigners Act 1906, s 1(4).

Subordinate Legislation

Consular Fees Regulations 1981, SI 1981/476; Consular Fees Order 2012, SI 2012/798; Consular Fees (Amendment) Order 2012, SI 2012/1752; Consular Fees (Amendment) Order 2013, SI 2013/535; Consular Fees (Amendment) Regulations 2013, SI 2013/762; Consular Fees (Amendment) (No 2) Order 2013, SI 2013/1720; Consular Fees (Amendment) Order 2014, SI 2014/509.

[SENIOR COURTS ACT 1981]

1981 c 54

An Act to consolidate with amendments the Supreme Court of Judicature (Consolidation) Act 1925 and other enactments relating to the Supreme Court in England and Wales and the administration of justice therein; to repeal certain obsolete or unnecessary enactments so relating; to amend Part VIII of the Mental Health Act 1959, the Courts-Martial (Appeals) Act 1968, the Arbitration Act 1979 and the law relating to county courts; and for connected purposes

[28 July 1981]

Amendment

Act title (originally Supreme Court Act 1981) substituted by the Constitutional Reform Act 2005, s 59(5), Sch 11, Pt 1, para 1, as from 1 October 2009: see SI 2009/1604, art 2(d).

PART II
JURISDICTION

THE HIGH COURT

Other particular fields of jurisdiction

[**31A Transfer of judicial review applications to Upper Tribunal**
(1) This section applies where an application is made to the High Court—
  (a)   for judicial review, or
  (b)   for permission to apply for judicial review.
(2) If Conditions 1, 2 [and 3] are met, the High Court must by order transfer the application to the Upper Tribunal.
[(2A)   . . .]
(3) If Conditions 1 [and 2] are met, but Condition 3 is not, the High Court may by order transfer the application to the Upper Tribunal if it appears to the High Court to be just and convenient to do so.
(4) Condition 1 is that the application does not seek anything other than—
  (a)   relief under section 31(1)(a) and (b);
  (b)   permission to apply for relief under section 31(1)(a) and (b);
  (c)   an award under section 31(4);
  (d)   interest;
  (e)   costs.
(5) Condition 2 is that the application does not call into question anything done by the Crown Court.
(6) Condition 3 is that the application falls within a class specified under section 18(6) of the Tribunals, Courts and Enforcement Act 2007.
(7)   . . .
[(8)   . . .]]

Amendment
  Inserted by the Tribunals, Courts and Enforcement Act 2007, s 19(1).
  Sub-s (2): words in square brackets substituted by the Crime and Courts Act 2013, s 22(1)(a). Date in force: 1 November 2013: see SI 2013/2200, art 5.
  Sub-s (2A): inserted by the Borders, Citizenship and Immigration Act 2009, s 53(1)(a); repealed by the Crime and Courts Act 2013, s 22(1)(b). Date in force: 1 November 2013: see SI 2013/2200, art 5.
  Sub-s (3): words in square brackets substituted by the Crime and Courts Act 2013, s 22(1)(c). Date in force: 1 November 2013: see SI 2013/2200, art 5.
  Sub-s (7): repealed by the Crime and Courts Act 2013, s 22(1)(d). Date in force: 1 November 2013: see SI 2013/2200, art 5.
  Sub-s (8): inserted by the Borders, Citizenship and Immigration Act 2009, s 53(1)(b); repealed by the Crime and Courts Act 2013, s 22(1)(d). Date in force: 1 November 2013: see SI 2013/2200, art 5.

BRITISH NATIONALITY ACT 1981

1981 c 61

An Act to make fresh provision about citizenship and nationality, and to amend the Immigration Act 1971 as regards the right of abode in the United Kingdom

[30 October 1981]

PART I
BRITISH CITIZENSHIP

Acquisition after commencement

1 Acquisition by birth or adoption

(1)   A person born in the United Kingdom after commencement[, or in a qualifying territory on or after the appointed day,] shall be a British citizen if at the time of the birth his father or mother is—

    (a)   a British citizen; or

    (b)   settled in the United Kingdom [or that territory].

[(1A)   A person born in the United Kingdom or a qualifying territory on or after the relevant day shall be a British citizen if at the time of the birth his father or mother is a member of the armed forces.]

(2)   A new-born infant who, after commencement, is found abandoned in the United Kingdom[, or on or after the appointed day is found abandoned in a qualifying territory,] shall, unless the contrary is shown, be deemed for the purposes of subsection (1)—

    (a)   to have been born in the United Kingdom after commencement [or in that territory on or after the appointed day]; and

    (b)   to have been born to a parent who at the time of the birth was a British citizen or settled in the United Kingdom [or that territory].

(3)   A person born in the United Kingdom after commencement who is not a British citizen by virtue of subsection (1)[, (1A) or (2)] shall be entitled to be registered as a British citizen if, while he is a minor—

    (a)   his father or mother becomes a British citizen or becomes settled in the United Kingdom; and

    (b)   an application is made for his registration as a British citizen.

[(3A)   A person born in the United Kingdom on or after the relevant day who is not a British citizen by virtue of subsection (1), (1A) or (2) shall be entitled to be registered as a British citizen if, while he is a minor—

    (a)   his father or mother becomes a member of the armed forces; and

    (b)   an application is made for his registration as a British citizen.]

(4)   A person born in the United Kingdom after commencement who is not a British citizen by virtue of subsection (1)[, (1A)] or (2) shall be entitled, on an application for his registration as a British citizen made at any time after he has attained the age of ten years, to be registered as such a citizen if, as regards each of the first ten years of that person's life, the number of days on which he was absent from the United Kingdom in that year does not exceed 90.

[(5)   Where—

    (a)   any court in the United Kingdom [or, on or after the appointed day, any court in a qualifying territory] makes an order authorising the adoption of a minor who is not a British citizen; or

    (b)   a minor who is not a British citizen is adopted under a Convention adoption, [effected under the law of a country or territory outside the United Kingdom,]

that minor shall, if the requirements of subsection (5A) are met, be a British citizen as from the date on which the order is made or the Convention adoption is effected, as the case may be.

(5A)   Those requirements are that on the date on which the order is made or the Convention adoption is effected (as the case may be)—

    (a)   the adopter or, in the case of a joint adoption, one of the adopters is a British citizen; and

(b)   in a case within subsection (5)(b), the adopter or, in the case of a joint adoption, both of the adopters are habitually resident in the United Kingdom [or in a designated territory].]

(6)   Where an order [or a Convention adoption] in consequence of which any person became a British citizen by virtue of subsection (5) ceases to have effect, whether on annulment or otherwise, the cesser shall not affect the status of that person as a British citizen.

(7)   If in the special circumstances of any particular case the Secretary of State thinks fit, he may for the purposes of subsection (4) treat the person to whom the application relates as fulfilling the requirement specified in that subsection although, as regards any one or more of the first ten years of that person's life, the number of days on which he was absent from the United Kingdom in that year or each of the years in question exceeds 90.

(8)   In this section and elsewhere in this Act "settled" has the meaning given by section 50 [. . .].

[(9)   The relevant day for the purposes of subsection (1A) or (3A) is the day appointed for the commencement of section 42 of the Borders, Citizenship and Immigration Act 2009 (which inserted those subsections).]

Amendment

Sub-s (1): words ", or in a qualifying territory on or after the appointed day," in square brackets inserted by the British Overseas Territories Act 2002, s 5, Sch 1, para 1(1), (2)(a).

Sub-s (1): in para (b) words "or that territory" in square brackets inserted by the British Overseas Territories Act 2002, s 5, Sch 1, para 1(1), (2)(b).

Sub-s (1A): inserted by the Borders, Citizenship and Immigration Act 2009, s 42(1), (2).

Sub-s (2): words ", or on or after the appointed day is found abandoned in a qualifying territory," in square brackets inserted by the British Overseas Territories Act 2002, s 5, Sch 1, para 1(1), (3)(a).

Sub-s (2): in para (a) words "or in that territory on or after the appointed day" in square brackets inserted by the British Overseas Territories Act 2002, s 5, Sch 1, para 1(1), (3)(b).

Sub-s (2): in para (b) words "or that territory" in square brackets inserted by the British Overseas Territories Act 2002, s 5, Sch 1, para 1(1), (3)(c).

Sub-s (3): reference to ", (1A)" in square brackets inserted by the Borders, Citizenship and Immigration Act 2009, s 42(1), (3).

Sub-s (3A): inserted by the Borders, Citizenship and Immigration Act 2009, s 42(1), (4).

Sub-s (4): reference to ", (1A)" in square brackets inserted by the Borders, Citizenship and Immigration Act 2009, s 42(1), (5).

Sub-ss (5), (5A): substituted, for sub-s (5) as originally enacted, by the Adoption (Intercountry Aspects) Act 1999, s 7(1).

Sub-s (5): in para (a) words "or, on or after the appointed day, any court in a qualifying territory" in square brackets inserted by the British Overseas Territories Act 2002, s 5, Sch 1, para 1(1), (4).

Sub-s (5): in para (b) words "effected under the law of a country or territory outside the United Kingdom" in square brackets inserted by the Adoption and Children Act 2002, s 137(3), (4)(a).

Sub-s (5A): in para (b) words "or in a designated territory" in square brackets inserted by the Adoption and Children Act 2002, s 137(3), (4)(b).

Sub-s (6): words "or a Convention adoption" in square brackets inserted by the Adoption (Intercountry Aspects) Act 1999, s 7(2).

Sub-s (8): words omitted in square brackets inserted by the Adoption (Intercountry Aspects) Act 1999, s 7(3).

Sub-s (8): words omitted repealed by the Adoption and Children Act 2002, ss 137(3), (4)(c), 139(3), Sch 5.

Sub-s (9): inserted by the Borders, Citizenship and Immigration Act 2009, s 42(1), (6).

See Further

See further, in relation to the application of this section, with modifications, to the arrangements by which a parental order may be obtained under the Human Fertilisation and Embryology Act 2008, s 54: the Human Fertilisation and Embryology (Parental Orders) Regulations 2010, SI 2010/985, reg 5, Sch 4.

2 Acquisition by descent

(1) A person born outside the United Kingdom [and the qualifying territories] after commencement shall be a British citizen if at the time of the birth his father or mother—

- (a) is a British citizen otherwise than by descent; or
- (b) is a British citizen and is serving outside the United Kingdom [and the qualifying territories] in service to which this paragraph applies, his or her recruitment for that service having taken place in the United Kingdom [or a qualifying territory]; or
- (c) is a British citizen and is serving outside the United Kingdom [and the qualifying territories] in service under [an EU] institution, his or her recruitment for that service having taken place in a country which at the time of the recruitment was a member of the [European Union].

(2) Paragraph (b) of subsection (1) applies to—

- (a) Crown service under the government of the United Kingdom [or of a qualifying territory]; and
- (b) service of any description for the time being designated under subsection (3).

(3) For the purposes of this section the Secretary of State may by order made by statutory instrument designate any description of service which he considers to be closely associated with the activities outside the United Kingdom [and the qualifying territories] of Her Majesty's government in the United Kingdom [or in a qualifying territory].

(4) Any order made under subsection (3) shall be subject to annulment in pursuance of a resolution of either House of Parliament.

Amendment

Sub-s (1): words "and the qualifying territories" in each place they occur and words "or a qualifying territory" in square brackets inserted by the British Overseas Territories Act 2002, s 5, Sch 1, para 2(1), (2); for effect see Sch 1, para 2(1) thereto.

Sub-s (1): in para (c) words "an EU" and "European Union" in square brackets substituted by SI 2011/1043, arts 4(1), 6(1)(c), (3). Date in force: 22 April 2011: see SI 2011/1043, art 2; for transitional savings see art 3(3) thereof.

Sub-s (2): in para (a) words "or of a qualifying territory" in square brackets inserted by the British Overseas Territories Act 2002, s 5, Sch 1, para 2(1), (3); for effect see Sch 1, para 2(1) thereto.

Sub-s (3): words "and the qualifying territories" and "or in a qualifying territory" in square brackets inserted by the British Overseas Territories Act 2002, s 5, Sch 1, para 2(1), (4); for effect see Sch 1, para 2(1) thereto.

Subordinate Legislation

British Citizenship (Designated Service) Order 2006, SI 2006/1390.
British Citizenship (Designated Service) (Amendment) Order 2007, SI 2007/744.

3 Acquisition by registration: minors

(1) If while a person is a minor an application is made for his registration as a British citizen, the Secretary of State may, if he thinks fit, cause him to be registered as such a citizen.

(2) A person born outside the United Kingdom [and the qualifying territories] shall be entitled, on an application for his registration as a British citizen made [while he is a minor], to be registered as such a citizen if the requirements specified in subsection (3) or, in the case of a person born stateless, the requirements specified in paragraphs (a) and (b) of that subsection, are fulfilled in the case of either that person's father or his mother ("the parent in question").

(3) The requirements referred to in subsection (2) are—

- (a) that the parent in question was a British citizen by descent at the time of the birth; and

    (b)   that the father or mother of the parent in question—

        (i)   was a British citizen otherwise than by descent at the time of the birth of the parent in question; or

        (ii)   became a British citizen otherwise than by descent at commencement, or would have become such a citizen otherwise than by descent at commencement but for his or her death; and

    (c)   that, as regards some period of three years ending with a date not later than the date of the birth—

        (i)   the parent in question was in the United Kingdom [or a qualifying territory] at the beginning of that period; and

        (ii)   the number of days on which the parent in question was absent from the United Kingdom [and the qualifying territories] in that period does not exceed 270.

(4) ...

(5) A person born outside the United Kingdom [and the qualifying territories] shall be entitled, on an application for his registration as a British citizen made while he is a minor, to be registered as such a citizen if the following requirements are satisfied, namely—

    (a)   that at the time of that person's birth his father or mother was a British citizen by descent; and

    (b)   subject to subsection (6), that that person and his father and mother were in the United Kingdom [or a qualifying territory] at the beginning of the period of three years ending with the date of the application and that, in the case of each of them, the number of days on which the person in question was absent from the United Kingdom [and the qualifying territories] in that period does not exceed 270; and

    (c)   subject to subsection (6), that the consent of his father and mother to the registration has been signified in the prescribed manner.

(6) In the case of an application under subsection (5) of the registration of a person as a British citizen—

    (a)   if his father or mother died, or their marriage [or civil partnership] was terminated, on or before the date of the application, or his father and mother were legally separated on that date, the references to his father and mother in paragraph (b) of that subsection shall be read either as references to his father or as references to his mother; [and]

    (b)   if his father or mother died on or before that date, the reference to his father and mother in paragraph (c) of that subsection shall be read as a reference to either of them; ...

    (c)   ...

Amendment

    Sub-s (2): words "and the qualifying territories" in square brackets inserted by the British Overseas Territories Act 2002, s 5, Sch 1, para 3(1), (2); for effect see Sch 1, para 3(1) thereto.

    Sub-s (2): words "while he is a minor" in square brackets substituted by the Borders, Citizenship and Immigration Act 2009, s 43(1), (2).

    Sub-s (3): in para (c) words "or a qualifying territory" and "and the qualifying territories" in square brackets inserted by the British Overseas Territories Act 2002, s 5, Sch 1, para 3(1), (3); for effect see Sch 1, para 3(1) thereto.

    Sub-s (4): repealed by the Borders, Citizenship and Immigration Act 2009, ss 43(1), (3), 56, Schedule, Pt 2.

    Sub-s (5): words "and the qualifying territories" in both places they occur and "or a qualifying territory" in square brackets inserted by the British Overseas Territories Act 2002, s 5, Sch 1, para 3(1), (4); for effect see Sch 1, para 3(1) thereto.

    Sub-s (6): in para (a) words "or civil partnership" in square brackets inserted by the Civil Partnership Act 2004, s 261(1), Sch 27, para 71.

Sub-s (6): in para (a) word "and" in square brackets inserted by the Nationality, Immigration and Asylum Act 2002, s 9(2)(a).

Sub-s (6): in para (b) word omitted repealed by the Nationality, Immigration and Asylum Act 2002, ss 9(2)(b), 161, Sch 9.

Sub-s (6): para (c) repealed by the Nationality, Immigration and Asylum Act 2002, ss 9(2)(c), 161, Sch 9.

4 Acquisition by registration: [British overseas territories citizens] etc

(1)   This section applies to any person who is a [British overseas territories citizen], [a British National (Overseas),] a British Overseas citizen, a British subject under this Act or a British protected person.

(2)   A person to whom this section applies shall be entitled, on an application for his registration as a British citizen, to be registered as such a citizen if the following requirements are satisfied in the case of that person, namely—

(a)   subject to subsection (3), that he was in the United Kingdom at the beginning of the period of five years ending with the date of the application and that the number of days on which he was absent from the United Kingdom in that period does not exceed 450; and

(b)   that the number of days on which he was absent from the United Kingdom in the period of twelve months so ending does not exceed 90; and

(c)   that he was not at any time in the period of twelve months so ending subject under the immigration laws to any restriction on the period for which he might remain in the United Kingdom; and

(d)   that he was not at any time in the period of five years so ending in the United Kingdom in breach of the immigration laws.

(3)   So much of subsection (2)(a) as requires the person in question to have been in the United Kingdom at the beginning of the period there mentioned shall not apply in relation to a person who was settled in the United Kingdom immediately before commencement.

(4)   If in the special circumstances of any particular case the Secretary of State thinks fit, he may for the purposes of subsection (2) do all or any of the following things, namely—

(a)   treat the person to whom the application relates as fulfilling the requirement specified in subsection (2)(a) or subsection (2)(b), or both, although the number of days on which he was absent from the United Kingdom in the period there mentioned exceeds the number there mentioned;

(b)   disregard any such restriction as is mentioned in subsection (2)(c), not being a restriction to which that person was subject on the date of the application;

(c)   treat that person as fulfilling the requirement specified in subsection (2)(d) although he was in the United Kingdom in breach of the immigration laws in the period there mentioned.

(5)   If, on an application for registration as a British citizen made by a person to whom this section applies, the Secretary of State is satisfied that the applicant has at any time served in service to which this subsection applies, he may, if he thinks fit in the special circumstances of the applicant's case, cause him to be registered as such a citizen.

(6)   Subsection (5) applies to—

(a)   Crown service under the government of a [British overseas territory]; and

(b)   paid or unpaid service (not falling within paragraph (a)) as a member of any body established by law in a [British overseas territory] members of which are appointed by or on behalf of the Crown.

Amendment

Section heading: words "British overseas territories citizens" in square brackets substituted by the British Overseas Territories Act 2002, s 2(2)(b).

Sub-s (1): words "British overseas territories citizen" in square brackets substituted by the British Overseas Territories Act 2002, s 2(2)(b).

Sub-s (1): words "a British National (Overseas)," in square brackets inserted by SI 1986/948, art 7.

Sub-s (6): words "British overseas territory" in square brackets in both places they occur substituted by the British Overseas Territories Act 2002, s 1(1)(b).

See Further

See further, in relation to the construction of the reference to being in the United Kingdom "in breach of the immigration laws" in sub-ss (2), (4) above: the Nationality, Immigration and Asylum Act 2002, s 11.

[4A Acquisition by registration: further provision for British overseas territories citizens]

[(1)   If an application is made to register as a British citizen a person who is a British overseas territories citizen, the Secretary of State may if he thinks fit cause the person to be so registered.

(2)   Subsection (1) does not apply in the case of a British overseas territories citizen who—

(a)   is such a citizen by virtue only of a connection with the Sovereign Base Areas of Akrotiri and Dhekelia; or

(b)   has ceased to be a British citizen as a result of a declaration of renunciation.]

Amendment

Inserted by the British Overseas Territories Act 2002, s 4.

[4B Acquisition by registration: certain persons without other citizenship]

[(1)   This section applies to a person who has the status of—

(a)   British Overseas citizen,

(b)   British subject under this Act, . . .

(c)   British protected person[, or

(d)   British National (Overseas)].

(2)   A person to whom this section applies shall be entitled to be registered as a British citizen if—

(a)   he applies for registration under this section,

(b)   the Secretary of State is satisfied that the person does not have, apart from the status mentioned in subsection (1), any citizenship or nationality, and

(c)   the Secretary of State is satisfied that the person has not after [the relevant day] renounced, voluntarily relinquished or lost through action or inaction any citizenship or nationality.]

[(3)   For the purposes of subsection (2)(c), the "relevant day" means—

(a)   in the case of a person to whom this section applies by virtue of subsection (1)(d) only, 19th March 2009, and

(b)   in any other case, 4th July 2002.]

Amendment

Inserted by the Nationality, Immigration and Asylum Act 2002, s 12(1).

Sub-s (1): in para (b) word omitted repealed by the Borders, Citizenship and Immigration Act 2009, ss 44(1), (2)(a), 56, Schedule, Pt 2.

Sub-s (1): para (d) and word ", or" immediately preceding it inserted by the Borders, Citizenship and Immigration Act 2009, s 44(1), (2)(b).

Sub-s (2): in para (c) words "the relevant day" in square brackets substituted by the Borders, Citizenship and Immigration Act 2009, s 44(1), (3).

Sub-s (3): inserted by the Borders, Citizenship and Immigration Act 2009, s 44(1), (4).

[4C Acquisition by registration: certain persons born between 1961 and 1983]

[(1) A person is entitled to be registered as a British citizen if—

    (a) he applies for registration under this section, and

    (b) he satisfies each of the following conditions.

(2) The first condition is that the applicant was born . . . before 1st January 1983.

[(3) The second condition is that the applicant would at some time before 1st January 1983 have become a citizen of the United Kingdom and Colonies—

    (a) under section 5 of, or paragraph 3 of Schedule 3 to, the 1948 Act if assumption A had applied,

    (b) under section 12(3), (4) or (5) of that Act if assumption B had applied and as a result of its application the applicant would have been a British subject immediately before 1st January 1949, or

    (c) under section 12(2) of that Act if one or both of the following had applied—

        (i) assumption A had applied;

        (ii) assumption B had applied and as a result of its application the applicant would have been a British subject immediately before 1st January 1949.

(3A) Assumption A is that—

    (a) section 5 or 12(2) of, or paragraph 3 of Schedule 3 to, the 1948 Act (as the case may be) provided for citizenship by descent from a mother in the same terms as it provided for citizenship by descent from a father, and

    (b) references in that provision to a father were references to the applicant's mother.

(3B) Assumption B is that—

    (a) a provision of the law at some time before 1st January 1949 which provided for a nationality status to be acquired by descent from a father provided in the same terms for its acquisition by descent from a mother, and

    (b) references in that provision to a father were references to the applicant's mother.

(3C) For the purposes of subsection (3B), a nationality status is acquired by a person ("P") by descent where its acquisition—

    (a) depends, amongst other things, on the nationality status of one or both of P's parents, and

    (b) does not depend upon an application being made for P's registration as a person who has the status in question.

(3D) For the purposes of subsection (3), it is not to be assumed that any registration or other requirements of the provisions mentioned in that subsection or in subsection (3B) were met.]

(4) The third condition is that immediately before 1st January 1983 the applicant would have had the right of abode in the United Kingdom by virtue of section 2 of the Immigration Act 1971 (c 77) had he become a citizen of the United Kingdom and Colonies as described in subsection (3) above.]

[(5) For the purposes of the interpretation of section 5 of the 1948 Act in its application in the case of assumption A to a case of descent from a mother, the reference in the proviso to subsection (1) of that section to "a citizen of the United Kingdom and Colonies by descent only" includes a reference to a female person who became a citizen of the United Kingdom and Colonies by virtue of—

    (a) section 12(2), (4) or (6) only of the 1948 Act,

    (b) section 13(2) of that Act,

    (c) paragraph 3 of Schedule 3 to that Act, or

(d)   section 1(1)(a) or (c) of the British Nationality (No 2) Act 1964.]

Amendment

Inserted by the Nationality, Immigration and Asylum Act 2002, s 13(1).

Sub-s (2): words omitted repealed by the Borders, Citizenship and Immigration Act 2009, ss 45(1), (2), 56, Schedule Pt 2.

Sub-ss (3), (3A)–(3D): substituted, for sub-s (3) as originally enacted, by the Borders, Citizenship and Immigration Act 2009, s 45(1), (3).

Sub-s (5): inserted by the Borders, Citizenship and Immigration Act 2009, s 45(1), (4).

[4D Acquisition by registration: children of members of the armed forces]

[(1) A person ("P") born outside the United Kingdom and the qualifying territories on or after the relevant day is entitled to be registered as a British citizen if—

    (a)   an application is made for P's registration under this section; and

    (b)   each of the following conditions is satisfied.

(2) The first condition is that, at the time of P's birth, P's father or mother was—

    (a)   a member of the armed forces; and

    (b)   serving outside the United Kingdom and the qualifying territories.

(3) The second condition is that, if P is a minor on the date of the application, the consent of P's father and mother to P's registration as a British citizen has been signified in the prescribed manner.

(4) But if P's father or mother has died on or before the date of the application, the reference in subsection (3) to P's father and mother is to be read as a reference to either of them.

(5) The Secretary of State may, in the special circumstances of a particular case, waive the need for the second condition to be satisfied.

(6) The relevant day for the purposes of this section is the day appointed for the commencement of section 46 of the Borders, Citizenship and Immigration Act 2009 (which inserted this section).]

Amendment

Inserted by the Borders, Citizenship and Immigration Act 2009, s 46.

[4E The general conditions

For the purposes of sections 4F to 4I, a person ("P") meets the general conditions if—

    (a)   P was born before 1 July 2006;

    (b)   at the time of P's birth, P's mother—

        (i)   was not married, or

        (ii)   was married to a person other than P's natural father;

    (c)   no person is treated as the father of P under section 28 of the Human Fertilisation and Embryology Act 1990; and

    (d)   P has never been a British citizen.]

Amendment

Inserted by the Immigration Act 2014, s 65, as from a day to be appointed.

[4F Person unable to be registered under other provisions of this Act

(1) A person ("P") is entitled to be registered as a British citizen on an application made under this section if—

    (a)   P meets the general conditions; and

    (b)   P would be entitled to be registered as a British citizen under—

        (i)   section 1(3),

        (ii)   section 3(2),

        (iii)   section 3(5),

        (iv)   paragraph 4 of Schedule 2, or

        (v)   paragraph 5 of Schedule 2,

had P's mother been married to P's natural father at the time of P's birth.

(2)   In the following provisions of this section "relevant registration provision" means the provision under which P would be entitled to be registered as a British citizen (as mentioned in subsection (1)(b)).

(3)   If the relevant registration provision is section 3(2), a person who is registered as a British citizen under this section is a British citizen by descent.

(4)   If the relevant registration provision is section 3(5), the Secretary of State may, in the special circumstances of the particular case, waive the need for any or all of the parental consents to be given.

(5)   For that purpose, the "parental consents" are—

    (a)   the consent of P's natural father, and

    (b)   the consent of P's mother,

insofar as they would be required by section 3(5)(c) (as read with section 3(6)(b)), had P's mother been married to P's natural father at the time of P's birth.]

Amendment

    Inserted by the Immigration Act 2014, s 65, as from a day to be appointed.

[4G Person unable to become citizen automatically after commencement

(1)   A person ("P") is entitled to be registered as a British citizen on an application made under this section if—

    (a)   P meets the general conditions; and

    (b)   at any time in the period after commencement, P would have automatically become a British citizen at birth by the operation of any provision of this Act or the British Nationality (Falkland Islands) Act 1983, had P's mother been married to P's natural father at the time of P's birth.

(2)   A person who is registered as a British citizen under this section is a British citizen by descent if the British citizenship which the person would have acquired at birth (as mentioned in subsection (1)(b)) would (by virtue of section 14) have been British citizenship by descent.

(3)   If P is under the age of 18, no application may be made unless the consent of P's natural father and mother to the registration has been signified in the prescribed manner.

(4)   But if P's natural father or mother has died on or before the date of the application, the reference in subsection (3) to P's natural father and mother is to be read as a reference to either of them.

(5)   The Secretary of State may, in the special circumstances of a particular case, waive the need for any or all of the consents required by subsection (3) (as read with subsection (4)) to be given.

(6)   The reference in this section to the period after commencement does not include the time of commencement (and, accordingly, this section does not apply to any case in which a person was unable to become a British citizen at commencement).]

Amendment

    Inserted by the Immigration Act 2014, s 65, as from a day to be appointed.

[4H Citizen of UK and colonies unable to become citizen at commencement

(1)   A person ("P") is entitled to be registered as a British citizen on an application made under this section if—

    (a)   P meets the general conditions;

    (b)   P was a citizen of the United Kingdom and Colonies immediately before commencement; and

    (c)   P would have automatically become a British citizen at commencement, by the operation of any provision of this Act, had P's mother been married to P's natural father at the time of P's birth.

(2)   A person who is registered as a British citizen under this section is a British citizen by descent if the British citizenship which the person would have acquired at commencement (as mentioned in subsection (1)(c)) would (by virtue of section 14) have been British citizenship by descent.]

Amendment

Inserted by the Immigration Act 2014, s 65, as from a day to be appointed.

[4I Other person unable to become citizen at commencement

(1)   A person ("P") is entitled to be registered as a British citizen on an application made under this section if—

- (a)   P meets the general conditions;
- (b)   P is either—
  - (i)   an eligible former British national, or
  - (ii)   an eligible non-British national; and
- (c)   had P's mother been married to P's natural father at the time of P's birth, P—
  - (i)   would have been a citizen of the United Kingdom and Colonies immediately before commencement, and
  - (ii)   would have automatically become a British citizen at commencement by the operation of any provision of this Act.

(2)   P is an "eligible former British national" if P was not a citizen of the United Kingdom and Colonies immediately before commencement and either—

- (a)   P ceased to be a British subject or a citizen of the United Kingdom and Colonies by virtue of the commencement of any independence legislation, but would not have done so had P's mother been married to P's natural father at the time of P's birth, or
- (b)   P was a British subject who did not automatically become a citizen of the United Kingdom and Colonies at commencement of the British Nationality Act 1948 by the operation of any provision of it, but would have done so had P's mother been married to P's natural father at the time of P's birth.

(3)   P is an "eligible non-British national" if—

- (a)   P was never a British subject or citizen of the United Kingdom and Colonies; and
- (b)   had P's mother been married to P's natural father at the time of P's birth, P would have automatically become a British subject or citizen of the United Kingdom and Colonies—
  - (i)   at birth, or
  - (ii)   by virtue of paragraph 3 of Schedule 3 to the British Nationality Act 1948 (child of male British subject to become citizen of the United Kingdom and Colonies if the father becomes such a citizen).

(4)   A person who is registered as a British citizen under this section is a British citizen by descent if the British citizenship which the person would have acquired at commencement (as mentioned in subsection (1)(c)(ii)) would (by virtue of section 14) have been British citizenship by descent.

(5)   In determining for the purposes of subsection (1)(c)(i) whether P would have been a citizen of the United Kingdom and Colonies immediately before commencement, it must be assumed that P would not have—

- (a)   renounced or been deprived of any notional British nationality, or
- (b)   lost any notional British nationality by virtue of P acquiring the nationality of a country or territory outside the United Kingdom.

(6)   A "notional British nationality" is—

(a) in a case where P is an eligible former British national, any status as a British subject or a citizen of the United Kingdom and Colonies which P would have held at any time after P's nationality loss (had that loss not occurred and had P's mother had been married to P's natural father at the time of P's birth);

(b) in a case where P is an eligible non-British national—

    (i) P's status as a British subject or citizen of the United Kingdom and Colonies mentioned in subsection (3)(b), and

    (ii) any other status as a British subject or citizen of the United Kingdom and Colonies which P would have held at any time afterwards (had P's mother been married to P's natural father at the time of P's birth).

(7) In this section—

"British subject" has any meaning which it had for the purposes of the British Nationality and Status of Aliens Act 1914;

"independence legislation" means an Act of Parliament or any subordinate legislation (within the meaning of the Interpretation Act 1978) forming part of the law in the United Kingdom (whenever passed or made, and whether or not still in force)—

    (a) providing for a country or territory to become independent from the United Kingdom, or

    (b) dealing with nationality, or any other ancillary matters, in connection with a country or territory becoming independent from the United Kingdom;

"P's nationality loss" means P's—

    (a) ceasing to be a British subject or citizen of the United Kingdom and Colonies (as mentioned in subsection (2)(a)), or

    (b) not becoming a citizen of the United Kingdom and Colonies (as mentioned in subsection (2)(b)).]

Amendment

Inserted by the Immigration Act 2014, s 65, as from a day to be appointed.

[4J Sections 4E to 4I: supplementary provision

(1) In sections 4E to 4I and this section, a person's "natural father" is a person who satisfies the requirements as to proof of paternity that are prescribed in regulations under section 50(9B).

(2) The power under section 50(9B) to make different provision for different circumstances includes power to make provision for the purposes of any provision of sections 4E to 4I which is different from other provision made under section 50(9B).

(3) The following provisions apply for the purposes of sections 4E to 4I.

(4) A reference to a person automatically becoming a British citizen, or a citizen of the United Kingdom and Colonies, is a reference to the person becoming such a citizen without the need for—

(a) the person to be registered as such a citizen by the Secretary of State or any other minister of the Crown;

(b) the birth of the person to be registered by a diplomatic or consular representative of the United Kingdom; or

(c) the person to be naturalised as such a citizen.

(5) If the mother of a person could not actually have been married to the person's natural father at the time of the person's birth (for whatever reason), that fact does not prevent an assumption being made that the couple were married at the time of the birth.]

Amendment

Inserted by the Immigration Act 2014, s 65, as from a day to be appointed.

5 Acquisition by registration: nationals for purposes of the [EU] treaties

A [British overseas territories citizen] who falls to be treated as a national of the United Kingdom for the purposes of the [EU] Treaties shall be entitled to be registered as a British citizen if an application is made for his registration as such a citizen.

Amendment

References to "EU" in square brackets substituted by SI 2011/1043, art 6(1)(a). Date in force: 22 April 2011: see SI 2011/1043, art 2; for transitional savings see art 3(3) thereof.

Words "British overseas territories citizen" in square brackets substituted by the British Overseas Territories Act 2002, s 2(2)(b).

6 Acquisition by naturalisation

(1) If, on an application for naturalisation as a British citizen made by a person of full age and capacity, the Secretary of State is satisfied that the applicant fulfils the requirements of Schedule 1 for naturalisation as such a citizen under this subsection, he may, if he thinks fit, grant to him a certificate of naturalisation as such a citizen.

(2) If, on an application for naturalisation as a British citizen made by a person of full age and capacity who on the date of the application *is married to a British citizen [or is the civil partner of a British citizen]* [has a relevant family association], the Secretary of State is satisfied that the applicant fulfils the requirements of Schedule 1 for naturalisation as such a citizen under this subsection, he may, if he thinks fit, grant to him a certificate of naturalisation as such a citizen.

[(3) For the purposes of this section and Schedule 1, a person ("A") has a relevant family association if A has a connection of a prescribed description to a person of a prescribed description.

(4) If in the special circumstances of any particular case the Secretary of State thinks fit, the Secretary of State may for the purposes of subsection (3) treat A as having a relevant family association on the date of the application although the relevant family association ceased to exist before that date.]

Amendment

Sub-s (2): words "is married to a British citizen or is the civil partner of a British citizen" in italics repealed and subsequent words in square brackets substituted by the Borders, Citizenship and Immigration Act 2009, s 40(1), as from a day to be appointed.

Sub-s (2): words "or is the civil partner of a British citizen" in square brackets inserted by the Civil Partnership Act 2004, s 261(1), Sch 27, para 72.

Sub-ss (3), (4): inserted by the Borders, Citizenship and Immigration Act 2009, s 40(2), as from a day to be appointed.

Acquisition after commencement: special cases

7–9

(*Repealed by the Nationality, Immigration and Asylum Act 2002, ss 15, 161, Sch 2, para 1(a)–(c), Sch 9.*)

10 Registration following renunciation of citizenship of UK and Colonies

(1) Subject to subsection (3), a person shall be entitled, on an application for his registration as a British citizen, to be registered as such a citizen if immediately before commencement he would (had he applied for it) have been entitled under section 1(1) of the British Nationality Act 1964 (resumption of citizenship) to be registered as a citizen of the United Kingdom and Colonies by virtue of having an appropriate qualifying connection with the United Kingdom or. . . by virtue of having been married before commencement to a person who has, or would if living have, such a connection.

(2) On an application for his registration as a British citizen made by a person of full capacity who had before commencement ceased to be a citizen of the United Kingdom

and Colonies as a result of a declaration of renunciation, the Secretary of State may, if he thinks fit, cause that person to be registered as a British citizen if that person—

    (a)   has an appropriate qualifying connection with the United Kingdom; or

    (b)   . . . has been married to[, or has been the civil partner of,] a person who has, or would if living have, such a connection.

(3)   A person shall not be entitled to registration under subsection (1) on more than one occasion.

(4)   For the purposes of this section a person shall be taken to have an appropriate qualifying connection with the United Kingdom if he, his father or his father's father—

    (a)   was born in the United Kingdom; or

    (b)   is or was a person naturalised in the United Kingdom; or

    (c)   was registered as a citizen of the United Kingdom and Colonies in the United Kingdom or in a country which at the time was mentioned in section 1(3) of the 1948 Act.

Amendment

Sub-s (1): words omitted repealed by the Nationality, Immigration and Asylum Act 2002, ss 5(a), 161, Sch 9.

Sub-s (2): in para (b) words omitted repealed by the Nationality, Immigration and Asylum Act 2002, ss 5(a), 161, Sch 9.

Sub-s (2): in para (b) words ", or has been the civil partner of," in square brackets inserted by the Civil Partnership Act 2004, s 261(1), Sch 27, para 73.

Acquisition at commencement

11 Citizens of UK and Colonies who are to become British citizens at commencement

(1)   Subject to subsection (2), a person who immediately before commencement—

    (a)   was a citizen of the United Kingdom and Colonies; and

    (b)   had the right of abode in the United Kingdom under the Immigration Act 1971 as then in force,

shall at commencement become a British citizen.

(2)   A person who was registered as a citizen of the United Kingdom and Colonies under section 1 of the British Nationality (No 2) Act 1964 (stateless persons) on the ground mentioned in subsection (1)(a) of that section (namely that his mother was a citizen of the United Kingdom and Colonies at the time when he was born) shall not become a British citizen under subsection (1) unless—

    (a)   his mother becomes a British citizen under subsection (1) or would have done so but for her death; or

    (b)   immediately before commencement he had the right of abode in the United Kingdom by virtue of section 2(1)(c) of the Immigration Act 1971 as then in force (settlement in United Kingdom, combined with five or more years' ordinary residence there as a citizen of the United Kingdom and Colonies).

(3)   A person who—

    (a)   immediately before commencement was a citizen of the United Kingdom and Colonies by virtue of having been registered under subsection (6) of section 12 of the 1948 Act (British subjects before commencement of 1948 Act becoming citizens of United Kingdom and Colonies) under arrangements made by virtue of subsection (7) of that section (registration in independent Commonwealth country by United Kingdom High Commissioner); and

    (b)   was so registered on an application under the said subsection (6) based on the applicant's descent in the male line from a person ("the relevant person") possessing one of the qualifications specified in subsection (1)(a) and (b) of that section (birth or naturalisation in the United Kingdom and Colonies),

shall at commencement become a British citizen if the relevant person was born or naturalised in the United Kingdom.

Renuciation and resumption

12 Renunciation

(1) If any British citizen of full age and capacity makes in the prescribed manner a declaration of renunciation of British citizenship, then, subject to subsections (3) and (4), the Secretary of State shall cause the declaration to be registered.

(2) On the registration of a declaration made in pursuance of this section the person who made it shall cease to be a British citizen.

(3) A declaration made by a person in pursuance of this section shall not be registered unless the Secretary of State is satisfied that the person who made it will after the registration have or acquire some citizenship or nationality other than British citizenship; and if that person does not have any such citizenship or nationality on the date of registration and does not acquire some such citizenship or nationality within six months from that date, he shall be, and be deemed to have remained, a British citizen notwithstanding the registration.

(4) The Secretary of State may withhold registration of any declaration made in pursuance of this section if it is made during any war in which Her Majesty may be engaged in right of Her Majesty's government in the United Kingdom.

(5) For the purposes of this section any person who has been married[, or has formed a civil partnership,] shall be deemed to be of full age.

Amendment

Sub-s (5): words ", or has formed a civil partnership," in square brackets inserted by the Civil Partnership Act 2004, s 261(1), Sch 27, para 74.

See Further

See further, in relation to British Nationals (Overseas) and their status: the Hong Kong (British Nationality) Order 1986, SI 1986/948, art 7(10).

13 Resumption

(1) Subject to subsection (2), a person who has ceased to be a British citizen as a result of a declaration of renunciation shall be entitled, on an application for his registration as a British citizen, to be registered as such a citizen if—

    (a)   he is of full capacity; and

    (b)   his renunciation of British citizenship was necessary to enable him to retain or acquire some other citizenship or nationality.

(2) A person shall not be entitled to registration under subsection (1) on more than one occasion.

(3) If a person of full capacity who has ceased to be a British citizen as a result of a declaration of renunciation (for whatever reason made) makes an application for his registration as such a citizen, the Secretary of State may, if he thinks fit, cause him to be registered as such a citizen.

Supplementary

14 Meaning of British citizen "by descent"

(1) For the purposes of this Act a British citizen is a British citizen "by descent" if and only if—

(a)   he is a person born outside the United Kingdom after commencement who is a British citizen by virtue of section 2(1)(a) only or by virtue of registration under section 3(2) or 9; or

(b)   subject to subsection (2), he is a person born outside the United Kingdom before commencement who became a British citizen at commencement and immediately before commencement—

(i)   was a citizen of the United Kingdom and Colonies by virtue of section 5 of the 1948 Act (citizenship by descent); or

(ii)   was a person who, under any provision of the British Nationality Acts 1948 to 1965, was deemed for the purposes of the proviso to section 5(1) of the 1948 Act to be a citizen of the United Kingdom and Colonies by descent only, or would have been so deemed if male; or

(iii)   had the right of abode in the United Kingdom by virtue only of paragraph (b) of subsection (1) of section 2 of the Immigration Act 1971 as then in force (connection with United Kingdom through parent or grandparent), or by virtue only of that paragraph and paragraph (c) of that subsection (settlement in United Kingdom with five years' ordinary residence there), or by virtue only of being or having been the wife of a person who immediately before commencement had that right by virtue only of the said paragraph (b) or the said paragraphs (b) and (c); or

(iv)   being a woman, was a citizen of the United Kingdom and Colonies as a result of her registration as such a citizen under section 6(2) of the 1948 Act by virtue of having been married to a man who at commencement became a British citizen by descent or would have done so but for having died or ceased to be a citizen of the United Kingdom and Colonies as a result of a declaration of renunciation; or

(c)   he is a British citizen by virtue of registration under section 3(1) and either—

(i)   his father or mother was a British citizen at the time of the birth; or

(ii)   his father or mother was a citizen of the United Kingdom and Colonies at that time and became a British citizen at commencement, or would have done so but for his or her death; or

(d)   he is a British citizen by virtue of registration under [section 4B[, 4C] or 5]; or

[(da)   the person is a British citizen by descent by virtue of section 4F(3), 4G(2), 4H(2) or 4I(4); or]

(e)   subject to subsection (2), being a woman born outside the United Kingdom before commencement, she is a British citizen as a result of her registration as such a citizen under section 8 by virtue of being or having been married to a man who at commencement became a British citizen by descent or would have done so but for his having died or ceased to be a citizen of the United Kingdom and Colonies as a result of a declaration of renunciation; or

(f)   he is a British citizen by virtue of registration under section 10 who, having before commencement ceased to be a citizen of the United Kingdom and Colonies as a result of a declaration of renunciation, would, if he had not so ceased, have at commencement become a British citizen by descent by virtue of paragraph (b); or

(g)   he is a British citizen by virtue of registration under section 13 who, immediately before he ceased to be a British citizen as a result of a declaration of renunciation, was such a citizen by descent; or

(h)   he is a person born in a [British overseas territory] after commencement who is a British citizen by virtue of paragraph 2 of Schedule 2.

(2)   A person born outside the United Kingdom before commencement is not a British citizen "by descent" by virtue of subsection (1)(b) or (e) if his father was at the time of his birth serving outside the United Kingdom—

(a)   in service of a description mentioned in subsection (3), his recruitment for the service in question having taken place in the United Kingdom; or

(b)   in service under [an EU] institution, his recruitment for that service having taken place in a country which at the time of the recruitment was a member of the [European Union].

(3)   The descriptions of service referred to in subsection (2) are—

(a)   Crown service under the government of the United Kingdom; and

(b)   service of any description at any time designated under section 2(3).

Amendment

Sub-s (1): in para (d) words in square brackets beginning with the words "section 4B or 5" substituted by the Nationality, Immigration and Asylum Act 2002, s 12(2).

Sub-s (1): in para (d) reference to ", 4C" in square brackets inserted by the Nationality, Immigration and Asylum Act 2002, s 13(2).

Sub-s (1): para (da) inserted by the Immigration Act 2014, s 73, Sch 9, Pt 9, para 70(1), (2), as from a day to be appointed.

Sub-s (1): in para (h) words "British overseas territory" in square brackets substituted by the British Overseas Territories Act 2002, s 1(1)(b).

Sub-s (2): in para (b) words "an EU" and "European Union" in square brackets substituted by SI 2011/1043, arts 4(1), 6(1)(c), (3). Date in force: 22 April 2011: see SI 2011/1043, art 2; for transitional savings see art 3(3) thereof.

PART II
[BRITISH OVERSEAS TERRITORIES CITIZENSHIP]

Amendment

Words "British Overseas Territories Citizenship" in square brackets substituted by the British Overseas Territories Act 2002, s 2(2)(a).

Acquisition after commencement

15 Acquisition by birth or adoption

(1)   A person born in a [British overseas territory] after commencement shall be a [British overseas territories citizen] if at the time of the birth his father or mother is—

(a)   a [British overseas territories citizen]; or

(b)   settled in a [British overseas territory].

(2)   A new-born infant who, after commencement, is found abandoned in a [British overseas territory] shall, unless the contrary is shown, be deemed for the purposes of subsection (1)—

(a)   to have been born in that territory after commencement; and

(b)   to have been born to a parent who at the time of the birth was a [British overseas territories citizen] or settled in a [British overseas territory].

(3)   A person born in a [British overseas territory] after commencement who is not a [British overseas territories citizen] by virtue of subsection (1) or (2) shall be entitled to be registered as such a citizen if, while he is a minor—

(a)   his father or mother becomes such a citizen or becomes settled in a [British overseas territory]; and

(b)   an application is made for his registration as such a citizen.

(4)   A person born in a [British overseas territory] after commencement who is not a [British overseas territories citizen] by virtue of subsection (1) or (2) shall be entitled, on an application for registration as a [British overseas territories citizen] made at any time after he has attained the age of ten years, to be registered as such a citizen if, as regards each of the first ten years of that person's life, the number of days on which he was absent from that territory in that year does not exceed 90.

(5)   Where after commencement an order authorising the adoption of a minor who is not a [British overseas territories citizen] is made by a court in any [British overseas territory], he shall be a [British overseas territories citizen] as from the date on which the order is made if the adopter or, in the case of a joint adoption, one of the adopters, is a [British overseas territories citizen] on that date.

[(5A)   Where—

    (a)   a minor who is not a British overseas territories citizen is adopted under a Convention adoption,

    (b)   on the date on which the adoption is effected—

        (i)   the adopter or, in the case of a joint adoption, one of the adopters is a British overseas territories citizen, and

        (ii)   the adopter or, in the case of a joint adoption, both of the adopters are habitually resident in a designated territory, and

    (c)   the Convention adoption is effected under the law of a country or territory outside the designated territory,

the minor shall be a British overseas territories citizen as from that date.]

(6)   Where an order [or a Convention adoption] in consequence of which any person became a [British overseas territories citizen] by virtue of subsection (5) ceases to have effect, whether on annulment or otherwise, the cesser shall not affect the status of that person as such a citizen.

(7)   If in the special circumstances of any particular case the Secretary of State thinks fit, he may for the purposes of subsection (4) treat the person to whom the application relates as fulfilling the requirements specified in that subsection although, as regards any one or more of the first ten years of that person's life, the number of days on which he was absent from the [British overseas territory] there mentioned in that year or each of the years in question exceeds 90.

Amendment

Sub-s (1): words "British overseas territory" in square brackets in both places they occur substituted by the British Overseas Territories Act 2002, s 1(1)(b).

Sub-s (1): words "British overseas territories citizen" in square brackets in both places they occur substituted by the British Overseas Territories Act 2002, s 2(2)(b).

Sub-s (2): words "British overseas territory" in square brackets in both places they occur substituted by the British Overseas Territories Act 2002, s 1(1)(b).

Sub-s (2): words "British overseas territories citizen" in square brackets substituted by the British Overseas Territories Act 2002, s 2(2)(b).

Sub-s (3): words "British overseas territory" in square brackets in both places they occur substituted by the British Overseas Territories Act 2002, s 1(1)(b).

Sub-s (3): words "British overseas territories citizen" in square brackets substituted by the British Overseas Territories Act 2002, s 2(2)(b).

Sub-s (4): words "British overseas territory" in square brackets substituted by the British Overseas Territories Act 2002, s 1(1)(b).

Sub-s (4): words "British overseas territories citizen" in square brackets in both places they occur substituted by the British Overseas Territories Act 2002, s 2(2)(b).

Sub-s (5): words "British overseas territories citizen" in square brackets in each place they occur substituted by the British Overseas Territories Act 2002, s 2(2)(b).

Sub-s (5): words "British overseas territory" in square brackets substituted by the British Overseas Territories Act 2002, s 1(1)(b).

Sub-s (5A): inserted by the Adoption and Children Act 2002, s 137(3), (5)(a).

Sub-s (6): words "or a Convention adoption" in square brackets inserted by the Adoption and Children Act 2002, s 137(3), (5)(b).

Sub-s (6): words "British overseas territories citizen" in square brackets substituted by the British Overseas Territories Act 2002, s 2(2)(b).

Sub-s (7): words "British overseas territory" in square brackets substituted by the British Overseas Territories Act 2002, s 1(1)(b).

16 Acquisition by descent

(1)   A person born outside the [British overseas territories] after commencement shall be a [British overseas territories citizen] if at the time of the birth his father or mother—

    (a)   is such a citizen otherwise than by descent; or

    (b)   is such a citizen and is serving outside the [British overseas territories] in service to which this paragraph applies, his or her recruitment for that service having taken place in a [British overseas territory].

(2)   Paragraph (b) of subsection (1) applies to—

    (a)   Crown service under the government of a [British overseas territory]; and

    (b)   service of any description for the time being designated under subsection (3).

(3)   For the purposes of this section the Secretary of State may by order made by statutory instrument designate any description of service which he considers to be closely associated with the activities outside the [British overseas territories] of the government of any [British overseas territory].

(4)   Any order made under subsection (3) shall be subject to annulment in pursuance of a resolution of either House of Parliament.

Amendment

Sub-s (1): words "British overseas territory" and words "British overseas territories" in square brackets in both places they occur substituted by the British Overseas Territories Act 2002, s 1(1)(b).

Sub-s (1): words "British overseas territories citizen" in square brackets substituted by the British Overseas Territories Act 2002, s 2(2)(b).

Sub-s (2): in para (a) words "British overseas territory" in square brackets substituted by the British Overseas Territories Act 2002, s 1(1)(b).

Sub-s (3): words "British overseas territories" and "British overseas territory" in square brackets substituted by the British Overseas Territories Act 2002, s 1(1)(b).

Subordinate Legislation

British Dependent Territories Citizenship [British Overseas Territories Citizenship] (Designated Service) Order 1982, SI 1982/1710.

British Overseas Territories Citizenship (Designated Service) (Amendment) Order 2008, SI 2008/1207.

17 Acquisition by registration: minors

(1)   If while a person is a minor an application is made for his registration as a British Territories citizen the Secretary of State may, if he thinks fit, cause him to be registered as such a citizen.

(2)   A person born outside the [British overseas territories] shall be entitled, on an application for his registration as a [British overseas territories citizen] made within the period of twelve months from the date of the birth, to be registered as such a citizen if the requirements specified in subsection (3) or, in the case of a person born stateless, the requirements specified in paragraphs (a) and (b) of that subsection, are fulfilled in the case of either that person's father or mother ("the parent in question").

(3)   The requirements referred to in subsection (2) are—

    (a)   that the parent in question was a [British overseas territores citizen] by descent at the time of the birth; and

    (b)   that the father or mother of the parent in question—

        (i)   was a [British overseas territories citizen] otherwise than by descent at the time of birth of the parent in question; or

      (ii)   became a [British overseas territories citizen] otherwise than by descent at commencement, or would have become such a citizen otherwise than by descent at commencement but for his or her death; and

  (c)   that, as regards some period of three years ending with a date not later than the date of the birth—

      (i)   the parent in question was in a [British overseas territory] at the beginning of that period; and

      (ii)   the number of days on which the parent in question was absent from that territory in that period does not exceed 270.

(4) If in the special circumstances of any particular case the Secretary of State thinks fit, he may treat subsection (2) as if the reference to twelve months were a reference to six years.

(5) A person born outside the [British overseas territories] shall be entitled, on an application for his registration as a [British overseas territories citizen] made while he is a minor, to be registered as such a citizen if the following requirements are satisfied, namely—

  (a)   that at the time of that person's birth his father or mother was a [British overseas territories citizen] by descent; and

  (b)   subject to subsection (6), that that person and his father and mother were in one and the same [British overseas territory] (no matter which) at the beginning of the period of three years ending with the date of the application and that, in the case of each of them, the number of days on which the person in question was absent from the last-mentioned territory in that period does not exceed 270; and

  (c)   subject to subsection (6), that the consent of his father and mother to the registration has been signified in the prescribed manner.

(6) In the case of an application under subsection (5) for the registration of a person as a [British overseas territories citizen]—

  (a)   if his father or mother died, or their marriage [or civil partnership] was terminated, on or before the date of the application, or his father and mother were legally separated on that date, the references to his father and mother in paragraph (b) of that subsection shall be read either as references to his father or as references to his mother; [and]

  (b)   if his father or mother died on or before that date, the reference to his father and mother in paragraph (c) of that subsection shall be read as a reference to either of them; . . .

  (c)   . . .

Amendment

Sub-s (2): words "British overseas territories" in square brackets substituted by the British Overseas Territories Act 2002, s 1(1)(b).

Sub-s (2): words "British overseas territories citizen" in square brackets substituted by the British Overseas Territories Act 2002, s 2(2)(b).

Sub-s (3): words "British overseas territories citizen" in square brackets in each place they occur substituted by the British Overseas Territories Act 2002, s 2(2)(b).

Sub-s (3): in para (c)(ii) words "British overseas territory" in square brackets substituted by the British Overseas Territories Act 2002, s 1(1)(b).

Sub-s (5): words "British overseas territories" in square brackets substituted by the British Overseas Territories Act 2002, s 1(1)(b).

Sub-s (5): words "British overseas territories citizen" in square brackets in both places they occur substituted by the British Overseas Territories Act 2002, s 2(2)(b).

Sub-s (5): in para (b) words "British overseas territory" in square brackets substituted by the British Overseas Territories Act 2002, s 1(1)(b).

Sub-s (6): words "British overseas territories citizen" in square brackets substituted by the British Overseas Territories Act 2002, s 2(2)(b).

Sub-s (6): in para (a) words "or civil partnership" in square brackets inserted by the Civil Partnership Act 2004, s 261(1), Sch 27, para 75.

Sub-s (6): in para (a) word "and" in square brackets inserted by the Nationality, Immigration and Asylum Act 2002, s 9(3)(a).

Sub-s (6): in para (b) word omitted repealed by the Nationality, Immigration and Asylum Act 2002, ss 9(3)(b), 161, Sch 9.

Sub-s (6): para (c) repealed by the Nationality, Immigration and Asylum Act 2002, ss 9(3)(c), 161, Sch 9.

18 Acquisition by naturalisation

(1) If, on an application for naturalisation as a [British overseas territories citizen] made by a person of full age and capacity, the Secretary of State is satisfied that the applicant fulfils the requirements of Schedule 1 for naturalisation as such a citizen under this subsection, he may, if he thinks fit, grant to him a certificate of naturalisation as such a citizen.

(2) If, on an application for naturalisation as a [British overseas territories citizen] made by a person of full age and capacity who on the date of the application is married to such a citizen [or is the civil partner of such a citizen], the Secretary of State is satisfied that the applicant fulfils the requirements of Schedule 1 for naturalisation as such a citizen under this subsection, he may, if he thinks fit, grant to him a certificate of naturalisation as such a citizen.

(3) Every application under this section shall specify the [British overseas territory] which is to be treated as the relevant territory for the purposes of that application; and, in relation to any such application, references in Schedule 1 to the relevant territory shall be construed accordingly.

Amendment

Sub-s (1): words "British overseas territories citizen" in square brackets substituted by the British Overseas Territories Act 2002, s 2(2)(b).

Sub-s (2): words "British overseas territories citizen" in square brackets substituted by the British Overseas Territories Act 2002, s 2(2)(b).

Sub-s (2): words "or is the civil partner of such a citizen" in square brackets inserted by the Civil Partnership Act 2004, s 261(1), Sch 27, para 76.

Sub-s (3): words "British overseas territory" in square brackets substituted by the British Overseas Territories Act 2002, s 1(1)(b).

Acquisition after commencement: special cases

19–21

(Repealed by the Nationality, Immigration and Asylum Act 2002, ss 15, 161, Sch 2, para 1(d)–(f), Sch 9.)

22 Right to registration replacing right to resume citizenship of UK and colonies

(1) Subject to subsection (3), a person shall be entitled, on an application for his registration as a [British overseas territories citizen], to be registered as such a citizen if immediately before commencement he would (had he applied for it) have been entitled under section 1(1) of the British Nationality Act 1964 (resumption of citizenship) to be registered as a citizen of the United Kingdom and Colonies by virtue of having an appropriate qualifying connection with a [British overseas territory] or. . . by virtue of having been married before commencement to a person who has, or would if living have, such a connection.

(2) On an application for his registration as a [British overseas territories citizen] made by a person of full capacity who had before commencement ceased to be a citizen of the United Kingdom and Colonies as a result of a declaration of

renunciation, the Secretary of State may, if he thinks fit, cause that person to be registered as a [British overseas territories citizen] if that person—

    (a)   has an appropriate qualifying connection with a [British overseas territory]; or

    (b)   . . . has been married to[, or has been the civil partner of,] a person who has, or would if living have, such a connection.

(3) A person shall not be entitled to registration under subsection (1) on more than one occasion.

(4) For the purposes of this section a person shall be taken to have an appropriate qualifying connection with a [British overseas territory] if he, his father or his father's father—

    (a)   was born in that territory; or

    (b)   is or was a person naturalised in that territory; or

    (c)   was registered as a citizen of the United Kingdom and Colonies in that territory; or

    (d)   became a British subject by reason of the annexation of any territory included in that territory.

Amendment

Sub-s (1): words "British overseas territories citizen" in square brackets substituted by the British Overseas Territories Act 2002, s 2(2)(b).

Sub-s (1): words "British overseas territory" in square brackets substituted by the British Overseas Territories Act 2002, s 1(1)(b).

Sub-s (1): words omitted repealed by the Nationality, Immigration and Asylum Act 2002, ss 5(b), 161, Sch 9.

Sub-s (2): words "British overseas territories citizen" in square brackets in both places they occur substituted by the British Overseas Territories Act 2002, s 2(2)(b).

Sub-s (2): in para (a) words "British overseas territory" in square brackets substituted by the British Overseas Territories Act 2002, s 1(1)(b).

Sub-s (2): in para (b) words omitted repealed by the Nationality, Immigration and Asylum Act 2002, ss 5(b), 161, Sch 9.

Sub-s (2): in para (b) words ", or has been the civil partner of," in square brackets inserted by the Civil Partnership Act 2004, s 261(1), Sch 27, para 77.

Sub-s (4): words "British overseas territory" in square brackets substituted by the British Overseas Territories Act 2002, s 1(1)(b).

Acquisition at commencement

23 Citizens of UK and Colonies who are to become [British overseas territories citizens] at commencement

(1) A person shall at commencement become a [British overseas territories citizen] if—

    (a)   immediately before commencement he was a citizen of the United Kingdom and Colonies who had that citizenship by his birth, naturalisation or registration in a [British overseas territory]; or

    (b)   he was immediately before commencement a citizen of the United Kingdom and Colonies, and was born to a parent—

        (i)   who at the time of the birth ("the material time") was a citizen of the United Kingdom and Colonies; and

        (ii)   who either had that citizenship at the material time by his birth, naturalisation or registration in a [British overseas territory] or was himself born to a parent who at the time of that birth so had that citizenship; or

    (c)   being a woman, she was immediately before commencement a citizen of the United Kingdom and Colonies and either was then, or had at any time been, the wife of a man who under paragraph (a) or (b) becomes a [British overseas territories citizen] at commencement or would have done so but for his death.

(2)   A person shall at commencement become a [British overseas territories citizen] if—

    (a)   immediately before commencement he was a citizen of the United Kingdom and Colonies by virtue of registration under section 7 of the 1948 Act (minor children) or section 1 of the British Nationality (No. 2) Act 1964 (stateless persons); and

    (b)   he was so registered otherwise than in a [British overseas territory]; and

    (c)   his father or mother (in the case of a person registered under the said section 7) or his mother (in the case of a person registered under the said section 1)—

        (i)   was a citizen of the United Kingdom and Colonies at the time of the registration or would have been such a citizen at that time but for his or her death; and

        (ii)   becomes a [British overseas territories citizen] at commencement or would have done so but for his or her death.

(3)   A person who—

    (a)   immediately before commencement was a citizen of the United Kingdom and Colonies by virtue of having been registered under subsection (6) of section 12 of the 1948 Act (British subjects before commencement of 1948 Act becoming citizens of United Kingdom and Colonies) otherwise than in a [British overseas territory]; and

    (b)   was so registered on an application under that subsection based on the applicant's descent in the male line from a person ("the relevant person") possessing one of the qualifications specified in subsection (1) of that section (birth or naturalisation in the United Kingdom and Colonies, or acquisition of the status of British subject by reason of annexation of territory),

shall at commencement become a [British overseas territories citizen] if the relevant person—

        (i)   was born or naturalised in a [British overseas territory]; or

        (ii)   became a British subject by reason of the annexation of any territory included in a [British overseas territory].

(4)   A person who—

    (a)   immediately before commencement was a citizen of the United Kingdom and Colonies by virtue of registration under section 1 of the British Nationality Act 1964 (resumption of citizenship); and

    (b)   was so registered otherwise than in a [British overseas territory]; and

    (c)   was so registered by virtue of having an appropriate qualifying connection with a [British overseas territory] or, if a woman, by virtue of having been married to a person who at the time of the registration had or would, if then living, have had such a connection,

shall at commencement become a [British overseas territories citizen].

(5)   For the purposes of subsection (4) a person shall be taken to have an appropriate qualifying connection with a [British overseas territory] if he, his father or his father's father—

    (a)   was born in a [British overseas territory]; or

    (b)   is or was a person naturalised in a [British overseas territory]; or

    (c)   was registered as a citizen of the United Kingdom and Colonies in a [British overseas territory]; or

    (d)   became a British subject by reason of the annexation of any territory included in a [British overseas territory].

(6) For the purposes of subsection (1)(b) references to citizenship of the United Kingdom and Colonies shall, in relation to a time before the year 1949, be construed as references to British nationality.

Amendment

Section heading: words "British overseas territories citizens" in square brackets substituted by the British Overseas Territories Act 2002, s 2(2)(b).

Sub-s (1): words "British overseas territories citizen" in square brackets in both places they occur substituted by the British Overseas Territories Act 2002, s 2(2)(b).

Sub-s (1): words "British overseas territory" in square brackets in both places they occur substituted by the British Overseas Territories Act 2002, s 1(1)(b).

Sub-s (2): words "British overseas territories citizen" in square brackets in both places they occur substituted by the British Overseas Territories Act 2002, s 2(2)(b).

Sub-s (2): in para (b) words "British overseas territory" in square brackets substituted by the British Overseas Territories Act 2002, s 1(1)(b).

Sub-s (3): words "British overseas territory" in square brackets in each place they occur substituted by the British Overseas Territories Act 2002, s 1(1)(b).

Sub-s (3): words "British overseas territories citizen" in square brackets substituted by the British Overseas Territories Act 2002, s 2(2)(b).

Sub-s (4): words "British overseas territory" in square brackets in both places they occur substituted by the British Overseas Territories Act 2002, s 1(1)(b).

Sub-s (4): words "British overseas territories citizen" in square brackets substituted by the British Overseas Territories Act 2002, s 2(2)(b).

Sub-s (5): words "British overseas territory" in square brackets in each place they occur substituted by the British Overseas Territories Act 2002, s 1(1)(b).

Renunciation and resumption

24 Renunciation and resumption

The provisions of sections 12 and 13 shall apply in relation to [British overseas territories citizens] and [British overseas territories citizenship] as they apply in relation to British citizens and British citizenship.

Amendment

Words "British overseas territories citizens" in square brackets substituted by the British Overseas Territories Act 2002, s 2(2)(b).

Words "British overseas territories citizenship" in square brackets substituted by the British Overseas Territories Act 2002, s 2(2)(a).

Supplementary

25 Meaning of [British overseas territories citizen] "by descent"

(1) For the purposes of this Act a [British overseas territories citizen] is such a citizen "by descent" if and only if—

(a) he is a person born outside the [British overseas territories] after commencement who is a [British overseas territories citizen] by virtue by section 16(1)(a) only or by virtue of registration under section 17(2) or 21; or

(b) subject to subsection (2), he is a person born outside the [British overseas territories] before commencement who became a [British overseas territories citizen] at commencement and immediately before commencement—

(i) was a citizen of the United Kingdom and Colonies by virtue of section 5 of the 1948 Act (citizenship by descent); or

(ii) was a person who, under any provision of the British Nationality Acts 1948 to 1965, was deemed for the purposes of the proviso to section 5(1) of the 1948 Act to be a citizen of the United Kingdom and Colonies by descent only, or would have been so deemed if male; or

(c) he is a [British overseas territories citizen] by virtue of registration under section 17(1) and either—

    (i) his father or mother was a [British overseas territories citizen] at the time of the birth; or

    (ii) his father or mother was a citizen of the United Kingdom and Colonies at that time and became a [British overseas territories citizen] at commencement, or would have done so but for his or her death; or

(d) subject to subsection (2), he is a person born outside the [British overseas territories] before commencement who became a [British overseas territories citizen] at commencement under section 23(1)(b) only; or

(e) subject to subsection (2), being a woman, she became a [British overseas territories citizen] at commencement under section 23(1)(c) only, and did so only by virtue of having been, immediately before commencement or earlier, the wife of a man who immediately after commencement was, or would but for his death have been, a [British overseas territories citizen] by descent by virtue of paragraph (b) or (d) of this subsection; or

(f) subject to subsection (2), being a woman born outside the [British overseas territories] before commencement, she is a [British overseas territories citizen] as such a citizen by virtue of her registration as such a citizen under section 20 by virtue of being or having been married to a man who at commencement became such a citizen by descent or would have done so but for his having died or ceased to be a citizen of the United Kingdom and Colonies as a result of a declaration of renunciation; or

(g) he is a [British overseas territories citizen] by virtue of registration under section 22 who, having before commencement ceased to be a citizen of the United Kingdom and Colonies as a result of a declaration of renunciation, would, if he had not so ceased, have at commencement become a [British overseas territories citizen] by descent by virtue of paragraph (b), (d) or (e); or

(h) he is a [British overseas territories citizen] by virtue of registration under section 13 (as applied by section 24) who, immediately before he ceased to be a [British overseas territories citizen] as a result of a declaration of renunciation, was such a citizen by descent; or

(i) he is a person born in the United Kingdom after commencement who is a [British overseas territories citizen] by virtue of paragraph 1 of Schedule 2.

(2) A person born outside the [British overseas territories] before commencement is not a [British overseas territories citizen] "by descent" by virtue of subsection (1)(b), (d), (e) or (f) if his father was at the time of his birth serving outside the [British overseas territories] in service of a description mentioned in subsection (3), his recruitment for the service in question having taken place in a [British overseas territory].

(3) The descriptions of service referred to in subsection (2) are—

(a) Crown service under the government of a [British overseas territory]; and

(b) service of any description at any time designated under section 16(3).

Amendment

Section heading: words "British overseas territories citizen" in square brackets substituted by the British Overseas Territories Act 2002, s 2(2)(b).

Sub-s (1): words "British overseas territories citizen" in square brackets in each place they occur substituted by the British Overseas Territories Act 2002, s 2(2)(b).

Sub-s (1): words "British overseas territories" in square brackets in each place they occur substituted by the British Overseas Territories Act 2002, s 1(1)(b).

Sub-s (2): words "British overseas territory" and words "British overseas territories" in square brackets in both places they occur substituted by the British Overseas Territories Act 2002, s 1(1)(b).

Sub-s (2): words "British overseas territories citizen" in square brackets substituted by the British Overseas Territories Act 2002, s 2(2)(b).

Sub-s (3): words "British overseas territory" in square brackets substituted by the British Overseas Territories Act 2002, s 1(1)(b).

PART III
BRITISH OVERSEAS CITIZENSHIP

26 Citizens of UK and Colonies who are to become British Overseas citizens at commencement

Any person who was a citizen of the United Kingdom and Colonies immediately before commencement and who does not at commencement become either a British citizen or a [British overseas territories citizen] shall at commencement become a British Overseas citizen.

Amendment

Words "British overseas territories citizen" in square brackets substituted by the British Overseas Territories Act 2002, s 2(2)(b).

27 Registration of minors

(1)   If while a person is a minor an application is made for his registration as a British Overseas citizen, the Secretary of State may, if he thinks fit, cause him to be registered as such a citizen.

(2)   . . .

Amendment

Sub-s (2): repealed by the Nationality, Immigration and Asylum Act 2002, ss 15, 161, Sch 2, para 1(g), Sch 9.

28

(Repealed by the Nationality, Immigration and Asylum Act 2002, ss 15, 161, Sch 2, para 1(h), Sch 9.)

29 Renunciation

The provisions of section 12 shall apply in relation to British Overseas citizens and British Overseas citizenship as they apply in relation to British citizens and British citizenship.

PART IV
BRITISH SUBJECTS

30 Continuance as British subjects of existing British subjects of certain descriptions

A person who immediately before commencement was—

(a)   a British subject without citizenship by virtue of section 13 to 16 of the 1948 Act; or

(b)   a British subject by virtue of section 1 of the British Nationality Act 1965 (registration of alien women who have been married to British subjects of certain descriptions),

shall as from commencement be a British subject by virtue of this section.

31 Continuance as British subjects of certain former citizens of Eire

(1) A person is within this subsection if immediately before 1st January 1949 he was both a citizen of Eire and a British subject.

(2) A person within subsection (1) who immediately before commencement was a British subject by virtue of section 2 of the 1948 Act (continuance of certain citizens of Eire as British subjects) shall as from commencement be a British subject by virtue of this subsection.

(3) If at any time after commencement a citizen of the Republic of Ireland who is within subsection (1) but is not a British subject by virtue of subsection (2) gives notice in writing to the Secretary of State claiming to remain a British subject on either or both of the following grounds, namely—

(a) that he is or has been in Crown Service under the government of the United Kingdom; and

(b) that he has associations by way of descent, residence or otherwise with the United Kingdom or with any [British overseas territory],

he shall as from that time be a British subject by virtue of this subsection.

(4) A person who is a British subject by virtue of subsection (2) or (3) shall be deemed to have remained a British subject from 1st January 1949 to the time when (whether already a British subject by virtue of the said section 2 or not) he became a British subject by virtue of that subsection.

Amendment

Sub-s (3): in para (b) words "British overseas territory" in square brackets substituted by the British Overseas Territories Act 2002, s 1(1)(b).

32 Registration of minors

If while a person is a minor an application is made for his registration as a British subject, the Secretary of State may, if he thinks fit, cause him to be registered as a British subject.

33

(*Repealed by the Nationality, Immigration and Asylum Act 2002, ss 15, 161, Sch 2, para 1(i), Sch 9.*)

34 Renunciation

The provisions of section 12 shall apply in relation to British subjects and the status of a British subject as they apply in relation to British citizens and British citizenship.

35 Circumstances in which British subjects are to lose that status

A person who under this Act is a British subject otherwise than by virtue of section 31 shall cease to be such a subject if, in whatever circumstances and whether under this Act or otherwise, he acquires any other citizenship or nationality whatever.

PART V
MISCELLANEOUS AND SUPPLEMENTARY

36 Provisions for reducing statelessness

The provisions of Schedule 2 shall have effect for the purpose of reducing statelessness.

37 Commonwealth citizenship

(1) Every person who—

(a) under [the British Nationality Acts 1981 and 1983] [or the British Overseas Territories Act 2002] is a British citizen, a [British overseas territories citizen], [a British National (Overseas),] a British Overseas citizen or a British subject; or

(b)   under any enactment for the time being in force in any country mentioned in Schedule 3 is a citizen of that country,

shall have the status of a Commonwealth citizen.

(2)   Her Majesty may by Order in Council amend Schedule 3 by the alteration of any entry, the removal of any entry, or the insertion of any additional entry.

(3)   Any Order in Council made under this section shall be subject to annulment in pursuance of a resolution of either House of Parliament.

(4)   After commencement no person shall have the status of a Commonwealth citizen or the status of a British subject otherwise than under this Act.

Amendment

Sub-s (1): in para (a) words the British Nationality Acts 1981 and 1983? in square brackets substituted by the British Nationality (Falkland Islands) Act 1983, s 4(3).

Sub-s (1): in para (a) words "or the British Overseas Territories Act 2002" in square brackets inserted by the British Overseas Territories Act 2002, s 5, Sch 1, para 4.

Sub-s (1): in para (a) words "British overseas territories citizen" in square brackets substituted by the British Overseas Territories Act 2002, s 2(2)(b).

Sub-s (1): in para (a) words "a British National (Overseas)," in square brackets inserted by SI 1986/948, art 7.

Modification

Modification: in sub-s (1) reference to the British Nationality Act 1981 modified to include the Hong Kong (British Nationality) Order 1986, by the Hong Kong (British Nationality) Order 1986, SI 1986/948, art 7(3).

See Further

See further: the British Nationality (Hong Kong) Act 1990, s 2.

Subordinate Legislation

British Nationality (Brunei) Order 1983, SI 1983/1699; British Nationality (Pakistan) Order 1989, SI 1989/1331; British Nationality (Namibia) Order 1990, SI 1990/1502; British Nationality (Cameroon and Mozambique) Order 1998, SI 1998/3161; British Nationality (Rwanda) Order 2010, SI 2010/246.

38 British protected persons

(1)   Her Majesty may by Order in Council made in relation to any territory which was at any time before commencement—

(a)   a protectorate or protected state for the purposes of the 1948 Act; or

(b)   a United Kingdom trust territory within the meaning of that Act,

declare to be British protected persons for the purposes of this Act any class of person who are connected with that territory and are not citizens of any country mentioned in Schedule 3 which consists of or includes that territory.

(2)   Any Order in Council made under this section shall be subject to annulment in pursuance of a resolution of either House of Parliament.

Subordinate Legislation

British Protectorates, Protected States and Protected Persons Order 1982, SI 1982/1070.
British Nationality (Brunei) Order 1983, SI 1983/1699.

39 Amendment of Immigration Act 1971

(1)–(5) . . .

(6)   Schedule 4 (which contains further amendments of the Immigration Act 1971) shall have effect.

(7) . . .

(8)   A certificate of patriality issued under the Immigration Act 1971 and in force immediately before commencement shall have effect after commencement as if it were a certificate of entitlement issued under that Act [as in force after commencement], unless at commencement the holder ceases to have right of abode in the United Kingdom.

Amendment

Sub-ss (1), (2), (4): substitute the Immigration Act 1971, s 2, and insert s 8(5A) thereof.

Sub-ss (3), (5): repealed by the Immigration Act 1988, s 3(3).

Sub-s (7): amends the Mental Health Act 1959, s 90, and the Mental Health (Scotland) Act 1960, s 82; repealed in part by the Mental Health Act 1983, s 148(3), Sch 6.

Sub-s (8): words in square brackets substituted by the Immigration Act 1988, s 3(3).

See Further

See further, the extension of this section to the Isle of Man: the Immigration (Isle of Man) Order 2008, SI 2008/680, art 8(1), (2)(a), (b).

[40 Deprivation of citizenship

(1)   In this section a reference to a person's "citizenship status" is a reference to his status as—

- (a)   a British citizen,
- (b)   a British overseas territories citizen,
- (c)   a British Overseas citizen,
- (d)   a British National (Overseas),
- (e)   a British protected person, or
- (f)   a British subject.

[(2)   The Secretary of State may by order deprive a person of a citizenship status if the Secretary of State is satisfied that deprivation is conducive to the public good.]

(3)   The Secretary of State may by order deprive a person of a citizenship status which results from his registration or naturalisation if the Secretary of State is satisfied that the registration or naturalisation was obtained by means of—

- (a)   fraud,
- (b)   false representation, or
- (c)   concealment of a material fact.

(4)   The Secretary of State may not make an order under subsection (2) if he is satisfied that the order would make a person stateless.

[(4A)   But that does not prevent the Secretary of State from making an order under subsection (2) to deprive a person of a citizenship status if—

- (a)   the citizenship status results from the person's naturalisation,
- (b)   the Secretary of State is satisfied that the deprivation is conducive to the public good because the person, while having that citizenship status, has conducted him or herself in a manner which is seriously prejudicial to the vital interests of the United Kingdom, any of the Islands, or any British overseas territory, and
- (c)   the Secretary of State has reasonable grounds for believing that the person is able, under the law of a country or territory outside the United Kingdom, to become a national of such a country or territory.]

(5)   Before making an order under this section in respect of a person the Secretary of State must give the person written notice specifying—

- (a)   that the Secretary of State has decided to make an order,
- (b)   the reasons for the order, and
- (c)   the person's right of appeal under section 40A(1) or under section 2B of the Special Immigration Appeals Commission Act 1997 (c 68).

(6)   Where a person acquired a citizenship status by the operation of a law which applied to him because of his registration or naturalisation under an enactment having effect before commencement, the Secretary of State may by order deprive the person of the citizenship status if the Secretary of State is satisfied that the registration or naturalisation was obtained by means of—

- (a)   fraud,
- (b)   false representation, or
- (c)   concealment of a material fact.]

Amendment

Substituted, together with s 40A for this section as originally enacted, by the Nationality, Immigration and Asylum Act 2002, s 4(1); for transitional provisions see sub-s (4) thereof.

Sub-s (2): substituted by the Immigration, Asylum and Nationality Act 2006, s 56(1).

Sub-s (4A): inserted by the Immigration Act 2014, s 66(1), as from 28 July 2014.

See Further

See further, in relation to British Nationals (Overseas) and their status: the Hong Kong (British Nationality) Order 1986, SI 1986/948, art 7(11).

See further: the British Nationality (Hong Kong) Act 1990, s 2.

See further: the British Nationality (Hong Kong) Act 1997, s 2.

[40A Deprivation of citizenship: appeal]

[(1)   A person who is given notice under section 40(5) of a decision to make an order in respect of him under section 40 may appeal against the decision to [the First-tier Tribunal].

(2)   Subsection (1) shall not apply to a decision if the Secretary of State certifies that it was taken wholly or partly in reliance on information which in his opinion should not be made public—

    (a)   in the interests of national security,

    (b)   in the interests of the relationship between the United Kingdom and another country, or

    (c)   otherwise in the public interest.

[(3)   The following provisions of the Nationality, Immigration and Asylum Act 2002 (c 41) shall apply in relation to an appeal under this section as they apply in relation to an appeal under section 82 . . . of that Act—

    (a)   *section 87 (successful appeal: direction) (for which purpose a direction may, in particular, provide for an order under section 40 above to be treated as having had no effect),*

    (b)   . . .

    (c)   section 106 (rules), . . .

    (d)   section 107 (practice directions)[, and

    (e)   section 108 (forged document: proceedings in private)].]

(6)   . . .

(7)   . . .

(8)   . . .]

Amendment

Substituted, together with s 40 for s 40 as originally enacted, by the Nationality, Immigration and Asylum Act 2002, s 4(1).

Sub-s (1): words "the First-tier Tribunal" in square brackets substituted by SI 2010/21, art 5(1), Sch 1, para 7(a).

Sub-s (3): substituted, for sub-ss (3)–(5), by the Asylum and Immigration (Treatment of Claimants, etc) Act 2004, s 26(7), Sch 2, Pt 1, para 4(b); for transitional provisions see s 26(7), Sch 2, Pt 2 thereto.

Sub-s (3): words ", 83 or 83A" (omitted in the first place) repealed by the Immigration Act 2014, s 73, Sch 9, Pt 4, para 25(a), as from 20 October 2014 (see SI 2014/2771, art 2), subject to savings in SI 2014/2771, arts 9–11.

Sub-s (3): para (a) repealed by the Immigration Act 2014, s 73, Sch 9, Pt 4, para 25(b), as from 20 October 2014 (see SI 2014/2771, art 2), subject to savings in SI 2014/2771, arts 9–11.

Sub-s (3): para (b) repealed by SI 2010/21, art 5(1), Sch 1, para 7(b).

Sub-s (3): in para (c) word omitted repealed by the Immigration, Asylum and Nationality Act 2006, ss 56(2), 61, Sch 3.

Sub-s (3): para (e) and word ", and" immediately preceding it inserted by the Immigration, Asylum and Nationality Act 2006, s 56(2).

Sub-ss (6)–(8): repealed by the Asylum and Immigration (Treatment of Claimants, etc) Act 2004, ss 26(7), 47, Sch 2, Pt 1, para 4(c), Sch 4; for transitional provisions see s 26(7), Sch 2, Pt 2 thereto.

Subordinate Legislation
Asylum and Immigration Tribunal (Fast Track Procedure) Rules 2005, SI 2005/560.

[40B Review of power under section 40(4A)

(1)   The Secretary of State must arrange for a review of the operation of the relevant deprivation power to be carried out in relation to each of the following periods—

(a)   the initial one year period;

(b)   each subsequent three year period.

(2)   The "relevant deprivation power" is the power to make orders under section 40(2) to deprive persons of a citizenship status in the circumstances set out in section 40(4A).

(3)   A review must be completed as soon as practicable after the end of the period to which the review relates.

(4)   As soon as practicable after a person has carried out a review in relation to a particular period, the person must—

(a)   produce a report of the outcome of the review, and

(b)   send a copy of the report to the Secretary of State.

(5)   The Secretary of State must lay before each House of Parliament a copy of each report sent under subsection (4)(b).

(6)   The Secretary of State may, after consultation with the person who produced the report, exclude a part of the report from the copy laid before Parliament if the Secretary of State is of the opinion that it would be contrary to the public interest or prejudicial to national security for that part of the report to be made public.

(7)   The Secretary of State may—

(a)   make such payments as the Secretary of State thinks appropriate in connection with the carrying out of a review, and

(b)   make such other arrangements as the Secretary of State thinks appropriate in connection with the carrying out of a review (including arrangements for the provision of staff, other resources and facilities).

(8)   In this section—

"initial one year period" means the period of one year beginning with the day when section 40(4A) comes into force;

"subsequent three year period" means a period of three years beginning with the first day after the most recent of—

(a)   the initial one year period, or

(b)   the most recent subsequent three year period.]

Amendment
Inserted by the Immigration Act 2014, s 66(3), as from 28 July 2014.

41 Regulations and Orders in Council

(1)   The Secretary of State may by regulations make provision generally for carrying into effect the purposes of this Act, and in particular provision—

(a)   for prescribing anything which under this Act is to be prescribed;

(b)   for prescribing the manner in which, and the persons to and by whom, applications for registration or naturalisation under any provision of this Act may or must be made;

[(bza) requiring an application for registration or naturalisation of a person as a British citizen to be accompanied by biometric information, or enabling an authorised person to require an individual to whom such an application relates to provide biometric information;]

[(ba)   for determining whether a person has sufficient knowledge of a language for the purpose of an application for naturalisation;

(bb)   for determining whether a person has sufficient knowledge about life in the United Kingdom for the purpose of an application for naturalisation;]

[(bc)   for amending paragraph 4B(3)(a) or (b) or (4)(a) or (b) of Schedule 1 to substitute a different number for the number for the time being specified there;

(bd)   for determining whether a person has, for the purposes of an application for naturalisation under section 6, participated in activities prescribed for the purposes of paragraph 4B(5)(a) of Schedule 1;

(be)   for determining whether a person is to be treated for the purposes of such an application as having so participated;]

(c)   for the registration of anything required or authorised by or under this Act to be registered;

[(d)   for the time within which an obligation to make a citizenship oath and pledge at a citizenship ceremony must be satisfied;

(da)   for the time within which an obligation to make a citizenship oath or pledge must be satisfied;

(db)   for the content and conduct of a citizenship ceremony;

(dc)   for the administration and making of a citizenship oath or pledge;

(dd)   for the registration and certification of the making of a citizenship oath or pledge;

(de)   for the completion and grant of a certificate of registration or naturalisation;]

(e)   for the giving of any notice required or authorised to be given to any person under this Act;

(f)   for the cancellation of the registration of, and the cancellation and amendment of certificates of naturalisation relating to persons deprived of citizenship [or of the status of a British National (Overseas)] under this Act, and for requiring such certificates to be delivered up for those purposes;

(g)   for the births and deaths of persons of any class or description born or dying in a country mentioned in Schedule 3 to be registered . . . ;

(h)   for the births and deaths of persons of any class or description born or dying in a foreign country to be registered . . . ;

(i)   . . .

[(j)   as to the consequences of failure to comply with provision made under any of paragraphs (a) to (i)].

[(1ZA) In subsection (1)(bza) "authorised person" and "biometric information" have the same meaning as in section 126 of the Nationality, Immigration and Asylum Act 2002.

(1ZB) Section 126(4) to (7) of that Act applies to regulations under subsection (1)(bza) as it applies to regulations under section 126(1) of that Act.

(1ZC) Section 8 of the UK Borders Act 2007 (power to make regulations about use and retention of biometric information) applies to biometric information provided in accordance with regulations under subsection (1)(bza) as it applies to biometric information provided in accordance with regulations under section 5(1) of that Act.

(1ZD) But (despite section 8(5)(b) of that Act) regulations made by virtue of subsection (1ZC) may provide for photographs of a person who is registered or naturalised as a British citizen to be retained until the person is issued with a United Kingdom passport describing the person as a British citizen.]

[(1A)   Regulations under subsection (1)(ba) or (bb) may, in particular—

(a)   make provision by reference to possession of a specified qualification;

(b)   make provision by reference to possession of a qualification of a specified kind;

(c)   make provision by reference to attendance on a specified course;

(d)   make provision by reference to attendance on a course of a specified kind;

(e)   make provision by reference to a specified level of achievement;

    (f)   enable a person designated by the Secretary of State to determine sufficiency of knowledge in specified circumstances;

    (g)   enable the Secretary of State to accept a qualification of a specified kind as evidence of sufficient knowledge of a language.]

[(1B)   Regulations under subsection (1)(bc) may make provision so that—

    (a)   the number specified in sub-paragraph (3)(a) of paragraph 4B of Schedule 1 is the same as the number specified in sub-paragraph (4)(a) of that paragraph;

    (b)   the number specified in sub-paragraph (3)(b) of that paragraph is the same as the number specified in sub-paragraph (4)(b) of that paragraph.

(1C)   Regulations under subsection (1)(bd) or (be)—

    (a)   may make provision that applies in relation to time before the commencement of section 41 of the Borders, Citizenship and Immigration Act 2009;

    (b)   may enable the Secretary of State to make arrangements for such persons as the Secretary of State thinks appropriate to determine whether, in accordance with those regulations, a person has, or (as the case may be) is to be treated as having, participated in an activity.]

(2)   ...

(3)   Regulations under subsection (1) . . . may make different provision for different circumstances; and—

    (a)   regulations under subsection (1) may provide for the extension of any time-limit for the [making of oaths and pledges of citizenship]; and

    (b)   . . .

[(3A)   Regulations under subsection (1)(d) to (de) may, in particular—

    (a)   enable the Secretary of State to designate or authorise a person to exercise a function (which may include a discretion) in connection with a citizenship ceremony or a citizenship oath or pledge;

    (b)   require, or enable the Secretary of State to require, a local authority to provide specified facilities and to make specified arrangements in connection with citizenship ceremonies;

    (c)   impose, or enable the Secretary of State to impose, a function (which may include a discretion) on a local authority or on a registrar.

(3B)   In subsection (3A)—

"local authority" means—

        (a)   in relation to England and Wales, a county council, a county borough council, a metropolitan district council, a London Borough Council and the Common Council of the City of London, and

        (b)   in relation to Scotland, a council constituted under section 2 of the Local Government etc (Scotland) Act 1994 (c 39), and

"registrar" means—

        (a)   in relation to England and Wales, a superintendent registrar of births, deaths and marriages (or, in accordance with section 8 of the Registration Service Act 1953 (c 37), a deputy superintendent registrar), and

        (b)   in relation to Scotland, a district registrar within the meaning of section 7(12) of the Registration of Births, Deaths and Marriages (Scotland) Act 1965 (c 49).]

(4)   Her Majesty may by Order in Council provide for any Act or Northern Ireland legislation to which this subsection applies to apply, with such adaptations and modifications as appear to Her necessary, to births and deaths registered—

(a)   in accordance with regulations made in pursuance of subsection (1)(g) [and (h)] of this section or subsection (1)(f) and (g) of section 29 of the 1948 Act; or

(b)   at a consulate of Her Majesty in accordance with regulations made under the British Nationality and Status of Aliens Act 1914 to 1943 or in accordance with instructions of the Secretary of State; or

(c)   by a High Commissioner for Her Majesty's government in the United Kingdom or members of his official staff in accordance with instructions of the Secretary of State;

and an Order in Council under this subsection may exclude, in relation to births and deaths so registered, any of the provisions of section 45.

(5) Subsection (4) applies to—

(a)   the Births and Deaths Registration Act 1953, the Registration Service Act 1953 and the Registration of Births, Deaths and Marriages (Scotland) Act 1965; and

(b)   so much of any Northern Ireland legislation for the time being in force (whether passed or made before or after commencement) as relates to the registration of births and deaths.

(6) The power to make regulations under subsection (1) or (2) shall be exercisable by statutory instrument.

(7) Any regulations or Order in Council made under this section [(other than regulations referred to in subsection (8))] shall be subject to annulment in pursuance of a resolution of either House of Parliament.

[(8) Any regulations (whether alone or with other provision)—

(a)   under subsection (1)(a) for prescribing activities for the purposes of paragraph 4B(5)(a) of Schedule 1; or

(b)   under subsection [(1)(bza), (bc)], (bd) or (be),

may not be made unless a draft has been laid before and approved by a resolution of each House of Parliament.]

Amendment

Sub-s (1): para (bza) inserted by the Immigration Act 2014, s 10(1), (2), as from 28 July 2014.

Sub-s (1): paras (ba), (bb) inserted by the Nationality, Immigration and Asylum Act 2002, s 1(3).

Sub-s (1): paras (bc)–(be) inserted by the Borders, Citizenship and Immigration Act 2009, s 41(2), as from a day to be appointed.

Sub-s (1): paras (d), (da)–(de) substituted, for para (d) as originally enacted, by the Nationality, Immigration and Asylum Act 2002, s 3, Sch 1, paras 3, 4.

Sub-s (1): in para (f) words in square brackets inserted by SI 1986/948, art 7(4)(b).

Sub-s (1): words omitted from paras (g), (h) repealed and para (i) repealed by SI 2014/542, art 2(a), as from 1 April 2014.

Sub-s (1): para (j) inserted by the Immigration, Asylum and Nationality Act 2006, s 50(4).

Sub-ss (1ZA)–(1ZD): inserted by the Immigration Act 2014, s 10(1), (3), as from 28 July 2014.

Sub-s (1A): inserted by the Nationality, Immigration and Asylum Act 2002, s 1(4).

Sub-ss (1B), (1C): inserted by the Borders, Citizenship and Immigration Act 2009, s 41(3), as from a day to be appointed.

Sub-s (2): repealed by the Immigration, Asylum and Nationality Act 2006, ss 52(7), 61, Sch 2, para 1(a), Sch 3.

Sub-s (3): words omitted repealed by the Immigration, Asylum and Nationality Act 2006, ss 52(7), 61, Sch 2, para 1(b)(i), Sch 3.

Sub-s (3): in para (a) words "making of oaths and pledges of citizenship" in square brackets substituted by the Nationality, Immigration and Asylum Act 2002, s 3, Sch 1, paras 3, 6.

Sub-s (3): para (b) repealed by the Immigration, Asylum and Nationality Act 2006, ss 52(7), 61, Sch 2, para 1(b)(ii), Sch 3.

Sub-ss (3A), (3B): inserted by the Nationality, Immigration and Asylum Act 2002, s 3, Sch 1, paras 3, 7.

Sub-s (4): words in square brackets in para (a) substituted by SI 2014/542, art 2(b), as from 1 April 2014.

Sub-s (7): words "(other than regulations referred to in subsection (8))" in square brackets inserted by the Borders, Citizenship and Immigration Act 2009, s 41(4), as from a day to be appointed.

Sub-s (8): inserted by the Borders, Citizenship and Immigration Act 2009, s 41(5), as from a day to be appointed.

Sub-s (8): words in square brackets in para (b) substituted by the Immigration Act 2014, s 10(1), (4), as from 28 July 2014.

Modification

Modification: references to the British Nationality Act 1981 modified to include the Hong Kong (British Nationality) Order 1986, by the Hong Kong (British Nationality) Order 1986, SI 1986/948, art 7(4).

The Northern Ireland Act 1998 makes new provision for the government of Northern Ireland for the purpose of implementing the Belfast Agreement (the agreement reached at multi-party talks on Northern Ireland and set out in Command Paper 3883). As a consequence of that Act, any reference in this section to the Parliament of Northern Ireland or the Assembly established under the Northern Ireland Assembly Act 1973, s 1, certain office-holders and Ministers, and any legislative act and certain financial dealings thereof, shall, for the period specified, be construed in accordance with Sch 12, paras 1–11 to the 1998 Act.

See Further

See further: the British Nationality (Hong Kong) Act 1990, s 2.

See further: the British Nationality (Hong Kong) Act 1997, s 2.

Subordinate Legislation

Registration (Entries of Overseas Births and Deaths) Order 1982, SI 1982/1526; Registration of Overseas Births and Deaths (Amendment) Regulations 1982, SI 1982/1647; British Nationality (Hong Kong) Regulations 1986, SI 1986/2175; British Nationality (Hong Kong) Regulations 1986, SI 1986/2175; British Nationality (Hong Kong) (Amendment) Regulations 2003, SI 2003/540; British Nationality (General) Regulations 2003, SI 2003/548; British Nationality (General) (Amendment) Regulations 2003, SI 2003/3158; British Nationality (General) (Amendment) Regulations 2005, SI 2005/2785; British Nationality (General and Hong Kong) (Amendment) Regulations 2007, SI 2007/3137; British Nationality (British Overseas Territories) Regulations 2007, SI 2007/3139; British Nationality (General) (Amendment) Regulations 2009, SI 2009/3363; British Nationality (General) (Amendment) Regulations 2010, SI 2010/785; British Nationality (General) (Amendment) Regulations 2012, SI 2012/1588; British Nationality (General) (Amendment) Regulations 2013, SI 2013/2541; Registration of Overseas Births and Deaths Regulations 2014, SI 2014/511.

[41A Registration: requirement to be of good character]

[(1) An application for registration of an adult or young person as a British citizen under section 1(3), (3A) or (4), 3(1), (2) or (5), 4(2) or (5), 4A, 4C, 4D, [4F, 4G, 4H, 4I,] 5, 10(1) or (2) or 13(1) or (3) must not be granted unless the Secretary of State is satisfied that the adult or young person is of good character.

(2) An application for registration of an adult or young person as a British overseas territories citizen under section 15(3) or (4), 17(1) or (5), 22(1) or (2) or 24 must not be granted unless the Secretary of State is satisfied that the adult or young person is of good character.

(3) An application for registration of an adult or young person as a British Overseas citizen under section 27(1) must not be granted unless the Secretary of State is satisfied that the adult or young person is of good character.

(4) An application for registration of an adult or young person as a British subject under section 32 must not be granted unless the Secretary of State is satisfied that the adult or young person is of good character.

(5) In this section, "adult or young person" means a person who has attained the age of 10 years at the time when the application is made.]

Amendment

Inserted by the Borders, Citizenship and Immigration Act 2009, s 47(1).

Date in force: 13 January 2010: see SI 2009/2731, art 4(f).

Sub-s (1): figures in square brackets inserted by the Immigration Act 2014, s 73, Sch 9, Pt 9, para 70(1), (3), as from a day to be appointed.

[42 Registration and naturalisation: citizenship ceremony, oath and pledge]

[(1)   A person of full age shall not be registered under this Act as a British citizen unless he has made the relevant citizenship oath and pledge specified in Schedule 5 at a citizenship ceremony.

(2)   A certificate of naturalisation as a British citizen shall not be granted under this Act to a person of full age unless he has made the relevant citizenship oath and pledge specified in Schedule 5 at a citizenship ceremony.

(3)   A person of full age shall not be registered under this Act as a British overseas territories citizen unless he has made the relevant citizenship oath and pledge specified in Schedule 5.

(4)   A certificate of naturalisation as a British overseas territories citizen shall not be granted under this Act to a person of full age unless he has made the relevant citizenship oath and pledge specified in Schedule 5.

(5)   A person of full age shall not be registered under this Act as a British Overseas citizen or a British subject unless he has made the relevant citizenship oath specified in Schedule 5.

(6)   Where the Secretary of State thinks it appropriate because of the special circumstances of a case he may—

   (a)   disapply any of subsections (1) to (5), or

   (b)   modify the effect of any of those subsections.

(7)   Sections 5 and 6 of the Oaths Act 1978 (c 19) (affirmation) apply to a citizenship oath; and a reference in this Act to a citizenship oath includes a reference to a citizenship affirmation.]

Amendment

Substituted, together with ss 42A, 42B for this section as originally enacted, by the Nationality, Immigration and Asylum Act 2002, s 3, Sch 1, para 1.

See Further

See further: the British Nationality (Hong Kong) Act 1990, s 2.

See further, in relation to citizens of Mauritius: the Mauritius Republic Act 1992, s 1.

See further: the British Nationality (Hong Kong) Act 1997, s 2.

42A

(*Substituted, together with ss 42, 42B for s 42 as originally enacted, by the Nationality, Immigration and Asylum Act 2002, s 3, Sch 1, para 1. Repealed by the Immigration, Asylum and Nationality Act 2006, ss 52(7), 61, Sch 2, para 2, Sch 3, 2 April 2007: see SI 2007/1109, arts 4, 5, Schedule.*)

[42B Registration and naturalisation: timing]

[(1)   A person who is registered under this Act as a citizen of any description or as a British subject shall be treated as having become a citizen or subject—

   (a)   immediately on making the required citizenship oath and pledge in accordance with section 42, or

   (b)   where the requirement for an oath and pledge is disapplied, immediately on registration.

(2)   A person granted a certificate of naturalisation under this Act as a citizen of any description shall be treated as having become a citizen—

> (a) immediately on making the required citizenship oath and pledge in accordance with section 42, or
>
> (b) where the requirement for an oath and pledge is disapplied, immediately on the grant of the certificate.

(3) In the application of subsection (1) to registration as a British Overseas citizen or as a British subject the reference to the citizenship oath and pledge shall be taken as a reference to the citizenship oath.]

Amendment

Substituted, together with ss 42, 42A for s 42 as originally enacted, by the Nationality, Immigration and Asylum Act 2002, s 3, Sch 1, para 1.

43 Exercise of functions of Secretary of State by Governors and others

(1) Subject to subsection (3), the Secretary of State may, in the case of any of his functions under this Act with respect to any of the matters mentioned in subsection (2), make arrangements for that function to be exercised—

> (a) in any of the Islands, by the Lieutenant-Governor in cases concerning British citizens or British citizenship;
>
> (b) in any [British overseas territory] . . ., by the Governor in cases concerning [British overseas territories citizens] or [British overseas territories citizenship] [and in cases concerning British Nationals (Overseas) or the status of a British National (Overseas)].

(2) The said matters are—

> (a) registration and naturalisation; and
>
> (b) renunciation, resumption and deprivation of British citizenship or [British overseas territories citizenship]
>
> [(c) renunciation and deprivation of the status of a British National (Overseas)].

(3) Nothing in this section applies in the case of any power to make regulations or rules conferred on the Secretary of State by this Act.

(4) Arrangements under subsection (1) may provide for any such function as is there mentioned to be exercisable only with the approval of the Secretary of State.

AMENDMENT

Sub-s (1): in para (b) words "British overseas territory" in square brackets substituted by the British Overseas Territories Act 2002, s 1(1)(b).

Sub-s (1): in para (b) words omitted repealed by the British Overseas Territories Act 2002, s 7, Sch 2.

Sub-s (1): in para (b) words "British overseas territories citizens" in square brackets substituted by the British Overseas Territories Act 2002, s 2(2)(b).

Sub-s (1): in para (b) words "British overseas territories citizenship" in square brackets substituted by the British Overseas Territories Act 2002, s 2(2)(a).

Sub-s (1): in para (b) words from and in cases? to British National (Overseas)? in square brackets inserted by SI 1986/948, art 7(6)(b).

Sub-s (2): in para (b) words "British overseas territories citizenship" in square brackets substituted by the British Overseas Territories Act 2002, s 2(2)(a).

Sub-s (2): para (c) inserted by SI 1986/948, art 7.

Modification

Modification: references to the British Nationality Act 1981 modified to include the Hong Kong (British Nationality) Order 1986, by the Hong Kong (British Nationality) Order 1986, SI 1986/948, art 7(6).

44 Decisions involving exercise of discretion

(1) Any discretion vested by or under this Act in the Secretary of State, a Governor or a Lieutenant-Governor shall be exercised without regard to the race, colour or religion of any person who may be affected by its exercise.

(2) . . .

(3) . . .

Amendment

Sub-ss (2), (3): repealed by the Nationality, Immigration and Asylum Act 2002, ss 7(1), 161, Sch 9.

See Further

See further: the British Nationality (Hong Kong) Act 1990, s 2.

[44A Waiver of requirement for full capacity]

[Where a provision of this Act requires an applicant to be of full capacity, the Secretary of State may waive the requirement in respect of a specified applicant if he thinks it in the applicant's best interests.]

Amendment

Inserted by the Immigration, Asylum and Nationality Act 2006, s 49.

45 Evidence

(1)   Every document purporting to be a notice, certificate, order or declaration, or an entry in a register, or a subscription of an oath of allegiance, given, granted or made under this Act or any of the former nationality Acts shall be received in evidence and shall, unless the contrary is provided, be deemed to have been given, granted or made by or on behalf of the person by whom or on whose behalf it purports to have been given, granted or made.

(2)   Prima facie evidence of any such document may be given by the production of a document purporting to be certified as a true copy of it by such person and in such manner as may be prescribed.

(3)   Any entry in a register made under this Act or any of the former nationality Acts shall be received as evidence (and in Scotland as sufficient evidence) of the matters stated in the entry.

(4)   A certificate given by or on behalf of the Secretary of State that a person was at any time in Crown service under the government of the United Kingdom or that a person's recruitment for such service took place in the United Kingdom shall, for the purposes of this Act, be conclusive evidence of that fact.

Modification

Modification: references to the British Nationality Act 1981 modified to include the Hong Kong (British Nationality) Order 1986, by the Hong Kong (British Nationality) Order 1986, SI 1986/948, art 7(7).

See Further

See further: the British Nationality (Hong Kong) Act 1990, s 2.
See further: the British Nationality (Hong Kong) Act 1997, s 2.

46 Offences and proceedings

(1)   Any person who for the purpose of procuring anything to be done or not to be done under this Act—

    (a)   makes any statement which he knows to be false in a material particular; or

    (b)   recklessly makes any statement which is false in a material particular,

shall be liable on summary conviction in the United Kingdom to imprisonment for a term not exceeding *three months* [51 weeks] or to a fine [not exceeding level 5 on the standard scale], or both.

(2)   Any person who without reasonable excuse fails to comply with any requirement imposed on him by regulations made under this Act with respect to the delivering up of certificates of naturalisation shall be liable on summary conviction in the United Kingdom to a fine [not exceeding level 4 on the standard scale].

(3)   In the case of an offence under subsection (1)—

(a)   any information relating to the offence may in England and Wales be tried by a magistrates' court if it is laid within six months after the commission of the offence, or if it is laid within three years after the commission of the offence and not more than two months after the date certified by a chief officer of police to be the date on which evidence sufficient to justify proceedings came to the notice of an officer of his police force; and

(b)   summary proceedings for the offence may in Scotland be commenced within six months after the commission of the offence, or within three years after the commission of the offence and not more than two months after the date on which evidence sufficient in the opinion of the Lord Advocate to justify proceedings came to his knowledge; and

(c)   a complaint charging the commission of the offence may in Northern Ireland be heard and determined by a magistrates' court if it is made within six months after the commission of the offence, or if it is made within three years after the commission of the offence and not more than two months after the date certified by an officer of police not below the rank of assistant chief constable to be the date on which evidence sufficient to justify the proceedings came to the notice of the police in Northern Ireland.

(4) For the purposes of subsection (3)(b) proceedings shall be deemed to be commenced on the date on which a warrant to apprehend or to cite the accused is granted, if such warrant is executed without undue delay; and a certificate of the Lord Advocate as to the date on which such evidence as is mentioned in subsection (3)(b) came to his knowledge shall be conclusive evidence.

(5) For the purposes of the trial of a person for an offence under subsection (1) or (2), the offence shall be deemed to have been committed either at the place at which it actually was committed or at any place at which he may be.

(6) In their application to the Bailiwick of Jersey subsections (1) and (2) shall have effect with the omission of the words "on summary conviction".

Amendment

Sub-s (1): words "three months" in italics repealed and subsequent words in square brackets substituted by the Criminal Justice Act 2003, s 280(2), (3), Sch 26, para 29, as from a day to be appointed.

Sub-s (1): maximum fine converted to a level on the standard scale by the Criminal Justice Act 1982, ss 37, 46.

Sub-s (2): maximum fine converted to a level on the standard scale by the Criminal Justice Act 1982, ss 37, 46.

Modification

Modification: in sub-s (1) reference to the British Nationality Act 1981 modified to include the Hong Kong (British Nationality) Order 1986, by the Hong Kong (British Nationality) Order 1986, SI 1986/948, art 7(7).

See Further

odification: in sub-s (1) reference to the British Nationality Act 1981 modified to include the Hong Kong (British Nationality) Order 1986, by the Hong Kong (British Nationality) Order 1986, SI 1986/948, art 7(7).

See further: the British Nationality (Hong Kong) Act 1997, s 2.

Transfer of Functions

By virtue of the Scotland Act 1998, s 44(1)(c), the Lord Advocate ceased, on 20 May 1999 (see SI 1998/3178), to be a Minister of the Crown and became a member of the Scottish Executive. Accordingly, certain functions of the Lord Advocate are transferred to the Secretary of State (or as the case may be the Secretary of State for Scotland), or the Advocate General for Scotland: see the Transfer of Functions (Lord Advocate and Secretary of State) Order 1999, SI 1999/678 and the Transfer of Functions (Lord Advocate and Advocate General for Scotland) Order 1999, SI 1999/679.

(Repealed by the Nationality, Immigration and Asylum Act 2002, ss 9(4), 161, Sch 9.)

48 Posthumous children

Any reference in this Act to the status or description of the father or mother of a person at the time of that person's birth shall, in relation to a person born after the death of his father or mother, be construed as a reference to the status or description of the parent in question at the time of that parent's death; and where that death occurred before, and the birth occurs after, commencement, the status or description which would have been applicable to the father or mother had he or she died after commencement shall be deemed to be the status or description applicable to him or her at the time of his or her death.

Modification

Modification: references to the British Nationality Act 1981 modified to include the Hong Kong (British Nationality) Order 1986, by the Hong Kong (British Nationality) Order 1986, SI 1986/948, art 7(7).

See Further

See further: the British Nationality (Hong Kong) Act 1990, s 2.

See further: the British Nationality (Hong Kong) Act 1997, s 2.

49

(Repealed by the British Nationality Act 1981, s 52(8), Sch 9 . . . .)

50 Interpretation

(1) In this Act, unless the context otherwise requires—

"the 1948 Act" means the British Nationality Act 1948;

"alien" means a person who is neither a Commonwealth citizen nor a British protected person nor a citizen of the Republic of Ireland;

["appointed day" means the day appointed by the Secretary of State under section 8 of the British Overseas Territories Act 2002 for the commencement of Schedule 1 to that Act;]

"association" means an unincorporated body of persons;

["British National (Overseas)" means a person who is a British National (Overseas) under the Hong Kong (British Nationality) Order 1986, and "status of a British National (Overseas)" shall be construed accordingly;]

"British Overseas citizen" includes a person who is a British Overseas citizen under the Hong Kong (British Nationality) Order 1986;]

["British overseas territory" means a territory mentioned in Schedule 6;]

"British protected person" means a person who is a member of any class of person declared to be British protected persons by an Order in Council for the time being in force under section 38 or is a British protected person by virtue of the Solomon Islands Act 1978;

"commencement", without more, means the commencement of this Act;

"Commonwealth citizen" means a person who has the status of a Commonwealth citizen under this Act;

"company" means a body corporate;

["Convention adoption" means an adoption effected under the law of a country or territory in which the Convention is in force, and certified in pursuance of Article 23(1) of the Convention;]

"Crown service" means the service of the Crown, whether within Her Majesty's dominions or elsewhere;

"Crown service under the government of the United Kingdom" means Crown service under Her Majesty's government in the United Kingdom or under Her Majesty's government in Northern Ireland [or under the Scottish Administration] [or under the Welsh Assembly Government];

. . .

["designated territory" means a qualifying territory, or the Sovereign Base Areas of Akrotiri and Dhekelia, which is designated by Her Majesty by Order in Council under subsection (14);]

"enactment" includes an enactment comprised in Northern Ireland legislation;

"foreign country" means a country other than the United Kingdom, a [British overseas territory], a country mentioned in Schedule 3 and the Republic of Ireland;

"the former nationality Acts" means—

    (a)   the British Nationality Acts 1948 to 1965;

    (b)   the British Nationality and Status of Aliens Acts 1914 to 1943; and

    (c)   any Act repealed by the said Acts of 1914 to 1943 or by the Naturalization Act 1870;

"Governor", in relation to a [British overseas territory], includes the officer for the time being administering the government of that territory;

"High Commissioner" includes an acting High Commissioner;

"immigration laws"—

    (a)   in relation to the United Kingdom, means the Immigration Act 1971 and any law for purposes similar to that Act which is for the time being or has at any time been in force in any part of the United Kingdom;

    (b)   in relation to a [British overseas territory], means any law for purposes similar to the Immigration Act 1971 which is for the time being or has at any time been in force in that territory;

"the Islands" means the Channel Islands and the Isle of Man;

"minor" means a person who has not attained the age of eighteen years;

"prescribed" means prescribed by regulations made under section 41;

["qualifying territory" means a British overseas territory other than the Sovereign Base Areas of Akrotiri and Dhekelia;]

"settled" shall be construed in accordance with subsections (2) to (4);

"ship" includes a hovercraft;

"statutory provision" means any enactment or any provision contained in—

    (a)   subordinate legislation (as defined in section 21(1) of the Interpretation Act 1978); or

    (b)   any instrument of a legislative character made under any Northern Ireland legislation;

"the United Kingdom" means Great Britain, Northern Ireland and the Islands, taken together;

"United Kingdom consulate" means the office of a consular officer of Her Majesty's government in the United Kingdom where a register of the births is kept or, where there is no such office, such office as may be prescribed.

[(1A)   Subject to subsection (1B), references in this Act to being a member of the armed forces are references to being—

    (a)   a member of the regular forces within the meaning of the Armed Forces Act 2006, or

(b)   a member of the reserve forces within the meaning of that Act subject to service law by virtue of paragraph (a), (b) or (c) of section 367(2) of that Act.

(1B)   A person is not to be regarded as a member of the armed forces by virtue of subsection (1A) if the person is treated as a member of a regular or reserve force by virtue of—

(a)   section 369 of the Armed Forces Act 2006, or

(b)   section 4(3) of the Visiting Forces (British Commonwealth) Act 1933.]

(2)   Subject to subsection (3), references in this Act to a person being settled in the United Kingdom or in a [British overseas territory] are references to his being ordinarily resident in the United Kingdom or, as the case may be, in that territory without being subject under the immigration laws to any restriction on the period for which he may remain.

(3)   Subject to subsection (4), a person is not to be regarded for the purposes of this Act—

(a)   as having been settled in the United Kingdom at any time when he was entitled to an exemption under section 8(3) or (4)(b) or (c) of the Immigration Act 1971 or, unless the order under section 8(2) of that Act conferring the exemption in question provides otherwise, to an exemption under the said section 8(2), or to any corresponding exemption under the former immigration laws; or

(b)   as having been settled in a [British overseas territory] at any time when he was under the immigration laws entitled to any exemption corresponding to any such exemption as is mentioned in paragraph (a) (that paragraph being for the purposes of this paragraph read as if the words from "unless" to "otherwise" were omitted).

(4)   A person to whom a child is born in the United Kingdom after commencement is to be regarded for the purposes of section 1(1) as being settled in the United Kingdom at the time of the birth if—

(a)   he would fall to be so regarded but for being at that time entitled to an exemption under section 8(3) of the Immigration Act 1971; and

(b)   immediately before he became entitled to that exemption he was settled in the United Kingdom; and

(c)   he was ordinarily resident in the United Kingdom from the time when he became entitled to that exemption to the time of the birth;

but this subsection shall not apply if at the time of the birth the child's father or mother is a person on whom any immunity from jurisdiction is conferred by or under the Diplomatic Privileges Act 1964.

(5)   It is hereby declared that a person is not to be treated for the purpose of any provision of this Act as ordinarily resident in the United Kingdom or in a [British overseas territory] at a time when he is in the United Kingdom or, as the case may be, in that territory in breach of the immigration laws.

(6)   For the purposes of this Act—

(a)   a person shall be taken to have been naturalised in the United Kingdom if, but only if, he is—

(i)   a person to whom a certificate of naturalisation was granted under any of the former nationality Acts by the Secretary of State or, in any of the Islands, by the Lieutenant-Governor; or

(ii)   a person who by virtue of section 27(2) of the British Nationality and Status of Aliens Act 1914 was deemed to be a person to whom a certificate of naturalisation was granted, if the certificate of naturalisation in which his name was included was granted by the Secretary of State; or

(iii)   a person who by virtue of section 10(5) of the Naturalization Act 1870 was deemed to be a naturalised British subject by reason of his residence with his father or mother;

(b)   a person shall be taken to have been naturalised in a [British overseas territory] if, but only if, he is—

(i)   a person to whom a certificate of naturalisation was granted under any of the former nationality Acts by the Governor of that territory or by a person for the time being specified in a direction given in relation to that territory under paragraph 4 of Schedule 3 to the West Indies Act 1967 or for the time being holding an office so specified; or

(ii)   a person who by virtue of the said section 27(2) was deemed to be a person to whom a certificate of naturalisation was granted, if the certificate of naturalisation in which his name was included was granted by the Governor of that territory; or

(iii)   a person who by the law in force in that territory enjoyed the privileges of naturalisation within that territory only;

and references in this Act to naturalisation in the United Kingdom or in a [British overseas territory] shall be construed accordingly.

(7) For the purposes of this Act a person born outside the United Kingdom aboard a ship or aircraft—

(a)   shall be deemed to have been born in the United Kingdom if—

(i)   at the time of the birth his father or mother was a British citizen; or

(ii)   he would, but for this subsection, have been born stateless,

and (in either case) at the time of the birth the ship or aircraft was registered in the United Kingdom or was an unregistered ship or aircraft of the government of the United Kingdom; but

(b)   subject to paragraph (a), is to be regarded as born outside the United Kingdom, whoever was the owner of the ship or aircraft at the time, and irrespective of whether or where it was then registered.

[(7A) For the purposes of this Act a person born outside a qualifying territory aboard a ship or aircraft—

(a)   shall be deemed to have been born in that territory if—

(i)   at the time of the birth his father or mother was a British citizen or a British overseas territories citizen; or

(ii)   he would, but for this subsection, have been born stateless,

and (in either case) at the time of the birth the ship or aircraft was registered in that territory or was an unregistered ship or aircraft of the government of that territory; but

(b)   subject to paragraph (a), is to be regarded as born outside that territory, whoever was the owner of the ship or aircraft at the time, and irrespective of whether or where it was then registered.

(7B) For the purposes of this Act a person born outside a British overseas territory, other than a qualifying territory, aboard a ship or aircraft—

(a)   shall be deemed to have been born in that territory if—

(i)   at the time of the birth his father or mother was a British overseas territories citizen; or

(ii)   he would, but for this subsection, have been born stateless,

and (in either case) at the time of the birth the ship or aircraft was registered in that territory or was an unregistered ship or aircraft of the government of that territory; but

(b)   subject to paragraph (a), is to be regarded as born outside that territory, whoever was the owner of the ship or aircraft at the time, and irrespective of whether or where it was then registered.]

(8)   For the purposes of this Act an application under any provision thereof shall be taken to have been made at the time of its receipt by a person authorised to receive it on behalf of the person to whom it is made; and references in this Act to the date of such an application are references to the date of its receipt by a person so authorised.

[(9)   For the purposes of this Act a child's mother is the woman who gives birth to the child.

(9A)   For the purposes of this Act a child's father is—

(a)   the husband, at the time of the child's birth, of the woman who gives birth to the child, or

[(b)   where a person is treated as the father of the child under section 28 of the Human Fertilisation and Embryology Act 1990 or section 35 or 36 of the Human Fertilisation and Embryology Act 2008, that person, or

(ba)   where a person is treated as a parent of the child under section 42 or 43 of the Human Fertilisation and Embryology Act 2008, that person, or

(c)   where none of paragraphs (a) to (ba) applies, a person who satisfies prescribed requirements as to proof of paternity].

(9B)   In subsection (9A)(c) "prescribed" means prescribed by regulations of the Secretary of State; and the regulations—

(a)   may confer a function (which may be a discretionary function) on the Secretary of State or another person,

(b)   may make provision which applies generally or only in specified circumstances,

(c)   may make different provision for different circumstances,

(d)   must be made by statutory instrument, and

(e)   shall be subject to annulment in pursuance of a resolution of either House of Parliament.

(9C)   The expressions "parent", "child" and "descended" shall be construed in accordance with subsections (9) and (9A).]

(10)   For the purposes of this Act—

(a)   a period "from" or "to" a specified date includes that date; and

(b)   any reference to a day on which a person was absent from the United Kingdom or from a [British overseas territory] or from the [British overseas territories] is a reference to a day for the whole of which he was so absent.

(11)   For the purposes of this Act—

(a)   a person is of full age if he has attained the age of eighteen years, and of full capacity if he is not of unsound mind; and

(b)   a person attains any particular age at the beginning of the relevant anniversary of the date of his birth.

(12)   References in this Act to any country mentioned in Schedule 3 include references to the dependencies of that country.

(13)   Her Majesty may by Order in Council subject to annulment in pursuance of a resolution of either House of Parliament amend Schedule 6 in any of the following circumstances, namely—

(a)   where the name of any territory mentioned in it is altered; or

(b)   where any territory mentioned in it is divided into two or more territories.

[(14)   For the purposes of the definition of "designated territory" in subsection (1), an Order in Council may—

(a)   designate any qualifying territory, or the Sovereign Base Areas of Akrotiri and Dhekelia, if the Convention is in force there, and

(b)   make different designations for the purposes of section 1 and section 15; and, for the purposes of this subsection and the definition of "Convention adoption" in subsection (1), "the Convention" means the Convention on the Protection of Children and Co-operation in respect of Intercountry Adoption, concluded at the Hague on 29th May 1993.

An Order in Council under this subsection shall be subject to annulment in pursuance of a resolution of either House of Parliament.]

Amendment

Sub-s (1): definition "appointed day" inserted by the British Overseas Territories Act 2002, s 5, Sch 1, para 5(1), (2).

Sub-s (1): definitions British National (Overseas)? and British Overseas citizen? inserted by SI 1986/948, art 7.

Sub-s (1): definition "British overseas territory" inserted by the British Overseas Territories Act 2002, s 1(1)(a).

Sub-s (1): definition "Convention adoption" inserted by the Adoption and Children Act 2002, s 137(3), (6)(a).

Sub-s (1): in definition "Crown service under the government of the United Kingdom" words "or under the Scottish Administration" in square brackets inserted by SI 1999/1042, art 3, Sch 1, para 10.

Sub-s (1): in definition "Crown service under the government of the United Kingdom" words "or under the Welsh Assembly Government" in square brackets inserted by SI 2009/2958, art 3.

Date in force: 6 November 2009: see SI 2009/2958, art 1(2).

Sub-s (1): definition "dependent territory" (omitted) repealed by the British Overseas Territories Act 2002, s 7, Sch 2.

Sub-s (1): definition "designated territory" inserted by the Adoption and Children Act 2002, s 137(3), (6)(b).

Sub-s (1): in definitions "foreign country", "Governor" and "immigration laws" words "British overseas territory" in square brackets substituted by the British Overseas Territories Act 2002, s 1(1)(b).

Sub-s (1): definition "qualifying territory" inserted by the British Overseas Territories Act 2002, s 5, Sch 1, para 5(1), (2).

Sub-ss (1A), (1B): inserted by the Borders, Citizenship and Immigration Act 2009, s 49(1).

Date in force: 13 January 2010: see SI 2009/2731, art 4(h).

Sub-s (2): words "British overseas territory" in square brackets substituted the British Overseas Territories Act 2002, s 1(1)(b).

Sub-s (3): in para (b) words "British overseas territory" in square brackets substituted by the British Overseas Territories Act 2002, s 1(1)(b).

Sub-s (5): words "British overseas territory" in square brackets substituted by the British Overseas Territories Act 2002, s 1(1)(b).

Sub-s (6): words "British overseas territory" in square brackets in both places they occur substituted by the British Overseas Territories Act 2002, s 1(1)(b).

Sub-ss (7A), (7B): substituted, for sub-s (7) proviso as originally enacted, by the British Overseas Territories Act 2002, s 5, Sch 1, para 5(1), (3).

Sub-ss (9), (9A)–(9C): substituted, for sub-s (9) as originally enacted, by the Nationality, Immigration and Asylum Act 2002, s 9(1).

Sub-s (9A): paras (b), (ba), (c) substituted for sub-paras (b), (c) as originally enacted, by the Human Fertilisation and Embryology Act 2008, s 56, Sch 6, Pt 1, para 22.

Sub-s (10): in para (b) words "British overseas territory" and "British overseas territories" in square brackets substituted by the British Overseas Territories Act 2002, s 1(1)(b).

Sub-s (14): inserted by the Adoption and Children Act 2002, s 137(3), (7).

Modification

The Northern Ireland Act 1998 makes new provision for the government of Northern Ireland for the purpose of implementing the Belfast Agreement (the agreement reached at multi-party talks on Northern Ireland and set out in Command Paper 3883). As a consequence of that Act, any reference in this section to the Parliament of Northern Ireland or the Assembly established under the Northern Ireland Assembly Act 1973, s 1, certain office-holders and Ministers, and any legislative act and certain financial dealings thereof, shall, for the period specified, be construed in accordance with Sch 12, paras 1–11 to the 1998 Act.

See Further

See further: the British Nationality (Hong Kong) Act 1990, s 2.

See further: the British Nationality (Hong Kong) Act 1997, s 2.

See further, in relation to the construction of the reference to being in the United Kingdom "in breach of the immigration laws" in sub-s (5) above: the Nationality, Immigration and Asylum Act 2002, s 11.

See further, in relation to the modification of this section, in so far as references to an office-holder in the Scottish Administration are to be taken to include a reference to the Scottish Court Service established by the Judiciary and Courts (Scotland) Act 2008, s 60(1): see the Judiciary and Courts (Scotland) Act 2008 (Consequential Provisions and Modifications) Order 2009, SI 2009/2231, art 3.

Subordinate Legislation

British Nationality Act 1981 (Amendment of Schedule 6) Order 2001, SI 2001/3497.

British Nationality (Proof of Paternity) Regulations 2006, SI 2006/1496.

British Nationality Act 1981 (Amendment of Schedule 6) Order 2009, SI 2009/2744.

[50A Meaning of references to being in breach of immigration laws]

[(1)   This section applies for the construction of a reference to being in the United Kingdom "in breach of the immigration laws" in—

    (a)   section 4(2) or (4);

    (b)   section 50(5); or

    (c)   Schedule 1.

(2)   It applies only for the purpose of determining on or after the relevant day—

    (a)   whether a person born on or after the relevant day is a British citizen under section 1(1),

    (b)   whether, on an application under section 1(3) or 4(2) made on or after the relevant day, a person is entitled to be registered as a British citizen, or

    (c)   whether, on an application under section 6(1) or (2) made on or after the relevant day, the applicant fulfils the requirements of Schedule 1 for naturalisation as a British citizen under section 6(1) or (2).

(3)   But that is subject to section 48(3)(d) and (4) of the Borders, Citizenship and Immigration Act 2009 (saving in relation to section 11 of the Nationality, Immigration and Asylum Act 2002).

(4)   A person is in the United Kingdom in breach of the immigration laws if (and only if) the person—

    (a)   is in the United Kingdom;

    (b)   does not have the right of abode in the United Kingdom within the meaning of section 2 of the Immigration Act 1971;

    (c)   does not have leave to enter or remain in the United Kingdom (whether or not the person previously had leave);

    (d)   does not have a qualifying CTA entitlement;

    (e)   is not entitled to reside in the United Kingdom by virtue of any provision made under section 2(2) of the European Communities Act 1972 (whether or not the person was previously entitled);

    (f)   is not entitled to enter and remain in the United Kingdom by virtue of section 8(1) of the Immigration Act 1971 (crew) (whether or not the person was previously entitled); and

    (g)   does not have the benefit of an exemption under section 8(2) to (4) of that Act (diplomats, soldiers and other special cases) (whether or not the person previously had the benefit of an exemption).

(5)   For the purposes of subsection (4)(d), a person has a qualifying CTA entitlement if the person—

    (a)   is a citizen of the Republic of Ireland,

    (b)   last arrived in the United Kingdom on a local journey (within the meaning of the Immigration Act 1971) from the Republic of Ireland, and

(c) on that arrival, was a citizen of the Republic of Ireland and was entitled to enter without leave by virtue of section 1(3) of the Immigration Act 1971 (entry from the common travel area).

(6) Section 11(1) of the Immigration Act 1971 (person deemed not to be in the United Kingdom before disembarkation, while in controlled area or while under immigration control) applies for the purposes of this section as it applies for the purposes of that Act.

(7) This section is without prejudice to the generality of—

(a) a reference to being in a place outside the United Kingdom in breach of immigration laws, and

(b) a reference in a provision other than one specified in subsection (1) to being in the United Kingdom in breach of immigration laws.

(8) The relevant day for the purposes of subsection (2) is the day appointed for the commencement of section 48 of the Borders, Citizenship and Immigration Act 2009 (which inserted this section).]

Amendment

Inserted by the Borders, Citizenship and Immigration Act 2009, s 48(1); for savings see s 48(4) thereof.

Date in force: 13 January 2010: see SI 2009/2731, art 4(g).

51 Meaning of certain expressions relating to nationality in other Acts and instruments

(1) Without prejudice to subsection (3)(c), in any enactment or instrument whatever passed or made before commencement "British subject" and "Commonwealth citizen" have the same meaning, that is—

(a) in relation to any time before commencement—

(i) a person who under the 1948 Act was at that time a citizen of the United Kingdom and Colonies or who, under any enactment then in force in a country mentioned in section 1(3) of that Act as then in force, was at that time a citizen of that country; and

(ii) any other person who had at that time the status of a British subject under that Act or any other enactment then in force;

(b) in relation to any time after commencement, a person who has the status of a Commonwealth citizen under this Act.

(2) In any enactment or instrument whatever passed or made after commencement—

"British subject" means a person who has the status of a British subject under this Act;

"Commonwealth citizen" means a person who has the status of a Commonwealth citizen under this Act.

(3) In any enactment or instrument whatever passed or made before commencement—

(a) "citizen of the United Kingdom and Colonies"—

(i) in relation to any time before commencement, means a person who under the 1948 Act was at that time a citizen of the United Kingdom and Colonies;

(ii) in relation to any time after commencement, means a person who under [the British Nationality Acts 1981 and 1983] [or the British Overseas Territories Act 2002] is a British citizen, a [British overseas territories citizen] or a British Overseas citizen [or who under the Hong Kong (British Nationality) Order 1986 is a British National (Overseas)];

(b) any reference to ceasing to be a citizen of the United Kingdom and Colonies shall, in relation to any time after commencement, be construed as a reference to becoming a person who is neither a British citizen nor a [British overseas territories citizen] [nor a British National (Overseas)] nor a British Overseas citizen;

(c)   any reference to a person who is a British subject (or a British subject without citizenship) by virtue of section 2, 13, or 16 of the 1948 Act or by virtue of, or of section 1 of, the British Nationality Act 1965 shall, in relation to any time after commencement, be construed as a reference to a person who under this Act is a British subject.

(4)   In any statutory provision, whether passed or made before or after commencement, and in any other instrument whatever made after commencement "alien", in relation to any time after commencement, means a person who is neither a Commonwealth citizen nor a British protected person nor a citizen of the Republic of Ireland.

(5)   The preceding provisions of this section—

(a)   shall not apply in cases where the context otherwise requires; and

(b)   shall not apply to this Act or to any instrument made under this Act.

Amendment

Sub-s (3): in para (a)(ii) words the British Nationality Acts 1981 and 1983? in square brackets substituted by the British Nationality (Falkland Islands) Act 1983, s 4(3).

Sub-s (3): in para (a)(ii) words "or the British Overseas Territories Act 2002" in square brackets inserted by the British Overseas Territories Act 2002, s 5, Sch 1, para 6.

Sub-s (3): words "British overseas territories citizen" in square brackets in both places they occur substituted by the British Overseas Territories Act 2002, s 1(1)(b).

Sub-s (3): in para (a)(ii) words the British Nationality Acts 1981 and 1983? in square brackets substituted by the British Nationality (Falkland Islands) Act 1983, s 4(3).

See Further

See further: the British Nationality (Hong Kong) Act 1997, s 2.

52 Consequential amendments, transitional provisions, repeals and savings

(1)   In any enactment or instrument whatever passed or made before commencement, for any reference to section 1(3) of the 1948 Act (list of countries whose citizens are Commonwealth citizens under that Act) there shall be substituted a reference to Schedule 3 to this Act, unless the context makes that substitution inappropriate.

(2)   Subject to subsection (3), Her Majesty may by Order in Council make such consequential modifications of—

(a)   any enactment of the Parliament of the United Kingdom passed before commencement;

(b)   any provision contained in any Northern Ireland legislation passed or made before commencement; or

(c)   any instrument made before commencement under any such enactment or provision,

as appear to Her necessary or expedient for preserving after commencement the substantive effect of that enactment, provision or instrument.

(3)   Subsection (2) shall not apply in relation to—

(a)   the Immigration Act 1971; or

(b)   any provision of this Act not contained in Schedule 7.

(4)   Any Order in Council made under subsection (2) shall be subject to annulment in pursuance of a resolution of either House of Parliament.

(5)   Any provision made by Order in Council under subsection (2) after commencement may be made with retrospective effect as from commencement or any later date.

(6)   The enactments specified in Schedule 7 shall have effect subject to the amendments there specified, being amendments consequential on the provisions of this Act.

(7) This Act shall have effect subject to the transitional provisions contained in Schedule 8.

(8) The enactments mentioned in Schedule 9 are hereby repealed to the extent specified in the third column of that Schedule.

(9) Without prejudice to section 51, nothing in this Act affects the operation, in relation to any time before commencement, of any statutory provision passed or made before commencement.

(10) Nothing in this Act shall be taken as prejudicing the operation of sections 16 and 17 of the Interpretation Act 1978 (which relate to the effect of repeals).

(11) In this section "modifications" includes additions, omissions and alterations.

Modification

The Northern Ireland Act 1998 makes new provision for the government of Northern Ireland for the purpose of implementing the Belfast Agreement (the agreement reached at multi-party talks on Northern Ireland and set out in Command Paper 3883). As a consequence of that Act, any reference in this section to the Parliament of Northern Ireland or the Assembly established under the Northern Ireland Assembly Act 1973, s 1, certain office-holders and Ministers, and any legislative act and certain financial dealings thereof, shall, for the period specified, be construed in accordance with Sch 12, paras 1–11 to the 1998 Act.

Subordinate Legislation

British Nationality (Modification of Enactments) Order 1982, SI 1982/1832.

53 Citation, commencement and extent

(1) This Act may be cited as the British Nationality Act 1981.

(2) This Act, except the provisions mentioned in subsection (3), shall come into force on such day as the Secretary of State may by order made by statutory instrument appoint; and references to the commencement of this Act shall be construed as references to the beginning of that day.

(3) Section 49 and this section shall come into force on the passing of this Act.

(4) This Act extends to Northern Ireland.

(5) The provisions of this Act, except those mentioned in subsection (7), extend to the Islands and all [British overseas territories]; and section 36 of the Immigration Act 1971 (power to extend provisions of that Act to Islands) shall apply to the said excepted provisions as if they were provisions of that Act.

(6) . . .

(7) The provisions referred to in subsections (5) . . . are—

  (a) section 39 and Schedule 4;

  (b) section 52(7) and Schedule 8 so far as they relate to the Immigration Act 1971; and

  (c) section 52(8) and Schedule 9 so far as they relate to provisions of the Immigration Act 1971 other than Schedule 1.

Amendment

Sub-s (5): words "British overseas territories" in square brackets substituted by the British Overseas Territories Act 2002, s 1(1)(b).

Sub-s (6): repealed by the Statute Law (Repeals) Act 1995.

Sub-s (7): words omitted repealed by the Statute Law (Repeals) Act 1995.

Subordinate Legislation

British Nationality Act 1981 (Commencement) Order 1982, SI 1982/933.

SCHEDULE 1

REQUIREMENTS FOR NATURALISATION

Sections 6, 18

Naturalisation as a British citizen under section 6(1)

1

(1) Subject to paragraph 2, the requirements for naturalisation as a British citizen under section 6(1) are, in the case of any person who applies for it—

(a) the requirements specified in sub-paragraph (2) of this paragraph, *or the alternative requirement specified in sub-paragraph (3) of this paragraph*; and

(b) that he is of good character; and

(c) that he has a sufficient knowledge of the English, Welsh or Scottish Gaelic language; and

[(ca) that he has sufficient knowledge about life in the United Kingdom; and]

(d) that either—

(i) his intentions are such that, in the event of a certificate of naturalisation as a British citizen being granted to him, his home or (if he has more than one) his principal home will be in the United Kingdom; or

(ii) he intends, in the event of such a certificate being granted to him, to enter into, or continue in, Crown service under the government of the United Kingdom, or service under an international organisation of which the United Kingdom or Her Majesty's government therein is a member, or service in the employment of a company or association established in the United Kingdom.

(2) *The requirements referred to in sub-paragraph (1)(a) of this paragraph are—*

(a) *that the applicant was in the United Kingdom at the beginning of the period of five years ending with the date of the application, and that the number of days on which he was absent from the United Kingdom in that period does not exceed 450; and*

(b) *that the number of days on which he was absent from the United Kingdom in the period of twelve months so ending does not exceed 90; and*

(c) *that he was not at any time in the period of twelve months so ending subject under the immigration laws to any restriction on the period for which he might remain in the United Kingdom; and*

(d) *that he was not at any time in the period of five years so ending in the United Kingdom in breach of the immigration laws.*

[(2) The requirements referred to in sub-paragraph (1)(a) of this paragraph are—

(a) that the applicant ("A") was in the United Kingdom at the beginning of the qualifying period;

(b) that the number of days on which A was absent from the United Kingdom in each year of the qualifying period does not exceed 90;

(c) that A had a qualifying immigration status for the whole of the qualifying period;

(d) that on the date of the application A has probationary citizenship leave, permanent residence leave, a qualifying CTA entitlement, a Commonwealth right of abode or a permanent EEA entitlement;

(e) that, where on the date of the application A has probationary citizenship leave granted for the purpose of taking employment in the United

Kingdom, A has been in continuous employment since the date of the grant of that leave; and

(f)   that A was not at any time in the qualifying period in the United Kingdom in breach of the immigration laws.]

(3)   *The alternative requirement referred to in sub-paragraph (1)(a) of this paragraph is that on the date of the application he is serving outside the United Kingdom in Crown service under the government of the United Kingdom.*

2

[(1)]   If in the special circumstances of any particular case the Secretary of State thinks fit, he may for the purposes of paragraph 1 do all or any of the following things, namely—

(a)   *treat the applicant as fulfilling the requirement specified in paragraph 1(2)(a) or paragraph 1(2)(b), or both, although the number of days on which he was absent from the United Kingdom in the period there mentioned exceeds the number there mentioned;*

[(a)   treat the applicant as fulfilling the requirement specified in paragraph 1(2)(b) although the number of days on which the applicant was absent from the United Kingdom in a year of the qualifying period exceeds 90;]

(b)   treat the applicant as having been in the United Kingdom for the whole or any part of any period during which he would otherwise fall to be treated under paragraph 9(1) as having been absent;

[(ba)   treat the applicant as fulfilling the requirement specified in paragraph 1(2)(c) where the applicant has had a qualifying immigration status for only part of the qualifying period;

(bb)   treat the applicant as fulfilling the requirement specified in paragraph 1(2)(d) where the applicant has had probationary citizenship leave but it expired in the qualifying period;]

(c)   *disregard any such restriction as is mentioned in paragraph 1(2)(c), not being a restriction to which the applicant was subject on the date of the application;*

[(ca)   treat the applicant as fulfilling the requirement specified in paragraph 1(2)(e) although the applicant has not been in continuous employment since the date of the grant mentioned there;]

(d)   treat the applicant as fulfilling the requirement specified in paragraph 1(2)(d) [1(2)(f)] although he was in the United Kingdom in breach of the immigration laws in the *period there mentioned* [qualifying period];

(e)   waive the need to fulfil [either or both of the requirements specified in paragraph 1(1)(c) and (ca)] if he considers that because of the applicant's age or physical or mental condition it would be unreasonable to [expect him to fulfil that requirement or those requirements].

[(2)   If in the special circumstances of a particular case that is an armed forces case or an exceptional Crown service case the Secretary of State thinks fit, the Secretary of State may for the purposes of paragraph 1 waive the need to fulfil all or any of the requirements specified in paragraph 1(2).

(3)   An armed forces case is a case where, on the date of the application, the applicant is or has been a member of the armed forces.

(4)   An exceptional Crown service case is a case where—

(a)   the applicant is, on the date of the application, serving outside the United Kingdom in Crown service under the government of the United Kingdom; and

(b)   the Secretary of State considers the applicant's performance in the service to be exceptional.]

[(5) In paragraph 1(2)(e) and sub-paragraph (1)(ca) of this paragraph, "employment" includes self-employment.]

[2A

(1) A person has a qualifying immigration status for the purposes of paragraph 1(2) if the person has—

    (a)   qualifying temporary residence leave;

    (b)   probationary citizenship leave;

    (c)   permanent residence leave;

    (d)   a qualifying CTA entitlement;

    (e)   a Commonwealth right of abode; or

    (f)   a temporary or permanent EEA entitlement.

(2) A person who is required for those purposes to have a qualifying immigration status for the whole of the qualifying period need not have the same qualifying immigration status for the whole of that period.]

Naturalisation as a British citizen under section 6(2)

3

Subject to paragraph 4, the requirements for naturalisation as a British citizen under section 6(2) are, in the case of any person who applies for it—

    (a)   *that he was in the United Kingdom at the beginning of the period of three years ending with the date of the application, and that the number of days on which he was absent from the United Kingdom in that period does not exceed 270; and*

    (b)   *that the number of days on which he was absent from the United Kingdom in the period of twelve months so ending does not exceed 90; and*

    (c)   *that on the date of the application he was not subject under the immigration laws to any restriction on the period for which he might remain in the United Kingdom; and*

    (d)   *that he was not at any time in the period of three years ending with the date of the application in the United Kingdom in breach of the immigration laws; and*

    (e)   *the [requirements specified in paragraph 1(1)(b), (c) and (ca)].*

[3

(1) Subject to paragraph 4, the requirements for naturalisation as a British citizen under section 6(2) are, in the case of any person ("A") who applies for it—

    (a)   the requirements specified in sub-paragraph (2) of this paragraph;

    (b)   the requirement specified in sub-paragraph (3) of this paragraph;

    (c)   that A is of good character;

    (d)   that A has a sufficient knowledge of the English, Welsh or Scottish Gaelic language; and

    (e)   that A has sufficient knowledge about life in the United Kingdom.

(2) The requirements referred to in sub-paragraph (1)(a) are—

    (a)   that A was in the United Kingdom at the beginning of the qualifying period;

    (b)   that the number of days on which A was absent from the United Kingdom in each year of the qualifying period does not exceed 90;

    (c)   that, subject to sub-paragraph (5)—

        (i)   A had a relevant family association for the whole of the qualifying period, and

(ii) A had a qualifying immigration status for the whole of that period;

(d) that on the date of the application—

(i) A has probationary citizenship leave, or permanent residence leave, based on A's having the relevant family association referred to in section 6(2), or

(ii) A has a qualifying CTA entitlement or a Commonwealth right of abode; and

(e) that A was not at any time in the qualifying period in the United Kingdom in breach of the immigration laws.

(3) The requirement referred to in sub-paragraph (1)(b) is—

(a) that A's intentions are such that, in the event of a certificate of naturalisation as a British citizen being granted to A, A's home or (if A has more than one) A's principal home will be in the United Kingdom;

(b) that A intends, in the event of such a certificate being granted to A, to enter into, or continue in, service of a description mentioned in sub-paragraph (4); or

(c) that, in the event of such a certificate being granted to A—

(i) the person with whom A has the relevant family association referred to in section 6(2) ("B") intends to enter into, or continue in, service of a description mentioned in sub-paragraph (4); and

(ii) A intends to reside with B for the period during which B is in the service in question.

(4) The descriptions of service referred to in sub-paragraph (3) are—

(a) Crown service under the government of the United Kingdom;

(b) service under an international organisation of which the United Kingdom, or Her Majesty's government in the United Kingdom, is a member; or

(c) service in the employment of a company or association established in the United Kingdom.

(5) Where the relevant family association referred to in section 6(2) is (in accordance with regulations under section 41(1)(a)) that A is the partner of a person who is a British citizen or who has permanent residence leave—

(a) the requirement specified in sub-paragraph (2)(c)(i) is fulfilled only if A was that person's partner for the whole of the qualifying period, and

(b) for the purposes of sub-paragraph (2)(c)(ii), A can rely upon having a qualifying immigration status falling within paragraph 4A(1)(a), (b) or (c) only if that partnership is the relevant family association upon which the leave to which the status relates is based.

(6) For the purposes of sub-paragraph (5), A is a person's partner if—

(a) that person is A's spouse or civil partner or is in a relationship with A that is of a description that the regulations referred to in that sub-paragraph specify, and

(b) the marriage, civil partnership or other relationship satisfies the conditions (if any) that those regulations specify.

(7) For the purposes of sub-paragraph (5), the relationship by reference to which A and the other person are partners need not be of the same description for the whole of the qualifying period.]

4

Paragraph 2 shall apply in relation to paragraph 3 with the following modifications namely—

(a) *the reference to the purposes of paragraph 1 shall be read as a reference to the purposes of paragraph 3;*

(b) the references to paragraphs *1(2)(a)*, *1(2)(b)* and *1(2)(d)* shall be read as references to paragraphs *3(a)*, *3(b)* and *3(d)* respectively;

(c) paragraph *2(c)* .... shall be omitted; and

(d) after paragraph *(e)* there shall be added—

"(f) *waive the need to fulfil all or any of the requirements specified in paragraph 3(a) and (b) if on the date of the application the person to whom the applicant is married [, or of whom the applicant is the civil partner,] is serving in service to which section 2(1)(b) applies, that person's recruitment for that service having taken place in the United Kingdom".*

[4

If in the special circumstances of any particular case the Secretary of State thinks fit, the Secretary of State may for the purposes of paragraph 3 do all or any of the following, namely—

(a) treat A as fulfilling the requirement specified in paragraph 3(2)(b), although the number of days on which A was absent from the United Kingdom in a year of the qualifying period exceeds 90;

(b) treat A as having been in the United Kingdom for the whole or any part of any period during which A would otherwise fall to be treated under paragraph 9(1) as having been absent;

(c) treat A as fulfilling the requirement specified in paragraph 3(2)(c)(i) (including where it can be fulfilled only as set out in paragraph 3(5)) where a relevant family association of A's has ceased to exist;

(d) treat A as fulfilling the requirement specified in paragraph 3(2)(c)(ii) (including where it can be fulfilled only as set out in paragraph 3(5)) where A has had a qualifying immigration status for only part of the qualifying period;

(e) treat A as fulfilling the requirement specified in paragraph 3(2)(d) where A has had probationary citizenship leave but it expired in the qualifying period;

(f) treat A as fulfilling the requirement specified in paragraph 3(2)(e) although A was in the United Kingdom in breach of the immigration laws in the qualifying period;

(g) waive the need to fulfil either or both of the requirements specified in paragraph 3(1)(d) and (e) if the Secretary of State considers that because of A's age or physical or mental condition it would be unreasonable to expect A to fulfil that requirement or those requirements;

(h) waive the need to fulfil all or any of the requirements specified in paragraph 3(2)(a), (b), (c) or (d) (including where paragraph 3(2)(c) can be fulfilled only as set out in paragraph 3(5)) if—

(i) on the date of the application, the person with whom A has the relevant family association referred to in section 6(2) is serving in service to which section 2(1)(b) applies, and

(ii) that person's recruitment for that service took place in the United Kingdom.]

[4A

(1) Subject to paragraph 3(5), a person has a qualifying immigration status for the purposes of paragraph 3 if the person has—

(a) qualifying temporary residence leave based on a relevant family association;

(b) probationary citizenship leave based on a relevant family association;

(c) permanent residence leave based on a relevant family association;

(d) a qualifying CTA entitlement; or

(e)   a Commonwealth right of abode.

(2)   For the purposes of paragraph 3 and this paragraph, the leave mentioned in sub-paragraph (1)(a), (b) or (c) is based on a relevant family association if it was granted on the basis of the person having a relevant family association.

(3)   A person who is required for the purposes of paragraph 3 to have, for the whole of the qualifying period, a qualifying immigration status and a relevant family association need not, for the whole of that period—

    (a)   have the same qualifying immigration status; or

    (b)   (subject to paragraph 3(5)) have the same relevant family association.

(4)   Where, by virtue of sub-paragraph (3)(a), a person relies upon having more than one qualifying immigration status falling within sub-paragraph (1)(a), (b) or (c)—

    (a)   subject to paragraph 3(5), it is not necessary that the leave to which each status relates is based on the same relevant family association, and

    (b)   in a case where paragraph 3(5) applies, the relationship by reference to which the persons referred to in paragraph 3(5) are partners need not be of the same description in respect of each grant of leave.]

[The qualifying period for naturalisation as a British citizen under section 6

4B

(1)   The qualifying period for the purposes of paragraph 1 or 3 is a period of years which ends with the date of the application in question.

(2)   The length of the period is determined in accordance with the following provisions of this paragraph.

(3)   In the case of an applicant who does not meet the activity condition, the number of years in the period is—

    (a)   8, in a case within paragraph 1;

    (b)   5, in a case within paragraph 3.

(4)   In the case of an applicant who meets the activity condition, the number of years in the period is—

    (a)   6, in a case within paragraph 1;

    (b)   3, in a case within paragraph 3.

(5)   The applicant meets the activity condition if the Secretary of State is satisfied that the applicant—

    (a)   has participated otherwise than for payment in prescribed activities; or

    (b)   is to be treated as having so participated.]

Naturalisation as a [British overseas territories citizen] under section 18(1)

5

(1)   Subject to paragraph 6, the requirements for naturalisation as a [British overseas territories citizen] under section 18(1) are, in the case of any person who applies for it—

    (a)   the requirements specified in sub-paragraph (2) of this paragraph, or the alternative specified in sub-paragraph (3) of this paragraph; and

    (b)   that he is of good character; and

    (c)   that he has a sufficient knowledge of the English language or any other language recognised for official purposes in the relevant territory; and

    (d)   that either—

        (i)   his intentions are such that, in the event of a certificate of naturalisation as a [British overseas territories citizen] being granted to him, his home or (if he has more than one) his principal home will be in the relevant territory; or

(ii)   he intends, in the event of such a certificate being granted to him, to enter into, or continue in, Crown service under the government of that territory, or service under an international organisation of which that territory or the government of that territory is a member, or service in the employment of a company or association established in that territory.

(2)   The requirements referred to in sub-paragraph (1)(a) of this paragraph are—

(a)   that he was in the relevant territory at the beginning of the period of five years ending with the date of the application, and that the number of days on which he was absent from that territory in that period does not exceed 450; and

(b)   that the number of days on which he was absent from that territory in the period of twelve months so ending does not exceed 90; and

(c)   that he was not at any time in the period of twelve months so ending subject under the immigration laws to any restriction on the period for which he might remain in that territory; and

(d)   that he was not at any time in the period of five years so ending in that territory in breach of the immigration laws.

(3)   The alternative requirement referred to in sub-paragraph (1)(a) of this paragraph is that on the date of the application he is serving outside the relevant territory in Crown service under the government of that territory.

6

If in the special circumstances of any particular case the Secretary of State thinks fit, he may for the purposes of paragraph 5 do all or any of the following things, namely—

(a)   treat the applicant as fulfilling the requirement specified in paragraph 5(2)(a) or paragraph 5(2)(b), or both, although the number of days on which he was absent from the relevant territory in the period there mentioned exceeds the number there mentioned;

(b)   treat the applicant as having been in the relevant territory for the whole or any part of any period during which he would otherwise fall to be treated under paragraph 9(2) as having been absent;

(c)   disregard any such restriction as is mentioned in paragraph 5(2)(c), not being a restriction to which the applicant was subject on the date of the application;

(d)   treat the applicant as fulfilling the requirement specified in paragraph 5(2)(d) although he was in the relevant territory in breach of the immigration laws in the period there mentioned;

(e)   waive the need to fulfil the requirement specified in paragraph 5(1)(c) if he considers that because of the applicant's age or physical or mental condition it would be unreasonable to expect him to fulfil it.

Naturalisation as a [British overseas territories citizen] under section 18(2)

7

Subject to paragraph 8. the requirements for naturalisation as a [British overseas territories citizen] under section 18(2) are, in the case of any person who applies for it—

(a)   that he was in the relevant territory at the beginning of the period of three years ending with the date of the application, and that the number of days on which he was absent from that territory in that period does not exceed 270; and

(b)   that the number of days on which he was absent from that territory in the period of twelve months so ending does not exceed 90; and

(c)   that on the date of the application he was not subject under the immigration laws to any restriction on the period for which he might remain in that territory; and

(d)   that he was not at any time in the period of three years ending with the date of the application in that territory in breach of the immigration laws; and

(e)   the [requirements specified in paragraph 5(1)(b) and (c)].

8

Paragraph 6 shall apply in relation to paragraph 7 with the following modifications, namely—

(a)   the reference to the purposes of paragraph 5 shall be read as a reference to the purposes of paragraph 7;

(b)   the references to paragraphs 5(2)(a), and 5(2)(b) and 5(2)(d) shall be read as references to paragraph 7(a), 7(b) and 7(d) respectively;

(c)   paragraph 6(c) . . . shall be omitted; and

(d)   after paragraph (e) there shall be added—

"(f)   waive the need to fulfil all or any of the requirements specified in paragraph 7(a) and (b) if on the date of the application the person to whom the applicant is married[, or of whom the applicant is the civil partner,] is serving in service to which section 16(1)(b) applies, that person's recruitment for that service having taken place in a [British overseas territory]".

Periods to be treated as periods of absence from U.K. or a [British overseas territory]

9

(1) For the purposes of this Schedule a person shall (subject to *paragraph 2(b)* [paragraph 2(1)(b) or 4(b)]) be treated as having been absent from the United Kingdom during any of the following periods, that is to say—

(a)   any period when he was in the United Kingdom and either was entitled to an exemption under section 8(3) or (4) of the Immigration Act 1971 (exemptions for diplomatic agents etc and members of the forces) or was a member of the family and formed part of the household of a person so entitled;

(b)   any period when he was detained—

(i)   in any place of detention in the United Kingdom in pursuance of a sentence passed on him by a court in the United Kingdom or elsewhere for any offence;

(ii)   in any hospital in the United Kingdom under a hospital order made under [Part III of the Mental Health Act 1983] or section 175 or 376 of the Criminal Procedure (Scotland) Act 1975 or Part III of the Mental Health [(Northern Ireland) Order 1986], being an order made in connection with his conviction of an offence; or

(iii)   under any power of detention conferred by the immigration laws of the United Kingdom;

(c)   any period when, being liable to be detained as mentioned in paragraph (b)(i) or (ii) of this sub-paragraph, he was unlawfully at large or absent without leave and for that reason liable to be arrested or taken into custody;

(d)   any period when, his actual detention under any such power as is mentioned in paragraph (b)(iii) of this sub-paragraph being required or specifically authorised, he was unlawfully at large and for that reason liable to be arrested.

(2) For the purposes of this Schedule a person shall (subject to paragraph 6(b)) be treated as having been absent from any particular [British overseas territory] during any of the following periods, that is to say—

(a) any period when he was in that territory and either was entitled to an exemption under the immigration laws of that territory corresponding to any such exemption as is mentioned in sub-paragraph (1)(a) or was a member of the family and formed part of the household of a person so entitled;

(b) any period when he was detained—

(i) in any place of detention in the relevant territory in pursuance of a sentence passed on him by a court in that territory or elsewhere for any offence;

(ii) in any hospital in that territory under a direction (however described) made under any law for purposes similar to [Part III of the Mental Health Act 1983] which was for the time being in force in that territory, being a direction made in connection with his conviction of an offence and corresponding to a hospital order under that Part; or

(iii) under any power of detention conferred by the immigration laws of that territory;

(c) any period when, being liable to be detained as mentioned in paragraph (b)(i) or (ii) of this sub-paragraph, he was unlawfully at large or absent without leave and for that reason liable to be arrested or taken into custody;

(d) any period when, his actual detention under any such power as is mentioned in paragraph (b)(iii) of this sub-paragraph being required or specifically authorised, he was unlawfully at large and for that reason liable to be arrested.

Interpretation

10

In this Schedule "the relevant territory" has the meaning given by section 18(3).

[11

(1) This paragraph applies for the purposes of this Schedule.

(2) A person has qualifying temporary residence leave if—

(a) the person has limited leave to enter or remain in the United Kingdom, and

(b) the leave is granted for a purpose by reference to which a grant of probationary citizenship leave may be made.

(3) A person has probationary citizenship leave if—

(a) the person has limited leave to enter or remain in the United Kingdom, and

(b) the leave is of a description identified in rules under section 3 of the Immigration Act 1971 as "probationary citizenship leave",

and the reference in sub-paragraph (2) to a grant of probationary citizenship leave is to be construed accordingly.

(4) A person has permanent residence leave if the person has indefinite leave to enter or remain in the United Kingdom.

(5) A person has a qualifying CTA entitlement if the person—

(a) is a citizen of the Republic of Ireland,

(b) last arrived in the United Kingdom on a local journey (within the meaning of the Immigration Act 1971) from the Republic of Ireland, and

(c) on that arrival, was a citizen of the Republic of Ireland and was entitled to enter without leave by virtue of section 1(3) of the Immigration Act 1971 (entry from the common travel area).

(6) A person has a Commonwealth right of abode if the person has the right of abode in the United Kingdom by virtue of section 2(1)(b) of the Immigration Act 1971.

(7) A person has a permanent EEA entitlement if the person is entitled to reside in the United Kingdom permanently by virtue of any provision made under section 2(2) of the European Communities Act 1972.

(8) A person has a temporary EEA entitlement if the person does not have a permanent EEA entitlement but is entitled to reside in the United Kingdom by virtue of any provision made under section 2(2) of the European Communities Act 1972.

(9) A reference in this paragraph to having leave to enter or remain in the United Kingdom is to be construed in accordance with the Immigration Act 1971.]

Amendment

Para 1: in sub-para (1)(a) words ", or the alternative requirement specified in sub-paragraph (3) of this paragraph" in italics repealed by the Borders, Citizenship and Immigration Act 2009, ss 39(1), 56, Schedule, Pt 2, as from a day to be appointed.

Para 1: sub-para (1)(ca) inserted by the Nationality, Immigration and Asylum Act 2002, s 1(1).

Para 1: sub-para (2) substituted by the Borders, Citizenship and Immigration Act 2009, s 39(2), as from a day to be appointed.

Para 1: sub-para (3) repealed by the Borders, Citizenship and Immigration Act 2009, ss 39(3), 56, Schedule, Pt 2, as from a day to be appointed.

Para 2: sub-para (1) numbered as such by the Borders, Citizenship and Immigration Act 2009, s 39(4), as from a day to be appointed.

Para 2: sub-para (1)(a) substituted by the Borders, Citizenship and Immigration Act 2009, s 39(4). as from a day to be appointed.

Para 2: sub-para (1)(ba), (bb) inserted by the Borders, Citizenship and Immigration Act 2009, s 39(5), as from a day to be appointed.

Para 2: sub-para (1)(c) repealed by the Borders, Citizenship and Immigration Act 2009, ss 39(6), 56, Schedule, Pt 2, as from a day to be appointed.

Para 2: sub-para (1)(ca) inserted by the Borders, Citizenship and Immigration Act 2009, s 39(7), as from a day to be appointed.

Para 2: in sub-para (1)(d) reference to "1(2)(d)" in italics repealed and subsequent reference in square brackets substituted by the Borders, Citizenship and Immigration Act 2009, s 39(8)(a), as from a day to be appointed.

Para 2: in sub-para (1)(d) words "period there mentioned" in italics repealed and subsequent words in square brackets substituted by the Borders, Citizenship and Immigration Act 2009, s 39(8)(b), as from a day to be appointed.

Para 2: in sub-para (1)(e) words "either or both of the requirements specified in paragraph 1(1)(c) and (ca)" in square brackets substituted by the Nationality, Immigration and Asylum Act 2002, s 1(2)(a).

Para 2: in sub-para (1)(e) words "expect him to fulfil that requirement or those requirements" in square brackets substituted by the Nationality, Immigration and Asylum Act 2002, s 1(2)(b).

Para 2: sub-paras (2)–(4) inserted by the Borders, Citizenship and Immigration Act 2009, s 39(9), as from a day to be appointed.

Para 2: sub-para (5) inserted by the Borders, Citizenship and Immigration Act 2009, s 39(10), as from a day to be appointed.

Para 2A: inserted by the Borders, Citizenship and Immigration Act 2009, s 39(11), as from a day to be appointed.

Para 3: substituted by the Borders, Citizenship and Immigration Act 2009, s 40(3), as from a day to be appointed.

Para 3: in sub-para (e) words "requirements specified in paragraph 1(1)(b), (c) and (ca)" in square brackets substituted by the Nationality, Immigration and Asylum Act 2002, s 2(1)(a).

Para 4: substituted by the Borders, Citizenship and Immigration Act 2009, s 40(4), as from a day to be appointed.

Para 4: in sub-para (c) words omitted repealed by the Nationality, Immigration and Asylum Act 2002, ss 2(1)(b), 161, Sch 9.

Para 4: in sub-para (d) words ", or of whom the applicant is the civil partner," in square brackets inserted by the Civil Partnership Act 2004, s 261(1), Sch 27, para 78.

Para 4A: inserted by the Borders, Citizenship and Immigration Act 2009, s 40(5).

Date in force: to be appointed: see the Borders, Citizenship and Immigration Act 2009, s 58(2).

Para 4B: inserted by the Borders, Citizenship and Immigration Act 2009, s 41(1).

Date in force: to be appointed: see the Borders, Citizenship and Immigration Act 2009, s 58(2).

Para 5 heading: words "British overseas territories citizen" in square brackets substituted by the British Overseas Territories Act 2002, s 2(2)(b).

Para 5: words "British overseas territories citizen" in square brackets in both places they occur substituted by the British Overseas Territories Act 2002, s 2(2)(b).

Para 7 heading: words "British overseas territories citizen" in square brackets substituted by the British Overseas Territories Act 2002, s 2(2)(b).

Para 7: words "British overseas territories citizen" in square brackets substituted by the British Overseas Territories Act 2002, s 2(2)(b).

Para 7: in sub-para (e) words "requirements specified in paragraph 5(1)(b) and (c)" in square brackets substituted by the Nationality, Immigration and Asylum Act 2002, s 2(2)(a).

Para 8: in sub-para (c) words omitted repealed by the Nationality, Immigration and Asylum Act 2002, ss 2(2)(b), 161, Sch 9.

Para 8: in sub-para (d) words ", or of whom the applicant is the civil partner," in square brackets inserted by the Civil Partnership Act 2004, s 261(1), Sch 27, para 78.

Para 8: in sub-para (d) words "British overseas territory" in square brackets substituted by the British Overseas Territories Act 2002, s 1(1)(b).

Para 9 heading: words "British overseas territory" in square brackets substituted by the British Overseas Territories Act 2002, s 1(1)(b).

Para 9: in sub-para (1) words "paragraph 2(b)" in italics repealed and subsequent words in square brackets substituted by the Borders, Citizenship and Immigration Act 2009, s 49(2).

Date in force: to be appointed: see the Borders, Citizenship and Immigration Act 2009, s 58(2).

Para 9: in sub-para (1)(b)(ii) words Part III of the Mental Health Act 1983? in square brackets substituted by the Mental Health Act 1983, s 148, Sch 4, para 60(a).

Para 9: in sub-para (1)(b)(ii) words (Northern Ireland) Order 1986? in square brackets substituted by SI 1986/596, art 8.

Para 9: in sub-para (2) words "British overseas territory" in square brackets substituted by the British Overseas Territories Act 2002, s 1(1)(b).

Para 9: in sub-para (2)(b)(ii) words Part III of the Mental Health Act 1983? in square brackets substituted by the Mental Health Act 1983, s 148, Sch 4, para 60(b)

Para 11: inserted by the Borders, Citizenship and Immigration Act 2009, s 49(3).

Date in force: to be appointed: see the Borders, Citizenship and Immigration Act 2009, s 58(2).

See Further

See further, in relation to the construction of references to being in the United Kingdom "in breach of the immigration laws" in paras 1(2)(d), 2(d), 3(d), 5(2)(d), 6(d), 7(d) above: the Nationality, Immigration and Asylum Act 2002, s 11.

SCHEDULE 2
PROVISIONS FOR REDUCING STATELESSNESS

Section 36

Persons born in the United Kingdom after commencement

1

(1) Where a person born in the United Kingdom after commencement would, but for this paragraph, be born stateless, then, subject to sub-paragraph (3)—

    (a)   if at the time of the birth his father or mother is a citizen or subject of a description mentioned in sub-paragraph (2), he shall be a citizen or subject of that description; and accordingly

     (b)   if . . . at the time of the birth each of his parents is a citizen or subject of a different description so mentioned, he shall be a citizen or subject of the same description so mentioned as each of them is respectively at that time.

(2)   The descriptions referred to in sub-paragraph (1) are a [British overseas territories citizen], a British Overseas citizen and a British subject under this Act.

(3)   A person shall not be a British subject by virtue of this paragraph if by virtue of it he is a citizen of a description mentioned in sub-paragraph (2).

Persons born in a [British overseas territory] after commencement

2

(1)   Where a person born in a [British overseas territory] after commencement would, but for this paragraph, be born stateless, then, subject to sub-paragraph (3)—

     (a)   if at the time of the birth his father or mother is a citizen or subject of a description mentioned in sub-paragraph (2), he shall be a citizen or subject of that description; and accordingly

     (b)   if . . . at the time of the birth each of his parents is a citizen or subject of a different description so mentioned, he shall be a citizen or subject of the same description so mentioned as each of them is respectively at that time.

(2)   The descriptions referred to in sub-paragraph (1) are a British citizen, a British Overseas citizen and a British subject under this Act.

(3)   A person shall not be a British subject by virtue of this paragraph if by virtue of it he is a citizen of a description mentioned in sub-paragraph (2).

Persons born in the United Kingdom or a [British overseas territory]
after commencement

3

(1)   A person born in the United Kingdom or a [British overseas territory] after commencement shall be entitled, on an application for his registration under this paragraph, to be so registered if the following requirements are satisfied in his case, namely—

     (a)   that he is and always has been stateless; and

     (b)   that on the date of the application he . . . was under the age of twenty-two; and

     (c)   that he was in the United Kingdom or a [British overseas territory] (no matter which) at the beginning of the period of five years ending with that date and that (subject to paragraph 6) the number of days on which he was absent from both the United Kingdom and the [British overseas territories] in that period does not exceed 450.

(2)   A person entitled to registration under this paragraph—

     (a)   shall be registered under it as a British citizen if, in the period of five years mentioned in sub-paragraph (1), the number of days wholly or partly spent by him in the United Kingdom exceeds the number of days wholly or partly spent by him in the [British overseas territories];

     (b)   in any other case, shall be registered under it as a [British Overseas Territories] citizen.

Persons born outside the United Kingdom and the [British overseas territories] after commencement

4

(1)   A person born outside the United Kingdom and the [British overseas territories] after commencement shall be entitled, on an application for his registration under this paragraph, to be so registered if the following requirements are satisfied, namely—

    (a)   that that person is and always has been stateless; and

    (b)   that at the time of that person's birth his father or mother was a citizen or subject of a description mentioned in sub-paragraph (4); and

    (c)   that that person was in the United Kingdom or a [British overseas territory] (no matter which) at the beginning of the period of three years ending with the date of the application and that (subject to paragraph 6) the number of days on which he was absent from both the United Kingdom and the [British overseas territories] in that period does not exceed 270.

(2)   A person entitled to registration under this paragraph—

    (a)   shall be registered under it as a citizen or subject of a description available to him in accordance with sub-paragraph (3); and

    (b)   if more than one description is so available to him, shall be registered under this paragraph as a citizen of whichever one or more of the descriptions so available to him is or are stated in the application under this paragraph to be wanted.

(3)   For the purposes of this paragraph the descriptions of citizen or subject available to a person entitled to registration under this paragraph are—

    (a)   in the case of a person whose father or mother was at the time of that person's birth a citizen of a description mentioned in sub-paragraph (4), any description of citizen so mentioned which applied to his father or mother at that time;

    (b)   in any other case, a British subject under this Act.

(4)   The descriptions referred to in sub-paragraphs (1) to (3) are a British citizen, a [British overseas territories citizen], a British Overseas citizen and a British subject under this Act.

Persons born stateless before commencement

5

(1)   A person born before commencement shall be entitled, on an application for his registration under this paragraph, to be so registered if the circumstances are such that, if—

    (a)   this Act had not been passed, and the enactments repealed or amended by this Act had continued in force accordingly; and

    (b)   an application for the registration of that person under section 1 of the British Nationality (No 2) Act 1964 (stateless persons) as a citizen of the United Kingdom and Colonies had been made on the date of the application under this paragraph,

that person would have been entitled under that section to be registered as such a citizen.

(2)   A person entitled to registration under this paragraph shall be registered under it as such a citizen as he would have become at commencement if, immediately before commencement, he had been registered as a citizen of the United Kingdom and Colonies under section 1 of the British Nationality (No 2) Act 1964 on whichever of the grounds mentioned in subsection (1)(a) to (c) of that section he would have been

entitled to be so registered on in the circumstances described in sub-paragraph (1)(a) and (b) of this paragraph.

Supplementary

6

If in the special circumstances of any particular case the Secretary of State thinks fit, he may for the purposes of paragraph 3 or 4 treat the person who is the subject of the application as fulfilling the requirement specified in sub-paragraph (1)(c) of that paragraph although the number of days on which he was absent from both the United Kingdom and the [British overseas territories] in the period there mentioned exceeds the number there mentioned.

Amendment

Para 1: in sub-para (1)(b) words omitted repealed by the Nationality, Immigration and Asylum Act 2002, ss 9(5)(a), 161, Sch 9.

Para 1: in sub-para (2) words "British overseas territories citizen" in square brackets substituted by the British Overseas Territories Act 2002, s 2(2)(b).

Para 2 heading: words "British overseas territory" in square brackets substituted by the British Overseas Territories Act 2002, s 1(1)(b).

Para 2: in sub-para (1) words "British overseas territory" in square brackets substituted by the British Overseas Territories Act 2002, s 1(1)(b).

Para 2: in sub-para (1)(b) words omitted repealed by the Nationality, Immigration and Asylum Act 2002, ss 9(5)(b), 161, Sch 9.

Para 3 heading: words "British overseas territory" in square brackets substituted by the British Overseas Territories Act 2002, s 1(1)(b).

Para 3: words "British overseas territory" and "British overseas territories" in square brackets in each place they occur substituted by the British Overseas Territories Act 2002, s 1(1)(b).

Para 3: in sub-para (1)(b) words omitted repealed by the Nationality, Immigration and Asylum Act 2002, ss 8, 161, Sch 9.

Para 4 heading: words "British overseas territories" in square brackets substituted by the British Overseas Territories Act 2002, s 1(1)(b).

Para 4: words "British overseas territory" and words "British overseas territories" in both places they occur in square brackets substituted by the British Overseas Territories Act 2002, s 1(1)(b).

Para 4: in sub-para (4) words "British overseas territories citizen" in square brackets substituted by the British Overseas Territories Act 2002, s 2(2)(b).

Para 6: words "British overseas territories" in square brackets substituted by the British Overseas Territories Act 2002, s 1(1)(b).

SCHEDULE 3
COUNTRIES WHOSE CITIZENS ARE COMMONWEALTH CITIZENS

Section 37
Antigua and Barbuda
Australia
The Bahamas
Bangladesh
Barbados
Belize
Botswana
[Brunei]
[Cameroon]
Canada
Republic of Cyprus
Dominica
Fiji

The Gambia
Ghana
Grenada
Guyana
India
Jamaica
Kenya
Kiribati
Lesotho
Malawi
Malaysia
[Maldives]
Malta
Mauritius
[Mozambique]
[Namibia]
Nauru
New Zealand
Nigeria
[Pakistan]
Papua New Guinea
[Rwanda]
[Saint Christopher and Nevis]
Saint Lucia
Saint Vincent and the Grenadines
Seychelles
Sierra Leone
Singapore
Solomon Islands
[South Africa]
Sri Lanka
Swaziland
Tanzania
Tonga
Trinidad and Tobago
Tuvalu
Uganda
Vanuatu
Western Samoa
Zambia
Zimbabwe

Amendment

Para 9: in sub-para (2)(b)(ii) words Part III of the Mental Health Act 1983? in square brackets substituted by the Mental Health Act 1983, s 148, Sch 4, para 60(b)

Entry "Cameroon" inserted by SI 1998/3161, art 2.

Entry "Maldives" inserted by the Brunei and Maldives Act 1985, s 1, Schedule.

Entry "Mozambique" inserted by SI 1998/3161, art 2.

Entry "Namibia" inserted by SI 1990/1502, art 2.

Entry "Pakistan" inserted by SI 1989/1331, art 2.

Entry "Rwanda" inserted by SI 2010/246, art 2. Date in force: 10 March 2010: see SI 2010/246, art 1.

Entry "Saint Christopher and Nevis" inserted by SI 1983/882, art 2.

Entry "South Africa" inserted by SI 1994/1634, art 2.

SCHEDULE 4

(Sch 4 amends various provisions of the Immigration Act 1971; these amendments have been incorporated at the appropriate place in this work.)

[SCHEDULE 5
CITIZENSHIP OATH AND PLEDGE

Section 42(1)

1

The form of citizenship oath and pledge is as follows for registration of or naturalisation as a British citizen—

Oath

"I, *[name]*, swear by Almighty God that, on becoming a British citizen, I will be faithful and bear true allegiance to Her Majesty Queen Elizabeth the Second, Her Heirs and Successors according to law."

Pledge

"I will give my loyalty to the United Kingdom and respect its rights and freedoms. I will uphold its democratic values. I will observe its laws faithfully and fulfil my duties and obligations as a British citizen."

2

The form of citizenship oath and pledge is as follows for registration of or naturalisation as a British overseas territories citizen—

Oath

"I, *[name]*, swear by Almighty God that, on becoming a British overseas territories citizen, I will be faithful and bear true allegiance to Her Majesty Queen Elizabeth the Second, Her Heirs and Successors according to law."

Pledge

"I will give my loyalty to *[name of territory]* and respect its rights and freedoms. I will uphold its democratic values. I will observe its laws faithfully and fulfil my duties and obligations as a British overseas territories citizen."

3

The form of citizenship oath is as follows for registration of a British Overseas citizen—

I, *[name]*, swear by Almighty God that, on becoming a British Overseas citizen, I will be faithful and bear true allegiance to Her Majesty Queen Elizabeth the Second, Her Heirs and Successors according to law."

4

The form of citizenship oath is as follows for registration of a British subject—

"I, *[name]*, swear by Almighty God that, on becoming a British subject, I will be faithful and bear true allegiance to Her Majesty Queen Elizabeth the Second, Her Heirs and Successors according to law.".]

Amendment

Substituted by the Nationality, Immigration and Asylum Act 2002, s 3, Sch 1, para 2.

SCHEDULE 6
[BRITISH OVERSEAS TERRITORIES]

Amendment

Schedule heading: "British Overseas Territories" in square brackets substituted by the British Overseas Territories Act 2002, s 1(1)(c).

Section 50(1)

Anguilla

Bermuda

British Antarctic Territory

British Indian Ocean Territory

Cayman Islands

Falkland Islands . . .

Gibraltar

. . .

Montserrat

Pitcairn, Henderson, Ducie and Oeno Islands

. . .

[St Helena, Ascension and Tristan da Cunha]

[South Georgia and the South Sandwich Islands]

The Sovereign Base Areas of Akrotiri and Dhekelia (that is to say the areas mentioned in section 2(1) of the Cyprus Act 1960)

Turks and Caicos Islands

Virgin Islands.

Amendment

Entry "Falkland Islands": words omitted repealed by SI 2001/3497, art 2(a).

First entry omitted repealed by SI 1986/948, art 5.

Second entry omitted repealed by SI 1983/882, art 2.

Entry "St Helena, Ascension and Tristan da Cunha" substituted, for entry "St Helena and Dependencies" as originally enacted, by SI 2009/2744, art 2.

Entry "South Georgia and the South Sandwich Islands" inserted by SI 2001/3497, art 2(b).

SCHEDULE 7

(Sch 7 contains consequential amendments which, in so far as relevant to this work, have been incorporated at the appropriate place.)

SCHEDULE 8
TRANSITIONAL PROVISIONS

Section 52(7)

Applications for naturalisation or registration pending at commencement

1

(1) This paragraph applies to any application—

    (a)   for registration under any provision of the British Nationality Acts 1948 to 1965 as a citizen of the United Kingdom and Colonies or as a British subject; or

    (b)   for a certificate of naturalisation under section 10 of the 1948 Act,

which is received before commencement by a person authorised to receive it on behalf of the person to whom it is made but which at commencement has not been determined.

(2)   In relation to any application to which this paragraph applies—

   (a)   the British Nationality Acts 1948 to 1965 and all regulations and arrangements in force under them immediately before commencement shall (so far as applicable) continue to apply; and

   (b)   this Act shall not apply;

but on the granting of such an application and the taking under those Acts of such other steps as are necessary for the person in question to become—

   (i)   a citizen of the United Kingdom and Colonies by virtue of any provision of those Acts; or

   (ii)   a British subject by virtue of registration under any provision of those Acts,

that person, instead of becoming a citizen or subject of that description, shall become under this Act such a citizen or subject as he would have become at commencement if, immediately before commencement, he had been such a citizen or subject as is mentioned in paragraph (i) or (ii), as the case may be.

(3)   Sub-paragraph (2) shall have effect as if the references in it to the British Nationality Acts 1948 to 1965 did, and as if the reference in paragraph (b) of it to this Act did not, include section 49 of this Act.

2

Where a person who has been registered or to whom a certificate of naturalisation has been granted before the passing of this Act has at commencement not yet taken the oath of allegiance, paragraph 1(2) shall apply as if the application on which he was registered or the certificate was granted were an application to which paragraph 1 applies.

Registration at U.K. consulate, after commencement, of certain births occurring in foreign countries less than a year before commencement

3

(1)   This paragraph applies to a person born less than a year before commencement if—

   (a)   the birth occurred in a place in a foreign country (within the meaning of the 1948 Act); and

   (b)   at the time of the birth his father was a citizen of the United Kingdom and Colonies by descent only; and

   (c)   the birth was not registered at a United Kingdom consulate before commencement.

(2)   If the birth of a person to whom this paragraph applies is registered at a United Kingdom consulate within one year of its occurrence, he shall be deemed for the purposes of this Act to have been, immediately before commencement, a citizen of the United Kingdom and Colonies by virtue of section 5 of the 1948 Act (citizenship by descent).

(3)   References in this paragraph to the 1948 Act are references to that Act as in force at the time of the birth in question.

Declarations by certain persons who by virtue of an Order in Council under section 4 of the Cyprus Act 1960 have ceased to be citizens of the United Kingdom and Colonies

4

(1)   Where—

   (a)   a person has before commencement duly made a declaration under section 4(2) of the Cyprus Act 1960 of his intention to resume citizenship of the United Kingdom and Colonies; but

(b)   at commencement the declaration has not been registered,

the Secretary of State shall cause the declaration to be registered.

(2)   If—

    (a)   a person who in consequence of anything done before he attained the age of sixteen years ceased by virtue of an Order in Council under section 4 of the Cyprus Act 1960 to be a citizen of the United Kingdom and Colonies makes, in such a manner as the Secretary of State may direct, a declaration of his intention to accept the citizenship available to him under this paragraph; and

    (b)   the declaration is made by him after commencement and within one year after his attaining the age of twenty-one years,

the Secretary of State shall cause the declaration to be registered.

(3)   On the registration under sub-paragraph (1) or (2) of any such declaration as is there mentioned the person who made it shall become under this Act such a citizen as he would have become at commencement if, immediately before commencement, he had been a citizen of the United Kingdom and Colonies by virtue of section 4(2) of the Cyprus Act 1960.

Applications for certificates of patriality pending at commencement

5

Any application for a certificate of patriality under the Immigration Act 1971 duly made but not determined before commencement shall be treated as if it were an application for a certificate of entitlement under that Act as amended by this Act.

Appeals under Part II of Immigration Act 1971

6

Where a person who has been refused a certificate of patriality under the Immigration Act 1971 before commencement has immediately before commencement a right of appeal under Part II (appeals) of that Act against the refusal, the provisions of that Part shall have effect in relation to the refusal as if he had applied for, and been refused, a certificate of entitlement under that Act as amended by this Act.

7

Any appeal under Part II of the Immigration Act 1971 against a refusal of a certificate of patriality under that Act which is pending immediately before commencement shall be treated as if it were an appeal against a refusal of a certificate of entitlement under that Act as amended by this Act.

8

In relation to appeals against any decision taken or other thing done under the Immigration Act 1971 before commencement, other than a refusal of a certificate of patriality under that Act, the provisions of that Act shall continue to apply as in force immediately before commencement, and not as amended by this Act.

SCHEDULE 9

(Sch 9 contains repeals which, in so far as relevant to this work, have been incorporated at the appropriate place.)

FINANCE (NO 2) ACT 1987

1987 c 51

An Act to grant certain duties, to alter other duties, and to amend the law relating to the National Debt and the Public Revenue, and to make further provision in connection with Finance

[23 July 1987]

PART III
MISCELLANEOUS AND SUPPLEMENTARY

102 Government fees and charges

(1)   This section applies where a Minister of the Crown or any other person has power under any enactment (whenever passed) to require the payment of, or to determine by subordinate legislation the amount of, any fee or charge (however described), which is payable to the Minister or to any other person who is required to pay the fee or charge into the Consolidated Fund (whether the obligation is so expressed or is expressed as a requirement to make the payment into the Exchequer).

(2)   In the following provisions of this section, a power falling within subsection (1) above is referred to as a "power to fix a fee" and, in relation to such a power,—

    (a)   "fee" includes charge;

    (b)   "the appropriate authority" means, if the power is exercisable by a Minister of the Crown or any Commissioners, that Minister or those Commissioners and, in any other case, such Minister of the Crown as the Treasury may determine; and

    (c)   "the recipient" means the Minister or other person to whom the fee is payable.

(3)   In relation to any power to fix a fee, the appropriate authority or any Minister of the Crown with the consent of the appropriate authority may, by order made by statutory instrument, specify functions, whether of the recipient or any other person and whether arising under any enactment, by virtue of any [EU] obligation or otherwise, the costs of which, in addition to any other matters already required to be taken into account, are to be taken into account in determining the amount of the fee.

(4)   In relation to any functions the costs of which fall to be taken into account on the exercise of any power to fix a fee (whether by virtue of subsection (3) above or otherwise), the appropriate authority or any Minister of the Crown with the consent of the appropriate authority may, by order made by statutory instrument, specify matters which, in addition to any matters already required to be taken into account, are to be taken into account in determining those costs, and, without prejudice to the generality of the power conferred by this subsection, those matters may include deficits incurred before as well as after the exercise of that power, a requirement to secure a return on an amount of capital and depreciation of assets.

(5)   No order shall be made under subsection (3) or subsection (4) above unless a draft of the order has been laid before, and approved by a resolution of, the House of Commons.

(6)   An order under subsection (3) or subsection (4) above has effect in relation to any exercise of the power to fix the fee concerned after the making of the order; but no earlier exercise of that power shall be regarded as having been invalid if, had the order been made before that exercise of the power, the exercise would have been validated by the order.

(7)   In this section—

    (a)   "Minister of the Crown" has the same meaning as in the Ministers of the Crown Act 1975;

(b)   "Commissioners" means the Commissioners of Customs and Excise or the Commissioners of Inland Revenue;

(c)   "enactment" does not include Northern Ireland legislation, as defined in section 24(5) of the Interpretation Act 1978; and

(d)   subject to paragraph (c) above, "subordinate legislation" has the same meaning as in the Interpretation Act 1978.

(8)   An Order in Council under paragraph 1(1)(b) of Schedule 1 to the Northern Ireland Act 1974 (legislation for Northern Ireland in the interim period) which states that it is made only for purposes corresponding to those of this section—

(a)   shall not be subject to sub-paragraphs (4) and (5) of paragraph 1 of that Schedule (affirmative resolution of both Houses of Parliament); but

(b)   shall be subject to annulment in pursuance of a resolution of either House.

Amendment

Amendment Sub-s (3): reference to "EU" in square brackets substituted by SI 2011/1043, art 6(1)(e). Date in force: 22 April 2011: see SI 2011/1043, art 2; for transitional savings see art 3(3) thereof.

Subordinate Legislation

Immigration (Application Fees) Order 2005, SI 2005/582; Consular Fees Act 1980 (Fees) Order 2005, SI 2005/2112; Consular Fees Act 1980 (Fees) (No 2) Order 2005, SI 2005/3198. Other statutory instruments made under this section are not relevant to this work.

CHILDREN ACT 1989

1989 c 41

An Act to reform the law relating to children; to provide for local authority services for children in need and others; to amend the law with respect to children's homes, community homes, voluntary homes and voluntary organisations; to make provision with respect to fostering, child minding and day care for young children and adoption; and for connected purposes

[16 November 1989]

PART III
LOCAL AUTHORITY SUPPORT FOR CHILDREN AND FAMILIES

Provision of services for children and their families

17 Provision of services for children in need, their families and others

(1)   It shall be the general duty of every local authority (in addition to the other duties imposed on them by this Part)—

(a)   to safeguard and promote the welfare of children within their area who are in need; and

(b)   so far as is consistent with that duty, to promote the upbringing of such children by their families,

by providing a range and level of services appropriate to those children's needs.

(2)   For the purpose principally of facilitating the discharge of their general duty under this section, every local authority shall have the specific duties and powers set out in Part I of Schedule 2.

(3)   Any service provided by an authority in the exercise of functions conferred on them by this section may be provided for the family of a particular child in need or for

any member of his family, if it is provided with a view to safeguarding or promoting the child's welfare.

(4) The [appropriate national authority] may by order amend any provision of Part I of Schedule 2 or add any further duty or power to those for the time being mentioned there.

[(4A) Before determining what (if any) services to provide for a particular child in need in the exercise of functions conferred on them by this section, a local authority shall, so far as is reasonably practicable and consistent with the child's welfare—

- (a) ascertain the child's wishes and feelings regarding the provision of those services; and
- (b) give due consideration (having regard to his age and understanding) to such wishes and feelings of the child as they have been able to ascertain.]

(5) Every local authority—

- (a) shall facilitate the provision by others (including in particular voluntary organisations) of services which *the authority have power* [it is a function of the authority] to provide by virtue of this section, or section 18, 20, [23 [22A to 22C], 23B to 23D, 24A or 24B]; and
- (b) may make such arrangements as they see fit for any person to act on their behalf in the provision of any such service.

(6) The services provided by a local authority in the exercise of functions conferred on them by this section may include [providing accommodation and] giving assistance in kind or . . . in cash.

(7) Assistance may be unconditional or subject to conditions as to the repayment of the assistance or of its value (in whole or in part).

(8) Before giving any assistance or imposing any conditions, a local authority shall have regard to the means of the child concerned and of each of his parents.

(9) No person shall be liable to make any repayment of assistance or of its value at any time when he is in receipt [of universal credit (except in such circumstances as may be prescribed)] *of income support* [under] [*Part VII of the Social Security Contributions and Benefits Act 1992*] [, *of any element of child tax credit other than the family element, of working tax credit*][, *of an income-based jobseeker's allowance or of an income-related employment and support allowance*].

(10) For the purposes of this Part a child shall be taken to be in need if—

- (a) he is unlikely to achieve or maintain, or to have the opportunity of achieving or maintaining, a reasonable standard of health or development without the provision for him of services by a local authority under this Part;
- (b) his health or development is likely to be significantly impaired, or further impaired, without the provision for him of such services; or
- (c) he is disabled,

and "family", in relation to such a child, includes any person who has parental responsibility for the child and any other person with whom he has been living.

(11) For the purposes of this Part, a child is disabled if he is blind, deaf or dumb or suffers from mental disorder of any kind or is substantially and permanently handicapped by illness, injury or congenital deformity or such other disability as may be prescribed; and in this Part—

"development" means physical, intellectual, emotional, social or behavioural development; and

"health" means physical or mental health.

[(12) *The Treasury may by regulations prescribe circumstances in which a person is to be treated for the purposes of this Part (or for such of those purposes as are prescribed) as in receipt of any element of child tax credit other than the family element or of working tax credit.*]

Amendment

Sub-s (4): words "appropriate national authority" in square brackets substituted by the Children and Young Persons Act 2008, s 39, Sch 3, paras 1, 2.

Sub-s (4A): inserted by the Children Act 2004, s 53(1).

Sub-s (5): in para (a) words "the authority have power" in italics repealed and subsequent words in square brackets substituted by the Children and Young Persons Act 2008, s 8(2), Sch 1, para 1(a). Date in force (in relation to England): 1 April 2011: see SI 2010/2981, art 4(a). Date in force (in relation to Wales): to be appointed: see the Children and Young Persons Act 2008, s 44(3), (4), (5)(a).

Sub-s (5): in para (a) words "23, 23B to 23D, 24A or 24B" in square brackets substituted by the Children (Leaving Care) Act 2000, s 7(1), (2), as from 1 October 2001: see SI 2001/2191, art 2 and SI 2001/2878, art 2.

Sub-s (5): in para (a) reference to "23" in italics repealed and subsequent words in square brackets substituted by the Children and Young Persons Act 2008, s 8(2), Sch 1, para 1(b).Date in force (in relation to England): 1 April 2011: see SI 2010/2981, art 4(a). Date in force (in relation to Wales): to be appointed: see the Children and Young Persons Act 2008, s 44(3), (4), (5)(a).

Sub-s (6): words in square brackets inserted by the Adoption and Children Act 2002, s 116(1).

Sub-s (6): words omitted repealed by the Children and Young Persons Act 2008, ss 24, 42, Sch 4. Date in force (in relation to England): 1 April 2011: see SI 2010/2981, art 4(i), (l). Date in force (in relation to Wales): 19 June 2012: see SI 2012/1553, art 2(c).

Sub-s (9): words "of universal credit (except in such circumstances as may be prescribed)," in square brackets inserted by the Welfare Reform Act 2012, s 31, Sch 2, para 1(a). Date in force: 29 April 2013: see SI 2013/983, art 3(1)(b)(i).

Sub-s (9): words "of income support under Part VII of the Social Security Contributions and Benefits Act 1992," in italics repealed by the Welfare Reform Act 2009, ss 9(3)(b), 58(1), Sch 7, Pt 1; for further provision in relation to this repeal see s 9(1), (2), (4)–(10) thereof,

Sub-s (9): words from "of income support" to the end repealed by the Welfare Reform Act 2012, s 147, Sch 14, Pt 1, as from a day to be appointed.

Sub-s (9): word "under" in square brackets substituted by the Tax Credits Act 2002, s 47, Sch 3, paras 15, 16(1), (2)(a).

Sub-s (9): words "Part VII of the Social Security Contributions and Benefits Act 1992" in square brackets substituted by the Social Security (Consequential Provisions) Act 1992, s 4, Sch 2, para 108(a).

Sub-s (9): words from ", of any element" to "working tax credit" in square brackets inserted by the Tax Credits Act 2002, s 47, Sch 3, paras 15, 16(1), (2)(b).

Sub-s (9): words from ", of an income-based" to "and support allowance" in square brackets substituted by the Welfare Reform Act 2007, s 28(1), Sch 3, para 6(1), (2).

Sub-s (12): inserted by the Tax Credits Act 2002, s 47, Sch 3, paras 15, 16(1), (3), as from 6 April 2003: see SI 2003/962, art 2(1), (3)(b), (d)(iii). Repealed by the Welfare Reform Act 2012, s 147, Sch 14, Pt 1, as from a day to be appointed.

Subordinate Legislation

Children Act 1989, Section 17(12) Regulations 2003, SI 2003/2077.

Provision of accommodation for children

20 Provision of accommodation for children: general

(1) Every local authority shall provide accommodation for any child in need within their area who appears to them to require accommodation as a result of—

    (a)   there being no person who has parental responsibility for him;

    (b)   his being lost or having been abandoned; or

    (c)   the person who has been caring for him being prevented (whether or not permanently, and for whatever reason) from providing him with suitable accommodation or care.

(2) Where a local authority provide accommodation under subsection (1) for a child who is ordinarily resident in the area of another local authority, that other local authority may take over the provision of accommodation for the child within—

(a)   three months of being notified in writing that the child is being provided with accommodation; or

(b)   such other longer period as may be prescribed.

(3)   Every local authority shall provide accommodation for any child in need within their area who has reached the age of sixteen and whose welfare the authority consider is likely to be seriously prejudiced if they do not provide him with accommodation.

(4)   A local authority may provide accommodation for any child within their area (even though a person who has parental responsibility for him is able to provide him with accommodation) if they consider that to do so would safeguard or promote the child's welfare.

(5)   A local authority may provide accommodation for any person who has reached the age of sixteen but is under twenty-one in any community home which takes children who have reached the age of sixteen if they consider that to do so would safeguard or promote his welfare.

(6)   Before providing accommodation under this section, a local authority shall, so far as is reasonably practicable and consistent with the child's welfare—

(a)   ascertain the child's wishes [and feelings] regarding the provision of accommodation; and

(b)   give due consideration (having regard to his age and understanding) to such wishes [and feelings] of the child as they have been able to ascertain.

(7)   A local authority may not provide accommodation under this section for any child if any person who—

(a)   has parental responsibility for him; and

(b)   is willing and able to—

(i)   provide accommodation for him; or

(ii)   arrange for accommodation to be provided for him,

objects.

(8)   Any person who has parental responsibility for a child may at any time remove the child from accommodation provided by or on behalf of the local authority under this section.

(9)   Subsections (7) and (8) do not apply while any person—

[(a)   who is named in a child arrangements order as a person with whom the child is to live;]

[(aa)   who is a special guardian of the child; or]

(b)   who has care of the child by virtue of an order made in the exercise of the High Court's inherent jurisdiction with respect to children,

agrees to the child being looked after in accommodation provided by or on behalf of the local authority.

(10)   Where there is more than one such person as is mentioned in subsection (9), all of them must agree.

(11)   Subsections (7) and (8) do not apply where a child who has reached the age of sixteen agrees to being provided with accommodation under this section.

Amendment

Sub-s (6): in paras (a), (b) words "and feelings" in square brackets inserted by the Children Act 2004, s 53(2).

Sub-s (9): para (a) substituted by the Children and Families Act 2014, s 12(4), Sch 2, Pt 1, paras 1, 28. Date in force: 22 April 2014: see SI 2014/889, art 4(b), (f).

Sub-s (9): para (aa) inserted by the Adoption and Children Act 2002, s 139(1), Sch 3, paras 54, 59.

See Further

In relation to the Isles of Scilly, any reference in this section to a "local authority" is to be construed as a reference to the Council of the Isles of Scilly: see the Isles of Scilly (Children Act 1989) Order 2010, SI 2010/1116, art 2.

Duties of local authorities in relation to children looked after by them

22 General duty of local authority in relation to children looked after by them

(1) In this Act, any reference to a child who is looked after by a local authority is a reference to a child who is—

(a)   in their care; or

(b)   provided with accommodation by the authority in the exercise of any functions (in particular those under this Act) which [are social services functions within the meaning of] the Local Authority Social Services Act 1970[, apart from functions under sections [17], 23B and 24B].

(2) In subsection (1) "accommodation" means accommodation which is provided for a continuous period of more than 24 hours.

(3) It shall be the duty of a local authority looking after any child—

(a)   to safeguard and promote his welfare; and

(b)   to make such use of services available for children cared for by their own parents as appears to the authority reasonable in his case.

[(3A) The duty of a local authority under subsection (3)(a) to safeguard and promote the welfare of a child looked after by them includes in particular a duty to promote the child's educational achievement.]

[(3B) A local authority in England must appoint at least one person for the purpose of discharging the duty imposed by virtue of subsection (3A).

(3C) A person appointed by a local authority under subsection (3B) must be an officer employed by that authority or another local authority in England.]

(4) Before making any decision with respect to a child whom they are looking after, or proposing to look after, a local authority shall, so far as is reasonably practicable, ascertain the wishes and feelings of—

(a)   the child;

(b)   his parents;

(c)   any person who is not a parent of his but who has parental responsibility for him; and

(d)   any other person whose wishes and feelings the authority consider to be relevant,

regarding the matter to be decided.

(5) In making any such decision a local authority shall give due consideration—

(a)   having regard to his age and understanding, to such wishes and feelings of the child as they have been able to ascertain;

(b)   to such wishes and feelings of any person mentioned in subsection (4)(*b*) to (*d*) as they have been able to ascertain; and

(c)   to the child's religious persuasion, racial origin and cultural and linguistic background.

(6) If it appears to a local authority that it is necessary, for the purpose of protecting members of the public from serious injury, to exercise their powers with respect to a child whom they are looking after in a manner which may not be consistent with their duties under this section, they may do so.

(7) If the [appropriate national authority] considers it necessary, for the purpose of protecting members of the public from serious injury, to give directions to a local authority with respect to the exercise of their powers with respect to a child whom they are looking after, [the appropriate national authority] may give such directions to [the local authority].

(8) Where any such directions are given to an authority they shall comply with them even though doing so is inconsistent with their duties under this section.

Amendment

Sub-s (1): in para (b) words "are social services functions within the meaning of" in square brackets substituted by the Local Government Act 2000, s 107, Sch 5, para 19.

Sub-s (1): in para (b) words ", apart from functions under sections 23B and 24B" in square brackets inserted by the Children (Leaving Care) Act 2000, s 2(1), (2).

Sub-s (1): in para (b) reference to "17" in square brackets inserted by the Adoption and Children Act 2002, s 116(2).

Sub-s (3A): inserted by the Children Act 2004, s 52.

Sub-ss (3B), (3C): inserted by the Children and Families Act 2014, s 99. Date in force: 13 May 2014: see SI 2014/889, art 5(e).

Sub-s (7): words "appropriate national authority" in both places in square brackets substituted by the Children and Young Persons Act 2008, s 39, Sch 3, paras 1, 6(a), (b).

Sub-s (7): words "the local authority" in square brackets substituted by the Children and Young Persons Act 2008, s 39, Sch 3, paras 1, 6(c).

Modification

Sub-ss (4)(b), (c), (5)(b): modified, in relation to England, in so far as relating to adoption, by the Adoption Agencies Regulations 2005, SI 2005/389, reg 45(1), (2)(a)–(c).

Sub-ss (4)(b), (c), (5)(b): modified, in relation to Wales, in so far as relating to adoption, by the Adoption Agencies (Wales) Regulations 2005, SI 2005/1313, reg 46(1), (2)(a)–(c).

See Further

In relation to the Isles of Scilly, any reference in this section to a "local authority" is to be construed as a reference to the Council of the Isles of Scilly: see the Isles of Scilly (Children Act 1989) Order 2010, SI 2010/1116, art 2.

[22A Provision of accommodation for children in care

When a child is in the care of a local authority, it is their duty to provide the child with accommodation.]

Amendment

Substituted, together with ss 22B–22F, for s 23 as originally enacted, by the Children and Young Persons Act 2008, s 8(1).

Date in force (in relation to England): 1 April 2011: see SI 2010/2981, art 4(a). Date in force (in relation to Wales): to be appointed: see the Children and Young Persons Act 2008, s 44(3), (4), (5)(a).

See Further

In relation to the Isles of Scilly, any reference in this section to a "local authority" is to be construed as a reference to the Council of the Isles of Scilly: see the Isles of Scilly (Children Act 1989) Order 2010, SI 2010/1116, art 2.

[22B Maintenance of looked after children

It is the duty of a local authority to maintain a child they are looking after in other respects apart from the provision of accommodation.]

Extent

This section does not extend to Scotland: see s 108(11).

Amendment

Substituted, together with ss 22A, 22C–22F, for s 23 as originally enacted, by the Children and Young Persons Act 2008, s 8(1).

Date in force (in relation to England): 1 April 2011: see SI 2010/2981, art 4(a). Date in force (in relation to Wales): to be appointed: see the Children and Young Persons Act 2008, s 44(3), (4), (5)(a).

See Further

In relation to the Isles of Scilly, any reference in this section to a "local authority" is to be construed as a reference to the Council of the Isles of Scilly: see the Isles of Scilly (Children Act 1989) Order 2010, SI 2010/1116, art 2.

[22C Ways in which looked after children are to be accommodated and maintained

(1) This section applies where a local authority are looking after a child ("C").

(2) The local authority must make arrangements for C to live with a person who falls within subsection (3) (but subject to subsection (4)).

(3) A person ("P") falls within this subsection if—

(a) P is a parent of C;

(b) P is not a parent of C but has parental responsibility for C; or

(c) in a case where C is in the care of the local authority and there was [a child arrangements order] in force with respect to C immediately before the care order was made, P was a person [named in the child arrangements order as a person with whom C was to live].

(4) Subsection (2) does not require the local authority to make arrangements of the kind mentioned in that subsection if doing so—

(a) would not be consistent with C's welfare; or

(b) would not be reasonably practicable.

(5) If the local authority are unable to make arrangements under subsection (2), they must place C in the placement which is, in their opinion, the most appropriate placement available.

(6) In subsection (5) "placement" means—

(a) placement with an individual who is a relative, friend or other person connected with C and who is also a local authority foster parent;

(b) placement with a local authority foster parent who does not fall within paragraph (a);

(c) placement in a children's home in respect of which a person is registered under Part 2 of the Care Standards Act 2000; or

(d) subject to section 22D, placement in accordance with other arrangements which comply with any regulations made for the purposes of this section.

(7) In determining the most appropriate placement for C, the local authority must, subject to [subsection (9B) and] the other provisions of this Part (in particular, to their duties under section 22)—

(a) give preference to a placement falling within paragraph (a) of subsection (6) over placements falling within the other paragraphs of that subsection;

(b) comply, so far as is reasonably practicable in all the circumstances of C's case, with the requirements of subsection (8); and

(c) comply with subsection (9) unless that is not reasonably practicable.

(8) The local authority must ensure that the placement is such that—

(a) it allows C to live near C's home;

(b) it does not disrupt C's education or training;

(c) if C has a sibling for whom the local authority are also providing accommodation, it enables C and the sibling to live together;

(d) if C is disabled, the accommodation provided is suitable to C's particular needs.

(9) The placement must be such that C is provided with accommodation within the local authority's area.

[(9A) Subsection (9B) applies (subject to subsection (9C)) where the local authority are a local authority in England and—

(a) are considering adoption for C, or

(b) are satisfied that C ought to be placed for adoption but are not authorised under section 19 of the Adoption and Children Act 2002 (placement with parental consent) or by virtue of section 21 of that Act (placement orders) to place C for adoption.

(9B) Where this subsection applies—

(a) subsections (7) to (9) do not apply to the local authority,

(b)   the local authority must consider placing C with an individual within subsection (6)(a), and

(c)   where the local authority decide that a placement with such an individual is not the most appropriate placement for C, the local authority must consider placing C with a local authority foster parent who has been approved as a prospective adopter.

(9C)   Subsection (9B) does not apply where the local authority have applied for a placement order under section 21 of the Adoption and Children Act 2002 in respect of C and the application has been refused.]

(10)   The local authority may determine—

(a)   the terms of any arrangements they make under subsection (2) in relation to C (including terms as to payment); and

(b)   the terms on which they place C with a local authority foster parent (including terms as to payment but subject to any order made under section 49 of the Children Act 2004).

(11)   The appropriate national authority may make regulations for, and in connection with, the purposes of this section.

(12)   In this Act "local authority foster parent" means a person who is approved as a local authority foster parent in accordance with regulations made by virtue of paragraph 12F of Schedule 2.]

Amendment

Substituted, together with ss 22A, 22B, 22D–22F, for s 23 as originally enacted, by the Children and Young Persons Act 2008, s 8(1).

Date in force (in relation to England for certain purposes): 1 September 2009: see SI 2009/2273, art 2(2)(a)(i).

Date in force (in relation to Wales for certain purposes): 26 April 2010: see SI 2010/1329, art 2(a)(i).

Date in force (in relation to England for remaining purposes): 1 April 2011: see SI 2010/2981, art 4(a).

Date in force (in relation to Wales for remaining purposes): to be appointed: see the Children and Young Persons Act 2008, s 44(3), (4), (5)(a).

Sub-s (3): in para (c) words in square brackets substituted by the Children and Families Act 2014, s 12(4), Sch 2, Pt 1, paras 1, 29. Date in force: 22 April 2014: see SI 2014/889, art 4(b), (f).

Sub-s (7): words in square brackets inserted by the Children and Families Act 2014, s 2(1), (2). Date in force: 25 July 2014: see SI 2014/889, art 6(b).

Sub-ss (9A)–(9C): inserted by the Children and Families Act 2014, s 2(1), (3). Date in force: 25 July 2014: see SI 2014/889, art 6(b).

See Further

In relation to the Isles of Scilly, any reference in this section to a "local authority" is to be construed as a reference to the Council of the Isles of Scilly: see the Isles of Scilly (Children Act 1989) Order 2010, SI 2010/1116, art 2.

Subordinate Legislation

Care Planning, Placement and Case Review (England) Regulations 2010, SI 2010/959; Fostering Services (England) Regulations 2011, SI 2011/581; Adoption Agencies and Independent Review of Determinations (Amendment) Regulations 2011, SI 2011/589; Care Planning, Placement and Case Review (England) (Miscellaneous Amendments) Regulations 2013, SI 2013/706; Care Planning, Placement and Case Review and Fostering Services (Miscellaneous Amendments) Regulations 2013, SI 2013/984; Adoption Agencies (Miscellaneous Amendments) Regulations 2013, SI 2013/985; Children's Homes and Looked after Children (Miscellaneous Amendments) (England) Regulations 2013, SI 2013/3239; Adoption and Care Planning (Miscellaneous Amendments) Regulations 2014, SI 2014/1556; Care Planning and Care Leavers (Amendment) Regulations 2014, SI 2014/1917.

[22D Review of child's case before making alternative arrangements for accommodation

(1) Where a local authority are providing accommodation for a child ("C") other than by arrangements under section 22C(6)(d), they must not make such arrangements for C unless they have decided to do so in consequence of a review of C's case carried out in accordance with regulations made under section 26.

(2) But subsection (1) does not prevent a local authority making arrangements for C under section 22C(6)(d) if they are satisfied that in order to safeguard C's welfare it is necessary—

    (a)   to make such arrangements; and

    (b)   to do so as a matter of urgency.]

Amendment

Substituted, together with ss 22A–22C, 22E, 22F, for s 23 as originally enacted, by the Children and Young Persons Act 2008, s 8(1).

Date in force (in relation to England): 1 April 2011: see SI 2010/2981, art 4(a).

Date in force (in relation to Wales): to be appointed: see the Children and Young Persons Act 2008, s 44(3), (4), (5)(a).

See Further

In relation to the Isles of Scilly, any reference in this section to a "local authority" is to be construed as a reference to the Council of the Isles of Scilly: see the Isles of Scilly (Children Act 1989) Order 2010, SI 2010/1116, art 2.

[22E Children's homes provided by appropriate national authority

Where a local authority place a child they are looking after in a children's home provided, equipped and maintained by an appropriate national authority under section 82(5), they must do so on such terms as that national authority may from time to time determine.]

Amendment

Substituted, together with ss 22A–22D, 22F, for s 23 as originally enacted, by the Children and Young Persons Act 2008, s 8(1).

Date in force (in relation to England): 1 April 2011: see SI 2010/2981, art 4(a).

Date in force (in relation to Wales): to be appointed: see the Children and Young Persons Act 2008, s 44(3), (4), (5)(a).

See Further

In relation to the Isles of Scilly, any reference in this section to a "local authority" is to be construed as a reference to the Council of the Isles of Scilly: see the Isles of Scilly (Children Act 1989) Order 2010, SI 2010/1116, art 2.

[22F Regulations as to children looked after by local authorities

Part 2 of Schedule 2 has effect for the purposes of making further provision as to children looked after by local authorities and in particular as to the regulations which may be made under section 22C(11).]

Amendment

Substituted, together with ss 22A–22E, for s 23 as originally enacted, by the Children and Young Persons Act 2008, s 8(1).

Date in force (in relation to England): 1 September 2009: see SI 2009/2273, art 2(2)(a)(ii).

Date in force (in relation to Wales): 26 April 2010: see SI 2010/1329, art 2(a)(ii).

See Further

In relation to the Isles of Scilly, any reference in this section to a "local authority" is to be construed as a reference to the Council of the Isles of Scilly: see the Isles of Scilly (Children Act 1989) Order 2010, SI 2010/1116, art 2.

[22G General duty of local authority to secure sufficient accommodation for looked after children

(1) It is the general duty of a local authority to take steps that secure, so far as reasonably practicable, the outcome in subsection (2).

(2) The outcome is that the local authority are able to provide the children mentioned in subsection (3) with accommodation that—

    (a)   is within the authority's area; and

    (b)   meets the needs of those children.

(3) The children referred to in subsection (2) are those—

    (a)   that the local authority are looking after,

    (b)   in respect of whom the authority are unable to make arrangements under section 22C(2), and

    (c)   whose circumstances are such that it would be consistent with their welfare for them to be provided with accommodation that is in the authority's area.

(4) In taking steps to secure the outcome in subsection (2), the local authority must have regard to the benefit of having—

    (a)   a number of accommodation providers in their area that is, in their opinion, sufficient to secure that outcome; and

    (b)   a range of accommodation in their area capable of meeting different needs that is, in their opinion, sufficient to secure that outcome.

(5) In this section "accommodation providers" means—

local authority foster parents; and

children's homes in respect of which a person is registered under Part 2 of the Care Standards Act 2000.]

Amendment

Inserted by the Children and Young Persons Act 2008, s 9.

Date in force (in relation to England): 1 April 2011: see SI 2010/2981, art 4(b).

Date in force (in relation to Wales): to be appointed: see the Children and Young Persons Act 2008, s 44(3), (4), (5)(a).

See Further

In relation to the Isles of Scilly, any reference in this section to a "local authority" is to be construed as a reference to the Council of the Isles of Scilly: see the Isles of Scilly (Children Act 1989) Order 2010, SI 2010/1116, art 2.

HUMAN RIGHTS ACT 1998

1998 c 42

An Act to give further effect to rights and freedoms guaranteed under the European Convention on Human Rights; to make provision with respect to holders of certain judicial offices who become judges of the European Court of Human Rights; and for connected purposes.

[9 November 1998]

Introduction

1 The Convention Rights

(1) In this Act "the Convention rights" means the rights and fundamental freedoms set out in—

    (a)   Articles 2 to 12 and 14 of the Convention,

    (b)   Articles 1 to 3 of the First Protocol, and

    (c)   [Article 1 of the Thirteenth Protocol],

as read with Articles 16 to 18 of the Convention.

(2) Those Articles are to have effect for the purposes of this Act subject to any designated derogation or reservation (as to which see sections 14 and 15).

(3) The Articles are set out in Schedule 1.

(4) The [Secretary of State] may by order make such amendments to this Act as he considers appropriate to reflect the effect, in relation to the United Kingdom, of a protocol.

(5) In subsection (4) "protocol" means a protocol to the Convention—

    (a)   which the United Kingdom has ratified; or

    (b)   which the United Kingdom has signed with a view to ratification.

(6) No amendment may be made by an order under subsection (4) so as to come into force before the protocol concerned is in force in relation to the United Kingdom.

Amendment

Sub-s (1): in para (c) words "Article 1 of the Thirteenth Protocol" in square brackets substituted by SI 2004/1574, art 2(1).

Sub-s (4): words "Secretary of State" in square brackets substituted by SI 2003/1887, art 9, Sch 2, para 10(1).

Subordinate Legislation

Human Rights Act 1998 (Amendment) Order 2004, SI 2004/1574.

2 Interpretation of Convention rights

(1) A court or tribunal determining a question which has arisen in connection with a Convention right must take into account any—

    (a)   judgment, decision, declaration or advisory opinion of the European Court of Human Rights,

    (b)   opinion of the Commission given in a report adopted under Article 31 of the Convention,

    (c)   decision of the Commission in connection with Article 26 or 27(2) of the Convention, or

    (d)   decision of the Committee of Ministers taken under Article 46 of the Convention,

whenever made or given, so far as, in the opinion of the court or tribunal, it is relevant to the proceedings in which that question has arisen.

(2) Evidence of any judgment, decision, declaration or opinion of which account may have to be taken under this section is to be given in proceedings before any court or tribunal in such manner as may be provided by rules.

(3) In this section "rules" means rules of court or, in the case of proceedings before a tribunal, rules made for the purposes of this section—

    (a)   by < . . . > [the Lord Chancellor or] the Secretary of State, in relation to any proceedings outside Scotland;

    (b)   by the Secretary of State, in relation to proceedings in Scotland; or

    (c)   by a Northern Ireland department, in relation to proceedings before a tribunal in Northern Ireland—

        (i)   which deals with transferred matters; and

       (ii)   for which no rules made under paragraph (a) are in force.

Amendment

Sub-s (3): in para (a) words omitted repealed by SI 2003/1887, art 9, Sch 2, para 10(2).

Sub-s (3): in para (a) words "the Lord Chancellor or" in square brackets inserted by SI 2005/3429, art 8, Schedule, para 3.

Legislation

3 Interpretation of legislation

(1)   So far as it is possible to do so, primary legislation and subordinate legislation must be read and given effect in a way which is compatible with the Convention rights.

(2)   This section—

    (a)   applies to primary legislation and subordinate legislation whenever enacted;

    (b)   does not affect the validity, continuing operation or enforcement of any incompatible primary legislation; and

    (c)   does not affect the validity, continuing operation or enforcement of any incompatible subordinate legislation if (disregarding any possibility of revocation) primary legislation prevents removal of the incompatibility.

4 Declaration of incompatibility

(1)   Subsection (2) applies in any proceedings in which a court determines whether a provision of primary legislation is compatible with a Convention right.

(2)   If the court is satisfied that the provision is incompatible with a Convention right, it may make a declaration of that incompatibility.

(3)   Subsection (4) applies in any proceedings in which a court determines whether a provision of subordinate legislation, made in the exercise of a power conferred by primary legislation, is compatible with a Convention right.

(4)   If the court is satisfied—

    (a)   that the provision is incompatible with a Convention right, and

    (b)   that (disregarding any possibility of revocation) the primary legislation concerned prevents removal of the incompatibility,

it may make a declaration of that incompatibility.

(5)   In this section "court" means—

    [(a)   the Supreme Court;]

    (b)   the Judicial Committee of the Privy Council;

    (c)   the [Court Martial Appeal Court];

    (d)   in Scotland, the High Court of Justiciary sitting otherwise than as a trial court or the Court of Session;

    (e)   in England and Wales or Northern Ireland, the High Court or the Court of Appeal;

    [(f)   the Court of Protection, in any matter being dealt with by the President of the Family Division, the [Chancellor of the High Court] or a puisne judge of the High Court].

(6)   A declaration under this section ("a declaration of incompatibility")—

    (a)   does not affect the validity, continuing operation or enforcement of the provision in respect of which it is given; and

    (b)   is not binding on the parties to the proceedings in which it is made.

Amendment

Sub-s (5): para (a) substituted by the Constitutional Reform Act 2005, s 40(4), Sch 9, Pt 1, para 66(1), (2).

Sub-s (5): in para (c) words "Courts-Martial Appeal Court" in italics repealed and subsequent words in square brackets substituted by the Armed Forces Act 2006, s 378(1), Sch 16, para 156.

Sub-s (5): para (f) inserted by the Mental Capacity Act 2005, s 67(1), Sch 6, para 43.

Sub-s (5): in para (f) words in square brackets substituted by the Crime and Courts Act 2013, s 21(4), Sch 14, Pt 3, para 5(5). Date in force: 1 October 2013: see SI 2013/2200, art 3(g).

5 Right of Crown to intervene

(1)   Where a court is considering whether to make a declaration of incompatibility, the Crown is entitled to notice in accordance with rules of court.

(2)   In any case to which subsection (1) applies—

(a)   a Minister of the Crown (or a person nominated by him),

(b)   a member of the Scottish Executive,

(c)   a Northern Ireland Minister,

(d)   a Northern Ireland department,

is entitled, on giving notice in accordance with rules of court, to be joined as a party to the proceedings.

(3)   Notice under subsection (2) may be given at any time during the proceedings.

(4)   A person who has been made a party to criminal proceedings (other than in Scotland) as the result of a notice under subsection (2) may, with leave, appeal to the [Supreme Court] against any declaration of incompatibility made in the proceedings.

(5)   In subsection (4)—

"criminal proceedings" includes all proceedings before the *Courts-Martial Appeal Court* [Court Martial Appeal Court]; and

"leave" means leave granted by the court making the declaration of incompatibility or by the [Supreme Court].

Amendment

Sub-s (4): words "Supreme Court" in square brackets substituted by the Constitutional Reform Act 2005, s 40(4), Sch 9, Pt 1, para 66(1), (3).

Sub-s (5): in definition "criminal proceedings" words "Courts-Martial Appeal Court" in italics repealed and subsequent words in square brackets substituted by the Armed Forces Act 2006, s 378(1), Sch 16, para 157.

Date in force (for certain purposes): 28 March 2009: see SI 2009/812, art 3(a), (b).

Date in force (for remaining purposes): to be appointed: see the Armed Forces Act 2006, s 383(2).

Sub-s (5): in definition "leave" words "Supreme Court" in square brackets substituted by the Constitutional Reform Act 2005, s 40(4), Sch 9, Pt 1, para 66(1), (3).

Transfer of Functions

The function under sub-s (2) shall be exercisable by the National Assembly for Wales concurrently with any Minister of the Crown by whom it is exercisable, in so far as it relates to any proceedings in which a court is considering whether to make a declaration of incompatibility within the meaning of s 4 of this Act, in respect of subordinate legislation made by the National Assembly, and subordinate legislation made, in relation to Wales, by a Minister of the Crown in the exercise of a function which is exercisable by the National Assembly: see the National Assembly for Wales (Transfer of Functions) (No 2) Order 2000, SI 2000/1830, art 2.

Subordinate Legislation

Act of Adjournal (Criminal Procedure Rules Amendment No 2) (Human Rights Act 1998) 2000, SSI 2000/315; Act of Sederunt (Rules of the Court of Session Amendment No 6) (Human Rights Act 1998) 2000, SSI 2000/316.

Public authorities

6 Acts of public authorities

(1)   It is unlawful for a public authority to act in a way which is incompatible with a Convention right.

(2)   Subsection (1) does not apply to an act if—

(a)   as the result of one or more provisions of primary legislation, the authority could not have acted differently; or

(b)   in the case of one or more provisions of, or made under, primary legislation which cannot be read or given effect in a way which is compatible with the Convention rights, the authority was acting so as to give effect to or enforce those provisions.

(3)   In this section "public authority" includes—

(a)   a court or tribunal, and

(b)   any person certain of whose functions are functions of a public nature, but does not include either House of Parliament or a person exercising functions in connection with proceedings in Parliament.

(4) ...

(5) In relation to a particular act, a person is not a public authority by virtue only of subsection (3)(b) if the nature of the act is private.

(6) "An act" includes a failure to act but does not include a failure to—

    (a)   introduce in, or lay before, Parliament a proposal for legislation; or

    (b)   make any primary legislation or remedial order.

Amendment

Sub-s (4): repealed by the Constitutional Reform Act 2005, ss 40(4), 146, Sch 9, Pt 1, para 66(1), (4), Sch 18, Pt 5.

7 Proceedings

(1) A person who claims that a public authority has acted (or proposes to act) in a way which is made unlawful by section 6(1) may—

    (a)   bring proceedings against the authority under this Act in the appropriate court or tribunal, or

    (b)   rely on the Convention right or rights concerned in any legal proceedings, but only if he is (or would be) a victim of the unlawful act.

(2) In subsection (1)(a) "appropriate court or tribunal" means such court or tribunal as may be determined in accordance with rules; and proceedings against an authority include a counterclaim or similar proceeding.

(3) If the proceedings are brought on an application for judicial review, the applicant is to be taken to have a sufficient interest in relation to the unlawful act only if he is, or would be, a victim of that act.

(4) If the proceedings are made by way of a petition for judicial review in Scotland, the applicant shall be taken to have title and interest to sue in relation to the unlawful act only if he is, or would be, a victim of that act.

(5) Proceedings under subsection (1)(a) must be brought before the end of—

    (a)   the period of one year beginning with the date on which the act complained of took place; or

    (b)   such longer period as the court or tribunal considers equitable having regard to all the circumstances,

but that is subject to any rule imposing a stricter time limit in relation to the procedure in question.

(6) In subsection (1)(b) "legal proceedings" includes—

    (a)   proceedings brought by or at the instigation of a public authority; and

    (b)   an appeal against the decision of a court or tribunal.

(7) For the purposes of this section, a person is a victim of an unlawful act only if he would be a victim for the purposes of Article 34 of the Convention if proceedings were brought in the European Court of Human Rights in respect of that act.

(8) Nothing in this Act creates a criminal offence.

(9) In this section "rules" means—

    (a)   in relation to proceedings before a court or tribunal outside Scotland, rules made by ... [the Lord Chancellor or] the Secretary of State for the purposes of this section or rules of court,

    (b)   in relation to proceedings before a court or tribunal in Scotland, rules made by the Secretary of State for those purposes,

    (c)   in relation to proceedings before a tribunal in Northern Ireland—

        (i)   which deals with transferred matters; and

        (ii)   for which no rules made under paragraph (a) are in force,

rules made by a Northern Ireland department for those purposes, and includes provision made by order under section 1 of the Courts and Legal Services Act 1990.

(10)   In making rules, regard must be had to section 9.

(11)   The Minister who has power to make rules in relation to a particular tribunal may, to the extent he considers it necessary to ensure that the tribunal can provide an appropriate remedy in relation to an act (or proposed act) of a public authority which is (or would be) unlawful as a result of section 6(1), by order add to—

> (a)   the relief or remedies which the tribunal may grant; or
>
> (b)   the grounds on which it may grant any of them.

(12)   An order made under subsection (11) may contain such incidental, supplemental, consequential or transitional provision as the Minister making it considers appropriate.

(13)   "The Minister" includes the Northern Ireland department concerned.

Amendment
    Sub-s (9): in para (a) words omitted repealed by SI 2003/1887, art 9, Sch 2, para 10(2).
    Sub-s (9): in para (a) words "the Lord Chancellor or" in square brackets inserted by SI 2005/3429, art 8, Schedule, para 3.

8 Judicial remedies

(1)   In relation to any act (or proposed act) of a public authority which the court finds is (or would be) unlawful, it may grant such relief or remedy, or make such order, within its powers as it considers just and appropriate.

(2)   But damages may be awarded only by a court which has power to award damages, or to order the payment of compensation, in civil proceedings.

(3)   No award of damages is to be made unless, taking account of all the circumstances of the case, including—

> (a)   any other relief or remedy granted, or order made, in relation to the act in question (by that or any other court), and
>
> (b)   the consequences of any decision (of that or any other court) in respect of that act,

the court is satisfied that the award is necessary to afford just satisfaction to the person in whose favour it is made.

(4)   In determining—

> (a)   whether to award damages, or
>
> (b)   the amount of an award,

the court must take into account the principles applied by the European Court of Human Rights in relation to the award of compensation under Article 41 of the Convention.

(5)   A public authority against which damages are awarded is to be treated—

> (a)   in Scotland, for the purposes of section 3 of the Law Reform (Miscellaneous Provisions) (Scotland) Act 1940 as if the award were made in an action of damages in which the authority has been found liable in respect of loss or damage to the person to whom the award is made;
>
> (b)   for the purposes of the Civil Liability (Contribution) Act 1978 as liable in respect of damage suffered by the person to whom the award is made.

(6)   In this section—

> "court" includes a tribunal;
>
> "damages" means damages for an unlawful act of a public authority; and
>
> "unlawful" means unlawful under section 6(1).

9 Judicial acts

(1)   Proceedings under section 7(1)(a) in respect of a judicial act may be brought only—

(a)   by exercising a right of appeal;

(b)   on an application (in Scotland a petition) for judicial review; or

(c)   in such other forum as may be prescribed by rules.

(2) That does not affect any rule of law which prevents a court from being the subject of judicial review.

(3) In proceedings under this Act in respect of a judicial act done in good faith, damages may not be awarded otherwise than to compensate a person to the extent required by Article 5(5) of the Convention.

(4) An award of damages permitted by subsection (3) is to be made against the Crown; but no award may be made unless the appropriate person, if not a party to the proceedings, is joined.

(5) In this section—

"appropriate person" means the Minister responsible for the court concerned, or a person or government department nominated by him;

"court" includes a tribunal;

"judge" includes a member of a tribunal, a justice of the peace [(or, in Northern Ireland, a lay magistrate)] and a clerk or other officer entitled to exercise the jurisdiction of a court;

"judicial act" means a judicial act of a court and includes an act done on the instructions, or on behalf, of a judge; and

"rules" has the same meaning as in section 7(9).

Amendment

Sub-s (5): in definition "judge" words "(or, in Northern Ireland, a lay magistrate)" in square brackets inserted by the Justice (Northern Ireland) Act 2002, s 10(6), Sch 4, para 39.

Remedial action

10 Power to take remedial action

(1) This section applies if—

(a)   a provision of legislation has been declared under section 4 to be incompatible with a Convention right and, if an appeal lies—

(i)   all persons who may appeal have stated in writing that they do not intend to do so;

(ii)   the time for bringing an appeal has expired and no appeal has been brought within that time; or

(iii)   an appeal brought within that time has been determined or abandoned; or

(b)   it appears to a Minister of the Crown or Her Majesty in Council that, having regard to a finding of the European Court of Human Rights made after the coming into force of this section in proceedings against the United Kingdom, a provision of legislation is incompatible with an obligation of the United Kingdom arising from the Convention.

(2) If a Minister of the Crown considers that there are compelling reasons for proceeding under this section, he may by order make such amendments to the legislation as he considers necessary to remove the incompatibility.

(3) If, in the case of subordinate legislation, a Minister of the Crown considers—

(a)   that it is necessary to amend the primary legislation under which the subordinate legislation in question was made, in order to enable the incompatibility to be removed, and

(b)   that there are compelling reasons for proceeding under this section,

he may by order make such amendments to the primary legislation as he considers necessary.

(4) This section also applies where the provision in question is in subordinate legislation and has been quashed, or declared invalid, by reason of incompatibility with a Convention right and the Minister proposes to proceed under paragraph 2(b) of Schedule 2.

(5) If the legislation is an Order in Council, the power conferred by subsection (2) or (3) is exercisable by Her Majesty in Council.

(6) In this section "legislation" does not include a Measure of the Church Assembly or of the General Synod of the Church of England.

(7) Schedule 2 makes further provision about remedial orders.

Subordinate Legislation

Marriage Act 1949 (Remedial) Order 2007, SI 2007/438; Asylum and Immigration (Treatment of Claimants, etc) Act 2004 (Remedial) Order 2011, SI 2011/1158; Sexual Offences Act 2003 (Remedial) Order 2012, SI 2012/1883.

Other rights and proceedings

11 Safeguard for existing human rights

A person's reliance on a Convention right does not restrict—

- (a) any other right or freedom conferred on him by or under any law having effect in any part of the United Kingdom; or
- (b) his right to make any claim or bring any proceedings which he could make or bring apart from sections 7 to 9.

12 Freedom of expression

(1) This section applies if a court is considering whether to grant any relief which, if granted, might affect the exercise of the Convention right to freedom of expression.

(2) If the person against whom the application for relief is made ("the respondent") is neither present nor represented, no such relief is to be granted unless the court is satisfied—

- (a) that the applicant has taken all practicable steps to notify the respondent; or
- (b) that there are compelling reasons why the respondent should not be notified.

(3) No such relief is to be granted so as to restrain publication before trial unless the court is satisfied that the applicant is likely to establish that publication should not be allowed.

(4) The court must have particular regard to the importance of the Convention right to freedom of expression and, where the proceedings relate to material which the respondent claims, or which appears to the court, to be journalistic, literary or artistic material (or to conduct connected with such material), to—

- (a) the extent to which—
  - (i) the material has, or is about to, become available to the public; or
  - (ii) it is, or would be, in the public interest for the material to be published;
- (b) any relevant privacy code.

(5) In this section—

"court" includes a tribunal; and

"relief" includes any remedy or order (other than in criminal proceedings).

13 Freedom of thought, conscience and religion

(1) If a court's determination of any question arising under this Act might affect the exercise by a religious organisation (itself or its members collectively) of the Convention right to freedom of thought, conscience and religion, it must have particular regard to the importance of that right.

(2) In this section "court" includes a tribunal.

Derogations and reservations

14 Derogations

(1) In this Act "designated derogation" means—

. . .

any derogation by the United Kingdom from an Article of the Convention, or of any protocol to the Convention, which is designated for the purposes of this Act in an order made by the [Secretary of State].

(2) . . .

(3) If a designated derogation is amended or replaced it ceases to be a designated derogation.

(4) But subsection (3) does not prevent the [Secretary of State] from exercising his power under subsection (1) . . . to make a fresh designation order in respect of the Article concerned.

(5) The [Secretary of State] must by order make such amendments to Schedule 3 as he considers appropriate to reflect—

    (a)   any designation order; or

    (b)   the effect of subsection (3).

(6) A designation order may be made in anticipation of the making by the United Kingdom of a proposed derogation.

Amendment

Sub-s (1): words omitted repealed by SI 2001/1216, art 2(a).

Sub-s (1): words "Secretary of State" in square brackets substituted by SI 2003/1887, art 9, Sch 2, para 10(1).

Sub-s (2): repealed by SI 2001/1216, art 2(b).

Sub-s (4): words "Secretary of State" in square brackets substituted by SI 2003/1887, art 9, Sch 2, para 10(1).

Sub-s (4): reference omitted repealed by SI 2001/1216, art 2(c).

Sub-s (5): words "Secretary of State" in square brackets substituted by SI 2003/1887, art 9, Sch 2, para 10(1).

15 Reservations

(1) In this Act "designated reservation" means—

    (a)   the United Kingdom's reservation to Article 2 of the First Protocol to the Convention; and

    (b)   any other reservation by the United Kingdom to an Article of the Convention, or of any protocol to the Convention, which is designated for the purposes of this Act in an order made by the [Secretary of State].

(2) The text of the reservation referred to in subsection (1)(a) is set out in Part II of Schedule 3.

(3) If a designated reservation is withdrawn wholly or in part it ceases to be a designated reservation.

(4) But subsection (3) does not prevent the [Secretary of State] from exercising his power under subsection (1)(b) to make a fresh designation order in respect of the Article concerned.

(5) The [Secretary of State] must by order make such amendments to this Act as he considers appropriate to reflect—

    (a)   any designation order; or

    (b)   the effect of subsection (3).

Amendment

Sub-s (1): in para (b) words "Secretary of State" in square brackets substituted by SI 2003/1887, art 9, Sch 2, para 10(1).

Sub-s (4): words "Secretary of State" in square brackets substituted by SI 2003/1887, art 9, Sch 2, para 10(1).

Sub-s (5): words "Secretary of State" in square brackets substituted by SI 2003/1887, art 9, Sch 2, para 10(1).

16 Period for which designated derogations have effect

(1) If it has not already been withdrawn by the United Kingdom, a designated derogation ceases to have effect for the purposes of this Act—

. . .

at the end of the period of five years beginning with the date on which the order designating it was made.

(2) At any time before the period—

    (a)   fixed by subsection (1) . . . , or

    (b)   extended by an order under this subsection,

comes to an end, the [Secretary of State] may by order extend it by a further period of five years.

(3) An order under section 14(1) . . . ceases to have effect at the end of the period for consideration, unless a resolution has been passed by each House approving the order.

(4) Subsection (3) does not affect—

    (a)   anything done in reliance on the order; or

    (b)   the power to make a fresh order under section 14(1) . . . .

(5) In subsection (3) "period for consideration" means the period of forty days beginning with the day on which the order was made.

(6) In calculating the period for consideration, no account is to be taken of any time during which—

    (a)   Parliament is dissolved or prorogued; or

    (b)   both Houses are adjourned for more than four days.

(7) If a designated derogation is withdrawn by the United Kingdom, the [Secretary of State] must by order make such amendments to this Act as he considers are required to reflect that withdrawal.

Amendment

Sub-s (1): words omitted repealed by SI 2001/1216, art 3(a).

Sub-s (2): in para (b) words omitted repealed by SI 2001/1216, art 3(b).

Sub-s (2): words "Secretary of State" in square brackets substituted by SI 2003/1887, art 9, Sch 2, para 10(1).

Sub-s (3): reference omitted repealed by SI 2001/1216, art 3(c).

Sub-s (4): in para (b) reference omitted repealed by SI 2001/1216, art 3(d).

Sub-s (7): words "Secretary of State" in square brackets substituted by SI 2003/1887, art 9, Sch 2, para 10(1).

17 Periodic review of designated reservations

(1) The appropriate Minister must review the designated reservation referred to in section 15(1)(a)—

    (a)   before the end of the period of five years beginning with the date on which section 1(2) came into force; and

    (b)   if that designation is still in force, before the end of the period of five years beginning with the date on which the last report relating to it was laid under subsection (3).

(2) The appropriate Minister must review each of the other designated reservations (if any)—

    (a)   before the end of the period of five years beginning with the date on which the order designating the reservation first came into force; and

    (b)   if the designation is still in force, before the end of the period of five years beginning with the date on which the last report relating to it was laid under subsection (3).

(3)   The Minister conducting a review under this section must prepare a report on the result of the review and lay a copy of it before each House of Parliament.

Judges of the European Court of Human Rights

18 Appointment to European Court of Human Rights

(1)   In this section "judicial office" means the office of—

    (a)   Lord Justice of Appeal, Justice of the High Court or Circuit judge, in England and Wales;

    (b)   judge of the Court of Session or sheriff, in Scotland;

    (c)   Lord Justice of Appeal, judge of the High Court or county court judge, in Northern Ireland.

(2)   The holder of a judicial office may become a judge of the European Court of Human Rights ("the Court") without being required to relinquish his office.

(3)   But he is not required to perform the duties of his judicial office while he is a judge of the Court.

(4)   In respect of any period during which he is a judge of the Court—

    (a)   a Lord Justice of Appeal or Justice of the High Court is not to count as a judge of the relevant court for the purposes of section 2(1) or 4(1) of the [Senior Courts Act 1981] (maximum number of judges) nor as a judge of the [Senior Courts] for the purposes of section 12(1) to (6) of that Act (salaries etc);

    (b)   a judge of the Court of Session is not to count as a judge of that court for the purposes of section 1(1) of the Court of Session Act 1988 (maximum number of judges) or of section 9(1)(c) of the Administration of Justice Act 1973 ("the 1973 Act") (salaries etc);

    (c)   a Lord Justice of Appeal or judge of the High Court in Northern Ireland is not to count as a judge of the relevant court for the purposes of section 2(1) or 3(1) of the Judicature (Northern Ireland) Act 1978 (maximum number of judges) nor as a judge of the [Court of Judicature] of Northern Ireland for the purposes of section 9(1)(d) of the 1973 Act (salaries etc);

    (d)   a Circuit judge is not to count as such for the purposes of section 18 of the Courts Act 1971 (salaries etc);

    (e)   a sheriff is not to count as such for the purposes of section 14 of the Sheriff Courts (Scotland) Act 1907 (salaries etc);

    (f)   a county court judge of Northern Ireland is not to count as such for the purposes of section 106 of the County Courts Act (Northern Ireland) 1959 (salaries etc).

(5)   If a sheriff principal is appointed a judge of the Court, section 11(1) of the Sheriff Courts (Scotland) Act 1971 (temporary appointment of sheriff principal) applies, while he holds that appointment, as if his office is vacant.

(6)   Schedule 4 makes provision about judicial pensions in relation to the holder of a judicial office who serves as a judge of the Court.

(7)   The Lord Chancellor or the Secretary of State may by order make such transitional provision (including, in particular, provision for a temporary increase in the maximum number of judges) as he considers appropriate in relation to any holder of a judicial office who has completed his service as a judge of the Court.

[(7A)   The following paragraphs apply to the making of an order under subsection (7) in relation to any holder of a judicial office listed in subsection (1)(a)—

   (a)   before deciding what transitional provision it is appropriate to make, the person making the order must consult the Lord Chief Justice of England and Wales;

   (b)   before making the order, that person must consult the Lord Chief Justice of England and Wales.

(7B)   The following paragraphs apply to the making of an order under subsection (7) in relation to any holder of a judicial office listed in subsection (1)(c)—

   (a)   before deciding what transitional provision it is appropriate to make, the person making the order must consult the Lord Chief Justice of Northern Ireland;

   (b)   before making the order, that person must consult the Lord Chief Justice of Northern Ireland.

(7C)   The Lord Chief Justice of England and Wales may nominate a judicial office holder (within the meaning of section 109(4) of the Constitutional Reform Act 2005) to exercise his functions under this section.

(7D)   The Lord Chief Justice of Northern Ireland may nominate any of the following to exercise his functions under this section—

   (a)   the holder of one of the offices listed in Schedule 1 to the Justice (Northern Ireland) Act 2002;

   (b)   a Lord Justice of Appeal (as defined in section 88 of that Act).]

Amendment

Sub-s (4): in para (a) words in both pairs of square brackets substituted by the Constitutional Reform Act 2005, s 59(5), Sch 11, Pt 1, para 1(2), Pt 2, para 4(1), (3).

Sub-s (4): in para (c) words in square brackets substituted by the Constitutional Reform Act 2005, s 59(5), Sch 11, Pt 3, para 6(1), (3).

Sub-ss (7A)–(7D): inserted by the Constitutional Reform Act 2005, s 15(1), Sch 4, Pt 1, para 278.

Subordinate Legislation

Judicial Pensions (European Court of Human Rights) Order 1998, SI 1998/2768; Judicial Pensions (European Court of Human Rights) (Amendment) Order 2012, SI 2012/489.

Parliamentary procedure

19 Statements of compatibility

(1)   A Minister of the Crown in charge of a Bill in either House of Parliament must, before Second Reading of the Bill—

   (a)   make a statement to the effect that in his view the provisions of the Bill are compatible with the Convention rights ("a statement of compatibility"); or

   (b)   make a statement to the effect that although he is unable to make a statement of compatibility the government nevertheless wishes the House to proceed with the Bill.

(2)   The statement must be in writing and be published in such manner as the Minister making it considers appropriate.

Supplemental

20 Orders etc under this Act

(1)   Any power of a Minister of the Crown to make an order under this Act is exercisable by statutory instrument.

(2) The power of . . . [the Lord Chancellor or] the Secretary of State to make rules (other than rules of court) under section 2(3) or 7(9) is exercisable by statutory instrument.

(3) Any statutory instrument made under section 14, 15 or 16(7) must be laid before Parliament.

(4) No order may be made by . . . [the Lord Chancellor or] the Secretary of State under section 1(4), 7(11) or 16(2) unless a draft of the order has been laid before, and approved by, each House of Parliament.

(5) Any statutory instrument made under section 18(7) or Schedule 4, or to which subsection (2) applies, shall be subject to annulment in pursuance of a resolution of either House of Parliament.

(6) The power of a Northern Ireland department to make—

    (a)   rules under section 2(3)(c) or 7(9)(c), or

    (b)   an order under section 7(11),

is exercisable by statutory rule for the purposes of the Statutory Rules (Northern Ireland) Order 1979.

(7) Any rules made under section 2(3)(c) or 7(9)(c) shall be subject to negative resolution; and section 41(6) of the Interpretation Act (Northern Ireland) 1954 (meaning of "subject to negative resolution") shall apply as if the power to make the rules were conferred by an Act of the Northern Ireland Assembly.

(8) No order may be made by a Northern Ireland department under section 7(11) unless a draft of the order has been laid before, and approved by, the Northern Ireland Assembly.

Amendment

Sub-s (2): words omitted repealed by SI 2003/1887, art 9, Sch 2, para 10(2).

Sub-s (2): words "the Lord Chancellor or" in square brackets inserted by SI 2005/3429, art 8, Schedule, para 3.

Sub-s (4): words omitted repealed by SI 2003/1887, art 9, Sch 2, para 10(2).

Sub-s (4): words "the Lord Chancellor or" in square brackets inserted by SI 2005/3429, art 8, Schedule, para 3.

21 Interpretation, etc

(1) In this Act—

"amend" includes repeal and apply (with or without modifications);

"the appropriate Minister" means the Minister of the Crown having charge of the appropriate authorised government department (within the meaning of the Crown Proceedings Act 1947);

"the Commission" means the European Commission of Human Rights;

"the Convention" means the Convention for the Protection of Human Rights and Fundamental Freedoms, agreed by the Council of Europe at Rome on 4th November 1950 as it has effect for the time being in relation to the United Kingdom;

"declaration of incompatibility" means a declaration under section 4;

"Minister of the Crown" has the same meaning as in the Ministers of the Crown Act 1975;

"Northern Ireland Minister" includes the First Minister and the deputy First Minister in Northern Ireland;

"primary legislation" means any—

    (a)   public general Act;

    (b)   local and personal Act;

    (c)   private Act;

    (d)   Measure of the Church Assembly;

    (e)   Measure of the General Synod of the Church of England;

    (f)   Order in Council—

(i) made in exercise of Her Majesty's Royal Prerogative;

(ii) made under section 38(1)(a) of the Northern Ireland Constitution Act 1973 or the corresponding provision of the Northern Ireland Act 1998; or

(iii) amending an Act of a kind mentioned in paragraph (a), (b) or (c);

and includes an order or other instrument made under primary legislation (otherwise than by the [Welsh Ministers, the First Minister for Wales, the Counsel General to the Welsh Assembly Government], a member of the Scottish Executive, a Northern Ireland Minister or a Northern Ireland department) to the extent to which it operates to bring one or more provisions of that legislation into force or amends any primary legislation;

"the First Protocol" means the protocol to the Convention agreed at Paris on 20th March 1952;

. . .

"the Eleventh Protocol" means the protocol to the Convention (restructuring the control machinery established by the Convention) agreed at Strasbourg on 11th May 1994;

["the Thirteenth Protocol" means the protocol to the Convention (concerning the abolition of the death penalty in all circumstances) agreed at Vilnius on 3rd May 2002;]

"remedial order" means an order under section 10;

"subordinate legislation" means any—

(a) Order in Council other than one—

 (i) made in exercise of Her Majesty's Royal Prerogative;

 (ii) made under section 38(1)(a) of the Northern Ireland Constitution Act 1973 or the corresponding provision of the Northern Ireland Act 1998; or

 (iii) amending an Act of a kind mentioned in the definition of primary legislation;

(b) Act of the Scottish Parliament;

[(ba) Measure of the National Assembly for Wales;

(bb) Act of the National Assembly for Wales;]

(c) Act of the Parliament of Northern Ireland;

(d) Measure of the Assembly established under section 1 of the Northern Ireland Assembly Act 1973;

(e) Act of the Northern Ireland Assembly;

(f) order, rules, regulations, scheme, warrant, byelaw or other instrument made under primary legislation (except to the extent to which it operates to bring one or more provisions of that legislation into force or amends any primary legislation);

(g) order, rules, regulations, scheme, warrant, byelaw or other instrument made under legislation mentioned in paragraph (b), (c), (d) or (e) or made under an Order in Council applying only to Northern Ireland;

(h) order, rules, regulations, scheme, warrant, byelaw or other instrument made by a member of the Scottish Executive[, Welsh Ministers, the First Minister for Wales, the Counsel General to the Welsh Assembly Government], a Northern Ireland Minister or a Northern Ireland department in exercise of prerogative or other executive functions of Her Majesty which are exercisable by such a person on behalf of Her Majesty;

"transferred matters" has the same meaning as in the Northern Ireland Act 1998; and "tribunal" means any tribunal in which legal proceedings may be brought.

(2) The references in paragraphs (b) and (c) of section 2(1) to Articles are to Articles of the Convention as they had effect immediately before the coming into force of the Eleventh Protocol.

(3) The reference in paragraph (d) of section 2(1) to Article 46 includes a reference to Articles 32 and 54 of the Convention as they had effect immediately before the coming into force of the Eleventh Protocol.

(4) The references in section 2(1) to a report or decision of the Commission or a decision of the Committee of Ministers include references to a report or decision made as provided by paragraphs 3, 4 and 6 of Article 5 of the Eleventh Protocol (transitional provisions).

(5) . . .

Amendment

Sub-s (1): in definition "primary legislation" words from "Welsh Ministers, the" to "Welsh Assembly Government" in square brackets substituted by the Government of Wales Act 2006, s 160(1), Sch 10, para 56(1), (2).

Sub-s (1): definition "the Sixth Protocol" (omitted) repealed by SI 2004/1574, art 2(2).

Sub-s (1): definition "the Thirteenth Protocol" inserted by SI 2004/1574, art 2(2).

Sub-s (1): in definition "subordinate legislation" paras (ba), (bb) inserted by the Government of Wales Act 2006, s 160(1), Sch 10, para 56(1), (3).

Sub-s (1): in definition "subordinate legislation" in para (h) words from ", Welsh Ministers, the" to "Welsh Assembly Government," in square brackets inserted by the Government of Wales Act 2006, s 160(1), Sch 10, para 56(1), (4).

Sub-s (5): repealed by the Armed Forces Act 2006, s 378(2), Sch 17.

22 Short title, commencement, application and extent

(1) This Act may be cited as the Human Rights Act 1998.

(2) Sections 18, 20 and 21(5) and this section come into force on the passing of this Act.

(3) The other provisions of this Act come into force on such day as the Secretary of State may by order appoint; and different days may be appointed for different purposes.

(4) Paragraph (b) of subsection (1) of section 7 applies to proceedings brought by or at the instigation of a public authority whenever the act in question took place; but otherwise that subsection does not apply to an act taking place before the coming into force of that section.

(5) This Act binds the Crown.

(6) This Act extends to Northern Ireland.

(7) . . .

Amendment

Sub-s (7): repealed by the Armed Forces Act 2006, s 378(2), Sch 17.

Subordinate Legislation

Human Rights Act 1998 (Commencement) Order 1998, SI 1998/2882.

Human Rights Act 1998 (Commencement No 2) Order 2000, SI 2000/1851.

SCHEDULE 1
THE ARTICLES

Section 1(3)

PART I
THE CONVENTION

RIGHTS AND FREEDOMS

ARTICLE 2
Right to life

1

Everyone's right to life shall be protected by law. No one shall be deprived of his life intentionally save in the execution of a sentence of a court following his conviction of a crime for which this penalty is provided by law.

2

Deprivation of life shall not be regarded as inflicted in contravention of this Article when it results from the use of force which is no more than absolutely necessary:

(a) in defence of any person from unlawful violence;

(b) in order to effect a lawful arrest or to prevent the escape of a person lawfully detained;

(c) in action lawfully taken for the purpose of quelling a riot or insurrection.

ARTICLE 3
Prohibition of torture

No one shall be subjected to torture or to inhuman or degrading treatment or punishment.

ARTICLE 4
Prohibition of slavery and forced labour

1

No one shall be held in slavery or servitude.

2

No one shall be required to perform forced or compulsory labour.

3

For the purpose of this Article the term "forced or compulsory labour" shall not include:

(a) any work required to be done in the ordinary course of detention imposed according to the provisions of Article 5 of this Convention or during conditional release from such detention;

(b) any service of a military character or, in case of conscientious objectors in countries where they are recognised, service exacted instead of compulsory military service;

(c) any service exacted in case of an emergency or calamity threatening the life or well-being of the community;

(d) any work or service which forms part of normal civic obligations.

ARTICLE 5
Right to liberty and security

1

Everyone has the right to liberty and security of person. No one shall be deprived of his liberty save in the following cases and in accordance with a procedure prescribed by law:

(a)   the lawful detention of a person after conviction by a competent court;

(b)   the lawful arrest or detention of a person for non-compliance with the lawful order of a court or in order to secure the fulfilment of any obligation prescribed by law;

(c)   the lawful arrest or detention of a person effected for the purpose of bringing him before the competent legal authority on reasonable suspicion of having committed an offence or when it is reasonably considered necessary to prevent his committing an offence or fleeing after having done so;

(d)   the detention of a minor by lawful order for the purpose of educational supervision or his lawful detention for the purpose of bringing him before the competent legal authority;

(e)   the lawful detention of persons for the prevention of the spreading of infectious diseases, of persons of unsound mind, alcoholics or drug addicts or vagrants;

(f)   the lawful arrest or detention of a person to prevent his effecting an unauthorised entry into the country or of a person against whom action is being taken with a view to deportation or extradition.

2

Everyone who is arrested shall be informed promptly, in a language which he understands, of the reasons for his arrest and of any charge against him.

3

Everyone arrested or detained in accordance with the provisions of paragraph 1(c) of this Article shall be brought promptly before a judge or other officer authorised by law to exercise judicial power and shall be entitled to trial within a reasonable time or to release pending trial. Release may be conditioned by guarantees to appear for trial.

4

Everyone who is deprived of his liberty by arrest or detention shall be entitled to take proceedings by which the lawfulness of his detention shall be decided speedily by a court and his release ordered if the detention is not lawful.

5

Everyone who has been the victim of arrest or detention in contravention of the provisions of this Article shall have an enforceable right to compensation.

ARTICLE 6
Right to a fair trial

1

In the determination of his civil rights and obligations or of any criminal charge against him, everyone is entitled to a fair and public hearing within a reasonable time by an independent and impartial tribunal established by law. Judgment shall be pronounced publicly but the press and public may be excluded from all or part of the trial in the interest of morals, public order or national security in a democratic society, where the interests of juveniles or the protection of the private life of the parties so require, or to the extent strictly necessary in the opinion of the court in special circumstances where publicity would prejudice the interests of justice.

2

Everyone charged with a criminal offence shall be presumed innocent until proved guilty according to law.

3

Everyone charged with a criminal offence has the following minimum rights:

(a) to be informed promptly, in a language which he understands and in detail, of the nature and cause of the accusation against him;

(b) to have adequate time and facilities for the preparation of his defence;

(c) to defend himself in person or through legal assistance of his own choosing or, if he has not sufficient means to pay for legal assistance, to be given it free when the interests of justice so require;

(d) to examine or have examined witnesses against him and to obtain the attendance and examination of witnesses on his behalf under the same conditions as witnesses against him;

(e) to have the free assistance of an interpreter if he cannot understand or speak the language used in court.

ARTICLE 7
No punishment without law

1

No one shall be held guilty of any criminal offence on account of any act or omission which did not constitute a criminal offence under national or international law at the time when it was committed. Nor shall a heavier penalty be imposed than the one that was applicable at the time the criminal offence was committed.

2

This Article shall not prejudice the trial and punishment of any person for any act or omission which, at the time when it was committed, was criminal according to the general principles of law recognised by civilised nations.

ARTICLE 8
Right to respect for private and family life

1

Everyone has the right to respect for his private and family life, his home and his correspondence.

2

There shall be no interference by a public authority with the exercise of this right except such as is in accordance with the law and is necessary in a democratic society in the interests of national security, public safety or the economic well-being of the country, for the prevention of disorder or crime, for the protection of health or morals, or for the protection of the rights and freedoms of others.

ARTICLE 9
Freedom of thought, conscience and religion

1

Everyone has the right to freedom of thought, conscience and religion; this right includes freedom to change his religion or belief and freedom, either alone or in community with others and in public or private, to manifest his religion or belief, in worship, teaching, practice and observance.

2

Freedom to manifest one's religion or beliefs shall be subject only to such limitations as are prescribed by law and are necessary in a democratic society in the interests of public safety, for the protection of public order, health or morals, or for the protection of the rights and freedoms of others.

ARTICLE 10
Freedom of expression

1

Everyone has the right to freedom of expression. This right shall include freedom to hold opinions and to receive and impart information and ideas without interference by public authority and regardless of frontiers. This Article shall not prevent States from requiring the licensing of broadcasting, television or cinema enterprises.

2

The exercise of these freedoms, since it carries with it duties and responsibilities, may be subject to such formalities, conditions, restrictions or penalties as are prescribed by law and are necessary in a democratic society, in the interests of national security, territorial integrity or public safety, for the prevention of disorder or crime, for the protection of health or morals, for the protection of the reputation or rights of others, for preventing the disclosure of information received in confidence, or for maintaining the authority and impartiality of the judiciary.

ARTICLE 11
Freedom of assembly and association

1

Everyone has the right to freedom of peaceful assembly and to freedom of association with others, including the right to form and to join trade unions for the protection of his interests.

2

No restrictions shall be placed on the exercise of these rights other than such as are prescribed by law and are necessary in a democratic society in the interests of national security or public safety, for the prevention of disorder or crime, for the protection of health or morals or for the protection of the rights and freedoms of others. This Article shall not prevent the imposition of lawful restrictions on the exercise of these rights by members of the armed forces, of the police or of the administration of the State.

ARTICLE 12
Right to marry

Men and women of marriageable age have the right to marry and to found a family, according to the national laws governing the exercise of this right.

ARTICLE 14
Prohibition of discrimination

The enjoyment of the rights and freedoms set forth in this Convention shall be secured without discrimination on any ground such as sex, race, colour, language, religion, political or other opinion, national or social origin, association with a national minority, property, birth or other status.

ARTICLE 16
Restrictions on political activity of aliens

Nothing in Articles 10, 11 and 14 shall be regarded as preventing the High Contracting Parties from imposing restrictions on the political activity of aliens.

ARTICLE 17
Prohibition of abuse of rights

N
person g in this Convention may be interpreted as implying for any State, group or of any of right to engage in any activity or perform any act aimed at the destruction extent than rights and freedoms set forth herein or at their limitation to a greater vided for in the Convention.

ARTICLE 18
itation on use of restrictions on rights

The restrictions permitte nder this Convention to the said rights and freedoms shall not be applied for any urpose other than those for which they have been prescribed.

THE FIRST RT II ROTOCOL
ARTICLE
Protection of prope y

Every natural or legal person is entitled to the peacefu njoyment of his possessions. No one shall be deprived of his possessions except in the public interest and subject to the conditions provided for by law and by the general principles of international law.

The preceding provisions shall not, however, in any way impair the right of a State to enforce such laws as it deems necessary to control the use of property in accordance with the general interest or to secure the payment of taxes or other contributions or penalties.

ARTICLE 2
Right to education

No person shall be denied the right to education. In the exercise of any functions which it assumes in relation to education and to teaching, the State shall respect the right of parents to ensure such education and teaching in conformity with their own religious and philosophical convictions.

ARTICLE 3
Right to free elections

The High Contracting Parties undertake to hold free elections at reasonable intervals by secret ballot, under conditions which will ensure the free expression of the opinion of the people in the choice of the legislature.

[PART III
ARTICLE 1 OF THE THIRTEENTH PROTOCOL]

[Abolition of the Death Penalty

The death penalty shall be abolished. No one shall be condemned to such penalty or executed.]

Amendment
Substituted by SI 2004/1574, art 2(3).

SCHEDULE 2
REMEDIAL ORDERS

Section 10

Orders

1

(1) A remedial order may—

    (a)   contain such incidental, supplemental, consequential or ~~transitional~~ provision as the person making it considers appropriate; on which it is

    (b)   be made so as to have effect from a date earlier than made;

    (c)   make provision for the delegation of specific fu~~nctions~~;

    (d)   make different provision for different cases.

(2) The power conferred by sub-paragraph (1)(a) inc~~ludes~~—

    (a)   power to amend primary legislation (i~~nclu~~ding primary legislation other than that which contains the incom~~pat~~ible provision); and

    (b)   power to amend or revoke subor~~din~~ate legislation (including subordinate legislation other than that w~~hich~~ contains the incompatible provision).

(3) A remedial order may be made s~~o a~~s to have the same extent as the legislation which it affects.

(4) No person is to be guilty of ~~an~~ offence solely as a result of the retrospective effect of a remedial order.

Procedure

2

No remedial order may be made unless—

    (a)   a draft of the order has been approved by a resolution of each House of Parliament made after the end of the period of 60 days beginning with the day on which the draft was laid; or

    (b)   it is declared in the order that it appears to the person making it that, because of the urgency of the matter, it is necessary to make the order without a draft being so approved.

Orders laid in draft

3

(1) No draft may be laid under paragraph 2(a) unless—

    (a)   the person proposing to make the order has laid before Parliament a document which contains a draft of the proposed order and the required information; and

    (b)   the period of 60 days, beginning with the day on which the document required by this sub-paragraph was laid, has ended.

(2) If representations have been made during that period, the draft laid under paragraph 2(a) must be accompanied by a statement containing—

    (a)   a summary of the representations; and

    (b)   if, as a result of the representations, the proposed order has been changed, details of the changes.

Urgent cases

4

(1) If a remedial order ("the original order") is made without being approved in draft, the person making it must lay it before Parliament, accompanied by the required information, after it is made.

(2) If representations have been made during the period of 60 days beginning with the day on which the original order was made, the person making it must (after the end of that period) lay before Parliament a statement containing—

    (a)   a summary of the representations; and

    (b)   if, as a result of the representations, he considers it appropriate to make changes to the original order, details of the changes.

(3) If paragraph (2)(b) applies, the person making the statement must—

    (a)   make such changes to the original order; and

    (b)   lay a further remedial order replacing the original order; and lay the replacement order before Parliament.

(4) If, at the end of the period of 120 days beginning with the day on which the original order was made, a resolution has not been passed by each House approving the original or replacement order, the order ceases to have effect (but without that affecting anything previously done under either order or the power to make a fresh remedial order).

Definitions

5

In this Schedule—

    "representations" means representations about a remedial order (or proposed remedial order) made to the person making (or proposing to make) it and includes any relevant Parliamentary report or resolution; and

    "required information" means—

    (a)   an explanation of the incompatibility which the order (or proposed order) seeks to remove, including particulars of the relevant declaration, finding or order; and

    (b)   a statement of the reasons for proceeding under section 10 and for making an order in those terms.

Calculating periods

6

In calculating any period for the purposes of this Schedule, no account is to be taken of any time during which—

    (a)   Parliament is dissolved or prorogued; or

    (b)   both Houses are adjourned for more than four days.

[7

(1) This paragraph applies in relation to—

    (a)   any remedial order made, and any draft of such an order proposed to be made,—

        (i)   by the Scottish Ministers; or

        (ii)   within devolved competence (within the meaning of the Scotland Act 1998) by Her Majesty in Council; and

    (b)   any document or statement to be laid in connection with such an order (or proposed order).

(2) This Schedule has effect in relation to any such order (or proposed order), document or statement subject to the following modifications.

(3) Any reference to Parliament, each House of Parliament or both Houses of Parliament shall be construed as a reference to the Scottish Parliament.
(4) Paragraph 6 does not apply and instead, in calculating any period for the purposes of this Schedule, no account is to be taken of any time during which the Scottish Parliament is dissolved or is in recess for more than four days.]

Amendment

Para 7: inserted by SI 2000/2040, art 2(1), Schedule, Pt I, para 21.

Subordinate Legislation

Marriage Act 1949 (Remedial) Order 2007, SI 2007/438; Asylum and Immigration (T of Claimants, etc) Act 2004 (Remedial) Order 2011, SI 2011/1158.

SCHEDULE 3
DEROGATION AND RESERVATION

Sections 14 and 15

PART I
. . .

Amendment

Original Pt I repealed by SI 2001/1216, art   New Pt I inserted by SI 2001/4032, art 2,
Schedule and repealed by SI 2005/1071, art

PART II
RESERVATION

At the time of signing the present (First) Protocol, I declare that, in view of certain provisions of the Education Acts in the United Kingdom, the principle affirmed in the second sentence of Article 2 is accepted by the United Kingdom only so far as it is compatible with the provision of efficient instruction and training, and the avoidance of unreasonable public expenditure.

Dated 20 March 1952. Made by the United Kingdom Permanent Representative to the Council of Europe.

SCHEDULE 4
JUDICIAL PENSIONS

Section 18(6)

Duty to make orders about pensions

1

(1) The appropriate Minister must by order make provision with respect to pensions payable to or in respect of any holder of a judicial office who serves as an ECHR judge.
(2) A pensions order must include such provision as the Minister making it considers is necessary to secure that—

    (a)   an ECHR judge who was, immediately before his appointment as an ECHR judge, a member of a judicial pension scheme is entitled to remain as a member of that scheme;

    (b)   the terms on which he remains a member of the scheme are those which would have been applicable had he not been appointed as an ECHR judge; and

    (c)   entitlement to benefits payable in accordance with the scheme continues to be determined as if, while serving as an ECHR judge, his salary was that which would (but for section 18(4)) have been payable to him in respect of his continuing service as the holder of his judicial office.

Contributions

2

A pensions order may, in particular, make provision—

    (a)   for any contributions which are payable by a person who remains a member of a scheme as a result of the order, and which would otherwise be payable by deduction from his salary, to be made otherwise than by deduction from his salary as an ECHR judge; and

    (b)   for such contributions to be collected in such manner as may be determined by the administrators of the scheme.

Amendments of other enactments

3

A pensions order may amend any provision of, or made under, a pensions Act in such manner and to such extent as the Minister making the order considers necessary or expedient to ensure the proper administration of any scheme to which it relates.

Definitions

4

In this Schedule—

    "appropriate Minister" means—

        (a)   in relation to any judicial office whose jurisdiction is exercisable exclusively in relation to Scotland, the Secretary of State; and

        (b)   otherwise, the Lord Chancellor;

    "ECHR judge" means the holder of a judicial office who is serving as a judge of the Court;

    "judicial pension scheme" means a scheme established by and in accordance with a pensions Act;

    "pensions Act" means—

        (a)   the County Courts Act (Northern Ireland) 1959;

        (b)   the Sheriffs' Pensions (Scotland) Act 1961;

        (c)   the Judicial Pensions Act 1981; or

        (d)   the Judicial Pensions and Retirement Act 1993; and

        [(e)   the Public Service Pensions Act 2013;] and

    "pensions order" means an order made under paragraph 1.

Amendment

Para 4: in definition "pensions Act" para (e) inserted by the Public Service Pensions Act 2013, s 27, Sch 8, para 26. Date in force: 1 April 2014: see SI 2014/839, art 4(2)(k).

Subordinate Legislation

Judicial Pensions (European Court of Human Rights) Order 1998, SI 1998/2768; Judicial Pensions (European Court of Human Rights) (Amendment) Order 2012, SI 2012/489.

BRITISH OVERSEAS TERRITORIES ACT 2002

2002 c 8

An Act to make provision about the name "British overseas territories" and British citizenship so far as relating to the British overseas territories.

[26 February 2002]

Change of names

1 British overseas territories

(1)   As the territories mentioned in Schedule 6 to the British Nationality Act 1981 (c 61) are now known as "British overseas territories"—

- (a)   in section 50(1) of that Act (definitions), at the appropriate place insert— ""British overseas territory" means a territory mentioned in Schedule 6;",
- (b)   for "dependent territory" (or "dependent territories"), wherever occurring in that Act, substitute "British overseas territory" (or "British overseas territories"), and
- (c)   in the heading to that Schedule, for "British Dependent Territories" substitute "British Overseas Territories".

(2)   In any other enactment passed or made before the commencement of this section (including an enactment comprised in subordinate legislation), any reference to a dependent territory within the meaning of the British Nationality Act 1981 shall be read as a reference to a British overseas territory.

(3)   In the Interpretation Act 1978 (c 30), at the appropriate place in Schedule 1 (list of definitions) insert—

>   ""British overseas territory" has the same meaning as in the British Nationality Act 1981;".

2 British overseas territories citizenship

(1)   Pursuant to section 1, British Dependent Territories citizenship is renamed "British overseas territories citizenship"; and a person having that citizenship is a "British overseas territories citizen".

(2)   Accordingly, in the British Nationality Act 1981 (c 61)—

- (a)   for "British Dependent Territories citizenship", wherever occurring, substitute "British overseas territories citizenship", and
- (b)   for "British Dependent Territories citizen" (or "British Dependent Territories citizens"), wherever occurring, substitute "British overseas territories citizen" (or "British overseas territories citizens").

(3)   In any other enactment passed or made before the commencement of this section (including an enactment comprised in subordinate legislation), any reference to British Dependent Territories citizenship, or a British Dependent Territories citizen, shall be read as a reference to British overseas territories citizenship, or a British overseas territories citizen.

British citizenship

3 Conferral on British overseas territories citizens

(1)   Any person who, immediately before the commencement of this section, is a British overseas territories citizen shall, on the commencement of this section, become a British citizen.

(2)   Subsection (1) does not apply to a person who is a British overseas territories citizen by virtue only of a connection with the Sovereign Base Areas of Akrotiri and Dhekelia.

(3)   A person who is a British citizen by virtue of this section is a British citizen by descent for the purposes of the British Nationality Act 1981 if, and only if—

- (a)   he was a British overseas territories citizen by descent immediately before the commencement of this section, and
- (b)   if at that time he was a British citizen as well as a British overseas territories citizen, he was a British citizen by descent

4

(Inserts the British Nationality Act 1981, s 4A.)

5 Acquisition by reference to the British overseas territories

Schedule 1 (which makes provision about the acquisition of British citizenship by reference to the British overseas territories) has effect.

Supplementary

6 The Ilois: citizenship

(1) A person shall become a British citizen on the commencement of this section if—

(a) he was born on or after 26 April 1969 and before 1 January 1983,

(b) he was born to a woman who at the time was a citizen of the United Kingdom and Colonies by virtue of her birth in the British Indian Ocean Territory, and

(c) immediately before the commencement of this section he was neither a British citizen nor a British overseas territories citizen.

(2) A person who is a British citizen by virtue of subsection (1) is a British citizen by descent for the purposes of the British Nationality Act 1981 (c 61).

(3) A person shall become a British overseas territories citizen on the commencement of this section if—

(a) subsection (1)(a) and (b) apply in relation to him, and

(b) immediately before the commencement of this section he was not a British overseas territories citizen.

(4) A person who is a British overseas territories citizen by virtue of subsection (3) is such a citizen by descent for the purposes of the British Nationality Act 1981.

7 Repeals

The enactments mentioned in Schedule 2 (which include some which are spent or effectively superseded) are repealed to the extent specified there.

8 Short title, commencement and extent

(1) This Act may be cited as the British Overseas Territories Act 2002.

(2) The following provisions of this Act are to come into force on such day as the Secretary of State may by order made by statutory instrument appoint—

(a) sections 3 to 5 and Schedule 1,

(b) section 6, and

(c) section 7 and Schedule 2, so far as relating to the British Nationality (Falkland Islands) Act 1983 (c 6).

(3) An order under subsection (2) may—

(a) include different days for different purposes, and

(b) appoint such transitional provision as the Secretary of State considers expedient.

(4) This Act extends to—

(a) the United Kingdom,

(b) the Channel Islands and the Isle of Man, and

(c) the British overseas territories.

Subordinate Legislation

British Overseas Territories Act 2002 (Commencement) Order 2002, SI 2002/1252.

SCHEDULES 1, 2

(Sch 1 amends the British Nationality Act 1981, ss 1–3, 37, 50, 51; Sch 2 contains repeals which, in so far as relevant to this work, have been incorporated at the appropriate place.)

CONSTITUTIONAL REFORM ACT 2005

2005 c 4

An Act to make provision for modifying the office of Lord Chancellor, and to make provision relating to the functions of that office; to establish a Supreme Court of the United Kingdom, and to abolish the appellate jurisdiction of the House of Lords; to make provision about the jurisdiction of the Judicial Committee of the Privy Council and the judicial functions of the President of the Council; to make other provision about the judiciary, their appointment and discipline; and for connected purposes.

[24 March 2005]

PART 2
ARRANGEMENTS TO MODIFY THE OFFICE OF LORD CHANCELLOR

Continued judicial independence

3 Guarantee of continued judicial independence

(1)   The Lord Chancellor, other Ministers of the Crown and all with responsibility for matters relating to the judiciary or otherwise to the administration of justice must uphold the continued independence of the judiciary.

(2)   Subsection (1) does not impose any duty which it would be within the legislative competence of the Scottish Parliament to impose.

(3)   A person is not subject to the duty imposed by subsection (1) if he is subject to the duty imposed by section 1(1) of the Justice (Northern Ireland) Act 2002 (c 26).

(4)   The following particular duties are imposed for the purpose of upholding that independence.

(5)   The Lord Chancellor and other Ministers of the Crown must not seek to influence particular judicial decisions through any special access to the judiciary.

(6)   The Lord Chancellor must have regard to—

    (a)   the need to defend that independence;

    (b)   the need for the judiciary to have the support necessary to enable them to exercise their functions;

    (c)   the need for the public interest in regard to matters relating to the judiciary or otherwise to the administration of justice to be properly represented in decisions affecting those matters.

(7)   In this section "the judiciary" includes the judiciary of any of the following—

    (a)   the Supreme Court;

    (b)   any other court established under the law of any part of the United Kingdom;

    (c)   any international court.

[(7A)   In this section "the judiciary" also includes every person who—

    (a)   holds an office listed in Schedule 14 or holds an office listed in subsection (7B), and

(3) A holder of the office of Senior President of Tribunals must, in carrying out the functions of that office, have regard to—

    (a)   the need for tribunals to be accessible,

    (b)   the need for proceedings before tribunals—

        (i)   to be fair, and

        (ii)   to be handled quickly and efficiently,

    (c)   the need for members of tribunals to be experts in the subject-matter of, or the law to be applied in, cases in which they decide matters, and

    (d)   the need to develop innovative methods of resolving disputes that are of a type that may be brought before tribunals.

(4) In subsection (3) "tribunals" means—

    (a)   the First-tier Tribunal,

    (b)   the Upper Tribunal,

    (c)   employment tribunals, [and]

    (d)   the Employment Appeal Tribunal, . . .

    (e)   . . .

Amendment

Sub-s (4): in para (c) word in square brackets inserted, and para (e) and word omitted immediately preceding it repealed, by SI 2010/21, art 5(1), Sch 1, paras 36, 37.

CHAPTER 2

FIRST-TIER TRIBUNAL AND UPPER TRIBUNAL
Establishment

3 The First-tier Tribunal and the Upper Tribunal

(1) There is to be a tribunal, known as the First-tier Tribunal, for the purpose of exercising the functions conferred on it under or by virtue of this Act or any other Act.

(2) There is to be a tribunal, known as the Upper Tribunal, for the purpose of exercising the functions conferred on it under or by virtue of this Act or any other Act.

(3) Each of the First-tier Tribunal, and the Upper Tribunal, is to consist of its judges and other members.

(4) The Senior President of Tribunals is to preside over both of the First-tier Tribunal and the Upper Tribunal.

(5) The Upper Tribunal is to be a superior court of record.

Members and composition of tribunals

4 Judges and other members of the First-tier Tribunal

(1) A person is a judge of the First-tier Tribunal if the person—

    (a)   is a judge of the First-tier Tribunal by virtue of appointment under paragraph 1(1) of Schedule 2,

    (b)   is a transferred-in judge of the First-tier Tribunal (see section 31(2)),

    (c)   is a judge of the Upper Tribunal,

    [(ca)   is within section 6A,]

    (d)   . . . or

    (e)   is a member of a panel of [Employment Judges].

(2) A person is also a judge of the First-tier Tribunal, but only as regards functions of the tribunal in relation to appeals such as are mentioned in subsection (1) of section 5 of the Criminal Injuries Compensation Act 1995 (c 53), if the person is an adjudicator appointed under that section by the Scottish Ministers.

(3) A person is one of the other members of the First-tier Tribunal if the person—

(a)   is a member of the First-tier Tribunal by virtue of appointment under paragraph 2(1) of Schedule 2,

(b)   is a transferred-in other member of the First-tier Tribunal (see section 31(2)),

(c)   is one of the other members of the Upper Tribunal, or

(d)   is a member of a panel of members of employment tribunals that is not a panel of [Employment Judges].

(4) Schedule 2—

contains provision for the appointment of persons to be judges or other members of the First-tier Tribunal, and

makes further provision in connection with judges and other members of the First-tier Tribunal.

Amendment

Sub-s (1): para (ca) inserted by the Crime and Courts Act 2013, s 21(4), Sch 14, Pt 4, paras 6, 7. Date in force: 1 October 2013: see SI 2013/2200, art 3(b), (g).

Sub-s (1): in para (d) words omitted repealed by SI 2010/21, art 5(1), Sch 1, paras 36, 38.

Date in force: 15 February 2010: see SI 2010/21, art 1; for transitional provisions and savings see art 5(4), Sch 4, paras 14–18, 21 thereto.

Sub-s (1): in para (e) words "Employment Judges" in square brackets substituted by the Crime and Courts Act 2013, s 21(4), Sch 14, Pt 7, para 13(1). Date in force: 1 October 2013: see SI 2013/2200, art 3(b), (g).

Sub-s (3): in para (d) words "Employment Judges" in square brackets substituted by the Crime and Courts Act 2013, s 21(4), Sch 14, Pt 7, para 13(1). Date in force: 1 October 2013: see SI 2013/2200, art 3(b), (g).

5 Judges and other members of the Upper Tribunal

(1) A person is a judge of the Upper Tribunal if the person—

(a)   is the Senior President of Tribunals,

(b)   is a judge of the Upper Tribunal by virtue of appointment under paragraph 1(1) of Schedule 3,

(c)   is a transferred-in judge of the Upper Tribunal (see section 31(2)),

(d)   . . .

(e)   is the Chief Social Security Commissioner, or any other Social Security Commissioner, appointed under section 50(1) of the Social Security Administration (Northern Ireland) Act 1992 (c 8),

(f)   is a Social Security Commissioner appointed under section 50(2) of that Act (deputy Commissioners),

(g)   is within section 6(1),

(h)   is a deputy judge of the Upper Tribunal (whether under paragraph 7 of Schedule 3 or under section 31(2)), or

(i)   is a Chamber President or a Deputy Chamber President, whether of a chamber of the Upper Tribunal or of a chamber of the First-tier Tribunal, and does not fall within any of paragraphs (a) to (h).

(2) A person is one of the other members of the Upper Tribunal if the person—

(a)   is a member of the Upper Tribunal by virtue of appointment under paragraph 2(1) of Schedule 3,

(b)   is a transferred-in other member of the Upper Tribunal (see section 31(2)), [or]

(c)   is a member of the Employment Appeal Tribunal appointed under section 22(1)(c) of the Employment Tribunals Act 1996 (c 17) . . .

(d)   . . .

(3) Schedule 3—

contains provision for the appointment of persons to be judges (including deputy judges), or other members, of the Upper Tribunal, and makes further provision in connection with judges and other members of the Upper Tribunal.

Amendment

Sub-s (1): para (d) repealed by SI 2010/21, art 5(1), Sch 1, paras 36, 39(a).

Date in force: 15 February 2010: see SI 2010/21, art 1; for transitional provisions and savings see art 5(4), Sch 4, paras 14–18, 21 thereto.

Sub-s (2): in para (b) word "or" in square brackets inserted by SI 2010/21, art 5(1), Sch 1, paras 36, 39(b)(i).

Date in force: 15 February 2010: see SI 2010/21, art 1; for transitional provisions and savings see art 5(4), Sch 4, paras 14–18, 21 thereto.

Sub-s (2): para (d) and word omitted immediately preceding it repealed by SI 2010/21, art 5(1), Sch 1, paras 36, 39(b)(ii).

Date in force: 15 February 2010: see SI 2010/21, art 1; for transitional provisions and savings see art 5(4), Sch 4, paras 14–18, 21 thereto.

6 Certain judges who are also judges of First-tier Tribunal and Upper Tribunal

(1) A person is within this subsection (and so, by virtue of sections 4(1)(c) and 5(1)(g), is a judge of the First-tier Tribunal and of the Upper Tribunal) if the person—

[(za) is the Lord Chief Justice of England and Wales,

(zb) is the Master of the Rolls,

(zc) is the President of the Queen's Bench Division of the High Court in England and Wales,

(zd) is the President of the Family Division of the High Court in England and Wales,

(ze) is the Chancellor of the High Court in England and Wales,]

(a) is an ordinary judge of the Court of Appeal in England and Wales (including the vice-president, if any, of either division of that Court),

(b) is a Lord Justice of Appeal in Northern Ireland,

(c) is a judge of the Court of Session,

(d) is a puisne judge of the High Court in England and Wales or Northern Ireland,

[(da) is a deputy judge of the High Court in England and Wales,

(db) is the Judge Advocate General,]

(e) is a circuit judge,

(f) is a sheriff in Scotland,

(g) is a county court judge in Northern Ireland,

(h) is a district judge in England and Wales or Northern Ireland, or

(i) is a District Judge (Magistrates' Courts).

(2) References in subsection (1)(c) to (i) to office-holders do not include deputies or temporary office-holders.

Amendment

Sub-s (1): paras (za)–(ze) inserted by the Crime and Courts Act 2013, s 21(4), Sch 14, Pt 4, paras 6, 8(1), (2). Date in force: 1 October 2013: see SI 2013/2200, art 3(b), (g).

Sub-s (1): paras (da), (db) inserted by the Crime and Courts Act 2013, s 21(4), Sch 14, Pt 4, paras 6, 8(1), (3). Date in force: 1 October 2013: see SI 2013/2200, art 3(b), (g).

[6A Certain judges who are also judges of the First-tier Tribunal

A person is within this section (and so, by virtue of section 4(1)(ca), is a judge of the First-tier Tribunal) if the person—

(a) is a deputy Circuit judge,

(b) is a Recorder,

(c) is a person who holds an office listed—

(i) in the first column of the table in section 89(3C) of the Senior Courts Act 1981 (senior High Court Masters etc), or

(ii)   in column 1 of Part 2 of Schedule 2 to that Act (High Court Masters etc),

(d)   is a deputy district judge appointed under section 102 of that Act or section 8 of the County Courts Act 1984,

(e)   is a Deputy District Judge (Magistrates' Courts), or

(f)   is a person appointed under section 30(1)(a) or (b) of the Courts-Martial (Appeals) Act 1951 (assistants to the Judge Advocate General).]

Amendment

Inserted by the Crime and Courts Act 2013, s 21(4), Sch 14, Pt 4, paras 6, 9. Date in force: 1 October 2013: see SI 2013/2200, art 3(b), (g).

7 Chambers: jurisdiction and Presidents

(1) The Lord Chancellor may, with the concurrence of the Senior President of Tribunals, by order make provision for the organisation of each of the First-tier Tribunal and the Upper Tribunal into a number of chambers.

(2) There is—

(a)   for each chamber of the First-tier Tribunal, and

(b)   for each chamber of the Upper Tribunal,

to be a person, or two persons, to preside over that chamber.

(3) A person may not at any particular time preside over more than one chamber of the First-tier Tribunal and may not at any particular time preside over more than one chamber of the Upper Tribunal (but may at the same time preside over one chamber of the First-tier Tribunal and over one chamber of the Upper Tribunal).

(4) A person appointed under this section to preside over a chamber is to be known as a Chamber President.

(5) Where two persons are appointed under this section to preside over the same chamber, any reference in an enactment to the Chamber President of the chamber is a reference to a person appointed under this section to preside over the chamber.

(6) The Senior President of Tribunals may (consistently with subsections (2) and (3)) appoint a person who is the Chamber President of a chamber to preside instead, or to preside also, over another chamber.

(7) The [Senior President of Tribunals] may (consistently with subsections (2) and (3)) appoint a person who is not a Chamber President to preside over a chamber.

(8) Schedule 4 (eligibility for appointment under subsection (7), appointment of Deputy Chamber Presidents and Acting Chamber Presidents, assignment of judges and other members of the First-tier Tribunal and Upper Tribunal, and further provision about Chamber Presidents and chambers) has effect.

(9) Each of the Lord Chancellor and the Senior President of Tribunals may, with the concurrence of the other, by order—

(a)   make provision for the allocation of the First-tier Tribunal's functions between its chambers;

(b)   make provision for the allocation of the Upper Tribunal's functions between its chambers;

(c)   amend or revoke any order made under this subsection.

Amendment

Sub-s (7): words "Senior President of Tribunals" in square brackets substituted by the Crime and Courts Act 2013, s 20, Sch 13, Pt 4, paras 42, 43. Date in force: 1 October 2013: see SI 2013/2200, art 3(a), (e).

8 Senior President of Tribunals: power to delegate

(1) The Senior President of Tribunals may delegate any function he has in his capacity as Senior President of Tribunals—

(a)   to any judge, or other member, of the Upper Tribunal or First-tier Tribunal;

(b)   to staff appointed under section 40(1).

[(1A)   A function under paragraph 1(1) or 2(1) of Schedule 2 may be delegated under subsection (1) only to a Chamber President of a chamber of the Upper Tribunal.]

(2)   Subsection (1) does not apply to functions of the Senior President of Tribunals [under any of the following—

section 7(7);

section 7(9);

paragraph 2(1) of Schedule 3;

paragraph 7(1) of Schedule 3;

paragraph 2 of Schedule 4;

paragraph 5(1) and (3) of Schedule 4;

paragraph 5(5) to (8) of Schedule 4;

paragraph 5A(2)(a) of Schedule 4;

paragraph 5A(3)(a) of Schedule 4].

(3)   A delegation under subsection (1) is not revoked by the delegator's becoming incapacitated.

(4)   Any delegation under subsection (1) that is in force immediately before a person ceases to be Senior President of Tribunals continues in force until varied or revoked by a subsequent holder of the office of Senior President of Tribunals.

(5)   The delegation under this section of a function shall not prevent the exercise of the function by the Senior President of Tribunals.

Amendment

Sub-s (1A): inserted by the Crime and Courts Act 2013, s 20, Sch 13, Pt 4, paras 42, 44(1). Date in force: 1 October 2013: see SI 2013/2200, art 3(a), (e).

Sub-s (2): words in square brackets substituted by the Crime and Courts Act 2013, s 20, Sch 13, Pt 4, paras 42, 44(2). Date in force: 1 October 2013: see SI 2013/2200, art 3(a), (e).

Review of decisions and appeals

9 Review of decision of First-tier Tribunal

(1)   The First-tier Tribunal may review a decision made by it on a matter in a case, other than a decision that is an excluded decision for the purposes of section 11(1) (but see subsection (9)).

(2)   The First-tier Tribunal's power under subsection (1) in relation to a decision is exercisable—

(a)   of its own initiative, or

(b)   on application by a person who for the purposes of section 11(2) has a right of appeal in respect of the decision.

(3)   Tribunal Procedure Rules may—

(a)   provide that the First-tier Tribunal may not under subsection (1) review (whether of its own initiative or on application under subsection (2)(b)) a decision of a description specified for the purposes of this paragraph in Tribunal Procedure Rules;

(b)   provide that the First-tier Tribunal's power under subsection (1) to review a decision of a description specified for the purposes of this paragraph in Tribunal Procedure Rules is exercisable only of the tribunal's own initiative;

(c)   provide that an application under subsection (2)(b) that is of a description specified for the purposes of this paragraph in Tribunal Procedure Rules may be made only on grounds specified for the purposes of this paragraph in Tribunal Procedure Rules;

(d)   provide, in relation to a decision of a description specified for the purposes of this paragraph in Tribunal Procedure Rules, that the First-tier

Tribunal's power under subsection (1) to review the decision of its own initiative is exercisable only on grounds specified for the purposes of this paragraph in Tribunal Procedure Rules.

(4) Where the First-tier Tribunal has under subsection (1) reviewed a decision, the First-tier Tribunal may in the light of the review do any of the following—

(a) correct accidental errors in the decision or in a record of the decision;

(b) amend reasons given for the decision;

(c) set the decision aside.

(5) Where under subsection (4)(c) the First-tier Tribunal sets a decision aside, the First-tier Tribunal must either—

(a) re-decide the matter concerned, or

(b) refer that matter to the Upper Tribunal.

(6) Where a matter is referred to the Upper Tribunal under subsection (5)(b), the Upper Tribunal must re-decide the matter.

(7) Where the Upper Tribunal is under subsection (6) re-deciding a matter, it may make any decision which the First-tier Tribunal could make if the First-tier Tribunal were re-deciding the matter.

(8) Where a tribunal is acting under subsection (5)(a) or (6), it may make such findings of fact as it considers appropriate.

(9) This section has effect as if a decision under subsection (4)(c) to set aside an earlier decision were not an excluded decision for the purposes of section 11(1), but the First-tier Tribunal's only power in the light of a review under subsection (1) of a decision under subsection (4)(c) is the power under subsection (4)(a).

(10) A decision of the First-tier Tribunal may not be reviewed under subsection (1) more than once, and once the First-tier Tribunal has decided that an earlier decision should not be reviewed under subsection (1) it may not then decide to review that earlier decision under that subsection.

(11) Where under this section a decision is set aside and the matter concerned is then re-decided, the decision set aside and the decision made in re-deciding the matter are for the purposes of subsection (10) to be taken to be different decisions.

10 Review of decision of Upper Tribunal

(1) The Upper Tribunal may review a decision made by it on a matter in a case, other than a decision that is an excluded decision for the purposes of section 13(1) (but see subsection (7)).

(2) The Upper Tribunal's power under subsection (1) in relation to a decision is exercisable—

(a) of its own initiative, or

(b) on application by a person who for the purposes of section 13(2) has a right of appeal in respect of the decision.

(3) Tribunal Procedure Rules may—

(a) provide that the Upper Tribunal may not under subsection (1) review (whether of its own initiative or on application under subsection (2)(b)) a decision of a description specified for the purposes of this paragraph in Tribunal Procedure Rules;

(b) provide that the Upper Tribunal's power under subsection (1) to review a decision of a description specified for the purposes of this paragraph in Tribunal Procedure Rules is exercisable only of the tribunal's own initiative;

(c) provide that an application under subsection (2)(b) that is of a description specified for the purposes of this paragraph in Tribunal Procedure Rules may be made only on grounds specified for the purposes of this paragraph in Tribunal Procedure Rules;

(d)   provide, in relation to a decision of a description specified for the purposes of this paragraph in Tribunal Procedure Rules, that the Upper Tribunal's power under subsection (1) to review the decision of its own initiative is exercisable only on grounds specified for the purposes of this paragraph in Tribunal Procedure Rules.

(4) Where the Upper Tribunal has under subsection (1) reviewed a decision, the Upper Tribunal may in the light of the review do any of the following—

    (a)   correct accidental errors in the decision or in a record of the decision;

    (b)   amend reasons given for the decision;

    (c)   set the decision aside.

(5) Where under subsection (4)(c) the Upper Tribunal sets a decision aside, the Upper Tribunal must re-decide the matter concerned.

(6) Where the Upper Tribunal is acting under subsection (5), it may make such findings of fact as it considers appropriate.

(7) This section has effect as if a decision under subsection (4)(c) to set aside an earlier decision were not an excluded decision for the purposes of section 13(1), but the Upper Tribunal's only power in the light of a review under subsection (1) of a decision under subsection (4)(c) is the power under subsection (4)(a).

(8) A decision of the Upper Tribunal may not be reviewed under subsection (1) more than once, and once the Upper Tribunal has decided that an earlier decision should not be reviewed under subsection (1) it may not then decide to review that earlier decision under that subsection.

(9) Where under this section a decision is set aside and the matter concerned is then re-decided, the decision set aside and the decision made in re-deciding the matter are for the purposes of subsection (8) to be taken to be different decisions.

11 Right to appeal to Upper Tribunal

(1) For the purposes of subsection (2), the reference to a right of appeal is to a right to appeal to the Upper Tribunal on any point of law arising from a decision made by the First-tier Tribunal other than an excluded decision.

(2) Any party to a case has a right of appeal, subject to subsection (8).

(3) That right may be exercised only with permission (or, in Northern Ireland, leave).

(4) Permission (or leave) may be given by—

    (a)   the First-tier Tribunal, or

    (b)   the Upper Tribunal,

on an application by the party.

(5) For the purposes of subsection (1), an "excluded decision" is—

    (a)   any decision of the First-tier Tribunal on an appeal made in exercise of a right conferred by the Criminal Injuries Compensation Scheme in compliance with section 5(1)(a) of the Criminal Injuries Compensation Act 1995 (c 53) (appeals against decisions on reviews),

   [(aa) any decision of the First-tier Tribunal on an appeal made in exercise of a right conferred by the Victims of Overseas Terrorism Compensation Scheme in compliance with section 52(3) of the Crime and Security Act 2010,]

    (b)   any decision of the First-tier Tribunal on an appeal under section 28(4) or (6) of the Data Protection Act 1998 (c 29) (appeals against national security certificate),

    (c)   any decision of the First-tier Tribunal on an appeal under section 60(1) or (4) of the Freedom of Information Act 2000 (c 36) (appeals against national security certificate),

    (d)   a decision of the First-tier Tribunal under section 9—

        (i)   to review, or not to review, an earlier decision of the tribunal,

      (ii)   to take no action, or not to take any particular action, in the light of a review of an earlier decision of the tribunal,

      (iii)   to set aside an earlier decision of the tribunal, or

      (iv)   to refer, or not to refer, a matter to the Upper Tribunal,

  (e)   a decision of the First-tier Tribunal that is set aside under section 9 (including a decision set aside after proceedings on an appeal under this section have been begun), or

  (f)   any decision of the First-tier Tribunal that is of a description specified in an order made by the Lord Chancellor.

(6) A description may be specified under subsection (5)(f) only if—

  (a)   in the case of a decision of that description, there is a right to appeal to a court, the Upper Tribunal or any other tribunal from the decision and that right is, or includes, something other than a right (however expressed) to appeal on any point of law arising from the decision, or

  (b)   decisions of that description are made in carrying out a function transferred under section 30 and prior to the transfer of the function under section 30(1) there was no right to appeal from decisions of that description.

(7) Where—

  (a)   an order under subsection (5)(f) specifies a description of decisions, and

  (b)   decisions of that description are made in carrying out a function transferred under section 30,

the order must be framed so as to come into force no later than the time when the transfer under section 30 of the function takes effect (but power to revoke the order continues to be exercisable after that time, and power to amend the order continues to be exercisable after that time for the purpose of narrowing the description for the time being specified).

(8) The Lord Chancellor may by order make provision for a person to be treated as being, or to be treated as not being, a party to a case for the purposes of subsection (2).

Amendment

  Sub-s (5): para (aa) inserted by the Crime and Security Act 2010, s 48(4), Sch 2, para 5.

  Date in force: 8 April 2010: see the Crime and Security Act 2010, s 59(2)(b).

12 Proceedings on appeal to Upper Tribunal

(1) Subsection (2) applies if the Upper Tribunal, in deciding an appeal under section 11, finds that the making of the decision concerned involved the making of an error on a point of law.

(2) The Upper Tribunal—

  (a)   may (but need not) set aside the decision of the First-tier Tribunal, and

  (b)   if it does, must either—

      (i)   remit the case to the First-tier Tribunal with directions for its reconsideration, or

      (ii)   re-make the decision.

(3) In acting under subsection (2)(b)(i), the Upper Tribunal may also—

  (a)   direct that the members of the First-tier Tribunal who are chosen to reconsider the case are not to be the same as those who made the decision that has been set aside;

  (b)   give procedural directions in connection with the reconsideration of the case by the First-tier Tribunal.

(4) In acting under subsection (2)(b)(ii), the Upper Tribunal—

  (a)   may make any decision which the First-tier Tribunal could make if the First-tier Tribunal were re-making the decision, and

  (b)   may make such findings of fact as it considers appropriate.

13 Right to appeal to Court of Appeal etc

(1) For the purposes of subsection (2), the reference to a right of appeal is to a right to appeal to the relevant appellate court on any point of law arising from a decision made by the Upper Tribunal other than an excluded decision.

(2) Any party to a case has a right of appeal, subject to subsection (14).

(3) That right may be exercised only with permission (or, in Northern Ireland, leave).

(4) Permission (or leave) may be given by—

    (a)   the Upper Tribunal, or

    (b)   the relevant appellate court,

on an application by the party.

(5) An application may be made under subsection (4) to the relevant appellate court only if permission (or leave) has been refused by the Upper Tribunal.

(6) The Lord Chancellor may, as respects an application under subsection (4) that falls within subsection (7) and for which the relevant appellate court is the Court of Appeal in England and Wales or the Court of Appeal in Northern Ireland, by order make provision for permission (or leave) not to be granted on the application unless the Upper Tribunal or (as the case may be) the relevant appellate court considers—

    (a)   that the proposed appeal would raise some important point of principle or practice, or

    (b)   that there is some other compelling reason for the relevant appellate court to hear the appeal.

[(6A) Rules of court may make provision for permission not to be granted on an application under subsection (4) to the Court of Session that falls within subsection (7) unless the court considers—

    (a)   that the proposed appeal would raise some important point of principle, or

    (b)   that there is some other compelling reason for the court to hear the appeal.]

(7) An application falls within this subsection if the application is for permission (or leave) to appeal from any decision of the Upper Tribunal on an appeal under section 11.

(8) For the purposes of subsection (1), an "excluded decision" is—

    (a)   any decision of the Upper Tribunal on an appeal under section 28(4) or (6) of the Data Protection Act 1998 (c 29) (appeals against national security certificate),

    (b)   any decision of the Upper Tribunal on an appeal under section 60(1) or (4) of the Freedom of Information Act 2000 (c 36) (appeals against national security certificate),

    (c)   any decision of the Upper Tribunal on an application under section 11(4)(b) (application for permission or leave to appeal),

    (d)   a decision of the Upper Tribunal under section 10—

        (i)   to review, or not to review, an earlier decision of the tribunal,

        (ii)   to take no action, or not to take any particular action, in the light of a review of an earlier decision of the tribunal, or

        (iii)   to set aside an earlier decision of the tribunal,

    (e)   a decision of the Upper Tribunal that is set aside under section 10 (including a decision set aside after proceedings on an appeal under this section have been begun), or

    (f)   any decision of the Upper Tribunal that is of a description specified in an order made by the Lord Chancellor.

(9) A description may be specified under subsection (8)(f) only if—

    (a)   in the case of a decision of that description, there is a right to appeal to a court from the decision and that right is, or includes, something other than a right (however expressed) to appeal on any point of law arising from the decision, or

    (b)   decisions of that description are made in carrying out a function transferred under section 30 and prior to the transfer of the function under section 30(1) there was no right to appeal from decisions of that description.

(10)   Where—

    (a)   an order under subsection (8)(f) specifies a description of decisions, and

    (b)   decisions of that description are made in carrying out a function transferred under section 30,

the order must be framed so as to come into force no later than the time when the transfer under section 30 of the function takes effect (but power to revoke the order continues to be exercisable after that time, and power to amend the order continues to be exercisable after that time for the purpose of narrowing the description for the time being specified).

(11)   Before the Upper Tribunal decides an application made to it under subsection (4), the Upper Tribunal must specify the court that is to be the relevant appellate court as respects the proposed appeal.

(12)   The court to be specified under subsection (11) in relation to a proposed appeal is whichever of the following courts appears to the Upper Tribunal to be the most appropriate—

    (a)   the Court of Appeal in England and Wales;

    (b)   the Court of Session;

    (c)   the Court of Appeal in Northern Ireland.

(13)   In this section except subsection (11), "the relevant appellate court", as respects an appeal, means the court specified as respects that appeal by the Upper Tribunal under subsection (11).

(14)   The Lord Chancellor may by order make provision for a person to be treated as being, or to be treated as not being, a party to a case for the purposes of subsection (2).

(15)   Rules of court may make provision as to the time within which an application under subsection (4) to the relevant appellate court must be made.

Amendment

   Sub-s (6A): inserted by the Crime and Courts Act 2013, s 23. Date in force: 15 July 2013: see SI 2013/1725, art 2(b).

14 Proceedings on appeal to Court of Appeal etc

(1)   Subsection (2) applies if the relevant appellate court, in deciding an appeal under section 13, finds that the making of the decision concerned involved the making of an error on a point of law.

(2)   The relevant appellate court—

    (a)   may (but need not) set aside the decision of the Upper Tribunal, and

    (b)   if it does, must either—

        (i)   remit the case to the Upper Tribunal or, where the decision of the Upper Tribunal was on an appeal or reference from another tribunal or some other person, to the Upper Tribunal or that other tribunal or person, with directions for its reconsideration, or

        (ii)   re-make the decision.

(3)   In acting under subsection (2)(b)(i), the relevant appellate court may also—

    (a)   direct that the persons who are chosen to reconsider the case are not to be the same as those who—

        (i)   where the case is remitted to the Upper Tribunal, made the decision of the Upper Tribunal that has been set aside, or

        (ii)   where the case is remitted to another tribunal or person, made the decision in respect of which the appeal or reference to the Upper Tribunal was made;

    (b)   give procedural directions in connection with the reconsideration of the case by the Upper Tribunal or other tribunal or person.

(4) In acting under subsection (2)(b)(ii), the relevant appellate court—

    (a)   may make any decision which the Upper Tribunal could make if the Upper Tribunal were re-making the decision or (as the case may be) which the other tribunal or person could make if that other tribunal or person were re-making the decision, and

    (b)   may make such findings of fact as it considers appropriate.

(5) Where—

    (a)   under subsection (2)(b)(i) the relevant appellate court remits a case to the Upper Tribunal, and

    (b)   the decision set aside under subsection (2)(a) was made by the Upper Tribunal on an appeal or reference from another tribunal or some other person,

the Upper Tribunal may (instead of reconsidering the case itself) remit the case to that other tribunal or person, with the directions given by the relevant appellate court for its reconsideration.

(6) In acting under subsection (5), the Upper Tribunal may also—

    (a)   direct that the persons who are chosen to reconsider the case are not to be the same as those who made the decision in respect of which the appeal or reference to the Upper Tribunal was made;

    (b)   give procedural directions in connection with the reconsideration of the case by the other tribunal or person.

(7) In this section "the relevant appellate court", as respects an appeal under section 13, means the court specified as respects that appeal by the Upper Tribunal under section 13(11).

"Judicial review"

15 Upper Tribunal's "judicial review" jurisdiction

(1) The Upper Tribunal has power, in cases arising under the law of England and Wales or under the law of Northern Ireland, to grant the following kinds of relief—

    (a)   a mandatory order;

    (b)   a prohibiting order;

    (c)   a quashing order;

    (d)   a declaration;

    (e)   an injunction.

(2) The power under subsection (1) may be exercised by the Upper Tribunal if—

    (a)   certain conditions are met (see section 18), or

    (b)   the tribunal is authorised to proceed even though not all of those conditions are met (see section 19(3) and (4)).

(3) Relief under subsection (1) granted by the Upper Tribunal—

    (a)   has the same effect as the corresponding relief granted by the High Court on an application for judicial review, and

    (b)   is enforceable as if it were relief granted by the High Court on an application for judicial review.

(4) In deciding whether to grant relief under subsection (1)(a), (b) or (c), the Upper Tribunal must apply the principles that the High Court would apply in deciding whether to grant that relief on an application for judicial review.

(5) In deciding whether to grant relief under subsection (1)(d) or (e), the Upper Tribunal must—

    (a)   in cases arising under the law of England and Wales apply the principles that the High Court would apply in deciding whether to grant that relief under section 31(2) of the [Senior Courts Act 1981] (c 54) on an application for judicial review, and

    (b)   in cases arising under the law of Northern Ireland apply the principles that the High Court would apply in deciding whether to grant that relief on an application for judicial review.

(6) For the purposes of the application of subsection (3)(a) in relation to cases arising under the law of Northern Ireland—

    (a)   a mandatory order under subsection (1)(a) shall be taken to correspond to an order of mandamus,

    (b)   a prohibiting order under subsection (1)(b) shall be taken to correspond to an order of prohibition, and

    (c)   a quashing order under subsection (1)(c) shall be taken to correspond to an order of certiorari.

Amendment

Sub-s (5): in para (a) words "Senior Courts Act 1981" in square brackets substituted by the Constitutional Reform Act 2005, s 59(5), Sch 11, Pt 1, para 1(2).

16 Application for relief under section 15(1)

(1) This section applies in relation to an application to the Upper Tribunal for relief under section 15(1).

(2) The application may be made only if permission (or, in a case arising under the law of Northern Ireland, leave) to make it has been obtained from the tribunal.

(3) The tribunal may not grant permission (or leave) to make the application unless it considers that the applicant has a sufficient interest in the matter to which the application relates.

(4) Subsection (5) applies where the tribunal considers—

    (a)   that there has been undue delay in making the application, and

    (b)   that granting the relief sought on the application would be likely to cause substantial hardship to, or substantially prejudice the rights of, any person or would be detrimental to good administration.

(5) The tribunal may—

    (a)   refuse to grant permission (or leave) for the making of the application;

    (b)   refuse to grant any relief sought on the application.

(6) The tribunal may award to the applicant damages, restitution or the recovery of a sum due if—

    (a)   the application includes a claim for such an award arising from any matter to which the application relates, and

    (b)   the tribunal is satisfied that such an award would have been made by the High Court if the claim had been made in an action begun in the High Court by the applicant at the time of making the application.

(7) An award under subsection (6) may be enforced as if it were an award of the High Court.

(8) Where—

    (a)   the tribunal refuses to grant permission (or leave) to apply for relief under section 15(1),

    (b)   the applicant appeals against that refusal, and

    (c)   the Court of Appeal grants the permission (or leave),

the Court of Appeal may go on to decide the application for relief under section 15(1).

(9) Subsections (4) and (5) do not prevent Tribunal Procedure Rules from limiting the time within which applications may be made.

17 Quashing orders under section 15(1): supplementary provision

(1) If the Upper Tribunal makes a quashing order under section 15(1)(c) in respect of a decision, it may in addition—

    (a)   remit the matter concerned to the court, tribunal or authority that made the decision, with a direction to reconsider the matter and reach a decision in accordance with the findings of the Upper Tribunal, or

    (b)   substitute its own decision for the decision in question.

(2) The power conferred by subsection (1)(b) is exercisable only if—

    (a)   the decision in question was made by a court or tribunal,

    (b)   the decision is quashed on the ground that there has been an error of law, and

    (c)   without the error, there would have been only one decision that the court or tribunal could have reached.

(3) Unless the Upper Tribunal otherwise directs, a decision substituted by it under subsection (1)(b) has effect as if it were a decision of the relevant court or tribunal.

18 Limits of jurisdiction under section 15(1)

(1) This section applies where an application made to the Upper Tribunal seeks (whether or not alone)—

    (a)   relief under section 15(1), or

    (b)   permission (or, in a case arising under the law of Northern Ireland, leave) to apply for relief under section 15(1).

(2) If Conditions 1 to 4 are met, the tribunal has the function of deciding the application.

(3) If the tribunal does not have the function of deciding the application, it must by order transfer the application to the High Court.

(4) Condition 1 is that the application does not seek anything other than—

    (a)   relief under section 15(1);

    (b)   permission (or, in a case arising under the law of Northern Ireland, leave) to apply for relief under section 15(1);

    (c)   an award under section 16(6);

    (d)   interest;

    (e)   costs.

(5) Condition 2 is that the application does not call into question anything done by the Crown Court.

(6) Condition 3 is that the application falls within a class specified for the purposes of this subsection in a direction given in accordance with Part 1 of Schedule 2 to the Constitutional Reform Act 2005 (c 4).

(7) The power to give directions under subsection (6) includes—

    (a)   power to vary or revoke directions made in exercise of the power, and

    (b)   power to make different provision for different purposes.

(8) Condition 4 is that the judge presiding at the hearing of the application is either—

    (a)   a judge of the High Court or the Court of Appeal in England and Wales or Northern Ireland, or a judge of the Court of Session, or

    (b)   such other persons as may be agreed from time to time between the Lord Chief Justice, the Lord President, or the Lord Chief Justice of Northern Ireland, as the case may be, and the Senior President of Tribunals.

(9) Where the application is transferred to the High Court under subsection (3)—

    (a)   the application is to be treated for all purposes as if it—

        (i)   had been made to the High Court, and

        (ii)   sought things corresponding to those sought from the tribunal, and

     (b)   any steps taken, permission (or leave) given or orders made by the tribunal in relation to the application are to be treated as taken, given or made by the High Court.

(10)   Rules of court may make provision for the purpose of supplementing subsection (9).

(11)   The provision that may be made by Tribunal Procedure Rules about amendment of an application for relief under section 15(1) includes, in particular, provision about amendments that would cause the application to become transferrable under subsection (3).

(12)   For the purposes of subsection (9)(a)(ii), in relation to an application transferred to the High Court in Northern Ireland—

     (a)   an order of mandamus shall be taken to correspond to a mandatory order under section 15(1)(a),

     (b)   an order of prohibition shall be taken to correspond to a prohibiting order under section 15(1)(b), and

     (c)   an order of certiorari shall be taken to correspond to a quashing order under section 15(1)(c).

19 Transfer of judicial review applications from High Court

(1)   . . .

(2)   . . .

(3)   Where an application is transferred to the Upper Tribunal under 31A of the [Senior Courts Act 1981] (c 54) or section 25A of the Judicature (Northern Ireland) Act 1978 (transfer from the High Court of judicial review applications)—

     (a)   the application is to be treated for all purposes as if it—

         (i)   had been made to the tribunal, and

         (ii)   sought things corresponding to those sought from the High Court,

     (b)   the tribunal has the function of deciding the application, even if it does not fall within a class specified under section 18(6), and

     (c)   any steps taken, permission given, leave given or orders made by the High Court in relation to the application are to be treated as taken, given or made by the tribunal.

(4)   Where—

     (a)   an application for permission is transferred to the Upper Tribunal under section 31A of the [Senior Courts Act 1981] (c 54) and the tribunal grants permission, or

     (b)   an application for leave is transferred to the Upper Tribunal under section 25A of the Judicature (Northern Ireland) Act 1978 (c 23) and the tribunal grants leave,

the tribunal has the function of deciding any subsequent application brought under the permission or leave, even if the subsequent application does not fall within a class specified under section 18(6).

(5)   Tribunal Procedure Rules may make further provision for the purposes of supplementing subsections (3) and (4).

(6)   For the purposes of subsection (3)(a)(ii), in relation to an application transferred to the Upper Tribunal under section 25A of the Judicature (Northern Ireland) Act 1978—

     (a)   a mandatory order under section 15(1)(a) shall be taken to correspond to an order of mandamus,

     (b)   a prohibiting order under section 15(1)(b) shall be taken to correspond to an order of prohibition, and

     (c)   a quashing order under section 15(1)(c) shall be taken to correspond to an order of certiorari.

Amendment

Sub-s (1): inserts the Senior Courts Act 1981, s 31A.

Sub-s (2): inserts the Judicature (Northern Ireland) Act 1978, s 25A.

Sub-s (3): words "Senior Courts Act 1981" in square brackets substituted by the Constitutional Reform Act 2005, a 59(5), Sch 11, Pt 1, para 1(2).

Sub-s (4): in para (a) words "Senior Courts Act 1981" in square brackets substituted by the Constitutional Reform Act 2005, s 59(5), Sch 11, Pt 1, para 1(2).

20 Transfer of judicial review applications from the Court of Session

(1) Where an application is made to the supervisory jurisdiction of the Court of Session, the Court—

  (a)   must, if Conditions 1 [and 2 are met, and], . . .

  [(aa)   . . .]

  (b)   may, if Conditions [and 3] are met, but Condition 2 is not,

by order transfer the application to the Upper Tribunal.

(2) Condition 1 is that the application does not seek anything other than an exercise of the supervisory jurisdiction of the Court of Session.

(3) Condition 2 is that the application falls within a class specified for the purposes of this subsection by act of sederunt made with the consent of the Lord Chancellor.

(4) Condition 3 is that the subject matter of the application is not a devolved Scottish matter.

(5)   . . .

[(5A)   . . .]

(6) There may not be specified under subsection (3) any class of application which includes an application the subject matter of which is a devolved Scottish matter.

(7) For the purposes of this section, the subject matter of an application is a devolved Scottish matter if it—

  (a)   concerns the exercise of functions in or as regards Scotland, and

  (b)   does not relate to a reserved matter within the meaning of the Scotland Act 1998 (c 46).

(8) In subsection (2), the reference to the exercise of the supervisory jurisdiction of the Court of Session includes a reference to the making of any order in connection with or in consequence of the exercise of that jurisdiction.

Amendment

Sub-s (1): in para (a) word omitted repealed by the Borders, Citizenship and Immigration Act 2009, s 53(3)(a). Date in force: 8 August 2011: see SI 2011/1741, art 2.

Sub-s (1): in para (a) words in square brackets substituted by the Crime and Courts Act 2013, s 22(2)(a)(i). Date in force: 1 November 2013: see SI 2013/2200, art 5.

Sub-s (1): para (aa) inserted by the Borders, Citizenship and Immigration Act 2009, s 53(3)(a) and repealed by the Crime and Courts Act 2013, s 22(2)(a)(ii). Date in force: 1 November 2013: see SI 2013/2200, art 5.

Sub-s (1): in para (b) words in square brackets substituted by the Crime and Courts Act 2013, s 22(2)(a)(iii). Date in force: 1 November 2013: see SI 2013/2200, art 5.

Sub-s (5): repealed by the Crime and Courts Act 2013, s 22(2)(b). Date in force: 1 November 2013: see SI 2013/2200, art 5.

Sub-s (5A): inserted by the Borders, Citizenship and Immigration Act 2009, s 53(3)(b) and repealed by the Crime and Courts Act 2013, s 22(2)(b). Date in force: 1 November 2013: see SI 2013/2200, art 5.

21 Upper Tribunal's "judicial review" jurisdiction: Scotland

(1) The Upper Tribunal has the function of deciding applications transferred to it from the Court of Session under section 20(1).

(2) The powers of review of the Upper Tribunal in relation to such applications are the same as the powers of review of the Court of Session in an application to the supervisory jurisdiction of that Court.

(3)   In deciding an application by virtue of subsection (1), the Upper Tribunal must apply principles that the Court of Session would apply in deciding an application to the supervisory jurisdiction of that Court.

(4)   An order of the Upper Tribunal by virtue of subsection (1)—

    (a)   has the same effect as the corresponding order granted by the Court of Session on an application to the supervisory jurisdiction of that Court, and

    (b)   is enforceable as if it were an order so granted by that Court.

(5)   Where an application is transferred to the Upper Tribunal by virtue of section 20(1), any steps taken or orders made by the Court of Session in relation to the application (other than the order to transfer the application under section 20(1)) are to be treated as taken or made by the tribunal.

(6)   Tribunal Procedure Rules may make further provision for the purposes of supplementing subsection (5).

Miscellaneous

22 Tribunal Procedure Rules

(1)   There are to be rules, to be called "Tribunal Procedure Rules", governing—

    (a)   the practice and procedure to be followed in the First-tier Tribunal, and

    (b)   the practice and procedure to be followed in the Upper Tribunal.

(2)   Tribunal Procedure Rules are to be made by the Tribunal Procedure Committee.

(3)   In Schedule 5—

Part 1 makes further provision about the content of Tribunal Procedure Rules,

Part 2 makes provision about the membership of the Tribunal Procedure Committee,

Part 3 makes provision about the making of Tribunal Procedure Rules by the Committee, and

Part 4 confers power to amend legislation in connection with Tribunal Procedure Rules.

(4)   Power to make Tribunal Procedure Rules is to be exercised with a view to securing—

    (a)   that, in proceedings before the First-tier Tribunal and Upper Tribunal, justice is done,

    (b)   that the tribunal system is accessible and fair,

    (c)   that proceedings before the First-tier Tribunal or Upper Tribunal are handled quickly and efficiently,

    (d)   that the rules are both simple and simply expressed, and

    (e)   that the rules where appropriate confer on members of the First-tier Tribunal, or Upper Tribunal, responsibility for ensuring that proceedings before the tribunal are handled quickly and efficiently.

(5)   In subsection (4)(b) "the tribunal system" means the system for deciding matters within the jurisdiction of the First-tier Tribunal or the Upper Tribunal.

23 Practice directions

(1)   The Senior President of Tribunals may give directions—

    (a)   as to the practice and procedure of the First-tier Tribunal;

    (b)   as to the practice and procedure of the Upper Tribunal.

(2)   A Chamber President may give directions as to the practice and procedure of the chamber over which he presides.

(3)   A power under this section to give directions includes—

    (a)   power to vary or revoke directions made in exercise of the power, and

(b)   power to make different provision for different purposes (including different provision for different areas).

(4)   Directions under subsection (1) may not be given without the approval of the Lord Chancellor.

(5)   Directions under subsection (2) may not be given without the approval of—

(a)   the Senior President of Tribunals, and

(b)   the Lord Chancellor.

(6)   Subsections (4) and (5)(b) do not apply to directions to the extent that they consist of guidance about any of the following—

(a)   the application or interpretation of the law;

(b)   the making of decisions by members of the First-tier Tribunal or Upper Tribunal.

(7)   Subsections (4) and (5)(b) do not apply to directions to the extent that they consist of criteria for determining which members of the First-tier Tribunal or Upper Tribunal may be chosen to decide particular categories of matter; but the directions may, to that extent, be given only after consulting the Lord Chancellor.

24 Mediation

(1)   A person exercising power to make Tribunal Procedure Rules or give practice directions must, when making provision in relation to mediation, have regard to the following principles—

(a)   mediation of matters in dispute between parties to proceedings is to take place only by agreement between those parties;

(b)   where parties to proceedings fail to mediate, or where mediation between parties to proceedings fails to resolve disputed matters, the failure is not to affect the outcome of the proceedings.

(2)   Practice directions may provide for members to act as mediators in relation to disputed matters in a case that is the subject of proceedings.

(3)   The provision that may be made by virtue of subsection (2) includes provision for a member to act as a mediator in relation to disputed matters in a case even though the member has been chosen to decide matters in the case.

(4)   Once a member has begun to act as a mediator in relation to a disputed matter in a case that is the subject of proceedings, the member may decide matters in the case only with the consent of the parties.

(5)   Staff appointed under section 40(1) may, subject to their terms of appointment, act as mediators in relation to disputed matters in a case that is the subject of proceedings.

(6)   In this section—

"member" means a judge or other member of the First-tier Tribunal or a judge or other member of the Upper Tribunal;

"practice direction" means a direction under section 23(1) or (2);

"proceedings" means proceedings before the First-tier Tribunal or proceedings before the Upper Tribunal.

25 Supplementary powers of Upper Tribunal

(1)   In relation to the matters mentioned in subsection (2), the Upper Tribunal—

(a)   has, in England and Wales or in Northern Ireland, the same powers, rights, privileges and authority as the High Court, and

(b)   has, in Scotland, the same powers, rights, privileges and authority as the Court of Session.

(2)   The matters are—

(a)   the attendance and examination of witnesses,

(b)   the production and inspection of documents, and

(c)   all other matters incidental to the Upper Tribunal's functions.

(3) Subsection (1) shall not be taken—
  (a) to limit any power to make Tribunal Procedure Rules;
  (b) to be limited by anything in Tribunal Procedure Rules other than an express limitation.

(4) A power, right, privilege or authority conferred in a territory by subsection (1) is available for purposes of proceedings in the Upper Tribunal that take place outside that territory (as well as for purposes of proceedings in the tribunal that take place within that territory).

26 First-tier Tribunal and Upper Tribunal: sitting places

Each of the First-tier Tribunal and the Upper Tribunal may decide a case—
  (a) in England and Wales,
  (b) in Scotland, or
  (c) in Northern Ireland,
even though the case arises under the law of a territory other than the one in which the case is decided.

27 Enforcement

(1) A sum payable in pursuance of a decision of the First-tier Tribunal or Upper Tribunal made in England and Wales—
  (a) shall be recoverable as if it were payable under an order of [the county court] in England and Wales;
  (b) shall be recoverable as if it were payable under an order of the High Court in England and Wales.

(2) An order for the payment of a sum payable in pursuance of a decision of the First-tier Tribunal or Upper Tribunal made in Scotland (or a copy of such an order certified in accordance with Tribunal Procedure Rules) may be enforced as if it were an extract registered decree arbitral bearing a warrant for execution issued by the sheriff court of any sheriffdom in Scotland.

(3) A sum payable in pursuance of a decision of the First-tier Tribunal or Upper Tribunal made in Northern Ireland—
  (a) shall be recoverable as if it were payable under an order of a county court in Northern Ireland;
  (b) shall be recoverable as if it were payable under an order of the High Court in Northern Ireland.

(4) This section does not apply to a sum payable in pursuance of—
  (a) an award under section 16(6), or
  (b) an order by virtue of section 21(1).

(5) The Lord Chancellor may by order make provision for subsection (1) or (3) to apply in relation to a sum of a description specified in the order with the omission of one (but not both) of paragraphs (a) and (b).

(6) Tribunal Procedure Rules—
  (a) may make provision as to where, for purposes of this section, a decision is to be taken to be made;
  (b) may provide for all or any of subsections (1) to (3) to apply only, or not to apply except, in relation to sums of a description specified in Tribunal Procedure Rules.

Amendment

Sub-s (1): in para (a) words in square brackets substituted by the Crime and Courts Act 2013, s 17(5), Sch 9, Pt 3, para 52(1)(b), (2). Date in force: 22 April 2014: see SI 2014/954, art 2(a), (c).

28 Assessors

(1) If it appears to the First-tier Tribunal or the Upper Tribunal that a matter before it requires special expertise not otherwise available to it, it may direct that in dealing

with that matter it shall have the assistance of a person or persons appearing to it to have relevant knowledge or experience.

(2) The remuneration of a person who gives assistance to either tribunal as mentioned in subsection (1) shall be determined and paid by the Lord Chancellor.

(3) The Lord Chancellor may—

    (a)   establish panels of persons from which either tribunal may (but need not) select persons to give it assistance as mentioned in subsection (1);

    (b)   under paragraph (a) establish different panels for different purposes;

    (c)   after carrying out such consultation as he considers appropriate, appoint persons to a panel established under paragraph (a);

    (d)   remove a person from such a panel.

29 Costs or expenses

(1) The costs of and incidental to—

    (a)   all proceedings in the First-tier Tribunal, and

    (b)   all proceedings in the Upper Tribunal,

shall be in the discretion of the Tribunal in which the proceedings take place.

(2) The relevant Tribunal shall have full power to determine by whom and to what extent the costs are to be paid.

(3) Subsections (1) and (2) have effect subject to Tribunal Procedure Rules.

(4) In any proceedings mentioned in subsection (1), the relevant Tribunal may—

    (a)   disallow, or

    (b)   (as the case may be) order the legal or other representative concerned to meet,

the whole of any wasted costs or such part of them as may be determined in accordance with Tribunal Procedure Rules.

(5) In subsection (4) "wasted costs" means any costs incurred by a party—

    (a)   as a result of any improper, unreasonable or negligent act or omission on the part of any legal or other representative or any employee of such a representative, or

    (b)   which, in the light of any such act or omission occurring after they were incurred, the relevant Tribunal considers it is unreasonable to expect that party to pay.

(6) In this section "legal or other representative", in relation to a party to proceedings, means any person exercising a right of audience or right to conduct the proceedings on his behalf.

(7) In the application of this section in relation to Scotland, any reference in this section to costs is to be read as a reference to expenses.

CHAPTER 3

TRANSFER OF TRIBUNAL FUNCTIONS

30 Transfer of functions of certain tribunals

(1) The Lord Chancellor may by order provide for a function of a scheduled tribunal to be transferred—

    (a)   to the First-tier Tribunal,

    (b)   to the Upper Tribunal,

    (c)   to the First-tier Tribunal and the Upper Tribunal with the question as to which of them is to exercise the function in a particular case being determined by a person under provisions of the order,

    (d)   to the First-tier Tribunal to the extent specified in the order and to the Upper Tribunal to the extent so specified,

(e)   to the First-tier Tribunal and the Upper Tribunal with the question as to which of them is to exercise the function in a particular case being determined by, or under, Tribunal Procedure Rules,

(f)   to an employment tribunal,

(g)   to the Employment Appeal Tribunal,

(h)   to an employment tribunal and the Employment Appeal Tribunal with the question as to which of them is to exercise the function in a particular case being determined by a person under provisions of the order, or

(i)   to an employment tribunal to the extent specified in the order and to the Employment Appeal Tribunal to the extent so specified.

(2)   In subsection (1) "scheduled tribunal" means a tribunal in a list in Schedule 6 that has effect for the purposes of this section.

(3)   The Lord Chancellor may, as respects a function transferred under subsection (1) or this subsection, by order provide for the function to be further transferred as mentioned in any of paragraphs (a) to (i) of subsection (1).

(4)   An order under subsection (1) or (3) may include provision for the purposes of or in consequence of, or for giving full effect to, a transfer under that subsection.

(5)   A function of a tribunal may not be transferred under subsection (1) or (3) if, or to the extent that, the provision conferring the function—

(a)   would be within the legislative competence of the Scottish Parliament if it were included in an Act of that Parliament, or

(b)   would be within the legislative competence of the Northern Ireland Assembly if it were included in an Act of that Assembly.

(6)   Subsection (5) does not apply to—

(a)   the Secretary of State's function of deciding appeals under section 41 of the Consumer Credit Act 1974 (c 39),

(b)   functions of the Consumer Credit Appeals Tribunal,

(c)   the Secretary of State's function of deciding appeals under section 7(1) of the Estate Agents Act 1979 (c 38), or

(d)   functions of an adjudicator under section 5 of the Criminal Injuries Compensation Act 1995 (c 53) (but see subsection (7)).

(7)   Functions of an adjudicator under section 5 of the Criminal Injuries Compensation Act 1995 (c 53), so far as they relate to Scotland, may be transferred under subsection (1) or (3) only with the consent of the Scottish Ministers.

(8)   A function of a tribunal may be transferred under subsection (1) or (3) only with the consent of the Welsh Ministers if any relevant function is exercisable in relation to the tribunal by the Welsh Ministers (whether by the Welsh Ministers alone, or by the Welsh Ministers jointly or concurrently with any other person).

(9)   In subsection (8) "relevant function", in relation to a tribunal, means a function which relates—

(a)   to the operation of the tribunal (including, in particular, its membership, administration, staff, accommodation and funding, and payments to its members or staff), or

(b)   to the provision of expenses and allowances to persons attending the tribunal or attending elsewhere in connection with proceedings before the tribunal.

31 Transfers under section 30: supplementary powers

(1)   The Lord Chancellor may by order make provision for abolishing the tribunal by whom a function transferred under section 30(1) is exercisable immediately before its transfer.

(2)   The Lord Chancellor may by order make provision, where functions of a tribunal are transferred under section 30(1), for a person—

(a)   who is the tribunal (but is not the Secretary of State), or

      (b)   who is a member of the tribunal, or

      (c)   who is an authorised decision-maker for the tribunal,

to (instead or in addition) be the holder of an office specified in subsection (3).

(3)   Those offices are—

      (a)   transferred-in judge of the First-tier Tribunal,

      (b)   transferred-in other member of the First-tier Tribunal,

      (c)   transferred-in judge of the Upper Tribunal,

      (d)   transferred-in other member of the Upper Tribunal, and

      (e)   deputy judge of the Upper Tribunal.

(4) Where functions of a tribunal are transferred under section 30(1), the Lord Chancellor must exercise the power under subsection (2) so as to secure that each person who immediately before the end of the tribunal's life—

      (a)   is the tribunal,

      (b)   is a member of the tribunal, or

      (c)   is an authorised decision-maker for the tribunal,

becomes the holder of an office specified in subsection (3) with effect from the end of the tribunal's life (if the person is not then already the holder of such an office).

(5)   Subsection (4) does not apply in relation to a person—

      (a)   by virtue of the person's being the Secretary of State, or

      (b)   by virtue of the person's being a Commissioner for the general purposes of the income tax;

and a reference in subsection (4) to the end of a tribunal's life is to when the tribunal is abolished or (without being abolished) comes to have no functions.

(6)   For the purposes of this section, a person is an "authorised decision-maker" for a tribunal if—

      (a)   the tribunal is listed in column 1 of an entry in the following Table, and

      (b)   the person is of the description specified in column 2 of that entry.

(1) *Tribunal*	*(2)* *Authorised decision-maker*
Adjudicator to Her Majesty's Land Registry	Member of the Adjudicator's staff who is authorised by the Adjudicator to carry out functions of the Adjudicator which are not of an administrative character
The Secretary of State as respects his function of deciding appeals under section 41 of the Consumer Credit Act 1974 (c 39)	Person who is a member of a panel under regulation 24 of the Consumer Credit Licensing (Appeals) Regulations 1998 (SI 1998/1203)
The Secretary of State as respects his function of deciding appeals under section 7(1) of the Estate Agents Act 1979 (c 38)	Person appointed, at any time after 2005, under regulation 19(1) of the Estate Agents (Appeals) Regulations 1981 (SI 1981/1518) to hear an appeal on behalf of the Secretary of State

(7) Where a function of a tribunal is transferred under section 30(1), the Lord Chancellor may by order provide for procedural rules in force immediately before the transfer to have effect, or to have effect with appropriate modifications, after the transfer (and, accordingly, to be capable of being varied or revoked) as if they were—

      (a)   Tribunal Procedure Rules, or

      (b)   employment tribunal procedure regulations, or Appeal Tribunal procedure rules, within the meaning given by section 42(1) of the Employment Tribunals Act 1996 (c 17).

(8)   In subsection (7)—

"procedural rules" means provision (whether called rules or not)—

(a)   regulating practice or procedure before the tribunal, and

(b)   applying for purposes connected with the exercise of the function;

"appropriate modifications" means modifications (including additions and omissions) that appear to the Lord Chancellor to be necessary to secure, or expedient in connection with securing, that the procedural rules apply in relation to the exercise of the function after the transfer.

(9)   The Lord Chancellor may, in connection with provision made by order under section 30 or the preceding provisions of this section, make by order such incidental, supplemental, transitional or consequential provision, or provision for savings, as the Lord Chancellor thinks fit, including provision applying only in relation to cases selected by a member—

(a)   of the First-tier Tribunal,

(b)   of the Upper Tribunal,

(c)   of the Employment Appeal Tribunal, or

(d)   of a panel of members of employment tribunals.

(10)   Subsections (1), (2) and (7) are not to be taken as prejudicing the generality of subsection (9).

32 Power to provide for appeal to Upper Tribunal from tribunals in Wales

(1)   Subsection (2) applies if—

(a)   a function is transferred under section 30(1)(a), (c), (d) or (e) in relation to England but is not transferred under section 30(1) in relation to Wales, or

(b)   a function that is not exercisable in relation to Wales is transferred under section 30(1)(a), (c), (d) or (e) in relation to England and, although there is a corresponding function that is exercisable in relation to Wales, that corresponding function is not transferred under section 30(1) in relation to Wales.

(2)   The Lord Chancellor may by order—

(a)   provide for an appeal against a decision to be made to the Upper Tribunal instead of to the court to which an appeal would otherwise fall to be made where the decision is made in exercising, in relation to Wales, the function mentioned in subsection (1)(a) or (as the case may be) the corresponding function mentioned in subsection (1)(b);

(b)   provide for a reference of any matter to be made to the Upper Tribunal instead of to the court to which a reference would otherwise fall to be made where the matter arises in exercising, in relation to Wales, the function mentioned in subsection (1)(a) or (as the case may be) the corresponding function mentioned in subsection (1)(b).

(3)   The Lord Chancellor may by order provide for an appeal against a decision of a scheduled tribunal to be made to the Upper Tribunal, instead of to the court to which an appeal would otherwise fall to be made, where the decision is made by the tribunal in exercising a function in relation to Wales.

(4)   In subsection (3) "scheduled tribunal" means a tribunal in a list in Schedule 6 that has effect for the purposes of that subsection.

(5)   An order under subsection (2) or (3)—

(a)   may include provision for the purposes of or in consequence of, or for giving full effect to, provision made by the order;

(b)   may include such incidental, supplemental, transitional or consequential provision or savings as the Lord Chancellor thinks fit.

33 Power to provide for appeal to Upper Tribunal from tribunals in Scotland

(1)   Subsection (2) applies if—

(a) a function is transferred under section 30(1)(a), (c), (d) or (e) in relation to England (whether or not also in relation to Wales) but is not transferred under section 30(1) in relation to Scotland,

(b) an appeal may be made to the Upper Tribunal against any decision, or any decision of a particular description, made in exercising the transferred function in relation to England, and

(c) no appeal may be made against a corresponding decision made in exercising the function in relation to Scotland.

(2) The Lord Chancellor may by order provide for an appeal against any such corresponding decision to be made to the Upper Tribunal.

(3) An order under subsection (2)—

(a) may include provision for the purposes of or in consequence of, or for giving full effect to, provision made by the order;

(b) may include such incidental, supplemental, transitional or consequential provision or savings as the Lord Chancellor thinks fit.

(4) An order under subsection (2) does not cease to have effect, and power to vary or revoke the order does not cease to be exercisable, just because either or each of the conditions in subsection (1)(b) and (c) ceases to be satisfied in relation to the function and decisions concerned.

34 Power to provide for appeal to Upper Tribunal from tribunals in Northern Ireland

(1) Subsection (2) applies if—

(a) a function is transferred under section 30(1)(a), (c), (d) or (e) in relation to England (whether or not also in relation to Wales) but is not transferred under section 30(1) in relation to Northern Ireland,

(b) an appeal may be made to the Upper Tribunal against any decision, or any decision of a particular description, made in exercising the transferred function in relation to England, and

(c) no appeal may be made against a corresponding decision made in exercising the function in relation to Northern Ireland.

(2) The Lord Chancellor may by order provide for an appeal against any such corresponding decision to be made to the Upper Tribunal.

(3) An order under subsection (2)—

(a) may include provision for the purposes of or in consequence of, or for giving full effect to, provision made by the order;

(b) may include such incidental, supplemental, transitional or consequential provision or savings as the Lord Chancellor thinks fit.

(4) An order under subsection (2) does not cease to have effect, and power to vary or revoke the order does not cease to be exercisable, just because either or each of the conditions in subsection (1)(b) and (c) ceases to be satisfied in relation to the function and decisions concerned.

35 Transfer of Ministerial responsibilities for certain tribunals

(1) The Lord Chancellor may by order—

(a) transfer any relevant function, so far as that function is exercisable by a Minister of the Crown—

(i) to the Lord Chancellor, or

(ii) to two (or more) Ministers of the Crown of whom one is the Lord Chancellor;

(b) provide for any relevant function that is exercisable by a Minister of the Crown other than the Lord Chancellor to be exercisable by the other Minister of the Crown concurrently with the Lord Chancellor;

(c) provide for any relevant function that is exercisable by the Lord Chancellor concurrently with another Minister of the Crown to cease to be exercisable by the other Minister of the Crown.

(2) In this section "relevant function" means a function, in relation to a scheduled tribunal, which relates—

    (a)   to the operation of the tribunal (including, in particular, its membership, administration, staff, accommodation and funding, and payments to its members or staff), or

    (b)   to the provision of expenses and allowances to persons attending the tribunal or attending elsewhere in connection with proceedings before the tribunal.

(3) In subsection (2) "scheduled tribunal" means a tribunal in a list in Schedule 6 that has effect for the purposes of this section.

(4) A relevant function may not be transferred under subsection (1) if, or to the extent that, the provision conferring the function—

    (a)   would be within the legislative competence of the Scottish Parliament if it were included in an Act of that Parliament, or

    (b)   would be within the legislative competence of the Northern Ireland Assembly if it were included in an Act of that Assembly.

(5) Subsection (4) does not apply to any relevant function of the Secretary of State—

    (a)   under section 41 of the Consumer Credit Act 1974 (c 39) (appeals), or

    (b)   under section 7 of the Estate Agents Act 1979 (c 38) (appeals).

(6) Any reference in subsection (1) to a Minister of the Crown includes a reference to a Minister of the Crown acting jointly.

(7) An order under subsection (1)—

    (a)   may relate to a function either wholly or in cases (including cases framed by reference to areas) specified in the order;

    (b)   may include provision for the purposes of, or in consequence of, or for giving full effect to, the transfer or (as the case may be) other change as regards exercise;

    (c)   may include such incidental, supplementary, transitional or consequential provision or savings as the Lord Chancellor thinks fit;

    (d)   may include provision for the transfer of any property, rights or liabilities of the person who loses functions or whose functions become shared with the Lord Chancellor.

(8) An order under subsection (1), so far as it—

    (a)   provides under paragraph (a) for the transfer of a function, or

    (b)   provides under paragraph (b) for a function to become exercisable by the Lord Chancellor, or

    (c)   provides under paragraph (c) for a function to cease to be exercisable by a Minister of the Crown other than the Lord Chancellor,

may not, after that transfer or other change has taken place, be revoked by another order under that subsection.

(9) Section 1 of the 1975 Act (power to transfer Ministerial functions) does not apply to a function of the Lord Chancellor—

    (a)   so far as it is a function transferred to the Lord Chancellor under subsection (1)(a),

    (b)   so far as it is a function exercisable by the Lord Chancellor as a result of provision under subsection (1)(b), or

    (c)   so far as it is a function that has become exercisable by the Lord Chancellor alone as a result of provision under subsection (1)(c).

(10) In this section—

"Minister of the Crown" has the meaning given by section 8(1) of the 1975 Act but includes the Commissioners for Her Majesty's Revenue and Customs;

"the 1975 Act" means the Ministers of the Crown Act 1975 (c 26).

36 Transfer of powers to make procedural rules for certain tribunals

(1) The Lord Chancellor may by order transfer any power to make procedural rules for a scheduled tribunal to—

    (a)   himself, or

    (b)   the Tribunal Procedure Committee.

(2) A power may not be transferred under subsection (1) if, or to the extent that, the provision conferring the power—

    (a)   would be within the legislative competence of the Scottish Parliament if it were included in an Act of that Parliament, or

    (b)   would be within the legislative competence of the Northern Ireland Assembly if it were included in an Act of that Assembly.

(3) Subsection (2) does not apply to—

    (a)   power conferred by section 40A(3) . . . of the Consumer Credit Act 1974 (c 39) (power to make provision with respect to appeals), or

    (b)   power conferred by section 7(3) of the Estate Agents Act 1979 (c 38) (duty of Secretary of State to make regulations with respect to appeals under section 7(1) of that Act).

(4) An order under subsection (1)(b)—

    (a)   may not alter any parliamentary procedure relating to the making of the procedural rules concerned, but

    (b)   may otherwise include provision for the purpose of assimilating the procedure for making them to the procedure for making Tribunal Procedure Rules.

(5) An order under subsection (1)(b) may include provision requiring the Tribunal Procedure Committee to make procedural rules for purposes notified to it by the Lord Chancellor.

(6) An order under this section—

    (a)   may relate to a power either wholly or in cases (including cases framed by reference to areas) specified in the order;

    (b)   may include provision for the purposes of or in consequence of, or for giving full effect to, the transfer;

    (c)   may include such incidental, supplementary, transitional or consequential provision or savings as the Lord Chancellor thinks fit.

(7) A power to make procedural rules for a tribunal that is exercisable by the Tribunal Procedure Committee by virtue of an order under this section must be exercised by the committee with a view to securing—

    (a)   that the system for deciding matters within the jurisdiction of that tribunal is accessible and fair,

    (b)   that proceedings before that tribunal are handled quickly and efficiently,

    (c)   that the rules are both simple and simply expressed, and

    (d)   that the rules where appropriate confer on persons who are, or who are members of, that tribunal responsibility for ensuring that proceedings before that tribunal are handled quickly and efficiently.

(8) In this section—

    "procedural rules", in relation to a tribunal, means provision (whether called rules or not) regulating practice or procedure before the tribunal;

    "scheduled tribunal" means a tribunal in a list in Schedule 6 that has effect for the purposes of this section.

Amendment

    Sub-s (3): in para (a) words omitted repealed by s 146, Sch 23, Pt 1 hereto.

37 Power to amend lists of tribunals in Schedule 6

(1) The Lord Chancellor may by order amend Schedule 6—

(a)   for the purpose of adding a tribunal to a list in the Schedule;

(b)   for the purpose of removing a tribunal from a list in the Schedule;

(c)   for the purpose of removing a list from the Schedule;

(d)   for the purpose of adding to the Schedule a list of tribunals that has effect for the purposes of any one or more of sections 30, 32(3), 35 and 36.

(2)   The following rules apply to the exercise of power under subsection (1)—

(a)   a tribunal may not be added to a list, or be in an added list, if the tribunal is established otherwise than by or under an enactment;

(b)   a tribunal established by an enactment passed or made after the last day of the Session in which this Act is passed must not be added to a list, or be in an added list, that has effect for the purposes of section 30;

(c)   if any relevant function is exercisable in relation to a tribunal by the Welsh Ministers (whether by the Welsh Ministers alone, or by the Welsh Ministers jointly or concurrently with any other person), the tribunal may be added to a list, or be in an added list, only with the consent of the Welsh Ministers;

(d)   a tribunal may be in more than one list.

(3)   In subsection (2)(c) "relevant function", in relation to a tribunal, means a function which relates—

(a)   to the operation of the tribunal (including, in particular, its membership, administration, staff, accommodation and funding, and payments to its members or staff), or

(b)   to the provision of expenses and allowances to persons attending the tribunal or attending elsewhere in connection with proceedings before the tribunal.

(4)   In subsection (1) "tribunal" does not include an ordinary court of law.

(5)   In this section "enactment" means any enactment whenever passed or made, including an enactment comprised in subordinate legislation (within the meaning of the Interpretation Act 1978 (c 30)).

38 Orders under sections 30 to 36: supplementary

(1)   Provision in an order under any of sections 30 to 36 may take the form of amendments, repeals or revocations of enactments.

(2)   In this section "enactment" means any enactment whenever passed or made, including an enactment comprised in subordinate legislation (within the meaning of the Interpretation Act 1978).

(3)   Any power to extend enactments to a territory outside the United Kingdom shall have effect as if it included—

(a)   power to extend those enactments as they have effect with any amendments and repeals made in them by orders under any of sections 30 to 36, and

(b)   power to extend those enactments as if any amendments and repeals made in them under those sections had not been made.

CHAPTER 4

ADMINISTRATIVE MATTERS IN RESPECT OF CERTAIN TRIBUNALS

39 The general duty

(1)   The Lord Chancellor is under a duty to ensure that there is an efficient and effective system to support the carrying on of the business of—

(a)   the First-tier Tribunal,

(b)   the Upper Tribunal,

(c)   employment tribunals, [and]

(d)   the Employment Appeal Tribunal. . .

(e) . . .

and that appropriate services are provided for those tribunals (referred to in this section and in sections 40 and 41 as "the tribunals").

(2) Any reference in this section, or in section 40 or 41, to the Lord Chancellor's general duty in relation to the tribunals is to his duty under subsection (1).

(3) The Lord Chancellor must annually prepare and lay before each House of Parliament a report as to the way in which he has discharged his general duty in relation to the tribunals.

Amendment

Sub-s (1): in para (c) word "and" in square brackets inserted by SI 2010/21, art 5(1), Sch 1, paras 36, 40(a).

Date in force: 15 February 2010: see SI 2010/21, art 1; for transitional provisions and savings see art 5(4), Sch 4, paras 14–18, 21 thereto.

Sub-s (1): para (e) and word omitted immediately preceding it repealed by SI 2010/21, art 5(3), Sch 1, paras 36, 40(b).

Date in force: 15 February 2010: see SI 2010/21, art 1; for transitional provisions and savings see art 5(4), Sch 4, paras 14–18, 21 thereto.

40 Tribunal staff and services

(1) The Lord Chancellor may appoint such staff as appear to him appropriate for the purpose of discharging his general duty in relation to the tribunals.

(2) Subject to subsections (3) and (4), the Lord Chancellor may enter into such contracts with other persons for the provision, by them or their sub-contractors, of staff or services as appear to him appropriate for the purpose of discharging his general duty in relation to the tribunals.

(3) The Lord Chancellor may not enter into contracts for the provision of staff to discharge functions which involve making judicial decisions or exercising any judicial discretion.

(4) The Lord Chancellor may not enter into contracts for the provision of staff to carry out the administrative work of the tribunals unless an order made by the Lord Chancellor authorises him to do so.

(5) Before making an order under subsection (4) the Lord Chancellor must consult the Senior President of Tribunals as to what effect (if any) the order might have on the proper and efficient administration of justice.

(6) An order under subsection (4) may authorise the Lord Chancellor to enter into contracts for the provision of staff to discharge functions—

(a)   wholly or to the extent specified in the order,

(b)   generally or in cases or areas specified in the order, and

(c)   unconditionally or subject to the fulfilment of conditions specified in the order.

41 Provision of accommodation

(1) The Lord Chancellor may provide, equip, maintain and manage such tribunal buildings, offices and other accommodation as appear to him appropriate for the purpose of discharging his general duty in relation to the tribunals.

(2) The Lord Chancellor may enter into such arrangements for the provision, equipment, maintenance or management of tribunal buildings, offices or other accommodation as appear to him appropriate for the purpose of discharging his general duty in relation to the tribunals.

(3) The powers under—

(a)   section 2 of the Commissioners of Works Act 1852 (c 28) (acquisition by agreement), and

(b)   section 228(1) of the Town and Country Planning Act 1990 (c 8) (compulsory acquisition), to acquire land necessary for the public service are to be treated as including power to acquire land for the purpose of its provision under arrangements entered into under subsection (2).

(4) In this section "tribunal building" means any place where any of the tribunals sits, including the precincts of any building in which it sits.

42 Fees

(1) The Lord Chancellor may by order prescribe fees payable in respect of—

    (a)   anything dealt with by the First-tier Tribunal,

    (b)   anything dealt with by the Upper Tribunal,

    (c)   . . .

    (d)   anything dealt with by an added tribunal, and

    (e)   mediation conducted by staff appointed under section 40(1).

(2) An order under subsection (1) may, in particular, contain provision as to—

    (a)   scales or rates of fees;

    (b)   exemptions from or reductions in fees;

    (c)   remission of fees in whole or in part.

(3) In subsection (1)(d) "added tribunal" means a tribunal specified in an order made by the Lord Chancellor.

(4) A tribunal may be specified in an order under subsection (3) only if—

    (a)   it is established by or under an enactment, whenever passed or made, and

    (b)   is not an ordinary court of law.

(5) Before making an order under this section, the Lord Chancellor must consult—

    (a)   the Senior President of Tribunals . . .

    (b)   . . .

(6) The making of an order under subsection (1) requires the consent of the Treasury except where the order contains provision only for the purpose of altering amounts payable by way of fees already prescribed under that subsection.

(7) The Lord Chancellor must take such steps as are reasonably practicable to bring information about fees under subsection (1) to the attention of persons likely to have to pay them.

(8) Fees payable under subsection (1) are recoverable summarily as a civil debt.

(9) Subsection (8) does not apply to the recovery in Scotland of fees payable under this section.

(10) . . .

Amendment

Sub-s (1): para (c) repealed by SI 2010/21, art 5(1), Sch 1, paras 36, 41.

Date in force: 15 February 2010: see SI 2010/21, art 1; for transitional provisions and savings see art 5(4), Sch 4, paras 14–18, 21 thereto.

Sub-s (5): para (b) and word omitted immediately preceding it repealed by SI 2013/2042, art 2(2), Schedule, paras 31, 32(a). Date in force: 19 August 2013: see SI 2013/2042, art 1(2).

Sub-s (10): repealed by SI 2013/2042, art 2(2), Schedule, paras 31, 32(b). Date in force: 19 August 2013: see SI 2013/2042, art 1(2).

Subordinate Legislation

Upper Tribunal (Immigration and Asylum Chamber) (Judicial Review) (England and Wales) Fees Order 2011, SI 2011/2344.

43 Report by Senior President of Tribunals

(1) Each year the Senior President of Tribunals must give the Lord Chancellor a report covering, in relation to relevant tribunal cases—

    (a)   matters that the Senior President of Tribunals wishes to bring to the attention of the Lord Chancellor, and

    (b)   matters that the Lord Chancellor has asked the Senior President of Tribunals to cover in the report.

(2)   The Lord Chancellor must publish each report given to him under subsection (1).

(3)   In this section "relevant tribunal cases" means—

> (a)   cases coming before the First-tier Tribunal,
>
> (b)   cases coming before the Upper Tribunal,
>
> (c)   cases coming before the Employment Appeal Tribunal, . . . [and]
>
> (d)   cases coming before employment tribunals[. . .
>
> (e)   . . .].

Amendment

Sub-s (3): in para (c) word omitted repealed by the UK Borders Act 2007, s 58, Schedule.

Sub-s (3): in para (c) word "and" in square brackets inserted by SI 2010/21, art 5(1), Sch 1, paras 36, 42(a).

Date in force: 15 February 2010: see SI 2010/21, art 1; for transitional provisions and savings see art 5(4), Sch 4, paras 14–18, 21 thereto.

Sub-s (3): para (e) and word omitted immediately preceding it inserted by the UK Borders Act 2007, s 56(1).

Sub-s (3): para (e) and word omitted immediately preceding it repealed by SI 2010/21, art 5(1), Sch 1, paras 36, 42(b).

Date in force: 15 February 2010: see SI 2010/21, art 1; for transitional provisions and savings see art 5(4), Sch 4, paras 14–18, 21 thereto.

44, 45

((Chapter 5) Outside the scope of this work.)

CHAPTER 6

SUPPLEMENTARY

46 Delegation of functions by Lord Chief Justice etc

(1)   The Lord Chief Justice of England and Wales may nominate a judicial office holder (as defined in section 109(4) of the Constitutional Reform Act 2005) to exercise any of his functions under the provisions listed in subsection (2).

(2)   The provisions are—

paragraphs 3(4) and 6(3)(a) of Schedule 2;

paragraphs 3(4) and 6(3)(a) of Schedule 3;

paragraphs 2(2) and 5(5) of Schedule 4;

paragraphs 21(2), 22, 24 and 25(2)(a) of Schedule 5.

(3)   The Lord President of the Court of Session may nominate any of the following to exercise any of his functions under the provisions listed in subsection (4)—

> (a)   a judge who is a member of the First or Second Division of the Inner House of the Court of Session;
>
> (b)   the Senior President of Tribunals.

(4)   The provisions are—

paragraphs 3(2) and 6(3)(b) of Schedule 2;

paragraphs 3(2) and 6(3)(b) of Schedule 3;

paragraphs 2(3) and 5(6) of Schedule 4;

paragraphs 23, 24, 25(2)(b) and (c) and 28(1)(b) of Schedule 5.

(5)   The Lord Chief Justice of Northern Ireland may nominate any of the following to exercise any of his functions under the provisions listed in subsection (6)—

> (a)   the holder of one of the offices listed in Schedule 1 to the Justice (Northern Ireland) Act 2002 (c 26);
>
> (b)   a Lord Justice of Appeal (as defined in section 88 of that Act);
>
> (c)   the Senior President of Tribunals.

(6)   The provisions are—
   paragraphs 3(3) and 6(3)(c) of Schedule 2;
   paragraphs 3(3) and 6(3)(c) of Schedule 3;
   paragraphs 2(4) and 5(7) of Schedule 4;
   paragraphs 24 and 25(2)(c) of Schedule 5.

[(7)   In Schedules 2 to 4 "senior judge" mean
   (a)   the Lord Chief Justice of England and Wales,
   (b)   the Lord President of the Court of Session,
   (c)   the Lord Chief Justice of Northern Ireland, or
   (d)   the Senior President of Tribunals.]

Amendment
   Sub-s (7): inserted by the Crime and Courts Act 2013, s 20, Sch 13, Pt 4, paras 42, 44(3). Date in force: 1 October 2013: see SI 2013/2200, art 3(a), (e).

47 Co-operation in relation to judicial training, guidance and welfare

(1)   Persons with responsibilities in connection with a courts-related activity, and persons with responsibilities in connection with the corresponding tribunals activity, must co-operate with each other in relation to the carrying-on of those activities.

(2)   In this section "courts-related activity" and "corresponding tribunals activity" are to be read as follows—
   (a)   making arrangements for training of judiciary of a territory is a courts-related activity, and the corresponding tribunals activity is making arrangements for training of tribunal members;
   (b)   making arrangements for guidance of judiciary of a territory is a courts-related activity, and the corresponding tribunals activity is making arrangements for guidance of tribunal members;
   (c)   making arrangements for the welfare of judiciary of a territory is a courts-related activity, and the corresponding tribunals activity is making arrangements for the welfare of tribunal members.

(3)   Subsection (1) applies to a person who has responsibilities in connection with a courts-related activity only if—
   (a)   the person is the chief justice of the territory concerned, or
   (b)   what the person does in discharging those responsibilities is done (directly or indirectly) on behalf of the chief justice of that territory.

(4)   Subsection (1) applies to a person who has responsibilities in connection with a corresponding tribunals activity only if—
   (a)   the person is the Senior President of Tribunals, or
   (b)   what the person does in discharging those responsibilities is done (directly or indirectly) on behalf of the Senior President of Tribunals.

(5)   For the purposes of this section—
   (a)   "territory" means—
      (i)   England and Wales,
      (ii)   Scotland, or
      (iii)   Northern Ireland;
   (b)   the "chief justice"—
      (i)   of England and Wales is the Lord Chief Justice of England and Wales,
      (ii)   of Scotland is the Lord President of the Court of Session, and
      (iii)   of Northern Ireland is the Lord Chief Justice of Northern Ireland;
   (c)   a person is a "tribunal member" if the person is—
      (i)   a judge, or other member, of the First-tier Tribunal or Upper Tribunal,

> (ii) a judge, or other member, of the Employment Appeal Tribunal, [or]
>
> (iii) a member of a panel of members of employment tribunals (whether or not a panel of [Employment Judges]) ...
>
> (iv) ...

Amendment

Sub-s (5): in para (c)(ii) word "or" in square brackets inserted by SI 2010/21, art 5(1), Sch 1, paras 36, 43(a).

Date in force: 15 February 2010: see SI 2010/21, art 1; for transitional provisions and savings see art 5(4), Sch 4, paras 14–18, 21 thereto.

Sub-s (5): in para (c)(iii) words "Employment Judges" in square brackets substituted by the Crime and Courts Act 2013, s 21(4), Sch 14, Pt 7, para 13(1). Date in force: 1 October 2013: see SI 2013/2200, art 3(b), (g).

Sub-s (5): para (c)(iv) and word omitted immediately preceding it repealed by SI 2010/21, art 5(3), Sch 1, paras 36, 43(b).

Date in force: 15 February 2010: see SI 2010/21, art 1; for transitional provisions and savings see art 5(4), Sch 4, paras 14–18, 21 thereto.

48

(This section introduces Schs 8, 9 to the Act.)

49 Orders and regulations under Part 1: supplemental and procedural provisions

(1) Power—

    (a) of the Lord Chancellor to make an order, or regulations, under this Part,

    (b) of the Senior President of Tribunals to make an order under section 7(9), or

    (c) of the Scottish Ministers, or the Welsh Ministers, to make an order under paragraph 25(2) of Schedule 7,

is exercisable by statutory instrument.

(2) The Statutory Instruments Act 1946 (c 36) shall apply in relation to the power to make orders conferred on the Senior President of Tribunals by section 7(9) as if the Senior President of Tribunals were a Minister of the Crown.

(3) Any power mentioned in subsection (1) includes power to make different provision for different purposes.

(4) Without prejudice to the generality of subsection (3), power to make an order under section 30 or 31 includes power to make different provision in relation to England, Scotland, Wales and Northern Ireland respectively.

(5) No order mentioned in subsection (6) is to be made unless a draft of the statutory instrument containing it (whether alone or with other provision) has been laid before, and approved by a resolution of, each House of Parliament.

(6) Those orders are—

    (a) an order under section 11(8), 13(6) or (14), 30, 31(1), 32, 33, 34, 35, 36, 37 or 42(3);

    (b) an order under paragraph 15 of Schedule 4;

    (c) an order under section 42(1)(a) to (d) that provides for fees to be payable in respect of things for which fees have never been payable;

    (d) an order under section 31(2), (7) or (9), or paragraph 30(1) of Schedule 5, that contains provision taking the form of an amendment or repeal of an enactment comprised in an Act.

(7) A statutory instrument that—

    (a) contains—

        (i) an order mentioned in subsection (8), or

        (ii) regulations under Part 3 of Schedule 9, and

    (b)   is not subject to any requirement that a draft of the instrument be laid before, and approved by a resolution of, each House of Parliament,

is subject to annulment in pursuance of a resolution of either House of Parliament.

(8) Those orders are—

    (a)   an order made by the Lord Chancellor under this Part;

    (b)   an order made by the Senior President of Tribunals under section 7(9).

(9) A statutory instrument that contains an order made by the Scottish Ministers under paragraph 25(2) of Schedule 7 is subject to annulment in pursuance of a resolution of the Scottish Parliament.

(10) A statutory instrument that contains an order made by the Welsh Ministers under paragraph 25(2) of Schedule 7 is subject to annulment in pursuance of a resolution of the National Assembly for Wales.

PART 2
JUDICIAL APPOINTMENTS

50 Judicial appointments: "judicial-appointment eligibility condition"

(1) Subsection (2) applies for the purposes of any statutory provision that—

    (a)   relates to an office or other position, and

    (b)   refers to a person who satisfies the judicial-appointment eligibility condition on an N-year basis (where N is the number stated in the provision).

(2) A person satisfies that condition on an N-year basis if—

    (a)   the person has a relevant qualification, and

    (b)   the total length of the person's qualifying periods is at least N years.

(3) In subsection (2) "qualifying period", in relation to a person, means a period during which the person—

    (a)   has a relevant qualification, and

    (b)   gains experience in law (see section 52).

(4) For the purposes of subsections (2) and (3), a person has a relevant qualification if the person—

    (a)   is a solicitor or a barrister (but see section 51), or

    (b)   holds a qualification that under section 51(1) is a relevant qualification in relation to the office, or other position, concerned.

(5) In this section—

"barrister" means barrister in England and Wales;

"solicitor" means solicitor of the Senior Courts of England and Wales;

"statutory provision" means—

    (a)   a provision of an Act, or

    (b)   a provision of subordinate legislation (within the meaning given by section 21(1) of the Interpretation Act 1978 (c 30)).

(6) Schedule 10, which makes amendments—

for the purpose of substituting references to satisfying the judicial-appointment eligibility condition in place of references to having a qualification mentioned in section 71 of the Courts and Legal Services Act 1990 (c 41),

for the purpose of reducing qualifying periods for eligibility for appointment to certain judicial offices from ten and seven years to seven and five years respectively, and

for connected purposes,

has effect.

(7) At any time before the coming into force of section 59(1) of the Constitutional Reform Act 2005 (c 4) (renaming of Supreme Court), the reference to the Senior Courts in subsection (5) is to be read as a reference to the Supreme Court.

51 "Relevant qualification" in section 50: further provision

(1)   The Lord Chancellor may by order provide for a qualification specified in the order to be a relevant qualification for the purposes of section 50(2) and (3) in relation to an office or other position specified in the order.

(2)   A qualification may be specified under subsection (1) only if it is one
[awarded by a body which, for the purposes of the Legal Services Act 2007, is an approved regulator in relation to the exercise of a right of audience or the conduct of litigation (within the meaning of that Act)].

(3)   An order under subsection (1) may, in relation to a qualification specified in the order, include provision as to when a person who holds the qualification is, for the purposes of section 50, to be taken first to have held it.

(4)   Where—

    (a)   a qualification is specified under subsection (1),

    (b)   the qualification is one awarded by a body such as is mentioned in subsection [(2)], and

    (c)   after the qualification is specified under subsection (1), it becomes the case that

[, for the purposes of the Legal Services Act 2007, the body—

        (i)   is not an approved regulator in relation to the exercise of a right of audience (within the meaning of that Act), and

        (ii)   is not an approved regulator in relation to the conduct of litigation (within the meaning of that Act),]

the provision under subsection (1) specifying the qualification ceases to have effect, subject to any provision made under [section 46 of the Legal Services Act 2007 (transitional etc provision in consequence of cancellation of designation as approved regulator)].

(5)   For the purposes of section 50 and this section, a person shall be taken first to become a solicitor when the person's name is entered on the roll kept under section 6 of the Solicitors Act 1974 (c 47) (Law Society to keep list of all solicitors) for the first time after the person's admission as a solicitor.

(6)   For the purposes of section 50 and this section, a person shall be taken first to become a barrister—

    (a)   when the person completes pupillage in connection with becoming a barrister, or

    (b)   in the case of a person not required to undertake pupillage in connection with becoming a barrister, when the person is called to the Bar of England and Wales.

(7)   For the purposes of section 50—

    (a)   a barrister,

    (b)   a solicitor, or

    (c)   a person who holds a qualification specified under subsection (1),

shall be taken not to have a relevant qualification at times when, as a result of disciplinary proceedings, he is prevented from practising as a barrister or (as the case may be) as a solicitor or as a holder of the specified qualification.

(8)   The Lord Chancellor may by order make provision supplementing or amending subsections (5) to (7).

(9)   Before making an order under subsection (1) or (8), the Lord Chancellor must consult—

    (a)   the Lord Chief Justice of England and Wales, and

    (b)   the Judicial Appointments Commission.

(10)   The Lord Chief Justice of England and Wales may nominate a judicial office holder (as defined in section 109(4) of the Constitutional Reform Act 2005 (c 4)) to exercise his function under subsection (9)(a).

(11) In this section—

"barrister" means barrister in England and Wales;

"solicitor" means solicitor of the Senior Courts of England and Wales.

(12) Power to make an order under this section is exercisable by statutory instrument.

(13) An order under this section may make different provision for different purposes.

(14) No order may be made under this section unless a draft of the statutory instrument containing it (whether alone or with other provision) has been laid before, and approved by a resolution of, each House of Parliament.

(15) At any time before the coming into force of section 59(1) of the Constitutional Reform Act 2005 (renaming of Supreme Court), the reference to the Senior Courts in subsection (11) is to be read as a reference to the Supreme Court.

Amendment

Sub-s (2): words from "awarded by a" to "of that Act)" in square brackets substituted by the Legal Services Act 2007, s 208(1), Sch 21, paras 162(1), (2).

Sub-s (4): in para (b) reference to "(2)" in square brackets substituted by the Legal Services Act 2007, s 208(1), Sch 21, paras 162(1), (3)(a).

Sub-s (4): in para (c) words from ", for the purposes" to "as approved regulator)" in square brackets substituted by the Legal Services Act 2007, s 208(1), Sch 21, paras 162(1), (3)b).

Sub-s (4): in para (c) words from "section 46 of" to "as approved regulator)" in square brackets substituted by the Legal Services Act 2007, s 208(1), Sch 21, paras 162(1), (3)(c).

52 Meaning of "gain experience in law" in section 50

(1) This section applies for the purposes of section 50.

(2) A person gains experience in law during a period if the period is one during which the person is engaged in law-related activities.

(3) For the purposes of subsection (2), a person's engagement in law-related activities during a period is to be disregarded if the engagement is negligible in terms of the amount of time engaged.

(4) For the purposes of this section, each of the following is a "law-related activity"—

    (a)   the carrying-out of judicial functions of any court or tribunal;

    (b)   acting as an arbitrator;

    (c)   practice or employment as a lawyer;

    (d)   advising (whether or not in the course of practice or employment as a lawyer) on the application of the law;

    (e)   assisting (whether or not in the course of such practice) persons involved in proceedings for the resolution of issues arising under the law;

    (f)   acting (whether or not in the course of such practice) as mediator in connection with attempts to resolve issues that are, or if not resolved could be, the subject of proceedings;

    (g)   drafting (whether or not in the course of such practice) documents intended to affect persons' rights or obligations;

    (h)   teaching or researching law;

    (i)   any activity that, in the relevant decision-maker's opinion, is of a broadly similar nature to an activity within any of paragraphs (a) to (h).

(5) For the purposes of this section, an activity mentioned in subsection (4) is a "law-related activity" whether it—

    (a)   is done on a full-time or part-time basis;

    (b)   is or is not done for remuneration;

    (c)   is done in the United Kingdom or elsewhere.

(6) In subsection (4)(i) "the relevant decision-maker", in relation to determining whether a person satisfies the judicial-appointment eligibility condition on an N-year basis in a particular case, means—

    (a)   where the condition applies in respect of appointment by Her Majesty to an office or other position, the person whose function it is to recommend the exercise of Her Majesty's function of making appointments to that office or position;

    (b)   where the condition applies in respect of appointment, by any person other than Her Majesty, to an office or other position, that person.

(7)   In subsection (6) "appointment", in relation to an office or position, includes any form of selection for that office or position (whether called appointment or selection, or not).

53–61

(These sections contain amendments only. In so far as relevant to this work, they have been incorporated at the appropriate place.)

PARTS 3–7

62–143

(Outside the scope of this work.)

PART 8
GENERAL

144

(Amends legislation outside the scope of this work.)

145 Power to make supplementary or other provision

(1)   The Lord Chancellor (or, in relation to Chapter 3 of Part 5 only, the Secretary of State) may by order make any supplementary, incidental, consequential, transitory, transitional or saving provision which he considers necessary or expedient for the purposes of, in consequence of, or for giving full effect to, any provision of this Act.

(2)   An order under this section may in particular—

    (a)   provide for any provision of this Act which comes into force before another to have effect, until that other provision has come into force, with modifications specified in the order;

    (b)   amend, repeal or revoke any enactment other than one contained in an Act or instrument passed or made after the Session in which this Act is passed.

(3)   The amendments that may be made by an order under this section are in addition to those made by or under any other provision of this Act.

(4)   An order under this section may make different provision for different purposes.

(5)   The power to make an order under this section is exercisable by statutory instrument.

(6)   A statutory instrument containing an order under this section, unless it is an order to which subsection (7) applies, is subject to annulment in pursuance of a resolution of either House of Parliament.

(7)   No order amending or repealing an enactment contained in an Act may be made under this section unless a draft of the order has been laid before and approved by a resolution of each House of Parliament.

146

(This section introduces Sch 23 (repeals) to the Act.)

147 Extent

(1)   Parts 1, 2 and 6 and this Part extend to England and Wales, Scotland and Northern Ireland.

(2)   The other provisions of this Act extend only to England and Wales.

(3)   Subsections (1) and (2) are subject to subsections (4) and (5).

(4)   Unless provided otherwise, amendments, repeals and revocations in this Act extend to any part of the United Kingdom to which the provisions amended, repealed or revoked extend.

(5)   The following extend also to the Isle of Man—

    (a)   section 143(1) and (2),

    (b)   the repeal by this Act of any provision specified in Part 6 of Schedule 23 that extends to the Isle of Man,

    (c)   sections 145 and 148(5) to (7) so far as relating to—

        (i)   section 143(1) and (2), and

        (ii)   the provisions of this Act by which the repeals mentioned in paragraph (b) are effected, and

    (d)   this section and section 149.

148 Commencement

(1)   Section 60 comes into force at the end of the period of two months beginning with the day on which this Act is passed.

(2)   The provisions of Chapter 3 of Part 5 come into force in accordance with provision made by the Lord Chancellor or the Secretary of State by order.

(3)   The provisions of Part 6 come into force, except as provided by subsection (4), in accordance with provision made by the Secretary of State by order.

(4)   The provisions of Part 6 come into force, in so far as they extend to Scotland, in accordance with provision made by the Scottish Ministers by order.

(5)   The remaining provisions of this Act, except sections 53, 55, 56, 57, 145, 147, 149, this section and Schedule 11, come into force in accordance with provision made by the Lord Chancellor by order.

(6)   An order under this section may make different provision for different purposes.

(7)   The power to make an order under this section is exercisable by statutory instrument.

Subordinate Legislation

Tribunals, Courts and Enforcement Act 2007 (Commencement No 1) Order 2007, SI 2007/2709; Tribunals, Courts and Enforcement Act 2007 (Commencement No 2) Order 2007, SI 2007/3613; Tribunals, Courts and Enforcement Act 2007 (Commencement No 3) Order 2008, SI 2008/749; Tribunals, Courts and Enforcement Act 2007 (Commencement No 4) Order 2008, SI 2008/1158; Tribunals, Courts and Enforcement Act 2007 (Commencement) (Scotland) Order 2008, SSI 2008/150; Tribunals, Courts and Enforcement Act 2007 (Commencement No 5 and Transitional Provisions) Order 2008, SI 2008/1653; Tribunals, Courts and Enforcement Act 2007 (Commencement No 6 and Transitional Provisions) Order 2008, SI 2008/2696; Tribunals, Courts and Enforcement Act 2007 (Commencement No 7) Order 2009, SI 2009/382; Tribunals, Courts and Enforcement Act 2007 (Commencement No 8) Order 2012, SI 2012/1312; Tribunals, Courts and Enforcement Act 2007 (Commencement No 9) Order 2013, SI 2013/1739; Tribunals, Courts and Enforcement Act 2007 (Commencement No 10) Order 2013, SI 2013/2043; Tribunals, Courts and Enforcement Act 2007 (Commencement No 11) Order 2014, SI 2014/768.

149 Short title

This Act may be cited as the Tribunals, Courts and Enforcement Act 2007.

SCHEDULE 1

SENIOR PRESIDENT OF TRIBUNALS

Section 2

PART 1

RECOMMENDATIONS FOR APPOINTMENT

Duty to fill vacancies

1

(1) If there is a vacancy in the office of Senior President of Tribunals, the Lord Chancellor must recommend a person for appointment to that office.

(2) Sub-paragraph (1) does not apply to a vacancy while the Lord Chief Justice of England and Wales agrees that it may remain unfilled.

The two routes to a recommendation: agreement under this paragraph or selection under Part 2

2

(1) Before the Lord Chancellor may recommend a person for appointment to the office of Senior President of Tribunals, the Lord Chancellor must consult—

    (a)   the Lord Chief Justice of England and Wales,

    (b)   the Lord President of the Court of Session, and

    (c)   the Lord Chief Justice of Northern Ireland.

(2) Sub-paragraphs (3) and (4) apply if—

    (a)   the outcome of consultation under sub-paragraph (1) is agreement between—

        (i)   the Lord Chancellor,

        (ii)   the Lord Chief Justice of England and Wales,

        (iii)   the Lord President of the Court of Session, and

        (iv)   the Lord Chief Justice of Northern Ireland,

    as to the person to be recommended, and

    (b)   the person is—

        (i)   an ordinary judge of the Court of Appeal in England and Wales,

        (ii)   a judge of the Court of Session who is a member of the First or Second Division of the Inner House of that Court, or

        (iii)   a Lord Justice of Appeal in Northern Ireland.

(3) The Lord Chancellor must recommend the person for appointment to the office of Senior President of Tribunals, subject to sub-paragraph (4).

(4) Where the person—

    (a)   declines to be recommended, or does not agree within a time specified to him for that purpose, or

    (b)   is otherwise not available within a reasonable time to be recommended,

the Lord Chancellor must, instead of recommending the person for appointment, consult afresh under sub-paragraph (1).

(5) If the Lord Chancellor has consulted under sub-paragraph (1) but sub-paragraphs (3) and (4) do not apply following that consultation, the Lord Chancellor must make a request to the Judicial Appointments Commission for a person to be selected for recommendation for appointment to the office of Senior President of Tribunals.

PART 2
SELECTION BY THE JUDICIAL APPOINTMENTS COMMISSION

Eligibility for selection

3

A person is eligible for selection in pursuance of a request under paragraph 2(5) only if—

- (a) he satisfies the judicial-appointment eligibility condition on a 7-year basis,
- (b) he is an advocate or solicitor in Scotland of at least seven years' standing, or
- (c) he is a barrister or solicitor in Northern Ireland of at least seven years' standing.

4, 5

. . .

Amendment

Paras 4, 5 amend legislation outside the scope of this work.

PART 3
TERMS OF OFFICE

Tenure, removal, resignation etc

6

(1) If—

- (a) a person appointed to the office of Senior President of Tribunals is appointed on terms that provide for him to retire from the office at a particular time specified in those terms ("the end of the fixed-term"), and
- (b) the end of the fixed-term is earlier than the time at which the person is required by the 1993 Act to retire from the office,

the person shall, if still holding the office at the end of the fixed-term, vacate the office at the end of the fixed-term.

(2) Subject to sub-paragraph (1) (and to the 1993 Act), a person appointed to the office of Senior President of Tribunals shall hold that office during good behaviour, subject to a power of removal by Her Majesty on an address presented to Her by both Houses of Parliament.

(3) It is for the Lord Chancellor to recommend to Her Majesty the exercise of the power of removal under sub-paragraph (2).

(4) In this paragraph "the 1993 Act" means the Judicial Pensions and Retirement Act 1993 (c 8).

7

(1) Sub-paragraph (2) applies to a person appointed to the office of Senior President of Tribunals on a recommendation made under paragraph 2(3).

(2) The person ceases to be Senior President of Tribunals if he ceases to fall within paragraph 2(2)(b).

8

A person who holds the office of Senior President of Tribunals may at any time resign that office by giving the Lord Chancellor notice in writing to that effect.

9

(1)   The Lord Chancellor, if satisfied by means of a medical certificate that a person holding the office of Senior President of Tribunals—

    (a)   is disabled by permanent infirmity from the performance of the duties of the office, and

    (b)   is for the time being incapacitated from resigning the office,

may, subject to sub-paragraph (2), by instrument under his hand declare the person to have vacated the office; and the instrument shall have the like effect for all purposes as if the person had on the date of the instrument resigned the office.

(2)   A declaration under sub-paragraph (1) with respect to a person shall be of no effect unless it is made with the concurrence of—

    (a)   the Lord Chief Justice of England and Wales,

    (b)   the Lord President of the Court of Session, and

    (c)   the Lord Chief Justice of Northern Ireland.

Remuneration, allowances and expenses

10

The Lord Chancellor may pay to the Senior President of Tribunals such amounts (if any) as the Lord Chancellor may determine by way of—

    (a)   remuneration;

    (b)   allowances;

    (c)   expenses.

Oaths

11

(1)   A person appointed to the office of Senior President of Tribunals must take the required oaths in the presence of—

    (a)   the Lord Chief Justice of England and Wales, or

    (b)   another holder of high judicial office (as defined in section 60(2) of the Constitutional Reform Act 2005 (c 4)) who is nominated by the Lord Chief Justice of England and Wales for the purpose of taking the oaths from the person.

(2)   Sub-paragraph (1) applies whether or not the person has previously taken the required oaths after accepting another office.

(3)   In this paragraph "the required oaths" means—

    (a)   the oath of allegiance, and

    (b)   the judicial oath,

as set out in the Promissory Oaths Act 1868 (c 72).

PART 4
CERTAIN FUNCTIONS OF THE SENIOR PRESIDENT

Meaning of "tribunal member"

12

(1)   For the purposes of this Part of this Schedule, each of the following is a "tribunal member"—

    (a)   a judge, or other member, of the First-tier Tribunal or Upper Tribunal,

    (b)   . . .

    (c)   a member of a panel of members of employment tribunals (whether or not a panel of [Employment Judges]),

    (d)   a judge, or other member, of the Employment Appeal Tribunal, and

    (e)   a person who is, or is a member of, a tribunal in a list in Schedule 6 that has effect for the purposes of section 30.

(2)   In this Part of this Schedule "tribunals" means—

    (a)   the First-tier Tribunal,

    (b)   the Upper Tribunal,

    (c)   ...

    (d)   employment tribunals,

    (e)   the Employment Appeal Tribunal, and

    (f)   any tribunal in a list in Schedule 6 that has effect for the purposes of section 30.

Representations to Parliament

13

The Senior President of Tribunals may lay before Parliament written representations on matters that appear to him to be matters of importance relating—

    (a)   to tribunal members, or

    (b)   otherwise to the administration of justice by tribunals.

Representation of views of tribunal members

14

The Senior President of Tribunals is responsible for representing the views of tribunal members to Parliament, to the Lord Chancellor and to Ministers of the Crown generally.

Amendment

Para 12: sub-para (1)(b) repealed by SI 2010/21, art 5(1), Sch 1, paras 36, 44.

Date in force: 15 February 2010: see SI 2010/21, art 1; for transitional provisions and savings see art 5(4), Sch 4, paras 14–18, 21 thereto.

Para 12: in sub-para (1)(c) words "Employment Judges" in square brackets substituted by the Crime and Courts Act 2013, s 21(4), Sch 14, Pt 7, para 13(1). Date in force: 1 October 2013: see SI 2013/2200, art 3(b), (g).

Para 12: sub-para (2)(c) repealed by SI 2010/21, art 5(1), Sch 1, paras 36, 44.

Date in force: 15 February 2010: see SI 2010/21, art 1; for transitional provisions and savings see art 5(4), Sch 4, paras 14–18, 21 thereto.

SCHEDULE 2

JUDGES AND OTHER MEMBERS OF THE FIRST-TIER TRIBUNAL

Section 4

Power to appoint judges of First-tier Tribunal

1

(1)   The [Senior President of Tribunals] may appoint a person to be one of the judges of the First-tier Tribunal

(2)   A person is eligible for appointment under sub-paragraph (1) only if the person—

    (a)   satisfies the judicial-appointment eligibility condition on a 5-year basis,

    (b)   is an advocate or solicitor in Scotland of at least five years' standing,

    (c)   is a barrister or solicitor in Northern Ireland of at least five years' standing, or

(d) in the [opinion of the Senior President of Tribunals], has gained experience in law which makes the person as suitable for appointment as if the person satisfied any of paragraphs (a) to (c).

(3) Section 52(2) to (5) (meaning of "gain experience in law") apply for the purposes of sub-paragraph (2)(d), but as if section 52(4)(i) referred to the [Senior President of Tribunals] instead of to the relevant decision-maker.

Power to appoint other members of First-tier Tribunal

2

(1) The [Senior President of Tribunals] may appoint a person to be one of the members of the First-tier Tribunal who are not judges of the tribunal.

(2) A person is eligible for appointment under sub-paragraph (1) only if the person has qualifications prescribed in an order made by the Lord Chancellor with the concurrence of the Senior President of Tribunals.

Appointed and transferred-in judges and other members: removal from office

3

(1) This paragraph applies to any power by which—

(a) a person appointed under paragraph 1(1) or 2(1),

(b) a transferred-in judge of the First-tier Tribunal, or

(c) a transferred-in other member of the First-tier Tribunal,

may be removed from office.

(2) If the person exercises functions wholly or mainly in Scotland, the power may be exercised only with the concurrence of the Lord President of the Court of Session.

(3) If the person exercises functions wholly or mainly in Northern Ireland, the power may be exercised only with the concurrence of the Lord Chief Justice of Northern Ireland.

(4) If neither of sub-paragraphs (2) and (3) applies, the power may be exercised only with the concurrence of the Lord Chief Justice of England and Wales.

Terms of appointment

4

(1) This paragraph applies—

(a) to a person appointed under paragraph 1(1) or 2(1),

(b) to a transferred-in judge of the First-tier Tribunal, and

(c) to a transferred-in other member of the First-tier Tribunal.

(2) If the terms of the person's appointment provide that he is appointed on a salaried (as opposed to fee-paid) basis, the person may be removed from office—

(a) only by the Lord Chancellor (and in accordance with paragraph 3), and

(b) only on the ground of inability or misbehaviour.

(2A) [If the terms of the person's appointment provide that the person is appointed on a fee-paid basis, the person may be removed from office—

(a) only by the Lord Chancellor (and in accordance with paragraph 3), and

(b) only on—

(i) the ground of inability or misbehaviour, or

(ii) a ground specified in the person's terms of appointment.

(2B) If the period (or extended period) for which the person is appointed ends before—

(a) the day on which the person attains the age of 70, or

(b)   if different, the day that for the purposes of section 26 of the Judicial Pensions and Retirement Act 1993 is the compulsory retirement date for the office concerned in the person's case,

then, subject to sub-paragraph (2C), the Lord Chancellor must extend the period of the person's appointment (including a period already extended under this sub-paragraph) before it ends.

(2C)   Extension under sub-paragraph (2B)—

(a)   requires the person's agreement,

(b)   is to be for such period as the Lord Chancellor considers appropriate, and

(c)   may be refused on—

(i)   the ground of inability or misbehaviour, or

(ii)   a ground specified in the person's terms of appointment,

but only with any agreement of a senior judge (see section 46(7)), or a nominee of a senior judge, that may be required by those terms.]

(3)   Subject to [the preceding provisions of this paragraph (but subject in the first place] to the Judicial Pensions and Retirement Act 1993 (c 8)), the person is to hold and vacate office in accordance with the terms of his appointment[, which are to be such as the Lord Chancellor may determine].

Remuneration, allowances and expenses

5

(1)   Sub-paragraph (2) applies—

(a)   to a person appointed under paragraph 1(1) or 2(1),

(b)   to a transferred-in judge of the First-tier Tribunal, and

(c)   to a transferred-in other member of the First-tier Tribunal.

(2)   The Lord Chancellor may pay to a person to whom this sub-paragraph applies such amounts (if any) as the Lord Chancellor may determine by way of—

(a)   remuneration;

(b)   allowances;

(c)   expenses.

Certain judges neither appointed under paragraph 1(1) nor transferred in

6

(1)   In this paragraph "judge by request of the First-tier Tribunal" means a person who is a judge of the First-tier Tribunal but who—

(a)   is not the Senior President of Tribunals,

(b)   is not a judge of the First-tier Tribunal appointed under paragraph 1(1),

(c)   is not a transferred-in judge of the First-tier Tribunal,

(d)   is not a Chamber President, or Acting Chamber President or Deputy Chamber President, of a chamber of the First-tier Tribunal,

(e)   is not a judge of the First-tier Tribunal by virtue of section 4(1)(e) ([Employment Judge]),

(f)   . . . and

(g)   is not a judge of the First-tier tribunal by virtue of section 4(2) (criminal injuries compensation adjudicator appointed by the Scottish Ministers).

(2)   A judge by request of the First-tier Tribunal may act as a judge of the First-tier Tribunal only if requested to do so by the Senior President of Tribunals.

(3)   Such a request made to a person who is a judge of the First-tier Tribunal by virtue of the combination of sections 4(1)(c) and 5(1)(g) may be made only with—

(a)   the concurrence of the Lord Chief Justice of England and Wales where the person is—

        (i)   an ordinary judge of the Court of Appeal in England and Wales,
        (ii)   a puisne judge of the High Court in England and Wales,
        (iii)   a circuit judge,
        (iv)   a district judge in England and Wales, . . .
        (v)   a District Judge (Magistrates' Courts);
        (vi)   the Master of the Rolls,
        (vii) the President of the Queen's Bench Division of the High Court of England and Wales,
        (viii) the President of the Family Division of that court,
        (ix)   the Chancellor of that court,
        (x)   a deputy judge of that court, or
        (xi)   the Judge Advocate General];
   (b)   the concurrence of the Lord President of the Court of Session where the person is—
        (i)   a judge of the Court of Session, or
        (ii)   a sheriff;
   (c)   the concurrence of the Lord Chief Justice of Northern Ireland where the person is—
        (i)   a Lord Justice of Appeal in Northern Ireland,
        (ii)   a puisne judge of the High Court in Northern Ireland,
        (iii)   a county court judge in Northern Ireland, or
        (iv)   a district judge in Northern Ireland.

[(3A) A request made under sub-paragraph (2) to a person who is a judge of the First-tier Tribunal by virtue of section 4(1)(ca) may be made only with the concurrence of the Lord Chief Justice of England and Wales.]

(4) Sub-paragraph (5) applies—
   (a)   to a judge by request of the First-tier Tribunal, [and]
   (b)   to a person who is a judge of the First-tier Tribunal by virtue of section 4(1)(e) ([Employment Judge]). . .
   (c)   . . .

(5) The Lord Chancellor may pay to a person to whom this sub-paragraph applies such amounts (if any) as the Lord Chancellor may determine by way of—
   (a)   remuneration;
   (b)   allowances;
   (c)   expenses.

Other members neither appointed under paragraph 2(1) nor transferred in

7

(1) In this paragraph "ex officio member of the First-tier Tribunal" means a person who is a member of the First-tier Tribunal by virtue of—
   (a)   section 4(3)(d) (members of employment tribunals who are not [Employment Judges]), [or]
   (b)   the combination of sections 4(3)(c) and 5(2)(c) (members of Employment Appeal Tribunal appointed under section 22(1)(c) of the Employment Tribunals Act 1996). . .
   (c)   . . .

(2) The Lord Chancellor may pay to an ex officio member of the First-tier Tribunal such amounts (if any) as the Lord Chancellor may determine by way of—
   (a)   remuneration;
   (b)   allowances;
   (c)   expenses.

Training etc

8

The Senior President of Tribunals is responsible, within the resources made available by the Lord Chancellor, for the maintenance of appropriate arrangements for the training, guidance and welfare of judges and other members of the First-tier Tribunal (in their capacities as such judges and other members).

Oaths

9

(1)   Sub-paragraph (2) applies to a person ("J")—

    (a)   who is appointed under paragraph 1(1) or 2(1), or

    (b)   who becomes a transferred-in judge, or a transferred-in other member, of the First-tier Tribunal and has not previously taken the required oaths after accepting another office.

(2)   J must take the required oaths before—

    (a)   the Senior President of Tribunals, or

    (b)   an eligible person who is nominated by the Senior President of Tribunals for the purpose of taking the oaths from J.

(3)   A person is eligible for the purposes of sub-paragraph (2)(b) if any one or more of the following paragraphs applies to him—

    (a)   he holds high judicial office (as defined in section 60(2) of the Constitutional Reform Act 2005 (c 4));

    (b)   he holds judicial office (as defined in section 109(4) of that Act);

    (c)   he holds (in Scotland) the office of sheriff.

(4)   In this paragraph "the required oaths" means (subject to sub-paragraph (5))—

    (a)   the oath of allegiance, and

    (b)   the judicial oath,

as set out in the Promissory Oaths Act 1868 (c 72).

(5)   Where it appears to the Lord Chancellor that J will carry out functions as a judge or other member of the First-tier Tribunal wholly or mainly in Northern Ireland, the Lord Chancellor may direct that in relation to J "the required oaths" means—

    (a)   the oath as set out in section 19(2) of the Justice (Northern Ireland) Act 2002 (c 26), or

    (b)   the affirmation and declaration as set out in section 19(3) of that Act.

Amendment

Para 1: in sub-paras (1, (2)(d), (3) words in square brackets substituted by the Crime and Courts Act 2013, s 20, Sch 13, Pt 4, paras 42, 45(1)–(4). Date in force: 1 October 2013: see SI 2013/2200, art 3(a), (e).

Para 2: in sub-para (1) words "Senior President of Tribunals" in square brackets substituted by the Crime and Courts Act 2013, s 20, Sch 13, Pt 4, paras 42, 45(1), (2). Date in force: 1 October 2013: see SI 2013/2200, art 3(a), (e).

Para 4: sub-paras (2A)–(2C) inserted by the Crime and Courts Act 2013, s 20, Sch 13, Pt 4, paras 42, 45(1), (5). Date in force: 1 October 2013: see SI 2013/2200, art 3(a), (e).

Para 4: in sub-para (3) words "the preceding provisions of this paragraph (but subject in the first place" in square brackets substituted by the Crime and Courts Act 2013, s 20, Sch 13, Pt 4, paras 42, 45(1), (6)(a). Date in force: 1 October 2013: see SI 2013/2200, art 3(a), (e).

Para 4: in sub-para (3) words ", which are to be such as the Lord Chancellor may determine" in square brackets inserted by the Crime and Courts Act 2013, s 20, Sch 13, Pt 4, paras 42, 45(1), (6)(b). Date in force: 1 October 2013: see SI 2013/2200, art 3(a), (e).

Para 6: in sub-para (1)(e) words "Employment Judge" in square brackets substituted by virtue of the Crime and Courts Act 2013, s 21(4), Sch 14, Pt 7, para 13(2). Date in force: 1 October 2013: see SI 2013/2200, art 3(b), (g).

Para 6: in sub-para (1)(f) words omitted repealed by SI 2010/21, art 5(1), Sch 1, paras 36, 45(a)(i).

Date in force: 15 February 2010: see SI 2010/21, art 1; for transitional provisions and savings see art 5(4), Sch 4, paras 14–18, 21 thereto.

Para 6: in sub-para (3)(a)(iv) word omitted repealed by the Crime and Courts Act 2013, s 21(4), Sch 14, Pt 4, paras 6, 10(1). Date in force: 1 October 2013: see SI 2013/2200, art 3(b), (g).

Para 6: sub-para (3)(a)(vi)–(xi) inserted by the Crime and Courts Act 2013, s 21(4), Sch 14, Pt 4, paras 6, 10(1). Date in force: 1 October 2013: see SI 2013/2200, art 3(b), (g).

Para 6: sub-para (3A) inserted by the Crime and Courts Act 2013, s 21(4), Sch 14, Pt 4, paras 6, 10(2). Date in force: 1 October 2013: see SI 2013/2200, art 3(b), (g).

Para 6: in sub-para (4)(a) word "and" in square brackets inserted by SI 2010/21, art 5(1), Sch 1, paras 36, 45(a)(ii)(aa).

Date in force: 15 February 2010: see SI 2010/21, art 1; for transitional provisions and savings see art 5(4), Sch 4, paras 14–18, 21 thereto.

Para 6: in sub-para (4)(b) words "Employment Judge" in square brackets substituted by virtue of the Crime and Courts Act 2013, s 21(4), Sch 14, Pt 7, para 13(2). Date in force: 1 October 2013: see SI 2013/2200, art 3(b), (g).

Para 6: sub-para (4)(c) and word omitted immediately preceding it repealed by SI 2010/21, art 5(1), Sch 1, paras 36, 45(a)(ii)(bb).

Date in force: 15 February 2010: see SI 2010/21, art 1; for transitional provisions and savings see art 5(4), Sch 4, paras 14–18, 21 thereto.

Para 7: in sub-para (1)(a) words "Employment Judges" in square brackets substituted by the Crime and Courts Act 2013, s 21(4), Sch 14, Pt 7, para 13(1). Date in force: 1 October 2013: see SI 2013/2200, art 3(b), (g).

Para 7: in sub-para (1)(a) word "or" in square brackets inserted by SI 2010/21, art 5(1), Sch 1, paras 36, 45(b)(i).

Date in force: 15 February 2010: see SI 2010/21, art 1; for transitional provisions and savings see art 5(4), Sch 4, paras 14–18, 21 thereto.

Para 7: sub-para (1)(c) and word omitted immediately preceding it repealed by SI 2010/21, art 5(1), Sch 1, paras 36, 45(b)(ii).

Date in force: 15 February 2010: see SI 2010/21, art 1; for transitional provisions and savings see art 5(4), Sch 4, paras 14–18, 21 thereto.

Subordinate Legislation

Qualifications for Appointment of Members to the First-tier Tribunal and Upper Tribunal Order 2008, SI 2008/2692.

Qualifications for Appointment of Members to the First-tier Tribunal and Upper Tribunal (Amendment) Order 2009, SI 2009/1592.

SCHEDULE 3
JUDGES AND OTHER MEMBERS OF THE UPPER TRIBUNAL
Section 5

Power to appoint judges of Upper Tribunal

1

(1)   Her Majesty, on the recommendation of the Lord Chancellor, may appoint a person to be one of the judges of the Upper Tribunal.

(2)   A person is eligible for appointment under sub-paragraph (1) only if the person—

    (a)   satisfies the judicial-appointment eligibility condition on a 7-year basis,

    (b)   is an advocate or solicitor in Scotland of at least seven years' standing,

    (c)   is a barrister or solicitor in Northern Ireland of at least seven years' standing, or

    (d)   in the [opinion of the Senior President of Tribunals], has gained experience in law which makes the person as suitable for appointment as if the person satisfied any of paragraphs (a) to (c).

(3) Section 52(2) to (5) (meaning of "gain experience in law") apply for the purposes of sub-paragraph (2)(d), but as if section 52(4)(i) referred to the Lord Chancellor instead of to the relevant decision-maker.

Power to appoint other members of Upper Tribunal

2

(1) The [Senior President of Tribunals] may appoint a person to be one of the members of the Upper Tribunal who are not judges of the tribunal.

(2) A person is eligible for appointment under sub-paragraph (1) only if the person has qualifications prescribed in an order made by the Lord Chancellor with the concurrence of the Senior President of Tribunals.

Appointed and transferred-in judges and other members: removal from office

3

(1) This paragraph applies to any power by which—

    (a)   a person appointed under paragraph 1(1) or 2(1),

    (b)   a transferred-in judge of the Upper Tribunal,

    [(ba)   a person who is a deputy judge of the Upper Tribunal (whether by appointment under paragraph 7(1) or as a result of provision under section 31(2)),] or

    (c)   a transferred-in other member of the Upper Tribunal,

may be removed from office.

(2) If the person exercises functions wholly or mainly in Scotland, the power may be exercised only with the concurrence of the Lord President of the Court of Session.

(3) If the person exercises functions wholly or mainly in Northern Ireland, the power may be exercised only with the concurrence of the Lord Chief Justice of Northern Ireland.

(4) If neither of sub-paragraphs (2) and (3) applies, the power may be exercised only with the concurrence of the Lord Chief Justice of England and Wales.

Terms of appointment

4

(1) This paragraph applies—

    (a)   to a person appointed under paragraph 1(1) or 2(1),

    (b)   to a transferred-in judge of the Upper Tribunal, and

    (c)   to a transferred-in other member of the Upper Tribunal.

(2) If the terms of the person's appointment provide that he is appointed on a salaried (as opposed to fee-paid) basis, the person may be removed from office—

    (a)   only by the Lord Chancellor (and in accordance with paragraph 3), and

    (b)   only on the ground of inability or misbehaviour.

(2A) [If the terms of the person's appointment provide that the person is appointed on a fee-paid basis, the person may be removed from office—

    (a)   only by the Lord Chancellor (and in accordance with paragraph 3), and

    (b)   only on—

        (i)   the ground of inability or misbehaviour, or

        (ii)   a ground specified in the person's terms of appointment.

(2B) If the period (or extended period) for which the person is appointed ends before—

    (a)   the day on which the person attains the age of 70, or

    (b)   if different, the day that for the purposes of section 26 of the Judicial Pensions and Retirement Act 1993 is the compulsory retirement date for the office concerned in the person's case,

then, subject to sub-paragraph (2C), the Lord Chancellor must extend the period of the person's appointment (including a period already extended under this sub-paragraph) before it ends.

(2C)   Extension under sub-paragraph (2B)—

    (a)   requires the person's agreement,

    (b)   is to be for such period as the Lord Chancellor considers appropriate, and

    (c)   may be refused on—

        (i)   the ground of inability or misbehaviour, or

        (ii)   a ground specified in the person's terms of appointment,

but only with any agreement of a senior judge (see section 46(7)), or a nominee of a senior judge, that may be required by those terms.]

(3)   Subject to [the preceding provisions of this paragraph (but subject in the first place] to the Judicial Pensions and Retirement Act 1993 (c 8)), the person is to hold and vacate office as a judge, or other member, of the Upper Tribunal in accordance with the terms of his appointment[, which are to be such as the Lord Chancellor may determine].

Remuneration, allowances and expenses

5

(1)   Sub-paragraph (2) applies—

    (a)   to a person appointed under paragraph 1(1) or 2(1),

    (b)   to a transferred-in judge of the Upper Tribunal, and

    (c)   to a transferred-in other member of the Upper Tribunal.

(2)   The Lord Chancellor may pay to a person to whom this sub-paragraph applies such amounts (if any) as the Lord Chancellor may determine by way of—

    (a)   remuneration;

    (b)   allowances;

    (c)   expenses.

Certain judges neither appointed under paragraph 1(1) nor transferred in

6

(1)   In this paragraph "judge by request of the Upper Tribunal" means a person who is a judge of the Upper Tribunal but—

    (a)   is not the Senior President of Tribunals,

    (b)   is not a judge of the Upper Tribunal appointed under paragraph 1(1),

    (c)   is not a transferred-in judge of the Upper Tribunal,

    (d)   . . .

    (e)   is not a deputy judge of the Upper Tribunal, and

    (f)   is not a Chamber President, or Acting Chamber President or Deputy Chamber President, of a chamber of the Upper Tribunal.

(2)   A judge by request of the Upper Tribunal may act as a judge of the Upper Tribunal only if requested to do so by the Senior President of Tribunals.

(3)   Such a request made to a person who is a judge of the Upper Tribunal by virtue of section 5(1)(g) may be made only with—

    (a)   the concurrence of the Lord Chief Justice of England and Wales where the person is—

        (i)   an ordinary judge of the Court of Appeal in England and Wales,

        (ii)   a puisne judge of the High Court in England and Wales,

	(iii)	a circuit judge,
	(iv)	a district judge in England and Wales, . . .
	(v)	a District Judge (Magistrates' Courts);
	(vi)	the Master of the Rolls,
	(vii)	the President of the Queen's Bench Division of the High Court of England and Wales,
	(viii)	the President of the Family Division of that court,
	(iv)	the Chancellor of that court,
	(x)	a deputy judge of that court, or
	(xi)	the Judge Advocate General];

(b) the concurrence of the Lord President of the Court of Session where the person is—

    (i) a judge of the Court of Session, or

    (ii) a sheriff;

(c) the concurrence of the Lord Chief Justice of Northern Ireland where the person is—

    (i) a Lord Justice of Appeal in Northern Ireland,

    (ii) a puisne judge of the High Court in Northern Ireland,

    (iii) a county court judge in Northern Ireland, or

    (iv) a district judge in Northern Ireland.

(4) The Lord Chancellor may pay to a judge by request of the Upper Tribunal, or a person who is a judge of the Upper Tribunal by virtue of section 5(1)(d), such amounts (if any) as the Lord Chancellor may determine by way of—

    (a) remuneration;

    (b) allowances;

    (c) expenses.

Deputy judges of the Upper Tribunal

7

(1) The [Senior President of Tribunals] may appoint a person to be a deputy judge of the Upper Tribunal for such period as the Lord Chancellor considers appropriate.

(2) A person is eligible for appointment under sub-paragraph (1) only if he is eligible to be appointed under paragraph 1(1) (see paragraph 1(2)).

(3) [The following provisions of this paragraph] apply—

    (a) to a person appointed under sub-paragraph (1), and

    (b) to a person who becomes a deputy judge of the Upper Tribunal as a result of provision under section 31(2).

[(3A) [The person may be removed from office—

    (a) only by the Lord Chancellor (and in accordance with paragraph 3), and

    (b) only on—

        (i) the ground of inability or misbehaviour, or

        (ii) a ground specified in the person's terms of appointment.

(3B) If the period (or extended period) for which the person is appointed ends before—

    (a) the day on which the person attains the age of 70, or

    (b) if different, the day that for the purposes of section 26 of the Judicial Pensions and Retirement Act 1993 is the compulsory retirement date for the office concerned in the person's case,

then, subject to sub-paragraph (3C), the Lord Chancellor must extend the period of the person's appointment (including a period already extended under this sub-paragraph) before it ends.

(3C) Extension under sub-paragraph (3B)—

    (a)   requires the person's agreement,

    (b)   is to be for such period as the Lord Chancellor considers appropriate, and

    (c)   may be refused on—

           (i)   the ground of inability or misbehaviour, or

           (ii)   a ground specified in the person's terms of appointment,

but only with any agreement of a senior judge (see section 46(7)), or a nominee of a senior judge, that may be required by those terms.

(4) Subject to the previous provisions of this paragraph (but subject in the first place to the Judicial Pensions and Retirement Act 1993), a person is to hold and vacate office as a deputy judge of the Upper Tribunal in accordance with the person's terms of appointment, which are to be such as the Lord Chancellor may determine.]

(5) The Lord Chancellor may pay to a person to whom this sub-paragraph applies such amounts (if any) as the Lord Chancellor may determine by way of—

    (a)   remuneration;

    (b)   allowances;

    (c)   expenses.

Other members neither appointed under paragraph 2(1) nor transferred in

8

(1) In this paragraph "ex officio member of the Upper Tribunal" means—

    (a)   a person who is a member of the Upper Tribunal by virtue of section 5(2)(c) (member of Employment Appeal Tribunal appointed under section 22(1)(c) of the Employment Tribunals Act 1996 (c 17))...

    (b)   ...

(2) The Lord Chancellor may pay to an ex officio member of the Upper Tribunal such amounts (if any) as the Lord Chancellor may determine by way of—

    (a)   remuneration;

    (b)   allowances;

    (c)   expenses.

Training etc

9

The Senior President of Tribunals is responsible, within the resources made available by the Lord Chancellor, for the maintenance of appropriate arrangements for the training, guidance and welfare of judges and other members of the Upper Tribunal (in their capacities as such judges and other members).

Oaths

10

(1) Sub-paragraph (2) applies to a person ("J")—

    (a)   who is appointed under paragraph 1(1), 2(1) or 7(1), or

    (b)   who—

           (i)   becomes a transferred-in judge, or a transferred-in other member, of the Upper Tribunal, or

           (ii)   becomes a deputy judge of the Upper Tribunal as a result of provision under section 31(2),

and has not previously taken the required oaths after accepting another office.

(2) J must take the required oaths before—

    (a)   the Senior President of Tribunals, or

    (b)   an eligible person who is nominated by the Senior President of Tribunals for the purpose of taking the oaths from J.

(3)   A person is eligible for the purposes of sub-paragraph (2)(b) if any one or more of the following paragraphs applies to him—

    (a)   he holds high judicial office (as defined in section 60(2) of the Constitutional Reform Act 2005 (c 4));

    (b)   he holds judicial office (as defined in section 109(4) of that Act);

    (c)   he holds (in Scotland) the office of sheriff.

(4)   In this paragraph "the required oaths" means (subject to sub-paragraph (5))—

    (a)   the oath of allegiance, and

    (b)   the judicial oath,

as set out in the Promissory Oaths Act 1868 (c 72).

(5)   Where it appears to the Lord Chancellor that J will carry out functions as a judge or other member of the Upper Tribunal wholly or mainly in Northern Ireland, the Lord Chancellor may direct that in relation to J "the required oaths" means—

    (a)   the oath as set out in section 19(2) of the Justice (Northern Ireland) Act 2002 (c 26), or

    (b)   the affirmation and declaration as set out in section 19(3) of that Act.

Amendment

Para 1: in sub-para (2)(d) words in square brackets substituted by the Crime and Courts Act 2013, s 20, Sch 13, Pt 4, para 30(1), (2). Date in force: 1 October 2013: see SI 2013/2200, art 3(e).

Para 2: in sub-para (1) words "Senior President of Tribunals" in square brackets substituted by the Crime and Courts Act 2013, s 20, Sch 13, Pt 4, paras 42, 46(1), (2). Date in force: 1 October 2013: see SI 2013/2200, art 3(e).

Para 3: sub-para (1)(ba) inserted by the Crime and Courts Act 2013, s 20, Sch 13, Pt 4, paras 42, 46(1), (3). Date in force: 1 October 2013: see SI 2013/2200, art 3(e).

Para 4: sub-paras (2A)–(2C) inserted by the Crime and Courts Act 2013, s 20, Sch 13, Pt 4, paras 42, 46(1), (4). Date in force: 1 October 2013: see SI 2013/2200, art 3(e).

Para 4: in sub-para (3) words "the preceding provisions of this paragraph (but subject in the first place" in square brackets substituted by the Crime and Courts Act 2013, s 20, Sch 13, Pt 4, paras 42, 46(1), (5)(a). Date in force: 1 October 2013: see SI 2013/2200, art 3(e).

Para 4: in sub-para (3) words ", which are to be such as the Lord Chancellor may determine" in square brackets inserted by the Crime and Courts Act 2013, s 20, Sch 13, Pt 4, paras 42, 46(1), (5)(b). Date in force: 1 October 2013: see SI 2013/2200, art 3(e).

Para 6: sub-para (1)(d) repealed by SI 2010/21, art 5(1), Sch 1, paras 36, 46(a).

Date in force: 15 February 2010: see SI 2010/21, art 1; for transitional provisions and savings see art 5(4), Sch 4, paras 14–18, 21 thereto.

Para 6: in sub-para (3)(a)(iv) word omitted repealed by the Crime and Courts Act 2013, s 21(4), Sch 14, Pt 4, paras 6, 10(1). Date in force: 1 October 2013: see SI 2013/2200, art 3(b), (g).

Para 6: sub-para (3)(a)(vi)–(xi) inserted by the Crime and Courts Act 2013, s 21(4), Sch 14, Pt 4, paras 6, 10(1). Date in force: 1 October 2013: see SI 2013/2200, art 3(b), (g).

Para 7: in sub-para (1) words "Senior President of Tribunals" in square brackets substituted by the Crime and Courts Act 2013, s 20, Sch 13, Pt 4, paras 42, 46(1), (6). Date in force: 1 October 2013: see SI 2013/2200, art 3(e).

Para 7: in sub-para (3) words "The following provisions of this paragraph" in square brackets substituted by the Crime and Courts Act 2013, s 20, Sch 13, Pt 4, paras 42, 46(1), (7). Date in force: 1 October 2013: see SI 2013/2200, art 3(e).

Para 7: sub-paras (3A)–(3C), (4) substituted, for sub-para (4) as originally enacted, by the Crime and Courts Act 2013, s 20, Sch 13, Pt 4, paras 42, 46(1), (8). Date in force: 1 October 2013: see SI 2013/2200, art 3(e).

Para 8: sub-para (1)(b) and word omitted immediately preceding it repealed by SI 2010/21, art 5(1), Sch 1, paras 36, 46(b).

Date in force: 15 February 2010: see SI 2010/21, art 1; for transitional provisions and savings see art 5(4), Sch 4, paras 14–18, 21 thereto.

Subordinate Legislation

Qualifications for Appointment of Members to the First-tier Tribunal and Upper Tribunal Order 2008, SI 2008/2692.

Qualifications for Appointment of Members to the First-tier Tribunal and Upper Tribunal (Amendment) Order 2009, SI 2009/1592.

SCHEDULE 4

CHAMBERS AND CHAMBER PRESIDENTS: FURTHER PROVISION

Section 7

PART 1

CHAMBER PRESIDENTS: APPOINTMENT, DELEGATION, DEPUTIES AND FURTHER PROVISION

Eligibility for appointment as Chamber President [under section 7(7)]

1

A person is eligible for appointment under section 7(7) only if—

    (a)   he is a judge of the Upper Tribunal, or

    (b)   he does not fall within paragraph (a) but is eligible to be appointed under paragraph 1(1) of Schedule 3 as a judge of the Upper Tribunal (see paragraph 1(2) of that Schedule).

Appointment as Chamber President [under section 7(7)]: consultation and nomination

2

(1)   The [Senior President of Tribunals must consult the Lord Chancellor before the Senior President of Tribunals] appoints under section 7(7) a person within—

    section 6(1)(a) (ordinary judge of Court of Appeal in England and Wales),

    section 6(1)(b) (Lord Justice of Appeal in Northern Ireland),

    section 6(1)(c) (judge of the Court of Session), or

    section 6(1)(d) (puisne judge of the High Court in England and Wales or Northern Ireland).

(2)   If the [Senior President of Tribunals], in exercise of his power under section 7(7) in a particular case, wishes that the person appointed should be drawn from among the ordinary judges of the Court of Appeal in England and Wales or the puisne judges of the High Court in England and Wales, the Lord Chancellor must first ask the Lord Chief Justice of England and Wales to nominate one of those judges for the purpose.

(3)   If the [Senior President of Tribunals], in exercise of his power under section 7(7) in a particular case, wishes that the person appointed should be drawn from among the judges of the Court of Session, the Lord Chancellor must first ask the Lord President of the Court of Session to nominate one of those judges for the purpose.

(4)   If the [Senior President of Tribunals], in exercise of his power under section 7(7) in a particular case, wishes that the person appointed should be drawn from among the Lords Justices of Appeal in Northern Ireland or the puisne judges of the High Court in Northern Ireland, the Lord Chancellor must first ask the Lord Chief Justice of Northern Ireland to nominate one of those judges for the purpose.

[(4A)   The Senior President of Tribunals may make a request under sub-paragraph (2), (3) or (4) only with the Lord Chancellor's concurrence.]

(5)   If a judge is nominated under sub-paragraph (2), (3) or (4) in response to a request under that sub-paragraph, the [Senior President of Tribunals] must appoint the nominated judge as Chamber President of the chamber concerned.

Chamber Presidents: duration of appointment, remuneration etc

3

(1) A Chamber President is to hold and vacate office as a Chamber President in accordance with the terms of his appointment as a Chamber President [but subject to paragraph 5A (and subject in the first place] to the Judicial Pensions and Retirement Act 1993 (c 8))[, and those terms are to be such as the Lord Chancellor may determine].

(2) The Lord Chancellor may pay to a Chamber President such amounts (if any) as the Lord Chancellor may determine by way of—

  (a) remuneration;
  (b) allowances;
  (c) expenses.

Delegation of functions by Chamber Presidents

4

(1) The Chamber President of a chamber of the First-tier Tribunal or Upper Tribunal may delegate any function he has in his capacity as the Chamber President of the chamber—

  (a) to any judge, or other member, of either of those tribunals;
  (b) to staff appointed under section 40(1).

(2) A delegation under sub-paragraph (1) is not revoked by the delegator's becoming incapacitated.

(3) Any delegation made by a person under sub-paragraph (1) that is in force immediately before the person ceases to be the Chamber President of a chamber continues in force until subsequently varied or revoked by another holder of the office of Chamber President of that chamber.

(4) The delegation under sub-paragraph (1) of a function shall not prevent the exercise of the function by the Chamber President of the chamber concerned.

(5) In this paragraph "delegate" includes further delegate.

Deputy Chamber Presidents

5

(1) The [Senior President of Tribunals] may appoint a person who is not a Deputy Chamber President of a chamber to be a Deputy Chamber President of a chamber.

(2) The Senior President of Tribunals may appoint a person who is a Deputy Chamber President of a chamber to be instead, or to be also, a Deputy Chamber President of another chamber.

(3) The power under sub-paragraph (1) is exercisable in any particular case only if the [Senior President of Tribunals]—

  (a) has consulted the [Lord Chancellor] about whether a Deputy Chamber President should be appointed for the chamber concerned, and
  (b) considers, in the light of the consultation, that a Deputy Chamber President of the chamber should be appointed.

(4) A person is eligible for appointment under sub-paragraph (1) only if—

  (a) he is a judge of the Upper Tribunal by virtue of appointment under paragraph 1(1) of Schedule 3,
  (b) he is a transferred-in judge of the Upper Tribunal (see section 31(2)),
  (c) he is a judge of the Upper Tribunal by virtue of—

   . . .

    section 5(1)(e) (Social Security Commissioner for Northern Ireland), section 5(1)(g) (certain judges of courts in the United Kingdom), or

section 5(1)(h) (deputy judge of the Upper Tribunal), or

(d)   he falls within none of paragraphs (a) to (c) but is eligible to be appointed under paragraph 1(1) of Schedule 3 as a judge of the Upper Tribunal (see paragraph 1(2) of that Schedule).

(5) If the [Senior President of Tribunals], in exercise of his power under sub-paragraph (1) in a particular case, wishes that the person appointed should be drawn from among the ordinary judges of the Court of Appeal in England and Wales or the puisne judges of the High Court in England and Wales, the [Senior President of Tribunals] must first ask the Lord Chief Justice of England and Wales to nominate one of those judges for the purpose.

(6) If the [Senior President of Tribunals], in exercise of his power under sub-paragraph (1) in a particular case, wishes that the person appointed should be drawn from among the judges of the Court of Session, the [Senior President of Tribunals] must first ask the Lord President of the Court of Session to nominate one of those judges for the purpose.

(7) If the [Senior President of Tribunals], in exercise of his power under sub-paragraph (1) in a particular case, wishes that the person appointed should be drawn from among the Lords Justices of Appeal in Northern Ireland or the puisne judges of the High Court in Northern Ireland, the [Senior President of Tribunals] must first ask the Lord Chief Justice of Northern Ireland to nominate one of those judges for the purpose.

[(7A)   The Senior President of Tribunals may make a request under sub-paragraph (5), (6) or (7) only with the Lord Chancellor's concurrence.]

(8) If a judge is nominated under sub-paragraph (5), (6) or (7) in response to a request under that sub-paragraph, the [Senior President of Tribunals] must appoint the nominated judge as a Deputy Chamber President of the chamber concerned.

(9) A Deputy Chamber President is to hold and vacate office as a Deputy Chamber President in accordance with the terms of his appointment [but subject to paragraph 5A (and subject in the first place] to the Judicial Pensions and Retirement Act 1993 (c 8))[, and those terms are to be such as the Lord Chancellor may determine].

(10)   The Lord Chancellor may pay to a Deputy Chamber President such amounts (if any) as the Lord Chancellor may determine by way of—

(a)   remuneration;

(b)   allowances;

(c)   expenses.

(11) In sub-paragraphs (1) and (2) "chamber" means chamber of the First-tier Tribunal or chamber of the Upper Tribunal.

*[Chamber Presidents and Deputies: removal from office and extension
of appointment*

5A

(1) This paragraph applies to a person—

(a)   appointed under section 7(6) or (7) as a Chamber President, or

(b)   appointed under paragraph 5(1) or (2) as a Deputy Chamber President of a chamber.

(2) If the terms of the person's appointment provide that the person is appointed otherwise than on a fee-paid basis, the person may be removed from office—

(a)   only by the Lord Chancellor with the concurrence of the Senior President of Tribunals, and

(b)   only on the ground of inability or misbehaviour.

(3) If the terms of the person's appointment provide that the person is appointed on a fee-paid basis, the person may be removed from office—

    (a)   only by the Lord Chancellor with the concurrence of the Senior President of Tribunals, and

    (b)   only on—

        (i)   the ground of inability or misbehaviour, or

        (ii)   a ground specified in the person's terms of appointment.

(4) If the period (or extended period) for which the person is appointed ends before—

    (a)   the day on which the person attains the age of 70, or

    (b)   if different, the day that for the purposes of section 26 of the Judicial Pensions and Retirement Act 1993 is the compulsory retirement date for the office concerned in the person's case,

then, subject to sub-paragraph (5), the Lord Chancellor must extend the period of the person's appointment (including a period already extended under this sub-paragraph) before it ends.

(5) Extension under sub-paragraph (4)—

    (a)   requires the person's agreement,

    (b)   is to be for such period as the Lord Chancellor considers appropriate, and

    (c)   may be refused on—

        (i)   the ground of inability or misbehaviour, or

        (ii)   a ground specified in the person's terms of appointment,

but only with any agreement of a senior judge (see section 46(7)), or a nominee of a senior judge, that may be required by those terms.]

Acting Chamber Presidents

6

(1) If in the case of a particular chamber of the First-tier Tribunal or Upper Tribunal there is no-one appointed under section 7 to preside over the chamber, the Senior President of Tribunals may appoint a person to preside over the chamber during the vacancy.

(2) A person appointed under sub-paragraph (1) is to be known as an Acting Chamber President.

(3) A person who is the Acting Chamber President of a chamber is to be treated as the Chamber President of the chamber for all purposes other than—

    (a)   the purposes of this paragraph of this Schedule, and

    (b)   the purposes of the Judicial Pensions and Retirement Act 1993 (c 8).

(4) A person is eligible for appointment under sub-paragraph (1) only if he is eligible for appointment as a Chamber President.

(5) An Acting Chamber President is to hold and vacate office as an Acting Chamber President in accordance with the terms of his appointment.

(6) The Lord Chancellor may pay to an Acting Chamber President such amounts (if any) as the Lord Chancellor may determine by way of—

    (a)   remuneration;

    (b)   allowances;

    (c)   expenses.

Guidance

7

The Chamber President of a chamber of the First-tier Tribunal or the Upper Tribunal is to make arrangements for the issuing of guidance on changes in the law and practice as they relate to the functions allocated to the chamber.

Oaths

8

(1) Sub-paragraph (2) applies to a person ("the appointee")—

    (a)   appointed under section 7(7) as a Chamber President,

    (b)   appointed under paragraph 5(1) as a Deputy Chamber President of a chamber, or

    (c)   appointed as an Acting Chamber President.

(2) The appointee must take the required oaths before—

    (a)   the Senior President of Tribunals, or

    (b)   an eligible person who is nominated by the Senior President of Tribunals for the purpose of taking the oaths from the appointee.

(3) A person is eligible for the purposes of sub-paragraph (2)(b) if any one or more of the following paragraphs applies to him—

    (a)   he holds high judicial office (as defined in section 60(2) of the Constitutional Reform Act 2005 (c 4));

    (b)   he holds judicial office (as defined in section 109(4) of that Act);

    (c)   he holds (in Scotland) the office of sheriff.

(4) Sub-paragraph (2) does not apply to the appointee if he has previously taken the required oaths in compliance with a requirement imposed on him under paragraph 9 of Schedule 2 or paragraph 10 of Schedule 3.

(5) In this paragraph "the required oaths" means (subject to sub-paragraph (6))—

    (a)   the oath of allegiance, and

    (b)   the judicial oath,

as set out in the Promissory Oaths Act 1868 (c 72).

(6) Where it appears to the Lord Chancellor that the appointee will carry out functions under his appointment wholly or mainly in Northern Ireland, the Lord Chancellor may direct that in relation to the appointee "the required oaths" means—

    (a)   the oath as set out in section 19(2) of the Justice (Northern Ireland) Act 2002 (c 26), or

    (b)   the affirmation and declaration as set out in section 19(3) of that Act.

Amendment

Para 1 heading: words in square brackets substituted by the Crime and Courts Act 2013, s 20, Sch 13, Pt 4, paras 42, 47(1), (2). Date in force: 1 October 2013: see SI 2013/2200, art 3(a), (e).

Para 2 heading: words in square brackets substituted by the Crime and Courts Act 2013, s 20, Sch 13, Pt 4, paras 42, 47(1), (2). Date in force: 1 October 2013: see SI 2013/2200, art 3(a), (e).

Para 2: in sub-para (1) words from "Senior President of" to "President of Tribunals" in square brackets substituted by the Crime and Courts Act 2013, s 20, Sch 13, Pt 4, paras 42, 47(1), (3). Date in force: 1 October 2013: see SI 2013/2200, art 3(a), (e).

Para 2: in sub-paras (2)–(5) words "Senior President of Tribunals" in square brackets substituted by the Crime and Courts Act 2013, s 20, Sch 13, Pt 4, paras 42, 47(1), (4). Date in force: 1 October 2013: see SI 2013/2200, art 3(a), (e).

Para 2: sub-para (4A) inserted by the Crime and Courts Act 2013, s 20, Sch 13, Pt 4, paras 42, 47(1), (5). Date in force: 1 October 2013: see SI 2013/2200, art 3(a), (e).

Para 3: in sub-para (1) words "but subject to paragraph 5A (and subject in the first place" in square brackets substituted by the Crime and Courts Act 2013, s 20, Sch 13, Pt 4, paras 42, 47(1), (7)(a). Date in force: 1 October 2013: see SI 2013/2200, art 3(a), (e).

Para 3: in sub-para (1) words ", and those terms are to be such as the Lord Chancellor may determine" in square brackets inserted by the Crime and Courts Act 2013, s 20, Sch 13, Pt 4, paras 42, 47(1), (7)(b). Date in force: 1 October 2013: see SI 2013/2200, art 3(a), (e).

Para 5: in sub-paras (1), (3), (5)–(7), words "Senior President of Tribunals" in square brackets substituted by the Crime and Courts Act 2013, s 20, Sch 13, Pt 4, paras 42, 47(1), (8), (9). Date in force: 1 October 2013: see SI 2013/2200, art 3(a), (e).

Para 5: in sub-para (3)(a) words "Lord Chancellor" in square brackets substituted by the Crime and Courts Act 2013, s 20, Sch 13, Pt 4, paras 42, 47(1), (10). Date in force: 1 October 2013: see SI 2013/2200, art 3(a), (e).

Para 5: in sub-para (4)(c) words omitted repealed by SI 2010/21, art 5(1), Sch 1, paras 36, 47(a). Date in force: 15 February 2010: see SI 2010/21, art 1; for transitional provisions and savings see art 5(4), Sch 4, paras 14–18, 21 thereto.

Para 5: sub-para (7A) inserted by the Crime and Courts Act 2013, s 20, Sch 13, Pt 4, paras 42, 47(1), (11). Date in force: 1 October 2013: see SI 2013/2200, art 3(a), (e).

Para 5: in sub-para (8) words "Senior President of Tribunals" in square brackets substituted by the Crime and Courts Act 2013, s 20, Sch 13, Pt 4, paras 42, 47(1), (12). Date in force: 1 October 2013: see SI 2013/2200, art 3(a), (e).

Para 5: in sub-para (9) words "but subject to paragraph 5A (and subject in the first place" in square brackets substituted by the Crime and Courts Act 2013, s 20, Sch 13, Pt 4, paras 42, 47(1), (13)(a). Date in force: 1 October 2013: see SI 2013/2200, art 3(a), (e).

Para 5: in sub-para (9) words ", and those terms are to be such as the Lord Chancellor may determine" in square brackets inserted by the Crime and Courts Act 2013, s 20, Sch 13, Pt 4, paras 42, 47(1), (13)(b). Date in force: 1 October 2013: see SI 2013/2200, art 3(a), (e).

Para 5A: inserted by the Crime and Courts Act 2013, s 20, Sch 13, Pt 4, paras 42, 47(1), (14). Date in force: 1 October 2013: see SI 2013/2200, art 3(a), (e).

Subordinate Legislation
First-tier Tribunal and Upper Tribunal (Composition of Tribunal) Order 2008, SI 2008/2835.

PART 2
JUDGES AND OTHER MEMBERS OF CHAMBERS: ASSIGNMENT AND JURISDICTION

Assignment is function of Senior President of Tribunals

9

(1)   The Senior President of Tribunals has—

    (a)   the function of assigning judges and other members of the First-tier Tribunal (including himself) to chambers of the First-tier Tribunal, and

    (b)   the function of assigning judges and other members of the Upper Tribunal (including himself) to chambers of the Upper Tribunal.

(2)   The functions under sub-paragraph (1) are to be exercised in accordance with the following provisions of this Part of this Schedule.

Deemed assignment of Chamber Presidents and Deputy Chamber Presidents

10

(1)   The Chamber President, or a Deputy Chamber President, of a chamber—

    (a)   is to be taken to be assigned to that chamber;

    (b)   may be assigned additionally to one or more of the other chambers;

    (c)   may be assigned under paragraph (b) to different chambers at different times.

(2)   Paragraphs 11(1) and (2) and 12(2) and (3) do not apply to assignment of a person who is a Chamber President or a Deputy Chamber President.

(3)   In sub-paragraph (1) "chamber" means chamber of the First-tier Tribunal or the Upper Tribunal.

Assigning members of First-tier Tribunal to its chambers

11

(1)   Each person who is a judge or other member of the First-tier Tribunal by virtue of appointment under paragraph 1(1) or 2(1) of Schedule 2 or who is a transferred-in judge, or transferred-in other member, of the First-tier Tribunal—

    (a)   is to be assigned to at least one of the chambers of the First-tier Tribunal, and

    (b)   may be assigned to different chambers of the First-tier Tribunal at different times.

(2)   A judge or other member of the First-tier Tribunal to whom sub-paragraph (1) does not apply—

    (a)   may be assigned to one or more of the chambers of the First-tier Tribunal, and

    (b)   may be assigned to different chambers of the First-tier Tribunal at different times.

(3)   The Senior President of Tribunals may assign a judge or other member of the First-tier Tribunal to a particular chamber of the First-tier Tribunal only with the concurrence—

    (a)   of the Chamber President of the chamber, and

    (b)   of the judge or other member.

(4)   The Senior President of Tribunals may end the assignment of a judge or other member of the First-tier Tribunal to a particular chamber of the First-tier Tribunal only with the concurrence of the Chamber President of the chamber.

(5)   Sub-paragraph (3)(a) does not apply where the judge, or other member, concerned is not assigned to any of the chambers of the First-tier Tribunal.

(6)   Sub-paragraphs (3)(a) and (4) do not apply where the judge concerned is within section 6(1)(a) to (d) (judges of Courts of Appeal, Court of Session and High Courts).

(7)   Sub-paragraphs (3) and (4) do not apply where the judge concerned is the Senior President of Tribunals himself.

Assigning members of Upper Tribunal to its chambers

12

(1)   Sub-paragraph (2) applies to a person if—

    (a)   he is a judge of the Upper Tribunal by virtue of appointment under paragraph 1(1) of Schedule 3, or

    (b)   he is a transferred-in judge of the Upper Tribunal, or

    (c)   he is a deputy judge of the Upper Tribunal, or

    (d)   he is a member of the Upper Tribunal by virtue of appointment under paragraph 2(1) of Schedule 3, or

    (e)   he is a transferred-in other member of the Upper Tribunal.

(2)   Each person to whom this sub-paragraph applies—

    (a)   is to be assigned to at least one of the chambers of the Upper Tribunal, and

    (b)   may be assigned to different chambers of the Upper Tribunal at different times.

(3)   A judge or other member of the Upper Tribunal to whom sub-paragraph (2) does not apply—

    (a)   may be assigned to one or more of the chambers of the Upper Tribunal, and

    (b)   may be assigned to different chambers of the Upper Tribunal at different times.

(4)   The Senior President of Tribunals may assign a judge or other member of the Upper Tribunal to a particular chamber of the Upper Tribunal only with the concurrence—

    (a)   of the Chamber President of the chamber, and

    (b)   of the judge or other member.

(5)   The Senior President of Tribunals may end the assignment of a judge or other member of the Upper Tribunal to a particular chamber of the Upper Tribunal only with the concurrence of the Chamber President of the chamber.

(6)   Sub-paragraph (4)(a) does not apply where the judge, or other member, concerned is not assigned to any of the chambers of the Upper Tribunal.

(7)   Sub-paragraphs (4)(a) and (5) do not apply where the judge concerned is within section 6(1)(a) to (d) (judges of Courts of Appeal, Court of Session and High Courts).

(8)   Sub-paragraphs (4) and (5) do not apply where the judge concerned is the Senior President of Tribunals himself.

Policy of Senior President of Tribunals as respects assigning members to chambers etc

13

(1)   The Senior President of Tribunals must publish a document recording the policy adopted by him in relation to—

    (a)   the assigning of persons to chambers in exercise of his functions under paragraph 9,

    (b)   . . . and

    (c)   the nominating of persons to act as members of panels of members of employment tribunals in exercise of his functions under any such provision as is mentioned in section 5D(1) of the Employment Tribunals Act 1996 (c 17).

(2)   That policy must be such as to secure—

    (a)   that appropriate use is made of the knowledge and experience of the judges and other members of the First-tier Tribunal and Upper Tribunal, and

    (b)   that, in the case of a chamber (of the First-tier Tribunal or Upper Tribunal) whose business consists of, or includes, cases likely to involve the application of the law of Scotland or Northern Ireland, sufficient knowledge and experience of that law is to be found among persons assigned to the chamber.

(3)   No policy may be adopted by the Senior President of Tribunals for the purposes of sub-paragraph (1) unless the Lord Chancellor concurs in the policy.

(4)   The Senior President of Tribunals must keep any policy adopted for the purposes of sub-paragraph (1) under review.

Choosing members to decide cases

14

(1)   The First-tier Tribunal's function, or the Upper Tribunal's function, of deciding any matter in a case before the tribunal is to be exercised by a member or members of the chamber of the tribunal to which the case is allocated.

(2)   The member or members must be chosen by the Senior President of Tribunals.

(3)   A person choosing under sub-paragraph (2)—

    (a)   must act in accordance with any provision under paragraph 15;

    (b)   may choose himself.

(4)   In this paragraph "member", in relation to a chamber of a tribunal, means a judge or other member of the tribunal who is assigned to the chamber.

Composition of tribunals

15

(1)   The Lord Chancellor must by order make provision, in relation to every matter that may fall to be decided by the First-tier Tribunal or the Upper Tribunal, for determining the number of members of the tribunal who are to decide the matter.

(2)   Where an order under sub-paragraph (1) provides for a matter to be decided by a single member of a tribunal, the order—

(a)   must make provision for determining whether the matter is to be decided by one of the judges, or by one of the other members, of the tribunal, and

(b)   may make provision for determining, if the matter is to be decided by one of the other members of the tribunal, what qualifications (if any) that other member must have.

(3)   Where an order under sub-paragraph (1) provides for a matter to be decided by two or more members of a tribunal, the order—

(a)   must make provision for determining how many (if any) of those members are to be judges of the tribunal and how many (if any) are to be other members of the tribunal, and

(b)   may make provision for determining—

(i)   if the matter is to be decided by persons who include one or more of the other members of the tribunal, or

(ii)   if the matter is to be decided by two or more of the other members of the tribunal,

what qualifications (if any) that other member or any of those other members must have.

(4)   A duty under sub-paragraph (1), (2) or (3) to provide for the determination of anything may be discharged by providing for the thing to be determined by the Senior President of Tribunals, or a Chamber President, in accordance with any provision made under that sub-paragraph.

(5)   Power under paragraph (b) of sub-paragraph (2) or (3) to provide for the determination of anything may be exercised by giving, to the Senior President of Tribunals or a Chamber President, power to determine that thing in accordance with any provision made under that paragraph.

(6)   Where under sub-paragraphs (1) to (4) a matter is to be decided by two or more members of a tribunal, the matter may, if the parties to the case agree, be decided in the absence of one or more (but not all) of the members chosen to decide the matter.

(7)   Where the member, or any of the members, of a tribunal chosen to decide a matter does not have any qualification that he is required to have under sub-paragraphs (2)(b), or (3)(b), and (5), the matter may despite that, if the parties to the case agree, be decided by the chosen member or members.

(8)   Before making an order under this paragraph, the Lord Chancellor must consult the Senior President of Tribunals.

(9)   In this paragraph "qualification" includes experience.

Amendment

Para 13: in sub-para (1)(b) words omitted repealed by SI 2010/21, art 5(1), Sch 1, paras 36, 47(b).

Date in force: 15 February 2010: see SI 2010/21, art 1; for transitional provisions and savings see art 5(4), Sch 4, paras 14–18, 21 thereto.

SCHEDULE 5
PROCEDURE IN FIRST-TIER TRIBUNAL AND UPPER TRIBUNAL
Section 22

PART 1
TRIBUNAL PROCEDURE RULES

Introductory

1

(1) This Part of this Schedule makes further provision about the content of Tribunal Procedure Rules.

(2) The generality of section 22(1) is not to be taken to be prejudiced by—

    (a)   the following paragraphs of this Part of this Schedule, or

    (b)   any other provision (including future provision) authorising or requiring the making of provision by Tribunal Procedure Rules.

(3) In the following paragraphs of this Part of this Schedule "Rules" means Tribunal Procedure Rules.

Concurrent functions

2

Rules may make provision as to who is to decide, or as to how to decide, which of the First-tier Tribunal and Upper Tribunal is to exercise, in relation to any particular matter, a function that is exercisable by the two tribunals on the basis that the question as to which of them is to exercise the function is to be determined by, or under, Rules.

Delegation of functions to staff

3

(1) Rules may provide for functions—

    (a)   of the First-tier Tribunal, or

    (b)   of the Upper Tribunal,

to be exercised by staff appointed under section 40(1).

(2) In making provision of the kind mentioned in sub-paragraph (1) in relation to a function, Rules may (in particular)—

    (a)   provide for the function to be exercisable by a member of staff only if the member of staff is, or is of a description, specified in exercise of a discretion conferred by Rules;

    (b)   provide for the function to be exercisable by a member of staff only if the member of staff is approved, or is of a description approved, for the purpose by a person specified in Rules.

Time limits

4

Rules may make provision for time limits as respects initiating, or taking any step in, proceedings before the First-tier Tribunal or the Upper Tribunal.

Repeat applications

5

Rules may make provision restricting the making of fresh applications where a previous application in relation to the same matter has been made.

Tribunal acting of its own initiative

6

Rules may make provision about the circumstances in which the First-tier Tribunal, or the Upper Tribunal, may exercise its powers of its own initiative.

Hearings

7

Rules may—

    (a)   make provision for dealing with matters without a hearing;

    (b)   make provision as respects allowing or requiring a hearing to be in private or as respects allowing or requiring a hearing to be in public.

Proceedings without notice

8

Rules may make provision for proceedings to take place, in circumstances described in Rules, at the request of one party even though the other, or another, party has had no notice.

Representation

9

Rules may make provision conferring additional rights of audience before the First-tier Tribunal or the Upper Tribunal.

Evidence, witnesses and attendance

10

(1) Rules may make provision about evidence (including evidence on oath and administration of oaths).

(2) Rules may modify any rules of evidence provided for elsewhere, so far as they would apply to proceedings before the First-tier Tribunal or Upper Tribunal.

(3) Rules may make provision, where the First-tier Tribunal has required a person—

    (a)   to attend at any place for the purpose of giving evidence,

    (b)   otherwise to make himself available to give evidence,

    (c)   to swear an oath in connection with the giving of evidence,

    (d)   to give evidence as a witness,

    (e)   to produce a document, or

    (f)   to facilitate the inspection of a document or any other thing (including any premises),

for the Upper Tribunal to deal with non-compliance with the requirement as though the requirement had been imposed by the Upper Tribunal.

(4) Rules may make provision for the payment of expenses and allowances to persons giving evidence, producing documents, attending proceedings or required to attend proceedings.

Use of information

11

(1) Rules may make provision for the disclosure or non-disclosure of information received during the course of proceedings before the First-tier Tribunal or Upper Tribunal.

(2) Rules may make provision for imposing reporting restrictions in circumstances described in Rules.

Costs and expenses

12

(1) Rules may make provision for regulating matters relating to costs, or (in Scotland) expenses, of proceedings before the First-tier Tribunal or Upper Tribunal.

(2) The provision mentioned in sub-paragraph (1) includes (in particular)—

    (a)   provision prescribing scales of costs or expenses;

    (b)   provision for enabling costs to undergo detailed assessment in England and Wales by [the county court] or the High Court;

    (c)   provision for taxation in Scotland of accounts of expenses by an Auditor of Court;

    (d)   provision for enabling costs to be taxed in Northern Ireland in a county court or the High Court;

    (e)   provision for costs or expenses—

        (i)   not to be allowed in respect of items of a description specified in Rules;

        (ii)   not to be allowed in proceedings of a description so specified;

    (f)   provision for other exceptions to either or both of subsections (1) and (2) of section 29.

Set-off and interest

13

(1) Rules may make provision for a party to proceedings to deduct, from amounts payable by him, amounts payable to him.

(2) Rules may make provision for interest on sums awarded (including provision conferring a discretion or provision in accordance with which interest is to be calculated).

Arbitration

14

Rules may provide for [any of the provisions of sections 1 to 15 of and schedule 1 to the Arbitration (Scotland) Act 2010 (which extends to Scotland) or] Part 1 of the Arbitration Act 1996 (c 23) (which extends to England and Wales, and Northern Ireland, but not Scotland) not to apply, or not to apply except so far as is specified in Rules, where the First-tier Tribunal, or Upper Tribunal, acts as arbitrator.

Correction of errors and setting-aside of decisions on procedural grounds

15

(1) Rules may make provision for the correction of accidental errors in a decision or record of a decision.

(2) Rules may make provision for the setting aside of a decision in proceedings before the First-tier Tribunal or Upper Tribunal—

(a)   where a document relating to the proceedings was not sent to, or was not received at an appropriate time by, a party to the proceedings or a party's representative,

(b)   where a document relating to the proceedings was not sent to the First-tier Tribunal or Upper Tribunal at an appropriate time,

(c)   where a party to the proceedings, or a party's representative, was not present at a hearing related to the proceedings, or

(d)   where there has been any other procedural irregularity in the proceedings.

(3)   Sub-paragraphs (1) and (2) shall not be taken to prejudice, or to be prejudiced by, any power to correct errors or set aside decisions that is exercisable apart from rules made by virtue of those sub-paragraphs.

Ancillary powers

16

Rules may confer on the First-tier Tribunal, or the Upper Tribunal, such ancillary powers as are necessary for the proper discharge of its functions.

Rules may refer to practice directions

17

Rules may, instead of providing for any matter, refer to provision made or to be made about that matter by directions under section 23.

Presumptions

18

Rules may make provision in the form of presumptions (including, in particular, presumptions as to service or notification).

Differential provision

19

Rules may make different provision for different purposes or different areas.

Amendment

Para 12: in sub-para (2)(b) words "the county court" in square brackets substituted by the Crime and Courts Act 2013, s 17(5), Sch 9, Pt 3, para 52(1)(b), (2). Date in force: 22 April 2014: see SI 2014/954, art 2(a), (c); for transitional provision see art 3.

Para 14: words from "any of the" to "to Scotland) or" in square brackets inserted by SSI 2010/220, art 2, Schedule, para 8.

Date in force: 5 June 2010: see SSI 2010/220, art 1.

Subordinate Legislation

Tribunal Procedure (First-tier Tribunal) (Social Entitlement Chamber) Rules 2008, SI 2008/2685.

Tribunal Procedure (First-tier Tribunal) (War Pensions and Armed Forces Compensation Chamber) Rules 2008, SI 2008/2686.

Tribunal Procedure (Upper Tribunal) Rules 2008, SI 2008/2698.

Tribunal Procedure (First-tier Tribunal) (Health, Education and Social Care Chamber) Rules 2008, SI 2008/2699.

Tribunal Procedure (First-tier Tribunal) (Tax Chamber) Rules 2009, SI 2009/273.

Tribunal Procedure (Amendment) Rules 2009, SI 2009/274.

Tribunal Procedure (Amendment No 2) Rules 2009, SI 2009/1975.

Tribunal Procedure (First-tier Tribunal) (General Regulatory Chamber) Rules 2009, SI 2009/1976.

Tribunal Procedure (Amendment) Rules 2010, SI 2010/43.

Tribunal Procedure (Amendment No 2) Rules 2010, SI 2010/44.

Tribunal Procedure (Upper Tribunal) (Amendment) Rules 2010, SI 2010/747.

Tribunal Procedure (Upper Tribunal) (Lands Chamber) Rules 2010, SI 2010/2600

Tribunal Procedure (Amendment No 3) Rules 2010, SI 2010/2653.

Tribunal Procedure (Amendment) Rules 2011, SI 2011/651.

Tribunal Procedure (Upper Tribunal) (Amendment) Rules 2011, SI 2011/2343.

PART 2
TRIBUNAL PROCEDURE COMMITTEE

Membership

20

The Tribunal Procedure Committee is to consist of—

    (a)   the Senior President of Tribunals or a person nominated by him,

    (b)   the persons currently appointed by the Lord Chancellor under paragraph 21,

    (c)   the persons currently appointed by the Lord Chief Justice of England and Wales under paragraph 22,

    (d)   the person currently appointed by the Lord President of the Court of Session under paragraph 23, and

    (e)   any person currently appointed under paragraph 24 at the request of the Senior President of Tribunals.

Lord Chancellor's appointees

21

(1)   The Lord Chancellor must appoint—

    (a)   three persons each of whom must be a person with experience of—

        (i)   practice in tribunals, or

        (ii)   advising persons involved in tribunal proceedings, . . .

    (b)   . . .

(2)   Before making an appointment under sub-paragraph (1), the Lord Chancellor must consult the Lord Chief Justice of England and Wales.

(3)   . . .

Lord Chief Justice's appointees

22

(1)   The Lord Chief Justice of England and Wales must appoint—

    (a)   one of the judges of the First-tier Tribunal,

    (b)   one of the judges of the Upper Tribunal, and

    (c)   one person who is a member of the First-tier Tribunal, or is a member of the Upper Tribunal, but is not a judge of the First-tier Tribunal and is not a judge of the Upper Tribunal.

(2)   Before making an appointment under sub-paragraph (1), the Lord Chief Justice of England and Wales must consult the Lord Chancellor.

Lord President's appointee

23

(1)   The Lord President of the Court of Session must appoint one person with experience in and knowledge of the Scottish legal system.

(2)   Before making an appointment under sub-paragraph (1), the Lord President of the Court of Session must consult the Lord Chancellor.

Persons appointed at request of Senior President of Tribunals

24

(1)   At the request of the Senior President of Tribunals, an appropriate senior judge may appoint a person or persons with experience in and knowledge of—

(a)   a particular issue, or

(b)   a particular subject area in relation to which the First-tier Tribunal or the Upper Tribunal has, or is likely to have, jurisdiction,

for the purpose of assisting the Committee with regard to that issue or subject area.

(2)   In sub-paragraph (1) "an appropriate senior judge" means any of—

(a)   the Lord Chief Justice of England and Wales,

(b)   the Lord President of the Court of Session, and

(c)   the Lord Chief Justice of Northern Ireland.

(3)   The total number of persons appointed at any time under sub-paragraph (1) must not exceed four.

(4)   Before making an appointment under sub-paragraph (1), the person making the appointment must consult the Lord Chancellor.

(5)   The terms of appointment of a person appointed under sub-paragraph (1) may (in particular) authorise him to act as a member of the Committee only in relation to matters specified by those terms.

Power to amend paragraphs 20 to 24

25

(1)   The Lord Chancellor may by order—

(a)   amend any of paragraphs 20, 21(1), 22(1), 23(1) and 24(1), and

(b)   make consequential amendments in any other provision of paragraphs 21 to 24 or in paragraph 28(7).

(2)   The making of an order under this paragraph—

(a)   requires the concurrence of the Lord Chief Justice of England and Wales,

(b)   if the order amends paragraph 23(1), requires also the concurrence of the Lord President of the Court of Session, and

(c)   if the order amends paragraph 24(1), requires also the concurrence of the Lord President of the Court of Session and the Lord Chief Justice of Northern Ireland.

Committee members' expenses

26

The Lord Chancellor may reimburse members of the Tribunal Procedure Committee their travelling and out-of-pocket expenses.

Amendment

Para 21: sub-para (1)(b) and word omitted immediately preceding it repealed by SI 2013/2042, art 2(2), Schedule, paras 31, 35(a). Date in force: 19 August 2013: see SI 2013/2042, art 1(2).

Para 21: sub-para (3) repealed by SI 2013/2042, art 2(2), Schedule, paras 31, 35. Date in force: 19 August 2013: see SI 2013/2042, art 1(2).

Subordinate Legislation

Tribunal Procedure (First-tier Tribunal) (Social Entitlement Chamber) Rules 2008, SI 2008/2685.

Tribunal Procedure (First-tier Tribunal) (War Pensions and Armed Forces Compensation Chamber) Rules 2008, SI 2008/2686.

Tribunal Procedure (First-tier Tribunal) (Health, Education and Social Care Chamber) Rules 2008, SI 2008/2699.

Tribunal Procedure (First-tier Tribunal) (Tax Chamber) Rules 2009, SI 2009/273.

Tribunal Procedure (Amendment) Rules 2009, SI 2009/274.

Tribunal Procedure (Amendment No 2) Rules 2009, SI 2009/1975.

Tribunal Procedure (First-tier Tribunal) (General Regulatory Chamber) Rules 2009, SI 2009/1976.

Tribunal Procedure (Amendment) Rules 2010, SI 2010/43.

Tribunal Procedure (Amendment No 2) Rules 2010, SI 2010/44.

Tribunal Procedure (Upper Tribunal) (Amendment) Rules 2010, SI 2010/747.

Tribunal Procedure (Upper Tribunal) (Lands Chamber) Rules 2010, SI 2010/2600

Tribunal Procedure (Amendment No 3) Rules 2010, SI 2010/2653.

Tribunal Procedure (Amendment) Rules 2011, SI 2011/651.

Tribunal Procedure (Upper Tribunal) (Amendment) Rules 2011, SI 2011/2343.

PART 3
MAKING OF TRIBUNAL PROCEDURE RULES BY TRIBUNAL PROCE-DURE COMMITTEE

Meaning of "Rules" and "the Committee"

27

In the following provisions of this Part of this Schedule—

"the Committee" means the Tribunal Procedure Committee;

"Rules" means Tribunal Procedure Rules.

Process for making Rules

28

(1) Before the Committee makes Rules, the Committee must—

    (a)   consult such persons (including such of the Chamber Presidents) as it considers appropriate,

    (b)   consult the Lord President of the Court of Session if the Rules contain provision relating to proceedings in Scotland, and

    (c)   meet (unless it is inexpedient to do so).

(2) Rules made by the Committee must be—

    (a)   signed by a majority of the members of the Committee, and

    (b)   submitted to the Lord Chancellor.

(3) The Lord Chancellor may allow or disallow Rules so made.

(4) If the Lord Chancellor disallows Rules so made, he must give the Committee written reasons for doing so.

(5) Rules so made and allowed—

    (a)   come into force on such day as the Lord Chancellor directs, and

    (b)   are to be contained in a statutory instrument to which the Statutory Instruments Act 1946 (c 36) applies as if the instrument contained rules made by a Minister of the Crown.

(6) A statutory instrument containing Rules made by the Committee is subject to annulment in pursuance of a resolution of either House of Parliament.

(7) In the case of a member of the Committee appointed under paragraph 24, the terms of his appointment may (in particular) provide that, for the purposes of sub-paragraph (2)(a), he is to count as a member of the Committee only in relation to matters specified in those terms.

Power of Lord Chancellor to require Rules to be made

29

(1) This paragraph applies if the Lord Chancellor gives the Committee written notice that he thinks it is expedient for Rules to include provision that would achieve a purpose specified in the notice.

(2) The Committee must make such Rules, in accordance with paragraph 28, as it considers necessary to achieve the specified purpose.

(3) Those Rules must be made—

    (a) within such period as may be specified by the Lord Chancellor in the notice, or

    (b) if no period is so specified, within a reasonable period after the Lord Chancellor gives the notice to the Committee.

Subordinate Legislation

Tribunal Procedure (First-tier Tribunal) (Social Entitlement Chamber) Rules 2008, SI 2008/2685.

Tribunal Procedure (First-tier Tribunal) (War Pensions and Armed Forces Compensation Chamber) Rules 2008, SI 2008/2686.

Tribunal Procedure (First-tier Tribunal) (Health, Education and Social Care Chamber) Rules 2008, SI 2008/2699.

Tribunal Procedure (First-tier Tribunal) (Tax Chamber) Rules 2009, SI 2009/273.

Tribunal Procedure (Amendment) Rules 2009, SI 2009/274.

Tribunal Procedure (Amendment No 2) Rules 2009, SI 2009/1975.

Tribunal Procedure (First-tier Tribunal) (General Regulatory Chamber) Rules 2009, SI 2009/1976.

Tribunal Procedure (Amendment) Rules 2010, SI 2010/43.

Tribunal Procedure (Amendment No 2) Rules 2010, SI 2010/44.

Tribunal Procedure (Upper Tribunal) (Amendment) Rules 2010, SI 2010/747.

Tribunal Procedure (Upper Tribunal) (Lands Chamber) Rules 2010, SI 2010/2600

Tribunal Procedure (Amendment No 3) Rules 2010, SI 2010/2653.

Tribunal Procedure (Amendment) Rules 2011, SI 2011/651.

Tribunal Procedure (Upper Tribunal) (Amendment) Rules 2011, SI 2011/2343.

PART 4
POWER TO AMEND LEGISLATION IN CONNECTION WITH TRIBUNAL PROCEDURE RULES

Lord Chancellor's power

30

(1) The Lord Chancellor may by order amend, repeal or revoke any enactment to the extent he considers necessary or desirable—

    (a) in order to facilitate the making of Tribunal Procedure Rules, or

    (b) in consequence of—

        (i) section 22,

        (ii) Part 1 or 3 of this Schedule, or

        (iii) Tribunal Procedure Rules.

(2) In this paragraph "enactment" means any enactment whenever passed or made, including an enactment comprised in subordinate legislation (within the meaning of the Interpretation Act 1978 (c 30)).

Subordinate Legislation

Tribunals, Courts and Enforcement Act 2007 (Transitional and Consequential Provisions) Order 2008, SI 2008/2683.

Tribunal Procedure (First-tier Tribunal) (Social Entitlement Chamber) Rules 2008, SI 2008/2685.

Tribunal Procedure (First-tier Tribunal) (War Pensions and Armed Forces Compensation Chamber) Rules 2008, SI 2008/2686.

Tribunal Procedure (First-tier Tribunal) (Health, Education and Social Care Chamber) Rules 2008, SI 2008/2699.

Transfer of Tribunal Functions Order 2008, SI 2008/2833.

Transfer of Tribunal Functions and Revenue and Customs Appeals Order 2009, SI 2009/56.

Tribunal Procedure (First-tier Tribunal) (Tax Chamber) Rules 2009, SI 2009/273.

Tribunal Procedure (Amendment) Rules 2009, SI 2009/274.

Transfer of Functions of the Charity Tribunal Order 2009, SI 2009/1834.

Transfer of Functions of the Consumer Credit Appeals Tribunal Order 2009, SI 2009/1835.

Transfer of Functions (Transport Tribunal and Appeal Panel) Order 2009, SI 2009/1885.

Tribunal Procedure (Amendment No 2) Rules 2009, SI 2009/1975.

Tribunal Procedure (First-tier Tribunal) (General Regulatory Chamber) Rules 2009, SI 2009/1976.

Transfer of Tribunal Functions Order 2010, SI 2010/22.

Tribunal Procedure (Amendment) Rules 2010, SI 2010/43.

Tribunal Procedure (Amendment No 2) Rules 2010, SI 2010/44.

Tribunal Procedure (Upper Tribunal) (Amendment) Rules 2010, SI 2010/747.

Tribunal Procedure (Upper Tribunal) (Lands Chamber) Rules 2010, SI 2010/2600

Tribunal Procedure (Amendment No 3) Rules 2010, SI 2010/2653.

Tribunal Procedure (Amendment) Rules 2011, SI 2011/651.

Tribunal Procedure (Upper Tribunal) (Amendment) Rules 2011, SI 2011/2343.

SCHEDULE 6
TRIBUNALS FOR THE PURPOSES OF SECTIONS 30 TO 36

Sections 30 to 37

PART 1
TRIBUNALS FOR THE PURPOSES OF SECTIONS 30, 35 AND 36

Tribunal	Enactment
Appeal tribunal	Chapter 1 of Part 1 of the Social Security Act 1998 (c 14)
Child Support Commissioner	Section 22 of the Child Support Act 1991 (c 48)
The Secretary of State as respects his function of deciding appeals under:	Section 41 of the Consumer Credit Act 1974 (c 39)
The Secretary of State as respects his function of deciding appeals under:	Section 7(1) of the Estate Agents Act 1979 (c 38)
Foreign Compensation Commission	Section 1 of the Foreign Compensation Act 1950 (c 12)
Commissioner for the general purposes of the income tax	Section 2 of the Taxes Management Act 1970 (c 9)
Information Tribunal	Section 6 of the Data Protection Act 1998 (c 29)
Meat Hygiene Appeals Tribunal	Regulation 6 of the Fresh Meat (Hygiene and Inspection) Regulations 1995 (SI 1995/539)

Meat Hygiene Appeals Tribunal	Regulation 6 of the Poultry Meat, Farmed Game Bird Meat and Rabbit Meat (Hygiene and Inspection) Regulations 1995 (SI 1995/540)
Meat Hygiene Appeals Tribunal	Regulation 5 of the Wild Game Meat (Hygiene and Inspection) Regulations 1995 (SI 1995/2148)
Mental Health Review Tribunal for a region of England	Section 65(1) and (1A)(a) of the Mental Health Act 1983 (c 20)
Reinstatement Committee	Paragraph 1 of Schedule 2 to the Reserve Forces (Safeguard of Employment) Act 1985 (c 17)
Reserve forces appeal tribunal	Section 88 of the Reserve Forces Act 1996 (c 14)
Sea Fish Licence Tribunal	Section 4AA of the Sea Fish (Conservation) Act 1967 (c 84)
Social Security Commissioner	Schedule 4 to the Social Security Act 1998 (c 14)
Special Educational Needs and Disability Tribunal	Section 333 of the Education Act 1996 (c 56)
Transport Tribunal	Schedule 4 to the Transport Act 1985 (c 67)
Umpire or deputy umpire	Paragraph 5 of Schedule 2 to the Reserve Forces (Safeguard of Employment) Act 1985
VAT and duties tribunal	Schedule 12 to the Value Added Tax Act 1994 (c 23)

Amendment

Entries relating to "Agricultural Land Tribunals for areas in England" and "Rent assessment committees for areas in England" (omitted) inserted by SI 2013/1034; outside the scope of this work.

PART 2
TRIBUNALS FOR THE PURPOSES OF SECTIONS 30 AND 35

Tribunal	Enactment
Adjudicator	Section 5 of the Criminal Injuries Compensation Act 1995 (c 53)

PART 3
TRIBUNALS FOR THE PURPOSES OF SECTIONS 30 AND 36

Tribunal	Enactment
Adjudicator to Her Majesty's Land Registry	Section 107 of the Land Registration Act 2002 (c 9)
Charity Tribunal	Section 2A of the Charities Act 1993 (c 10)
Consumer Credit Appeals Tribunal	Section 40A of the Consumer Credit Act 1974 (c 39)
. . .	. . .
Gambling Appeals Tribunal	Section 140 of the Gambling Act 2005 (c 19)
Immigration Services Tribunal	Section 87 of the Immigration and Asylum Act 1999 (c 33)

Lands Tribunal	Section 1(1)(b) of the Lands Tribunal Act 1949 (c 42)
Pensions Appeal Tribunal in England and Wales	Paragraph 1(1) of the Schedule to the Pensions Appeal Tribunals Act 1943 (c 39)
Pensions Regulator Tribunal	Section 102 of the Pensions Act 2004 (c 35)
Commissioner for the special purposes of the Income Tax Acts	Section 4 of the Taxes Management Act 1970 (c 9)

Amendment

Entry relating to "Financial Services and Markets Tribunal" (omitted) repealed by the Financial Services Act 2012, s 114(2), Sch 19. Date in force: 1 April 2013: see SI 2013/423, art 3, Schedule.

PART 4
TRIBUNALS FOR THE PURPOSES OF SECTION 30

Tribunal	Enactment
. . .	. . .
. . .	. . .
Antarctic Act Tribunal	Regulation 11 of the Antarctic Regulations 1995 (SI 1995/490)
Appeal tribunal	Part 2 of Schedule 9 to the Scheme set out in Schedule 2 to the Firefighters' Pension Scheme Order 1992 (SI 1992/129)
[Asylum and Immigration Tribunal	Section 81 of the Nationality, Immigration and Asylum Act 2002]
Asylum Support Adjudicator	Section 102 of the Immigration and Asylum Act 1999
Case tribunal, or interim case tribunal, drawn from the Adjudication Panel for England	Section 76 of the Local Government Act 2000 (c 22)
[Claims Management Services Tribunal	Section 12 of the Compensation Act 2006 (c 29)]
Family Health Services Appeal Authority	Section 49S of the National Health Service Act 1977 (c 49)
[Gender Recognition Panel	Section 1(3) of the Gender Recognition Act 2004 (c 7)]
Insolvency Practitioners Tribunal	Section 396(1) of the Insolvency Act 1986 (c 45)
[Panel	Section 189(6) of the Greater London Authority Act 1999]
Appeals Tribunal	Part 3 of the Local Authorities (Code of Conduct) (Local Determination) Regulations 2003 (SI 2003/1483)
Plant Varieties and Seeds Tribunal	Section 42 of the Plant Varieties Act 1997 (c 66)
Tribunal	Rule 6 of the model provisions with respect to appeals as applied with modifications by the Chemical Weapons (Licence Appeal Provisions) Order 1996 (SI 1996/3030)
Tribunal	Health Service Medicines (Price Control Appeals) Regulations 2000 (SI 2000/124)
Tribunal	Section 706 of the Income and Corporation Taxes Act 1988 (c 1)
[Tribunal	Section 704 of the Income Tax Act 2007 (c 3)]

Tribunal	Enactment
Tribunal	Section 150 of the Mines and Quarries Act 1954 (c 70)
Tribunal	Part 1 of Schedule 3 to the Misuse of Drugs Act 1971 (c 38)
Tribunal	Regulation H6(3) of the Police Pensions Regulations 1987 (SI 1987/257)
Tribunal	Section 9 of the Protection of Children Act 1999 (c 14)

Amendment

Entry relating to "Agricultural Land Tribunal" repealed by SI 2013/1034, art 3. Date in force: 29 April 2013.

Entry relating to "Aircraft and Shipbuilding Industries Arbitration Tribunal" (omitted) repealed by SI 2013/686, art 3, Sch 1, para 9. Date in force: 22 March 2013: see SI 2013/686, art 1(2).

Entry relating to "Section 81 of the Nationality, Immigration and Asylum Act 2002" inserted by SI 2010/20, art 2.

Date in force: 14 February 2010: see SI 2010/20, art 1.

Entry relating to "Section 12 of the Compensation Act 2006" inserted by SI 2008/2833, art 2.

Entry relating to "Section 1(3) of the Gender Recognition Act 2004" inserted by SI 2008/2833, art 2.

Entry relating to "Section 189(6) of the Greater London Authority Act 1999" inserted by SI 2009/1836, art 4.

Entry relating to "Section 704 of the Income Tax Act 2007" inserted by SI 2008/2833, art 2.

Transfer of Functions

Functions of the Asylum and Immigration Tribunal under this Part of this Schedule transferred to the First-tier Tribunal, by the Transfer of Functions of the Asylum and Immigration Tribunal Order 2010, SI 2010/21, art 2; for transitional provisions and savings see art 5(4), Sch 4, paras 14–18, 21 thereto.

PART 5

TRIBUNALS FOR THE PURPOSES OF SECTIONS 35 AND 36

Tribunal	Enactment
Employment Appeal Tribunal	Section 20 of the Employment Tribunals Act 1996 (c 17)

PART 6

TRIBUNALS FOR THE PURPOSES OF SECTION 35

Tribunal	Enactment
Employment tribunal	Section 1 of the Employment Tribunals Act 1996

PART 7
TRIBUNALS FOR THE PURPOSES OF SECTION 32(3)

Tribunal	Enactment
Case tribunal, or interim case tribunal, drawn from the Adjudication Panel for Wales	Section 76 of the Local Government Act 2000 (c 22)
Appeals Tribunal	Local Government Investigations (Functions of Monitoring Officers and Standards Committees) (Wales) Regulations 2001 (SI 2001/2281)
Mental Health Review Tribunal for Wales	Section 65(1) and (1A)(b) of the Mental Health Act 1983 (c 20)
Special Educational Needs Tribunal for Wales	Section 336ZA of the Education Act 1996 (c 56)
Tribunal	Section 27 of, and Schedule 3 to, the Education Act 2005 (c 18)

Amendment

Entries relating to "Agricultural Land Tribunal for Wales" and "Rent assessment committees for areas in Wales" (omitted) inserted by SI 2013/1034; outside the scope of this work.

SCHEDULES 7, 8

(Sch 7 outside the scope of this work; Sch 8 contains amendments which, in so far as relevant to this work, have been incorporated at the appropriate place.)

SCHEDULE 9
TRIBUNALS: TRANSITIONAL PROVISION

Section 48(2)

PART 1
GENERAL AND MISCELLANEOUS

Introductory

1

The following provisions of this Schedule are to be taken not to prejudice the generality of sections 31(9) and 145(1).

Membership of Tribunal Procedure Committee

2

(1) The Lord Chancellor may by order make provision for a person—

(a) who is a scheduled tribunal, or

(b) who is a member of a scheduled tribunal,

to be treated for the purposes of sub-paragraph (1) of paragraph 22 of Schedule 5 as falling within paragraph (a), (b) or (c) of that sub-paragraph.

(2) In sub-paragraph (1) "scheduled tribunal" means a tribunal in a list in Schedule 6 that has effect for the purposes of section 30.

(3)   The power under sub-paragraph (1) may not be exercised so as to provide for the Secretary of State to be treated as mentioned in that sub-paragraph.

Subordinate Legislation

Membership of the Tribunal Procedure Committee Transitional Order 2008, SI 2008/1149.

PART 2
JUDGES AND OTHER MEMBERS OF FIRST-TIER AND UPPER TRIBUNALS: RETIREMENT DATES

Interpretation of Part 2 of Schedule

3

(1)   For the purposes of this Part of this Schedule—

  (a)   "relevant judicial office" means—

   (i)   the office of transferred-in judge, or transferred-in other member, of the First-tier Tribunal or of the Upper Tribunal (see section 31(2)),

   (ii)   an office to which a person is appointed under paragraph 1(1) or 2(1) of Schedule 2 or 3 (judge, or other member, of the First-tier Tribunal or of the Upper Tribunal),

   (iii)   the office of deputy judge of the Upper Tribunal (whether under section 31(2) or under paragraph 7 of Schedule 3),

   (iv)   the office of Chamber President, or Deputy Chamber President, of a chamber of the First-tier Tribunal or of the Upper Tribunal, or

   (v)   the office of Senior President of Tribunals;

  (b)   "relevant day", in relation to a person who holds a relevant judicial office, means the day when he was appointed to that office or, if he holds that office as the latest in an unbroken succession of different relevant judicial offices, the day when he was appointed to the first of the offices in that succession;

  (c)   an office is a "qualifying office" at any particular time (but see sub-paragraph (2)) if—

   (i)   the office is that of member of a tribunal which at that time is in a list in Schedule 6, or

   (ii)   the office itself is at that time in a list in Schedule 6,

  and (in either case) the list has effect at that time for the purposes of section 30;

  (d)   "the 1993 Act" means the Judicial Pensions and Retirement Act 1993 (c 8).

(2)   Where—

  (a)   a person held two or more qualifying offices ("the actual offices") immediately before the relevant day, and

  (b)   at that time the person held at least one of the actual offices on a salaried basis and held at least one of the actual offices on a non-salaried basis,

the person shall be treated for the purposes of paragraphs 6 and 7 as not having held immediately before the relevant day any of the actual offices that the person held on a non-salaried basis at that time.

(3)   For the purposes of sub-paragraph (2)—

  (a)   a person holds an office on a salaried basis at any particular time if, at that time, the person's service in the office is remunerated by payment of a salary, and

  (b)   a person holds an office on a non-salaried basis at any particular time if, at that time, the person's service in the office—

   (i)   is remunerated by the payment of fees,

      (ii)   is remunerated by the payment of a supplement to the salary payable to him in respect of his service in another office, or

      (iii)   is unremunerated.

Retirement from First-tier and Upper Tribunals: application of paragraphs 5 to 8

4

Paragraphs 5 to 8 apply where a person holds a relevant judicial office.

Retirement later than age 70 in certain cases where office previously held in another tribunal

5

(1) Subject to paragraph 8(1) (persons who held certain judicial offices on 30th March 1995), sub-paragraphs (3) and (4) apply where the person has a personal retirement date under either or both of paragraphs 6 and 7.

(2) In sub-paragraphs (3) and (4) and paragraph 8(1) and (2)—

    (a)   if the person has a personal retirement date under just one of paragraphs 6 and 7 or has the same personal retirement date under each of those paragraphs, "the special date" means that date;

    (b)   if the person has a personal retirement date under each of those paragraphs and those dates are different, "the special date" means the later of those dates.

(3) Subsection (1) of section 26 of the 1993 Act shall have effect (subject to the following provisions of that section) as if it provided for the person to vacate the relevant judicial office on the special date.

(4) The special date is to be taken for the purposes of that section to be the compulsory retirement date for the relevant judicial office in the person's case.

Cases where retirement from existing office would be after age 70

6

(1) Sub-paragraphs (2) and (3) apply where, immediately before the relevant day, the person—

    (a)   held a qualifying office, and

    (b)   was required to vacate the qualifying office on a day later than the day on which he attains the age of 70.

(2) The person's personal retirement date under this paragraph is the later day mentioned in sub-paragraph (1)(b), subject to sub-paragraph (3).

(3) If—

    (a)   there are two or more qualifying offices each of which is one that, immediately before the relevant day, the person—

        (i)   held, and

        (ii) was required to vacate on a day later than the day on which he attains the age of 70, and

    (b)   the later day mentioned in paragraph (a)(ii) is not the same for each of those offices,

the person's personal retirement date under this paragraph is the latest (or later) of those later days.

Cases where no requirement to retire from existing office

7

(1) Sub-paragraph (2) applies where—

    (a) immediately before the relevant day, the person held, on an unlimited basis, a qualifying office or two or more qualifying offices, and

    (b) the relevant day falls after the day on which the person attains the age of 69.

(2) The person's personal retirement date under this paragraph is the last day of the 12 months beginning with the day after the relevant day.

(3) For the purposes of this paragraph, a person holds an office on an unlimited basis at a particular time if at that time he is not required to vacate the office at any particular later time.

Interaction between rules under paragraph 5, and rules under Schedule 7 to the 1993 Act, in cases where office held on 30th March 1995

8

(1) If—

    (a) sub-paragraph (2) of paragraph 2 of Schedule 7 to the 1993 Act (transitional provision where person held salaried relevant office on 30th March 1995) has effect in relation to retirement from the relevant judicial office in the person's case, and

    (b) the date that, for the purposes of that paragraph, is the person's potential retirement date by reference to his pre-commencement office ("the retirement date preserved in 1995") is the same as, or later than, the special date,

paragraph 5(3) and (4) do not apply.

(2) If the special date is later than the retirement date preserved in 1995, paragraph 2(2)(b) of Schedule 7 to the 1993 Act does not have effect in relation to relevant judicial office in the person's case.

(3) Accordingly, in paragraph 1 of Schedule 7 to the 1993 Act, after sub-paragraph (5) insert—

"(6) Paragraph 2(2) has effect subject to paragraph 8(2) of Schedule 9 to the Tribunals, Courts and Enforcement Act 2007 (certain cases where the post-commencement office is that of judge, or other member, of the First-tier Tribunal or the Upper Tribunal)."

Eligibility for appointment after having attained age of 70

9

(1) Sub-paragraph (3) applies in respect of a person on each day that—

    (a) is, or is later than, the day on which the person attains the age of 70,

    (b) is a day on which the person holds a qualifying office, and

    (c) is earlier than the day on which the person is required to vacate the qualifying office.

(2) Sub-paragraph (3) also applies in respect of a person on each day that—

    (a) is, or is later than, the day on which the person attains the age of 70, and

    (b) is a day on which the person holds, on an unlimited basis, a qualifying office.

(3) Where this sub-paragraph applies in respect of a person on a day, the fact that the person has attained the age of 70 shall not (by itself) render him ineligible for appointment (or re-appointment) on that day to a relevant judicial office.

(4)   For the purposes of this paragraph, a person holds an office on an unlimited basis at a particular time if at that time he is not required to vacate the office at any particular later time.

PART 3
JUDGES AND OTHER MEMBERS OF FIRST-TIER AND UPPER TRIBUNALS: PENSIONS WHERE OFFICE ACQUIRED UNDER SECTION 31(2)

Interpretation of Part 3 of Schedule

10

For the purposes of this Part of this Schedule—
- (a)   "new office" means—
    - (i)   the office of judge of the First-tier Tribunal by virtue of being a transferred-in judge of the First-tier Tribunal,
    - (ii)   the office of other member of the First-tier Tribunal by virtue of being a transferred-in other member of the First-tier Tribunal,
    - (iii) the office of judge of the Upper Tribunal by virtue of being a transferred-in judge of the Upper Tribunal, and
    - (iv)   the office of other member of the Upper Tribunal by virtue of being a transferred-in other member of the Upper Tribunal;
- (b)   a person holds an office "on a salaried basis" if and so long as, and to the extent that—
    - (i)   the person's service in the office is remunerated by payment of a salary, and
    - (ii)   the salary is not subject to terms which preclude rights to pensions and other benefits accruing by reference to it;
- (c)   a person shall be regarded as holding "qualifying judicial office" at any time when he holds, on a salaried basis, any one or more of the offices specified in Schedule 1 to the 1993 Act, and any reference to a "qualifying judicial office" is a reference to any office specified in that Schedule if it is held on a salaried basis;
- (d)   "the 1993 Act" means the Judicial Pensions and Retirement Act 1993 (c 8).

Right to opt in to Part 1 of the 1993 Act where qualifying judicial office not previously held

11

(1)   Sub-paragraphs (2) and (3) apply where—
- (a)   a person becomes, as a result of provision under section 31(2), the holder of a new office,
- (b)   before that, the person has never held qualifying judicial office, and
- (c)   the person, on becoming the holder of the new office, holds the new office on a salaried basis.

(2)   Section 1(1)(a) of the 1993 Act (Part 1 of the 1993 Act applies to a person who first holds qualifying judicial office on or after 31st March 1995) does not have effect in relation to the person.

(3)   The person is entitled, subject to paragraph 12, to elect for Part 1 of the 1993 Act (judicial pensions) to apply to him.

(4)   Part 1 of the 1993 Act applies to a person who makes an election under sub-paragraph (3).

(5)   Sub-paragraph (4) is subject to sections 1(5) and 13 of the 1993 Act (where person has opted out of Part 1 of the 1993 Act then, except as provided by section 13 of that Act, that Part does not apply to the person).

Election under paragraph 11(3) for pension under Part 1 of the 1993 Act

12

(1)   In this paragraph "opt-in election" means an election under paragraph 11(3).

(2)   An opt-in election may be made only in such circumstances, within such time and in such manner as the Lord Chancellor may by regulations prescribe.

(3)   An opt-in election is irrevocable.

(4)   Regulations under sub-paragraph (2) may permit the making of an opt-in election even though the person in respect of whom the opt-in election is made—

    (a)   has ceased (whether by virtue of dying or otherwise) to hold the office mentioned in paragraph 11(1)(a), or

    (b)   has ceased to hold that office on a salaried basis without having ceased to hold that office.

(5)   Where regulations under sub-paragraph (2) permit the making of an opt-in election in respect of a person who has died, the right to make that election is exercisable by the person's personal representatives.

(6)   The Lord Chancellor may by regulations provide for a person in respect of whom an opt-in election is made to be treated for such purposes as may be prescribed by the regulations as if the person had, at such times as may be prescribed by the regulations, been a person to whom Part 1 of the 1993 Act applies.

(7)   An opt-in election may not be made in respect of a person at any time when an election made under section 13 of the 1993 Act (election to opt out of Part 1 of the 1993 Act) is in force in respect of the person.

Continuation of existing public service pension arrangements in certain cases

13

(1)   Sub-paragraph (2) applies if—

    (a)   a person, as a result of provision under section 31(2), becomes the holder of a new office,

    (b)   either—

        (i)   the person held qualifying judicial office immediately before 31st March 1995, or

        (ii)   before becoming the holder of the new office, the person has never held qualifying judicial office,

    (c)   immediately before the person becomes the holder of the new office—

        (i)   the person holds an office within paragraph (a), (b) or (c) of section 31(2) (the "old office"), and

        (ii)   the person's service in the old office is subject to a public service pension scheme,

    (d)   the person, on becoming the holder of the new office, holds the new office on a salaried basis, and

    (e)   immediately after the person becomes the holder of the new office, the person—

        (i)   is not a person to whom Part 1 of the 1993 Act applies, and

        (ii)   is not a person to whom that Part would apply but for section 13 of that Act.

(2)   The person's service in the new office, so far as it is service during the continuity period—

(a)   shall be subject to that public service pension scheme, and

(b)   shall be subject to that scheme in a way that corresponds to the way in which the person's service in the old office was subject to that scheme.

(3)   In sub-paragraph (2) "the continuity period" means the period—

(a)   that begins when the person becomes the holder of the new office on a salaried basis, and

(b)   that ends with whichever of the following first happens after that—

(i)   the person's ceasing to hold the new office,

(ii)   the person's ceasing to hold the new office on a salaried basis without ceasing to hold the new office,

(iii)   the person's becoming a person to whom Part 1 of the 1993 Act applies, and

(iv)   the person's becoming a person to whom Part 1 of the 1993 Act would apply but for section 13 of that Act.

(4)   For the purposes of sub-paragraph (1)(c)(ii), the person's service in the old office is not to be treated as subject to a public service pension scheme at a time when the scheme does not apply to him as a result of his having exercised a right to elect for the scheme not to apply to him.

(5)   A public service pension scheme which, apart from sub-paragraph (2), would not be a judicial pension scheme for the purposes of the 1993 Act does not become a judicial pension scheme for those purposes if it is only as a result of sub-paragraph (2) that pensions and other benefits are payable under the scheme in respect of service in qualifying judicial office.

(6)   In this paragraph "public service pension scheme" means any public service pension scheme, as defined in—

(a)   section 1 of the Pension Schemes Act 1993 (c 48), or

(b)   section 1 of the Pension Schemes (Northern Ireland) Act 1993 (c 49).

Subordinate Legislation

Tribunals, Courts and Enforcement Act 2007 (Transitional Judicial Pensions Provisions) Regulations 2008, SI 2008/2697.

PART 4

(Amends legislation outside the scope of this work.)

SCHEDULES 10–20

(Outside the scope of this work.)

SCHEDULE 21
REGULATIONS UNDER SECTIONS 111 AND 113

Sections 111 and 113

1

The first column of this table lists the matters referred to in sections 111(3) and 113(5).

2

A matter listed in the first column includes the aspects set out in the appropriate part of the second column.

Matter about which particular provision may be made:	Including these aspects:
1 The scheme operator.	(a) The constitution of the scheme operator.
	(b) The governance of the scheme operator.
	(c) The size of the scheme operator's undertaking.
	(d) The financial standing of the scheme operator.
	(e) Whether or not a scheme operator is a profit-making organisation.
2 The terms of a debt management scheme.	(a) The non-business debtors to whom the scheme is open.
	(b) The kinds of debts which may be specified in a plan arranged in accordance with the scheme.
3 The operation of a debt management scheme.	(a) How decisions are made about whether debt repayment plans are to be arranged.
	(b) How debt repayment plans are arranged.
	(c) How decisions are made about the terms of debt repayment plans, including decisions about—
	(i) what payments will be required in relation to the specified debts;
	(ii) the amounts, times and recipients of payments;
	(iii) the duration of the plan.
	(d) The format of debt repayment plans.
	(e) When debt repayment plans begin to have effect.
	(f) How changes are to be made to debt repayment plans (including the specification of debts after a plan has been arranged).
	(g) How decisions are made about whether debt repayment plans are to be terminated.
	(h) How debt repayment plans are terminated.
4 Changes that affect the scheme operator.	
5 Changes to— (i) the terms of a debt management scheme; (ii) the operation of a debt management scheme	(a) Whether changes may be made. (b) How changes are made.
6 The transfer of the operation of a debt management scheme to another body.	(a) Whether the operation of the scheme may be transferred.
	(b) How the operation of the scheme is transferred.

Commencement

To be appointed: see s 148(5).

SCHEDULES 22, 23

(Sch 22 contains amendments to legislation outside the scope of this work; Sch 23 contains repeals which, in so far as relevant to this work, have been incorporated at the appropriate place.)

Appendix 3

IMMIGRATION RULES

IMMIGRATION RULES

Notes

Laid before Parliament: 23 May 1994.

Authority: Immigration Act 1971, s 3(2).

Further updates to these Rules can be found at www.gov.uk/government/collections/immigration-rules.

Contents

The following Immigration Rules incorporate amending Statements of Change laid before, or presented to, Parliament on:	
20 September 1994	Cmnd 2663
26 October 1995	HC 797
4 January 1996	Cmnd 3073
7 March 1996	HC 274
2 April 1996	HC 329
30 August 1996	Cmnd 3365
31 October 1996	HC 31
27 February 1997	HC 338
29 May 1997	Cmnd 3669
5 June 1997	HC 26
30 July 1997	HC 161
11 May 1998	Cmnd 3953
8 October 1998	Cmnd 4065
18 November 1999	HC 22
28 July 2000	HC 704
20 September 2000	Cmnd 4851
27 August 2001	Cmnd 5253
16 April 2002	HC 735
27 August 2002	Cmnd 5597
7 November 2002	HC 1301
26 November 2002	HC 104
8 January 2003	HC 180
10 February 2003	HC 389
31 March 2003	HC 538
30 May 2003	Cmnd 5829
25 August 2003	Cmnd 5949
12 November 2003	HC 1224
17 December 2003	HC 95
12 January 2004	HC 176
26 February 2004	HC 370
31 March 2004	HC 464
1 May 2004	HC 523
3 August 2004	Cm 6297
24 September 2004	Cm 6339
18 October 2004	HC 1112
20 December 2004	HC 164
11 January 2005	HC 194
7 February 2005	HC 302
22 February 2005	HC 346
24 March 2005	HC 486
15 June 2005	HC 104
12 July 2005	HC 299
24 October 2005	HC 582
30 November 2005	HC 645

9 January 2006	HC 769
12 February 2006	HC 819
22 March 2006	HC 949
3 April 2006	HC 974 HC 1016
30 April 2006	HC 1053
20 July 2006	HC 1337
9 October 2006	Cm 6918
8 November 2006	HC 1702
1 January 2007	HC 130
19 March 2007	HC 398
3 April 2007	Cm 7074
4 April 2007	Cm 7075
7 November 2007	HC 82
13 November 2007	HC 40
19 November 2007	HC 82
29 February and 1 April 2008	HC 321
7 April 2008	HC 420
9 June 2008	HC 607
15 July 2008	HC 971
4 November 2008	HC 1113
9 February 2009	HC 227
9 September	HC 413
1 October 2009	Cm 7701
1 October 2009	Cm 7711
10 December 2009	HC 120
10 February 2010	HC 367
18 March 2010	HC 439
15 July 2010	HC 96
28 June 2010	HC 59
22 July 2010	HC 382
19 August 2010	Cmnd 7929
22 October 2010	Cm 7944
21 December 2010	HC 698
16 March 2011	HC 863
31 March 2011	HC 908
13 June 2011	HC 1148
19 August 2011	HC 1436
10 October 2011	HC 1511
8 December 2011	HC 1693
20 December 2011	HC 1719
19 January 2012	HC 1733
15 March 2012	HC 1888
4 April 2012	Cm 8337
9 July 2012	HC 194
20 July 2012	Cm 8423
6 September 2012	HC 565

1 October 2012	HC 194
13 December 2012	HC 760
12 December 2012	HC 820
20 December 2012	HC 847
30 January 2013	HC 943
7 February 2013	HC 967
11 March 2013	HC 1038
14 March 2013	HC 1039
April 2013	Cm 8599
1 July 2013	HC 244
6 September 2013	HC 628
1 December 2013	HC 803
1 January 2014	HC 889
13 March 2014	HC 1138
1 April 2014	HC 1201
10 July 2014	HC 532
16 October 2014	HC 693

INTRODUCTION

1. The Home Secretary has made changes in the Rules laid down by him as to the practice to be followed in the administration of the Immigration Acts for regulating entry into and the stay of persons in the United Kingdom and contained in the statement laid before Parliament on 23 March 1990 (HC 251) (as amended). This statement contains the Rules as changed and replaces the provisions of HC 251 (as amended).

2. Immigration Officers, Entry Clearance Officers and all staff of the Home Office Immigration and Nationality [Directorate] will carry out their duties without regard to the race, colour or religion of persons seeking to enter or remain in the United Kingdom [and in compliance with the provisions of the Human Rights Acts 1998].

3. In these Rules words importing the masculine gender include the feminine unless the contrary intention appears.

Note

Words in square brackets inserted by Cm 4851.

Implementation and transitional provisions

4. These Rules come into effect on 1 October 1994 and will apply to all decisions taken on or after that date save that any application made before 1 October 1994 for entry clearance, leave to enter or remain or variation of leave to enter or remain [, other than an application for leave by a person seeking asylum,] shall be decided under the provisions of HC 251, as amended, as if these Rules had not been made.

Application

5. [Save where expressly indicated, these Rules do not apply to those persons who are entitled to enter or remain in the United Kingdom by virtue of the provisions of the 2006 EEA Regulations. But any person who is not entitled to rely on the provisions of those Regulations is covered by these Rules.]

Note

Substituted by Cm 4851.

Interpretation

6. In these Rules the following interpretations apply:

["the **Immigration Acts**" has the same meaning as it has in the Interpretation Act 1978.]

"**the 1993 Act**" is the Asylum and Immigration Appeals Act 1993.

["**the 1996 Act**" is the Asylum and Immigration Act 1996.]

["**the 2006 EEA Regulations**" are the Immigration (European Economic Area) Regulations 2006.]

"**adoption**" unless the contrary intention appears, includes a de facto adoption in accordance with the requirements of paragraph 309A of these Rules, and "adopted" and "adoptive parent" should be construed accordingly.

[In Appendix FM references to "**application for leave to remain**" include an application for variation of leave to enter or remain of a person in the UK.]

"**Approved Destination Status Agreement with China**" means the Memorandum of Understanding on visa and related issues concerning tourist groups from the People's Republic of China to the United Kingdom as a approved destination, signed on 21 January 2005.

"**a** *bona fide* **private education institution**" is a private education institution which:

(a)   maintains satisfactory records of enrolments and attendance of students, and supplies these to the Border and Immigration Agency when requested;

(b)   provides courses which involve a minimum of 15 hours organised daytime study per week;

(c)   ensures a suitably qualified tutor is present during the hours of study to offer teaching and instruction to the students;

(d)   offers courses leading to qualifications recognised by the appropriate accreditation bodies;

(e)   employs suitably qualified staff to provide teaching, guidance and support to the students;

(f)   provides adequate accommodation, facilities, staffing levels and equipment to support the numbers of students enrolled at the institution; and

(g)   if it offers tuition support to external students at degree level, ensures that such students are registered with the UK degree awarding body.

["**Business day**" means any day other than Saturday or Sunday, a day which is bank holiday under the Banking and Financial Dealings Act 1971 in the part of the United Kingdom to which the notice is sent, Christmas Day or Good Friday.]

"**civil partner**" means a civil partnership which exists under or by virtue of the Civil Partnership Act 2004 (and any deference to a civil partner is to be read accordingly);

["**conviction**" means conviction for a criminal offence in the UK or any other country.]

[**curtailment,** in relation to the curtailment of a person's leave to enter or remain in the UK, means curtailing their leave such that they will have a shorter period of, or no, leave remaining.]

"**degree level study**" means a course which leads to a recognised United Kingdom degree at bachelor's level or above, or an equivalent qualification at level 6 or above of the revised National Qualifications Framework, or levels 9 or above of the Scottish Credit and Qualifications Framework;

[Under Part 8 of these Rules, "**post-graduate level study**" means a course at level 7 or above of the revised National Qualifications Framework or Qualifications and Credit Framework, or level 11 or above of the Scottish Credit and Qualifications Framework, which leads to a recognised United Kingdom postgraduate degree at Master's level or above, or an equivalent qualification at the same level.]

["**foundation degree**" means a programme of study which lead to a qualification awarded by [an English higher education institution with degree awarding powers which is at a minimum of level 5 on the revised National Qualifications Framework, or awarded on a directly equivalent basis in the devolved administrations.]

["**primary degree**" means a qualification obtained from a course of degree level study, which did not feature as an entry requirement a previous qualification obtained from degree level study. An undergraduate degree is a primary degree. A Masters degree that has a Bachelor degree as an entry requirement is not a primary degree.]

[A "**UK recognised body**" is an institution that has been granted degree awarding powers by either a Royal Charter, an Act of Parliament or the Privy Council.

[For the purposes of these Rules we will consider the Foundation Programme Office [, South London Local Education and Training Board] and the Yorkshire and Humber Strategic Health Authority as equivalent to UK Recognised Bodies.]

[A "**UK listed body**" is an institution that is not a UK recognised body but which provides full courses that lead to the award of a degree by a UK recognised body.]

["**EEA National**" has the meaning given in regulation 2(1) of the 2006 EEA Regulations.]

"an external student" is a student studying for a degree from a UK degree awarding body without any requirement to attend the UK degree awarding body's premises or a UK Listed Body's premises for lectures and tutorials.

"United Kingdom passport" bears the meaning it has in the Immigration Act 1971.

"a UK Bachelors degree" means

(a)   A programme of study or research which leads to the award, by or on behalf of a university, college or other body which is authorised by Royal Charter or by or under an Act of Parliament to grant degrees, of a qualification designated by the awarding institution to be of Bachelors degree level; or

(b)   A programme of study or research, which leads to a recognised award for the purposes of section 214(2)(c) of the Education Reform Act 1988, of a qualification designated by the awarding institution to be of Bachelors degree level.

"Immigration Officer" includes a Customs Officer acting as an Immigration Officer.

"Multiple Entry work permit employment" is work permit employment where the person concerned does not intend to spend a continuous period in the United Kingdom in work permit employment.

[**"public funds"** means

(a)   housing under Part VI or VII of the Housing Act 1996 and under Part II of the Housing Act 1985, Part I or II of the Housing (Scotland) Act 1987, Part II of the Housing (Northern Ireland) Order 1981 or Part II of the Housing (Northern Ireland) Order 1988;

(b)   attendance allowance, severe disablement allowance, [carer's allowance] and disability living allowance under Part III of the Social Security Contribution and Benefits Act 1992; income support . . . council tax benefit . . . and housing benefit under Part VII of that Act; a social fund payment under Part VIII of that Act; child benefit under Part IX of that Act; income based jobseeker's allowance under the Jobseekers Act 1995, [income related allowance under Part 1 of the Welfare Reform Act 2007 (employment and support allowance)] [; state pension credit under the State Pension Credit Act 2002; or child tax credit and working tax credit under Part 1 of the Tax Credits Act 2002].

(c)   attendance allowance, severe disablement allowance, [carer's allowance] and disability living allowance under Part III of the Social Security Contribution and Benefits (Northern Ireland) Act 1992; income support . . . council tax benefit [and] . . . housing benefit under Part VII of that Act; a social fund payment under Part VIII of that Act; child benefit under Part IX of that Act; ... income based jobseeker's allowance under the Jobseekers (Northern Ireland) Order 1995 [or income related allowance under Part 1 of the Welfare Reform Act (Northern Ireland) 2007].

(d)   [Universal Credit under Part 1 of the Welfare Reform Act 2012 or Personal Independence Payment under Part 4 of that Act;]

(e)   Universal Credit, Personal Independence Payment or any domestic relief under the Northern Ireland Welfare Reform Act 2013]

(f)   a council tax reduction under a council tax reduction scheme under section 13A of the Local Government Finance Act 1992 in relation to England and Wales or a council tax reduction pursuant to the Council Tax Reduction (Scotland) Regulations 2012 or the Council Tax Reduction (State pension Credit) (Scotland) Regulations 2012.]

"settled in the United Kingdom" means that the person concerned:

(a)   is free from any restriction on the period for which he may remain save that a person entitled to an exemption under Section 8 of the Immigration Act 1971 (otherwise than as a member of the home forces) is not to be regarded as settled in the United Kingdom except in so far as Section 8(5A) so provides; and

(b) is either:
  (i) ordinarily resident in the United Kingdom without having entered or remained in breach of the immigration laws; or
  (ii) despite having entered or remained in breach of the immigration laws, has subsequently entered lawfully or has been granted leave to remain and is ordinarily resident.

"a parent" includes:

(a) the stepfather of a child whose father is dead (and the reference to stepfather includes a relationship arising through civil partnership);
(b) the stepmother of a child whose mother is dead (and the reference to stepmother includes a relationship arising through civil partnership);
(c) the father as well as the mother of an illegitimate child where he is proved to be the father;
(d) [an adoptive parent, where a child was adopted in accordance with a decision taken by the competent administrative authority or court in a country whose adoption orders are recognised by the United Kingdom or where a child is the subject of a de facto adoption in accordance with the requirements of paragraph 309A of these Rules (except that an adopted child or child who is the subject of a de facto adoption may not make an application for leave to enter or remain in order to accompany, join or remain with an adoptive parent under paragraphs 297–303); and]
(e) in the case of a child born in the United Kingdom who is not a British citizen, a person to whom there has been a genuine transfer of parental responsibility on the ground of the original parent(s)' inability to care for the child.

["date of application" means the date of application determined in accordance with paragraph 30 or 34G of these rules as appropriate.

"a valid application" means an application made in accordance with the requirements of Part 1 of these Rules.

"refugee leave" means limited leave granted pursuant to paragraph 334 or 335 of these rules and has not been revoked pursuant to paragraph 339A or 339B of these rules.

"humanitarian protection" means limited leave granted pursuant to paragraph 339C of these rules and has not been revoked pursuant to paragraph 339G or 339H of these rules.

"a period of imprisonment" referred to in these rules has the same meaning as set out in section 38(2) of the UK Borders Act 2007.

"Overstayed" or "Overstaying" means the applicant has stayed in the UK beyond the latest of:
(i) the time limit attached to the last period of leave granted, or
(ii) beyond the period that his leave was extended under sections 3C or 3D of the Immigration Act 1971, ...
(iii) the date that an applicant receives the notice of invalidity declaring that an application for leave to remain is not a valid application, provided the application was submitted before the time limit attached to the last period of leave expired.

["intention to live permanently with the other" or "intend to live together permanently" means an intention to live together, evidenced by a clear commitment from both parties that they will live together permanently in the United Kingdom immediately following the outcome of the application in question or as soon as circumstances permit thereafter. However, where an application is made under Appendix Armed Forces the words "in the UK" in this definition do not apply.]]

[Where an application is made under Appendix FM and the sponsor is a permanent member of HM Diplomatic Service, or a comparable UK-based staff member of the British Council, the Department for International Development or the Home Office on a tour of duty outside the UK, the words "in the UK" in this definition do not apply.]

[["**present and settled**" or "**present and settled in the UK**" means that the person concerned is settled in the United Kingdom and, at the time that an application under these Rules is made, is physically present here or is coming here with or to join the applicant and intends to make the UK their home with the applicant if the application is successful.

Where the person concerned is a British Citizen or settled in the UK and is:

(i)   a member of HM Forces serving overseas, or
(ii)   a permanent member of HM Diplomatic Service, or a comparable UK-based staff member of the British Council, the Department for International Development or the Home Office on a tour of duty outside the UK, and the applicant has provided the evidence specified in paragraph 26A of Appendix FM-SE,

then for the purposes of Appendix FM the person is to be regarded as present and settled in the UK, and in paragraphs R-LTRP.1.1.(a) and R-ILRP.1.1.(a) of Appendix FM the words "and their partner must be in the UK" are to be disregarded.

For the purposes of an application as a fiancé(e) or proposed civil partner under paragraphs 289AA to 295 or Appendix FM, an EEA national who holds a document certifying permanent residence issued under the 2006 EEA Regulations is to be regarded as present and settled in the UK.]]

["**sponsor**" means the person in relation to whom an applicant is seeking leave to enter or remain as their spouse, fiancé, civil partner, proposed civil partner, unmarried partner or same-sex partner, as the case may be, under paragraphs 277 to 295O or 317 to 319][or the person in relation to whom an applicant is seeking entry clearance or leave as their partner or dependent relative under Appendix FM.]

["**overcrowded**" means overcrowded within the meaning of the Housing Act 1985, the Housing (Scotland) Act 1987 or the Housing (Northern Ireland) Order 1988 (as appropriate).

"**working illegally**" means working in breach of conditions of leave or working when in the UK without valid leave where such leave is required.

"**in breach of immigration laws**" means without valid leave where such leave is required, or in breach of the conditions of leave.

[["**adequate**" and "**adequately**" in relation to a maintenance and accommodation requirement shall mean that, after income tax, national insurance contributions and housing costs have been deducted, there must be available to the family the level of income that would be available to them if the family was in receipt of income support.]]

"**occupy exclusively**" in relation to accommodation shall mean that part of the accommodation must be for the exclusive use of the [family].

["**must not be leading an independent life**" or "**is not leading an independent life**" means that the applicant does not have a partner as defined in Appendix FM; is living with their parents (except where they are at boarding school, college or university as part of their full-time education); is not employed full-time (unless aged 18 years or over); is wholly or mainly dependent upon their parents for financial support (unless aged 18 years or over); and is wholly or mainly dependent upon their parents for emotional support.]

[Where a relative other than a parent may act as the sponsor of the applicant, references in this definition to "parents" shall be read as applying to that other relative.]

["**prohibited degree of relationship**" has the same meaning as in the Marriage Act 1949, the Marriage (Prohibited Degrees of Relationship) Act 1986 and the Civil Partnership Act 2004.]

"**visa nationals**" are the persons specified in [Appendix 1] to these Rules who need a visa for the United Kingdom.

"**non-visa nationals**" are persons who are not specified in Appendix 1 to these Rules.

"**specified nationals**" is a person specified in Appendix 3 to these Rules who seeks leave to enter the United Kingdom for a period of more than 6 months.

"**employment**" unless the contrary intention appears, includes paid and unpaid employment [paid and unpaid work placements undertaken as part of a course or period of study,] self-employment and engaging in business or any professional activity.

[. . .]

["**the Human Rights Convention**" means the Convention for the Protection of Human Rights and Fundamental Freedoms, agreed by the Council of Europe at Rome on 4th November 1950 as it has effect for the time being in relation to the United Kingdom.]

["**Immigration employment document**" means a work permit or any other document which relates to employment and is issued for the purpose of these Rules or in connection with leave to enter or remain in the United Kingdom.]

["**Employment as a Doctor or Dentist in Training**" means employment in a medical post or programme which has been approved by the Postgraduate Medical Education and Training Board, or employment in a postgraduate training programme in dentistry.]

"**these Rules**" means these Immigration rules (HC 395) made under section 3(2) of the Immigration Act 1971.

["**A refugee**" is a refugee as defined in regulation 2 of The Refugee or Person in Need of International Protection (Qualification) Regulation 2006.]

[In part 6A of these Rules, "relevant grant allocation period" means a specified period of time, which will be published by the Secretary of State on the [visas and immigration pages of the gov.uk] website, during which applications for entry clearance or leave to enter in respect of a particular route may be granted subject to the grant allocation for that period;

[In part 6A of these Rules, "grant allocation period" means a limit, details of which will be published by the Secretary of State on the [visas and immigration pages of the gov.uk] website, on the number of grants of entry clearance or leave to enter which may be granted in respect of a particular route during the grant allocation for that period;]

Under Part 6A of these Rules, "**Highly Skilled Migrant**" means a migrant who is granted leave under paragraphs 135A to 135G of the Rules in force before 30th June 2008.

Under Part 6A of these Rules, "**Highly Skilled Migrant Programme Approval Letter**" means a letter issued by the Home Office confirming that the applicant meets the criteria specified by the Secretary of State for entry to or stay in the UK under the Highly Skilled Migrant Programme.

Under Part 6A of these Rules, "**Innovator**" means a migrant who is granted leave under paragraphs 210A to 210F of the Rules in force before 30th June 2008.

. . ..

Under Part 6A of these Rules, **"Participant in the Fresh Talent Working in Scotland Scheme"** means a migrant who is granted leave under paragraphs 143A to 143F of the Rules in force before 30th June 2008.

Under Part 6A of these Rules, **"Participant in the International Graduates Scheme"** means a migrant who is granted leave under paragraphs 135O to 135T of the Rules in force before 30th June 2008.

Under Part 6A of these Rules, **"Postgraduate Doctor or Dentist"** means a migrant who is granted leave under paragraphs 70 to 75 of these Rules.

Under Part 6A of these Rules, **"Self-Employed"** means an applicant is registered as self-employed with HM Revenue & Customs, or is employed by a company of which the applicant is a controlling shareholder.

Under Part 6A of these Rules, **"Student"** means a migrant who is granted leave under paragraphs 57 to 62 of these Rules.

Under Part 6A of these Rules, **"Student Nurse"** means a migrant who is granted leave under paragraphs 63 to 69 of these Rules.

Under Part 6A of these Rules, **"Student Re-Sitting an Examination"** means a migrant who is granted leave under paragraphs 69A to 69F of these Rules.

Under Part 6A of these Rules, **"Student Writing-Up a Thesis"** means a migrant who is granted leave under paragraphs 69G to 69L of these Rules.

Under Part 6A of these Rules, **"Work Permit Holder"** means a migrant who is granted leave under paragraphs 128 to 133 of these Rules.

Under Part 6A of these Rules, **"Prospective Student"** means a migrant who is granted leave under paragraphs 128 to 133 of these Rules.

[Under Part 6A of these Rules, an **"A-rated Sponsor"** is a Sponsor which is recorded as being "A-rated" on the register of licensed Sponsors maintained by the United Kingdom Border Agency.

[Under Part 6A and Appendix A of these Rules, a **"B-Rated Sponsor"** is a Sponsor which is recorded as being "B-Rated" on the register of licensed Sponsors maintained by the United Kingdom Border Agency.]

[Under Part 6A of these Rules, an **"Highly Trusted Sponsor"** means a sponsor which is recorded as being "Highly Trusted" on the register of licensed sponsors maintained by the United Kingdom Border Agency.]

[Under paragraph 34K of these Rules, a **"Premium Sponsor"** is a sponsor recorded as holding Premium status on the register of licensed Sponsors maintained by the United Kingdom Border Agency.]

Under Part 6A of these Rules, **"Certificate of Sponsorship"** means an authorisation issued by the Secretary of State to a Sponsor in respect of one or more applications, or potential applications, for entry clearance, leave to enter or remain [as a Tier 2 migrant or a Tier 5 migrant] in accordance with these Rules.

[Under Part 6A and Appendix A of these Rules, **"Confirmation of Acceptance for Studies"** means a unique reference number electronically issued by a Sponsor via the Sponsor Management System to an applicant for entry clearance, leave to enter or remain as a Tier 4 Migrant in accordance with these Rules.]

Under [Parts 6A and 9] of these Rules, **"Certificate of Sponsorship Checking Service"** means a computerised interface with the Points Based System computer database which allows a United Kingdom Border Agency caseworker or entry clearance officer assessing a migrant's application for entry clearance, leave to enter or leave to remain to access and review details of the migrant's Certificate of Sponsorship, including details of the migrant's Sponsor, together with details of the job . . .

[Under Part 6A and Appendix A of these Rules, **"length of the period of engagement"** is the period beginning with the employment start date as recorded on the Certificate of Sponsorship Checking Service entry which relates to the Certificate of Sponsorship reference number for which the migrant was awarded points under Appendix A and ending on the employment end date as recorded in the same entry.

[Under Part 6A and Appendix A of these Rules, a **"genuine vacancy"** is a vacancy which exists in practice (or would exist in practice were it not filled by the applicant) for a position which:

(a)   requires the jobholder to undertake the specific duties and responsibilities, for the weekly hours and length of the period of engagement, described by the Sponsor in the Certificate of Sponsorship relating to the applicant; and

(b)   does not include dissimilar and/or unequally skilled duties such that the Standard Occupational Classification (SOC) code used by the Sponsor as stated in the Certificate of Sponsorship relating to the applicant is inappropriate.]

[Under Part 6A and Appendix A of these Rules, working for **"the same employer"** or **"the same Sponsor"** includes working for a different employer or Sponsor in circumstances which constitute a "relevant transfer" under Regulation 3(1) of the Transfer of Undertakings (Protection of Employment) Regulations 2006, or similar protection, provided the worker's duties remain unchanged.]

Under Part 6A and Appendix A of these Rules, **"Designated Competent Body"** means an organisation which has been approved by the UK Border Agency to endorse applicants as a Tier 1 (Exceptional Talent) Migrant.

[Under Part 6A and Appendix A of these Rules, **"Tier 1 (Exceptional Talent) Unique Reference Number"** means a unique reference number issued for the purposes of managing the Tier 1 (Exceptional Talent) Limit and provided by the UK Border Agency to an applicant prior to making his application as a Tier 1 (Exceptional Talent) Migrant.]

For the purpose of para 320(7B) of these Rules "Removal Decision" means (a) a decision to remove in accordance with section 10 of the Immigration and Asylum Act 1999; (b) a decision to remove an illegal entrant by way of directions under paragraphs 8 to 10 of Schedule 2 to the Immigration Act 1971 or (c) a decision to remove in accordance with section 47 of the Immigration, Asylum and Nationality Act 2006.

Pending appeal has the same meaning as in section 104 of the Nationality, Immigration and Asylum Act 2002.]

[Under Part 6A of these Rules "**Confirmation of Acceptance for Studies Checking Service**" means a computerised interface with the Points Based System computer database which allows a United Kingdom Border Agency caseworker or entry clearance officer assessing a migrant's application for entry clearance, leave to enter or leave to remain as a Tier 4 migrant under these Rules to access and review details of the migrant's Confirmation of Acceptance for Studies, including details of the migrant's Sponsor, together with details of the course of study and other details associated with the circumstances in which the Confirmation of Acceptance for Studies was issues.]

Under Part 6A of these Rules, **"Established Entertainer"** means an applicant who is applying for leave to remain as a Tier 2 (General) Migrant or a Tier 2 (Intra-Company Transfer) Migrant in respect of whom the following conditions are satisfied:

(a)   the Certificate of Sponsorship Checking Service entry to which the applicant's Certificate of Sponsorship reference number relates, records that the applicant is being sponsored in an occupation which is defined in the United Kingdom Border Agency's Transitional Guidance as being a job in the entertainment sector,

(b)   the applicant has, or has previously had, entry clearance, leave to enter or leave to remain in the UK as a Work Permit Holder, and the work permit that led to that grant was issued in the sports and entertainment category to enable him to work in the occupation in which he is, at the date of the application for leave to remain, currently being sponsored,

(c)   [the applicant's last grant of leave was as:

    (i)   as a Work Permit Holder in the sports and entertainment category, provided the work permit on the basis of which that leave was granted was issued in the sports and entertainment category to enable him to work either in the occupation in which he is, at the date of the current application for leave to remain, currently being sponsored, or in another occupation which is defined in the UK Border Agency's Transitional Guidance as being a job in the entertainment sector, or

    (ii)   leave to remain as a Tier 2 (General) Migrant or a Tier 2 (Intra-Company Transfer) Migrant, provided (in either case):

        (1)   he previously had leave as a Work Permit Holder in the sports and entertainment category to work as described in (i) above,

        (2)   he has not been granted entry clearance in this or any other route since his last grant of leave as a Work Permit Holder, and

        (3)   his last grant of leave was made to enable him to work either in the occupation in which he is, at the date of the current application for leave to remain, currently being sponsored or in another occupation which is defined in the UK Border Agency's Transitional Guidance as being a job in the entertainment sector,]

(d)   the Certificate of Sponsorship Checking Service entry to which the applicant's Certificate of Sponsorship reference number relates records:

    (i)   that the applicant will be paid a salary for the job that is at or above the appropriate entertainments industry rate, as listed in the United Kingdom Border Agency's Transitional Guidance; and

    (ii)   that before agreeing to employ the applicant, the Sponsor consulted with such bodies as the United Kingdom Border Agency's Transitional Guidance indicates that it should consult with before employing someone in this capacity, and

(e)   the applicant has not spent a period of 5 years or more in the UK, beginning with the last grant of entry clearance, as a Qualifying Work Permit Holder, Tier 2 (General) Migrant or Tier 2 (Intra-Company Transfer) Migrant, or in any combination of these.

Under Part 6A of these Rules, **"Qualifying Work Permit Holder"** means a Work Permit Holder who was issued a work permit in the business and commercial or sports and entertainment work permit categories.

Under Part 6A of these Rules, **"Senior Care Worker"** means an applicant who is applying for leave to remain as a Tier 2 (General) Migrant or a Tier 2 (Intra-Company Transfer) Migrant in respect of whom the following conditions are satisfied:

(a)   [the Certificate of Sponsorship Checking Service entry to which the applicant's Certificate of Sponsorship reference number relates, records that the applicant is being sponsored in an occupation which is defined in the codes of practice for Tier 2 Sponsors published by the UK Border Agency as being a senior care worker role,

(b)   the applicant's last grant of leave was:

    (i)   as a Qualifying Work Permit Holder, or

    (ii)   leave to remain as a Tier 2 (General) Migrant or a Tier 2 (Intra-Company Transfer) Migrant, provided (in either case):

(1)   he previously had leave as a Qualifying Work Permit Holder, and

(2)   he has not been granted entry clearance in this or any other route since his last grant of leave as a Qualifying Work Permit Holder.]

(c)   the work permit or Certificate of Sponsorship that led to the last grant of leave was issued to enable the applicant to work as a senior care worker, and

(d)   the applicant has not spent a period of 5 years or more in the UK, beginning with the last grant of entry clearance, as a Qualifying Work Permit Holder, Tier 2 (General) Migrant or Tier 2 (Intra-Company Transfer) Migrant, or in any combination of these.

Under Part 6A of these Rules, **"Sponsor"** means the person or Government that the Certificate of Sponsorship Checking Service [or Confirmation of Acceptance for Studies Checking Service] records as being the Sponsor for a migrant.

[In Part 6A and Appendices A and J of these Rules, **"settled worker"** means a person who:

(i)   is a national of the UK,

(ii)   [is a person with a right of residence in accordance with the Immigration (European Economic Area) Regulations 2006 or, except where that person is subject to worker authorisation, the regulations made under section 2 of the European Union (Accessions) Act 2006 in combination with section 292) of the European Communities Act 1972 or the regulations made under section 4 of the European Union (Croation Accession and Irish Protocol) Act 2013,],

(iii)   . . .

(iv)   is a Commonwealth citizen with leave to enter or remain granted on the basis of UK Ancestry (paragraphs 186 to 193 of these Rules), or

(v)   has settled status in the UK within the meaning of the Immigration Act 1971, as amended by the Immigration and Asylum Act 1999, and the Nationality and Asylum Act 2002.]

Under Part 6A of these Rules, a reference to a **"sponsor licence"** means a licence granted by the Secretary of State to a person who, by virtue of such a grant, is licensed as a Sponsor under Tiers 2, 4 or 5 of the Points Based System.

Under Part 6A of these Rules, **"supplementary employment"** means [other employment in a job which appears on the Shortage Occupation List in Appendix K, or in the same profession and at the same professional level] as that which the migrant is being sponsored to do provided that:

(a)   the migrant remains working for the Sponsor in the employment that the Certificate of Sponsorship Checking Service records that the migrant is being sponsored to do,

(b)   the other employment does not exceed 20 hours per week and takes place outside of the hours when the migrant is contracted to work for the Sponsor in the employment the migrant is being sponsored to do.]

[Under part 6A and Appendix A of these Rules, **"overseas higher education institution"** means an institution which holds overseas accreditation confirmed by UK NARIC as offering degree programmes which are equivalent to UK degree level qualifications, and which teach no more than half of a degree programme in the UK as a study abroad programme.]

"Business person" means a migrant granted leave under paragraphs 200 to 208 of the Rules in force before 30th June 2008

"Investor" means a migrant granted leave under paragraphs 224 to 229 of the Rules in force before 30th June 2008.

"Self-employed Lawyer" means a migrant granted entry clearance, or leave to enter or remain, outside the Rules under the concession for Self-employed lawyers that formerly appeared in Chapter 6, Section 1 Annex D of the Immigration Directorate Instructions.

["**Points Based System Migrant**" means a migrant applying for granted leave as a Tier 1 Migrant, a Tier 2 Migrant, a Tier 4 Migrant or a Tier 5 Migrant;

"**Tier 1 Migrant**" means a migrant who is granted leave as a Tier 1 (Exceptional Talent) Migrant, a Tier 1 (General) Migrant, a Tier 1 (Entrepreneur) Migrant, a Tier 1 (Investor) Migrant, a Tier 1 (Graduate Entrepreneur) Migrant or a Tier 1 (Post-Study Work Migrant.

"**Tier 1 (Exceptional Talent) Migrant**" means a migrant who is granted leave under paragraphs 245B to 245BF of these Rules.

"**Tier 1 (General) Migrant**" means a migrant who is granted leave under paragraphs 245C to 245CE of these Rules.

"**Tier 1 (Entrepreneur) Migrant**" means a migrant who is granted leave under paragraphs 245D to 245DF of these Rules.

"**Tier 1 (Investor) Migrant**" means a migrant who is granted leave under paragraphs 245E to 245EF of these Rules.

"**Tier 1 (Graduate Entrepreneur) Migrant**" means a migrant who is granted leave under paragraphs 245F to 245FB of these Rules in place on or after 6 April 2012.

"**Tier 1 (Post-Study Work) Migrant**" means a migrant who is granted leave under paragraphs 245F to 245FE of these Rules in place before 6 April 2012.

"**Tier 2 Migrant**" means a migrant who is granted leave as a Tier 2 (Intra-Company Transfer) Migrant, a Tier 2 (General) Migrant, a Tier 2 (Minister of Religion) Migrant or a Tier 2 (Sportsperson) Migrant.

"**Tier 2 (Intra-Company Transfer) Migrant**" means a migrant granted leave under paragraphs 245G to 245GF of these Rules.

"**Tier 2 (General) Migrant**" means a migrant granted leave under paragraphs 245H to 245HF of these Rules and who obtains points under paragraphs 76 to 84A of Appendix A.

"**Tier 2 (Minister of Religion) Migrant**" means a migrant granted leave under paragraphs 245H to 245HF of these Rules and who obtains points under paragraphs 85 to 92 of Appendix A.

"**Tier 2 (Sportsperson) Migrant**" means a migrant granted leave under paragraphs 245H to 245HF of these Rules and who obtains points under paragraphs 93 to 100 of Appendix A.]

["Tier 4 (General) Student" means a migrant granted leave under paragraphs 245ZT to 245ZY of these Rules;

"Tier 4 (Child) Student" means a migrant granted leave under paragraphs 245ZZ to 245ZZD of these Rules;

"Tier 4 Migrant" means a Tier 4 (General) Student or a Tier 4 (Child) Student;]

["expected end date of a course leading to the award of a PhD" means the date the PhD is expected to be formally confirmed, by the sponsor, as completed to the standard required for the award of a PhD and recorded on the confirmation of acceptance for studies accompanying the application for leave to remain as a Tier 4 (General) Student on the doctorate extension scheme.]

"Tier 5 (Youth Mobility) Temporary Migrant" means a migrant granted leave under paragraphs 245ZI to 245ZL of these Rules.

"Tier 5 (Temporary Worker) Migrant" means a migrant granted leave under paragraphs 245ZM to [245ZS] of these Rules.

["deemed sponsorship status" means that the country or territory is not required to issue its nationals or passport holders with a Certificate of Sponsorship in order to enable a successful application under the Tier 5 Youth Mobility Scheme and is held by a country or territory listed as such at Appendix G of these Rules.]

"Tier 5 Migrant" means a migrant who is either a Tier 5 (Temporary Worker) Migrant or a Tier 5 (Youth Mobility) Temporary Migrant;

[Under Part 6A of these Rules **"Government Authorised Exchange Scheme"** means a scheme under the Tier 5 (Temporary Worker) Government Authorised Exchange sub-category which is endorsed by a Government Department in support of Government objectives and provides temporary work in an occupation which appears on the list of occupations skilled to National Qualifications Framework level 3, as stated in the codes of practice for Tier 2 Sponsors published by the UK Border Agency, and where the migrant will be supernumerary.

Under Part 6A of these Rules **"Work Experience Programme"** means work experience including volunteering and job-shadowing, internships and work exchange programmes under a Government Authorised Exchange Scheme.

Under Part 6A of these Rules **"Research Programme"** means research programmes and fellowships under a Government Authorised Exchange Scheme where the migrant is working on a scientific, academic, medical, or government research project/s at either a UK Higher Education Institution or another research institution operating under the authority and/or financial sponsorship of a relevant Government Department,

Under Part 6A of these Rules **"Training Programme"** means a training programme under a Government Authorised Exchange Scheme where the migrant either receives formal, practical training in the fields of science and/or medicine[, or will be trained by HM Armed Forces or by UK emergency services] or meets the requirements of paragraph 245ZQ(b)(vi)(2) to (4).

[Under Part 6A of these Rules **"Overseas Government Language Programme"** means an overseas Government sponsored professional language development programme under the Government Authorised Exchange Scheme where the migrant delivers language training and participates in a cultural exchange programme that is fully or partially paid for by the overseas government or an organisation affiliated to an overseas government.]

Under Part 6A of these Rules **"Temporary Engagement as a Sports Broadcaster"** means providing guest expert commentary on a particular sporting event.]

[**"Contractual Service Supplier"** means a migrant who is granted entry clearance, leave to enter or leave to remain under paragraphs 245ZP(e) and 245ZR(b)(ii)(3) of these Rules on the basis that the circumstances in which such leave is sought engage the United Kingdom's commitments in respect of contractual service suppliers under the relevant provisions of one of the agreements specified in paragraph 111(f)(i) of Appendix A of these Rules.]

[. . .]

[**"Independent Professional"** means a migrant who is granted entry clearance, leave to enter or leave to remain under paragraphs 245ZP(e) and 245ZR(b)(ii)(3) of these Rules on the basis that the circumstances in which such leave is sought engage the United Kingdom's commitments in respect of independent professionals under the relevant provisions of one of the agreements specified in paragraph 111(f)(i) of Appendix A of these Rules.]

"Jewish Agency Employee" means a migrant granted leave outside of these Rules under the concession that formerly appeared in Chapter 17 Section 5 Part 2 of the Immigration Directorate Instructions.

"Member of the Operational Ground Staff of an Overseas-owned Airline" means a migrant granted leave under paragraphs 178 to 185 of the Rules in force before 27 November 2008.

"Minister of Religion, Missionary or Member of a Religious Order" means a migrant granted leave under paragraphs 170 to 177A of the Rules in force before 27 November 2008.

"Overseas Qualified Nurse or Midwife" means a migrant granted leave under paragraphs 69M to 69R of the Rules in force before 27 November 2008.

"Participant in the Science and Engineering Graduates Scheme" means a migrant granted leave under paragraphs 135O to 135T of the Rules in force before 1 May 2007.

"Representative of an Overseas Newspaper, News Agency or Broadcasting Organisation" means a migrant granted leave under paragraphs 136 to 143 of the Rules in force before 27 November 2008.

"Student Union Sabbatical Officer" means a migrant granted leave under paragraphs 87A to 87F of the Rules in force before 27 November 2008.

"Working Holidaymaker" means a migrant granted leave under paragraphs 95 to 97 of the Rules in force before 27 November 2008.

[A **"visitor"** is a person granted leave to enter or remain in the UK under paragraphs 40-56Z, 75A-M or 82–87 of these Rules.]

A **"Business Visitor"** is a person granted leave to enter or remain in the UK under paragraphs 46G-46L, 75A-F or 75G-M of these Rules.

An **"Academic Visitor"** is a person who is from an overseas academic institution or who is highly qualified within his own field of expertise seeking leave to enter the UK to carry out research and associated activities for his own purposes.

A **"Visiting Professor"** is a person who is seeking leave to enter the UK as an academic professor to accompany students who are studying here on Study Abroad Programmes.

A **"Sports Visitor"** is a person granted leave to enter or remain in the UK under paragraphs 46M-46R of these Rules.

An **"Amateur"** is a person who engages in a sport or creative activity solely for personal enjoyment and who is not seeking to derive a living from the activity.

A **"Series of events"** is two or more linked events, such as a tour, or rounds of a competition, which do not add up to a league or a season.

An **"Entertainer Visitor"** is a person granted leave to enter or remain in the UK under paragraphs 46S-46X of these Rules.

A **"Special Visitor"** is a person granted leave for a short-term visit in the following circumstances:

(a)   A person granted leave to enter or remain in the UK as a visitor for private medical treatment under paragraphs 51 – 56 of these Rules

(b)   A person granted leave to enter or remain in the UK for the purpose of marriage or to enter into civil partnership under paragraphs 56D – 56F of these Rules

(c)   A person granted leave to enter or remain in the UK as a Parent of a child at school under paragraphs 56A – 56C of these Rules

(d)   A person granted leave to enter or remain in the UK as a Child Visitor under paragraphs 46A–46F of these Rules

(e)   A person granted leave to enter or remain in the UK as a Student Visitor under paragraphs 56K – 56M of these Rules

(f)   A person granted leave to enter or remain in the UK as a Prospective Student under paragraphs 82-87 of these Rules

(g)   A person granted leave to enter the UK as a Visitor in transit under paragraphs 47-50 of these Rules[, or

(h)   A person granted entry clearance, leave to enter or leave to remain in the UK as a Prospective Entrepreneur under paragraphs 56N – 56Q of these Rules.]

["**A visitor undertaking permitted paid engagements**" is someone who is granted leave to enter under paragraphs 56X-56Z of these Rules.]

. . .]

"**Writer, Composer or Artist**" means a migrant granted leave under paragraphs 232 to 237 of the Rules in force before 30th June 2008.

"In paragraph 320(7B) and paragraph 320(11) of these Rules:

"**Deception**" means making false representations or submitting false documents (whether or not material to the application), or failing to disclose material facts.

"**Illegal Entrant**" has the same definition as in section 33(1) of the Immigration Act 1971.

[In paragraph 320(22) and 322(12) of these Rules and in paragraphs S-EC.2.3., S-LTR.2.3. and S-ILR 2.3 of Appendix FM to these Rules.

["**relevant NHS Body**" means

(a)   in relation to England-
   (i)   a National Health Service Trust established under section 26 of the National Health Service Act 2006,
   (ii)   a NHS foundation trust.
(b)   in relation to Wales-
   (i)   a Local Health Board established under section 11 of the National Health Service Act 2006,
   (ii)   a National Health Service Trust established under section 18 of the National Health Service (Wales) Act 2006,
   (iii)   a Special Health Authority established under 22 of the National Health Service (Wales) Act 2006.
(c)   in relation to Scotland-
   (i)   a Health Board or Special Health Board established under section 2 of the National Health Service (Scotland) Act 1978 (c. 29),
   (ii)   the Commons Services Agency for the Scottish Health Service established under section 10 of that Act,
   (iii)   Healthcare Improvement Scotland established under section 10A of that Act.
(d)   in relation to Northern Ireland-
   (i)   the Regional Health and Social Care Board established under the Health and Social Care (Reform) Act (Northern Ireland) 2009
   (ii)   a Health and Social Care trust established under the Health and Personal Social Services (Northern Ireland) Order 1991 (S.I. 1991/194) (N.I. 1)) and renamed under the Health and Social Care (Reform) Act (Northern Ireland) 2009

"**relevant NHS regulations**" means

(i)   The National Health Service (Charges to Overseas Visitors) (Amendment) (Wales) Regulations 2004 (2004 No 1433):

(ii)   The National Health Service (Charges to Overseas Visitors) (Scotland) Regulations 1989 as amended (1989 No 364);

(iii)   The Health and Personal Social Services (Provision of Health Services to Persons not Ordinarily Resident) Regulations 2005 (2005 No 551); or

(iv)   The National Health Service (Charges to Overseas Visitors) Regulations (2011 No 1556).]

"administrative review" means a review conducted in accordance with Appendix AR of these Rules;

"eligible decision" means a decision eligible for administrative review as referred to in paragraph AR3.2 of Appendix AR of these Rules;

"working day" means a business day in the part of the UK in which the applicant resides or (as the case may be) is detained.

[. . .]

Note

Word "or" deleted by HC 693, para 1 as from 20 October 2014. Amended by HC 693, para 2 as from 6 November 2014. Amended by HC 693, para 3 as from 6 November 2014. Amended by HC 693, para 4 as from 6 November 2014. Amended by HC 693, para 5 as from 6 November 2014. Amended by HC 693, para 6 as from 6 November 2014, save that if an application has been made for entry clearance or leave to enter or remain before 6 November 2014, the application will be decided in accordance with the Rules in force on 5 November 2014. Amended by HC 693, para 7 as from 20 October 2014.

6A.   [For the purpose of these Rules, a person (P) is not to be regarded as having (or potentially having) recourse to public funds merely because P is (or will be) reliant in whole or in part on public funds provided to P's sponsor unless, as a result of P's presence in the United Kingdom, the sponsor is (or would be) entitled to increased or additional public funds (save where such entitlement to increased or additional public funds is by virtue of P and the sponsor's joint entitlement to benefits under the regulations referred to in paragraph 6B).

6B.   Subject to paragraph 6C, a person (P) shall not be regarded as having recourse to public funds if P is entitled to benefits specified under section 115 of the Immigration and Asylum Act 1999 by virtue of regulations made under sub-sections (3) and (4) of that section or section 42 of the Tax Credits Act 2002.

6C.   A person (P) making an application from outside the United Kingdom will be regarded as having recourse to public funds where P relies upon the future entitlement to any public funds that would be payable to P or to P's sponsor as a result of P's presence in the United Kingdom, (including those benefits to which P or the sponsor would be entitled as a result of P's presence in the United Kingdom under the regulations referred to in paragraph (6B).]

Note

Frequent amendments to this paragraph makes it important to note the following. Before 4 April 1996 the definition covered: housing under the Housing Act 1985; income support family credit, council tax benefit and housing benefit. After 3 April 1996, HC 329 added: attendance allowance, severe disablement allowance, invalid care allowance, disability living allowance, disability working allowance. The position (as at March 1997) is that since 30 October 1996 HC 31 has added child benefit. It also replaces income support with income-based jobseeker's allowance (JSA). This definition does not include contributions-based JSA. The definition of 'visa national' was amended with effect from 11 May 1998 (Cmnd 3953). On each occasion the definitions have included the equivalent provisions under legislation for Scotland and Northern Ireland. Words in square brackets beginning 'the 2000 EEA Regulations' substituted by Cmnd 4851. Definition of 'family member' omitted by CM 4851. Words in square brackets beginning 'the Human Rights Convention' inserted by Cmnd 4851. Definition of 'Department of Employment' following definition of 'public funds' deleted by Cmnd 5253. Definitions of 'EEA National', 'Immigration employment document' and 'Public funds' inserted by Cmnd 5597. In definition 'Public funds' words in square brackets inserted and words deleted by HC 346. Definition of 'adoption' inserted and sub-paragraph (d) in definition of 'a parent' substituted by HC 538. Definitions of 'intention to live permanently with the other' and 'present and settled' inserted by HC 538. Definition of 'specified national' inserted by HC 1224. Definition of 'Accession State national' inserted by HC 523. Definition of 'degree level study' inserted and definition of 'sponsor' substituted by Cm 6339. Inserted by HC 346. Definition of 'Approved Destination Status Agreement with China' inserted by HC 486. Definitions of 'a bona fide private education institution' and 'an external student' inserted by Cm 7074. Definition 'employment' amended by HC 40. Definitions for 'Businessperson', 'Investor', 'Self-employed Lawyer', 'Tier 1 (General) Migrant', Tier 1 (Entrepreneur) Migrant', Tier 1 (Investor) Migrant', Tier 1 (Post-Study Work) Migrant' and 'Worker, Composer or Artist' inserted by HC 607. Paragraphs (6A)-(6C) substituted by HC 314. Definition 'foundation degree' inserted by HC 367, para 1 as from 3 March 2010; words in square brackets substituted by HC 439, para 1 as from 6 April 2010. Definitions 'UK recognised body' and 'UK listed body' inserted by HC 439, para 2 as from 6 April 2010. Definition 'Employment as a Doctor or Dentist in Training' inserted by HC 439, para 3 as from 6 April 2010. Definition 'Highly Trusted Sponsor' inserted by HC 439, para 4 as from 6 April 2010. Definition 'relevant grant allocation period' and 'grant allocation' inserted by HC 59, para 1 as from 19 July 2010. Amended by Cm 7944, paras 1–2 as from 22 October 2010. 'Tier 2 Interim Limit' and 'Exceptional Consideration Process' inserted by HC 698, para 1 as from 21 December 2010. Definitions 'length of the period of engagement', 'working for the same employer', 'Designated Competent Body', 'Removal Decision' and Pending appeal inserted by HC 863, para 1 as from 6 April 2011. Definition of 'Established Entertainer' amended by HC 863, para 2 as from 6 April 2011. Definition of 'Senior Care Worker' amended by HC 863, para 3 as from 6 April 2011. Definition of 'Special Visitor' amended by HC 863, paras 4 and 5 as from 6 April 2011. Definitions of 'B-Rated Sponsor' and 'Confirmation of Acceptance for Studies' by HC 908, paras 1 and 2 as from 21 April 2011. Further amended by HC 1148, paras 1 and 2 as from 4 July 2011. Further amended by HC 1436, para 1 as from 9 August 2011. Further amended by HC 1511, para 1 as from 31 October 2011. "Relevant NHS body" and "relevant NHS regulations" inserted by HC 1511, para 2 as from 31 October 2011. "Deemed sponsorship status" inserted by HC 1693, para 1 as from 1 January 2012. Further amended by HC 194, para 1 as from 9 July 2012. Further amended by Cm 8423, paras 1–3 as from 20 July 2012. Further amended by HC 565, paras 1–4 as from 6 September 2012. Further amended by HC 760, paras 1–5 as from 13 December 2012. Further amended by HC 1038, para 1 as from 1 April 2013 and HC 1039, paras 1–3: where an applicant has made an application for entry clearance or leave before 6 April 2013 and the application has not been decided before that date, it will be decided in accordance with the rules in force on 5 April 2013. Further amended by HC 244, para 1 as from 1 July 2013. Further amended by HC 628, paras 1, 2 and if applicant has made an application for entry clearance or leave before 1 October 2012, the application will be decided in accordance with the Rules in force on 30 September 2013. Further amended by HC 803, paras 1 and 2 as from 1 December 2013. Further amended by HC 1138, para 1 shall apply to all applications decided on or after 6 April 2014. Amended by HC 1138, para 2 as from 6 April 2014. Further amended by HC 1138, para 3 as from 6 April 2014. Amended by HC 1138, para 3 as from 6 April 2014. Amended by HC 1138, para 4 as from 6 April 2014. Amended by HC 1138, para 5 as from 6 April 2014. Amended by HC 1138, para 6 as from 6 April 2014. Deleted by HC 1138, para 7 as from 6 April 2014.

PART 1 — GENERAL PROVISIONS REGARDING LEAVE TO ENTER OR REMAIN IN THE UNITED KINGDOM

Leave to enter the United Kingdom

7.   [A person who is neither a British citizen nor a Commonwealth citizen with the right of abode nor a person who is entitled to enter or remain in the United Kingdom by virtue of the provisions of the 2006 EEA Regulations requires leave to enter the United Kingdom.]

Note

Substituted by CM 4851.

8.   [Under Sections 3 and 4 of the Immigration Act 1971 an Immigration Officer when admitting to the United Kingdom a person subject to control under that Act may give leave to enter for a limited period and, if he does, may impose all or any of the following conditions:

(i)   a condition restricting employment or occupation in the United Kingdom;

(ii)   a condition requiring the person to maintain and accommodate himself, and any dependants of his, without recourse to public funds; and

(iii)   a condition requiring the person to register with the police.

He may also require him to report to the appropriate Medical Officer of Environmental Health. Under Section 24 of the 1971 Act it is an offence knowingly to remain beyond the time limit or to fail to comply with such a condition or requirement.]

9. [The time limit and any conditions attached will normally be made known to the person concerned:

(i)   by written notice given to him or endorsed by the Immigration Officer in his passport or travel document; or

(ii)   in any other manner permitted by the Immigration (Leave to Enter and Remain) Order 2000.]

Note

Paragraph 9 substituted by HC 704.

[Exercise of the power to refuse leave to enter the United Kingdom or to cancel leave to enter or remain which is in force]

10. The power to refuse leave to enter the United Kingdom [or to cancel leave to enter or remain which is already in force] is not to be exercised by an Immigration Officer acting on his own. The authority of a Chief Immigration Officer or of an Immigration Inspector must always be obtained.

[Suspension of leave to enter or remain in the United Kingdom

10A. Where a person has arrived in the United Kingdom with leave to enter or remain which is in force but which was given to him before his arrival he may be examined by an Immigration Officer under paragraph 2A of Schedule 2 to the Immigration Act 1971. An Immigration Officer examining a person under paragraph 2A may suspend that person's leave to enter or remain in the United Kingdom until the examination is completed.

Cancellation of leave to enter or remain in the United Kingdom

10B. Where a person arrived in the United Kingdom with leave to enter or remain in the United Kingdom which is already in force, an Immigration Officer may cancel that leave.]

Note

Sub-heading of paragraph 10 substituted, words in square brackets in para 10 inserted and paragraphs 10A and B inserted by HC 704.

Requirement for persons arriving in the United Kingdom or seeking entry through the Channel Tunnel to produce evidence of identity and nationality

11. A person must, on arrival in the United Kingdom or when seeking entry through the Channel Tunnel, produce on request by the Immigration Officer:

(i)   a valid national passport or other document satisfactorily establishing his identity and nationality; and

(ii)   such information as may be required to establish whether he requires leave to enter the United Kingdom and, if so, whether and on what terms leave to enter should be given.

Note

See *MC (Gambia)* [2008] UKAIT 00030.

This para reproduces the powers of Immigration Officers contained in the Immigration Act 1971, Sch 2, para 4.

Requirement for a person not requiring leave to enter the United Kingdom to prove that he has the right of abode

12. A person claiming to be a British citizen must prove that he has the right of abode in the United Kingdom by producing either:

(i)   a United Kingdom passport describing him as a British citizen or as a citizen of the United Kingdom and Colonies having the right of abode in the United Kingdom; or

(ii)   a certificate of entitlement duly issued by or on behalf of the Government of the United Kingdom certifying that he has the right of abode.

Note

This para reproduces the requirements of the Immigration Act 1971, s 3(9) as substituted by the British Nationality Act 1981 and the Immigration Act 1988.

13. A person claiming to be a Commonwealth citizen with the right of abode in the United Kingdom must prove that he has the right of abode by producing a certificate of entitlement duly issued to him by or on behalf of the Government of the United Kingdom certifying that he has the right of abode.

14. A Commonwealth citizen who has been given limited leave to enter the United Kingdom may later claim to have the right of abode. The time limit on his stay may be removed if he is able to establish a claim to the right of abode, for example by showing that:

(i)   immediately before the commencement of the British Nationality Act 1981 he was a Commonwealth citizen born to or legally adopted by a parent who at the time of his birth had citizenship of the United Kingdom and Colonies by his birth in the United Kingdom or any of the Islands; and

(ii)   he has not ceased to be a Commonwealth citizen in the meanwhile.

Note

An application for a certificate can be made to the UKBA in the UK or to an ECO. See the Immigration Directorate Instructions on the Right of Abode in Chapter 1, Section 1, at: www.bia. homeoffice.gov.uk/sitecontent/documents/policyandlaw/IDIs/idischapter1

and *R v Secretary of State for the Home Department, ex p Phansopkar* [1976] QB 606, [1975] All ER 497, CA.

Common Travel Area

15. The United Kingdom, the Channel Islands, the Isle of Man and the Republic of Ireland collectively form a common travel area. A person who has been examined for the purpose of immigration control at the point at which he entered the area does not normally require leave to enter any other part of it. However certain persons subject to the Immigration (Control of Entry through the Republic of Ireland) Order 1972 (as amended) who enter the United Kingdom through the Republic of Ireland do require leave to enter. This includes:

(i)   those who merely passed through the Republic of Ireland;
(ii)   persons requiring visas;
(iii)   persons who entered the Republic of Ireland unlawfully;
(iv)   persons who are subject to directions given by the Secretary of State for their exclusion from the United Kingdom on the ground that their exclusion is conducive to the public good;
(v)   persons who entered the Republic from the United Kingdom and Islands after entering there unlawfully or overstaying their leave.

Note

See the Immigration Directorate Instructions on the Common Travel Area in Chapter 1, Section 2, at: www.bia.homeoffice.gov.uk/sitecontent/documents/policyandlaw/IDIs/idischapter1

Admission of certain British passport holders

16. A person in any of the following categories may be admitted freely to the United Kingdom on production of a United Kingdom passport issued in the United Kingdom and Islands or the Republic of Ireland prior to 1 January 1973, unless his passport has been endorsed to show that he was subject to immigration control:

(i)   a British Dependent Territories citizen;
(ii)   a British National (Overseas);
(iii)   a British Overseas citizen;
(iv)   a British protected person;
(v)   a British subject by virtue of Section 30(a) of the British Nationality Act 1981, (who, immediately before the commencement of the 1981 Act, would have been a British subject not possessing citizenship of the United Kingdom and Colonies or the citizenship of any other Commonwealth country or territory).

17. British Overseas citizens who hold United Kingdom passports wherever issued and who satisfy the Immigration Officer that they have, since 1 March 1968, been given indefinite leave to enter or remain in the United Kingdom may be given indefinite leave to enter.

[Persons outside the United Kingdom

17A. Where a person is outside the United Kingdom but wishes to travel to the United Kingdom an Immigration Officer may give or refuse him leave to enter. An Immigration Officer may exercise these powers whether or not he is, himself, in the United Kingdom. However, an Immigration Officer is not obliged to consider an application for leave to enter from a person outside the United Kingdom.

17B. Where a person, having left the common travel area, has leave to enter the United Kingdom which remains in force under article 13 of the Immigration (Leave to Enter and Remain) Order 2000, an Immigration Officer may cancel that leave. An Immigration Officer mat exercise these powers whether or not he is, himself, in the United Kingdom. If a person outside the United Kingdom has leave to remain in the United Kingdom which is in force in this way, the Secretary of State may cancel that leave.]

Note

Paragraphs 17A and 17B inserted by HC 704.

Returning Residents

18. A person seeking leave to enter the United Kingdom as a returning resident may be admitted for settlement provided the Immigration Officer is satisfied that the person concerned:

(i)   had indefinite leave to enter or to remain in the United Kingdom when he last left; and
(ii)   has not been away from the United Kingdom for more than 2 years; and
(iii)   did not receive assistance from public funds towards the cost of leaving the United Kingdom; and
(iv)   now seeks admission for the purpose of settlement.

19 A person who does not benefit from the preceding paragraph by reason only of having been away from the United Kingdom too long may nevertheless be admitted as a returning resident if, for example, he has lived here for most of his life.

19A. [Where a person who has indefinite leave to enter or remain in the United Kingdom accompanies, on a tour of duty abroad, a spouse, civil partner, unmarried partner or same-sex partner who is a member of HM Forces serving overseas, or a permanent member of HM Diplomatic Service, or a comparable United Kingdom-based staff member of the British Council, or a staff member of the Department for International Development who is a British Citizen or is settled in the United Kingdom, sub-paragraphs (ii) and (iii) of paragraph 18 shall not apply.]

General note

See the Immigration Directorate Instructions at Chapter 1, Section 3 (including annexes K–O) for case working instructions on returning residents, including for those residents who have been outside the country for more than two years: www.ukba.homeoffice.gov.uk/sitecontent/documents/policyandlaw/IDIs/idischapter1 /section1/section1.pdf?view=Binary.

Note

Substituted by Cm 5597.

20.   The leave of a person whose stay in the United Kingdom is subject to a time limit lapses on his going to a country or territory outside the common travel area [if the leave was given for a period of six months or less or conferred by a visit visa. In other cases, leave lapses on the holder remaining outside the United Kingdom for a continuous period of more than two years]. [A person whose leave has lapsed and] who returns after a temporary absence abroad within the period of this earlier leave has no claim to admission as a returning resident. His application to re-enter the United Kingdom should be considered in the light of all the relevant circumstances. The same time limit and any conditions attached will normally be reimposed if he meets the requirements of these Rules, unless he is seeking admission in a different capacity from the one in which he was last given leave to enter or remain.

Note

Words in first set of square brackets in paragraph 20 inserted and those in second set of square brackets substituted by HC 704.

[Non-lapsing leave

20A.   Leave to enter or remain in the United Kingdom will usually lapse on the holder going to a country or territory outside the common travel area. However, under article 13 of the Immigration (Leave to Enter and Remain) Order 2000 such leave will not lapse where it was given for a period exceeding six months or where it was conferred by means of an entry clearance (other than a visit visa).]

Note

Inserted by HC 704.

Holders of restricted travel documents and passports

21.   The leave to enter or remain in the United Kingdom of the holder of a passport or travel document whose permission to enter another country has to be exercised before a given date may be restricted so as to terminate at least 2 months before that date.

22.   If his passport or travel document is endorsed with a restriction on the period for which he may remain outside his country of normal residence, his leave to enter or remain in the United Kingdom may be limited so as not to extend beyond the period of authorised absence.

23.   The holder of a travel document issued by the Home Office should not be given leave to enter or remain for a period extending beyond the validity of that document. This paragraph and paragraphs 21–22 do not apply to a person who is eligible for admission for settlement or to a spouse or civil partner who is eligible for admission under paragraph 282 or to a person who qualifies for the removal of the time limit on his stay.

Leave to enter granted on arrival in the United Kingdom

23A.   [A person who is not a visa national and who is seeking leave to enter on arrival in the United Kingdom for a period not exceeding 6 months for a purpose for which prior entry clearance is not required under these Rules may be granted such leave, for a period not exceeding 6 months. This paragraph does not apply where the person is a British National (Overseas), a British overseas territories citizen, a British Overseas citizen, a British protected person, or a person who under the British Nationality Act 1981 is a British subject].

23B. A person who is a British National (Overseas), a British overseas territories citizen, a British Overseas citizen, a British protected person, or a person who under the British Nationality Act 1981 is a British subject, and who is seeking leave to enter on arrival in the United Kingdom for a purpose for which prior entry clearance is not required under these Rules may be granted such leave, irrespective of the period of time for which he seeks entry, for a period not exceeding 6 months.

Note

Paragraph 23A inserted by HC 1224, para 2 as from 13 November 2003.

Entry clearance

24. The following must produce to the Immigration Officer a valid passport or other identity document endorsed with a United Kingdom entry clearance issued to him for the purpose for which he seeks entry:

(i)   a visa national;
(ii)   any other person (other than British Nationals (Overseas), a British overseas territories citizen, a British Overseas citizen, a British protected person or a person who under the British Nationality Act 1981 is a British subject) who is seeking entry for a period exceeding six months or is seeking entry for a purpose for which prior entry clearance is required under these Rules.

Such a person will be refused leave to enter if he has no such current entry clearance. Any other person who wishes to ascertain in advance whether he is eligible for admission to the United Kingdom may apply for the issue of an entry clearance.

Note

For a current list of visa countries, see Appendix 1 of the Immigration Rules.

25. Entry clearance takes the form of a visa (for visa nationals) or an entry certificate (for non-visa nationals). These documents are to be taken as evidence of the holder's eligibility for entry into the United Kingdom, and accordingly accepted as "entry clearances" within the meaning of the Immigration Act 1971.

25A [An entry clearance which satisfies the requirements set out in article 3 of the Immigration (Leave to Enter and Remain) Order 2000 will have effect as leave to enter the United Kingdom. The requirements are that the entry clearance must specify the purpose for which the holder wants to enter the United Kingdom and should be endorsed with the conditions to which it is subject or with a statement that it has effect as indefinite leave to enter the United Kingdom. The holder of such an entry clearance will not require leave to enter on arrival in the United Kingdom and, for the purposes of the Rules, will be treated as a person who has arrived in the United Kingdom with leave to enter the United Kingdom which is in force but which was given to him before his arrival.]

Note

Words in square brackets in para 24 inserted by HC 1224. Paragraph 25A inserted by HC 704.

26. An application for entry clearance will be considered in accordance with the provisions in these Rules governing the grant or refusal of leave to enter. Where appropriate, the term "Entry Clearance Officer" should be substituted for "Immigration Officer".

27. An application of entry clearance is to be decided in the light of the circumstances existing at the time of the decision, except that an applicant will not be refused an entry clearance where entry is sought in one of the categories contained in paragraphs 296–316 [or paragraph EC-C of Appendix FM] solely on account of his attaining the age of 18 years between receipt of his application and the date of the decision on it.

Note

As to the position in relation to applications for leave to remain, see the Immigration Directorate Instructions at Chapter 8, Section 5a, Annex M at paragraph 2.3: www.ukba.homeoffice.gov.uk/

Note

Paragraphs 32 and 33 deleted by HC 321, para 2 as from 29 February 2008.

Paragraph 33B-33G deleted by HC 628, para 3.

Specified forms and procedures for applications or claims in connection with immigration

A34. [An application for leave to remain in the United Kingdom . . . under . . . these Rules . . . must be made either by completing the relevant online application process in accordance with paragraph A34 (iii) or by using the specified application form in accordance with paragraphs 34A to 34D.

(i) "The relevant online application process" means the application process accessible via the [visas and immigration pages of the gov.uk] website and identified there as relevant for applications for leave to remain [for the immigration category under which the applicant wishes to apply].

(ii) "Specified" in relation to the relevant online application process means specified in the online guidance accompanying that process.

(iii) When the application is made via the relevant online application process:

    (a) any specified fee in connection with the application must be paid in accordance with the method specified;

    (b) if the online application process requires the applicant to provide biometric information that information must be provided as specified;

    (c) if the online application process requires supporting documents to be submitted by post then any such documents specified as mandatory must be submitted in the specified manner within 15 working days of submission of the online application;

    (d) if the online application process requires the applicant to make an appointment to attend a public enquiry office of the United Kingdom Border Agency the applicant must, within 45 working days of submission of the online application, make and attend that appointment; and comply with any specified requirements in relation to the provision of biometric information and documents specified as mandatory.]

Note

Paragraph A34 inserted by HC 1733, para 1 as from 13 February 2012. Further amended by HC 760, paras 6–8 as from 13 December 2012. Amended by HC 1138, para 9 as from 6 April 2014. Deleted by HC 693, para 8 as from 6 November 2014, save that if an application has been made for entry clearance or leave to enter or remain before 6 November 2014, the application will be decided in accordance with the Rules in force on 5 November 2014.

34. An application form is specified when:

(i) it is posted on the [visas and immigration pages of the gov.uk] website,

(ii) it is marked on the form that it is a specified form for the purpose of the immigration rules,

(iii) it comes into force on the date specified on the form and/or in any accompanying announcement.

Note

Amended by HC 1138, para 10 as from 6 April 2014.

34A. [Subject to paragraph A34] where an application form is specified, the application or claim must also comply with the following requirements:

(i) the application or claim must be made using the specified form,

(ii) any specified fee in connection with the application or claim must be paid in accordance with the method specified in the application form, separate payment form and/or related guidance notes, as applicable,

(iii) any section of the form which is designated as mandatory in the application form and/or related guidance notes must be completed as specified,

(iv)   if the application form and/or related guidance notes require the applicant to provide [biometric] . . . information, such information must be provided as specified,

(v)   an appointment for the purposes stated in subparagraph (iv) must be made and must take place by the dates specified in any subsequent notification by the Secretary of State following receipt of the application, or as agreed by the Secretary of State,

(vi)   where the application or claim is made by post or courier, or submitted in person:

    (a)   the application or claim must be accompanied by the photographs and documents specified as mandatory in the application form and/or related guidance notes, . . .

        [(ab)   those photographs must be in the same format specified as mandatory in the application form and/or related guidance notes, and]

    (b)   the form must be signed by the applicant, and where applicable, the applicant's spouse, civil partner, same-sex partner or unmarried partner, save that where the applicant is under the age of eighteen, the form may be signed by the parent or legal guardian of the applicant on his behalf.

Note

Words in sub-paragraph (i) inserted by HC 1733, para 2 as from 13 February 2012. Sub-paragraph (vii) omitted by HC 1733, para 3 as from 13 February 2012. Amended by HC 693, para 9 as from 6 November 2014, save that if an application has been made for entry clearance or leave to enter or remain before 6 November 2014, the application will be decided in accordance with the Rules in force on 5 November 2014.

34B. [Where an application form is specified, it must be sent by prepaid post to the Home Office at the address specified on the application form for such purposes, or submitted in person at a Home Office premium service centre. Application types permitted in person at a Home Office premium service centre are listed on the visa and immigration pages of the gov.uk website.]

[(i)]   an application may be sent by courier to the ... Home Office [at the address specified on the application form for such purposes] if it is an application for:

    (a)   limited or indefinite leave to remain as a sole representative, retired person of independent means, or as a [Tier 1 (Migrant or Tier 2 Migrant];

    (b)   limited leave to remain for work permit employment, as a seasonal agricultural worker, for the purpose of employment under the Sectors-Based Scheme . . . ,

    (c)   Indefinite leave to remain as a businessperson, investor or innovator [, or

    [(d)   limited leave to remain as a Tier 5 (Temporary Worker) Migrant.]

[[(ii)]   an applicant may submit an application online where this option is available on the [visas and immigration pages of the gov.uk] website.]

[(iii)]   an application must not be sent by pre-paid post, and must not be made online if it is an application for a Tier 2, Tier 4 or Tier 5 (Temporary Worker) Sponsorship licence.

Note

Words "Subject to paragraph 34" inserted by HC 1733, para 2 as from 13 February 2012. Words in square brackets and words omitted by HC 607. Words 'United Kingdom Border Agency' substituted by HC 1113, para 4 as from 27 November 2008. Words in 34A 'or biometric' in sub-paragaph (iv) deleted by HC 1113, para 5 as from 25 November 2008. Sub-paragraphs 34(vi)(ab) and 34(vii)(ab) inserted by HC 1113, paras 7, 9 as from 25 November 2008. Words deleted in para 34B(i)(a) by HC 314 as from 31 March 2009. Paragraph (ba) inserted by HC 314 as from 31 March 2009. Words in sub-para (i)(ba) substituted by HC 1888, para 7 as from 6 April 2012. Paragraph (i)(f) inserted by HC 120, para 1 as from 1 January 2010. Paragraph (iv) amended by Cm 7944, para 3 as from 22 October 2010. Paragraph (vii) deleted by HC 1733, para 3 as from 13 February 2012. Further amended by HC 1039, paras 4–6: where an applicant has made an application for entry clearance or leave before 6 April 2013 and the application has not been decided before that date, it will be decided in accordance with the Rules in force on 5 April 2013. Amended by HC 1138, para 11 as from 6 April 2014. Amended by HC 693, para 10 as from 6 November 2014, save that if an application has been made for entry clearance or leave to enter or remain before 6 November 2014, the application will be decided in accordance with the Rules in force on 5 November 2014. Deleted by HC 693, para 11 as from 6 November 2014, save that if an application has been made for entry clearance or leave to enter or remain before 6 November 2014, the application will be decided in accordance with the Rules in force on 5 November 2014. Word "United Kingdom Border Agency of the" deleted by HC 693, para 12 as from 6 November 2014, save that if an application has been made for entry clearance or leave to enter or remain before 6 November 2014, the application will be decided in accordance with the Rules in force on 5 November 2014. Amended by HC 693, para 12 as from 6 November 2014, save that if an application has been made for entry clearance or leave to enter or remain before 6 November 2014, the application will be decided in accordance with the Rules in force on 5 November 2014. Sub-paragraphs (ii), (iii) and (iv) renumbered as (i), (ii) and (iii) by HC 693, para 13 as from 6 November 2014, save that if an application has been made for entry clearance or leave to enter or remain before 6 November 2014, the application will be decided in accordance with the Rules in force on 5 November 2014.

[34C. Where an application or claim in connection with immigration for which an application form is specified does not comply with the requirements in paragraph 34A, or where an application for leave to remain in the United Kingdom is made by completing the relevant online application process, and does not comply with the requirements of paragraph A34(iii), the following provisions apply:
(a) Subject to sub-paragraph (b), the application will be invalid if it does not comply with the relevant requirements of A34(iii) or 34A, as applicable, and will not be considered. Notice of invalidity will be given in writing and deemed to be received on the date it is given, except where it is sent by post, in which case it will be deemed to be received on the second day after it was posted excluding any day which is not a business day, unless the contrary is proved.
(b) The decision maker may contact the applicant or their representative in writing and give the applicant a single opportunity to correct any omission or error which renders the application invalid. The amended application and/or any requested documents must be received at the address specified in the request within 10 business days of the date on which the request was sent.]

Note

Words in square brackets inserted by HC 194, para 3 as from 9 July 2012. Substituted by HC 693, para 14 as from 6 November 2014, save that if an application has been made for entry clearance or leave to enter or remain before 6 November 2014, the application will be decided in accordance with the Rules in force on 5 November 2014.

34D. Where the main applicant wishes to include applications or claims by any members of his family as his dependants on his own application form, the applications or claims of the dependants must meet the following requirements or they will be invalid and will not be considered:
(i) the application form must expressly permit the applications or claims of dependants to be included, and
[(ii) such dependants must be:
(a) the spouse, civil partner, unmarried or same-sex partner of the main applicant; and/or
(b) children of the main applicant aged under 18; and/or
(c) where permitted by the Rules for the immigration category under which the applicant wishes to apply, any dependants of the main applicant aged 18 or over.]

Note

Para 34CA deleted. Paras 34A–D: For the general position on the effect of non-compliance with procedural requirements, see *R v Immigration Appeal Tribunal, ex p Jeyeanthan; Ravichandran v Secretary of State for the Home Department* [1999] 3 All ER 231, [2000] Imm AR 10; [2000] INLR 241 for UKBA guidance on prescribed forms and procedures see: www.ukba.homeoffice. gov.uk/sitecontent/documents/policyandlaw/modernised/applications/specified-forms-procedures. pdf?view=Binary; see also the General note on Part 6A of the Rules. Amended by HC 693, para 15 as from 6 November 2014, save that if an application has been made for entry clearance or leave to enter or remain before 6 November 2014, the application will be decided in accordance with the Rules in force on 5 November 2014.

Variation of Applications or Claims for Leave to Remain

34E. If a person wishes to vary the purpose of an application or claim for leave to remain in the United Kingdom and an application form is specified for such new purpose[, or paragraph A34 applies,], the variation must comply with the requirements of paragraph 34A [or paragraph A34] (as they apply at the date the variation is made) as if the variation were a new application or claim, or the variation will be invalid and will not be considered.

Note

Words in square brackets inserted by HC 1733, para 5 as from 13 February 2012.

34F. Any valid variation of a leave to remain application will be decided in accordance with the immigration rules in force at the date such variation is made.

Determination of the date of an application or claim (or variation of an application or claim) in connection with immigration

34G. For the purposes of these rules, the date on which an application or claim (or a variation in accordance with paragraph 34E) is made is as follows:
(i)   where the application form is sent by post, the date of posting,
(ii)   where the application form is submitted in person, the date on which it is accepted by a ... Home Office [premium service centre],
(iii) where the application form is sent by courier, the date on which it is delivered to the ... Home Office, or
(iv) [where the application is made via the online application process, on the date on which the online application is submitted.]

Note

Sub-paragraph (iv) substituted by HC 1733, para 6 as from 13 February 2012. Word "public enquiry office of the United Kingdom Border Agency of the" deleted by HC 693, para 16 as from 6 November 2014, save that if an application has been made for entry clearance or leave to enter or remain before 6 November 2014, the application will be decided in accordance with the Rules in force on 5 November 2014. Amended by HC 693, para 16 as from 6 November 2014, save that if an application has been made for entry clearance or leave to enter or remain before 6 November 2014, the application will be decided in accordance with the Rules in force on 5 November 2014. Word "United Kingdom Border Agency of the" deleted by HC 693, para 17 as from 6 November 2014, save that if an application has been made for entry clearance or leave to enter or remain before 6 November 2014, the application will be decided in accordance with the Rules in force on 5 November 2014.

34H. Applications or claims for leave to remain made before 29 February 2008 for which a form was prescribed prior to 29 February 2008 shall be subject to the forms and procedures as in force on the date on which the application or claim was made.

34I. Where an application or claim is made no more than 21 days after the date on which a form is specified under the immigration rules and on a form that was permitted for such application or claim immediately prior to the date of such specification, the application or claim shall be deemed to have been made on the specified form.

Note

Words deleted by Cmnd 4851. Paragraphs 34-34J substituted by HC 321. Paragraph 34G: words "United Kingdom Border Agency" substituted by HC 1113.

Withdrawn applications and claims for leave to remain in the United Kingdom

34J. Where a person whose application or claim for leave to remain is being considered requests the return of his passport for the purpose of travel outside the common travel area, the application for leave shall, provided it has not already been determined, be treated as withdrawn as soon as the passport is returned in response to that request.

34K. [Paragraph 34J does not apply to an applicant who is applying as a Tier 2 Migrant or a Tier 5 Migrant and whose application is supported by a Certificate of Sponsorship from a Premium Sponsor.]

Note

Paragraph 34K inserted by HC 1888, para 8 as from 6 April 2012.

[Specified forms and procedures in connection with applications for administrative review

Notice of an eligible decision

34L.

(1)   Unless sub-paragraph (2) applies, written notice must be given to a person of any eligible decision. The notice given must:
  (a)   include or be accompanied by a statement of reasons for the decision to which it relates, and
  (b)   include information on how to apply for an administrative review and the time limit for making an application.
(2)   Sub-paragraph (1) does not apply where the eligible decision is a grant of leave to remain.

Note

Inserted by HC 693, para 18 as from 20 October 2014.

Making an application

34M.

(1)   Unless sub-paragraph (2) applies only one valid application for administrative review may be made in respect of an eligible decision.
(2)   A further application for administrative review in respect of an eligible decision may be made where the outcome of the administrative review is as set out in paragraph AR2.2(d) of Appendix AR of these Rules.

Note

Inserted by HC 693, para 18 as from 20 October 2014.

34N.   An application for administrative review must be made in accordance with the requirements set out in paragraphs 34O to 34S. If it is not it will be invalid and will not be considered.

Note

Inserted by HC 693, para 18 as from 20 October 2014.

34O.   The application must be made in accordance with paragraph 34U or paragraph 34V.

Note

Inserted by HC 693, para 18 as from 20 October 2014.

34P.   The application must be made in relation to an eligible decision.

Note

Inserted by HC 693, para 18 as from 20 October 2014.

34Q.   The application must be made while the applicant is in the UK.

Note

Inserted by HC 693, para 18 as from 20 October 2014.

34R.

(1)   The application must be made:
  (a)   where the applicant is not detained, no more than 14 calendar days after receipt by the applicant of the notice of the eligible decision; or
  (b)   where the applicant is in detention under the Immigration Acts, no more than 7 calendar days after receipt by the applicant of the notice of the eligible decision.

(2) But the application may be accepted out of time if the Secretary of State is satisfied that it would be unjust not to waive the time limit and the application was made as soon as reasonably practicable.

(3) For the purposes of this paragraph, where notice of the eligible decision is sent by post to an address in the UK, it is deemed to have been received, unless the contrary is shown, on the second working day after the day on which it was posted.

(4) For provision about when an application is made see paragraph 34W.

Note

Inserted by HC 693, para 18 as from 20 October 2014.

34S. An application may only include an application on behalf of a dependant of the applicant if that dependant was also a dependant on the application which resulted in the eligible decision.

Note

Inserted by HC 693, para 18 as from 20 October 2014.

Notice of invalidity

34T.

(1) A notice informing an applicant that their application is invalid will be given in writing (which includes, where an email address has been provided for correspondence, by electronic mail).

(2) A notice of invalidity is deemed to have been received, unless the contrary is shown:

 (a) where it is sent by post, on the second working day after the day on which it was posted;

 (b) where it is sent by electronic mail, on the day on which it is sent; and

 (c) where it is given in person, on the day on which it is given.

Note

Inserted by HC 693, para 18 as from 20 October 2014.

Online applications for administrative review

34U.

(1) In this paragraph:

- "the relevant online application process" means the application process accessible via the gov.uk website and identified there as relevant for applications for administrative review; and
- "specified" in relation to the relevant online application process means specified in the online guidance accompanying that process.

(2) An application may be made online by completing the relevant online application process.

(3) Where an application is made online:

 (a) any specified fee in connection with the application must be paid in accordance with the method specified;

 (b) any section of the online application which is designated as mandatory must be completed as specified; and

 (c) documents specified as mandatory on the online application or in the related guidance must be submitted either electronically with the online application and in the specified manner, where this is permitted, or received by post and in the specified manner no more than 7 working days after the day on which the online application is submitted.

Note

Inserted by HC 693, para 18 as from 20 October 2014.

Postal applications for administrative review

34V.
(1)   An application may be made by post or courier in accordance with this paragraph.
(2)   Where an application is made by post or courier:
    (a)   it must be made on the application form as specified within the meaning of paragraph 34 (but see paragraph 34Y);
    (b)   any specified fee in connection with the application must be paid in accordance with the method specified in the application form, separate payment form or related guidance notes (as applicable);
    (c)   any section of the application form which is designated as mandatory in the form itself or related guidance notes must be completed;
    (d)   the form must be signed by the applicant or their representative;
    (e)   the application must be accompanied by the documents specified as mandatory in the application form or related guidance notes; and
    (f)   the application must be sent to the address specified on the form.

Note

Inserted by HC 693, para 18 as from 20 October 2014.

Determining the date of an application

34W.
(1)   An application for administrative review is made:
    (a)   where it is made by post in accordance with paragraph 34V, on the marked date of posting;
    (b)   where it is made by courier in accordance with paragraph 34V, on the date on which it is delivered; and
    (c)   where it is made online in accordance with paragraph 34U, on the date on which it is submitted.
(2)   Accepting an application has been made does not mean that it is accepted as being valid.

Note

Inserted by HC 693, para 18 as from 20 October 2014.

Withdrawal of applications

34X.
(1)   An application which has not been determined will be treated as withdrawn if the applicant requests the return of their passport for the purpose of travel outside the UK.
(2)   An application which may only be brought from within the UK and which has not been determined will be treated as withdrawn if the applicant leaves the UK.
(3)   The application for administrative review may be withdrawn by the applicant. A request to withdraw an application must be made in writing to the Home Office at the address provided for that purpose on the visas and immigration pages of the gov.uk website. The application will be treated as withdrawn on the date on which the request is received.

Note

Inserted by HC 693, para 18 as from 20 October 2014.

Transitional arrangements for specified forms used in postal and courier applications

34Y.   Where an application is made no more than 21 days after the date on which a form is specified (within the meaning of paragraph 34) and on a form that was specified immediately prior to the date of the new specification, the application is deemed to have been made on the specified form (and is therefore not to be treated as invalid by reason only of being made on the "wrong" form).]

Note

Inserted by HC 693, para 18 as from 20 October 2014.

Undertakings

35.   A sponsor of a person seeking leave to enter . . . or remain in the United Kingdom may be asked to give an undertaking in writing to be responsible for that person's [maintenance, accommodation and (as appropriate) personal care] for the period of any leave granted, including any further variation [, or for a period of 5 years from date of grant where indefinite leave to enter or remain is granted]. Under the Social Security Administration Act 1992 and the Social Security Administration (Northern Ireland) Act 1992, the Department of Social Security or, as the case may be, the Department of Health and Social Services in Northern Ireland may seek to recover from the person giving such an undertaking any income support paid to meet the needs of the person in respect of whom the undertaking has been given. [Under the Immigration and Asylum Act 1999 the Home Office may seek to recover from the person giving such an undertaking amounts attributable to any support provided under section 95 of the Immigration and Asylum Act 1999 (support for asylum seekers) to, or in respect of, the person in respect of whom the undertaking has been given. Failure by the sponsor to maintain that person on accordance with the undertaking, may also be an offence under section 105 of the Social Security Administration Act 1992 and/or under section 108 of the Immigration and Asylum Act 1999 if, as a consequence asylum support and/or income support is provided to or in respect of, that person.]

Note

Words in square brackets inserted by Cmnd 4851. Words deleted, substituted and inserted by HC 194, para 5 as from 9 July 2012.

The particular form required of an undertaking is not proscribed in the Immigration rules; the substance not the form of the undertaking will determine its effect: see *Shah v Secretary of State for Social Security* [2002] EWCA Civ 285, [2002] All ER (D) 419 (Feb).) A form for sponsorship undertakings is available at: www.ukba.homeoffice.gov.uk/policyandlaw/guidance/ecg/ecb/ecb12

Medical

36.   A person who intends to remain in the United Kingdom for more than 6 months should normally be referred to the Medical Inspector for examination. If he produces a medical certificate he should be advised to hand it to the Medical Inspector. Any person seeking entry who mentions health or medical treatment as a reason for his visit, or who appears not to be in good mental or physical health, should also be referred to the Medical Inspector; and the Immigration Officer has discretion, which should be exercised sparingly, to refer for examination in any other case.

37.   Where the Medical Inspector advises that a person seeking entry is suffering from a specified disease or condition which may interfere with his ability to support himself or his dependants, the Immigration Officer should take account of this, in conjunction with other factors, in deciding whether to admit that person. The Immigration Officer should also take account of the Medical Inspector's assessment of the likely course of treatment in deciding whether a person seeking entry for private medical treatment has sufficient means at his disposal.

38.   A returning resident should not be refused leave to enter [or have existing leave to enter or remain cancelled] on medical grounds. But where a person would be refused leave to enter [or to cancel existing leave to enter or remain] on medical grounds if he were not a returning resident, or in any case where it is decided on compassionate grounds not to exercise the power to refuse leave to enter, or in any other case where the Medical Inspector so recommends, the Immigration Officer should give the person concerned a notice requiring him to report to the Medical Officer of Environmental Health designated by the Medical Inspector with a view to further examination and any necessary treatment.

[A39.   Any person from a country listed in Appendix T Part 1 making an application for entry clearance to come to the UK for more than six months or as a fiance(e) or proposed civil partner applying for leave to enter under Section EC-P: Entry clearance as a partner under Appendix FM or leave to enter under paragraphs 290–291 in Part 8 of these Rules, must present at the time of application, a valid medical certificate issued by a medical practitioner listed in Appendix T Part 2 confirming that they have undergone screening for active pulmonary tuberculosis and that this tuberculosis is not present in the applicant.]

Note

Substituted by Cm 8599, para 1 as from 30 April 2013.

B39. Applicants seeking leave to enter as a returning resident under paragraph 1 of these rules, having been absent from the United Kingdom for more than two years are also subject to the requirements in paragraph A39.]

Note

Paras 36–39: See, Immigration Directorate Instructions at Chapter 1, Section 8 at paras 2.9–10 for possible exemptions or waivers of the requirement: www.bia.homeoffice.gov.uk/sitecontent/docu ments/policyandlaw/IDIs/idischapter1/section8/section8.pdf?view=Binary. See also para 320(17), for a possible general basis of refusal.

Paras 7–39 replace HC 251, paras 6–21 and 58–60. Words in square brackets in para 38 inserted by HC 704. Paragraphs A39 and B39 inserted by HC 565, para 8 as from 6 September 2012.

[Students

39A. An application for a variation of leave to enter or remain made by a student who is sponsored by a government or international sponsorship agency may be refused if the sponsor has not given written consent to the proposed variation.]

[Specified Documents

39B.
(a) Where these Rules state that specified documents must be provided, that means documents specified in these Rules as being specified documents for the route under which the applicant is applying. If the specified documents are not provided, the applicant will not meet the requirement for which the specified documents are required as evidence.
(b) Where these Rules specify documents that are to be provided, those documents are considered to be specified documents, whether or not they are named as such, and as such are subject to the requirements in (c) to (f) below.
(c) If the Entry Clearance Officer or Secretary of State has reasonable cause to doubt the genuineness of any document submitted by an applicant which is, or which purports to be, a specified document under these Rules, and having taken reasonable steps to verify the document is unable to verify that it is genuine, the document will be discounted for the purpose of this application.
(d) Specified documents must be originals, not copies, except where stated otherwise.
(e) Specified documents must contain, or the applicant must provide, full contact details to allow each document to be verified.
(f) [Where any specified documents provided are not in English or Welsh, the applicant must provide the original and a full translation that can be independently verified by the Entry Clearance Officer, Immigration Officer or the Secretary of State.
   The translation must be dated and include:
   (i) confirm that it is an accurate translation of the original document;
   (ii) the full name and original signature of the translator or an authorised official of the translation company;
   (iii) the translator or translation company's contact details; and
   (iv) if the applicant is applying for leave to remain or indefinite leave to remain, certification by a qualified translator and details of the translator or translation company's credentials.]

Note

Paragraph 39B inserted by Cm 8423, para 4 as from 20 July 2012. Amended by HC 628, para 4 and if applicant has made an application for entry clearance or leave before 1 October 2012, the application will be decided in accordance with the Rules in force on 30 September 2013.

See para 245AA and Appendix FM-SE at para 1(K) for the circumstances in which the UKBA will contact the applicant where specified documents are not provided.

[Indefinite leave to enter or remain

39C.

(a) An applicant for indefinite leave to enter or remain must, unless the applicant provides a reasonable explanation, comply with any request made by the Secretary of State to attend an interview.

(b) If the decision-maker has reasonable cause to doubt (on examination or interview or on any other basis) that any document submitted by an applicant for the purposes of satisfying the requirements of Appendix KoLL of these Rules was genuinely obtained, that document may be discounted for the purposes of the application.

(c) Where sub-paragraph (b) applies, the decision-maker may request the applicant to provide additional evidence of knowledge of the English language and/or knowledge about life in the UK (as set out in paragraphs 3.2(b)(ii) and 3.3 of Appendix KoLL) for the purposes of demonstrating sufficient knowledge of the English language requirement and sufficient knowledge about life in the United Kingdom in accordance with Appendix KoLL.

(d) A decision-maker will not request evidence under sub-paragraph (c) where the decision-maker does not anticipate that the supply of that evidence will lead to a grant of leave to enter or remain in the United Kingdom because the application may be refused for other reasons.

Inserted by HC 693, para 19 as from 6 November 2014.

PART 2 — PERSONS SEEKING TO ENTER OR REMAIN IN THE UNITED KINGDOM FOR VISITS

Visitors

[Requirements for leave to enter as a general visitor]

40. For the purpose of paragraphs 41–46 a general visitor includes a person living and working outside the United Kingdom who comes to the United Kingdom as a tourist. A person seeking leave to enter the United Kingdom as a Business Visitor, which includes Academic Visitors, must meet the requirements of paragraph 46G. A person seeking entry as a Sports Visitor must meet the requirements of paragraph 46M. A person seeking entry as an Entertainment Visitor must meet the requirements of paragraph 46S. [A visitor seeking leave to enter for the purpose of marriage or to enter into a civil partnership must meet the requirements of paragraph 56D. [A person seeking enter to study as a student visitor must meet the requirements of paragraph 56K.]]

Note

Words in square brackets substituted by HC 314, para 7 as from 6 April 2009. Heading substituted by HC 1113, para 21 as from 27 November 2008. Final sentence inserted by HC 628, para 5 and shall apply to all applications decided on or after 1 October 2013.

41. The requirements to be met by a person seeking leave to enter the United Kingdom as a [general visitor] are that he:

(i) is genuinely seeking entry as a [general visitor] for a limited period as stated by him, not exceeding 6 months [or not exceeding 12 months in the case of a person seeking entry to accompany an academic visitor, provided in the latter case the visitor accompanying the academic visitor [(as their child, spouse or partner)] has entry clearance]; and

(ii)   intends to leave the United Kingdom at the end of the period of the visit as stated by him; and [does not intend to live for extended periods in the United Kingdom through frequent or successive visits; and]

(iii)   does not intend to take employment in the United Kingdom; and

(iv)   does not intend to produce goods or provide services within the United Kingdom, including the selling of goods or services direct to members of the public; and

(v)   [save to the extent provided by paragraph 43A,] does not intend to [undertake a course of study]; and

(vi)   will maintain and accommodate himself and any dependants adequately out of resources available to him without recourse to public funds or taking employment; or will, with any dependants, be maintained and [/or] accommodated adequately by relatives or friends [who can demonstrate they are able and intend to do so, and are legally present in the United Kingdom, or will be at the time of their visit; and]

(vii)   can meet the cost of the return or onward journey; and

(viii)   is not a child under the age of 18.

(ix)   [does not intend to do any of the activities provided for in paragraphs 46G(iii), 46M(iii) or 46S(iii); and

(x)   does not, during his visit, intend to marry or form a civil partnership, or to give notice of marriage or civil partnership; and

(xi)   does not intend to receive private medical treatment during his visit; and

(xii)   is not in transit to a country outside the common travel area.]

(xiii)   [where he is seeking leave to enter as a general visitor to take part in archaeological excavations, provides a letter from the director o organiser of he excavation stating the length of their visit and, where appropriate, what arrangements have been made for their accommodation and maintenance.]

Note

Words in square brackets in sub-para (v) inserted by Cm 7074, para 2 as from 1 September 2007. Sub-para (v) amended by HC 628, para 6 as from. Sub-paragraphs (ix)-(xii) inserted by HC 1113. Words in square brackets in sub-para (i) inserted by HC 314, para 8 as from 6 April 2009. Sub-paragraph (xiii) inserted by Cm 8423, para 5 as from 20 July 2012. Further amended by HC 1039, paras 7–9: where an applicant has made an application for entry clearance or leave before 6 April 2013 and the application has not been decided before that date, it will be decided in accordance with the rules in force on 5 April 2013. Further amended by HC 628, para 6 and shall apply to all applications decided on or after 1 October 2013. Amended by HC 693, para 20 as from 6 November 2014, save that if an application has been made for entry clearance or leave to enter or remain before 6 November 2014, the application will be decided in accordance with the Rules in force on 5 November 2014.

41A.   The requirements to be met by a person seeking leave to enter the United Kingdom as a general visitor who is acting as an organ donor, or is to be assessed as a suitable organ donor, are that the person:

(a)   meets the requirements in paragraph 41 (i) to (xii); and

(b)   genuinely intends to donate an organ, or be assessed as a suitable organ donor to an identified recipient in the UK, with whom the visitor has a genetic or pre-existing emotional relationship; and

(c)   is confirmed as a donor match to the identified recipient through medical tests, or is undergoing further tests to be assessed as a potential donor to the intended recipient; and

(d)   provides a letter, dated no more than three months prior to the person's intended date of arrival in the UK, from either:

(i)   the lead nurse or coordinator of the UK's NHS Trust's Living Donor Kidney Transplant team; or

(ii)   a UK registered medical practitioner who holds an NHS consultant post or who appears in the Specialist Register of the General Medical Council; which:

(aa)   confirms that the visitor meets the requirements in subparagraphs (b) and (c); and

(bb)   confirms when and where the planned organ transplant or medical tests will take place; and

(e)   can demonstrate, if required to do so, that the identified recipient is legally present in the United Kingdom or will be at the time of the visitor's planned organ transplant.

Note

Inserted by HC 693, para 21 as from 6 November 2014, save that if an application has been made for entry clearance or leave to enter or remain before 6 November 2014, the application will be decided in accordance with the Rules in force on 5 November 2014.

General note

For detailed, consolidated guidance on the categories of visitor in Part 2, see Modernised Guidance at: www.ukba.homeoffice.gov.uk/sitecontent/documents/policyandlaw/modernised/visiting/

The current visitor regime as set out in Part 2 is structured on the basis of a category for 'general visits' and for a number of other specific purposes. The Modernised Guidance contains full guidance on each of these categories:

41(i): the maximum duration of the general visit visa will normally be six months (and see para 44 below), save as specified in para 41(i); see also page 7 of the Modernised Guidance on General visitors for the discretion to grant for a longer period in exceptional compassionate cases; details of the Carers concession can be found in the IDIs at Chapter 17, Section 2. While the general period of leave granted is six months, shorter periods may also be granted. An immigration officer is entitled, in setting the period of entry, to take in to account a visitor's financial and other circumstances: see *Immigration Officer, London (Heathrow Airport) v Schönenburger* [1975] Imm AR 7. For the possibility of extending leave as a visitor: see para 44.

The IDI also indicates that no specified period must have elapsed between visits, but a visitor should not normally spend more than 6 out of any 12–month period in the UK as a visitor: but see *Sawmynaden (Family visitors - considerations) Mauritius* [2012] UKUT 161 (IAC) as to the proper approach to multiple successive visits. On the jurisdiction of the First-tier Tribunal to consider family visit appeals see: *Ajakaiye (visitor appeals - right of appeal) Nigeria* [2011] UKUT 375 (IAC). See also the Immigration Appeals (Family Visitor) Regulations 2012 and the UKBA's plans to end visit appeals from 2014 at: www.ukba.homeoffice.gov.uk/sitecontent/newsar ticles/2012/june/25-family-visit-visa-appeal

41(ii): An immigration officer will need to be satisfied that the visitor will return after the period of leave given, and will not overstay or otherwise act incompatibly with his or her status as a visitor, for example by taking employment.

The fact that a visitor will leave but not necessarily within the required period does not necessarily mean that the visitor is not intending a genuine visit: *Visa Officer, Cairo v Malek* [1979–80] Imm AR 111; nor should a visitor be refused because they may seek an extension of their leave: *R v Secretary of State for the Home Department, ex p Arjumand* [1979–80] Imm AR 111.

A visitor's economic, social and familial circumstances in their home country, as an indicator of an incentive to return, may be relevant in assessing intention, as well as the individual and family immigration history (see, inter alia, Chapter 2 at 2.1.6). However, in assessing what a visitor says about their visit, it is important to draw a distinction between a wish and an intention: *Masood v Immigration Appeal Tribunal* [1992] Imm AR 69. An expression of a wish may not be fatal to the proof of intention.

41(iii): Other conditions may be imposed: see the Immigration Act 1971, s 3 (1) (c) as amended;

41(vi): Recourse to public funds means no additional recourse: per para 6A of HC 395. An undertaking from a sponsor may also be required where there are concerns about how maintenance will be provided: see para 35 of HC 395 (and also para 320(14) for a general refusal on that basis).

[Leave to enter as a general visitor

42.   A person seeking leave to enter the United Kingdom as a general visitor may be admitted for a period not exceeding 6 months [or not exceeding 12 months in the case of a person accompanying an academic visitor [(as their child, spouse or partner)]], subject to a condition prohibiting employment[, ... and recourse to public funds], provided the Immigration Officer is satisfied that each or the requirements of paragraph 41 is met.]

Note

Substituted by HC 1113, para 27 as from 27 November 2008. Words in square brackets inserted by HC 314, para 9 as from 6 April 2009. Words ", study and recourse to public funds" inserted by HC 565, para 9 as from 6 September 2012. Word ", study" deleted by HC 628, para 7 and shall apply to all applications decided on or after 1 October 2013. Further amended by HC 693, para 20 as from 6 November 2014, save that if an application has been made for entry clearance or leave to enter or remain before 6 November 2014, the application will be decided in accordance with the Rules in force on 5 November 2014.

[Refusal of leave to enter as a general visitor

43. Leave to enter as a general visitor is to be refused if the Immigration Officer is not satisfied that each of the requirements of paragraph 41 is met.]

Note

Substituted by HC 1113, para 27 as from 27 November 2008.

Permitted study as a general visitor

43A. [
(1) A person who has been granted leave to enter the United Kingdom under paragraph 42 may undertake a course of study to the extent permitted by this paragraph.
(2) A course of study is permitted under this paragraph if it-
   (a) does not exceed 30 days in duration (either alone or taken together with any other course and whether continuous or otherwise); and
   (b) is a recreational course; but
   (c) is not an English language course.
(3) A course of study is also permitted under this paragraph if it-
   (a) does not exceed 30 days in duration (either alone or taken together with any other course and whether continuous or otherwise); and
   (b) is provided by an institution which is-
      (i) the holder of a Sponsor licence for Tier 4 of the Points-Based System,
      (ii) the holder of valid accreditation from Accreditation UK, the Accreditation Body for Language Services (ABLS), the British Accreditation Council (BAC), or the Accreditation service for International Colleges (ASIC),
      (iii) the holder of a valid and satisfactory full institutional inspection, review or audit by the Bridge Schools Inspectorate, the Education and Training Inspectorate, Estyn, Education Scotland, the Independent Schools Inspectorate, Office for Standards in Education, the Quality Assurance Agency for Higher Education, the Schools Inspection Service or the Education and Training Inspectorate Northern Ireland, or
      (iv) an overseas higher education institution offering only part of its programmes in the united Kingdom, holding its own nationals accreditation and offering programmes that are an equivalent level to a United Kingdom degree.
(4) For the purposes of this paragraph a "recreational course" is one which a person undertakes purely for leisure purposes.]

Note

Inserted by HC 628, para 8 and shall apply to all applications decided on or after 1 October 2013.

[Requirements for an extension of stay as a general visitor

44. Six months is the maximum permitted leave which may be granted to a general visitor. The requirements for an extension of stay as a general visitor are that the applicant:
(i) meets the requirements of paragraph 41(ii)–(vii) and (ix)-(xii); and

(ii)   has not already spent, or would not as a result of an extension of stay spend, more than 6 months in total in the United Kingdom [or not more than 12 months in the case of a person accompanying an academic visitor] as a general visitor. [Any periods spent as a child visitor are to be counted as a period spent as a general visitor;] [and

(iii)   has, or was last granted, entry clearance, leave to enter or leave to remain as a general visitor or as a child visitor.][; and

(iv)   must not be in the UK in breach of immigration laws except that any period of overstaying for a period of 28 days or less will be disregarded.]

Note

Words in square brackets inserted by HC 486 and Cm 7074 as from 1 September 2007. Substituted by HC 1113, para 27 as from 27 November 2008. Words in square brackets in (ii) inserted by HC 314, para 10 as from 31 March 2010. Sub-para (iv) inserted by HC 194, para 6 as from 1 October 2012.

[Extension of stay as a general visitor

45. An extension of stay as a general visitor may be granted, subject to a condition prohibiting employment[...and recourse to public funds], provided the Secretary of State is satisfied that each of the requirements of paragraph 44 is met.

Note

Substituted by HC 1113, para 27 as from 27 November 2008. Words ", study and recourse to public funds" inserted by HC 565, para 10 as from 6 September 2012. Words ", study" deleted by HC 628, para 9 and shall apply to all applications decided on or after 1 October 2013.

[Refusal of extension of stay as a general visitor

46. An extension of stay as a general visitor is to be refused if the Secretary of State is not satisfied that each of the requirements of paragraph 44 is met.]

Note

Substituted by HC 1113, para 27 as from 27 November 2008.

Child visitors

[Requirements for leave to enter as a child visitor

46A [(1) The requirements to be met by a person seeking leave to enter the United Kingdom as a child visitor are that the applicant:

(i)   is genuinely seeking entry as a child visitor for a limited period as stated, not exceeding 6 months or not exceeding 12 months to accompany an academic visitor, provided in the latter case the applicant has entry clearance; and

(ii)   meets the requirements of paragraph 41(ii)-(iv), (vi)-(vii) and (x)-(xii); and

(iii)   is under the age of 18; and

(iv)   can demonstrate that suitable arrangements have been made for their travel to, and reception and care in the United Kingdom . . . [; and]

(v)   has a parent or guardian in his home country or country of habitual residence who is responsible for their care and who confirms that they consent to the arrangements for the applicant's travel, reception and care in the United Kingdom; and

(vi)   if a visa national:

    (a)   the applicant holds a valid United Kingdom entry clearance for entry as an accompanied child visitor and is travelling in the company of the adult identified on his entry clearance, who is on the same occasion being admitted to the United Kingdom; or

(b)   the applicant holds a valid United Kingdom entry clearance for entry as an unaccompanied child visitor; and

(vii)   if the applicant has been accepted for a course of study, this is to be provided by an institution which is outside the maintained sector and is:]

(vii)   [if the applicant has been accepted for [or intends to follow] a course of study, this is to be provided by an institution which is outside the maintained sector and is:]

    (a)   the holder of a Sponsor Licence for Tier 4 of the Points Based System, or

    (b)   the holder of valid accreditation from [Accreditation UK; the Accreditation Body for Language Services (ABLS); the British Accreditation Council (BAC) or the Accreditation Service for International Colleges (ASIC), or], or

    [(c)   the holder of a valid and satisfactory full institutional inspection, review or audit by one of the following bodies: the Bridge Schools Inspectorate; the Education and Training Inspectorate; Estyn; Education Scotland; the Independent Schools Inspectorate; Office for Standards in Education; the Schools Inspection Service or the Education and Training Inspectorate Northern Ireland.]

[(viii) if the applicant is undertaking an exchange or educational visit only, this is to be provided by one of the following schools:

    (a)   For England and Wales, maintained schools as defined under section 20(7) of the School Standards and Framework Act 1998; non-maintained special schools approved under section 342 of the Education Act 1996; independent schools as defined under section 463 of the Education Act 1996 and registered independent schools entered on the register of independent schools maintained under section 18 of the Education Act 2002; academies as defined in section 1(10) of the Academies Act 2010; city technologies colleges and city colleges for technology of the arts as established under the Education Act 1996 and treated as academies under section 1594) of the Academies Act.

    (b)   For Scotland, [public] schools, grant-aided schools and independent fee paying schools as defined under Section 135 of the Education (Scotland) Act 1980.

    (c)   For Northern Ireland, grant-aided schools as defined under Articles 10 and 11 of and Schedules 4 to 7 to the Education and Libraries (NI) Order in Council 1986; grant maintained integrated schools as defined under Article 69 and Schedule 5 to the Education Reform (NI) Order 1989; independent fee paying schools as defined under Article 38 of the Education and Libraries (NI) Order 1986.]

[(2) In sub-paragraph (1)(via), a "maintained school" is one which provides a free education and is primarily funded from public funds.]

Note

Substituted by HC 120, para 2 as from 1 January 2010. Words substituted in sub-para (iv) and (iv)(a)(1)-(2) inserted by Cm 8423, paras 6–8 as from 20 July 2012. Further amended by HC 565, paras, 12, 12, 14–16 as from 6 September 2012. Further amended by HC 803, paras 4–6 as from 1 December 2013.

See www.ukba.homeoffice.gov.uk/sitecontent/documents/policyandlaw/modernised/visiting/child-visitor.pdf?view=BinaryIDI for detailed guidance.

Leave to enter as a child visitor

46B [An applicant] seeking leave to enter the United Kingdom as a child visitor may be admitted for a period not exceeding 6 months, [or not exceeding 12 months in the case of a child visitor accompanying an academic visitor] subject to a condition prohibiting employment [and recourse to public funds], providing that the Immigration Officer is satisfied that each of the requirements of paragraph 46A is met.

Note

Words in square brackets substituted by HC 314, para 14 as from 31 March 2009. Words at beginning substituted by HC 120, para 3 as from 1 January 2010. Words "and recourse to public funds" inserted by HC 565, para 17 as from 6 September 2012.

Refusal of leave to enter as a child visitor

46C   Leave to enter as a child visitor is to be refused if the Immigration Officer is not satisfied that each of the requirements of paragraph 46A is met.

Requirements for an extension of stay as a child visitor

46D   Six months is the maximum permitted leave which may be granted to a child visitor. The requirements for an extension of stay as a child visitor are that the applicant:
(i)   [meets the requirements of paragraph 41 (ii) to (vii) [and (x)-(xii)], [and
(ii)   is under the age of 18; and
(iii)   can demonstrate that there are suitable arrangements for his care in the United Kingdom. [If a foster carer or relative (not a parent or guardian) will be responsible for the care of the applicant, the arrangements must meet the requirements [as set out in paragraph 46A(iv)(a)]]; and
(iv)   has a parent or guardian in his home country or country of habitual residence who is responsible for his care, [and who confirms that they consent to the arrangements for the applicant's travel, reception and care in the United Kingdom]; and
(v)   has not already spent, or would not as a result of an extension of stay spend, more than 6 months in total in the United Kingdom [or not more than 12 months in total in the case of a child visitor accompanying an academic visitor[, and
(vi)   has, or was last granted, entry clearance, leave to enter or leave to remain as a child visitor][; and
(vii)   must not be in the UK in breach of immigration laws except that any period of overstaying for a period of 28 days or less will be disregarded.]

Note

Paragraph (i) substituted by HC 314, para 15 as from 31 March 2009. Words in square brackets in paragraph (i), (iii), (iv) inserted by HC 120, paras 3–6 as from 1 January 2010. Words "as set out in paragraph 46A(iv)(a)" substituted by Cm 8423, para 9 as from 20 July 2012. Words in square brackets in paragraph (v) inserted by HC 314, para 16 as from 31 March 2009. Paragraph (vii) inserted by HC 194, para 7 as from 1 October 2012.

Extension of stay as a child visitor

46E   An extension of stay as a child visitor may be granted, subject to a condition prohibiting employment [and recourse to public funds], provided the Secretary of State is satisfied that each of the requirements of paragraph 46D is met.

Note

Words "and recourse to public funds" inserted by HC 565, para 18 as from 6 September 2012.

Refusal of extension of stay as a child visitor

46F   An extension of stay as a child visitor is to be refused if the Secretary of State is not satisfied that each of the requirements of paragraph 46D is met.

Business Visitors

Requirements for leave to enter as a Business Visitor

46G The requirements to be met by a person seeking leave to enter the United Kingdom as a business visitor are that he:

(i)   is genuinely seeking entry as a Business Visitor for a limited period as stated by him:

        (a)   not exceeding 6 months; or

        (b)   not exceeding 12 months if seeking entry as an Academic Visitor

(ii)   meets the requirements of paragraph 41(iii)-(iv), subject to [paragraphs 46HA(v), (vii)-(viii) and (x)-(xii)]

(iii)   intends to do one or more of the following during his visit:

        (a)   [to carry out one of the following activities;

            (i)   to attend meetings, conferences and interviews, provided they were arranged before arrival in the UK and, if the applicant is a board-level director attending board meetings in the UK, provided they are not employed by a UK company (although they may be paid a fee for attending the meeting);

            (ii)   to attend trade fairs for promotional work only, provided they are not directly selling;

            (iii)   to arrange deals, or negotiating or signing trade agreements or contracts;

            (iv)   to carry out fact-finding missions;

            (v)   to conduct site visits;

            (vi)   to work as a driver on a genuine international route delivering goods or passengers from abroad;

            (vii)   to work as a tour group courier, providing the applicant is contracted to a firm with headquarters outside the UK, is seeking entry to accompany a tour group, and will depart with that tour, or another tour organised by the same company;

            (viii)   to speak at a one-off conference which is not organised as a commercial concern, and is not making a profit for the organiser;

            (ix)   to represent a foreign manufacturer by:

                (i)   carrying out installing, debugging or enhancing work for computer software companies,

                (ii)   servicing or repairing the manufacturer's products within the initial guarantee period, or

                (iii)   being briefed on the requirements of a UK customer, provided this is limited to briefing and does not include work involving use of the applicant's expertise to make a detailed assessment of a potential customer's requirements;

            (x)   to represent a foreign machine manufacturer, as part of the contract of purchase and supply, in erecting and installing machinery too heavy to be delivered in one piece;

            (xi)   to act as an interpreter or translator for visiting business people, provided they are all employed by, and doing the business of, the same overseas company;

            (xii)   to erect, dismantle, install, service, repair or advise on the development of foreign-made machinery, provided the will only do so in the UK for up to six months;

        (b)   to take part in a location shoot as a member of a film crew [meaning he is a film actor, producer, director or technician paid or employed by an overseas firm other than one established in the UK and is coming to the UK for location sequences only for an overseas film];

        (c)   to represent overseas news media including as a journalist, correspondent, producer or cameraman provided he is employed or paid by an overseas company and is gathering information for an overseas publication [; or]

        (d)   to act as an Academic Visitor but only if[;

            (1)   he is an academic who is:

  (a) on sabbatical leave from an overseas academic institution to carry out research;

  (b) taking part in formal exchange arrangements with UK counterparts (including doctors);

  (c) coming to share knowledge or experience, or to hold informal discussions with their UK counterparts, or

  (d) taking part in a single conference or seminar that is not a commercial or non-profit venture;

  (e) an eminent senior doctor or dentist taking part in research, teaching or clinical practice; and

  (2) he has been working as an academic in an institution of higher education overseas or in the field of their academic expertise immediately prior to seeking entry;]

(e) to act as a Visiting Professor [subject to undertaking only a small amount of teaching for the institution hosting the students he is supervising, being employed and paid by the overseas academic institution and not intending to base himself or seek employment in the UK];

(f) [To be a secondee to a UK company which is directly contracted with the visitor's overseas company, with which it has no corporate relationship, to provide goods or services, provided the secondee remains employed and paid by the overseas company throughout the secondee's visit];

(g) to undertake some preaching or pastoral work as a religious worker, provided his base is abroad and he is not taking up an office, post or appointment;

(h) [To act as an adviser, consultant, trainer[, internal auditor] or trouble shooter, to the UK branch of the same group of companies as the visitor's overseas company, provided the visitor remains employed and paid by the overseas company and does not undertake work, paid or unpaid with the UK company's clients];

(i) [Specific, one-off training on techniques and work practices used in the UK where:

  (a) the training is to be delivered by the UK branch of the same group of companies to which the individual's employer belongs; or

  (b) the training is to be provided by a UK company contracted to provide goods or services to the overseas company; or

  (c) a UK company is contracted to provide training facilities only, to an overseas company.]

  (d) the training is corporate training which is being delivered by an outside provider to overseas and UK employees of the same group of companies; or]

  (e) the training is corporate training provided for the purposes of the person's employment overseas and delivered by a UK company that is neither part of the person's employer's corporate group nor whose main activity is the provision of training.]

[(j) To share knowledge or experience relevant to, or advise on, an international project that is being led from the UK as an overseas scientist or researcher, provided the visitor remains paid and employed overseas and is not carrying out research in the United Kingdom;

(k) To advise a UK client on litigation and/or international transactions as an employee of an international law firm which has offices in the UK, provided the visitor remains paid and employed overseas.]

Note

Inserted by HC 1113, para 32 as from 27 November 2008. Paragraphs (iii)(f)-(i) substituted by HC 314, paras 17–19 as from 31 March 2009. Further amended by Cm 8423, paras 10–12 as from 20 July 2012. Further amended by HC 565, para 19 as from 6 September 2012. Further amended by HC 628, paras 10–12 and shall apply to all applications decided on or after 1 October 2013. Amended by HC 693, para 22 as from 6 November 2014, save that if an application has been made for entry clearance or leave to enter or remain before 6 November 2014, the application will be decided in accordance with the Rules in force on 5 November 2014.

See www.ukba.homeoffice.gov.uk/sitecontent/documents/policyandlaw/modernised/visiting/busin ess-visitors.pdf?view=Binary for detailed guidance

Leave to enter as a business visitor

46H   A person seeking leave to enter to the United Kingdom as a Business Visitor may be admitted for a period not exceeding 6 months, subject to a condition prohibiting employment[.... and recourse to public funds], provided the Immigration Officer is satisfied that each of the requirements of paragraph 46G is met. A person seeking leave to enter the United Kingdom as an Academic Visitor who does not have entry clearance may, if otherwise eligible, be admitted for a period not exceeding 6 months, subject to a condition prohibiting employment, provided the Immigration Officer is satisfied that each of the requirements of paragraph 46G are met. An Academic Visitor who has entry clearance may be admitted for up to 12 months subject to a condition prohibiting employment.

Note

Inserted by HC 1113, para 32 as from 27 November 2008. Words ", study and recourse to public funds" inserted by HC 565, para 22 as from 6 September 2012. Words ", study" deleted by HC 628, para 13 and shall apply to all applications decided on or after 1 October 2013.

Permitted study as a business visitor

[**46HA**   A person granted leave to enter under paragraph 46H may undertake a course of study to the same extent permitted by paragraph 43A.].

Note

Inserted by HC 628, para 14 and shall apply to all applications decided on or after 1 October 2013.

Refusal of leave to enter as a Business Visitor

46I   Leave to enter as a Business Visitor is to be refused if the Immigration Officer is not satisfied that each of the requirements of paragraph 46G are met.

Note

Inserted by HC 1113, para 32 as from 27 November 2008.

Requirements for an extension of stay as a Business Visitor

46J   Twelve months is the maximum permitted leave which may be granted to an Academic Visitor and six months is the maximum that may be granted to any other form of Business Visitor. The requirements for an extension of stay as a Business Visitor are that the applicant:
(i)   meets the requirements of paragraph 46G(ii)-(iii); and
(ii)   if he is a Business Visitor other than an Academic Visitor, has not already spent, or would not as a result of an extension of stay spend, more than 6 months in total in the United Kingdom as a Business Visitor; and
(iii) if he is an Academic Visitor, has not already spent, or would not as a result of an extension of stay spend, more than 12 months in total in the United Kingdom as a Business Visitor; and
(iv)   has, or was last granted, entry clearance, leave to enter or leave to remain as a Business Visitor[; and
(v)   must not be in the UK in breach of immigration laws except that any period of overstaying for a period of 28 days or less will be disregarded.]

Note

Inserted by HC 1113, para 32 as from 27 November 2008. Paragraph (v) inserted by HC 194, para 8 as from 1 October 2012.

Extension of stay as a Business Visitor

46K   An extension of stay as a Business Visitor may be granted, subject to a condition prohibiting employment[... and recourse to public funds], provided the Secretary of State is satisfied that each of the requirements of paragraph 46J is met.

Note

Inserted by HC 1113, para 32 as from 27 November 2008. Words ", study and recourse to public funds" inserted by HC 565, para 23 as from 6 September 2012. Words ", study" deleted by HC 628, para 15 and shall apply to all applications decided on or after 1 October 2013.

Refusal of extension of stay as a Business Visitor

46L An extension of stay as a Business Visitor is to be refused if the Secretary of State is not satisfied that each of the requirements of paragraph 46J is met.

Note

Inserted by HC 1113, para 32 as from 27 November 2008.

Sports Visitors

Requirements for leave to enter as a Sports Visitor

46M The requirements to be met by a person seeking leave to enter the United Kingdom as a Sports Visitor are that he:
(i)   is genuinely seeking entry as a Sports Visitor for a limited period as stated by him, not exceeding six months; and
(ii)   meets the requirements of paragraphs 41(ii)-(viii) and (x)-(xii) [(except that the requirement in paragraph 41(v) is to be read as if it were not qualified by paragraph 43A)]; and
(iii) intends to do one or more of the following during his visit:
     (a)   [to take part in a sports tournament, a particular sporting event or series of sporting evens in which the applicant is either:
         (i)   taking part, either as an individual or as part of a team;
         (ii)   making personal appearances and promotions, such as book signings, television interviews, guest commentaries, negotiating contracts, or to discuss sponsorship deals;
         (iii) taking part in 'trials', providing it is not in front of an audience, either paying or non-paying;
         (iv) undertaking short periods of training, either as an individual or part of a team, providing the applicant is not intending to settle in the UK, being paid by a UK sporting body, or joining a UK team where they are involved in friendly or exhibition matches.]
     (b)   To take part in a specific one off charity sporting event, provided no payment is received other than for travelling and other expenses;
     (c)   To join, as an Amateur, a wholly or predominantly amateur team provided no payment is received other than for board and lodging and reasonable expenses;
     (d)   To serve as a member of the technical or personal staff, or as an official, attending the same event as a visiting sportsperson coming for one or more of the purposes listed in (a), (b) or (c)[, or attending the same event as a sports-person carrying out permitted paid engagements as a visitor].

Note

Inserted by HC 1113, para 32 as from 27 November 2008. Words in square brackets in sub-para (iii)(d) inserted by HC 1888, para 9 as from 6 April 2012. Sub-paragraph (iii)(a) substituted by HC 565, para 24 as from 6 September 2012. Further amended by HC 628, para 16 and shall apply to all applications decided on or after 1 October 2013.

See www.ukba.homeoffice.gov.uk/sitecontent/documents/policyandlaw/modernised/visiting/sport s-visitors.pdf?view=Binary for detailed guidance.

Leave to enter as a Sports Visitor

46N A person seeking leave to enter to the United Kingdom as a Sports Visitor may be admitted for a period not exceeding 6 months, subject to a condition prohibiting employment[, study and recourse to public funds], provided the Immigration Officer is satisfied that each of the requirements of paragraph 46M is met.

Note

Inserted by HC 1113, para 32 as from 27 November 2008. Words ", study and recourse to public funds" inserted by HC 565, para 25 as from 6 September 2012.

Refusal of leave to enter as a Sports Visitor

46O   Leave to enter as a Sports Visitor is to be refused if the Immigration Officer is not satisfied that each of the requirements of paragraph 46M is met.

Note

Inserted by HC 1113, para 32 as from 27 November 2008.

Requirements for an extension of stay as a Sports Visitor

46P   Six months is the maximum permitted leave which may be granted to a Sports Visitor. The requirements for an extension of stay as a sports visitor are that the applicant:
(i)   meets the requirements of paragraph 46M(ii)-(iii); and
(ii)   has not already spent, or would not as a result of an extension of stay spend, more than 6 months in total in the United Kingdom as a Sports Visitor; and
(iii)   has, or was last granted, entry clearance, leave to enter or leave to remain as a Sports Visitor[; and
(iv)   must not be in the UK in breach of immigration laws except that any period of overstaying for a period of 28 days or less will be disregarded.]

Note

Inserted by HC 1113, para 32 as from 27 November 2008. Paragraph (iv) inserted by HC 194, para 9 as from 1 October 2012.

Extension of stay as a Sports Visitor

46Q   An extension of stay as a Sports Visitor may be granted, subject to a condition prohibiting employment[, study and recourse to public funds], provided the Secretary of State is satisfied that each of the requirements of paragraph 46P is met.

Note

Inserted by HC 1113, para 32 as from 27 November 2008. Words ", study and recourse to public funds" inserted by HC 565, para 26 as from 6 September 2012.

Refusal of extension of stay as a Sports Visitor

46R   An extension of stay as a Sports Visitor is to be refused if the Secretary of State is not satisfied that each of the requirements of paragraph 46P is met.

Note

Inserted by HC 1113, para 32 as from 27 November 2008.

Entertainer Visitors

Requirements for leave to enter as an Entertainer Visitor

46S   The requirements to be met by a person seeking leave to enter the United Kingdom as an Entertainer Visitor are that he:
(i)   is genuinely seeking entry as an Entertainer Visitor for a limited period as stated by him, not exceeding six months and
(ii)   meets the requirements of paragraphs 41(ii)-(viii) and (x)-(xii) [(except that the requirement in paragraph 41(v) is to be read as if it were not qualified by paragraph 43A)] and
(iii)   intends to do one or more of the following during his visit:
(a)   to take part as a professional entertainer in one or more music competitions; and/or

(b)   to fulfil one or more specific engagements as either an individual Amateur entertainer or as an Amateur group; and/or

(c)   [to take part, as an amateur or professional entertainer, in one or more cultural events or festivals on the list of permit free festivals at Appendix R to these Rules.]

(d)   serve as a member of the technical or personal staff, or of the production team, of an entertainer coming for one or more of the purposes listed in (a), (b), or (c)[, or attending the same event as an entertainer carrying out permitted paid engagements as a visitor].

Note

Inserted by HC 1113, para 32 as from 27 November 2008. Words in square brackets in sub-para (iii)(d) inserted by HC 1888, para 10 as from 6 April 2012. Sub-para (iii)(c) substituted by HC 565, para 27 as from 6 September 2012. Further amended by HC 628, para 17 and shall apply to all applications decided on or after 1 October 2013.

See www.ukba.homeoffice.gov.uk/sitecontent/documents/policyandlaw/modernised/visiting/entert ainer-visitors.pdf?view=Binary for detailed guidance.

Leave to enter as an Entertainer Visitor

46T   A person seeking leave to enter to the United Kingdom as an Entertainer Visitor may be admitted for a period not exceeding 6 months, subject to a condition prohibiting employment[, study and recourse to public funds], provided the Immigration Officer is satisfied that each of the requirements of paragraph 46S is met.

Note

Inserted by HC 1113, para 32 as from 27 November 2008. Words ", study and recourse to public funds" inserted by HC 565, para 28 as from 6 September 2012.

Refusal of leave to enter as an Entertainer Visitor

46U   Leave to enter as an Entertainer Visitor is to be refused if the Immigration Officer is not satisfied that each of the requirements of paragraph 46S is met.

Note

Inserted by HC 1113, para 32 as from 27 November 2008.

Requirements for an extension of stay as an Entertainer Visitor

46V   Six months is the maximum permitted leave which may be granted to an Entertainer Visitor. The requirements for an extension of stay as an Entertainer Visitor are that the applicant:

(i)   meets the requirements of paragraph 46S(ii)-(iii); and

(ii)   has not already spent, or would not as a result of an extension of stay spend, more than 6 months in total in the United Kingdom as an Entertainer Visitor; and

(iii)   has, or was last granted, entry clearance, leave to enter or leave to remain as an Entertainer Visitor[; and

(iv)   must not be in the UK in breach of immigration laws except that any period of overstaying for a period of 28 days or less will be disregarded.]

Note

Inserted by HC 1113, para 32 as from 27 November 2008. Paragraph (iv) inserted by HC 194, para 10 as from 1 October 2012.

Extension of stay as an Entertainer Visitor

46W   An extension of stay as an Entertainer Visitor may be granted, subject to a condition prohibiting employment[, study and recourse to public funds], provided the Secretary of State is satisfied that each of the requirements of paragraph 46V is met.

Note

Inserted by HC 1113, para 32 as from 27 November 2008. Words ", study and recourse to public funds" inserted by HC 565, para 29 as from 6 September 2012.

Refusal of extension of stay as an Entertainer Visitor

46X An extension of stay as an Entertainer Visitor is to be refused if the Secretary of State is not satisfied that each of the requirements of paragraph 46V is met.]

Note

Inserted by HC 1113, para 32 as from 27 November 2008.

Visitors in transit

Transit by visa nationals

47ZA. A visa national who seeks to enter the UK for the purpose of transit (that is, to travel via the UK en route to another destination country) must be in possession of a visa enabling their admission to the United Kingdom as a visitor in transit under paragraph 47, or must meet the requirements for admission under the transit without visa scheme provided for by paragraphs 50A to 50D when seeking leave to enter the UK.

Inserted by HC 693, para 23 as from 1 December 2014.

Requirements for admission as a visitor in transit to another country

47. The requirements to be met by a person (not being a member of the crew of a ship, aircraft, hovercraft, hydrofoil or train) seeking leave to enter the United Kingdom as visitor in transit to another country are that he:
(i) is [genuinely] in transit to a country outside the common travel area; and
(ii) has both the means and the intention of proceeding at once to another country; and
(iii) is assured of entry there; and
(iv) intends and is able to leave the United Kingdom within 48 hours.

Note

See www.ukba.homeoffice.gov.uk/sitecontent/documents/policyandlaw/modernised/visiting/transit-visitor.pdf?view=BinaryIDI for detailed guidance. Amended by HC 693, para 24 as from 1 December 2014.

Leave to enter as a visitor in transit

48. A person seeking leave to enter the United Kingdom as a visitor in transit may be admitted for a period not exceeding 48 hours with a prohibition on employment [, study and recourse to public funds] provided the Immigration Officer is satisfied that each of the requirements of paragraph 47 is met.

Note

Words ", study and recourse to public funds" inserted by HC 565, para 30 as from 6 September 2012.

Refusal of leave to enter as a visitor in transit

49. Leave to enter as a visitor in transit is to be refused if the Immigration Officer is not satisfied that each of the requirements of paragraph 47 is met.

Extension of stay as a visitor in transit

50. The maximum permitted leave which may be granted to a visitor in transit is 48 hours. An application for an extension of stay beyond 48 hours from a person admitted in this category is to be refused.

Note

[See HC 251, paras 25 and 105.]

These paras introduce a separate category for visitors admitted in transit for up to 48 hours.

[Transit without visa scheme

50A. A visa national must meet the requirements in paragraphs 50B and 50C when seeking leave to enter the UK in order to be granted leave to enter under the transit without visa scheme.

Note

Inserted by HC 693, para 25 as from 1 December 2014.

50B. The requirements to be met by a visa national seeking leave to enter the United Kingdom under the transit without visa scheme are that he:
(i) has arrived and will depart by air; and
(ii) is genuinely in transit to another country, meaning the purpose of his visit is to travel via the UK en route to another destination country, and he is taking a reasonable transit route; and
(iii) does not intend to access public funds, undertake employment or study in the UK; and
(iv) intends and is able to leave the UK before 23:59 hours on the day after the day when he arrived; and
(v) has a confirmed booking on a flight departing the UK before 23:59 hours on the day after the day when he arrived; and
(vi) is assured entry to his country of destination and any other countries he is transiting through on his way there.

Note

Inserted by HC 693, para 25 as from 1 December 2014.

50C. The visa national must also:
(i) be travelling to (or on part of a reasonable journey to) Australia, Canada, New Zealand or the USA and have a valid visa for that country; or
(ii) be travelling from (or on part of a reasonable journey from) Australia, Canada, New Zealand or the USA and it is less than 6 months since he last entered that country with a valid entry visa; or
(iii) hold a valid residence permit issued by either:
    (a) Australia;
    (b) Canada, issued after 28 June 2002;
    (c) New Zealand;
    (d) USA, issued after 21 April 1998 including: a valid USA I-551 Temporary Immigrant visa (a wet-ink stamp version will NOT be accepted by UK border control); a permanent residence card; an expired I-551 Permanent Residence card provided it is accompanied by a valid I-797 letter authorising extension; a standalone US Immigration Form 155A/155B; or
    (e) an EEA state or Switzerland; or
(iv) hold a valid uniform format category D visa for entry to a state in the European Economic Area (EEA) or Switzerland; or
(v) be travelling on to the Republic of Ireland and have a valid Irish biometric visa; or
(vi) be travelling from the Republic of Ireland and it is less than 3 months since the applicant was last given permission to land or be in the Republic by the Irish authorities with a valid Irish biometric visa.

Note

Inserted by HC 693, para 25 as from 1 December 2014.

Leave to enter under the transit without visa scheme

50D. A person seeking leave to enter the United Kingdom on arrival under the transit without visa scheme may be admitted for a period ending no later than 23:59 hours on the day after the day on which he arrived, with a prohibition on employment, study and recourse to public funds, provided the Immigration Officer is satisfied that the requirements of paragraphs 50B and 50C are met.

Note

Inserted by HC 693, para 25 as from 1 December 2014.

Refusal of leave to enter under the transit without visa scheme

50E. Leave to enter under the transit without visa scheme is to be refused if the Immigration Officer is not satisfied that the requirements of paragraphs 50B and 50C are met.

Note

Inserted by HC 693, para 25 as from 1 December 2014.

Extension of stay under the transit without visa scheme

50F. The maximum permitted leave which may be granted to a person under the transit without visa scheme is for a period ending no later than 23:59 hours on the day after the day on which they arrived. An application for an extension of stay beyond this period by a person admitted in this category is to be refused.]

Note

Inserted by HC 693, para 25 as from 1 December 2014.

Visitors seeking to enter or remain for private medical treatment

Requirements for leave to enter as a visitor for private medical treatment

[**51.** The requirements to be met by a person seeking leave to enter the UK as a visitor for private medical treatment are that the person:

(i)   is genuinely seeking entry as a visitor who will be receiving private medical treatment in the UK for an initial period as stated by him that is:
  (a)   not exceeding six months; or
  (b)   not exceeding 11 months, where the visitor's medical practitioner has confirmed that the period of treatment is likely to exceed six months and provided the person has entry clearance as a visitor; and
(ii)   meets the requirements set out in paragraph 41(iii)–(vii), (ix)-(x) and (xii) (except that the requirement in paragraph 41(v) is to be read as if it were not qualified by paragraph 43A for entry as a general visitor); and
(iii)   in the case of a person suffering from a communicable disease, has satisfied the Medical Inspector that there is no danger to public health; and
(iv)   can show, if required to do so, that any proposed course of treatment is of finite duration; and
(v)   intends to leave the UK at the end of the treatment; and
(vi)   can produce satisfactory evidence, if required to do so, of:
  (a)   the medical condition requiring consultation or treatment; and
  (b)   satisfactory arrangements for the necessary consultation or treatment at his own expense; and
  (c)   the estimated costs of such consultation or treatment; and
  (d)   the likely duration of the treatment; and
  (e)   sufficient funds available to the person in the UK to meet the estimated costs and the person's undertaking to do so.]

Note

Sub-paragraph (i) substituted by HC 1113, para 33 as from 27 November 2008. Further amended by HC 628, para 18 and shall apply to all applications decided on or after 1 October 2013. Substituted by HC 693, para 26 as from 6 November 2014, save that if an application has been made for entry clearance or leave to enter or remain before 6 November 2014, the application will be decided in accordance with the Rules in force on 5 November 2014.

See www.ukba.homeoffice.gov.uk/sitecontent/documents/policyandlaw/modernised/visiting/medic al-visitor.pdf?view=Binary for detailed guidance. It is necessary for the applicant to show, if required to do so, that any proposed course of treatment is for a finite period.

Leave to enter as a visitor for private medical treatment

[52.   A person seeking leave to enter the UK as a visitor for private medical treatment may be admitted for a period not exceeding six months, or for a period not exceeding 11 months where paragraph 51(i)(b) applies, subject to a condition prohibiting employment, study and recourse to public funds, provided the Immigration Officer is satisfied that each of the requirements of paragraph 51 is met.]

Note

Words ", study and recourse to public funds" inserted by HC 565, para 31 as from 6 September 2012. Substituted by HC 693, para 27 as from 6 November 2014, save that if an application has been made for entry clearance or leave to enter or remain before 6 November 2014, the application will be decided in accordance with the Rules in force on 5 November 2014.

Refusal of leave to enter as a visitor for private medical treatment

53.   Leave to enter as a visitor for private medical treatment is to be refused if the Immigration Officer is not satisfied that each of the requirements of paragraph 51 is met.

Requirements for an extension of stay as a visitor for private medical treatment

54.   The requirements for an extension of stay as a visitor to undergo or continue private medical treatment are that the applicant:
(i)   [meets the requirements set out in paragraph 41(iii)–(vii), (ix)-(x) and paragraph 51(ii)–(v); and]
(ii)   [has produced evidence [in the form of a letter on headed notepaper giving a private practice or hospital address] from a registered medical practitioner who holds an NHS consultant post or who appears in the Specialist Register of the General Medical Council of [that provides full details of the:
         (a)   nature of the illness;
         (b)   proposed or continuing treatment;
         (c)   frequency of consultations;
         (d)   probable duration of the treatment;
         (e)   details of the cost of treatment and confirmation that all expenses are being met; and
         (f)   where treatment amounts to private visits to a consultant for a relatively minor ailment, details of the progress being made.]
(iii)   [has provided evidence that] he has met, out of the resources available to him, any costs and expenses incurred in relation to his treatment in the United Kingdom; and
(iv)   [provided evidence that he has] sufficient funds available to him in the United Kingdom[, or if relying on funds from abroad has provided evidence that those funds a fully transferable to the United Kingdom,] has provided evidence to meet the likely costs of his treatment and intends to meet those costs; [and
(v)   was not last admitted to the United Kingdom under the Approved Destination Status Agreement with China.][; and
(vi)   must not be in the UK in breach of immigration laws except that any period of overstaying for a period of 28 days or less will be disregarded.]

Note

Para 54(ii) substituted by Cmnd 4851. Para 54(v) inserted by HC 486. Sub-paragraph (i) substituted by HC 1113, para 34 as from 27 November 2008. Further amended by Cm 8423, paras 13–17 as from 20 July 2012. Paragraph (vi) inserted by HC 194, para 11 as from 1 October 2012.

Extension of stay as a visitor for private medical treatment

[55.   An extension of stay to undergo or continue private medical treatment may be granted for a period not exceeding six months, with a prohibition on employment, study and recourse to public funds, provided the Secretary of State is satisfied that each of the requirements of paragraph 54 is met.]

Note

Words ", study and recourse to public funds" inserted by HC 565, para 32 as from 6 September 2012. Substituted by HC 693, para 28 as from 6 November 2014, save that if an application has been made for entry clearance or leave to enter or remain before 6 November 2014, the application will be decided in accordance with the Rules in force on 5 November 2014.

Refusal of extension of stay as a visitor for private medical treatment

56.   An extension of stay as a visitor to undergo or continue private medical treatment is to be refused if the Secretary of State is not satisfied that each of the requirements of paragraph 54 is met.

[Parent of a child at school

Requirements for leave to enter or remain as the parent of a child at school

56A.   The requirements to be met by a person seeking leave to enter or remain in the United Kingdom as the parent of a child at school are that:

   [(i)   the parent meets the requirements set out in paragraph [41] (ii)-(xii) [(except that the requirement in paragraph 41(v) is to be read as if it were not qualified by paragraph 43A)]; and]

   (1)   if the child has leave under paragraphs 57 to 62 of these Rules, the child is attending an independent fee paying day school and meets the requirements set out in paragraph 57(i) to (ix), or

   (2)   if the child is a Tier 4 (Child) Student, the child is attending an independent fee paying day school and meets the requirements set out in paragraph 245ZZA (if seeking leave to enter) or 245ZZC (if seeking leave to remain); and]

   (iii)   the child is under 12 years of age; and

   (iv)   the parent can provide satisfactory evidence of adequate and reliable funds for maintaining a second home in the United Kingdom; and

   (v)   the parent is not seeking to make the United Kingdom his main home; [and

   (vi)   the parent was not last admitted to the United Kingdom under the Approved Destination Status Agreement with China][; and

   (vii)   if seeking leave to remain must not be in the UK in breach of immigration laws except that any period of overstaying for a period of 28 days or less will be disregarded.]

Note

Para 56A(vi) inserted by HC 486. Words in square brackets amended by HC 40. Sub-paragraph (i) substituted by HC 1113, para 35 as from 27 November 2008. Figure '41' added to paragraph (i) by HC 314, para 20 as from 31 March 2009. Sub-paragraph (ii) substituted by HC 314. Paragraph (vii) inserted by HC 194, para 12 as from 1 October 2012. Further amended by HC 628, para 19 and shall apply to all applications decided on or after 1 October 2013.

See www.ukba.homeoffice.gov.uk/sitecontent/documents/policyandlaw/modernised/visiting/parent-child.pdf?view=Binary for detailed guidance.

Leave to enter or remain as the parent of a child at school

56B.   A person seeking leave to enter or remain in the United Kingdom as the parent of a child at school may be admitted or allowed to remain for a period not exceeding 12 months, subject to a condition prohibiting employment[, study and recourse to public funds], providing the Immigration Officer or, in the case of an application for limited leave to remain, the Secretary of State is satisfied that each of the requirements of paragraph 56A is met.

Note

Words ", study and recourse to public funds" inserted by HC 565, para 33 as from 6 September 2012.

Refusal of leave to enter or remain as the parent of a child at school

56C. Leave to enter or remain in the United Kingdom as the parent of a child at school is to be refused if the Immigration Office or, in the case of an application for limited leave to remain, the Secretary of State, is not satisfied that each of the requirements of paragraph 56A is met.]

Notes

[Paras 51–56 replace HC 251, paras 23 and 106.]

Words in square brackets inserted by Cmnd 4851.

[Visitors seeking to enter for the purposes of marriage or to enter into a civil partnership]

[Requirements for leave to enter as a visitor for marriage or to enter into a civil partnership]

56D. [The requirements to be met by a person seeking leave to enter the United Kingdom as a visitor for marriage or civil partnership are that he:
- (i) meets the requirements set out in paragraph 41 [(i)-(ix) and (xi)-(xii)] [(except that the requirement in paragraph 41(v) is to be read as if it were not qualified by paragraph 43A)]; and
- (ii) can show that he intends to give notice of marriage or civil partnership, or marry or form a civil partnership, in the United Kingdom within the period for which entry is sought; and
- (iii) can produce satisfactory evidence, if required to do so, of the arrangements for giving notice of marriage or civil partnership, or for his wedding or civil partnership . . . to take place, in the United Kingdom during the period for which entry is sought; and
- [(iv) does not intend to enter into a sham marriage or sham civil partnership within the meaning of sections 24(5) and 24A(5) of the Immigration and Asylum Act 1999; and]]
- [(v) holds a valid UK entry clearance for entry in this capacity]

NOTES

Inserted by HC 346 as from 15 March 2005. Words in sub-paragraph (i) substituted by HC 314, para 23 as from 31 March 2009. Headings substituted by HC 314, para 21 as from 31 March 2009. Further amended by HC 628, para 20 and shall apply to all applications decided on or after 1 October 2013. Further amended by HC 693, para 29 as from 6 November 2014, save that if an application has been made for entry clearance or leave to enter or remain before 6 November 2014, the application will be decided in accordance with the Rules in force on 5 November 2014. Amended by HC 693, para 30 as from 6 November 2014, save that if an application has been made for entry clearance or leave to enter or remain before 6 November 2014, the application will be decided in accordance with the Rules in force on 5 November 2014.

See www.ukba.homeoffice.gov.uk/sitecontent/documents/policyandlaw/modernised/visiting/marriage-visitor.pdf?view=Binary for detailed guidance.

[Leave to enter as a visitor for marriage or civil partnership]

56E. [A person seeking leave to enter the United Kingdom as a visitor for marriage or civil partnership may be admitted for a period not exceeding 6 months, subject to a condition prohibiting employment[, study and recourse to public funds], provided the Immigration Officer is satisfied that each of the requirements of paragraph 56D is met.]

Notes

Inserted by HC 346 as from 15 March 2005. Words ", study and recourse to public funds" inserted by HC 565, para 34 as from 6 September 2012.

[Refusal of leave to enter as a visitor for marriage or civil partnership]

56F. [Leave to enter as a visitor for marriage or civil partnership is to be refused if the Immigration Officer is not satisfied that each of the requirements of paragraph 56D is met.]

Notes

Inserted by HC 346 as from 15 March 2005.

[Visitors seeking leave to enter under the Approved Destination Status (ADS) Agreement with China]

[Requirements for leave to enter as a visitor under the Approved Destination Status Agreement with China ('ADS Agreement')]

56G. [The requirements to be met by a person seeking leave to enter the United Kingdom as a visitor under the ADS agreement with China are that he:
(i)   [meets the requirements set out in paragraph 41 (ii)–(xii) [(except that the requirement in paragraph 41(v) is to be read as if it were not qualified by paragraph 43A)]; and]
(ii)   is a national of the People's Republic of China; and
(iii)   is genuinely seeking entry as a visitor for a limited period as stated by him, not exceeding 30 days; and
(iv)   intends to enter, leave and travel within the territory of the United Kingdom as a member of a tourist group under the ADS agreement; and
(v)   holds a valid ADS agreement visit visa.]

Note

Inserted by HC 486. Sub-paragraph (i) substituted by HC 1113, para 37 as from 27 November 2008. Further amended by HC 628, para 21 and shall apply to all applications decided on or after 1 October 2013.

See www.ukba.homeoffice.gov.uk/sitecontent/documents/policyandlaw/modernised/visiting/ads.pdf?view=Binary for detailed guidance.

[Leave to enter as a visitor under the ADS agreement with China]

56H. [A person seeking leave to enter the United Kingdom as a visitor under the ADS Agreement may be admitted for a period not exceeding 30 days, subject to a condition prohibiting employment[, study and recourse to public funds], provided they hold an ADS Agreement visit visa.]

Note

Inserted by HC 486. Inserted by HC 346. Words ", study and recourse to public funds" inserted by HC 565, para 35 as from 6 September 2012.

[Refusal of leave to enter as a visitor under the ADS agreement with China]

56I [Leave to enter as a visitor under the ADS agreement with China is to be refused if the person does not hold an ADS Agreement visit visa.]

Note

Inserted by HC 486.

[Extension of stay as a visitor under the ADS agreement with China]

56J [Any application for an extension of stay as a visitor under the ADS Agreement with China is to be refused.]

Notes

Inserted by HC 486.

Student visitors

Requirements for leave to enter as a student visitor

56K (1) The requirements to be met by a person seeking leave to enter the United Kingdom as a student visitor are that he:

(i)   is genuinely seeking entry as a student visitor for a limited period as stated by him, not exceeding six months; and

(ii)   has been accepted on a course of study which is to be provided by an institution which is

    (a)   the holder of a Sponsor licence for Tier 4 of the Points Based System, or

    (b)   Accreditation UK, the Accreditation Body for Language Services (ABLS), the British Accreditation Council (BAC) or the Accreditation Service for International Colleges (ASIC)], or

    (c)   the holder of a valid and satisfactory full institutional inspection, review or audit by one of the following bodies: the Bridge Schools Inspectorate; the Education and Training Inspectorate; Estyn; Education Scotland; the Independent Schools Inspectorate; Office for Standards in Education; the Schools Inspection Service or the Education and Training Inspectorate Northern Ireland, or]

    (d)   an overseas Higher Education Institution offering only part of their programmes in the United Kingdom, holding its own national accreditation and offering programmes that are an equivalent level to a United Kingdom degree, [or:]

    (iia)-

        (a)   is enrolled on a course of study abroad equivalent to at least UK degree level study, and

        (b)   has been accepted by a UK recognised body or a body in receipt of public funding as a higher education institution from the Department fro Employment and Learning in Northern Ireland, the Higher Education Funding Council for England, the Higher Education Funding Council for Wales or the Scottish Funding Council to undertake research or research tuition at the UK institution, providing that-

        (c)   the overseas course provider confirms that the research or research tuition is part of or relevant to the course of study mentioned in sub-paragraph (a) above, and

        (d)   the student is not to be employed as a sponsored researcher under the relevant Tier 5 Government Authorised Exchange scheme, or under Tier 2 of the Points-Based System, at the UK institution; and

(iii)   intends to leave the United Kingdom at the end of his visit as stated by him; and

(iv)   does not intend to take employment in the United Kingdom; and

(v)   does not intend to engage in business, to produce goods or provide services within the United Kingdom, including the selling of goods or services direct to members of the public; and

(vi)   does not intend to study at a maintained school; and

(vii)   will maintain and accommodate himself and any dependants adequately out of resources available to him without recourse to public funds or taking employment; or will, with any dependants, be maintained and accommodated adequately by relatives or friends; and

(viii)   can meet the cost of the return or onward journey; and

(ix)   is not a child under the age of 18.

(x)   [meets the requirements set out in paragraph 41(ix)-(xii)].

[(2) In sub-paragraph (1)(iia) "research tuition" means tuition given to the applicant about hoe to conduct research.]

Part 2 — Persons seeking to enter or remain in the United Kingdom for visits

Notes

Inserted by Cm 7074, para 6 as from 1 September 2007. Amended by HC 40. Paragraph (x) inserted by HC 314, para 24 as from 31 March 2009. Paragraph (ii) substituted by HC 120, para 7 as from 1 January 2010. Sub-para (ii)(b), (c) substituted by HC 565, paras 36, 37 as from 6 September 2012. Further amended by HC 628, paras 22, 23 and shall apply to all applications decided on or after 1 October 2013.

See www.ukba.homeoffice.gov.uk/sitecontent/documents/policyandlaw/modernised/visiting/student-visitors.pdf?view=Binary for detailed guidance. Note the *English language concession* at page 12 of the Guidance which provides for the grant of a maximum of 11 months outside the rules for student visitors seeking entry to do an English language course.

Leave to enter as a student visitor

56L A person seeking leave to enter to the United Kingdom as a student visitor may be admitted for a period not exceeding 6 months, subject to a condition prohibiting employment[, and recourse to public funds], provided the Immigration Officer is satisfied that each of the requirements of paragraph 56K is met.

Notes

Inserted by Cm 7074, para 6 as from 1 September 2007. Words ", and recourse to public funds" inserted by HC 565, para 38 as from 6 September 2012.

Refusal of leave to enter as a student visitor

56M Leave to enter as a student visitor is to be refused if the Immigration Officer is not satisfied that each of the requirements of paragraph 56K is met.

Notes

Inserted by Cm 7074, para 6 as from 1 September 2007.

[Prospective Entrepreneurs

Purpose

56N. This Special Visitor route is to enable individuals who are at the time of applying for leave under this route in discussions with:
(i) one or more registered venture capitalist firms regulated by the [Financial Conduct Authority], and/or
(ii) one or more UK entrepreneurial seed funding competitions which is listed as endorsed on the UK Trade & Investment website, and/or
(iii) one or more UK Government Departments,

to secure funding in order to join, set up or take over, and be actively involved in the running of, a business in the UK.]

Notes

Inserted by HC 863, para 8 as from 6 April 2011. Amended by HC 628, para 25 as from

[Requirements for leave to enter as a Prospective Entrepreneur

56O. The requirements to be met by a person seeking leave to enter the United Kingdom as a Prospective Entrepreneur are that:
(a) The applicant must provide an original, . . . letter on headed paper [signed by an authorised official of that institution] supporting the application form:
(i) one or more registered venture capitalist firms regulated by the [Financial Conduct Authority],
(ii) one or more UK entrepreneurial seed funding competitions which is listed as endorsed on the UK Trade & Investment website, or
(iii) one or more UK Government Departments;
(b) The letter referred to in (a) must be dated no earlier than three months before the date of the application, be signed by an authorised official, and contain:

(i)   a description of the nature of the individual(s) and/or organisation(s) supporting the application;

(ii)   a description of the background and nature of the proposed business;

(iii)   a description of the applicant's suitability to be involved with the proposed business;

(iv)   a commitment by the individual(s) and/or organisation(s) supporting the applicant [to make a decision whether to provide a minimum of £50,000 funding] for the proposed business within 6 months of the applicant entering the UK. (If more than one individual and/or organisation is supporting the applicant, each amount proposed may be less than £50k, provided that the total amount is a minimum of £50k);

(v)   a commitment by the individual(s) or organisation(s) supporting the applicant that the proposed business will be set up and run from the UK;

(vi)   details of a contact name, telephone number and e-mail address for the individual(s) and/or organisation(s) supporting the applicant; and

(vii)   confirmation that the individual(s) and/or organisation(s) supporting the applicant is content to be contacted about the applicant;

(c)   The applicant's primary intention in applying as a Prospective Entrepreneur is to secure funding in order to join, set up or take over, and be actively involved in the running of a business in the UK;

(d)   The applicant intends to carry out one of the activities as listed [in paragraph 56O(d)(i)], specifying the activities that a Prospective Entrepreneur may undertake during a visit to the UK;

(i)   The permitted activities are:

(1)   attending meetings, including meetings arranged while in the UK, interviews arranged before arriving in the UK and conferences;

(2)   attending trade fairs provided this is restricted to promotional work and does not involve selling directly to members of the public;

(3)   arranging deals and negotiating or signing trade agreements and contracts;

(4)   conducting site visits;

(5)   speaking at a one-off conference which is not organised as a commercial concern;

(6)   undertaking fact finding missions;

(7)   purchasing, checking the details of examining goods;

(8)   recruiting staff for the proposed business activity which is the object of the visa

(e)   The applicant intends to leave the United Kingdom at the end of the period of the visit as stated by him, unless he makes a successful application for leave to remain as a Tier 1 (Entrepreneur) Migrant before the end of the period of the visit;

(f)   The applicant will maintain and accommodate himself and any dependants adequately out of resources available to him without recourse to public funds or taking employment; or will, with any dependants, be maintained and accommodated adequately by relatives or friends;

(g)   The applicant does not intend during his visit to:

(i)   take employment in the United Kingdom;

(ii)   produce goods or provide services within the United Kingdom, including the selling of goods or services direct to members of the public;

(iii)   undertake a course of study;

(iv)   marry or form a civil partnership, or to give notice of marriage or civil partnership; or

(v)   receive private medical treatment,

(h)   The applicant is not under the age of 18;

(i)   The applicant is not in transit to a country outside the common travel area; and

(j)   The applicant holds a valid United Kingdom entry clearance for entry in this capacity.]

Notes

Inserted by HC 863, para 8 as from 6 April 2011. Words in square brackets in (b)(iv) substituted by HC 908, para 3 as from 21 April 2011. Further amended by Cm 8423, para 20 as from 20 July

2012. Further amended by HC 628, para 25 and shall apply to all applications decided on or after 1 October 2013.

See www.ukba.homeoffice.gov.uk/sitecontent/documents/policyandlaw/modernised/visiting/ prospective-entrepreneur.pdf?view=Binary for detailed guidance.

[Leave to enter as a Prospective Entrepreneur

56P. A person seeking leave to enter to the United Kingdom as a Prospective Entrepreneur may be admitted for a period not exceeding 6 months, subject to a condition prohibiting employment[, study and recourse to public funds], provided the Secretary of State is satisfied that each of the requirements of paragraph 56O is met.]

Notes

Inserted by HC 863, para 8 as from 6 April 2011. Words ", study and recourse to public funds" inserted by HC 565, para 39 as from 6 September 2012.

[Refusal of leave to enter as a Prospective Entrepreneur

56Q. Leave to enter as a Prospective Entrepreneur is to be refused if the Secretary of State is not satisfied that each of the requirements of paragraph 56O is met.]

Notes

Inserted by HC 863, para 8 as from 6 April 2011.

Rules 56R-56W DELETED.

Visitors undertaking permitted paid engagements

Requirements for leave to enter as a visitor undertaking permitted paid engagements

56X. The requirements to be met by a person seeking leave to enter the United Kingdom as a visitor undertaking permitted paid engagements are that the applicant:
(i) is genuinely seeking enter as a visitor undertaking a permitted paid engagement for a limited period, not exceeding one month; and
(ii) meets the requirements of paragraphs 41(ii), (v), (vii), (viii), (x)-(xii) (except that the requirement in paragraph 41(v) is to be read as if it were not qualified by paragraph 43A); and
(iii) intends to do one of the following pre-arranged paid engagements which can be evidenced by a formal invitation, and can show that the engagement relates to his or her area of expertise and/or qualifications, and full-time occupation overseas:
   (a) examine students and/or participants in or chair selection panels as a visiting academic, who is highly qualified within this or her field of expertise, invited by a United Kingdom Higher Education Institution or a United Kingdom based research or arts organisation as part of that institution or organisation's quality assurance processes;
   (b) give one or more lectures in his or her field of expertise as a visitor lecturer, invited by a United Kingdom Higher Education Institution or a United Kingdom based research or arts organisation provided this is not in a formal teaching role;
   (c) as an overseas designated pilot examiner, assess United Kingdom based pilots to ensure they meet the national aviation regulatory requirements of other countries, by invitation of an approved training organisation based in the United Kingdom that is regulated by the United Kingdom Civil Aviation Authority for that purpose;
   (d) provide advocacy in a particular area of law as a qualified lawyer for the purposes of a court or tribunal hearing, arbitration or other form of alternative dispute resolution for legal proceedings within the United Kingdom, at the invitation of a client in the United Kingdom or foreign based client:

      (e)   undertake an activity relating to the arts, entertainment or sporting professions, by invitation of an arts or sports organisation or broadcaster based in the United Kingdom; and

(iv)   does not intend to take employment, produce goods or provide services within the United Kingdom, including the selling of goods or services direct to members of the public other than as permitted for by the pre-arranged paid engagement; and

(v)   will maintain and accommodate him or herself adequately out of resource available to the applicant without recourse to public funds or taking employment; or will be maintained and accommodated adequately by relatives or friends.

Leave to enter as a visitor undertaking permitted paid engagements

56Y. A person seeking leave to enter the United Kingdom as a visitor undertaking permitted paid engagements may be admitted for a single entry and for a period not exceeding 1 month, with a condition prohibiting study and recourse to public funds provided the Immigration Officer is satisfied that each of the requirements of paragraph 56X are met.

Refusal of leave to enter as a visitor undertaking permitted paid engagements

56Z. Leave to enter as a visitor undertaking permitted paid engagements is to be refused if the Immigration Officer is not satisfied that each of the requirements of paragraph 56X are met.

[Commonwealth Games Family Member Visitor

Period for which these rules have effect

56ZA. ...

Deleted by HC 693, para 31 as from 6 November 2014, save that if an application has been made for entry clearance or leave to enter or remain before 6 November 2014, the application will be decided in accordance with the Rules in force on 5 November 2014.

Requirements for leave to enter or remain as a Commonwealth Games Family Member Visitor

56ZB. ...

Deleted by HC 693, para 31 as from 6 November 2014, save that if an application has been made for entry clearance or leave to enter or remain before 6 November 2014, the application will be decided in accordance with the Rules in force on 5 November 2014.

Leave to enter or remain as a Commonwealth Games Family Member Visitor

56ZC. ...

Deleted by HC 693, para 31 as from 6 November 2014, save that if an application has been made for entry clearance or leave to enter or remain before 6 November 2014, the application will be decided in accordance with the Rules in force on 5 November 2014.

Refusal of leave to enter or remain as a Commonwealth Games Family Member

56ZD. ...

Deleted by HC 693, para 31 as from 6 November 2014, save that if an application has been made for entry clearance or leave to enter or remain before 6 November 2014, the application will be decided in accordance with the Rules in force on 5 November 2014.

Requirements for leave to enter or remain as a Commonwealth Games Family Child Visitor

56ZE. ...

Deleted by HC 693, para 31 as from 6 November 2014, save that if an application has been made for entry clearance or leave to enter or remain before 6 November 2014, the application will be decided in accordance with the Rules in force on 5 November 2014.

Leave to enter or remain as a Commonwealth Games Family Member Child Visitor

56ZF. ...

Deleted by HC 693, para 31 as from 6 November 2014, save that if an application has been made for entry clearance or leave to enter or remain before 6 November 2014, the application will be decided in accordance with the Rules in force on 5 November 2014.

Refusal of leave to enter or remain as a Commonwealth Games Family Member Child Visitor

56ZG. ...

Deleted by HC 693, para 31 as from 6 November 2014, save that if an application has been made for entry clearance or leave to enter or remain before 6 November 2014, the application will be decided in accordance with the Rules in force on 5 November 2014.

Meaning of employment related to the Commonwealth Games

56ZH. ...

Notes

Inserted by HC 628, para 26. Deleted by HC 693, para 31 as from 6 November 2014, save that if an application has been made for entry clearance or leave to enter or remain before 6 November 2014, the application will be decided in accordance with the Rules in force on 5 November 2014.

PART 3 — PERSONS SEEKING TO ENTER OR REMAIN IN THE UNITED KINGDOM FOR STUDIES

Paragraphs 57–75 DELETED.

Student nurses

[Postgraduate doctors, dentists and trainee general practitioners]

[[Requirements for leave to enter the United Kingdom to take the Professional and Linguistic Assessments Board (PLAB Test) or an Objective Structured Clinical Examination (OSCE).]]

75A. [The requirements to be met by a person seeking leave to enter in order to take the PLAB Test [or an OSCE] are that the applicant:
[(i)   is a graduate of a medical school and intends to take the PLAB Test, or is a graduate of an overseas nursing school and intends to take an OSCE, in the UK; and
(ii)   can provide documentary evidence of a confirmed test date or of his eligibility to take the PLAB Test by way of a letter or email from the General Medical Council or a test admission card; or can provide evidence of a confirmed test date or of his eligibility to take an OSCE by way of a letter from the Nursing and Midwifery Council; and
(iii)   meets the requirements of paragraph 41(ii)-(viii) and (x)-(xi) for entry as a visitor; and]

(iv)   [intends to leave the United Kingdom at the end of his leave granted under this paragraph unless he is successful in the PLAB Test and granted leave to remain to undertake a clinical attachment in accordance with paragraphs 75G to 75M of these Rules.]]

Note

Paras 75A–75M inserted by HC 346, para 7 as from 5 March 2005. Paragraph (iv) substituted by HC 314, para 28 as from 31 March 2009. Para (ii): words in square brackets inserted by HC 565, para 42 as from 6 September 2012. Further amended by HC 693, para 32 as from 6 November 2014, save that if an application has been made for entry clearance or leave to enter or remain before 6 November 2014, the application will be decided in accordance with the Rules in force on 5 November 2014. Amended by HC 693, para 33 as from 6 November 2014, save that if an application has been made for entry clearance or leave to enter or remain before 6 November 2014, the application will be decided in accordance with the Rules in force on 5 November 2014. Amended by HC 693, para 34 as from 6 November 2014, save that if an application has been made for entry clearance or leave to enter or remain before 6 November 2014, the application will be decided in accordance with the Rules in force on 5 November 2014.

[Leave to enter to take the PLAB Test [or an OSCE]]

75B.   [A person seeking leave to enter the United Kingdom to take the PLAB Test [or an OSCE] may be admitted for a period not exceeding 6 months [subject to a condition prohibiting employment, study and recourse to public funds], provided the Immigration Officer is satisfied that each of the requirements of paragraph 75A is met.]

Note

Paras 75A–75M inserted by HC 346, para 7 as from 5 March 2005. Words in square brackets inserted by HC 565, para 43 as from 6 September 2012. Further amended by HC 693, para 35 as from 6 November 2014, save that if an application has been made for entry clearance or leave to enter or remain before 6 November 2014, the application will be decided in accordance with the Rules in force on 5 November 2014. Further amended by HC 693, para 36 as from 6 November 2014, save that if an application has been made for entry clearance or leave to enter or remain before 6 November 2014, the application will be decided in accordance with the Rules in force on 5 November 2014.

[Refusal of leave to enter to take the PLAB Test [or an OSCE]]

75C.   [Leave to enter the United Kingdom to take the PLAB Test [or an OSCE] is to be refused if the Immigration Officer is not satisfied that each of the requirements of paragraph 75A is met.]

Note

Paras 75A–75M inserted by HC 346, para 7 as from 5 March 2005. Further amended by HC 693, para 37 as from 6 November 2014, save that if an application has been made for entry clearance or leave to enter or remain before 6 November 2014, the application will be decided in accordance with the Rules in force on 5 November 2014. Further amended by HC 693, para 38 as from 6 November 2014, save that if an application has been made for entry clearance or leave to enter or remain before 6 November 2014, the application will be decided in accordance with the Rules in force on 5 November 2014.

[Requirements for an extension of stay in order to take the PLAB Test]

75D.   [The requirements for an extension of stay in the United Kingdom in order to take the PLAB Test are that the applicant:

(i)   was given leave to enter the United Kingdom for the purposes of taking the PLAB Test in accordance with paragraph 75B of these Rules; and

(ii)   intends to take the PLAB Test and can provide documentary evidence of a confirmed test date [by way of a letter or email from the General Medical Council or a test admission card]; and

(iii)   meets the requirements set out in paragraph 41 (iii)–(vii); and

(iv)   intends to leave the United Kingdom at the end of his leave granted under this paragraph unless he is successful in the PLAB Test and granted leave to remain:

        (a)   as a postgraduate doctor or trainee general practitioner in accordance with paragraphs 70 to 75; or

        (b)   to undertake a clinical attachment in accordance with paragraphs 75G to 75M of these Rules; or

           . . .

(v)   would not as a result of an extension of stay spend more than 18 months in the United Kingdom for the purpose of taking the PLAB Test][; and

(vi)   must not be in the UK in breach of immigration laws except that any period of overstaying for a period of 28 days or less will be disregarded.]

Note

Paras 75A–75M inserted by HC 346, para 7 as from 15 March 2005. Sub-para (ii): words in square brackets inserted by HC 565, para 44 as from 6 September 2012. Sub-paragraph (iv)(d) deleted by HC 321, para 6 as from 29 February 2008. Sub-paragraph (iv)(c) deleted by HC 1113, para 39(c) as from 27 November 2008. Sub-paragraph (vi) inserted by HC 194, para 13 as from 1 October 2012.

[Extension of stay to take the PLAB Test]

75E. [A person seeking leave to remain in the United Kingdom to take the PLAB Test may be granted an extension of stay for a period not exceeding 6 months [subject to a condition prohibiting employment, study and recourse to public funds], provided the Secretary of State is satisfied that each of the requirements of paragraph 75D is met.]

Note

Paras 75A–75M inserted by HC 346, para 7 as from 5 March 2005. Words in square brackets inserted by HC 565, para 45 as from 6 September 2012.

[Refusal of extension of stay to take the PLAB Test]

75F. [Leave to remain in the United Kingdom to take the PLAB Test is to be refused if the Secretary of State is not satisfied that each of the requirements of paragraph 75D is met.]

[Requirements for leave to enter to undertake a clinical attachment or dental observer post]

75G. The requirements to be met by a person seeking leave to enter to undertake a clinical attachment or dental observer post are that the applicant:

(i)   is a graduate from a medical or dental school and intends to undertake a clinical attachment or dental observer post in the United Kingdom; and

(ii)   can provide documentary evidence of the clinical attachment or dental observer post which will:

        (a)   be unpaid; and

        (b)   only involve observation, not treatment, of patients; and

(iii)   meets the requirements of paragraph 41 (iii)–(vii) of these Rules; and

(iv)   [intends to leave the United Kingdom at the end of his leave granted under this paragraph;]

(v)   if he has previously been granted leave in this category, is not seeking leave to enter which, when amalgamated with those previous periods of leave, would total more than 6 months.

Note

Paras 75A–75M inserted by HC 346, para 7 as from 5 March 2005. Sub-paragraph (iv)(c) deleted by HC 321, para 8 as from 29 February 2008. Paragraph (iv) substituted by HC 314, para 30 as from 31 March 2009.

[Leave to enter to undertake a clinical attachment or dental observer post]

75H. [A person seeking leave to enter the United Kingdom to undertake a clinical attachment or dental observer post may be admitted for the period of the clinical attachment or dental observer post, [up to a maximum of 3 months at a time] or

6 months in total in this category, [subject to a condition prohibiting employment, study and recourse to public funds,] provided the Immigration Officer is satisfied that each of the requirements of paragraph 75G is met.]

Note

Paras 75A–75M inserted by HC 346, para 7 as from 5 March 2005. Amended by HC 1039, para 11 as from 6 April 2014: where an applicant has made an application for entry clearance or leave before 6 April 2013 and the application has not been decided before that date, it will be decided in accordance with the Rules in force on 5 April.

[Refusal of leave to enter to undertake a clinical attachment or dental observer post]

75J. [Leave to enter the United Kingdom to undertake a clinical attachment or dental observer post is to be refused if the Immigration Officer is not satisfied that each of the requirements of paragraph 75G is met.]

Note

Paras 75A–75M inserted by HC 346, para 7 as from 5 March 2005.

[Requirements for an extension of stay in order to undertake a clinical attachment or dental observer post]

75K. [The requirements to be met by a person seeking an extension of stay to undertake a clinical attachment or dental observer post are that the applicant:
(i) was given leave to enter or remain in the United Kingdom to undertake a clinical attachment or dental observer post or:
    (a) for the purposes of taking the PLAB Test in accordance with paragraphs 75A to 75F and has passed both parts of the PLAB Test;
    (b) as a postgraduate doctor, dentist or trainee general practitioner in accordance with paragraphs 70 to 75; or
    (c) as a work permit holder for employment in the UK as a doctor or dentist in accordance with paragraphs 128 to 135; and
(ii) is a graduate from a medical or dental school and intends to undertake a clinical attachment or dental observer post in the United Kingdom; and
(iii) can provide documentary evidence of the clinical attachment or dental observer post which will:
    (a) be unpaid; and
    (b) only involve observation, not treatment, of patients; and
(iv) [intends to leave the United Kingdom at the end of his period of leave granted under this paragraph; and]
(v) meets the requirements of paragraph 41 (iii)–(vii) of these Rules] and;
(vi) if he has previously been granted leave in this category, is not seeking an extension of stay which, when amalgamated with those previous periods of leave, would total more than 6 months[; and
(vii) must not be in the UK in breach of immigration laws except that any period of overstaying for a period of 28 days or less will be disregarded.]

Note

Paras 75A–75M inserted by HC 346, para 7 as from 5 March 2005. Paragraph (iv) substituted by HC 314, para 31 as from 31 March 2009. Paragraph (vii) inserted by HC 194, para 14 as from 1 October 2012.

[Extension of stay to undertake a clinical attachment or dental observer post]

75L. [A person seeking leave to remain in the United Kingdom to undertake a clinical attachment or dental observer post may be granted an extension of stay for the period of their clinical attachment or dental observer post, [up to a maximum of 3 weeks at a time] or 6 months in total in this category [subject to a condition prohibiting employment, study and recourse to public funds] provided that the Secretary of State is satisfied that each of the requirements of paragraph 75K is met.]

Note

Paras 75A–75M inserted by HC 346, para 7 as from 5 March 2005. Words in square brackets inserted by HC 565, para 47 as from 6 September 2012. Further amended by HC 1039, para 11: where an applicant has made an application for entry clearance or leave before 6 April 2013 and the application has not been decided before that date, it will be decided in accordance with the Rules in force on 5 April 2013.

[Refusal of extension of stay to undertake a clinical attachment or dental observer post]

75M. [Leave to remain in the United Kingdom to undertake a clinical attachment or dental observer post is to be refused if the Secretary of State is not satisfied that each of the requirements of paragraph 75K is met.]

Note

Paras 75A–75M inserted by HC 346, para 7 as from 5 March 2005.

[Spouses or civil partners of students or civil partners of prospective students granted leave under this part of the Rules]

Note

Heading substituted by HC 314.

Requirements for leave to enter or remain as the spouse or civil partner of a student and for leave to remain as the spouse or civil partner of a prospective student]

76. The requirements to be met by a person seeking leave to enter or remain in the United Kingdom as the spouse or civil partner of a student or [leave to remain as a spouse or civil partner of] a prospective student are that:

(i)   the applicant is married to or the civil partner of a person admitted to or allowed to remain in the United Kingdom under paragraphs 57–75 [or 82–87F]; and

(ii)   each of the parties intends to live with the other as his or her spouse or civil partner during the applicant's stay and the marriage or the civil partnership is subsisting; and

(iii)   there will be adequate accommodation for the parties and any dependants without recourse to public funds; and

(iv)   the parties will be able to maintain themselves and any dependants adequately without recourse to public funds; and

(v)   the applicant does not intend to take employment except as permitted under paragraph 77 below; and

(vi)   the applicant intends to leave the United Kingdom at the end of any period of leave granted to him[; and

(vii) if seeking leave to remain must not be in the UK in breach of immigration laws except that any period of overstaying for a period of 28 days or less will be disregarded.]

Note

Paragraph (vii) inserted by HC 194, para 15 as from 1 October 2012. Amended by HC 628, para 28 and if applicant has made an application for entry clearance or leave before 1 October 2012, the application will be decided in accordance with the Rules in force on 30 September 2013.

Note

Unmarried partners are not included: see para 76(i). On para 76(iii), see *PA (Student's family: third-party support) Bangladesh* [2008] UKAIT 00016 disallowing the possibility of support from a third party, but see *Mahad (previously referred to as AM) (Ethiopia) v Entry Clearance Officer* [2009] UKSC 16, [2010] 2 All ER 535 overruling a prohibition on third party support under similarly worded provisions in Part 8 of the rules (dealing with applications for settlement).

Leave to enter or remain as the spouse or civil partner of a student [or leave to remain as the spouse or civil partner of a] prospective student]

77.   A person seeking leave to enter or remain in the United Kingdom as the spouse or civil partner of a student or [leave to remain as the spouse or civil partner of a] prospective student may be admitted or allowed to remain for a period not in excess of that granted to the student provided the Immigration Officer or, in the case of an application for limited leave to remain, the Secretary of State, is satisfied that each of the requirements of paragraph 76 is met. [Employment may be permitted] where the period of leave being granted is[, or was,] 12 months or more.

Note

Words in square brackets substituted and inserted by Cmnd 4851. Heading amended by HC 628, paras 29, 30 and if applicant has made an application for entry clearance or leave before 1 October 2013, the application will be decided in accordance with the Rules in force on 30 September 2013.

Refusal of leave to enter or remain as the spouse or civil partner of a student [or leave to remain as the spouse or civil partner of a prospective student]

78.   Leave to enter or remain as the spouse of a student or [leave to remain as the spouse or civil partner of a] prospective student is to be refused if the Immigration Officer or, in the case of an application for limited leave to remain, the Secretary of State is not satisfied that each of the requirements of paragraph 76 is met.

Note

Amended by HC 628, paras 30, 31 and if applicant has made an application for entry clearance or leave before 1 October 2013, the application will be decided in accordance with the Rules in force on 30 September 2013.

Children of students or prospective students [granted leave under this part of the Rules]

[Requirements for leave to enter or remain as the child of a student and for leave to remain as the child of a prospective student]

79.   The requirements to be met by a person seeking leave to enter or remain in the United Kingdom as the child of a student or leave to remain as the child of a prospective student are that he:
(i)   is the child of a parent admitted to or allowed to remain in the United Kingdom as a student under the paragraphs 57–75 [or 82–87F]; and
(ii)   is under the age of 18 or has current leave to enter or remain in this capacity; and
(iii)   [is not married or in a civil partnership], has not formed an independent family unit and is not leading an independent life; and
(iv)   can, and will, be maintained and accommodated adequately without recourse to public funds;
(v)   will not stay in the United Kingdom beyond any period of leave granted to his parent[, and]
(vi)   [meets the requirements of paragraph 79A][; and
(vii)   if seeking leave to remain must not be in the UK in breach of immigration laws except that any period of overstaying for a period of 28 days or less will be disregarded.

Note

Paragraphs (iv)-(vi) amended by HC 314, paras 34–36 as from 31 March 2009. Words in square brackets in sub-paragraph (iii) inserted by HC 1888, para 13 as from 6 April 2012. Sub-paragraph (vii) inserted by HC 194, para 16 as from 1 October 2012.

79A.   [Both of the applicant's parents must either be lawfully present in the UK, or being granted entry clearance or leave to remain at the same time as the applicant [or one parent must be lawfully present in the UK and the other being granted entry clearance or leave to remain at the same time as the applicant], unless:

(i)   The student or prospective student is the applicant's sole surviving parent, or

(ii)   The student or prospective student has and has had sole responsibility for the applicant's upbringing, or

(iii)   there are serious or compelling family or other considerations which would make it desirable not to refuse the application and suitable arrangements have been made in the UK for the applicant's care.]

Note

Paragraph 79 inserted by HC 314, para 37 as from 31 March 2009. Words in square brackets inserted by HC 1888, para 14 as from 6 April 2012.

Leave to enter or remain as the child of a student [or [leave to remain as the child of a] prospective student]

80.   [A person seeking leave to enter or remain in the United Kingdom as the child of a student or [leave to remain as he child of a] prospective student may be admitted or allowed to remain for a period not in excess of that granted to the student or prospective student provided the Immigration Officer or, in the case of an application for limited leave to remain, the Secretary of State is satisfied that each of the requirements of paragraph 79 is met. Employment may be permitted where the period of leave being granted is, or was, 12 months or more.]

Note

Substituted by Cmnd 4851. Amended by HC 628, paras 35, 36 and if applicant has made an application for entry clearance or leave before 1 October 2013, the application will be decided in accordance with the Rules in force on 30 September 2013.

Refusal of leave to enter or remain as the child of a student [or prospective student]

81.   Leave to enter or remain in the United Kingdom as the child of a student or [leave to remain as the child of a] prospective student is to be refused if the Immigration Officer or, in the case of an application for limited leave to remain, the Secretary of State, is not satisfied that each of the requirements of paragraph 79 is met.

Note

[Paras 76–81 replace HC 251, paras 31 and 116.]

Amended by HC 628, paras 37, 38.

The husband of a female student is able to qualify as a dependant spouse in the same way as a wife of a male student. Spouses and children are prohibited from taking employment unless the leave to enter or remain is for 12 months or more.

Prospective students

Requirements for leave to enter as a prospective student

[A82   In this Part "prospective student" means a person who was granted leave to enter as a prospective student under paragraph 83 as it was at 30 September 2013 (and see further Part 5 of Appendix F to these Rules)]

Notes

Inserted by HC 628, para 38.

Paragraphs 82–84 deleted by HC 628, para 39 and if applicant has made an application for entry clearance or leave before 1 October 2013, the application will be decided in accordance with the Rules in force on 30 September 2013.

Requirements for extension of stay as a prospective student

85.   Six months is the maximum permitted leave which may be granted to a prospective student. The requirements for an extension of stay as a prospective student are that the applicant:

(i) was admitted to the United Kingdom with a valid prospective student entry clearance; and
(ii) meets the requirements of paragraph 82; and
(iii) would not, as a result of an extension of stay, spend more than 6 months in the United Kingdom[; and
(iv) must not be in the UK in breach of immigration laws except that any period of overstaying for a period of 28 days or less will be disregarded.]

Note

Paragraph 85(i) amended by Cmnd 3953 and Cm 7074, para 18 as from 1 September 2007. Paragraph (iv) inserted by HC 194, para 17 as from 1 October 2012.

Extension of stay as a prospective student

86. An extension of stay as a prospective student may be granted, with a prohibition on employment, provided the Secretary of State is satisfied that each of the requirements of paragraph 85 is met.

Refusal of extension of stay as a prospective student

87. An extension of stay as a prospective student is to be refused if the Secretary of State is not satisfied that each of the requirements of paragraph 85 is met.

Note

Paragraphs 87A-87F deleted by HC 314, para 27(f) as from 31 March 2009. Paragraphs 88–94 deleted by HC 1113, para 39(d) and if applicant has made an application for entry clearance or leave before 1 October 2013, the application will be decided in accordance with the Rules in force on 30 September 2013.

PART 4 — PERSONS SEEKING TO ENTER OR REMAIN IN THE UNITED KINGDOM IN AN 'AU PAIR' PLACEMENT, AS A WORKING HOLIDAYMAKER OR FOR TRAINING OR WORK EXPERIENCE

Paragraphs 104–110 deleted by HC 1888, para 15 as from 6 April 2012.

Requirements for leave to enter as a teacher or language assistant under an approved exchange scheme

. . . . .

Note

Deleted by HC 1888, para 15 as from 6 April 2012.

Spouses or civil partners of persons with limited leave to enter or remain under paragraphs 110–121

Requirements for leave to enter or remain as the spouse or civil partner of a person with limited leave to enter or remain in the United Kingdom under paragraphs 110–121

122. The requirements to be met by a person seeking leave to enter or remain in the United Kingdom as the spouse or civil partner of a person with limited leave to enter or remain in the United Kingdom under paragraphs 110–121 are that:
(i) the applicant is married to or the civil partner of a person with limited leave to enter or remain in the United Kingdom under paragraphs 110–121; and
(ii) each or the parties intends to live with the other as his or her spouse or civil partner during the applicant's stay and the marriage or civil partnership is subsisting; and
(iii) there will be adequate accommodation for the parties and any dependants without recourse to public funds in accommodation which they own or occupy exclusively; and

(iv)   the parties will be able to maintain themselves and any dependants adequately without recourse to public funds; and

(v)   the applicant does not intend to stay in the United Kingdom beyond any period of leave granted to his spouse; and

(vi)   if seeking leave to enter, the applicant holds a valid United Kingdom entry clearance for entry in this capacity or, if seeking leave to remain, was admitted with a valid United Kingdom entry clearance for entry in this capacity[; or

(vii)   if seeking leave to remain, must not be in the UK in breach of immigration laws except that any period of overstaying for a period of 28 days or less will be disregarded.]

Note

Paragraph (vii) inserted by HC 194, para 18 as from 1 October 2012.

Leave to enter or remain as the spouse or civil partner of a person with limited leave to enter or remain in the United Kingdom under paragraphs 110–121

123.   A person seeking leave to enter or remain in the United Kingdom as the spouse or civil partner of a person with limited leave to enter or remain in the United Kingdom under paragraphs 110–121 may be given leave to enter or remain in the United Kingdom for a period of leave not in excess of that granted to the person with limited leave to enter or remain under paragraphs 110–121 provided that, in relation to an application for leave to enter, he is able, on arrival, to produce to the Immigration Officer a valid United Kingdom entry clearance for entry in this capacity or, in the case of an application for limited leave to remain, was admitted with a valid United Kingdom entry clearance for entry in this capacity and is able to satisfy the Secretary of State that each of the requirements of paragraph 122(i)–(v) [and (vii)] is met.

Note

Words "and (vii)" inserted by HC 194, para 19 as from 1 October 2012.

Refusal of leave to enter or remain as the spouse of a person with limited leave to enter or remain in the United Kingdom under paragraphs 110–121

124.   Leave to enter or remain in the United Kingdom as the spouse or civil partner of a person with limited leave to enter or remain in the United Kingdom under paragraphs 110–121 is to be refused if, in relation to an application for leave to enter, a valid United Kingdom entry clearance for entry in this capacity is not produced, the Immigration Officer on arrival or, in the case of an application for limited leave to remain, if the applicant was not admitted with a valid United Kingdom entry clearance for entry in this capacity or is unable to satisfy the Secretary of State that each of the requirements of paragraph 122(i)–(v) [and (vii)] is met.

Note

Words "and (vii)" inserted by HC 194, para 20 as from 1 October 2012.

Children of persons admitted or allowed to remain under paragraphs 110–121

Requirements for leave to enter or remain as the child of a person with limited leave to enter or remain in the United Kingdom under paragraphs 110–121

125.   The requirements to be met by a person seeking leave to enter or remain in the United Kingdom as the child of a person with limited leave to enter or remain in the United Kingdom under paragraphs 110–121 are that:

(i)   he is the child of a parent who has limited leave to enter or remain in the United Kingdom under paragraphs 110–121; and

(ii)   he is under the age of 18 or has current leave to enter or remain in this capacity; and

(iii)   he is unmarried and is not a civil partner, has not formed an independent family unit and is not leading an independent life; and

(iv)   he can, and will, be maintained and accommodated adequately without recourse to public funds in accommodation which his parent(s) own or occupy exclusively; and

(v)   he will not stay in the United Kingdom beyond any period of leave granted to his parent(s); and

(vi)   both parents are being or have been admitted to or allowed to remain in the United Kingdom save where:

   (a)   the parent he is accompanying or joining is his sole surviving parent; or

   (b)   the parent he is accompanying or joining has had sole responsibility for his upbringing; or

   (c)   there are serious and compelling family or other considerations which make exclusion from the United Kingdom undesirable and suitable arrangements have been made for his care; and

(vii)   if seeking leave to enter, he holds a valid United Kingdom entry clearance for entry in this capacity of, if seeking leave to remain, was admitted with a valid United Kingdom entry clearance for entry in this capacity[; or

(viii)   if seeking leave to remain, must not be in the UK in breach of immigration laws except that any period of overstaying for a period of 28 days or less will be disregarded.]

Note

Paragraph (viii) inserted by HC 194, para 21 as from 1 October 2012.

Leave to enter or remain as the child of a person with limited leave to enter or remain in the United Kingdom under paragraphs 110–121

126.   A person seeking leave to enter or remain in the United Kingdom as the child of a person with limited leave to enter or remain in the United Kingdom under paragraphs 110–121 may be given leave to enter or remain in the United Kingdom for a period of leave not in excess of that granted to the person with limited leave to enter or remain under paragraphs 110–121 provided that, in relation to an application for leave to enter, he is able, on arrival, to produce to the Immigration Officer a valid United Kingdom entry clearance for entry in this capacity or, in the case of an application for limited leave to remain, he was admitted with a valid United Kingdom entry clearance for entry in this capacity and is able to satisfy the Secretary of State that each of the requirements of paragraph 125(i)–(vi) [and (viii)] is met.

Note

Words "and (viii)" inserted by HC 194, para 22 as from 1 October 2012.

Refusal of leave to enter or remain as the child of a person with limited leave to enter or remain in the United Kingdom under paragraphs 110–121

127.   Leave to enter or remain in the United Kingdom as the child of a person with limited leave to enter or remain in the United Kingdom under paragraphs 110–121 is to be refused if, in relation to an application for leave to enter, a valid United Kingdom entry clearance for entry in this capacity is not produced to the Immigration Officer on arrival or, in the case of an application for limited leave to remain, if the applicant was not admitted with a valid United Kingdom entry clearance for entry in this capacity or is unable to satisfy the Secretary of State that each of the requirements of paragraph 125(i)–(vi) [and (viii)] is met.

Note

Words "and (viii)" inserted by HC 194, para 23 as from 1 October 2012.

PART 5 — PERSONS SEEKING TO ENTER OR REMAIN IN THE UNITED KINGDOM FOR EMPLOYMENT

Work permit employment

[General requirements for indefinite leave to remain

128A. [For the purposes of references in this Part to requirements for indefinite leave to remain:

(a) "continuous period of 5 years or 4 years lawfully in the UK" means[, subject to paragraph (aa)] residence in the United Kingdom for an unbroken period with valid leave, and for these purposes a period shall not be considered to have been broken where:

    [(aa) For the purposes of paragraph (a), time spent with valid leave in the Bailiwick of Guernsey, Bailiwick of Jersey or the Isle of Man may be included in the continuous period of 5 or 4 years residence in the UK, provided that:

        (i) the leave granted in the Bailiwick of Guernsey, Bailiwick of Jersey or the Isle of Man was granted in a category equivalent to those specified in the indefinite leave to remain provisions in this Part; and

        (ii) any period of leave granted in the Bailiwick of Guernsey, Bailiwick of Jersey or the Isle of Man as a work permit holder was for employment:

            (a) in a job which appears on the list of occupations skilled to National Qualifications Framework level 3 or above, as stated in the Codes of Practice in Appendix J, or

            (b) in a job which appears in the Creative Sector Codes of Practice in Appendix J, or

            (c) as a professional sportsperson (including a sports coach); and

        (iii) in the case of leave granted in the Bailiwick of Guernsey, Bailiwick of Jersey or the Isle of Man as an overseas domestic worker in a private household it was granted before 6 April 2012; and

        (iv) the most recent period of leave in the relevant continuous period of 5 years or 4 years has been granted in the United Kingdom.]

    (i) the applicant has been absent from the UK for a period of 180 days or less in any of the five consecutive 12 calendar month periods (or four consecutive 12 calendar month periods [where the applicant received a Highly Skilled Migrant Programme approval letter issued on the basis of an application made before 3 April 2006, and was subsequently granted entry clearance or leave to remain on the basis of that letter]) preceding the date of the application for indefinite leave to remain; and

    (ii) the applicant has existing limited leave to enter or remain upon their departure and return, except that where that leave expired no more than 28 days prior to a further application for entry clearance, that period and any period pending the determination of that application shall be disregarded; and

    (iii) the applicant has any period of overstaying between periods of entry clearance, leave to enter or leave to remain of up to 28 days and any period of overstaying pending the determination of an application made within that 28 day period disregarded.

(b) Except for periods when the applicant had leave as a highly skilled migrant, a self-employed lawyer, a writer, composer or artist, an innovator or on the grounds of his UK Ancestry[, and subject to paragraph (ba)]:

[(ba) For the purposes of paragraph (b), continuous employment in the UK may include employment in the Bailiwick of Guernsey, Bailiwick of Jersey or the Isle of Man under the terms of his work permit or in the employment for which he was given leave to enter or remain, provided that the most recent work permit or period of leave was granted in the UK; and, in any such case, paragraph (b) shall apply to employment in the Bailiwick of Guernsey, Bailiwick of Jersey or the Isle of Man in the same way as it applies to employment in the UK.]

(i)   the applicant must have been employed in the UK continuously throughout the five years, under the terms of his work permit or in the employment for which he was given leave to enter or remain, except that any breaks in employment in which he applied for leave as a work permit holder or as an employee under any provision of this section to work for a new employer shall be disregarded provided this is within 60 days of the end of his employment with his previous employer.

(ii)   any absences from the UK must have been for a purpose that is consistent with the continuous permitted employment in (i), including paid annual leave or for serious or compelling reasons.]

Note

Amended by HC 1039, paras 12–15 as from on or after 6 April 2013.

Paragraphs 128–133 deleted and paragraph 128 substituted by HC 1888, para 16 as from 6 April 2012 except insofar as relevant to paragraphs 134 to 135. Amended by HC 1138, para 12 as from 6 April 2014.

Requirements for leave to enter the United kingdom for work permit employment

128.   A person coming to the UK to seek or take employment must be otherwise eligible for admission under these Rules or eligible for admission as a seaman under contract to join a ship due to leave British waters. The requirements for applications for work permit employment set out in paragraphs 128 to 133 of these Rules were deleted on 6 April 2012 by Statement of Changes HC 1888 except insofar as relevant to paragraphs 134 to 135.

[Indefinite leave to remain for a work permit holder

134.   Indefinite leave to remain may be granted on application . . . provided [the applicant]:

(i)   . . . has spent a continuous period of 5 years lawfully in the UK, of which the most recent period must have been spent with leave as a work permit holder (under paragraphs 128 to 133 of these rules), and the remainder must be . . . [any combination of] leave as a work permit holder or leave as a highly skilled migrant (under paragraphs 135A to 135F of these rules) [or leave as a self-employed lawyer (under the concession that appeared in Chapter 6, Section I Annex D of the Immigration Directorate Instructions), or leave as a writer, composer or artist (under paragraphs 232 to 237 of these rules);]

(ii)   . . . has met the requirements of paragraph 128(i) to (v) throughout [their] leave as a work permit holder, and has met the requirements of paragraph 135G(ii) throughout any leave as a highly skilled migrant;

(iii)   . . . is still required for the employment in question, as certified by [the] employer; [and

(iv)   [provides certification from the employer] that [the applicant] is paid at or above the appropriate rate for the job as stated in [the Codes of Practice in Appendix J][or, where the applicant is on maternity, paternity or adoption leave at the time of the application and not being paid the appropriate rate, the date that leave started and that they were paid at the appropriate rate immediately before the start of that leave], and

(v)   [. . . provided [the specified documents in paragraph 134–SD] to evidence the employer's certification in sub-section (iv) [and the reason for the absences set out in paragraph 128A], and][

(vi)   [has demonstrated sufficient knowledge of the English language and sufficient knowledge about life in the United Kingdom, in accordance with Appendix KoLL; and]

(vii)   [does not fall for refusal under the general grounds for refusal]][; and

(viii) must not be in the UK in breach of immigration laws except that any period of overstaying for a period of 28 days or less will be disregarded.]

Note

Para 134 substituted by HC 321, para 11 as from 29 February 2008. Words in square brackets inserted by HC 607. Para 9, (iv) substituted by, and (v) and (vi) added by, HC 863, para 10 as from

6 April 2011. Further amended by HC 1511, para 7 as from 31 October 2011. Further amended by Cm 8423, paras 21–22 as from 20 July 2012. Paragraph (viii) inserted by HC 194, para 24 as from 1 October 2012. Further amended by HC 760, paras 11–18 as from 13 December 2012. Further amended by HC 1039, para 16 as from on or after 6 April 2013. Further amended by HC 628, para 40 and if applicant has made an application for entry clearance or leave before 1 October 2013, the application will be decided in accordance with the Rules in force on 30 September 2013.

[**Specified documents**

134-SD   The specified documents referred to in paragraph 134(v) are [A, B and C below]:

A. Either a payslip and a personal bank or building society statement, or a payslip and a building society pass book.
(a)   Payslips must be:
   (i)   the applicant's most recent payslip,
   (ii)   dated no earlier than one calendar month before the date of the application, and
   (iii)   either:
      (1)   an original payslip,
      (2)   on company-headed paper, or
      (3)   accompanied by a letter from the applicant's Sponsor, on company headed paper and signed by a senior official, confirming the payslip is authentic.
(b)   Personal bank or building society statements must:
   (i)   be the most applicant's most recent statement,
   (ii)   be dated no earlier than one calendar month before the date of the application,
   (iii)   clearly show:
      (1)   the applicant's name,
      (2)   the applicant's account number,
      (3)   the date of the statement,
      (4)   the financial institution's name,
      (5)   the financial institution's logo, and
      (6)   transactions by the Sponsor covering the period no earlier than one calendar month before the date of the application, including the amount shown on the specified payslip as at 134–SD A (a),
   (iv)   be either:
      (1)   printed on the bank's or building society's letterhead,
      (2)   electronic bank or building society statements ..., accompanied by a supporting letter from the bank or building society, on company headed paper, confirming the statement provided is authentic, or
      (3)   electronic bank or building society statements ..., bearing the official stamp of the bank or building society on every page,
      and
   (v)   not be mini-statements from automatic teller machines (ATMs).
(c)   Building society pass books must
   (i)   clearly show:
      (1)   the applicant's name,
      (2)   the applicant's account number,
      (3)   the financial institution's name,
      (4)   the financial institution's logo, and
      (5)   transactions by the sponsor covering the period no earlier than one calendar month before the date of the application, including the amount shown on the specified payslip as at 134–SD A (a), and
      and
   (ii)   be either:

(1) the original pass book, or
(2) a photocopy of the pass book which has been certified by the issuing building society on company headed paper, confirming the statement provided is authentic.

B. A letter from the employer detailing the purpose and period of absences in connection with the employment, including periods of annual leave. Where the absence was sue to a serious or compelling reason, a personal letter from the applicant which includes all details of the reason for the absences and all original supporting documents in relation to those reasons — e.g. medical certificates, birth/death certificates, information about the reasons which led to the absence from the UK.]

[C. Where the applicant is not being paid the appropriate rate in Appendix J due to maternity, paternity or adoption leave:
(a) Payslips must be:
(i) the applicant's payslip from the month immediately preceding the leave,
(ii) the applicant's payslips for each month of the period of the leave,
(iii) as set out in A(a)(iii) above.
(b) Bank or building society statements must be:
(i) the applicant's statement from the month immediately preceding the leave,
(ii) the applicant's statement for each month of the period of the leave,
(iii) as set out in A(b)(iii) above.]

Note

Inserted by HC 760, para 19 as from 13 December 2012. Further amended by HC 1039, paras 17, 18 as from on or after 6 April 2013. Further amended by HC 628, paras 41, 42 and if applicant has made an application for entry clearance or leave before 1 October 2013, the application will be decided in accordance with the Rules in force on 30 September 2013.

Refusal of indefinite leave to remain for a work permit holder

135. Indefinite leave to remain in the United Kingdom for a work permit holder is to be refused if the Secretary of State is not satisfied that each of the requirements of paragraph 134 is met.

Note

[*Paras 128–135 replace HC 251, paras 34, 35, 122 and 139(a).*]

[Highly skilled migrants]

Note

Paragraph 135A–135F DELETED.

[Requirements for indefinite leave to remain as a highly skilled migrant

135G. The requirements for indefinite leave to remain for a person who has been granted leave as a highly skilled migrant are that the applicant:
(a) has spent a continuous period of 5 years (or 4 years where the applicant received a Highly Skilled Migrant Programme approval letter issued on the basis of an application made before 3 April 2006, and was subsequently granted entry clearance or leave to remain on the basis of that letter) lawfully in the United Kingdom; and
(b) on the date that the continuous period of 5 years (or 4 years as appropriate, as set out in (a)) ends, has leave as a highly skilled migrant, and has spent the remainder of the period with leave as a highly skilled migrant, a work permit holder or an Innovator; and
(c) throughout the 5 years (or 4 years where applicable, as set out in (a)) spent in the United Kingdom, has maintained and accommodated himself and any dependants adequately without recourse to public funds; and

(d)   is lawfully economically active in the United Kingdom in employment, self-employment or a combination of both; and

(e)   has demonstrated sufficient knowledge of the English language and sufficient knowledge about life in the United Kingdom, in accordance with Appendix KoLL, unless the applicant received a Highly Skilled Migrant Programme approval letter issued on the basis of an application made before 7 November 2006, and was subsequently granted entry clearance or leave to remain on the basis of that letter; and

(f)   does not fall for refusal under the general grounds for refusal, except that paragraph 322(1C) shall not apply if the applicant received a Highly Skilled Migrant Programme approval letter issued on the basis of an application made before 7 November 2006, and was subsequently granted entry clearance or leave to remain on the basis of that letter; and

(g)   must not be in the UK in breach of immigration laws except that any period of overstaying for a period of 28 days or less will be disregarded, unless the applicant received a Highly Skilled Migrant Programme approval letter issued on the basis of an application made before 7 November 2006, and was subsequently granted entry clearance or leave to remain on the basis of that letter; and

(h)   has made the application for indefinite leave to remain before 6 April 2018.]

Note

Words in square brackets in (i) inserted by Cm 7701, para 2 as from 1 October 2009. Words in square brackets in (i) inserted by Cm 7701, para 3 as from 1 October 2009. Words in sub-paras (i), (ii), (iv), (v) "set out in Appendix S" substituted by HC 565, paras 48–51 as from 6 September 2012. Words in square brackets in (iv) inserted by Cm 7701, para 4 as from 1 October 2009. Words in square brackets in (iv) inserted by HC 863, para 11 as from 6 April 2011, (v) added by HC 863, para 12 as from 6 April 2011. Paragraph (vi) inserted by HC 194, para 25 as from 1 October 2012. Further amended by HC 760, para 20 as from 13 December 2012. Further amended by HC 628, para 43 and if applicant has made an application for entry clearance or leave before 1 October 2013, the application will be decided in accordance with the Rules in force on 30 September 2013. Paragraph 135G deleted and Substituted by HC 1138, para 13 as from 13 March 2014. Substituted by HC 1138, para 13 as from 6 April 2014.

Indefinite leave to remain as a highly skilled migrant

135GA.   Indefinite leave to remain may be granted provided that the Secretary of State is satisfied that each of the requirements of paragraph 135G is met and that the application does not fall for refusal under paragraph 135HA.

Note

Inserted by HC 538.

Refusal of indefinite leave to remain as a highly skilled migrant

135H.   Indefinite leave to remain in the United Kingdom is to be refused if the Secretary of State is not satisfied that each of the requirements of paragraph 135G is met or if the application falls for refusal under paragraph 135HA.

Note

Inserted by HC 538.

Additional grounds for refusal for highly skilled migrants

135HA.   [An application under paragraphs 135A–135C or 135G–135H of these Rules is to be refused, even if the applicant meets all the requirements of those paragraphs, if the Immigration Officer or Secretary of State has cause to doubt the genuineness of any document submitted by the applicant and, having taken reasonable steps to verify the document, has been unable to verify that it is genuine.]

Note

Substituted by HC 321, para 14 as from 29 February 2008.

Paragraphs 135KJ-135N deleted by HC 314, para 27(g) as from 31 March 2009.

Paragraphs 135I-135T DELETED.

Representatives of overseas newspapers, news agencies and broadcasting organisations

Requirements for leave to enter as a representative of an overseas newspaper, news agency or broadcasting organisation

136.

Note

Deleted on 27 November 2008 by paragraphs 39 of Statement of Changes HC 1113 except insofar as they are relevant to paragraph 142 and 143,

Indefinite leave to remain for a representative of an overseas newspaper, news agency or broadcasting organisation

142.   Indefinite leave to remain may be granted, on application, to a representative of an overseas newspaper, news agency or broadcasting organisation provided [the applicant]:

(i)   . . . has spent a continuous period of 5 years [lawfully] in the United Kingdom in this capacity; and

(ii)   . . . has met the requirements of paragraph 139 throughout the 5 year period; and

(iii)   . . . is still required for the employment in question, as certified by [the] employer; and

(iv)   [has demonstrated sufficient knowledge of the English language and sufficient knowledge about life in the United Kingdom in accordance with Appendix KoLL; and]

(v)   [does not fall for refusal under the general grounds for refusal][; and

(vi)   . . . is not in the UK in breach of immigration laws except that any period of overstaying for a period of 28 days or less will be disregarded.]

(vii) [provides the specified documents in paragraph 142–SD to evidence the reason for the absences set out in paragraph 128A.]

Note

Words in square brackets inserted by HC 863, paras 13 and 14 as from 6 April 2011. Paragraph (vi) inserted by HC 194, para 26 as from 1 October 2012. Further amended by HC 760, paras 21–28 as from 13 December 2012. Further amended by HC 628, para 44 and if applicant has made an application for entry clearance or leave before 1 October 2013, the application will be decided in accordance with the Rules in force on 30 September 2013.

[Specified documents

142-SD   The specified documents referred to in paragraph 142(vii) are:

(a)   A letter from the employer detailing the purpose and period of absences in connection with the employment, including periods of annual leave.

(b)   Where the absence was due to a serious or compelling reason, a personal letter from the applicant which includes full details of the reason for the absences and all original supporting documents in relation to those reasons — e.g. medical certificates, birth/death certificates, information about the reasons which led to the absence from the UK.]

Note

Inserted by HC 760, para 29 as from 13 December 2012.

143. Indefinite leave to remain in the United Kingdom for a representative of an overseas newspaper, news agency or broadcasting organisation is to be refused if the Secretary of State is not satisfied that each of the requirements of paragraph 142 is met.

Note

Heading deleted by Cm 7701, para 5 as from 1 October 2009.

Paragraphs 143A-143F DELETED.

Representatives of overseas businesses

[Requirements for leave to enter as a representative of an overseas business

144. The requirements to be met by a person seeking leave to enter the United Kingdom as a representative are that he:
(i)   has been recruited and taken on as an employee outside the United Kingdom of a business which has its headquarters and principal place of business outside the United Kingdom; and
(ii)   is seeking entry to the United Kingdom:
    (a)   as a senior employee [of an overseas business which has no branch, subsidiary or other representative in the United Kingdom] with full authority to take operational decisions on behalf of the overseas business for the purpose of representing it in the United Kingdom by establishing and operating a registered branch or wholly owned subsidiary of that overseas business, the branch or subsidiary of which he will be concerned with same type of business activity as the overseas business; or
    (b)   as an employee of an overseas newspaper, news agency or broadcasting organisation being posted on a long-term assignment as a representative of their overseas employer.
(iii)   where entry is sought under (ii)(a), the person:
    (a)   will be the sole representative of the employer present in the United Kingdom under the terms of this paragraph;
    (b)   intends to be employed full time as a representative of that overseas business; and
    (c)   is not a majority shareholder in that overseas business.
(iv)   where entry is sought under (ii)(b), the person intends to work full-time as a representative of their overseas employer.
(v)   does not intend to take employment except within the terms of this paragraph; and
(vi)   has competence in the English language to the required standard on the basis that
    (a)   [the applicant is a national of one of the following countries: Antigua and Barbuda; Australia; the Bahamas; Barbados; Belize; Canada; Dominica; Grenada; Guyana; Jamaica; New Zealand; St Kitts and Nevis; St Lucia; St Vincent and the Grenadines; Trinidad and Tobago; United States of America [and provides the specified documents in paragraph 144–SD(a)]; or]
    (b)   [the applicant has a knowledge of English equivalent to level A1 or above or above of the Council of Europe's Common European Framework for Language Learning, and]
        (1)   [provides the specified documents from an English language test provider approved by the Secretary of State for these purposes, as listed in Appendix O, which clearly show] the applicants's name, the qualification obtained (which must meet or exceed [the standard described above]) and the date of the award, or
        (2)   [has obtained an academic qualification (not a professional or vocational qualification) which is deemed by UK NARIC to meet the recognised standard of a Bachelor's degree in the UK, and
        (i)   provides [the specified documents in paragraph 144–SD(b)] to show he has the qualification, and

        (ii)   UK NARIC has confirmed that the qualification was taught or researched in English to level C1 of the Council of Europe's Common European Framework for Language learning or above, or

     (3)   has obtained an academic qualification (not a professional or vocational qualification) which is deemed by UK NARIC to meet or exceed the recognised standard of a Bachelor's or Master's degree in the UK, and provides [the specified documents in paragraph 144–SD(c)] to show that:

        (i)   he has the qualification, and

        (ii)   the qualification was taught or researched in English,] [or

     (4)   [has obtained an academic qualification (not a professional or vocational qualification), which is deemed by UK NARIC to meet the recognised standard of a Bachelor's or Master's degree or PhD in the UK, from an educational establishment in one of the following countries: Antigua and Barbuda; Australia; The Bahamas; Barbados; Belize; Dominica; Grenada; Guyana; Ireland; Jamaica; New Zealand; St Kitts and Nevis; St Lucia; St Vincent and The Grenadines; Trinidad and Tobago; the UK; the USA; and provides [the specified documents in paragraph 144–SD(b)].]

(vii)   can maintain and accommodate himself and any dependants adequately without recourse to public funds; and

(viii) holds a valid United Kingdom entry clearance for entry in this capacity.

Note

Heading, sub-paras (i) and (ii)(a) amended by HC 439, paras 9–10 as from 6 April 2010. Sub-para (vi)(a), (b) substituted by HC 1888, paras 17, 18 as from 6 April 2012. Sub-para (vi)(b)(2) substituted by HC 863, para 15 as from 6 April 2011. Sub-para (vi)(b)(4) and word "or" preceding inserted by HC 1888, paras 19, 20 as from 6 April 2012. Further amended by Cm 8423, paras 24–29 as from 20 July 2012. Further amended by HC 628, para 45 and if applicant has made an application for entry clearance or leave before 1 October 2013, the application will be decided in accordance with the Rules in force on 30 September 2013.

[Specified documents

144.SD

(a)   The specified documents in paragraph 144(vi)(a) as evidence of nationality are the applicant's current valid original passport or travel document. If the applicant is unable to provide these, the UK Border Agency may exceptionally consider this requirement to have been met where the applicant provides full reasons in the passport section of the application form, and either:

    (1)   a current national identity document, or

    (2)   an original letter from his home government or embassy, on the letterheaded paper of the government or embassy, which has been issued by an authorised official of that institution and confirms the applicant's full name, date of birth and nationality.

(b)   The specified documents in paragraph 144(vi)(b)(2)(i) and paragraph 144(vi)(4) as evidence of qualifications taught in English are:

    (1)   the original certificate of the award, or

    (2)   if the applicant is awaiting graduation having successfully completed the qualification, or no longer has the certificate and the awarding institution is unable to provide a replacement, an academic transcript (or original letter in the case of a PhD qualification) from the awarding institution on its official headed paper, which clearly shows:

        (a)   the applicant's name,

        (b)   the name of the awarding institution,

        (c)   the title of the award,

        (d)   confirmation that the qualification has been or will be awarded, and

        (e)   the date that the certificate will be issued (if the applicant has not yet graduated) or confirmation that the institution is unable to reissue the original certificate or award.

(c)   The specified documents in paragraph 144(vi)(b)(3)(i) as evidence of qualifications taught in English are:

    (1)   the specified documents in (b) above, and

    (2)   an original letter from the awarding institution on its official headed paper, which clearly shows:

        (a)   the applicant's name,

        (b)   the name of the awarding institution,

        (c)   the title of the award,

        (d)   the date of the award, and

        (e)   confirmation that the qualification was taught in English.]

Note

Inserted by Cm 8423, para 30 as from 20 July 2012.

Leave to enter as a representative of an overseas business

145.   A person seeking leave to enter the United Kingdom as a representative of an overseas business may be admitted for a period not exceeding 3 years provided he is able to produce to the Immigration Officer, on arrival, a valid United Kingdom entry clearance for entry in this capacity, and his leave may be subject to the following conditions:

(i)   no recourse to public funds,

(ii)   registration with the police, if this is required by paragraph 326 of these Rules, and

(iii)   no employment other than working for business which the applicant has been admitted to represent.]

Refusal of leave to enter as a representative of an overseas business

146.   Leave to enter as a representative is to be refused if a valid United Kingdom entry clearance for entry in this capacity is not produced to the Immigration Officer on arrival

Requirements for an extension of stay as a representative of an overseas business

147.   The requirements for an extension of stay as a representative of an overseas business are that the applicant:

(i)   entered the United Kingdom with a valid United Kingdom entry clearance as:

    (a)   a sole representative of an overseas business, including entry under the rules providing for the admission of sole representatives in force prior to 1 October 2009; or

    (b)   a representative of an overseas newspaper, news agency or broadcasting organisation;

(ii)   the person was admitted in accordance with paragraph 144(ii)(a) and can show that:

    (a)   the overseas business still has its headquarters and principal date of business outside the United Kingdom; and

    (b)   he is employed full time as a representative of that overseas business has established and is in charge of its registered branch or wholly owned subsidiary; and

    (c)   he is still required for the employment in question, as certified by his employer;

(iii)   the person was admitted in accordance with paragraph 1444(iii)(b) and can show that:

    (a)   he is still engaged in the employment for which the entry clearance was granted; and

    (b)   he is still engaged for the employment in question, as certified by his employer:

(iv)   does not intend to take employment except within the terms of this paragraph; and

(v)   can maintain and accommodate himself and any dependants adequately without recourse to public funds][[; and

(vi)   must not be in the UK in breach of immigration laws except that any period of overstaying for a period of 28 days or less will be disregarded.]

Note

Paragraph (vi) inserted by HC 194, para 27 as from 1 October 2012.

Extension of stay as a representative of an overseas business

148. An extension of stay as a representative of an overseas business may be granted provided the Secretary of State is satisfied that each of the requirements of paragraph 147 is met. The extension of stay will be granted for:
(i)   a period not exceeding 2 years, unless paragraph (ii) applies.
(ii)   a period not exceeding 3 years, if the applicant was last granted leave prior to 1 October 2009, and will be subject to the following conditions:
    (i)   no recourse to public funds,
    (ii)   registration with the police, if this is required by paragraph 326 of these Rules, and
    (iii)   no employment other than working for the business which the applicant has been admitted to represent.]

Refusal of extension of stay as a representative of an overseas business

149. An extension of stay as a representative of an overseas business is to be refused if the Secretary of State is not satisfied that each of the requirements of paragraph 147 is met.

Indefinite leave to remain for a representative of an overseas business

150. Indefinite leave to remain may be granted, on application, to a representative of an overseas business provided [the applicant]:
(i)   . . . has spent a continuous period of 5 years [lawfully] in the United Kingdom in this capacity; and
(ii)   . . . has met the requirements of paragraph 147 throughout the 5 year period; and
(iii)   . . . is still required for the employment in question, as certified by [the] employer; and
(iv)   [has demonstrated sufficient knowledge of the English language and sufficient knowledge about life in the United Kingdom, in accordance with Appendix KoLL, and]
(v)   [does not fall for refusal under the general grounds for refusal]][; and
(vi)   . . . is not in the UK in breach of immigration laws except that any period of overstaying for a period of 28 days or less will be disregarded.]
(vii)   [provides the specified documents in paragraph 150–SD to evidence the reason for the absences set out in paragraph 128A.]

Note

Words in square brackets inserted by HC 863, paras 16 and 17 as from 6 April 2011. Paragraph (vi) inserted by HC 194, para 28 as from 1 October 2012. Further amended by HC 760, paras 30–37 as from 13 December 2012. Further amended by HC 628, para 46 and if applicant has made an application for entry clearance or leave before 1 October 2013, the application will be decided in accordance with the Rules in force on 30 September 2013.

[Specified documents

150-SD The specified documents referred to in paragraph 150(vii) are:
(a)   A letter from the employer detailing the purpose and period of absences in connection with the employment, including periods of annual leave.
(b)   Where the absence was due to a serious or compelling reason, a personal letter from the applicant which includes full details of the reason for the absences and all original supporting documents in relation to those reasons —e.g. medical certificates, birth/death certificates, information about the reasons which led to the absence from the UK.]

Note

Inserted by HC 760, paras 38 as from 13 December 2012.

Refusal of indefinite leave to remain for a sole representative of an overseas business

151. Indefinite leave to remain in the United Kingdom for a representative of an overseas business is to be refused if the Secretary of State is not satisfied that each of the requirements of paragraph 150 is met.]

Note

Paras 144–151 replace HC 251, paras 39, 124 and 139(b). Paras 144 to 151 deleted by Cm 7701, para 5 as from 1 October 2009. Paras 144 to 151 substituted by Cm 7701, para 6 as from 1 October 2009.

For guidance, see the Modernised Guidance at: www.ukba.homeoffice.gov.uk/sitecontent/docume nts/policyandlaw/modernised/working/ outside-pbs/overseas-businesses.pdf?view=Binary

Private servants in diplomatic households

Requirements for leave to enter as a private servant in a diplomatic household

152.

Note

Deleted on 27 November 2007 by paragraph 39 of Statement of Changes HC 1113 except insofar as relevant to paragraph 158 and 159.

Indefinite leave to remain for a servant in a diplomatic household

158. Indefinite leave to remain may be granted, on application, to a private servant in a diplomatic household provided [the applicant]:
(i)   . . . has spent a continuous period of 5 years [lawfully] in the United Kingdom in this capacity; and
(ii)   . . . has met the requirements of paragraph 155 throughout the 5 year period; and
(iii)   . . . is still required for the employment in question, as certified by [the] employer
(iv)   [has demonstrated sufficient knowledge of the English language and sufficient knowledge about life in the United Kingdom, in accordance with Appendix KoLL; and]
(v)   [does not fall for refusal under the general grounds for refusal]][; and
(vi)   . . . is not in the UK in breach of immigration laws except that any period of overstaying for a period of 28 days or less will be disregarded.]
(vii)   [provides the specified documents in paragraph 158-SD to evidence the reason for the absences set out in paragraph 128A.]

Note

Words in square brackets inserted by HC 863, para 19 as from 6 April 2011. Words "in accordance with paragraph 33B of these Rules" inserted in sub-para (iv) by HC 1888, para 21 as from 6 April 2012. Paragraph (vi) inserted by HC 194, para 29 as from 1 October 2012. Further amended by HC 760, paras 39–46 as from 13 December 2012. Further amended by HC 628, para 47 and if an applicant has made an application for entry clearance or leave before 1 October 2013, the application will be decided in accordance with the Rules in force on 30 September 2013.

[Specified documents

[158-SD   The specified documents referred to in paragraph 158(vii) are:
(a)   A letter from the employer detailing the purpose and period of absences in connection with the employment, including periods of annual leave.
(b)   Where the absence was due to a serious or compelling reason, a personal letter from the applicant which includes full details of the reason for the absences and all original supporting documents in relation to those reasons —e.g. medical certificates, birth/death certificates, information about the reasons which led to the absence from the UK.]

Note

Inserted by HC 760, para 47 as from 13 December 2012.

Appendix 3 — Immigration Rules

Refusal of indefinite leave to remain for a servant in a diplomatic household

159. Indefinite leave to remain in the United Kingdom for a private servant in a diplomatic household is to be refused if the Secretary of State is not satisfied that each of the requirements of paragraph 158 is met.

Note

[Paras 152–159 replace HC 251, paras 40(a) and 123.]

The age has been raised from 16 to 18 and now private servants can qualify for settlement.

[Domestic workers in private households]

Requirements for leave to enter as a domestic worker in a private household

[**159A.** The requirements to be met by a person seeking leave to enter the United Kingdom as a domestic worker in a private household are that the applicant:
(i)   is aged 18-65 inclusive;
(ii)   has been employed as a domestic worker for one year or more immediately prior to the application for entry clearance under the same roof as the employer or in a household that the employer uses for himself on a regular basis and where evidence . . . is produced to demonstrate the connection between employer and employee [in the form of:
    (a)   a letter from the employer confirming that the domestic worker has been employed by them in that capacity for the twelve months immediately prior to the date of application; and
    (b)   on of the following documents covering the same period of employment as that in (a):]
        (i)   payslips or bank statements showing payment of salary;
        (ii)   confirmation of tax paid;
        (iii)   confirmation of health insurance paid;
        (iv)   contract of employment;
        (v)   work visa, residence permit or equivalent passport endorsement for the country in which the domestic worker has been employed by that employer; or
        (vi)   visas or equivalent passport endorsement to confirm that the domestic worker has travelled with the employer; and
    and
(iii)   intends to work for the employer whilst the employer is in the United Kingdom and intends to travel in the company of either;
    (a)   a British or EEA national employer, or that employer's British or EEA national spouse, civil partner or child, where the employer's usual place of residence is outside the UK and where the employer does not intend to remain in the UK beyond six months; or
    (b)   a British or EEA national employer's foreign national spouse, civil partner or child where the employers does not intend to remain in the UK beyond six months; or
    (c)   a foreign national employer or the employer's spouse, civil partner or child where the employer is seeking or has been granted entry clearance or leave to enter under Part 2 of these Rules; and
(iv)   intends to leave the UK at the end of six months in the United Kingdom or at the same time as the employer, whichever is the earlier[, and does not intend to live for extended periods in the United Kingdom through frequent or successive visits; and]
(v)   has agreed in writing terms and conditions of employment in the UK, with the employer, [evidence of this in the form set out in Appendix 7], including specifically that the applicant will be paid in accordance with the National

798

Minimum Wage Act 1998 and any regulations made under it, and provides this with the entry clearance application; and

(vi)   will not take employment other than within the terms of this paragraph to work full time as a domestic worker for the employer in a household that the employer intends to live in; and

(vii)   can maintain and accommodate himself adequately without recourse to public funds; and

(viii)   holds a valid United Kingdom entry clearance for entry in this capacity.]

Note

Main heading and paras 159A–159H inserted by Cmnd 5597. Paragraph 159A substituted by HC 1888, para 22 as from 6 April 2012. Further amended by HC 565, paras 52, 53 as from 6 September 2012.

For guidance, see the Modernised Guidance at: www.ukba.homeoffice.gov.uk/sitecontent/docume nts/policyandlaw/modernised/working/outside-pbs/domestic-workers.pdf?view=

On the interpretation of the requirements in para 159A(ii), see *Wusa (para 159A(ii): Connection) Nigeria* [2011] UKUT 482 (IAC). Amended by HC 693, para 39 as from 6 November 2014, save that if an application has been made for entry clearance or leave to enter or remain before 6 November 2014, the application will be decided in accordance with the Rules in force on 5 November 2014.

[Leave to enter as a domestic worker in a private household

159B.   A person seeking leave to enter the United Kingdom as a domestic worker in a private household may be given leave to enter for that purpose for a period not exceeding [6] months provided he is able to produce to the Immigration Officer, on arrival, a valid United Kingdom entry clearance for entry in this capacity.]

Note

Main heading and paras 159A–159H inserted by Cmnd 5597. Figure substituted by HC 1888, para 23 as from 6 April 2012.

[Refusal of leave to enter as a domestic worker in a private household

159C.   Leave to enter as a domestic worker in a private household is to be refused if a valid United Kingdom entry clearance for entry in this capacity is not produced to the Immigration Officer on arrival.]

Note

Main heading and paras 159A–159H inserted by Cmnd 5597.

[Requirements for extension of stay as a domestic worker in a private household

159D.   The requirements for an extension of stay as a domestic worker in a private household are that the applicant:

(i)   entered the United Kingdom with a valid entry clearance as a domestic worker in a private household; and

(ii)   was granted less than 6 months leave to enter in this capacity; and

(iii)   has continued to be employed for the duration of leave granted as a domestic worker in the private household of the employer with whom the applicant entered or joined in the UK; and

(iv)   continues to be required for employment for the period of the extension sought as a domestic worker in a private household that the employer lives in [where there is evidence of this in the form of written terms and conditions of employment in the UK as set out in Appendix 7 and evidence that the employer is living in the UK]; and

(v)   does not intend to take employment except as a domestic worker in the private household of the employer; and

(vi)   meets each of the requirements of paragraph 159A(iv) and (vii)][; and

(vii)   must not be in the UK in breach of immigration laws except that any period of overstaying for a period of 28 days or less will be disregarded.]

Note

Main heading and paras 159A–159H inserted by Cmnd 5597. Paragraph 159A substituted by HC 1888, para 24 as from 6 April 2012. Paragraph (vii) inserted by HC 19, para 30 as from 1 October 2012. Words in square brackets in sub-para (iv) inserted by HC 565, para 54 as from 6 September 2012.

[**Extension of stay as a domestic worker in a private household**

159E. An extension of stay as a domestic worker in a private household may be granted for a period of six months less than the period already spent in the UK in this capacity.]

Note

Main heading and paras 159A–159H inserted by Cmnd 5597. Paragraph 159E and accompanying heading substituted by HC 1888, para 25 as from 6 April 2012.

[**Requirements for extension of stay as a domestic worker in a private household for applicants who entered the United Kingdom under the Rules in place before 6 April 2012**

159EA. The requirements for an extension of stay as a domestic worker in a private household for applicants who entered the United Kingdom under Rules in place before 6 April 2012 are that the applicant:

(i)   [last] entered the UK with a valid entry clearance as a domestic worker in a private household under Rules in place before 6 April 2012; and

(ii)   has continued to be employed for the duration of leave granted as a domestic worker in a private household; and

(iii)   continues to be required for employment for the period of the extension sough as a [full time] domestic worker in a private household under the same roof as the employer or in the same household that the employer lived in and where [evidence of this in the form of written terms and conditions of employment in the UK as set out in Appendix 7 and evidence that the employer resides in the UK]; and

(iv)   [does not intend to take employment except as a full time domestic worker in a private household referred to in paragraph 159EA (iii); and]

(v)   meets the requirements of paragraph 159A(i) and (vii)][; and

(vi)   must not be in the UK in breach of immigration laws except that any period of overstaying for a period of 28 days or less will be disregarded.]

Note

Paragraph 159EA and accompanying heading substituted by HC 1888, para 25 as from 6 April 2012. Words in square brackets in sub-para (ii) substituted by HC 565, para 55 as from 6 September 2012. Paragraph (vi) inserted by HC 194, para 31 as from 1 October 2012. Amended by HC 628, paras 48–50 and if applicant has made an application for entry clearance or leave before 1 October 2013, the application will be decided in accordance with the Rules in force on 30 September 2013.

[**Extension of stay as a domestic worker in a private household for applicants who entered into the United Kingdom under the Rules in place before 6 April 2012**

159EB. (i) An extension of stay as a domestic worker in a private household may be granted for a period not exceeding 12 months at a time provided the Secretary of State is satisfied that each of the requirements of paragraph 159EA are met.]

(ii) An extension of stay as a domestic worker in a private household may be granted for a period not exceeding 12 months at a time provided the Secretary of State is satisfied that each of the requirements of paragraph 159EA are met.]

Note

Paragraph 159EB and accompanying heading substituted by HC 1888, para 25 as from 6 April 2012.

[Refusal of extension of stay as a domestic worker in a private household.

159F. An extension of stay as a domestic worker may be refused if the Secretary of State is not satisfied that each of the requirements of [either paragraph 159D or, where applicable, ... [either paragraph 159D or where applicable, paragraph 159EA, is met.]]

Note

Main heading and paras 159A–159H inserted by Cmnd 5597. Words deleted and inserted in paragraph 159F by HC 1888, para 26 as from 6 April 2012.

[Indefinite leave to remain for a domestic worker in a private household.

159G. The requirements for indefinite leave to remain as a domestic worker in a private household are that the applicant:
(i)   entered the United Kingdom with a valid entry clearance as a domestic worker in a private household under the Rules in place before 6 April 2012; and
(ii)   has spent a continuous period of 5 years [lawfully] in the United Kingdom employed in this capacity; and
(iii)   he has met the requirements of paragraph 159A(vi) and (vii) throughout the 5 years [lawfully] period; and
(iv)   continues to be required for employment as a domestic worker in a private household as certified by the current employer; and
(v)   [has demonstrated sufficient knowledge of the English language and sufficient knowledge about life in the United Kingdom, in accordance Appendix KoLL; and]
(vi)   [fall for refusal under the general grounds for refusal]][; and
(vii)   must not be in the UK in breach of immigration laws except that any period of overstaying for a period of 28 days or less will be disregarded.]
(viii) [provides the specified documents in paragraph 159G-SD to evidence the reason for the absences set out in paragraph 128A.]

Note

Main heading and paras 159A–159H inserted by Cmnd 5597. Paragraph 159G substituted by HC 1888, para 27 as from 6 April 2012. Paragraph (vii) inserted by HC 194, para 32 as from 1 October 2012. Further amended by HC 760, paras 48–50 as from 13 December 2012. Further amended by HC 628, para 52 and if applicant has made an application for entry clearance or leave before 1 October 2013, the application will be decided in accordance with the Rules in force on 30 September 2013.

[Specified documents

159G-SD The specified documents referred to in paragraph 159G(viii) are:
(a)   A letter from the employer detailing the purpose and period of absences in connection with the employment, including periods of annual leave.
(b)   Where the absence was due to a serious or compelling reason, a personal letter from the applicant which includes full details of the reason for the absences and all original supporting documents in relation to those reasons —e.g. medical certificates, birth/death certificates, information about the reasons which led to the absence from the UK.]

Note

Inserted by HC 760, para 51 as from 13 December 2012.

[Refusal of indefinite leave to remain for a domestic worker in a private household

159H. Indefinite leave to remain in the United Kingdom for a domestic worker in a private household is to be refused if the Secretary of State is not satisfied that each of the requirements of paragraph 159G is met.]

Note

Main heading and paras 159A–159H inserted by Cmnd 5597.

Overseas government employees

Requirements for leave to enter as an overseas government employee

160. Deleted on 27 November 2008 by paragraph 39 of Statement of Changes HC 1113 except insofar as they are relevant to paragraph 167 and 168.

Indefinite leave to remain for an overseas government employee

167. Indefinite leave to remain may be granted, on application, to an overseas government employee provided [the applicant]:

(i)   . . . has spent a continuous period of 5 years [lawfully] in the United Kingdom in this capacity; and

(ii)   . . . has met the requirements of paragraph 164 throughout the 5 year period; and

(iii)   . . . is still required for the employment in question, as certified by [the] employer; and

(iv)   [has demonstrated sufficient knowledge of the English language and sufficient knowledge about life in the United Kingdom, in accordance with Appendix KoLL; and]

(v)   [does not fall for refusal under the grounds for refusal]][; and

(vi)   . . . is not in the UK in breach of immigration laws except that any period of overstaying for a period of 28 days or less will be disregarded.]

(vii)   [provides the specified documents in paragraph 167–SD to evidence the reason for the absences set out in paragraph 128A.]

Note

Words in square brackets inserted by HC 863, paras 20 and 21 as from 6 April 2011. Paragraph (vi) inserted by HC 194, para 33 as from 1 October 2012. Further amended by HC 760, paras 52–59 as from 13 December 2012. Further amended by HC 628, para 53 and if applicant has made an application for entry clearance or leave before 1 October 2013, the application will be decided in accordance with the Rules in force on 30 September 2013.

[Specified documents

167-SD   The specified documents referred to in paragraph 167(vii) are:

(a)   A letter from the employer detailing the purpose and period of absences in connection with the employment, including periods of annual leave.

(b)   Where the absence was due to a serious or compelling reason, a personal letter from the applicant which includes full details of the reason for the absences and all original supporting documents in relation to those reasons —e.g. medical certificates, birth/death certificates, information about the reasons which led to the absence from the UK.]

Note

Inserted by HC 760, para 60 as from 13 December 2012.

Refusal of indefinite leave to remain for an overseas government employee

168. Indefinite leave to remain in the United Kingdom for an overseas government employee is to be refused if the Secretary of State is not satisfied that each of the requirements of paragraph 167 is met.

Note

[Paras 160–168 replace HC 251, paras 40(b), 123 and 139(b).]

169. For the purposes of these Rules:

(i)   a minister of religion means a religious functionary whose main regular duties comprise the leading of a congregation in performing the rites and rituals of the faith and in preaching the essentials of the creed;

(ii)   a missionary means a person who is directly engaged in spreading a religious doctrine and whose work is not in essence administrative or clerical;

(iii)   a member of a religious order means a person who is coming to live in a community run by that order.

Requirements for leave to enter as a minister or religion, missionary or member of a religious order

170.   Amended by Cm 6297, para 1 as from 23 August 2004 and Cm 7074, para 19 as from 19 April 2007. Deleted on 27 November 2008 by paragraph 39 of Statement of Changes 1113 except insofar as they are relevant to paragraph 176 and 177.

Refusal of extension of stay as a minister of religion, missionary or member of a religious order

175.   An extension of stay as a minister of religion, missionary or member of a religious order is to be refused if the Secretary of State is not satisfied that each of the requirements of paragraph 173 [or 174A] is met.

Note

Words in square brackets inserted by Cm 6297, para 6 as from 23 August 2004.

Indefinite leave to remain for a minister of religion, missionary or member of a religious order

176.   Indefinite leave to remain may be granted, on application, to a person admitted as a minister of religion, missionary or member of a religious order provided [the applicant]:
(i)   . . . has spent a continuous period of 5 years [lawfully] in the United Kingdom in this capacity; and
(ii)   . . . has met the requirements of paragraph 173 [or 174A] throughout the 5 year period; and
(iii)   . . . is still required for the employment in question as certified by the leadership of [the] congregation, [the] employer or the head of the religious order to which [the applicant] belongs; and
(iv)   [has demonstrated sufficient knowledge of the English language and sufficient knowledge about life in the United Kingdom, in accordance Appendix KoLL; and]
(v)   [does not fall for refusal under the general grounds for refusal]][; and
(vi)   . . . is not in the UK in breach of immigration laws except that any period of overstaying for a period of 28 days or less will be disregarded.]
(vii)   [provides the specified documents in paragraph 176–SD to evidence the reason for the absences set out in paragraph 128A.]

Note

Words in square brackets inserted by Cm 6297, para 7 as from 23 August 2004. Words in square brackets in sub-paras (iv) and (v) inserted by HC 863, paras 22 and 23 as from 6 April 2011. Paragraph (vi) inserted by HC 194, para 34 as from 1 October 2012. Further amended by HC 760, paras 61–68 as from 13 December 2012. Further amended by HC 628, para 54 and if applicant has made an application for entry clearance or leave before 1 October 2013, the application will be decided in accordance with the Rules in force on 30 September 2013.

[Specified documents

176-SD   The specified documents referred to in paragraph 176(vii) are:
(a)   A letter from the leadership of the congregation, the employer or the head of the religious order to which the applicant belongs, detailing the purpose and period of absences in connection with the employment, including periods of annual leave.
(b)   Where the absence was due to a serious or compelling reason, a personal letter from the applicant which includes full details of the reason for the absences and all original supporting documents in relation to those reasons —e.g. medical certificates, birth/death certificates, information about the reasons which led to the absence from the UK.]

Note
Inserted by HC 760, para 69 as from 13 December 2012.

Refusal of indefinite leave to remain for a minister of religion, missionary or member of a religious order

177. Indefinite leave to remain in the United Kingdom for a minister of religion, missionary or member of a religious order is to be refused if the Secretary of State is not satisfied that each of the requirements of paragraph 176 is met.

. . .

Note
Paragraph 177A deleted by HC 1113.

Requirements for leave to enter the United Kingdom as a visiting religious worker or a religious worker in a non-pastoral role

Note
Paragraph 177B deleted by HC 1113.

Leave to enter as a visiting religious worker or a religious worker in a non-pastoral role

Note
Paragraph 177C deleted by HC 1113.

Refusal of leave to enter as a visiting religious worker or a religious worker in a non-pastoral role

Note
Paragraph 177D deleted by HC 1113.

Requirements for an extension of stay as a visiting religious worker or a religious worker in a non pastoral role

Note
Paragraph 177E deleted by HC 1113.

Extension of stay as a visiting religious worker or a religious worker in a non-pastoral role

Note
Paragraph 177F deleted by HC 1113.

Refusal of an extension of stay as a visiting religious worker or a religious worker in a non pastoral role

Note
Paragraph 177G deleted by HC 1113.

Airport-based operational ground staff of overseas-owned airlines

Paragraphs 178–183 deleted on 27 November 2008 by paragraph 39 of Statement of Changes HC 1113 except insofar as they are relevant to paragraph 184 and 185.

Indefinite leave to remain for a member of the operational ground staff of an overseas-owned airline

184. Indefinite leave to remain may be granted, on application, to a member of the operational ground staff of an overseas-owned airline provided [the applicant]:

(i)   . . . has spent a continuous period of 5 years [lawfully] in the United Kingdom in this capacity; and

(ii)   . . . has met the requirements of paragraph 181 throughout the 5 year period; and

(iii)   . . . is still required for the employment in question, as certified by the employer; and

(iv)   [has demonstrated sufficient knowledge of the English language and sufficient knowledge about life in the United Kingdom, in accordance Appendix KoLL; and]

(v)   [does not fall for refusal under the general grounds for refusal]][; and

(vi)   . . . is not in the UK in breach of immigration laws except that any period of overstaying for a period of 28 days or less will be disregarded.]

(vii) [provides the specified documents in paragraph 184–SD to evidence the reason for the absences set out in paragraph 128A.]

Note

Words in square brackets inserted by HC 863, paras 24 and 25 as from 6 April 2011. Paragraph (vi) inserted by HC 194, para 35 as from 1 October 2012. Further amended by HC 760, paras 70–77 as from 13 December 2012. Further amended by HC 628, para 55 and if applicant has made an application for entry clearance or leave before 1 October 2013, the application will be decided in accordance with the Rules in force on 30 September 2013.

[Specified documents

184-SD The specified documents referred to in paragraph 184(vii) are:

(a)   A letter from the employer detailing the purpose and period of absences in connection with the employment, including periods of annual leave.

(b)   Where the absence was due to a serious or compelling reason, a personal letter from the applicant which includes full details of the reason for the absences and all original supporting documents in relation to those reasons —e.g. medical certificates, birth/death certificates, information about the reasons which led to the absence from the UK.]

Note

Inserted by HC 760, para 78 as from 13 December 2012.

Refusal of indefinite leave to remain for a member of the operational ground staff of an overseas-owned airline

185. Indefinite leave to remain in the United Kingdom for a member of the operational ground staff of an overseas-owned airline is to be refused if the Secretary of State is not satisfied that each of the requirements of paragraph 184 is met.

Note

[Paras 178–185 replace HC 251, paras 40(e), 123 and 139(b).]

The new Rules clarify the requirements to be met and limit the posts to certain managerial grades.

Persons with United Kingdom ancestry

Requirements for leave to enter on the grounds of United Kingdom ancestry

186. The requirements to be met by a person seeking leave to enter the United Kingdom on the grounds of his United Kingdom ancestry are that he:

(i)   is a Commonwealth citizen; and

(ii)   is aged 17 or over; and

(iii)   is able to provide proof that one of his grandparents was born in the United Kingdom and Islands [and that any such grandparent is the applicant's blood grandparent or grandparent by reason of an adoption recognised by the laws of the United Kingdom relating to adoption]; and

(iv)　is able to work and intends to take or seek employment in the United Kingdom; and

(v)　will be able to maintain and accommodate himself and any dependants adequately without recourse to public funds; and

(vi)　holds a valid United Kingdom entry clearance for entry in this capacity.

Note

Words in square brackets in sub-para (iii) inserted by Cmnd 5949.

Leave to enter the United Kingdom on the grounds of United Kingdom ancestry

187.　A person seeking leave to enter the United Kingdom on the grounds of his United Kingdom ancestry may be given leave to enter for a period not exceeding 5 years provided he is able to produce to the Immigration Officer, on arrival, a valid United Kingdom entry clearance for entry in this capacity.

Refusal of leave to enter on the grounds of United Kingdom ancestry

188.　Leave to enter the United Kingdom on the grounds of United Kingdom ancestry is to be refused if a valid United Kingdom entry clearance for entry in this capacity is not produced to the Immigration Officer on arrival.

Requirements for an extension of stay on the grounds of United Kingdom ancestry

189　[The requirements to be met by a person seeking an extension of stay on the grounds of United Kingdom ancestry are that:

(i)　he is able to meet each of the requirements of paragraph 186 (i)–(v); and

(ii)　he was admitted to the United Kingdom on the grounds of United Kingdom ancestry in accordance with paragraphs 186 to 188 or has been granted an extension of stay in this capacity][; and

(iii)　he is not in the UK in breach of immigration laws except that any period of overstaying for a period of 28 days or less will be disregarded.]

Note

Para 189 substituted by HC 1112. Paragraph (iii) inserted by HC 194, para 36 as from 1 October 2012.

Extension of stay on the grounds of United Kingdom ancestry

190.　An extension of stay on the grounds of United Kingdom ancestry may be granted for a period not exceeding 3 years provided the Secretary of State is satisfied that each of the requirements of [paragraph 189] is met.

Note

Words in square brackets substituted by HC 1112.

Refusal of extension of stay on the grounds of United Kingdom ancestry

191.　An extension of stay on the grounds of United Kingdom ancestry is to be refused if the Secretary of State is not satisfied that each of the requirements of [paragraph 189] is met.

Note

Words in square brackets substituted by HC 1112.

Indefinite leave to remain on the grounds of United Kingdom ancestry

192.　Indefinite leave to remain may be granted, on application, to a Commonwealth citizen with a United Kingdom born grandparent provided [the applicant]:

(i)   . . . meets the requirements of paragraph 186(i)–(v); and
(ii)   . . . has spent a continuous period of 5 years [lawfully] in the United Kingdom in this capacity[; and
(iii)   [has demonstrated sufficient knowledge of the English language and sufficient knowledge about life in the United Kingdom, in accordance with Appendix KoLL; and]
(iv)   [does not fall for refusal under the general grounds for refusal]][; and
(v)   . . . is not in the UK in breach of immigration laws except that any period of overstaying for a period of 28 days or less will be disregarded.]
(vi)   [provides the specified documents in paragraph 192–SD to evidence the reason for the absences set out in paragraph 128A, where the absence was due to a serious or compelling reason.]

Note

Words in square brackets inserted by HC 863, para 26 as from 6 April 2011. Paragraph (v) inserted by HC 194, para 37 as from 1 October 2012. Further amended by HC 760, paras 79–85 as from 13 December 2012. Further amended by HC 628, para 56 and if applicant has made an application for entry clearance or leave before 1 October 2013, the application will be decided in accordance with the Rules in force on 30 September 2013.

[Specified documents

192-SD   The specified documents referred to in paragraph 192(vi) are:

A personal letter from the applicant which includes full details of the reason for the absences and all original supporting documents in relation to those reasons —e.g. medical certificates, birth/death certificates, information about the reasons which led to the absence from the UK.]

Note

Inserted by HC 760, para 86 as from 13 December 2012.

Refusal of indefinite leave to remain on the grounds of United Kingdom ancestry

193.   Indefinite leave to remain in the United Kingdom on the grounds of a United Kingdom born grandparent is to be refused if the Secretary of State is not satisfied that each of the requirements of paragraph 192 is met.

Note

[Paras 186–193 replace HC 251, paras 36 and 139(g).]

For guidance on paras 186–193, see the Modernised Guidance at: www.ukba.homeoffice.gov.uk/ sitecontent/documents/policyandlaw/modernised/working/ outside-pbs/uk-ancestry.pdf?view=Binary

[Partners] of persons who have or have had leave to enter or remain under paragraphs 128-193 (but not paragraphs 135I-135K)

[193A.   Nothing in paragraphs 194–194F is to be construed as allowing a person to be granted entry clearance, leave to enter, leave to remain or variation of leave as a [partner] of a person granted entry clearance or leave to enter under Paragraph 159A where that entry clearance or leave to enter was granted under 159A on or after 6 April 2012.]

Note

Paragraph 193A inserted by HC 1888, para 28 as from 6 April 2012. Heading amended by HC 628, para 57 and if applicant has made an application for entry clearance or leave before 1 October 2013, the application will be decided in accordance with the Rules in force on 30 September 2013.

Requirements for leave to enter as the [partner] of a person with limited leave to enter or remain in the United Kingdom under paragraphs 128-193 (but not paragraphs 135I-135K)

194. The requirements to be met by a person seeking leave to enter the United Kingdom as the [partner] of a person with limited leave to enter or remain in the United Kingdom under paragraphs 128-193 (but not paragraphs 135I-135K) are that:

(i) the applicant [is the spouse, civil partner, unmarried or same-sex partner of] a person with limited leave to enter in the United Kingdom under paragraphs 128-193 (but not paragraphs 135I-135K); and

(ii) [if an unmarried or same-sex partner:

  (1) any previous marriage or civil partnership (or similar relationship) by either partner has permanently broken down; and

  (2) the parties are not involved in a consanguineous relationship with one another; and

  (3) the parties have been living together in a relationship akin to marriage or civil partnership which has subsisted for 2 years or more; and

(iii) each of the parties intends to live with the other as his or her partner during the applicant's stay and the relationship is subsisting; and

(iv) there will be adequate accommodation for the parties and any dependants without recourse to public funds in accommodation which they own or occupy exclusively; and

(v) the parties will be able to maintain themselves and any dependants adequately without recourse to public funds; and

(vi) the applicant does not intend to stay in the United Kingdom beyond any period of leave granted to his partner; and

(vii) the applicant does not fall for refusal under the general grounds for refusal; and

(viii) the applicant holds a valid United Kingdom entry clearance for entry in this capacity.]

Note

Amended by HC 628, paras 58–60 and if applicant has made an application for entry clearance or leave before 1 October 2013, the application will be decided in accordance with the Rules in force on 30 September 2013.

Leave to enter as the [partner] of a person with limited leave to enter or remain in the United Kingdom under paragraphs 128-193 (but not paragraphs 135I-135K)

195. A person seeking leave to enter the United Kingdom as the spouse or civil partner of a person with limited leave to enter or remain in the United Kingdom under paragraphs 128-193 (but not paragraphs 135I-135K) may be given leave to enter for a period not in excess of that granted to the person with limited leave to enter or remain under paragraphs 128-193 (but not paragraphs 135I-135K) provided the Immigration Officer is satisfied that each of the requirements of paragraph 194 is met. [If the person is seeking leave to enter as the spouse or civil partner of a Highly Skilled Migrant, leave which is granted will be subject to a condition [prohibiting Employment as a Doctor or Dentist in Training, unless the applicant has obtained a degree in medicine or dentistry at bachelor's level or above from a UK institution that is a UK recognised or listed body, or which holds a sponsor licence under Tier 4 of the Points Based System[, and provides evidence of this degree.]]

Note

Words in square brackets inserted by HC 321, para 17 as from 29 February 2008 and further amended by HC 439, para 11 as from 6 April 2010. Words "and provides evidence of this degree" substituted by Cm 8423, para 31 as from 20 July 2012. Heading amended by HC 628, para 58 and if applicant has made an application for entry clearance or leave before 1 October 2013, the application will be decided in accordance with the Rules in force on 30 September 2013.

Refusal of leave to enter as the [partner] of a person with limited leave to enter or remain in the United Kingdom under paragraphs 128-193 (but not paragraphs 135I-135K)

196. Leave to enter the United Kingdom as the [partner] of a person with limited leave to enter or remain in the United Kingdom under paragraphs 128-193 (but not paragraphs 135I-135K) is to be refused if the Immigration Officer is not satisfied that each of the requirements of paragraph 194 is met.

Note

Heading amended by HC 628, para 58 and if applicant has made an application for entry clearance or leave before 1 October 2013, the application will be decided in accordance with the Rules in force on 30 September 2013.

Requirements for extension of stay as the [partner] of a person who has or has had leave to enter or remain in the United Kingdom under paragraphs 128-193 (but not paragraphs 135I-135K)

196A. The requirements to be met by a person seeking an extension of stay in the United Kingdom as the [partner] of a person who has or has had leave to enter or remain in the United Kingdom under paragraphs 128-193 (but not paragraphs 135I-135K) are that the applicant:

(i) [is the spouse, civil partner, unmarried or same-sex partner of a person who:
  (1) has limited leave to enter or remain in the United Kingdom under paragraphs 128–193 (but not paragraphs 135I-135K); or
  (2) has indefinite leave to remain in the United Kingdom or has become a British citizen, and who had limited leave to enter or remain in the United Kingdom under paragraphs 128-193 (but not paragraphs 135I-135K) immediately before being granted indefinite leave to remain;
(ii) meets the requirements of paragraph 194(ii)-(vii); and
(iii) was not granted:
  (1) entry clearance or leave as a visitor,
  (2) temporary admission, or
  (3) temporary release; and
(iv) must not be in the UK in breach of immigration laws except that any period of overstaying for a period of 28 days or less will be disregarded.]

Note

Paragraph (vi) inserted by HC 194, para 38 as from 1 October 2012. Heading amended by HC 628, paras 58–61 and if applicant has made an application for entry clearance or leave before 1 October 2013, the application will be decided in accordance with the Rules in force on 30 September 2013.

Extension of stay as the [partner] of a person who has or has had leave to enter or remain in the United Kingdom under paragraphs 128-193 (but not paragraphs 135I-135K)

196B. An extension of stay in the United Kingdom as:

(i) the [partner] of a person who has limited leave to enter or remain under paragraphs 128-193 (but not paragraphs 135I-135K) may be granted for a period not in excess of that granted to the person with limited leave to enter or remain; or
(ii) the [partner] of a person who is being admitted at the same time for settlement, or the [partner] of a person who has indefinite leave to remain [or has become a British citizen], may be granted for a period not exceeding 2 years, in both instances, provided the Secretary of State is satisfied that each of the requirements of paragraph 196A is met.

[If the person is seeking an extension of stay as the [partner], of a Highly Skilled Migrant, leave which is granted will be subject to a condition prohibiting Employment as a Doctor or Dentist in Training, unless the applicant:

(1) has obtained a [primary degree] in medicine or dentistry at bachelor's level or above from a UK institution that is a UK recognised or listed body, or which holds a sponsor licence under Tier 4 of the Points Based System; or
(2) [has, or has last been granted, entry clearance, leave to enter or leave to remain that was not subject to any condition restricting him from taking employment as a Doctor in Training, and has been employed during that leave as a Doctor in Training; or

(3)   has, or has last been granted, entry clearance, leave to enter or leave to remain that was not subject to any condition restricting him from taking employment as a Dentist in Training, and has been employed during that leave as a Dentist in Training.]

Note

Words at end in square brackets inserted by HC 321, para 18 as from 29 February 2008 and further amended by HC 439, para 12 as from 6 April 2010. Words in sub-para (1) inserted by HC 863, para 27 as from 6 April 2011. Sub-para (2) substituted by, and sub-para (3) inserted by, HC 863, para 28 as from 6 April 2011. Heading and sub-para (ii) amended by HC 628, paras 58, 62 and if applicant has made an application for entry clearance or leave before 1 October 2013, the application will be decided in accordance with the Rules in force on 30 September 2013.

Refusal of extension of stay as the [partner] of a person who has or has had leave to enter or remain in the United Kingdom under paragraphs 128-193 (but not paragraphs 135I-135K)

196C.   An extension of stay in the United Kingdom as the [partner] of a person who has or has had leave to enter or remain in the United Kingdom under paragraphs 128-193 (but not paragraphs 135I-135K) is to be refused if the Secretary of State is not satisfied that each of the requirements of paragraph 196A is met.

Note

Heading amended by HC 628, para 58 and if applicant has made an application for entry clearance or leave before 1 October 2013, the application will be decided in accordance with the Rules in force on 30 September 2013.

Requirements for indefinite leave to remain for the [partner] of a person who has or has had leave to enter or remain in the United Kingdom under paragraphs 128-193 (but not paragraphs 135I-135K)

196D.   The requirements to be met by a person seeking indefinite leave to remain in the United Kingdom as the [partner] of a person who has or has had leave to enter or remain in the United Kingdom under paragraphs 128-193 (but not paragraphs 135I-135K) are that the applicant:
(i)   [is the spouse, civil partner, unmarried or same-sex partner of a person who:
        (1)   has limited leave to enter or remain in the United Kingdom under paragraphs 128–193 (but not paragraphs 135I-135K) and who is being granted indefinite leave to remain at the same time; or
        (2)   is the spouse, civil partner, unmarried or same-sex partner of a person who has indefinite leave to remain in the United Kingdom or has become a British citizen, and who had limited leave to enter or remain in the United Kingdom under paragraphs 128–193 (but not paragraphs 135I-135K) immediately before being granted indefinite leave to remain; and
(ii)   meets the requirements of paragraph 194(ii)-(vii); and
(iii)   has demonstrated sufficient knowledge of the English language and sufficient knowledge about life in the United Kingdom, [in accordance with Appendix KoLL]; and
(iv)   was not last granted:
        (1)   entry clearance or leave as a visitor,
        (2)   temporary admission, or
        (3)   temporary release; and
(v)   must not be in the UK in breach of immigration laws except that any period of overstaying for a period of 28 days or less will be disregarded.]

Note

Words in square brackets inserted by HC 863, para 29 as from 6 April 2011. Paragraph (vii) inserted by HC 194, para 39 as from 1 October 2012. Paragraph (vi) substituted by HC 760, para 87 as from 13 December 2012. Amended by HC 628, paras 58, 59, 63, 64 and if applicant has made an application for entry clearance or leave before 1 October 2013, the application will be decided in accordance with the Rules in force on 30 September 2013.

Indefinite leave to remain as the [partner] of a person who has or has had leave to enter or remain in the United Kingdom under paragraphs 128-193 (but not paragraphs 135I-135K)

196E. Indefinite leave to remain in the United Kingdom [as] the [partner] of a person who has or has had leave to enter or remain in the United Kingdom under paragraphs 128-193 (but not paragraphs 135I-135K) may be granted provided the Secretary of State is satisfied that each of the requirements of paragraph 196D is met.

Note

Amended by HC 628, paras 58, 65 and if applicant has made an application for entry clearance or leave before 1 October 2013, the application will be decided in accordance with the Rules in force on 30 September 2013.

Refusal of indefinite leave to remain as the [partner] of a person who has or has had leave to enter or remain in the United Kingdom under paragraphs 128-193 (but not paragraphs 135I-135K)

196F. Indefinite leave to remain in the United Kingdom [as] the [partner] of a person who has or has had limited leave to enter or remain in the United Kingdom under paragraphs 128-193 (but not paragraphs 135I-135K) is to be refused if the Secretary of State is not satisfied that each of the requirements of [paragraph 196D] is met.

Note

Words in square brackets substituted by Cm 7944 as from 22 October 2010. Heading amended by HC 628, paras 58, 66 and if applicant has made an application for entry clearance or leave before 1 October 2013, the application will be decided in accordance with the Rules in force on 30 September 2013.

Children of persons with limited leave to enter or remain in the United Kingdom under paragraphs 128–193 [(but not paragraphs 135I–135K)]

Requirements for leave to enter or remain as the child of a person with limited leave to enter or remain in the United Kingdom under paragraphs 128–193 [(but not paragraphs 135I–135K)]

[**196G.** Nothing in paragraphs 197–199 is to be construed as allowing a person to be granted entry clearance, leave to enter, leave to remain or variation of leave as he child of a person granted entry clearance or leave to enter under Paragraph 159A where that entry clearance or leave to enter was granted under 19A on or after 6 April 2012.]

Note

Paragraph 196G inserted by HC 1888, para 29 as from April 2012.

197. The requirements to be met by a person seeking leave to enter or remain in the United Kingdom as a child of a person with limited leave to enter or remain in the United Kingdom under paragraphs 128–193 [(but not paragraphs 135I–135K)] are that:

(i) he is the child of a parent with limited leave to enter or remain in the United Kingdom under paragraphs 128–193 [(but not paragraphs 135I–135K) [or, in respect of applications for leave to remain only, of a parent who has indefinite leave to remain in the UK but who immediately before that grant had limited leave to enter or remain under those paragraphs]]; and

(ii) he is under the age of 18 or has current leave to enter or remain in this capacity; and

(iii) he is unmarried and is not a civil partner, has not formed an independent family unit and is not leading an independent life; and

(iv) he can and will be maintained and accommodated adequately without recourse to public funds in accommodation which his parent(s) own or occupy exclusively; and

(v) he will not stay in the United Kingdom beyond any period of leave granted to his parent(s); and

(vi)   both parents are being or have been admitted to or allowed to remain in the
         United Kingdom save where:
         (a)   the parent he is accompanying or joining is his sole surviving parent; or
         (b)   the parent he is accompanying or joining has had sole responsibility for
                 his upbringing; or
         (c)   there are serious and compelling family or other considerations which
                 make exclusion from the United Kingdom undesirable and suitable
                 arrangements have been made for his care; and
(vii)   [if seeking leave to enter, he holds a valid United Kingdom entry clearance for
         entry in this capacity or, if seeking leave to remain, he was not last granted:
         (1)   entry clearance or leave as a visitor,
         (2)   temporary admission, or
         (3)   temporary release; and]
(viii)   if seeking leave to remain, must not be in the UK in breach of immigration laws
         except that any period of overstaying for a period of 28 days or less will be
         disregarded.]

Note

Words in square brackets inserted by Cmnd 5829. Paragraph (viii) inserted by HC 194, para 40
as from 1 October 2012. Amended by HC 628, paras 67, 68 and if applicant has made an
application for entry clearance or leave before 1 October 2013, the application will be decided in
accordance with the Rules in force on 30 September 2013.

**[Leave to enter or remain as the child of a person with limited leave to enter or remain
in the United Kingdom under paragraphs 128–193 (but not paragraphs 135I–135K)**

198.   (a) A person seeking leave to enter or remain in the United Kingdom as the child
of a person with limited leave to enter or remain in the United Kingdom under
paragraphs 128–193 (but not paragraphs 135I–135K) may be given leave to enter or
remain in the United Kingdom for a period of leave not in excess of that granted to the
person with limited leave to enter or remain under paragraphs 128–193 (but not
paragraphs 135I–135K) provided that:
(i)   in relation to an application for leave to enter, he is able to produce to the
         Immigration Officer, on arrival, a valid United Kingdom entry clearance for
         entry in this capacity; or
(ii)   in the case of an application for limited leave to reman, he was not last granted:
         (1)   entry clearance or leave as a visitor,
         (2)   temporary admission, or
         (3)   temporary release,

and is able to satisfy the Secretary of State that each of the requirements of
paragraph 197(i)-(vi) and (viii) is met.

(b) A person seeking leave to remain as the child of a parent who has indefinite leave
to remain in the UK and who had limited leave under paragraphs 128–193 (but not
paragraphs 135I-135K) immediately before being granted indefinite leave maybe given
leave to remain in the UK for a period of 30 months provided he is in the UK with valid
leave under paragraph 198 and is able to satisfy the Secretary of State that each of the
requirements of paragraph 197(i) and 197(ii)-(vi) and (viii) is met.]

Note

Words in square brackets inserted by Cmnd 5829. Words "and (viii)" inserted by HC 194, para 41
as from 1 October 2012. Substituted and amended by HC 628, para 69, 70 and if applicant has
made an application for entry clearance or leave before 1 October 2013, the application will be
decided in accordance with the Rules in force on 30 September 2013.

812

[Refusal of leave to enter or remain as the child of a person with limited leave to enter or remain in the United Kingdom under paragraphs 128–193 (but not paragraphs 135I–135K)

198A. Leave to enter or remain in the United Kingdom as the child of a person with limited leave to enter or remain in the United Kingdom under paragraphs 128–193 (but not paragraphs 135I–135K) is to be refused if:
(i) in relation to an application for leave to enter, a valid United Kingdom entry clearance for entry in this capacity is not produced to the Immigration Officer on arrival; or
(ii) in the case of an application for limited leave to reman, he was not last granted:
    (1) entry clearance or leave as a visitor,
    (2) temporary admission, or
    (3) temporary release,

or is unable to satisfy the Secretary of State that each of the requirements of paragraph 197(i)-(vi) and (viii) is met.

Note

Substituted and amended by HC 628, para 69 and if applicant has made an application for entry clearance or leave before 1 October 2013, the application will be decided in accordance with the Rules in force on 30 September 2013.

[Requirements for indefinite leave to remain as the child of a person who has or has had leave to enter or remain in the United Kingdom under paragraphs 128–193 (but not paragraphs 135I–135K)

199. The requirements to be met by a person seeking indefinite leave to remain in the United Kingdom as the child of a person who has or has had leave to enter or remain in the United Kingdom under paragraphs 128–193 (but not paragraphs 135I–135K) are that the applicant:
(i) is the child of a person who:
    (1) has limited leave to enter or remain in the United Kingdom under paragraphs 128–193 (but not paragraphs 135I–135K) and who is being granted indefinite leave to remain at the same time; or
    (2) has indefinite leave to enter or remain in the United Kingdom and who had limited leave to enter or remain in the United Kingdom under paragraphs 128–193 (but not paragraphs 135I–135K) immediately before granted indefinite leave to remain; and
(ii) meets the requirements of paragraph 197(i)-(v) and (vii); and
(iii) was not last granted:
    (1) entry clearance or leave as a visitor,
    (2) temporary admission, or
    (3) temporary release,
(iv) does not fall for refusal under the general grounds for refusal; and
(v) must not be in the UK in breach of immigration laws except that any period of overstaying for a period of 28 days or less will be disregarded[; and]
(vi) has demonstrated sufficient knowledge of the English language and sufficient knowledge about life in the United Kingdom, in accordance with Appendix KoLL, unless he is under the age of 18 at the date on which the application is made.]

Note

Substituted and amended by HC 628, paras 69, 71, 72 and if applicant has made an application for entry clearance or leave before 1 October 2013, the application will be decided in accordance with the Rules in force on 30 September 2013.

[Indefinite leave to remain as the child of a person who has or has had leave to enter or remain in the United Kingdom under paragraphs 128–193 (but not paragraphs 135I-135K)

199A. Indefinite leave to remain as the child of a person who has or has had leave to enter or remain in the United Kingdom under paragraphs 128–193 (but not paragraphs 135I-135K) may be granted provided the Secretary of State is satisfied that each of the requirements of paragraph 199 is met.]

Note

Substituted by HC 628, para 69 and if applicant has made an application for entry clearance or leave before 1 October 2013, the application will be decided in accordance with the Rules in force on 30 September 2013.

[Refusal of indefinite leave to remain as the child of a person who has or has had leave to enter or remain in the United Kingdom under paragraphs 128–193 (but not paragraphs 135I-135K)

199B. Indefinite leave to remain as the child of a person who has or has had leave to enter or remain in the United Kingdom under paragraphs 128–193 (but not paragraphs 135I-135K) is to be refused if the Secretary of State is not satisfied that each of the requirements of paragraph 1999 is met.]

Note

Substituted by HC 628, para 69 and if applicant has made an application for entry clearance or leave before 1 October 2013, the application will be decided in accordance with the Rules in force on 30 September 2013.

PART 6 — PERSONS SEEKING TO ENTER OR REMAIN IN THE UNITED KINGDOM AS A BUSINESSMAN, SELF-EMPLOYED PERSON, INVESTOR, WRITER, COMPOSER OR ARTIST

[General requirements for indefinite leave to remain

200A. ...

Note

Inserted by HC 760, para 88 as from 13 December 2012. Further amended by HC 1039, paras 19–22 as from on or after 6 April 2013. Deleted by HC 628, para 73 and if applicant has made an application for entry clearance or leave before 1 October 2013, the application will be decided in accordance with the Rules in force on 30 September 2013.

Persons intending to establish themselves in business

Requirements for leave to enter the United Kingdom as a person intending to establish himself in business

200. Deleted on 30 June 2008 by paragraph 17 of the Statement of Changes HC 607 except insofar as relevant to paragraph 209. Please see Appendix F for the wording of these Rules in a case in which they are relevant.

201. Deleted on 30 June 2008 by paragraph 17 of the Statement of Changes HC 607 except insofar as relevant to paragraph 209. Please see Appendix F for the wording of these Rules in a case in which they are relevant.

202. Deleted on 30 June 2008 by paragraph 17 of the Statement of Changes HC 607 except insofar as relevant to paragraph 209. Please see Appendix F for the wording of these Rules in a case in which they are relevant.

203. Deleted on 30 June 2008 by paragraph 17 of the Statement of Changes HC 607 except insofar as relevant to paragraph 209. Please see Appendix F for the wording of these Rules in a case in which they are relevant.

Leave to enter the United Kingdom as a person seeking to establish himself in business

204.   Deleted on 30 June 2008 by paragraph 17 of the Statement of Changes HC 607 except insofar as relevant to paragraph 209. Please see Appendix F for the wording of these Rules in a case in which they are relevant.

Refusal of leave to enter the United Kingdom as a person seeking to establish himself in business

205.   Deleted on 30 June 2008 by paragraph 17 of the Statement of Changes HC 607 except insofar as relevant to paragraph 209. Please see Appendix F for the wording of these Rules in a case in which they are relevant.

Requirements for an extension of stay in order to remain in business

206.   Deleted on 30 June 2008 by paragraph 17 of the Statement of Changes HC 607 except insofar as relevant to paragraph 209. Please see Appendix F for the wording of these Rules in a case in which they are relevant

206B.   [Deleted on 30 June 2008 by paragraph 17 of the Statement of Changes HC 607 except insofar as relevant to paragraph 209. Please see Appendix F for the wording of these Rules in a case in which they are relevant

206C.   [Deleted on 30 June 2008 by paragraph 17 of the Statement of Changes HC 607 except insofar as relevant to paragraph 209. Please see Appendix F for the wording of these Rules in a case in which they are relevant

206D.   [Deleted on 30 June 2008 by paragraph 17 of the Statement of Changes HC 607 except insofar as relevant to paragraph 209. Please see Appendix F for the wording of these Rules in a case in which they are relevant

206E.   [Deleted on 30 June 2008 by paragraph 17 of the Statement of Changes HC 607 except insofar as relevant to paragraph 209. Please see Appendix F for the wording of these Rules in a case in which they are relevant

206F.   [Deleted on 30 June 2008 by paragraph 17 of the Statement of Changes HC 607 except insofar as relevant to paragraph 209. Please see Appendix F for the wording of these Rules in a case in which they are relevant

206G.   [Deleted on 30 June 2008 by paragraph 17 of the Statement of Changes HC 607 except insofar as relevant to paragraph 209. Please see Appendix F for the wording of these Rules in a case in which they are relevant.

206H   [Deleted on 30 June 2008 by paragraph 17 of the Statement of Changes HC 607 except insofar as relevant to paragraph 209. Please see Appendix F for the wording of these Rules in a case in which they are relevant.

206I.   [Deleted on 30 June 2008 by paragraph 17 of the Statement of Changes HC 607 except insofar as relevant to paragraph 209. Please see Appendix F for the wording of these Rules in a case in which they are relevant.

Extension of stay in order to remain in business

207.   [Deleted on 30 June 2008 by paragraph 17 of the Statement of Changes HC 607 except insofar as relevant to paragraph 209. Please see Appendix F for the wording of these Rules in a case in which they are relevant.

Refusal of extension of stay in order to remain in business

208.   [Deleted on 30 June 2008 by paragraph 17 of the Statement of Changes HC 607 except insofar as relevant to paragraph 209. Please see Appendix F for the wording of these Rules in a case in which they are relevant.

Indefinite leave to remain for a person established in business

209.   ...

Note

Deleted by HC 628, para 73.

[Specified documents

209-SD ....

Note

Inserted by HC 760, para 94 as from 13 December 2012. Deleted by HC 628, para 73.

Refusal of indefinite leave to remain for a person established in business

210. ...

Note

Deleted by HC 628, para 73.

Innovators

[Requirements for leave to enter the United Kingdom as an innovator

210A. ....

Note

Deleted by HC 628, para 73.

[Leave to enter as an innovator

210B. ....

Note

Deleted by HC 628, para 73.

[Refusal of leave to enter as an innovator

210C. ...

Note

Deleted by HC 628, para 73.

Requirements for an extension of stay as an innovator

210D-210G. ...

Note

Paras 210D–210G deleted by HC 628, para 73.

[Specified documents

210G-SD ....

Note

Inserted by HC 760, para 101 as from 13 December 2012. Deleted by HC 628, para 73.

[Refusal of indefinite leave to remain as an innovator

210H. ...

Note

Inserted by HC 538. Deleted by HC 628, para 73.

Persons intending to establish themselves in business under provisions of EC association agreements

Requirements for leave to enter the United Kingdom as a person intending to establish himself in business under the provisions of an EC Association Agreement

Note

Paragraph 211–214 deleted by HC 130.

Paragraphs 211–221 DELETED.

Paragraphs 212–223A DELETED.

Paras 227–242F deleted by HC 628, para 73.

[PART 6A POINTS-BASED SYSTEM

This General note relates to all of the separate categories within Part 6A of the rules.

Part 6A implements the Points Based System (PBS). The separate categories in the rules in Part 6A (hyperlinks to the relevant Guidance documents on the UKBA website are also set out) are:

Tier 1 (Exceptional Talent) Migrants [245B–245BF]

www.bia.homeoffice.gov.uk/sitecontent/applicationforms/pbs/t1-exceptional-talent-guide.pdf

Tier 1 (General) Migrants [245C–235CE]

www.ukba.homeoffice.gov.uk/sitecontent/applicationforms/pbs/t1-general-guidance.pdf

Tier 1 (Entrepreneur) Migrants [245D–245DF]

www.bia.homeoffice.gov.uk/sitecontent/applicationforms/pbs/tier1entrepreneurguidance1.pdf

Tier 1 (Investor) Migrants [245E–245EF]

www.ukba.homeoffice.gov.uk/sitecontent/applicationforms/pbs/tier1investorguidance1.pdf

Tier 1 (Graduate Entrepreneur) Migrants [245F-245FB]

www.ukba.homeoffice.gov.uk/sitecontent/applicationforms/pbs/t1-ge-guidance.pdf

Tier 2 (Intra-Company Transfer) Migrants [245G–245GF]

www.ukba.homeoffice.gov.uk/sitecontent/documents/policyandlaw/modernised/working/pbs/tier2?view=Binary

Tier 2 (General) Migrants; (Minister of Religion) Migrants; (Sportsperson) Migrants [245H–245HF]

www.bia.homeoffice.gov.uk/sitecontent/applicationforms/pbs/tier2-guidance.pdf

www.ukba.homeoffice.gov.uk/sitecontent/documents/policyandlaw/modernised/working/pbs/tier2?view=Binary

Tier 4 (General) Student [245ZT–245ZY]

www.bia.homeoffice.gov.uk/sitecontent/applicationforms/pbs/Tier4migrantguidance1.pdf

Tier 4 (Child) Student [245ZZ–245ZZD]

www.bia.homeoffice.gov.uk/sitecontent/applicationforms/pbs/Tier4migrantguidance1.pdf

Tier 5 (Youth Mobility scheme) Temporary Migrants [245ZI–245ZL]

www.bia.homeoffice.gov.uk/sitecontent/applicationforms/pbs/tier5youthmobilityguidance1.pdf

www.ukba.homeoffice.gov.uk/sitecontent/documents/policyandlaw/modernised/working/pbs/tier5-youthmobilityscheme?view=Binary

Tier 5 (Temporary Worker) Migrants [245ZN–245ZS]

www.bia.homeoffice.gov.uk/sitecontent/applicationforms/pbs/tier5temporaryworkerguidance1.pdf

www.ukba.homeoffice.gov.uk/sitecontent/documents/policyandlaw/modernised/working/pbs/tier5-temporaryworker?view=Binary

The structure of the requirements in the rules

Requirements in the body of the rules must be read in conjunction with:

- Appendices A – I setting out the detail of the requirements referred to in the text of the rules).
- Guidance documents (providing further detail on procedure in applying the rules)

The Guidance is subject to periodic amendment, and where it is important to know the precise content of a Guidance document as at the time of an application or decision, earlier versions of the documents (along with all other UKBA internal instructions) can be found on the National Archive Website: www.webarchive.nationalarchives.gov.uk/ and www.ukba.homeoffice.gov.uk/policyandlaw/

Relationship between the Immigration Rules and the Guidance

As to the relationship between the Guidance and the substantive requirements in the rules see *R (on the application of Alvi) v Secretary of State for the Home Department* [2012] UKSC 33. See also *Secretary of State for the Home Department v Pankina* [2010] EWCA Civ 719, [2010] 1 All ER 1043; see also *R (on the application of English UK Ltd) v Secretary of State for the Home Department* [2010] EWHC 1726 (Admin); and for the general applicability of *Pankina* in the interpretation of the rules by the Tribunal, see *FA and AA (PBS: effect of Pankina) Nigeria* [2010] UKUT 304 (IAC). The Guidance cannot purport to impose substantive requirements not found in the immigration rules. *Pankina* reversed the Tribunal's approach in *NA (Tier 1 Post-Study work funds)* [2009] UKAIT 00025, to the effect the structure of the Immigration rules read with the Guidance was a new form of hybrid provision where the Guidance was entitled to set out mandatory requirements.

A rule within the meaning of s 3(2) of the Immigration Act 1971 is to be defined as any requirement which, if not satisfied, will lead to an application for leave to enter or to remain being refused. A provision which is of that character is a rule within the ordinary meaning of that word. So a fair reading of s 3(2) requires that it be laid before Parliament: *R (on the application of Alvi) v Secretary of State for the Home Department* [2012] UKSC 33, [2012] All ER (D) 173 (Jul).

While the contents of Guidance which is not articulated in the Immigration rules (read with the relevant appendices) cannot be used adversely by Secretary of State for the Home Department in consideration of an application, the Tribunal have suggested in *HM (PBS – legitimate expectation – paragraph 245ZX (l) Malawi)* [2010] 446 UKUT (IAC) (although this decision has been expressly over ruled on its central reasoning by *QI (Pakistan) v Secretary of State for the Home Department* [2011] EWCA Civ 614;

Patel (revocation of sponsor licence – fairness) India [2011] UKUT 211 (IAC)) that an applicant may have a legitimate expectation that the guidance is followed where the contents of the Guidance assist an applicant's claim.

Following *Pankina*, many of the substantive requirements of the various PBS routes which were previously laid out in the Guidance have now been moved into the rules. As some of these amendments have been made in response to particular reported judgments of the courts, it's important to consider whether the case remains relevant notwithstanding the rule changes.

At the time of writing, in a very quick response to *Alvi*, the Secretary of State has signalled a statement of changes (HC514) is to be brought in with immediate effect to transfer further large quantities of guidance into the rules.

Fairness

On general issues of fairness in decision making under the PBS (with wider application), see *Patel (revocation of sponsor licence–fairness) India* [2011] UKUT 211 (IAC), and *Thakur (PBS decision–common law fairness) Bangladesh* [2011] UKUT 151 (IAC)(and see also *R (on the application of Q) v Secretary of State for the Home Department* [2003] EWCA Civ 364, [2003] 2 All ER 905). Immigration judges have jurisdiction to consider whether decisions on variation of leave applications are in accordance with the law, where issues of fairness arise.

It would be unfair to refuse an application for further leave where an applicant has had no prior knowledge of the revocation of a sponsor's licence and has been otherwise compliant with the provisions of the rules, and an applicant should be given an adequate opportunity to find another college at which to study; see *Patel* also for a general analysis of applications that have not been lawfully refused, and where there may be an opportunity to make a further application that constitutes an application for variation of leave; see also *QI (Pakistan) v Secretary of State for the Home Department* [2011] EWCA Civ 614(overruling *HM (PBS – legitimate expectation – paragraph 245ZX (l) Malawi)* [2010] 446 UKUT (IAC); and *QI (Pakistan) (para 245ZX (l) considered) Pakistan* [2010] UKUT 217 (IAC) on the basis that leave to remain granted by of the IA 1971, s 3C is relevant leave for the purposes of the Immigration Rules).

Where a sponsor's licence is revoked UKBA Guidance generally operates, where a student has more that six months' of the original leave granted remaining, to restrict remaining leave to 60 days. The period runs from the date on which the student received notice of the revocation (*Patel (Tier 4 – no '60 day extension') India* [2011] UKUT 187 (IAC); see also *JA (revocation of registration - Secretary of State's policy) India* [2011] UKUT 52 (IAC).

The UKBA's system of processing payments with postal applications risks falling into procedural unfairness *Basnet (validity of application – respondent) Nepal* [2012] UKUT 113 (IAC). If the UKBA asserts that an application was not accompanied by a fee, and so was not valid, the UKBA has the onus of proof.

The Secretary of State for the Home Department, drawing on practice (not contained in published policy) was found to have acted unfairly and irrationally in refusing applications sent together where the accompanying fees were sufficient to validate the applications of two of the three applicants (*US and MV (PBS – applicants from the same family) Malaysia* [2010] UKUT 167 (IAC). Where, however, a failure to provide documents clearly specified in the rules (photographs of an applicant; per para 34A of the rules) invalidated the application, the Secretary of State for the Home Department's treatment of the application was lawful (*R (on the application of Fu) v Secretary of State for the Home Department* [2010] EWHC 2922 (Admin)).

Article 8 of the ECtHR

On the possibility that a claim that failed under the PBS provisions in the Immigration rules might succeed under art 8 of the ECtHR, see *Secretary of State for the Home*

Department v Pankina [2010] EWCA Civ 719, [2011] 1 All ER 1043; *MB (Article 8 – near miss) Pakistan* [2010] UKUT 282 (IAC); the nature and degree of the non-compliance with the rules will be highly material in balancing the disruption of private and family life when set against the need to maintain immigration control. In *Pankina*, Sedley LJ said [paras 45-6]:

> There appears to me, in this situation, to be no escape from the proposition that in exercising her powers, whether within or outside the rules of practice for the time being in force, the Home Secretary must have regard and give effect to applicants' Convention rights. This will mean in most cases evaluating the extent and quality of their family and private life in the United Kingdom and the implications, both for them and for the United Kingdom, of truncating their careers here.' [45] 'That in turn will require consideration of the significance of the criteria by which their eligibility has been gauged and found wanting. It is one thing to expect an applicant to have the necessary academic and linguistic qualifications: here a miss is likely to be as good as a mile. It is another for an applicant to fall marginally or momentarily short of a financial criterion which in itself has no meaning: its significance is as a rough and ready measure of the applicant's ability to continue to live without reliance on public funds ... The Home Office has to exercise some common sense about this if it is not to make decisions which disproportionately deny respect to the private and family lives of graduates who by definition have been settled here for some years and are otherwise eligible for Tier 1 entry. [46].

Article 8 of the ECHR does not, however, create a free-standing right to depart from the requirements of the Immigration Rules. It will be particularly relevant, in weighing the balance under art 8 in a PBS case, that a person has come to the UK for temporary purposes and has no prior nexus with the UK. However, a person admitted for the purpose of studying who has not come to the end of their course which he/she is unable to complete by reason of non-compliance with the rules at that stage, depending on the reasons for the non-compliance, and where there are no countervailing considerations may have accrued private life that is worthy of respect: *CDS (PBS - 'available' - Article 8) Brazil* [2010] UKUT 00305 (IAC); see also *SAB (students – serious breach of conditions – Article 8) Ghana* [2010] UKUT 441 (IAC) for a case that fell the other side of the line because of persistent breaches of the rules by working in excess of hours permitted under the student rules. In *MM and SA (Pankina: near-miss) Pakistan* [2010] UKUT 481 (IAC), the Tribunal emphasised that the fact that an application was a 'near miss' under the Immigration rules had to be set in proper context and the weight accruing to maintaining orderly and consistent immigration control had to be properly considered. In *MM and SA*, less weight accrued to the position of an appellant who had sought to undertake a completely new course, rather than completing an existing one.

Procedure on appeal

Section 85A of Nationality, Immigration and Asylum Act 2002, inserted by s 19 of the UK Borders Act 2007, may have the effect of restricting the evidence that may be considered on appeal to that which was before Secretary of State for the Home Department at the time of application.

The Tribunal has considered the substantive requirements in the PBS rules in the following cases:

- Funds under the control of an applicant in an overseas bank account were available funds: *HM (PBS – legitimate expectation – paragraph 245ZX (l) Malawi* [2010] 446 UKUT (IAC). In *Rana (PBS – Appendix C – overdraft facility) India* [2011] UKUT 245 (IAC), the Tribunal accepted that an overdraft facility, with the ability to withdraw funds required under the Rules, constituted 'available funds'. The requirement that funds be 'available' was not be paraphrased (*Ejifugha (Tier 4 – funds – credit) Nigeria* [2011] UKUT 244 (IAC); funds could take the form of a credit card limit. In *CDS (PBS – 'available' – Article 8) Brazil* [2010] UKUT 00305 (IAC); third party sponsorship was accepted as being permissible. In *FA and AA (PBS: effect of Pankina) Nigeria* [2010] UKUT 00304 (IAC), funds in the bank account of the applicant's husband were funds available to her. A joint account, bearing the name of the applicant also met the requirements of funds under Tier 1: *AM and SS (PBS – Tier 1 – joint accounts) Pakistan* [2010] UKUT 169 (IAC).

- Tier 1 (General) migrants: work undertaken in the UK for a company based overseas, where the applicant was also paid in that country, absent an express provision in the rules that the work had also to be undertaken overseas, attracted the 'uplift provisions' for the calculation in Annex A (*Aleem (Pankina – Uplift for overseas earnings) Sri Lanka* [2011] UKUT 120 (IAC).

- For an interpretation of the requirement in Appendix A, Table 10(a) (for applications by Tier 1 (Post study) migrants: The applicant studied for his award at a UK institution that is a UK recognised or listed body, or which holds a sponsor licence under Tier 4 of the Points Based System'), see *Adubiri – Gyimah (post-study work – listed institution) Ghana* [2011] UKUT 123 (IAC); the requirement is that the institution must have been licenced at the time that the student studied.

- For a Tier 4 applicant wishing the rely on 'established presence' under Appendix C, the student must have been studying on a course within the last four months, and that course must itself have lasted for more than six months. The course may still be continuing, but if it came to an end within the last four months, and the student is embarking on another course (or repeating the same course), it is immaterial whether he was successful on the previous course. Appendix C requires the course to have been 'completed' no more than four months before; that does not mean 'successfully completed' (*DN (student – course 'completed' – established presence) Kenya* [2010] UKUT 443 (IAC).

[General requirements for indefinite leave to remain

245AAA. For the purposes of references in this Part to requirements for indefinite leave to remain, except for those in paragraphs 245BF, 245DF and 245EF:

(a)   "continuous period of 5 years lawfully in the UK" means [subject to paragraphs 245CD, 245GF and 245HF,] residence in the United Kingdom for an unbroken period with valid leave, and for these purposes a period shall not be considered to have been broken where:

    (i)   the applicant has been absent from the UK for a period of 180 days or less in any of the five consecutive 12 month periods preceding the date of the application for leave to remain;

    (ii)   the applicant has existing limited leave to enter or remain upon their departure and return except that where that leave expired no more than 28 days prior to a further application for entry clearance, that period and any period pending the determination of an application made within that 28 day period shall be disregarded; and

    (iii)   the applicant has any period of overstaying between periods of entry clearance, leave to enter or leave to remain of up to 28 days and any period of overstaying pending the determination of an application made within that 28 day period disregarded.

[(b)   Except for periods when the applicant had leave as a Tier 1 (General) Migrant, a Tier 1 (Investor) Migrant, a Tier 1 (Entrepreneur) Migrant, a Tier 1 (Exceptional Talent) Migrant, a highly skilled migrant, a businessperson, an Innovator, an Investor, a self-employed lawyer or a writer, composer or artist, the applicant must have been employed in the UK continuously throughout the five years, under the terms of their Certificate of Sponsorship, work permit or in the employment for which they ere given leave to enter or remain, except that any breaks in employment in which they applied for leave as a Tier 2 Migrant, or, under Tier 5 Temporary Worker (International Agreement) Migrant as a private sector in a diplomatic household, where in the latter case they applied to enter the UK before 6 April 2012, to work for a new employer shall be disregarded, provided this is within 60 days of the end of their employment with their previous employer or Sponsor.

(c)　Except for periods where the applicant had leave as a Tier 1 (Investor) Migrant, a Tier 1 (Entrepreneur) Migrant, a Tier 1 (Exceptional Talent) Migrant or a highly-skilled migrant, any absences form the UK during the five years must have been for a purpose that is consistent with the applicant's basis of stay here, including paid annual leave, or for serious or compelling reasons.]

Note

Inserted by HC 760, para 116 as from 13 December 2012. Further amended by HC 1039, paras 23–34 as from on or after 6 April 2013.

[Documents not submitted with applications

245AA.
(a)　Where Part 6A or any appendices referred to in Part 6A state that specified documents must be provided, [the Entry Clearance Officer, Immigration Officer or the Secretary of State] will only consider documents that have been submitted with the application, and will only consider documents submitted after the application [where they are substituted in accordance with subparagraph (b)].
(b)　[If the applicant has submitted specified documents in which:
　(i)　Some of the documents in a sequence have been omitted (for example, if one bank statement from a series if missing);
　(ii)　A document is in the wrong format (for example, if a letter is not on letterhead paper as specified); or
　(iii)　A document is a copy and not an original document; or
　(iv)　A document does not contain all of the specified information.
　the Entry Clearance officer, Immigration Officer or the Secretary of State may contact the applicant or his representative in writing, and request the correct documents. The requested documents must be received at the address specified in the request within 7 working days of the date of the request.
(c)　Documents will not be requested where a specified document has not been submitted (for example an English language certificate is missing), or where the Entry Clearance Officer, Immigration Officer or the Secretary of State does not anticipate that addressing the omission or error referred to in subparagraph (b) will lead to a grant because the application will be refused for other reasons.
(d)　If the applicant has submitted a specified document:
　(i)　in the wrong format, or
　(ii)　which is a copy and not an original document; or
　(iii)　which does not contain all of the specified information, but the missing information is verifiable from:
　　(1)　other documents submitted with the application
　　(2)　the website of the organisation which issued the document, or
　　(3)　the website of the appropriate regulatory body;
　the application may be granted exceptionally, provided the Entry Clearance Officer, Immigration Officer or the Secretary of State is satisfied that the specified documents are genuine and the applicant meets all the other requirements. The Entry Clearance Officer, Immigration Officer or the Secretary of State reserves the right to request the specified original documents in the correct format in all cases where (b) applies, and to refuse applications if these documents are not provided as set out in (b).]

Note

Inserted by HC 565, para 56 as from 6 September 2012. Further amended by HC 760, paras 117–120 as from 13 December 2012. Further amended by HC 628, paras 74, 75 and shall apply to all applications decided on or after 1 October 2013.

[Specified documents for students previously sponsored by an overseas government or international scholarship agency

245A.　Where Part 6A of these Rules state that specified documents must be provided to show that a sponsoring government or international scholarship agency has provided its unconditional written consent to the application, the specified documents are original letters, on the official letter-headed paper or stationery of the organisation(s), bearing the official stamp of that organisation and issued by an authorised official of that organisation. The documents must confirm that the organisation gives the applicant unconditional consent to remain in or re-enter the UK for an unlimited time.]

Note

Inserted by Cm 8423, para 32 as from 20 July 2012.

[Tier 1 (Exceptional Talent) Migrants

Purpose

245B. [This route is for exceptionally talented individuals [in particular fields], who wish to work in the UK. These individuals are those who are already internationally recognised at the highest level as world leaders in their particular field, or who have already demonstrates exceptional promise . . . and are likely to become world leaders in their particular area.]

Note

Substituted by HC 1436, para 2 as from 9 August 2011. Words deleted by HC 628, para 76 and if an applicant has made an application for entry clearance or leave before 1 October 2013, the application will be decided in accordance with the Rules in force on 30 September 2013. Amended by HC 1138, para 14 as from 6 April 2014.

Entry to the UK

245BA. All migrants arriving in the UK and wishing to enter as a Tier 1 (Exceptional Talent) Migrant must have a valid entry clearance for entry under this route. If they do not have a valid entry clearance, entry will be refused.

Note

Inserted by HC 863, para 42 as from 6 April 2011.

Requirements for entry clearance

245BB. To qualify for entry clearance as a Tier 1 (Exceptional Talent) Migrant, an applicant must meet the requirements listed below. If the applicant meets these requirements, entry clearance will be granted. If the applicant does not meet these requirements, the application will be refused.

Requirements:
(a)   The applicant must not fall for refusal under the general grounds for refusal.
(b)   . . .
(c)   The applicant must have a minimum of 75 points under paragraphs 1 to 6 of Appendix A.
(d)   An applicant who has, or was last granted, leave as a Student or a Postgraduate Doctor or Dentist, a Student Nurse, a Student Writing-Up a Thesis, a Student Re-Sitting an Examination or as a Tier 4 Migrant and:
   (i)   is currently being sponsored by a government or international scholarship agency, or
   (ii)   was being sponsored by a government or international scholarship agency, and that sponsorship came to an end 12 months ago or less,

must provide the unconditional written consent of the sponsoring Government or agency to the application and must provide [the specified documents as set out in paragraph 245A above], to show that this requirement has been met.

Note

Inserted by HC 863, para 42 as from 6 April 2011. Amended by HC 1436, paras 3, 4 as from 9 August 2011. Words "the specified documents as set out in paragraph 245A above" substituted by Cm 8423, para 33 as from 20 July 2012. Sub-para (b) deleted by HC 565, para 224 as from 1 October 2012.

Period and conditions of grant

245BC. [Entry clearance will be granted for a period of 5 years and 4 months] and will be subject to the following conditions:
(i)   no recourse to public funds,
(ii)   registration with the police, if this is required by paragraph 326,
(iii)   no employment as a Doctor or Dentist in Training, and
(iv)   no employment as a professional sportsperson (including as a sports coach).

Note

Inserted by HC 863, para 42 as from 6 April 2011. Amended by HC 1138, para 15 as from 6 April 2014. Amended by HC 693, para 40 as from 6 November 2014, save that if an application has been made for entry clearance or leave to enter or remain before 6 November 2014, the application will be decided in accordance with the Rules in force on 5 November 2014.

Requirements for leave to remain

245BD. To qualify for leave to remain as a Tier 1 (Exceptional Talent) Migrant, an applicant must meet the requirements listed below. If the applicant meets these requirements, leave to remain will be granted. If the applicant does not meet these requirements, the application will be refused.

Requirements:
(a)   The applicant must not fall for refusal under the general grounds for refusal, and must not be an illegal entrant.
(b)   The applicant must have a minimum of 10 points under paragraphs 1 to 15 of Appendix A.
[(c)]   The applicant must have, or have last been granted, entry clearance, leave to enter or remain as:
　　(i)   [a Tier 1 Migrant]
　　(ii)   a Tier 2 Migrant, or
　　(iii)   as a Tier 5 (Temporary Worker) Migrant, sponsored in the Government Authorised Exchange sub-category in an exchange scheme for sponsored researchers.
[(d)]   The applicant must not be in the UK in breach of immigration laws except that any period of overstaying for a period of 28 days or less will be disregarded.]

Note

Inserted by HC 863, para 42 as from 6 April 2011. Sub-paragraph (c) substituted by HC 1436, para 5 as from 9 August 2011. Words in sub-para (c) "paragraphs 1 to 15" substituted by HC 1888, para 31 as from April 2012. Sub-para (c) inserted by HC 565, para 225 as from 1 October 2012. Sub-para (e) inserted by HC 194, para 53 as from 1 October 2012. Para (d)(ii) substituted by HC 1039, para 25 as from 6 April 2013. Amended by HC 1138, para 16 as from 6 April 2014. Deleted by HC 693, para 41 as from 6 November 2014, save that if an application has been made for entry clearance or leave to enter or remain before 6 November 2014, the application will be decided in accordance with the Rules in force on 5 November 2014. Sub-paragraphs (d) and (e) renumbered as (c) and (d) by HC 693, para 42 as from 6 November 2014, save that if an application has been made for entry clearance or leave to enter or remain before 6 November 2014, the application will be decided in accordance with the Rules in force on 5 November 2014.

[Period and conditions of grant

245BE.
[(a)   Leave to remain will be granted for a period of 5 years.]
　　(i)   for a period of 2 years, to an applicant who has, or was last granted, leave as a Tier 1) (Exceptional Talent) Migrant, or
　　(ii)   for a period of 3 years, to any other applicant.
(b)   Leave to remain under this route will be subject to the following conditions:
　　(i)   no recourse to public funds,
　　(ii)   registration with the police, if this is required by paragraph 326,

(iii)   no employment as a Doctor or Dentist in Training, and

(iv)   no employment as a professional sportsperson (including as a sports coach).]

Note

Substituted by HC 760, para 121 as from 13 December 2012. Substituted by HC 693, para 43 as from 6 November 2014, save that if an application has been made for entry clearance or leave to enter or remain before 6 November 2014, the application will be decided in accordance with the Rules in force on 5 November 2014.

Requirements for indefinite leave to remain

245BF. To qualify for indefinite leave to remain, a Tier 1 (Exceptional Talent) Migrant must meet the requirements listed below. If the applicant meets these requirements, indefinite leave to remain will be granted. If the applicant does not meet these requirements, the application will be refused.

Requirements:

(a)   . . .

(b)   The applicant must not fall for refusal under the general grounds for refusal, and must not be an illegal entrant.

(c)   [The applicant must have spent a continuous period of 5 years lawfully in the UK as follows:

    (i)   The applicant must have, or have last been granted, leave as a Tier 1 (Exceptional Talent) Migrant;

    (ii)   The 5 years must have been spent with leave as a Tier 1 Migrant (excluding as a Tier 1 (Graduate Entrepreneur) Migrant or Tier 1 (Post-Study Work) Migrant) or as a Tier 2 Migrant (excluding as a Tier 2 (Intra-Company Transfer) Migrant); and

    (iii)   The applicant must have had absences from the UK of no more than 180 days in any 12 calendar months during the 5 years.]

(d)   The applicant must have a minimum of 75 points under paragraphs 1 to 6 of Appendix A.

(e)   [The applicant must have demonstrated sufficient knowledge of the English language and sufficient knowledge about life in the United Kingdom, in accordance with Appendix KoLL].

(f)   [The applicant must not be in the UK in breach of immigration laws except that any period of overstaying for a period of 28 days or less will be disregarded.]

Note

Inserted by HC 863, para 42 as from 6 April 2011. Sub-para (f) inserted by HC 194, para 54 as from 1 October 2012. Further amended by HC 760, paras 122, 123 as from 13 December 2012. Sub-para (e) substituted by HC 628, para 77 and if an applicant has made an application for entry clearance or leave before 1 October 2013, the application will be decided in accordance with the Rules in force on 30 September 2013. Amended by HC 1138, para 17 as from 6 April 2014.

Tier 1 (General) Migrants

Purpose

245C. This route is for highly skilled migrants who wish to work, or become self-employed, to extend their stay in the UK.

Note

Substituted by HC 863, para 42 as from 6 April 2011.

Requirements for leave to remain

245CA. To qualify for leave to remain as a Tier 1 (General) Migrant, an applicant must meet the requirements listed below. If the applicant meets these requirements, leave to remain will be granted. If the applicant does not meet these requirements, the application will be refused.

Requirements:

(a) The applicant must not fall for refusal under the general grounds for refusal, and must not be an illegal entrant.

(b) If the applicant has, or has had, leave as a Highly Skilled Migrant, as a Writer, Composer or Artist, Self-employed Lawyer, or as a Tier 1 (General) Migrant under the Rules in place before 19 July 2010, and has not been granted leave in any categories other than these under the Rules in place since 19 July 2010, the applicant must have 75 points under paragraphs 7 to 34 of Appendix A.

(c) In all cases other than those referred to in (b) above, the applicant must have 80 points under paragraphs 7 to 34 of Appendix A.

(d) The applicant must have 10 points under [paragraphs 1 to 15] of Appendix B.

(e) The applicant must have 10 points under paragraphs 1 to 3 of Appendix C.

(f) The applicant must have, or have last been granted, entry clearance, leave to enter or remain:

    (i) as a Tier 1 (General) Migrant,

    (ii) as a Highly Skilled Migrant,

    (iii) as a Writer, Composer or Artist, or

    (iv) as a Self-Employed Lawyer.

(g) [The applicant must not be in the UK in breach of immigration laws except that any period of overstaying for a period of 28 days or less will be disregarded.]

[(h) The application for leave to remain must have been made before 6 April 2015.]

Note

Inserted by HC 863, para 42 as from 6 April 2011. Words in sub-para (d) "paragraphs 1 to 15" substituted by HC 1888, para 32 as from April 2012. Sub-para (g) inserted by HC 194, para 55 as from 1 October 2011. Amended by HC 1138, para 18 as from 6 April 2014.

Period and conditions of grant

245CB.

[(a) Leave to remain will be granted for:

    (i) a period of 3 years, or

    (ii) the period the applicant needs to take his total leave granted in this category to 5 years,

whichever is the longer.

(b) DELETED.]

(c) Leave to remain under this route will be subject to the following conditions:

    (i) no recourse to public funds,

    (ii) registration with the police, if this is required by paragraph 326, and

    (iii) [no Employment as a Doctor or Dentist in Training, unless the applicant:

        (1) has obtained a primary degree in medicine or dentistry at bachelor's level or above from a UK institution that is a UK recognised or listed body, or which holds a sponsor licence under Tier 4 of the Points Based system;

        (2) has, or has last been granted, entry clearance, leave to enter or leave to remain that was not subject to any condition restricting him from taking employment as a Doctor in Training, and has been employed during that leave as a Doctor in Training; or

        (3) has, or has last been granted, entry clearance, leave to enter or leave to remain that was not subject to any condition restricting him from taking employment as a dentist in Training, and has been employed during that leave as a Dentist in Training,]

    (iv) no employment as a professional sportsperson (including as a sports coach).

Note

Inserted by HC 863, para 42 as from 6 April 2011. Sub-para (c)(iii) substituted by Cm 8423, para 34 as from 20 July 2012. Further amended by HC 760, paras 124, 125 as from 13 December 2012. Sub-paras (a) and (b) substituted by HC 693, para 44 as from 6 November 2014, save that if an application has been made for entry clearance or leave to enter or remain before 6 November 2014, the application will be decided in accordance with the Rules in force on 5 November 2014.

Requirements for indefinite leave to remain

245CD. To qualify for indefinite leave to remain, a Tier 1 (General) Migrant must meet the requirements listed below. If the applicant meets these requirements, indefinite leave to remain will be granted. If the applicant does not meet these requirements, the application will be refused.

Requirements:

(a)   . . .

(b)   The applicant must not fall for refusal under the general grounds for refusal [(except that paragraph 322(1C) shall not apply if the applicant meets the conditions in (f)(i)-(iii) below)], and must not be an illegal entrant.

(c)   [The applicant must have spent a continuous period as specified in (d) lawfully in the UK,] of which the most recent period must have been spent with leave as a Tier 1 (General) Migrant, in any combination of the following categories:

(i)   as a Tier 1 (General) Migrant,

(ii)   as a Highly Skilled Migrant,

(iii)   as a Work Permit Holder,

(iv)   as an Innovator,

(v)   as a Self-Employed Lawyer,

(vi)   as a Writer, Composer or Artist,

(vii)   as a Tier 2 (General) Migrant, a Tier 2 (Minister of Religion) Migrant or a Tier 2 (Sportsperson) Migrant, or

(viii) as a Tier 2 (Intra-Company Transfer) Migrant, provided the continuous period of 5 years spent lawfully in the UK includes a period of leave as a Tier 2 (Intra-Company Transfer) Migrant granted under the Rules in place before 6 April 2010[, or as a Work Permit Holder where the work permit was granted because the applicant was the subject of an Intra-Company Transfer.]

(d)   [The continuous period in (c) is:

(i)   4 years, if the applicant:

(1)   received a Highly Skilled Migrant Programme approval letter issued on the basis of an application made before 3 April 2006,

(2)   was subsequently granted entry clearance or leave to remain on the basis of that letter, and

(3)   has not since been granted entry clearance or leave to remain in any category other than as a Highly Skilled Migrant or Tier 1 (General) Migrant; or

(ii)   5 years, in all other cases.

(e)   If the applicant has or has had leave as a Highly Skilled Migrant, a Writer, Composer or artist, a self-employed lawyer or as a Tier 1 (General) Migrant under the Rules in place before 19 July 2010, and has not been granted leave in any categories other than these under the Rules in place since 19 July 2010, the applicant must have 75 points under paragraphs 7 to 34 of Appendix A.

(f)   Where the applicant:

(i)   received a Highly Skilled Migrant Programme approval letter issued on the basis of an application made before 7 November 2006,

(ii)   was subsequently granted entry clearance or leave to remain on the basis of that letter, and

827

(iii)   has not since been granted entry clearance or leave to remain in any category other than as a Highly Skilled Migrant or Tier 1 (General) Migrant,

the applicant must be economically active in the UK, in employment or self-employment or both.

(g)   in all cases other than those referred to in (e) or (f) above, the applicant must have 80 points under paragraphs 7 to 34 of Appendix A.

(h)   The applicant must have sufficient knowledge of the English language and sufficient knowledge about life in the United Kingdom, in accordance with Appendix KoLL of these Rules, unless the applicant meets the conditions in (f)(i)-(iii) above.

(i)   The applicant must not be in the UK in breach of immigration laws except that any period of overstaying for a period of 28 days or less will be disregarded, unless the applicant meets the conditions in (f)(i)-(iii) above.

(j)   The applicant must provide the specified documents in paragraph 245CD-SD to evidence the reason for the absences set out in paragraph 245AAA, unless the applicant meets the conditions in (f)(i)-(iii) above.]

(k)   [For the purposes of sub-paragraph (c), time spent with valid leave on the Bailiwick of Guernsey, the Bailiwick of Jersey or the Isle of Man in the category equivalent to those set out in (c)(i) to (viii) may be included in the continuous period of 5 years lawful residence in the UK, provided that:

    (i)   the most recent period of leave was granted in the UK as a Tier (General) Migrant; and

    (ii)   any period of leave granted in the Bailiwick of Guernsey, the Bailiwick of Jersey or the Isle of Man as a work permit holder or a Tier 2 Migrant was for employment:

        (a)   in a job which appears on the list of occupations skilled to National Qualifications Framework level 3 or above (or from 6 April 2011, National Qualifications Framework level 4 or above or from 14 June 2012, National Qualifications Framework level 6 or above), as stated in the Codes of Practice in Appendix J, or

        (b)   in a job which appears in the Creative Sector Codes of Practice in Appendix J, or

        (c)   as a professional sportsperson (including as a sports coach).

    (iii)   In any such case, references to the "UK" in paragraph 245AA shall include a reference to the Bailiwick of Guernsey, Bailiwick of Jersey or the Isle of Man, as the case may be.

(l)   For the purposes of paragraph (e), time spent with valid leave in the Bailiwick of Guernsey, the Bailiwick of Jersey and the Isle of Man in a category equivalent to those set out in (e)(i) to (iv) may be included in the continuous period of [5 years (or 4 years as the case may be)] lawful residence in the UK, provided that:

    (i)   the most recent period of leave was granted in the UK as a Tier 1 (General) Migrant; and

    (ii)   any period of leave was granted in the Bailiwick of Guernsey, the Bailiwick of Jersey or the Isle of Man as a work permit holder or a Tier 2 Migrant was for employment:

        (a)   in a job which appears on the list of occupations skilled to National Qualifications Framework level 3 or above (or from 6 April 2011, National Qualifications Framework level 4 or above or from 14 June 2012, National Qualifications Framework level 6 or above), as stated in the Codes of Practice in Appendix J, or

        (b)   in a job which appears in the Creative Sector Codes of Practice in Appendix J, or

        (c)   as a professional sportsperson (including as a sports coach).

(f)   [Except where the applicant has had entry clearance, leave to enter or leave to remain as a Tier 1(Entrepreneur) Migrant, a Businessperson or an Innovator in the 12 months immediately before the date of application and is being assessed under Table 5 of Appendix A, the Entry Clearance Officer must be satisfied that:

    (i)   the applicant genuinely intends and is able to establish, take over or become a director of one or more businesses in the UK within the next six months;

    (ii)   the applicant genuinely intends to invest the money referred to in Table 4 of Appendix 4 in the business or businesses referred to in (i);

    (iii)   [that the money referred to in Table 4 of Appendix A is genuinely available to the applicant, and will remain available to him until such time as it is spent for the purposes of his business or businesses.]

    (iv)   that the applicant does not intend to take employment in the United Kingdom other than under the terms of paragraph 245DC;

(g)   In making the assessment in (f), the Entry Clearance Officer will assess the balance of probabilities. The Entry Clearance Officer may take into account the following factors:

    (i)   the evidence the applicant has submitted;

    (ii)   the viability and credibility of the source of the money referred to in Table 4 of Appendix A;

    (iii)   the viability and credibility of the applicant's business plans and market research into their chosen business sector;

    (iv)   the applicant's previous educational and business experience (or lack thereof);

    (v)   the applicant's immigration history and previous activity in the UK; and

    (vi)   any other relevant information.

(h)   The Entry Clearance Officer reserves the right to request additional information and evidence to support the assessment in (f), and to refuse the application if the information or evidence is not provided. Any requested documents must be received by the UK Border Agency at the address specified in the request within [28 calendar days] of the date of the request.

(i)   If the Entry Clearance Officer is not satisfied with the genuineness of the application in relation to a points-scoring requirement in Appendix A, those points will not be awarded.

(j)   The Entry Clearance Officer [may decide not to carry out] the assessment in (f) if the application already falls for refusal on other grounds, but reserves the right to carry out this assessment in any reconsideration of the decision.]

[(k)   The applicant must be at least 16 years old.

(l)   Where the applicant is under 18 years of age, the application must be supported by the applicant's parents or legal guardian or by one parent if that parent has sole legal responsibility for the child.

(m)   Where the applicant is under 18 years of age, the applicant's parents or legal guardian, or one parent if that parent has sole legal responsibility for the child, must confirm that they consent to the arrangements for the applicant's care in the UK.]

Note

Words "paragraphs 1 to 3 of" and "paragraphs 1 to 2 of" in sub-paragraphs (c) and (d) inserted by HC 1113, paras 52, 53 as from 27 November 2008. Words "paragraphs 1 to 15" substituted by HC 1888, para 33 as from 6 April 2012. Sub-paragraph (e) inserted by HC 1113, para 54 as from 27 November 2008. Words in square brackets in sub-paragraph (e) substituted by HC 314. Words "as set out in paragraph 245A above" inserted by Cm 8423, para 39 as from 20 July 2012. Old para 245J renumbered as 245DB by HC 863, para 47 as from 6 April 2011. Words 'paragraphs 35 to 53 of Appendix A' in sub-paragraph (b) substituted by HC 863, para 48 as from 6 April 2011. Sub-paragraphs (f)-(j) inserted by HC 943, para 1 as from 31 January 2013. Sub-paragraph (j) amended by HC 628, para 80 and shall apply to all applications decided on or after 1 October 2013. Amended by HC 1138, para 26 shall apply to all applications decided on or after 6 April 2014. Amended by HC 1138, para 27 as from 6 April 2014. Amended by HC 693, para 45 as from 6 November 2014, save that if an application has been made for entry clearance or leave to enter or remain before 6 November 2014, the application will be decided in accordance with the Rules in force on 5 November 2014.

Period and conditions of grant

245DC.

(a)   Entry clearance will be granted for a period of 3 years [and four months] and will be subject to the following conditions:

(i)   no recourse to public funds,

(ii)   registration with the police, if this is required by paragraph 326 of these Rules, and

(iii)   no employment other than working for the business(es) the applicant has established, joined or taken over[, [but working for such business(es) does not include anything undertaken by the applicant pursuant to a contract of service or apprenticeship, whether express or implied and whether oral or written, with another business,] and

(iv)   no employment as a professional sportsperson (including as a sports coach).]

Note

Old para 245K renumbered as 245DC by HC 863, para 47 as from 6 April 2011. Words in square brackets inserted by HC 863, paras 49 and 50 as from 6 April 2011. Further amended by HC 532, para 1 as from 11 July 2014. However, if an applicant has made an application for entry clearance or leave before 11 July 2014 and the application has not been decided before that date, it will be decided in accordance with the Rules in force on 10 July 2014.

Requirements for leave to remain

245DD.
To qualify for leave to remain as a Tier 1 (Entrepreneur) Migrant under this rule, an applicant must meet the requirements listed below. If the applicant meets these requirements, leave to remain will be granted. If the applicant does not meet these requirements, the application will be refused.

Requirements:

(a)   [The applicant must not fall for refusal under the general grounds for refusal, except that paragraph 322(10) shall not apply, and must not be an illegal entrant.]

(b)   The applicant must have a minimum of 75 points under [paragraphs 35 to 53 of Appendix A].

(c)   The applicant must have a minimum of 10 points under [paragraphs 1 to 15] of] Appendix B.

(d)   The applicant must have a minimum of 10 points under [paragraphs 1 to 2 of] Appendix C.

(e)   The applicant who is applying for leave to remain must have, or have last been granted, entry clearance, leave to enter or remain:

(i)   as a Highly Skilled Migrant,

(ii)   as a Tier 1 (General) Migrant,

(iii)   as a Tier 1 (Entrepreneur) Migrant,

(iv)   as a Tier 1 (Investor) Migrant,

(v)   [as a Tier 1 (Graduate Entrepreneur) Migrant,]

(vi)   as a Tier 1 (Post-Study Work) Migrant,

(vii)   as a Businessperson,

(viii)   as an Innovator,

(ix)   as an Investor,

(x)   as a Participant in the Fresh Talent: Working in Scotland Scheme,

(xi)   as a Participant in the International Graduates Scheme (or its predecessor, the Science and Engineering Graduates Scheme),

(xii)   as a Postgraduate Doctor or Dentist,

(xiii)   as a Self-employed Lawyer,

(xiv)   as a Student,

(xv)   as a Student Nurse,

(xvi)   as a Student Re-Sitting an Examination,

(xvii)   as a Student Writing Up a Thesis,

(xviii)   as a Work Permit Holder, . . .

(xix)   as a Writer, Composer or Artist [. . .

(xx)   as a Tier 2 Migrant] . . .

(xxi)   as a Tier 4 Migrant[, or

(xxii)   as a Prospective Entrepreneur]

(f)   An applicant who has, or was last granted, leave as a Student or a Postgraduate Doctor or Dentist, [Student Nurse, Student Re-Sitting and Examination[, a Student Writing-Up a Thesis or as a Tier 4 Migrant]] and:

    (i)   is currently being sponsored by a government or international scholarship agency, or

    (ii)   was being sponsored by a government or international scholarship agency, and that sponsorship came to an end 12 months ago or less,

must provide the [unconditional] written consent of the sponsoring Government or agency to the application [and must provide the specified documents [as set out in paragraph 245A above] to show that this requirement has been met].

(g)   [The applicant must not be in the UK in breach of immigration laws except that any period of overstaying for a period of 28 days or less will be disregarded.]

(h)   [Except where the applicant has, or was last granted, leave as a Tier 1 (Entrepreneur) Migrant, a Businessperson or an Innovator and is being assessed under Table 5 of Appendix A, [the Secretary of State] must be satisfied that:

    (i)   the applicant genuinely:

        (1)   intends and is able to establish, take over or become a director of one or more businesses in the UK within the next six months, or

        (2)   has established, taken over or become a director of one or more businesses in the UK and continues to operate that business or businesses; and

    (ii)   the applicant genuinely intends to invest the money referred to in Table 4 of Appendix A in the business or businesses referred to in (i);

    (iii)   [the money referred to in Table 4 of Appendix A is genuinely available to the applicant, and will remain available to him until such time as it is spent for the purposes of his business or businesses.]

    (iv)   that the applicant does not intend to take employment in the United Kingdom other than under the terms of paragraph 245DE.

(i)   In making the assessment in (h), [the Secretary of State] will assess the balance of probabilities. [The Secretary of State] may take into account the following factors:

    (i)   the evidence the applicant has submitted;

    (ii)   the viability and credibility of the money referred to in Table 4 of Appendix A;

    (iii)   the viability and credibility of the applicant's business plans and market research into their chosen business sector;

    (iv)   the applicant's previous educational and business experience (or lack thereof);

    (v)   the applicant's immigration history and previous activity in the UK;

    (vi)   where the applicant has already registered in the UK as self-employed or as the director of a business, and the nature of the business requires mandatory accreditation, registration and/or insurance, whether that accreditation, registration and/or insurance has been obtained; and

    (vii)   any other relevant information.

(j)   [The Secretary of State] reserves the right to request additional information and evidence to support the assessment in (h), and to refuse the application if the information or evidence is not provided. Any requested documents must be received by the UK Border Agency at the address specified in the request within [28 calendar days] of the date of request.

(k)   If [the Secretary of State] is not satisfied with the genuineness of the application in relation to a points-scoring requirement in Appendix A, those points will not be awarded.

(l)   [The Secretary of State] [may decide not to carry out] the assessment in (h) if the applicant falls for refusal on other grounds, but reserves the right to carry out this assessment in any reconsideration of the decision.]

(m)   [The applicant must, unless he provides a reasonable explanation, comply with any request made by [the Secretary of State] to attend for interview.]

[(n)   The applicant must be at least 16 years old.

(o)   Where the applicant is under 18 years of age, the application must be supported by the applicant's parents or legal guardian or by one parent if that parent has sole legal responsibility for the child.

(p)   Where the applicant is under 18 years of age, the applicant's parents or legal guardian, or one parent if that parent has sole legal responsibility for the child, must confirm that they consent to the arrangements for the applicant's care in the UK.]

Note

Words in sub-paragraphs substituted and inserted by HC 1113, paras 55–62 as from 27 November 2008. Further amended by HC 314. Old para 245L renumbered as 245DD by HC 863, para 47 as from 6 April 2011. Words in sub-paragraphs (b), (e)(xix) and (e)(xx) substituted and inserted by HC 863, paras 52–55 as from 6 April 2011. Words in square brackets in sub-paragraph (c) and sub-paragraph (e)(v) inserted and following sub-paragraphs renumbered to (vi) to (xii) by HC 1888, paras 34–36 as from 6 April 2012. Words in sub-para (f) 'as set out in paragraph 245A above' inserted by Cm 8423, para 40 as from 20 July 2012. Sub-paragraph (g) inserted by HC 194, para 58 as from 1 October 2012. Sub-paragraphs (h)-(l) inserted by HC 943, para 2 as from 31 January 2013. Further amended by HC 1039, paras 30, 31: where an applicant has made an application for entry clearance or leave before 6 April 2013 and the application has not been decided before that date, it will be decided in accordance with the rules in force on 5 April 2013. Further amended by HC 628, paras 81, 82 and shall apply to all applications decided on or after 1 October 2013. Amended by HC 1138, para 28 shall apply to all applications decided on or after 6 April 2014. Amended by HC 1138, para 29 as from 6 April 2014. Amended by HC 693, para 46 as from 6 November 2014, save that if an application has been made for entry clearance or leave to enter or remain before 6 November 2014, the application will be decided in accordance with the Rules in force on 5 November 2014.

[Period, conditions and curtailment of grant]

245DE.

(a)   Leave to remain will be granted:

    (i)   for a period of 2 years, to an applicant who has, or was last granted, leave as a Tier 1 (Entrepreneur) Migrant,

    (ii)   for a period of 3 years, to any other applicant.

(b)   Leave to remain under this route will be subject to the following conditions:

    (i)   no recourse to public funds,

    (ii)   registration with the police, if this is required by paragraph 326 of these Rules, and

    (iii)   no employment, other than working for the business or businesses which he has established, joined or taken over[, [but working for such business(es) does not include anything undertaken by the applicant pursuant to a contract of service or apprenticeship, whether express or implied and whether oral or written, with another business,] and

    (iv)   no employment as a professional sportsperson (including as a sports coach).]

[(c)   Without prejudice to the grounds for curtailment in paragraph 323 of these Rules, leave to enter or remain granted to a Tier 1 (Entrepreneur) Migrant may be curtailed if:

    (i)   within 6 months of the date specified in paragraph (d), the applicant has not done one or more of the following things:

          (1)   registered with HM Revenue and Customs as self-employed,

          (2)   registered a new business in which he is a director, or

          (3)   registered as a director of an existing business; or

    (ii)   [the funds referred to in the relevant sections of Appendix A cease to be available to him, except where they have been spent for the purposes of his business or businesses.]

(d)   The date referred to in paragraph (c) is:

    (i)   the date of the applicant's entry to the UK, in the case of an applicant granted entry clearance as a Tier 1 (Entrepreneur) Migrant where there is evidence to establish the applicant's date of entry to the UK,

    (ii)   the date of the grant of entry clearance to the applicant, in the case of an applicant granted entry clearance as a Tier 1 (Entrepreneur) Migrant where there is no evidence to establish the applicant's date of entry to the UK, or

    (iii)   the date of the grant of leave to remain to the applicant, in any other case.

(e)   Paragraph [245DE(c)] does not apply where the applicant's last grant of leave prior to the grant of the leave that he currently has was as a Tier 1 (Entrepreneur) Migrant, a Businessperson or an Innovator.]

Note

Heading amended and sub-paragraph (c)–(e) inserted by HC 1113, paras 63–64 as from 27 November 2008. Old para 245M renumbered as 245DE by HC 863, para 47 as from 6 April 2011. Words in square brackets inserted and substituted by HC 863, paras 56–59 as from 6 April 2011. Sub-paragraph (c) substituted by HC 943, para 3 as from 31 January 2013. Amended by HC 1138, para 30 shall apply to all applications decided on or after 6 April 2014. Further amended by HC 532, para 2 as from 11 July 2014. However, if an applicant has made an application for entry clearance or leave before 11 July 2014 and the application has not been decided before that date, it will be decided in accordance with the Rules in force on 10 July 2014.

[Requirements for indefinite leave to remain

245DF.   To qualify for indefinite leave to remain as a Tier 1 (Entrepreneur) Migrant, an applicant must meet the requirements listed below. If the applicant meets these requirements, indefinite leave to remain will be granted. If the applicant does not meet these requirements, the application will be refused.

Requirements:

(a)   . . .

(b)   The applicant must not fall for refusal under the general grounds for refusal, and must not be an illegal entrant.

(c)   The applicant must have a minimum of 75 points under paragraphs 35 to 53 of Appendix A.

(d)   [The applicant must have demonstrated sufficient knowledge of the English language and sufficient knowledge about life in the United Kingdom, in accordance with Appendix KoLL.]

(e)   [The applicant must not be in the UK in breach of immigration laws except that any period of overstaying for a period of 28 days or less will be disregarded.]

Note

Old para 245N substituted by 245DF by HC 863, para 60 as from 6 April 2011. Sub-para (e) inserted by HC 194, para 59 as from 1 October 2012. Sub-paragraph (a) deleted by HC 760, para 129 as from 13 December 2012. sub-paragraph (d) substituted by HC 628, para 83 and if an applicant has made an application for entry clearance or leave before 1 October 2013, the application will be decided in accordance with the Rules in force on 30 September 2013.

Tier 1 (Investor) Migrants

Purpose

245E. This route is for high net worth individuals making a substantial financial investment to the UK.

Note

Old para 245O renumbered as 245E by HC 863, para 61 as from 6 April 2011.

Entry to the UK

245EA. All migrants arriving in the UK and wishing to enter as a Tier 1 (Investor) Migrant must have a valid entry clearance for entry under this route. If they do not have a valid entry clearance, entry will be refused.

Note

Old para 245P renumbered as 245EA by HC 863, para 62 as from 6 April 2011.

Requirements for entry clearance

245EB. To qualify for entry clearance or leave to remain as a Tier 1 (Investor) Migrant, an applicant must meet the requirements listed below. If the applicant meets these requirements, entry clearance will be granted. If the applicant does not meet these requirements, the application will be refused.

Requirements:
(a)   The applicant must not fall for refusal under the general grounds for refusal.
(b)   The applicant must have a minimum of 75 points under [[paragraphs 54 to 65-SD of Appendix A]].
(c)   [An applicant who has, or was last granted, leave as a Student or a Postgraduate Doctor or Dentist, a Student Nurse[, a Student Re-Sitting an Examination, a Student Writing-up a Thesis or as Tier 4 Migrant] and:
    (i)   is currently being sponsored by a government or international scholarship agency, or
    (ii)   was being sponsored by a government or international scholarship agency, and that scholarship came to an end 12 months ago or less must provide the unconditional written consent of the sponsoring Government or agency to the application and must provide the specified documents [as set out in paragraph 245A] to show that this requirement has been met.]
[(d)   The applicant must be at least 16 years old and the assets and investment he is claiming points for must be wholly under his control.
(e)   Where the applicant is under 18 years of age, the application must be supported by the applicant's parents or legal guardian or by one parent if that parent has sole legal responsibility for the child.
(f)   Where the applicant is under 18 years of age, the applicant's parents or legal guardian, or one parent if that parent has sole legal responsibility for the child, must confirm that they consent to the arrangements for the applicant's care in the UK.]
[(g)   The Entry Clearance Officer must not have reasonable grounds to believe that:
    (i)   notwithstanding that the applicant has provided the relevant specified documents required under Appendix A, the applicant is not in control of and at liberty to freely invest the money specified in their application for the purposes of meeting the requirements of Table 7 of Appendix A to these Rules (where relevant); or
    (ii)   any of the money specified in the application for the purposes of meeting the requirements of Table 7 of Appendix A to these Rules held by:
        (1)   the applicant; or

(2)   where any of the specified money has been made available to the
applicant by another party, that party,

has been acquired by means of conduct which is unlawful in the UK, or
would constitute unlawful conduct if it occurred in the UK; or

(iii)   where any of the money specified in the application for the purposes of
meeting the requirements of Table 7 of Appendix A to these Rules has
been made available by another party, the character, conduct or associations of that party are such that approval of the application would not be
conducive to the public good,

and where the Entry Clearance Officer does have reasonable grounds to believe one or
more of the above applies, no points from Table 7 (where relevant) will be awarded.]

Note

Old para 245Q renumbered as 245EB by HC 863, para 62 as from 6 April 2011. Words in
sub-paragraph (b) substituted by HC 863, para 63 as from 6 April 2011. Sub-paragraph (c)
inserted by HC 1113, para 65 as from 27 November 2008. Words in sub-paragraph (c) substituted
by HC 314. Words in sub-para (c) "as set out in paragraph 245A" inserted by Cm 8423, para 41
as from 20 July 2012. Amended by HC 1138, para 31 as from 6 April 2014. Further amended by
HC 693, para 47 as from 6 November 2014, save that if an application has been made for entry
clearance or leave to enter or remain before 6 November 2014, the application will be decided in
accordance with the Rules in force on 5 November 2014. Amended by HC 693, para 48 as from
6 November 2014, save that if an application has been made for entry clearance or leave to enter
or remain before 6 November 2014, the application will be decided in accordance with the Rules
in force on 5 November 2014.

Period and conditions of grant

245EC.
(a)   Entry clearance will be granted for a period of 3 years[and 4 months] and will
be subject to the following conditions:
(i)   no recourse to public funds,
(ii)   registration with the police, if this is required by paragraph 326 of these
Rules, . . .
(iii)   [no Employment as a Doctor or Dentist in Training, unless the applicant
has obtained a [primary degree] in medicine or dentistry at bachelor's level or above from a UK institution that is a UK recognised or
listed body, or which holds a sponsor licence under Tier 4 of the Points
Based System[, and]]
(iv)   no employment as a professional sportsperson (including as a sports
coach).]

Note

Sub-paragraph (iii) substituted by HC 439 as from 6 April 2010. Words in square brackets
substituted by HC 863, para 66 as from 6 April 2011. Old para 245R renumbered as 245EC by
HC 863, para 62 as from 6 April 2011. Words in sub-paragraph (a) substituted by HC 863,
para 64 as from 6 April 2011. Further amended by HC 760, paras 130–132 as from 13 December
2012.

Requirements for leave to remain

245ED.   To qualify for leave to remain as a Tier 1 (Investor) Migrant, an applicant
must meet the requirements listed below. If the applicant meets these requirements,
leave to remain will be granted. If the applicant does not meet these requirements, the
application will be refused.

Requirements:
(a)   The applicant must not fall for refusal under the general grounds for refusal, and
must not be an illegal entrant.
(b)   The applicant must have a minimum of 75 points under [[paragraphs 54 to
65-SD of Appendix A]].

(c)   The applicant must have, or have last been granted, entry clearance, leave to enter or remain:

    (i)   as a Highly Skilled Migrant,

    (ii)   as a Tier 1 (General) Migrant,

    (iii)   as a Tier 1 (Entrepreneur) Migrant,

    (iv)   as a Tier 1 (Investor) Migrant,

    (v)   as a Tier 1 (Post-Study Work) Migrant,

    (vi)   as a Businessperson,

    (vii)   as an Innovator,

    (viii)   as an Investor,

    (ix)   as a Student,

    (x)   as a Student Nurse,

    (xi)   as a Student Re-Sitting an Examination,

    (xii)   as a Student Writing Up a Thesis,

    (xiii)   as a Work Permit Holder, or

    (xiv)   as a Writer, Composer or Artist, [. . .]

    (xv)   as a Tier 2 Migrant, [or]

    [(xvi) as a Tier 4 Migrant.]

(d)   An applicant who has, or was last granted, leave as a [Student,] Student Nurse, Student Re-Sitting an Examination[, Student Writing-Up a Thesis or as a Tier 4 Migrant] and:

    (i)   is currently being sponsored by a government or international scholarship agency, or

    (ii)   was being sponsored by a government or international scholarship agency, and that sponsorship came to an end 12 months ago or less,

    must provide the [unconditional] written consent of the sponsoring Government or agency to the application [and must provide the specified documents [as set out in paragraph 245A] to show that this requirement has been met.]

[(e)   The applicant must be at least 16 years old and the assets and investment he is claiming points for must be wholly under his control.

(f)   Where the applicant is under 18 years of age, the application must be supported by the applicant's parents or legal guardian or by one parent if that parent has sole legal responsibility for the child.

(g)   Where the applicant is under 18 years of age, the applicant's parents or legal guardian, or one parent if that parent has sole legal responsibility for the child, must confirm that they consent to the arrangements for the applicant's care in the UK.]

[(h)   The applicant must not be in the UK in breach of immigration laws except that any period of overstaying for a period of 28 days or less will be disregarded.]

[(i)   The Secretary of State must not have reasonable grounds to believe that:

    (i)   notwithstanding that the applicant has provided the relevant specified documents required under Appendix A, the applicant is not in control of and at liberty to freely invest the money specified in their application for the purposes of meeting the requirements of Table 7 of Appendix A to these Rules (where relevant); or

    (ii)   any of the money specified in the application for the purposes of meeting the requirements of Table 7 of Appendix A to these Rules held by:

        (1)   the applicant; or

        (2)   where any of the specified money has been made available to the applicant by another party, that party,

    has been acquired by means of conduct which is unlawful in the UK, or would constitute unlawful conduct if it occurred in the UK; or

    (iii)   where any of the money specified in the application for the purposes of meeting the requirements of Table 7 of Appendix A to these Rules has been made available by another party, the character, conduct or associations of that party are such that approval of the application would not be conducive to the public good,

and where the Secretary of State does have reasonable grounds to believe one or more of the above applies, no points from Table 7 (where relevant) will be awarded.

Note

Amended by HC 1113, paras 66–71 as from 27 November 2008. Further amended by HC 314. Old para 245S renumbered as 245ED by HC 863, para 62 as from 6 April 2011. Words in sub-paragraph (b) substituted by HC 863, para 65 as from 6 April 2011. Sub-para (c)(xiv) renumbered as (xvi) by HC 1888, para 37 as from 6 April 2012. Word "Student" inserted by sub-para (d) by HC 1888, para 38 as from 6 April 2012. Words in sub-para (d) "as set out in paragraph 245A" inserted by Cm 8423, para 42 as from 20 July 2012. Sub-para (e) inserted by HC 194, para 60 as from 1 October 2012. Inserted para 245ED(e)–(g) by HC 1138, para 32 as from 13 March 2014. Amended by HC 1138, para 32 as from 6 April 2014. Further amended by HC 1138, para 33 as from 6 April 2014. Further amended by HC 693, para 49 as from 6 November 2014, save that if an application has been made for entry clearance or leave to enter or remain before 6 November 2014, the application will be decided in accordance with the Rules in force on 5 November 2014. Amended by HC 693, para 50 as from 6 November 2014, save that if an application has been made for entry clearance or leave to enter or remain before 6 November 2014, the application will be decided in accordance with the Rules in force on 5 November 2014.

[Period, conditions and curtailment of grant

245EE.
(a)   Leave to remain will be granted:
    (i)   for a period of 2 years, to an applicant who has, or was last granted, leave as a Tier 1 (Investor) Migrant,
    (ii)   for a period of 3 years, to any other applicant.
(b)   Leave to remain under this route will be subject to the following conditions:
    (i)   no recourse to public funds,
    (ii)   registration with the police, if this is required by paragraph 326 of these Rules, . . .
    (iii)   [no Employment as a Doctor in Training, unless the applicant:
        (1)   has obtained a primary degree in medicine or dentistry at bachelor's level or above from a UK institution that is a UK recognised or listed body, or which holds a sponsor licence under Tier 4 of the Points Based System, and provides evidence of this degree; or]
        (2)   has, or has last been granted, entry clearance, leave to enter or leave to remain that was not subject to any condition restricting him from taking employment as a Doctor in Training, has been employed during that leave as a Doctor in Training, and provides a letter from the Postgraduate Deanery or NHS Trust employing them which confirms that they have been working in a post or programme that has been approved by [the General Medical Council] as a training programme or post; or
        (3)   has, or has last been granted, entry clearance, leave to enter or leave to remain that was not subject to any condition restricting him from taking employment as a Dentist in Training, has been employed during that leave as a Dentist in Training, and provides a letter from the Postgraduate Deanery or NHS Trust employing them which confirms that they have been working in a post or programme that has been approved by [the Joint Committee for Postgraduate Training in Dentistry] as a training programme or post[, and]]
    (iv)   [no employment as a professional sportsperson (including as a sports coach).]
(c)   [Without prejudice to the grounds for curtailment in paragraph 323 of these Rules, leave to enter or remain as a Tier 1 (Investor) Migrant may be curtailed if:

    (i)   within 3 months of the date specified in paragraph (d), the applicant has not invested, or had invested on his behalf, at least [the amount of capital specified in paragraph (e)] in the UK by way of UK Government bonds, share capital or loan capital in active and trading UK registered companies other than those principally engaged in property investment, or

    (ii)   [the applicant does not maintain at least the level of investment] in (i) throughout the remaining period of hi leave.]

(d)   The date referred to in paragraph (c) is:

    (i)   the date of the applicant's entry to the UK, in the case of an applicant granted entry clearance as a Tier 1 (Investor) Migrant where there is evidence to establish the applicant's date of entry to the UK,

    (ii)   the date of the grant of entry clearance to the applicant, in the case of an applicant granted entry clearance as a Tier 1 (Investor) Migrant where there is no evidence to establish the applicant's date of entry to the UK, or

    (iii)   the date of the grant of leave to remain to the applicant, in any other case.

[(e)   The amount of capital referred to in paragraph (c) is:

    (i)   at least £2 million if the applicant was last granted leave under the Rules in place from 6 November 2014 and was awarded points as set out in Table 7 or Table 8A of Appendix A to these Rules in that last grant, or

    (ii)   at least £750,000 if the applicant was last granted leave under the Rules in place before 6 November 2014 or was awarded points as set out in Table 8B of Appendix A to these Rules in his last grant.

(f)   Paragraph 245EE(c) does not apply where the applicant's two most recent grants of leave were either as a Tier 1 (Investor) Migrant and / or as an Investor.]

Note

Amended by HC 1113. Sub-para (b)(iii) substituted by HC 439, para 17 as from 6 April 2010. Old para 245T renumbered as 245EE by HC 863, para 62 as from 6 April 2011. Words in sub-paragraph (b)(iii)(2), (3) and (e) substituted by HC 863, paras 67 and 68 as from 6 April 2011. Sub-para (b)(iii) substituted by Cm 8423, para 43 as from 20 July 2012. Further amended by HC 760, paras 133–138 as from 13 December 2012. Amended by HC 693, para 51 as from 6 November 2014, save that if an application has been made for entry clearance or leave to enter or remain before 6 November 2014, the application will be decided in accordance with the Rules in force on 5 November 2014. Amended by HC 693, para 52 as from 6 November 2014, save that if an application has been made for entry clearance or leave to enter or remain before 6 November 2014, the application will be decided in accordance with the Rules in force on 5 November 2014. Amended by HC 693, para 53 as from 6 November 2014, save that if an application has been made for entry clearance or leave to enter or remain before 6 November 2014, the application will be decided in accordance with the Rules in force on 5 November 2014.

[Requirements for indefinite leave to remain

245EF. To qualify for indefinite leave to remain, a Tier 1 (Investor) Migrant must meet the requirements listed below. If the applicant meets these requirements, indefinite leave to remain will be granted. If the applicant does not meet these requirements, the application will be refused.

Requirements:

(a)   . . .

(b)   The applicant must not fall for refusal under the general grounds for refusal, and must not be an illegal entrant.

(c)   The applicant must have a minimum of 75 points under [paragraphs 54 to 65-SD of Appendix A]

(d)   [The applicant must have demonstrated sufficient knowledge of the English language and sufficient knowledge about life in the United Kingdom, in accordance Appendix KoLL.]

(e)   [The applicant must not be in the UK in breach of immigration laws except that any period of overstaying for a period of 28 days or less will be disregarded.]

Note

Old para 245U substituted by 245EF by HC 863, para 69 as from 6 April 2011. Sub-para (e) inserted by HC 194, para 61 as from 1 October 2012. Sub-paragraph (a) deleted by HC 760, para 139 as from 13 December 2012. Sub-paragraph (d) substituted by HC 628, para 84 and if an applicant has made an application for entry clearance or leave before 1 October 2013, the application will be decided in accordance with the Rules in force on 30 September 2013. Amended by HC 693, para 54 as from 6 November 2014, save that if an application has been made for entry clearance or leave to enter or remain before 6 November 2014, the application will be decided in accordance with the Rules in force on 5 November 2014.

[Tier 1 (Graduate Entrepreneur) Migrants]

Purpose of this route and meaning of business

245F.

(a)   [This route is for:

    (i)   UK graduates who have been identified by Higher Education Institutions as having developed genuine and credible business ideas and entrepreneurial skills to extend their stay in the UK after graduation to establish one or more businesses in the UK;

    (ii)   Graduates who have been identified by UK Trade and Investment as elite global graduate entrepreneurs to establish one or more businesses in the UK.]

(b)   For the purpose of paragraphs 245F to [245FC] and paragraphs 66 to 72 of Appendix A 'Business' means an enterprise as:

    (i)   a sole trader,

    (ii)   a partnership, or

    (iii)   a company registered in the UK.

Note

Paragraph 245F to 245FE deleted and 245F, 245FA and 245FB substituted by HC 1888, para 39 as from 6 April 2012. Further amended by HC 1039, paras 32, 33: where an applicant has made an application for entry clearance or leave before 6 April 2013 and the application has not been decided before that date, it will be decided in accordance with the rules in force on 5 April 2013. Amended by HC 1138, para 34 as from 6 April 2014.

Entry to the UK

[**245FA.** All migrants arriving in the UK and wishing to enter as a Tier 1 (Graduate Entrepreneur) Migrant must have a valid entry clearance for entry under this route. If they do not have a valid entry clearance, entry will be refused.]

Requirements for entry clearance or leave to remain

[**245FB.** To qualify entry clearance for leave to remain as a Tier 1 (Graduate Entrepreneur) Migrant, an applicant must meet the requirements listed below. If the applicant meets these requirements, leave to remain will be granted. If the applicant does not meet these requirements, the application will be refused.]

Requirements:

(a)   The applicant must not fall for refusal under the general grounds for refusal, and must not be an illegal entrant.

(b)   The applicant must have a minimum of 75 points under paragraphs 66 to 72 of Appendix A.

(c)   The applicant must have a minimum of 10 points under [paragraphs 1 to 15 of Appendix B].

(d)   The applicant must have a minimum of 10 points under paragraphs 1 to 2 of Appendix C.

(e)   [If applying for leave to remain, the applicant] must have, or have last been granted, entry clearance, leave to enter or remain:

    (i)   as a Tier 4 Migrant,

    (ii)   as a Student,

    (iii)   as a Student Nurse,

      (iv)   as a Student Re-Sitting an Examination,

      (v)   as a Student Writing Up a Thesis,

      (vi)   as a Postgraduate Doctor or Dentist, . . .

      (vii)   as a Tier 1 (Graduate Entrepreneur) Migrant[, or

      (viii) [as a Tier 2 (General) Migrant.

(f)   [[An applicant who is applying for leave to remain and has], or was last granted, entry clearance or leave to remain as a Tier 2 (General) Migrant must have been granted leave to work as a post-doctoral researcher for the same institution which is endorsing his application as a Tier 1 (Graduate Entrepreneur) Migrant.]

(g)   The applicant must not have previously been granted entry clearance, leave to enter or remain as a Tier 1 (Post-Study Work) Migrant, a Participant in the Fresh Talent: Working in Scotland Scheme, or a Participant in the International Graduates Scheme (or its predecessor, the Science and Engineering Graduates Scheme).

(h)   The applicant must not previously have been granted leave as a Tier 1 (Graduate Entrepreneur) Migrant on more than 1 occasion.

(i)   An applicant who does not have, or was not last granted, leave to remain as a Tier 1 (Graduate Entrepreneur) Migrant and:

      (i)   is currently being sponsored in his studies by a government or international scholarship agency, or

      (ii)   was being sponsored in his studies by a government or international scholarship agency, and that sponsorship came to an end 12 months ago or less,

      must provide the unconditional written consent of the sponsoring government or agency to the application and must provide the specified documents [as set out in paragraph 245A above] to show that this requirement has been met.

(j)   [The applicant must not be in the UK in breach of immigration laws except that any period of overstaying for a period of 28 days or less will be disregarded.]

Note

Paragraphs 245F to 245FE deleted and 245F, 245FA and 245FB substituted by HC 1888, para 39 as from 6 April 2012. Words in sub-para (h) "as set out in paragraph 245A above" inserted by Cm 8423, para 44 as from 20 July 2012. Sub-para (i) inserted by HC 194, para 62 as from 1 October 2012. Further amended by HC 1039, paras 34–42: where an applicant has made an application for entry clearance or leave before 6 April 2013 and the application has not been decided before that date, it will be decided in accordance with the rules in force on 5 April 2013. Substituted para 245FB(f) by HC 1138, para 35 as from 13 March 2014. Amended by HC 532, para 3 of this statement takes effect on 11 July 2014.

[Period and conditions of grant

[245FC.]   Leave to remain will be granted for a period of 1 year and will be subject to the following conditions:

(i)   no recourse to public funds,

(ii)   registration with the police, if this is required by paragraph 326 of these Rules,

(iii)   no employment as a Doctor or Dentist in Training, and

(iv)   no employment as a professional sportsperson (including as a sports coach).]

Note

Paragraphs 245F to 245FE deleted and 245F, 245FA and 245FB substituted by HC 1888, para 39 as from 6 April 2012. Further amended by HC 1039, para 43: where an applicant has made an application for entry clearance or leave before 6 April 2013 and the application has not been decided before that date, it will be decided in accordance with the rules in force on 5 April 2013.

Tier 2 Migrants
[Tier 2 (Intra-Company Transfer) Migrants]

Purpose of this route and definitions

245G. This route enables multinational employers to transfer their existing employees from outside the EEA to their UK branch for training purposes or to fill a specific vacancy that cannot be filled by a British or EEA worker. There are four sub-categories in this route:

(i) Short Term Staff: for established employees of multi-national companies who are being transferred to a skilled job in the UK for 12 months or less that could not be carried out by a new recruit from the resident workforce;

(ii) Long Term Staff: for established employees of multi-national companies who are being transferred to a skilled job in the UK which will, or may, last for more than 12 months and could not be carried out by a new recruit from the resident workforce;

(iii) Graduate Trainee: for recent graduate recruits of multi-national companies who are being transferred to the UK branch of the same organisation as part of a structured graduate training programme, which clearly defines progression towards a managerial or specialist role;

(iv) Skills Transfer: for overseas employees of multi-national companies who are being transferred to the UK branch of the same organisation in a graduate occupation to learn the skills and knowledge they will need to perform their jobs overseas, or to impart their specialist skills to the UK workforce.

Note

This para substituted for old para 245ZB by HC 863, para 76 as from 6 April 2011.

Entry clearance

245GA. All migrants arriving in the UK and wishing to enter as a Tier 2 (Intra-Company Transfer) Migrant must have a valid entry clearance for entry under this route. If they do not have a valid entry clearance, entry will be refused.

Note

This para substituted for old para 245ZC by HC 863, para 76 as from 6 April 2011.

Requirements for entry clearance

245GB. To qualify for entry clearance as a Tier 2 (Intra-Company Transfer) Migrant, an applicant must meet the requirements listed below. If the applicant meets these requirements, entry clearance will be granted. If the applicant does not meet these requirements, the application will be refused.

Requirements:

(a) The applicant must not fall for refusal under the general grounds for refusal.

(b) The applicant must have a minimum of 50 points under paragraphs 73 to 75E of Appendix A.

(c) The applicant must have a minimum of 10 points under paragraphs 4 to 5 of Appendix C.

(d) The applicant must not have had entry clearance or leave to remain as a [Tier 2 Migrant] at any time during the 12 months immediately before the date of the application, . . . unless paragraph (e) below applies.

(e) Paragraph (d) above does not apply to an applicant who:

    (i) was not in the UK with leave as a Tier 2 migrant at any time during the above 12–month period, and provides evidence to show this[,]

    (ii) is applying under the Long Term Staff sub-category and who has, or last had entry clearance or leave to remain as a Tier 2 (Intra-Company Transfer) Migrant in the Short Term staff, Graduate Trainee or Skills Transfer sub-categories, or under the Rules in place before 6 April 2011[, or]]

(iii)   [will be paid a gross annual salary (as recorded by the Certificate of Sponsorship Checking Service entry, and including such allowances as are specified as acceptable for this purpose in paragraph 75 of Appendix A) of [£153,500] or higher.]

(f)   An applicant who has, or was last granted, leave as a Student, a Student Nurse, a Student Re-Sitting an Examination, a Student Writing-Up a Thesis, a Postgraduate Doctor or Dentist or a Tier 4 Migrant and:

(i)   is currently being sponsored by a government or international scholarship agency, or

(ii)   was being sponsored by a government or international scholarship agency, and that sponsorship came to an end 12 months ago or less,

must provide the unconditional written consent of the sponsoring Government or agency to the application and must provide the specified documents [as set out in paragraph 245A above,] to show that this requirement has been met.

(g)   The applicant must be at least 16 years old.

(h)   Where the applicant is under 18 years of age, the application must be supported by the applicant's parents or legal guardian, or by one parent if that parent has sole legal responsibility for the child.

(i)   Where the applicant is under 18 years of age, the applicant's parents or legal guardian, or just one parent if that parent has sole responsibility for the child, must confirm that they consent to the arrangements for the applicant's travel to, and reception and care in, the UK.

Note

This para substituted for old para 245ZD by HC 863, para 76 as from 6 April 2011. Words "Tier 2 Migrant" substituted in sub-para (d) by HC 1888, para 40 as from 6 April 2012. Further amended by Cm 8423, para 45 as from 20 July 2012. Further amended by HC 760, paras 140, 141 as from 13 December 2012. Further amended by HC 1039, paras 44–46: where an applicant has made an application for entry clearance or leave before 6 April 2013 and the application has not been decided before that date, it will be decided in accordance with the rules in force on 5 April 2013. Further amended by HC 1138, para 36 and if an applicant has made an application for entry clearance or leave on or after 6 April 2014 using a Certificate of Sponsorship that was assigned to him by his Sponsor before 6 April 2014, the application will be decided in accordance with the rules in force on 5 April 2014.

[**Period and conditions of grant**

245GC.

(a)   Entry clearance will be granted for whichever is the shorter of:

(i)   a period equal to the length of the period of engagement plus 1 month, or

(ii)   the maximum time, as set out in (b).

(b)   The maximum time referred to in (a)(ii) is:

(i)   6 months, if the applicant is applying in the Skills Transfer sub-category,

(ii)   12 months, if the applicant is applying in either of the Graduate Trainee or Short Term Staff sub-categories, or

(iii)   5 years and 1 month, if the applicant is applying in the Long Term Staff sub-category.]

(c)   Entry clearance will be granted with effect from 14 days before the date that the Certificate of Sponsorship Checking Service records as the start date for the applicant's employment in the UK, unless entry clearance is being granted less than 14 days before that date, in which case it will be granted with immediate effect.

(d)   Entry clearance will be subject to the following conditions:

(i)   no recourse to public funds,

(ii)   registration with the police, if this is required by paragraph 326, and

(iii)   no employment except:

(1)   working for the Sponsor in the employment that the Certificate of Sponsorship Checking Service records that the migrant is being

sponsored to do, [subject to any notification of a change to the details of that employment , other than prohibited changes as defined in paragraph 323AA,],

    (2)   supplementary employment, and

    (3)   voluntary work.

Note

This para substituted for old para 245ZE by HC 863, para 76 as from 6 April 2011. Further amended by Cm 8423, para 46 as from 20 July 2012. Further amended by HC 1138, para 37–38 as from 6 April 2014.

Requirements for leave to remain

245GD. To qualify for leave to remain as a Tier 2 (Intra-Company Transfer) Migrant under this rule, an applicant must meet the requirements listed below. If the applicant meets these requirements, leave to remain will be granted. If the applicant does not meet these requirements, the application will be refused.

Requirements:

    (a)   The applicant must not fall for refusal under the general grounds for refusal, and must not be an illegal entrant.

    (b)   If the applicant is applying for leave to remain as a Tier 2 (Intra-Company Transfer) Migrant in the Long Term Staff sub-category:

        (i)   the applicant must have, or have last been granted, entry clearance, leave to enter or leave to remain as either:

            (1)   a Tier 2 (Intra-Company Transfer) Migrant in the Long Term Staff sub-category, or

            (2)   a Tier 2 (Intra-Company Transfer) Migrant in the Established Staff sub-category under the Rules in place before 6 April 2011, or

            (3)   a Tier 2 (Intra-Company Transfer) Migrant granted under the Rules in place before 6 April 2010, or

            (4)   a Qualifying Work Permit Holder, provided that the work permit was granted because the applicant was the subject of an intra-company transfer, or

            (5)   as a Representative of an Overseas Business, and

        (ii)   the applicant must still be working for the same employer as he was at the time of that earlier grant of leave.

    (c)   If the applicant is applying for leave to remain as a Tier 2 (Intra-Company Transfer) Migrant in the Short Term Staff sub-category:

        (i)   the applicant must have, or have last been granted, entry clearance, leave to enter or leave to remain as a Tier 2 (Intra-Company Transfer) Migrant in the Short Term Staff sub-category, and

        (ii)   the applicant must still be working for the same employer as he was at the time of that earlier grant of leave.

    (d)   If the applicant is applying for leave to remain as a Tier 2 (Intra-Company Transfer) Migrant in the Graduate Trainee sub-category:

        (i)   the applicant must have, or have last been granted, entry clearance, leave to enter or leave to remain as a Tier 2 (Intra-Company Transfer) Migrant in the Graduate Trainee sub-category, and

        (ii)   the applicant must still be working for the same employer as he was at the time of that earlier grant of leave.

    (e)   If the applicant is applying for leave to remain as a Tier 2 (Intra-Company Transfer) Migrant in the Skills Transfer sub-category:

        (i)   the applicant must have, or have last been granted, entry clearance, leave to enter or leave to remain as a Tier 2 (Intra-Company Transfer) Migrant in the Skills Transfer sub-category, and

(ii) the applicant must still be working for the same employer as he was at the time of that earlier grant of leave.

(f) In all cases the applicant must have a minimum of 50 points under paragraphs 73 to 75E of Appendix A.

(g) ...

(h) The applicant must have a minimum of 10 points under paragraphs 4 to 5 of Appendix C.

(i) The applicant must be at least 16 years old.

(j) Where the applicant is under 18 years of age, the application must be supported by the applicant's parents or legal guardian, or by one parent if that parent has sole legal responsibility for the child.

(k) Where the applicant is under 18 years of age, the applicant's parents or legal guardian, or one parent if that parent has sole legal responsibility for the child, must confirm that they consent to the arrangements for the applicant's care in the UK.

[(l) The applicant must not be in the UK in breach of immigration laws except that any period of overstaying for a period of 28 days or less will be disregarded.]

Note

This para substituted for old para 245ZF by HC 863, para 76 as from 6 April 2011. Words "paragraphs 1 to 16" in sub-para (g) substituted by HC 1888, para 41 as from 6 April 2012. Sub-paragraph (l) inserted by HC 194, para 63 as from 1 October 2012. Further amended by HC 1039, para 47: where an applicant has made an application for entry clearance or leave before 6 April 2013 and the application has not been decided before that date, it will be decided in accordance with the rules in force on 5 April 2013. Sub-paragraph (g) deleted by HC 628, para 85 and if an applicant has made an application for entry clearance or leave before 1 October 2013, the application will be decided in accordance with the Rules in force on 30 September 2013.

[Period and conditions of grant

245GE.

(a) Leave to remain will be granted for whichever of the following is the shortest:
   (i) the length of the period of engagement plus 14 days,
   (ii) 5 years, or
   (iii) the difference between the continuous period of leave that the applicant has already been granted (notwithstanding any breaks between periods of leave of up to 28 days) as a Tier 2 (Intra-Company Transfer) Migrant, and the maximum time, as set out in (b).
   If the calculation of period of leave comes to zero or a negative number, leave to remain will be refused.

(b) The maximum time referred to in (a)(iii) is:
   (i) 6 months, if the applicant is applying in the Skills Transfer sub-category,
   (ii) 12 months, if the applicant is applying in either of the Graduate Trainee or Short Term Staff sub-categories,
   (iii) 5 years, if:
      (1) the applicant is applying in the Long Term Staff sub-category,
      (2) the Certificate of Sponsorship Checking Service entry records that the applicant's gross annual salary (including such allowances as are specified as acceptable for this purpose in paragraph 75 of Appendix A) to be paid by the Sponsor is less than £153,500, (or £152,100 if the Certificate of Sponsorship used in support of the application was assigned to him before 6 April 2014) and
      (3) Paragraph (v) below does not apply,
   (iv) 9 years, if:
      (1) the applicant is applying in the Long Term Staff sub-category,
      (2) the Certificate of Sponsorship Checking Service entry records that the applicant's gross annual salary (including such allowances as are specified as acceptable for this purpose in paragraph 75 of Appendix A) to be paid by the Sponsor is £153,500, (or £152,100

if the Certificate of Sponsorship used in support of the application was assigned to him before 6 April 2014) or higher, and

(3)   Paragraph (v) below does not apply,

or

(v)   No limit, if the applicant:

    (1)   is applying in the Long Term Staff sub-category,

    (2)   previously had leave as a Tier 2 (Intra-Company Transfer) Migrant under the Rules in place before 6 April 2011 [or as a Qualifying Work Permit Holder], and

    (3)   has not been granted entry clearance in this or any other route since the grant of leave referred to in (2) above.

(c)   In addition to the period in (a), leave to remain will be granted for the period between the date that the application is decided and the date that the Certificate of Sponsorship Checking Service records as the start date of employment in the UK, provided this is not a negative value.

(d)   Leave to remain will be granted subject to the following conditions:

    (i)   no recourse to public funds,

    (ii)   registration with the police, if this is required by paragraph 326, and

    (iii)   no employment except:

        (1)   working for the sponsor in the employment that the Certificate of Sponsorship Checking Service records that the migrant is being sponsored to do, subject to any notification of a change to the details of that employment, other than prohibited changes as defined in paragraph 323AA,

        (2)   supplementary employment, and

        (3)   voluntary work.]

Note

This para substituted for old para 245ZG by HC 863, para 76 as from 6 April 2011. Sub-paragraph (c) substituted by HC 1888, para 42 as from 6 April 2012. Words in square brackets in (g) and (h) inserted by HC 908, paras 6 and 7 as from 21 April 2011. Sub-paragraph (f) substituted by HC 1148, para 3 as from 4 July 2011. Figure substituted in sub-para (h)(ii) by HC 244, para 2 as from 1 July 2013. Words substituted in sub-para (h)(iii)(1) by Cm 8423, para 47 as from 20 July 2012. Further amended by HC 760, paras 142–145 as from 13 December 2012. Further amended by HC 244, para 2 as from 1 July 2013. Further amended by HC 1138, para 39 as from 6 April 2014.

Requirements for indefinite leave to remain

245GF.   To qualify for indefinite leave to remain as a Tier 2 (Intra-Company Transfer) Migrant, an applicant must meet the requirements listed below. If the applicant meets these requirements, indefinite leave to remain will be granted. If the applicant does not meet these requirements, the application will be refused.

Requirements:

(a)   . . .

(b)   The applicant must not fall for refusal under the general grounds for refusal, and must not be an illegal entrant.

(c)   The applicant must have spent a continuous period of 5 years lawfully in the UK, of which the most recent period must have been spent with leave as a Tier 2 (Intra-Company Transfer) Migrant, in any combination of the following categories:

    (i)   as a Tier 2 (Intra-Company Transfer) Migrant,

    (ii)   as a Qualifying Work Permit Holder, or

    (iii)   as a representative of an overseas Business.

(d)   The continuous period of 5 years referred to in paragraph [(c)] must include a period of leave as:

    (i)   a Tier 2 (Intra-Company Transfer) Migrant granted under the Rules in place before 6 April 2010, or

       (ii)   a Qualifying Work Permit Holder, provided that the work permit was granted because the applicant was the subject of an Intra-Company Transfer.

(e)   [The Sponsor that issued the Certificate of Sponsorship that led to the applicant's last grant of leave must:

       (i)   still hold, or have applied for a renewal of, a Tier 2 (Intra-Company Transfer) Sponsor licence; and

       (ii)   certify in writing that:

           (1)   he still requires the applicant for the employment in question, and

           (2)   the applicant is paid at or above the appropriate rate for the job as stated in the Codes of Practice in Appendix J, or where the applicant is not paid at that rate only due to maternity, paternity or adoption leave, the date that leave started and that the applicant was paid at the appropriate rate immediately before the leave.]

(f)   [The applicant provides the specified documents in paragraph 245GF-SD to evidence the sponsor's certification in sub-section (e)(ii) [and to evidence the reason for the absences set out in paragraph 245AAA.]]

(g)   [The applicant must have sufficient knowledge of the English language and sufficient knowledge about life in the United Kingdom, in accordance with Appendix KoLL.]

(h)   [The applicant must not be in the UK in breach of immigration laws except that any period of overstaying for a period of 28 days or less will be disregarded.]

(i)   [For the purposes of sub-paragraph (c), time spent with valid leave in the Bailiwick of Guernsey, the Bailiwick of Jersey or the Isle of Man in a category equivalent to the categories set out in (c)(i) to (iii) above, may be included in the continuous period of 5 years lawful residence, provided that:

       (i)   the continuous period of 5 years includes a period of leave as a Tier 2 (Intra-Company Transfer) Migrant granted before 6 April 2010, or a Qualifying Work Permit Holder (provided the work permit was granted because the applicant was the subject of an Intra-Company Transfer); and

       (ii)   any period of leave granted in the Bailiwick of Guernsey, the Bailiwick of Jersey or the Isle of Man as a work-permit holder or as a Tier 2 Migrant was for employment:

           (a)   in a job which appears on the list of occupations skilled to National Qualifications Framework level 3 or above (or from 6 April 2011, National Qualifications Framework level 4 or above or from 14 June 2012, National Qualifications Framework level 6 or above), as stated in the Codes of Practice in Appendix J, or

           (b)   in a job which appears in the Creative Sector Codes of Practice in Appendix J, or

           (c)   as a professional sportsperson (including as a sports coach); and

       (iii)   the most recent period of leave was granted in the UK as a Tier 2 (Intra-Company Transfer) Migrant.

In such cases, references to the "UK" in paragraph 245AAA shall include a reference to the Bailiwick of Guernsey, the Bailiwick of Jersey or the Isle of Man, as the case may be.]

Note

This para substituted for old para 245ZH by HC 863, para 76 as from 6 April 2011. Words in square brackets in sub-para (e)(ii) deleted by HC 1511, para 9 as from 31 October 2011. Words "the Codes of Practice for in Appendix J" in sub-para (e)(ii) substituted by Cm 8423, para 48 as from 20 July 2012. New sub-paragraph (f) inserted by HC 1511, para 11 as from 31 October 2011. Sub-paragraph (f) renumbered as sub-paragraph (g) by HC 1511, para 10 as from 31 October 2011. Sub-paragraph (h) inserted by HC 194, para 64 as from 1 October 2012. Further amended by HC 760, paras 146–148 as from 13 December 2012. Further amended by HC

1039, paras 48, 49 as from on or after 6 April 2013. Sub-paragraphs (e) and (g) substituted by HC 628, para 86, 87 and if an applicant has made an application for entry clearance or leave before 1 October 2013, the application will be decided in accordance with the Rules in force on 30 September 2013.

[Specified documents

245GF-SD The specified documents referred to in paragraph 245GF(f) are set out in [A, B and C below]:

A. Either a payslip and a personal bank or building society statement, or a payslip and a building society pass book.
(a) Payslips must be:
    (i) the applicant's most recent payslip,
    (ii) dated no earlier than one calendar month before the date of the application, and
    (iii) either:
        (1) an original payslip,
        (2) on company-headed paper, or
        (3) accompanied by a letter from the applicant's Sponsor, on company headed paper and signed by a senior official, confirming the payslip is authentic.
(b) Personal bank or building society statements must:
    (i) be the most applicant's most recent statement,
    (ii) be dated no earlier than one calendar month before the date of the application,
    (iii) clearly show:
        (1) the applicant's name,
        (2) the applicant's account number,
        (3) the date of the statement,
        (4) the financial institution's name,
        (5) the financial institution's logo, and
        (6) transactions by the Sponsor covering the period no earlier than one calendar month before the date of the application, including the amount shown on the specified payslip as at 245GF-SD A.(a)
    (iv) be either:
        (1) printed on the bank's or building society's letterhead,
        (2) electronic bank or building society statements ...., accompanied by a supporting letter from the bank or building society, on company headed paper, confirming the statement provided is authentic, or
        (3) electronic bank or building society statements ..., bearing the official stamp of the bank or building society on every page,
        and
    (v) not be mini-statements from automatic teller machines (ATMs).
(c) Building society pass books must
    (i) clearly show:
        (1) the applicant's name,
        (2) the applicant's account number,
        (3) the financial institution's name,
        (4) the financial institution's logo, and
        (5) transactions by the sponsor covering the period no earlier than one calendar month before the date of the application, including the amount shown on the specified payslip as at 245GF-SD A.(a)
        and
    (ii) be either:
        (1) the original pass book, or

(2)   a photocopy of the pass book which has been certified by the issuing building society on company headed paper, confirming the statement provided is authentic.

B. A letter from the employer detailing the purpose and period of absences in connection with the employment, including periods of annual leave. Where the absence was due to a serious or compelling reason, a personal letter from the applicant which includes full details of the reason for the absences and all original supporting documents in relation to those reasons — e.g. medical certificates, birth/death certificates, information about the reasons which led to the absence from the UK.]

[C. Where the applicant is not being paid the appropriate rate in Appendix J due to maternity, paternity or adoption leave:

(a)   Payslips must be:
  (i)   the applicant's payslip from the month immediately preceding the leave,
  (ii) the applicant's payslips for each month of the period of the leave,
  (iii) as set out in A(a)(iii) above.
(b)   Bank or building society statements must be:
  (i)   the applicant's statement from the month immediately preceding the leave,
  (ii) the applicant's statement for each month of the period of the leave,
  (iii) as set out in A(b)(iii) above.]

Note

Inserted by HC 760, para 149 as from 13 December 2012. Further amended by HC 1039, paras 50, 51 as from on or after 6 April 2013. Sub-para (iv)(2), (3) amended by HC 628, paras 88, 89 and if an applicant has made an application for entry clearance or leave before 1 October 2013, the application will be decided in accordance with the Rules in force on 30 September 2013.

Tier 2 (General) Migrants, Tier 2 (Minister of Religion) Migrants and Tier 2 (Sportsperson) Migrants

Purpose of these routes and definitions

245H.   These routes enable UK employers to recruit workers from outside the EEA to fill a particular vacancy that cannot be filled by a British or EEA worker.

Note

This para inserted by HC 863, para 76 as from 6 April 2011.

Entry clearance

245HA.   All migrants arriving in the UK and wishing to enter as a Tier 2 (General) Migrant, Tier 2 (Minister of Religion) Migrant or Tier 2 (Sportsperson) Migrant must have a valid entry clearance for entry under the relevant one of these routes. If they do not have a valid entry clearance, entry will be refused.

Note

This para inserted by HC 863, para 76 as from 6 April 2011.

Requirements for entry clearance

245HB.   To qualify for entry clearance as a Tier 2 (General) Migrant, Tier 2 (Minister of Religion) Migrant or Tier 2 (Sportsperson) Migrant, an applicant must meet the requirements listed below. If the applicant meets these requirements, entry clearance will be granted. If the applicant does not meet these requirements, the application will be refused.

Requirements:
(a)   The applicant must not fall for refusal under the general grounds for refusal.

(b)   If applying as a Tier 2 (General) Migrant, the applicant must have a minimum of 50 points under paragraphs 76 to 84A of Appendix A.

(c)   If applying as a Tier 2 (Minister of Religion) Migrant, the applicant must have a minimum of 50 points under paragraphs 85 to [92A] of Appendix A.

(d)   If applying as a Tier 2 (Sportsperson) Migrant, the applicant must have a minimum of 50 points under paragraphs 93 to 100 of Appendix A.

(e)   The applicant must have a minimum of 10 points under [paragraphs 1 to 18] of Appendix B.

(f)   The applicant must have a minimum of 10 points under paragraphs 4 to 5 of Appendix C.

(g)   [The applicant must not have had entry clearance or leave to remain as a Tier 2 Migrant at any time during the 12 months immediately before the date of the application, unless the applicant:

    (i)   was not in the UK with leave as a Tier 2 Migrant during this period, and provides evidence to show this, or

    (ii)   will be paid a gross annual salary (as recorded by the Certificate of Sponsorship Checking Service entry, and including such allowances as are specified as acceptable for this purpose in paragraph 79 of Appendix A) of [£153,500] or higher.]

(h)   An applicant who has, or was last granted, leave as a Student, a Student Nurse, a Student Re-Sitting an Examination, a Student Writing-Up a Thesis, a Postgraduate Doctor or Dentist or a Tier 4 Migrant and:

    (i)   is currently being sponsored by a government or international scholarship agency, or

    (ii)   was being sponsored by a government or international scholarship agency, and that sponsorship came to an end 12 months ago or less,

must provide the unconditional written consent of the sponsoring Government or agency to the application and must provide the specified documents [as set out in paragraph 245A above,] to show that this requirement has been met.

(i)   The applicant must be at least 16 years old.

(j)   Where the applicant is under 18 years of age, the application must be supported by the applicant's parents or legal guardian, or by one parent if that parent has sole legal responsibility for the child.

(k)   Where the applicant is under 18 years of age, the applicant's parents or legal guardian, or just one parent if that parent has sole responsibility for the child, must confirm that they consent to the arrangements for the applicant's travel to, and reception and care in, the UK.

(l)   If the Sponsor is a limited company, the applicant must not own more than 10% of its shares[, unless the gross annual salary (as recorded by the Certificate of Sponsorship Checking Service entry, and including such allowances as are specified as acceptable for this purpose in paragraph 79 of Appendix A) is £153,500 or higher.].

(m)   [If the applicant is applying as a Tier 2 (Minister of Religion) Migrant, the Entry Clearance Officer must be satisfied that the applicant:

    (i)   genuinely intends to undertake, and is capable of undertaking, the role recorded by the Certificate of Sponsorship Checking Service; and

    (ii)   will not undertake employment in the United Kingdom other than under the terms of [paragraph 245HC(d)(iii)].

(n)   To support the assessment in paragraph 245HB(m), the Entry Clearance Officer may:

    (i)   request additional information and evidence, and refuse the application if the information or evidence is not provided. Any requested documents must be received by the Home Office at the address specified in the request with [28 calendar days] of the date the request is sent, and

(ii) request the applicant attends an interview, and refuse the application if the applicant fails to comply with any such request without providing a reasonable explanation.

(o) If the Entry Clearance Officer is not satisfied following the assessment in paragraph 245HB(m), no points will be awarded under paragraphs 85 to 92A of Appendix A.

(p) The Entry Clearance Officer may decide not to carry out the assessment in paragraph 245HB(m) of the application already falls for refusal on other grounds, but reserves the right to carry out this assessment in any reconsideration of the decision.]

Note

This para inserted by HC 863, para 76 as from 6 April 2011. Words in square brackets in sub-para (e), sub-paragraphs (g) to (k) renumbered as (h) to (l) and (g) inserted by HC 1888, paras 43–45 as from 6 April 2012. Sub-para (h) words "as set out in paragraph 245A above," inserted by Cm 8423, para 51 as from 20 July 2012. Sub-para (h) words substituted by HC 760, para 150 as from 13 December 2012. Further amended by HC 1039, paras 52: where an applicant has made an application for entry clearance or leave before 6 April 2013 and the application has not been decided before that date, it will be decided in accordance with the rules in force on 5 April 2013. Further amended by HC 628, paras 90–92 and if an applicant has made an application for entry clearance or leave before 1 October 2013, the application will be decided in accordance with the Rules in force on 30 September 2013. Further amended by HC 1138 para 40 and if an applicant has made an application for entry clearance or leave on or after 6 April 2014 using a Certificate of Sponsorship that was assigned to him by his Sponsor before 6 April 2014, the application will be decided in accordance with the rules in force on 5 April 2014. Further amended by HC 1138, para 41 and if an applicant has made an application for entry clearance or leave on or after 6 April 2014 using a Certificate of Sponsorship that was assigned to him by his Sponsor before 6 April 2014, the application will be decided in accordance with the rules in force on 5 April 2014. Further amended by HC 693, para 55 as from 6 November 2014, save that if an application has been made for entry clearance or leave to enter or remain before 6 November 2014, the application will be decided in accordance with the Rules in force on 5 November 2014. Further amended by HC 693, para 56 as from 6 November 2014, save that if an application has been made for entry clearance or leave to enter or remain before 6 November 2014, the application will be decided in accordance with the Rules in force on 5 November 2014.

[**Period and conditions of grant**

245HC.

(a) Entry clearance will be granted for whichever of the following is the shorter:
 (i) a period equal to the length of the period of engagement plus 1 month, or
 (ii) the maximum time, as set out in (b).

(b) The maximum time referred to in (a)(ii) is:
 (i) 5 years and 1 month, if the applicant is applying as a Tier 2 (General) Migrant; or
 (ii) 3 years and 1 month, if the applicant is applying as a Tier 2 (Minister of Religion) Migrant or a Tier 2 (Sportsperson) Migrant.]

(c) Entry clearance will be granted with effect from 14 days before the date that the Certificate of Sponsorship Checking Service records as the start date for the applicant's employment in the UK, unless entry clearance is being granted less than 14 days before that date, in which case it will be granted with immediate effect.

(d) Entry clearance will be subject to the following conditions:
 (i) no recourse to public funds,
 (ii) registration with the police, if this is required by paragraph 326 of these Rules, and
 (iii) no employment except:
  (1) working for the Sponsor in the employment that the Certificate of Sponsorship Checking Service records that the migrant is being sponsored to do, [subject to any notification of a change to the details of that employment, other than prohibited changes as defined in paragraph 323AA,],

        (2)   supplementary employment,

        (3)   voluntary work, and

        (4)   if the applicant is applying as a Tier 2 (Sportsperson) Migrant, employment as a sportsperson for his national team while his national team is in the UK [and Temporary Engagement as a Sports Broadcaster.]

(i)   Applicants who meet the requirements for entry clearance and who obtain points under paragraphs 76 to 79D of Appendix A shall be granted entry clearance as a Tier 2 (General) Migrant.

(ii)   Applicants who meet the requirements for entry clearance and who obtain points under paragraphs 85 to 92 of Appendix A shall be granted entry clearance as a Tier 2 (Minister of Religion) Migrant.

(iii)   Applicants who meet the requirements for entry clearance and who obtain points under paragraphs 93 to 100 of Appendix A shall be granted entry clearance as a Tier 2 (Sportsperson) Migrant.

Note

This para inserted by HC 863, para 76 as from 6 April 2011. Further amended By Cm 8423, para 52 as from 20 July 2012. Further amended by HC 1138, para 42 as from 6 April 2014. Further amended by HC 1138, para 43 as from 6 April 2014. Amended by HC 693, para 57 as from 6 November 2014, save that if an application has been made for entry clearance or leave to enter or remain before 6 November 2014, the application will be decided in accordance with the Rules in force on 5 November 2014.

Requirements for leave to remain

245HD. To qualify for leave to remain as a Tier 2 (General) Migrant, Tier 2 (Minister of Religion Migrant or Tier 2 (Sportsperson) Migrant under this rule, an applicant must meet the requirements listed below. If the applicant meets these requirements, leave to remain will be granted. If the applicant does not meet these requirements, the application will be refused.

Requirements:

(a)   The applicant must not fall for refusal under the general grounds for refusal, and must not be an illegal entrant.

[(b)   the applicant must:

    (i)   have, or have last been granted, entry clearance, leave to enter or leave to remain as:

        (1)   a Tier 1 Migrant,

        (2)   a Tier 2 Migrant,

        (3)   a Highly Skilled Migrant,

        (4)   an Innovator,

        (5)   a Jewish Agency Employee,

        (6)   a Member of the Operational Ground Staff of an Overseas-owned Airline,

        (7)   a Minister of Religion, Missionary or Member of a Religious Order,

        (8)   a Participant in the Fresh Talent: Working in Scotland Scheme,

        (9)   a Participant in the International Graduates Scheme (or its predecessor, the Science and Engineering Graduates Scheme),

        (10)   a Qualifying Work Permit Holder,

        (11)   a Representative of an Overseas Business

        (12)   a Representative of an Overseas Newspaper, News Agency or Broadcasting Organisation,

        (13)   a Tier 5 (Temporary Worker) Migrant, or

        (14)   the partner of a Relevant Points Based System Migrant if the Relevant Points Based System Migrant is a Tier 4 Migrant, or

    (ii)   [have, or have last been granted, entry clearance, leave to enter or leave to remain as:]

        (1)   a Tier 4 Migrant,

        (2)   a Student,

        (3)   a Student Nurse,

        (4)   a Student Re-Sitting an Examination,

        (5)   a Person Writing Up a Thesis,

        (6)   an Overseas Qualified Nurse or Midwife,

        (7)   a Postgraduate Doctor or Dentist, or

        (8)   a Student Union Sabbatical Officer.]

(c)   An applicant who has, or was last granted leave as a Tier 2 (Inter-Company Transfer Migrant must

    (i)   have previously had leave as a Tier 2 (Intra-Company Transfer) Migrant under the Rules in place before 6 April 2010, or in the Established Staff sub-category under the Rules in place before 6 April 2011,

    (ii)   not have been granted entry clearance in this or any other route since the grant of leave referred to in (i) above; and

    (iii)   not be applying to work for the same sponsor as sponsored him when he was last granted leave.

[(d)   An applicant under the provisions in (b)(ii) above must met the following requirements:

    (i)   The applicant must have completed and passed:

        (1)   a UK recognised [bachelor's or master's degree] (not a qualification of equivalent level which is not a degree).

        (2)   a UK Postgraduate Certificate in Education or professional Graduate Diploma of Education (not a qualification of equivalent level).

        or the applicant must have completed a minimum of 12 months study in the UK towards a UK PhD.

    (ii)   The applicant must have studied for the course in (d)(i) at a UK institution that is a UK recognised or listed body, or which hosts a sponsor licence under Tier 4 of the Points Based System.

    (iii)   The applicant must have studied the course referred to in (d)(i) during:

        (1)   his last grant of leave, or

        (2)   a period of continuous leave which includes his last grant of leave [(For these purposes continuous leave will not be considered to have been broken if any of the circumstances set out in paragraphs 245AAA(a)(i) to (iii) of these Rules apply.)]

    (iv)   The applicant's periods of UK study and/or research towards the course in (i) must have been undertaken whilst he had entry clearance, leave to enter or leave to remain in the UK that was not subject to a restriction preventing him from undertaking that course of study and/or research.

    (v)   If the institution studied at is removed from the Tier 4 Sponsor Register, the applicant's qualification must not have been obtained on or after the date of removal from the Sponsor Register.

    (vi)   If the applicant:

        (1)   is currently being sponsored by a government or international scholarship agency, or

        (2)   was being sponsored by a government or international sponsorship agency, and that sponsorship came to an end 12 months ago or less,

        the applicant must provide the unconditional written consent of the sponsoring Government or agency to the application and must provide the specified documents [as set out in paragraph 245A above,] to show that this requirement has been met.

    (vii)   [The applicant must provide an original degree certificate, academic transcript or an academic reference on official headed paper of the institution, which clearly shows:

        (1)   The applicant's name,

      (2)   the course title/award,

      (3)   [the course duration (except on the case of a degree certificate), and]

      (4)   [unless the course is a PhD course, the date of course completion and pass (or the date of award in the case of a degree certificate).]

(e) An applicant who was last granted leave as a Tier 5 (Temporary Worker) Migrant must have been granted such leave in the Creative and Sporting sub-category of Tier 5 in order to allow the applicant to work as a professional footballer, . . .[, and the applicant must be applying for leave to remain as a Tier 2 (Sportsperson) Migrant.]

(f) If applying as a Tier 2 (General) Migrant, the applicant must have a minimum of 50 points under paragraphs 76 to 79D of Appendix A.

(g) If applying as a Tier 2 (Minister of Religion) Migrant, the applicant must have a minimum of 50 points under paragraphs 85 to [92A] of Appendix A.

(h) If applying as a Tier 2 (Sportsperson) Migrant, the applicant must have a minimum of 50 points under paragraphs 93 to 100 of Appendix A.

(i) The applicant must have a minimum of 10 points under [paragraphs 1 to 16] of Appendix B.

(j) The applicant must have a minimum of 10 points under paragraphs 4 to 5 of Appendix C.

[(k) The applicant must not have had entry clearance or leave to remain as a Tier 2 Migrant at any time during the 12 months immediately before the date of the application, unless:]

      (i)   the applicant's last grant of leave was as a Tier 2 migrant, . . .

      (ii) the applicant was not in the UK with leave as a Tier 2 Migrant during this period, and provides evidence to show this[, or]]

      (iii) [the applicant will be paid a gross annual salary As recorded by the Certificate of Sponsorship Checking Service entry, and including such allowances as are specified as acceptable for this purpose in paragraph 79 of Appendix A) of [£153,500] or higher.]]

(l) The applicant must be at least 16 years old.

(m) Where the applicant is under 18 years of age, the application must be supported by the applicant's parents or legal guardian, or by one parent if that parent has sole legal responsibility for the child.

(n) Where the applicant is under 18 years of age, the applicant's parents or legal guardian, or one parent if that parent has sole legal responsibility for the child, must confirm that they consent to the arrangements for the applicant's care in the UK.

(o) If the Sponsor is a limited company, the applicant must not own more than 10% of its shares[, unless the gross annual salary (as recorded by the Certificate of Sponsorship Checking Service entry, and including such allowances as are specified as acceptable for this purpose in paragraph 79 of Appendix A) is [£153,500] or higher.]

[(p) The applicant must not be in the UK in breach of immigration laws except that any period of overstaying for a period of 28 days or less will be disregarded.]

[(q) If the applicant is applying as a Tier 2 (Minister of Religion) Migrant, the Secretary of State must be satisfied that the applicant:

      (i)   genuinely intends to undertake, and is capable of undertaking, the role recorded by the Certificate of Sponsorship Checking Service; and

      (ii) will not undertake employment in the United Kingdom other than under the terms of [paragraph 245HE(d)(iii)].

(r) To support the assessment in paragraph 245HD(q), the Secretary of State may:

      (i)   request additional information and evidence, and refuse the application if the information or evidence is not provided. Any requested documents must be received by the Home Office at the address specified in the request within [28 calendar days] of the date the request is sent, and

(ii) request the applicant attends an interview, and refuse the application if the applicant fails to comply with any such request without providing a reasonable explanation.

(s) If the Secretary of State is not satisfied following the assessment in paragraph 245HD(q), no points will be awarded under paragraphs 85 to 92A of Appendix A.

(t) The Secretary of State may decide not to carry out the assessment in paragraph 245HD(q) if the application already falls for refusal on other grounds, but reserves the right to carry out this assessment in any reconsideration of the decision.]

Note

This para inserted by HC 863, para 76 as from 6 April 2011. Further amended by HC 1888, para 46–53 as from 6 April 2012. Further amended by Cm 8423, paras 53–55 as from 20 July 2012. Sub-para (p) inserted by HC 194, para 65 as from 1 October 2012. Further amended by HC 760, paras 151, 152 as from 13 December 2012. Further amended by HC 1039, paras 53–58: where an applicant has made an application for entry clearance or leave before 6 April 2013 and the application has not been decided before that date, it will be decided in accordance with the rules in force on 5 April 2013. Further amended by HC 628, paras 93–95 as from. Further amended by HC 1138, para 44 and if an applicant has made an application for entry clearance or leave on or after 6 April 2014 using a Certificate of Sponsorship that was assigned to him by his Sponsor before 6 April 2014, the application will be decided in accordance with the rules in force on 5 April 2014. Further amended by HC 1138, para 45 and if an applicant has made an application for entry clearance or leave on or after 6 April 2014 using a Certificate of Sponsorship that was assigned to him by his Sponsor before 6 April 2014, the application will be decided in accordance with the rules in force on 5 April 2014. Amended by HC 693, para 58 as from 6 November 2014, save that if an application has been made for entry clearance or leave to enter or remain before 6 November 2014, the application will be decided in accordance with the Rules in force on 5 November 2014. Amended by HC 693, para 59 as from 6 November 2014, save that if an application has been made for entry clearance or leave to enter or remain before 6 November 2014, the application will be decided in accordance with the Rules in force on 5 November 2014.

[**Period and conditions of grant**

245HE.

[(a) Leave to remain will be granted for whichever of the following is the shortest:
(i) the length of the period of engagement plus 14 days,
(ii) 5 years if the applicant is applying as a Tier 2 (General) Migrant, or
(iii) 3 years if the applicant is applying as a Tier 2 (Minister of Religion) Migrant or a Tier 2 (Sportsperson) Migrant, or
(iv) except where (b) applies, the difference between the continuous period of leave that the applicant has already been granted (notwithstanding any breaks between periods of leave of up to 28 days) as a Tier 2 Migrant [(other than as a Tier 2 (Intra-Company Transfer) Migrant)], and 6 years.
If the calculation of period of leave comes to zero or a negative number, leave to remain will be refused.

(b) The 6 year restriction set out in (a)(iv) will not apply if the applicant:
(i) previously had leave under the Rules in place before 6 April 2011 as:
(1) a Tier 2 (General) Migrant,
(2) a Tier 2 (Minister of Religion) Migrant,
(3) a Tier 2 (Sportsperson) Migrant,
(4) a Jewish Agency Employee,
(5) a Member of the Operational Ground Staff of an Overseas-owned Airline,
(6) a Minister of Religion, Missionary or Member of a Religious Order,
(7) a Qualifying Work Permit Holder, or
(8) a Representative of an Overseas Newspaper, News Agency or Broadcasting Organisation,
and

(ii)   has not been granted entry clearance as a Tier 2 (General) Migrant, Tier 2 (Minister of Religion) Migrant or Tier 2 (Sportsperson) Migrant under the Rules in place from 6 April 2011, and

(iii)   has not been granted entry clearance, leave to enter or leave to remain in any other category since the grant of leave referred to in (i) above.

(c)   In addition to the period in (a), leave to remain will be granted for the period between the date that the application is decided and the date that the Certificate of Sponsorship Checking Service records as the start date of employment in the UK, provided this is not a negative value.]

(d)   Leave to remain will be granted subject to the following conditions:

    (i)   no recourse to public funds,

    (ii)   registration with the police, if this is required by paragraph 326 of these Rules, and

    (iii)   no employment except:

        (1)   working for the Sponsor in the employment that the Certificate of Sponsorship Checking Service records that the migrant is being sponsored to do, [subject to any notification of a change to the details of that employment as defined in paragraph 323AA,],

        (2)   supplementary employment,

        (3)   voluntary work, . . .

        (4)   [until the start date of the period of engagement, any employment which the applicant was lawfully engaged in on the date of the application, and]

        (5)   if the applicant is applying as a Tier 2 (Sportsperson) Migrant, employment as a sportsperson for his national team while his national team is in the UK [and Temporary Engagement as a Sports Broadcaster.]

    (i)   Applicants who meet the requirements for leave to remain and who obtain points under paragraphs 76 to 79D of Appendix A shall be granted leave to remain as a Tier 2 (General) Migrant.

    (ii)   Applicants who meet the requirements for leave to remain and who obtain points under paragraphs 85 to 92 of Appendix A shall be granted leave to remain as a Tier 2 (Minister of Religion) Migrant.

    (iii)   Applicants who meet the requirements for leave to remain and who obtain points under paragraphs 93 to 100 of Appendix A shall be granted leave to remain as a Tier 2 (Sportsperson) Migrant.

Note

Inserted by HC 863, para 76 as from 6 April 2011. Further amended by HC 1888, para 54 as from 6 April 2012. Words in sub-para (g)(iii)(1) "subject to any notification of a change to the details of that employment as defined in paragraph 323AA," substituted by Cm 8423, para 56 as from 20 July 2012. Further amended by HC 1138, para 46 as from 6 April 2014. Further amended by HC 1138, para 47 as from 6 April 2014. Amended by HC 693, para 60 as from 6 November 2014, save that if an application has been made for entry clearance or leave to enter or remain before 6 November 2014, the application will be decided in accordance with the Rules in force on 5 November 2014. Amended by HC 693, para 61 as from 6 November 2014, save that if an application has been made for entry clearance or leave to enter or remain before 6 November 2014, the application will be decided in accordance with the Rules in force on 5 November 2014.

Requirements for indefinite leave to remain

245HF.   To qualify for indefinite leave to remain as a Tier 2 (General) Migrant, Tier 2 (Minister of Religion) Migrant or Tier 2 (Sportsperson) Migrant, an applicant must meet the requirements listed below. If the applicant meets these requirements, indefinite leave to remain will be granted. If the applicant does not meet these requirements, the application will be refused.

Requirements:

(a)   . . .

(b)   The applicant must not fall for refusal under the general grounds for refusal, and must not be an illegal entrant.

(c)   The applicant must have spent a continuous period of 5 years Lawfully in the UK, of which the most recent period must have been spent with leave as a Tier 2 Migrant, in any combination of the following categories:

    (i)   as a Member of the Operational Ground Staff of an Overseas-owned Airline,

    (ii)   as a Minister of Religion, Missionary or Member of a Religious Order,

    (iii)   as a Qualifying Work Permit Holder,

    (iv)   as a Representative of an Overseas Business,

    (v)   as a Representative of an Overseas Newspaper, News Agency or Broadcasting Organisation,

    (vi)   as a Tier 1 Migrant, other than a Tier 1 (Post Study Work) Migrant,

    (vii)   as a Highly Skilled Migrant,

    (viii)   as an Innovator,

    (ix)   as a Tier 2 (General) Migrant, a Tier 2 (Minister of Religion) Migrant or a Tier 2 (Sportsperson) Migrant, or

    (x)   as a Tier 2 (Intra-Company Transfer) Migrant, provided the continuous period of 5 years spent lawfully in the UK includes a period of leave as:

        (1)   a Tier 2 (Intra-Company Transfer) Migrant granted under the Rules in place before 6 April 2010, or

        (2)   a Qualifying Work Permit Holder, provided that the work permit was granted because the applicant was the subject of an intra-company transfer.

(d)   [The Sponsor that issued the Certificate of Sponsorship that led to the applicant's last grant of leave must:

    (i)   still hold, or have applied for a renewal of, a Tier 2 Sponsor licence in the relevant category; and

    (ii)   certify in writing that:

        (1)   he still requires the applicant for the employment in question, and

        (2)   in the case if a Tier 2 (General) Migrant applying for settlement, the applicant is paid at or above the appropriate rate for the job as stated in the Codes of Practice in Appendix J, or where the applicant is not paid at that rate only due to maternity, paternity or adoption leave, the date that leave started and that the applicant was paid at the appropriate rate immediately before the leave.]

(e)   [The applicant provides [the specified documents in paragraph 245HF-SD] to evidence the sponsor's certification in subsection (d)(ii)] [and to evidence the reason for the absences set out in paragraph 245AAA.]

(f)   [The applicant must have sufficient knowledge of the English language and sufficient knowledge about life in the United Kingdom, in accordance Appendix KoLL.]

(g)   [The applicant must not be in the UK in breach of immigration laws except that any period of overstaying for a period of 28 days or less will be disregarded.]

(h)   [For the purposes of sub-paragraph (c), time spent with valid leave in the Bailiwick of Guernsey, the Bailiwick of Jersey or the Isle of Man in a category equivalent to any of the categories set out in (c)(i) to (x), may be included in the continuous period of 5 years lawful residence, provided that:

    (i)   where the leave is in category (x), the continuous period of 5 years includes a period of leave as a Tier 2 (Intra-Company Transfer) Migrant granted before 6 April 2010, or a Qualifying Work Permit Holder (provided the work permit was granted because the applicant was the subject of an Intra-Company Transfer); and

    (ii)   any period of leave granted in the Bailiwick of Guernsey, the Bailiwick of Jersey or the Isle of Man as a work permit holder or as a Tier 2 Migrant was for employment:

(a)   in a job which appears on the list of occupations skilled to National Qualifications Framework level 3 or above (or from 6 April 2011, National Qualifications Framework level 4 or above or from 14 June 2012, National Qualifications Framework level 6 or above), as stated in the Codes of Practice in Appendix J, or

(b)   in a job which appears in the Creative Sector Codes of Practice in Appendix J, or

(c)   as a professional sportsperson (including as a sports coach); and

(iii)   the most recent period of leave was granted in the UK as a Tier 2 Migrant.

In any such case, references to the "UK" in paragraph 245AAA shall include a reference to the Bailiwick of Guernsey, Bailiwick of Jersey or the Isle of MAn, as the case may be.]

Note

This para inserted by HC 863, para 76 as from 6 April 2011. Sub-para (d)(ii) words in square brackets substituted by HC 565, para 62 as from 6 September 2012. Sub-paragraph (e) renumbered as (f) and new (e) inserted by HC 1511, paras 12,13 as from 31 October 2011. Words in square brackets in sub-para (e) substituted by Cm 8423, para 57 as from 20 July 2012. Sub-para (g) inserted by HC 194, para 66 as from 1 October 2012. Further amended by HC 760, paras 153, 154 as from 13 December 2012. Further amended by HC 1039, paras 59, 60 as from on or after 6 April 2013. Further amended by HC 628, paras 96, 97 and if an applicant has made an application for entry clearance or leave before 1 October 2013, the application will be decided in accordance with the Rules in force on 30 September 2013.

[Specified documents

245HF-SD   The specified documents referred to in paragraph 245HF(e) are set out in [A, B or C below]:

A. Either a payslip and a personal bank or building society statement, or a payslip and a building society pass book.

(a)   Payslips must be:

   (i)   the applicant's most recent payslip,

   (ii)   dated no earlier than one calendar month before the date of the application, and

   (iii)   either:

      (1)   an original payslip,

      (2)   on company-headed paper, or

      (3)   accompanied by a letter from the applicant's Sponsor, on company headed paper and signed by a senior official, confirming the payslip is authentic.

(b)   Personal bank or building society statements must:

   (i)   be the most applicant's most recent statement,

   (ii)   be dated no earlier than one calendar month before the date of the application,

   (iii)   clearly show:

      (1)   the applicant's name,

      (2)   the applicant's account number,

      (3)   the date of the statement,

      (4)   the financial institution's name,

      (5)   the financial institution's logo, and

      (6)   transactions by the Sponsor covering the period no earlier than one calendar month before the date of the application, including the amount shown on the specified payslip as at 245HF-SD A.(a)

   (iv)   be either:

      (1)   printed on the bank's or building society's letterhead,

      (2)   electronic bank or building society statements ..., accompanied by a supporting letter from the bank or building society, on company headed paper, confirming the statement provided is authentic, or

        (3)   electronic bank or building society statements ..., bearing the official stamp of the bank or building society on every page,

      and

    (v)   not be mini-statements from automatic teller machines (ATMs).

(c)   Building society pass books must

    (i)   clearly show:

        (1)   the applicant's name,

        (2)   the applicant's account number,

        (3)   the financial institution's name,

        (4)   the financial institution's logo, and

        (5)   transactions by the sponsor covering the period no earlier than one calendar month before the date of the application, including the amount shown on the specified payslip as at 245HF-SD A.(a)

      and

    (ii)   be either:

        (1)   the original pass book, or

        (2)   a photocopy of the pass book which has been certified by the issuing building society on company headed paper, confirming the statement provided is authentic.

B. A letter from the employer detailing the purpose and period of absences in connection with the employment, including periods of annual leave. Where the absence was due to a serious or compelling reason, a personal letter from the applicant which includes full details of the reason for the absences and all original supporting documents in relation to those reasons — e.g. medical certificates, birth/death certificates, information about the reasons which led to the absence from the UK.]

[C. Where the applicant is not being paid the appropriate rate in Appendix J due to maternity, paternity or adoption leave:

(a)   Payslips must be:

    (i)   the applicant's payslip from the month immediately preceding the leave,

    (ii)   the applicant's payslips for each month of the period of the leave,

    (iii)   as set out in A(a)(iii) above.

(b)   Bank or building society statements must be:

    (i)   the applicant's statement from the month immediately preceding the leave,

    (ii)   the applicant's statements for each month of the period of the leave,

    (iii)   as set out in A(b)(iii) above.]

Note

Inserted by HC 760, para 155 as from 13 December 2012. Further amended by HC 1039, paras 60, 61 as from on or after 6 April 2013. Further amended by HC 628, paras 98, 99 and if an applicant has made an application for entry clearance or leave before 1 October 2013, the application will be decided in accordance with the Rules in force on 30 September 2013.

Tier 5 (Youth Mobility Scheme) Temporary Migrants

Purpose of this route

245ZI. This route is for sponsored young people from participating countries [and territories] who wish to live and work temporarily in the UK.

Note

Words in square brackets inserted by HC 1693, para 2 as from 1 January 2012.

Entry clearance

245ZJ. All migrants arriving in the UK and wishing to enter as a Tier 5 (Youth Mobility Scheme) Temporary Migrant must have a valid entry clearance for entry under this route. [If a migrant does not] have a valid entry clearance, entry will be refused.

Note

Words in square brackets inserted by HC 1693, para 3 as from 1 January 2012.

Requirements for entry clearance

245ZK. To qualify for entry clearance as a Tier 5 (Youth Mobility Scheme) Temporary Migrant, an applicant must meet the requirements listed below. However, whether or not the requirements listed below are met, if a citizen of a country [or the rightful holder of a passport issued by a territory] listed in Appendix G makes an application for entry clearance which, if granted, would mean that the annual allocation of places under this route [as specified in Appendix G for citizens of that country or rightful holders of passports issued by that territory would be exceeded, the application will be refused.] The applicant will also be refused if the requirements listed below are not met.

Requirements:
- (a) The applicant must not fall for refusal under the general grounds for refusal [; and
- (b) The applicant must be:
  - (i) a citizen of a country [or rightful holder of a passport issued by a territory] listed in Appendix G to these Rules, or
  - (ii) a British Overseas Citizen, British Overseas Territories Citizen or British National (Overseas), as defined by the British Nationality Act 1981 and must provide [a valid passport] to show that this requirement has been met[; and
- (c) [The applicant must be sponsored by his country of citizenship or the territory of which he is a rightful passport holder as follows:
  - (i) If the applicant is a citizen of a country or the rightful holder of a passport issued by a territory that does not have Deemed Sponsorship Status, the applicant must hold a valid Certificate of Sponsorship issued by that country or territory and must use that Certificate of Sponsorship in support of an application lodged in the country or territory of issue; or
  - (ii) If the applicant is a citizen of a country or the rightful holder of a passport issued by a territory that has Deemed Sponsorship Status, his valid passport issued by the country or territory holding such status will stand as evidence of sponsorship and the application for leave may be made at any post worldwide; and]
- [(ca) A Certificate of Sponsorship will only be considered to be valid if:
  - (i) the country or territory issued it to the applicant no more than 3 months before the application for entry clearance is made, and
  - (ii) it has not have been cancelled by the county or territory since it was issued.]
- (d) The applicant must have a minimum of 40 points under paragraphs 101 to 104 of Appendix A[; and]
- (e) The applicant must have a minimum of 10 points under paragraphs 6 to 7 of Appendix C[; and]
- (f) The applicant must have no children under the age of 18 who are either living with him or for whom he is financially responsible[; and]
- (g) The applicant must not previously have spent time in the UK as a Working Holidaymaker or a Tier 5 (Youth Mobility Scheme) Temporary Migrant.

Note

Words in square brackets inserted by HC 1693, paras 4–9 as from 1 January 2012. Words in square brackets in sub-para (b)(ii) substituted by Cm 8423, para 59 as from 20 July 2012. Further amended by HC 760, para 156 as from 13 December 2012.

Period and conditions of grant

245ZL.   Entry clearance will be granted for a period of 2 years subject to the following conditions:
(a)   no recourse to public funds,
(b)   registration with the police, if this is required by paragraph 326 of these Rules,
(c)   no employment as a professional sportsperson (including as a sports coach), [...] and
(d)   [no employment as a Doctor or Dentist in Training, unless the applicant has obtained a degree in medicine or dentistry at bachelor's level or above from a UK institution that is a UK recognised or listed body, or which holds a sponsor licence under Tier 4 of the Points Based System[, and provides evidence of this degree]]
(e)   no self employment, except where the following conditions are met:
  (i)   the migrant has no premises which he owns, other than his home, from which he carries out his business,
  (ii)   the total value of any equipment used in the business does not exceed £5,000, and
  (iii)   the migrant has no employees.

Note

Sub-para (c) amended, sub-para (d) inserted, and existing sub-para (d) renumbered as sub-para (e) by HC 439, paras 35–37 as from 6 April 2010. Words in square brackets in sub-para (d) substituted by Cm 8423, para 60 as from 20 July 2012.

Tier 5 (Temporary Worker) Migrants

Purpose of this route and definitions

245ZM.
(a)   This route is for certain types of temporary worker whose entry helps to satisfy cultural, charitable, religious or international objectives[, including volunteering and job shadowing].
(b)   For the purposes of paragraphs 245ZM to [245ZS] and paragraphs 105 to [112] of Appendix A:
   a migrant has "consecutive engagements" if:
(i)   more than one Certificate of Sponsorship reference number has been allocated in respect of the migrant,
(ii)   there is no gap of more than 14 days between any of the periods of engagement, and
(iii)   all the Certificate of Sponsorship Checking Service references record that the migrant is being sponsored in the creative and sporting subcategory of the Tier 5 (Temporary Worker) Migrant route.

"Period of engagement" means a period beginning with the employment start date as recorded on the Certificate of Sponsorship Checking Service entry which relates to the Certificate of Sponsorship reference number for which the migrant was awarded points under paragraphs 105 to 111 of Appendix A, and ending on the employment end date as recorded in the same entry.

Note

Para (b) amended by HC 314, paras 80, 81 as from 31 March 2009. Words "including volunteering and job shadowing" in sub-para (a) inserted by HC 1888, para 59 as from 6 April 2012.

Entry clearance

245ZN.

(a) Subject to paragraph (b), all migrants arriving in the UK and wishing to enter as a Tier 5 (Temporary Worker) Migrant must have a valid entry clearance for entry under this route. If they do not have a valid entry clearance, entry will be refused.

(b) A migrant arriving in the UK and wishing to enter as a Tier 5 (Temporary Worker) Migrant who does not have a valid entry clearance will not be refused entry if the following conditions are met:

(i) the migrant is not a visa national,

(ii) the Certificate of Sponsorship reference number provided by the migrant leading to points being obtained under Appendix A links to an entry in the Certificate of Sponsorship Checking Service recording that their Sponsor has sponsored them in the creative and sporting subcategory of the Tier 5 (Temporary Worker) Migrant route,

(iii) if the migrant has consecutive engagements, the total length of all the periods of engagement, together with any gap between those engagements, is 3 months or less,

(iv) if the migrant does not have consecutive engagements, the total length of the period of engagement is 3 months or less, and

(v) the migrant meets the requirements in paragraph 245ZO below.

Requirements for entry clearance or leave to enter

245ZO. To qualify for entry clearance or, as the case may be, leave to enter, as a Tier 5 (Temporary Worker) Migrant, an applicant must meet the requirements listed below. If the applicant meets these requirements, entry clearance will be granted. If the applicant does not meet these requirements, the application will be refused.

Requirements:

(a) The applicant must not fall for refusal under the general grounds for refusal.

(b) The applicant must have a minimum of 30 points under paragraphs 105 to [112] of Appendix A.

(c) The applicant must have a minimum of 10 points under paragraphs 8 to 9 of Appendix C.

(d) [Where the applicant is under 18 years of age, the application must be supported by the applicant's parents or legal guardian, or by just one parent if that parent has sole legal responsibility for the child.

(e) Where the applicant is under 18 years of age, the applicant's parents or legal guardian, or just one parent if that parent has sole responsibility for the child, must confirm that they consent to the arrangements for the applicant's travel to, and reception and care in, the UK.]

(f) [An applicant being sponsored in the international agreement sub-category of Tier 5 (Temporary Workers) as a private servant in a diplomatic household must:

(i) be no less than 18 years of age at the time of application, and

(ii) provide evidence of agreed written terms and conditions of employment in the UK with his employer, . . .[including specifically that the applicant will be paid in accordance with the National Minimum Wage Act 1998 and regulations made under that Act, in the form set out in Appendix Q.]]

(g) [The employer referred to in (f)(ii) must be:

(i) a diplomat, or

(ii) an employee of an international organisation recognised by Her Majesty's Government, who enjoys certain privileges or immunity under UK or international law.]

(h) Where the Certificate of Sponsorship Checking Service reference number for which the applicant was awarded points under Appendix A records that the applicant is being sponsored as a Contractual Service Supplier [or Independent

Professional] in the International Agreement sub-category of the Tier 5 (Temporary Worker) Migrant route, the grant of leave to enter will not result in the applicant being granted leave to enter or remain as a Contractual Service Supplier [or Independent Professional] under the International Agreement sub-category of the Tier 5 (Temporary Worker) Migrant route for a cumulative period exceeding 6 months in any 12 month period ending during the period of leave to enter requested.]

(i) [The Entry Clearance Officer or Immigration Officer must be satisfied that the applicant:

    (i) genuinely intends to undertake, and is capable of undertaking, the role recorded by the Certificate of Sponsorship Checking Service; and

    (ii) will not undertake employment in the United Kingdom other than under the terms of paragraph 245ZP(f)(iii).

(j) To support the assessment in paragraph 245ZO(i), the Entry Clearance Officer or Immigration Officer may:

    (i) request additional information and evidence, and refuse the application if the information or evidence is not provided. Any requested documents must be received by the Home Office at the address specified in the request within [28 calendar days] of the date the request is sent, and

    (ii) request the applicant attends an interview , and refuse the application if the applicant fails to comply with any such request without providing a reasonable explanation.

(k) If the Entry Clearance Officer or Immigration Officer is not satisfied following the assessment in paragraph 245ZO(i), no points will be awarded under paragraphs 105 to 112 of Appendix A.

(l) The Entry Clearance Officer or Immigration officer may decide not to carry out the assessment in paragraph 245ZO(i) if the application already falls for refusal on other grounds, but reserves the right to carry out this assessment in any reconsideration of the decision.]

Note

Para (b) amended by HC 314, para 80 as from 31 March 2009. Sub-paras (d) and (e) inserted by HC 439, para 38 as from 6 April 2010. Sub-para (f) inserted by HC 1888, para 60 as from 6 April 2012. Words in square brackets in sub-para (f)(ii) deleted by Cm 8423, para 61 as from 20 July 2012. Words in square brackets in sub-para (f)(ii) inserted by HC 565, para 63 as from 6 September 2012. Further amended by HC 760, paras 157,158 as from 13 December 2012. Further amended by HC 1039, para 63: where an applicant has made an application for entry clearance or leave before 6 April 2013 and the application has not been decided before that date, it will be decided in accordance with the rules in force on 5 April 2013. Further amended by HC 628, para 100 shall apply to all applications decided on or after 1 October 2013. Amended by HC 693, para 62 as from 6 November 2014, save that if an application has been made for entry clearance or leave to enter or remain before 6 November 2014, the application will be decided in accordance with the Rules in force on 5 November 2014.

Period and conditions of grant

245ZP.

(a) Where paragraph 245ZN(b) applies and the applicant has consecutive engagements, leave to enter will be granted not more for:

    (i) a period commencing not more than 14 days before the beginning of the first period of engagement and ending 14 days after the end of the last period of engagement, or

    (ii) 3 months

    whichever is the shorter.

(b) Where paragraph 245ZN(b) applies and the applicant does not have consecutive engagements, leave to enter will be granted for:

    (i) a period commencing not more than 14 days before the beginning of the period of engagement and ending 14 days after the end of that period of engagement, or

       (ii)   3 months whichever is the shorter.

(c)   Where paragraph 255ZN(b) does not apply and the Certificate of Sponsorship Checking Service reference number for which the applicant was awarded points under Appendix A records that the applicant is being [sponsored in the Creative and Sporting subcategory, the Government Authorised Exchange subcategory for a Work Experience programme, or the Charity Workers sub-category of the Tier 5 (Temporary Worker) Migrant route, entry clearance or leave to enter will be granted for:]

       (i)   a period commencing 14 days before the beginning of the period of engagement (or of the first period of engagement, where the applicant has consecutive engagements) and ending 14 days after the end of that period of engagement (or of the last period of engagement, where the applicant has consecutive engagements), or

       (ii)   12 months

    whichever of (i) or (ii) is the shorter.

(d)   [Where paragraph 245ZN(b) does not apply and the Certificate of Sponsorship Checking Service reference number for which the applicant was awarded points under Appendix A records that the applicant is being sponsored in the religious workers, [the Government Authorised Exchange subcategory [for a Research Programme, Training Programme or Overseas Government Language Programme]] or, other than as a Contractual Service Supplier [or Independent Professional], in the international agreement subcategory of the Tier 5 (Temporary Worker) Migrant route, entry clearance will be granted for:

       (i)   a period commencing 14 days before the beginning of the period of engagement and ending 14 days after the end of that period of engagement, or

       (ii)   2 years,

    whichever is the shorter.]

(e)   Where paragraph 245ZN(b) does not apply and the Certificate of Sponsorship Checking Service reference number for which the applicant was awarded points under Appendix A records that the applicant is being sponsored as a Contractual Service Supplier [or Independent Professional] in the International Agreement sub-category of the Tier 5 (Temporary Worker) Migrant route, entry clearance will be granted for:

       (i)   a period commencing 14 days before the beginning of the period of engagement and ending 14 days after the end of that period of engagement, or

       (ii)   6 months,

    whichever is the shorter.]

(f)   Leave to enter and entry clearance will be granted subject to the following conditions:

       (i)   no recourse to public funds,

       (ii)   registration with the police if this is required by paragraph 326 of these Rules, and

       (iii)   no employment except:

           (1)   unless paragraph (2) applies, working for the person who for the time being is the Sponsor in the employment that the Certificate of Sponsorship Checking Service records that the migrant is being sponsored to do for that Sponsor,

           (2)   [in the case of a migrant whom the Certificate of Sponsorship Checking Service records as being sponsored in the Government Authorised Exchange subcategory of Tier 5 (Temporary Workers), he work, volunteering or job shadowing authorised by the Sponsor and that the Certificate of Sponsorship Checking Service records that the migrant is being sponsored to do,]

           (3)   supplementary employment[, except in the case of a migrant whom the Certificate of Sponsorship Checking Service records as being sponsored in the international agreement sub-category, to work as a private servant in a diplomatic household [or as a Contractual Service Supplier [or Independent Professional]],]

           (4)   in the case of a migrant whom the Certificate of Sponsorship Checking Service records as being sponsored in the creative and

> sporting subcategory of Tier 5 (Temporary Workers), employment as a sportsperson for his national team while his national team is in the UK [and Temporary Engagement as a Sports Broadcaster,]
>
> (iv) [in the case of an applicant whom the Certificate of Sponsorship Checking Service records as being sponsored in the international agreement sub-category of Tier 5 (Temporary Workers), to work as a private servant in a diplomatic household, the employment in (iii)(1) above means working only in the household of the employer recorded by the Certificate of Sponsorship Checking Service.]

Note

Amended by HC 439, para 39 as from 6 April 2010. Further amended by HC 1888, paras 61–66 as from 6 April 2012. Further amended by HC 760, paras 159–162 as from 13 December 2012. Further amended by HC 1039, paras 64–67: where an applicant has made an application for entry clearance or leave before 6 April 2013 and the application has not been decided before that date, it will be decided in accordance with the rules in force on 5 April 2013. Further amended by HC 1138, para 48 as from 6 April 2014.

Requirements for leave to remain

245ZQ. To qualify for leave to remain as a Tier 5 (Temporary Worker) Migrant under this rule, an applicant must meet the requirements listed below. Subject to paragraph 245ZR(a), if the applicant meets these requirements, leave to remain will be granted. If the applicant does not meet these requirements, the application will be refused.

Requirements:
(a)   The applicant must not fall for refusal under the general grounds for refusal, and must not be an illegal entrant.
(b)   [The applicant must have, or have last been granted:]
    (i)   [entry clearance or leave to remain as a Tier 5 (Temporary Worker) Migrant, or]
    (ii)   [entry clearance, leave to enter or leave to remain as] a Sports Visitor or Entertainer Visitor, provided:
        (1)   the Certificate of Sponsorship Checking Service reference for which he is being awarded points in this application shows that he is being sponsored in the creative and sporting subcategory; and
        (2)   the Certificate of Sponsorship reference number was allocated to the applicant before he entered the UK as a Sports Visitor or Entertainer Visitor, [or
    (iii)   [entry clearance, leave to enter or leave to remain as] a Overseas Government Employee, provided
        (a)   the Certificate of Sponsorship Checking Service reference for which he is being awarded points in this application shows that he is being sponsored in the international sub-category; and
        (b)   the applicant is continuing employment with the same overseas government or international organisation for which earlier leave was granted, or
    (iv)   [entry clearance, leave to enter or leave to remain as] a Qualifying Work Permit Holder, provided
        (a)   the applicant was previously issued with a work permit for the purpose of employment by an overseas government, and
        (b)   the Certificate of Sponsorship reference for which he is being awarded points in this application shows he is being sponsored in the international agreement sub-category, and
        (c)   the applicant is continuing employment with the same overseas government or international organisation for which earlier leave was granted] [,or]

    (v)   [entry clearance, leave to enter or leave to remain as] [a Qualifying Work Permit Holder, provided

        (1)   the applicant was previously issued with a work permit for the purpose of employment as a sponsored researcher, and

        (2)   the Certificate of Sponsorship Checking Service reference for which he is being awarded points in this application shows he is being sponsored in the government authorised exchange sub-category, and

        (3)   the applicant is continuing employment with the same organisation for which his most recent period of leave was granted][, or]

    (vi)   [entry clearance, leave to enter or leave to remain as a Student, a Student Re-Sitting an Examination, a Person Writing Up a Thesis, a Postgraduate Doctor or Dentist, a Student Nurse, a Student Union Sabbatical Officer, or a Tier 4 (General) Migrant, provided the Certificate of Sponsorship Checking Service reference for which he is being awarded points in this application confirms:

        (1)   he is being sponsored in the government authorised exchange sub-category, and

        (2)   he lawfully obtained a UK recognised bachelor or postgraduate degree (not a qualification of equivalent level which is not a degree) during his grant of leave, and

        (3)   [he is being sponsored to:

            (a)   [undertake a period of postgraduate professional training or work experience which is required to obtain a professional qualification or professional registration in the same professional field as the qualification in (2) above, and will not be filling a permanent vacancy, such that the employer he is directed to work for by the Sponsor does not intend to employ him in the UK once the training or work experience for which he is being sponsored has concluded, or

            (b)   undertake an internship for up to 12 months which directly relates to the qualification in (2) above, and will not be filling a permanent vacancy such that the employer he is directed to work for by the Sponsor does not intend to employ him in the UK once the training or work experience for which he is being sponsored has concluded,]

        [and the applicant provides an original degree certificate, academic transcript or an academic reference on official headed paper of the institution, which clearly shows his name, the course title/award, and the date of course completion and pass (Or the date of award in the case of a degree certificate).]

(c)   The applicant must have a minimum of 30 points under paragraphs 105 to [112] of Appendix A.

(d)   The applicant must have a minimum of 10 points under paragraphs 8 to 9 of Appendix C.

(e)   [The Certificate of Sponsorship Checking Service reference number for which points under Appendix A were awarded related must:

    (i)   record that the applicant is being sponsored in the same subcategory of the Tier 5 (Temporary Worker) Migrant route as the one in which he was being sponsored to work for when he was last granted entry clearance or leave to remain as a Tier 5 (Temporary Worker) Migrant), and

    (ii)   in the case of an applicant who the Certificate of Sponsorship Checking Service records as being sponsored in the international agreement sub-category of Tier 5 (Temporary Workers), to work as a private servant in a diplomatic household, who entered the UK with a valid entry clearance in that capacity under the Rules in place from 6 April 2012, record that the applicant is being sponsored to work for the same employer [as set out in paragraph 245ZO(g) who] he was being sponsored for when he was last granted entry clearance or leave to remain as a Tier 5 (Temporary Worker) Migrant, and the applicant must have continued to work for that employer throughout his period of leave and must provide evidence of agreed terms and conditions of employment in the UK with his employer, . . .[in the form set out in Appendix Q]]

(f) Where the applicant is under 18 years of age, the application must be supported by the applicant's parents or legal guardian, or by just one parent if that parent has sole legal responsibility for the child.

(g) Where the applicant is under 18 years of age, the applicant's parents or legal guardian, or just one parent if that parent has sole legal responsibility for the child, must confirm that they consent to the arrangements for the applicant's care in the UK.

(h) [An applicant who has, or was last granted, leave as a Student, a Student Re-Sitting and Examination, a Person Writing Up a Thesis, a Postgraduate Doctor or Dentist, a Student Nurse, a Student Union Sabbatical Officer or a Tier 4 (General) Migrant and:

    (i) is currently being sponsored by a government or international scholarship agency,

    (ii) was being sponsored by a government or international scholarship agency, and that sponsorship came to an end 12 months ago or less

must provide the unconditional written consent of the sponsoring Government or agency to the application and must provide the specified documents [as set out in paragraph 245A above,] to show that this requirement has been met.]

[(i) The applicant must not be in the UK in breach of immigration laws except that any period of overstaying for a period of 28 days or less will be disregarded.]

[(j) Where the Certificate of Sponsorship Checking Service reference number for which the applicant was awarded points under Appendix A records that the applicant is being sponsored as a Contractual Service Supplier [or Independent Professional] in the International Agreement subcategory of the Tier 5 (Temporary Worker) Migrant route, the grant of leave to remain will not result in the applicant being granted leave to enter or remain as a Contractual Service Supplier [or Independent Professional] under the international agreement subcategory of the Tier 5 (Temporary Worker) Migrant route for a cumulative period exceeding 6 months in any 12 month period ending during the period of leave requested.]

[(k) The Secretary of State must be satisfied that the applicant:

    (i) genuinely intends to undertake, and is capable of undertaking, the role recorded by the Certificate of Sponsorship Checking Service; and

    (ii) will not undertake employment in the United Kingdom other than under the terms of paragraph 245ZR(h)(iii).

(l) To support the assessment in paragraph 245ZQ(k), the Secretary of State may:

    (i) request additional information and evidence, and refuse the application if the information or evidence is not provided. Any requested documents must be received by the Home Office at the address specified in the request within [28 calendar days] of the date the request is sent, and

    (ii) request the applicant attends an interview, and refuse the application if the applicant fails to comply with any such request without providing a reasonable explanation.

(m) If the Secretary of State is not satisfied following the assessment in paragraph 245ZQ(k), no points will be awarded under paragraphs 1505 to 112 of Appendix A.

(n) The Secretary of State may decide not to carry out the assessment in paragraph 245ZQ(k) if the application already falls for refusal on other grounds, but reserves the right to carry out this assessment in any reconsideration of the decision.]

Note

Amended by HC 314. Words in square brackets after (b)(ii)(2) inserted by HC 120, para 8 as from 1 January 2010. Sub-paras (b)(iv), (f) and (g) inserted by HC 439, paras 40 and 41 as from 6 April 2010. Words in square brackets in (b) and (b)(i)–(v) substituted by HC 863, paras 77–79 as from 6 April 2011. Further amended by HC 1888, paras 67–71 as from 6 April 2012. Words in square brackets in sub-para (e)(ii) substituted by Cm 8423, para 62 as from 20 July 2012. Words in square brackets in sub-para (h) inserted by Cm 8423, para 63 as from 20 July 2012. Sub-para (i) inserted by HC 194, para 67 as from 1 October 2012. Words "in the form set out in Appendix Q" in sub-para (e)(ii) inserted by HC 565, para 64 as from 6 September 2012. Further amended by HC 760, paras 163–166 as from 13 December 2012. Further amended by HC 1039, paras 68: where an applicant has made an application for entry clearance or leave before 6 April 2013 and the application has not been decided before that date, it will be decided in accordance with the rules in force on 5 April 2013. Further amended by HC 628, paras 102, 103. Amended by HC 693, para 63 as from 6 November 2014, save that if an application has been made for entry clearance or leave to enter or remain before 6 November 2014, the application will be decided in accordance with the Rules in force on 5 November 2014.

Period and conditions of grant

245ZR.

(a)   If any calculation of period of leave comes to zero or a negative number, leave to remain will be refused.

(b)   Subject to paragraphs (c) to (f) below, leave to remain will be granted for:

    (i)   the length of the period of engagement, as recorded in the Certificate of Sponsorship Checking Service entry, plus 14 days (or, where the applicant has consecutive engagements, a period beginning on the first day of the first period of engagement and ending 14 days after the last day of the last period of engagement) or

    (ii)   [the difference between the period that the applicant has already spent in the UK since his last grant of entry clearance or leave to enter as a Tier 5 (Temporary Worker) Migrant and:

        (1)   12 months, if he is being sponsored in the Government Authorised exchange sub-category for a Work Experience Programme where the initial grant of leave was granted under the Rules in place from 6 April 2012, the Creative and Sporting subcategory, or the Charity Workers subcategory, or

        (2)   2 years, if he is being sponsored in the Government Authorised exchange sub-category where the initial grant of leave was granted under the Rules in place from 6 April 2012 or the Research Programme[, Training Programme or Overseas Government Language Programme], the Religious Workers subcategory, or the International Agreement subcategory [other than as a Contractual Service Supplier [or Independent Professional]], [or]

        (3)   [6 months, if the applicant is being sponsored in the International Agreement subcategory and is a Contractual Service Supplier [or Independent Professional],]

    whichever of (i) or (ii) is the shorter.

(c)   Where the provisions in paragraph 245ZQ(b)(ii) apply, the migrant will be granted leave to remain for:

    (i)   the period of engagement plus 14 days (or, where the applicant has consecutive engagements, a period beginning on the first day of the first period of engagement and ending 14 days after the last day of the last period of engagement), or

    (ii)   12 months

    whichever of (i) or (ii) is the shorter.

(d)   Where the Certificate of Sponsorship Checking Service reference records that the migrant is being sponsored in the international agreement subcategory of the Tier 5 (Temporary Worker) Migrant route as an overseas government employee[, employee of an international organisation] or a private servant in a diplomatic household [where in the case of the latter he entered the UK with a valid entry clearance in that capacity under the Rules in place before 6 April 2012,], leave to remain will be granted for:

(i)   the period of engagement plus 14 days, or

(ii)   [24 months],

whichever of (i) or (ii) is the shorter, unless at the date of the application for leave to remain the applicant has spent more than [4 years] continuously in the UK with leave as a Tier 5 (Temporary Worker) Migrant, in which case leave to remain will be granted for:

(iii)   the period of engagement plus 14 days, or

(iv)   a period equal to 6 years less X, where X is the period of time, beginning with the date on which the applicant was last granted entry clearance or leave to enter as a Tier 5 (Temporary Worker) Migrant, that the applicant has already spent in the UK as a Tier 5 (Temporary Worker) Migrant

whichever of (iii) or (iv) is the shorter.

(e)   [Where the Certificate of Sponsorship Checking Service reference records that the applicant is being sponsored in the international agreement sub-category of the Tier 5 (Temporary Worker) Migrant route as a private servant in a diplomatic household to work in a domestic category in the household of a named individual and where he entered the UK with a valid entry clearance in that capacity under the Rules in place from 6 April 2012, leave to remain will be granted for:

(i)   the period of engagement plus 14 days, or

(ii)   [24 months],

whichever of (i) or (ii) is the shorter, unless at the date of the application the applicant has spent more than [3 years] continuously in the UK with leave as a Tier 5 (Temporary Worker) Migrant, in which case leave will be granted for:

(iii)   the period of engagement plus 14 days, or

(iv)   a period equal to 5 years or less X, where X is the period of time, beginning with the date on which the applicant was first granted entry clearance as a Tier 5 (Temporary Worker) Migrant, that the applicant has already spent in the UK as a Tier 5 (Temporary Worker) Migrant

whichever of (iii) or (iv) is the shorter. Where the calculation at (iv) above results in zero or a negative number, the application for leave to remain will be refused.]

(f)   Where:

(i)   the Certificate of Sponsorship Checking Service reference number records that the applicant is being sponsored in the creative and sporting subcategory of the Tier 5 (Temporary Worker) Migrant route as a creative worker, and

(ii)   the Sponsor is the Sponsor who sponsored the applicant when he received his last grant of leave, leave to remain will be granted for the period set out [in paragraph (g)] below.

(g)   Where the conditions [in paragraph (f)] above] are met, leave to remain will be granted for:

(i)   the period of engagement plus 14 days (or, where the applicant has consecutive engagements, a period beginning on the first day of the first period of engagement and ending 14 days after the last day of the last period of engagement), or

(ii)   12 months

whichever of (i) or (ii) is the shorter, unless the applicant has spent more than 1 year continuously in the UK with leave as a Tier 5 (Temporary Worker) Migrant, in which case leave to remain will be granted for:

(iii)   the period of engagement plus 14 days (or, where the applicant has consecutive engagements, a period beginning on the first day of the first period of engagement and ending 14 days after the last day of the last period of engagement), or

(iv)   a period equal to 2 years less X, where X is the period of time, beginning with the date on which the applicant was last granted entry clearance or leave to enter as a Tier 5 (Temporary Worker) Migrant, that the applicant has already spent in the UK as a Tier 5 (Temporary Worker) Migrant whichever of (iii) or (iv) is the shorter.

(h)   Leave to remain will be granted subject to the following conditions:

    (i)   no recourse to public funds,

    (ii)   registration with the police if this is required by paragraph 326 of these Rules, and

    (iii)   no employment except:

        (1)   unless paragraph (2) applies, working for the person who for the time being is the Sponsor in the employment that the Certificate of Sponsorship Checking Service records that the migrant is being sponsored to do for that Sponsor,

        (2)   [in the case of a migrant whom the Certificate of Sponsorship Checking Service records as being sponsored in the government authorised exchange subcategory of Tier 5 (Temporary Workers), the work, volunteering or job shadowing authorised by the Sponsor and that the Certificate of Sponsorship Checking Service records that the migrant is being sponsored to do,]

        (3)   supplementary employment, [and

        (4)   in the case of a migrant whom the Certificate of Sponsorship Checking Service records as being sponsored in the creative and sporting subcategory of Tier 5 (Temporary Workers), employment as a sportsperson for his national team while his national team is in the UK [and Temporary Engagement as a Sports Broadcaster.]

    (iv)   [in the case of a migrant whom the Certificate of Sponsorship Checking Service records as being sponsored in the international agreement sub-category of Tier 5 (Temporary Workers), to work as a private servant in a diplomatic household, the employment in (iii)(1) above means working only in the household of the employer recorded by the Certificate of Sponsorship Checking Service.]

Note

Amended by HC 439, para 42 as from 6 April 2010. Further amended by HC 1888, paras 72–78 as from 6 April 2012. Further amended by HC 760, paras 167–169 as from 13 December 2012. Further amended by HC 1039, paras 69–74: where an applicant has made an application for entry clearance or leave before 6 April 2013 and the application has not been decided before that date, it will be decided in accordance with the rules in force on 5 April 2013. Further amended by HC 244, para 3 as from 1 July 2013. Further amended by HC 1138, para 49 as from 6 April 2014.

[Requirements for indefinite leave to remain

245ZS. To qualify for indefinite leave to remain as a Tier 5 (Temporary Worker) Migrant, an applicant must meet the requirements listed below. If the applicant meets these requirements, indefinite leave to remain will be granted. If the applicant does not meet these requirements, the application will be refused.

Requirements:

[(aa) . . . .]

(a)   The applicant must not fall for refusal under the general grounds for refusal and must not be an illegal entrant.

(b)   The applicant must have spent a continuous period of 5 years lawfully in the UK with leave in the international agreement sub-category of Tier 5 and working as a private servant in a diplomatic household [and have last been granted entry clearance in this capacity under the Rules in place before 6 April 2012].

(c)   [The applicant must have sufficient knowledge of the English language and sufficient knowledge about life in the United Kingdom, in accordance with Appendix KoLL.]

(d)   [The applicant must not be in the UK in breach of immigration laws except that any period of overstaying for a period of 28 days or less will be disregarded.]

(e)   [the applicant must provide a letter from the employer detailing the purpose and period of absences in connection with the employment, including periods of annual leave. Where the absence was due to a serious or compelling reason, the applicant must provide a personal letter which includes full details of the reason for the absences and all original supporting documents in relation to those reasons —e.g. medical certificates, birth/death certificates, information about the reasons which led to the absence from the UK.]

Note

Inserted by HC 314, para 82 as from 31 March 2009. Sub-para (aa) inserted by HC 863, para 80 as from 6 April 2011. Words in square brackets in sub-para (b) inserted by HC 1888, para 79 as from 6 April 2012. Sub-para (c) substituted by HC 628, para 101 as from. Sub-para (d) inserted by HC 194, para 68 as from 1 October 2012. Further amended by HC 760, paras 170, 171 as from 13 December 2012. Further amended by HC 628, para 101 and if an applicant has made an application for entry clearance or leave before 1 October 2013, the application will be decided in accordance with the Rules in force on 30 September 2013.

Tier 4 (General) Student

[Purpose of this route

245ZT. This route is for migrants aged 16 or over who wish to study in the UK.

[Entry clearance

245ZU. All migrants arriving in the UK and wishing to enter as a Tier 4 (General) Student must have a valid entry clearance for entry under this route. If they do not have a valid entry clearance, entry will be refused.

[Requirements for entry clearance

245ZV. To qualify for entry clearance as a Tier 4 (General) Student, an application must meet the requirements listed below. If the applicant meets these requirements, entry clearance will be granted. If the applicant does not meet these requirements, the application will be refused.

Requirements:
(a) The applicant must not fall for refusal under the General Grounds for Refusal.
(b) The applicant must have a minimum of 30 points under [paragraphs 113 to 120] of Appendix A.
(c) The applicant must have a minimum of 10 points under paragraphs 10 to [14] of Appendix C.
(ca) . . . The applicant must, if required to do so on examination or interview, be able to demonstrate without the assistance of an interpreter English language proficiency of a standard to be expected from an individual who has reached the standard specified in a Confirmation of Acceptance for Studies assigned in accordance with Appendix A paragraph [118(b)] (for the avoidance of doubt, the applicant will not be subject to a test at the standard set out in Appendix A, paragraph [118(b)].]
(da) If the applicant wishes to undertake course:
   (i) undergraduate or postgraduate studies leading to a Doctorate or Masters degree by research in one of the disciplines listed in paragraph 1 of Appendix 6 to these Rules, or
   (ii) undergraduate or postgraduate studies leading to a taught Masters degree in one of the disciplines listed in paragraph 2 of Appendix 6 to these Rules, or
   (iii) a period of study or research in excess of 6 months in one of the disciplines listed in paragraphs 1 or 2 of Appendix 6 to these Rules at an institution of higher education where this forms part of an overseas postgraduate qualification
the applicant must hold a valid Academic Technology Approval Scheme clearance certificate from the Counter-Proliferation Department of the Foreign and Common-wealth Office which relates to the course, or area of research, that the applicant will be

taking and at the institution at which the applicant wishes to undertake it and must provide [a print-out of his Academic Technology Approval Scheme Clearance certificate] to show that these requirements have been met.

(e) If the applicant wishes to be a postgraduate doctor or dentist on a recognised Foundation Programme:

    (i)   the applicant must have successfully completed a recognised UK degree in medicine or dentistry from:

        (1)   an institution with a Tier 4 General Sponsor License,

        (2)   a UK publicly funded institution of further or higher education or

        (3)   a UK bona fide private education institution which maintains satisfactory records of enrolment and attendance,

    (ii)   the applicant must have previously been granted leave:

        (1)   as a Tier 4 (General) Student, or as a Student, for the final academic year of the studies referred to in paragraph (i) above, and

        (2)   as a Tier 4 (General) Student, or as a Student, for at least one other academic year (aside from the final year) of the studies referred to in paragraph (i) above,

    (iii)   if the applicant has previously been granted leave as a Postgraduate Doctor or Dentist, the applicant must not be seeking entry clearance or leave to enter or remain to a date beyond 3 years from the date on which he was first granted leave to enter or remain in that category, and

    (iv)   if the applicant has previously been granted leave as Tier 4 (General) Student to undertake a course as a postgraduate doctor or dentist, the applicant must not be seeking entry clearance or leave to enter or remain to a date beyond 3 years from the date on which the applicant was first granted leave to undertake such a course.

(f) If the applicant is currently being sponsored by a Government or international scholarship agency, or within the last 12 months has come to the end of such a period of sponsorship, the applicant must provide the written consent of the sponsoring Government or agency to the application and must provide the specified documents [as set out in paragraph 245 above,] to show that this requirement has been met.

(g) If the course is below degree level, the grant of entry clearance the applicant is seeking must not lead to the applicant having spent more than 3 years in the UK as a Tier 4 Migrant since the age of 18 studying courses that did not consist of degree level study [. . .]

(ga) If the course is at degree level or above, the grant of entry clearance the applicant is seeking must not lead to the applicant having spent more than 5 years in the UK as a Tier 4 (General) Migrant, or as a Student, studying courses at degree level or above unless:

    (i)   the applicant has successfully completed a course at degree level in the UK of a minimum duration of 4 academic years, and will follow a course of study at Master's degree level sponsored by a Sponsor that is a Recognised Body or a body in receipt of public funding as a higher education institution from the Department of Employment and Learning in Northern Ireland, the Higher Education Funding Council for England, the Higher Education Funding Council for Wales or the Scottish Funding Council, and the grant of entry release must not lead to the applicant having spent more than 6 years in the UK as a Tier 4 (General) Migrant [, or as a Student,] studying courses at degree level or above; or

    (ii)   the grant of entry clearance is to follow a course leading to the award of a PhD, and the applicant is sponsored by a Sponsor that is a Recognised Body or a body in receipt of public funding as a higher education institution from the Department of Employment and Learning in Northern Ireland, the Higher Education Funding Council for England, the Higher Education Funding Council for Wales or the Scottish Funding Council; or

(iii)   the applicant is following a course of study in:

(1)   Architecture;

(2)   Medicine;

(3)   Dentistry;

(4)   [Law, where the applicant has completed a course at degree level in the UK and is progressing to:

    (a)   a law conversion course validated by the Joint Academic Stage Board in England and Wales, a Masters in Legal Science (MLegSc) in Northern Ireland, or an accelerated graduate LLB in Scotland; or

    (b)   the Legal Practice Course in England and Wales, the Solicitors Course in Northern Ireland, or a Diploma in Professional Legal Practice in Scotland or; or

    (c)   the Bar Professional Training Course in England and Wales, or the Bar Course In Northern Ireland.]

(5)   Veterinary Medicine & Science; or

(6)   Music at a music college that is a member of Conservatoires UK (CUK).

(gb)   If the applicant has completed a course leading to the award of a PhD in the UK, the grant of entry clearance the applicant is seeking must not lead to the applicant having spent more than 8 years in the UK as a Tier 4 (General) Migrant [, or as a Student].]

(h)   The applicant must be at least 16 years old.

(i)   Where the applicant is under 18 years of age, the application must be supported by the applicant's parents or legal guardian, or by just one parent if that parent has sole legal responsibility for the child.

(j)   Where the applicant is under 18 years of age, the applicants' parents or legal guardian, or just one parent if that parent has sole legal responsibility for the child, must confirm that they consent to the arrangements for the applicant's travel to, and reception and care in, the UK.

[(k)   The Entry Clearance Officer must be satisfied that the applicant is a genuine student.

[. . .]]

Note

Words in sub-para (b) substituted by Cm 7701, para 35 as from 1 October 2009. Sub-para (g) amended by HC 439, para 43 as from 6 April 2010. Words in square brackets in (c) substituted by, and (ca) inserted by, HC 908, paras 8 and 9 as from 21 April 2011. Sub-paragraph (g) (1), (2) deleted by HC 1148, para 6 as from 4 July 2011. Further amended by HC 1888, paras 80-84 as from 6 April 2012, Cm 8337, paras 1–2 as from 6 April 2012. Further amended by Cm 8423, paras 64, 65 as from 20 July 2012. Sub-para (k) and following paragraph inserted by HC 514, para 1 as from 29 July 2012. Further amended by HC 760, para 172, 173 as from 13 December 2012. Further amended by HC 244, para 4 as from 1 July 2013. Deleted by HC 1138, para 50 as from 6 April 2014.

[**Period and conditions of grant**

245ZW.

(a)   Subject to paragraph (b), entry clearance will be granted for the duration of the course.

(b)   In addition to the period of entry clearance granted in accordance with paragraph (a), entry clearance will also be grated for the periods set out in the following table. Notes to accompany the table appear below the table.

Type of course	Period of entry clearance to be granted before the course starts	Period of entry clearance to be granted before the course ends
12 months or more	1 month	4 months
6 months or more but less than 12 months	1 month	2 months
Pre-sessional course of less than 6 months	1 month	1 month
Course of less than 6 months that is not a pre-sessional course	7 days	7 days
Postgraduate doctor or dentist	1 month	1 month

Notes

(i)   If the grant of entry clearance is made less than 1 month or, in the case of a course of less than 6 months that is not a pre-sessional course, less than 7 days before the start of the course, entry clearance will be granted with immediate effect.

(ii)   A pre-sessional course is a course which prepares a student for the student's main course of study in the UK.

(iii)   The additional periods of entry clearance granted further to the table above will be disregarded for the purposes of calculating whether a migrant has exceeded the limits specified at 245ZV(g) to 245ZV(gb).

(c)   Entry clearance will be granted subject to the following conditions:

(i)   no recourse to public funds,

(ii)   registration with the police, if this is required by paragraph 326 of these Rules,

(iii)   no employment except:

(1)   [employment during term time of no more than 20 hours per week and employment (of any duration) during vacations, where the student is following a course of degree level study or a foundation degree level study and is either

(a)   sponsored by a Sponsor that is a Recognised Body or a body in receipt of public funding as a higher education institution from the Department of Employment and Learning in Northern Ireland, the Higher Education Funding Council for England, the Higher Education Funding Council for Wales or the Scottish Funding Council; or

(b)   sponsored by an overseas higher education institution to undertake a short-term Study Abroad Programme in the United Kingdom.

(2)   employment during term time of no more than 10 hours per week and any employment (of any duration) during vacations, where the student is following a course of below degree level study and is sponsored by a Sponsor that is a Recognised Body or a body in receipt of public funding as a higher education institution from the Department of Employment and Learning in Northern Ireland, the Higher Education Funding Council for England, the Higher Education Funding Council for Wales or the Scottish Funding Council,

(3)   employment during term time of no more than 10 hours per week and employment (of any duration) during vacations, where the student is following a course of study at any academic level and is

> sponsored by a Sponsor that is a publicly funded education college.]

(4)   employment as part of a course-related work placement which forms an assessed part of the applicant's course and provided that any period that the applicant spends on that placement does not exceed [one third] of the total length of the course undertaken in the UK [except].

   (i)   [where it is a United Kingdom statutory requirement that the placement should exceed one third of the total length of the course; or

   (ii)   where the placement does not exceed one half of the total length of the course undertaken in the UK and the student is following a course of degree level study and is either:

     (a)   sponsored by a Sponsor that is a Recognised Body or a body in receipt of public funding as a higher education institution from the Department of Employment and Learning in Northern Ireland, the Higher Education Funding Council for England, the Higher Education Funding Council for Wales or the Scottish Funding Council; or

     (b)   sponsored by an overseas higher education institution to undertake a short-term Study Abroad Programme in the United Kingdom.]

(5)   employment as a Student Union Sabbatical Officer, for up to 2 years, provided the post is elective and is at the institution which is the applicant's Sponsor [or they must be elected to a national Nation Union of Students (NUS) position].

(6)   employment as a postgraduate doctor or dentist on a recognised Foundation Programme

(7)   [until such time as a decision is received from the UK Border Agency on an application which is supported by a Certificate of Sponsorship assigned by a licensed Tier 2 Sponsor and which is made following successful completion of course at degree level or above at a Sponsor that is a Recognised Body or a body in receipt of public funding as a higher education institution from the Department of Employment and Learning in Northern Ireland, the Higher Education Funding Council for England, the Higher Education Funding Council for Wales or the Scottish Funding Council and while the applicant has extant leave, and any appeal [or administrative review] against that decision has been determined, employment with the Tier 2 Sponsor, in the role for which they assigned the Certificate of Sponsorship to the Tier 4 migrant[,]]

(8)   [self-employment, providing the migrant has made an application for leave to remain as a Tier 1 (Graduate Entrepreneur) Migrant which:

   (a)   is supported by an endorsement from a qualifying Higher Education Institution,

   (b)   is made following successful completion of a UK recognised Bachelor degree, Masters degree or PhD (not a qualification of equivalent level which is not a degree) course at a Sponsor that is a Recognised Body or body in receipt of public funding as a higher education institution from the Department of Employment and Learning in Northern Ireland, the Higher Education Funding Council for England, the Higher Education Funding Council for Wales or the Scottish Funding Council, and

(c)   is made while the applicant has extant leave,

until such time as a decision is received from the UK Border Agency on that application and any appeal [or administrative review] against that decision has been determined,]

provided that the migrant is not [self-employed other than under the conditions of (8) above, or employed as a Doctor or Dentist in Training other than under the conditions of (v) below,] professional sportsperson (including a sports coach) or an entertainer, and provided that the migrant's employment would not fill a [permanent] full time vacancy other than [under the conditions of (7) above, or] a vacancy on a recognised Foundation Programme or as a sabbatical officer]; and

[(iv)   no study except:

(1)   study at the institution that the Confirmation of Acceptance for Studies Checking Service records as the migrant's Sponsor, or where the migrant was awarded points for a visa letter, study at the institution which issued that visa letter unless the migrant is studying at an institution which is a partner institution of the migrant's Sponsor;

(2)   until such time as a decision is received from the Home Office on an application which is supported by a Confirmation of Acceptance for Studies assigned by a Highly Trusted Sponsor and which is made while the applicant has extant leave, and any appeal or administrative review against that decision has been determined, study at the Highly Trusted Sponsor institution which the Confirmation of Acceptance for Studies Checking Service records as having assigned a Confirmation of Acceptance for Studies to the Tier 4 migrant;

(3)   supplementary study;

(4)   study of the course, or courses where a pre-sessional is included, for which the Confirmation of Acceptance for Studies was assigned or the visa letter was issued, unless the student:

(a)   has yet to complete the course for which the Confirmation of Acceptance for Studies was assigned or the visa letter was issued;

(b)   continues studying at the institution referred to in (1) above; and

(c)   begins studying a new course, instead of the course for which the Confirmation of Acceptance for Studies was assigned or the visa letter was issued, that represents academic progress (as set out paragraph 120A(b) of Appendix A to these Rules) on the course(s) preceding the migrant's last grant of Tier 4 (General) Student or Student leave, and:

(i)   the new course is either:

(1)   at a higher or the same level as the course for which the Confirmation of Acceptance for Studies was assigned or the visa letter was issued; or

(2)   at a lower level than the course for which the Confirmation of Acceptance for Studies was assigned or the visa letter was issued, provided that the requirements and conditions of the migrant's grant of leave as at the date of commencement of the new course are

the same requirements and conditions to which the migrant's leave would have been subject had he made an application to study at that lower level under the Rules in force at the time of commencement of the new course; and

(ii) where the new course (or period of research) is of a type specified in paragraph 245ZV(da), the student obtains an Academic Technology Approval Scheme clearance certificate from the Counter-Proliferation Department of the Foreign and Commonwealth Office relating to that new course (or area of research) prior to commencing the new course.

(5) in the case of a course (or period of research) of a type specified in paragraph 245ZV(da), study or research to which the Academic Technology Approval Scheme certificate issued to the migrant relates. If the migrant's course (or research) completion date reported on the Confirmation of Acceptance for Studies is postponed for a period of more than three calendar months, or if there are any changes to the course contents (or the research proposal), the migrant must apply for a new Academic Technology Approval Scheme certificate within 28 calendar days.]

(v) no employment as a Doctor or Dentist in training unless:

(1) the course that the migrant is being sponsored to do (as recorded by the Confirmation of Acceptance for Studies Checking Service) is a recognised Foundation Programme, or

(2) the migrant has made an application as a Tier 4 (General) Student which is supported by a Confirmation of Acceptance for Studies assigned by a Highly Trusted Sponsor to sponsor the applicant to do a recognised Foundation Programme, and this study satisfies the requirements of (iv)(2) above, or

(3) the migrant has made an application as a Tier 2 (General) Migrant which is supported by a Certificate of Sponsorship assigned by a licensed Tier 2 Sponsor to sponsor the applicant to work as a Doctor or Dentist in Training, and this employment satisfies the conditions of (ii)(7) above.]

(4) [study at the same or a higher level of course as that stated on the confirmation of acceptance for studies, or at a lower level where the same requirements or conditions of leave would have applied if the application had been to study at that lower level.]

Note

Words in sub-para (c) amended by Cm 7701, paras 36-39 as from 1 October 2009. Sub-paragraphs (c)(iii) (1), (2) and (3) substituted by HC 1148, para 7 as from 4 July 2011. Para (c)(iv)(2), (3) substituted by HC 382, para 1 as from 23 July 2010. Words in square brackets in (c)(iv)(1) inserted by HC 908, para 10 as from 21 April 2011. Further amended by HC 1888, para 85–90 as from 6 April 2012. Further amended by HC 760, paras 174–180 as from 13 December 2012. Further amended by HC 1039, para 76: where an applicant has made an application for entry clearance or leave before 6 April 2013 and the application has not been decided before that date, it will be decided in accordance with the rules in force on 5 April 2013. Further amended by HC 693, para 64 as from 20 October 2014. Amended by HC 693, para 64 as from 20 October 2014. Amended by HC 693, para 64 as from 20 October 2014. Amended by HC 693, para 65 as from 6 November 2014, save that if an application has been made for entry clearance or leave to enter or remain before 6 November 2014, the application will be decided in accordance with the Rules in force on 5 November 2014.

[Requirements for leave to remain

245ZX.   To qualify for leave to remain as a Tier 4 (General) Student under this rule, an applicant must meet the requirements listed below. If the applicant meets those requirements, leave to remain will be granted. If the applicant does not meet those requirements, the applicant will be refused.

Requirements:

(a)   The applicant must not fall for refusal under the general grounds for refusal and must not be an illegal entrant.

(b)   The applicant must have, or have last been granted, entry clearance, leave to enter or leave to remain:

    (i)   as a Tier 4 (General) Student,

    (ii)   as a Tier 4 (Child) Student,

    (iii)   as a Tier 1 (Post-study Work) Migrant,

    (iv)   as a Tier 2 Migrant,

    (v)   as a Participant in the International Graduates Scheme (or its predecessor, the Science Engineering Graduates Scheme),

    (vi)   as a Participant in the Fresh Talent: Working in Scotland Scheme,

    (vii)   as a Postgraduate Doctor or Dentist,

    (viii)   as a Prospective Student,

    (ix)   as a Student,

    (x)   as a Student Nurse,

    (xi)   as a Student Re-sitting an Examination,

    (xii)   as a Student Writing Up a Thesis,

    (xiii)   as a Student Union Sabbatical Officer, or

    (xiv)   as a Work Permit Holder.

(c)   The applicant must have a minimum of 30 points under paragraphs 113 to 120 of Appendix A.

(d)   The applicant must have a minimum of 10 points under paragraphs 10 to [14] of Appendix C.

[(da)   The applicant must, if required to do son examination or interview, be able to demonstrate without the assistance of an interpreter English language proficiency of a standard to be expected from an individual who has reached the standard specified in a Confirmation of Acceptance for Studies assigned in accordance with Appendix A paragraph 118(b) (for the avoidance of doubt, the applicant will not be subject to a test at the standard set out in Appendix A, paragraph 118(b)).]

(e)   . . .

(ea)   if the applicant wishes to undertake a course . . . which is:

    (i)   undergraduate or postgraduate studies leading to a Doctorate or Masters degree by search in one of the disciplines listed in paragraph 1 of Appendix 6 of these Rules, or

    (ii)   undergraduate or postgraduate studies leading to a taught Masters degree or other postgraduate qualification in one of the disciplines listed in paragraph 2 of Appendix 6 of these Rules, or

    (iii)   a period of study or research in excess of 6 months in one of the disciplines listed in paragraphs 1 or 2 of Appendix 6 of these Rules at an institution of higher education where this forms part of an overseas postgraduate qualification

    the applicant must hold a valid Academic Technology Approval Scheme clearance certificate from the Counter-Proliferation Department of the Foreign and Commonwealth office which relates to he course, or area of research, that the applicant will be taking and at the institution at which the applicant wishes to undertake it and must provide [a print-out of his Academic Technology Approved Scheme clearance certificate] to show that these requirements have been met.

[Applicants applying for Leave to remain under the Doctorate Extension Scheme must, where required, meet the conditions of paragraph 245ZX(ea), unless they are applying for a course of study of 28 days or less.]

(f)   If the applicant wishes to be a postgraduate doctor or dentist on a recognised Foundation Programme:

    (i)   the applicant must have successfully completed a recognised UK degree in medicine or dentistry from:

        (1)   an institution with a Tier 4 General Sponsor Licence,

        (2)   a UK publicly funded institution of further or higher education or

        (3)   a UK bona fide private education institution which maintains satisfactory records of enrolment and attendance,

    (ii)   the applicant must have previously been granted leave:

        (1)   as a Tier 4 (General) Student, or as a Student, for the final academic year of the studies referred to in paragraph (i) above, and

        (2)   as a Tier 4 (General) Student, or as a Student, for at least one other academic year (aside from the final year) of the studies referred to in paragraph (i) above.

    (iii)   if the applicant has previously been granted leave as a Postgraduate Doctor or Dentist the applicant must not be seeking entry clearance or leave to enter or remain to a date beyond 3 years from the date on which he was first granted leave to enter or remain in that category, and

    (iv)   if the applicant has previously been granted leave as a Tier 4 (General) Student to undertake a course as a postgraduate doctor or dentist, the applicant must not be seeking entry clearance or leave to enter or remain to a date beyond 3 years from the date on which he was first granted leave to undertake such a course.

(g)   If the applicant is currently being sponsored by a Government or international scholarship agency, or within the last 12 months has come to the end of such a period of sponsorship, the applicant must provide the unconditional written consent of the sponsoring Government or agency to the application and must provide the specified documents [as set out in paragraph 245A above,] to show that this requirement has been met.

(h)   [If the course is below degree level the grant of leave to remain the applicant is seeking must not lead to the applicant having spent more than 3 years in the UK as a Tier 4 Migrant since the age of 18 studying courses that did not consist of degree level study . . .

[(ha)   If the course is at degree level or above, the grant of leave to remain the applicant is seeking must not lead to the applicant having spent more than 5 years in the UK as a Tier 4 (General) Migrant, or as a Student, studying courses at degree level or above unless:

    (i)   the applicant has successfully completed a course at degree level in the UK of a minimum duration of 4 academic years, and will follow a course of study at Master's degree level sponsored by a Sponsor that is a recognised Body or a body in receipt of public funding as a higher education institution from the Department of Employment and Learning in Northern Ireland, the Higher Education Funding Council for England, the Higher Education Funding Council for Wales or the Scottish Funding Council, and the grant of leave to remain must not lead to the applicant having spent more than 6 years in the UK as a Tier 4 (General) Migrant [, or a Student,] studying courses at degree level or above; or

    (ii)   the grant of leave to remain is to follow a course leading to the award of a PhD and the applicant is sponsored by a Sponsor that is a Recognised Body or a body in receipt of public funding as a higher education institution from the Department of Employment and Learning in Northern Ireland, the Higher Education Funding Council for England, the Higher Education Funding Council for Wales or the Scottish Funding Council; or

- (iii) the applicant is following a course of study in:
  - (1) Architecture;
  - (2) Medicine;
  - (3) Dentistry;
  - (4) [Law, where the applicant has completed a course at degree level in the UK and is progressing to:
    - (a) a law conversion course validated by the Joint Academic Stage Board in England and Wales, a Masters in Legal Science (MLegSc) in Northern Ireland, or an accelerated graduate LLB in Scotland; or; or;
    - (b) the Legal Practice Course in England and Wales, the Solicitors Course in Northern Ireland, or a Diploma in Professional Legal Practice in Scotland; or
    - (c) the Bar Professional Training Course in England and Wales, or the Bar Course in Northern Ireland.]
  - (5) Veterinary Medicine & Science; or
  - (6) Music at a music college that is a member of Conservatories UK (CUK).

- (hb) If the applicant has completed a course leading to the award of a PhD in the UK, the grant of leave to remain the applicant is seeking must not lead to the applicant having spent more than 8 years in the UK as a Tier 4 (General) Migrant[, or a Student].]

- (i) The applicant must be at least 16 years old.

- (j) Where the applicant is under 18 years of age, the application must be supported by the applicant's parents or legal guardian, or by just one parent if that parent has sole legal responsibility for the child.

- (k) Where the applicant is under 18 years of age, the applicant's parents or legal guardian, or just one parent if that parent has sole legal responsibility for the child, must confirm that they consent to the arrangements for the applicant's care in the UK.

- (l) [[Unless applying for leave to remain as a Tier 4 (General) Student on the doctorate extension scheme, the applicant] must be applying for leave to remain for the purpose of studies which would commence within 28 days of the expiry of the applicant's current leave to enter or remain or, where the applicant has overstayed, within 28 days of when that period of overstaying began.]

- (m) [The applicant must not be in the UK in breach of immigration laws except that any period of overstaying for a period of 28 days or less will be disregarded.]

- (n) [Where the applicant is applying for leave to remain as a Tier 4 (General) Student on the doctorate extension scheme:
  - (i) leave to remain as a Tier 4 (General) Student on the doctorate extension scheme must not have previously been granted;
  - (ii) the applicant must be following a course leading to the award of a PhD;
  - (iii) the applicant must be sponsored by a Sponsor that is a Recognised Body or a body in receipt of public funding as a higher education institution from the Department of Employment and Learning in Northern Ireland, the Higher Education Funding Council for England, the Higher Education Funding Council for Wales or the Scottish Funding Council and that sponsor will be the sponsor awarding the PhD; and;
  - (iv) the date of the application must be within 60 days of the expected end date of a course leading to the award of a PhD.]

- (o) [the Secretary of State must be satisfied that the applicant is a genuine student. [. . .]]

Note

Words in sub-para (c) amended by Cm 7711, paras 1 as from 1 October 2009. Figure substituted in sub-para (d) by HC 908, para 11 as from 21 April 2011. Sub-para (h) substituted by HC 439, para 45 as from 6 April 2010. Sub-paragraph (h)(1), (2) deleted by HC 1148, para 10 as from 4 July 2011. Words in square brackets in (l) inserted by HC 908, para 12 as from 21 April 2011. Further amended by HC 1888, paras 91–93 as from 6 April 2012 and Cm 8337, paras 3–4 as from 6 April 2012. Further amended by Cm 8423, paras 66, 67 as from 20 July 2012. Sub-para (l), (m) inserted by HC 194, paras 69, 70 as from 1 October 2012. Further amended by HC 760, para 181 as from 13 December 2012. Further amended by HC 1039, paras 77, 78: where an applicant has made an application for entry clearance or leave before 6 April 2013 and the application has not been decided before that date, it will be decided in accordance with the rules in force on 5 April 2013. Further amended by HC 244, para 5 as from 1 July 2013. Sub-paragraphs (da), (o) inserted by HC 628, paras 104, 105. Amended by HC 1138, para 51 as from 6 April 2014. Further amended by HC 1138, para 52 as from 6 April 2014.

[Period and conditions of grant

245ZY.
(a)   Subject to paragraphs (b) [(ba)] and (c) below, leave to remain will be granted for the duration of the course.
(b)   In addition to the period of leave to remain granted in accordance with paragraph (a), leave to remain will also be granted for the periods set out in the following table. Notes to accompany the table appear below the table.

Type of course	Period of leave to remain to be granted before the course starts	Period of leave to remain to be granted after the course ends
12 months or more	1 month	4 months
6 months or more but less than 12 months	1 month	2 months
Pre-sessional course of less than 6 months	1 month	1 month
Course of less than 6 months that is not a pre-sessional course	7 days	7 days
Postgraduate doctor or dentist	1 month	1 month

Notes
(i)   If the grant of leave to remain is being made less than 1 month or, in the case of a course of less than 6 months that is not a pre-sessional course, less than 7 days before the start of the course, leave to remain will be granted with immediate effect.
(ii)   A pre-sessional course is a course which prepares a student for the student's main course of study in the UK.
(iii)   [The additional periods of [leave to remain] granted further to the table above will be disregarded for the purposes of calculating whether a migrant has exceeded the limits specified at 245ZX(h) to 245Z(hb).]
[(ba) Leave to remain as a Tier 4 (General) Student on the doctorate extension scheme will be granted for 12 months, commencing on the expected end date of a course leading to the award of a PhD.]
[(bb) Leave to remain as a Tier 4 (General) Student on the doctorate extension scheme will not be subject to the conditions on the limited time that can be spent as a Tier 4 (General) Student or as a student, specified at 245ZX(hb).]
(c)   Leave to remain will be granted subject to the following conditions:
    (i)   no recourse to public funds,

    (ii)   registration with the police, if this is required by paragraph 326 of these Rules,

    (iii)   no employment except:

        (1)   [employment during term time of no more than 20 hours per week and employment (of any duration) during vacations, where the student is following a course of degree level study and is either:

            (a)   sponsored by a Sponsor that is a recognised Body or a body in receipt of public funding as a higher education institution from the Department of Employment and Learning in Northern Ireland, the Higher Education Funding Council for England, the Higher Education Funding Council for Wales or the Scottish Funding Council; or

            (b)   sponsored by an overseas higher education institution to undertake a short-term Study Abroad Programme in the United Kingdom.

        (2)   employment during term time of no more than 10 hours per week and employment (of any duration) during vacations, where the student is following a course of below degree level study and is sponsored by a Sponsor that is a Recognised Body or a body in receipt of public funding as a higher education institution from the Department of Employment and Learning in Northern Ireland, the Higher Education Funding Council for England, the Higher Education Funding Council for Wales or the Scottish Funding Council,

        (3)   employment during term time of no more than 10 hours per week and employment (of any duration) during vacations, where the student is following a course of study at any academic level and is sponsored by a Sponsor that is a publicly funded further education college,]

        (4)   employment as part of a course-related work placement which forms an assessed part of the applicant's course and provided that any period that the applicant spends on that placement does not exceed [one third] of the total length of the course undertaken in the UK [except[:].

            (i)   where it is a United Kingdom statutory requirement that the placement should exceed one third of the total length of the course; or

            (ii)   where the placement does not exceed one half of the total length of the course undertaken in the UK and the student is following a course of degree level study and is either:

                (a)   sponsored by a Sponsor that is a recognised Body of a body in receipt of public funding as a higher education institution from the Department of Employment and Learning in Northern Ireland, the Higher Education Funding Council for England, the Higher Education Funding Council for Wales or the Scottish Funding Council; or

                (b)   sponsored by an overseas higher education institution to undertake a short-term Study Abroad Programme in the United Kingdom.]

        (5)   employment as a Student Union Sabbatical Officer for up to 2 years provided the post is elective and is at the institution which is the applicant's Sponsor [or they must be elected to a National Union of Students (NUS) position]

        (6)   employment as a postgraduate doctor or dentist on a recognised Foundation Programme provided that the migrant is not self-

employed, [or employed as a Doctor or Dentist in Training] other than a vacancy on a recognised Foundation Programme, a professional sportsperson (including a sports coach) or an entertainer, and provided that the migrant's employment would not fill a [permanent] full time vacancy other than a vacancy on a recognised Foundation Programme [or as a sabbatical officer]

(7) [until such time as a decision is received from the UK Border Agency on an application which is supported by a Certificate of Sponsorship assigned by a licensed Tier 2 Sponsor and which is made following successful completion of course at degree level or above at a Sponsor that is a Recognised Body or a body in receipt of public funding as a higher education institution from the he Department of Employment and Learning in Northern Ireland, the Higher Education Funding Council for England, the Higher Education Funding Council for Wales or the Scottish Funding Council and while the applicant has extant leave, and any appeal [or administrative review] against that decision has been determined, employment with the Tier 2 Sponsor institution, in the role for which they assigned the Certificate of Sponsorship to the Tier 4 migrant[,]]

(8) [self-employment, providing the migrant has made an application for leave to remain as a Tier 1 (Graduate Entrepreneur) Migrant which is supported by an endorsement from a qualifying Higher Education Institution and which is made following successful completion of a course at degree level or above at a Sponsor that is a Recognised Body or a body in receipt of public funding as a higher education institution from the Department of Employment and Learning in Northern Ireland, the Higher Education Council for England, the Higher Education Funding Council for Wales or the Scottish Funding Council and while the applicant has extant leave, until such time as a decision is received from the UK Border Agency on an application and any appeal [or administrative review] against that decision has been determined,]

provided that the migrant is not [self-employed other than under the conditions of (8) above, or employed as a Doctor or Dentist in Training other than under the conditions of (v) below,], a professional sportsperson (including a sports coach) or an entertainer, and provided that the migrant's employment would not fill a permanent full time vacancy other than under the conditions of (7) above, or a vacancy on a recognised Foundation programme or as a sabbatical officer.

[(9) where, during the current period of leave, the migrant has successfully completed a PhD at a Sponsor that is a Recognised Body or body in receipt of public funding as a higher education institution from the Department of Employment and Learning in Northern Ireland, the Higher Education Council for England, the Higher Education Funding Council for Wales or the Scottish Funding Council, and has been granted leave to remain as a Tier 4 (General) Student on the doctorate extension scheme or has made a valid application for leave to remain as a Tier 4 (General) Student on the doctorate extension scheme but has not yet received a decision from the UK Border Agency on that application, there will be no limitation on the type of employment that may be taken, except for:

(a) no employment as a Doctor or Dentist in Training other than under the conditions of (v) below;

        (b)   no employment as a professional sportsperson (including a sports coach).]

[(iv) no study except:

      (1)   study at the institution that the Confirmation of Acceptance for Studies Checking Service records as the migrant's Sponsor, or where the migrant was awarded points for a visa letter, study at the institution which issued that visa letter unless the migrant is studying at an institution which is a partner institution of the migrant's Sponsor;

      (2)   until such time as a decision is received from the Home Office on an application which is supported by a Confirmation of Acceptance for Studies assigned by a Highly Trusted Sponsor and which is made while the applicant has extant leave, and any appeal or administrative review against that decision has been determined, study at the Highly Trusted Sponsor institution which the Confirmation of Acceptance for Studies Checking Service records as having assigned a Confirmation of Acceptance for Studies to the Tier 4 migrant;

      (3)   supplementary study;

      (4)   study of the course, or courses where a pre-sessional is included, for which the Confirmation of Acceptance for Studies was assigned or the visa letter was issued, unless the student:

          (a)   has yet to complete the course for which the Confirmation of Acceptance for Studies was assigned or the visa letter was issued;

          (b)   continues studying at the institution referred to in (1) above; and

          (c)   begins studying a new course, instead of the course for which the Confirmation of Acceptance for Studies was assigned or the visa letter was issued, that represents academic progress (as set out paragraph 120A(b) of Appendix A to these Rules) on the course(s) preceding the migrant's last grant of Tier 4 (General) Student or Student leave, and:

             (i)   the new course is either:

                (1)   at a higher or the same level as the course for which the Confirmation of Acceptance for Studies was assigned or the visa letter issued; or

                (2)   at a lower level than the course for which the Confirmation of Acceptance for Studies was assigned or the visa letter was issued, provided that the requirements and conditions of the migrant's grant of leave as at the date of commencement of the new course are the same requirements and conditions to which the migrant's leave would have been subject had he made an application to study at that lower level under the Rules in force at the time of commencement of the new course; and

             (ii)   where the new course (or period of research) is of a type specified in paragraph 245ZX(ea), the student obtains an Academic Technology Approval Scheme clearance certificate from the Counter-Proliferation Department of the Foreign and Commonwealth

(5) in the case of a course (or period of research) of a type specified in paragraph 245ZX(ea), study or research to which the Academic Technology Approval Scheme certificate issued to the migrant relates. If the migrant's course (or research) completion date reported on the Confirmation of Acceptance for Studies is postponed for a period of more than three calendar months, or if there are any changes to the course contents (or the research proposal), the migrant must apply for a new Academic Technology Approval Scheme certificate within 28 calendar days.]

[(v) no employment as a Doctor or Dentist in Training unless:

(1) the course that the migrant is being sponsored to do (as recorded by the Confirmation of Acceptance for Studies Checking Service) is a recognised Foundation Programme, or

(2) the migrant has made an application as a Tier 4 (General) Student which is supported by a Confirmation of Acceptance for Studies assigned by a Highly Trusted Sponsor to sponsor the applicant to do a recognised Foundation programme, and this study satisfies the requirements of (iv)(2) above, or

(3) the migrant has made an application as a Tier 2 (General) Student which is supported by a certificate of Sponsorship assigned by a licensed Tier 2 Sponsor to sponsor the applicant to work as a Doctor or Dentist in Training, and this employment satisfies the conditions of (iii)(7) above.]

(4) . . . .]

Note

Words in sub-para (c) amended by Cm 7701, paras 40-42 as from 1 October 2009. Sub-paragraph (c)(iv)(1)-(3) substituted by HC 1148, para 11 as from 4 July 2011. Further amended by HC 1888, paras 94–99 as from 6 April 2012. Further amended by HC 760, paras 182–188 as from 13 December 2012. Further amended by HC 1039, paras 79–83: where an applicant has made an application for entry clearance or leave before 6 April 2013 and the application has not been decided before that date, it will be decided in accordance with the rules in force on 5 April 2013. Sub-para (bb) and (c)(iv)(4) inserted by HC 244, paras 6, 8 as from 1 July 2013. Sub-para (c) (v)(4) deleted by HC 244, para 7 as from 1 July 2013. Further amended by HC 693, para 66 as from 20 October 2014. Further amended by HC 693, para 66 as from 20 October 2014. Further amended by HC 693, para 66 as from 20 October 2014. Amended by HC 693, para 67 as from 6 November 2014, save that if an application has been made for entry clearance or leave to enter or remain before 6 November 2014, the application will be decided in accordance with the Rules in force on 5 November 2014.

Tier 4 (Child) Student

[Purpose of route

245ZZ. This route is for children at least 4 years old and under the age of 18 who wish to be educated in the UK.

[Entry clearance

245ZZA. All migrants arriving in the UK and wishing to enter a Tier 4 (Child) Student must have a valid entry clearance for entry under this route. If they do not have a valid entry clearance, entry will be refused.

Requirements:

(a) The applicant must not fall for refusal under the general grounds for refusal.

(b) The applicant must have a minimum of 30 points under [paragraphs 121 to 126] of Appendix A.

(c)   The applicant must have a minimum of 10 points under paragraphs [15 to 22] of Appendix C.

(d)   The applicant must be at least 4 years old and under the age of 18.

(e)   The applicant must have no children under the age of 18 who are either living with the applicant or for whom the applicant is financially responsible.

(f)   [If a foster carer or a relative (not a parent or guardian) of the applicant will be responsible for the care of the applicant:

    (i)   the arrangements for the care of the applicant by the foster carer or relative must meet the requirements in paragraph 245ZZE and the applicant must provide the specified documents in paragraph 245ZZE to show that this requirement has been met, and

    (ii)   the applicant must provide details of the care arrangements in paragraph 245ZZE.].

(g)   The application must be supported by the applicant's parents or legal guardian, or by just one parent if that parent has sole legal responsibility for the child.

(h)   The applicant's parents or legal guardian, or by just one parent if that parent has sole legal responsibility for the child, must confirm that they consent to the arrangements of the applicant's travel to, and reception and care in, the UK.

(i)   [If the applicant is currently being sponsored by a Government or international scholarship agency, or within the last 12 months has come to the end of such a period of sponsorship, the applicant must provide the written consent of the sponsoring Government or agency to the application and must provide the specified documents [as set out in paragraph 245A above,] to show that this requirement has been met.]

Note

Words in sub-para (b) substituted by Cm 7701, para 43 as from 1 October 2009. Sub-para (i) inserted by Cm 7701, para 44 as from 1 October 2009. Words in square brackets in (c) substituted by HC 908, para 14 as from 21 April 2011. Further amended by Cm 8423, para 68, 69 as from 20 July 2012.

[Period and conditions of grant

245ZZB.

(a)   Where the applicant is under the age of 16, entry clearance will be granted for:

    (i)   a period of no more than 1 month before the course starts, plus

    (ii)   a period:

        (1)   requested by the applicant,

        (2)   equal to the length of the programme the applicant is following, or

        (3)   of 6 years

        whichever is the shorter, plus

    (iii)   4 months.

(b)   Where the applicant is aged 16 or over, entry clearance will be granted for:

    (i)   a period of no more than 1 month before the course starts, plus

    (i)   a period of no more than 1 month before the course starts, plus

    (ii)   a period:

        (1)   requested by the applicant,

        (2)   equal to the length of the programme the applicant is following, or

        (3)   of [3] years

        whichever is the shorter, plus

    (iii)   4 months.

(c)   Entry clearance will be granted subject to the following conditions:

    (i)   no recourse to public funds,

    (ii)   registration with the police, if this is required by paragraph 326 of these Rules,

    (iii)   no employment whilst the migrant is aged under 16,

    (iv)   no employment whilst the migrant is aged 16 or over except:

        (1)   employment during term time of no more than [10] hours per week,

        (2)   employment (of any duration) during vacations,

    (3)   employment as a part of a course-related work placement which forms an assessed part of the applicant's course and provided that any period that the applicant spend on that placement does not exceed half of the total length of the course undertaken in the UK [except where it is a United Kingdom statutory requirement that the placement should exceed half the total length of the course].

    (4)   employment as a Student Union Sabbatical Officer for up to 2 years provided the post is elective and is at the institution which is the applicant's Sponsor [or they must be elected to a National Union of Students (NUS) position,]

provided that the migrant is not self-employed, or employed as a Doctor in Training, a professional sportsperson (including a sports coach) or an entertainer, and provided that the migrant's employment would not fill a [permanent full time vacancy other than a vacancy as a sabbatical officer].

[(v)   no study except:

    (1)   study at the institution that the Confirmation of Acceptance for Studies Checking Service records as the migrant's Sponsor, or where the migrant was awarded points for a visa letter, study at the institution which issued that visa letter unless the migrant is studying at an institution which is a partner institution of the migrant's Sponsor;

    (2)   until such time as a decision is received from the Home Office on an application which is supported by a Confirmation of Acceptance for Studies assigned by a Highly Trusted Sponsor and which is made while the applicant has extant leave, and any appeal or administrative review against that decision has been determined, study at the Highly Trusted Sponsor institution which the Confirmation of Acceptance for Studies Checking Service records as having assigned a Confirmation of Acceptance for Studies to the Tier 4 migrant;

    (3)   supplementary study;

    (4)   study of the course, or courses where a pre-sessional is included, for which the Confirmation of Acceptance for Studies was assigned or the visa letter was issued, unless the student:

        (a)   has yet to complete the course for which the Confirmation of Acceptance for Studies was assigned or the visa letter was issued;

        (b)   continues studying at the institution referred to in (1) above; and

        (c)   begins studying a new course, instead of the course for which the Confirmation of Acceptance for Studies was assigned or the visa letter was issued, and the new course is either:

            (1)   at a higher or the same level as the course for which the Confirmation of Acceptance for Studies was assigned or the visa letter issued; or

            (2)   at a lower level than the course for which the Confirmation of Acceptance for Studies was assigned or the visa letter was issued, provided that the requirements and conditions of the migrant's grant of leave as at the date of commencement of the new course are the same requirements and conditions to which the migrant's leave would have been subject had he made an application to study at that lower level under the Rules in force at the time of commencement of the new course.]

Note

Sub-para (c) amended by Cm 7701, paras 45-47 as from 1 October 2009. Sub-paragraph (b)(ii)(3) amended by HC 439, para 23 as from 6 April 2010. Sub-paragraph (c)(iv)(1) amended by HC 367 as from 3 March 2010. Sub-paragraph (c)(v)(2) amended by HC 382, para 3 as from 23 July 2010. Words in square brackets in sub-paragraph (c)(v)(1) inserted by HC 1148, para 12 as from 1 July 2011. Further amended by HC 760, paras 189, 190 as from 13 December 2012. Further amended by HC 1039, para 84: where an applicant has made an application for entry clearance or leave before 6 April 2013 and the application has not been decided before that date, it will be decided in accordance with the rules in force on 5 April 2013. Amended by HC 693, para 68 as from 6 November 2014, save that if an application has been made for entry clearance or leave to enter or remain before 6 November 2014, the application will be decided in accordance with the Rules in force on 5 November 2014.

[Requirements for leave to remain

245ZZC. To qualify for leave to remain as Tier 4 (Child) student under this rule, an applicant must meet the requirements listed below. If the applicant meets these requirements, leave to remain will be granted. If the applicant does not meet these requirements, leave to remain will be refused.

Requirements:

(a) The applicant must not fall for refusal under the general grounds for refusal and must not be an illegal entrant.

(b) The applicant must have, or have last been granted, entry clearance, leave to enter or leave to remain:

  (i)   as a Tier 4 [Migrant],

  (ii) as a Student, or

  (iii) as a Prospective Student.

(c) The applicant must have a minimum of 30 points under [paragraphs 121 to 126] of Appendix A.

(d) The applicant must have a minimum of 10 points under paragraphs [15 to 22] of Appendix C.

(e) The applicant must be under the age of 18.

(f) The applicant must have no children under the age of 18 who are either living with the applicant or for whom the applicant is financially responsible.

(g) [If a foster carer or a relative (not a parent or guardian) of the applicant will be responsible for the care of the applicant:

  (i)   the arrangements for the care of the applicant by the foster carer or relative must meet the requirements in paragraph 245ZZE and the applicant must provide the specified documents in paragraph 25ZZE to show that this requirement has been met, and

  (ii) the applicant must provide details of the care arrangements as specified in paragraph 25ZZE].

(h) The application must be supported by the applicant's parents or legal guardian, or by just one parent if that parent has sole legal responsibility for the child.

(i) The applicant's parents or legal guardian, or just one parent if that parent has sole legal responsibility for the child, must confirm that they consent to the arrangements for the applicant's care in the UK.

(j) [The applicant must be applying for leave to remain for the purpose of studies which commence within 28 days of the expiry of the applicant's current leave to enter or remain or, where the applicant has overstayed, within 28 days of when that period of overstaying began.]

(k) [If the applicant is currently being sponsored by a Government or international scholarship agency, or within the last 12 months has come to the end of such a period of sponsorship, the applicant must provide the written consent of the sponsoring Government or agency to the application and must provide the specified documents [as set out in paragraph 245A above,] [to show that this requirement has been met.]

(l) [The applicant must not be in the UK in breach of immigration laws except that any period of overstaying for a period of 28 days or less will be disregarded.]

Note

Sub-para (k) inserted by Cm 7701, para 48 as from 1 October 2009. Words in square brackets in sub-para (g) substituted by Cm 7944, para 5 as from 22 October 2010. Words in square brackets in (b)(i), (d) and (j) substituted and inserted by HC 908, paras 15 to 17 as from 21 April 2011.

Further amended by Cm 8423, paras 70, 71 as from 20 July 2012. Sub-paras (j), (k) inserted by HC 194, paras 71, 72 as from 1 October 2012.

[Period and conditions of grant

245ZZD.
(a)   Where the applicant is under the age of 16, leave to remain will be granted for:
    (ii)   a period of no more than 1 month before the course starts, plus
    (ii)   a period:
        (1)   requested by the applicant,
        (2)   equal to the length of the programme the applicant is following, or
        (3)   of 6 years,
        whichever is the shorter, plus
    (iii)   4 months.
(b)   Where the applicant is aged 16 or over, leave to remain will be granted for:
    (i)   a period of no more than 1 month before the course starts, plus
    (ii)   a period:
        (1)   requested by the applicant,
        (2)   equal to the length of the programme the applicant is following, or
        (3)   of [3] years,
        whichever is the shorter, plus
    (iii)   4 months.
(c)   Leave to remain will be granted subject to the following conditions:
    (i)   no recourse to public funds,
    (ii)   registration with the police, if this required by paragraph 326 of these Rules,
    (iii)   no employment whilst the migrant is aged under 16,
    (iv)   no employment whilst the migrant is aged 16 or over except:
        (1)   employment during term time of no more than [10] hours per week,
        (2)   employment (of any duration) during vacations,
        (3)   employment as part of a course-related work placement which forms an assessed part of the applicant's course, and provided that any period that the applicant spend on that placement does not exceed half of the total length of the course undertaken in the UK [except where it is United Kingdom statutory requirement that the placement should exceed half the total length of the course],
        (4)   employment as a Student Union Sabbatical Officer for up to 2 years provided the post is elective and is at the institution which is the applicant's Sponsor [or they must be elected to a National Union of Students (NUS) position],
        provided that the migrant is not self-employed, or employed as a Doctor in Training, a professional sportsperson (including a sports coach) or an entertainer, and provided that the migrant's employment would not fill a [permanent full time vacancy other than a vacancy as a sabbatical officer.]
    [(v)   no study except:
        (1)   study at the institution that the Confirmation of Acceptance for Studies Checking Service records as the migrant's Sponsor, or where the migrant was awarded points for a visa letter, study at the institution which issued that visa letter unless the migrant is studying at an institution which is a partner institution of the migrant's Sponsor;
        (2)   until such time as a decision is received from the Home Office on an application which is supported by a Confirmation of Acceptance for Studies assigned by a Highly Trusted Sponsor and which is made while the applicant has extant leave, and any appeal or administrative review against that decision has been determined, study at the Highly Trusted Sponsor institution which the Confirmation of Acceptance for Studies Checking Service records as having assigned a Confirmation of Acceptance for Studies to the Tier 4 migrant;

(3)   supplementary study;

(4)   study of the course, or courses where a pre-sessional is included, for which the Confirmation of Acceptance for Studies was assigned or the visa letter was issued, unless the student:

    (a)   has yet to complete the course for which the Confirmation of Acceptance for Studies was assigned or the visa letter was issued;

    (b)   continues studying at the institution referred to in (1) above; and

    (c)   begins studying a new course, instead of the course for which the Confirmation of Acceptance for Studies was assigned or the visa letter was issued, and the new course is either:

        (1)   at a higher or the same level as the course for which the Confirmation of Acceptance for Studies was assigned or the visa letter issued; or

        (2)   at a lower level than the course for which the Confirmation of Acceptance for Studies was assigned or the visa letter was issued, provided that the requirements and conditions of the migrant's grant of leave as at the date of commencement of the new course are the same requirements and conditions to which the migrant's leave would have been subject had he made an application to study at that lower level under the Rules in force at the time of commencement of the new course.]

Note

Amended by Cm 7701, paras 49-51 as from 1 October 2009. Sub-paragraph (b)(ii)(3) amended by HC 439, para 34 as from 6 April 2010. Sub-paragraph (c)(iv) (1) amended by HC 367, para 9 as from 3 March 2010. Sub-paragraph (c)(v)(2), (3) substituted by HC 382, para 4 as from 23 July 2010. Words in square brackets in (c)(v)(1) inserted by HC 1148, para 13 as from 4 July 2011. Further amended by HC 760, paras 191,192 as from 13 December 2012. Further amended by HC 1039, para 85: where an applicant has made an application for entry clearance or leave before 6 April 2013 and the application has not been decided before that date, it will be decided in accordance with the rules in force on 5 April 2013. Amended by HC 693, para 69 as from 6 November 2014, save that if an application has been made for entry clearance or leave to enter or remain before 6 November 2014, the application will be decided in accordance with the Rules in force on 5 November 2014.

[Specified documents, details and requirements of care arrangements

245ZZE The specified documents, details and requirements of care arrangements referred to in paragraph 245ZZA(f) and paragraph 245ZZC(g) are:

(i)   The applicant must provide a written letter of undertaking from the intended carer confirming the care arrangement, which shows:

    (1)   the name, current address and contact details of the intended carer,

    (2)   the address where the carer and the Tier 4 (Child) student will be living in the UK if different from the intended carer's current address,

    (3)   confirmation that the accommodation offered to the Tier 4 (Child) student is a private address, and not operated as a commercial enterprise, such as a hotel or a youth hostel,

    (4)   the nature of the relationship between the Tier 4 (Child) student's parent(s) or legal guardian and the intended carer,

    (5)   that the intended carer agrees to the care arrangements for the Tier 4 (Child) student,

    (6)   that the intended carer has at least £500 per month (up to a maximum of nine months) available to look after and accommodate the Tier 4 (Child) student for the length of the course,

    (7)   a list of any other people that the intended carer has offered support to, and

    (8)   the signature and date of the undertaking.

(ii)   The applicant must provide a letter from his parent(s) or legal guardian confirming the care arrangement, which shows:

    (1)   the nature of their relationship with the intended carer,

    (2)   the address in the UK where the Tier 4 (Child) student and the Tier 4 (Child) student's intended carer will be living,

    (3)   that the parent(s) or legal guardian support the application, and authorise the intended carer to take responsibility for the care of the Tier 4 (Child) student during his stay in the UK,

    (4)   the intended carer's current passport, travel document or certificate of naturalisation, confirming that they are [settled] in the UK. The UK Border Agency will accept a notarised copy of the original passport or travel document, but reserves the right to request the original.

(iii)   If the applicant will be staying in a private foster care arrangement, he must receive permission from the private foster carer's UK local authority, as set out in the Children (Private Arrangements for Fostering) Regulations 2005.

(iv)   If the applicant will be staying in a private foster care arrangement and is under 16 years old, he must provide:

    (1)   a copy of the letter of notification from his parent(s), legal guardian or intended carer to the UK local authority, which confirms that the applicant will be in the care of a private foster carer while in the UK, and

    (2)   the UK local authority's confirmation of receipt, which confirms that the local authority has received notification of the foster care arrangement.]

Note

Inserted by Cm 8423, para 72 as from 20 July 2012. Further amended by HC 1138, para 53 as from 6 April 2014.

PART 7 — OTHER CATEGORIES

...

[Requirements for leave to enter the United Kingdom as a person exercising rights of access to a child resident in the United Kingdom

[A246.   Paragraphs 246 to 248F apply only to a person who has made an application before 9 July 2012 for leave to enter or remain or indefinite leave to remain as a person exercising rights of access to a child resident in the UK[, or who before 9 July 2012 has been granted leave to enter or remain as a person exercising rights of access to a child resident in the UK.]

AB246.   Where an application for leave to enter or remain is made on or after 9 July 2012 as a person exercising rights of access to a child resident in the UK Appendix FM will apply.]

Note

Paragraphs A246, AB 246 inserted by HC 194, para 73 as from 9 July 2012. Words in square brackets inserted by HC 565, para 65 as from 6 September 2012.

246.   The requirements to be met by a person seeking leave to enter the United Kingdom to exercise access rights to a child resident in the United Kingdom are that:

(i)   the applicant is the parent of a child who is resident in the United Kingdom; and

(ii)   the parent or carer with whom the child permanently resides is resident in the United Kingdom; and

(iii)   the applicant produces evidence that he has access rights to the child in the form of:

    (a)   a Residence Order or a Contact Order granted by a Court in the United Kingdom; or

    (b)   a certificate issued by a district judge confirming the applicant's intention to maintain contact with the child; and

(iv)   the applicant intends to continue to take an active role in the child's upbringing; and

(v)   the child is under the age of 18; and

(vi)   there will be adequate accommodation for the applicant and any dependants without recourse to public funds in accommodation which the applicant owns or occupies exclusively; and

(vii)   the applicant will be able to maintain himself and any dependants adequately without recourse to public funds; and

(viii)   the applicant holds a valid United Kingdom entry clearance for entry in this capacity.

Leave to enter the United Kingdom as a person exercising rights of access to a child resident in the United Kingdom

247.   Leave to enter as a person exercising access rights to a child resident in the United Kingdom may be granted for 12 months in the first instance, provided that a valid United Kingdom entry clearance for entry in this capacity is produced to the Immigration Officer on arrival.

Refusal of leave to enter the United Kingdom as a person exercising rights of access to a child resident in the United Kingdom

248.   Leave to enter as a person exercising rights of access to a child resident in the United Kingdom is to be refused if a valid United Kingdom entry clearance for entry in this capacity is not produced to the Immigration Officer on arrival.]

[Requirements for leave to remain in the United Kingdom as a person exercising rights of access to a child resident in the United Kingdom

248A.   The requirements to be met by a person seeking leave to remain in the United Kingdom to exercise access rights to a child resident in the United Kingdom are that:

(i)   the applicant is the parent of a child who is resident in the United Kingdom; and

(ii)   the parent or carer with whom the child permanently resides is resident in the United Kingdom; and

(iii)   the applicant produces evidence that he has access rights to the child in the form of:

    (a)   a Residence Order or a Contact Order granted by a Court in the United Kingdom; or

    (b)   a certificate issued by a district judge confirming the applicant's intention to maintain contact with the child; or

    (c)   a statement from the child's other parent (or, if contact is supervised, from the supervisor) that the applicant is maintaining contact with the child; and

(iv)   the applicant takes and intends to continue to take an active role in the child's upbringing; and

(v)   the child visits or stays with the applicant on a frequent and regular basis and the applicant intends this to continue; and

(vi)   the child is under the age of 18; and

(vii)   the applicant has limited leave to remain in the United Kingdom as the spouse or unmarried partner of a person present and settled in the United Kingdom who is the other parent of the child; and

(viii)   the applicant has not remained in breach of the immigration laws; and

(ix)   there will be adequate accommodation for the applicant and any dependants without recourse to public funds in accommodation which the applicant owns or occupies exclusively; and

(x)   the applicant will be able to maintain himself and any dependants adequately without recourse to public funds.

Leave to remain in the United Kingdom as a person exercising rights of access to a child resident in the United Kingdom

248B.   Leave to remain as a person exercising access rights to a child resident in the United Kingdom may be granted for 12 months in the first instance, provided the Secretary of State is satisfied that each of the requirements of paragraph 248A is met.

Refusal of leave to remain in the United Kingdom as a person exercising rights of access to a child resident in the United Kingdom

248C. Leave to remain as a person exercising rights of access to a child resident in the United Kingdom is to be refused if the Secretary of State is not satisfied that each of the requirements of paragraph 248A is met.

Indefinite leave to remain in the United Kingdom as a person exercising rights of access to a child resident in the United Kingdom

248D. The requirements for indefinite leave to remain in the United Kingdom as a person exercising rights of access to a child resident in the United Kingdom are that:
(i) the applicant was admitted to the United Kingdom or granted leave to remain in the United Kingdom for a period of 12 months as a person exercising rights of access to a child and has completed a period of 12 months as a person exercising rights of access to a child; and
(ii) the applicant takes and intends to continue to take an active role in the child's upbringing; and
(iii) the child visits or stays with the applicant on a frequent and regular basis and the applicant intends this to continue; and
(iv) there will be adequate accommodation for the applicant and any dependants without recourse to public funds in accommodation which the applicant owns or occupies exclusively; and
(v) the applicant will be able to maintain himself and any dependants adequately without recourse to public funds; and
(vi) the child is under 18 years of age; and
[(vi) the applicant has sufficient knowledge of the English language and sufficient knowledge about life in the United Kingdom, unless he is under the age of 18 or aged 65 or over at the time he makes his application; and
[(vii) The applicant must have demonstrated sufficient knowledge of the English language and sufficient knowledge about life in the United Kingdom, in accordance with Appendix KoLL; and]
(viii) the applicant does not fall for refusal under the general grounds for refusal.]

Note

Inserted by HC 314, para 82 as from 31 March 2009. Sub-para (vii) inserted by HC 863, para 81 as from 6 April 2011. Further amended by HC 760, para 193 as from 13 December 2012. Sub-paragraph (vii) substituted by HC 628, para 106 and if an applicant has made an application for entry clearance or leave before 1 October 2013, the application will be decided in accordance with the Rules in force on 30 September 2013.

Indefinite leave to remain as a person exercising rights of access to a child resident in the United Kingdom

248E. Indefinite leave to remain as a person exercising rights of access to a child may be granted provided the Secretary of State is satisfied that each of the requirements of paragraph 248D is met.

Refusal of indefinite leave to remain in the United Kingdom as a person exercising rights of access to a child resident in the United Kingdom

248F. Indefinite leave to remain as a person exercising rights of access to a child is to be refused if the Secretary of State is not satisfied that each of the requirements of paragraph 248D is met.]

General note on paras 246–248

Paragraphs 246–248 substituted by Cmnd 4851. Paragraphs 248A–248F inserted by Cmnd 4851.

See the Modernised Guidance at www.ukba.homeoffice.gov.uk/sitecontent/documents/policyandla w/modernised/family/child-resident?view=Binary

For the ECtHR context for such rules: see, *Berrehab v Netherlands (Application 10730/84)* (1988) 11 EHRR 322; *Ciliz v Netherlands (Application 29192/95)*[2000] 2 FLR 469,

[2000] ECHR 365. See also *MS (Ivory Coast) v Secretary of State for the Home Department* [2007] EWCA Civ 133; *DH (Jamaica) v Secretary of State for the Home Department* [2010] EWCA Civ 207. On para 246(iii)(b) see Modernised Guidance at pages 9-10:

> However, it is now impossible to provide the evidence required by paragraph 246 (iii)(b). Until the Immigration Rules are changed, you can accept in place of this option, a sworn affidavit from the UK resident parent or carer of the child. The affidavit must:
>
> * confirm the parent applying can have access to the child
> * describe in detail the arrangements to allow for this. If contact is supervised, the supervisor must swear the statement, and
> * be sworn before, and certified by a legal officer.

This is not the same option as exists at para 248A(iii)(c) of the Rules.

Holders of special vouchers

[. . . .]

Note

Paragraphs 249–254 deleted by Cmnd 5597.

EEA nationals and their families

Settlement

255.   DELETED.

Note

Substituted by Cmnd 4851. But this is subject to the transitional provision in paragraph 5 continues to apply for the purpose of determining an application made before 30 April 2006 for an endorsement under paragraph 255.

255A.   DELETED.

Note

Paragraph 255A inserted by Cmnd 5597. But this is subject to the transitional provision in paragraph 5 continues to apply for the purpose of determining an application made before 30 April 2006 for an endorsement under paragraph 255.

255B.   DELETED.

Note

Paragraph 255B inserted by HC 523. But this is subject to the transitional provision in paragraph 5 continues to apply for the purpose of determining an application made before 30 April 2006 for an endorsement under paragraph 255.

256   DELETED.

Note

Paragraph 256 deleted by Cmnd 4851.

Notes

Words deleted and words in square brackets inserted by CM 4851. Words in square brackets in definition of 'member of the family' inserted by Cmnd 5597. Definition of 'EEA national' substituted and sub-para (b) inserted by HC 523.

257A.   DELETED.

Note

Para 257A inserted by Cmnd 5597. But this is subject to the transitional provision in paragraph 5 continues to apply for the purpose of determining an application made before 30 April 2006 for an endorsement under paragraph 255.

257B.   DELETED.

Note

Para 257B inserted by HC 523. But this is subject to the transitional provision in paragraph 5 continues to apply for the purpose of determining an application made before 30 April 2006 for an endorsement under paragraph 255.

[Requirements for leave to enter or remain as the primary carer or relative of an EEA national self-sufficient child]

257C. DELETED.

Note

Paragraph 257C deleted by HC 1039, para 86 as from 6 April 2013.

On para 257C (iii) (b), and the meaning of 'leading an independent life', see *NM ('leading an independent life') Zimbabwe* [2007] UKAIT 00051:

'Where a child (who may be over 18) is seeking limited leave to remain as the child of a parent with limited leave, in order to establish that he is not "leading an independent life" he must not have formed through choice a separate (and therefore independent) social unit from his parents' family unit whether alone or with others. A child who, for example, chooses to live away from home may be "leading an independent life" despite some continuing financial and/or emotional dependence upon his parents.'; *BM and AL (352D(iv); meaning of 'family unit') Colombia* [2007] UKAIT 00055 and *MI (Paragraph 298(iii): 'independent life') Pakistan* [2007] UKAIT 00052 (no requirement that the dependency must be one of necessity:

'The fact that one leads the life one does out of choice does not prevent it from being a dependent one: there is no requirement that the dependency must be one of necessity. The fact that one lives with one's parents as a matter of custom is in my view equally irrelevant: all one need show is that one is not leading an independent life, not why' [at para 3]).

[Leave to enter or remain as the primary carer or relative of an EEA national self-sufficient child]

257D. . . .]

Note

Paragraph 257D deleted by HC 1039, para 87 as from 6 April 2013..

[Refusal of leave to enter or remain as the primary carer or relative of an EEA national self-sufficient child]

257E. . . .

Note

Paragraph 257E deleted by HC 1039, para 88 as from 6 April 2013.

258 [. . .]

Note

Paragraph 259–261 deleted by Cmnd 4851.

Registration with the police for family members of EEA nationals

262. [. . .]

Note

Deleted with effect from 11 May 1998 by Cmnd 3953.

Retired persons of independent means

Requirements for leave to enter the United Kingdom as a retired person of independent means

263. . . .

Note

Deleted by HC 1113.

Leave to enter as a retired person of independent means

264. . . .

Note

Deleted by HC 1113.

Refusal of leave to enter as a retired person of independent means

Note

Deleted by HC 1113.

. . .

Requirements for an extension of stay as a retired person of independent means

266. [The requirements for an extension of stay as a retired person of independent means are that the applicant:

(i)   entered the United Kingdom with a valid United Kingdom entry clearance as a retired person of independent means; and

(ii)   meets the following requirements:

    (a)   has under his control and disposable in the United Kingdom an income of his own of not less than £25,000 per annum; and

    (b)   is able and willing to maintain and accommodate himself and any dependants indefinitely in the United Kingdom from his own resources with no assistance from any other person and without taking employment or having recourse to public funds; and

    (c)   can demonstrate a close connection with the United Kingdom; and

(iii)   has made the United Kingdom his main home[; and

[(iv)   must not be in the UK in breach of immigration laws, except that any period of overstaying for a period of 28 days or less will be disregarded.]

Note

Inserted by HC 1113. Sub-para (iv) inserted by HC 194, para 74 as from 1 October 2012.

[Extension of stay as a retired person of independent means]

. . .

Note

Paragraphs 266A-266E deleted by HC 1113.

267. [An extension of stay as a retired person of independent means, with a prohibition on the taking of employment, may be granted so as to bring the person's stay in this category up to a maximum of 5 years in aggregate, provided the Secretary of State is satisfied that each of the requirements of paragraph 266 is met.]

Note

Substituted by HC 1113.

Refusal of extension of stay as a retired person of independent means

268. [An extension of stay as a retired person of independent means is to be refused if the Secretary of State is not satisfied that each of the requirements of paragraph 266 is met.]

Note

Substituted by HC 1113.

Indefinite leave to remain for a retired person of independent means

269. Indefinite leave to remain may be granted, on application, to a person admitted as a retired person of independent means provided [the applicant]:
(i)   has spent a continuous period of 5 years [lawfully] in the United Kingdom in this capacity; and
(ii)   has met the requirements of paragraph 266 throughout the 5 year period and continues to do so[; and
(iii)   does not [fall for refusal under the general grounds for refusal]][; and
(iv)   must not be in the UK in breach of immigration laws, except that any period of overstaying for a period of 28 days or less will be disregarded.]
[(v)   in the case of absences for serious or compelling reasons, submits a personal letter which includes full details of the reason for the absences and all original supporting documents in relation to those reasons — e.g. medical certificates, birth/death certificates, information about the reasons which led to the absence from the UK.]

[continuous period of 5 years lawfully in the UK means residence in the United Kingdom for an unbroken period with valid leave, and for these purposes a period shall not be considered to have been broken where:
(i)   the applicant has been absent from the UK for a period of 180 days or less in any of the five consecutive 12 calendar month periods preceding the date of the application for indefinite leave to remain; and
(ii)   the applicant has existing limited leave to enter or remain upon their departure and return, except that where that leave expired no more than 28 days prior to a further application for entry clearance, that period and any period pending the determination of an application made within that 28 day period shall be disregarded; and
(iii)   the applicant has any period of overstaying between periods of entry clearance, leave to enter or leave to remain of up to 28 days and any period of overstaying pending the determination of an application made within that 28 day period disregarded.]

Note

Words in square brackets inserted by HC 863, para 82 as from 6 April 2011. Sub-para (iv) inserted by HC 194, para 75 as from 1 October 2012. Further amended by HC 760, paras 194–198 as from 13 December 2012.

Refusal of indefinite leave to remain for a retired person of independent means

270. Indefinite leave to remain in the United Kingdom for a retired person of independent means is to be refused if the Secretary of State is not satisfied that each of the requirements of paragraph 26[9] is met.

Note

The retired persons of independent means replaces the former independent means category (HC 251, para 44). For applications for settlement from persons of independent means who were admitted under HC 251.

[Partners] of persons who have or have had leave to enter or remain in the United Kingdom as retired persons of independent means

Requirements for leave to enter as the [partners] of a person with limited leave to enter or remain in the United Kingdom as a retired person of independent means

271. The requirements to be met by a person seeking leave to enter the United Kingdom as the [partner] of a person with limited leave to enter or remain in the United Kingdom as a retired person of independent means are that:

(i) the applicant [is the spouse, civil partner, unmarried or same-sex partner of] a person with limited leave to enter or remain in the United Kingdom as a retired person of independent means; and

[(ii) if an unmarried or same-sex partner:

    (1) any previous marriage or civil partnership (or similar relationship) by either partner has permanently broken down; and

    (2) the parties are not involved in a consanguineous relationship with one another; and

    (3) the parties have been living together in a relationship akin to marriage or civil partnership which has subsisted for 2 years or more; and

(iii) each of the parties intends to live with the other as his or her spouse or civil partners during the applicant's stay and the marriage or civil partnership is subsisting; and

(iv) there will be adequate accommodation for the parties and any dependants without recourse to public funds in accommodation which they own or occupy exclusively; and

(v) the parties will be able to maintain themselves and any dependants adequately without recourse to public funds; and

(vi) the applicant does not fall for refusal under the general grounds for refusal; and

(vii) the applicant does not intend to stay in the United Kingdom beyond any period of leave granted to his partner; and

(viii) the applicant holds a valid United Kingdom entry clearance for entry in this capacity.]

Note

Amended by HC 628, paras 107–110 and if an applicant has made an application for entry clearance or leave before 1 October 2013, the application will be decided in accordance with the Rules in force on 30 September 2013.

Leave to enter as the [partner] of a person with limited leave to enter or remain in the United Kingdom as a retired person of independent means

272. A person seeking leave to enter the United Kingdom as the [partner] of a person with limited leave to enter or remain in the United Kingdom as a retired person of independent means may be given leave to enter for a period not in excess of that granted to the person with limited leave to enter or remain as a retired person of independent means, provided the Immigration Officer is satisfied that each of the requirements of paragraph 271 is met.

Note

Amended by HC 628, para 108 and if an applicant has made an application for entry clearance or leave before 1 October 2013, the application will be decided in accordance with the Rules in force on 30 September 2013.

Refusal of leave to enter as the [partner] of a person with limited leave to enter or remain in the United Kingdom as a retired person of independent means

273. Leave to enter as the [partner] of a person with limited leave to enter or remain in the United Kingdom as a retired person of independent means is to be refused if the Immigration Officer is not satisfied that each of the requirements of paragraph 271 is met.

Note

Amended by HC 628, para 108 and if an applicant has made an application for entry clearance or leave before 1 October 2013, the application will be decided in accordance with the Rules in force on 30 September 2013.

Requirements for extension of stay as the [partner] of a person who has or has had leave to enter or remain in the United Kingdom as a retired person of independent means

273A. The requirements to be met by a person seeking an extension of stay in the United Kingdom as the [partner] of a person who has or has had leave to enter or remain in the United Kingdom as a retired person of independent means are that the applicant:

[(i)   is the spouse, civil partner, unmarried or same-sex partner of a person who:

    (1)   has limited leave to enter or remain in the United Kingdom as a retired person of independent means; or

    (2)   has indefinite leave to remain in the United Kingdom or has become a British citizen, and who had limited leave to enter or remain in the United Kingdom as a retired person of independent means immediately before being granted indefinite leave to remain; and

(ii)   meets the requirements of paragraph 271(ii) – (vii); and

(iii)   was not last granted:

    (1)   entry clearance or leave as a visitor,

    (2)   temporary admission, or

    (3)   temporary release; and

(iv)   must not be in the UK in breach of immigration laws, except that any period of overstaying for a period of 28 days or less will be disregarded.]

Note

Sub-para (vi) inserted by HC 194, para 76 as from 1 October 2012. Further amended by HC 628, paras 108, 111 and if an applicant has made an application for entry clearance or leave before 1 October 2013, the application will be decided in accordance with the Rules in force on 30 September 2013.

Extension of stay as the [partner] of a person who has or has had leave to enter or remain in the United Kingdom as a retired person of independent means

273B. An extension of stay in the United Kingdom as:

(i)   [partner] of a person who has limited leave to enter or remain as a retired person of independent means may be granted for a period not in excess of that granted to the person with limited leave to enter or remain; or

(ii)   the [partner] of a person who is being admitted at the same time for settlement or the [partner] of a person who has indefinite leave to remain [or has become a British citizen] may be granted for a period not exceeding 2 years, in both instances, provided the Secretary of State is satisfied that each of the requirements of paragraph 273A is met.

Note

Amended by HC 628, paras 108, 112 and if an applicant has made an application for entry clearance or leave before 1 October 2013, the application will be decided in accordance with the Rules in force on 30 September 2013.

Refusal of extension of stay as the [partner] of a person who has or has had leave to enter or remain in the United Kingdom as a retired person of independent means

273C. An extension of stay in the United Kingdom as the [partner] of a person who has or has had leave to enter or remain in the United Kingdom as a retired person of independent means is to be refused if the Secretary of State is not satisfied that each of the requirements of paragraph 273A is met.

Note

Amended by HC 628, para 108 and if an applicant has made an application for entry clearance or leave before 1 October 2013, the application will be decided in accordance with the Rules in force on 30 September 2013.

Requirements for indefinite leave to remain for the [partner] of a person who has or has had leave to enter or remain in the United Kingdom as a retired person of independent means

273D.   The requirements to be met by a person seeking indefinite leave to remain in the United Kingdom as the [partner] of a person who has or has had leave to enter or remain in the United Kingdom as a retired person of independent means are that the applicant:

[(i)   is the spouse, civil partner, unmarried or same-sex partner of a person who:
- (1)   has limited leave to enter or remain in the United Kingdom as a retired person of independent means and who is being granted indefinite leave to remain at the same time; or
- (2)   is the spouse, civil partner, unmarried or same-sex partner of a person who has indefinite leave to remain in the United Kingdom or has become a British citizen, and who had limited leave to enter or remain as a retired person of independent means immediately before being granted indefinite leave to remain; and

(ii)   meets the requirements of paragraph 271(ii) – (vii); and

(iii)   has demonstrated sufficient knowledge of the English language and sufficient knowledge about life in the United Kingdom, [in accordance with Appendix KoLL]; and

(iv)   was not last granted:
- (1)   entry clearance or leave as a visitor,
- (2)   temporary admission, or
- (3)   temporary release; and

(v)   must not be in the UK in breach of immigration laws, except that any period of overstaying for a period of 28 days or less will be disregarded.]

Note

Words in square brackets inserted by HC 863, para 83 as from 6 April 2011. Sub-para (vi) amended by HC 760, para 199 as from 13 December 2012. Sub-para (vii) inserted by HC 194, para 77 as from 1 October 2012. Further amended by HC 760, para 1999 as from 13 December 2012. Further amended by HC 628, paras 108, 113, 114 and if an applicant has made an application for entry clearance or leave before 1 October 2013, the application will be decided in accordance with the Rules in force on 30 September 2013.

Indefinite leave to remain as the [partner] of a person who has or has had leave to enter or remain in the United Kingdom as a retired person of independent means

273E.   Indefinite leave to remain in the United Kingdom [as] the [partner] of a person who has or has had leave to enter or remain in the United Kingdom as a retired person of independent means may be granted provided the Secretary of State is satisfied that each of the requirements of paragraph 273D is met.

Note

Amended by HC 628, paras 108, 115 and if an applicant has made an application for entry clearance or leave before 1 October 2013, the application will be decided in accordance with the Rules in force on 30 September 2013.

Refusal of indefinite leave to remain as the [partner] of a person who has or has had leave to enter or remain in the United Kingdom as a retired person of independent means

273F.   Indefinite leave to remain in the United Kingdom [as] the [partner] of a person who has or has had leave to enter or remain in the United Kingdom as a retired person of independent means is to be refused if the Secretary of State is not satisfied that each of the requirements of paragraph 273D is met.

Note

Amended by HC 628, paras 108, 116 and if an applicant has made an application for entry clearance or leave before 1 October 2013, the application will be decided in accordance with the Rules in force on 30 September 2013.

Children of persons with limited leave to enter or remain in the United Kingdom as retired persons of independent means

Requirements for leave to enter or remain as the child of a person with limited leave to enter or remain in the United Kingdom as a retired person of independent means

274. The requirements to be met by a person seeking leave to enter or remain in the United Kingdom as the child of a person with limited leave to enter or remain in the United Kingdom as a retired person of independent means [or, for applications for leave to remain, of a parent with indefinite leave to remain in the UK and who had limited leave as a retired person of independent means immediately before being granted indefinite leave; and] are that:

(i) he is the child of a parent who has been admitted to or allowed to remain in the United Kingdom as a retired person of independent means[or, for applications for leave to remain, of a parent with indefinite leave to remain in the UK and who had limited leave as a retired person of independent means immediately before being granted indefinite leave; and];

(ii) he is under the age of 18 or has current leave to enter or remain in this capacity; and

(iii) he is unmarried and is not a civil partner, has not formed an independent family unit and is not leading an independent life; and

(iv) he can, and will, be maintained and accommodated adequately without recourse to public funds in accommodation which his parent(s) own or occupy exclusively; and

(v) he will not stay in the United Kingdom beyond any period of leave granted to his parent(s); and

(vi) both parents are being or have been admitted to or allowed to remain in the United Kingdom save where:

    (a) the parent he is accompanying or joining is his sole surviving parent; or

    (b) the parent he is accompanying or joining has had sole responsibility for his upbringing; or

    (c) there are serious and compelling family or other considerations which make exclusion from the United Kingdom undesirable and suitable arrangements have been made for his care; and

[(vii) if seeking leave to enter, he holds a valid United Kingdom entry clearance for entry in this capacity or, if seeking leave to remain, he was not last granted:

    (1) entry clearance or leave as a visitor,

    (2) temporary admission, or

    (3) temporary release; and]

(viii) if seeking leave to remain, must not be in the UK in breach of immigration laws, except that any period of overstaying for a period of 28 days or less will be disregarded.]

Note

Sub-para (viii) inserted by HC 194, para 78 as from 1 October 2012. Further amended by HC 628, paras 117, 118 and if an applicant has made an application for entry clearance or leave before 1 October 2013, the application will be decided in accordance with the Rules in force on 30 September 2013.

Leave to enter or remain as the child of a person with limited leave to enter or remain in the United Kingdom as a retired person of independent means

[275. (a) A person seeking leave to enter or remain in the United Kingdom as the child of a person with limited leave to enter or remain in the United Kingdom as a retired person of independent means "may be given leave to enter or remain in the United Kingdom for a period of leave not in excess of that granted to the person with limited leave to enter or remain as a retired person of independent means if:

(i)   in relation to an application for leave to enter, he is able to produce to the Immigration Officer, on arrival, a valid United Kingdom entry clearance for entry in this capacity; or

(ii)   in the case of an application for limited leave to remain, he was not last granted:
    (1)   entry clearance or leave as a visitor,
    (2)   temporary admission, or
    (3)   temporary release; and]
    and is able to satisfy the Secretary of State that each of the requirements of paragraph 274(i)-(vi) and (viii) is met.

(b) A person seeking limited leave to remain as the child of a parent who has indefinite leave to remain in the UK and who had limited leave as a retired person of independent means immediately before being granted indefinite leave may be given leave to remain in the UK for a period of 30 months provided he is in the UK with valid leave under paragraph 275 and is able to satisfy the Secretary of State that each of the requirements of paragraph 274(i) to (vi) and (viii) are satisfied.]

Note

Substituted by HC 628, para 119 and if an applicant has made an application for entry clearance or leave before 1 October 2013, the application will be decided in accordance with the Rules in force on 30 September 2013.

[275A.   An application for indefinite leave to remain in this category may be granted provided the applicant meets the requirements listed below. If the applicant meets these requirements, indefinite leave to remain will be granted. If the applicant does not meet these requirements, the application will be refused.

Requirements

(i)   he is the child of a parent with limited leave to enter or remain in the United Kingdom as a retired person of independent means who is, at the same time, been granted indefinite leave to remain, or he is the child of a parent who has indefinite leave to remain in the United Kingdom and who had limited leave under paragraphs 263–269 immediately before being granted indefinite leave; and

(ii)   he is under the age of 18 or has current leave to enter or remain in this capacity; and

(iii)   he is unmarried and is not a civil partner, has not formed an independent family unit and is not leading an independent life; and

(iv)   he can and will be maintained adequately without recourse to public funds in accommodation which his parent(s) own or occupy exclusively; and

(v)   he will not stay in the United Kingdom beyond any period of leave granted to his parent(s); and

(vi)   both parents are being or have been admitted to or allowed to remain in the United Kingdom save where:
    (a)   the parent he is accompanying or joining is his sole surviving parent; or
    (b)   the parent he is accompanying or joining has had sole responsibility for his upbringing; or
    (c)   there are serious and compelling family or other considerations which make exclusion from the United Kingdom undesirable and suitable arrangements have been made for his care;

(vii)   he must not be in the UK in breach of immigration laws except that any period of overstaying for a period of 28 days or less will be disregarded;

(viii)   if aged 18 years or over, he has sufficient knowledge of the English language and sufficient knowledge about life in the United Kingdom in accordance with Appendix KoLL of these Rules;

(ix)   indefinite leave to remain is, at the same time, being granted to the person with limited leave as a retired person of independent means unless, at the time when indefinite leave to remain was granted to that person, the applicant was aged 18 or over and unable to satisfy paragraph 275A(viii) and the applicant has continued to be in the United Kingdom with leave to remain as a child of that person.]

Note

Inserted by HC 628, para 120 and if an applicant has made an application for entry clearance or leave before 1 October 2013, the application will be decided in accordance with the Rules in force on 30 September 2013.

Refusal of leave to enter or remain as the child of a person with limited leave to enter or remain in the United Kingdom as a retired person of independent means

276. Leave to enter or remain in the United Kingdom as the child of a person with limited leave to enter or remain in the United Kingdom as a retired person of independent means is to be refused if, in relation to an application for leave to enter, a valid United Kingdom entry clearance for entry in this capacity is not produced to the Immigration Officer on arrival, or in the case of an application for limited leave to remain, if the applicant was not admitted with a valid United Kingdom entry clearance for entry in this capacity or is unable to satisfy the Secretary of State that each of the requirements of paragraph 274(i)–(vi) [and (viii)] is met. [An application for indefinite leave to remain in this category is to be refused if the applicant was not admitted with a valid United Kingdom entry clearance for entry in this capacity or is unable to satisfy the Secretary of State that each of the requirements of paragraph 275 is met.]

Note

Words "and (viii)" in both places inserted by HC 194, para 80 as from 1 October 2012. Amended by HC 628, para 121 and if an applicant has made an application for entry clearance or leave before 1 October 2013, the application will be decided in accordance with the Rules in force on 30 September 2013.

[Paras 263–276 replace HC 251, paras 44, 129 and 139(f).]

The former category of person of independent means is now restricted to *retired* persons aged 60 years or over who have a 'close connection' with the UK. There is now no provision for applicants without a 'close connection' whose presence in the UK would be in the 'general interest' of the UK. In addition, applicants must have under their control and disposable in the UK an *income* of not less than £25,000. This is a substantial increase in the old financial requirement of £200,000 capital or £20,000 income. In order to demonstrate an income of £25,000 at current interest rates the applicant's capital would have to be at least double the former capital requirement. Applicants must also intend to make the UK their 'main home'.

Long residence

[Long residence in the United Kingdom

276A. For the purposes of paragraphs 276B to 276D [, [276ADE(1)] . . . .]
(a)   "continuous residence" means residence in the United Kingdom for an unbroken period, and for these purposes a period shall not be considered to have been broken where an applicant is absent from the United Kingdom for a period of 6 months or less at any one time, provided that the applicant in question has existing limited leave to enter or remain upon their departure and return, but shall be considered to have been broken if the applicant:
   (i)   has been removed under Schedule 2 of the 1971 Act, section 10 of the 1999 Act, has been deported or has left the United Kingdom having been refused leave to enter or remain here; or
   (ii)   has left the United Kingdom and, on doing so, evidenced a clear intention not to return; or
   (iii)   left the United Kingdom in circumstances in which he could have had no reasonable expectation at the time of leaving that he would lawfully be able to return; or
   (iv)   has been convicted of an offence and was sentenced to a period of imprisonment or was directed to be detained in an institution other than

a prison (including, in particular, a hospital or an institution for young offenders), provided that the sentence in question was not a suspended sentence; or

(v)   has spent a total of more than 18 months absent from the United Kingdom during the period in question.

(b)   "lawful residence" means residence which is continuous residence pursuant to:

(i)   existing leave to enter or remain; or

(ii)   temporary admission within section 11 of the 1971 Act where leave to enter or remain is subsequently granted; or

(iii)   an exemption from immigration control, including where an exemption ceases to apply if it is immediately followed by a grant of leave to enter or remain.]

[(c)   'lived continuously' and 'living continuously' mean 'continuous residence', except that paragraph 276(a)(iv) shall not apply.]

Note

Inserted by HC 538. Words "and 276ADE" inserted by HC 194, para 81 as from 9 July 2012. Words ", 276ADE and 399A" and sub-para (c) inserted by HC 565, paras 66, 67 as from 6 September 2012. Word "and 399A" deleted by HC 532, para 4 of this statement take effect on 28 July 2014 and apply to all applications to which paragraphs 276ADE to 276DH and Appendix FM apply (or can be applied by virtue of the Immigration Rules), and to any other ECHR Article 8 claims (save for those from foreign criminals), and which are decided on or after that date. Further amended by HC 693, para 70 as from 6 November 2014.

[**276A0.**   For the purposes of paragraph 276ADE(1) the requirement to make a valid application will not apply when the Article 8 claim is raised:

(i)   as part of an asylum claim, or as part of a further submission in person after an asylum claim has been refused;

(ii)   where a migrant is in immigration detention. A migrant in immigration detention or their representative must submit any application or claim raising Article 8 to a prison officer, a prisoner custody officer, a detainee custody officer or a member of Home Office staff at the migrant's place of detention; or

(iii)   in an appeal (subject to the consent of the Secretary of State where applicable).]

Note

Substituted by HC 693, para 71 as from 6 November 2014.

[**276A00.**   Where leave to remain is granted under paragraphs 276ADE-276DH, or where an applicant does not meet the requirements in paragraph 276ADE(1) but the Secretary of State grants leave to remain outside the rules on Article 8 grounds, (and without prejudice to the specific provision that is made in paragraphs 276ADE-276DH in respect of a no recourse to public funds condition), that leave may be subject to such conditions as the Secretary of State considers appropriate in a particular case.]

Note

Inserted by HC 532, para 5 of this statement take effect on 28 July 2014 and apply to all applications to which paragraphs 276ADE to 276DH and Appendix FM apply (or can be applied by virtue of the Immigration Rules), and to any other ECHR Article 8 claims (save for those from foreign criminals), and which are decided on or after that date.

Requirements for an extension of stay on the ground of long residence in the United Kingdom

[**276A1.**   The requirement to be met by a person seeking an extension of stay on the ground of long residence in the United Kingdom is that the applicant meets each of the requirements in paragraph 276B(i)-(ii) [and (v)].]

Note

Words "and (v)" inserted by HC 194, para 82 as from 1 October 2012.

Extension of stay on the ground of long residence in the United Kingdom

276A2.   An extension of stay on the ground of long residence in the United Kingdom may be granted for a period not exceeding 2 years provided that the Secretary of State is satisfied that the requirement in paragraph 276A1 is met[, and a person granted such an extension of stay following an application made before 9 July 2012 will remain subject to the rules in force on 8 July 2012.]

Note

Words inserted by HC 565, para 68 as from September 2012.

Conditions to be attached to extension of stay on the ground of long residence in the United Kingdom

276A3. Where an extension of stay is granted under paragraph 276A2:

(i) if the applicant has spent less than [20] years in the UK, the grant of leave should be subject to the same conditions attached to his last period of lawful leave, or

(ii) if the applicant has spent [20] years or more in the UK, the grant of leave should not contain any restriction on employment.

Note

Figures substituted by HC 194, para 83 as from 9 July 2012.

Refusal of extension of stay on the ground of long residence in the United Kingdom

276A4. An extension of stay on the ground of long residence in the United Kingdom is to be refused if the Secretary of State is not satisfied that the requirement in paragraph 276A1 is met.

Requirements for indefinite leave to remain on the ground of long residence in the United Kingdom

276B. The requirements to be met by an applicant for indefinite leave to remain on the ground of long residence in the United Kingdom are that:

(i)
    (a) he has had at least 10 years continuous lawful residence in the United Kingdom; . . .
    [(b) . . .

(ii) having regard to the public interest there are no reasons why it would be undesirable for him to be given indefinite leave to remain on the ground of long residence, taking into account his:
    (a) age; and
    (b) strength of connections in the United Kingdom; and
    (c) personal history, including character, conduct, associations and employment record; and
    (d) domestic circumstances; and
    [(e)] compassionate circumstances; and
    [(f)] any representations received on the person's behalf; [and

(iii) the applicant does not [fall for refusal under the general grounds for refusal].]

[(iv) the applicant has demonstrated sufficient knowledge of the English language and sufficient knowledge about life in the United Kingdom, in accordance with Appendix KoLL.]

[(v) the applicant must not be in the UK in breach of immigration laws except that any period of overstaying for a period of 28 days or less will be disregarded[, as will any period of overstaying between periods of entry clearance, leave to enter or leave to remain of up to 28 days and any period of overstaying pending the determination of an application made within that 28 day period.]

Note

Inserted by HC 538. Sub-para (i)(b) substituted by CM 6339. Words and numbers in square brackets substituted and inserted by HC 863, paras 84–88 as from 6 April 2011. Further amended by HC 194, paras 84, 85 as from 9 July 2012. Sub-para (iii) amended by HC 760, para 200 as from 13 December 2012. Sub-para (v) inserted by HC 194, para 86 as from 1 October 2012. Further amended by HC 760, para 200 as from 13 December 2012. Further amended by HC 1039, para 90 as from on or after 6 April 2013. Further amended by HC 628, para 123 and if an applicant has made an application for entry clearance or leave before 1 October 2013, the application will be decided in accordance with the Rules in force on 30 September 2013.

[Indefinite leave to remain on the ground of long residence in the United Kingdom

276C. Indefinite leave to remain on the ground of long residence in the United Kingdom may be granted provided that the Secretary of State is satisfied that each of the requirements of paragraph 276B is met.]

Note

Inserted by HC 538. Amended by HC 565, para 73 as from 6 September 2012.

[Refusal of indefinite leave to remain on the ground of long residence in the United Kingdom

276D. Indefinite leave to remain on the ground of long residence in the United Kingdom is to be refused if the Secretary of State is not satisfied that each of the requirements of paragraph 276B is met.]

Note

Inserted by HC 538.

General note on paras 276A-D

See the Modernised Guidance at: www.ukba.homeoffice.gov.uk/sitecontent/documents/policyandl aw/modernised/other-categories/long-residence.pdf?view=Binary

Until 9 July 2012 there were two regimes:
  (a)   on the basis of lawful residence of at least ten years; and
  (b)   with a public interest proviso built in to the structure of the rule, 14 years' residence where the residence is of any quality.

The 14 year route was closed as of 9 July 2012, replaced by the new 'private life' category in para 276ADE. Applications submitted before that date will be considered under the old rule, but subject to the new 'suitability' requirements if decided on or after that date. Those granted or applying for limited leave under the 14 year rule before that date will still be able to apply for ILR under the old rules. See the guidance on transitional provisions at: www.ukba.homeoffice.gov.uk/sitecontent/documents/policyandlaw/IDIs/idischapter8/transition/transition.pdf?view=Binary

In relation to residency of at least ten years

Prior to the incorporation of the long residence provisions in to the Immigration Rules, the Secretary of State for the Home Department had a policy outside of the rules. The policy was withdrawn in March 2006, following the Tribunal's determination in *OS (10 years' lawful residence) Hong Kong* [2006] UKAIT 00031 (see also *FH (Bangladesh) v Secretary of State for the Home Department* [2009] EWCA Civ 385; *SA (Long residence concession) Bangladesh* [2009] UKAIT 00051) but the policy came back in to the IDIs in April 2009 (and continues in the Modernised Guidance).

In *OS (10 years' lawful residence) Hong Kong* [2006] UKAIT 00031, the Tribunal summarised the inter-relationship between the policy and the rules thus:

'Paragraphs 276A-D of HC 395 stand alongside the published concession in long residence cases. The terms of the concession are not to be used as an aid to interpretation of the rules. The rules mean what they say and a person who does not meet the requirements of the rules may have the benefit of the Secretary of State's exercise of discretion in his favour under the concession.'

There are important difference between the policy and the rule; inter alia, the policy permits the exercise of discretion where there is one short break of no more than ten calendar days and, exceptionally, multiple gaps in continuity (see page 19 of the Modernised Guidance).

In *R v Secretary of State for the Home Department, ex p Popatia; Chew v Secretary of State for the Home Department* [2001] Imm AR 46, a deportation order that remained on file and had not come to the attention of the applicant did not stop time running for the purposes of the rule.

Continuity of residence per para 276A(a), was not broken where an applicant had left the UK at a time when their existing leave to remain was extant and obtained further leave from an entry clearance officer: *TT (Long residence – 'continuous residence' – interpretation) British Overseas Citizen* [2008] UKAIT 00038.

On the provisions relating to residence of at least 14 years

See *ZH (Bangladesh) v Secretary of State for the Home Department* [2009] EWCA Civ 8, [2009] All ER (D) 118 (Jan) in relation to the examination of the public interest proviso in para 276B(ii). Since the rule is directed to applicants who have remained unlawfully for 14 years, that assessment must take proper account of that fact; eg the use of a false identity because of the fear of being detected as an overstayer is very different to possession of an identity for the purposes of committing fraud: see Sedley LJ at para 18:

> 'The opening words of Rule 276B, which postulate that the requirements of the rule are to be met by the applicant, place a formal onus on him under paragraph (ii) to show that there are no reasons which render a grant of ILR undesirable; but once the evidence has been heard on both sides, the practical question for the immigration judge is whether there are any reasons in the public interest why the appellant, despite his prolonged evasion of immigration controls, should not now be allowed to stay. To use the evasion itself as a reason is to defeat the purpose of the rule.'

See also *Aissaoui v Secretary of State for the Home Department* [2008] EWCA Civ 37, [2008] All ER (D) 92 (Feb); *FH (Bangladesh) v Secretary of State for the Home Department* [2009] EWCA Civ 385.

[Private life

Requirements to be met by an applicant for leave to remain on the grounds of private life

276ADE. [(1)] The requirements to be met by an applicant for leave to remain on the grounds of private life in the UK are that at the date of application, the applicant:
(i) does not fall for refusal under any of the grounds in Section S-LTR 1.2 to S-LTR [2.3. and S-LTR.3.1.] in Appendix FM; and
(ii) [has made a valid application for leave to remain on the grounds of private life in the UK; and]
(iii) has lived continuously in the UK for at least 20 years (discounting any period of imprisonment); or
(iv) is under the age of 18 years and has lived continuously in the UK for at least 7 years (discounting any period of imprisonment) [, and it would not be reasonable to expect the applicant to leave the UK]; or
(v) is aged 18 years or above and under 25 years and has spent at least half of his life [living] continuously in the UK (discounting any period of imprisonment); or
(vi) [subject to paragraph (2),] is aged 18 years or above, has lived continuously in the UK for less than 20 years (discounting any period of imprisonment) but [there would be very significant obstacles to the applicant's integration into] the country to which he would have to go if required to leave the UK.

[(2) Sub-paragraph (1)(v) does not apply, and may not relied upon, in circumstances in which it is proposed to return a person to a third country pursuant to Schedule 3 to the Asylum and Immigration (Treatment of Claimants, etc) Act 2004.]

Note

Amended by HC 565, paras 69–72 as from 6 September 2012. Sub-para (iv) Sub-para (i) substituted by HC 1039, para 91 as from 6 April 2013. Sub-para (iv) amended by HC 760, para 201 as from 13 December 2012. Further amended by HC 803, paras 7–9 as from 1 December 2013. Amended by HC 532, para 6 of this statement take effect on 28 July 2014 and apply to all applications to which paragraphs 276ADE to 276DH and Appendix FM apply (or can be applied by virtue of the Immigration Rules), and to any other ECHR Article 8 claims (save for those from foreign criminals), and which are decided on or after that date.

Leave to remain on the grounds of private life in the UK

276BE.
[(1)] Limited leave to remain on the grounds of private life in the UK may be granted for a period not exceeding 30 months provided that the Secretary of State is satisfied that the requirements in paragraph [276ADE(1)] are met [or in respect

of the requirements in paragraph [276ADE(1)(iv) and (v)], were met in a previous application which led to a grant of limited leave to remain under [this sub-paragraph].] Such leave shall be given subject to [a condition of no recourse to public funds unless the Secretary of State considers that the person should not be subject to such a condition] appropriate.

[(2) Where an applicant does not meet the requirements in paragraph 276ADE(1) but the Secretary of State grants leave to remain outside the rules on Article 8 grounds, the applicant will normally be granted leave for a period not exceeding 30 months and subject to a condition of no recourse to public funds unless the Secretary of State considers that the person should not be subject to such a condition.]

[(3) Where an applicant has extant leave at the date of decision, the remaining period of that extant leave up to a maximum of 28 days will be added to the period of limited leave to remain granted under paragraph 276BE(1) or 276BE(2) (which may therefore exceed 30 months).]

Note

Amended by HC 565, para 73 as from 6 September 2012. Amended by HC 532, para 7 of this statement take effect on 28 July 2014 and apply to all applications to which paragraphs 276ADE to 276DH and Appendix FM apply (or can be applied by virtue of the Immigration Rules), and to any other ECHR Article 8 claims (save for those from foreign criminals), and which are decided on or after that date. Substituted by HC 532, para 8 of this statement take effect on 28 July 2014 and apply to all applications to which paragraphs 276ADE to 276DH and Appendix FM apply (or can be applied by virtue of the Immigration Rules), and to any other ECHR Article 8 claims (save for those from foreign criminals), and which are decided on or after that date. Amended by HC 532, para 9 of this statement take effect on 28 July 2014 and apply to all applications to which paragraphs 276ADE to 276DH and Appendix FM apply (or can be applied by virtue of the Immigration Rules), and to any other ECHR Article 8 claims (save for those from foreign criminals), and which are decided on or after that date. Inserted by HC 532, para 10 of this statement take effect on 28 July 2014 and apply to all applications to which paragraphs 276ADE to 276DH and Appendix FM apply (or can be applied by virtue of the Immigration Rules), and to any other ECHR Article 8 claims (save for those from foreign criminals), and which are decided on or after that date. Amended by HC 693, para 72 as from 6 November 2014. Amended by HC 693, para 73 as from 6 November 2014. Amended by HC 693, para 74 as from 6 November 2014.

Refusal of limited leave to remain on the grounds of private life in the UK

276CE. Limited leave to remain on the grounds of private life in the UK is to be refused if the Secretary of State is not satisfied that the requirements in paragraph [276ADE(1)] are met.

Note

Amended by HC 693, para 75 as from 6 November 2014.

Requirements for indefinite leave to remain on the grounds of private life in the UK

276DE. The requirements to be met for the grant of indefinite leave to remain on the grounds of private life in the UK are that:

(a) the applicant has been in the UK with continuous leave on the grounds of private life for a period of at least 120 months;
[This continuous leave will disregard any period of overstaying between periods of leave on the grounds of private life where the application was made no later than 28 days after the expiry of the previous leave. Any period pending the determination of the application will also be disregarded].

(b) the applicant meets the requirements of paragraph [276ADE(1)];
[or, in respect of the requirements, in paragraph [276ADE(1)(iv) and (v)], the applicant met the requirements in a previous application which led to a grant of limited leave to remain under paragraph [276BE(1)];]

(c) [does not fall for refusal under any of the grounds in Section S-ILR Suitability — indefinite leave to remain in Appendix FM];

[(d)   the applicant has demonstrated sufficient knowledge of the English language and sufficient knowledge about life in the United Kingdom, in accordance wit Appendix KoLL; and]

(e)   there are no reasons why it would be undesirable to grant the applicant indefinite leave to remain based on the applicant's conduct, character or associations or because the applicant represents a threat to national security.

Note

Amended by HC 760, para 202, 203 as from 13 December 2012. Sub-para (b) amended by HC 1039, para 92 as from 6 April 2013. Amended by HC 628, para 124 and if an applicant has made an application for entry clearance or leave before 1 October 2013, the application will be decided in accordance with the Rules in force on 30 September 2013. Amended by HC 693, para 76 as from 6 November 2014. Amended by HC 693, para 77 as from 6 November 2014. Amended by HC 693, para 78 as from 6 November 2014.

Indefinite leave to remain on the grounds of private life in the UK

276DF.   Indefinite leave to remain on the grounds of private life in the UK may be granted provided that the Secretary of State is satisfied that each of the requirements of paragraph 276DE is met.]

276DG.   If the applicant does not meet the requirements for indefinite leave to remain on the grounds of private life in the UK only for one or both of the following reasons-
[(a)   paragraph S-ILR.1.5. or S-ILR.1.6. in Appendix FM applies;]
(b)   the applicant has not met the requirements of paragraphs 33B to 33G of these Rules,

the applicant may be granted further limited leave to remain on the grounds of private life in the UK for a period not exceeding 30 months, and subject to [a condition of no recourse to public funds unless the Secretary of State considers that the person should not be subject to such a condition].

Note

Sub–para (a) substituted by HC 760, para 204 as from 13 December 2012. Amended by HC 532, para 11 of this statement take effect on 28 July 2014 and apply to all applications to which paragraphs 276ADE to 276DH and Appendix FM apply (or can be applied by virtue of the Immigration Rules), and to any other ECHR Article 8 claims (save for those from foreign criminals), and which are decided on or after that date.

Refusal of indefinite leave to remain on the grounds of private life in the UK

276DH.   Indefinite leave to remain on the grounds of private life in the UK is to be refused if the Secretary of State is not satisfied that each of the requirements of paragraph 276DE is met, subject to paragraph 276DG.]

Note

Paragraphs 276ADE to 276DH inserted by HC 194, para 87 as from 9 July 2012.

Guidance on the private life category is at: www.ukba.homeoffice.gov.uk/sitecontent/documents/p olicyandlaw/modernised /other-categories/long-residence.pdf?view=Binary

[HM Forces]

[Transitional provisions and interaction between paragraphs 276E to 276AI of Part 7 and Appendix Armed Forces

276DI.   From 1 December 2013, Appendix Armed Forces will apply to all applications to which paragraphs 276E to 276AI of this Part applied on or after 30 November 2013, except where the provisions of 276E to 276AI are preserved and continue to apply in accordance with paragraph 276DL.

276DJ.   The requirements to be met under paragraphs 276E to 276AI from 1 December 2013 may be modified or supplemented by the requirements in Appendix Armed Forces or Appendix FM-SE.

276DK. The requirements in paragraphs 8 and 9 of Appendix Armed Forces apply to applications made under paragraphs 276E to 276AI where the decision is made on pot after 1 December 2013 (and irrespective of the date of the application).

276DL. Paragraphs 276E–276AI also continue to apply to applications:
(i) made before 1 December 2013 under paragraphs 276E to 276AI but which have not been decided before that date; and
(ii) by persons who have been granted entry clearance or limited leave to enter or remain under paragraphs 276E to 276AI before 1 December 2013 or in accordance with sub-paragraph (i) above and, where it is a requirement of Part 7, that leave to enter or remain is extant.]

Note

Inserted by HC 803, para 10 as from 1 December 2013.

[Definition of Gurkha]

276E. [For the purposes of these Rules the term 'Gurkha' means a citizen or national of Nepal who has served in the Brigade of Gurkhas of the British Army under the Brigade of Gurkhas' terms and conditions of service.]

Note

Inserted by HC 1112 as from 25 October 2004.

[Leave to enter or remain in the United Kingdom as a Gurkha discharged from the British Army]

[Requirements for indefinite leave to enter the United Kingdom as a Gurkha discharged from the British Army]

276F. [The requirements for indefinite leave to enter the United Kingdom as a Gurkha discharged from the British Army are that:
(i) the applicant has completed at least four years' service as a Gurkha with the British Army; and
(ii) was discharged from the British Army in Nepal on completion of engagement on or after 1 July 1997; and
(iii) was not discharged from the British Army more than 2 years prior to the date on which the application is made; and
(iv) holds a valid United Kingdom entry clearance for entry in this capacity] [; and
(v) does not [fall for refusal under the general grounds for refusal.]

Note

Inserted by HC 1112 as from 25 October 2004. Words in square brackets in (iv) and (v) inserted by HC 863, para 89 as from 6 April 2011. Further amended by HC 760, para 205 as from 13 December 2012.

[Indefinite leave to enter the United Kingdom as a Gurkha discharged from the British Army]

276G. [A person seeking indefinite leave to enter the United Kingdom as a Gurkha discharged from the British Army may be granted indefinite leave to enter provided a valid United Kingdom entry clearance for entry in this capacity is produced to the Immigration Officer on arrival.]

Note

Inserted by HC 1112 as from 25 October 2004.

[Refusal of indefinite leave to enter the United Kingdom as a Gurkha discharged from the British Army]

276H. [Indefinite leave to enter the United Kingdom as a Gurkha discharged from the British Army is to be refused if a valid United Kingdom entry clearance for entry in this capacity is not produced to the Immigration Officer on arrival.]

Note

Inserted by HC 1112 as from 25 October 2004.

[Requirements for indefinite leave to remain in the United Kingdom as a Gurkha discharged from the British Army]

276I. [The requirements for indefinite leave to remain in the United Kingdom as a Gurkha discharged from the British Army are that [the applicant]:
(i)   . . . has completed at least four years' service as a Gurkha with the British Army; and
(ii)   was discharged from the British Army in Nepal on completion of engagement on or after 1 July 1997; and
(iii)   was not discharged from the British Army more than 2 years prior to the date on which the application is made [unless they are applying following a grant of limited leave to remain under paragraph 276KA]; and
[(iv)   is not in the UK in breach of immigration laws except that any period of overstaying for a period of 28 days or less will be disregarded; and
(v)   does not fall for refusal under the general grounds for refusal.]

Note

Inserted by HC 1112 as from 25 October 2004. Words in square brackets in (iv) and (v) inserted by HC 863, para 90 as from 6 April 2011. Sub-para (iv) inserted by HC 194, para 88 as from 1 October 2012. Further amended by HC 760, paras 206–209 as from 13 December 2012.

[Indefinite leave to remain in the United Kingdom as a Gurkha discharged from the British Army]

276J. [A person seeking indefinite leave to remain in the United Kingdom as a Gurkha discharged from the British Army may be granted indefinite leave to remain provided the Secretary of State is satisfied that each of the requirements of paragraph 276I is met.]

Note

Inserted by HC 1112 as from 25 October 2004.

[Refusal of indefinite leave to remain in the United Kingdom as a Gurkha discharged from the British Army]

276K. [Indefinite leave to remain in the United Kingdom as a Gurkha discharged from the British Army is to be refused if the Secretary of State is not satisfied that each of the requirements of paragraph 276I is met.]

Note

Inserted by HC 1112 as from 25 October 2004.

General note on paras 276E-K

See the IDIs at Chapter 15, Section 2A www.bia.homeoffice.gov.uk/sitecontent/documents/policya ndlaw/IDIs/idischapter15/section2a/section2a.pdf?view=Binary

For the background to changes leading to the current policy, see *R (on the application of Limbu) v Secretary of State for the Home Department* [2008] EWHC 2261 (Admin), [2008] All ER (D) 122 (Sep).

[Leave to remain in the United Kingdom as a Gurka discharged from the British Army

276KA. If a Gurka discharged from the British Army does not meet the requirements for indefinite leave to remain only because paragraph 322(1C)(iii) or 322(1C)(iv) applies, the applicant may be granted limited leave to remain for a period not exceeding 30 months.]

Note

Inserted by HC 760, para 210 as from 13 December 2012.

[Leave to enter or remain in the United Kingdom as a foreign or Commonwealth citizen discharged from HM Forces]

[Requirements for indefinite leave to enter the United Kingdom as a foreign or Commonwealth citizen discharged from HM Forces]

276L. [The requirements for indefinite leave to enter the United Kingdom as a foreign or Commonwealth citizen discharged from HM Forces are that [the applicant]:
(i)   . . . has completed at least four years' service with HM Forces; and
(ii)   was discharged from HM Forces on completion of engagement; and
(iii)   was not discharged from HM Forces more than 2 years prior to the date on which the application is made; and
(iv)   holds a valid United Kingdom entry clearance for entry in this capacity[; and
(v)   does not [fall for refusal under the general grounds for refusal].]

Note

Inserted by HC 1112 as from 25 October 2004. Words in square brackets in (iv) and (v) inserted by HC 863, para 91 as from 6 April 2011. Further amended by HC 760, paras 211–213 as from 13 December 2012.

[Indefinite leave to enter the United Kingdom as a foreign or Commonwealth citizen discharged from HM Forces]

276M. [A person seeking indefinite leave to enter the United Kingdom as a foreign or Commonwealth citizen discharged from HM Forces may be granted indefinite leave to enter provided a valid United Kingdom entry clearance for entry in this capacity is produced to the Immigration Officer on arrival.]

Note

Inserted by HC 1112 as from 25 October 2004.

[Refusal of indefinite leave to enter the United Kingdom as a foreign or Commonwealth citizen discharged from HM Forces]

276N. [Indefinite leave to enter the United Kingdom as a foreign or Commonwealth citizen discharged from HM Forces is to be refused if a valid United Kingdom entry clearance for entry in this capacity is not produced to the Immigration Officer on arrival.]

Note

Inserted by HC 1112 as from 25 October 2004.

[Requirements for indefinite leave to remain in the United Kingdom as a foreign or Commonwealth citizen discharged from HM Forces]

276O. [The requirements for indefinite leave to remain in the United Kingdom as a foreign or Commonwealth citizen discharged from HM Forces are that [the applicant]:
(i)   . . . has completed at least four years' service with HM Forces; and
(ii)   was discharged from HM Forces on completion of engagement; and
(iii)   was not discharged from HM Forces more than 2 years prior to the date on which the application is made [unless they are applying following a grant of limited leave to remain under paragraph 276QA]; and

(iv)   [is not in the UK in breach of immigration laws except that any period of overstaying for a period of 28 days or less will be disregarded][; and

[(v)   does not fall for refusal under the general grounds for refusal.]

Note

Inserted by HC 1112 as from 25 October 2004. Words in square brackets in (iv) and (v) inserted by HC 863, para 92 as from 6 April 2011. Sub-para (iv) inserted by HC 194, para 89 as from 1 October 2012. Further amended by HC 760, paras 214–217 as from 13 December 2012.

[Indefinite leave to remain in the United Kingdom as a foreign or Commonwealth citizen discharged from HM Forces]

276P.   [A person seeking indefinite leave to remain in the United Kingdom as a foreign or Commonwealth citizen discharged from HM Forces may be granted indefinite leave to remain provided the Secretary of State is satisfied that each of the requirements of paragraph 276O is met.]

Note

Inserted by HC 1112 as from 25 October 2004.

[Refusal of indefinite leave to remain in the United Kingdom as a foreign or Commonwealth citizen discharged from HM Forces]

276Q.   [Indefinite leave to remain in the United Kingdom as a foreign or Commonwealth citizen discharged from HM Forces is to be refused if the Secretary of State is not satisfied that each of the requirements of paragraph 276O is met.]

Note

Inserted by HC 1112 as from 25 October 2004.

General note on paras 276L-Q

For UKBA interpretation, see: IDIs at Chapter 15, Section 2A; www.bia.homeoffice.gov.uk/siteco ntent/documents/policyandlaw/IDIs/idischapter15/section2a/ section2a.pdf?view=Binary

[Leave to remain in the United Kingdom as a foreign or Commonwealth citizen discharged from HM Forces

276QA.   If a foreign or Commonwealth citizen discharged from HM Forces does not meet the requirements for indefinite leave to remain only because paragraph 322(1C)(iii) or 322(1C)(iv) applies, the applicant may be granted limited leave to remain for a period not exceeding 30 months.]

Note

Sub-heading and paragraph 276QA inserted by HC 760, para 218 as from 13 December 2012.

[Spouses, civil partners, unmarried or same-sex partners of persons settled or seeking settlement in the United Kingdom in accordance with paragraphs 276E to 276Q (HM Forces rules) or of members of HM forces who are exempt from immigration control under section 8(4)(a) of the Immigration Act 1971 and have at least 5 years' continuous service]

[Leave to enter or remain in the UK as the spouse, civil partner, unmarried or same-sex partner of a person present and settled in the United Kingdom or being granted settlement on the same occasion in accordance with paragraphs 276E to 276Q or of a member of the HM Forces who is exempt from immigration control under section 8(4)(a) of the Immigration Act 1971 and have at least 5 years' continuous service.

[Requirements for indefinite leave to enter the United Kingdom as the spouse, civil partner, unmarried or same-sex partner of a person present and settled in the United Kingdom or being granted settlement on the same occasion in accordance with paragraphs 276E to 276Q or of a member of the HM Forces who is exempt from immigration control under section 8(4)(a) of the Immigration Act 1971 and have at least 5 years' continuous service

]

276R. [The requirements to be met by a person seeking indefinite leave to enter the United Kingdom as the spouse of a person present and settled in the United Kingdom or being admitted on the same occasion for settlement in accordance with paragraphs 276E to 276Q or of a member of the HM Forces who is exempt from immigration control under section 8(4)(a) of the Immigration Act 1971 and have at least 5 years' continuous service are that:

(i)   the applicant is married to, or the civil partner, unmarried or same-sex partner of a person present and settled in the United Kingdom or who is being admitted on the same occasion for settlement in accordance with paragraphs 276E to 276Q or of a member of the HM Forces who is exempt from immigration control under section 8(4)(a) of the Immigration Act 1971 and have at least 5 years' continuous service; and

(ii)   the parties to the marriage, civil partnership or relationship akin to marriage or civil partnership have met; and

(iii)   the parties were married or formed a civil partnership or a relationship akin to marriage or civil partnership at least 2 years ago; and

(iv)   each of the parties intends to live permanently with the other as his or her spouse, civil partner, unmarried or same-sex partner and

(v)   the marriage, civil partnership or relationship akin to marriage or civil partnership is subsisting; and

(vi)   the applicant holds a valid United Kingdom entry clearance for entry in this capacity[; and

(vii) the applicant does not [fall for refusal under the general grounds for refusal.]

Note

Paras 276R–276Z and 276AA–276AC inserted by HC 164 as from 1 January 2005. Inserted by HC 314, para 86 as from 31 March 2009. Words in square brackets in (vi) and (vii) inserted by HC 863, para 93 as from 6 April 2011. Further amended by HC 760, paras 219, 220 as from 13 December 2012.

[Indefinite leave to enter the United Kingdom as the spouse, civil partner, unmarried or same-sex partner of a person present and settled in the United Kingdom or being granted settlement on the same occasion in accordance with paragraphs 276E to 276Q or of a member of the HM Forces who is exempt from immigration control under section 8(4)(a) of the Immigration Act 1971 and have at least 5 years' continuous service]

276S. [A person seeking leave to enter the United Kingdom as the spouse, civil partner, unmarried or same-sex partner of a person present and settled in the United Kingdom or being admitted on the same occasion for settlement in accordance with paragraphs 276E to 276Q or of a member of HM Forces who is exempt from immigration control under section 8(4)(a) of the Immigration Act 1971 and has at least 5 years' continuous service may be granted indefinite leave to enter provided a valid United Kingdom entry clearance for entry in this capacity is produced to the Immigration Officer on arrival.]

Note

Paras 276R–276Z and 276AA–276AC inserted by HC 164 as from 1 January 2005. Inserted by HC 314, para 86 as from 31 March 2009.

[Refusal of indefinite leave to enter the United Kingdom as the spouse or civil partner of a person present and settled in the UK or being admitted on the same occasion for settlement in accordance with paragraphs 276E to 276Q or of a member of HM Forces who is exempt from immigration control under section 8(4)(a) of the Immigration Act 1971 and has at least 5 years' continuous service]

276T. [Leave to enter the United Kingdom as the spouse or civil partner of a person present and settled in the United Kingdom or being admitted on the same occasion for settlement in accordance with paragraphs 276E to 276Q or of a member of HM Forces who is exempt from immigration control under section 8(4)(a) of the Immigration Act 1971 and has at least 5 years' continuous service is to be refused if a valid United Kingdom entry clearance for entry in this capacity is not produced to the Immigration Officer on arrival.]

Note

Paras 276R–276Z and 276AA–276AC inserted by HC 164 as from 1 January 2005. Inserted by HC 314, para 86 as from 31 March 2009.

General note on paras 276R-T

See IDIs at Chapter 15, Section 2A: www.bia.homeoffice.gov.uk/sitecontent/documents/policyand law/IDIs/ idischapter15/section2a/section2a.pdf?view=Binary

[Requirements for indefinite leave to remain in the United Kingdom as the spouse or civil partner of a person present and settled in the United Kingdom or being granted settlement on the same occasion in accordance with paragraphs 276E to 276Q or of a member of HM Forces who is exempt from immigration control under section 8(4)(a) of the Immigration Act 1971 and has at least 5 years' continuous service]

276U. [The requirements to be met by a person seeking indefinite leave to remain in the United Kingdom as the spouse, civil partner, unmarried or same-sex partner of a person present and settled in the United Kingdom or being granted settlement on the same occasion in accordance with paragraphs 276E to 276Q or of a member of HM Forces who is exempt from immigration control under section 8(4)(a) of the Immigration Act 1971 and has at least 5 years' continuous service are that:

(i)   the applicant is married to or the civil partner or unmarried or same-sex partner of a person present and settled in the United Kingdom or being granted settlement on the same occasion in accordance with paragraphs 276E to 276Q or of a member of HM Forces who is exempt from immigration control under section 8(4)(a) of the Immigration Act 1971 and has at least 5 years' continuous service; and

(ii)   the parties to the marriage, civil partnership or relationship akin to marriage or civil partnership have met; and

(iii)   the parties were married or formed a civil partnership or relationship akin to marriage or civil partnership at least 2 years ago; and

(iv)   each of the parties intends to live permanently with the other as his or her spouse, civil partner, unmarried or same-sex partner; and

(v)   the marriage, civil partnership or relationship akin to marriage or civil partnership is subsisting; and

(vi)   has, or has been granted, leave to enter or remain in the United Kingdom as the spouse, civil partner, unmarried or same sex partner[; and

[(vii)   the applicant does not fall for refusal under the general grounds for refusal].]

Note

Paras 276R–276Z and 276AA–276AC inserted by HC 164 as from 1 January 2005. Inserted by HC 314, para 86 as from 31 March 2009. Words in square brackets in (vi) and (vii) inserted by HC 863, para 94 as from 6 April 2011. Further amended by HC 760, para 221 as from 13 December 2012.

[Indefinite leave to remain in the United Kingdom as the spouse or civil partner of a person present and settled in the United Kingdom or being granted settlement on the same occasion in accordance with paragraphs 276E to 276Q or of a member of HM Forces who is exempt from immigration control under section 8(4)(a) of the Immigration Act 1971 and has at least 5 years' continuous service]

276V. [Indefinite leave to remain in the United Kingdom as the spouse, civil partner, unmarried or same-sex partner of a person present and settled in the United Kingdom or being granted settlement on the same occasion in accordance with paragraphs 276E to 276Q or of a member of HM Forces who is exempt from immigration control under section 8(4)(a) of the Immigration Act 1971 and has at least 5 years' continuous service may be granted provided the Secretary of State is satisfied that each of the requirements of paragraph 276U is met.]

Note

Paras 276R–276Z and 276AA–276AC inserted by HC 164 as from 1 January 2005. Inserted by HC 314, para 86 as from 31 March 2009.

[Refusal of indefinite leave to remain in the United Kingdom as the spouse, civil partner, unmarried or same-sex partner of a person present and settled in the United Kingdom or being granted settlement on the same occasion in accordance with paragraphs 276E to 276Q or of a member of HM Forces who is exempt from immigration control under section 8(4)(a) of the Immigration Act 1971 and has at least 5 years' continuous service]

276W. [Indefinite leave to remain in the United Kingdom as the spouse, civil partner, unmarried or same sex partner of a person present and settled in the United Kingdom or being granted settlement on the same occasion in accordance with paragraphs 276E to 276Q or of a member of HM Forces who is exempt from immigration control under section 8(4)(a) of the Immigration Act 1971 and has at least 5 years' continuous service is to be refused if the Secretary of State is not satisfied that each of the requirements of paragraph 276U is met.]

Note

Paras 276R–276Z and 276AA–276AC inserted by HC 164 as from 1 January 2005. Inserted by HC 314, para 86 as from 31 March 2009.

General note on paras 276U–W

See IDIs at Chapter 15, Section 2A: www.bia.homeoffice.gov.uk/sitecontent/documents/policyand law/IDIs/idischapter15/section2a/ section2a.pdf?view=Binary

[Children of a parent, parents or a relative settled or seeking settlement in the United Kingdom under paragraphs 276E to 276Q (HM Forces Rules) or of a member of HM Forces who is exempt from immigration control under section 8(4)(a) of the Immigration Act 1971 and has at least 5 years' continuous service]

[Leave to enter or remain in the United Kingdom as the child of a parent, parents or a relative present and settled in the United Kingdom or being granted settlement on the same occasion in accordance with paragraphs 276E to 276Q or of a member of HM Forces who is exempt from immigration control under section 8(4)(a) of the Immigration Act 1971 and has at least 5 years' continuous service]

[Requirements for indefinite leave to enter the United Kingdom as the child of a parent, parents or a relative present and settled in the United Kingdom or being admitted for settlement on the same occasion in accordance with paragraphs 276E to 276Q or of a member of HM Forces who is exempt from immigration control under section 8(4)(a) of the Immigration Act 1971 and has at least 5 years' continuous service]

276X. [The requirements to be met by a person seeking indefinite leave to enter the United Kingdom as the child of a parent, parents or a relative present and settled in the United Kingdom or being admitted for settlement on the same occasion in accordance with paragraphs 276E to 276Q or of a member of HM Forces who is exempt from immigration control under section 8(4)(a) of the Immigration Act 1971 and has at least 5 years' continuous service are that:

(i)   the applicant is seeking indefinite leave to enter to accompany or join a parent, parents or a relative in one of the following circumstances:

    (a)   both parents are present and settled in the United Kingdom; or

    (b)   both parents are being admitted on the same occasion for settlement; or

    (c)   one parent is present and settled in the United Kingdom or is a member of HM Forces who is exempt from immigration control under section 8(4)(a) of the Immigration Act 1971 and has at least 5 years' continues service and the other is being admitted on the same occasion for settlement or is a member of HM Forces who is exempt from immigration control under section 8(4)(a) of the Immigration Act 1971 and has at least 5 years' continuous service; or

    (d)   one parent is present and settled in the United Kingdom or being admitted on the same occasion for settlement or is a member of HM Forces who is exempt from immigration control under section 8(4)(a) of the Immigration Act 1971 and has at least 5 years' continuous service and the other parent is dead; or

    (e)   one parent is present and settled in the United Kingdom or being admitted on the same occasion for settlement or is a member of HM Forces who is exempt from immigration control under section 8(4)(a) of the Immigration Act 1971 and has at least 5 years' continuous service and has had sole responsibility for the child's upbringing; or

    (f)   one parent or a relative is present and settled in the United Kingdom or being admitted on the same occasion for settlement or is a member of HM Forces who is exempt from immigration control under section 8(4)(a) of the Immigration Act 1971 and has at least 5 years' continuous service and there are serious and compelling family or other considerations which make exclusion of the child undesirable and suitable arrangements have been made for the child's care; and

(ii)   is under the age of 18; and

(iii)   is not leading an independent life, is unmarried and is not a civil partner, and has not formed an independent family unit; and

(iv)   holds a valid United Kingdom entry clearance for entry in this capacity[; and

(v)   the applicant does not [fall for refusal under the general grounds for refusal.]

Note

Paras 276R–276Z and 276AA–276AC inserted by HC 164 as from 1 January 2005. Inserted by HC 314, para 87 as from 31 March 2009. Words in square brackets in (iv) and (v) inserted by HC 863, para 95 as from 6 April 2011. Amended by HC 760, para 222 as from 13 December 2012.

[Indefinite leave to enter the United Kingdom as the child of a parent, parents or a relative present and settled in the United Kingdom or being admitted for settlement on the same occasion in accordance with paragraphs 276E to 276Q or of a member of HM Forces who is exempt from immigration control under section 8(4)(a) of the Immigration Act 1971 and has at least 5 years' continuous service]

276Y. [Indefinite leave to enter the United Kingdom as the child of a parent, parents or a relative present and settled in the United Kingdom or being admitted for settlement on the same occasion in accordance with paragraphs 276E to 276Q or of a member of HM Forces who is exempt from immigration control under section 8(4)(a) of the Immigration Act 1971 and has at least 5 years' continuous service may be granted provided a valid United Kingdom entry clearance for entry in this capacity is produced to the Immigration Officer on arrival.]

Note

Paras 276R–276Z and 276AA–276AC inserted by HC 164 as from 1 January 2005. Inserted by HC 314, para 87 as from 31 March 2009.

[Refusal of indefinite leave to enter the United Kingdom as the child of a parent, parents or a relative present and settled in the United Kingdom or being admitted for settlement on the same occasion in accordance with paragraphs 276E to 276Q or of a member of HM Forces who is exempt from immigration control under section 8(4)(a) of the Immigration Act 1971 and has at least 5 years' continuous service]

276Z. [Indefinite leave to enter the United Kingdom as the child of a parent, parents, or a relative present and settled in the United Kingdom or being admitted for settlement on the same occasion in accordance with paragraphs 276E to 276Q or of a member of HM Forces who is exempt from immigration control under section 8(4)(a) of the Immigration Act 1971 and has at least 5 years' continuous service is to be refused if a valid United Kingdom entry clearance for entry in this capacity is not produced to the Immigration Officer on arrival.]

Note

Paras 276R–276Z and 276AA–276AC inserted by HC 164 as from 1 January 2005. Inserted by HC 314, para 87 as from 31 March 2009.

[Requirements for indefinite leave to remain in the United Kingdom as the child of a parent, parents or a relative present and settled in the United Kingdom or being granted settlement on the same occasion in accordance with paragraphs 276E to 276Q or of a member of HM Forces who is exempt from immigration control under section 8(4)(a) of the Immigration Act 1971 and has at least 5 years' continuous service]

276AA. [The requirements to be met by a person seeking indefinite leave to remain in the United Kingdom as the child of a parent, parents or a relative present and settled in the United Kingdom or being granted settlement on the same occasion in accordance with paragraphs 276E to 276Q or is a member of HM Forces who is exempt from immigration control under section 8(4)(a) of the Immigration Act 1971 and has at least 5 years' continuous service are that:

(i)   the applicant is seeking indefinite leave to remain with a parent, parents or a relative in one of the following circumstances:

    (a)   both parents are present and settled in the United Kingdom or being granted settlement on the same occasion; or

    (ab)   one parent is present and settled in the United Kingdom or is a member of HM Forces who is exempt from immigration control under section 8(4)(a) of the Immigration Act 1971 and has at least 5 years' continuous service and the other is being granted settlement on the same occasion or of a member of HM Forces who is exempt from immigration control under section 8(4)(a) of the Immigration Act 1971 and has at least 5 years' continuous service; or

    (b)   one parent is present and settled in the United Kingdom or being granted settlement on the same occasion or is a member of HM Forces who is exempt from immigration control under section 8(4)(a) of the Immigration Act 1971 and has at least 5 years' continuous service and the other parent is dead; or

    (c)   one parent is present and settled in the United Kingdom or being granted settlement on the same occasion or of a member of HM Forces who is exempt from immigration control under section 8(4)(a) of the Immigration Act 1971 and has at least 5 years' continuous service and has had sole responsibility for the child's upbringing; or

    (d)   one parent or a relative is present and settled in the United Kingdom or being granted settlement on the same occasion or is a member of HM Forces who is exempt from immigration control under section 8(4)(a) of the Immigration Act 1971 and has at least 5 years' continuous service and there are serious and compelling family or other considerations which make exclusion of the child undesirable and suitable arrangements have been made for the child's care; and

(ii)   is under the age of 18; and

(iii)   is not leading an independent life, is unmarried and is not a civil partner, and has not formed an independent family unit; and

(iv)   [is not in the UK in breach of immigration laws except that any period of overstaying for a period of 28 days or less will be disregarded.]

(v)   the applicant does not [fall for refusal under the general grounds for refusal.]

Note

Paras 276R–276Z and 276AA–276AC inserted by HC 164 as from 1 January 2005. Inserted by HC 314, para 87 as from 31 March 2009. Words in square brackets in (iv) and (v) inserted by HC 863, para 96 as from 6 April 2011. Sub-para (iv) inserted by HC 194, para 90 as from 1 October 2012. Further amended by HC 760, para 223 as from 13 December 2012.

[Indefinite leave to remain in the United Kingdom as the child of a parent, parents or a relative present and settled in the United Kingdom or being granted settlement on the same occasion in accordance with paragraphs 276E to 276Q or of a member of HM Forces who is exempt from immigration control under section 8(4)(a) of the Immigration Act 1971 and has at least 5 years' continuous service]

276AB.   [Indefinite leave to remain in the United Kingdom as the child of a parent, parents or a relative present and settled in the United Kingdom or being granted settlement on the same occasion in accordance with paragraphs 276E to 276Q or of a member of HM Forces who is exempt from immigration control under section 8(4)(a) of the Immigration Act 1971 and has at least 5 years' continuous service may be granted if the Secretary of State is satisfied that each of the requirements of paragraph 276AA is met.]

Note

Paras 276R–276Z and 276AA–276AC inserted by HC 164 as from 1 January 2005. Amended by HC 314, para 87 as from 31 March 2009.

[Refusal of indefinite leave to remain in the United Kingdom as the child of a parent, parents or a relative present and settled in the United Kingdom or being granted settlement on the same occasion in accordance with paragraphs 276E to 276Q or of a member of HM Forces who is exempt from immigration control under section 8(4)(a) of the Immigration Act 1971 and has at least 5 years' continuous service]

276AC.   [Indefinite leave to remain in the United Kingdom as the child of a parent, parents or a relative present and settled in the United Kingdom or being granted settlement on the same occasion in accordance with paragraphs 276E to 276Q or of a member of HM Forces who is exempt from immigration control under section 8(4)(a) of the Immigration Act 1971 and has at least 5 years' continuous service is to be refused if the Secretary of State is not satisfied that each of the requirements of paragraph 276AA is met.]

Note

Paras 276R–276Z and 276AA–276AC inserted by HC 164 as from 1 January 2005. Inserted by HC 314, para 87 as from 31 March 2009.

Spouses, civil partners, unmarried or same-sex partners of armed forces members who are exempt from Immigration Control under section 8(4) of the Immigration Act 1971]

[Requirements for leave to enter or remain as the spouse, civil partner unmarried or same-sex partner of an armed forces member who is exempt from immigration control under section 8(4) of the Immigration Act 1971]

276AD.   [The requirements to be met by a person seeking leave to enter or remain in the United Kingdom as the spouse. civil partner, unmarried or same-sex partner of an armed forces member who is exempt from immigration control under section 8(4) of the Immigration Act 1971 are that:

(i)   the applicant is married to or the civil partner, unmarried or same-sex partner of an armed forces member who is exempt from immigration control under section 8(4) of the Immigration Act 1971; and

(ii)   each of the parties intends to live with the other as his or her spouse or civil partner, unmarried or same-sex partner during the applicant's stay and the marriage or civil partnership, or relationship akin to a marriage is subsisting; and

(iii)   there will be adequate accommodation for the parties and any dependants without recourse to public funds in accommodation which they own or occupy exclusively; and

(iv)   the parties will be able to maintain themselves and any dependants adequately without recourse to public funds; and

(v)   the applicant does not intend to stay in the United Kingdom beyond his or her spouse's, civil partner's, unmarried or same-sex partner's enlistment in the home forces, or period of posting or training in the United Kingdom; and]

(vi)   where the applicant is the unmarried or same-sex partner of an armed forces member who is exempt from immigration control under section 8(4) of the Immigration Act 1971, the following requirements are also met:

    (a)   any previous marriage or civil partnership or relationship akin to a marriage by the applicant or the *exempt armed forces member* must have permanently broken down,

    (b)   the applicant and the *exempt armed forces member* must not be so closely related that they would be prohibited from marrying each other in the UK, and

    (c)   the applicant and the *exempt armed forces member* must have been living together in a relationship akin to marriage or civil partnership for a period of at least 2 years.

Note

Paras 276AD–276AI inserted by HC 346, para 20 as from 15 March 2005. Inserted by HC 314, para 88 as from 31 March 2009.

[Leave to enter or remain as the spouse, civil partner, unmarried or same-sex partner of an armed forces member who is exempt from immigration control under section 8(4) of the Immigration Act 1971]

276AE.   [A person seeking leave to enter or remain in the United Kingdom as the spouse, civil partner, unmarried or same-sex partner of an armed forces member who is exempt from immigration control under section 8(4) of the Immigration Act 1971 may be given leave to enter or remain in the United Kingdom for a period not exceeding 4 years or the expected duration of the enlistment, posting or training of his or her spouse, civil partner, unmarried or same-sex partner, whichever is shorter, provided that the Immigration Officer, or in the case of an application for leave to remain, the Secretary of State, is satisfied that each of the requirements of paragraph 276AD(i)–(vi) is met.]

Note

Paras 276AD–276AI inserted by HC 346, para 20 as from 15 March 2005. Inserted by HC 314, para 88 as from 31 March 2009.

[Refusal of leave to enter or remain as the spouse, civil partner, unmarried or same-sex partner of an armed forces member who is exempt from immigration control under section 8(4) of the Immigration Act 1971]

276AF.   [Leave to enter or remain in the United Kingdom as the spouse, civil partner, unmarried or same-sex partner of an armed forces member who is exempt from immigration control under section 8(4) of the Immigration Act 1971 is to be refused if the Immigration Officer, or in the case of an application for leave to remain, the Secretary of State, is not satisfied that each of the requirements of paragraph 276AD (i)-(vi) is met.]

Note

Paras 276AD–276AI inserted by HC 346, para 20 as from 15 March 2005. Inserted by HC 314, para 88 as from 31 March 2009.

[**Children of armed forces members who are exempt from immigration control under section 8(4) of the Immigration Act 1971**]

[**Requirements for leave to enter or remain as the child of an armed forces member exempt from immigration control under section 8(4) of the Immigration Act 1971**]

276AG. [The requirements to be met by a person seeking leave to enter or remain in the United Kingdom as the child of an armed forces member exempt from immigration control under section 8(4) of the Immigration Act 1971 are that:

(i) he is the child of a parent who is an armed forces member exempt from immigration control under section 8(4) of the Immigration Act 1971; and

(ii) he is under the age of 18 or has current leave to enter or remain in this capacity; and

(iii) he is unmarried and is not a civil partner, has not formed an independent family unit and is not leading an independent life; and (iv) he can and will be maintained and accommodated adequately without recourse to public funds in accommodation which his parent(s) own or occupy exclusively; and

(v) he will not stay in the United Kingdom beyond the period of his parent's enlistment in the home forces, or posting or training in the United Kingdom; and

(vi) his other parent is being or has been admitted to or allowed to remain in the United Kingdom save where:

    (a) the parent he is accompanying or joining is his sole surviving parent; or

    (b) the parent he is accompanying or joining has had sole responsibility for his upbringing; or

    (c) there are serious and compelling family or other considerations which make exclusion from the United Kingdom undesirable and suitable arrangements have been made for his care.]

Note

Paras 276AD–276AI inserted by HC 346, para 20 as from 15 March 2005.

[**Leave to enter or remain as the child of an armed forces member exempt from immigration control under section 8(4) of the Immigration Act 1971**]

276AH. [A person seeking leave to enter or remain in the United Kingdom as the child of an armed forces member exempt from immigration control under section 8(4) of the Immigration Act 1971 may be given leave to enter or remain in the United Kingdom for a period not exceeding 4 years or the duration of the enlistment, posting or training of his parent, whichever is the shorter, provided that the Immigration Officer, or in the case of an application for leave to remain, the Secretary of State, is satisfied that each of the requirements of 276AG (i)–(vi) is met.]

Note

Paras 276AD–276AI inserted by HC 346, para 20 as from 15 March 2005.

[**Refusal of leave to enter or remain as the child of an armed forces member exempt from immigration control under section 8(4) of the Immigration Act 1971**]

276AI. [The requirement to be met by a person seeking an extension of stay on the ground of long residence in the United Kingdom is that the applicant meets each of the requirements in paragraph 276B(i)–(ii)].]

Note

Paras 276AD–276AI inserted by HC 346, para 20 as from 15 March 2005. Paragraph 27A1 substituted by HC 1888, para 100 as from 6 April 2012.

[Limited leave to enter for relevant Afghan citizens

Limited leave to enter the United Kingdom as a relevant Afghan citizen

276BA1. Limited leave to enter the United Kingdom for a period not exceeding 5 years will be granted to relevant Afghan citizens, unless the application falls for refusal under paragraph 276BC1.

Note

Inserted by HC 628, para 122 and if an applicant has made an application for entry clearance or leave before 1 October 2013, the application will be decided in accordance with the Rules in force on 30 September 2013.

Definition of a "relevant Afghan citizen"

276BB1. A relevant Afghan citizen is a person who:
(i)   is in Afghanistan;
(ii)   is an Afghan citizen;
(iii)   is aged 18 years or over;
(iv)   was employed in Afghanistan directly by the Ministry of Defence, the Foreign And Commonwealth Office or the Department for International Development;
(v)   was made redundant on or after 19 December 2012; and
(vi)   the Ministry of Defence, the Foreign and Commonwealth Office, or the Department for International Development has determined should qualify for the resettlement redundancy package as descried in the written Ministerial statement of the Secretary of State for Defence dated 4th June 2013.

Note

Inserted by HC 628, para 122 and if an applicant has made an application for entry clearance or leave before 1 October 2013, the application will be decided in accordance with the Rules in force on 30 September 2013.

Refusal of limited leave to enter the United Kingdom as a relevant Afghan citizen

276BC1. An applicant will be refused leave to enter as a relevant Afghan citizen if:
(i)   their application fails for refusal under the general grounds of refusal contained in Part 9 of these Rules;
(ii)   there are serious reasons for considering that the applicant has committed a crime against peace, a war crime, a crime against humanity, or any other serious crime or instigated or otherwise participated in such crimes;
(iii)   there are serious reasons for considering that the applicant is guilty of acts contrary to the purposes and principles of the United Nations or has committed, prepared or instigated such acts or encouraged or induced others to commit, prepare or instigate such acts; or
(iv)   there are serious reasons for considering that the applicant constitutes a danger to the community or to the security of the United Kingdom.

Note

Inserted by HC 628, para 122 and if an applicant has made an application for entry clearance or leave before 1 October 2013, the application will be decided in accordance with the Rules in force on 30 September 2013.

Curtailment of leave to enter the United Kingdom as a relevant Afghan citizen

276BD1. Limited leave to enter the United Kingdom as a relevant Afghan citizen under paragraph 276BA1 may be curtailed where the person is a danger to the security or public order of the United Kingdom or leave may be curtailed where:
(i)   the relevant Afghan citizen has made false representation or failed to disclose any material fact for the purpose of obtaining leave to enter; and/or
(ii)   it is undesirable to permit the relevant Afghan citizen to remain in the United Kingdom in the light of his conduct, character or associations or the fact that he represents a threat to national security.

Note

Inserted by HC 628, para 122 and if an applicant has made an application for entry clearance or leave before 1 October 2013, the application will be decided in accordance with the Rules in force on 30 September 2013.

Dependants of a relevant Afghan citizen

276BE1. A relevant Afghan citizen may include a partner or minor dependant child in his or her application for limited leave to enter as his or her dependants.

Note

Inserted by HC 628, para 122 and if an applicant has made an application for entry clearance or leave before 1 October 2013, the application will be decided in accordance with the Rules in force on 30 September 2013.

276BF1. All dependants included in the application for limited leave to enter the United Kingdom must be:
(i)   Afghan citizens; and
(ii)   in Afghanistan.

Note

Inserted by HC 628, para 122 and if an applicant has made an application for entry clearance or leave before 1 October 2013, the application will be decided in accordance with the Rules in force on 30 September 2013.

276BG1. The application must include the details of all dependants seeking relocation at the time the application is made. Additional dependants cannot normally be added after the application has been made.

Note

Inserted by HC 628, para 122 and if an applicant has made an application for entry clearance or leave before 1 October 2013, the application will be decided in accordance with the Rules in force on 30 September 2013.

276BH1. If the application is successful, the relevant Afghan citizen and his eligible dependants must all travel at the same time.

Note

Inserted by HC 628, para 122 and if an applicant has made an application for entry clearance or leave before 1 October 2013, the application will be decided in accordance with the Rules in force on 30 September 2013.

276BI1. If the relevant Afghan citizen is in a polygamous marriage, his or her application for limited leave may only include one partner.

Note

Inserted by HC 628, para 122 and if an applicant has made an application for entry clearance or leave before 1 October 2013, the application will be decided in accordance with the Rules in force on 30 September 2013.

Limited leave to enter the United Kingdom as the partner of a relevant Afghan citizen

276BJ1. Limited leave to enter the United Kingdom for a period not exceeding 5 years will be granted to the partner of a relevant Afghan citizen where:
(i)   the relationship requirements under paragraph 276BL1 are met; and; and
(ii)   the application does not fall for refusal under paragraph 276BM1.

Note

Inserted by HC 628, para 122 and if an applicant has made an application for entry clearance or leave before 1 October 2013, the application will be decided in accordance with the Rules in force on 30 September 2013.

Definition of "partner" of a relevant Afghan citizen

276BK1. For the purposes of this section a partner of a relevant Afghan citizen (the principal applicant) is a person who:
(i)   is the principal applicant's spouse; or
(ii)   is the principal applicant's civil partner; or
(iii)   has been living together with the principal applicant is a relationship akin to a marriage or civil partnership for at least two years prior to the date of the application.

Note

Inserted by HC 628, para 122 and if an applicant has made an application for entry clearance or leave before 1 October 2013, the application will be decided in accordance with the Rules in force on 30 September 2013.

Relationship requirements for a partner of a relevant Afghan citizen

276BL1. The relationship requirements for a partner of a relevant Afghan citizen (the principal applicant) are that:
(i)   they are aged 18 or over at the date of application;
(ii)   they are in a relationship with the principal applicant that is not within the prohibited degree of relationship;
(iii)   they have met the principal applicant in person;
(iv)   they are in a genuine and subsisting relationship with the principal applicant;
(v)   if the principal applicant and partner are married or in a civil partnership, they must be in a valid marriage or civil partnership and must provide reasonable evidence to the equivalent of a marriage certificate or civil partnership certificate issued in the United Kingdom and valid under the law in force in the relevant country;
(vi)   any previous relationship of the principal applicant or their partner must have broken down permanently, unless it is a relationship which falls with paragraph 278(i) of these Rules; and
(vii)   they must intend to live together permanently in the UK with the principal applicant.

Note

Inserted by HC 628, para 122 and if an applicant has made an application for entry clearance or leave before 1 October 2013, the application will be decided in accordance with the Rules in force on 30 September 2013.

Refusal of limited leave to enter the United Kingdom as the partner of a relevant Afghan citizen

276BM1. A partner of a relevant Afghan citizen (the principal applicant) will be refused limited leave to enter the United Kingdom if:
(i)   their application falls for refusal under the general grounds of refusal contained in Part 9 of these Rules;
(ii)   there are serious reasons for considering that the partner of the principal applicant has committed a crime against peace, a war crime, a crime against humanity, or any other serious crime or instigated or otherwise participated in such crimes;
(iii)   there are serious reasons for considering that the partner of the principal applicant is guilty of acts contrary to the purposes and principles of the United Nations or has committed, prepared or instigated such acts or encouraged or induced others to commit, prepare or instigate such acts; or
(iv)   there are serious reasons for considering that the partner of the principal applicant constitutes a danger to the community or to the security of the United Kingdom.

Note

Inserted by HC 628, para 122 and if an applicant has made an application for entry clearance or leave before 1 October 2013, the application will be decided in accordance with the Rules in force on 30 September 2013.

Curtailment of limited leave to enter the United Kingdom as the partner of a relevant Afghan citizen

276BN1. Limited leave to enter the United Kingdom as the partner of a relevant Afghan citizen and who has been granted leave in accordance with paragraph 276BJ1 may be curtailed where the person is a danger to the security or public order of the United Kingdom or leave may be curtailed where:

(i)   the partner of a relevant Afghan citizen has made false representations or failed to disclose any material fact for the purpose of obtaining leave to enter; and/or

(ii)   it is undesirable to permit the partner of a relevant Afghan citizen to remain in the United Kingdom in the light of his conduct, character or associations or the fact that he represents a threat to national security.

Limited leave to enter the United Kingdom as the minor dependant child of a relevant Afghan citizen or their partner

276BO1. Limited leave to enter the United Kingdom for a period not exceeding 5 years will be granted to the minor dependant child of a relevant Afghan citizen or their partner where:

(i)   the relationship requirements under paragraph 276BQ1 are met; and

(ii)   the application does not fall for refusal under paragraph 276BR1.

Definition of "minor dependant child" of a relevant Afghan citizen or their partner

276BP1. For the purposes of paragraphs 276BO1, 276BQ1, 276BR1 and 276BS1 a minor dependant child of a relevant Afghan citizen (the principal applicant) or their partner is a person who:

(i)   is the child of the principal applicant or the partner of the principal applicant who is also seeking leave to enter the United Kingdom on the same application; and who

(ii)   was under the age of 18 at 19 December 2012;

(iii)   is not married or in a civil partnership;

(iv)   has not formed an independent family unit; and

(v)   must not be leading an independent life.

Relationship requirements for a minor dependant child of a relevant Afghan citizen or their partner

276BQ1. The relationship requirements for a minor dependant child of a relevant Afghan citizen (the principal applicant) or their partner are that the person:

(i)   is the child of the principal applicant and the child's other parent is the principal applicant's partner; or

(ii)   is the child of the principal applicant; and

     (a)   the child's other parent is dead, or

     (b)   the principal applicant has sole responsibility for the child's upbringing; or

(iii)   is the child of the principal applicant's partner; and

     (a)   the child's other parent is dead, or

     (b)   the principal applicant's partner has sole responsibility for the child's upbringing; or

(iv)   is the adopted child of the principal applicant as defined at paragraph 309A or 309B of these Rules and where the requirements at paragraph 310(vi)-(xi) of these Rules are fulfilled; or

(v)   is the adopted child of the principal applicant's partner who is also seeking leave to enter the UK on the same application as defined at paragraph 309A or 309B of these Rules and where the requirements at paragraph 310(vi)-(xi) of these Rules are fulfilled.

Refusal of limited leave to enter the United Kingdom as the minor dependant child of a relevant Afghan citizen or their partner

276BR1. A minor dependant child of a relevant Afghan citizen (the principal applicant) or their partner will be refused leave to enter the United Kingdom if:

(i)   their application falls for refusal under the general grounds of refusal contained in Part 9 of these Rules;

(ii)   there are serious compelling reasons for considering that the minor dependant child of the principal applicant or their partner has committed a crime against peace, a war crime, a crime against humanity, or any other serious crime or instigated or otherwise participated in such crimes;

(iii)   there are serious reasons for considering that the minor dependant child of the principal applicant or their partner is guilty of acts contrary to the purposes and principles of the United Nations or has committed, prepared or instigated such acts or encouraged or induced others to commit, prepare or instigate such acts; or

(iv)   there are serious reasons for considering that the minor dependant child of the principal applicant or their partner constitutes a danger to the community or to the security of the United Kingdom.

Curtailment of limited leave to enter the United Kingdom as the minor dependant child of a relevant Afghan citizen or their partner

276BS1.   Limited leave to enter the United Kingdom as the minor dependant child of a relevant Afghan citizen or their partner and who has been granted leave in accordance with paragraph 276BO1 may be curtailed where the person is a danger to the security or public order of the United Kingdom or leave may be curtailed where:

(i)   the minor dependant child of a relevant Afghan citizen has made false representation or failed to disclose any material fact for the purpose of obtaining leave to enter; and/or

(ii)   it is undesirable to permit the minor dependant child of a relevant Afghan citizen to remain in the United Kingdom in the light of his conduct, character or associations or the fact that he represents a threat to national security.]

PART 8 — FAMILY MEMBERS

[Transitional provisions and interaction between Part 8[, Appendix FM and Appendix FM-SE]

A277.   From 9 July 2012 Appendix FM will apply to all applications to which Part 8 of these rules applied on or before 8 July 2012 except where the provisions of Part 8 are preserved and continue to apply, as set out in [paragraphs A280 to A280B].

Note

Amended by HC 693, para 79 as from 6 November 2014.

[**A277A.**   Where the Secretary of State is considering [an application for limited leave to remain or indefinite leave to remain] to which Part 8 of these rules continues to apply (excluding an application from a family member of a Relevant Points Based System Migrant), and where the applicant:

(a)   does not meet the requirements of Part 8 for indefinite leave to remain [(where the application is for indefinite leave to remain)], and

(b)   [meets or continues to meet the requirements for limited leave to remain under Part 8 in force at the date of decision,] further leave to remain under Part 8 may be granted of such a period and subject to such conditions as the Secretary of State deems appropriate.

[For the purposes of thus sub-paragraph an applicant last granted limited leave to enter under Part 8 will be considered as if they had last been granted limited leave to remain under Part 8.]

(c)   if the applicant does not meet the requirements of Part 8 for indefinite leave to remain as a bereaved partner [(where the application is for indefinite leave to remain as a bereaved partner)] only because paragraph 322(1C)(iii) or 322(1C)(iv) of these rules applies, the applicant will be granted limited leave to remain under Part 8 for a period not exceeding 30 months and subject to such conditions as the Secretary of State deems appropriate.]

Note

Amended by HC 693, para 80 as from 6 November 2014. Amended by HC 693, para 81 as from 6 November 2014. Amended by HC 693, para 81 as from 6 November 2014. Amended by HC 693, para 82 as from 6 November 2014. Amended by HC 693, para 83 as from 6 November 2014.

A277B. Where the Secretary of State is considering [an application for limited leave to remain or indefinite leave to remain] to which Part 8 of these rules continues to apply (excluding an application from a family member of a Relevant Points Based System Migrant) and where the application does not meet [the requirements for indefinite leave to remain (where the application is for indefinite leave to remain) or limited leave to remain under Part 8 in force at the date of decision:]

(a)   the application will also be considered under paragraphs R-LTRP.1.1.(a), (b) and (d), R-LTRPT.1.1.(a), (b) and (d) and EX.1. of Appendix FM (family life) and paragraphs 276ADE to 276DH (private life) of these rules;

(b)   if the applicant meets the requirements for leave under those paragraphs of Appendix FM or paragraphs 276ADE to 276DH (except the requirement for a valid application under that route), the applicant will be granted leave under those provisions; and

(c)   if the applicant is granted leave under those provisions, the period of the applicant's continuous leave under Part 8 at the date of application will be counted towards the period of continuous leave which must be completed before the applicant can apply for [indefinite leave to remain under paragraph 276B].

[(d)   Except sub-paragraph (c) does not apply to a person last granted leave as the family member of a Relevant Points Based System Migrant.

Note

Amended by HC 1138, para 54 shall apply to all applications decided on or after 6 April 2014. Amended by HC 693, para 84 as from 6 November 2014. Amended by HC 693, para 85 as from 6 November 2014. Amended by HC 693, para 86 as from 6 November 2014.

A277C. Subject to paragraphs A277 to [A280B][, paragraph 276A0] and paragraph GEN.1.9. of Appendix FM of these rules, where the Secretary of State [deems it appropriate, the Secretary of State will consider] any application to which the provisions of Appendix FM (family life) and paragraphs 276ADE to 276DH (private life) of these rules do not already apply [under paragraphs R-LTRP.1.1. (a), (b) and (d), R-LTRPT.1.1.(a), (b) and (d) and EX.1. of Appendix FM (family life) and [paragraph 276ADE(1)] (private life) of these rules. If the applicant meets the requirements for leave under those provisions (except the requirement for a valid application) the applicant will be granted leave under paragraph D-LTRP.1.2. or D-LTRPT.1.2 of Appendix FM or under [paragraph 276BE(1)] of these rules.]]

Note

Amended by HC 760, paras 226, 227 as from 13 December 2012. Paragraph A277C amended by HC 1039, para 93 as from 6 April 2013. Amended by HC 532, para 12 of this statement take effect on 28 July 2014 and apply to all applications to which paragraphs 276ADE to 276DH and Appendix FM apply (or can be applied by virtue of the Immigration Rules), and to any other ECHR Article 8 claims (save for those from foreign criminals), and which are decided on or after that date. Amended by HC 693, para 87 as from 6 November 2014. Amended by HC 693, para 88 as from 6 November 2014.

A278 The requirements to be met under Part 8 after 9 July 2012 may be modified or supplemented by the requirements in Appendix FM [and Appendix FM-SE].

A279. [Paragraphs 398-399D apply to all immigration decisions made further to applications under Part 8 and paragraphs 276A-276D where a decision is made on or after 28 July 2014, irrespective of the date the application was made.]

Note

Amended by HC 7860, para 228 as from 13 December 2012. Substituted by HC 532, para 13 of this statement takes effect on 28 July 2014.

A280. The following provisions of Part 8 apply in the manner and circumstances specified:

(a)   The following paragraphs apply in respect of all applications made under Part 8 [and Appendix FM], irrespective of the date of application or decision:

277–280
289AA
295AA
296

(b)   The following paragraphs of Part 8 continue to apply to all applications made on or after 9 July 2012. The paragraphs apply in their current form unless an additional requirement by reference to Appendix FM is specified:

Paragraph number	Additional requirement
295J	None
297 – 300	None
304-309	None
309[A] – 316F	[Where: (1) the applicant:] • falls under paragraph 314(i)(a); or • falls under paragraph 316A(i)(d) or (e); and • is applying on or after 9 July 2012[; and (2) the "other parent" mentioned in paragraph 314(i)(a), or one of the prospective parents mentioned in paragraph 316A(i)(d) or (e), has or is applying for entry clearance or limited leave to remain as a partner under Appendix FM, the application must also meet the requirements of paragraphs E-ECC 2.1-2.3 (entry clearance applications) or E-LTRC 2.1-2.3 (leave to remain applications) of Appendix FM, Where the applicant: • falls under paragraph 314(i)(d); • is applying on or after 9 July 2012; and • has two parents or prospective parents and one of the applicant's parents or prospective parents does not have right of abode, indefinite leave to enter or remain, is not present and settled in the UK or being admitted for settlement on the same occasion as the applicant is seeking admission[, but otherwise has or is applying for entry clearance or limited leave to remain as a partner under Appendix FM,] the application must also meet the requirements of paragraphs E-ECC 2.1-2.3 (entry clearance applications) or E-LTRC 2.1-2.3 (leave to remain applications) of Appendix FM.
319X	None

(c)   The following provisions of Part 8 continue to apply. . . on or after 9 July 2012, and are not subject to any additional requirement listed in (b) above:
 (i)   [to] persons who have made an application before 9 July 2012 under Part 8 which was not decided as at 9 July 2012; and
 (ii)   [to applications made] by persons [in the UK] who have been granted entry clearance or limited leave to enter or remain under Part 8 before

9 July 2012[and[, where this is a requirement of Part 8,] this leave to enter or limited leave to remain is extant]:

281-289
289A-289C
290-295
295A-295O
297-316F
317-319
319L-319U
319V-319Y

(d) [(i)] The following provisions of Part 8 continue to apply to applications made [in the period beginning with 9 July 2012 and ending on 30 November 2013, including those that have not been decided before 1 December 2013,] , and are not subject to any additional requirement listed in (b) above, by persons who have made an application for entry clearance, leave to enter or remain as the fiancé(e), proposed civil partner, spouse, civil partner, unmarried partner, same sex partner, or child or other dependant relative of a British citizen or settled person who is a full-time member of HM Forces:

281-289
289A-289C
290-295
295A-295O
297-316F
317-319

[(ii) Subject to the following provisions, from 1 December 2013, Appendix Armed Forces applies to all applications for entry clearance, leave to enter or remain as the fiance(e), proposed civil partner, spouse, civil partner, unmarried partner, same sex partner or child of a British citizen or settled person who is a full-time member of HM Forces.

[(iii) Except, from 1 December 2013, the provisions in paragraph A280(d)(i) continue to apply to persons who were granted entry clearance, limited leave to enter or remain under Part 8 before 1 December 2013, and where it is a requirement of Part 8, that leave is extant.]

(iv) Applications may continue to be made under paragraphs 297 to 316F of Part 8 by the child of a British citizen or settled person who is a full-time member of HM Forces regardless of the date of application and paragraph A280(b) continues to apply to these applications as appropriate.

(v) A new application by a dependent relative of a British citizen or settled person who is a full time member of HM Forces may no longer be made under paragraphs 317–319 on or after 1 December 2013. Those applications must meet the requirements of Appendix FM unless an application was submitted on or before 30 November 2013. An application made by a dependent relative of a British citizen or settled person who is a full time member of HM Forces on or after 30 November 2013 will be considered under the relevant paragraphs 317–319 which apply.

(vi) For the avoidance of doubt, paragraph A280(e) will continue to apply to the spouse, civil partner, unmarried partner or same sex partner of a British citizen or settled person who is a full-time member of HM Armed Forces who was admitted to the UK under paragraph 282(c) or 295(c) who has not yet applied for indefinite leave to remain, including where an application relying on paragraph 280(e) is made on or after 1 December 2013.

(vii) The requirements in paragraphs 8 and 9 of Appendix Armed Forces apply to applications for entry clearance, leave to enter or remain as the fiance(e), proposed civil partner, spouse, civil partner, unmarried partner, same sex partner, or child or other dependent relative of a British citizen or settled person who is a full-time member of HM Forces making an application under Part 8 (where paragraph A280(d) has permitted such an application) where the decision is made on or after 1 December 2013 (and irrespective of the date of the application).]

(e) The following provisions of Part 8 shall continue to apply to applications made on or after 9 July 2012, and are not subject to any additional requirement listed in (b) above, by a spouse, civil partner, unmarried partner or same sex partner who was admitted to the UK before 9 July 2012 further to paragraph 282(c) or 295B(c) of these Rules who has not yet applied for indefinite leave to remain:

284-286
287(a)(i)(c)
287(a)(ii)-(vii)
287(b)
288-289
289A-289C
295D-295F
295G(i)(c)
295G(ii)-(vii)
295H-295I]

[(f) Paragraphs 301–303F continue to apply to applications made under this route on or after 9 July 2012, and are not subject to any additional requirement listed in (b) above, by a child of a person to whom those paragraphs relate who has been granted limited leave to enter or remain or an extension of stay following an application made before 9 July 2012,

(g) For the avoidance of doubt, notwithstanding the introduction Appendix FM, paragraphs 319AA-319J of Part 8 continue to apply, and are not subject to any additional requirement listed in paragraph (b) above, to applications for entry clearance or leave to enter or remain as the spouse, civil partner, unmarried partner, same sex partner, or child of a Relevant Points Based System Migrant.]

Note

Paragraphs A277 to A280 inserted by HC 194, para 91 as from 9 July 2012. Paragraph A280 amended by HC 1039, paras 94, 95 as from 6 April 2013. Further amended by HC 803, paras 11,12 as from 1 December 2013. Sub-paragraph (d)(iii) substituted by HC 889, para 1. Further amended by HC 1138, para 55 shall apply to all applications decided on or after 6 April 2014.

[A280A. The sponsor of an applicant under Part 8 for limited or indefinite leave to remain as a spouse, civil partner, unmarried partner or same sex partner must be the same person as the sponsor of the applicant's last grant of leave in that category.

Note

Amended by HC 693, para 90 as from 6 November 2014.

[A280B. An applicant aged 18 or over may not rely on paragraph A280 where, since their last grant of limited leave to enter or remain under Part 8, they have been granted or refused leave under Appendix FM, Appendix Armed Forces or paragraph 276BE to CE of these rules, or been granted limited leave to enter or remain in a category outside their original route to settlement.]

Note

Inserted by HC 693, para 90 as from 6 November 2014.

[A281. In Part 8 "specified" means specified in Appendix FM-SE, unless otherwise stated, and "English language test provider approved by the Secretary of State" means a provider specified in Appendix O.]

Note

Paragraph A281 inserted by HC 565, para 85 as from 6 September 2012.

Guidance on the transitional provisions is at: www.ukba.homeoffice.gov.uk/sitecontent/document s/policyandlaw/IDIs/idischapter8/transition/transition.pdf?view=Binary

Guidance on the old family rules, and on issues unaffected by the July changes is at: www.ukba.h omeoffice.gov.uk/sitecontent/documents/policyandlaw/IDIs/idischapter8/

Guidance on the new rules (Appendix FM), including the remaining Part 8 categories, is at: www.ukba.homeoffice.gov.uk/sitecontent/documents/policyandlaw/IDIs/chp8-annex/

Spouses and civil partners

277. Nothing in these Rules shall be construed as permitting a person to be granted entry clearance, leave to enter, leave to remain or variation of leave as a spouse of another if [either the applicant] [or the sponsor will be aged under [18]] [. . .] on the date of arrival in the United Kingdom or (as the case may be) on the date on which the leave to remain or variation of leave would be granted. [In these rules the term "sponsor" includes "partner" as defined in GEN 1.2 of Appendix FM.]

Note

Figure "21" deleted and figure "18" substituted and words deleted by HC 1622, paras 1, 2 as from 28 November 2011. Final sentence inserted by HC 194, para 92 as from 9 July 2012.

As to the earlier requirement that an applicant must not be aged under 21, see *R (on the application of Aguilar Quila) v Secretary of State for the Home Department; R (on the application of Bibi) v same* [2011] UKSC 45, [2012] AC 621, [2012] 1 All ER 101. In considering applications involving marriage to British nationals, and where Secretary of State for the Home Department's rationale for having increased the age requirement to 21 related to attempts to deal with forced marriage, the rule, depending on the facts in an individual case, should be disapplied in the particular case, and there was no need for it to be struck down. As to the rationale for the policy, see the IDIs at Chapter 8, Section 1, Annex A2: www.ukba.homeoffice.gov.uk/sitecontent/docum ents/policyandlaw/IDIs/idischapter8/ section1/annexa2.pdf?view=Binary

278. [Nothing in these Rules shall be construed as allowing a person to be granted entry clearance, leave to enter, leave to remain or variation of leave as the spouse and civil partner of a man or woman (the sponsor) if:
(i)　　his or her marriage or civil partnership to the sponsor is polygamous; and
(ii)　　there is another person living who is the husband or wife of the sponsor and who:
　　(a)　　is, or at any time since his or her marriage or civil partnership to the sponsor has been, in the United Kingdom; or
　　(b)　　has been granted a certificate of entitlement in respect of the right of abode mentioned in Section 2(1)(a) of the Immigration Act 1988 or an entry clearance to enter the United Kingdom as the husband or wife of the sponsor.
For the purpose of this paragraph a marriage or civil partnership may be polygamous although at its inception neither party had any other spouse or civil partner.]

Note

In para 277 words in first square brackets substituted by HC 164; words in second square brackets substituted and inserted by HC 538. Paragraph 278 substituted by Cmnd 4851. Words '(or aged under 18 if either party is a serving member of HM Forces)' inserted by HC 439, para 47 as from 6 April 2010.

Note

See the IDIs at Chapter 8, Section 1, Annex C: www.bia.homeoffice.gov.uk/sitecontent/document s/policyandlaw/IDIs/idischapter8/section1/ annexc.pdf?view=Binary

279. [Paragraph 278 does not apply to any person who seeks entry clearance, leave to enter, leave to remain or variation of leave where:
(i)　　he or she has been in the United Kingdom before 1 August 1988 having been admitted for the purpose of settlement as the husband or wife of the sponsor; or

(ii)   he or she has, since their marriage or civil partnership to the sponsor, been in the United Kingdom at any time when there was no such other spouse or civil partner living as is mentioned in paragraph 278 (ii).

But where a person claims that paragraph 278 does not apply to them because they have been in the United Kingdom in circumstances which cause them to fall within sub-paragraphs (i) or (ii) of that paragraph, it shall be for them to prove that fact.]

Note

Paragraph 279 substituted by Cmnd 4851.

280. [For the purposes of paragraphs 278 and 279 the presence of any wife or husband in the United Kingdom in any of the following circumstances shall be disregarded:
(i)   as a visitor; or
(ii)   an illegal entrant; or
(iii) in circumstances whereby a person is deemed by Section 11(1) of the Immigration Act 1971 not to have entered the United Kingdom.]

Note

Paragraph 280 substituted by Cmnd 4851.

Spouses or civil partners of persons present and settled in the United Kingdom or being admitted on the same occasion for settlement

...

Requirements for leave to enter the United Kingdom with a view to settlement as the spouse or civil partner of a person present and settled in the United Kingdom or being admitted on the same occasion for settlement.

Note

See Appendix FM for applications not subject to the transitional provisions (ie for those making an application as a partner (including spouses, civil partners and unmarried partners) after 9 July 2012.

281. [The requirements to be met by a person seeking leave to enter the United Kingdom with a view to settlement as the spouse or civil partner of a person present and settled in the United Kingdom or who is on the same occasion being admitted for settlement are that:
[(i)(a)(i)the applicant is married to or the civil partner of a person present and settled in the United Kingdom or who is on the same occasion being admitted for settlement; and
[(ii)   the applicant provides an original English language test certificate in speaking and listening from an English language test provider approved by the Secretary of State for these purposes, which clearly shows the applicant's name and the qualification obtained (which must meet or exceed level A1 of the Common European Framework of Reference) unless:
      (a)   the applicant is aged 65 or over at the time he makes his application; or
      (b)   the [. . .] the applicant has a physical or mental condition that would prevent him from meeting the requirement; or
      (c)   [. . .] there are exceptional compassionate circumstances that would prevent the applicant from meeting the requirement; or
(iii) the applicant is a national of one of the following countries: Antigua and Barbuda; Australia; the Bahamas; Barbados; Belize; Canada; Dominica; Grenada; Guyana; Jamaica; New Zealand; St Kitts and Nevis: St Lucia; St Vincent and the Grenadines; Trinidad and Tobago; United States of America; or
(iv)   the applicant has obtained an academic qualification (not a professional or vocational qualification), which is deemed by UK NARIC to meet the recognised standard of a Bachelor's [or Masters] degree [or PhD] in the UK, from an educational establishment in one of the following countries: Antigua and Barbuda; Australia; The Bahamas; Barbados; Belize; Canada; Dominica; Gre-

nada; Guyana; Jamaica; New Zealand; St Kitts and Nevis: St Lucia; St Vincent and the Grenadines; Trinidad and Tobago; the UK; the USA; and provides the specified documents; or

(v)   the applicant has obtained an academic qualification (not a professional or vocational qualification) which is deemed by UK NARIC to meet the recognised standard of a Bachelor's [or Master's] degree [or PhD] in the UK, and
    (1)   provides the specified evidence to show he has the qualification, and
    (2)   UK NARIC has confirmed that the [qualification] was taught or researched in English, or

(vi)   the applicant has obtained an academic qualification (not a professional or vocational qualification) which is deemed by UK NARIC to meet the recognised standard of a Bachelor's [or Master's] degree [or PhD] in the UK, and provides the specified evidence to show:
    (1)   he has the qualification, and
    (2)   that the qualification was taught or researched in English] or

(b)(i)   the applicant is married to or the civil partner of a person who has a right of abode in the United Kingdom or indefinite leave to enter or remain in the United Kingdom and is on the same occasion seeking admission to the United Kingdom for the purposes of settlement and the parties were married or formed a civil partnership at least 4 years ago, since which time they have been living together outside the United Kingdom; and

[(b)(ii)the applicant has demonstrated sufficient knowledge of the English language and sufficient knowledge about life in the United Kingdom, in accordance with Appendix KoLL; and]

[(b)(iii). . .]

(ii)   the parties to the marriage or civil partnership have met; and

(iii)   each of the parties intends to live permanently with the other as his or her spouse or civil partner and the marriage or civil partnership is subsisting; and

(iv)   there will be adequate accommodation for the parties and any dependants without recourse to public funds in accommodation which they own or occupy exclusively; and

(v)   the parties will be able to maintain themselves and any dependants adequately without recourse to public funds; and

(vi)   the applicant holds a valid United Kingdom entry clearance for entry in this capacity [...]

[(vii)   the applicant does not fall for refusal under the general grounds for refusal.]

[For the purposes of this paragraph and paragraphs 282-289 a member of HM Forces serving overseas, or a permanent member of HM Diplomatic Service or a comparable UK-based staff member of the British Council on a tour of duty abroad, or a staff member of the Department for International Development who is a British Citizen or is settled in the United Kingdom, is to be regarded as present and settled in the United Kingdom.]

Note

As with all references in the rules to 'public funds' it will be essential to note here the dates of changes in the definition as contained in para 6: see note at para [304].

Substituted by HC 26, para 1 with effect from 5 June 1997. Words in first set of square brackets substituted by HC 538. Words in second set of square brackets substituted by Cmnd 5597. Further amended by Cm 7944, paras 6–8 as from 29 November 2010. Words in square brackets in (vi) and (vii) inserted by HC 863, para 97 as from 6 April 2011. Sub-para (i)(b)(iii) inserted by HC 908, para 15 to 18 as from 6 April 2011. Word in (vi) and para (vii) deleted by HC 908, paras 19 and 20 as from 6 April 2011. Words in (i)(a)(ii)(b)(c), (iv), (v) inserted, substituted and deleted by HC 1148, paras 14–19 as from 4 July 2011. Further amended by HC 760, paras 229, 230 as from 13 December 2012. Further amended by HC 628, para 125 and if an applicant has made an application for entry clearance or leave before 1 October 2013, the application will be decided in accordance with the Rules in force on 30 September 2013.

General note

For UKBA policy in relation to marriage and civil partnership, unmarried and same-sex partnerships, go to the index page (Chapter 8 of the IDIs) at www.bia.homeoffice.gov.uk/sitecont ent/documents/policyandlaw/IDIs/idischapter8/

On the validity of marriage, see Chapter 8, Section 1, Annex B: www.bia.homeoffice.gov.uk/sitec ontent/documents/policyandlaw/IDIs/idischapter8/section1/annexb.pdf?view=Binary

See also, *FI (Bangladesh – presumptions – marriage – legitimacy) Bangladesh* [2005] UKAIT 00016; *CB (Validity of marriage: proxy marriage) Brazil* [2008] UKAIT 00080.

On the language requirements in para 281(i)(a), and the exceptions to the general requirements in para 281(ii), see www.bia.homeoffice.gov.uk/sitecontent/documents/policyandlaw/IDIs/idischapte r8/section1/annexa3.pdf?view=Binary. On para 281(iii), see the IDI, Chapter 8, Section 1: www.ukba.homeoffice.gov.uk/sitecontent/documents/policyandlaw/IDIs/idischapter8/section1/sec tion1.pdf?view=Binary at para 2.2:

> ' "Intention to live permanently with the other" means an intention to live together, evidenced by a clear commitment from both parties that they will live together permanently in the United Kingdom immediately following the outcome of the application in question or as soon as circumstances permit thereafter, and "intends to live permanently with the other" shall be construed accordingly.'

See also *GA ('subsisting' marriage) Ghana* [2006] UKAIT 00046.

On para 281(iv) & (v):

In relation to the maintenance and accommodation requirements in para 281(iv), see the IDI at Chapter 8, Section 1 & 2, Annex F: www.bia.homeoffice.gov.uk/sitecontent/documents/policyand law/IDIs/idischapter8/section1/annexf.pdf?view=Binary

Maintenance and accommodation need to be available at the date of arrival, not the date of application (see the IDI). In examining the adequacy of maintenance and accommodation, what would be provided to a couple by income support is a relevant comparator: see, inter alia, *KA (adequacy of maintenance) Pakistan* [2006] UKAIT 00065; *Byron Lee French v Entry Clearance Officer (Kingston)* [2011] EWCA Civ 35, [2011] All ER (D) 232 (Jan).

Third party support and joint sponsorship in providing maintenance is permitted: see *Mahad (previously referred to as AM) (Ethiopia) v Entry Clearance Officer* [2009] UKSC 16, [2010] 2 All ER 535 with the viability of the arrangement to be determined on the evidence (eg by provision of a formal undertaking). As the Court commented in *Mahad*, the Supreme Court's approach to the maintenance provisions brings permissible sources of maintenance in to line with the position on accommodation, which it was accepted could be provided by a third party.

On the adequacy of accommodation, see the IDI at Section 6; see also *KJ ('Own or occupy exclusively') Jamaica* [2008] UKAIT 00006:

> 'The requirement in the Immigration Rules that a person "own or occupy exclusively" property does not carry any technical legal meaning of exclusive occupation. It is sufficient if there is a defined place where the person lives and which he has as his home, with the implication of stability that that implies.'

What constituted 'adequate' accommodation may involve a factual judgement: see *S (Pakistan)* [2004] UKIAT 00006. As to housing that cannot be taken in to account because of the prohibition on public funds in para 6 of the Immigration Rules, see *KA (Public funds: housing) Iraq* [2007] UKAIT 00081.

Leave to enter as the spouse or civil partner of a person present and settled in the United Kingdom or being admitted for settlement on the same occasion

282. A person seeking leave to enter the United Kingdom as the spouse or civil partner of a person present and settled in the United Kingdom or who is on the same occasion being admitted for settlement may:

(a)   in the case of a person [who meets the requirements of paragraph 281(i)(a)(i) and one of the requirements of paragraph 281(i)(a)(ii)-(vi)] be admitted for an initial period not exceeding [27 months], or

(b)   in the case of a person who meets [all] of the requirements in paragraph 281(i)(b), be granted indefinite leave to enter, or

(c)   in the case of a person who meets the requirement in paragraph 281(i)(b)(i), but not the requirement in paragraph 281(i)(b)(ii) to have sufficient knowledge of the English language and about life in the United Kingdom, be admitted for an initial period not exceeding [27 months], in all cases provided the Immigration Officer is satisfied that each of the relevant requirements of paragraph 281 is met.

Note

Words in square brackets inserted by HC 538. Word 'in' in final square brackets substituted by Cmnd 5949. Words in square brackets substituted by HC 971. Words in square brackets in sub-para (a) substituted by Cm 7944, para 9 as from 29 November 2010. Word in (b) substituted by HC 908, para 21 as from 6 April 2011.

Refusal of leave to enter as the spouse or civil partner of a person present and settled in the United Kingdom or being admitted on the same occasion for settlement

283. Leave to enter the United Kingdom as the spouse or civil partner of a person present and settled in the United Kingdom or who is on the same occasion being admitted for settlement is to be refused if the Immigration Officer is not satisfied that each of the requirements of paragraph 281 is met.

Requirements for an extension of stay as the spouse or civil partner of a person present and settled in the United Kingdom

Note

See Appendix FM for applications not subject to the transitional provisions (ie for those making an application for an extension of stay as a partner (including spouses, civil partners and unmarried partners) after 9 July 2012, unless previously granted leave in this category or as a fiancé or proposed civil partner on an application made before that date.

284. [The requirements for an extension of stay as the spouse or civil partner of a person present and settled in the United Kingdom are that:

(i) [the applicant has or was last granted limited leave to enter or remain in the United Kingdom which meets the following requirements:

    (a) The leave was given in accordance with any of the provisions of these Rules; and

    (b) The leave was granted for a period of 6 months or more, unless it was granted as a fiancé(e) or proposed civil partner; and

    (c) The leave was not as the spouse, civil partner, unmarried or same-sex partner of a Relevant Points Based System Migrant; and]

(ii) [the applicant] is married to or the civil partner of a person present and settled in the United Kingdom; and

(iii) the parties to the marriage or civil partnership have met; and

(iv) the applicant has not remained in breach of the immigration laws[, disregarding any period of overstaying for a period of 28 days or less]; and

(v) the marriage or civil partnership has not taken place after a decision has been made to deport the applicant or he has been recommended for deportation or been given notice under Section 6(2) of the Immigration Act 1971 [or been given directions for his removal under section 10 of the Immigration and Asylum Act 1999]; and

(vi) each of the parties intends to live permanently with the other as his or her spouse or civil partner and the marriage or civil partnership is subsisting; and

(vii) there will be adequate accommodation for the parties and any dependants without recourse to public funds in accommodation which they own or occupy exclusively; and

(viii) the parties will be able to maintain themselves and any dependants adequately without recourse to public funds;] [and

(ix)(a) the applicant provides an original English language test certificate in speaking and listening from an English test provider approved by the Secretary of State for these purposes, which clearly shows the applicant's name and qualification obtained (which must meet or exceed level A1 of the Common European Framework of Reference) unless:]

    (i) the applicant is aged 65 or over at the time he makes his application; or

    (ii) [. . .] the applicant has a physical or mental condition that would prevent him from meeting the requirement; or;

(iii)   [. . .] there are exceptional compassionate circumstances that would prevent the applicant from meeting the requirement; or]

(ix)(b) the applicant is a national of one of the following countries: Antigua and Barbuda; Australia; the Bahamas; Barbados; Belize; Canada; Dominica; Grenada; Guyana; Jamaica; New Zealand; St Kitts and Nevis: St Lucia; St Vincent and the Grenadines; Trinidad and Tobago; United States of America; or

(ix)(c) the applicant has obtained an academic qualification (not a professional or vocational qualification), which is deemed by UK NARIC to meet the recognised standard of a Bachelor's [or Master's] degree [or PhD] in the UK, from an educational establishment in one of the following countries: Antigua and Barbuda; Australia; The Bahamas; Barbados; Belize; Canada; Dominica; Grenada; Guyana; Ireland; Jamaica; New Zealand; St Kitts and Nevis: St Lucia; St Vincent and the Grenadines; Trinidad and Tobago; the UK; the USA; and provides the specified documents; or

(ix)(d) the applicant has obtained an academic qualification (not a professional or vocational qualification) which is deemed by UK NARIC to meet the recognised standard of a Bachelor's [or Master's] degree [or Phd] in the UK, and

  (1)   provides the specified evidence to show he has the qualification, and

  (2)   UK NARIC has confirmed that the [qualification] was taught or researched in English, or

(ix)(e) has obtained an academic qualification (not a professional or vocational qualification) which is deemed by the UK NARIC to meet the recognised standard of a Bachelor's [or Master's] degree [or PhD] in the UK, and provides the specified documents to show:

  (1)   he has the qualification, and

  (2)   that the qualification was taught or researched in English.]

Note

Substituted by HC 26, para 2 with effect from 5 June 1997. Sub-para (i) substituted by Cmnd 5949. Words in square brackets within sub-para (i) inserted by Cm 6339. Words in square brackets inserted by HC 971, para 2 as from 22 July 2008. Further amended by Cm 7944, paras 10–11 with effect from 29 November 2010. Words in (i) deleted by HC 863, para 98 as from 6 April 2011. Words in (ix) inserted, deleted and substituted by HC 1148, paras 20–25 as from 4 July 2011. Sub-paragraphs (i)(a), (b) substituted by HC 1511, para 14 as from 31 October 2011. Further amended by HC 1039, paras 96, 97 as from on or after 6 April 2013. Further amended by HC 244, paras 9,10 as from 1 July 2013. Further amended by HC 1138, para 56 as from 6 April 2014.

Extension of stay as the spouse or civil partner of a person present and settled in the United Kingdom

285.   An extension of stay as the spouse or civil partner of a person present and settled in the United Kingdom may be granted for a period of [2 years] in the first instance, provided the Secretary of State is satisfied that each of the requirements of paragraph 284 is met.

Note

Words in square brackets inserted by HC 538.

Refusal of extension of stay as the spouse or civil partner of a person present and settled in the United Kingdom

286.   An extension of stay as the spouse or civil partner of a person present and settled in the United Kingdom is to be refused if the Secretary of State is not satisfied that each of the requirements of paragraph 284 is met.

Requirements for indefinite leave to remain for the spouse or civil partner of a person present and settled in the United Kingdom

287.   [

(a)   The requirements for indefinite leave to remain for the spouse or civil partner of a person present and settled in the United Kingdom are that:

[(i)
- (a) the applicant was admitted to the United Kingdom for a period not exceeding 27 months or given an extension of stay for a period of 2 years in accordance with paragraphs 281 to 286 of these Rules and has completed a period of 2 years as the spouse or civil partner of a person present and settled in the United Kingdom; or]
- [(b) the applicant was admitted to the United Kingdom for a period not exceeding 27 months or given an extension of stay for a period of 2 years in accordance with paragraphs 295AA to 295F of these Rules and during that period married or formed a civil partnership with the person whom he or she was admitted or granted an extension of stay to join and has completed a period of 2 years as the unmarried or same-sex partner and then the spouse or civil partner of a person present and settled in the United Kingdom; or]
- (c) was admitted to the United Kingdom in accordance with leave granted under paragraph 282(c) of these rules; [[or]
- [(d) the applicant was admitted to the UK or given an extension of stay as the spouse or civil partner of a Relevant Points Based System Migrant; and then obtained an extension of stay under paragraphs 281 to 286 of these Rules and has completed a period of 2 years as the spouse or civil partner of the person who is now present and settled here; or]
- [(e) the applicant was admitted to the UK or given an extension of stay as the unmarried or same-sex partner of a Relevant Points Based System Migrant and during that period married or formed a civil partnership with the person whom he or she was admitted or granted an extension of stay to join and has completed a period of 2 years as the unmarried or same-sex partner and then the spouse or civil partner of the person who is now present and settled in the UK; or]
- (f) the applicant was admitted into the UK in accordance with paragraph 319L and has completed a period of 2 years limited leave as the spouse or civil partner of a refugee or beneficiary of humanitarian protection who is now present and settled in the UK or as the spouse or civil partner of a former refugee or beneficiary of humanitarian protection who is now a British Citizen.]
- (ii) the applicant is still the spouse or civil partner of the person he or she was admitted or granted an extension of stay to join and the marriage or civil partnership is subsisting; and
- (iii) each of the parties intends to live permanently with the other as his or her spouse or civil partner; and
- (iv) there will be adequate accommodation for the parties and any dependants without recourse to public funds in accommodation which they own or occupy exclusively; and
- (v) the parties will be able to maintain themselves and any dependants adequately without recourse to public funds; and
- [(vi) the applicant has demonstrated sufficient knowledge of the English language and sufficient knowledge about life in the United Kingdom, in accordance with Appendix KoLL; and]
- (vii) the applicant does not [fall for refusal under the general grounds for refusal.]

(b) The requirements for indefinite leave to remain for the bereaved spouse or civil partner of a person who was present and settled in the United Kingdom are that:
[(i)
- (a) the applicant was admitted to the United Kingdom for a period not exceeding 27 months or given an extension of stay for a period of 2 years as the spouse or civil partner of a person present and settled in the United Kingdom in accordance with paragraphs 281 to 286 of these Rules; or]
- [(b) the applicant was admitted to the United Kingdom for a period not exceeding 27 months or given an extension of stay for a period of 2 years as the unmarried partner of a person present and settled in

938

the United Kingdom in accordance with paragraphs 295AA to 295F of these Rules and during that period married or formed a civil partnership with the person whom he or she was admitted or granted an extension of stay to join; and]]

(ii) the person whom the applicant was admitted or granted an extension of stay to join died during that period; and

(iii) the applicant was still the spouse or civil partner of the person he or she was admitted or granted an extension of stay to join at the time of the death; and

(iv) each of the parties intended to live permanently with the other as his or her spouse or civil partner and the marriage or civil partnership was subsisting at the time of the death.]
[; and

(v) the applicant does not [fall for refusal under the general grounds for refusal].]

Note

Paragraph 287 substituted by Cmnd 4851. Words in square brackets substituted by HC 538. Sub-para (a)(i)(a), (b) substituted by Cm 6339. Sub-para (b)(i)(a), (b) substituted by Cm 6339, para 15 as from 1 October 2004. Sub-paragraphs (a)(i)(d), (e) inserted by HC 321. Words in (a)(i)(c)–(e) substituted and inserted by HC 863, paras 99–103 as from 6 April 2011. Word in (a)(vi) and sub-para (a)(vii) inserted by HC 908, para 22 as from 6 April 2011. Word in (b)(iv) and sub-para (b)(v) inserted by HC 908, para 23 as from 6 April 2011. Further amended by HC 760, paras 231, 232 as from 13 December 2012. Further amended by HC 1039, paras 98, 99: where an applicant has made an application for entry clearance or leave before 6 April 2013 and the application has not been decided before that date, it will be decided in accordance with the rules in force on 5 April 2013. Further amended by HC 628, para 126 and if an applicant has made an application for entry clearance or leave before 1 October 2013, the application will be decided in accordance with the Rules in force on 30 September 2013. Further amended by HC 693, para 91 as from 6 November 2014.

Indefinite leave to remain for the spouse of a person present and settled in the United Kingdom

288. Indefinite leave to remain for the spouse of a person present and settled in the United Kingdom may be granted provided the Secretary of State is satisfied that each of the requirements of paragraph 287 is met.

Refusal of indefinite leave to remain for the spouse of a person present and settled in the United Kingdom

289. Indefinite leave to remain for the spouse or civil partner of a person present and settled in the United Kingdom is to be refused if the Secretary of State is not satisfied that each of the requirements of paragraph 287 is met.

General note on paras 284-9

See note on para 281.

Victims of domestic violence

[Requirements for indefinite leave to remain in the United Kingdom as the victim of domestic violence

Note

See Appendix FM for the domestic violence rules for those who first applied for leave as a partner after 9 July 2012 and for those without extant leave (see para A280 for transitional provisions).

289A. The requirements to be met by a person who is the victim of domestic violence and who is seeking indefinite leave to remain in the United Kingdom are that the applicant:
[(i)

(a)   the applicant was last admitted to the UK for a period not exceeding 27 months in accordance with sub-paragraph 282(a), 282(c), 295B(a) or 295B(c) of these Rules; or

(b)   the applicant was last granted leave to remain as the spouse or civil partner or unmarried partner or same-sex partner of a person present and settled in the UK in accordance with paragraph 285 or 295E of these Rules, except where that leave extends leave originally granted to the applicant as the partner of a Relevant Points Based System Migrant; or

(c)   the applicant was last granted leave to enable access to public funds pending an application under paragraph 289A and the preceding grant of leave was given in accordance with paragraph 282(a), 282(c), 285, 295B(a), 295B(c) or 295E of these Rules, except where that leave extends leave originally granted to the applicant as the partner of a Relevant Points Based System Migrant; and

(ii)   the relationship with their spouse or civil partner or unmarried partner or same-sex partner, as appropriate, was subsisting at the beginning of the last period of leave granted in accordance with paragraph 282(a), 282(c), 285, 295B(a), 295B(c) or 295E of these Rules; and]

[(iii)] is able to produce [evidence] to establish that the relationship was caused to permanently break down before the end of that period as a result of domestic violence.]
[; and ...]

Note

Inserted by HC 104. Words in brackets in (i) and (ii) substituted by HC 538. Sub-paragraphs (i) and (ii) substituted by HC 971, para 4 as from 22 July 2008. Word in (iv) and sub-para (v) inserted by HC 908, para 24 as from 21 April 2011. Word "evidence" substituted in sub-para (iv) by HC 565, para 86 as from 6 September 2012. Further amended by HC 760, para 233 as from 13 December 2012. Amended by HC 693, para 92 as from 6 November 2014. Sub-paragraph (iv) renumbered as sub-paragraph (iii) by HC 693, para 92 as from 6 November 2014. Deleted by HC 693, para 92 as from 6 November 2014.

[Indefinite leave to remain as the victim of domestic violence

289B. Indefinite leave to remain as the victim of domestic violence may be granted provided the Secretary of State is satisfied that each of the requirements of paragraph 289A is met.]

Note

Inserted by HC 538.

[Refusal of indefinite leave to remain as the victim of domestic violence

289C. Indefinite leave to remain as the victim of domestic violence is to be refused if the Secretary of State is not satisfied that each of the requirements of paragraph 289A is met.]

Note

Inserted by HC 538.

General note on paras 289A–C

See the Modernised Guidance at: www.ukba.homeoffice.gov.uk/sitecontent/documents/policyandl aw/modernised/family/section4.pdf?view=Binary

The definition of domestic violence applied by UKBA is 'any incident of threatening behaviour, violence or abuse (psychological, physical, sexual, financial or emotional) between adults who are or have been intimate partners or family members, regardless of gender or sexuality' (see the IDI at para 1.3])); see also Sections 2-3 for the requirements for evidence (para 289A(iv)). Revised guidance in the IDIs follows the judgment in *Ishtiaq v Secretary of State for the Home Department* [2007] EWCA Civ 386, containing powerful statements as to the overarching purpose of the rule, and the need to interpret evidence submitted in support in an application in that context (per Dyson LJ:

'... In my judgment para 289A(iv) should be construed so as to further the policy of enabling persons whose relationships had permanently broken down as a result of domestic violence before the end of the probationary period to be granted indefinite leave to remain. A construction which precludes an applicant, whose relationship has in fact broken down as a result of domestic violence, from proving her case by producing cogent relative evidence would defeat the evident purpose of the Rule'; 'Spouses and partners who are the victims of domestic violence should not feel constrained to remain in an abusive relationship for two years solely in order to qualify for indefinite leave to remain').

As to the requirement that the relationship broke down because of domestic violence (para 289A(iv), see *LA (para 289A: causes of breakdown) Pakistan* [2009] UKAIT 00019), there is a need to look at the evidence and the history of the relationship as a whole; see also *R (on the application of B) v Secretary of State for the Home Department* [2002] EWCA Civ 1797, as the approach on causation, where domestic violence was 'a significant contributory factor to what happened' in the breakdown of the relationship.

An application on this basis should be made on the proscribed form, but may be made when an applicant has no extant leave: see *JL (Domestic violence: evidence and procedure) India* [2006] UKAIT 00058 (in part, and on other grounds, disapproved in *Ishtiaq v Secretary of State for the Home Department* [2007] EWCA Civ 386).

For confirmation that the domestic violence rule applies only to those granted leave under the spouse, civil partner and unmarried partner rules, see *Guzman-Barrios (domestic violence DLR - Article 14 ECHR) Colombia* [2011] UKUT 352 (IAC), though domestic violence.

[289D. If the applicant does not meet the requirements for indefinite leave to remain as a victim of domestic violence only because paragraph 322(1C)(iii) or 322(1C)(iv) applies, they may be granted further limited leave to remain for a period not exceeding 30 months and subject to such conditions as the Secretary of State deems appropriate.]

Note

Inserted by HC 760, para 234 as from 13 December 2012.

Fiancé(e)s and proposed civil partners

Fiancé(e)s and proposed civil partners

Note

See Appendix FM for applications made after 9 July 2012, unless previously granted leave in this category.

289AA. [Nothing in these Rules shall be construed as permitting a person to be granted entry clearance, leave to enter or variation of leave as a fiancé(e) or proposed civil partner if [either the applicant] or the sponsor will aged under [18] [. . .] on the date of arrival of the applicant in the United Kingdom or (as the case may be) on the date on which the leave to enter or variation of leave would be granted.]

Note

Para 289AA inserted by HC 538. Words in square brackets substituted by HC 164. Word "21" substituted by HC 1113. Words "(or aged under 18 if either party is a serving member of HM Forces)" inserted by HC 439, para 48 as from 6 April 2010. Figure "21" deleted and figure "18" substituted and words "(or aged under 18 if either party is a serving member of HM Forces)" deleted by HC 1622, paras 3, 4 as from 28 November 2011.

As to the rationale for the policy, see the IDIS at Chapter 8, Section 1, Annex A2: www.bia.home office.gov.uk/sitecontent/documents/policyandlaw/IDIs/idischapter8/section1/ annexa2.pdf?view=Binary

Requirements for leave to enter the United Kingdom as a fiancé(e) or proposed civil partner (i.e. with a view to marriage or civil partnership and permanent settlement in the United Kingdom)

290. [The requirements to be met by a person seeking leave to enter the United Kingdom as a fiancé(e) or proposed civil partner are that:

(i)   the applicant is seeking leave to enter the United Kingdom for marriage or civil partnership to a person present and settled in the United Kingdom or who is on the same occasion being admitted for settlement; and

(ii)   the parties to the proposed marriage or civil partnership have met; and

(iii)   each of the parties intends to live permanently with the other as his or her spouse or civil partner after the marriage or civil partnership; and

(iv)   adequate maintenance and accommodation without recourse to public funds will be available for the applicant until the date of the marriage or civil partnership; and

(v)   there will, after the marriage or civil partnership, be adequate accommodation for the parties and any dependants without recourse to public funds in accommodation which they own or occupy exclusively; and

(vi)   the parties will be able after the marriage or civil partnership to maintain themselves and any dependants adequately without recourse to public funds; and

[(vii)(a)the applicant provides an original language test certificate in speaking and listening from an English language test provider approved by the Secretary of State for these purposes, which clearly shows the applicant's name and qualification obtained (which must meet or exceed level A1 of the Common European Framework of Reference unless:

    (i)   the applicant is aged 65 or over at the time he makes his application; or

    (ii)   [. . .] that the applicant has a physical or mental condition that would prevent him from meeting the requirement; or;

    (iii)   [. . .] there are exceptional circumstances that would prevent the applicant from meeting the requirement; or

(vii)(b)the applicant is a national of one of the following countries: Antigua and Barbuda; Australia; the Bahamas; Barbados; Belize; Canada; Dominica; Grenada; Guyana; Jamaica; New Zealand; St Kitts and Nevis: St Lucia; St Vincent and the Grenadines; Trinidad and Tobago; United States of America; or

(vii)(c)the applicant has obtained an academic qualification (not a professional or vocational qualification), which is deemed by UK NARIC to meet the recognised standard of a Bachelor's [or Master's] degree [or PhD] in the UK, from an educational establishments in one of the following countries: Antigua and Barbuda; Australia; the Bahamas; Barbados; Belize; Dominica; Grenada; Guyana; Ireland; Jamaica; New Zealand; St Kitts and Nevis: St Lucia; St Vincent and the Grenadines; Trinidad and Tobago; the UK; the USA; or

(vii)(d)the applicant has obtained an academic qualification (not a professional or vocational qualification), which is deemed by UK NARIC to meet the recognised standard of a Bachelor's [or Master's] degree [or PhD] in the UK, and

    (1)   provides the specified evidence to show he has the qualification, and

    (2)   UK NARIC has confirmed that the [qualification] was taught or researched in English, or

(vii)(e)has obtained an academic qualification (not a professional or vocational qualification), which is deemed by UK NARIC to meet the recognised standard of a Bachelor's [or Master's] degree [or PhD] in the UK, and provides the specified evidence to show:

    (1)   he has the qualification, and

    (2)   that the qualification was taught or researched in English

(viii)   the applicant holds a valid United Kingdom entry clearance for entry in this capacity.]

Note

Substituted by HC 26, para 3 with effect from 5 June 1997. Further amended by Cm 7944, paras 12,13 with effect from 29 November 2010. words in sub-paragraph (vii) inserted, deleted and substituted by HC 1148, paras 26–31 as from 4 July 2011.

290A. [. . .]

Note

Para 290A inserted by Cmnd 5597. Further amended by HC 1138, para 57 as from 6 April 2014.

Leave to enter as a fiancé(e) or proposed civil partner

291. A person seeking leave to enter the United Kingdom as a fiancé(e) or proposed civil partner may be admitted, with a prohibition on employment, for a period not exceeding 6 months to enable the marriage or civil partnership to take place provided a valid United Kingdom entry clearance for entry in this capacity is produced to the Immigration Officer on arrival.

Refusal of leave to enter as a fiancé(e) or civil partner

292. Leave to enter the United Kingdom as a fiancé(e) or civil partner is to be refused if a valid United Kingdom entry clearance for entry in this capacity is not produced to the Immigration Officer on arrival.

Requirements for an extension of stay as a fiancé(e) or civil partner

293. The requirements for an extension of stay as a fiancé(e) or civil partner are that:
(i)   the applicant was admitted to the United Kingdom with a valid United Kingdom entry clearance as a fiancé(e) or proposed civil partner; and
(ii)   good cause is shown why the marriage or civil partnership did not take place within the initial period of leave granted under paragraph 291; and
(iii)   there is satisfactory evidence that the marriage or civil partnership will take place at an early date; and
(iv)   the requirements of paragraph [290(ii)–(vii)] are met.]

Note

Sub-para (iv) substituted by HC 26, para 4 with effect from 5 June 1997. Words in sub-para (iv) substituted by Cm 7944, para 14 with effect from 29 November 2010.

Extension of stay as a fiancé(e) or proposed civil partner

294. An extension of stay as a fiancé(e) or proposed civil partner may be granted for an appropriate period with a prohibition on employment to enable the marriage or civil partnership to take place provided the Secretary of State is satisfied that each of the requirements of paragraph 293 is met.

Refusal of extension of stay as a fiancé(e) or proposed civil partner

295. An extension of stay is to be refused if the Secretary of State is not satisfied that each of the requirements of paragraph 293 is met.

Note

See Modernised Guidance at: www.ukba.homeoffice.gov.uk/sitecontent/documents/policyandlaw/modernised/family/fiance-civilpartners.pdf?view=Binary

Note

[Paras 290–295 replace HC 251, paras 2–4, 50–51, 131–132, 47 and 130.]

The effect of the rules on family members is outlined at **IV[1]**.

See also European decisions.

Unmarried and same sex partners

[Leave to enter as the unmarried or same-sex partner of a person present and settled in the United Kingdom or being admitted on the same occasion for settlement

Note

See Appendix FM for applications not subject to the transitional provisions (ie for those making an application as a partner (including unmarried partners) after 9 July 2012.

295AA. [Nothing in these Rules shall be construed as permitting a person to be granted entry clearance, leave to enter or variation of leave as an unmarried or same-sex partner if [either the applicant] or the sponsor will aged under [21] [(or aged under 18 if either party is a serving member of HM Forces)] on the date of arrival of the applicant in the United Kingdom or (as the case may be) on the date on which the leave to enter or variation of leave would be granted.]

Note

Para 295AA inserted by HC 538. Words in square brackets substituted by HC 164. Figure '21' substituted by HC 1113. Words inserted by HC 439, para 49 with effect from 6 April 2010. Figure "21" deleted and figure "18" substituted and words "(or aged under 18 if either party is a serving member of HM Forces)" deleted by HC 1622, paras 5, 6 as from 28 November 2011.

Requirements for leave to enter the United Kingdom with a view to settlement as the unmarried or same-sex partner of a person present and settled in the United Kingdom or being admitted on the same occasion for settlement

295A. The requirements to be met by a person seeking leave to enter the United Kingdom with a view to settlement as the unmarried or same-sex partner of a person present and settled in the United Kingdom or being admitted on the same occasion for settlement, are that:

    (a)[(i)]the applicant is the unmarried or same-sex partner of a person present and settled in the United Kingdom or who is on the same occasion being admitted for settlement and the parties have been living together in a relationship akin to marriage or civil partnership which has subsisted for two years or more; or

    [(ii) the applicant provides an original English language certificate in speaking and listening from an English language test provider approved by the Secretary of State for these purposes, which clearly shows the applicant's name and qualification obtained (which must meet or exceed level A1 of the Common European Framework of Reference) unless:

        (a)   the applicant is aged 65 or over at the time he makes his application; or

        (b)   [. . .] the applicant has a physical or mental condition that would prevent him from meeting the requirement; or;

        (c)   [. . .] there are exceptional compassionate circumstances that would prevent the applicant from meeting the requirement; or

    (iii) the applicant is a national of one of the following countries: Antigua and Barbuda; Australia; the Bahamas; Barbados; Belize; Canada; Dominica; Grenada; Guyana; Jamaica; New Zealand; St Kitts and Nevis; St Lucia: St Vincent and the Grenadines; Trinidad and Tobago; United States of America; or

    (iv) the applicant has obtained an academic qualification (not a professional or vocational qualification), which is deemed by UK NARIC to meet the recognised standard of a Bachelor's [or Master's] degree [or PhD] in the UK, from an educational establishment in one of the following countries: Antigua and Barbuda; Australia; The Bahamas; Barbados; Belize; Dominica; Grenada; Guyana; Ireland; Jamaica; New Zealand; St Kitts and Nevis; St Lucia; St Vincent and the Grenadines; Trinidad and Tobago; the UK; the USA; and provides the specified documents; or

    (v) the applicant has obtained an academic qualification (not a professional or vocational qualification) which is deemed by UK NARIC to meet the recognised standard of a Bachelor's [or Master's] degree [or PhD] in the UK, and

        (1)   provides the specified evidence to show he has the qualification, and

        (2)   UK NARIC has confirmed that the [qualification] was taught or researched in English, or

    (vi) has obtained an academic qualification (not a professional or vocational qualification) which is deemed by UK NARIC to meet the recognised standard of a Bachelor's [or Master's] degree [or PhD] in the UK, and provides the specified evidence to show:

        (1)   he has the qualification, and

        (2)   that the degree was taught or researched in English, or]

(b)(i) the applicant is the unmarried or same-sex partner of a person who has a right of abode in the United Kingdom or indefinite leave to enter or remain in the United Kingdom and is on the same occasion seeking admission to the United Kingdom for the purposes of settlement and the parties have been living together outside the United Kingdom in a relationship akin to marriage or civil partnership which has subsisted for 4 years or more; and

[(b)(ii)the applicant has demonstrated sufficient knowledge of the English language and sufficient knowledge about life in the United Kingdom, in accordance with Appendix KoLL; and]

[(b)(iii). . .]

(ii) any previous marriage or civil partnership (or similar relationship) by either partner has permanently broken down; and

[(iii) the parties are not involved in a consanguineous relationship with one another; and]

(iv) . . .

(v) there will be adequate accommodation for the parties and any dependants without recourse to public funds in accommodation which they own or occupy exclusively; and

(vi) the parties will be able to maintain themselves and any dependants adequately without recourse to public funds; and

(vii) the parties intend to live together permanently; and

(viii) the applicant holds a valid United Kingdom entry clearance for entry in this capacity [...][; and

[(ix) the applicant does not fall for refusal under the general grounds for refusal.]

[For the purposes of this paragraph and paragraphs 295B–295I, a member of HM Forces serving overseas, or a permanent member of HM Diplomatic Service or a comparable UK-based staff member of the British Council on a tour of duty abroad, or a staff member of the Department for International Development who is a British Citizen or is settled in the United Kingdom, is to be regarded as present and settled in the United Kingdom.]

Note

Sub-para (i)(a) and (b) substituted and sub-para (iv) deleted by HC 538. Sub-para (iii) inserted by Cmnd 5949. Final paragraph inserted by Cm 5597. Further amended by Cm 7944, paras 15–17 with effect from 29 November 2010. Words in (viii) and (ix) inserted by HC 863, para 104 as from 6 April 2011. Sub-para (b)(iii) inserted by HC 908, para 25 as from 6 April 2011. Word in (viii) and para (ix) deleted by HC 908, paras 26 and 27 as from 6 April 2011. Words in square brackets inserted, deleted and substituted by HC 1148, paras 32–37 as from 4 July 2011. Further amended by HC 760, paras 235, 236 as from 13 December 2012. Further amended by HC 628, para 127 and if an applicant has made an application for entry clearance or leave before 1 October 2013, the application will be decided in accordance with the Rules in force on 30 September 2013.

General note

See General note on para 281.

On para 295(a)(i), as a matter of construction, it is suggested that the two year period refers to the length of the relationship rather than the period of cohabitation.

Leave to enter the United Kingdom with a view to settlement as the unmarried or same-sex partner of a person present and settled in the United Kingdom or being admitted on the same occasion for settlement

295B. A person seeking leave to enter the United Kingdom as the unmarried or same-sex partner of a person present and settled in the United Kingdom or who is on the same occasion being admitted for settlement may:

(a) in the case of a person [who meets the requirements of paragraph 295A(i)(a)(i), and one of the requirements of paragraph 295A(i)(a)(ii)-(vi)] be admitted for an initial period not exceeding [27 months], or

(b) in the case of a person who meets [all] of the requirements in paragraph 295A(i)(b), be granted indefinite leave to enter, or

(c)   in the case of a person who meets the requirement in paragraph 295A(i)(b)(i), but not the requirement in paragraph 295A(i)(b)(ii) to have sufficient knowledge of the English language and about life in the United Kingdom, be admitted for an initial period not exceeding [27 months], in all cases provided the Immigration Officer is satisfied that each of the relevant requirements of paragraph 295A is met.

Note

Words in square brackets inserted and substituted by HC 538. Word 'in' in last square brackets substituted by Cmnd 5949. Words '27 months' in sub-paras (a) and (c) substituted by HC 971. Words in sub-para (a) substituted by Cm 7944, para 18 with effect from 29 November 2010. Word in (b) substituted by HC 908, para 28 as from 6 April 2011.

Refusal of leave to enter the United Kingdom with a view to settlement as the unmarried or same-sex partner of a person present and settled in the United Kingdom or being admitted on the same occasion for settlement

295C.   Leave to enter the United Kingdom with a view to settlement as the unmarried or same-sex partner of a person present and settled in the United Kingdom or being admitted on the same occasion for settlement, is to be refused if the Immigration Officer is not satisfied that each of the requirements of paragraph 295A is met.

Leave to remain as the unmarried or same-sex partner of a person present and settled in the United Kingdom

Requirements for leave to remain as the unmarried or same-sex partner of a person present and settled in the United Kingdom

Note

See Appendix FM for applications not subject to the transitional provisions (ie for those making an application for an extension of stay as a partner (including unmarried partners) after 9 July 2012, unless previously granted leave in this category on an application made before that date.

295D.   The requirements to be met by a person seeking leave to remain as the unmarried or same-sex partner of a person present and settled in the United Kingdom are that:

(i)   [the applicant has or was last granted limited leave to enter or remain in the United Kingdom which was given in accordance with any of the provisions of these Rules, unless:

    (a)   as a result of that leave he would not have been in the United Kingdom beyond 6 months from the date on which he was admitted to the United Kingdom; or

    (b)   the leave was granted as the unmarried or same-sex partner of a Relevant Points Based System Migrant; and]

(ii)   any previous marriage or civil partnership (or similar relationship) by either partner has permanently broken down; and

(iii)   the applicant is the unmarried or same-sex partner of a person who is present and settled in the United Kingdom; and

(iv)   the applicant has not remained in breach of the immigration laws[, disregarding any period of overstaying for a period of 28 days or less]; and

[(v)   the parties are not involved in a consanguineous relationship with one another; and]

(vi)   the parties have been living together in a relationship akin to marriage or civil partnership which has subsisted for two years or more; and

(vii)   the parties' relationship pre-dates any decision to deport the applicant, recommend him for deportation, give him notice under Section 6(2) of the Immigration Act 1971, or give directions for his removal under section 10 of the Immigration and Asylum Act 1999; and

(viii)   there will be adequate accommodation for the parties and any dependants without recourse to public funds in accommodation which they own or occupy exclusively; and

(ix)   the parties will be able to maintain themselves and any dependants adequately without recourse to public funds; and

(x)   the parties intend to live together permanently; and

(xi)(a)the applicant provides an original English language test certificate in speaking and listening from an English language test provider approved by the Secretary of State for these purposes, which clearly shows the applicant's name and the qualification obtained (which must meet or exceed level A1 of the Common European Framework of reference) unless

(i)   the applicant is aged 65 or over at the time he makes his application; or

(ii)   [. . .] the applicant has a physical or mental condition that would prevent him from meeting the requirement; or;

(iii)   [. . .] there are exceptional compassionate circumstances that would prevent the applicant from meeting the requirement;

(xi)(b)the applicant is a national of one of the following countries: Antigua and Barbuda; Australia; the Bahamas; Barbados; Belize; Canada; Dominica; Grenada; Guyana; Jamaica; New Zealand; St Kitts and Nevis;St Lucia: St Vincent and the Grenadines; Trinidad and Tobago; United States of America;

(xi)(c)the applicant has obtained an academic qualification (not a professional or vocational qualification), which is deemed by UK NARIC to meet the recognised standard of a Bachelor's [or Master's] degree [or PhD] in the UK, from an educational establishment in one of the following countries: Antigua and Barbuda; Australia; The Bahamas; Barbados; Belize; Dominica; Grenada; Guyana; Ireland; Jamaica; New Zealand; St Kitts and Nevis; St Lucia: St Vincent and the Grenadines; Trinidad and Tobago; the UK; the USA; and provides the specified documents; or

(xi)(d)the applicant has obtained an academic qualification (not a professional or vocational qualification) which is deemed by UK NARIC to meet the recognised standard of a Bachelor's [or Masters's] degree [or PhD] in the UK, and

(1)   provides the specified evidence to show he has the qualification, and

(2)   UK NARIC has confirmed that the [qualification] was taught or researched in English, or

(xi)(e)has obtained an academic qualification (not a professional or vocational qualification) which is deemed by UK NARIC to meet the recognised standard of a Bachelor's [or Master's] degree [or PhD] in the UK, and provides the specified evidence to show:

(1)   he has the qualification, and

(2)   that the degree was taught or researched in English.]

Note

Sub-para (v) inserted by Cmnd 5949, para 9 as from 25 August 2003. Words in square brackets in sub-para (i) inserted by Cm 6339. Further amended by Cm 7944, paras 19–20 with effect from 29 November 2010. Further amended by HC 148, paras 38–43 as from 4 July 2011. Further amended by HC 1511, para 16 as from 31 October 2011. Words ", disregarding any period of overstaying for a period of 28 days or less" inserted by HC 1039, para 101 as from on or after 6 April 2013. Further amended by HC 1039, para 100: where an applicant has made an application for entry clearance or leave before 6 April 2013 and the application has not been decided before that date, it will be decided in accordance with the rules in force on 5 April 2013. Further amended by HC 244, para 11 as from 1 July 2013. Further amended by HC 1138, para 58 as from 6 April 2014.

General note

See General note on para 281. On para 295D(vi), as a matter of construction, it is suggested that the two year period refers to the length of the relationship rather than the period of cohabitation.

Leave to remain as the unmarried or same-sex partner of a person present and settled in the United Kingdom

295E.   Leave to remain as the unmarried or same-sex partner of a person present and settled in the United Kingdom may be granted for a period of 2 years in the first instance provided that the Secretary of State is satisfied that each of the requirements of paragraph 295D are met.

947

Refusal of leave to remain as the unmarried or same-sex partner of a person present and settled in the United Kingdom

295F. Leave to remain as the unmarried or same-sex partner of a person present and settled in the United Kingdom is to be refused if the Secretary of State is not satisfied that each of the requirements of paragraph 295D is met.

Indefinite leave to remain as the unmarried or same-sex partner of a person present and settled in the United Kingdom

Requirements for indefinite leave to remain as the unmarried or same-sex partner of a person present and settled in the United Kingdom

295G. The requirements to be met by a person seeking indefinite leave to remain as the unmarried or same-sex partner of a person present and settled in the United Kingdom are that:

(a) the applicant was admitted to the United Kingdom [for a period not exceeding 27 months] or given an extension of stay for a period of 2 years in accordance with paragraphs 295AA to 295F of these Rules and has completed a period of 2 years as the unmarried or same-sex partner of a person present and settled here; or

[(b) the applicant was admitted to the UK or given an extension of stay as the unmarried or same-sex partner of a Relevant Points Based System Migrant; and then obtained an extension of stay under paragraphs 295AA to 295F of these Rules; and has completed a period of 2 years as the unmarried or same-sex partners of the person who is now present and settled here; or]

(c) the applicant was admitted to the United Kingdom in accordance with leave granted under paragraph 295B(c) of these Rules[; or

(d) the applicant was admitted into the UK in accordance with paragraph 319O and has completed a period of 2 years limited leave as the unmarried or same-sex partner of a refugee or beneficiary of humanitarian protection who is now present and settled in the UK or as the unmarried or same-sex partner of a former refugee or beneficiary of humanitarian protection who is now a British Citizen.

(ii) the applicant is still the unmarried or same-sex partner of the person he was admitted or granted an extension of stay to join and the relationship is still subsisting; and

(iii) each of the parties intends to live permanently with the other as his partner; and

(iv) there will be adequate accommodation for the parties and any dependants without recourse to public funds in accommodation which they own or occupy exclusively; and

(v) the parties will be able to maintain themselves and any dependants adequately without recourse to public funds and;

[(vi) the applicant has demonstrated sufficient knowledge of the English language and sufficient knowledge about life in the United Kingdom, in accordance with Appendix KoLL; and]

(vii) the applicant does not [fall for refusal under the general grounds for refusal.]

Note

Words in square brackets in sub para (i) inserted by Cm 6339, para 17 as from 25 October 2004. Sub-para (i)(b) inserted by HC 321. Words in square brackets in sub para (i)(a) inserted by HC 971. Words in (i)(b)–(d), (vi) and (vii) substituted and inserted by HC 863, paras 105–107, 109 as from 6 April 2011. Further amended by HC 760, para 237 as from 13 December 2012. Further amended by HC 1039, para 102: where an applicant has made an application for entry clearance or leave before 6 April 2013 and the application has not been decided before that date, it will be decided in accordance with the rules in force on 5 April 2013. Further amended by HC 628, para 128 and if an applicant has made an application for entry clearance or leave before 1 October 2013, the application will be decided in accordance with the Rules in force on 30 September 2013.

Indefinite leave to remain as the unmarried or same-sex partner of a person present and settled in the United Kingdom

295H. Indefinite leave to remain as the unmarried or same-sex partner of a person present and settled in the United Kingdom may be granted provided that the Secretary of State is satisfied that each of the requirements of paragraph 295G is met.

Refusal of indefinite leave to remain as the unmarried or same-sex partner of a person present and settled in the United Kingdom

295I. Indefinite leave to remain as the unmarried or same-sex partner of a person present and settled in the United Kingdom is to be refused if the Secretary of State is not satisfied that each of the requirements of paragraph 295G is met.

Leave to enter or remain as the unmarried or same-sex partner of a person with limited leave to enter or remain in the United Kingdom under paragraphs 128-193; 200-239; or 263-270

Indefinite leave to remain for the bereaved unmarried or same-sex partner of a person present and settled in the United Kingdom

Requirements for indefinite leave to remain for the bereaved unmarried or same-sex partner of a person present and settled in the United Kingdom

295J-295L DELETED.

295M. The requirements to be met by a person seeking indefinite leave to remain as the bereaved unmarried or same-sex partner of a person present and settled in the United Kingdom, are that:
(i)   the applicant was admitted to the United Kingdom [for a period not exceeding 27 months] or given an extension of stay for a period of 2 years [in accordance with paragraphs 295AA to 295F of these Rules] as the unmarried or same-sex partner of a person present and settled in the United Kingdom; and
(ii)   the person whom the applicant was admitted or granted an extension of stay to join died during that [period of leave]; and
(iii) the applicant was still the unmarried or same-sex partner of the person he was admitted or granted extension of stay to join at the time of the death; and
(iv)   each of the parties intended to live permanently with the other as his partner and the relationship was subsisting at the time of the death[; and
(v)   the applicant does not [fall for refusal under the general grounds for refusal.]

Note

Words in square brackets in sub-para (i) inserted by Cm 6339, para 18 as from 1 October 2004. Further amended by HC 971, para 7 as from 22 July 2008. Words in (iv) and (v) inserted by HC 863, para 111 as from 6 April 2011. Further amended by HC 760, para 240 as from 13 December 2012.

Indefinite leave to remain for the bereaved unmarried or same-sex partner of a person present and settled in the United Kingdom

295N. Indefinite leave to remain for the bereaved unmarried or same-sex partner of a person present and settled in the United Kingdom, may be granted provided that the Secretary of State is satisfied that each of the requirements of paragraph 295M is met.

Refusal of indefinite leave to remain for the bereaved unmarried or same-sex partner of a person present and settled in the United Kingdom

295O. Indefinite leave to remain for the bereaved unmarried or same-sex partner of a person present and settled in the United Kingdom, is to be refused if the Secretary of State is not satisfied that each of the requirements of paragraph 295M is met.]

Note

Paragraphs 295A–295O inserted by Cmnd 4851.

Note

On the interpretation of terms in paras 295A–O: see note after para 281.

Children

Children

296.   [Nothing in these Rules shall be construed as permitting a child to be granted entry clearance, leave to enter or remain, or variation of leave where his mother is party to a polygamous marriage or civil partnership and any application by that parent for admission or leave to remain for settlement or with a view to settlement would be refused pursuant to paragraphs 278 or 278A].

Note

Paragraphs 296 substituted by Cmnd 4851.

Leave to enter or remain in the United Kingdom as the child of a parent, parents or a relative present and settled or being admitted for settlement in the United Kingdom

Requirements for indefinite leave to enter the United Kingdom as the child of a parent, parents or a relative present and settled or being admitted for settlement in the United Kingdom

297.   The requirements to be met by a person seeking indefinite leave to enter the United Kingdom as the child of a parent, parents or a relative present and settled or being admitted for settlement in the United Kingdom are that he:
(i)   is seeking leave to enter to accompany or join a parent, parents or a relative in one of the following circumstances:
   (a)   both parents are present and settled in the United Kingdom; or
   (b)   both parents are being admitted on the same occasion for settlement; or
   (c)   one parent is present and settled in the United Kingdom and the other is being admitted on the same occasion for settlement; or
   (d)   one parent is present and settled in the United Kingdom or being admitted on the same occasion for settlement and the other parent is dead; or
   (e)   one parent is present and settled in the United Kingdom or being admitted on the same occasion for settlement and has had sole responsibility for the child's upbringing; or
   (f)   one parent or a relative is present and settled in the United Kingdom or being admitted on the same occasion for settlement and there are serious and compelling family or other considerations which make exclusion of the child undesirable and suitable arrangements have been made for the child's care; and
(ii)   is under the age of 18; and
(iii)   is not leading an independent life, is unmarried, and is not a civil partner, and has not formed an independent family unit; and
[(iv)   can, and will, be accommodated adequately by the parent, parents or relative the child is seeking to join without recourse to public funds in accommodation which the parent, parents or relative the child is seeking to join, own or occupy exclusively; and
(v)   can, and will, be maintained adequately by the parent, parents or relative the child is seeking to join, without recourse to public funds; and
(vi)   holds a valid United Kingdom entry clearance for entry in this capacity[; and
(vii)   does not have [fall for refusal under the general grounds for refusal.]

Note

Paragraph 297 (iv)-(v) substituted and paragraph 297 (vi) inserted by CM 485. Words in (vi) and (vii) inserted by HC 863, para 112 as from 6 April 2011. Further amended by HC 760, para 241 as from 13 December 2012.

General note on paras 297-302

See the IDIs on children at Chapter 8, Section 5A: www.ukba.homeoffice.gov.uk/sitecontent/docuuments/policyandlaw/IDIs/idischapter8/section5a/section5A.pdf?view=Binary and, in particular, Annex M: www.ukba.homeoffice.gov.uk/sitecontent/documents/policyandlaw/IDIs/idischapter8/section5a/annex-m?view=Binary

In relation to the meaning of sole responsibility in para 297(i)(e), see the IDI at Annex M, Section 4 (in particular para 4.3): a question of fact on the evidence, to determine 'usually for a substantial period of time' (emphasis added) that the sponsor has been:

'the chief person exercising parental responsibility for the major decisions relating to the child's upbringing, and provides the child with the majority of the financial and emotional support he requires. It must also be shown that he has had and continues to have care and control of the child'

(taking account of the fact that the child and sponsor may be geographically separated) (para 4.1). Relevant factors, in the Secretary of State for the Home Department's analysis, in determining the existence of sole responsibility are set out at para 4.3; see also *Nmaju v Entry Clearance Officer* [2000] EWCA Civ 505, [2000] All ER (D) 2569 (also providing a summary of earlier relevant authority). In determining the existence of sole responsibility, the period over which it is exercised cannot be a *decisive* factor; *Nmaju*; *NA (Bangladesh) v Secretary of State for the Home Department* [2007] EWCA Civ 128, [2007] All ER (D) 189 (Jan) and *TD (Paragraph 297(i)(e): 'sole responsibility') Yemen* [2006] UKAIT 00049 (containing a summary of existing authority on the meaning of sole responsibility).

On para 297(i)(f) ('serious and compelling family or other considerations'), see Annex M at Section 1: provision to be read in accordance with obligations under the Borders, Citizenship and Immigration Act 2009, s 55. However, and so far as the purpose of the rule, Secretary of State for the Home Department states:

The objective of this provision is to allow a child to join a parent or relative in this country only where that child could not be adequately cared for by his parents or relatives in his own country. It has never been the intention of the Rules that a child should be admitted here due to the wish of or for the benefit of other relatives in this country.

This approach is entirely consistent with the internationally accepted principle that a child should first and foremost be cared for by his natural parent(s) or, if this is not possible, by his natural relatives in the country in which he lives. Only if the parent(s) or relative(s) in his own country cannot care for him should consideration be given to him joining relatives in another country. It is also consistent with the provisions of the European Convention on Human Rights, and the resolution on the harmonization of family reunification agreed by EU Ministers in June 1993.

In relation to para 297(iii), and the meaning of 'leading an independent life', see *NM ('leading an independent life') Zimbabwe* [2007] UKAIT 00051:

'Where a child (who may be over 18) is seeking limited leave to remain as the child of a parent with limited leave, in order to establish that he is not "leading an independent life" he must not have formed through choice a separate (and therefore independent) social unit from his parents' family unit whether alone or with others. A child who, for example, chooses to live away from home may be "leading an independent life" despite some continuing financial and/or emotional dependence upon his parents.'

See *BM and AL (352D(iv); meaning of 'family unit') Colombia* [2007] UKAIT 00055 and *MI (Paragraph 298(iii): 'independent life') Pakistan* [2007] UKAIT 00052 (no requirement that the dependency must be one of necessity:

'The fact that one leads the life one does out of choice does not prevent it from being a dependent one: there is no requirement that the dependency must be one of necessity. The fact that one lives with one's parents as a matter of custom is in my view equally irrelevant: all one need show is that one is not leading an independent life, not why' (at para 3)).

In relation to para 297(iv) & (v), maintenance and accommodation need to be available at the date of arrival, not the date of application. In examining the adequacy of maintenance and accommodation, what would be provided by income support is a relevant comparator: see, inter alia, *KA (adequacy of maintenance) Pakistan* [2006] UKAIT 00065; *Byron Lee French v Entry Clearance Officer (Kingston)* [2011] EWCA Civ 35, [2011] All ER (D) 232 (Jan).

Third party support and joint sponsorship in providing maintenance is permitted: see *Mahad (previously referred to as AM) (Ethiopia) v Entry Clearance Officer* [2009] UKSC 16, [2010] 2 All ER 535 with the viability of the arrangement to be determined on the evidence (eg by provision of a formal undertaking).

On the adequacy of accommodation, see *KJ ('Own or occupy exclusively') Jamaica* [2008] UKAIT 00006:

> 'The requirement in the Immigration Rules that a person "own or occupy exclusively" property does not carry any technical legal meaning of exclusive occupation. It is sufficient if there is a defined place where the person lives and which he has as his home, with the implication of stability that that implies'.

What constituted 'adequate' accommodation may involve a factual judgement see *S (Pakistan)* [2004] UKIAT 00006. As to housing that cannot be taken in to account because of the prohibition on public funds in para 6 of the Immigration Rules, see *KA (Public funds: housing) Iraq* [2007] UKAIT 00081.

Requirements for indefinite leave to remain in the United Kingdom as the child of a parent, parents or a relative present and settled or being admitted for settlement in the United Kingdom

298. The requirements to be met by a person seeking indefinite leave to remain in the United Kingdom as the child of a parent, parents or a relative present and settled in the United Kingdom are that he:
(i)   is seeking to remain with a parent, parents or a relative in one of the following circumstances:
    (a)   both parents are present and settled in the United Kingdom; or
    (b)   one parent is present and settled in the United Kingdom and the other parent is dead; or
    (c)   one parent is present and settled in the United Kingdom and has had sole responsibility for the child's upbringing [or the child normally lives with this parent and not their other parent]; or
    (d)   one parent or a relative is present and settled in the United Kingdom and there are serious and compelling family or other considerations which make exclusion of the child undesirable and suitable arrangements have been made for the child's care; and
(ii)   has [or has had] limited leave to enter or remain in the United Kingdom, and
    (a)   is under the age of 18; or
    (b)   was given leave to enter or remain with a view to settlement under paragraph 302 [or Appendix FM][; or
    (c)   was admitted into the UK in accordance with paragraph 319R and has completed a period of 2 years limited leave as the child of a refugee or beneficiary of humanitarian protection who is now present and settled in the UK or as the child of a former refugee or beneficiary of humanitarian protection who is now a British Citizen.]
    [(d)   the applicant [. . .] [has limited leave to enter or remain in] the United Kingdom in accordance with paragraph 319X, as the child of a relative with limited leave to remain as a refugee or beneficiary of humanitarian protection in the United Kingdom and who is now present and settled here][; or
    (e)   was last given limited leave to remain under paragraph 298A; and]
(iii)   is not leading an independent life, is unmarried and has not formed an independent family unit; and

[(iv)   can, and will, be accommodated adequately by the parent, parents or relative the child was admitted to join, without recourse to public funds in accommodation which the parent, parents or relative the child was admitted to join, own or occupy exclusively; and

(v)   can, and will, be maintained adequately by the parent, parents or relative the child was admitted to join, without recourse to public funds[; and

(vi)   does not [fall for refusal under the general grounds for refusal][; and.]

[(vii)   if aged 18 or over, was admitted to the United Kingdom under paragraph 302, or Appendix FM, or 319R or 319X and has demonstrated sufficient knowledge of the English language and sufficient knowledge about life in the United Kingdom in accordance with Appendix KoLL.]

Note

Paragraph 298(iv) substituted and paragraph 298(v) inserted by Cmnd 4851. Words in (ii)(b), (c), (vi) and (vii) substituted and inserted by HC 863, paras 113–115 as from 6 April 2011. Sub-paragraph (ii)(d) inserted by HC 1148, para 45 as from 4 July 2011. Further amended by HC 1511, para 17 as from 31 October 2011. Words "or Appendix FM" in sub-para (ii)(b) inserted by HC 565, para 87 as from 6 September 2012. Further amended by HC 760, paras 242–244 as from 13 December 2012. Further amended by HC 628, para 130 and if an applicant has made an application for entry clearance or leave before 1 October 2013, the application will be decided in accordance with the Rules in force on 30 September 2013. Amended by HC 1138, para 59 shall apply to all applications decided on or after 6 April 2014. Further amended by HC 1138, para 61 shall apply to all applications decided on or after 6 April 2014. Amended by HC 1138, para 62 shall apply to all applications decided on or after 6 April 2014.

298A. [If an applicant does not meet the requirements of paragraph 298 only because:

(a)   the applicant does not meet the requirement in paragraph 298(vi) by reason of a sentence or disposal of a type mentioned in paragraph 322(1C)(iii) or (iv); or

(b)   an applicant aged 18 or over does not meet the requirement in paragraph 298(vii); or

(c)   the applicant would otherwise be refused indefinite leave to remain under paragraph 322(1C)(iii) or (iv),

the applicant may be granted limited leave to remain for a period not exceeding 30 months and subject to a condition of no recourse to public funds.]

Note

Paragraph 298A inserted by HC 1138, para 62 as from 6 April 2014

Indefinite leave to enter or remain in the United Kingdom as the child of a parent, parents or a relative present and settled or being admitted for settlement in the United Kingdom

299. Indefinite leave to enter the United Kingdom as the child of a parent, parents or a relative present and settled or being admitted for settlement in the United Kingdom may be granted provided a valid United Kingdom entry clearance for entry in this capacity is produced to the Immigration Officer on arrival. Indefinite leave to remain in the United Kingdom as the child of a parent, parents or a relative present and settled in the United Kingdom may be granted provided the Secretary of State is satisfied that each of the requirements of paragraph 298 is met.

Refusal of indefinite leave to enter or remain in the United Kingdom as the child of a parent, parents or a relative present and settled or being admitted for settlement in the United Kingdom

300. Indefinite leave to enter the United Kingdom as the child of a parent, parents or a relative present and settled or being admitted for settlement in the United Kingdom is to be refused if a valid United Kingdom entry clearance for entry in this capacity is not produced to the Immigration Officer on arrival. Indefinite leave to remain in the United Kingdom as the child of a parent, parents or a relative present and settled in the United Kingdom is to be refused if the Secretary of State is not satisfied that each of the requirements of paragraph 298 is met.

Requirements for limited leave to enter or remain in the United Kingdom with a view to settlement as the child of a parent or parents given limited leave to enter or remain in the United Kingdom with a view to settlement

Note

See transitional provisions for paras 301-303F at A280(f).

301.   The requirements to be met by a person seeking limited leave to enter or remain in the United Kingdom with a view to settlement as the child of a parent or parents given limited leave to enter or remain in the United Kingdom with a view to settlement are that he:

(i)   is seeking leave to enter to accompany or join or remain with a parent or parents in one of the following circumstances:

    (a)   one parent is present and settled in the United Kingdom or being admitted on the same occasion for settlement and the other parent is being or has been given limited leave to enter or remain in the United Kingdom with a view to settlement; or

    (b)   one parent is being or has been given limited leave to enter or remain in the United Kingdom with a view to settlement and has had sole responsibility for the child's upbringing; or

    (c)   one parent is being or has been given limited leave to enter or remain in the United Kingdom with a view to settlement and there are serious and compelling family or other considerations which make exclusion of the child undesirable and suitable arrangements have been made for the child's care; and

(ii)   is under the age of 18; and

(iii)   is not leading an independent life, is unmarried and is not a civil partner, and has not formed an independent family unit; and

[(iv)   can, and will, be accommodated adequately without recourse to public funds, in accommodation which the parent or parents own or occupy exclusively; and

(iva)   can, and will, be maintained adequately by the parent or parents without recourse to public funds; and]

[(ivb)   does not qualify for limited leave to enter as a child of a parent or parents given limited leave to enter or remain as a refugee or beneficiary of humanitarian protection under paragraph 319R; and]

(v)   (where an application is made for limited leave to remain with a view to settlement) has limited leave to enter or remain in the United Kingdom; and

(vi)   if seeking leave to enter, holds a valid United Kingdom entry clearance for entry in this capacity . . ..

Note

Paragraph 301(iv) substituted and paragraph 301(iva) inserted by Cmnd 4851. Sub-para (ivb) inserted by HC 863, para 116 as from 6 April 2011. Words deleted by HC 244, para 12 as from 1 July 2013.

Note

See General note after para 297.

Limited leave to enter or remain in the United Kingdom with a view to settlement as the child of a parent or parents given limited leave to enter or remain in the United Kingdom with a view to settlement

302.   A person seeking limited leave to enter the United Kingdom with a view to settlement as the child of a parent or parents given limited leave to enter or remain in the United Kingdom with a view to settlement may be admitted for a period not exceeding [27 months] provided he is able, on arrival, to produce to the Immigration Officer a valid United Kingdom entry clearance for entry in this capacity. A person seeking limited leave to remain in the United Kingdom with a view to settlement as the child of a parent or parents given limited leave to enter or remain in the United Kingdom with a view to settlement may be given limited leave to remain for a period not exceeding [27] months provided the Secretary of State is satisfied that each of the requirements of paragraph 301(i)–(v) is met.

Note

Words in square brackets substituted by HC 971, para 8 as from 22 July 2008.

Refusal of limited leave to enter or remain in the United Kingdom with a view to settlement as the child of a parent or parents given limited leave to enter or remain in the United Kingdom with a view to settlement

303. Limited leave to enter the United Kingdom with a view to settlement as the child of a parent or parents given limited leave to enter or remain in the United Kingdom with a view to settlement is to be refused if a valid United Kingdom entry clearance for entry in this capacity is not produced to the Immigration Officer on arrival. Limited leave to remain in the United Kingdom with a view to settlement as the child of a parent or parents given limited leave to enter or remain in the United Kingdom with a view to settlement is to be refused if the Secretary of State is not satisfied that each of the requirements of paragraph 301(i)–(v) is met.

[Leave to enter and extension of stay in the United Kingdom as the child of a parent who is being, or has been admitted to the United Kingdom as a fiancé(e) or proposed civil partner

Requirements for limited leave to enter the United Kingdom as the child of a fiancé(e) or proposed civil partner

Note

See transitional provisions for paras 301-303F at A280(f).

303A. The requirements to be met by a person seeking limited leave to enter the United Kingdom as the child of a fiancé(e) or proposed civil partner, are that:
(i) he is seeking to accompany or join a parent who is, on the same occasion that the child seeks admission, being admitted as a fiancé(e) or proposed civil partner, or who has been admitted as a fiancé(e) or proposed civil partner; and
(ii) he is under the age of 18; and
(iii) he is not leading an independent life, is unmarried and is not a civil partner, and has not formed an independent family unit; and
(iv) he can, and will, be maintained and accommodated adequately without recourse to public funds with the parent admitted or being admitted as a fiancé(e) or proposed civil partner; and
(v) there are serious and compelling family or other considerations which make the child's exclusion undesirable, that suitable arrangements have been made for his care in the United Kingdom, and there is no other person outside the United Kingdom who could reasonably be expected to care for him; and
(vi) he holds a valid United Kingdom entry clearance for entry in this capacity.

Note

See General note after para 297.

Limited leave to enter the United Kingdom as the child of a parent who is being, or has been admitted to the United Kingdom as a fiancé(e) or proposed civil partner

303B. A person seeking limited leave to enter the United Kingdom as the child of a fiancé(e) or proposed civil partner, may be granted limited leave to enter the United Kingdom for a period not in excess of that granted to the fiancé(e) or proposed civil partner, provided that a valid United Kingdom entry clearance for entry in this capacity is produced to the Immigration Officer on arrival. Where the period of limited leave granted to a fiancé(e) or proposed civil partner will expire in more than 6 months, a person seeking limited leave to enter as the child of the fiancé(e) or proposed civil partner should be granted leave for a period not exceeding six months.

Refusal of limited leave to enter the United Kingdom as the child of a parent who is being, or has been admitted to the United Kingdom as a fiancé(e) or proposed civil partner

303C. Limited leave to enter the United Kingdom as the child of a fiancé(e) or proposed civil partner, is to be refused if a valid United Kingdom entry clearance for entry in this capacity is not produced to the Immigration Officer on arrival.

Requirements for an extension of stay in the United Kingdom as the child of a fiancé(e) or proposed civil partner

303D. The requirements to be met by a person seeking an extension of stay in the United Kingdom as the child of a fiancé(e) or proposed civil partner are that:
(i)   the applicant was admitted with a valid United Kingdom entry clearance as the child of a fiancé(e) or proposed civil partner; and
(ii)   the applicant is the child of a parent who has been granted limited leave to enter, or an extension of stay, as a fiancé(e) or proposed civil partner; and
(iii) the requirements of paragraph 303A (ii)-(v) are met.

Extension of stay in the United Kingdom as the child of a fiancé(e) or proposed civil partner

303E. An extension of stay as the child of a fiancé(e) or proposed civil partner may be granted provided that the Secretary of State is satisfied that each of the requirements of paragraph 303D is met.

Refusal of an extension of stay in the United Kingdom as the child of a fiancé(e) or proposed civil partner

303F. An extension of stay as the child of a fiancé(e) or proposed civil partner is to be refused if the Secretary of State is not satisfied that each of the requirements of paragraph 303D is met.]

Note

Paragraphs 303A-303F inserted by Cmnd 4851.

Children born in the United Kingdom who are not British citizens

Note

Paras 304-309 remain unaffected by the rule changes of 9 July 2012 (para A280(b)).

304. This paragraph and paragraphs 305–309 apply only to dependent children under 18 years of age who are unmarried and are not civil partners and who were born in the United Kingdom on or after 1 January 1983 (when the British Nationality Act 1981 came into force) but who, because neither of their parents was a British citizen or settled in the United Kingdom at the time of their birth, are not British citizens and are therefore subject to immigration control. Such a child requires leave to enter where admission to the United Kingdom is sought, and leave to remain where permission is sought for the child to be allowed to stay in the United Kingdom. If he qualifies for entry clearance, leave to enter or leave to remain under any other part of these Rules, a child who was born in the United Kingdom but is not a British citizen may be granted entry clearance, leave to enter or leave to remain in accordance with the provisions of that other part.

Requirements for leave to enter or remain in the United Kingdom as the child of a parent or parents given leave to enter or remain in the United Kingdom

305. The requirements to be met by a child born in the United Kingdom who is not a British citizen who seeks leave to enter or remain in the United Kingdom as the child of a parent or parents given leave to enter or remain in the United Kingdom are that he:
(a)   is accompanying or seeking to join or remain with a parent or parents who have, or are given, leave to enter or remain in the United Kingdom; or

(b)   is accompanying or seeking to join or remain with a parent or parents one of whom is a British citizen or has the right of abode in the United Kingdom; or

(c)   is a child in respect of whom the parental rights and duties are vested solely in a local authority; and

(ii)   is under the age of 18; and

(iii)   was born in the United Kingdom; and

(iv)   is not leading an independent life, is unmarried and is not a civil partner, and has not formed an independent family unit; and

(v)   (where an application is made for leave to enter) has not been away from the United Kingdom for more than 2 years.

Note

In relation to para 305(iv), and the meaning of 'leading an independent life', see *NM ('leading an independent life') Zimbabwe* [2007] UKAIT 00051:

> 'Where a child (who may be over 18) is seeking limited leave to remain as the child of a parent with limited leave, in order to establish that he is not "leading an independent life" he must not have formed through choice a separate (and therefore independent) social unit from his parents' family unit whether alone or with others. A child who, for example, chooses to live away from home may be "leading an independent life" despite some continuing financial and/or emotional dependence upon his parents.'; *BM and AL (352D(iv); meaning of 'family unit') Colombia* [2007] UKAIT 00055 and *MI (Paragraph 298(iii): 'independent life') Pakistan* [2007] UKAIT 00052 (no requirement that the dependency must be one of necessity:

>> 'The fact that one leads the life one does out of choice does not prevent it from being a dependent one: there is no requirement that the dependency must be one of necessity. The fact that one lives with one's parents as a matter of custom is in my view equally irrelevant: all one need show is that one is not leading an independent life, not why' (at para 3)).

Leave to enter or remain in the United Kingdom

306. A child born in the United Kingdom who is not a British citizen and who requires leave to enter or remain in the circumstances set out in paragraph 304 may be given leave to enter for the same period as his parent or parents where paragraph 305 (i)(a) applies, provided the Immigration Officer is satisfied that each of the requirements of paragraph 305 (ii)–(v) is met. Where leave to remain in sought, the child may be granted leave to remain for the same period as his parent or parents where paragraph 305 (i)(a) applies, provided the Secretary of State is satisfied that each of the requirements of paragraph 305 (ii)–(iv) is met. Where the parent or parents have or are given periods of leave of different duration, the child may be given leave to whichever period is longer except that if the parents are living apart the child should be given leave for the same period as the parent who has day to day responsibility for him.

307. If a child does not qualify for leave to enter or remain because neither of his parents has a current leave (and neither of them is a British citizen or has the right of abode), he will normally be refused leave to enter or remain, even if each of the requirements of paragraph 305 (ii)–(v) has been satisfied. However, he may be granted leave to enter or remain for a period not exceeding 3 months if both of his parents are in the United Kingdom and it appears unlikely that they will be removed in the immediate future, and there is no other person outside the United Kingdom who could reasonably be expected to care for him.

308. A child born in the United Kingdom who is not a British citizen and who requires leave to enter or remain in the United Kingdom in the circumstances set out in paragraph 304 may be given indefinite leave to enter where paragraph 305 (i)(b) or (i)(c) applies provided the Immigration Officer is satisfied that each of the requirements of paragraph 305 (ii)–(v) is met. Where an application is for leave to remain, such a child may be granted indefinite leave to remain where paragraph 305 (i)(b) or (i)(c) applies, provided the Secretary of State is satisfied that each of the requirements of paragraph 305 (ii)–(iv) is met.

Refusal of leave to enter or remain in the United Kingdom

309. Leave to enter the United Kingdom where the circumstances set out in paragraph 304 apply is to be refused if the Immigration Officer is not satisfied that each of the requirements of paragraph 305 is met. Leave to remain for such a child is to be refused if the Secretary of State is not satisfied that each of the requirements of paragraph 305 (i)–(iv) is met.

Adopted children

309A. [For the purposes of adoption under paragraphs 310-316C a de facto adoption shall be regarded as having taken place if:

(a)   at the time immediately preceding the making of the application for entry clearance under these Rules the adoptive parent or parents have been living abroad (in applications involving two parents both must have lived abroad together) for at least a period of time equal to the first period mentioned in sub-paragraph (b)(i) and must have cared for the child for at least a period of time equal to the second period material in that sub-paragraph; and

(b)   during their time abroad, the adoptive parent or parents have:

    (i)   lived together for a minimum period of 18 months, of which the 12 months immediately preceding the application for entry clearance must have been spent living together with the child; and

    (ii)   have assumed the role of the child's parents, since the beginning of the 18 month period, so that there has been a genuine transfer of parental responsibility.]

Note

Inserted by HC 538.

Note

On the general relationship between the rules relating to adoption and art 8 of the ECHR, see *Singh v Entry Clearance Officer, New Delhi* [2004] EWCA Civ 1075, [2005] QB 608 (an appeal on an application pre-dating the insertion of para 309A in to the Immigration Rules), considered by the AIT in *SK ('Adoption' not recognised in UK) India* [2006] UKAIT 00068.

For a discussion of the requirements of para 309A, see also *SK; MK (Somalia) v Entry Clearance Officer* [2008] EWCA Civ 1453, [2009] 2 FLR 138.

[**309B.** Inter-country adoptions which ae not a de facto adoption under paragraph 309A are subject to the Adoption and Children Act 2002 and the Adoptions with a Foreign Element Regulations 2005. As such all prospective adopters must be assessed as suitable to adopt by a competent authority in the UK, and obtain a Certificate of Eligibility from the Department for Education, before travelling abroad to identify a child for adoption. This Certificate of Eligibility must be provided with all entry clearance adoption applications under paragraphs 310–316F.]

Note

Inserted by HC 565, para 88 as from 6 September 2012.

Requirements for indefinite leave to enter the United Kingdom as the adopted child of a parent or parents present and settled or being admitted for settlement in the United Kingdom

310. The requirements to be met in the case of a child seeking indefinite leave to enter the United Kingdom as the adopted child of a parent or parents present and settled or being admitted for settlement in the United Kingdom are that he:

(i)   is seeking leave to enter to accompany or join an adoptive parent or parents in one of the following circumstances:

    (a)   both parents are present and settled in the United Kingdom; or

    (b)   both parents are being admitted on the same occasion for settlement; or

    (c)   one parent is present and settled in the United Kingdom and the other is being admitted on the same occasion for settlement; or

    (d)   one parent is present and settled in the United Kingdom or being admitted on the same occasion for settlement and the other parent is dead; or

(e)   one parent is present and settled in the United Kingdom or being admitted on the same occasion for settlement and has had sole responsibility for the child's upbringing; or

(f)   one parent is present and settled in the United Kingdom or being admitted on the same occasion for settlement and there are serious and compelling family or other considerations which make exclusion of the child undesirable and suitable arrangements have been made for the child's care; [or]

[(g)   in the case of a de facto adoption one parent has a right of abode in the United Kingdom or indefinite leave to enter or remain in the United Kingdom and is seeking admission to the United Kingdom on the same occasion for the purposes of settlement; and]

(ii)   is under the age of 18; and

(iii)   is not leading an independent life, is unmarried and is not a civil partner, and has not formed an independent family unit; and

[(iv)   can, and will, be accommodated [and maintained] adequately without recourse to public funds in accommodation which the adoptive parent or parents own or occupy exclusively; and]

[(v)   . . .]

(a)   was adopted in accordance with a decision taken by the competent administrative authority or court in his country of origin or the country in which he is resident [, being a country whose adoption orders are recognised by the United Kingdom]; or

(b)   is the subject of a de facto adoption; and]

(vii)   was adopted at a time when:

(a)   both adoptive parents were resident together abroad; or

(b)   either or both adoptive parents were settled in the United Kingdom; and

(viii)   has the same rights and obligations as any other child of the [adoptive parent's or parents' family]; and

(ix)   was adopted due to the inability of the original parent(s) or current carer(s) to care for him and there has been a genuine transfer of parental responsibility to the adoptive parents; and

(x)   has lost or broken his ties with his family of origin; and

(xi)   was adopted, but the adoption is not one of convenience arranged to facilitate his admission to or remaining in the United Kingdom; and

(xii)   holds a valid United Kingdom entry clearance for entry in this capacity[; and

(xiii)   does not [fall for refusal under the general grounds for refusal.]

Note

Paragraph 310(iv) substituted, paragraph 310(v) inserted and subsequent paragraphs renumbered by Cmnd 4851. Words in square brackets in sub-para (i)(f), (i)(g), (iv), (vi) and (viii) substituted and sub-para (v) deleted by HC 538. Words in square brackets in (vi)(a) inserted by Cmnd 5253. Words in (xii), (xiii) inserted by HC 863, para 117 as from 6 April 2011. Further amended by HC 760, para 245 as from 13 December 2012.

On the interpretation of para 310(ix), see *Radhika Sharma v Entry Clearance Officer (New Delhi)* [2005] EWCA Civ 89.

On the interpretation of para 310(x), see *VB v Entry Clearance Officer, Ghana* [2002] UKIAT 1323.

Requirements for indefinite leave to remain in the United Kingdom as the adopted child of a parent or parents present and settled in the United Kingdom

311.   The requirements to be met in the case of a child seeking indefinite leave to remain in the United Kingdom as the adopted child of a parent or parents present and settled in the United Kingdom are that he:

(i)   is seeking to remain with an adoptive parent or parents in one of the following circumstances:

(a)   both parents are present and settled in the United Kingdom; or

(b)   one parent is present and settled in the United Kingdom and the other parent is dead; or

(c)   one parent is present and settled in the United Kingdom and has had sole responsibility for the child's upbringing; or

    (d)   one parent is present and settled in the United Kingdom and there are serious and compelling family or other considerations which make exclusion of the child undesirable and suitable arrangements have been made for the child's care; [or]

    [(e)   in the case of a de facto adoption one parent has a right of abode in the United Kingdom or indefinite leave to enter or remain in the United Kingdom and is seeking admission to the United Kingdom on the same occasion for the purpose of settlement; and]

(ii)   has limited leave to enter or remain in the United Kingdom, and

    (a)   is under the age of 18; or

    (b)   was given leave to enter or remain with a view to settlement under paragraph 315 [or paragraph 316B]; and

(iii)   is not leading an independent life, is unmarried and is not a civil partner, and has not formed an independent family unit; and

[(iv)   can, and will, be accommodated [and maintained] adequately without recourse to public funds in accommodation which the adoptive parent or parents own or occupy exclusively; and]

[(v)   . . . .]

    (a)   was adopted in accordance with a decision taken by the competent administrative authority or court in his country of origin or the country in which he is resident [, being a country whose adoption orders are recognised by the United Kingdom]; or

    (b)   is the subject of a de facto adoption; and]

(vii)   was adopted at a time when:

    (a)   both adoptive parents were resident together abroad; or

    (b)   either or both adoptive parents were settled in the United Kingdom; and

(viii)   has the same rights and obligations as any other child of the [adoptive parent's or parents' family]; and

(ix)   was adopted due to the inability of the original parent(s) or current carer(s) to care for him and there has been a genuine transfer of parental responsibility to the adoptive parents; and

(x)   has lost or broken his ties with his family of origin; and

(xi)   was adopted, but the adoption is not one of convenience arranged to facilitate his admission to or remaining in the United Kingdom[; and

(xii)   does not [fall for refusal under the general grounds for refusal.]

Note

Words in square brackets in paragraph 311(ii)(b) inserted, paragraph 311(iv) substituted and subsequent paragraphs renumbered by Cmnd 4851. Words in square brackets in sub-para (i)(d), (i)(e), (iv), (vi) and (viii) substituted and (v) deleted by HC 538. Words in square brackets in (vi)(a) inserted by Cmnd 5253. Words in (xi), (xii) inserted by HC 863, para 118 as from 6 April 2011. Further amended by HC 760, para 246 as from 13 December 2012.

Indefinite leave to enter or remain in the United Kingdom as the adopted child of a parent or parents present and settled or being admitted for settlement in the United Kingdom

312.   Indefinite leave to enter the United Kingdom as the adopted child of a parent or parents present and settled or being admitted for settlement in the United Kingdom may be granted provided a valid United Kingdom entry clearance for entry in this capacity is produced to the Immigration Officer on arrival. Indefinite leave to remain in the United Kingdom as the adopted child of a parent or parents present and settled in the United Kingdom may be granted provided the Secretary of State is satisfied that each of the requirements of paragraph 311 is met.

Refusal of indefinite leave to enter or remain in the United Kingdom as the adopted child of a parent or parents present and settled or being admitted for settlement in the United Kingdom

313.   Indefinite leave to enter the United Kingdom as the adopted child of a parent or parents present and settled or being admitted for settlement in the United Kingdom is to be refused if a valid United Kingdom entry clearance for entry in this capacity is not produced to the Immigration Officer on arrival. Indefinite leave to remain in the United Kingdom as the adopted child of a parent or parents present and settled in the United Kingdom is to be refused if the Secretary of State is not satisfied that each of the requirements of paragraph 311 is met.

Requirements for limited leave to enter or remain in the United Kingdom with a view to settlement as the adopted child of a parent or parents given limited leave to enter or remain in the United Kingdom with a view to settlement

314. The requirements to be met in the case of a child seeking limited leave to enter or remain in the United Kingdom with a view to settlement as the adopted child of a parent or parents given limited leave to enter or remain in the United Kingdom with a view to settlement are that he:

(i)   is seeking leave to enter to accompany or join or remain with a parent or parents in one of the following circumstances:

    (a)   one parent is present and settled in the United Kingdom or being admitted on the same occasion for settlement and the other parent is being or has been given limited leave to enter or remain in the United Kingdom with a view to settlement; or

    (b)   one parent is being or has been given limited leave to enter or remain in the United Kingdom with a view to settlement and has had sole responsibility for the child's upbringing; or

    (c)   one parent is being or has been given limited leave to enter or remain in the United Kingdom with a view to settlement and there are serious and compelling family or other considerations which make exclusion of the child undesirable and suitable arrangements have been made for the child's care; or

    [(d)   in the case of a de facto adoption one parent has a right of abode in the United Kingdom or indefinite leave to enter or remain in the United Kingdom and is seeking admission to the United Kingdom on the same occasion for the purpose of settlement; and]

(ii)   is under the age of 18; and

(iii)   is not leading an independent life, is unmarried and is not a civil partner, and has not formed an independent family unit; and

[(iv)   can, and will, be accommodated [and maintained] adequately without recourse to public funds in accommodation which the adoptive parent or parents own or occupy exclusively; and]

    (a)   was adopted in accordance with a decision taken by the competent administrative authority or court in his country of origin or the country in which he is resident[, being a country whose adoption orders are recognised by the United Kingdom]; or

    (b)   is the subject of a de facto adoption; and]

(vi)   was adopted at a time when:

    (a)   both adoptive parents were resident together abroad; or

    (b)   either or both adoptive parents were settled in the United Kingdom; and

(vii)   has the same rights and obligations as any other child of the [adoptive parent's or parents' family]; and

(viii)   was adopted due to the inability of the original parent(s) or current carer(s) to care for him and there has been a genuine transfer of parental responsibility to the adoptive parents; and

(ix)   has lost or broken his ties with his family of origin; and

(x)   was adopted, but the adoption is not one of convenience arranged to facilitate his admission to the United Kingdom; and

(xi)   (where an application is made for limited leave to remain with a view to settlement) has limited leave to enter or remain in the United Kingdom; and

(xii)   if seeking leave to enter, holds a valid United Kingdom entry clearance for entry in this capacity.

Note

Paragraph 314(iv) substituted by Cmnd 4851. Words in square brackets in sub-para (i)(c), (i)(d), (iv), (v) and (vii) substituted and (iva) deleted by HC 538. Words in square brackets in (v)(a) inserted by Cmnd 5253.

The transitional provisions at para A280(b) state:

'Where the applicant:

- falls under paragraph 314(i)(a); or
- falls under paragraph 316A(i)(d) or (e); and
- is applying on or after 9 July 2012

the application must also meet the requirements of paragraphs E-ECC 2.1-2.3 (entry clearance applications) or E-LTRC 2.1-2.3 (leave to remain applications) of Appendix FM.

Where the applicant:

- falls under paragraph 314(i)(d);
- is applying on or after 9 July 2012; and
- has two parents or prospective parents and one of the applicant's parents or prospective parents does not have right of abode, indefinite leave to enter or remain, is not present and settled in the UK or being admitted for settlement on the same occasion as the applicant is seeking admission

the application must also meet the requirements of paragraphs E-ECC 2.1-2.3 (entry clearance applications) or E-LTRC 2.1-2.3 (leave to remain applications) of Appendix FM.'

Limited leave to enter or remain in the United Kingdom with a view to settlement as the adopted child of a parent or parents given limited leave to enter or remain in the United Kingdom with a view to settlement

315. A person seeking limited leave to enter the United Kingdom with a view to settlement as the adopted child of a parent or parents given limited leave to enter or remain in the United Kingdom with a view to settlement may be admitted for a period not exceeding 12 months provided he is able, on arrival, to produce to the Immigration Officer a valid United Kingdom entry clearance for entry in this capacity. A person seeking limited leave to remain in the United Kingdom with a view to settlement as the adopted child of a parent or parents given limited leave to enter or remain in the United Kingdom with a view to settlement may be granted limited leave for a period not exceeding 12 months provided the Secretary of State is satisfied that each of the requirements of paragraph 314(i)–(xi) is met.

Refusal of limited leave to enter or remain in the United Kingdom with a view to settlement as the adopted child of a parent or parents given limited leave to enter or remain in the United Kingdom with a view to settlement

316. Limited leave to enter the United Kingdom with a view to settlement as the adopted child of a parent or parents given limited leave to enter or remain in the United Kingdom with a view to settlement is to be refused if a valid United Kingdom entry clearance for entry in this capacity is not produced to the Immigration Officer on arrival. Limited leave to remain in the United Kingdom with a view to settlement as the adopted child of a parent or parents given limited leave to enter or remain in the United Kingdom with a view to settlement is to be refused if the Secretary of State is not satisfied that each of the requirements of paragraph 314(i)–(xi) is met.

Note

[Paras 310–316 replace HC 251, paras 53–55, 133–137 and 139.]

The concession in HC 251, para 55 relating to fully dependent daughters over 18 and under 21 has been removed.

Paras 310–316 have been introduced to take account of European harmonisation in this area. Article 2 of The Resolution on the Harmonisation of National Policies on Family Reunification agreed by EC Ministers (Copenhagen, 1993) states that Member States will normally grant admission to 'children adopted by both the resident and his or her spouse while they were resident together in a third country . . . and where the adopted children have the same rights and obligations as the other children and there has been a definitive break with the family of origin.'

The adoption must have taken place in accordance 'with a decision taken by the competent administrative authority or court in his country of origin or country in which he is resident.' – paras 310(v), 311(v), and 314(v).

The effect of the rules on children is outlined at **IV[1]**.

See note under para 314 for the transitional provisions relating to para 316.

[Requirements for limited leave to enter the United Kingdom with a view to settlement as a child for adoption

316A. The requirements to be satisfied in the case of a child seeking limited leave to enter the United Kingdom for the purpose of being adopted [(which, for the avoidance of doubt, does not include a de facto adoption)] in the United Kingdom are that he:

(i) is seeking limited leave to enter to accompany or join a person or persons who wish to adopt him in the United Kingdom (the 'prospective parent(s)'), in one of the following circumstances:

    (a) both prospective parents are present and settled in the United Kingdom; or

    (b) both prospective parents are being admitted for settlement on the same occasion that the child is seeking admission; or

    (c) one prospective parent is present and settled in the United Kingdom and the other is being admitted for settlement on the same occasion that the child is seeking admission; or

    (d) one prospective parent is present and settled in the United Kingdom and the other is being given limited leave to enter or remain in the United Kingdom with a view to settlement on the same occasion that the child is seeking admission, or has previously been given such leave; or

    (e) one prospective parent is being admitted for settlement on the same occasion that the other is being granted limited leave to enter with a view to settlement, which is also on the same occasion that the child is seeking admission; or

    (f) one prospective parent is present and settled in the United Kingdom or is being admitted for settlement on the same occasion that the child is seeking admission, and has had sole responsibility for the child's upbringing; or

    (g) one prospective parent is present and settled in the United Kingdom or is being admitted for settlement on the same occasion that the child is seeking admission, and there are serious and compelling family or other considerations which would make the child's exclusion undesirable, and suitable arrangements have been made for the child's care; and

(ii) is under the age of 18; and

(iii) is not leading an independent life, is unmarried and is not a civil partner, and has not formed an independent family unit; and

(iv) can, and will, be maintained and accommodated adequately without recourse to public funds in accommodation which the prospective parent or parents own or occupy exclusively; and

(v) will have the same rights and obligations as any other child of the marriage or civil partnership; and

(vi) is being adopted due to the inability of the original parent(s) or current carer(s) (or those looking after him immediately prior to him being physically transferred to his prospective parent or parents) to care for him, and there has been a genuine transfer of parental responsibility to the prospective parent or parents; and

(vii) has lost or broken or intends to lose or break his ties with his family of origin; and

(viii) will be adopted in the United Kingdom by his prospective parent or parents [in accordance with the law relating to adoption in the United Kingdom], but the proposed adoption is not one of convenience arranged to facilitate his admission to the United Kingdom.

Note

Words in square brackets inserted by HC 538.

Limited leave to enter the United Kingdom with a view to settlement as a child for adoption

316B. A person seeking limited leave to enter the United Kingdom with a view to settlement as a child for adoption may be admitted for a period not exceeding [24 months] provided he is able, on arrival, to produce to the Immigration Officer a valid United Kingdom entry clearance for entry in this capacity.

Note

Words in square brackets inserted by Cmnd 5829.

Refusal of limited leave to enter the United Kingdom with a view to settlement as a child for adoption

316C. Limited leave to enter the United Kingdom with a view to settlement as a child for adoption is to be refused if a valid United Kingdom entry clearance for entry in this capacity is not produced to the Immigration Officer on arrival.]

Note

Paragraphs 316A–316C inserted by Cmnd 4851.

[Requirements for limited leave to enter the United Kingdom with a view to settlement as a child for adoption under the Hague Convention

316D. The requirements to be satisfied in the case of a child seeking limited leave to enter the United Kingdom for the purpose of being adopted in the United Kingdom under the Hague Convention are that he:
(i) is seeking limited leave to enter to accompany one or two people each of whom are habitually resident in the United Kingdom and who wish to adopt him under the Hague Convention ("the prospective parents");
(ii) is the subject of an agreement made under Article 17(c) of the Hague Convention; and
(iii) has been entrusted to the prospective parents by the competent administrative authority of the country from which he is coming to the United Kingdom for adoption under the Hague Convention; and
(iv) is under the age of 18; and
(v)* can, and will, be maintained and accommodated adequately without recourse to public funds in accommodation which the prospective parent or parents own or occupy exclusively; and
(vi)* holds a valid United Kingdom entry clearance for entry in this capacity.]

Note

Paragraphs 316D–316F inserted by Cmnd 5829.

* Please note that in the printed version of Cmnd 5829 these points appear in error numbered as an alternative version of 316D (iii) and (iv).

[Limited leave to enter the United Kingdom with a view to settlement as a child for adoption under the Hague Convention

316E. A person seeking limited leave to enter the United Kingdom with a view to settlement as a child for adoption under the Hague Convention may be admitted for a period not exceeding 24 months provided he is able, on arrival, to produce to the Immigration Officer a valid United Kingdom entry clearance for entry in this capacity.]

Note

Paragraphs 316D–316F inserted by Cmnd 5829.

[Refusal of limited leave to enter the United Kingdom with a view to settlement as a child for adoption under the Hague Convention

316F. Limited leave to enter the United Kingdom with a view to settlement as a child for adoption under the Hague Convention is to be refused if a valid United Kingdom entry clearance for entry in this capacity is not produced to the Immigration Officer on arrival.]

Note

Paragraphs 316D–316F inserted by Cmnd 5829.

General note

The regime on adoption, as reflected by the structure of the rules, is complicated. See current guidance at: www.ukba.homeoffice.gov.uk/sitecontent/documents/policyandlaw/modernised/famil y/adopted-children.pdf?view=Binary

The types of adoption and corresponding immigration routes are set out at page 7 of the Modernised Guidance on Adopted children

The route to adoption, as set out in the rules, is summarised at para 3.1 of Annex Q to Section 5B (September 2009).

The rules on adoption exist side-by-side with the general rules on the admission of children (see General note on para 297). As the IDI notes at para 6 of Chapter 8, Section 5B, an application involving a child would first be considered under the para 297 regime where the sponsor (ie person adopting) is a blood relative (and see *SK ('Adoption' not recognised in UK) India* [2006] UKAIT 00068). It is only if the application falls to be refused under those provisions, in cases of blood relatives, that consideration shifts to the position under the rules on adoption.

On the general relationship between the rules relating to adoption and art 8 of the ECtHR, see *Singh v Entry Clearance Officer, New Delhi* [2004] EWCA Civ 1075, [2005] QB 608; considered by the AIT in *SK ('Adoption' not recognised in UK) India* [2006] UKAIT 00068.

For a discussion of the requirements of para 309A, see also *SK; MK (Somalia) v Entry Clearance Officer* [2008] EWCA Civ 1453, [2009] 2 FLR 138.

On the interpretation of para 310(ix), see *Radhika Sharma v Entry Clearance Officer (New Delhi)* [2005] EWCA Civ 89.

On the interpretation of para 310(x), see *VB v Entry Clearance Officer, Ghana* [2002] UKIAT 1323.

Parents, grandparents and other dependent relatives of persons present and settled in the United Kingdom

Requirements for indefinite leave to enter or remain in the United Kingdom as the parent, grandparent or other dependent relative of a person present and settled in the United Kingdom

Note

This category has been closed for those applying after 9 July 2012. Those applying as adult dependent relatives after that date will be applying under Appendix FM.

317. The requirements to be met by a person seeking indefinite leave to enter or remain in the United Kingdom as the parent, grandparent or other dependent relative of a person present and settled in the United Kingdom are that the person:
(i)   is related to a person present and settled in the United Kingdom in one of the following ways:
    (a)   [. . .] [parent or grandparent who is divorced, widowed, single or separated] aged 65 years or over; or
    [(b)]   parents or grandparents travelling together of whom at least one is aged 65 or over; or
    [(c)]   a parent or grandparent aged 65 or over who has entered into a second relationship but cannot look to the spouse, civil partner or children of

> that second relationship for financial support; and where the person settled in the United Kingdom is able and willing to maintain the parent or grandparent and any spouse or civil partner or child of the second relationship who would be admissible as a dependant; or

[(d) parent or grandparent under the age of 65 if living alone outside the United Kingdom in the most exceptional compassionate circumstances; or]

[(e) parents or grandparents travelling together who are both under the age of 65 if living in the most exceptional compassionate circumstances; or]

[(f) the son, daughter, sister, brother, uncle or aunt over the age of 18 if living alone outside the United Kingdom in the most exceptional compassionate circumstances; and

(ii) is joining or accompanying a person who is present and settled in the United Kingdom or who is on the same occasion being admitted for settlement; and

(iii) is financially wholly or mainly dependent on the relative present and settled in the United Kingdom; and

[(iv) can, and will, be accommodated adequately, together with any dependants, without recourse to public funds, in accommodation which the sponsor owns or occupies exclusively; and

(iva) can, and will, be maintained adequately, together with any dependants, without recourse to public funds; and]

(v) has no other close relatives in his own country to whom he could turn for financial support; and

(vi) if seeking leave to enter, holds a valid United Kingdom entry clearance for entry in this capacity[; and

(vii) does not [fall for refusal under the general grounds for refusal.]

Note

Paragraph 317(iv) substituted and paragraph 317(iva) inserted by Cmnd 4851. Words in (vi), (vii) inserted by HC 863, para 119 as from 6 April 2011. Further amended by HC 1511, paras 18–24 as from 31 October 2011. Further amended by HC 760, para 247 as from 13 December 2012.

General note

For relevant guidance, see the IDIs at Chapter 8, Section 6: Index page at www.bia.homeoffice.go v.uk/sitecontent/documents/policyandlaw/IDIs/idischapter8/

Applications can be made prior to entry, as an application to an entry clearance officer, or in-country. Where the application is made in-country, the approach is that set out in *MB (Para 317: in country applications) Bangladesh* [2006] UKAIT 00091 at para 9:

> '.... the question is not what the position was before the applicant left her home country. But nor is it simply what the applicant's position is now, whilst she is in the United Kingdom. The correct question is what the applicant's position would be if, instead of being in the United Kingdom, she were in her own country. That is the way in which the Rule is applied in equal terms to those who are in the United Kingdom and those who are not ...'

In para 317(i)(a) and (b), a separated parent can be equated with a widow: see *R v Immigration Appeal Tribunal, ex p Zanib Bibi* [1987] Imm AR 392. As to the limitations on a purposive interpretation of the rule to bring other relatives within its ambit, see *MB (Somalia) v Entry Clearance Officer* [2008] EWCA Civ 102.

In para 317(iii), the applicant (as opposed, for example, to a wider family unit which has particular needs and is supported by the UK sponsor) must be dependent, looking at the applicant's circumstances in the round. Emotional dependency may tip the balance in a marginal case. The dependency must be of necessity (*Zaman v Entry Clearance Officer, Lahore* [1973] Imm AR 71).

In relation to para 317(iv) & (iva), maintenance and accommodation need to be available at the date of arrival, not the date of application. In examining the adequacy of maintenance and accommodation, what would be provided by income support is a relevant comparator: see, inter alia, *KA (adequacy of maintenance) Pakistan* [2006] UKAIT 00065; *Byron Lee French v Entry Clearance Officer (Kingston)* [2011] EWCA Civ 35,[2011] All ER (D) 232 (Jan)

Third party support and joint sponsorship in providing maintenance is permitted: see *Mahad (previously referred to as AM) (Ethiopia) v Entry Clearance Officer* [2009] UKSC 16, [2010]

2 All ER 535 with the viability of the arrangement to be determined on the evidence (eg by provision of a formal undertaking).

On the adequacy of accommodation, see *KJ ('Own or occupy exclusively') Jamaica* [2008] UKAIT 00006:

'The requirement in the Immigration Rules that a person "own or occupy exclusively" property does not carry any technical legal meaning of exclusive occupation. It is sufficient if there is a defined place where the person lives and which he has as his home, with the implication of stability that that implies'.

What constituted 'adequate' accommodation may involve a factual judgement: see *S (Pakistan)* [2004] UKIAT 00006. As to housing that cannot be taken in to account because of the prohibition on public funds in para 6 of the Immigration Rules, see *KA (Public funds: housing) Iraq* [2007] UKAIT 00081.

In relation to para 317(v), see the IDI, Chapter 8, Annex V at para 2: the test is that the relatives are *able* and *willing* to provide support:

'... If there is a relative in the applicant's own country who is able and willing to support him, then it would not be unreasonable to expect him to turn to that relative for support, even if the sponsor in the United Kingdom is financially in a better position to do so.

Close relatives **may** be sons, daughters, brothers, sisters, grandchildren, uncles, aunts, and possibly nephews, nieces, or in-laws. However it should be noted that this will largely depend on their culture. For example, in the Indian sub-continent, married women are unlikely to be **able** to provide support. Alternatively if there are several close relatives there is no reason why it cannot be a collective ability among them to support the applicant.

Although the onus is on the applicant to demonstrate that he has no close relative to turn to any refusal on that basis should be backed up with sound evidence that this is not the case. On occasions it may be necessary to make local enquiries.

Applications from married couples should not be refused solely on the basis that they have each other to turn to. Account should be taken of the age and health of the applicants as well as the ability of other relatives to visit them regularly' (emphasis in the original).'

In relation to an interpretation of 'living alone outside the United Kingdom in the most exceptional compassionate circumstances', the wording imposes a test with a high threshold: *SS (Entry Clearance Officer Art 8) Malaysia v ECO, KUala Lumper* [2004] UKIAT 00091; *Senanayake v Secretary of State for the Home Department* [2005] EWCA Civ 1530, [2005] All ER (D) 215 (Nov)

The IDI at Chapter 8, Section 6, Annex V states:

'Each application must be considered on the individual merits of the case, it is therefore not possible to list every possible circumstance which may arise, however, illness, incapacity, isolation [so the implication is that 'alone' needs to be construed in that sense rather than its purely literal meaning] and poverty are of all compassionate circumstances which should be considered.'

The IDI, Section 8 (para 3.2) notes:

'Where the applicant is a young single or divorced woman, living in a country where it is claimed that it is socially unacceptable for her to live there alone, this may be taken into account. But such a situation is not on its own a sufficiently compelling reason to grant leave to enter or remain.'

Indefinite leave to enter or remain as the parent, grandparent or other dependent relative of a person present and settled in the United Kingdom

318. Indefinite leave to enter the United Kingdom as the parent, grandparent or other dependent relative of a person present and settled in the United Kingdom may be granted provided a valid United Kingdom entry clearance for entry in this capacity is produced to the Immigration Officer on arrival. Indefinite leave to remain in the United

Kingdom as the parent, grandparent or other dependent relative of a person present and settled in the United Kingdom may be granted provided the Secretary of State is satisfied that each of the requirements of paragraph 317(i)–(v) is met.

Refusal of indefinite leave to enter or remain in the United Kingdom as the parent, grandparent or other dependent relative of a person present and settled in the United Kingdom

319.   Indefinite leave to enter the United Kingdom as the parent, grandparent or other dependent relative of a person settled in the United Kingdom is to be refused if a valid United Kingdom entry clearance for entry in this capacity is not produced to the Immigration Officer on arrival. Indefinite leave to remain in the United Kingdom as the parent, grandparent or other dependent relative of a person present and settled in the United Kingdom is to be refused if the Secretary of State is not satisfied that each of the requirements of paragraph 317(i)–(v) is met.

Note

[Paras 317–319 replace HC 251, paras 56–57 and 139.]

The only change of policy is that the admission of widowed parents and grandparents is now limited to those of 65 years of age, unless he or she, although under 65, is 'living alone outside the UK in the most exceptional compassionate circumstances and mainly dependent financially on relatives settled in the UK.' Other relatives who can qualify for admission under this paragraph, if they are living alone in the most exceptional compassionate circumstances and mainly dependent financially on relatives in the UK, are sons, daughters, sisters, brothers, uncles and aunts.

[Family members of relevant points-based system migrants]

Partners of relevant points-based system migrants

Purpose

319AA.   [In paragraphs 319A to 319K and Appendix E 'Relevant Points Based System Migrant' means a migrant granted leave as a Tier 1 Migrant, a Tier 2 Migrant[, a [Tier 4 (General) Student] or a Tier 5 (Temporary Worker) Migrant.]]

Note

Words in square brackets substituted by HC 314, para 89 as from 31 March 2009. Words 'Tier 4 (General) Student' substituted by HC 908, para 29 as from 21 April 2011.

319A.   This route is for the spouse, civil partner, unmarried or same-sex partner of a [Relevant Points Based System Migrant] (Partner of a Relevant Points Based System Migrant). Paragraphs 277 to 280 of these Rules apply to spouses or civil partners of Relevant Points Based System Migrant; paragraph 277 of these Rules applies to civil partners of Relevant Points Based System Migrant; and paragraph 295AA of these Rules applies to unmarried and same-sex partners of Relevant Points Based System Migrant.

Note

Amended by HC 1113, para 88 as from 25 November 2008.

Entry to the UK

319B.
[(a)   Subject to paragraph (b), all migrants all migrants arriving in the UK and wishing to enter as the Partner of a [Relevant Points Based System Migrant] must have a valid entry clearance for entry under this route. If they do not have a valid entry clearance, entry will be refused.]
[(b)   A migrant arriving in the UK, and wishing to enter as a partner of a Tier 5 (Temporary Worker) Migrant, who does not have a valid entry clearance will not be refused entry if the following conditions are met:
    (i)   the migrant wishing to enter as a partner is not a visa national,

(ii)   the migrant wishing to enter as a Partner is accompanying an applicant who at the same time is being granted leave to enter under paragraph 245ZN(b), and

(iii)   the migrant wishing to enter as a Partner meets the requirements of entry clearance in paragraph 319C.]

Note

Amended by HC 1113, paras 90–92 as from 25 November 2008.

Requirements for entry clearance or leave to remain

319C. To qualify for entry clearance or leave to remain as the Partner of a [Relevant Points Based System Migrant], an applicant must meet the requirements listed below. If the applicant meets these requirements, entry clearance or leave to remain will be granted. If the applicant does not meet these requirements, the application will be refused.

Requirements:

(a)   The applicant must not fall for refusal under the general grounds for refusal, and if applying for leave to remain, must not be an illegal entrant.

(b)   The applicant must be the spouse or civil partner, unmarried or same-sex partner of a person who:

    (i)   has valid leave to enter or remain as a [Relevant Points Based System Migrant], or

    (ii)   is, at the same time, being granted entry clearance or leave to remain as a [Relevant Points Based System Migrant][, or]

    (iii)   has indefinite leave to remain as a Relevant Points Based System Migrant, or is... at the same time being granted indefinite leave to remain as a Relevant Points Based System Migrant, where the applicant is applying for further leave to remain[, or has been refused indefinite leave to remain solely because the applicant has not met the requirements of paragraph 319E(g),] and was last granted leave:

        (1)   as the partner of that same Relevant Points Based System Migrant; or

        (2)   as the spouse or civil partner, unmarried or same sex partner of that person at a time when that person had leave under another category of these Rules; or

    (iv)   has become a British Citizen where prior to that they held indefinite leave to remain as a Relevant Points Based System Migrant and where the applicant is applying for further leave to remain and was last granted leave:

        (1)   as the partner of that same Relevant Points Based System Migrant, or

        (2)   as the spouse or civil partner, unmarried or same sex partner of that person at a time when that person had leave under another category of these Rules.]

(c)   An applicant who is the unmarried or same-sex partner of a [Relevant Points Based System Migrant] must also meet the following requirements:

    (i)   any previous marriage or similar relationship by the applicant or the [Relevant Points Based System Migrant] with another person must have permanently broken down,

    (ii)   the applicant and the [Relevant Points Based System Migrant] must not be so closely related that they would be prohibited from marrying each other in the UK, and

    (iii)   the applicant and the [Relevant Points Based System Migrant] must have been living together in a relationship similar to marriage or civil partnership for a period of at least 2 years.

(d)   The marriage or civil partnership, or relationship similar to marriage or civil partnership, must be subsisting at the time the application is made.

(e)   The applicant and the [Relevant Points Based System Migrant] must intend to live with the other as their spouse or civil partner, unmarried or same-sex partner throughout the applicant's stay in the UK.

(f)   The applicant must not intend to stay in the UK beyond any period of leave granted to the [Relevant Points Based System Migrant].

(g)   [Unless the [Relevant Points Based System Migrant] is a Tier 1 (Investor) Migrant [or a Tier 1 (Exceptional Talent) Migrant], there] must be a sufficient level of funds available to the applicant, as set out in Appendix E.

[(h)   An applicant who is applying for leave to remain must not have last been granted:

    (i)   entry clearance or leave as a visitor, unless the relevant Points Based System Migrant has, or is being granted, leave to remain as a Tier 5 (Temporary worker) Migrant in the creative and sporting subcategory on the basis of having met the requirement at paragraph 245ZQ(b)(ii);

    (ii)   temporary admission; or

    (iii) temporary release.]

[(i)   Where the relevant Points Based System Migrant is applying for, or has been granted, entry clearance, leave to enter, or leave to remain in the United Kingdom as a Tier 4 (General) Student either:

    (i)   the relevant Points Based System Migrant must be a government sponsored student who is applying for, or who has been granted, entry clearance or leave to remain to undertake a course of study longer than six months;

    (ii)   the relevant Points Based System Migrant must:

        (1)   be applying for, or have been granted entry clearance or leave to remain in order to undertake a course of study at post-graduate level [that is 12 months or longer in duration]; and

        (2)   be sponsored by a sponsor who is a Recognised Body or a body in receipt of funding as a higher education institution from either:

            (a)   the Department for Employment in Northern Ireland;

            (b)   the Higher Education Funding Council for England;

            (c)   the Scottish Funding Council;

    (iii) the relevant Points Based System Migrant must be applying for, or have been granted leave to remain as a Tier 4 (General) Student on the doctorate extension scheme; or

    (iv)   the following conditions must be met:

        (1)   the relevant Points Based System Migrant must be applying for entry clearance, leave to enter, or leave to remain, to undertake a course of study that is longer than six months and either:

            (a)   have entry clearance, leave to enter, or leave to remain as a Tier 4 (General) Student or as a student to undertake a course of study longer than six months; or

            (b)   have last had entry clearance, leave to enter, or leave to remain within the three months preceding the application as a Tier 4 (General) Student or as a student to undertake a course of study longer than six months; and

        (2)   the Partner must either

            (a)   have entry clearance, leave to enter, or leave to remain as the Partner of a Tier 4 (General) Student or a student with entry clearance, leave to enter, or leave to remain, to undertake a course of study longer than six months; or

            (b)   have last had entry clearance, leave to enter, or leave to remain within the three months preceding the application as the Partner of a Tier 4 (General) Student or as a student to undertake a course of study longer than six months; and

under the Rules in place before 9 July 2012, and since then has had continuous leave as the Partner of that Relevant Points based System Migrant, the specified period is 2 years

(ii)   If (i) does not apply, [the specified period is a continuous period of 5 years], during which the applicant must:

(a)   have been in a relationship with the same Relevant Points Based System Migrant for this entire period,

(b)   have spent the most recent part of the 5 year period with leave as the Partner of that Relevant Points Based System Migrant, and during that part of the period have met all of the requirements of paragraph 319C(a) to (e), and

(c)   have spent the remainder of the 5 year period, where applicable, [with leave] as the spouse or civil partner, unmarried or same-sex partner of that person at a time when that person had leave under another category of these Rules.]

(e)   The marriage or civil partnership or relationship similar to marriage or civil partnership, must be subsisting at the time the application is made.

(f)   The applicant and the Relevant Points Based System Migrant must intend to live permanently with the other as their spouse or civil partner.

[(g)   The applicant had demonstrated sufficient knowledge of the English language and sufficient knowledge about life in the United Kingdom, in accordance with Appendix KoLL.]

(h)   . . .

(i)   The applicant must not be in the UK in breach of immigration laws except that any period of overstaying for a period of 28 days will be disregarded.

Note

Amended by HC 439, para 52 as from 7 April 2010. Words in (g) and (h) inserted by HC 863, para 122 as from 6 April 2011. Further amended by HC 194, paras 94–96 as from 9 July 2012. Further amended by HC 565, para 92 as from 6 September 2012. Further amended by HC 194, paras 97, 98 as from 1 October 2012. Further amended by HC 760, para 250 as from 13 December 2012. Further amended by HC 628, paras 133–135 and if an applicant has made an application for entry clearance or leave before 1 October 2013, the application will be decided in accordance with the Rules in force on 30 September 2013.

Those making their first application for leave as a partner of a PBS migrant after 9 July 2012 will now have to spend five years in the partner category before being entitled to apply for ILR. Where the PBS migrant has been granted ILR prior to the partner, the partner will be able to apply for extensions or ILR under the PBS dependant rules rather than switch into Appendix FM.

Children of [Relevant Points Based System Migrant]

Purpose

319F. This route is for the children of [a] [Relevant Points Based System Migrant] who are under the age of 18 when they apply to enter under this route. Paragraph 296 of these Rules applies to children of [Relevant Points Based System Migrants].

Note

Amended by HC 565, para 93 as from 6 September 2012.

Entry to the UK

319G.

[(a)   Subject to paragraph (b), all migrants arriving] in the UK and wishing to enter as the Child of a [Relevant Points Based System Migrant] must have a valid entry clearance for entry under this route. If they do not have a valid entry clearance, entry will be refused.

[(b)   A migrant arriving in the UK and wishing to enter as the child of a Tier 5 (Temporary Worker) Migrant who does not have a valid entry clearance will not be refused entry if the following conditions are met:
    (i)   the migrant wishing to enter as [a] child is not a visa national,
    (ii)   the migrant wishing to enter as the child is accompanying an applicant who at the same time is being granted leave to enter under 245ZN(b), and
    (iii)   the migrant wishing to enter as the Child meets the requirements of entry clearance in paragraph 319H.]

Note

Amended by HC 1113, paras 93, 94 as from 25 November 2008. Further amended by HC 565, para 94 as from 6 September 2011.

Requirements for entry clearance or leave to remain

319H.   To qualify for entry clearance or leave to remain under this route, an applicant must meet the requirements listed below. If the applicant meets these requirements, entry clearance or leave to remain will be granted. If the applicant does not meet these requirements, the application will be refused.

Requirements:
(a)   The applicant must not fall for refusal under the general grounds for refusal, and if applying for leave to remain, must not be an illegal entrant.
(b)   [The applicant must be the child of a parent who has, or is at the same time being granted, valid entry clearance, leave to enter or remain, or indefinite leave to remain, as:
    (i)   a Relevant Points Based System Migrant, or
    (ii)   the partner of a Relevant Points Based System Migrant,
or who has obtained British citizenship having previously held indefinite leave to remain as above.]
(c)   The applicant must be under the age of 18 on the date the application is made, or if over 18 and applying for leave to remain, must have, or have last been granted, leave as the Child of a [**Relevant Points Based System Migrant**] [or as the child of the parent who had leave under another category of these Rules and who has since been granted, or is at the time being granted, leave to remain as a Relevant Points Based System Migrant].
(d)   The applicant must not be married or in a civil partnership, must not have formed an independent family unit, and must not be leading an independent life[, and, if he is over the age of 16 on the date the application is made, he must provide the specified documents and information in paragraph 319H-SD to show that this requirement is met.]
(e)   The applicant must not intend to stay in the UK beyond any period of leave granted to the [Relevant Points Based System Migrant] parent.
[(f)   Both of the applicant's parents must either be lawfully present in the UK, or being granted entry clearance or leave to remain at the same time as the applicant or one parent must be lawfully present in the UK and the other is being granted entry clearance or leave to remain at the same time as the applicant, unless:
    (i)   The Relevant Points Based System Migrant is the applicant's sole surviving parent, or
    (ii)   The Relevant Points Based System Migrant parent has and has had sole responsibility for the applicant's upbringing, or
    (iii)   there are serious and compelling family or other considerations which would make it desirable not to refuse the application and suitable arrangements have been made in the UK for the applicant's care.]
(g)   [Unless the [Relevant Points Based System Migrant] is [a Tier 1 (Investor) Migrant or a Tier 1 (Exceptional Talent) Migrant], there] must be a sufficient level of funds available to the applicant, as set out in Appendix E.
[(h)   An applicant who is applying for leave to remain must not have last been granted:

(i)   entry clearance or leave as a visitor, unless the Relevant Points Based System Migrant has, or is being granted, leave to remain as a Tier 5 (Temporary Worker) Migrant in the creative and sporting subcategory on the basis of having met the requirement at paragraph 245ZQ(b)(ii);

(ii)   temporary admission; or

(iii)   temporary release.]

[(i) Where the relevant Points Based System Migrant is applying for, or has been granted, entry clearance, leave to enter, or leave to remain in the United Kingdom as a Tier 4 (General) Student either:

    (i)   the relevant Points Based System Migrant must be a government sponsored student who is applying for, or who has been granted, entry clearance or leave to remain to undertake a course of study longer than six months;

    (ii)   the relevant Points Based System Migrant must:

        (1)   be applying for, or have been granted entry clearance or leave to remain in order to undertake a course of study at post-graduate level [that is 12 months or longer in duration]; and

        (2)   be sponsored by a sponsor who is a Recognised Body or a body in receipt of funding as a higher education institution from either:

            (a)   the Department for Employment and Learning in Northern Ireland;

            (b)   the Higher Education Funding Council for England;

            (c)   the Higher Education Funding Council for Wales; or

            (d)   the Scottish Funding Council;

    (iii)   the relevant Points Based System Migrant must be applying for, or have been granted leave to remain as a Tier 4 (General) Student on the doctorate extension scheme; or

    (iv)   the following conditions must be met:

        (1)   the relevant Points Based System Migrant must be applying for Entry Clearance, leave to enter, or leave to remain, to undertake a course of study that is longer than six months and either:

            (a)   have entry clearance, leave to enter, or leave to remain as a Tier 4 (General) Student or as a student to undertake a course of study longer than six months; or

            (b)   have last had entry clearance, leave to enter, or leave to remain within the three months preceding the application as a Tier 4 (General) Student or as a student to undertake a course of study longer than six months; and

        (2)   the Child must either:

            (a)   have entry clearance, leave to enter, or leave to remain as the Child of a Tier 4 (General) Student or a student with entry clearance, leave to enter, or leave to remain, to undertake a course of study longer than six months; or

            (b)   have last had entry clearance, leave to enter, or leave to remain within the three months preceding the application as the Child of a Tier 4 (General) Student or as a student to undertake a course of study longer than six months; or

        (3)   the relevant Points Based System Migrant and the Child must be applying at the same time.]

(j)   A Child whose parent is a Relevant Points Based System Migrant, who is a Tier 4 (General) Student or Student, and who does not otherwise meet the requirements of paragraph 319H(i):

    (1)   must have been born during the Relevant Points Based System Migrant's most recent grant of entry clearance, leave to enter or leave to remain as a Tier 4 (General) Student or Student with leave for a course of more than six months duration; or

> (2) where the Relevant Points Based System Migrant's most recent grant of entry clearance, leave to enter or leave to remain was to re-sit examinations or repeat a module of a course, must either have been born during a period of leave granted for the purposes of re-sitting examinations or repeating a module of a course or during the Relevant Points Based System Migrant's grant of leave for a course of more than six months, where that course is the same as the one for which the most recent grant of leave was to re-sit examinations or repeat a module; or
>
> (3) must have been born than three months after the expiry of that most recent grant of leave; and
>
> (4) must be applying for entry clearance.]

[(k) If the applicant is a child born in the UK to a Relevant Points Based System migrant and their partner, the applicant must provide a full UK birth certificate showing the names of both parents.

(l) All arrangements for the child's care and accommodation in the UK must comply with relevant UK legislation and regulations.

(m) The applicant must not be in the UK in breach of immigration laws except that any period of overstaying for a period of 28 days will be disregarded.]

Note

Amended by HC 1113, para 95 as from 25 November 2008. Further amended by HC 314, paras 96–98 as from 31 March 2009. Sub-paragraph (i) inserted by HC 367, para 12 as from 3 March 2010. New sub-para (h) inserted by HC 863, para 123 as from 6 April 2011. Words in square brackets in (f)-(h) substituted and inserted by HC 1888, paras 102–104 as from 6 April 2012. Words in square brackets in (i) substituted by HC 908, para 32 as from 21 April 2011. Further amended by HC 1148, para 48 as from 4 July 2011. Further amended by HC 194, para 99 as from 9 July 2012. Sub-paras (k)-(l) inserted by Cm 8423, para 75 as from 20 July 2012. Sub-para (f) deleted by Cm 565, para 9 as from 6 September 2012. Further amended by HC 760, paras 251–253 as from 13 December 2012. Further amended by HC 1039, paras 108, 110–114: where an applicant has made an application for entry clearance or leave before 6 April 2013 and the application has not been decided before that date, it will be decided in accordance with the rules in force on 5 April 2013. Further amended by HC 244, para 14 as from 1 July 2013. Further amended by Cm 8690, para 2 as from 1 August 2013. Further amended by HC 628, para 136 and if an applicant has made an application for entry clearance or leave before 1 October 2013, the application will be decided in accordance with the Rules in force on 30 September 2013. Further amended by HC 1138, para 64 as from 6 April 2014.

[Specified documents and information

319H-SD Applicants who are over the age of 16 on the date the application is made must provide the following specified documents and information:

(a) The applicant must provide two items from the list below confirming his residential address:
   (i) bank statements,
   (ii) credit card bills,
   (iii) driving licence,
   (iv) NHS Registration document,
   (v) letter from his current school, college or university, on official headed paper and bearing the official stamp of that organisation, and issued by an authorised official of that organisation.

(b) The documents submitted must be from two separate sources and dated no more than one calendar month before the date of the application.

(c) If the applicant pays rent or board, he must provide details of how much this amounts to each calendar month.

(d) If the applicant is residing separately from the Relevant Points Based System Migrant, he must provide:
   (i) reasons for residing away fro the family home. Where this is due to academic endeavours he must provide confirmation from his university or college confirming his enrolment and attendance on the specific course,

on official headed paper and bearing the official stamp of that organisation, and issued by an authorised official of that organisation,

(ii) the following evidence that he has been supported financially by his parents whilst residing away from the family home:

(1) bank statements for the applicant covering the three months before the date of the application clearly showing the origin of the deposit; and

(2) bank statements for the applicant's parent covering the three months before the date of the application also showing corroborating payments out of their account.]

Note

Inserted by HC 1039, para 109 as from 6 April 2013.

Period and conditions of grant

319I.

(a) [Entry clearance and leave to remain will be granted for:

(i) a period which expires on the same day as the leave granted to the parent whose leave expires first, or

(ii) where both parents have, or are at the same time being granted, indefinite leave to remain, or have since become British citizens, leave to remain will be granted to the applicant for a period of 3 years.]

(b) Entry clearance and leave to remain under this route will be subject to the following conditions:

(i) no recourse to public funds, [. . .]

(ii) registration with the police, if this is required under paragraph 326 of these Rules, [and]

[(iii) if the Relevant Points Based System Migrant is a Tier 4 (General) Student and the Child meets the requirements of paragraph [319H(i)(iv)(1),(2) and (3)] or 319H(j):

(1) the Relevant Points Based System Migrant is a Tier 4 (General) Student applying for leave for less than 12 months, no employment, or

(2) the Relevant Points Based System Migrant is a Tier 4 (General) Student who is following a course of below degree level study, no employment.]

Note

Amended by HC 314, paras 99–101 as from 31 March 2009. Words in square brackets in sub-para (a) inserted by HC 565, para 97 as from 6 September 2012. Sub-paragraph (b)(iv) inserted by HC 367, para 13 as from 3 March 2010. Sub-paragraph (iii) substituted by HC 1148, para 49 as from 4 July 2011. Further amended by HC 628, para 137 and if an applicant has made an application for entry clearance or leave before 1 October 2013, the application will be decided in accordance with the Rules in force on 30 September 2013. Further amended by HC 1138, para 65 as from 6 April 2014.

Requirements for indefinite leave to remain

319J. To qualify for indefinite leave to remain under this route, an applicant must meet the requirements listed below. If the applicant meets these requirements, indefinite leave to remain will be granted. If the applicant does not meet these requirements, the application will be refused [...].

Requirements:

(a) The applicant must not fall for refusal under the general grounds for refusal, and must not be an illegal entrant.

[(b) The applicant must be the child of a parent who has, or is at the same time being granted, indefinite leave to remain as:

(i) a Relevant Points Based System Migrant; or

(ii) the partner of a Relevant Points Based System Migrant.]

(c)   The applicant must have, or have last been granted, leave as the child of[, or have been born in the United Kingdom to,] the [Points Based System Migrant][, or the partner of a Points Based System migrant] who is being granted indefinite leave to remain.

(d)   The applicant must not be married or in a civil partnership, must not have formed an independent family unit, and must not be leading an independent life[, and, if he is over the age of 16 on the date the application is made, he must provide the specified documents and information in paragraph 319H-SD to show that this requirement is met.]

(e)   Both of an applicant's parents must either be lawfully [settled] in the UK, or being granted . . . indefinite leave to remain at the same time as the applicant, unless:

   (i)   The [Points Based System Migrant] is the applicant's sole surviving parent, or

   (ii)   The [Points Based System Migrant] parent has and has had sole responsibility for the applicant's upbringing, or

   (iii)   there are [serious and compelling] family or other considerations which would make it desirable not to refuse the application and suitable arrangements have been made for the applicant's care[; or

   [(iv)   One parent is, at the same time, being granted indefinite leave to remain as a Relevant Points Based System Migrant, the other parent is lawfully present in the UK or being granted leave at the same time as the applicant, and the applicant was granted leave as the child of a Relevant Points Based System Migrant under these Rules in place before 9 July 2012.]

[(f)   The applicant has demonstrated sufficient knowledge of the English language and sufficient knowledge about life in the United Kingdom, in accordance with Appendix KoLL, unless he is under the age of 18 at the date on which the application is made.]

[(g)   If the applicant is a child born in the UK to a Relevant Points Based System migrant and their partner, the applicant must provide a full UK birth certificate showing the names of both parents;

(h)   All arrangements for the child's care and accommodation in the UK must comply with relevant UK legislation and regulations.

(i)   The applicant must not be in the UK in breach of immigration laws except thatt any period of overstaying for a period of 28 days will be disregarded.]

Note

Amended by HC 1113. Further amended by HC 439, para 53 as from 7 April 2010. Words in square brackets in sub-paragraph (c) inserted by HC 1888, para 105 as from 6 April 2012. Words in (f) and (g) inserted by HC 863, para 124 as from 6 April 2011. Further amended by HC 194, para 101 as from 9 July 2012. Sub-paras (h), (i) inserted by Cm 8423, para 7 as from 20 July 2012. Further amended by HC 565, para 98 as from 6 September 2012. Further amended by HC 194, para 102 as from 1 October 2012. Further amended by HC 760, paras 254–259 as from 13 December 2012. Further amended by HC 1039, para 115: where an applicant has made an application for entry clearance or leave before 6 April 2013 and the application has not been decided before that date, it will be decided in accordance with the rules in force on 5 April 2013. Further amended by HC 628, para 138 and if an applicant has made an application for entry clearance or leave before 1 October 2013, the application will be decided in accordance with the Rules in force on 30 September 2013

Documentary evidence

319K. . . .

Note

Deleted by Cm 8423, para 77 as from 20 July 2012.

[Other family members of persons with limited leave to enter or remain in the United Kingdom as a refugee or beneficiary of humanitarian protection]

Requirements for leave to enter the United Kingdom as the spouse or civil partner of a person with limited leave to enter or remain in the United Kingdom as a refugee or beneficiary of humanitarian protection.

Note

See transitional provisions at A280(c). Those making their first applications in these categories (paras 319L to 319Y) after 9 July 2012 will be applying under Appendix FM.

319L. [The requirements to be met by a person seeking leave to enter the United Kingdom as the spouse or civil partner of a person with limited leave to enter or remain in the United Kingdom as a refugee or beneficiary of humanitarian protection, are that:

(a)   the applicant is married to or the civil partner of a person who has limited leave to enter or remain in the United Kingdom as a refugee or beneficiary of humanitarian protection granted such status under the immigration rules and the parties are married or have formed a civil partnership after the person granted asylum or humanitarian protection left the country of his former habitual residence in order to seek asylum or humanitarian protection; and

(b)   the applicant provides an original English language test certificate in speaking and listening from an English language test provider approved by the Secretary of State for these purposes, which clearly shows the applicant's name and the qualification obtained (which must meet or exceed level A1 of the Common European Framework of Reference) unless:

(i)   the applicant is aged 65 or over at the date he makes his application; or

(ii)   the Secretary of State or Entry Clearance Officer considers that the applicant has a physical or mental condition that would prevent him from meeting the requirement; or

(iii)   the Secretary of State or Entry Clearance Officer considers there are exceptional compassionate circumstances that would prevent the applicant from meeting the requirement; or

(iv)   the applicant is a national of one of the following countries: Antigua and Barbuda; Australia; the Bahamas; Barbados; Belize; Canada; Dominica; Grenada; Guyana; Jamaica; New Zealand; St Kitts and Nevis; St Lucia; St Vincent and the Grenadines; Trinidad and Tobago; USA; or

(v)   the applicant has obtained an academic qualification (not a professional or vocational qualification), which is deemed by UK NARIC to meet the recognised standard of a Bachelor's or Masters degree or PhD in the UK, from an educational establishment in one of the following countries: Antigua and Barbuda; Australia; The Bahamas; Barbados; Belize; Dominica; Grenada; Guyana; Ireland; Jamaica; New Zealand; St Kitts and Nevis; St Lucia; St Vincent and The Grenadines; Trinidad and Tobago; the UK; the USA; and provides the specified documents; or

(vi)   the applicant has obtained an academic qualification (not a professional or vocational qualification) which is deemed by UK NARIC to meet the recognised standard of a Bachelor's or Masters degree or PhD in the UK, and

(1)   provides the specified evidence to show he has the qualification, and

(2)   UK NARIC has confirmed that the degree was taught or researched in English, or

(vii)   has obtained an academic qualification (not a professional or vocational qualification) which is deemed by UK NARIC to meet the recognised standard of a Bachelor's or Masters degree or PhD in the UK, and provides the specified evidence to show:

(1)   he has the qualification, and

          (2)   that the qualification was taught or researched in English; and

(ii)   the parties to the marriage or civil partnership have met; and

(iii)   each of the parties intends to live permanently with the other as his or her spouse or civil partner and the marriage or civil partnership is subsisting; and

(iv)   there will be adequate accommodation for the parties and any dependants without recourse to public funds in accommodation which they own or occupy exclusively; and

(v)   the parties will be able to maintain themselves and any dependants adequately without recourse to public funds; and

(vi)   the applicant holds a valid United Kingdom entry clearance for entry in this capacity.]

Note

Paras 319L–319U inserted by HC 863, para 127 as from 6 April 2011.

319M. [Leave to enter the United Kingdom as the spouse or civil partner of a refugee or beneficiary of humanitarian protection may be granted for 63 months provided the Immigration Officer is satisfied that each of the requirements of paragraph 319L (i)–(vi) are met.]

Note

Paras 319L–319U inserted by HC 863, para 127 as from 6 April 2011.

319N. [Leave to enter the United Kingdom as the spouse or civil partner of a refugee or beneficiary of humanitarian protection is to be refused if the Immigration Officer is not satisfied that each of the requirements of paragraph [319L(i)–(vi)] are met.]

Note

Paras 319L–319U inserted by HC 863, para 127 as from 6 April 2011. Words in square brackets substituted by HC 1148, para 50 as from 4 July 2011.

[Requirements for leave to enter the United Kingdom as the unmarried or same-sex partner of a person with limited leave to enter or remain in the United Kingdom as a refugee or beneficiary of humanitarian protection.

319O. The requirements to be met by a person seeking leave to enter the United Kingdom as the unmarried or same-sex partner of a person with limited leave to enter or remain in the United Kingdom as a refugee or beneficiary of humanitarian protection, are that:

(a)   the applicant is the unmarried or same-sex partner of a person who has limited leave to enter or remain in the United Kingdom as a refugee or beneficiary of humanitarian protection granted such status under the immigration rules, and the parties have been living together in a relationship akin to either a marriage or civil partnership subsisting for two years or more after the person granted asylum or humanitarian protection left the country of his former habitual residence in order to seek asylum or humanitarian protection; and

(b)   the applicant provides an original English language test certificate in speaking and listening from an English language test provider approved by the Secretary of State for these purposes, which clearly shows the applicant's name and the qualification obtained (which must meet or exceed level A1 of the Common European Framework of Reference) unless:

       (i)   the applicant is aged 65 or over at the time he makes his application;

      (ii)   the Secretary of State or Entry Clearance Officer considers that the applicant has a physical or mental condition that would prevent him from meeting the requirement; or

     (iii) the Secretary of State or Entry Clearance Officer considers there are exceptional compassionate circumstances that would prevent the applicant from meeting the requirement;

(iv)   the applicant is a national of one of the following countries: Antigua and Barbuda; Australia; the Bahamas; Barbados; Belize; Canada; Dominica; Grenada; Guyana; Jamaica; New Zealand; St Kitts and Nevis; St Lucia; St Vincent and the Grenadines; Trinidad and Tobago; USA;

(v)   the applicant has obtained an academic qualification(not a professional or vocational qualification), which is deemed by UK NARIC to meet the recognised standard of a Bachelor's or Masters degree or PhD in the UK, from an educational establishment in one of the following countries: Antigua and Barbuda; Australia; The Bahamas; Barbados; Belize; Dominica; Grenada; Guyana; Ireland; Jamaica; New Zealand; St Kitts and Nevis; St Lucia; St Vincent and The Grenadines; Trinidad and Tobago; the UK; the USA; and provides the specified documents; or

(vi)   the applicant has obtained an academic qualification (not a professional or vocational qualification) which is deemed by UK NARIC to meet the recognised standard of a Bachelor's or Masters degree or PhD in the UK, and

    (1)   provides the specified evidence to show he has the qualification, and

    (2)   UK NARIC has confirmed that the degree was taught or researched in English, or

(vii)   has obtained an academic qualification (not a professional or vocational qualification) which is deemed by UK NARIC to meet the recognised standard of a Bachelor's or Masters degree or PhD in the UK, and provides the specified evidence to show:

    (1)   he has the qualification, and

    (2)   that the qualification was taught or researched in English; and

(ii)   any previous marriage or civil partnership (or similar relationship) by either partner has permanently broken down; and

(iii)   the parties are not involved in a consanguineous relationship with one another; and

(iv)   there will be adequate accommodation for the parties and any dependants without recourse to public funds in accommodation which they own or occupy exclusively; and

(v)   the parties will be able to maintain themselves and any dependants adequately without recourse to public funds; and

(vi)   the parties intend to live together permanently; and

(vii)   the applicant holds a valid United Kingdom entry clearance for entry in this capacity.]

Note

Paras 319L–319U inserted by HC 863, para 127 as from 6 April 2011.

319P. [Leave to enter the United Kingdom as the unmarried or same-sex partner of a refugee or beneficiary of humanitarian protection may be granted for 63 months provided the Immigration Officer is satisfied that each of the requirements of paragraph 319O (i)–(vii) are met.]

Note

Paras 319L–319U inserted by HC 863, para 127 as from 6 April 2011.

319Q. [Leave to enter the United Kingdom as the unmarried or same-sex partner of a refugee or beneficiary of humanitarian protection is to be refused if the Immigration Officer is not satisfied that each of the requirements of paragraph 319O (i)–(vii) are met.]

Note

Paras 319L–319U inserted by HC 863, para 127 as from 6 April 2011.

[Requirements for leave to enter the United Kingdom as the child of a parent or parents given limited leave to enter or remain in the United Kingdom as a refugee or beneficiary of humanitarian protection

319R. The requirements to be met by a person seeking leave to enter the United Kingdom as the child of a parent or parents given limited leave to enter or remain in the United Kingdom as a refugee or beneficiary of humanitarian protection, are that the applicant:

(i)   is the child of a parent or parents granted limited leave to enter or remain as a refugee or beneficiary of humanitarian protection granted as such under the immigration rules; and

(ii)   is under the age of 18, and

(iii)   is not leading an independent life, is unmarried, is not in a civil partnership, and has not formed an independent family unit; and

(iv)   was conceived after the person granted asylum or humanitarian protection left the country of his habitual residence in order to seek asylum in the UK; and

(v)   can, and will, be accommodated adequately by the parent or parents the child is seeking to join without recourse to public funds in accommodation which the parent or parents the child is seeking to join, own or occupy exclusively; and

(vi)   can, and will, be maintained adequately by the parent or parents the child is seeking to join, without recourse to public funds; and

(vii) if seeking leave to enter, holds a valid United Kingdom entry clearance for entry in this capacity.]

Note

Paras 319L–319U inserted by HC 863, para 127 as from 6 April 2011.

319S. [Limited leave to enter the United Kingdom as the child of a refugee or beneficiary of humanitarian protection may be granted for 63 months provided the Immigration Officer is satisfied that each of the requirements in paragraph 319R (i)–(vii) are met.]

Note

Paras 319L–319U inserted by HC 863, para 127 as from 6 April 2011.

319T. [Limited leave to enter the United Kingdom as the child of a refugee or beneficiary humanitarian protection is to be refused if the Immigration Officer is not satisfied that each of the requirements in paragraph 319R (i)–(vii) are met.]

Note

Paras 319L–319U inserted by HC 863, para 127 as from 6 April 2011.

[Requirements for indefinite leave to remain in the United Kingdom as the spouse or civil partner, unmarried or same-sex partner or child of a refugee or beneficiary of humanitarian protection present and settled in the United Kingdom

319U. To qualify for indefinite leave to remain in the UK, an applicant must meet the requirements set out in paragraph 287 if the applicant is a spouse or civil partner, paragraph 295G if they are an unmarried or same-sex partner, or 298 if the applicant is a child and the sponsor must be present and settled in the United Kingdom at the time the application is made. If an applicant meets the requirements as set out in the relevant paragraphs, indefinite leave to remain will be granted. If the applicant does not meet these requirements, the application will be refused.]

Note

Paras 319L–319U inserted by HC 863, para 127 as from 6 April 2011.

[PARENTS, GRANDPARENTS AND OTHER DEPENDENT RELATIVES OF PERSONS WITH
LIMITED LEAVE TO ENTER OR REMAIN IN THE UNITED KINGDOM AS A REFUGEE OR
BENEFICIARY OF HUMANITARIAN PROTECTION]

[REQUIREMENTS FOR LEAVE TO ENTER OR REMAIN IN THE UNITED KINGDOM AS THE
PARENT, GRANDPARENT OR OTHER DEPENDENT RELATIVE OF A PERSON WITH LIMITED
LEAVE TO ENTER OR REMAIN IN THE UNITED KINGDOM AS A REFUGEE OR BENEFICIARY
OF HUMANITARIAN PROTECTION

319V. The requirements to be met by a person seeking leave to enter or remain in the United Kingdom as the parent, grandparent or other dependent relative of a person with limited leave to enter or remain in the United Kingdom as a refugee or beneficiary of humanitarian protection are that the person:

(i)   is related to a refugee or beneficiary of humanitarian protection with limited leave to enter or remain in the United Kingdom in one of the following ways:

   (a)   [. . .] [parent or grandparent who is divorced, widowed, single or separated] aged 65 years or over; or

   (b)   parents or grandparents travelling together of whom at least one is aged 65 or over; or

   (c)   a parent or grandparent aged 65 or over who has entered into a second relationship of marriage or civil partnership but cannot look to the spouse, civil partner or children of that second relationship for financial support; and where the person with limited leave to enter or remain in the United Kingdom is able and willing to maintain the parent or grandparent and any spouse or civil partner or child of the second relationship who would be admissible as a dependant; or

   (d)   a parent or grandparent under the age of 65 if living alone outside the United Kingdom in the most exceptional compassionate circumstances [. . .]; or

   (e)   parents or grandparents travelling together who are both under the age of 65 if living in the most exceptional compassionate circumstances; or]

   (f)   the son, daughter sister, brother, uncle or aunt over the age of 18 if living alone outside the United Kingdom in the most exceptional circumstances [. . .]; and

(ii)   is joining a refugee or beneficiary of humanitarian protection with limited leave to enter or remain in the United Kingdom; and

(iii)   is financially wholly or mainly dependent on the relative who has limited leave to enter or remain as a refugee or beneficiary of humanitarian protection in the United Kingdom; and

(iv)   can, and will, be accommodated adequately, together with any dependants, without recourse to public funds, in accommodation which the sponsor owns or occupies exclusively; and

(v)   can, and will, be maintained adequately, together with any dependants, without recourse to public funds; and

(vi)   has no other close relatives in his own country to whom he could turn for financial support; and

(vii)   if seeking leave to enter, holds a valid United Kingdom entry clearance for entry in this capacity[or, if seeking leave to remain, holds valid leave to remain in another capacity][.]

Note

Amended by HC 1511, paras 25–33 as from 31 October 2011.

319VA. Limited leave to enter the United Kingdom as the parent, grandparent or other dependent relative of a refugee or beneficiary of humanitarian protection with limited leave to enter or remain in the United Kingdom may be granted for 5 years provided a valid United Kingdom entry clearance for entry in this capacity is produced to the Immigration Officer on arrival. Limited leave to remain in the United Kingdom as the parent, grandparent or other dependent relative of a refugee or beneficiary of humanitarian protection with limited leave to enter or remain in the United Kingdom may be granted provided the Secretary of State is satisfied that each of the requirements of paragraph [319V(i)-(vii)] is met.

Note

Amended by HC 1511, para 34 as from 31 October 2011.

319VB. Limited leave to enter the United Kingdom as the parent, grandparent or other dependent relative of a refugee or beneficiary of humanitarian protection with limited leave to enter or remain in the United Kingdom is to be refused if a valid United Kingdom entry clearance for entry in this capacity is not produced to the Immigration Officer on arrival. Limited leave to remain in the United Kingdom as the parent, grandparent or other dependent relative of a refugee or beneficiary of humanitarian protection with limited leave to enter or remain in the United Kingdom is to be refused if the Secretary of State is satisfied that each of the requirements of paragraph [319V(i)-(vii)] is met.

Note

Amended by HC 1511, para 35 as from 31 October 2011.

REQUIREMENTS FOR INDEFINITE LEAVE TO REMAIN IN THE UNITED KINGDOM AS THE PARENT, GRANDPARENT OR OTHER DEPENDENT RELATIVE OF A REFUGEE OR BENEFICIARY OF HUMANITARIAN PROTECTION WHO IS PRESENT AND SETTLED IN THE UNITED KINGDOM OR OF A FORMER REFUGEE OR BENEFICIARY HUMANITARIAN PROTECTION, WHO IS NOW A BRITISH CITIZEN.

319W. The requirements for indefinite leave to remain in the United Kingdom as the parent, grandparent or other dependent relative of a refugee or beneficiary of humanitarian protection who is now present and settled in the United Kingdom or who is now a British Citizen are that:

(i)   the applicant [has limited leave to enter or remain in] [. . .] the United Kingdom in accordance with paragraph 319V as a dependent relative of a refugee or beneficiary of humanitarian protection with limited leave to enter or remain in the United Kingdom; and

(ii)   the sponsor the applicant was admitted to join is now present and settled in the United Kingdom, or is now a British Citizen; and

(iii)   the applicant is financially wholly or mainly dependent on the relative who is present and settled in the United Kingdom; and

(iv)   the applicant can, and will, be accommodated adequately, together with any dependants, without recourse to public funds, in accommodation which the sponsor owns or occupies exclusively; and

(v)   the applicant can, and will, be accommodated adequately, together with any dependants, without recourse to public funds; and

(vi)   the applicant has no other close relatives in their country of former habitual residence to whom he could turn for financial support; and

(vii)   does not [fall for refusal under the general grounds for refusal].

Note

Amended by HC 1511, para 36 as from 31 October 2011. Sub-paragaph (vii) amended by HC 760, para 260 as from 13 December 2012.

319WA. Indefinite leave to remain in the United Kingdom as the parent, grandparent or other dependent relative of a refugee or beneficiary of humanitarian protection who is present and settled in the United Kingdom, or who is now a British Citizen may be granted provided the Secretary of State is satisfied that each of the requirements of paragraph 319W(i)-(vii) is met.

319WB. Indefinite leave to remain in the United Kingdom as the parent, grandparent or other dependent relative of a person present and settled in the United Kingdom is to be refused if the Secretary of State is not satisfied that each of the requirements of paragraph 319W(i)-(vii) is met.

REQUIREMENTS FOR LEAVE TO ENTER OR REMAIN IN THE UNITED KINGDOM AS THE CHILD OF A RELATIVE WITH LIMITED LEAVE TO ENTER OR REMAIN IN THE UNITED KINGDOM AS A REFUGEE OR BENEFICIARY OF HUMANITARIAN PROTECTION

319X. The requirements to be met by a person seeking leave to enter or remain in the United Kingdom as the child of a relative with limited leave to remain as a refugee or beneficiary of humanitarian protection in the United Kingdom are that:

(i)   the applicant is seeking leave to enter [or remain] to [. . .] join a relative with limited leave to enter or remain as a refugee or person with humanitarian protection; and:

(ii)   the relative has limited leave in the United Kingdom as a refugee or beneficiary of humanitarian protection and there are serious and compelling family or other considerations which make exclusion of the child undesirable and suitable arrangements have been made for the child's care; and

(iii)   the relative is not the parent of the child who is seeking leave to enter or remain in the United Kingdom; and

(iv)   the applicant is under the age of 18; and

(v)   the applicant is not leading an independent life, is unmarried and is not a civil partner, and has not formed an independent family unit; and

(vi)   the applicant can, and will, be accommodated adequately by the relative the child is seeking to join without recourse to public funds in accommodation which the relative in the United Kingdom owns or occupies exclusively; and

(vii)   the applicant, and will, be maintained adequately by the relative in the United Kingdom without recourse to public funds; and

(viii)   if seeking leave to enter, the applicant holds a valid United Kingdom entry clearance for entry in this capacity or, if seeking leave to remain, holds valid leave to remain in [this or] another capacity.]

Note

Amended by HC 1511, paras 37–39 as from 31 October 2011. Further amended by HC 693, para 96 as from 6 November 2014.

319XA. Limited leave to enter the United Kingdom as the child of a relative with limited leave to enter or remain as a refugee or beneficiary of humanitarian protection in the United Kingdom may be granted for 5 years provided that a valid United Kingdom entry clearance for entry in this capacity is produced to the Immigration Officer on arrival. Limited leave to remain in the United Kingdom as the child of a relative with limited leave to enter or remain as a refugee or beneficiary of humanitarian protection in the United Kingdom may be granted provided the Secretary of State is satisfied that each of the requirements of paragraph [319X(i)-(viii)] is met.

Note

Amended by HC 1511, para 40 as from 31 October 2011.

319XB. Limited leave to enter the United Kingdom as the child of a relative with limited leave to enter or remain as a refugee or beneficiary of humanitarian protection in the United Kingdom is to be refused if a valid United Kingdom entry clearance for entry in this capacity is not produced to the Immigration Officer on arrival. Limited leave to remain in the United Kingdom as the child of a relative with limited leave to enter or remain as a refugee or beneficiary of humanitarian protection in the United Kingdom is to be refused if the Secretary of State is not satisfied that each of the requirements of paragraph [319X(i)-(viii)] is met.

Note

Amended by HC 1511, para 41 as from 31 October 2011.

[REQUIREMENTS FOR INDEFINITE LEAVE TO REMAIN IN THE UNITED KINGDOM AS THE CHILD OF A RELATIVE WHO IS PRESENT AND SETTLED IN THE UNITED KINGDOM OR AS A FORMER REFUGEE OR BENEFICIARY OF HUMANITARIAN PROTECTION WHO IS NOW A BRITISH CITIZEN.

319Y. To qualify for indefinite leave to remain as the child of a relative who is present and settled in the United Kingdom, an applicant must meet the requirements set out in paragraph [298].]

Note

Paras 319V–319Y inserted by HC 1148, para 51, 52 as from 4 July 2011. Words in square brackets substituted by HC 1511, para 42 as from 31 October 2011.

[PART 9 — GENERAL GROUNDS FOR THE REFUSAL OF ENTRY CLEARANCE, LEAVE TO ENTER, LEAVE TO REMAIN, VARIATION OF LEAVE TO ENTER OR REMAIN AND CURTAILMENT OF LEAVE IN THE UNITED KINGDOM]

Note

Heading substituted by HC 382, para 5 as from 12 August 2010.

[**A320**   Paragraphs 320 (except subparagraph (3), (10) and (11)) and 322 do not apply to an application for entry clearance, leave to enter or leave to remain as a Family Member under Appendix FM, and Part 9 (except for paragraph 322(1)) does not apply to an application for leave to remain on the grounds of private life under paragraphs 276ADE-276DH.].]

Note

Paragraph A320 inserted by HC 194, para 104 as from 9 July 2012. Words in square brackets inserted by HC 565, para 99 as from 6 September 2012.

[**B320.**   (1) Subject to paragraph (2), paragraphs 320 (except sub-paragraphs (3), (7B), (10) and (11)) and 322 (except sub-paragraphs (2) and (3)) do not apply to an application for entry clearance, leave to enter or leave to remain under Appendix Armed Forces.

(2) As well as the sub-paragraphs mentioned above, sub-paragraph (13) of paragraph 320 also applies to applications for entry clearance, leave to enter or leave to remain under Part 9 or 10 of Appendix Armed Forces.

Note

Inserted by HC 887, para 2 as from 30 December 2013.

Refusal of entry clearance or leave to enter the United Kingdom

320.   In addition to the grounds for refusal of entry clearance or leave to enter set out in Parts 2–8 of these Rules, and subject to paragraph 321 below, the following grounds for the refusal of entry clearance or leave to enter apply:

Grounds on which entry clearance or leave to enter the United Kingdom is to be refused

(1)   the fact that entry is being sought for a purpose not covered by these Rules;

[(2)   the fact that the person seeking entry to the United Kingdom:
- (a)   is currently the subject of a deportation order; or
- (b)   has been convicted of an offence for which they have been sentenced to a period of imprisonment of at least 4 years; or
- (c)   has been convicted of an offence for which they have been sentenced to a period of imprisonment of at least 12 months but less than 4 years, unless a period of 10 years has passed since the end of the sentence; or
- (d)   has been convicted of an offence for which they have been sentenced to a period of imprisonment of less than 12 months, unless a period of 5 years has passed since the end of the sentence.

Where this paragraph applies, unless refusal would be contrary to the Human Rights Convention or the Convention and Protocol relating to the Status of Refugees, it will only be in exceptional circumstances that the public interest in maintaining refusal will be outweighed by compelling factors.]

(3)   failure by the person seeking entry to the United Kingdom to produce to the Immigration Officer a valid national passport or other document satisfactorily establishing his identity and nationality;

(4)   failure to satisfy the Immigration Officer, in the case of a person arriving in the United Kingdom or seeking entry through the Channel Tunnel with the intention of entering any other part of the common travel area, that he is acceptable to the immigration authorities there;

(5)   failure, in the case of a visa national, to produce to the Immigration Officer a passport or other identity document endorsed with a valid and current United Kingdom entry clearance issued for the purpose for which entry is sought;

(6)   where the Secretary of State has personally directed that the exclusion of a person from the United Kingdom is conducive to the public good;

(7)   save in relation to a person settled in the United Kingdom or where the Immigration Officer is satisfied that there are strong compassionate reasons justifying admission, confirmation from the Medical Inspector that, for medical reasons, it is undesirable to admit a person seeking leave to enter the United Kingdom.

[(7A) where false representations have been made or false documents [or information] have been submitted (whether or not material to the application, and whether or not to the applicant's knowledge), or material facts have not been disclosed, in relation to the application [, or in order to obtain documents from the Secretary of State or a third party required in support of the application].]

[(7B) [where the applicant has previously breached the UK's immigration laws (and was [18 or over] at the time of his most recent breach) by]:

(a)   Overstaying;

(b)   breaching a condition attached to his leave;

(c)   being an Illegal Entrant;

(d)   using Deception in an application for entry clearance, leave to enter or remain[, or in order to obtain documents from the Secretary of State or a third party required in support of the application] (whether successful or not);

unless the applicant:

(i)   Overstayed for [90 days] or less and left the UK voluntarily, not at the expense (directly or indirectly) of the Secretary of State;

(ii)   used Deception in an application for entry clearance more than 10 years ago;

(iii) left the UK voluntarily, not at the expense (directly or indirectly) of the Secretary of State, more than 12 months ago;

[(iv) left the UK voluntarily, at the expense (directly or indirectly) of the Secretary of State, more than 2 years ago; and the date the person left the UK was no more than 6 months after the date on which the person was given notice of the removal decision, or no more than 6 months after the date on which the person no longer had a pending appeal [or administrative review]; whichever is the later;

(v)   left the UK voluntarily, at the expense (directly or indirectly) of the Secretary of State, more than 5 years ago; . . .

(vi)   was removed or deported from the UK more than 10 years ago[; or]

(vii) left or was removed from the UK as a condition of a caution issued in accordance with [section 22 of the Criminal Justice Act 2003] more than five years ago.]

Where more than one breach of the UK's immigration laws has occurred, only the breach which leads to the longest period of absence from the UK will be relevant under this paragraph.

[(7C) . . .

[(7D) failure, without providing a reasonable explanation, to comply with a request made on behalf of the Entry Clearance Officer to attend for interview.]

Note

Sub-paras (7A) inserted by HC 321, para 33 as from 29 February 2008. Words in square brackets in sub-paragraph (7A) inserted by HC 1113, para 97 as from 27 November 2008. Sub-s (7A) further amended by HC 1888, para 106 as from 6 April 2012. Words in square brackets in sub-para (d) inserted by HC 1888, para 107 as from April 2012. Sub–paras (7B)(iv), (v) and (vi) substituted and inserted by HC 863, para 128 as from 6 April 2011. Further amended by HC 194, para 105 as from 9 July 2012. Para (7B)(d)(i): words "90 days" inserted by HC 194, para 10 as from 1 October 2012. Para (7D): inserted by HC 514, para 2 as from 29 July 2012. Further amended by HC 1039, para 116: where an applicant has made an application for entry clearance or leave before 6 April 2013 and the application has not been decided before that date, it will be decided in accordance with the rules in force on 5 April 2013. Further amended by HC 803, para 14 as from 1 December 2013. Further amended by HC 693, para 97 as from 20 October 2014.

Sub-para (7C), the exemption for those seeking to enter under the family categories, has been replaced by para A320.

For guidance on how Secretary of State for the Home Department applies these provisions, see the Modernised Guidance at: www.ukba.homeoffice.gov.uk/sitecontent/documents/policyandlaw/modernised/general-grounds-refusing/

Grounds on which entry clearance or leave to enter the United Kingdom should normally be refused

(8)   failure by a person arriving in the United Kingdom to furnish the Immigration Officer with such information as may be required for the purpose of deciding whether he requires leave to enter and, if so, whether and on what terms leave should be given;

[(8A) where the person seeking leave is outside the United Kingdom, failure by him to supply any information, documents, copy documents or medical report requested by an Immigration Officer;]

(9)   failure by a person seeking leave to enter as a returning resident to satisfy the Immigration Officer that he meets the requirements of paragraph 18 of these Rules [or that he seeks leave to enter for the same purpose as that for which his earlier leave was granted];

(10)   production by the person seeking leave to enter the United Kingdom of a national passport or travel document issued by a territorial entity or authority which is not recognised by Her Majesty's Government as a state or is not dealt with as a government by them, or which does not accept valid United Kingdom passports for the purpose of its own immigration control; or a passport or travel document which does not comply with international passport practice;

[(11)   where the applicant has previously contrived in a significant way to frustrate the intentions of the Rules by:

    (i)   overstaying; or

    (ii)   breaching a condition attached to his leave; or

    (iii)   being an illegal entrant; or

    (iv)   using deception in an application for entry clearance, leave to enter or remain or in order to obtain documents from the Secretary of State or a third party required in support of the application (whether successful or not); and

there are aggravating circumstances, such as absconding, not meeting temporary admission/reporting restrictions or bail conditions, using an assumed identity or multiple identities, switching nationality, making frivolous applications or not complying with the re-documentation process.]

(12)   . . .

(13)   failure, except by a person eligible for admission to the United Kingdom for settlement . . ., to satisfy the Immigration Officer that he will be admitted to another country after a stay in the United Kingdom;

(14)   refusal by a sponsor of a person seeking leave to enter the United Kingdom to give, if requested to do so, an undertaking in writing to be responsible for that person's maintenance and accommodation for the period of any leave granted;

(15)   . . .];

(16)   failure, in the case of a child under the age of 18 years seeking leave to enter the United Kingdom otherwise than in conjunction with an application made by his parent(s) or legal guardian, to provide the Immigration Officer, if required to do so, with written consent to the application from his parent(s) or legal guardian;

save that the requirement as to written consent does not apply in the case of a child seeking admission to the United Kingdom as an asylum seeker;

(17) save in relation to a person settled in the United Kingdom, refusal to undergo a medical examination when required to do so by the Immigration Officer;

(18) . . .

[(18A)[within the 12 months prior to the date on which the application is decided], the person had been convicted of or admitted an offence for which they received a non-custodial sentence or other out of court disposal that is recorded on their criminal record;

(18B) in the view of the Secretary of State:

    (a)   the person's offending has caused serious harm; or

    (b)   the person is a persistent offender who shows a particular disregard for the law.]

(19) [The immigration officer deems the exclusion of the person from the United Kingdom to be conducive to the public good. For example, because the person's conduct (including convictions which do not fall within paragraph 320(2)), character, associations, or other reasons, make it undesirable to grant them leave to enter.]

[(20) failure by a person seeking entry into the United Kingdom to comply with a requirement relating to the provision of physical data to which he is subject by regulations made under section 126 of the Nationality, Immigration and Asylum Act 2002.]

(21) . . . .

[(22) Where one or more relevant NHS body has notified the Secretary of State that the person seeking entry or leave to enter has failed to pay a charge or charges with a total value of at least £1000 in accordance with the relevant NHS regulations on charges to overseas visitors.]

Note

See General note below.

See the IDIs at Chapter 9, Section 2, and the Entry Clearance Guidance RFL3 (hyperlinks in general note below).

On the specific provisions, and the guidance contained in Chapter 9, Section 2.

Para 320(10) see IDI, at section 12; see also *NA (Iraq) v Secretary of State for the Home Department* [2007] EWCA Civ 759. Special provisions apply in relation to holders of documents from TRNC, Taiwan, and Palestine.

Para 320(11) is not intended to be used punitively; eg a minor period of overstaying would not suffice.

Para 320(18) & (19) should not be invoked where an offence has become spent under the Rehabilitation of Offenders Act 1974.

Sub-para (8A) inserted by HC 704. Words in square brackets in sub-para (11) inserted by HC 1888, para 108 as from 6 April 2012. Sub-para (11) substituted by HC 565, para 100 as from 6 September 2012. Sub-para (15) deleted by HC 1888, para 109 as from 6 April 2012. Words in square brackets in sub-para 911) inserted by HC 1888, para 108 as from 6 April 2012. Sub-para (20) inserted by HC 370. Words in square brackets in sub-para (15) substituted by Cm 6339. Sub-para (21) inserted by HC 1112, para 16 as from 25 October 2004. Sub-para (21) deleted by HC 321, para 34 as from 29 February 2008. Sub-para (22) inserted by HC 1511, para 43 as from 31 October 2011. Sub-para (13): words deleted by HC 194, para 108 as from 9 July 2012. Further amended by HC 760, paras 264–266 as from 13 December 2012. Further amended by HC 803, para 15 as from 1 December 2013.

Refusal of leave to enter in relation to a person in possession of an entry clearance

321. A person seeking leave to enter the United Kingdom who holds an entry clearance which was duly issued to him and is still current may be refused leave to enter only where the Immigration Officer is satisfied that:

[(i)   False representations were made or false documents [or information] were submitted (whether or not material to the application, and whether or not to the holder's knowledge), or material facts were not disclosed, in relation to the application for entry clearance[, or in order to obtain documents from the Secretary of State or a third party required in support of the application]; or]

(ii)   a change of circumstances since it was issued has removed the basis of the holder's claim to admission, except where the change of circumstances amounts solely to the person becoming over age for entry in one of the categories contained in paragraphs 296–316 of these Rules since the issue of the entry clearance; or

(iii)   refusal is justified on grounds of restricted returnability; on medical grounds; [on grounds which would have led to a refusal under paragraphs 320(2), 320(6), 320(18A), 320(18B) or 320(19)] (except where this sub-paragraph applies in respect of an entry clearance issued under Appendix Armed Forces it is to be read as if for "paragraphs 320(2), 320(6), 320(18A), 320(18B) or 320(19)" it said "paragraph 8(a), (b), (c) or (g) and paragraph 9(d)"].

Note

Sub-para (i) substituted by HC 321, para 35 as from 29 February 2008. Words in square brackets in sub-paragraph (i) inserted by HC 1113, para 99 as from 25 November 2008. Words in square brackets ", or in order" to "of the application" in sub-paragraph (i) inserted by HC 1888, para 110 as from 6 April 2012. Further amended by HC 760, para 267 as from 13 December 2012. Words in sub-paragraph (iii) in square brackets inserted by HC 887, para 3 as from 30 December 2013.

See Note on para 320 and General note below.

[Grounds on which leave to enter or remain which is in force is to be cancelled at port or while the holder is outside the United Kingdom

321A.   The following grounds for the cancellation of a person's leave to enter or remain which is in force on his arrival in, or whilst he is outside, the United Kingdom apply:

(1)   there has been such a change in the circumstances of that person's case, since the leave was given, that it should be cancelled; or

[(2)   false representations were made or false documents were submitted (whether or not material to the application, and whether or not to the holder's knowledge), or material facts were not disclosed, in relation to the application for leave[, or in order to obtain documents from the Secretary of State or a third party required in support of the application]; [or

(3)   save in relation to a person settled in the United Kingdom or where the Immigration Officer or the Secretary of State is satisfied that there are strong compassionate reasons justifying admission, where it is apparent that, for medical reasons, it is undesirable to admit that person to the United Kingdom; or

(4)   where the Secretary of State has personally directed that the exclusion of that person from the United Kingdom is conducive to the public good; or

[(4A)   Grounds which would have led to a refusal under paragraphs 320(2),320(6), 320(18A), 320(18B) or 320(19) if the person concerned were making a new application for leave to enter or remain] [except where this sub-paragraph applies in respect of leave to enter or remain granted under Appendix Armed Forces it is to be read as if for "paragraphs 320(2), 320(6), 320(18A), 320(18B) or 320(19)" it said "paragraph 8(a), (b), (c) or (g) and paragraph 9(d)"].

(5)   [The Immigration officer or the Secretary of State deems the exclusion of the person from the United Kingdom to be conducive to the public good. For example, because the person's conduct (including convictions which do not fall within paragraph 320(2)), character, associations, or other reasons, make it undesirable to grant them leave to enter the United Kingdom; or]

(6)   where that person is outside the United Kingdom, failure by that person to supply any information, documents, copy documents or medical report requested by an Immigration Officer or the Secretary of State.]

Note

Para 321 replaces HC 251, para 17, which did not come under the sub-heading General in Pt IX of HC 251. Paragraph 321A inserted by HC 704. Sub-para (2) substituted by HC 321, para 36 as from 29 February 2008. Words in square brackets in sub-paragraphs (2) inserted by HC 1888, para 111 as from 6 April 2012. Further amended by HC 760, paras 268–270 as from 13 December 2012. Words in square brackets in sub-paragraph (4A) inserted by HC 887, para 4 as from 30 December 2013.

See Note on para 320 and General note below.

[Refusal of leave to remain, variation of leave to enter or remain or curtailment of leave]

322. In addition to the grounds for refusal of extension of stay set out in Parts 2–8 of these Rules, the following provisions apply in relation to the refusal of an application for [leave to remain,] variation of leave to enter or remain or, where appropriate, the curtailment of leave:

[Grounds on which leave to remain and variation of leave to enter or remain in the United Kingdom are to be refused]

(1)   the fact that variation of leave to enter or remain is being sought for a purpose not covered by these Rules.

[(1A) where false representations have been made or false documents have been submitted (whether or not material to the application, and whether or not to the applicant's knowledge), or material facts have not been disclosed, in relation to the application[, or in order to obtain documents from the Secretary of State or a third party required in support of the application].]

[(1B) the applicant is, at the date of application, the subject of a deportation order or a decision to make a deportation order;

[(1C) where the person is seeking leave to enter or remain:

(i)   they have been convicted of an offence for which they have been sentenced to imprisonment for at least 4 years; or

(ii)   they have been convicted of an offence for which they have been sentenced to imprisonment for at least 12 months but less than 4 years, unless a period of 15 years has passed since the end of the sentence; or

(iii) they have been convicted of an offence for which they have been sentenced to imprisonment for at least 12 months, unless a period of 7 years has passed since the end of the sentence; or

(iv)   they have, within the 24 months [prior to the date on which the application is decided], been convicted or admitted an offence for which they have received a non-custodial sentence or other out of court disposal that is recorded on their criminal record.]

[(1D) . . .]

Note

Sub-paragraph (1A) inserted by HC 321, para 39 as from 29 February 2008. Words in square brackets in sub-paragraph (1A) inserted by HC 1113. Headings substituted by HC 382, paras 6–9 as from 12 August 2010. Words in square brackets inserted by HC 382, para 7 as from 12 August 2010. Further amended by HC 1888, para 112 as from 6 April 2012. Further amended by HC 760, para 271 as from 13 December 2012. Sub-paragraph (1D) inserted by HC 943, para 4 as from 31 January 2013. Further amended by HC 1039, para 117: where an applicant has made an application for entry clearance or leave before 6 April 2013 and the application has not been decided before that date, it will be decided in accordance with the rules in force on 5 April 2013. Further amended by HC 803, para 16 as from 1 December 2013. Further amended by HC 1138, para 66 as from 6 April 2014.

[Grounds on which leave to remain and variation of leave to enter or remain in the United Kingdom should normally be refused]

(2) the making of false representations or the failure to disclose any material fact for the purpose of obtaining leave to enter or a previous variation of leave[, or in order to obtain documents from the Secretary of State or a third party required in support of the application for leave to enter or a previous variation of leave];

[(2A) the making of false representations or the failure to disclose any material fact for the purpose of obtaining a document from the Secretary of State that indicates the person has a right to reside in the United Kingdom.]

(3) failure to comply with any conditions attached to the grant of leave to enter or remain;

(4) failure by the person concerned to maintain or accommodate himself and any dependants without recourse to public funds;

(5) the undesirability of permitting the person concerned to remain in the United Kingdom in the light of his [conduct (including convictions which do not fall within paragraph 322(1C)), character or associations] or the fact that he represents a threat to national security;

[(5A) it is undesirable to permit the person concerned to enter or remain in the United Kingdom because, in the view of the Secretary of State:
(a) their offending has caused serious harm; or
(b) they are a persistent offender who shows a particular disregard for the law.]

(6) refusal by a sponsor of the person concerned to give, if requested to do so, an undertaking in writing to be responsible for his maintenance and accommodation in the United Kingdom or failure to honour such an undertaking once given;

(7) failure by the person concerned to honour any declaration or undertaking given orally or in writing as to the intended duration and/or purpose of his stay;

(8) failure, except by a person who qualifies for settlement in the United Kingdom or by the spouse or civil partner of a person settled in the United Kingdom, to satisfy the Secretary of State that he will be returnable to another country if allowed to remain in the United Kingdom for a further period;

[(9) failure by an applicant to produce within a reasonable time information, documents or other evidence required by the Secretary of State to establish his claim to remain under these Rules;]

(10) failure, without providing a reasonable explanation, to comply with a request made on behalf of the Secretary of State to attend for interview;

(11) failure, in the case of a child under the age of 18 years seeking a variation of his leave to enter or remain in the United Kingdom otherwise than in conjunction with an application by his parent(s) or legal guardian, to provide the Secretary of State, if required to do so, with written consent to the application from his parent(s) or legal guardian; save that the requirement as to written consent does not apply in the case of a child who has been admitted to the United Kingdom as an asylum seeker.

[(12) Where one or more relevant NHS body has notified the Secretary of State that the person seeking leave to remain or a variation of leave to enter or remain has failed to pay a charge or charges with a total value of at least £1000 in accordance with the relevant NHS regulations on charges to overseas visitors.]

Note

See Note on para 320 and General note below.

Heading substituted by HC 321. Sub-paragraph inserted by HC 321. Words in square brackets in sub-paragraph (1A) inserted by HC 1113. Sub-para (2) amended by HC 1888, para 113 as from 6 April 2012. Sub-para (9) substituted by HC 104. Sub-paras (10) and (11) are also new. Heading substituted by HC 321. Sub-para (12) inserted by HC 1511, para 44 as from 31 October 2011.

Further amended by HC 760, paras 272–273 as from 13 December 2012. Paragraph 322(2A) inserted by HC 1138, para 66 as from 13 March 2014.

Grounds on which leave to enter or remain may be curtailed

323. [A person's leave to enter or remain may be curtailed:
(i) on any of the grounds set out in paragraph 322 (2)–[(5A)] above [(except where this paragraph applies in respect of a person granted leave under Appendix Armed Forces "paragraph 322(2)-(5A) above" is to be read as if it said "paragraph 322(2) and (3) above and paragraph 8(e) and (g) of Appendix Armed Forces")]; or
[(ia) if he uses deception in seeking (whether successfully or not) leave to remain or a variation of leave to remain; or]
(ii) if he ceases to meet the requirements of the Rules under which his leave to enter or remain was granted; or
(iii) if he is the dependant, or is seeking leave to remain as the dependant, of an asylum applicant whose claim has been refused and whose leave has been curtailed under section 7 of the 1993 Act, and he does not qualify for leave to remain in his own right[; or]
(iv) on any of the grounds set out in paragraph 339A (i)-(vi) and paragraph 339G (i)-(vi)[; or
[(v) where a person has, within the first 6 months of being granted leave to enter, committed an offence for which they are subsequently sentenced to a period of imprisonment][, or
(vi) if he was granted his current period of leave as the dependent of a person ("P") and P's leave to enter or remain is being, or has been, curtailed]

Note

See Note on para 320 and General note below.

Amended by HC 760, paras 274, 275 as from 13 December 2012. Sub-para (i) amended by HC 628, para 139 and if an applicant has made an application for entry clearance or leave before 1 October 2013, the application will be decided in accordance with the Rules in force on 30 September 2013. Words in sub-paragraph (i) inserted by HC 887, para 5 as from 30 December 2013. Further amended by HC 1138, para 67 of this statement takes effect on the day on which section 1 of the Immigration Act 2014 comes into force. Further amended by HC 1138, para 68 as from 6 April 2014.

[Curtailment of leave . . . in relation to a Tier 2 Migrant[, a Tier 5 Migrant or a Tier 5 Migrant]

[323A. In addition to the grounds specified in paragraph 323, the leave to enter or remain of a Tier 2 Migrant, a Tier 4 Migrant or a Tier 5 Migrant:
(a) is to be curtailed . . . if:
(i) in the case of a Tier 2 Migrant or a Tier 5 Migrant:
(1) [the migrant fails to commence, or]
(2) [the migrant ceases, or will cease, before the end date recorded on the Certificate of Sponsorship Checking Service,
the employment, volunteering, training or job shadowing (as the case may be) that the migrant has been sponsored to do.]
(ii) in the case of a Tier 4 Migrant:

(1) the migrant fails to commence studying with the Sponsor, or
(2) [the Sponsor has excluded or withdrawn the migrant, or the migrant has withdrawn, from the course of studies, or]
[(2A) the migrant's course of study has ceased, or will cease, before the end date recorded on the Certificate of Sponsorship Checking Service, or]
(3) the Sponsor withdraws their sponsorship of a migrant on the doctorate extension scheme[, or]]
(4) [the Sponsor withdraws their sponsorship of a migrant who, having completed a pre-sessional course as provided in

> paragraph 120(b)(i) of Appendix A, does not have a knowledge of English equivalent to level B2 of the Council of Europe's Common European Framework for Language Learning in all four components (reading, writing, speaking and listening) or above.]]

(b)   may be curtailed . . . if:

    (i)   the migrant's Sponsor ceases to have a sponsor licence (for whatever reason); or

    (ii)   the migrant's Sponsor transfers the business for which the migrant worked, or at which the migrant is studying, to another person; and

        (1)   that person does not have a sponsor licence; and

        (2)   fails to apply for a sponsor licence within 28 days of the date of the transfer of the business; or

        (3)   applies for a sponsor licence but is refused; or

        (4)   makes a successful application for a sponsor licence, but the Sponsor licence granted is not in a category that would allow the Sponsor to issue a Certificate of Sponsorship [or Confirmation of Acceptance for Studies] to the migrant:

    (iii)   [in the case of a Tier 2 Migrant or a Tier 5 Migrant, if the employment that the certificate of Sponsorship Checking Service records that the migrant is being sponsored to do undergoes a prohibited change as specified in paragraph 323AA]:

        (1)   maternity leave

        (2)   paternity leave

        (3)   adoption leave, or

        (4)   sick leave;

    (iv)   paragraph (a) above applies but:

        (1)   the migrant is under the age of 18;

        (2)   the migrant has a dependant child under the age of 18;

        (3)   leave is to be varied such that when the variation takes effect the migrant will have leave to enter or remain and the migrant has less than 60 days extant leave remaining;

        (4)   the migrant has ben granted leave to enter to remain with another Sponsor or under immigration category; or

        (5)   the migrant has a pending application for leave to remain, or variation of leave, with the UK Border Agency, or has a pending appeal under Section 82 of the Nationality, Immigration and Asylum Act 2002[, or has a pending administrative review].]

Note

Substituted by HC 1888, para 114 as from 6 April 2012. Sub-para (iii) substituted by Cm 8423, para 78 as from 20 July 2012. Further amended by HC 1039, paras 118, 119: where an applicant has made an application for entry clearance or leave before 6 April 2013 and the application has not been decided before that date, it will be decided in accordance with the rules in force on 5 April 2013. Further amended by HC 628, para 140 shall apply to all applications decided on or after 1 October 2013. Further amended by HC 1138, para 70–75 as from 6 April 2014. Further amended by HC 693, para 98 as from 20 October 2014.

General note: For guidance on the application of the mandatory and discretionary refusals, see the Modernised Guidance at: www.ukba.homeoffice.gov.uk/sitecontent/documents/policyandlaw/mo dernised/general-grounds-refusing/

See also UK Entry Clearance guidance on Refusals of Entry Clearance; at www.ukba.homeoffice. gov.uk/policyandlaw/guidance/ecg/rfl/

The ambit of the provisions of Section 9, and the approach to be taken to them, have been considered in *R (Mauritius) v Entry Clearance Officer Port Louis* [2003] UKIAT 00030; *RM (Kwok on Tong): HC 395 para 320) India* [2006] UKAIT 00039; and *JC (Part 9 HC 395 - burden of proof) China* [2007] UKAIT 00027; see also *R (on the application of NA (Iraq)) v Secretary of State for Foreign and Commonwealth Affairs* [2007] EWCA Civ 759. Part 9 deals with applications being determined in-country by Secretary of State for the Home Department and by an ECO, outside of the UK. Where the decision must be made by the ECO, then the decision on an application is for him or her, and Secretary of State for the Home Department cannot, by issuing guidance, take away or remove the ECO's decision making power, although any guidance issued will be relevant to that decision (see *R (on the application of NA (Iraq)) v Secretary of State for the Home Department* [2007] EWCA Civ 759). An application may be refused by Secretary of State for the Home Department or an ECO on the basis that it fails to meet the substantive requirements of the rules and or alternatively, even if it does, on the basis that refusal may also be justified under the provisions of Part 9. Refusal under Part 9 can therefore serve as a stand alone refusal. The importance of invoking both substantive provisions and the mandatory or discretionary rules on refusal under Part 9 is highlighted in the guidance issued to ECOs in RFL3, given the view expressed in the instruction [RFL 3.1]:

> 'If appropriate, the ECO also needs to refuse the application under the category of the application applied for, as well as the general rules. If an ECO only refuses under para 320 and an appeal is allowed, they cannot then consider the substantive application and entry clearance will have to be issued'

[but see *JC (Part 9 HC 395 - burden of proof) China*]. The provisions of para 9 are, as the AIT have commented, a 'mixed bag' of provisions. The most important division in the scheme of these rules is between mandatory refusals (' . . . is to be refused'); and refusals where an element of discretion is maintained, so that the refusal may not be automatic (' . . . should normally be refused'). The IDIs contain some blurring of the applicability of mandatory refusal and the suggestion that residual discretion may still be exercised: see Chapter 2, Section 9 at para 1: 'Sub paragraphs (1)–(7) of para 320 set out grounds on which refusal of entry clearance is mandatory. In practice, however, entry clearance or leave to enter, as applicable, is normally refused on these grounds . . . ' Furthermore, even where the application would fall to be refused on a mandatory basis, and a decision to grant could not be in accordance with the scheme of the Immigration rules and would not therefore be in accordance with the law (see *RM (Kwon on Tong: HC 395 Para 320) India*) at para 14), a residual consideration to grant the application outside the Immigration rules is still maintained. Where an application falls to be refused on discretionary or mandatory grounds under para 9, the ECO should refer the case to Home Office for a decision outside the rules see, RFL3 at para 3.1:

> As with any application, an ECO needs to consider if there are any human rights grounds (in particular right to family life under Article 8) or any exceptional, compelling circumstances which would justify the issue of entry clearance. If there are exceptional, compelling circumstances, the application must be referred to the Referred Casework Unit (RCU), using the HO Referrals process, for a decision to be made outside of the Rules.

So far as general guidance to the application of Part 9 is concerned: see *JC (Part 9 HC 395, burden of proof) China*:

(1) The burden in showing that any precedent fact needed to invoke Part 9 lies on the decision-maker.

(2) There is no 'fixed' evidential standard, but it is likely to be on the higher end of the spectrum of balance of probability, particularly where there is an allegation of deception or quasi or actual criminal conduct; the more serious the allegation or its consequences, the stronger the evidence must generally be to make out the allegation.

(3) If the allegation is made out, then the burden then shifts to the applicant to prove that the appeal succeeds.

(4) There is no hard and fast rule as to the order in which substantive and general grounds of refusal should be considered.

(5) Where an immigration judge concludes that one of the mandatory refusal provisions properly applied then the appeal would fall to be dismissed (*RM (Kwok on Tong: HC 395 Para 320) India*).

(6) Where the application of Part 9 involves the application of a Discretionary provision the it is incumbent on the ECO and Immigration Judge to examine carefully all of the relevant facts (*R (Mauritius) v ECO-Port Louis*).

The IDIs: see, inter alia, Chapter 9, Section 1, acknowledge that refusal must be based on the existence of cogent evidence, and cannot rely merely on a decision maker's suspicion. It would not, for example, be acceptable to rely on an anonymous denunciation. Where an inappropriate application is made (the example cited in the IDI is of an applicant applying for ILR on the basis of marriage, when they would only be entitled to apply for probationary leave) and it is obvious that there would be entitlement on another basis, the application should not generally be refused on that basis, and clarification from the applicant should be sought (Chapter 9, Section 1 at section 6); similarly, applications that appeared to be made on a basis not covered by the Immigration rules might not be refused if they were in reality applications for a visit (section 9.1); and there remains a residual discretion to grant the application outside of the rules because of the existence of exceptional circumstances (para 9.2). Where an application falls to be refused on the basis of a failure to disclose material facts, this cannot be raised unless there had been some indication to the applicant of the kind of information or evidence that was required for the application (RFL3 at para 3.2.5).

[Prohibited changes to employment for Tier 2 Migrants and Tier 5 Migrants

323AA.

The following are prohibited changes, unless a further application for leave to remain is granted which expressly permits the changes:

(a)　The migrant is absent from work without pay for one calendar month or more in total (whether over a single period or more than one period), during any calendar year (1 January to 31 December), unless the absence from work is due solely to:

　　(i)　　maternity leave,
　　(ii)　paternity leave,
　　(iii)　adoption leave, or
　　(iv)　long term sick leave of one calendar month or more during any one period.

(b)　The employment changes such that the migrant is working for a different employer or Sponsor, unless:

　　(i)　　the migrant is a Tier 5 (Temporary Worker) Migrant in the Government Authorised Exchange sub-category and the change of employer is authorised by the Sponsor and under the terms of the work, volunteering or job shadowing that the Certificate of Sponsorship Checking Service records that the migrant is being sponsored to do, . . .

　　(ii)　the migrant is working for a different Sponsor under arrangements covered by the Transfer of Undertakings (Protection of Employment) Regulations 2006 or similar protection to continue in the same job[, or]

　　[(iii)　the migrant is a Tier 2 (Sportsperson) Migrant or a Tier 5 (Temporary Worker) Migrant in the creative and sporting sub-category and the following conditions are met:

　　　　(1)　　The migrant's sponsor is a sports club;
　　　　(2)　　The migrant is sponsored as a player only and is being temporarily loaned as a player to another sports club;
　　　　(3)　　Player loans are specifically permitted in rules set down by the relevant sports governing body listed in Appendix M;
　　　　(4)　　The migrant's sponsor has made arrangements with the loan club to enable the sponsor to continue to meet its sponsor duties; and
　　　　(5)　　The migrant will return to working for the sponsor at the end of the loan.]

(c)　The employment changes to a job in a different Standard Occupational Classification (SOC) code to that recorded by the Certificate of Sponsorship Checking Service.

(d)　If the migrant is a Tier 2 (Intra-Company Transfer) Migrant or a Tier 2 (General) Migrant, the employment changes to a different job in the same Standard Occupational Classification code to that recorded by the Certificate of Sponsorship Checking Service, and the gross annual salary (including such allowances as are specified as acceptable for this purpose in Appendix A) is below the appropriate salary rate for that job as specified in the Codes of Practice in Appendix J.

(e)   If the migrant was required to be Sponsored for a job at a minimum National Qualifications framework level in the application which led to his last grant of entry clearance or leave to remain, the employment changes to a job which the Codes of Practice in Appendix J record as being at a lower level.

(f)   If the migrant is a Tier 2 (General) Migrant and scored points from the shortage occupation provisions of Appendix A, the employment changes to a job which does appear in the Shortage Occupation List in Appendix K.

(g)   Except where (h) applies, the gross annual salary (including such allowances as are specified as acceptable for this purpose in Appendix A) reduces below:

   (i)   any minimum salary threshold specified in Appendix A of these Rules, where the applicant was subject to or relied on that threshold in the application which led to his current grant of entry clearance or leave to remain, or

   (ii)   the appropriate salary rate for the job as specified in the Codes of Practice in Appendix J, or

   (iii)   in cases where there is no applicable threshold in Appendix A and no applicable salary rate in Appendix J, the salary recorded by the Certificate of Sponsorship Checking Service.

(h)   Other reductions in salary are permitted if the reduction coincides with a period of:

   (i)   maternity leave,

   (ii)   paternity leave,

   (iii)   adoption leave,

   (iv)   long term sick leave of one calendar month or more, . . .

   [(v)   working for the sponsor's organisation while the migrant is not physically present in the UK, if the migrant is a Tier 2 (Intra-Company Transfer) Migrant, or]

   [(vi)   undertaking professional examinations before commencing work for the sponsor, where such examinations are a regulatory requirement of the job the migrant is being sponsored to do, and providing the migrant continues to be sponsored during that period.]]

Note

Inserted by Cm 8423, para 79 as from 20 July 2012. Substituted by HC 1039, para 120: where an applicant has made an application for entry clearance or leave before 6 April 2013 and the application has not been decided before that date, it will be decided in accordance with the rules in force on 5 April 2013. Word "or" deleted by HC 1138, para 76 as from 6 April 2014. Further amended by HC 1138, para 77 as from 6 April 2014. Further amended by HC 1138, para 78 as from 6 April 2014. Word "or" deleted by HC 1138, para 79 as from 6 April 2014. Further amended by HC 1138, para 80 as from 6 April 2014. Further amended by HC 1138, para 81 as from 6 April 2014. Further amended by HC 693, para 99 as from 6 November 2014, save that if an application has been made for entry clearance or leave to enter or remain before 6 November 2014, the application will be decided in accordance with the Rules in force on 5 November 2014.

323B.   [In addition to the grounds specified in paragraph 323, the leave to enter or remain of a Tier 1 (Exceptional Talent) Migrant may be curtailed if the Designated Competent Body that endorsed the application which led to the migrant's current grant of leave withdraws its endorsement of the migrant.]

Note

Inserted by HC 1436, para 6 as from 9 August 2011.

Curtailment of leave in relation to a Tier 1 (Graduate Entrepreneur) Migrant

[**323C.**   In addition to the grounds specified in paragraph 323, the leave to enter or remain of a Tier 1 (Graduate Entrepreneur) Migrant may be curtailed if the [endorsing body] that endorsed the application which led to the migrant's current grant of leave:

(a)   loses its status as an endorsing institution for Tier 1 (Graduate Entrepreneur) Migrants,

(b)   loses its status as a Highly Trusted Sponsor under Tier 4 of the Points-Based System (for whatever reason);

(c)   ceases to be an A-rated Sponsor under Tier 2 or Tier 5 of the Points-Based System because its Tier 2 or Tier 5 Sponsor licence is downgraded or revoked by the UK Border Agency, or

(d)   withdraws its endorsement of the migrant.]

Note

Inserted by HC 1888, para 115 as from 6 April 2012. Further amended by HC 1039, para 121: where an applicant has made an application for entry clearance or leave before 6 April 2013 and the application has not been decided before that date, it will be decided in accordance with the rules in force on 5 April 2013.

Crew members

324.   A person who has been given leave to enter to join a ship, aircraft, hovercraft, hydrofoil or international train service as a member of its crew, or a crew member who has been given leave to enter for hospital treatment, repatriation or transfer to another ship, aircraft, hovercraft, hydrofoil or international train service in the United Kingdom, is to be refused leave to remain unless an extension of stay is necessary to fulfil the purpose for which he was given leave to enter or unless he meets the requirements for an extension of stay as a spouse or civil partner in paragraph 284.

Note

Paras 320–324 replace HC 251, paras 78–86, 99–102.

PART 10 — REGISTRATION WITH THE POLICE

324A.   [. . .

325.   For the purposes of paragraph 326, a 'relevant foreign national' is a person aged 16 or over who is:

(i)   a national or citizen of a country or territory listed in Appendix 2 to these Rules;

(ii)   a stateless person; or

(iii)   a person holding a non-national travel document.

326.

(1)   Subject to sub-paragraph (2) below, a condition requiring registration with the police should normally be imposed on any relevant foreign national who is:

    (i)   given limited leave to enter the United Kingdom for longer than six months; or

    (ii)   given limited leave to remain which has the effect of allowing him to remain in the United Kingdom for longer than six months, reckoned from the date of his arrival (whether or not such a condition was imposed when he arrived).

(2)   Such a condition should not normally be imposed where the leave is given:

    (i)   as a seasonal agricultural worker;

    (ii)   as a [Tier 5 (Temporary Worker) Migrant, provided the Certificate of Sponsorship Checking System reference for which points were awarded records that the applicant is being sponsored as an overseas government employee or a private servant in a diplomatic household];

    (iii)   as a [Tier 2 (Minister of Religion) Migrant];

    (iv)   on the basis of marriage to or civil partnership with a person settled in the United Kingdom or as the unmarried same-sex partner of a person settled in the United Kingdom;

    (v)   as a person exercising access rights to a child resident in the United Kingdom;

    (vi)   as the parent of a child at school; or

    (vii)   following the grant of asylum.

(3)   Such a condition should also be imposed on any foreign national given limited leave to enter the United Kingdom where, exceptionally, the Immigration Officer considers it necessary to ensure that he complies with the terms of the leave.]

Note

Para 324A deleted and paras 325 and 326 substituted by HC 194 as from 4 February 2005. Words in square brackets in sub-paragraph (2)(ii) and (iii) substituted by HC 1113, paras 101 and 102 as from 27 November 2008.

PART 11 — ASYLUM

Procedure

[**326A.** The procedures set out in these Rules shall apply to the consideration of asylum and humanitarian protection.]

Note

Inserted by HC 82, para 1 as from 1 December 2007.

[**326B** Where the Secretary of State is considering a claim for asylum or humanitarian protection under this Part, she will consider any Article 8 elements of that claim in line with the provisions of Appendix FM (family life) [which are relevant to those elements and in line with] paragraphs 276ADE to 276DH (private life) of these Rules [unless the person is someone to whom Part 13 of these Rules applies].]

Note

Paragraph 326B inserted by HC 194, para 109 as from 9 July 2012. Words in square brackets substituted by HC 760, para 276 as from 13 December 2012 and shall apply to all applications decided on or after 13 December 2012, regardless of the date the application was made. Further amended by HC 532, para 14 of this statement take effect on 28 July 2014 and apply to all ECHR Article 8 claims from foreign criminals which are decided on or after that date.

Definition of asylum applicant

327. Under the Rules an asylum applicant is a person either:

(a) who makes a request to be recognised as a refugee under the Geneva Convention on the basis that it would be contrary to the United Kingdom's obligations under the Geneva Convention for him to be removed from or required to leave the United Kingdom, or

(b) otherwise makes a request for international protection. "Application for asylum" shall be construed accordingly".

Note

The definition is widely framed, so it is presumably capable of including non-Art 3 ECHR human rights cases, and all other claims intended to lead to grants of Discretionary, Humanitarian or Temporary protection. Where an asylum claim is limited, for other purposes, to claims that engage the Geneva Convention or Art 3 of ECHR, this is specifically indicated in statute: see, for example, s 94 of the Immigration and Asylum Act 1999; and s 113 of the Nationality, Immigration and Asylum Act 2002. Secretary of State for the Home Department's position: see the API on Withdrawal of Applications: www.bia.homeoffice.gov.uk/sitecontent/documents/policyandlaw/as ylumpolicyinstructions/apis/withdrawalofapplications.pdf, is that a claim within the ambit of para 327 is limited to a claim raising Geneva Convention grounds or Art 2 or Art 3 ECHR (in non-medical cases)).

327A. Every person has the right to make an application for asylum on his own behalf.

Applications for asylum

328. All asylum applications will be determined by the Secretary of State in accordance with the United Kingdom's obligations under the Geneva Convention. Every asylum application made by a person at a port or airport in the United Kingdom will be referred by the Immigration Officer for determination by the Secretary of State in accordance with these Rules.

328A. [The Secretary of State shall ensure that authorities which are likely to be addressed by someone who wishes to make an application for asylum are able to advise that person how and where such an application may be made.]

329. [Until an asylum application has been determined by the Secretary of State or the Secretary of State has issued a certificate under Part 2, 3, 4 or 5 of Schedule 3 to the Asylum and Immigration (Treatment of Claimants, etc.) Act 2004 no action will be taken to require the departure of the asylum applicant or his dependants from the United Kingdom.]

Note

Para 328A inserted by HC 82, para 4 as from 1 December 2007. Para 329 substituted by HC 1112, para 17 as from 25 October 2004.

330. If the Secretary of State decides to grant asylum and the person has not yet been given leave to enter, the Immigration Officer will grant limited leave to enter.

Note

This will normally be for five years: see para 339Q.

331. [[If a person seeking leave to enter is refused asylum [or their application for asylum is withdrawn or treated as withdrawn under paragraph 333C of these Rules], the Immigration Officer will consider whether or not he is in a position to decide to give or refuse leave to enter without interviewing the person further. If the Immigration Officer decides that a further interview is not required he may serve the notice giving or refusing leave to enter by post. If the Immigration Officer decides that a further interview is required, he will then resume his examination to determine whether or not to grant the person] leave to enter under any other provision of these Rules. If the person fails at any time to comply with a requirement to report to an Immigration Officer for examination, the Immigration Officer may direct that the person's examination shall be treated as concluded at that time. The Immigration Officer will then consider any outstanding applications for entry on the basis of any evidence before him.]

Note

Para 331 substituted by Cm 3365. Words in further square brackets inserted by HC 704. Words from "or their application" etc inserted by HC 420 as from 7 April 2008.

332. If a person who has been refused leave to enter applies for asylum and that application is refused [or withdrawn or treated as withdrawn under paragraph 333C of these Rules], leave to enter will again be refused unless the applicant qualifies for admission under any other provision of these Rules.

[**333.** Written notice of decisions on applications for asylum shall be given in reasonable time. Where the applicant is legally represented, notice may instead be given to the representative. Where the applicant has no legal representative and free legal assistance is not available, he shall be informed of the decision on the application for asylum and, if the application is rejected, how to challenge the decision, in a language that he may reasonably be supposed to understand.]

Note

Inserted by HC 82, para 5 as from 1 December 2007.

[**333A.** The Secretary of State shall ensure that a decision is taken by him on each application for asylum as soon as possible, without prejudice to an adequate and complete examination.

Where a decision on an application for asylum cannot be taken within six months of the date it was recorded, the Secretary of State shall either:
(a)   inform the applicant of the delay; or
(b)   if the applicant has made a specific written request for it, provide information on the time-frame within which the decision on his application is to be expected. The provision of such information shall not oblige the Secretary of State to take a decision within the stipulated time-frame.]

Note

Inserted by HC 82, para 6 as from 1 December 2007.

[**333B.** Applicants for asylum shall be allowed an effective opportunity to consult, at their own expense or at public expense in accordance with provision made for this by the Legal Services Commission or otherwise, a person who is authorised under Part V of the Immigration and Asylum Act 1999 to give immigration advice. This paragraph shall also apply where the Secretary of State is considering revoking a person's refugee status in accordance with these Rules.]

Note

Inserted by HC 82, para 7 as from 1 December 2007.

Withdrawal of application

333C. [If an application for asylum is withdrawn either explicitly or implicitly, consideration of it may be discontinued. An application will be treated as explicitly withdrawn if the applicant signs the relevant form provided by the Secretary of State. An application may be treated as impliedly withdrawn if an applicant fails to attend the personal interview as provided in paragraph 339A of these Rules unless the applicant demonstrates within a reasonable time that that failure was due to circumstances beyond his or her control. The Secretary of State will indicate on the applicant's asylum file that the application for asylum has been withdrawn and consideration of it has been discontinued.]

Note

Para 333 deleted by Cmnd 4851. Para 333–333C inserted by HC 82, paras 5–8 as from 1 December 2007. Further amended by HC 420.

For Secretary of State for the Home Department's policy (what constitutes implicit and explicit withdrawal; and the circumstances under which an explicit withdrawal will not be accepted), see API on withdrawal: www.bia.homeoffice.gov.uk/sitecontent/documents/policyandlaw/asylumpolicyinstructions/apis/withdrawalofapplications.pdf

Grant of asylum

334. An asylum applicant will be granted asylum in the United Kingdom if the Secretary of State is satisfied that:

(i) he is in the United Kingdom or has arrived at a port of entry in the United Kingdom;

(ii) he is a refugee, as defined in regulation 2 of The Refugee or Person in Need of International Protection (Qualification) Regulations 2006;

(iii) there are no reasonable grounds for regarding him as a danger to the security of the United Kingdom;

(iv) he does not, having been convicted by a final judgment of a particularly serious crime, constitute danger to the community of the United Kingdom; and

(v) refusing his application would result in him being required to go (whether immediately or after the time limited by any existing leave to enter or remain) in breach of the Geneva Convention, to a country in which his life or freedom would be threatened on account of his race, religion, nationality, political opinion or membership of a particular social group.

335. If the Secretary of State decides to grant asylum to a person who has been given leave to enter (whether or not the leave has expired) or to a person who has entered without leave, the Secretary of State will vary the existing leave or grant limited leave to remain.

Refusal of asylum

336. An application which does not meet the criteria set out in paragraph 334 will be refused. [Where an application for asylum is refused, the reasons in fact and law shall be stated in the decision and information provided in writing on how to challenge the decision.]

337. DELETED

338. When a person in the United Kingdom is notified that his asylum application has been refused he may, if he is liable to removal as an illegal entrant[, removal under section 10 of the Immigration and Asylum Act 1999] or to deportation, at the same

time be notified of removal directions, served with a notice of intention to make a deportation order, or served with a deportation order, as appropriate.

Note

Words in square brackets inserted in para 338 by Cmnd 4851.

339. . . .

Note

Para 339 deleted by Cmnd 4851.

Revocation or refusal to renew a grant of asylum

339A. A person's grant of asylum under paragraph 334 will be revoked or not renewed if the Secretary of State is satisfied that:

(i)   he has voluntarily re-availed himself of the protection of the country of nationality;

(ii) having lost his nationality, he has voluntarily re-acquired it; or

(iii) he has acquired a new nationality, and enjoys the protection of the country of his new nationality;

(iv) he has voluntarily re-established himself in the country which he left or outside which he remained owing to a fear of persecution;

(v)   he can no longer, because the circumstances in connection with which he has been recognised as a refugee have ceased to exist, continue to refuse to avail himself of the protection of the country of nationality;

(vi) being a stateless person with no nationality, he is able, because the circumstances in connection with which he has been recognised a refugee have ceased to exist, to return to the country of former habitual residence;

(vii) he should have been or is excluded from being a refugee in accordance with regulation 7 of The Refugee or Person in Need of International Protection (Qualification) Regulations 2006;

(viii) his misrepresentation or omission or facts, including the use of false documents, were decisive for the grant of asylum;

(ix) there are reasonable grounds for regarding him as a danger to the security of the United Kingdom; or

(x)   having been convicted by a final judgment of a particularly serious crime he constitutes danger to the community of the United Kingdom.

In considering (v) and (vi), the Secretary of State shall have regard to whether the change of circumstances is of such a significant and non-temporary nature that the refugee's fear of persecution can no longer be regarded as well-founded.

Where an application for asylum was made on or after the 21st October 2004, the Secretary of State will revoke or refuse to renew a person's grant of asylum where he is satisfied that at least one of the provisions in sub-paragraph (i)-(vi) apply.

Note

There is an important distinction between a grant of asylum and the Immigration leave that may have been granted as a consequence of the grant of that status. Limited leave, as para 339B makes clear, may also be curtailed if asylum status is revoked. For Secretary of State for the Home Department's approach to revocation, see APIs: 'Cancellation, Cessation and Revocation of Refugee Status' at: www.bia.homeoffice.gov.uk/sitecontent/documents/policyandlaw/asylumpolicy instructions/apis/cessation.pdf?view=Binary Exclusion: arts IF and 33 (2) of the Refugee Convention at: www.bia.homeoffice.gov.uk/sitecontent/documents/policyandlaw/asylumpolicyinstruction s/apis/exclusion.pdf. The Secretary of State for the Home Department considers that UNHCR should generally have the opportunity to comment on individual cases: see the API on cancellation and cessation (para 2.4). Dependants on the original application may be treated in-line, but there may be compelling reasons for not so doing (para 2.6). For the standards that the rule implements, see arts 11-14 of Directive 2004/83/EC. Paragraph 339A(i) – (vi) relate to cessation, under art 1c of the Geneva Convention, as defined in art 11 of 2004/83/EC; see also the Nationality, Immigration and Asylum Act 2002, s 76(3) for the basis on which Indefinite leave granted to a refugee may be revoked. For the general approach to cessation, see *R (on the application of B) v Secretary of State for the Home Department; R (on the application of Hoxha) v Secretary of State for the Home Department* [2005] UKHL 19, [2005] 4 All ER 580 and *RD (Cessation-burden of proof-procedure) Algeria* [2007] UKAIT 00066; see also the UNHCR Handbook at paras 111-39; and DL (DRC); ZN *(Afghanistan) v Entry Clearance Officer, Karachi* [2008] EWCA Civ 1420, for the possibility that cessation may be automatic, with no procedural steps required of Secretary of State for the Home Department for it to apply (In the cases considered by the Court, because of the acquisition of British nationality). Paragraph 339(vii) relates to Exclusion under arts 1D–F of the Geneva Convention. On the interpretation of art 1D, see *El-Ali v Secretary of State for the Home Department; Daraz v Secretary of State for the Home Department* [2002] EWCA Civ 1103, [2003] Imm AR 179. On art 1F: see art 7 of the Refugee in Need of International Protection Regulations 2006, which interprets art 1F(b) to include exclusion on the basis of a non-political crime to include 'a particularly cruel action even if committed with an allegedly political objective', and provides for exclusion on the basis that the action has been committed up to and including the date on which a residence permit is issued. In relation to what comes within the ambit of art 1F(c), see also the Immigration, Asylum and Nationality Act 2006 (terrorism, as defined in the Terrorism Act 2000, s 55 constitutes an action contrary to the purposes and principles of the United Nations under art 1F(c); but see *Al-Sirri v Secretary of State for the Home Department* [2009] EWCA Civ 222, [2009] All ER (D) 220 (Mar)). There is no bar to exclusion being raised, even when it has not raised at the outset: see *A (Iraq) v Secretary of State for the Home Department* [2005] EWCA Civ 1438. For the interpretation of the ambit of exclusion under art 1F (a)–(c), see *T v Secretary of State for the Home Department* [1996] 2 All ER 865, [1996] Imm AR 443, HL; *KJ (Sri Lanka) v Secretary of State for the Home Department* [2009] EWCA Civ 292, [2009] All ER (D) 41 (Apr); *R (on the application of JS (Sri Lanka) v Secretary of State for the Home Department* [2009] EWCA Civ 364, [2009] All ER (D) 235 (Apr); *Al-Sirri v Secretary of State for the Home Department (United Nations High Comr for Refugees intervening)* [2009] EWCA Civ 222, [2009] All ER (D) 220 (Mar); *MT (Article 1F (a) - aiding and abetting) Zimbabwe* [2012] UKUT 15 (IAC); *CM (Article 1F(a) - superior orders) Zimbabwe* [2012] UKUT 236 (IAC); *SK (Zimbabwe) v Secretary of State for the Home Department* [2012] EWCA Civ 807, [2012] All ER (D) 119 (Jun); *KK (Article 1F(c)), Turkey* [2004] UKIAT 00101; and the starred determination *Gurung v Secretary of State for the Home Department* [2003] UKIAT 4870, [2003] Imm AR 115 (partly disapproved by Toulson LJ in *JS (Sri Lanka)*). In relation to para 339(ix), see *Secretary of State for the Home Dept v Rehman* [2001] UKHL 47, [2002] Imm AR 98, [2002] INLR 92, [2002] 1 All ER 122. In para 339A(x), what constitutes a 'particularly serious crime' has now been placed on a statutory footing: see Nationality, Immigration and Asylum Act 2002, s 72. The presumptions that the crime was particularly serious and that the individual constitutes a danger to the community must be capable of being rebutted: see *EN (Serbia) v Secretary of State for the Home Department; KC (South Africa) v Secretary of State for the Home Department* [2009] EWCA Civ 630, [2010] QB 633.

339B. When a person's grant of asylum is revoked or not renewed any limited leave which they have may be curtailed.

[**339BA.** Where the Secretary of State is considering revoking refugee status in accordance with these Rules, the person concerned shall be informed in writing that the Secretary of State is reconsidering his qualification for refugee status and the reasons for the reconsideration. That person shall be given the opportunity to submit, in a personal interview or in a written statement, reasons as to why his refugee status should not be revoked. If there is a personal interview, it shall be subject to the safeguards set out in these Rules.] [However, where a person acquires British citizenship status, his refugee status is automatically revoked in accordance with paragraph 3339A(iii) upon acquisition of that status without the need to follow the procedure set out above.]

Note

Para 339BA inserted by HC 82, para 10 as from 1 December 2007. Final sentence inserted by Cm 7944, para 21 as from 22 October 2010.

This rule originates in the detailed provisions contained in art 38 of Directive 2005/85/EC; see also API on Cancellation, cessation and revocation: www.bia.homeoffice.gov.uk/sitecontent/document s/policyandlaw/asylumpolicyinstructions/ apis/cessation.pdf?view=Binary

Grant of humanitarian protection

339C. A person will be granted humanitarian protection in the United Kingdom if the Secretary of State is satisfied that:
(i)   he is in the United Kingdom or has arrived at a port of entry in the United Kingdom;

(ii)   he does not qualify as a refugee as defined in regulation 2 of The Refugee or Person in Need of International Protection (Qualification) Regulations 2006;

(iii)   substantial grounds have been shown for believing that the person concerned, if he returned to the country of return, would face a real risk of suffering serious harm and is unable, or, owing to such risk, unwilling to avail himself of the protection of that country; and

(iv)   he is not excluded from a grant of humanitarian protection.

Serious harm consists of:

(i)   the death penalty or execution;

(ii)   unlawful killing;

(iii)   torture or inhuman or degrading treatment or punishment of a person in the country of return; or

(iv)   serious and individual threat to a civilian's life or person by reason of indiscriminate violence in situations of international or internal armed conflict.

Note

See Directive 2004/83/EC at arts 15-19. See API on Humanitarian protection: www.ukba.home office.gov.uk/sitecontent/documents/policyandlaw/asylumpolicyinstructions/apis/humanitarianpr otection.pdf?view=Binar. In relation to what constitutes 'serious and individual threat to a civilian's life or person by reason of indiscriminate violence in situations of international or internal armed conflict' (transposing art 15(c) of Directive 2004/83/EC), see *Elgafaji v Staatssecretaris van Justitie* (C-465/07) [2009] All ER (EC) 651, [2009] 1 WLR 2100; ECJ (Grand Chamber); *QD (Iraq) v Secretary of State for the Home Dept (UNHCR intervener); AH (Iraq) v Secretary of State for the Home Dept (UNHCR intervener)* [2009] EWCA Civ 620, [2009] All ER (D) 256 (Jun).

Exclusion from humanitarian protection

339D. A person is excluded from a grant of humanitarian protection under paragraph 339C (iv) where the Secretary of State is satisfied that:

(i)   there are serious reasons for considering that he has committed a crime against peace, a war crime, a crime against humanity, or any other serious crime or instigated or otherwise participated in such crimes;

(ii)   there are serious reasons for considering that he is guilty of acts contrary to the purposes and principles of the United Nations or has committed, prepared or instigated such acts or encouraged or induced others to commit, prepare or instigate such acts;

(iii)   there are serious reasons for considering that he constitutes a danger to the community or to the security of the United Kingdom; [...] [or]

(iv)   prior to his admission to the United Kingdom the person committed a crime outside the scope of (i) and (ii) that would be punishable by imprisonment were it committed in the United Kingdom and the person left his country of origin solely in order to avoid sanctions resulting from the crime.

Note

See note on para 339A. Sub-para (iii) amended by HC 439, para 54 as from 6 April 2010.

339E. If the Secretary of State decides to grant humanitarian protection and the person has not yet been given leave to enter, the Secretary of State or an Immigration Officer will grant limited leave to enter. If the Secretary of State decides to grant humanitarian protection to a person who has been given limited leave to enter (whether or not that leave has expired) or a person who has entered without leave, the Secretary of State will vary the existing leave or grant limited leave to remain.

Refusal of humanitarian protection

339F. Where the criteria set out in paragraph 339C is not met humanitarian protection will be refused.

Revocation of humanitarian protection

339G. A person's humanitarian protection granted under paragraph 339C will be revoked or not renewed if the Secretary of State is satisfied that at least one of the following applies:

(i)   the circumstances which led to the grant of humanitarian protection have ceased to exist or have changed to such a degree that such protection is no longer required;

(ii)   the person granted humanitarian protection should have been or is excluded from humanitarian protection because there are serious reasons for considering that he has committed a crime against peace, a war crime, a crime against humanity, or any other serious crime or instigated or otherwise participated in such crimes;

(iii)   the person granted humanitarian protection should have been or is excluded from humanitarian protection because there are serious reasons for considering that he is guilty of acts contrary to the purposes and principles of the United Nations or has committed, prepared or instigated such acts or encouraged or induced others to commit, prepare or instigate such acts;

(iv)   the person granted humanitarian protection should have been or is excluded from humanitarian protection because there are serious reasons for considering that he constitutes a danger to the community or to the security of the United Kingdom;

(v)   the person granted humanitarian protection misrepresented or omitted facts, including the use of false documents, which were decisive to the grant of humanitarian protection; or

(vi)   the person granted humanitarian protection should have been or is excluded from humanitarian protection because prior to his admission to the United Kingdom the person committed a crime outside the scope of (ii) and (iii) that would be punishable by imprisonment had it been committed in the United Kingdom and the person left his country of origin solely in order to avoid sanctions resulting from the crime.

In applying (i) the Secretary of State shall have regard to whether the change of circumstances is of such a significant and non-temporary nature that the person no longer faces a real risk of serious harm;

Note

See note on para 339A.

339H. When a person's humanitarian protection is revoked or not renewed any limited leave which they have may be curtailed.

Consideration of applications

339HA. [The Secretary of State shall ensure that the personnel examining applications for asylum and taking decisions on his behalf have the knowledge with respect to relevant standards applicable in the field of asylum and refugee law.]

339I. When the Secretary of State considers a person's asylum claim, eligibility for a grant of humanitarian protection or human rights claim it is the duty of the person to submit to the Secretary of State as soon as possible all material factors needed to substantiate the asylum claim or establish that he is a person eligible for humanitarian protection or substantiate the human rights claim, which the Secretary of State shall assess in cooperation with the person.

The material factors include:

(i)   the person's statement on the reasons for making an asylum claim or on eligibility for a grant of humanitarian protection or for making a human rights claim;

(ii)   all documentation at the person's disposal regarding the person's age, background (including background details of relevant relatives), identity, nationality(ies), country(ies) and place(s) of previous residence, previous asylum applications, travel routes; and

(iii)   identity and travel documents.

339IA.   For the purposes of examining individual applications for asylum

(i)   Information provided in support of an application and the fact that an application has been made shall not be disclosed to the alleged actor(s) of persecution of the applicant, and

(ii)   information shall not be obtained from the alleged actors(s) of persecution that would result in their being directly informed that an application for asylum has been made by the applicant in question and would jeopardise the physical integrity of the applicant and his dependants, or the liberty and security of his family members still living in the country of origin.

This paragraph shall also apply where the Secretary of State is considering revoking a person's refugee status in accordance with these Rules.]

Note

Paras 339HA, 339IA inserted by HC 82, paras 11, 12 as from 1 December 2007.

339J.   The assessment by the Secretary of State of an asylum claim, eligibility for a grant of humanitarian protection or a human rights claim will be carried out on an individual[, objective and impartial] basis. This will include taking into account in particular:

(i)   all relevant facts as they relate to the country of origin or country of return at the time of taking a decision on the grant; including laws and regulations of the country of origin or country of return and the manner in which they are applied;

(ii)   relevant statements and documentation presented by the person including information on whether the person has been or may be subject to persecution or serious harm;

(iii)   the individual position and personal circumstances of the person, including factors such as background, gender and age, so as to assess whether, on the basis of the person's personal circumstances, the acts to which the person has been or could be exposed would amount to persecution or serious harm;

(iv)   whether the person's activities since leaving the country of origin or country of return were engaged in for the sole or main purpose of creating the necessary conditions for making an asylum claim or establishing that he is a person eligible for humanitarian protection or a human rights claim, so as to assess whether these activities will expose the person to persecution or serious harm if he returned to that country; and

(v)   whether the person could reasonably be expected to avail himself of the protection of another country where he could assert citizenship.

Note

Amended by HC 82, para 13 as from 1 December 2007.

Country conditions or the fact that an applicant is a member of a group systematically exposed to a risk of ill-treatment may go to demonstrate risk beyond the requirement in (iii) to relate the assessment to individual experience: see *Batayav v Secretary of State for the Home Department* [2003] EWCA Civ 1489, [2003] All ER (D) 60 (Nov); *Hariri v Secretary of State for the Home Department* [2003] EWCA Civ 807; see, in particular, *NA v United Kingdom* App no. 25904/07 (2008) ECHR 616 at paras 108-117. In relation to para 339J(iv), and the significance of sur place activities, see *Danian v Secretary of State for the Home Department* [1999] EWCA Civ 3000, [2000] Imm AR 96, [1999] INLR 533; *YB (Eritrea) v Secretary of State for the Home Department* [2008] EWCA Civ 360, [2008] All ER (D) 195 (Apr).

339JA.   [Reliable and up-to-date information shall be obtained from various sources as to the general situation prevailing in the countries of origin of applicants for asylum and, where necessary, in countries through which they have transited. Such information shall be made available to the personnel responsible for examining applications and taking decisions and may be provided to them in the form of a consolidated country information report.

This paragraph shall also apply where the Secretary of State is considering revoking a person's refugee status in accordance with these Rules.]

Note

Paragraph 339JA inserted by HC 82, para 14 as from 1 December 2007.

For country reports compiled by the Country of Origin Information Service in the Border Agency, see: www.bia.homeoffice.gov.uk/policyandlaw/guidance/coi/. For Secretary of State for the Home Department's Country policy bulletins and Operational guidance Notes (OGN) see: www.bia.hom eoffice.gov.uk/sitecontent/documents/policyandlaw/countryspecificasylum policyogns/

339K. The fact that a person has already been subject to persecution or serious harm, or to direct threats of such persecution or such harm, will be regarded as a serious indication of the person's well-founded fear of persecution or real risk of suffering serious harm, unless there are good reasons to consider that such persecution or serious harm will not be repeated.

Note

See also *Demirkaya v Secretary of State for the Home Department* [1999] EWCA Civ 1654, [1999] INLR 441, [1999] Imm AR 498.

339L. It is the duty of the person to substantiate the asylum claim or establish that he is a person eligible for humanitarian protection or substantiate his human rights claim. Where aspects of the person's statements are not supported by documentary or other evidence, those aspects will not need confirmation when all of the following conditions are met:
(i) the person has made a genuine effort to substantiate his asylum claim or establish that he is a person eligible for humanitarian protection or substantiate his human rights claim;
(ii) all material factors at the person's disposal have been submitted, and a satisfactory explanation regarding any lack of other relevant material has been given;
(iii) the person's statements are found to be coherent and plausible and do not run counter to available specific and general information relevant to the person's case;
(iv) the person has made an asylum claim or sought to establish that he is a person eligible for humanitarian protection or made a human rights claim at the earliest possible time, unless the person can demonstrate good reason for not having done so; and
(v) the general credibility of the person has been established.

339M. The Secretary of State may consider that a person has not substantiated his asylum claim or established that he is a person eligible for humanitarian protection or substantiated his human rights claim [and thereby reject his application for asylum, determine that he is not eligible for humanitarian protection or reject his human rights claim,] if he fails, without reasonable explanation, to make a prompt and full disclosure of material facts, either orally or in writing, or otherwise to assist the Secretary of State in establishing the facts of the case; this includes, for example, . . . failure to report to a designated place to be fingerprinted, failure to complete an asylum questionnaire or failure to comply with a requirement to report to an immigration officer for examination.

339MA. [Applications for asylum shall be neither rejected nor excluded from examination on the sole ground that they have not been made as soon as possible.]

Note

Words in square brackets inserted by HC 82, para 15 as from 1 December 2007. Para 339MA inserted by HC 82, para 16 as from 1 December 2007. Words deleted by HC 420 as from 7 April 2008.

339N. In determining whether the general credibility of the person has been established the Secretary of State will apply the provisions in s 8 of the Asylum and Immigration (Treatment of Claimants, etc.) Act 2004.

Note

On paras 339HA–MA: see Directive 2004/83/EC.

[Personal interview

339NA Before a decision is taken on the application for asylum, the applicant shall be given the opportunity of a personal interview on his application for asylum with a representative of the Secretary of State who is legally competent to conduct such an interview.

The personal interview may be omitted where:

(i)   the Secretary of State is able to take a positive decision on the basis of evidence available;

(ii)   the Secretary of State has already had a meeting with the applicant for the purpose of assisting him with completing his application and submitting the essential information regarding the application;

(iii) the applicant, in submitting his application and presenting the facts, has only raised issues that are not relevant or of minimal relevance to the examination of whether he is a refugee, as defined in regulation 2 of the Refugee or person in need of International Protection (Qualification) Regulations 2006;

(iv) the applicant has made inconsistent, contradictory, improbable or insufficient representations which make his claim clearly unconvincing in relation to his having been the object of persecution;

(v)   the applicant has submitted a subsequent application which does not raise any relevant new elements with respect to his particular circumstances or to the situation in his country of origin;

(vi) the applicant is making an application merely in order to delay or frustrate the enforcement of an earlier or imminent decision which would result in his removal; and

(vii) it is not reasonably practicable, in particular where the Secretary of State is of the opinion that the applicant is unfit or unable to be interviewed owing to enduring circumstances beyond his control.

The omission of a personal interview shall not prevent the Secretary of State from taking a decision on the application.

Where the personal interview is omitted, the applicant and dependants shall be given a reasonable opportunity to submit further information.]

339NB. [

(i)   The personal interview mentioned in paragraph 339NA above shall normally take place without the presence of the applicant's family members unless the Secretary of State considers it necessary for an appropriate examination to have other family members present.

(ii)   The personal interview shall take place under conditions which ensure appropriate confidentiality.]

339NC. [

(i)   A written report shall be made of every personal interview containing at least the essential information regarding the asylum application as presented by the applicant in accordance with paragraph 339I of these Rules.

(ii)   The Secretary of State shall ensure that the applicant has timely access to the report of the personal interview and that access is possible as soon as necessary for allowing an appeal to be prepared and lodged in due time.]

339ND. [The Secretary of State shall provide at public expense an interpreter for the purpose of allowing the applicant to submit his case, wherever necessary. The Secretary of State shall select an interpreter who can ensure appropriate communication between the applicant and the representative of the Secretary of State who conducts the interview.]

Note

Heading and paras 339NA, 339NB, 339NC, 339ND inserted by HC 82, paras 18–21 as from 1 December 2007.

Paragraph 339NC(iii) and (iv) deleted by HC 439, para 55 as from 6 April 2010.

See arts 12-14 of Directive 2005/85/EC; Secretary of State for the Home Department's policy is set out in the APG on Interviewing: www.bia.homeoffice.gov.uk/sitecontent/documents/policyandla w/asylumpolicyinstructions/apis/interviewing.pdf. Where an applicant's representative or inter-preter are unable to attend the interview, the high standards of fairness applicable in the asylum context may require that the interview be tape-recorded: *R (on the application of Dirshe) v Secretary of State for the Home Department* [2005] EWCA Civ 421, [2005] 1 WLR 2685. *Dirshe* though is not authority for the proposition that where a claimant requests tape-recording of an interview, but that is not carried out, the record is inadmissible: *MB (admissible evidence; interview records) Iran (Rev 1)* [2012] UKUT 119 (IAC).

Internal relocation

339O
(i)   The Secretary of State will not make:
    (a)   a grant of asylum if in part of the country of origin a person would not have a well founded fear of being persecuted, and the person can reasonably be expected to stay in that part of the country; or
    (b)   a grant of humanitarian protection if in part of the country of return a person would not face a real risk of suffering serious harm, and the person can reasonably be expected to stay in that part of the country.
(ii)   In examining whether a part of the country of origin or country of return meets the requirements in (i) the Secretary of State, when making his decision on whether to grant asylum or humanitarian protection, will have regard to the general circumstances prevailing in that part of the country and to the personal circumstances of the person.
(iii)   (i) applies notwithstanding technical obstacles to return to the country of origin or country of return.

Note

See API on Internal Relocation www.bia.homeoffice.gov.uk/sitecontent/documents/policyandlaw /asylumpolicyinstructions/apis/internalrelocation.pdf. For the source of the current rule, see art 8 of Directive 2004/83/EC; see also para 91 of the UNHCR handbook. The approach applicable in assessing whether internal relocation is reasonable in all the circumstances is set out in *Januzi v Secretary of State for the Home Department* [2006] UKHL 5, [2006] 2 AC 426, [2006] 3 All ER 305; see also *R v Secretary of State for the Home Department, ex p Robinson v Secretary of State for the Home Department* [1997] EWCA Civ 3090, [1998] QB 929, [1997] Imm AR 568, [1997] 4 All ER 210; the starred determination in *Dyli v Secretary of State for the Home Department* [2000] UKIAT 0001, [2000] Imm AR 652, [2000] INLR 372; *Canaj v Secretary of State for the Home Department; Vallaj v Special Adjudicator* [2001] EWCA Civ 782, [2001] INLR 342; [2000] EWCA Civ 11, [2000] 3 All ER 449, [2000] Imm AR 271, [2000] INLR 122 and *E v Secretary of State for the Home Department* [2003] EWCA Civ 1032, [2004] QB 531, [2003] Imm AR 609, [2003] INLR 475. An asylum seeker must demonstrate the existence of a well-founded fear in their home area; the question of whether the option of internal relocation exists, which is an exacting test, is to be assessed on all of the facts, and on the basis of whether it is reasonable in all the circumstances: it must be reasonably practicable and safe to reach the area of proposed relocation; in deciding what is reasonable, standards in the country in which asylum has been sought do not provide a relevant comparator; internal relocation does not require a guarantee of international socio, economic and political rights in that area; it is relevant to compare the situation and socio-economic and other conditions in the home area and other parts of the country with circumstances in the area of proposed relocation; reasonableness depends on all of the circum-stances, but where, inter alia, an individual relocating might not be able to access basic subsistence needs, or conditions would expose them to danger, then it might not be viable for them to relocate; where the state, or its agents, is the source of the persecution in the home area, there is no presumption that internal relocation does not exist as an alternative to seeking international protection, and whether internal relocation exists as a viable possibility must be assessed on the basis of all of the facts including the likely impact of or reach of state actors; and socio-economic or other considerations in an applicant's country of origin, or the circumstances of the applicant in the country in which they have sought asylum, may be relevant to a claim that they should not be returned on humanitarian or human rights grounds.

Sur place claims

339P. A person may have a well-founded fear of being persecuted or a real risk of suffering serious harm based on events which have taken place since the person left the country of origin or country of return and/or activates which have been engaged in by a person since he left he country of origin or country of return, in particular where it is established that the activities relied upon constitute the expression and continuation of convictions or orientations held in the country of origin or country of return.

Note

See *Danian v Secretary of State for the Home Department* [1999] EWCA Civ 3000, [2000] Imm AR 96, [1999] INLR 533; *YB (Eritrea) v Danian v Secretary of State for the Home Department* [2008] EWCA Civ 360, [2008] All ER (D) 195 (Apr).

Residence Permits

339Q.
(i)   The Secretary of State will issue to a person granted asylum in the United Kingdom a United Kingdom Residence Permit (UKRP) as soon as possible after the grant of asylum. The UKRP will be valid for five years and renewable, unless compelling reasons of national security or public order otherwise require or where there are reasonable grounds for considering that the applicant is a danger to the security of the UK or having been convicted by a final judgment of a particularly serious crime, the applicant constitutes a danger to the community of the UK.

(ii)   The Secretary of State will issue to a person granted humanitarian protection in the United Kingdom a UKRP as soon as possible after the grant of humanitarian protection. The UKRP will be valid for five years and renewable, unless compelling reasons of national security or public order otherwise require or where there are reasonable grounds for considering that the person granted humanitarian protection is a danger to the security of the UK or having been convicted by a final judgment of a serious crime, this person constitutes a danger to the community of the UK.

(iii)   The Secretary of State will issue a UKRP to a family member of a person granted asylum or humanitarian protection where the family member does not qualify for such status. A UKRP will be granted for a period of five years. The UKRP is renewable on the terms set out in (i) and (ii) respectively. ["Family member" for the purposes of this sub-paragraph refers only to those who are treated as dependants for the purposes of paragraph 349].

(iv)   The Secretary of State may revoke or refuse to renew a person's UKRP where their grant of asylum or humanitarian protection is revoked under the provisions in the immigration rules.

Note

Inserted by HC 628, para 141.

[Requirements for indefinite leave to remain for persons granted asylum or humanitarian protection

339R. The requirements for indefinite leave to remain for a person granted asylum or humanitarian protection, or their dependants ranted asylum or humanitarian protection in line with the main applicant, are that:

(i)   the applicant has held a UK Residence Permit (UKRP) issued under paragraph 339Q for a continuous period of five years in the UK; and

(ii)   the applicant's UKRP has not been revoked or not renewed under paragraphs 339A or 339G of the immigration rules; and

(iii)   the applicant has not:
    (a)   been convicted of an offence for which they have been sentenced to imprisonment for at least 4 years; or
    (b)   been convicted of an offence for which they have been sentenced to imprisonment for at least 12 months but less than 4 years, unless a period of 15 years has passed since the end of the sentence; or

(c)   been convicted of an offence for which they have been sentenced to imprisonment for at least 12 months, unless a period of 7 years has passed since the end of the sentence; or

(d)   been convicted of an offence for which they have received a non-custodial sentence or other out of court disposal that is recorded on their criminal record, unless a period of 24 months has passed since they received their sentence; or

(e)   in the view of the Secretary of State persistently offended and shown a particular disregard for the law, unless a period of seven years has passed since the most recent sentence was received.]

Note

Inserted by HC 628, para 141 and if an applicant has made an application for entry clearance or leave before 1 October 2013, the application will be decided in accordance with the Rules in force on 30 September 2013.

[Indefinite leave to remain for a person granted asylum or humanitarian protection

339S. Indefinite leave to remain for a person granted asylum or humanitarian protection will be granted where each of the requirements in paragraph 339R is met.]

Note

Inserted by HC 628, para 141 and if an applicant has made an application for entry clearance or leave before 1 October 2013, the application will be decided in accordance with the Rules in force on 30 September 2013.

[Refusal of indefinite leave to remain for a person granted asylum or humanitarian protection

339T. (i) Indefinite leave to remain for a person granted asylum or humanitarian protection is to be refused if any of the requirements in paragraph 339R is not met.

(ii) An applicant refused indefinite leave to remain under paragraph 339T(i) may apply to have their UK Residence Permit extended in accordance with paragraph 339Q.]

Note

Inserted by HC 628, para 141 and if an applicant has made an application for entry clearance or leave before 1 October 2013, the application will be decided in accordance with the Rules in force on 30 September 2013.

[Consideration of asylum applications and human rights claims]

340. . . .

Note

Para 340 deleted by Cm 6918.

341. [. . .]

Note

Para 341 deleted by Cm 6918.

342. The actions of anyone acting as an agent of the asylum applicant [or human rights claimant] may also be taken into account in regard to the matters set out in paragraphs 340 and 341.

Note

Words in square brackets inserted by HC 299.

343. . . .

Note

Para 343 deleted by Cm 6918.

344. . . .

Note

Para 344 deleted by Cm 6918.

Travel documents

344A.

(i)   After having received a complete application for a travel document, the Secretary of State will issue to a person granted asylum in the United Kingdom and their family members travel documents, in the form set out in the Schedule to the Geneva Convention, for the purpose of travel outside the United Kingdom, unless compelling reasons of national security or public order otherwise require.

(ii)   After having received a complete application for a travel document, the Secretary of State will issue travel documents to a person granted humanitarian protection in the United Kingdom where that person is unable to obtain a national passport or other identity documents which enable him to travel, unless compelling reasons of national security or public order otherwise require.

(iii)   Where the person referred to in (ii) can obtain a national passport or identity documents but has not done so, the Secretary of State will issue that person with a travel document where he can show that he has made reasonable attempts to obtain a national passport or identity document and there are serious humanitarian reasons for travel.

Note

In relation to para 344A (ii), the terms of an earlier policy, requiring applicants for travel documents who had been granted leave on non-asylum grounds to produce evidence that they had attempted to obtain renewal of their own passports, was unsuccessfully challenged in *R v Secretary of State for the Home Department, ex p Najem* [1998] EWHC 829 (Admin), [1999] Imm AR 107, although a challenge might be made where an applicant or their family might be exposed to risk as a result of making an application for a travel document from their national authorities.

Access to Employment

344B.   The Secretary of State will not impose conditions restricting the employment or occupation in the United Kingdom of a person granted asylum or humanitarian protection.

Information

344C.   A person who is granted asylum or humanitarian protection will be provided with access to information in a language that they may reasonably be supposed to understand which sets out the rights and obligations relating to that status. The Secretary of State will provide the information as soon as possible after the grant of asylum or humanitarian protection.

Third country cases

345.

[(1)   In a case where the Secretary of State is satisfied that the conditions set out in paragraphs 4 and 5(1), 9 and 10(1), 14 and 15(1) or 17 of Schedule 3 to the Asylum and Immigration (Treatment of Claimants, etc) Act 2004 are fulfilled, he will normally decline to examine the asylum application substantively and issue a certificate under Part 2, 3, 4 or 5 of Schedule 3 to the Asylum and Immigration (Treatment of Claimants, etc.) Act 2004 as appropriate.

(2)   The Secretary of State shall not issue a certificate under Part 2, 3, 4 or 5 of Schedule 3 to the Asylum and Immigration (Treatment of Claimants, etc) Act 2004 unless:

(i)   the asylum applicant has not arrived in the United Kingdom directly from the country in which he claims to fear persecution and has had an opportunity at the border or within the third country or territory to make contact with the authorities of that third country or territory in order to seek their protection; or

(ii)   there is other clear evidence of his admissibility to a third country or territory.

[Provided that he is satisfied that a case meets these criteria, the Secretary of State is under no obligation to consult the authorities of the third country or territory before the removal of an asylum applicant to that country or territory.]

[(2A) Where a certificate is issued under Part 2, 3, 4 or 5 of Schedule 3 to the Asylum and Immigration (Treatment of Claimants, etc.) Act 2004 the asylum applicant shall:

    (i)   be informed in a language that he may reasonably be expected to understand regarding his removal to a safe third country;

    (ii)   be provided with a document informing the authorities of the safe and third country, in the language of that country, that the asylum application has not been examined in substance by the authorities in the United Kingdom;

    (iii)   sub-paragraph 345(2A)(ii) shall not apply if removal takes place with reference to the arrangements set out in Regulation (EC) No. 343/2003 [or Regulation (EC) No 604/2013] (the Dublin Regulation); and

    (iv)   if an asylum applicant removed under this paragraph is not admitted to the safe third country (not being a country to which the Dublin Regulation applies as specified in paragraph 345(2A)(iii), subject to determining and resolving the reasons for his non-admission, the asylum applicant shall be admitted to the asylum procedure in the United Kingdom.]

(3)   Where a certificate is issued under Part 2, 3, 4 or 5 of Schedule 3 to the Asylum and Immigration (Treatment of Claimants, etc) Act 2004 in relation to the asylum claim and the person is seeking leave to enter the Immigration Officer will consider whether or not he is in a position to decide to give or refuse leave to enter without interviewing the person further. If the Immigration Officer decides that a further interview is not required he may serve the notice giving or refusing leave to enter by post. If the Immigration Officer decides that a further interview is required, he will then resume his examination to determine whether or not to grant the person leave to enter under any other provision of these Rules. If the person fails at any time to comply with a requirement to report to an Immigration Officer for examination, the Immigration Officer may direct that the person's examination shall be treated as concluded at that time. The Immigration Officer will then consider any outstanding applications for entry on the basis of any evidence before him.

(4)   Where a certificate is issued under Part 2, 3, 4 or 5 of Schedule 3 to the Asylum and Immigration (Treatment of Claimants, etc) Act 2004 the person may, if liable to removal as an illegal entrant, or removal under section 10 of the Immigration and Asylum Act 1999 or to deportation, at the same time be notified of removal directions, served with a notice of intention to make a deportation order, or served with a deportation order, as appropriate.]

Note

Para 345 substituted by HC 1112, para 18 as from 25 October 2004. Sub-paragraph (2A) inserted by HC 82, para 22 as from 1 December 2007. Further amended by HC 803, para 17 as from 1 December 2013.

Previously rejected applications

346.   . . . .

347.   . . .

Note

Para 346 deleted by HC 1112, para 19 as from 25 October 2004.

Rights of appeal

348.   . . .

Note

Para 348 deleted by Cmnd 4851.

Dependants

349. [A spouse, civil partner, unmarried or same-sex partner, or minor child accompanying a principal applicant may be included in his application for asylum as his dependant, [provided, in the case of an adult dependant with legal capacity, the dependant consents to being treated as such at the time the application is lodged.] A spouse, civil partner, unmarried or same-sex partner or minor child may also claim asylum in his own right. If the principal applicant is granted asylum and leave to enter or remain any spouse, civil partner, unmarried or same-sex partner or minor child will be granted leave to enter or remain for the same duration. The case of any dependant who claims asylum in his own right will be [also] considered individually in accordance with paragraph 334 above. An applicant under this paragraph, including an accompanied child, may be interviewed where he makes a claim as a dependant or in his own right.

If the spouse, civil partner, unmarried or same-sex partner, or minor child in question has a claim in his own right, that claim should be made at the earliest opportunity. Any failure to do so will be taken into account and may damage credibility if no reasonable explanation for it is given. Where an asylum [or humanitarian protection] application is unsuccessful, at the same time that asylum [or humanitarian protection] is refused the applicant may be notified of removal directions or served with a notice of the Secretary of State's intention to deport him, as appropriate. In this paragraph and paragraphs 350-352 a child means a person who is under 18 years of age or who, in the absence of documentary evidence establishing age, appears to be under that age. An unmarried or same sex partner for the purposes of this paragraph, is a person who has been living together with the principal applicant in a subsisting relationship akin to marriage or a civil partnership for two years or more.]

Note

Para 324 substituted by Cmnd 5597. Words in square brackets inserted by HC 28, paras 2–4 as from 8 November 2007. Words from "Provided" to "application is lodged" and word "also" inserted by HC 82, para 24 as from 1 December 2007.

The API on Dependants is currently under review.

Unaccompanied children

350. Unaccompanied children may also apply for asylum and, in view of their potential vulnerability, particular priority and care is to be given to the handling of their cases.

351. A person of any age may qualify for refugee status under the Convention and the criteria in paragraph 334 apply to all cases. However, account should be taken of the applicant's maturity and in assessing the claim of a child more weight should be given to objective indications of risk than to the child's state of mind and understanding of his situation. An asylum application made on behalf of a child should not be refused solely because the child is too young to understand his situation or to have formed a well founded fear of persecution. Close attention should be given to the welfare of the child at all times.

352. [Any child over the age of 12 who has claimed asylum in his own right shall be interviewed about the substance of his claim unless the child is unfit or unable to be interviewed. When an interview takes place it shall be conducted in the presence of a parent, guardian, representative or another adult independent of the Secretary of State who has responsibility for the child. The interviewer shall have specialist training in the interviewing of children and have particular regard to the possibility that a child will feel inhibited or alarmed. The child shall be allowed to express himself in his own way and at his own speed. If he appears tired or distressed,] [the interview will be suspended. The interviewer should then consider whether it would be appropriate for the interview to be resumed the same day or on another day].

352ZA. [The Secretary of State shall as soon as possible after an unaccompanied child makes an application for asylum take measures to ensure that a representative represents and/or assists the unaccompanied child with respect to the examination of the application and ensure that the representative is given the opportunity to inform the unaccompanied child about the meaning and possible consequences of the interview and, where appropriate, how to prepare himself for the interview. The representative shall have the right to be present at the interview and ask questions and make comments in the interview, within the framework set by the interviewer.]

352ZB. [The decision on the application for asylum shall be taken by a person who is trained to deal with asylum claims from children.]

Note

Words in square brackets substituted by Cmnd 5597. Paragraph 352 replaced by HC 82, para 25 as from 1 December 2007. Paragraph 352 amended by HC 439, para 56 as from 6 April 2010. Paragraphs 352ZA and 352ZB inserted by HC 82, paras 26, 27 as from 1 December 2007. Paragraphs 352ZC-ZF inserted by HC 1039, para 122 as from 6 April 2013.

See Asylum Process Instruction 'Processing asylum applications from children': www.bia.homeo ffice.gov.uk/sitecontent/documents/policyandlaw/asylumprocessguidance/specialcases/guidance/pr ocessingasylumapplication1.pdf. On the consequences of non-compliance with the rules, see *AA (Afghanistan) v Secretary of State for the Home Department* [2007] EWCA Civ 12, [2007] All ER (D) 250 (Jan); see also *CL (Vietnam) v Secretary of State for the Home Department* [2008] EWCA Civ 1551, [2009] 1 WLR 1873 on the approach in assessing the existence or adequacy of reception arrangements for unaccompanied minors in the country of return. Adjudicator Guidance note No 8 (April 2004) provides guidance on the approach of the AIT in hearing appeals involving unaccompanied children:
www.justice.gov.uk/downloads/tribunals/immigration-and-asylum/lower/GuideNoteNo8.pdf

Requirements for limited leave to remain as an unaccompanied asylum seeking child

352ZC. The requirements to be met in order for a grant of limited leave to remain to be made in relation to an unaccompanied asylum seeking child under paragraph 352ZE are:
(a)   the applicant is an unaccompanied asylum seeking child under the age of 17 and a half years throughout the duration of leave to be granted in this capacity;
(b)   the applicant must have applied for asylum and been refused Refugee Leave and Humanitarian Protection;
(c)   there are no adequate reception arrangements in the country to which they would be returned if leave to remain was not granted;
(d)   the applicant must not be excluded from a grant of asylum under Regulation 7 of the refugee or person in Need of International Protection (Qualification) Regulations 2006 or excluded from a grant of Humanitarian Protection under paragraph 339D or both;
(e)   there are no reasonable grounds for regarding the applicant as a danger to the security of the United Kingdom;
(f)   the applicant has not been convicted by a final judgment of a particularly serious crime, and the applicant does not constitute a danger to the community of the United Kingdom; and
(g)   the applicant is not, at the date of their application, the subject of a deportation order or a decision to make a deportation order.

352ZD. An unaccompanied asylum seeking child is a person who:
(a)   is under 18 years of age when the asylum application is submitted.
(b)   is applying for asylum in their own right; and
(c)   is separated from both parents and is not being cared for by an adult who in law or by custom has responsibility to do so.

352ZE. Limited leave to remain should be granted for a period of 30 months or until the child is 17 and a half years of age whichever is shorter, provided that the Secretary of State is satisfied that the requirements in paragraph 352ZC are met.

352ZF. Limited leave granted under this provision will cease if
(a)   any one or more of the requirements listed in paragraph 352ZC cease to be met, or

(b) a misrepresentation or omission of facts, including the use of false documents, were decisive for the grant of leave under 352ZE.]

Requirements for limited leave to remain as an unaccompanied asylum seeking child

352A. [The requirements to be met by a person seeking leave to enter or remain in the United Kingdom as the spouse or civil partner of a refugee are that:

(i) the applicant is married to or the civil partner of a person [who is currently a refugee granted status as such under the immigration rules] in the United Kingdom; and

(ii) the marriage or civil partnership did not take place after the person granted asylum left the country of his former habitual residence in order to seek asylum; and

(iii) the applicant would not be excluded from protection by virtue of article 1F of the United Nations Convention and Protocol relating to the Status of Refugees if he were to seek asylum in his own right; and

[(iv) each of the parties intends to live permanently with the other as his or her spouse or civil partner and the marriage is subsisting; and]

[(v)] if seeking leave to enter, the applicant holds a valid United Kingdom entry clearance for entry in this capacity.

Note

Words in square brackets in sub-para (i) inserted by Cm 7944, para 22 as from 22 October 2010. Paragraphs 352ZC-352ZF inserted by HC 1039, para 122 as from 6 April 2013.

See General note at para 352F. On para 352F (ii), see *A (Somalia) v Entry Clearance Officer, Pretoria* [2004] UKIAT 00031. On para 352F(iii), see the note at para 339A.

352AA. The requirements to be met by a person seeking leave to enter or remain in the United Kingdom as the unmarried or the same-sex partner of a refugee are that:

(i) the applicant is the unmarried or same-sex partner of a person[who is currently a refugee granted status as such under the immigration rules in the United Kingdom and was granted that status] on or after 9th October 2006; and

(ii) the parties have been living together in a relationship akin to either a marriage or a civil partnership which has subsisted for two years or more; and

(iii) the relationship existed before the person granted asylum left the country of his former habitual residence in order to seek asylum; and

(iv) the applicant would not be excluded from protection by virtue of paragraph 334(iii) or

(v) of these Rules or article 1F of the Geneva Convention if he were to seek asylum in his own right; and

[(vi) the parties are not involved in a consanguineous relationship with one another; and]

[(vii)] each of the parties intends to live permanently with the other as his or her unmarried or same-sex partner and the relationship is subsisting; and

[(viii)]if seeking leave to enter, the applicant holds a valid United Kingdom entry clearance for entry in this capacity.

Note

Words in square brackets in sub-para (i) inserted by Cm 7944, para 23 as from 22 October 2010. Sub-para (vi) inserted by HC 863, para 129 as from 6 April 2011. Old sub–paras (vi) and (vii) renumbered by HC 863, para 130 as from 6 April 2011.

See General note at para 352F. In relation to para 352AA(ii), it must be arguable that the requirement of the rule is that the couple have been living together in a relationship akin to marriage or a civil partnership, in a relationship which has subsisted for two years (even though the period of cohabitation may not have been of the same duration). On para 352AA(iv) and (v), see the note at para 339A.

352B. Limited leave to enter the United Kingdom as the spouse or civil partner of a refugee may be granted provided a valid United Kingdom entry clearance for entry in this capacity is produced to the Immigration Officer on arrival. Limited leave to remain in the United Kingdom as the spouse or civil partner of a refugee may be granted provided the Secretary of State is satisfied that each of the requirements of paragraph [352A(i)–(iv)] are met.

Note

Words in square brackets substituted by HC 863, para 131 as from 6 April 2011.

352BA Limited leave to enter the United Kingdom as the unmarried or same-sex partner of a refugee may be granted provided a valid United Kingdom entry clearance for entry in this capacity is produced to the Immigration Officer on arrival. Limited leave to remain in the United Kingdom as the unmarried or same sex partner of a refugee may be granted provided the Secretary of State is satisfied that each of the requirements of paragraph [352AA(i)–(vii)] are met.

Note

Words in square brackets substituted by HC 863, para 132 as from 6 April 2011.

352C. Limited leave to enter the United Kingdom as the spouse or civil partner of a refugee is to be refused if a valid United Kingdom entry clearance for entry in this capacity is not produced to the Immigration Officer on arrival. Limited leave to remain as the spouse or civil partner of a refugee is to be refused if the Secretary of State is not satisfied that each of the requirements of paragraph [352A(i)–(v)] are met.

Note

Words in square brackets substituted by HC 863, para 133 as from 6 April 2011.

352CA Limited leave to enter the United Kingdom as the unmarried or same-sex partner of a refugee is to be refused if a valid United Kingdom entry clearance for entry in this capacity is not produced to the Immigration Officer on arrival. Limited leave to remain as the unmarried or same sex partner of a refugee is to be refused if the Secretary of State is not satisfied that each of the requirements of paragraph [352AA(i)–(vi)] are met.

Note

Words in square brackets substituted by HC 863, para 134 as from 6 April 2011.

352D. The requirements to be met by a person seeking leave to enter or remain in the United Kingdom [in order to join or remain with the parent [who is currently a refugee granted status as such under the immigration rules] in the United Kingdom] are that the applicant:

(i)   is the child of a parent [who is currently a refugee granted status as such under the immigration rules] in the United Kingdom; and

(ii)   is under the age of 18, and

(iii)   is not leading an independent life, is unmarried and is not a civil partner, and has not formed an independent family unit; and

(iv)   was part of the family unit of the person granted asylum at the time that the person granted asylum left the country of his habitual residence in order to seek asylum; and

(v)   would not be excluded from protection by virtue of article 1F of the United Nations Convention and Protocol relating to the Status of Refugees if he were to seek asylum in his own right; and

(vi)   if seeking leave to enter, holds a valid United Kingdom entry clearance for entry in this capacity.

Note

Words in square brackets inserted by Cm 7944, paras 24, 25 as from 22 October 2010.

See General note at para 352F. For the definition of 'parent' in para 352D(i), see para 6 of the rules. See also *MK (Somalia) v Entry Clearance Officer* [2008] EWCA Civ 1453, [2009] 2 FLR 138; de facto adoption is not within the ambit of the rule. For the meaning of 'not leading an independent life', see *NM ('leading an independent life') Zimbabwe* [2007] UKAIT 00051; [2007] UKAIT 00052: an applicant must not have formed, through choice, a separate (and independent) social unit from his or her parents' family unit, either alone or with others. The dependency on an applicant's parents' family unit may be of choice and need not be of necessity. The existence of 'Family' in para 352D(iv) is a question of fact: see *BM and AL (352D (iv); meaning of 'family unit') Colombia* [2007] UKAIT 00055.

352E. Limited leave to enter the United Kingdom as the child of a refugee may be granted provided a valid United Kingdom entry clearance for entry in this capacity is produced to the Immigration Officer on arrival. Limited leave to remain in the United Kingdom as the child of a refugee may be granted provided the Secretary of State is satisfied that each of the requirements of paragraph 352D (i)–(v) are met.

352F. Limited leave to enter the United Kingdom as the child of a refugee is to be refused if a valid United Kingdom entry clearance for entry in this capacity is not produced to the Immigration Officer on arrival. Limited leave to remain as the child of a refugee is to be refused if the Secretary of State is not satisfied that each of the requirements of paragraph 352D(i)–(v) are met.]

General Note

These provisions incorporate Secretary of State for the Home Department's general interpretation of the principle of family unity annexed to the Geneva Convention: see paras 181-188 of the UNHCR Handbook. The rules for entry for the family of refugees and those with humanitarian protection are divided into two parts. The rules in Part 11 are made under 'refugee family reunion' principles (ie for pre-flight partners and minor children). Those in Appendix FM are for post-flight partners and children, and adult dependent relatives, and are the same as for settled and British citizen sponsors. There is no longer a family reunion policy operating outside the rules.

For Guidance on Family Reunion see: www.ukba.homeoffice.gov.uk/policyandlaw/guidance/ecg/s et/set10/ and for post-flight families see: www.ukba.homeoffice.gov.uk/policyandlaw/guidance/ecg/set/set18/

352FA. [The requirements to be met by a person seeking leave to enter or remain in the United Kingdom as the spouse or civil partner of a person [who is currently a beneficiary of humanitarian protection granted under the immigration rules in the United Kingdom and was granted that status] on or after 30 August 2005 are that:

(i)   the applicant is married to or the civil partner of a person [who is currently a beneficiary of humanitarian protection granted under the immigration rules and was granted that status] on or after 30 August 2005; and

(ii)   the marriage or civil partnership did not take place after the person granted humanitarian protection left the country of his former habitual residence in order to seek asylum in the UK; and

(iii)   the applicant would not be excluded from a grant of humanitarian protection for any of the reason's in paragraph 339D; and

(iv)   each of the parties intend to live permanently with the other as his or her spouse or civil partner and the marriage or civil partnership is subsisting; and

(v)   if seeking leave to enter, the applicant holds a valid United Kingdom entry clearance for entry in this capacity.

Note

Words in square brackets inserted by Cm 7944, paras 26, 27 as from 22 October 2010.

352FB. Limited leave to enter the United Kingdom as the spouse or civil partner of a person granted humanitarian protection may be granted provided a valid United Kingdom entry clearance for entry in this capacity is produced to the Immigration Officer on arrival. Limited leave to remain in the United Kingdom as the spouse or civil partner of a person granted humanitarian protection may be granted provided the Secretary of State is satisfied that each of the requirements in sub-paragraph 353FA(i)–(iv) are met.

352FC. Limited leave to enter the United Kingdom as the spouse or civil partner of a person granted humanitarian protection is to be refused if a valid United Kingdom entry clearance for entry in this capacity is not produced to the Immigration Officer on arrival. Limited leave to remain in the United Kingdom as the spouse or civil partner as a person granted humanitarian protection may be granted provided the Secretary of State is satisfied that each of the requirements in sub-paragraph 353FA(i)–(iv) are met.

352FD. The requirements to be met by a person seeking leave to enter or remain in the United Kingdom as the unmarried or same-sex partner of a person [who is currently a beneficiary of humanitarian protection granted under the immigration rules] in the United Kingdom are that:

(i)   the applicant is the unmarried or same-sex partner of a person [who is currently a beneficiary of humanitarian protection granted under the immigration rules in the United Kingdom and was granted that status] on or after 9th October 2006; and

(ii)   the parties have been living together in a relationship akin to either a marriage or a civil partnership which has subsisted for two years or more; and

(iii)   the relationship existed before the person granted humanitarian protection left the country of his former habitual residence in order to seek asylum; and

(iv)   the applicant would not be excluded from a grant of humanitarian protection for any of the reasons in paragraph 339D; and

(v)   each of the parties intends to live permanently with the other as his or her unmarried or same-sex partner and the relationship is subsisting; and

[(vi)   the parties are not involved in a consanguineous relationship with one another; and]

[(vii)]   if seeking leaver to enter, the applicant holds a valid United Kingdom entry clearance for entry in this capacity.

Note

Words in square brackets inserted by Cm 7944, paras 28, 29 as from 22 October 2010. New sub–para (vi) inserted by HC 863, para 135 as from 6 April 2011. Old sub–para (vi) renumbered by HC 863, para 136 as from 6 April 2011.

352FE.   Limited leave to enter the United Kingdom ad the unmarried or same-sex partner of a person granted humanitarian protection may be granted provided a valid United Kingdom entry clearance for entry in this capacity is produced to the Immigration Officer on arrival. Limited leave to remain in the United Kingdom as the unmarried or same sex partner of a person granted humanitarian protection may be granted provided the Secretary of State is satisfied that each of the requirements in subparagraphs [352FD (i)-(vi)] are met.

Note

Words in square brackets substituted by HC 863, para 137 as from 6 April 2011.

352FF.   Limited leave to enter the United Kingdom ad the unmarried or same-sex partner of a person granted humanitarian protection is to be refused if a valid United Kingdom entry clearance for entry in this capacity is not produced to the Immigration Officer on arrival. Limited leave to remain in the United Kingdom as the unmarried or same sex partner of a person granted humanitarian protection is to be refused if the Secretary of State is not satisfied that each of the requirements in subparagraphs [352FD (i)-(vi)] are met.

Note

Words in square brackets substituted by HC 863, para 138 as from 6 April 2011.

352FG.   The requirements to be met by a person seeking leave to enter or remain in the United Kingdom in order to join or remain with their parent [who is currently a beneficiary of humanitarian protection granted under the immigration rules in the United Kingdom and was granted that status] on or after 30 August 2005 are that the applicant:

(i)   is the child of a parent [who is currently a beneficiary of humanitarian protection granted under the immigration rules in the United Kingdom and was granted that status] on or after 30 August 2005; and

(ii)   is under the age of 18, and

(iii)   is not leading an independent life, is unmarried or is not in a civil partnership, and has not formed an independent family unit; and

(iv)   was part of the family unit of the person who has been granted humanitarian protection at the time that the person granted humanitarian protection left the country of his habitual residence in order to seek asylum in the UK; and

(v)   would not be excluded from a grant of humanitarian protection for any of the reasons in paragraph 339D; and

(vi)   if seeking leave to enter, holds a valid United Kingdom entry clearance for entry in this capacity.

Note

Words in square brackets inserted by Cm 7944, paras 30, 31 as from 22 October 2010.

352FH.   Limited leave to enter the United Kingdom as the child of a person granted humanitarian protection may be granted provided a valid United Kingdom entry clearance for entry in this capacity is produced to the Immigration Officer on arrival. Limited leave to remain in the United Kingdom as the child of a person granted humanitarian protection may be granted provided the Secretary of State is satisfied that each of the requirements in subparagraphs 352FG(i)-(v) are met.

352FI.   Limited leave to enter the United Kingdom as the child of a person granted humanitarian protection is to be refused if a valid United Kingdom entry clearance for entry in this capacity is not produced to the Immigration Officer on arrival. Limited leave to remain in the United Kingdom as the child of a person granted humanitarian protection is to be refused if the Secretary of State is not satisfied that each of the requirements in subparagraphs 352FG(i)-(v) are met.]

Note

Paragraphs 352FA-352FI inserted by HC 28, para 5 as from 8 November 2007.

In relation to paras 352FA-FL, see notes at paras 352A-D.

352FJ.   Nothing in paragraphs 352A-352FI shall allow a person to be granted leave to enter or remain in the United Kingdom as the spouse or civil partner, unmarried or same sex partner or child of a refugee, or of a person granted humanitarian protection under the immigration rules in the United Kingdom on or after 30 August 2005, if the refugee or, as the case may be, person granted humanitarian protection, is a British Citizen.]

Note

Inserted by Cm 7944, para 32 with effect from 22 October 2010.

Interpretation

352G.   For the purposes of this Part:
(a)   "Geneva Convention" means the United Nations Convention and Protocol relating to the Status of Refugees;
(b)   "Country of return" means a country or territory listed in paragraph 8(c) of Schedule 2 of the Immigration Act 1971;
(c)   "Country of origin" means the country or countries of nationality or, for a stateless person, or former habitual residence.

Note

Paras 352A–352F inserted by Cmnd 4851. In para 352A sub-para (iv) inserted and (v) renumbered by Cmnd 5597. Words in square brackets in 352D substituted by Cmnd 5597.

[PART 11A — TEMPORARY PROTECTION]

[Definition of Temporary Protection Directive]

354.   [For the purposes of paragraphs 355 to 356B, 'Temporary Protection Directive' means Council Directive 2001/55/EC of 20 July 2001 regarding the giving of temporary protection by Member States in the event of a mass influx of displaced persons.]

Note

Paragraphs 354–356B inserted by HC 164 as from 1 January 2005.

As para 354 indicates, the source of these provisions is Directive 2001/55/EC.

[Grant of temporary protection]

355.   [An applicant for temporary protection will be granted temporary protection if the Secretary of State is satisfied that:
(i)   the applicant is in the United Kingdom or has arrived at a port of entry in the United Kingdom; and
(ii)   the applicant is a person entitled to temporary protection as defined by, and in accordance with, the Temporary Protection Directive; and

(iii)   the applicant does not hold an extant grant of temporary protection entitling him to reside in another Member State of the European Union. This requirement is subject to the provisions relating to dependants set out in paragraphs 356 to 356B and to any agreement to the contrary with the Member State in question; and

(iv)   the applicant is not excluded from temporary protection under the provisions in paragraph 355A.

355A.   An applicant or a dependant may be excluded from temporary protection if:

(i)   there are serious reasons for considering that:

    (a)   he has committed a crime against peace, a war crime, or a crime against humanity, as defined in the international instruments drawn up to make provision in respect of such crimes; or

    (b)   he has committed a serious non-political crime outside the United Kingdom prior to his application for temporary protection; or

    (c)   he has committed acts contrary to the purposes and principles of the United Nations, or

(ii)   there are reasonable grounds for regarding the applicant as a danger to the security of the United Kingdom or, having been convicted by a final judgment of a particularly serious crime, to be a danger to the community of the United Kingdom.

Consideration under this paragraph shall be based solely on the personal conduct of the applicant concerned. Exclusion decisions or measures shall be based on the principle of proportionality.

355B.   If temporary protection is granted to a person who has been given leave to enter or remain (whether or not the leave has expired) or to a person who has entered without leave, the Secretary of State will vary the existing leave or grant limited leave to remain.

355C.   A person to whom temporary protection is granted will be granted limited leave to enter or remain, which is not to be subject to a condition prohibiting employment, for a period not exceeding 12 months. On the expiry of this period, he will be entitled to apply for an extension of this limited leave for successive periods of 6 months thereafter.

355D.   A person to whom temporary protection is granted will be permitted to return to the United Kingdom from another Member State of the European Union during the period of a mass influx of displaced persons as established by the Council of the European Union pursuant to Article 5 of the Temporary Protection Directive.

355E.   A person to whom temporary protection is granted will be provided with a document in a language likely to be understood by him in which the provisions relating to temporary protection and which are relevant to him are set out. A person with temporary protection will also be provided with a document setting out his temporary protection status.

355F.   The Secretary of State will establish and maintain a register of those granted temporary protection. The register will record the name, nationality, date and place of birth and marital status of those granted temporary protection and their family relationship to any other person who has been granted temporary protection.

355G.   If a person who makes an asylum application is also eligible for temporary protection, the Secretary of State may decide not to consider the asylum application until the applicant ceases to be entitled to temporary protection.]

[Dependants]

356.   [In this part:

'dependant' means a family member or a close relative.

'family member' means:

(i)   the spouse or civil partner of an applicant for, or a person who has been granted, temporary protection; or (ii)　the unmarried or same-sex partner of an applicant for, or a person who has been granted, temporary protection where the parties have been living together in a relationship akin to marriage or civil partnership which has subsisted for 2 years or more; or

(iii)　the minor child (who is unmarried and not a civil partner), parent or grandparent of an applicant for, or a person who has been granted, temporary protection or his spouse,

who lived with the principal applicant as part of the family unit in the country of origin immediately prior to the mass influx.

'close relative' means:

(i)　the parent, grandparent or unmarried adult child of an applicant for, or person who has been granted, temporary protection; or

(ii)　the sibling (who is unmarried and not a civil partner) or the uncle or aunt of an applicant for, or person who has been granted, temporary protection, who lived with the principal applicant as part of the family unit in the country of origin immediately prior to the mass influx and was wholly or mainly dependent upon the principal applicant at that time, and would face extreme hardship if reunification with the principal applicant did not take place.

356A.　A dependant may apply for temporary protection. Where the dependant falls within paragraph 356 and does not fall to be excluded under paragraph 355A, he will be granted temporary protection for the same duration and under the same conditions as the principal applicant.

356B.　When considering any application by a dependant child, the Secretary of State shall take into consideration the best interests of that child.]

Note

Paragraphs 354–356B inserted by HC 164, para 8 as from 1 January 2005.

[PART 11B] — ASYLUM

[Reception Conditions for non-EU asylum applicants]

357.　[Part 11B only applies to asylum applicants (within the meaning of these Rules) who are not nationals of a member State.]

Note

Paragraphs 357–361 inserted by HC 194, para 3 as from 4 February 2005.

[Information to be provided to asylum applicants]

357A.　[The Secretary of State shall inform asylum applicants in a language they may be reasonably be supposed to understand and within a reasonable time after their claim for asylum has been recorded of the procedure to be followed, their rights and obligations during the procedure, and the possible consequences of non-compliance and non-co-operation. They shall be informed of the likely timeframe for consideration of the application and the means at their disposal for submitting all relevant information.]

358.　[The Secretary of State shall inform asylum applicants within a reasonable time not exceeding fifteen days after their claim for asylum has been recorded of the benefits and services that they may be eligible to receive and of the rules and procedures with which they must comply relating to them. The Secretary of State shall also provide information on non-governmental organisations and persons that provide legal assistance to asylum applicants and which may be able to help asylum applicants or provide information on available benefits and services.

358A.　The Secretary of State shall ensure that the information referred to in paragraph 358 is available in writing and, to the extent possible, will provide the information in a language that asylum applicants may reasonably be supposed to understand. Where appropriate, the Secretary of State may also arrange for this information to be supplied orally.]

Note

Paragraphs 357–361 inserted by HC 194, para 3 as from 4 February 2005. Para 357A inserted by HC 82.

[Information to be provided by asylum applicants]

358B. [An asylum applicant must notify the Secretary of State of his current address and of any change to his address or residential status. If not notified beforehand, any change must be notified to the Secretary of State without delay after it occurs.]

Note

Paragraphs 357–361 inserted by HC 194, para 3 as from 4 February 2005.

[The United Nations High Commissioner for Refugees

358C. A representative of the United Nations High Commissioner for refugees (UNHCR) or an organisation working in the United Kingdom on behalf of the UNHCR pursuant to an agreement with the government shall:
(a)   have access to applicants for asylum, including those in detention;
(b)   have access to information on individual applications for asylum, on the course of the procedure and on the decisions taken on applications for asylum, provided that the applicant for asylum agrees thereto;
(c)   be entitled to present his views, in the exercise of his supervisory responsibilities under Article 35 of the Geneva Convention, to the Secretary of State regarding individual applications for asylum at any stage of the procedure.

This paragraph shall also apply where the Secretary of State is considering revoking a person's refugee status in accordance with these Rules.]

Note

Heading and para 358C inserted by HC 82, paras 30, 31 as from 1 December 2007.

[Documentation]

359. [The Secretary of State shall ensure that, within three working days of recording an asylum application, a document is made available to that asylum applicant, issued in his own name, certifying his status as an asylum applicant or testifying that he is allowed to remain in the United Kingdom while his asylum application is pending. For the avoidance of doubt, in cases where the Secretary of State declines to examine an application it will no longer be pending for the purposes of this rule.

359A. The obligation in paragraph 359 above shall not apply where the asylum applicant is detained under the Immigration Acts, the Immigration and Asylum Act 1999 or the Nationality, Immigration and Asylum Act 2002.

359B. A document issued to an asylum applicant under paragraph 359 does not constitute evidence of the asylum applicant's identity.

359C. In specific cases the Secretary of State or an Immigration Officer may provide an asylum applicant with evidence equivalent to that provided under rule 359. This might be, for example, in circumstances in which it is only possible or desirable to issue a time-limited document.]

Note

Paragraphs 357–361 inserted by HC 194, para 3 as from 4 February 2005.

[Right to request permission to take up employment]

360. [An asylum applicant may apply to the Secretary of State for permission to take up employment if a decision at first instance has not been taken on the applicant's asylum application within one year of the date on which it was recorded. The Secretary of State shall only consider such an application if, in the Secretary of State's opinion, any delay in reaching a decision at first instance cannot be attributed to the applicant.

360A. If permission to take up employment is granted under paragraph 360, that permission will be subject to the following restrictions:
(i) employment may only be taken up in a post which is, at the time an offer of employment is accepted, included on the list of shortage occupations published by the United Kingdom Border Agency (as that list is amended from time to time);
(ii) no work in a self-employed capacity; and
(iii) no engagement in setting up a business.

360B. If an asylum applicant is granted permission to take up employment under paragraph 360 this shall only be until such time as his asylum application has been finally determined.

360C. Where an individual makes further submissions which raise asylum grounds and which fall to be considered under paragraph 353 of these Rules, that individual may apply to the Secretary of State for permission to take up employment if a decision pursuant to paragraph 353 of these Rules has not been taken on the further submissions within one year of the date on which they were recorded. The Secretary of State shall only consider such an application if, in the Secretary of States's opinion, any delay in reaching a decision pursuant to paragraph 353 of these Rules cannot be attributed to the individual.

360D. If permission to take up employment is granted under paragraph 360C, that permission will be subject to the following restrictions:
(i) employment may only be taken up in a post which is, at the time an offer of employment is accepted, included on the list of shortage occupations published by the United Kingdom Border Agency (as that list is amended from time to time):
(ii) no work in a self-employed capacity; and
(iii) no engagement in setting up a business.

360E. Where permission to take up employment is granted pursuant to paragraph 360C, that shall only be until such time as:
(i) a decision has been taken pursuant to paragraph 353 that the further submissions do not amount to a fresh claim; or
(ii) where the further submissions are considered to amount to a fresh claim for asylum pursuant to paragraph 353, all rights of appeal from the immigration decision made in consequence of the rejection of the further submissions have been exhausted.]

Note

Paragraphs 357–361 inserted by HC 194, para 3 as from 4 February 2005. Paragraphs 360– 360E substituted by Cmnd 7929, para 1 as from 20 August 2010.

[Interpretation]

361. [For the purposes of this Part:
(a) 'working day' means any day other than a Saturday or Sunday, a bank holiday, Christmas day or Good Friday;
(b) 'member State' has the same meaning as in Schedule 1 to the European Communities Act 1972.]

Note

Paragraphs 357–361 inserted by HC 194, para 3 as from 4 February 2005.

For the source of the provisions in paras 357-361, see Directives 2003/9/EC and 2005/85/EC.

[PART 12 — PROCEDURE AND RIGHTS OF APPEAL]

[Fresh Claims]

353. [When a human rights or asylum claim has been refused [or withdrawn or treated as withdrawn under paragraph 333C of these Rules] and any appeal relating to that claim is no longer pending, the decision maker will consider any further submissions and, if rejected, will then determine whether they amount to a fresh claim. The submissions will amount to a fresh claim if they are significantly different from the material that has previously been considered. The submissions will only be significantly different if the content:

(i) had not already been considered; and

(ii) taken together with the previously considered material, created a realistic prospect of success, notwithstanding its rejection.

This paragraph does not apply to claims made overseas.]

353A. [Consideration of further submissions shall be subject to the procedures set out in these Rules. An applicant who has made further submissions shall not be removed before the Secretary of State has considered the submissions under paragraph 353 or otherwise.

This paragraph does not apply to submissions made overseas.]

Exceptional circumstances

353B. [Where further submissions have been made and the decision maker has established whether or not they amount to a fresh claim under paragraph 353 of these Rules, or in cases with no outstanding further submissions whose appeal rights have been exhausted and which are subject to a review, the decision maker will also have regard to the migrant's:

(i) character, conduct and associations including any criminal record and the nature of any offence of which the migrant concerned has been convicted;

(ii) compliance with any conditions attached to any previous grant of leave to enter or remain and compliance with any conditions of temporary admission or immigration bail where applicable;

(iii) length of time spent in the United Kingdom spent for reasons beyond the migrant's control after the human rights or asylum claim has been submitted or refused; in deciding whether there are exceptional circumstances which mean that removal from the United Kingdom is no longer appropriate.]

[This paragraph does not apply where the person is liable to deportation.]

Note

Paragraph 353B inserted by HC 1733, para 7 as from 13 February 2012. Final sentence inserted by HC 194 as from 9 July 2012.

354-361 [. . .]

Note

Paragraphs 354 to 361 deleted by Cmnd 4851. Para 353 inserted by HC 1112. Para 353 amended by HC 420 as from 7 April 2008. Para 353A inserted by HC 82, para 28 as from 1 December 2007.

On Secretary of State for the Home Department's general approach and procedure in considering whether a claim fulfils the requirements of para 353, see the API on further submissions. Further submissions have to be delivered in person to the Further Submissions Unit in Liverpool or, in some cases, to the Local Immigration Team. As para 353A makes clear, an applicant cannot be removed until a decision on whether material constitutes a fresh claim has been taken by Secretary of State for the Home Department. When a decision is taken to refuse the fresh claim, a written explanation of Secretary of State for the Home Department's reasons must also be given. The origin of the Immigration rules relating to fresh claims is in *R v Secretary of State for the Home Department, ex p Onibiyo* [1996] EWCA Civ 1338, [1996] QB 768, [1996] 2 All ER 901, [1996] Imm AR 370 in which Bingham MR identified the overarching requirement: 'The acid test must always be whether, comparing the new claim with that earlier rejected, and excluding material on which the claimant could reasonably have been expected to rely in the earlier claim [the current formulation in para 353 imposes no such explicit requirement], the new claim is sufficiently different from the earlier claim to admit of a realistic prospect that a favourable view could be taken of the new claim despite the unfavourable conclusion reached on the earlier claim.' Bingham MR also emphasised that there need not necessarily be a change in the nature of the claim actually advanced, so that the new evidence could simply cast the reliability of significance of an existing claim or evidence in a new light: see also *R (on the application of Senkoy) v Secretary of State for the Home Department* [2001] EWCA Civ 328. 'Submissions' need not take any particular form: see *R (on the application of AK Sri Lanka) v Secretary of State for the Home Department* [2009] EWCA Civ 447. As emphasised in *Onibiyo*, the question of whether the further evidence constitutes a fresh claim is in the first instance a matter for Secretary of State for the Home Department, so that the reviewing Court is not coming to its own conclusions on the merits but assessing whether any refusal of a fresh claim is susceptible to challenge on public law grounds. In reviewing Secretary of State for the Home Department's decisions, the correct point of departure is not whether Secretary of State for the Home Department himself thinks that the fresh material is a good, viable claim but whether the AIT, giving anxious scrutiny to the material (and applying the relatively modest burden that must be discharged by an appellant), could find in the applicant's favour: see *WM (Democratic Republic of Congo); AR (Afghanistan) v Secretary of State for the Home Department* [2006] EWCA Civ 1495; *ZT (Kosovo) v Secretary of State for the Home Department* [2009] UKHL 6; [2009] 3 All ER 976; see also *AK (Sri Lanka) v Secretary of State for the Home Department* [2009] EWCA Civ 447. The Court will need to be satisfied (and this will frequently be the basis of challenge in judicial review proceedings) that Secretary of State for the Home Department has considered all of the material, in conducting that assessment, on the basis of anxious scrutiny, and the Court may intervene if Secretary of State for the Home Department has not done so: see *WM (Democratic Republic of Congo); AR (Afghanistan) v Secretary of State for the Home Department* [2006] EWCA Civ 1495 at para 11. The fact that an appellant has been disbelieved in the past does not mean, per se, that on a later occasion, further evidence will be incapable of being accepted: *R v Secretary of State for the Home Department, ex p Boybeyi* [1997] EWCA Civ 1689, [1997] Imm AR 491 (the submission of a previous document, found to be a forgery, did not mean, per se, that a further document submitted would also be found not to be genuine). The evidence in support of the claim must be apparently credible although not incontrovertible: *Haile v Immigration Appeal Tribunal* [2001] EWCA Civ 663, [2002] Imm AR 170. Where the evidence submitted in support of the fresh claim could have an important influence on the outcome, and unless Secretary of State for the Home Department was able to show that that it was not apparently credible, there might be an obligation to conclude that the further material did meet the fresh claim threshold: *R v Secretary of State for the Home Department, ex p Boybeyi* [1997] EWCA Civ 1689, [1997] Imm AR 491. The same approach has also been applied (under the old para 346 which referred only to a fresh claim for asylum) in determining whether further representations constitute a fresh human rights claim: see *R (on the application of Ratnam) v Secretary of State for the Home Department* [2003] EWHC 398 (Admin). In some instances, considerations of fairness may dictate that a further right of appeal be given (see the API on further representations: section 'Applicant is asking UK Border Agency for discretion to afford a further right of appeal aside from para 353 on the grounds of fairness'; which refers to Secretary of State for the Home Department's earlier policy, cited in *R v Secretary of State for the Home Department, ex p Kazmi* (CO/2230/94), [1995] Imm AR 73).

PART 13 — DEPORTATION

Where Article 8 is raised in the context of deportation under Part 13 of these Rules, the claim under Article 8 will only succeed where the requirements of these rules as at [28 July 2014] are met, regardless of when the notice of intention to deport or the deportation order, as appropriate, was served.]

Note

Paragraph A262 inserted by HC 194, para 111 as from 9 July 2012. Amended by HC 532, para 15 of this statement take effect on 28 July 2014 and apply to all ECHR Article 8 claims from foreign criminals which are decided on or after that date.

A deportation order

362. A deportation order requires the subject to leave the United Kingdom and authorises his detention until he is removed. It also prohibits him from re-entering the

country for as long as it is in force and invalidates any leave to enter or remain in the United Kingdom given him before the order was made or while it is in force.

363. [The circumstances in which a person is liable to deportation include:
(i)   where the Secretary of State deems the person's deportation to be conducive the public good;
(ii)   where the person is the spouse or civil partner or child under 18 of a person ordered to be deported; and
(iii) where a court recommends deportation in the case of a person over the age of 17 who has been convicted of an offence punishable with imprisonment.]

363A [Prior to 2 October 2000, a person would have been liable to deportation in certain circumstances in which he is now liable to administrative removal.. . . However, such a person remains liable to deportation, rather than administrative removal where:
(i)   a decision to make a deportation order against him was taken before 2 October 2000; or
(ii)   the person has made a valid application under the Immigration (Regularisation Period for Overstayers) Regulations 2000.]

Note

Words deleted by HC 1039, para 123 as from 6 April 2013.

364 . . .

Note

Deportation on the basis that such is 'conducive to the Public good' is not limited to criminal conviction, and may extend to other situations, such as consideration of national security, or where the individual's presence is not considered desirable but the individual cannot be administratively removed because they hold extant leave. For detailed guidance on deportation and enforcement in general, see Secretary of State for the Home Department's Enforcement Guidance and Instructions (EGI) at www.bia.homeoffice.gov.uk/policyandlaw/guidance/enforcem ent para 364 was amended with effect from 20 July 2006. Prior to that date, and while the stated aim of the rule was to maintain consistency of approach as between individual cases in which deportation action was being pursued, Secretary of State for the Home Department was required to look at the merits of the individual case in deciding whether to pursue deportation action. This approach is preserved in relation to certain cases where administrative removal is pursued: see para 395C of the Immigration Rules (below). However, while the general presumption is that deportation action should be pursued in the cases of criminal conviction (the threshold being, in the case of a non-EEA national, a custodial sentence of 12 months or cumulatively, when aggregating 2 or 3 offences over the preceding five years; or a custodial sentence of any length in cases of a drugs conviction (non-possession); or a conviction of any length in relation to an offence in the list set out at para 11.2.1 of Chapter 11 of the EIG), Chapter 12 of the EIG recognises that age; length of residence; strength of connection; links with the country of origin; and domestic circumstances are relevant in deciding whether to pursue deportation action. Furthermore, such considerations may be wider than human rights considerations (para 12.3.1): see Chapter 11 & 12 at: www.bia.homeoffice.gov.uk/sitecontent/documents/policyandlaw/enforcement/oemsection b/chapter11; www.bia.homeoffice.gov.uk/sitecontent/documents/policyandlaw/enforcement/oems ectionb/chapter12. As to the general approach in an appeal under para 364, see *EO (Deportation appeals: scope and process) Turkey v Secretary of State for the Home Department* [2007] UKAIT 00062. In determining an appeal against a deportation decision made on 'conducive' grounds by the Secretary of State for the Home Department on or after 20 July 2006 the AIT should:
(a)   confirm that the appellant is liable to deportation (because the sentencing judge recommended deportation or because the Secretary of State has deemed deportation to be conducive to the public good);
(b)   if so, consider whether deportation would breach the appellant's rights under the Refugee Convention or the ECHR; if not
(c)   consider para 364.

On that basis 'exceptional circumstances', only become relevant once the claim has failed on asylum or ECHR grounds. Proper weight must be given to Secretary of State for the Home Department's policy on deportation: see *Samaroo v Secretary of State for the Home Department* [2001] EWCA Civ 1139; *N (Kenya) v Secretary of State for the Home Department* [2004] EWCA Civ 1094, [2004] INLR 612 at para 64 (these cases were concerned with the old formulation of para 364: the presumption that the public interest requires deportation is now effectively in the text of the current wording of the rule):

'Where a person who is not a British citizen commits a number of very serious crimes, the public interest side of the balance will include importantly, although not exclusively, the public policy need to deter and to express society's revulsion at the seriousness of the criminality. It is for the adjudicator in the exercise of his discretion to weigh all relevant factors, but an individual adjudicator is no better able to judge the critical public interest factor than is the court. In the first instance, that is a matter for the Secretary of State. The adjudicator should then take proper account of the Secretary of State's public interest view'

and see *OP (Jamaica) v Secretary of State for the Home Department* [2008] EWCA Civ 440, indicating that the assessment must be taken as a given unless it is palpably wrong and to hold otherwise would amount to an error of law; see also *OH (Serbia) v Secretary of State for the Home Department* [2008] EWCA Civ 694, [2009] INLR 109. However, deterrence may, in cases where an individual was assessed as being at low risk of re-offending, and there was no serious and deliberate wrong doing, be of less significance in considering the public interest: *AS (Pakistan) v Secretary of State for the Home Department* [2008] EWCA Civ 1118. In addressing the human rights framework in deportation appeals under art 8 of the ECHR, the Grand Chamber of the ECtHR has set down important framework guidance in *Uner v Netherlands* (Application 46410/99)[2006] ECHR 873, (2006) 45 EHRR 421, [2007] Imm AR 303, [2007] INLR 273; and *Maslov v Austria* (Application 1638/03) [2008] ECHR 546, [2009] INLR 47. To date, these two important framework decisions have apparently received little direct attention from the Higher Courts in the UK and appear to be fairly frequently overlooked by decision makers. The guidance provided by these two judgments would suggest that the evaluation is more factually nuanced than perhaps contemplated by many decision makers. In considering where the balance lies, both judgments indicate that particular attention must be given to the position of migrants who have arrived in the signatory state at an early stage and who have then spent there formative years there: see *Uner* at para 58:

'... it is self-evident that the Court will have regard to the special situation of aliens who have spent most, if not all, their childhood in the host country, were brought up there and received their education there; and at para 59 '... Regardless of the existence or otherwise of a "family life", therefore, the Court considers that the expulsion of a settled migrant constitutes interference with his or her right to respect for private life. It will depend on the circumstances of the particular case whether it is appropriate for the Court to focus on the "family life" rather than the "private life" aspect.'

Exclusion of long-term resident migrants following a criminal conviction should be seen as preventive rather than punitive in nature (para 56). In *Maslov*, and in the case of such a settled migrant, the Court indicated that 'very serious reasons are required to justify expulsion. This is all the more so where the person concerned committed the offences underlying the expulsion measure as a juvenile' (para 75). Similar considerations might apply where the deportee had arrived as an adult, but they had a spouse or children who were settled migrants and they could not be reasonably expected to follow if deportation were to be implemented: see *Sezen v Netherlands* (Application 50252/99) (2006) 43 EHRR 30, [2006] ECHR 87, 43 EHRR 30. So far as the framework in considering whether the balance lay in expulsion, the Court in *Uner* set out a number of relevant factors (paras 57-8):

(a)   the nature and seriousness of the offence committed by the applicant;
(b)   the length of the applicant's stay in the country from which he or she is to be expelled;
(c)   the time elapsed since the offence was committed and the applicant's conduct during that period;
(d)   the nationalities of the various persons concerned;
(e)   the applicant's family situation, such as the length of the marriage, and other factors expressing the effectiveness of a couple's family life;
(f)   whether the spouse knew about the offence at the time when he or she entered into a family relationship;
(g)   whether there are children of the marriage, and if so, their age;
(h)   the seriousness of the difficulties which the spouse is likely to encounter in the country to which the applicant is to be expelled;
(i)   the best interests and well-being of the children, in particular the seriousness of the difficulties which any children of the applicant are likely to encounter in the country to which the applicant is to be expelled; and
(j)   the solidity of social, cultural and family ties with the host country and with the country of destination.

In *Maslov*, and in cases of settled migrants who were too young to have formed their own family unit, the Grand Chamber indicated that the relevant considerations were:

(a)   the nature and seriousness of the offence committed by the applicant;

(b)   the length of the applicant's stay in the country from which he or she is to be expelled;

(c)   the time elapsed since the offence was committed and the applicant's conduct during that period; and

(d)   the solidity of social, cultural and family ties with the host country and with the country of destination.

As an example of a case which falls the other side of the balance, see *Konstatinov v Netherlands* (Application 16351/03) [2007] 2 FCR 194, [2007] ECHR 336, where the Court upheld an expulsion where the applicant had never had leave to remain, or met the requirements of domestic immigration law; developed family life at a time when they should have realised that their status was uncertain; and had committed a number of offences. For the deportation of EEA nationals and their family members see Chapter 8 of the European Casework Instructions: www.bia.homeoffice. gov.uk/sitecontent/documents/policyandlaw/ecis/chapter8.pdf and Immigration (European Economic Area) Regulations 2006 at regs 19-21; and see Directive 2004/38/EC at arts 27-33; see also *R v Bouchereau: 30/77* [1978] QB 732, [1981] 2 All ER 924n, ECJ; *LG (Italy) v Secretary of State for the Home Department* [2008] EWCA Civ 190, [2008] All ER (D) 262 (Mar); *Bulale Hussein v Secretary of State for the Home Department* [2008] EWCA Civ 806, [2009] QB 536; *HR (Portugal) v Secretary of State for the Home Department* [2009] EWCA Civ 371, [2010]1 All ER 144, [2009] 3 CMLR 295; *LG & CC (EEA Reg: residence; imprisonment; removal) Italy* [2009] UKAIT 00024. As to the special position of Irish nationals, who are now only deported in exceptional circumstances, see Liam Bryne's written statement (Hansard, 19 Feb 2007: Column WS54):

'Irish citizens will be considered for deportation only where a court has recommended deportation in sentencing or where the Secretary of State concludes that, due to the exceptional circumstances of the case, the public interest requires deportation. In reviewing our approach in this area we have taken into account the close historical, community and political ties between the United Kingdom and Ireland, along with the existence of the Common Travel Area ...'

See also chapter 15 of the Deportations and Criminal Caseworking Manual at para 15.9: www.bia.homeoffice.gov.uk/sitecontent/documents/policyandlaw/enforcement/oemsectionb/For the position of Turkish nationals under the Ankara agreement, see *Nazli v Stadt Nürnberg C-340/97* [2000] ECR I-957, ECJ.

364A.   . . .

Note

Words in square brackets in the title to Part 13 inserted by Cmnd 4851. Paragraph 363 substituted and paragraph 363A and words in square brackets in paragraph 364 inserted by Cmnd 4851.

Para 364 indicates that the parallel regime of 'automatic deportation' brought in by the UK Borders Act 2007, will be the applicable regime, rather than para 364, when deportation is initiated under the provisions contained in the UK Borders Act 2007.

Paragraphs 364, 364A deleted by HC 194, para 112 as from 9 July 2012.

Deportation of family members

365.   [... The Secretary of State will not normally decide to deport the spouse or civil partner of a deportee [under section 5 of the Immigration Act 1971] where:
(i)   he has qualified for settlement in his own right; or
(ii)   he has been living apart from the deportee.]

Note

Further amended by HC 693, para 100 as from 20 October 2014.

366.   [The Secretary of State will not normally decide to deport the child of a deportee [under section 5 of the Immigration Act 1971] where:
(i)   he and his mother or father are living apart from the deportee; or
(ii)   he has left home and established himself on an independent basis; or
(iii)   he married or formed a civil partnership before deportation came into prospect.]

Note

Further amended by HC 693, para 101 as from 20 October 2014.

367. ....

368 ...

Note

See the Enforcement Instructions and Guidance at Chapter 13: www.bia.homeoffice.gov.uk/sitec
ontent/documents/policyandlaw/enforcement/oemsectionb/chapter13. See also: Chapter 53, particularly in relation to the operation of earlier Concessions such as DP3 & 5/96 at: www.bia.hom
eoffice.gov.uk/sitecontent/documents/policyandlaw/enforcement/detention and removals/chapter
53.

Paragraph 367 deleted by HC 194, para 112 as from 9 July 2012. Deleted by HC 693, para 102
as from 20 October 2014.

Right of appeal against destination

369. DELETED

Restricted right of appeal against deportation in cases of breach of limited leave

370. DELETED

Exemption to the restricted right of appeal

371. DELETED

372. DELETED

A deportation order made on the recommendation of a Court

373. DELETED

Where deportation is deemed to be conductive to the public good

374. DELETED

375. DELETED

Note

Paragraph 369 to 374 deleted by Cmnd 4851.

Hearing of appeals

376. . . .

377. . . .

378. [...]

Note

Paragraph 377 deleted and paragraph 378 substituted by Cmnd 4851. Further amended by HC
532, para 16 of this statement take effect on 28 July 2014 and apply to all ECHR Article 8 claims
from foreign criminals which are decided on or after that date. Deleted by HC 693, para 103 as
from 20 October 2014.

Persons who have claimed asylum

379-379A. [. . . .]:

Note

Paragraphs 379 and 379A deleted by Cmnd 4851.

380. . . .

Note

Deleted by HC 194, para 112 as from 9 July 2012.

Procedure

381. When a decision to make a deportation order has been taken (otherwise than on the recommendation of a court) a notice will be given to the person concerned informing him of the decision ... [. . .].

Notes

Phrase "and of his right of appeal" deleted by HC 693, para 104 as from 20 October 2014.

382. [Following the issue of such a notice the Secretary of State may authorise detention or make an order restricting a person as to residence, employment or occupation and requiring him to report to the police, pending the making of a deportation order.]

383. [. . .].

384. ...

Notes

Words in paragraph 381 deleted, paragraph 382 substituted, paragraph 383 deleted and words in square brackets in paragraph 384 inserted by Cmnd 4851. Deleted by HC 693, para 105 as from 20 October 2014.

Arrangements for removal

385. A person against whom a deportation order has been made will normally be removed from the United Kingdom. The power is to be exercised so as to secure the person's return to the country of which he is a national, or which has most recently provided him with a travel document, unless he can show that another country will receive him. In considering any departure from the normal arrangements, regard will be had to the public interest generally, and to any additional expense that may fall on public funds.

386. ...

Notes

Amended by HC 532, para 17 of this statement take effect on 28 July 2014 and apply to all ECHR Article 8 claims from foreign criminals which are decided on or after that date. Deleted by HC 693, para 106 as from 20 October 2014.

Supervised departure

387. [. . .].

Note

Paragraph 387 deleted by Cmnd 4851.

Returned deportees

388. Where a person returns to [the UK] when a deportation order is in force against him, he may be deported under the original order. The Secretary of State will consider every such case in the light of all the relevant circumstances before deciding whether to enforce the order.

Note

See *Al-Sawaf v Secretary of State for the Home Department* [1988] Imm AR 410. See also Enforcement Instructions and Guidance at Chapter 5 :www.bia.homeoffice.gov.uk/sitecontent/do cuments/policyandlaw/enforcement/oemsectiona/ chapter5

Amended by HC 693, para 107 as from 20 October 2014.

Returned family members

389. Persons deported in the circumstances set out in paragraph 365–368 above (deportation of family members) may be able to seek re-admission to the United Kingdom under the Immigration Rules where:

(i)   a child reaches 18 (when he ceases to be subject to the deportation order); or

(ii)   in the case of a spouse or civil partner, the marriage or civil partnership comes to an end.

Revocation of deportation order

390. An application for revocation of a deportation order will be considered in the light of all the circumstances including the following:

(i)   the grounds on which the order was made;

(ii)   any representations made in support of revocation;

(iii)   the interests of the community, including the maintenance of an effective immigration control;

(iv)   the interests of the applicant, including any compassionate circumstances.

390A. Where paragraph 398 applies the Secretary of State . . . will consider whether paragraph 399 or 399A applies, and, if it does not, it will only be in exceptional circumstances that the public interest in maintaining the deportation order will be outweighed by other factors.

Note

Amended by HC 760, para 277 as from 13 December 2012.

[**391.** In the case of a person who has been deported following conviction for a criminal offence, the continuation of a deportation order against that person will be the proper course:

(a)   in the case of a conviction for an offence for which the person was sentenced to a period of imprisonment of less than 4 years, unless 10 years have elapsed since the making of the deportation order, [when, if an application for revocation is received, consideration will be given on a case by case basis to whether the deportation order should be maintained] or

(b)   in the case of a conviction for an offence for which the person was sentenced to a period of imprisonment of at least 4 years, at any time,

Unless, in either case, the continuation would be contrary to the Human Rights Convention or the Convention and protocol relating to the Status of Refugees, or there are other exceptional circumstances that mean the continuation is outweighed by compelling factors.]

Note

Substituted by HC 760, para 278 as from 13 December 2012. Further amended by HC 693, para 108 as from 20 October 2014.

[**391A.** In other cases, revocation of the order will not normally be authorised unless the situation has been materially altered, wither by a change in circumstances since the order was made, or by fresh information coming to light which was not before the appellate authorities or the Secretary of State. The passage of time since the person was deported may also in itself amount to such a change of circumstances as to warrant revocation of the order.]

Note

Inserted by HC 760, para 279 as from 13 December 2012.

392. Revocation of a deportation order does not entitle the person concerned to re-enter the United Kingdom; it renders him eligible to apply for admission under the Immigration Rules. Application for revocation of the order may be made to the Entry Clearance Officer or direct to the Home Office.

Note

For general guidance in the Immigration Directorate Instructions, see Chapter 13, Section 5. The effect of para 391 is that, in cases where the custodial sentence that lead to the decision to deport is longer than 30 months deportation, will normally lead to permanent exclusion, because such a conviction does not become spent. This is a significant shift from the previous formulation of para 391 which provided:

'In the case of an applicant with a serious criminal record continued exclusion for a long term of years will normally be the proper course. In other cases revocation of the order will not normally be authorised unless the situation has been materially altered, either by a change of circumstances since the order was made, or by fresh information coming to light which was not before the court which made the recommendation or the appellate authorities or the Secretary of State. The passage of time since the person was deported may also in itself amount to such a change of circumstances as to warrant revocation of the order. However, save in the most exceptional circumstances, the Secretary of State will not revoke the order unless the person has been absent from the United Kingdom for a period of at least 3 years since it was made.'

Chapter 13, Section 15 indicates that, in addition to considerations relating to human rights or asylum, there may be other 'exceptional' reasons for revoking an order in cases where the deportation order was made on account of a criminal offence. The intention to exclude permanently clearly has an impact on the assessment of proportionality when the original deportation decision is challenged: see also *AS (Pakistan) v Secretary of State for the Home Department* [2008] EWCA Civ 1118 at para 27, in relation to Secretary of State for the Home Department's change in policy on the duration of exclusion via the amendment of para 391:

'The duration of exclusion is a factor to be taken into account when considering the question of proportionality: see *Maslov v Austria (Application 1638/03)* paragraph 98. It seems likely that under the policy previously in force ... the appellant could have hoped to make a successful application for the revocation of the deportation order after at the most ten years' absence from the United Kingdom, whereas under the current policy he could expect to be excluded from this country permanently. As [SSHD] accepted, this change in policy since the order was made provides the appellant with grounds for making a fresh appeal against his deportation order . . .'

As to the general possibility of seeking to apply to revoke a deportation order in-country, if the order has been signed but no removal has been implemented, see *R (on the application of BA (Nigeria)) v Secretary of State for the Home Department; R (on the application of PE (Cameroon)) v Secretary of State for the Home Department* [2009] EWCA Civ 119, [2009] QB 686. For EEA nationals, an intention, per se, to impose permanent exclusion of an EEA national coming within the terms of the Directive would be incompatible with the terms of 2004/38/EC at Preamble 27 and art 32. The expelling state must allow such an individual to challenge their continued exclusion within a reasonable period after expulsion, and at any event, within three years, on the basis that there has been a material change in circumstances. The Immigration (European Economic Area) Regulations 2006 now contain a provision permitting applications for revocation to be made on the basis of a material change in circumstances (reg 24A, inserted as from 1 June 2009 by SI 2009/1117).

Heading 'Administrative removal' deleted by HC 1733, para 8 as from 13 February 2012. Paragraphs 395A-F deleted by HC 1733, para 9 as from 13 February 2012.

Rights of appeal in relation to a decision not to revoke a deportation order

393-394 [. . .].

395. ...

Note

Deleted by HC 693, para 109 as from 20 October 2014.

[396. Where a person is liable to deportation the presumption shall be that the public interest requires deportation. It is in the public interest to deport where the Secretary of State must make a deportation order in accordance with section 32 of the UK Borders Act 2007.

397. A deportation order will not be made if the person's removal pursuant to the order would be contrary to the UK's obligations under the Refugee Convention or the

Human Rights Convention. Where deportation would not be contrary to these obligations, it will only be in exceptional circumstances that the public interest in deportation is outweighed.

[Deportation and Article 8]

[A398. These rules apply where:
(a)   a foreign criminal liable to deportation claims that his deportation would be contrary to the United Kingdom's obligations under Article 8 of the Human Rights Convention;
(b)   a foreign criminal applies for a deportation order made against him to be revoked.]

Note

Inserted by HC 532, para 18 of this statement take effect on 28 July 2014 and apply to all ECHR Article 8 claims from foreign criminals which are decided on or after that date.

398. Where a person claims that their deportation would be contrary to the UK's obligations under Article 8 of the Human Rights Convention, and
(a)   the deportation of the person from the UK is conducive to the public good [and in the public interest] because they have been convicted of an offence for which they have been sentenced to a period of imprisonment of at least 4 years;
(b)   the deportation of the person from the UK is conducive to the public good [and in the public interest] because they have been convicted of an offence for which they have been sentenced to a period of imprisonment of less than 4 years but at least 12 months; or
(c)   the deportation of the person from the UK is conducive to the public good [and in the public interest] because, in the view of the Secretary of State, their offending has caused serious harm or they are a persistent offender who shows a particular disregard for the law,

the Secretary of State in assessing that claim will consider whether paragraph 399 or 399A applies and, if it does not, [the public interest in deportation will only be outweighed by other factors where there are very compelling circumstances over and above those described in paragraphs 399 and 399A].

Note

Amended by HC 532, para 19 of this statement take effect on 28 July 2014 and apply to all ECHR Article 8 claims from foreign criminals which are decided on or after that date. Amended by HC 532, para 20 of this statement take effect on 28 July 2014 and apply to all ECHR Article 8 claims from foreign criminals which are decided on or after that date. Amended by HC 532, para 21 of this statement take effect on 28 July 2014 and apply to all ECHR Article 8 claims from foreign criminals which are decided on or after that date. Amended by HC 532, para 22 of this statement take effect on 28 July 2014 and apply to all ECHR Article 8 claims from foreign criminals which are decided on or after that date.

399. This paragraph applies where paragraph 398 (b) or (c) applies if –

(a)   the person has a genuine and subsisting parental relationship with a child under the age of 18 years who is in the UK, and
(i)   the child is a British Citizen; or
(ii)   the child has lived in the UK continuously for at least the 7 years immediately preceding the date of the immigration decision; and in either case
     (a)   [it would be unduly harsh for the child to live in the country to which the person is to be deported]; and
     (b)   [it would be unduly harsh for the child to remain in the UK without the person who is to be deported]; or
(b)   the person has a genuine and subsisting relationship with a partner who is in the UK and is a [British Citizen or settled in the UK], and
     [(i)   the relationship was formed at a time when the person (deportee) was in the UK lawfully and their immigration status was not precarious; and

> (ii)   it would be unduly harsh for that partner to live in the country to which the person is to be deported, because of compelling circumstances over and above those described in paragraph EX.2. of Appendix FM; and
>
> (iii)   it would be unduly harsh for that partner to remain in the UK without the person who is to be deported.]

Note

Amended by HC 532, para 23 of this statement take effect on 28 July 2014 and apply to all ECHR Article 8 claims from foreign criminals which are decided on or after that date. Amended by HC 532, para 24 of this statement take effect on 28 July 2014 and apply to all ECHR Article 8 claims from foreign criminals which are decided on or after that date. Amended by HC 532, para 25 of this statement take effect on 28 July 2014 and apply to all ECHR Article 8 claims from foreign criminals which are decided on or after that date. Amended by HC 532, para 26 of this statement take effect on 28 July 2014 and apply to all ECHR Article 8 claims from foreign criminals which are decided on or after that date.

399A.   This paragraph applies where paragraph 398(b) or (c) applies if –
[(a)   the person has been lawfully resident in the UK for most of his life; and
(b)   he is socially and culturally integrated in the UK; and
(c)   there would be very significant obstacles to his integration into the country to which it is proposed he is deported.]

Note

Amended by HC 532, para 27 of this statement take effect on 28 July 2014 and apply to all ECHR Article 8 claims from foreign criminals which are decided on or after that date.

399B.   [Where an Article 8 claim from a foreign criminal is successful:
(a)   in the case of a person who is in the UK unlawfully or whose leave to enter or remain has been cancelled by a deportation order, limited leave may be granted for periods not exceeding 30 months and subject to such conditions as the Secretary of State considers appropriate;
(b)   in the case of a person who has not been served with a deportation order, any limited leave to enter or remain may be curtailed to a period not exceeding 30 months and conditions may be varied to such conditions as the Secretary of State considers appropriate;
(c)   indefinite leave to enter or remain may be revoked under section 76 of the 2002 Act and limited leave to enter or remain granted for a period not exceeding 30 months subject to such conditions as the Secretary of State considers appropriate;
(d)   revocation of a deportation order does not confer entry clearance or leave to enter or remain or re-instate any previous leave.]

Note

Substituted by HC 532, para 28 of this statement take effect on 28 July 2014 and apply to all ECHR Article 8 claims from foreign criminals which are decided on or after that date.

[**399C.**   Where a foreign criminal who has previously been granted a period of limited leave under this Part applies for further limited leave or indefinite leave to remain his deportation remains conducive to the public good and in the public interest notwithstanding the previous grant of leave.]

Note

Inserted by HC 532, para 29 of this statement take effect on 28 July 2014 and apply to all ECHR Article 8 claims from foreign criminals which are decided on or after that date.

[**399D.**   Where a foreign criminal has been deported and enters the United Kingdom in breach of a deportation order enforcement of the deportation order is in the public interest and will be implemented unless there are very exceptional circumstances.]

Note

Inserted by HC 532, para 30 of this statement take effect on 28 July 2014 and apply to all ECHR Article 8 claims from foreign criminals which are decided on or after that date.

[400. Where a person claims that their removal under paragraphs 8 to 10 of Schedule 2 to the Immigration Act 1971, section 10 of the Immigration and Asylum Act 1999 or section 47 of the Immigration, Asylum and Nationality Act 2006 would be contrary to the UK's obligations under Article 8 of the Human Rights Convention, the Secretary of State may require an application under paragraph 276ADE(1) (private life) or under paragraphs R-LTRP.1.1.(a), (b) and (d), R-LTRPT.1.1.(a), (b) and (d) and EX.1. of Appendix FM (family life as a partner or parent) of these rules. Where an application is not required, in assessing that claim the Secretary of State or an immigration officer will, subject to paragraph 353, consider that claim against the requirements to be met (except the requirement to make a valid application) under paragraph 276ADE(1) (private life) or paragraphs R-LTRP.1.1.(a), (b) and (d), R-LTRPT.1.1.(a), (b) and (d) and EX.1. of Appendix FM (family life as a partner or parent) of these rules as appropriate and if appropriate the removal decision will be cancelled.]

Note

Amended by HC 760, paras 28–282 as from 13 December 2012. Substituted by HC 693, para 110 as from 6 November 2014.

Paragraphs 398 and 399 represent the limits that the Secretary of State has set for assessing whether deportation will be in breach of Article 8. For guidance on the application of paragraph 399 – consideration of a child's best interests in cases where there is criminality - see: www.ukba.homeoffice.gov.uk/sitecontent/documents/policyandlaw/IDIs/chp8-annex/399a-guidance-.pdf?view=Binary

These provisions have been considered by the Upper Tribunal in *MF (Article 8 - new rules) Nigeria* [2012] UKUT 393 (IAC). The Upper Tribunal decided that its approach to assessing an Article 8 claim in the context of the new Rules is much the same as it was before the Rules were changed.

Whilst the transitional provision at para A362 states:

'Where Article 8 is raised in the context of deportation under Part 13 of these Rules, the claim under Article 8 will only succeed where the requirements of these rules as at 9 July 2012 are met, regardless of when the notice of intention to deport or the deportation order, as appropriate, was served', the Upper Tribunal doubted in MF that the new Rules could be applied to a case already considered by the First-Tier Tribunal before the date of the Rule change.'

[PART 14. STATELESS PERSONS

Definition of a stateless person

401. For the purposes of this Part a stateless person is a person who:
(a) satisfies the requirements of Article 1(1) of the 1954 United Nations Convention relating to the Status of Stateless Persons, as a person who is not considered as a national by any State under the operation of its law;
(b) is in the United Kingdom; and
(c) is not excluded from recognition as a Stateless person under paragraph 402.

Note

Inserted by HC 1039, para 124: where an applicant has made an application for entry clearance or leave before 6 April 2013 and the application has not been decided before that date, it will be decided in accordance with the rules in force on 5 April 2013.

Exclusion from recognition as a stateless person

402. A person is excluded from recognition as a stateless person if there are serious reasons for considering that they:
(a) are at present receiving from organs or agencies of the United Nations, other than the United Nations High Commissioner for Refugees, protection or assistance, so long as they are receiving such protection or assistance;
(b) are recognised by the competent authorities of the county of their former habitual residence as having the rights and obligations which are attached to the possession of that nationality of that country;

(c)   have committed a crime against peace, a war crime, or a crime against humanity, as defined in the international instruments drawn up to make provisions in respect of such crimes;

(d)   have committed a serious non-political crime outside the UK prior to their arrival in the UK;

(e)   have been guilty of acts contrary to the purposes and principles of the United Nations.

Note

Inserted by HC 1039, para 125: where an applicant has made an application for entry clearance or leave before 6 April 2013 and the application has not been decided before that date, it will be decided in accordance with the rules in force on 5 April 2013.

Requirements for limited leave to remain as a stateless person

403.   The requirements for leave to remain in the United Kingdom as a stateless person are that the applicant:

(a)   has made a valid application to the Secretary of State for limited leave to remain as a stateless person;

(b)   is recognised as a stateless person by the Secretary of State in accordance with paragraph 401;

(c)   is not admissible to their country of former habitual residence or any other country; and

(d)   has obtained and submitted all reasonably available evidence to enable the Secretary of State to determine whether they are stateless.

Note

Inserted by HC 1039, para 126: where an applicant has made an application for entry clearance or leave before 6 April 2013 and the application has not been decided before that date, it will be decided in accordance with the rules in force on 5 April 2013.

Refusal of limited leave to remain as a stateless person

404.   An applicant will be refused leave to remain in the United Kingdom as stateless person if:

(a)   they do not meet the requirements of paragraph 403;

(b)   there are reasonable grounds for considering that they are:

     (i)   a danger to the security of the United Kingdom;

     (ii)   a danger to the public order of the United Kingdom; or

(c)   their application would fall to be refused under any of the grounds set out in paragraph 322 of these Rules.

Note

Inserted by HC 1039, para 127: where an applicant has made an application for entry clearance or leave before 6 April 2013 and the application has not been decided before that date, it will be decided in accordance with the rules in force on 5 April 2013.

Grant of limited leave to remain to a stateless person

405.   Where an applicant meets the requirements of paragraph 403 they may be granted limited leave to remain in the United Kingdom for a period not exceeding 30 months.

Note

Inserted by HC 1039, para 128: where an applicant has made an application for entry clearance or leave before 6 April 2013 and the application has not been decided before that date, it will be decided in accordance with the rules in force on 5 April 2013.

Curtailment of limited leave to remain as a stateless person

406.   Limited leave to remain as a stateless person under paragraph 405 may be curtailed where the stateless person is a danger to the security or public order of the

United Kingdom or where leave would be curtailed pursuant to paragraph 323 of these Rules.

Note

Inserted by HC 1039, para 129: where an applicant has made an application for entry clearance or leave before 6 April 2013 and the application has not been decided before that date, it will be decided in accordance with the rules in force on 5 April 2013.

Requirements for indefinite limited leave to remain as a stateless person

407. The requirements for indefinite leave to remain as a stateless person are that the applicant:

(a)   has made a valid application to the Secretary of State for indefinite leave to remain as a stateless person;

(b)   was last granted limited leave to remain as a stateless person in accordance with paragraph 405;

(c)   has spent a continuous period of five years in the United Kingdom with lawful leave, except that any period of overstaying for a period of 28 days or less will be disregarded;

(d)   continues to meet the requirements of paragraph 403.

Note

Inserted by HC 1039, para 130: where an applicant has made an application for entry clearance or leave before 6 April 2013 and the application has not been decided before that date, it will be decided in accordance with the rules in force on 5 April 2013.

Grant of indefinite leave remain as a stateless person

408. Where an applicant meets the requirements of paragraph 407 they may be granted indefinite leave to remain.

Note

Inserted by HC 1039, para 131: where an applicant has made an application for entry clearance or leave before 6 April 2013 and the application has not been decided before that date, it will be decided in accordance with the rules in force on 5 April 2013.

Refusal of indefinite leave remain as a stateless person

409. An applicant will be refused indefinite leave to remain if:

(a)   the applicant does not meet the requirements of paragraph 407;

(b)   there are reasonable grounds for considering that the applicant is:

    (i)   a danger to the security of the United Kingdom;

    (ii)   a danger to the public order of the United Kingdom; or

(c)   the application would fall to be refused under any of the grounds set out in paragraph 322 of these Rules.

Note

Inserted by HC 1039, para 132: where an applicant has made an application for entry clearance or leave before 6 April 2013 and the application has not been decided before that date, it will be decided in accordance with the rules in force on 5 April 2013.

Requirements for limited leave to enter or remain as a family member of as stateless person

410. For the purposes of this Part a family member of a stateless person means their:

(a)   spouse;

(b)   civil partner;

(c)   unmarried or same sex partner with whom they have lived together in a subsisting relationship akin to marriage or a civil partnership for two years or more;

(d)   child under 18 years of age who:

    (i)   is not leading an independent life;

    (ii)   is not married or a civil partner; and

    (iii)   has not formed an independent family unit.

Note

Inserted by HC 1039, para 133: where an applicant has made an application for entry clearance or leave before 6 April 2013 and the application has not been decided before that date, it will be decided in accordance with the rules in force on 5 April 2013.

411. The requirements for leave to enter or remain in the United Kingdom as the family member of a stateless person are that the applicant:

(a)   has made a valid application to the Secretary of State for leave to enter or remain as the family member of a stateless person;

(b)   is the family member of a person granted leave to remain under paragraphs 405 or 408;

(c)   is seeking leave to enter, holds a valid United Kingdom entry clearance for entry in this capacity.

Note

Inserted by HC 1039, para 134: where an applicant has made an application for entry clearance or leave before 6 April 2013 and the application has not been decided before that date, it will be decided in accordance with the rules in force on 5 April 2013.

Refusal of leave to enter or remain as the family member of a stateless person

412. A family member will be refused leave to enter or remain if:

(a)   they do not meet the requirements of paragraph 411;

(b)   there are reasonable grounds for considering that:

    (i)   they are a danger to the security of the United Kingdom;

    (ii)   they are a danger to the public order of the United Kingdom; or

(c)   their application would fall to be refused under any of the grounds set out in paragraph 320, 321 or 322 of these Rules.

Note

Inserted by HC 1039, para 135: where an applicant has made an application for entry clearance or leave before 6 April 2013 and the application has not been decided before that date, it will be decided in accordance with the rules in force on 5 April 2013.

Grant of leave to enter or remain as the family member of a stateless person

413. A person who meets the requirements of paragraph 411 may be granted leave to enter or remain for a period not exceeding 30 months.

Note

Inserted by HC 1039, para 136: where an applicant has made an application for entry clearance or leave before 6 April 2013 and the application has not been decided before that date, it will be decided in accordance with the rules in force on 5 April 2013.

Curtailment of limited leave to enter or remain as the family member of a stateless person

414. Limited leave to remain as the family member of a stateless person under paragraph 413 may be curtailed where the family member is a danger to the security or public order of the United Kingdom or where leave would be curtailed pursuant to paragraph 323 of these Rules.

Note

Inserted by HC 1039, para 137: where an applicant has made an application for entry clearance or leave before 6 April 2013 and the application has not been decided before that date, it will be decided in accordance with the rules in force on 5 April 2013.

Requirements for indefinite leave to remain as the family member of a stateless person

415. The requirements for indefinite leave to enter or remain as the family member of a stateless person are that the applicant:

(a)   has made a valid application to the Secretary of State for indefinite leave to remain as the family member of a stateless person;

(b)   was last granted limited leave to remain as a family member of a stateless person in accordance with paragraph 413; and

    (i)   is still a family member of a stateless person; or

    (ii)   is over 18 and was last granted leave as the family member of a stateless person; and

        (a)   is not leading an independent life;

        (b)   is not married or a civil partner; and

        (c)   has not formed an independent family unit.

(c)   has spent a continuous period of five years with lawful leave in the United Kingdom, except that any period of overstaying for a period of 28 days or less will be disregarded.

Note

Inserted by HC 1039, para 138: where an applicant has made an application for entry clearance or leave before 6 April 2013 and the application has not been decided before that date, it will be decided in accordance with the rules in force on 5 April 2013.

Refusal of indefinite leave to remain as the family member of a stateless person

416. An applicant will be refused indefinite leave to remain as a family member of a stateless person if:

(a)   they do not meet the requirements of paragraph 415;

(b)   there are reasonable grounds for considering that:

    (i)   they are a danger to the security of the United Kingdom;

    (ii)   they are a danger to the public order of the United Kingdom; or

(c)   their application would fall to be refused under any of the grounds set out in paragraph 322 of these Rules.]

Note

Inserted by HC 1039, para 139: where an applicant has made an application for entry clearance or leave before 6 April 2013 and the application has not been decided before that date, it will be decided in accordance with the rules in force on 5 April 2013.

[APPENDIX 1
VISA REQUIREMENTS FOR THE UNITED KINGDOM]

1.   Subject to paragraph 2 below the following persons need a visa for the United Kingdom:

    (a)   Nationals or citizens of the following countries or territorial entities:

Afghanistan	Georgia	Philippines
Albania	Ghana	[Qatar (except those referred to in sub-paragraphs 2(k) and (u) of this Appendix)]
Algeria	Guinea	[. . .]
Angola	Guinea-Bissau	Russia
Armenia	Guyana	Rwanda
Azerbaijan	Haiti	Sao Tome e Principe
Bahrain [(except those referred to in sub-paragraph 2(w) of this Appendix).]	India	Saudi Arabia

Bangladesh	Indonesia	Senegal
Belarus	Iran	Sierra Leone
Benin	Iraq	[. . .]
Bhutan	Ivory Coast	Somalia
Bolivia		
Bosnia-Herzegovina	Jamaica	South Africa (. . .)
[. . .]	Jordan	[South Sudan]
Burkina Faso	Kazakhstan	Sri Lanka
Burma	Kenya	Sudan
		Surinam
Burundi	Kirgizstan	Swaziland
		Syria
Cambodia	Korea (North)	Taiwan (except those referred to in sub paragraph 2(h) of this Appendix)
Cameroon	Laos	[. . .]
Cape Verde	Lebanon	Tajikistan
	Lesotho	Tanzania
Central African Republic	Liberia	Thailand
Chad	Libya	Togo
[People's Republic of China (except those referred to in sub-paragraph 2(d) and (e) of this Appendix)]	Macedonia	Tunisia
[Colombia]	Madagascar	Turkey [(except those referred to in sub-paragraph 2(q) of this Appendix)]
Comoros	Malawi	Turkmenistan
Congo	Mali	Uganda
	Mauritania	Ukraine
Cuba	Moldova	[United Arab Emirates (except those referred to in sub-paragraphs 2(l) and (u) of this Appendix)]
[Democratic Republic of the Congo (Zaire)]	Mongolia	Uzbekistan
		Venezuela . . .
Djibouti	Morocco	Vietnam
Dominican Republic	Mozambique	Yemen
Ecuador	Nepal	The territories formerly comprising the Socialist Federal Republic of Yugoslavia excluding Croatia and Slovenia
Egypt	Niger	Zambia
Equatorial Guinea	Nigeria	Zimbabwe

Eritrea	[Oman (except those re-ferred to in sub-paragraphs 2(j) and (u) of this Appendix)]
Ethiopia	Pakistan
Fiji	. . .
Gabon	Peru

(b) Persons who hold passports or travel documents issued by the former Soviet Union or by the former Socialist Federal Republic of Yugoslavia.

(c) Stateless persons.

(d) [Persons travelling on any document other than a national passport, regardless of whether the document is issued by, or evidences nationality of, a state not listed in paragraph (a), except where that document has been issued by the UK].

2. The following persons do not need a visa for the United Kingdom:

   (a) those who qualify for admission to the United Kingdom as returning residents in accordance with paragraph 18;

   [(b) those who seek leave to enter the United Kingdom within the period of their earlier leave and for the same purpose as that for which leave was granted, unless it:

     (i) was for a period of six months or less; or

     (ii) was extended by statutory instrument [or by section 3C of the Immigration Act 1971 (inserted by section 3 of the Immigration and Asylum Act 1999];]

    . . .

   [(d) those nationals or citizens of the People's Republic of China holding passports issued by Hong Kong Special Administrative Region; or

   (e) those nationals or citizens of the People's Republic of China holding passports issued by Macao Special Administrative Region;]

   [(f) those who arrive in the United Kingdom with leave to enter which is in force but which was given before arrival, so long as those in question arrive within the period of their earlier leave and for the same purpose as that for which leave was granted, unless that leave—

     (i) was for a period of six months or less, or

     (ii) was extended by statutory instrument or by section 3C of the Immigration Act 1971 (inserted by section 3 of the Immigration and Asylum Act 1999).]

    [(. . .]

   [(h) those nationals or citizens of Taiwan who hold a passport issued by Taiwan that includes the number of his identification card issued by the competent authority in Taiwan in it.

   [(i) . . .]

   [(j) those nationals or citizens of Oman, who hold diplomatic and special passports issued by Oman when travelling to the UK for the purpose of a general visit in accordance with paragraph 41,

   (k) those nationals or citizens of Qatar who hold diplomatic and special passports issued by Qatar when travelling to the UK for the purpose of a general visit in accordance with paragraph 41,

   (l) those nationals or citizens of the United Arab Emirates who hold diplomatic and special passports issued by the United Arab Emirates when travelling to the UK for the purpose of a general visit in accordance with paragraph 41.]

   [(m) DELETED;

   (n) DELETED;

   (o) DELETED;

   (p) DELETED]

   [(q) those nationals of Turkey, who hold diplomatic passports issued by Turkey when travelling to the UK for the purpose of a general visit in accordance with paragraph 41.]

[(r) those nationals of Kuwait who hold diplomatic and special passports issued by Kuwait when travelling to the UK for the purpose of a general visit in accordance with paragraph 41.]

[(s) for the period beginning with 4 March 2014 and ending with 3 August 2014, nationals or citizens of the countries or territorial entities listed in paragraph 1 who hold a XX (20th) Commonwealth Games Identity and Accreditation Card issued by the Organising Committee of the Commonwealth Games (Glasgow 2014 Ltd) save for those who are accredited under (and whose card indicates accreditation under) category code WKF or S,

(t) for the period beginning with 4 March 2014 and ending with 3 September 2014 nationals or citizens of the countries or territorial entities listed in paragraph 1 who hold Commonwealth Games Identity and Accreditation Card issued by Glasgow 2014 Ltd unless

   (i) the holder is accredited under (and the card indicates accreditation under)category code WKF or S; or

   (ii) the holder had not had leave to enter, leave to remain or entry clearance under paragraph 56ZC or 56ZF at any time during the period beginning with 4 March 2013 and ending with 3 August 2014.]

[(u) those passport holders of Oman, Qatar or the United Arab Emirates who hold and use an Electronic Visa Waiver ("EVW") Document in accordance with paragraphs 3 to 9. Where the passport holder does not hold and use an EVW Document in accordance with paragraphs 3 to 9, the passport holder is a visa national and requires entry clearance.

(v) persons who hold Service, Temporary Service and Diplomatic passports issued by the Holy See.

[(w) "those nationals or citizens of Bahrain who hold diplomatic and special passports issued by Bahrain when travelling to the UK for the purpose of a general visit in accordance with paragraph 41."]

Note

Further amended by HC 693, para 111 as from 6 November 2014, save that if an application has been made for entry clearance or leave to enter or remain before 6 November 2014, the application will be decided in accordance with the Rules in force on 5 November 2014.

EXCEPTION WHERE THE APPLICANT HOLDS AN ELECTRONIC VISA WAIVER DOCUMENT (OMAN, QATAR AND UNITED ARAB EMIRATES PASSPORT HOLDERS ONLY

3. To obtain an Electronic Visa Waiver ("EVW") Document, a person (the "holder") or their agent must provide the required biographic and travel information at the Visa4UK website established by the United Kingdom Government at www.visa4uk.fc o.gov.uk/home/evw. The ECW Document must also specify:

(a) the flight, train or ship on which the holder intends to arrive in the United Kingdom, including the port of departure and arrival, and the scheduled date and time of departure and arrival, unless (b) or (c) applies;

(b) where the holder is seeking to arrive in the UK by entering a control zone in France or Belgium or supplementary control zone in France, the train or ship on which the holder intends to arrive in the United Kingdom, including:

   (i) the railway station or port where the holder enters the control zone or supplementary control zone and from which the holder intends to depart for the United Kingdom, and

   (ii) the railway station or port at which the holder intends to leave the train or ship after arrival in the United Kingdom, and

   (iii) the scheduled date and time of departure from, and of arrival at, the specified railway stations or ports; or

(c) where the holder intends to cross the land border from the Republic of Ireland to the United Kingdom by train, car or any other means, the place at which it is intended to cross and the intended date and time of arrival in the United Kingdom.

When the EVW Document is issued it must be printed in a legible form and in English.

4. An EVW Document is only valid if issued at least 48 hours before the holder departs on a flight, train or ship to the United Kingdom or crosses the United Kingdom land border from the Republic of Ireland by train, car or any other means. An EVW Document may not be issued more than 3 months before the date of the holder's scheduled departure to the United Kingdom as specified in the EVW Document or, where the holder intends to cross the land border with the Republic of Ireland, before the intended date of the holder's arrival in the United Kingdom as specified on the EVW Document.

5. An EVW Document relates to one person and may only be used for one application for leave to enter the United Kingdom or, where applicable, one crossing of the land border from the Republic of Ireland. A child must have a separate EVW Document.

6. The holder must present the EVW Document to an Immigration Officer on request upon the holder's arrival in the United Kingdom or, where the holder is seeking to arrive in the United Kingdom by entering a control zone in France or Belgium or a supplementary control zone in France, upon arrival in that zone. The EVW Document must be surrendered to an Immigration Officer upon request.

7. The holder will be a visa national, and so will require entry clearance, if the biographic details on the EVW Document do not match those on the valid national passport also presented to the Immigration Officer.

8. The holder will be a visa national, and so will require entry clearance, unless:
(a)   the holder travels on the flight, train or ship specified on the EVW Document; or
(b)   save where paragraphs (c) or (d) apply, the holder travels on a different flight, train or ship which departs from the same port and arrives at the same United Kingdom port as specified on the EVW Document, and which departs after the departure time specified on the EVW Document but arrives in the United Kingdom no more than 8 hours after the arrival time specified on the EVW Document; or
(c)   where the holder is seeking to arrive in the United Kingdom by entering a control zone in France or Belgium or a supplementary control zone in France, the holder travels on a different ship or train which departs from the same railway station or port and arrives in the same United Kingdom railway station or port as specified on the EVW Document, and which departs after, but no more than 8 hours after, the departure time specified on the EVW Document; or
(d)   where the holder is seeking to arrive in the United Kingdom by crossing the land border from the Republic of Ireland, the holder crosses the border at the time specified on the EVW Document or no more than 8 hours after the time specified on the EVW Document.

9. For the purposes of paragraphs 3, 6 and 8, "control zone" means a control zone defined by Article 2(1) and Schedule 1 to the Channel Tunnel (International Arrangements) Order 1993 (SI 1993/1813) and Article 2 of the Nationality and Immigration and Asylum Act 2002 (Juxtaposed Controls) Order 2003 (SI 2003/2818), and "supplementary control zone" means a supplementary control zone defined by Article 2(1) and Schedule 1 to the Channel Tunnel (International Arrangements) Order 1993 (SI 1993/1813).]

Note

Appendix amended by Statement of Changes in Immigration Rules with effect from 4 April 1996. Renamed Appendix 1 with effect from 11 May 1998 (Cmnd 3953). Republic of Croatia added by HC 22. People's Republic of China amended by HC 735. Maldives, Mauritius and Papua New Guinea deleted by HC 104. Jamaica inserted by HC 180. Zimbabwe inserted by HC 1301. Slovak Republic deleted by HC 95. Sub-paras 2(d) and (e) inserted by HC 735. Sub-para 2(c) deleted by HC 389. Words in square brackets in sub–paragraph 2(b)(ii) and sub-paragraphs (f)(i) and (ii) inserted by HC 104. Sub-paragraph 1(a) amended and sub-paragraph (g) inserted by HC 227.

Sub-paragraph 1(a) amended and sub-para (h) and (i) inserted by HC 413. Oman, Qatar and United Arab Emirates entries amended by HC 863, paras 139–141 as from 6 April 2011. Sub-paras (2)(j)-(l) inserted by HC 863, para 142 as from 6 April 2011. Sub-paragraphs 2 (m)-(p) inserted by HC 1511, para 45 as from 31 October 2011. Entry in sub-paragraph 1(A) "South Sudan" inserted and words in square brackets in entry "Turkey" by HC 1719, paras 2,3 as from 9 January 2012. Sub-paragraph 2(q) inserted by HC 1719, paras 4 as from 9 January 2012. Sub-paragraphs 2(r), (s) inserted by HC 628, para 144 and if an applicant has made an application for entry clearance or leave before 1 October 2013, the application will be decided in accordance with the Rules in force on 30 September 2013. Entries relating to the Oman, Qatar and the United Arab Emirates amended by HC 887, para 6 as from 30 December 2013. Sub-paragraph 2(u), (v) and sub-paragraph 3 inserted by HC 887, para 7 as from 1 January 2014. Paragraphs 3–9 inserted by HC 887, para 7 as from 1 January 2014. Further amended by HC 1138, para 82 as from 6 April 2014. Further amended by HC 1138, para 83 as from 6 April 2014. Further amended by HC 1138, para 84 of this statement comes into force on 5 May 2014. Paragraph "(i)" deleted by HC 1138, para 85 as from 6 April 2014.

[APPENDIX 2
COUNTRIES OR TERRITORIES WHOSE NATIONALS OR CITIZENS ARE RELEVANT FOREIGN NATIONALS FOR THE PURPOSES OF PART 10 OF THESE RULES

Registration with the police

Afghanistan	Iran	Qatar
Algeria	Iraq	Russia
Argentina	Israel	Saudi Arabia
Armenia	Jordan	Sudan
Azerbaijan	Kazakhstan	Syria
Bahrain	Kirgizstan	Tajikistan
Belarus	Kuwait	Tunisia
Bolivia	Lebanon	Turkey
Bhutan	Libya	Turkmenistan
Brazil	Moldova	United Arab Emirates
China	Morocco	Ukraine
Colombia	North Korea	Uzbekistan
Cuba	Oman	Yemen]
Egypt	Palestine	
Georgia	Peru	

Note

Inserted by Cmnd 3953 as from 11 May 1998.

APPENDIX 3
LIST OF COUNTRIES PARTICIPATING IN THE WORKING HOLIDAYMAKER SCHEME

DELETED.

[APPENDIX 7
STATEMENT OF THE TERMS AND CONDITIONS OF EMPLOYMENT OF AN OVERSEAS DOMESTIC WORKER IN A PRIVATE HOUSEHOLD IN THE UNITED KINGDOM

Please complete this form in capitals

Name of employee:

Name of employer:

1. Job Title:

2. Duties/Responsibilities:

3. Date of start of employment in the UK:

4. Employer's address in the UK:

5. Employee's address in the UK (if different from 4 please explain):

6. Employee's place of work in the UK (if different from 4 please explain):

7. Rate of Pay per week/month:

Note: By signing this document, the employer is declaring that the employee will be paid in accordance with the National Minimum Wage Act 1998 and any Regulations made under it for the duration of the employment

8. Hours of work per day/week:

Free periods per day

Free periods per week

9. Details of sleeping accommodation:

10. Details of Holiday entitlement:

11. Ending the employment:

Employee must give . . . . . . weeks notice if he/she decides to leave his/her job.

Employee is entitled to . . . . . . weeks notice if the employer decides to dismiss him/her.

Employee is employed on a fixed-term contract until (date) [if applicable].

Signed . . . . . . Date . . . . . . (Employer)

I confirm that the above reflects my condition of employment:

Signed . . . . . . Date . . . . . . (Employee)]

Note

Inserted by HC 565, para 101 as from 6 September 2012.

APPENDIX A
ATTRIBUTES

[Attributes for Tier 1 (Exceptional Talent) Migrants

1. [An applicant applying for entry clearance, leave to remain or indefinite leave to remain as a Tier 1 (Exceptional Talent) Migrant must score 75 points for attributes.]

Note

This paragraph substituted by HC 863, para 143 as from 6 April 2011.

2. [Available points are shown in Table 1.]

Note

This paragraph substituted by HC 863, para 143 as from 6 April 2011.

3. [Notes to accompany the table are shown below the table.]

Note

This paragraph substituted by HC 863, para 143 as from 6 April 2011.

[Table 1

Applications for entry clearance and leave to remain where the applicant does not have, or has not last had, leave as a Tier 1 (Exceptional Talent) Migrant]

Criterion	Points
Endorsed by Designated Competent Body according to that body's criteria as set out in Appendix L.	75

[All other applications for entry clearance and leave to remain and applications for indefinite leave to remain]

Criterion	Points
(i) During his most recent period of leave as a Tier 1 (Exceptional Talent) Migrant, the applicant has earned money in the UK as a result of employment or self-employment in his expert field as previously endorsed by a Designated Competent Body; and (ii) That Designated Competent Body has not withdrawn its endorsement of the applicant.]	75

Note

Table 1 substituted by HC 565, para 227 as from 1 October 2012. Appendix A Table 1 first and second section heading substituted by HC 1138, paras 86, 87 as from 13 March 2014. Further amended by HC 1138, para 86 as from 6 April 2014. Further amended by HC 1138, para 87 as from 6 April 2014.

Notes

Tier 1 (Exceptional Talent) Limit

4.
(a) The Secretary of State shall be entitled to limit the total number of Tier 1 (Exceptional Talent) endorsements Designated Competent Bodies may make in support of successful applications [for entry clearance and leave to remain] in a particular period, to be referred to a the Tier 1 (Exceptional Talent) Limit.
(b) [The Tier 1 (Exceptional Talent) Limit is 1,000 endorsements in total per year (beginning on 6 April and ending on 5 April) which will be allocated to the Designated Competent Bodies as follows:
   (i) 250 endorsements to the Arts Council for the purpose of endorsing applicants with exceptional talent in the fields of arts and culture;
   (ii) 250 endorsements to the Royal Society for the purpose of endorsing applicants with exceptional talent in the fields of natural sciences and medical science research;
   (iii) 150 endorsements to the Royal Academy of Engineering for the purpose of endorsing applicants with exceptional talent in the field of engineering;

(iv)   150 endorsements to the British Academy for the purpose of endorsing applicants with exceptional talent in the fields of humanities and social sciences; and

(v)   200 endorsements to Tech City UK for the purpose of endorsing applicants with exceptional talent in the field of digital technology.]

(c)   [The Tier 1 (Exceptional Talent) Limit will be operated according to the practice set out in paragraph 5 below.]

(d)   If a Designated Competent Body chooses to transfer part of its unused allocation of endorsements to another Designated Competent Body by mutual agreement of both sides and the Secretary of State, the allocations of both bodies will be adjusted accordingly and the adjusted allocations will be published on the [visas and immigration pages of the gov.uk] website.

Note

Sub-paragraph (c) substituted by HC 565, para 228 as from 1 October 2012. Further amended by HC 1138, para 88 as from 6 April 2014. Further amended by HC 1138, para 89 as from 6 April 2014.

. . .

5.

(a)   [Before an applicant applies for entry clearance or leave to remain (unless he has, or last had, leave as a Tier 1 (Exceptional Talent) Migrant), he must make an application for a Designated Competent Body endorsement, and this application must:

    (i)   be made to the UK Border Agency using the specified form,

    (ii)   state which Designated Competent Body he wishes to endorse his application, and

    (iii)   provide the specified evidence set out in Appendix L.]

(b)   A number of endorsements will be made available for each Designated Competent Body, as follows:

    (i)   From 6 April to 30 September each year, half that body's allocated endorsements under paragraph 4 above.

    (ii)   From 1 October to 5 April each ear, that body's remaining unused allocated endorsements under paragraph 4 above.

(c)   Unused endorsements will not be carried over from one year to the next.

(d)   [If a Designated Competent Body endorses an application for an endorsement, the applicant subsequently uses that endorsement to make an application for entry clearance or leave to remain which is refused, and that refusal is not subsequently overturned, the used endorsement will be returned to the number of endorsements available for the relevant Designated Competent Body, providing the end of the period (6 April to 5 April) to which it relates has not yet passed.

(e)   An application for a Designated Competent Body endorsement will be refused if the Designated Competent Body has reached or exceeded the number of endorsements available to it.]

(f)   [The number of endorsements available for each Designated Competent Body to endorse Tier 1 (Exceptional Talent) applicants in a particular period, will be reduced by one for each Croation national that body endorses in that period for the purposes of applying to be deemed a highly skilled person under the Accession of Croatian (Immigration and Worker Authorisation) Regulations 2013.]]

Note

Paragraph 5 substituted by HC 55, para 230 as from 1 October 2012. Sub-paragraph (f) inserted by HC 628, para 145 and if an applicant has made an application for entry clearance or leave before 1 October 2013, the application will be decided in accordance with the Rules in force on 30 September 2013.

Endorsement by the relevant Designated Competent Body

[6. Points will only be awarded in an application for entry clearance or leave to remain (except where the applicant has, or last had, leave as a Tier 1 (Exceptional Talent) Migrant) for an endorsement from the relevant Designated Competent Body if:

(a)   the applicant provides a valid approval letter from the UK Border Agency for a Designated Competent Body endorsement, which was granted to him no more than three months before the date of the application for entry clearance or leave to remain, and

(b)   the endorsement has not been withdrawn by the relevant Designated Competent Body at the time the application is considered by the UK Border Agency.]

Note

Paragraphs 4–6 substituted by HC 1436, para 9 as from 9 August 2011. Paras 4(b), 5(b)(i), (ii), (d)(i), (e)(i) amended by HC 1888, paras 116–120 as from 6 April 2012.

[Money earned in the UK

6A. Points will only be awarded from money earned in the UK if the applicant provides the following specified documents:

(a)   If the applicant is a salaried employee, the specified documents are at least one of the following:

    (i)   payslips confirming his earnings, which must be either:

        (1)   [original formal payslips issued by the employer and showing the employer's name, or],

        (2)   accompanied by a letter from the applicant's employer, on company headed paper and signed by a senior official, confirming the payslips are authentic; or

    (ii)   personal bank statements on official bank stationery showing the payments made to the applicant; or

    (iii)   electronic bank statements ..., which either:

        (1)   are accompanied by a supporting letter from the bank on company headed paper confirming that the documents are authentic

        (2)   beat the official stamp of the issuing bank on every page of the document; or

    (iv)   an official tax document produced by HM Revenue & Customs or the applicant's employer, which shows earnings on which tax has been paid or will be paid in a tax year, and is either:

        (1)   a document produced by HM Revenue & Customs that shows details of declarable income on which tax has been paid or will be paid in a tax year, such as a tax refund letter or tax demand,

        (2)   a P60 document produced by an employer as an official return to HM Revenue & Customs, showing details of earnings on which tax has been paid in a tax year, or

        (3)   a document produced by a person, business, or company as an official return to HM Revenue & Customs, showing details of earnings on which tax has been paid or will be paid in a tax year, and which has been approved, registered, or stamped by HM Revenue & Customs; or

    (v)   Dividend vouchers, confirming the gross and net dividend paid by a company to the applicant, normally from its profits. The applicant must provide a separate dividend voucher or payment advice slip for each dividend payment.

(b)   If the applicant has worked in self-employed capacity, the specified documents are at least one of the following:

    (i)   A letter from the applicant's accountant (who must be either a fully qualified chartered accountant or a certified accountant who is a member of a registered body in the UK), on headed paper, which shows a breakdown of the gross and net earnings. The letter should give a breakdown of salary, dividends, profits, tax credits and dates of net payments earned. if the applicant's earnings are a share of the net profit of the company, the letter should also explain this; or

    (ii)   Company or business accounts that meet statutory requirements and clearly show:

        (1)   the net profit of the company or business made over the earnings period to be assessed,

        (2)   both a profit and loss account (or income and expenditure account if the organisation is not trading for profit), and

        (3)   a balance sheet signed by a director; or

    (iii) If the applicant has worked as a sponsored researcher, a letter on official headed paper to the applicant from the institution providing the funding, which confirms:

        (1)   the applicant's name,

        (2)   the name of the sponsoring institution providing the funding,

        (3)   the name of the host institution where the applicant's sponsored research is based,

        (4)   the title of the post, and

        (5)   details of the funding provided.

(c)   All applicants must also provide at least one of the following specified documents:

    (i)   A contract of service or work between the applicant and a UK employer or UK institution which indicates the field of work he has undertaken; or

    (ii)   A letter from a UK employer or UK institution on its official headed paper, confirming that the applicant has earned money in his expert field.]

Note

This paragraph substituted by HC 565, para 231 as from 1 October 2012. Amended by HC 628, paras 146–148 and if an applicant has made an application for entry clearance or leave before 1 October 2013, the application will be decided in accordance with the Rules in force on 30 September 2013.

[Attributes for Tier 1 (General) Migrants

7.   An applicant applying for leave to remain or indefinite leave to remain as a Tier 1 (General) Migrant must score 75 points for attributes, if the applicant has, or has had, leave as a Highly Skilled Migrant, as a Writer, Composer or Artist, Self-employed Lawyer, or as a Tier 1 (General) Migrant under the rules in place before 19 July 2010, and has not been granted leave in any categories other than these under the rules in place since 19 July 2010.]

Note

This paragraph substituted by HC 863, para 143 as from 6 April 2011.

8.   [An applicant applying for leave to remain or indefinite leave to remain as a Tier 1 (General) Migrant who does not fall within the scope of paragraph 7 above or paragraph 9 below must score 80 points for attributes.]

Note

This paragraph substituted by HC 863, para 143 as from 6 April 2011.

9.   [An applicant applying for indefinite leave to remain as a Tier 1 (General) Migrant is not required to score points for attributes if he:

(a)   received a Highly Skilled Migrant Programme approval letter issued on the basis of an application made before 7 November 2006,

(b)   was subsequently granted entry clearance or leave to remain on the basis of that letter, and

(c)   has not since been granted entry clearance or leave to remain in any category other than as a Highly Skilled Migrant or Tier 1 (General) Migrant.]

Note

This paragraph substituted by HC 863, para 143 as from 6 April 2011. Words in square brackets substituted by HC 565, para 102 as from 6 September 2012. Further amended by HC 1138, para 90 as from 6 April 2014.

10.   [Available points are shown in Table 2 and Table 3 below. Only one set of points will be awarded per column in each table. For example, points will only be awarded for one qualification.]

Note

This paragraph substituted by HC 863, para 143 as from 6 April 2011.

11.   [Notes to accompany Table 2 and Table 3 appear below Table 3.]

Note

This paragraph substituted by HC 863, para 143 as from 6 April 2011.

[Table 2 – Applications for leave to remain and indefinite leave to remain where the applicant has, or has had, leave as a Highly Skilled Migrant, as a Writer, Composer or Artist, Self-employed Lawyer, or as a Tier 1 (General) Migrant under the rules in place before 6 April 2010, and has not been granted leave in any categories other than these since 6 April 2010

Qualification	Points	Previous earnings	Points	UK Experience	Points	Age (at date of application for first grant)	Points
Bachelor's degree (see paragraph 13 below)	30	£16,000-£17,999.99 (see paragraph 18 below)	5	If £16,000 or more of the previous earnings for which points are claimed were earned in the UK	5	Under 28 years of age	20
Master's degree	35	£18,000-£19,999.99 (see paragraph 18 below)	10	If £16,000 or more of the previous earnings for which points are claimed were earned in the UK		28 or 29 years of age	10
PhD	50	£20,000-£22,999.99	15			30 or 31 years of age	5
		£23,000-£25,999.99	20				
		£26,000-£28,999.99	25				
		£29,000-£31,999.99	30				
		£32,000-£34,999.99	35				
		£35,000-£39,999.99	40				
		£40,000 or more	45				

Table 3 - All other applications for leave to remain and indefinite leave to remain

Qualification	Points	Previous earnings	Points	UK Experience	Points	Age (at date of application for first grant)	Points
Bachelor's degree	30	£25,000-£29,999.99	5	if £25,000 or more of the previous earnings for which points are claimed were earned in the UK	5	Under 30 years of age	20
Master's degree	35	£30,000-£34,999.99	15			30 to 34 years of age	10
PhD	45	£35,000-£39,999.99	20			5 to 39 years of age	5
		£40,000-£49,999.99	5 15 20				
		£50,000-£54,999.99	30				
		£55,000-£64,999.99	35				
		£65,000-£74,999.99	40				
		£75,000-£149,999.99	45				
		£150,000 or more	80				

12. Qualifications and/or earnings will not be taken into account if the applicant was in breach of the UK's immigration laws at the time those qualifications were studied for or those earnings were made.]

Note

This paragraph substituted by HC 863, para 143 as from 6 April 2011.

13. An applicant will be awarded no points for a Bachelor's degree if:
(a) his last grant of entry clearance was as a Tier 1 (General) Migrant under the Rules in place between 31 March 2009 and 5 April 2010, or
    (i) he has had leave to remain as a Tier 1 (General) Migrant under the Rules in place between 31 March 2009 and 5 April 2010, and
    (ii) his previous entry clearance, leave to enter or leave to remain before that leave was not as a Highly Skilled Migrant, as a Writer, Composer or artist, as a Self-Employed Lawyer, or as a Tier 1 (General) Migrant.]

Note

This paragraph substituted by HC 863, para 143 as from 6 April 2011.

14. [[The specified documents in paragraph 14–SD must be provided] must be provided as evidence of the qualification, unless the applicant has, or was last granted, leave as a Highly Skilled Migrant or a Tier 1 (General) Migrant and previously scored points for the same qualification in respect of which points are being claimed in this application.]

Note

This paragraph substituted by HC 863, para 143 as from 6 April 2011. Words in square brackets substituted by Cm 8423, para 81 as from 20 July 2012. Further amended by HC 1138, para 91 as from 6 April 2014.

14-SD.
[(a)   the specified documents in paragraph 14 are
    (i)   the original certificate of award of the qualification, which clearly shows the:
        (1)   applicant's name,
        (2)   title of the award,
        (3)   date of the award, and
        (4)   name of the awarding institution, or
    (ii)   if:
        (1)   the applicant is awaiting graduation having successfully completed his degree, or
        (2)   the applicant no longer has the certificate and the institution who issued the certificate is unable to produce a replacement.
        an original academic reference to in (a) (ii) must be on the official headed paper of the institution and clearly show the that it is awarding the degree together with an original accompanying transcript, unless (d) applies.
(b)   The academic reference referred to in (a)(ii) must on the official headed paper of the institution and clearly show the:
    (1)   applicant's name,
    (2)   title of the award,
    (3)   date of the award, confirming that it has been or will be awarded, and
    (4)   either the date that the certificate will be issued (if the applicant has not yet graduated) or confirmation that the institution is unable to re-issue the original certificate or award.
(c)   The academic transcript referred to in (a)(ii) must on the official headed paper of the institution and clearly show the:
    (1)   applicant's name,
    (2)   name of the awarding institution,
    (3)   course title, and
    (4)   confirmation of the award.
(d)   If the applicant cannot provide his original certificate for one of the reasons given in (a)(ii) and is claiming points for a qualification with a significant research bias, such as a doctorates, an academic transcript is not required, providing the applicant provides an academic reference which includes all the information detailed in (b) above.
(e)   Where an applicant cannot find details of his academic qualification on the points based calculator on the [visas and immigration pages of the gov.uk] website, he must, in addition to the document or documents in (a), provide an original letter or certificate from UK NARIC confirming the equivalency of the level of his qualification.
(f)   Where an applicant cannot find details of his professional or vocational qualification on the points based calculator on the UK Border Agency website, he must, in addition to the document or documents in (a), provide an original letter from the appropriate UK professional body confirming the equivalency of the level of his qualification, which clearly shows:
    (1)   the name of the qualification, including the country and awarding body, and
    (2)   confirmation of which UK academic level the qualification is equivalent to.]

Note

This paragraph inserted by Cm 8423, para 82 as from 20 July 2012. Words in Appendix A paragraph 14-SD(e) substituted by HC 1138, para 91 as from 13 March 2014.

15. [Points will only be awarded for an academic qualification if an applicant's qualification is deemed by the National Academic Recognition Information Centre for the United Kingdom (UK NARIC) to meet or exceed the recognised standard of a Bachelor's or Master's degree or a PhD, as appropriate, in the UK.]

Note

This paragraph substituted by HC 863, para 143 as from 6 April 2011.

[Previous earnings: notes

18. An applicant will be awarded no points for previous earnings of less than £20,000 if:
- (a) his last grant of entry clearance was as a Tier 1 (General) Migrant under the Rules in place between 31 March 2009 and 5 April 2010, or
  - (i) he has had leave to remain as a Tier 1 (General) Migrant under the Rules in place between 31 March 2009 and 5 April 2010, and
  - (ii) his previous entry clearance, leave to enter or leave to remain before that leave was not as a Highly Skilled Migrant, as a Writer, Composer or Artist, as a Self-Employed Lawyer, or as a Tier 1 (General) Migrant.]

Note

This paragraph substituted by HC 863, para 143 as from 6 April 2011.

[19.
- [(a) In all cases, the applicant must provide at least two different types of the specified documents in paragraph 19–SD(a) from two or more separate sources as evidence for each source of previous earnings.
- (b) If the applicant is claiming points for self-employed earnings made in the UK, he must also provide the specified documents in paragraph 19–SD(b) to show that:
  - (i) he is registered as self-employed,
  - (ii) he was registered as self-employed during the period(s) of self-employment used to claim points, and
  - (iii) he was paying Class 2 National Insurance contributions during the period(s) of self-employment used to claim points.
- (c) Each piece of supporting evidence must support all the other evidence and, where appropriate, be accompanied by any information or explanation of the documents submitted, including further documents such as a letter of explanation from the applicant's accountant, so that together the documents clearly prove the earnings claimed.
- (d) Full contact details must be provided for each supporting document for verification purposes.
- (e) Where an applicant in providing bank statements as evidence, the bank statements must:
  - (i) be on official bank stationery, and must show each of the payments that the applicant is claiming, or
  - (ii) electronic bank statements ..., which either
    - (1) are accompanied by a supporting letter from the bank on company headed paper confirming that the documents are authentic, or
    - (2) bear the official stamp of the issuing bank on every page of the statement.
- (f) Where an applicant is providing official tax documents as evidence, the documents must be:
  - (i) a document produced by a tax authority that shows details of declarable income on which tax has been paid or will be paid in a tax year (for example a tax refund letter or tax demand),
  - (ii) a document produced by an employer as an official return to a tax authority, showing details of earnings on which tax has been paid in a tax year (for example a P60 in the United Kingdom), or

(iii)   a document produced by a person, business, or company as an official return to a tax authority, showing details of earnings on which tax has been paid, or will be paid in a tax year, and which has been approved, registered, or stamped by the tax authority.

(i)   Where an applicant is providing evidence from an accountant or accountancy firm, the accountant must be a fully qualified chartered accountant or a certified accountant who is a member of a registered body.

(ii)   if the earnings were for work done while the applicant was in the UK, such evidence must come from an accountant or accountancy firm in the UK who is member of one of the following recognised supervisory bodies:

    (1)   The Institute of Chartered Accountants in England and Wales (ICAEW),

    (2)   The Institute of Chartered Accountants in Scotland (ICAS),

    (3)   The Institute of Chartered Accountants in Ireland (ICAI),

    (4)   The Association of Chartered Certified Accountants (ACCA),

    (5)   The Chartered Institute of Public Finance and Accountancy (CIPFA),

    (6)   The Institute of Financial Accountants (IFA),

    (7)   The Chartered Institute of Management Accountants (CIMA)[, or]

    [(8)   [The Association of International Accountants (AIA).]

(iii)   If the earnings were made while the applicant was not in the UK, the evidence must come from an accountant or accountancy firm which meets the requirements in (ii) or appears on the list of full members given on the website of the International Federation of Accountants.

[(h)   if the applicant has exchanged some of his UK employment rights for shares as an employee-owner, the value of those shares will not be included when calculating the applicant's previous earnings.]

[(i)   The Secretary of State must be satisfied that the earnings are from genuine employment. If the Secretary of State is not satisfied, points for those earnings will not be awarded.

(j)   In making the assessment in paragraph 19(i), the Secretary of State will assess on the balance of probabilities and may take into account the following factors:

    (i)   the evidence the applicant has submitted;

    (ii)   whether the money appears to have been earned through genuine employment, rather than being borrowed, gifted, or otherwise shown in the applicant's financial transactions or records without being earned;

    (iii)   whether the business from which the earnings are claimed can be shown to exist and be lawfully and genuinely trading;

    (iv)   verification of previous earnings claims with declarations made in respect of the applicant to other Government Departments, including declarations made in respect of earnings claimed by the applicant in previous applications;

    (v)   the applicant's previous educational and business experience (or lack thereof) in relation to the claimed business activity;

    (vi)   the applicant's immigration history and previous activity in the UK;

    (vii)   where the nature of the applicant's employment or business requires him to have mandatory accreditation, registration or insurance, whether that accreditation, registration or insurance has been obtained;

    (viii)   any payments made by the applicant to other parties; and

    (ix)   any other relevant information.

(k)   To support the assessment in paragraph 19(i), the secretary of State may:

    (i)   request additional information and evidence, and refuse the application if the information or evidence is not provided. Any requested documents must be received by the Secretary of State at the address specified in the request within [28 calendar days] of the date the request is sent, and

    (ii)   request the applicant attends an interview, and refuse the application if the applicant fails to comply with any such request without providing a reasonable explanation.

(l)   The Secretary of State may decide not to carry out the assessment in paragraph 19(i) of the application already falls for refusal on other grounds, but reserves the right to carry out this assessment in any reconsideration of the decision.]

Note

Sub-para (h) inserted by HC 1039 para 146 as from 6 April 2013. Amended by HC 628, paras 149, 150 as from. Further amended by HC 1138, para 93 as from 6 April 2014. Amended by HC 1138, para 94 as from 6 April 2014. Further amended by HC 693, para 112 as from 6 November 2014, save that if an application has been made for entry clearance or leave to enter or remain before 6 November 2014, the application will be decided in accordance with the Rules in force on 5 November 2014.

[**19-SD.**   (a) The specified documents in paragraph 19(a) are:
[(i)   Payslips covering the whole period claimed, which must be either:
    (1)   original formal payslips issued by the employer and showing the employer's name, or
    (2)   accompanied by a letter from the applicant's employer, on the company's head paper and signed by a senior official, confirming the payslips are authentic;]
(ii)   Personal bank statements showing the payments made to the applicant;
(iii)   A letter from the applicant's employer(s) during the period claimed (or in the case of winnings, the relevant awarding body), on company headed paper, which:
    (1)   is dated after the period for which earnings are being claimed, and
    (2)   clearly confirms the applicant's gross and net earnings during the period claimed, and the date and amount of each payment;
(iv)   Official tax document produced by the relevant tax authority or employer, showing earnings on which tax has been paid or will be paid in a tax year;
(v)   Dividend vouchers which show the amount of money paid by the company to the applicant, normally from its profits, and which confirm both the gross and net dividend paid. The applicant must provide a separate dividend voucher or payment advice slip for each dividend payment, to cover the whole period claimed;
(vi)   If the applicant is claiming points for self-employed earnings, a letter from his accountant on headed paper, confirming that the applicant received the exact amount he is claiming, or the net profit to which he is entitled. This is a letter from the applicant's accountant on headed paper confirming the gross and net pay for the period claimed. The letter should give a breakdown of salary, dividends, profits, tax credits and dates of net payments earned. If the applicant's earnings are a share of the net profit of the company, the letter should also explain this;
(vii)   Invoice explanations or payment summaries from the applicant's accountant, which include a breakdown of the gross salary, tax deductions and dividend payments made to the applicant, and which enable the UK Border Agency to check that the total gross salary and dividend payments correspond with the net payments into the applicant's personal bank account.
(viii) Company or business accounts that meet statutory requirements and clearly show:
    (1)   the net profit of the company or business made over the earnings period to be assessed,
    (2)   both a profit and loss account (or income and expenditure account if the organisation is not trading for profit), and
    (3)   a balance sheet signed by a director;
(ix)   Business bank statements showing the payments made to the applicant;
(x)   If the applicant provides a combination of bank statements and a letter or invoice summary from his accountant, he must also provide any invoices generated during the period for which earnings are being claimed.

(b) The specified documents in paragraph 19(b) are:
(i)   If the applicant's National Insurance is paid by bill, the original bill from the billing period immediately before the application.
(ii)   If the applicant's National Insurance is paid by direct debit, the most recent bank statement issued before the application, showing the direct debit payment of National Insurance to HM Revenue & Customs.
(iii)   If the applicant has low earnings, an original small earnings exception certificate issued by HM Revenue & Customs for the most recent return date.

(iv)   If the applicant has not yet received the documents in (i) to (iii), the original, dated welcome letter from HM Revenue & Customs containing the applicant's unique taxpayer reference number.]

[Period for assessment

20.   Applicants should indicate in the application form for which 12-month period their earnings should be assessed.]

Note

This paragraph substituted by HC 863, para 143 as from 6 April 2011. Amended by HC 628, paras 151 and if an applicant has made an application for entry clearance or leave before 1 October 2013, the application will be decided in accordance with the Rules in force on 30 September 2013.

[**21.**
(a)   [For all applicants the period for assessment of earnings must:
        (i)   consist of no more than 12 months which must run consecutively, and
        (ii)   fall within the 15 months immediately preceding the application.
(b)   If the applicant:
        (i)   has been on maternity or adoption leave at some point within the 12 months preceding the application, and
        (ii)   has provided the specified documents [in paragraph 21–SD], or where due to exceptional circumstances the specified documents are not available, has provided alternative documents which show that the circumstances provided for in (i) apply,

the applicant may choose for a period of no more than 12 months spent on maternity or adoption leave to be disregarded when calculating both the 12-month and 15-month period.]

Note

This paragraph substituted by HC 863, para 143 as from 6 April 2011. Words in square brackets inserted by Cm 8423, para 84 as from 20 July 2012.

[**21-SD**   (a) Where paragraph 21(b)(ii) states that specified documents must be provided, the applicant must provide:
(i)   The document in (b) below, if it has been issued, and
(ii)   If the document in (b) has been issued and is provided, the documents in either (c)(i) or (c)(ii) below, or
(iii) If the document in (b) has not been issued, the documents in both (c)(i) and (ii) below, or
(iv)   If the applicant is unable to satisfy (ii) or (iii) above:
        (1)   the documents in either (b) or (c)(i) or (c)(ii),
        (2)   a satisfactory explanation as to why the other types of document cannot be provided, and
        (3)   one of the types of documents in (d) below.

The specified documents are:

(b) The original full birth certificate or original full certificate of adoption (as appropriate), containing the names of parents or adoptive parents of the child for whom the period of maternity or adoption-related absence was taken;

(c)
(i)   An original letter from the applicant's employer, on the company headed paper, which confirms the start and end dates of the period of maternity or adoption-related absence;
(ii)   Original payslips or other payment or remittance documents, on the official letter-headed paper of the issuing authority, and covering the entire period for which the maternity or adoption-related absence is being claimed and showing the statutory maternity or adoption payments to the applicant;

(d) One of the following documents, from an official source and which is independently verifiable:

(i)   official adoption papers issued by the relevant authority;

(ii)   any relevant medical documents

(iii)   a relevant extract from a register of birth accompanied by an original letter from the issuing authority.]

22. [If the applicant has not indicated a period for assessment of earnings, or has indicated a period which does not meet the conditions [in paragraph 21 above], their earnings will be assessed against the 12-month period immediately preceding their application, assuming the specified documents [in paragraph 19–SD above] have been provided. Where the specified documents [in paragraph 19–SD above] have not been provided, points will not be awarded for previous earnings.]

Note

This paragraph substituted by HC 863, para 143 as from 6 April 2011. Amended by Cm 8423, paras 83, 86, 87 as from 20 July 2012.

[**Earnings**

23. Earnings include, but are not limited to:

(a)   salaries (includes full-time, part-time and bonuses),

(b)   earnings derived through self-employment,

(c)   earnings derived through business activities,

(d)   statutory and contractual maternity pay, statutory and contractual adoption pay,

(e)   allowances (such as accommodation, schooling or car allowances) which form part of an applicant's remuneration package and are specified in the applicant's payslips,

(f)   dividends paid by a company in which the applicant is active in the day-to-day management, or where the applicant receives the dividend as part or all of their remuneration package,

(g)   property rental income, where this constitutes part of the applicant's business, and (h) payments in lieu of notice.]

Note

This paragraph substituted by HC 863, para 143 as from 6 April 2011.

24. [Where the earnings take the form of a salary or wages, they will be assessed before tax (i.e. gross salary).]

Note

This paragraph substituted by HC 863, para 143 as from 6 April 2011.

25. [Where the earnings are the profits of a business derived through self-employment or other business activities:

(a)   the earnings that will be assessed are the profits of the business before tax. Where the applicant only has a share of the business, the earnings that will be assessed are the profits of the business before tax to which the applicant is entitled, and

(b)   the applicant must be registered as self-employed in the UK, and must provide the specified evidence.]

Note

This paragraph substituted by HC 863, para 143 as from 6 April 2011.

26. [Earnings do not include unearned sources of income, such as:

(a)   allowances (such as accommodation, schooling or car allowances) which are paid as reimbursement for monies the applicant has previously paid,

(b)   any other allowances, unless part of the applicant's remuneration package and specified in the applicant's payslips,

(c)   dividends, unless paid by a company in which the applicant is active in the day-to-day management, or unless the applicant receives the dividend as part or all of their remuneration package,

(d)   property rental income, unless this constitutes part of the applicant's business,

(e)   interest on savings and investments,

(f)   funds received through inheritance,
(g)   [employer pension contributions or monies paid to the applicant as a pension,]
(h)   expenses where the payment constitutes a reimbursement for monies the applicant has previously outlaid,
(i)   redundancy payment,
(j)   sponsorship for periods of study,
(k)   state benefits, or
(l)   prize money or competition winnings, other than where they are directly related to the applicant's main profession or occupation.]

Note

This paragraph substituted by HC 863, para 143 as from 6 April 2011. Amended by HC 760, para 285 as from 13 December 2012.

[Converting foreign currencies

27.   Earnings in a foreign currency will be converted to pound sterling (£) using the closing spot exchange rate for the last day of the period for which the applicant has claimed earnings in that currency.]

Note

This paragraph substituted by HC 863, para 143 as from 6 April 2011.

28.   [If the applicant's earnings fall either side of a period of maternity or adoption leave, earnings in a foreign currency will be converted to pounds sterling (£) using the closing spot exchange rate which exists:
(a)   for the earnings earned before maternity or adoption leave, on the last day of the period before maternity leave, and
(b)   for the earnings earned after maternity or adoption leave, on the last day of the period after maternity leave.]

Note

This paragraph substituted by HC 863, para 143 as from 6 April 2011.

29.   [The spot exchange rate which will be used is that which appears on www.oand a.com*]

Note

This paragraph substituted by HC 863, para 143 as from 6 April 2011.

30.   [Where the previous earnings claimed are in different currencies, any foreign currencies will be converted before being added together, and then added to any UK earnings, to give a total amount.]

Note

This paragraph substituted by HC 863, para 143 as from 6 April 2011.

[UK Experience: notes

31.   Previous earnings will not be taken into account for the purpose of awarding points for UK experience if the applicant was not physically present in the UK at the time those earnings were made.]

Note

This paragraph substituted by HC 863, para 143 as from 6 April 2011.

32.   [Previous earnings will not be taken into account for the purpose of awarding points for UK experience if the applicant was physically present in the Isle of Man or the Channel Islands at the time those earnings were made.]

Note

This paragraph substituted by HC 863, para 143 as from 6 April 2011.

[Age: notes

33. If the applicant was first granted leave in the categories of Highly Skilled Migrant, Writer, Composer or Artist, Self-employed lawyer or Tier 1 (General) Migrant and has not been granted leave in any category other than those listed here since the first grant of leave, points will be awarded based on the applicant's age at the date of the application for that first grant of leave. If the applicant has been granted leave since his first grant of leave in a category not listed in this paragraph, points will be awarded based on his age at the date of application for a grant of leave in a category listed in this paragraph where leave has not been granted in any category not listed in this paragraph between that grant of leave and the current application.]

Note

This paragraph substituted by HC 863, para 143 as from 6 April 2011.

34. [[The specified documents in paragraph 34–SD must be provided] as evidence of age.

are shown in Table 6.]

Note

This paragraph substituted by HC 863, para 143 as from 6 April 2011. Further amended by Cm 8423, para 88 as from 20 July 2012.

34-SD. The specified documents in paragraph 34 are:
(i)   The applicant's Biometric Residence Permit, which contains the date of approval of the last grant of leave and the age of the applicant; or
(ii)   The applicant's current valid original passport or travel document containing the last [entry clearance] granted to the applicant.]

Note

This paragraph inserted by Cm 8423, para 89 as from 20 July 2012. Amended by HC 760, para 286 as from 13 December 2012.

[Attributes for Tier 1 (Entrepreneur) Migrants

35. An applicant applying for entry clearance, leave to remain or indefinite leave to remain as a Tier 1 (Entrepreneur) Migrant must score 75 points for attributes.]

Note

This paragraph substituted by HC 863, para 143 as from 6 April 2011.

36. [Subject to paragraph 37, available points for applications for entry clearance or leave to remain are shown in Table 4.]

Note

This paragraph substituted by HC 863, para 143 as from 6 April 2011.

[36A. An applicant who is applying for leave to remain and has, or was last granted, entry clearance, leave to enter or leave to remain as:
(i)   a Tier 4 Migrant,
(ii)   a Student,
(iii)   a Student Nurse,
(iv)   a Student Re-sitting an Examination, or
(v)   a Student Writing Up a Thesis,

will only be awarded points under [the provisions in (b)(ii) or (b)(iii)] in Table 4.]

Note

This paragraph inserted by HC 760, para 287 as from 13 December 2012. Amended by HC 532, para 31 as from 11 July 2014. However, if an applicant has made an application for entry clearance or leave before 11 July 2014 and the application has not been decided before that date, it will be decided in accordance with the Rules in force on 10 July 2014.

[36B. An applicant who is applying for leave to remain and has, or was last granted, entry clearance, leave to enter or leave to remain as a Tier 1 (Post-Study Work) Migrant will only be awarded points under the provisions in (b)(ii), (b)(iii) or (d) in Table 4.]

Note

Inserted by HC 532, para 32 as from 11 July 2014. However, if an applicant has made an application for entry clearance or leave before 11 July 2014 and the application has not been decided before that date, it will be decided in accordance with the Rules in force on 10 July 2014.

37. [Available points are shown in Table 5 for an applicant who
(a) has had entry clearance, leave to enter or leave to remain as a Tier 1 (Entrepreneur) Migrant, a Businessperson or an Innovator in the 12 months immediately before the date of application, or
(b) is applying for leave to remain and has, or was last granted, entry clearance, leave to enter or leave to remain as a Tier 1 (Entrepreneur) Migrant, a Businessperson or an Innovator.]

Note

Substituted by HC 1888, para 121 as from 6 April 2012.

38. [Available points for applications for indefinite leave to remain are shown in Table 6.]

Note

This paragraph substituted by HC 863, para 143 as from 6 April 2011.

[Investment and business activity: notes

39.
(a) Notes to accompany Table 4 appear below Table 4.
(b) [Notes to accompany Tables 4, 5 and 6 appear below Table 6].

Note

This paragraph substituted by HC 863, para 143 as from 6 April 2011. Sub-para (b) substituted by HC 1888, para 122 as from 6 April 2012.

[40. In all cases, an applicant cannot use the same funds to score points for attributes under this Appendix and to score points for maintenance funds for himself or his dependants under Appendices C or E.]

[Table 4: Applications for entry clearance or leave to remain referred to in paragraph 36

Investment and business activity	Points
(a) The applicant has access to not less than £200,000, or	25
(b) The applicant has access to not less than £50,000 from:	
(i) one or more registered venture capitalist firms [regulated by the Financial Conduct Authority (FCA)],	
(ii) one or more UK Entrepreneurial seed funding competitions which is listed as endorsed on the UK Trade & Investment website, or	
(iii) one or more UK Government Departments [or Devolved Government Departments in Scotland, Wales or Northern Ireland,] and made available by the Department(s) for the specific purpose of establishing or expanding a UK business, or	
(c) The applicant:	
(i) is applying for leave to remain	
(ii) has, or was last granted, leave as a Tier 1 (Graduate Entrepreneur) migrant, and	
(iii) has access to not less than £50,000, or	
(d) the applicant:	
(i) is applying for leave to remain,	

Investment and business activity	Points
(ii) has, or was last granted leave as a Tier 1 (Post-Study Work) Migrant,	
(iii) [since before 11 July 2014 and up to the date of his application, has been continuously engaged in business activity which was not, or did not amount to, activity pursuant to a contract of service with a business other than his own and, during such period, has been continuously:	
(1) registered with HM Revenue & Customs as self-employed, or	
(2) registered with Companies House as a director of a new or an existing business. Directors who are on the list of disqualified directors provided by Companies House will not be awarded points,]	
[(iv) [since before 11 July 2014 and up to the date of his application, has continuously been working] in an occupation which appears on the list of occupations skilled to National Qualifications Framework level 4 or above, as stated in the Codes of Practice in Appendix J, and provides the specified evidence in paragraph 41–SD. "Working" in this context means that the core service his business provides to its customers or clients involves the business delivering a service in an occupation at this level. It excludes any work involved in administration, marketing or website functions for the business.]	
(v) has access to not less than £50,000	
The money is held in one or more regulated financial institutions	25
[The money is disposable in the UK. If the applicant is applying for leave to remain, the money must be held in the UK.]	25

Note

Amended by Cm 8423, para 90 as from 20 July 2012. This paragraph deleted by Cm 8423, para 91 as from 20 July 2012. Further amended by HC 760, paras 288, 289 as from 13 December 2012. Further amended by HC 244, para 15 as from 1 July 2013. This paragraph inserted by HC 628, para 152 and if an applicant has made an application for entry clearance or leave before 1 October 2013, the application will be decided in accordance with the Rules in force on 30 September 2013. Amended by HC 532, para 33 as from 11 July 2014. However, if an applicant has made an application for entry clearance or leave before 11 July 2014 and the application has not been decided before that date, it will be decided in accordance with the Rules in force on 10 July 2014. Amended by HC 532, para 34 as from 11 July 2014. However, if an applicant has made an application for entry clearance or leave before 11 July 2014 and the application has not been decided before that date, it will be decided in accordance with the Rules in force on 10 July 2014. Further amended by HC 693, para 113 as from 6 November 2014, save that if an application has been made for entry clearance or leave to enter or remain before 6 November 2014, the application will be decided in accordance with the Rules in force on 5 November 2014.

41. [An applicant will only be considered to have access to funds if:
[(a) [The specified documents in paragraph 41-SD are provided] to show cash money to the amount required (this must not be in the form of assets [and, where multiple documents are provided, they must show the total amount required is available on the same date]);
(b) The specified documents are provided to show that the applicant has permission to use the money to invest in a business in the UK; [. . ..]
(c) The money is either held in a UK regulated financial institution or is transferable to the UK[; and]]
[(d) [The money will remain available to the applicant until such time as it is spent for the purposes of the applicant's business or businesses. The Secretary of State

reserves the right to request further evidence or otherwise verify that the money will remain available, and to refuse the application if this evidence is not provided or it is unable to satisfactorily verify.]

    (1)   in his own possession,

    (2)   in the financial accounts of a UK incorporated business of which he is the director, or

    (3)   available from the third party or parties named in the application under the terms of the declaration(s) referred to in paragraph 41-SD(b) of Appendix A.]

Note

This paragraph substituted by HC 863, para 143 as from 6 April 2011. Further amended by Cm 8423, para 91 as from 20 July 2012. Sub-paragraphs (b), (c) amended and sub-paragraph (d) inserted by HC 943, para 7 as from 31 January 2013. Further amended by HC 1138, para 95 shall apply to all applications decided on or after 6 April 2014. Further amended by HC 693, para 114 as from 6 November 2014, save that if an application has been made for entry clearance or leave to enter or remain before 6 November 2014, the application will be decided in accordance with the Rules in force on 5 November 2014.

[41-SD.   The specified documents in Table 4 and paragraph 41 and paragraph 41, and associated definitions, are as follows:

(a)   Where this paragraph refers to funding being available, unless stated otherwise, this means funding available to:

    (i)   the applicant;

    (ii)   the entrepreneurial team, if the applicant is applying under the provisions in paragraph 52 of this Appendix; or

    (iii)   the applicant's business.

[(b)   Where sub-paragraph (a)(iii) above applies and this paragraph refers to the applicant's business, the business must be a company and the applicant must be registered as a director of that business in the UK, and provide a Companies House document showing the address of the registered office in the UK, or head office in the UK if it has no registered office, and the applicant's name, as it appears on the application form, as a director.]

(c)   The specified documents to show evidence of the money available to [invest, whether from the applicant's own funds or from one or more third parties,] are one or more of the following specified documents:

    (i)   A letter from each financial institution holding the funds, to confirm the amount of money available. Each letter must:

        (1)   be an original document and not a copy,

        (2)   be on the institution's official headed paper,

        (3)   have been issued by an authorised official of that institution,

        (4)   have been produced within the three months immediately before the date of application,

        (5)   confirm that the institution is regulated by the appropriate body,

        (6)   state the applicant's name, and his team partner's name where relevant,

        (7)   show the account number and

        (8)   state the date of the document,

        (9)   confirm the amount of money available from the applicant's own funds (if applicable) that are held in that institution,

        (10)   [for money available from any third party (if applicable) that is held in that institution, confirm that the third party has informed the institution of the amount of money it intends to make available, and that the institution is not aware of the third party having promised to make that money available to any other person,]

        (11)   confirm the name of each third party and their contact details, including their full address including postal code and where available, landline phone number and any email address, and

        (12)   confirm that if the money is not in an institution regulated by the Financial Conduct Authority (FCA) and the Prudential Regulation Authority (PRA), the money cannot be transferred into the UK; or

(ii) For money held in the UK only, a recent personal bank or building society statement from each UK financial institution holding the funds, which confirms the amount of money available. Each statement must satisfy the following requirements:

  (1) the statements must be original documents and not copies;

  (2) the bank or building society holding the money must be based in the UK and regulated by the Financial Conduct Authority (FCA) and the Prudential Regulation Authority (PRA);

  (3) the money must be in cash in the account, not Individual Savings Accounts or assets such as stocks and shares;

  (4) the account must be in the applicant's own name only (or both names for an entrepreneurial team [or where it is a joint account with the applicant's spouse, civil partner or partner as set out in paragraph 53 below]), not in the name of a business or third party;

  (5) each statement must be on the institution's official stationary showing the institution's name and logo, and confirm the applicant's name and, where relevant, the applicant's entrepreneurial team partner's name), the account number and the date of the statement;

  (6) each statement must have been issued by an authorised official of that institution and produced within the three months immediately before the date of the application; and

  (7) If the statements are printouts of electronic statements they must either be accompanied by a supporting letter from the bank, on the bank's headed paper, confirming the authenticity of the statements, or bear the official stamp of the bank in question on each page of the statement;

 or

(iii) For £50,000 from a Venture Capital firm, Seed Funding Competition or UK Government Department only, a recent letter from an accountant, who is a member of a recognised UK supervisory body, or other authorised official in the case of a UK Government Department, confirming the amount of money made available. Each letter must:

  (1) be an original document and not a copy,

  (2) be on the institution's official headed paper,

  (3) have been issued by an accountant engaged by the Venture Capital firm, Seed Funding Competition or UK Government Department or other official of the UK Government Department authorised to provide the information,

  (4) have been produced within the three months immediately before the date of the application,

  (5) state the applicant's name, and his team partner's name where relevant, or the name of the applicant's business,

  (6) state the date of the document,

  (7) confirm the amount of money available to the applicant, the entrepreneurial team or the applicant's business from the Venture Capital firm, Seed funding competition or UK Government Department, and

  (8) confirm the name of the Venture Capital firm, Seed funding competition or UK Government Department and the contact details of an official of that organisation, including their full address, postal code, and, where available, landline phone number and any email address,

(d) If the applicant is applying using money from a third party, he must provide all of the following specified documents[, in addition to the specified documents in (c) above.]:

(i) An original declaration from every third party that they have made the money available for the applicant to invest in a business in the United Kingdom, containing:

  (1) the names of the third party and the applicant (and his team partner's name where relevant) or the name of the applicant's business,

(2)   the date of the declaration;

(3)   the applicant's signature and the signature of the third party (and the signature of the applicant's team partner where relevant),

(4)   the amount of money available in pounds sterling,

(5)   the relationship(s) of the third party to the applicant,

(6)   if the third party is a venture capitalist firm, confirmation of whether [this body is registered with the Financial Conduct Authority (FCA) and its entry in the register includes a permission to arrange, deal in or manage investments, or to manage alternative investment funds],

(7)   if the third party is a UK Seed Funding Competition, confirmation that the applicant, the entrepreneurial team or the applicant's business has been awarded money and that the competition is listed as endorsed on the UK Trade & Investment website, together with the amount of the award and naming the applicant, the entrepreneurial team or the applicant's business as a winner,

(8)   if the third party is a UK Government Department, confirmation that it has made money available to the applicant for the specific purpose of establishing or expanding a UK business, and the amount[; ...

[(9)   if the third party is another business in which the applicant is self-employed or a director, evidence of the applicant's status within that business and that the applicant is the sole controller of that business's finances, or, where the applicant is not the sole controller, the letter must be signed by another authorised official of that business who is not the applicant, and]

[[(10)]confirmation that the money will remain available until such time as it is transferred to the applicant or the applicant's business] and

(ii)   A letter from a legal representative [who is independent from the third party or third parties,] confirming the validity of signatures on each third-party declaration provided, which confirms that the declaration(s) from the third party/parties contains the signatures of the people stated. It can be a single letter covering all third-party permissions, or several letters from several legal representatives. It must be an original letter and not a copy, and it must be from a legal representative permitted to practise in the country where the third party or the money is. The letter must clearly show the following:

(1)   the name of the legal representative confirming the details,

(2)   the registration or authority of the legal representative to practise legally in the country in which the permission or permissions was/were given,

(3)   the date of the confirmation letter,

(4)   the applicant's name (and the name of the applicant's team partners name where relevant), and where (b) applies, that the applicant is a director of the business named in each third party declaration,]

(5)   [the third party's name (which cannot be the legal representative themselves or their client),]

(6)   that the declaration from the third party is signed and valid, and

(7)   if the third party is not a Venture Capitalist Firm, Seed Funding Competition or UK Government Department, the number of the third party's identity document (such as a passport or national identity card), the place of issue and dates of issue and expiry.

(e)   If the applicant is applying under the provisions in (d) in Table 4, he must provide:

(i)   his job title,

(ii)   the Standard Occupational Classification (SOC) code of the occupation that the applicant [has been working in since before 11 July 2014 up to the date of his application], which must appear on the list of occupations skilled to National Qualifications Framework level 4 or above, as stated in the Codes of practice in Appendix J,

      (iii) one or more of the following specified documents [covering (either together or individually) a continuous period commencing before 11 July 2014 up to no earlier than three months before the date of his application:]

          (1) advertising or marketing material, including printouts of online advertising, that has been published locally or nationally, showing the applicant's name (and the name of the business if applicable) together with the business activity, where his business is trading online, confirmation of this ownership of the domain, name of the business's website,

          (2) article(s) or online links to article(s) in a newspaper or other publication showing the applicant's name (and the name of the business if applicable) together with the business activity,

          (3) information from a trade fair(s), at which the applicant has had a stand or given a presentation to market his business, showing the applicant's name (and the name of the business if applicable) together with the business activity, or

          (4) personal registration with a UK trade's body linked to the applicant's occupation.;

        and

    [(iv) one or more of the following documents showing trading, which must cover (either together or individually) a continuous period commencing before 11 July 2014 up to no earlier than three months before the date of his application:

          (1) one or more contracts for service. If a contract is not an original the applicant must sign each page. Each contract must show:

             (a) the applicant's name and the name of the business;

             (b) the service provided by the applicant's business;

             (c) the name of the other party or parties involved in the contract and their contact details, including their full address, postal code and, where available, landline phone number and any email address; and

             (d) the duration of the contract; or

          (2) one or more original letters from UK-regulated financial institutions with which the applicant has a business bank account, on the institution's headed paper, confirming the dates the business was trading during the period referred to at (iv) above;

          (1) if claiming points for being self-employed, the following specified documents to show the applicant's compliance with National Insurance requirements:

             (a) the original bills covering the continuous billing period during which the applicant claims to have been self-employed, if his Class 2 National Insurance is paid by bill;

             (b) bank statements covering the continuous period during which the applicant claims to have been self-employed, showing the direct debit payment of Class 2 National Insurance to HM Revenue & Customs;

             (c) all original small earnings exception certificates issued to the applicant by HM Revenue & Customs covering the continuous tax period during which the applicant claims to have been self-employed, if he has low earnings; or

             (d) if applying before 31 January 2015, the original, dated welcome letter from HM Revenue & Customs containing the applicant's unique taxpayer reference number, if he has not yet become liable for paying National Insurance, or has not yet received the documents in (c);

            or

          (2)

             (a) if claiming points for being a director of a UK company at the time of his application, a printout of a Current Appointment Report from Companies House, dated no earlier than three months before the date of the application, listing the applicant as a director of a company that is actively trading and not dormant, or struck-off, or dissolved or in liquidation, and showing the date of his appointment as a director of that company; and

(b)   if claiming points for being a director of a UK company other than the company referred to in (a) above, at any time before the date of his application, a printout from Companies House of the applicant's appointments history, showing that the applicant has held directorships continuously during the period in which he claims to have been a director;

and the evidence at (1) and (2) above must cover (either together or individually) a continuous period commencing before 11 July 2014 up to no earlier than three months before the date of his application, unless the applicant is claiming points for being self-employed at the time of his application and the evidence consists of documents issued by HM Revenue & Customs referred to at (v)(1)(a), (c) or (d) above, in which case the applicant must submit the most recent document issued before the date of his application;
and]

[(vi) if the applicant is currently a director, the following evidence that his business has business premises in the UK and is subject to UK taxation:

(1)   a printout of a Companies House document showing the address of the registered office in the UK, or head office in the UK if it has no registered office, and the applicant's name, as it appears on the application form, as a director; and

(2)   documentation from HM Revenue & Customs which confirms that the business is registered for corporation tax;

and

(vii) the following evidence that the business has a UK bank account of which the applicant is a signatory:

(1)   if the applicant is currently self employed, a personal bank statement showing transactions for his business (which must be currently active), or a business bank statement, or a letter from [the UK bank in question, on its headed paper,] confirming that he has a business and acts through that bank for the purposes of that business, or

(2)   if the applicant is currently a director, a company bank statement showing that the company has a UK account, or a letter from [the UK bank in question, on its headed paper,] confirming that the company has a bank account and the applicant is a signatory of that account,

and the evidence at (vi) and (vii)(2) above must relate to a company that is actively trading and not dormant, or struck-off, or dissolved or in liquidation.]

Note

Substituted by HC 628, paras 153 and if an applicant has made an application for entry clearance or leave before 1 October 2013, the application will be decided in accordance with the Rules in force on 30 September 2013. Further amended by HC 1138, para 96 shall apply to all applications decided on or after 6 April 2014. Further amended by HC 1138, para 97 shall apply to all applications decided on or after 6 April 2014. Further amended by HC 1138, para 98 shall apply to all applications decided on or after 6 April 2014. Further amended by HC 1138, para 99 as from 6 April 2014. Further amended by HC 1138, para 100 as from 6 April 2014. Amended by HC 532, para 35 as from 11 July 2014. However, if an applicant has made an application for entry clearance or leave before 11 July 2014 and the application has not been decided before that date, it will be decided in accordance with the Rules in force on 10 July 2014. Amended by HC 532, para 36 as from 11 July 2014. However, if an applicant has made an application for entry clearance or leave before 11 July 2014 and the application has not been decided before that date, it will be decided in accordance with the Rules in force on 10 July 2014. Amended by HC 532, para 37 as from 11 July 2014. However, if an applicant has made an application for entry clearance or leave before 11 July 2014 and the application has not been decided before that date, it will be decided in accordance with the Rules in force on 10 July 2014. Amended by HC 532, para 38 as from 11 July 2014. However, if an applicant has made an application for entry clearance or leave before 11 July 2014 and the application has not been decided before that date, it will be decided in accordance with the Rules in force on 10 July 2014. Further amended or Amended by HC 532, para 39 as from 11 July 2014. However, if an applicant has made an application for entry clearance or leave before 11 July 2014 and the application has not been decided before that date, it will be decided in accordance with the Rules in force on 10 July 2014. Further amended by HC 693, para 115 as from 6 November 2014, save that if an application has been made for entry clearance or leave to enter or remain before 6 November 2014, the application will be decided in accordance with the Rules in force on 5 November 2014. Further amended by HC 693, para 116 as from 6 November 2014, save that if an application has been made for entry clearance or leave to enter or remain before 6 November 2014, the application will be decided in accordance with the Rules in force on 5 November 2014. Word "and" deleted by HC 693, para 117 as from 6 November 2014, save that if an application has been made for entry clearance or leave to enter or remain before 6 November 2014, the application will be decided in accordance with the Rules in force on 5 November 2014. Inserted by HC 693, para 118 as from 6 November 2014, save that if an application has been made for entry clearance or leave to enter or remain before 6 November 2014, the application will be decided in accordance with the Rules in force on 5 November 2014. Paragraph 41-SD(d)(i)(9), subparagraph (9) renumber as (10) by HC 693, para 119 as from 6 November 2014, save that if an application has been made for entry clearance or leave to enter or remain before 6 November 2014, the application will be decided in accordance with the Rules in force on 5 November 2014. Further amended by HC 693, para 120 as from 6 November 2014, save that if an application has been made for entry clearance or leave to enter or remain before 6 November 2014, the application will be decided in accordance with the Rules in force on 5 November 2014. Further amended by HC 693, para 121 as from 6 November 2014, save that if an application has been made for entry clearance or leave to enter or remain before 6 November 2014, the application will be decided in accordance with the Rules in force on 5 November 2014.

42. [[Subject to paragraphs 36A and 36B above, points will only be awarded] to an applicant to whom Table 4, paragraph (b) applies if the total sum of those funds derives from one or more of the sources listed in (b)(i) to (iii) in Table 4.]

Note

This paragraph substituted by HC 863, para 143 as from 6 April 2011. Amended by HC 532, para 40 as from 11 July 2014. However, if an applicant has made an application for entry clearance or leave before 11 July 2014 and the application has not been decided before that date, it will be decided in accordance with the Rules in force on 10 July 2014.

43. [A regulated financial institution is one which is regulated by the appropriate regulatory body for the country in which the financial institution operates.]

Note

This paragraph substituted by HC 863, para 143 as from 6 April 2011.

44. [Money is disposable in the UK if all of the money is held in a UK based financial institution or if the money is freely transferable to the UK and convertible to sterling. Funds in a foreign currency will be converted to pounds sterling (£) using the spot exchange rate which appeared on www.oanda.com* on the date on which the application was made.]

Note

This paragraph substituted by HC 863, para 143 as from 6 April 2011.

[**45.** If the applicant has invested the money referred to in Table 4 in the UK before the date of the application, points will be awarded for funds available as if the applicant had not yet invested the funds, providing:

(a)   the investment was made no more than 12 months (or 24 months if the applicant was last granted leave as a Tier 1 (Graduate Entrepreneur) Migrant) before the date of the application; and

(b)   all of the specified documents required in paragraphs 46-SD(a) to (g) are provided to show:

    (i)   the amount of money invested; and

    (ii)   that the applicant has established a business in the UK, in which the money was invested.

Note

This paragraph substituted by HC 863, para 143 as from 6 April 2011. Amended by Cm 8423, para 95 as from 20 July 2012. Further amended by HC 1138, para 101 as from 6 April 2014. Substituted by HC 693, para 122 as from 6 November 2014, save that if an application has been made for entry clearance or leave to enter or remain before 6 November 2014, the application will be decided in accordance with the Rules in force on 5 November 2014.

[45A. No points will be awarded where the specified documents show that the funds are held in a financial institution listed in Appendix P as being an institution with which the UK Border Agency is unable to make satisfactory verification checks.]

Note

Inserted by HC 760, para 292 as from 13 December 2012.

[**Table 5: Applications for entry clearance or leave to remain referred to in paragraph 37**]

Investment and business activity	Points
The applicant has invested, or had invested on his behalf, not less than £200,000 (or £50,000 if, in his last grant of leave, he was awarded points for funds of £50,000 [. . .]) in cash directly into one or more businesses in the UK.	20
The applicant has: (a) registered with HM Revenue and Customs as self-employed, or [(b) registered with Companies House as a director of a new or an existing business. Directors who are on the list of disqualified directors provided by Companies House will not be awarded points.] Where the applicant's last grant of entry clearance, leave to enter or leave to remain was as a Tier 1 (Entrepreneur) Migrant, the above condition must have been met within 6 months of his entry to the UK (if he was granted entry clearance as a Tier 1 (Entrepreneur) Migrant and there is evidence to establish his date of arrival to the UK), or, in any other case, the date of the grant of leave to remain.	20
On a date no earlier than three months prior to the date of application, the applicant was: (a) registered with HM Revenue and Customs as self-employed, or [(b) registered with Companies House as a director of a new or an existing business. Directors who are on the list of disqualified directors provided by Companies House will not be awarded points.]	15
The applicant has: (a) established a new business or businesses that has or have created the equivalent of at least two new full time jobs for persons settled in the UK, or (b) taken over or invested in an existing business or businesses and his services or investment have resulted in a net increase in the employment provided by the business or businesses for persons settled in the UK by creating the equivalent of at least two new full time jobs. Where the applicant's last grant of entry clearance or leave to enter or remain was as a Tier 1 (Entrepreneur) Migrant, the jobs must have existed for at least 12 months of the period for which the previous leave was granted.	20

Note

Table heading substituted by HC 760, para 293 as from 13 December 2012. Word "as set out in Table 4 above" deleted by HC 532, para 41 as from 11 July 2014. However, if an applicant has made an application for entry clearance or leave before 11 July 2014 and the application has not been decided before that date, it will be decided in accordance with the Rules in force on 10 July 2014. Amended by HC 532, paras 42, 43 as from 11 July 2014. However, if an applicant has made an application for entry clearance or leave before 11 July 2014 and the application has not been decided before that date, it will be decided in accordance with the Rules in force on 10 July 2014.

[Table 6: Applications for indefinite leave to remain as referred to in paragraph 38]

Row	Investment and business activity	Points
[1.	The applicant has invested, or had invested on his behalf, not less than £200,000 (or £50,000 if, in his last grant of leave, he was awarded points for funds of £50,000) in cash directly into one or more businesses in the UK. The applicant will not need to provide evidence of this investment if he was awarded points for it, as set out in Table 5, in his previous grant of entry clearance or leave to remain as a Tier 1 (Entrepreneur) Migrant.]	20
[2.]	On a date no earlier than three months prior to the date of application, the applicant was: (a) registered with HM Revenue and Customs as self-employed, or [(b) registered with Companies House as a director of a new or an existing business. Directors who are on the list of disqualified directors provided by Companies House will not be awarded points.]	20
[3.]	The applicant has: (a) established a new UK business or businesses that has or have created the equivalent of X new full time jobs for persons settled in the UK, or (b) taken over or invested in an existing UK business or businesses and his services or investment have resulted in a net increase in the employment provided by the business or businesses for persons settled in the UK by creating the equivalent of X new full time jobs where X is at least 2. Where the applicant's last grant of entry clearance or leave to enter or remain was as a Tier 1 (Entrepreneur) Migrant, the jobs must have existed for [for at least 12 months during that last grant of leave].	20
[4.]	The applicant has spent the specified continuous period lawfully in the UK, with absences from the UK of no more than 180 days in any 12 calendar months during that period. The specified period must have been spent with leave as a Tier 1 (Entrepreneur) Migrant, as a Businessperson and/or as an Innovator, of which the most recent period must have been spent with leave as a Tier (1) (Entrepreneur) Migrant. The specified continuous period is: (a) 3 years if the number of new full time jobs, X, referred to in [row 3 above] is at least 10, [or] (b) 3 years if the applicant has:	35

Row	Investment and business activity	Points
	(i) established a new UK business that has had an income from business activity of at least £5 million during a 3 year period in which the applicant has had leave as a Tier 1 (Entrepreneur) Migrant, or (ii) taken over or invested in an existing UK business and his services or investment have resulted in a net increase in income from business activity to that business of £5 million during a 3 year period in which the applicant has had leave as a Tier 1 (Entrepreneur) Migrant, when compared to the immediately preceding 3 year period, or (c) 5 years in all other cases. [Time spent with valid leave in the Bailiwick of Guernsey, the Bailiwick of Jersey or the Isle of Man in a category equivalent to the categories set out above may be included in the continuous period of lawful residence, provided the most recent period of leave was a Tier 1 (Entrepreneur) Migrant in the UK. In any such case, the applicant must have absences from the Bailiwick of Guernsey, the Bailiwick of Jersey or the Isle of Man (as the case may be) of no more than 180 days in any 12 calendar months during the specified continuous period.]	

Note

Table 6 amended by HC 1039, para 147 as from 6 April 2013 on applications decided on or after 6 April 2013. Further amended by HC 628, para 154 and if an applicant has made an application for entry clearance or leave before 1 October 2013, the application will be decided in accordance with the Rules in force on 30 September 2013. Amended by HC 532, para 44 as from 11 July 2014. However, if an applicant has made an application for entry clearance or leave before 11 July 2014 and the application has not been decided before that date, it will be decided in accordance with the Rules in force on 10 July 2014. Amended by HC 693, para 123 as from 6 November 2014, save that if an application has been made for entry clearance or leave to enter or remain before 6 November 2014, the application will be decided in accordance with the Rules in force on 5 November 2014. Subsequent rows 1 to 3 of Table 6 renumbered as 2 to 4 by HC 693, para 124 as from 6 November 2014, save that if an application has been made for entry clearance or leave to enter or remain before 6 November 2014, the application will be decided in accordance with the Rules in force on 5 November 2014. Further amended by HC 693, para 125 as from 6 November 2014, save that if an application has been made for entry clearance or leave to enter or remain before 6 November 2014, the application will be decided in accordance with the Rules in force on 5 November 2014. Further amended by HC 693, para 126 as from 6 November 2014, save that if an application has been made for entry clearance or leave to enter or remain before 6 November 2014, the application will be decided in accordance with the Rules in force on 5 November 2014.

Investment and business activity: notes

[46. Documentary evidence must be provided in all cases. The specified documents in paragraph 46-SD must be provided as evidence of any investment and business activity that took place when the applicant had leave as a Tier 1 (Entrepreneur) Migrant or a Tier 1 (Post-Study Work) Migrant, and any investment made no more than 12 months [(or 24 months if the applicant was last granted leave as a Tier 1 (Graduate Entrepreneur) Migrant)] before the date of the application for which the applicant is claiming points.]

Note

Substituted by Cm 8423, para 96 as from 20 July 2012. Further amended by HC 1138, para 102 as from 6 April 2014.

[46-SD   The specified documents in paragraphs 45 and 46 are as follows:

(a)   The applicant must provide all the appropriate specified documents needed to establish the amount of money he has invested from the following list:

  (i)   If the applicant's business is a registered company that is required to produce audited accounts, the audited accounts must be provided;

  (ii)   [If the applicant's business is not required to produce audited accounts, unaudited accounts and an accounts compilation report must be provided from an accountant who is a member of a UK Recognised Supervisory Body (as defined in the Companies Act 2006);]

  (iii)   If the applicant has made the investment in the form of a director's loan, it must be shown in the relevant set of accounts provided, and the applicant must also provide a legal agreement, between the applicant (in the name that appears on his application) and the company, showing:

    (1)   the terms of the loan,

    (2)   any interest that is payable,

    (3)   the period of the loan, and

    (4)   that the loan is unsecured and subordinated in favour of third-party creditors.

  [(iv)   If the applicant is claiming points for investing £50,000 from a Venture Capital firm, Seed Funding Competition or UK Government Department, and has not been awarded points in a previous application for having those funds available, he must provide a letter as specified in paragraph 41-SD(c)(iii) (except that the letter does not need to have been produced within the three months immediately before the date of the application) as evidence of the source of those funds.]

(b)   Audited or unaudited accounts must show the investment in money made directly by the applicant, in his own name [or on his behalf (and showing his name)]. If he has invested by way of share capital the business accounts must show the shareholders, the amount and value of the shares (on the date of purchase) in the applicant's name as it appears on his application. If the value of the applicant's share capital is not shown in the accounts, then share certificates must be submitted as documentary evidence. The accounts must clearly show the name of the accountant, the date the accounts were produced, and how much the applicant has invested in the business. [The accounts must be prepared and signed off in accordance with statutory requirements,]

(c)   The applicant must provide the following specified documents to show that he has established a UK business:

  (i)   Evidence that the business has business premises in the United Kingdom:

    (1)   If the applicant is self employed, his registration with HM Revenue and Customs to show that the business is based in the UK, or

    (2)   If the applicant is a director, printout of a Companies House document showing the address of the registered office in the UK, or head office in the UK if it has no registered office, and the applicant's name, as it appears on the application form, as a director,

    and

  [(ii)   Evidence that the business has a UK bank account of which the applicant is a signatory:

    (1)   If the applicant is self employed, a personal bank statement showing transactions for his business, or a business bank statement, or a letter from a UK-regulated financial institution, on the institution's headed paper, confirming that he has a business and acts through that bank for the purposes of that business, or

    (2)   If the applicant is a director, a company bank statement showing that the company has a UK account, or a letter from a UK-regulated financial institution, on the institution's headed paper, confirming that the company has a bank account and the applicant is a signatory of that account,

    and]

      (iii)   Evidence that the business is subject to UK taxation:

            (1)   If the applicant is self-employed, he must be registered as self-employed for National Insurance assessment and provide either the welcome letter from HM Revenue & Customs, the Small Earnings Exception certificate, a copy of the National Insurance bill from HM Revenue & Customs, or the applicant's bank statement showing that National Insurance is taken by HM Revenue & Customs by direct debit, or

           [(2)   If the applicant is a director of a business, the business must be registered for corporation tax and the applicant must provide documentation from HM Revenue & Customs which confirms this.]

(d)   If the applicant has bought property that includes residential accommodation the value of this part of the property will not be counted towards the amount of the business investment. The applicant must provide an estimate of the value of the living accommodation if it is part of the premises also used for the business, from a surveyor who is a member of the Royal Institution of Chartered Surveyors. This valuation must be produced in the three months prior to the date of application.

(e)   If some of the money has been invested into a business in the UK, the balance of funds must be held in a regulated financial institution and disposable in the UK, and the applicant must provide the specified documents required in paragraph 41-SD for the previous investment of money together with the specified documents required in paragraph 41-SD required for his access to the balance of sufficient funds.

(f)   Where Table 5 applies and the applicant's last grant of entry clearance, leave to enter or leave to remain was as a Tier 1 (Entrepreneur) Migrant [...,] he must provide the following specified documents as evidence of his registration as self-employed or as a director within the 6 months after the specified date [in the relevant table]:

      (i)   If the applicant was self-employed, he must provide one of the following:

           (1)   an original, dated welcome letter from HM Revenue & Customs containing the applicant's unique taxpayer reference number [dated no more than 8 months from the specified date in the relevant table,]

           (2)   an original Exception Certificate from HM Revenue & Customs, dated no more than 8 months from the specified date [in the relevant table],

           (3)   an original National Insurance bill from the HM Revenue & Customs dated during the 6 months after the specified date [in the relevant table], or

           (4)   a bank statement dated in the 6 months after the specified date [in the relevant table], showing the direct debit payment of National Insurance to HM Revenue & Customs.

      (ii)   If the applicant was a director of a new or existing company, he must provide a Current Appointment Report from Companies House, listing the applicant as the Director of the company and the date of his appointment, which must be no more than 8 months after the specified date [in the relevant table].

(g)   The applicant must provide the following specified documents as evidence of his current registration as self-employed or as a director:

      (i)   If the applicant is claiming points for being currently self-employed, he must provide the following specified documents to show that he is paying Class 2 National Insurance contributions:

           (1)   the original bill from the billing period immediately before the application, if his Class 2 National Insurance is [paid by bill],

           (2)   the most recent bank statement issued before the application, showing the direct debit payment of National Insurance to HM Revenue & Customs, if his National Insurance is paid by direct debit,

        (3)   an original small earnings exception certificate issued by HM Revenue & Customs for the most recent return date, if he has low earnings, or

        (4)   the original, dated welcome letter from HM Revenue & Customs containing the applicant's unique taxpayer reference number, if he has not yet received the documents in (1) to (3).

    (ii)   If the applicant is claiming points for currently being a director of a UK company, he must provide a printout of a Current Appointment Report from Companies House, dated no earlier than three months before the date of the application, listing the applicant as a director of the company, and confirming the date of his appointment. The company must be actively trading and not struck-off, or dissolved or in liquidation on the date that the printout was produced. . . .

(h)   If the applicant is required to score points for creating the net increase in employment in Table 5 or Table 6, he must provide the following information and specified documents:

    (i)   A HM Revenue & Customs [Employee Payment Record]), showing details of the earnings for the settled worker for each week that he worked for the applicant, and signed and dated by the applicant;

    (ii)   If the date of the start of the employment is not shown in the [Employee Payment Record], an original HM Revenue & Customs form P45 or form P46 (also called a Full Payment Submission) for the settled worker, showing the starting date of the employment;

    (iii)   If the employer is taking part in the Real Time Initiative pilot, printouts of the Full Payment Submission, sent to HM Revenue & Customs, which include the start date of the settled worker and are initialled by the applicant;

    (iv)   Duplicate payslips or wage slips for each settled worker for whom points are being claimed, covering the full period of the employment for which points are being claimed;

    (v)   Confirmation of the hourly rate for each settled worker used to claim points, including any changes in the hourly rate and the dates of the changes, enabling calculation of the hours of work created for each settled worker;

    (vi)   Documents which show that the employment was created for settled workers, such as the passport pages from a UK passport that contain the employee's personal details, and the page containing the UK Government stamp or endorsement, if appropriate, or the worker's full birth certificate, showing the name of at least one parent;

    (vii)   If the applicant was a director of a company, the information from the Companies House Current Appointment Report to confirm that he was a Director of the company that employed the settled worker at the time that he was employed;

    (viii) If the applicant was self-employed, the specified documents in (c) above showing the dates that the applicant became self-employed, the names on the [Employee Payment Record] and bank account, and the address of the business;

    (ix)   If the applicant took over or joined a business that employed workers before he joined it, he must also provide one of the following types of payroll documentation:

        (1)   a duplicate HM Revenue & Customs [Full Payment Submission] for the year before the jobs were created and the year that the jobs were created, showing the net increase in employment, and signed and dated by the applicant (If the posts were created too recently for a [Full Payment Submission] to have been produced, the applicant must provide a draft copy), or

        (2)   a printout of the information sent to HM Revenue & Customs, initialled by the applicant, if the employer is taking part in the Real Time Initiative pilot;

    (x)   If the applicant took over or joined a business that employed workers before he joined it, he must also provide an original accountant's letter verifying the net increase in employment and confirming the number of posts. The accountant must be a member of the Institute of Chartered Accountants in England and Wales, the Institute of Chartered Accountants in Scotland, the Institute of Chartered Accountants in Ireland, the Association of Chartered Certified Accountants, or the Association of Authorised Public Accountants. The letter must contain:

(1) the name and contact details of the business,
(2) the applicant's status in the business,
(3) the number of posts created in the business and the hours worked,
(4) the dates of the employment created,
(5) the registration or permission of the accountant to operate in the United Kingdom,
(6) the date that the accountant created the letter on the applicant's behalf, and
(7) that the accountant will confirm the content of the letter to the UK Border Agency on request.]

Note

Inserted by Cm 8423, para 97 as from 20 July 2012. Amended by HC 760, paras 294–297 as from 13 December 2012. Further amended by HC 628, paras 155–161 and if an applicant has made an application for entry clearance or leave before 1 October 2013, the application will be decided in accordance with the Rules in force on 30 September 2013. Further amended by HC 1138, paras 103–105 as from 6 April 2014. Amended by HC 532, paras 45, 46 as from 11 July 2014. However, if an applicant has made an application for entry clearance or leave before 11 July 2014 and the application has not been decided before that date, it will be decided in accordance with the Rules in force on 10 July 2014. Paragraph "Directors who are on the list of disqualified directors provided by Companies House will not be awarded points." deleted by HC 532, para 47 as from 11 July 2014. However, if an applicant has made an application for entry clearance or leave before 11 July 2014 and the application has not been decided before that date, it will be decided in accordance with the Rules in force on 10 July 2014.

[47. For the purposes of Tables 4, 5 and 6, "investment and business activity" does not include investment in any residential accommodation, property development or property management, and must not be in the form of a director's loan unless it is unsecured and subordinated in favour of the business. "Property development or property management" in this context means any development of property owned by the applicant or his business to increase the value of the property with a view to earning a return either through rent or a future sale or both, or management of property (whether or not it is owned by the applicant or his business) for the purposes of renting it out or resale.]

Note

This paragraph substituted by HC 863, para 143 as from 6 April 2011. Substituted by HC 693, para 127 as from 6 November 2014, save that if an application has been made for entry clearance or leave to enter or remain before 6 November 2014, the application will be decided in accordance with the Rules in force on 5 November 2014.

[48. Points will only be awarded in respect of a UK business or businesses.

(a) A business will be considered to be a UK business if:
(i) it is trading within the UK economy, and
(ii) it has a registered office in the UK, except where the applicant is registered with HM Revenue & Customs as self-employed and does not have a business office, and
(iii) it has a UK bank account, and
(iv) it is subject to UK taxation.

(b) Multinational companies that are registered as UK companies with either a registered office or head office in the UK are considered to be UK businesses for the purposes of Tables 4, 5 and 6.

(c) Subject to (d) below, a business will only be considered to be a "new" business for the purposes of Tables 5 and 6 if it was established no earlier than 12 months before the start of a period throughout which the applicant has had continuous leave as a Tier 1 (Entrepreneur) Migrant, and which includes the applicant's last grant of leave. (For these purposes continuous leave will not be considered to have been broken if any of the circumstances set out in paragraphs 245AAA(a)(i) to (iii) of these Rules apply.)

(d)   If the applicant held entry clearance or leave to remain as a Tier 1 (Graduate Entrepreneur) Migrant no more than 28 days before the application which led to the start of the period of continuous leave as a Tier 1 (Entrepreneur) Migrant referred to in (c) above, a business will only be considered to be a "new" business for the purposes of Tables 5 and 6 if it was established no earlier than 24 months before the start of the period in (c).]

Note

This paragraph substituted by HC 863, para 143 as from 6 April 2011. Substituted by HC 693, para 127 as from 6 November 2014, save that if an application has been made for entry clearance or leave to enter or remain before 6 November 2014, the application will be decided in accordance with the Rules in force on 5 November 2014.

49. [A full time job is one involving at least 30 hours' of work a week. Two or more part time jobs that add up to 30 hours a week will count as one full time job but one full time job of more than 30 hours work a week will not count as more than one full time job.]

Note

This paragraph substituted by HC 863, para 143 as from 6 April 2011.

50. [Where the applicant's last grant of entry clearance or leave was as a Tier 1 (Entrepreneur) Migrant, the jobs must have existed for a total of at least 12 months during the period in which the migrant had leave in that category. This need not consist of 12 consecutive months and the jobs need not exist at the date of application, provided they existed for at least 12 months during the period in which the migrant had leave as a Tier 1 (Entrepreneur) Migrant.]

Note

This paragraph substituted by HC 863, para 143 as from 6 April 2011.

51. [The jobs must comply with all relevant UK legislation including, but not limited to, the National Minimum Wage and the Working Time Directive.]

Note

This paragraph inserted by HC 863, para 143 as from 6 April 2011.

[Entrepreneurial teams: Notes]

52. Two applicant[, and no more than two applicants] may claim points for the same investment and business activity in Tables 4, 5 or 6 providing the following requirements are met.

Requirements:

(a)   The applicants have equal level of control over the funds and/or the business or businesses in question;

(b)   The applicants are both shown by name in each other's applications and in the specified evidence required in the relevant table; and

(c)   Neither applicant has previously been granted leave as a Tier 1 (Entrepreneur) Migrant on the basis of investment and/or business activity linked in this way with any applicant other than each other if the same funds are being relied on as in a previous application.]

Note

This paragraph inserted by HC 863, para 143 as from 6 April 2011. Amended by HC 628, para 162 and if an applicant has made an application for entry clearance or leave before 1 October 2013, the application will be decided in accordance with the Rules in force on 30 September 2013.

[53.

[(a)   No points will be awarded for funds that are made available to any individual other than the applicant, except:

(i)   under the terms of paragraph 52 above; or

(ii)   where the money is held in a joint account with the applicant's [spouse, civil partner or partner (defined as a person who has been living together with the applicant in a relationship akin to a marriage or civil partnership for at least two years prior to the date of application)], and that spouse or partner is not (or is not applying to be) another Tier 1 (Entrepreneur) Migrant.

(b) No points will be awarded for investment and business activity shared with another Tier 1 (Entrepreneur) applicant, except under the terms of paragraph 52 above.

(c) If the applicant is not the sole partner or director in the business, he must state:
  (i) the names of the other partners or directors,
  (ii) whether any of the other partners or directors are also Tier 1 (Entrepreneur) Migrants, and
  (iii) if so:
    (1) the dates they became partners or directors,
    (2) whether they are applying under the provisions in paragraph 52 above, and
    (3) if they have made (or are making at the same time) an application in which they claimed points for creating jobs, the names of the jobholders in question.]

Note

Substituted by HC 760, para 298 as from 13 December 2012. Amended by HC 1138, para 106 as from 6 April 2014. Amended by HC 532, para 48 as from 11 July 2014. However, if an applicant has made an application for entry clearance or leave before 11 July 2014 and the application has not been decided before that date, it will be decided in accordance with the Rules in force on 10 July 2014.

[Attributes for Tier 1 (Investor) Migrants

54. An applicant applying for entry clearance, leave to remain or indefinite leave to remain as a Tier 1 (Investor) Migrant must score 75 points for attributes.]

Note

This paragraph inserted by HC 863, para 143 as from 6 April 2011.

[**55.** Except where paragraph 56 applies, available points for applications for entry clearance or leave to remain are shown in Table 7.]

Note

This paragraph inserted by HC 863, para 143 as from 6 April 2011. Substituted by HC 693, para 128 as from 6 November 2014, save that if an application has been made for entry clearance or leave to enter or remain before 6 November 2014, the application will be decided in accordance with the Rules in force on 5 November 2014.

[**56.**
(a) Available points for entry clearance or leave to remain are shown in Table 8A for an applicant who:
  (i) has had entry clearance, leave to enter or leave to remain as a Tier 1 (Investor) Migrant, which was granted under the Rules in place from 6 November 2014, in the 12 months immediately before the date of application, or
  (ii) is applying for leave to remain and has, or was last granted, entry clearance, leave to enter or leave to remain as a Tier 1 (Investor) Migrant, which was granted under the Rules in place from 6 November 2014.
(b) Available points for entry clearance or leave to remain are shown in Table 8B for an applicant who:
  (i) has had entry clearance, leave to enter or leave to remain as a Tier 1 (Investor) Migrant, under the Rules in place before 6 November 2014, or as an Investor, in the 12 months immediately before the date of application;, or
  (ii) is applying for leave to remain and has, or was last granted, entry clearance, leave to enter or leave to remain as a Tier 1 (Investor) Migrant, under the Rules in place before 6 November 2014, or as an Investor.]

Note

This paragraph substituted by HC 1888, para 127 as from 6 April 2012. Substituted by HC 693, para 128 as from 6 November 2014, save that if an application has been made for entry clearance or leave to enter or remain before 6 November 2014, the application will be decided in accordance with the Rules in force on 5 November 2014.

[57.

(a) Available points for applications for indefinite leave to remain are shown in Table 9A for an applicant who was last granted as a Tier 1 (Investor) Migrant under the Rules in place from 6 November 2014, and was awarded points as set out in Table 7 or Table 8A of Appendix A to these Rules in that last grant.

(b) Available points for applications for indefinite leave to remain are shown in Table 9B for an applicant who was last granted as a Tier 1 (Investor) Migrant under the Rules in place before 6 November 2014, or was awarded points as set out in Table 8B of Appendix A in his last grant.]

Note

This paragraph inserted by HC 863, para 143 as from 6 April 2011. Substituted by HC 693, para 128 as from 6 November 2014, save that if an application has been made for entry clearance or leave to enter or remain before 6 November 2014, the application will be decided in accordance with the Rules in force on 5 November 2014.

[58. Notes to accompany Tables 7 to Table 9B appear below Table 9B.]

Note

This paragraph inserted by HC 863, para 143 as from 6 April 2011. Substituted by HC 693, para 128 as from 6 November 2014, save that if an application has been made for entry clearance or leave to enter or remain before 6 November 2014, the application will be decided in accordance with the Rules in force on 5 November 2014.

[Table 7: Applications for entry clearance or leave to remain referred to in paragraph 55

Money to invest in the UK	Points
The applicant has money of his own under his control held in a regulated financial institution and disposable in the UK amounting to not less than £2 million.]	75

Note

Table amended by HC 628, para 164.

Amended by HC 693, para 129 as from 6 November 2014, save that if an application has been made for entry clearance or leave to enter or remain before 6 November 2014, the application will be decided in accordance with the Rules in force on 5 November 2014.

[Table 8A: Applications for entry clearance or leave to remain from applicants who initially applied to enter the category from 6 November 2014 as referred to in paragraph 56(a)

Money and investment	Points
The applicant has invested not less than £2 million in the UK by way of UK Government bonds, share capital or loan capital in active and trading UK registered companies, subject to the restrictions set out in paragraph 65 below.	75
The investment referred to above was made:	
(1) within 3 months of the applicant's entry to the UK, if he was granted entry clearance as a Tier 1 (Investor) Migrant and there is evidence to establish his date of entry to the UK, unless there are exceptionally compelling reasons for the delay in investing, or	

Money and investment	Points
(2) where there is no evidence to establish his date of entry in the UK or where the applicant was granted entry clearance in a category other than Tier 1 (Investor) Migrant, within 3 months of the date of the grant of entry clearance or leave to remain as a Tier 1 (Investor) Migrant, unless there are exceptionally compelling reasons for the delay in investing, or	
(3) where the investment was made prior to the application which led to the first grant of leave as a Tier 1 (Investor) Migrant, no earlier than 12 months before the date of such application,	
and in each case the level of investment has been at least maintained for the whole of the remaining period of that leave.	
"Compelling reasons for the delay in investing" must be unforeseeable and outside of the applicant's control. Delays caused by the applicant failing to take timely action will not be accepted. Where possible, the applicant must have taken reasonable steps to mitigate such delay.]	

Note

Table heading substituted by HC 760, para 299 as from 13 December 2012. Amended by HC 628, para 165 and if an applicant has made an application for entry clearance or leave before 1 October 2013, the application will be decided in accordance with the Rules in force on 30 September 2013. Amended by HC 1138, para 107 as from 6 April 2014. Amended by HC 693, para 130 as from 6 November 2014, save that if an application has been made for entry clearance or leave to enter or remain before 6 November 2014, the application will be decided in accordance with the Rules in force on 5 November 2014.

[Table 8B: Applications for entry clearance or leave to remain from applicants who initially applied to enter the category before 6 November 2014 as referred to in paragraph 56(b)

Money and investment	Points
The applicant:	30
(a) has money of his own under his control in the UK amounting to not less than £1 million, or	
(b) (i) owns personal assets which, taking into account any liabilities to which they are subject, have a value of not less than £2 million; and	
(ii) has money under his control and disposable in the UK amounting to not less than £1 million which has been loaned to him by a UK regulated financial institution.	
The applicant has invested not less than £750,000 of his capital in the UK by way of UK Government bonds, share capital or loan capital in active and trading UK registered companies, subject to the restrictions set out in paragraph 65 below and has invested the remaining balance of £1,000,000 in the UK by the purchase of assets or by maintaining the money on deposit in a UK regulated financial institution.	30
(i) The investment referred to above was made:	15

Money and investment	Points
(1) within 3 months of the applicant's entry to the UK, if he was granted entry clearance as a Tier 1 (Investor) Migrant and there is evidence to establish his date of entry to the UK, unless there are exceptionally compelling reasons for the delay in investing; or	
(2) where there is no evidence to establish his date of entry in the UK or where the applicant was granted entry clearance in a category other than Tier 1 (Investor) Migrant, within 3 months of the date of the grant of entry clearance or leave to remain as a Tier 1 (Investor) Migrant, unless there are exceptionally compelling reasons for the delay in investing; or	
(3) where the investment was made prior to the application which led to the first grant of leave as a Tier 1 (Investor) Migrant, no earlier than 12 months before the date of such application,	
and in each case the level of investment has been at least maintained for the whole of the remaining period of that leave; or	
(ii) The migrant has, or was last granted, entry clearance, leave to enter or leave to remain as an Investor.	
"Compelling reasons for the delay in investing" must be unforeseeable and outside of the applicant's control. Delays caused by the applicant failing to take timely action will not be accepted. Where possible, the applicant must have taken reasonable steps to mitigate such delay.]	

Note

Amended by HC 693, para 130 as from 6 November 2014, save that if an application has been made for entry clearance or leave to enter or remain before 6 November 2014, the application will be decided in accordance with the Rules in force on 5 November 2014.

[**Table 9A: Applications for indefinite leave to remain from applicants who initially applied to enter the category from 6 November 2014 as referred to in paragraph 57(a)**

Row	Money and investment	Points
1.	The applicant has invested money of his own under his control amounting to at least: (a) £10 million; or (b) £5 million; or (c) £2 million in the UK by way of UK Government bonds, share capital or loan capital in active and trading UK registered companies, subject to the restrictions set out in paragraph 65 below.	40
2.	The applicant has spent the specified continuous period lawfully in the UK, with absences from the UK of no more than 180 days in any 12 calendar months during that period. The specified continuous period must have been spent with leave as a Tier 1 (Investor) Migrant. The specified continuous period is:	20

Row	Money and investment	Points
	(a) 2 years if the applicant scores points from row 1(a) above;	
	(b) 3 years if the applicant scores points from row 1(b) above; or	
	(c) 5 years if the applicant scores points from row 1(c) above.	
	Time spent with valid leave in the Bailiwick of Guernsey, the Bailiwick of Jersey or the Isle of Man in a category equivalent to the categories set out above may be included in the continuous period of lawful residence, provided the most recent period of leave was as a Tier 1 (Investor) Migrant in the UK. In any such case, the applicant must have absences from the Bailiwick of Guernsey, the Bailiwick of Jersey or the Isle of Man (as the case may be) of no more than 180 days in any 12 calendar months during the specified continuous period.	
3.	The investment referred to above was made no earlier than 12 months before the date of the application which led to the first grant of leave as a Tier 1 (Investor) Migrant.	15
	The level of investment has been at least maintained throughout the relevant specified continuous period referred to in row 2, other than in the first 3 months of that period, and the applicant has provided the specified documents to show that this requirement has been met.	
	When calculating the specified continuous period, the first day of that period will be taken to be the later of:	
	(a) the date the applicant first entered the UK as a Tier 1 (Investor) Migrant, (or the date entry clearance was granted as a Tier 1 (Investor) Migrant) or the date the applicant first entered the Bailiwick of Guernsey, the Bailiwick of Jersey or the Isle of Man with leave in a category equivalent to Tier 1 (Investor) if this is earlier; or	
	(b) the date 3 months before the full specified amount was invested in the UK, or before the full required amount in an equivalent category was invested in the Bailiwick of Guernsey, the Bailiwick of Jersey or the Isle of Man.]	

Note

Table 9 amended by HC 760, para 300 as from 13 December 2012. Amended by HC 1039, para 149 as from 6 April 2013 and apply to all applications decided on or after 6 April 2013. Further amended by HC 628, para 166 and if an applicant has made an application for entry clearance or leave before 1 October 2013, the application will be decided in accordance with the Rules in force on 30 September 2013. Amended by HC 693, para 131 as from 6 November 2014, save that if an application has been made for entry clearance or leave to enter or remain before 6 November 2014, the application will be decided in accordance with the Rules in force on 5 November 2014.

[Table 9B: Applications for indefinite leave to remain from applicants who initially applied to enter the category before 6 November 2014 as referred to in paragraph 57(b)]

Row	Money and investment	Points
1.	The applicant:	20
	(a) (i) has money of his own under his control in the UK amounting to not less than £10 million; or	
	(ii) (1) owns personal assets which, taking into account any liabilities to which they are subject, have a value of not less than £20 million; and	
	(2) has money under his control and disposable in the UK amounting to not less than £10 million which has been loaned to him by a UK regulated financial institution, or	
	(b) (i) has money of his own under his control in the UK amounting to not less than £5 million; or	
	(ii) (1) owns personal assets which, taking into account any liabilities to which they are subject, have a value of not less than £10 million; and	
	(2) has money under his control and disposable in the UK amounting to not less than £5 million which has been loaned to him by a UK regulated financial institution; or	
	(c) (i) has money of his own under his control in the UK amounting to not less than £1 million; or	
	(ii) (1) owns personal assets which, taking into account any liabilities to which they are subject, have a value of not less than £2 million; and	
	(2) has money under his control and disposable in the UK amounting to not less than £1 million which has been loaned to him by a UK regulated financial institution.	
2.	The applicant has invested not less than 75% of the specified invested amount of his capital in the UK by way of UK Government bonds, share capital or loan capital in active and trading UK registered companies, subject to the restrictions set out in paragraph 65 below, and has invested the remaining balance of the specified invested amount in the UK by the purchase of assets or by maintaining the money on deposit in a UK regulated financial institution.	20
	The specified invested amount is:	
	(a) £10,000,000 if the applicant scores points from row 1(a) above,	
	(b) £5,000,000 if the applicant scores points from row 1(b) above, or	
	(c) £1,000,000 if the applicant scores points from row 1(c) above.	
3.	The applicant has spent the specified continuous period lawfully in the UK, with absences from the UK of no more than 180 days in any 12 calendar months during that period.	20
	The specified continuous period must have been spent with leave as a Tier 1 (Investor) Migrant and/or as an Investor, of which the most recent period must have been spent with leave as a Tier 1 (Investor) Migrant.	

Row	Money and investment	Points
	The specified continuous period is: (a) 2 years if the applicant scores points from row 1(a) above, (b) 3 years if the applicant scores points from row 1(b) above, or (c) 5 years if the applicant scores points from row 1(c) above. Time spent with valid leave in the Bailiwick of Guernsey, the Bailiwick of Jersey or the Isle of Man in a category equivalent to the categories set out above may be included in the continuous period of lawful residence, provided the most recent period of leave was as a Tier 1 (Investor) Migrant in the UK. In any such case, the applicant must have absences from the Bailiwick of Guernsey, the Bailiwick of Jersey or the Isle of Man (as the case may be) of no more than 180 days in any 12 calendar months during the specified continuous period.	
4.	The investment referred to above was made no earlier than 12 months before the date of the application which led to the first grant of leave as a Tier 1 (Investor) Migrant. The level of investment has been at least maintained throughout the time spent with leave as a Tier 1 (Investor) Migrant in the UK in the relevant specified continuous period referred to in row 3, other than in the first 3 months of that period. In relation to time spent with leave as a Tier 1 (Investor) Migrant in the UK, the applicant has provided the specified documents to show that this requirement has been met. When calculating the specified continuous period, the first day of that period will be taken to be the later of: (a) the date the applicant first entered the UK as a Tier 1 (Investor) Migrant (or the date entry clearance was granted as a Tier 1 (Investor) Migrant), or the date the applicant first entered the Bailiwick of Guernsey, the Bailiwick of Jersey or the Isle of Man with leave in a category equivalent to Tier 1 (Investor) if this is earlier, or (b) the date 3 months before the full specified amount was invested in the UK, or before the full required amount in an equivalent category was invested in the Bailiwick of Guernsey, the Bailiwick of Jersey or the Isle of Man.]	15

Note

Amended by HC 693, para 131 as from 6 November 2014, save that if an application has been made for entry clearance or leave to enter or remain before 6 November 2014, the application will be decided in accordance with the Rules in force on 5 November 2014.

[Money and assets: notes]

59. DELETED.]

Note

This paragraph inserted by HC 863, para 143 as from 6 April 2011 and deleted by Cm 8423, para 98 as from 20 July 2012. New sub-heading inserted by HC 693, para 132 as from 6 November 2014, save that if an application has been made for entry clearance or leave to enter or remain before 6 November 2014, the application will be decided in accordance with the Rules in force on 5 November 2014.

60. [Money is disposable in the UK if all of the money is held in a UK based financial institution or if the money is freely transferable to the UK and convertible to sterling. funds in a foreign currency will be converted to pounds sterling (£) using the spot exchange rate which appeared on www.oanda.com* on the date on which the application was made.]

Note

This paragraph inserted by HC 863, para 143 as from 6 April 2011.

61. ['Money of his own', 'personal assets' and 'his capital' include money or assets belonging to the applicant's spouse, civil partner or unmarried or same-sex partner, provided that:
(a) the applicant's spouse, civil partner or unmarried or same-sex partner meets the requirements of [paragraphs 319C(c) and (d)] of these Rules [and the specified documents in paragraph 61–SD are provided,] and
(b) specified documents [in paragraph 61–SD] are provided to show that the money or assets are under the applicant's control and that he is free to invest them.]

Note

This paragraph inserted by HC 863, para 143 as from 6 April 2011. Further amended by HC 1888, para 130 as from 6 April 2012. Further amended by Cm 8423, paras 99, 100 as from 20 July 2012.

[61A. [In Tables 7 to 9B]. "money of his own under his control" and "money under his control" exclude money that a loan has been secured against, where another party would have a claim on the money if loan repayments were not met[, except where]
(i) the applicant made an application before 13 December 2012 which is undecided or which led to a grant of entry clearance or leave to remain as an Investor or a Tier 1 (Investor) migrant,
(ii) the applicant has not been granted entry clearance, leave to enter or leave to remain in any other category since the grant referred to in (i), and
(iii) the money is under the applicant's control, except for the fact that the loan referred to [in paragraph (b) in Table 8B or row 1 in Table 9B] has been secured against it.]

Note

Inserted by HC 760, para 301 as from 13 December 2012. Words in square brackets substituted by HC 820, para 3 as from 13 December 2012. Further amended by HC 693, para 133 as from 6 November 2014, save that if an application has been made for entry clearance or leave to enter or remain before 6 November 2014, the application will be decided in accordance with the Rules in force on 5 November 2014. Further amended by HC 693, para 134 as from 6 November 2014, save that if an application has been made for entry clearance or leave to enter or remain before 6 November 2014, the application will be decided in accordance with the Rules in force on 5 November 2014.

[61-SD   The specified documents in paragraph 61, as evidence of the relationship and to show that the money or assets are under the applicant's control and that he is free to invest them, are as follows:
(a)   The applicant must provide:
    (i) The original certificate of marriage or civil partnership, to confirm the relationship, which includes the name of the applicant and the husband, wife or civil partner, or
    (ii) At least three of the following types of specified documents to demonstrate a relationship similar in nature to marriage or civil partnership, including unmarried and same-sex relationships, covering a full two-year period immediately before the date of the application:
        (1) a bank statement or letter from a bank confirming a joint bank account held in both names,
        (2) an official document such as a mortgage agreement showing a joint mortgage,

(3)　official documents such as deeds of ownership or a mortgage agreement showing a joint investment, such as in property or business,

(4)　a joint rent (tenancy) agreement,

(5)　any other official correspondence linking both partners to the same address, such as example bills for council tax or utilities,

(6)　a life insurance policy naming the other partner as beneficiary,

(7)　birth certificates of any children of the relationship, showing both partners as parents, or

(8)　any other evidence that adequately demonstrates the couple's long-term commitment to one another.

(b)　The applicant must provide an original declaration from the applicant's husband, wife, civil partner, or unmarried or same-sex partner that he will permit all joint or personal money used to claim points for the application to be under the control of the applicant in the UK, known as a gift of beneficial ownership of the money while retaining the legal title, which clearly shows:

(1)　the names of husband, wife, civil partner, or unmarried or same-sex partner and the applicant,

(2)　the date of the declaration,

(3)　the signatures of the husband, wife, civil partner, or unmarried or same-sex partner and applicant,

(4)　the amount of money available, and

(5)　a statement that the husband, wife, civil partner, or unmarried or same-sex partner agrees that the applicant has sole control over the money.

(c)　The applicant must provide a letter, from a legal adviser who is permitted to practise in the country where the declaration was made, confirming that the declaration is valid and which clearly shows:

(1)　the name of the legal adviser confirming that the declaration is valid,

(2)　the registration or authority of the legal adviser to practise legally in the country in which the document was drawn up,

(3)　the date of the confirmation of the declaration,

(4)　the names of the applicant and husband, wife, civil partner, or unmarried or same-sex partner, and

(5)　that the declaration is signed and valid according to the laws of the country in which it was made.]

Note

Inserted by Cm 8423, para 101 as from 20 July 2012.

62.　["Regulated financial institution" is defined in paragraph 43, Appendix A.]

Note

This paragraph inserted by HC 863, para 143 as from 6 April 2011.

62A.　[...]

Note

This paragraph inserted by Cm 8423, para 102 as from 20 July 2012. Deleted by HC 693, para 135 as from 6 November 2014, save that if an application has been made for entry clearance or leave to enter or remain before 6 November 2014, the application will be decided in accordance with the Rules in force on 5 November 2014.

[**63.**　In the case of an application where Table 7 applies, where the money referred to in Table 7 has already been invested in the UK before the date of application, points will only be awarded if it was invested in the UK no more than 12 months before the date of application.]

Note

This paragraph inserted by HC 863, para 143 as from 6 April 2011. Substituted by HC 693, para 136 as from 6 November 2014, save that if an application has been made for entry clearance or leave to enter or remain before 6 November 2014, the application will be decided in accordance with the Rules in force on 5 November 2014.

[Source of money: notes]

64. [In the case of an application where Table 7 applies, points will only be awarded if the applicant:

(a)   has had the money ... referred to in Table 7 for a consecutive 90-day period of time, ending no earlier than one calendar month before the date of application, [and provides the specified documents in paragraph 64-SD]; or

(b)   [provides additional specified documents in paragraph 64A-SD].]

Note

This paragraph inserted by HC 863, para 143 as from 6 April 2011. Further amended by Cm 8423, paras 103,104 as from 20 July 2012. New sub-heading inserted by HC 693, para 137 as from 6 November 2014, save that if an application has been made for entry clearance or leave to enter or remain before 6 November 2014, the application will be decided in accordance with the Rules in force on 5 November 2014. Phrase "or assets" deleted by HC 693, para 138 as from 6 November 2014, save that if an application has been made for entry clearance or leave to enter or remain before 6 November 2014, the application will be decided in accordance with the Rules in force on 5 November 2014.

64-SD The specified document requirements in paragraph 64(a), as evidence of having held the money ... for the specified 90-day period, are as follows:

(a)   [The applicant must provide:]

(i)   A portfolio report produced by a UK regulated financial institution, or a breakdown of investments in an original letter produced by a UK regulated financial institution, on the official letter-headed paper of the institution, issued by an authorised official of that institution. The portfolio report or letter must cover the three consecutive months before the date of application. The report must be no more than one calendar month old at the time of application. The portfolio report or letter must confirm all the following:

(1)   the amount of the money held in the investments,

(2)   the beneficial owner of the funds,

(3)   the date of the investment period covered,

(4)   that the institution is a UK regulated financial institution, with the details of the registration shown on the documentation, and

(5)   that the money can be transferred into the UK should the application be successful, if it is held abroad, or that the money has already been invested in the UK in the form of UK Government bonds, share capital or loan capital in active and trading UK registered companies, and the dates of these investments;

(ii)   If the applicant manages his own investments, or has a portfolio manager who does not operate in the UK and is not therefore [regulated by the Financial Conduct Authority (FCA) and the Prudential Regulation Authority (PRA) where applicable], he must provide one or more of the documents from the list below, as relevant to their type of investments, covering the three consecutive months in the period immediately before the date of application:

(1)   certified copies of bond documents showing the value of the bonds, the date of purchase and the owner;

(2)   share documents showing the value of the shares, the date of purchase and the owner,

(3)   the latest audited annual accounts of the organisation in which the investment has been made, clearly showing the amount of money held in the investments, the name of the applicant (or applicant and/or husband, wife, civil partner, or unmarried or same-sex partner), and the date of investment, or, if no accounts have been produced, a certificate from an accountant showing the amount of money held in the investments, and

(4)   original trust fund documents from a legal adviser showing the amount of money in the fund, the date that the money is available and the beneficial owner, and including the name and contact details of the legal adviser and at least one of the trustees;

(iii)   Original personal bank statements on the official bank stationery from a bank that is regulated by the official regulatory body for the country in which the institution operates and the funds are located, showing the amount of money available in the name of the applicant (or applicant and/or husband, wife, civil partner, or unmarried or same-sex partner), covering the three full consecutive months before the date of application. The most recent statement must be no more than one calendar month old at the date of application. Electronic bank statements ... must be accompanied by a supporting letter from the bank on the institution's official headed paper, issued by an authorising official of that institution, confirming the content and that the document is genuine;

(iv)   If the applicant cannot provide bank statements, an original letter from a bank that is regulated by the official regulatory body for the country in which the institution operates and the funds are located, on the institution's official headed paper, issued by an authorised official of that institution, stating that the account has held the required amount of money on the day the letter was produced and for the three full consecutive months immediately before the date of the letter. The letter must be dated no more than one calendar month before the date of application. The letter must confirm:

(1)   the name of the applicant (or applicant and/or husband, wife, civil partner, or unmarried or same-sex partner), and that the money is available in their name(s),

(2)   that the bank is regulated by the official regulatory body for the country in which the institution operates and the funds are located,

(3)   the dates of the period covered, including both the day the letter was produced and three full consecutive months immediately before the date of the letter, and

(4)   the balance of the account to cover the amount claimed as a credit balance on the date of the letter and the three full consecutive months before the date of the letter;

(v)   If the funds are not held in the UK, the applicant must provide an original letter from a bank or financial institution that is regulated by the official regulatory body for the country in which the institution operates and the funds are located, on the institution's official headed paper, issued by an authorised official of that institution, which confirms:

(1)   the name of the beneficial owner, which should be the applicant (or applicant and/or husband, wife, civil partner, or unmarried or same-sex partner),

(2)   the date of the letter,

(3)   the amount of money to be transferred,

(4)   that the money can be transferred to the UK if the application is successful, and

(5)   that the institution will confirm the content of the letter to the UK Border Agency on request.

[(b)]   If specified documents are provided from accountants, the accountant must:

(i)   if based in the UK, be a member of the Institute of Chartered Accountants in England and Wales, the Institute of Chartered Accountants in Scotland, the Institute of Chartered Accountants in Ireland, the Association of Chartered Certified Accountants, or the Association of Authorised Public Accountants, or

(ii)   if not based in the UK, be a member of an equivalent, appropriate supervisory or regulatory body in the country in which they operate.

Note

Words "or assets" deleted by HC 693, para 140 as from 6 November 2014, save that if an application has been made for entry clearance or leave to enter or remain before 6 November 2014, the application will be decided in accordance with the Rules in force on 5 November 2014. Further amended by HC 693, para 141 as from 6 November 2014, save that if an application has been made for entry clearance or leave to enter or remain before 6 November 2014, the application will be decided in accordance with the Rules in force on 5 November 2014. Deleted by HC 693, para 142 as from 6 November 2014, save that if an application has been made for entry clearance or leave to enter or remain before 6 November 2014, the application will be decided in accordance with the Rules in force on 5 November 2014. Sub-paragraph (c) as (b) renumbered by HC 693, para 143 as from 6 November 2014, save that if an application has been made for entry clearance or leave to enter or remain before 6 November 2014, the application will be decided in accordance with the Rules in force on 5 November 2014.

64A-SD. Where paragraph 64(b) states that specified documents are required as evidence [that the money is under the applicant's control and that he is free to invest it], the applicant must provide all the specified documents from the following list, with contact details that enable verification:

(a)   Original documents in the form of:

   (i)   Money given to the applicant (or applicant and/or husband, wife, civil partner, or unmarried or same-sex partner) within the three months immediately before the application must be shown in an irrevocable memorandum of gift, which clearly shows:

   (1)   the name and signature of the person receiving the gift,
   (2)   the name and signature of the person giving the gift,
   (3)   the date of the memorandum,
   (4)   the amount of money being given,
   (5)   a statement that the legal ownership of the gift is transferred and that the document is the memorandum of transfer,
   (6)   a clear description of the gift, and
   (7)   a statement that the gift is irrevocable;

   (ii)   If a memorandum of gift in (i) is provided, it must be accompanied by an original confirmation letter from a legal adviser permitted to practise in the country where the gift was made, which clearly shows:

   (1)   the name of the legal adviser who is confirming the details,
   (2)   the registration or authority of the legal adviser to practise legally in the country in which the gift was made,
   (3)   the date of the confirmation of the memorandum,
   (4)   the names of the person giving the gift and the person receiving it,
   (5)   the amount of money given,
   (6)   the date that the money was transferred to the applicant, or to the husband, wife, civil partner, or unmarried partner or same-sex partner of the applicant,
   (7)   that the memorandum is signed and valid,
   (8)   that the gift is irrevocable, and
   (9)   that the memorandum is binding according to the laws of the country in which it was made;

   (iii)   Deeds of sale of assets such as business or property, if the applicant has generated these funds within the three months immediately before the date of application, which meet the relevant legal requirements of the country of sale and clearly show:

   (1)   the name of the applicant (or applicant and/or husband, wife, civil partner, or unmarried or same-sex partner),
   (2)   the amount of money raised, and
   (3)   the date of the sale;

   (iv)   If a deed of sale in (iii) is provided, it must be accompanied by an original confirmation letter from a legal adviser permitted to practise in the country where the sale was made, which clearly shows:

   (1)   the name of the legal adviser confirming the details,
   (2)   the registration or authority of the legal adviser to practise legally in the country in which the sale was made,
   (3)   the date of the sale,
   (4)   the date of production of the letter confirming the sale,
   (5)   the details of what was sold and the amount of money received from the sale,
   (6)   the name of the person receiving the money from the sale,
   (7)   the date that the money was transferred, and
   (8)   that the sale was valid according to the laws of the country in which it was made;

   (v)   If the funds are currently held in the applicant's business (or the business of the applicant and/or the applicant's husband, wife, civil partner, or unmarried or same-sex partner), the applicant must provide business accounts, which:

(1)   are profit and loss accounts (or income and expenditure accounts if the organisation is not trading for profit),

(2)   are prepared and signed off in accordance with statutory requirements, and

(3)   clearly show the amount of money available for investment;

(vi)   If business accounts in (v) are provided, they must be accompanied by an original letter from a legal adviser who is permitted to practise in the country where business was operating, confirming that the applicant (or applicant and/or husband, wife, civil partner, or unmarried or same-sex partner) can lawfully extract the money from the business, which clearly shows:

(1)   the name of the legal adviser who is confirming the details,

(2)   the registration or authority of the legal adviser to practise legally in the country in which the business is operating,

(3)   the date on which the details are confirmed, and

(4)   that the applicant (or applicant and/or husband, wife, civil partner, or unmarried or same-sex partner) can lawfully extract the money from the business in question;

(vii)   If the applicant (or applicant and/or husband, wife, civil partner, or unmarried or same sex partner) has been the beneficiary of a will within the three months before making the application, and has received money as a result, the applicant must provide a notarised copy of the will. If the applicant (or applicant and/or husband, wife, civil partner, or unmarried or same-sex partner) has received possessions or assets, rather than money, then the applicant (or applicant and/or husband, wife, civil partner, or unmarried or same-sex partner) may not use estimates of the value of the items as evidence of funds for investment. The notarised copy of the will must clearly show:

(1)   the date of the will,

(2)   the beneficiary of the will (this should be the applicant or applicant and/or husband, wife, civil partner, or unmarried or same-sex partner),

(3)   the amount of money that the applicant (or applicant and/or husband, wife, civil partner, or unmarried or same-sex partner) has inherited, and

(4)   the names of any executors, plus any codicils (additions) to the will that affect the amount of money that was received;

(viii)   If a notarised copy of a will in (vii) is provided, it must be accompanied by an original confirmation letter from a legal adviser who is permitted to practise in the country where will was made, confirming the validity of the will, which clearly shows:

(1)   the name of the legal adviser confirming the details,

(2)   the registration or authority of the legal adviser to practise legally in the country in which the will was made,

(3)   the date of the document produced by the legal adviser confirming the will,

(4)   the date that the applicant received the money as a result of the settlement of the will,

(5)   the names of the person making the will and the beneficiary,

(6)   confirmation of the amount of money received by the applicant (or applicant and/or husband, wife, civil partner, or unmarried or same-sex partner).

(7)   that the will is signed and valid, and

(8)   that the will is valid according to the laws of the country in which it was made;

(ix)   If the applicant (or applicant and/or husband, wife, civil partner, or unmarried or same-sex partner) has obtained money as a result of a divorce settlement within the three months immediately before the date of application, the applicant must provide a notarised copy of a financial agreement following a divorce. If the applicant (or applicant and/or husband, wife, civil partner, or unmarried or same-sex partner) has received possessions or assets, rather than money, estimates of the value of the items will not be accepted as evidence of money for investment.

(x) If a divorce settlement in (ix) is provided, it must be accompanied by an original confirmation letter from a legal adviser who is permitted to practise in the country where the divorce took place, which clearly shows:

    (1) the name of the legal adviser confirming the details,

    (2) the registration or authority of the legal adviser to practise legally in the country in which the divorce took place,

    (3) the date of the document produced by the legal adviser confirming the divorce settlement,

    (4) the date that the applicant received the money as a result of the settlement,

    (5) the names of the persons who are divorced,

    (6) confirmation of the amount of money received by the applicant (or applicant and/or husband, wife, civil partner, or unmarried or same-sex partner,

    (7) that the divorce settlement is complete and valid, and

    (8) that the divorce settlement is valid according to the laws of the country in which it was made;

(xi) If the applicant is relying on a financial award or winnings as a source of funds, he must provide an original letter from the organisation issuing the financial award or winnings, which clearly shows:

    (1) the name of the applicant (or applicant and/or husband, wife, civil partner, or unmarried or same-sex partner),

    (2) the date of the award,

    (3) the amount of money won,

    (4) the winnings are genuine, and

    (5) the contact details for the organisation issuing the award or winnings;

(xii) If a letter showing a financial award or winnings in (xi) is provided, it must be accompanied by an original confirmation letter from a legal adviser who is permitted to practise in the country where the award was made, which clearly shows:

    (1) the name of the legal adviser confirming the details,

    (2) the registration or authority of the legal adviser to practise legally in the country in which the award was made,

    (3) the date of the letter of confirmation,

    (4) the date of the award,

    (5) the name of the recipient of the award,

    (6) the amount of the winnings,

    (7) the source of the winnings, and

    (8) the date that the money was transferred to the applicant, or husband, wife, civil partner, or unmarried or same-sex partner;

(xiii) If the applicant (or applicant and/or husband, wife, civil partner, or unmarried or same-sex partner) has received money from a source not listed above, the applicant must provide relevant original documentation as evidence of the source of the money, together with independent supporting evidence, which both clearly confirm:

    (1) the amount of money received,

    (2) the date that the money was received,

    (3) the source of the money, and

    (4) that the applicant (or applicant and/or husband, wife, civil partner, or unmarried or same-sex partner) was the legal recipient of the money.]

Note

Further amended by HC 244, para 19 as from 1 July 2013. Amended by HC 628, paras 163, 167. Further amended by HC 693, para 144 as from 6 November 2014, save that if an application has been made for entry clearance or leave to enter or remain before 6 November 2014, the application will be decided in accordance with the Rules in force on 5 November 2014.

[Source of additional money (Table 9A and Table 9B): notes]

[64B-SD. In the case of an application where Table 9A, row 1 (a) or (b), or Table 9B, row 1 (a)(i) or (b)(i) applies, points will only be awarded if the applicant:

(a)

    (i)   has had the additional money (or the additional assets in respect of an application to which either row 1 (a)(i) or (b)(i) of Table 9B applies) that he was not awarded points for in his previous grant of leave for a consecutive 90-day period of time, ending on the date(s) this additional capital was invested (as set out in row 1 of Table 9A or row 2 of Table 9B), and

    (ii)   provides the specified documents in paragraph 64-SD (or the additional assets in respect of an application to which either row 1 (a)(i) or (b)(i) of Table 9B applies), with the difference that references to "date of application" in that paragraph are taken to read "date of investment"; or

(b)   provides the additional specified documents in paragraph 64A-SD of the source of the additional money (with the difference that references to "date of application" in that paragraph are taken to read "date of investment").]

Note

This paragraph inserted by HC 760, para 302 as from 13 December 2012. New sub-heading inserted by HC 693, para 145 as from 6 November 2014, save that if an application has been made for entry clearance or leave to enter or remain before 6 November 2014, the application will be decided in accordance with the Rules in force on 5 November 2014. Substituted by HC 693, para 146 as from 6 November 2014, save that if an application has been made for entry clearance or leave to enter or remain before 6 November 2014, the application will be decided in accordance with the Rules in force on 5 November 2014.

[64C-SD. In the case of an application where Table 9B, row 1 (a)(ii) or (b)(ii) applies, points will only be awarded if the applicant provides an original letter of confirmation from each UK regulated financial institution the applicant has taken out a loan with to obtain the additional funds that he was not awarded points for in his previous grant of leave. The letter must have been issued by an authorised official, on the official letter-headed paper of the institution(s), and confirm:

(i)   the amount of money that the institution(s) has loaned to the applicant,

(ii)   the date(s) the loan(s) was taken out by the applicant, which must be no later than the date(s) this additional capital was invested (as set out in Table 9B, row 2),

(iii) that the institution is a UK regulated financial institution for the purpose of granting loans,

(iv) that the applicant has personal assets with a net value of at least £2 million, £10 million or £20 million (as appropriate), and

(v)   that the institution(s) will confirm the content of the letter to the Home Office on request.]

Note

Inserted by HC 693, para 147 as from 6 November 2014, save that if an application has been made for entry clearance or leave to enter or remain before 6 November 2014, the application will be decided in accordance with the Rules in force on 5 November 2014.

[Qualifying investments (Table 8A to Table 9B): notes]

65. [Investment excludes investment by the applicant by way of:

(a)   An offshore company or trust [or investments that are held in offshore custody] [except that investments held in offshore custody shall not be excluded where the applicant made an application before 13 December 2012 which is undecided or which led to a grant of entry clearance or leave to remain as an Investor or a Tier 1 (Investor) migrant and has not since been granted entry clearance, leave to enter or leave to remain in any other category.]

(b)   Open-ended investment companies, investment trust companies or pooled investment vehicles,

(c)   Companies mainly engaged in property investment, property management or property development,

(d)   Deposits with a bank, building society or other enterprise whose normal course of business includes the acceptance of deposits,

(e)   ISAs, premium bonds and saving certificates issued by the national savings and investment agency (ns&i), for an applicant who has, or last had leave as a Tier 1 (Investor) Migrant, or

[(f)   Leveraged investment funds, except where the leverage in question is the security against the loan referred to in paragraph (b) in Table 8B or row 1 of Table 9B (as appropriate), and paragraph 61A(i)-(iii) apply.]

Note

This paragraph inserted by HC 863, para 143 as from 6 April 2011. Amended by HC 760, para 303 as from 13 December 2012. Words in square brackets in sub-paras (a), (f) substituted by HC 820, paras 4, 5 as from 13 December 2012. New sub-heading inserted by HC 693, para 148 as from 6 November 2014, save that if an application has been made for entry clearance or leave to enter or remain before 6 November 2014, the application will be decided in accordance with the Rules in force on 5 November 2014. Further amended by HC 693, para 149 as from 6 November 2014, save that if an application has been made for entry clearance or leave to enter or remain before 6 November 2014, the application will be decided in accordance with the Rules in force on 5 November 2014.

[65A.   "Active and trading UK registered companies" means companies which:
(a)   have a registered office or head office in the UK;
(b)   have a UK bank account showing current business transactions; and
(c)   are subject to UK taxation.]

Note

Inserted by HC 760, para 304 as from 13 December 2012. Substituted by HC 693, para 150 as from 6 November 2014, save that if an application has been made for entry clearance or leave to enter or remain before 6 November 2014, the application will be decided in accordance with the Rules in force on 5 November 2014.

[65B.   No points will be awarded where the specified documents show that the funds are held in a financial institution listed in Appendix P as being an institution with which the Home Office is unable to make satisfactory verification checks.]

Note

Inserted by HC 693, para 150 as from 6 November 2014, save that if an application has been made for entry clearance or leave to enter or remain before 6 November 2014, the application will be decided in accordance with the Rules in force on 5 November 2014.

[65C.
(a)   In the case of an application where Table 8A or Table 9A applies, points for maintaining the level of investment for the specified continuous period of leave will only be awarded:
      (i)   if the applicant has maintained a portfolio of qualifying investments for which he paid a total purchase price of at least £2 million (or £5 million or £10 million, as appropriate) throughout such period; and
      (ii)   if the applicant sells any part of the portfolio of qualifying investments during the specified continuous period of leave such that the price he paid for the remaining portfolio falls below the purchase price referred to in (i) above, the shortfall is fully corrected within the same reporting period by the purchase of further qualifying investments.
(b)   In the case of an application where Table 8B or Table 9B applies, points for maintaining the level of investment for the relevant period of leave will only be awarded if:
      (i)   the applicant has maintained a portfolio of qualifying investments with a market value of at least £750,000 (or £3,750,000 or £7,500,000 as appropriate);
      (ii)   any fall in the market value of the portfolio below the amount in (i) is corrected by the next reporting period by the purchase of further qualifying investments with a market value equal to the amount of any such fall; and
      (iii)   the applicant has maintained a total level of investment (including the qualifying investments at (i) and (ii) above) of £1,000,000.]

Note

Inserted by HC 693, para 150 as from 6 November 2014, save that if an application has been made for entry clearance or leave to enter or remain before 6 November 2014, the application will be decided in accordance with the Rules in force on 5 November 2014.

[65-SD] The following specified documents must be provided as evidence of investment:

(a) The applicant must provide a portfolio of investments certified as correct by a UK regulated financial institution, which must:

    (i) Cover the required period, beginning no later than the end of the 3 month timescale specified in [the relevant table];

    (ii) Continue to the last reporting date of the most recent billing period of the year directly before the date of the application;

    (iii) Include the value of the investments;

    (iv) Show that any shortfall in investments below the specified investment amount was made up by the next reporting period [as required by paragraph 65C (a) or (b) as applicable];

    (v) Show the dates that the investments were made;

    (vi) Show the destination of the investments;

    (vii) Include, for investments made as loan funds to companies, audited accounts or unaudited accounts with an [accounts compilation report] for the investments made, giving the full details of the applicant's investment. The accountant must be a member of the Institute of Chartered Accountants in England and Wales, the Institute of Chartered Accountants in Scotland, the Institute of Chartered Accountants in Ireland, the Association of Chartered Certified Accountants, or the Association of Authorised Public Accountants;

    (viii) Show the name and contact details of the financial institution that has certified the portfolio as correct, and confirmation that this institution is [regulated by the Financial Conduct Authority (FCA) (and the Prudential Regulation Authority (PRA) where applicable)];

    (ix) Show that the investments were made in the applicant's name and/or that of his spouse, civil partner, unmarried or same-sex partner and not in the name of an offshore company or trust even if this is wholly owned by the applicant;

    (x) include the date that the portfolio was certified by the financial institution; and

    (xi) state that the institution will confirm the content of the letter to the [Home Office] on request.

(b) [Where the applicant is applying under Table 8B or Table 9B, previously had leave as an Investor and is unable to provide the evidence listed above because he manages his own investments, or because he has a portfolio manager who does not operate in the UK] and is therefore not [regulated by the Financial Conduct Authority (FCA) (and the Prudential Regulation Authority (PRA) where applicable)], the applicant must provide the following specified documents showing his holdings used to claim points, as relevant to the type of investment:

    (i) Certified copies of bond documents showing the value of the bonds, the date of purchase and the owner;

    (ii) Share documents showing the value of the shares, the date of purchase and the owner;

    (iii) The latest audited annual accounts of the organisation in which the investment has been made, [which have been prepared and signed off in accordance with statutory requirements, and clearly show:]

        (1) the amount of money held in the investments,

        (2) the name of the applicant (or applicant and/or husband, wife, civil partner, or unmarried or same-sex partner), and

        (3) the date of investment.

    (iv) If the organisation in (iii) is not required to produce accounts, the applicant must provide a certificate showing the amount of money held in the investments, from an accountant who is a member of the Institute of Chartered Accountants in England and Wales, the Institute of Chartered Accountants in Scotland, the Institute of Chartered Accountants in

Ireland, the Association of Chartered Certified Accountants, or the Association of Authorised Public Accountants.

(c) [Where the applicant is applying under Table 8B or Table 9B and has invested] at least 75% of the specified investment amount but less than 100%, he must provide one or more of the following specified documents as evidence of the balance of the funds required to bring his total investment in the UK up to the specified investment amount:

(i) Documents confirming the purchase of assets in the UK, showing the assets purchased, the value of these assets and the dates of purchase. When using property only the unmortgaged portion of the applicant's own home can be considered and the valuation must be provided on a report issued by a surveyor (who is a member of the Royal Institution of Chartered Surveyors) in the six months prior to the date of application;

(ii) If the applicant maintained money on deposit in the UK, a statement or statements of account on the official stationery of the institution that holds the funds. These statements must be in the name of the applicant (or applicant and/or the husband, wife, civil partner, or unmarried or same-sex partner of the applicant) and confirm the dates and amount of money held. The applicant must ensure that the institution will confirm the content of the statement to the [Home Office] on request;

(iii) An original letter from the financial institution that holds the cash on deposit, on the institution's official headed paper, issued by an authorised official of that institution, which confirms the dates and amount of money held and that the institution will confirm the content of the letter to the UK Border Agency on request.

(d) If the applicant wishes the start of the 3 month timescale specified in [Table 8A, Table 8B, Table 9A or Table 9B] to be taken as the date he entered the UK, he must provide evidence which proves this date, such as a stamp in the applicant's passport, or an aircraft boarding card.

(e) Evidence of the investment having been maintained, from the date that the funds were invested for the full period of remaining leave, will be determined using the portfolio provided in (a).]

Note

Amended by HC 244, paras 20, 21 as from 1 July 2013. Amended by HC 1138, para 108 as from 6 April 2014. Amended by HC 1138, para 109 as from 6 April 2014. Further amended by HC 693, para 151 as from 6 November 2014, save that if an application has been made for entry clearance or leave to enter or remain before 6 November 2014, the application will be decided in accordance with the Rules in force on 5 November 2014. Amended by HC 693, para 152 as from 6 November 2014, save that if an application has been made for entry clearance or leave to enter or remain before 6 November 2014, the application will be decided in accordance with the Rules in force on 5 November 2014. Further amended by HC 693, para 153 as from 6 November 2014, save that if an application has been made for entry clearance or leave to enter or remain before 6 November 2014, the application will be decided in accordance with the Rules in force on 5 November 2014. Further amended by HC 693, para 154 as from 6 November 2014, save that if an application has been made for entry clearance or leave to enter or remain before 6 November 2014, the application will be decided in accordance with the Rules in force on 5 November 2014. Further amended by HC 693, para 155 as from 6 November 2014, save that if an application has been made for entry clearance or leave to enter or remain before 6 November 2014, the application will be decided in accordance with the Rules in force on 5 November 2014. Further amended by HC 693, para 156 as from 6 November 2014, save that if an application has been made for entry clearance or leave to enter or remain before 6 November 2014, the application will be decided in accordance with the Rules in force on 5 November 2014. Further amended by HC 693, para 157 as from 6 November 2014, save that if an application has been made for entry clearance or leave to enter or remain before 6 November 2014, the application will be decided in accordance with the Rules in force on 5 November 2014.

[Attributes for Tier 1 (Graduate Entrepreneur) Migrants]

66. An applicant applying [for entry clearance or leave to remain] as a Tier 1 (Graduate Entrepreneur) Migrant must score 75 points for attributes.

Note

Further amended by HC 693, para 158 as from 6 November 2014, save that if an application has been made for entry clearance or leave to enter or remain before 6 November 2014, the application will be decided in accordance with the Rules in force on 5 November 2014.

67. Available points are shown in Table 10.

68. Notes to accompany the table appear below the table.

[TABLE 10

Criterion			Points
(a)		The applicant has been endorsed by a UK Higher Education Institution which:	
	(i)	has Highly Trusted Sponsor status under Tier 4 of the Points-Based System,	
	(ii)	is an A-rated Sponsor under Tier 2 of the Points-Based System if a Tier 2 licence is held,	
	(iii)	is an A-rated Sponsor under Tier 5 of the Points-Based System if a Tier 5 licence is held,	25
	(iv)	has degree-awarding powers, and	
	(v)	has established processes and competence for identifying, nurturing and developing entrepreneurs among its undergraduate and postgraduate population;	
or			
(b)		The applicant has been endorsed by UK Trade and Investment.	
The applicant has been awarded a degree qualification (not a qualification of equivalent level which is not a degree) which meets or exceeds the recognised standard of a Bachelor's degree in the UK. For overseas qualifications, the standard must be confirmed by UK NARIC.			25
The endorsement must confirm that the endorsing body has assessed the applicant and considers that:			
(a)		the applicant has a genuine and credible business idea, and	
(b)		the applicant will spend the majority of his working time on developing business ventures, and	25
(c)		if the applicant is applying for leave to remain and his last grant of leave was as a Tier 1 (Graduate Entrepreneur), he has made satisfactory progress in developing his business since that leave was granted.]	

Note

Amended by HC 314, para 111 as from 31 March 2009. This paragraph and old *Table 9* renumbered by HC 863, paras 144 and 146 as from 6 April 2011. Words in square brackets in (b) inserted by HC 863, para 147 as from 6 April 2011. Table 10 substituted by HC 1039, para 150 as from 6 April 2013. Table 10 amended by HC 887, paras 8–10 as from 30 December 2013. Amended by HC 1138, para 110 as from 6 April 2014.

Tier 1 (Graduate Entrepreneur) Limit: notes

69.

(a) The Secretary of State shall be entitled to limit the total number of Tier 1 (Graduate Entrepreneur) endorsements qualifying [endorsing bodies] may make in support of successful applications in a particular period, to be referred to as the Tier 1 (Graduate Entrepreneur) Limit.

(b) [The Tier 1 (Graduate Entrepreneur) Limit is 2,000 places per year (beginning on 6 April and ending on 5 April), which will be allocated as follows:

(i) 1,900 places will be allocated to qualifying Higher Education Institutions as set out in (c) below; and

(ii) 100 places will be allocated to UK Trade and Investment.]

(c) [Places for qualifying Higher Education Institutions will be allocated as follows:

   (i) The Secretary of State will, on an annual basis, invite all UK Higher Education Institutions which meet the requirements in (a)(i) to (iv) in the first row of Table 10 to take part as endorsing bodies, with responses required by 5 April for the year beginning the next day.

   (ii) The endorsements will be allocated between all invited Higher Education Institutions who confirm that:

     (1) They wish to take part, and

     (2) They meet the requirement in (a)(v) in the first row of Table 10 above.

   (iii) Each qualifying body in (ii) will be allocated the smallest of:

     (1) The number of [endorsements] it has requested,

     (2) Its equal share of the number of endorsements available (If the result is not an integer it will be rounded down to the next lowest integer), or

     (3) 20 endorsements.

   (iv) If the result of (i) to (iii) is that there are fewer than 1,850 endorsements allocated to qualifying Higher Education Institutions for the year, the Home Office will invite all UK Higher Education Institutions which meet the requirements in (a)(i) to (iv) in the first row of Table 10 to request the remaining endorsements for the year ending 5 April, with responses required by 30 September.

   (v) The remaining endorsements will be allocated between all invited Higher Education Institutions who meet the criteria in (ii), regardless of whether they were previously allocated endorsements for the year.

   (vi) If all requests can be met without exceeding the number of remaining places available, each Higher Education Institution in (v) will be allocated the number of endorsements it has requested.

   (vii) If all requests cannot be met without exceeding the number of remaining places available, each Higher Education Institution in (v) will be allocated the smaller of:

     (1) The number of endorsements it has requested, or

     (2) Its equal share of the remaining number of endorsements available (If the result is not an integer it will be rounded down to the next lowest integer).

   (viii) If the result of (iv) to (vii) is that there are still remaining places in the Tier 1 (Graduate Entrepreneur) Limit for the year, those places will not be allocated.]

(d) If:

   (i) an applicant does not make a valid application within 3 months of the date of his endorsement, or

   (ii) an application is refused, and that refusal is not subsequently overturned, the endorsement used in that application will be cancelled and the relevant endorsing body's unused allocation of endorsements will be increased by one, providing the end of the period (6 April to 5 April) to which it relates has not yet passed.

(e) The Tier 1 (Graduate Entrepreneur) limit will not apply to applications for leave to remain where the applicant has, or last had, leave to remain as a Tier 1 (Graduate Entrepreneur).

(f) Endorsements which have not been used by endorsing bodies cannot be carried over from one year (beginning on 6 April and ending on 5 April) to the next.]

Note

Amended by HC 1138, para 111 as from 6 April 2014. Further amended by HC 693, para 159 as from 6 November 2014, save that if an application has been made for entry clearance or leave to enter or remain before 6 November 2014, the application will be decided in accordance with the Rules in force on 5 November 2014.

Endorsement

70. Points will only be awarded for an endorsement if:

(a)   the endorsement was issued to the applicant no more than 3 months before the date of application,
(b)   the endorsement has not been withdrawn by the [relevant endorsing body] at the time the application is considered by [the entry clearance officer or the Secretary of State], and
(c)   [the applicant provides an original endorsement from the [relevant endorsing body,] which shows:
          (i)   the endorsement reference number,
          (ii)   the date of issue (including a statement on how long the letter is valid for),
          (iii)   the applicant's name,
          (iv)   the applicant's date of birth,
          (v)   the applicant's nationality,
          (vi)   the applicant's current passport number,
          (vii)   details of any dependants of the applicant who are already in the UK or who the applicant intends to bring to the UK,
          (viii) [the name of the endorsing body,]
          (ix)   the name and contact details of the authorising official of the endorsing body,
          (x)   [the name, level and date of award of the applicant's qualification, unless this was shown in a previous successful Tier 1 (Graduate Entrepreneur) application,]
          (xi)   the applicant's intended business sector or business intention,
          (xii)   what has led the endorsing body to endorse the application, and
          (xiii) [if the applicant is applying for leave to remain and was last granted leave] as a Tier 1 (Graduate Entrepreneur) Migrant, confirmation that the endorsing body is satisfied that he has made satisfactory progress.]

Note

Amended by HC 1138, para 112 as from 6 April 2014. Amended by HC 1138, para 113 as from 6 April 2014. Further amended by HC 693, para 160 as from 6 November 2014, save that if an application has been made for entry clearance or leave to enter or remain before 6 November 2014, the application will be decided in accordance with the Rules in force on 5 November 2014.

[**Qualifications**

71.   [Points will be awarded for a degree qualification if the endorsement:
(a)   is by the UK Higher Education Institution which awarded the qualification; and
(b)   contains the specified details of the qualification, as set out in paragraph 70(c).]

Note

Paragraphs 66–72 and Table 10 substituted by HC 1888, para 131 as from 6 April 2012. Further amended by Cm 8423, paras 107,108 as from 20 July 2012. Amended by HC 1138, para 114 as from 6 April 2014.

[**72.**
(a)   [In cases other than those in paragraph 71, points will only be awarded for a degree qualification if the applicant provides the following specified documents:]
          (i)   The original certificate of award for the qualification, which clearly shows the:
                    (1)   applicant's name,
                    (2)   title of the award,
                    (3)   date of the award, and
                    (4)   name of the awarding institution, or
          (ii)   if:
                    (1)   the applicant is awaiting graduation having successfully completed his degree, or
                    (2)   the applicant no longer has the certificate and the institution who issued the certificate is unable to produce a replacement, an original academic reference from the institution that is awarding, or has awarded, the degree together with an original academic transcript, unless (d) applies.

(b)   The academic reference referred to in (a)(ii) must be on official headed paper of the institution and clearly show the:
    (1)   applicant's name,
    (2)   title of award,
    (3)   date of award confirming that it has been or will be awarded, and,
    (4)   either the date that the certificate will be issued (if the applicant has not yet graduated) or confirmation that the institution is unable to re-issue the original certificate or award.

(c)   The academic transcript referred to in (a)(ii) must be on the institution's offical paper and must show the:
    (1)   applicant's name,
    (2)   name of the academic institution,
    (3)   course title, and
    (4)   confirmation of the award.

(d)   If the applicant cannot provide his original certificate for one of the reasons given in (a)(ii) and is claiming points for a qualification with a significant research bias, such as a doctorate, an academic transcript is not required, providing the applicant provides an academic reference which includes all the information detailed in (b) above.

(e)   [Where the degree is an overseas qualification and an applicant cannot find details of it on the points based calculator on the visas and immigration pages of the gov.uk website, he must, in addition to the document or documents in (a), provide an original letter or certificate from UK NARIC confirming the equivalency of the level of his qualification.]]

Note

Amended by HC 1138, para 115 as from 6 April 2014. Amended by HC 1138, para 116 as from 6 April 2014.

Attributes for Tier 2 (Intra-Company Transfer) Migrants

73.   [An applicant applying for entry or leave to remain as a Tier 2 (Intra-Company Transfer) Migrant must score 50 points for attributes.]

Note

This paragraph inserted by HC 863, para 150 as from 6 April 2011.

73A.   [Available points for entry clearance or leave to remain are shown in Table 11].

Note

This paragraph inserted by HC 863, para 150 as from 6 April 2011.

73B.   [Notes to accompany Table 11 appear below the table.]

Note

This paragraph inserted by HC 863, para 150 as from 6 April 2011.

[Table 11

Criterion	Points
Certificate of Sponsorship	30
Appropriate salary	20

Notes

Certificate of Sponsorship

74.   In order to obtain points for a Certificate of Sponsorship, the applicant must provide a valid Certificate of Sponsorship reference number.]

Note

This paragraph inserted by HC 863, para 150 as from 6 April 2011.

74A.   [A Certificate of Sponsorship reference number will only be considered to be valid if:
(a)   the number supplied links to a Certificate of Sponsorship Checking Service entry that names the applicant as the migrant and confirms that the Sponsor is sponsoring him as a Tier 2 (Intra-Company Transfer) Migrant and specifies the sub-category of Tier 2 (Intra-Company Transfer) under which he is applying,
(b)   the Sponsor assigned the Certificate of Sponsorship reference number to the migrant no more than 3 months before the application for entry clearance or leave to remain is made,
(c)   the application for entry clearance or leave to remain is made no more than 3 months before the start of the employment as stated on the Certificate of Sponsorship,
(d)   The migrant must not previously have applied for entry clearance, leave to enter or leave to remain using the same Certificate of Sponsorship reference number, if that application was either approved or refused (not rejected as an invalid application [, declared void] or withdrawn), [...]
(e)   that reference number must not have been withdrawn or cancelled by the Sponsor or by the UK Border Agency since it was assigned, including where it has been cancelled by the UK Border Agency due to having been used in a previous application][, and
(f)   the Sponsor is an A-rated Sponsor, unless the application is for leave to remain and the applicant has, or was last granted, leave as a Tier 2 (Intra-Company) Migrant or a Qualifying Work Permit Holder.]

Note

This paragraph inserted by HC 863, para 150 as from 6 April 2011. Words in square brackets in (d) deleted by HC 908, para 37 as from 21 April 2011. Words in square brackets in (e) and sub-para (f) inserted by HC 908, paras 38 and 39 as from 21 April 2011. Further amended by HC 1888, para 132 as from 6 April 2012.

[74B.   No points will be awarded for a Certificate of Sponsorship unless:
(a)   the job that the Certificate of Sponsorship Checking Service entry records that the person is being sponsored to do appears on:
    (i)   the list of occupations skilled to National Qualifications Framework level 6 or above, as stated in [the Codes of Practice in Appendix J], or
    (ii)   [one of the following creative sector occupations skilled to National Framework Qualifications Framework level 4 or above:
        (1)   3411 Artists,
        (2)   3412 Authors, writers and translators,
        (3)   3413 Actors, entertainers and presenters,
        (4)   3414 Dancers and choreographers, or
        (5)   3422 Product, clothing and related designers, or]]
(b)   :
    (i)   the applicant is applying for leave to remain,
    (ii)   the applicant previously had leave as a Tier 2 (Intra-Company Transfer) Migrant under the Rules in place between 6 April 2011 and [13 June 2012], and has not since been granted leave to remain in any other route, or entry clearance or leave to enter in any route, and
    (iii)   the job that the Certificate of Sponsorship Checking Service entry records that the person is being sponsored to do appears on the list of occupations skilled to National Qualifications Framework level 4 or above, as stated in [the Codes of Practice in Appendix J,] . . .
(c)   :
    (i)   the applicant is applying for leave to remain as a Tier 2 (Intra-Company Transfer) Migrant in the Long Term Staff sub-category,
    (ii)   the applicant previously had leave as:
        (1)   a Tier 2 (Intra-Company Transfer) Migrant under the rules in place before 6 April 2011, or
        (2)   a Qualifying Work permit Holder,

and has not since been granted leave to remain in any other route, or entry clearance or leave to enter in any route, and

(iii)   the job that the Certificate of Sponsorship Checking Service entry records that the person is being sponsored to do appears on the list of occupations skilled to National Qualifications Framework level 3 or above, as stated in [the Codes of Practice in Appendix J,], or the applicant is a Senior Care Worker or an Established Entertainer as defined in paragraph 6 of these Rules[, or]]

(d) :

(i)   the applicant was last granted entry clearance or leave as a Tier 2 (Intra-Company Transfer) Migrant,

(ii)   the applicant is applying for leave to remain to work in the same occupation for the same Sponsor as in the application which led to his previous grant of leave,

(iii)   the Certificate of Sponsorship used in support of the applicant's previous application was assigned by the Sponsor before 6 April 2013, and

(iv)   the occupation fails to meet the required skill level in (a) to (c) above solely due to reclassification from the SOC 2000 system to the 2010 system.]

Note

This paragraph inserted by Cm 8337, para 5 as from 6 April 2012. Further amended by Cm 8423, paras 109–112 as from 20 July 2012. Further amended by HC 760, para 305 as from 13 December 2012. Word "or" deleted by HC 1138, para 117 as from 6 April 2014. Amended by HC 1138, para 118 as from 6 April 2014.

74C.

[(a)   if the applicant is applying as a Tier 2 (Intra-Company Transfer) Migrant in either the Short Term Staff or Long Term Staff sub-categories, no points will be awarded for a Certificate of Sponsorship unless:

(i)   the Certificate of Sponsorship Checking Service entry confirms that the applicant has been working for the Sponsor for at least 12 months as specified in paragraphs (b) and (c) below,

(ii)   the applicant provides, if requested to do so, the specified documents as set out in paragraph 74C-SD(a) below, unless he was last granted leave to work for the same Sponsor in the same sub-category as he is currently applying under. The application may be granted without these specified documents, but the Home Office reserves the right to request the specified documents, and to refuse applications if these documents are not received at the address specified in the request within 7 working days of the date of the request.

(b)   Throughout the 12 months referred to in paragraph (a)(i) above, the applicant must have been working for the Sponsor:

(i)   outside the UK, or

(ii)   in the UK, provided he had leave to work for the Sponsor as:

    (1)   a Tier 2 (Intra-Company Transfer) Migrant in either of the Short Term Staff or Long Term Staff sub-categories,

    (2)   a Tier 2 (Intra-Company Transfer) Migrant in the established staff sub-category under the rules in place before 6 April 2011,

    (3)   a Tier 2 (Intra-Company Transfer) Migrant under the rules in place before 6 April 2010,

    (4)   a Qualifying Work Permit Holder (provided that the work permit was granted because the holder was the subject of an Intra-Company Transfer), and/or

    (5)   a representative of an Overseas Business, and

(c)   The 12 months referred to in paragraph (a)(i) above is:

(i)   a continuous period of 12 months immediately prior to the date of application, or

(ii)   an aggregated period of at least 12 months within the 24 month period immediately prior to the date of application, if at some point within the 12 months preceding the date of application, the applicant has been:

    (1)   on maternity, paternity or adoption leave,

    (2)   on long-term sick leave lasting one month or longer, or

(3) working for the Sponsor in the UK as a Tier 2 (Intra-Company Transfer) Migrant in either of the Graduate Trainee or Skills Transfer sub-categories,

and if requested to provide the specified documents set out in paragraph 74C-SD(a) below, also provides, at the same time, the specified documents as set out in paragraph 74C-SD(c) below, or

(iii) an aggregated period of at least 12 months during the time the applicant has been continuously working for the Sponsor, if at some point within the 12 months preceding the date of application, the applicant has been working in the UK for the Sponsor lawfully under any other category of these Rules not listed in paragraph (b)(ii) above.]

Note

This paragraph inserted by HC 863, para 150 as from 14 June 2011. Further amended by Cm 8423, paras 113, 114 as from 20 July 2012. Amended by HC 1138, para 119 as from 6 April 2014.

[74C-SD (a) The specified documents in paragraph 74C(a) are:

(i) [Original formal payslips issued by the employer and showing the employer's name] covering the full specified period (The most recent payslip must be dated no earlier than 31 days before the date of the application);

(ii) [Other payslips] covering the full specified period (The most recent payslip must be dated no earlier than 31 days before the date of the application), accompanied by a letter from the Sponsor, on company headed paper and signed by a senior official, confirming the authenticity of the payslips;

(iii) Personal bank or building society statements covering the full specified period, which clearly show:
 (1) the applicant's name,
 (2) the account number,
 (3) the date of the statement (The most recent statement must be dated no earlier than 31 days before the date of the application),
 (4) the financial institution's name and logo, and
 (5) transactions by the Sponsor covering the full specified period; [or]

(iv) A building society pass book, which clearly shows:
 (1) the applicant's name,
 (2) the account number,
 (3) the financial institution's name and logo, and
 (4) transactions by the Sponsor covering the full specified period.

(b) If the applicant provides the bank or building society statements in (a)(iii):

(i) The statements must:
 (1) be printed on paper bearing the bank or building society's letterhead,
 (2) bear the official stamp of the bank on every page, or
 (3) be accompanied by a supporting letter from the issuing bank or building society, on company headed paper, confirming the authenticity of the statements provided;

(ii) The statements must not be mini-statements obtained from an Automated Teller Machine.

(c) The specified documents as evidence of periods of maternity, paternity or adoption leave, as required in paragraph 74C(b), are:

(i) The original full birth certificate or original full certificate of adoption (as appropriate) containing the names of the parents or adoptive parents of the child for whom the leave was taken, if this is available; and

(ii) At least one (or both, if the document in (i) is unavailable) of the following, if they are available:
 (1) An original letter from the applicant and his sponsor, on company headed paper, confirming the start and end dates of the applicant's leave,
 (2) One of the types of documents set out in (a) above, covering the entire period of leave, and showing the maternity, paternity or adoption payments.

and

(iii)   If the applicant cannot provide two of the types of specified document in (i) and (ii), at least one of the types of specified documents in either (i) or (ii), a full explanation of why the other documents cannot be provided, and at least one of the following specified documents, from an official source and which is independently verifiable:

    (1)   official adoption papers issued by the relevant authority,

    (2)   any relevant medical documents, or

    (3)   a relevant extract from a register of birth which is accompanied by an original letter from the issuing authority.

(d) The specified documents as evidence of periods of long term sick leave, as required in paragraph 74C(b), are:

(i)   An original letter from the applicant's Sponsor, on company headed paper, confirming the start and end dates of the applicant's leave, if this is available;

(ii)   One of the types of documents set out in (a) above, covering the entire period of leave, and showing the statutory sick pay and/or sick pay from health insurance, if these documents are available; and

(iii)   If the applicant cannot provide the specified documents in both (i) and (ii), the specified documents in either (i) or (ii), a full explanation of why the other documents cannot be provided, and any relevant medical documents, from an official source and which are independently verifiable.]

Note

This paragraph inserted by Cm 8423, paras 115 as from 20 July 2012. Amended by HC 628, paras 168–170 and if an applicant has made an application for entry clearance or leave before 1 October 2013, the application will be decided in accordance with the Rules in force on 30 September 2013.

74D.   [If the applicant is applying as a Tier 2 (Intra-Company Transfer) Migrant in the Graduate Trainee sub-category, no points will be awarded for a Certificate of Sponsorship unless:

(a)   the job that the Certificate of Sponsorship Checking service entry records that the person is being sponsored to do is part of a structured graduate training programme [with clearly defined progression towards a managerial or specialist role within the organisation,]

(b)   the Sponsor has assigned Certificates of Sponsorship to 5 applicants or fewer, including the applicant in question, under the Graduate Trainee sub-category in the current year, beginning [6 April and ending 5 April each year] and

(c)   [the Certificate of Sponsorship Checking Service entry confirms that the applicant has been working for the Sponsor outside the UK for a continuous period of 3 months immediately prior to the date of application and, if requested to do so, the applicant provides the specified documents in paragraph 74C-SD(a) above to prove this. The application may be granted without these specified documents, but the UK Border Agency reserves the right to request the specified documents, and to refuse applications if these documents are not received at the address specified in the request within 7 working days of the date of the request.]

Note

This paragraph inserted by HC 863, para 150 as from 6 April 2011. Words in square brackets substituted by Cm 8337, para 6 as from 6 April 2012. Sub-paras (a), (c) amended by Cm 8423, paras 116, 117 as from 20 July 2012.

74E.   [If the applicant is applying as a Tier 2 (Intra-Company Transfer) Migrant in the Skills Transfer subcategory, no points will be awarded for a Certificate of Sponsorship unless the job that the Certificate of Sponsorship Checking Service entry records that the person is being sponsored to do is for the sole purpose of transferring skills to or from the Sponsor's UK work environment. The appointment must be additional to staffing requirements, that is the role in the UK would not exist but for the need for skills transfer.]

Note

This paragraph inserted by HC 863, para 150 as from 6 April 2011.

74F. [An applicant cannot score points for a Certificate of Sponsorship from Table 11 if the job that the Certificate of Sponsorship Checking Service entry records that he is being sponsored to do is as a Sports person or a Minister of Religion.]

Note

This paragraph inserted by HC 863, para 150 as from 6 April 2011.

[**74G.** No points will be awarded for a Certificate of Sponsorship if the job that the Certificate of Sponsorship Checking Service entry records that the applicant is being sponsored to do amounts to:
(a) the hire of the applicant to a third party who is not the sponsor to fill a position with that party, whether temporary or permanent, or
(b) contract work to undertake an ongoing routine role or to provide an ongoing routine service for a third party who is not the sponsor,

regardless of the nature or length of any arrangement between the sponsor and the third party.]

Note

Inserted by HC 693, para 161 as from 6 November 2014, save that if an application has been made for entry clearance or leave to enter or remain before 6 November 2014, the application will be decided in accordance with the Rules in force on 5 November 2014.

[**74H.** No points will be awarded for a Certificate of Sponsorship if the Entry Clearance Officer or the Secretary of State has reasonable grounds to believe, notwithstanding that the applicant has provided the evidence required under the relevant provisions of Appendix A, that:
(a) the job as recorded by the Certificate of Sponsorship Checking Service is not a genuine vacancy, if the applicant is applying as a Tier 2 (Intra-Company Transfer) Migrant in either of the Short Term Staff or Long Term Staff subcategories, or
(b) the applicant is not appropriately qualified to do the job in question.]

Note

Inserted by HC 693, para 161 as from 6 November 2014, save that if an application has been made for entry clearance or leave to enter or remain before 6 November 2014, the application will be decided in accordance with the Rules in force on 5 November 2014.

[**74I.** To support the assessment in paragraph 74H, the Entry Clearance Officer or the Secretary of State may request additional information and evidence from the applicant or the Sponsor, and refuse the application if the information or evidence is not provided. Any requested documents must be received by the Entry Clearance Officer or the Secretary of State at the address specified in the request within 28 calendar days of the date the request is sent.]

Note

Inserted by HC 693, para 161 as from 6 November 2014, save that if an application has been made for entry clearance or leave to enter or remain before 6 November 2014, the application will be decided in accordance with the Rules in force on 5 November 2014.

[Appropriate salary

75. The points awarded for appropriate salary will be based on the applicant's gross annual salary to be paid by the Sponsor, as recorded in the Certificate of Sponsorship Checking Service entry to which the applicant's Certificate of Sponsorship reference number relates, subject to the following conditions:
(i) Points will be awarded based on basic pay (excluding overtime);
(ii) Allowances will be included in the salary for the awarding of points where they are part of the guaranteed salary package and:
  (1) would be paid to a local settled worker in similar circumstances, or
  (2) are paid to cover the additional cost of living in the UK;
(iii) Where allowances are made available solely for the purpose of accommodation, they will only be included up to a value of:

(1)   40% of the total salary package for which points are being awarded, if the applicant is applying in either the Short Term Staff, Graduate Trainee or skills Transfer sub-categories, or

(2)   30% of the total salary package for which points are being awarded, if the applicant is applying in the Long Term Staff sub-category;

(iv)   [Other allowances and benefits, such as bonus or incentive pay, employer pension contributions, and allowances] to cover business expenses, including (but not limited to) travel to and from the sending country, will not be included.]

(v)   [If the applicant has exchanged some of his UK employment rights for shares as an employee-owner, the value of those shares will not be included.]

Note

This paragraph inserted by HC 863, para 150 as from 6 April 2011. Amended by HC 760, para 306 as from 13 December 2012.

[**75A.** No points will be awarded if the salary referred to in paragraph 75 above is less than [£41,000] per year where the applicant is applying in the Long Term Staff sub-category, unless the applicant is applying for leave to remain and previously had leave as:

(i)   a Qualifying Work Permit Holder, or

(ii)   a Tier 2 (Intra-Company Transfer) Migrant under the Rules in place before 6 April 2011.

and has not been granted entry clearance in this or any other route since that grant of leave.]

Note

This paragraph substituted by HC 760, para 307 as from 13 December 2012. Amended by HC 1138, para 120 and if an applicant has made an application for entry clearance or leave on or after 6 April 2014 using a Certificate of Sponsorship that was assigned to him by his Sponsor before 6 April 2014, the application will be decided in accordance with the rules in force on 5 April 2014.

75B. [No points will be awarded if the salary referred to in paragraph 75 above is less than [£24,500] per year where the applicant is applying in the Short Term Staff, Graduate Trainee or Skills Transfer sub-categories, unless the applicant is applying for leave to remain and has, or last had entry clearance, leave to enter or leave to remain as a Tier 2 (Intra-Company Transfer) Migrant under the Rules in place before 6 April 2011.]

Note

This paragraph inserted by HC 863, para 150 as from 6 April 2011. Amended by HC 1138, para 121 and if an applicant has made an application for entry clearance or leave on or after 6 April 2014 using a Certificate of Sponsorship that was assigned to him by his Sponsor before 6 April 2014, the application will be decided in accordance with the rules in force on 5 April 2014.

75C. [No points will be awarded if the salary referred to in paragraph 75 above is less than the appropriate rate for the job as stated in [the Codes of Practice in Appendix J], unless the applicant is an Established Entertainer as defined in paragraph 6 of these Rules.]

Note

This paragraph inserted by HC 863, para 150 as from 6 April 2011. Words "the Codes of Practice in Appendix J" substituted by Cm 8423, para 118 as from 20 July 2012.

75D. [Where the applicant is paid hourly, the appropriate salary consideration will be based on earnings up to a maximum of 48 hours a week, even if the applicant works for longer than this. For example, an applicant who works 60 hours a week for £8 per hour be considered to have a salary of £19,968 (8x48x52) and not £25,960 (8x60x52), and will therefore not be awarded points for appropriate salary.]

Note

This paragraph inserted by HC 863, para 150 as from 6 April 2011.

75E. [No points will be awarded for appropriate salary if the applicant does not provide a valid Certificate of Sponsorship reference number with his application.]

Note

This paragraph inserted by HC 863, para 150 as from 6 April 2011.

[Attributes for Tier 2 (General) Migrants

76. An applicant applying for entry or leave to remain as a Tier 2 (General) Migrant must score 50 points for attributes.]

Note

This paragraph inserted by HC 863, para 150 as from 6 April 2011.

76A. [Available points for entry clearance or leave to remain are shown in Table 11A.]

Note

This paragraph inserted by HC 863, para 150 as from 6 April 2011.

76B. [Notes to accompany Table 11A appear below the table.]

Note

This paragraph inserted by HC 863, para 150 as from 6 April 2011.

[Table 11A

Certificate of Sponsorship	Points	Appropriate salary	Points
Job offer passes Resident Labour Market Test	30	Appropriate salary	20
Resident Labour Market Test exemption applies	30		
Continuing to work in the same occupation for the same Sponsor	30		

Notes

Certificate of Sponsorship

77. Points may only be scored for one entry in the Certificate of Sponsorship column.]

Note

This paragraph inserted by HC 863, para 150 as from 6 April 2011.

77A. [In order to obtain points for a Certificate of Sponsorship, the applicant must provide a valid Certificate of Sponsorship reference number.]

Note

This paragraph inserted by HC 863, para 150 as from 6 April 2011.

77B. [The only Certificates of Sponsorship to be allocated to Sponsors for applicants to be sponsored as Tier 2 (General) Migrants [. . .] are:

(a) Certificates of Sponsorship to be assigned to applicants . . . as a Tier 2 (General) Migrant, as allocated to Sponsors under the Tier 2 (General) limit, which is set out in paragraphs 80 to 84A below.

(b) Certificates of Sponsorship to be assigned to [specified applicants for leave to remain as a Tier 2 (General) Migrant, as set out in paragraph 77D of Appendix A,]

(c) Certificates of Sponsorship to be assigned to an applicant to do a job for which the gross annual salary (including such allowances as are specified as acceptable for this purpose [in paragraph 79 of this Appendix]) is [£153,500 (or £152,100, if the recruitment took place before 6 April 2014)].

Note

This paragraph inserted by HC 863, para 150 as from 6 April 2011. Words in square brackets substituted and deleted by Cm 8337, paras 7–9 as from 6 April 2012. Amended by HC 628, para 171 and if an applicant has made an application for entry clearance or leave before 1 October 2013, the application will be decided in accordance with the Rules in force on 30 September 2013. Amended by HC 1138, para 122 as from 6 April 2014.

77C. [A Certificate of Sponsorship reference number will only be considered to be valid if:
(a)   the number supplied links to a Certificate of Sponsorship Checking Service entry that names the applicant as the migrant and confirms that the Sponsor is sponsoring him as a Tier 2 (General) Migrant,
(b)   the Sponsor assigned that reference number to the migrant no more than 3 months after the Sponsor was allocated the Certificate of Sponsorship, if the Certificate of Sponsorship was allocated to the Sponsor under the Tier 2 (General) limit,
(c)   the Sponsor assigned that reference number to the migrant no more than 3 months before the application for entry clearance or leave to remain is made,
(d)   the application for entry clearance or leave to remain is made no more than 3 months before the start of the employment as stated on the Certificate of Sponsorship,
(e)   [the migrant must not previously have applied for entry clearance, leave to enter or leave to remain using the same Certificate of Sponsorship reference number, if that application was either approved or refused (Not rejected as an invalid application, declared void or withdrawn),]
(f)   that reference number must not have been withdrawn or cancelled by the Sponsor or by the UK Border Agency since it was assigned, including where it has been cancelled by the UK Border Agency due to having been used in a previous application[, and
(g)   the Sponsor is an A-rated Sponsor, unless:
        (1)   the application is for leave to remain, and
        (2)   the applicant has, or was last granted, leave as a Tier 2 (General) Migrant, a Jewish Agency Employee, a Member of the Operational Ground Staff of an Overseas-owned Airline, a Representative of an Overseas Newspaper, News Agency or Broadcasting Organisation, or a Qualifying Work Permit Holder, and
        (3)   the applicant is applying to work for the same employer named on the Certificate of Sponsorship or Work Permit document which led to his last grant of leave or, in the case of an applicant whose last grant of leave was as a Jewish Agency Employee, a Member of the Operational Ground Staff of an Overseas-owned Airline, a Representative of an Overseas Newspaper, News Agency or Broadcasting Organisation, the same employer for whom the applicant was working or stated he was intending to work when last granted leave.]

Note

This paragraph inserted by HC 863, para 150 as from 6 April 2011. Words in square brackets in (e) deleted by HC 908, para 40 as from 21 April 2011. Words in square brackets in (f) and sub-para (g) inserted by HC 908, paras 41 and 42 as from 21 April 2011. Sub-paragraph (e) substituted by HC 1888, para 135 as from 6 April 2012.

77D. [No points will be awarded for a Certificate of Sponsorship unless:
(a)   in the case of a Certificate of Sponsorship which was allocated to the Sponsor under the Tier 2 (General) limit, the number supplied links to a Certificate of Sponsorship Checking Service entry which contains the same job and at least the same salary details as stated in the Sponsor's application for that Certificate of Sponsorship,
(b)   in the case of a Certificate of Sponsorship which was not allocated to the Sponsor under the Tier 2 (General) limit:
        [(i)   the applicant:
                (1)   is applying for leave to remain, and

(2)   does not have, or was not last granted, entry clearance, leave to enter or leave to remain as the Partner of a Relevant Points Based System Migrant,

    or]

(ii)   the number supplied links to a Certificate of Sponsorship Checking Service entry which shows that the applicant's gross annual salary (including such allowances as are specified as acceptable for this purpose in paragraph 79 of this Appendix) to be paid by the Sponsor is [£153,500 (or £152,100, if the recruitment took place before 6 April 2014)].

Note

This paragraph inserted by HC 863, para 150 as from 6 April 2011. Sub-paragraph (b)(i) substituted by Cm 8337, para 10 as from 6 April 2012. Amended by HC 1138, para 123 as from 6 April 2014. Further amended by HC 693, para 162 as from 6 November 2014, save that if an application has been made for entry clearance or leave to enter or remain before 6 November 2014, the application will be decided in accordance with the Rules in force on 5 November 2014.

[77E.   No points will be awarded for a Certificate of Sponsorship unless

(a)   the job that the Certificate of Sponsorship Checking Service entry records that the person is being sponsored to do appears on

    (i)   the list of occupations skilled to National Qualifications Framework level 6 or above, as stated in [the Codes of Practice in Appendix J], or

    (ii)   [one of the following creative sector occupations skilled to National Qualifications Framework level 4 or above:

        (1)   3411 Artists,

        (2)   3412 Authors, writers and translators,

        (3)   3413 Actors, entertainers and presenters,

        (4)   3414 Dancers and choreographers, or

        (5)   3422 Product, clothing and related designers, or]

(b)   the job that the Certificate of Sponsorship Checking Service entry records that the person is being sponsored to do is skilled to National Qualifications Framework level 4 or above, and appears on [the Shortage Occupation List in Appendix K], or

(c)   :

    (i)   the applicant is applying for leave to remain,

    (ii)   the applicant previously had leave as a Tier 2 (General) Migrant or a Qualifying Work Permit Holder, and has not since been granted leave to remain in any other route, or entry clearance or leave to enter in any route,

    (iii)   at the time a Certificate of Sponsorship or Work Permit which led to a grant of leave in (ii) was issued, the job referred to in that Certificate of Sponsorship or Work Permit appeared on [the Shortage Occupation List in Appendix K,] and

    (iv)   the job that the Certificate of Sponsorship Checking Service entry records that the person is being sponsored to do in his current application is the same job referred to in (iii), for either the same or a different employer, or

(d)   :

    (i)   the applicant is applying for leave to remain,

    (ii)   the applicant previously had leave as a Tier 2 (General) Migrant under the Rules in place between 6 April 2011 and [13 June 2012], and has not since been granted leave to remain in any other route, or entry clearance or leave to enter in any route, and

    (iii)   the job that the Certificate of Sponsorship Checking Service entry records that the person is being sponsored to do appears on the list of occupations skilled to National Qualifications Framework level 4 or above, as stated in [the Codes of Practice in Appendix J], or

(e)   :

    (i)   the applicant is applying for leave to remain,

    (ii)   the applicant previously had leave as:

        (1)   a Tier 2 (General) Migrant under the rules in place before 6 April 2011,

        (2)   a Qualifying Work Permit Holder,

> (3)   a Representative of an Overseas Newspaper, News Agency or Broadcasting Organisation,
>
> (4)   a Member of the Operational Ground Staff of an Overseas-owned Airline
>
> (5)   a Jewish Agency Employee
>
> and has not since been granted leave to remain in any other route, or entry clearance or leave to enter in any route, and

(iii)   the job that the Certificate of Sponsorship Checking Service entry records that the person is being sponsored to do appears on the list of occupations skilled to National Qualifications Framework level 3 or above, as stated in [the Codes of Practice in Appendix J,] or the applicant is Senior Care Worker or an Established Entertainer as defined in paragraph 6 of these Rules.]

(f)   :

(i)   the applicant was last granted as a Tier 2 (General) Migrant,

(ii)   the applicant is applying for leave to remain to work in the same occupation for the same Sponsor as in the application which led to his previous grant of leave,

(iii)   the Certificate of Sponsorship used in support of the applicant's previous application was assigned by the Sponsor before 6 April 2013, and

(iv)   the occupation fails to meet the required skill level (a) to (e) above solely due to classification from the SOC 2000 system to the SOC 2010 system.]

Note

Substituted by Cm 8337, para 11 as from 14 June 2012. Further amended by Cm 8423, paras 119–124 as from 20 July 2012. Further amended by HC 760, para 308 as from 13 December 2012.

77F. [An applicant cannot score points for a Certificate of Sponsorship from Table 11A if the job that the Certificate of Sponsorship Checking Service entry records that he is being sponsored to do is as a Sports person or a Minister of Religion.]

Note

This paragraph inserted by HC 863, para 150 as from 6 April 2011.

[**77G.**   No points will be awarded for a Certificate of Sponsorship if the job that the Certificate of Sponsorship Checking Service entry records that the applicant is being sponsored to do amounts to:

(a)   the hire of the applicant to a third party who is not the sponsor to fill a position with that party, whether temporary or permanent, or

(b)   contract work to undertake an ongoing routine role or to provide an ongoing routine service for a third party who is not the sponsor,

regardless of the nature or length of any arrangement between the sponsor and the third party.]

Note

Inserted by HC 693, para 163 as from 6 November 2014, save that if an application has been made for entry clearance or leave to enter or remain before 6 November 2014, the application will be decided in accordance with the Rules in force on 5 November 2014.

[**77H.**   No points will be awarded for a Certificate of Sponsorship if the Entry Clearance Officer or the Secretary of State has reasonable grounds to believe, notwithstanding that the applicant has provided the evidence required under the relevant provisions of Appendix A, that:

(a)   the job as recorded by the Certificate of Sponsorship Checking Service is not a genuine vacancy,

(b)   the applicant is not appropriately qualified or registered to do the job in question (or will not be, by the time they begin the job), or

(c)   the stated requirements of the job as recorded by the Certificate of Sponsorship Checking Service and in any advertisements for the job are inappropriate for the job on offer and / or have been tailored to exclude resident workers from being recruited.]

Note

Inserted by HC 693, para 163 as from 6 November 2014, save that if an application has been made for entry clearance or leave to enter or remain before 6 November 2014, the application will be decided in accordance with the Rules in force on 5 November 2014.

[77I. To support the assessment in paragraph 77H(b), if the applicant is not yet appropriately qualified or registered to do the job in question, he must provide evidence with his application showing that he can reasonably be expected to obtain the appropriate qualifications or registrations by the time he begins the job, for example, a letter from the relevant body providing written confirmation that the applicant has registered to sit the relevant examinations.]

Note

Inserted by HC 693, para 163 as from 6 November 2014, save that if an application has been made for entry clearance or leave to enter or remain before 6 November 2014, the application will be decided in accordance with the Rules in force on 5 November 2014.

[77J. To support the assessment in paragraph 77H(a)-(c), the Entry Clearance Officer or the Secretary of State may request additional information and evidence from the applicant or the Sponsor, and refuse the application if the information or evidence is not provided. Any requested documents must be received by the Entry Clearance Officer or the Secretary of State at the address specified in the request within 28 calendar days of the date the request is sent.]

Note

Inserted by HC 693, para 163 as from 6 November 2014, save that if an application has been made for entry clearance or leave to enter or remain before 6 November 2014, the application will be decided in accordance with the Rules in force on 5 November 2014.

[Job offer passes Resident Labour Market Test

78. Points will only be awarded for a job offer that passes the Resident Labour Market Test:
(a)   the Sponsor has advertised (or had advertised on its behalf) the job as set out in Tables 11B and 11C below; and,
(b)   The advertisements have stated:
    (i)   the job title,
    (ii)   the main duties and responsibilities of the job (job description),
    (iii)   the location of the job,
    (iv)   an indication of the salary package or salary range or terms on offer,
    (v)   the skills, qualifications and experience required for the job, and
    (vi)   the closing date for applications, unless it is part of the Sponsor's rolling recruitment programme, in which case the advertisement should show the period of the recruitment programme; and
(c)   The advertisements were published in English (or Welsh if the job is based in Wales); and
(d)   The Sponsor can show that no suitable settled worker is available to fill the job unless the job is in a PhD-level occupation listed in Appendix J. Settled workers will not be considered unsuitable on the basis that they lack qualifications, experience or skills (including language skills) that were not specifically required in the job advertisement; and
(e)   The Certificate of Sponsorship Checking Service entry contains full details of when and where the job was advertised, and any advertisement reference numbers, including the Universal Jobmatch (or other Jobcentre Plus online service) or JobCentre Online vacancy reference number where relevant.

[Table 11B: Advertising methods and duration which satisfy the Resident Labour Market Test

Type of job	Methods of advertising / recruitment	Duration / timing of advertising
New graduate jobs or internships	• University milkround visits to at least 3 UK universities (or all UK universities which provide the relevant course, whichever is the lower number), • At least one of the following websites: – www.jobs.ac.uk, – www.milkround.com, – www.prospects.ac.uk, or – www.targetjobs.co.uk and • At least one other medium listed in Table 11C	At least 28 days within the **4 years** immediately before the Sponsor assigned the Certificate of Sponsorship to the applicant
Pupillages for trainee barristers	• At least two media (or one medium if the job was advertised before 6 April 2013) listed in Table 11C	At least 28 days within the **2 years** immediately before the Sponsor assigned the Certificate of Sponsorship to the applicant
Jobs in PhD-level occupations as listed in Appendix J	• At least two media (or one medium if the job was advertised before 6 April 2013) listed in Table 11C	At least 28 days within the **1 year** immediately before the Sponsor assigned the Certificate of Sponsorship to the applicant
Jobs where the appropriate salary, as determined by paragraphs 79 to 79D of Appendix A, is [at least £71,600 per year (or £71,000 per year if the job was advertised before 6 April 2014)] or there is a stock exchange disclosure requirement	• At least two media (or one medium if the job was advertised before 6 April 2013) listed in Table 11C	At least 28 days within the **6 months** immediately before the Sponsor assigned the Certificate of Sponsorship to the applicant
Creative sector jobs covered by Table 9 of Appendix J	• As set out in Table 9 of Appendix J	As set out in Table 9 of Appendix J
Orchestral musicians	• Universal Jobmatch (or other Jobcentre Plus online service) for jobs based in England, Scotland or Wales, or JobCentre Online for jobs based in Northern Ireland, and	At least 28 days within the **2 years** immediately before the Sponsor assigned the Certificate of Sponsorship to the applicant

Type of job	Methods of advertising / recruitment	Duration / timing of advertising
	• At least one other medium listed in Table 11C	
Positions in the NHS where the Resident Labour Market Test includes advertising on NHS Jobs between 19 November 2012 and [6 April 2015]	• NHS Jobs	At least 28 days within the **6 months** immediately before the Sponsor assigned the Certificate of Sponsorship to the applicant
All other jobs	• Universal Jobmatch (or other Jobcentre Plus online service) for jobs based in England, Scotland or Wales, or JobCentre Online for jobs based in Northern Ireland, and	At least 28 days within the **6 months** immediately before the Sponsor assigned the Certificate of Sponsorship to the applicant
	• At least one other medium listed in Table 11C	

Note

This table amended by HC 628, para 172 and if an applicant has made an application for entry clearance or leave before 1 October 2013, the application will be decided in accordance with the Rules in force on 30 September 2013. Amended by HC 1138, para 124 as from 6 April 2014. Amended by HC 1138, para 125 as from 6 April 2014. Further amended by HC 693, para 164 as from 6 November 2014, save that if an application has been made for entry clearance or leave to enter or remain before 6 November 2014, the application will be decided in accordance with the Rules in force on 5 November 2014.

Table 11C: Advertising media which satisfy the Resident Labour Market Test

Type of medium	Criteria for suitable media
Newspaper	Must be: • marketed throughout the UK or throughout the whole of the devolved nation in which the job is located, and • published at least once a week
Professional journal	Must be: • available nationally through retail outlets or through subscription, • published at least once a month, and • related to the nature of the job i.e. a relevant trade journal, official journal of a professional occupational body, or subject-specific publication
Website	Must be one of the following: • Universal Jobmatch (or other Jobcentre Plus online service), for jobs based in England, Scotland or Wales, • JobCentre Online, for jobs based in Northern Ireland, • an online version of a newspaper or professional journal which would satisfy the criteria above,

Type of medium	Criteria for suitable media
	• the website of a prominent professional or recruitment organisation, which does not charge a fee to jobseekers to view job advertisements or to apply for jobs via those advertisements, or • if the Sponsor is a multinational organisation or has over 250 permanent employees in the UK, the Sponsor's own website]

Note

Tables 11B, 11C substituted by HC 1039, para 173 as from 6 April 2013 if an applicant has made an application for entry clearance or leave on or after 6 April 2013 using a Certificate of Sponsorship that was assigned to him by his Sponsor before 6 April 2013, the application will be decided in accordance with the rules in force on 5 April 2013.

Resident Labour Market Test exemption applies

Shortage occupation

78A. In order for a Resident Labour Market Test exemption to apply for a job offer in a shortage occupation:
(a) the job must, at the time the Certificate of Sponsorship was assigned to the applicant, have appeared on the shortage occupation list in Appendix K,
(b) in all cases, contracted working hours must be for at least 30 hours a week, and,
(c) in all cases, if the UK Border Agency list of shortage occupations indicates that the job appears on the 'Scotland only' shortage occupation list, the job offer must be for employment in which the applicant will be working at a location in Scotland.

Post-Study Work

78B. In order for a Resident Labour Market Test exemption to apply for post-study work:
(a) the applicant must be applying for leave to remain,
(b) the applicant must have, or have last been granted, entry clearance, leave to enter or leave to remain as:
(1) [a Tier 1 (Graduate Entrepreneur) Migrant.]
(2) a Tier 1 (Post-Study Work) Migrant,
(3) a Participant in the International Graduates Scheme (or its predecessor, the Science and Engineering Graduates Scheme),
(4) a Participant in the Fresh Talent: Working in Scotland Scheme,
(5) a Tier 4 Migrant,
(6) a Student,
(7) a Student Nurse,
(8) a Student Re-Sitting an Examination,
(9) a Person Writing Up a Thesis,
(10) an Overseas Qualified Nurse or Midwife,
(11) a Postgraduate Doctor or Dentist, or,
(12) a Student Union Sabbatical Officer, and
(c) Where (b)[(5) to (12)] apply, the applicant must meet the requirements of paragraph 245HD(d) of these Rules.

Note

Amended by HC 628, paras 173–175 and if an applicant has made an application for entry clearance or leave before 1 October 2013, the application will be decided in accordance with the Rules in force on 30 September 2013.

OTHER EXEMPTIONS

78C. In order for another Resident Labour Market Test exemption to apply, either:
(a)   the Certificate of Sponsorship Checking Service entry must show that the applicant's gross annual salary (including such allowances as are specified as acceptable for this paragraph in paragraph 79 of this appendix) to be paid by the Sponsor is [£153,500 (or £152,100, if the recruitment took place before 6 April 2014)] or higher; or
(b)   [the job offer must be in a supernumerary research position where the applicant has been issued a scientific research Award or Fellowship by an external organisation which is not the Sponsor, meaning that the role is over and above the Sponsor's normal requirements and if the applicant was not there, the role would not be filled by anyone else; or]
(c)   the job offer must be to continue working as a Doctor or Dentist in training, under the same NHS Training Number which was assigned to the applicant for previous lawful employment as a Doctor or Dentist in Training in the UK; or
(d)   the job offer must be as a Doctor in Speciality Training where the applicant's salary and the costs of his training are being met by the government of another country under an agreement with that country and the United Kingdom Government[; or]
[(e)   the job offer must be to resume a post in a Higher Education Institution, working for the same Sponsor as in a previous grant of entry clearance or leave to remain as a Tier 2 (General) Migrant, where the break in employment is due solely to a period of academic leave;]

and the Certificate of Sponsorship Checking Service entry must provide full details why an exemption applies.]

Note

Sub-para (b) substituted by HC 244, para 22 as from 1 July 2013: if an applicant has made an application for entry clearance or leave using a Certificate of Sponsorship that was assigned to him by his Sponsor before 1 July 2013, the application will be decided in accordance with the rules in force on 30 June 2013. Amended by HC 1138, para 126 as from 6 April 2014. Amended by HC 1138, para 127 as from 6 April 2014. Amended by HC 1138, para 128 as from 6 April 2014.

[Continuing to work in the [same occupation] for the same Sponsor

78D. In order for the applicant to be awarded points for continuing to work in the [same occupation] for the same Sponsor:
(a)   the applicant must be applying for leave to remain,
(b)   the applicant must have [, or have last been granted,] entry clearance or leave to remain as:
    (i)   a Tier 2 (General) Migrant,
    (ii)   a Qualifying Work Permit Holder,
    (iii)   a Representative of an Overseas Newspaper, News Agency or Broadcasting Organisation,
    (iv)   a Member of the Operational Ground Staff of an Overseas-owned Airline or
    (v)   a Jewish Agency Employee,
(c)   the Sponsor must be the same employer:
    (i)   as the Sponsor on the previous application that was granted, in the case of an applicant whose last grant of leave was as a Tier 2 (General) Migrant,
    (ii)   that the work permit was issued to, in the case of an applicant whose last grant of leave was as a Qualifying Work Permit Holder,
    (iii)   for whom the applicant was working or stated he was intending to work when last granted leave, in the case of an applicant whose last grant of leave was a Representative of an Overseas Newspaper, News Agency or Broadcasting Organisation, a Member of the Operational Ground Staff of an Overseas-owned Airline, or a Jewish Agency Employee.
(d)   the job that the Certificate of Sponsorship Checking Service entry records the applicant as having been engaged to do must be the [same occupation]:

(i)   in respect of which the Certificate of Sponsorship that led to the previous grant was issued, in the case of an applicant whose last grant of leave was as a Tier 2 (General) Migrant,

(ii)   in respect of which the previous work permit was issued, in the case of an applicant whose last grant of leave was as a Qualifying Permit Holder, or

(iii)   that the applicant was doing, or intended to do, when he received his last grant of leave, in the case of an applicant whose last grant of leave was a Representative of an Overseas Newspaper, News Agency or Broadcasting Organisation, a Member of the Operational Ground Staff of an Overseas-owned Airline, or a Jewish Agency Employee.]

(iv)   [If the applicant has exchanged some of his UK employment rights for shares as an employee-owner, the value of those shares will not be included.]

Note

This paragraph inserted by HC 863, para 150 as from 6 April 2011. Amended by HC 693, para 165 as from 6 November 2014, save that if an application has been made for entry clearance or leave to enter or remain before 6 November 2014, the application will be decided in accordance with the Rules in force on 5 November 2014.

[Appropriate salary

79.   The points awarded for appropriate salary will be based on the applicant's gross annual salary to be paid by the Sponsor, as recorded in the Certificate of Sponsorship Checking Service entry to which the applicant's Certificate of Sponsorship reference number relates, subject to the following conditions:

(i)   Points will be awarded based on basic pay (excluding overtime);

(ii)   Allowances, such as London weighting, will be included in the salary for the awarding of points where they are part of the guaranteed salary package and would be paid to a local settled worker in similar circumstances;

(iii)   Other allowances and benefits, such as bonus or incentive pay, [employer pension contributions,] travel and subsistence (including travel to and from the applicant's home country), will not be included.]

(iv)   [If the applicant has exchanges some of his UK employment rights for shares as an employee-owner, the value of those shares will not be included.]

Note

This paragraph inserted by HC 863, para 150 as from 6 April 2011. Further amended by HC 760, para 312 as from 13 December 2012. Sub-para (iv) inserted by HC 1039, para 177 as from 6 April 2013.

[**79A.**   No points will be awarded if the salary referred to in paragraph 79 above is less than £20,500 per year, unless:

(a)   the applicant:

     (i)   is applying for leave to remain, and

     (ii)   previously had leave as:

         (1)   a Qualifying Work Permit Holder,

         (2)   a Representative of an Overseas Newspaper, News Agency or Broadcasting Organisation,

         (3)   a Member of the operational Ground Staff of an Overseas-owned Airline,

         (4)   a Jewish Agency Employee, or

         (5)   a Tier 2 (General) Migrant under the Rules in place before 6 April 2011; and

     (iii)   has not been granted entry clearance in this or any other route since that grant of leave; or

(b)   the Certificate of Sponsorship checking service entry records that the applicant:

     (i)   obtained a Nursing and Midwifery Council permission before 30 March 2015 to undertake the Overseas Nursing Programme or the Adaptation to Midwifery Programme;

     (ii)   is being sponsored as a nurse or midwife in a supervised practice placement approved by the Nursing and Midwifery Council;

(iii)   will continue to be sponsored as a registered nurse or midwife by the Sponsor after achieving Nursing and Midwifery Council registration;, and

(iv)   will be paid at least £20,500 per year once that registration is achieved, and the applicant provides evidence of the above, if requested to do so.]

Note

This paragraph is substituted by HC 1039, para 178 as from 6 April 2013 but if an applicant has made an application for entry clearance or leave on or after 6 April 2013 using a Certificate of Sponsorship that was assigned to him by his Sponsor before 6 April 2013, the application will be decided in accordance with the rules in force on 5 April 2013. Word in Appendix paragraph 79A and (b) substituted by HC 1138, paras 129, 130 as from 5 April 2014. Substituted by HC 693, para 166 as from 6 November 2014, save that if an application has been made for entry clearance or leave to enter or remain before 6 November 2014, the application will be decided in accordance with the Rules in force on 5 November 2014.

79B.   [No points will be awarded for appropriate salary if the salary referred to in paragraph 79 above is less than the appropriate rate for the job as stated in [the Codes of Practice in Appendix J,] unless the applicant is an Established Entertainer as defined in paragraph 6 of these Rules.]

Note

This paragraph inserted by HC 863, para 150 as from 6 April 2011. Words "the Codes of Practice in Appendix J," substituted by Cm 8423, para 127 as from 20 July 2012.

79C.   [Where the applicant is paid hourly, the appropriate salary consideration will be based on earnings up to a maximum of 48 hours a week, even if the applicant works for longer than this. For example, an applicant who works 60 hours a week for £8 per hour be considered to have a salary of £19,968 (8x48x52) and not £25,960 (8x60x52), and will therefore not be awarded points for appropriate salary.]

Note

This paragraph inserted by HC 863, para 150 as from 6 April 2011.

79D.   [No points will be awarded for appropriate salary if the applicant does not provide a valid Certificate of Sponsorship reference number with his application.]

Note

This paragraph inserted by HC 863, para 150 as from 6 April 2011. Amended by HC 1138, para 129 and if an applicant has made an application for entry clearance or leave on or after 6 April 2014 using a Certificate of Sponsorship that was assigned to him by his Sponsor before 6 April 2014, the application will be decided in accordance with the rules in force on 5 April 2014. Amended by HC 1138, para 130 and if an applicant has made an application for entry clearance or leave on or after 6 April 2014 using a Certificate of Sponsorship that was assigned to him by his Sponsor before 6 April 2014, the application will be decided in accordance with the rules in force on 5 April 2014.

[Tier 2 (General) limit

Overview

80.   The Secretary of State shall be entitled to limit the number of Certificates of Sponsorship available to be allocated to Sponsors in any specific period under the Tier 2 (General) limit referred to in paragraph 77B(a) above;]

Note

This paragraph inserted by HC 863, para 150 as from 6 April 2011.

[**80A.**   The Tier 2 (General) limit is 20,700 Certificates of Sponsorship in each year (beginning on 6 April and ending on 5 April).]

Note

This paragraph substituted by Cm 8337, para 12 as from 6 April 2012.

[**80B.**   The process by which Certificates of Sponsorship shall be allocated to Sponsors under the Tier 2 (General) limit is set out in paragraphs 80C to 84A and [Table 11D].]

Note

This paragraph inserted by HC 863, para 150 as from 6 April 2011.

80C. [A Sponsor must apply to the Secretary of State for a Certificate of Sponsorship.]

Note

This paragraph inserted by HC 863, para 150 as from 6 April 2011.

80D. [Available points for an application for a Certificate of Sponsorship are shown in Table [11D]. No application will be granted unless it scores a minimum of 30 points under the heading "Type of Job" and a minimum of 2 points under the heading "Salary on Offer".]

Note

This paragraph inserted by HC 863, para 150 as from 6 April 2011.

80E. [Notes to accompany Table [11D] appear below the table.]

Note

This paragraph inserted by HC 863, para 150 as from 6 April 2011.

[Table 11D
Applications for Certificates of Sponsorship under the Tier 2 (General) limit

Type of job	Points	Salary on offer	Points
Shortage Occupation	75	[[£20,500]-£20,999.99]	2
PhD-level occupation code and job passes Resident Labour Market Test	50	£21,000-£21,999.99	3
Job passes Resident Labour Market Test [or an exemption applies as set out in [paragraphs 78B or 78C]]	30	£22,000-£22,999.99	4
		£23,000-£23,999.99	5
		£24,000-£24,999.99	6
		£25,000-£25,999.99	7
		£26,000-£26,999.99	8
		£27,000-£27,999.99	9
		£28,000-£31,999.99	10
		£32,000-£45,999.99	15
		£46,000-£74,999.99	20
		£75,000-£99,999.99	25
		[£100,000-[£153,499.99]]	30

Note

This paragraph amended by HC 628, para 176 and if an applicant has made an application for entry clearance or leave before 1 October 2013, the application will be decided in accordance with the Rules in force on 30 September 2013. Amended by HC 1138, para 131 shall apply to all applications decided on or after 6 April 2014. Amended by HC 1138, para 132 shall apply to all applications decided on or after 6 April 2014.

Notes

81. Points may only be scored for one entry in each column.]

Note

This paragraph inserted by HC 863, para 150 as from 6 April 2011.

[**81A.** No points will be awarded under the heading "Type of Job" unless the job described in the sponsor's application for a Certificate of Sponsorship:

(a) appears on:
    (i) the list of occupations skilled to National Qualifications Framework level 6 or above, as stated in [the Codes of Practice in Appendix J,] or
    (ii) [one of the following creative sector occupations skilled to National Qualifications Framework level 4 or above:
        (1) 3411 Artists,
        (2) 3412 Authors, writers and translators,
        (3) 3413 Actors, entertainers and presenters
        (4) 3414 Dancers and choreographers, or
        (5) 3422 Product, clothing and related designers, or]
(b) is skilled to National Qualifications Framework level 4 or above, and appears on [the Shortage Occupation List in Appendix K] published by the UK Border Agency.]

Note

Substituted by Cm 8337, para 13 as from 14 June 2012. Further amended by Cm 8423, paras 128–130 as from 20 July 2012.

81B. [In order for the Sponsor's application to be awarded points for a job in a shortage occupation, the job must, at the time the application for a Certificate of Sponsorship is decided, appear on [the Shortage Occupation List in Appendix K,] and contracted working hours must be for at least 30 hours a week. Furthermore, if the UK Border Agency list of shortage occupations indicates that the job appears on the 'Scotland only' shortage occupation list, the job must be for employment in Scotland.]

Note

This paragraph inserted by HC 863, para 150 as from 6 April 2011. Words "the Shortage Occupation List in Appendix K," substituted by Cm 8423, para 131 as from 20 July 2012.

81C. [In order for the Sponsor's application to be awarded points for a job in a PhD-level occupation code, the job must be in an occupation code which appears on the list of PhD-level occupation codes as stated in [the Codes of Practice in Appendix J]. The Sponsor's application must also meet the requirements of paragraph 81D.]

Note

This paragraph inserted by HC 863, para 150 as from 6 April 2011. Words "the Codes of practice in Appendix J" substituted by Cm 8423, para 132 as from 20 July 2012.

81D. [In order for the Sponsor's application to be awarded points for a job that passes the resident labour market test, or an exemption applies, the Sponsor must certify that it has met the requirements of that test, as defined [in paragraph 79B of this Appendix] in respect of the job, or that are one of the exemptions set out [in [paragraphs 78B or 78C] of this Appendix,] applies.]

Note

This paragraph substituted by HC 1888, para 142 as from 6 April 2012. Words "in paragraph 79B of this Appendix," substituted by Cm 8423, para 133 as from 20 July 2012. Words "paragraphs 78B or 78C" substituted by HC 628, para 177 and if an applicant has made an application for entry clearance or leave before 1 October 2013, the application will be decided in accordance with the Rules in force on 30 September 2013.

81E. [The points awarded under the heading "Salary on Offer" will be based on the gross annual salary on offer to be paid by the Sponsor, as stated in the Sponsor's application, subject to the following conditions:
(i) Points will be awarded based on basic pay (excluding overtime);
(ii) Allowances, such as London weighting, will be included in the salary for the awarding of points where they are part of the guaranteed salary package and would be paid to a local settled worker in similar circumstances;
(iii) Other allowances and benefits, such as bonus or incentive pay, travel and subsistence (including travel to and from the applicant's home country), will not be included.]

Note

This paragraph inserted by HC 863, para 150 as from 6 April 2011.

81F. [No points will be awarded for the salary on offer if the salary referred to in paragraph 81E above is less than the appropriate rate for the job as stated in [the Codes of Practice in Appendix J].]

Note

This paragraph inserted by HC 863, para 150 as from 6 April 2011. Words "the Codes of Practice in Appendix J" substituted by Cm 8423, para 134 as from 20 July 2012.

81G. [Where the salary on offer will be paid hourly, the salary on offer will be calculated on the basis of earnings up to a maximum of 48 hours a week, even if the jobholder works for longer than this.]

Note

This paragraph inserted by HC 863, para 150 as from 6 April 2011.

[**81H.** No points will be awarded for a Certificate of Sponsorship if the Secretary of State has reasonable grounds to believe that:
(a)   the job described in the application is not a genuine vacancy, or
(b)   the stated requirements of the job described in the application and in any advertisements for the job are inappropriate for the job on offer and / or have been tailored to exclude resident workers from being recruited.]

Note

Inserted by HC 693, para 167 as from 6 November 2014, save that if an application has been made for entry clearance or leave to enter or remain before 6 November 2014, the application will be decided in accordance with the Rules in force on 5 November 2014.

[**81I.** To support the assessment in paragraph 81H, the Secretary of State may request additional information and evidence from the Sponsor. This request will follow the procedure for verification checks as set out in paragraph 82C.]

Note

Inserted by HC 693, para 167 as from 6 November 2014, save that if an application has been made for entry clearance or leave to enter or remain before 6 November 2014, the application will be decided in accordance with the Rules in force on 5 November 2014.

Monthly allocations

82. [The Tier 2 (General) limit will be divided into monthly allocations.]

[**82A.**
(i)   There will be a monthly allocation specifying the number of Certificates of Sponsorship available to be allocated in respect of applications for Certificates of Sponsorship received during each previous month.
(ii)   The monthly allocation and allocation periods begin on the 6th date of each calendar month and end on the 5th date of the next calendar month.
(iii)   The provisional monthly allocation, subject to the processes set out in paragraphs 83 to 84a below, is 1,725 Certificates of Sponsorship each month.

82B. Applications by Sponsors for Certificates of Sponsorship each month will be accepted for consideration against each monthly allocation in the following month.

82C.
(i)   An application that would fall to be considered as having been received in a particular month may be deferred for consideration as if it had been received in the following month if the Secretary of State considers that the information stated in the application requires verification checks, and may be refused if the information cannot be verified or is confirmed as false.
(ii)   If the verification checks are prolonged due to the failure of the Sponsor to co-operate with the verification process such that the application cannot be considered as if it had been received in the next month, the application will be refused.

82D. [These provisional monthly allocations may be adjusted according to the processes set out in paragraphs 83 to 84A below.]

83. In paragraphs 83A to 84A below:
(a) "number of applications" means the number of applications by Sponsors for a certificate of Sponsorship under the Tier 2 (General) limit in a single monthly application period.
(b) "monthly applications" means 1,725 Certificates of Sponsorship, adjusted according to the processes set out in these paragraphs following the assigning of Certificates of Sponsorship under the Tier 2 (General) limit, or to Croation nationals as set out in (c) below, in the previous monthly period.
(c) (i) Subject to (ii) and (iii) below, each monthly allocation will be reduced by the number of Certificates of Sponsorship assigned by Tier 2 (General) Sponsors to Croation nationals in the previous monthly allocation period.
(ii) Paragraph (i) does not apply to the first monthly allocation under the Tier 2 (General) limit to 6 April to 5 April each year, to which the application period of 6 March to 5 April relates, or to Certificates of Sponsorship assigned by Tier 2 (General) Sponsors to Croation nationals before 1 July 2013.]

Notes

83A. [Subject to paragraph 83E below, if the number of applications is equal to or less than the monthly allocation:
(a) All applications by Sponsors which score 32 points or more from the points available in Table [11D] above will be granted, and
(b) If the number of applications granted under (a) above is less than the monthly allocation, the next monthly allocation will be increased by a number equivalent to the Certificates of Sponsorship remaining for allocation in the undersubscribed current month.]

Note

This paragraph inserted by HC 863, para 150 as from 6 April 2011.

83B. [Subject to paragraph 83E below, if the number of applications is greater than the monthly allocation:
(a) The minimum points level at which applications for Certificates of Sponsorship will be granted will be calculated as follows:
(i) If the number of applications scoring 32 points or more is no more than 100 greater than the monthly allocation, all applications which score 32 points or more will be granted.
(ii) If the number of applications scoring 32 points or more is more than 100 greater than the monthly allocation, X (being both the number of points scored in Table [11D] above and the minimum number of points required for an application to be granted) will be increased by 1 point incrementally until the number of applications scoring X points is:
(1) less than or equal to the monthly allocation; or
(2) on long-term sick leave lasting one month or longer
whichever results in the higher value of X, at which stage all applications which score X points or more will be granted.
(b) If the number of applications granted under (a) above is less than the monthly allocation, the number remaining under the monthly allocation will be added to the next monthly allocation.
(c) If the number of applications granted under (a) above is more than the monthly allocation, the number by which the monthly allocation is exceeded will be subtracted from the next monthly allocation.]

Note

This paragraph inserted by HC 863, para 150 as from 6 April 2011.

83C. [If a Sponsor is allocated one or more Certificates of Sponsorship under the Tier 2 (General) limit which it then elects not to assign to a migrant it may return them to the Secretary of State and the Secretary of State will subsequently add such Certificates of Sponsorship to the following monthly allocation.]

83D. [If:
(i) a Sponsor is allocated one or more Certificates of Sponsorship under the Tier 2 (General) limit; and

(ii)   the application(s) by the Sponsor scored points from [Table 11D] for a job in a shortage occupation; and

(iii)   the Sponsor has not assigned the Certificate(s) of Sponsorship to a migrant(s); and

(iv)   the job(s) in question no longer appear on the list of shortage occupations published by the UK Border Agency,
the Certificate(s) of Sponsorship in question will be cancelled and the Secretary of State will subsequently add such Certificates of Sponsorship to the following monthly allocation.]

Note

This paragraph inserted by HC 863, para 150 as from 6 April 2011.

83E. [With regard to the final monthly allocation under the Tier 2 (General) limit [for 6 April to 5 April each year, to which the application period of 6 February to 5 March relates:]

(i)   Paragaphs 83A(b), 83B(b) and 83B(c) do not apply to this monthly allocation, such that no adjustments will be made to the next monthly allocation, and

(ii)   References to "more than 100 greater than the monthly allocation" in paragraphs 83B(a)(ii) to (iii) are amended to 'greater than the monthly allocation', such that the total Tier 2 (General) limit in the period 6 April to 5 April each year will not be exceeded.

Note

This paragraph inserted by HC 863, para 150 as from 6 April 2011. Words in square brackets substituted by Cm 8337, paras 15, 16 as from 6 April 2012.

84. [The Secretary of State is entitled (but not required) to grant an application for a Certificate of Sponsorship under the Tier 2 (General) limit exceptionally outside of the processes set out in paragraphs 82A to 83B above if:

(a)   the application is considered by the Secretary of State to require urgent treatment when considered in line with the Tier 2 (Sponsor) guidance published on the [visas and immigration pages of the gov.uk website], and

(b)   the application scores enough points from Table [11D] above that it would have met the requirements to be granted under the previous monthly allocation.]

Note

This paragraph inserted by HC 863, para 150 as from 6 April 2011. Amended by HC 1138, para 133 as from 6 April 2014.

84A. [For each Certificate of Sponsorship application granted under the urgent treatment process set out in paragraph 84 above:

(i)   the current monthly allocation for granting Certificates of Sponsorship further to requests for urgent treatment will be reduced by one, if the current monthly allocation has not yet been reached; or

(ii)   in all other cases, the subsequent monthly allocation for granting Certificates of Sponsorship further to requests for urgent treatment will be reduced by one.]

Note

This paragraph inserted by HC 863, para 150 as from 6 April 2011.

Attributes for Tier 2 (Ministers of Religion) Migrants

85. An applicant applying for entry clearance or leave to remain as a Tier 2 (Minister of Religion) Migrant must score 50 points for attributes.

86. Available points are shown in Table 12 below.

87. Notes to accompany Table 12 appear below that table.

Table 12

Criterion	Points
Certificate of Sponsorship	50

Notes

88. In order to obtain points for sponsorship, the applicant will need to provide a valid Certificate of Sponsorship reference number for sponsorship in this category.

89. [A Certificate of Sponsorship reference number will only be considered to be valid for the purposes of this sub-category if:
(a) the number supplied links to a Certificate of Sponsorship Checking Service entry that names the applicant as the Migrant and confirms that the Sponsor is sponsoring him as a Tier 2 (Minister of Religion) Migrant, and
(b) the Sponsor is an A-rated Sponsor, unless:
    (1) the application is for leave to remain, and
    (2) the applicant has, or was last granted, leave as a Tier 2 (Minister of Religion) Migrant, a Minister of Religion, Missionary or Member of a Religious Order, and
    (3) the applicant is applying to work for the same employer named on the Certificate of Sponsorship which led to his last grant of leave or, in the case of an applicant whose last grant of leave was as a Minister of Religion, Missionary or Member of a Religious Order, the same employer for whom the applicant was working or stated he was intending to work when last granted leave.]

Note

This paragraph substituted by HC 908, para 43 as from 21 April 2011.

90. The Sponsor must have assigned the Certificate of Sponsorship reference number to the migrant no more than 3 months before the application is made and the reference number must not have been cancelled by the Sponsor or by the United Kingdom Border Agency since then.

[**91.** The migrant must not previously have been granted entry clearance, leave to enter or leave to remain using the same Certificate of Sponsorship reference number, if that application was either approved or refused (not rejected as an invalid application, declared void or withdrawn).].

Note

This paragraph substituted by HC 1888, para 143 as from 6 April 2012.

92. In addition, the Certificate of Sponsorship Checking Service entry [must]
[(a) confirm that the applicant is being sponsored to preform religious duties, which:
    (i) must be work which is within the Sponsor's organisation, or directed by the Sponsor's organisation,
    (ii) may include preaching, pastoral work and non pastoral work, and
    (iii) must not involve mainly non-pastoral duties such as school training, media production. domestic work, or administrative or clerical work, unless the role is a senior position in the sponsor's organisation and]
(b) provide an outline of the duties in (a).
(c) if the Sponsor's organisation is a religious order, confirm that the applicant is a member of that order.
(d) confirm that the applicant will receive pay and conditions at least equal to those given to settled workers in the same role, that the remuneration complies with or is exempt from National Minimum Wage regulations, and provide details of the remuneration,
(e) confirm that the requirements of the resident labour market test, [as set out in paragraph 92A below,] in respect of the job, have been complied with, unless the applicant is applying for leave to remain and the Sponsor is the same sponsor as in his last grant of leave,]
[(f) confirm that the migrant:
    (i) is qualified to do the job in respect of which he is seeking leave as a Tier 2 (Minister of Religion) Migrant,
    (ii) intends to base himself in the UK, and
    (iii) will comply with the conditions of his leave, if his application is successful, and

(g)   confirm that the Sponsor will maintain or accommodate the migrant.]

Note

Word in square brackets "must" substituted by HC 1888, para 144 as from 6 April 2012. Further amended by Cm 8423, paras 135,136 a from 20 July 2012. Further amended by HC 760, para 313 as from 13 December 2012.

[**92A.**   To confirm that the Resident Labour Market Test has been passed or the role is exempt from the test, and for points to be awarded, the Certificate of Sponsorship Checking Service entry must confirm:

(a)   That the role is supernumerary, such that it is over and above the Sponsor's normal staffing requirements and if the person filling the role was not there, it would not need to be filled by anyone else, with a full explanation of why it is supernumerary; or

(b)   That the role involves living mainly within and being a member of a religious order, which must be a lineage of communities or of people who live in some way set apart from society in accordance with their specific religious devotion, for example an order of nuns or monks; or

(c)   That the Sponsor holds national records of all available individuals, details of those records and confirmation that the records show that no suitable settled worker is available to fill the role; or

(d)   That a national recruitment search was undertaken, including the following details:

    (i)   Where the role was advertised, which must be at least one of the following:

        (1)   a national form of media appropriate to the Sponsor's religion or denomination,

        (2)   the Sponsor's own website, if that is how the Sponsor usually reaches out to its community on a national scale, that is where it normally advertises vacant positions, and the pages containing the advertisement are free to view without paying a subscription fee or making a donation, or

        (3)   Jobcentre Plus (or in Northern Ireland, JobCentre Online) or in the employment section of a national newspaper, if there is no suitable national form of media appropriate to the Sponsor's religion or denomination;

    (ii)   any reference numbers of the advertisements;

    (iii)   the period the role was advertised for, which must include at least 28 days during the 6 month period immediately before the date the Sponsor assigned the Certificate of Sponsorship to the applicant; and

    (iv)   confirmation that no suitable settled workers are available to be recruited for the role.

or the applicant must be applying for leave to remain and the Sponsor must be the same Sponsor as in his last grant of leave.]

Note

Substituted by HC 244, para 23 as from 1 July 2013.

Attributes for Tier 2 (Sportsperson) Migrants

93.   An applicant applying for entry clearance or leave to remain as a Tier 2 (Sportsperson) Migrant must score 50 points for attributes.

94.   Available points are shown in Table 13 below.

95.   Notes to accompany Table 13 appear below that table.

Criterion	Points
Certificate of Sponsorship	50

Notes

96. In order to obtain points for sponsorship, the applicant will need to provide a valid Certificate of Sponsorship reference number for sponsorship in this subcategory.

97. [A Certificate of Sponsorship reference number will only be considered to be valid for the purposes of this sub-category if:
(a)   the number supplied links to a Certificate of Sponsorship Checking Service entry that names the applicant as the Migrant and confirms that the Sponsor is sponsoring him as a Tier 2 (Sportsperson) Migrant, and
(b)   the Sponsor is an A-rated Sponsor, unless:
    (1)   the application is for leave to remain, and
    (2)   the applicant has, or was last granted, leave as a Tier 2 (Sportsperson) Migrant or a Qualifying Work Permit Holder, and
    (3)   the applicant is applying to work for the same employer named on the Certificate of Sponsorship or Work Permit document which led to his last grant of leave.]

Note

This paragraph substituted by HC 908, para 44 as from 21 April 2011.

98. The Sponsor must have assigned the Certificate of Sponsorship reference number to the migrant no more than 3 months before the application is made and the reference number must not have been cancelled by the Sponsor or by the United Kingdom Border Agency since then.

[**99.** The migrant must not previously have applied for entry clearance, leave to enter or leave to remain using the same Certificate of Sponsorship reference number, if that application was either approved or refused (not rejected as an invalid application, declared void or withdrawn).].

Note

Substituted by HC 1888, para 147 as from 6 April 2012.

100. In addition, the Certificate of Sponsorship Checking Service entry must confirm that the migrant:
(a)   is qualified to do the job in question,
(b)   has been endorsed by the Governing Body for his sport (that is, the organisation which is [specified in Appendix M] as being the Governing Body for the sport in question),
[(c)   The endorsement referred to in (b) above must confirm that the player or coach is internationally established at the highest level whose employment will make a significant contribution to the development of his sport at the highest level in the UK, and that the post could not be filled by a suitable settled worker,]
[(d)]   intends to base himself in the UK, and
[(e)]   will comply with the conditions of his leave, if his application is successful.

Note

Words in square brackets inserted and substituted by HC 863, paras 151 and 152 as from 6 April 2011. sub-para (b) words "specified in Appendix M" substituted by Cm 8423, para 138 as from 20 July 2012.

Attributes for Tier 5 (Youth Mobility Scheme) Temporary Migrants

101. An applicant applying for entry clearance as a Tier 5 (Youth Mobility Scheme) Temporary Migrant must score 40 points for attributes.

102. Available points are shown in Table 14 below.

103. Notes to accompany Table 14 appear below that table.

Table 14

Criterion	Points
Citizen of a country [or rightful holder of a passport issued by a territory listed] in Appendix G	30

or

is a British Overseas Citizen, British Territories Overseas Citizen or British National (Overseas.)

Will be 18 or over when his entry clearance becomes valid for use and was under the age of 31 on the date his application was made.   10

Notes

Note

Words in square brackets inserted by HC 1693, para 14 as from 1 January 2012.

[104.   The applicant must provide a valid passport as evidence of all of the above.]

Note

Substituted by Cm 8423, para 139 as from 20 July 2012.

Attributes for Tier 5 (Temporary Worker) Migrants

105.   An applicant applying for entry clearance or leave enter or remain as a Tier 5 (Temporary Worker) Migrant must score 30 points for attributes.

106.   Available points are shown in Table 15 below.

107.   Notes to accompany Table 15 appear below that table.

Criterion	Points awarded
Holds a Tier 5 (Temporary Worker) Certificate of Sponsorship	30

Notes

108.   In order to meet the "holds a Certificate of Sponsorship" requirement, the applicant will need to provide a valid Certificate of Sponsorship reference number for sponsorship in this category.

109.   A Certificate of Sponsorship reference number will only be considered to be valid if the number supplied links to a Certificate of Sponsorship Checking Service reference that names the applicant as the migrant and confirms that the Sponsor is sponsoring him as a Tier 5 (Temporary Worker) Migrant in the subcategory indicated by the migrant in his application for entry clearance or leave [. . .].

109A.   [A Certificate of Sponsorship reference number will only be considered to be valid if:

(a)   the Sponsor assigned the reference number to the migrant no more than 3 months before the application for entry clearance or leave to remain is made [unless the migrant is applying for leave to enter and has previously been granted leave to enter using the same Certificate of Sponsorship reference number],

(b)   the application for entry clearance or leave to remain is made no more than 3 months before the start date of the employment as stated on the Certificate of Sponsorship, [..]

(c)   that reference number must not have been cancelled by the Sponsor or by the United Kingdom Border Agency since it was assigned[, and

(d)   the Sponsor is an A-rated Sponsor, unless the application is for leave to remain and the applicant has, or was last granted, leave as a Tier 5 Migrant, an Overseas Government Employee or a Qualifying Work Permit Holder.]

Note

Inserted by HC 314, para 121 as from 31 March 2009. Word in square brackets in (b) deleted by HC 908, para 45 as from 21 April 2011. Words in square brackets in (c) and sub-para (d) inserted by HC 908, paras 41 and 42 as from 21 April 2011.

[110.   The migrant must not previously have applied for entry clearance or leave to remain using the same Certificate of Sponsorship reference number, if that application was either approved or refused (not rejected as an invalid application, declared void or withdrawn).]

Note

Substituted by HC 1888, para 148 as from 6 April 2012.

[**111.** In addition, a Certificate of Sponsorship reference number will only be considered to be valid:

(a)   where the Certificate of Sponsorship Checking Service shows that the Certificate of Sponsorship has been issued in the Creative and Sporting subcategory to enable the applicant to work as a sportsperson, if:

    (i)   The Certificate of Sponsorship Checking Service entry shows that the applicant has been endorsed by the Governing Body for his sport (that is, the organisation which is [specified in Appendix M] as being the Governing Body for the sport in question), and

    (ii)   The endorsement referred to in (i) above confirms that the player or coach is internationally established at the highest level and/or will make a significant contribution to he development of his sport at the highest level in the UK, and that the post could not be filled by a settled worker.

(b)   [where the Certificate of Sponsorship Checking Service entry shows that the Certificate of Sponsorship has been issued in the Creative and Sporting subcategory to enable the applicant to work as a creative worker, if the entry confirms that:

    (i)   where a relevant creative sector Codes of Practice exists in Appendix J, the Sponsor has complied with that Code of Practice; or

    (ii)   where no relevant creative sector Codes of practice exists in Appendix J, the Sponsor has otherwise taken into account the needs of the resident labour labour market in that field, and the work could not be carried out by a suitably settled worker.]

(c)   where the Certificate of Sponsorship Checking Service entry shows that the Certificate of Sponsorship has been issued in the Charity Workers subcategory, if the work the applicant is being sponsored to do is:

    (i)   voluntary fieldwork directly related to the purpose of the charity which is sponsoring him,

    (ii)   not paid (except reasonable expenses outlined in section 44 of the National Minimum Wage Act), and

    (iii)   not a permanent position.

(d)   where the Certificate of Sponsorship Checking Service entry shows that the Certificate of Sponsorship has been issued in the Religious Workers subcategory, if the entry confirms:

    (i)   that the applicant is being sponsored to perform religious duties, which:

        (1)   must be work which is within the Sponsor's organisation, or directed by the Sponsor's organisation,

        (2)   may include preaching, pastoral work and non pastoral work, and

    (ii)   an outline of the duties in (i),

    (iii)   if the Sponsor's organisation is a religious order, that the applicant is a member of that order;

    (iv)   that the applicant will receive pay and conditions at least equal to those given to settled workers in the same role,

    (v)   that the remuneration complies with or is exempt from National Minimum Wage regulations, and provides details of the remuneration,

    (vi)   [details of the resident labour market test has been complied with or why the role is exempt from the test, as set out in paragraph 92A of this Appendix.]

(e)   where the Certificate of Sponsorship Checking Service entry shows that the Certificate of Sponsorship has been issued in the Government Authorised Exchange subcategory, if the entry confirms that the work, volunteering or job shadowing the applicant is being sponsored to do:

    (i)   meets the requirements of the individual exchange scheme, [as set out in Appendix N,],

    (ii)   does not fill a vacancy in the workforce,

    (iii)   is skilled to National Qualifications Framework level 3, as stated in [the Codes of Practice in Appendix J,] unless the applicant is being sponsored under an individual exchange scheme set up as part of the European Commission's Lifelong Learning Programme,

(iv)   conforms with all relevant UK and EU legislation, such as the National Minimum Wage Act and the Working Time Directive,

(f)   [where the Certificate of Sponsorship Checking Service entry shows that the Certificate of Sponsorship has been issued in the International Agreement subcategory and the applicant is applying for entry clearance or leave to enter or remain for the purpose of work as a Contractual Service Supplier [or Independent Professional], if either:

(i)   the work is pursuant to a contract to supply services to the sponsor in the United Kingdom by an overseas undertaking established on the territory of a party to the General Agreement on Trade in Services or a similar trade agreement which has been concluded between the EU and another party or parties and which is in force, and which has no commercial presence in the European Union; and

(ii)   the service which that undertaking is contracted to supply to the sponsor in the United Kingdom is a service falling within the scope of the sectors specified in the relevant commitments in respect of Contractual Service Suppliers [or Independent Professionals] as set out in the agreements mentioned at (i) above; and

(iii)   the sponsor has, through an open tendering procedure or other procedure which guarantees the bona fide character of the contract, awarded a services contract for a period not exceeding 12 months to the applicant's employer; and

(iv)   the sponsor will be the final consumer of the services provided under that contract; and

(v)   the applicant is a national of the country in which the overseas undertaking is established; and

(vi)   [where the applicant is a Contractual Service Supplier, he possesses:

    (1)   a university degree or a technical qualification demonstrating knowledge of an equivalent level, and provides the original certificate of his qualification, except where (4) applies;

    (2)   where they are required by any relevant law, regulations or requirements in force in the United Kingdom in order to exercise the activity in question, professional qualifications;

    (3)   3 years' professional experience in the sector concerned, except:

        (a)   (4) in the case of advertising and translation services, relevant qualifications and 3 years' professional experience, and provides the original certificate of those qualifications;

        (b)   in the case of management consulting services and services related to management consulting (managers and senior consultants), a university degree and 3 years professional experience, and provides the original certificate of that qualification;

        (c)   in the case of technical testing and analysis services, a university degree or technical qualifications demonstrating technical knowledge and 3 years professional experience, and provides the original certificate of that qualification;

        (d)   in the case of fashion model services and entertainment services other than audiovisual services, 3 years' relevant experience;

        (e)   in the case of chef de cuisine services, an advanced technical qualification and 6 years' relevant experience at the level of chef de cuisine, and provides the original certificate of that qualification;

(vii)   where the applicant is a Contractual Service Supplier, he has been employed, and provides the specified documents in paragraph 111–SD to show that he has been employed, by the service supplier for a period of at least one year immediately prior to the date of application; or

(viii)   where the applicant is an Independent Professional, he possesses:

    (1)   a university degree or a technical qualification demonstrating knowledge of an equivalent level, and provide the original certificate of that qualification,

(2) where they are required by any relevant law, regulations or requirements in force in the United Kingdom in order to exercise the activity in question, professional qualifications; and

(3) at least six years professional experience in the sector concerned; or

(ix) the applicant is applying for leave to remain and holds a Certificate of Sponsorship issued in the International Agreement sub-category by the same sponsor, and for the purposes of the same contract to supply services, as was the case when the applicant was last granted entry clearance, leave to enter or remain.]

(g) where the Certificate of Sponsorship Checking Service entry shows that the Certificate of Sponsorship has been issued in the International Agreement subcategory and the applicant is coming for a purpose other than work as a Contractual Service Supplier [or Independent Professional], if the entry confirms that applicant is being sponsored:

(i) as an employee of an overseas government, or

(ii) as an employee of an international organisation established by international treaty signed by the UK or European Union, or

(iii) as a private servant in a diplomatic household under the provisions of the Vienna Convention on Diplomatic Relations, 1961, or in the household of an employee of an international organisation recognised by Her Majesty's Government, who enjoys a certain privileges or immunity under UK or international law, and confirms the name of the individual who is employing them.]

Note

Paragraph substituted by HC 1888, para 148 as from 6 April 2012. Further amended by Cm 8423, paras 140–144 as from 20 July 2012. Further amended by HC 760, para 314 as from 13 December 2012. Sub-para (d)(vi) substituted by HC 244, para 24 as from 1 July 2013. Further amended by HC 628, para 178 and if an applicant has made an application for entry clearance or leave before 1 October 2013, the application will be decided in accordance with the Rules in force on 30 September 2013. Amended by HC 1138, para 134 as from 6 April 2014.

[111–SD

(a) Where paragraph 111(f)(vii) refers to specified documents, those specified documents are:

[(i) original formal payslips issued by the employer and showing the employer's name; or

(ii) payslips accompanied by a letter from the applicant's employer, on the employer's headed paper and signed by a senior official, confirming the payslips are authentic; or]

(iii) Personal bank or building society statements covering the full specified period, which clearly show:

(1) the applicant's name,

(2) the account number,

(3) the date of the statement (The most recent statement must be dated no earlier than 31 days before the date of the application),

(4) the financial institution's name and logo, and

(5) transactions by the service supplier covering the full specified period; or

(iv) A building society pass book, which clearly shows:

(1) the applicant's name,

(2) the account number,

(3) the financial institution's name and logo, and

(4) transactions by the service supplier covering the full specified period.

(b) If the applicant provides the bank or building society statements in (a)(iii):

(i) The statements must:

> (1)   be printed on paper bearing the bank or building society's letter-head,
>
> (2)   bear the official stamp of the bank on every page, or
>
> (3)   be accompanied by a supporting letter from the issuing bank or building society, on company headed paper, confirming the authenticity of the statements provided;
>
> (ii)   The statements must not be mini-statements obtained from an Automated Teller Machine.]

Note

Inserted by HC 760, para 315 as from 13 December 2012. Further amended by HC 628, para 179 and if an applicant has made an application for entry clearance or leave before 1 October 2013, the application will be decided in accordance with the Rules in force on 30 September 2013.

112. [Points will not be awarded for a Tier 5 (Temporary Worker) Certificate of Sponsorship where the claimed basis for its issuance are the provisions under Mode 4 of the General Agreement on Trade in Services relating to intra-corporate transfers.]

Note

Words in square brackets inserted by HC 1113. Amended by Cm 7701. Paragraph 12 inserted by HC 314, para 122 as from 31 March 2009.

[Attributes for Tier 4 (General) Students

113. An applicant applying for entry clearance or leave to remain as a Tier 4 (General Student) must score 30 points for attributes.

114. Available points are shown in Table 16 below.

115. Notes to accompany Table 16 appear before that tables.

Table 16

[Criterion	Points awarded
Confirmation of Acceptance for Studies	30]

Notes

115A. [In order to obtain points for a Confirmation of Acceptance for Studies, the applicant must provide a valid Confirmation of Acceptance for Studies reference number.]

Note

This paragraph inserted by HC 908, para 48 as from 21 April 2011.

[Tier 4 Interim Limit

115B. *The Secretary of State shall be entitled to limit the number of Confirmations of Acceptance for Studies allocated to any specific Sponsor in any one period.*]

Note

This paragraph inserted by HC 908, para 48 as from 21 April 2011. Deleted by HC 760, para 316 as from 1 January 2013.

115C. [*The limit on the number of Confirmations of Acceptance for Studies allocated to specific Sponsors shall be known as the Tier 4 Interim Limit.*]

Note

This paragraph inserted by HC 908, para 48 as from 21 April 2011. Deleted by HC 760, para 317 as from 1 January 2013.

[**115CA.** *The interim limit implemented by HC908 and effective in relation to Tier 4 between 21 April 2011 and April 2012 shall be known as the Former Interim Limit.*]

Note

This paragraph inserted by HC 1888, para 149 as from 6 April 2012. Deleted by HC 760, para 318 as from 1 January 2013.

115D. [*The Tier 4 Interim Limit will apply from [6 April 2012 to 31 December 2012] (inclusive) (the "Tier 4 Interim Limit Period").*]

Note

This paragraph inserted by HC 908, para 48 as from 21 April 2011. Words in square brackets substituted by HC 1888, para 150 as from 6 April 2012. Deleted by HC 760, para 319 as from 1 January 2013.

115E. [*The Tier 4 Interim Limit will be applied to any Tier 4 Sponsor that does not satisfy both of the following criteria throughout the Tier 4 Interim Limit Period:*
(i)   *has Highly Trusted Sponsor status; and*
(ii)   *is subject to and holds a valid and satisfactory full institutional inspection, review or audit by one of the following bodies:*
    (a)   *the Bridge Schools Inspectorate; or*
    (b)   *the Education and Training Inspectorate; or*
    (c)   *Estyn; or*
    (d)   *[Education Scotland]; or*
    (e)   *the Independent Schools Inspectorate; or*
    (f)   *Ofsted; or*
    (g)   *the Quality Assurance Agency for Higher Education; or*
    (h)   *The Schools Inspection Service;*
    or is not: . . .
(iii)   *the Foundation Programme Office;*
(iv)   *the Yorkshire and Humber Strategic Health Authority; [. . .]*
(v)   *a Tier 4 Sponsor that applied for a Tier 4 Sponsor licence on or after 21 April 2011 and meets the requirements of (ii) (but not (i)) above] [and has not yet to receive a first decision on it application for Highly Trusted Sponsor status;]*
(vi)   *an overseas higher education institution which has Highly Trusted Sponsor Status.]*
(vii)   *[a licensed sponsor, who did not have a licence on 5 April 2012, and was granted a licence on or after 6 April 2012 and has yet to receive a first decision on its application for Highly Trusted Sponsor status.]*

Note

This paragraph inserted by HC 908, para 48 as from 21 April 2011. Sub-paragraph (iii) deleted and (iv) to (vii) renumbered as (iii) to (vi) by HC 1888, paras 151,152 as from 6 April 2012. Words in square brackets in sub-para (v) inserted by HC 1888, para 153 as from 6 April 2012. Sub-paragraph (vii) inserted by HC 1888, para 154 as from 6 April 2012. Words "Education Scotland" substituted by HC 1511, para 46 as from 31 October 2011. Deleted by HC 760, para 330 as from 1 January 2013.

[**115F.** *A Tier 4 Sponsor who does not satisfy the requirements of paragraph 115E and is therefore subject to the Tier 4 Interim Limit is known as a Limited Sponsor.*]

Note

This paragraph inserted by HC 908, para 48 as from 21 April 2011. Deleted by HC 760, para 321 as from 1 January 2013.

[**115FA.** *No Confirmations of Acceptance for Studies will be allocated to a Limited Sponsor where:*
(i)   *The Limited Sponsor did not apply for inspection, review or audit by the appropriate specified body by the relevant deadline, as listed below: or*

Specified body	Deadline
Qualified Assurance Agency	9 September 2011
Independent Schools Inspectorate	9 September 2011
Bridge Schools Inspectorate	7 October 2011
School Inspection Service	7 October 2011

Education Scotland	11 November 2011

(ii)   *The Limited Sponsor applied by the deadline specified in (i) above, and failed to meet the required standard to obtain a full institutional audit, inspection or review; or*

(iii)   *The Limited Sponsor applied for Highly Trusted Sponsor status on two occasions and has not been granted Highly Trusted Sponsor status.*

Note

Inserted by HC 1888, para 155 as from 6 April 2012. Deleted by HC 760, para 322 as from 1 January 2013.

[115FB. *A Limited Sponsor that is allocated no Confirmations of Acceptance for Studies further to paragraph 11FA is known as a Legacy Sponsor.*]

Note

Inserted by HC 1888, para 155 as from 6 April 2012. Deleted by HC 760, para 323 as from 1 January 2013.

[115G. *All Confirmations of Acceptance for Studies allocated by the Secretary of State to Limited Sponsors prior to [6 April 2012] and which have not been assigned to an applicant for entry clearance, leave to enter or leave to remain under Tier 4 prior to [6 April 2012] are withdrawn and the only Confirmations of Acceptance for Studies allocated to a Limited Sponsor are the Confirmations of Acceptance for Studies allocated in accordance with paragraph 115H below.*]

Note

This paragraph inserted by HC 908, para 48 as from 21 April 2011. Words in square brackets " 6 April 2012" substituted by HC 1888, paras 156, 157 as from 6 April 2012. Deleted by HC 760, para 324 as from 1 January 2013.

115H.   [*The Tier 4 Interim Limit will be calculated as follows:*

(i)   *A Limited Sponsor who has that status as at 6 April 2012 will be allocated:*

    (a)   *where the Limited Sponsor was subject to the Former Tier 4 Interim Limit for the entirety of the period 21 April 2011 to 5 April 2012, a number of Confirmations of Acceptance for Studies equal to three quarters of the number of Confirmations of Acceptance for Studies allocated to that Limited Sponsor for the period 21 April 2011 to 5 April 2012;*

    (b)   *where the Limited Sponsor had a Tier 4 Sponsor Licence for only part of the period 21 April 2011 to 5 April 2012, and was subject to the Former Tier 4 Interim Limit from the date on which it was granted a sponsor licence, a number of Confirmations of Acceptance for Studies equal to:*

        (i)   *the number of Confirmations of Acceptance for Studies allocated to that Limited Sponsor for the period it was licensed between 21 April 2011 to 5 April 2012;*

        (ii)   *multiplied by the appropriate factor such that the figure in (i) is equal to the number of Confirmations of Acceptance for Studies that would have been granted to that Limited Sponsor for a period of 9 months;*

    (c)   *where the Limited Sponsor had a Tier 4 Sponsor licence for the entirety of the period 21 April 2011 to 6 April 2012 and was subject to the Former Tier 4 Interim Limit for only part of that period, a number of Confirmations of Acceptance for Studies equal to:*

        (i)   *the number of Confirmations of Acceptance for Studies allocated to that Limited Sponsor under the Tier 4 Interim Limit;*

        (ii)   *multiplied by the appropriate factor such that the figure in (i) is equal to the number of Confirmations of Acceptance for Studies that would have been granted to that Limited Sponsor for a period of 9 months;*

    (d)   *where the calculation in paragraphs (a) to (c) above results in 0 or a negative number, the Limited Sponsor will be allocated 0 Confirmations of Acceptance for Studies under the Tier 4 Interim Limit;*

    (e)   *where the calculation in paragraphs (a) to (c) does not result in a whole number, the Limited Sponsor will be allocated a number of Confirmations of Acceptance for Studies equal to the nearest whole number (fractions will be rounded up to the nearest whole number).*

(ii)   *A Limited Sponsor who acquires that status after 6 April 2012 will be allocated a number of Confirmations of Acceptance for Studies:*

    (a)   *equal to the result of the calculation appropriate for the Limited Sponsor's circumstances as set out in 115H(i) above; and*

    (b)   *subject where appropriate to a reduction equal to the number of Confirmations of Acceptance for Studies assigned by the Limited Sponsor to Tier 4 Migrants since 6 April 2012 which were used for an application for entry clearance, leave to enter or leave to remain since 6 April 2012;*

    (c)   *divided by the appropriate factor such that the figure resulting from (a) and (b) is proportionate to the period of the Tier 4 Interim Limit remaining.]*

Note

Inserted by HC 1888, para 158 as from 6 April 2012. Deleted by HC 760, para 325 as from 1 January 2013.

[115B. The Secretary of State shall be entitled to limit the number of Confirmations of Acceptance for Studies allocated to any specific Sponsor in any one period.

115C. The limit on the number of Confirmations of Acceptance for Studies allocated to specific Sponsors shall be known as the Tier 4 Interim Limit.

115CA. The interim limit implemented by HC1888 and effective in relation to Tier 4 between 6 April 2012 and 31 December 2012 shall be known as the Former Interim Limit.

115D. The Tier 4 Interim Limit will apply from 1 January 2013 to 30 June 2013 (inclusive) (the "Tier 4 Interim Limit Period").

115E. The Tier 4 Interim Limit will be applied to any Tier 4 Sponsor who

(i)   is still subject to the former interim limit on 31 December 2012 and has applied for but not yet achieved HTS status and a valid and satisfactory full institutional inspection, review or audit from one of the following bodies:

    (a)   the Bridge Schools Inspectorate; or

    (b)   the Education and Training Inspectorate; or

    (c)   Estyn; or

    (d)   Education Scotland; or

    (e)   the Independent Schools Inspectorate; or

    (f)   Ofsted; or

    (g)   the Quality Assurance Agency for Higher Education; or

    (h)   The Schools Inspection Service; or is not:

(ii)   the Foundation Programme Office;

(iii)   the Yorkshire and Humber Strategic Health Authority;

(iv)   an overseas higher education institution which has Highly Trusted Sponsor Status.

115F. A Tier 4 Sponsor who does not satisfy the requirements of paragraph 115E and is therefore subject to the Tier 4 Interim Limit is known as a Limited Sponsor.

115FA. No Confirmations of Acceptance for Studies will be allocated to a Limited Sponsor where:

(i)   The Limited Sponsor did not apply for inspection, review or audit by the appropriate specified body by the relevant deadline, as listed below:

Specified body	Deadline
Quality Assurance Agency	9 September 2011

Specified body	Deadline
Independent Schools Inspectorate	9 September 2011
Bridge Schools Inspectorate	7 October 2011
School Inspection Service	7 October 2011
Education Scotland	11 November 2011
Education and Training Inspectorate N.I.	30 April 2012

or

(ii) The Limited Sponsor applied by the deadline specified in (i) above, and failed to meet the required standard to obtain a full institutional audit, inspection or review, except for where The Limited Sponsor requires a second institutional audit, inspection or review within 6 months of the initial audit, inspection or review as determined by the relevant body listed above; or

(iii) The Limited Sponsor applied for Highly Trusted Sponsor status on two occasions and has not been granted Highly Trusted Sponsor status.

115FB. A Limited Sponsor that is allocated no Confirmations of Acceptance for Studies further to paragraph 115FA is known as a Legacy Sponsor

115G. All Confirmations of Acceptance for Studies allocated by the Secretary of State to Limited Sponsors prior to 1 January 2013 and which have not been assigned to an applicant for entry clearance, leave to enter or leave to remain under Tier 4 prior to 1 January 2013 are withdrawn and the only Confirmations of Acceptance for Studies allocated to a Limited Sponsor are the Confirmations of Acceptance for Studies allocated in accordance with paragraph 115H below.

115H. The Tier 4 Interim Limit will be calculated as follows:

(i) A Limited Sponsor who has that status as at 1 January 2013 will be allocated:

    (a) where the Limited Sponsor was subject to the Former Tier 4 Interim Limit for the entirety of the period 6 April 2012 to 31 December 2012, a number of Confirmations of Acceptance for Studies equal to two thirds of the number of Confirmations of Acceptance for Studies allocated to that Limited Sponsor for the period 6 April 2012 to 31 December 2012;

    (b) where the Limited Sponsor had a Tier 4 Sponsor Licence for only part of the period 6 April 2012 to 31 December 2012, and was subject to the Former Tier 4 Interim Limit from the date on which it was granted a sponsor licence, a number of Confirmations of Acceptance for Studies equal to:

        (i) the number of Confirmations of Acceptance for Studies allocated to that Limited Sponsor for the period it was licenced between 6 April 2012 to 31 December 2012;

        (ii) multiplied by the appropriate factor such that the figure in (i) is equal to the number of Confirmations of Acceptance for Studies that would have been granted to that Limited Sponsor for a period of 6 months;

    (c) where the Limited Sponsor had a Tier 4 Sponsor Licence for the entirety of the period 6 April 2012 to 31 December 2012 and was subject to the Former Tier 4 Interim Limit for only part of that period, a number of Confirmations of Acceptance for Studies equal to:

        (i) the number of Confirmations of Acceptance for Studies allocated to that Limited Sponsor under the Tier 4 Interim Limit;

        (ii) multiplied by the appropriate factor such that the figure in (i) is equal to the number of Confirmations of Acceptance for Studies that would have been granted to that Limited Sponsor for a period of 6 months;

    (d) where the calculation in paragraphs (a) to (c) results in 0 or a negative number, the Limited Sponsor will be allocated 0 Confirmations of Acceptance for Studies under the Tier 4 Interim Limit;

(e) where the calculation in paragraphs (a) to (c) does not result in a whole number, the Limited Sponsor will be allocated a number of Confirmations of Acceptance for Studies equal to the nearest whole number (fractions will be rounded up to the nearest whole number).

115I. A Limited Sponsor will, on provision to the UK Border Agency of evidence that it meets the criteria set out in paragraph 115E above, be exempt from the Tier 4 Interim Limit from the date the UK Border Agency provides written confirmation that it is so exempt.]

Note

Paragraphs 115B-115I inserted by HC 760, para 326 as from 1 January 2013.

115I. [A Limited Sponsor will, on provision to the UK Border Agency of evidence that it meets the criteria set out in paragraph 115E above, be exempt from the Tier 4 Interim Limit from the date the UK Border Agency provides written confirmation that it is so exempt.]

Note

This paragraph inserted by HC 908, para 48 as from 21 April 2011.

116. A . . . Confirmation of Acceptance for Studies will only be considered to be valid
(a) it was issued no more than 6 months before the application is made,
(b) the application for entry clearance or leave to remain is made no more than 3 months before the start date of the course of study as stated on the . . . Confirmation of Acceptance for Studies,
(c) the Sponsor has not withdrawn the offer since the . . . Confirmation of Acceptance for Studies was issued,
(d) it was issued by an institution with a Tier 4 (General) Student Sponsor Licence,
[(da) where the application for entry clearance or leave to remain is for the applicant to commence a new course of study, not for completion of a course already commenced by way of re-sitting examinations or repeating a module of a course, the Sponsor must hold an A-rated or Highly Trusted Sponsor Licence [and must not be a Legacy Sponsor],]
[(db) where the Confirmation of Acceptance for Studies is issued by a Legacy Sponsor or a B-rated sponsor, the Confirmation of Acceptance for Studies will only be valid if it is issued for completion of a course already commenced by way of re-sitting examinations or repeating a module of a course and the Confirmation of Acceptance for Studies must be for the same course for which the last period of leave was granted to study with the same sponsor,]
(e) the institution must still hold such a licence at the time the application for entry clearance or leave to remain is determined,] [..]
[(ea) the migrant must not previously have applied for entry clearance, leave to enter or leave to remain using the same Confirmation of Acceptance for Studies reference number where that application was either approved or refused (not rejected as an invalid application[, declared void] or withdrawn),]
[(f) it contains the following mandatory information:
  (i) the applicant's:
    (1) name,
    (2) date of birth,
    (3) gender,
    (4) nationality, and
    (5) passport number;
  (ii) the course:
    (1) title,
    (2) level,
    (3) start and end dates, and
    (4) hours per week, including confirmation that the course is full-time;
  (iii) confirmation if the course is one in which the applicant must hold a valid Academic Technology Approval Scheme clearance certificate from the Counter-Proliferation Department of the Foreign and Commonwealth Office;

(iv)   confirmation of the course is a recognised Foundation programme for postgraduate doctors or dentists, and requires a certificate from the Postgraduate Dean;

(v)   the main study address;

(vi)   details of how the Tier 4 Sponsor has assessed the applicant's English language ability including, where relevant, the applicant's English language test scores in all four components (reading, writing, speaking and listening);

(vii)   details of any work placements relating to the course;

(viii)   accommodation, fees and boarding costs;

(ix)   details of any partner institution, if the course will be provided by an education provider that is not the Tier 4 Sponsor; and

(x)   the name and address of he overseas higher education institution, if the course is part of a study abroad programme.]

[(g)   ... . it was not issued for a course of studies, it was issued for a full-time, salaried, elected executive position as a student union sabbatical officer to an applicant who is part-way through their studies or who is being sponsored to fill the position in the academic year immediately after their graduation[; or]

[(h)   it was not issued for a course of studies, it was issued within 60 days of the expected end date of a course leading to the award of a PhD and the migrant is sponsored by a Sponsor that is a Recognised Body or a body in receipt of public funding as a higher education institution from the Department of Employment and learning in Northern Ireland, the Higher Education Funding Council for England, the Higher Education Funding Council for Wales or the Scottish Funding Council, to enable the migrant to remain in the UK as a Tier 4 (General) Student on the doctorate extension scheme.]

Note

Words deleted by HC 120, paras 10–12 as from 1 January 2010. Sub-paragraph (g) inserted by HC 382, para 16 as from 23 July 2010. Sub-paras (da) and (ea) inserted by HC 908, paras 49 and 50 as from 21 April 2011. Further amended by HC 1888, paras 159–161 as from 6 April 2012. Further amended by HC 565, para 107 as from 6 September 2012.

117.   A Confirmation of Acceptance for Studies reference number will only be considered to be valid if:

(a)   the number supplied links to a Confirmation of Acceptance for Studies Checking Service entry that names the applicant as the migrant and confirms that the Sponsor us sponsoring him I the Tier 4 category indicated by the migrant in his application for leave to remain (that is, as a Tier 4 (General) Student or a Tier 4 (Child) Student), and

[(b)   that reference number must not have been withdrawn or cancelled by the Sponsor or the UK Border Agency since it was assigned.]

Note

Words deleted by HC 120, paras 10–12 as from 1 January 2010. Sub-paragraph (g) inserted by HC 382, para 16 as from 23 July 2010. Sub-para (b) substituted by HC 908, para 51 as from 21 April 2011.

118.   [No points will be awarded for a Confirmation of Acceptance for Studies unless:

(a)   the applicant supplies, as evidence of previous qualifications, [the specified documents, as set out in paragraph 120–SD(a), that the applicant] used to obtain the offer of a place on a course from the Sponsor [unless the applicant is sponsored by a Highly Trusted Sponsor, is a national of one of the countries [or the rightful holder of a qualifying passport issued by one of the relevant competent authorities, as appropriate,] listed in Appendix H, and is applying for entry clearance in his country of nationality [or in the territory related to the passport he holds, as appropriate,] or leave to remain in the UK. The UK Border Agency reserves the right to request the specified documents from these applicants. The application will be refused if the specified documents are not provided in accordance with the request made]; and

(b)   [[One], of the requirements in (i) to (iii) below is met:

(i)   the course is degree level study and the Confirmation of Acceptance for Studies has been assigned by a Sponsor which is a Recognised Body or a body in receipt of funding as a higher education institution from the

Department for Employment and Learning in Northern Ireland, the Higher Education Funding Council for England, the Higher Education Funding Council for Wales, or the Scottish Funding Council, and:

(1)   the applicant is a national of one of the following countries: Antigua and Barbuda; Australia; The Bahamas; Barbados; Belize; Canada; Dominica; Grenada; Guyana; Jamaica; New Zealand; St Kitts and Nevis; St Lucia; St Vincent and the Grenadines; Trinidad and Tobago; United States of America, and provides the specified documents [set out in paragraph 120–SD(b)]; or

(2)   has obtained an academic qualification (not a professional or vocational qualification), which is deemed by UK NARIC to meet or exceed the recognised standard of a Bachelor's or Master's degree or a PhD in the UK, from an educational establishment in one of the following countries: Antigua and Barbuda; Australia; The Bahamas; Barbados; Belize; Dominica; Grenada; Guyana; Ireland; Jamaica; New Zealand; St Kitts and Nevis; St Lucia; St Vincent and The Grenadines; Trinidad and Tobago; the UK; the USA, and provides the specified documents [set out in paragraph 120–SD(a)]; or

(3)   the applicant has successfully completed a course as a Tier 4 (Child) Student (or under the student rules that were in force before 31 March 2009, where the student was granted permission [to] stay whilst he was under 18 years old) which:

(i)   was at least six months in length, and

(ii)   ended within two years of the date the sponsor assigned the Confirmation of Acceptance for Studies; or

(4)   the Confirmation of Acceptance for Studies Checking Service entry confirms that the applicant has a knowledge of English equivalent to level B2 of the Council of Europe's Common European Framework for Language Learning in all four components (reading, writing, speaking and listening), or above [or that the Sponsor is satisfied that on completion of a pre-sessional course as provided for in paragraph 120(b)(i) of this Appendix, the applicant will have a knowledge of English as set out in this paragraph][; or]

(ii) the course is degree level study and the Confirmation of Acceptance for Studies has been assigned by a Sponsor which is not a Recognised Body or is not a body in receipt of funding as a higher education institution from the Department for Employment and Learning in Northern Ireland, the Higher Education Funding Council for England, the Higher Education Funding Council for Wales, or the Scottish Funding Council, and:

(1)   the applicant is a national of one of the following countries: Antigua and Barbuda; Australia; The Bahamas; Barbados; Belize; Canada; Dominica; Grenada; Guyana; Jamaica; New Zealand; St Kitts and Nevis; St Lucia; St Vincent and the Grenadines; Trinidad and Tobago; United States of America, and provides the specified documents [set out in paragraph 120–SD(b)]; or

(2) has obtained an academic qualification (not a professional or vocational qualification), which is deemed by UK NARIC to meet or exceed the recognised standard of a Bachelor's or Master's degree or a PhD in the UK, from an educational establishment in one of the following countries: Antigua and Barbuda; Australia; The Bahamas; Barbados; Belize; Dominica; Grenada; Guyana; Ireland; Jamaica; New Zealand; St Kitts and Nevis; St Lucia; St Vincent and The Grenadines; Trinidad and Tobago; the UK; the USA, and provides the specified documents [set out in paragraph 120–SD(a)]; or

(3) the applicant has successfully completed a course as a Tier 4 (Child) Student (or under the student rules that were in force before 31 March 2009, where the student was granted permission [to] stay whilst he was under 18 years old) which:

(i) was at least six months in length, and

(ii) ended within two years of the date the sponsor assigned the Confirmation of Acceptance for Studies; or

[(4)   the applicant provides the specified documents from an English language test provider approved by the Secretary of State for these purposes as listed in Appendix O, which clearly show:

    (i)   the applicant's name,

    (ii)   that the applicant has achieved or exceeded level B2 of the Council of Europe's Common European Framework for Language learning in all four components (reading, writing, speaking and listening), unless exempted from sitting a component on the basis of the applicant's disability,

    (iii)   the date of the award, and

    (iv)   that the test is within its validity date (where applicable).] Or

(iii)   the course is for below degree level study and:

(1)   the applicant is a national of one of the following countries: Antigua and Barbuda; Australia; The Bahamas; Barbados; Belize; Canada; Dominica; Grenada; Guyana; Jamaica; New Zealand; St Kitts and Nevis; St Lucia; St Vincent and the Grenadines; Trinidad and Tobago; United States of America, and provides the specified documents [set out in paragraph 120–SD(b)]; or

(2)   has obtained an academic qualification (not a professional or vocational qualification), which is deemed by UK NARIC to meet or exceed the recognised standard of a Bachelor's or Master's degree or a PhD in the UK, from an educational establishment in one of the following countries: Antigua and Barbuda; Australia; The Bahamas; Barbados; Belize; Dominica; Grenada; Guyana; Ireland; Jamaica; New Zealand; St Kitts and Nevis; St Lucia; St Vincent and The Grenadines; Trinidad and Tobago; the UK; the USA, and provides the specified documents [set out in paragraph 120–SD(a)]; or

(3)   the applicant has successfully completed a course as a Tier 4 (Child) Student (or under the student rules that were in force before 31 March 2009, where the student was granted permission [to] stay whilst he was under 18 years old) which:

    (i)   was at least six months in length, and

    (ii)   ended within two years of the date the sponsor assigned the Confirmation of Acceptance for Studies; or

(4)   the applicant provides an original English language test certificate from an English language test provider approved by the Secretary of State for these purposes [as listed in Appendix O,] which is within its validity date, and clearly shows:

    (i)   the applicant's name,

    (ii)   that the applicant has achieved or exceeded level B1 of the Council of Europe's Common European Framework for Language Learning in all four components (reading, writing, speaking and listening), unless exempted from sitting a component on the basis of the applicant's disability, and

    (iii)   the date of the award.]

    (iv)   that the test is within its validity date (where applicable)]

Note

Words deleted by HC 120, para 13 as from 1 January 2010. Paragraph 118 substituted by HC 382, para 17 as from 12 August 2010. Words in sub-para (a) inserted by HC 1511. Words in (b) substituted by HC 908, para 52 as from 21 April 2011. Sub-para (c) inserted by HC 908, para 53 as from 21 April 2011. Words in square brackets further inserted by HC 1148, para 57 as from 4 July 2011. Further amended by HC 1511, paras 47–48 as from 31 October 2011. Further amended by HC 1888, paras 163–167 as from 6 April 2012. Further amended by Cm 8423, paras 145–158 as from 20 July 2012. Further amended by HC 565, para 108 as from 6 September 2012. Further amended by HC 244, paras 25, 26 as from 1 July 2013. Further amended by HC 628, para 180 as from

119.   [If the applicant is re-sitting examinations or repeating a module of a course, the applicant must not previously have re-sat the same examination or repeated the same module more than once, unless the Sponsor is a Highly Trusted Sponsor. If this requirement is not met then no points will be awarded for the Confirmation of Acceptance for Studies, unless the Sponsor is a Highly Trusted Sponsor.]

Note

Paragraph 119 substituted by HC 439, para 79 as from 6 April 2010.

[120] [Points will only be awarded for a Confirmation of Acceptance for Studies . . . (even if all the requirements in paragraphs 116 to 119 above are met) if the course in respect of which it is issued meets each of the following requirements:

(a)   The course must meet the following minimum academic requirements:

    (i)   for applicants applying to study in England, Wales or Northern Ireland, the course must be at National Qualifications Framework (NQF) / Qualifications and Credit Framework (QCF) Level 3 or above if the Sponsor is a Highly Trusted Sponsor; or

    (ii)   for applicants applying to study in England, Wales or Northern Ireland, the course must be at National Qualifications Framework (NQF) / Qualifications and Credit Framework (QCF) Level 4 or above if the Sponsor is an A-Rated Sponsor or a B-Rated Sponsor; or

    (iii)   for applicants applying to study in Scotland, the course must be accredited at Level 6 or above in the Scottish Credit and Qualifications Framework (SCQF) by the Scottish Qualifications Authority and the Sponsor must be a Highly Trusted Sponsor; or

    (iv)   for applicants applying to study in Scotland, the course must be accredited at Level 7 or above in the Scottish Credit and Qualifications Framework (SCQF) by the Scottish Qualifications Authority if the Sponsor is an A-Rated Sponsor or B-Rated Sponsor; or

    (v)   the course must be a short-term Study Abroad Programme in the United Kingdom as part of the applicant's qualification at an overseas higher education institution, and that qualification must be confirmed as the same as a United Kingdom degree level by the National Recognition Information Centre for the United Kingdom (UK NARIC); or

    (vi)   the course must be an English language course at level B2 or above of the Common European Framework of Reference for Languages; or

    (vii)   the course must be a recognised Foundation Programme for postgraduate doctors or dentists;

(b)   The Confirmation of Acceptance for Studies must be for a single course of study except where the Confirmation of Acceptance for Studies is:

    (i)   issued by a Sponsor which is a Recognised Body or a body in receipt of funding as a higher education institution from the Department for Employment and Learning in Northern Ireland, the Higher Education Funding Council for England, the Higher Education Funding Council for Wales, or the Scottish Funding Council to cover both a pre-sessional course of no longer than three months' duration and a course of degree level study at that Sponsor; and

    (ii)   the applicant has an unconditional offer of a place on a course of degree level study at that Sponsor[, or that where the offer is made in respect of an applicant whose knowledge of English is not at B2 level of the Council of Europe's Common European Framework for Language Learning in all four components (reading, writing, speaking and listening) or above, the Sponsor is satisfied that on completion of a pre-sessional course as provided for in (i) above, the applicant will have knowledge of English at as set out in this paragraph]; and

    (iii)   the course of degree level study commences no later than one month after the end date of the pre-sessional course.

(c)   The course must, except in the case of a pre-sessional course, lead to an approved qualification . . . .

    [(ca) If a student is specifically studying towards an Association of Certified Chartered Accountants (ACCA) qualification or an ACCA Foundation in Accountancy . . . qualification, the sponsor must be an ACCA approved learning partner — student tuition (ALP-st) at either Gold or Platinum level.]

    (cb) An approved qualification as that is:

    (1)   validated by Royal Charter,

    (2)   awarded by a body that is on the list of recognised bodies produced by the Department for Business, Innovation and Skills,

    (3)   recognised by one or more recognised bodies through a formal articulation agreement with the awarding body,

    (4)   in England, Wales and Northern Ireland, on the Register of Regulated Qualifications register.ofqual.gov.uk/) at National Qualifications Framework (NQF) / Qualifications and Credit Framework (QCF) level 3 or above,

    (5)   in Scotland, accredited at Level 6 or above in the Scottish Credit and Qualifications Framework (SCQF) by the Scottish Qualifications Authority,

    (6)   an overseas qualification that UK NARIC assesses as valid and equivalent to National Qualifications Framework (NQF) / Qualifications and Credit Framework (QCF) level 3 or above, or

    (7)   covered by a formal legal agreement between a UK-recognised body and another education provider or awarding body. An authorised signatory for institutional agreements within the recognised body must sign this. The agreement must confirm the recognised body's own independent assessment of the level of the Tier 4 Sponsor's or the awarding body's programme compared to the National Qualifications Framework (NQF) / Qualifications and Credit Framework (QCF) or its equivalents. It must also state that the recognised body would admit any student who successfully completed the Tier 4 Sponsor's or the awarding body's named course onto a specific or a range of degree-level courses it offers.

(d)   Other than when the applicant is on a course-related work placement or a pre-sessional course, all study that forms part of the course must take place on the premises of the sponsoring educational institution or an institution which is a partner institution of the migrant's Sponsor.

(e)   The course must meet one of the following requirements:

    (i)   be a full time course of degree level study that leads to an approved qualification [as defined in (cb) above];

    (ii)   be an overseas course of degree level study that is recognised as being equivalent to a UK Higher Education course and is being provided by an overseas Higher Education Institution; or

    (iii)   be a full time course of study involving a minimum of 15 hours per week organised daytime study and, except in the case of a pre-sessional course, lead to an approved qualification, below bachelor degree level [as defined in (cb) above].

(f)   [Where the student is following a course of below degree level study including course-related work placement, the course can only be offered if the Sponsor is a Highly Trusted Sponsor. If the course contains a course-related work placement, any period that the applicant will be spending on that placement must not exceed one third of the total length of the course spent in the United Kingdom except:]

    (i)   where it is a United Kingdom statutory requirement that the placement should exceed one third of the total length of the course; or

    (ii)   where the placement does not exceed one half of the total length of the course undertaken in the UK and the student is following a degree level study and is either:

        (a)   sponsored by a Sponsor that is a recognised Body or a body in receipt of public funding as a higher education institution from the Department of Employment and learning in Northern Ireland, the Higher Education Funding Council for England, the Higher Education Funding Council for Wales or the Scottish Funding Council; or

        (b)   sponsored by an overseas higher education institution to undertake a short-term Study Abroad programme in the United Kingdom.]

Note

This paragraph inserted by HC 908, para 55 as from 21 April 2011. Sub-para (ca) inserted by HC 1148, para 58 as from 4 July 2011. Sub-paragraph (f) substituted by HC 1888, paras 169, 170 as from 6 April 2012. Renumbered by HC 1888, paras 172 as from 6 April 2012. Further amended by HC 565, para 109 as from 6 September 2012. Further amended by HC 760, para 327 as from 13 December 2012. Further amended by HC 628, para 181 and shall apply to all applications decided on or after 1 October 2013.

[Specified documents

120-SD Where paragraphs 118 to 120 of this Appendix refer to specified documents, those specified documents are as follows:

[(a) In the case of evidence relating to previous qualifications, the applicant must provide, for each qualification, either:

    (i) The original certificate(s) of qualification, which clearly shows:
  - (1) the applicant's name,
  - (2) the title of the award,
  - (3) the date of the award, and
  - (4) the name of the awarding institution;

    (ii) The transcript of results, which clearly shows:
  - (1) the applicant's name,
  - (2) the name of the academic institution,
  - (3) their course title, and
  - (4) confirmation of the award;

This transcript must be original unless the applicant has applied for their course through UCAS (Universities and Colleges Admissions Service), and:

    (a) the applicant is applying in the UK to study at a Higher Education Institution which has Highly Trusted Sponsor status, and

    (b) the qualification is issued by the UK awarding body for a course that the applicant has studied in the UK;

or

    (iii) If the applicant's Tier 4 sponsor has assessed the applicant by using one or more references, and the Confirmation of Acceptance for Studies Checking Service entry includes details of the references assessed, the original reference(s) (or a copy, together with an original letter from the Tier 4 sponsor confirming it is a true copy of the reference they assessed), which must contain:
  - (1) the applicant's name,
  - (2) confirmation of the type and level of course or previous experience; and dates of study or previous experience,
  - (3) date of the letter, and
  - (4) contact details of the referee.]

(b) In the case of evidence of the applicant's nationality, the specified documents are the applicant's current valid original passport or travel document. If the applicant is unable to provide this, the UK Border Agency may exceptionally consider this requirement to have been met where the applicant provides full reasons in the passport section of the application form, and either:

    (1) a current national identity document, or

    (2) an original letter from his home government or embassy, on the letter-headed paper of the government or embassy, which has been issued by an authorised official of that institution and confirms the applicant's full name, date of birth and nationality.]

Note

Sub-para (a) substituted by HC 244, para 27 as from 1 July 2013.

[120A.] (a)

[Points will only be awarded for a valid Confirmation of Acceptance for Studies . . . (even if all the requirements in paragraphs 116 to 120A above are met) if the Sponsor has confirmed that the course for which the Confirmation of Acceptance for Studies has been assigned represents academic progress from previous study[, as defined in (b) below] undertaken during the last period of leave as a Tier 4 (General) Student or as a Student [where the applicant has had such leave], except where:

(i) the applicant is re-sitting examinations or repeating modules in accordance with paragraph 119 above, or

(ii) the applicant is making a first application to move to a new institution to complete a course commenced elsewhere.]

[(b) For a course to represent academic progress from previous study, the course must:

(i)   be above the level of the previous course for which the applicant was granted leave as a Tier 4 (General) Student or as a Student, or

(ii)   involve further study at the same level, which the Tier 4 Sponsor confirms as complementing the previous course for which the applicant was granted leave as a Tier 4 (General) Student or as a Student.]

Note

Inserted by HC 1148, para 59 as from 4 July 2011. Words omitted by HC 1888, para 171 as from 6 April 2012. Renumbered by HC 1888, paras 172 as from 6 April 2012. Further amended by Cm 8423, paras 159–163 as from 20 July 2012.

Attributes for Tier 4 (Child) Students

121. An applicant applying for entry Clearance or leave to remain as a Tier 4 (Child) Student must score 30 points for attributes.

122. Available points are shown in Table 17 below.

123. Notes to accompany Table 17 appear below that table.

Table 17

[Criterion	Points awarded
Confirmation of Acceptance for Studies	30]

Notes

Note

Table 17 substituted by HC 120, para 17 as from 1 January 2010.

[**123A.** In order to obtain points for a Confirmation of Acceptance for Studies, the applicant must provide a valid Confirmation of Acceptance for Studies reference number.]

Note

Paragraph 123A inserted by HC 1888, para 173 as from 6 April 2012.

124. A . . . Confirmation of Acceptance for Studies will be considered to be valid only if:

(a)   where the applicant is under 16, it was issued by an independent, fee paying school,

(b)   it was issued no more than 6 months before the application is made,

(c)   the application for entry clearance or leave to remain is made no more than 3 months before the start date of the course of study as stated in the . . . Confirmation of Acceptance for Studies,

(d)   the Sponsor has not withdrawn the offer since the . . . Confirmation of Acceptance for Studies was issued,

(e)   it was issued by an institution with a Tier 4 (Child) Student Sponsor Licence, and

(f)   the institution must still hold such a licence at the time the application for entry clearance or leave to remain is determined.

[(fa) the migrant must not previously have applied for entry clearance, leave to enter or leave to remain using the same Confirmation of Acceptance for Studies reference number, if that application was either approved or refused (not rejected as an invalid application[, declared void] or withdrawn), and]

(g)   it contains such information as is specified as mandatory in [these immigration rules].

Note

Words deleted by HC 120, paras 18–20 as from 1 January 2010. Sub-para (fa) inserted by HC 908, para 56 as from 21 April 2011. Words in square brackets ", declared void" inserted by HC 1888, para 174 as from 6 April 2012. Words "these immigration rules" substituted by HC 760, para 328 as from 13 December 2012.

125. A Confirmation of Acceptance for Studies reference number will only be considered to be valid if:

(a) the number supplied links to a Confirmation of Acceptance for Studies Checking Service entry that names the applicant as the migrant and confirms that the Sponsor is sponsoring him in the Tier 4 category indicated by the migrant in his application for leave to remain (that is, as a Tier 4 (General) Student or a Tier 4 (Child) Student), . . .

[(b) that reference number must not have been withdrawn or cancelled by the Sponsor or the UK Border Agency since it was assigned, [or]]

[(c) where the application for entry clearance or leave to remain is for the applicant to commence a new course of study, not for completion of a course already commenced by way of re-sitting examinations or repeating a module of a course, the Sponsor must hold an A-rated or Highly Trusted Sponsor Licence and must not be a Legacy Sponsor,

(d) where the Confirmation of Acceptance for Studies is issued by a legacy Sponsor or a B-rated Sponsor, the Confirmation of Acceptance for Studies will only be valid if it is issued for completion of a course already commenced by way of re-sitting examinations or repeating a module of a course and the Confirmation of Acceptance for Studies must be for the same course as the course for which the last period of leave was granted to study with the same sponsor.],

Note

Sub-para (b) substituted by HC 908, para 57 as from 21 April 2011. Sub-paragraphs (c)-(d) inserted by HC 1888, para 176 as from 6 April 2012.

125A. [Points will only be awarded for a Confirmation of Acceptance for Studies if the applicant:

(a) supplies, as evidence of previous qualifications, [the specified documents set out in paragraph 125–SD] that the applicant used to obtain the offer of a place on a course from the Sponsor, or

(b) is sponsored by a Highly Trusted Sponsor, is a national of one of the countries [or the rightful holder of a qualifying passport issued by one of the relevant competent authorities, as appropriate,] listed in Appendix H and is applying for entry clearance in his country of nationality [or in the territory related to the passport he holds, as appropriate,] or leave to remain in the UK. The UK Border Agency reserves the right to request the specified documents [set out in paragraph 125–SD] from these applicants. The application will be refused of the specified documents are not provided in accordance with the request made][or

(c) where the application for entry clearance or leave to remain is for the applicant to commence a new course of study, not for completion of a course already commenced by way of re-sitting examinations or repeating a module of a course, the Sponsor must hold an A-rated or Highly Trusted Sponsor Licence and must not be a Legacy Sponsor,

(d) where the Confirmation of Acceptance for Studies is issued by a legacy Sponsor or a B-rated sponsor, the Confirmation of Acceptance for Studies will only be valid if it is issued for completion of a course already commenced by way of re-sitting examinations or repeating a module of a course and the Confirmation of Acceptance for Studies must be the same course as the course for which the last period of leave was granted to study with the same sponsor.]

Note

Inserted by HC 1148, para 60 as from 4 July 2011. Words in square brackets in sub-para (b) inserted by HC 1511, paras 50–51 as from 31 October 2011. Sub-paragraphs (c), (d) inserted by HC 1888, para 176 as from 6 April 2012. Further amended by Cm 8423, paras 164, 165 as from 20 July 2012.

[Specified documents

125-SD Where paragraph 125 of this Appendix refers to specified documents evidence relating to previous qualifications, those specified documents are:

(i) The original certificate(s) of qualification, which clearly shows:

  (1) the applicant's name,

  (2) the title of the award,

(3)　　the date of the award, and
(4)　　the name of the awarding institution;
(ii)　The original transcript of results, which clearly shows:
　　　(1)　　the applicant's name,
　　　(2)　　the name of the academic institution,
　　　(3)　　their course title, and
　　　(4)　　confirmation of the award.]

Note

Inserted by Cm 8423, paras 166 as from 20 July 2012.

126.　Points will not be awarded under Table 17 unless the course that the student will be pursuing meets one of the following requirements:
(a)　　be taught in accordance with the National Curriculum,
(b)　　be taught in accordance with the National Qualification Framework (NQF),
(c)　　be accepted as being of equivalent status to (a) or (b) above by Ofsted (England), the Education and Training Inspectorate (Northern Ireland), Her Majesty's Inspectorate of Education (Scotland) or Estyn (Wales),
(d)　　be provided as required by prevailing independent school education inspection standards.]
[(e)　is a single course of study, except where the Confirmation of Acceptance for Studies is:
　　　(i)　　issued by an independent school to cover both a pre-sessional course and a course at an independent school; and
　　　(ii)　　the applicant has an unconditional offer of a place at the independent school; and
　　　(iii)　　the duration of the pre-sessional course and period of study at the independent school does not exceed the maximum period of entry clearance or leave to remain that can be granted under paragraphs 245ZZB and 245ZZD of the Immigration Rules.]

Note

Sub-para (e) inserted by HC 908, para 58 as from 21 April 2011. Paragraph 125A inserted by HC 1148, para 60 as from 4 July 2011. Further amended by HC 1039, paras 141–194.

[APPENDIX AR
ADMINISTRATIVE REVIEW

Introduction

Administrative review is available where an eligible decision has been made. Decisions eligible for administrative review are listed in paragraph AR3.2 of this Appendix.

Administrative review will consider whether an eligible decision is wrong because of a case working error and, if it is considered to be wrong, the decision will be withdrawn or amended as set out in paragraph AR2.2 of this Appendix.

Rules about how to make a valid application for administrative review are set out at paragraphs 34M to 34Y of these Rules.

Definitions

AR1.1 For the purpose of this Appendix the following definitions apply:

Applicant	the individual applying for administrative review.
Case working error	an error in decision-making listed in paragraph AR3.4 (for administrative review in the UK).
Valid application	an application for administrative review made in accordance with paragraphs 34M to 34Y of these Rules.

Pending	as defined in paragraph AR2.9.
Reviewer	the Home Office case worker or Immigration Officer conducting the administrative review.
Original decision maker	the Home Office case worker or Immigration Officer who made the *eligible decision*.

General Principles

WHAT IS ADMINISTRATIVE REVIEW?

AR2.1   Administrative review is the review of an *eligible decision* to decide whether the decision is wrong due to a *case working error*.

OUTCOME OF ADMINISTRATIVE REVIEW

AR2.2   The outcome of an administrative review will be:
(a)   Administrative review succeeds and the *eligible decision* is withdrawn; or
(b)   Administrative review does not succeed and the *eligible decision* remains in force and all of the reasons given for the decision are maintained; or
(c)   Administrative review does not succeed and the *eligible decision* remains in force but one or more of the reasons given for the decision are withdrawn; or
(d)   Administrative review does not succeed and the *eligible decision* remains in force but with different or additional reasons to those specified in the decision under review.

WHAT WILL BE CONSIDERED ON ADMINISTRATIVE REVIEW?

AR2.3   The *eligible decision* will be reviewed to establish whether there is a *case working error*, either as identified in the application for administrative review, or identified by the *Reviewer* in the course of conducting the administrative review.

AR2.4   The *Reviewer* will not consider any evidence that was not before the *original decision maker* except where evidence that was not before the *original decision maker* is submitted to demonstrate that a *case working error* as defined in paragraph AR3.4 (e), (g), (h) and (j) has been made.

AR2.5   If the *applicant* has identified a *case working error* as defined in paragraph AR3.4 (e), (g), (h) and (j), the *Reviewer* may contact the applicant or his representative in writing, and request relevant evidence. The requested evidence must be received at the address specified in the request within 7 working days of the date of the request.

AR2.6   The *Reviewer* will not consider whether the applicant is entitled to leave to remain on some other basis and nothing in these rules shall be taken to mean that the *applicant* may make an application for leave or vary an existing application for leave, or make a protection or human rights claim, by seeking administrative review.

APPLYING FOR ADMINISTRATIVE REVIEW

AR2.7   The rules setting out the process to be followed for making an application for administrative review are at 34M to 34Y of these Rules.

EFFECT OF PENDING ADMINISTRATIVE REVIEW ON LIABILITY FOR REMOVAL

AR2.8   Where administrative review is pending (as defined in AR2.9) the Home Office will not seek to remove the *applicant* from the United Kingdom.

WHEN IS ADMINISTRATIVE REVIEW PENDING?

AR2.9   Administrative review is pending for the purposes of sections 3C(2)(d) and 3D(2)(c) of the Immigration Act 1971:

(a) While an application for administrative review can be made in accordance with 34M to 34Y of these Rules, ignoring any possibility of an administrative review out-of-time under paragraph 34R(2);

(b) While a further application for administrative review can be made in accordance with paragraph 34M(2) of these Rules following a notice of outcome at AR2.2(d) served in accordance with Articles 8ZA to 8ZC of the Immigration (Leave to Enter and Remain) Order 2000 (SI 2000/1161) (as amended);

(c) When an application for administrative review has been made until:

    (i) the application for administrative review is rejected as invalid because it does not meet the requirements of paragraph 34N to 34S of these Rules;

    (ii) the application for administrative review is withdrawn in accordance with paragraph 34X; or

    (iii) the notice of outcome at AR2.2(a), (b) or (c) is served in accordance with Articles 8ZA to 8ZC of the Immigration (Leave to Enter and Remain) Order 2000 (SI 2000/1161) (as amended).

AR2.10 Administrative review is not pending when an administrative review waiver form has been signed by an individual in respect of whom an *eligible decision* has been made. An administrative review waiver form is a form where the person can declare that although they can make an application in accordance with paragraphs 34M to 34Y of these Rules, they will not do so.

Administrative Review in the UK

DECISIONS ELIGIBLE FOR ADMINISTRATIVE REVIEW IN THE UNITED KINGDOM

AR3.1 Administrative review is only available where an *eligible decision* has been made.

AR3.2

(a) An *eligible decision* is a refusal of an application made on or after 20th October 2014 for:

    (i) leave to remain as a Tier 4 Migrant under the Points Based System; or

    (ii) leave to remain as the partner of a Tier 4 Migrant under paragraph 319C of the Immigration Rules; or

    (iii) leave to remain as the child of a Tier 4 Migrant under paragraph 319H of the Immigration Rules.

(b) An eligible decision is also a decision to grant leave to remain in relation to an application referred to in sub-paragraph (a) where a review is requested of the period of leave granted.

AR3.3 Any decision not listed in AR3.2. is not an *eligible decision* and administrative review is not available in respect of that decision.

WHAT IS A CASE WORKING ERROR?

AR3.4 The following is a complete list of case working errors for the purposes of these Rules:

(a) Where the *original decision maker* applied the wrong Immigration Rules;

(b) Where the *original decision maker* applied the Immigration Rules incorrectly;

(c) Where the *original decision maker* incorrectly added up the points to be awarded under the Immigration Rules;

(d) Where there has been an error in calculating the correct period of immigration leave either held or to be granted;

(e) Where the *original decision maker* has not considered all the evidence that was submitted as evidenced in the *eligible decision*;

(f) Where the *original decision maker* has considered some or all of the evidence submitted incorrectly as evidenced in the *eligible decision*;

(g) Where the Immigration Rules provide for the *original decision maker* to consider the credibility of the applicant in deciding the application and the *original decision maker* has reached an unreasonable decision on the credibility of the applicant;

(h)   Where the *original decision maker*'s decision to refuse an application on the basis that the supporting documents were not genuine was incorrect;

(i)   Where the *original decision maker*'s decision to refuse an application on the basis that the supporting documents did not meet the requirements of the Immigration Rules was incorrect;

(j)   Where the *original decision maker* has incorrectly refused an application on the basis that it was made more than 28 days after leave expired; and

(k)   Where the *original decision maker* failed to apply the Secretary of State's relevant published policy and guidance in relation to the application.]

Note

Inserted by HC 693, para 168 as from 20 October 2014.

APPENDIX ARMED FORCES

PART 1
GENERAL

WHO THESE RULES APPLY TO

1.   The rules contained in this Appendix apply to those seeking to enter or remain in the United Kingdom as:

(a)   a foreign or Commonwealth member of HM Forces (on discharge);

(b)   a partner or child of a member of HM Forces;

(c)   a partner or child of a member of non-HM Forces who is exempt from immigration control by virtue of section 8(4)(b) or (c) of the Immigration Act 1971;

(d)   a member of non-HM Forces who is not exempt from immigration control; . . .

(e)   a partner or child of a member of non-HM Forces who is not exempt from immigration control[;]

[(f)   a Relevant Civilian Employee as defined in paragraph 2(ja); and

(g)   a partner or child of a Relevant Civilian Employee.]

Note

Word "and" deleted by HC 1138, para 135 as from 6 April 2014. Amended by HC 1138, para 135 as from 6 April 2014. Amended by HC 1138, para 135 as from 6 April 2014.

INTERPRETATION AND GENERAL PROVISIONS

2.   In this Appendix (including as it applies to applications under Part 7 or 8 of these Rules):

(a)   an application for leave to enter or remain includes an application for variation of leave to enter or remain;

(b)   a reference to a British Citizen in the United Kingdom includes:

(i)   a British Citizen who is coming to the United Kingdom with the applicant as the applicant's partner or parent; and

(ii)   a British Citizen who has naturalised having accrued 5 years' reckonable service in HM Forces;

[(ba)   a reference to a civilian employee of NATO includes an employee of the American National Red Cross working with US Forces in the United Kingdom;]

(c)   "Gurkha" means a member of HM Forces who is serving or has served in the Brigade of Gurkhas of the British Army under the Brigade of Gurkhas' terms and conditions of service;

(d)   "a member of HM Forces" is a person who, subject to sub-paragraphs (e) and (f), is a member of the regular forces within the meaning of the Armed Forces Act 2006;

(e)   a person is not to be regarded as a member of HM Forces if the person is treated as a member of a regular force by virtue of:

   (i) section 369 of the Armed Forces Act 2006, or

   (ii) section 4(3) of the Visiting Forces (British Commonwealth) Act 1933;

 (f) a reference to a member of HM Forces includes a person who was a member of HM Forces but was discharged within the period of 2 years prior to the date of the application under these Rules made in relation to that member;

 (g) "a member of non-HM Forces" means a member of other armed forces who is:

   (i) exempt from immigration control under section 8(4)(b) or (c) of the Immigration Act 1971, or

   (ii) not exempt from immigration control;

 (h) "partner" means [(unless a different meaning of partner applies elsewhere in this Appendix)]:

   (i) the applicant's spouse;

   (ii) the applicant's civil partner;

   (iii) the applicant's fiancé(e) or proposed civil partner; or

   (iv) a person who has been living together with the applicant in a relationship akin to a marriage or civil partnership for at least 2 years prior to the date of the application;

 (i) a reference to a person who is present and settled in the UK includes a person who is being admitted for settlement on the same occasion as the applicant;

 (j) "reckonable service" is the service which counts towards pension, which starts from the first day of paid service in HM Forces;

 [(ja) a reference to a Relevant Civilian Employee means a civilian who is being employed to work in the United Kingdom by:

   (i) [a NATO force];

   (ii) a company under contract to [a NATO force]; or

   (iii) the Australian Department of Defence;]

 (k) "specified" means specified in Appendix FM-SE and Appendix O to these Rules;

 (l) where a financial or maintenance requirement applies in this Appendix, paragraphs A. to 21 of Appendix FM-SE to these Rules shall apply as appropriate.

3. If an Entry Clearance Officer, or the Secretary of State, has reasonable cause to doubt the genuineness of any document submitted in support of an application, and having taken reasonable steps to verify the document, is unable to verify that it is genuine, the document will be discounted for the purposes of the application.

4. A reference to an application being considered under this Appendix includes, where relevant, an application considered under Part 7 or 8 of these Rules which requires compliance with this Appendix.

5. Paragraphs 277-280, 289AA, 295AA and 296 of Part 8 of these Rules apply to applications made under this Appendix.

Note

Appendix Armed Forces paragraph 2(b) inserted by HC 1138, para 136 as from 13 March 2014. Amended by HC 1138, para 136 as from 6 April 2014. Amended by HC 1138, para 137 shall apply to all applications decided on or after 6 April 2014. Amended by HC 1138, para 138 as from 6 April 2014. Amended by HC 693, para 169 as from 6 November 2014, save that if an application has been made for entry clearance or leave to enter or remain before 6 November 2014, the application will be decided in accordance with the Rules in force on 5 November 2014.

LEAVE TO ENTER

6. The requirements to be met by a person seeking leave to enter the United Kingdom under this Appendix are that the person:

    (a)   must have a valid entry clearance for entry in a route under this Appendix[, unless they are:
        (i)   a non-visa national;
        (ii)   not seeking entry for a period exceeding 6 months; and
        (iii)   applying for leave to enter under paragraphs 56, 61B or 64 of this Appendix; and]

    (b)   must produce to the Immigration Officer on arrival a valid national passport or other document satisfactorily establishing their identity and nationality.

7.   If a person does not meet the requirements of paragraph 6, entry will be refused.

Note

Amended by HC 693, para 170 as from 6 November 2014, save that if an application has been made for entry clearance or leave to enter or remain before 6 November 2014, the application will be decided in accordance with the Rules in force on 5 November 2014.

PART 2
SUITABILITY REQUIREMENTS

8.   An application under this Appendix will be refused on the grounds of suitability if any of the provisions in this paragraph apply:

    (a)   in respect of applications for entry clearance, the Secretary of State has personally directed that the exclusion of the applicant from the United Kingdom is conducive to the public good;

    (b)   the applicant is currently the subject of a deportation order;

    (c)   subject to sub-paragraph (d), permitting the applicant to enter, or remain in, the United Kingdom is not conducive to the public good because he or she has been convicted of an offence for which he or she has been sentenced to a period of imprisonment of:
        (i)   at least 4 years; or
        (ii)   at least 12 months, but less than 4 years, unless:
            (aa)   in respect of applications for entry clearance: a period of 10 years has passed since the end of the sentence; or
            (bb)   in respect of applications for indefinite leave to remain: a period of 15 years has passed since the end of the sentence; or
        (iii)   in respect of applications for entry clearance or indefinite leave to remain, less than 12 months, unless:
            (aa)   in respect of applications for entry clearance: a period of 5 years has passed since the end of the sentence; or
            (bb)   in respect of applications for indefinite leave to remain: a period of 7 years has passed since the end of the sentence;

    (d)   in respect of applications for entry clearance, where sub-paragraph (c) applies, unless refusal would be contrary to the Human Rights Convention or the Convention and Protocol Relating to the Status of Refugees, it will only be in exceptional circumstances that the public interest in maintaining refusal will be outweighed by compelling factors;

    (e)   in respect of applications for limited leave to remain or indefinite leave to remain, in the view of the Secretary of State,
        (i)   the applicant's offending has caused serious harm; or
        (ii)   the applicant is a persistent offender who shows a particular disregard for the law;

    (f)   in respect of applications for indefinite leave to remain, the applicant has, within the 24 months prior to the date on which the application is decided, been convicted of or admitted an offence for which they received a non-custodial sentence or other out of court disposal that is recorded on their criminal record;

(g)   permitting the applicant to enter, or remain in, the UK is not conducive to the public good because, for example, their conduct (including convictions which do not fall within sub-paragraph (c) or (f) as appropriate, character, associations, or other reasons, make it undesirable to grant them entry clearance or allow them to remain in the UK;

(h)   in respect of applications for entry clearance, the applicant left or was removed from the United Kingdom pursuant to a condition attached to a conditional caution given under section 22 of the Criminal Justice Act 2003 less than 5 years before the date on which the application is decided;

(i)   the applicant has failed without reasonable excuse to comply with a requirement to:

    (i)   attend an interview;

    (ii)   provide information;

    (iii)   provide physical data; or

    (iv)   undergo a medical examination or provide a medical report; or

(j)   it is undesirable to grant entry clearance to the applicant for medical reasons.

9.   An application under this Appendix will normally be refused on the grounds of suitability if any of the provisions in this paragraph apply:

(a)   whether or not to the applicant's knowledge:

    (i)   false information, representations or documents have been submitted in relation to the application (including false information submitted to any person to obtain a document used in support of the application); or

    (ii)   there has been a failure to disclose material facts in relation to the application;

(b)   one or more relevant NHS bodies (within the meaning of paragraph 6 of these Rules) has notified the Secretary of State that:

    (i)   the applicant has failed to pay charges in accordance with the relevant NHS regulations on charges to overseas visitors; and

    (ii)   the outstanding charges have a total value of at least £1000;

(c)   a maintenance and accommodation undertaking has been requested or required under this Appendix or paragraph 35 of these Rules or otherwise and has not been provided;

(d)   in respect of applications for entry clearance, the exclusion of the applicant from the United Kingdom is conducive to the public good because:

    (i)   within the 12 months prior to the date on which the application is decided, the person has been convicted of or admitted an offence for which they received a non-custodial sentence or other out of court disposal that is recorded on their criminal record; or

    (ii)   in the view of the Secretary of State:

       (aa)   the person's offending has caused serious harm; or

       (bb)   the person is a persistent offender who shows a particular disregard for the law.

10.   In respect of applications for limited leave to remain or indefinite leave to remain, when considering whether the presence of the applicant in the UK is not conducive to the public good any legal or practical reasons why the applicant cannot presently be removed from the United Kingdom must be ignored.

PART 3
DISCHARGED MEMBERS OF HM FORCES

GENERAL ELIGIBILITY REQUIREMENTS

11.　The general eligibility requirements to be met for entry clearance (and limited or indefinite leave to enter) or for limited or indefinite leave to remain as a discharged member of HM Forces are that:

(a)　the applicant:

    (i)　has completed at least 4 years' reckonable service in HM Forces; or

    (ii)　meets the medical discharge criteria in paragraph 12; and

(b)　on the date on which the application is made:

    (i)　the applicant has been discharged from HM Forces for a period of less than 2 years; or

    (ii)　in the case of an applicant who was medically discharged more than 2 years before, new information regarding his or her prognosis is being considered by the Secretary of State; or

    (iii)　the applicant has been granted his or her most recent period of limited leave:

        (aa)　under paragraph 15 or 19 of this Appendix as a foreign or Commonwealth citizen who has been discharged from HM Forces; or

        (bb)　under paragraph 276KA or 276QA of these Rules; or

        (cc)　under the concession which existed outside these Rules, whereby the Secretary of State exercised her discretion to grant leave to enter or remain to members of HM Forces who have been medically discharged; and

(c)　in relation to an application made by a Gurkha, the Gurkha is a citizen or national of Nepal.

MEDICAL DISCHARGE

12.　The medical discharge criteria are satisfied where the applicant was medically discharged from HM Forces:

(a)　where the cause was attributable to service in HM Forces and it came about owing to deployment in an operational theatre; or

(b)　where the cause was attributable to service in HM Forces, it did not come about owing to deployment in an operational theatre but it is appropriate to grant leave to enter or remain in the United Kingdom following an assessment of the following factors:

    (i)　the seriousness of the illness or injury;

    (ii)　the need for further medical treatment in relation to the illness or injury and the availability of such medical treatment in the applicant's country of origin;

    (iii)　the prognosis for recovery, including whether the injury or illness will affect the applicant's ability to support themselves in their country of origin; and

    (iv)　the length of reckonable service in HM Forces at the time of the applicant's discharge.

INDEFINITE LEAVE TO ENTER

13.　Entry clearance and indefinite leave to enter as a foreign or Commonwealth citizen discharged from HM Forces will be granted to an applicant who:

(a)　is outside the United Kingdom;

(b)　has made a valid application for entry clearance and indefinite leave to enter as a foreign or Commonwealth citizen discharged from HM Forces;

(c)　does not fall to be refused on the grounds of suitability under paragraph 8 or 9; and (d)　　meets the general eligibility requirements in paragraph 11.

LEAVE TO REMAIN

14.　Limited leave to remain as a foreign or Commonwealth citizen discharged from HM Forces will be granted to an applicant who:

(a)　　is in the United Kingdom;

(b)　　is not in breach of immigration laws, except that any period of overstaying for a period of 28 days or less will be disregarded;

(c)　　has made a valid application for limited leave to remain as a foreign or Commonwealth citizen discharged from HM Forces;

(d)　　does not fall to be refused on the grounds of suitability under paragraph 8 or 9; and

(e)　　meets the general eligibility requirements in paragraph 11.

15.　Limited leave to remain granted under paragraph 14 will normally be granted for a period not exceeding 30 months and will be subject to such conditions as the Secretary of State considers appropriate.

INDEFINITE LEAVE TO REMAIN

16.　Indefinite leave to remain as a foreign or Commonwealth citizen discharged from HM Forces will be granted to an applicant who:

(a)　　is in the United Kingdom;

(b)　　is not in breach of immigration laws, except that any period of overstaying for a period of 28 days or less will be disregarded;

(c)　　has made a valid application for indefinite leave to remain as a foreign or Commonwealth citizen discharged from HM Forces;

(d)　　does not fall to be refused on the grounds of suitability under paragraph 8 or 9; and

(e)　　meets the general eligibility requirements in paragraph 11.

CIRCUMSTANCES IN WHICH LIMITED LEAVE TO REMAIN MAY BE GRANTED TO APPLICANTS FOR INDEFINITE LEAVE TO REMAIN UNDER PARAGRAPH 16

17.　Limited leave to remain as a foreign or Commonwealth citizen discharged from HM Forces may be granted to a person who fails to meet the requirements for indefinite leave to remain in paragraph 16 of this Appendix by reason only of failing to meet the suitability requirements in paragraph 8 or 9 in respect of a grant of indefinite leave to remain (but not a grant of limited leave to remain).

18.　Limited leave to remain as a foreign or Commonwealth citizen discharged from HM Forces may be granted to a person (P) who fails to meet the requirements for indefinite leave to remain in paragraph 16 of this Appendix by reason only of being unable to meet the medical discharge criteria in paragraph 12, provided that the following conditions are met:

(a)　　P has been medically discharged from HM Forces;

(b)　　the cause of P's discharge was attributable to service in HM Forces; and

(c)　　before P can return to P's country of origin it is appropriate to grant limited leave to remain to facilitate:

(i)　　further medical treatment for P; or

(ii)　　a period of recovery for P.

19.　Limited leave to remain granted under paragraph 17 or 18 will normally be granted for a period not exceeding 30 months and will be subject to such conditions as the Secretary of State considers appropriate.

PART 4
PARTNERS OF MEMBERS OF HM FORCES

GENERAL ELIGIBILITY REQUIREMENTS

20. The general eligibility requirements to be met by the partner (P) of a member of HM Forces are that on the date the application is made:

    (a) P's sponsor is a member of HM Forces (as defined in paragraph 2(d) of this Appendix) who:

        (i) is exempt from immigration control; or

        (ii) has leave to enter or remain under paragraphs 13-19 of this Appendix or paragraphs 276E-QA of these Rules [or under the concession which existed outside these Rules whereby the Secretary of State exercised her discretion to grant leave to enter or remain to a member of HM Forces who has been medically discharged]; or

        (iii) is being granted leave to enter or remain under paragraphs 13-19 of this Appendix or paragraphs 276E-QA of these Rules at the same time as P; or

        (iv) is a British Citizen;

    (b) P and P's sponsor:

        (i) are both aged 18 or over;

        (ii) must not be within a prohibited degree of relationship;

        (iii) must intend to live together permanently; and

        (iv) must have met in person;

    (c) the relationship between P and P's sponsor is genuine and subsisting; and

    (d) any previous relationship of P or P's sponsor must have broken down permanently, unless it is a relationship which falls within paragraph 278(i) of these Rules.

21. If P and P's sponsor are married or in a civil partnership, it must be a valid marriage or civil partnership as specified in Appendix FM-SE.

22. If P is the fiancé(e) or proposed civil partner of P's sponsor, P must be seeking entry to the UK to enable their marriage or civil partnership to take place.

LEAVE TO ENTER

23. Entry clearance and leave to enter as the partner of a member of HM Forces will be granted to an applicant who:

    (a) is outside the United Kingdom;

    (b) has made a valid application for entry clearance and leave to enter as the partner of a member of HM Forces;

    (c) does not fall to be refused on the grounds of suitability under paragraph 8 or 9;

    (d) meets the general eligibility requirements in paragraph 20;

    (e) meets the English language requirement in Part 11 of this Appendix; and

    (f) meets the financial requirements in Part 12 of this Appendix.

24. Entry clearance and leave to enter granted under paragraph 23 will normally be:

    (a) for whichever is the shortest period of:

        (i) 5 years;

        (ii) the remaining duration of the applicant's partner's enlistment;

        (iii) the remaining duration of the applicant's partner's extant leave under paragraph 276KA or 276QA of these Rules or paragraph 15 or 19 of this Appendix or under the concession which existed outside these Rules whereby the Secretary of State exercised her discretion to grant leave to enter or remain to a member of HM Forces who has been medically discharged; or

        (iv) in the case of a fiancé(e) or proposed civil partner, a period not exceeding 6 months; and

    (b)   subject to the following conditions:
        (i)   no recourse to public funds; and
        (ii)   in the case of a fiancé(e) or proposed civil partner, a prohibition on employment.

INDEFINITE LEAVE TO ENTER

25.   Entry clearance and indefinite leave to enter as the partner of a member of HM Forces will be granted to an applicant who:

    (a)   is outside the United Kingdom;

    (b)   has made a valid application for entry clearance and indefinite leave to enter as the partner of a member of HM Forces;

    (c)   has a partner who:
        (i)   is a foreign or Commonwealth citizen who is a member of HM Forces with at least 5 years' reckonable service in HM Forces; or
        (ii)   has been granted indefinite leave to enter or remain under paragraph 13 or 16 of this Appendix or paragraphs 276E-Q of these Rules and is in the United Kingdom; or
        (iii)   is a British Citizen;

    (d)   does not fall to be refused on the grounds of suitability under paragraph 8 or 9;

    (e)   meets the general eligibility requirements in paragraph 20;

    (f)   can demonstrate sufficient knowledge of the English language and sufficient knowledge about life in the UK in accordance with the requirements of Appendix KoLL to these Rules;

    (g)   meets the financial requirements in Part 12 of this Appendix; and

    (h)   has completed a continuous period of 60 months with leave under this Appendix as the partner of the same member of HM Forces, excluding any period of entry clearance or limited leave as a fiancé(e) or proposed civil partner.

26.   Entry clearance and limited leave to enter as a partner (excluding as a fiancé(e) or proposed civil partner) of a member of HM Forces for a period of 30 months may be granted:

    (a)   where an applicant fails to meet the requirements of paragraph 25 by reason only of failing to meet the requirements of paragraph 25(c)(i) or (ii), provided that the applicant's sponsor has been granted leave to enter or remain under paragraph 15 or 19 of this Appendix; or

    (b)   where an applicant fails to meet the requirements of paragraph 25 by reason only of failing to meet the requirements of paragraph 25(f).

27.   Entry clearance and limited leave to enter granted under paragraph 26 will be subject to a condition of no recourse to public funds.

LEAVE TO REMAIN

28.   Limited leave to remain as the partner of a member of HM Forces will be granted to an applicant who:

    (a)   is in the United Kingdom, but not:
        (i)   as a visitor;
        (ii)   with valid leave that was granted for a period of 6 months or less, unless that leave:
            (aa)   is as a fiancé(e) or proposed civil partner; or
            (bb)   was granted pending the outcome of family court or divorce proceedings; or
        (iii)   on temporary admission or temporary release;

    (b)   is not in breach of immigration laws, except that any period of overstaying for a period of 28 days or less is to be disregarded;

    (c)   has made a valid application for limited leave to remain as the partner of a member of HM Forces;

(d)   does not fall to be refused on the grounds of suitability under paragraph 8 or 9;

(e)   meets the general eligibility requirements in paragraph 20;

(f)   is not a fiancé(e) or proposed civil partner of the member of HM Forces, unless:

    (i)   the applicant is in the United Kingdom with leave as a fiancé(e) or proposed civil partner under paragraph 23 (and that earlier leave was granted in respect of the current sponsor);

    (ii)   there is good reason why the marriage or civil partnership has not taken place during that period of leave; and

    (iii)   there is evidence that the marriage or civil partnership will take place within the next 6 months;

(g)   meets the English language requirement in Part 11 of this Appendix; and

(h)   meets the financial requirements in Part 12 of this Appendix.

29.   Limited leave to remain granted under paragraph 28 will normally be granted:

(a)   for whichever is the shortest period of:

    (i)   5 years;

    (ii)   the remaining duration of the applicant's partner's enlistment; or

    (iii)   the remaining duration of the applicant's partner's extant leave under paragraph 276KA or 276QA of these Rules or paragraph 15 or 19 of this Appendix or under the concession which existed outside these Rules whereby the Secretary of State exercised her discretion to grant leave to enter or remain to a member of HM Forces who has been medically discharged; or

    (iv)   in the case of a fiancé(e) or proposed civil partner, a period not exceeding 6 months; and

(b)   subject to the following conditions:

    (i)   no recourse to public funds; and

    (ii)   in the case of a fiancé(e) or proposed civil partner, a prohibition on employment.

30.   An applicant granted limited leave to remain under paragraph 29 will be eligible to apply for settlement after a continuous period of 60 months with such leave under this Appendix as the partner of the same member of HM Forces, excluding any period of entry clearance or limited leave as a fiancé(e) or proposed civil partner.

INDEFINITE LEAVE TO REMAIN

31.   Indefinite leave to remain as the partner of a member of HM Forces will be granted to an applicant who:

(a)   is in the United Kingdom;

(b)   is not in breach of immigration laws, except that any period of overstaying for a period of 28 days or less is to be disregarded;

(c)   has a partner who:

    (i)   is a foreign or Commonwealth citizen who is a member of HM Forces with at least 5 years' reckonable service in HM Forces; or

    (ii)   has been granted, or is being granted at the same time as the applicant, indefinite leave to enter or remain under paragraph 13 or 16 of this Appendix or paragraphs 276E-Q of these Rules; or

    (iii)   is a British Citizen;

(d)   does not fall to be refused on the grounds of suitability under paragraph 8 or 9;

(e)   meets the general eligibility requirements in paragraph 20;

(f)   can demonstrate sufficient knowledge of the English language and sufficient knowledge about life in the UK in accordance with the requirements of Appendix KoLL to these Rules;

(g)   meets the financial requirements in Part 12 of this Appendix; and

    (h)   has completed a continuous period of 60 months with leave under this Appendix as the partner of the same member of HM Forces, excluding any period of entry clearance or limited leave as a fiancé(e) or proposed civil partner.

32.   Limited leave to remain as the partner (excluding as a fiancé(e) or proposed civil partner) of a member of HM Forces for a period of 30 months may be granted where the applicant fails to meet the requirements for indefinite leave to remain in paragraph 31:

    (a)   by reason only of failing to satisfy the suitability requirements in paragraph 8 or 9 in respect of a grant of indefinite leave to remain (but not a grant of limited leave to remain); or

    (b)   by reason only of failing to meet the requirements of paragraph 31(c)(i) or (ii), provided that the applicant's sponsor has been granted leave to enter or remain under paragraph 15 or 19 of this Appendix; or

    (c)   by reason only of failing to meet the requirements of paragraph 31(f).

33.   Limited leave to remain granted under paragraph 32 will be subject to a condition of no recourse to public funds.

PART 5
BEREAVED PARTNERS OF MEMBERS OF HM FORCES

GENERAL ELIGIBILITY REQUIREMENTS

34.   The general eligibility requirements to be met by a bereaved partner of a member of HM Forces are that:

    (a)   the applicant's partner at the time of the applicant's last grant of leave as a partner (other than as a fiancé(e) or proposed civil partner) was:

        (i)   a foreign or Commonwealth citizen who was a serving member of HM Forces; or

        (ii)   a discharged member of HM Forces who had been granted, or was seeking at the same time as the applicant, leave to enter or remain under paragraphs 13-19 of this Appendix or paragraphs 276E-QA of these Rules; or

        (iii)   a British Citizen in HM Forces;

    (b)   the applicant's partner has died;

    (c)   at the time of the applicant's partner's death the applicant and the partner:

        (i)   were both aged 18 or over;

        (ii)   were not within a prohibited degree of relationship; and

        (iii)   had met in person; and

    (d)   at the time of the applicant's partner's death the relationship between the applicant and the partner was genuine and subsisting and each of the parties intended to live together permanently.

INDEFINITE LEAVE TO ENTER

35.   Entry clearance and indefinite leave to enter as a bereaved partner of a member of HM Forces will be granted to an applicant who:

    (a)   is outside the United Kingdom as a result of accompanying their sponsor on an overseas posting;

    (b)   has made a valid application for entry clearance and indefinite leave to enter as the bereaved partner of a member of HM Forces;

    (c)   does not fall to be refused on the grounds of suitability under paragraph 8 or 9; and

    (d)   meets the general eligibility requirements in paragraph 34.

INDEFINITE LEAVE TO REMAIN

36.   Indefinite leave to remain as a bereaved partner of a member of HM Forces will be granted to an applicant who:

(a)   is in the United Kingdom;

(b)   has made a valid application for indefinite leave to remain as the bereaved partner of a member of HM Forces;

(c)   does not fall to be refused on the grounds of suitability under paragraph 8 or 9; and

(d)   meets the general eligibility requirements in paragraph 34.

37.   Limited leave to remain as a bereaved partner of a member of HM Forces for a period of 30 months may be granted to a person who fails to meet the requirements for indefinite leave to remain in paragraph 36 by reason only of failing to meet the suitability requirements in paragraph 8 or 9 in respect of a grant of indefinite leave to remain (but not a grant of limited leave to remain).

38.   Limited leave to remain granted under paragraph 37 will be subject to a condition of no recourse to public funds.

PART 6
PARTNERS OF MEMBERS OF HM FORCES WHO ARE THE VICTIM OF DOMESTIC VIOLENCE

GENERAL ELIGIBILITY REQUIREMENTS

39.   The general eligibility requirements to be met by the partner of a member of HM Forces who is a victim of domestic violence are that:

(a)   the applicant is in the UK and was:

(i)   last admitted to the UK under paragraph 276AD of these Rules or paragraph 23, 26, 28 or 32 of this Appendix; or

[(ii)   last granted leave to enable access to public funds pending an application under this paragraph and the preceding grant of leave was given in accordance with paragraph 276AD of these Rules or paragraph 23, 26, 28 or 32 of this Appendix;]

(b)   the leave referred to in sub-paragraph (a) [(i) or, where applicable, the preceding grant of leave referred to in subparagraph (a)(ii)] was as the partner (other than a fiancé(e) or proposed civil partner) of a member of HM Forces who is:

(i)   a British Citizen; or

(ii)   a foreign or Commonwealth citizen with at least 4 years' reckonable service in HM Forces at the date of application under this paragraph;

(c)   the applicant does not fall to be refused on grounds of suitability under paragraph 8 or 9;

(d)   the applicant has made a valid application for indefinite leave to remain as a victim of domestic violence; and

(e)   the applicant must provide evidence that during the last period of limited leave as a partner the applicant's relationship with their partner broke down permanently as a result of domestic violence.

Note

Amended by HC 693, para 171 as from 6 November 2014. Further amended by HC 693, para 171 as from 6 November 2014.

INDEFINITE LEAVE TO REMAIN

40.   Indefinite leave to remain as the partner of a member of HM Forces who is a victim of domestic violence will be granted to an applicant who meets the general eligibility requirements in paragraph 39.

41.   Limited leave to remain for a period of 30 months may be granted to a partner of a member of HM Forces who is a victim of domestic violence who fails to meet the requirements for indefinite leave to remain in paragraph 40 by reason only of failing to meet the suitability requirements in paragraph 8 or 9 in respect

of a grant of indefinite leave to remain (but not a grant of limited leave to remain). This will be subject to such conditions as the Secretary of State considers appropriate.

PART 7
CHILDREN OF MEMBERS OF HM FORCES

GENERAL ELIGIBILITY REQUIREMENTS

42. The general eligibility requirements to be met by the child of a member of HM Forces are that:
    (a) the applicant is the child of a parent who is:
        (i) a foreign or Commonwealth citizen who is a serving member of HM Forces; or
        (ii) a discharged member of HM Forces who has been granted, or who is being granted at the same time as the applicant, leave to enter or remain under paragraphs 13-19 of this Appendix or paragraphs 276E-QA of these Rules [or under the concession which existed outside these Rules whereby the Secretary of State exercised her discretion to grant leave to enter or remain to a member of HM Forces who has been medically discharged]; or
        (iii) a member of HM Forces who is a British Citizen; and
    (b) the applicant meets one of the following criteria:
        (i) the applicant's other parent must:
            (aa) also come within paragraph 42(a); or
            (bb) have been granted leave to enter or remain under paragraphs 23-33 of this Appendix or paragraph 276S, 276V or 276AE of these Rules; or
            (cc) be being granted leave to enter or remain under paragraphs 23-33 of this Appendix or paragraph 276S, 276V or 276AE of these Rules at the same time as the applicant; or
            (dd) have died; or
        (ii) the parent under paragraph 42(a) has sole responsibility for the applicant's upbringing; or
        (iii) there are serious and compelling family or other considerations which make the applicant's exclusion from the United Kingdom undesirable and suitable arrangements have been made for their care.

LEAVE TO ENTER

43. Entry clearance and leave to enter as the child of a member of HM Forces will be granted to an applicant who:
    (a) was either:
        (i) under 18 years of age at the date of application; or
        (ii) aged 18 or over at the date of application; and was last granted leave to remain under paragraph 43 or 47 of this Appendix or paragraph 276AH of these Rules;
    (b) is outside the United Kingdom;
    (c) is not married or in a civil partnership;
    (d) has not formed an independent family unit;
    (e) is not leading an independent life;
    (f) has made a valid application for entry clearance and leave to enter as the child of a member of HM Forces;
    (g) does not fall to be refused on the grounds of suitability under paragraph 8 or 9;
    (h) meets the general eligibility requirements in paragraph 42;
    [(i) either:
        (a) meets the financial requirement in Part 12 of this Appendix; or

(b) in a case in which sub-paragraph (b)(i)(aa), (b)(i)(dd) or (b)(ii) of paragraph 42 applies will be:

(i) accommodated adequately by the parent or parents the applicant will be joining without recourse to public funds in accommodation which the parent or parents own or occupy exclusively; and

(ii) maintained adequately by that parent or those parents without recourse to public funds;]

(j) has not applied and does not qualify for indefinite leave to enter under paragraph 45.

44. Entry clearance and leave to enter granted under paragraph 43 will be granted:

(a) for whichever is the shortest period of:

(i) 5 years; or

(ii) the remaining duration of the applicant's parent's enlistment; or

(iii) the remaining duration of the applicant's parent's leave; and

(b) subject to a condition of no recourse to public funds.

INDEFINITE LEAVE TO ENTER

45. Entry clearance and indefinite leave to enter as the child of a member of HM Forces will be granted to an applicant who:

(a) was either:

(i) under 18 years of age at the date of application; or

(ii) aged 18 or over at the date of application and was last granted leave to remain under paragraph 43 or 47 of this Appendix or paragraph 276AH of these Rules;

(b) is outside the United Kingdom;

(c) is not married or in a civil partnership;

(d) has not formed an independent family unit;

(e) is not leading an independent life;

(f) has made a valid application for entry clearance and indefinite leave to enter as the child of a member of HM Forces;

(g) is the child of:

(i) a foreign or Commonwealth citizen who is a serving member of HM Forces who has completed at least 5 years' reckonable service; or

(ii) a person who has been granted indefinite leave to enter or remain under paragraph 13 or 16 of this Appendix or paragraphs 276E-Q of these Rules and is in the UK; or

(iii) a member of HM Forces who is a British Citizen;

(h) meets one of the following criteria:

(i) the applicant's other parent must:

(aa) come within paragraph 45(g); or

(bb) have been granted indefinite leave to enter or remain under paragraph 25 or 31 of this Appendix or paragraph 276S or 276V of these Rules; or

(cc) be being granted indefinite leave to enter or remain under paragraph 25 or 31 of this Appendix or paragraph 276S or 276V of these Rules at the same time as the applicant; or

(dd) have died; or

(ii) the parent under paragraph 45(g) has sole responsibility for the applicant's upbringing; or

(iii) there are serious and compelling family or other considerations which make the applicant's exclusion from the United Kingdom undesirable and suitable arrangements have been made for their care;

     (i)   does not fall to be refused on the grounds of suitability under paragraph 8 or 9;

     (j)   meets the general eligibility requirements in paragraph 42;

     (k)   where the applicant is aged 18 or over, can demonstrate sufficient knowledge of the English language and about life in the United Kingdom, in accordance with the requirements of Appendix KoLL to these Rules;

     (l)   will be accommodated adequately by the parent or parents the applicant is seeking to join without recourse to public funds in accommodation which the parent or parents the applicant is seeking to join, own or occupy exclusively; and

     (m)   will be maintained adequately by the parent or parents the applicant is seeking to join, without recourse to public funds.

46.   Entry clearance and limited leave to enter as a child of a member of HM Forces for a period of 30 months may be granted subject to a condition of no recourse to public funds where:

     a)   an applicant fails to meet the requirements for indefinite leave to enter in paragraph 45 by reason solely of failing to meet the requirements of paragraph 45(k); or

     b)   an applicant fails to meet the requirements of paragraph 45 by reason only of failing to meet the requirements of paragraph 45(g)(i) or (ii), provided that the applicant's sponsor has been granted leave to enter or remain under paragraph 15 or 19 of this Appendix.

LEAVE TO REMAIN

47.   Limited leave to remain as the child of a member of HM Forces will be granted to an applicant who:

     (a)   was either:

         (i)   under 18 years of age at the date of application; or

         (ii)   aged 18 or over at the date of application and who was last granted leave under paragraph 43 or 47 of this Appendix or paragraph 276AH of these Rules;

     (b)   is not married or in a civil partnership;

     (c)   has not formed an independent family unit;

     (d)   is not leading an independent life;

     (e)   is not in breach of immigration laws, except that any period of overstaying for 28 days or less will be disregarded;

     (f)   is in the United Kingdom;

     (g)   has made a valid application for leave to remain as the child of a member of HM Forces;

     (h)   does not fall to be refused on the grounds of suitability under paragraph 8 or 9;

     (i)   meets:

         (aa) the general eligibility requirements in paragraph 42; or

         (bb) meets those general eligibility requirements, except that subparagraph (b)(ii) does not apply but the parent of the applicant falls under paragraph 49(h) and the applicant normally lives with this parent and not their other parent; and

     [(i)   either:

         (a)   meets the financial requirement in Part 12 of this Appendix; or

         (b)   in a case in which sub-paragraph (b)(i)(aa), (b)(i)(dd) or (b)(ii) of paragraph 42 applies (and including the application of sub-paragraph b(ii) as modified by sub-paragraph (i) above) will be:

            (i)   accommodated adequately by the parent or parents the applicant is seeking to remain with without recourse to public funds in accommodation which the parent or parents own or occupy exclusively; and

(ii)   maintained adequately by that parent or those parents without recourse to public funds.]

48.   Leave to remain granted under paragraph 47 will be:

(a)   for whichever is the shortest period of:

    (i)   5 years; or

    (ii)   the remaining duration of the applicant's parent's enlistment; or

    (iii)   the remaining duration of the applicant's parent's leave; and

(b)   subject to a condition of no recourse to public funds.

INDEFINITE LEAVE TO REMAIN

49.   Indefinite leave to remain as the child of a member of HM Forces will be granted to an applicant who has or has had leave to enter or remain under paragraph 43 or 47 of this Appendix or paragraph 276AH of these Rules and who:

(a)   was either:

    (i)   under 18 years of age at the date of application; or

    (ii)   aged 18 or over at the date of application and who was last granted leave under paragraph 43 or 47 of this Appendix or paragraph 276AH of these Rules;

(b)   is not married or in a civil partnership;

(c)   has not formed an independent family unit;

(d)   is not leading an independent life;

(e)   is in the United Kingdom;

(f)   has made a valid application for indefinite leave to remain as the child of a member of HM Forces;

(g)   is not in breach of immigration laws, except that any period of overstaying for 28 days or less will be disregarded;

(h)   is the child of:

    (i)   a foreign or Commonwealth citizen who is a serving member of HM Forces who has completed at least 5 years' reckonable service; or

    (ii)   a person who has been granted, or is being granted at the same time as the applicant, indefinite leave to enter or remain under paragraph 13 or 16 of this Appendix or paragraphs 276E-Q of these Rules; or

    (iii)   a member of HM Forces who is a British Citizen;

(i)   meets one of the following criteria:

    (i)   the applicant's other parent must:

        (aa)   also come within paragraph 49(h); or

        (bb)   have been granted indefinite leave to enter or remain under paragraph 25 or 31 of this Appendix or paragraph 276S or 276V of these Rules; or

        (cc)   be being granted indefinite leave to enter or remain under paragraph 25 or 31 of this Appendix or paragraph 276S or 276V of these Rules at the same time as the applicant; or

        (dd)   have died; or

    (ii)   the parent under paragraph 49(h) has sole responsibility for the applicant's upbringing or the applicant normally lives with this parent and not their other parent; or

    (iii)   there are serious and compelling family or other considerations which make the applicant's exclusion from the United Kingdom undesirable and suitable arrangements have been made for their care;

(j)   does not fall to be refused on the grounds of suitability under paragraph 8 or 9;

(k)   meets the general eligibility requirements in paragraph 42;

    (l)   where the applicant is aged 18 or over, can demonstrate sufficient knowledge of the English language and about life in the United Kingdom, in accordance with the requirements of Appendix KoLL to these Rules;

    (m)   will be accommodated adequately by the parent or parents the applicant is seeking to remain with without recourse to public funds in accommodation which the parent or parents the applicant is seeking to join own or occupy exclusively; and

    (n)   will be maintained adequately by the parent or parents the applicant is seeking to join, without recourse to public funds.

50.   Limited leave to remain as a child of a member of HM Forces for a period of 30 months and subject to a condition of no recourse to public funds will be granted:

    (a)   where an applicant fails to meet the requirements for indefinite leave to remain in paragraph 49 by reason only of failing to satisfy the suitability requirements in paragraph 8 or 9 in respect of a grant of indefinite leave to remain (but not a grant of limited leave to remain); or

    (b)   where an applicant fails to meet the requirements for indefinite leave to remain by reason only of failing to meet the requirements in paragraph 49(l); or

    (c)   by reason only of failing to meet the requirements of paragraph 49(h)(i) or (ii), provided that the applicant's sponsor has been granted leave to enter or remain under paragraph 15 or 19 of this Appendix.

PART 8
BEREAVED CHILDREN OF MEMBERS OF HM FORCES

GENERAL ELIGIBILITY REQUIREMENTS

51.   The general eligibility requirements to be met by a bereaved child of a member of HM Forces are that:

    (a)   one of their parents has died and at the time of their death was:

        (i)   a foreign or Commonwealth citizen who was a serving member of HM Forces; or

        (ii)   a discharged member of HM Forces who had been granted, or was seeking at the same time as the applicant, leave to enter or remain under paragraphs 13-19 of this Appendix or paragraphs 276E-QA of these Rules; or

        (iii)   a British Citizen who was a member of HM Forces; and

    (b)   they meet one of the following criteria:

        (i)   their other parent must:

            (aa)   also come within sub-paragraph 51(a); or

            (bb)   have been granted, or be being granted at the same time as the applicant, leave to enter or remain under paragraphs 23-33 or 35-37 of this Appendix, under paragraph 276S, 276V or 276AE of these Rules or under any concession that existed outside these Rules whereby the Secretary of State exercised her discretion to grant leave to enter or remain to bereaved partners of foreign or Commonwealth members of HM Forces; or

            (cc)   have died; or

        (ii)   the parent referred to in sub-paragraph (a) had sole responsibility for their upbringing; or

        (iii)   there are serious and compelling family or other considerations which make exclusion of the applicant from the United Kingdom undesirable and suitable arrangements have been made for their care.

INDEFINITE LEAVE TO ENTER

52.   Entry clearance and indefinite leave to enter as a bereaved child of a member of HM Forces will be granted to an applicant who:
- (a)   was either:
  - (i)   under 18 years of age at the date of application; or
  - (ii) aged 18 or over at the date of application and was last granted leave to enter or remain under paragraph 43 or 47 of this Appendix or paragraph 276AH of these Rules;
- (b)   is outside the United Kingdom;
- (c)   is not married or in a civil partnership;
- (d)   has not formed an independent family unit;
- (e)   is not leading an independent life;
- (f)   has made a valid application for entry clearance and indefinite leave to enter as the bereaved child of a member of HM Forces;
- (g)   does not fall to be refused on the grounds of suitability under paragraph 8 or 9; and
- (h)   meets the general eligibility requirements in paragraph 51.

INDEFINITE LEAVE TO REMAIN

53.   Indefinite leave to remain as a bereaved child of a member of HM Forces will be granted to an applicant who:
- (a)   is in the United Kingdom;
- (b)   was either:
  - (i)   under 18 years of age at the date of application; or
  - (ii) aged 18 or over at the date of application and was last granted leave to remain under paragraph 43 or 47 of this Appendix or paragraph 276AH of these Rules; and
- (c)   is not married or in a civil partnership;
- (d)   has not formed an independent family unit;
- (e)   is not leading an independent life;
- (f)   has made a valid application for indefinite leave to remain as the bereaved child of a member of HM Forces;
- (g)   does not fall to be refused on the grounds of suitability under paragraph 8 or 9; and
- (h)   meets the general eligibility requirements in paragraph 51.

54.   Limited leave to remain as a bereaved child of a member of HM Forces for a period of 30 months will be granted subject to a condition of no recourse to public funds to an applicant who fails to meet the requirements for indefinite leave to remain in paragraph 53 by reason solely of failing to meet the suitability requirements in paragraph 8 or 9 in respect of a grant of indefinite leave (but not a grant of limited leave to remain).

PART 9
MEMBERS OF ARMED FORCES WHO ARE NOT EXEMPT FROM IMMIGRATION CONTROL

GENERAL ELIGIBILITY REQUIREMENTS

55.   The general eligibility requirements for members of armed forces who are not exempt from immigration control are that they:
- (a)   are a member of a foreign armed force;
- (b)   have been invited by:
  - (i)   HM Forces to undergo training in the United Kingdom which HM Forces will provide; or
  - (ii) the Ministry of Defence to study, or become familiarised with military equipment being supplied by a firm in the United Kingdom;

(c)   will leave the United Kingdom after the period of training, study or familiarisation;

(d)   can provide evidence that they are able to maintain themselves and any dependants adequately in the United Kingdom without recourse to public funds;

(e)   can provide evidence that there will be adequate accommodation, without recourse to public funds, for themselves and any dependants in the United Kingdom, including any other dependants who are not included in the application but who will live in the same household in the United Kingdom, which the applicant and their dependants own or occupy exclusively: accommodation will not be regarded as adequate if:

    (i)   it is, or will be, overcrowded; or

    (ii)   it contravenes public health regulations.

LEAVE TO ENTER

56.   [Entry clearance and/or leave to enter] as a member of an armed force not exempt from immigration control will be granted to an applicant who:

    (a)   is outside the United Kingdom;

    (b)   has made a valid application for entry clearance and leave to enter as a member of an armed force not exempt from immigration control;

    (c)   does not fall to be refused on the grounds of suitability under paragraph 8 or 9; and

    (d)   meets the general eligibility requirements in paragraph 55.

57.   [Entry clearance and/or leave to enter] granted under paragraph 56 will be granted:

    (a)   for whichever is the shorter period of:

        (i)   4 years; and

        (ii)   the duration of the training, study or familiarisation; and

    (b)   subject to the following conditions:

        (i)   no recourse to public funds; and

        (ii)   a prohibition on employment other than that for the purposes for which the applicant was granted leave to enter.

58.   [Entry clearance and/or leave to enter] granted under paragraph 56 may be granted subject to the conditions in paragraph 57(b) for an additional period of 3 months beyond the end of the training, study or familiarisation where:

    (a)   such leave is required in order to enable the applicant to meet third country transit regulations which require passengers to have 3 months' extant leave in the United Kingdom;

    (b)   travel to the third country forms part of the training, study or familiarisation; and

    (c)   the total period of leave granted does not exceed 4 years.

Note

Amended by HC 693, para 172 as from 6 November 2014, save that if an application has been made for entry clearance or leave to enter or remain before 6 November 2014, the application will be decided in accordance with the Rules in force on 5 November 2014.

LEAVE TO REMAIN

59.   Limited leave to remain as a member of an armed force not exempt from immigration control will be granted to an applicant who:

    (a)   is in the United Kingdom;

    (b)   was last granted leave to enter or remain under paragraph 56 or 59 of this Appendix or under the concession which existed outside these Rules whereby the Secretary of State exercised her discretion to grant leave to enter or remain to members of armed forces who are not exempt from immigration control;

    (c)   is not in breach of immigration laws, except that any period of overstaying for 28 days or less will be disregarded;

    (d)   has made a valid application for leave to remain as a member of an armed force not exempt from immigration control;

    (e)   does not fall to be refused on the grounds of suitability under paragraph 8 or 9; and

    (f)   meets the general eligibility requirements in paragraph 55.

60.   Limited leave to remain granted under paragraph 59 will be granted:

    (a)   for whichever is the shorter period of:

        (i)   4 years; or

        (ii)   the duration of the training, study or familiarisation; and

        provided the total period of leave granted (including any leave granted under paragraph 57 or 59) does not exceed 4 years; and

    (b)   subject to the following conditions:

        (i)   no recourse to public funds; and

        (ii)   a prohibition on employment other than that for the purposes for which the applicant was granted leave to remain.

61.   Limited leave to remain granted under paragraph 59 may be granted subject to the conditions in paragraph 60(b) for an additional 3 months beyond the end of the training, study or familiarisation where:

    (a)   such leave is required in order to enable the applicant to meet third country transit regulations which require passengers to have 3 months' extant leave in the United Kingdom;

    (b)   travel to the third country forms part of the training, study or familiarisation; and

    (c)   the total period of leave granted (including any leave granted under paragraph 57 or 59 [or the concession which existed outside these Rules whereby the Secretary of State exercised her discretion to grant leave to enter or remain to members of armed forces who are not exempt from immigration control] does not exceed 4 years.

[PART 9A
RELEVANT CIVILIAN EMPLOYEES

GENERAL ELIGIBILITY REQUIREMENTS

61A.   The general eligibility requirements for Relevant Civilian Employees are that the applicant:

    (a)   is a Relevant Civilian Employee;

    (b)   will leave the United Kingdom at the end of their period of employment;

    (c)   can provide evidence that they are able to maintain themselves and any dependants adequately in the United Kingdom without recourse to public funds; and

    (d)   can provide evidence that there will be adequate accommodation, without recourse to public funds, for themselves and any dependants in the United Kingdom, including any other dependants who are not included in the application but who will live in the same household in the United Kingdom, which the applicant and their dependants own or occupy exclusively: accommodation will not be regarded as adequate if:

        (i)   it is, or will be, overcrowded; or

        (ii)   it contravenes public health regulations.

Note

Inserted by HC 1138, para 139 as from 6 April 2014. Inserted by HC 1138, para 139 as from 6 April 2014. Inserted by HC 1138, para 139 as from 6 April 2014.

LEAVE TO ENTER

61B. Entry clearance and/or leave to enter as a Relevant Civilian Employee will be granted to an applicant who:

(a) is outside the United Kingdom;

(b) has made a valid application for entry clearance and/or leave to enter as a Relevant Civilian Employee;

(c) does not fall to be refused on the grounds of suitability under paragraph 8 or 9; and

(d) meets the general eligibility requirements in paragraph 61A.

61C. Entry clearance and/or leave to enter granted under paragraph 61B will be granted:

[(a) for

(i) in respect of an application from a civilian employee of a NATO force or the Australian Department of Defence:

(aa) 6 months, where the duration of their period of employment in the United Kingdom does not exceed 6 months; or

(bb) five years, where the duration of their period of employment in the United Kingdom exceeds 6 months; or

(ii) in respect of a civilian employee of a company under contract to a NATO force, the duration of their period of employment in the United Kingdom or, if the shorter period, 4 years; and]

(b) subject to the following conditions:

(i) no recourse to public funds; and

(ii) a prohibition on employment other than for the purposes for which the applicant was last granted leave to enter.

Note

Amended by HC 693, para 173 as from 6 November 2014, save that if an application has been made for entry clearance or leave to enter or remain before 6 November 2014, the application will be decided in accordance with the Rules in force on 5 November 2014.

LEAVE TO REMAIN

61D. Leave to remain as a Relevant Civilian Employee will be granted to an applicant who:

(a) is in the United Kingdom;

[(b) was last:

(i) granted leave to enter or remain under paragraph 61C or 61E of this Appendix or under the concessions which existed outside these Rules whereby the Secretary of State exercised her discretion to grant leave to enter or remain to Relevant Civilian Employees; or

(ii) exempt from control under section 8(4)(b) of the Immigration Act 1971 and has been offered employment as a Relevant Civilian Employee;]

(c) is not in breach of any immigration laws, except that any period of overstaying for 28 days or less will be disregarded;

(d) has made a valid application for leave to remain as a Relevant Civilian Employee;

(e) does not fall to be refused on the grounds of suitability under paragraph 8 or 9; and

(f) meets the general eligibility requirements set out in paragraph 61A.

61E. Leave to remain granted under paragraph 61D will be granted:

(a) ...:

(i) in respect of an application from a civilian employee of NATO or the Australian Department of Defence, five years; or

(ii)   in respect of an application from a civilian employee of a company under contract to NATO, [the duration of their period of employment in the United Kingdom, or, if the shorter period, four years; and]

(b)   subject to the following conditions:

    (i)   no recourse to public funds; and

    (ii)   a prohibition on employment other than for the purposes for which the applicant was last granted leave to enter or remain]

Note

Appendix Armed Forces Part 9A inserted by HC 1138, para 139 as from 13 March 2014. Amended by HC 693, para 174 as from 6 November 2014, save that if an application has been made for entry clearance or leave to enter or remain before 6 November 2014, the application will be decided in accordance with the Rules in force on 5 November 2014. Phrase "whichever is the shorter period of" deleted by HC 693, para 175 as from 6 November 2014, save that if an application has been made for entry clearance or leave to enter or remain before 6 November 2014, the application will be decided in accordance with the Rules in force on 5 November 2014. Amended by HC 693, para 175 as from 6 November 2014, save that if an application has been made for entry clearance or leave to enter or remain before 6 November 2014, the application will be decided in accordance with the Rules in force on 5 November 2014. Deleted by HC 693, para 175 as from 6 November 2014, save that if an application has been made for entry clearance or leave to enter or remain before 6 November 2014, the application will be decided in accordance with the Rules in force on 5 November 2014.

PART 10
DEPENDANTS OF NON-HM [AND OF RELEVANT CIVILIAN EMPLOYEES] FORCES

GENERAL ELIGIBILITY REQUIREMENTS

62.   The general eligibility requirements to be met by dependants of a member of non-HM Forces [or of a Relevant Civilian Employee] are that:

(a)   the applicant is sponsored by:

    (i)   a serving armed forces member who is exempt from immigration control under section 8(4)(b) or (c) of the Immigration Act 1971; or

    (ii)   a serving armed forces member who:

        (aa)   has leave to enter or remain under paragraph 56 or 59 of this Appendix or under any concession that existed outside these Rules whereby the Secretary of State exercised her discretion to grant leave to enter or remain to members of armed forces who are not exempt from immigration control; or

        (bb)   is being granted leave to enter or remain under paragraph 56 or 59 of this Appendix at the same time as the applicant; [or]

    (iii)   a Relevant Civilian Employee who:

        (aa)   has been granted leave to enter or remain under paragraph 61B or 61D or under the concession which existed outside these Rules whereby the Secretary of State exercised her discretion to grant leave to enter or remain to a Relevant Civilian Employee; or

        (bb)   is being granted leave to enter or remain under paragraph 61B or 61D at the same time as the applicant;

(b)   the applicant's sponsor is:

    (i)   the applicant's partner (except a fiancé(e) or proposed civil partner) where:

        (aa)   both parties are aged 18 or over;

                  (bb)   both parties intend to live with the other during their stay in the United Kingdom; and

                  (cc)   the relationship is genuine and subsisting; or

      [(ii)   the applicant's parent and the applicant:

                  (aa)   is under 18 years of age at the date of application;

                  (bb)   is not married or in a civil partnership;

                  (cc)   has not formed an independent family unit; and

                  (dd)   is not living an independent life; or

      (iii)   a serving armed forces member who is exempt from immigration control under section 8(4)(b) or (c) of the Immigration Act 1971 or a civilian employed to work in the UK by a NATO force or the Australian Department of Defence and the applicant: (aa) is a dependant other than a partner within the meaning of section 12(4)(b) of the Visiting Forces Act 1952 or Article I(c) of the NATO Status of Forces Agreement; and (bb) is listed as a dependant of the sponsor on the sponsor's military movement orders or equivalent civilian posting letter;]

  (c)   the applicant must provide evidence that their [sponsor] is able to maintain and accommodate themselves, the applicant and any dependants adequately in the United Kingdom without recourse to public funds;

  (d)   the applicant must provide evidence that there will be adequate accommodation, without recourse to public funds, for the applicant, the applicant's sponsor and any other family members of the applicant, including other family members who are not included in the application but who will live in the same household, which the applicant, the applicant's sponsor and the other family members own or occupy exclusively: accommodation will not be regarded as adequate if-

      (i)   it is, or will be, overcrowded; or

      (ii)   it contravenes public health regulations; and

  (e)   the applicant intends to leave the United Kingdom at the end of their sponsor's period of posting, [employment,] training, study or familiarisation in the United Kingdom.

Note

Further amended by HC 1138, para 141 as from 6 April 2014. Amended by HC 1138, para 142 as from 6 April 2014. Further amended by HC 1138, para 143 as from 6 April 2014. Amended by HC 693, para 176 as from 6 November 2014, save that if an application has been made for entry clearance or leave to enter or remain before 6 November 2014, the application will be decided in accordance with the Rules in force on 5 November 2014. Amended by HC 693, para 177 as from 6 November 2014, save that if an application has been made for entry clearance or leave to enter or remain before 6 November 2014, the application will be decided in accordance with the Rules in force on 5 November 2014.

63.   Where the sponsor is the applicant's parent, the applicant must meet one of the following criteria:

  (a)   their other parent must:

      (i)   also meet the criteria set out in paragraph 62(a)(i)[, (ii) or (iii)]; or

      (ii)   either:

                  (aa)   have been granted leave to enter or remain as a partner in relation to that member of non-HM Forces [or Relevant Civilian Employee] under [paragraph 64 or 66] of this Appendix or paragraph 276AE of these Rules or under any concession that existed outside these Rules whereby the Secretary of State exercised her discretion to grant leave to enter or remain to partners of non-exempt members of armed forces [or Relevant Civilian Employees]; or

<ul>
<li>(bb) be being granted leave to enter or remain under paragraph 64 or 66 at the same time as the applicant; or</li>
<li>(iii) have died; or</li>
<li>(b) the parent they are joining in paragraph 62(a) has sole responsibility for their upbringing; or</li>
<li>(c) there are serious and compelling family or other considerations which make the applicant's exclusion from the United Kingdom undesirable and suitable arrangements have been made for their care.</li>
</ul>

Note

Further amended by HC 1138, para 144 as from 6 April 2014. Further amended by HC 1138, para 145 as from 6 April 2014. Further amended by HC 1138, para 146 as from 6 April 2014.

Note

Further amended by HC 1138, para 140 as from 6 April 2014.

LEAVE TO ENTER

64. Entry clearance and[/or] leave to enter as the dependant of a member [or of a Relevant Civilian Employee] will be granted to an applicant who:
<ul>
<li>(a) is outside the United Kingdom;</li>
<li>[(b)] has made a valid application for entry clearance and[/or] leave to enter as the dependant of a member of non-HM Forces [or of a Relevant Civilian Employee];</li>
<li>[(c)] does not fall to be refused on the grounds of suitability under paragraph 8 or 9; and</li>
<li>[(d)] meets the general eligibility requirements in paragraph 62 and where relevant one of the criteria in paragraph 63.</li>
</ul>

Note

Further amended by HC 1138, para 147 as from 6 April 2014. Further amended by HC 1138, para 148 as from 6 April 2014. Delete paragraph 64(b) and re-number subparagraphs (c), (d) and (e) as subparagraphs (b), (c) and (d) accordingly by HC 693, para 178 as from 6 November 2014, save that if an application has been made for entry clearance or leave to enter or remain before 6 November 2014, the application will be decided in accordance with the Rules in force on 5 November 2014.

65. Entry clearance and[/or] leave to enter granted under paragraph 64 will be granted:
<ul>
<li>[(a) for
<ul>
<li>(i) in respect of an application from the dependant of an armed forces member who is not exempt from immigration control or of a civilian employee of a company under contract to a NATO force, the duration of the sponsor's period of posting, employment, training, study or familiarisation in the United Kingdom or, if the shorter period, 4 years; or</li>
<li>(ii) in respect of an application from the dependant of an armed forces member who is exempt from immigration control under section 8(4)(b) or (c) of the Immigration Act 1971 or of a civilian employee of a NATO force or the Australian Department of Defence: (aa) 6 months, where the duration of the sponsor's period of posting, employment, training, study or familiarisation in the United Kingdom does not exceed 6 months; or (bb) a maximum of 5 years, where the duration of the sponsor's period of posting, employment, training, study or familiarisation in the United Kingdom exceeds 6 months; and]</li>
</ul>
</li>
<li>(b) subject to the following conditions:
<ul>
<li>(i) no recourse to public funds; and</li>
</ul>
</li>
</ul>

(ii)   in respect of applications from dependants [of Relevant Civilian Employees or] of armed forces members who are not exempt from immigration control and are being granted leave to enter for less than 6 months, a prohibition on employment.

Note

Further amended by HC 1138, para 149 as from 6 April 2014. Further amended by HC 1138, para 150 as from 6 April 2014. Further amended by HC 1138, para 151 as from 6 April 2014. Further amended by HC 1138, para 152 as from 6 April 2014. Further amended by HC 1138, para 153 as from 6 April 2014. Amended by HC 693, para 179 as from 6 November 2014, save that if an application has been made for entry clearance or leave to enter or remain before 6 November 2014, the application will be decided in accordance with the Rules in force on 5 November 2014.

LEAVE TO REMAIN

66.   Leave to remain as the dependant of a member of non-HM Forces [or of a Relevant Civilian Employee] will be granted to an applicant who:
(a)   is in the United Kingdom;
[(b)   in relation to an application to which sub-paragraph 62(a)(ii) applies, was last granted leave to enter or remain under paragraph 64 or 66 of this Appendix or under the concession which existed outside these Rules whereby the Secretary of State exercised her discretion to grant leave to enter or remain to the dependant of a member of the armed forces who is not exempt from immigration control;]
(i)   was under 18 years of age at the date of application; or
(ii)   was aged 18 or over at the date of application and was last granted leave to remain as a dependant in relation to that member of non-HM Forces [or Relevant Civilian Employee] under paragraph 64 or 66 of this Appendix or paragraph 276AH of these Rules or under any concession that existed outside these Rules whereby the Secretary of State exercised her discretion to grant leave to enter or remain to children of non-exempt members of armed forces [or of Relevant Civilian Employees];
(c)   is not in breach of immigration laws, except that any period of overstaying for 28 days or less will be disregarded;
(d)   has made a valid application for leave to remain as the dependant of a member of non-HM Forces [or of a Relevant Civilian Employee];
(e)   does not fall to be refused on the grounds of suitability under paragraph 8 or 9; and
[(f)   meets the general eligibility criteria in paragraph 62 and, where the sponsor is the applicant's parent, one of the criteria in paragraph 63, except that the applicant does not need to be under 18 years of age at the date of application where:
(i)   paragraph 66(b) applies; or
(ii)   sub-paragraph 62(a)(iii) applies and the applicant was last granted leave to enter or remain under paragraph 64 or 66 of this Appendix or under the concession which existed outside these Rules whereby the Secretary of State exercised her discretion to grant leave to enter or remain to the dependant of an employee of a company under contract to a NATO force.]

Note

Further amended by HC 1138, para 154 as from 6 April 2014. Further amended by HC 1138, para 155 as from 6 April 2014. Further amended by HC 1138, para 156 as from 6 April 2014. Amended by HC 693, para 180 as from 6 November 2014, save that if an application has been made for entry clearance or leave to enter or remain before 6 November 2014, the application will be decided in accordance with the Rules in force on 5 November 2014. Amended by HC 693, para 180 as from 6 November 2014, save that if an application has been made for entry clearance or leave to enter or remain before 6 November 2014, the application will be decided in accordance with the Rules in force on 5 November 2014.

67. Leave to remain granted under paragraph 66 will be granted:

    (a) for ...:

        (i) in respect of an application from the dependant of an armed forces member who is not exempt from immigration control [or of a civilian employee of a company under contract to NATO], [the duration of the sponsor's period of posting, employment, training, study or familiarisation in the United Kingdom, or, if the shorter period, 4 years; or]

        (ii) in respect of an application from the dependant of an armed forces member who is exempt from immigration control under section 8(4)(b) or (c) of the Immigration Act 1971 [or of a civilian employee of NATO or the Australian Department of Defence], [a maximum of 5 years; and]

    (b) subject to the following conditions:

        (i) no recourse to public funds; and

        (ii) in respect of applications from dependants [of Relevant Civilian Employees or] of armed forces members who are not exempt from immigration control and are being granted leave to remain for less than 6 months, a prohibition on employment.

Note

Further amended by HC 1138, para 157 as from 6 April 2014. Further amended by HC 1138, para 158 as from 6 April 2014. Further amended by HC 1138, para 159 as from 6 April 2014. Further amended by HC 1138, para 160 as from 6 April 2014. Phrase "whichever is the shorter period of" deleted by HC 693, para 181 as from 6 November 2014, save that if an application has been made for entry clearance or leave to enter or remain before 6 November 2014, the application will be decided in accordance with the Rules in force on 5 November 2014. Amended by HC 693, para 181 as from 6 November 2014, save that if an application has been made for entry clearance or leave to enter or remain before 6 November 2014, the application will be decided in accordance with the Rules in force on 5 November 2014. Amended by HC 693, para 181 as from 6 November 2014, save that if an application has been made for entry clearance or leave to enter or remain before 6 November 2014, the application will be decided in accordance with the Rules in force on 5 November 2014. Deleted by HC 693, para 181 as from 6 November 2014, save that if an application has been made for entry clearance or leave to enter or remain before 6 November 2014, the application will be decided in accordance with the Rules in force on 5 November 2014.

PART 11
ENGLISH LANGUAGE REQUIREMENT

MEETING THE ENGLISH LANGUAGE REQUIREMENT IN APPLICATIONS FOR LEAVE TO ENTER OR REMAIN

68. Where an English language requirement applies to an application for leave to enter or remain made by a partner under this Appendix, and if the applicant has not met the requirement in a previous application for leave as a partner, the applicant must provide specified evidence set out in Appendix FM-SE and Appendix O that they:

    (a) are a national of a majority English speaking country listed in paragraph 70 of this Part;

    (b) have passed an English language test in speaking and listening at a minimum of level A1 of the Common European Framework of Reference for Languages with a provider approved by the Secretary of State;

    (c) have an academic qualification recognised by UK NARIC to be equivalent to the standard of a Bachelor's or Master's degree or PhD in the UK, which was taught in English; or

(d) are exempt from the English language requirement under paragraph 69 of this Part.

EXEMPTIONS FROM THE ENGLISH LANGUAGE REQUIREMENT

69. The applicant is exempt from the English language requirement if at the date of application:
   (a) the applicant is aged 65 or over;
   (b) the applicant has a disability (physical or mental condition) which prevents the applicant from meeting the requirement; or
   (c) there are exceptional circumstances which prevent the applicant from being able to meet the requirement, which for an application for entry clearance is prior to entry to the UK.

MAJORITY ENGLISH SPEAKING COUNTRIES

70. For the purposes of paragraph 68(a) of this Part the applicant must be a national of:
   Antigua and Barbuda,
   Australia,
   the Bahamas,
   Barbados,
   Belize,
   Canada,
   Dominica,
   Grenada,
   Guyana,
   Jamaica,
   New Zealand,
   St Kitts and Nevis,
   St Lucia,
   St Vincent and the Grenadines,
   Trinidad and Tobago,
   or the United States of America.

PART 12
FINANCIAL REQUIREMENTS

This Part applies where the financial requirements in Part 12 must be met in an application for leave to enter or remain [or for indefinite leave to enter or remain] made under this Appendix by a partner or child of a member of HM Forces. Paragraphs A. to 21 of Appendix FM-SE to these Rules apply to applications to which this Part applies. References in this Part to the applicant's parent or the applicant's parent's partner relate only to applications made by a child under this Appendix. References in this Part to a partner or to the applicant's partner do not refer to the partner of a child making an application under this Appendix.

Note

Further amended by HC 1138, para 161 shall apply to all applications decided on or after 6 April 2014.

FINANCIAL REQUIREMENTS FOR APPLICATIONS FOR LEAVE TO ENTER

71. The applicant must provide specified evidence, from the sources listed in paragraph 73, of:
   (a) a specified gross annual income of at least:
      (i) £18,600;
      (ii) an additional £3,800 for the first child; and
      (iii) an additional £2,400 for each additional child; alone or in combination with
   (b) specified savings of:

(i)   £16,000; and

(ii)   additional savings of an amount equivalent to the difference – multiplied by the length in years of the period of limited leave for which the applicant has applied [(or by the part-year equivalent if the applicant has applied for less than 12 months' limited leave)] – between the gross annual income from the sources listed in paragraph 73(a)-(f) and the total amount required under paragraph 71(a); or

(c)   the requirements in paragraph 74 are met.

Note

Further amended by HC 1138, para 162 shall apply to all applications decided on or after 6 April 2014.

72.   In paragraph 71 "child" means a dependent child of the applicant or of the applicant's parent who is:

(a)   under the age of 18 years, or who was under the age of 18 years when they were first granted entry under this route;

(b)   applying for entry clearance or has limited leave to enter or remain in the United Kingdom under this Appendix;

(c)   not a British Citizen or settled in the United Kingdom; and

(d)   not an EEA national with a right to be admitted under the Immigration (EEA) Regulations 2006.

73.   When determining whether the financial requirements in paragraph 71 are met only the following sources will be taken into account:

(a)   income of the applicant's partner or the applicant's parent's partner from specified employment or self-employment, which, in respect of a partner (or applicant's parent's partner) returning to the United Kingdom with the applicant, can include specified employment or self-employment overseas and in the United Kingdom;

(b)   income of the applicant's parent from specified employment or self-employment if they are in the United Kingdom unless they are working illegally;

(c)   specified pension income of the applicant and their partner or of the applicant's parent and that parent's partner;

(d)   any specified maternity allowance or bereavement benefit in the UK, or any specified benefit relating to service in HM Forces, received by the applicant and their partner or by the applicant's parent and that parent's partner;

(e)   other specified income of the applicant and their partner or of the applicant's parent and that parent's partner; and

(f)   income from the sources at sub-paragraphs (b), (d) and (e) of a dependent child of the applicant or the applicant's parent under paragraph 72 who is aged 18 or over; and

(g)   specified savings of the applicant and their partner; or of the applicant's parent and that parent's partner; or of a dependent child of the applicant or the applicant's parent under paragraph 72 who is aged 18 or over.

74.   The requirements to be met under this paragraph are:

(a)   the applicant's partner or the applicant's parent's partner must be receiving one or more of the following:

(i)   Disability Living Allowance;

(ii)   Severe Disablement Allowance;

(iii)   Industrial Injury Disablement Benefit;

(iv)   Attendance Allowance;

(v)   Carer's Allowance;

(vi)   Personal Independence Payment;

      (vii)   Armed Forces Independence Payment or Guaranteed Income Payment under the Armed Forces Compensation Scheme; or

      (viii) Constant Attendance Allowance, Mobility Supplement or War Disablement Pension under the War Pensions Scheme; and

  (b)   the applicant must provide evidence that their partner (or their parent's partner) is able to maintain and accommodate themselves, the applicant (and their parent) and any dependants adequately in the UK without recourse to public funds.

75.   The applicant must provide evidence that there will be adequate accommodation, without recourse to public funds, for the family, including other family members who are not included in the application but who live in the same household, which the family own or occupy exclusively: accommodation will not be regarded as adequate if:

  (a)   it is, or will be, overcrowded; or

  (b)   it contravenes public health regulations.

FINANCIAL REQUIREMENTS FOR APPLICATIONS FOR LEAVE TO REMAIN

76.   The applicant must provide specified evidence, from the sources listed in paragraph 78, of:

  (a)   a specified gross annual income of at least:

      (i)   £18,600;

      (ii) an additional £3,800 for the first child; and

      (iii) an additional £2,400 for each additional child; alone or in combination with

  (b)   specified savings of:

      (i)   £16,000; and

      (ii) additional savings of an amount equivalent to the difference – multiplied by the length in years of any period of limited leave for which the applicant has applied [(or by the part-year equivalent if the applicant has applied for less than 12 months' limited leave)] – between the gross annual income from the sources listed in paragraph 78(a)-(f) and the total amount required under paragraph 76(a); or

  (c)   the requirements in paragraph 79 are met.

Note

   Further amended by HC 1138, para 163 shall apply to all applications decided on or after 6 April 2014.

77.   In paragraph 76, "child" means a dependent child of the applicant or of the applicant's parent who is:

  (a)   under the age of 18 years, or who was under the age of 18 years when they were first granted entry under this route;

  (b)   applying for entry clearance or is in the United Kingdom;

  (c)   not a British Citizen or settled in the United Kingdom; and

  (d)   not an EEA national with a right to remain in the United Kingdom under the Immigration (EEA) Regulations 2006.

78.   When determining whether the financial requirements in paragraph 76 are met only the following sources may be taken into account:

  (a)   income of the applicant's partner or of the applicant's parent's partner from specified employment or self-employment;

  (b)   income of the applicant (where aged 18 or over) or of the applicant's parent from specified employment or self-employment unless they are working illegally;

  (c)   specified pension income of the applicant and their partner or of the applicant's parent and that parent's partner;

(d) any specified maternity allowance or bereavement benefit in the UK, or any specified benefit relating to service in HM Forces, received by the applicant or their partner or by the applicant's parent and that parent's partner;

(e) other specified income of the applicant and their partner or of the applicant's parent and that parent's partner;

(f) income from the sources at sub-paragraphs (b), (d) or (e) of a dependent child of the applicant or their parent under paragraph 77 who is aged 18 years or over; and

(g) specified savings of the applicant and their partner; of the applicant's parent and that parent's partner; or of a dependent child of the applicant or the applicant's parent under paragraph 77 who is aged 18 or over.

79. The requirements to be met under this paragraph are:

(a) the applicant's partner or the applicant's parent's partner must be receiving one or more of the following:

(i) Disability Living Allowance;

(ii) Severe Disablement Allowance;

(iii) Industrial Injury Disablement Benefit;

(iv) Attendance Allowance;

(v) Carer's Allowance;

(vi) Personal Independence Payment;

(vii) Armed Forces Independence Payment or Guaranteed Income Payment under the Armed Forces Compensation Scheme; or

(viii) Constant Attendance Allowance, Mobility Supplement or War Disablement Pension under the War Pensions Scheme; and

(b) the applicant must provide evidence that their partner (or their parent's partner) is able to maintain and accommodate themselves, the applicant (and their parent) and any dependants adequately in the UK without recourse to public funds.

80. The applicant must provide evidence that there will be adequate accommodation, without recourse to public funds, for the family, including other family members who are not included in the application but who live in the same household, which the family own or occupy exclusively: accommodation will not be regarded as adequate if:

(a) it is, or will be, overcrowded; or

(b) it contravenes public health regulations.]

[FINANCIAL REQUIREMENTS FOR APPLICATIONS FOR INDEFINITE LEAVE TO ENTER OR REMAIN

81. The applicant must meet all of the requirements of paragraphs 71 to 75 (for indefinite leave to enter) or paragraphs 76 to 80 (for indefinite leave to remain), except that instead of the requirement in paragraph 71(b) or 76(b) the applicant must provide specified evidence from the sources listed in paragraph 73 or 78 (as the case may be) of specified savings of:

(i) £16,000; and

(ii) additional savings of an amount equivalent to the difference between the gross annual income from the sources listed in paragraph 73(a)-(f) or 78(a)-(f) and the total amount required under paragraph 71(a) or 76(a).]

Note

Inserted by HC 803, para 19 as from 1 December 2013. Further amended by HC 877, paras 11–15 as from 30 December 2013. Further amended by HC 1138, para 164 shall apply to all applications decided on or after 6 April 2014.

[APPENDIX B
ENGLISH LANGUAGE

[1.   An applicant applying as a Tier 1 Migrant or Tier 2 Migrant must have 10 points for English language, unless applying for entry clearance or leave to remain:
(i)   as a Tier 1 (Exceptional Talent) Migrant,
(ii)   as a Tier 1 (Investor) Migrant, or
(iii)   as a Tier 2 (Intra-Company Transfer) Migrant.]

Note

Amended by HC 628, para 182 and if an applicant has made an application for entry clearance or leave before 1 October 2013, the application will be decided in accordance with the Rules in force on 30 September 2013. Substituted by HC 693, para 182 as from 6 November 2014, save that if an application has been made for entry clearance or leave to enter or remain before 6 November 2014, the application will be decided in accordance with the Rules in force on 5 November 2014.

2.   The levels of English language required are shown in Table 1.

3.   Available points for English language are shown in Table 2.

4.   Notes to accompany the tables are shown below each table.

Table 1 Level of English language require to score points

Row	Category	Applications	Level of English language required
A	Tier 1 (General)	Entry clearance and leave to remain	A knowledge of English equivalent to level C1 or above of the Council of Europe's Common European Framework for Language Learning
B.	Tier 1 (Entrepreneur)	Entry clearance and leave to remain	A knowledge of English equivalent to [level B1] or above of the Council of Europe's Common European Framework for Language Learning
C.	Tier 1 (Graduate Entrepreneur)	[Entry clearance and leave to remain]	A knowledge of English equivalent to [level B1] or above of the Council of Europe's Common European Framework for Language Learning

Tier 2

Row	Category	Applications	Level of English language required
E	Tier 2 (Minister of Religion)	Entry clearance and leave to remain	A knowledge of English equivalent to level B2 or above of the Council of Europe's Common European Framework for Language Learning
F.	Tier 2 (General)	Entry clearance and leave to remain, other than the cases in paragraph 5	A knowledge of English equivalent to level B1 or above of the Council of Europe's Common European Framework for Language Learning
[G].	Tier 2 (General)	Leave to remain cases in paragraph 5 below.	A knowledge of English equivalent to level A1 or above of the Council of Europe's Common European Framework for Language Learning
[H].	Tier 2 (Sportsperson)	Entry clearance and leave to remain	A knowledge of English equivalent to level A1 or above of the Council of Europe's Common European Framework for Language Learning

Note

Amended by HC 628, para 183 and if an applicant has made an application for entry clearance or leave before 1 October 2013, the application will be decided in accordance with the Rules in force on 30 September 2013. Table row deleted by HC 693, para 183 as from 6 November 2014, save that if an application has been made for entry clearance or leave to enter or remain before 6 November 2014, the application will be decided in accordance with the Rules in force on 5 November 2014.

Notes

5. An applicant applying for leave to remain as a Tier 2 (General) Migrant must have competence of English to level A1 or above as set out in Table 1 above if:
(i)   he previously had leave as:
    (1)   a Tier 2 (General) Migrant under the rules in place before 6 April 2011,
    (2)   a Qualifying Work Permit Holder,
    (3)   a representative of an overseas newspaper, news agency or Broadcasting organisation,
    (4)   a member of the Operational Ground Staff of an Overseas-owned Airline, or

(5)   a Jewish Agency Employee, and
(ii)   he has not been granted leave to remain in any other routes, or entry clearance or leave to enter in any route, since the grant of leave referred to in (i) above.

Table 2 Points available for English language

Factor	Points
National of a majority English speaking country	10
Degree taught in English	10
Passed an English language test	10
Met requirement in a previous grant of leave	10
Transitional arrangements	10

National of a majority English speaking country

6.   10 points will only be awarded for being a national of a majority English speaking country if the applicant has the relevant level of English language shown in Table 1 and:
(i)   is a national of one of the following countries:
Antigua and Barbuda
Australia
The Bahamas
Barbados
Belize
Canada
Dominica
Grenada
Guyana
Jamaica
New Zealand
St Kitts and Nevis
St Lucia
St Vincent and the Grenadines
Trinidad and Tobago
USA, and
[(ii)   provides his current valid original passport or travel document to show that this requirement is met. If the applicant is unable to do so, the UK Border agency may exceptionally consider his requirement to have been met where the applicant provides full reasons in the passport section of the application form, and either:
(1)   a current identity document, or
(2)   an original letter from his home government or embassy, on the letter-headed paper of the government or embassy, which has been issued by an authorised official of that institution and confirms the applicant's full name, date of birth and nationality.]

Degree taught in English

7.   10 points will be awarded for a degree taught in English if the applicant has the relevant level of English language shown in Table 1 and:
(i)   has obtained an academic qualification (not a professional or vocational qualification) which either:
(1)   is deemed by UK NARIC to meet the recognised standard of a Bachelor's degree (not a Master's degree or a PhD) in the UK, and UK NARIC has confirmed that the degree was taught or researched in English to level C1 of the Council of Europe's Common European Framework for Language learning or above or:
(2)   is deemed by UK NARIC to meet or exceed the recognised standard of a Bachelor's degree or Master's degree or a PhD) in the UK, and is from an educational establishment in one of the following countries:
Antigua and Barbuda

> Australia
> The Bahamas
> Barbados
> Belize
> Dominica
> Grenada
> Guyana
> Ireland
> Jamaica
> New Zealand
> St Kitts and Nevis
> St Lucia
> St Vincent and the Grenadines
> Trinidad and Tobago
> the UK
> the USA,

and

(ii) [provides the specified evidence to show he has the qualification:

    (i) provides the following specified documents to show he has the qualification:

        (1) the original certificate of the award, or

        (2) if the applicant is awaiting graduation having successfully completed the qualification, or no longer has the certificate and the awarding institution is unable to provide a replacement, an academic transcript (or original letter in the case of a PhD qualification) from the awarding institution on its official headed paper, which clearly shows:

            (a) the applicant's name,

            (b) the name of the awarding institution,

            (c) the title of the award,

            (d) confirmation that the qualification has been or will be awarded, and

            (e) the date that the certificate will be issued (if the applicant has not yet graduated) or confirmation that the institution is unable to reissue the original certificate or award.]

8. If the applicant is required to have competence of English to level A1 as set out in Table 1 above [(rows G and H)], 10 points will be awarded for a degree taught in English if the applicant has the relevant level of English language shown in Table 1 and:

(i) has obtained an academic qualification (not a professional or vocational qualification) which is deemed by UK NARIC to meet or exceed the recognised standard of a Bachelor's or Master's degree or a PhD in the UK, . . .

(ii) [provides the specified documents in paragraph 7(ii) evidence to show that he has the qualification, and;

(iii) provides an original letter from the awarding institution on its official headed paper, which clearly shows:

    (1) the applicant's name,

    (2) the name of the awarding institution,

    (3) the title of the award,

    (4) the date of the award, and

    (5) confirmation that the qualification was taught in English.]

Note

Amended by HC 628, para 184 and if an applicant has made an application for entry clearance or leave before 1 October 2013, the application will be decided in accordance with the Rules in force on 30 September 2013.

[9. [An applicant for entry clearance or leave to remain as a Tier 1 (Graduate Entrepreneur) Migrant does not need to provide evidence of a qualification taught in English if:

(a) the applicant scores points from Appendix A for an endorsement by the UK Higher Education Institution which awarded the qualification; and

(b) the endorsement letter contains the specified details of the qualification, as set out in paragraph 70(c) of Appendix A.]]

Note

Further amended by HC 1138, para 165 as from 6 April 2014.

[Passed an English language test

10. 10 Points will only be awarded for passing an English language test if the applicant has the relevant level of English language shown in Table 1 and provides the specified documents from an English language test provider approved by the Secretary of State for these purposes as listed in Appendix O, which clearly show:
(1)   the applicant's name,
(2)   the qualification obtained, which must meet or exceed the relevant level shown in Table 1 in all four components (reading, writing, speaking and listening), unless the applicant was exempted from sitting a component on the basis of his disability,
(3)   the date of the award, and
(4)   that the test is within its validity date (where applicable).]

Note

Substituted by HC 244, para 28 as from 1 July 2013.

Met requirement in a previous grant of leave

11. Subject to [paragraph 15 below], 10 points will be awarded for meeting the requirement in a previous grant of leave if the applicant:
(i)   [has ever been granted leave as a Tier 1 (General) Migrant, a Tier 1 (Entrepreneur) Migrant or Business person, or a Tier 1 (Post-Study Work) Migrant, or]
(ii)   has ever been granted leave as a Highly Skilled Migrant under the Rules in place on or after 5 December 2006.

Note

Substituted by HC 628, para 185 and if an applicant has made an application for entry clearance or leave before 1 October 2013, the application will be decided in accordance with the Rules in force on 30 September 2013. Further amended by HC 1138, para 166 as from 6 April 2014.

[**12.** Subject to paragraph 15 below, where the application falls under [rows B to H] of Table 1 above, 10 points will be awarded for meting the requirement in a previous grant of leave if the applicant has ever been granted leave:
(a)   as a Minister of Religion (not as a Tier 2 (Minister of Religion) Migrant) under the Rules in place on or after 19 April 2007,
(b)   as a Tier 2 (Minister of Religion) Migrant, provided that when he was granted that leave he obtained points for English language for being a national of a majority English speaking country, a degree taught in English, or passing an English language test, or
(c)   as a Tier 4 (General) student, and the Confirmation of Acceptance for Studies used to support that application was assigned on or after 21 April 2011 for a course of at least degree level study.]

Note

Substituted and amended by HC 628, paras 186, 187 and if an applicant has made an application for entry clearance or leave before 1 October 2013, the application will be decided in accordance with the Rules in force on 30 September 2013.

[**13.** Subject to paragraph 15 below, where the application falls under rows B to C or rows F to H of Table 1 above, 10 points will be awarded for meeting the requirement in a previous grant of leave if the applicant has ever been granted leave:
(a)   as a Tier 1 (Graduate Entrepreneur) Migrant,
(b)   as a Tier 2 (General) Migrant under the Rules in place on or after 6 April 2011, or
(c)   as a Tier 4 (General) student, and the Confirmation of Acceptance for Studies used to support that application was assigned on or after 21 April 2011,

provided that when he was granted that leave he obtained points for having knowledge of English equivalent to level B1 of the Council of Europe's Common European Framework for Language Learning or above.]

Note

Substituted by HC 628, para 188 and if an applicant has made an application for entry clearance or leave before 1 October 2013, the application will be decided in accordance with the Rules in force on 30 September 2013. Further amended by HC 1138, para 167 as from 6 April 2014. Further amended by HC 1138, para 168 as from 6 April 2014. Substituted by HC 693, para 184 as from 6 November 2014, save that if an application has been made for entry clearance or leave to enter or remain before 6 November 2014, the application will be decided in accordance with the Rules in force on 5 November 2014.

14. [Subject to paragraph 15 below, where the application] falls under [rows G and H] of table 1 above, 10 points will be awarded for meeting the requirement in a previous grant of leave if the applicant has ever been granted:
(i)   leave as a Minister of Religion (not as Tier 2 (Minister of Religion) Migrant) under the Rules in place on or after 23 August 2004,
(ii)   leave as a Tier 2 Migrant, provided that when he was granted that leave he obtained points for English language for being a national of a majority English speaking country, a degree taught in English, or passing an English language test.

Note

Amended by HC 628, paras 189, 190 and if an applicant has made an application for entry clearance or leave before 1 October 2013, the application will be decided in accordance with the Rules in force on 30 September 2013.

15. No points will be awarded for meeting the requirement in a previous grant of leave if false representations were made of false documents or information were submitted (whether or not to the applicant's knowledge) in relation to the requirement in the application for that previous grant of leave.

Transitional arrangements

16. 10 Points will only be awarded for English if the applicant:
(a)   is applying for leave to remain as [a Tier 2 (General) Migrant], and
(b)   has previously been granted entry clearance, leave to enter or leave to remain as:
(i)   a Jewish Agency Employee,
(ii)   a Member of the Operational Ground Staff of an Overseas-owned Airline,
(iii)   a Minister of Religion, Missionary or Member of a Religious Order,
(iv)   a Qualifying Work Permit Holder,
(v)   a Representative of an Overseas Newspaper, News Agency or Broadcasting Organisation and
(c)   has not been granted leave in any categories other than Tier 2 (General), Tier 2 (Intra-Company Transfer) and those listed in (b) above under the Rules in place since 28 November 2008.

Note

Amended by HC 628, para 191 and if an applicant has made an application for entry clearance or leave before 1 October 2013, the application will be decided in accordance with the Rules in force on 30 September 2013.

17. 10 points will be awarded for English language if the applicant:
(a)   is applying for leave to remain as a Tier 2 (Minister of Religion) Migrant,
(b)   has previously been granted entry clearance, leave to enter and/or leave to remain as a Minister of Religion, Missionary or Member of a Religious Order, and
(c)   has not been granted leave in any categories other than Tier 2 (Minister of Religion) and those listed in (b) above under the Rules in place since 28 November 2008.

18. 10 points will be awarded for English language if the applicant:
(a)   is applying for leave to remain as a Tier 2 (Sportsperson) Migrant,

(b)   has previously been granted entry clearance, leave to enter and/or leave to remain as a Qualifying Work Permit Holder, and

(c)   has not been granted leave in any categories other than Tier 2 (Sportsperson) and as a Qualifying Work Permit Holder under the Rules in place since 28 November 2008.]

Note

Appendix B substituted by HC 1888, para 177 as from 6 April 2012. Further amended by Cm 8423, paras 167–171 as from 20 July 2012. Further amended by HC 760, paras 329–333 as from 13 December 2012. Further amended by HC 1039, paras 195–199.

APPENDIX C
MAINTENANCE (FUNDS)

1A.   [In all cases where an applicant is required to obtain points under Appendix C, the applicant must meet the requirements listed below:

(a)   The applicant must have the funds specified in the relevant part of Appendix C at the date of the application.

(b)   [If the applicant is applying as a Tier 1 Migrant, a Tier 2 Migrant or a Tier 5 (Temporary Worker) Migrant, the applicant must have had the funds referred to in (a) above for a consecutive 90–day period of time, unless applying as a Tier 1 (Exceptional Talent) Migrant or a Tier 1 (Investor) Migrant;

(c)   If the applicant is applying as a Tier 4 Migrant, the applicant must have had the funds referred to in (a) above for a consecutive 28–day period of time;]

[(ca) If thee applicant is applying for entry clearance or leave to remain as a Tier 4 Migrant, he must confirm that the funds referred yo in (a) above are:

(i) available in the manner specified in paragraph 13 below for his use in studying and living in the UK; and

(ii) that the funds will remain available in the manner specified in paragraph 13 below unless used to pay for course fees and living costs;]

(d)   If the funds were obtained when the applicant was in the UK, the funds must have been obtained while the applicant had valid leave and was not acting in breach of any conditions attached to that leave; [...]

(e)   [. . .];

(f)   Where the applicant is applying as a Tier 1 Migrant, a Tier 2 Migrant or a Tier 5 Migrant, the funds must have been under his own control on the date of the application and for the period specified in (b) above; and

(g)   Where the application is made at the same time as applications by the partner or child of the applicant (such that the applicant is a Relevant Points Based System migrant for the purposes of paragraph 319AA), each applicant must have the total requisite funds specified in the relevant parts of Appendices C and E. If each applicant does not individually meet the requirements of Appendices C and / or E, as appropriate, all the applications (the application by the Relevant Points Based System Migrant and applications as the partner or child of that Relevant Points Based System Migrant) will be refused.]

(h)   [the end date of the 90–day and 28–day periods referred to in (b) and (c) above will be taken as the date of the closing balance on the most recent of the specified documents [(Where specified documents from two or more accounts are submitted, this will be the end date for the account that most favours the applicant)], and must be no earlier than 31 days before the date of application.]

(i)   [No points will be awarded where the specified documents show that the funds are held in a financial institution listed in Appendix P as being an institution with which the UK Border Agency is unable to make satisfactory verification checks.]

(j)   [maintenance must be in the form of cash funds. Other accounts or financial instruments such as shares, bonds, [credit cards,] pension funds etc, regardless of notice period are not acceptable.

(k)   If the applicant wishes to rely on a join account as evidence of available funds, the applicant (or for children under 18 ears of age, the applicant's parent or legal guardian who is legally present in the United Kingdom) must be named on he account as one of the account holders.]

(l)   [Overdraft facilities will not be considered towards funds that are available or under an applicant's own control.]

Note
Word in square brackets in (e) deleted by HC 863, para 160 as from 6 April 2011. Sub-paras (f)–(h) inserted by HC 863, para 161 as from 6 April 2011. Sub-paragraphs (b)-(c), (ca), (i) amended by HC 1148, paras 61, 63 as from 4 July 2011. Sub-paragraph (j) inserted by HC 1888, para 178 as from 6 April 2012. Further amended by Cm 8423, paras 172–176 as from 20 July 2012. Further amended by HC 565, para 110 as from 6 September 2012. Further amended by HC 1039, para 200. Further amended by HC 1138, para 169 shall apply to all applications decided on or after 6 April 2014.

1B [In all cases where Appendix C or Appendix E states that an applicant is required to provide specified documents, the specified documents are:

(a) Personal bank or building society statements which satisfy the following requirements:

   (i) The statements must cover:

      (1) a consecutive 90-day period of time, if the applicant is applying as a Tier 1 Migrant, a Tier 2 Migrant a Tier 5 (Temporary Worker) Migrant, or the Partner or Child of a Relevant Points Based System Migrant in any of these categories,

      (2) a single date within 31 days of the date of the application, if the applicant is applying as a Tier 5 (Youth Mobility Scheme) Migrant, or

      (3) a consecutive 28-day period of time, if the applicant is applying as a Tier 4 Migrant or the Partner or Child of a Relevant Points Based System Migrant who is a Tier 4 Migrant

   (ii) The most recent statement must be dated no earlier than 31 days before the date of the application;

   (iii) The statements must clearly show:

      (1) the name of:

         i. the applicant,

         ii the applicant's parent(s) or legal guardian's name, if the applicant is applying as Tier 4 Migrant,

         iii. the name of the Relevant Points-Based System Migrant, if the applicant is applying as a Partner or Child of a Relevant Points-Based System Migrant, or

         iv. the name of the applicant's other parent who is legally present in the UK, if the applicant is applying as a Child of a Relevant Points-Based System Migrant,

      (2) the account number,

      (3) the date of each statement,

      (4) the financial institution's name,

      (5) the financial institution's logo,

      (6) any transactions during the specified period, and

      (7) that the funds in the account have been at the required level throughout the specified period;

   (iv) The statements must be either:

      (1) printed on the bank's or building society's letterhead,

      (2) electronic bank or building society statements ..., accompanied by a supporting letter from the bank or building society, on company headed paper, confirming the statement provided is authentic, or

      (3) electronic bank or building society statements ..., bearing the official stamp of the bank or building society on every page,

   (v) The statements must not be mini-statements from automatic teller machines (ATMs);

   or

(b) A building society pass book which satisfies the following requirements:

   (i) The building society pass book must cover:

      (1) a consecutive 90-day period of time, if the applicant is applying as a Tier 1 Migrant, a Tier 2 Migrant a Tier 5 (Temporary Worker) Migrant, or the Partner or Child of a Relevant Points Based System Migrant in any of these categories,

      (2) a single date within 31 days of the date of the application, if the applicant is applying as a Tier 5 (Youth Mobility Scheme) Migrant, or

      (3)   a consecutive 28-day period of time, if the applicant is applying as a Tier 4 Migrant or the Partner or Child of a Relevant Points Based System Migrant who is a Tier 4 Migrant

  (ii)   The period covered by the building society pass book must end no earlier than 31 days before the date of the application;

  (iii) The building society pass book must clearly show:

     (1)   the name of:

        _i.   the applicant,

        _ii   the applicant's parent(s) or legal guardian's name, if the applicant is applying as Tier 4 Migrant,

        _iii. the name of the Relevant Points-Based System Migrant, if the applicant is applying as a Partner or Child of a Relevant Points-Based System Migrant, or

        _iv. the name of the applicant's other parent who is legally present in the UK, if the applicant is applying as a Child of a Relevant Points-Based System Migrant,

     (2)   the account number,

     (3)   the building society's name and logo,

     (4)   any transactions during the specified period, and

     (5)   that there have been enough funds in the applicant's account throughout the specified period;

    or

 (c)   A letter from the applicant's bank or building society, or a letter from a financial institution [regulated by the Financial Conduct Authority (FCA) and the Prudential Regulation Authority (PRA)] or, for overseas accounts, the official regulatory body for the country in which the institution operates and the funds are located, which satisfies the following requirements:

  (i)   The letter must confirm the level of funds and that they have been held for:

     (1)   a consecutive 90-day period of time, if the applicant is applying as a Tier 1 Migrant, a Tier 2 Migrant a Tier 5 (Temporary Worker) Migrant, or the Partner or Child of a Relevant Points Based System Migrant in any of these categories,

     (2)   a single date within 31 days of the date of the application, if the applicant is applying as a Tier 5 (Youth Mobility Scheme) Migrant, or

     (3)   a consecutive 28-day period of time, if the applicant is applying as a Tier 4 Migrant or the Partner or Child of a Relevant Points Based System Migrant who is a Tier 4 Migrant;

  (ii)   The period covered by the letter must end no earlier than 31 days before the date of the application;

  (iii) The letter must be dated no earlier than 31 days before the date of the application;

  (iv) The letter must be on the financial institution's letterhead or official stationery;

  (v)   The letter must clearly show:

     (1)   the name of:

        _i.   the applicant,

        _ii   the applicant's parent(s) or legal guardian's name, if the applicant is applying as Tier 4 Migrant,

        _iii. the name of the Relevant Points-Based System Migrant, if the applicant is applying as a Partner or Child of a Relevant Points-Based System Migrant, or

        _iv. the name of the applicant's other parent who is legally present in the UK, if the applicant is applying as a Child of a Relevant Points-Based System Migrant,

     (2)   the account number,

     (3)   the date of the letter,

(4)   the financial institution's name and logo,
(5)   the funds held in the applicant's account, and
(5)   confirmation that there have been enough funds in the applicant's account throughout the specified period;

or

(d)   If the applicant is applying as Tier 4 Migrant, an original loan letter from a financial institution [regulated by the Financial Conduct Authority (FCA) and the Prudential Regulation Authority (PRA)] or, in the case of overseas accounts, the official regulatory body for the country the institution is in and where the money is held, which is dated no more than 6 months before the date of the application and clearly shows:

(1)   the applicant's name,
(2)   the date of the letter,
(3)   the financial institution's name and logo,
(4)   the money available as a loan,
(5)   for applications for entry clearance, that the loan funds are or will be available to the applicant before he travels to the UK, unless the loan is an academic or student loan from the applicant's country's national government and will be released to the applicant on arrival in the UK, and
(6)   there are no conditions placed upon the release of the loan funds to the applicant, other than him making a successful application as a Tier 4 Migrant.]

Note

Inserted by Cm 8423, para 176 as from 20 July 2012. Further amended by HC 244, paras 29, 30 as from 1 July 2013. Further amended by HC 628, paras 192, 193 and if an applicant has made an application for entry clearance or leave before 1 October 2013, the application will be decided in accordance with the Rules in force on 30 September 2013.

Tier 1 Migrants

1.   [An applicant applying for entry clearance or leave to remain as a Tier 1 Migrant must score 10 points for funds, unless applying as a Tier 1 (Exceptional Talent) Migrant or a Tier 1 (Investor) Migrant.]

Note

Substituted by HC 1148, para 64 as from 4 July 2011.

2.   10 points will only be awarded if an applicant:

(a)   applying for entry clearance, has the level of funds shown in the table below and provides the specified documents [in paragraph 1B above], or

Category	Level of funds	Points
Tier 1 (Entrepreneur)	[£3,310]	10
Tier 1 (Graduate Entrepreneur)	[£1,890]	10

(b)   applying for leave to remain, has the level of funds shown in the table below and provides the specified documents [in paragraph 1B above][, or]

Level of funds	Points
[£945]	10

[(c)   applying as a Tier 1 (Graduate Entrepreneur) Migrant scores points from Appendix A [for an endorsement from UK Trade and Investment], and UK Trade and Investment has confirmed in the endorsement letter that it has awarded funding of [at least £1,890 (for entry clearance applications) or £945 (for leave to remain applications)] to the applicant.]

Note

Figures substituted by HC 1888, paras 179, 180 as from 14 June 2012. Words in square brackets inserted by Cm 8423, paras 177, 178 as from 20 July 2012. Further amended by HC 1039, paras 201–203. Further amended by HC 1138, para 170 as from 1 July 2014. However, if an applicant has made an application for entry clearance or leave before 1 July 2014, the application will be decided in accordance with the Rules in force on 30 June 2014. Further amended by HC 1138, para 171 as from 1 July 2014. However, if an applicant has made an application for entry clearance or leave before 1 July 2014, the application will be decided in accordance with the Rules in force on 30 June 2014. Further amended by HC 1138, para 172 as from 1 July 2014. However, if an applicant has made an application for entry clearance or leave before 1 July 2014, the application will be decided in accordance with the Rules in force on 30 June 2014. Further amended by HC 1138, para 173 as from 1 July 2014. However, if an applicant has made an application for entry clearance or leave before 1 July 2014, the application will be decided in accordance with the Rules in force on 30 June 2014. Further amended by HC 1138, para 174 as from 1 July 2014. However, if an applicant has made an application for entry clearance or leave before 1 July 2014, the application will be decided in accordance with the Rules in force on 30 June 2014.

[3. Where he applicant is applying as a Tier 1 (Entrepreneur) Migrant, he cannot use the same funds to score points for attributes under Appendix A and to score points for maintenance funds for himself or his dependants under this Appendix or Appendix E.]

Note

Inserted by HC 628, para 194 and if an applicant has made an application for entry clearance or leave before 1 October 2013, the application will be decided in accordance with the Rules in force on 30 September 2013.

Tier 2 Migrants

4. An applicant applying for entry clearance or leave to enter or remain as a Tier 2 Migrant must score 10 points for Funds.

5. 10 points will only be awarded if:
(a) the applicant has the level of funds shown in the table below and provides the specified documents [in paragraph 1B above][, or]:

Level of funds	Points awarded
[£945]	10

(b) the applicant has [. . .] entry clearance, leave to enter or leave to remain as:
    (i) a Tier 2 Migrant,
    (ii) a Jewish Agency Employee,
    (iii) a Member of the Operational Ground Staff of an Overseas- owned Airline,
    (iv) a Minister of Religion, Missionary or Member of a Religious Order,
    (v) a Representative of an Overseas Newspaper, News Agency or Broadcasting Organisation, or
    (vi) a Work Permit Holder, or
[(c) the Sponsor is an A rated Sponsor and has certified on the Certificate of Sponsorship that, should it become necessary, it will maintain and accommodate the migrant up to the end of the first month of his employment. The sponsor may limit the amount of the undertaking but any limit must be at least [£945]. Points will only be awarded if the applicant provides a valid Certificate of Sponsorship reference number with his application.]

Note

Words in square brackets in (a) inserted by Cm 8423, para 179 as from 20 July 2012. Words in square brackets in (c) and sub-para (d) substituted by HC 863, paras 163 and 164 as from 6 April 2011. Further amended by HC 1888, paras 181, 183 as from 14 June 2016, paras 182, 184 as from 6 April 2012. Further amended by HC 1138, para 175 as from 1 July 2014. However, if an applicant has made an application for entry clearance or leave before 1 July 2014, the application will be decided in accordance with the Rules in force on 30 June 2014. Further amended by HC 1138, para 176 as from 1 July 2014. However, if an applicant has made an application for entry clearance or leave before 1 July 2014, the application will be decided in accordance with the Rules in force on 30 June 2014.

Tier 5 (Youth Mobility) Temporary Migrants

6. An applicant applying for entry clearance as a Tier 5 (Youth Mobility) Temporary Migrant must score 10 points for Funds.

7. 10 points will only be awarded if an applicant has the level of funds shown in the table below and provides the specified documents [in paragraph 1B above]:

Level of funds	Points awarded
[£1,890]	10

Note

Figure amended by HC 1888, para 185 as from 6 April 2012. Words in square brackets inserted by Cm 9423, para 180 as from 20 July 2012. Further amended by HC 1138, para 177 as from 1 July 2014. However, if an applicant has made an application for entry clearance or leave before 1 July 2014, the application will be decided in accordance with the Rules in force on 30 June 2014.

Tier 5 (Temporary Worker) Migrants

8. A migrant applying for entry clearance or leave to remain as a Tier 5 (Temporary Worker) Migrant must score 10 points for Funds.

9. 10 points will only be awarded if the applicant has the level of funds shown in the table below and provides the specified documents [in paragraph 1B above]:

Criterion	Points awarded
meets one of the following criteria:	10
• Has [£945]; or	
• The Sponsor is an A rated Sponsor and the Certificate of Sponsorship Checking Service confirms that the Sponsor has certified that that the applicant will not claim public funds during his period of leave as a Tier 5 (Temporary Worker) Migrant. [Points will only be awarded if the applicant provides a valid Certificate of Sponsorship reference number with his application].	

Note

Words in square brackets inserted by HC 863, para 165 as from 6 April 2011. Figure amended by HC 1888, para 186 as from 14 June 2012. Words "in paragraph 1B above" inserted by Cm 8423, para 181 as from 20 July 2012. Further amended by HC 1138, para 178 as from 1 July 2014. However, if an applicant has made an application for entry clearance or leave before 1 July 2014, the application will be decided in accordance with the Rules in force on 30 June 2014.

Tier 4 (General) Students

10. A Tier 4 (General) Student must score 10 points for funds.

11. [10 points will only be awarded if the funds shown in the table below are available in the manner specified in paragraph 13 [and 13A] below to the applicant. The applicant must either:
(a)   provide the specified documents [in paragraph 1B above] to show that the funds are available to him, or
(b)   where the applicant is sponsored by a Highly Trusted Sponsor, is a national of one of the countries [or the rightful holder of a qualifying passport issued by one of the relevant competent authorities, as appropriate,] listed in Appendix H, and is applying for entry clearance in his country of nationality [or in the territory related to the passport he holds, as appropriate,] or leave to remain in the UK,

confirm that the funds are available to him in the specified manner. The UK Border Agency reserves the right to request the specified documents [in paragraph 1B above] from these applicants to support this confirmation. The application will be refused if the specified documents are not provided in accordance with the request made.]

[Criterion	Points
If studying in inner London:	10
(i) Where the applicant does not have an established presence studying in the United Kingdom, the applicant must have funds amounting to the full course fees for the first academic year of the course, or for the entire course if it is less than a year long, plus [£1,020] for each month of the course up to a maximum of nine months.	
(ii) Where the applicant has an established presence studying in the United Kingdom, the applicant must have funds amounting to the course fees required either for the remaining academic year if the applicant is applying part-way through, or for the next academic year if the applicant will continue or commence a new course at the start of the next academic year, or for the entire course if it is less than a year long, plus [£1,020] for each month of the course up to a maximum of two months.	
If studying in outer London and elsewhere in the United Kingdom	
(iii) Where the applicant does not have an established presence studying in the United Kingdom, the applicant must have funds amounting to the full course fees for the first academic year of the course, or for the entire course if it is less than a year long, plus [£820] for each month of the course up to a maximum of nine months.	
(iv) Where the applicant has an established presence studying in the United Kingdom, the applicant must have funds amounting to the course fees required either for the remaining academic year if the applicant is applying part-way through, or for the next academic year if the applicant will continue or commence a new course at the start of the next academic year, or for the entire course if it is less than a year long, plus [£820] for each month of the course up to a maximum of two months.]	

Note

Words "and 13A" inserted by HC 1888, para 187 as from 6 April 2012 and figures amended by HC 1888, paras 188, 189 as from 6 April 2012. Words "in paragraph 1B above" in sub-paras (a), (b) inserted by Cm 8423, paras 182, 183 as from 20 July 2012. Further amended by HC 1138, para 179 as from 1 July 2014. However, if an applicant has made an application for entry clearance or leave before 1 July 2014, the application will be decided in accordance with the Rules in force on 30 June 2014. Further amended by HC 1138, para 180 as from 1 July 2014. However, if an applicant has made an application for entry clearance or leave before 1 July 2014, the application will be decided in accordance with the Rules in force on 30 June 2014.

Notes

12. An applicant will be considered to be studying in [inner London] if the institution, or branch of the institution, at which the applicant will be studying is situated [in any of the London boroughs of Camden, City of London, Hackney, Hammersmith and Fulham, Haringey, Islington, Kensington and Chelsea, Lambeth, Lewisham, Newham

Southwark, Tower Hamlets, Wandswoth, or Westminster]. If the applicant will be studying at more than one site, one or more of which is in [inner London] and one or more outside, then the applicant will be considered to be studying in [inner London] if the applicant's . . . [Confirmation of Acceptance for Studies] states that the applicant will be spending the majority of time studying at a site or sites situated in [inner London].

Note

Words in square brackets inserted by HC 903, para 59 as from 21 April 2011. Words in square brackets in paragraph 11 substituted by HC 1148, para 65 as from 4 July 2011. Words "or the rightful holder of a qualifying passport issued by one of the relevant competent authorities, as appropriate," and "or in the territory related to the passport he holds, as appropriate," inserted by HC 1511, paras 52–53 as from 31 October 2011. Further amended by Cm 8423, para 184 as from 20 July 2012.

[**12A.** If the length of the applicant's course includes a part of a month, the time will be rounded up to the next full month.]

Note

Paragraph inserted by HC 908, para 60 as from 21 April 2011.

[**13.** Funds will be available to the applicant only where the specified documents show [or, where permitted by these Rules, the applicant confirms that] the funds are held or provided by:
(i)   the applicant (whether as a sole or joint account holder); and/or
(ii)   the applicant's parent(s) or legal guardian(s), and the parent(s) or legal guardian(s) have provided written consent that their funds may be used by the applicant in order to study in the UK; and/or
(iii)   an official financial sponsor which must be Her Majesty's Government, the applicant's home government, the British Council or any international organisation, international company, University or Independent school.]

Note

Paragraph substituted by HC 908, para 61 as from 21 April 2011. Words in square brackets inserted by HC 1148, para 66 as from 4 July 2011.

[**13A.** In assessing whether the requirements of Appendix C, paragraph 11 are met, where an applicant pays a deposit on account to the sponsor for accommodation costs this amount, up to a maximum of [£1,020], can be offset against the total maintenance requirement if he will be staying in accommodation arranged by the Tier 4 sponsor and he has paid this money to that Tier 4 sponsor.]

Note

Substituted by HC 760, para 335 as from 13 December 2012. Further amended by HC 1138, para 181 as from 1 July 2014. However, if an applicant has made an application for entry clearance or leave before 1 July 2014, the application will be decided in accordance with the Rules in force on 30 June 2014.

[**13B.** If the applicant is relying on the provisions in paragraph 13(ii) above, he must provide:
(a)   one of the following original (or notarised copy) documents:
        (i)   his birth certificate showing names of his parent(s),
        (ii)   his certificate of adoption showing the names of both parent(s) or legal guardian, or
        (iii)   a Court document naming his legal guardian; and
(b)   a letter from his parent(s) or legal guardian, confirming:
        (1)   the relationship between the applicant and his parent(s) or legal guardian, and
        (2)   that the parent(s) or legal guardian give their consent to the applicant using their funds to study in the UK.

13C. If the applicant has already paid all or part of the course fees to his Tier 4 Sponsor:
(a)   the Confirmation of Acceptance for Studies Checking Service entry must confirm details of the fees already paid; or

(b)   the applicant must provide an original paper receipt issued by the Tier 4 Sponsor, confirming details of the fees already paid.

13D.   If the applicant has an official financial sponsor as set out in paragraph 13(iii) above:

(a)   the Confirmation of Acceptance for Studies Checking Service entry must confirm details of the official financial sponsorship, if it is the Tier 4 Sponsor who is the official financial sponsor; or

(b)   the applicant must provide a letter of confirmation from his official financial sponsor, on official letter-headed paper or stationery of that organisation and bearing the official stamp of that organisation, which clearly shows:

(1)   the applicant's name,

(2)   the name and contact details of the official financial sponsor,

(3)   the date of the letter,

(4)   the length of the official financial sponsorship, and

(5)   the amount of money the official financial sponsor is giving to the applicant, or a statement that the official financial sponsor will cover all of the applicant's fees and living costs.]

Note

Inserted by Cm 8423, para 185 as from 20 July 2012.

[**14.**   An applicant will have an established presence studying in the UK if the applicant has current entry clearance, leave to enter or leave to remain as a Tier 4 migrant, Student or as a Postgraduate Doctor or Dentist and at the date of application:

(i)   has finished a single course that was at least six months long within the applicant's last period of entry clearance, leave to enter or leave to remain, or

(ii)   is applying for continued study on a single course where the applicant has completed at least six months of that course[; or]]

(iii) [is applying for leave to remain as a Tier 4 (General) Student on the doctorate extension scheme.]

Note

Paragraph substituted by HC 908, para 62 as from 21 April 2011. Further amended by HC 1039, paras 204, 205.

Tier 4 (Child) Students

15.   A Tier 4 (Child) Student must score 10 points for funds.

16.   [10 points will only be awarded if the funds shown in the table below are available in the manner specified in paragraph 21 [and 21A] below to the applicant. The applicant must either:

(a)   provide the specified documents [in paragraph 1B above] to show that the funds are available to him, or

(b)   where the applicant is sponsored by a Highly Trusted Sponsor, is national of one of the countries [or the rightful holder of a qualifying passport issued by one of the relevant competent authorities, as appropriate,] listed in Appendix H, and is applying for entry clearance in his country of nationality [or in the territory related to the passport he holds, as appropriate,] or leave to remain in the UK, confirm that the funds are available to him in the specified manner. The UK Border Agency reserves the right to request the specified documents [in paragraph 1B above] from these applicants to support this confirmation. The application will be refused if the specified documents are not provided in accordance with the request made.]

[Criterion	Points
Where the child is (or will be) studying at a residential independent school: sufficient funds are available to the applicant to pay boarding fees (being course fees plus board/lodging fees) for an academic year.	10

Where the child is (or will be) studying at a non-residential independent school and is in a private foster care arrangement (see notes below) or staying with and cared for by a close relative (see notes below): sufficient funds are available to the applicant to pay school fees for an academic year, the foster carer or relative [(who must meet the requirements specified in paragraph 19 of this Appendix]) has undertaken to maintain and accommodate the child for the duration of the course, and that foster carer or relative has funds equivalent to at least [£560] per month, for up to a maximum of nine months, to support the child while he is in the United Kingdom.	10
Where the child is (or will be) studying at a non-residential independent school, is under the age of 12 and is (or will be) accompanied by a parent,, sufficient funds are available to the applicant to pay school fees for an academic year, plus:	10
— if no other children are accompanying the applicant and the parent, [£1,535] per month of stay up to a maximum of nine months; or — if other children are accompanying the applicant and the parent, [[£1,535] per month, plus [£615] per month] for each additional child, up to a maximum of nine months.	
Where the child is aged 16 or 17 years old and is living independently and studying in inner London:	10
i) Where the applicant does not have an established presence studying in the United Kingdom, the applicant must have funds amounting to the full course fees for the first academic year of the course, or for the entire course if it is less than a year long, plus [£920] for each month of the course up to a maximum of nine months.	
ii) Where the applicant has an established presence studying in the United Kingdom, the applicant must have funds amounting to the course fees required either for the remaining academic year if the applicant is applying part-way through, or for the next academic year if the applicant will continue or commence a new course at the start of the next academic year, or for the entire course if it is less than a year long, plus [£920] for each month of the course up to a maximum of two months.	
Where the child is aged 16 or 17 years old, is living independently and studying in outer London or elsewhere in the United Kingdom:	10
iii) Where the applicant does not have an established presence studying in the United Kingdom, the applicant must have funds amounting to the full course fees for the first academic year of the course, or for the entire course if it is less than a year long, plus [£715] for each month of the course up to a maximum of nine months.	

iv)	Where the applicant has an established presence studying in the United Kingdom, the applicant must have funds amounting to the course fees required either for the remaining academic year if the applicant is applying part-way through, or for the next academic year if the applicant will continue or commence a new course at the start of the next academic year, or for the entire course if it is less than a year long, plus [£715] for each month of the course up to a maximum of two months.]

Note

Amended by HC 1138, paras 183–186 as from 1 July 2014. Further amended by HC 1138, para 182 as from 1 July 2014. However, if an applicant has made an application for entry clearance or leave before 1 July 2014, the application will be decided in accordance with the Rules in force on 30 June 2014. Further amended by HC 1138, para 183 as from 1 July 2014. However, if an applicant has made an application for entry clearance or leave before 1 July 2014, the application will be decided in accordance with the Rules in force on 30 June 2014. Further amended by HC 1138, para 184 as from 1 July 2014. However, if an applicant has made an application for entry clearance or leave before 1 July 2014, the application will be decided in accordance with the Rules in force on 30 June 2014. Further amended by HC 1138, para 185 as from 1 July 2014. However, if an applicant has made an application for entry clearance or leave before 1 July 2014, the application will be decided in accordance with the Rules in force on 30 June 2014. Further amended by HC 1138, para 186 as from 1 July 2014. However, if an applicant has made an application for entry clearance or leave before 1 July 2014, the application will be decided in accordance with the Rules in force on 30 June 2014.

17. Children (under 16, or under 18 if disabled) are privately fostered when they are cared for on a full-time basis by a person or persons aged 18 or over, who are not their parents or a close relative, for a period of 28 days or more.

18. A close relative is a grandparent, brother, sister, step-parent, uncle (brother or half-brother of the child's parent) or aunt (sister or half-sister of the child's parent) who is aged 18 or over.

[**19.** The care arrangement made for the child's care in the UK must comply with the following requirements:
(a) In all cases, the applicant must provide a letter from their parent(s) or legal guardian, confirming:
    (1) the relationship between the parent(s) or legal guardian and the applicant,
    (2) that the parent(s) or legal guardian have given their consent to the application,
    (3) that the parent(s) or legal guardian agrees to the applicant's living arrangements in the UK, and
    (4) if the application is for entry clearance, that the parent(s) or legal guardian agrees to the arrangements made for the applicant's travel to and reception in the UK,
    (5) if a parent(s) or legal guardian has legal custody or sole responsibility for the applicant,
    (6) that each parent or legal guardian with legal custody or responsibility for the applicant agrees to the contents of the letter, and signs the letter, and
    (7) the applicant's parent(s) or legal guardian's consent to the applicant travelling to and living in the UK independently, if the applicant is 16 or 17 years old and living independently.
(b) If the applicant is under 16 years old or is not living in the UK independently, the applicant must provide:
    (i) a written letter of undertaking from his intended carer confirming the care arrangement, which clearly shows:
        (1) the name, current address and contact details of the intended carer,
        (2) the address where the carer and the applicant will be living in the UK if different from the intended carer's current address,

        (3)   confirmation that the accommodation offered to the applicant is a private address, and not operated as a commercial enterprise, such as a hotel or a youth hostel,

        (4)   the nature of the relationship between the applicant's parent(s) or legal guardian and the intended carer,

        (5)   that the intended carer agrees to the care arrangements for the applicant,

        (6)   that the intended carer has at least [£560] per month (up to a maximum of nine months) available to look after and accommodate the applicant for the length of the course,

        (7)   a list of any other people that the intended carer has offered support to, and

        (8)   the carer's signature and date of the undertaking;

    (ii)   A letter from his parent(s) or legal guardian, which confirms the care arrangement and clearly shows:

        (1)   the nature of parent(s) or legal guardian's relationship with the intended carer,

        (2)   the address in the UK where the applicant and the intended carer will be living,

        (3)   that the parent(s) or legal guardian support the application, and authorise the intended carer to take responsibility for the care of the applicant during his stay in the UK;

        and

    (iii)   The intended carer's original (or notarised copy, although the UK Border Agency reserves the right to request the original):

        (1)   current UK or European Union passport,

        (2)   current passport or travel document to confirm that they are [settled in the United Kingdom], or

        (3)   certificate of naturalisation.

(c)   If the applicant is staying in a private foster care arrangement, he must receive permission from the private foster carer's UK local authority, as set out in the Children (Private Arrangements for Fostering) Regulations 2005.

(d)   If the applicant is staying in a private foster care arrangement and is under 16 years old, he must provide:

    (i)   A copy of the letter of notification from his parent(s), legal guardian or intended carer to the UK local authority, confirming that the applicant will be in the care of a private foster carer while in the UK, and

    (ii)   The UK local authority's confirmation of receipt, confirming that the local authority has received notification of the foster care arrangement.]

Note

Amended by HC 1138, para 187 as from 1 July 2014. However, if an applicant has made an application for entry clearance or leave before 1 July 2014, the application will be decided in accordance with the Rules in force on 30 June 2014.

[**19A.** (a) An applicant will be considered to be studying in inner London if the institution, or branch of the institution, at which the applicant will be studying is situated in any of the London boroughs of Camden, City of London, Hackney, Hammersmith and Fulham, Haringey, Islington, Kensington and Chelsea, Lambeth, Lewisham, Newham Southwark, Tower Hamlets, Wandsworth, or Westminster.

(b) If the applicant will be studying at more than one site, one or more of which is in inner London and one or more outside, then the applicant will be considered to be studying in inner London if the applicant's Confirmation of Acceptance for Studies states that the applicant will be spending the majority of time studying at a site or sites situated in inner London.]

20. [If the length of the applicant's course includes a part of a month, the time will be rounded up to the next full month.]

Note

Paragraphs 14–18 renumbered as 15–19, table after paragraph 16 deleted and replaced, and paragraph 20 inserted by HC 439, paras 89–91 as from 6 April 2010. Paragraph substituted by HC 908, para 63 as from 21 April 2011. Paragraph substituted by HC 908, para 63 as from

21 April 2011. Words in square brackets in paragraph 16 substituted by HC 1148, para 68 as from 4 July 2011. Words "or the rightful holder of a qualifying passport issued by one of the relevant competent authorities, as appropriate," and "or in the territory related to the passport he holds, as appropriate," inserted by HC 1511, paras 54–55 as from 31 October 2011. Paragraph 16 further amended by HC 1888, paras 191–198 as from 6 April 2012. Words "in paragraph 1B above" inserted by Cm 8423, para 188 as from 20 July 2012. Further amended by Cm 8423, paras 186–189 as from 20 July 2012. Further amended by HC 565, para 111 as from 6 September 2012. Further amended by HC 1039, para 206. Further amended by HC 1138, para 187 as from 1 July 2014.

21. [Funds will be available to the applicant only where the specified documents show [or, where permitted by these Rules, the applicant confirms that] the funds are held or provided by:

(i)   the applicant (whether as a sole or joint account holder); and/or

(ii)   the applicant's parent(s) or legal guardian(s), and the parent(s) or legal guardian(s) have provided written consent that their funds may be used by the applicant in order to study in the UK; and/or

(iii)   an official financial sponsor which must be Her Majesty's Government, the applicant's home government, the British Council or any international organisation, international company, University or Independent school.]

Note

Paragraph inserted by HC 908, para 63 as from 21 April 2011. Words in square brackets inserted by HC 1148, para 69 as from 4 July 2011.

[**21A.** In assessing whether the requirements of Appendix C, paragraph 16 are met, where an applicant pays a deposit on account to the sponsor for accommodation costs this amount, up to a maximum of [£1,020], can be offset against the total maintenance requirement if he will be staying in accommodation arranged by the Tier 4 sponsor and he has paid this money to that Tier 4 sponsor.]

Note

Paragraph substituted by HC 760, para 336 as from 13 December 2012. Further amended by HC 1138, para 188 as from 1 July 2014. However, if an applicant has made an application for entry clearance or leave before 1 July 2014, the application will be decided in accordance with the Rules in force on 30 June 2014.

21B. [If the applicant has already paid all or part of the course fees to his Tier 4 Sponsor:

(a)   the Confirmation of Acceptance for Studies Checking Service entry must confirm details of the fees already paid; or

(b)   the applicant must provide an original paper receipt issued by the Tier 4 Sponsor, confirming details of the fees already paid.

21C. If the applicant has an official financial sponsor as set out in paragraph 21(iii) above:

(a)   the Confirmation of Acceptance for Studies Checking Service entry must confirm details of the official financial sponsorship, if it is the Tier 4 Sponsor who is the official financial sponsor; or

(b)   the applicant must provide a letter of confirmation from his official financial sponsor, on official letter-headed paper or stationery of that organisation and bearing the official stamp of that organisation, which clearly shows:

(1)   the applicant's name,

(2)   the name and contact details of the official financial sponsor,

(3)   the date of the letter,

(4)   the length of the official financial sponsorship, and

(5)   the amount of money the official financial sponsor is giving to the applicant, or a statement that the official financial sponsor will cover all of the applicant's fees and living costs.]

Note

Paragraph inserted Cm 8423, para 190 as from 20 July 2012.

22. [An applicant will have an established presence studying in the UK if the applicant has current entry clearance, leave to enter or leave to remain as a Tier 4 migrant or Student and at the date of application:

(i)   has finished a single course that was at least six months long within the applicant's last period of entry clearance, leave to enter or leave to remain, or

(ii)   is applying for continued study on a single course where the applicant has completed at least six months of that course.]

Note

Paragraph inserted by HC 908, para 63 as from 21 April 2011.

APPENDIX D
IMMIGRATION RULES FOR LEAVE TO ENTER AS A HIGHLY SKILLED MIGRANT AS AT 31 MARCH 2008, AND IMMIGRATION RULES FOR LEAVE TO REMAIN AS A HIGHLY SKILLED MIGRANT AS AT 23 FEBRUARY

Requirements for an extension of stay as a highly skilled migrant

135A. The requirements to be met by a person seeking leave to enter as a highly skilled migrant are that the applicant:

(i)   must produce a valid document issued by the Home Office confirming that he meets, at the time of the issue of that document, the criteria specified by the Secretary of State for entry to the United Kingdom under the Highly Skilled Migrant Programme; and

(ii)   intends to make the United Kingdom his main home; and

(iii)   is able to maintain and accommodate himself and any dependants adequately without recourse to public funds; and

(iv)   holds a valid United Kingdom entry clearance for entry in this capacity.

Leave to enter as a highly skilled migrant

135B. A person seeking leave to enter the United Kingdom as a highly skilled migrant may be admitted for a period not exceeding 2 years, subject to a condition prohibiting Employment as a Doctor in Training, (unless the applicant has submitted with this application a valid Highly Skilled Migrant Programme Approval Letter, where the application for that approval letter was made on or before 6 February 2008), provided the Immigration Officer is satisfied that each of the requirements of paragraph 135A is met and that the application does not fall for refusal under paragraph 135HA.

Refusal of leave to enter as a highly skilled migrant

135C. Leave to enter as a highly skilled migrant is to be refused if the Immigration Officer is not satisfied that each of the requirements of paragraph 135A is met or if the application falls for refusal under paragraph 135HA.

135D. The requirements for an extension of stay as a highly skilled migrant for a person who has previously been granted entry clearance or leave in this capacity, are that the applicant:

(i)   entered the United Kingdom with a valid United Kingdom entry clearance as a highly skilled migrant, or has previously been granted leave in accordance with paragraphs 135DA–135DH of these Rules; and

(ii)   has achieved at least 75 points in accordance with the criteria specified in Appendix 4 of these Rules, having provided all the documents which are set out in Appendix 5 (Part I) of these Rules which correspond to the points which he is claiming; and

(a)   has produced an International English Language Testing System certificate issued to him to certify that he has achieved at least band 6 competence in English; or

(b)   has demonstrated that he holds a qualification which was taught in English and which is of an equivalent level to a UK Bachelors degree by providing both documents which are set out in Appendix 5 (Part II) of these Rules; and

(iv)   meets the requirements of paragraph 135A(ii)–(iii).

135DA The requirements for an extension of stay as a highly skilled migrant for a work permit holder are that the applicant:
(i) entered the United Kingdom or was given leave to remain as a work permit holder in accordance with paragraphs 128 to 132 of these Rules; and
(ii) meets the requirements of paragraph 135A (i)-(iii).

135DB The requirements for an extension of stay as a highly skilled migrant for a student are that the applicant:
(i) entered the United Kingdom or was given leave to remain as a student in accordance with paragraphs 57 to 62 of these Rules; and
(ii) has obtained a degree qualification on a recognised degree course at either a United Kingdom publicly funded further or higher education institution or a bona fide United Kingdom private education institution which maintains satisfactory records of enrolment and attendance; and
(iii) has the written consent of his official sponsor to remain as a highly skilled migrant if he is a member of a government or international scholarship agency sponsorship and that sponsorship is either ongoing or has recently come to an end at the time of the requested extension; and
(iv) meets the requirements of paragraph 135A(i)-(iii).

135DC. The requirements for an extension of stay as a highly skilled migrant for a postgraduate doctor or postgraduate dentist are that the applicant:
(i) entered the United Kingdom or was given leave to remain as a postgraduate doctor or a postgraduate dentist in accordance with paragraphs 70 to 75 of these Rules; and
(ii) has the written consent of his official sponsor to such employment if he is a member of a government or international scholarship agency sponsorship and that sponsorship is either ongoing or has recently come to an end at the time of the requested extension; and
(iii) meets the requirements of paragraph 135A(i)-(iii).

135DD The requirements for an extension of stay as a highly skilled migrant for a working holidaymaker are that the applicant:
(i) entered the United Kingdom as a working holidaymaker in accordance with paragraphs 95 to 96 of these Rules; and
(ii) meets the requirements of paragraph 135A(i)-(iii).

135DE The requirements for an extension of stay as a highly skilled migrant for a participant in the Science and Engineering Graduates Scheme or International Graduates Scheme are that the applicant:
(i) entered the United Kingdom or was given leave to remain as a participant in the Science and Engineering Graduates Scheme or International Graduates Scheme in accordance with paragraphs 135O to 135T of these Rules; and
(ii) meets the requirements of paragraph 135A(i)-(iii).

135DF. The requirements for an extension of stay as a highly skilled migrant for an innovator are that the applicant:
(i) entered the United Kingdom or was given leave to remain as an innovator in accordance with paragraphs 210A to 210E of these Rules; and
(ii) meets the requirements of paragraph 135A(i)-(iii).

135DG. Deleted.

135DH. The requirements for an extension of stay as a highly skilled migrant for a participant in the Fresh Talent: Working in Scotland scheme are that the applicant:
(i) entered the United Kingdom or was given leave to remain as a Fresh Talent: Working in Scotland scheme participant in accordance with paragraphs 143A to 143F of these Rules; and
(ii) has the written consent of his official sponsor to such employment if the studies which led to him being granted leave under the Fresh Talent: Working in Scotland scheme in accordance with paragraphs 143A to 143F of these Rules, or any studies he has subsequently undertaken, were sponsored by a government or international scholarship agency; and
(iii) meets the requirements of paragraph 135A(i)-(iii).

Extension of stay as a highly skilled migrant

135E. An extension of stay as a highly skilled migrant may be granted for a period not exceeding 3 years, provided that the Secretary of State is satisfied that each of the requirements of paragraph 135D, 135DA, 135DB, 135DC, 135DD, 135DE, 135DF or 135DH is met and that the application does not fall for refusal under paragraph 135HA.

Refusal of extension of stay as a highly skilled migrant

135F. An extension of stay as a highly skilled migrant is to be refused if the Secretary of State is not satisfied that each of the requirements of paragraph 135D, 135DA, 135DB, 135DC, 135DD, 135DE, 135DF or 135DH is met or if the application falls for refusal under paragraph 135HA.

Additional grounds for refusal for highly skilled migrants

135HA. An application under paragraphs 135A-135H of these Rules is to be refused, even if the applicant meets all the requirements of those paragraphs, if:

(i) the applicant submits any document which, whether or not it is material to his application, is forged or not genuine, unless the Immigration Officer or Secretary of State is satisfied that the applicant is unaware that the document is forged or not genuine; or

(ii) the Immigration Officer or Secretary of State has cause to doubt the genuineness of any document submitted by the applicant and, having taken reasonable steps to verify the document, has been unable to verify that it is genuine.

APPENDIX E
MAINTENANCE (FUNDS) FOR THE FAMILY OF RELEVANT BASED SYSTEM MIGRANTS

A sufficient level of funds must be available to an applicant applying as the Partner or Child of a Tier 1 Migrant [or a Tier 1 (Exceptional Talent) Migrant]. A sufficient level of funds will only be available if the requirements below are met.

[(aa) Paragraphs 1A and 1B of Appendix C also apply to this Appendix.]

[(ab) Where the application is connected to a Tier 1 (Entrepreneur) Migrant, the applicant cannot use the same funds to score points for maintenance funds from this Appendix as the Tier 1 (Entrepreneur) Migrant used to score points for attributes under Appendix A.]

[(a) Where the application is connected to a Tier 1 (Investor) Migrant) who is outside the UK or who has been in the UK for a period of less than 12 months [there must be:

    (i) [£1,260] in funds, where the applicant is connected to a Tier 1 (Graduate Entrepreneur) Migrant;

    (ii) [£1,890] in funds in other cases.]

[(b) Where:

    (i) paragraph (a) does not apply, and

    (ii) the application is connected to a Relevant Points Based System Migrant who is not a Tier 1 (Investor) Migrant[, a Tier 1 (Exceptional Talent) Migrant] or a [Tier 4 (General) Student].

there must be [£630] in funds.]

    (i) Where the application is connected to a [Tier 4 (General) Student]:

        (1) if the [Tier 4 (General) Student] is studying in [inner London (as defined in paragraph 12 of Appendix C)], there must be [£615] in funds for each month for which the applicant would, if successful, be granted leave under paragraph 319D(a), up to a maximum of [£5,535], [or]

        (2) if the [Tier 4 (General) Student] is not studying in [inner] London, there must be [£460] in funds for each month for which the

1195

applicant would, if successful, be granted leave under paragraph 319D(a), up to a maximum of [£4,140]][, and in each case

(3) the applicant must confirm that the funds are referred to in (1) or (2) above are:

  (i) available in the manner specified in paragraph (f) below for use in living costs in the UK; and

  (ii) that the funds will remain available in the manner specified in paragraph (f) below unless used to pay for living costs.]

(c) Where the applicant is applying as the Partner of a Relevant Points Based System Migrant, the relevant amount of funds must be available to either the applicant or the Relevant Points Based System Migrant

(d) Where the applicant is applying as the Child of a Relevant Points Based System Migrant, the relevant amount of funds must be available to the applicant, the Relevant Points Based System Migrant, or the applicant's other parent who is Lawfully present in the UK or being granted entry clearance, or leave to enter or remain, at the same time.

(e) Where the Relevant Points Based System Migrant is applying for entry clearance or leave to remain at the same time as the applicant, the amount of funds available to the applicant must be in addition to the level of funds required separately of the Relevant Points Based System Migrant.

[(f) In all cases, the funds in question must be available to:

  (i) the applicant, or

  (ii) where he is applying as the partner of a Relevant Points Based System Migrant, either to him or to that Relevant Points Based System Migrant, or

  (iii) where he is applying as the child of a Relevant Points Based System Migrant, either to him, to the Relevant Points Based System Migrant or to the child's other parent who is lawfully present in the UK or being granted entry clearance, or leave to enter or remain, at the same time;

[(g) The funds in question must be available to the person referred to in [(f)] above [on the date of application and]) for:

  (i) a consecutive 90–day period of time, ..., if the applicant is applying as the Partner or Child of a Tier 1 Migrant (other than a Tier 1 (Investor) Migrant), [or a Tier 1 (Exceptional Talent) Migrant] a Tier 2 Migrant or a Tier 5 (Temporary Worker) Migrant;

  (ii) a consecutive 28–day period of time, ..., if the applicant is applying as the Partner or Child of a [Tier 4 (General) Student];

(h) If the funds in question were obtained when the person referred to in [(f)] above was in the UK, the funds must have been obtained while that person had valid leave and was not acting in breach of any conditions attached to that leave; and

(i) In the following cases, sufficient funds will be deemed to be available where all of the following conditions are met:

  (1) the Relevant Points Based System Migrant to whom the application is connected has, or is being granted, leave as a Tier 2 Migrant.

  (2) the Sponsor of that Relevant Points Based System Migrant is A-rated, and.

  (3) [that Sponsor has certified on the Certificate of Sponsorship that, should it become necessary, it will maintain and accommodate the dependants of the Relevant Points Based System Migrant up to the end of [the first month of the dependant's leave, if granted]. The undertaking may be limited provided the limit is at least [£630] per dependant. If the Relevant Points Based System Migrant is applying at the same time as the applicant, points will only be awarded if the Relevant Points Based System Migrant provides a valid Certificate of Sponsorship reference number with his application.]

[(ia)   Sufficient funds will not be deemed to be available to the Partner or Child if the specified documents. as set out in paragraph 1B of Appendix C, show that the funds are held in a financial institution listed in Appendix P. as being an institution with which the UK Border Agency is unable to make satisfactory verification checks.]

[(ib)   Sufficient funds will not be deemed to be available where the application is connected to a Tier 1 (Graduate Entrepreneur) Migrant who scores, or scored, points from Appendix A [for an endorsement from UK Trade and Investment], and UK Trade and Investment has confirmed in the endorsement letter that it has awarded funding that is at least sufficient to cover the required maintenance funds for the Tier 1 (Graduate Entrepreneur) Migrant, the applicant and any other dependants.]

(j)   In all cases the applicant must provide the specified documents [as set out in paragraph 1B of Appendix C][, unless the applicant is applying at the same time as the Relevant Points Based System Migrant who is a Tier 4 (General) Student sponsored by a Highly Trusted Sponsor, is a national of one of the countries [or the rightful holder of a qualifying passport issued by one of the relevant competent authorities, as appropriate,] listed in Appendix H, and is applying for entry clearance in his country of nationality [or in the territory related to the passport he holds, as appropriate,] or leave to remain in the UK, and the applicant is also a national of the same country, and confirms these requirements are met, in which case the specified documents shall not be required. The UK Border Agency reserves the right to request the specified documents from these applicants. The application will be refused if the specified documents are not provided in accordance with the request made.]

[(k)   Where the funds are in one or more foreign currencies, the applicant must have the specified level of funds when converted to pound sterling (£) using the spot exchange rate which appears on www.oanda.com* for the date of the application.

(l)   Where the application is one of a number of applications made at the same time as a partner or child of a Relevant Points Based System Migrant (as set out in paragraphs 319A and 319F) each applicant, including the Relevant Points Based System migrant if applying at the same time, must have the total requisite funds specified in the relevant parts of Appendices C and E. If each applicant does not individually meet the requirements of Appendices C and / or E, as appropriate, all the applications (the application by the Relevant Points Based System Migrant and applications as the partner or child of that Relevant Points Based System Migrant) will be refused.]

[(m)   The end of the 90–day and 28–day periods referred to in (g) above will be taken as the date of the closing balance on the most recent of specified documents [(Where specified documents from two or more accounts are submitted, this will be the end date for the account that most favours the applicant)] [as set out in paragraph 1B of Appendix C,] and must be no earlier than 31 days before the date of application.]

[(n)   If:
    (i)   the Relevant Points-Based System is a Tier 4 (General) Student who has official financial sponsorship as set out in paragraph 13(iii) of Appendix C, and
    (ii)   this sponsorship is intended to cover costs of the Relevant Points Bases System Migrant's family member(s).

the applicant must provide a letter of confirmation from the Tier 4 (General) Student's official financial sponsor which satisfies the requirements in paragraph 13D of Appendix C, and confirms that the sponsorship will cover costs of the applicant in addition to costs of the Relevant Points Bases System Migrant.]

[(o)   Where the Relevant Points Based System Migrant is applying for entry clearance or leave to remain at the same time as the applicant, and is not required to provide evidence of maintenance funds because of the provisions in paragraph 5(B) of Appendix C, the applicant is also not required to provide evidence of maintenance funds.]

[(p)   Overdraft facilities will not be considered towards funds that are available or under an applicant's own control.]

Note

Sub-para (iv) substituted by HC 26, para 4 with effect from 5 June 1997. Paragraphs (f)-(j) substituted by HC 382, para 22 as from 23 July 2010. Words in square brackets in paragraphs (f) and (g) substituted by Cm 7929, para 2 as from 20 August 2010. Words in square brackets in (a), (b)(ii) and (g) inserted by HC 863, paras 168–170 as from 6 April 2011. Sub-para (i)(3) inserted by HC 863, para 171 as from 6 April 2011. Words in sub-para (j) "or the rightful holder of a qualifying passport issued by one of the relevant competent authorities, as appropriate," and "or in the territory related to the passport he holds, as appropriate," inserted by HC 1511, paras 56–57 as from 31 October 2011. Sub-paras (k) and (l) inserted by HC 863, para 172 as from 6 April 2011. Further amended by HC 1148, paras 71–77 as from 4 July 2011. In paragraph (a) figure "£1,800" substituted by HC 1888, para 200 as from 14 June 2012. In paragraph (b)(ii) figure "£600" substituted by HC 1888, para 201 as from 14 June 2012. In paragraph (i)(3) figure "£600" substituted by HC 1888, para 210 as from 14 June 2012. Further amended by HC 1888, paras 203–209, 211, 212 as from 6 April 2012. Further amended by Cm 8423, paras 191–195 as from 20 July 2012. Further amended by HC 565, para 112 as from 6 September 2012. Further amended by HC 1039, paras 207–209. Further amended by HC 1138, para 189 as from 1 July 2014. However, if an applicant has made an application for entry clearance or leave before 1 July 2014, the application will be decided in accordance with the Rules in force on 30 June 2014. Further amended by HC 1138, para 190 as from 1 July 2014. However, if an applicant has made an application for entry clearance or leave before 1 July 2014, the application will be decided in accordance with the Rules in force on 30 June 2014. Further amended by HC 1138, para 191 as from 1 July 2014. However, if an applicant has made an application for entry clearance or leave before 1 July 2014, the application will be decided in accordance with the Rules in force on 30 June 2014. Further amended by HC 1138, para 192 as from 1 July 2014. However, if an applicant has made an application for entry clearance or leave before 1 July 2014, the application will be decided in accordance with the Rules in force on 30 June 2014. Further amended by HC 1138, para 193 as from 1 July 2014. However, if an applicant has made an application for entry clearance or leave before 1 July 2014, the application will be decided in accordance with the Rules in force on 30 June 2014. Further amended by HC 1138, para 194 as from 1 July 2014. However, if an applicant has made an application for entry clearance or leave before 1 July 2014, the application will be decided in accordance with the Rules in force on 30 June 2014. Further amended by HC 1138, para 195 as from 1 July 2014. However, if an applicant has made an application for entry clearance or leave before 1 July 2014, the application will be decided in accordance with the Rules in force on 30 June 2014. Further amended by HC 1138, para 196 as from 1 July 2014. However, if an applicant has made an application for entry clearance or leave before 1 July 2014, the application will be decided in accordance with the Rules in force on 30 June 2014. Further amended by HC 1138, para 197 as from 6 April 2014.

APPENDIX F
ARCHIVED IMMIGRATION RULES]

[Part 1 Immigration Rules relating to highly skilled migrants, the International Graduates Scheme, the Fresh talent: Working in Scotland Scheme, businesspersons, innovators, Investors and Writers, Composers and artists as at 29 June 2008]

Highly skilled migrants

Requirements for leave to enter the United Kingdom as a highly skilled migrant

135A.   The requirements to be met by a person seeking leave to enter as a highly skilled migrant are that the applicant:

(i)   must produce a valid document issued by the Home Office confirming that he meets, at the time of the issue of that document, the criteria specified by the

Secretary of State for entry to the United Kingdom under the Highly Skilled Migrant Programme; and

(ii)   intends to make the United Kingdom his main home; and

(iii)   is able to maintain and accommodate himself and any dependants adequately without recourse to public funds; and

(iv)   holds a valid United Kingdom entry clearance for entry in this capacity; and

(v)   if he makes an application for leave to enter on or after 29 February 2008, is not applying in India.

Immigration Officers at port should not refuse entry to passengers on the basis that they applied in India, if those passengers have a valid entry clearance for entry in this capacity

Leave to enter as a highly skilled migrant

135B.   A person seeking leave to enter the United Kingdom as a highly skilled migrant may be admitted for a period not exceeding 2 years, subject to a condition prohibiting Employment as a Doctor in Training (unless the applicant has submitted with this application a valid Highly Skilled Migrant Programme Approval Letter, where the application for that approval letter was made on or before 6 February 2008), provided the Immigration Officer is satisfied that each of the requirements of paragraph 135A is met and that the application does not fall for refusal under paragraph 135HA.

Refusal of leave to enter as a highly skilled migrant

135C.   Leave to enter as a highly skilled migrant is to be refused if the Immigration Officer is not satisfied that each of the requirements of paragraph 135A is met or if the application falls for refusal under paragraph 135HA.

International Graduates Scheme

Requirements for leave to enter as a participant in the International Graduates Scheme

135O.   The requirements to be met by a person seeking leave to enter as a participant in the International Graduates Scheme are that he:

(i)   has successfully completed and obtained either:

(a)   a recognised UK degree (with second class honours or above) in a subject approved by the Department for Education and Skills for the purposes of the Science and Engineering Graduates scheme, completed before 1 May 2007; or

(b)   a recognised UK degree, Master's degree, or PhD in any subject completed on or after 1 May 2007; or

(c)   a postgraduate certificate or postgraduate diploma in any subject completed on or after 1 May 2007;

at a UK education institution which is a recognised or listed body.

(ii)   intends to seek and take work during the period for which leave is granted in this capacity; (Hi) can maintain and accommodate himself and any dependants without recourse to public funds;

(iv)   completed his degree, Master's degree, PhD or postgraduate certificate or diploma, in the last 12 months;

(v)   if he has previously spent time in the UK as a participant in the Science and Engineering Graduates Scheme or International Graduates Scheme, is not seeking leave to enter to a date beyond 12 months from the date he was first given leave to enter or remain under the Science and Engineering Graduates Scheme or the International Graduates Scheme;

(vi)   intends to leave the United Kingdom if, on expiry of his leave under this scheme, he has not been granted leave to remain in the United Kingdom in accordance with paragraphs 128-135, 200-210H or 245A-245G of these Rules;

(vii)   has the written consent of his official sponsor to enter or remain in the United Kingdom under the Science and Engineering Graduates Scheme or International

Graduates Scheme if his approved studies, or any studies he has subsequently undertaken, were sponsored by a government or international scholarship agency; and
(viii) holds a valid entry clearance for entry in this capacity except where he is a British National (Overseas),a British overseas territories citizen, a British Overseas citizen, a British protected person or a person who under the British Nationality Act 1981 is a British subject.

Leave to enter as a participant in the International Graduates Scheme

135P. A person seeking leave to enter the United Kingdom as a participant in the International Graduates Scheme may be admitted for a period not exceeding 12 months provided he is able to produce to the Immigration Officer, on arrival, a valid United Kingdom entry clearance for entry in this capacity.

Refusal of leave to enter as a participant in the International Graduates Scheme

135Q. Leave to enter as a participant in the International Graduates Scheme is to be refused if the Immigration Officer is not satisfied that each of the requirements of paragraph 135O is met.

Requirements for leave to remain as a participant in the International Graduates Scheme

135R. The requirements to be met by a person seeking leave to remain as a participant in the International Graduates Scheme are that he:
(i) meets the requirements of paragraph 135O(i) to (vii); and
(ii) has leave to enter or remain as a student or as a participant in the Science and Engineering Graduates Scheme or International Graduates Scheme in accordance with paragraphs 57-69L or 135O-135T of these Rules;
(iii) would not, as a result of an extension of stay, remain in the United Kingdom as a participant in the International Graduates Scheme to a date beyond 12 months from the date on which he was first given leave to enter or remain in this capacity or under the Science and Engineering Graduates Scheme.

Leave to remain as a participant in the International Graduates Scheme

135S. Leave to remain as a participant in the International Graduates Scheme may be granted if the Secretary of State is satisfied that the applicant meets each of the requirements of paragraph 135R.

Refusal of leave to remain as a participant in the International Graduates Scheme

135T. Leave to remain as a participant in the International Graduates Scheme is to be refused if the Secretary of State is not satisfied that each of the requirements of paragraph 135R is met.

Requirements for leave to enter the United Kingdom as a Fresh Talent: Working in Scotland scheme participant

143A. The requirements to be met by a person seeking leave to enter as a Fresh Talent: Working in Scotland scheme participant are that the applicant:
(i) has been awarded:
(a) a HND, by a Scottish publicly funded institution of further or higher education, or a Scottish bona fide private education institution; or
(b) a recognised UK undergraduate degree, Master's degree or PhD or postgraduate certificate or diploma, by a Scottish education institution which is a recognised or listed body; and
(ii) has lived in Scotland for an appropriate period of time whilst studying for the HND, undergraduate degree, Master's degree PhD or postgraduate certificate or diploma referred to in (i) above; and

(iii)   intends to seek and take employment in Scotland during the period of leave granted under this paragraph; and

(iv)   is able to maintain and accommodate himself and any dependants adequately without recourse to public funds; and

(v)   has completed the HND, undergraduate degree, Master's degree PhD or postgraduate certificate or diploma referred to in (i) above in the last 12 months; and

(vi)   intends to leave the United Kingdom if, on expiry of his leave under this paragraph, he has not been granted leave to remain in the United Kingdom as:

    (a)   a work permit holder in accordance with paragraphs 128-135 of these Rules; or

    (b)   a Tier 1 (General) Migrant; or

    (c)   a person intending to establish themselves in business in accordance with paragraphs 200-210 of these Rules; or

    (d)   an innovator in accordance with paragraphs 21OA-21OH of these Rules; and

(vii)   has the written consent of his official sponsor to enter or remain in the United Kingdom as a Fresh Talent: Working in Scotland scheme participant, if the studies which led to his qualification under (i) above (or any studies he has subsequently undertaken) were sponsored by a government or international scholarship agency; and

(viii)   if the has previously been granted leave as either:

    (a)   a Fresh Talent: Working in Scotland scheme participant in accordance with this paragraph; and/or

    (b)   a participant in the Science and Engineering Graduates Scheme or International Graduates Scheme in accordance with paragraphs 135O-135T of these Rules is not seeking leave to enter under this paragraph which, when amalgamated with any previous periods of leave granted in either of these two categories, would total more than 24 months; and

(ix)   holds a valid entry clearance for entry in this capacity except where he is a British National (Overseas), a British overseas territories citizen, a British Overseas citizen, a British protected person or a person who under the British Nationality Act 1981 is a British subject.

Leave to enter as a Fresh Talent: Working in Scotland scheme participant

143B.   A person seeking leave to enter the United Kingdom as a Fresh Talent: Working in Scotland scheme participant may be admitted for a period not exceeding 24 months provided the Immigration Officer is satisfied that each of the requirements of paragraph 143A is met.

Refusal of leave to enter as a Fresh Talent: Working in Scotland scheme participant

143C.   Leave to enter as a Fresh Talent: Working in Scotland scheme participant is to be refused if the Immigration Officer is not satisfied that each of the requirements of paragraph 143A is met.

Requirements for an extension of stay as a Fresh Talent: Working in Scotland scheme participant

143D.   The requirements to be met by a person seeking an extension of stay as a Fresh Talent: Working in Scotland scheme participant are that the applicant:

(i)   meets the requirements of paragraph 143A (i) to (vii); and

(ii)   has leave to enter or remain in the United Kingdom as either:

    (a)   a student in accordance with paragraphs 57-69L of these Rules; or

    (b)   a participant in the Science and Engineering Graduates Scheme or International Graduates Scheme in accordance with paragraphs 135O-135T of these Rules; or

    (c)   a Fresh Talent: Working in Scotland scheme participant in accordance with paragraphs 143A-143F of these Rules; and

(iii)   if he has previously been granted leave as either:

    (a)   a Fresh Talent: Working in Scotland scheme participant in accordance with paragraphs 143A-143F of these Rules; and/or

(b)   a Science and Engineering Graduates Scheme or International Graduates Scheme participant in accordance with paragraphs 1350-135T of these Rules is not seeking leave to remain under this paragraph which, when amalgamated with any previous periods of leave granted in either of these two categories, would total more than 24 months.

Extension of stay as a Fresh Talent: Working in Scotland scheme participant

143E.   An extension of stay as a Fresh Talent: Working in Scotland scheme participant may be granted for a period not exceeding 24 months if the Secretary of State is satisfied that each of the requirements of paragraph 143D is met.

Refusal of extension of stay as a Fresh Talent: Working in Scotland scheme participant

143F.   An extension of stay as a Fresh Talent: Working in Scotland scheme participant is to be refused if the Secretary of State is not satisfied that each of the requirements of paragraph 143D is met.

Persons intending to establish themselves in business

Requirements for leave to enter the United Kingdom as a person intending to establish himself in business

200.   For the purpose of paragraphs 201-210 a business means an enterprise as:

a sole trader; or

a partnership; or

a company registered in the United Kingdom.

201.   The requirements to be met by a person seeking leave to enter the United Kingdom to establish himself in business are:
(i)   that he satisfies the requirements of either paragraph 202 or paragraph 203; and
(ii)   that he has not less than £200,000 of his own money under his control and disposable in the United Kingdom which is held in his own name and not by a trust or other investment vehicle and which he will be investing in the business in the United Kingdom; and
(iii)   that until his business provides him with an income he will have sufficient additional funds to maintain and accommodate himself and any dependants without recourse to employment (other than his work for the business) or to public funds; and
(iv)   that he will be actively involved full time in trading or providing services on his own account or in partnership, or in the promotion and management of the company as a director; and
(v)   that his level of financial investment will be proportional to his interest in the business; and
(vi)   that he will have either a controlling or equal interest in the business and that any partnership or directorship does not amount to disguised employment; and
(vii)   that he will be able to bear his share of liabilities; and
(vii)   that there is a genuine need for his investment and services in the United Kingdom; and
(ix)   that his share of the profits of the business will be sufficient to maintain and accommodate himself and any dependants without recourse to employment (other than his work for the business) or to public funds; and
(x)   that he does not intend to supplement his business activities by taking or seeking employment in the United Kingdom other than his work for the business; and
(xi)   that he holds a valid United Kingdom entry clearance for entry in this capacity.

202.   There a person intends to take over or join as a partner or director an existing business in the United Kingdom he will need, in addition to meeting the requirements at paragraph 201, to produce:

(i)   a written statement of the terms on which he is to take over or join the business; and

(ii)   audited accounts for the business for previous years; and

(iiii) evidence that his services and investment will result in a net increase in the employment provided by the business to persons settled here to the extent of creating at least 2 new full time jobs.

203. There a person intends to establish a new business in the United Kingdom he will need, in addition to meeting the requirements at paragraph 201 above, to produce evidence:

(i)   that he will be bringing into the country sufficient funds of his own to establish a business; and

(ii)   that the business will create full time paid employment for at least 2 persons already settled in the United Kingdom.

Leave to enter the United Kingdom as a person seeking to establish himself in business

204. A person seeking leave to enter the United Kingdom to establish himself in business may be admitted for a period not exceeding 2 years with a condition restricting his freedom to take employment provided he is able to produce to the Immigration Officer, on arrival, a valid United Kingdom entry clearance for entry in this capacity.

Refusal of leave to enter the United Kingdom as a person seeking to establish himself in business

205. Leave to enter the United Kingdom as a person seeking to establish himself in business is to be refused if a valid United Kingdom entry clearance for entry in this capacity is not produced to the Immigration Officer on arrival.

Requirements for an extension of stay in order to remain in business

206. The requirements for an extension of stay in order to remain in business in the United Kingdom are that the applicant can show:

(i)   that he entered the United Kingdom with a valid United Kingdom entry clearance as a businessman; and

(ii)   audited accounts which show the precise financial position of the business and which confirm that he has invested not less than £200,000 of his own money directly into the business in the United Kingdom; and

(iii) that he is actively involved on a full time basis in trading or providing services on his own account or in partnership or in the promotion and management of the company as a director; and

(iv) that his level of financial investment is proportional to his interest in the business; and

(v)   that he has either a controlling or equal interest in the business and that any partnership or directorship does not amount to disguised employment; and

(vi) that he is able to bear his share of any liability the business may incur; and

(vii) that there is a genuine need for his investment and services in the United Kingdom; and

      (a)   that where he has established a new business, new full time paid employment has been created in the business for at least 2 persons settled in the United Kingdom; or

      (b)   that where he has taken over or joined an existing business, his services and investment have resulted in a net increase in the employment provided by the business to persons settled here to the extent of creating at least 2 new full time jobs; and

(ix) that his share of the profits of the business is sufficient to maintain and accommodate him and any dependants without recourse to employment (other than his work for the business) or to public funds; and

(x)   that he does not and will not have to supplement his business activities by taking or seeking employment in the United Kingdom other than his work for the business.

206A. The requirements for an extension of stay as a person intending to establish himself in business in the United Kingdom for a person who has leave to enter or remain for work permit employment are that the applicant:
(i)   entered the United Kingdom or was given leave to remain as a work permit holder in accordance with paragraphs 128 to 133 of these Rules; and
(ii)   meets each of the requirements of paragraph 201 (i)-(x).

206B. The requirements for an extension of stay as a person intending to establish himself in business in the United Kingdom for a highly skilled migrant are that the applicant:
(i)   entered the United Kingdom or was given leave to remain as a highly skilled migrant in accordance with paragraphs 135A to 135F of these Rules; and
(ii)   meets each of the requirements of paragraph 201 (i)-(x).

206C. The requirements for an extension of stay as a person intending to establish himself in business in the United Kingdom for a participant in the Science and Engineering Graduates Scheme or International Graduates Scheme are that the applicant:
(i)   entered the United Kingdom or was given leave to remain as a participant in the Science and Engineering Graduates Scheme or International Graduates Scheme in accordance with paragraphs 135O to 135T of these Rules; and
(ii)   meets each of the requirements of paragraph 201 (i)-(x).

206D. The requirements for an extension of stay as a person intending to establish himself in business in the United Kingdom for an innovator are that the applicant:
(i)   entered the United Kingdom or was given leave to remain as an innovator in accordance with paragraphs 210A to 210F of these Rules; and
(ii)   meets each of the requirements of paragraph 201 (i)-(x).

206E. The requirements for an extension of stay as a person intending to establish himself in business in the United Kingdom for a student are that the applicant:
(i)   entered the United Kingdom or was given leave to remain as a student in accordance with paragraphs 57 to 62 of these Rules; and
(ii)   has obtained a degree qualification on a recognised degree course at either a United Kingdom publicly funded further or higher education institution or a bona fide United Kingdom private education institution which maintains satisfactory records of enrolment and attendance; and
(iii)   has the written consent of his official sponsor to such self employment if he is a member of a government or international scholarship agency sponsorship and that sponsorship is either ongoing or has recently come to an end at the time of the requested extension; and
(iv)   meets each of the requirements of paragraph 201 (i)-(x).

206F. The requirements for an extension of stay as a person intending to establish himself in business in the United Kingdom for a working holidaymaker are that the applicant:
(i)   entered the United Kingdom or was given leave to remain as a working holidaymaker in accordance with paragraphs 95 to 100 of these Rules; and
(ii)   has spent more than 12 months in total in the UK in this capacity; and
(iii)   meets each of the requirements of paragraph 201 (i)-(x).

206G. The requirements for an extension of stay as a person intending to establish himself in business in the United Kingdom in the case of a person who has leave to enter or remain as a Fresh Talent: Working in Scotland scheme participant are that the applicant:
(i)   entered the United Kingdom or was given leave to remain as a Fresh Talent: Working in Scotland scheme participant in accordance with paragraphs 143A to 143F of these Rules; and
(ii)   has the written consent of his official sponsor to such employment if the studies which led to him being granted leave under the Fresh Talent: Working in Scotland scheme in accordance with paragraphs 143A to 143F of these Rules, or any studies he has subsequently undertaken, were sponsored by a government or international scholarship agency; and
(iii)   meets each of the requirements of paragraph 201 (i)-(x).

206H. The requirements for an extension of stay as a person intending to establish himself in business in the United Kingdom for a Postgraduate Doctor or Dentist are that the applicant:

(i)   entered the United Kingdom or was given leave to remain as a Postgraduate Doctor or Dentist in accordance with paragraphs 70 to 75 of these Rules; and

(ii)   has the written consent of his official sponsor to such self employment if he is a member of a government or international scholarship agency sponsorship and that sponsorship is either ongoing or has recently come to an end at the time of the requested extension; and

(iii)   meets each of the requirements of paragraph 201 (i)-(x).

206I. The requirements for an extension of stay as a person intending to establish himself in business in the United Kingdom for a Tier 1 (General) Migrant are that the applicant:

(i)   entered the United Kingdom or was given leave to remain as a Tier 1 (General) Migrant; and

(ii)   meets each of the requirements of paragraph 201(i)-(x).

Extension of stay in order to remain in business

207. An extension of stay in order to remain in business with a condition restricting his freedom to take employment may be granted for a period not exceeding 3 years at a time provided the Secretary of State is satisfied that each of the requirements of paragraph 206, 206A, 206B, 206C, 206D, 206E, 206F, 206G, 206H or 206I is met.

Refusal of extension of stay in order to remain in business

210. An extension of stay in order to remain in business is to be refused if the Secretary of State is not satisfied that each of the requirements of paragraph 206, 206A, 206B, 206C, 206D,206E, 206F, 206G, 206H or 206I is met.

Innovators

Requirements for leave to enter the United Kingdom as an innovator

210A. The requirements to be met by a person seeking leave to enter as an innovator are that the applicant:

(i)   is approved by the Home Office as a person who meets the criteria specified by the Secretary of State for entry under the innovator scheme at the time that approval is sought under that scheme;

(ii)   intends to set up a business that will create full-time paid employment for at least 2 persons already settled in the UK; and

(iii)   intends to maintain a minimum five per cent shareholding of the equity capital in that business, once it has been set up, throughout the period of his stay as an innovator; and

(iv)   will be able to maintain and accommodate himself and any dependants adequately without recourse to public funds or to other employment; and

(v)   holds a valid United Kingdom entry clearance for entry in this capacity.

Leave to enter as an innovator

210B. A person seeking leave to enter the United Kingdom as an innovator may be admitted for a period not exceeding 2 years, provided the Immigration Officer is satisfied that each of the requirements of paragraph 210A is met.

Refusal of leave to enter as an innovator

210C. Leave to enter as an innovator is to be refused if the Immigration Officer is not satisfied that each of the requirements of paragraph 210A are met.

Requirements for an extension of stay as an innovator

210D. The requirements for an extension of stay in the United Kingdom as an innovator, in the case of a person who was granted leave to enter under paragraph 21OA, are that the applicant:

(i)   has established a viable trading business, by reference to the audited accounts and trading records of that business; and

(ii)   continues to meet the requirements of paragraph 21OA (i) and (iv); and has set up a business that will create full-time paid employment for at least 2 persons already settled in the UK; and

(iii)   has maintained a minimum five per cent shareholding of the equity capital in that business, once it has been set up, throughout the period of his stay.

210DA. The requirements for an extension of stay in the United Kingdom as an innovator, in the case of a person who has leave for the purpose of work permit employment are that the applicant:

(i)   entered the United Kingdom or was given leave to remain as a work permit holder in accordance with paragraphs 128 to 132 of these Rules; and

(ii)   meets the requirements of paragraph 210A (i)-(iv).

210DB. The requirements for an extension of stay in the United Kingdom as an innovator in the case of a person who has leave as a student are that the applicant:

(i)   entered the United Kingdom or was given leave to remain as a student in accordance with paragraphs 57 to 62 of these Rules; and

(ii)   has obtained a degree qualification on a recognised degree course at either a United Kingdom publicly funded further or higher education institution or a bona fide United Kingdom private education institution which maintains satisfactory records of enrolment and attendance; and

(iii)   has the written consent of his official sponsor to remain under the Innovator category if he is a member of a government or international scholarship agency sponsorship and that sponsorship is either ongoing or has recently come to an end at the time of the requested extension; and

(iv)   meets the requirements of paragraph 21O(i)-(iv).

210DC. The requirements to be met for an extension of stay as an innovator, for a person who has leave as a working holidaymaker are that the applicant:

(i)   entered the United Kingdom as a working holidaymaker in accordance with paragraphs 95 to 96 of these Rules; and

(ii)   meets the requirements of paragraph 21OA(i)-(iv).

210DD. The requirements to be met for an extension of stay as an innovator, for a postgraduate doctor, postgraduate dentist or trainee general practitioner are that the applicant:

(i)   entered the United Kingdom or was given leave to remain as a postgraduate doctor, postgraduate dentist or trainee general practitioner in accordance with paragraphs 70 to 75 of these Rules; and

(ii)   has the written consent of his official sponsor to remain under the innovator category if he is a member of a government or international scholarship agency sponsorship and that sponsorship is either ongoing or has recently come to an end at the time of the requested extension; and

(iii)   meets the requirements of paragraph 21O(i)-(iv).

210DE. The requirements to be met for an extension of stay as an innovator, for a participant in the Science and Engineering Graduate Scheme or International Graduates Scheme are that the applicant:

(i)   entered the United Kingdom or was given leave to remain as a participant in the Science and Engineering Graduate Scheme or International Graduates Scheme in accordance with paragraphs 1350 to 135T of these Rules; and

(ii)   meets the requirements of paragraph 21OA(i)-(iv).

210DF The requirements to be met for an extension of stay as an innovator, for a highly skilled migrant are that the applicant:

(i)   entered the United Kingdom or was given leave to remain as a highly skilled migrant in accordance with paragraphs 135A to 135E of these Rules; and

(ii)   meets the requirements of paragraph 21OA(i)-(iv)

Requirements for leave to enter the United Kingdom as an investor

224. The requirements to be met by a person seeking leave to enter the United Kingdom as an investor are that he:

(i)	(a) has money of his own under his control in the United Kingdom amounting to no less than £1 million; or (b) (i) owns personal assets which, taking into account any liabilities to which he is subject, have a value exceeding £2 million; and
(ii)	has money under his control in the United Kingdom amounting to no less than £1 million, which may include money loaned to him provided that it was loaned by a financial institution regulated by the Financial Services Authority; and
(ii)	intends to invest not less than £750,000 of his capital in the United Kingdom by way of United Kingdom Government bonds, share capital or loan capital in active and trading United Kingdom registered companies (other than those principally engaged in property investment and excluding investment by the applicant by way of deposits with a bank, building society or other enterprise whose normal course of business includes the acceptance of deposits); and
(iii)	intends to make the United Kingdom his main home; and
(iv)	is able to maintain and accommodate himself and any dependants without taking employment (other than self employment or business) or recourse to public funds; and
(v)	holds a valid United Kingdom entry clearance for entry in this capacity.

Leave to enter as an investor

225. A person seeking leave to enter the United Kingdom as an investor may be admitted for a period not exceeding 2 years with a restriction on his right to take employment, provided he is able to produce to the Immigration Officer, on arrival, a valid United Kingdom entry clearance for entry in this capacity.

Refusal of leave to enter as an investor

226. Leave to enter as an investor is to be refused if a valid United Kingdom entry clearance for entry in this capacity is not produced to the Immigration Officer on arrival.

Requirements for an extension of stay as an investor

EXTENSION OF STAY AS AN INVESTOR

227. The requirements for an extension of stay as an investor are that the applicant:

(i)	entered the United Kingdom with a valid United Kingdom entry clearance as an investor; and (ii) (a) has money of his own under his control in the United Kingdom amounting to no less than £1 million; or (b) (i) owns personal assets which, taking into account any liabilities to which he is subject, have a value exceeding £2 million; and
(ii)	has money under his control in the United Kingdom amounting to no less than £1 million, which may include money loaned to him provided that it was loaned by a financial institution regulated by the Financial Services Authority; and
(iii)	has invested not less than £750,000 of his capital in the United Kingdom on the terms set out in paragraph 224 (ii) above and intends to maintain that investment on the terms set out in paragraph 224 (ii); and
(iv)	has made the United Kingdom his main home; and
(v)	is able to maintain and accommodate himself and any dependants without taking employment (other than his self employment or business) or recourse to public funds.

227A. The requirements to be met for an extension of stay as an investor, for a person who has leave to enter or remain in the United Kingdom as a work permit holder are that the applicant:

(i)	entered the United Kingdom or was granted leave to remain as a work permit holder in accordance with paragraphs 128 to 133 of these Rules; and

(ii)   meets the requirements of paragraph 224 (i)-(iv).

227B.   The requirements to be met for an extension of stay as an investor, for a person in the United Kingdom as a highly skilled migrant are that the applicant:
(i)   entered the United Kingdom or was granted leave to remain as a highly skilled migrant in accordance with paragraphs 135A to 135F of these Rules; and
(ii)   meets the requirements of paragraph 224 (i)-(iv).

227C.   The requirements to be met for an extension of stay as an investor, for a person in the United Kingdom to establish themselves or remain in business are that the applicant:
(i)   entered the United Kingdom or was granted leave to remain as a person intending to establish themselves or remain in business in accordance with paragraphs 201 to 208 of these Rules; and
(ii)   meets the requirements of paragraph 224 (i)-(iv).

227D.   The requirements to be met for an extension of stay as an investor, for a person in the United Kingdom as an innovator are that the applicant:
(i)   entered the United Kingdom or was granted leave to remain as an innovator in accordance with paragraphs 210A to 210F of these Rules; and
(ii)   meets the requirements of paragraph 224 (i)-(iv).

227E.   The requirements to be met for an extension of stay as an investor, for a person in the United Kingdom as a Tier 1 (General) Migrant are that the applicant:
(i)   entered the United Kingdom or was granted leave to remain as a Tier 1 (General) Migrant; and
(ii)   meets the requirements of paragraph 224(i)-(iv).

228.   An extension of stay as an investor, with a restriction on the taking of employment, may be granted for a period not exceeding 3 years at a time of 3 years, provided the Secretary of State is satisfied that each of the requirements of paragraph 227, 227A, 227B, 227C, 227D or 227E is met.

REFUSAL OF EXTENSION OF STAY AS AN INVESTOR

229.   An extension of stay as an investor is to be refused if the Secretary of State is not satisfied that each of the requirements of paragraph 227, 227A, 227B, 227C, 227D or 227E is met.

Writers, composers and artists

Requirements for leave to enter the United Kingdom as a writer, composer or artist

232.   The requirements to be met by a person seeking leave to enter the United Kingdom as a writer, composer or artist are that he:
(i)   has established himself outside the United Kingdom as a writer, composer or artist primarily engaged in producing original work which has been published (other than exclusively in newspapers or magazines), performed or exhibited for its literary, musical or artistic merit; and
(ii)   does not intend to work except as related to his self employment as a writer, composer or artist; and
(iii) has for the preceding year been able to maintain and accommodate himself and any dependants from his own resources without working except as a writer, composer or artist; and
(iv)   will be able to maintain and accommodate himself and any dependants from his own resources without working except as a writer, composer or artist and without recourse to public funds; and
(v)   holds a valid United Kingdom entry clearance for entry in this capacity.

Leave to enter as a writer, composer or artist

233.   A person seeking leave to enter the United Kingdom as a writer, composer or artist may be admitted for a period not exceeding 2 years, subject to a condition restricting his freedom to take employment, provided he is able to produce to the Immigration Officer, on arrival, a valid United Kingdom entry clearance for entry in this capacity.

Refusal of leave to enter as a writer, composer or artist

234. Leave to enter as a writer, composer or artist is to be refused if a valid United Kingdom entry clearance for entry in this capacity is not produced to the Immigration Officer on arrival.

Requirements for an extension of stay as a writer, composer or artist

235. The requirements for an extension of stay as a writer, composer or artist are that the applicant:
(i)   entered the United Kingdom with a valid United Kingdom entry clearance as a writer, composer or artist; and
(ii)   meets the requirements of paragraph 232 (ii)-(iv).

Extension of stay as a writer, composer or artist

236. An extension of stay as a writer, composer or artist may be granted for a period not exceeding 3 years with a restriction on his freedom to take employment, provided the Secretary of State is satisfied that each of the requirements of paragraph 235 is met.

Refusal of extension of stay as a writer, composer or artist

237. An extension of stay as a writer, composer or artist is to be refused if the Secretary of State is not satisfied that each of the requirements of paragraph 235 is met.

Part 2 Immigration rules as at 26 November 2008 relating to routes deleted on 27 November 2008

A) Requirements for leave to enter as an overseas qualified nurse or midwife

69M. The requirements to be met by a person seeking leave to enter as an overseas qualified nurse or midwife are that the applicant:
(i)   has obtained confirmation from the Nursing and Midwifery Council that he is eligible:
    (a)   for admission to the Overseas Nurses Programme; or
    (b)   to undertake a period of supervised practice; or
    (c)   to undertake an adaptation programme leading to registration as a midwife; and
(ii)   has been offered:
    (a)   a supervised practice placement through an education provider that is recognised by the Nursing and Midwifery Council; or
    (b)   a supervised practice placement in a setting approved by the Nursing and Midwifery Council; or
    (c)   a midwifery adaptation programme placement in a setting approved by the Nursing and Midwifery Council; and
(iii)   did not obtain acceptance of the offer referred to in paragraph 69 (ii) by misrepresentation; and
(iv)   is able and intends to undertake the supervised practice placement or midwife adaptation programme; and
(v)   does not intend to engage in business or take employment, except:
    (a)   in connection with the supervised practice placement or midwife adaptation programme; or
    (b)   part-time work of a similar nature to the work undertaken on the supervised practice placement or midwife adaptation programme; and
(vi)   is able to maintain and accommodate himself and any dependants without recourse to public funds.

Leave to enter the United Kingdom as an overseas qualified nurse or midwife

69N. Leave to enter the United Kingdom as an overseas qualified nurse or midwife may be granted for a period not exceeding 18 months, provided the Immigration Officer is satisfied that each of the requirements of paragraph 69M is met.

Refusal of leave to enter as an overseas qualified nurse or midwife

69O. Leave to enter the United Kingdom as an overseas qualified nurse or midwife is to be refused if the Immigration Officer is not satisfied that each of the requirements of paragraph 69M is met.

B) Requirements for an extension of stay as an overseas qualified nurse or midwife

69P. The requirements to be met by a person seeking an extension of stay as an overseas qualified nurse or midwife are that the applicant:

(i) has leave to enter or remain in the United Kingdom as a prospective student in accordance with paragraphs 82 — 87 of these Rules; or

(ii) has leave to enter or remain in the United Kingdom as a student in accordance with paragraphs 57 to 69L of these Rules; or

(iii)(a) has leave to enter or remain in the United Kingdom as a work permit holder in accordance with paragraphs 128 to 135 of these Rules; or

C) Requirements for leave to enter the United Kingdom to take the PLAB Test

75A. The requirements to be met by a person seeking leave to enter in order to take the PLAB Test are that the applicant:

(iv) intends to leave the United Kingdom at the end of his leave granted under this paragraph unless he is successful in the PLAB Test and granted leave to remain:

    (c) as a work permit holder for employment in the United Kingdom as a doctor in accordance with paragraphs 128 to 135.

Requirements for an extension of stay in order to take the PLAB Test

75D. The requirements for an extension of stay in the United Kingdom in order to take the PLAB Test are that the applicant:

(iv) intends to leave the United Kingdom at the end of his leave granted under this paragraph unless he is successful in the PLAB Test and granted leave to remain:

    (c) as a work permit holder for employment in the United Kingdom as a doctor in accordance with paragraphs 128 to 135; *and*

Requirements for leave to enter to undertake a clinical attachment or dental observer post

75G. The requirements to be met by a person seeking leave to enter to undertake a clinical attachment or dental observer post are that the applicant:

(iv) intends to leave the United Kingdom at the end of his leave granted under this paragraph unless he is granted leave to remain:

    (b) as a work permit holder for employment in the United Kingdom as a doctor or dentist in accordance with paragraphs 128 to 135; and

Requirements for an extension of stay in order to undertake a clinical attachment or dental observer post

75K. The requirements to be met by a person seeking an extension of stay to undertake a clinical attachment or dental observer post are that the applicant:

(iv) intends to leave the United Kingdom at the end of his period of leave granted under this paragraph unless he is granted leave to remain:

    (b) as a work permit holder for employment in the United Kingdom as a doctor or dentist in accordance with paragraphs 128 to 135; and

D) Definition of an "au pair" placement

88. For the purposes of these Rules an "au pair" placement is an arrangement whereby a young person:

(a)   comes to the United Kingdom for the purpose of learning the English language; and

(b)   lives for a time as a member of an English speaking family with appropriate opportunities for study; and

(c)   helps in the home for a maximum of 5 hours per day in return for a reasonable allowance and with two free days per week.

Requirements for leave to enter as an "au pair"

89. The requirements to be met by a person seeking leave to enter the United Kingdom as an "au pair" are that he:

(i)   is seeking entry for the purpose of taking up an arranged placement which can be shown to fall within the definition set out in paragraph 88; and

(ii)   is aged between 17-27 inclusive or was so aged when first given leave to enter in this capacity; and

(iii)   is unmarried and is not a civil partner; and

(iv)   is without dependants; and

(v)   is a national of one of the following countries: Andorra, Bosnia-Herzegovina, Croatia, The Faroes, Greenland, Macedonia, Monaco, San Marino or Turkey; and

(vi)   does not intend to stay in the United Kingdom for more than 2 years as an "au pair"; and

(vii)   intends to leave the United Kingdom on completion of his stay as an "au pair"; and

(viii)   if he has previously spent time in the United Kingdom as an "au pair", is not seeking leave to enter to a date beyond 2 years from the date on which he was first given leave to enter the United Kingdom in this capacity; and

(ix)   is able to maintain and accommodate himself without recourse to public funds.

Leave to enter as an "au pair"

90. A person seeking leave to enter the United Kingdom as an "au pair" may be admitted for a period not exceeding 2 years with a prohibition on employment except as an "au pair" provided the Immigration Officer is satisfied that each of the requirements of paragraph 89 is met. (A non visa national who wishes to ascertain in advance whether a proposed "au pair" placement is likely to meet the requirements of paragraph 89 is advised to obtain an entry clearance before travelling to the United Kingdom).

Refusal of leave to enter as an "au pair"

91. An application for leave to enter as an "au pair" is to be refused if the Immigration Officer is not satisfied that each of the requirements of paragraph 89 is met.

E) Working holidaymakers

Requirements for leave to enter as a working holidaymaker

95. The requirements to be met by a person seeking leave to enter the United Kingdom as a working holidaymaker are that he:

(i)   is a national or citizen of a country listed in Appendix 3 of these Rules, or a British Overseas Citizen; a British Overseas Territories Citizen; or a British National (Overseas); and

(ii)   is aged between 17 and 30 inclusive or was so aged at the date of his application for leave to enter; and

    (a)   is unmarried and is not a civil partner, or

    (b)   is married to, or the civil partner of, a person who meets the requirements of this paragraph and the parties to the marriage or civil partnership intend to take a working holiday together; and

(iv)   has the means to pay for his return or onward journey, and

(v)   is able and intends to maintain and accommodate himself without recourse to public funds; and

(vi)   is intending only to take employment incidental to a holiday, and not to engage in business, or to provide services as a professional sportsperson, and in any event not to work for more than 12 months during his stay; and

(vii) does not have dependent children any of whom are 5 years of age or over or who will reach 5 years of age before the applicant completes his working holiday; and

(viii) intends to leave the UK at the end of his working holiday: and

(ix)   has not spent time in the United Kingdom on a previous working holidaymaker entry clearance; and

(x)   holds a valid United Kingdom entry clearance, granted for a limited period not exceeding 2 years, for entry in this capacity.

Leave to enter as a working holidaymaker

96. A person seeking to enter the United Kingdom as a working holidaymaker may be admitted provided he is able to produce on arrival a valid United Kingdom entry clearance granted for a period not exceeding 2 years for entry in this capacity.

Refusal of leave to enter as a working holidaymaker

97. Leave to enter as a working holidaymaker is to be refused if a valid United Kingdom entry clearance for entry in this capacity is not produced to the Immigration Officer on arrival.

F) Children of working holidaymakers

Requirements for leave to enter or remain as the child of a working holidaymaker

101. The requirements to be met by a person seeking leave to enter or remain in the United Kingdom as the child of a working holidaymaker are that:

(i)   he is the child of a parent admitted to, and currently present in, the United Kingdom as a working holidaymaker; and

(ii)   he is under the age of 5 and will leave the United Kingdom before reaching that age; and

(iii) he can and will be maintained and accommodated adequately without recourse to public funds or without his parent(s) engaging in employment except as provided by paragraph 95 above; and

(iv)   both parents are being or have been admitted to the United Kingdom, save where:

   (a)   the parent he is accompanying or joining is his sole surviving parent; or

   (b)   the parent he is accompanying or joining has had sole responsibility for his upbringing; or

   (c)   there are serious and compelling family or other considerations which make exclusion from the United Kingdom undesirable and suitable arrangements have been made for his care; and

(v)   he holds a valid United Kingdom entry clearance for entry in this capacity or, if seeking leave to remain, was admitted with a valid United Kingdom entry clearance for entry in this capacity, and is seeking leave to a date not beyond the date to which his parent(s) have leave to enter in the working holidaymaker category.

Leave to enter or remain as the child of a working holidaymaker

102. A person seeking to enter the United Kingdom as the child of working holidaymaker/s must be able to produce on arrival a valid United Kingdom entry clearance for entry in this capacity.

Refusal of leave to enter or remain as the child of a working holidaymaker

103. Leave to enter or remain in the United Kingdom as the child of a working holidaymaker is to be refused if, in relation to an application for leave to enter, a valid United Kingdom entry clearance for entry in this capacity is not produced to the

Immigration Officer on arrival or, in the case of an application for leave to remain, the applicant was not admitted with a valid United Kingdom entry clearance for entry in this capacity or is unable to satisfy the Secretary of State that each of the requirements of paragraph 101 (i)-(iv) is met.

G) Requirements for leave to enter as a teacher or language assistant under an approved exchange scheme

110. The requirements to be met by a person seeking leave to enter the United Kingdom as a teacher or language assistant on an approved exchange scheme are that he:
(i) is coming to an educational establishment in the United Kingdom under an exchange scheme approved by the Department for Education and Skills, the Scottish or Welsh Office of Education or the Department of Education, Northern Ireland, or administered by the British Council's Education and Training Group or the League for the Exchange of Commonwealth Teachers; and
(ii) intends to leave the United Kingdom at the end of his exchange period; and
(iii) does not intend to take employment except in the terms of this paragraph; and
(iv) is able to maintain and accommodate himself and any dependants without recourse to public funds; and
(v) holds a valid United Kingdom entry clearance for entry in this capacity.

Leave to enter as a teacher or language assistant under an exchange scheme

111. A person seeking leave to enter the United Kingdom as a teacher or language assistant under an approved exchange scheme may be given leave to enter for a period not exceeding 12 months provided he is able to produce to the Immigration Officer, on arrival, a valid United Kingdom entry clearance for entry in this capacity.

Refusal of leave to enter as a teacher or language assistant under an approved exchange scheme

112. Leave to enter the United Kingdom as a teacher or language assistant under an approved exchange scheme is to be refused if a valid United Kingdom entry clearance for entry in this capacity is not produced to the Immigration Officer on arrival.

Requirements for extension of stay as a teacher or language assistant under an approved exchange scheme

113. The requirements for an extension of stay as a teacher or language assistant under an approved exchange scheme are that the applicant:
(i) entered the United Kingdom with a valid United Kingdom entry clearance as a teacher or language assistant; and
(ii) is still engaged in the employment for which his entry clearance was granted; and
(iii) is still required for the employment in question, as certified by the employer; and
(iv) meets the requirements of paragraph 110 (ii)-(iv); and
(v) would not, as a result of an extension of stay, remain in the United Kingdom as an exchange teacher or language assistant for more than 2 years from the date on which he was first given leave to enter the United Kingdom in this capacity.

Extension of stay as a teacher or language assistant under an approved exchange scheme

114. An extension of stay as a teacher or language assistant under an approved exchange scheme may be granted for a further period not exceeding 12 months provided the Secretary of State is satisfied that each of the requirements of paragraph 113 is met.

Refusal of extension of stay as a teacher or language assistant under an approved exchange scheme

115. An extension of stay as a teacher or language assistant under an approved exchange scheme is to be refused if the Secretary of State is not satisfied that each of the requirements of paragraph 113 is met.

H) Requirements for leave to enter for Home Office approved training or work experience

116. The requirements to be met by a person seeking leave to enter the United Kingdom for Home Office approved training or work experience are that he:

(i)   holds a valid work permit from the Home Office issued under the Training and Work Experience Scheme; and

(ii)   DELETED

(iii) is capable of undertaking the training or work experience as specified in his work permit; and

(iv) intends to leave the United Kingdom on the completion of his training or work experience; and

(v)   does not intend to take employment except as specified in his work permit; and

(vi) is able to maintain and accommodate himself and any dependants adequately without recourse to public funds; and

(vii) holds a valid United Kingdom entry clearance for entry in this capacity except where he holds a work permit valid for 6 months or less or he is a British National (Overseas), a British overseas territories citizen, a British Overseas citizen, a British protected person or a person who under the British Nationality Act 1981 is a British subject.

Leave to enter for Home Office approved training or work experience

117. A person seeking leave to enter the United Kingdom for the purpose of approved training or approved work experience under the Training or Work Experience Scheme may be admitted to the United Kingdom for a period not exceeding the period of training or work experience approved by the Home Office for this purpose (as specified in his work permit), subject to a condition restricting him to that approved employment, provided he is able to produce to the Immigration Officer, on arrival, a valid United Kingdom entry clearance for entry in this capacity or, where entry clearance is not required, provided the Immigration Officer is satisfied that each of the requirements of paragraph 116(i)-(vi) is met.

Refusal of leave to enter for Home Office approved training or work experience

118. Leave to enter the United Kingdom for Home Office approved training or work experience under the Training and Work Experience scheme is to be refused if a valid United Kingdom entry clearance for entry in this capacity is not produced to the Immigration Officer on arrival or, where entry clearance is not required, if the Immigration Officer is not satisfied that each of the requirements of paragraph 116(i)-(vi) is met.

Requirements for extension of stay for Home Office approved training or work experience

119. The requirements for an extension of stay for Home Office approved training or work experience are that the applicant:

(i)   entered the United Kingdom with a valid work permit under paragraph 117 or was admitted or allowed to remain in the United Kingdom as a student; and

(ii)   has written approval from the Home Office for an extension of stay in this category; and

(iii) meets the requirements of paragraph 116 (ii)-(vi).

Extension of stay for Home Office approved training or work experience

120. An extension of stay for approved training or approved work experience under the Training and Work Experience scheme may be granted for a further period not exceeding the extended period of training or work experience approved by the Home Office for this purpose (as specified in his work permit), provided that in each case the Secretary of State is satisfied that the requirements of paragraph 119 are met. An extension of stay is to be subject to a condition permitting the applicant to take or change employment only with the permission of the Home Office.

Refusal of extension of stay for Home Office approved training or work experience

121. An extension of stay for approved training or approved work experience under the Training and Work Experience scheme is to be refused if the Secretary of State is not satisfied that each of the requirements of paragraph 119 is met.

I) Representatives of overseas newspapers, news agencies and broadcasting organisations

Requirements for leave to enter as a representative of an overseas newspaper, news agency or broadcasting organisation

136. The requirements to be met by a person seeking leave to enter the United Kingdom as a representative of an overseas newspaper, news agency or broadcasting organisation are that he:
(i)   has been engaged by that organisation outside the United Kingdom and is being posted to the United Kingdom on a long term assignment as a representative; and
(ii)   intends to work full time as a representative of that overseas newspaper, news agency or broadcasting organisation; and
(iii)   does not intend to take employment except within the terms of this paragraph; and
(iv)   can maintain and accommodate himself and any dependants adequately without recourse to public funds; and
(v)   holds a valid United Kingdom entry clearance for entry in this capacity.

Leave to enter as a representative of an overseas newspaper, newsagency or broadcasting organisation

137. A person seeking leave to enter the United Kingdom as a representative of an overseas newspaper, news agency or broadcasting organisation may be admitted for a period not exceeding 2 years, provided he is able to produce to the Immigration Officer, on arrival, a valid United Kingdom entry clearance for entry in this capacity.

Refusal of leave to enter as a representative of an overseas newspaper, news agency or broadcasting organisation

138. Leave to enter as a representative of an overseas newspaper, news agency or broadcasting organisation is to be refused if a valid United Kingdom entry clearance for entry in this capacity is not produced to the Immigration Officer on arrival.

Requirements for an extension of stay as a representative of an overseas newspaper, news agency or broadcasting organisation

139. The requirements for an extension of stay as a representative of an overseas newspaper, news agency or broadcasting organisation are that the applicant:
(i)   entered the United Kingdom with a valid United Kingdom entry clearance as a representative of an overseas newspaper, news agency or broadcasting organisation; and
(ii)   is still engaged in the employment for which his entry clearance was granted; and
(iii)   is still required for the employment in question, as certified by his employer; and
(iv)   meets the requirements of paragraph 136 (ii)-(iv).

Extension of stay as a representative of an overseas newspaper, news agency or broadcasting organisation

140. An extension of stay as a representative of an overseas newspaper, news agency or broadcasting organisation may be granted for a period not exceeding 3 years provided the Secretary of State is satisfied that each of the requirements of paragraph 139 is met.

Refusal of extension of stay as a representative of an overseas newspaper, news agency or broadcasting organisation

141. An extension of stay as a representative of an overseas newspaper, news agency or broadcasting organisation is to be refused if the Secretary of State is not satisfied that each of the requirements of paragraph 139 is met.

J) Private servants in diplomatic households

Requirements for leave to enter as a private servant in a diplomatic household

152. The requirements to be met by a person seeking leave to enter the United Kingdom as a private servant in a diplomatic household are that he:
(i)   is aged 18 or over; and
(ii)   is employed as a private servant in the household of a member of staff of a diplomatic or consular mission who enjoys diplomatic privileges and immunity within the meaning of the Vienna Convention on Diplomatic and Consular Relations or a member of the family forming part of the household of such a person; and
(iii)   intends to work full time as a private servant within the terms of this paragraph; and
(iv)   does not intend to take employment except within the terms of this paragraph; and
(v)   can maintain and accommodate himself and any dependants adequately without recourse to public funds; and
(vi)   holds a valid United Kingdom entry clearance for entry in this capacity.

Leave to enter as a private servant in a diplomatic household

153. A person seeking leave to enter the United Kingdom as a private servant in a diplomatic household may be given leave to enter for a period not exceeding 12 months provided he is able to produce to the Immigration Officer, on arrival, a valid United Kingdom entry clearance for entry in this capacity.

Refusal of leave to enter as a private servant in a diplomatic household

154. Leave to enter as a private servant in a diplomatic household is to be refused if a valid United Kingdom entry clearance for entry in this capacity is not produced to the Immigration Officer on arrival.

Requirements for an extension of stay as a private servant in a diplomatic household

155. The requirements for an extension of stay as a private servant in a diplomatic household are that the applicant:
(i)   entered the United Kingdom with a valid United Kingdom entry clearance as a private servant in a diplomatic household; and
(ii)   is still engaged in the employment for which his entry clearance was granted; and
(iii)   is still required for the employment in question, as certified by the employer; and
(iv)   meets the requirements of paragraph 152 (iii)-(v).

Extension of stay as a private servant in a diplomatic household

156. An extension of stay as a private servant in a diplomatic household may be granted for a period not exceeding 12 months at a time provided the Secretary of State is satisfied that each of the requirements of paragraph 155 is met.

Refusal of extension of stay as a private servant in a diplomatic household

157. An extension of stay as a private servant in a diplomatic household is to be refused if the Secretary of State is not satisfied that each of the requirements of paragraph 155 is met.

K) Overseas government employees

Requirements for leave to enter as an ...

160. For the purposes of these Rules *...overnment employee* person coming for employment by an over...eas government employee means a Nations Organisation or other international...rnment or employed by the United is a member. ...tion of which the United Kingdom

161. The requirements to be met by a per... Kingdom as an overseas government employee king leave to enter the United
(i)   is able to produce either a valid United Kin...t he:
        capacity or satisfactory docu...ntary evi...ntry clearance for entry in this
        government employee; and ...of his status as an overseas
(ii)   intends to work full time for the gover...ment
(iii)   does not intend to take employment except w...anisation concerned; and
        and ...e terms of this paragraph;
(iv)   can maintain and accommodate himself and any c...
        recourse to public funds. ...ants adequately without

Leave to enter as an overseas government employee

162. A person seeking leave to enter the United Kingdom as a ...rseas government employee may be given leave to enter for a period not exceeding...ears, provided he is able, on arrival, to produce to the Immigration Officer a valid U... Kingdom entry clearance for entry in this capacity or satisfy the Immigration Offic...hat each of the requirements of paragraph 161 is met.

Refusal of leave to enter as an overseas government employee

163. Leave to enter as an overseas government employee is to be refuse...if a valid United Kingdom entry clearance for entry in this capacity is not produced to the Immigration Officer on arrival or if the Immigration Officer is not satisfied that each of the requirements of paragraph 161 is met.

Requirements for an extension of stay as an overseas government employee

164. The requirements to be met by a person seeking an extension of stay as an overseas government employee are that the applicant:
(i)   was given leave to enter the United Kingdom under paragraph 162 as an overseas government employee; and
(ii)   is still engaged in the employment in question; and
(iii)   is still required for the employment in question, as certified by the employer; and
(iv)   meets the requirements of paragraph 161 (ii)-(iv).

Extension of stay as an overseas government employee

165. An extension of stay as an overseas government employee may be granted for a period not exceeding 3 years provided the Secretary of State is satisfied that each of the requirements of paragraph 164 is met.

Refusal of extension of stay as an overseas government employee

166. An extension of stay as an overseas government employee is to be refused if the Secretary of State is not satisfied that each of the requirements of paragraph 164 is met.

L) Requirements for leave to enter as a minister of religion, missionary, or member of a religious order

170. The requirements to be met by a person seeking leave to enter the United Kingdom as a minister of religion, missionary or member of a religious order are that he:

(a)   ....nister of Religion has either been working
if seeking leave to ent.....inister of religion in any of the 5 years
for at least one yea.... on which the application is made or, where
immediately prior t.... religious faith as the sole means of entering
ordination is presc....ned as a minister of religion following at least
the ministry, has b.... years' part time training for the ministry; or
one year's full tim....s a missionary has been trained as a missionary

(b)   if seeking leave ....sionary and is being sent to the United Kingdom
or has worked ....ation; or

(c)   by an overseas....r as a member of a religious order is coming to live
if seeking leav....intained by the r....ligious order of which he is a
in a commun....ending to teach ....does not intend to do so save at an
member and....ntained by h....s order; and

(ii)   establishme....as a min....ter of religion, missionary or for the religious
intends to work f....member; and

(iii)   order of which he employment except within the terms of this paragraph;
does not intend

(iv)   and   ....commo....ate himself and any dependants adequately without
can maintain ....funds; and

(iva)   recourse to p....s a Minister of Religion can produce an International English
if seeking leg.....System certificate issued to him to certify that he has achieved
Language ....nce in spoken and written English and that it is dated not more
level 6 co....s prior to the date on which the application is made.
than two

(v)   holds a ....l United Kingdom entry clearance for entry in this capacity.

Leave to ent ....*as a minister of religion, missionary, or member of a religious order*

171.   A p....on seeking leave to enter the United Kingdom as a minister of religion,
missionar....or member of a religious order may be admitted for a period not exceeding
2 years p....vided he is able to produce to the Immigration Officer, on arrival, a valid
United ....ingdom entry clearance for entry in this capacity.

*Refusal of leave to enter as a minister of religion, missionary or member of a
religious or....er*

172.   Le....ve to enter as a minister of religion, missionary or member of a religious
order i.... to be refused if a valid United Kingdom entry clearance for entry in this
capacity is not produced to the Immigration Officer on arrival.

*Requirements for an extension of stay as a minister of religion where entry to the
United Kingdom was granted in that capacity*

173.   The requirements for an extension of stay as a minister of religion, where entry
to the United Kingdom was granted in that capacity, missionary or member of a
religious order are that the applicant:
(i)   entered the United Kingdom with a valid United Kingdom entry clearance as a
minister of religion, missionary or member of a religious order; and
(ii)   is still engaged in the employment for which his entry clearance was granted; and
(iii)   is still required for the employment in question as certified by the leadership of
his congregation, his employer or the head of his religious order; and
(a)   if he entered the United Kingdom as a minister of religion, missionary or
member of a religious order in accordance with sub paragraph (i) prior to
23 August 2004 meets the requirements of paragraph 170(ii) — (iv); or
(b)   if he entered the United Kingdom as a minister of religion, missionary or
member of a religious order in accordance with sub paragraph (i), on or
after 23 August 2004 but prior to 19 April 2007, or was granted leave to
remain in accordance with paragraph 174B between those dates, meets
the requirements of paragraph 170 (ii) — (iv), and if a minister of religion
met the requirement to produce an International English Language
Testing System certificate certifying that he achieved level 4 competence in
spoken English at the time he was first granted leave in this capacity; or

Refusal of leave to enter as a visiting religious worker or a religious worker in a non-pastoral role

177D. Leave to enter as a visiting religious worker or a religious worker in a non pastoral role is to be refused if the Immigration Officer is not satisfied that each of the requirements of paragraph 177B is met.

Requirements for an extension of stay as a visiting religious worker or a religious worker in a non pastoral role

177E. The requirements to be met by a person seeking an extension of stay as a visiting religious worker or a religious worker in a non-pastoral role are that the applicant:

(i)   entered the United Kingdom with a valid entry clearance in this capacity or was given leave to enter as a visiting religious worker or a religious worker in a non-pastoral role; and

(ii) intends to continue employment as a visiting religious worker or a religious worker in a nonpastoral role; and

(iii) if seeking an extension of stay as a visiting religious worker:
    (a)   meets the requirement of paragraph 177B(i)(a)(i) above; and
    (b)   submits a letter from a senior member or senior representative of one or more local religious communities in the UK confirming that he is still wanted to perform religious duties as a visiting religious worker at one or more locations in the UK and confirming the expected duration of that employment; and
    (c)   would not, as the result of an extension of stay, be granted leave as a visiting religious worker which, when amalgamated with his previous periods of leave in this category in the last 12 months, would total more than 6 months; or

(iv) if seeking an extension of stay as a religious worker in a non-pastoral role:
    (a)   meets the requirements of paragraph 177B(i)(b)(i) and (ii); and
    (b)   submits a letter from a senior member or senior representative of the local religious community for which he works in the UK confirming that his employment as a religious worker in a non-pastoral role in that religious community will continue, and confirming the duration of that employment; and
    (c)   would not, as the result of an extension of stay, remain in the UK for a period of more than 24 months as a religious worker in a non-pastoral role; and

(v)   meets the requirements of paragraph 177B (ii) to (v); and

Extension of stay as a visiting religious worker or a religious worker in a non-pastoral role

177F. An extension of stay as a visiting religious worker or a religious worker in a non-pastoral role may be granted:

(a)   as a visiting religious worker, for a period not exceeding 6 months; or

(b)   as a religious worker in a non-pastoral role, for a period not exceeding 24 months; if the Secretary of State is satisfied that each of the requirements of paragraph 177E is met.

Refusal of an extension of stay as a visiting religious worker or a religious worker in a non pastoral role

177G. An extension of stay as a visiting religious worker or a religious worker in a non-pastoral role is to be refused if the Secretary of State is not satisfied that each of the requirements of paragraph 177E is met.

N) Airport based operational ground staff of overseas-owned airlines

Requirements for leave to enter the United Kingdom as a member of the operational ground staff of an overseas-owned airline

178. The requirements to be met by a person seeking leave to enter the United Kingdom as a member of the operational ground staff of an overseas owned airline are that he:

(i)   has been transferred to the United Kingdom by an overseas-owned airline operating services to and from the United Kingdom to take up duty at an international airport as station manager, security manager or technical manager; and

(ii)   intends to work full time for the airline concerned; and

(iii)   does not intend to take employment except within the terms of this paragraph; and

(iv)   can maintain and accommodate himself and any dependants without recourse to public funds; and

(v)   holds a valid United Kingdom entry clearance for entry in this capacity.

Leave to enter as a member of the operational ground staff of an overseas owned airline

179. A person seeking leave to enter the United Kingdom as a member of the operational ground staff of an overseas owned airline may be given leave to enter for a period not exceeding 2 years, provided he is able to produce to the Immigration Officer, on arrival, a valid United Kingdom entry clearance for entry in this capacity.

Refusal of leave to enter as a member of the operational ground staff of an overseas owned airline

180. Leave to enter as a member of the operational ground staff of an overseas owned airline is to be refused if a valid United Kingdom entry clearance for entry in this capacity is not produced to the Immigration Officer on arrival.

Requirements for an extension of stay as a member of the operational ground staff of an overseas owned airline

181. The requirements to be met by a person seeking an extension of stay as a member of the operational ground staff of an overseas owned airline are that the applicant:

(i)   entered the United Kingdom with a valid United Kingdom entry clearance as a member of the operational ground staff of an overseas owned airline; and

(ii)   is still engaged in the employment for which entry was granted; and

(iii)   is still required for the employment in question, as certified by the employer; and

(iv)   meets the requirements of paragraph 178 (ii)-(iv).

Extension of stay as a member of the operational ground staff of an overseas owned airline

182. An extension of stay as a member of the operational ground staff of an overseas owned airline may be granted for a period not exceeding 3 years, provided the Secretary of State is satisfied that each of the requirements of paragraph 181 is met.

Refusal of extension of stay as a member of the operational ground staff of an overseas owned airline

183. An extension of stay as a member of the operational ground staff of an overseas owned airline is to be refused if the Secretary of State is not satisfied that each of the requirements of paragraph 181 is met.

O) Retired persons of independent means

Requirements for leave to enter the United Kingdom as a retired person of independent means

263. The requirements to be met by a person seeking leave to enter the United Kingdom as a retired person of independent means are that he:
(i)   is at least 60 years old; and
(ii)   has under his control and disposable in the United Kingdom an income of his own of not less than £25,000 per annum; and
(iii)   is able and willing to maintain and accommodate himself and any dependants indefinitely in the United Kingdom from his own resources with no assistance from any other person and without taking employment or having recourse to public funds; and
(iv)   can demonstrate a close connection with the United Kingdom; and
(v)   intends to make the United Kingdom his main home; and
(vi)   holds a valid United Kingdom entry clearance for entry in this capacity.

Leave to enter as a retired person of independent means

264. A person seeking leave to enter the United Kingdom as a retired person of independent means may be admitted subject to a condition prohibiting employment for a period not exceeding 5 years, provided he is able to produce to the Immigration Officer, on arrival, a valid United Kingdom entry clearance for entry in this capacity.

Refusal of leave to enter as a retired person of independent means

265. Leave to enter as a retired person of independent means is to be refused if a valid United Kingdom entry clearance for entry in this capacity is not produced to the Immigration Officer on arrival.

Requirements for an extension of stay as a retired person of independent means

266. The requirements for an extension of stay as a retired person of independent means are that the applicant:
(i)   entered the United Kingdom with a valid United Kingdom entry clearance as a retired person of independent means; and
(ii)   meets the requirements of paragraph 263 (ii)-(iv); and
(iii)   has made the United Kingdom his main home.

Extension of stay as a retired person of independent means

266A. The requirements for an extension of stay as a retired person of independent means for a person in the United Kingdom as a work permit holder are that the applicant:
(i)   entered the United Kingdom or was granted leave to remain as a work permit holder in accordance with paragraphs 128 to 133 of these Rules; and
(ii)   meets the requirements of paragraph 263 (i) -(v).

266B. The requirements for an extension of stay as a retired person of independent means for a person in the United Kingdom as a highly skilled migrant are that the applicant:
(i)   entered the United Kingdom or was granted leave to remain as a highly skilled migrant in accordance with paragraphs 135A to 135F of these Rules; and
(ii)   meets the requirements of paragraph 263 (i) — (v).

266C. The requirements for an extension of stay as a retired person of independent means for a person in the United Kingdom to establish themselves or remain in business are that the applicant:
(i)   entered the United Kingdom or was granted leave to remain as a person intending to establish themselves or remain in business in accordance with paragraphs 201 to 208 of these Rules; and

(ii)   meets the requirements of paragraph 263 (i) — (v).

266D.   The requirements for an extension of stay as a retired person of independent means for a person in the United Kingdom as an innovator are that the applicant:
(i)   entered the United Kingdom or was granted leave to remain as an innovator in accordance with paragraphs 210A to 210F of these Rules; and
(ii)   meets the requirements of paragraph 263 (i) — (v).

266E.   The requirements for an extension of stay as a retired person of independent means for a person in the UK as a Tier 1 (General) Migrant, Tier 1 (Entrepreneur) Migrant or Tier 1 (Investor) Migrant are that the applicant:
(i)   entered the UK or was granted leave to remain as a Tier 1 (General) Migrant, Tier 1 (Entrepreneur) Migrant or Tier 1 (Investor) Migrant; and
(ii)   meets the requirements of paragraphs 263(i) to (v).

267.   An extension of stay as a retired person of independent means, with a prohibition on the taking of employment, may be granted so as to bring the person's stay in this category up to a maximum of 5 years in aggregate, provided the Secretary of State is satisfied that each of the requirements of paragraph 266 is met. An extension of stay as a retired person of independent means, with a prohibition on the taking of employment, may be granted for a maximum period of 5 years, provided the Secretary of State is satisfied that each of the requirements of paragraph 266A, 266B, 266C, 266D or 266E is met.

Refusal of extension of stay as a retired person of independent means

268.   An extension of stay as a retired person of independent means is to be refused if the Secretary of State is not satisfied that each of the requirements of paragraph 266, 266A, 266B, 266C, 266D or 266E is met.

Indefinite leave to remain for a retired person of independent means

269.   Indefinite leave to remain may be granted, on application, to a person admitted as a retired person of independent means provided he:
(i)   has spent a continuous period of 5 years in the United Kingdom in this capacity; and
(ii)   has met the requirements of paragraph 266 throughout the 5 year period and continues to do so.

Refusal of indefinite leave to remain for a retired person of independent means

270.   Indefinite leave to remain in the United Kingdom for a retired person of independent means is to be refused if the Secretary of State is not satisfied that each of the requirements of paragraph 269 is met.

Part 3 Immigration rules as at 30 March 2009 relating to Students, Student Nurses, Students Re-sitting an Examination, Students Writing Up a Thesis, Postgraduate Doctors or Dentists, Sabbatical Officers and applicants under the Sectors-Based Scheme

Specified forms and procedures for applications or claims in connection with immigration

34B.   Where an application form is specified, it must be sent by prepaid post to the United Kingdom Border Agency of the Home Office, or submitted in person at a public enquiry office of the United Kingdom Border Agency of the Home Office, save for the following exceptions:
(i)   an application may not be submitted at a public enquiry office of the United Kingdom Border Agency of the Home Office if it is an application for:
(f)   limited leave to remain as a Tier 5 (Temporary Worker) Migrant.

Requirements for leave to enter as a student

57. The requirements to be met by a person seeking leave to enter the United Kingdom as a student are that he:
(i)   has been accepted for a course of study, or a period of research, which is to be provided by or undertaken at an organistion which is included on the Register of Education and Training Providers, and is at either;
    (a)   a publicly funded institution of further or higher education which maintains satisfactory records of enrolment and attendance of students and supplies these to the United Kingdom Border Agency when requested; or
    (b)   a bona fide private education institution; or
    (c)   an independent fee paying school outside the maintained sector which maintains satisfactory records of enrolment and attendance of students and supplies these to the United Kingdom Border Agency when requested; and
(ii)   is able and intends to follow either:
    (a)   a recognised full-time degree course or postgraduate studies at a publicly funded institution of further or higher education; or
    (b)   a period of study and/or research in excess of 6 months at a publicly funded institution of higher education where this forms part of an overseas degree course; or
    (c)   a weekday full-time course involving attendance at a single institution for a minimum of 15 hours organised daytime study per week of a single subject, or directly related subject; or
    (d)   a full-time course of study at an independent fee paying school; and
(iii) if under the age of 16 years is enrolled at an independent fee paying school on a full time course of studies which meets the requirements of the Education Act 1944; and
(iv)   if he has been accepted to study externally for a degree at a private education institution, he is also registered as an external student with the UK degree awarding body; and
(v)   he holds a valid Academic Technology Approval Scheme (ATAS) clearance certificate from the Counter-Proliferation Department of the Foreign and Commonwealth Office which relates to the course, or area of research, he intends to undertake and the institution at which he wishes to undertake it; if he intends to undertake either.
    (i)   postgraduate studies leading to a Doctorate or Masters degree by research in one of the disciplines listed in paragraph 1 of Appendix 6 to these Rules; or
    (ii)   postgraduate studies leading to a taught Masters degree in one of the disciplines listed in paragraph 2 of Appendix 6 to these Rules; or
    (iii) a period of study or research, as described in paragraph 57(ii)(b), in one of the disciplines listed in paragraph 1 or 2 of Appendix 6 to these Rules, that forms part of an overseas postgraduate qualification; and
    (vi)   intends to leave the United Kingdom at the end of his studies; and
    (vii) does not intend to engage in business or to take employment, except part-time or vacation work undertaken with the consent of the Secretary of State; and
    (viii) is able to meet the costs of his course and accommodation and the maintenance of himself and any dependants without taking employment or engaging in business or having recourse to public funds; and
    (ix)   holds a valid United Kingdom entry clearance for entry in this capacity.

Leave to enter as a student

58. A person seeking leave to enter the United Kingdom as a student may be admitted for an appropriate period depending on the length of his course of study and his means, and with a condition restricting his freedom to take employment, provided he is able to produce to the Immigration Officer on arrival a valid United Kingdom entry clearance for entry in this capacity.

Refusal of leave to enter as a student

59. Leave to enter as a student is to be refused if the Immigration Officer is not satisfied that each of the requirements of paragraph 57 is met.

Requirements for an extension of stay as a student

60. The requirements for an extension of stay as a student are that the applicant:

(a) was last admitted to the United Kingdom in possession of a valid student entry clearance in accordance with paragraphs 57-62 of valid prospective student entry clearance in accordance with paragraphs 82-87 of these Rules; or

(b) has previously been granted leave to enter or remain in the United Kingdom to re-sit an examination in accordance with paragraphs 69A-69F of these Rules, or

(c) if he has been accepted on a course of study at degree level or above, has previously been granted leave to enter or remain in the United Kingdom in accordance with paragraphs 87A-87F, 128-135, 135O-135T and 143A *to 143F or 345V to 245ZA* of these Rules; or

(d) has valid leave as a student in accordance with paragraphs 57-62 of these Rules; and

(ii) meets the requirements for admission as a student set out in paragraph 57(i)-(viii); and

(iii) has produced evidence of his enrolment on a course which meets the requirements of paragraph 57; and

(iv) can produce satisfactory evidence of regular attendance during any course which he has already begun; or any other course for which he has been enrolled in the past; and

(v) can show evidence of satisfactory progress on his course of study including the taking and passing of any relevant examinations; and

(vi) would not, as a result of an extension of stay, spend more than 2 years on short courses below degree level (ie courses of less than 1 years duration, or longer courses broken off before completion): and

(vii) has not come to the end of a period of government or international scholarship agency sponsorship, or has the written consent of his official sponsor for a further period of study in the United Kingdom and satisfactory evidence that sufficient sponsorship funding is available.

Extension of stay as a student

61. An extension of stay as a student may be granted subject to a restriction on his freedom to take employment, provided the Secretary of State is satisfied that the applicant meets each of the requirements of paragraph 60.

Extension of stay as a student

62. An extension of stay as a student is to be refused if the Secretary of State is not satisfied that each of the requirements of paragraph 60 is met.

Student nurses

Definition of student nurse

63. For the purposes of these Rules the term student means a person accepted for training as a student nurse or midwife leading to a registered nursing qualification.

Requirements for leave to enter as a student nurse

64. The requirements to be met by a person seeking leave to enter the United Kingdom as a student nurse are that the person:

(i) comes within the definition set out in paragraph 63 above; and

(ii) has been accepted for a course of study in recognised nursing educational establishment offering nursing training which meets the requirements of the Nursing and Midwifery Council.

(iii) did not obtain acceptance on the course of study referred to in (ii) above by misrepresentation;

(iv) is able and intends to follow the course; and

(v) does not intend to engage in business or to take employment except in connection with the training course and

(vi) intends to leave the United Kingdom at the end of the course; and

(vii) has sufficient funds available for accommodation and maintenance for himself and any dependants without engaging in business or taking employment (except in connection with the training course) or having recourse to public funds. The possession of a Department of Health bursary may be taken into account in assessing whether the student meets the maintenance requirement.

Leave to enter the United Kingdom as a student nurse

65. A person seeking leave to enter the United Kingdom as a student nurse may be admitted for the duration of the course, with a restriction on his freedom to take employment, provided the Immigration Officer is satisfied that each of the requirements of paragraph 64 is met.

Refusal of leave to enter as a student nurse

66. leave to enter as a student nurse is to be refused of the Immigration Officer is not satisfied that each of the requirements of paragraph 64 is met.

Refusal for an extension of stay as a student nurse

67. The requirements for an extension of stay as a student nurse are that the applicant:

(i) was last admitted to the United Kingdom in possession of a valid student entry clearance, or valid prospective student entry clearance in accordance with paragraphs 82 to 87 of these Rules, if he is a person specified in Appendix 1 to these Rules; and

(ii) meets the requirements set out in paragraph 64(i)-(vii)); and

(iii) has produced evidence of enrolment at a recognised nursing educational establishment; and

(iv) can provide satisfactory evidence of regular attendance during any course which he has already begun; or any other course for which he has been enrolled in the past; and

(v) would not, as a result of an extension of stay, spend more than 4 years in obtaining the relevant qualification; and

(vi) has not come to the end of a period of government or international scholarship agency sponsorship, or has the written consent of his official sponsor for a further period of study in the United Kingdom and evidence that sufficient sponsorship funding is available.

Extension of stay as a student nurse

68. An extension of stay as a student nurse may be granted, subject to a restriction on his freedom to take employment, provided the Secretary of State is satisfied that the applicant meets each of the requirements of paragraph 67.

Refusal of stay as a student nurse

69. An extension of stay as a student nurse is to be refused if the Secretary of State is not satisfied that each of the requirements of paragraph 67 is met.

Re-sits of examinations

Requirements for leave to enter to re-sit an examination

69A. The requirements to be met by a person seeking leave to enter the United Kingdom in order to re-sit an examination are that the applicant:

(a)   meets the requirements for admission as a student set out in paragraph 57(i)-(viii); or

(b)   met the requirements for admission as a student set out in paragraph 57(i)-(viii) in the previous academic year and continues to meet the requirements of paragraph 57(iv)-(viii)

(i)   save for the purposes of paragraphs (i)(a) or (b) above, where leave was last granted in accordance with paragraphs 57-62 of these Rules before 30 November 2007, the requirements of paragraph 57(v) do not apply; and

(ii)   has produced written confirmation from the education institution or independent fee paying school which he attends or attended in the previous academic year that he is required to re-sit an examination; and

(iii)   can provide satisfactory evidence of regular attendance during any course which he has already begun; or any other course for which he has been enrolled in the past; and

(iv)   has not come to the end of a period of government or international scholarship agency sponsorship, or has the written consent of his official sponsor for a further period of study in the United Kingdom and satisfactory evidence that sufficient sponsorship funding is available; and

(v)   has not previously been granted leave to re-sit an examination.

Leave to enter to re-sit an examination

69B. A person seeking leave to enter the United Kingdom in order to re-sit an examination may be submitted for a period sufficient to enable him to re-sit the examination at the first available opportunity with a condition restricting his freedom to take employment, provided the Immigration officer is satisfied that each of the requirements of paragraph 69A is met.

Refusal of leave to enter to re-sit an examination

69C. Leave to enter to re-sit an examination is to be refused if the Immigration officer is not satisfied that each of the requirements of paragraph 69A is met.

Requirements for an extension of stay to re-sit an examination

69D. The requirements for an extension of stay to re-sit an examination are that the applicant:

(i)   was admitted to the United Kingdom with a valid student entry clearance if he was then a visa national;

(ii)   meets the requirements set out in paragraph 69A(i)-(v).

Extension of stay to re-sit an examination

69E. An extension of stay to re-sit an examination may be granted for a period sufficient to enable the applicant to re-sit the examination at the first available opportunity, subject to a restriction on his freedom to take employment, provided the Immigration officer is satisfied that each of the requirements of paragraph 69D is met.

Refusal of extension of stay to re-sit an examination

69F. An extension of stay to re-sit an examination is to be refused if the Immigration officer is not satisfied that each of the requirements of paragraph 69D is met.

Writing up a thesis

Requirements for leave to enter to write up a thesis

69G. The requirements to be met by a person seeking leave to enter the United Kingdom in order to write up a thesis are that the applicant:

(a)   meets the requirements for admission as a student set out in paragraph 57(i)-(viii); or

     (b)   met the requirements for admission as a student set out in paragraph 57(i)-(iii) in the previous academic year and continues to meet the requirements of paragraph 57(iv)-(viii)

(i)   save, for the purpose of paragraph (i)(a) or (b) above, where leave was last granted in accordance with paragraphs 57-62 of these Rules before 30 November 2007, the requirements of paragraph 57(v) do not apply; and

(ii)   can provide satisfactory evidence that he is a postgraduate student enrolled at an education institution either a full time, part time or writing up student; and

(iii)   can demonstrate that his application is supported by the education institution; and

(iv)   has not come to the end of a period of government or international scholarship agency sponsorship, or has the written consent of his official sponsor for a further period of study in the United Kingdom and satisfactory evidence that sufficient sponsorship funding is available; and

(v)   has not previously been granted 12 months leave to write up the same thesis.

Requirements for leave to enter to write up a thesis

69H. A person seeking leave to enter the United Kingdom in order to write up a thesis may be admitted for 12 months with a condition restricting his freedom to take employment, provided the Immigration officer is satisfied that each of the requirements of paragraph 69G is met.

Refusal of leave to enter to write up a thesis

69I. Leave to enter to write up a thesis is to be refused if the Immigration officer is not satisfied that each of the requirements of paragraph 69G is met.

Requirements for an extension of stay to write up a thesis

69J. The requirements for an extension of stay to write up a thesis are that the applicant:

(i)   was admitted to the United Kingdom with a valid student entry clearance if he as then a visa national; and

(ii)   meets the requirements set out in paragraph 69(G)(i)-(v),

Extension of stay to write up a thesis

69K. An extension of stay to write up a thesis may be granted for 12 months subject to a restriction on his freedom to take employment, provided the Secretary of State is satisfied that the applicant meets each of the requirements of paragraph 69J.

Refusal of extension of stay to write up a thesis

69L. An extension of stay to write up a thesis is to be refused if the Secretary of State is not satisfied that each of the requirements of paragraph 69J is met.

Postgraduate doctors, dentists and trainee general practitioners

Requirements for leave to enter the United Kingdom as a postgraduate doctor or dentist

70. The requirements to be met by a person seeking leave to enter the UK as a postgraduate doctor or dentist are that the applicant:

(i)   has successfully completed and obtained a recognised UK degree in medicine or dentistry from either:

    (a)   a UK publicly funded institution of further or higher education; or

    (b)   a UK bona fide private education institution which maintains satisfactory records of enrolment and attendance;

(ii)   has previously been granted leave:

    (a)   in accordance with paragraphs 57 to 69L of these Rules for the final academic year of the studies referred to in (i) above; and

     (b)   as a student under paragraphs 57 to 62 of these Rules for at least one other academic year (aside from the final year) of the studies referred to in (i) above; and

(iii)   holds a letter from the Postgraduate Dean confirming he has a full-time place on a recognised Foundation programme; and

(iv)   intends to train in his post on the Foundation programme; and

(v)   is able to maintain and accommodate himself any dependants without recourse to public funds; and

(vi)   intends to leave the United Kingdom if, on expiry of his leave under this paragraph, he has not been granted leave to remain in the United Kingdom as:

     (a)   a doctor or dentist undertaking a period of clinical attachment or a dental observer post in accordance with paragraphs 75G to 75M of these Rules; or

     (b)   a Tier 2 Migrant

     (c)   a Tier 1 (General) Migrant or Tier (1) (Entrepreneur) Migrant; and

(vii)   if his study at medical school or dental school, or any subsequent studies he has undertaken, were sponsored by a government or international scholarship agency, he has written consent of his sponsor to enter or remain in the United Kingdom as a postgraduate doctor or dentist; and

(viii)   if he has not previously been granted leave in this category has completed his medical or dental degree in the 12 months preceding this application; and

(ix)   if he has previously been granted leave as a postgraduate doctor or dentist, is not seeking leave to enter to a date beyond 3 years from that date on which he was first granted leave to enter or remain in this category; and

(x)   holds a valid entry clearance for entry in this capacity except where he is British National (Overseas), a British Overseas Territories Citizen, a British Overseas Citizen, a British Protected Person or a person who under the British Nationality Act 1981 is a British Subject.

Leave to enter as a postgraduate doctor or dentist

71.   Leave to enter the United Kingdom as a postgraduate doctor or dentist may be granted for the duration of the Foundation Programme, for a period not exceeding 26 months, provided the Immigration officer is satisfied that each of the requirements of paragraph 70 is met.

Refusal of leave to enter as a postgraduate doctor or dentist

72.   Leave to enter as a postgraduate doctor or dentist is to be refused if the Immigration Officer is not satisfied that each of the requirements of paragraph 70 is met.

Requirements for an extension of stay as a postgraduate doctor or dentist

73.   The requirements to be met by a person seeking an extension as a postgraduate doctor or dentist are that the applicant:

(i)   meets the requirements of paragraph 70(i)-(vii); and

(ii)   has leave to enter or remain in the United Kingdom as either

     (a)   a student in accordance with paragraphs 57 to 69L of these Rules; or

     (b)   as a postgraduate doctor or dentist in accordance with paragraphs 70 to 75 of these Rules; or

     (c)   as a doctor or dentist undertaking a period of clinical attachment or a dental observer post in accordance with paragraphs 75G to 75M of these Rules.

(iii)   if he has not previously been granted leave in this category, has completed his medical or dental degree in the last 12 months;

(iv)   would not, as a result of an extension of stay, remain in the United Kingdom as a postgraduate doctor or dentist to a date beyond 3 years from the date on which he was first given leave to enter or remain in this capacity.

Extension of stay as a postgraduate doctor or dentist

74.   An extension of stay as a postgraduate doctor or dentist may be granted for the duration of the Foundation Programme, for a period not exceeding 3 years, provided the Secretary of State is satisfied that each of the requirements of paragraph 73 is met.

Refusal of an extension of stay as a postgraduate doctor or dentist

75. An extension of stay as a postgraduate doctor or dentist is to be refused if the Secretary of State is not satisfied that each of the requirements of paragraph 73 is met.

Requirements for leave to enter the United Kingdom to take the PLAB Test

75A. The requirements to be met by a person seeking leave to enter in order to take the PLAB Test are that the applicant:
(i) is a graduate from a medical school and intends to take the PLAB Test in the United Kingdom; and
(ii) can provide documentary evidence of a confirmed test date or of his eligibility to take the PLAB Test; and
(iii) meets the requirements of paragraph 41(iii)-(vii) for entry as a visitor; and
(iv) intends to leave the United Kingdom at the end of his leave granted under this paragraph unless he is successful in the PLAB Test and granted leave to remain:
    (a) as a postgraduate doctor or trainee general practitioner in accordance with paragraphs 70 to 75; or
    (b) to undertake a clinical attachment in accordance with paragraphs 75G to 75M of these Rules; or

Leave to enter to take the PLAB Test

75B. A person seeking leave to enter the United Kingdom to take the PLAB Test may be admitted for a period not exceeding 6 months, provided the Immigration officer is satisfied that each of the requirements of paragraph 75A is met.

Refusal of leave to enter to take the PLAB Test

75C. Leave to enter the United Kingdom to take the PLAB Test is to be refused if the Immigration Officer is not satisfied that each of the requirements of paragraph 75A is met.

Requirements for an extension to stay in order to take the PLAB Test

75D. The requirements for an extension of stay in the United Kingdom in order to take the PLAB Test are that the applicant:
(i) was given leave to enter the United Kingdom for the purposes of taking the PLAB Test in accordance with paragraph 75B of these Rules; and
(ii) intends to take the PLAB Test and can provide documentary evidence of a confirmed test date; and
(iii) meets the requirements set out in paragraph 41(iii)-(vii); and
(iv) intends to leave the United Kingdom at the end of his leave granted under this paragraph unless he is successful in the PLAB Test and granted leave to remain:
    (a) as a postgraduate doctor or trainee general practitioner in accordance with paragraphs 70 to 75; or
    (b) to undertake a clinical attachment in accordance with paragraphs 75G to 75M of these Rules; or
(v) would not as a result of an extension of stay spend more than 18 months in the United Kingdom for the purpose of taking the PLAB Test.

Extension of stay to take the PLAB Test

75E. A person seeking leave to remain in the United Kingdom to take the PLAB Test may be granted an extension of stay for a period not exceeding 6 months, provided the Secretary of State is satisfied that each of the requirements of paragraph 75D is met.

Refusal of extension of stay to take the PLAB Test

75F. Leave to remain in the United Kingdom to take the PLAB Test is to be refused if the Secretary of State is not satisfied that each of the requirements of paragraph 75D is met.

Requirements for leave to enter to undertake a clinical attachment or dental observer post

75G. The requirements to be met by a person seeking leave to enter to undertake a clinical attachment or dental observer post are that the applicant:

(i)   is a graduate from a medical or dental school and intends to undertake a clinical attachment or dental observer post in the United Kingdom; and

(ii)   can provide documentary evidence of the clinical attachment or dental observer post which will:

    (a)   be unpaid; and

    (b)   only involve observation, not treatment, of patients; and

(iii)   meets the requirements of paragraph 41(iii)-(vii) of these Rules; and

(iv)   intends to leave the United Kingdom at the end of his leave granted under this paragraph unless he is granted leave to remain:

    (a)   as a postgraduate doctor, dentist or trainee general practitioner in accordance with paragraphs 70 to 75;

(v)   if he has previously been granted leave in this category, is not seeking leave to enter which, when amalgamated with those previous periods of leave, would total more than 6 months.

Leave to enter to undertake a clinical attachment or dental observer post

75H. A person seeking leave to enter the United Kingdom to undertake a clinical attachment or dental observer post may be admitted for the period of the clinical attachment or dental observer post, up to a maximum of 6 weeks at a time or 6 months in total in this category, provided the Immigration officer is satisfied that each of the requirements of paragraph 75G is met.

Refusal of leave to enter to undertake a clinical attachment or dental observer post

75J. Leave to enter the United Kingdom to undertake a clinical attachment or dental observer post is to refused if the Immigration officer is not satisfied that each of the requirements of paragraph 75G is met.

Requirements for an extension of stay in order to undertake a clinical attachment or dental observer post

75K. The requirements to be met by a person seeking an extension of stay to undertake a clinical attachment or dental observer post are that the applicant:

(i)   was given leave to enter or remain ion the United Kingdom to undertake a clinical attachment or dental observer post or;

    (a)   for the purposes of taking the PLAB Test in accordance with paragraphs 75A to 75F and has passed both parts of the PLAB Test:

    (b)   as a postgraduate doctor, dentist or trainee general practitioner in accordance with paragraphs 70 to 75; or

    (c)   as a work permit holder for employment in the UK as a doctor or dentist in accordance with paragraphs 128 to 135; and

(ii)   is a graduate from a medical or dental school and intends to undertake a clinical attachment or dental observer post in the United Kingdom; and

(iii)   can provide documentary evidence of the clinical attachment or dental observer post which will:

    (a)   be unpaid; and

    (b)   only involve observation, not treatment, of patients; and

(iv)   intends to leave the United Kingdom at the end of his period of leave granted under this paragraph unless he is granted leave to remain:

    (a)   as a postgraduate doctor, dentist or trainee general practitioner in accordance with paragraphs 70 to 75; or

(v)   meets the requirements of paragraph 41(iii)-(vii) of these Rules; and

(vi)   if he has previously been granted leave in this category, is not seeking an extension of stay which, when amalgamated with those previous periods of leave, would total more than 6 months.

Extension of stay to undertake a clinical attachment or dental observer post

75L. A person seeking leave to remain in the United Kingdom to undertake a clinical attachment or dental observer post up to a maximum of 6 weeks at a time or 6 months in total in this category, may be granted an extension of stay for the period of their clinical attachment or dental observer post, provided that the Secretary of State is satisfied that each of the requirements of paragraph 75K is met.

Refusal of extension of stay to undertake a clinical attachment or dental observer post

75M. Leave to remain in the United Kingdom to undertake a clinical attachment or dental observer post is to be refused of the Secretary of State is not satisfied that each of the requirements of paragraph 75K is met.

Requirements for leave to enter as a prospective student

82. The requirements to be met by a person seeking leave to enter the United Kingdom as a prospective student are that he:
(i)   can demonstrate a genuine and realistic intention of undertaking, within 6 months of his date of entry:
    (b)   a supervised practice placement or midwife adaption course which would meet the requirements for an extension of stay as an overseas qualified nurse or midwife under paragraphs 69P to 69R of these Rules; and
(ii)   intends to leave the United Kingdom on completion of his studies or on the expiry of his leave to enter if he is not able to meet the requirements for an extension of stay:
    (b)   as an overseas qualified nurse or midwife in accordance with paragraph 69P of these Rules; and

Student's unions sabbatical officers

Requirements for leave to enter as a sabbatical officer

87A. The requirements to be met by a person seeking leave to enter the United Kingdom as a sabbatical officer are that the person:
(i)   has been elected to a full-time salaried post as a sabbatical officer at an educational establishment at which he is registered as a student;
(ii)   meets the requirements set out in paragraph 57(i)-(ii) or met the requirements set out in paragraph 57(i)-(ii) in the academic year prior to the one in which he took up or intends to take up the sabbatical office; and
(iii)   does not intend to engage in business or take employment except in connection with his sabbatical post; and
(iv)   is able to maintain and accommodate himself and any dependants adequately without recourse to public funds; and
(v)   at the end of the sabbatical post he intends to:
    (a)   complete a course of study which he has already begun; or
    (b)   take up a further course of study which has been deferred to enable the applicant to take up the sabbatical post; or
    (c)   leave the United Kingdom; and
(vi)   has not come to the end of a period of government or international scholarship sponsorship, or has the written consent of his official sponsor to take up a sabbatical post in the United Kingdom; and
(vii)   has not already completed 2 years as a sabbatical officer.

Leave to enter the United Kingdom as a sabbatical officer

87B. A person seeking leave to enter the United Kingdom as a sabbatical officer may be admitted for a period not exceeding 12 months on conditions specifying his employment provided the Immigration Officer is satisfied that each of the requirements of paragraph 87A is met.

Refusal of leave to enter the United Kingdom as a sabbatical officer

87C.   Leave to enter as a sabbatical officer is to be refused if the Immigration Officer is not satisfied that each of the requirements of paragraph 87A is met.

Requirements for an extension of stay as a sabbatical officer

87D.   The requirements for an extension of stay as a sabbatical officer are that the applicant:
(i)   was admitted to the United Kingdom with a valid student entry clearance if he was then a visa national; and
(ii)   meets the requirements set out in paragraph 87A(i)-(vi); and
(iii)   would not, as a result of an extension of stay, remain in the United Kingdom as a sabbatical officer to a date beyond 2 years from the date on which he was first given leave to enter the United Kingdom in this capacity.

Extension of stay as a sabbatical officer

87E.   An extension of stay as a sabbatical officer may be granted for a period not exceeding 12 months on conditions specifying his employment provided the Secretary of State is satisfied that the applicant meets each of the requirements of paragraph 87D.

Refusal of extension of stay as a sabbatical officer

87F.   An extension of stay as a sabbatical officer is to refused if the Secretary of State is not satisfied that each of the requirements of paragraph 87D is met.

Requirements for leave to enter the United Kingdom for the purpose of employment under the Sectors-Based Scheme

135I.   The requirements to be met by a person seeking leave to enter the United Kingdom for the purpose of employment under the Sector-Based Scheme are that he:
(i)   holds a valid Home Office immigration employment document issued under the Sector-Based Scheme; and
(ii)   is aged 18 and 30 inclusive or was so aged at the date of his application for leave to enter; and
(iii)   is capable of undertaking the employment specified in the immigration employment document; and
(iv)   does not intend to take employment except as specified in the immigration employment document; and
(v)   is able to maintain and accommodate himself adequately without recourse to public funds; and
(vi)   intends to leave the United Kingdom at the end of his approved employment; and
(vii)   holds a valid United Kingdom entry clearance for entry in this capacity.

Leave to enter for the purpose of employment under the Sectors-Based Scheme

135J.   A person seeking leave to enter the United Kingdom for the purpose of employment under the Sectors-Based Scheme may be admitted for a period not exceeding 12 months (normally as specified in his work permit), subject to a condition restricting him to employment approved by the Home Office, provided the Immigration Officer is satisfied that each of the requirements of paragraph 135I is met.

Refusal of leave to enter for the purpose of employment under the Sectors-Based Scheme

135K.   Leave to enter the United Kingdom for the purpose of employment under the Sectors-Based Scheme is to be refused if the Immigration Officer is not satisfied that each of the requirements of paragraph 135I is met.

Requirements for an extension of stay for Sector-Based employment

135L. The requirements for an extension of stay for Sector-Based employment are that the applicant:
(i)   entered the United Kingdom with a valid Home Office immigration employment document issued under the sectors-Based Scheme and;
(ii)   has written approval from the Home Office for the continuation of his employment under the Sectors-Based Scheme; and
(iii) meets the requirements of paragraph 135(1)(ii) to (vi); and
(iv) would not, as a result of the extension of stay sought, remain in the United Kingdom for Sector-Based Scheme employment to a date beyond 12 months from the date on which he was given leave to enter the United Kingdom on this occasion in this capacity.

Extension of stay for Sector-Based employment

135M. An extension of stay for Sectors-Based Scheme employment may be granted for a period not exceeding the period of approved employment recommended by the Home Office provided the Secretary of State is satisfied that each of the requirements of paragraph 135L are met. An extension of stay is to be subject to a condition restricting the applicant to employment approved by the Home Office.

Refusal of extension of stay for Sector-Based employment

135N. An extension of stay for Sectors-Based Scheme employment is to be refused if the Secretary of State is not satisfied that each of the requirements of paragraph 135L is met.

Period and conditions of grant

245ZG.
(b)   The cases referred to in paragraph (a) are those where the applicant has, or was last granted, entry clearance, leave to enter or leave to remain as:
(iii)   a Minister of Religion, Missionary or Member of a Religious Order; provided he is still working for the same employer;

Attributes for Tier 1 (Investor) Migrants

47. A regulated financial institution is one which is regulated by the appropriate regulatory body for the country in which the financial institution operates. For example, where a financial institution does business in the UK, the appropriate regulator id the Financial Services Authority.]

Part 4 Immigration Rules as at 5 April 2012 relating to Overseas qualified nurses or midwives, seasonal agricultural workers, Work permit employment, Multiple Entry work permit Employment, and Tier 1 (Post Study Work) Migrants

Overseas qualified nurse or midwife

Requirements for leave to enter as an overseas qualified nurse or midwife

69M. Deleted on 27 November 2008 by paragraph 39 of Statement of Changes HC 1113 except insofar as relevant to paragraph 69P.

Leave to enter the United Kingdom as an overseas qualified nurse or midwife

69N. DELETED.

Refusal of leave to enter as an overseas qualified nurse or midwife

69O. DELETED.

Requirements for an extension of stay as an overseas qualified nurse or midwife

69P. The requirements to be met by a person seeking an extension of stay as an overseas qualified nurse or midwife are that the applicant:
(i)   Deleted by HC 1113
(ii)   Deleted by HC 1113
(iii)   Deleted by HC 1113
(iv)   has leave to enter or remain as an overseas qualified nurse or midwife in accordance with paragraphs 69M-69R of these Rules; and
(v)   meets the requirements set out in paragraph 69M (i)-(vi); and
(vi)   can provide satisfactory evidence of regular attendance during any previous period of supervised practice or midwife adaptation course; and
(vii)   if he has previously been granted leave:
  (a)   as an overseas qualified nurse or midwife under paragraphs 69M-69R of these Rules, or
  (b)   to undertake an adaptation course as a student nurse under paragraphs 63–69 of these Rules; and is not seeking an extension of stay in this category which, when amalgamated with those previous periods of leave, would total more than 18 months; and
(viii) if his previous studies, supervised practice placement or midwife adaptation programme placement were sponsored by a government or international scholarship agency, he has the written consent of his official sponsor to remain in the United Kingdom as an overseas qualified nurse or midwife.

Extension of stay as an overseas qualified nurse or midwife

69Q. An extension of stay as an overseas qualified nurse or midwife may be granted for a period not exceeding 18 months, provided that the Secretary of State is satisfied that each of the requirements of paragraph 69P is met.

Refusal of extension of stay as an overseas qualified nurse or midwife

69R. An extension of stay as an overseas qualified nurse or midwife is to be refused if the Secretary of State is not satisfied that each of the requirements of paragraph 69P is met.

Seasonal agricultural workers

Requirements for leave to enter as a seasonal agricultural worker

104. The requirements to be met by a person seeking leave to enter the United Kingdom as a seasonal agricultural worker are that he:
(i)   is a student in full time education aged 18 or over; and
(ii)   holds an immigration employment document in the form of a valid Home Office work card issued by the operator of a scheme approved by the Secretary of State; and
(iii)   intends to leave the United Kingdom at the end of his period of leave as a seasonal worker; and
(iv)   does not intend to take employment except as permitted by his work card and within the terms of this paragraph; and
(v)   is not seeking leave to enter on a date not less than 3 months from the date on which an earlier period of leave to enter or remain granted to him in this capacity expired; and
(vi)   is able to maintain and accommodate himself without recourse to public funds.

Leave to enter as a seasonal agricultural worker

105. A person seeking leave to enter the United Kingdom as a seasonal agricultural worker may be admitted with a condition restricting his freedom to take employment for a period not exceeding 6 months providing the Immigration officer is satisfied that each of the requirements of paragraph 104 is met.

Refusal of leave to enter as a seasonal agricultural worker

106. Leave to enter the United Kingdom as a seasonal agricultural worker is to be refused if the Immigration Officer is not satisfied that each of the requirements of paragraph 104 is met.

Requirements for extension of stay as a seasonal agricultural worker

107. The requirements for an extension of stay as a seasonal agricultural worker are that the applicant:
(i)   entered the United Kingdom as a seasonal agricultural worker under paragraph 105; and
(ii)   meets the requirements of paragraph 104 (iii)-(vi); and
(iii) would not, as a result of an extension of stay sought, remain in the United Kingdom as a seasonal agricultural worker beyond 6 months from the date on which he was given leave to enter the United Kingdom on this occasion in this capacity.

Extension of stay as a seasonal agricultural worker

108. An extension of stay as a seasonal agricultural worker may be granted with a condition restricting his freedom to take employment for a period which does not extend beyond 6 months from the date on which he was given leave to enter the United Kingdom on this occasion in this capacity, provided the Secretary of State is satisfied that the applicant meets each of the requirements of paragraph 107.

Refusal of extension of stay as a seasonal worker

109. An extension of stay as a seasonal worker is to be refused if the Secretary of State is not satisfied that each of the requirements of paragraph 107 is met.

Work permit employment

Requirements for leave to enter the United Kingdom for work permit employment

128. The requirements to be met by a person coming to the United Kingdom to seek or take employment (unless he is otherwise eligible for admission for employment under these Rules or is eligible for admission as a seaman under contract to join a ship due to leave British waters) are that he:
(i)   holds a valid Home Office work permit; and
(ii)   is not of an age which puts him outside the limits for employment; and
(iii)   is capable of undertaking the employment specified in the work permit; and
(iv)   does not intend to take employment except as specified in his work permit; and
(v)   is able to maintain and accommodate himself and any dependants adequately without recourse to public funds; and
(vi)   in the case of a person in possession of a work permit which is valid for a period of 12 months or less, intends to leave the United Kingdom at the end of his approved employment; and
(vii)   holds a valid United Kingdom entry clearance for entry in this capacity except where he holds a work permit valid for 6 months or less or he is a British National (Overseas), a British overseas territories citizen, a British Overseas citizen, a British protected person or a person who under the British Nationality Act 1981 is a British subject.

Leave to enter for work permit employment

129. A person seeking leave to enter the United Kingdom for the purpose of work permit employment may be admitted for a period not exceeding the period of employment approved by the Home Office (as specified in his work permit), subject to a condition restricting him to that approved employment, provided he is able to produce to the Immigration Officer, on arrival, a valid United Kingdom entry clearance for entry in this capacity or, where entry clearance is not required, provided the Immigration Officer is satisfied that each of the requirements of paragraph 128(i)-(vi) is met.

Refusal of leave to enter for employment

130.   Leave to enter the United Kingdom for the purpose of work permit employment is to be refused if a valid United Kingdom entry clearance for entry in this capacity is not produced to the Immigration Officer on arrival or, where entry clearance is not required, if the Immigration Officer is not satisfied that each of the requirements of paragraph 128(i)-(vi) is met.

Requirements for an extension of stay for work permit employment

131.   The requirements for an extension of stay to seek or take employment (unless the applicant is otherwise eligible for an extension of stay for employment under these Rules) are that the applicant:
(i)   entered the United Kingdom with a valid work permit under paragraph 129; and
(ii)   has written approval from the Home Office for the continuation of his employment; and
(iii)   meets the requirements of paragraph 128 (ii)-(v).

131A.   The requirements for an extension of stay to take employment (unless the applicant is otherwise eligible for an extension of stay for employment under these Rules) for a student are that the applicant:
(i)   entered the United Kingdom or was given leave to remain as a student in accordance with paragraphs 57 to 62 of these Rules; and
(ii)   has obtained a degree qualification on a recognised degree course at either a United Kingdom publicly funded further or higher education institution or a bona fide United Kingdom private education institution which maintains satisfactory records of enrolment and attendance; and
(iii)   holds a valid Home Office immigration employment document for employment; and
(iv)   has the written consent of his official sponsor to such employment if he is a member of a government or international scholarship agency sponsorship and that sponsorship is either ongoing or has recently come to an end at the time of the requested extension; and
(v)   meets each of the requirements of paragraph 128 (ii) to (vi).

131B.   The requirements for an extension of stay to take employment (unless the applicant is otherwise eligible for an extension of stay for employment under these Rules) for a student nurse overseas qualified nurse or midwife, postgraduate doctor or postgraduate dentist are that the applicant:
(i)   entered the United Kingdom or was given leave to remain as a student nurse in accordance with paragraphs 63 to 69 of these Rules; or
(ia)   entered the United Kingdom or was given leave to remain as an overseas qualified nurse or midwife in accordance with paragraphs 69M to 69R of these Rules; and
(ii)   entered the United Kingdom or was given leave to remain as a postgraduate doctor or a postgraduate dentist in accordance with paragraphs 70 to 75 of these Rules; and
(iii)   holds a valid Home Office immigration employment document for employment as a nurse, doctor or dentist; and
(iv)   has the written consent of his official sponsor to such employment if he is a member of a government or international scholarship agency sponsorship and that sponsorship is either ongoing or has recently come to an end at the time of the requested extension; and
(v)   meets each of the requirements of paragraph 128 (ii) to (vi).

131C.   The requirements for an extension of stay to take employment for a Science and Engineering Graduate Scheme participant are that the applicant:
(i)   entered the United Kingdom or was given leave to remain as a Science and Engineering Graduate Scheme or International Graduates Scheme participant in accordance with paragraphs 135O to 135T of these Rules; and

(ii)   holds a valid Home Office immigration employment document for employment; and

(iii)   meets each of the requirements of paragraph 128 (ii) to (vi).

131D. The requirements for an extension of stay to take employment (unless the applicant is otherwise eligible for an extension of stay for employment under these Rules) for a working holidaymaker are that the applicant:

(i)   entered the United Kingdom as a working holidaymaker in accordance with paragraphs 95 to 96 of these Rules; and

(ii)   he has spent more than 12 months in total in the UK in this capacity; and

(iii)   holds a valid Home Office immigration employment document for employment in an occupation listed on the Work Permits (UK) shortage occupations list; and

(iv)   meets each of the requirements of paragraph 128 (ii) to (vi).

131E. The requirements for an extension of stay to take employment for a highly skilled migrant are that the applicant:

(i)   entered the United Kingdom or was given leave to remain as a highly skilled migrant in accordance with paragraphs 135A to 135E of these Rules; and

(ii)   holds a valid work permit; and

(iii)   meets each of the requirements of paragraph 128 (ii) to (vi).

131F. The requirements for an extension of stay to take employment (unless the applicant is otherwise eligible for an extension of stay for employment under these Rules) for an Innovator are that the applicant:

(i)   entered the United Kingdom or was given leave to remain as an Innovator in accordance with paragraphs 210A to 210E of these Rules; and

(ii)   holds a valid Home Office immigration employment document for employment; and

(iii)   meets each of the requirements of paragraph 128 (ii) to (vi).

131G. The requirements for an extension of stay to take employment (unless the applicant is otherwise eligible for an extension of stay for employment under these Rules) for an individual who has leave to enter or remain in the United Kingdom to take the PLAB Test or to undertake a clinical attachment or dental observer post are that the applicant:

(i)   entered the United Kingdom or was given leave to remain for the purposes of taking the PLAB Test in accordance with paragraphs 75A to 75F of these Rules; or

(ii)   entered the United Kingdom or was given leave to remain to undertake a clinical attachment or dental observer post in accordance with paragraphs 75G to 75M of these Rules; and

(iii)   holds a valid Home Office immigration employment document for employment as a doctor or dentist; and

(iv)   meets each of the requirements of paragraph 128 (ii) to (vi).

131H. The requirements for an extension of stay to take employment (unless the applicant is otherwise eligible for an extension of stay for employment under these Rules) in the case of a person who has leave to enter or remain as a Fresh Talent: Working in Scotland scheme participant are that the applicant:

(i)   entered the United Kingdom or was given leave to remain as a Fresh Talent: Working in Scotland scheme participant in accordance with paragraphs 143A to 143F of these Rules; and

(ii)   holds a valid Home Office immigration employment document for employment in Scotland; and

(iii)   has the written consent of his official sponsor to such employment if the studies which led to him being granted leave under the Fresh Talent: Working in Scotland scheme in accordance with paragraphs 143A to 143F of these Rules, or any studies he has subsequently undertaken, were sponsored by a government or international scholarship agency; and

(iv)   meets each of the requirements of paragraph 128 (ii) to (vi).

131I. The requirements for an extension of stay to take employment for a Tier 1 Migrant are that the applicant:

(i)   entered the UK or was given leave to remain as a Tier 1 Migrant, and

(ii)   holds a valid work permit; and

(iii)   meets each of the requirements of paragraph 128 (ii) to (vi).

Extension of stay for work permit employment

132.   An extension of stay for work permit employment may be granted for a period not exceeding the period of approved employment recommended by the Home Office provided the Secretary of State is satisfied that each of the requirements of paragraphs 131, 131A, 131B, 131C, 131D, 131E, 131F, 131G, 131H or 131I is met. An extension of stay is to be subject to a condition restricting the applicant to employment approved by the Home Office.

133.   An extension of stay for employment is to be refused if the Secretary of State is satisfied that each of the requirements of paragraphs 131, 131A, 131B, 131C, 131D, 131E, 131F, 131G, 131H or 131I is met (unless the applicant is otherwise eligible for an extension of stay for employment under these Rules).

Multiple Entry work permit employment

Requirements for leave to enter for Multiple Entry work permit employment

199A.   The requirements to be met by a person coming to the United Kingdom to seek or take Multiple Entry work permit employment are that he:
(i)   holds a valid work permit;
(ii)   is not of an age which puts him outside the limits for employment;
(iii)   is capable of undertaking the employment specified in the work permit;
(iv)   does not intend to take employment except as specified in his work permit;
(v)   is able to maintain and accommodate himself adequately without recourse to public funds; and
(vi)   intends to leave the United Kingdom at the end of the employment covered by the Multiple Entry work permit and holds a valid United Kingdom Entry clearance for entry into this capacity except where he holds a work permit valid for 6 months or less or he is a British National (Overseas), a British overseas territories citizen, a British Overseas citizen, a British protected person or a person who under the British Nationality Act 1981 is a British subject.

Leave to enter for Multiple Entry work permit employment

199B.   A person seeking leave to enter the United Kingdom for the purpose of Multiple Entry work permit employment may be admitted for a period not exceeding 2 years provided that the Immigration Officer is satisfied that each of the requirements of paragraph 199A are met.

Refusal of leave to enter for Multiple Entry work permit employment

199C.   Leave to enter for the purpose of Multiple Entry work permit employment is to be refused if the Immigration Officer is not satisfied that each of the requirements of paragraph 199A is met.

Tier 1 (Post-Study work) Migrants

245F.   Purpose

The purpose of this route is to encourage international graduates who have studied in the UK to stay on and do skilled or highly skilled work.

245FA.   Entry to the UK

All migrants arriving in the UK and wishing to enter as a Tier 1 (Post-Study Work) Migrant must have a valid entry clearance for entry under this route. If they do not have a valid entry clearance, entry will be refused.

245FB.   Requirements for entry clearance

To qualify for entry clearance as a Tier 1 (Post-Study Work) Migrant, an applicant must meet the requirements listed below. If the applicant meets these requirements, entry clearance will be granted. If the applicant does not meet these requirements, the application will be refused.

Requirements:

(a) The applicant must not fall for refusal under the general grounds for refusal.

(b) The applicant must not previously have been granted entry clearance or leave to remain as a Tier 1 (Post-Study Work) Migrant as a Participant in the International Graduates Scheme (or its predecessor, the Science and Engineering Graduates Scheme), or as a Participant in the Fresh Talent: Working in Scotland Scheme.

(c) The applicant must have a minimum of 75 points under paragraphs 66 to 72 of Appendix A.

(d) The applicant must have a minimum of 10 points under paragraphs 1 to 3 of Appendix B.

(e) The applicant must have a minimum of 10 points under paragraphs 1 to 2 of Appendix C.

(f) If:

    (i) the studies that led to the qualification for which the applicant obtains points under paragraphs 6 to 72 of Appendix A were sponsored by a Government or international scholarship agency, and

    (ii) those studies came to an end 12 months ago or less the applicant must provide the unconditional written consent of the sponsoring Government or agency to the application and must provide the specified documents to show that this requirement has been met.

Note

Ameded by HC 1138, para 35 as from 6 April 2014.

245FC. Period and conditions of grant

Entry clearance will be granted for a period of 2 years and will be subject to the following conditions:

(a) no recourse to public funds,

(b) registration with the police, if this is required by paragraph 326 of these Rules, and

(c) no Employment as a Doctor or Dentist in Training, unless the applicant has obtained a degree in medicine or dentistry at bachelor's level or above from a UK institution that is a UK Recognised or listed body, or which holds a sponsor licence under Tier 4 of the Points Based System.

245FD. Requirements for leave to remain

To qualify for leave to remain as a Tier 1 (Post-Study Work) Migrant, an applicant must meet the requirements listed below. Subject to paragraph 245FE(a)(i), if the applicant meets those requirements, leave to remain will be granted. If the applicant does not meet these requirements, the application will be refused.

Requirements:

(a) The applicant must not fall for refusal under the general grounds for refusal, and must not be an illegal entrant.

(b) The applicant must not previously have been granted entry clearance or leave to remain as a Tier 1 (Post-Study Work) migrant.

(c) The applicant must have a minimum of 75 points under paragraphs 66 to 72 of Appendix A.

(d) The applicant must have a minimum of 10 points under paragraphs 1 to 3 of Appendix B.

(e) The applicant must have a minimum of 10 points under paragraphs 1 to 2 of Appendix C.

(f) The applicant must have, or have last been granted, entry clearance, leave to enter or leave to remain:

    (i)   as a Participant in the Fresh Talent: Working in Scotland Scheme,

    (ii)   as a Participant in the International Graduates Scheme (or its predecessor, the Science and Engineering Graduates Scheme),

    (iii)   as a Student, provided the applicant has not previously been granted leave in any of the categories referred to in paragraphs (i) and (ii) above,

    (iv)   as a Student Nurse, provided the applicant has not previously been granted leave in any of the categories referred to in paragraphs (i) and (ii) above,

    (v)   as a Student Re-Sitting an Examination, provided the applicant has not previously been granted leave in any of the categories referred to in paragraphs (i) and (ii) above,

    (vi)   as a Student Writing Up a Thesis, provided the applicant has not previously been granted leave as a Tier 1 Migrant or in any of the categories referred to in paragraphs (i) and (ii) above,

    (vii)   as a Tier 4 Migrant, provided the applicant has not previously been granted leave as a Tier 1 (Post-Study Work) Migrant or in any of the categories referred to in paragraphs (i) and (ii) above,

    (viii) as a Postgraduate Doctor or Dentist, provided the applicant has not previously been granted leave as a Tier 1 (Post-Study Work) Migrant or in any of the categories referred to in paragraphs (i) and (ii) above,

(g)   An applicant who has, or was last granted leave as a Participant in the Fresh Talent: Working in Scotland Scheme must be a British National (Overseas), British overseas territories citizen, British Overseas citizen, British protected person or a British subject as defined in the British Nationality Act 1981.

(h)   If:

    (i)   the studies that led to the qualification for which the applicant obtains points under paragraphs 66 to 72 of Appendix A were sponsored by a Government or international scholarship agency, and

    (ii)   those studies came to an end 12 months ago or less the applicant must provide the unconditional written consent of the sponsoring Government or agency to the application and must provide the specified documents to show that this requirement has been met.

245FE. Period and conditions of grant

(a)   Leave to remain will be granted:

    (i)   for a period of the difference between 2 years and the period of the last grant of entry clearance, leave to enter or remain, to an applicant who has or was last granted leave as a Participant in the Fresh Talent: Working in Scotland Scheme, as a Participant in the International Graduates Scheme (or its predecessor the Science and Engineering Graduates Scheme). If this calculation results in no grant of leave then leave to remain is to be refused;

    (ii)   for a period of 2 years, to any other applicant.

(b)   Leave to remain under this route will be subject to the following conditions:

    (i)   no access to public funds,

    (ii)   registration with the police, if this is required by paragraph 326 of these Rules, and

    (iii)   no Employment as a Doctor or Dentist in training, unless the applicant:

        (1)   has obtained a primary degree in medicine or dentistry at bachelor's level or above from a UK institution hat is a UK recognised or listed body, or which holds a sponsor licence under Tier 4 of the Points Based System; or

        (2)   has, or has last been granted, entry clearance, leave to enter or leave to remain that was not subject to any condition restricting him from taking employment as a Doctor in Training, and has been employed during that leave as a Doctor in Training; or

        (3)   has, or has last been granted, entry clearance, leave to enter to leave or remain that was not subject to any condition restricting

him from taking employment as a Dentist in Training, and has been employed during that leave as a Dentist in Training.

Appendix A Attributed for Tier 1 (Post-Study Work) Migrants

66. An applicant applying for entry clearance or leave to remain as a Tier 1(Post-Study Work) Migrant must score 75 points for attributes.

67. Available points are shown in Table 10.

68. Notes to accompany the table appear below the table.

Table 10

Qualifications	Points
The applicant has been awarded: (a) a UK recognised bachelor or postgraduate degree, or (b) a UK postgraduate certificate in education or professional Graduate Diploma of Education, or (c) a Higher National Diploma ('HND') from a Scottish Institution.	20
(a) The applicant studied for his award at a UK institution that is a UK recognised or listed body, or which holds a sponsor licence under Tier 4 of the Points Based System, or (b) If the applicant is claiming points for having been awarded a Higher National Diploma from a Scottish Institution, he studied for that diploma at a Scottish publicly funded institution of further or higher education, or a Scottish bona fide private education institution which maintains satisfactory records of enrolment and attendance.	20
The Scottish institution must: (i) be on the list of Education and Training providers list on the Department of Business, Innovation and Skills website, or (ii) hold a Sponsor licence under Tier 4 of the Points Based System.	
The applicant's periods of UK study and/or research towards his eligible award were undertaken whilst he had entry clearance, leave to enter or leave to remain in the UK that was not subject to a restriction preventing him from undertaking a course of study and/or research.	20
The applicant made the application for entry clearance or leave to remain as a Tier 1 (Post-Study Work) Migrant within 12 months of obtaining the relevant qualification or within 12 months of completing a United Kingdom Foundation Programme as a postgraduate doctor or dentist.	15
The applicant is applying for leave to remain and has, or was last granted, leave as a Participant in the International Graduates Scheme (or its predecessor, the Science and Engineering Graduates Scheme) or as a Participant in the Fresh Talent: Working in Scotland Scheme.	75

Qualification: notes

69. Specified documents must be provided as evidence of the qualification and, where relevant, completion of the United Kingdom Foundation Programme Office affiliated Foundation Programme as a postgraduate doctor or dentist.

70. A qualification will have been deemed to have been 'obtained' on the date on which the applicant was first notified in writing, by the awarding institution, that the qualification has been awarded.

71. If the institution studied at is removed from one of the relevant lists referred to in Table 10, or from the Tier 4 Sponsor Register, no points will be awarded for a qualification obtained on or after the date the institution was removed from the relevant list or from the Tier 4 Sponsor Register.

72. To qualify as an HND from a Scottish institution, a qualification must be at level 8 on he Scottish Credit and Qualifications Framework.

Part 5 Immigration rules relating to prospective students as at 30 September 2013

Requirements for leave to enter as a prospective student

82. The requirements to be met by a person seeking leave to enter the United Kingdom as a prospective student are that he:
(i)   can demonstrate a genuine and realistic intention of undertaking, within 6 months of his date of entry:
    (a)   a course of study which would meet the requirements for an extension of stay as a student under paragraph 245ZX or paragraph 245ZZC; and
    (b)   DELETED
(ii)   intends to leave the United Kingdom on completion of his studies or on the expiry of his leave to enter if he is not able to meet the requirements for an extension of stay:
    (a)   as a student in accordance with paragraph 245ZX or paragraph 245ZZC; and
    (b)   DELETED
(iii)   is able without working or recourse to public funds to meet the costs of his intended course and accommodation and the maintenance of himself and any dependants while making arrangements to study and during the course of his studies; and
(iv)   holds a valid United Kingdom entry clearance for entry in this capacity.

Leave to enter as a prospective student

83. A person seeking leave to enter the United Kingdom as a prospective student may be admitted for a period not exceeding 6 months with a condition prohibiting employment, provided he is able to produce to the Immigration officer on arrival a valid United Kingdom entry clearance for entry in this capacity.

Refusal of leave to enter as a prospective student

84. Leave to enter as a prospective student is to be refused if the Immigration Officer is not satisfied that each of the requirements of paragraph 82 is met.

[APPENDIX FM
FAMILY MEMBERS

This Appendix applies to applications under this route made on or after 9 July 2012 and to applications under Part 8 as set out in the Statement of Changes laid on 13 June 2012 (HC 194), except as otherwise set out at paragraphs A277-A280.

The sections of this Appendix are set out in the following order –

General

Section GEN: General

Family life as a partner

Section EC-P: Entry clearance as a partner

Section S-EC: Suitability-entry clearance

Section E-ECP: Eligibility for entry clearance as a partner

Section D-ECP: Decision on application for entry clearance as a partner

Section R-LTRP: Requirements for limited leave to remain as a partner

Section S-LTR: Suitability-leave to remain

Section E-LTRP: Eligibility for limited leave to remain as a partner

Section D-LTRP: Decision on application for limited leave to remain as a partner

Section R-ILRP: Requirements for indefinite leave to remain (settlement) as a partner

[Section S-ILR: Suitability-indefinite leave to remain]

Section E-ILRP: Eligibility for indefinite leave to remain as a partner

Section D-ILRP: Decision on application for indefinite leave to remain as a partner

Exception

Section EX: Exception

Bereaved partner

Section BPILR: Indefinite leave to remain (settlement) as a bereaved partner

Section E-BPILR: Eligibility for indefinite leave to remain as a bereaved partner

Section D-BPILR: Decision on application for indefinite leave to remain as a bereaved partner

Victim of domestic violence

Section DVILR: Indefinite leave to remain (settlement) as a victim of domestic violence

Section E-DVILR: Eligibility for indefinite leave to remain as a victim of domestic violence

Section D-DVILR: Decision on application for indefinite leave to remain as a victim of domestic violence

Family life as a child of a parent with limited leave as a partner or parent

Section EC-C: Entry clearance as a child

Section E-ECC: Eligibility for entry clearance as a child

Section D-ECC: Decision on application for entry clearance as a child

Section [R-LTRC]: Requirements for leave to remain as a child

Section E-LTRC: Eligibility for leave to remain as a child

Section D-LTRC: Decision on application for leave to remain as a child

Family life as a parent

Section EC-PT: Entry clearance as a parent

Section E-ECPT: Eligibility for entry clearance as a parent

Section D-ECPT: Decision on application for entry clearance as a parent

Section R-LTRPT: Requirements for limited leave to remain as a parent

Section E-LTRPT: Eligibility for limited leave to remain as a parent

Section D-LTRPT: Decision on application for limited leave to remain as a parent

Section R-ILRPT: Requirements for indefinite leave to remain (settlement) as a parent

Section E-ILRPT: Eligibility for indefinite leave to remain as a parent

Section D-ILRPT: Decision on application for indefinite leave to remain as a parent

Adult dependent relatives

Section EC-DR: Entry clearance as an adult dependent relative

Section E-ECDR: Eligibility for entry clearance as an adult dependent relative

Section D-ECDR: Decision on application for entry clearance as an adult dependent relative

Section R-ILRDR: Requirements for indefinite leave to remain as an adult dependent relative

Section E-ILRDR: Eligibility for indefinite leave to remain as an adult dependent relative

Section D-ILRDR: Decision on application for indefinite leave to remain as an adult dependent relative

General

Section GEN: General

Purpose

GEN.1.1. This route is for those seeking to enter or remain in the UK on the basis of their family life with a person who is a British Citizen, is settled in the UK, or is in the UK with limited leave as a refugee or person granted humanitarian protection [(and the applicant cannot seek leave to enter or remain in the UK as their family member under Part 11 of these rules)]. It sets out the requirements to be met and, in considering applications under this route, it reflects how, under Article 8 of the Human Rights Convention, the balance will be struck between the right to respect for private and family life and the legitimate aims of protecting national security, public safety and the economic well-being of the UK; the prevention of disorder and crime; the protection of health or morals; and the protection of the rights and freedoms of others [(and in doing so also reflects the relevant public interest considerations as set out in Part 5A of the Nationality, Immigration and Asylum Act 2002)]. It also takes into account the need to safeguard and promote the welfare of children in the UK[, in line with the Secretary of State's duty under section 55 of the Borders, Citizenship and Immigration Act 2009].

Note

Amended by HC 532, para 49 of this statement take effect on 28 July 2014 and apply to all applications to which paragraphs 276ADE to 276DH and Appendix FM apply (or can be applied by virtue of the Immigration Rules), and to any other ECHR Article 8 claims (save for those from foreign criminals), and which are decided on or after that date. Amended by HC 532, para 50 of this statement take effect on 28 July 2014 and apply to all applications to which paragraphs 276ADE to 276DH and Appendix FM apply (or can be applied by virtue of the Immigration Rules), and to any other ECHR Article 8 claims (save for those from foreign criminals), and which are decided on or after that date.

Definitions

GEN.1.2. For the purposes of this Appendix "partner" means-
(i)   the applicant's spouse;
(ii)   the applicant's civil partner;
(iii)   the applicant's fiancé(e) or proposed civil partner; or
(iv)   a person who has been living [together] with the applicant in a relationship akin to a marriage or civil partnership for at least two years prior to the date of application,

[unless a different meaning of partner applies elsewhere in this Appendix.]

Note

Amended by HC 1138, para 198 shall apply to all applications decided on or after 6 April 2014.

GEN.1.3. For the purposes of this Appendix-
(a)   "application for leave to remain" also includes an application for variation of leave to enter or remain by a person in the UK;
(b)   references to a person being present and settled in the UK also include a person who is being admitted for settlement on the same occasion as the applicant; and
(c)   references to a British Citizen in the UK also include a British Citizen who is coming to the UK with the applicant as their partner or parent.

GEN.1.4. In this [Appendix] "specified" means specified in the application or related guidance.

GEN.1.5. If the Entry Clearance Officer, or Secretary of State, has reasonable cause to doubt the genuineness of any document submitted in support of an application, and having taken reasonable steps to verify the document, is unable to verify that it is genuine, the document will be discounted for the purposes of the application.

GEN.1.6. For the purposes of paragraph E-ECP.4.1.(a); E-LTRP.4.1.(a); E-ECPT.4.1(a) and E-LTRPT.5.1.(a) the applicant must be a national of Antigua and Barbuda; Australia; the Bahamas; Barbados; Belize; Canada; Dominica; Grenada; Guyana; Jamaica; New Zealand; St Kitts and Nevis; St Lucia; St Vincent and the Grenadines; Trinidad and Tobago; or the United States of America.

GEN.1.7. In this Appendix references to paragraphs are to paragraphs of this Appendix unless the context otherwise requires.

GEN.1.8. Paragraphs 277-280, 289AA, 295AA and 296 of Part 8 of these Rules shall apply to this Appendix.

[GEN.1.9. In this Appendix:
(a)   the requirement to make a valid application will not apply when the Article 8 claim is raised:
    (i)   as part of an asylum claim, or as part of a further submission in person after an asylum claim has been refused;
    (ii)   where a migrant is in immigration detention. A migrant in immigration detention or their representative must submit any application or claim raising Article 8 to a prison officer, a prisoner custody officer, a detainee custody officer or a member of Home Office staff at the migrant's place of detention; or
    (iii)   in an appeal (subject to the consent of the Secretary of State where applicable); and
(b)   where an application or claim raising Article 8 is made in any of the circumstances specified in paragraph GEN.1.9.(a), or is considered by the Secretary of State under paragraph A277C of these rules, the requirements of paragraphs R-LTRP.1.1.(c) and R-LTRPT.1.1.(c) are not met.]

[GEN.1.10. Where an applicant does not meet the requirements of this Appendix as a partner or parent but the decision-maker grants entry clearance or leave to enter or remain outside the rules on Article 8 grounds, the applicant will normally be granted entry clearance for a period not exceeding 33 months, or leave to enter or remain for a period not exceeding 30 months, and subject to a condition of no recourse to public funds unless the decision-maker considers that the person should not be subject to such a condition.

GEN.1.11. Where entry clearance or leave to enter or remain is granted under this Appendix, or where an applicant does not meet the requirements of this Appendix as a partner or parent but the decision-maker grants entry clearance or leave to enter or remain outside the rules on Article 8 grounds, (and without prejudice to the specific provision that is made in this Appendix in respect of a no recourse to public funds condition), that leave may be subject to such conditions as the decision-maker considers appropriate in a particular case.

GEN.1.12. In paragraphs GEN.1.10. and GEN.1.11. "decision-maker" refers to the Secretary of State or an Entry Clearance Officer.]

[GEN.1.13. For the purposes of paragraphs D-LTRP.1.1., D-LTRP.1.2., DILRP.1.2., D-LTRPT.1.1., D-LTRPT.1.2., and D-ILRPT.1.2. (excluding a grant of limited leave to remain as a fiancé(e) or proposed civil partner), where the applicant has extant leave at the date of decision, the remaining period of that extant leave up to a maximum of 28 days will be added to the period of limited leave to remain granted under that paragraph (which may therefore exceed 30 months).]

Note

Inserted by HC 532, para 51 of this statement take effect on 28 July 2014 and apply to all applications to which paragraphs 276ADE to 276DH and Appendix FM apply (or can be applied by virtue of the Immigration Rules), and to any other ECHR Article 8 claims (save for those from foreign criminals), and which are decided on or after that date. Inserted by HC 532, para 51 of this statement take effect on 28 July 2014 and apply to all applications to which paragraphs 276ADE to 276DH and Appendix FM apply (or can be applied by virtue of the Immigration Rules), and to any other ECHR Article 8 claims (save for those from foreign criminals), and which are decided on or after that date. Inserted by HC 532, para 51 of this statement take effect on 28 July 2014 and apply to all applications to which paragraphs 276ADE to 276DH and Appendix FM apply (or can be applied by virtue of the Immigration Rules), and to any other ECHR Article 8 claims (save for those from foreign criminals), and which are decided on or after that date. Substituted by HC 693, para 185 as from 6 November 2014. Inserted by HC 693, para 186 as from 6 November 2014.

Leave to enter

GEN.2.1. The requirements to be met by a person seeking leave to enter the UK under this route are that the person-
(a)   must have a valid entry clearance for entry under this route; and
(b)   must produce to the Immigration Officer on arrival a valid national passport or other document satisfactorily establishing their identity and nationality.

GEN.2.2. If a person does not meet the requirements of paragraph GEN.2.1. entry will be refused.

Family life with a Partner

Section EC-P: Entry clearance as a partner

EC-P.1.1. The requirements to be met for entry clearance as a partner are that-
(a)   the applicant must be outside the UK;
(b)   the applicant must have made a valid application for entry clearance as a partner;
(c)   the applicant must not fall for refusal under any of the grounds in Section S-EC: Suitability–entry clearance; and
(d)   the applicant must meet all of the requirements of Section E-ECP: Eligibility for entry clearance as a partner.

Section S-EC: Suitability-entry clearance

[S-EC.1.1. The applicant will be refused entry clearance on grounds of suitability if any of paragraphs S-EC.1.2. to 1.8. apply.]

S-EC.1.2. The Secretary of State has personally directed that the exclusion of the applicant from the UK is conducive to the public good.

S-EC.1.3. The applicant is [currently] the subject of a deportation order.

Note
Amended by HC 803, para 20 as from 1 December 2013.

S-EC.1.4. The exclusion of the applicant from the UK is conducive to the public good because they have been convicted of an offence for which they have[:

(a)   been convicted of an offence for which they have been sentenced to a period of imprisonment of at least 4 years; or

(b)   been convicted of an offence for which they have been sentenced to a period of imprisonment of at least 12 months but less than 4 years, unless a period of 10 years has passed since the end of the sentence; or

(c)   been convicted of an offence for which they have been sentenced to a period of imprisonment of at less than 12 months, unless a period of 5 years has passed since the end of the sentence.

Where this paragraph applies, unless refusal would be contrary to the Human Tights Convention or the Convention and Protocol Relating to the Status of Refugees, it will only be in exceptional circumstances that the public interest in maintaining refusal will be outweighed by compelling factors.]

S-EC.1.5. The exclusion of the applicant from the UK is conducive to the public good . . . because, for example, the applicant's conduct (including convictions which do not fall within paragraph S-EC.1.4.), character, associations, or other reasons, make it undesirable to grant them entry clearance.

[S-EC.1.6. The applicant has failed without reasonable excuse to [comply with a requirement to]-

[(a)] attend an interview

[(b)] provide . . . information

[(c)] provide . . . physical data; or

[(d)] undergo a medical examination or provide a medical report,

. . .]

S-EC.1.7. It is undesirable to grant entry clearance to the applicant for medical reasons.

[S-EC.1.8. The applicant left or was removed from the UK as a condition of a caution issued in accordance with [section 22 of the Criminal Justice Act 2003] less than 5 years prior to the date on which the application is decided.]

Note
Amended by HC 803, para 21 as from 1 December 2013.

S-EC.2.1. The applicant will normally be refused on grounds of suitability if any of paragraphs S-EC.2.2. to [2.5. apply].

S-EC.2.2. Whether or not to the applicant's knowledge –

(a)   false information, representations or documents have been submitted in relation to the application (including false information submitted to any person to obtain a document used in support of the application); or

(b)   there has been a failure to disclose material facts in relation to the application.

S-EC.2.3. One or more relevant NHS body has notified the Secretary of State that the applicant has failed to pay charges in accordance with the relevant NHS regulations on charges to overseas visitors and the outstanding charges have a total value of at least £1000.

S-EC.2.4. A maintenance and accommodation undertaking has been requested or required under paragraph 35 of these Rules or otherwise and has not been provided.

[S-EC.2.5. The exclusion of the applicant from the UK is conducive to the public good because:
(a)   [within the 12 months prior to the date on which the application is decided,] the person has been convicted of or admitted an offence for which they received a non-custodial sentence or other out of court disposal that is recorded on their criminal record; or
(b)   in the view of the Secretary of State:
    (i)   the person's offending has caused serious harm; or
    (ii)   the person is a persistent offender who shows a particular disregard for the law.]

Note
Amended by HC 803, para 22 as from 1 December 2013.

Section E-ECP: Eligibility for entry clearance as a partner

E-ECP.1.1. To meet the eligibility requirements for entry clearance as a partner all of the requirements in paragraphs E-ECP.2.1. to 4.2. must be met.

Relationship requirements

E-ECP.2.1. The applicant's partner must be-
(a)   a British Citizen in the UK[, subject to paragraph GEN.1.3.(c)]; or
(b)   present and settled in the UK[, subject to paragraph GEN.1.3.(b)]; or
(c)   in the UK with refugee leave or with humanitarian protection.

E-ECP.2.2. The applicant must be aged 18 or over at the date of application.

E-ECP.2.3. The partner must be aged 18 or over at the date of application.

E-ECP.2.4. The applicant and their partner must not be within the prohibited degree of relationship.

E-ECP.2.5. The applicant and their partner must have met in person.

E-ECP.2.6. The relationship between the applicant and their partner must be genuine and subsisting.

E-ECP.2.7. If the applicant and partner are married or in a civil partnership it must be a valid marriage or civil partnership, as specified.

E-ECP.2.8. If the applicant is a fiancé(e) or proposed civil partner they must be seeking entry to the UK to enable their marriage or civil partnership to take place.

E-ECP.2.9. Any previous relationship of the applicant or their partner must have broken down permanently, unless it is a relationship which falls within paragraph 278(i) of these Rules.

E-ECP.2.10. The applicant and partner must intend to live together permanently in the UK.

Financial requirements

E-ECP.3.1. The applicant must provide specified evidence, from the sources listed in paragraph E-ECP.3.2., of-
(a)   a specified gross annual income of at least-
    (i)   £18,600;
    (ii)   an additional £3,800 for the first child; and
    (iii)   an additional £2,400 for each additional child; alone or in combination with
(b)   specified savings of-
    (i)   £16,000; and

(ii)   additional savings of an amount equivalent to 2.5 times the amount which is the difference between the gross annual income from the sources listed in paragraph E-ECP.3.2.(a)-(d) and the total amount required under paragraph E-ECP.3.1.(a); or

(c)   the requirements in paragraph E-ECP.3.3.being met.

In this paragraph "child" means a dependent child of the applicant who is-

(a)   under the age of 18 years, or who was under the age of 18 years when they were first granted entry under this route;

(b)   applying for entry clearance as a dependant of the applicant, or has limited leave to enter or remain in the UK;

(c)   not a British Citizen or settled in the UK; and

(d)   not an EEA national with a right to be admitted under the Immigration (EEA) Regulations 2006.

E-ECP.3.2. When determining whether the financial requirement in paragraph E-ECP.3.1. is met only the following sources will be taken into account-

(a)   income of the partner from specified employment or self-employment, which, in respect of a partner returning to the UK with the applicant, can include specified employment or self-employment overseas and in the UK;

(b)   specified pension income of the applicant and partner;

(c)   any specified maternity allowance or bereavement benefit received by the partner in the UK [or any specified payment relating to service in HM Forces received by the applicant or partner];

(d)   other specified income of the applicant and partner; and

(e)   specified savings of the applicant and partner.

Note

Amended by HC 803, para 23 as from 1 December 2013.

E-ECP.3.3. The requirements to be met under this paragraph are-

(a)   the applicant's partner must be receiving one or more of the following -

    (i)   disability living allowance;

    (ii)   severe disablement allowance;

    (iii)   industrial injury disablement benefit;

    (iv)   attendance allowance; . . .

    (v)   carer's allowance; [....

    [(vi)   personal independence payment; ....]

    [(vii)   Armed Forces Independence Payment or Guaranteed Income Payment under the Armed Forces Compensation Scheme; or

    (viii)   Constant Attendance Allowance, Mobility Supplement or War Disablement pension under the War Pensions Scheme; and]

(b)   the applicant must provide . . . evidence that their partner is able to maintain and accommodate themselves, the applicant and any dependants adequately in the UK without recourse to public funds.

Note

Amended by HC 803, paras 24–26 as from 1 December 2013.

E-ECP.3.4. The applicant must provide . . . evidence that there will be adequate accommodation, without recourse to public funds, for the family, including other family members who are not included in the application but who live in the same household, which the family own or occupy exclusively: accommodation will not be regarded as adequate if-

(a)   it is, or will be, overcrowded; or

(b)   it contravenes public health regulations.

English language requirement

E-ECP.4.1. The applicant must provide specified evidence that they-

(a)   are a national of a majority English speaking country listed in paragraph [GEN.1.6].;

(b)   have passed an English language test in speaking and listening at a minimum of level A1 of the Common European Framework of Reference for Languages with a provider approved by the [Secretary of State];

(c)   have an academic qualification recognised by [UK NARIC] to be equivalent to the standard of a Bachelor's or Master's degree or PhD in the UK, which was taught in English; or

(d)   are exempt from the English language requirement under paragraph [E-ECP.4.2.]

Note

Amended by HC 628, para 197. Further amended by HC 693, para 187 as from 6 November 2014.

E-ECP.4.2. The applicant is exempt from the English language requirement if at the date of application-

(a)   the applicant is aged 65 or over;

(b)   the applicant has a disability (physical or mental condition) which prevents the applicant from meeting the requirement; or

(c)   there are exceptional circumstances which prevent the applicant from being able to meet the requirement prior to entry to the UK.

Section D-ECP: Decision on application for entry clearance as a partner

D-ECP.1.1. If the applicant meets the requirements for entry clearance as a partner the applicant will be granted entry clearance for an initial period not exceeding 33 months, and subject to a condition of no recourse to public funds; or, where the applicant is a fiancé(e) or proposed civil partner, the applicant will be granted entry clearance for a period not exceeding 6 months, and subject to a condition of no recourse to public funds and a prohibition on employment.

D-ECP.1.2. Where the applicant does not meet the requirements for entry clearance as a partner the application will be refused.

Section R-LTRP: Requirements for limited leave to remain as a partner

R-LTRP.1.1. The requirements to be met for limited leave to remain as a partner are-

(a)   the applicant and their partner must be in the UK;

(b)   the applicant must have made a valid application for limited [or indefinite] leave to remain as a partner; and either

(i)   the applicant must not fall for refusal under Section S-LTR: Suitability leave to remain; and

(ii)   the applicant [meets] all of the requirements of Section E-LTRP: Eligibility for leave to remain as a partner; [or]

(iii)   . . .

(i)   the applicant [must not fall for refusal under] Section S-LTR: Suitability leave to remain; and

[(ii)   the applicant meets the requirements of paragraphs E-LTRP.1.2–1.12 and E-LTRP.2.1.]; and

(iii)   paragraph EX.1. applies.

Section S-LTR: Suitability-leave to remain

S-LTR.1.1. The applicant will be refused limited leave to remain on grounds of suitability if any of paragraphs S-LTR.1.2. to 1.7. apply.

S-LTR.1.2. The applicant is [currently] the subject of a deportation order.

Note

Amended by HC 803, para 27 as from 1 December 2013.

S-LTR.1.3. The presence of the applicant in the UK is not conducive to the public good because they have been convicted of an offence for which they have been sentenced to imprisonment for at least 4 years.

S-LTR.1.4. The presence of the applicant in the UK is not conducive to the public good because they have been convicted of an offence for which they have been sentenced to imprisonment for less than 4 years but at least 12 months.

S-LTR.1.5. The presence of the applicant in the UK is not conducive to the public good because, in the view of the Secretary of State, their offending has caused serious harm or they are a persistent offender who shows a particular disregard for the law.

S-LTR.1.6. The presence of the applicant in the UK is not conducive to the public good because their conduct (including convictions which do not fall within paragraphs S-LTR.1.3. to 1.5.), character, associations, or other reasons, make it undesirable to allow them to remain in the UK.

[S-LTR.1.7. The applicant has failed without reasonable excuse to [comply with a requirement to] -

[(a)] attend an interview;

[(b)] provide . . . information;

[(c)] provide . . . physical data; or

[(d)] undergo a medical examination or provide a medical report,

. . .]

S-LTR.2.1. The applicant will normally be refused on grounds of suitability if any of paragraphs S-LTR.2.2. to 2.4. apply.

S-LTR.2.2. Whether or not to the applicant's knowledge –
(a)   false information, representations or documents have been submitted in relation to the application (including false information submitted to any person to obtain a document used in support of the application); or
(b)   there has been a failure to disclose material facts in relation to the application.

S-LTR.2.3. One or more relevant NHS body has notified the Secretary of State that the applicant has failed to pay charges in accordance with the relevant NHS regulations on charges to overseas visitors and the outstanding charges have a total value of at least £1000.

S-LTR.2.4. A maintenance and accommodation undertaking has been requested under paragraph 35 of these Rules and has not been provided.

S-LTR.3.1. When considering whether the presence of the applicant in the UK is not conducive to the public good any legal or practical reasons why the applicant cannot presently be removed from the UK must be ignored.

Section E-LTRP: Eligibility for limited leave to remain as a partner

E-LTRP.1.1. To qualify for limited leave to remain as a partner all of the requirements of paragraphs E-LTRP.1.2. to 4.2. must be met.

Relationship requirements

E-LTRP.1.2. The applicant's partner must be-
(a)   a British Citizen in the UK;
(b)   present and settled in the UK; or
(c)   in the UK with refugee leave or as a person with humanitarian protection.

E-LTRP.1.3. The applicant must be aged 18 or over at the date of application.

E-LTRP.1.4. The partner must be aged 18 or over at the date of application.

E-LTRP.1.5. The applicant and their partner must not be within the prohibited degree of relationship.

E-LTRP.1.6. The applicant and their partner must have met in person.

E-LTRP.1.7. The relationship between the applicant and their partner must be genuine and subsisting.

E-LTRP.1.8. If the applicant and partner are married or in a civil partnership it must be a valid marriage or civil partnership, as specified.

E-LTRP.1.9. Any previous relationship of the applicant or their partner must have broken down permanently, unless it is a relationship which falls within paragraph 278(i) of these Rules.

E-LTRP.1.10. The applicant and their partner must intend to live together permanently in the UK[and, in any application for further leave to remain as a partner (except where the applicant is in the UK as a fiancé(e) or proposed civil partner) and in any application for indefinite leave to remain as a partner, the applicant must provide evidence that, since entry clearance as a partner was granted under paragraph D-ECP1.1. or since the last grant of limited leave to remain as a partner, the applicant and their partner have lived together in the UK or there is good reason, consistent with a continuing intention to live together permanently in the UK, for any period in which they have not done so].

E-LTRP.1.11. If the applicant is in the UK with leave as a fiancé(e) or proposed civil partner [and the marriage or civil partnership did not take place during that period of leave] there must be good reason why . . . and evidence that it will take place within the next 6 months.

[E-LTRP.1.12. The applicant's partner cannot be the applicant's fiancé(e) or proposed civil partner, unless the applicant was granted entry clearance as that person's fiancé(e) or proposed civil partner.]

Immigration status requirements

E-LTRP.2.1. The applicant must not be in the UK-
(a)   as a visitor; [or]
(b)   with valid leave granted for a period of 6 months or less, unless that leave is as a fiancé(e) or proposed civil partner[, or was granted pending the outcome of family court of divorce proceedings]. . .
. . .

Note

Amended by HC 532, para 52 of this statement take effect on 28 July 2014 and apply to all applications to which paragraphs 276ADE to 276DH and Appendix FM apply (or can be applied by virtue of the Immigration Rules), and to any other ECHR Article 8 claims (save for those from foreign criminals), and which are decided on or after that date. Word "; or" deleted by HC 532, para 53 of this statement take effect on 28 July 2014 and apply to all applications to which paragraphs 276ADE to 276DH and Appendix FM apply (or can be applied by virtue of the Immigration Rules), and to any other ECHR Article 8 claims (save for those from foreign criminals), and which are decided on or after that date. Deleted by HC 532, para 54 of this statement take effect on 28 July 2014 and apply to all applications to which paragraphs 276ADE to 276DH and Appendix FM apply (or can be applied by virtue of the Immigration Rules), and to any other ECHR Article 8 claims (save for those from foreign criminals), and which are decided on or after that date.

[E-LTRP.2.2. The applicant must not be in the UK –
(a)   on temporary admission or temporary release, unless paragraph EX.1. applies; or
(b)   in breach of immigration laws (disregarding any period of overstaying for a period of 28 days or less), unless paragraph EX.1. applies.]

Note

Substituted by HC 532, para 55 of this statement take effect on 28 July 2014 and apply to all applications to which paragraphs 276ADE to 276DH and Appendix FM apply (or can be applied by virtue of the Immigration Rules), and to any other ECHR Article 8 claims (save for those from foreign criminals), and which are decided on or after that date.

Financial requirements

E-LTRP.3.1. The applicant must provide specified evidence, from the sources listed in paragraph E-LTRP.3.2., of-

(a) a specified gross annual income of at least-
  (i) £18,600;
  (ii) an additional £3,800 for the first child; and
  (iii) an additional £2,400 for each additional child; alone or in combination with

(b) specified savings of-
  (i) £16,000; and
  (ii) additional savings of an amount equivalent to 2.5 times the amount which is the difference between the gross annual income from the sources listed in paragraph E-LTRP.3.2.(a)-(f) and the total amount required under paragraph E-LTRP.3.1.(a); or

(c) the requirements in paragraph E-LTRP.3.3. being met, unless paragraph EX.1. applies.

In this paragraph "child" means a dependent child of the applicant who is-

(a) under the age of 18 years, or who was under the age of 18 years when they were first granted entry under this route;

(b) applying for entry clearance or is in the UK as a dependant of the applicant;

(c) not a British Citizen or settled in the UK; and

(d) not an EEA national with a right to remain in the UK under the Immigration (EEA) Regulations 2006.

E-LTRP.3.2. When determining whether the financial requirement in paragraph E-LTRP.3.1. is met only the following sources may be taken into account-

(a) income of the partner from specified employment or self-employment;

(b) income of the applicant from specified employment or self-employment unless they are working illegally;

(c) specified pension income of the applicant and partner;

(d) any specified maternity allowance or bereavement benefit received by the applicant and partner in the UK [or any specified payment relating to service in HM Forces received by the applicant or partner]

(e) other specified income of the applicant and partner;

(f) income from the sources at (b), (d) or (e) of a dependent child of the applicant under paragraph E-LTRP.3.1. who is aged 18 years or over; and

(g) specified savings of the applicant, partner and a dependent child of the applicant under paragraph E-LTRP.3.1. who is aged 18 years or over.

Note

Amended by HC 803, para 28 as from 1 December 2013.

E-LTRP.3.3. The requirements to meet this paragraph are-

(a) the applicant's partner must be receiving one or more of the following -
  (i) disability living allowance;
  (ii) severe disablement allowance;
  (iii) industrial injury disablement benefit;
  (iv) attendance allowance; . . .
  (v) carer' allowance; [...
  [(vi) personal independence payment; ...
  [(vii) Armed Forces Independence Payment or Guaranteed Income Payment under the Armed Forces Compensation Scheme; or

(viii) Constant Attendance Allowance, Mobility Supplement or War Disablement pension under the War Pensions Scheme; and]
(b) the applicant must provide . . . evidence that their partner is able to maintain and accommodate themselves, the applicant and any dependants adequately in the UK without recourse to public funds.

Note

Amended by HC 803, paras 29–31 as from 1 December 2013.

E-LTRP.3.4. The applicant must provide . . . evidence that there will be adequate accommodation, without recourse to public funds, for the family, including other family members who are not included in the application but who live in the same household, which the family own or occupy exclusively[, unless paragraph EX.1. applies]: accommodation will not be regarded as adequate if-
(a) it is, or will be, overcrowded; or
(b) it contravenes public health regulations.

English language requirement

E-LTRP.4.1. If the applicant has not met the requirement in a previous application for leave as a partner [or parent], the applicant must provide specified evidence that they-
(a) are a national of a majority English speaking country listed in paragraph [GEN.1.6];
(b) have passed an English language test in speaking and listening at a minimum of level A1 of the Common European Framework of Reference for Languages with a provider approved by the [Secretary of State];
(c) have an academic qualification recognised by [UK NARIC] to be equivalent to the standard of a Bachelor's or Master's degree or PhD in the UK, which was taught in English; or
(d) are exempt from the English language requirement under paragraph [E-LTRP.4.2.;]

unless paragraph EX.1. applies.

Note

Amended by HC 628, para 198. Further amended by HC 1138, para 199 as from 6 April 2014. Further amended by HC 693, para 188 as from 6 November 2014.

E-LTRP.4.2. The applicant is exempt from the English language requirement if at the date of application-
(a) the applicant is aged 65 or over;
(b) the applicant has a disability (physical or mental condition) which prevents the applicant from meeting the requirement; or
(c) there are exceptional circumstances which prevent the applicant from being able to meet the requirement.

Section D-LTRP: Decision on application for limited leave to remain as a partner

D-LTRP.1.1. If the applicant meets the requirements in paragraph R-LTRP.1.1.(a) to (c) for limited leave to remain as a partner the applicant will be granted limited leave to remain for a period not exceeding 30 months, and subject to a condition of no recourse to public funds, and they will be eligible to apply for settlement after [a continuous period of at least 60 months with such leave or in the UK with entry clearance as a partner under paragraph D-ECP1.1. (excluding in all cases any period of entry clearance or limited leave as a fiancé(e) or proposed civil partner)]; or, if paragraph E-LTRP.1.11. applies, the applicant will be granted limited leave for a period not exceeding 6 months and subject to a condition of no recourse to public funds and a prohibition on employment.

D-LTRP.1.2. If the applicant meets the requirements in paragraph R-LTRP.1.1.(a), (b) and (d) for limited leave to remain as a partner they will be granted leave to remain for a period not exceeding 30 months [and subject to a condition of no recourse to public funds [unless the Secretary of State considers that the person should not be subject to such a condition],] and [they] will be eligible to apply for settlement after [a continuous period of at least 120 months with such leave, with limited leave as a partner under paragraph D-LTRP.1.1., or in the UK with entry clearance as a partner under paragraph D-ECP1.1. (excluding in all cases any period of entry clearance or limited leave as a fiancé(e) or proposed civil partner)], or, if paragraph E-LTRP.1.11. applies, the applicant will be granted limited leave for a period not exceeding 6 months and subject to a condition of no recourse to public funds and a prohibition on employment.

D-LTRP.1.3. If the applicant does not meet the requirements for limited leave to remain as a partner the application will be refused.

Note

Amended by HC 532, para 56 of this statement take effect on 28 July 2014 and apply to all applications to which paragraphs 276ADE to 276DH and Appendix FM apply (or can be applied by virtue of the Immigration Rules), and to any other ECHR Article 8 claims (save for those from foreign criminals), and which are decided on or after that date.

Section R-ILRP: Requirements for indefinite leave to remain (settlement) as a partner

[R-ILRP.1.1. The requirements to be met for indefinite leave to remain as a partner are that-
(a)   the applicant and their partner must be in the UK;
(b)   the applicant must have made a valid application for indefinite leave to remain as a partner;
(c)   the applicant must not fall for refusal under any of the grounds in Section S-ILR: Suitability for indefinite leave to remain;
(d)   the applicant:
  (i)   must meet all of the requirements of Section E-LTRP: Eligibility for leave to remain as a partner (but in applying paragraph E-LTRP.3.1.(b)(ii) delete the words "2.5 times"); or
  (ii)   must meet the requirements of paragraphs E-LTRP.1.2.-1.12. and E-LTRP.2.1. and paragraph EX.1. applies; and
(e)   the applicant must meet all of the requirements of Section E-ILRP: Eligibility for indefinite leave to remain as a partner.]

Note

Substituted by HC 693, para 189 as from 6 November 2014.

[Section S-ILR: Suitability for indefinite leave to remain

S-ILR.1.1. The applicant will be refused indefinite leave to remain on grounds of suitability if any of paragraphs S-ILR.1.2. to 1.9. apply.

S-ILR.1.2. The applicant is [currently] the subject of a deportation order.

Note

Amended by HC 803, para 32 as from 1 December 2013.

S-ILR.1.3. The presence of the applicant in the UK is not conducive to the public good because they have been convicted of an offence for which they have been sentenced to imprisonment for at least 4 years.

S-ILR.1.4. The presence of the applicant in the UK is not conducive to the public good because they have been convicted of an offence for which they have been sentenced to imprisonment for less than 4 years but at least 12 months, unless a period of 15 years has passed since the end of the sentence.

S-ILR.1.5. The presence of the applicant in the UK is not conducive to the public good because they have been convicted of an offence for which they have been sentenced to imprisonment for less than 12 months, unless a period of 7 years has passed since the end of the sentence.

S-ILR.1.6. The applicant has, within the 24 months [prior to the date on which the application is decided,] been convicted of or admitted an offence for which they received a non-custodial sentence or other out of court disposal that is recorded on their criminal record.

Note
Amended by HC 803, para 33 as from 1 December 2013.

S-ILR.1.7. The presence of the applicant in the UK is not conducive to the public good because, in the view of the Secretary of State, their offending has caused serious harm or they are a persistent offender who shows a particular disregard for the law.

S-ILR.1.8. The presence of the applicant in the UK is not conducive to the public good because their conduct (including convictions which do not fall within paragraphs S-ILR.1.3. to 1.6.), character, associations, or other reasons, make it undesirable to allow them to remain in the UK.

S-ILR.1.9. The applicant has failed without reasonable excuse to comply with a requirement to-
(a)   attend an interview;
(b)   provide information;
(c)   provide physical data; or
(d)   undergo a medical examination or provide a medical report.

S-ILR.2.1. The applicant will normally be refused on grounds of suitability if any of paragraphs S-ILR.2.2. to 2.4. apply.

S-ILR.2.2. Whether or not to the applicant's knowledge –
(a)   false information, representations or documents have been submitted in relation to the application (including false information submitted to any person to obtain a document used in support of the application); or
(b)   there has been a failure to disclose material facts in relation to the application.

S-ILR.2.3. One or more relevant NHS body has notified the Secretary of State that the applicant has failed to pay charges in accordance with the relevant NHS regulations on charges to overseas visitors and the outstanding charges have a total value of at least £1000.

S-ILR.2.4. A maintenance and accommodation undertaking has been requested under paragraph 35 of these Rules and has not been provided.

S-ILR.3.1. When considering whether the presence of the applicant in the UK is not conducive to the public good, any legal or practical reasons why the applicant cannot presently be removed from the UK must be ignored.]

Section E-ILRP: Eligibility for indefinite leave to remain as a partner

E-ILRP.1.1. To meet the eligibility requirements for indefinite leave to remain as a partner all of the requirements of paragraphs E-ILRP.1.2. to 1.6. must be met.

E-ILRP.1.2. The applicant must be in the UK with valid leave to remain as a partner (disregarding any period of overstaying for a period of 28 days or less).

E-ILRP.1.3. The applicant must have completed a continuous period of at least 60 months with limited leave as a partner under paragraph R-LTRP.1.1.(a) to (c) [or in the UK with entry clearance as a partner under paragraph D-ECP.1.1.;] or a continuous period of at least 120 months with limited leave as a partner under paragraph R-LTR.P.1.1(a), (b) and (d) [or in the UK with entry clearance as a partner under paragraph D-ECP.1.1.;] or a continuous period of at least 120 months with limited leave as a partner under a combination of these paragraphs[, excluding in all cases any period of entry clearance or limited leave as a fiancé(e) or proposed civil partner.]

E-ILRP.1.4. In calculating the periods under paragraph E-ILRP.1.3. only the periods when the applicant's partner is the same person as the applicant's partner for the previous period of limited leave shall be taken into account.

[E-ILRP.1.5. In calculating the periods under paragraph E-ILRP.1.3. the words "in the UK" in that paragraph shall not apply to any period(s) to which the evidence in paragraph 26A of Appendix FM-SE applies.]

E-ILRP.1.6. The applicant must have [demonstrated] sufficient knowledge of the English language and sufficient knowledge about life in the [United Kingdom] in accordance with the requirements of [Appendix KoLL] of these Rules.

Note

Amended by HC 628, para 199. Substituted by HC 693, para 190 as from 6 November 2014.

Section D-ILRP: Decision on application for indefinite leave to remain as a partner

D-ILRP.1.1. If the applicant meets all of the requirements for indefinite leave to remain as a partner the applicant will be granted indefinite leave to remain.

D-ILRP.1.2. If the applicant does not meet the requirements for indefinite leave to remain as a partner only for one or both of the following reasons-
(a)   [paragraph S-ILR.1.5 or S-ILR.1.6. applies];
[(b)   the applicant has not demonstrated sufficient knowledge of the English language or about life in the United Kingdom in accordance with Appendix KoLL,],

the applicant will be granted further limited leave to remain as a partner for a period not exceeding 30 months, and subject to a condition of no recourse to public funds.

Note

Amended by HC 628, para 200.

D-ILRP.1.3. If the applicant does not meet [all the eligibility requirements for indefinite leave to remain as a partner, and does not qualify for] further limited leave to remain as a partner under paragraph D-ILRP.1.2., the application will be refused[, [unless the applicant meets the requirements in paragraph R-LTRP.1.1.(a), (b) and (d) for limited leave to remain as a partner. Where they do,] the applicant will be granted further limited leave to remain as a partner for a period not exceeding 30 months under paragraph D-LTRP.1.2. [and subject to a condition of no recourse to public funds [unless the Secretary of State considers that the person should not be subject to such a condition].]

Note

For guidance on the partner route see:www.ukba.homeoffice.gov.uk/sitecontent/documents/policy andlaw/IDIs/chp8-annex/ partners.pdf?view=Binary

For guidance on how the UKBA will assess whether a relationship is 'genuine and subsisting' see: www.ukba.homeoffice.gov.uk/sitecontent/documents/policyandlaw/IDIs/chp8-annex/ section-FM 2.1.pdf?view=Binary

For guidance on the financial requirements see: www.ukba.homeoffice.gov.uk/sitecontent/docume nts/policyandlaw/IDIs/chp8-annex/ section-FM-1.7.pdf?view=Binary

Where the partner is in receipt of specified benefits see: www.ukba.homeoffice.gov.uk/sitecontent /documents/policyandlaw/IDIs/chp8-annex/ maintenance.pdf?view=Binary

Note also the requirements for specified evidence (ie evidence of meeting the financial requirements, of marriage or civil partnership, and of meeting the English language requirement is set out in Appendix FM.

Amended by HC 532, para 57 of this statement take effect on 28 July 2014 and apply to all applications to which paragraphs 276ADE to 276DH and Appendix FM apply (or can be applied by virtue of the Immigration Rules), and to any other ECHR Article 8 claims (save for those from foreign criminals), and which are decided on or after that date.

[Section EX: Exceptions to certain eligibility requirements for leave to remain as a partner or parent]

EX.1. This paragraph applies if

(a)

(i) the applicant has a genuine and subsisting parental relationship with a child who-

    (aa) is under the age of 18 years[, or was under the age of 18 years when the applicant was first granted leave on the basis that this paragraph applied];

    (bb) is in the UK;

    (cc) is a British Citizen or has lived in the UK continuously for at least the 7 years immediately preceding the date of application; and

(ii) it would not be reasonable to expect the child to leave the UK; or

(b) the applicant has a genuine and subsisting relationship with a partner who is in the UK and is a British Citizen, settled in the UK or in the UK with refugee leave or humanitarian protection, and there are insurmountable obstacles to family life with that partner continuing outside the UK.

Note

For guidance on EX1 as regard to children's best interests see: www.ukba.homeoffice.gov.uk/sitec ontent/documents/policyandlaw/IDIs/chp8-annex/ ex1-guidance-1.pdf?view=Binary

Amended by HC 532, para 58 of this statement take effect on 28 July 2014 and apply to all applications to which paragraphs 276ADE to 276DH and Appendix FM apply (or can be applied by virtue of the Immigration Rules), and to any other ECHR Article 8 claims (save for those from foreign criminals), and which are decided on or after that date.

[EX.2. For the purposes of paragraph EX.1.(b) "insurmountable obstacles" means the very significant difficulties which would be faced by the applicant or their partner in continuing their family life together outside the UK and which could not be overcome or would entail very serious hardship for the applicant or their partner.]

Note

Inserted by HC 532, para 59 of this statement take effect on 28 July 2014 and apply to all applications to which paragraphs 276ADE to 276DH and Appendix FM apply (or can be applied by virtue of the Immigration Rules), and to any other ECHR Article 8 claims (save for those from foreign criminals), and which are decided on or after that date.

Bereaved partner

Section BPILR: Indefinite leave to remain (settlement) as a bereaved partner

BPILR.1.1. The requirements to be met for indefinite leave to remain in the UK as a bereaved partner are that-

(a) the applicant must be in the UK;

(b) the applicant must have made a valid application for indefinite leave to remain as a bereaved partner;

(c) the applicant must not fall for refusal under any of the grounds in [Section S-ILR: Suitability-indefinite leave to remain]; and

(d) the applicant must meet all of the requirements of Section E-BPILR: Eligibility for indefinite leave to remain as a bereaved partner.

Section E-BPILR: Eligibility for indefinite leave to remain as a bereaved partner

E-BPILR.1.1. To meet the eligibility requirements for indefinite leave to remain as a bereaved partner all of the requirements of paragraphs E-BPILR1.2. to [1.4.] must be met.

E-BPILR.1.2. The applicant's last grant of limited leave must have been as-

(a) a partner (other than a fiancé(e) or proposed civil partner) of a British Citizen or a person settled in the UK; or

(b) a bereaved partner.

E-BPILR.1.3. The person who was the applicant's partner at the time of the last grant of limited leave as a partner must have died.

E-BPILR.1.4. At the time of the partner's death the relationship between the applicant and the partner must have been genuine and subsisting and each of the parties must have intended to live permanently with the other in the UK.

. . . .

Section D-BPILR: Decision on application for indefinite leave to remain as a bereaved partner

D-BPILR.1.1. If the applicant meets all of the requirements for indefinite leave to remain as a bereaved partner the applicant will be granted indefinite leave to remain.

D-BPILR.1.2. If the applicant does not meet the requirements for indefinite leave to remain as a bereaved partner only because [paragraphs S-ILR.1.5 or S-ILR.1.6 applies], the applicant will be granted further limited leave to remain for a period not exceeding 30 months, and subject to a condition of no recourse to public funds.

D-BPILR.1.3. If the applicant does not meet the requirements for indefinite leave to remain as a bereaved partner, or limited leave to remain as a bereaved partner under paragraph D-BPILR.1.2., the application will be refused.

Victim of domestic violence

Section DVILR: Indefinite leave to remain (settlement) as a victim of domestic violence

DVILR.1.1. The requirements to be met for indefinite leave to remain in the UK as a victim of domestic violence are that-
(a)   the applicant must be in the UK;
(b)   the applicant must have made a valid application for indefinite leave to remain as a victim of domestic violence;
(c)   the applicant must not fall for refusal under any of the grounds in [Section S-ITR: Suitability-indefinite leave to remain]; and
(d)   the applicant must meet all of the requirements of Section E-DVILR: Eligibility for indefinite leave to remain as a victim of domestic violence.

Section E-DVILR: Eligibility for indefinite leave to remain as a victim of domestic violence

E-DVILR.1.1. To meet the eligibility requirements for indefinite leave to remain as a victim of domestic violence all of the requirements of paragraphs E-DVILR.1.2. [and 1.3.] must be met.

E-DVILR.1.2. [The applicant's first grant of limited leave under this Appendix must have been as a partner (other than a fiancé(e) or proposed civil partner) of a British Citizen or a person settled in the UK under paragraph D-ECP.1.1., D-LTRP.1.1. or D-LTRP.1.2. of this Appendix and any subsequent grant of limited leave must have been:]
[(a)   granted as a partner (other than a fiancé(e) or proposed civil partner) of a British Citizen or a person settled in the UK under paragraph D-ECP.1.1., D-LTRP.1.1. or D-LTRP.1.2. of this Appendix; or
(b)   granted to enable access to public funds pending an application under DVILR and the preceding grant of leave was granted as a partner (other than a fiancé(e) or proposed civil partner) of a British Citizen or a person settled in the UK under paragraph D-ECP.1.1., D-LTRP.1.1. or D-LTRP.1.2. of this Appendix; or]

E-DVILR.1.3. The applicant must provide . . . evidence that during the last period of limited leave as a partner [of a British Citizen or a person settled in the UK under paragraph D-ECP.1.1., D-LTRP.1.1. or D-LTRP.1.2. of this Appendix] the applicant's relationship with their partner broke down permanently as a result of . . . domestic violence.

. . . .

Note

Further amended by HC 693, para 191 as from 6 November 2014. Amended by HC 693, para 191 as from 6 November 2014. Amended by HC 693, para 192 as from 6 November 2014.

Section D-DVILR: Decision on application for indefinite leave to remain as a victim of domestic violence

D-DVILR.1.1. If the applicant meets all of the requirements for indefinite leave to remain as a victim of domestic violence the applicant will be granted indefinite leave to remain.

D-DVILR.1.2. If the applicant does not meet the requirements for indefinite leave to remain as a victim of domestic violence only because [paragraph S-ILR.1.5. or S-ILR.1.6. applies,] the applicant will be granted further limited leave to remain for a period not exceeding 30 months.

D-DVILR.1.3. If the applicant does not meet the requirements for indefinite leave to remain as a victim of domestic violence, or further limited leave to remain under paragraph D-DVILR.1.2. the application will be refused.

Note

Guidance on the Domestic Violence category is at: www.ukba.homeoffice.gov.uk/sitecontent/docu ments/policyandlaw/modernised/family/ section4.pdf?view=Binary

Family life as a child of a person with limited leave as a partner or parent

This route is for a child whose parent is applying for entry clearance or leave, or who has limited leave, as a partner or parent. For further provision on a child seeking to enter or remain in the UK for the purpose of their family life see Part 8 of these Rules.

Section EC-C: Entry clearance as a child

EC-C.1.1. The requirements to be met for entry clearance as a child are that-
(a)   the applicant must be outside the UK;
(b)   the applicant must have made a valid application for entry clearance as a child;
(c)   the applicant must not fall for refusal under any of the grounds in Section S-EC: Suitability for entry clearance; and
(d)   the applicant must meet all of the requirements of Section E-ECC: Eligibility for entry clearance as a child.

Section E-ECC: Eligibility for entry clearance as a child

E-ECC.1.1. To meet the eligibility requirements for entry clearance as a child all of the requirements of paragraphs E-ECC.1.2. to 2.4. must be met.

Relationship requirements

E-ECC.1.2. The applicant must be under the age of 18 at the date of application.

E-ECC.1.3. The applicant must not be married or in a civil partnership.

E-ECC.1.4. The applicant must not have formed an independent family unit.

E-ECC.1.5. The applicant must not be leading an independent life.

E-ECC.1.6. One of the applicant's parents must be in the UK with limited leave to enter or remain, [or be applying, or have applied, for entry clearance as] a partner or a parent under this Appendix (referred to in this section as the "applicant's parent")[, and
(a)   the applicant's parent partner under Appendix FM is also a parent of the applicant; or

(b)   the applicant's parent has had and continues too have sole responsibility for the child's upbringing; or

(c)   there are serious and compelling family or other considerations which make exclusion of the child undesirable and suitable arrangements have been made for the child's care.]

Financial requirement

E-ECC.2.1. The applicant must provide specified evidence, from the sources listed in paragraph E-ECC.2.2., of-

(a)   a specified gross annual income of at least-
    (i)   £18,600;
    (ii)   an additional £3,800 for the first child; and
    (iii)   an additional £2,400 for each additional child; alone or in combination with

(b)   specified savings of
    (i)   £16,000; and
    (ii)   additional savings of an amount equivalent to 2.5 times the amount which is the difference between the gross annual income from the sources listed in paragraph E-ECC.2.2.(a)-(f) and the total amount required under paragraph E-ECC.2.1.(a); or

(c)   the requirements in paragraph E-ECC.2.3. being met.

In this paragraph "child" means the applicant and any other dependent child of the applicant's parent who is -

(a)   under the age of 18 years, or who was under the age of 18 years when they were first granted entry under this route;

(b)   in the UK;

(c)   not a British Citizen or settled in the UK; and

(d)   not an EEA national with a right to remain in the UK under the Immigration (EEA) Regulations 2006.

E-ECC.2.2. When determining whether the financial requirement in paragraph E-ECC.2.1. is met only the following sources may be taken into account-

(a)   income of the applicant's parent's partner from specified employment or self-employment[, which, in respect of an applicant's parent's partner returning to the UK with the applicant, can include specified employment or self-employment overseas and in the UK;]

(b)   income of the applicant's parent from specified employment or self-employment if they are in the UK unless they are working illegally;

(c)   specified pension income of the applicant's parent and that parent's partner;

(d)   any specified maternity allowance or bereavement benefit received by the applicant's parent and that parent's partner in the UK [or any specified payment relating to service in HM Forces received by the applicant's parent and that parent's partner];

(e)   other specified income of the applicant's parent and that parent's partner. . .;

(f)   income from the sources at (b), (d) or (e) of a dependent child of the applicant's parent under paragraph E-ECC.2.1. who is aged 18 years or over; and

(g)   specified savings of the applicant's parent, that parent's partner and a dependent child of the applicant's parent under paragraph E-ECC.2.1. who is aged 18 years or over.

Note

Amended by HC 803, para 34 as from 1 December 2013.

E-ECC.2.3. The requirements to be met under this paragraph are-

(a)   the applicant's parent's partner must be receiving one or more of the following-
    (i)   disability living allowance;

(ii)   severe disablement allowance;
(iii) industrial injury disablement benefit;
(iv)   attendance allowance; . . .
(v)   carer's allowance; [...]
[(vi) personal independence payment; ...]
[(vii) Armed Forces Independence Payment or Guaranteed Income Payment under the Armed Forces Compensation Scheme; or
(viii) Constant Attendance Allowance, Mobility Supplement or War Disablement Pension under the War Pensions Scheme; and]]

(b)   the applicant must provide . . . evidence that their parent's partner is able to maintain and accommodate themselves, the applicant's parent, the applicant and any dependants adequately in the UK without recourse to public funds.

Note

Amended by HC 803, paras 35–37 as from 1 December 2013.

E-EEC.2.4. The applicant must provide . . . evidence that there will be adequate accommodation, without recourse to public funds, for the family, including other family members who are not included in the application but who live in the same household, which the family own or occupy exclusively: accommodation will not be regarded as adequate if-
(a)   it is, or will be, overcrowded; or
(b)   it contravenes public health regulations.

Section D-ECC: Decision on application for entry clearance as a child

D-ECC.1.1. If the applicant meets the requirements for entry clearance as a child they will be granted entry clearance of a duration which will expire at the same time as the leave granted to the applicant's parent, and subject to a condition of no recourse to public funds.

D-ECC.1.2. If the applicant does not meet the requirements for entry clearance as a child the application will be refused.

[Section R-LTRC:] Requirements for leave to remain as a child

[R-LTRC.1.1.] The requirements to be met for leave to remain as a child are that-
(a)   the applicant must be in the UK;
(b)   the applicant must have made a valid application for leave to remain as a child;
      (i)   the applicant must not fall for refusal under any of the grounds in Section S-LTR: Suitability-leave to remain; and
      (ii)   the applicant meets all of the requirements of Section E-LTRC: Eligibility for leave to remain as a child; or
      (i)   the applicant must not fall for refusal under any of the grounds in Section S-LTR: Suitability-leave to remain; and
      (ii)   the applicant meets all of the requirements of paragraphs E-LTRC.1.2.-1.6.; and
      (iii) a parent of the applicant has been or is at the same time being granted leave to remain under paragraph D-LTRP.1.2. or D-LTRPT.1.2. or indefinite leave to remain under this Appendix (except as an adult dependent relative).]

Section E-LTRC: Eligibility for leave to remain as a child

E-LTRC.1.1. To qualify for limited leave to remain as a child all of the requirements of Section E-LTRC.1.2. to 2.4. must be met [(except where paragraph R-LTRC.1.1.(d)(ii) applies).]

Relationship requirements

E-LTRC.1.2. The applicant must be under the age of 18 at the date of application or when first granted leave as a child under this route.

E-LTRC.1.3. The applicant must not be married or in a civil partnership.

E-LTRC.1.4. The applicant must not have formed an independent family unit.

E-LTRC.1.5. The applicant must not be leading an independent life.

[E-LTRC.1.6. One of the applicant's parents (referred to in this section as the "applicant's parent") must be in the UK and have leave to enter or remain or indefinite leave to remain, or is at the same time being granted leave to remain or indefinite leave to remain, under this Appendix (except as an adult dependent relative), and
(a)   the applicant's parent's partner under Appendix FM is also a parent of the applicant; or
(b)   the applicant's parent has had and continues to have sole responsibility for the child's upbringing or the applicant normally lives with this parent and not their other parent; or
(c)   there are serious and compelling family and other considerations which make exclusion of the child undesirable and suitable arrangements have been made for the child's care.]

Financial requirements

E-LTRC.2.1. The applicant must provide specified evidence, from the sources listed in paragraph E-LTRC.2.2., of -
(a)   a specified gross annual income of at least-
      (i)   £18,600;
      (ii)   an additional £3,800 for the first child; and
      (iii) an additional £2,400 for each additional child; alone or in combination with
(b)   specified savings of-
      (i)   £16,000; and
      (ii)   additional savings of an amount equivalent to 2.5 times (or if the parent is applying for indefinite leave to remain 1 times) the amount which is the difference between the gross annual income from the sources listed in paragraph E-LTRC.2.2.(a)-(f) and the total amount required under paragraph E-LTRC.2.1.(a); or
(c)   the requirements in paragraph E-LTRC.2.3. being met.

In this paragraph "child" means the applicant and any other dependent child of the applicant's parent who is-
(i)   under the age of 18 years, or who was under the age of 18 years when they were first granted entry under this route;
(ii)   in the UK;
(iii) not a British Citizen or settled in the UK; and
(iv)   not an EEA national with a right to remain in the UK under the Immigration (EEA) Regulations 2006.

E-LTRC.2.2. When determining whether the financial requirement in paragraph E-LTRC.2.1. is met only the following sources may be taken into account-
(a)   income of the applicant's parent's partner from specified employment or self-employment;
(b)   income of the applicant's parent from specified employment or self-employment;
(c)   specified pension income of the applicant's parent and that parent's partner;
(d)   any specified maternity allowance or bereavement benefit received by the applicant's parent and that parent's partner in the UK [or any specified payment relating to service in HM Forces received by the applicant's parent and that parent's partner];
(e)   other specified income of the applicant's parent and that parent's partner . . .;
(f)   income from the sources at (b), (d) or (e) of a dependent child of the applicant's parent under paragraph E-LTRC.2.1. who is aged 18 years or over; and

(g)   specified savings of the applicant's parent, that parent's partner and a dependent child of the applicant's parent under paragraph E-ECC.2.1. who is aged 18 years or over.

Note

Amended by HC 803, para 38 as from 1 December 2013.

E-LTRC.2.3. The requirements to be met under this paragraph are-

(a)   the applicant's parent's partner must be receiving one or more of the following -

    (i)   disability living allowance;
    (ii)   severe disablement allowance;
    (iii)   industrial injury disablement benefit;
    (iv)   attendance allowance; . . .
    (v)   carer's allowance; [...]
    [(vi)   personal independence payment; ...]
    [(vii)   Armed Forces Independence Payment or Guaranteed Income Payment under the Armed Forces Compensation Scheme; or
    (viii)   Constant Attendance Allowance, Mobility Supplement or War Disablement Pension under the War pensions Scheme; and]

(b)   the applicant must provide . . . evidence that their parent's partner is able to maintain and accommodate themselves, the applicant's parent, the applicant and any dependants adequately in the UK without recourse to public funds.

Note

Amended by HC 803, paras 39–41 as from 1 December 2013.

E-LTRC2.4. The applicant must provide . . . evidence that there will be adequate accommodation in the UK, without recourse to public funds, for the family, including other family members who are not included in the application but who live in the same household, which the family own or occupy exclusively: accommodation will not be regarded as adequate if-

(a)   it is, or will be, overcrowded; or

(b)   it contravenes public health regulations.

Section D-LTRC: Decision on application for leave to remain as a child

D-LTRC.1.1. If the applicant meets the requirements for leave to remain as a child the applicant will be granted leave to remain of a duration which will expire at the same time as the leave granted to the applicant's parent, and subject to a condition of no recourse to public funds [. To qualify for indefinite leave to remain as a child of a person with indefinite leave to remain as a partner or parent, the applicant must meet the requirements of paragraph 298 of these rules.]

D-LTRC.1.2. If the applicant does not meet the requirements for leave to remain as a child the application will be refused.

Note

Specified evidence for the financial requirement is set out in Appendix FM-SE.

Family life as a parent of a child in the UK

Section EC-PT: Entry clearance as a parent of a child in the UK

EC-PT.1.1. The requirements to be met for entry clearance as a parent are that-

(a)   the applicant must be outside the UK;

(b)   the applicant must have made a valid application for entry clearance as a parent;

(c)   the applicant must not fall for refusal under any of the grounds in Section S-EC: Suitability–entry clearance; and

(d)   the applicant must meet all of the requirements of Section E-ECPT: Eligibility for entry clearance as a parent.

Section E-ECPT: Eligibility for entry clearance as a parent

E-ECPT.1.1. To meet the eligibility requirements for entry clearance as a parent all of the requirements in paragraphs E-ECPT.2.1. to 4.2. must be met.

Relationship requirements

E-ECPT.2.1. The applicant must be aged 18 years or over.

E-ECPT.2.2. The child of the applicant must be-
(a) under the age of 18 years at the date of application;
(b) living in the UK; and
(c) a British Citizen or settled in the UK.

E-ECPT.2.3. Either -
(a) the applicant must have sole parental responsibility for the child; or
(b) the parent or carer with whom the child normally lives must be-
(i) a British Citizen in the UK or settled in the UK;
(ii) not the partner of the applicant; and
(iii) the applicant must not be eligible to apply for entry clearance as a partner under this Appendix.

E-ECPT.2.4.
(a) The applicant must provide . . . evidence that they have either-
(i) sole parental responsibility for the child; or
(ii) access rights to the child; and
(b) The applicant must provide specified evidence that they are taking, and intend to continue to take, an active role in the child's upbringing.

Financial requirements

E-ECPT.3.1. The applicant must provide . . . evidence that they will be able to adequately maintain and accommodate themselves and any dependants in the UK without recourse to public funds

E-ECPT.3.2. The applicant must provide . . . evidence that there will be adequate accommodation in the UK, without recourse to public funds, for the family, including other family members who are not included in the application but who live in the same household, which the family own or occupy exclusively: accommodation will not be regarded as adequate if-
(a) it is, or will be, overcrowded; or
(b) it contravenes public health regulations.

English language requirement

E-ECPT.4.1. The applicant must provide specified evidence that they-
(a) are a national of a majority English speaking country listed in paragraph [GEN.1.6];
(b) have passed an English language test in speaking and listening at a minimum of level A1 of the Common European Framework of Reference for Languages with a provider approved by the [Secretary of State];
(c) have an academic qualification recognised by [UK NARIC] to be equivalent to the standard of a Bachelor's or Master's degree or PhD in the UK, which was taught in English; or
(d) are exempt from the English language requirement under paragraph [E-ECPT.4.2.]

Note

Amended by HC 628, para 201. Further amended by HC 693, para 193 as from 6 November 2014.

E-ECPT.4.2. The applicant is exempt from the English language requirement if at the date of application-

(a)   the applicant is aged 65 or over;

(b)   the applicant has a disability (physical or mental condition) which prevents the applicant from meeting the requirement; or

(c)   there are exceptional circumstances which prevent the applicant from being able to meet the requirement prior to entry to the UK.

Section D-ECPT: Decision on application for entry clearance as a parent

[D-ECPT.1.1.] If the applicant meets the requirements for entry clearance as a parent they will be granted entry clearance for an initial period not exceeding 33 months, and subject to a condition of no recourse to public funds.

D-ECPT.1.2. If the applicant does not meet the requirements for entry clearance as a parent the application will be refused.

Section R-LTRPT: Requirements for limited leave to remain as a parent

R-LTRPT.1.1. The requirements to be met for limited leave to remain as a parent are-

(a)   the applicant and the child must be in the UK;

(b)   the applicant must have made a valid application for limited [or indefinite] leave to remain as a parent [or partner]; and either

    (c) (i) the applicant must not fall for refusal under Section S-LTR: Suitability leave to remain; and

    (ii)   the applicant [meets] all of the requirements of Section E-LTRPT: Eligibility for leave to remain as a parent, [or

    (iii)   .....

    (d) (i) the applicant [must not fall for refusal under] Section S-LTR: Suitability leave to remain; and

    [(ii)   the applicant meets the requirements of paragraphs E-LTRPT.2.2–2.4. and E-LTRPT.3.1.]; and

    (iii)   paragraph EX.1. applies.

Section E-LTRPT: Eligibility for limited leave to remain as a parent

E-LTRPT.1.1. To qualify for limited leave to remain as a parent all of the requirements of paragraphs E-LTRPT.2.2. to 5.2. must be met.

Relationship requirements

E-LTRPT.2.2. The child of the applicant must be-

(a)   under the age of 18 years at the date of application[, or where the child has turned 18 years of age since the applicant was first granted entry clearance or leave to remain as a parent under this Appendix, must not have formed an independent family unit or be leading an independent life];

(b)   living in the UK; and

(c)   a British Citizen or settled in the UK[; or

(d)   has lived in the UK continuously for at least the 7 years immediately preceding the date of application and paragraph EX.1. applies.]

E-LTRPT.2.3. Either-

(a)   the applicant must have sole parental responsibility for the child [or the child normally lives with the applicant and not their other parent (who is a British Citizen or settled in the UK)]; or

(b)   the parent or carer with whom the child normally lives must be-

    (i)   a British Citizen in the UK or settled in the UK;

    (ii)   not the partner of the applicant [(which here includes a person who has been in a relationship with the applicant for less than two years prior to the date of application)]; and

    (iii)   the applicant must not be eligible to apply for leave to remain as a partner under this Appendix.

E-LTRPT.2.4.
(a)   The applicant must provide . . . evidence that they have either-
       (i)   sole parental responsibility for the child[, or that the child normally lives
              with them]; or
       (ii)   access rights to the child; and
(b)   The applicant must provide . . . evidence that they are taking, and intend to
       continue to take, an active role in the child's upbringing.

Note

Amended by HC 628, para 202.

Immigration status requirement

E-LTRPT.3.1. The applicant must not be in the UK-
(a)   as a visitor; [or]
(b)   with valid leave granted for a period of 6 months or less[, unless that leave was
       granted pending the outcome of family court or divorce proceedings];
. . .

Note

Amended by HC 532, para 60 of this statement take effect on 28 July 2014 and apply to all
applications to which paragraphs 276ADE to 276DH and Appendix FM apply (or can be applied
by virtue of the Immigration Rules), and to any other ECHR Article 8 claims (save for those from
foreign criminals), and which are decided on or after that date. Deleted by HC 532, para 61 of this
statement take effect on 28 July 2014 and apply to all applications to which paragraphs 276ADE
to 276DH and Appendix FM apply (or can be applied by virtue of the Immigration Rules), and
to any other ECHR Article 8 claims (save for those from foreign criminals), and which are decided
on or after that date.

[E-LTRPT.3.2. The applicant must not be in the UK –
(a)   on temporary admission or temporary release, unless paragraph EX.1. applies;
       or
(b)   in breach of immigration laws (disregarding any period of overstaying for a
       period of 28 days or less), unless paragraph EX.1. applies.]

Note

Substituted by HC 532, para 62 of this statement take effect on 28 July 2014 and apply to all
applications to which paragraphs 276ADE to 276DH and Appendix FM apply (or can be applied
by virtue of the Immigration Rules), and to any other ECHR Article 8 claims (save for those from
foreign criminals), and which are decided on or after that date.

Financial requirements

E-LTRPT.4.1. The applicant must provide . . . evidence that they will be able to
adequately maintain and accommodate themselves and any dependants in the UK
without recourse to public funds[, unless paragraph EX.1. applies].

E-LTRPT.4.2. The applicant must provide . . . evidence that there will be adequate
accommodation in the UK, without recourse to public funds, for the family, including
other family members who are not included in the application but who live in the same
household, which the family own or occupy exclusively[, unless paragraph EX.1.
applies]: accommodation will not be regarded as adequate if-
(a)   it is, or will be, overcrowded; or
(b)   it contravenes public health regulations.

English language requirement

E-LTRPT.5.1. [If the applicant has not met the requirement in a previous application for
leave as a parent or partner, the applicant] must provide specified evidence that they-
(a)   are a national of a majority English speaking country listed in paragraph
       [GEN.1.6];
(b)   have passed an English language test in speaking and listening at a minimum of
       level A1 of the Common European Framework of Reference for Languages with
       a provider approved by the [Secretary of State];

(c) have an academic qualification recognised by [UK NARIC] to be equivalent to the standard of a Bachelor's or Master's degree or PhD in the UK, which was taught in English; or

(d) are exempt from the English language requirement under paragraph [E-LTRPT.5.2.;]

[, unless paragraph EX.1. applies.]

Note

Further amended by HC 1138, para 200 as from 6 April 2014. Further amended by HC 693, para 194 as from 6 November 2014.

E-LTRPT.5.2. The applicant is exempt from the English language requirement if at the date of application-

(a) the applicant is aged 65 or over;

(b) the applicant has a disability (physical or mental condition) which prevents the applicant from meeting the requirement; or

(c) there are exceptional circumstances which prevent the applicant from being able to meet the requirement.

Section D-LTRPT: Decision on application for limited leave to remain as a parent

D-LTRPT.1.1. If the applicant meets the requirements in paragraph [R-]LTRPT.1.1. (a) to (c) for limited leave to remain as a parent the applicant will be granted limited leave to remain for a period not exceeding 30 months, and subject to a condition of no recourse to public funds, and they will be eligible to apply for settlement after [a continuous period of at least 60 months with such leave or in the UK with entry clearance as a parent under paragraph D-ECPT.1.1.].

Note

Amended by HC 1138, para 201 as from 6 April 2014.

D-LTRPT.1.2. If the applicant meets the requirements in paragraph [R-]LTRPT.1.1. (a), (b) and (d) for limited leave to remain as a parent they will be granted leave to remain for a period not exceeding 30 months [and subject to a condition of no recourse to public funds [unless the Secretary of State considers that the person should not be subject to such a condition],] and [they] will be eligible to apply for settlement after [a continuous period of at least 120 months with such leave, with limited leave as a parent under paragraph D-LRPT.1.1, or in the UK with entry clearance as a parent under paragraph D-ECPT.1.1.].

D-LTRPT.1.3. If the applicant does not meet the requirements for limited leave to remain as a parent the application will be refused.

Note

Amended by HC 1138, para 202 as from 6 April 2014. Amended by HC 532, para 63 of this statement take effect on 28 July 2014 and apply to all applications to which paragraphs 276ADE to 276DH and Appendix FM apply (or can be applied by virtue of the Immigration Rules), and to any other ECHR Article 8 claims (save for those from foreign criminals), and which are decided on or after that date.

Section R-ILRPT: Requirements for indefinite leave to remain (settlement) as a parent

R-ILRPT.1.1. The requirements to be met for indefinite leave to remain as a parent are that-

(a) the applicant must be in the UK;

(b) the applicant must have made a valid application for indefinite leave to remain as a parent;

(c) the applicant must not fall for refusal under any of the grounds in [Section S-ILR: Suitability-indefinite leave to remain];

(d) the applicant must meet all of the requirements of Section E-LTRPT: Eligibility for leave to remain as a parent; and

(e) the applicant must meet all of the requirements of Section E-ILRPT: Eligibility for indefinite leave to remain as a parent.

Section E-ILRPT: Eligibility for indefinite leave to remain as a parent

E-ILRPT.1.1. To meet the eligibility requirements for indefinite leave to remain as a parent all of the requirements of paragraphs E-ILRPT.1.2. to 1.5. must be met.

E-ILRPT.1.2. The applicant must be in the UK with valid leave to remain as a parent (disregarding any period of overstaying for 28 days or less).

E-ILRPT.1.3. The applicant must have completed a continuous period of at least 60 months with limited leave as a parent under paragraph R-LTRPT.1.1.(a) to (c) [or in the UK with entry clearance as a parent under paragraph D-ECPT.1.1] or a continuous period of at least 120 months with limited leave a parent, under paragraphs R-LTRPT.1.1(a), (b) and (d) [or in the UK with entry clearance as a parent under paragraph D-ECPT.1.1] or a continuous period of at least 120 months with limited leave as a [parent] under a combination of these paragraphs.

E-ILRPT.1.4. DELETED.

[E-ILRPT.1.5]. The applicant must have [demonstrated] sufficient knowledge of the English language and sufficient knowledge about life in the [United Kingdom] in accordance with the requirements of [Appendix KoLL] of these Rules.

Note

Amended by HC 628, para 204.

Section D-ILRPT: Decision on application for indefinite leave to remain as a parent

D-ILRPT.1.1. If the applicant meets all of the requirements for indefinite leave to remain as a parent the applicant will be granted indefinite leave to remain.

D-ILRPT.1.2. If the applicant does not meet the requirements for indefinite leave to remain as a parent only for one or both of the following reasons-

(a) [paragraph S-ILR.1.5 or S-ILR.1.6 applies]; or

[(b) The applicant has not demonstrated sufficient knowledge of the English language or about life in the United Kingdom in accordance with Appendix KoLL.],

the applicant will be granted further limited leave to remain as a parent for a period not exceeding 30 months, and subject to a condition of no recourse to public funds.

Note

Amended by HC 628, para 205.

D-ILRPT.1.3. If the applicant does not meet [all the eligibility requirements for indefinite leave to remain as a parent, and does not qualify for] further limited leave to remain under paragraph D-ILRPT.1.2., the application will be refused [, [unless the applicant meets the requirements in paragraph R-LTRPT.1.1. (a), (b) and (d) for limited leave to remain as a parent. Where they do,] the applicant will be granted further limited leave to remain as a parent fr a period not exceeding 30 months under paragraph D-LTRPT.1.2. [and subject to a condition of no recourse to public funds [unless the Secretary of State considers that the person should not be subject to such a condition].]

Note

Specified evidence for the financial requirement is set out in Appendix FM-SE. Amended by HC 532, para 64 of this statement take effect on 28 July 2014 and apply to all applications to which paragraphs 276ADE to 276DH and Appendix FM apply (or can be applied by virtue of the Immigration Rules), and to any other ECHR Article 8 claims (save for those from foreign criminals), and which are decided on or after that date.

Adult Dependent Relative

Section EC-DR: Entry clearance as an adult dependent relative

EC-DR.1.1. The requirements to be met for entry clearance as an adult dependent relative are that-

(a)   the applicant must be outside the UK;

(b)   the applicant must have made a valid application for entry clearance as an adult dependent relative;

(c)   the applicant must not fall for refusal under any of the grounds in Section S-EC: Suitability for entry clearance; and

(d)   the applicant must meet all of the requirements of Section E-ECDR: Eligibility for entry clearance as an adult dependent relative.

Section E-ECDR: Eligibility for entry clearance as an adult dependent relative

E-ECDR.1.1. To meet the eligibility requirements for entry clearance as an adult dependent relative all of the requirements in paragraphs E-ECDR.2.1. to 3.2. must be met.

Relationship requirements

E-ECDR.2.1. The applicant must be the-

(a)   parent aged 18 years or over;

(b)   grandparent;

(c)   brother or sister aged 18 years or over; or

(d)   son or daughter aged 18 years or over

of a person ("the sponsor") who is in the UK.

E-ECDR.2.2. If the applicant is the sponsor's parent or grandparent they must not be in a subsisting relationship with a partner unless that partner is also the sponsor's parent or grandparent and is applying for entry clearance at the same time as the applicant.

E-ECDR.2.3. The sponsor must at the date of application be-

(a)   aged 18 years or over; and

(i)   a British Citizen in the UK; or

(ii)   present and settled in the UK; or

(iii)   in the UK with refugee leave or humanitarian protection.

E-ECDR.2.4. The applicant or, if the applicant and their partner are the sponsor's parents or grandparents, the applicant's partner, must as a result of age, illness or disability require long-term personal care to perform everyday tasks.

E-ECDR.2.5. The applicant or, if the applicant and their partner are the sponsor's parents or grandparents, the applicant's partner, must be unable, even with the practical and financial help of the sponsor, to obtain the required level of care in the country where they are living, because-

(a)   it is not available and there is no person in that country who can reasonably provide it; or

(b)   it is not affordable.

Financial requirements

E-ECDR.3.1. The applicant must provide . . . evidence that they can be adequately maintained, accommodated and cared for in the UK by the sponsor without recourse to public funds.

E-ECDR.3.2. If the applicant's sponsor is a British Citizen or settled in the UK, the applicant must provide an undertaking signed by the sponsor confirming that the applicant will have no recourse to public funds, and that the sponsor will be responsible for their maintenance, accommodation and care, for a period of 5 years from the date the applicant enters the UK if they are granted indefinite leave to enter.

Section D-ECDR: Decision on application for entry clearance as an adult dependent relative

D-ECDR.1.1. If the applicant meets the requirements for entry clearance as an adult dependent relative of a British Citizen or person settled in the UK they will be granted indefinite leave to enter.

D-ECDR.1.2. If the applicant meets the requirements for entry clearance as an adult dependent relative and the sponsor has limited leave the applicant will be granted limited leave of a duration which will expire at the same time as the sponsor's limited leave, and subject to a condition of no recourse to public funds. If the sponsor applies for further limited leave, the applicant may apply for further limited leave of the same duration, if the requirements in EC-DR.1.1. (c) and (d) continue to be met, and subject to no recourse to public funds.

D-ECDR.1.3. If the applicant does not meet the requirements for entry clearance as an adult dependent relative the application will be refused.

Section R-ILRDR: Requirements for indefinite leave to remain as an adult dependent relative

R-ILRDR.1.1. The requirements to be met for indefinite leave to remain as an adult dependent relative are that-
(a)   the applicant is in the UK;
(b)   the applicant must have made a valid application for indefinite leave to remain as an adult dependent relative;
(c)   the applicant must not fall for refusal under any of the grounds in [Section S-ILR: Suitability-indefinite leave to remain]; and
(d)   the applicant must meet all of the requirements of Section E-ILRDR: Eligibility for indefinite leave to remain as an adult dependent relative.

Section E-ILRDR: Eligibility for indefinite leave to remain as an adult dependent relative

E-ILRDR.1.1. To qualify for indefinite leave to remain as an adult dependent relative all of the requirements of paragraphs E-ILRDR. 1.2. to [1.5]. must be met.

E-ILRDR.1.2. The applicant must be in the UK with valid leave to remain as an adult dependent relative (disregarding any period of overstaying for a period of 28 days or less).

E-ILRDR.1.3. The applicant's sponsor must at the date of application be
(a)   present and settled in the UK; or
(b)   in the UK with refugee leave or as a person with humanitarian protection and have made an application for indefinite leave to remain.

E-ILRDR.1.4. The applicant must provide . . . . evidence that they can be adequately maintained, accommodated and cared for in the UK by the sponsor without recourse to public funds.

E-ILRDR.1.5. The applicant must provide an undertaking signed by the sponsor confirming that the applicant will have no recourse to public funds, and that the sponsor will be responsible for their maintenance, accommodation and care, for a period ending 5 years from the date the applicant entered the UK with limited leave as an adult dependent relative.

Section D-ILRDR: Decision on application for indefinite leave to remain as an adult dependent relative

D-ILRDR.1.1. If the applicant meets the requirements for indefinite leave to remain as an adult dependent relative and the applicant's sponsor is settled in the UK, the applicant will be granted indefinite leave to remain as an adult dependent relative.

D-ILRDR.1.2. If the applicant does not meet the requirements for indefinite leave to remain as an adult dependent relative because [paragraph S-ILR.1.5. or S-ILR.1.6. applies], the applicant will be granted further limited leave to remain as an adult dependent relative for a period not exceeding 30 months, and subject to a condition of no recourse to public funds.

D-ILRDR.1.3. If the applicant's sponsor has made an application for indefinite leave to remain and that application is refused, the applicant's application for indefinite leave to remain will be refused. If the sponsor is granted limited leave, the applicant will be granted further limited leave as an adult dependent relative of a duration which will expire at the same time as the sponsor's further limited leave, and subject to a condition of no recourse to public funds.

D-ILRDR.1.4. Where an applicant does not meet the requirements for indefinite leave to remain, or further limited leave to remain under paragraphs D-ILRDR.1.2. or 1.3., the application will be refused.

Note

For Guidance on the Adult Dependent Relatives category see: www.ukba.homeoffice.gov.uk/sitecontent/documents/policyandlaw/IDIs/chp8-annex/section-FM-6.0.pdf?view=Binary

Evidential requirements are set out in Appendix FM-SE.

Deportation and Removal

Where the Secretary of State or an immigration officer is considering deportation or removal of a person who claims that their deportation or removal from the UK would be a breach of the right to respect for private and family life under Article 8 of the Human Rights Convention that person may be required to make an application under this Appendix or paragraph [276ADE(1)], but if they are not required to make an application Part 13 of these Rules will apply.]

Note

Appendix FM Inserted by HC 194, para 115 as from 9 July 2012. Further amended by Cm 8423, paras 209–234 as from 20 July 2012 and HC 565, para 113–156 as from 6 September 2012. Further amended by HC 760, paras 338–398 as from 13 December 2012. Further amended by HC 1039, paras 210–227 as from on or after 6 April 2013. Further amended by HC 693, para 195 as from 6 November 2014.

[APPENDIX FM-SE
FAMILY MEMBERS — SPECIFIED EVIDENCE

:

A.   This Appendix sets out the specified evidence applicants need to provide to meet the requirements of rules contained in Appendix FM [and, where those requirements are also contained in other rules[, including Appendix Armed Forces,] and unless otherwise stated, the specified evidence applicants need to provide to meet the requirements of those rules.]

B.   Where evidence is not specified by Appendix FM, but is of a type covered by this Appendix, the requirements of this Appendix shall apply.

C.   In this Appendix references to paragraphs are to paragraphs of this Appendix unless the context otherwise requires

    (a)   In deciding an application in relation to which this appendix states that specified documents must be provided, the Entry Clearance Officer or Secretary of State ("the decision-maker") will consider documents that have been submitted with the application, and will only consider documents submitted after the application where sub-paragraph (b) or (e) applies.

    (b)   if the applicant:

        (i)   Has submitted:

         (aa) A sequence of documents and some of the documents in the sequence have been omitted (e.g. if one bank statement from a series is missing);

         (bb) A document in the wrong format [(for example, if a letter is not on letterhead paper as specified)]; or

         (cc) A document that is a copy and not an original document; or

         [(dd) A document which does not contain all of the specified information; or]

  (ii) has not submitted a specified document

      the decision-maker may contact the applicant or his representative in writing or otherwise, and request the document(s) or the correct version(s). the material requested must be received ... at the address specified in the request within a reasonable timescale in the request.

(c)   The decision-maker will not request documents where he or she does not anticipate that addressing the error or omission referred to in sub-paragraph (b) will lead to a grant because the application will be refused for other reasons.

(d)   If the applicant has submitted:

  (i)   A document in the wrong format; or

  (ii) A document that is a copy and not an original document,

      the application may be granted exceptionally, providing the decision-maker is satisfied that the document(s) is genuine and that the applicant meets the requirement to which the document relates. the decision-maker reserves the right to request the specified original document(s) in the correct format in all cases where sub-paragraph (b) applies, and to refuse applications if this material is not provided as set out in sub-paragraph (b).

(e)   Where the decision-maker is satisfied that there is a valid reason why a specified document(s) cannot be supplied, e.g. because it is not issued in a particular country or has been permanently lost. he or she may exercise discretion not to apply the requirement for the document(s) or to request alternative or additional information or document(s) be submitted by the applicant.]

(f)   [Before making a decision under Appendix FM or this Appendix, the decision-maker may contact the applicant or their representative in writing or otherwise to request further information or documents. The material requested must be received ... at the address specified in the request within a reasonable timescale in the request.]

Note

Amended by HC 628, paras 206–210. Further amended by HC 803, para 42 as from 1 December 2013.

Evidence of Financial Requirements [under Appendix FM]

[**A1.** To meet the financial requirements under paragraphs E-ECP.3.1., E-LTRP.3.1., E-ECC.2.1. and E-LTRC.2.1. of Appendix FM, the applicant must meet:

(a)   The level of financial requirement applicable to the application under Appendix FM; and

(b)   The requirements specified in Appendix FM and this Appendix as to:

  (i)   The permitted sources of income and savings;

  (ii) The time periods and permitted combinations of sources applicable to each permitted source relied upon; and

  (iii) The evidence required for each permitted source relied upon.]

1.   In relation to evidencing the financial requirements in Appendix FM the following general provisions shall apply:

(a)   . . . bank statements must:

      (i)   be from a financial institution regulated by the appropriate regulatory body for the country in which that institution is operating.

      (ii)   not be from a financial institution on the list of excluded institutions in Appendix P of these rules.

      (iii) [in relation to personal bank statements,] be only in the name of:

          (1)   the applicant's partner, the applicant or both as appropriate; or

          (2)   if the applicant is a child the applicant parent's partner, the applicant's parent or both as appropriate; or

          (3)   if the applicant is an adult dependent relative, the applicant's sponsor [or the applicant],

          unless otherwise stated.

     [(iv) cover the period(s) specified.

      (v)   be:

          (1)   on official bank stationery; or

          (2)   electronic bank statements ... which are either accompanied by a letter from the bank on its headed stationery confirming that the documents are authentic or which bear the official stamp of the issuing bank on every page.]

[(aa) Where a bank statement is specified in this Appendix, a building society statement, a building society pass book, a letter from the applicant's bank or building society, or a letter from a financial institution regulated by the Financial Services Authority or, for overseas accounts, the appropriate regulatory body for the country in which the institution operates and the funds are located, may be submitted as an alternative to a bank statement(s) provided that:

      (1)   the requirements in paragraph 1(a)(i)-(iv) are met as if the document were a bank statement; and

      (2)   a building society pass book must clearly show:

          (i)   the account number;

          (ii)   the building society's name and logo; and

          (iii) the information required on transactions, funds held and time period(s) or as otherwise specified in this Appendix in relation to bank statements; and/or

      (3)   a letter must be on the headed stationery of the bank, building society or other financial institution and must clearly show:

          (i)   the account number;

          (ii)   the date of the letter;

          (iii) the financial institutions's name and logo; and

          (iv) the information required on transactions, funds held and time period(s) or as otherwise specified in this Appendix in relation to bank statements.]

  (b)   [Promises of third party support will not be accepted. Third party support will only be accepted in the form of:]

      (i)   [payments from a former partner of the applicant for the maintenance of the applicant or any children of the applicant and the former partner, and payments from a former partner of the applicant's partner for the maintenance of that partner.]

      (ii)   income from a dependent child who has turned 18, remains in the same UK household as the applicant and continues to be counted towards the financial requirement under Appendix FM; ...

      (iii) [gift of cash savings (whose source must be declared)] evidenced at paragraph 1(a)(iii), provided that the cash savings have been held by the person or persons at paragraph 1(a)(iii) for at least 6 months prior to the date of application and are under their control[; and

(iv) a maintenance grant or stipend associated with undergraduate study or postgraduate study or research.]

[(bb) Payslips must be:

(i) original formal payslips issued by the employer and showing the employer's name; or

(ii) accompanied by a letter from the employer, on the employer's headed paper and signed by a senior official, confirming the payslips are authentic.]

(c) The [employment or self-employment income of an applicant] will only be taken into account if they are in the UK, aged 18 years or over and working legally[, and prospective employment income will not be taken into account (except that of an applicant's partner or parent's partner who is returning to employment or self-employment in the UK at paragraphs E-ECP.3.2.(a) and E-ECC.2.2(a) of Appendix FM).]

[(cc) The income of an applicant or sponsor working in the UK in salaried or non-salaried employment or in self-employment can include income from work undertaken overseas, provided paragraph E-LTRP.1.10 of Appendix FM and the other requirements of this Appendix are met.]

(d) All income and savings must be lawfully derived.

(e) Savings must be held in cash.

(f) Income or cash savings in a foreign currency will be converted to pounds sterling using the closing spot exchange rate which appears on www.oanda.com* on the date of application.

(g) Where there is income or cash savings in different foreign currencies, each will be converted into pounds sterling before being added together, and then added to any UK income or savings to give a total amount.

(h) All documentary evidence must be original, unless otherwise stated.

(i) Evidence of profit from the sale of a business, property, investment, bond, stocks, shares or other asset will:

(i) not be accepted as evidence of income, but

(ii) the associated funds will be accepted as cash savings subject to the requirements of this Appendix and Appendix FM.

[(j) Where any specified documents are not in English or Welsh, the applicant must provide the original and a full translation that can be independently verified by the Entry Clearance Officer, Immigration Officer or the Secretary of State. The translation must be dated and include

(i) confirmation that it is an accurate translation of the original document;

(ii) the full name and original signature of the translator or an authorised official of the translation company;

(iii) the translator or translation company's company details; and

(iv) if the applicant is applying for leave to remain or indefinite leave to remain, certification by a qualified translator and details of the translator or translation company's credentials.]

(k) . . .

[(l) Where this Appendix requires the applicant to provide specified evidence relating to a period which ends with the date of application, that evidence, or the most recently dated part of it, must be dated no earlier than 28 days before the date of application.]

[(m) Cash income on which the correct tax has been paid may be counted as income under this Appendix, subject to the relevant evidential requirements of this Appendix.]

[(n) The gross amount of any cash income may be counted where the person's specified bank statements show the net amount which relates to the gross amount shown on their payslips (or in the relevant specified evidence provided in addition to the specified bank statements in relation to non-employment income). Otherwise, only the net amount shown on the specified bank statements may be counted.]

[(o) In this Appendix, a reference to the "average" is a reference to the mean average.]

[2. In respect of salaried employment in the UK [(except where paragraph 9 applies)], all of the following evidence must be provided:

(a) [Payslips] covering:

(i) a period of 6 months prior to the date of application if the [person] has been employed by their current employer for at least 6 months (and where paragraph 13(b) of this Appendix does not apply); or

(ii) any period of salaried employment in the] period of 12 months prior to the date of application if the [person] has been employed by their current employer for less than 6 months (or at least 6 months but the person does not rely on paragraph 13(a) of this Appendix), or in the financial year(s) relied upon by a self-employed person.

(b) A letter from the employer(s) who issued the [payslips] at paragraph 2(a) confirming:

(i) the person's employment and gross annual salary;

(ii) the length of their employment;

(iii) the period over which they have been or were paid the level of salary relied upon in the application; and

(iv) the type of employment (permanent, fixed-term contract or agency).

(c) Personal bank statements corresponding to the same period(s) as the [payslips] at paragraph 2(a), showing that the salary has been paid into an account in the name of the person or in the name of the person and their partner jointly.]

[(d) Where the person is a director of a limited company based in the UK, evidence that the company is not of a type specified in paragraph 9(a). This can include the latest Annual Return filed at Companies House.]]

[2A.

(i) In respect of salaried employment in the UK (paragraph 2 of this Appendix), statutory or contractual maternity, paternity, adoption or sick pay in the UK (paragraph 5 or 6 of this Appendix), or a director's salary paid to a self-employed person (paragraph 9 of this Appendix), the applicant may, in addition to the [payslips] and personal bank statements required under that paragraph, submit the P60 for the relevant period(s) of employment relied upon (if issued). If they do not, the Entry Clearance Officer or Secretary of State may grant the application if otherwise satisfied that the requirements of this Appendix relating to that employment are met. The Entry Clearance Officer or Secretary of State may request that the applicant submit the document(s) in accordance with paragraph D of this Appendix.

(ii) In respect of salaried employment in the UK (paragraph 2 of this Appendix), or statutory or contractual, maternity, paternity, adoption or sick pay in the UK (paragraph 5 or 6 of this Appendix), the applicant may, in addition to the letter from the employer(s) required under that paragraph, submit a signed contract of employment. Of they do not, the Entry Clearance Officer or Secretary of State may grant the application if otherwise satisfied that the requirements of this Appendix relating to that employment are met. The Entry Clearance Officer or Secretary of State may request that the applicant submit the document(s) in accordance with paragraph D of this Appendix.]

3. In respect of salaried employment outside of the UK, evidence should be a reasonable equivalent to that set out in paragraph 2 [and (where relevant) paragraph 2A]. [In respect of an equity partner whose income from the partnership is treated as salaried employment under paragraph 17, the payslips and employer's letter referred to in paragraph 2 may be replaced by other evidence providing the relevant information in paragraph 2 (which may include, but is not confined to, a letter on official stationery from an accountant, solicitor or business manager acting for the partnership).]

4. In respect of a job offer in the UK [(for an applicant's partner or parent's partner returning to salaried employment in the UK at paragraphs E-ECP.3.2(a) and E-ECC.2.2.(a) of Appendix FM)] a letter from the employer must be provided:

 (a) confirming the job offer, the gross annual salary and the starting date of the employment which must be within 3 months of the applicant's partner's return to the UK; or

 (b) enclosing a signed contract of employment, which must have a starting date within 3 months of the applicant's partner's return to the UK.

5. In respect of statutory or contractual maternity, paternity or adoption pay . . . all of the following[, and in respect of parental leave in the UK only the evidence at paragraph 5(c),] must be provided:

 [(a) Personal bank statements corresponding to the same period(s) as the [payslips] at paragraph 5(b), showing that the salary has been paid into an account in the name of the person or in the name of the person and their partner jointly.]

 (b) [Payslips] covering:

  (i) a period of 6 months prior to [the date of application or to] the commencement of the maternity, paternity or adoption leave, if the applicant has been employed by their current employer for at least 6 months [(and where paragraph 13(b) does not apply)]; or

  (ii) [any period of salaried employment in the] period of 12 months prior to [the date of application or to] the commencement of the maternity, paternity or adoption leave, if the applicant has been employed by their current employer for less than 6 months [(or at least 6 months but the person does not rely on paragraph 13(a))].

 (c) A letter from the employer confirming:

  (i) the length of the person's employment;

  (ii) the gross annual salary and the period over which it has been paid at this level;

  (iii) the entitlement to maternity, paternity[, parental] or adoption leave; and

  (iv) the date of commencement and the end-date of the maternity, paternity[, parental] or adoption leave.

6. In respect of statutory or contractual sick pay in the UK all of the following must be provided:

 [(a) Personal bank statements corresponding to the same period(s) as the [payslips] at paragraph 6(b), showing that the salary has been paid into an account in the name of the person or in the name of the person and their partner jointly.]

 (b) [Payslips] covering:

  (i) a period of 6 months prior to [the date of application or to] the commencement of the sick leave, if the applicant has been employed by their current employer for at least 6 months [(and where paragraph 13(b) does not apply)]; or,

  (ii) [any period of salaried employment in the] period of 12 months prior to [the date of application or to] the commencement of the sick leave, if the applicant has been employed by their current employer for less than 6 months [(or at least 6 months but the person does not rely on paragraph 13(a))].

(c) A letter from employer confirming:

    (i) the length of the person's employment;

    (ii) the gross annual salary and the period over which it has been paid at this level;

    (iii) that the person is in receipt of statutory or contractual sick pay; and

    (iv) the date of commencement of the sick leave.

7. In respect of self-employment in the UK as a partner, as a sole trader or in a franchise all of the following must be provided:

    (a) Evidence of the amount of tax payable, paid and unpaid for the last [full] financial year.

    (b) [The following documents for the last full financial year, or for the last two such years (where those documents show the necessary level of gross income as an average of those two years):

        (i) annual self-assessment tax return to HMRC (a copy or print-out); and

        (ii) Statement of Account (SA300 or SA302).]

    (c) Proof of registration with HMRC as self-employed [if available.] . . . .

    (d) Each partner's Unique Tax Reference Number (UTR) and/or the UTR of the partnership or business.

    (e) Where the person holds or held a separate business bank account(s), . . . bank statements for the same 12-month period as the tax return(s).

    (f) . . . personal bank statements for the same 12-month period as the tax return(s) showing that the income from self-employment has been paid into an account in the name of the person or in the name of the person and their partner jointly.

    [(g) Evidence of ongoing self-employment through evidence of payment of Class 2 National Insurance contributions[, or (where the person has reached state pension age) through alternative evidence (which may include, but is not confined to, evidence of ongoing payment of business rates, business-related insurance premiums, employer National Insurance contributions or franchise payments to the parent company)].]

    (h) One of the following documents must also be submitted:

        [(i) (aa) If the [business] is required to produce annual audited accounts, [such accounts for the last full financial year]; or

        (bb) If the . . . business is not required to produce annual audited accounts, [unaudited accounts for the last full financial year] and an accountant's certificate of confirmation, from an accountant who is a member of a UK Recognised Supervisory Body (as defined in the Companies Act 2006);]

        (ii) A certificate of VAT registration and the . . . VAT return [for the last full financial year] [(a copy or print-out)] confirming the VAT registration number, if turnover is in excess of [£79,000 or was in excess of the threshold which applied during the last full financial year];

        (iii) Evidence to show appropriate planning permission or local planning authority consent is held to operate the type/class of business at the trading address (where this is a local authority requirement); or

        (iv) A franchise agreement signed by both parties.

    (i) The document referred to in paragraph [7](h)(iv) must be provided if the organisation is a franchise.

8. In respect of self-employment outside of the UK, evidence should be a reasonable equivalent to that set out in paragraph 7.

[9. In respect of income from employment and/or shares in a limited company based in the UK of a type specified in paragraph 9(a), the requirements of paragraph 9(b)-(d) shall apply in place of the requirements of paragraph 2 and 10(b).

(a) The specified type of limited company is one in which:

  (i)   the person is a director of the company (or another company within the same group); and

  (ii) shares are held (directly or indirectly) by the person, their partner or the following family members of the person or their partner: parent, grandparent, child, stepchild, grandchild, brother, sister, uncle, aunt, nephew, niece or first cousin; and

  (iii) any remaining shares are held (directly or indirectly) by fewer than five other persons.

(b) All of the following must be provided:

  (i)   Company Tax return CT600 (a copy or print-out) for the last full financial year and evidence this has been files with HMRC, such as electronic or written acknowledgment from HMRC.

  (ii) Evidence of registration with the Registrar of Companies at Companies House.

  (iii) If the company is required to produce annual audited accounts, [such accounts for the last full financial year].

  (iv) If the company is not required to produce annual audited accounts, [unaudited accounts for the last full financial year] and an accountant's certificate of confirmation, from an accountant who is a member of a UK Recognized Supervisory Body (as defined in the Companies Act 2006).

  (v)   Corporate/business bank statements covering the same 12–month period as the Company Tax Return CT600.

  (vi) A current Appointment Report from Companies House.

  (vii) One of the following documents must also be provided:

    (1) A certificate of VAT registration and the . . . VAT return [for the last full financial year] (a copy or print-out) confirming the VAT registration number, if turnover is in excess of [£79,000 or was in excess of the threshold which applied during the last full financial year].

    (2) proof of ownership or lease of business premises.

    (3) Original proof of ownership with HMRC as an employer for the purposes of PAYE and National Insurance, proof of PAYE reference number and Accounts office reference number. This evidence may be in the form of a certified copy of the documentation issued by HMRC.

(c) Where the person is listed as a director of the company and receives a salary from the company, all of the following documents must also be provided:

  (i)   [Payslips] and P60 (if issued) covering the same period as the Company Tax Return CT600.

  (ii) Personal bank statements covering the same 12–month period as the Company Tax Return CT600 showing that the salary as a director was paid into an account in the name of the person or in the name of the person and their partner jointly.

(d) Where the person receives dividends from the company, all of the following documents must be provided:

  (i)   Dividend vouchers for all dividends declared in favour of the person during or in respect of the period covered by the Company

Tax Return CT600 showing the company's and the person's details with the person's net dividend amount and tax credit.

(ii) Personal bank statement(s) showing that those dividends were paid into an account in the name of the person or in the name of the person and their partner jointly.]

10. In respect of non-employment income all the following evidence, in relation to the form of income relied upon, must be provided:

(a) To evidence property rental income:

(i) Confirmation that [the person or the person and their partner jointly] own the property for which the rental income is received, through:

[(1) A copy of the title deeds of the property or of the title register from the Land Registry (or overseas equivalent); or]

(2) A mortgage statement.

(ii) . . . personal bank statements for the 12-month period prior to the date of application showing the rental income was paid into an account in the name of the person or of the person and their partner jointly.

(iii) A rental agreement or contract.

(b) To evidence dividends [(except where paragraph 9 applies)] or other income from investments, stocks, shares, bonds or trust funds:

(i) A certificate showing proof of ownership and the amount(s) of any investment(s).

(ii) A portfolio report (for a financial institution regulated by [regulated by the Financial Conduct Authority (FCA) and the Prudential Regulation Authority (PRA) where applicable] in the UK [or a dividend voucher showing the company and person's details with the person's net dividend amount and tax credit].

(iii) . . . personal bank statements for the 12-month period prior to the date of application showing that the income relied upon was paid into an account in the name of the person or of the person and their partner jointly.

[(iv) Where the person is a director of a limited company based in the UK, evidence that the company is not of a type specified in paragraph 9(a). This can include the latest Annual Return filed at Companies House.]

(c) To evidence interest from savings:

(i) . . . personal bank statements for the 12-month period prior to the date of application showing the amount of the savings held and that the interest was paid into an account in the name of the person or of the person and their partner jointly.

(d) To evidence maintenance payments (from a former partner [of the applicant] to maintain their and the applicant's child or children [or the applicant[, or from a former partner of the applicant's partner to maintain the applicant's partner]]):

(i) Evidence of a maintenance agreement through any of the following:

(1) A court order;

(2) Written voluntary agreement; or

(3) Child Support Agency documentation.

(ii) . . . personal bank statements for the 12-month period prior to the date of application showing the income relied upon was paid into an account in the name of the applicant.

(e) To evidence a pension:

(i) Official documentation from:

> > (1)   [The Department for Work and Pensions] (in respect of the Basic State Pension and the Additional or Second State Pension) [or other government department or agency[, including the Veterans Agency]];
> > (2)   An overseas pension authority; or
> > (3)   A pension company,
> > confirming pension entitlement and amount.
>
> (ii)   At least one [. . . personal bank statement in the 12–month period prior to the date of application] showing payment of the pension into the person's account.
>
> [(iii)   For the purposes of sub-paragraph (i), War Disablement Pension, War Widow's/Widower's Pension and any other pension or equivalent payment for life made under the War Pensions Scheme, the Armed Forces Compensation Scheme or the Armed Forces Attributable benefits Scheme may be treated as a pension, unless excluded under paragraph 21 of this Appendix.]

(f)   To evidence UK Maternity Allowance, Bereavement Allowance, Bereavement Payment and Widowed Parent's Allowance:

> (i)   Department for Work and Pensions documentation confirming [the person or their partner] is or was in receipt of the benefit [in the 12–month period prior to the date of application].
>
> (ii)   . . . personal bank statements for the 12-month period prior to the date of application showing the income was paid into the person's account.

[(ff)   Subject to paragraph 12, to evidence payments under the War Pensions Scheme, the Armed Forces Compensation Scheme or the Armed Forces Attributable Benefits Scheme which are not treated as a pension for the purposes of paragraph 10(e)(i):

> (i)   Veterans Agency or Department for Work and Pensions documentation in the form of an award notification letter confirming the person or their partner is or was in receipt of the payment at the date of the application.
>
> (ii)   personal bank statements for the 12–month period prior to the date of application showing the income was paid into the person's account.]

[(g)   To evidence a maintenance grant or stipend (not a loan) associated with undergraduate study or postgraduate study or research:

> (i)   Documentation from the body or company awarding the grant or stipend confirming that the person is currently in receipt of the grant or stipend or will not be within 3 months of the date of application, confirming that the grant or stipend will be paid for at least 12 months [or for at least one full academic year] from the date of application or from the date on which payment of the grant or stipend will commence, and confirming the annual amount of the grant or stipend. [Where the grant or stipend is or will be paid on a tax-free basis, the amount of the gross equivalent may be counted as income under this Appendix.]
>
> (ii)   . . . personal bank statements for any part of the 12–month period prior to the date of the application during which the person has been in receipt of the grant or stipend showing the income was paid into the person's account.]

[(h)   To evidence ongoing insurance payments (such as, but not exclusively, payments received under an income protection policy):

> (i)   documentation from the insurance company confirming:

            (a)   that in the 12 months prior to the date of application the person has been in receipt of insurance payments and the amount and frequency of the payments.

            (b)   the reason for the payments and their expected duration.

            (c)   that, provided any relevant terms and conditions continue to be met, the payment(s) will continue for at least the 12 months following the date of application.

      (ii)   personal bank statements for the 12-month period prior to the date of application showing the insurance payments were paid into the person's account.

  (i)   To evidence ongoing payments (other than maintenance payments under paragraph 10(d)) arising from a structured legal settlement (such as, but not exclusively, one arising from settlement of a personal injury claim):

      (i)   documentation from a court or the person's legal representative confirming:

            (a)   that in the 12 months prior to the date of application the person has been in receipt of structured legal settlement payments and the amount and frequency of those payments.

            (b)   the reason for the payments and their expected duration.

            (c)   that the payment(s) will continue for at least the 12 months following the date of application.

      (ii)   personal bank statements for the 12-month period prior to the date of application showing the payments were paid into the person's account, either directly or via the person's legal representative.]

11.   In respect of cash savings the following must be provided:

  [(a)   personal bank statements showing that at least the level of cash savings relied upon in the application has been held have in an account(s) in the name of the person or of the person and their partner jointly throughout the period of 6 months prior to the date of application.]

  [(b)   A declaration by the account holder(s) of the source(s) of the cash savings.]

[11A. In respect of cash savings:

  (a)   The savings may be held in any form of bank/savings account [(whether a deposit or investment account)], provided that the account allows the savings to be accessed immediately (with or without a penalty for withdrawing funds without notice). This can include. . . , savings held in a pension savings account which can be immediately withdrawn.

  (b)   Paid out competition winnings or a legacy which has been paid can contribute to cash savings.]

  [(c)   Funds held as cash savings by the applicant, their partner or both jointly at the date of application can have been transferred from investments, stocks, shares, bonds or trust funds within the period of 6 months prior to the date of application, provided that:

      (i)   The funds have been in the ownership and under the control of the applicant, their partner or both jointly for at least the period of 6 months prior to the date of application.

      (ii)   The ownership of the funds in the form of investments, stocks, shares, bonds or trust funds; the cash value of the funds in that form at or before the beginning of the period of 6 months prior to the date of application; and the transfer of the funds into cash, are evidenced by a portfolio report or other relevant documentation from a financial institution regulated by the appropriate regulatory body for the country in which that institution is operating.

    (iii)   The requirements of this Appendix in respect of cash savings held at the date of application are met, except that the period of ... 6 months prior to the date of application in paragraph 11(a) will be reduced by the amount of that period in which the relevant funds were held in the form of investments, stocks, shares, bonds or trust funds.]

   [(iv) For the purposes of sub-paragraph 11A(c), "investments" includes funds held in an investment account which does not meet the requirements of paragraphs 11 and 11A(a).]

[(d)   Funds held as cash savings by the applicant, their partner or both jointly at the date of application can be from the proceeds of the sale of property, in the form only of a dwelling, other building or land, which took lace within the period of 6 months prior to the date of application, provided that:

    (i)   The property (or relevant share of the property) was owned at the beginning of the period of 6 months prior to the date of application and at the date of sale by the applicant, their partner or both jointly.

    (ii) Where ownership of the property was shared with a third party, only the proceeds of the sale of the share of the property owned by the applicant, their partner or both jointly may be counted.

    (iii) The funds deposited as cash savings are the net proceeds of the sale, once any mortgage or loan secured on the property (or relevant share of the property) has been repaid and once any taxes and professional fees associated with the sale have been paid.

    (iv) The decision-maker is satisfied that the requirements in sub-paragraphs (i)-(iii) are met on the basis of information and documents submitted in support of the application. These may include for example:

       (1)   Registration information or documentation (or a copy of this) from the Land Registry (or overseas equivalent).

       (2)   A letter from a solicitor (or other relevant professional, if the sale takes place overseas) instructed in the sale of the property confirming the sale price and other relevant information.

       (3)   A letter from a lender (a bank or building society) on its headed stationery regarding the repayment of a mortgage or loan secured on the property.

       (4)   Confirmation of payment of taxes or professional fees associated with the sale.

       (5)   Any other relevant evidence that the requirements in sub-paragraphs (i)-(iii) are met.

    (v)   The requirements of this Appendix in respect of cash savings held at the date of application are met, except that the period of 6 months mentioned in paragraph 11(a) will be reduced by the amount of time which passed between the start of that 6–month period and the deposit of the sale in an account mentioned in paragraph 11(a).]

12.   Where [a person] is in receipt of Carer's Allowance, Disability Living Allowance, Severe Disablement Allowance, Industrial Injuries Disablement Benefit[,] Attendance Allowance [or Personal Independence Payment] [or Armed Forces Independence Payment or Guaranteed Income Payment under the Armed Forces Compensation Scheme or Constant Attendance Allowance, Mobility Supplement or War Disablement Pension under the War Pensions Scheme.], all the following must be provided:

(a) Official documentation from the Department for Work and Pensions [or Veterans Agency] confirming [the current entitlement and the amount currently received].

(b) At least one [. . . personal bank statement in the 12–month period prior to the date of application] showing [payment of the amount of the benefit or allowance to which the person is currently entitled into their account].

[12A. Where the financial requirement the applicant must met under Appendix FM relates to adequate maintenance, paragraphs 2 to 12 apply only to the extent and in the manner specified by this paragraph. Where such a financial requirement applies, the applicant must provide the following evidence:

(a) Where the current salaried employment in the UK of the applicant or their partner, parent, parent's partner or sponsor is relied upon:

(i) A letter from the employer confirming the employment, the gross annual salary and the annual salary after income tax and National Insurance contributions have been paid, how long the employment has been held, and the type of employment (permanent, fixed-term contract or agency).

(ii) [Payslips] covering the period of 6 months prior to the date of application or such shorter period as the current employment has been held.

(iii) . . . personal bank statements covering the same period as the [payslips], showing that the salary has been paid into an account in the name of the person or in the name of the person and their partner jointly.

(b) Where statutory or contractual maternity, paternity, adoption or sick pay in the UK of the applicant or their partner, parent, parent's partner or sponsor are relied upon, paragraph 5(b)(i) and (c) or paragraph 6(b)(i) and (c) apply as appropriate.

(c) Where self-employment in the UK of the applicant or their partner, parent, parent's partner or sponsor[, or income from employment and/or shares in a limited company based in the UK of a type to which paragraph 9 applies,] is relied upon, paragraph 7 or 9 applies as appropriate.

(d) Where non-employment income of the applicant or their partner, parent, parent's partner or sponsor is relied upon, paragraph 10 applies and paragraph 10(f) shall apply as if it referred to any UK welfare benefit or tax credit relied upon and to HMRC as well as Department for Work and Pensions [or other official] documentation.

(e) Where the cash savings of the applicant or their partner, parent, parent's partner or sponsor are relied upon, paragraphs 11 and 11A apply.

(f) The monthly housing and Council Tax costs for he accommodation in the UK in which the applicant (and any other family members who are or will be part of the same household) lives or will live if the application is granted.

(g) Where the applicant is an adult dependent relative applying for entry clearance, the applicant must in addition provide details of the care arrangements in the UK planned for them by their sponsor (which can involve other family members in the UK), of the cost of these arrangements and of how that cost will be met by the sponsor.]

[12B. Where the financial requirement an applicant must meet under Part 8 (excluding an applicant who is a family member of a Relevant Points Based System Migrant) or under Appendix FM relates to adequate maintenance and where cash savings are relied upon to meet the requirement in full or in part, the decision-maker will:

(a) Establish the total cash savings which meet the requirements of paragraphs 11 and 11A;

(b)   Divide this figure by the number of weeks of limited leave which would be issued if the application were granted, or by 52 if the application is for indefinite leave to enter or remain;

(c)   Add the figure in sub-paragraph 12B(b) to the weekly net income (before the deduction of housing costs) available to meet the requirement.]

Note

Further amended by HC 693, para 196 as from 6 November 2014. Further amended by HC 693, para 197 as from 6 November 2014. Amended by HC 693, para 198 as from 6 November 2014. Further amended by HC 693, para 199 as from 6 November 2014. Amended by HC 693, para 200 as from 6 November 2014. Further amended by HC 693, para 201 as from 6 November 2014. Further amended by HC 693, para 202 as from 6 November 2014. Further amended by HC 693, para 203 as from 6 November 2014. Amended by HC 693, para 204 as from 6 November 2014.

Calculating Gross Annual Income [under Appendix FM]

13.   Based on evidence that meets the requirements of this Appendix, and can be taken into account with reference to the applicable provisions of Appendix FM, gross annual income under paragraphs E-ECP.3.1., E-LTRP.3.1., E-ECC.2.1. and E-LTRC.2.1. will be calculated in the following ways:

     (a)   Where the person is in salaried employment in the UK at the date of application[,] has been employed by their current employer for at least 6 months [and has been paid throughout the period of 6 months prior to the date of application at a level of gross annual salary which equals or exceeds the level relied upon in paragraph 13(a)(i),] their gross annual income will be [(where paragraph 13(b) does not apply)] the total of:

         (i)   [The level of gross annual salary relied upon in the application];

         (ii)   The gross amount of any specified non-employment income [(other than pension income)] received by them or their partner in the 12 months prior to the date of application; and

         (iii)   The gross annual income from a UK or foreign State pension or a private pension received by them or their partner.

     (b)   Where the person is in salaried employment in the UK at the date of application and has been employed by their current employer for less than 6 months [(or at least 6 months but the person does not rely on paragraph 13(a)),] their gross annual income will be the total of:

         (i)   The gross annual salary from employment as it was at the date of application;

         (ii)   The gross amount of any specified non-employment income [(other than pension income)] received by them or their partner in the 12 months prior to the date of application; and

         (iii)   The gross annual income from a UK or foreign State pension or a private pension received by them or their partner.

         [In addition, the requirements of paragraph 15 must be met.]

     (c)   Where the person is the applicant's partner, is in salaried employment outside of the UK at the date of application, has been employed by their current employer for at least 6 months, and is returning to the UK to take up salaried employment in the UK starting within 3 months of their return, the person's gross annual income will be calculated:

         (i)   On the basis set out in paragraph 13(a); and also

         (ii)   On that basis but substituting for the gross annual salary at paragraph 13(a)(i) the gross annual salary in the salaried employment in the UK to which they are returning.

     (d)   Where the person is the applicant's partner, has been in salaried employment outside of the UK within 12 months of the date of application, and is returning to the UK to take up salaried employment in the UK starting within 3 months of their return, the person's gross annual income will be calculated:

    (i)   On the basis set out in paragraph 13(a) but substituting for the gross annual salary at paragraph 13(a)(i) the gross annual salary in the salaried employment in the UK to which they are returning; and also

    (ii)   On the basis set out in paragraph 15(b).

(e)   Where the person is self-employed, their gross annual income will be the total of their gross income from their self-employment, [from any salaried or non-salaried employment they have had or their partner has had (if their partner is in the UK with permission to work),] from specified non-employment income received by them or their partner, and from income from a UK or foreign State pension or a private pension received by them or their partner, in the last full financial year or as an average of the last two full financial years. [The requirements of this Appendix for specified evidence relating to these forms of income shall apply as if references to the date of application were references to the end of the relevant financial year(s).] [The relevant financial year(s) cannot be combined with any financial year(s) to which paragraph 9 applies and vice versa.]

(f)   Where the person is self-employed, they cannot combine their gross annual income at paragraph 13(e) with specified savings in order to meet the level of income required under Appendix FM.

[(g)   Where the person is not relying on income from salaried employment or self-employment, their gross annual income will be the total of:

    (i)   The gross amount of any specified non-employment income (other than pension income) received by them or their partner in the 12 months prior to the date of application; and

    (ii)   The gross annual income from a UK or foreign State pension or a private pension received by them or their partner.]

[(h)   Where the person is the applicant's partner and is in self-employment outside the UK at the date of application and is returning to the UK to take up salaried employment in the UK starting within 3 months of their return, the person's gross annual income will be calculated:

    (i)   On the basis set out in paragraph 13(a) but substituting for the gross annual salary at paragraph 13(a)(i) the gross annual salary in the salaried employment in the UK to which they are returning; and also

    (ii)   On the basis set out in paragraph 13(e).]

[(i)   Any period of unpaid maternity, paternity, adoption, parental or sick leave in the 12 months prior to the date of application will not be counted towards any period relating to employment, or any period relating to income from employment, for which this Appendix provides.]

[(j)   The provisions of paragraph 13 which apply to self-employment also apply to income from employment and/or shares in a limited company based in the UK of a type to which paragraph 9 applies and to a person in receipt of such income.]

[(k)   Where the application relies on the employment income of the applicant and the sponsor, all of that income must be calculated either under sub-paragraph 13(a) or under sub-paragraph 13(b) and paragraph 15, and not under a combination of these methods.]

14.   Where the requirements of this Appendix and Appendix FM are met by the combined income or cash savings of more than one person, the income or the cash savings must only be counted once unless stated otherwise.

15.   In respect of paragraph 13(b) [and paragraph 13(d)], the provisions in this paragraph also apply:

(a) In order to evidence the level of gross annual income required by Appendix FM, the person must meet the requirements in paragraph 13(b) [and paragraph 13(d)(i)]; and

(b) The person must also meet the level of gross annual income required by Appendix FM on the basis that their income is the total of:

    (i) The gross income from salaried employment [in the UK or overseas] earned by the person in the 12 months prior to the date of application;

    (ii) The gross amount of any specified non-employment income [(other than pension income)] received by the person or their partner in the 12 months prior to the date of application;

    (iii) The gross amount received from a UK or foreign State pension or a private pension by the person or their partner in the 12 months prior to the date of application; and

    (iv) The person cannot combine he gross annual income at paragraph 15(b)(i)-(iii) with specified savings in order to meet the level of income required.

    (v) . . .

16. Where a person is in receipt of maternity, paternity, adoption or sick pay [or has been so in the 6 months prior to the date of application,] this paragraph applies:

(a) the relevant date for considering the length of employment with their current employer will be the date that the maternity, paternity, adoption or sick leave commenced [or] the date of application; and

(b) the relevant period for calculating income from their salaried employment will be the period prior to the commencement of the maternity, paternity, adoption or sick pay [or to] the date of application.

17. If a person is an equity partner, for example in a law firm, the income they draw from the partnership will be treated as salaried employment for the purposes of this Appendix and Appendix FM.

[17A. Where a person is a subcontractor under the Construction Industry Scheme administered by HMRC and dies not rely on paragraph 139(e), the income they receive as a subcontractor under the Construction Industry Scheme may be treated as income from salaried employment for the purposes of this Appendix and Appendix FM. In that case, the requirements for specified evidence in paragraph 2 must be met, subject to applying those requirements so as to reflect the person's status as a subcontractor under thw Construction Industry Scheme.].

18. When calculating income from salaried employment under paragraphs [12A and] 13 to 16, this paragraph applies:

(a) Basic pay, skills-based allowances, and UK location-based allowances will be counted as income provided that:

    (i) They are contractual; and

    (ii) Where these allowances make up more than 30% of the total salary, only the amount up to 30% is counted.

(b) Overtime, commission-based pay and bonuses [(which can include tips and gratuities paid via a tronc scheme registered with HMRC)] will be counted as income[, where they have been received in the relevant period(s) of employment or self-employment relied upon in the application.].

[(bb) In respect of a person in salaried employment at the date of application, the amount of income in sub-paragraph (b) which may be added to their gross annual salary, and counted as part of that figure for the purposes of paragraph 13(a)(i) or 13(b)(i), is the annual equivalent of the person's average gross monthly income from that income in their current employment in the 6 months prior to the date of application.]

(c) UK and overseas travel, subsistence and accommodation allowances, and allowances relating to the cost of living overseas will not be counted as income.

[(d) Gross income from non-salaried employment will be calculated on the same basis as income from salaried employment, except as provided in paragraph 18(e) and 18(f), and the requirements of this Appendix for specified evidence relating to salaried employment shall apply as if references to salary were references to income from non-salaried employment. Non-salaried employment includes that paid at an hourly or other rate [(and the number and/or pattern of hours required to be worked may vary),] or paid an amount which varies according to the work undertaken[, whereas salaried employment includes that paid at a minimum fixed rate (usually annual) and is subject usually to a contractual minimum number of hours to be worked.].

(e) For the purpose of paragraph 13(a)(i), in respect of a person in non-salaried employment at the date of application "the level of gross annual salary relied upon in the application" shall be no greater than the annual equivalent of the person's average gross monthly income from non-salaried employment in the 6 months prior to the date of application, where that employment was held throughout that period.

(f) For the purpose of paragraph 13(B)(i), "the gross annual salary from employment as it was at the date of application" of a person in non-salaried employment at the date of application shall be considered to be the annual equivalent of the person's average gross monthly income from non-salaried employment in the 6 months prior to the date of application, regardless of whether that employment as held throughout that period.]

[(g) For the purposes of paragraphs 13(c)(ii) and 13(d)(i), "the gross annual salary in the salaried employment in the UK to which they are returning" of a person who is returning to the UK to take up non-salaried employment in the UK starting within 3 months of their return is the gross annual income from that employment, based on the rent or amount of pay,a nd the standard or core hours of work, set out in the document(s) from the employer provided under paragraph 4. Notwithstanding paragraph 18(b), this may include the gross "on-target" earnings which may be expected from satisfactory performance in the standard or core hours of work.]

19. When calculating income from self-employment[, and (where income from salaried employment is also relied upon or where paragraph 9(c) applies) ongoing employment,] under [paragraphs 12A and 13(e)][, and in relation to income from employment and/or shares in a limited company based in the UK of a type to which paragraph 9 applies,] this paragraph applies:

(a) There must be evidence of ongoing self-employment[, and (where income from salaried employment is also relied upon or where paragraph 9(c) applies) ongoing employment,] at the date of application.

(b) Where the self-employed person is a sole trader or is in a partnership or franchise agreement, the income will be:
(i) the gross taxable profits from their share of the business; and
(ii) allowances or deductible expenses which are not taxed will not be counted towards income.

[(c)] Where [income to which paragraph 19 applies] is being used to meet the financial requirement for an initial application for leave to remain as a partner under Appendix FM by an applicant who used such income to meet that requirement in an application for entry clearance as a fiance(e) or proposed civil partner under that Appendix in the last 12 months, the Secretary of State may continue to accept the same level and evidence of [income to which paragraph 19 applies] that was accepted in granting the application for entry clearance, provided that there is evidence of on-going self-employment[, and where income from salaried employment is also relied upon or where paragraph 9(c) applies) ongoing employment,] at the date of the application for leave to remain.]

[(d) The financial year(s) to which paragraph 7 refers is the period of the last full financial year(s) to which the required Statement(s) of Account (SA300 or SA302) relates.]

[(e) The financial year(s) to which paragraph 9 refers is the period of the last full financial year(s) to which the required Company Tax Return(s) CT600 relates.]

20. When calculating income from specified non-employment sources under [paragraphs 12A and 13 to 15], this paragraph applies:

(a) Assets or savings must be in the name of the person, or jointly with their partner.

(b) [Any asset or savings on which income is based] must be held [or owned] by the person at the date of application.

(c) Any rental income from property, in the UK or overseas, must be from a property that is:

(i) owned by the person;

(ii) not their main residence [and will not be so if the application is granted, except in the circumstances specified in paragraph 20(e)]; and

(iii) if ownership of the property is shared with a third party, only income received from their share of the property can be counted.

[(cc) The amount of rental income from property received before any management fee was deducted may be counted.]

(d) Equity in a property cannot be used to meet the financial requirement.

[(e) Where the applicant and their partner are resident outside the UK at the date of application, rental income from a property in the UK that will become their main residence if the application is granted may only be counted under paragraph 13(c)(i) and paragraph 13(d)(ii).]

[(f) Any future entitlement to a maintenance grant or stipend of the type specified in paragraph 10(g) may be counted as though the person had received the annual amount of that grant or stipend in the 12 months prior to the date of application.]

[20A. When calculating the gross annual income from pension under paragraph 13, the gross annual amount of any pension received may be counted where the pension has become a source of income at least 28 days prior to the date of application.]

21. When calculating income under paragraphs 13 to 16, the following sources will not be counted:

(a) Loans and credit facilities.

(b) Income-related benefits: Income Support, income-related Employment and Support Allowance, Pension Credit, Housing Benefit, Council Tax Benefit and income-based Jobseeker's Allowance.

(c) The following contributory benefits: contribution-based Jobseeker's Allowance, contribution-based Employment and Support Allowance and Incapacity Benefit.

[(cc) Unemployability Allowance, Allowance for a Lowered Standard of Occupation and Invalidity Allowance under the War Pension Scheme.]

(d) Child Benefit.

(e) Working Tax Credit.

(f) Child Tax Credit.

(g) Any other source of income not specified in this appendix.

Note

Amended by HC 693, para 205 as from 6 November 2014.

Evidence of Marriage or Civil Partnerships

22. A claim to have been married in the United Kingdom must be evidenced by a marriage certificate.

23. A claim to be divorced in the United Kingdom must be evidenced by a decree absolute from a civil court.

24. A civil partnership in the United Kingdom must be evidenced by a civil partnership certificate.

25. The dissolution of a civil partnership in the UK must be evidenced by a final order of civil partnership dissolution from a civil court.

26. Marriages, civil partnerships or evidence of divorce or dissolution from outside the UK must be evidenced by a reasonable equivalent to the evidence detailed in paragraphs 22 to 25, valid under the law in force in the relevant country.

[Evidence of the Applicant Living Overseas with a Crown Servant

26A. Where

   (a) An applicant for entry clearance, limited leave to enter or remain or indefinite leave to remain as a partner under Appendix FM (except as a fiancé(e) or proposed civil partner) intends to enter or remain in the UK to begin their probationary period (or has done so) and then to live outside the UK for the time being with their sponsor (or is doing so or has done so) before the couple live together permanently in the UK; and

   (b) The sponsor, who is a British Citizen or settled in the UK, is a permanent member of HM Diplomatic Service or a comparable UK-based staff member of the British Council, the Department for International Development or the Home Office on a tour of duty outside the UK,

the applicant must provide a letter on official stationery from the sponsor's head of mission confirming the information at (a) and (b) and confirming the start date and expected end date of the sponsor's tour of duty outside the UK.]

Note

Inserted by HC 693, para 206 as from 6 November 2014.

Evidence of English Language Requirements

27. Evidence of passing an English language test in speaking and listening must take the form of either:

   (a) a certificate [and/or other document(s) for the relevant test as specified in Appendix O] that:

      (i) is from an English language test provider approved by the Secretary of State for these purposes as specified in Appendix O of these rules

      (ii) is a test approved by the Secretary of State for these purposes as specified in Appendix O of these rules

      (iii) shows the applicant's name;

      (iv) shows the qualification obtained (which must meet or exceed level A1 of the Common European Framework of Reference); and,

      (v) shows the date of award.

      Or,

   (b) a print out of the online score from a PTE (Pearson) test which:

      (i) is a test approved by the Secretary of State for these purposes as specified in Appendix O of these rules;

      (ii) can be used to show that the qualification obtained (which must meet or exceed level A1 of the Common European Framework of Reference); and,

      (iii) is from an English language test provider approved by the Secretary of State for these purposes as specified in Appendix O of these rules

28. The evidence required to show that a person is a citizen or national of a majority English speaking country is a valid passport or travel document, unless paragraphs 29 and 30 apply. A dual national may invoke either of their nationalities.

29. If the applicant has not provided their passport or travel document other evidence of nationality can be supplied in the following circumstances only (as indicated by the applicant on their application form):

(a)   where the passport [or travel document] has been lost or stolen;

(b)   where the passport [or travel document] has expired and been returned to the relevant authorities; or

(c)   where the passport [or travel document] is with another part of the [Home Office].

30. Alternative evidence as proof of nationality, if acceptable, must be either:

(a)   A current national identity document; or

(b)   An original letter from the applicant's [national government, Embassy or High Commission] confirming the applicant's full name, date of birth and nationality.

31. Evidence of an academic qualification (recognised by [UK NARIC] to be equivalent to the standard of a Bachelor's or Master's degree or PhD in the UK) and was taught in English must be either:

(a)   A certificate issued by the relevant institution confirming the award of the academic qualification showing:

(i)   the applicant's name;

(ii)   the title of award;

(iii) the date of award;

(iv)   the name of the awarding institution; and,

(v)   that the qualification was taught in English

Or,

(b)   If the applicant is awaiting graduation or no longer has the certificate and cannot get a new one, the evidence must be:

(i)   an original academic reference from the institution awarding the academic qualification that;

(1)   is on official letter headed paper;

(2)   shows the applicant's name;

(3)   shows the title of award;

(4)   confirms that the qualification was taught in English;

(5)   explains when the academic qualification has been, or will be awarded; and

(6)   states either the date that the certificate will be issued (if the applicant has not yet graduated) or confirms that the institution is unable to re-issue the original certificate of award.

or

(ii)   an original academic transcript that

(1)   is on official letter headed paper

(2)   shows the applicant's name;

(3)   the name of the academic institution;

(4)   the course title;

(5)   confirms that the qualification was taught in English; and,

(6)   provides confirmation of the award.

32. If the qualification was taken in one of the following countries, it will be assumed for the purpose of paragraph 31 that it was taught in English: Antigua and Barbuda, Australia, the Bahamas, Barbados, Belize, Dominica, Grenada, Guyana, Ireland, Jamaica, New Zealand, St Kitts and Nevis, St Lucia, St Vincent and the Grenadines, Trinidad and Tobago, the UK, the USA.

[32A. For the avoidance of doubt paragraphs 27 to 32D of this Appendix apply to fiancé(e), proposed civil partner, spouse, civil partner, unmarried partner and same sex partner applications for limited leave to enter or remain made under Part 8 of these Rules where English language requirements apply, regardless of the date of application. Paragraphs 27 to 32D of this Appendix also apply to spouse, civil partner, unmarried partner and same sex partner applications which do not meet the requirements of Part 8 of these Rules for indefinite leave to remain (where the application is for indefinite leave to remain) and are being considered for a grant of limited leave to remain where paragraph A277A(b) of these Rules applies. Any references in paragraphs 27 to 32D of this Appendix to "limited leave to enter or remain" shall therefore be read as referring to all applicants referred to in this paragraph.]

[32B. Where the decision-maker has:

    (a) reasonable cause to doubt that an English language test in speaking and listening at a minimum of level A1 of the Common Framework of Reference for Languages relied on at any time to meet a requirement for limited leave to enter or remain in Part 8 or Appendix FM was genuinely obtained; or

    (b) information that the test certificate or result awarded to the applicant has been withdrawn by the test provider for any reason,

the decision-maker may discount the document and the applicant must provide a new test certificate or result from an approved provider which shows that they meet the requirement, if they are not exempt from it.]

[32C. If an applicant applying for limited leave to enter or remain under Part 8 or Appendix FM submits an English language test certificate or result which has ceased by the date of application to be:

    (a) from an approved test provider, or

    (b) in respect of an approved test,

the decision-maker will not accept that certificate or result as valid, unless the decision-maker does so in accordance with paragraph 32D of this Appendix and subject to any transitional arrangements made in respect of the test provider or test in question.]

[32D. If an applicant applying for limited leave to enter or remain under Part 8 or Appendix FM submits an English language test certificate or result and the Home Office has already accepted it as part of a successful previous partner or parent application (but not where the application was refused, even if on grounds other than the English language requirement), the decision-maker may accept that certificate or result as valid if it is:

    (a) from a provider which is no longer approved, or

    (b) from a provider who remains approved but the test the applicant has taken with that provider is no longer approved, or

    (c) past its validity date (if a validity date is required under Appendix O), provided that when the subsequent application is made:

        (i) the applicant has had continuous leave (disregarding any period of overstaying of no more than 28 days) as a partner or parent since the Home Office accepted the test certificate as valid; and

        (ii) the award to the applicant does not fall within the circumstances set out in paragraph 32B of this Appendix.]

Note

Amended by HC 693, para 207 as from 6 November 2014. Amended by HC 693, para 208 as from 6 November 2014. Amended by HC 693, para 209 as from 6 November 2014. Further amended or Amended by HC 693, para 210 as from 6 November 2014.

Adult dependent relatives

33. Evidence of the family relationship between the applicant(s) and the sponsor should take the form of birth or adoption certificates, or other documentary evidence.

34. Evidence that, as a result of age, illness or disability, the applicant requires long-term personal care should take the form of:
    (a) [Independent] medical evidence that the applicant's physical or mental condition means that they cannot perform everyday tasks; and
    (b) This must be from a doctor or other health professional.

35. [Independent] evidence that the applicant is unable, even with the practical and financial help of the sponsor in the UK, to obtain the required level of care in the country where they are living should be from:
    (a) a central or local health authority;
    (b) a local authority; or
    (c) a doctor or other health professional.

36. If the applicant's required care has previously been provided through a private arrangement, the applicant must provide details of that arrangement and why it is no longer available.]

[37. If the applicant's required level of care is not, or is no longer, affordable because payment previously made for arranging this care is no longer being made, the applicant must provide records of that payment and an explanation of why that payment cannot continue. If financial support has been provided by the sponsor or other close family in the UK, the applicant must provide an explanation of why this cannot continue or is no longer sufficient to enable the required level of care to be provided.]

Note

Inserted by Cm 8323, para 23 as from 20 July 2012. Further amended by HC 565, paras 157–210 as from 6 September 2012. Further amended by HC 760, paras 399–441 as from 13 December 2012. Further amended by HC 1039, paras 228–279 as from on or after 6 April 2013. Further amended by HC 244, paras 32–35 as from 1 July 2013. Further amended by HC 628, paras 211–237. Further amended by HC 803, paras 42–50 as from 1 December 2013. Further amended by HC 1138, para 203–222 as from 6 April 2014. Further amended by HC 1138, para 223 shall apply to all applications decided on or after 6 April 2014.

[APPENDIX G:
COUNTRIES AND TERRITORIES PARTICIPATING IN THE TIER 5 YOUTH MOBILITY SCHEME AND ANNUAL ALLOCATIONS OF PLACES FOR 2015

Places available for use by Countries and Territories with Deemed Sponsorship Status:
- Australia – 38,000 places
- Canada – 5,000 places
- Japan – 1,000 places
- New Zealand – 11,000 places
- Monaco –1,000 places

Places available for use by Countries and Territories without Deemed Sponsorship Status:
- Taiwan – 1,000 places
- South Korea – 1,000 places
- Hong Kong – 1,000 places]

Note

Inserted by HC 1113, para 1693, para 15 as from 1 January 2012. Amended by HC 194, para 116 as from 9 July 2012. Substituted by HC 693, para 212 as from 1 January 2015.

[APPENDIX H
[APPLICANTS WHO] ARE SUBJECT TO DIFFERENT DOCUMENTARY
REQUIREMENTS UNDER TIER 4 OF THE POINTS BASED SYSTEM

[An applicant will be subject to different documentary requirements under Tier 4 of the Points Based System where he is a national of one of the following countries and he is applying for entry clearance in his country of nationality or leave to remain in the UK:]

Argentina

Australia

[Barbados]

[Botswana]

[. . .]

Brunei

Canada

Chile

...

[....]

Japan

[Malaysia]

New Zealand

[Oman]

[Qatar]

Singapore

South Korea

[. . .]

Trinidad and Tobago

[United Arab Emirates]

United States of America

Where an applicant is a dual national, and only one of their nationalities is listed above, he will be able to apply using the different documentary requirements that apply to these nationals, provided he is applying either for entry clearance in his country of nationality listed above or for leave to remain in the UK.]

An applicant will be subject to different documentary requirements under Tier 4 of the Points Based System where he is the rightful holder of one of the following passports, which has been issued by the relevant competent authority, and where he is applying for leave to remain in the UK or for entry clearance in the territory related to the passport he holds:[

- British National (Overseas)
- Hong Kong
- Taiwan (those who hold a passport issued by Taiwan that includes the number of the identification card issued by the competent authority in Taiwan)

Where an applicant is the rightful holder of a passport issued by a relevant competent authority listed above and also holds another passport or is the national of a country not listed above, he will be able to apply using the different documentary requirements that apply to rightful holders of those passports listed in this Appendix provided he is applying either for entry clearance in the territory related to the passport he holds or for leave to remain in the UK.]]

Note

Inserted by HC 1148, para 78 as from 4 July 2011. Amended by HC 1511, paras 58–63 as from 31 October 2011. Botswana and Malaysia inserted by HC 565, para 232 as from 1 October 2012. Further amended by HC 1138, para 224–226 as from 6 April 2014.

[APPENDIX I PAY REQUIREMENTS WHICH THE SECRETARY OF STATE INTENDS TO APPLY TO APPLICATIONS FOR INDEFINITE LEAVE TO REMAIN FROM TIER 2 (GENERAL) AND TIER 2 (SPORTSPERSONS) MIGRANTS MADE ON OR AFTER 6 APRIL 2016

Pay requirements which the Secretary of State intends to apply to applications for indefinite leave to remain from Tier 2 (General) and Tier 2 (Sportspersons) migrants made on or after 6 April 2016. The Immigration Rules are subject to change and applicants will need to meet the rules in force at the date of application. However, it is the Secretary of State's intention that these rules, as they relate to apply, will replace 245HF from that date.

245HF. Requirements for indefinite leave to remain as a Tier 2 (General) or Tier 2 (Sportsperson) Migrant

To qualify for indefinite leave to remain as a Tier 2 (General) Migrant or Tier 2 (Sportsperson) Migrant an applicant must meet the requirements listed below. If the applicant meets these requirements, indefinite leave to remain will be granted. If the applicant does not meet these requirements, the application will be refused.

Requirements:

(a)   The applicant must not have one or more unspent convictions within the meaning of the Rehabilitation of Offenders Act 1974.

(b)   The applicant must not fall for refusal under the general grounds for refusal, and must not be an illegal entrant.

(c)   The applicant must have a continuous period of 5 years lawfully in the UK, in any combination of the following categories of which the most recent period must have been spent with leave as a Tier 2 Migrant either:

    (i)   as a Tier 1 Migrant, other than a Tier 1 (Post Study Work) Migrant.

    (ii)   as a Tier 2 (General) Migrant, a Tier 2 (Minister of Religion) Migrant or a Tier 2 (Sportsperson) Migrant.

(d)   The Sponsor that issued the Certificate of Sponsorship that led to the applicant's last grant of leave must certify in writing:

    (i)   that he still requires the applicant for the employment in question, and

    (ii)   subject to sub-paragraph (iii), in the case of a Tier 2 (General) or Tier 2 (Sportsperson) Migrant applying for settlement, that they are being paid for the employment in question either:

        (1)   at or above the appropriate rate for the job, as stated in [the Codes of Practice in Appendix J], or

        (2)   [a gross annual salary of at least:]

            (a)   £35,000 if applying on or after 6 April 2016,

            (b)   £35,500 if applying on or after 6 April 2018,

            (c)   £35,800 if applying on or after 6 April 2019,]

whichever is higher, where the appropriate rate or salary includes basic pay and allowances as set out in paragraph 79E or paragraph 100A of Appendix A.

(iii)   where a Tier 2 (General) Migrant applying for settlement is recorded (at the time of application for settlement) by the Certificate of Sponsorship Checking Service as being sponsored to do a job that either:

(1)   appears on [the Shortage Occupation List in Appendix K], or has appeared on that list during any time the applicant was being sponsored to do that job and during the continuous period of 5 years referred to in paragraph (c) above, or

(2)   appears on [the occupations skilled to PhD-level as stated in the Codes of Practice in Appendix J], or has appeared on that list during any time the applicant was being sponsored to do that job and during the continuous period of 5 years referred to in paragraph (c) above, or

sub-paragraph (d)(ii) does not apply and the Sponsor that issued the Certificate of Sponsorship for the employment in question must certify that the Tier 2 (General) migrant applying for Indefinite Leave to Remain is being paid at or above the appropriate rate for the job as stated in [the Codes of Practice in Appendix J], where the appropriate rate or salary includes basic pay and allowances as set out in paragraph 79E of Appendix A.

(e)   [The applicant provides the specified documents in paragraph 245HF-SD to evidence the sponsor's certification in subsection (d)(ii)]

(f)   The applicant must have sufficient knowledge of the English language and sufficient knowledge about life in the United Kingdom, in accordance with paragraph 33BA of these Rules, unless the applicant is under the age of 18 or aged 65 or over at the time the application is made.

Note

Amended by HC 1138, para 227 as from 6 April 2014.

245HG.   Requirements for indefinite leave to remain as a Tier 2 (Minister of Religion) Migrant

To qualify for indefinite leave to remain as a Tier 2 (Minister of Religion) Migrant, an applicant must meet the requirements listed below. If the applicant meets these requirements, indefinite leave to remain will be granted. If the applicant does not meet these requirements, the application will be refused.

Requirements:

(a)   The applicant must not have one or more unspent convictions within the meaning of the Rehabilitation of Offenders Act 1974.

(b)   The applicant must not fall for refusal under the general grounds for refusal, and must not be an illegal entrant.

(c)   The applicant must have spent a continuous period of 5 years lawfully in the UK, in any combination of the following categories of which the most recent period must have been spent with leave as a Tier 2 Migrant (Minister of Religion):

(i)   as a Tier 1 Migrant, other than a Tier 1 (Post Study Work) Migrant, or

(ii)   as a Tier 2 (General) Migrant, a Tier 2 (Minister of Religion) Migrant or a Tier 2 (Sportsperson) Migrant,

(d)   The Sponsor that issued the Certificate of Sponsorship that led to the applicant's last grant of leave must certify in writing that he still requires the applicant for the employment in question, and

(e)   The applicant must have sufficient knowledge of the English language and sufficient knowledge about life in the United Kingdom, in accordance with paragraph 33BA of these Rules, unless the applicant is under the age of 18 or aged over 65 or over at the time the application is made.

2. In Appendix A — Attributes, after 79D insert:

79E.   Appropriate salary for indefinite leave to remain

An applicant applying for Indefinite Leave to Remain under paragraph 245HF is expected to demonstrate that he is being paid either at or above the appropriate rate for the job, as stated in [the Codes of Practice in Appendix J], or [a gross annual salary as set out in paragraph 245HF(d)(ii)(2)], whichever is higher. The appropriate rate [or gross annual salary as set out in paragraph 245HF(d)(ii)(2)] will be based on the applicant's gross annual salary to be paid by the Sponsor, as recorded in the Certificate of Sponsorship Checking Service entry to which the applicant's Certificate of Sponsorship reference number relates, subject to the following conditions:

(i)   Salary will be based on basic pay (excluding overtime);
(ii)   Allowances, such as London weighting, will be included in the salary where they are part of the guaranteed salary package and would be paid to a local settled worker in similar circumstances;
(iii) Other allowances and benefits, such as bonus or incentive pay, travel expenses and subsistence (including travel to and from the applicant's home country), will not be included.

3. In Appendix A — Attributes, after paragraph 100 insert:

Appropriate salary for indefinite leave to remain

Note

Amended by HC 1138, para 228 as from 6 April 2014. Further amended by HC 1138, para 229 as from 6 April 2014.

100A. An applicant applying for Indefinite Leave to Remain under 245HF is expected to demonstrate that he is being paid either at or above the appropriate rate for the job, as stated in [the Codes of Practice in Appendix J], or [a gross annual salary as set out in paragraph 245HF(d)(ii)(2)], whichever is higher. The appropriate rate [or gross annual salary as set out in paragraph 245HF(d)(ii)(2)] will be based on the applicant's gross annual salary to be paid by the Sponsor, as recorded in the Certificate of Sponsorship Checking Service entry to which the applicant's Certificate of Sponsorship reference number relates, subject to the following conditions:

(i)   Salary will be based on basic pay (excluding overtime);
(ii)   Allowances, such as London weighting, will be included in the salary where they are part of the guaranteed salary package and would be paid to a local settled worker in similar circumstances;
(iii) Other allowances and benefits, such as bonus or incentive pay, travel expenses and subsistence (including travel to and from the applicant's home country), will not be included.

Note

Inserted by HC 1888, para 214 as from 6 April 2016. Further amended by Cm 8423, paras 196–201 as from 20 July 2012. Further amended by HC 565, para 211 as from 6 September 2012. Further amended by HC 1138, para 230–231 as from 6 April 2014.

APPENDIX J CODES OF PRACTICE FOR TIER 2 SPONSORS, TIER 5 SPONSORS AND EMPLOYERS OF WORK PERMIT HOLDERS

APPENDIX K SHORTAGE OCCUPATION LIST

APPENDIX KOLL

APPENDIX L DESIGNATED COMPETENT BODY CRITERIA FOR TIER 1 (EXCEPTIONAL TALENT) APPLICATIONS

APPENDIX M SPORTS GOVERNING BODIES FOR TIER 2 (SPORTSPERSON) AND TIER 5 (TEMPORARY WORKER — CREATIVE AND SPORTING) APPLICATIONS

APPENDIX N APPROVED TIER 5 GOVERNMENT AUTHORISED EXCHANGE SCHEME

APPENDIX O LIST OF ENGLISH LANGUAGE TESTS THAT HAVE BEEN ASSESSED AS MEETING THE UK BORDER AGENCY'S REQUIREMENTS

APPENDIX P LISTS OF FINANCIAL INSTITUTIONS THAT DO NOT SATISFACTORILY VERIFY FINANCIAL STATEMENTS, OR WHOSE FINANCIAL STATEMENTS ARE ACCEPTED

APPENDIX Q STATEMENT OF WRITTEN TERMS AND CONDITIONS OF EMPLOYMENT REQUIRED IN PARAGRAPH 245ZO(F)(II) AND PARAGRAPH 245 ZQ (E)(II)

APPENDIX R LIST OF RECOGNISED FESTIVALS FOR WHICH ENTRY BY AMATEUR AND PROFESSIONAL ENTERTAINER VISITORS IS PERMITTED

Appendix 4

PROCEDURE RULES, PRACTICE DIRECTIONS ETC

Contents

CIVIL PROCEDURE RULES 1998

(SI 1998/3132)

Made: 10 December 1998.

Authority: Civil Procedure Act 1997, s 2.

Commencement: 26 April 1999.

[PART 54
[JUDICIAL REVIEW AND STATUTORY REVIEW]]

Amendment

Part 54 inserted by SI 2000/2092, r 22, Schedule. Date in force: 2 October 2000: see SI 2000/2092, r 1.

Part heading: substituted by SI 2003/364, r 3. Date in force: 1 April 2003: see SI 2003/364, r 1 and SI 2003/754, art 2(1), Sch 1.

[SECTION I—JUDICIAL REVIEW]

Amendment

Section heading: inserted by SI 2003/364, r 4, Schedule, Pt 1. Date in force: 1 April 2003: see SI 2003/364, r 1 and SI 2003/754, art 2(1), Sch 1.

[Rule 54.1 Scope and interpretation

(1)　[This Section of this Part] contains rules about judicial review.

(2)　[In this Section]—

　　(a)　a "claim for judicial review" means a claim to review the lawfulness of—

　　　　(i)　an enactment; or

(ii)   a decision, action or failure to act in relation to the exercise of a public function.

(b)   . . .

(c)   . . .

(d)   . . .

(e)   "the judicial review procedure" means the Part 8 procedure as modified by [this Section];

(f)   "interested party" means any person (other than the claimant and defendant) who is directly affected by the claim; and

(g)   "court" means the High Court, unless otherwise stated.

(Rule 8.1(6)(b) provides that a rule or practice direction may, in relation to a specified type of proceedings, disapply or modify any of the rules set out in Part 8 as they apply to those proceedings)]

Amendment

Inserted by SI 2000/2092, r 22, Schedule.

Date in force: 2 October 2000: see SI 2000/2092, r 1.

Para (1): words "This section of this part" in square brackets substituted by SI 2003/364, r 5(a). Date in force: 1 April 2003: see SI 2003/364, r 1 and SI 2003/754, art 2(1), Sch 1.

Para (2): words "In this Section" in square brackets substituted by SI 2003/364, r 5(b)(i). Date in force: 1 April 2003: see SI 2003/364, r 1 and SI 2003/754, art 2(1), Sch 1.

Para (2): sub-paras (b)–(d) revoked by SI 2003/3361, r 12. Date in force: 1 May 2004: see SI 2003/3361, r 1(d).

Para (2): in sub-para (e) words "this Section" in square brackets substituted by SI 2003/364, r 5(b)(ii). Date in force: 1 April 2003: see SI 2003/364, r 1 and SI 2003/754, art 2(1), Sch 1.

[Rule 54.1A Who may exercise the powers of the High Court

(1)   A court officer assigned to the Administrative Court office who is—

(*a*)   a barrister; or

(*b*)   a solicitor,

may exercise the jurisdiction of the High Court with regard to the matters set out in paragraph (2) with the consent of the President of the Queen's Bench Division.

(2)   The matters referred to in paragraph (1) are—

(*a*)   any matter incidental to any proceedings in the High Court;

(*b*)   any other matter where there is no substantial dispute between the parties; and

(*c*)   the dismissal of an appeal or application where a party has failed to comply with any order, rule or practice direction.

(3)   A court officer may not decide an application for—

(*a*)   permission to bring judicial review proceedings;

(*b*)   an injunction;

(*c*)   a stay of any proceedings, other than a temporary stay of any order or decision of the lower court over a period when the High Court is not sitting or cannot conveniently be convened, unless the parties seek a stay by consent.

(4)   Decisions of a court officer may be made without a hearing.

(5)   A party may request any decision of a court officer to be reviewed by a judge of the High Court.

(6)   At the request of a party, a hearing will be held to reconsider a decision of a court officer, made without a hearing.

(7)   A request under paragraph (5) or (6) must be filed within 7 days after the party is served with notice of the decision.]

Amendment

Inserted by SI 2012/2208, rr 2, 9(b). Date in force: 1 October 2012: see SI 2012/2208, r 1.

[Rule 54.2 When this [Section] must be used
The judicial review procedure must be used in a claim for judicial review where the claimant is seeking—

(a) a mandatory order;

(b) a prohibiting order;

(c) a quashing order; or

(d) an injunction under section 30 of the [Senior Courts Act 1981] (restraining a person from acting in any office in which he is not entitled to act).]

Amendment

Inserted by SI 2000/2092, r 22, Schedule. Date in force: 2 October 2000: see SI 2000/2092, r 1.

Provision heading: word "Section" in square brackets substituted by SI 2003/364, r 5(c).

Date in force: 1 April 2003: see SI 2003/364, r 1 and SI 2003/754, art 2(1), Sch 1.

In para (d) words "Senior Courts Act 1981" in square brackets substituted by the Constitutional Reform Act 2005, s 59(5), Sch 11, Pt 1, para 1(2). Date in force: 1 October 2009: see SI 2009/1604, art 2(d).

[Rule 54.3 When this [Section] may be used
(1) The judicial review procedure may be used in a claim for judicial review where the claimant is seeking—

(a) a declaration; or

(b) an injunction(GL).

(Section 31(2) of the [Senior Courts Act 1981] sets out the circumstances in which the court may grant a declaration or injunction in a claim for judicial review)

(Where the claimant is seeking a declaration or injunction in addition to one of the remedies listed in rule 54.2, the judicial review procedure must be used)

(2) A claim for judicial review may include a claim for damages[, restitution or the recovery of a sum due] but may not seek [such a remedy] alone.

(Section 31(4) of the [Senior Courts Act 1981] sets out the circumstances in which the court may award damages[, restitution or the recovery of a sum due] on a claim for judicial review)]

Amendment

Inserted by SI 2000/2092, r 22, Schedule. Date in force: 2 October 2000: see SI 2000/2092, r 1.

Provision heading: word "Section" in square brackets substituted by SI 2003/364, r 5(c). Date in force: 1 April 2003: see SI 2003/364, r 1 and SI 2003/754, art 2(1), Sch 1.

Para (1): words "Senior Courts Act 1981" in square brackets substituted by the Constitutional Reform Act 2005, s 59(5), Sch 11, Pt 1, para 1(2). Date in force: 1 October 2009: see SI 2009/1604, art 2(d).

Para (2): words ", restitution or the recovery of a sum due" in square brackets in both places they occur inserted by SI 2003/3361, r 13(a)(i), (b). Date in force: 1 May 2004: see SI 2003/3361, rule 1(d).

Para (2): words "such a remedy" in square brackets substituted by SI 2003/3361, r 13(b). Date in force: 1 May 2004: see SI 2003/3361, rule 1(d).

Para (2): words "Senior Courts Act 1981" in square brackets substituted by the Constitutional Reform Act 2005, s 59(5), Sch 11, Pt 1, para 1(2). Date in force: 1 October 2009: see SI 2009/1604, art 2(d).

[Rule 54.4 Permission required
The court's permission to proceed is required in a claim for judicial review whether started under this [Section] or transferred to the Administrative Court.]

Amendment

Inserted by SI 2000/2092, r 22, Schedule. Date in force: 2 October 2000: see SI 2000/2092, r 1.

Word "Section" in square brackets substituted by SI 2003/364, r 5(d). Date in force: 1 April 2003: see SI 2003/364, r 1 and SI 2003/754, art 2(1), Sch 1.

[Rule 54.5 Time limit for filing claim form
(A1) In this rule—
"the planning acts" has the same meaning as in section 336 of the Town and Country Planning Act 1990; "decision governed by the Public Contracts Regulations 2006" means any decision the legality of which is or may be affected by a duty owed to an economic operator by virtue of regulation 47A of those Regulations (and for this purpose it does not matter that the claimant is not an economic operator); and
"economic operator" has the same meaning as in regulation 4 of the Public Contracts Regulations 2006.
(1) The claim form must be filed—
(a) promptly; and
(b) in any event not later than 3 months after the grounds to make the claim first arose.
(2) The time limits in this rule may not be extended by agreement between the parties.
(3) This rule does not apply when any other enactment specifies a shorter time limit for making the claim for judicial review.
[(4) Paragraph (1) does not apply in the cases specified in paragraphs (5) and (6).
(5) Where the application for judicial review relates to a decision made by the Secretary of State or local planning authority under the planning acts, the claim form must be filed not later than six weeks after the grounds to make the claim first arose.
(6) Where the application for judicial review relates to a decision governed by the Public Contracts Regulations 2006, the claim form must be filed within the time within which an economic operator would have been required by regulation 47D(2) of those Regulations (and disregarding the rest of that regulation) to start any proceedings under those Regulations in respect of that decision.]]

Amendment
Inserted by SI 2000/2092, r 22, Schedule. Date in force: 2 October 2000: see SI 2000/2092, r 1.
Para (A1): inserted by SI 2013/1412, r 4(a)(i). Date in force: 1 July 2013: see SI 2013/1412, r 1; for transitional provision see r 5(2) thereof.
Para (2): word "limits" in square brackets substituted by SI 2013/1412, r 4(a)(ii). Date in force: 1 July 2013: see SI 2013/1412, r 1; for transitional provision see r 5(2) thereof.
Paras (4)–(6): inserted by SI 2013/1412, r 4(a)(iii). Date in force: 1 July 2013: see SI 2013/1412, r 1; for transitional provision see r 5(2) thereof.

[Rule 54.6 Claim form
(1) In addition to the matters set out in rule 8.2 (contents of the claim form) the claimant must also state—
(a) the name and address of any person he considers to be an interested party;
(b) that he is requesting permission to proceed with a claim for judicial review; . . .
(c) any remedy (including any interim remedy) he is claiming[; and
(d) where appropriate, the grounds on which it is contended that the claim is an Aarhus Convention claim].
[(Rules 45.41 to 45.44 make provision about costs in Aarhus Convention claims.)]
(Part 25 sets out how to apply for an interim remedy)
(2) The claim form must be accompanied by the documents required by [Practice Direction 54A].]

Amendment

Inserted by SI 2000/2092, r 22, Schedule. Date in force: 2 October 2000: see SI 2000/2092, r 1.

Para (1): word omitted from sub-para (b) revoked and sub-para (d) and word "; and" immediately preceding it inserted by SI 2013/262, r 18). Date in force: 1 April 2013: see SI 2013/262, r 2; for transitional provisions see r 22(8) thereof.

Para (1): words "(Rules 45.41 to 45.44 make provision about costs in Aarhus Convention claims.)" in square brackets inserted by SI 2013/262, r 18(c). Date in force: 1 April 2013: see SI 2013/262, r 2; for transitional provisions see r 22(8) thereof.

Para (2): words "Practice Direction 54A" in square brackets substituted by SI 2009/3390, r 29(b).

Date in force: 6 April 2010: see SI 2009/3390, r 1(2).

[Rule 54.7 Service of claim form

The claim form must be served on—

(a)   the defendant; and

(b)   unless the court otherwise directs, any person the claimant considers to be an interested party,

within 7 days after the date of issue.]

Amendment

Inserted by SI 2000/2092, r 22, Schedule. Date in force: 2 October 2000: see SI 2000/2092, r 1.

[Rule 54.7A Judicial review of decisions of the Upper Tribunal

(1)   This rule applies where an application is made, following refusal by the Upper Tribunal of permission to appeal against a decision of the First Tier Tribunal, for judicial review—

(*a*)   of the decision of the Upper Tribunal refusing permission to appeal; or

(*b*)   which relates to the decision of the First Tier Tribunal which was the subject of the application for permission to appeal.

(2)   Where this rule applies—

(*a*)   the application may not include any other claim, whether against the Upper Tribunal or not; and

(*b*)   any such other claim must be the subject of a separate application.

(3)   The claim form and the supporting documents required by paragraph (4) must be filed no later than 16 days after the date on which notice of the Upper Tribunal's decision was sent to the applicant.

(4)   The supporting documents are—

(*a*)   the decision of the Upper Tribunal to which the application relates, and any document giving reasons for the decision;

(*b*)   the grounds of appeal to the Upper Tribunal and any documents which were sent with them;

(*c*)   the decision of the First Tier Tribunal, the application to that Tribunal for permission to appeal and its reasons for refusing permission; and

(*d*)   any other documents essential to the claim.

(5)   The claim form and supporting documents must be served on the Upper Tribunal and any other interested party no later than 7 days after the date of issue.

(6)   The Upper Tribunal and any person served with the claim form who wishes to take part in the proceedings for judicial review must, no later than 21 days after service of the claim form, file and serve on the applicant and any other party an acknowledgment of service in the relevant practice form.

(7)   The court will give permission to proceed only if it considers—

(*a*)   that there is an arguable case, which has a reasonable prospect of success, that both the decision of the Upper Tribunal refusing permission to appeal and the decision of the First Tier Tribunal against which permission to appeal was sought are wrong in law; and (*b*)   that either—

    (i)   the claim raises an important point of principle or practice; or

    (ii)   there is some other compelling reason to hear it.

(8) If the application for permission is refused on paper without an oral hearing, rule 54.12(3) (request for reconsideration at a hearing) does not apply.

(9) If permission to apply for judicial review is granted—

    (*a*)   if the Upper Tribunal or any interested party wishes there to be a hearing of the substantive application, it must make its request for such a hearing no later than 14 days after service of the order granting permission; and

    (*b*)   if no request for a hearing is made within that period, the court will make a final order quashing the refusal of permission without a further hearing.

(10) The power to make a final order under paragraph (9)(*b*) may be exercised by the Master of the Crown Office or a Master of the Administrative Court.]

Amendment

Inserted by SI 2012/2208, rr 2, 9(c). Date in force: 1 October 2012: see SI 2012/2208, r 1.

[Rule 54.8 Acknowledgement of service

(1) Any person served with the claim form who wishes to take part in the judicial review must file an acknowledgement of service in the relevant practice form in accordance with the following provisions of this rule.

(2) Any acknowledgement of service must be—

    (a)   filed not more than 21 days after service of the claim form; and

    (b)   served on—

    (i)   the claimant; and

    (ii)   subject to any direction under rule 54.7(b), any other person named in the claim form,

as soon as practicable and, in any event, not later than 7 days after it is filed.

(3) The time limits under this rule may not be extended by agreement between the parties.

(4) The acknowledgement of service—

    (a)   must—

    (i)   where the person filing it intends to contest the claim, set out a summary of his grounds for doing so; and

    (ii)   state the name and address of any person the person filing it considers to be an interested party; and

    (b)   may include or be accompanied by an application for directions.

(5) Rule 10.3(2) does not apply.]

Amendment

Inserted by SI 2000/2092, r 22, Schedule.

Date in force: 2 October 2000: see SI 2000/2092, r 1.

[Rule 54.9 Failure to file acknowledgement of service

(1) Where a person served with the claim form has failed to file an acknowledgement of service in accordance with rule 54.8, he—

    (a)   may not take part in a hearing to decide whether permission should be given unless the court allows him to do so; but

    (b)   provided he complies with rule 54.14 or any other direction of the court regarding the filing and service of—

    (i)   detailed grounds for contesting the claim or supporting it on additional grounds; and

    (ii)   any written evidence,

may take part in the hearing of the judicial review.

(2)   Where that person takes part in the hearing of the judicial review, the court may take his failure to file an acknowledgement of service into account when deciding what order to make about costs.

(3)   Rule 8.4 does not apply.]

Amendment

Inserted by SI 2000/2092, r 22, Schedule.

Date in force: 2 October 2000: see SI 2000/2092, r 1.

[Rule 54.10 Permission given

(1)   Where permission to proceed is given the court may also give directions.]

[(2)   Directions under paragraph (1) may include—

(a)   a stay (GL) of proceedings to which the claim relates;

(b)   directions requiring the proceedings to be heard by a Divisional Court.]

Amendment

Inserted by SI 2000/2092, r 22, Schedule.

Date in force: 2 October 2000: see SI 2000/2092, r 1.

Para (2): substituted by SI 2010/2577, r 3.

Date in force: 20 October 2010: see SI 2010/2577, r 1(2).

[Rule 54.11 Service of order giving or refusing permission

The court will serve—

(a)   the order giving or refusing permission; and

(b)   any directions,

on—

(i)   the claimant;

(ii)   the defendant; and

(iii)   any other person who filed an acknowledgement of service.]

Amendment

Inserted by SI 2000/2092, r 22, Schedule.

Date in force: 2 October 2000: see SI 2000/2092, r 1.

[Rule 54.12 Permission decision without a hearing

(1)   This rule applies where the court, without a hearing—

(a)   refuses permission to proceed; or

(b)   gives permission to proceed—

(i)   subject to conditions; or

(ii)   on certain grounds only.

(2)   The court will serve its reasons for making the decision when it serves the order giving or refusing permission in accordance with rule 54.11.

(3)   [Subject to paragraph (7), the] claimant may not appeal but may request the decision to be reconsidered at a hearing.

(4)   A request under paragraph (3) must be filed within 7 days after service of the reasons under paragraph (2).

(5)   The claimant, defendant and any other person who has filed an acknowledgement of service will be given at least 2 days' notice of the hearing date.

[(6)   The court may give directions requiring the proceedings to be heard by a Divisional Court.]

[(7)   Where the court refuses permission to proceed and records the fact that the application is totally without merit in accordance with rule 23.12, the claimant may not request that decision to be reconsidered at a hearing.]]

Amendment

Inserted by SI 2000/2092, r 22, Schedule. Date in force: 2 October 2000: see SI 2000/2092, r 1.

Para (3): words in square brackets substituted by SI 2013/1412, r 4(b)(i). Date in force: 1 July 2013: see SI 2013/1412, r 1; for transitional provision see r 5(1) thereof.

Para (6): inserted by SI 2010/2577, r 4.

Date in force: 20 October 2010: see SI 2010/2577, r 1(2).

Para (7): inserted by SI 2013/1412, r 4(b)(ii). Date in force: 1 July 2013: see SI 2013/1412, r 1; for transitional provision see r 5(1) thereof.

[Rule 54.13 Defendant etc may not apply to set aside(GL)

Neither the defendant nor any other person served with the claim form may apply to set aside(GL) an order giving permission to proceed.]

Amendment

Inserted by SI 2000/2092, r 22, Schedule.

Date in force: 2 October 2000: see SI 2000/2092, r 1.

[Rule 54.14 Response

(1)　A defendant and any other person served with the claim form who wishes to contest the claim or support it on additional grounds must file and serve—

　　(a)　detailed grounds for contesting the claim or supporting it on additional grounds; and

　　(b)　any written evidence,

within 35 days after service of the order giving permission.

(2)　The following rules do not apply—

　　(a)　rule 8.5(3) and 8.5(4) (defendant to file and serve written evidence at the same time as acknowledgement of service); and

　　(b)　rule 8.5(5) and 8.5(6) (claimant to file and serve any reply within 14 days).]

Amendment

Inserted by SI 2000/2092, r 22, Schedule.

Date in force: 2 October 2000: see SI 2000/2092, r 1.

[Rule 54.15 Where claimant seeks to rely on additional grounds

The court's permission is required if a claimant seeks to rely on grounds other than those for which he has been given permission to proceed.]

Amendment

Inserted by SI 2000/2092, r 22, Schedule.

Date in force: 2 October 2000: see SI 2000/2092, r 1.

[Rule 54.16 Evidence

(1)　Rule 8.6[(1)] does not apply.

(2)　No written evidence may be relied on unless—

　　(a)　it has been served in accordance with any—

　　　　(i)　rule under this [Section]; or

　　　　(ii)　direction of the court; or

　　(b)　the court gives permission.]

Amendment

Inserted by SI 2000/2092, r 22, Schedule.

Date in force: 2 October 2000: see SI 2000/2092, r 1.

Para (1): reference to "(1)" in square brackets inserted by SI 2002/2058, r 21.

Date in force: 2 December 2002: see SI 2002/2058, r 1(b).

Para (2): in sub-para (a)(i) word "Section" in square brackets substituted by SI 2003/364, r 5(d).

Date in force: 1 April 2003 : see SI 2003/364, r 1 and SI 2003/754, art 2(1), Sch 1.

[Rule 54.17 Court's powers to hear any person

(1) Any person may apply for permission—

    (a)   to file evidence; or

    (b)   make representations at the hearing of the judicial review.

(2) An application under paragraph (1) should be made promptly.]

Amendment

Inserted by SI 2000/2092, r 22, Schedule.

Date in force: 2 October 2000: see SI 2000/2092, r 1.

[Rule 54.18 Judicial review may be decided without a hearing

The court may decide the claim for judicial review without a hearing where all the parties agree.]

Amendment

Inserted by SI 2000/2092, r 22, Schedule.

Date in force: 2 October 2000: see SI 2000/2092, r 1.

[Rule 54.19 Court's powers in respect of quashing orders

(1) This rule applies where the court makes a quashing order in respect of the decision to which the claim relates.

[(2) The court may—

    (a)

        (i)   remit the matter to the decision-maker; and

        (ii)   direct it to reconsider the matter and reach a decision in accordance with the judgment of the court; or

    (b)   in so far as any enactment permits, substitute its own decision for the decision to which the claim relates.

(Section 31 of the Supreme Court Act 1981 enables the High Court, subject to certain conditions, to substitute its own decision for the decision in question.)]

(3) . . .]

Amendment

Inserted by SI 2000/2092, r 22, Schedule.

Date in force: 2 October 2000: see SI 2000/2092, r 1.

Para (2): substituted by SI 2007/3543, r 7(b).

Date in force: 6 April 2008: see SI 2007/3543, r 1(b).

Para (3): revoked by SI 2007/3543, r 7(c).

Date in force: 6 April 2008: see SI 2007/3543, r 1(b).

[Rule 54.20 Transfer

The court may—

    (a)   order a claim to continue as if it had not been started under this [Section]; and

    (b)   where it does so, give directions about the future management of the claim.

(Part 30 (transfer) applies to transfers to and from the Administrative Court)]

Amendment

Inserted by SI 2000/2092, r 22, Schedule.

Date in force: 2 October 2000: see SI 2000/2092, r 1.

In para (a) word "Section" in square brackets substituted by SI 2003/364, r 5(e).

Date in force: 1 April 2003 (being the date on which the Nationality, Immigration and Asylum Act 2002, ss 81–117 came into force): see SI 2003/364, r 1 and SI 2003/754, art 2(1), Sch 1; for transitional provisions see SI 2003/754, art 3, and Sch 2, para 1(4A), (4B) (as amended by SI 2003/1339, art 4) and (5).

SECTION II—STATUTORY REVIEW UNDER THE NATIONALITY, IMMIGRATION AND ASYLUM ACT 2002

Rules 54.21–54.27

(Revoked by SI 2007/3543, r 7(d)(ii). Date in force: 6 April 2008: see SI 2007/3543, r 1(b).)

SECTION III—APPLICATIONS FOR STATUTORY REVIEW UNDER SECTION 103A OF THE NATIONALITY, IMMIGRATION AND ASYLUM ACT 2002

Rules 54.28–54.36

(Revoked by SI 2009/3390, r 29(c). Date in force: 15 February 2010: see SI 2009/3390, r 1(4).)

SPECIAL IMMIGRATION APPEALS COMMISSION (PROCEDURE) RULES 2003

(SI 2003/1034)

Made: 1 April 2003.

Authority: Special Immigration Appeals Commission Act 1997, ss 5, 8; Anti-terrorism, Crime and Security Act 2001, ss 24(3), 27(5); Special Immigration Appeals Commission Act 1997, ss 5(9), 8(4).

Commencement: 1 April 2003 (see r 1).

PART 1
INTRODUCTION

1 Citation and commencement

These Rules may be cited as the Special Immigration Appeals Commission (Procedure) Rules 2003 and shall come into force forthwith.

2 Interpretation

(1) In these Rules—

"the 1997 Act" means the Special Immigration Appeals Commission Act 1997;

. . .

"the 2002 Act" means the Nationality, Immigration and Asylum Act 2002; ["the 2004 Act" means the Asylum and Immigration (Treatment of Claimants, etc) Act 2004;

"the 2006 Act" means the Immigration, Asylum and Nationality Act 2006;] "appellant" means a person appealing to the Commission [or, as the case may be, making an application to the Commission for review under section 2C or section 2D of the 1997 Act], and in Part 7 is to be interpreted as additionally including—

(i)　　in relation to applications for permission to appeal or applications for bail, the applicant;　. . .

(ii)　. . .

. . .

"chairman" means the chairman of the Commission;

"Commission" means the Special Immigration Appeals Commission;

["application to the Commission for review under section 2C or section 2D of the 1997 Act" means an application to the Commission under subsection 2C(2) of the 1997 Act to set aside a direction to which that subsection applies, or an application to the Commission under subsection 2D(2) of the 1997 Act to set aside a decision to which that subsection applies, and, unless the contrary intention appears, "applying for review" and "application for review" are to be read accordingly;]

["exculpatory material" means material which adversely affects the Secretary of State's case or supports the appellant's case;]

["Immigration Acts" means the Acts referred to in section 64(2) of the 2006 Act;]

"proceedings" means any appeal or application to　. . .　the Commission;

"relevant law officer" has the meaning given by section 6(2) of the 1997 Act;

. . .

"special advocate" means a person appointed under section 6(1) of the 1997 Act to represent the interests of a party to proceedings;

"United Kingdom Representative" means the United Kingdom Representative of the United Nations High Commissioner for Refugees.

(2)　In relation to an appeal to the Commission under section 2B of the 1997 Act against a decision which was made by a person exercising the functions of the Secretary of State pursuant to section 43 of the British Nationality Act 1981, references in these Rules to the Secretary of State are to be read as if they referred to the person who made the decision.

Amendment

Para (1): definition "the 2001 Act" (omitted) revoked by SI 2007/1285, r 2(a). Date in force: 7 May 2007: see SI 2007/1285, r 1(1); for transitional provisions see r 35 thereof.

Para (1): definitions "the 2004 Act", "the 2006 Act" and "exculpatory material" inserted by SI 2007/1285, r 2(b), (e). Date in force: 7 May 2007: see SI 2007/1285, r 1(1); for transitional provisions see r 35 thereof.

Para (1): in definition "appellant" para (ii) and word omitted immediately preceding it revoked by SI 2007/1285, r 2(c). Date in force: 7 May 2007: see SI 2007/1285, r 1(1); for transitional provisions see r 35 thereof.

Para (1): words in square brackets in definition "appellant" inserted and definition "application to the Commission" inserted by SI 2013/2995, r 2, as from 28 November 2013.

Para (1): definitions "certification" and "review" (omitted) revoked by SI 2007/1285, r 2(d), (h). Date in force: 7 May 2007: see SI 2007/1285, r 1(1); for transitional provisions see r 35 thereof.

Para (1): defintion "Immigration Acts" substituted by SI 2007/1285, r 2(f). Date in force: 7 May 2007: see SI 2007/1285, r 1(1); for transitional provisions see r 35 thereof.

Para (1): in definition "proceedings" words omitted revoked by SI 2007/1285, r 2(g). Date in force: 7 May 2007: see SI 2007/1285, r 1(1); for transitional provisions see r 35 thereof.

3 Scope of these Rules

These Rules apply to the following proceedings—

(a)　　appeals to the Commission;

[(aa)　applications to the Commission for review under section 2C or section 2D of the 1997 Act;]

(b)　　. . .

    (c)   applications to the Commission for leave to appeal to the Court of Appeal, the Court of Session or the Court of Appeal in Northern Ireland; and

    (d)   applications to the Commission for bail.

Amendment

Para (aa): inserted by SI 2013/2995, r 3, as from 28 November 2013.

Para (b) revoked by SI 2007/1285, r 3. Date in force: 7 May 2007: see SI 2007/1285, r 1(1); for transitional provisions see r 35 thereof.

4 General duty of Commission

(1) When exercising its functions, the Commission shall secure that information is not disclosed contrary to the interests of national security, the international relations of the United Kingdom, the detection and prevention of crime, or in any other circumstances where disclosure is likely to harm the public interest.

(2) Where these Rules require information not to be disclosed contrary to the public interest, that requirement is to be interpreted in accordance with paragraph (1).

(3) Subject to paragraphs (1) and (2), the Commission must satisfy itself that the material available to it enables it properly to determine proceedings.

5 Delegated powers

(1) The powers of the Commission under the following provisions of these Rules may be exercised by the chairman or by any other member of the Commission who falls within paragraph 5(a) or (b) of Schedule 1 to the 1997 Act—

    (a)   rule 8(5) (extensions of time for appealing [or applying for review]);

    [(aa)   rule 9A (directions hearing);]

    (b)   [rule 11(1)] (applications for leave to vary grounds of appeal [or review]);

    (c)   . . .

    (d)   Part 5 (applications for leave to appeal to Court of Appeal, Court of Session or Court of Appeal in Northern Ireland);

    (e)   Part 6 (bail);

    (f)   rule 37(5) (applications for leave to amend or supplement material filed by Secretary of State);

    (g)   rule 39 (directions);

    (h)   rule 40(1) (orders upon failure to comply with directions);

    (i)   rule 45 (issue of witness summons); and

    (j)   rule 46 (orders that two or more proceedings be heard together).

(2) Anything of an administrative nature which is required or permitted to be done by the Commission under these Rules may be done by a member of the Commission's staff.

Amendment

Para (1): in sub-paras (a), (b), words "or applying for review" and "or review" inserted by SI 2013/2995, r 4, as from 28 November 2013.

Para (1): sub-para (aa) inserted by SI 2007/1285, r 4(a). Date in force: 7 May 2007: see SI 2007/1285, r 1(1); for transitional provisions see r 35 thereof.

Para (1): in sub-para (b) words "rule 11(1)" in square brackets substituted by SI 2007/1285, r 4(b). Date in force: 7 May 2007: see SI 2007/1285, r 1(1); for transitional provisions see r 35 thereof.

Para (1): sub-para (c) revoked by SI 2007/1285, r 4(c). Date in force: 7 May 2007: see SI 2007/1285, r 1(1); for transitional provisions see r 35 thereof.

PART 2

[APPEALS TO AND REVIEWS BY THE COMMISSION UNDER THE 1997 ACT]

[6 Scope of this Part

This Part applies to—

(a) appeals to the Commission under section 2 or 2B of the 1997 Act and section 97A(3) of the 2002 Act; and

(b) applications to the Commission for review under section 2C or 2D of the 1997 Act.]

Amendment

Part heading: substituted by SI 2013/2995, r 5, as from 28 November 2013.

Substituted by SI 2013/2995, r 6, as from 28 November 2013.

7 Starting an appeal [or application for review]

(1) An appeal to the Commission under the 1997 Act [or section 97A(3) of the 2002 Act] must be made by giving notice of appeal in accordance with these Rules.

[(1A) An application to the Commission for review under the 1997 Act must be made by giving notice of application in accordance with these Rules.]

(2) Subject to paragraph (3), notice of appeal [or notice of application for review] must be given by filing it with the Commission.

(3) A person who is in detention under the Immigration Acts . . . may give notice of appeal [or notice of application for review] either—

(a) in accordance with paragraph (2); or

(b) by serving it on the person having custody of him.

(4) When a person files a notice of appeal [or notice of application for review] in accordance with paragraph (2), he must at the same time serve a copy of the notice and any accompanying documents on the Secretary of State.

(5) Where notice of appeal [or notice of application for review] is given in accordance with paragraph (3)(b)—

(a) the person having custody of the appellant must endorse on the notice the date that it is served on him and forward it to the Commission; and

(b) the Commission must serve a copy of the notice and any accompanying documents on the Secretary of State.

Amendment

Rule heading: words in square brackets inserted by SI 2013/2995, r 7, as from 28 November 2013.

Para (1): words "or section 97A(3) of the 2002 Act" in square brackets inserted by SI 2007/1285, r 6(a). Date in force: 7 May 2007: see SI 2007/1285, r 1(1); for transitional provisions see r 35 thereof.

Para (1A): inserted by SI 2013/2995, r 8(a), as from 28 November 2013.

Paras (2)–(5): words "or notice of application for review" in each place they appear, inserted by SI 2013/2995, r 8(b)–(e), as from 28 November 2013.

Para (3): words omitted revoked by SI 2007/1285, r 6(b). Date in force: 7 May 2007: see SI 2007/1285, r 1(1); for transitional provisions see r 35 thereof.

8 Time limit for appealing [or for applying for review]

(1) Subject to the following paragraphs of this rule, a notice of appeal to the Commission under the 1997 Act [or section 97A(3) of the 2002 Act] [or a notice of application for review under the 1997 Act] must be given—

(a) if the appellant is in detention under the Immigration Acts . . . when he is served with notice of the decision against which he wishes to appeal [or direction or decision in respect of which he wishes to apply for review], not later than 5 days after he is served with that notice;

(b) otherwise—

(i) if the appellant is in the United Kingdom, not later than 10 days; or

(ii) if the appellant is outside the United Kingdom, not later than 28 days,

after the appellant is served with notice of the decision against which he wishes to appeal [or direction or decision in respect of which he wishes to apply for review].

(2) Where the appellant—

    (a)   is in the United Kingdom when he is served with notice of the decision against which he wishes to appeal; and

    (b)   may not appeal against the decision while in the United Kingdom by reason of section 2(5) of the 1997 Act,

a notice of appeal against the decision must be given not later than 28 days after his departure from the United Kingdom.

(3) Paragraph (4) applies where—

    (a)   the appellant has given notice of appeal under Part 5 of the 2002 Act against a decision ("the previous appeal"); and

    (b)   the previous appeal has lapsed due to a certificate being issued under section 97 of the 2002 Act while the appeal was pending.

(4) Where this paragraph applies, a notice of appeal to the Commission against the decision which was the subject of the previous appeal must be given—

    (a)   if the appellant is in detention under the Immigration Acts . . . when he is served with notice that the previous appeal has lapsed, not later than 5 days after he is served with that notice;

    (b)   otherwise—

        (i)   if the appellant is in the United Kingdom, not later than 10 days; or

        (ii)   if the appellant is outside the United Kingdom, not later than 28 days,

after the appellant is served with notice that the previous appeal has lapsed.

[(4A) Where a person is served with notice of certification under section 2C(1)(a) or section 2D(1)(b) of the 1997 Act, the date from which the time limit for giving a notice of application for review under paragraph (1) begins is the later of the following—

    (a)   the date he is served with that notice of certification; or

    (b)   the date on which this paragraph came into force.]

(5) The Commission may extend the time limits in this rule if satisfied that by reason of special circumstances it would be unjust not to do so.

Amendment

Rule heading: words in square brackets inserted by SI 2013/2995, r 9, as from 28 November 2013.

Para (1): words in first pair of square brackets inserted by SI 2007/1285, r 7(a). Date in force: 7 May 2007: see SI 2007/1285, r 1(1); for transitional provisions see r 35 thereof. Words in second pair of square brackets inserted by SI 2013/2995, r 10(a), as from 28 November 2013.

Para (1): in sub-para (a) words omitted revoked by SI 2007/1285, r 7(b). Date in force: 7 May 2007: see SI 2007/1285, r 1(1); for transitional provisions see r 35 thereof.

Para (1): words in square brackets in sub-paras (a), (b) inserted by SI 2013/2995, r 10(b), (c), as from 28 November 2013.

Para (4): in sub-para (a) words omitted revoked by SI 2007/1285, r 7(b). Date in force: 7 May 2007: see SI 2007/1285, r 1(1); for transitional provisions see r 35 thereof.

Para (4A): inserted by SI 2013/2995, r 10(d), as from 28 November 2013.

9 Contents of notice of appeal [or notice of application for review]

(1) The notice of appeal must set out the grounds for the appeal and give reasons in support of those grounds.

[(1A) The notice of application for review must—

    (a)   specify, by reference to the principles which would be applied in an application for judicial review, the grounds for applying for a review;

    (b)   give reasons in support of those grounds; and

    (c)   specify the order or relief sought.]

(2) The notice of appeal [or application for review] must state the name and address of—

    (a)   the appellant; and

    (b)   any representative of the appellant.

(3) The notice of appeal [or application for review] must be signed by the appellant or his representative, and dated.

(4) If the notice of appeal [or application for review] is signed by the appellant's representative, the representative must certify in the notice of appeal that he has completed the notice of appeal in accordance with the appellant's instructions.

(5) The appellant must attach to the notice of appeal [or application for review] a copy of the notice of decision against which he is appealing and any other document which was served on him containing reasons for that decision.

Amendment

Rule heading: words in square brackets inserted by SI 2013/2995, r 11, as from 28 November 2013.

Para (1A): inserted by SI 2013/2995, r 12(a), as from 28 November 2013.

Paras (2)–(5): words in square brackets inserted by SI 2013/2995, r 12(b)–(e), as from 28 November 2013.

9A Directions hearing

[(1) The Commission must, unless it orders otherwise, fix a directions hearing as soon as reasonably practicable after notice of appeal [or notice of application for review] is filed under rule 7, at which the parties and their representatives, and any special advocate, may be present.

(2) At a directions hearing the Commission may give directions as to the order in which, and the time within which, the following documents are to be filed and served—

    (a)   the statement and any material to be filed by the Secretary of State under rule 10(1);

    (b)   any statement to be filed and served by the appellant under rule 10A(1);

    (c)   any application to be made by the appellant or the special advocate under rule 10A(5);

    (d)   any statement or material to be filed under rule 10A(2) or pursuant to a direction under rule 10A(7), or served under rule 10A(8), by the Secretary of State;

    (e)   closed material, to be served by the Secretary of State on the special advocate under rule 10(4), 10A(8)(a) or 37(3);

    (f)   any reply by the special advocate under rule 38(4)(a) to any objection by the Secretary of State to disclosure;

    (g)   any response by the Secretary of State under rule 38(4)(b) to the special advocate's reply;

    (h)   any skeleton arguments on behalf of the parties and the special advocate.

(3) The Commission may also give directions as to the date of—

    (a)   any hearing of an application for bail under Part 6 of these Rules;

    (b)   any hearing under rule 38;

    (c)   the hearing of the appeal [or application for review] under rule 12.]

Amendment

Inserted by SI 2007/1285, r 8. Date in force: 7 May 2007: see SI 2007/1285, r 1(1); for transitional provisions see r 35 thereof.

Paras (1), (3) : words in square brackets inserted by SI 2013/2995, r 13, as from 28 November 2013.

10 Secretary of State's reply [to an appeal]

[(A1)   This rule does not apply to an application to the Commission for review under section 2C or 2D of the 1997 Act.]

[(1)   Where the Secretary of State intends to oppose an appeal, he must file with the Commission—

    (a)   a statement of the evidence on which he relies in opposition to the appeal; and

    (b)   any exculpatory material of which he is aware.]

(2)   Unless the Secretary of State objects to the statement being disclosed to the appellant or his representative, he must serve a copy of the statement of evidence on the appellant at the same time as filing it.

(3)   Where the Secretary of State objects to a statement filed under paragraph (1) being disclosed to the appellant or his representative, rules 37 and 38 shall apply.

[(4)   Where a special advocate is appointed, the Secretary of State must serve on him a copy of the statement and material filed under paragraph (1).]

Amendment

Rule heading: words in square brackets inserted by SI 2013/2995, r 14, as from 28 November 2013.

Para (A1): inserted by SI 2013/2995, r 15, as from 28 November 2013.

Para (1): substituted by SI 2007/1285, r 9(a). Date in force: 7 May 2007: see SI 2007/1285, r 1(1); for transitional provisions see r 35 thereof.

Para (4): inserted by SI 2007/1285, r 9(b). Date in force: 7 May 2007: see SI 2007/1285, r 1(1); for transitional provisions see r 35 thereof.

10A Further material [in relation to an appeal]

[(A1)   This rule does not apply to an application to the Commission for review under section 2C or 2D of the 1997 Act.]

[(1)   Where the appellant wishes to rely on evidence in support of his appeal, he must file with the Commission and serve on the Secretary of State and on any special advocate a statement of that evidence.

(2)   Where the appellant serves a statement under paragraph (1), the Secretary of State must—

    (a)   make a reasonable search for exculpatory material;

    (b)   notify the appellant of the extent of that search, subject to paragraph (4);

    (c)   file with the Commission any exculpatory material; and

    (d)   if he wishes to rely on further evidence, file with the Commission a statement of that evidence.

(3)   The factors relevant in deciding the reasonableness of a search include the following—

    (a)   the number of documents involved;

    (b)   the nature and complexity of the proceedings;

    (c)   whether the documents are in the control of the Secretary of State;

    (d)   the ease and expense of retrieval of any particular document;

    (e)   the significance of any document which is likely to be located during the search.

(4)   Where the Secretary of State considers that the disclosure of particular information in the notification under paragraph (2)(b) would be contrary to the public interest, he must—

    (a)   omit that information from the notification to be served on the appellant; and

    (b)   serve a copy of the notification, including that information, on the special advocate.

(5) Both the appellant and any special advocate may apply to the Commission for a direction requiring the Secretary of State to file further information about his case, or other information.

(6) An applicant under paragraph (5) must indicate why the information sought is necessary for the determination of the appeal.

(7) The Commission may make a direction on an application under paragraph (5) where it considers that the information sought—

    (a)   is necessary for the determination of the appeal; and

    (b)   may be provided without disproportionate cost, time or effort.

(8) The Secretary of State must serve a copy of any statement or material filed under paragraph (2) or of information filed pursuant to a direction under paragraph (7), at the same time as filing it, on—

    (a)   any special advocate; and

    (b)   the appellant, unless he objects to the disclosure of the statement, material or information to the appellant or his representative.

(9) Where the Secretary of State objects to any such disclosure, rules 37 and 38 apply.

(10) Any duty to file material or a statement of evidence continues until the appeal has been determined.

(11) Where material or a statement to which that duty extends comes to a party's attention before the appeal has been determined, he must immediately—

    (a)   file it with the Commission; and

    (b)   serve it on the other party and on any special advocate, except that paragraphs (8) and (9) apply to that material or statement as they apply to the material and statement referred to in those paragraphs.]

Amendment

Rule heading: words in square brackets inserted by SI 2013/2995, r 16, as from 28 November 2013.

Para (A1): inserted by SI 2013/2995, r 17, as from 28 November 2013.

Inserted by SI 2007/1285, r 10. Date in force: 7 May 2007: see SI 2007/1285, r 1(1); for transitional provisions see r 35 thereof.

[10B Secretary of State's reply to an application for review

(1) Where the Secretary of State intends to oppose an application for review, he must file with the Commission—

    (a)   a statement of the evidence on which he relies in opposition to the application for review; and

    (b)   material relevant to the issues in the application for review.

(2) Unless the Secretary of State objects to the statement and material filed under paragraph (1), or to part thereof, being disclosed to the appellant or his representative, he must serve a copy of the statement and material, or as much of the statement and material as he does not object to disclosing to the appellant or his representative, on the appellant at the same time as filing it.

(3) Where the Secretary of State objects to the statement and material filed under paragraph (1), or to part thereof, being disclosed to the appellant or his representative, rules 37 and 38 shall apply in respect of the statement and material, or the part thereof which the Secretary of State objects to disclosing to the appellant or his representative.

(4) Where a special advocate is appointed, the Secretary of State must serve on him a copy of the statement and material filed under paragraph (1).]

Amendment

Inserted by SI 2013/2995, r 18, as from 28 November 2013.

11 Variation of grounds of appeal [or application for review]
(1)   Subject to section 85(2) of the 2002 Act, the appellant may vary the grounds of appeal [or application for review] only with the leave of the Commission.
(2)   The appellant must file any proposed variation of the grounds of appeal [or application for review] with the Commission and serve a copy on the Secretary of State.

Amendment
Rule heading: words in square brackets inserted by SI 2013/2995, r 19, as from 28 November 2013.
Paras (1), (2): words in square brackets inserted by SI 2013/2995, r 20, as from 28 November 2013.

[11A Withdrawal of appeal [or application for review]
(1)   An appellant may withdraw an appeal [or application for review]—
    (a)   orally, at a hearing; or
    (b)   at any time, by filing written notice with the Commission.
(2)   An appeal [or application for review] shall be treated as withdrawn if the Secretary of State notifies the Commission that the decision to which the appeal relates has been withdrawn.
(3)   If an appeal [or application for review] is withdrawn or treated as withdrawn, the Commission must serve on the parties and on any special advocate a notice that the appeal has been recorded as having been withdrawn.]

Amendment
Inserted by SI 2007/1285, r 11. Date in force: 7 May 2007: see SI 2007/1285, r 1(1); for transitional provisions see r 35 thereof.
Rule heading: words in square brackets inserted by SI 2013/2995, r 21, as from 28 November 2013.
Paras (1)–(3): words in square brackets inserted by SI 2013/2995, r 22, as from 28 November 2013.

[11B Striking out
The Commission may strike out—
    (a)   a notice of appeal, a notice of application for review or a reply by the Secretary of State, if it appears to the Commission that it discloses no reasonable grounds for bringing or defending the appeal or for seeking or opposing the application for review, as the case may be; or
    (b)   a notice of appeal or a notice of application for review, if it appears to the Commission that it is an abuse of the Commission's process.]

Amendment
Inserted by SI 2007/1285, r 11. Date in force: 7 May 2007: see SI 2007/1285, r 1(1); for transitional provisions see r 35 thereof.
Substituted by SI 2013/2995, r 23, as from 28 November 2013.

12 Hearing of appeal [or application for review]
Every appeal [and every application for review] must be determined at a hearing before the Commission, except where—
    (a)   the appeal—
        (i)   is treated as abandoned pursuant to section 2(4) of the 1997 Act or [section 104(4) to (4C)] of the 2002 Act;
        (ii)   is treated as finally determined pursuant to section 104(5) of the 2002 Act; or
        (iii)   is withdrawn by the appellant;
    [(aa)   the application for review is withdrawn by the appellant;]
    [(b)   the Secretary of State consents to—
        (i)   the appeal being allowed; or

  (ii) the granting of the order or the relief sought in an application for review; or]

 (c) the appellant is outside the United Kingdom or it is impracticable to give him notice of a hearing and, in either case, he is unrepresented.

Amendment

Rule heading: words in square brackets inserted by SI 2013/2995, r 24, as from 28 November 2013.

First words in square brackets inserted, para (aa) inserted and para (b) substituted by SI 2013/2995, r 25, as from 28 November 2013.

In para (a)(i) words "section 104(4) to (4C)" in square brackets substituted by SI 2007/1285, r 12. Date in force: 7 May 2007: see SI 2007/1285, r 1(1); for transitional provisions see r 35 thereof.

13–25

((*Pts 3, 4) Revoked by SI 2007/1285, r 13. Date in force: 7 May 2007: see SI 2007/1285, r 1(1); for transitional provisions see r 35 thereof.*)

PART 5
APPLICATIONS FOR LEAVE TO APPEAL FROM COMMISSION

[26 Scope of this Part

This Part applies to applications to the Commission for leave to appeal to the Court of Appeal, the Court of Session or the Court of Appeal in Northern Ireland from a final determination by the Commission—

 (a) of an appeal, on a question of law; or

 (b) of an application for review under section 2C or 2D of the 1997 Act.]

Amendment

Substituted by SI 2013/2995, r 26, as from 28 November 2013.

27 Application for leave to appeal

(1) An application for leave to appeal must be made by filing with the Commission an application in writing.

[(2) Subject to paragraph (2B), the appellant must file any application for permission to appeal with the Commission—

 (a) if he is in detention under the Immigration Acts when he is served with the Commission's determination [under rule 47(3)], not later than 5 days after he is so served; and

 (b) otherwise, not later than 10 days after he is so served.

(2A) Subject to paragraph (2B), the Secretary of State must file any application for permission to appeal with the Commission [not later than 10 days after he is served with the Commission's determination under rule 47(3)].

(2B) The Commission may accept an application filed after the expiry of the relevant period in paragraph (2) or (2A) if it is satisfied that, by reason of special circumstances, it would be unjust not to do so.]

(3) The application must—

 (a) state the grounds of appeal; and

 (b) be signed by the applicant or his representative, and dated.

(4) The applicant must serve a copy of the application notice on every other party.

(5) The Commission may decide an application for leave without a hearing unless it considers that there are special circumstances which make a hearing necessary or desirable.

Amendment

Paras (2), (2A), (2B): substituted, for para (2) as originally enacted, by SI 2007/1285, r 15. Date in force: 7 May 2007: see SI 2007/1285, r 1(1); for transitional provisions see r 35 thereof.

Para (2): in sub-para (a) words "under rule 47(3)" in square brackets inserted by SI 2007/3370, r 2(a). Date in force: 1 December 2007: see SI 2007/3370, r 1(1).

Para (2A): words from "not later than" to "under rule 47(3)" in square brackets substituted by SI 2007/3370, r 2(b). Date in force: 1 December 2007: see SI 2007/3370, r 1(1).

PART 6
BAIL

28 Scope of this Part and interpretation

This Part applies to applications to the Commission under—

    (a)   the Immigration Acts; . . .

    (b)   . . .

by persons detained under those Acts, to be released on bail.

Amendment

Para (b) and word omitted immediately preceding it revoked by SI 2007/1285, r 16. Para (b) and word omitted immediately preceding it revoked by SI 2007/1285, r 16.

29 Application for bail

(1) An application to be released on bail must be made by filing with the Commission an application in writing.

(2) The application must contain the following details—

    (a)   the applicant's—

        (i)   full name;

        (ii)   date of birth; and

        (iii)   date of arrival in the United Kingdom;

    (b)   the address of the place where the applicant is detained;

    (c)   whether there are pending before the Commission any proceedings to which the applicant is a party;

    (d)   the address where the applicant will reside if his application for bail is granted or, if he is unable to give such an address, the reason why an address is not given;

    (e)   the amount of the recognizance in which he will agree to be bound;

    (f)   the full names, addresses, occupations and dates of birth of any persons who have agreed to act as sureties for the applicant if bail is granted, and the amounts of the recognizances in which they will agree to be bound;

    [(fa)   where the applicant is a person aged 18 or over, whether he will, if required, agree as a condition of bail to co-operate with electronic monitoring under section 36 of the 2004 Act;]

    (g)   the grounds on which the application is made and, where a previous application has been refused, full details of any change in circumstances which has occurred since the refusal; and

    (h)   whether the applicant requires an interpreter at the hearing and, if so, for what language and dialect.

(3) The application must be signed by the applicant or his representative or, in the case of an applicant who is a child or is for any other reason incapable of acting, by a person acting on his behalf.

Amendment

Para (2): sub-para (fa) inserted by SI 2007/1285, r 17. Date in force: 7 May 2007: see SI 2007/1285, r 1(1); for transitional provisions see r 35 thereof.

30 Bail hearing and decision

(1) Where an application for bail is filed, the Commission must—

    (a)   as soon as reasonably practicable, serve a copy of the application on the Secretary of State; and

    (b)   fix a hearing [, unless a hearing has already been fixed under rule 9A(3)(a)].

(2)   If the Secretary of State wishes to contest the application, he must file with the Commission a written statement of his reasons for doing so—

    (a)   not later than 2.00 pm the day before the hearing; or

    (b)   where he received notice of the hearing less than 24 hours before that time, as soon as reasonably practicable.

(3)   If the Secretary of State objects to a statement filed under paragraph (2) being disclosed to the applicant or his representative, rules 37 and 38 shall apply.

(4)   The Commission must serve written notice of—

    (a)   its decision upon an application for bail; and

    (b)   if and to the extent that it is possible to do so without disclosing information contrary to the public interest, the reasons for its decision,

on the applicant, the Secretary of State, and the person having custody of the applicant.

(5)   Where bail is granted, the notice must include—

    (a)   the conditions of bail; and

    (b)   the amounts in which the applicant and any sureties are to be bound.

(6)   The recognizance of the applicant or of a surety must be in writing and must state—

    (a)   the amount in which he agrees to be bound; and

    (b)   that he has read and understood the bail decision and that he agrees to pay that amount of money if the applicant fails to comply with the conditions set out in the bail decision.

(7)   The recognizance must be—

    (a)   signed by the applicant or surety; and

    (b)   filed with the Commission.

(8)   The person having custody of an applicant must release him upon—

    (a)   being served with a copy of the decision to grant bail; and

    (b)   being satisfied that any recognizances required as a condition of that decision have been entered into.

Amendment

Para (1): in sub-para (b) words ", unless a hearing has already been fixed under rule 9A(3)(a)" in square brackets inserted by SI 2007/1285, r 18. Date in force: 7 May 2007: see SI 2007/1285, r 1(1); for transitional provisions see r 35 thereof.

31 Application of this Part to Scotland

(1)   Rules 29 and 30 shall apply to Scotland with the following modifications—

    (a)   in rule 29, in paragraph (2), for sub-paragraphs (e) and (f) substitute—

        "(e)   the amount, if any, to be deposited if bail is granted;

        (f)   the full names, addresses, occupations and dates of birth of any persons offering to act as cautioners if the application for bail is granted;";

    (b)   in rule 30—

        (i)   in paragraph (5), for sub-paragraph (b) substitute—

        "(b)   the amount (if any) to be deposited by the applicant and any cautioners.";

        (ii)   paragraphs (6) and (7) do not apply; and

        (iii)   in paragraph (8), for sub-paragraph (b) substitute—

        "(b)   being satisfied that the amount to be deposited, if any, has been deposited.".

PART 7
GENERAL PROVISIONS

32 Parties

(1)   Subject to rule 2(2) and to paragraph (2) of this rule, the parties to proceedings shall be the appellant and the Secretary of State.

(2)   The United Kingdom Representative may give written notice to the Commission that he wishes to be treated as a party to proceedings, and where he gives such notice he shall be treated as a party from the date of the notice.

(3)   Any restriction imposed by or under these Rules in relation to the appellant as to—

(a)   the disclosure of material;

(b)   attendance at hearings;

(c)   notification of orders, directions or determinations; and

(d)   communication from the special advocate,

shall also apply to the United Kingdom Representative where he is a party.

33 Representation of parties

(1)   The appellant may act in person or be represented by—

(a)   a person having a qualification referred to in section 6(3) of the 1997 Act;

(b)   . . .

(c)   with the leave of the Commission, any other person,

provided that the person referred to in [sub-paragraph (a) to (c)] is not prohibited from providing immigration services by section 84 of the Immigration and Asylum Act 1999.

(2)   The Secretary of State and the United Kingdom Representative may be represented by any person authorised by them to act on their behalf.

Amendment

Para (1): sub-para (b) revoked by SI 2007/1285, r 19(a). Date in force: 7 May 2007: see SI 2007/1285, r 1(1); for transitional provisions see r 35 thereof.

Para (1): words "sub-paragraph (a) or (c)" in square brackets substituted by SI 2007/1285, r 19(b). Date in force: 7 May 2007: see SI 2007/1285, r 1(1); for transitional provisions see r 35 thereof.

34 Appointment of special advocate

(1)   Subject to paragraph (2), the Secretary of State must, upon being served with a copy of a notice of [appeal, application for review or other application] under these Rules, give notice of the proceedings to the relevant law officer.

(2)   Paragraph (1) applies unless—

(a)   the Secretary of State does not intend to—

(i)   oppose the appeal or application; or

(ii)   object to the disclosure of any material to the appellant; or

(b)   a special advocate has already been appointed to represent the interests of the appellant in the proceedings.

(3)   Where notice is given to the relevant law officer under paragraph (1), the relevant law officer may appoint a special advocate to represent the interests of the appellant in proceedings before the Commission.

(4)   Where any proceedings before the Commission are pending but no special advocate has been appointed, the appellant or the Secretary of State may at any time request the relevant law officer to appoint a special advocate.

Amendment

Para (1): words in square brackets substituted by SI 2013/2995, r 27, as from 28 November 2013.

35 Functions of special advocate

The functions of a special advocate are to represent the interests of the appellant by—

(a)   making submissions to the Commission at any hearings from which the appellant and his representatives are excluded;

(b)   [adducing evidence and] cross-examining witnesses at any such hearings; and

(c)   making written submissions to the Commission.

Amendment

In para (b) words "adducing evidence and" in square brackets inserted by SI 2007/1285, r 20. Date in force: 7 May 2007: see SI 2007/1285, r 1(1); for transitional provisions see r 35 thereof.

36 Special advocate: communicating about proceedings

(1)   The special advocate may communicate with the appellant or his representative at any time before the Secretary of State serves material on him which he objects to being disclosed to the appellant.

(2)   After the Secretary of State serves material on the special advocate as mentioned in paragraph (1), the special advocate must not communicate with any person about any matter connected with the proceedings, except in accordance with paragraph (3) [or (6)(b)] or a direction of the Commission pursuant to a request under paragraph (4).

(3)   The special advocate may, without directions from the Commission, communicate about the proceedings with—

(a)   the Commission;

(b)   the Secretary of State, or any person acting for him;

(c)   the relevant law officer, or any person acting for him;

(d)   any other person, except for the appellant or his representative, with whom it is necessary for administrative purposes for him to communicate about matters not connected with the substance of the proceedings.

(4)   The special advocate may request directions from the Commission authorising him to communicate with the appellant or his representative or with any other person.

(5)   Where the special advocate makes a request for directions under paragraph (4)—

(a)   the Commission must notify the Secretary of State of the request; and

(b)   the Secretary of State must, within a period specified by the Commission, file with the Commission and serve on the special advocate notice of any objection which he has to the proposed communication, or to the form in which it is proposed to be made.

(6)   Paragraph (2) does not prohibit the appellant from communicating with the special advocate after the Secretary of State has served material on him as mentioned in paragraph (1), but—

(a)   the appellant may only communicate with the special advocate through a legal representative in writing; and

(b)   the special advocate must not reply to the communication other than in accordance with directions of the Commission, except that he may without such directions send a written acknowledgment of receipt to the appellant's legal representative.

Amendment

Para (2): words "or (6)(b)" in square brackets inserted by SI 2007/1285, r 21. Date in force: 7 May 2007: see SI 2007/1285, r 1(1); for transitional provisions see r 35 thereof.

37 Closed material

[(1)   In this rule, "closed material" means material which the Secretary of State would otherwise be required to disclose to the appellant or his representative under rule 10, 10A or 10B, but which the Secretary of State objects to disclosing to the appellant or his representative.]

(2) The Secretary of State may not rely upon closed material unless a special advocate has been appointed to represent the interests of the appellant.

(3) Where the Secretary of State [is required by rule [10(2), 10A(8) or 10B(2)] to serve on the appellant, or wishes to rely upon,] closed material and a special advocate has been appointed, the Secretary of State must file with the Commission and serve on the special advocate—

    (a)   a copy of the closed material;

    (b)   a statement of his reasons for objecting to its disclosure; and

    (c)   if and to the extent that it is possible to do so without disclosing information contrary to the public interest, a statement of the material in a form which can be served on the appellant.

(4) The Secretary of State must, at the same time as filing it, serve on the appellant any statement filed under paragraph (3)(c).

[(4A) Where the Secretary of State serves on the special advocate any closed material which he has redacted on grounds other than those of legal professional privilege—

    (a)   he must file the material with the Commission in an unredacted form, together with an explanation of the redactions; and

    (b)   the Commission must give a direction to the Secretary of State as to what he may redact.]

(5) The Secretary of State may, with the leave of the Commission [or the agreement of the special advocate], at any time amend or supplement material filed under this rule.

Amendment

Para (1): substituted by SI 2013/2995, r 28(a), as from 28 November 2013.

Para (3): words in outer square brackets substituted by SI 2007/1285, r 22(b). Date in force: 7 May 2007: see SI 2007/1285, r 1(1); for transitional provisions see r 35 thereof.

Para (3): words in second inner square brackets substituted by SI 2013/2995, r 28(b), as from 28 November 2013.

Para (3): in sub-para (a) words ", if he has not already done so" in square brackets inserted by SI 2007/1285, r 22(c). Date in force: 7 May 2007: see SI 2007/1285, r 1(1); for transitional provisions see r 35 thereof.

Para (4A): inserted by SI 2007/1285, r 22(d). Para (4A): inserted by SI 2007/1285, r 22(d).

Para (5): words "or the agreement of the special advocate" in square brackets inserted by SI 2007/1285, r 22(e). Date in force: 7 May 2007: see SI 2007/1285, r 1(1); for transitional provisions see r 35 thereof.

38 Consideration of Secretary of State's objection

(1) Where the Secretary of State makes an objection under rule 36(5)(b) or rule 37, the Commission must decide in accordance with this rule whether to uphold the objection.

(2) The Commission must fix a hearing for the Secretary of State and the special advocate to make oral representations, unless—

    (a)   the special advocate gives notice to the Commission that he does not challenge the objection;

    (b)   the Commission has previously considered an objection by the Secretary of State [relating to the same or substantially the same communication or material], and is satisfied that it would be just to uphold the objection without a hearing; or

    (c)   the Secretary of State and the special advocate consent to the Commission deciding the issue without an oral hearing.

(3) If the special advocate does not challenge the objection, he must give notice of that fact to the Commission and the Secretary of State within 14 days after the Secretary of State serves on him a notice under rule 36(5)(b) or material under rule 37(3).

[(4) Where the Commission fixes a hearing under this rule—

(a)   the special advocate may file with the Commission and serve on the Secretary of State a reply to the Secretary of State's objection;

(b)   the Secretary of State may file with the Commission and serve on the special advocate a response to the special advocate's reply;

(c)   the Secretary of State and the special advocate must file with the Commission a schedule identifying the issues which cannot be agreed between them, which must—

    (i)   list the items or issues in dispute;

    (ii)   give brief reasons for their contentions on each; and

    (iii)   set out any proposals for the Commission to resolve the issues in dispute.]

(5)   A hearing under this rule shall take place in the absence of the appellant and his representative.

[(6)   The Commission may uphold or overrule the Secretary of State's objection.

(7)   The Commission must uphold the Secretary of State's objection under rule 37 where it considers that the disclosure of the material would be contrary to the public interest.

(8)   Where the Commission upholds the Secretary of State's objection under rule 37, it must—

(a)   consider whether to direct the Secretary of State to serve a summary of the closed material on the appellant; and

(b)   approve any such summary, to secure that it does not contain any information or other material the disclosure of which would be contrary to the public interest.

(9)   Where the Commission overrules the Secretary of State's objection under rule 37 or directs him to serve a summary of the closed material on the appellant—

(a)   the Secretary of State shall not be required to serve that material or summary; but

(b)   if he does not do so, the Commission may at a hearing at which the Secretary of State and the special advocate may make representations—

    (i)   if it considers that the material or anything that is required to be summarised might adversely affect the Secretary of State's case or support the appellant's case, direct that the Secretary of State shall not rely on such points in his case, or shall make such concessions or take such other steps, as the Commission may specify; or

    (ii)   in any other case, direct that the Secretary of State shall not rely in the proceedings on that material or (as the case may be) on that which is required to be summarised.]

Amendment

Para (2): in sub-para (b) words "relating to the same or substantially the same communication or material" in square brackets substituted by SI 2007/1285, r 23(a). Date in force: 7 May 2007: see SI 2007/1285, r 1(1); for transitional provisions see r 35 thereof.

Para (4): substituted by SI 2007/1285, r 23(b). Date in force: 7 May 2007: see SI 2007/1285, r 1(1); for transitional provisions see r 35 thereof.

Paras (6)–(9): substituted, for paras (6), (7) as originally enacted, by SI 2007/1285, r 23(c). Date in force: 7 May 2007: see SI 2007/1285, r 1(1); for transitional provisions see r 35 thereof.

[**38A Other redactions**

In any proceedings before the Commission, where the Secretary of State serves on the appellant any statement or material which he has redacted on grounds other than those of legal professional privilege, he must—

(a)   notify the appellant that the statement or material has been redacted and on what grounds it has been redacted; and

(b)   file the statement or material with the Commission in an unredacted form, together with an explanation of the redactions.]

Amendment

Inserted by SI 2007/1285, r 24. Date in force: 7 May 2007: see SI 2007/1285, r 1(1); for transitional provisions see r 35 thereof.

39 Directions

(1)   The Commission may [, in addition to its power to give directions under rule 9A(2),] give directions relating to the conduct of any proceedings.

(2)   The power to give directions is to be exercised subject to—

(a)   these Rules, including in particular the obligation in rule 4(1) to ensure that information is not disclosed contrary to the public interest; and

(b)   any decision which the Commission makes under rule 38(6).

(3)   Directions under this rule may be given orally or in writing.

(4)   Subject to rule 48, the Commission must serve notice of any written directions on every party.

(5)   Directions given under this rule may in particular—

(a)   specify the length of time allowed for anything to be done;

(b)   vary any time limit;

(c)   require any party to file and serve—

(i)   further details of his case, or any other information which appears to be necessary for the determination of the appeal or application;

(ii)   witness statements;

(iii)   written submissions;

(iv)   a statement of any interpretation requirements; or

(v)   any other document;

(d)   provide for—

(i)   a particular matter to be dealt with as a preliminary issue; or

(ii)   a pre-hearing review to be held;

(e)   relate to any matter concerning the preparation for a hearing;

(f)   specify—

(i)   the manner in which any evidence is to be given; and

(ii)   the witnesses, if any, to be heard;

(g)   provide for a hearing to be conducted or evidence given or representations made by video link or by other electronic means; and

(h)   make provision to secure the anonymity of the appellant or a witness.

(6)   The power to give directions may be exercised in the absence of the parties.

Amendment

Para (1): words ", in addition to its power to give directions under rule 9A(2)," in square brackets inserted by SI 2007/1285, r 25. Date in force: 7 May 2007: see SI 2007/1285, r 1(1); for transitional provisions see r 35 thereof.

40 Failure to comply with directions

(1)   Where a party or the special advocate fails to comply with a direction, the Commission may serve on him a notice which states—

(a)   the respect in which he has failed to comply with the direction;

(b)   a time limit for complying with the direction; and

[(c)   that the Commission may—

(i)   proceed to determine the appeal [or application for review] on the material available to it if the party or special advocate fails to comply with the direction within the time specified; or

(ii)   strike out the notice of appeal[, notice of application for review] or the Secretary of State's reply, as the case may be].

(2)   Where a party or special advocate [who has been served with such a notice fails to comply with a direction] fails to comply with such a notice, the Commission may proceed in accordance with paragraph (1)(c).

[(3) Where the Commission has struck out a notice of appeal, notice of application for review or the Secretary of State's reply under paragraph (1)(c)(ii), it may subsequently reinstate the notice or reply if it is satisfied that circumstances outside the control of the appellant or the Secretary of State (as the case may be) made it impracticable for the appellant or the Secretary of State to comply with the direction.]

Amendment

Para (1): sub-para (c) substituted by SI 2007/1285, r 26(a). Date in force: 7 May 2007: see SI 2007/1285, r 1(1); for transitional provisions see r 35 thereof.

Para (1): words in square brackets in sub-para (c) inserted by SI 2013/2995, r 29(a), (b), as from 28 November 2013.

Para (2): words "who has been served with such a notice fails to comply with a direction" in square brackets substituted by SI 2007/1285, r 26(b). Date in force: 7 May 2007: see SI 2007/1285, r 1(1); for transitional provisions see r 35 thereof.

Para (3): inserted by SI 2013/2995, r 29(c), as from 28 November 2013.

41 Notification of hearing

Unless the Commission orders otherwise, it must serve notice of the date, time and place fixed for any hearing on—

(a)   every party, whether or not entitled to attend that hearing; and

(b)   the special advocate, if one has been appointed.

42 Adjournment of hearing

The Commission may adjourn the hearing of any proceedings.

43 Hearings in private

(1) If the Commission considers it necessary for the appellant and his representative to be excluded from a hearing or part of a hearing in order to secure that information is not disclosed contrary to the public interest, it must—

(a)   direct accordingly; and

(b)   conduct the hearing, or that part of it from which the appellant and his representative are excluded, in private.

(2) The Commission may conduct a hearing or part of a hearing in private for any other good reason.

[43A Interpreters

[n appellant is entitled to the services of an interpreter for bringing his appeal [or application for review]—

(a)   when giving evidence; and

(b)   in such other circumstances as the Commission considers necessary.]

Amendment

Inserted by SI 2007/3370, r 3. Date in force: 1 December 2007: see SI 2007/3370, r 1(1).

Words in square brackets inserted by SI 2013/2995, r 30, as from 28 November 2013.

44 Evidence

(1) Subject to these Rules, the evidence of witnesses may be given either—

(a)   orally, before the Commission;

(b)   in writing, in which case it shall be given in such a manner and at such time as the Commission directs.

(2) The Commission may also receive evidence in documentary or any other form.

(3) The Commission may receive evidence that would not be admissible in a court of law.

(4) No person shall be compelled to give evidence or produce a document which he could not be compelled to give or produce on the trial of a civil claim in the part of the United Kingdom in which the proceedings before the Commission are taking place.

(5) Every party shall be entitled to adduce evidence and to cross-examine witnesses during any part of a hearing from which he and his representative are not excluded.
[(5A) The special advocate shall be entitled to adduce evidence and to cross-examine witnesses.]
(6) The Commission may require a witness to give evidence on oath.

Amendment

Para (5A): inserted by SI 2007/1285, r 27. Date in force: 7 May 2007: see SI 2007/1285, r 1(1); for transitional provisions see r 35 thereof.

45 Summoning of witnesses

(1) Subject to these Rules, the Commission may, by issuing a summons, require any person in the United Kingdom—

    (a) to attend as a witness at the hearing of any proceedings before the Commission; and

    (b) at the hearing, to answer any questions or produce any documents in his custody or under his control which relate to any matter in issue in the proceedings.

(2) No person shall be required to attend a hearing in compliance with a summons issued under paragraph (1) unless—

    (a) the summons is served on him; and

    (b) the necessary expenses of his attendance are paid or tendered to him.

(3) Where a summons is issued at the request of a party, that party must pay or tender the expenses of the witness.

46 Hearing two or more proceedings together

(1) Where two or more appeals [or applications] are pending at the same time, the Commission may direct them to be heard together if—

    (a) some common question of law or fact arises in each of them;

    (b) they relate to decisions or action taken in respect of persons who are members of the same family; or

    (c) for some other reason it is desirable for the proceedings to be heard together.

(2) Except where [paragraph (3)] applies, the Commission must give all the parties who would be entitled to attend the hearing of the proceedings an opportunity to make representations before hearing proceedings together under this rule.

[(3) Where two or more appeals which relate to decisions or action taken in respect of the same person are pending at the same time, the Commission must so far as is reasonably practicable hear the appeals together, unless to do so would cause unreasonable delay to any of the appeals.]

Amendment

Para (1): words "or applications" in square brackets substituted by SI 2007/1285, r 28(a). Date in force: 7 May 2007: see SI 2007/1285, r 1(1); for transitional provisions see r 35 thereof.

Para (2): words "paragraph (3)" in square brackets substituted by SI 2007/1285, r 28(b). Date in force: 7 May 2007: see SI 2007/1285, r 1(1); for transitional provisions see r 35 thereof.

Para (3): inserted by SI 2007/1285, r 28(c). Date in force: 7 May 2007: see SI 2007/1285, r 1(1); for transitional provisions see r 35 thereof.

47 Giving of determination

(1) This rule applies when the Commission determines any proceedings.

(2) The Commission must record its decision and the reasons for it.

(3) The Commission must [, within a reasonable time,] serve on the parties a written determination containing its decision and, if and to the extent that it is possible to do so without disclosing information contrary to the public interest, the reasons for it.

(4) Where the determination under paragraph (3) does not include the full reasons for its decision, the Commission must serve on the Secretary of State and the special advocate a separate determination including those reasons.

[(5) Where the Commission serves a separate determination under paragraph (4), the special advocate may apply to the Commission to amend that determination and the determination under paragraph (3) on the grounds that the separate determination contains material the disclosure of which would not be contrary to the public interest.

(6) The special advocate must serve a copy of an application under paragraph (5) on the Secretary of State.

(7) The Commission must give the special advocate and the Secretary of State an opportunity to make representations and may determine the application with or without a hearing.]

Amendment

Para (3): words ", within a reasonable time," in square brackets inserted by SI 2007/3370, r 4. Date in force: 1 December 2007: see SI 2007/3370, r 1(1).

Paras (5)–(7): inserted by SI 2007/1285, r 29. Date in force: 7 May 2007: see SI 2007/1285, r 1(1); for transitional provisions see r 35 thereof.

48 [Application by Secretary of State to amend determination etc]

(1) This rule applies where the Commission proposes to serve [on the appellant]—
    (a)   [notice of] any order or direction made or given in the absence of the Secretary of State; or
    (b)   its determination of the proceedings.

(2) Before the Commission serves [any such document] on the appellant, it must first serve notice on the Secretary of State [and any special advocate] of its intention to do so.

(3) The Secretary of State may, within 5 days of being served with notice under paragraph (2), apply to the Commission to [amend the order, direction or proposed determination] if he considers that—
    (a)   his compliance with the order or direction; or
    (b)   the notification to the appellant of any matter contained in the order, direction or determination,
would cause information to be disclosed contrary to the public interest.

(4) Where the Secretary of State makes an application under paragraph (3), he must at the same time serve a copy of it on the special advocate, if one has been appointed.

[(5) The Commission must give the special advocate and the Secretary of State an opportunity to make representations and may determine the application with or without a hearing.]

(6) The Commission must not serve [any document] on the appellant as mentioned in paragraph (1) before the time for the Secretary of State to make an application under paragraph (3) has expired [or, where such an application is made, before it has been determined].

Amendment

Provision heading: substituted by SI 2007/1285, r 30(a). Date in force: 7 May 2007: see SI 2007/1285, r 1(1); for transitional provisions see r 35 thereof.

Para (1): words "on the appellant" in square brackets substituted by SI 2007/1285, r 30(b). Date in force: 7 May 2007: see SI 2007/1285, r 1(1); for transitional provisions see r 35 thereof.

Para (1): in sub-para (a) words "notice of" in square brackets inserted by SI 2007/1285, r 30(c). Date in force: 7 May 2007: see SI 2007/1285, r 1(1); for transitional provisions see r 35 thereof.

Para (2): words "any such document" in square brackets substituted by SI 2007/1285, r 30(d). Date in force: 7 May 2007: see SI 2007/1285, r 1(1); for transitional provisions see r 35 thereof.

Para (2): words "and any special advocate" in square brackets inserted by SI 2007/1285, r 30(e). Date in force: 7 May 2007: see SI 2007/1285, r 1(1); for transitional provisions see r 35 thereof.

Para (3): words "amend the order, direction or proposed determination" in square brackets substituted by SI 2007/1285, r 30(f). Date in force: 7 May 2007: see SI 2007/1285, r 1(1); for transitional provisions see r 35 thereof.

Para (5): substituted by SI 2007/1285, r 30(g). Date in force: 7 May 2007: see SI 2007/1285, r 1(1); for transitional provisions see r 35 thereof.

Para (6): words "any document" in square brackets substituted by SI 2007/1285, r 30(h). Date in force: 7 May 2007: see SI 2007/1285, r 1(1); for transitional provisions see r 35 thereof.

Para (6): words "or, where such an application is made, before it has been determined" in square brackets inserted by SI 2007/1285, r 30(i). Date in force: 7 May 2007: see SI 2007/1285, r 1(1); for transitional provisions see r 35 thereof.

49 Filing and service of documents

(1) Any document which is required or permitted by these Rules or by an order of the Commission to be filed with the Commission or served on any person may be—

    (a)   delivered or sent by post to [a postal address];

    (b)   sent by fax to a fax number; . . .

    (c)   sent by e-mail to an e-mail address [; or

    (d)   sent through a document exchange to a document exchange number or address],

specified for that purpose by the Commission or the person to which the document is directed.

(2) A document to be served on an individual may be served personally by leaving it with that individual.

(3) Subject to paragraph (4), if any document is served on a person who has notified the Commission that he is acting as the representative of a party, it shall be deemed to have been served on that party.

(4) Paragraph (3) does not apply if the Commission directs that a document is to be served on both a party and his representative.

(5) Any document that is served on a person in accordance with this rule shall, unless the contrary is proved, be deemed to be served—

    (a)   where the document is sent by post [or through a document exchange] from and to a place within the United Kingdom, on the second day after it was sent;

    (b)   where the document is sent by post from or to a place outside the United Kingdom, on the twenty-eighth day after it was sent; and

    (c)   in any other case, on the day on which the document was sent or delivered to, or left with, that person.

(6) Any document which is filed with the Commission shall be treated as being filed on the day on which it is received by the Commission.

Amendment

Para (1): in sub-para (a) words "a postal address" in square brackets substituted by SI 2007/1285, r 31(a)(i). Date in force: 7 May 2007: see SI 2007/1285, r 1(1); for transitional provisions see r 35 thereof.

Para (1): in sub-para (b) word omitted revoked by SI 2007/1285, r 31(a)(ii). Date in force: 7 May 2007: see SI 2007/1285, r 1(1); for transitional provisions see r 35 thereof.

Para (1): sub-para (d) and word "; or" immediately preceding it inserted by SI 2007/1285, r 31(a)(iii). Date in force: 7 May 2007: see SI 2007/1285, r 1(1); for transitional provisions see r 35 thereof.

Para (5): in sub-para (a) words "or through a document exchange" in square brackets inserted by SI 2007/1285, r 31(b). Date in force: 7 May 2007: see SI 2007/1285, r 1(1); for transitional provisions see r 35 thereof.

50 Address for service

(1) Every party, and any person representing a party or acting as special advocate, must notify the Commission of a postal address at which documents may be served on him and of any changes to that address.

(2) Until a party, representative or special advocate notifies the Commission of a change of address, any document served on him at the most recent [postal] address he has given to the Commission shall be deemed to have been properly served on him.

Amendment

Para (2): word "postal" in square brackets inserted by SI 2007/1285, r 32. Date in force: 7 May 2007: see SI 2007/1285, r 1(1); for transitional provisions see r 35 thereof.

51 Calculation of time

(1) Where a period of time for doing any act is specified by these Rules or by a direction of the Commission, that period is to be calculated—
- (a) excluding the day on which the period begins; and
- (b) where the period is 10 days or less, excluding any day which is not a business day.

(2) Where the time specified by these Rules or by a direction of the Commission for doing any act ends on a day which is not a business day, that act is done in time if it is done on the next business day.

(3) In this rule, "business day" means any day other than a Saturday or Sunday, a bank holiday, Christmas Day, 27th to 31st December or Good Friday.

52 Signature of documents

Any requirement in these Rules for a document to be signed shall be satisfied, in the case of a document which is filed or served by e-mail in accordance with these Rules, by the person who is required to sign the document typing his name in it [or producing it by computer or other mechanical means].

Amendment

Words "or producing it by computer or other mechanical means" in square brackets inserted by SI 2007/1285, r 33. Date in force: 7 May 2007: see SI 2007/1285, r 1(1); for transitional provisions see r 35 thereof.

53 Errors of procedure

Where in any proceedings, before they have been determined by the Commission, there has been an error of procedure such as a failure to comply with a rule—
- (a) subject to these Rules, the error does not invalidate any step taken in the proceedings unless the Commission so orders; and
- (b) the Commission may make an order or take any other step that it considers appropriate to remedy the error.

54 Correction of orders and determinations

(1) The Commission may at any time amend an order or determination to correct a clerical error or other accidental slip or omission.

(2) Where an order or determination is amended under this rule—
- (a) [subject to rule 48(1)(b) and (2),] the Commission must serve the amended order or determination on every person on whom the original order or determination was served; and
- (b) the time within which a party may apply for permission to appeal against an amended determination runs from the date on which the party is served with the amended determination.

Amendment

Para (2): in sub-para (a) words "subject to rule 48(1)(b) and (2)," in square brackets inserted by SI 2007/1285, r 34. Date in force: 7 May 2007: see SI 2007/1285, r 1(1); for transitional provisions see r 35 thereof.

PART 8
REVOCATIONS AND TRANSITIONAL PROVISIONS

55 Revocations

The following Rules are revoked—

    (a)   the Special Immigration Appeals Commission (Procedure) Rules 1998 ("the 1998 Rules"); and

    (b)   the Special Immigration Appeals Commission (Procedure) (Amendment) Rules 2000.

56 Transitional provisions

(1)   These Rules shall apply—

    (a)   with appropriate modifications, to any proceedings pending on the date on which they come into force, to which immediately before that date the 1998 Rules applied; and

    (b)   to any appeal under section 2B of the 1997 Act pending on the date on which these Rules come into force.

(2)   In relation to any proceedings pending on the date on which these Rules come into force, anything done or any direction given before that date under the 1998 Rules or under any other powers of the Commission shall be treated as if done or given under these Rules.

(3)   If—

    (a)   a notice of appeal is given or an application is made to the Commission within 5 days of the date on which these Rules come into force; and

    (b)   the notice of appeal or application would have been given or made in time if these Rules had not come into force,

the notice of appeal or application shall be treated as being given or made in time, notwithstanding any time limit in these Rules.

FIRST TIER AND UPPER TRIBUNAL
CHILD, VULNERABLE ADULT AND SENSITIVE WITNESSES
PRACTICE DIRECTION: 30 OCTOBER 2008

1.   In this Practice Direction:

(a)   "child" means a person who has not attained the age of 18;

(b)   "vulnerable adult" has the same meaning as in the Safeguarding Vulnerable Groups Act 2006;

(c)   "sensitive witness" means an adult witness where the quality of evidence given by the witness is likely to be diminished by reason of fear or distress on the part of the witness in connection with giving evidence in the case.

CIRCUMSTANCES UNDER WHICH A CHILD, VULNERABLE ADULT OR SENSITVE WITNESS MAY GIVE EVIDENCE

2.   A child, vulnerable adult or sensitive witness will only be required to attend as a witness and give evidence at a hearing where the Tribunal determines that the evidence is necessary to enable the fair hearing of the case and their welfare would not be prejudiced by doing so.

3.   In determining whether it is necessary for a child, vulnerable adult or sensitive witness to give evidence to enable the fair hearing of a case the Tribunal should have regard to all the available evidence and any representations made by the parties.

4.   In determining whether the welfare of the child, vulnerable adult or sensitive witness would be prejudiced it may be appropriate for the Tribunal to invite submissions from interested persons, such as a child's parents.

5.   The Tribunal may decline to issue a witness summons under the Tribunal Procedure Rules or to permit a child, vulnerable adult or sensitive witness to give

evidence where it is satisfied that the evidence is not necessary to enable the fair hearing of the case and must decline to do so where the witness's welfare would be prejudiced by them giving evidence.

MANNER IN WHICH EVIDENCE IS GIVEN

6.   The Tribunal must consider how to facilitate the giving of any evidence by a child, vulnerable adult or sensitive witness.

7.   It may be appropriate for the Tribunal to direct that the evidence should be given by telephone, video link or other means directed by the Tribunal, or to direct that a person be appointed for the purpose of the hearing who has the appropriate skills or experience in facilitating the giving of evidence by a child, vulnerable adult or sensitive witness.

8.   This Practice Direction is made by the Senior President of Tribunals with the agreement of the Lord Chancellor. It is made in the exercise of powers conferred by the Tribunals, Courts and Enforcement Act 2007.

LORD JUSTICE CARNWATH

SENIOR PRESIDENT OF TRIBUNALS

30 October 2008

FORM OF DECISIONS AND NEUTRAL CITATION FIRST-TIER TRIBUNAL AND UPPER TRIBUNAL ON OR AFTER 3 NOVEMBER 2008
PRACTICE STATEMENT: 31 OCTOBER 2008

1.   This Practice Statement sets out the arrangements for the neutral citation of decisions or written reasons (referred to in this Practice Statement simply as "decisions") of the First-tier Tribunal and Upper Tribunal from 3 November 2008. It follows international practice designed to facilitate their publication on the World Wide Web and their subsequent use by those who have access to it.

FORM OF DECISIONS

2.   First-tier Tribunal and Upper Tribunal decisions must be prepared for delivery, or issued as approved decisions, with paragraph numbering.

NEUTRAL CITATIONS

3.   In the Upper Tribunal a unique number will be issued for a decision, on request, by the Upper Tribunal Office. In the First-tier Tribunal requests for a unique number for a decision should be made to the Chamber President. If the Chamber President considers it appropriate, the decision will then be referred to the Upper Tribunal and a unique number will be issued by the Upper Tribunal Office.

4.   The decisions will be numbered in the following way:

Upper Tribunal (Administrative Appeals Chamber): [200n] UKUT 1 (AAC) First-tier Tribunal (Health Education and Social Care Chamber): [200n] UKFTT 1 (HESC) First-tier Tribunal (Social Entitlement Chamber): [200n] UKFTT 2 (SEC) First-tier Tribunal (War Pensions and Armed Forces Compensation Chamber): [200n] UKFTT 3 (WPAFCC)

5.   There will be consecutive numbering of decisions in each of the First-tier Tribunal and the Upper Tribunal. Thus, the first three decisions of [2000n] delivered by the First-tier Tribunal would be numbered 1, 2, 3 irrespective of whether the case was allocated to HESC, SEC or WPAFCC.

6.   Under these arrangements, paragraph 77 in Jones v Secretary of State for the Department of Work and Pensions, the tenth numbered decision of the year in the Upper Tribunal, would be cited:

Jones v Secretary of State for the Department of Work and Pensions [200n] UKUT 10 (AAC) at [77]

7. The paragraph number allotted by the Upper Tribunal Office should be used in all references to that decision.

8. Where anonymity was previously given to a party in a tribunal case, that practice will continue pending further review.

9. The neutral citation will be the official number attributed to the decision by the Tribunal and must always be used on at least one occasion when the decision is cited in a later decision or judgment. Once the decision is reported, the neutral citation will appear in front of any citation from the law report series. Thus:

Jones v Secretary of State for the Department of Work and Pensions [200n] UKUT 10 (AAC) at [77], [200n] 2 All ER 364, R(AF) 3/08

10. Given that this form of citation contains the official number given to each decision it is hoped that it will be reproduced wherever the decision is published.

LORD JUSTICE CARNWATH

SENIOR PRESIDENT OF TRIBUNALS

31 October 2008

TRIBUNAL PROCEDURE (FIRST-TIER TRIBUNAL) (SOCIAL ENTITLEMENT CHAMBER) RULES 2008

(SI 2008/2685)

Made: 9 October 2008.

Authority: Social Security Act 1998, s 20(2), (3); Tribunals, Courts and Enforcement Act 2007, ss 9(3), 22, 29(3), Sch 5.

Commencement: 3 November 2008.

PART 1
INTRODUCTION

1 Citation, commencement, application and interpretation

(1) These Rules may be cited as the Tribunal Procedure (First-tier Tribunal) (Social Entitlement Chamber) Rules 2008 and come into force on 3rd November 2008.

[(2) These Rules apply to proceedings before the Social Entitlement Chamber of the First-tier Tribunal.]

(3) In these Rules—

"the 2007 Act" means the Tribunals, Courts and Enforcement Act 2007;

"appeal" includes an application under section 19(9) of the Tax Credits Act 2002;

"appellant" means a person who makes an appeal to the Tribunal, or a person substituted as an appellant under rule 9(1) (substitution of parties);

"asylum support case" means proceedings concerning the provision of support for an asylum seeker [, a failed asylum seeker or a person designated under section 130 of the Criminal Justice and Immigration Act 2008 (designation), or the dependants of any such person];

"criminal injuries compensation case" means proceedings concerning the payment of compensation under a scheme made under the Criminal Injuries Compensation Act 1995 [or section 47 of the Crime and Security Act 2010];

"decision maker" means the maker of a decision against which an appeal has been brought;

"dispose of proceedings" includes, unless indicated otherwise, disposing of a part of the proceedings;

"document" means anything in which information is recorded in any form, and an obligation under these Rules to provide or allow access to a document or a copy of a document for any purpose means, unless the Tribunal directs otherwise, an obligation to provide or allow access to such document or copy in a legible form or in a form which can be readily made into a legible form;

"hearing" means an oral hearing and includes a hearing conducted in whole or in part by video link, telephone or other means of instantaneous two-way electronic communication;

"legal representative" means [a person who, for the purposes of the Legal Services Act 2007, is an authorised person in relation to an activity which constitutes the exercise of a right of audience or the conduct of litigation within the meaning of that Act], an advocate or solicitor in Scotland or a barrister or solicitor in Northern Ireland;

"party" means—

    (a)   a person who is an appellant or respondent in proceedings before the Tribunal;

    (b)   a person who makes a reference to the Tribunal under section 28D of the Child Support Act 1991;

    (c)   a person who starts proceedings before the Tribunal under paragraph 3 of Schedule 2 to the Tax Credits Act 2002; or

    (d)   if the proceedings have been concluded, a person who was a party under paragraph (a), (b) or (c) when the Tribunal finally disposed of all issues in the proceedings;

"practice direction" means a direction given under section 23 of the 2007 Act;

"respondent" means—

    (a)   in an appeal against a decision, the decision maker and any person other than the appellant who had a right of appeal against the decision;

    (b)   in a reference under section 28D of the Child Support Act 1991—

        (i)   the absent parent or non-resident parent;

        (ii)   the person with care; and

        (iii)   in Scotland, the child if the child made the application for a departure direction or a variation;

    (c)   in proceedings under paragraph 3 of Schedule 2 to the Tax Credits Act 2002, a person on whom it is proposed that a penalty be imposed; or

    (d)   a person substituted or added as a respondent under rule 9 (substitution and addition of parties);

"social security and child support case" means any case allocated to the Social Entitlement Chamber except an asylum support case or a criminal injuries compensation case;

"Tribunal" means the First-tier Tribunal.

Amendment

Para (2): substituted by SI 2010/2653, r 5(1), (2). Date in force: 29 November 2010: see SI 2010/2653, r 1.

Para (3): in definition "asylum support case" words in square brackets substituted by SI 2009/274, r 2. Date in force: 1 April 2009: see SI 2009/274, r 1.

Para (3): in definition "criminal injuries compensation case" words in square brackets inserted by SI 2013/477, rr 22, 23. Date in force: 8 April 2013: see SI 2013/477, r 1(2)(a).

Para (3): in definition "legal representatives" words from "a person who" to "of that Act" in square brackets substituted by SI 2010/43, reg 3. Date in force: 18 January 2010: see SI 2010/43, r 1.

Para (3): definition "Social Entitlement Chamber" (omitted) revoked by SI 2011/651, r 4(1), (2)(a). Date in force: 1 April 2011: see SI 2011/651, r 1(2)(a).

Para (3): in definition "social security and child support case" words "of the First-tier Tribunal" in square brackets inserted by SI 2011/651, r 4(1), (2)(b). Date in force: 1 April 2011: see SI 2011/651, r 1(2)(a).

2 Overriding objective and parties' obligation to co-operate with the Tribunal

(1)   The overriding objective of these Rules is to enable the Tribunal to deal with cases fairly and justly.

(2)   Dealing with a case fairly and justly includes—

(a)   dealing with the case in ways which are proportionate to the importance of the case, the complexity of the issues, the anticipated costs and the resources of the parties;

(b)   avoiding unnecessary formality and seeking flexibility in the proceedings;

(c)   ensuring, so far as practicable, that the parties are able to participate fully in the proceedings;

(d)   using any special expertise of the Tribunal effectively; and

(e)   avoiding delay, so far as compatible with proper consideration of the issues.

(3)   The Tribunal must seek to give effect to the overriding objective when it—

(a)   exercises any power under these Rules; or

(b)   interprets any rule or practice direction.

(4)   Parties must—

(a)   help the Tribunal to further the overriding objective; and

(b)   co-operate with the Tribunal generally.

3 Alternative dispute resolution and arbitration

(1)   The Tribunal should seek, where appropriate—

(a)   to bring to the attention of the parties the availability of any appropriate alternative procedure for the resolution of the dispute; and

(b)   if the parties wish and provided that it is compatible with the overriding objective, to facilitate the use of the procedure.

(2)   Part 1 of the Arbitration Act 1996 does not apply to proceedings before the Tribunal.

PART 2
GENERAL POWERS AND PROVISIONS

4 Delegation to staff

(1)   Staff appointed under section 40(1) of the 2007 Act (tribunal staff and services) may, with the approval of the Senior President of Tribunals, carry out functions of a judicial nature permitted or required to be done by the Tribunal.

(2)   The approval referred to at paragraph (1) may apply generally to the carrying out of specified functions by members of staff of a specified description in specified circumstances.

(3)   Within 14 days after the date on which the Tribunal sends notice of a decision made by a member of staff under paragraph (1) to a party, that party may apply in writing to the Tribunal for that decision to be considered afresh by a judge.

5 Case management powers

(1) Subject to the provisions of the 2007 Act and any other enactment, the Tribunal may regulate its own procedure.

(2) The Tribunal may give a direction in relation to the conduct or disposal of proceedings at any time, including a direction amending, suspending or setting aside an earlier direction.

(3) In particular, and without restricting the general powers in paragraphs (1) and (2), the Tribunal may—

    (a) extend or shorten the time for complying with any rule, practice direction or direction;

    [(aa) extend the time within which an appeal must be brought under regulation 28(1) of the Child Benefit and Guardian's Allowance (Decisions and Appeals) Regulations 2003;]

    (b) consolidate or hear together two or more sets of proceedings or parts of proceedings raising common issues, or treat a case as a lead case (whether in accordance with rule 18 (lead cases) or otherwise);

    (c) permit or require a party to amend a document;

    (d) permit or require a party or another person to provide documents, information, evidence or submissions to the Tribunal or a party;

    (e) deal with an issue in the proceedings as a preliminary issue;

    (f) hold a hearing to consider any matter, including a case management issue;

    (g) decide the form of any hearing;

    (h) adjourn or postpone a hearing;

    (i) require a party to produce a bundle for a hearing;

    (j) stay (or, in Scotland, sist) proceedings;

    (k) transfer proceedings to another court or tribunal if that other court or tribunal has jurisdiction in relation to the proceedings and—

        (i) because of a change of circumstances since the proceedings were started, the Tribunal no longer has jurisdiction in relation to the proceedings; or

        (ii) the Tribunal considers that the other court or tribunal is a more appropriate forum for the determination of the case; or

    (l) suspend the effect of its own decision pending the determination by the Tribunal or the Upper Tribunal of an application for permission to appeal against, and any appeal or review of, that decision.

Amendment

Para (3): sub-para (aa) inserted by SI 2013/2067, rr 22, 23. Date in force: 1 November 2013: see SI 2013/2067, r 1.

6 Procedure for applying for and giving directions

(1) The Tribunal may give a direction on the application of one or more of the parties or on its own initiative.

(2) An application for a direction may be made—

    (a) by sending or delivering a written application to the Tribunal; or

    (b) orally during the course of a hearing.

(3) An application for a direction must include the reason for making that application.

(4) Unless the Tribunal considers that there is good reason not to do so, the Tribunal must send written notice of any direction to every party and to any other person affected by the direction.

(5) If a party or any other person sent notice of the direction under paragraph (4) wishes to challenge a direction which the Tribunal has given, they may do so by applying for another direction which amends, suspends or sets aside the first direction.

7 Failure to comply with rules etc

(1) An irregularity resulting from a failure to comply with any requirement in these Rules, a practice direction or a direction, does not of itself render void the proceedings or any step taken in the proceedings.

(2) If a party has failed to comply with a requirement in these Rules, a practice direction or a direction, the Tribunal may take such action as it considers just, which may include—

    (a)   waiving the requirement;

    (b)   requiring the failure to be remedied;

    (c)   exercising its power under rule 8 (striking out a party's case); or

    (d)   exercising its power under paragraph (3).

(3) The Tribunal may refer to the Upper Tribunal, and ask the Upper Tribunal to exercise its power under section 25 of the 2007 Act in relation to, any failure by a person to comply with a requirement imposed by the Tribunal—

    (a)   to attend at any place for the purpose of giving evidence;

    (b)   otherwise to make themselves available to give evidence;

    (c)   to swear an oath in connection with the giving of evidence;

    (d)   to give evidence as a witness;

    (e)   to produce a document; or

    (f)   to facilitate the inspection of a document or any other thing (including any premises).

8 Striking out a party's case

(1) The proceedings, or the appropriate part of them, will automatically be struck out if the appellant has failed to comply with a direction that stated that failure by a party to comply with the direction would lead to the striking out of the proceedings or that part of them.

(2) The Tribunal must strike out the whole or a part of the proceedings if the Tribunal—

    (a)   does not have jurisdiction in relation to the proceedings or that part of them; and

    (b)   does not exercise its power under rule 5(3)(k)(i) (transfer to another court or tribunal) in relation to the proceedings or that part of them.

(3) The Tribunal may strike out the whole or a part of the proceedings if—

    (a)   the appellant has failed to comply with a direction which stated that failure by the appellant to comply with the direction could lead to the striking out of the proceedings or part of them;

    (b)   the appellant has failed to co-operate with the Tribunal to such an extent that the Tribunal cannot deal with the proceedings fairly and justly; or

    (c)   the Tribunal considers there is no reasonable prospect of the appellant's case, or part of it, succeeding.

(4) The Tribunal may not strike out the whole or a part of the proceedings under paragraph (2) or (3)(b) or (c) without first giving the appellant an opportunity to make representations in relation to the proposed striking out.

(5) If the proceedings, or part of them, have been struck out under paragraph (1) or (3)(a), the appellant may apply for the proceedings, or part of them, to be reinstated.

(6) An application under paragraph (5) must be made in writing and received by the Tribunal within 1 month after the date on which the Tribunal sent notification of the striking out to the appellant.

(7) This rule applies to a respondent as it applies to an appellant except that—

    (a)   a reference to the striking out of the proceedings is to be read as a reference to the barring of the respondent from taking further part in the proceedings; and

(b)   a reference to an application for the reinstatement of proceedings which have been struck out is to be read as a reference to an application for the lifting of the bar on the respondent from taking further part in the proceedings.

(8) If a respondent has been barred from taking further part in proceedings under this rule and that bar has not been lifted, the Tribunal need not consider any response or other submission made by that respondent [and may summarily determine any or all issues against that respondent].

Amendment

Para (8): words "and may summarily determine any or all issues against that respondent" in square brackets inserted by SI 2010/2653, r 5(1), (3). Date in force: 29 November 2010: see SI 2010/2653, r 1.

9 Substitution and addition of parties

(1) The Tribunal may give a direction substituting a party if—

    (a)   the wrong person has been named as a party; or

    (b)   the substitution has become necessary because of a change in circumstances since the start of proceedings.

(2) The Tribunal may give a direction adding a person to the proceedings as a respondent.

(3) If the Tribunal gives a direction under paragraph (1) or (2) it may give such consequential directions as it considers appropriate.

10 No power to award costs

The Tribunal may not make any order in respect of costs (or, in Scotland, expenses).

11 Representatives

(1) A party may appoint a representative (whether a legal representative or not) to represent that party in the proceedings.

(2) Subject to paragraph (3), if a party appoints a representative, that party (or the representative if the representative is a legal representative) must send or deliver to the Tribunal written notice of the representative's name and address.

(3) In a case to which rule 23 (cases in which the notice of appeal is to be sent to the decision maker) applies, if the appellant (or the appellant's representative if the representative is a legal representative) provides written notification of the appellant's representative's name and address to the decision maker before the decision maker provides its response to the Tribunal, the appellant need not take any further steps in order to comply with paragraph (2).

(4) If the Tribunal receives notice that a party has appointed a representative under paragraph (2), it must send a copy of that notice to each other party.

(5) Anything permitted or required to be done by a party under these Rules, a practice direction or a direction may be done by the representative of that party, except signing a witness statement.

(6) A person who receives due notice of the appointment of a representative—

    (a)   must provide to the representative any document which is required to be provided to the represented party, and need not provide that document to the represented party; and

    (b)   may assume that the representative is and remains authorised as such until they receive written notification that this is not so from the representative or the represented party.

(7) At a hearing a party may be accompanied by another person whose name and address has not been notified under paragraph (2) or (3) but who, with the permission of the Tribunal, may act as a representative or otherwise assist in presenting the party's case at the hearing.

(8)   Paragraphs (2) to (6) do not apply to a person who accompanies a party under paragraph (7).

12 Calculating time

(1)   Except in asylum support cases, an act required by these Rules, a practice direction or a direction to be done on or by a particular day must be done by 5pm on that day.

(2)   If the time specified by these Rules, a practice direction or a direction for doing any act ends on a day other than a working day, the act is done in time if it is done on the next working day.

(3)   In this rule "working day" means any day except a Saturday or Sunday, Christmas Day, Good Friday or a bank holiday under section 1 of the Banking and Financial Dealings Act 1971.

13 Sending and delivery of documents

(1)   Any document to be provided to the Tribunal under these Rules, a practice direction or a direction must be—

(a)   sent by pre-paid post or delivered by hand to the address specified for the proceedings;

(b)   sent by fax to the number specified for the proceedings; or

(c)   sent or delivered by such other method as the Tribunal may permit or direct.

(2)   Subject to paragraph (3), if a party provides a fax number, email address or other details for the electronic transmission of documents to them, that party must accept delivery of documents by that method.

(3)   If a party informs the Tribunal and all other parties that a particular form of communication (other than pre-paid post or delivery by hand) should not be used to provide documents to that party, that form of communication must not be so used.

(4)   If the Tribunal or a party sends a document to a party or the Tribunal by email or any other electronic means of communication, the recipient may request that the sender provide a hard copy of the document to the recipient. The recipient must make such a request as soon as reasonably practicable after receiving the document electronically.

(5)   The Tribunal and each party may assume that the address provided by a party or its representative is and remains the address to which documents should be sent or delivered until receiving written notification to the contrary.

14 Use of documents and information

(1)   The Tribunal may make an order prohibiting the disclosure or publication of—

(a)   specified documents or information relating to the proceedings; or

(b)   any matter likely to lead members of the public to identify any person whom the Tribunal considers should not be identified.

(2)   The Tribunal may give a direction prohibiting the disclosure of a document or information to a person if—

(a)   the Tribunal is satisfied that such disclosure would be likely to cause that person or some other person serious harm; and

(b)   the Tribunal is satisfied, having regard to the interests of justice, that it is proportionate to give such a direction.

(3)   If a party ("the first party") considers that the Tribunal should give a direction under paragraph (2) prohibiting the disclosure of a document or information to another party ("the second party"), the first party must—

(a)   exclude the relevant document or information from any documents that will be provided to the second party; and

(b)   provide to the Tribunal the excluded document or information, and the reason for its exclusion, so that the Tribunal may decide whether the document or information should be disclosed to the second party or should be the subject of a direction under paragraph (2).

(4) The Tribunal must conduct proceedings as appropriate in order to give effect to a direction given under paragraph (2).

(5) If the Tribunal gives a direction under paragraph (2) which prevents disclosure to a party who has appointed a representative, the Tribunal may give a direction that the documents or information be disclosed to that representative if the Tribunal is satisfied that—

- (a) disclosure to the representative would be in the interests of the party; and
- (b) the representative will act in accordance with paragraph (6).

(6) Documents or information disclosed to a representative in accordance with a direction under paragraph (5) must not be disclosed either directly or indirectly to any other person without the Tribunal's consent.

15 Evidence and submissions

(1) Without restriction on the general powers in rule 5(1) and (2) (case management powers), the Tribunal may give directions as to—

- (a) issues on which it requires evidence or submissions;
- (b) the nature of the evidence or submissions it requires;
- (c) whether the parties are permitted or required to provide expert evidence;
- (d) any limit on the number of witnesses whose evidence a party may put forward, whether in relation to a particular issue or generally;
- (e) the manner in which any evidence or submissions are to be provided, which may include a direction for them to be given—
  - (i) orally at a hearing; or
  - (ii) by written submissions or witness statement; and
- (f) the time at which any evidence or submissions are to be provided.

(2) The Tribunal may—

- (a) admit evidence whether or not—
  - (i) the evidence would be admissible in a civil trial in the United Kingdom; or
  - (ii) the evidence was available to a previous decision maker; or
- (b) exclude evidence that would otherwise be admissible where—
  - (i) the evidence was not provided within the time allowed by a direction or a practice direction;
  - (ii) the evidence was otherwise provided in a manner that did not comply with a direction or a practice direction; or
  - (iii) it would otherwise be unfair to admit the evidence.

(3) The Tribunal may consent to a witness giving, or require any witness to give, evidence on oath, and may administer an oath for that purpose.

16 Summoning or citation of witnesses and orders to answer questions or produce documents

(1) On the application of a party or on its own initiative, the Tribunal may—

- (a) by summons (or, in Scotland, citation) require any person to attend as a witness at a hearing at the time and place specified in the summons or citation; or
- (b) order any person to answer any questions or produce any documents in that person's possession or control which relate to any issue in the proceedings.

(2) A summons or citation under paragraph (1)(a) must—

- (a) give the person required to attend 14 days' notice of the hearing or such shorter period as the Tribunal may direct; and

(b)   where the person is not a party, make provision for the person's necessary expenses of attendance to be paid, and state who is to pay them.

(3)   No person may be compelled to give any evidence or produce any document that the person could not be compelled to give or produce on a trial of an action in a court of law in the part of the United Kingdom where the proceedings are due to be determined.

(4)   A summons, citation or order under this rule must—

(a)   state that the person on whom the requirement is imposed may apply to the Tribunal to vary or set aside the summons, citation or order, if they have not had an opportunity to object to it; and

(b)   state the consequences of failure to comply with the summons, citation or order.

17 Withdrawal

(1)   Subject to paragraph (2), a party may give notice of the withdrawal of its case, or any part of it—

(a)   . . . by sending or delivering to the Tribunal a written notice of withdrawal; or

(b)   orally at a hearing.

(2)   In the circumstances described in paragraph (3), a notice of withdrawal will not take effect unless the Tribunal consents to the withdrawal.

(3)   The circumstances referred to in paragraph (2) are where a party gives notice of withdrawal—

(a)   in a criminal injuries compensation case; or

[(b)   in a social security and child support case where the Tribunal has directed that notice of withdrawal shall take effect only with the Tribunal's consent; or

(c)   at a hearing].

(4)   A party who has withdrawn their case may apply to the Tribunal for the case to be reinstated.

(5)   An application under paragraph (4) must be made in writing and be received by the Tribunal within 1 month after—

(a)   the date on which the Tribunal received the notice under paragraph (1)(a); or

(b)   the date of the hearing at which the case was withdrawn orally under paragraph (1)(b).

(6)   The Tribunal must notify each party in writing [that a withdrawal has taken effect] under this rule.

Amendment

Para (1): in sub-para (a) words omitted revoked by SI 2013/477, rr 22, 24(a). Date in force: 8 April 2013: see SI 2013/477, r 1(2)(a).

Para (3): in sub-para (a) words omitted revoked by SI 2013/477, rr 22, 24(b). Date in force: 8 April 2013: see SI 2013/477, r 1(2)(a).

Para (3): sub-paras (b), (c) substituted, for sub-para (b) as originally enacted, by SI 2013/477, rr 22, 24(c). Date in force: 8 April 2013: see SI 2013/477, r 1(2)(a).

Para (6): words in square brackets substituted by SI 2013/477, rr 22, 24(d). Date in force: 8 April 2013: see SI 2013/477, r 1(2)(a).

18 Lead cases

(1)   This rule applies if—

(a)   two or more cases have been started before the Tribunal;

(b)   in each such case the Tribunal has not made a decision disposing of the proceedings; and

(c)   the cases give rise to common or related issues of fact or law.

(2)   The Tribunal may give a direction—

    (a)   specifying one or more cases falling under paragraph (1) as a lead case or lead cases; and

    (b)   staying (or, in Scotland, sisting) the other cases falling under paragraph (1) ("the related cases").

(3)   When the Tribunal makes a decision in respect of the common or related issues—

    (a)   the Tribunal must send a copy of that decision to each party in each of the related cases; and

    (b)   subject to paragraph (4), that decision shall be binding on each of those parties.

(4)   Within 1 month after the date on which the Tribunal sent a copy of the decision to a party under paragraph (3)(a), that party may apply in writing for a direction that the decision does not apply to, and is not binding on the parties to, a particular related case.

(5)   The Tribunal must give directions in respect of cases which are stayed or sisted under paragraph (2)(b), providing for the disposal of or further directions in those cases.

(6)   If the lead case or cases lapse or are withdrawn before the Tribunal makes a decision in respect of the common or related issues, the Tribunal must give directions as to—

    (a)   whether another case or other cases are to be specified as a lead case or lead cases; and

    (b)   whether any direction affecting the related cases should be set aside or amended.

19 Confidentiality in child support or child trust fund cases

(1)   Paragraph (3) applies to proceedings under the Child Support Act 1991 in the circumstances described in paragraph (2), other than an appeal against a reduced benefit decision (as defined in section 46(10)(b) of the Child Support Act 1991, as that section had effect prior to the commencement of section 15(b) of the Child Maintenance and Other Payments Act 2008).

(2)   The circumstances referred to in paragraph (1) are that the absent parent, non-resident parent or person with care would like their address or the address of the child to be kept confidential and has given notice to that effect—

    [(a)   in the notice of appeal or when notifying the Secretary of State or the Tribunal of any subsequent change of address; or

    (b)   within 14 days after an enquiry is made by the recipient of the notice of appeal or the notification referred to in sub-paragraph (a)].

(3)   Where this paragraph applies, the Secretary of State . . . and the Tribunal must take appropriate steps to secure the confidentiality of the address, and of any information which could reasonably be expected to enable a person to identify the address, to the extent that the address or that information is not already known to each other party.

(4)   Paragraph (6) applies to proceedings under the Child Trust Funds Act 2004 in the circumstances described in paragraph (5).

(5)   The circumstances referred to in paragraph (4) are that a relevant person would like their address or the address of the eligible child to be kept confidential and has given notice to that effect, or a local authority with parental responsibility in relation to the eligible child would like the address of the eligible child to be kept confidential and has given notice to that effect—

    (a)   to HMRC in the notice of appeal or when notifying any subsequent change of address;

    (b)   to HMRC within 14 days after an enquiry by HMRC; or

    (c)   to the Tribunal when notifying any change of address.

(6) Where this paragraph applies, HMRC and the Tribunal must take appropriate steps to secure the confidentiality of the address, and of any information which could reasonably be expected to enable a person to identify the address, to the extent that the address or that information is not already known to each other party.

(7) In this rule—

"eligible child" has the meaning set out in section 2 of the Child Trust Funds Act 2004;

"HMRC" means Her Majesty's Revenue and Customs;

"non-resident parent" and "parent with care" have the meanings set out in section 54 of the Child Support Act 1991;

"parental responsibility" has the meaning set out in section 3(9) of the Child Trust Funds Act 2004; and

"relevant person" has the meaning set out in section 22(3) of the Child Trust Funds Act 2004.

Amendment

Para (2): in sub-paras (a), (b) substituted, for sub-paras (a)–(c) as originally enacted, by SI 2013/2067, rr 22, 24. Date in force: 1 November 2013: see SI 2013/2067, r 1.

Para (3): words omitted revoked by SI 2012/2007, art 3(2), Schedule, Pt 2, para 117(c). Date in force: 1 August 2012: see SI 2012/2007, art 1(2

20 Expenses in criminal injuries compensation cases

(1) This rule applies only to criminal injuries compensation cases.

(2) The Tribunal may meet reasonable expenses—

(a) incurred by the appellant, or any person who attends a hearing to give evidence, in attending the hearing; or

(b) incurred by the appellant in connection with any arrangements made by the Tribunal for the inspection of the appellant's injury.

21 Expenses in social security and child support cases

(1) This rule applies only to social security and child support cases.

(2) The Secretary of State may pay such travelling and other allowances (including compensation for loss of remunerative time) as the Secretary of State may determine to any person required to attend a hearing in proceedings under section 20 of the Child Support Act 1991, section 12 of the Social Security Act 1998 or paragraph 6 of Schedule 7 to the Child Support, Pensions and Social Security Act 2000.

PART 3
PROCEEDINGS BEFORE THE TRIBUNAL

CHAPTER 1

BEFORE THE HEARING

22 Cases in which the notice of appeal is to be sent to the Tribunal

[(1) This rule applies to all cases except those to which—

(a) rule 23 (cases in which the notice of appeal is to be sent to the decision maker), or

(b) rule 26 (social security and child support cases started by reference or information in writing),

applies.]

(2) An appellant must start proceedings by sending or delivering a notice of appeal to the Tribunal so that it is received—

(a) in asylum support cases, within 3 days after the date on which the appellant received written notice of the decision being challenged;

    (b)   in criminal injuries compensation cases, within 90 days after the date of the decision being challenged.

    (c)   in appeals under the Vaccine Damage Payments Act 1979, at any time;

    (d)   in other cases—

        (i)   if mandatory reconsideration applies, within 1 month after the date on which the appellant was sent notice of the result of mandatory reconsideration;

        (ii)   if mandatory reconsideration does not apply, within the time specified in Schedule 1 to these Rules (time specified for providing notices of appeal)].

(3)   The notice of appeal must be in English or Welsh, must be signed by the appellant and must state—

    (a)   the name and address of the appellant;

    (b)   the name and address of the appellant's representative (if any);

    (c)   an address where documents for the appellant may be sent or delivered;

    (d)   the name and address of any respondent [other than the decision maker];

    (e)   . . . ; and

    (f)   the grounds on which the appellant relies.

(4)   The appellant must provide with the notice of appeal—

    [(a)   a copy of—

        (i)   the notice of the result of mandatory reconsideration, in any social security and child support case to which mandatory reconsideration applies;

        (ii)   the decision being challenged, in any other case;]

    (b)   any statement of reasons for that decision that the appellant has[; and]

    (c)   any documents in support of the appellant's case which have not been supplied to the respondent . . .

    (d)   . . .

(5)   In asylum support cases the notice of appeal must also—

    (a)   state whether the appellant will require an interpreter at any hearing, and if so for which language or dialect; and

    (b)   state whether the appellant intends to attend or be represented at any hearing.

(6)   If the appellant provides the notice of appeal to the Tribunal later than the time required by paragraph (2) or by an extension of time allowed under rule 5(3)(a) (power to extend time)—

    (a)   the notice of appeal must include a request for an extension of time and the reason why the notice of appeal was not provided in time; and

    (b)   [subject to paragraph (8)] unless the Tribunal extends time for the notice of appeal under rule 5(3)(a) (power to extend time) the Tribunal must not admit the notice of appeal.

(7)   The Tribunal must send a copy of the notice of appeal and any accompanying documents to each other party—

    (a)   in asylum support cases, on the day that the Tribunal receives the notice of appeal, or (if that is not reasonably practicable) as soon as reasonably practicable on the following day;

    (b)   in [all other] cases, as soon as reasonably practicable after the Tribunal receives the notice of appeal.

[(8)   Where an appeal in a social security and child support case is not made within the time specified in paragraph (2)—

    (a)   it will be treated as having been made in time, unless the Tribunal directs otherwise, if it is made within not more than 12 months of the time specified and neither the decision maker nor any other respondent objects;

(b)   the time for bringing the appeal may not be extended under rule 5(3)(a) by more than 12 months.

(9)   For the purposes of this rule, mandatory reconsideration applies where the notice of the decision being challenged includes a statement to the effect that there is a right of appeal in relation to the decision only if the decision-maker has considered an application for the revision, reversal, review or reconsideration (as the case may be) of the decision being challenged.]

Amendment

Para (1): substituted by SI 2013/477, rr 22, 25(a). Date in force: 8 April 2013: see SI 2013/477, r 1(2)(a).

Para (2): sub-paras (c), (d) inserted by SI 2013/477, rr 22, 25(b). Date in force: 8 April 2013: see SI 2013/477, r 1(2)(a).

Para (3): in sub-para (d) words "other than the decision maker" in square brackets inserted and sub-para (e) revoked by SI 2013/477, rr 22, 25(c). Date in force: 8 April 2013: see SI 2013/477, r 1(2)(a).

Para (4): sub-para (a) substituted, in sub-para (b) word "; and" in square brackets substituted, in sub-para (c) word omitted revoked and sub-para (d) revoked by SI 2013/477, rr 22, 25(d)). Date in force: 8 April 2013: see SI 2013/477, r 1(2)(a).

Para (6): words omitted in each place they occur revoked by SI 2014/514, rr 21, 22. Date in force: 6 April 2014: see SI 2014/514, r 1.

Para (6): in sub-para (b) words "subject to paragraph (8)" in square brackets inserted by SI 2013/477, rr 22, 25(e). Date in force: 8 April 2013: see SI 2013/477, r 1(2)(a).

Para (7): in sub-para (b) words "all other" in square brackets substituted by SI 2013/477, rr 22, 25(f).Date in force: 8 April 2013: see SI 2013/477, r 1(2)(a).

Paras (8), (9): inserted by SI 2013/477, rr 22, 25(g). Date in force: 8 April 2013: see SI 2013/477, r 1(2)(a).

23 Cases in which the notice of appeal is to be sent to the decision maker

[(1)   This rule applies to social security and child support cases in which the notice of decision being challenged informs the appellant that any appeal must be sent to the decision maker.]

(2)   An appellant must start proceedings by sending or delivering a notice of appeal to the decision maker so that it is received within the time specified in Schedule 1 to these Rules (time limits for providing notices of appeal to the decision maker).

(3)   If the appellant provides the notice of appeal to the decision maker later than the time required by paragraph (2) the notice of appeal must include the reason why the notice of appeal was not provided in time.

(4)   Subject to paragraph (5), where an appeal is not made within the time specified in Schedule 1, it will be treated as having been made in time [if neither the decision maker nor any other respondent objects].

(5)   No appeal may be made more than 12 months after the time specified in Schedule 1.

(6)   The notice of appeal must be in English or Welsh, must be signed by the appellant and must state—

(a)   the name and address of the appellant;

(b)   the name and address of the appellant's representative (if any);

(c)   an address where documents for the appellant may be sent or delivered;

(d)   details of the decision being appealed; and

(e)   the grounds on which the appellant relies.

(7)   The decision maker must refer the case to the Tribunal immediately if—

(a)   the appeal has been made after the time specified in Schedule 1 and the decision maker [or any other respondent] objects to it being treated as having been made in time; or

> (b)   the decision maker considers that the appeal has been made more than 12 months after the time specified in Schedule 1.

[(8)   Notwithstanding rule 5(3)(a) [or (aa)] (case management powers) and rule 7(2) (failure to comply with rules etc), the Tribunal must not extend the time limit in paragraph (5).]

Amendment

Para (1): substituted by SI 2013/477, rr 22, 26. Date in force: 8 April 2013: see SI 2013/477, r 1(2)(a).

Para (4): words in square brackets substituted by SI 2012/500, r 4(1), (2)(a). Date in force: 6 April 2012: see SI 2012/500, r 1(2).

Para (7): in sub-para (a) words in square brackets inserted by SI 2012/500, r 4(1), (2)(b). Date in force: 6 April 2012: see SI 2012/500, r 1(2).

Para (8): inserted by SI 2009/1975, rr 2, 3. Date in force: 1 September 2009: see SI 2009/1975, r 1.

Para (8): words "or (aa)" in square brackets inserted by SI 2013/2067, rr 22, 26. Date in force: 1 November 2013: see SI 2013/2067, r 1.

24 Responses and replies

(1)   When a decision maker receives a copy of a notice of appeal from the Tribunal under rule 22(7), the decision maker must send or deliver a response to the Tribunal—

> (a)   in asylum support cases, so that it is received within 3 days after the date on which the Tribunal received the notice of appeal;
> (b)   in—
>> (i)   criminal injuries compensation cases,
>> (ii)   appeals under the Child Support Act 1991, or
>> (iii)   appeals under the Child Trust Funds Act 2004,
>
> within 42 days after the date on which the decision maker received the copy of the notice of appeal; and
> (c)   in other cases, within 28 days after the date on which the decision maker received the copy of the notice of appeal.

(1A)   Where a decision maker receives a notice of appeal from an appellant under rule 23(2), the decision maker must send or deliver a response to the Tribunal so that it is received as soon as reasonably practicable after the decision maker received the notice of appeal.]

(2)   The response must state—

> (a)   the name and address of the decision maker;
> (b)   the name and address of the decision maker's representative (if any);
> (c)   an address where documents for the decision maker may be sent or delivered;
> (d)   the names and addresses of any other respondents and their representatives (if any);
> (e)   whether the decision maker opposes the appellant's case and, if so, any grounds for such opposition which are not set out in any documents which are before the Tribunal; and
> (f)   any further information . . . required by a practice direction or direction.

(3)   The response may include a submission as to whether it would be appropriate for the case to be disposed of without a hearing.

(4)   The decision maker must provide with the response—

> (a)   a copy of any written record of the decision under challenge, and any statement of reasons for that decision, if they were not sent with the notice of appeal;
> (b)   copies of all documents relevant to the case in the decision maker's possession, unless a practice direction or direction states otherwise; and

    (c)   in cases to which rule 23 (cases in which the notice of appeal is to be sent to the decision maker) applies, a copy of the notice of appeal, any documents provided by the appellant with the notice of appeal and (if they have not otherwise been provided to the Tribunal) the name and address of the appellant's representative (if any).

(5)   The decision maker must provide a copy of the response and any accompanying documents to each other party at the same time as it provides the response to the Tribunal.

(6)   The appellant and any other respondent may make a written submission and supply further documents in reply to the decision maker's response.

(7)   Any submission or further documents under paragraph (6) must be provided to the Tribunal within 1 month after the date on which the decision maker sent the response to the party providing the reply, and the Tribunal must send a copy to each other party.

Amendment

Paras (1), (1A): substituted, for para (1) as originally enacted, by SI 2013/477, rr 22, 27(a). Date in force: 1 October 2014: see SI 2013/477, r 1(2)(b).

Para (2): in sub-para (f) words omitted revoked by SI 2013/477, rr 22, 27(b). Date in force: 1 October 2014: see SI 2013/477, r 1(2)(b).

25 Medical and physical examination in appeals under section 12 of the Social Security Act 1998

(1)   This rule applies only to appeals under section 12 of the Social Security Act 1998.

(2)   At a hearing an appropriate member of the Tribunal may carry out a physical examination of a person if the case relates to—

    (a)   the extent of that person's disablement and its assessment in accordance with section 68(6) of and Schedule 6 to, or section 103 of, the Social Security Contributions and Benefits Act 1992; or

    (b)   diseases or injuries prescribed for the purpose of section 108 of that Act.

(3)   If an issue which falls within Schedule 2 to these Rules (issues in relation to which the Tribunal may refer a person for medical examination) is raised in an appeal, the Tribunal may exercise its power under section 20 of the Social Security Act 1998 to refer a person to a health care professional approved by the Secretary of State for—

    (a)   the examination of that person; and

    (b)   the production of a report on the condition of that person.

(4)   Neither paragraph (2) nor paragraph (3) entitles the Tribunal to require a person to undergo a physical test for the purpose of determining whether that person is unable to walk or virtually unable to do so.

26 Social security and child support cases started by reference or information in writing

(1)   This rule applies to proceedings under section 28D of the Child Support Act 1991 and paragraph 3 of Schedule 2 to the Tax Credits Act 2002.

(2)   A person starting proceedings under section 28D of the Child Support Act 1991 must send or deliver a written reference to the Tribunal.

(3)   A person starting proceedings under paragraph 3 of Schedule 2 to the Tax Credits Act 2002 must send or deliver an information in writing to the Tribunal.

(4)   The reference or the information in writing must include—

    (a)   an address where documents for the person starting proceedings may be sent or delivered;

    (b)   the names and addresses of the respondents and their representatives (if any); and

    (c)   a submission on the issues that arise for determination by the Tribunal.

(5) Unless a practice direction or direction states otherwise, the person starting proceedings must also provide a copy of each document in their possession which is relevant to the proceedings.

(6) Subject to any obligation under rule 19(3) (confidentiality in child support cases), the person starting proceedings must provide a copy of the written reference or the information in writing and any accompanying documents to each respondent at the same time as they provide the written reference or the information in writing to the Tribunal.

(7) Each respondent may send or deliver to the Tribunal a written submission and any further relevant documents within one month of the date on which the person starting proceedings sent a copy of the written reference or the information in writing to that respondent.

CHAPTER 2

HEARINGS

27 Decision with or without a hearing

(1) Subject to the following paragraphs, the Tribunal must hold a hearing before making a decision which disposes of proceedings unless—

    (a)   each party has consented to, or has not objected to, the matter being decided without a hearing; and

    (b)   the Tribunal considers that it is able to decide the matter without a hearing.

(2) This rule does not apply to decisions under Part 4.

(3) The Tribunal may in any event dispose of proceedings without a hearing under rule 8 (striking out a party's case).

(4) In a criminal injuries compensation case—

    (a)   the Tribunal may make a decision which disposes of proceedings without a hearing; and

    (b)   subject to paragraph (5), if the Tribunal makes a decision which disposes of proceedings without a hearing, any party may make a written application to the Tribunal for the decision to be reconsidered at a hearing.

(5) An application under paragraph (4)(b) may not be made in relation to a decision—

    (a)   not to extend a time limit;

    (b)   not to set aside a previous decision;

    (c)   not to allow an appeal against a decision not to extend a time limit; or

    (d)   not to allow an appeal against a decision not to reopen a case.

(6) An application under paragraph (4)(b) must be received within 1 month after the date on which the Tribunal sent notice of the decision to the party making the application.

28 Entitlement to attend a hearing

Subject to rule 30(5) (exclusion of a person from a hearing), each party to proceedings is entitled to attend a hearing.

29 Notice of hearings

(1) The Tribunal must give each party entitled to attend a hearing reasonable notice of the time and place of the hearing (including any adjourned or postponed hearing) and any changes to the time and place of the hearing.

(2) The period of notice under paragraph (1) must be at least 14 days except that—

    (a)   in an asylum support case the Tribunal must give at least 1 day's and not more than 5 days' notice; and

    (b)   the Tribunal may give shorter notice—
        (i)   with the parties' consent; or
        (ii)   in urgent or exceptional circumstances.

30 Public and private hearings

(1)   Subject to the following paragraphs, all hearings must be held in public.

(2)   A hearing in a criminal injuries compensation case must be held in private unless—

    (a)   the appellant has consented to the hearing being held in public; and
    (b)   the Tribunal considers that it is in the interests of justice for the hearing to be held in public.

(3)   The Tribunal may give a direction that a hearing, or part of it, is to be held in private.

(4)   Where a hearing, or part of it, is to be held in private, the Tribunal may determine who is permitted to attend the hearing or part of it.

(5)   The Tribunal may give a direction excluding from any hearing, or part of it—

    (a)   any person whose conduct the Tribunal considers is disrupting or is likely to disrupt the hearing;
    (b)   any person whose presence the Tribunal considers is likely to prevent another person from giving evidence or making submissions freely;
    (c)   any person who the Tribunal considers should be excluded in order to give effect to a direction under rule 14(2) (withholding information likely to cause harm); or
    (d)   any person where the purpose of the hearing would be defeated by the attendance of that person.

(6)   The Tribunal may give a direction excluding a witness from a hearing until that witness gives evidence.

31 Hearings in a party's absence

If a party fails to attend a hearing the Tribunal may proceed with the hearing if the Tribunal—

    (a)   is satisfied that the party has been notified of the hearing or that reasonable steps have been taken to notify the party of the hearing; and
    (b)   considers that it is in the interests of justice to proceed with the hearing.

CHAPTER 3

DECISIONS

32 Consent orders

(1)   The Tribunal may, at the request of the parties but only if it considers it appropriate, make a consent order disposing of the proceedings and making such other appropriate provision as the parties have agreed.

(2)   Notwithstanding any other provision of these Rules, the Tribunal need not hold a hearing before making an order under paragraph (1), or provide reasons for the order.

33 Notice of decisions

(1)   The Tribunal may give a decision orally at a hearing.

(2)   Subject to rule 14(2) (withholding information likely to cause harm), the Tribunal must provide to each party as soon as reasonably practicable after making [a decision (other than a decision under Part 4) which finally disposes of all issues in the proceedings or of a preliminary issue dealt with following a direction under rule 5(3)(e)]—

    (a)   a decision notice stating the Tribunal's decision;

(b)   where appropriate, notification of the right to apply for a written statement of reasons under rule 34(3); and

(c)   notification of any right of appeal against the decision and the time within which, and the manner in which, such right of appeal may be exercised.

(3)   In asylum support cases the notice and notifications required by paragraph (2) must be provided at the hearing or sent on the day that the decision is made.

Amendment

Para (2): words in square brackets substituted by SI 2013/477, rr 22, 28. Date in force: 8 April 2013: see SI 2013/477, r 1(2)(a).

34 Reasons for decisions

(1)   In asylum support cases the Tribunal must send a written statement of reasons for a decision which disposes of proceedings (except a decision under Part 4) to each party—

(a)   if the case is decided at a hearing, within 3 days after the hearing; or

(b)   if the case is decided without a hearing, on the day that the decision is made.

(2)   In all other cases the Tribunal may give reasons for a decision which disposes of proceedings (except a decision under Part 4)—

(a)   orally at a hearing; or

(b)   in a written statement of reasons to each party.

(3)   Unless the Tribunal has already provided a written statement of reasons under paragraph (2)(b), a party may make a written application to the Tribunal for such statement following a decision [which finally disposes of—

(a)   all issues in the proceedings; or

(b)   a preliminary issue dealt with following a direction under rule 5(3)(e)].

(4)   An application under paragraph (3) must be received within 1 month of the date on which the Tribunal sent or otherwise provided to the party a decision notice relating to the decision . . .

(5)   If a party makes an application in accordance with paragraphs (3) and (4) the Tribunal must, subject to rule 14(2) (withholding information likely to cause harm), send a written statement of reasons to each party within 1 month of the date on which it received the application or as soon as reasonably practicable after the end of that period.

Amendment

Para (3): words from "which finally disposes" to "under rule 5(3)(e)" in square brackets substituted by SI 2013/477, rr 22, 29(a). Date in force: 8 April 2013: see SI 2013/477, r 1(2)(a).

Para (4): words omitted revoked by SI 2013/477, rr 22, 29(b). Date in force: 8 April 2013: see SI 2013/477, r 1(2)(a.

PART 4
CORRECTING, SETTING ASIDE, REVIEWING AND APPEALING TRIBUNAL DECISIONS

35 Interpretation

In this Part—

"appeal" means the exercise of a right of appeal—

(a)   under paragraph 2(2) or 4(1) of Schedule 2 to the Tax Credits Act 2002;

(b)   under section 21(10) of the Child Trust Funds Act 2004; or

(c)   on a point of law under section 11 of the 2007 Act; and

"review" means the review of a decision by the Tribunal under section 9 of the 2007 Act.

36 Clerical mistakes and accidental slips or omissions

The Tribunal may at any time correct any clerical mistake or other accidental slip or omission in a decision, direction or any document produced by it, by—

    (a)   sending notification of the amended decision or direction, or a copy of the amended document, to all parties; and

    (b)   making any necessary amendment to any information published in relation to the decision, direction or document.

37 Setting aside a decision which disposes of proceedings

(1) The Tribunal may set aside a decision which disposes of proceedings, or part of such a decision, and re-make the decision, or the relevant part of it, if—

    (a)   the Tribunal considers that it is in the interests of justice to do so; and

    (b)   one or more of the conditions in paragraph (2) are satisfied.

(2) The conditions are—

    (a)   a document relating to the proceedings was not sent to, or was not received at an appropriate time by, a party or a party's representative;

    (b)   a document relating to the proceedings was not sent to the Tribunal at an appropriate time;

    (c)   a party, or a party's representative, was not present at a hearing related to the proceedings; or

    (d)   there has been some other procedural irregularity in the proceedings.

(3) A party applying for a decision, or part of a decision, to be set aside under paragraph (1) must make a written application to the Tribunal so that it is received no later than 1 month after the date on which the Tribunal sent notice of the decision to the party.

38 Application for permission to appeal

(1) This rule does not apply to asylum support cases or criminal injuries compensation cases.

(2) A person seeking permission to appeal must make a written application to the Tribunal for permission to appeal.

(3) An application under paragraph (2) must be sent or delivered to the Tribunal so that it is received no later than 1 month after the latest of the dates that the Tribunal sends to the person making the application—

[(za)   the relevant decision notice;]

    (a)   written reasons for the decision[, if the decision disposes of—

        (i)   all issues in the proceedings; or

        (ii)   subject to paragraph (3A), a preliminary issue dealt with following a direction under rule 5(3)(e)];

    (b)   notification of amended reasons for, or correction of, the decision following a review; or

    (c)   notification that an application for the decision to be set aside has been unsuccessful.

[(3A) The Tribunal may direct that the 1 month within which a party may send or deliver an application for permission to appeal against a decision that disposes of a preliminary issue shall run from the date of the decision that disposes of all issues in the proceedings.]

(4) The date in paragraph (3)(c) applies only if the application for the decision to be set aside was made within the time stipulated in rule 37 (setting aside a decision which disposes of proceedings) or any extension of that time granted by the Tribunal.

(5) If the person seeking permission to appeal sends or delivers the application to the Tribunal later than the time required by paragraph (3) or by any extension of time under rule 5(3)(a) (power to extend time)—

    (a)   the application must include a request for an extension of time and the reason why the application was not provided in time; and

    (b)   unless the Tribunal extends time for the application under rule 5(3)(a) (power to extend time) the Tribunal must not admit the application.

(6) An application under paragraph (2) must—

    (a)   identify the decision of the Tribunal to which it relates;

    (b)   identify the alleged error or errors of law in the decision; and

    (c)   state the result the party making the application is seeking.

(7) If a person makes an application under paragraph (2) [in respect of a decision that disposes of proceedings or of a preliminary issue dealt with following a direction under rule 5(3)(e)] when the Tribunal has not given a written statement of reasons for its decision—

    (a)   if no application for a written statement of reasons has been made to the Tribunal, the application for permission must be treated as such an application;

    (b)   unless the Tribunal decides to give permission and directs that this sub-paragraph does not apply, the application is not to be treated as an application for permission to appeal; and

    (c)   if an application for a written statement of reasons has been, or is, refused because of a delay in making the application, the Tribunal must only admit the application for permission if the Tribunal considers that it is in the interests of justice to do so.

Amendment

Para (3): sub-para (za) inserted by SI 2013/477, rr 22, 30(a). Date in force: 8 April 2013: see SI 2013/477, r 1(2)(a).

Para (3): in sub-para (a) words in square brackets inserted by SI 2013/477, rr 22, 30(b). Date in force: 8 April 2013: see SI 2013/477, r 1(2)(a).

Para (3A): inserted by SI 2013/477, rr 22, 30(c). Date in force: 8 April 2013: see SI 2013/477, r 1(2)(a).

Para (7): words in square brackets inserted by SI 2013/477, rr 22, 30(d). Date in force: 8 April 2013: see SI 2013/477, r 1(2)(a).

39 Tribunal's consideration of application for permission to appeal

(1) On receiving an application for permission to appeal the Tribunal must first consider, taking into account the overriding objective in rule 2, whether to review the decision in accordance with rule 40 (review of a decision).

(2) If the Tribunal decides not to review the decision, or reviews the decision and decides to take no action in relation to the decision, or part of it, the Tribunal must consider whether to give permission to appeal in relation to the decision or that part of it.

(3) The Tribunal must send a record of its decision to the parties as soon as practicable.

(4) If the Tribunal refuses permission to appeal it must send with the record of its decision—

    (a)   a statement of its reasons for such refusal; and

    (b)   notification of the right to make an application to the Upper Tribunal for permission to appeal and the time within which, and the method by which, such application must be made.

(5) The Tribunal may give permission to appeal on limited grounds, but must comply with paragraph (4) in relation to any grounds on which it has refused permission.

40 Review of a decision

(1) This rule does not apply to asylum support cases or criminal injuries compensation cases.

(2) The Tribunal may only undertake a review of a decision—

(a) pursuant to rule 39(1) (review on an application for permission to appeal); and

(b) if it is satisfied that there was an error of law in the decision.

(3) The Tribunal must notify the parties in writing of the outcome of any review, and of any right of appeal in relation to the outcome.

(4) If the Tribunal takes any action in relation to a decision following a review without first giving every party an opportunity to make representations, the notice under paragraph (3) must state that any party that did not have an opportunity to make representations may apply for such action to be set aside and for the decision to be reviewed again.

41 Power to treat an application as a different type of application
The Tribunal may treat an application for a decision to be corrected, set aside or reviewed, or for permission to appeal against a decision, as an application for any other one of those things.

SCHEDULE 1

TIME LIMITS FOR PROVIDING NOTICES OF APPEAL . . .

Rule 23

Type of proceedings	Time for providing notice of appeal
[Cases other than those listed below	the latest of—

the latest of—

(a) one month after the date on which notice of the decision being challenged was sent to the appellant;

(b) if a written statement of reasons for the decision was requested within that month, 14 days after the later of—

    (i) the end of that month; or

    (ii) the date on which the written statement of reasons was provided; or

[(c) if the appellant made an application for revision of the decision under—

    (i) regulation 14 of the Child Support Maintenance Calculation Regulations 2012;

    (ii) regulation 3(1) or (3) of the Social Security and Child Support (Decision and Appeals) Regulations 1999;

    (iii) egulation 4 of the Housing Benefit and Council Tax Benefit (Decisions and Appeals) Regulations 2001;

    (iv) regulation 17(1)(a) of the Child Support (Maintenance Assessment Procedure) Regulations 1992 (where still applicable to the particular case); or

    (v) regulation 3A(1) of the Social Security and Child Support (Decisions and Appeals) Regulations 1999 (where still applicable to the particular case),

and that application was unsuccessful, 1 month after the date on which notice that the decision would not be revised was sent to the appellant].]

Type of proceedings	Time for providing notice of appeal

appeal against a certificate of NHS charges under section 157(1) of the Health and Social Care (Community Health and Standards) Act 2003	(a) 3 months after the latest of—
	
	   (i) the date on the certificate;
	
	   (ii) the date on which the compensation payment was made;
	
	   (iii) if the certificate has been reviewed, the date the certificate was confirmed or a fresh certificate was issued; or
	
	   (iv) the date of any agreement to treat an earlier compensation payment as having been made in final discharge of a claim made by or in respect of an injured person and arising out of the injury or death; or
	
	 (b) if the person to whom the certificate has been issued makes an application under section 157(4) of the Health and Social Care (Community Health and Standards) Act 2003, one month after—
	
	   (i) the date of the decision on that application; or
	
	   (ii) if the person appeals against that decision under section 157(6) of that Act, the date on which the appeal is decided or withdrawn

appeal against a waiver decision under section 157(6) of the Health and Social Care (Community Health and Standards) Act 2003	one month after the date of the decision
appeal against a certificate of NHS charges under section 7 of the Road Traffic (NHS Charges) Act 1999	3 months after the latest of— (a) the date on which the liability under section 1(2) of the Road Traffic (NHS Charges) Act 1999 was discharged; (b) if the certificate has been reviewed, the date the certificate was confirmed or a fresh certificate was issued; or (c) the date of any agreement to treat an earlier compensation payment as having been made in final discharge of a claim made by or in respect of a traffic casualty and arising out of the injury or death
appeal against a certificate of recoverable benefits under section 11 of the Social Security (Recovery of Benefits) Act 1997	one month after the latest of— (a) the date on which any payment to the Secretary of State required under section 6 of the Social Security (Recovery of Benefits) Act 1997 was made; (b) if the certificate has been reviewed, the date the certificate was confirmed or a fresh certificate was issued; or (c) the date of any agreement to treat an earlier compensation payment as having been made in final discharge of a claim made by or in respect of an injured person and arising out of the accident, injury or disease

Type of proceedings	Time for providing notice of appeal
appeal under the Vaccine Damage Payments Act 1979	no time limit
appeal under the Tax Credits Act 2002	as set out in the Tax Credits Act 2002
appeal under the Child Trust Funds Act 2004	as set out in the Child Trust Funds Act 2004
appeal against a decision in respect of a claim for child benefit or guardian's allowance under section 12 of the Social Security Act 1998	as set out in regulation 28 of the Child Benefit and Guardian's Allowance (Decisions and Appeals) Regulations 2003

Amendment

Schedule heading: words omitted revoked by SI 2013/477, rr 22, 31(a). Date in force: 8 April 2013: see SI 2013/477, r 1(2)(a).

Table: first entry substituted by SI 2010/2653, r 5(1), (4). Date in force: 29 November 2010: see SI 2010/2653, r 1.

Table: in first entry para (c) substituted by SI 2013/477, rr 22, 31(b). Date in force: 8 April 2013: see SI 2013/477, r 1(2)(a).

SCHEDULE 2

ISSUES IN RELATION TO WHICH THE TRIBUNAL MAY REFER A PERSON FOR MEDICAL EXAMINATION UNDER SECTION 20(2) OF THE SOCIAL SECURITY ACT 1998

Rule 25(3)

An issue falls within this Schedule if the issue—

(a) is whether the claimant satisfies the conditions for entitlement to—

    (i) an attendance allowance specified in section 64 and 65(1) of the Social Security Contributions and Benefits Act 1992;

    (ii) severe disablement allowance under section 68 of that Act;

    (iii) the care component of a disability living allowance specified in section 72(1) and (2) of that Act;

    (iv) the mobility component of a disability living allowance specified in section 73(1), (8) and (9) of that Act; . . .

    (v) a disabled person's tax credit specified in section 129(1)(b) of that Act.

    [(vi) the daily living component of personal independence payment specified in section 78 of the Welfare Reform Act 2012; or

    (vii) the mobility component of personal independence payment specified in section 79 of the Welfare Reform Act 2012].

(b) relates to the period throughout which the claimant is likely to satisfy the conditions for entitlement to an attendance allowance or a disability living allowance;

(c) is the rate at which an attendance allowance is payable;

(d) is the rate at which the care component or the mobility component of a disability living allowance is payable;

(e) is whether a person is incapable of work for the purposes of the Social Security Contributions and Benefits Act 1992;

(f)   relates to the extent of a person's disablement and its assessment in accordance with Schedule 6 to the Social Security Contributions and Benefits Act 1992;

(g)   is whether the claimant suffers a loss of physical or mental faculty as a result of the relevant accident for the purposes of section 103 of the Social Security Contributions and Benefits Act 1992;

(h)   relates to any payment arising under, or by virtue of a scheme having effect under, section 111 of, and Schedule 8 to, the Social Security Contributions and Benefits Act 1992 (workmen's compensation);

(i)   is whether a person has limited capability for work or work-related activity for the purposes of the Welfare Reform Act 2007;

(j)   is the rate at which the daily living component or mobility component of personal independence payment is payable].

Amendment

In para (a)(iv) word omitted revoked by SI 2013/477, rr 22, 32(a). Date in force: 8 April 2013: see SI 2013/477, r 1(2)(a).

Para (a)(vi), (vii) inserted by SI 2013/477, rr 22, 32(b). Date in force: 8 April 2013: see SI 2013/477, r 1(2)(a).

Para (j) inserted by SI 2013/477, rr 22, 32(c). Date in force: 8 April 2013: see SI 2013/477, r 1(2)(a).

TRIBUNAL PROCEDURE (UPPER TRIBUNAL) RULES 2008

(SI 2008/2698)

Made: 9 October 2008.

Authority: Tribunals, Courts and Enforcement Act 2007, ss 10(3), 16(9), 22, 29(3), (4),Sch 5.

Commencement: 3 November 2008.

PART 1
INTRODUCTION

1 Citation, commencement, application and interpretation

(1)   These Rules may be cited as the Tribunal Procedure (Upper Tribunal) Rules 2008 and come into force on 3rd November 2008.

(2)   These Rules apply to proceedings before the Upper Tribunal [except proceedings in the Lands Chamber].

(3)   In these Rules—

"the 2007 Act" means the Tribunals, Courts and Enforcement Act 2007;

["appellant" means—

(a)   a person who makes an appeal, or applies for permission to appeal, to the Upper Tribunal;

(b)   in proceedings transferred or referred to the Upper Tribunal from the First-tier Tribunal, a person who started the proceedings in the First-tier Tribunal; or

(c)   a person substituted as an appellant under rule 9(1) (substitution and addition of parties);]

["applicant" means—

(a)   a person who applies for permission to bring, or does bring, judicial review proceedings before the Upper Tribunal and, in judicial review proceedings transferred to the Upper Tribunal from a court, includes a person who was a claimant or petitioner in the proceedings immediately before they were transferred; or

(b)   a person who refers a financial services case [or a wholesale energy case] to the Upper Tribunal;]

["appropriate national authority" means, in relation to an appeal, the Secretary of State, the Scottish Ministers[, the Department of the Environment in Northern Ireland] or the Welsh Ministers, as the case may be;]

["asylum case" means proceedings before the Upper Tribunal on appeal against a decision in proceedings under section 82, 83 or 83A of the Nationality, Immigration and Asylum Act 2002 in which a person claims that removal from, or a requirement to leave, the United Kingdom would breach the United Kingdom's obligations under the Convention relating to the Status of Refugees done at Geneva on 28 July 1951 and the Protocol to the Convention;]

["authorised person" means—

(a)   an examiner appointed by the Secretary of State under section 66A of the Road Traffic Act 1988;

(b)   an examiner appointed by the Department of the Environment in Northern Ireland under Article 74 of the Road Traffic (Northern Ireland) Order 1995; or

(c)   any person authorised in writing by the Department of the Environment in Northern Ireland for the purposes of the Goods Vehicles (Licensing of Operators) Act (Northern Ireland) 2010;

and includes a person acting under the direction of such an examiner or other authorised person, who has detained the vehicle to which an appeal relates;]

. . .

"dispose of proceedings" includes, unless indicated otherwise, disposing of a part of the proceedings;

"document" means anything in which information is recorded in any form, and an obligation under these Rules or any practice direction or direction to provide or allow access to a document or a copy of a document for any purpose means, unless the Upper Tribunal directs otherwise, an obligation to provide or allow access to such document or copy in a legible form or in a form which can be readily made into a legible form;

["fast-track case" means an asylum case or an immigration case where the person who appealed to the First-tier Tribunal—

(a)   was detained under the Immigration Acts at a place specified in Schedule 2 to the Asylum and Immigration Tribunal (Fast Track Procedure) Rules 2005 when the notice of decision that was the subject of the appeal to the First-tier Tribunal was served on the appellant;

(b)   remains so detained; and

(c)   the First-tier Tribunal or the Upper Tribunal has not directed that the case cease to be treated as a fast-track case;]

. . .

"hearing" means an oral hearing and includes a hearing conducted in whole or in part by video link, telephone or other means of instantaneous two-way electronic communication;

["immigration case" means proceedings before the Upper Tribunal on appeal against a decision in proceedings under section 40A of the British Nationality Act 1981, section 82 of the Nationality, Immigration and Asylum Act 2002, or regulation 26 of the Immigration (European Economic Area) Regulations 2006 that are not an asylum case;]

["immigration judicial review proceedings" means judicial review proceedings which are designated as an immigration matter—

- (a) in a direction made in accordance with Part 1 of Schedule 2 to the Constitutional Reform Act 2005 specifying a class of case for the purposes of section 18(6) of the 2007 Act; or
- (b) in an order of the High Court in England and Wales made under section 31A(3) of the Senior Courts Act 1981, transferring to the Upper Tribunal an application of a kind described in section 31A(1) of that Act;]

"interested party" means—

- (a) a person who is directly affected by the outcome sought in judicial review proceedings, and has been named as an interested party under rule 28 or 29 (judicial review), or has been substituted or added as an interested party under rule 9 [(addition, substitution and removal of parties)]; . . .
- (b) in judicial review proceedings transferred to the Upper Tribunal under section 25A(2) or (3) of the Judicature (Northern Ireland) Act 1978 or section 31A(2) or (3) of the [Senior Courts Act 1981], a person who was an interested party in the proceedings immediately before they were transferred to the Upper Tribunal; [and
- (c) in a financial services case [or a wholesale energy case], any person other than the applicant who could have referred the case to the Upper Tribunal and who has been added or substituted as an interested party under rule 9 (addition, substitution and removal of parties);]

"judicial review proceedings" means proceedings within the jurisdiction of the Upper Tribunal pursuant to section 15 or 21 of the 2007 Act, whether such proceedings are started in the Upper Tribunal or transferred to the Upper Tribunal;

. . .

"mental health case" means proceedings before the Upper Tribunal on appeal against a decision in proceedings under the Mental Health Act 1983 or paragraph 5(2) of the Schedule to the Repatriation of Prisoners Act 1984;

["national security certificate appeal" means an appeal under section 28 of the Data Protection Act 1998 or section 60 of the Freedom of Information Act 2000 (including that section as applied and modified by regulation 18 of the Environmental Information Regulations 2004);]

"party" means a person who is an appellant, an applicant, a respondent or an interested party in proceedings before the Upper Tribunal, a person who has referred a question [or matter] to the Upper Tribunal or, if the proceedings have been concluded, a person who was an appellant, an applicant, a respondent or an interested party when the [Upper] Tribunal finally disposed of all issues in the proceedings;

"permission" includes leave in cases arising under the law of Northern Ireland;

"practice direction" means a direction given under section 23 of the 2007 Act;

["reference", in a financial services case, includes an appeal;]

["relevant minister" means the Minister or designated person responsible for the signing of the certificate to which a national security certificate appeal relates;]

"respondent" means—

- (a) in an appeal, or application for permission to appeal, against a decision of another tribunal, any person other than the appellant who—
  - (i) was a party before that other tribunal;

(ii) . . .

(iii) otherwise has a right of appeal against the decision of the other tribunal and has given notice to the Upper Tribunal that they wish to be a party to the appeal;

(b) in an appeal [other than a road transport case], the person who made the decision;

(c) in judicial review proceedings—

(i) in proceedings started in the Upper Tribunal, the person named by the applicant as the respondent;

(ii) in proceedings transferred to the Upper Tribunal under section 25A(2) or (3) of the Judicature (Northern Ireland) Act 1978 or section 31A(2) or (3) of the [Senior Courts Act 1981], a person who was a defendant in the proceedings immediately before they were transferred;

(iii) in proceedings transferred to the Upper Tribunal under section 20(1) of the 2007 Act, a person to whom intimation of the petition was made before the proceedings were transferred, or to whom the Upper Tribunal has required intimation to be made;

[(ca) in proceedings transferred or referred to the Upper Tribunal from the First-tier Tribunal, a person who was a respondent in the proceedings in the First-tier Tribunal;]

(d) in a reference under the Forfeiture Act 1982, the person whose eligibility for a benefit or advantage is in issue; . . .

[(da) in a financial services case—

(i) where the case is a multiple regulator case, both the primary and secondary regulator as defined in Schedule 3 to these rules (but subject to the operation of paragraph 4A(3) of that Schedule);

(ii) where the case is a single regulator case, the maker of the decision in respect of which a reference has been made; or]

[(db) in a wholesale energy case, in relation to Great Britain, the Gas and Electricity Markets Authority or, in relation to Northern Ireland, the Northern Ireland Authority for Utility Regulation; or]

(e) a person substituted or added as a respondent under rule 9 (substitution and addition of parties);

. . .

["road transport case" means an appeal against a decision of a traffic commissioner or the Department of the Environment in Northern Ireland;]

["tribunal" does not include a traffic commissioner;]

"working day" means any day except a Saturday or Sunday, Christmas Day, Good Friday or a bank holiday under section 1 of the Banking and Financial Dealings Act 1971.

Amendment

Para (2): words "except proceedings in the Lands Chamber" in square brackets inserted by SI 2009/1975, rr 7, 8(a). Date in force: 1 September 2009: see SI 2009/1975, r 1.

Para (3): definition "appellant" substituted by SI 2009/274, rr 3, 5(a). Date in force: 1 April 2009: see SI 2009/274, r 1.

Para (3): definition "applicant" substituted by SI 2010/747, rr 2, 4(a).Date in force: 6 April 2010: see SI 2010/747, r 1.

Para (3): in definition "applicant" words in square brackets inserted by SI 2014/514, rr 2, 4(a). Date in force: 6 April 2014: see SI 2014/514, r 1.

Para (3): definition "appropriate national authority" inserted by SI 2009/1975, rr 7, 8(b)(i). Date in force: 1 September 2009: see SI 2009/1975, r 1. Words in square brackets in that definition inserted by SI 2012/1363, r 5(a), as from 1 July 2012.

Para (3): definition "asylum case" inserted by SI 2010/44, rr 2, 3(a).Date in force: 15 February 2010: see SI 2010/44, r 1.

Para (3): definition "authorised person" inserted by SI 2009/1975, rr 7, 8(b)(i) and substituted by SI 2012/1363, r 5(b), as from 1 July 2012.

Para (3): definition "disability discrimination in schools case" (omitted) revoked by SI 2009/274, rr 3, 5(b). Date in force: 1 April 2009: see SI 2009/274, r 1.

Para (3): definition "fast-track case" inserted by SI 2010/44, rr 2, 3(c).Date in force: 15 February 2010: see SI 2010/44, r 1.

Para (3): definition "financial services case" inserted by SI 2010/747, rr 2, 4(b). Date in force: 6 April 2010: see SI 2010/747, r 1.

Para (3): definition "financial services case" (omitted) outside the scope of this work.

Para (3): definition "fresh claim proceedings" (omitted) inserted by SI 2011/2343, rr 2, 4 and revoked by SI 2013/2067, rr 2, 4(a). Date in force: 1 November 2013: see SI 2013/2067, r 1.

Para (3): definition "immigration case" inserted by SI 2010/44, rr 2, 3(b). Date in force: 15 February 2010: see SI 2010/44, r 1.

Para (3): definition "immigration judicial review proceedings" inserted by SI 2013/2067, rr 2, 4(b). Date in force: 1 November 2013: see SI 2013/2067, r 1.

Para (3): in definition "interested party" in sub-para (a) words "(addition, substitution and removal of parties)" in square brackets substituted by SI 2010/747, rr 2, 4(c)(i). Date in force: 6 April 2010: see SI 2010/747, r 1.

Para (3): in definition "interested party" in sub-para (b) word omitted revoked by SI 2010/747, rr 2, 4(c)(ii). Date in force: 6 April 2010: see SI 2010/747, r 1.

Para (3): in definition "interested party" in sub-para (b) words "Senior Courts Act 1981" in square brackets substituted by the Constitutional Reform Act 2005, s 59(5), Sch 11, Pt 1, para 1(2).Date in force: 1 October 2009: see the Constitutional Reform Act 2005 (Commencement No 11) Order 2009, art 2(d).

Para (3): in definition "interested party" sub-para (c) and word "and" immediately preceding it inserted by SI 2010/747, rr 2, 4(c)(iii). Date in force: 6 April 2010: see SI 2010/747, r 1.

Para (3): definition "legal representative" (omitted) revoked by SI 2009/274, rr 3, 5(c). Date in force: 1 April 2009: see SI 2009/274, r 1.

Para (3): in definition "interested party" words in square brackets in sub-para (c) inserted by SI 2014/514, rr 2, 4(c). Date in force: 6 April 2014: see SI 2014/514, r 1.

Para (3): definition "national security certificate appeal" inserted by SI 2010/43, rr 5, 6(a). Date in force: 18 January 2010: see SI 2010/43, r 1.

Para (3): in definition "party" words "or matter" in square brackets inserted by SI 2010/747, rr 2, 4(d). Date in force: 6 April 2010: see SI 2010/747, r 1.

Para (3): in definition "party" word "Upper" in square brackets inserted by SI 2013/2067, rr 2, 4(c). Date in force: 1 November 2013: see SI 2013/2067, r 1.

Para (3): definition "reference" inserted by SI 2010/747, rr 2, 4(e). Date in force: 6 April 2010: see SI 2010/747, r 1.

Para (3): definition "relevant minister" inserted by SI 2010/43, rr 5, 6(b). Date in force: 18 January 2010: see SI 2010/43, r 1.

Para (3): in definition "respondent" sub-para (a)(ii) revoked by SI 2009/274, rr 3, 5(d)(i).Date in force: 1 April 2009: see SI 2009/274, r 1

Para (3): in definition "respondent" in sub-para (b) words in square brackets substituted by SI 2012/1363, r 5(c), as from 1 July 2012.

Para (3): in definition "respondent" in sub-para (c)(ii) words "Senior Courts Act 1981" in square brackets substituted by the Constitutional Reform Act 2005, s 59(5), Sch 11, Pt 1, para 1(2). Date in force: 1 October 2009: see the Constitutional Reform Act 2005 (Commencement No 11) Order 2009, art 2(d).

Para (3): in definition "respondent" sub-para (ca) inserted by SI 2009/274, rr 3, 5(d)(ii). Date in force: 1 April 2009: see SI 2009/274, r 1.

Para (3): in definition "respondent" in sub-para (d) word omitted revoked by SI 2010/747, rr 2, 4(f)(i). Date in force: 6 April 2010: see SI 2010/747, r 1.

Para (3): in definition "respondent" sub-para (da) (as inserted by SI 2010/747, rr 2, 4(f)(ii)) substituted by SI 2013/606, r 2(1), (2)(b). Date in force: 1 April 2013: see SI 2013/606, r 1.

Para (3): in definition "respondent" para (db) inserted by SI 2014/514, rr 2, 4(d). Date in force: 6 April 2014: see SI 2014/514, r 1.

Para (3): definition "road transport case" inserted by SI 2012/1363, r 5(d), as from 1 July 2012.

Para (3): definition "special educational needs case" (omitted) revoked by SI 2009/274, rr 3, 5(e).Date in force: 1 April 2009: see SI 2009/274, r 1.

Para (3): definition "tribunal" inserted by SI 2009/1975, rr 7, 8(b)(iii). Date in force: 1 September 2009: see SI 2009/1975, r 1.

Para (3): definition "wholesale energy case" (omitted) outside the scope of this work.

2 Overriding objective and parties' obligation to co-operate with the Upper Tribunal

(1)   The overriding objective of these Rules is to enable the Upper Tribunal to deal with cases fairly and justly.

(2)   Dealing with a case fairly and justly includes—

   (a)   dealing with the case in ways which are proportionate to the importance of the case, the complexity of the issues, the anticipated costs and the resources of the parties;

   (b)   avoiding unnecessary formality and seeking flexibility in the proceedings;

   (c)   ensuring, so far as practicable, that the parties are able to participate fully in the proceedings;

   (d)   using any special expertise of the Upper Tribunal effectively; and

   (e)   avoiding delay, so far as compatible with proper consideration of the issues.

(3)   The Upper Tribunal must seek to give effect to the overriding objective when it—

   (a)   exercises any power under these Rules; or

   (b)   interprets any rule or practice direction.

(4)   Parties must—

   (a)   help the Upper Tribunal to further the overriding objective; and

   (b)   co-operate with the Upper Tribunal generally.

3 Alternative dispute resolution and arbitration

(1)   The Upper Tribunal should seek, where appropriate—

   (a)   to bring to the attention of the parties the availability of any appropriate alternative procedure for the resolution of the dispute; and

   (b)   if the parties wish and provided that it is compatible with the overriding objective, to facilitate the use of the procedure.

(2)   Part 1 of the Arbitration Act 1996 does not apply to proceedings before the Upper Tribunal.

PART 2
GENERAL POWERS AND PROVISIONS

4 Delegation to staff

(1)   Staff appointed under section 40(1) of the 2007 Act (tribunal staff and services) may, with the approval of the Senior President of Tribunals, carry out functions of a judicial nature permitted or required to be done by the Upper Tribunal.

(2)   The approval referred to at paragraph (1) may apply generally to the carrying out of specified functions by members of staff of a specified description in specified circumstances.

(3)   Within 14 days after the date on which the Upper Tribunal sends notice of a decision made by a member of staff under paragraph (1) to a party, that party may apply in writing to the Upper Tribunal for that decision to be considered afresh by a judge.

5 Case management powers

(1)   Subject to the provisions of the 2007 Act and any other enactment, the Upper Tribunal may regulate its own procedure.

(2)   The Upper Tribunal may give a direction in relation to the conduct or disposal of proceedings at any time, including a direction amending, suspending or setting aside an earlier direction.

(3)   In particular, and without restricting the general powers in paragraphs (1) and (2), the Upper Tribunal may—

(a)   extend or shorten the time for complying with any rule, practice direction or direction;

(b)   consolidate or hear together two or more sets of proceedings or parts of proceedings raising common issues, or treat a case as a lead case;

(c)   permit or require a party to amend a document;

(d)   permit or require a party or another person to provide documents, information, evidence or submissions to the Upper Tribunal or a party;

(e)   deal with an issue in the proceedings as a preliminary issue;

(f)   hold a hearing to consider any matter, including a case management issue;

(g)   decide the form of any hearing;

(h)   adjourn or postpone a hearing;

(i)   require a party to produce a bundle for a hearing;

(j)   stay (or, in Scotland, sist) proceedings;

(k)   transfer proceedings to another court or tribunal if that other court or tribunal has jurisdiction in relation to the proceedings and—

(i)   because of a change of circumstances since the proceedings were started, the Upper Tribunal no longer has jurisdiction in relation to the proceedings; or

(ii)   the Upper Tribunal considers that the other court or tribunal is a more appropriate forum for the determination of the case;

(l)   suspend the effect of its own decision pending an appeal or review of that decision;

(m)   in an appeal, or an application for permission to appeal, against the decision of another tribunal, suspend the effect of that decision pending the determination of the application for permission to appeal, and any appeal;

[(n)   require any person, body or other tribunal whose decision is the subject of proceedings before the Upper Tribunal to provide reasons for the decision, or other information or documents in relation to the decision or any proceedings before that person, body or tribunal].

[(4)   The Upper Tribunal may direct that a fast-track case cease to be treated as a fast-track case if—

(a)   all the parties consent;

(b)   the Upper Tribunal is satisfied that there are exceptional circumstances which suggest that the appeal or application could not be justly determined if it were treated as a fast-track case; or

(c)   the Secretary of State for the Home Department has failed to comply with a provision of these Rules or a direction of the First-tier Tribunal or the Upper Tribunal, and the Upper Tribunal is satisfied that the other party would be prejudiced if the appeal or application were treated as a fast-track case.]

[(5)   In a financial services case, the Upper Tribunal may direct that the effect of the decision in respect of which the reference has been made is to be suspended pending the determination of the reference, if it is satisfied that to do so would not prejudice—

(a)   the interests of any persons (whether consumers, investors or otherwise) intended to be protected by that notice; . . .

(b)   the smooth operation or integrity of any market intended to be protected by that notice[; or

(c)   the stability of the financial system of the United Kingdom].

(6) Paragraph (5) does not apply in the case of a reference in respect of a decision of the Pensions Regulator.]

[(7) In a wholesale energy case, the Upper Tribunal may direct that the effect of the decision in respect of which the reference has been made is to be suspended pending the determination of the reference.]

Amendment

Para (3): sub-para (n) substituted by SI 2009/1975, rr 7, 9. Date in force: 1 September 2009: see SI 2009/1975, r 1.

Para (4): inserted by SI 2010/44, rr 2, 4. Date in force: 15 February 2010: see SI 2010/44, r 1.

Paras (5), (6): inserted by SI 2010/747, rr 2, 5. Date in force: 6 April 2010: see SI 2010/747, r 1.

Para (5): in sub-para (a) word omitted revoked by SI 2013/606, r 2(1), (3)(a). Date in force: 1 April 2013: see SI 2013/606, r 1.

Para (5): sub-para (c) and word preceding it inserted by SI 2013/606, r 2(1), (3)(b), (c). Date in force: 1 April 2013: see SI 2013/606, r 1.

Para (7): inserted by SI 2014/514, rr 2, 5. Date in force: 6 April 2014: see SI 2014/514, r 1.

6 Procedure for applying for and giving directions

(1) The Upper Tribunal may give a direction on the application of one or more of the parties or on its own initiative.

(2) An application for a direction may be made—

    (a) by sending or delivering a written application to the Upper Tribunal; or

    (b) orally during the course of a hearing.

(3) An application for a direction must include the reason for making that application.

(4) Unless the Upper Tribunal considers that there is good reason not to do so, the Upper Tribunal must send written notice of any direction to every party and to any other person affected by the direction.

(5) If a party or any other person sent notice of the direction under paragraph (4) wishes to challenge a direction which the Upper Tribunal has given, they may do so by applying for another direction which amends, suspends or sets aside the first direction.

7 Failure to comply with rules etc

(1) An irregularity resulting from a failure to comply with any requirement in these Rules, a practice direction or a direction, does not of itself render void the proceedings or any step taken in the proceedings.

(2) If a party has failed to comply with a requirement in these Rules, a practice direction or a direction, the Upper Tribunal may take such action as it considers just, which may include—

    (a) waiving the requirement;

    (b) requiring the failure to be remedied;

    (c) exercising its power under rule 8 (striking out a party's case); or

    (d) except in [a mental health case, an asylum case or an immigration case], restricting a party's participation in the proceedings.

(3) Paragraph (4) applies where the First-tier Tribunal has referred to the Upper Tribunal a failure by a person to comply with a requirement imposed by the First-tier Tribunal—

    (a) to attend at any place for the purpose of giving evidence;

    (b) otherwise to make themselves available to give evidence;

    (c) to swear an oath in connection with the giving of evidence;

    (d) to give evidence as a witness;

    (e) to produce a document; or

    (f) to facilitate the inspection of a document or any other thing (including any premises).

(4) The Upper Tribunal may exercise its power under section 25 of the 2007 Act (supplementary powers of the Upper Tribunal) in relation to such non-compliance as if the requirement had been imposed by the Upper Tribunal.

Amendment

Para (2): in sub-para (d) words "a mental health case, an asylum case or an immigration case" in square brackets substituted by SI 2010/44, rr 2, 5.

Date in force: 15 February 2010: see SI 2010/44, r 1.

8 Striking out a party's case

[(1A) Except for paragraph (2), this rule does not apply to an asylum case or an immigration case.]

[(1) The proceedings, or the appropriate part of them, will automatically be struck out—

- (a) if the appellant or applicant has failed to comply with a direction that stated that failure by the appellant or applicant to comply with the direction would lead to the striking out of the proceedings or part of them; or

- [(b) in immigration judicial review proceedings, when a fee has not been paid, as required, in respect of an application under rule 30(4) or upon the grant of permission].]

(2) The Upper Tribunal must strike out the whole or a part of the proceedings if the Upper Tribunal—

- (a) does not have jurisdiction in relation to the proceedings or that part of them; and

- (b) does not exercise its power under rule 5(3)(k)(i) (transfer to another court or tribunal) in relation to the proceedings or that part of them.

(3) The Upper Tribunal may strike out the whole or a part of the proceedings if—

- (a) the appellant or applicant has failed to comply with a direction which stated that failure by the appellant or applicant to comply with the direction could lead to the striking out of the proceedings or part of them;

- (b) the appellant or applicant has failed to co-operate with the Upper Tribunal to such an extent that the Upper Tribunal cannot deal with the proceedings fairly and justly; or

- (c) in proceedings which are not an appeal from the decision of another tribunal or judicial review proceedings, the Upper Tribunal considers there is no reasonable prospect of the appellant's or the applicant's case, or part of it, succeeding.

(4) The Upper Tribunal may not strike out the whole or a part of the proceedings under paragraph (2) or (3)(b) or (c) without first giving the appellant or applicant an opportunity to make representations in relation to the proposed striking out.

(5) If the proceedings have been struck out under paragraph (1) or (3)(a), the appellant or applicant may apply for the proceedings, or part of them, to be reinstated.

(6) An application under paragraph (5) must be made in writing and received by the Upper Tribunal within 1 month after the date on which the Upper Tribunal sent notification of the striking out to the appellant or applicant.

(7) This rule applies to a respondent [or an interested party] as it applies to an appellant or applicant except that—

- (a) a reference to the striking out of the proceedings is to be read as a reference to the barring of the respondent [or interested party] from taking further part in the proceedings; and

- (b) a reference to an application for the reinstatement of proceedings which have been struck out is to be read as a reference to an application for the lifting of the bar on the respondent [or interested party] . . . taking further part in the proceedings.

(8)   If a respondent [or an interested party] has been barred from taking further part in proceedings under this rule and that bar has not been lifted, the Upper Tribunal need not consider any response or other submission made by that respondent [or interested party, and may summarily determine any or all issues against that respondent or interested party].

Amendment
    Para (1A): inserted by SI 2010/44, rr 2, 6.
    Date in force: 15 February 2010: see SI 2010/44, r 1.
    Para (1): substituted by SI 2011/2343, rr 2, 5.
    Date in force: 17 October 2011: see SI 2011/2343, r 1.
    Para (1): sub-para (b) substituted by SI 2013/2067, rr 2, 5. Date in force: 1 November 2013: see SI 2013/2067, r 1.
    Para (7): words "or an interested party" in square brackets inserted by SI 2009/274, rr 3, 6(1), (2)(a).
    Date in force: 1 April 2009: see SI 2009/274, r 1.
    Para (7): in sub-paras (a), (b) words "or interested party" in square brackets inserted by SI 2009/274, rr 3, 6(1), (2)(b).
    Date in force: 1 April 2009: see SI 2009/274, r 1.
    Para (7): in sub-para (b) word omitted revoked by SI 2009/274, rr 3, 6(1), (2)(c).
    Date in force: 1 April 2009: see SI 2009/274, r 1.
    Para (8): words "or an interested party" in square brackets inserted by SI 2009/274, rr 3, 6(1), (3)(a).
    Date in force: 1 April 2009: see SI 2009/274, r 1.
    Para (8): words from "or interested party," to "or interested party" in square brackets inserted by SI 2009/274, rr 3, 6(1), (3)(b).
    Date in force: 1 April 2009: see SI 2009/274, r 1.

[9 Addition, substitution and removal of parties]
[(1)   The Upper Tribunal may give a direction adding, substituting or removing a party as an appellant, a respondent or an interested party.
(2)   If the Upper Tribunal gives a direction under paragraph (1) it may give such consequential directions as it considers appropriate.
(3)   A person who is not a party may apply to the Upper Tribunal to be added or substituted as a party.
(4)   If a person who is entitled to be a party to proceedings by virtue of another enactment applies to be added as a party, and any conditions applicable to that entitlement have been satisfied, the Upper Tribunal must give a direction adding that person as a respondent or, if appropriate, as an appellant.]
[(5)   In an asylum case, the United Kingdom Representative of the United Nations High Commissioner for Refugees ("the United Kingdom Representative") may give notice to the Upper Tribunal that the United Kingdom Representative wishes to participate in the proceedings.
(6)   If the United Kingdom Representative gives notice under paragraph (5)—
    (i)   the United Kingdom Representative is entitled to participate in any hearing; and
    (ii)   all documents which are required to be sent or delivered to parties must be sent or delivered to the United Kingdom Representative.]

Amendment
    Substituted by SI 2009/1975, rr 7, 10.
    Date in force: 1 September 2009: see SI 2009/1975, r 1.
    Paras (5), (6): inserted by SI 2010/44, rr 2, 7.
    Date in force: 15 February 2010: see SI 2010/44, r 1.

[10 Orders for costs]

[(1) The Upper Tribunal may not make an order in respect of costs (or, in Scotland, expenses) in proceedings [transferred or referred by, or on appeal from,] another tribunal except—

[(aa) in a national security certificate appeal, to the extent permitted by paragraph (1A);]

(a) in proceedings [transferred by, or on appeal from,] the Tax Chamber of the First-tier Tribunal; or

(b) to the extent and in the circumstances that the other tribunal had the power to make an order in respect of costs (or, in Scotland, expenses).

[(1A) In a national security certificate appeal—

(a) the Upper Tribunal may make an order in respect of costs or expenses in the circumstances described at paragraph (3)(c) and (d);

(b) if the appeal is against a certificate, the Upper Tribunal may make an order in respect of costs or expenses against the relevant Minister and in favour of the appellant if the Upper Tribunal allows the appeal and quashes the certificate to any extent or the Minister withdraws the certificate;

(c) if the appeal is against the application of a certificate, the Upper Tribunal may make an order in respect of costs or expenses—

(i) against the appellant and in favour of any other party if the Upper Tribunal dismisses the appeal to any extent; or

(ii) in favour of the appellant and against any other party if the Upper Tribunal allows the appeal to any extent.]

(2) The Upper Tribunal may not make an order in respect of costs or expenses under section 4 of the Forfeiture Act 1982.

(3) In other proceedings, the Upper Tribunal may not make an order in respect of costs or expenses except—

(a) in judicial review proceedings;

(b) . . .

(c) under section 29(4) of the 2007 Act (wasted costs) [and costs incurred in applying for such costs]; . . .

(d) if the Upper Tribunal considers that a party or its representative has acted unreasonably in bringing, defending or conducting the proceedings;[;][or

(e) if, in a financial services case [or a wholesale energy case], the Upper Tribunal considers that the decision in respect of which the reference was made was unreasonable].

(4) The Upper Tribunal may make an order for costs (or, in Scotland, expenses) on an application or on its own initiative.

(5) A person making an application for an order for costs or expenses must—

(a) send or deliver a written application to the Upper Tribunal and to the person against whom it is proposed that the order be made; and

(b) send or deliver with the application a schedule of the costs or expenses claimed sufficient to allow summary assessment of such costs or expenses by the Upper Tribunal.

(6) An application for an order for costs or expenses may be made at any time during the proceedings but may not be made later than 1 month after the date on which the Upper Tribunal sends—

(a) a decision notice recording the decision which finally disposes of all issues in the proceedings; or

[(b) notice under rule 17(5) that a withdrawal which ends the proceedings has taken effect].

(7) The Upper Tribunal may not make an order for costs or expenses against a person (the "paying person") without first—

(a) giving that person an opportunity to make representations; and

(b) if the paying person is an individual and the order is to be made under paragraph (3)(a), (b) or (d), considering that person's financial means.

(8) The amount of costs or expenses to be paid under an order under this rule may be ascertained by—

(a) summary assessment by the Upper Tribunal;

(b) agreement of a specified sum by the paying person and the person entitled to receive the costs or expenses[, including the costs or expenses of the assessment,] ("the receiving person"); or

(c) assessment of the whole or a specified part of the costs or expenses incurred by the receiving person, if not agreed.

(9) Following an order for assessment under paragraph (8)(c), the paying person or the receiving person may apply—

(a) in England and Wales, to the High Court or the Costs Office of the Supreme Court (as specified in the order) for a detailed assessment of the costs on the standard basis or, if specified in the order, on the indemnity basis; and the Civil Procedure Rules 1998 shall apply, with necessary modifications, to that application and assessment as if the proceedings in the tribunal had been proceedings in a court to which the Civil Procedure Rules 1998 apply;

(b) in Scotland, to the Auditor of the Court of Session for the taxation of the expenses according to the fees payable in that court; or

(c) in Northern Ireland, to the Taxing Office of the High Court of Northern Ireland for taxation on the standard basis or, if specified in the order, on the indemnity basis.]

[(10) Upon making an order for the assessment of costs, the [Upper] Tribunal may order an amount to be paid on account before the costs or expenses are assessed.]

Amendment

Substituted by SI 2009/274, rr 3, 7.

Date in force: 1 April 2009: see SI 2009/274, r 1.

Para (1): words "transferred or referred by, or on appeal from," in square brackets substituted by SI 2009/1975, rr 7, 11(a)(i).

Date in force: 1 September 2009: see SI 2009/1975, r 1.

Para (1): sub-para (aa) inserted by SI 2010/43, rr 5, 7(a).

Date in force: 18 January 2010: see SI 2010/43, r 1.

Para (1): in sub-para (a) words "transferred by, or on appeal from," in square brackets substituted by SI 2009/1975, rr 7, 11(a)(ii).

Date in force: 1 September 2009: see SI 2009/1975, r 1.

Para (1A): inserted by SI 2010/43, rr 5, 7(b).

Date in force: 18 January 2010: see SI 2010/43, r 1.

Para (3): sub-para (b) revoked by SI 2009/1975, rr 7, 11(b).

Date in force: 1 September 2009: see SI 2009/1975, r 1.

Para (3): in sub-para (c) word omitted revoked by SI 2010/747, rr 2, 6(a).

Date in force: 6 April 2010: see SI 2010/747, r 1.

Para (3): in sub-para (c) words "and costs incurred in applying for such costs" in square brackets inserted by SI 2013/477, rr 49, 50. Date in force: 1 April 2013: see SI 2013/477, r 1(2)(c).

Para (3): sub-para (e) and word "or" immediately preceding it inserted by SI 2010/747, rr 2, 6(b). Date in force: 6 April 2010: see SI 2010/747, r 1.

Para (3): in sub-para (e) words "or a wholesale energy case" in square brackets inserted by SI 2014/514, rr 2, 6. Date in force: 6 April 2014: see SI 2014/514, r 1.

Para (6): sub-para (b) substituted by SI 2013/477, rr 49, 51. Date in force: 1 April 2013: see SI 2013/477, r 1(2)(c).

Para (8): in sub-para (c) words ", including the costs or expenses of the assessment," in square brackets inserted by SI 2013/477, rr 49, 52. Date in force: 1 April 2013: see SI 2013/477, r 1(2)(c)

Para (10): inserted by SI 2013/477, rr 49, 53. Date in force: 1 April 2013: see SI 2013/477, r 1(2)(c).

Para (10): word "Upper" in square brackets inserted by SI 2013/2067, rr 2, 6. Date in force: 1 November 2013: see SI 2013/2067, r 1.

11 Representatives

(1) [Subject to paragraph (5A),] a party may appoint a representative (whether a legal representative or not) to represent that party in the proceedings [save that a party in an asylum or immigration case may not be represented by any person prohibited from representing by section 84 of the Immigration and Asylum Act 1999].

(2) If a party appoints a representative, that party (or the representative if the representative is a legal representative) must send or deliver to the Upper Tribunal . . . written notice of the representative's name and address.

[(2A) If the Upper Tribunal receives notice that a party has appointed a representative under paragraph (2), it must send a copy of that notice to each other party.]

(3) Anything permitted or required to be done by a party under these Rules, a practice direction or a direction may be done by the representative of that party, except signing a witness statement.

(4) A person who receives due notice of the appointment of a representative—

    (a)   must provide to the representative any document which is required to be provided to the represented party, and need not provide that document to the represented party; and

    (b)   may assume that the representative is and remains authorised as such until they receive written notification that this is not so from the representative or the represented party.

(5) [Subject to paragraph (5B),] at a hearing a party may be accompanied by another person whose name and address has not been notified under paragraph (2) but who, subject to paragraph (8) and with the permission of the Upper Tribunal, may act as a representative or otherwise assist in presenting the party's case at the hearing.

[(5A) In [immigration judicial review] proceedings, a party may appoint as a representative only a person authorised under the Legal Services Act 2007 to undertake the conduct of litigation in the High Court.

(5B) At a hearing of [immigration judicial review] proceedings, rights of audience before the Upper Tribunal are restricted to persons authorised to exercise those rights in the High Court under the Legal Services Act 2007.]

(6) Paragraphs (2) to (4) do not apply to a person who accompanies a party under paragraph (5).

(7) In a mental health case if the patient has not appointed a representative the Upper Tribunal may appoint a legal representative for the patient where—

    (a)   the patient has stated that they do not wish to conduct their own case or that they wish to be represented; or

    (b)   the patient lacks the capacity to appoint a representative but the Upper Tribunal believes that it is in the patient's best interests for the patient to be represented.

(8) In a mental health case a party may not appoint as a representative, or be represented or assisted at a hearing by—

    (a)   a person liable to be detained or subject to guardianship or after-care under supervision, or who is a community patient, under the Mental Health Act 1983; or

    (b)   a person receiving treatment for mental disorder at the same hospital home as the patient.

[(9) In this rule "legal representative" means [a person who, for the purposes of the Legal Services Act 2007, is an authorised person in relation to an activity which constitutes the exercise of a right of audience or the conduct of litigation within the meaning of that Act], [a qualified person as defined in section 84(2) of the Immigration and Asylum Act 1999,] an advocate or solicitor in Scotland or a barrister or solicitor in Northern Ireland.]

[(10)   In an asylum case or an immigration case, an appellant's representative before the First-tier Tribunal will be treated as that party's representative before the Upper Tribunal, unless the Upper Tribunal receives notice—

    (a)   of a new representative under paragraph (2) of this rule; or

    (b)   from the appellant stating that they are no longer represented.]

Amendment

Para (1): words "Subject to paragraph (5A)," in square brackets inserted by SI 2011/2343, rr 2, 6(a).

Date in force: 17 October 2011: see SI 2011/2343, r 1.

Para (1): words from "save that a" to "the Immigration and Asylum Act 1999" in square brackets inserted by SI 2010/44, rr 2, 8(a).

Date in force: 15 February 2010: see SI 2010/44, r 1.

Para (2): words omitted revoked by SI 2009/274, rr 3, 8(a).

Date in force: 1 April 2009: see SI 2009/274, r 1.

Para (2A): inserted by SI 2009/274, rr 3, 8(b).

Date in force: 1 April 2009: see SI 2009/274, r 1.

Para (5): words "Subject to paragraph (5B)," in square brackets inserted by SI 2011/2343, rr 2, 6(b).

Date in force: 17 October 2011: see SI 2011/2343, r 1.

Paras (5A), (5B): inserted by SI 2011/2343, rr 2, 6(c). Date in force: 17 October 2011: see SI 2011/2343, r 1.

Paras (5A), (5B): words "immigration judicial review" in square brackets substituted by SI 2013/2067, rr 2, 7. Date in force: 1 November 2013: see SI 2013/2067, r 1.

Para (9): inserted by SI 2009/274, rr 3, 8(c).

Date in force: 1 April 2009: see SI 2009/274, r 1.

Para (9): words from "a person who," to "of that Act" in square brackets substituted by SI 2010/43, rr 5, 8.

Date in force: 18 January 2010: see SI 2010/43, r 1.

Para (9): words from "a qualified person" to "the Immigration and Asylum Act 1999," in square brackets inserted by SI 2010/44, rr 2, 8(b).

Date in force: 15 February 2010: see SI 2010/44, r 1.

Para (10): inserted by SI 2010/44, rr 2, 8(c).

Date in force: 15 February 2010: see SI 2010/44, r 1.

12 Calculating time

(1)   An act required by these Rules, a practice direction or a direction to be done on or by a particular day must be done by 5pm on that day.

(2)   If the time specified by these Rules, a practice direction or a direction for doing any act ends on a day other than a working day, the act is done in time if it is done on the next working day.

(3)   In a special educational needs case or a disability discrimination in schools case, the following days must not be counted when calculating the time by which an act must be done—

    (a)   25th December to 1st January inclusive; and

    (b)   any day in August.

[(3A)   In an asylum case or an immigration case, when calculating the time by which an act must be done, in addition to the days specified in the definition of "working days" in rule 1 (interpretation), the following days must also not be counted as working days—

    (a)   27th to 31st December inclusive; and

    (b)   in a fast-track case, 24th December, Maundy Thursday, or the Tuesday after the last Monday in May.]

(4)   Paragraph (3) [or (3A)] does not apply where the Upper Tribunal directs that an act must be done by or on a specified date.

[(5)   In this rule—

"disability discrimination in schools case" means proceedings concerning disability discrimination in the education of a child or related matters; and

"special educational needs case" means proceedings concerning the education of a child who has or may have special educational needs.]

Amendment

Para (3A): inserted by SI 2010/44, rr 2, 9(a).

Date in force: 15 February 2010: see SI 2010/44, r 1.

Para (4): words "or (3A)" in square brackets inserted by SI 2010/44, rr 2, 9(b).

Date in force: 15 February 2010: see SI 2010/44, r 1.

Para (5): inserted by SI 2009/274, rr 3, 9.

Date in force: 1 April 2009: see SI 2009/274, r 1.

13 Sending and delivery of documents

(1)   Any document to be provided to the Upper Tribunal under these Rules, a practice direction or a direction must be—

   (a)   sent by pre-paid post or [by document exchange, or delivered by hand,] to the address specified for the proceedings;

   (b)   sent by fax to the number specified for the proceedings; or

   (c)   sent or delivered by such other method as the Upper Tribunal may permit or direct.

(2)   Subject to paragraph (3), if a party provides a fax number, email address or other details for the electronic transmission of documents to them, that party must accept delivery of documents by that method.

(3)   If a party informs the Upper Tribunal and all other parties that a particular form of communication, other than pre-paid post or delivery by hand, should not be used to provide documents to that party, that form of communication must not be so used.

(4)   If the Upper Tribunal or a party sends a document to a party or the Upper Tribunal by email or any other electronic means of communication, the recipient may request that the sender provide a hard copy of the document to the recipient. The recipient must make such a request as soon as reasonably practicable after receiving the document electronically.

(5)   The Upper Tribunal and each party may assume that the address provided by a party or its representative is and remains the address to which documents should be sent or delivered until receiving written notification to the contrary.

[(6)   Subject to paragraph (7), if a document submitted to the Upper Tribunal is not written in English, it must be accompanied by an English translation.

(7)   In proceedings that are in Wales or have a connection with Wales, a document or translation may be submitted to the [Upper] Tribunal in Welsh.]

Amendment

Para (1): in sub-para (a) words "by document exchange, or delivered by hand," in square brackets substituted by SI 2009/274, rr 3, 10. Date in force: 1 April 2009: see SI 2009/274, r 1.

Paras (6), (7): inserted by SI 2010/44, rr 2, 10. Date in force: 15 February 2010: see SI 2010/44, r 1.

Para (7): word "Upper" in square brackets inserted by SI 2013/2067, rr 2, 8. Date in force: 1 November 2013: see SI 2013/2067, r 1.

14 Use of documents and information

(1)   The Upper Tribunal may make an order prohibiting the disclosure or publication of—

   (a)   specified documents or information relating to the proceedings; or

   (b)   any matter likely to lead members of the public to identify any person whom the Upper Tribunal considers should not be identified.

(2) The Upper Tribunal may give a direction prohibiting the disclosure of a document or information to a person if—

(a) the Upper Tribunal is satisfied that such disclosure would be likely to cause that person or some other person serious harm; and

(b) the Upper Tribunal is satisfied, having regard to the interests of justice, that it is proportionate to give such a direction.

(3) If a party ("the first party") considers that the Upper Tribunal should give a direction under paragraph (2) prohibiting the disclosure of a document or information to another party ("the second party"), the first party must—

(a) exclude the relevant document or information from any documents that will be provided to the second party; and

(b) provide to the Upper Tribunal the excluded document or information, and the reason for its exclusion, so that the Upper Tribunal may decide whether the document or information should be disclosed to the second party or should be the subject of a direction under paragraph (2).

(4) ...

(5) If the Upper Tribunal gives a direction under paragraph (2) which prevents disclosure to a party who has appointed a representative, the Upper Tribunal may give a direction that the documents or information be disclosed to that representative if the Upper Tribunal is satisfied that—

(a) disclosure to the representative would be in the interests of the party; and

(b) the representative will act in accordance with paragraph (6).

(6) Documents or information disclosed to a representative in accordance with a direction under paragraph (5) must not be disclosed either directly or indirectly to any other person without the Upper Tribunal's consent.

(7) Unless the Upper Tribunal gives a direction to the contrary, information about mental health cases and the names of any persons concerned in such cases must not be made public.

[(8) The Upper Tribunal may, on its own initiative or on the application of a party, give a direction that certain documents or information must or may be disclosed to the Upper Tribunal on the basis that the Upper Tribunal will not disclose such documents or information to other persons, or specified other persons.

(9) A party making an application for a direction under paragraph (8) may withhold the relevant documents or information from other parties until the Upper Tribunal has granted or refused the application.

(10) In a case involving matters relating to national security, the Upper Tribunal must ensure that information is not disclosed contrary to the interests of national security.

(11) The Upper Tribunal must conduct proceedings and record its decision and reasons appropriately so as not to undermine the effect of an order made under paragraph (1), a direction given under paragraph (2) or (8) or the duty imposed by paragraph (10).]

Amendment

Para (4): revoked by SI 2009/1975, rr 7, 13(a).

Date in force: 1 September 2009: see SI 2009/1975, r 1.

Paras (8)–(11): inserted by SI 2009/1975, rr 7, 13(b).

Date in force: 1 September 2009: see SI 2009/1975, r 1.

15 Evidence and submissions

(1) Without restriction on the general powers in rule 5(1) and (2) (case management powers), the Upper Tribunal may give directions as to—

(a) issues on which it requires evidence or submissions;

(b) the nature of the evidence or submissions it requires;

(c) whether the parties are permitted or required to provide expert evidence, and if so whether the parties must jointly appoint a single expert to provide such evidence;

(d) any limit on the number of witnesses whose evidence a party may put forward, whether in relation to a particular issue or generally;

(e) the manner in which any evidence or submissions are to be provided, which may include a direction for them to be given—

(i) orally at a hearing; or

(ii) by written submissions or witness statement; and

(f) the time at which any evidence or submissions are to be provided.

(2) The Upper Tribunal may—

(a) admit evidence whether or not—

(i) the evidence would be admissible in a civil trial in the United Kingdom; or

(ii) the evidence was available to a previous decision maker; or

(b) exclude evidence that would otherwise be admissible where—

(i) the evidence was not provided within the time allowed by a direction or a practice direction;

(ii) the evidence was otherwise provided in a manner that did not comply with a direction or a practice direction; or

(iii) it would otherwise be unfair to admit the evidence.

[(2A) In an asylum case or an immigration case—

(a) if a party wishes the Upper Tribunal to consider evidence that was not before the First-tier Tribunal, that party must send or deliver a notice to the Upper Tribunal and any other party—

(i) indicating the nature of the evidence; and

(ii) explaining why it was not submitted to the First-tier Tribunal; and

(b) when considering whether to admit evidence that was not before the First-tier Tribunal, the Upper Tribunal must have regard to whether there has been unreasonable delay in producing that evidence.]

(3) The Upper Tribunal may consent to a witness giving, or require any witness to give, evidence on oath, and may administer an oath for that purpose.

Amendment

Para (2A): inserted by SI 2010/44, rr 2, 11.

Date in force: 15 February 2010: see SI 2010/44, r 1.

16 Summoning or citation of witnesses and orders to answer questions or produce documents

(1) On the application of a party or on its own initiative, the Upper Tribunal may—

(a) by summons (or, in Scotland, citation) require any person to attend as a witness at a hearing at the time and place specified in the summons or citation; or

(b) order any person to answer any questions or produce any documents in that person's possession or control which relate to any issue in the proceedings.

(2) A summons or citation under paragraph (1)(a) must—

(a) give the person required to attend 14 days' notice of the hearing or such shorter period as the Upper Tribunal may direct; and

(b) where the person is not a party, make provision for the person's necessary expenses of attendance to be paid, and state who is to pay them.

(3) No person may be compelled to give any evidence or produce any document that the person could not be compelled to give or produce on a trial of an action in a court

of law in the part of the United Kingdom where the proceedings are due to be determined.

[(4) A person who receives a summons, citation or order may apply to the Upper Tribunal for it to be varied or set aside if they did not have an opportunity to object to it before it was made or issued.

(5) A person making an application under paragraph (4) must do so as soon as reasonably practicable after receiving notice of the summons, citation or order.

(6) A summons, citation or order under this rule must—

(a)   state that the person on whom the requirement is imposed may apply to the Upper Tribunal to vary or set aside the summons, citation or order, if they did not have an opportunity to object to it before it was made or issued; and

(b)   state the consequences of failure to comply with the summons, citation or order.]

Amendment

Paras (4)–(6): substituted, for para (4) as originally enacted, by SI 2009/274, rr 3, 11.

Date in force: 1 April 2009: see SI 2009/274, r 1.

17 Withdrawal

(1) Subject to paragraph (2), a party may give notice of the withdrawal of its case, or any part of it—

(a)   . . . by sending or delivering to the Upper Tribunal a written notice of withdrawal; or

(b)   orally at a hearing.

(2) Notice of withdrawal will not take effect unless the Upper Tribunal consents to the withdrawal except in relation to an application for permission to appeal.

(3) A party which has withdrawn its case may apply to the Upper Tribunal for the case to be reinstated.

(4) An application under paragraph (3) must be made in writing and be received by the Upper Tribunal within 1 month after—

(a)   the date on which the Upper Tribunal received the notice under paragraph (1)(a); or

(b)   the date of the hearing at which the case was withdrawn orally under paragraph (1)(b).

(5) The Upper Tribunal must notify each party in writing [that a withdrawal has taken effect] under this rule.

[(6) Paragraph (3) does not apply to a financial services case other than a reference against a penalty.]

Amendment

Para (1): in sub-para (a) words omitted revoked by SI 2013/477, rr 49, 54(a). Date in force: 1 April 2013: see SI 2013/477, r 1(2)(c).

Para (5): words "that a withdrawal has taken effect" in square brackets substituted by SI 2013/477, rr 49, 54(b). Date in force: 1 April 2013: see SI 2013/477, r 1(2)(c).

Para (6): inserted by SI 2010/747, rr 2, 7. Date in force: 6 April 2010: see SI 2010/747, r 1.

[17A Appeal treated as abandoned or finally determined in an asylum case or an immigration case]

[(1) A party to an asylum case or an immigration case before the Upper Tribunal must notify the [Upper] Tribunal if they are aware that—

(a)   the appellant has left the United Kingdom;

(b)   the appellant has been granted leave to enter or remain in the United Kingdom;

(c)   a deportation order has been made against the appellant; or

(d)   a document listed in paragraph 4(2) of Schedule 2 to the Immigration (European Economic Area) Regulations 2006 has been issued to the appellant.

(2)   Where an appeal is treated as abandoned pursuant to section 104(4) or (4A) of the Nationality, Immigration and Asylum Act 2002 or paragraph 4(2) of Schedule 2 to the Immigration (European Economic Area) Regulations 2006, or as finally determined pursuant to section 104(5) of the Nationality, Immigration and Asylum Act 2002, the Upper Tribunal must send the parties a notice informing them that the appeal is being treated as abandoned or finally determined.

(3)   Where an appeal would otherwise fall to be treated as abandoned pursuant to section 104(4A) of the Nationality, Immigration and Asylum Act 2002, but the appellant wishes to pursue their appeal, the appellant must send or deliver a notice, which must comply with any relevant practice directions, to the Upper Tribunal and the respondent so that it is received within thirty days of the date on which the notice of the grant of leave to enter or remain in the United Kingdom was sent to the appellant.

(4)   Where a notice of grant of leave to enter or remain is sent electronically or delivered personally, the time limit in paragraph (3) is twenty eight days.

(5)   Notwithstanding rule 5(3)(a) (case management powers) and rule 7(2) (failure to comply with rules etc), the Upper Tribunal must not extend the time limits in paragraph (3) and (4).]

Amendment

Inserted by SI 2010/44, rr 2, 12. Date in force: 15 February 2010: see SI 2010/44, r 1.

Para (1): word "Upper" in square brackets inserted by SI 2013/2067, rr 2, 9. Date in force: 1 November 2013: see SI 2013/2067, r 1.

18 Notice of funding of legal services

If a party is granted funding of legal services at any time, that party must as soon as practicable—

(a)
   (i)   if [civil legal services (within the meaning of section 8 of the Legal Aid, Sentencing and Punishment of Offenders Act 2012) are provided under arrangements made for the purposes of Part 1 of that Act or by] the Northern Ireland Legal Services Commission, send a copy of the [certificate or] funding notice to the Upper Tribunal; or
   (ii)   if funding is granted by the Scottish Legal Aid Board, send a copy of the legal aid certificate to the Upper Tribunal; and

(b)   notify every other party in writing that funding has been granted.

Amendment

In para (a)(i) words from "civil legal services" to "Act or by" in square brackets substituted by SI 2013/477, rr 49, 55(a). Date in force: 1 April 2013: see SI 2013/477, r 1(2)(c); for savings see SI 2013/534, regs 2, 14(3).

In para (a)(i) words "certificate or" in square brackets inserted by SI 2013/477, rr 49, 55(b). Date in force: 1 April 2013: see SI 2013/477, r 1(2)(c); for savings see SI 2013/534, regs 2, 14(3).

19 Confidentiality in child support or child trust fund cases

(1)   Paragraph (3) applies to an appeal against a decision of the First-tier Tribunal in proceedings under the Child Support Act 1991 in the circumstances described in paragraph (2), other than an appeal against a reduced benefit decision (as defined in section 46(10)(b) of the Child Support Act 1991, as that section had effect prior to the commencement of section 15(b) of the Child Maintenance and Other Payments Act 2008).

(2)   The circumstances referred to in paragraph (1) are that—

(a)   in the proceedings in the First-tier Tribunal in respect of which the appeal has been brought, there was an obligation to keep a person's address confidential; or

(b)   a person whose circumstances are relevant to the proceedings would like their address (or, in the case of the person with care of the child, the child's address) to be kept confidential and has given notice to that effect—

    (i)   to the Upper Tribunal in an application for permission to appeal or notice of appeal;

    (ii)   to the Upper Tribunal within 1 month after an enquiry by the Upper Tribunal; or

    (iii)   to the Secretary of State . . . or the Upper Tribunal when notifying a change of address after proceedings have been started.

(3)   Where this paragraph applies, the Secretary of State . . . and the Upper Tribunal must take appropriate steps to secure the confidentiality of the address, and of any information which could reasonably be expected to enable a person to identify the address, to the extent that the address or that information is not already known to each other party.

(4)   Paragraph (6) applies to an appeal against a decision of the First-tier Tribunal in proceedings under the Child Trust Funds Act 2004 in the circumstances described in paragraph (5).

(5)   The circumstances referred to in paragraph (4) are that—

(a)   in the proceedings in the First-tier Tribunal in respect of which the appeal has been brought, there was an obligation to keep a person's address confidential; or

(b)   a person whose circumstances are relevant to the proceedings would like their address (or, in the case of the person with care of the eligible child, the child's address) to be kept confidential and has given notice to that effect—

    (i)   to the Upper Tribunal in an application for permission to appeal or notice of appeal;

    (ii)   to the Upper Tribunal within 1 month after an enquiry by the Upper Tribunal; or

    (iii)   to HMRC or the Upper Tribunal when notifying a change of address after proceedings have been started.

(6)   Where this paragraph applies, HMRC and the Upper Tribunal must take appropriate steps to secure the confidentiality of the address, and of any information which could reasonably be expected to enable a person to identify the address, to the extent that the address or that information is not already known to each other party.

(7)   In this rule—

"eligible child" has the meaning set out in section 2 of the Child Trust Funds Act 2004; and

"HMRC" means Her Majesty's Revenue and Customs.

Amendment

Paras (2), (3): words omitted revoked by SI 2012/2007, art 3(2), Schedule, Pt 2, para 118. Date in force: 1 August 2012: see SI 2012/2007, art 1(2).

20 Power to pay expenses and allowances

(1)   In proceedings brought under section 4 of the Safeguarding Vulnerable Groups Act 2006 . . . ., the Secretary of State may pay such allowances for the purpose of or in connection with the attendance of persons at hearings as the Secretary of State may, with the consent of the Treasury, determine.

(2)   Paragraph (3) applies to proceedings on appeal from a decision of—

(a)   the First-tier Tribunal in proceedings under the Child Support Act 1991, section 12 of the Social Security Act 1998 or paragraph 6 of Schedule 7 to the Child Support, Pensions and Social Security Act 2000;

(b)   the First-tier Tribunal in a war pensions and armed forces case (as defined in the Tribunal Procedure (First-tier Tribunal) (War Pensions and Armed Forces Compensation Chamber) Rules 2008); or

(c)   a Pensions Appeal Tribunal for Scotland or Northern Ireland.

(3)   The Lord Chancellor (or, in Scotland, the Secretary of State) may pay to any person who attends any hearing such travelling and other allowances, including compensation for loss of remunerative time, as the Lord Chancellor (or, in Scotland, the Secretary of State) may determine.

Amendment
Para (1): words omitted revoked by SI 2009/274, rr 3, 12.
Date in force: 1 April 2009: see SI 2009/274, r 1.

[20A Procedure for applying for a stay of a decision pending an appeal]
[(1)   This rule applies where another enactment provides in any terms for the Upper Tribunal to stay or suspend, or to lift a stay or suspension of, a decision which is or may be the subject of an appeal to the Upper Tribunal ("the substantive decision") pending such appeal.

(2)   A person who wishes the Upper Tribunal to decide whether the substantive decision should be stayed or suspended must make a written application to the Upper Tribunal which must include—

(a)   the name and address of the person making the application;

(b)   the name and address of any representative of that person;

(c)   the address to which documents for that person should be sent or delivered;

(d)   the name and address of any person who will be a respondent to the appeal;

(e)   details of the substantive decision and any decision as to when that decision is to take effect, and copies of any written record of, or reasons for, those decisions; and

(f)   the grounds on which the person making the application relies.

(3)   In the case of an application under paragraph (2) [in a road transport case]—

(a)   the person making the application must notify the [decision maker]when making the application;

(b)   within 7 days of receiving notification of the application the [decision maker] must send or deliver written reasons for refusing or withdrawing the stay—

(i)   to the Upper Tribunal; and

(ii)   to the person making the application, if the [decision maker] has not already done so.

(4)   If the Upper Tribunal grants a stay or suspension following an application under this rule—

(a)   the Upper Tribunal may give directions as to the conduct of the appeal of the substantive decision; and

(b)   the Upper Tribunal may, where appropriate, grant the stay or suspension subject to conditions.

(5)   Unless the Upper Tribunal considers that there is good reason not to do so, the Upper Tribunal must send written notice of any decision made under this rule to each party.]

Amendment
Inserted by SI 2009/1975, rr 7, 14. Date in force: 1 September 2009: see SI 2009/1975, r 1.
Para (3): words in square brackets substituted by SI 2012/1363, r 6, as from 1 July 2012.

PART 3
[PROCEDURE FOR CASES IN] THE UPPER TRIBUNAL

Amendment
Part heading: words "Procedure for Cases in" in square brackets substituted by SI 2009/274, rr 3, 13.
Date in force: 1 April 2009: see SI 2009/274, r 1.

21 Application to the Upper Tribunal for permission to appeal

(1)   . . .

(2)   A person may apply to the Upper Tribunal for permission to appeal to the Upper Tribunal against a decision of another tribunal only if—

  (a)   they have made an application for permission to appeal to the tribunal which made the decision challenged; and

  (b)   that application has been refused or has not been admitted [or has been granted only on limited grounds].

(3)   An application for permission to appeal must be made in writing and received by the Upper Tribunal no later than—

  (a)   in the case of an application under section 4 of the Safeguarding Vulnerable Groups Act 2006, 3 months after the date on which written notice of the decision being challenged was sent to the appellant; . . .

  [(aa)   subject to paragraph (3A), in an asylum case or an immigration case where the appellant is in the United Kingdom at the time that the application is made—

      (i)   seven working days after the date on which notice of the First-tier Tribunal's refusal of permission was sent to the appellant; or

      (ii)   if the case is a fast-track case, four working days after the date on which notice of the First-tier Tribunal's refusal of permission was sent to the appellant;

  (ab)   subject to paragraph (3A), in an asylum case or an immigration case where the appellant is outside the United Kingdom at the time that the application is made, fifty six days after the date on which notice of the First-tier Tribunal's refusal of permission was sent to the appellant; or]

  (b)   otherwise, a month after the date on which the tribunal that made the decision under challenge sent notice of its refusal of permission to appeal, or refusal to admit the application for permission to appeal, to the appellant.

[(3A)   Where a notice of decision is sent electronically or delivered personally, the time limits in paragraph (3)(aa) and (ab) are—

  (a)   in sub-paragraph (aa)(i), five working days;

  (b)   in sub-paragraph (aa)(ii), two working days; and

  (c)   in sub-paragraph (ab), twenty eight days.]

(4)   The application must state—

  (a)   the name and address of the appellant;

  (b)   the name and address of the representative (if any) of the appellant;

  (c)   an address where documents for the appellant may be sent or delivered;

  (d)   details (including the full reference) of the decision challenged;

  (e)   the grounds on which the appellant relies; and

  (f)   whether the appellant wants the application to be dealt with at a hearing.

(5)   The appellant must provide with the application a copy of—

  (a)   any written record of the decision being challenged;

  (b)   any separate written statement of reasons for that decision; and

  (c)   if the application is for permission to appeal against a decision of another tribunal, the notice of refusal of permission to appeal, or notice of refusal to admit the application for permission to appeal, from that other tribunal.

(6) If the appellant provides the application to the Upper Tribunal later than the time required by paragraph (3) or by an extension of time allowed under rule 5(3)(a) (power to extend time)—

(a) the application must include a request for an extension of time and the reason why the application was not provided in time; and

(b) unless the Upper Tribunal extends time for the application under rule 5(3)(a) (power to extend time) the Upper Tribunal must not admit the application.

(7) If the appellant makes an application to the Upper Tribunal for permission to appeal against the decision of another tribunal, and that other tribunal refused to admit the appellant's application for permission to appeal because the application for permission or for a written statement of reasons was not made in time—

(a) the application to the Upper Tribunal for permission to appeal must include the reason why the application to the other tribunal for permission to appeal or for a written statement of reasons, as the case may be, was not made in time; and

(b) the Upper Tribunal must only admit the application if the Upper Tribunal considers that it is in the interests of justice for it to do so.

[(8) In this rule, a reference to notice of a refusal of permission to appeal is to be taken to include a reference to notice of a grant of permission to appeal on limited grounds.]

Amendment

Para (1): revoked by SI 2009/1975, rr 7, 15.

Date in force: 1 September 2009: see SI 2009/1975, r 1.

Para (2): in sub-para (b) words "or has been granted only on limited grounds" in square brackets inserted by SI 2014/514, rr 2, 7(a). Date in force: 6 April 2014: see SI 2014/514, r 1.

Para (3): in sub-para (a) word omitted revoked by SI 2010/44, rr 2, 13(a)(i).

Date in force: 15 February 2010: see SI 2010/44, r 1.

Para (3): sub-paras (aa), (ab) inserted by SI 2010/44, rr 2, 13(a)(ii).

Date in force: 15 February 2010: see SI 2010/44, r 1.

Para (3A): inserted by SI 2010/44, rr 2, 13(b).

Date in force: 15 February 2010: see SI 2010/44, r 1.

Para (8): inserted by SI 2014/514, rr 2, 7(b). Date in force: 6 April 2014: see SI 2014/514, r 1.

22 Decision in relation to permission to appeal

(1) [Subject to rule 40A,] if the Upper Tribunal refuses permission to appeal [or refuses to admit a late application for permission], it must send written notice of the refusal and of the reasons for the refusal to the appellant.

(2) If the Upper Tribunal gives permission to appeal—

(a) the Upper Tribunal must send written notice of the permission, and of the reasons for any limitations or conditions on such permission, to each party;

(b) subject to any direction by the Upper Tribunal, the application for permission to appeal stands as the notice of appeal and the Upper Tribunal must send to each respondent a copy of the application for permission to appeal and any documents provided with it by the appellant; and

(c) the Upper Tribunal may, with the consent of the appellant and each respondent, determine the appeal without obtaining any further response.

[(3) Paragraph (4) applies where the Upper Tribunal, without a hearing, determines an application for permission to appeal—

(a) against a decision of—

(i) the Tax Chamber of the First-tier Tribunal;

  (ii) the Health, Education and Social Care Chamber of the First-tier Tribunal;

  [(iia) the General Regulatory Chamber of the First-tier Tribunal;]

  [(iib) the Property Chamber of the First-tier Tribunal;]

  (iii) the Mental Health Review Tribunal for Wales; or

  (iv) the Special Educational Needs Tribunal for Wales; or

 (b) under section 4 of the Safeguarding Vulnerable Groups Act 2006.]

(4) In the circumstances set out at paragraph (3) the appellant may apply for the decision to be reconsidered at a hearing if the Upper Tribunal—

 (a) refuses permission to appeal [or refuses to admit a late application for permission]; or

 (b) gives permission to appeal on limited grounds or subject to conditions.

(5) An application under paragraph (4) must be made in writing and received by the Upper Tribunal within 14 days after the date on which the Upper Tribunal sent written notice of its decision regarding the application to the appellant.

Amendment

Para (1): words "Subject to rule 40A," in square brackets inserted by SI 2014/1505, rr 2, 3. Date in force: 30 June 2014: see SI 2014/1505, r 1.

Para (1): words "or refuses to admit a late application for permission" in square brackets inserted by SI 2014/514, rr 2, 8(a). Date in force: 6 April 2014: see SI 2014/514, r 1.

Para (3): substituted by SI 2009/274, rr 3, 14. Date in force: 1 April 2009: see SI 2009/274, r 1.

Para (3): in sub-para (a)(iia) inserted by SI 2009/1975, rr 7, 16. Date in force: 1 September 2009: see SI 2009/1975, r 1.

Para (3): sub-para (a)(iib) inserted by SI 2014/514, rr 2, 8(b). Date in force: 6 April 2014: see SI 2014/514, r 1.

Para (4): in sub-para (a) words "or refuses to admit a late application for permission" in square brackets inserted by SI 2014/514, rr 2, 8(c). Date in force: 6 April 2014: see SI 2014/514, r 1.

23 Notice of appeal

[(1) This rule applies—

 (a) to proceedings on appeal to the Upper Tribunal for which permission to appeal is not required, except proceedings to which rule 26A [or 26B] applies;

 (b) if another tribunal has given permission for a party to appeal to the Upper Tribunal; or

 (c) subject to any other direction by the Upper Tribunal, if the Upper Tribunal has given permission to appeal and has given a direction that the application for permission to appeal does not stand as the notice of appeal.

[(1A) In an asylum case or an immigration case in which the First-tier Tribunal has given permission to appeal, subject to any direction of the First-tier Tribunal or the Upper Tribunal, the application for permission to appeal sent or delivered to the First-tier Tribunal stands as the notice of appeal and accordingly paragraphs (2) to (6) of this rule do not apply.]

(2) The appellant must provide a notice of appeal to the Upper Tribunal so that it is received within 1 month after—

 (a) the date that the tribunal that gave permission to appeal sent notice of such permission to the appellant; or

 (b) if permission to appeal is not required, the date on which notice of decision to which the appeal relates was sent to the appellant.]

(3) The notice of appeal must include the information listed in rule 21(4)(a) to (e) (content of the application for permission to appeal) and, where the Upper Tribunal has given permission to appeal, the Upper Tribunal's case reference.

(4) If another tribunal has granted permission to appeal, the appellant must provide with the notice of appeal a copy of—

(a) any written record of the decision being challenged;

(b) any separate written statement of reasons for that decision; and

(c) the notice of permission to appeal.

(5) If the appellant provides the notice of appeal to the Upper Tribunal later than the time required by paragraph (2) or by an extension of time allowed under rule 5(3)(a) (power to extend time)—

(a) the notice of appeal must include a request for an extension of time and the reason why the notice was not provided in time; and

(b) unless the Upper Tribunal extends time for the notice of appeal under rule 5(3)(a) (power to extend time) the Upper Tribunal must not admit the notice of appeal.

[(6) When the Upper Tribunal receives the notice of appeal it must send a copy of the notice and any accompanying documents—

(a) to each respondent; or

[(b) in a road transport case, to—

(i) the decision maker;

(ii) the appropriate national authority; and

(iii) in a case relating to the detention of a vehicle, the authorised person.]]

Amendment

Paras (1), (2): substituted by SI 2009/1975, rr 7, 17(a).

Date in force: 1 September 2009: see SI 2009/1975, r 1.

Para (1): in sub-para (a) words "or 26B" in square brackets inserted by SI 2010/747, rr 2, 8.

Date in force: 6 April 2010: see SI 2010/747, r 1.

Para (1A): inserted by SI 2010/44, rr 2, 14.

Date in force: 15 February 2010: see SI 2010/44, r 1.

Para (6): substituted by SI 2009/1975, rr 7, 17(b).

Date in force: 1 September 2009: see SI 2009/1975, r 1.

Para (6): sub-para (b) substituted by SI 2012/1363, r 7, as from 1 July 2012.

24 Response to the notice of appeal

[(1) This rule and rule 25 do not apply to [a road transport case], in respect of which Schedule 1 makes alternative provision.

(1A) Subject to any direction given by the Upper Tribunal, a respondent may provide a response to a notice of appeal.]

(2) Any response provided under paragraph [(1A)] must be in writing and must be sent or delivered to the Upper Tribunal so that it is received—

[(a) if an application for permission to appeal stands as the notice of appeal, no later than one month after the date on which the respondent was sent notice that permission to appeal had been granted;]

[(aa) in a fast-track case, one day before the hearing of the appeal; or]

(b) in any other case, no later than 1 month after the date on which the Upper Tribunal sent a copy of the notice of appeal to the respondent.

(3) The response must state—

(a) the name and address of the respondent;

(b) the name and address of the representative (if any) of the respondent;

(c) an address where documents for the respondent may be sent or delivered;

(d) whether the respondent opposes the appeal;

(e) the grounds on which the respondent relies, including [(in the case of an appeal against the decision of another tribunal)] any grounds on which the respondent was unsuccessful in the proceedings which are the subject of the appeal, but intends to rely in the appeal; and

(f) whether the respondent wants the case to be dealt with at a hearing.

(4) If the respondent provides the response to the Upper Tribunal later than the time required by paragraph (2) or by an extension of time allowed under rule 5(3)(a) (power to extend time), the response must include a request for an extension of time and the reason why the [response] was not provided in time.

(5) When the Upper Tribunal receives the response it must send a copy of the response and any accompanying documents to the appellant and each other party.

Amendment

Paras (1), (1A): substituted, for para (1) as originally enacted, by SI 2009/1975, rr 7, 18(a).

Date in force: 1 September 2009: see SI 2009/1975, r 1.

Para (1): words in square brackets substituted by SI 2012/1363, r 8, as from 1 July 2012.

Para (2): reference to "(1A)" in square brackets substituted by SI 2010/43, rr 5, 9.

Date in force: 18 January 2010: see SI 2010/43, r 1.

Para (2): sub-para (a) substituted by SI 2010/44, rr 2, 15(a).

Date in force: 15 February 2010: see SI 2010/44, r 1.

Para (2): sub-para (aa) inserted by SI 2010/44, rr 2, 15(c).

Date in force: 15 February 2010: see SI 2010/44, r 1.

Para (3): in sub-para (e) words "(in the case of an appeal against the decision of another tribunal)" in square brackets inserted by SI 2009/1975, rr 7, 18(c).

Date in force: 1 September 2009: see SI 2009/1975, r 1.

Para (4): word "response" in square brackets substituted by SI 2009/274, rr 3, 15.

Date in force: 1 April 2009: see SI 2009/274, r 1.

25 Appellant's reply

(1) Subject to any direction given by the Upper Tribunal, the appellant may provide a reply to any response provided under rule 24 (response to the notice of appeal).

(2) [Subject to paragraph (2A), any] reply provided under paragraph (1) must be in writing and must be sent or delivered to the Upper Tribunal so that it is received within one month after the date on which the Upper Tribunal sent a copy of the response to the appellant.

[(2A) In an asylum case or an immigration case, the time limit in paragraph (2) is—

    (a)   one month after the date on which the Upper Tribunal sent a copy of the response to the appellant, or five days before the hearing of the appeal, whichever is the earlier; and

    (b)   in a fast-track case, the day of the hearing.]

(3) When the Upper Tribunal receives the reply it must send a copy of the reply and any accompanying documents to each respondent.

Amendment

Para (2): words "Subject to paragraph (2A), any" in square brackets substituted by SI 2010/44, rr 2, 16(a).

Date in force: 15 February 2010: see SI 2010/44, r 1.

Para (2A): inserted by SI 2010/44, rr 2, 16(b).

Date in force: 15 February 2010: see SI 2010/44, r 1.

26 References under the Forfeiture Act 1982

(1) If a question arises which is required to be determined by the Upper Tribunal under section 4 of the Forfeiture Act 1982, the person to whom the application for the relevant benefit or advantage has been made must refer the question to the Upper Tribunal.

(2) The reference must be in writing and must include—

    (a)   a statement of the question for determination;

    (b)   a statement of the relevant facts;

    (c)   the grounds upon which the reference is made; and

    (d)   an address for sending documents to the person making the reference and each respondent.

(3) When the Upper Tribunal receives the reference it must send a copy of the reference and any accompanying documents to each respondent.

(4) Rules 24 (response to the notice of appeal) and 25 (appellant's reply) apply to a reference made under this rule as if it were a notice of appeal.

[26A Cases transferred or referred to the Upper Tribunal, applications made directly to the Upper Tribunal and proceedings without notice to a respondent]

[[(1) Paragraphs (2) and (3) apply to—

    (a)   a case transferred or referred to the Upper Tribunal from the First-tier Tribunal; . . .

    [(aa)   in a reference under Schedule 1D of the Charities Act 1993, the Upper Tribunal may give directions providing for an application to join the proceedings as a party and the time within which it may be made; and]

    (b)   a case, other than an appeal or a case to which rule 26 (references under the Forfeiture Act 1982) applies, which is started by an application made directly to the Upper Tribunal.]

(2) In a case to which this paragraph applies—

    (a)   the Upper Tribunal must give directions as to the procedure to be followed in the consideration and disposal of the proceedings; and

    (b)   the preceding rules in this Part will only apply to the proceedings to the extent provided for by such directions.

(3) If a case or matter to which this paragraph applies is to be determined without notice to or the involvement of a respondent—

    (a)   any provision in these Rules requiring a document to be provided by or to a respondent; and

    (b)   any other provision in these Rules permitting a respondent to participate in the proceedings

does not apply to that case or matter.

[(4) Schedule 2 makes further provision for national security certificate appeals transferred to the Upper Tribunal.]]

Amendment

Inserted by SI 2009/274, rr 3, 16.

Date in force: 1 April 2009: see SI 2009/274, r 1.

Para (1): substituted by SI 2009/1975, rr 7, 19.

Date in force: 1 September 2009: see SI 2009/1975, r 1.

Para (2): word from sub-para (a) revoked and sub-para (aa) inserted by SI 2012/500, r 5. Date in force: 6 April 2012: see SI 2012/500, r 1(2).

Para (4): inserted by SI 2010/43, rr 5, 10.

Date in force: 18 January 2010: see SI 2010/43, r 1.

26B

(*Financial services cases and wholesale energy cases; outside the scope of this work.*)

PART 4
JUDICIAL REVIEW PROCEEDINGS IN THE UPPER TRIBUNAL

27 Application of this Part to judicial review proceedings transferred to the Upper Tribunal

(1) When a court transfers judicial review proceedings to the Upper Tribunal, the Upper Tribunal—

    (a)   must notify each party in writing that the proceedings have been transferred to the Upper Tribunal; and

    (b)   must give directions as to the future conduct of the proceedings.

(2) The directions given under paragraph (1)(b) may modify or disapply for the purposes of the proceedings any of the provisions of the following rules in this Part.

(3) In proceedings transferred from the Court of Session under section 20(1) of the 2007 Act, the directions given under paragraph (1)(b) must—

    (a)   if the Court of Session did not make a first order specifying the required intimation, service and advertisement of the petition, state the Upper Tribunal's requirements in relation to those matters;

    (b)   state whether the Upper Tribunal will consider summary dismissal of the proceedings; and

    (c)   where necessary, modify or disapply provisions relating to permission in the following rules in this Part.

28 Applications for permission to bring judicial review proceedings

(1) A person seeking permission to bring judicial review proceedings before the Upper Tribunal under section 16 of the 2007 Act must make a written application to the Upper Tribunal for such permission.

(2) Subject to paragraph (3), an application under paragraph (1) must be made promptly and, unless any other enactment specifies a shorter time limit, must be sent or delivered to the Upper Tribunal so that it is received no later than 3 months after the date of the decision[, action or omission] to which the application relates.

(3) An application for permission to bring judicial review proceedings challenging a decision of the First-tier Tribunal may be made later than the time required by paragraph (2) if it is made within 1 month after the date on which the First-tier Tribunal sent—

    (a)   written reasons for the decision; or

    (b)   notification that an application for the decision to be set aside has been unsuccessful, provided that that application was made in time.

(4) The application must state—

    (a)   the name and address of the applicant, the respondent and any other person whom the applicant considers to be an interested party;

    (b)   the name and address of the applicant's representative (if any);

    (c)   an address where documents for the applicant may be sent or delivered;

    (d)   details of the decision challenged (including the date, the full reference and the identity of the decision maker);

    (e)   that the application is for permission to bring judicial review proceedings;

    (f)   the outcome that the applicant is seeking; and

    (g)   the facts and grounds on which the applicant relies.

(5) If the application relates to proceedings in a court or tribunal, the application must name as an interested party each party to those proceedings who is not the applicant or a respondent.

(6) The applicant must send with the application—

    (a)   a copy of any written record of the decision in the applicant's possession or control; and

    (b)   copies of any other documents in the applicant's possession or control on which the applicant intends to rely.

(7) If the applicant provides the application to the Upper Tribunal later than the time required by paragraph (2) or (3) or by an extension of time allowed under rule 5(3)(a) (power to extend time)—

    (a)   the application must include a request for an extension of time and the reason why the application was not provided in time; and

    (b)   unless the Upper Tribunal extends time for the application under rule 5(3)(a) (power to extend time) the Upper Tribunal must not admit the application.

(8) [Except where rule 28A(2)(a) (special provisions for [immigration judicial review] proceedings) applies,] when the Upper Tribunal receives the application it must send a copy of the application and any accompanying documents to each person named in the application as a respondent or interested party.

Amendment
 Para (2): words ", action or omission" in square brackets inserted by SI 2009/274, rr 3, 17.
 Date in force: 1 April 2009: see SI 2009/274, r 1.
 Para (8): words "Except where rule 28A(2)(a) (special provisions for fresh claim proceedings) applies," in square brackets inserted by SI 2011/2343, rr 2, 7.
 Date in force: 17 October 2011: see SI 2011/2343, r 1.
 Para (8): words "immigration judicial review" in square brackets substituted by SI 2013/2067, rr 2, 10.
 Date in force: 1 November 2013: see SI 2013/2067, r 1.

[28A Special provisions for [immigration judicial review] proceedings]
[(1) The Upper Tribunal must not accept an application for permission to bring [immigration judicial review] proceedings unless it is either accompanied by any required fee or the Upper Tribunal accepts an undertaking that the fee will be paid.
(2) Within 9 days of making an application referred to in paragraph (1), an applicant must provide—
   (a)   a copy of the application and any accompanying documents to each person named in the application as a respondent or an interested party; and
   (b)   the Upper Tribunal with a written statement of when and how this was done.]

Amendment
 Inserted by SI 2011/2343, rr 2, 8. Date in force: 17 October 2011: see SI 2011/2343, r 1.
 Provision heading: words "immigration judicial review" in square brackets substituted by SI 2013/2067, rr 2, 11(a). Date in force: 1 November 2013: see SI 2013/2067, r 1.
 Para (1): words "immigration judicial review" in square brackets substituted by SI 2013/2067, rr 2, 11(b). Date in force: 1 November 2013: see SI 2013/2067, r 1

29 Acknowledgment of service
(1) A person who is sent [or provided with] a copy of an application for permission under rule 28(8) (application for permission to bring judicial review proceedings) [or rule 28A(2)(a) (special provisions for [immigration judicial review] proceedings)] and wishes to take part in the proceedings must [provide] to the Upper Tribunal an acknowledgment of service so that it is received no later than 21 days after the date on which the Upper Tribunal sent[, or in [immigration judicial review] proceedings the applicant provided,] a copy of the application to that person.
(2) An acknowledgment of service under paragraph (1) must be in writing and state—
   (a)   whether the person intends to [support or] oppose the application for permission;
   (b)   their grounds for any [support or] opposition under sub-paragraph (a), or any other submission or information which they consider may assist the Upper Tribunal; and
   (c)   the name and address of any other person not named in the application as a respondent or interested party whom the person providing the acknowledgment considers to be an interested party.
[(2A) In [immigration judicial review] proceedings, a person who provides an acknowledgement of service under paragraph (1) must also provide a copy to—
   (a)   the applicant; and
   (b)   any other person named in the application under rule 28(4)(a) or acknowledgement of service under paragraph (2)(c)

no later than the time specified in paragraph (1).]

(3)   A person who is [provided with] a copy of an application for permission under rule 28(8) [or 28A(2)(a)] but does not provide an acknowledgment of service [to the Upper Tribunal] may not take part in the application for permission [unless allowed to do so by the Upper Tribunal], but may take part in the subsequent proceedings if the application is successful.

Amendment

Para (1): words "or provided with" in square brackets inserted by SI 2011/2343, rr 2, 9(a)(i). Date in force: 17 October 2011: see SI 2011/2343, r 1.

Para (1): words "or rule 28A(2)(a) (special provisions for fresh claim proceedings)" in square brackets inserted by SI 2011/2343, rr 2, 9(a)(ii).

Date in force: 17 October 2011: see SI 2011/2343, r 1.

Para (1): word "provide" in square brackets substituted by SI 2011/2343, rr 2, 9(a)(iii). Date in force: 17 October 2011: see SI 2011/2343, r 1.

Para (1): words "immigration judicial review" in square brackets in both places they occur substituted by SI 2013/2067, rr 2, 12(a). Date in force: 1 November 2013: see SI 2013/2067, r 1

Para (2): in sub-para (a) words "support or" in square brackets inserted by SI 2009/274, rr 3, 18(a).

Date in force: 1 April 2009: see SI 2009/274, r 1.

Para (1): words ", or in fresh claim proceedings the applicant provided," in square brackets inserted by SI 2011/2343, rr 2, 9(a)(iv).

Date in force: 17 October 2011: see SI 2011/2343, r 1.

Para (2): in sub-para (b) words "support or" in square brackets inserted by SI 2009/274, rr 3, 18(b).

Date in force: 1 April 2009: see SI 2009/274, r 1.

Para (2A): inserted by SI 2011/2343, rr 2, 9(b).

Date in force: 17 October 2011: see SI 2011/2343, r 1.

Para (2A): words "immigration judicial review" in square brackets substituted by SI 2013/2067, rr 2, 12(b). Date in force: 1 November 2013: see SI 2013/2067, r 1.

Para (3): words "provided with" in square brackets substituted by SI 2011/2343, rr 2, 9(c)(i). Date in force: 17 October 2011: see SI 2011/2343, r 1.

Para (3): words "or 28A(2)(a)" in square brackets inserted by SI 2011/2343, rr 2, 9(c)(ii). Date in force: 17 October 2011: see SI 2011/2343, r 1.

Para (3): words "to the Upper Tribunal" in square brackets inserted by SI 2011/2343, rr 2, 9(c)(iii).

Date in force: 17 October 2011: see SI 2011/2343, r 1.

Para (3): words "unless allowed to do so by the Upper Tribunal" in square brackets inserted by SI 2011/651, r 8(1), (3)(3).

Date in force: 1 April 2011: see SI 2011/651, r 1(2)(a).

30 Decision on permission or summary dismissal, and reconsideration of permission or summary dismissal at a hearing

(1)   The Upper Tribunal must send to the applicant, each respondent and any other person who provided an acknowledgment of service to the Upper Tribunal, and may send to any other person who may have an interest in the proceedings, written notice of—

    (a)   its decision in relation to the application for permission; and

    [(b)   the reasons for any—

        (i)   refusal of the application or refusal to admit the late application, or

        (ii)   limitations or conditions on permission].

(2)   In proceedings transferred from the Court of Session under section 20(1) of the 2007 Act, where the Upper Tribunal has considered whether summarily to dismiss of the proceedings, the Upper Tribunal must send to the applicant and each respondent, and may send to any other person who may have an interest in the proceedings, written notice of—

(a)   its decision in relation to the summary dismissal of proceedings; and

(b)   the reasons for any decision summarily to dismiss part or all of the proceedings, or any limitations or conditions on the continuation of such proceedings.

(3)   Paragraph (4) applies where the Upper Tribunal, without a hearing—

[(a)   determines an application for permission to bring judicial review proceedings by—

(i)   refusing permission or refusing to admit the late application, or

(ii)   giving permission on limited grounds or subject to conditions]; or

(b)   in proceedings transferred from the Court of Session, summarily dismisses part or all of the proceedings, or imposes any limitations or conditions on the continuation of such proceedings.

(4)   [Subject to paragraph (4A), in the circumstances specified in paragraph (3) the applicant may apply for the decision to be reconsidered at a hearing.

[(4A)   Where the Upper Tribunal refuses permission to bring immigration judicial review proceedings [or refuses to admit a late application for permission to bring such proceedings] and considers the application to be totally without merit, it shall record that fact in its decision notice and, in those circumstances, the applicant may not request the decision to be reconsidered at a hearing.]

(5)   An application under paragraph (4) must be made in writing and must be sent or delivered to the Upper Tribunal so that it is received within 14 days[, or in fresh claim proceedings 9 days,] after the date on which the Upper Tribunal sent written notice of its decision regarding the application to the applicant.

Amendment

Para (1): sub-para (b) substituted by SI 2014/514, rr 2, 11(a). Date in force: 6 April 2014: see SI 2014/514, r 1.

Para (3): sub-para (a) substituted by SI 2014/514, rr 2, 11(b). Date in force: 6 April 2014: see SI 2014/514, r 1.

Para (4): words "Subject to paragraph (4A), in" in square brackets substituted by SI 2013/2067, rr 2, 13(a). Date in force: 1 November 2013: see SI 2013/2067, r 1; for transitional provisions see r 29 thereof.

Para (4A): inserted by SI 2013/2067, rr 2, 13(b). Date in force: 1 November 2013: see SI 2013/2067, r 1; for transitional provisions see r 29 thereof.

Para (4A): words from "or refuses to" to "bring such proceedings" in square brackets inserted by SI 2014/514, rr 2, 11(c). Date in force: 6 April 2014: see SI 2014/514, r 1.

Para (5): words in outer square brackets inserted by SI 2011/2343, rr 2, 10. Date in force: 17 October 2011: see SI 2011/2343, r 1; words in inner square brackets substituted by SI 2013/2067, rr 2, 13(c). Date in force: 1 November 2013: see SI 2013/2067, r 1.

31 Responses

(1)   Any person to whom the Upper Tribunal has sent notice of the grant of permission under rule 30(1) (notification of decision on permission), and who wishes to contest the application or support it on additional grounds, must provide detailed grounds for contesting or supporting the application to the Upper Tribunal.

(2)   Any detailed grounds must be provided in writing and must be sent or delivered to the Upper Tribunal so that they are received not more than 35 days after the Upper Tribunal sent notice of the grant of permission under rule 30(1).

32 Applicant seeking to rely on additional grounds

The applicant may not rely on any grounds, other than those grounds on which the applicant obtained permission for the judicial review proceedings, without the consent of the Upper Tribunal.

33 Right to make representations

Each party and, with the permission of the Upper Tribunal, any other person, may—

(a)   submit evidence, except at the hearing of an application for permission;

(b)   make representations at any hearing which they are entitled to attend; and

(c)   make written representations in relation to a decision to be made without a hearing.

[33A Amendments and additional grounds resulting in transfer of proceedings to the High Court in England and Wales]

[(1)   This rule applies only to judicial review proceedings arising under the law of England and Wales.

(2)   In relation to such proceedings—

(a)   the powers of the Upper Tribunal to permit or require amendments under rule 5(3)(c) extend to amendments which would, once in place, give rise to an obligation or power to transfer the proceedings to the High Court in England and Wales under section 18(3) of the 2007 Act or paragraph (3);

(b)   except with the permission of the Upper Tribunal, additional grounds may not be advanced, whether by an applicant or otherwise, if they would give rise to an obligation or power to transfer the proceedings to the High Court in England and Wales under section 18(3) of the 2007 Act or paragraph (3).

(3)   Where the High Court in England and Wales has transferred judicial review proceedings to the Upper Tribunal under any power or duty and subsequently the proceedings are amended or any party advances additional grounds—

(a)   if the proceedings in their present form could not have been transferred to the Upper Tribunal under the relevant power or duty had they been in that form at the time of the transfer, the Upper Tribunal must transfer the proceedings back to the High Court in England and Wales;

(b)   subject to sub-paragraph (a), where the proceedings were transferred to the Upper Tribunal under section 31A(3) of the Senior Courts Act 1981 (power to transfer judicial review proceedings to the Upper Tribunal), the Upper Tribunal may transfer proceedings back to the High Court in England and Wales if it appears just and convenient to do so.]

Amendment
Inserted by SI 2011/2343, rr 2, 11. Date in force: 17 October 2011: see SI 2011/2343, r 1.

PART 5
HEARINGS

34 Decision with or without a hearing

(1)   Subject to [paragraphs (2) and (3)], the Upper Tribunal may make any decision without a hearing.

(2)   The Upper Tribunal must have regard to any view expressed by a party when deciding whether to hold a hearing to consider any matter, and the form of any such hearing.

(3)   In immigration judicial review proceedings, the Upper Tribunal must hold a hearing before making a decision which disposes of proceedings.

(4)   Paragraph (3) does not affect the power of the Upper Tribunal to—

(a)   strike out a party's case, pursuant to rule 8(1)(b) or 8(2);

(b)   consent to withdrawal, pursuant to rule 17;

(c)   determine an application for permission to bring judicial review proceedings, pursuant to rule 30; or

(d)   make a consent order disposing of proceedings, pursuant to rule 39,

without a hearing.]

Amendment

Para (1): words "paragraphs (2) and (3)" in square brackets substituted by SI 2013/2067, rr 2, 14(a). Date in force: 1 November 2013: see SI 2013/2067, r 1.

Paras (3), (4): inserted by SI 2013/2067, rr 2, 14(b). Date in force: 1 November 2013: see SI 2013/2067, r 1.

35 Entitlement to attend a hearing

[(1)] Subject to rule 37(4) (exclusion of a person from a hearing), each party is entitled to attend a hearing.

[(2) In a national security certificate appeal the relevant Minister is entitled to attend any hearing.]

Amendment

Para (1): numbered as such by SI 2010/43, rr 5, 11(a).

Date in force: 18 January 2010: see SI 2010/43, r 1.

Para (2): inserted by SI 2010/43, rr 5, 11(b).

Date in force: 18 January 2010: see SI 2010/43, r 1.

36 Notice of hearings

(1) The Upper Tribunal must give each party entitled to attend a hearing reasonable notice of the time and place of the hearing (including any adjourned or postponed hearing) and any change to the time and place of the hearing.

(2) The period of notice under paragraph (1) must be at least 14 days except that—

    (a)   in applications for permission to bring judicial review proceedings, the period of notice must be at least 2 working days; . . .

    [(aa) in a fast-track case the period of notice must be at least one working day; and]

    (b)   [in any case other than a fast-track case] the Upper Tribunal may give shorter notice—

        (i)   with the parties' consent; or

        (ii)   in urgent or exceptional cases.

Amendment

Para (2): in sub-para (a) word omitted revoked by SI 2010/44, rr 2, 17(a)(i).

Date in force: 15 February 2010: see SI 2010/44, r 1.

Para (2): sub-para (aa) inserted by SI 2010/44, rr 2, 17(a)(ii).

Date in force: 15 February 2010: see SI 2010/44, r 1.

Para (2): in sub-para (b) words "in any case other than a fast-track case" in square brackets inserted by SI 2010/44, rr 2, 17(b).

Date in force: 15 February 2010: see SI 2010/44, r 1.

[36A Special time limits for hearing an appeal in a fast-track case]

[(1) Subject to rule 36(2)(aa) (notice of hearings) and paragraph (2) of this rule, where permission to appeal to the Upper Tribunal has been given in a fast-track case, the Upper Tribunal must start the hearing of the appeal not later than—

    (a)   four working days after the date on which the First-tier Tribunal or the Upper Tribunal sent notice of its grant of permission to appeal to the appellant; or

    (b)   where the notice of its grant of permission to appeal is sent electronically or delivered personally, two working days after the date on which the First-tier Tribunal or the Upper Tribunal sent notice of its grant of permission to appeal to the appellant.

(2) If the Upper Tribunal is unable to arrange for the hearing to start within the time specified in paragraph (1), it must set a date for the hearing as soon as is reasonably practicable.]

Amendment
Inserted by SI 2010/44, rr 2, 18.
Date in force: 15 February 2010: see SI 2010/44, r 1.

37 Public and private hearings

(1)   Subject to the following paragraphs, all hearings must be held in public.

(2)   The Upper Tribunal may give a direction that a hearing, or part of it, is to be held in private.

[(2A)   In a national security certificate appeal, the Upper Tribunal must have regard to its duty under rule 14(10) (no disclosure of information contrary to the interests of national security) when considering whether to give a direction that a hearing, or part of it, is to be held in private.]

(3)   Where a hearing, or part of it, is to be held in private, the Upper Tribunal may determine who is entitled to attend the hearing or part of it.

(4)   The Upper Tribunal may give a direction excluding from any hearing, or part of it—

   (a)   any person whose conduct the Upper Tribunal considers is disrupting or is likely to disrupt the hearing;

   (b)   any person whose presence the Upper Tribunal considers is likely to prevent another person from giving evidence or making submissions freely;

   (c)   any person who the Upper Tribunal considers should be excluded in order to give effect to [the requirement at rule 14(11) (prevention of disclosure or publication of documents and information)]; . . .

   (d)   any person where the purpose of the hearing would be defeated by the attendance of that person[; or

   (e)   a person under the age of eighteen years].

(5)   The Upper Tribunal may give a direction excluding a witness from a hearing until that witness gives evidence.

Amendment
Para (2A): inserted by SI 2010/43, rr 5, 12.
Date in force: 18 January 2010: see SI 2010/43, r 1.
Para (4): in sub-para (c) words from "the requirement at" to "documents and information)" in square brackets substituted by SI 2009/1975, rr 7, 20.
Date in force: 1 September 2009: see SI 2009/1975, r 1.
Para (4): in sub-para (c) word omitted revoked by SI 2009/274, rr 3, 19(a).
Date in force: 1 April 2009: see SI 2009/274, r 1.
Para (4): sub-para (e) and word "; or" immediately preceding it inserted by SI 2009/274, rr 3, 19(b).
Date in force: 1 April 2009: see SI 2009/274, r 1.

38 Hearings in a party's absence

If a party fails to attend a hearing, the Upper Tribunal may proceed with the hearing if the Upper Tribunal—

   (a)   is satisfied that the party has been notified of the hearing or that reasonable steps have been taken to notify the party of the hearing; and

   (b)   considers that it is in the interests of justice to proceed with the hearing.

PART 6
DECISIONS

39 Consent orders

(1)   The Upper Tribunal may, at the request of the parties but only if it considers it appropriate, make a consent order disposing of the proceedings and making such other appropriate provision as the parties have agreed.

(2)   Notwithstanding any other provision of these Rules, the [Upper] Tribunal need not hold a hearing before making an order under paragraph (1) . . .

Amendment
    Para (2): word "Upper" in square brackets inserted by SI 2013/2067, rr 2, 15. Date in force: 1 November 2013: see SI 2013/2067, r 1.
    Para (2): words omitted revoked by SI 2009/274, rr 3, 20. Date in force: 1 April 2009: see SI 2009/274, r 1.

40 Decisions
(1)   The Upper Tribunal may give a decision orally at a hearing.
[(1A)   Subject to paragraph (1B), in immigration judicial review proceedings, a decision which disposes of proceedings shall be given at a hearing.
(1B)   Paragraph (1A) does not affect the power of the Upper Tribunal to—

    (a)   strike out a party's case, pursuant to rule 8(1)(b) or 8(2);
    (b)   consent to withdrawal, pursuant to rule 17;
    (c)   determine an application for permission to bring judicial review proceedings, pursuant to rule 30; or
    (d)   make a consent order disposing of proceedings, pursuant to rule 39,

without a hearing.]
(2)   . . . [Except where rule 40A (special procedure for providing notice of a decision relating to an asylum case) applies,] the Upper Tribunal must provide to each party as soon as reasonably practicable after making [a decision (other than a decision under Part 7) which finally disposes of all issues in the proceedings or of a preliminary issue dealt with following a direction under rule 5(3)(e)]—

    (a)   a decision notice stating the Tribunal's decision; and
    (b)   notification of any rights of review or appeal against the decision and the time and manner in which such rights of review or appeal may be exercised.

(3)   [Subject to rule [14(11) (prevention of disclosure or publication of documents and information)],] the Upper Tribunal must provide written reasons for its decision with a decision notice provided under paragraph (2)(a) unless—

    (a)   the decision was made with the consent of the parties; or
    (b)   the parties have consented to the Upper Tribunal not giving written reasons.

(4)   The [Upper] Tribunal may provide written reasons for any decision to which paragraph (2) does not apply.
[(5)   In a national security certificate appeal, when the Upper Tribunal provides a notice or reasons to the parties under this rule, it must also provide the notice or reasons to the relevant Minister and the Information Commissioner, if they are not parties.]

Amendment
    Paras (1A), (1B): inserted by SI 2013/2067, rr 2, 16. Date in force: 1 November 2013: see SI 2013/2067, r 1.
    Para (2): words omitted revoked by SI 2009/274, rr 3, 21(a).
    Date in force: 1 April 2009: see SI 2009/274, r 1.
    Para (2): words from "Except where rule" to "asylum case) applies," in square brackets inserted by SI 2010/44, rr 2, 19. Date in force: 15 February 2010: see SI 2010/44, r 1.
    Para (2): words from "a decision (other" to "under rule 5(3)(e)" in square brackets substituted by SI 2013/477, rr 49, 56(a). Date in force: 1 April 2013: see SI 2013/477, r 1(2)(c).
    Para (2): in sub-para (a) word "Upper" in square brackets inserted by SI 2013/477, rr 49, 56(b).Date in force: 1 April 2013: see SI 2013/477, r 1(2)(c).
    Para (3): words in square brackets beginning with the words "Subject to rule" inserted by SI 2009/274, rr 3, 21(b).
    Date in force: 1 April 2009: see SI 2009/274, r 1.

Para (3): words "14(11) (prevention of disclosure or publication of documents and information)" in square brackets substituted by SI 2009/1975, rr 7, 21(a).
Date in force: 1 September 2009: see SI 2009/1975, r 1.
Para (4): word "Upper" in square brackets inserted by SI 2009/1975, rr 7, 21(b).
Date in force: 1 September 2009: see SI 2009/1975, r 1.
Para (5): inserted by SI 2010/43, rr 5, 13.
Date in force: 18 January 2010: see SI 2010/43, r 1.

[40A Special procedure for providing notice of a decision relating to an asylum case
[(1) This rule applies to a decision of the Upper Tribunal in an asylum case—

    (a)   to refuse (or not to admit) an application for permission to appeal to the Upper Tribunal made by the person who appealed to the First-tier Tribunal; or

    (b)   on an appeal under section 11 of the 2007 Act,
    where—

        (i)   at the time the application or appeal (as the case may be) is made the person who appealed to the First-tier Tribunal is in the United Kingdom; and

        (ii)   the decision is not made in a fast track case.]

(2) The Upper Tribunal must provide to the Secretary of State for the Home Department as soon as reasonably practicable—

    (a)   a decision notice stating the Upper Tribunal's decision; and

    (b)   a statement of any right of appeal against the decision and the time and manner in which such a right of appeal may be exercised.

(3) The Secretary of State must, subject to paragraph (5)—

    (a)   send the documents listed in paragraph (2) to the other party not later than 30 days after the Upper Tribunal sent them to the Secretary of State for the Home Department; and

    (b)   as soon as practicable after sending the documents listed in paragraph (2), notify the Upper Tribunal on what date and by what means they were sent.

(4) If the Secretary of State does not notify the Upper Tribunal under paragraph (3)(b) within 31 days after the documents listed in paragraph (2) were sent, the Upper Tribunal must send the notice of decision to the other party as soon as reasonably practicable.

(5) If the Secretary of State applies for permission to appeal under section 13 of the 2007 Act, the Secretary of State must send the documents listed in paragraph (2) to the other party no later than the date on which the application for permission is sent to the Upper Tribunal.]

Amendment
Inserted by SI 2010/44, rr 2, 20. Date in force: 15 February 2010: see SI 2010/44, r 1.
Para (1): substituted by SI 2014/1505, rr 2, 4. Date in force: 30 June 2014: see SI 2014/1505, r 1.

PART 7
CORRECTING, SETTING ASIDE, REVIEWING AND APPEALING DECISIONS
OF THE UPPER TRIBUNAL

41 Interpretation
In this Part—

    "appeal"[, except in rule 44(2) (application for permission to appeal),] means the exercise of a right of appeal under section 13 of the 2007 Act; and

    "review" means the review of a decision by the Upper Tribunal under section 10 of the 2007 Act.

Amendment

In definition "appeal" words ", except in rule 44(2) (application for permission to appeal)," in square brackets inserted by SI 2009/274, rr 3, 22.

Date in force: 1 April 2009: see SI 2009/274, r 1.

42 Clerical mistakes and accidental slips or omissions

The Upper Tribunal may at any time correct any clerical mistake or other accidental slip or omission in a decision or record of a decision by—

(a)   sending notification of the amended decision, or a copy of the amended record, to all parties; and

(b)   making any necessary amendment to any information published in relation to the decision or record.

43 Setting aside a decision which disposes of proceedings

(1)   The Upper Tribunal may set aside a decision which disposes of proceedings, or part of such a decision, and re-make the decision or the relevant part of it, if—

(a)   the Upper Tribunal considers that it is in the interests of justice to do so; and

(b)   one or more of the conditions in paragraph (2) are satisfied.

(2)   The conditions are—

(a)   a document relating to the proceedings was not sent to, or was not received at an appropriate time by, a party or a party's representative;

(b)   a document relating to the proceedings was not sent to the Upper Tribunal at an appropriate time;

(c)   a party, or a party's representative, was not present at a hearing related to the proceedings; or

(d)   there has been some other procedural irregularity in the proceedings.

(3)   [Except where paragraph (4) applies,] a party applying for a decision, or part of a decision, to be set aside under paragraph (1) must make a written application to the Upper Tribunal so that it is received no later than 1 month after the date on which the [Upper] Tribunal sent notice of the decision to the party.

[(4)   In an asylum case or an immigration case, the written application referred to in paragraph (3) must be sent or delivered so that it is received by the Upper Tribunal—

(a)   where the person who appealed to the First-tier Tribunal is in the United Kingdom at the time that the application is made, no later than twelve days after the date on which the Upper Tribunal or, as the case may be in an asylum case, the Secretary of State for the Home Department, sent notice of the decision to the party making the application; or

(b)   where the person who appealed to the First-tier Tribunal is outside the United Kingdom at the time that the application is made, no later than thirty eight days after the date on which the Upper Tribunal sent notice of the decision to the party making the application.

(5)   Where a notice of decision is sent electronically or delivered personally, the time limits in paragraph (4) are ten working days.]

Amendment

Para (3): words "Except where paragraph (4) applies," in square brackets inserted by SI 2010/44, rr 2, 21(a).

Date in force: 15 February 2010: see SI 2010/44, r 1.

Para (3): word "Upper" in square brackets inserted by SI 2013/2067, rr 2, 17. Date in force: 1 November 2013: see SI 2013/2067, r 1.

Paras (4), (5): inserted by SI 2010/44, rr 2, 21(b).

Date in force: 15 February 2010: see SI 2010/44, r 1.

44 Application for permission to appeal

(1) [Subject to [paragraphs (4A) and (4B)],] a person seeking permission to appeal must make a written application to the Upper Tribunal for permission to appeal.

(2) Paragraph (3) applies to an application under paragraph (1) in respect of a decision—

- (a) on an appeal against a decision in a social security and child support case (as defined in the Tribunal Procedure (First-tier Tribunal) (Social Entitlement Chamber) Rules 2008);
- (b) on an appeal against a decision in proceedings in the War Pensions and Armed Forces Compensation Chamber of the First-tier Tribunal; . . .
- [(ba) on an appeal against a decision of a Pensions Appeal Tribunal for Scotland or Northern Ireland; or]
- (c) in proceedings under the Forfeiture Act 1982.

(3) Where this paragraph applies, the application must be sent or delivered to the Upper Tribunal so that it is received within 3 months after the date on which the Upper Tribunal sent to the person making the application—

- (a) written notice of the decision;
- (b) notification of amended reasons for, or correction of, the decision following a review; or
- (c) notification that an application for the decision to be set aside has been unsuccessful.

[(3A) An application under paragraph (1) in respect of a decision in an asylum case or an immigration case must be sent or delivered to the Upper Tribunal so that it is received within the appropriate period after the Upper Tribunal or, as the case may be in an asylum case, the Secretary of State for the Home Department, sent any of the documents in paragraph (3) to the party making the application.

(3B) The appropriate period referred to in paragraph (3A) is as follows—

- (a) where the person who appealed to the First-tier Tribunal is in the United Kingdom at the time that the application is made—
  - (i) [twelve working days]; or
  - (ii) if the party making the application is in detention under the Immigration Acts, seven working days; and
- (b) where the person who appealed to the First-tier Tribunal is outside the United Kingdom at the time that the application is made, thirty eight days.

(3C) Where a notice of decision is sent electronically or delivered personally, the time limits in paragraph (3B) are—

- (a) in sub-paragraph (a)(i), ten working days;
- (b) in sub-paragraph (a)(ii), five working days; and
- (c) in sub-paragraph (b), ten working days.]

[(3D) An application under paragraph (1) in respect of a decision in a financial services case must be sent or delivered to the Upper Tribunal so that it is received within 14 days after the date on which the Upper Tribunal sent to the person making the application—

- (a) written notice of the decision;
- (b) notification of amended reasons for, or correction of, the decision following a review; or
- (c) notification that an application for the decision to be set aside has been unsuccessful.]

(4) Where paragraph (3)[, (3A)[, (3D) or (4C)]]] does not apply, an application under paragraph (1) must be sent or delivered to the Upper Tribunal so that it is received within 1 month after the latest of the dates on which the Upper Tribunal sent to the person making the application—

- (a) written reasons for the decision;

(b)   notification of amended reasons for, or correction of, the decision following a review; or

(c)   notification that an application for the decision to be set aside has been unsuccessful.

[(4A)   Where a decision that disposes of immigration judicial review proceedings is given at a hearing, a party may apply at that hearing for permission to appeal, and the Upper Tribunal must consider at the hearing whether to give or refuse permission to appeal.

(4B)   Where a decision that disposes of immigration judicial review proceedings is given at a hearing and no application for permission to appeal is made at that hearing—

(a)   the Upper Tribunal must nonetheless consider at the hearing whether to give or refuse permission to appeal; and

(b)   if permission to appeal is given to a party, it shall be deemed for the purposes of section 13(4) of the 2007 Act to be given on application by that party.

(4C)   Where a decision that disposes of immigration judicial review proceedings is given pursuant to rule 30 and the Upper Tribunal records under rule 30(4A) that the application is totally without merit, an application under paragraph (1) must be sent or delivered to the Upper Tribunal so that it is received within 7 days after the later of the dates on which the Upper Tribunal sent to the applicant—

(a)   written reasons for the decision; or

(b)   notification of amended reasons for, or correction of, the decision following a review.]

(5)   The date in paragraph (3)(c) or (4)(c) applies only if the application for the decision to be set aside was made within the time stipulated in rule 43 (setting aside a decision which disposes of proceedings) or any extension of time granted by the Upper Tribunal.

(6)   If the person seeking permission to appeal provides the application to the Upper Tribunal later than the time required by paragraph (3)[, (3A)][, (3D)] or (4), or by any extension of time under rule 5(3)(a) (power to extend time)—

(a)   the application must include a request for an extension of time and the reason why the application notice was not provided in time; and

(b)   unless the Upper Tribunal extends time for the application under rule 5(3)(a) (power to extend time) the Upper Tribunal must refuse the application.

(7)   An application under paragraph (1) [or (4A)(a)] must—

(a)   identify the decision of the [Upper] Tribunal to which it relates;

(b)   identify the alleged error or errors of law in the decision; and

(c)   state the result the party making the application is seeking.

Amendment

Para (1): words in square brackets beginning with the words "Subject to" inserted by SI 2012/2890, rr 2, 3(a). Date in force: 11 December 2012: see SI 2012/2890, r 1.

Para (1): words "paragraphs (4A) and (4B)" in square brackets substituted by SI 2013/2067, rr 2, 18(a). Date in force: 1 November 2013: see SI 2013/2067, r 1.

Para (2): in sub-para (a) word omitted revoked by SI 2009/274, rr 3, 23(a).

Date in force: 1 April 2009: see SI 2009/274, r 1.

Para (2): sub-para (ba) inserted by SI 2009/274, rr 3, 23(b).

Date in force: 1 April 2009: see SI 2009/274, r 1.

Paras (3A)–(3C): inserted by SI 2010/44, rr 2, 22(1), (2).

Date in force: 15 February 2010: see SI 2010/44, r 1.

Para (3B): in sub-para (a)(i) words "twelve working days" in square brackets substituted by SI 2011/651, r 8(1), (4).

Date in force: 1 April 2011: see SI 2011/651, r 1(2)(a).

Para (3D): inserted by SI 2010/747, rr 2, 10(a).

Date in force: 6 April 2010: see SI 2010/747, r 1.

Para (4): words ", (3A) or (3D)" in square brackets substituted by SI 2010/747, rr 2, 10(b).

Date in force: 6 April 2010: see SI 2010/747, r 1.

Para (4): words ", (3D) or (4C)" in square brackets substituted by SI 2013/2067, rr 2, 18(b).
Date in force: 1 November 2013: see SI 2013/2067, r 1.

Paras (4A)–(4C): substituted, for para (4A), by SI 2013/2067, rr 2, 18(c). Date in force:
1 November 2013: see SI 2013/2067, r 1.

Para (6): reference to ", (3A)" in square brackets inserted by SI 2010/44, rr 2, 22(1), (4).

Date in force: 15 February 2010: see SI 2010/44, r 1.

Para (6): reference to ", (3D)" in square brackets inserted by SI 2010/747, rr 2, 10(c).

Date in force: 6 April 2010: see SI 2010/747, r 1.

Para (7): words "or (4A)(a)" in square brackets inserted by SI 2012/2890, rr 2, 3(c). Date in
force: 11 December 2012: see SI 2012/2890, r 1.

Para (7): in sub-para (a) word "Upper" in square brackets inserted by SI 2013/2067, rr 2,
18(d). Date in force: 1 November 2013: see SI 2013/2067, r 1.

45 Upper Tribunal's consideration of application for permission to appeal

(1) On receiving an application for permission to appeal the Upper Tribunal may
review the decision in accordance with rule 46 (review of a decision), but may only do
so if—

> (a)   when making the decision the Upper Tribunal overlooked a legislative
> provision or binding authority which could have had a material effect on
> the decision; or
>
> (b)   since the Upper Tribunal's decision, a court has made a decision which is
> binding on the Upper Tribunal and which, had it been made before the
> Upper Tribunal's decision, could have had a material effect on the
> decision.

(2) If the Upper Tribunal decides not to review the decision, or reviews the decision
and decides to take no action in relation to the decision or part of it, the Upper
Tribunal must consider whether to give permission to appeal in relation to the decision
or that part of it.

(3) The Upper Tribunal must [provide] a record of its decision to the parties as soon
as practicable.

(4) If the Upper Tribunal refuses permission to appeal it must [provide] with the
record of its decision—

> (a)   a statement of its reasons for such refusal; and
>
> (b)   notification of the right to make an application to the relevant appellate
> court for permission to appeal and the time within which, and the
> method by which, such application must be made.

(5) The Upper Tribunal may give permission to appeal on limited grounds, but must
comply with paragraph (4) in relation to any grounds on which it has refused
permission.

Amendment

Paras (3), (4): word "provide" in square brackets substituted by SI 2013/2067, rr 2, 19. Date
in force: 1 November 2013: see SI 2013/2067, r 1.

46 Review of a decision

[(1) The Upper Tribunal may only undertake a review of a decision pursuant to
rule 45(1) (review on an application for permission to appeal).]

(2) The Upper Tribunal must notify the parties in writing of the outcome of any
review and of any rights of review or appeal in relation to the outcome.

(3) If the Upper Tribunal decides to take any action in relation to a decision
following a review without first giving every party an opportunity to make

representations, the notice under paragraph (2) must state that any party that did not have an opportunity to make representations may apply for such action to be set aside and for the decision to be reviewed again.

Amendment

Para (1): substituted by SI 2011/2343, rr 2, 12. Date in force: 17 October 2011: see SI 2011/2343, r 1.

47 [Setting aside] a decision in proceedings under the Forfeiture Act 1982

(1)   A person who referred a question to the Upper Tribunal under rule 26 (references under the Forfeiture Act 1982) must refer the Upper Tribunal's previous decision in relation to the question to the Upper Tribunal if they—

(a)   consider that the decision should be [set aside and re-made under this rule]; or

(b)   have received a written application for the decision to be [set aside and re-made under this rule] from the person to whom the decision related.

(2)   The Upper Tribunal may [set aside the decision, either in whole or in part, and re-make it] if—

(a)   . . .

(b)   the decision was made in ignorance of, or was based on a mistake as to, some material fact; or

(c)   there has been a relevant change in circumstances since the decision was made.

[(3)   Rule 26(2) to (4), Parts 5 and 6 and this Part apply to a reference under this rule as they apply to a reference under rule 26(1).]

Amendment

Provision heading: words "Setting aside" in square brackets substituted by SI 2011/2343, rr 2, 13(a).

Date in force: 17 October 2011: see SI 2011/2343, r 1.

Para (1): in sub-para (a) words "set aside and re-made under this rule" in square brackets substituted by SI 2011/2343, rr 2, 13(b).

Date in force: 17 October 2011: see SI 2011/2343, r 1.

Para (1): in sub-para (b) words "set aside and re-made under this rule" in square brackets substituted by SI 2011/2343, rr 2, 13(c).

Date in force: 17 October 2011: see SI 2011/2343, r 1.

Para (2): words "set aside the decision, either in whole or in part, and re-make it" in square brackets substituted by SI 2011/2343, rr 2, 13(d).

Date in force: 17 October 2011: see SI 2011/2343, r 1.

Para (2): sub-para (a) revoked by SI 2011/2343, rr 2, 13(e).

Date in force: 17 October 2011: see SI 2011/2343, r 1.

Para (3): substituted, for paras (3)–(5) as originally enacted, by SI 2011/2343, rr 2, 13(f).

Date in force: 17 October 2011: see SI 2011/2343, r 1.

[48   Power to treat an application as a different type of application]

[The [Upper] Tribunal may treat an application for a decision to be corrected, set aside or reviewed, or for permission to appeal against a decision, as an application for any other one of those things.]

Amendment

Inserted by SI 2010/2653, r 8. Date in force: 29 November 2010: see SI 2010/2653, r 1.

Word "Upper" in square brackets inserted by SI 2013/2067, rr 2, 20. Date in force: 1 November 2013: see SI 2013/2067, r 1.

SCHEDULES 1–3

(Sch 1 relates to procedure after the Notice of Appeal in road transport cases; Sch 2 relates to additional procedure in National Security Certificate cases and Sch 3 relates to procedure in

Financial Services Cases (all outside the scope of this work).)

APPEALS (EXCLUDED DECISIONS) ORDER 2009

(SI 2009/275)

Made: 5 February 2009.

Authority: Tribunals, Courts and Enforcement Act 2007, ss 11(5)(f), 13(8)(f).

Commencement: 1 April 2009.

1 Citation and commencement

This Order may be cited as the Appeals (Excluded Decisions) Order 2009 and comes into force on 1st April 2009.

[2 Excluded decisions

For the purposes of section 11(1) of the Tribunals, Courts and Enforcement Act 2007, the following decisions of the First-tier Tribunal are excluded decisions—

(a)   a decision under section 103 of the Immigration and Asylum Act 1999 (appeals); and

(b)   a decision under paragraphs 22, 23, 24, 29, 30, 31, 32 and 33 of Schedule 2 to the Immigration Act 1971.]

Amendment

Substituted by SI 2010/41, arts 2, 3. Date in force: 15 February 2010: see SI 2010/41, art 1.

3

For the purposes of sections 11(1) and 13(1) of the Tribunals, Courts and Enforcement Act 2007, the following decisions of the First-tier Tribunal or the Upper Tribunal are excluded decisions—

(a)   any decision under section 20(7), (8B) or (8G)(b) (power to call for documents of taxpayer and others), 20B(1B) or (6) (restrictions on powers under sections 20 and 20A) or 20BB(2)(a) (falsification etc of documents) of the Taxes Management Act 1970;

(b)   any decision under section 35A(2) (variation of undertakings), 79A(2) (variation of undertakings) or 219(1A) (power to require information) of the Inheritance Tax Act 1984;

(c)   any decision under section 152(5) (notification of taxable amount of certain benefits) or 215(7) (advance clearance by Board of distributions and payments) of the Income and Corporation Taxes Act 1988;

(d)   any decision under section 138(4) of the Taxation of Chargeable Gains Act 1992 (procedure for clearance in advance);

(e)   any decision under section 187(5) or (6) (returns and information) of, or paragraph 3(2) or 6(2) of Schedule 21 (restrictions on powers under section 187) to, the Finance Act 1993;

(f)   any decision under paragraph 91(5) of Schedule 15 to the Finance Act 2000 (corporate venturing scheme: advance clearance);

(g)   any decision under paragraph 88(5) of Schedule 29 to the Finance Act 2002 (gains and losses from intangible fixed assets: transfer of business or trade);

(h)   any decision under paragraph 2, 4, 7, 9, 10, 11 or 24 of Schedule 13 to the Finance Act 2003 (stamp duty land tax: information powers);

(i)   any decision under section 306A (doubt as to notifiability), 308A (supplemental information), 313B (reasons for non-disclosure:

supporting information) or 314A (order to disclose) of the Finance Act 2004;

(j)   any decision under section 697(4) of the Income Tax Act 2007 (opposed notifications: determinations by tribunal);

(k)   any decision under regulation 10(3) of the Venture Capital Trust (Winding up and Mergers) (Tax) Regulations 2004 (procedure for Board's approval);

(l)   any decision under regulation 5A (doubt as to notifiability), 7A (supplemental information), 12B (reasons for non-disclosure: supporting information) or 12C (order to disclose) of the National Insurance Contributions (Application of Part 7 of the Finance Act 2004) Regulations 2007;

[(m)   any procedural, ancillary or preliminary decision made in relation to an appeal against a decision under section 40A of the British Nationality Act 1981, section 82, 83 or 83A of the Nationality, Immigration and Asylum Act 2002, or regulation 26 of the Immigration (European Economic Area) Regulations 2006].

Amendment

Para (m) inserted by SI 2010/41, arts 2, 4. Date in force: 15 February 2010: see SI 2010/41, art 1.

4 Revocations

The Appeals (Excluded Decisions) Order 2008 and the Appeals (Excluded Decisions) (Amendment) Order 2008 are revoked.

TRANSFER OF FUNCTIONS OF THE ASYLUM AND IMMIGRATION TRIBUNAL ORDER 2010

(SI 2010/21)

Made: 6 January 2010.

Authority: Tribunals, Courts and Enforcement Act 2007, ss 30(1), (4), 31(1), (2), (7), (9), 38.

Commencement: 15 February 2010.

1 Citation and commencement

This Order may be cited as the Transfer of Functions of the Asylum and Immigration Tribunal Order 2010 and comes into force on 15th February 2010.

2 Transfer of functions and abolition of tribunal

(1)   The functions of the Asylum and Immigration Tribunal are transferred to the First-tier Tribunal.

(2)   The Asylum and Immigration Tribunal is abolished.

3 Transfer of persons into the First-tier Tribunal and the Upper Tribunal

A person who, immediately before this Order comes into force, holds an office listed in column (1) of the following table is to hold the office or offices listed in the corresponding entry in column (2) of the table.

(1) *Office held*	(2) *Office to be held*
Deputy President of the Asylum and Immigration Tribunal appointed under paragraph 5(1)(b) of Schedule 4 to the Nationality, Immigration and Asylum Act 2002	Transferred-in judge of the Upper Tribunal
Legally qualified member of the Asylum and Immigration Tribunal appointed under paragraphs 1 and 2(1)(a) to (d) of Schedule 4 to the Nationality, Immigration and Asylum Act 2002 and specified by the Lord Chancellor as a Senior Immigration Judge pursuant to the Asylum and Immigration Tribunal (Judicial Titles) Order 2005	Transferred-in judge of the Upper Tribunal
Legally qualified member of the Asylum and Immigration Tribunal appointed under paragraphs 1 and 2(1)(a) to (d) of Schedule 4 to the Nationality, Immigration and Asylum Act 2002 and specified by the Lord Chancellor as a Designated Immigration Judge pursuant to the Asylum and Immigration Tribunal (Judicial Titles) Order 2005	Transferred-in deputy judge of the Upper Tribunal; transferred-in judge of the First-tier Tribunal
Legally qualified member of the Asylum and Immigration Tribunal appointed under paragraphs 1 and 2(1)(a) to (d) of Schedule 4 to the Nationality, Immigration and Asylum Act 2002	Transferred-in judge of the First-tier Tribunal
Other member of the Asylum and Immigration Tribunal appointed under paragraphs 1 and 2(1)(e) of Schedule 4 to the Nationality, Immigration and Asylum Act 2002	Transferred-in other member of the Upper Tribunal

4 Transfer of Rules

The Asylum and Immigration Tribunal (Procedure) Rules 2005 and the Asylum and Immigration Tribunal (Procedure) (Fast-track) Rules 2005 have effect as if they were Tribunal Procedure Rules.

5 Consequential and transitional provisions

(1)   Schedule 1 contains consequential amendments to primary legislation as a consequence of the transfers effected by this Order.

(2)   Schedule 2 contains consequential amendments to secondary legislation as a consequence of the transfers effected by this Order.

(3)   Schedule 3 contains repeals and revocations as a consequence of the amendments in Schedules 1 and 2.

(4)   Schedule 4 contains transitional and saving provisions.

SCHEDULE 4

TRANSITIONAL AND SAVING PROVISIONS

Article 5(4)

Appeals and applications for bail

1

An appeal under section 40A of the British Nationality Act 1981, section 82, 83 or 83A of the 2002 Act or regulation 26 of the Immigration (European Economic Area) Regulations 2006, or an application for bail under Schedule 2 to the Immigration Act 1971, made to the Asylum and Immigration Tribunal before 15 February 2010 but not determined before that date shall continue as an appeal or application before the First-tier Tribunal.

Section 103A applications

2

An application for review made to the Asylum and Immigration Tribunal under section 103A of the 2002 Act and Schedule 2 to the 2004 Act before 15 February 2010 but not determined before that date shall continue as an application to the First-tier Tribunal for permission to appeal to the Upper Tribunal under section 11 of the 2007 Act.

3

Where the Asylum and Immigration Tribunal or the appropriate court has made an order for reconsideration under section 103A of the 2002 Act before 15 February 2010, but reconsideration has not taken place before that date, the order for reconsideration shall be treated as an order granting permission to appeal to the Upper Tribunal under section 11 of the 2007 Act and sections 12 and 13 of the 2007 Act shall apply.

4

Where the reconsideration of an appeal by the Asylum and Immigration Tribunal under section 103A of the 2002 Act has commenced before 15 February 2010 but has not been determined, the reconsideration shall continue as an appeal to the Upper Tribunal under section 12 of the 2007 Act and section 13 of the 2007 Act shall apply.

5

An application for review made to the appropriate court under section 103A of the 2002 Act before 15 February 2010 but not determined before that date shall continue as an application for review under section 103A of the 2002 Act.

6

An order for reconsideration made by the appropriate court on or after 15 February 2010 which, if it had been made before that date would have been for reconsideration by the Asylum and Immigration Tribunal, shall be treated as an order granting permission to appeal to the Upper Tribunal under section 11 of the 2007 Act and sections 12 and 13 of the 2007 Act shall apply.

Section 103C references

7

A reference made by the appropriate court to the appropriate appellate court under section 103C of the 2002 Act before 15 February 2010 shall continue to be considered as a reference under section 103C of the 2002 Act.

8

A case remitted or restored by the appropriate appellate court on or after 15 February 2010 which, if it had been remitted or restored before that date would have been remitted to the Asylum and Immigration Tribunal or restored to the appropriate court, shall be remitted to the Upper Tribunal and sections 12 and 13 of the 2007 Act shall apply.

Section 103B and 103E applications

9

An application for permission to appeal to the appropriate appellate court made to the Asylum and Immigration Tribunal under section 103B or 103E of the 2002 Act before 15 February 2010 but not determined before that date shall continue as an application to the Upper Tribunal for permission to appeal to the relevant appellate court under section 13 of the 2007 Act.

10

An application for permission to appeal to the appropriate appellate court made to that court under section 103B or 103E of the 2002 Act before 15 February 2010 but not determined before that date shall continue as an application for permission to appeal to the appropriate appellate court under section 103B or 103E of the 2002 Act.

11

An appeal which is proceeding before the appropriate appellate court under section 103B or 103E of the 2002 Act before 15 February 2010 but which is not determined before that date shall continue as an appeal to the appropriate appellate court under section 103B or 103E of the 2002 Act.

12

A case remitted by the appropriate appellate court on or after 15 February 2010 which, if it had been remitted before that date would have been remitted to the Asylum and Immigration Tribunal, shall be remitted to the Upper Tribunal and sections 12 and 13 of the 2007 Act shall apply.

Time limits

13

(1)   Where the time period for making an appeal or application has begun but not expired before 15 February 2010, in the case of—

(a)   an appeal to the Asylum and Immigration Tribunal under section 40A of the British Nationality Act 1981, section 82, 83 or 83A of the 2002 Act or regulation 26 of the Immigration (European Economic Area) Regulations 2006, an appeal may be made within that period to the First-tier Tribunal;

(b)   an application to the Asylum and Immigration Tribunal for review under section 103A of the 2002 Act and Schedule 2 to the 2004 Act, an application for permission to appeal to the Upper Tribunal under section 11 of the 2007 Act may be made within that period to the First-tier Tribunal;

(c)   an application to the appropriate court for review under section 103A of the 2002 Act, an application may be made within that period under section 103A of the 2002 Act to the appropriate court;

(d)   an application to the Asylum and Immigration Tribunal for permission to appeal to the appropriate appellate court under section 103B or 103E of the 2002 Act, an application for permission to appeal to the relevant appellate court under section 13 of the 2007 Act may be made within that period to the Upper Tribunal; and

(e)   an application to the appropriate appellate court for permission to appeal to that court under section 103B or 103E of the 2002 Act, an application for permission to appeal to the relevant appellate court under section 13 of the 2007 Act may be made within that period to that court.

(2)   Where an appeal or application mentioned in sub-paragraphs (1)(a) to (e) is made after the time period in question has expired, it must be made and decided in accordance with the relevant procedural rules or other enactments, as they apply on and after the transfer date.

(3)   Where an appeal or application has been determined by the Asylum and Immigration Tribunal before the transfer date but the determination has not been served on the parties before that date, the determination shall be treated as if it were a determination of the First-tier Tribunal or (if it follows reconsideration) a determination of the Upper Tribunal, as the case may be, and the determination may be served accordingly.

(4)   Sub-paragraph (3) applies, subject to any necessary modifications, to any other decision of the Asylum and Immigration Tribunal that has been made but not served before the transfer date.

General

14

(1)   This paragraph applies where proceedings are commenced or continued in the First-tier Tribunal or the Upper Tribunal by virtue of the provisions of this Schedule.

(2)   The First-tier Tribunal or Upper Tribunal, as the case may be, may give any direction to ensure that the proceedings are dealt with fairly and, in particular, may apply any provision in procedural rules which applied to the proceedings before 15 February 2010.

(3)   In sub-paragraph (2) "procedural rules" includes any provision (whether called rules or not) regulating practice or procedure before the Asylum and Immigration Tribunal.

(4)   Any direction or order given or made in the proceedings which is in force immediately before 15 February 2010 remains in force on and after that date as if it were a direction or order of the First-tier Tribunal or Upper Tribunal, as the case may be, and may be varied accordingly.

(5)   A time period which has started to run before15 February 2010 and which has not expired shall continue to apply.

15

Any procedural, ancillary or preliminary matter before the Asylum and Immigration Tribunal before 15 February 2010 may, on or after that date, be considered by the First-tier Tribunal or the Upper Tribunal, as the case may be, as appropriate.

16

(1)   This paragraph applies when—

    (a)   the Asylum and Immigration Tribunal has started to reconsider or has reconsidered an appeal before 15 February 2010, but has not produced a determination before that date; and

    (b)   the reconsideration of the appeal continues as an appeal to the Upper Tribunal by virtue of paragraph 4.

(2)   A member of the Asylum and Immigration Tribunal who was hearing or otherwise considering the appeal may take all such steps as the member considers necessary to determine the appeal and produce a determination on or after 15 February 2010.

17

In any judicial review proceedings before the High Court, the Court of Session or the High Court of Northern Ireland before 15 February 2010 where a matter could be remitted to the Asylum and Immigration Tribunal, on or after that date the matter may be remitted to the First-tier Tribunal or the Upper Tribunal as the court considers appropriate.

18

Staff appointed to the Asylum and Immigration Tribunal before 15 February 2010 are to be treated on and after that date, for the purpose of any enactment, as if they had been appointed by the Lord Chancellor under section 40(1) of the Tribunals, Courts and Enforcement Act 2007 (tribunal staff and services).

Saving provisions

19

In accordance with the provisions of this Schedule, sections 87(3) and (4), 103A, 103B, 103C and 103E of the 2002 Act, shall continue to apply to proceedings to which paragraphs 5, 7, 10 to 12 and 13(1)(c) and (2) (in relation to sub-paragraph (1)(c)) apply as if the repeals in Schedule 1 in respect of those sections of the 2002 Act had not been made.

20

Section 103D of the 2002 Act and the Community Legal Service (Asylum and Immigration Appeals) Regulations 2005 ("the 2005 Regulations") (legal aid funding arrangements) shall continue to apply to proceedings to which paragraphs 2 to 8 and 13(1)(b), (c) and (2) (in relation to sub-paragraphs (1)(b) to (e)) apply until the proceedings are finally determined—

(a) as if the repeals in Schedule 1 in respect of sections 103A and 103D of the 2002 Act and rule 33 of the Asylum and Immigration Tribunal (Procedure) Rules 2005 ("the 2005 Rules"), and the repeals and revocations in Schedule 3 in respect of paragraph 30 of Schedule 2 to the 2004 Act and the 2005 Regulations had not been made;

(b) as if the references to the Tribunal in section 103D of the 2002 Act, paragraph 30 of Schedule 2 to the 2004 Act, the 2005 Regulations and rule 33 of the 2005 Rules were references to the First-tier Tribunal or the Upper Tribunal as appropriate, and the references to the appropriate court and the High Court were references to the Upper Tribunal where appropriate; and

(c) subject to any necessary modifications to the 2005 Regulations and the 2005 Rules.

Interpretation

21

In this Schedule—

"appropriate court" means—

(i) in relation to an appeal decided in England or Wales, the High Court;

(ii) in relation to an appeal decided in Scotland, the Outer House of the Court of Session; and

(iii) in relation to an appeal decided in Northern Ireland, the High Court of Northern Ireland;

"appropriate appellate court" means—

(iv) in relation to an appeal decided in England or Wales, the Court of Appeal;

(v) in relation to an appeal decided in Scotland, the Inner House of the Court of Session; and

(vi) in relation to an appeal decided in Northern Ireland, the Court of Appeal of Northern Ireland;

"the 2002 Act" means the Nationality, Immigration and Asylum Act 2002;

"the 2004 Act" means the Asylum and Immigration (Treatment of Claimants, etc) Act 2004; and

"the 2007 Act" means the Tribunals, Courts and Enforcement Act 2007.

FIRST-TIER TRIBUNAL AND UPPER TRIBUNAL (CHAMBERS) ORDER 2010

(SI 2010/2655)

Made: 28 October 2010.

Authority: Tribunals, Courts and Enforcement Act 2007, ss 7(1), (9).

Commencement: 29 November 2010.

1 Citation, commencement and revocations

(1) This Order may be cited as the First-tier Tribunal and Upper Tribunal (Chambers) Order 2010 and comes into force on 29th November 2010.

(2) The Orders listed in the first column of the Schedule to this Order are revoked to the extent specified in the second column.

2 First-tier Tribunal Chambers

The First-tier Tribunal shall be organised into the following chambers—

    (a)   the General Regulatory Chamber;

    (b)   the Health, Education and Social Care Chamber;

    (c)   the Immigration and Asylum Chamber;

    [(cc) the Property Chamber;]

    (d)   the Social Entitlement Chamber;

    (e)   the Tax Chamber;

    (f)   the War Pensions and Armed Forces Compensation Chamber.

Amendment

Para (cc) inserted by SI 2013/1187, arts 2, 3. Date in force: 1 July 2013: see SI 2013/1187, art 1.

3 Functions of the General Regulatory Chamber

To the General Regulatory Chamber are allocated all functions related to—

    (a)   proceedings in respect of the decisions and actions of regulatory bodies which are not allocated to the Health, Education and Social Care Chamber by article 4 or to the Tax Chamber by article 7;

    (b)   matters referred to the First-tier Tribunal under Schedule 1D to the Charities Act 1993 (references to Tribunal);

    (c)   the determination of remuneration for carrying mail-bags in a ship or aircraft.

4 Functions of the Health, Education and Social Care Chamber

To the Health, Education and Social Care Chamber are allocated all functions related to—

    (a)   an appeal against a decision related to children with special educational needs;

    (b)   a claim of disability discrimination in the education of a child;

    (c)   an application or an appeal against a decision or determination related to work with children or vulnerable adults;

    (d)   an appeal against a decision related to registration in respect of the provision of health or social care;

    (e)   an application in respect of, or an appeal against a decision related to, the provision of health care or health services;

    (f)   an appeal against a decision related to registration in respect of social workers and social care workers;

    (g)   an appeal against a decision related to the provision of childcare;

    (h)   an appeal against a decision related to an independent school or other independent educational institution;

    (i)   applications and references by and in respect of patients under the provisions of the Mental Health Act 1983 or paragraph 5(2) of the Schedule to the Repatriation of Prisoners Act 1984.

5 Functions of the Immigration and Asylum Chamber of the First-tier Tribunal

To the Immigration and Asylum Chamber of the First-tier Tribunal are allocated all functions related to immigration and asylum matters, with the exception of matters allocated to—

(a)   the Social Entitlement Chamber by article 6(a);

(b)   the General Regulatory Chamber by article 3(a).

[5A Functions of the Property Chamber

To the Property Chamber are allocated all functions conferred on the First-tier Tribunal relating to—

(a)   a reference by the Chief Land Registrar and any other application, matter or appeal under the Land Registration Act 2002;

(b)   proceedings under any of the enactments referred to in section 6A(2) of the Agriculture (Miscellaneous Provisions) Act 1954 or the Hill Farming Act 1946;

(c)   housing etc, under the Housing Act 2004;

(d)   leasehold property;

(e)   residential property;

(f)   rents;

(g)   the right to buy;

(h)   applications and appeals under the Mobile Homes Act 1983.]

Amendment

Inserted by SI 2013/1187, arts 2, 4. Date in force: 1 July 2013: see SI 2013/1187, art 1.

6 Functions of the Social Entitlement Chamber

To the Social Entitlement Chamber are allocated all functions related to appeals—

(a)   in cases regarding support for asylum seekers, failed asylum seekers, persons designated under section 130 of the Criminal Justice and Immigration Act 2008, or the dependants of any such persons;

(b)   in criminal injuries compensation cases;

(c)   regarding entitlement to, payments of, or recovery or recoupment of payments of, social security benefits, child support, vaccine damage payments, health in pregnancy grant and tax credits, with the exception of—

    (i)   appeals under section 11 of the Social Security Contributions (Transfer of Functions, etc) Act 1999 (appeals against decisions of Her Majesty's Revenue and Customs);

    (ii)   appeals in respect of employer penalties or employer information penalties (as defined in section 63(11) and (12) of the Tax Credits Act 2002);

    (iii)   appeals under regulation 28(3) of the Child Trust Funds Regulations 2004;

(d)   regarding saving gateway accounts with the exception of appeals against requirements to account for an amount under regulations made under section 14 of the Saving Gateway Accounts Act 2009;

(e)   regarding child trust funds with the exception of appeals against requirements to account for an amount under regulations made under section 22(4) of the Child Trust Funds Act 2004 in relation to section 13 of that Act;

(f)   regarding payments in consequence of diffuse mesothelioma;

(g)   regarding a certificate or waiver decision in relation to NHS charges;

(h)   regarding entitlement to be credited with earnings or contributions;

(i)   against a decision as to whether an accident was an industrial accident.

7 Functions of the Tax Chamber

To the Tax Chamber are allocated all functions, except those functions allocated to the Social Entitlement Chamber by article 6 or to the Tax and Chancery Chamber of the

Upper Tribunal by article 13, related to an appeal, application, reference or other proceeding in respect of—

(a)   a function of the Commissioners for Her Majesty's Revenue and Customs or an officer of Revenue and Customs;

(b)   the exercise by [the National Crime Agency] of general Revenue functions or Revenue inheritance tax functions (as defined in section 323 of the Proceeds of Crime Act 2002);

(c)   the exercise by the Director of Border Revenue of functions under section 7 of the Borders, Citizenship and Revenue Act 2009;

(d)   a function of the Compliance Officer for the Independent Parliamentary Standards Authority.

Amendment

In para (b) words "the National Crime Agency" in square brackets substituted by virtue of the Crime and Courts Act 2013, s 15(3), Sch 8, Pt 4, para 190. Date in force: 7 October 2013: see SI 2013/1682, art 3(v).

8 Functions of the War Pensions and Armed Forces Compensation Chamber

To the War Pensions and Armed Forces Compensation Chamber are allocated all functions related to appeals under the War Pensions (Administrative Provisions) Act 1919 and the Pensions Appeal Tribunals Act 1943.

9 Upper Tribunal Chambers

The Upper Tribunal shall be organised into the following chambers—

(a)   the Administrative Appeals Chamber;

(b)   the Immigration and Asylum Chamber of the Upper Tribunal;

(c)   the Lands Chamber;

(d)   the Tax and Chancery Chamber.

10 Functions of the Administrative Appeals Chamber

To the Administrative Appeals Chamber are allocated all functions related to—

(a)   an appeal—

     (i)   against a decision made by the First-tier Tribunal, except an appeal allocated to the Tax and Chancery Chamber by article 13(a) or the Immigration and Asylum Chamber of the Upper Tribunal by article 11(a);

     (ii)   under section 5 of the Pensions Appeal Tribunals Act 1943 (appeals against assessment of extent of disablement) against a decision of the Pensions Appeal Tribunal in Northern Ireland established under paragraph 1(3) of the Schedule to the Pensions Appeal Tribunals Act 1943 (constitution, jurisdiction and procedure of Pensions Appeal Tribunals);

     (iii)   against a decision of the Pensions Appeal Tribunal in Scotland established under paragraph 1(2) of the Schedule to the Pensions Appeal Tribunals Act 1943;

     (iv)   against a decision of the Mental Health Review Tribunal for Wales established under section 65 of the Mental Health Act 1983 (Mental Health Review Tribunals);

     (v)   against a decision of the Special Educational Needs Tribunal for Wales;

     (vi)   under section 4 of the Safeguarding Vulnerable Groups Act 2006 (appeals);

     (vii)   transferred to the Upper Tribunal from the First-tier Tribunal under Tribunal Procedure Rules, except an appeal allocated to the Tax and Chancery Chamber by article 13(1)(e);

     [(viii)   against a decision in a road transport case;]

(b)   an application, except an application allocated to another chamber by article 11(c)[, (d) or (e)], 12(c) or 13(g), for the Upper Tribunal—

    (i)   to grant the relief mentioned in section 15(1) of the Tribunals, Courts and Enforcement Act 2007 (Upper Tribunal's "judicial review" jurisdiction);

    (ii)   to exercise the powers of review under section 21(2) of that Act (Upper Tribunal's "judicial review" jurisdiction: Scotland);

(c)   a matter referred to the Upper Tribunal by the First-tier Tribunal—

    (i)   under section 9(5)(b) of the Tribunals, Courts and Enforcement Act 2007 (review of decision of First-tier Tribunal), or

    (ii)   under Tribunal Procedure Rules relating to non-compliance with a requirement of the First-tier Tribunal,

except where the reference is allocated to another chamber by article 11(b) or 13(f);

(d)   a determination or decision under section 4 of the Forfeiture Act 1982;

(e)   proceedings, or a preliminary issue, transferred under Tribunal Procedure Rules to the Upper Tribunal from the First-tier Tribunal, except those allocated to [the Lands Chamber by article 12(cc) or to] the Tax and Chancery Chamber by article 13(1)(e).

Amendment

Para (a)(viii) substituted by SI 2012/1673, arts 2, 3. Date in force: 20 July 2012: see SI 2012/1673, art 1.

In para (b) words ", (d) or (e)" in square brackets substituted by SI 2013/2068, arts 2, 3. Date in force: 1 November 2013: see SI 2013/2068, art 1.

In para (e) words "the Lands Chamber by article 12(cc) or to" in square brackets inserted by SI 2013/1187, arts 2, 5. Date in force: 1 July 2013: see SI 2013/1187, art 1.

11 Functions of the Immigration and Asylum Chamber of the Upper Tribunal

To the Immigration and Asylum Chamber of the Upper Tribunal are allocated all functions related to—

(a)   an appeal against a decision of the First-tier Tribunal made in the Immigration and Asylum Chamber of the First-tier Tribunal;

(b)   a matter referred to the Upper Tribunal under section 9(5)(b) of the Tribunals, Courts and Enforcement Act 2007 or under Tribunal Procedure Rules by the Immigration and Asylum Chamber of the First-tier Tribunal;

[(c)   an application for the Upper Tribunal to grant relief mentioned in section 15(1) of the Tribunals, Courts and Enforcement Act 2007 (Upper Tribunal's "judicial review" jurisdiction), or to exercise the power of review under section 21(2) of that Act (Upper Tribunal's "judicial review" jurisdiction: Scotland), which is made by a person who claims to be a minor from outside the United Kingdom challenging a defendant's assessment of that person's age;

(d)   an application for the Upper Tribunal to exercise the powers of review under section 21(2) of the Tribunals, Court and Enforcement Act (Upper Tribunal's "judicial review" jurisdiction: Scotland), which relates to a decision of the First-tier Tribunal mentioned in paragraph (a);

(e)   an application for the Upper Tribunal to grant relief mentioned in section 15(1) of the Tribunals, Courts and Enforcement Act 2007 (Upper Tribunal's "judicial review" jurisdiction), which is designated as an immigration matter—

    (i)   in a direction made in accordance with Part 1 of Schedule 2 to the Constitutional Reform Act 2005 specifying a class of case for the purposes of section 18(6) of the Tribunals, Courts and Enforcement Act 2007; or

(ii) in an order of the High Court in England and Wales made under section 31A(3) of the Senior Courts Act 1981, transferring to the Upper Tribunal an application of a kind described in section 31A(1) of that Act].

Amendment

Paras (c)–(e) substituted, for paras (c), (d), by SI 2013/2068, arts 2, 4. Date in force: 1 November 2013: see SI 2013/2068, art 1.

12 Functions of the Lands Chamber

To the Lands Chamber are allocated—

(a) all functions related to—

(i) compensation and other remedies for measures taken which affect the ownership, value, enjoyment or use of land or water, or of rights over or property in land or water;

[(ii) appeals from decisions of—

(aa) the First-tier Tribunal made in the Property Chamber other than appeals allocated to the Tax and Chancery Chamber by article 13(h);

(ab) leasehold valuation tribunals in Wales, residential property tribunals in Wales, rent assessment committees in Wales, the Agricultural Land Tribunal in Wales or the Valuation Tribunal for Wales;

(ac) the Valuation Tribunal for England;]

(iii) the determination of questions of the value of land or an interest in land arising in tax proceedings;

(iv) proceedings in respect of restrictive covenants, blight notices or the obstruction of light;

(b) the Upper Tribunal's function as arbitrator under section 1(5) of the Lands Tribunal Act 1949;

(c) an application for the Upper Tribunal to grant the relief mentioned in section 15(1) of the Tribunals, Courts and Enforcement Act 2007 (Upper Tribunal's "judicial review" jurisdiction) which relates to a decision of a tribunal mentioned in sub-paragraph (a)(ii);

[(cc) any case which may be transferred under Tribunal Procedure Rules to the Upper Tribunal from the Property Chamber of the First-tier Tribunal in relation to functions listed in article 5A(c) to (h);]

(d) any other functions transferred to the Upper Tribunal by the Transfer of Tribunal Functions (Lands Tribunal and Miscellaneous Amendments) Order 2009.

Amendment

Para (a)(ii) substituted by SI 2013/1187, arts 2, 6(a). Date in force: 1 July 2013: see SI 2013/1187, art 1.

Para (cc) inserted by SI 2013/1187, arts 2, 6(b). Date in force: 1 July 2013: see SI 2013/1187, art 1.

13 Functions of the Tax and Chancery Chamber

(1) To the Tax and Chancery Chamber are allocated all functions related to—

(a) an appeal against a decision of the First-tier Tribunal made—

(i) in the Tax Chamber;

(ii) in the General Regulatory Chamber in a charities case;

(b) a reference or appeal in respect of—

(i) a decision of the Financial Services Authority;

    (ii)   a decision of the Bank of England;

    (iii)   a decision of a person related to the assessment of any compensation or consideration under the Banking (Special Provisions) Act 2008;

    (iv)   a determination or dispute within the meaning of regulation 14(5) or 15 of the Financial Services and Management Act 2000 (Contribution to Costs of Special Resolution Regime) Regulations 2010;

(c)   a reference in respect of a decision of the Pensions Regulator;

(d)   an application under paragraph 50(1)(d) of Schedule 36 to the Finance Act 2008;

(e)   proceedings, or a preliminary issue, transferred to the Upper Tribunal under Tribunal Procedure Rules—

    (i)   from the Tax Chamber of the First-tier Tribunal;

    (ii)   from the General Regulatory Chamber of the First-tier Tribunal in a charities case;

(f)   a matter referred to the Upper Tribunal under section 9(5)(b) of the Tribunals, Courts and Enforcement Act 2007 or under Tribunal Procedure Rules relating to non-compliance with a requirement of the First-tier Tribunal—

    (i)   by the Tax Chamber of the First-tier Tribunal;

    (ii)   by the General Regulatory Chamber of the First-tier Tribunal in a charities case;

(g)   an application for the Upper Tribunal to grant the relief mentioned in section 15(1) of the Tribunals, Courts and Enforcement Act 2007 (Upper Tribunal's "judicial review" jurisdiction), or to exercise the powers of review under section 21(2) of that Act (Upper Tribunal's "judicial review" jurisdiction: Scotland), which relates to—

    (i)   a decision of the First-tier Tribunal mentioned in paragraph (1)(a)(i) or (ii);

    (ii)   a function of the Commissioners for Her Majesty's Revenue and Customs or an officer of Revenue and Customs, with the exception of any function in respect of which an appeal would be allocated to the Social Entitlement Chamber by article 6;

    (iii)   the exercise by [the National Crime Agency] of general Revenue functions or Revenue inheritance tax functions (as defined in section 323 of the Proceeds of Crime Act 2002), with the exception of any function in relation to which an appeal would be allocated to the Social Entitlement Chamber by article 6;

    (iv)   a function of the Charity Commission, or one of the bodies mentioned in sub-paragraph (b) or (c)[;

(h)   an appeal against a decision of the First-tier Tribunal made in the Property Chamber in a case mentioned in article 5A(a)].

(2)   In this article "a charities case" means an appeal or application in respect of a decision, order or direction of the Charity Commission, or a reference under Schedule 1D to the Charities Act 1993.

Amendment

    Para (1): in sub-para (g)(iii) words "the National Crime Agency" in square brackets substituted by virtue of the Crime and Courts Act 2013, s 15(3), Sch 8, Pt 4, para 190. Date in force: 7 October 2013: see SI 2013/1682, art 3(v).

    Para (1) sub-para (h) inserted by SI 2013/1187, arts 2, 7. Date in force: 1 July 2013: see SI 2013/1187, art 1.

14 Resolution of doubt or dispute as to chamber

If there is any doubt or dispute as to the chamber in which a particular matter is to be dealt with, the Senior President of Tribunals may allocate that matter to the chamber which appears to the Senior President of Tribunals to be most appropriate.

15 Re-allocation of a case to another chamber

At any point in the proceedings, the Chamber President of the chamber to which a case or any issue in that case has been allocated by or under this Order may, with the consent of the corresponding Chamber President, allocate that case or that issue to another chamber within the same tribunal, by giving a direction to that effect.

IMMIGRATION AND ASYLUM CHAMBERS OF THE FIRST-TIER TRIBUNAL AND THE UPPER TRIBUNAL PRACTICE DIRECTION: 10 FEBRUARY 2010

PART 1
PRELIMINARY

1 Interpretation, etc.

1.1 In these Practice Directions:-

"the 2002 Act" means the Nationality, Immigration and Asylum Act 2002;

"the 2007 Act" means the Tribunals, Courts and Enforcement Act 2007;

"adjudicator" means an adjudicator appointed, or treated as appointed, under section 81 of the 2002 Act (as originally enacted);

"AIT" means the Asylum and Immigration Tribunal;

"CMR hearing" means a case management review hearing;

"fast track appeal" means an appeal to which Part 2 of the Fast Track Rules applies;

"Fast Track Rules" means the Asylum and Immigration Tribunal (Fast Track Procedure) Rules 2005;

"First-tier rule", followed by a number, means the rule bearing that number in the Asylum and Immigration Tribunal (Procedure) Rules 2005;

"IAT" means the Immigration Appeal Tribunal;

"Practice Statements" means the Practice Statements — *Immigration and Asylum Chambers of the First-tier Tribunal and the Upper Tribunal* (dated 10 February 2010); and "Practice Statement", followed by a number, means the Statement bearing that number in the Practice Statements;

"Transfer of Functions Order" means the Transfer of Functions of the Asylum and Immigration Tribunal Order 2010 (SI/2010/21);

"The Tribunal" means the Immigration and Asylum Chamber of the First-tier Tribunal or of the Upper Tribunal, as the case may be;

"UT rule", followed by a number, means the rule bearing that number in the Tribunal Procedure (Upper Tribunal) Rules 2008.

1.2 Except where expressly stated to the contrary, any reference in these Practice Directions to an enactment is a reference to that enactment as amended by or under any other enactment.

1.3 Other expressions in these Practice Statements have the same meanings as in the 2007 Act.

1.4 These Practice Directions come into force on 15 February 2010.

1.5 These Practice Directions apply, as appropriate, in relation to transitional cases to which Schedule 4 to the Transfer of Functions Order applies; and references to the First-tier Tribunal and the Upper Tribunal shall be construed accordingly.

PART 2
PRACTICE DIRECTIONS FOR THE IMMIGRATION AND ASYLUM CHAMBER OF THE FIRST-TIER TRIBUNAL

2 Standard directions in fast track appeals

2.1   In the case of a fast track appeal, the parties must respectively serve the material specified in Practice Direction 7.5(a) and (b) either at the hearing or, if practicable, on the business day immediately preceding the date of the hearing.

2.2   Subject to the exception mentioned in Practice Direction 7.7, witness statements served in pursuance of paragraph 2.1 shall stand as evidence-in-chief at the hearing.

PART 3
PRACTICE DIRECTIONS FOR THE IMMIGRATION AND ASYLUM CHAMBER OF THE UPPER TRIBUNAL

3 Procedure on appeal

3.1   Where permission to appeal to the Upper Tribunal has been granted, then, unless and to the extent that they are directed otherwise, for the purposes of preparing for a hearing in the Upper Tribunal the parties should assume that:-

(a)   the Upper Tribunal will decide whether the making of the decision of the First-tier Tribunal involved the making of an error on a point of law, such that the decision should be set aside under section 12(2)(a) of the 2007 Act;

(b)   except as specified in Practice Statement 7.2 (disposal of appeals by Upper Tribunal), the Upper Tribunal will proceed to re-make the decision under section 12(2)(b)(ii), if satisfied that the original decision should be set aside; and

(c)   in that event, the Upper Tribunal will consider whether to re-make the decision by reference to the First-tier Tribunal's findings of fact and any new documentary evidence submitted under UT rule 15(2A) which it is reasonably practicable to adduce for consideration at that hearing.

3.2   The parties should be aware that, in the circumstances described in paragraph 3.1(c), the Upper Tribunal will generally expect to proceed, without any further hearing, to re-make the decision, where this can be undertaken without having to hear oral evidence. In certain circumstances, the Upper Tribunal may give directions for the giving of oral evidence at the relevant hearing, where it appears appropriate to do so. Such directions may be given before or at that hearing.

3.3   In a case where no oral evidence is likely to be required in order for the Upper Tribunal to re-make the decision, the Upper Tribunal will therefore expect any documentary evidence relevant to the re-making of the decision to be adduced in accordance with Practice Direction 4 so that it may be considered at the relevant hearing; and, accordingly, the party seeking to rely on such documentary evidence will be expected to show good reason why it is not reasonably practicable to adduce the same in order for it to be considered at that hearing.

3.4   If the Upper Tribunal nevertheless decides that it cannot proceed as described in paragraph 3.1(c) because findings of fact are needed which it is not in a position to make, the Upper Tribunal will make arrangements for the adjournment of the hearing, so that the proceedings may be completed before the same constitution of the Tribunal; or, if that is not reasonably practicable, for their transfer to a different constitution, in either case so as to enable evidence to be adduced for that purpose.

3.5   Where proceedings are transferred in the circumstances described in paragraph 3.4, any documents sent to or given by the Tribunal from which the proceedings are transferred shall be deemed to have been sent to or given by the Tribunal to which those proceedings are transferred.

3.6   Where such proceedings are transferred, the Upper Tribunal shall prepare written reasons for finding that the First-tier Tribunal made an error of law, such that its decision fell to be set aside, and those written reasons shall be sent to the parties before the next hearing.

3.7 The written reasons shall be incorporated **in full** in, and form part of, the determination of the Upper Tribunal that re-makes the decision. Only in very exceptional cases can the decision contained in those written reasons be departed from or varied by the Upper Tribunal which re-makes the decision under section 12(2)(b)(ii) of the 2007 Act.

3.8 Unless directed otherwise, the parties to any fast track appeal which is before the Upper Tribunal will be expected to attend with all necessary witnesses and evidence that may be required if the Upper Tribunal should decide that it is necessary to set aside the decision of the First-tier Tribunal and re-make the decision. It will be unusual for the Upper Tribunal to adjourn or transfer, but, if it does so, paragraph 3.6 and 3.7 will, so far as appropriate, apply.

3.9 In this Practice Direction and Practice Direction 4, "the relevant hearing" means a hearing fixed by the Upper Tribunal at which it will consider if the First-tier Tribunal made an error of law.

3.10 Without prejudice to the generality of paragraph 1.5, where, by virtue of any transitional provisions in Schedule 4 to the Transfer of Functions Order, the Upper Tribunal is undertaking the reconsideration of a decision of the AIT, references in this Practice Direction and Practice Direction 4 to the First-tier Tribunal shall be construed as references to the AIT.

4 Evidence

4.1 UT rule 15(2A) imposes important procedural requirements where the Upper Tribunal is asked to consider evidence that was not before the First-tier Tribunal. UT rule 15(2A) must be complied with in **every case** where permission to appeal is granted and a party wishes the Upper Tribunal to consider such evidence. Notice under rule 15(2A)(a), indicating the nature of the evidence and explaining why it was not submitted to the First-tier Tribunal, must be filed with the Upper Tribunal and served on the other party within the time stated in any specific directions given by the Upper Tribunal; or, if no such direction has been given, as soon as practicable after permission to appeal has been granted.

4.2 A party who wishes the Upper Tribunal to consider any evidence that was not before the First-tier Tribunal must indicate in the notice whether the evidence is sought to be adduced:-

(a) in connection with the issue of whether the First-tier Tribunal made an error of law, requiring its decision to be set aside; or

(b) in connection with the re-making of the decision by the Upper Tribunal, in the event of the First-tier Tribunal being found to have made such an error.

4.3 The notice must clearly indicate whether the party concerned wishes the evidence to be considered at the relevant hearing and state whether the evidence is in oral or documentary form.

4.4 Where a party wishes, in the circumstances described in paragraph 4.2(b), to adduce only documentary evidence, Practice Direction 3.3 will apply.

4.5 Where a party wishes, in the circumstances described in paragraph 4.2(b), to adduce oral evidence at the relevant hearing, the notice must explain why it is considered desirable to proceed in such a manner and give details of the oral evidence and a time estimate.

4.6 Where the Upper Tribunal acts under Practice Direction 3 to adjourn or transfer the hearing, it shall consider any notice given under UT rule 15(2A) and give any directions arising therefrom, if and to the extent that this has not already been done.

4.7 This Practice Direction does not apply in the case of a fast track appeal (as to which, see Practice Direction 3.8).

5 Pursuing appeal after grant of leave

5.1 This Practice Direction applies where:-

(a)   an appeal would otherwise fall to be treated as abandoned pursuant to section 104(4A) of the 2002 Act because the appellant is granted leave to remain in the United Kingdom; but

(b)   the appellant wishes, in pursuance of section 104(4B) or (4C), to pursue the appeal, insofar as it is brought on asylum grounds or on grounds of unlawful discrimination.

5.2   Where this Practice Direction applies, the appellant must comply with the following requirements (which are the relevant practice directions for the purposes of UT rule 17A(3)).

5.3   Where section 104(4B) of the 2002 Act (asylum grounds) applies, the notice required by UT rule 17A(3) to be sent or delivered to the Upper Tribunal must state:-

(a)   the appellant's full name and date of birth;
(b)   the Tribunal's reference number;
(c)   the Home Office reference number, if applicable;
(d)   the Foreign and Commonwealth Office reference number, if applicable;
(e)   the date on which the appellant was granted leave to enter or remain in the United Kingdom for a period exceeding 12 months; and
(f)   that the appellant wishes to pursue the appeal in so far as it is brought on the ground specified in section 84(1)(g) of the 2002 Act which relates to the Refugee Convention.

5.4   Where section 104(4C) of the 2002 Act (grounds of unlawful discrimination) applies, the notice required by UT rule 17A(3) to be sent or delivered to the Upper Tribunal must state:-

(a)   the appellant's full name and date of birth;
(b)   the Tribunal's reference number;
(c)   the Home Office reference number, if applicable;
(d)   the Foreign and Commonwealth Office reference number, if applicable;
(e)   the date on which the appellant was granted leave to enter or remain in the United Kingdom; and
(f)   that the appellant wishes to pursue the appeal in so far as it is brought on the ground specified in section 84(1)(b) of the 2002 Act which relates to section 19B of the Race Relations Act 1976 (discrimination by public authorities).

5.5   Where an appellant has sent or delivered a notice under UT rule 17A(3), the Upper Tribunal will notify the appellant of the date on which it received the notice.

5.6   The Upper Tribunal will send a copy of the notice issued under paragraph 5.5 to the respondent.

5.7   In this Practice Direction:-

"appellant" means the party who was the appellant before the First-tier Tribunal; and

"respondent" means the party who was the respondent before the First-tier Tribunal.

PART 4
PRACTICE DIRECTIONS FOR THE IMMIGRATION AND ASYLUM CHAMBER OF THE FIRST-TIER TRIBUNAL AND THE UPPER TRIBUNAL

6 Form of notice of appeal etc.

6.1   The form of notice approved for the purpose of:-

(a)   First-tier rule 8 (notice of appeal);
(b)   First-tier rule 24 (application for permission to appeal to the Upper Tribunal);
(c)   First-tier rule 38 (application for bail); and
(d)   UT rule 21 (application to the Upper Tribunal for permission to appeal).

as the case may be, is the appropriate form as displayed on the Tribunal's website at the time when the notice is given, or that form with any variations that circumstances may require.

7 Case management review hearings and directions

7.1 Where the Tribunal so directs, a CMR hearing will be held in the case of an appeal where the party who is or was the appellant before the First-tier Tribunal:-

(a)   is present in the United Kingdom; and
(b)   has a right of appeal whilst in the United Kingdom.

7.2 It is important that the parties and their representatives understand that a CMR hearing is a **hearing** in the appeal and that the appeal may be determined under the relevant Procedure Rules if a party does not appear and is not represented at that hearing.

7.3 In addition to any information required by First-tier rule 8 (form of contents and notice of appeal), the appellant before the First-tier Tribunal must provide that Tribunal and the respondent at the CMR hearing with:-

(a)   particulars of any application for permission to vary the grounds of appeal;
(b)   particulars of any amendments to the reasons in support of the grounds of appeal;
(c)   particulars of any witnesses to be called or whose written statement or report is proposed to be relied upon at the full hearing; and
(d)   the draft of any directions that the appellant is requesting the Tribunal to make at the CMR hearing.

7.4 In addition to any documents required by relevant Procedure Rules, the party who is or was the respondent before the First-tier Tribunal must provide the Tribunal and the other party at the CMR hearing with:-

(a)   any amendment that has been made or is proposed to be made to the notice of decision to which the appeal relates or to any other document served on the person concerned giving reasons for that decision; and
(b)   a draft of any directions that the Tribunal is requested to make at the CMR hearing.

7.5 In most cases, including those appeals where a CMR hearing is to be held, the Tribunal will normally have given to the parties the following directions with the notice of hearing:-

(a)   not later than 5 working days before the full hearing (or 10 days in the case of an out-of-country appeal) the appellant shall serve on the Tribunal and the respondent:
    (i)   witness statements of the evidence to be called at the hearing, such statements to stand as evidence in chief at the hearing;
    (ii)   a paginated and indexed bundle of all the documents to be relied on at the hearing with a schedule identifying the essential passages;
    (iii)   a skeleton argument, identifying all relevant issues including human rights claims and citing all the authorities relied upon; and
    (iv)   a chronology of events;
(b)   not later than 5 working days before the full hearing, the respondent shall serve on the Tribunal and the appellant a paginated and indexed bundle of all the documents to be relied upon at the hearing, with a schedule identifying the relevant passages, and a list of any authorities relied upon.

7.6 At the end of the CMR hearing, the Tribunal will give the parties any further written directions relating to the conduct of the appeal.

7.7 Although in normal circumstances a witness statement should stand as evidence-in-chief, there may be cases where it will be appropriate for appellants or witnesses to have the opportunity of adding to or supplementing their witness statements.

7.8 In addition to the directions referred to above, at the end of the CMR hearing the Tribunal will also give to the parties written confirmation of:-

(a)   any issues that have been agreed at the CMR hearing as being relevant to the determination of the appeal; and
(b)   any concessions made at the CMR hearing by a party.

8 Trial bundles

8.1 The parties must take all reasonably practicable steps to act in accordance with paragraph 8.2 to 8.6 in the preparation of trial bundles for hearings before the Tribunal.

8.2 The best practice for the preparation of bundles is as follows:-

(a) all documents must be relevant, be presented in logical order and be legible;

(b) where the document is not in the English language, a typed translation of the document signed by the translator, and certifying that the translation is accurate, must be inserted in the bundle next to the copy of the original document, together with details of the identity and qualifications of the translator;

(c) if it is necessary to include a lengthy document, that part of the document on which reliance is placed should, unless the passages are outlined in any skeleton argument, be highlighted or clearly identified by reference to page and/or paragraph number;

(d) bundles submitted must have an index showing the page numbers of each document in the bundle;

(e) the skeleton argument or written submission should define and confine the areas at issue in a numbered list of brief points and each point should refer to any documentation in the bundle on which the appellant proposes to rely (together with its page number);

(f) where reliance is placed on a particular case or text, photocopies of the case or text must be provided in full for the Tribunal and the other party; and

(g) large bundles should be contained in a ring binder or lever arch file, capable of lying flat when opened.

8.3 The Tribunal recognises the constraints on those representing the parties in appeals in relation to the preparation of trial bundles and this Practice Direction does not therefore make it mandatory in every case that bundles in exactly the form prescribed must be prepared. Where the issues are particularly complex it is of the highest importance that comprehensive bundles are prepared. If parties to appeals fail in individual cases to present documentation in a way which complies with the direction, it will be for the Tribunal to deal with any such issue.

8.4 Much evidence in immigration and asylum appeals is in documentary form. Representatives preparing bundles need to be aware of the position of the Tribunal, which may be coming to the case for the first time. The better a bundle has been prepared, the greater it will assist the Tribunal. Bundles should contain all the documents that the Tribunal will require to enable it to reach a decision without the need to refer to any other file or document. The Tribunal will not be assisted by repetitious, outdated or irrelevant material.

8.5 It may not be practical in many appeals to require there to be an agreed trial bundle but it nevertheless remains vital that the parties inform each other at an early stage of all and any documentation upon which they intend to rely.

8.6 The parties cannot rely on the Tribunal having any prior familiarity with any country information or background reports in relation to the case in question. If either party wishes to rely on such country or background information, copies of the relevant documentation must be provided.

9 Adjournments

9.1 Applications for the adjournment of appeals (other than fast track appeals) listed for hearing before the Tribunal must be made not later than 5.00p.m. one clear working day before the date of the hearing.

9.2 For the avoidance of doubt, where a case is listed for hearing on, for example, a Friday, the application must be received by 5.00p.m. on the Wednesday.

9.3 The application for an adjournment must be supported by full reasons and must be made in accordance with relevant Procedure Rules.

9.4 Any application made later than the end of the period mentioned in paragraph 9.1 must be made to the Tribunal at the hearing and will require the attendance of the party or the representative of the party seeking the adjournment.

9.5   It will be only in the most exceptional circumstances that a late application for an adjournment will be considered without the attendance of a party or representative.

9.6   Parties must not assume that an application, even if made in accordance with paragraph 9.1, will be successful and they must always check with the Tribunal as to the outcome of the application.

9.7   Any application for the adjournment of a fast track appeal must be made to the Tribunal at the hearing and will be considered by the Tribunal in accordance with relevant Procedure Rules.

9.8   If an adjournment is not granted and the party fails to attend the hearing, the Tribunal may in certain circumstances proceed with the hearing in that party's absence.

10 Expert evidence

10.1   A party who instructs an expert must provide clear and precise instructions to the expert, together with all relevant information concerning the nature of the appellant's case, including the appellant's immigration history, the reasons why the appellant's claim or application has been refused by the respondent and copies of any relevant previous reports prepared in respect of the appellant.

10.2   It is the duty of an expert to help the Tribunal on matters within the expert's own expertise. This duty is paramount and overrides any obligation to the person from whom the expert has received instructions or by whom the expert is paid.

10.3   Expert evidence should be the independent product of the expert uninfluenced by the pressures of litigation.

10.4   An expert should assist the Tribunal by providing objective, unbiased opinion on matters within his or her expertise, and should not assume the role of an advocate.

10.5   An expert should consider all material facts, including those which might detract from his or her opinion.

10.6   An expert should make it clear:-

(a)   when a question or issue falls outside his or her expertise; and
(b)   when the expert is not able to reach a definite opinion, for example because of insufficient information.

10.7   If, after producing a report, an expert changes his or her view on any material matter, that change of view should be communicated to the parties without delay, and when appropriate to the Tribunal.

10.8   An expert's report should be addressed to the Tribunal and not to the party from whom the expert has received instructions.

10.9   An expert's report must:-

(a)   give details of the expert's qualifications;
(b)   give details of any literature or other material which the expert has relied on in making the report;
(c)   contain a statement setting out the substance of all facts and instructions given to the expert which are material to the opinions expressed in the report or upon which those opinions are based;
(d)   make clear which of the facts stated in the report are within the expert's own knowledge;
(e)   say who carried out any examination, measurement or other procedure which the expert has used for the report, give the qualifications of that person, and say whether or not the procedure has been carried out under the expert's supervision;
(f)   where there is a range of opinion on the matters dealt with in the report:
   (i)   summarise the range of opinion, so far as reasonably practicable, and
   (ii)   give reasons for the expert's own opinion;
(g)   contain a summary of the conclusions reached;

(h)   if the expert is not able to give an opinion without qualification, state the qualification; and

(i)   contain a statement that the expert understands his or her duty to the Tribunal, and has complied and will continue to comply with that duty.

10.10   An expert's report must be verified by a Statement of Truth as well as containing the statements required in paragraph 10.9(h) and (j).

10.11   The form of the Statement of Truth is as follows:-

"I confirm that insofar as the facts stated in my report are within my own knowledge I have made clear which they are and I believe them to be true, and that the opinions I have expressed represent my true and complete professional opinion".

10.12   The instructions referred to in paragraph 10.9(c) are not protected by privilege but cross-examination of the expert on the contents of the instructions will not be allowed unless the Tribunal permits it (or unless the party who gave the instructions consents to it). Before it gives permission the Tribunal must be satisfied that there are reasonable grounds to consider that the statement in the report or the substance of the instructions is inaccurate or incomplete. If the Tribunal is so satisfied, it will allow the cross-examination where it appears to be in the interests of justice to do so.

10.13   In this Practice Direction:-

"appellant" means the party who is or was the appellant before the First-tier Tribunal; and

"respondent" means the party who is or was the respondent before the First-tier Tribunal.

11 Citation of unreported determinations

11.1   A determination of the Tribunal which has not been reported may not be cited in proceedings before the Tribunal unless:-

(a)   the person who is or was the appellant before the First-tier Tribunal, or a member of that person's family, was a party to the proceedings in which the previous determination was issued; or

(b)   the Tribunal gives permission.

11.2   An application for permission to cite a determination which has not been reported must:-

(a)   include a **full** transcript of the determination;

(b)   identify the proposition for which the determination is to be cited; and

(c)   certify that the proposition is not to be found in any reported determination of the Tribunal, the IAT or the AIT and had not been superseded by the decision of a higher authority.

11.3   Permission under paragraph 11.1 will be given only where the Tribunal considers that it would be materially assisted by citation of the determination, as distinct from the adoption in argument of the reasoning to be found in the determination. Such instances are likely to be rare; in particular, in the case of determinations which were unreportable (see Practice Statement 11 (reporting of determinations)). It should be emphasised that the Tribunal will not exclude good arguments from consideration but it will be rare for such an argument to be capable of being made only by reference to an unreported determination.

11.4   The provisions of paragraph 11.1 to 11.3 apply to unreported and unreportable determinations of the AIT, the IAT and adjudicators, as those provisions apply respectively to unreported and unreportable determinations of the Tribunal.

11.5   A party citing a determination of the IAT bearing a neutral citation number prior to [2003] (including all series of "bracket numbers") must be in a position to certify that the matter or proposition for which the determination is cited has not been the subject of more recent, reported, determinations of the IAT, the AIT or the Tribunal.

11.6 In this Practice Direction and Practice Direction 12, "determination" includes any decision of the AIT or the Tribunal.

12 Starred and Country Guidance determinations

12.1 Reported determinations of the Tribunal, the AIT and the IAT which are "starred" shall be treated by the Tribunal as authoritative in respect of the matter to which the "starring" relates, unless inconsistent with other authority that is binding on the Tribunal.

12.2 A reported determination of the Tribunal, the AIT or the IAT bearing the letters "CG" shall be treated as an authoritative finding on the country guidance issue identified in the determination, based upon the evidence before the members of the Tribunal, the AIT or the IAT that determine the appeal. As a result, unless it has been expressly superseded or replaced by any later "CG" determination, or is inconsistent with other authority that is binding on the Tribunal, such a country guidance case is authoritative in any subsequent appeal, so far as that appeal:-

(a)   relates to the country guidance issue in question; and
(b)   depends upon the same or similar evidence.

12.3 A list of current CG cases will be maintained on the Tribunal's website. Any representative of a party to an appeal concerning a particular country will be expected to be conversant with the current "CG" determinations relating to that country.

12.4 Because of the principle that like cases should be treated in like manner, any failure to follow a clear, apparently applicable country guidance case or to show why it does not apply to the case in question is likely to be regarded as grounds for appeal on a point of law.

13 Bail applications

13.1 An application for bail must if practicable be listed for hearing within three working days of receipt by the Tribunal of the notice of application.

13.2 Any such notice which is received by the Tribunal after 3.30 p.m. on a particular day will be treated for the purposes of this paragraph as if it were received on the next business day.

13.3 An Upper Tribunal judge may exercise bail jurisdiction under the Immigration Act 1971 by reason of being also a First-tier judge.

13.4 Notwithstanding paragraph 13.3, it will usually be appropriate for a bail application to be made to an Upper Tribunal judge only where the appeal in question is being heard by the Upper Tribunal, or where a hearing before the Upper Tribunal is imminent. In case of doubt, a potential applicant should consult the bails section of the First-tier Tribunal.

14 This Practice Direction is made by the Senior President of Tribunals with the agreement of the Lord Chancellor. It is made in the exercise of powers conferred by the Tribunals, Courts and Enforcement Act 2007.

LORD JUSTICE CARNWATH

SENIOR PRESIDENT OF TRIBUNALS

10 February 2010

IMMIGRATION AND ASYLUM CHAMBERS OF THE FIRST-TIER TRIBUNAL AND THE UPPER TRIBUNAL PRACTICE STATEMENT: 10 FEBRUARY 2010

PART 1
PRELIMINARY

1. Interpretation, etc.

1.1 In these Practice Statements:

"the 2007 Act" means the Tribunals, Courts and Enforcement Act 2007;

"the 2008 Order" means the First-tier Tribunal and Upper Tribunal (Composition of Tribunal) Order 2008;

"Chamber President" means the President of the Immigration and Asylum Chamber of the First-tier Tribunal or of the Upper Tribunal, as the case may be;

"CMR hearing" means a case management review hearing;

"First-tier rule", followed by a number, means the rule bearing that number in the Asylum and Immigration Tribunal (Procedure) Rules 2005;

"First-tier judge" means a judge of the First-tier Tribunal;

"other member" means a person who, immediately before the repeal by the Transfer of Functions Order of section 5(2)(d) of the 2007 Act, was a member of the Upper Tribunal by reason of that enactment;

"Practice Directions" means the Practice Directions — *Immigration and Asylum Chambers of the First-tier Tribunal and the Upper Tribunal* (dated 10 February 2010); and "Practice Direction", followed by a number, means the Direction bearing that number in the Practice Directions;

"Senior President" means the Senior President of Tribunals;

"Transfer of Functions Order" means the Transfer of Functions of the Asylum and Immigration Tribunal Order 2010 (SI/2010/21);

"The Tribunal" means the Immigration and Asylum Chamber of the First-tier Tribunal or of the Upper Tribunal, as the case may be;

"Upper Tribunal judge" means a judge of the Upper Tribunal;

"UT Rules" means the Tribunal Procedure (Upper Tribunal) Rules 2008; and "UT rule", followed by a number, means the rule bearing that number in the UT Rules.

1.2 Other expressions used in these Practice Statements have the same meanings as in the 2007 Act.

1.3 Any reference in these Practice Statements to an enactment is a reference to that enactment as amended by or under any other enactment.

1.4 These Practice Statements come into force on 15 February 2010.

1.5 These Practice Statements apply, as appropriate, in relation to transitional cases to which Schedule 4 to the Transfer of Functions Order applies; and references to the First-tier Tribunal and the Upper Tribunal shall be construed accordingly.

PART 2
PRACTICE STATEMENTS FOR THE IMMIGRATION AND ASYLUM CHAMBER OF THE FIRST-TIER TRIBUNAL

2. Composition of Immigration and Asylum Chamber of the First-tier Tribunal

2.1 Subject to paragraph 2.2, any decision that falls to be decided by the First-tier Tribunal in respect of any matter specified in the first column below is to be decided by the number and type of members specified in the second column.

(1)	Whether notice of appeal given in time/whether to extend time for appealing (except where First-tier rule 11 applies)/refusal to accept notice of appeal (First-tier rule 9)	One First-tier judge
(2)	Whether to extend time for appealing where First-tier rule 11 applies (special provisions for imminent removal cases)	One First-tier judge, from those approved by the Senior President to make such decisions
(3)	All appeals or other matters which are not specified below	One First-tier judge or a panel of two or three members, at least one of whom must be a First-tier judge and no more than one of whom may be an other member
(4)	The giving of any directions under First-tier rule 45(6)	The Chamber President
(5)	The giving of any other directions (whether or not at case management review or other hearings)	One First-tier judge
(6)	Appeals which are to be determined without a hearing	One First-tier judge
(7)	Applications for bail and other bail matters	One First-tier judge
(8)	Issue of a witness summons	One First-tier judge
(9)	Any determination that an appeal be dismissed as abandoned or finally determined	One First-tier judge
(10)	Review under First-tier rule 60(1A) and any resulting action under that paragraph	The Chamber President
(11)	Applications for permission to appeal to Upper Tribunal	One First-tier judge, from those approved by the Senior President to deal with such applications
(12)	Review under section 9 of the 2007 Act of a decision (consequent on an application for permission to appeal) and any resulting action under that section	One First-tier judge, from those approved by the Senior President to deal with section 9 matters

2.2 Any of the matters specified in paragraph 2.1(5), (7), (8), or (9) may be decided by the members of the Tribunal deciding an appeal or other matter pursuant to paragraph 2.1(3).

2.3 Any decision that an appeal or other matter is to be decided by more than one member pursuant to paragraph 2.1(3) is that of the Chamber President; but such a decision may be delegated to another First-tier judge.

3 Where the Tribunal may not accept a notice of appeal

3.1 First-tier rule 9 (where the Tribunal may not accept a notice of appeal) imposes a duty on the Tribunal not to accept an invalid notice of appeal (in the circumstances described in rule 9(1A)) and to serve notice to this effect on the person who gave the notice of appeal and on the respondent.

3.2 The Tribunal will scrutinise a notice of appeal as soon as practicable after it has been given. First-tier rule 9 makes no provision for the issue of validity to be determined by means of a hearing or by reference to any representations of the parties.

3.3 Once the Tribunal has served the notice described in paragraph 3.1, First-tier rule 9 provides that the Tribunal must take no further action in relation to the notice of appeal. The decision under First-tier rule 9 is, accordingly, a procedural or preliminary decision.

3.4 The fact that a hearing date may have been given to the parties does not mean that the appeal must be treated as valid. Accordingly, if at a hearing (including a CMR hearing) it transpires that the notice of appeal does not relate to a decision against which there is, in the circumstances, an exercisable right of appeal, the Tribunal must so find; but it will do so in the form of a determination, rather than by means of a notice under First-tier rule 9.

4 Review of decision of First-tier Tribunal

4.1 On an application to the First-tier Tribunal for permission to appeal under section 11 of the 2007 Act (right to appeal to Upper Tribunal) on a point of law arising from a decision, the First-tier Tribunal may review that decision pursuant to First-tier rule 26, only if it is satisfied that there was an error of law in that decision.

4.2 Following such a review, the First-tier Tribunal may (subject to section 9(10)) set the decision aside under section 9(4)(c) and re-decide the matter concerned under section 9(5)(a). The First-tier Tribunal is, however, likely to adopt this course only if it is satisfied that:-

(a)   the effect of any error of law has been to deprive a party before the First-tier Tribunal of a fair hearing or other opportunity for that party's case to be put to and considered by the First-tier Tribunal; or

(b)   there are highly compelling reasons why the matter should be re-decided by the First-tier Tribunal. (Such reasons are likely to be rare.)

4.3 Nothing in this Practice Statement affects the operation of First-tier rule 60 (correction of orders and determinations).

5 Record of proceedings

5.1 The Tribunal shall keep a record of proceedings of any hearing and attach that record to the Tribunal's case file.

PART 3
PRACTICE STATEMENTS FOR THE IMMIGRATION AND ASYLUM CHAMBER OF THE UPPER TRIBUNAL

6 Composition of Immigration and Asylum Chamber of the Upper Tribunal

6.1 Subject to paragraph 6.2 to 6.5, any matter that falls to be decided by the Upper Tribunal is to be decided by one Upper Tribunal judge.

6.2 Where the Senior President or the Chamber President considers that the matter involves a question of law of special difficulty or an important point of principle or practice, or that it is otherwise appropriate, the matter is to be decided by two or three Upper Tribunal judges.

6.3 Where the Senior President or the Chamber President considers that it is appropriate, the matter is to be decided by:-

(a)   one Upper Tribunal judge and one other member; or

(b)   two Upper Tribunal judges and one other member.

6.4   An application for permission to appeal to the Upper Tribunal is to be decided by one Upper Tribunal judge, from those approved by the Senior President or the Chamber President.

6.5   Nothing in paragraph 6.2 to 6.4 prevents any procedural or ancillary matter regarding the case concerned from being decided by any Upper Tribunal judge.

6.6   Any decision of the Chamber President pursuant to paragraph 6.2 or 6.3 may be delegated by the Chamber President to another Upper Tribunal judge.

7 Disposal of appeals in Upper Tribunal

7.1   Where under section 12(1) of the 2007 Act (proceedings on appeal to the Upper Tribunal) the Upper Tribunal finds that the making of the decision concerned involved the making of an error on a point of law, the Upper Tribunal may set aside the decision and, if it does so, must either remit the case to the First-tier Tribunal under section 12(2)(b)(i) or proceed (in accordance with relevant Practice Directions) to re-make the decision under section 12(2)(b)(ii).

7.2   The Upper Tribunal is likely on each such occasion to proceed to re-make the decision, instead of remitting the case to the First-tier Tribunal, unless the Upper Tribunal is satisfied that:-

(a)   the effect of the error has been to deprive a party before the First-tier Tribunal of a fair hearing or other opportunity for that party's case to be put to and considered by the First-tier Tribunal; or
(b)   there are highly compelling reasons why the decision should not be re-made by the Upper Tribunal. (Such reasons are likely to be rare.)

PART 4
PRACTICE STATEMENTS FOR THE IMMIGRATION AND ASYLUM CHAMBERS OF THE FIRST-TIER TRIBUNAL AND THE UPPER TRIBUNAL

8 Presiding member

8.1   Where more than one member of the Tribunal is to decide a matter, the presiding member for the purposes of article 7 of the 2008 Order and this Practice Statement is:-

(a)   the judge; or
(b)   the senior judge, where the Tribunal contains more than one judge.

9 Transfer of proceedings

9.1   Where:-

(a)   the Tribunal ("the original Tribunal") has started to hear an appeal but has not completed the hearing or given its determination; and
(b)   the Chamber President decides that it is not practicable for the original Tribunal to complete the hearing or give its determination without undue delay,

the Chamber President may direct the appeal to be heard by a differently constituted Tribunal ("the new Tribunal").

9.2   Where an appeal has been transferred under paragraph 9.1:-

(a)   any documents sent to or given by the original Tribunal shall be deemed to have been sent to or given by the new Tribunal; and
(b)   the new Tribunal will deal with the appeal as if it had been commenced before it.

9.3   Without prejudice to paragraph 9.1, the Chamber President may transfer proceedings in the circumstances described in Practice Direction 3 (procedure on appeal); and paragraph 9.2(a) shall apply in the case of such a transfer as it applies in the case of a transfer under paragraph 9.1.

10 Format etc of determinations

10.1 In order to ensure consistency in the formatting of determinations, every determination of the Tribunal must:-

(a)   state in the heading whether the appeal is being determined following a hearing or without a hearing;

(b)   be laid out in sequentially numbered paragraphs; and

(c)   be signed and dated at its end or employ such electronic or other methods as the Senior President or the Chamber President may approve for signifying that the determination is finalised.

10.2   Since Article 8 of the 2008 Order provides that the decision of the majority is the decision of the Tribunal (and that the presiding member has a casting vote), where the jurisdiction of the Tribunal is exercised by more than one member the resulting determination or other decision will not express any dissenting view or indicate that it is that of a majority.

11 Reporting of determinations

11.1   This Practice Statement is to be read in conjunction with Practice Direction 11 (citation of unreported determinations) and Practice Statement – *Form of decisions and neutral citation First-tier Tribunal and Upper Tribunal on or after 3 November 2008* (31 October 2008).

11.2   The decision whether to report a determination is that of the Tribunal and it is not perceived to be an issue in which the parties to the appeal have an interest.

11.3   A determination is reportable only if it follows a hearing or other consideration where the jurisdiction of the Tribunal was exercised by the Senior President, the Chamber President or an Upper Tribunal judge (whether or not sitting alone and, in the case of an Upper Tribunal judge, whether sitting as such or as a First-tier judge).

11.4   A determination which is reportable but not in fact reported will be anonymised (where appropriate), treated as an unreported determination for the purposes of the Tribunal's website and entered as such on that website.

11.5   Determinations not falling within paragraph 11.3 are unreportable. They will be sent to the parties (in accordance with the relevant Procedure Rules) but will not be published or archived in publicly accessible form.

11.6   The Tribunal's website is the only official source of the determinations of the Tribunal.

11.7   In this Practice Statement:

"determination" includes any decision of the Tribunal; and

"Upper Tribunal judge" does not include a deputy judge of the Upper Tribunal.

LORD JUSTICE CARNWATH

SENIOR PRESIDENT OF TRIBUNALS

10 February 2010

EUROPEAN COURT OF HUMAN RIGHTS: RULES OF COURT, RULES 39, 40, 45–47

TITLE II
PROCEDURE

CHAPTER I

GENERAL RULES

Rule 39 (Interim measures)
(1)   The Chamber or, where appropriate, its President may, at the request of a party or of any other person concerned, or of its own motion, indicate to the parties any interim measure which it considers should be adopted in the interests of the parties or of the proper conduct of the proceedings before it.
(2)   Notice of these measures shall be given to the Committee of Ministers.
(3)   The Chamber may request information from the parties on any matter connected with the implementation of any interim measure it has indicated.

Amendment
   As amended by the Court on 4 July 2005.

Rule 40 (Urgent notification of an application)
In any case of urgency the Registrar, with the authorisation of the President of the Chamber, may, without prejudice to the taking of any other procedural steps and by any available means, inform a Contracting Party concerned in an application of the introduction of the application and of a summary of its objects.

CHAPTER II
INSTITUTION OF PROCEEDINGS

Rule 45 (Signatures)
(1)   Any application made under Articles 33 or 34 of the Convention shall be submitted in writing and shall be signed by the applicant or by the applicant's representative.
(2)   Where an application is made by a non-governmental organisation or by a group of individuals, it shall be signed by those persons competent to represent that organisation or group. The Chamber or Committee concerned shall determine any question as to whether the persons who have signed an application are competent to do so.
(3)   Where applicants are represented in accordance with Rule 36, a power of attorney or written authority to act shall be supplied by their representative or representatives.

Rule 46 (Contents of an inter-State application)
Any Contracting Party or Parties intending to bring a case before the Court under Article 33 of the Convention shall file with the Registry an application setting out
   (a)   the name of the Contracting Party against which the application is made;
   (b)   a statement of the facts;
   (c)   a statement of the alleged violation(s) of the Convention and the relevant arguments;
   (d)   a statement on compliance with the admissibility criteria (exhaustion of domestic remedies and the six-month rule) laid down in Article 35 § 1 of the Convention;

(e)   the object of the application and a general indication of any claims for just satisfaction made under Article 41 of the Convention on behalf of the alleged injured party or parties; and

(f)   the name and address of the person or persons appointed as Agent;

and accompanied by

(g)   copies of any relevant documents and in particular the decisions, whether judicial or not, relating to the object of the application. 28

Rule 47 (Contents of an individual application)

(1) Any application under Article 34 of the Convention shall be made on the application form provided by the Registry, unless the President of the Section concerned decides otherwise. It shall set out

(a)   the name, date of birth, nationality, sex, occupation and address of the applicant;

(b)   the name, occupation and address of the representative, if any;

(c)   the name of the Contracting Party or Parties against which the application is made;

(d)   a succinct statement of the facts;

(e)   a succinct statement of the alleged violation(s) of the Convention and the relevant arguments;

(f)   a succinct statement on the applicant's compliance with the admissibility criteria (exhaustion of domestic remedies and the six-month rule) laid down in Article 35 § 1 of the Convention; and

(g)   the object of the application;

and be accompanied by

(h)   copies of any relevant documents and in particular the decisions, whether judicial or not, relating to the object of the application.

(2) Applicants shall furthermore

(a)   provide information, notably the documents and decisions referred to in paragraph 1 (h) of this Rule, enabling it to be shown that the admissibility criteria (exhaustion of domestic remedies and the six-month rule) laid down in Article 35 § 1 of the Convention have been satisfied; and

(b)   indicate whether they have submitted their complaints to any other procedure of international investigation or settlement.

(3) Applicants who do not wish their identity to be disclosed to the public shall so indicate and shall submit a statement of the reasons justifying such a departure from the normal rule of public access to information in proceedings before the Court. The President of the Chamber may authorise anonymity or grant it of his or her own motion.

(4) Failure to comply with the requirements set out in paragraphs 1 and 2 of this Rule may result in the application not being examined by the Court. 29

(5) The date of introduction of the application for the purposes of Article 35 § 1 of the Convention shall as a general rule be considered to be the date of the first communication from the applicant setting out, even summarily, the subject matter of the application, provided that a duly completed application form has been submitted within the time-limits laid down by the Court. The Court may for good cause nevertheless decide that a different date shall be considered to be the date of introduction.

(6) Applicants shall keep the Court informed of any change of address and of all circumstances relevant to the application.

Amendment

As amended by the Court on 17 June and 8 July 2002, 11 December 2007 and 22 September 2008.

PRACTICE DIRECTIONS
PRACTICE DIRECTION
REQUESTS FOR INTERIM MEASURES[1]

(RULE 39 OF THE RULES OF COURT)

By virtue of Rule 39 of the Rules of Court, the Court may issue interim measures which are binding on the State concerned. Interim measures are only applied in exceptional cases.

The Court will only issue an interim measure against a Member State where, having reviewed all the relevant information, it considers that the applicant faces a real risk of serious, irreversible harm if the measure is not applied.

Applicants or their legal representatives[2] who make a request for an interim measure pursuant to Rule 39 of the Rules of Court should comply with the requirements set out below.

Failure to do so may mean that the Court will not be in a position to examine such requests properly and in good time.

I. Accompanying information

Any request lodged with the Court must state *reasons*. The applicant must in particular specify in detail the grounds on which his or her particular fears are based the nature of the alleged risks and the Convention provisions alleged to have been violated.

A mere reference to submissions in other documents or domestic proceedings is not sufficient. It is essential that requests be accompanied by all necessary supporting documents, *in particular relevant domestic court, tribunal or other decisions*, together with any other material which is considered to substantiate the applicant's allegations.

The Court will not necessarily contact applicants whose request for interim measures is incomplete, and requests which do not include the information necessary to make a decision will not normally be submitted for a decision.

Where the case is already pending before the Court, reference should be made to the application number allocated to it.

In cases concerning extradition or deportation, details should be provided of the expected *date and time* of the removal, the applicant's address or place of detention and his or her official case-reference number. The Court must be notified of any change to those details (date and time of removal, address, etc.) as soon as possible.

The Court may decide to take a decision on the admissibility of the case at the same time as considering the request for interim measures.

II. Requests to be made by fax or letter[3]

Requests for interim measures under Rule 39 should be sent *by facsimile or by post*. *The Court will not deal with requests sent by e-mail.* The request should, where possible, be in one of the official languages of the Contracting Parties. All requests should be marked as follows in bold on the face of the request:

"*Rule 39 – Urgent*
Person to contact (name and contact details): . . .
[*In deportation or extradition cases*]
Date and time of removal and destination: . . . "

III. Making requests in good time

Requests for interim measures should normally be received as soon as possible after the final domestic decision has been taken, in order to enable the Court and its Registry to have sufficient time to examine the matter. The Court may not be able to deal with requests in removal cases received less than a working day before the planned time of removal.[4]

Where the final domestic decision is imminent and there is a risk of immediate enforcement, especially in extradition or deportation cases, applicants and their representatives should submit the request for interim measures without waiting for that decision, indicating clearly the date on which it will be taken and that the request is subject to the final domestic decision being negative.

Applicants and their representatives should be aware, however, that the Court cannot always examine in a timely and proper manner requests which are sent at the last moment, particularly when they are supported by a large number of documents. For that reason, where the final domestic decision is imminent and there is a risk of immediate enforcement, especially in extradition or deportation cases, applicants and their representatives should submit the request for interim measures without waiting for that decision, indicating clearly the date on which it will be taken and that the request is subject to the final domestic decision being negative.

Amendment

[1] Issued by the President of the Court in accordance with Rule 32 of the Rules of Court on 5 March 2003 and amended on 16 October 2009 and on 7 July 2011.

[2] It is essential that full contact details be provided.

[3] According to the degree of urgency and bearing in mind that requests by letter must not be sent by standard post.

[4] 1. The list of public and other holidays when the Court's Registry is closed can be consulted on the Court's internet site:www.echr.coe.int/ECHR/EN/Bottom/Contact/Holidays.htm.

IV Domestic measures with suspensive effect

The Court is not an appeal tribunal from domestic tribunals, and applicants in extradition and expulsion cases should pursue domestic avenues which are capable of suspending removal before applying to the Court for interim measures. Where it remains open to an applicant to pursue domestic remedies which have suspensive effect, the Court will not apply Rule 39 to prevent removal.

V Follow-up

Applicants who apply for an interim measure under Rule 39 should ensure that they reply to correspondence from the Court's Registry. In particular, where a measure has been refused, they should inform the Court whether they wish to pursue the application. Where a measure has been applied, they must keep the Court regularly and promptly informed about the state of any continuing domestic proceedings. Failure to do so may lead to the case being struck out of the Court's list of cases.

PRACTICE DIRECTION
INSTITUTION OF PROCEEDINGS[1,2]

(INDIVIDUAL APPLICATIONS UNDER ARTICLE 34 OF THE CONVENTION)

I. General

(1) An application under Article 34 of the Convention must be submitted in writing. No application may be made by telephone.

(2) An application must be sent to the following address:
The Registrar
European Court of Human Rights
Council of Europe
F-67075 Strasbourg Cedex.

(3) An application should normally be made on the form[3] referred to in Rule 47 § 1 of the Rules of Court and be accompanied by the documents and decisions mentioned in Rule 47 § 1 (h).

Where an applicant introduces his or her application in a letter, such letter must set out, at least in summary form, the subject matter of the application in order to interrupt the running of the six-month rule contained in Article 35 § 1 of the Convention.

(4) If an application has not been submitted on the official form or an introductory letter does not contain all the information referred to in Rule 47, the applicant may be required to submit a duly completed form. It must be sent within eight weeks from the date of the Registry's letter requesting the applicant to complete and return the form. Failure to comply with this time-limit will have implications for the date of introduction of the application and may therefore affect the applicant's compliance with the six-month rule contained in Article 35 § 1 of the Convention.

(5) Applicants may file an application by sending it by fax.[4] However, they must send the signed original by post within eight weeks from the date of the Registry's letter referred to in paragraph 4 above.

(6) Where, within six months of being asked to do so, an applicant has not returned a duly completed application form, the file will be destroyed.

(7) On receipt of the first communication setting out the subject-matter of the case, the Registry will open a file, whose number must be mentioned in all subsequent correspondence. Applicants will be informed thereof by letter. They may also be asked for further information or documents.

(8)

    (a)   An applicant should be diligent in conducting correspondence with the Court's Registry.

    (b)   A delay in replying or failure to reply may be regarded as a sign that the applicant is no longer interested in pursuing his or her application.

(9) Failure to provide further information or documents at the Registry's request (see paragraph 7) may result in the application not being examined by the Court or being declared inadmissible or struck out of the Court's list of cases.

II. Form and contents

(10) An application should be written legibly and, preferably, typed.

(11) Where, exceptionally, an application exceeds ten pages (excluding annexes listing documents), an applicant must also file a short summary.

(12) Where applicants produce documents in support of the application, they should not submit original copies. The documents should be listed in order by date, numbered consecutively and given a concise description (e.g., letter, order, judgment, appeal, etc.).

(13) An applicant who already has an application pending before the Court must inform the Registry accordingly, stating the application number.

(14)

    (a)   Where an applicant does not wish to have his or her identity disclosed, he or she should state the reasons for his or her request in writing, pursuant to Rule 47 § 3.

    (b)   The applicant should also state whether, in the event of anonymity being authorised by the President of the Chamber, he or she wishes to be designated by his or her initials or by a single letter (e.g., "X", "Y", "Z", etc.)

Amendment

[1]   Issued by the President of the Court in accordance with Rule 32 of the Rules of Court on 1 November 2003 and amended on 22 September 2008 and on 24 June 2009.

[2]   This practice direction supplements Rules 45 and 47.

[3]   The relevant form can be downloaded from the Court's website.

[4] Fax no. +33 (0)3 88 41 27 30; other fax numbers can be found on the Court's website.

JOINT PRESIDENTIAL GUIDANCE NOTE NO 2 OF 2010: CHILD, VULNERABLE ADULT AND SENSITIVE APPELLANT GUIDANCE

1. This guidance, which covers appellants and witnesses, has been developed for the First Tier Immigration and Asylum Chamber following the Guidance issued by the Senior President of Tribunals regarding Child, Vulnerable Adult and Sensitive Witnesses[1]. Although specific to these groups it is also a reminder of good judgecraft.

2. Although some individuals are by definition vulnerable[2] others are less easily identifiable. Factors to be taken into account include:

*   mental health problems
*   social or learning difficulties
*   religious beliefs and practices, sexual orientation, ethnic social and cultural background
*   domestic and employment circumstances
*   physical disability or impairment that may affect the giving of evidence

3. The consequences of such vulnerability differ according to the degree to which an individual is affected. It is a matter for you to determine the extent of an identified vulnerability, the effect on the quality of the evidence and the weight to be placed on such vulnerability in assessing the evidence before you, taking into account the evidence as a whole.

---

[1] Issued 30th October 2008, see Annex B for full copy.

[2] As defined in the Senior President's guidance "Child" means a person who has not attained the age of 18; "vulnerable adult" has the same meaning as in the Safeguarding Vulnerable Groups Act 2006; "sensitive witness" means an adult witness where the quality of evidence given by the witness is likely to be diminished by reason of fear or distress on the part of the witness in connection with giving evidence in the case. s59 Safeguarding Vulnerable Groups Act defines a vulnerable adult as follows:

(1) A person is a vulnerable adult if he has attained the age of 18 and

(a) he is in residential accommodation,

(b) he is in sheltered housing,

(c) he receives domiciliary care,

(d) he receives any form of health care,

(e) he is detained in lawful custody,

(f) he is by virtue of an order of a court under supervision by a person exercising functions for the purposes of Part 1 of the Criminal Justice and Court Services Act 2000 (c. 43),

(g) he receives a welfare service of a prescribed description,

(h) he receives any service or participates in any activity provided specifically for persons who fall within subsection (9),

(i) payments are made to him (or to another on his behalf) in pursuance of arrangements under section 57 of the Health and Social Care Act 2001 (c. 15), or

(j) he requires assistance in the conduct of his own affairs.

Some individuals are vulnerable because of what has happened to them eg they are victims of trafficking or have sustained serious harm or torture or are suffering from PTSD.

Paragraph 349 of Statement of Changes of Immigration Rules HC395 as amended ("the Rules") defines child as an individual who is under 18 years of age or who appears to be under that age.

BEFORE THE SUBSTANTIVE HEARING

4. In so far as it is possible potential issues and solutions should be identified at a CMRH or pre hearing review and the casepapers noted so that the substantive hearing can proceed with minimal exposure to trauma or further trauma of vulnerable witnesses or appellants. It is important not to assume that an individual will want specific or particular arrangements made.

5. Where there has not been a pre hearing review or CMHR or the parties were inadequately prepared these matters should in any event be considered at the commencement of the substantive hearing.

5.1 Generic

(i)   The primary responsibility for identifying vulnerable individuals lies with the party calling them but representatives may fail to recognise vulnerability.

(ii)   Establish precise details of any potential disability or medical condition to enable appropriate arrangements to be made for the Tribunal hearing room in terms of eg mobility in the hearing room, provision of an induction loop, adequate space for carers, re-arrangement of furniture to enable a child friendly or less formal structure eg all on the same level. Ensure the room is rearranged prior to sitting.

(iii)   Ensure the time estimate provided allows for special arrangements eg frequent breaks to ensure adequate concentration levels, access to toilets to accommodate special needs at the hearing.

(iv)   Record that the appeal is to be heard first in the list; it is undesirable that these cases are adjourned part heard.

(v)   Identify and record potential behavioural challenges or difficulties, consider and record appropriate hearing room arrangements.

(vi)   Identify and record whether the appellant is legally represented. If not consider whether an adjournment of the substantive hearing would enable representation to be obtained[3]. Bear in mind that legal aid may not be available.

(vii)   Consider whether expert evidence eg as to disability, age or mental health is required, particularly if there is a dispute on an issue over ability to participate in the proceedings; consider whether an adjournment would be appropriate to enable either party to obtain reports.

(viii)   Relevant policies and practices relied upon by either party should be disclosed eg protocols for victims of trafficking[4], interview protocols.

(ix)   Ensure adequate focussed and effective directions are issued.

---

[3]   Paragraph 21 Asylum and Immigration Tribunal (Procedure) Rules 2005, as amended. Para 352ZA the Rules

[4]   Further information on dealing with victims of trafficking can be found on the specific Victims of Trafficking policy guidance by UKBA and in the online trafficking toolkit at www.crimere duction.gov.uk/toolkits/tp00.htm Referral to the Competent Authority is made through the police or UKBA. You should talk to your RSIJ. The Record of proceedings should be noted accordingly and consideration given to an adjournment to enable further investigation.

5.2 Children

(i)   A minor appellant should have been identified by the IAC centre and the file noted accordingly.

(ii)   All unaccompanied asylum seeking children should have been referred to the Refugee Council's Panel of Advisors by UKBA but this may not be recorded in the papers before you; the Panel of Advisors can assist a minor appellant in finding legal representation.

(iii)   Identify and record whether a minor asylum seeking appellant has a responsible adult eg parent, social worker, teacher, foster parent who will be attending the substantive hearing to provide support. A legal representative is not and cannot be a responsible adult. It is advisable that a child has someone available at all hearings but it is not possible for you to direct a third party to attend[5].

(iv)   There is no provision in our jurisdiction for a Tribunal appointed guardian, intermediary or facilitator

(v)   If an appellant is 'age disputed' treat that appellant in accordance with these guidelines.

[5]   Para 352 of the Rules requires a responsible adult to be present at all interviews conducted by UKBA.

5.3 Vulnerable and sensitive witnesses

(i)   Consider any request for a single gender Tribunal but bear in mind that sensitive issues may not be the subject of questions or core to the evidence.

(ii)   There is no provision in our jurisdiction for support for vulnerable adults but you may consider it appropriate to suggest attendance by such an individual to assist the appellant in giving evidence.

6.   In the final analysis it is the Tribunal's decision whether specific arrangements are made, what those arrangements are and whether the hearing can proceed in their absence.

THE SUBSTANTIVE HEARING

7.   Enable the appellant to have adequate time prior to the commencement of the hearing to familiarise him/herself with the hearing room and give instructions to his/her representative.

8.   It may only be at the substantive hearing following service of all relevant documents including witness statements that you are able to assess whether oral evidence is required.

9.   Agreement between the parties in advance of oral evidence as to the matters agreed or in dispute enables questioning to be focussed, sensitive and minimises potential trauma. If the parties have not spoken to each other, identify areas of dispute and agreement prior to commencement of oral evidence.

10. Hearing evidence

10.1 At commencement of hearing

(i)   Introduce all individuals in the hearing room.

(ii)   Ensure there has been an adequate explanation of the hearing process and the issues at stake.

(iii)   Remind the appellant's representative and supporting adult, if any, of their responsibility to identify concerns they may have during the course of the hearing as to the appellant's wellbeing although you should continue to ensure by any appropriate means that the appellant understands what is happening

(iv)   Do not assume that a child or other vulnerable person wants a specific person eg parent with them during hearing

(v)   Exclude members of the public when a child is giving evidence;

(vi)   Consider restricting or barring members of the public/family members in other cases to enable oral evidence to be given freely and without covert intimidation. If, from reading the papers you suspect abuse or trafficking, you should consider excluding individuals not associated with the presentation of the case to enable the witness to give evidence unhindered. You may notice individuals in the Tribunal who have no apparent bearing on the hearing and you may consider closing the hearing to the public to enable evidence to be given, even if you do not suspect trauma.

10.2 During the hearing

(i) Speak clearly and directly to the appellant/witness. Demonstrate active listening.

(ii) Use plain English and avoid legal and other jargon; be sensitive to specific communication needs for reasons of language or disability,

(iii) Ensure questions asked are open ended wherever possible; broken down to avoid having more than one idea or point in each question and avoid suggesting a particular answer.

(iv) Curtail improper or aggressive cross examination; control the manner of questioning to avoid harassment, intimidation or humiliation. Ensure that questions are asked in an appropriate manner using a tone and vocabulary appropriate to the appellant's age, maturity, level of understanding and personal circumstances and attributes. Pay special attention to avoid re-traumatisation of a victim of crime, torture, sexual violence

(v) Be sensitive to the possibility that the witness/appellant has understood the question, and, if there is a risk of confusion, check this

(vi) Ensure that adequate breaks are given during the hearing; check at intervals throughout the hearing that the appellant is comfortable and understands the proceedings; don't wait to be asked.

(vii) If there is no or inadequate representation it is important that you obtain clarification of all matters of which you are unclear[6].

(viii) If an individual is, during the course of the hearing, identified as a vulnerable adult or sensitive witness, an adjournment may be required to enable expert evidence to be called as to the effect of this on the individual's ability to give cogent evidence of the events relied upon. Allow adequate time for the representative, if there is one, to consider and take instructions.

---

[6] Lord Woolf called for judges to take a more pro-active role in relation to unrepresented litigants; justice must not only be done but be seen to be done (Access to justice Interim Report pp99 and 119)

Be aware

(ix) A person with special needs may be more easily influenced by the way information and choices are presented and there may be a tendency to guess an answer rather than say "don't know".

(x) People with special needs may need more time to understand and think about a question. Ensure adequate time is given to understand the question; reassure the appellant that "don't understand", "don't know" "don't remember" are acceptable answers if true

(xi) People with special needs are not always used to having their views listened to and may be more easily influenced by others even when they have a different view themselves.

(xii) Apparently contradictory answers may indicate a lack of understanding; a question may need to be asked in various ways to ensure understanding.

(xiii) A possible power imbalance may exist between those asking the questions and the witness/appellant.

10. As evidence progresses and you become aware of changed circumstances, a short adjournment to later in the day may be appropriate to consider the format of the hearing, for both representatives to take further instructions, possibly for social services or the police to be informed. It may be that one or other of the parties is not represented and you may consider an adjournment for a longer period with an appropriate direction to enable representation in the light of the changed circumstances

10.3 Assessing evidence

Take account of potentially corroborative evidence

Be aware:

(i)   Children often do not provide as much detail as adults in recalling experiences and may often manifest their fears differently from adults;

(ii)   Some forms of disability cause or result in impaired memory;

(iii)   The order and manner in which evidence is given may be affected by mental, psychological or emotional trauma or disability;

(iv)   Comprehension of questioning may have been impaired.

Determination

11.   An appellant is entitled to a clear decision with reasons.

12.   Record whether the appellant had someone there to support him or her and the role played, if any.

13.   The weight to be placed upon factors of vulnerability may differ depending on the matter under appeal, the burden and standard of proof and whether the individual is a witness or an appellant.

14.   Consider the evidence, allowing for possible different degrees of understanding by witnesses and appellant compared to those are not vulnerable, in the context of evidence from others associated with the appellant and the background evidence before you. Where there were clear discrepancies in the oral evidence, consider the extent to which the age, vulnerability or sensitivity of the witness was an element of that discrepancy or lack of clarity.

15.   The decision should record whether the Tribunal has concluded the appellant (or a witness) is a child, vulnerable or sensitive, the effect the Tribunal considered the identified vulnerability had in assessing the evidence before it and thus whether the Tribunal was satisfied whether the appellant had established his or her case to the relevant standard of proof. In asylum appeals, weight should be given to objective indications of risk rather than necessarily to a state of mind[7].

---

[7]   Para 351 the Rules

ANNEX A

Why guidance is necessary?

16.   Effective communication is the bedrock of the legal process; everyone involved in legal proceedings must understand and be understood or the process of law will be seriously impeded. Judges must reduce the impact of misunderstandings in communication. Unless all parties to proceedings understand the material before them and the meaning of questions asked and answers given, the process of law is at best seriously impeded and at worst thrown seriously off course[8].

17.   All possible steps should be taken to assist a vulnerable individual to understand and participate in the proceedings and the ordinary process should, so far as necessary, be adapted to meet those ends.

18.   Documents, process and procedure which fail to take into account vulnerability may compromise the quality of the evidence produced; a failure to take into account procedural requirements may result in evidence being potentially inadmissible or unreliable[9].

---

[8]   Chapter 1.2 Equal Treatment Bench Book

[9]   The UKBA have a number of protocols and guidance documents which set out standards to

be complied with when interviewing children, victims of torture, traumatised victims, mentally disturbed individuals. These are available through the policy and law section of the UKBA website.

To whom does this guidance apply?

19. This guidance applies to individuals who may be appellants or witnesses. An individual may be vulnerable because of an innate characteristic (eg age), because of his or her personal characteristics (eg mental health problems) or because of events over which they had or have no control eg detention or torture.

20. This guidance applies to children and young persons under the age of 18, who appear to be under the age of 18 or claim to be under the age of 18, individuals who suffer from a mental disorder within the meaning of the Mental Health Act 1983 or who have any significant impairment of intelligence or social function such as to inhibit understanding and participation in proceedings or learning disability or as defined in the Safeguarding Vulnerable Groups Act 2006 or who are vulnerable because of external factors. Some individuals may be vulnerable because of a combination of factors.

21. It may only become apparent that an individual is vulnerable at the commencement of or during the substantive hearing. Many difficulties (eg dyslexia or dyspraxia) are 'hidden' and become apparent during questioning (eg because of lack of concentration, inability to understand a question or read a document, lack of co-ordination). Evidence of, eg, trafficking, rape and torture may be given for the first time on the day of the hearing.

Other Sources of Guidance

22. Chapter 5 of the Equal Treatment Bench Book[10] provides an overview of disability and sets out the requirement that the judiciary should be able to recognise disabilities when they exist, identify the implications, know what powers they have to compensate for the resulting disadvantage and understand how to use these powers without causing prejudice to other parties.

23. Practice Directions have been issued for Criminal Proceedings setting out the special arrangements to be made for vulnerable defendants. A Vulnerable Witnesses Guidance Pack was issued in Scotland in 2005 following the Vulnerable Witnesses (Scotland) Act 2004[11].

24. Section 55 Borders Citizen and Immigration Act 2009 sets out a statutory duty to ensure that UKBA functions are discharged having regard to the need to safeguard and promote the welfare of children who are in the UK[12].

25. The Council of Europe[13] has draft guidelines (May 2010) to ensure the effective implementation of existing binding European and international standards to protect and promote children's rights taking into account

26. The United Nations Convention on the Rights of the Child 1989 (CRC) provides a comprehensive framework for the responsibilities of States for all children within its borders and provides that in all actions concerning children the best interests of the child 'be a primary consideration'[14].

27. The UNHCR recognises the importance of States promoting an age, gender and diversity sensitive approach and emphasises the importance of particular attention being given to the vulnerability of women and children and those with disabilities[15]; affirm that children because of their age social status and physical and mental development are often more vulnerable than adults in situations of forced displacement and the principle that the best interest of the child shall be a primary consideration; recognise that sexual abuse and exploitation are a consequence of unequal power relationships.

---

[10]   www.jsboard.co.uk/etac/etbb/index.htm

[11]   www.scotland.gov.uk/topics/justice

[12]   The UKBA approach is set out in Arrangements to Safeguard and Promote the Welfare of Children for those Exercising UK Border Agency Functions and outlines the key principles: the best interests of the child will be a primary consideration; no child should be discriminated against through being a child, or on grounds of gender, race religion, disability, sexual orientation or culture; the views and wishes of the child should be sought and taken into account whenever decisions affecting them are made. This should be done in a way that takes account of the child's age and maturity.

[13]   www.coe.int/t/dghl/standardsetting/childjustice/CJ-S-CH%20_2010_%209%20E%20-%205TH%20DRAFT%20COE%20GUIDELINES%20ON%20CHILD-FRIENDLY%20JUSTICE.pdf

[14]   Article 3 CRC, ratified by every country in the world except the USA and Somalia.

[15]   Ex Comm No 98 of 2003, 107 of 2007, 108 of 2008

ANNEX B
PRACTICE DIRECTION
FIRST TIER AND UPPER TRIBUNAL
CHILD, VULNERABLE ADULT AND SENSITIVE WITNESSES

1.   In this Practice Direction:

(a)   "child" means a person who has not attained the age of 18;

(b)   "vulnerable adult" has the same meaning as in the Safeguarding Vulnerable Groups Act 2006;

(c)   "sensitive witness" means an adult witness where the quality of evidence given by the witness is likely to be diminished by reason of fear or distress on the part of the witness in connection with giving evidence in the case.

Circumstances under which a Child, Vulnerable Adult or Sensitive Witness May Give Evidence

2.   A child, vulnerable adult or sensitive witness will only be required to attend as a witness and give evidence at a hearing where the Tribunal determines that the evidence is necessary to enable the fair hearing of the case and their welfare would not be prejudiced by doing so.

3.   In determining whether it is necessary for a child, vulnerable adult or sensitive witness to give evidence to enable the fair hearing of a case the Tribunal should have regard to all the available evidence and any representations made by the parties.

4.   In determining whether the welfare of the child, vulnerable adult or sensitive witness would be prejudiced it may be appropriate for the Tribunal to invite submissions from interested persons, such as a child's parents.

5.   The Tribunal may decline to issue a witness summons under the Tribunal Procedure Rules or to permit a child, vulnerable adult or sensitive witness to give evidence where it is satisfied that the evidence is not necessary to enable the fair hearing of the case and must decline to do so where the witness's welfare would be prejudiced by them giving evidence.

Manner in which Evidence is Given

6.   The Tribunal must consider how to facilitate the giving of any evidence by a child, vulnerable adult or sensitive witness.

7.   It may be appropriate for the Tribunal to direct that the evidence should be given by telephone, video link or other means directed by the Tribunal, or to direct that a person be appointed for the purpose of the hearing who has the appropriate skills or experience in facilitating the giving of evidence by a child, vulnerable adult or sensitive witness.

8.   This Practice Direction is made by the Senior President of Tribunals with the agreement of the Lord Chancellor. It is made in the exercise of powers conferred by the Tribunals, Courts and Enforcement Act 2007.

LORD JUSTICE CARNWATH

SENIOR PRESIDENT OF TRIBUNALS

30 October 2008

IN THE SENIOR COURTS OF ENGLAND AND WALES
DIRECTION OF THE LORD CHIEF JUSTICE
CLASS OF CASES SPECIFIED FOR THE PURPOSES OF SECTION 18(6)
OF THE TRIBUNALS COURTS AND ENFORCEMENT ACT 2007

1.   The Lord Chief Justice hereby specifies the following class of case for the purposes of section 18(6) of the Tribunals Courts and Enforcement Act 2007 ("the 2007 Act"):

applications calling into question a decision of the Secretary of State not to treat submissions as an asylum claim or a human rights claim within the meaning of Part 5 of the Nationality, Immigration and Asylum Act 2002 wholly or partly on the basis that they are not significantly different from material that has previously been considered.

2.   An application also falls within the class specified in paragraph 1 if, in addition to calling into question a decision of the sort there described, it challenges:
(i)   a decision or decisions to remove (or direct the removal of) the applicant from the United Kingdom; or
(ii)   a failure or failures by the Secretary of State to make a decision on submissions said to support an asylum or human rights claim;

or both (i) and (ii); but not if it challenges any other decision.

3.   This direction takes effect on 17/10/11 in relation to applications made on or after that date to the High Court or Upper Tribunal for judicial review or for permission to apply for judicial review that seek relief of a kind mentioned in section 15(1) of the 2007 Act.

4.   For the avoidance of doubt,
(i)   a case which has been transferred under this direction continues to fall within the specified class of case and the Upper Tribunal has the function of deciding the application, where, after transfer, additional material is submitted to the Secretary of State for decision but no decision has been made upon that material;
(ii)   this direction does not have effect where an application seeks a declaration of incompatibility under section 4 of the Human Rights Act 1998, or where the applicant seeks to challenge detention.

5.   This direction is made by the Lord Chief Justice with the agreement of the Lord Chancellor. It is made in the exercise of powers conferred by section 18(6) and (7) of the 2007 Act and in accordance with Part 1 of Schedule 2 of the Constitutional Reform Act 2005.

The Right Honourable Lord Judge

Lord Chief Justice of England and Wales

IN THE SUPREME COURT OF ENGLAND AND WALES
DIRECTION OF THE LORD CHIEF JUSTICE
CLASSES OF CASES SPECIFIED UNDER SECTION 18(6) OF THE
TRIBUNALS, COURTS AND ENFORCEMENT ACT 2007

It is ordered as follows—

1.   The following direction takes effect in relation to an application made to the High Court or Upper Tribunal on or after 3 November 2008 that seeks relief of a kind mentioned in section 15(1) of the Tribunals, Courts and Enforcement Act 2007 ("the 2007 Act").

2. The following direction takes effect in relation to an application made to the High Court or Upper Tribunal on or after 3 November 2008 that seeks relief of a kind mentioned in section 15(1) of the Tribunals, Courts and Enforcement Act 2007 ("the 2007 Act"):

(a)　any decision of the First-Tier Tribunal on an appeal made in the exercise of a right conferred by the Criminal Injuries Compensation Scheme in compliance with section 5(1) of the Criminal Injuries Compensation Act 1995 (appeals against decisions on review); and

(b)　any decision of the First-tier Tribunal made under Tribunal Procedure Rules or section 9 of the 2007 Act where there is no right of appeal to the Upper Tribunal and that decision is not an excluded decision within paragraph (b), (c), or (f) of section 11(5) of the 2007 Act.

3. This Direction does not have effect where an application seeks (whether or not alone) a declaration of incompatibility under section 4 of the Human Rights Act 1998.

4. This Direction is made by the Lord Chief Justice with the agreement of the Lord Chancellor. It is made in the exercise of powers conferred by section 18(6) of the 2007 Act and in accordance with Part 1 of Schedule 2 to the Constitutional Reform Act 2005.

The Right Honourable Lord Judge

Lord Chief Justice of England and Wales

TRIBUNALS JUDICIARY – PRACTICE DIRECTIONS
FRESH CLAIM JUDICIAL REVIEW IN THE IMMIGRATION AND
ASYLUM CHAMBER OF THE UPPER TRIBUNAL

PART 1
PRELIMINARY

1. Interpretation

1.1　In these Practice Statements:

"applicant" has the same meaning as in the UT Rules;

"the application" means the written application under rule 28 for permission to bring judicial review proceedings;

"fresh claim proceedings" has the same meaning as in the UT Rules;

"party" has the same meaning as in the UT Rules;

"respondent" has the same meaning as in the UT Rules;

"the Tribunal" means the Immigration and Asylum Chamber of the Upper Tribunal;

"UKBA" means the UK Border Agency of the Home Office;

"UT Rules" means the Tribunal Procedure (Upper Tribunal) Rules 2008 and "rule", followed by a number, means the rule bearing that number in the UT Rules.

PART 2
SCOPE

2. Scope

2.1　Parts 3 and 4 of these Practice Directions apply to fresh claim proceedings.

2.2　Part 5 of these Practice Directions applies to proceedings to which Part 3 applies, where:

(a)   a person has been served with a copy of directions for that person's removal from the United Kingdom by UKBA and notified that Part 5 applies; and

(b)   that person makes an application to the Tribunal or a court for permission to bring judicial review proceedings or to apply for judicial review, before the removal takes effect.

2.3   In the case of proceedings transferred to the Tribunal by a court, the Tribunal will expect the applicant to have complied with all relevant Practice Directions of that court that applied up to the point of transfer. In the event of non-compliance, the Tribunal will make such directions pursuant to rule 27(1)(b) as are necessary and which may, in particular, include applying provisions of these Practice Directions.

PART 3
GENERAL PROVISIONS

The application to bring judicial review proceedings

3. Form of application

3.1   The application must be made using the form displayed on the Upper Tribunal's website at the time the application is made.

4. Additional materials to be filed with the application

4.1   Without prejudice to rule 28, the application must be accompanied by:

(a)   any written evidence on which it is intended to rely (but see paragraph 4.2 below);

(b)   copies of any relevant statutory material; and

(c)   a list of essential documents for advance reading by the Tribunal (with page references to the passages relied on).

4.2   The applicant may rely on the matters set out in the application as evidence under this Practice Direction if the application is verified by a statement of truth.

5. Bundle of documents to be sent etc. with the application

5.1   The applicant must file two copies of a paginated and indexed bundle containing all the documents required by rule 28 and these Practice Directions to be sent or delivered with the application.

6. Permission without a hearing

6.1   The Tribunal will generally, in the first instance, consider the question of permission without a hearing.

The substantive hearing

7. Additional grounds at the substantive hearing

7.1   Where an applicant who has been given permission to bring judicial review proceedings intends to apply under rule 32 to rely on additional grounds at the substantive hearing, the applicant must give written notice to the Tribunal and to any other person served with the application, not later than 7 working days before that hearing.

8. Skeleton arguments for the substantive hearing

8.1   The applicant must serve a skeleton argument on the Tribunal and on any other person served with the application, not later than 21 days before the substantive hearing.

8.2   The respondent and any other party wishing to make representations at the hearing must serve a skeleton argument on the Tribunal and on the applicant, not later than 14 days before the hearing.

8.3   Skeleton arguments must contain:

(a)   a time estimate for the complete hearing, including the giving of the decision by the Tribunal;
(b)   a list of issues;
(c)   a list of the legal points to be taken (together with any relevant authorities with page references to the passages relied on);
(d)   a chronology of events (with page references to the bundle of documents (see Practice Direction 9 below);
(e)   a list of essential documents for the advance reading of the Tribunal (with page references to the passages relied on) (if different from that served with the application) and a time estimate for that reading; and
(f)   a list of persons referred to.

9. Bundle of documents for the substantive hearing

9.1   The applicant must serve on the Tribunal and any other person served with the application a paginated and indexed bundle of all relevant documents required for the substantive hearing, when the applicant's skeleton argument is served.

9.2   The bundle must also include those documents required by the respondent and any other person who is expected to make representations at the hearing.

10. Agreed final order

10.1   If the parties agree about the final order to be made, the applicant must file at the Tribunal a document (with 2 copies) signed by all the parties setting out the terms of the proposed agreed order, together with a short statement of the matters relied on as justifying the proposed agreed order and copies of any authorities or statutory provisions relied on.

10.2   The Tribunal will consider the documents referred to in paragraph 10.1 above and will make the order if satisfied that the order should be made.

10.3   If the Tribunal is not satisfied that the order should be made, a hearing date will be set.

PART 4
URGENT APPLICATIONS FOR PERMISSION TO BRING JUDICIAL REVIEW PROCEEDINGS

11. Request for Urgent Consideration

11.1   Where it is intended to request the Tribunal to deal urgently with the application or where an interim injunction is sought, the applicant must serve with the application a written "Request for Urgent Consideration", in the form displayed on the Upper Tribunal's website at the time the application is made, which states:

(a)   the need for urgency;
(b)   the timescale sought for the consideration of the application (eg. within 72 hours or sooner if necessary); and
(c)   the date by which the substantive hearing should take place.

11.2   Where an interim injunction is sought, the applicant must, in addition, provide:

(a)   the draft order; and
(b)   the grounds for the injunction.

12. Notifying the other parties

12.1   The applicant must serve (by fax and post) the application form and the Request for Urgent Consideration on the respondent and interested parties, advising them of the application and that they may make representations.

12.2   Where an interim injunction is sought, the applicant must serve (by fax and post) the draft order and grounds for the injunction on the respondent and interested parties, advising them of the application and that they may make representations.

13. Consideration by Tribunal

13.1   The Tribunal will consider the application within the time requested and may make such order as it considers appropriate.

13.2   If the Tribunal specifies that a hearing shall take place within a specified time, the representatives of the parties must liaise with the Tribunal and each other to fix a hearing of the application within that time.

PART 5
APPLICATIONS WHICH CHALLENGE REMOVAL

14. General

14.1   The requirements contained in this Part are additional to those contained in Part 3 and (where applicable) Part 4 of these Practice Directions.

14.2   Nothing in these Practice Directions prevents a person from making the application after that person has been removed from the United Kingdom.

15. Special requirements regarding the application

15.1   Without prejudice to rule 28, the application must:

(a)   indicate on its face that this Part of these Practice Directions applies; and
(b)   be accompanied by:
    (i)   a copy of the removal directions and the decisions to which the application relates; and
    (ii)   any document served with the removal directions including any document which contains UKBA's factual summary of the case; and
(c)   contain or be accompanied by the detailed statement of the applicant's grounds for making the application.

15.2   If the applicant is unable to comply with paragraph 15.1(b) or (c) above, the application must contain or be accompanied by a statement of the reasons why.

15.3   Notwithstanding rule 28A, immediately upon issue of the application, the applicant must send copies of the issued application form and accompanying documents to the address specified by the United Kingdom Border Agency.

16. Referral in case of non-compliance

16.1   Where the applicant has not complied with Practice Direction 15.1(b) or (c) above and has provided reasons for not complying, and the Tribunal has issued the application form, the Tribunal's staff will:

(a)   refer the matter to a Judge for consideration as soon as practicable; and
(b)   notify the parties that they have done so.

17. Application clearly without merit

17.1   If, upon a refusal to grant permission to bring judicial review proceedings, the Tribunal indicates that the application is clearly without merit, that indication will be included in the order refusing permission.

These Practice Directions are made by the Senior President of Tribunals with the agreement of the Lord Chancellor. They are made in the exercise of powers conferred by the Tribunals, Courts and Enforcement Act 2007.

LORD JUSTICE CARNWATH

SENIOR PRESIDENT OF TRIBUNALS

17 October 2011

PRESIDENTIAL GUIDANCE NOTE NO 2 OF 2011: ANONYMITY DIRECTIONS IN THE FIRST-TIER TRIBUNAL (IAC)

1.   Applications for anonymity are made in the notice of appeal. There is a web link to the appropriate form for the appellant to complete. The appeal file will be marked accordingly. Either party may apply for anonymity at a later stage. Once an application is made the appeal will be anonymised and will remain so until further directions of the Tribunal.

2.   All asylum appeals will be anonymised at case creation.

3.   Once anonymity is granted the Tribunal will remove the appellant's name from all published documents that are in the public domain. The names will remain in full on the judicial cause list.

4.   The power to direct anonymity is derived from article 8 ECHR and such directions should be made where public knowledge of the person or the case might impact on that person's protected rights. An interim anonymity direction is more likely to be appropriate during initial stages of an appeal to enable the parties to prepare their cases without interference or hindrance. At the CMR or at the substantive hearing the Immigration Judge should review the application for anonymity and direct whether the appellant should be granted anonymity. There may well be appeals where no application is made by either party but the court will self direct that anonymity should be granted.

5.   Anonymity directions will often, if not always, be made where the appeal involves—

(i)   a child or vulnerable person
(ii)   evidence that the appeal concerns personal information about the lives of those under 18 and their welfare may be injured if such details are revealed and their names are known
(iii)   there is highly personal evidence in the appeal that should remain confidential
(iv)   there is a claim that the appellant would be at risk of harm and that by publishing their names and details it may cause them harm or put others at real risk of harm
(v)   publication of the determination may be used subsequently to support a *sur place* claim.

FIRST TIER

It is unusual, (but not unknown) for the determinations of the first tier to be published. If anonymity is granted the determination should give brief reasons why anonymity is granted with fuller reasons if either party objects.

The power to direct anonymity stems from rule 45(4)(i) of the Asylum and Immigration Tribunal (Procedure) Rules 2005. For the purpose of this rule the First-tier Tribunal is a "court"[1] and therefore s.11 of the Contempt of Court Act 1981[2] will apply to any direction so given.

In most appeals a direction in the determination, which should be clearly identified, could be made—

> "The appellant be granted anonymity throughout these proceedings, unless and until a tribunal or court directs otherwise, and be referred to as [initials of appellant]. No report of these proceedings shall directly or indirectly identify him/her or any member of their family. This direction applies both to the appellant and to the respondent. Failure to comply with this direction could lead to a contempt of court."

There may be other instances where the entire determination should be anonymised and the immigration judge should ensure that the determination in itself, even if publicised, would not identify the appellant. Examples of this could be where the appellant has been working for the security services. In other appeals only some part of the determination may need to be anonymised. This may arise where it is in the public interest for the appellant to be named, for example in a serious criminal deportation appeal, but their address should not be disclosed to prevent harm to him or his family.

---

1   Contempt of Court Act 1981, s. 19: Interpretation . . . "court" includes any tribunal or body exercising the judicial power of the State, and "legal proceedings" shall be construed accordingly;

2   Contempt of Court Act 1981, s.11: Publication of matters exempted from disclosure in court. In any case where a court (having power to do so) allows a name or other matter to be withheld from the public in proceedings before the court, the court may give such directions prohibiting the publication of that name or matter in connection with the proceedings as appear to the court to be necessary for the purpose for which it was so withheld.

HOLDING HEARINGS IN PRIVATE AND ANONYMITY DIRECTIONS

A direction for anonymity under rule 45(4)(i) would not automatically exclude members of the public to a hearing and judges should consider if it is necessary to make a further direction under rule 54 at the substantive hearing. Exclusion of the public from a hearing should be comparatively rare as long as the identity of the appellant and/or their family is protected.

Mr Michael Clements
President, First-tier Tribunal (Immigration and Asylum Chamber)

UPPER TRIBUNAL IMMIGRATION AND ASYLUM CHAMBER GUIDANCE NOTE 2011 NO 2
REPORTING DECISIONS OF THE UPPER TRIBUNAL IMMIGRATION AND ASYLUM CHAMBER

This guidance note is issued under Paragraph 7 of Schedule 4 to the Tribunals, Courts and Enforcement Act 2007. It was amended in February 2012, September 2013 and March 2014.

1.   The Upper Tribunal Immigration and Asylum Chamber (the Chamber) decides some 6000 appeals a year. Most decisions turn upon their particular facts and the application of the provisions of the Immigration Rules and statutory regime applicable to the case.

2.   The Chamber at present normally sits in constitutions of one either with a permanent or deputy judge of the Upper Tribunal. Occasionally the Chamber will sit as a panel with an Upper Tribunal Judge, the President or other senior judicial member of the Upper Tribunal presiding.

3.   Most decisions of the Chamber are unreported. It is not considered conducive to the overriding objective for thousands of fact sensitive decisions to be published, placing onerous obligations on advocates and litigants in person to search for decisions of potential relevance to their own.

4.   Following promulgation to the parties unreported decisions are stored electronically and may be accessed on the Chamber web site at www.judiciary.gov.uk/media/tribunal-decisions/immigrationasylum-chamber By the terms of the Senior President's Practice Direction 11 unreported decisions of the Chamber may not be cited as authority without permission of the judge that will only be granted sparingly where there is good reason to do so.

5.   The Chamber has a Reporting Committee, whose task is the selection of cases considered suitable for reporting applying the criteria set out in the appendix to this note. It normally convenes fortnightly.

6.   Decisions in which a permanent judge of the Chamber or visiting senior judge has participated are suitable for reporting. Decisions in which a panel of judges has sat may be considered more authoritative than decisions of a single judge of the Chamber.

7.   Promulgated determinations that a permanent judge of the Chamber considers meets the criteria for reporting may be nominated for consideration by the Reporting Committee. When such nomination is made the Committee reviews the determination for compliance with the criteria and may advise the determining judge on the words of the keywords and italicised summary that must accompany reported cases. Debatable cases are referred to the Chamber President for decision.

8.   Representatives may refer decisions they consider meet the reporting criteria to the Chair of the Committee for consideration but resources prevent the Chamber corresponding about reporting decisions.

9.   Where a decision is selected for reporting it is given a neutral citation number and placed on the Chamber website as soon as practicable thereafter. Both reported decisions and unreported decisions (since 1 June 2013) may be found on the web site. Both classes are searchable by title and subject matter (but see paragraph 4 above). Decisions of the Chamber are available on a number of other publicly available web sites and legal databases.

10.   In the event of diverging jurisprudence on an important question of law, a decision of a panel of the Chamber may be reported as a starred case, when it will become binding. In the absence of a starred case the common law doctrine of judicial precedent shall not apply and decisions of the AIT and one constitution of the Chamber do not as a matter of law bind later constitutions. Judges of the First-tier Tribunal Immigration and Asylum Chamber are, however, expected to follow the law set out in reported cases, unless persuaded that the decision failed to take into account an applicable legislative provision or a binding decision of a superior court. Where there is reasonable doubt about whether a decision of the AIT or the Chamber should continue to be followed permission to appeal to the Chamber may well be granted in appropriate cases. Further guidance on permission to appeal to the Chamber is given in the Presidential Guidance Note 2011 No 1 Permission to Appeal.

11.   Special arrangements are made for the reporting of country guidance cases. Before a case is promulgated and designated as a Country Guidance case it is considered by the relevant country convener and the Reporting Committee and advice may be tendered to the determining judges. Practice Direction 12.2 states:

> "A reported determination of the Tribunal, the AIT or the IAT bearing the letters CG shall be treated as authoritative finding on the country guidance issue identified in the determination, based on the evidence before the members of Tribunal . . . .that determine the appeal. As a result, unless it has been expressly superseded or replaced by any later CG determination, or is inconsistent with other authority that is binding on the Tribunal, such a country guidance case is authoritative in any subsequent appeal, so far as that appeal:-
> a)   relates to the country guidance issue in question; and
> b)   depends upon the same or similar evidence".

If there is credible fresh evidence relevant to the issue that has not been considered in the Country Guidance case or, if a subsequent case includes further issues that have not been considered in the CG case, the judge will reach the appropriate conclusion on the evidence, taking into account the conclusion in the CG case so far as it remains relevant.

12.   Country Guidance cases will remain as such on the Chamber web site unless and until replaced by fresh Country Guidance or reversed by a decision of a higher court. Where Country Guidance has become outdated by reason of developments in the country in question, it is anticipated that a judge of the First-tier Tribunal will have such credible fresh evidence as envisaged in paragraph 11 above. Where there is reasonable doubt as to whether Country Guidance is still applicable permission to appeal to the Chamber may well be given in an appropriate case.

13.   The criteria for reporting cases include cases where the factual findings may be of some general interest. As a general rule, cases deciding factual issues are selected for

reporting only if they meet the criteria for country guidance, but occasionally there may be cases where factual findings are likely to be of importance for other determinations where for one reason or another it has not been possible or appropriate to report the case as an authoritative Country Guidance one. These cases will be found on the recent decisions part of the Chamber web site without the letters CG. Reported decisions that are not Country Guidance cases are of persuasive value only on the facts.

14.   Judgments of the Chamber on applications for judicial review (following grant of permission) in immigration judicial review proceedings[3] are automatically given a neutral citation (which includes the letters "IJR") and reported, without keywords or italicised summary. The same procedure applies to judgments of the Chamber in "age assessment" judicial reviews[4] except that the neutral citation includes the letters "AAJR".

15.   Although every judicial review judgment that follows the grant of permission is given a neutral citation number and reported, such a judgment may, in addition, be given keywords and an italicised summary, if the judgment also meets the general criteria for reporting (including, where relevant, as a country guidance case). Other types of judicial review decision may also be reported, if they meet the general criteria for reporting, and will be given the appropriate neutral citation letters (see paragraph 14 above).

16.   The objective of this Guidance Note and of the practices of the Chamber with regard to reporting of decisions is to promote consistency of high-quality decision making in the field of immigration, asylum, free movement and related human rights law and transparency and ease of access by interested parties to the most significant of the Chamber's decisions. These practices are kept under regular review in the light of developing experience.

The Hon Mr JUSTICE

Blake

President

July 2011

(amended September 2013 and March 2014)

---

1   Currently Upper Tribunal Judge Peter Lane
2   See s.107(3)(b) of the Nationality, Immigration and Asylum Act 2002 and the Senior President's Practice Direction 12.1
3   See rule 1 of the Tribunal Procedure (Upper Tribunal) Rules 2008 (as amended) and the Lord Chief Justice's direction of 21 August 2013 at www.judiciary.gov.uk/publications-and-repor ts/practicedirections/tribunals/tribunals-pd..
4   See the First-tier Tribunal and Upper Tribunal Chambers Order 2010, article 11(c)

CRITERIA FOR REPORTING

1.   In deciding whether a decision should be reported the Reporting Committee shall apply the criteria set out below.

2.   A decision will be reported where:-

(a)   the Reporting Committee considers that it has general significance and utility in the development of the UT's law, is sufficiently well-reasoned and is consistent with binding statutory provisions or precedent of the senior courts; or

(b)   it is a decision which follows a substantive hearing of an application for judicial review.

3.   Decisions selected for reporting by virtue of paragraph 2(a) will have at least one, and normally than more than one, of the following features:

(a)   the Tribunal has considered previous decisions on the issue or issues and has had sufficient argument on them;

(b)   the decision considers a novel point of law, construction, procedure and practice, or develops previous decisions in the same area;

(c)   the decision gives guidance likely to be of general assistance to judges, the parties or practitioners;

(d)   the decision contains an assessment of facts of a kind that others ought to be aware of, because it is likely to be of assistance in other cases; or

(e)   there is some other compelling reason why the decision ought to be reported.

4.   A decision selected for reporting by virtue of paragraph 2(a) will be given key words and italic wording, summarising the matters in respect of which it is being reported.

5.   Where the Committee considers that a decision falling within paragraph 2(b) also meets the criteria set out in paragraph 2(a) (read with paragraph 3), the Committee will cause the decision to be given key words and italic wording, as described in paragraph 4.

UPPER TRIBUNAL (IMMIGRATION AND ASYLUM CHAMBER) (JUDICIAL REVIEW) (ENGLAND AND WALES) FEES ORDER 2011

(SI 2011/2344)

Made: 22 September 2011.

Authority: Tribunals, Courts and Enforcement Act 2007, s 42.

Commencement: 17 October 2011.

1 Citation, commencement, interpretation and extent

(1)   This Order may be cited as the Upper Tribunal (Immigration and Asylum Chamber) (Judicial Review) (England and Wales) Fees Order 2011 and shall come into force on 17 October 2011.

(2)   In this Order—

. . .

["immigration judicial review proceedings" means judicial review proceedings (within the meaning of the Tribunal Procedure (Upper Tribunal) Rules 2008), which are designated as an immigration matter—

(a)   in a direction made in accordance with Part 1 of Schedule 2 to the Constitutional Reform Act 2005 specifying a class of case for the purposes of section 18(6) of the Tribunals, Courts and Enforcement Act 2007; or

(b)   in an order of the High Court in England and Wales made under section 31A(3) of the Senior Courts Act 1981, transferring to the Upper Tribunal an application of a kind described in section 31A(1) of that Act;]

"LSC" means the Legal Services Commission established under section 1 of the Access to Justice Act 1999; and

"the Tribunal" means the Upper Tribunal.

(3)   This Order extends to England and Wales only.

Amendment

Para (2): definition "fresh claim proceedings" (omitted) revoked by SI 2013/2069, arts 3, 4(a). Date in force: 1 November 2013: see SI 2013/2069, art 1.

Para (2): definition "immigration judicial review proceedings" inserted by SI 2013/2069, arts 3, 4(b). Date in force: 1 November 2013: see SI 2013/2069, art 1.

2 Fees payable

Where [immigration judicial review] are issued in or transferred to the Tribunal, the fees set out in column 2 of Schedule 1 are payable in respect of items described in column 1 in accordance with and subject to the directions specified in that column.

Amendment

Words in square brackets substituted by SI 2013/2069, arts 3, 5. Date in force: 1 November 2013: see SI 2013/2069, art 1.

3

Where by any convention, treaty or other instrument entered into by Her Majesty with any foreign power it is provided that no fee is required to be paid in respect of any proceedings, the fees specified in this Order are not payable in respect of those proceedings.

4 Remissions and part remissions

Schedule 2 applies for the purpose of ascertaining whether a party is entitled to a remission or part remission of a fee prescribed by this Order.

SCHEDULE 1

FEES TO BE TAKEN IN [IMMIGRATION JUDICIAL REVIEW] PROCEEDINGS

Article 2

Number and description of fee	Amount of fee
1 Starting proceedings	
1.1 For permission to apply for judicial review.	[£140]
[1.1(a) on a request to reconsider at a hearing a decision on permission Where fee 1.1(a) has been paid and permission is granted at a hearing, [the amount payable under fee 1.2 is £350].]	[£350]
Where the Tribunal has made an order giving permission to proceed with an application for judicial review, there is payable by the applicant within 7 days of service on the applicant of that order:	
1.2 If the judicial review procedure has been started.	[£700]
1.3 If the claim for judicial review was started otherwise than by using the judicial review procedure.	[£140]
2 Other Fees charged	
2.1 On an application on notice where no other fee is specified.	£80
2.2 On an application by consent or without notice where no other fee is specified.	£45
Fee 2.2 is not payable in relation to an application by consent for an adjournment of a hearing where the application is received by the Tribunal at least 14 days before the date set for that hearing.	
2.3 On an application for a summons or order for a witness to attend the Tribunal.	£40
3 Copy Documents	
3.1 On a request for a copy of a document filed for the purposes of [immigration judicial review] proceedings in the Tribunal (other than where fee 3.2 applies):	
(a) for ten pages or less;	£5
(b) for each subsequent page.	50p
Note: The fee payable under fee 3.1 includes:	
where the Tribunal allows a party to fax to the Tribunal for the use of that party a document that has not been requested by the Tribunal and is not intended to be placed on the Tribunal's file;	

Number and description of fee	Amount of fee
where a party requests that the Tribunal fax a copy of a document from the Tribunal's file;	
the Tribunal provides a subsequent copy of a document which it has previously provided.	
3.2 On a request for a copy of a document on a computer disk or in other electronic form, for each such copy.	£5

Amendment

Schedule heading: words in square brackets substituted by SI 2013/2069, arts 3, 6. Date in force: 1 November 2013: see SI 2013/2069, art 1.

Fee 1.1: in column 2 sum "£140" in square brackets substituted by SI 2014/878, art 2(1), (2)(a). Date in force: 22 April 2014: see SI 2014/878, art 1.

Fee 1.1(a): inserted by SI 2013/2302, art 10(1), (2). Date in force: 7 October 2013: see SI 2013/2302, art 1; for transitional provisions see art 13 thereof.

Fee 1.1(a): in column 2 sum "£350" in square brackets substituted by SI 2014/878, art 2(1), (2)(b). Date in force: 22 April 2014: see SI 2014/878, art 1.

Fee 1.1(a) note: in column 1 words "the amount payable under fee 1.2 is £350" in square brackets substituted by SI 2014/878, art 2(1), (2)(c). Date in force: 22 April 2014: see SI 2014/878, art 1.

Fee 1.2: in column 2 sum "£700" in square brackets substituted by SI 2014/878, art 2(1), (2)(d). Date in force: 22 April 2014: see SI 2014/878, art 1.

Fee 1.3: in column 2 sum "£140" in square brackets substituted by SI 2014/878, art 2(1), (2)(e). Date in force: 22 April 2014: see SI 2014/878, art 1.

Fee 3.1: in column 1 words "immigration judicial review" in square brackets substituted by SI 2013/2069, arts 3, 6. Date in force: 1 November 2013: see SI 2013/2069, art 1.

[SCHEDULE 2
REMISSIONS AND PART REMISSIONS

Interpretation

1

(1) In this Schedule—
"child" means a person—
> (a) whose main residence is with a party and who is aged—
>> (i)   under 16 years; or
>> (ii) 16 to 19 years; and is—
>>> (aa) not married or in a civil partnership; and
>>> (bb) enrolled or accepted in full-time education that is not advanced education, or approved training; or
> (b) in respect of whom a party or their partner pays child support maintenance or periodic payments in accordance with a maintenance agreement,

and "full-time education", "advanced education" and "approved training" have the meaning given by the Child Benefit (General) Regulations 2006;

"child support maintenance" has the meaning given in section 3(6) of the Child Support Act 1991;

"couple" has the meaning given in section 3(5A) of the Tax Credits Act 2002;

"disposable capital" has the meaning given in paragraph 5;

"excluded benefits" means any of the following—
> (c) any of the following benefits payable under the Social Security Contributions and Benefits Act 1992 or the corresponding provisions of the Social Security Contributions and Benefits (Northern Ireland) Act 1992—

        (i)   attendance allowance under section 64;

        (ii)   severe disablement allowance;

        (iii)   carer's allowance;

        (iv)   disability living allowance;

        (v)   constant attendance allowance under section 104 as an increase to a disablement pension;

        (vi)   any payment made out of the social fund;

        (vii) housing benefit;

        (viii) widowed parents allowance;

    (d)   any of the following benefit payable under the Tax Credits Act 2002—

        (i)   any disabled child element or severely disabled child element of the child tax credit;

        (ii)   any childcare element of the child tax credit;

    (e)   any direct payment made under the Community Care, Services for Carers and Children's Services (Direct Payments) (England) Regulations 2009, the Community Care, Services for Carers and Children's Services (Direct Payments) (Wales) Regulations 2011, the Carers and Direct Payments Act (Northern Ireland) 2002, or section 12B(1) of the Social Work (Scotland) Act 1968;

    (f)   a back to work bonus payable under section 26 of the Jobseekers Act 1995, or article 28 of the Jobseekers (Northern Ireland) Order 1995;

    (g)   any exceptionally severe disablement allowance paid under the Personal Injuries (Civilians) Scheme 1983;

    (h)   any payments from the Industrial Injuries Disablement Benefit;

    (i)   any pension paid under the Naval, Military and Air Forces etc (Disablement and Death) Service Pension Order 2006;

    (j)   any payment made from the Independent Living Funds;

    (k)   any payment made from the Bereavement Allowance;

    (l)   any financial support paid under an agreement for the care of a foster child;

    (m)   any housing credit element of pension credit;

    (n)   any armed forces independence payment;

    (o)   any personal independence payment payable under the Welfare Reform Act 2012;

    (p)   any payment on account of benefit as defined in the Social Security (Payments on Account of Benefit) Regulations 2013;

    (q)   any of the following amounts, as defined by the Universal Credit Regulations 2013, that make up an award of universal credit—

        (i)   an additional amount to the child element in respect of a disabled child;

        (ii)   a housing costs element;

        (iii)   a childcare costs element;

        (iv)   a carer element;

        (v)   a limited capability for work or limited capacity for work and work -related activity element.

"family help (higher)" has the meaning given in paragraph 15(3) of the Civil Legal Aid (Merits Criteria) Regulations 2013;

"family help (lower)" has the meaning given in paragraph 15(2) of the Civil Legal Aid (Merits Criteria) Regulations 2013;

"gross monthly income" has the meaning given in paragraph 13;

"Independent Living Funds" means the funds listed at regulation 20(2)(b) of the Criminal Legal Aid (Financial Resources) Regulations 2013;

"legal representation" has the meaning given in paragraph 18(2) of the Civil Legal Aid (Merits Criteria) Regulations 2013;

"maintenance agreement" has the meaning given in subsection 9(1) of the Child Support Act 1991;

"partner" means a person with whom the party lives as a couple and includes a person with whom the party is not currently living but from whom the party is not living separate and apart;

"party" means the individual who would, but for this Schedule, be liable to pay a fee under this Order;

"restraint order" means—

    (a)   an order under section 42(1A) of the Senior Courts Act 1981;

    (b)   an order under section 33 of the Employment Tribunals Act 1996;

    (c)   a civil restraint order made under rule 3.11 of the Civil Procedure Rules 1998, or a practice direction made under that rule; or

    (d)   a civil restraint order under rule 4.8 of the Family Procedure Rules 2010, or the practice direction referred to in that rule.

(2) References to remission of a fee are to be read as including references to a part remission of a fee as appropriate and remit and remitted shall be construed accordingly.

Fee remission

2

If a party satisfies the disposable capital test, the amount of any fee remission is calculated by applying the gross monthly income test.

Disposable capital test

Disposable capital test

3

(1) Subject to paragraph 4, a party satisfies the disposable capital test if—

    (a)   the fee payable by the party and for which an application for remission is made, falls within a fee band set out in column 1 of Table 1; and

    (b)   the party's disposable capital is less than the amount in the corresponding row of column 2.

Table 1

Column 1 (fee band)	Column 2 (disposable capital)
Up to and including £1,000	£3,000
£1,001 to £1,335	£4,000
£1,336 to £1,665	£5,000
£1,666 to £2,000	£6,000
£2,001 to £2,330	£7,000
£2,331 to £4,000	£8,000
£4,001 to £5,000	£10,000
£5,001 to £6,000	£12,000
£6,001 to £7,000	£14,000
£7,001 or more	£16,000

4

Subject to paragraph 14, if a party or their partner is aged 61 or over, that party satisfies the disposable capital test if that party's disposable capital is less than £16,000.

Disposable capital

5

Subject to paragraph 14, disposable capital is the value of every resource of a capital nature belonging to the party on the date on which the application for remission is made, unless it is treated as income by this Order, or it is disregarded as excluded disposable capital.

Disposable capital—non-money resources

6

The value of a resource of a capital nature that does not consist of money is calculated as the amount which that resource would realise if sold, less—

(a) 10% of the sale value; and
(b) the amount of any borrowing secured against that resource that would be repayable on sale.

Disposable capital—resources held outside the United Kingdom

7

(1) Capital resources in a country outside the United Kingdom count towards disposable capital.

(2) If there is no prohibition in that country against the transfer of a resource into the United Kingdom, the value of that resource is the amount which that resource would realise if sold in that country, in accordance with paragraph 6.

(3) If there is a prohibition in that country against the transfer of a resource into the United Kingdom, the value of that resource is the amount that resource would realise if sold to a buyer in the United Kingdom.

Disposable capital—foreign currency resources

8

Where disposable capital is held in currency other than sterling, the cost of any banking charge or commission that would be payable if that amount were converted into sterling, is deducted from its value.

Disposable capital—jointly owned resources

9

Where any resource of a capital nature is owned jointly or in common, there is a presumption that the resource is owned in equal shares, unless evidence to the contrary is produced.

Excluded disposable capital

10

The following things are excluded disposable capital—

(a) a property which is the main or only dwelling occupied by the party;
(b) the household furniture and effects of the main or only dwelling occupied by the party;
(c) articles of personal clothing;
(d) any vehicle, the sale of which would leave the party, or their partner, without motor transport;
(e) tools and implements of trade, including vehicles used for business purposes;
(f) the capital value of the party's or their partner's business, where the party or their partner is self-employed;

(g) the capital value of any funds or other assets held in trust, where the party or their partner is a beneficiary without entitlement to advances of any trust capital;

(h) a jobseeker's back to work bonus;

(i) a payment made as a result of a determination of unfair dismissal by a court or tribunal, or by way of settlement of a claim for unfair dismissal;

(j) any compensation paid as a result of a determination of medical negligence or in respect of any personal injury by a court, or by way of settlement of a claim for medical negligence or personal injury;

(k) the capital held in any personal or occupational pension scheme;

(l) any cash value payable on surrender of a contract of insurance;

(m) any capital payment made out of the Independent Living Funds;

(n) any bereavement payment;

(o) any capital insurance or endowment lump sum payments that have been paid as a result of illness, disability or death;

(p) any student loan or student grant;

(q) any payments under the criminal injuries compensation scheme.

Gross monthly income test

Remission of fees—gross monthly income

11

(1) If a party satisfies the disposable capital test, no fee is payable under this Order if, at the time when the fee would otherwise be payable, the party or their partner has the number of children specified in column 1 of Table 2 and—

(a) if the party is single, their gross monthly income does not exceed the amount set out in the appropriate row of column 2; or

(b) if the party is one of a couple, the gross monthly income of that couple does not exceed the amount set out in the appropriate row of column 3.

Table 2

Column 1 Number of children of party	Column 2 Single	Column 3 Couple
no children	£1,085	£1,245
1 child	£1,330	£1,490
2 children	£1,575	£1,735

(2) If a party or their partner has more than 2 children, the relevant amount of gross monthly income is the appropriate amount specified in Table 2 for 2 children, plus the sum of £245 for each additional child.

(3) For every £10 of gross monthly income received above the appropriate amount in Table 2, including any additional amount added under sub-paragraph (2), the party must pay £5 towards the fee payable, up to the maximum amount of the fee payable.

(4) This paragraph is subject to paragraph 12.

Gross monthly income cap

12

(1) No remission is available if a party or their partner has the number of children specified in column 1 of Table 3 and—

(a) if the party is single, their gross monthly income exceeds the amount set out in the appropriate row of column 2 of Table 3; or

(b)   if the party is one of a couple, the gross monthly income of that couple exceeds the amount set out in the appropriate row of column 3 of Table 3.

Table 3

Column 1	Column 2	Column 3
Number of children of party	Single	Couple
no children	£5,085	£5,245
1 child	£5,330	£5,490
2 children	£5,575	£5,735

(2)   If a party or their partner has more than 2 children, the relevant amount of gross monthly income is the appropriate amount specified in Table 3 for 2 children, plus the sum of £245 for each additional child.

Gross monthly income

13

(1)   Subject to paragraph 14, gross monthly income means the total monthly income, for the month preceding that in which the application for remission is made, from all sources, other than receipt of any of the excluded benefits.

(2)   Income from a trade, business or gainful occupation other than an occupation at a wage or salary is calculated as—

(a)   the profits which have accrued or will accrue to the party; and

(b)   the drawings of the party;

in the month preceding that in which the application for remission is made.

(3)   In calculating profits under sub-paragraph (2)(a), all sums necessarily expended to earn those profits are deducted.

General

Resources and income treated as the party's resources and income

14

(1)   Subject to sub-paragraph (2), the disposable capital and gross monthly income of a partner of a party is to be treated as disposable capital and gross monthly income of the party.

(2)   Where the partner of a party has a contrary interest to the party in the matter to which the fee relates, the disposable capital and gross monthly income of that partner, if any, is not treated as the disposable capital and gross monthly income of the party.

Application for remission of a fee

15

(1)   An application for remission of a fee must be made at the time when the fee would otherwise be payable.

(2)   Where an application for remission of a fee is made, the party must—

(a)   indicate the fee to which the application relates;

(b)   declare the amount of their disposable capital; and

(c)   provide documentary evidence of their gross monthly income and the number of children relevant for the purposes of paragraphs 11 and 12.

(3)   Where an application for remission of a fee is made on or before the date on which a fee is payable, the date for payment of the fee is disapplied.

(4) Where an application for remission is refused, or if part remission of a fee is granted, the amount of the fee which remains unremitted must be paid within the period notified in writing to the party.

Remission in exceptional circumstances

16

A fee specified in this Order may be remitted where the Lord Chancellor is satisfied that there are exceptional circumstances which justify doing so.

Refunds

17

(1) Subject to sub-paragraph (3), where a party pays a fee at a time when that party would have been entitled to a remission if they had provided the documentary evidence required by paragraph 15, the fee, or the amount by which the fee would have been reduced as the case may be, must be refunded if documentary evidence relating to the time when the fee became payable is provided at a later date.

(2) Subject to sub-paragraph (3), where a fee has been paid at a time when the Lord Chancellor, if all the circumstances had been known, would have remitted the fee under paragraph 15, the fee or the amount by which the fee would have been reduced, as the case may be, must be refunded to the party.

(3) No refund shall be made under this paragraph unless the party who paid the fee applies within 3 months of the date on which the fee was paid.

(4) The Lord Chancellor may extend the period of 3 months mentioned in sub-paragraph (3) if the Lord Chancellor considers that there is a good reason for a refund being made after the end of the period of 3 months.

Legal Aid

18

A party is not entitled to a fee remission if, under Part 1 of the Legal Aid, Sentencing and Punishment of Offenders Act 2012, they are in receipt of the following civil legal services—

    (a)   Legal representation; or

    (b)   Family help (higher); or

    (c)   Family help (lower) in respect of applying for a consent order.

Vexatious litigants

19

(1) This paragraph applies where—

    (a)   a restraint order is in force against a party; and

    (b)   that party makes an application for permission to—

        (i)   issue proceedings or take a step in proceedings as required by the restraint order;

        (ii)   apply for amendment or discharge of the order; or

        (iii)   appeal the order.

(2) The fee prescribed by this Order for the application is payable in full.

(3) If the party is granted permission, they are to be refunded the difference between—

    (a)   the fee paid; and

    (b)   the fee that would have been payable if this Schedule had been applied without reference to this paragraph.

Exceptions

20

No remissions or refunds are available in respect of the fee payable for—

    (a)   copy or duplicate documents;

(b)   searches.]

Amendment

Substituted by SI 2013/2302, art 10(1), (3). Date in force: 7 October 2013: see SI 2013/2302, art 1; for transitional provisions see art 13 thereof.

FIRST-TIER TRIBUNAL (IMMIGRATION AND ASYLUM CHAMBER) FEES ORDER 2011

(SI 2011/2841)

Made: 18 December 2011.

Authority: Tribunals, Courts and Enforcement Act 2007, s 42.

Commencement: 19 December 2011.

1 Citation and commencement

This Order may be cited as the First-tier Tribunal (Immigration and Asylum Chamber) Fees Order 2011 and shall come into force on the day after the date on which it is made.

2 Interpretation

In this Order—

"an immigration or asylum matter" means a matter in respect of which functions are allocated to the Immigration and Asylum Chamber of the First-tier Tribunal under article 5 of the First-tier Tribunal and Upper Tribunal (Chambers) Order 2010;

"appellant" means any person identified in the notice of appeal as appealing in relation to an immigration and asylum matter to the First-tier Tribunal;

"BACS" means the method of payment known as "Banks Automated Clearing System" by which money is transferred from one bank in the United Kingdom to another by means of an automated system;

"international money transfer" means a method of payment by which money is transferred from a bank account outside the United Kingdom to a bank account in the United Kingdom by means of an automated system;

"the 1971 Act" means the Immigration Act 1971;

"the 1999 Act" means the Immigration and Asylum Act 1999;

"the 2002 Act" means the Nationality, Immigration and Asylum Act 2002.

3 Fees for appeals

(1)   A fee is payable in respect of an appeal to the First-tier Tribunal where the appeal relates to an immigration or asylum matter and the decision against which the appeal is made was taken on or after the coming into force of this Order.

(2)   The fee is payable by or in respect of each appellant on the date on which the Notice of Appeal is given.

(3)   The fee payable is—

(a)   where the appellant consents to the appeal being determined without a hearing, £80; or

(b)   where the appellant does not consent to the appeal being determined without a hearing, £140.

(4)   Subject to paragraph (5), where after making payment in accordance with paragraph (3)(a), the appellant withdraws their consent to the appeal being determined without a hearing, the difference between the amounts specified in

subparagraphs (a) and (b) of paragraph (3) ("the balance") becomes payable on the withdrawal of that consent.

(5) The balance referred to in paragraph (4) ceases to be payable if the Tribunal decides that the appeal can be justly determined without a hearing.

(6) This article is subject to articles 5, 6 and 7.

4 Method of paying fee

(1) The fee payable must be paid by one of the following methods—

    (a)   credit card;

    (b)   debit card;

    (c)   BACS; or

    (d)   international money transfer.

(2) For the purposes of enabling payment to be made by or in respect of the appellant—

    (a)   authorisation to take payment and details of the credit or debit card, or

    (b)   an undertaking by or on behalf of each appellant to pay by BACS or an international money transfer,

must be provided at the same time as the giving of the notice of appeal or the subsequent withdrawal of their consent to the appeal being determined without a hearing (as the case may be).

5 Exemption from fees

(1) No fee is payable for—

    (a)   an appeal against a decision made under—

        (i)   section 2A of the 1971 Act (deprivation of right of abode);

        (ii)   section 5(1) of the 1971 Act (a decision to make a deportation order);

        (iii)   paragraphs 8, 9,10, 10A or 12(2) of Schedule 2 to the 1971 Act (a decision that an illegal entrant, any family or seaman and aircrew is or are to be removed from the United Kingdom by way of directions);

        (iv)   section 40 of the British Nationality Act 1981 (deprivation of citizenship);

        (v)   section 10(1) of the 1999 Act (removal of certain persons unlawfully in the United Kingdom);

        (vi)   section 76 of the 2002 Act (revocation of indefinite leave to enter or remain in the United Kingdom);

        (vii)   section 47 of the Immigration, Asylum and Nationality Act 2006 (removal: persons with statutorily extended leave);

        (viii)   regulation 19(3) of the Immigration (European Economic Area) Regulations 2006 (a decision to remove an EEA national or the family member of such a national); or

    (b)   an appeal to which Part 2 of the Asylum and Immigration Tribunal (Fast Track Procedure) Rules 2005 applies.

(2) No fee is payable where, at the time the fee would otherwise become payable, the appellant is, under the 1999 Act—

    (a)   a "supported person" as defined in section 94(1); or

    (b)   provided with temporary support under section 98.

(3) No fee is payable where, for the purpose of proceedings before the Tribunal, the appellant is in receipt of—

    [(a)   civil legal services (within the meaning of Part 1 of the Legal Aid, Sentencing and Punishment of Offenders Act 2012) made available under arrangements made for the purposes of that Part of that Act;]

    (b)   legal aid under Part 2 of the Legal Aid, Advice and Assistance (Northern Ireland) Order 1981; or

    (c)   civil legal aid or advice and assistance under the Legal Aid (Scotland) Act 1986.

(4)   No fee is payable where the appellant is the person for whose benefit services are provided by a local authority under section 17 of the Children Act 1989.

(5)   Where by any convention, treaty or other instrument entered into by Her Majesty with any foreign power it is provided that no fee is required to be paid in respect of any proceedings, the fees specified in this Order are not payable in respect of those proceedings.

Amendment

Para (3): sub-para (a) substituted by SI 2013/534, reg 14(1), Schedule, Pt 2, para 23. Date in force: 1 April 2013: see SI 2013/534, reg 1; for savings see reg 14(2)

6 Power to defer payment in certain cases

The Lord Chancellor may defer payment of a fee where the appeal is brought on the grounds that the removal of the appellant from, or a requirement for the appellant to leave, the United Kingdom would breach the United Kingdom's obligations under either—

    (a)   the Convention relating to the Status of Refugees done at Geneva on 28 July 1951 and the Protocol to the Convention; or

    (b)   article 21 of Directive 2004/83/EC of the European Parliament and Council of 29 April 2004.

7 Reduction or remission of fees

A fee specified in this Order may be reduced or remitted where the Lord Chancellor is satisfied that there are exceptional circumstances which justify doing so.

8 Certificate of fee satisfaction

(1)   The Lord Chancellor must issue a certificate of fee satisfaction if satisfied that—

    (a)   the appropriate fee payable under article 3 has been paid;

    (b)   in view of an undertaking given by or on behalf of the appellant, payment will be promptly made by BACS or an international money transfer;

    (c)   no fee is payable;

    (d)   payment is to be deferred in accordance with article 6; or

    (e)   the appellant has, at the time a fee would otherwise be payable under article 3, applied for the fee to be reduced or remitted in accordance with article 7.

(2)   The issuing of such a certificate is without prejudice to the power to recover the amount of any payable fee or part of such fee which remains unpaid and unremitted.

(3)   The Lord Chancellor may revoke a certificate of fee satisfaction and if a certificate is revoked, the Tribunal shall be notified accordingly.

9 Refunds

(1)   Subject to paragraph (2)—

    (a)   where the fee payable under article 3(3)(b) has been paid but the appeal is determined without a hearing, the difference between the amounts specified in article 3(3)(a) and 3(3)(b) may be refunded; and

    (b)   where a fee has been paid which the Lord Chancellor, if all the circumstances had been known, would have reduced or remitted under article 7, the fee or the amount by which the fee would have been reduced, as the case may be, shall be refunded.

(2)   No refund will be made under this article unless the appellant applies in writing to the Lord Chancellor within 6 months of the date the fee becomes payable.

(3) The Lord Chancellor may extend the period of 6 months mentioned in paragraph (2) if the Lord Chancellor considers there is a good reason for the application being made after the end of the period of 6 months.

UPPER TRIBUNAL IMMIGRATION AND ASYLUM CHAMBER GUIDANCE NOTE 2013 NO 1: ANONYMITY ORDERS

This guidance note is issued by the Hon Mr Justice Blake, Chamber President under paragraph 7 of Schedule 4 to the Tribunals, Courts and Enforcement Act 2007.

I. INTRODUCTION

1. Rule 14(1) of the Tribunal Procedure (Upper Tribunal) Rules 2008 (the UT Procedure Rules) contains a power to make an order prohibiting the disclosure or publication of specified documents or information relating to the proceedings or of any matter likely to lead members of the public to identify any person whom the Upper Tribunal considers should not be identified. The effect of such an "anonymity order"[1] (as it will be called in this guidance note) may therefore be to prohibit *anyone* (not merely the parties in the case) from disclosing relevant information. Breach of the order may be punishable as a contempt of court (see further paragraph 25 below).

2. Rule 14 (2) of the UT Procedure Rules provides that the Upper Tribunal may give a direction prohibiting the disclosure of a document or information to a person if the Tribunal is satisfied that disclosure 'would be likely to cause that person or some other person serious harm' and that it is proportionate having regard to the interests of justice to give such a direction.

3. The work of the Upper Tribunal, Immigration and Asylum Chamber (UTIAC) makes it appropriate in certain classes of cases to exercise rule 14 powers to prevent certain information from entering the public domain[2].

4. All determinations of UTIAC are available on its web site, but in the past only Reported Decisions of the Upper Tribunal could be searched for by name, subject and other indicators. This has now changed and all Unreported Decisions made after 1 June 2013 can be searched for on the web site.

5. Such a development makes it particularly important that UTIAC judges follow a consistent practice where anonymity has been granted and that parties to an appeal and others are aware of the practice to be adopted.

---

[1] An example of an anonymity order is as follows:

> *Pursuant to rule 14 of the Tribunal Procedure (Upper Tribunal) Rules 2008, [the appellant] is granted anonymity throughout these proceedings. No report of these proceedings (in whatever form) shall directly or indirectly identify [the appellant]. Failure to comply with this order could lead to a contempt of court".*

[2] In addition to rule 14, the Upper Tribunal has, by virtue of section 25 of the TCEA, the same powers etc as the High Court (or, in Scotland, the Court of Session) as regards certain specified matters, which include all "matters incidental to the Upper Tribunal's functions". In certain circumstances, it may be appropriate for the Tribunal to utilise these powers, in cases with which this guidance note is concerned, instead of, or in addition to, rule 14.

II. PRINCIPLES TO BE APPLIED

6. The starting point for consideration of anonymity orders in UTIAC, as in all courts and tribunals, is open justice. This principle promotes the rule of law and public confidence in the legal system. UTIAC sits in open court with the public and press able to attend and nothing should be done to discourage the publication to the wider public of fair and accurate reports of proceedings that have taken place.

7. Given the importance of open justice, the general principle is that an anonymity order should only be made by UTIAC to the extent that the law requires it or it is found necessary to do so.

Cases where the law requires anonymity

8.   The law requires anonymity to be respected in certain circumstances, whether or not the Tribunal has made an order. These circumstances include:

(a)   Section 1 of the Sexual Offences Amendment Act 1992, as amended, requires anonymity for a victim or alleged victim of a sexual offence listed in section 2 of that Act.

(b)   Section 97 (2) of the Children Act 1989 requires anonymity for a child subject to family law proceedings and includes a prohibition on the disclosure of any information that might identify the address or school of that child.

(c)   Section 49 of the Children and Young Persons Act 1933 prohibits publication of the name, address, school or any other matter likely to identify a person under 18 as being concerned in proceedings before the Youth Courts. A child or young person is concerned in proceedings if they are a victim, witness or defendant.

(d)   Another jurisdiction has made an order forbidding disclosure of certain information, for example a temporary restraint on publication under section 4 of the Contempt of Court Act 1981.

Cases where the law permits anonymisation

General

9.   UTIAC has power to make an anonymity order or otherwise direct that information be not revealed, where such an order is necessary to protect human rights, whether (for example) the private life of a party subject to the jurisdiction or the life, liberty and bodily integrity of a witness or a person referred to in proceedings. The Tribunal may also make such an order where it is necessary in the interests of the welfare of a child or the interests of justice would otherwise be frustrated.

10.   Parties may apply for an anonymity order or UTIAC may consider making one of its own volition. Where anonymity is an issue, the UTIAC judge should deal with the matter as a preliminary issue and decide, first, the extent of any anonymity order made, if any.

11.   A decision to make an anonymity order where not required by law may require the weighing of the competing interests of an individual and their rights (for example, under Articles 3 or 8 of the ECHR or their ability to present their case in full without hindrance) against the need for open justice.

12.   An anonymity order will not be made because an appellant or witness has engaged in conduct that is considered socially embarrassing to reveal. In particular, that the fact that someone has committed a criminal offence will not justify the making of an anonymity order, even if it is known that such a person has children who may be more readily identified if the details of the person are known.

Asylum and other protection claims

13.   It is the present practice of the First-tier Tribunal, Immigration and Asylum Chamber that an anonymity order is made in all appeals raising asylum or other international protection claims. An appellant will be identified by initial and country in such cases unless and until a judge has decided that anonymity is not necessary. UTIAC will follow the same general practice, with the result that anonymity will remain, unless a UT judge decides it is unnecessary.

14.   Where details of witnesses or relatives abroad form part of a protection case, particular consideration should also be given as to whether publication of those details would be likely to cause serious harm.

Medical issues

15.   The revelation of the medical condition of an appellant will not normally require the making of an anonymity order unless disclosure of the fact of such a condition gives rise to a real likelihood of harm to a person, or UTIAC has required confidential medical details to be provided to it.

16. Rule 14 (7) of the Tribunal Procedure (Upper Tribunal) Rules 2008 contains a presumption that information about mental health cases and the names of the people concerned in such will not be disclosed in the absence of good reason.

17. It will not normally be necessary for the Tribunal to disclose intimate medical or other information about a witness or third party, but if it is then consideration should be given to whether the identity of the person concerned should not be disclosed.

Children etc

18. The identity of children whether they are appellants or the children of an appellant (or otherwise concerned with the proceedings), will not normally be disclosed nor will their school, the names of their teacher or any social worker or health professional with whom they are concerned, unless there are good reasons in the interests of justice to do so. Such good reasons will normally exist if a criminal court has directed that the identity of a child offender be disclosed.

19. Where the identity of a child is not to be revealed the name and address of a parent other than the appellant may also need to be withheld to preserve the anonymity of a child.

20. In other cases, UTIAC may need to make an order to protect the identity of a child or vulnerable person where there is good reason to do so. It will be necessary to do so where information about the child or family proceedings concerning a child has been supplied by the Family Court under the terms of the Joint Protocol between the President Family Division and the Senior President of Tribunals dated 19 July 2013.

III. UTIAC PRACTICE WHEN MAKING AN ANONYMITY ORDER

21. Where an anonymity order is made the title page of the UTIAC determination will refer to this immediately after the names of the parties as **ANONYMITY ORDER MADE** and a footnote or paragraph in the determination will explain the reasons for the order and its scope[3].

22. Where an anonymity order has been applied for or previously made, but it has been decided that no such order should be made, the title page will refer to this fact with the words **NO ANONYMITY ORDER MADE** and a footnote or paragraph in the determination will give any explanation.

23. Where an anonymity order has been made the determination shall refer to the person who is the subject of the order by initial or pseudonym.

24. Where an anonymity order has been made the judge will then be responsible for ensuring that determinations do not reveal information contrary to the terms of the order made (rule 14(11)).

25. Where an anonymity order has been made but a person with knowledge of the order has breached it by putting the information in the public domain, such conduct may be punishable as a contempt of court either by the Upper Tribunal exercising the powers of the High Court under section 25 (2) (c) of the Tribunals, Courts and Enforcement Act 2007 or by any other court of competent jurisdiction[4].

26. Where an anonymity order has been made but any party contends that the order should not have been made, an application can be made to the Office of the Chamber President giving reasons why the order should be set aside in whole or in part.

---

[3]   Unusually, UTIAC may decide to make an order under rule 14, the purpose of which is not to confer anonymity on a party or other person but merely to prohibit disclosure of specified information.

[4]   See fn 2 above.

Other useful links:

Presidential Guidance Note No 2 of 2011: Anonymity Directions in the FtT(IAC)

The Family Courts: Media Access & Reporting – July 2011

CPS Guidance on Contempt of Court and Reporting Restrictions

Family Court Practice Guidance issued by President of the Family Division — 16 January 2014

The Hon Mr Justice Blake

30 September 2013

UPPER TRIBUNAL IMMIGRATION AND ASYLUM CHAMBER GUIDANCE NOTE 2013 NO 2: VIDEO LINK HEARINGS

This guidance note is issued under paragraph 7 of Schedule 4 to the Tribunals, Courts and Enforcement Act 2007 ("the 2007 Act").

THE RELEVANT RULES

1. In rule 1 of the Tribunal Procedure (Upper Tribunal) Rules 2008 ("the Upper Tribunal Rules"), a "hearing" is defined as "an oral hearing and includes a hearing conducted in whole or in part by video link, telephone or other means of instantaneous two-way electronic communication".

2. Rule 2 states that the overriding objective of the UT Rules "is to enable the Upper Tribunal to deal with cases fairly and justly". Rule 2(2) explains that dealing with a case fairly and justly includes—

"(a) dealing with the case in ways that are proportionate to the importance of the case, the complexity of the issues, the anticipated costs and the resources of the parties;

(b) avoiding unnecessary formality and seeking flexibility in the proceedings;

(c) ensuring, so far as practicable, that the parties are able to participate fully in the proceedings;

(d) using any special expertise of the Upper Tribunal effectively; and

(e) avoiding delay, so far as compatible with proper consideration of the issues."

3. Rule 5 provides that, subject to the provisions of the 2007 Act and any other enactment, "the Upper Tribunal may regulate its own procedure, including by giving directions. Rule 5(3)(g) states that, in particular, the Upper Tribunal may "decide the form of any hearing".

GENERAL PRINCIPLES

4. The ideal form of hearing in UTIAC is where the appellant[1], the supporting witnesses and the advocates are all physically present in the same courtroom as the judge[2]. Such an arrangement gives the Tribunal the best opportunity to evaluate the appellant and witnesses as they give their evidence, receive new documentary information, and maintain an informed dialogue with the advocates.

5. However, it is recognised that there are occasions when all or part of the hearing may need to be conducted by video link in order to give effect to the overriding objective (see above); in particular, to ensure participation, avoid delay and avoid excessive cost.

6. The decision whether to conduct a hearing by video link is a matter for directions by a judge on an application duly made by a party.

7. UTIAC sits outside London at certain court and/or tribunal hearing centres. Where a party and his or her advocate reside (or are otherwise based) in the UK outside reasonable travelling distance from UTIAC's main hearing centre3, it may be appropriate to apply for a transfer of venue from London to one of those hearing centres, rather than to apply for a hearing by video link.

8.   An application to hear a party, witness or advocate by video link must be made by a party to UTIAC in writing, as soon as possible after permission to appeal to UTIAC has been granted, and in any event, must be made not later than 5 working days after the date the notice of hearing in UTIAC was sent out.

9.   Wherever possible, the party making the application should first consult with the other party, with a view to securing agreement as to the application (including its terms). In any event, the application should state whether the other party has been consulted and what views, if any, that other party has expressed concerning the application.

10.   Every application should explain:

(a)   why the application is made and why any alternatives would be impractical;
(b)   what arrangements are proposed and who will bear the costs of them; and
(c)   in the event that the application is granted, the latest time by which any consolidated and paginated bundle of documents to be used at the hearing will be available.

[1]   In this Guidance, references to the appellant are references to the person who was the appellant in the appeal before the First-tier Tribunal.

[2]   In this Guidance, references to a judge are references to the member or members of UTIAC assigned to hear the appeal.

[3]   Field House, 15 Breams Buildings, London, EC4A 1DZ

VIDEO LINKS BETWEEN SITES IN THE UK

11.   UTIAC prefers a video link to be between the hearing centre specified in the notice of hearing and another UTIAC hearing centre, convenient to the parties, where there is a court clerk to assist in the conduct of the proceedings. In such a situation, the expectation is that the appellant[4], witnesses, advocates (including the Home Office's presenting officer) and any Tribunal-appointed interpreter will all be present in the courtroom in the other hearing centre, together with any members of the public who wish to observe the proceedings[5].

12.   In certain circumstances, it may be possible for advocates to participate by video link with Field House from suitable professional premises (with the costs involved being borne by the party making the application). In such circumstances, the expectation described in paragraph 11 above may need to be modified; for example, by the other advocate being present in the courtroom in which the judge is present or in a suitable third location (provided that relevant technology is available and sufficiently reliable). It is unlikely that the use of professional premises as described in this paragraph will be appropriate where it is proposed that oral evidence should be taken from those premises.

[4]   See fn 1 above.

[5]   In certain circumstances, the Upper Tribunal may give a direction under rule 37 of the Upper Tribunal Rules that a hearing, or part of it, is to be held in private. Subject to that qualification, the public are also entitled to be present in the courtroom in which the judge is present.

VIDEO LINKS IN OVERSEAS CASES

13.   An application to receive oral evidence from an appellant[6] or witness who is overseas is unlikely to be granted unless it is established to UTIAC's satisfaction by the party making the application that:

(a)   the time and effort involved in making those arrangements are likely to be reasonable and proportionate, given the nature of the case (see paragraphs 2, 4 and 5 above);
(b)   technological and logistic arrangements are in place so that the evidence can be received at the time required;

(c)   The appellant or witness will be giving evidence from a location at which arrangements are in place to satisfy the Tribunal that the circumstances in which the evidence is given are appropriate;

(d)   the identity of the appellant or witness can be established satisfactorily;

(e)   the Tribunal can be satisfied as to who else will be present while that evidence is being given;

(f)   the costs of hearing the evidence will be borne by the party making the application; and

(g)   all such inquiries as may be required by paragraph 14 below have been made and that no objection has been forthcoming from the foreign government concerned.

14. It should not be presumed that all foreign governments are willing to allow their nationals or others within their jurisdiction to be examined before a tribunal in the United Kingdom by means of video link. If there is any doubt, the party making the application should make appropriate enquiries with the Foreign and Commonwealth Office (International Legal Matters Unit, Consular Division), with a view to ensuring that no objection will be taken at diplomatic level.

[6]   See fn 3 above.

CERTIFICATE OF COMPLIANCE

15. Where permission has been granted for a party, witness or advocate to participate in a hearing by video link, the party requesting that permission shall provide the Tribunal with written confirmation, to be received not less than 7 working days before the date of that hearing, that the arrangements specified in UTIAC's grant of permission are in place. Failure to comply with the requirement to submit a certificate of compliance is likely to result in permission to participate by video link being withdrawn.

The Hon Mr Justice Blake

30 September 2013

TRIBUNAL PROCEDURE (FIRST-TIER TRIBUNAL) (IMMIGRATION AND ASYLUM CHAMBER) RULES 2014

(SI 2014/2604)

Made: 24 September 2014.

Authority: Immigration Act 1971, Sch 2, para 25; British Nationality Act 1981, s 40A(3); Nationality, Immigration and Asylum Act 2002, s 106(3); Tribunals, Courts and Enforcement Act 2007, ss 9, 22, 29(3), (4), Sch 5; Immigration (European Economic Area) Regulations 2006, SI 2006/1003, Sch 1.

Commencement: 20 October 2014.

PART 1
INTRODUCTION

1 Citation, commencement, application and interpretation

(1) These Rules may be cited as the Tribunal Procedure (First-tier Tribunal) (Immigration and Asylum Chamber) Rules 2014 and come into force on 20th October 2014.

(2) They apply to proceedings before the Immigration and Asylum Chamber of the First-tier Tribunal.

(3) The Schedule of Fast Track Rules has effect in the circumstances and in the manner specified in that Schedule.

(4) In these Rules—

"the 1999 Act" means the Immigration and Asylum Act 1999;

"the 2002 Act" means the Nationality, Immigration and Asylum Act 2002;

"the 2004 Act" means the Asylum and Immigration (Treatment of Claimants, etc) Act 2004;

"the 2006 Regulations" means the Immigration (European Economic Area) Regulations 2006;

"the 2007 Act" means the Tribunals, Courts and Enforcement Act 2007;

"appealable decision" means a decision from which there is a right of appeal to the Immigration and Asylum Chamber of the First-tier Tribunal;

"appellant" means a person who has provided a notice of appeal to the Tribunal against an appealable decision in accordance with these Rules;

"asylum claim" has the meaning given in section 113(1) of the 2002 Act;

"certificate of fee satisfaction" means a certificate of fee satisfaction issued by the Lord Chancellor under article 8 of the Fees Order;

"decision maker" means the maker of a decision against which an appeal is brought;

"dispose of proceedings" includes, unless indicated otherwise, disposing of a part of the proceedings;

"document" means anything in which information is recorded in any form, and an obligation under these Rules to provide or allow access to a document or a copy of a document for any purpose means, unless the Tribunal directs otherwise, an obligation to provide or allow access to such document or copy in a legible form or in a form which can be readily made into a legible form;

"Fast Track Rules" means the rules contained in the Schedule to this statutory instrument;

"the Fees Order" means the First-tier Tribunal (Immigration and Asylum Chamber) Fees Order 2011;

"hearing" means an oral hearing and includes a hearing conducted in whole or in part by video link, telephone or other means of instantaneous two-way electronic communication;

"the Immigration Acts" means the Acts referred to in section 61 of the UK Borders Act 2007;

"party" means—

    (a)   an appellant or respondent to proceedings;

    (b)   a party to a bail application as provided for in rule 37(3) and 37(4); and

    (c)   the UNHCR where notice has been given to the Tribunal in accordance with rule 8(3);

"practice direction" means a direction given under section 23 of the 2007 Act;

"qualified representative" means a person who is a qualified person in accordance with section 84(2) of the 1999 Act;

"respondent" means—

    (a)   the decision maker specified in the notice of decision against which a notice of appeal has been provided; and

    (b)   a person substituted or added as a respondent in accordance with rule 8.

"Tribunal" means the First-tier Tribunal;

"the UNHCR" means the United Kingdom Representative of the United Nations High Commissioner for Refugees; and

"working day" means any day except—

    (a)   a Saturday or Sunday, Christmas Day, Good Friday or a bank holiday under section 1 of the Banking and Financial Dealings Act 1971; and

    (b)   27th to 31st December inclusive.

(5)   A rule or Part referred to by number alone, means a rule in, or Part of, these Rules.

2 Overriding objective and parties' obligation to co-operate with the Tribunal

(1)   The overriding objective of these Rules is to enable the Tribunal to deal with cases fairly and justly.

(2)   Dealing with a case fairly and justly includes—

    (a)   dealing with the case in ways which are proportionate to the importance of the case, the complexity of the issues, the anticipated costs and the resources of the parties and of the Tribunal;

    (b)   avoiding unnecessary formality and seeking flexibility in the proceedings;

    (c)   ensuring, so far as practicable, that the parties are able to participate fully in the proceedings;

    (d)   using any special expertise of the Tribunal effectively; and

    (e)   avoiding delay, so far as compatible with proper consideration of the issues.

(3)   The Tribunal must seek to give effect to the overriding objective when it—

    (a)   exercises any power under these Rules; or

    (b)   interprets any rule or practice direction.

(4)   Parties must—

    (a)   help the Tribunal to further the overriding objective; and

    (b)   co-operate with the Tribunal generally.

PART 2
GENERAL POWERS AND PROVISIONS

3 Delegation to staff

(1)   Anything of a formal or administrative nature which is required or permitted to be done by the Tribunal under these Rules may be done by a member of the Tribunal's staff.

(2)   Staff appointed by the Lord Chancellor may, with the approval of the Senior President of Tribunals, carry out functions of a judicial nature permitted or required to be done by the Tribunal.

(3)   The approval referred to at paragraph (2) may apply generally to the carrying out of specified functions by members of staff of a specified description in specified circumstances.

(4)   Within 14 days after the date on which the Tribunal sends notice of a decision made by a member of staff under paragraph (2) to a party, that party may apply in writing to the Tribunal for that decision to be considered afresh by a judge.

4 Case management powers

(1)   Subject to the provisions of the 2007 Act and any other enactment, the Tribunal may regulate its own procedure.

(2)   The Tribunal may give a direction in relation to the conduct or disposal of proceedings at any time, including a direction amending, suspending or setting aside an earlier direction.

(3)   In particular, and without restricting the general powers in paragraphs (1) and (2), the Tribunal may—

    (a)   extend or shorten the time for complying with any rule, practice direction or direction;

(b)   consolidate or hear together two or more sets of proceedings or parts of proceedings raising common issues;

(c)   permit or require a party to amend a document;

(d)   permit or require a party or another person to provide documents, information, evidence or submissions to the Tribunal or a party;

(e)   provide for a particular matter to be dealt with as a preliminary issue;

(f)   hold a hearing to consider any matter, including a case management issue;

(g)   decide the form of any hearing;

(h)   adjourn or postpone a hearing;

(i)   require a party to produce a bundle for a hearing;

(j)   stay (or, in Scotland, sist) proceedings;

(k)   transfer proceedings to another court or tribunal if that other court or tribunal has jurisdiction in relation to the proceedings and—

    (i)   because of a change of circumstances since the proceedings were started, the Tribunal no longer has jurisdiction in relation to the proceedings; or

    (ii)   the Tribunal considers that the other court or tribunal is a more appropriate forum for the determination of the case; or

(l)   suspend the effect of its own decision pending the determination by the Tribunal or the Upper Tribunal of an application for permission to appeal against, and any appeal or review of, that decision.

5 Procedure for applying for and giving directions

(1)   The Tribunal may give a direction on the application of one or more of the parties or on its own initiative.

(2)   An application for a direction may be made—

    (a)   by sending or delivering a written application to the Tribunal; or

    (b)   orally during the course of a hearing.

(3)   An application for a direction must include the reason for making that application.

(4)   Unless the Tribunal considers that there is good reason not to do so, the Tribunal must send written notice of any direction to every party and to any other person affected by the direction.

(5)   If a party or any other person sent notice of the direction under paragraph (4) wishes to challenge the direction which the Tribunal has given, they may do so by applying for another direction which amends, suspends or sets aside the first direction.

6 Failure to comply with rules etc

(1)   An irregularity resulting from a failure to comply with any requirement in these Rules, a practice direction or a direction does not of itself render void the proceedings or any step taken in the proceedings.

(2)   If a party has failed to comply with a requirement in these Rules, a practice direction or a direction, the Tribunal may take such action as it considers just, which may include—

    (a)   waiving the requirement;

    (b)   requiring the failure to be remedied; or

    (c)   exercising its power under paragraph (3).

(3)   The Tribunal may refer to the Upper Tribunal, and ask the Upper Tribunal to exercise its power under section 25 (supplementary powers of Upper Tribunal) of the 2007 Act in relation to, any failure by a person to comply with a requirement imposed by the Tribunal—

    (a)   to attend at any place for the purpose of giving evidence;

    (b)   otherwise to make themselves available to give evidence;

    (c)   to swear an oath in connection with the giving of evidence;

(d)   to give evidence as a witness;

(e)   to produce a document; or

(f)   to facilitate the inspection of a document or any other thing (including any premises).

7 Striking out of an appeal for non-payment of fee and reinstatement

(1)   Where the Tribunal is notified by the Lord Chancellor that a certificate of fee satisfaction has been revoked, the appeal shall automatically be struck out without order of the Tribunal and the Tribunal must notify each party that the appeal has been struck out.

(2)   Where an appeal has been struck out in accordance with paragraph (1), the appeal may be reinstated if—

(a)   the appellant applies to have the appeal reinstated; and

(b)   the Lord Chancellor has issued a new certificate of fee satisfaction.

(3)   An application made under paragraph (2)(a) must be made in writing and received by the Tribunal within 14 days, or if the appellant is outside the United Kingdom within 28 days, of the date on which the Tribunal sent notification of the striking out to the appellant.

8 Substitution and addition of parties

(1)   The Tribunal may give a direction substituting a respondent if—

(a)   the wrong person has been named as a respondent; or

(b)   the substitution has become necessary because of a change in circumstances since the start of proceedings.

(2)   The Tribunal may give a direction adding a person to the proceedings as a respondent.

(3)   The UNHCR may give notice to the Tribunal that they wish to participate in any proceedings where the appellant has made an asylum claim and on giving such notice becomes a party to the proceedings.

(4)   If—

(a)   the Tribunal gives a direction under paragraph (1) or (2); or

(b)   the UNHCR gives notice to the Tribunal under paragraph (3),

the Tribunal may give such consequential directions as it considers appropriate.

9 Orders for payment of costs and interest on costs (or, in Scotland, expenses)

(1)   If the Tribunal allows an appeal, it may order a respondent to pay by way of costs to the appellant an amount no greater than—

(a)   any fee paid under the Fees Order that has not been refunded; and

(b)   any fee which the appellant is or may be liable to pay under that Order.

(2)   The Tribunal may otherwise make an order in respect of costs only—

(a)   under section 29(4) of the 2007 Act (wasted costs) and costs incurred in applying for such costs; or

(b)   if a person has acted unreasonably in bringing, defending or conducting proceedings.

(3)   The Tribunal may make an order under this rule on an application or on its own initiative.

(4)   A person making an application for an order for costs—

(a)   must, unless the application is made orally at a hearing, send or deliver an application to the Tribunal and to the person against whom the order is sought to be made; and

(b)   may send or deliver together with the application a schedule of the costs claimed in sufficient detail to allow summary assessment of such costs by the Tribunal.

(5) An application for an order for costs may be made at any time during the proceedings but must be made within 28 days after the date on which the Tribunal sends—

    (a)   a notice of decision recording the decision which disposes of the proceedings; or

    (b)   notice that a withdrawal has taken effect under rule 17 (withdrawal).

(6) The Tribunal may not make an order for costs against a person (in this rule called the "paying person") without first giving that person an opportunity to make representations.

(7) The amount of costs to be paid under an order under this rule may be determined by—

    (a)   summary assessment by the Tribunal;

    (b)   agreement of a specified sum by the paying person and the person entitled to receive the costs (in this rule called the "receiving person");

    (c)   detailed assessment of the whole or a specified part of the costs (including the costs of the assessment) incurred by the receiving person, if not agreed.

(8) Except in relation to paragraph (9), in the application of this rule in relation to Scotland, any reference to costs is to be read as a reference to expenses.

(9) Following an order for detailed assessment made by the Tribunal under paragraph (7)(c) the paying person or the receiving person may apply—

    (a)   in England and Wales, to the county court for a detailed assessment of the costs on the standard basis or, if specified in the order, on the indemnity basis; and the Civil Procedure Rules 1998, section 74 (interest on judgment debts, etc) of the County Courts Act 1984 and the County Court (Interest on Judgment Debts) Order 1991 shall apply, with necessary modifications, to that application and assessment as if the proceedings in the Tribunal had been proceedings in a court to which the Civil Procedure Rules 1998 apply;

    (b)   in Scotland, to the Auditor of the Sheriff Court or the Court of Session (as specified in the order) for the taxation of the expenses according to the fees payable in that court; or

    (c)   in Northern Ireland, to the Taxing Office of the High Court of Northern Ireland for taxation on the standard basis or, if specified in the order, on the indemnity basis.

10 Representatives

(1) A party may be represented by any person not prohibited from representing by section 84 of the 1999 Act.

(2) Where a party is or has been represented by a person prohibited from representing by section 84 of the 1999 Act, that does not of itself render void the proceedings or any step taken in the proceedings.

(3) If a party appoints a representative, that party (or the representative if the representative is a qualified representative) must send or deliver to the Tribunal written notice of the representative's name and address, which may be done at a hearing.

(4) Anything permitted or required to be done by a party under these Rules, a practice direction or a direction may be done by the representative of that party, except signing a witness statement.

(5) A person who receives notice of the appointment of a representative—

    (a)   must provide to the representative any document which is required to be provided to the represented party, and need not provide that document to the represented party; and

    (b)   may assume that the representative is and remains authorised as such until they receive written notification that this is not so from the representative or the represented party.

(6)   As from the date on which a person has notified the Tribunal that they are acting as the representative of an appellant and has given an address for service, if any document is provided to the appellant a copy must also at the same time be provided to the appellant's representative.

11 Calculating time

(1)   An act required or permitted to be done on or by a particular day by these Rules, a practice direction or a direction must, unless otherwise directed, be done by midnight on that day.

(2)   Subject to the Tribunal directing that this paragraph does not apply, if the time specified by these Rules, a practice direction or a direction for doing any act ends on a day other than a working day, the act is done in time if it is done on the next working day.

12 Sending, delivery and language of documents

(1)   Any document to be provided to the Tribunal or any person under these Rules, a practice direction or a direction must be—

    (a)   delivered, or sent by post, to an address;

    (b)   sent via a document exchange to a document exchange number or address;

    (c)   sent by fax to a fax number;

    (d)   sent by e-mail to an e-mail address; or

    (e)   sent or delivered by any other method,

identified for that purpose by the Tribunal or person to whom the document is directed.

(2)   A document to be provided to an individual may be provided by leaving it with that individual.

(3)   If the respondent believes that the address specified under paragraph (1) for the provision of documents to the appellant is not appropriate for that purpose, the respondent must notify the Tribunal in writing of that fact and, if aware of it, an address which would be appropriate.

(4)   If any document is provided to a person who has notified the Tribunal that they are acting as the representative of a party, it shall be deemed to have been provided to that party.

(5)   Subject to paragraph (6)—

    (a)   any notice of appeal or application notice provided to the Tribunal must be completed in English; and

    (b)   if a document provided to the Tribunal is not written in English, it must be accompanied by an English translation.

(6)   In proceedings that are in Wales or have a connection with Wales, a document or translation may be provided to the Tribunal in Welsh.

13 Use of documents and information

(1)   The Tribunal may make an order prohibiting the disclosure or publication of—

    (a)   specified documents or information relating to the proceedings; or

    (b)   any matter likely to lead members of the public to identify any person whom the Tribunal considers should not be identified.

(2)   The Tribunal may give a direction prohibiting the disclosure of a document or information to a person if—

    (a)   the Tribunal is satisfied that such disclosure would be likely to cause that person or some other person serious harm; and

    (b)   the Tribunal is satisfied, having regard to the interests of justice, that it is proportionate to give such a direction.

(3) If a party ("the first party") considers that the Tribunal should give a direction under paragraph (2) prohibiting the disclosure of a document or information to another party ("the second party"), the first party must—

    (a)   exclude the relevant document or information from any documents to be provided to the second party; and

    (b)   provide to the Tribunal the excluded document or information, and the reason for its exclusion, so that the Tribunal may decide whether the document or information should be disclosed to the second party or should be the subject of a direction under paragraph (2).

(4) The Tribunal must conduct proceedings as appropriate in order to give effect to a direction given under paragraph (2).

(5) If the Tribunal gives a direction under paragraph (2) which prevents disclosure to a party who has appointed a representative, the Tribunal may give a direction that the documents or information be disclosed to that representative if the Tribunal is satisfied that—

    (a)   disclosure to the representative would be in the interests of the party; and

    (b)   the representative will act in accordance with paragraph (6).

(6) Documents or information disclosed to a representative in accordance with a direction under paragraph (5) must not be disclosed either directly or indirectly to any other person without the Tribunal's consent.

(7) The Tribunal may, on the application of a party or on its own initiative, give a direction that certain documents or information must or may be disclosed to the Tribunal on the basis that the Tribunal will not disclose such documents or information to other persons, or specified other persons.

(8) A party making an application for a direction under paragraph (7) may withhold the relevant documents or information from other parties until the Tribunal has granted or refused the application.

(9) In a case involving matters relating to national security, the Tribunal must ensure that information is not disclosed contrary to the interests of national security.

(10) The Tribunal must conduct proceedings and record its decision and reasons appropriately so as not to undermine the effect of an order made under paragraph (1), a direction given under paragraph (2), (5) or (7) or the duty imposed by paragraph (9).

14 Evidence and submissions

(1) Without restriction on the general powers in rule 4 (case management powers), the Tribunal may give directions as to—

    (a)   issues on which it requires evidence or submissions;

    (b)   the nature of the evidence or submissions it requires;

    (c)   whether the parties are permitted or required to provide expert evidence;

    (d)   any limit on the number of witnesses whose evidence a party may put forward, whether in relation to a particular issue or generally;

    (e)   the manner in which any evidence or submissions are to be provided, which may include a direction for them to be given—

        (i)   orally at a hearing; or

        (ii)   by witness statement or written submissions; and

    (f)   the time at which any evidence or submissions are to be provided.

(2) The Tribunal may admit evidence whether or not—

    (a)   the evidence would be admissible in a civil trial in the United Kingdom; or

    (b)   subject to section 85A(4) of the 2002 Act, the evidence was available to the decision maker.

(3) The Tribunal may consent to a witness giving, or require any witness to give, evidence on oath or affirmation, and may administer an oath or affirmation for that purpose.

15 Summoning or citation of witnesses and orders to answer questions or produce documents

(1)   On the application of a party or on its own initiative, the Tribunal may—

    (a)   by summons (or, in Scotland, citation) require any person to attend as a witness at a hearing at the time and place specified in the summons or citation; or

    (b)   order any person to answer any questions or produce any documents in that person's possession or control which relate to any issue in the proceedings.

(2)   A summons or citation under paragraph (1)(a) must—

    (a)   give the person required to attend 14 days' notice of the hearing or such shorter period as the Tribunal may direct; and

    (b)   where the person is not a party, make provision for the person's necessary expenses of attendance to be paid, and state who is to pay them.

(3)   No person may be compelled to give any evidence or produce any document that the person could not be compelled to give or produce on a trial of an action in a court of law in the part of the United Kingdom where the proceedings are to be determined.

(4)   A summons, citation or order under this rule must—

    (a)   state that the person on whom the requirement is imposed may apply to the Tribunal to vary or set aside the summons, citation or order, if they have not had an opportunity to object to it; and

    (b)   state the consequences of failure to comply with the summons, citation or order.

16 Appeal treated as abandoned or finally determined

(1)   A party must notify the Tribunal if they are aware that—

    (a)   the appellant has left the United Kingdom;

    (b)   the appellant has been granted leave to enter or remain in the United Kingdom;

    (c)   a deportation order has been made against the appellant; or

    (d)   a document listed in paragraph 4(2) of Schedule 2 to the 2006 Regulations has been issued to the appellant.

(2)   Where an appeal is treated as abandoned pursuant to section 104(4A) of the 2002 Act or paragraph 4(2) of Schedule 2 to 2006 Regulations, the Tribunal must send the parties a notice informing them that the appeal is being treated as abandoned or finally determined, as the case may be.

(3)   Where an appeal would otherwise fall to be treated as abandoned pursuant to section 104(4A) of the 2002 Act, but the appellant wishes to pursue their appeal, the appellant must provide a notice, which must comply with any relevant practice direction, to the Tribunal and each other party so that it is received within 28 days of the date on which the appellant was sent notice of the grant of leave to enter or remain in the United Kingdom or was sent the document listed in paragraph 4(2) of Schedule 2 to the 2006 Regulations, as the case may be.

17 Withdrawal

(1)   A party may give notice of the withdrawal of their appeal—

    (a)   by providing to the Tribunal a written notice of withdrawal of the appeal; or

    (b)   orally at a hearing,

and in either case must specify the reasons for that withdrawal.

(2)   The Tribunal must (save for good reason) treat an appeal as withdrawn if the respondent notifies the Tribunal and each other party that the decision (or, where the appeal relates to more than one decision, all of the decisions) to which the appeal relates has been withdrawn and specifies the reasons for the withdrawal of the decision.

(3) The Tribunal must notify each party in writing that a withdrawal has taken effect under this rule and that the proceedings are no longer regarded by the Tribunal as pending.

18 Certification of pending appeal

(1) The Secretary of State must, upon issuing a certificate under section 97 or 98 of the 2002 Act which relates to a pending appeal, provide notice of the certification to the Tribunal.

(2) Where a notice of certification is provided under paragraph (1), the Tribunal must—

    (a)   notify the parties; and

    (b)   take no further action in relation to the appeal.

PART 3

PROCEEDINGS BEFORE THE TRIBUNAL

CHAPTER 1

BEFORE THE HEARING

19 Notice of appeal

(1) An appellant must start proceedings by providing a notice of appeal to the Tribunal.

(2) If the person is in the United Kingdom, the notice of appeal must be received not later than 14 days after they are sent the notice of the decision against which the appeal is brought.

(3) If the person is outside the United Kingdom, the notice of appeal must be received—

    (a)   not later than 28 days after their departure from the United Kingdom if the person—

        (i)   was in the United Kingdom when the decision against which they are appealing was made, and

        (ii)   may not appeal while they are in the United Kingdom by reason of a provision of the 2002 Act; or

    (b)   in any other case, not later than 28 days after they receive the notice of the decision.

(4) The notice of appeal must—

    (a)   set out the grounds of appeal;

    (b)   be signed and dated by the appellant or their representative;

    (c)   if the notice of appeal is signed by the appellant's representative, the representative must certify in the notice of appeal that it has been completed in accordance with the appellant's instructions;

    (d)   state whether the appellant requires an interpreter at any hearing and if so for which language and dialect;

    (e)   state whether the appellant intends to attend at any hearing; and

    (f)   state whether the appellant will be represented at any hearing.

(5) The appellant must provide with the notice of appeal—

    (a)   the notice of decision against which the appellant is appealing or if it is not practicable to include the notice of decision, the reasons why it is not practicable;

    (b)   any statement of reasons for that decision;

    (c)   any documents in support of the appellant's case which have not been supplied to the respondent;

    (d)   an application for the Lord Chancellor to issue a certificate of fee satisfaction;

(e)   any further information or documents required by an applicable practice direction.

(6) The Tribunal must send a copy of the notice of appeal and the accompanying documents or information provided by the appellant to the respondent.

(7) An appellant may, with the permission of the Tribunal, vary the grounds on which they rely in the notice of appeal.

20 Late notice of appeal

(1) Where a notice of appeal is provided outside the time limit in rule 19, including any extension of time directed under rule 4(3)(a) (power to extend time), the notice of appeal must include an application for such an extension of time and the reason why the notice of appeal was not provided in time.

(2) If, upon receipt of a notice of appeal, the notice appears to the Tribunal to have been provided outside the time limit but does not include an application for an extension of time, the Tribunal must (unless it extends time of its own initiative) notify the person in writing that it proposes to treat the notice of appeal as being out of time.

(3) Where the Tribunal gives notification under paragraph (2), the person may by written notice to the Tribunal contend that—

(a)   the notice of appeal was given in time; or

(b)   time for providing the notice of appeal should be extended,

and, if so, that person may provide the Tribunal with written evidence in support of that contention.

(4) The Tribunal must decide any issue under this rule as to whether a notice of appeal was given in time, or whether to extend the time for appealing, as a preliminary issue, and may do so without a hearing.

(5) Where the Tribunal makes a decision under this rule it must provide to the parties written notice of its decision, including its reasons.

21 Special provision for imminent removal cases (late notice of appeal)

(1) This rule applies in any case to which rule 20 applies, where the respondent notifies the Tribunal that directions have been given for the removal of that person from the United Kingdom on a date within 5 days of the date on which the notice of appeal was received.

(2) The Tribunal must, if reasonably practicable, make any decision under rule 20 before the date and time proposed for the removal.

(3) Rule 20 shall apply, subject to the modifications that the Tribunal may—

(a)   give notification under rule 20(2) orally, which may include giving it by telephone,

(b)   direct a time for providing evidence under rule 20(3), and

(c)   direct that evidence in support of a contention under rule 20(3) is to be given orally, which may include requiring the evidence to be given by telephone, and hold a hearing for the purpose of receiving such evidence.

22 Circumstances in which the Tribunal may not accept a notice of appeal

(1) Where a person has provided a notice of appeal to the Tribunal and any of the circumstances in paragraph (2) apply, the Tribunal may not accept the notice of appeal.

(2) The circumstances referred to in paragraph (1) are that—

(a)   there is no appealable decision; or

(b)   the Lord Chancellor has refused to issue a certificate of fee satisfaction.

(3) Where the Tribunal does not accept a notice of appeal, it must—

(a)   notify the person providing the notice of appeal and the respondent; and

(b)   take no further action on that notice of appeal.

23 Response: entry clearance cases

(1)   This rule applies to an appeal against a refusal of entry clearance or a refusal of an EEA family permit (which has the meaning given in regulation 2(1) of the 2006 Regulations).

(2)   When a respondent is provided with a copy of a notice of appeal from a refusal of entry clearance or a refusal of an EEA family permit, the respondent must provide the Tribunal with—

(a)   the notice of the decision to which the notice of appeal relates and any other document the respondent provided to the appellant giving reasons for that decision;

(b)   a statement of whether the respondent opposes the appellant's case and, if so, the grounds for such opposition;

(c)   any statement of evidence or application form completed by the appellant;

(d)   any record of an interview with the appellant in relation to the decision being appealed;

(e)   any other unpublished document which is referred to in a document mentioned in sub-paragraph (a) or relied upon by the respondent; and

(f)   the notice of any other appealable decision made in relation to the appellant.

(3)   The respondent must send to the Tribunal and the other parties the documents listed in paragraph (2) within 28 days of the date on which the respondent received from the Tribunal a copy of the notice of appeal and any accompanying documents or information provided under rule 19(6).

24 Response: other cases

(1)   Except in appeals to which rule 23 applies, when a respondent is provided with a copy of a notice of appeal, the respondent must provide the Tribunal with—

(a)   the notice of the decision to which the notice of appeal relates and any other document the respondent provided to the appellant giving reasons for that decision;

(b)   any statement of evidence or application form completed by the appellant;

(c)   any record of an interview with the appellant in relation to the decision being appealed;

(d)   any other unpublished document which is referred to in a document mentioned in sub-paragraph (a) or relied upon by the respondent; and

(e)   the notice of any other appealable decision made in relation to the appellant.

(2)   The respondent must, if the respondent intends to change or add to the grounds or reasons relied upon in the notice or the other documents referred to in paragraph (1)(a), provide the Tribunal and the other parties with a statement of whether the respondent opposes the appellant's case and the grounds for such opposition.

(3)   The documents listed in paragraph (1) and any statement required under paragraph (2) must be provided in writing within 28 days of the date on which the Tribunal sent to the respondent a copy of the notice of appeal and any accompanying documents or information provided under rule 19(6).

CHAPTER 2

HEARINGS

25 Consideration of decision with or without a hearing

(1)   The Tribunal must hold a hearing before making a decision which disposes of proceedings except where—

(a)   each party has consented to, or has not objected to, the matter being decided without a hearing;

(b)   the appellant has not consented to the appeal being determined without a hearing but the Lord Chancellor has refused to issue a certificate of fee satisfaction for the fee payable for a hearing;

(c)   the appellant is outside the United Kingdom and does not have a representative who has an address for service in the United Kingdom;

(d)   it is impracticable to give the appellant notice of the hearing;

(e)   a party has failed to comply with a provision of these Rules, a practice direction or a direction and the Tribunal is satisfied that in all the circumstances, including the extent of the failure and any reasons for it, it is appropriate to determine the appeal without a hearing;

(f)   the appeal is one to which rule 16(2) or 18(2) applies; or

(g)   subject to paragraph (2), the Tribunal considers that it can justly determine the matter without a hearing.

(2)   Where paragraph (1)(g) applies, the Tribunal must not make the decision without a hearing without first giving the parties notice of its intention to do so, and an opportunity to make written representations as to whether there should be a hearing.

(3)   This rule does not apply to decisions under Part 4 or Part 5.

26 Notice of hearings

The Tribunal must give each party entitled to attend a hearing reasonable notice of the time and place of the hearing (including any adjourned or postponed hearing) and any changes to the time and place of the hearing.

27 Public and private hearings

(1)   Subject to the following paragraphs and to section 108 of the 2002 Act, all hearings must be held in public.

(2)   The Tribunal may give a direction that a hearing, or part of it, is to be held in private.

(3)   Where a hearing, or part of it, is to be held in private, the Tribunal may determine who is permitted to attend the hearing or part of it.

(4)   The Tribunal may give a direction excluding from any hearing, or part of it—

(a)   any person whose conduct the Tribunal considers is disrupting or is likely to disrupt the hearing;

(b)   any person whose presence the Tribunal considers is likely to prevent another person from giving evidence or making submissions freely;

(c)   any person who the Tribunal considers should be excluded in order to give effect to a direction under rule 13(2) (withholding a document or information likely to cause serious harm); or

(d)   any person where the purpose of the hearing would be defeated by the attendance of that person.

(5)   The Tribunal may give a direction excluding a witness from a hearing until that witness gives evidence.

28 Hearing in a party's absence

If a party fails to attend a hearing the Tribunal may proceed with the hearing if the Tribunal—

(a)   is satisfied that the party has been notified of the hearing or that reasonable steps have been taken to notify the party of the hearing; and

(b)   considers that it is in the interests of justice to proceed with the hearing.

CHAPTER 3

DECISIONS

29 Decisions and notice of decisions

(1)   The Tribunal may give a decision orally at a hearing.

(2)   Subject to rule 13(2) (withholding information likely to cause serious harm), the Tribunal must provide to each party as soon as reasonably practicable after making a decision (other than a decision under Part 4) which disposes of the proceedings—

(a)   a notice of decision stating the Tribunal's decision; and

(b)   notification of any right of appeal against the decision and the time within which, and the manner in which, such right of appeal may be exercised.

(3)   Where the decision of the Tribunal relates to—

(a)   an asylum claim or a humanitarian protection claim, the Tribunal must provide, with the notice of decision in paragraph (2)(a), written reasons for its decision;

(b)   any other matter, the Tribunal may provide written reasons for its decision but, if it does not do so, must notify the parties of the right to apply for a written statement of reasons.

(4)   Unless the Tribunal has already provided a written statement of reasons, a party may make a written application to the Tribunal for such statement following a decision which disposes of the proceedings.

(5)   An application under paragraph (4) must be received within 28 days of the date on which the Tribunal sent or otherwise provided to the party a notice of decision relating to the decision which disposes of the proceedings.

(6)   If a party makes an application in accordance with paragraphs (4) and (5) the Tribunal must, subject to rule 13(2) (withholding a document or information likely to cause serious harm), send a written statement of reasons to each party as soon as reasonably practicable.

PART 4
CORRECTING, SETTING ASIDE, REVIEWING AND APPEALING TRIBUNAL DECISIONS

30 Interpretation

In this Part—

"appeal" means the exercise of a right of appeal on a point of law under section 11 of the 2007 Act;

"review" means the review of a decision by the Tribunal under section 9 of the 2007 Act.

31 Clerical mistakes and accidental slips or omissions

The Tribunal may at any time correct any clerical mistake or other accidental slip or omission in a decision, direction or any document produced by it, by—

(a)   providing notification of the amended decision or direction, or a copy of the amended document, to all parties; and

(b)   making any necessary amendment to any information published in relation to the decision, direction or document.

32 Setting aside a decision which disposes of proceedings

(1)   The Tribunal may set aside a decision which disposes of proceedings, or part of such a decision, and re-make the decision, or the relevant part of it, if—

(a)   the Tribunal considers that it is in the interests of justice to do so; and

(b)   one or more of the conditions in paragraph (2) are satisfied.

(2)   The conditions are—

(a)   a document relating to the proceedings was not provided to, or was not received at an appropriate time by, a party or a party's representative;

(b)   a document relating to the proceedings was not provided to the Tribunal at an appropriate time;

(c)   a party, or a party's representative, was not present at a hearing related to the proceedings; or

(d)   there has been some other procedural irregularity in the proceedings.

(3)   An application for a decision, or part of a decision, to be set aside under paragraph (1) must be made—

(a)   if the appellant is outside the United Kingdom, within 28 days; or

(b)   in any other case, within 14 days,

of the date on which the party was sent the notice of decision.

33 Application for permission to appeal to the Upper Tribunal

(1)   A party seeking permission to appeal to the Upper Tribunal must make a written application to the Tribunal for permission to appeal.

(2)   Subject to paragraph (3), an application under paragraph (1) must be provided to the Tribunal so that it is received no later than 14 days after the date on which the party making the application was provided with written reasons for the decision.

(3)   Where an appellant is outside the United Kingdom, an application to the Tribunal under paragraph (1) must be provided to the Tribunal so that it is received no later than 28 days after the date on which the party making the application was provided with written reasons for the decision.

(4)   The time within which a party may apply for permission to appeal against an amended notice of decision runs from the date on which the party is sent the amended notice of decision.

(5)   An application under paragraph (1) must—

(a)   identify the decision of the Tribunal to which it relates;

(b)   identify the alleged error or errors of law in the decision; and

(c)   state the result the party making the application is seeking and include any application for an extension of time and the reasons why such an extension should be given.

(6)   If a person makes an application under paragraph (1) when the Tribunal has not given a written statement of reasons for its decision—

(a)   the Tribunal must, if no application for a written statement of reasons has been made, treat the application for permission as such an application; and

(b)   may—

(i)   direct under rule 36 that the application is not to be treated as an application for permission to appeal; or

(ii)   determine the application for permission to appeal.

(7)   If an application for a written statement of reasons has been, or is, refused because the application was received out of time, the Tribunal must only admit the application for permission if the Tribunal considers that it is in the interests of justice to do so.

34 Tribunal's consideration of an application for permission to appeal to the Upper Tribunal

(1)   On receiving an application for permission to appeal the Tribunal must first consider whether to review the decision in accordance with rule 35.

(2)   If the Tribunal decides not to review the decision, or reviews the decision and decides to take no action in relation to the decision, or part of it, the Tribunal must consider whether to give permission to appeal in relation to the decision or that part of it.

(3)   The Tribunal must send a record of its decision to the parties as soon as practicable.

(4)   If the Tribunal refuses permission to appeal it must send with the record of its decision—

   (a)   a statement of its reasons for such refusal; and

   (b)   notification of the right to make an application to the Upper Tribunal for permission to appeal and the time within which, and the manner in which, such application must be made.

(5)   The Tribunal may give permission to appeal on limited grounds, but must comply with paragraph (4) in relation to any grounds on which it has refused permission.

35 Review of a decision

(1)   The Tribunal may only undertake a review of a decision—

   (a)   pursuant to rule 34 (review on an application for permission to appeal); and

   (b)   if it is satisfied that there was an error of law in the decision.

(2)   The Tribunal must notify the parties in writing of the outcome of any review, and of any right of appeal in relation to the outcome.

(3)   If the Tribunal takes any action in relation to a decision following a review without first giving every party an opportunity to make representations—

   (a)   the notice under paragraph (2) must state that any party that did not have an opportunity to make representations may apply for such action to be set aside; and

   (b)   the Tribunal may regard the review as incomplete and act accordingly.

36 Power to treat an application as a different type of application

The Tribunal may treat an application for a decision to be corrected, set aside or reviewed, or for permission to appeal against a decision, as an application for any other one of those things.

PART 5
BAIL

37 Scope of this Part and interpretation

(1)   This Part applies to bail proceedings, meaning bail applications and any matter relating to bail which the Tribunal is considering on its own initiative.

(2)   In this Part, "bail party" means a person released on bail or applying to the Tribunal to be released on bail.

(3)   Except where paragraph (4) applies, the parties to bail proceedings are the bail party and the Secretary of State.

(4)   Where the proceedings concern forfeiture of a recognizance, the parties are the Secretary of State and any person who entered into the recognizance in question, whether as principal or surety.

38 Bail applications

(1)   A bail application must be made by sending or delivering to the Tribunal an application notice containing the information specified below.

(2) A bail application must specify whether it is for—

    (a)   the bail party to be released on bail;

    (b)   variation of bail conditions;

    (c)   continuation of bail; or

    (d)   forfeiture of a recognizance.

(3) Subject to paragraph (4), a bail application must contain the following details—

    (a)   the bail party's—

        (i)   full name;

        (ii)   date of birth; and

        (iii)   date of their most recent arrival in the United Kingdom;

    (b)   the address of any place where the bail party is detained;

    (c)   the address where the bail party will reside if the bail application is granted, or, if unable to give such an address, the reason why an address is not given;

    (d)   the amount of any recognizance in which the bail party is, or is proposed to be, bound;

    (e)   whether the bail party has a pending appeal to the Tribunal or any pending application for further appeal relating to such an appeal;

    (f)   the full name, address, date of birth and any occupation of any person who is acting or is proposed to act as a surety for the recognizance and the amount in which the surety is, or is proposed to be, bound;

    (g)   where the bail party is aged 18 or over, whether the bail party will, if required, agree as a condition of bail to co-operate with electronic monitoring under section 36 of the 2004 Act;

    (h)   the grounds on which the application is made and, where a previous application has been refused, when it was refused and details of any material change in circumstances since the refusal; and

    (i)   whether an interpreter will be required at the hearing, and in respect of what language and dialect.

(4) Where the application is for forfeiture of a recognizance, paragraph (3) applies except for sub-paragraphs (a)(iii), (b), (c), (e) and (g) of that paragraph.

(5) An application made by the bail party must be signed by the bail party or their representative.

(6) On receipt of a bail application, the Tribunal must record the date on which it was received and provide a copy of the application to the Secretary of State as soon as reasonably practicable.

39 Bail hearings

(1) Subject to paragraph (3), where a bail application is for the bail party to be released on bail, the Tribunal must, as soon as reasonably practicable, hold a hearing of the application.

(2) In all other bail proceedings, the Tribunal may determine the matter without a hearing if it considers it can justly do so.

(3) Where an application for release on bail is received by the Tribunal within 28 days after a Tribunal decision made at a hearing under paragraph (1) not to release the bail party on bail, the Tribunal—

    (a)   must determine whether the bail party has demonstrated that there has been a material change in circumstances since the decision;

    (b)   if the Tribunal so determines, must apply paragraph (1);

    (c)   otherwise, must dismiss the application without a hearing.

(4) Paragraph (3) has no effect until the date on which section 7(3)(c) of the Immigration Act 2014 (inserting paragraph 25(2) of Schedule 2 to the Immigration Act 1971) comes into force.

40 Response to a bail application

(1)   If the Secretary of State opposes a bail application, the Secretary of State must provide the Tribunal and the bail party with a written statement of the reasons for doing so—

(a)   not later than 2.00 pm on the working day before the hearing; or

(b)   if the Secretary of State was provided with notice of the hearing less than 24 hours before that time, as soon as reasonably practicable.

(2)   Where the Secretary of State's reasons for opposition include that directions are in force for the removal of the bail party from the United Kingdom, the Secretary of State must provide a copy of the notice of those directions.

41 Decision in bail proceedings

(1)   The Tribunal must provide written notice of its decision to—

(a)   the parties; and

(b)   if the bail application is for the bail party to be released on bail, the person having custody of the bail party.

(2)   Where bail is granted, varied or continued, the notice must state any bail conditions, including any amounts in which the bail party and any sureties are to be bound.

(3)   Where bail is refused or where the Tribunal orders forfeiture of the recognizance, the notice must include reasons for the decision.

(4)   Where, instead of granting or refusing bail, the Tribunal fixes the amount and conditions of the bail with a view to the recognizance being taken subsequently by a person specified by the Tribunal, the notice must include the matters stated in paragraph (2) and the name or office of the person so specified.

(5)   Paragraph (6) applies where the Tribunal determines that directions for the removal of the bail party from the United Kingdom are for the time being in force and the directions require the bail party to be removed from the United Kingdom within 14 days of the date of the decision to release the bail party on bail or under paragraph (4).

(6)   The notice provided under paragraph (1) must state—

(a)   the determination of the Tribunal under paragraph (5);

(b)   whether the Secretary of State has consented to the release of the bail party;

(c)   where the Secretary of State has not consented to that release, that the bail party must therefore not be released on bail.

42 Recognizances

(1)   Any recognizance must be in writing and must state—

(a)   the bail conditions, including the amount of the recognizance and any amount in which any surety agrees to be bound; and

(b)   that the bail party and any surety understand the bail conditions and that, if the bail party fails to comply with those conditions, they may be ordered to pay all or part of the amount in which they are bound.

(2)   The recognizance must be signed by the bail party and any surety and provided to the Tribunal, and a copy provided to—

(a)   the parties,

(b)   any person having custody of the bail party, and

(c)   any surety.

43 Release of bail party

The person having custody of the bail party must release the bail party upon—

(a)   being provided with a notice of decision to grant bail; or

(b)   being—

(i)   provided with a notice of decision fixing the amount and conditions of the bail, and

(ii)   satisfied that the recognizance required by that decision has been entered into.

44 Application of this Part to Scotland

This Part applies to Scotland with the following modifications—

(a)   in rule 37, for paragraph (4) substitute—

"(4)   Where the proceedings concern forfeiture of bail, the parties are the Secretary of State and any person who entered into the bail bond in question, whether that is the bail party or cautioner."

(b)   in rule 38—

(i)   for paragraph (2)(d) substitute—

"(d)   forfeiture of bail.";

(ii)   for paragraph (3)(d) substitute—

"(d)   the amount, if any, deposited or to be deposited if bail is granted;";

(iii)   for paragraph (3)(f) substitute—

"(f)   the full name, address, date of birth and any occupation of any person acting or offering to act as a cautioner if the application for bail is granted, and the amount, if any, deposited or to be deposited;"; and

(iv)   for paragraph (4) substitute—

"(4)   Where the application is for forfeiture of bail, paragraph (3) applies with the exception of sub-paragraphs (a)(iii) and (b), (c), (e) and (g) of that paragraph";

(c)   in rule 41, for paragraphs (2), (3) and (4) substitute—

"(2)   Where bail is granted, varied or continued, the notice must state any bail conditions, including the amounts (if any) to be deposited by the bail party and any cautioners.

(3)   Where bail is refused or where the Tribunal orders forfeiture of bail, the notice must include reasons for the decision.

(4)   Where, instead of granting or refusing bail, the Tribunal fixes the amount and conditions of bail with a view to a bail bond being entered into subsequently before a person specified by the Tribunal, the notice must include the matters stated in paragraph (2) and the name or office of the person so specified.";

(d)   for rule 42 substitute—

"42 Bail bond

(1)   Any bail bond of a bail party or cautioner must be in writing and, where the deposit of money is required as a condition of bail, must state—

(a)   the amount to be deposited; and

(b)   that the bail party and any cautioner understand that, if the bail party fails to answer to bail, all or part of the amount deposited may be forfeited.

(2)   The bail bond must be signed by the bail party and any cautioner and provided to the Tribunal, and a copy provided to—

(a)   the parties,

(b)   any person having custody of the bail party, and

(c)   any cautioner."

(e)   in rule 43, for sub-paragraph (b) substitute—

"(b)   being—

(i)   provided with the notice of decision fixing the amount and conditions of the bail, and

(ii)   satisfied that the amount, if any, to be deposited in accordance with those conditions has been deposited.".

PART 6
FINAL

45 Revocations

The statutory instruments listed in the left hand column of Table 1 below are revoked to the extent specified in the right hand column.

Revocations

Statutory Instrument	Extent of revocation
The Asylum and Immigration Tribunal (Procedure) Rules 2005 (SI 2005/230)	The entire Rules
The Asylum and Immigration Tribunal (Procedure) (Amendment) Rules 2006 (SI 2006/2788)	The entire Rules
The Asylum and Immigration Tribunal (Procedure) Rules 2007 (SI 2007/835)	The entire Rules
The Asylum and Immigration Tribunal (Procedure) (Amendment No 2) Rules 2007 (SI 2007/3170)	The entire Rules
The Asylum and Immigration Tribunal (Procedure) (Amendment) Rules 2008 (SI 2008/1088)	The entire Rules
The Tribunal Procedure (Amendment No 2) Rules 2010 (SI 2010/44)	Rules 23 to 28 inclusive
The Tribunal Procedure (Amendment No 3) Rules 2010 (SI 2010/2653)	Rule 4
The Tribunal Procedure (Amendment) (No 2) Rules 2011 (SI 2011/2840)	The entire Rules
The Asylum and Immigration Tribunal (Fast Track Procedure) Rules 2005 (SI 2005/560)	The entire Rules
The Asylum and Immigration Tribunal (Fast Track Procedure) (Amendment) Rules 2006 (SI 2006/2789)	The entire Rules
The Asylum and Immigration Tribunal (Fast Track Procedure) (Amendment) Rules 2008 (SI 2008/1089)	The entire Rules

46 Transitional provisions

(1)   The Tribunal may give any direction to ensure that proceedings are dealt with fairly and, in particular, may—

(a)   apply any provision of the Asylum and Immigration Tribunal (Procedure) Rules 2005 or the Asylum and Immigration Tribunal (Fast Track Procedure) Rules 2005 which applied to the proceedings immediately before the date these Rules came into force; or

(b)   disapply provisions of these Rules (including the Fast Track Rules).

(2)   A time period which has started to run before the date on which these Rules come into force and which has not expired shall continue to apply.

SCHEDULE
THE FAST TRACK RULES

Rule 1(3)

PART 1
INTRODUCTION AND SCOPE

Interpretation and relationship with the Principal Rules

1

(1)   The rules in this Schedule are the Fast Track Rules.

(2)   A rule or Part referred to in this Schedule by number alone means a rule in, or Part of, the Fast Track Rules.

(3)   In these Rules, the "Principal Rules" means rules 1 to 46 of the Tribunal Procedure (First-tier Tribunal) (Immigration and Asylum Chamber) Rules 2014.

(4)   The Principal Rules, except for those provisions referred to in Table 2 below apply for the purposes of and the interpretation of the Fast Track Rules.

(5)   Where the Fast Track Rules cease to apply to an appeal or application because—

   (a)   the condition referred to in rule 2(1)(b) ceases to apply; or

   (b)   the Tribunal makes an order under rule 14,

the Principal Rules shall apply to the appeal or application.

(6)   Where—

   (a)   a period of time for taking a step has started to run under a provision of the Fast Track Rules, and

   (b)   that provision ceases to apply in the circumstances to which paragraph (5) refers,

if the Principal Rules contain a time limit for taking such step, the time limit in the Principal Rules shall apply, and the relevant period of time shall be treated as running from the date on which the period of time under the Fast Track Rules started to run.

Principal Rules which do not apply in the fast track

Rule numbers refer to the Principal Rules	Notes
Rule 3(2)–(4) (delegation to staff)	
Rule 4(3)(a) (case management powers: reducing or extending time)	Rule 5(2)–(6) of the Fast Track Rules (time limits) applies
Rule 4(3)(h) (case management powers: adjourning or postponing hearing)	Rule 12 of the Fast Track Rules (adjournment) applies
Rule 4(3)(j) (case management powers: stay or sist proceedings)	
Rule 4(3)(k) (case management powers: transfer of proceedings)	
Rule 4(3)(l) (suspending effect of decision pending onward appeal etc)	
Rule 7 (striking out of appeal for non-payment of fee and reinstatement)	
Rule 9(1) (costs orders for payment of Tribunal fees)	
Rule 19 (notice of appeal)	Rules 3 to 6 of the Fast Track Rules apply

Rules 20 and 21 (late notice of appeal; special provision for imminent removal cases)	Rule 5 of the Fast Track Rules (time limits) applies
Rule 22, except for the purposes of paragraph (2)(a) (no appealable decision)	
Rules 23–24 (response: entry clearance and other cases)	Rule 7 of the Fast Track Rules (filing of documents by respondent) applies
Rule 29(2) to (6) (provision of written statement of reasons for Tribunal's decision)	Rule 10 of the Fast Track Rules (decisions and notice of decisions) applies
Rule 33(2) and (3) (time limit for applying to the Tribunal for permission to appeal to the Upper Tribunal)	Rule 11 of the Fast Track Rules (time limit for making an application for permission to appeal) applies
Rule 34(1) (Tribunal to consider first whether to review decision)	

Scope of Fast Track Rules

2

(1)   The Fast Track Rules apply to an appeal to the Tribunal or an application for permission to appeal to the Upper Tribunal where the appellant—

(a)   was detained under the Immigration Acts at a place specified in paragraph (3) when provided with notice of the appealable decision against which the appellant is appealing; and

(b)   has been continuously detained under the Immigration Acts at a place or places specified in paragraph (3) since that notice was served on the appellant.

(2)   An appellant does not, for the purposes of this rule, cease to satisfy the condition in paragraph (1)(b) by reason only of—

(a)   being transported from one place of detention specified in paragraph (3) to another place which is so specified; or

(b)   leaving and returning to such a place of detention for any purpose between the hours of 6 am and 10 pm.

(3)   The places specified for the purposes of this rule are—

(a)   Colnbrook House Immigration Removal Centre, Harmondsworth, Middlesex;

(b)   Harmondsworth Immigration Removal Centre, Harmondsworth, Middlesex;

(c)   Yarl's Wood Immigration Removal Centre, Clapham, Bedfordshire.

PART 2
APPEALS TO THE TRIBUNAL

Notice of appeal

3

(1)   An appellant must start proceedings by providing a notice of appeal to the Tribunal.

(2)   The notice of appeal must—

(a)   set out the grounds of appeal;

(b)   be signed and dated by the appellant or their representative;

(c)   if a notice of appeal is signed by the appellant's representative, the representative must certify in the notice of appeal that it has been completed in accordance with the appellant's instructions;

    (d)   state whether the appellant requires an interpreter at any hearing and if so for which language and dialect;

    (e)   state whether the appellant intends to attend at any hearing; and

    (f)   state whether the appellant will be represented at any hearing.

(3)   The appellant must provide with the notice of appeal—

    (a)   the notice of decision against which the appellant is appealing or if it is not practicable to include the notice of decision, the reasons why it is not practicable;

    (b)   any statement of reasons for that decision;

    (c)   any documents in support of the appellant's case which have not been supplied to the respondent;

    (d)   an application for the Lord Chancellor to issue a certificate of fee satisfaction;

    (e)   any further information or documents required by an applicable practice direction.

(4)   An appellant may, with the permission of the Tribunal, vary the grounds on which they rely in the notice of appeal.

Providing notice of appeal

4

(1)   An appellant may provide a notice of appeal to the Tribunal either—

    (a)   by providing it to the Tribunal; or

    (b)   by providing it to the person having custody of the appellant.

(2)   Where a notice of appeal is provided under paragraph (1)(b), the person having custody of the appellant must—

    (a)   endorse on the notice the date that it is provided to the person having custody of the appellant; and

    (b)   provide it to the Tribunal immediately.

Time limits

5

(1)   The notice of appeal must be provided not later than 2 working days after the day on which the appellant was provided with notice of the decision against which the appeal is brought.

(2)   Where a notice of appeal is provided outside the time limit in paragraph (1), the Tribunal must not extend the time for appealing unless it considers that it is in the interests of justice to do so.

(3)   Subject to paragraph (5), the Tribunal must consider any issue as to—

    (a)   whether a notice of appeal was given outside the time limit in paragraph (1); and

    (b)   whether to extend the time for appealing,

at the hearing fixed for the hearing of the appeal under the Fast Track Rules under rule 8, and rules 9, 12 and 14 apply to the consideration and decision of such an issue as they apply to the consideration and decision of an appeal.

(4)   Where a notice of appeal is provided outside the time limit in paragraph (1) and the respondent notifies the Tribunal that directions have been given for the removal of that person from the United Kingdom on a date within 5 working days of the date on which the notice of appeal was received, the Tribunal must, if reasonably practicable, make any decision on an issue referred to in paragraph (3) before the date and time proposed for the removal, and may do so as a preliminary issue.

(5)   Where the Tribunal decides that the notice of appeal was provided outside the time limit and does not extend the time for appealing, the Tribunal must provide to the parties notice of its decision, including its reasons, not later than 1 working day after

the date on which that decision was made, after which it shall take no further action in relation to the notice of appeal.

(6) In a case to which paragraph (5) applies, the notice of decision may be given orally at a hearing.

Service of notice of appeal etc on respondent

6

When the Tribunal receives a notice of appeal and any further documents or information from the appellant under rule 4, it must immediately provide a copy to the respondent.

Filing of documents by respondent

7

The respondent must, not later than 2 working days after the day on which the Tribunal provides the respondent with the notice of appeal, provide the following documents to the Tribunal—

- (a) the notice of the decision to which the notice of appeal relates, and any other document the respondent provided to the appellant giving reasons for that decision;
- (b) any statement of evidence or application form completed by the appellant;
- (c) any record of an interview with the appellant, in relation to the decision being appealed;
- (d) any other unpublished document which is referred to in a document mentioned in sub-paragraph (a) or relied upon by the respondent; and
- (e) the notice of any other appealable decision made in relation to the appellant.

Fixing date of appeal hearing

8

(1) The Tribunal must fix a date for the hearing of the appeal which is—

- (a) not later than 3 working days after the day on which the respondent provides the documents under rule 7; or
- (b) if the Tribunal is unable to arrange a hearing within that time, as soon as practicable.

(2) The Tribunal must provide notice of the date, time and place of the hearing to every party as soon as practicable and in any event not later than noon on the working day before the hearing.

(3) A practice direction may provide that, as regards—

- (a) all appellants detained at one of the places specified in rule 2(3); or
- (b) a class or category of appellants detained in any of those specified places,

a period of 6 working days shall apply instead of the period of 3 working days provided for in paragraph (1).

Consideration with or without a hearing

9

(1) The Tribunal must conclude the hearing of the appeal on the date fixed under the Fast Track Rules.

(2) Where—

- (a) the appeal—
  - (i) lapses pursuant to section 99 of the 2002 Act;
  - (ii) is treated as abandoned pursuant to section 104(4A) of the 2002 Act; or
  - (iii) is withdrawn by the appellant or treated as withdrawn in accordance with rule 17 of the Principal Rules;

    (b)   the Tribunal postpones or adjourns the hearing under rule 12 or 14(2)(a); or

    (c)   all of the parties to the appeal consent to the Tribunal deciding the appeal without a hearing;

the requirement referred to in paragraph (1) ceases.

Decisions and notice of decisions

10

(1)   Where the Tribunal decides an appeal, it must provide to each party—

    (a)   a notice of decision and the reasons for it;

    (b)   notification of any right of appeal against the decision and the time within which, and the manner in which, such right of appeal may be exercised.

(2)   The Tribunal must provide the notice and the notification—

    (a)   where rule 9(1) applies, not later than 2 working days after the day on which the hearing of the appeal was concluded; or

    (b)   in any other case, not later than 2 working days after the day on which the appeal was decided.

PART 3
APPEALS TO THE UPPER TRIBUNAL

Time limit for making an application for permission to appeal

11

An application for permission to appeal to the Upper Tribunal must be provided to the Tribunal so that it is received no later than 3 working days after the date on which the party making the application was provided with the notice of decision.

PART 4
GENERAL PROVISIONS

Adjournment

12

Unless the Tribunal makes an order under rule 14, the Tribunal may postpone or adjourn the hearing of the appeal only where the Tribunal is satisfied that—

    (a)   the appeal could not justly be decided if the hearing were to be concluded on the date fixed under the Fast Track Rules; and

    (b)   there is an identifiable future date, not more than 10 working days after the date so fixed, upon which the Tribunal can conclude the hearing and justly decide the appeal within the timescales provided for in the Fast Track Rules.

Correction of errors and determinations

13

Where a notice of decision is amended under the Principal Rules, the Tribunal must, not later than one working day after making the amendment, provide an amended version to every party to whom it provided the original.

PART 5
TRANSFER OUT OF FAST TRACK

Transfer out of fast track

14

(1)   Where the Fast Track Rules apply to an appeal or application, the Tribunal must order that the Fast Track Rules shall cease to apply—

    (a)   if all the parties consent; or

(b)   if the Tribunal is satisfied that the case cannot justly be decided within the timescales provided for in the Fast Track Rules.

(2)   When making an order under paragraph (1), the Tribunal may, notwithstanding rule 1(5) or (6) of the Fast Track Rules or the application of the Principal Rules—

(a)   postpone or adjourn any hearing of the appeal or application; and

(b)   give directions in relation to the conduct of the proceedings.

Appendix 5

STATUTORY INSTRUMENTS

Contents

1493

IMMIGRATION (CONTROL OF ENTRY THROUGH REPUBLIC OF IRELAND) ORDER 1972

(SI 1972/1610)

Made: 23 October 1972.

Authority: Immigration Act 1971, s 9(2), (6)

Commencement: 1 January 1973.

1

This Order may be cited as the Immigration (Control of Entry through Republic of Ireland) Order 1972 and shall come into operation on 1st January 1973.

2

(1)   In this Order—

"the Act" means the Immigration Act 1971; and

"visa national" means a person who, in accordance with the immigration rules, is required on entry into the United Kingdom to produce a passport or other document of identity endorsed with a United Kingdom visa and includes a stateless person.

(2)   In this Order any reference to an Article shall be construed as a reference to an Article of this Order and any reference in an Article to a paragraph as a reference to a paragraph of that Article.

(3)   The Interpretation Act 1889 shall apply to the interpretation of this Order as it applies to the interpretation of an Act of Parliament.

3

(1)   This Article applies to—

(a)   any person (other than a citizen of the Republic of Ireland) who arrives in the United Kingdom on an aircraft which began its flight in that Republic if he entered that Republic in the course of a journey to the United Kingdom which began outside the common travel area and was not given leave to land in that Republic in accordance with the law in force there;

(b)   any person (other than a person to whom sub-paragraph (a) of this paragraph applies) who arrives in the United Kingdom on a local journey from the Republic of Ireland if he satisfies any of the following conditions, that is to say:—

(i) he is a visa national who has no valid visa for his entry into the United Kingdom;

(ii) he entered that Republic unlawfully from a place outside the common travel area;

(iii) he entered that Republic from a place in the United Kingdom and Islands after entering there unlawfully, [or, if he had a limited leave to enter or remain there, after the expiry of the leave, provided that in either case] he has not subsequently been given leave to enter or remain in the United Kingdom or any of the Islands; or

(iv) he is a person in respect of whom directions have been given by the Secretary of State for him not to be given entry to the United Kingdom on the ground that his exclusion is conducive to the public good.

(2) In relation only to persons to whom this Article applies, the Republic of Ireland shall be excluded from section 1(3) of the Act (provisions relating to persons travelling on local journeys in the common travel area).

Amendment

Para (1): words in square brackets substituted by SI 1979/730, art 2.

4

(1) Subject to paragraph (2), this Article applies to [any person who does not have the right of abode in the United Kingdom under section 2 of the Act] and is not a citizen of the Republic of Ireland who enters the United Kingdom on a local journey from the Republic of Ireland after having entered that Republic—

(a) on coming from a place outside the common travel area; or

(b) after leaving the United Kingdom whilst having a limited leave to enter or remain there which has since expired.

(2) This Article shall not apply to any person [who arrives in the United Kingdom with leave to enter or remain in the United Kingdom which is in force but which was given to him before his arrival or] who requires leave to enter the United Kingdom by virtue of Article 3 or section 9(4) of the Act.

(3) A person to whom this Article applies by virtue only of paragraph (1)(a) shall, unless he is a visa national who has a visa containing the words "short visit", be subject to the restriction and to the condition set out in paragraph (4).

(4) The restriction and the condition referred to in paragraph (3) are—

(a) the period for which he may remain in the United Kingdom shall not be more than three months from the date on which he entered the United Kingdom; and

[(b) unless he is a national of a state which is a member of the European Economic Community he shall not engage in any occupation for reward; and

(c) unless he is a national of a state which is a member of the European Economic Community other than . . . [, Portugal or Spain] he shall not engage in any employment.]

(5) In relation to a person who is a visa national and has a visa containing the words "short visit" the restriction and the conditions set out in paragraph (6) shall have effect instead of the provisions contained in paragraph (4).

(6) The restriction and the conditions referred to in paragraph (5) are—

(a) the period for which he may remain in the United Kingdom shall not be more than one month from the date on which he entered the United Kingdom;

(b)   he shall not engage in any occupation for reward or any employment; and

(c)   he shall, unless he is under the age of 16 years, be required to register with the police.

(7)   The preceding provisions of this Article shall have effect in relation to a person to whom this Article applies by virtue of sub-paragraph (b) of paragraph (1) (whether or not he is also a person to whom this Article applies by virtue of sub-paragraph (a) thereof) as they have effect in relation to a person to whom this Article applies by virtue only of the said sub-paragraph (a), but as if for the references in paragraphs (4) and (6) to three months and one month respectively there were substituted a reference to seven days.

Amendment

Para (1): words in square brackets substituted by SI 1982/1028, art 2.

Para (2): words from "who arrives in" to "his arrival or" in square brackets inserted by SI 2000/1776, art 2. Date in force: 30 July 2000: see SI 2000/1776, art 1.

Para (4): sub-paras (b), (c) substituted, for sub-para (b) as originally enacted, by SI 1980/1859, art 2.

Para (4): in sub-para (c) word omitted revoked by SI 1987/2092, art 2.

Para (4): in sub-para (c) words ", Portugal or Spain" in square brackets inserted by SI 1985/1854, art 2.

IMMIGRATION (EXEMPTION FROM CONTROL) ORDER 1972

(SI 1972/1613)

Made: 24 October 1972.

Authority: Immigration Act 1971, s 8(2).

Commencement: 1 January 1973.

1

This Order may be cited as the Immigration (Exemption from Control) Order 1972 and shall come into operation on 1st January 1973.

2

(1)   In this Order—

"the Act" means the Immigration Act 1971; and

"consular employee" and "consular officer" have the meanings respectively assigned to them by Article 1 of the Vienna Convention on Consular Relations as set out in Schedule 1 to the Consular Relations Act 1968.

(2)   In this Order any reference to an Article or to the Schedule shall be construed as a reference to an Article of this Order or, as the case may be, to the Schedule thereto and any reference in an Article to a paragraph as a reference to a paragraph of that Article.

(3)   In this Order any reference to an enactment is a reference to it as amended, and includes a reference to it as applied, by or under any other enactment and any reference to an instrument made under or by virtue of any enactment is a reference to any such instrument for the time being in force.

(4)   The Interpretation Act 1889 shall apply to the interpretation of this Order as it applies to the interpretation of an Act of Parliament.

3

(1)   The following persons shall be exempt from any provision of the Act relating to those who are not [British citizens], that is to say:—

   (a)   any consular officer in the service of any of the states specified in the Schedule (being states with which consular conventions have been concluded by Her Majesty);

   (b)   any consular employee in such service as is mentioned in sub-paragraph (a) of this paragraph; and

   (c)   any member of the family of a person exempted under sub-paragraph (a) or (b) of this paragraph forming part of his household.

(2)   In paragraph (1) and in Article 4 any reference to a consular employee shall be construed as a reference to such an employee who is in the full-time service of the state concerned and is not engaged in the United Kingdom in any private occupation for gain.

Amendment

   Para (1): words in square brackets substituted by SI 1982/1649, art 2.

4

The following persons shall be exempt from any provision of the Act relating to those who are not [British citizens] except any provision relating to deportation, that is to say:—

   (a)   unless the Secretary of State otherwise directs, any member of the government of a country or territory outside the United Kingdom and Islands who is visiting the United Kingdom on the business of that government;

   (b)   any person entitled to immunity from legal process with respect to acts performed by him in his official capacity under any Order in Council made under section 3(1) of the Bretton Woods Agreements Act 1945 (which empowers Her Majesty by Order in Council to make provision relating to the immunities and privileges of the governors, executive directors, alternates, officers and employees of the International Monetary Fund and the International Bank for Reconstruction and Development);

   (c)   any person entitled to immunity from legal process with respect to acts performed by him in his official capacity under any Order in Council made under section 3(1) of the International Finance Corporation Act 1955 (which empowers Her Majesty by Order in Council to make provision relating to the immunities and privileges of the governors, directors, alternates, officers and employees of the International Finance Corporation);

   (d)   any person entitled to immunity from legal process with respect to acts performed by him in his official capacity under any Order in Council made under section 3(1) of the International Development Association Act 1960 (which empowers Her Majesty by Order in Council to make provision relating to the immunities and privileges of the governors, directors, alternates, officers and employees of the International Development Association);

   (e)   any person (not being a person to whom section 8(3) of the Act applies) who is the representative or a member of the official staff of the representative of the government of a country to which section 1 of the Diplomatic Immunities (Conferences with Commonwealth Countries and Republic of Ireland) Act 1961 applies (which provides for representatives of certain Commonwealth countries and their staff attending conferences in the United Kingdom to be entitled to diplomatic immunity) so long as he is included in a list compiled and published in accordance with that section;

(f) any person on whom any immunity from jurisdiction is conferred by any Order in Council made under section 12(1) of the Consular Relations Act 1968 (which empowers Her Majesty by Order in Council to confer on certain persons connected with the service of the government of Commonwealth countries or the Republic of Ireland all or any of the immunities and privileges which are conferred by or may be conferred under that Act on persons connected with consular posts);

(g) any person (not being a person to whom section 8(3) of the Act applies) on whom any immunity from suit and legal process is conferred by any Order in Council made under section 1(2), 5(1) or 6(2) of the International Organisations Act 1968 (which empower Her Majesty by Order in Council to confer certain immunities and privileges on persons connected with certain international organisations and international tribunals and on representatives of foreign countries and their staffs attending certain conferences in the United Kingdom) except any such person as is mentioned in section 5(2)(c) to (e) of the said Act of 1968 [or by any Order in Council continuing to have effect by virtue of section 12(5) of the said Act of 1968];

(h) any consular officer (not being an honorary consular officer) in the service of a state other than such a state as is mentioned in the Schedule;

(i) any consular employee in such service as is mentioned in paragraph (h);

[(j) any officer or servant of the Commonwealth Secretariat falling within paragraph 6 of the Schedule to the Commonwealth Secretariat Act 1966 (which confers certain immunities on those members of the staff of the Secretariat who are not entitled to full diplomatic immunity);

[(k) any person to whom any immunity from suit and legal process is conferred by the European Communities (Immunities and Privileges of the North Atlantic Salmon Conservation Organisation) Order 1985 (which confers certain immunities and privileges on the representatives and officers of the North Atlantic Salmon Conservation Organisation);

[(l) any member of the Hong Kong Economic and Trade Office as defined by paragraph 8 of the Schedule to the Hong Kong Economic and Trade Office Act 1996,

[(m)

(i) Any member or servant of the Independent International Commission on Decommissioning ("the Commission") established under an Agreement between the Government of the United Kingdom of Great Britain and Northern Ireland and the Government of the Republic of Ireland concluded on 26th August 1997,

(ii) in sub-paragraph (i) above, "servant" includes any agent of or person carrying out work for or giving advice to the Commission,

(n) any member of the family of a person exempted under any of the preceding paragraphs forming part of his household;]]]]

[(o) any person falling within article 4A below].

Amendment

Words "British citizens" in square brackets substituted by SI 1982/1649, art 2.

In para (g) words "or by any Order in Council continuing to have effect by virtue of section 12(5) of the said Act of 1968" in square brackets inserted by SI 1977/693, art 3(a).

Paras (j), (k) substituted for para (j) as originally enacted, by SI 1977/693, art 3(b).

Paras (k), (l) substituted for existing para (k), by SI 1985/1809, art 4.

Paras (l), (m) substituted for existing para (l), by SI 1997/1402, art 3.

Paras (m), (n) prospectively substituted for existing para (m), by SI 1997/2207, art 3, as from 1 September 1997.

Para (o) inserted by SI 2004/3171, art 2(1), (2). Date in force: this amendment shall come into force on the date on which the Agreement on the Privileges and Immunities of the International Criminal Court done at New York on 9 September 2002 enters into force in respect of the United Kingdom: see SI 2004/3171, art 1.

[4A
(1)   In relation to the court ("the ICC") established by the Rome Statute of the International Criminal Court done at Rome on 17th July 1998 ("the Rome Statute");
  (a)   except in so far as in any particular case the exemption given by this article is waived by the State or intergovernmental organisation they represent,
    (i)   any representative of a State party to the Rome Statute attending meetings of the Assembly or one of its subsidiary organs,
    (ii)   any representative of another State attending meetings of the Assembly or one of its subsidiary organs as an observer, and
    (iii) any representative of a State or of an intergovernmental organisation invited to a meeting of the Assembly or one of its subsidiary organs,
  while exercising their official functions and during their journey to and from the place of the meeting;
  (b)   except in so far as in any particular case the exemption given by this article is waived by the State they represent, any representative of a State participating in the proceedings of the ICC while exercising their official functions and during their journeys to and from the place of the proceedings of the ICC;
  (c)   except in so far as in any particular case the exemption given by this article is waived by an absolute majority of the judges, any judge and the Prosecutor, when engaged on or with respect to the business of the ICC;
  (d)   except in so far as in any particular case the exemption given by this article is waived by the Prosecutor, any Deputy Prosecutor, when engaged on or with respect to the business of the ICC;
  (e)   except in so far as in any particular case the exemption given by this article is waived by the Presidency, the Registrar, when engaged on or with respect to the business of the ICC;
  (f)   except in so far as in any particular case the exemption given by this article is waived by the Registrar, the Deputy Registrar, so far as necessary for the performance of his functions;
  (g)   except in so far as in any particular case the exemption given by this article is waived by the Prosecutor, any member of the staff of the office of the Prosecutor, so far as necessary for the performance of their functions;
  (h)   except in so far as in any particular case the exemption given by this article is waived by the Registrar, any member of the staff of the Registry, so far as necessary for the performance of their functions;
  (i)   except in so far as in any particular case the exemption given by this article is waived by the Presidency and subject to the production of the certificate under seal of the Registrar provided to counsel and persons assisting defence counsel upon appointment, counsel and any person assisting defence counsel, so far as necessary for the performance of their functions;
  (j)   except in so far as in any particular case the exemption given by this article is waived by the Presidency and subject to the production of a

document provided by the ICC certifying that the person's appearance before the ICC is required by the ICC and specifying a time period during which such appearance is necessary, any witness, to the extent necessary for their appearance before the ICC for the purposes of giving evidence;

(k) except in so far as in any particular case the exemption given by this article is waived by the Presidency and subject to the production of a document provided by the ICC certifying the participation of the person in the proceedings of the ICC and specifying a time period for that participation, any victim, to the extent necessary for their appearance before the ICC;

(l) except in so far as in any particular case the exemption given by this article is waived by the head of the organ of the ICC appointing the person and subject to the production of a document provided by the ICC certifying that the person is performing functions for the ICC and specifying a time period during which those functions will last, any expert performing functions for the ICC, to the extent necessary for the exercise of those functions;

(m) any member of the family of a person exempted under any of paragraphs (c) to (h) above forming part of their household.

(2) In paragraph (1) above:

"the Assembly" means the assembly of State parties to the Rome Statute;

"the Presidency" means the organ of the ICC composed of the president and the first and second vice-presidents of the ICC elected in accordance with article 38, paragraph 1, of the Rome Statute;

"the Prosecutor" and "Deputy Prosecutors" mean the prosecutor and deputy prosecutors respectively elected by the assembly of State parties to the Rome Statute in accordance with article 42, paragraph 4, of the Rome Statute;

"the Registrar" and "the Deputy Registrar" mean the registrar and deputy registrar respectively elected by the ICC in accordance with article 43, paragraph 4, of the Rome Statute.]

Amendment

Inserted by SI 2004/3171, art 2(1), (3). Date in force: this amendment shall come into force on the date on which the Agreement on the Privileges and Immunities of the International Criminal Court done at New York on 9 September 2002 enters into force in respect of the United Kingdom: see SI 2004/3171, art 1.

5

(1) Subject to the provisions of this Article the following persons who are not [British citizens] shall, on arrival in the United Kingdom, be exempt from the provisions of section 3(1)(a) of the Act (which requires persons who are not [British citizens] to obtain leave to enter the United Kingdom), that is to say—

(a) any citizen of the United Kingdom and Colonies who holds a passport issued to him in the United Kingdom and Islands and expressed to be a British Visitor's Passport;

(b) any Commonwealth citizen who is included in a passport issued in the United Kingdom by the Government of the United Kingdom or in one of the Islands by the Lieutenant-Governor thereof which is expressed to be a Collective Passport;

(c) any Commonwealth citizen or citizen of the Republic of Ireland returning to the United Kingdom from an excursion to France or Belgium [or the Netherlands] who holds a valid document of identity issued in accordance with arrangements approved by the United Kingdom Government and in a form authorised by the Secretary of State and enabling him to travel on such an excursion without a passport;

(d)   any Commonwealth citizen who holds a British seaman's card or any citizen of the Republic of Ireland if (in either case) he was engaged as a member of the crew of a ship in a place within the common travel area and, on arrival in the United Kingdom, is, or is to be, discharged from his engagement;

(e)   any person who, having left the United Kingdom after having been given a limited leave to enter, returns to the United Kingdom within the period for which he had leave as a member of the crew of an aircraft under an engagement requiring him to leave on that or another aircraft as a member of its crew within a period exceeding seven days.

(2)   Paragraph (1) shall not apply so as to confer any exemption on any person against whom there is a deportation order in force or who has previously entered the United Kingdom unlawfully and has not subsequently been given leave to enter or remain in the United Kingdom and sub-paragraphs (d) and (e) of that paragraph shall not apply to a person who is required by an immigration officer to submit to examination in accordance with Schedule 2 to the Act.

(3)   In this Article any reference to a Commonwealth citizen shall be construed as including a reference to a British protected person and in paragraph (1)(d) "British seaman's card" means a valid card issued under any regulations in force under section 70 of the Merchant Shipping Act 1970 or any card having effect by virtue of the said regulations as a card so issued and "holder of a British seaman's card" has the same meaning as in the said regulations.

Amendment

Para (1): first and second words in square brackets substituted by SI 1982/1649, art 2; final words in square brackets inserted by SI 1975/617, art 2.

[6

(1)   For the purposes of section 1(1) of the British Nationality Act 1981 (which relates to acquisition of British citizenship by birth in the United Kingdom), a person to whom a child is born in the United Kingdom on or after 1st January 1983 is to be regarded (notwithstanding the preceding provisions of this Order) as settled in the United Kingdom at the time of the birth if—

(a)   he would fall to be so regarded but for his being at that time entitled to an exemption by virtue of this Order; and

(b)   immediately before he became entitled to that exemption he was settled in the United Kingdom; and

(c)   he was ordinarily resident in the United Kingdom from the time when he became entitled to that exemption to the time of the birth;

but this Article shall not apply if at the time of the birth the child's father or mother is a person on whom any immunity from jurisdiction is conferred by or under the Diplomatic Privileges Act 1964.

(2)   Expressions used in this Article shall be construed in accordance with section 50 of the British Nationality Act 1981.]

Amendment

Inserted by SI 1982/1649, art 3.

SCHEDULE
STATES WITH WHICH CONSULAR CONVENTIONS HAVE BEEN CONCLUDED BY HER MAJESTY

Articles 3, 4

Austria

Belgium

Bulgaria

[Czechoslovakia]
Denmark
France
[German Democratic Republic]
Greece
Federal Republic of Germany
Hungary
Italy
Japan
Mexico
[Mongolia]
Norway
Poland
Roumania
Sweden
Spain
Union of Soviet Socialist Republics
United States of America
Yugoslavia

Amendment
Words in square brackets inserted by SI 1977/693, art 4.

IMMIGRATION (HOTEL RECORDS) ORDER 1972

(SI 1972/1689)

Made: 7 November 1972.
Authority: Immigration Act 1971, s 4(4).
Commencement: 1 January 1973.

1 Citation and commencement

This Order may be cited as the Immigration (Hotel Records) Order 1972 and shall come into operation on 1st January 1973.

2 Interpretation and transitional provisions

(1) In this Order the following expressions have the meanings hereby respectively assigned to them, that is to say:—

"alien" has the same meaning as in the [British Nationality Act 1981];

"certificate of registration" means a certificate issued, or treated as issued, in pursuance of regulations from time to time in force under section 4(3) of the Immigration Act 1971;

"keeper", in relation to any premises, includes any person who for reward receives any other person to stay in the premises, whether on his own behalf or as manager or otherwise on behalf of any other person;

"nationality" includes the status of a stateless alien;

"stay" means lodge or sleep, for one night or more, in accommodation provided for reward.

(2) The Interpretation Act 1889 shall apply to the interpretation of this Order as it applies to the interpretation of an Act of Parliament.

(3) Any information required by this Order to be given by or to any person may be given by or to any other person acting on his behalf.

(4)   Anything done under, or for the purposes of, Article 19 of the Aliens Order 1953, as amended, shall have effect as if done under, or for the purposes of, this Order and, in particular, any information given or record maintained under or for the purposes of the said Article 19 shall be treated as if it had been given or maintained under, or for the purposes of, this Order.

Amendment

Para (1): in definition "alien" words in square brackets substituted by SI 1982/1025, art 2.

3 Application of Order

This Order shall apply in the case of any hotel or other premises, whether furnished or unfurnished, where lodging or sleeping accommodation is provided for reward, not being premises certified by the chief officer of police of the area in which they are situate to be occupied for the purposes of a school, hospital, club or other institution or association.

4 Provision of information by visitors

(1)   Every person of or over the age of 16 years who stays at any premises to which this Order applies shall, on arriving at the premises, inform the keeper of the premises of his full name and nationality.

(2)   Every such person who is an alien shall also—

(a)   on arriving at the premises, inform the keeper of the premises of the number and place of issue of his passport, certificate of registration or other document establishing his identity and nationality; and

(b)   on or before his departure from the premises, inform the keeper of the premises of his next destination and, if it is known to him, his full address there.

5 Records to be maintained by keeper of premises

The keeper of any premises to which this Order applies shall—

(a)   require all persons of or over the age of 16 years who stay at the premises to comply with their obligations under the foregoing Article; and

(b)   keep for a period of at least 12 months a record in writing of the date of arrival of every such person and of all information given to him by any such person in pursuance of the foregoing Article;

and every record shall at all times be open to inspection by any constable or by any person authorised by the Secretary of State.

IMMIGRATION (REGISTRATION WITH POLICE) REGULATIONS 1972

(SI 1972/1758)

Made: 14 November 1972.

Authority: Immigration Act 1971, s 4(3).

Commencement: 1 January 1973.

1 Citation and commencement

These Regulations may be cited as the Immigration (Registration with Police) Regulations 1972 and shall come into operation on 1st January 1973.

2 Interpretation and transitional provisions

(1)   In these Regulations, except where the context otherwise requires, the following expressions have the meanings hereby respectively assigned to them, that is to say:—

"the Act" means the Immigration Act 1971;

"alien" has the same meaning as in the [British Nationality Act 1981];

"certificate of registration" means a certificate issued in pursuance of Regulation 10(1) to the alien concerned;

"local register" means a register kept in pursuance of Regulation 4;

"nationality" includes the status of a stateless alien;

"registration officer" and "appropriate registration officer" have the meanings assigned thereto by Regulation 4;

"a residence" means a person's private dwelling-house or other premises in which he is ordinarily resident but does not include any premises in which he is not ordinarily resident.

(2) In these Regulations any reference to a Regulation is a reference to a Regulation contained therein and any reference in a Regulation to a paragraph is a reference to a paragraph of that Regulation.

(3) Where an alien has failed to comply with any requirement made by a provision of these Regulations within a period specified in that provision he shall, without prejudice to any liability in respect of that failure under section 26(1)(f) of the Act, continue to be subject to that requirement notwithstanding the expiry of that period.

(4) The Interpretation Act 1889 shall apply to the interpretation of these Regulations as it applies to the interpretation of an Act of Parliament.

(5) Anything done, or having effect as if done, under or for the purposes of, any provision of the Aliens Order 1953, as amended, corresponding to a provision of these Regulations shall have effect as if done under, or for the purposes of, that corresponding provision and, in particular—

(a)   any register kept under Article 13 of the said Order shall be treated as part of the local register kept under Regulation 4(2);

(b)   particulars furnished under Article 14(2) of the said Order shall be treated as furnished under Regulation 5, and

(c)   a certificate of registration supplied in pursuance of Article 13(3)(b) of the said Order shall be treated as a certificate of registration issued in pursuance of Regulation 10(1).

Amendment

Para (1): in definition "alien" words in square brackets substituted by SI 1982/1024, reg 2.

3 Application of Regulations

These Regulations shall apply in the case of an alien who has a limited leave to enter or remain in the United Kingdom which is for the time being subject to a condition requiring him to register with the police and in the case of an alien who, by virtue of section 34 of the Act or paragraph 1 of Schedule 4 thereto, is treated as having such a limited leave.

4 Registration officers etc

(1) For the purposes of these Regulations the chief officer of police for each police area shall be the registration officer for that area, and the police area shall be the registration area; and any reference to the appropriate registration officer is a reference—

(a)   in the case of an alien who has a residence in the United Kingdom, to the registration officer for the area in which that residence is situated;

(b)   in any other case, to the registration officer for the area in which, for the time being, he happens to be.

(2) Every registration officer shall keep for his registration district a local register of aliens containing the particulars specified in the Schedule hereto:

Provided that if a registration officer is not satisfied as to the nationality of an alien he may describe that alien in the local register as being of uncertain nationality or may describe him as having such nationality as appears to that officer to be the probable nationality of the alien.

(3) Anything required or authorised by these Regulations to be done by or to a registration officer may be done by or to any constable or other person who is authorised by that officer to act for the purposes of these Regulations.

5 Duty to register etc

(1) Within 7 days of these Regulations becoming applicable to him, an alien shall, subject to Regulation 6, attend at the office of the appropriate registration officer and furnish to that officer such information, documents and other particulars (including a recent photograph) relating to him as are required by that officer for the purposes of the local register kept by him or the issue of a certificate of registration to the alien.

(2) Without prejudice to the generality of paragraph (1) an alien attending as aforesaid shall either—

(a)   produce to the appropriate registration officer a passport furnished with a photograph of himself or some other document satisfactorily establishing his identity and nationality; or

(b)   give to that officer a satisfactory explanation of the circumstances which prevent him from producing such a passport or document.

6 Exemption from registration in certain cases

(1) An alien shall not be required to attend and furnish particulars under Regulation 5 if—

(a)   immediately before these Regulations becoming applicable to him, he was ordinarily resident in the United Kingdom, and

(b)   he had previously, during that period of ordinary residence, attended and furnished particulars under Regulation 5.

(2) Without prejudice to paragraph (1) or the provisions of Regulation 2(5), an alien shall not be required to attend and furnish particulars under Regulation 5 if—

(a)   on the coming into operation of these Regulations they become applicable to him,

(b)   immediately before their coming into operation he was resident in the United Kingdom, and

(c)   he had previously, during that period of residence, attended and furnished particulars under Article 14(2) of the Aliens Order 1953, as amended.

7 Duty to notify changes of residence or address etc

(1) Every alien to whom these Regulations apply who has furnished particulars under Regulation 5 shall be under a duty to notify any changes therein in accordance with this Regulation.

(2) Such an alien who for the time being has a residence in the United Kingdom shall, if he adopts a new residence within the United Kingdom, report his arrival at his new residence to the appropriate registration officer before the expiration of the period of 7 days beginning with the day of his arrival.

(3) Such an alien who for the time being has a residence in the United Kingdom, if he is absent from his residence for a continuous period exceeding 2 months (without adopting a new residence)—

(a)   shall forthwith notify the appropriate registration officer of his address for the time being (whether within or outside the United Kingdom);

(b)   subject to paragraph (5), shall notify the appropriate registration officer of any subsequent change of address within the United Kingdom before the expiration of 8 days beginning with the day of his arrival at the new address; and

(c)   shall, on returning to his residence, notify the appropriate registration officer of his return (whether or not he has throughout the period of absence remained in the United Kingdom).

(4)   Subject to paragraphs (5) and (6), such an alien who for the time being has not a residence in the United Kingdom shall, if he moves from one address to another (in the same or a different registration district), notify the appropriate registration officer of his arrival thereat before the expiration of 8 days beginning with the day of his arrival.

(5)   Such an alien need not, under paragraph (3)(b) or (4), notify the appropriate registration officer of his address unless he remains or intends to remain at that address for a longer period than 7 days beginning with the day of his arrival thereat.

(6)   If such an alien who for the time being has not a residence in the United Kingdom supplies to a registration officer the name and address of a referee, being a person resident within the United Kingdom who is willing to act, and in the opinion of that officer is a suitable person to act, as a referee under this paragraph, the officer shall include the referee's name and address among the entries relating to the alien in the local register kept by him; and in such case, the following provisions shall apply in substitution for those of paragraph (4), that is to say:—

(a)   the alien shall keep the referee informed as to his address from time to time and shall notify the registration officer of any change in the referee's address; and

(b)   the referee shall, if so required by the registration officer, furnish to that officer any information in his possession as to the alien which is required by that officer for the purposes of his duties under these Regulations.

8 Duty to notify other changes in particulars etc

Every alien to whom these Regulations apply who has furnished particulars under Regulation 5—

(a)   shall notify the appropriate registration officer of any change in his case in the particulars specified as items 1, 3, 5, 6, 7 and 14 in the Schedule hereto, before the expiration of 8 days beginning with that on which the change, or the event occasioning the change, occurs; and

(b)   if so required by the appropriate registration officer, shall furnish to that officer by such date as he may specify such information, documents and other particulars (including, where so required, a recent photograph) relating to him which are required by that officer for the purposes of his duties under these Regulations.

9 Provisions supplemental to Regulations 5, 7 and 8

(1)   An alien required under Regulation 5(1) or 8(b) to furnish a photograph of himself shall furnish 2 copies of the same photograph; and, if he fails to furnish such copies, the registration officer may cause him to be photographed.

(2)   An alien required under Regulation 7 or 8(a) to notify the appropriate registration officer of any change in his residence or address or of any change in his case in the particulars mentioned in Rule 8(a) shall either attend for the purpose at the office of the registration officer or send written notice of the change to that officer by post so, however, that where written notice is given the alien shall also send to the registration officer his certificate of registration.

(3)   An alien required under Regulation 8(b) to furnish information, documents or other particulars to the appropriate registration officer (whether or not in connection with a change of which written notice has been given in pursuance of paragraph (2)) shall attend for the purpose at the office of the registration officer if that officer so requires.

[10 Issue of registration certificates

(1)   Every registration officer shall issue certificates of registration to aliens of whom particulars are entered in the local register kept by him.

(2)   A certificate of registration shall be independent of, and shall not be included in, any other document.

(3)   An alien to whom a certificate of registration is issued shall pay to the registration officer concerned a fee of [£34] except where the requirement to register is a condition of leave granted to an alien after an absence from the United Kingdom of a period of less than one year immediately following an earlier period of leave which was subject to the same condition.]

Amendment

Substituted by SI 1990/400, reg 2.

Para (3): sum in square brackets substituted by SI 1995/2928, reg 2.

11 Production of registration certificates

(1)   On the making of any alteration or addition to the local register, the registration officer may require the alien concerned to produce his certificate of registration in order that any necessary amendment may be made thereto.

(2)   Any immigration officer or constable may—

    (a)   require an alien to whom these Regulations apply, forthwith, to either produce a certificate of registration or give to the officer or constable a satisfactory reason for his failure to produce it;

    (b)   where the alien fails to produce a certificate of registration in pursuance of such a requirement (whether or not he gives a satisfactory reason for his failure), require him, within the following 48 hours, to produce a certificate of registration at a police station specified by the officer or constable,

so, however, that a requirement under sub-paragraph (b) to produce a certificate of registration at a police station shall have effect in substitution for the requirement under sub-paragraph (a) so as to cause that previous requirement to cease to have effect.

SCHEDULE

PARTICULARS TO BE ENTERED IN LOCAL REGISTER

1

Name in full.

2

Sex.

3

Matrimonial status (married or single).

4

    (a)   Date of birth.

    (b)   Country of birth.

5

    (a)   Present nationality.

    (b)   How and when acquired.

    (c)   Previous nationality (if any).

6

Particulars of passport or other document establishing nationality.

7

Business, profession or occupation.

8

Residence in the United Kingdom (or address if no residence).

9

Name and address of referee (if any) supplied under Regulation 7(b).

10

Last residence outside the United Kingdom.

11

(a)   Date of arrival in the United Kingdom.
(b)   Place of arrival in the United Kingdom.
(c)   Mode of arrival in the United Kingdom.

12

Duration of limited leave and conditions attached thereto.

13

Restrictions or conditions, if any, applicable by virtue of section 9(2) of the Act.

14

(a)   If employed in the United Kingdom—
    (i)   name and address of employer;
    (ii)   address at which employed, if different.
(b)   If engaged in business or profession in the United Kingdom—
    (i)   name under which business or profession is carried on;
    (ii)   address at which business or profession is carried on.

15

Signature (or fingerprints if unable to write in the characters of the English language).

16

Photograph.

SOCIAL SECURITY ([CARER'S ALLOWANCE]) REGULATIONS 1976

(SI 1976/409)

Made: 1 March 1976.

Authority: Social Security Contributions and Benefits Act 1992, ss 70, 90, 113(1), (2); National Insurance Act 1965, s 37(6).

Commencement: 12 April 1976.

Amendment

Title: words "Carer's Allowance" in square brackets substituted by virtue of SI 2002/2497, reg 3, Sch 2, paras 1, 2.

Date in force: 1 April 2003: see SI 2002/2497, reg 1(b).

PART I
GENERAL

1 Citation and commencement

These regulations may be cited as the Social Security (Invalid Care Allowance) Regulations 1976 and shall come into operation on 12th April 1976.

2 Interpretation

[(1) In these Regulations, "the Contributions and Benefits Act" means the Social Security Contributions and Benefits Act 1992.]

(2) Any reference in these regulation to any provision made by or contained in any enactment or instrument shall, except in so far as the context otherwise requires, be construed as a reference to that provision as amended or extended by any enactment or instrument and as including a reference to any provision which may re-enact or replace it, with or without modification.

(3) The rules for the construction of Acts of Parliament contained in the Interpretation Act 1889 shall apply for the purposes of the interpretation of these regulations as they apply for the purposes of the interpretation of an Act of Parliament.

Amendment
   Para (1): substituted by SI 1996/2744, reg 2(2).

[2A Disapplication of section 1(1A) of the Administration Act

Section 1(1A) of the Administration Act (requirement to state national insurance number) shall not apply—

   (a)   . . .
   (b)   to any claim for [carer's allowance] made or treated as made before 9th February 1998;
   (c)   to an adult dependant in respect of whom a claim for an increase of [carer's allowance] is made or treated as made before 5th October 1998;
   [(d)   to an adult dependant who—
         (i)   is a person in respect of whom a claim for an increase of carer's allowance is made;
         (ii)   is subject to immigration control within the meaning of section 115(9)(a) of the Immigration and Asylum Act 1999; and
         (iii) has not previously been allocated a national insurance number].]

Amendment
   Inserted by SI 1997/2676, reg 11.
   Para (a) revoked by SI 2003/937, reg 2(1).
   Date in force: 6 April 2003: see SI 2003/937, reg 1(a).
   In paras (b), (c) words "carer's allowance" in square brackets substituted by SI 2002/2497, reg 3, Sch 2, paras 1, 2.
   Date in force: 1 April 2003: see SI 2002/2497, reg 1(b).
   Para (d) inserted by SI 2009/471, reg 2.
   Date in force: 6 April 2009: see SI 2009/471, reg 1.

SOCIAL SECURITY (WIDOW'S BENEFIT AND RETIREMENT PENSIONS) REGULATIONS 1979

(SI 1979/642)

Made: 11 June 1979.

Authority: Social Security Contributions and Benefits Act 1992, ss 49(5), 54(1), (2), 60, 78, 79, 121, Sch 5, para 2(2), 3; Social Security Administration Act 1992, s 73.

Commencement: 10 July 1979.

10 Conditions for entitlement to a Category D retirement pension

The conditions for entitlement to a Category D retirement pension shall be that the person concerned—

[(a)   was resident in Great Britain for a period of at least 10 years in any continuous period of 20 years which included the day before that on which he attained the age of 80 or any day thereafter; and]

(b)   was ordinarily resident in Great Britain either—

(i)   on the day he attained the age of 80; or

(ii)   if he was not so ordinarily resident on that day and the date of his claim for the pension was later than that day, on the date of his claim, so however that where a person satisfies this condition under this head he shall be deemed to have satisfied it on the date that he became so ordinarily resident.

Amendment

Para (a): substituted by SI 1984/1704, reg 2.

IMMIGRATION (PORTS OF ENTRY) ORDER 1987

(SI 1987/177)

Made: 10 February 1987.

Authority: Immigration Act 1971, s 33(3).

Commencement: 1 March 1987.

1

(1)   This Order may be cited as the Immigration (Ports of Entry) Order 1987 and shall come into force on 1st March 1987.

(2)   . . .

Amendment

Para (2): revokes SI 1972/1668, SI 1975/2221 and SI 1979/1635.

2

The ports specified in the Schedule to this Order shall be ports of entry for the purposes of the Immigration Act 1971.

SCHEDULE
PORTS OF ENTRY

Article 2

Seaports and Hoverports

Dover	Plymouth
Felixstowe	Portsmouth
Folkestone	Ramsgate
Harwich	Sheerness

Hull	Southampton
London	Tyne
Newhaven	

Airports

Aberdeen	Leeds/Bradford
Belfast	Liverpool
Birmingham	Luton
Bournemouth (Hurn)	Manchester
Bristol	Newcastle
Cardiff (Wales)	Norwich
East Midlands	Prestwick
Edinburgh	Southampton
Gatwick–London	Southend
Glasgow	Stansted–London
Heathrow–London	Tees-side

INCOME SUPPORT (GENERAL) REGULATIONS

(SI 1987/1967)

Made: 20 November 1987.

Authority: Social Security Act 1975, ss 114, 166(1)–(3A); Social Security Act 1986, ss 20(1), (3)(d), (4), (9), (11), (12), 22(1), (2), (4), (5)–(9), 23(1), (3), (5), 51(1)(n), 84(1).

Commencement: 11 April 1988.

[21AA Special cases: supplemental—persons from abroad

(1) "Person from abroad" means, subject to the following provisions of this regulation, a claimant who is not habitually resident in the United Kingdom, the Channel Islands, the Isle of Man or the Republic of Ireland.

(2) No claimant shall be treated as habitually resident in the United Kingdom, the Channel Islands, the Isle of Man or the Republic of Ireland unless he has a right to reside in (as the case may be) the United Kingdom, the Channel Islands, the Isle of Man or the Republic of Ireland other than a right to reside which falls within paragraph (3).

(3) A right to reside falls within this paragraph if it is one which exists by virtue of, or in accordance with, one or more of the following—

(a) regulation 13 of the Immigration (European Economic Area) Regulations 2006;

(b) regulation 14 of those Regulations, but only in a case where the right exists under that regulation because the claimant is—

(i) a jobseeker for the purpose of the definition of "qualified person" in regulation 6(1) of those Regulations, or

(ii) a family member (within the meaning of regulation 7 of those Regulations) of such a jobseeker;

[(bb) regulation 15A(1) of those Regulations, but only in a case where the right exists under that regulation because the claimant satisfies the criteria in regulation 15A(4A) of those Regulations;]

(c) Article 6 of Council Directive No 2004/38/EC; . . .

(d) Article 39 of the Treaty establishing the European Community (in a case where the claimant is a person seeking work in the United Kingdom, the Channel Islands, the Isle of Man or the Republic of Ireland)[; or

(e) Article 20 of the Treaty on the Functioning of the European Union (in a case where the right to reside arises because a British citizen would otherwise be deprived of the genuine enjoyment of the substance of their rights as a European Union citizen)].

(4) A claimant is not a person from abroad if he is—

[(za) a qualified person for the purposes of regulation 6 of the Immigration (European Economic Area) Regulations 2006 as a worker or a self-employed person;

(zb) a family member of a person referred to in sub-paragraph (za) within the meaning of regulation 7(1)(a), (b) or (c) of those Regulations;

(zc) a person who has a right to reside permanently in the United Kingdom by virtue of regulation 15(1)(c), (d) or (e) of those Regulations;]

(g) a refugee within the definition in Article 1 of the Convention relating to the Status of Refugees done at Geneva on 28th July 1951, as extended by Article 1(2) of the Protocol relating to the Status of Refugees done at New York on 31st January 1967;

[(h) a person who has been granted leave or who is deemed to have been granted leave outside the rules made under section 3(2) of the Immigration Act 1971 where that leave is—

(i) discretionary leave to enter or remain in the United Kingdom;

(ii) leave to remain under the Destitution Domestic Violence concession; or

(iii) leave deemed to have been granted by virtue of regulation 3 of the Displaced Persons (Temporary Protection) Regulations 2005;]

(hh) a person who has humanitarian protection granted under those rules;] [or]

(i) a person who is not a person subject to immigration control within the meaning of section 115(9) of the Immigration and Asylum Act and who is in the United Kingdom as a result of his deportation, expulsion or other removal by compulsion of law from another country to the United Kingdom; . . .

(j) . . .

[(k) . . .]]

Amendment

Inserted by SI 2006/1026, reg 6(1), (3). Date in force: 30 April 2006: see SI 2006/1026, reg 1.

Para (3): sub-para (bb) inserted, word omitted from sub-para (c) revoked, and sub-para (e) and word "; or" immediately preceding it inserted by SI 2012/2587, reg 2. Date in force: 8 November 2012: see SI 2012/2587, reg 1.

Para (4): sub-paras (za)–(zc) substituted, for original sub-paras (a)–(f), by SI 2014/902, reg 2. Date in force: 31 May 2014: see SI 2014/902, reg 1.

Para (4): sub-paras (h), (hh) substituted, for sub-para (h) as originally enacted, by SI 2006/2528, reg 2. Date in force: 9 October 2006: see SI 2006/2528, reg 1.

Para (4): sub-para (h) further substituted and in sub-para (hh) word "or" in square brackets inserted, by SI 2013/2536, reg 4(1), (5)(a), (b). Date in force: 29 October 2013: see SI 2013/2536, reg 1(1).

Para (4): in sub-para (i) word omitted revoked by SI 2009/362, reg 2(1), (2). Date in force: 18 March 2009: see SI 2009/362, reg 1(2).

Para (4): sub-para (j), and sub-para (k) (as inserted by SI 2009/362, reg 2(1), (3)) revoked by SI 2013/2536, reg 4(1), (5)(c). Date in force: 29 October 2013: see SI 2013/2536, reg 1(1).

SOCIAL SECURITY (ATTENDANCE ALLOWANCE) REGULATIONS 1991

(SI 1991/2740)

Made: 5 December 1991.

Authority: Social Security Act 1975, ss 35(1), (2)(b), (2A), (4A), (6), 85(1)(b), 166(2), (3), Sch 20.

Commencement: 6 April 1992.

1 Citation, commencement and interpretation

(1) These Regulations may be cited as the Social Security (Attendance Allowance) Regulations 1991 and shall come into force on 6th April 1992.

(2) In these Regulations—

"the Act" means the Social Security Act 1975;

. . .

"the NHS Act of 1978" means the National Health Service (Scotland) Act 1978;

. . .

["the NHS Act of 2006" means the National Health Service Act 2006;

"the NHS (Wales) Act of 2006" means the National Health Service (Wales) Act 2006;]

"terminally ill" shall be construed in accordance with section 35(2C) of the Act.

(3) Unless the context otherwise requires, any reference in these Regulations to a numbered regulation is a reference to the regulation bearing that number in these Regulations and any reference in a regulation to a numbered paragraph is a reference to the paragraph of that regulation bearing that number.

Amendment

Para (2): definitions "the NHS Act of 1977" and "the NHS Act of 1990" (omitted) revoked by SI 2013/389, reg 3(1), (2)(a). Date in force: 8 April 2013: see SI 2013/389, reg 1(2).

Para (2): definitions "the NHS Act of 2006" and "the NHS (Wales) Act of 2006" inserted by SI 2013/389, reg 3(1), (2)(b). Date in force: 8 April 2013: see SI 2013/389, reg 1(2).

2 Conditions as to residence and presence in Great Britain

(1) Subject to the following provisions of this regulation [and regulations 2A and 2B], the prescribed conditions for the purposes of section 35(1) of the Act as to residence and presence in Great Britain in relation to any person on any day shall be that—

    (a)   on that day—

        (i)   he is [habitually] resident in [the United Kingdom, the Republic of Ireland, the Isle of Man or the Channel Islands], and

       [(ib)   he is not a person subject to immigration control within the meaning of section 115(9) of the Immigration and Asylum Act 1999 or section 115 of that Act does not apply to him for the purposes of entitlement to attendance allowance by virtue of regulation 2 of the Social Security (Immigration and Asylum) Consequential Amendments Regulations 2000, and]

       (ii)   he is present in Great Britain, and

(iii)   he has been present in Great Britain for a period of, or for periods amounting in the aggregate to, not less than [104] weeks in the [156] weeks immediately preceding that day; . . .

(b)   . . ..

[(1A)   . . .]

(2)   For the purposes of paragraph (1)(a)(ii) and (iii), notwithstanding that on any day a person is absent from Great Britain, he shall be treated as though he were present in Great Britain if his absence is by reason only of the fact that on that day—

(a)   he is abroad in his capacity as—

(i)   a serving member of the forces,

(ii)   an airman or mariner within the meaning of regulations [111 and 115] respectively of the Social Security (Contributions) Regulations [2001],

and for the purpose of this provision, the expression "serving members of the forces" has the same meaning as in regulation 1(2) of the Regulations of [2001]; or

(b)   he is in employment prescribed for the purposes of section 132 of the Act in connection with continental shelf operations; or

(c)   he is living with a person mentioned in sub-paragraph (a)(i) and is the spouse, [civil partner,] son, daughter, step-son, step-daughter, father, father-in-law, step-father, mother, mother-in-law or step-mother of that person; or

[(d)   he is temporarily absent from Great Britain and that absence has not lasted for a continuous period exceeding 13 weeks.]

(e)   . . .

(3)   Where a person is terminally ill and makes a claim for attendance allowance expressly on the ground that he is such a person, paragraph (1) shall apply to him as if head (iii) of sub-paragraph (a) was omitted.

[(3A)   A person shall be treated as habitually resident in Great Britain for the purpose of paragraph (1)(a)(i) where—

(a)   he is resident outside Great Britain in his capacity as a serving member of the forces and for this purpose "serving member of the forces" has the meaning given in regulation 1(2) of the Social Security (Contributions) Regulations 2001; or

(b)   he is living with a person mentioned in paragraph (a) and is the spouse, civil partner, son, daughter, step-son, step-daughter, father, father-in-law, step-father, mother, mother-in-law or step-mother of that person.

(3B)   Where a person is temporarily absent from Great Britain, he is treated as present in Great Britain for the purposes of paragraph (1)(a)(ii) and (iii) for the first 26 weeks of that absence, where—

(a)   this absence is solely in connection with arrangements made for the medical treatment of him for a disease or bodily or mental disablement which commenced before he left Great Britain; and

(b)   the arrangements referred to in sub-paragraph (a) relate to medical treatment—

(i)   outside Great Britain,

(ii)   during the period whilst he is temporarily absent from Great Britain, and

(iii)   by, or under the supervision of, a person appropriately qualified to carry out that treatment, and

"medical treatment" means medical, surgical or rehabilitative treatment (including any course or diet or regimen), and references to a person receiving or submitting to medical treatment are to be construed accordingly.]

(3C) For the purpose of paragraph (2)(d) and (3B) a person is "temporarily absent" if, at the beginning of the period of absence, that absence is unlikely to exceed 52 weeks.]

(4) . . .

Amendment

Para (1): words in first pair of square brackets inserted, words in square brackets in sub-para (a)(i) substituted, and numbers in square brackets in sub-para (a)(iii) substituted, by SI 2013/389, reg 3(1), (3)(a)–(c). Date in force: 8 April 2013: see SI 2013/389, reg 1(2).

Para (1): sub-para (a)(ib) substituted by SI 2000/636, reg 10(1), (2). Date in force: 3 April 2000: see SI 2000/636, reg 1(2).

Para (1): sub-para (b) and word omitted immediately preceding it revoked by SI 2006/2378, reg 7. Date in force: 1 October 2006: see SI 2006/2378, reg 1(2).

Para (1A) (as inserted by SI 1996/30, reg 2(b)): revoked by SI 2000/636, reg 10(1), (3). Date in force: 3 April 2000: see SI 2000/636, reg 1(2).

Para (2): in sub-para (a), words in square brackets substituted by SI 2013/389, reg 3(1), (3)(d). Date in force: 8 April 2013: see SI 2013/389, reg 1(2).

Para (2): in sub-para (c) words "civil partner," in square brackets inserted by SI 2005/2877, art 2(3), Sch 3, para 19. Date in force: 5 December 2005: see SI 2005/2877, art 1.

Para (2): sub-para (d) substituted by SI 2013/389, reg 3(1), (3)(e). Date in force: 8 April 2013: see SI 2013/389, reg 1(2).

Para (2): sub-para (e) revoked by SI 2013/389, reg 3(1), (3)(f). Date in force: 8 April 2013: see SI 2013/389, reg 1(2).

Paras (3A)–(3C): inserted by SI 2013/389, reg 3(1), (3)(g)–(i). Date in force: 8 April 2013: see SI 2013/389, reg 1(2).

Para (4): revoked by SI 2006/2378, reg 7. Date in force: 1 October 2006: see SI 2006/2378, reg 1(2).

SOCIAL SECURITY (DISABILITY LIVING ALLOWANCE) REGULATIONS 1991

(SI 1991/2890)

Made: 18 December 1991.

Authority: Social Security Act 1975, ss 37ZA(6), 37ZB(2), (3), (7), (8), 37ZC, 37ZD, 37ZE(2), 85(1), 114(1), 166(2)– (3A), Sch 20; Social Security (Miscellaneous Provisions) Act 1977, s 13; Disability Living Allowance and Disability Working Allowance Act 1991, s 5(1).

Commencement: 6 April 1992.

PART II
GENERAL

2 Conditions as to residence and presence in Great Britain

(1) Subject to the following provisions of this regulation [and regulations 2A and 2B], the prescribed conditions for the purposes of [section 71](6) of the Act as to residence and presence in Great Britain in relation to any person on any day shall be that—

    (a)   on that day—

        (i)   he is [ordinarily] resident in [the United Kingdom, the Republic of Ireland, the Isle of Man or the Channel Islands]; and

        [(ib)   he is not a person subject to immigration control within the meaning of section 115(9) of the Immigration and Asylum Act 1999 or section 115 of that Act does not apply to him for the purposes of entitlement to disability living allowance by virtue of regulation 2 of the Social Security (Immigration and Asylum) Consequential Amendments Regulations 2000, and]

(ii) he is present in Great Britain; and

(iii) he has been present in Great Britain for a period of, or for periods amounting in the aggregate to, not less than [104] weeks in the [156] weeks immediately preceding that day; . . .

(b) . . ..

[(1A) . . .]

(2) For the purposes of paragraph (1)(a)(ii) and (iii), notwithstanding that on any day a person is absent from Great Britain, he shall be treated as though he was present in Great Britain if his absence is by reason only of the fact that on that day—

(a) he is abroad in his capacity as—

(i) a serving member of the forces,

(ii) an airman or mariner within the meaning of regulations [111 and 115] respectively of the Social Security (Contributions) Regulations [2001],

and for the purpose of this provision, the expression "serving members of the forces" has the same meaning as in regulation 1(2) of the Regulations of [2001]; or

(b) he is in employment prescribed for the purposes of [section 120] of the Act in connection with continental shelf operations; or

(c) he is living with a person mentioned in sub-paragraph (a)(i) and is the spouse, [civil partner,] son, daughter, step-son, step-daughter, father, father-in-law, step-father, mother, mother-in-law or step-mother of that person; or

[(d) he is temporarily absent from Great Britain and that absence has not lasted for a continuous period exceeding 13 weeks.]

(e) . . .

(3) . . .

[(3A) A person shall be treated as habitually resident in Great Britain for the purpose of paragraph (1)(a)(i) where—

(a) he is resident outside Great Britain in his capacity as a serving member of the forces and for this purpose "serving member of the forces" has the meaning given in regulation 1(2) of the Social Security (Contributions) Regulations 2001; or

(b) he is living with a person mentioned in paragraph (a) and is the spouse, civil partner, son, daughter, step-son, step-daughter, father, father-in-law, step-father, mother, mother-in-law or step-mother of that person.

(3B) Where a person is temporarily absent from Great Britain, he is treated as present in Great Britain for the purposes of paragraph (1)(a)(ii) and (iii) for the first 26 weeks of that absence, where—

(a) this absence is solely in connection with arrangements made for the medical treatment of him for a disease or bodily or mental disablement which commenced before he left Great Britain; and

(b) the arrangements referred to in sub-paragraph (a) relate to medical treatment—

(i) outside Great Britain,

(ii) during the period whilst he is temporarily absent from Great Britain, and

(iii) by, or under the supervision of, a person appropriately qualified to carry out that treatment, and

"medical treatment" means medical, surgical or rehabilitative treatment (including any course or diet or regimen), and references to a person receiving or submitting to medical treatment are to be construed accordingly.]

(3C)   For the purpose of paragraph (2)(d) and (3B) a person is "temporarily absent" if, at the beginning of the period of absence, that absence is unlikely to exceed 52 weeks.]

(4)   Where a person is terminally ill and—

    (a)   makes a claim for disability living allowance; or

    (b)   an application is made for a [revision under section 9 of the 1998 Act or supersession under section 10 of that Act] of his award of disability living allowance,

expressly on the ground that he is such a person, paragraph (1) shall apply to him as if head (iii) of sub-paragraph (a) was omitted.

(5)   Paragraph (1) shall apply in the case of a child under the age of 6 months as if in head (iii) of sub-paragraph (a) for the reference to [104] weeks there was substituted a reference to 13 weeks.

(6)   Where in any particular case a child has by virtue of paragraph (5), entitlement to the care component immediately before the day he attains the age of 6 months, then until the child attains the age of 12 months, head (iii) of sub-paragraph (a) of paragraph (1) shall continue to apply in his case as if for the reference to [104] weeks there was substituted a reference to 13 weeks.

[(7)   Paragraph (1) shall apply in the case of a child who is over the age of 6 months but who has not exceeded the age of 36 months as if in head (iii) of sub-paragraph (a) for the reference to 104 weeks there was substituted a reference to 26 weeks.]

Amendment

Para (1): words in first pair of square brackets inserted, words in square brackets in sub-para (a)(i) substituted, and numbers in square brackets in sub-para (a)(iii) substituted, by SI 2013/389, reg 4(1), (3)(a)–(c). Date in force: 8 April 2013: see SI 2013/389, reg 1(2).

Para (1): words "section 71" in square brackets substituted by SI 1993/1939, reg 2(3).

Para (1): sub-para (a)(ib) substituted, for sub-para (a)(ia) (as inserted by SI 1996/30, reg 4(a)), by SI 2000/636, reg 11(1), (2). Date in force: 3 April 2000: see SI 2000/636, reg 1(2).

Para (1): sub-para (b) and word omitted immediately preceding it revoked by SI 2006/2378, reg 8. Date in force: 1 October 2006: see SI 2006/2378, reg 1(2).

Para (1A) (as inserted by SI 1996/30, reg 4(b)): revoked by SI 2000/636, reg 11(1), (3).

Para (2): in sub-para (a) words in square brackets substituted by SI 2013/389, reg 4(1), (3)(d), Date in force: 8 April 2013: see SI 2013/389, reg 1(2).

Para (2): in sub-para (b) words "section 120" in square brackets substituted by SI 1993/1939, reg 2(3).

Para (2): in sub-para (c) words "civil partner," in square brackets inserted by SI 2005/2877, art 2(3), Sch 3, para 20. Date in force: 5 December 2005: see SI 2005/2877, art 1.

Para (2): sub-para (d) substituted by SI 2013/389, reg 4(1), (3(e). Date in force: 8 April 2013: see SI 2013/389, reg 1(2).

Para (2): sub-para (e) revoked by SI 2013/389, reg 4(1), (3)(f). Date in force: 8 April 2013: see SI 2013/389, reg 1(2).

Para (3): revoked by SI 2006/2378, reg 8. Date in force: 1 October 2006: see SI 2006/2378, reg 1(2).

Paras (3A)–(3C): inserted by SI 2013/389, reg 4(1), (3)(g)–(i). Date in force: 8 April 2013: see SI 2013/389, reg 1(2).

Para (4): in sub-para (b) words in square brackets substituted by SI 1999/2860, art 3(7), Sch 7, para 2.

Para (5): reference to "104" in square brackets substituted by SI 2013/389, reg 4(1), (3)(j). Date in force: 8 April 2013: see SI 2013/389, reg 1(2).

Para (6): reference to "104" in square brackets substituted by SI 2013/389, reg 4(1), (3)(k). Date in force: 8 April 2013: see SI 2013/389, reg 1(2).

Para (7): inserted by SI 2013/389, reg 4(1), (3)(l). Date in force: 8 April 2013: see SI 2013/389, reg 1(2).

SOCIAL SECURITY (INCAPACITY BENEFIT) REGULATIONS 1994

(SI 1994/2946)

Made: 21 November 1994.

Authority: Social Security Contributions and Benefits Act 1992, ss 30B(7), 30C(3), (4)(a), (6), 30D(3), 30E(1), (2), 122, 175(1), (3).

[PART IV
ADDITIONAL CONDITIONS FOR PERSONS INCAPACITATED IN YOUTH]

Amendment
Inserted by SI 2000/3120, reg 2(1), (5).

Date in force: 6 April 2001 (except in relation to a person who is entitled to incapacity benefit before that date and continues, on or after that date, to be entitled to incapacity benefit, whether or not by virtue of s 30C of the Social Security Contributions and Benefits Act 1992): see SI 2000/3120, regs 1, 6.

[16 Conditions relating to residence or presence
(1) The prescribed conditions for the purposes of section 30A(2A)(d) of the Contributions and Benefits Act as to residence or presence in Great Britain in relation to any person on the relevant day shall be that on that day—

    (a)   he is ordinarily resident in Great Britain;

    (b)   he is not a person subject to immigration control within the meaning of section 115(9) of the Immigration and Asylum Act 1999 or he is a person to whom paragraph (5) applies;

    (c)   he is present in Great Britain; and

    (d)   he has been present in Great Britain for a period of, or for periods amounting in aggregate to, not less than 26 weeks in the 52 weeks immediately preceding that day.

(2) . . .

(3) . . .

(4) In determining whether a person satisfies paragraph (1), where a person is absent from Great Britain by reason only of the fact that—

    (a)   he is abroad in his capacity as a serving member of the forces, or he is the spouse, [civil partner,] son, daughter, father, father-in-law, mother or mother-in-law of, and living with, a serving member of the forces abroad;

    (b)   he is in employment prescribed for the purposes of section 120 of the Contributions and Benefits Act in connection with continental shelf operations; or

    (c)   he is abroad in his capacity as an airman within the meaning of regulation 81, or mariner within the meaning of regulation 86, of the Social Security (Contributions) Regulations 1979;

any day or period of absence shall be treated as a day on which, or period during which, the person is present or resident, as the case may be, in Great Britain; and for the purposes of this paragraph "serving member of the forces" has the same meaning as in regulation 1(2) of the Social Security (Contributions) Regulations 1979.

(5) This paragraph applies where a person is—

    (a)   a member of a family of a national of a State contracting party to the Agreement on the European Economic Area signed at Oporto on 2nd May 1992 as adjusted by the Protocol signed at Brussels on 17th March 1993;

    (b)   a person who is lawfully working in Great Britain and is a national of a State with which the [European Union] has concluded an agreement under [Article 217 of the Treaty on the Functioning of the European Union] providing, in the field of social security, for the equal treatment of workers who are nationals of the signatory State and their families;

(c) a person who is a member of a family of, and living with, a person specified in sub-paragraph (b); or

(d) a person who has been given leave to enter, or remain in, the United Kingdom by the Secretary of State upon an undertaking by another person or persons pursuant to the immigration rules within the meaning of the Immigration Act 1971 to be responsible for his maintenance and accommodation.

(6) A person shall be treated as having satisfied the residence or presence conditions on any subsequent day of incapacity for work falling within the same period of incapacity for work where the residence or presence conditions specified in paragraphs (1) to (4) are satisfied on the first relevant day.]

Amendment

Inserted by SI 2000/3120, reg 2(1), (5).

Date in force: 6 April 2001 (except in relation to a person who is entitled to incapacity benefit before that date and continues, on or after that date, to be entitled to incapacity benefit, whether or not by virtue of s 30C of the Social Security Contributions and Benefits Act 1992): see SI 2000/3120, regs 1, 6.

Paras (2), (3): revoked by SI 2006/2378, reg 10(1), (4).

Date in force: 1 October 2006: see SI 2006/2378, reg 1(2).

Para (4): in sub-para (a) words "civil partner," in square brackets inserted by SI 2005/2877, art 2(3), Sch 3, para 24.

Date in force: 5 December 2005: see SI 2005/2877, art 1.

Para (5): in sub-para (b) words "European Union" in square brackets substituted by SI 2011/1043, art 4(1).

Date in force: 22 April 2011: see SI 2011/1043, art 2; for transitional savings see art 3(3) thereof.

Para (5): in sub-para (b) words "Article 217 of the Treaty on the Functioning of the European Union" in square brackets substituted by SI 2011/1043, art 5.

Date in force: 22 April 2011: see SI 2011/1043, art 2; for transitional savings see art 3(3) thereof.

JOBSEEKER'S ALLOWANCE REGULATIONS 1996

(SI 1996/207)

Made: 1 February 1996.

Authority: Jobseekers Act 1995, ss 2(1)(c), 3, 4(1)(b), (2), (4), (5), (12), 5(3), 6, 7, 8, 9(1), (8), (10)–(12), 10(1), (6)(c) and (7), 11(2), (5), (7), 12, 13, 15(1), (2)(d), (5), (6), 17(1), 19(2), (4), (7), (8), (10)(c), 20, 21, 22, 23, 35(1), (3), 36, 40, Sch 1.,

PART VII
AMOUNTS

[85A Special cases: supplemental—persons from abroad

(1) "Person from abroad" means, subject to the following provisions of this regulation, a claimant who is not habitually resident in the United Kingdom, the Channel Islands, the Isle of Man or the Republic of Ireland.

[(2) No claimant shall be treated as habitually resident in the United Kingdom, the Channel Islands, the Isle of Man or the Republic of Ireland unless—

(a) the claimant has been living in any of those places for the past three months; and

(b)   the claimant has a right to reside in any of those places, other than a right to reside which falls within paragraph (3).]

(3)   A right to reside falls within this paragraph if it is one which exists by virtue of, or in accordance with, one or more of the following—

(a)   regulation 13 of the Immigration (European Economic Area) Regulations 2006; . . .

[(aa)   regulation 15A(1) of those Regulations, but only in a case where the right exists under that regulation because the claimant satisfies the criteria in regulation 15A(4A) of those Regulations;]

(b)   Article 6 of Council Directive No 2004/38/EC[; or

(c)   Article 20 of the Treaty on the Functioning of the European Union (in a case where the right to reside arises because a British citizen would otherwise be deprived of the genuine enjoyment of the substance of their rights as a European Union citizen)].

(4)   A claimant is not a person from abroad if he is—

[(za)   a qualified person for the purposes of regulation 6 of the Immigration (European Economic Area) Regulations 2006 as a worker or a self-employed person;

(zb)   a family member of a person referred to in sub-paragraph (za) within the meaning of regulation 7(1)(a), (b) or (c) of those Regulations;

(zc)   a person who has a right to reside permanently in the United Kingdom by virtue of regulation 15(1)(c), (d) or (e) of those Regulations;]

(g)   a refugee within the definition in Article 1 of the Convention relating to the Status of Refugees done at Geneva on 28th July 1951, as extended by Article 1(2) of the Protocol relating to the Status of Refugees done at New York on 31st January 1967;

[[(h)   a person who has been granted leave or who is deemed to have been granted leave outside the rules made under section 3(2) of the Immigration Act 1971 where that leave is—

    (i)   discretionary leave to enter or remain in the United Kingdom;

    (ii)   leave to remain under the Destitution Domestic Violence concession; or

    (iii)   leave deemed to have been granted by virtue of regulation 3 of the Displaced Persons (Temporary Protection) Regulations 2005;]

(hh)   a person who has humanitarian protection granted under those rules;] [or]

(i)   a person who is not a person subject to immigration control within the meaning of section 115(9) of the Immigration and Asylum Act and who is in the United Kingdom as a result of his deportation, expulsion or other removal by compulsion of law from another country to the United Kingdom; . . .

(j)   . . .

[(k)   . . .]

Amendment

Inserted by SI 2006/1026, reg 7(1), (3). Date in force: 30 April 2006: see SI 2006/1026, reg 1.

Para (2): substituted by SI 2013/3196, reg 2. Date in force: 1 January 2014: see SI 2013/3196, reg 1; for saving see reg 3 thereof.

Para (3): in sub-para (a) word omitted revoked, sub-para (aa) inserted, and sub-para (c) and word "; or" immediately preceding it inserted, by SI 2012/2587, reg 3(1), (2)–(4). Date in force: 8 November 2012: see SI 2012/2587, reg 1.

Para (4): sub-paras (za)–(zc) substituted, for sub-paras (a)–(f), by SI 2014/902, reg 3. Date in force: 31 May 2014: see SI 2014/902, reg 1.

Para (4): sub-paras (h), (hh) substituted, for para (h) as originally enacted, by SI 2006/2528, reg 3. Date in force: 9 October 2006: see SI 2006/2528, reg 1.

Para (4): sub-para (h) further substituted and in sub-para (hh) word "or" in square brackets inserted by SI 2013/2536, reg 6(1), (8)(a), (b). Date in force: 29 October 2013: see SI 2013/2536, reg 1(1).

Para (4): in sub-para (i) word omitted revoked by SI 2009/362, reg 3(1), (2). Date in force: 18 March 2009: see SI 2009/362, reg 1(2).

Para (4): sub-paras (j), (k) revoked by SI 2013/2536, reg 6(1), (8)(c).Date in force: 29 October 2013: see SI 2013/2536, reg 1(1).

Para (4): sub-para (k) inserted by SI 2009/362, reg 3(1), (3). Date in force: 18 March 2009: see SI 2009/362, reg 1(2).

See Further

See further, the Social Security (Persons from Abroad) Amendment Regulations 2006, SI 2006/1026, reg 10(f) which provides that para (4)(a)–(e) above shall apply in relation to a national of Norway, Iceland, Liechtenstein or Switzerland or a member of his family as if such a national were a national of a member State.

ASYLUM SUPPORT (INTERIM PROVISIONS) REGULATIONS 1999

(SI 1999/3056)

Made: 13 November 1999.

Authority: Immigration and Asylum Act 1999, ss 94,166, Sch 9, paras 1, 2, 4–7, 9, 11, 13–15.

Commencement: 6 December 1999.

1 Citation, commencement and extent

(1) These Regulations may be cited as the Asylum Support (Interim Provisions) Regulations 1999 and shall come into force on 6th December 1999.

(2) These Regulations do not extend to Scotland or Northern Ireland.

2 Interpretation

(1) In these Regulations—

"assisted person" means an asylum-seeker, or a dependant of an asylum-seeker, who has applied for support and for whom support is provided;

"dependant", in relation to an asylum-seeker, an assisted person or a person claiming support, means a person in the United Kingdom who:

    (a)   is his spouse [or civil partner];

    (b)   is a child of his, or of his spouse [or civil partner], who is under 18 and dependent on him;

    (c)   is under 18 and is a member of his, or his spouse's [or civil partner's], close family;

    (d)   is under 18 and had been living as part of his household:

        (i)   for at least six of the 12 months before the day on which his claim for support was made; or

        (ii)   since birth;

    (e)   is in need of care and attention from him or a member of his household by reason of a disability and would fall within sub-paragraph (c) or (d) but for the fact that he is not under 18;

    (f)   had been living with him as a member of an unmarried couple for at least two of the three years before the day on which his claim for support was made;

    [(ff)   had been living with him as a member of a same-sex couple for at least two of the three years before the day on which his claim for support was made;]

(g) is a person living as part of his household who was receiving assistance from a local authority under section 17 of the Children Act 1989 immediately before the beginning of the interim period;

(h) has made a claim for leave to enter or remain in the United Kingdom, or for variation of any such leave, which is being considered on the basis that he is dependent on the asylum-seeker; or

(i) in relation to an assisted person or a person claiming support who is himself a dependant of an asylum-seeker, is the asylum-seeker;

"eligible persons" means asylum-seekers or their dependants who appear to be destitute or to be likely to become destitute within 14 days;

"local authority" means:

(a) in England, a county council, a metropolitan district council, a district council with the functions of a county council, a London borough council, the Common Council of the City of London or the Council of the Isles of Scilly;

(b) in Wales, a county council or a county borough council.

(2) Any reference in these Regulations to support is to support under these Regulations.

(3) Any reference in these Regulations to assistance under section 21 of the National Assistance Act 1948 is to assistance, the need for which has arisen solely:

(a) because of destitution; or

(b) because of the physical effects, or anticipated physical effects, of destitution.

(4) Any reference in these Regulations to assistance under section 17 of the Children Act 1989 is to the provision of accommodation or of any essential living needs.

(5) The interim period begins on the day on which these Regulations come into force and ends on [3rd April 2006].

[(6) The period prescribed under section 94(3) of the Immigration and Asylum Act 1999 (day on which a claim for asylum is determined) for the purposes of Part VI of that Act is 28 days where paragraph (7) below applies, and 21 days in any other case.

(7) This paragraph applies where:

(a) the Secretary of State notifies the claimant that his decision is to accept the asylum claim;

(b) the Secretary of State notifies the claimant that his decision is to reject the asylum claim but at the same time notifies him that he is giving him limited leave to enter or remain in the United Kingdom; or

(c) an appeal by the claimant against the Secretary of State's decision has been disposed of by being allowed.]

Amendment

Para (1): in definition "dependant" in para (a) words "or civil partner" in square brackets inserted by SI 2005/2114, art 2(13), Sch 13, Pt 1, para 1(a). Date in force: 5 December 2005: see SI 2005/2114, art 1.

Para (1): in definition "dependant" in para (b) words "or civil partner" in square brackets inserted by SI 2005/2114, art 2(13), Sch 13, Pt 1, para 1(b). Date in force: 5 December 2005: see SI 2005/2114, art 1.

Para (1): in definition "dependant" in para (c) words "or civil partner's" in square brackets inserted by SI 2005/2114, art 2(13), Sch 13, Pt 1, para 1(c). Date in force: 5 December 2005: see SI 2005/2114, art 1.

Para (1): in definition "dependant" para (ff) inserted by SI 2005/2114, art 2(13), Sch 13, Pt 1, para 1(d). Date in force: 5 December 2005: see SI 2005/2114, art 1.

Para (5): words "3rd April 2006" in square brackets substituted by SI 2005/595, reg 2. Date in force: 3 April 2005: see SI 2005/595, reg 1.

Paras (6), (7): substituted, for para (6) as originally enacted, by SI 2002/471, reg 4. Date in force: 8 April 2002: see SI 2002/471, reg 1(2).

3 Requirement to provide support

(1) Subject to regulations 7 and 8:

    (a)   the local authority concerned, or

    (b)   the local authority to whom responsibility for providing support is transferred under regulation 9,

must provide support during the interim period to eligible persons.

(2) The question whether a person is an eligible person is to be determined by the local authority concerned.

(3) For the purposes of these Regulations, the local authority concerned are the local authority to whom a claim for support is made, except where a claim for support is transferred by a local authority in accordance with regulation 9, in which case the local authority concerned are the local authority to whom the claim is transferred.

4 Temporary support

(1) This regulation applies to support to be provided before it has been determined whether a person is an eligible person ("temporary support").

(2) Temporary support is to be provided to a person claiming support:

    (a)   by the local authority to whom the claim is made until such time (if any) as the claim is transferred under regulation 9;

    (b)   where the claim is so transferred, by the local authority to whom the claim is transferred.

(3) Temporary support must appear to the local authority by whom it is provided to be adequate for the needs of the person claiming support and his dependants (if any).

5 Provision of support

(1) Subject to paragraph (2), support is to be provided by providing:

    (a)   accommodation appearing to the local authority by whom it is provided to be adequate for the needs of the assisted person and his dependants (if any) ("accommodation"); and

    (b)   what appear to the local authority by whom it is provided to be essential living needs of the assisted person and his dependants (if any) ("essential living needs").

(2) Where an assisted person's household includes a child who is under 18 and a dependant of his, support is to be provided:

    (a)   in accordance with paragraph (1);

    (b)   by providing accommodation; or

    (c)   by providing essential living needs.

(3) Support is to be provided to enable the assisted person (if he is the asylum-seeker) to meet reasonable travel expenses incurred in attending:

    (a)   a hearing of an appeal on his claim for asylum; or

    (b)   an interview in connection with his claim for asylum which has been requested by the Secretary of State.

(4) Where the circumstances of a particular case are exceptional, support is to be provided in such other ways as are necessary to enable the assisted person and his dependants (if any) to be supported.

(5) . . .

(6) A local authority may provide support subject to conditions.

(7) Such conditions are to be set out in writing.

(8) A copy of the conditions is to be given to the assisted person.

Amendment

Para (5): revoked by SI 2002/471, reg 5. Date in force: 8 April 2002: see SI 2002/471, reg 1(2).

6 Matters to which the local authority are to have regard

(1)   In providing support, the local authority are to have regard to:

(a)   income which the assisted person has, or his dependants (if any) have, or might reasonably be expected to have;

(b)   support which is, or assets which are, or might reasonably be expected to be, available to the assisted person, or to his dependants (if any);

(c)   the welfare of the assisted person and his dependants (if any); and

(d)   the cost of providing support.

(2)   In providing accommodation under these Regulations, the local authority are not to have regard to any preference that the assisted person or his dependants (if any) may have as to:

(a)   the locality in which the accommodation is to be provided;

(b)   the nature of the accommodation to be provided; or

(c)   the nature and standard of fixtures and fittings in that accommodation.

7 Refusal of support

(1)   Unless this paragraph does not apply, support must be refused in the following circumstances:

(a)   where the person claiming support has intentionally made himself and his dependants (if any) destitute;

(b)   where the person claiming support has made a claim for support to another local authority, except where the claim is one to which regulation 9 applies;

(c)   where the claim for support is made by a person to a local authority other than one to whom, in the previous 12 months, he has made a claim for assistance under section 21 of the National Assistance Act 1948 or under section 17 of the Children Act 1989;

(d)   where the person claiming support—

(i)   is an asylum-seeker within the meaning of paragraph (3A)(a) or (aa) of regulation 70 of the Income Support (General) Regulations 1987 who has not ceased to be an asylum-seeker by virtue of sub-paragraph (b) of that paragraph;

(ii)   is a person who became an asylum-seeker under paragraph (3A)(a) of regulation 70 of the Income Support (General) Regulations 1987 and who has not ceased to be an asylum-seeker by virtue of sub-paragraph (b) of that paragraph, as saved by regulation 12(1) of the Social Security (Persons from Abroad) Miscellaneous Amendments Regulations 1996;

(iii) is not a person from abroad within the meaning of sub-paragraph (a) of regulation 21(3) of the Income Support (General) Regulations 1987 by virtue of the exclusions specified in that sub-paragraph;

(e)   where neither the person claiming support nor any of his dependants is an asylum-seeker or has made a claim for leave to enter or remain in the United Kingdom, or for variation of any such leave, which is being considered on the basis that he is dependent on an asylum-seeker.

(2)   For the purposes of paragraph (1)(a), a person has intentionally made himself destitute if he appears to be, or likely within 14 days to become, destitute as a result of an act or omission deliberately done or made by him or any dependant of his without reasonable excuse while in the United Kingdom.

(3)   Paragraph (1) does not apply where the local authority concerned did not know, or could not with reasonable diligence have known, of any circumstance set out in that paragraph.

8 Suspension and discontinuation of support

(1)   Support for the assisted person and his dependants (if any) must be discontinued as soon as the local authority by whom it is provided become aware of any circumstance which, if they had known of it when the claim was made, would have led to the claim being refused in accordance with regulation 7(1).

(2)   Support may be suspended or discontinued:

(a)   where the assisted person, or any dependant of his, fails without reasonable excuse to comply with any condition subject to which the support is provided;

(b)   where the assisted person, or any dependant of his, leaves accommodation provided as part of such support for more than seven consecutive days without reasonable excuse.

9 Transfer of a claim for support or responsibility for providing support by a local authority

A local authority may transfer a claim for support made to them, or responsibility for providing support, to another local authority on such terms as may be agreed between the two authorities.

10 Assistance to those providing support

Reasonable assistance to a local authority providing support is to be given by:

(a)   any district council for an area any part of which lies within the area of the local authority providing support, and

(b)   any [private registered provider of social housing or] registered social landlord, within the meaning of Part I of the Housing Act 1996, which manages any house or other property which is in the area of the local authority providing support,

who is requested to provide such assistance by the local authority providing support.

Amendment

In para (b) words in square brackets inserted by SI 2010/671, art 4, Sch 1, para 26. Date in force: 1 April 2010: see SI 2010/671, art 1(2), and SI 2010/862, art 2.

11 Transitional provision

Where an asylum-seeker or a dependant of an asylum-seeker is receiving assistance from a local authority under section 21 of the National Assistance Act 1948 or under section 17 of the Children Act 1989 immediately before the beginning of the interim period, he is to be taken to have been accepted for support by the local authority providing such assistance.

12 Entitlement to claim support

A person entitled to support under these Regulations is not entitled to assistance under section 17 of the Children Act 1989.

IMMIGRATION (REGULARISATION PERIOD FOR OVERSTAYERS) REGULATIONS 2000

(SI 2000/265)

Made: 7 February 2000.

Authority: Immigration and Asylum Act 1999, ss 9(1)–(3), 166(3), 167.

Commencement: 8 February 2000.

1 Citation, commencement and interpretation

(1) These Regulations may be cited as the Immigration (Regularisation Period for Overstayers) Regulations 2000 and shall come into force on the day after the day on which they are made.

(2) In these Regulations "the Act" means the Immigration and Asylum Act 1999.

2 Manner of application

(1) An application under section 9(1) of the Act shall be made in the following manner.

(2) The application shall be made in writing, setting out the information required by paragraph (4), and attaching the material required by paragraph (5).

(3) The application shall either:

   (a)   be sent by post to the following address:
      Regularisation Scheme for Overstayers
      Initial Consideration Unit
      Immigration and Nationality Directorate
      Block C
      Whitgift Centre
      Croydon
      CR9 1AT; or

   (b)   be delivered by hand to the Home Office at:
      The Public Caller Unit
      Immigration and Nationality Directorate
      Block C
      Whitgift Centre
      Wellesley Road
      Croydon.

(4) The information referred to in paragraph (2) is:

   (a)   the applicant's full name, date of birth and nationality;

   (b)   the applicant's home address or, if none, an address where he may be contacted;

   (c)   the name and address of any representative who is acting on behalf of the applicant;

   (d)   the date of each occasion on which leave to enter or remain has been granted to the applicant since his first arrival in the United Kingdom, if known;

   (e)   in relation to each date specified in accordance with sub-paragraph (d), the period for which leave was granted, if known;

   (f)   the applicant's Home Office reference, if known;

   (g)   the fact that the application is made under section 9 of the Act; and

   (h)   all the circumstances which the applicant wishes the Secretary of State to take into account when considering his application, including:

      (i)   his length of residence in the United Kingdom;

      (ii)   the strength of his connections with the United Kingdom;

      (iii)   his personal history, including character, conduct and employment record;

      (iv)   his domestic circumstances; and

      (v)   any compassionate circumstances.

(5) The material referred to in paragraph (2) is:

   (a)   the applicant's current passport, if he has one and it is available to him;

   (b)   any other passports (whether expired or not) which have been used by the applicant and which are available to him; and

   (c)   any document or copy document which the applicant considers is evidence supporting his application.

3 Prescribed days

(1)   The day prescribed for the purposes of section 9(2) of the Act (the start of the regularisation period) is the day on which these Regulations come into force or, if later, 1st February 2000.

(2)   The day prescribed for the purposes of section 9(3) of the Act (the end of the regularisation period in certain circumstances) is 1st October 2000.

4 Delivery of applications

(1)   Paragraph (2) applies to an application sent by recorded delivery, addressed to the address set out in regulation 2(3)(a).

(2)   Such an application shall be taken to have been delivered for the purposes of these Regulations and section 9 of the Act on the second day after the day on which it was posted, if not received earlier.

ASYLUM SUPPORT REGULATIONS 2000

(SI 2000/704)

Made: 6 March 2000.

Authority: Immigration and Asylum Act 1999, ss 94, 95, 97, 114, 166, 167, Sch 8.

Commencement: 3 April 2000.

General

1 Citation and commencement

These Regulations may be cited as the Asylum Support Regulations 2000 and shall come into force on 3rd April 2000.

2 Interpretation

(1)   In these Regulations—

"the Act" means the Immigration and Asylum Act 1999;

"asylum support" means support provided under section 95 of the Act;

["civil partnership couple" means two people of the same sex who are civil partners of each other and who are members of the same household;]

"dependant" has the meaning given by paragraphs (4) and (5);

"the interim Regulations" means the Asylum Support (Interim Provisions) Regulations 1999;

"married couple" means a man and woman who are married to each other and are members of the same household;

["same-sex couple" means two people of the same sex who, though not civil partners of each other, are living together as if they were;] and

"unmarried couple" means a man and woman who, though not married to each other, are living together as if married.

[(2)   The period prescribed under section 94(3) of the Act (day on which a claim for asylum is determined) for the purposes of Part VI of the Act is 28 days where paragraph (2A) applies, and 21 days in any other case.

(2A)   This paragraph applies where:

(a)   the Secretary of State notifies the claimant that his decision is to accept the asylum claim;

(b)   the Secretary of State notifies the claimant that his decision is to reject the asylum claim but at the same time notifies him that he is giving him limited leave to enter or remain in the United Kingdom; or

(c) an appeal by the claimant against the Secretary of State's decision has been disposed of by being allowed.]

(3) Paragraph (2) does not apply in relation to a case to which the interim Regulations apply (for which case, provision corresponding to paragraph (2) is made by regulation 2(6) of those Regulations).

(4) In these Regulations "dependant", in relation to an asylum-seeker, a supported person or an applicant for asylum support, means, subject to paragraph (5), a person in the United Kingdom ("the relevant person") who—

(a) is his spouse [or civil partner];

(b) is a child of his or of his spouse [or civil partner], is dependant on him and is, or was at the relevant time, under 18;

(c) is a member of his or his spouse's [or civil partner's] close family and is, or was at the relevant time, under 18;

(d) had been living as part of his household—

(i) for at least six of the twelve months before the relevant time, or

(ii) since birth,

and is, or was at the relevant time, under 18;

(e) is in need of care and attention from him or a member of his household by reason of a disability and would fall within sub-paragraph (c) or (d) but for the fact that he is not, and was not at the relevant time, under 18;

(f) had been living with him as a member of an unmarried couple for at least two of the three years before the relevant time;

[(fa) had been living with him as a member of a same-sex couple for at least two of the three years before the relevant time;]

(g) is living as part of his household and was, immediately before 6th December 1999 (the date when the interim Regulations came into force), receiving assistance from a local authority under section 17 of the Children Act 1989;

(h) is living as part of his household and was, immediately before the coming into force of these Regulations, receiving assistance from a local authority under—

(i) section 22 of the Children (Scotland) Act 1995; or

(ii) Article 18 of the Children (Northern Ireland) Order 1995; or

(i) has made a claim for leave to enter or remain in the United Kingdom, or for variation of any such leave, which is being considered on the basis that he is dependant on the asylum-seeker;

and in relation to a supported person, or an applicant for asylum support, who is himself a dependant of an asylum-seeker, also includes the asylum-seeker if in the United Kingdom.

(5) Where a supported person or applicant for asylum support is himself a dependant of an asylum-seeker, a person who would otherwise be a dependant of the supported person, or of the applicant, for the purposes of these Regulations is not such a dependant unless he is also a dependant of the asylum-seeker or is the asylum-seeker.

(6) In paragraph (4), "the relevant time", in relation to the relevant person, means—

(a) the time when an application for asylum support for him was made in accordance with regulation 3(3); or

(b) if he has joined a person who is already a supported person in the United Kingdom and sub-paragraph (a) does not apply, the time when he joined that person in the United Kingdom.

(7) Where a person, by falling within a particular category in relation to an asylum-seeker or supported person, is by virtue of this regulation a dependant of the asylum-seeker or supported person for the purposes of these Regulations, that category is also a prescribed category for the purposes of paragraph (c) of the definition of

"dependant" in section 94(1) of the Act and, accordingly, the person is a dependant of the asylum-seeker or supported person for the purposes of Part VI of the Act.

(8) Paragraph (7) does not apply to a person who is already a dependant of the asylum-seeker or supported person for the purposes of Part VI of the Act because he falls within either of the categories mentioned in paragraphs (a) and (b) of the definition of "dependant" in section 94(1) of the Act.

(9) Paragraph (7) does not apply for the purposes of any reference to a "dependant" in Schedule 9 to the Act.

Amendment

Para (1): definition "civil partnership couple" inserted by SI 2005/2114, art 2(13), Sch 13, Pt 1, para 2(1), (2)(a). Date in force: 5 December 2005: see SI 2005/2114, art 1.

Para (1): definition "same-sex couple" inserted by SI 2005/2114, art 2(13), Sch 13, Pt 1, para 2(1), (2)(b). Date in force: 5 December 2005: see SI 2005/2114, art 1.

Paras (2), (2A): substituted, for para (2) as originally enacted, by SI 2002/472, reg 3. Date in force: 8 April 2002: see SI 2002/472, reg 1.

Para (4): in sub-paras (a)–(c) words in square brackets inserted by SI 2005/2114, art 2(13), Sch 13, Pt 1, para 2(1), (3)(a)–(c). Date in force: 5 December 2005: see SI 2005/2114, art 1.

Para (4): sub-para (fa) inserted by SI 2005/2114, art 2(13), Sch 13, Pt 1, para 2(1), (3)(d). Date in force: 5 December 2005: see SI 2005/2114, art 1.

Initial application for support

3 Initial application for support: individual and group applications

(1) Either of the following—

    (a)   an asylum-seeker, or

    (b)   a dependant of an asylum-seeker,

may apply to the Secretary of State for asylum support.

(2) An application under this regulation may be—

    (a)   for asylum support for the applicant alone; or

    (b)   for asylum support for the applicant and one or more dependants of his.

(3) The application must be made by completing in full and in English the form for the time being issued by the Secretary of State for the purpose..

[(4) The application may not be entertained by the Secretary of State—

    (a)   where it is made otherwise than in accordance with paragraph (3); or

    (b)   where the Secretary of State is not satisfied that the information provided is complete or accurate or that the applicant is co-operating with enquiries made under paragraph (5).]

(5) The Secretary of State may make further enquiries of the applicant about any matter connected with the application.

[(5A) Where the Secretary of State makes further enquiries under paragraph (5) the applicant shall reply to those enquiries within five working days of his receipt of them.

(5B) The Secretary of State shall be entitled to conclude that the applicant is not co-operating with his enquiries under paragraph (5) if he fails, without reasonable excuse, to reply within the period prescribed by paragraph (5A).

(5C) In cases where the Secretary of State may not entertain an application for asylum support he shall also discontinue providing support under section 98 of the Act.]

(6) Paragraphs (3) and (4) do not apply where a person is already a supported person and asylum support is sought for a dependant of his for whom such support is not already provided (for which case, provision is made by regulation 15).

[(7) For the purposes of this regulation, working day means any day other than a Saturday, a Sunday, Christmas Day, Good Friday or a day which is a bank holiday under section 1 of the Banking and Financial Dealings Act 1971 in the locality in which the applicant is living.]

Amendment

Para (3): words omitted revoked by SI 2007/863, reg 2. Date in force: 9 April 2007: see SI 2007/863, reg 1.

Para (4): substituted by SI 2002/3110, reg 2. Date in force: 8 January 2003: see SI 2002/3110, reg 1.

Paras (5A)–(5C): inserted by SI 2005/11, regs 2, 3(a). Date in force: 5 February 2005: see SI 2005/11, reg 1.

Para (7): inserted by SI 2005/11, regs 2, 3(b). Date in force: 5 February 2005: see SI 2005/11, reg 1.

4 Persons excluded from support

(1) The following circumstances are prescribed for the purposes of subsection (2) of section 95 of the Act as circumstances where a person who would otherwise fall within subsection (1) of that section is excluded from that subsection (and, accordingly, may not be provided with asylum support).

(2) A person is so excluded if he is applying for asylum support for himself alone and he falls within paragraph (4) by virtue of any sub-paragraph of that paragraph.

(3) A person is so excluded if—

    (a)   he is applying for asylum support for himself and other persons, or he is included in an application for asylum support made by a person other than himself;

    (b)   he falls within paragraph (4) (by virtue of any sub-paragraph of that paragraph); and

    (c)   each of the other persons to whom the application relates also falls within paragraph (4) (by virtue of any sub-paragraph of that paragraph).

(4) A person falls within this paragraph if at the time when the application is determined—

    (a)   he is a person to whom interim support applies; or

    (b)   he is a person to whom social security benefits apply; or

    (c)   he has not made a claim for leave to enter or remain in the United Kingdom, or for variation of any such leave, which is being considered on the basis that he is an asylum-seeker or dependent on an asylum-seeker.

(5) For the purposes of paragraph (4), interim support applies to a person if—

    (a)   at the time when the application is determined, he is a person to whom, under the interim Regulations, support under regulation 3 of those Regulations must be provided by a local authority;

    (b)   sub-paragraph (a) does not apply, but would do so if the person had been determined by the local authority concerned to be an eligible person; or

    (c)   sub-paragraph (a) does not apply, but would do so but for the fact that the person's support under those Regulations was (otherwise than by virtue of regulation 7(1)(d) of those Regulations) refused under regulation 7, or suspended or discontinued under regulation 8, of those Regulations;

and in this paragraph "local authority", "local authority concerned" and "eligible person" have the same meanings as in the interim Regulations.

(6) For the purposes of paragraph (4), a person is a person to whom social security benefits apply if he is—

    (a)   a person who by virtue of regulation 2 of the Social Security (Immigration and Asylum) Consequential Amendments Regulations 2000 is not excluded by section 115(1) of the Act from entitlement to—

        (i)   income-based jobseeker's allowance under the Jobseekers Act 1995; . . .

        (ii)   income support, housing benefit or council tax benefit under the Social Security Contributions and Benefits Act 1992; [. . .

        (iii)   income-related employment and support allowance payable under Part 1 of the Welfare Reform Act 2007;][or

        (iv)   universal credit under Part 1 of the Welfare Reform Act 2012;]

  (b)   a person who, by virtue of regulation 2 of the Social Security (Immigration and Asylum) Consequential Amendments Regulations (Northern Ireland) 2000 is not excluded by section 115(2) of the Act from entitlement to—

        (i)   income-based jobseeker's allowance under the Jobseekers (Northern Ireland) Order 1995; . . .

        (ii)   income support or housing benefit under the Social Security Contributions and Benefits (Northern Ireland) Act 1992; [or

        (iii)   income-related employment and support allowance payable under Part 1 of the Welfare Reform Act (Northern Ireland) 2007.]

(7) A person is not to be regarded as falling within paragraph (2) or (3) if, when asylum support is sought for him, he is a dependant of a person who is already a supported person.

(8) The circumstances prescribed by paragraphs (2) and (3) are also prescribed for the purposes of section 95(2), as applied by section 98(3), of the Act as circumstances where a person who would otherwise fall within subsection (1) of section 98 is excluded from that subsection (and, accordingly, may not be provided with temporary support under section 98).

(9) For the purposes of paragraph (8), paragraphs (2) and (3) shall apply as if any reference to an application for asylum support were a reference to an application for support under section 98 of the Act.

Amendment

    Para (6): in sub-para (a)(i) word omitted revoked by SI 2008/1879, reg 11(a). Date in force: 27 October 2008: see SI 2008/1879, reg 1(1).

    Para (6): sub-para (a)(iii) and word "or" immediately preceding it inserted by SI 2008/1879, reg 11(b). Date in force: 27 October 2008: see SI 2008/1879, reg 1(1).

    Para (6): word omitted from sub-para (a)(ii) revoked and sub-para (a)(iv) and word "or" immediately preceding it inserted, by SI 2013/630, reg 59. Date in force: 29 April 2013: see SI 2013/630, reg 1(2).

    Para (6): word omitted from sub-para (b)(i) revoked and sub-para (b)(iii) and word "or" immediately preceding it inserted, by SR 2008/412, reg 9. Date in force: 27 October 2008: see SR 2008/412, reg 1.

Determining whether persons are destitute

5 Determination where application relates to more than one person, etc

(1) Subject to paragraph (2), where an application in accordance with regulation 3(3) is for asylum support for the applicant and one or more dependants of his, in applying section 95(1) of the Act the Secretary of State must decide whether the applicant and all those dependants, taken together, are destitute or likely to become destitute within the period prescribed by regulation 7.

(2) Where a person is a supported person, and the question falls to be determined whether asylum support should in future be provided for him and one or more other persons who are his dependants and are—

  (a)   persons for whom asylum support is also being provided when that question falls to be determined; or

  (b)   persons for whom the Secretary of State is then considering whether asylum support should be provided,

in applying section 95(1) of the Act the Secretary of State must decide whether the supported person and all those dependants, taken together, are destitute or likely to become destitute within the period prescribed by regulation 7.

6 Income and assets to be taken into account

(1) This regulation applies where it falls to the Secretary of State to determine for the purposes of section 95(1) of the Act whether—

(a) a person applying for asylum support, or such an applicant and any dependants of his, or

(b) a supported person, or such a person and any dependants of his,

is or are destitute or likely to become so within the period prescribed by regulation 7.

(2) In this regulation "the principal" means the applicant for asylum support (where paragraph (1)(a) applies) or the supported person (where paragraph (1)(b) applies).

(3) The Secretary of State must ignore—

(a) any asylum support, and

(b) any support under section 98 of the Act,

which the principal or any dependant of his is provided with or, where the question is whether destitution is likely within a particular period, might be provided with in that period.

(4) But he must take into account—

(a) any other income which the principal, or any dependant of his, has or might reasonably be expected to have in that period;

(b) any other support which is available to the principal or any dependant of his, or might reasonably be expected to be so available in that period; and

(c) any assets mentioned in paragraph (5) (whether held in the United Kingdom or elsewhere) which are available to the principal or any dependant of his otherwise than by way of asylum support or support under section 98, or might reasonably be expected to be so available in that period.

(5) Those assets are—

(a) cash;

(b) savings;

(c) investments;

(d) land;

(e) cars or other vehicles; and

(f) goods held for the purpose of a trade or other business.

(6) The Secretary of State must ignore any assets not mentioned in paragraph (5).

7 Period within which applicant must be likely to become destitute

The period prescribed for the purposes of section 95(1) of the Act is—

(a) where the question whether a person or persons is or are destitute or likely to become so falls to be determined in relation to an application for asylum support and sub-paragraph (b) does not apply, 14 days beginning with the day on which that question falls to be determined;

(b) where that question falls to be determined in relation to a supported person, or in relation to persons including a supported person, 56 days beginning with the day on which that question falls to be determined.

8 Adequacy of existing accommodation

(1) Subject to paragraph (2), the matters mentioned in paragraph (3) are prescribed for the purposes of subsection (5)(a) of section 95 of the Act as matters to which the Secretary of State must have regard in determining for the purposes of that section whether the accommodation of—

(a) a person applying for asylum support, or

(b) a supported person for whom accommodation is not for the time being provided by way of asylum support,

is adequate.

(2)   The matters mentioned in paragraph (3)(a) and (d) to (g) are not so prescribed for the purposes of a case where the person indicates to the Secretary of State that he wishes to remain in the accommodation.

(3)   The matters referred to in paragraph (1) are—

    (a)   whether it would be reasonable for the person to continue to occupy the accommodation;

    (b)   whether the accommodation is affordable for him;

    (c)   whether the accommodation is provided under section 98 of the Act, or otherwise on an emergency basis, only while the claim for asylum support is being determined;

    (d)   whether the person can secure entry to the accommodation;

    (e)   where the accommodation consists of a moveable structure, vehicle or vessel designed or adapted for human habitation, whether there is a place where the person is entitled or permitted both to place it and reside in it;

    (f)   whether the accommodation is available for occupation by the person's dependants together with him;

    (g)   whether it is probable that the person's continued occupation of the accommodation will lead to domestic violence against him or any of his dependants.

(4)   In determining whether it would be reasonable for a person to continue to occupy accommodation, regard may be had to the general circumstances prevailing in relation to housing in the district of the local housing authority where the accommodation is.

(5)   In determining whether a person's accommodation is affordable for him, the Secretary of State must have regard to—

    (a)   any income, or any assets mentioned in regulation 6(5) (whether held in the United Kingdom or elsewhere), which is or are available to him or any dependant of his otherwise than by way of asylum support or support under section 98 of the Act, or might reasonably be expected to be so available;

    (b)   the costs in respect of the accommodation; and

    (c)   the person's other reasonable living expenses.

(6)   In this regulation—

    (a)   "domestic violence" means violence from a person who is or has been a close family member, or threats of violence from such a person which are likely to be carried out; and

    (b)   "district of the local housing authority" has the meaning given by section 217(3) of the Housing Act 1996.

(7)   The reference in paragraph (1) to subsection (5)(a) of section 95 of the Act does not include a reference to that provision as applied by section 98(3) of the Act.

9 Essential living needs

(1)   The matter mentioned in paragraph (2) is prescribed for the purposes of subsection (7)(b) of section 95 of the Act as a matter to which the Secretary of State may not have regard in determining for the purposes of that section whether a person's essential living needs (other than accommodation) are met.

(2)   That matter is his personal preference as to clothing (but this shall not be taken to prevent the Secretary of State from taking into account his individual circumstances as regards clothing).

(3)   None of the items and expenses mentioned in paragraph (4) is to be treated as being an essential living need of a person for the purposes of Part VI of the Act.

(4)   Those items and expenses are—

    (a)   the cost of faxes;

    (b)   computers and the cost of computer facilities;

    (c)   the cost of photocopying;

   (d)   travel expenses, except the expense mentioned in paragraph (5);
   (e)   toys and other recreational items;
   (f)   entertainment expenses.

(5) The expense excepted from paragraph (4)(d) is the expense of an initial journey from a place in the United Kingdom to accommodation provided by way of asylum support or (where accommodation is not so provided) to an address in the United Kingdom which has been notified to the Secretary of State as the address where the person intends to live.

(6) Paragraph (3) shall not be taken to affect the question whether any item or expense not mentioned in paragraph (4) or (5) is, or is not, an essential living need.

(7) The reference in paragraph (1) to subsection (7)(b) of section 95 of the Act includes a reference to that provision as applied by section 98(3) of the Act and, accordingly, the reference in paragraph (1) to "that section" includes a reference to section 98.

Provision of support

10 Kind and levels of support for essential living needs

(1) This regulation applies where the Secretary of State has decided that asylum support should be provided in respect of the essential living needs of a person.

[(2) As a general rule, asylum support in respect of the essential living needs of that person may be expected to be provided weekly in the form of [cash, equal to] the amount shown in the second column of the following Table opposite the entry in the first column which for the time being describes that person . . .]

[TABLE	
Qualifying couple	£72.52
Lone parent aged 18 or over	£43.94
Single person aged 25 or over (where the decision to grant support was made prior to the 5th October 2009 and the person reached age 25 prior to that date)	£42.62
Any other single person aged 18 or over	£36.62
Person aged at least 16 but under 18 (except a member of a qualifying couple)	£39.80
Person aged under 16	£52.96]]

(3) In paragraph (1) and the provisions of paragraph (2) preceding the Table, "person" includes "couple".

[(3A) For the purposes of the table at regulation 10(2), a decision to grant support is made on the date recorded on the letter granting asylum support to the applicant.]

(4) In this regulation—
   [(a)   "qualifying couple" means a married couple, an unmarried couple, a civil partnership couple or a same-sex couple, at least one of whom is aged 18 or over and neither of whom is aged under 16;]
   [(b)   "lone parent" means a parent who is not a member of a married couple, an unmarried couple, a civil partnership couple or a same-sex couple;]
   (c)   "single person" means a person who is not a parent or a member of a qualifying couple; and

(d)   "parent" means a parent of a relevant child, that is to say a child who is aged under 18 and for whom asylum support is provided.

(5)   Where the Secretary of State has decided that accommodation should be provided for a person (or couple) by way of asylum support, and the accommodation is provided in a form which also meets other essential living needs (such as bed and breakfast, or half or full board), the amounts shown in the Table in paragraph (2) shall be treated as reduced accordingly.

(6)   . . .

Amendment

Para (2): substituted by SI 2002/472, reg 4(1). Date in force: 8 April 2002: see SI 2002/472, reg 1.

Para (2): words "cash, equal to" in square brackets substituted by SI 2004/1313, reg 2(a). Date in force: 4 June 2004: see SI 2004/1313, reg 1.

Para (2): words omitted revoked by SI 2004/1313, reg 2(b). Date in force: 4 June 2004: see SI 2004/1313, reg 1.

Para (2): Table: substituted by SI 2011/907, reg 2. Date in force: 18 April 2011: see SI 2011/907, reg 1.

Para (3A): inserted by SI 2009/1388, reg 2(1), (3). Date in force: 6 July 2009: see SI 2009/1388, reg 1.

Para (4): sub-para (a) substituted by SI 2005/2114, art 2(13), Sch 13, Pt 1, para 2(1), (4)(a). Date in force: 5 December 2005: see SI 2005/2114, art 1.

Para (4): sub-para (b) substituted by SI 2005/2114, art 2(13), Sch 13, Pt 1, para 2(1), (4)(b). Date in force: 5 December 2005: see SI 2005/2114, art 1.

Para (6): revoked by SI 2002/472, reg 4(2). Date in force: 8 April 2002: see SI 2002/472, reg 1.

[10A Additional support for pregnant women and children under 3

(1)   In addition to the [cash support which the Secretary of State may be expected to provide weekly as] described in regulation 10(2), in the case of any pregnant woman or child aged under 3 for whom the Secretary of State has decided asylum support should be provided, there shall, as a general rule, be added to the [cash support] for any week the amount shown in the second column of the following table opposite the entry in the first column which for the time being describes that person.

TABLE

Pregnant woman	£3.00
Child aged under 1	£5.00
Child aged at least 1 and under 3	£3.00

(2)   In this regulation, "pregnant woman" means a woman who has provided evidence to satisfy the Secretary of State that she is pregnant.]

Amendment

Inserted by SI 2003/241, reg 2. Date in force: 3 March 2003: see SI 2003/241, reg 1.

Para (1): words "cash support which the Secretary of State may be expected to provide weekly as" in square brackets substituted by SI 2004/1313, reg 3(a). Date in force: 4 June 2004: see SI 2004/1313, reg 1.

Para (1): words "cash support" in square brackets substituted by SI 2004/1313, reg 3(b). Date in force: 4 June 2004: see SI 2004/1313, reg 1.

11

(*Revoked by SI 2004/1313, reg 4. Date in force: 4 June 2004 (except in relation to payments to a person whose qualifying period ends on or before that date): see SI 2004/1313, regs 1, 4(2).*)

12 Income and assets to be taken into account in providing support

(1) This regulation applies where it falls to the Secretary of State to decide the level or kind of asylum support to be provided for—

    (a)   a person applying for asylum support, or such an applicant and any dependants of his; or

    (b)   a supported person, or such a person and any dependants of his.

(2) In this regulation "the principal" means the applicant for asylum support (where paragraph (1)(a) applies) or the supported person (where paragraph (1)(b) applies).

(3) The Secretary of State must take into account—

    (a)   any income which the principal or any dependant of his has or might reasonably be expected to have,

    (b)   support which is or might reasonably be expected to be available to the principal or any dependant of his, and

    (c)   any assets mentioned in regulation 6(5) (whether held in the United Kingdom or elsewhere) which are or might reasonably be expected to be available to the principal or any dependant of his,

otherwise than by way of asylum support.

13 Accommodation

(1) The matters mentioned in paragraph (2) are prescribed for the purposes of subsection (2)(b) of section 97 of the Act as matters to which regard may not be had when exercising the power under section 95 of the Act to provide accommodation for a person.

(2) Those matters are—

    (a)   his personal preference as to the nature of the accommodation to be provided; and

    (b)   his personal preference as to the nature and standard of fixtures and fittings;

but this shall not be taken to prevent the person's individual circumstances, as they relate to his accommodation needs, being taken into account.

14 Services

(1) The services mentioned in paragraph (2) may be provided or made available by way of asylum support to persons who are otherwise receiving such support, but may be so provided only for the purpose of maintaining good order among such persons.

(2) Those services are—

    (a)   education, including English language lessons,

    (b)   sporting or other developmental activities.

Change of circumstances

15 Change of circumstances

(1) If a relevant change of circumstances occurs, the supported person concerned or a dependant of his must, without delay, notify the Secretary of State of that change of circumstances.

(2) A relevant change of circumstances occurs where a supported person or a dependant of his—

    (a)   is joined in the United Kingdom by a dependant or, as the case may be, another dependant, of the supported person;

    (b)   receives or gains access to any money, or other asset mentioned in regulation 6(5), that has not previously been declared to the Secretary of State;

    (c)   becomes employed;

    (d)   becomes unemployed;

(e)   changes his name;
(f)   gets married;
[(fa)   forms a civil partnership;]
(g)   starts living with a person as if married to that person;
[(ga)   starts living with a person as if a civil partner of that person;]
(h)   gets divorced;
[(ha)   becomes a former civil partner on the dissolution of his civil partnership;]
(i)   separates from a spouse, or from a person with whom he has been living as if married to that person;
[(ia)   separates from his civil partner or from the person with whom he has been living as if a civil partner of that person;]
(j)   becomes pregnant;
(k)   has a child;
(l)   leaves school;
(m)   starts to share his accommodation with another person;
(n)   moves to a different address, or otherwise leaves his accommodation;
(o)   goes into hospital;
(p)   goes to prison or is otherwise held in custody;
(q)   leaves the United Kingdom; or
(r)   dies.

(3)   If, on being notified of a change of circumstances, the Secretary of State considers that the change may be one—

(a)   as a result of which asylum support should be provided for a person for whom it was not provided before, or
(b)   as a result of which asylum support should no longer be provided for a person, or
(c)   which may otherwise affect the asylum support which should be provided for a person,

he may make further enquiries of the supported person or dependant who gave the notification.

(4)   The Secretary of State may, in particular, require that person to provide him with such information as he considers necessary to determine whether, and if so, what, asylum support should be provided for any person.

Amendment

Para (2): sub-para (fa) inserted by SI 2005/2114, art 2(13), Sch 13, Pt 1, para 2(1), (5)(a). Date in force: 5 December 2005: see SI 2005/2114, art 1.

Para (2): sub-para (ga) inserted by SI 2005/2114, art 2(13), Sch 13, Pt 1, para 2(1), (5)(b). Date in force: 5 December 2005: see SI 2005/2114, art 1.

Para (2): sub-para (ha) inserted by SI 2005/2114, art 2(13), Sch 13, Pt 1, para 2(1), (5)(c). Date in force: 5 December 2005: see SI 2005/2114, art 1.

Para (2): sub-para (ia) inserted by SI 2005/2114, art 2(13), Sch 13, Pt 1, para 2(1), (5)(d). Date in force: 5 December 2005: see SI 2005/2114, art 1.

Contributions

16 Contributions

(1)   This regulation applies where, in deciding the level of asylum support to be provided for a person who is or will be a supported person, the Secretary of State is required to take into account income, support or assets as mentioned in regulation 12(3).

(2)   The Secretary of State may—

(a)   set the asylum support for that person at a level which does not reflect the income, support or assets; and

    (b)   require from that person payments by way of contributions towards the cost of the provision for him of asylum support.

(3) A supported person must make to the Secretary of State such payments by way of contributions as the Secretary of State may require under paragraph (2).

(4) Prompt payment of such contributions may be made a condition (under section 95(9) of the Act) subject to which asylum support for that person is provided.

Recovery of sums by Secretary of State

17 Recovery where assets become realisable

(1) This regulation applies where it appears to the Secretary of State at any time (the relevant time)—

    (a)   that a supported person had, at the time when he applied for asylum support, assets of any kind in the United Kingdom or elsewhere which were not capable of being realised; but

    (b)   that those assets have subsequently become, and remain, capable of being realised.

(2) The Secretary of State may recover from that person a sum not exceeding the recoverable sum.

(3) Subject to paragraph (5), the recoverable sum is a sum equal to whichever is the less of—

    (a)   the monetary value of all the asylum support provided to the person up to the relevant time; and

    (b)   the monetary value of the assets concerned.

(4) As well as being recoverable as mentioned in paragraph 11(2)(a) of Schedule 8 to the Act, an amount recoverable under this regulation may be recovered by deduction from asylum support.

(5) The recoverable sum shall be treated as reduced by any amount which the Secretary of State has by virtue of this regulation already recovered from the person concerned (whether by deduction or otherwise) with regard to the assets concerned.

[17A Recovery of asylum support

(1) The Secretary of State may require a supported person to refund asylum support if it transpires that at any time during which asylum support was being provided for him he was not destitute.

(2) If a supported person has dependants, the Secretary of State may require him to refund asylum support if it transpires that at any time during which asylum support was being provided for the supported person and his dependants they were not destitute.

(3) The refund required shall not exceed the monetary value of all the asylum support provided to the supported person or to the supported person and his dependants for the relevant period.

(4) In this regulation the relevant period is the time during which asylum support was provided for the supported person or the supported person and his dependants and during which he or they were not destitute.

(5) If not paid within a reasonable period, the refund required may be recovered from the supported person as if it were a debt due to the Secretary of State.]

Amendment

    Inserted by SI 2005/11, regs 2, 4. Date in force: 5 February 2005: see SI 2005/11, reg 1.

18 Overpayments: method of recovery

As well as being recoverable as mentioned in subsection (3) of section 114 of the Act, an amount recoverable under subsection (2) of that section may be recovered by deduction from asylum support.

Breach of conditions and suspension and discontinuation of support

19 Breach of conditions: decision whether to provide support

(1) When deciding—

(a) whether to provide, or to continue to provide, asylum support for any person or persons, or

(b) the level or kind of support to be provided for any person or persons,

the Secretary of State may take into account [the extent to which a] relevant condition has been complied with.

[(2) A relevant condition is one which makes the provision of asylum support subject to actual residence by the supported person or a dependant of his for whom support is being provided in a specific place or location.]

Amendment

Para (1): words "the extent to which a" in square brackets substituted by SI 2005/11, regs 2, 5(a). Date in force: 5 February 2005: see SI 2005/11, reg 1.

Para (2): substituted by SI 2005/11, regs 2, 5(b). Date in force: 5 February 2005: see SI 2005/11, reg 1.

[20 Suspension or discontinuation of support

(1) Asylum support for a supported person and any dependant of his or for one or more dependants of a supported person may be suspended or discontinued if—

(a) support is being provided for the supported person or a dependant of his in collective accommodation and the Secretary of State has reasonable grounds to believe that the supported person or his dependant has committed a serious breach of the rules of that accommodation;

(b) the Secretary of State has reasonable grounds to believe that the supported person or a dependant of his for whom support is being provided has committed an act of seriously violent behaviour whether or not that act occurs in accommodation provided by way of asylum support or at the authorised address or elsewhere;

(c) the supported person or a dependant of his has committed an offence under Part VI of the Act;

(d) the Secretary of State has reasonable grounds to believe that the supported person or any dependant of his for whom support is being provided has abandoned the authorised address without first informing the Secretary of State or, if requested, without permission;

(e) the supported person has not complied within a reasonable period, which shall be no less than five working days beginning with the day on which the request was received by him, with requests for information made by the Secretary of State and which relate to the supported person's or his dependant's eligibility for or receipt of asylum support including requests made under regulation 15;

(f) the supported person fails, without reasonable excuse, to attend an interview requested by the Secretary of State relating to the supported person's or his dependant's eligibility for or receipt of asylum support;

(g) the supported person or, if he is an asylum seeker, his dependant, has not complied within a reasonable period, which shall be no less than ten working days beginning with the day on which the request was received by him, with a request for information made by the Secretary of State relating to his claim for asylum;

(h) the Secretary of State has reasonable grounds to believe that the supported person or a dependant of his for whom support is being provided has concealed financial resources and that the supported person or a dependant of his or both have therefore unduly benefited from the receipt of asylum support;

(i)   the supported person or a dependant of his for whom support is being provided has not complied with a reporting requirement;

(j)   the Secretary of State has reasonable grounds to believe that the supported person or a dependant of his for whom support is being provided has made a claim for asylum ("the first claim") and before the first claim has been determined makes or seeks to make a further claim for asylum not being part of the first claim in the same or a different name; or

(k)   the supported person or a dependant of his for whom support is being provided has failed without reasonable excuse to comply with a relevant condition.

(2) If a supported person is asked to attend an interview of the type referred to in paragraph (1)(f) he shall be given no less than five working days notice of it.

(3) Any decision to discontinue support in the circumstances referred to in paragraph (1) above shall be taken individually, objectively and impartially and reasons shall be given. Decisions will be based on the particular situation of the person concerned and particular regard shall be had to whether he is a vulnerable person as described by Article 17 of Council Directive 2003/9/EC of 27th January 2003 laying down minimum standards for the reception of asylum seekers.

(4) No person's asylum support shall be discontinued before a decision is made under paragraph (1).

(5) Where asylum support for a supported person or his dependant is suspended or discontinued under paragraph (1)(d) or (i) and the supported person or his dependant are traced or voluntarily report to the police, the Secretary of State or an immigration officer, a duly motivated decision based on the reasons for the disappearance shall be taken as to the reinstatement of some or all of the supported person's or his dependant's or both of their asylum support.

(6) For the purposes of this regulation—

(a)   the authorised address is—

    (i)   the accommodation provided for the supported person and his dependants (if any) by way of asylum support; or

    (ii)   if no accommodation is so provided, the address notified by the supported person to the Secretary of State in his application for asylum support or, where a change of address has been notified to the Secretary of State under regulation 15 or under the Immigration Rules or both, the address for the time being so notified;

(b)   "collective accommodation" means accommodation which a supported person or any dependant of his for whom support is being provided shares with any other supported person and includes accommodation in which only facilities are shared;

(c)   "relevant condition" has the same meaning as in regulation 19(2);

(d)   "reporting requirement" is a condition or restriction which requires a person to report to the police, an immigration officer or the Secretary of State and is imposed under—

    (i)   paragraph 21 of Schedule 2 to the Immigration Act 1971 (temporary admission or release from detention);

    (ii)   paragraph 22 of that Schedule; or

    (iii)   paragraph 2 or 5 of Schedule 3 to that Act (pending deportation).

(e)   "working day" has the same meaning as in regulation 3(7) save that the reference to the applicant shall be a reference to the supported person or his dependant.]

Amendment

Substituted by SI 2005/11, regs 2, 6. Date in force: 5 February 2005: see SI 2005/11, reg 1.

[20A Temporary Support
Regulations 19 and 20 shall apply to a person or his dependant who is provided with temporary support under section 98 of the Act in the same way as they apply to a person and his dependant who is in receipt of asylum support and any reference to asylum support in regulations 19 and 20 shall include a reference to temporary support under section 98.]

Amendment
Inserted by SI 2005/11, regs 2, 7. Date in force: 5 February 2005: see SI 2005/11, reg 1.

21 Effect of previous suspension or discontinuation
(1) [Subject to regulation 20(5) where—]
- (a) an application for asylum support is made,
- (b) the applicant or any other person to whom the application relates has previously had his asylum support suspended or discontinued under regulation 20, and
- (c) there has been no material change of circumstances since the suspension or discontinuation,

the application need not be entertained unless the Secretary of State considers that there are exceptional circumstances which justify its being entertained.

(2) A material change of circumstances is one which, if the applicant were a supported person, would have to be notified to the Secretary of State under regulation 15.

(3) This regulation is without prejudice to the power of the Secretary of State to refuse the application even if he has entertained it.

Amendment
Para (1): words in square brackets substituted by SI 2005/11, regs 2, 8. Date in force: 5 February 2005: see SI 2005/11, reg 1.

Notice to quit

22 Notice to quit
(1) If—
- (a) as a result of asylum support, a person has a tenancy or licence to occupy accommodation,
- (b) one or more of the conditions mentioned in paragraph (2) is satisfied, and
- (c) he is given notice to quit in accordance with paragraph (3) or (4),

his tenancy or licence is to be treated as ending with the period specified in that notice, regardless of when it could otherwise be brought to an end.

(2) The conditions are that—
- (a) the asylum support is suspended or discontinued as a result of any provision of regulation 20;
- (b) the relevant claim for asylum has been determined;
- (c) the supported person has ceased to be destitute; or
- (d) he is to be moved to other accommodation.

(3) A notice to quit is in accordance with this paragraph if it is in writing and—
- (a) in a case where sub-paragraph (a), (c) or (d) of paragraph (2) applies, specifies as the notice period a period of not less than seven days; or
- (b) in a case where the Secretary of State has notified his decision on the relevant claim for asylum to the claimant, specifies as the notice period a period at least as long as whichever is the greater of—
  - (i) seven days; or

    (ii)   the period beginning with the date of service of the notice to quit and ending with the date of determination of the relevant claim for asylum (found in accordance with section 94(3) of the Act).

(4)   A notice to quit is in accordance with this paragraph if—

    (a)   it is in writing;

    (b)   it specifies as the notice period a period of less than seven days; and

    (c)   the circumstances of the case are such that that notice period is justified.

Meaning of "destitute" for certain other purposes

23 Meaning of "destitute" for certain other purposes

(1)   In this regulation "the relevant enactments" means—

    (a)   section 21(1A) of the National Assistance Act 1948;

    (b)   section 45(4A) of the Health Services and Public Health Act 1968;

    (c)   paragraph 2(2A) of Schedule 8 to the National Health Service Act 1977;

    (d)   sections 12(2A), 13A(4) and 13B(3) of the Social Work (Scotland) Act 1968;

    (e)   [article 14 of the Mental Health (Care and Treatment) (Scotland) Act 2003 (Consequential Provisions) Order 2005]; and

    (f)   Articles 7(3) and 15(6) of the Health and Personal Social Services (Northern Ireland) Order 1972.

(2)   The following provisions of this regulation apply where it falls to an authority, or the Department, to determine for the purposes of any of the relevant enactments whether a person is destitute.

(3)   Paragraphs (3) to (6) of regulation 6 apply as they apply in the case mentioned in paragraph (1) of that regulation, but as if references to the principal were references to the person whose destitution or otherwise is being determined and references to the Secretary of State were references to the authority or (as the case may be) Department.

(4)   The matters mentioned in paragraph (3) of regulation 8 (read with paragraphs (4) to (6) of that regulation) are prescribed for the purposes of subsection (5)(a) of section 95 of the Act, as applied for the purposes of any of the relevant enactments, as matters to which regard must be had in determining for the purposes of any of the relevant enactments whether a person's accommodation is adequate.

(5)   The matter mentioned in paragraph (2) of regulation 9 is prescribed for the purposes of subsection (7)(b) of section 95 of the Act, as applied for the purposes of any of the relevant enactments, as a matter to which regard may not be had in determining for the purposes of any of the relevant enactments whether a person's essential living needs (other than accommodation) are met.

(6)   Paragraphs (3) to (6) of regulation 9 shall apply as if the reference in paragraph (3) to Part VI of the Act included a reference to the relevant enactments.

(7)   The references in regulations 8(5) and 9(2) to the Secretary of State shall be construed, for the purposes of this regulation, as references to the authority or (as the case may be) Department.

Amendment

Para (1): in sub-para (e) words in square brackets substituted by SI 2005/2078, art 15, Sch 2, para 20. Date in force: 5 October 2005: see SI 2005/2078, art 1(1).

SCHEDULE

(Revoked by SI 2007/863, reg 4. Date in force: 9 April 2007: see SI 2007/863, reg 1.)

PERSONS SUBJECT TO IMMIGRATION CONTROL (HOUSING AUTHORITY ACCOMMODATION AND HOMELESSNESS) ORDER 2000

(SI 2000/706)

Made: 7 March 2000.

Authority: Immigration and Asylum Act 1999, ss 118, 119, 166(3).

Commencement: 3 April 2000.

1 Citation, commencement and extent

(1)   This Order may be cited as the Persons subject to Immigration Control (Housing Authority Accommodation and Homelessness) Order 2000 and shall come into force on 3rd April 2000.

(2)   This Order does not extend to Wales.

(3)   Article 4 extends to England only.

(4)   Articles 5 and 8 extend to Northern Ireland only.

(5)   Articles 6 and 9 extend to Scotland only.

(6)   Article 7 extends to Scotland and Northern Ireland only.

2 Interpretation

In this Order—

"the 1971 Act" means the Immigration Act 1971;

"the 1985 Act" means the Housing Act 1985;

. . . .

"the 1999 Act" means the Immigration and Asylum Act 1999;

"asylum-seeker" means a person who is not under 18 and who made a claim for asylum which is recorded by the Secretary of State as having been made on or before 2nd April 2000 but which has not been determined;

"child in need" means a child—

(a)   who is unlikely to achieve or maintain, or to have the opportunity of achieving or maintaining, a reasonable standard of health or development without the provision for him of services by a local authority under Part III of the Children Act 1989 (local authority support for children and families);

(b)   whose health or development is likely to be significantly impaired, or further impaired, without the provision for him of such services; or

(c)   who is blind, deaf or dumb or suffers from mental disorder of any kind or is substantially and permanently handicapped by illness, injury or congenital deformity or such other disability as may be prescribed by regulations made under section 17 of the Children Act 1989 (provision of services for children in need, their families and others);

"claim for asylum" means a claim that it would be contrary to the United Kingdom's obligations under the Refugee Convention for the claimant to be removed from, or required to leave, the United Kingdom;

"Common Travel Area" means the United Kingdom, the Channel Islands, the Isle of Man and the Republic of Ireland collectively;

"designated course" means a course of any kind designated by regulations made by the Secretary of State for the purposes of paragraph 10 of Schedule 1 to the 1985 Act (student lettings which are not secure tenancies);

"development" means physical, intellectual, emotional, social or behavioural development;

"educational establishment" means a university or institution which provides further education or higher education (or both); and for the purposes of this definition "further education" has the same meaning as in section 2 of the Education Act 1996 (definition of further education) and "higher education" means education provided by means of a course of any description mentioned in Schedule 6 to the Education Reform Act 1988 (courses of higher education);

"family", in relation to a child in need, includes any person who has parental responsibility for the child and any other person with whom he has been living;

"full-time course" means a course normally involving not less than 15 hours attendance a week in term time for the organised day-time study of a single subject or related subjects;

"health" means physical or mental health;

"the immigration rules" means the rules laid down as mentioned in section 3(2) of the 1971 Act (general provisions for regulation and control);

. . .

"the Refugee Convention" means the Convention relating to the Status of Refugees done at Geneva on 28th July 1951 as extended by Article 1(2) of the Protocol relating to the Status of Refugees done at New York on 31st January 1967;

"specified education institution" means—

(a) a university or other institution within the higher education sector within the meaning of section 91(5) of the Further and Higher Education Act 1992 (interpretation of Education Acts), in respect of a university or other institution in England, or section 56(2) of the Further and Higher Education (Scotland) Act 1992 (interpretation of Part II), in respect of a university or other institution in Scotland;

(b) an institution in England within the further education sector within the meaning of section 91(3) of the Further and Higher Education Act 1992;

(c) a college of further education in Scotland which is under the management of an education authority or which is managed by a board of management in terms of Part I of the Further and Higher Education (Scotland) Act 1992 (further education in Scotland);

(d) a central institution in Scotland within the meaning of section 135(1) of the Education (Scotland) Act 1980 (interpretation);

(e) an institution in England which provides a course qualifying for funding under Part I of the Education Act 1994 (teaching training);

(f) a higher education institution in Northern Ireland within the meaning of Article 30(3) of the Education and Libraries (Northern Ireland) Order 1993 (funding by Department of higher education); or

(g) an institution of further education in Northern Ireland within the meaning of Article 3 of the Further Education (Northern Ireland) Order 1997 (definition of "further education").

Amendment

Definitions "the 1995 Act" and "limited leave" (omitted) revoked by SI 2008/1768, art 2(1), (2). Date in force: 7 August 2008: see SI 2008/1768, art 1.

3 Housing authority accommodation—England, Scotland and Northern Ireland

The following are classes of persons specified for the purposes of section 118(1) of the 1999 Act (housing authority accommodation) in respect of England, Scotland and Northern Ireland—

(a) Class A—a person recorded by the Secretary of State as a refugee within the definition in Article 1 of the Refugee Convention;

(b) Class B—a person—

[(i) who has leave to enter or remain in the United Kingdom granted outside the provisions of the immigration rules; and]

(ii) whose leave is not subject to a condition requiring him to maintain and accommodate himself, and any person who is dependent on him, without recourse to public funds;

[(bb) Class BA—a person who has humanitarian protection granted under the immigration rules;]

(c) Class C—a person who has current leave to enter or remain in the United Kingdom which is not subject to any limitation or condition and who is habitually resident in the Common Travel Area other than a person—

(i) who has been given leave to enter or remain in the United Kingdom upon an undertaking given by another person (his "sponsor") in writing in pursuance of the immigration rules to be responsible for his maintenance and accommodation;

(ii) who has been resident in the United Kingdom for less than five years beginning on the date of entry or the date on which the undertaking was given in respect of him, whichever date is the later; and

(iii) whose sponsor or, where there is more than one sponsor, at least one of whose sponsors, is still alive;

(d) Class D—a person who left the territory of Montserrat after 1st November 1995 because of the effect on that territory of a volcanic eruption;

(e) . . .

(f) Class F—a person who is attending a full-time course at a specified education institution in a case where the housing accommodation which is or may be provided to him—

(i) is let by a housing authority to that specified education institution for the purposes of enabling that institution to provide accommodation for students attending a full-time course at that institution; and

(ii) would otherwise be difficult for that housing authority to let on terms which, in the opinion of the housing authority, are satisfactory.

Amendment

Para (b)(i) substituted by SI 2006/2521, art 2(1), (2)(a). Date in force: 9 October 2006: see SI 2006/2521, art 1.

Para (bb) inserted by SI 2006/2521, art 2(1), (2)(b). Date in force: 9 October 2006: see SI 2006/2521, art 1.

Para (e) revoked by SI 2008/1768, art 2(1), (3). Date in force: 7 August 2008: see SI 2008/1768, art 1; for transitional provisions see art 3(1) thereof.

4 Housing authority accommodation—England

(1) The following are classes of persons specified for the purposes of section 118(1) of the 1999 Act in respect of England—

(a)   Class G—a person who is owed a duty under section 21 of the National Assistance Act 1948 (duty of local authorities to provide accommodation);

(b)   Class H—a person who is either a child in need or a member of the family of a child in need;

(c)   Class I—a person—

   (i)   who is owed a duty under section 63(1) (interim duty to accommodate in case of apparent priority need), 65(2) or (3) (duties to persons found to be homeless) or 68(1) or (2) (duties to persons whose applications are referred) of the 1985 Act;

   (ii)   who is owed a duty under section 188(1) (interim duty to accommodate in case of apparent priority need), 190(2) (duties to persons becoming homeless intentionally), 193(2) (duty to persons with priority need who are not homeless intentionally), 195(2) (duties in case of threatened homelessness) or 200(1), (3) or (4) (duties to applicant whose case is considered for referral or referred) of the Housing Act 1996; or

   (iii)   in respect of whom a local housing authority are exercising their power under section 194(1) (power exercisable after minimum period of duty under section 193) of the Housing Act 1996;

(d)   Class J—an asylum-seeker to whom, or a dependant of an asylum-seeker to whom, a local authority is required to provide support in accordance with regulations made under Schedule 9 to the 1999 Act (asylum support: interim provisions);

(e)   Class K—a person who is attending a designated course, which is a full-time course, at an educational establishment in a case where the housing accommodation which is or may be provided him by a local housing authority—

   (i)   is not and will not be let to him as a secure tenancy by virtue of paragraph 10 of Schedule 1 to the 1985 Act (student lettings which are not secure tenancies); and

   (ii)   would otherwise be difficult for that local housing authority to let on terms which, in the opinion of the local housing authority, are satisfactory;

(f)   Class L—a person who has a secure tenancy within the meaning of section 79 of the 1985 Act (secure tenancies).

(2)   "Dependant", in relation to an asylum-seeker within paragraph (1)(d) (Class J), means a person in the United Kingdom who—

(a)   is his spouse;

(b)   is a child of his, or of his spouse, who is under 18 and dependent on him; or

(c)   falls within such additional category as may be prescribed under section 94(1) of the 1999 Act (interpretation of Part VI—support for asylum-seekers), for the purposes of regulations made under Schedule 9 to the 1999 Act (asylum support: interim provisions), in relation to an asylum-seeker.

5 Housing authority accommodation—Northern Ireland

The following are classes of persons specified for the purposes of section 118(1) of the 1999 Act in respect of Northern Ireland—

(a)   Class M—a person who is a secure tenant of the Northern Ireland Housing Executive or a registered housing association within the meaning of Article 25 of the Housing (Northern Ireland) Order 1983 (secure tenancies);

(b)   Class N—a person who is owed a duty under Article 8 (interim duty to accommodate in case of apparent priority need), 10(2) or (3) (duties to persons found to be homeless) or 11(2) (duties to persons found to be threatened with homelessness) of the Housing (Northern Ireland) Order 1988.

6 Housing authority accommodation—Scotland

The following are classes of persons specified for the purposes of section 118(1) of the 1999 Act in respect of Scotland—

(a)   Class O—a person who is a secure tenant within the meaning of Part III of the Housing (Scotland) Act 1987 (rights of public sector tenants);

(b)   Class P—a person who is owed a duty under section 29 (interim duty to accommodate in case of apparent priority need), 31 (duties to persons found to be homeless), 32 (duties to persons found to be threatened with homelessness) or 34 (duties to persons whose applications are referred to another local authority) of the Housing (Scotland) Act 1987.

7 Homelessness—Scotland and Northern Ireland

(1) The following are classes of persons specified for the purposes of section 119(1) of the 1999 Act (homelessness: Scotland and Northern Ireland) in respect of Scotland and Northern Ireland—

[(a)   the classes specified in article 3(a) to (d) (Class A, Class B, Class BA, Class C and Class D);]

(b)   Class Q—a person who is an asylum-seeker and who made a claim for asylum—

(i)   which is recorded by the Secretary of State as having been made on his arrival (other than on re-entry) in the United Kingdom from a country outside the Common Travel Area; and

(ii)   which has not been recorded by the Secretary of State as having been either decided (other than on appeal) or abandoned;

(c)   Class R—a person who is an asylum-seeker and—

(i)   who made a relevant claim for asylum on or before 4th February 1996; and

(ii)   who was, on 4th February 1996, entitled to benefit under regulation 7A of the Housing Benefit (General) Regulations 1987 (persons from abroad) or regulation 7A of the Housing Benefit (General) Regulations (Northern Ireland) 1987 (persons from abroad).

(2) In paragraph (1)(c)(i), a relevant claim for asylum is a claim for asylum which—

(a)   has not been recorded by the Secretary of State as having been either decided (other than on appeal) or abandoned; or

(b)   has been recorded as having been decided (other than on appeal) on or before 4th February 1996 and in respect of which an appeal is pending which—

(i)   was pending on 5th February 1996; or

(ii)   was made within the time limits specified in the rules of procedure made under section 22 of the 1971 Act (procedure).

Amendment

Para (1): sub-para (a) substituted by SI 2008/1768, art 2(1), (4). Date in force: 7 August 2008: see SI 2008/1768, art 1; for transitional provisions see art 3(2) thereof.

[8 Homelessness—Northern Ireland

The following is a class of person specified for the purposes of section 119(1) of the 1999 Act in respect of Northern Ireland—

Class T—a person who is an asylum-seeker and—

(a) who was in Northern Ireland when the Secretary of State made a declaration to the effect that the country of which that person is a national is subject to such a fundamental change in circumstances that he would not normally order the return of a person to that country;

(b) who made a claim for asylum which is recorded by the Secretary of State as having been made within a period of three months from the day on which that declaration was made; and

(c) whose claim for asylum has not been recorded by the Secretary of State as having been either decided (other than on appeal) or abandoned.]

Amendment

Substituted by SI 2008/1768, art 2(1), (5). Date in force: 7 August 2008: see SI 2008/1768, art 1; for transitional provisions see art 3(2) thereof.

[9 Homelessness—Scotland
The following is a class of person specified for the purposes of section 119(1) of the 1999 Act in respect of Scotland—

Class V—a person who is an asylum-seeker and—

(a) who was in Great Britain when the Secretary of State made a declaration to the effect that the country of which that person is a national is subject to such a fundamental change in circumstances that he would not normally order the return of a person to that country;

(b) who made a claim for asylum which is recorded by the Secretary of State as having been made within a period of three months from the day on which that declaration was made; and

(c) whose claim for asylum has not been recorded by the Secretary of State as having been either decided (other than on appeal) or abandoned.]

Amendment

Substituted by SI 2008/1768, art 2(1), (6). Date in force: 7 August 2008: see SI 2008/1768, art 1; for transitional provisions see art 3(2) thereof.

10 Revocation
The following Orders are revoked—

(a) the Housing Accommodation and Homelessness (Persons subject to Immigration Control) Order 1996, in so far as it extends to England and Scotland;

(b) the Homelessness (Persons subject to Immigration Control) (Amendment) Order 1997, in so far as it extends to England and Scotland;

(c) the Housing Accommodation and Homelessness (Persons subject to Immigration Control) (Amendment) Order 1998, in so far as it extends to England;

(d) the Housing Accommodation and Homelessness (Persons subject to Immigration Control) (Northern Ireland) Order 1998;

(e) the Housing Accommodation and Homelessness (Persons subject to Immigration Control) (Amendment) (Scotland) Order 1999; and

(f) the Housing Accommodation (Persons subject to Immigration Control) (Amendment) (England) Order 1999.

IMMIGRATION (LEAVE TO ENTER AND REMAIN) ORDER 2000

(SI 2000/1161)

Made: 19th April 2000.

Authority: Immigration Act 1971, ss 3A(1)–(4), (6), (10), 3B(2)(a), (c), (3)(a).

Commencement: see art 1.

PART I
GENERAL

1 Citation, commencement and interpretation

(1)   This Order may be cited as the Immigration (Leave to Enter and Remain) Order 2000.

(2)   Articles 1 to 12, 14 and 15(1) of this Order shall come into force on 28th April 2000 or, if later, on the day after the day on which it is made and articles 13 and 15(2) shall come into force on 30th July 2000.

(3)   In this Order—

"the Act" means the Immigration Act 1971;

["ADS Agreement with China" means the Memorandum of Understanding on visa and related issues concerning tourist groups from the People's Republic of China to the United Kingdom as an approved destination, signed on 21st January 2005;]

"control port" means a port in which a control area is designated under paragraph 26(3) of Schedule 2 to the Act;

["convention travel document" means a travel document issued pursuant to Article 28 of the Refugee Convention, except where that travel document was issued by the United Kingdom Government;]

["decision-maker" means—

(a)   the Secretary of State;

(b)   an immigration officer;]

"the Immigration Acts" means:

(a)   the Act;

(b)   the Immigration Act 1988;

(c)   the Asylum and Immigration Appeals Act 1993;

(d)   the Asylum and Immigration Act 1996; and

(e)   the Immigration and Asylum Act 1999;

["Refugee Convention" means the Convention relating to the Status of Refugees done at Geneva on 28th July 1951 and its Protocol;]

["representative" means a person who appears to the decision-maker—

(a)   to be the representative of the person referred to in article 8ZA(1); and

(b)   not to be prohibited from acting as a representative by section 84 of the Immigration and Asylum Act 1999;]

"responsible third party" means a person appearing to an immigration officer to be:

(a)   in charge of a group of people arriving in the United Kingdom together or intending to arrive in the United Kingdom together;

(b)   a tour operator;

(c)   the owner or agent of a ship, aircraft, train, hydrofoil or hovercraft;

    (d)   the person responsible for the management of a control port or his agent; or

    (e)   an official at a British Diplomatic Mission or at a British Consular Post or at the office of any person outside the United Kingdom and Islands who has been authorised by the Secretary of State to accept applications for entry clearance;

"tour operator" means a person who, otherwise than occasionally, organises and provides holidays to the public or a section of it; and

"visit visa" means an entry clearance granted for the purpose of entry to the United Kingdom as a visitor under the immigration rules.

Amendment

Para (3): definition "ADS Agreement with China" inserted by SI 2005/1159, arts 2, 3. Date in force: 1 April 2005: see SI 2005/1159, art 1.

Para (3): definition "convention travel document" inserted by SI 2004/475, arts 2, 3(a). Date in force: 27 February 2004: see SI 2004/475, art 1.

Para (3): definitions "decision-maker" and "representative" inserted by SI 2013/1749, arts 2, 3. Date in force: 12 July 2013: see SI 2013/1749, art 1.

Para (3): definition "Refugee Convention" inserted by SI 2004/475, arts 2, 3(b). Date in force: 27 February 2004: see SI 2004/475, art 1.

PART II
ENTRY CLEARANCE AS LEAVE TO ENTER

2 Entry clearance as Leave to Enter

Subject to article 6(3), an entry clearance which complies with the requirements of article 3 shall have effect as leave to enter the United Kingdom to the extent specified in article 4, but subject to the conditions referred to in article 5.

3 Requirements

[(1) Subject to paragraph (4), an entry clearance shall only have effect as leave to enter if it complies with the requirements of this article.]

(2) The entry clearance must specify the purpose for which the holder wishes to enter the United Kingdom.

(3) The entry clearance must be endorsed with:

    (a)   the conditions to which it is subject; or

    (b)   a statement that it is to have effect as indefinite leave to enter the United Kingdom.

[(4) Subject to paragraph (5), an entry clearance shall not have effect as leave to enter if it is endorsed on a convention travel document.

(5) An entry clearance endorsed on a convention travel document before 27th February 2004 shall have effect as leave to enter.]

Amendment

Para (1): substituted by SI 2004/475, arts 2, 4(a). Date in force: 27 February 2004: see SI 2004/475, art 1.

Paras (4), (5): inserted by SI 2004/475, arts 2, 4(b). Date in force: 27 February 2004: see SI 2004/475, art 1.

4 Extent to which Entry Clearance is to be Leave to Enter

(1) A visit visa [(other than a visit visa granted pursuant to the ADS Agreement with China) unless endorsed with a statement that it is to have effect as a single-entry visa], during its period of validity, shall have effect as leave to enter the United Kingdom on an unlimited number of occasions, in accordance with paragraph (2).

(2) On each occasion the holder arrives in the United Kingdom, he shall be treated for the purposes of the Immigration Acts as having been granted, before arrival, leave to enter the United Kingdom for a limited period beginning on the date of arrival, being:

    (a)   six months if six months or more remain of the visa's period of validity; or

    (b)   the visa's remaining period of validity, if less than six months.

[(2A) A visit visa granted pursuant to the ADS Agreement with China endorsed with a statement that it is to have effect as a dual-entry visa, shall have effect as leave to enter the United Kingdom on two occasions during its period of validity, in accordance with paragraph (2B).

(2B) On arrival in the United Kingdom on each occasion, the holder shall be treated for the purposes of the Immigration Acts as having been granted, before arrival, leave to enter the United Kingdom for a limited period, being the period beginning on the date on which the holder arrives in the United Kingdom and ending on the date of expiry of the entry clearance.]

(3) In the case of [any form of entry clearance to which this paragraph applies], it shall have effect as leave to enter the United Kingdom on one occasion during its period of validity; and, on arrival in the United Kingdom, the holder shall be treated for the purposes of the Immigration Acts as having been granted, before arrival, leave to enter the United Kingdom:

    (a)   in the case of an entry clearance which is endorsed with a statement that it is to have effect as indefinite leave to enter the United Kingdom, for an indefinite period; or

    (b)   in the case of an entry clearance which is endorsed with conditions, for a limited period, being the period beginning on the date on which the holder arrives in the United Kingdom and ending on the date of expiry of the entry clearance.

[(3A) Paragraph (3) applies to—

    (a)   a visit visa (other than a visit visa granted pursuant to the ADS Agreement with China) endorsed with a statement that it is to have effect as a single entry visa;

    (b)   a visit visa granted pursuant to the ADS Agreement with China unless endorsed with a statement to the effect that it is to have effect as a dual entry visa; and

    (c)   any other form of entry clearance.]

(4) In this article "period of validity" means the period beginning on the day on which the entry clearance becomes effective and ending on the day on which it expires.

Amendment

Para (1): words from "(other than a" to "single-entry visa" in square brackets inserted by SI 2005/1159, arts 2, 4(1), (2). Date in force: 1 April 2005: see SI 2005/1159, art 1.

Paras (2A), (2B): inserted by SI 2005/1159, arts 2, 4(1), (3). Date in force: 1 April 2005: see SI 2005/1159, art 1.

Para (3): words "any form of entry clearance to which this paragraph applies" in square brackets substituted by SI 2005/1159, arts 2, 4(1), (4). Date in force: 1 April 2005: see SI 2005/1159, art 1.

Para (3A): inserted by SI 2005/1159, arts 2, 4(1), (5). Date in force: 1 April 2005: see SI 2005/1159, art 1.

Modification

Modified, in its application to the Channel Tunnel, by the Channel Tunnel (International Arrangements) Order 1993, SI 1993/1813, art 7(1), Sch 4, para 4.

5 Conditions

An entry clearance shall have effect as leave to enter subject to any conditions, being conditions of a kind that may be imposed on leave to enter given under section 3 of the Act, to which the entry clearance is subject and which are endorsed on it.

6 Incidental, supplementary and consequential provisions

(1)   Where an immigration officer exercises his power to cancel leave to enter under paragraph 2A(8) of Schedule 2 to the Act or article 13(7) below in respect of an entry clearance which has effect as leave to enter, the entry clearance shall cease to have effect.

(2)   If the holder of an entry clearance—

> (a)   arrives in the United Kingdom before the day on which it becomes effective; or
>
> (b)   seeks to enter the United Kingdom for a purpose other than the purpose specified in the entry clearance,

an immigration officer may cancel the entry clearance.

(3)   If the holder of an entry clearance which does not, at the time, have effect as leave to enter the United Kingdom seeks leave to enter the United Kingdom at any time before his departure for, or in the course of his journey to, the United Kingdom and is refused leave to enter under article 7, the entry clearance shall not have effect as leave to enter.

Modification

Modified, in its application to the Channel Tunnel, by the Channel Tunnel (International Arrangements) Order 1993, SI 1993/1813, art 7(1), Sch 4, para 4.

PART III
FORM AND MANNER OF GIVING AND REFUSING LEAVE TO ENTER

7 Grant and refusal of leave to enter before arrival in the United Kingdom

(1)   An immigration officer, whether or not in the United Kingdom, may give or refuse a person leave to enter the United Kingdom at any time before his departure for, or in the course of his journey to, the United Kingdom.

(2)   In order to determine whether or not to give leave to enter under this article (and, if so, for what period and subject to what conditions), an immigration officer may seek such information, and the production of such documents or copy documents, as an immigration officer would be entitled to obtain in an examination under paragraph 2 or 2A of Schedule 2 to the Act.

(3)   An immigration officer may also require the person seeking leave to supply an up to date medical report.

(4)   Failure by a person seeking leave to supply any information, documents, copy documents or medical report requested by an immigration officer under this article shall be a ground, in itself, for refusal of leave.

[8 Oral grant or refusal of leave

(1)   A notice giving or refusing leave to enter the United Kingdom as a visitor may, instead of being given in writing as required by section 4(1) of the Act, be given orally, including by means of a telephone.

(2)   In paragraph (1), "leave to enter the United Kingdom as a visitor" means leave to enter as a visitor under the immigration rules for a period not exceeding six months, subject to conditions prohibiting employment and recourse to public funds (within the meaning of the immigration rules).]

Amendment

Articles 8, 8ZA, 8ZB, 8ZC substituted, for art 8 as originally enacted, by SI 2013/1749, arts 2, 4. Date in force: 12 July 2013: see SI 2013/1749, art 1.

[8ZA Grant, refusal or variation of leave by notice in writing

(1)   A notice in writing—

> (a)   giving leave to enter or remain in the United Kingdom;
>
> (b)   refusing leave to enter or remain in the United Kingdom;

    (c)   refusing to vary a person's leave to enter or remain in the United Kingdom; or

    (d)   varying a person's leave to enter or remain in the United Kingdom,

may be given to the person affected as required by section 4(1) of the Act as follows.

(2)   The notice may be—

    (a)   given by hand;

    (b)   sent by fax;

    (c)   sent by postal service to a postal address provided for correspondence by the person or the person's representative;

    (d)   sent electronically to an e-mail address provided for correspondence by the person or the person's representative;

    (e)   sent by document exchange to a document exchange number or address; or

    (f)   sent by courier.

(3)   Where no postal or e-mail address for correspondence has been provided, the notice may be sent—

    (a)   by postal service to—

        (i)   the last-known or usual place of abode, place of study or place of business of the person; or

        (ii)   the last-known or usual place of business of the person's representative; or

    (b)   electronically to—

        (i)   the last-known e-mail address for the person (including at the person's last-known place of study or place of business); or

        (ii)   the last-known e-mail address of the person's representative.

(4)   Where attempts to give notice in accordance with paragraphs (2) and (3) are not possible or have failed, when the decision-maker records the reasons for this and places the notice on file the notice shall be deemed to have been given.

(5)   Where a notice is deemed to have been given in accordance with paragraph (4) and then subsequently the person is located, the person shall as soon as is practicable be given a copy of the notice and details of when and how it was given.

(6)   A notice given under this article may, in the case of a person who is under 18 years of age and does not have a representative, be given to the parent, guardian or another adult who for the time being takes responsibility for the child.]

Amendment

   Articles 8, 8ZA, 8ZB, 8ZC substituted, for art 8 as originally enacted, by SI 2013/1749, arts 2, 4. Date in force: 12 July 2013: see SI 2013/1749, art 1.

[8ZB Presumptions about receipt of notice

(1)   Where a notice is sent in accordance with article 8ZA, it shall be deemed to have been given to the person affected, unless the contrary is proved—

    (a)   where the notice is sent by postal service—

        (i)   on the second day after it was sent by postal service in which delivery or receipt is recorded if sent to a place within the United Kingdom;

        (ii)   on the 28th day after it was posted if sent to a place outside the United Kingdom;

    (b)   where the notice is sent by fax, e-mail, document exchange or courier, on the day it was sent.

(2)   For the purposes of paragraph (1)(a) the period is to be calculated excluding the day on which the notice is posted.

(3)   For the purposes of paragraph (1)(a)(i) the period is to be calculated excluding any day which is not a business day.

(4) In paragraph (3) "business day" means any day other than a Saturday, a Sunday, Christmas Day, Good Friday or a day which is a bank holiday under the Banking and Financial Dealings Act 1971 in the part of the United Kingdom to which the notice is sent.]

Amendment

Articles 8, 8ZA, 8ZB, 8ZC substituted, for art 8 as originally enacted, by SI 2013/1749, arts 2, 4. Date in force: 12 July 2013: see SI 2013/1749, art 1.

[8ZC Notice not given

No notice under article 8(1) or 8ZA(1)(a) shall be given where a person is given leave to enter the United Kingdom by passing through an automated gate in accordance with article 8A.

Amendment

Articles 8, 8ZA, 8ZB, 8ZC substituted, for art 8 as originally enacted, by SI 2013/1749, arts 2, 4. Date in force: 12 July 2013: see SI 2013/1749, art 1.

[8A Automatic grant of leave

(1) An immigration officer may authorise a person to be a person who may obtain leave to enter the United Kingdom by passing through an automated gate.

(2) Such an authorisation may—

    (a)   only authorise a person to obtain leave to enter the United Kingdom as one of the categories of person under the immigration rules mentioned in paragraph (5);

    (b)   set out the conditions of use for an automated gate;

    (c)   list the automated gates for which the authorisation is valid;

    (d)   remain in force for up to 24 months; and

    (e)   be varied or withdrawn at any time, with or without notice being given to the person.

(3) Where a person passes through an automated gate—

    (a)   having been authorised under paragraph (1) as a person who may obtain leave to enter the United Kingdom by passing through an automated gate;

    (b)   in accordance with the conditions of use for an automated gate;

    (c)   which is an automated gate for which the authorisation is valid; and

    (d)   while the authorisation remains in force,

the person shall be given leave to enter the United Kingdom for six months as the category of person under the immigration rules for which the person has been authorised under paragraph (1).

(4) Such leave shall be subject to conditions prohibiting employment and recourse to public funds (within the meaning of the immigration rules).

(5) The categories of person under the immigration rules mentioned in this paragraph are—

    (a)   a general visitor;

    (b)   a business visitor;

    (c)   an academic visitor;

    (d)   a sports visitor;

    (e)   an entertainer visitor;

    (f)   a person seeking leave to enter as a visitor for private medical treatment;

    (g)   a person seeking leave to enter as the parent of a child at school in the United Kingdom.]

Amendment

Inserted by SI 2010/957, arts 2, 4. Date in force: 25 March 2010: see SI 2010/957, art 1.

9 Grant or refusal of leave by notice to a responsible third party

(1)   Leave to enter may be given or refused to a person by means of a notice given (in such form and manner as permitted by the Act or this Order for a notice giving or refusing leave to enter) to a responsible third party acting on his behalf.

(2)   A notice under paragraph (1) may refer to a person to whom leave is being granted or refused either by name or by reference to a description or category of persons which includes him.

10 Notice of refusal of leave

(1)   Where a notice refusing leave to enter to a person is given under [article 8(1)] or 9, an immigration officer shall as soon as practicable give to him a notice in writing stating that he has been refused leave to enter the United Kingdom and stating the reasons for the refusal.

(2)   Where an immigration officer serves a notice under the Immigration (Appeals) Notices Regulations 1984 or under regulations made under paragraph 1 of Schedule 4 to the Immigration and Asylum Act 1999 in respect of the refusal, he shall not be required to serve a notice under paragraph (1).

(3)   Any notice required by paragraph (1) to be given to any person may be [given in accordance with article 8ZA].

Amendment

Para (1): words in square brackets substituted by SI 2013/1749, arts 2, 5(a). Date in force: 12 July 2013: see SI 2013/1749, art 1.

Para (3): words in square brackets substituted by SI 2013/1749, arts 2, 5(b). Date in force: 12 July 2013: see SI 2013/1749, art 1.

11 Burden of proof

Where any question arises under the Immigration Acts as to whether a person has leave to enter the United Kingdom and he alleges that he has such leave by virtue of a notice given under [article 8(1)] or 9, [or by virtue of article 8A,] the onus shall lie upon him to show the manner and date of his entry into the United Kingdom.

Amendment

Words "article 8(1)" in square brackets substituted by SI 2013/1749, arts 2, 6. Date in force: 12 July 2013: see SI 2013/1749, art 1.

Words "or by virtue of article 8A," in square brackets inserted by SI 2010/957, arts 2, 5. Date in force: 25 March 2010: see SI 2010/957, art 1.

12

(1)   This article applies where—

    (a)   an immigration officer has commenced examination of a person ("the applicant") under paragraph 2(1)(c) of Schedule 2 to the Act (examination to determine whether or not leave to enter should be given);

    (b)   that examination has been adjourned, or the applicant has been required (under paragraph 2(3) of Schedule 2 to the Act) to submit to a further examination, whilst further inquiries are made (including, where the applicant has made an asylum claim, as to the Secretary of State's decision on that claim); and

    (c)   upon the completion of those inquiries, an immigration officer considers he is in a position to decide whether or not to give or refuse leave to enter without interviewing the applicant further.

(2)   Where this article applies, any notice giving or refusing leave to enter which is on any date thereafter sent by post to the applicant (or is communicated to him in such form or manner as is permitted by this Order) shall be regarded, for the purposes of the Act, as having been given within the period of 24 hours specified in paragraph 6(1) of Schedule 2 to the Act (period within which notice giving or refusing leave to enter must be given after completion of examination).

PART IV
LEAVE WHICH DOES NOT LAPSE ON TRAVEL OUTSIDE COMMON TRAVEL AREA

13

(1) In this article "leave" means—

    (a)   leave to enter the United Kingdom (including leave to enter conferred by means of an entry clearance under article 2); and

    (b)   leave to remain in the United Kingdom.

(2) Subject to paragraph (3), where a person has leave which is in force and which was:

    (a)   conferred by means of an entry clearance (other than a visit visa) under article 2; or

    (b)   given by an immigration officer or the Secretary of State for a period exceeding six months,

such leave shall not lapse on his going to a country or territory outside the common travel area.

(3) Paragraph (2) shall not apply:

    (a)   where a limited leave has been varied by the Secretary of State; and

    (b)   following the variation the period of leave remaining is six months or less.

(4) Leave which does not lapse under paragraph (2) shall remain in force either indefinitely (if it is unlimited) or until the date on which it would otherwise have expired (if limited), but—

    (a)   where the holder has stayed outside the United Kingdom for a continuous period of more than two years, the leave (where the leave is unlimited) or any leave then remaining (where the leave is limited) shall thereupon lapse; and

    (b)   any conditions to which the leave is subject shall be suspended for such time as the holder is outside the United Kingdom.

(5) For the purposes of paragraphs 2 and 2A of Schedule 2 to the Act (examination by immigration officers, and medical examination), leave to remain which remains in force under this article shall be treated, upon the holder's arrival in the United Kingdom, as leave to enter which has been granted to the holder before his arrival.

(6) Without prejudice to the provisions of section 4(1) of the Act, where the holder of leave which remains in force under this article is outside the United Kingdom, the Secretary of State may vary that leave (including any conditions to which it is subject) in such form and manner as permitted by the Act or this Order for the giving of leave to enter.

(7) Where a person is outside the United Kingdom and has leave which is in force by virtue of this article, that leave may be cancelled:

    (a)   in the case of leave to enter, by an immigration officer; or

    (b)   in the case of leave to remain, by the Secretary of State.

(8) In order to determine whether or not to vary (and, if so, in what manner) or cancel leave which remains in force under this article and which is held by a person who is outside the United Kingdom, an immigration officer or, as the case may be, the Secretary of State may seek such information, and the production of such documents or copy documents, as an immigration officer would be entitled to obtain in an examination under paragraph 2 or 2A of Schedule 2 to the Act and may also require the holder of the leave to supply an up to date medical report.

(9) Failure to supply any information, documents, copy documents or medical report requested by an immigration officer or, as the case may be, the Secretary of State under this article shall be a ground, in itself, for cancellation of leave.

(10)   Section 3(4) of the Act (lapsing of leave upon travelling outside the common travel area) shall have effect subject to this article.

PART V
CONSEQUENTIAL AND TRANSITIONAL PROVISIONS

14

Section 9(2) of the Act (further provisions as to common travel area: conditions applicable to certain arrivals on a local journey) shall have effect as if, after the words "British Citizens", there were inserted "and do not hold leave to enter or remain granted to them before their arrival".

15

(1)   Article 12 shall apply where an applicant's examination has begun before the date that article comes into force, as well as where it begins on or after that date.

(2)   Article 13 shall apply with respect to leave to enter or remain in the United Kingdom which is in force on the date that article comes into force, as well as to such leave given after that date.

IMMIGRATION (REMOVAL DIRECTIONS) REGULATIONS 2000

(SI 2000/2243)

Made: 16 August 2000.

Authority: Immigration and Asylum Act 1999, ss 10, 166(3), 167.

Commencement: 2 October 2000.

1 Citation and commencement
These Regulations may be cited as the Immigration (Removal Directions) Regulations 2000 and shall come into force on 2nd October 2000.

2 Interpretation
(1)   In these Regulations—

"the Act" means the Immigration and Asylum Act 1999;

"aircraft" includes hovercraft;

"captain" means master (of a ship) or commander (of an aircraft);

"international service" has the meaning given by section 13(6) of the Channel Tunnel Act 1987;

"ship" includes every description of vessel used in navigation; and

"the tunnel system" has the meaning given by section 1(7) of the Channel Tunnel Act 1987.

(2)   In these Regulations, a reference to a section number is a reference to a section of the Act.

3 Persons to whom directions may be given
For the purposes of section 10(6)(a) (classes of person to whom directions may be given), the following classes of person are prescribed—

(a)   owners of ships;

(b)   owners of aircraft;

(c)   agents of ships;

(d)   agents of aircraft;

(e)   captains of ships about to leave the United Kingdom;

(f)   captains of aircraft about to leave the United Kingdom; and

(g)   persons operating an international service.

4 Requirements that may be imposed by directions

(1) For the purposes of section 10(6)(b) (requirements that may be imposed by directions), the following kinds of requirements are prescribed—

(a)   in the case where directions are given to a captain of a ship or aircraft about to leave the United Kingdom, a requirement to remove the relevant person from the United Kingdom in that ship or aircraft;

(b)   in the case where directions are given to a person operating an international service, a requirement to make arrangements for the removal of the relevant person through the tunnel system;

(c)   in the case where directions are given to any other person who falls within a class prescribed in regulation 3, a requirement to make arrangements for the removal of the relevant person in a ship or aircraft specified or indicated in the directions; and

(d)   in all cases, a requirement to remove the relevant person in accordance with arrangements to be made by an immigration officer.

(2) Paragraph (1) only applies if the directions specify that the relevant person is to be removed to a country or territory being—

(i)   a country of which he is a national or citizen; or

(ii)   a country or territory to which there is reason to believe that he will be admitted.

(3) Paragraph (1)(b) only applies if the relevant person arrived in the United Kingdom through the tunnel system.

(4) "Relevant person" means a person who may be removed from the United Kingdom in accordance with section 10(1).

IMMIGRATION (DESIGNATION OF TRAVEL BANS) ORDER 2000

(SI 2000/2724)

Made: 3 October 2000.

Authority: Immigration Act 1971, s 8B(5), (6).

Commencement: 10 October 2000.

1

This Order may be cited as the Immigration (Designation of Travel Bans) Order 2000 and shall come into force on 10th October 2000.

2

The instruments listed in the Schedule to this Order are designated for the purposes of section 8B(4) and (5) of the Immigration Act 1971.

3

Section 8B(1), (2) and (3) of the Immigration Act 1971 shall not apply in any case where:

(a)   failure to apply these provisions would not be contrary to the United Kingdom's obligations under any of the instruments designated by article 2 of this Order,

(b)   to apply these provisions would be contrary to the United Kingdom's obligations under the Convention for the Protection of Human Rights and Fundamental Freedoms, agreed by the Council of Europe at Rome on 4th November 1950, or

(c)   to apply these provisions would be contrary to the United Kingdom's obligations under the Convention relating to the Status of Refugees done at Geneva on 28th July 1951 and the Protocol to that Convention.

[SCHEDULE

DESIGNATED INSTRUMENTS

Article 2

PART 1

RESOLUTIONS OF THE SECURITY COUNCIL OF THE UNITED NATIONS

Resolution 1988 (2011) of 17 June 2011 (Afghanistan).
Resolution 1989 (2011) of 17 June 2011 (Al Qaida).
Resolution 1390 (2002) of 16 January 2002 (Al Qaida and the Taliban).
Resolution 1735 (2006) of 22 December 2006 (Al Qaida and the Taliban).
Resolution 1822 (2008) of 30 June 2008 (Al Qaida and the Taliban).
Resolution 1904 (2009) of 17 December 2009 (Al Qaida and the Taliban).
Resolution 2134 (2014) of 28 January 2014 (Central African Republic).
Resolution 1572 (2004) of 15 November 2004 (Côte d'Ivoire).
Resolution 1893 (2009) of 29 October 2009 (Côte d'Ivoire).
Resolution 1946 (2010) of 15 October 2010 (Côte d'Ivoire).
Resolution 1975 (2011) of 30 March 2011 (Côte d'Ivoire).
Resolution 1980 (2011) of 28 April 2011 (Côte d'Ivoire).
Resolution 2045 (2012) of 26 April 2012 (Côte d'Ivoire).
Resolution 2153 (2014) of 29 April 2014 (Côte d'Ivoire).
Resolution 1596 (2005) of 18 April 2005 (Democratic Republic of the Congo).
Resolution 1649 (2005) of 21 December 2005 (Democratic Republic of the Congo).
Resolution 1698 (2006) of 31 July 2006 (Democratic Republic of the Congo).
Resolution 1807 (2008) of 31 March 2008 (Democratic Republic of the Congo).
Resolution 1857 (2008) of 22 December 2008 (Democratic Republic of the Congo).
Resolution 1896 (2009) of 30 November 2009 (Democratic Republic of the Congo).
Resolution 1952 (2010) of 29 November 2010 (Democratic Republic of the Congo).
Resolution 2021 (2011) of 29 November 2011 (Democratic Republic of the Congo).
Resolution 2136 (2014) of 30 January 2014 (Democratic Republic of the Congo).
Resolution 1718 (2006) of 14 October 2006 (Democratic People's Republic of Korea).
Resolution 1874 (2009) of 12 June 2009 (Democratic People's Republic of Korea).
Resolution 1928 (2010) of 7 June 2010 (Democratic People's Republic of Korea).
Resolution 1985 (2011) of 10 June 2011 (Democratic People's Republic of Korea).
Resolution 2094 (2013) of 7 March 2013 (Democratic People's Republic of Korea).
Resolution 1907 (2009) of 23 December 2009 (Eritrea).
Resolution 2048 (2012) of 18 May 2012 (Guinea-Bissau).
Resolution 1737 (2006) of 23 December 2006 (Iran).
Resolution 1747 (2007) of 24 March 2007 (Iran).
Resolution 1803 (2008) of 3 March 2008 (Iran).
Resolution 1929 (2010) of 9 June 2010 (Iran).
Resolution 1521 (2003) of 22 December 2003 (Liberia).
Resolution 1903 (2009) of 17 December 2009 (Liberia).
Resolution 1961 (2010) of 17 December 2010 (Liberia).

Resolution 2025 (2011) of 14 December 2011 (Liberia).

Resolution 1970 (2011) of 26 February 2011 (Libya).

Resolution 1973 (2011) of 17 March 2011 (Libya).

Resolution 1844 (2008) of 20 November 2008 (Somalia).

Resolution 2002 (2011) of 29 July 2011 (Somalia and Eritrea).

Resolution 2023 (2011) of 5 December 2011 (Somalia and Eritrea).

Resolution 1591 (2005) of 29 March 2005 (Sudan).

Resolution 1672 (2006) of 25 April 2006 (Sudan).

Resolution 1636 (2005) of 31 October 2005 (Syria and the Lebanon).

PART 2
INSTRUMENTS MADE BY THE COUNCIL OF THE EUROPEAN UNION

Council Decision 2011/486/CFSP of 1 August 2011 (Afghanistan) as implemented by Council Implementing Decision 2012/167/CFSP of 23 March 2012 (Afghanistan) and as implemented by Council Implementing Decision 2012/334/CFSP of 25 June 2012 (Afghanistan) and as implemented by Council Implementing Decision 2012/393/CFSP of 16 July 2012 (Afghanistan) and as implemented by Council Implementing Decision 2012/454/CFSP of 1 August 2012 (Afghanistan) and as implemented by Council Implementing Decision 2012/809/CFSP of 20 December 2012 (Afghanistan) and as implemented by Council Implementing Decision 2013/73/CFSP of 31 January 2013 (Afghanistan) and as implemented by Council Implementing Decision 2013/145/CFSP of 21 March 2013 (Afghanistan) and as implemented by Council Implementing Decision 2013/219/CFSP of 16 May 2013 (Afghanistan) and as implemented by Council Implementing Decision 2014/140/CFSP of 14 March 2014 (Afghanistan) and as implemented by Council Implementing Decision 2014/142/CFSP of 14 March 2014 (Afghanistan).

Common Position 2002/402/CFSP of 27 May 2002 as amended by Council Decision 2011/487/CFSP of 1 August 2011 (Al-Qaida).

Council Decision 2012/642/CFSP of 15 October 2012 (Belarus) as implemented by Council Implementing Decision 2013/248/CFSP of 29 May 2013 (Belarus) and as amended by Council Decision 2013/308/CFSP of 24 June 2013 (Belarus) and as amended by Council Decision 2013/534/CFSP of 29 October 2013 (Belarus).

Common Position 97/193/CFSP of 17 March 1997 (Bosnia-Herzegovina).

Council Decision 2011/173/CFSP of 21 March 2011 (Bosnia and Herzegovina) as amended by Council Decision 2012/158/CFSP of 19 March 2012 (Bosnia and Herzegovina) and as amended by Council Decision 2013/134/CFSP of 18 March 2013 (Bosnia and Herzegovina) and as amended by Council Decision 2014/157/CFSP of 20 March 2014 (Bosnia and Herzegovina).

Council Decision 2010/656/CFSP of 29 October 2010 (Côte d'Ivoire) as amended by Council Decision 2010/801/CFSP of 22 December 2010 (Côte d'Ivoire) and as amended by Council Decision 2011/221/CFSP of 6 April 2011 (Côte d'Ivoire) and as implemented by Council Implementing Decision 2012/144/CFSP of 8 March 2012 (Côte d'Ivoire) and as implemented by Council Implementing Decision 2014/271/CFSP of 12 May 2014 (Côte d'Ivoire).

Council Decision 2010/788/CFSP of 20 December 2010 (Democratic Republic of the Congo) as implemented by Council Implementing Decision 2011/699/CFSP of 20 October 2011 (Democratic Republic of the Congo) and as implemented by Council Implementing Decision 2011/848/CFSP of 16 December 2011 (Democratic Republic of the Congo)and as amended by Council Decision 2012/811/CFSP of 20 December 2012 (Democratic Republic of the Congo) and as implemented by Council Implementing Decision 2013/46/CFSP of 22 January 2013 (Democratic Republic of the Congo) and as amended by Council Decision 2014/147/CFSP of 17 March 2014 (Democratic Republic of the Congo).

Council Decision 2010/127/CFSP of 1 March 2010 (Eritrea) as amended by Council Decision 2010/414/CFSP of 26 July 2010 (Eritrea).

Council Decision 2010/638/CFSP of 25 October 2010 (Republic of Guinea) as amended by Council Decision 2011/169/CFSP of 21 March 2011 (Republic of Guinea) and as amended by Council Decision 2011/706/CFSP of 27 October 2011 (Republic of Guinea) and as amended by Council Decision 2013/515/CFSP of 21 October 2013 (Republic of Guinea).

Council Decision 2012/285/CFSP of 31 May 2012 (Republic of Guinea-Bissau) as implemented by Council Implementing Decision 2012/516/CFSP of 24 September 2012 (Republic of Guinea-Bissau) and as implemented by Council Implementing Decision 2013/293/CFSP of 18 June 2013 (Republic of Guinea-Bissau).

Council Decision 2010/413/CFSP of 26 July 2010 (Iran) as amended by Council Decision 2010/644/CFSP of 25 October 2010 (Iran) and as amended by Council Decision 2011/299/CFSP of 23 May 2011 (Iran) and as amended by Council Decision 2011/783/CFSP of 1 December 2011 (Iran) and as amended by Council Decision 2012/35/CFSP of 23 January 2012 (Iran) and as amended by Council Decision 2012/169/CFSP of 23 March 2012 (Iran) and as amended by Council Decision 2012/205/CFSP of 23 April 2012 (Iran) and as amended by Council Decision 2012/457/CFSP of 2 August 2012 (Iran) and as amended by Council Decision 2012/635/CFSP of 15 October 2012 (Iran) and as amended by Council Decision 2012/829/CFSP of 21 December 2012 (Iran)and as amended by Council Decision 2013/124/CFSP of 11 March 2013 (Iran) and as amended by Council Decision 2013/270/CFSP of 6 June 2013 (Iran) and as amended by Council Decision 2013/497/CFSP of 10 October 2013 (Iran) and as amended by Council Decision 2013/661/CFSP of 15 November 2013 (Iran).

Council Decision 2011/235/CFSP of 12 April 2011 (Iran) as implemented by Council Implementing Decision 2011/670/CFSP of 10 October 2011 (Iran) and as amended by Council Decision 2012/168/CFSP of 23 March 2012 (Iran) and as amended by Council Decision 2014/205/CFSP of 10 April 2014 (Iran).

Council Decision 2013/183/CFSP of 22 April 2013 (Democratic People's Republic of Korea) as amended by Council Decision 2014/212/CFSP of 14 April 2014 (Democratic People's Republic of Korea).

Common Position 2005/888/CFSP of 12 December 2005 (Lebanon).

Common Position 2008/109/CFSP of 12 February 2008 (Liberia).

Council Decision 2011/137/CFSP of 28 February 2011 (Libya) as amended by Council Decision 2011/178/CFSP of 23 March 2011 (Libya) and as implemented by Council Implementing Decision 2011/236/CFSP of 12 April 2011 (Libya) and as implemented by Council Implementing Decision 2011/300/CFSP of 23 May 2011 (Libya) and as amended by Council Decision 2013/182/CFSP of 22 April 2013 (Libya).

Council Decision 2013/184/CFSP of 22 April 2013 (Myanmar/Burma) as amended by Council Decision 2014/214/CFSP of 14 April 2014 (Myanmar/Burma).

Council Decision 2010/573/CFSP of 27 September 2010 (Republic of Moldova) as amended by Council Decision 2011/171/CFSP of 21 March 2011 (Republic of Moldova) and as amended by Council Decision 2011/641/CFSP of 29 September 2011 (Republic of Moldova) and as amended by Council Decision 2012/170/CFSP of 23 March 2012 (Republic of Moldova) and as amended by Council Decision 2012/527/CFSP of 27 September 2012 (Republic of Moldova) and as implemented by Council Implementing Decision 2013/477/CFSP of 27 September 2013 (Republic of Moldova).

Council Decision 2010/231/CFSP of 26 April 2010 (Somalia) as amended by Council Decision 2011/635/CFSP of 26 September 2011 (Somalia) and as amended by Council Decision 2012/388/CFSP of 16 July 2012 (Somalia) and as amended by Council Decision 2012/633/CFSP of 15 October 2012 (Somalia).

Council Decision 2014/449/CFSP of 10 July 2014 (South Sudan).

Council Decision 2014/450/CFSP of 10 July 2014 (Sudan)

Council Decision 2012/739/CFSP of 29 November 2012 (Syria) as amended by Council Decision 2013/109/CFSP of 28 February 2013 (Syria) and as implemented by Council Implementing Decision 2013/185/CFSP of 22 April 2013 (Syria).

Council Decision 2013/255/CFSP of 31 May 2013 (Syria) as amended by Council Decision 2014/309/CFSP of 28 May 2014 (Syria).

Council Decision 2014/145/CFSP of 17 March 2014 (Ukraine) as implemented by Council Implementing Decision 2014/151/CFSP of 21 March 2014 (Ukraine) and as implemented by Council Implementing Decision 2014/238/CFSP of 28 April 2014 (Ukraine) and as amended by Council Decision 2014/265/CFSP of 12 May 2014 (Ukraine) and as amended by Council Decision 2014/308/CFSP of 28 May 2014 (Ukraine) and as amended by Council Decision 2014/455/CFSP of 11 July 2014 (Ukraine).

Common Position 2000/696/CFSP of 10 November 2000 (Federal Republic of Yugoslavia) as amended by Common Position 2001/155/CFSP of 26 February 2001 (Federal Republic of Yugoslavia).

Council Decision 2011/101/CFSP of 15 February 2011 (Zimbabwe) as amended by Council Decision 2012/97/CFSP of 17 February 2012 (Zimbabwe) and as implemented by Council Implementing Decision 2012/124/CFSP of 27 February 2012 (Zimbabwe) and as amended by Council Decision 2013/89/CFSP of 18 February 2013 (Zimbabwe) and as amended by Council Decision 2013/160/CFSP of 27 March 2013 (Zimbabwe) and as implemented by Council Implementing Decision 2013/469/CFSP of 23 September 2013 (Zimbabwe) and as amended by Council Decision 2014/98/CFSP of 17 February 2014 (Zimbabwe).

Amendment
Schedule substituted by SI 2014/1849, art 2, Sch 1, as from 21 July 2014.

REPORTING OF SUSPICIOUS MARRIAGES AND REGISTRATION OF MARRIAGES (MISCELLANEOUS AMENDMENTS) REGULATIONS 2000

(SI 2000/3164)

Made: 29 November 2000.

Authority: Marriage Act 1949, ss 27(1), 27B(2)(b), 31(2), (5), (5D), 74; Registration Service Act 1953, s 20(a); Immigration and Asylum Act 1999, s 24(3).

Commencement: 1 January 2001.

1 Citation, commencement and interpretation

(1) These Regulations may be cited as the Reporting of Suspicious Marriages and Registration of Marriages (Miscellaneous Amendments) Regulations 2000 and shall come into force on 1st January 2001.

(2) In these Regulations, unless the context otherwise requires—

"registration officer" means one of the persons referred to in section 24(1)(a)[, (aa)] or (b) of the 1999 Act or a registrar of marriages as referred to in section 24(2)(a) of that Act;

"the 1949 Act" means the Marriage Act 1949;

"the 1970 Act" means the Marriage (Registrar General's Licence) Act 1970;

"the 1999 Act" means the Immigration and Asylum Act 1999;

"the Authorised Persons Regulations" means the Marriage (Authorised Persons) Regulations 1952;

"the principal Regulations" means the Registration of Marriages Regulations 1986; and "the Welsh Regulations" means the Registration of Marriages (Welsh Language) Regulations 1999.

Amendment

Para (2): figure in square brackets in definition "registration officer" inserted by SI 2014/1660, reg 2(a), as from 21 July 2014.

2 Reporting suspicious marriages

For the purposes of section 24 of the 1999 Act (reporting suspicious marriages) a registration officer shall—

(a) report his suspicions to the Secretary of State by making a report in writing or other permanent form giving the information specified in Schedule 1 to these Regulations [(to the extent that that information is available)], and

(b) forward that report to the Home Office, Immigration and Nationality Directorate, Intelligence Section, Status 3, 4 Nobel Drive, Hayes, Middlesex UB3 5EY or, where the Secretary of State has notified the Registrar General of another address to be used in relation to any particular registration district, that address.

Amendment

Words in square brackets inserted by SI 2014/1660, reg 2(b), as from 21 July 2014.

6 Transitional provision

Regulations 3, 4 and 5 shall not apply in respect of any marriage, notice of which has been entered in the marriage notice book for—

(a) the registration district referred to in section 27(1)(a) or (2) of the 1949 Act, or

(b) each registration district referred to in section 27(1)(b) of the 1949 Act, before 1st January 2001.

SCHEDULE 1

INFORMATION TO BE PROVIDED WHEN REPORTING A SUSPICIOUS MARRIAGE

Regulation 2

Name and surname of each party to the marriage

Date of birth and/or age of each party to the marriage

[Condition] of each party to the marriage

Address (and district of residence) of each party to the marriage

Nationality of each party to the marriage

Date of marriage

Place of marriage

Time of marriage

Nature of evidence produced in respect of—

(i) name and age

(ii) [condition]

(iii) nationality

of the parties to the marriage

Reason for making the report

Full name of registration officer making the report

Date report made

Amendment

Words "Condition" and "condition" in square brackets substituted by SI 2005/3177, reg 8. Date in force: 5 December 2005: see SI 2005/3177, reg 1.

DETENTION CENTRE RULES 2001

(SI 2001/238)

Notes

Made: 29 January 2001.

Authority: Immigration and Asylum Act 1999, ss 148(3), 149(6), 152(2), (3), 153, 166(3), Sch 11, para 2, Sch 12, paras 1–3, Sch 13, para 2.

Commencement: 2 April 2001.

See Further

See further, the Nationality, Immigration and Asylum Act 2002, s 66(4) which provides that the reference to a detention centre is to be construed as a reference to a removal centre as defined in the Immigration and Asylum Act 1999, Pt VIII.

PART I

1 Citation and commencement

These Rules may be cited as the Detention Centre Rules 2001 and shall come into force on 2nd April 2001.

2 Interpretation

In these Rules, where the context so admits, the expression—

"compact" has the meaning set out at rule 4(1);

"controlled drug" means any drug which is a controlled drug for the purposes of the Misuse of Drugs Act 1971;

"legal adviser" means, in relation to a detained person, his counsel, representative or solicitor, and includes a clerk acting on behalf of his solicitor;

"manager" means, in relation to any detention centre, the person appointed under section 148(1) of the Immigration and Asylum Act 1999;

"officer" means an officer of a detention centre (whether a Crown servant or an employee of the contractor or otherwise) and, for the purposes of rule 8(2), includes a detainee custody officer who is authorised to perform escort functions in accordance with section 154 of the Immigration and Asylum Act 1999 or a prison officer or prisoner custody officer performing those functions under that section.

PART II
DETAINED PERSONS

GENERAL

3 Purpose of detention centres

(1) The purpose of detention centres shall be to provide for the secure but humane accommodation of detained persons in a relaxed regime with as much freedom of movement and association as possible, consistent with maintaining a safe and secure environment, and to encourage and assist detained persons to make the most productive use of their time, whilst respecting in particular their dignity and the right to individual expression.

(2) Due recognition will be given at detention centres to the need for awareness of the particular anxieties to which detained persons may be subject and the sensitivity that this will require, especially when handling issues of cultural diversity.

ADMISSIONS AND DISCHARGE

4 Information to detained persons about these Rules and the detention centre

(1) The Secretary of State shall devise a document (to be known as the "compact") setting out certain rights to be enjoyed and responsibilities to be undertaken by detained persons during their stay at detention centres.

(2) The compact shall in no way prejudice any other rights or responsibilities of detained persons as set out in these Rules, the Human Rights Convention, or otherwise.

(3) Every detained person shall be provided, as soon as possible after his reception into a detention centre and (so far as reasonably practicable) in a language which he understands, with a copy of the compact together with information in writing about those provisions in these Rules and other matters about life in the detention centre which it is necessary that he should know (including information about the proper method of making requests and complaints at the centre).

(4) In the case of a detained person aged less than 18, or a detained person aged 18 or over who cannot read or appears to have difficulty in understanding the information so provided, the manager, or a member of staff deputed by him, shall so explain it to him in order that he can understand his rights and responsibilities.

(5) These Rules shall be translated into a variety of languages as directed by the Secretary of State.

(6) A copy of these Rules shall be made available to any detained person who requests it.

5 Record, photograph and fingerprinting

(1) For purposes of identification and welfare, a personal record for each detained person shall be prepared and maintained in such manner as the Secretary of State may direct.

(2) This record shall include such details and measurements of external physical characteristics as the Secretary of State may direct, but no copy of the record shall be given to any person not authorised to receive it by the Secretary of State.

(3) Every detained person may be photographed on reception and subsequently as many times as may be required by the Secretary of State, but no copy of any photographs taken shall be given to any person not authorised to receive it by the Secretary of State.

(4) Any detained person may have his fingerprints taken in accordance with section 141 of the Immigration and Asylum Act 1999 if specifically directed by the Secretary of State.

6 Detained persons' property

(1) Every detained person shall be entitled to retain all his personal property, other than cash, for his own use at the detention centre save where such retention is contrary to the interests of safety or security or is incompatible with the storage facilities provided at the centre.

(2) Anything, other than cash, which a detained person has at a detention centre and which he is not allowed to retain for his own use as a result of paragraph (1) shall be taken into the manager's custody.

(3) An inventory of a detained person's property shall be kept, and he shall be required to sign it, after having a proper opportunity to see that it is correct.

(4) A detained person may have supplied to him at his expense and retain for his own use books, newspapers, writing materials and other means of occupation, except any that appears objectionable to the manager or the Secretary of State on grounds that it is likely to give offence to others.

(5) Any cash that a detained person does not wish to keep in his possession, or which he is not entitled to keep in his possession, shall be deposited with the manager for

safekeeping and a receipt issued, which the detained person shall be required to sign, after having a proper opportunity to see that it is correct.

(6) A detained person shall be entitled to reasonable access to any cash deposited with the manager for safekeeping under paragraph (5).

(7) For the purposes of paragraph (5), a detained person shall not be entitled to keep in his possession any cash which is greater than an amount to be directed by the Secretary of State in the interests of prevention of loss or crime at the detention centre.

(8) Any property or cash which a detained person has deposited with, or surrendered to, the manager in accordance with these Rules shall be returned to the detained person upon his discharge from the detention centre.

(9) Any article belonging to a detained person which remains unclaimed for a period of more than one year after he is discharged from the detention centre, or dies, may be sold or otherwise disposed of and the net proceeds of any sale shall be applied, under the joint authority of the manager and the contract monitor, to purposes for the benefit of all detained persons.

(10) The manager may confiscate any unauthorised article found in the possession of a detained person after his reception into a detention centre, or concealed or deposited anywhere within a centre.

7 Search

(1) For reasons of security and safety, every detained person shall be searched when taken into custody by an officer, on his reception into a detention centre and subsequently as the manager thinks necessary, or as the Secretary of State may direct.

(2) A detained person shall be searched in as seemly a manner as is consistent with discovering anything concealed.

(3) No detained person shall be stripped and searched in the sight of another detained person, or in the sight or presence of an officer or other person not of the same sex.

(4) Paragraphs (2) and (3) apply to searches by officers acting in accordance with escort arrangements as well as to those exercising custodial functions.

8 Custody outside of detention centres

(1) A person being taken to or from a detention centre in custody shall be exposed as little as possible to public observation and proper care shall be taken to protect him from curiosity and insult.

(2) A detained person required to be taken in custody anywhere outside of a detention centre shall be kept in the custody of an officer appointed to escort him or a police officer.

9 Detention reviews and update of claim

(1) Every detained person will be provided, by the Secretary of State, with written reasons for his detention at the time of his initial detention, and thereafter monthly.

(2) The Secretary of State shall, within a reasonable time following any request to do so by a detained person, provide that person with an update on the progress of any relevant matter relating to him.

(3) For the purposes of paragraph (2) "relevant matter" means any of the following—

  (a) a claim for asylum;
  (b) an application for, or for the variation of, leave to enter or remain in the United Kingdom;
  (c) an application for British nationality;
  (d) a claim for a right of admission into the United Kingdom under a provision of [EU] law;
  (e) a claim for a right of residence in the United Kingdom under a provision of [EU] law;

    (f)   the proposed removal or deportation of the detained person from the United Kingdom;

    (g)   an application for bail under the Immigration Acts or under the Special Immigration Appeals Commission Act 1997;

    (h)   an appeal against, or an application for judicial review in relation to, any decision taken in connection with a matter referred to in paragraphs (a) to (g).

Amendment

Para (3): in sub-paras (d), (e) reference to "EU" in square brackets substituted by SI 2011/1043, art 6(2)(a). Date in force: 22 April 2011: see SI 2011/1043, art 2; for transitional savings see art 3(3) thereof.

10 Female detained persons

Female detained persons will be provided with sleeping accommodation separate from male detained persons, subject to rule 11.

11 Families and minors

(1) Detained family members shall be entitled to enjoy family life at the detention centre save to the extent necessary in the interests of security and safety.

(2) Detained persons aged under 18 and families will be provided with accommodation suitable to their needs.

(3) Everything reasonably necessary for detained persons' protection, safety and well-being and the maintenance and care of infants and children shall be provided.

WELFARE AND PRIVILEGES

12 Clothing

(1) All detained persons may wear clothing of their own if and insofar as it is suitable and clean, and shall be permitted to arrange for the supply to them from outside the detention centre of sufficient clean clothing.

(2) Where required all detained persons shall be provided with clothing adequate for warmth and health in accordance with arrangements approved by the Secretary of State.

(3) A detained person shall be provided, where necessary, with suitable and adequate clothing on his release.

(4) Facilities for the laundering of items of clothing shall be provided.

13 Food

(1) Subject to any directions of the Secretary of State, no detained person shall be allowed, except as authorised by the medical practitioner to have any food other than that ordinarily provided.

(2) No detained person shall be given less food than is ordinarily provided, except with his written consent and upon the written recommendation of the medical practitioner.

(3) The food provided shall:

    (a)   be wholesome, nutritious, well prepared and served, reasonably varied, sufficient in quantity and

    (b)   meet all religious, dietary, cultural and medical needs.

(4) The contract monitor at a contracted-out detention centre, or the manager at a directly managed detention centre, shall regularly inspect the food both before and after it is cooked and, in the case of the contract monitor, shall report any deficiency or defect to the manager.

(5) In this rule "food" includes drink.

14 Alcohol

No detained person shall be allowed to have any intoxicating liquor except:—

(a)   by written order of the medical practitioner, specifying the quantity and the name of the detained person and the medical reason for the order; or

(b)   for the observance of religious festivals, and for sacraments, with the prior agreement of the manager.

15 Certification of accommodation

(1)   The Secretary of State shall satisfy himself that in every detention centre sufficient accommodation is provided for all detained persons.

(2)   No room shall be used as sleeping accommodation for a detained person unless the Secretary of State has certified that:—

(a)   its size, lighting, heating, ventilation and fittings are adequate for health;

(b)   it has adequate storage facilities (consistent with interests of security and safety); and

(c)   it allows the detained person to communicate at any time with an officer.

(3)   No room shall be used for the purposes of:—

(a)   removal from association under rule 40;

(b)   temporary confinement under rule 42; or

(c)   application of special control or restraint under rule 43 unless the Secretary of State has certified that its lighting, heating, ventilation and fittings are adequate for health and that it allows the detained person to communicate at any time with an officer.

(4)   A certificate given under this rule in respect of any room shall specify the maximum number of detained persons who may be accommodated in the room.

16 Hygiene

(1)   Every detained person shall have proper regard for personal hygiene in their own interests and the interests of others.

(2)   Every detained person shall be provided with toilet articles necessary for his health and cleanliness, which shall be replaced as necessary.

(3)   Facilities shall be provided for every detained person to have a daily bath or shower.

(4)   Facilities shall be provided to male detained persons to permit daily shaving.

(5)   Facilities shall be provided to allow detained persons to have their hair cut on a regular basis.

(6)   No detained person shall be required to have his or her hair cut without consent.

17 Regime and paid activity

(1)   All detained persons shall be provided with an opportunity to participate in activities to meet, as far as possible, their recreational and intellectual needs and the relief of boredom.

(2)   Wherever reasonably possible the development of skills and of services to the centre and to the community should be encouraged.

(3)   Detained persons shall be entitled to undertake paid activities to the extent that the opportunity to do so is provided by the manager.

(4)   Detained persons undertaking activities under paragraph (3) shall be paid at rates approved by the Secretary of State, either generally or in relation to particular cases.

(5)   Every detained person able to take part in educational activities provided at a detention centre shall be encouraged to do so.

(6)   Programmes of educational classes shall be provided at every detention centre.

(7)   Arrangements shall be made for each detained person to have the opportunity of taking part in physical education or recreation, which shall consist of both sports and health-related activities.

(8)   A library shall be provided in every detention centre, which will meet a range of cultural, ethnic and linguistic needs and, subject to any direction of the Secretary

of State in any particular case, every detained person shall be allowed access to it at reasonable times.

18 Time in open air

(1)   Subject to paragraph (2), a detained person shall be given the opportunity to spend at least one hour in the open air every day.

(2)   Time in the open air may be refused in exceptional circumstances where necessary in the interests of safety or security.

19 Privileges

(1)   At every detention centre all detained persons shall have access to a system of privileges approved by the Secretary of State, which shall include arrangements under which they may spend their money within the detention centre.

(2)   Systems of privileges approved under paragraph (1) may include arrangements under which privileges may be granted to detained persons only in so far as they have met, and for so long as they continue to meet, specified standards of behaviour (whether under the compact, these Rules or otherwise).

(3)   Systems of privileges which include arrangements of the kind referred to in paragraph (2) shall include procedures to be followed in determining whether or not any of the privileges concerned shall be granted to a detained person and such procedures shall include a requirement that the detained person be given reasons for any decision adverse to him together with a statement of the means by which he may appeal against it.

(4)   This rule shall be without prejudice to any other provision of these Rules which provides that a privilege may be forfeited or otherwise lost or a detained person deprived of association with other detained persons.

RELIGION

20 Diversity of religion

The practice of religion in detention centres shall take account of the diverse cultural and religious background of detained persons.

21 Religious denomination

If a detained person wishes to declare himself to belong to a particular religion, the manager shall upon that person's reception at the detention centre record the religion to which the detained person wishes to belong.

22 Manager of religious affairs and ministers of religion

(1)   Every detention centre shall have a manager of religious affairs whose appointment shall be approved by the Secretary of State.

(2)   Where in any detention centre the number of detained persons who belong to a particular religion is such as in the opinion of the Secretary of State to require the appointment of a minister of that religion, the Secretary of State may appoint such a minister to that detention centre.

(3)   The manager of religious affairs shall make arrangements for a minister of religion to meet with every detained person of his religion individually soon after the detained person's reception into the detention centre if the detained person so wishes.

(4)   A minister of religion shall visit daily all detained persons of his religion who are sick, under restraint, in temporary confinement, or undergoing removal from association, as far as he reasonably can and to the extent that the detained person so wishes.

23 Regular visits by ministers of religion

(1)   The manager shall make arrangements for a minister of religion to visit detained persons of his religion as often as he reasonably can and to the extent that the detained person so wishes.

(2) Where a detained person belongs to a religion for which no minister of religion has been appointed the manager will do what he reasonably can, if so requested by the detained person, to arrange for him to be visited by a minister of that religion as often as he reasonably can and to the extent that the detained person so wishes.

24 Religious services

The manager shall make arrangements for ministers of religion to conduct religious services for detained persons of their religions at such times as may be arranged.

25 Religious books

There shall, so far as reasonably practicable, be available for the personal use of every detained person such religious books recognised by his religion as are approved by the Secretary of State for use in detention centres.

COMMUNICATIONS

26 Outside contacts

(1) In accordance with rules 27, 28 and 57, detained persons shall be entitled to enjoy family life by way of visits from, or communications with, family members living outside the detention centre, save to the extent necessary in the interests of security or safety.

(2) A detained person shall be entitled to establish and maintain, as far as are possible, such relations with persons and agencies outside the detention centre as he may wish, save to the extent that such relations prejudice interests of security or safety.

27 Correspondence

(1) Every detained person may send at his own expense and receive as many letters and facsimiles as he wishes.

(2) If a detained person does not have the necessary funds to do so, the Secretary of State may bear the postage expense of any reasonable number of letters which that person wishes to send.

(3) A detained person shall on request be provided with any writing materials necessary for the purposes of sending letters pursuant to paragraph (2).

(4) No letter or other communication to or from a detained person may be opened, read or stopped save where the manager has reasonable cause to believe that its contents may endanger the security of the detention centre or the safety of others or are otherwise of a criminal nature or where it is not possible to determine the addressee or sender without opening the correspondence.

(5) Detained persons will be given the opportunity of being present when any correspondence is opened or read and shall be given reasons in advance if any correspondence is to be opened, read or stopped under paragraph (4).

(6) Without prejudice to paragraph (2), if a detained person does not have the necessary funds to do so, the Secretary of State shall bear the postage expense of any letter to the European Court of Human Rights, the European Court of Justice, the High Court, the Court of Session, the Special Immigration Appeals Commission[, the First-tier Tribunal or the Upper Tribunal] (or any court entitled to hear an appeal against a decision of those bodies).

Amendment

Para (6): words in square brackets substituted by SI 2010/21, art 5(2), Sch 2, para 1. Date in force: 15 February 2010: see SI 2010/21, art 1; for transitional provisions and savings see art 5(4), Sch 4, paras 14–18, 21 thereto.

28 Visits

(1) Every detained person may receive as many visits as he wishes within such reasonable limits and subject to such reasonable conditions as the Secretary of State may direct, either generally or in a particular case.

(2) In the interests of security and safety, every visit to a detained person shall take place within sight of an officer, unless the Secretary of State otherwise directs.

(3) Every visit to a detained person shall take place out of the hearing of an officer unless the Secretary of State otherwise directs in a particular case in the interests of security or safety (in which case the detained person shall be given reasons for the direction in advance).

(4) No person visiting a detained person at a detention centre shall be permitted to take a photograph whilst there without the permission of the Secretary of State.

29 Official interviews

A police officer, immigration officer or any other government official may interview any detained person willing to see him or obliged to see him.

30 Legal advisers and representatives

The legal adviser or representative of any detained person in any legal proceedings shall be afforded reasonable facilities for interviewing him in confidence, save that any such interview may be in the sight of an officer.

31 Use of telephones

(1) All detained persons shall have access to public telephones at the detention centre.

(2) Information about tariffs shall be provided by the manager on request by detained persons.

(3) A separate telephone system shall be provided for incoming calls, and the manager shall ensure that detained persons are notified promptly of such calls.

(4) If a detained person does not have the necessary funds to do so, the Secretary of State may bear the expense of any telephone calls (within reasonable limits) which that person wishes to make.

32 Money and articles received by post or courier

(1) Any money or other article (other than a letter or other communication) sent to a detained person through the post or courier shall be dealt with in accordance with the provisions of this rule, and the detained person shall be informed of the manner in which it is dealt with.

(2) Any cash shall, at the discretion of the manager, be—

    (a)   dealt with in accordance with rule 6(5), (6) or (7); or

    (b)   returned to the sender (if known).

(3) Any security for money shall, at the discretion of the manager, be—

    (a)   delivered to the detained person or placed with his property at the centre; or

    (b)   returned to the sender (if known).

(4) Any other article to which this rule applies shall, at the discretion of the manager, be—

    (a)   delivered to the detained person or placed with his property at the detention centre; or

    (b)   returned to the sender (if known).

HEALTH CARE

33 Medical practitioner and health care team

(1) Every detention centre shall have a medical practitioner, who shall be vocationally trained as a general practitioner and a fully registered person within the meaning of the Medical Act 1983 [who holds a licence to practise].

(2) Every detention centre shall have a health care team (of which the medical practitioner will be a member), which shall be responsible for the care of the physical and mental health of the detained persons at that centre.

(3) Each member of the health care team shall (as far as they are qualified to do so) pay special attention to the need to recognise medical conditions which might be found among a diverse population and the cultural sensitivity appropriate when performing his duties.

(4) The health care team shall observe all applicable professional guidelines relating to medical confidentiality.

(5) Every request by a detained person to see the medical practitioner shall be recorded by the officer to whom it is made and forthwith passed to the medical practitioner or nursing staff at the detention centre.

(6) The medical practitioner may consult with other medical practitioners at his discretion.

(7) All detained persons shall be entitled to request that they are attended by a registered medical practitioner or dentist other than the medical practitioner or those consulted by him under paragraph (6), so long as—

    (a)   the detained person will pay any expense incurred;

    (b)   the manager is satisfied that there are reasonable grounds for the request; and

    (c)   the attendance is in consultation with the medical practitioner.

(8) The medical practitioner shall obtain, so far as reasonably practicable, any previous medical records located in the United Kingdom relating to each detained person in the detention centre.

(9) The health care team shall ensure that all medical records relating to a detained person are forwarded as appropriate following his transfer to another detention centre or a prison or on discharge from the detention centre.

(10) All detained persons shall be entitled, if they so wish, to be examined only by a registered medical practitioner of the same sex, and the medical practitioner shall ensure that all detained persons of the opposite sex are aware of that entitlement prior to any examination.

(11) Subject to any directions given in the particular case by the Secretary of State, a registered medical practitioner selected by or on behalf of a detained person who is party to legal proceedings shall be afforded reasonable facilities for examining him in connection with the proceedings.

Amendment

    Para (1): words in square brackets inserted by SI 2002/3135, art 16(1), Sch 1, Pt II, para 47. Date in force: 16 November 2009: see SI 2002/3135, art 1(2), (3) and the London Gazettes, 21 August 2009.

34 Medical examination upon admission and thereafter

(1) Every detained person shall be given a physical and mental examination by the medical practitioner (or another registered medical practitioner in accordance with rules 33(7) or (10)) within 24 hours of his admission to the detention centre.

(2) Nothing in paragraph (1) shall allow an examination to be given in any case where the detained person does not consent to it.

(3) If a detained person does not consent to an examination under paragraph (1), he shall be entitled to the examination at any subsequent time upon request.

35 Special illnesses and conditions (including torture claims)

(1) The medical practitioner shall report to the manager on the case of any detained person whose health is likely to be injuriously affected by continued detention or any conditions of detention.

(2) The medical practitioner shall report to the manager on the case of any detained person he suspects of having suicidal intentions, and the detained person shall be placed under special observation for so long as those suspicions remain, and a record of his treatment and condition shall be kept throughout that time in a manner to be determined by the Secretary of State.

(3) The medical practitioner shall report to the manager on the case of any detained person who he is concerned may have been the victim of torture.

(4) The manager shall send a copy of any report under paragraphs (1), (2) or (3) to the Secretary of State without delay.

(5) The medical practitioner shall pay special attention to any detained person whose mental condition appears to require it, and make any special arrangements (including counselling arrangements) which appear necessary for his supervision or care.

36 Notification of illness or death

(1) If a detained person dies, becomes seriously ill, sustains any severe injury or is removed to hospital on account of mental disorder, the manager shall inform the Secretary of State without delay and the Secretary of State shall at once inform:—

- (a) the detained person's spouse or next of kin (if he knows of their contact details); and
- (b) any other person who the detained person may reasonably have asked should be informed.

(2) In any case in which the Secretary of State is under a duty to inform the detained person's spouse or next of kin under paragraph (1), this shall be done in person by the appropriate officer wherever it is reasonably practicable to do so.

(3) Without prejudice to paragraph (1), if a detained person dies, the manager shall give notice immediately to the police, to the coroner or procurator fiscal having jurisdiction, to the visiting committee and to the Secretary of State.

37 Medical examinations required in the interests of others

(1) This rule applies where a detainee custody officer, acting under an authorisation given by the manager under Schedule 12 to the Immigration and Asylum Act 1999, requires a detained person to submit to a medical examination for the purposes of determining whether he is suffering from a disease specified by order under paragraph 3(7) of that Schedule to that Act.

(2) A detained person who has been required to submit to a medical examination shall, so far as is reasonably practicable, be asked to consent to the examination and be informed by the examining medical practitioner—

- (a) that he is being required to submit to a medical examination in accordance with Schedule 12 to the Immigration and Asylum Act 1999;
- (b) of the nature of the disease from which there are reasonable grounds to believe he is suffering; and
- (c) that a refusal, without reasonable excuse, to submit to the medical examination is an offence under that Act.

REQUESTS AND COMPLAINTS

38 Requests and complaints

(1) A request or complaint to the manager, visiting committee or the Secretary of State relating to a detained person's detention shall be made orally or in writing by the detained person in accordance with such procedures as may be approved by the Secretary of State.

(2) On every day the manager shall hear any requests and complaints that are made to him under paragraph (1).

(3) In the case of a contracted-out detention centre, any complaint involving allegations against any officer at that centre shall be brought to the attention of the contract monitor as soon as possible.

(4) A detained person may make a written request or complaint under paragraph (1) in his own language.

(5) Any written request or complaint made under paragraph (1) may be made in confidence and, if the detained person so wishes, shall be sealed in an envelope with the addressee clearly indicated.

PART III

MAINTENANCE OF SECURITY AND SAFETY

39 General security and safety

(1) Security shall be maintained, but with no more restriction than is required for safe custody and well ordered community life.

(2) A detained person shall not behave in any way which might endanger the health or personal safety of others.

(3) A detained person shall not behave in any way which is inconsistent with his responsibilities under the compact.

(4) A detained person shall not be employed in any disciplinary capacity.

40 Removal from association

(1) Where it appears necessary in the interests of security or safety that a detained person should not associate with other detained persons, either generally or for particular purposes, the Secretary of State (in the case of a contracted-out detention centre) or the manager (in the case of a directly managed detention centre) may arrange for the detained person's removal from association accordingly.

(2) In cases of urgency, the manager of a contracted-out detention centre may assume the responsibility of the Secretary of State under paragraph (1) but shall notify the Secretary of State as soon as possible after making the necessary arrangements.

(3) A detained person shall not be removed under this rule for a period of more than 24 hours without the authority of the Secretary of State.

(4) An authority under paragraph (3) shall be for a period not exceeding 14 days.

(5) Notice of removal from association under this rule shall be given without delay to a member of the visiting committee, the medical practitioner and the manager of religious affairs.

(6) Where a detained person has been removed from association he shall be given written reasons for such removal within 2 hours of that removal.

(7) The manager may arrange at his discretion for such a detained person as aforesaid to resume association with other detained persons, and shall do so if in any case the medical practitioner so advises on medical grounds.

(8) Particulars of every case of removal from association shall be recorded by the manager in a manner to be directed by the Secretary of State.

(9) The manager, the medical practitioner and (at a contracted-out detention centre) an officer of the Secretary of State shall visit all detained persons who have been removed from association at least once each day for so long as they remain so removed.

41 Use of force

(1) A detainee custody officer dealing with a detained person shall not use force unnecessarily and, when the application of force to a detained person is necessary, no more force than is necessary shall be used.

(2) No officer shall act deliberately in a manner calculated to provoke a detained person.

(3) Particulars of every case of use of force shall be recorded by the manager in a manner to be directed by the Secretary of State, and shall be reported to the Secretary of State.

42 Temporary confinement

(1) The Secretary of State (in the case of a contracted-out detention centre) or the manager (in the case of a directly managed detention centre) may order a refractory or

violent detained person to be confined temporarily in special accommodation, but a detained person shall not be so confined as a punishment, or after he has ceased to be refractory or violent.

(2) In cases of urgency, the manager of a contracted-out detention centre may assume the responsibility of the Secretary of State under paragraph (1) above but shall notify the Secretary of State as soon as possible after giving the relevant order.

(3) A detained person shall not be confined in special accommodation for longer than 24 hours without a direction in writing given by an officer of the Secretary of State (not being an officer of a detention centre).

(4) The direction shall state the grounds for the confinement and the time during which it may continue (not exceeding 3 days).

(5) A copy of the direction shall be given to the detained person before the 27th hour of the confinement.

(6) Notice of the direction shall be given without delay to a member of the visiting committee, the medical practitioner and the manager of religious affairs.

(7) Particulars of every case of temporary confinement shall be recorded by the manager in a manner to be directed by the Secretary of State.

(8) The manager, the medical practitioner and (at a contracted-out detention centre) an officer of the Secretary of State shall visit all detained persons in temporary confinement at least once each day for as long as they remain so confined.

43 Special control or restraint

(1) The Secretary of State (in the case of a contracted-out detention centre) or the manager (in the case of a directly managed detention centre) may order a detained person to be put under special control or restraint where this is necessary to prevent the detained person from injuring himself or others, damaging property or creating a disturbance.

(2) In cases of urgency, the manager of a contracted-out detention centre may assume the responsibility of the Secretary of State under paragraph (1) but shall notify the Secretary of State without delay after giving the relevant order.

(3) Notice of such an order shall be given without delay to a member of the visiting committee, the medical practitioner and the manager of religious affairs.

(4) On receipt of the notice the medical practitioner shall inform the manager whether there are any medical reasons why the detained person should not be put under special control or restraint and the manager shall give effect to any recommendation which the medical practitioner may make.

(5) A detained person shall not be kept under special control or restraint longer than necessary, nor shall he be so kept for longer than 24 hours without a direction in writing given by an officer of the Secretary of State (not being an officer of the detention centre).

(6) A direction given under paragraph (5) shall state the grounds for the special control or restraint and the time during which it may continue.

(7) A copy of the direction will be given to the detained person before the 27th hour of application of the special control or restraint.

(8) Particulars of every case of special control or restraint shall be recorded by the manager in a manner to be directed by the Secretary of State.

(9) The manager, the medical practitioner and (at a contracted-out detention centre) an officer of the Secretary of State shall visit any detained person placed under special control and restraint at reasonable intervals during every 24 hour period for so long as the special control or restraint continues to be applied.

(10) Except as provided by this rule no detained person shall be put under special control or restraint otherwise than for safe custody, to give effect to directions lawfully given for his removal from the United Kingdom, or on medical grounds by direction of the medical practitioner.

(11) No detained person shall be put under special control or restraint as a punishment.

(12) Any means of special control or restraint shall be of a pattern authorised by the Secretary of State, and shall be used in such manner and under such conditions as the Secretary of State may direct.

44 Compulsory testing for controlled drugs and alcohol

(1) This rule applies where a detainee custody officer, acting under an authorisation given by the Secretary of State under paragraph 2 of Schedule 12 to the Immigration and Asylum Act 1999, requires a detained person to provide a sample for the purpose of ascertaining whether he has a controlled drug or alcohol in his body.

(2) In this rule "sample" means a sample of urine or breath or any other description of sample specified in the authorisation.

(3) The detainee custody officer shall not require a sample to be taken unless there are reasonable grounds for believing that the detained person has a controlled drug or alcohol in his body.

(4) When requiring a detained person to provide a sample, the detainee custody officer shall inform the detained person that he is being required to provide a sample in accordance with paragraph 2 of Schedule 12 to the Immigration and Asylum Act 1999.

(5) The detainee custody officer shall require the detained person to provide a fresh sample, free from any adulteration.

(6) A detainee custody officer requiring a sample shall make such arrangements and give the detained person such instructions for its provision as may be reasonably necessary in order to prevent or detect its adulteration or falsification.

(7) A detained person who is required to provide a sample may be kept apart from other detained persons for a period not exceeding one hour to enable arrangements to be made for the provision of the sample.

(8) A detained person who is unable to provide a sample of urine when required to do so may be kept apart from other detained persons until he has provided the required sample, save that the detained person may not be kept apart under this paragraph for a period of more than 5 hours.

(9) A detained person required to provide a sample of urine shall be afforded such degree of privacy for the purposes of providing the sample as may be compatible with the need to prevent or detect any adulteration or falsification of the sample and in particular a detained person shall not be required to provide such a sample in the sight of a person of the opposite sex.

PART IV
OFFICERS OF DETENTION CENTRES

45 General duty of officers

(1) It shall be the duty of every officer to conform to these Rules and the rules and regulations of the detention centre, to assist and support the manager in their maintenance and to obey his lawful instructions.

(2) An officer shall inform the manager and the Secretary of State promptly of any abuse or impropriety which comes to his knowledge.

(3) Detainee custody officers exercising custodial functions shall pay special attention to their duty under paragraph 2(3)(d) of Schedule 11 to the Immigration and Asylum Act 1999 to attend to the well-being of detained persons.

(4) Detainee custody officers shall notify the health care team of any concern they have about the physical or mental health of a detainee.

(5) In managing detained persons, all officers shall seek by their own example and leadership to enlist their willing co-operation.

(6)   At all times the treatment of detained persons shall be such as to encourage their self-respect, a sense of personal responsibility and tolerance towards others.

46 Gratuities forbidden

No officer shall receive any unauthorised fee, gratuity or other consideration in connection with his office.

47 Transactions with detained persons

(1)   No officer shall take part in any business or pecuniary transaction with or on behalf of a detained person without the leave of the Secretary of State.

(2)   No officer shall without authority bring in or take out, or attempt to bring in or take out, or knowingly allow to be brought in or taken out, to or for a detained person, or deposit in any place with intent that it shall come into the possession of a detained person, any article whatsoever.

48 Contract monitor

(1)   The contract monitor at each contracted-out detention centre must investigate promptly any complaint made against any officer at that centre.

(2)   Paragraph (1) is without prejudice to the duties of the contract monitor under section 149(7) of the Immigration and Asylum Act 1999.

49 Contractors' staff

All contractors' staff employed at the detention centre shall facilitate the exercise by the contract monitor of his functions.

50 Search of officers

An officer shall submit himself to be searched in the detention centre if the manager so directs. Any such search shall be conducted in as seemly a manner as is consistent with discovering anything concealed.

51 Contact with former detained persons

No officer shall, without the authority of the Secretary of State, communicate with any person whom he knows to be a former detained person or a relative or friend of a detained person or former detained person in such a way as could compromise that officer in the execution of his duty or the safety, security or control of the centre.

52 Communication with the press

(1)   No officer shall make, directly or indirectly, any unauthorised communication to a representative of the press or any other person concerning matters which have become known to him in the course of his duty.

(2)   No officer shall, without authority, publish any matter or make any public pronouncement relating to the administration of any detention centre, short-term holding facility or prison or to any detained persons accommodated there.

PART V
PERSONS HAVING ACCESS TO DETENTION CENTRES

53 Authorisation for access

No person shall have access to a detention centre unless authorised by statute or the manager or the Secretary of State.

54 Prohibited articles

(1)   No person shall, without authority, convey into or throw into or deposit in a detention centre, or convey or throw out of a detention centre, or convey to a detained person, or deposit in any place with intent that it shall come into the possession of a detained person, any money, clothing, food, drink, tobacco, letter, paper, book, tool or other article whatever.

(2)   Anything so conveyed, thrown or deposited may be confiscated by the manager.

55 Control of persons and vehicles

(1) Any person or vehicle entering a detention centre may be stopped, examined and searched.

(2) Any search of a person under paragraph (1) shall be carried out in as seemly a manner as is consistent with discovering anything concealed.

(3) The manager may direct the removal from a detention centre of any person who does not leave on being required to do so.

56 Viewing of detention centres

No outside person shall be permitted to view inside a detention centre unless authorised to do so by statute or the Secretary of State.

57 Visitors

(1) Without prejudice to any other powers to prohibit or restrict entry to detention centres, and to his powers under rule 28, the Secretary of State may, with a view to ensuring safety and security or the prevention of crime or in the interests of any persons, impose prohibitions on visits by a person to a detention centre or to a detained person in a detention centre for such periods of time as he considers necessary.

(2) Paragraph (1) shall not apply in relation to any visits to a detention centre or detained person by a member of the visiting committee of the detention centre, or to prevent any visit by a legal adviser for the purposes of an interview under rule 30.

PART VI
VISITING COMMITTEES

58 Disqualification for membership

Any person interested in any contract for the supply of goods or services to a detention centre shall not be a member of the visiting committee for that detention centre and any member who becomes so interested in such a contract shall vacate office as a member.

59 Visiting committees

(1) A member of the visiting committee for a detention centre appointed by the Secretary of State under section 152 of the Immigration and Asylum Act 1999 shall, subject to paragraphs (3) and (4), hold office for three years, or such lesser period as the Secretary of State may appoint.

(2) A member—

  (a) appointed for the first time to the visiting committee for a particular detention centre; or

  (b) re-appointed to the committee following a gap of a year or more in his membership of it, shall, during the period of 12 months following the date on which he is so appointed or (as the case may be) re-appointed undertake such training as may be required by the Secretary of State.

(3) The Secretary of State may terminate the appointment of a member if he is satisfied that—

  (a) he has failed satisfactorily to perform his duties;

  (b) he has failed to undertake training he has been required to under paragraph (2), by the end of the period specified in that paragraph;

  (c) he is by reason of physical or mental illness, or for any other reason, incapable of carrying out his duties; or

  (d) he has been convicted of such a criminal offence, or his conduct has been such, that it is not in the Secretary of State's opinion fitting that he should remain a member.

(4) Where the Secretary of State:

(a)   has reason to suspect that a member of the visiting committee of a detention centre may have so conducted himself that his appointment may be liable to be terminated under paragraph (3)(a) or (d) above; and

(b)   is of the opinion that the suspected conduct is of such a serious nature that the member cannot be permitted to continue to perform his functions as a member of the committee pending the completion of the Secretary of State's investigations into the matter and any decision as to whether the member's appointment should be terminated,

he may suspend the member from office for such a period or periods as he may reasonably require in order to complete his investigations and determine whether or not the appointment of the member should be so terminated; and a member so suspended shall not, during the period of the suspension be regarded as being a member of the visiting committee, other than for the purposes of this paragraph and paragraphs (1) and (3).

(5)   A committee shall have a chairman and a vice-chairman, who shall be members of the committee.

(6)   The Secretary of State shall—

(a)   upon the constitution of a committee for the first time, appoint a chairman and a vice-chairman to hold office for a period not exceeding twelve months;

(b)   thereafter appoint, before the date of the first meeting of the committee in any year of office of the board, a chairman and a vice-chairman for that year, having first consulted the committee; and

(c)   promptly fill, after having first consulted the committee, any casual vacancy in the office of chairman or vice-chairman.

(7)   The Secretary of State may terminate the appointment of a member as chairman or vice-chairman of the committee if he is satisfied that the member has—

(a)   failed satisfactorily to perform his functions as chairman or (as the case may be) vice-chairman; or

(b)   has grossly misconducted himself whilst performing those functions.

60 Proceedings of visiting committees

(1)   The visiting committee of a detention centre shall meet at the detention centre once a month or, if they resolve for reasons specified in the resolution that less frequent meetings are sufficient, not fewer than eight times in twelve months.

(2)   The committee may fix a quorum of not fewer than three members for proceedings.

(3)   The committee shall keep minutes of their proceedings.

(4)   The proceedings of the committee shall not be invalidated by any vacancy in the membership or any defect in the appointment of a member.

61 General duties of visiting committees

(1)   The visiting committee of a detention centre shall satisfy themselves as to the state of the detention centre premises, the administration of the detention centre and the treatment of the detained persons.

(2)   The committee shall inquire into and report upon any matter into which the Secretary of State asks them to inquire.

(3)   The committee shall direct the attention of the manager to any matter which calls for his attention, and shall report to the Secretary of State any matter which they consider expedient to report.

(4)   The committee shall inform the Secretary of State immediately of any abuse which comes to their knowledge.

(5)   The committee shall bring to the attention of the Secretary of State any aspect of the process of consideration of the immigration status of any detained person that causes them concern insofar as it affects that detained person's continued detention.

(6) Subject to paragraph (5) the committee shall not concern themselves with any issue directly relating to the immigration status of any detained person under the Immigration Acts.

(7) Before exercising any power under these Rules the committee and any member of the committee shall consult the manager in relation to any matter which may affect safety and security.

62 Particular duties

(1) A member of the visiting committee shall visit any detained person who is subject for the time being to:—

    (a) removal from association under rule 40;

    (b) temporary confinement under rule 42; or

    (c) special control or restraint under rule 43 within 24 hours of his being made so subject, and thereafter as the Secretary of State may direct.

(2) The visiting committee for a detention centre and any member of the committee shall hear any complaint or request which a detained person wishes to make to them or him.

(3) The committee shall arrange for the food of the detained persons to be inspected by a member of the committee at frequent intervals.

(4) The committee shall inquire into any report made to them, whether or not by a member of the committee, that a detained person's health, mental or physical, is likely to be injuriously affected by any conditions of his detention.

63 Members visiting detention centres

(1) The members of the visiting committee for a detention centre shall (subject to paragraph (4)) visit the detention centre frequently, and the committee shall arrange a rota whereby at least one of its members visits the detention centre each week.

(2) A member of the committee shall have access at any time to every part of the detention centre and to every detained person, and he may interview any detained person out of the sight and hearing of officers.

(3) A member of the committee shall have access to the records of the detention centre.

(4) In exceptional circumstances, the Secretary of State may temporarily restrict visits by members of the committee in the interests of safety or security.

64 Annual report

(1) The visiting committee for a detention centre shall, in accordance with paragraphs (2) and (3), from time to time make a report to the Secretary of State concerning the state of the detention centre and its administration, including in it any advice and suggestions they consider appropriate.

(2) The committee shall comply with any directions given to them from time to time by the Secretary of State as to the following matters—

    (a) the period to be covered by the report under paragraph (1);

    (b) the frequency with which such a report is to be made; and

    (c) the length of time from the end of the period covered by such a report within which it is to be made,

either in respect of a particular report or generally, providing that no directions may be issued under this paragraph if they would have the effect of requiring a committee to make or deliver a report less frequently than once in every twelve months.

(3) Subject to any directions given to them under paragraph (2), the committee shall, under paragraph (1), make an annual report to the Secretary of State as soon as reasonably possible after 31st December each year, which shall cover the period of twelve months ending on that date or, in the case of a committee constituted for the first time during that period, such part of that period during which the committee has been in existence.

PART VII
SUPPLEMENTAL

65 Delegation by the Secretary of State
The manager of a detention centre may, with the leave of the Secretary of State, delegate any of the powers and duties under these Rules to another officer of that detention centre.

IMMIGRATION (LEAVE TO ENTER) ORDER 2001

(SI 2001/2590)

Made: 17 July 2001.

Authority: Immigration Act 1971, s 3A(1), (7), (8), (10).

Commencement: 18 July 2001.

1

(1) This Order may be cited as the Immigration (Leave to Enter) Order 2001 and shall come into force on the day after the day on which it is made.

(2) In this Order—

(a) "the 1971 Act" means the Immigration Act 1971; and

(b) "claim for asylum" and "the Human Rights Convention" have the meanings assigned by section 167 of the Immigration and Asylum Act 1999.

2

(1) Where this article applies to a person, the Secretary of State may give or refuse him leave to enter the United Kingdom.

(2) This article applies to a person who seeks leave to enter the United Kingdom and who—

(a) has made a claim for asylum; or

(b) has made a claim that it would be contrary to the United Kingdom's obligations under the Human Rights Convention for him to be removed from, or required to leave, the United Kingdom.

(3) This article also applies to a person who seeks leave to enter the United Kingdom for a purpose not covered by the immigration rules or otherwise on the grounds that those rules should be departed from in his case.

(4) In deciding whether to give or refuse leave under this article the Secretary of State may take into account any additional grounds which a person has for seeking leave to enter the United Kingdom.

(5) The power to give or refuse leave to enter the United Kingdom under this article shall be exercised by notice in writing to the person affected or in such manner as is permitted by the Immigration (Leave to Enter and Remain) Order 2000.

3

In relation to the giving or refusing of leave to enter by the Secretary of State under article 2, paragraphs 2 (examination by immigration officers, and medical examination), 4 (information and documents), 7(1), (3) and (4) (power to require medical examination after entry), 8 (removal of persons refused leave to enter), 9 (removal of illegal entrants) and 21 (temporary admission of persons liable to detention) of Schedule 2 to the 1971 Act shall be read as if references to an immigration officer included references to the Secretary of State.

4

(1) This article applies where—

  (a) an immigration officer has commenced examination of a person ("the applicant") under paragraph 2(1)(c) of Schedule 2 to the 1971 Act (examination to determine whether or not leave to enter should be given);

  (b) that examination has been adjourned, or the applicant has been required (under paragraph 2(3) of Schedule 2 to the Immigration Act 1971) to submit to a further examination;

  (c) the Secretary of State subsequently examines the applicant or conducts a further examination in relation to him; and

  (d) the Secretary of State thereafter gives or refuses the applicant leave to enter.

(2) Where this article applies, the notice giving or refusing leave to enter shall be regarded for the purposes of the 1971 Act as having been given within the period of 24 hours specified in paragraph 6(1) of Schedule 2 to that Act (period within which notice giving or refusing leave to enter must be given after completion of examination by an immigration officer).

STATE PENSION CREDIT REGULATIONS 2002

(SI 2002/1792)

Notes

Made: 11 July 2002.

Authority: Social Security Contributions and Benefits Act 1992, s 175(3)–(5); Social Security Fraud Act 2001, ss 7(4A), 9(4A), 11(1), (4); State Pension Credit Act 2002, ss 1(5), 2(3), (4), (6), 3(4)–(8), 4(3), 5, 6(2), 7(4), (7), 9(4), (5), 12(2) , (3), 15, 16(2), 17(1), (2).

Commencement: 6 October 2003.

PART II

ENTITLEMENT AND AMOUNT

2 Persons not in Great Britain]

[(1) A person is to be treated as not in Great Britain if, subject to the following provisions of this regulation, he is not habitually resident in the United Kingdom, the Channel Islands, the Isle of Man or the Republic of Ireland.

(2) No person shall be treated as habitually resident in the United Kingdom, the Channel Islands, the Isle of Man or the Republic of Ireland unless he has a right to reside in (as the case may be) the United Kingdom, the Channel Islands, the Isle of Man or the Republic of Ireland other than a right to reside which falls within paragraph (3).

(3) A right to reside falls within this paragraph if it is one which exists by virtue of, or in accordance with, one or more of the following—

  (a) regulation 13 of the Immigration (European Economic Area) Regulations 2006;

  (b regulation 14 of those Regulations, but only in a case where the right exists under that regulation because the person is—

   (i) a jobseeker for the purpose of the definition of "qualified person" in regulation 6(1) of those Regulations, or

   (ii) a family member (within the meaning of regulation 7 of those Regulations) of such a jobseeker;

[(bb) regulation 15A(1) of those Regulations, but only in a case where the right exists under that regulation because the claimant satisfies the criteria in regulation 15A(4A) of those Regulations;]

(c) Article 6 of Council Directive No 2004/38/EC; . . .

(d) [Article 45 of the Treaty on the Functioning of the European Union] (in a case where the person is seeking work in the United Kingdom, the Channel Islands, the Isle of Man or the Republic of Ireland)[; or

(e) Article 20 of the Treaty on the Functioning of the European Union (in a case where the right to reside arises because a British citizen would otherwise be deprived of the genuine enjoyment of the substance of their rights as a European Union citizen)].

(4) A person is not to be treated as not in Great Britain if he is—

(za) a qualified person for the purposes of regulation 6 of the Immigration (European Economic Area) Regulations 2006 as a worker or a self-employed person;

(zb) a family member of a person referred to in sub-paragraph (za) within the meaning of regulation 7(1)(a), (b) or (c) of those Regulations;

(zc) a person who has a right to reside permanently in the United Kingdom by virtue of regulation 15(1)(c), (d) or (e) of those Regulations;]

(g) a refugee within the definition in Article 1 of the Convention relating to the Status of Refugees done at Geneva on 28th July 1951, as extended by Article 1(2) of the Protocol relating to the Status of Refugees done at New York on 31st January 1967;

[[(h) a person who has been granted leave or who is deemed to have been granted leave outside the rules made under section 3(2) of the Immigration Act 1971 (where that leave is—

(i) discretionary leave to enter or remain in the United Kingdom;

(i) leave to remain under the Destitution Domestic Violence concession; or

(i) leave deemed to have been granted by virtue of regulation 3 of the Displaced Persons (Temporary Protection) Regulations 2005;]

(hh) a person who has humanitarian protection granted under those rules;] [or]

(i) a person who is not a person subject to immigration control within the meaning of section 115(9) of the Immigration and Asylum Act 1999 and who is in the United Kingdom as a result of his deportation, expulsion or other removal by compulsion of law from another country to the United Kingdom; . . .

(j) . . .

(k) . . .]

Amendment

Substituted by SI 2006/1026, reg 9. Date in force: 30 April 2006: see SI 2006/1026, reg 1.

Para (3): sub-para (bb) inserted by SI 2012/2587, reg 4(1), (2). Date in force: 8 November 2012: see SI 2012/2587, reg 1.

Para (3): in sub-para (c) word omitted revoked by SI 2012/2587, reg 4(1), (3). Date in force: 8 November 2012: see SI 2012/2587, reg 1.

Para (3): in sub-para (d) words "Article 45 of the Treaty on the Functioning of the European Union" in square brackets substituted by SI 2012/1809, art 3(1), Schedule, Pt 2. Date in force: 1 August 2012 (except in its application to things done before 1 December 2009, being the date on which the Treaty of Lisbon came into force): see SI 2012/1809, art 2.

Para (3): sub-para (e) and word "; or" immediately preceding it inserted by SI 2012/2587, reg 4(1), (4). Date in force: 8 November 2012: see SI 2012/2587, reg 1.

Para (4): sub-paras (za)–(zc) substituted, for sub-paras (a)–(f), by SI 2014/902, reg 4. Date in force: 31 May 2014: see SI 2014/902, reg 1.

Para (4): sub-paras (h), (hh) substituted, for sub-para (h) as originally enacted, by SI 2006/2528, reg 4. Date in force: 9 October 2006: see SI 2006/2528, reg 1.

Para (4): sub-para (h) substituted by SI 2013/2536, reg 10(1), (3)(a). Date in force: 29 October 2013: see SI 2013/2536, reg 1(1).

Para (4): in sub-para (hh) word "or" in square brackets inserted by SI 2013/2536, reg 10(1), (3)(b). Date in force: 29 October 2013: see SI 2013/2536, reg 1(1).

Para (4): in sub-para (i) word omitted revoked by SI 2009/362, reg 4(1), (2). Date in force: 18 March 2009: see SI 2009/362, reg 1(2).

Para (4): sub-paras (j), (k) revoked by SI 2013/2536, reg 10(1), (3)(c). Date in force: 29 October 2013: see SI 2013/2536, reg 1(1).

WITHHOLDING AND WITHDRAWAL OF SUPPORT (TRAVEL ASSISTANCE AND TEMPORARY ACCOMMODATION) REGULATIONS 2002

(SI 2002/3078)

Notes

Made: 13 December 2002.

Authority: Nationality, Immigration and Asylum Act 2002, s 54, Sch 3, paras 8–12, 16(2), 17.

Commencement: 8 January 2003.

1 Citation and commencement

These Regulations may be cited as the Withholding and Withdrawal of Support (Travel Assistance and Temporary Accommodation) Regulations 2002 and shall come into force on 8th January 2003.

2 Interpretation

(1) In these Regulations—

"the Act" means the Nationality, Immigration and Asylum Act 2002,

"person with refugee status abroad" means a person to whom paragraph 1 of Schedule 3 to the Act applies by virtue of paragraph 4 of that Schedule,

"EEA national" means a person to whom paragraph 1 of Schedule 3 to the Act applies by virtue of paragraph 5 of that Schedule,

"person unlawfully in the United Kingdom" means a person to whom paragraph 1 of Schedule 3 to the Act applies by virtue of paragraph 7 of that Schedule,

"relevant EEA State" means—

    (a)   in relation to a person with refugee status abroad, the EEA State the government of which has determined that he, or a person on whom he is dependent, is entitled to protection as a refugee under the Refugee Convention;

    (b)   in relation to an EEA national, the EEA State of which he, or a person on whom he is dependent, is a national;

"travel arrangements" means arrangements made under regulation 3(1).

(2) In these Regulations and for the purposes of Schedule 3 to the Act, a "dependant" of a person means a person who at the relevant time—

    (a)   is his spouse [or his civil partner];

    (b)   is a child of his or of his spouse [or his civil partner];

    (c)   is a member of his or his spouse's [or his civil partner's]close family and is under 18;

    (d)   has been living as part of his household—

    (i) for at least six of the twelve months before the relevant time, or

    (ii) since birth,

  and is under 18;

  (e) is in need of care and attention from him or a member of his household by reason of a disability and would fall under (c) or (d) but for the fact that he is not under 18;

  (f) has been living with him as [a couple] for at least two of the three years before the relevant time,

and "dependent" has the corresponding meaning.

(3) In paragraph (2)—

  "relevant time" means, in relation to any arrangements made by a local authority in respect of a person, the time when the local authority begins to make those arrangements;

  "unmarried couple" means a man and woman who, though not married to each other, are living together as if married;

  ["couple" means a man and woman who are not married to each other but are living together as if they are, or, two people of the same sex who are not civil partners of each other but are living together as if they are].

Amendment

 Para (2): in sub-para (a) words "or his civil partner" in square brackets inserted by SI 2005/2114, art 2(13), Sch 13, Pt 1, para 3(a). Date in force: 5 December 2005: see SI 2005/2114, art 1.

 Para (2): in sub-para (b) words "or of his civil partner" in square brackets inserted by SI 2005/2114, art 2(13), Sch 13, Pt 1, para 3(b). Date in force: 5 December 2005: see SI 2005/2114, art 1.

 Para (2): in sub-para (c) words "or his civil partner's" in square brackets inserted by SI 2005/2114, art 2(13), Sch 13, Pt 1, para 3(c). Date in force: 5 December 2005: see SI 2005/2114, art 1.

 Para (2): in sub-para (f) words "a couple" in square brackets substituted by SI 2005/2114, art 2(13), Sch 13, Pt 1, para 3(d). Date in force: 5 December 2005: see SI 2005/2114, art 1.

 Para (3): definition "couple" substituted, for definition "unmarried couple" as originally enacted, by SI 2005/2114, art 2(13), Sch 13, Pt 1, para 3(e). Date in force: 5 December 2005: see SI 2005/2114, art 1.

3 Power for local authorities to arrange travel and provide accommodation

(1) A local authority may make arrangements ("travel arrangements") enabling a person with refugee status abroad or who is an EEA national to leave the United Kingdom to travel to the relevant EEA State.

(2) A local authority may make arrangements for the accommodation of a person in respect of whom travel arrangements have been or are to be made pending the implementation of those arrangements.

(3) A local authority may make arrangements for the accommodation of a person unlawfully in the United Kingdom who has not failed to co-operate with removal directions issued in respect of him.

(4) Arrangements for a person by virtue of paragraph (2) or (3)—

  (a) may be made only if the person has with him a dependent child, and

  (b) may include arrangements for that child.

4 Requirements relating to travel and accommodation arrangements

(1) Travel arrangements and arrangements for accommodation must be made so as to secure implementation of those arrangements at the lowest practicable cost to the local authority.

(2) Subject to the requirements in paragraph (1), travel arrangements made in respect of a person must be made so that the person leaves the United Kingdom as soon as practicable.

(3)   Travel arrangements and arrangements for accommodation may not include cash payments to a person in respect of whom the arrangements are made and must be made in such a way as to prevent the obtaining of services or benefits other than those specified in the arrangements.

(4)   A local authority must have regard to guidance issued by the Secretary of State in making travel arrangements and arrangements for accommodation.

5 Failure to implement travel arrangements

Where a person with refugee status abroad or an EEA national refuses an offer of travel arrangements or fails to implement or co-operate with travel arrangements, a local authority may make new travel arrangements for him to travel to the relevant EEA State.

6

(1)   Where a person with refugee status abroad or an EEA national in respect of whom travel arrangements have been made by a local authority fails to implement or co-operate with those travel arrangements, neither that local authority nor any other local authority may make arrangements for the accommodation of that person except in accordance with the following provisions of this regulation.

(2)   Where paragraph (1) applies to a person because of his failure to travel as arranged, the relevant local authority or another local authority may make further arrangements for the accommodation of that person pending the implementation of revised travel arrangements if, but only if, the local authority considers that—

    (a)   the failure was for one or both of the reasons set out in paragraph (3) and for no other reason, and

    (b)   the person took all reasonable steps to travel as arranged,

and the person has provided or taken all reasonable steps to provide the explanations and evidence requested by the local authority as regards the matters referred to in sub-paragraphs (a) and (b).

(3)   The reasons referred to in paragraph (2) are—

    (a)   that the applicant or a person within his family group was medically unfit to travel as arranged;

    (b)   that despite his having taken all reasonable steps to ensure that he travelled as arranged, he was prevented from doing so by failure of a transport service.

(4)   Arrangements for accommodation pursuant to this regulation may only be made in accordance with the provisions of these Regulations, including this regulation.

(5)   In this regulation—

    (a)   "family group" in relation to a person means that person and those of his dependants who are to travel with him under arrangements made under these Regulations;

    (b)   "transport service" means a public transport service or any transport provided or arranged by the local authority.

ALLOCATION OF HOUSING (ENGLAND) REGULATIONS 2002

(SI 2002/3264)

Notes

Made: 18 December 2002.

Authority: Housing Act 1996, ss 160(4), 160A(3), (5), 172(4).

Commencement: 31 January 2003.

1 Citation, commencement and application

(1)   These Regulations may be cited as the Allocation of Housing (England) Regulations 2002 and shall come into force on 31st January 2003.

(2)   These Regulations apply in England only.

2 Interpretation

In these Regulations—

"the Act" means the Housing Act 1996;

"the Common Travel Area" means the United Kingdom, the Channel Islands, the Isle of Man and the Republic of Ireland collectively; and

["family intervention tenancy"—

(a)   in relation to a tenancy granted by a local housing authority, has the meaning given by paragraph 4ZA(3) of Schedule 1 to the Housing Act 1985;

(b)   in relation to a tenancy granted by a registered social landlord [or a private registered provider of social housing], has the meaning given by paragraph 12ZA(3) of Part 1 of Schedule 1 to the Housing Act 1988;]

"the immigration rules" means the rules laid down as mentioned in section 3(2) of the Immigration Act 1971 (general provisions for regulation and control).

Amendment

Definition "family intervention tenancy" inserted by SI 2008/3015, reg 2(1), (2). Date in force: 1 January 2009: see SI 2008/3015, reg 1(1).

In definition "family intervention tenancy" in para (b) words in square brackets inserted by SI 2010/671, art 4, Sch 1, para 29. Date in force: 1 April 2010: see SI 2010/671, art 1(2), and SI 2010/862, art 2; for transitional provisions and savings see SI 2010/671, art 5, Sch 2, paras 1, 2, 5, 6 and SI 2010/862, arts 2, 3, Schedule, paras 1–5.

3 Cases where the provisions of Part 6 of the Act do not apply

(1)   The provisions of Part 6 of the Act about the allocation of housing accommodation do not apply in the following cases.

(2)   They do not apply where a local housing authority secures the provision of suitable alternative accommodation under section 39 of the Land Compensation Act 1973 (duty to rehouse residential occupiers).

(3)   They do not apply in relation to the grant of a secure tenancy under sections 554 and 555 of the Housing Act 1985 (grant of tenancy to former owner-occupier or statutory tenant of defective dwelling-house).

[(4)   They do not apply in relation to the allocation of housing accommodation by a local housing authority to a person who lawfully occupies accommodation let on a family intervention tenancy.]

Amendment

Para (4): inserted by SI 2008/3015, reg 2(1), (3).

Date in force: 1 January 2009: see SI 2008/3015, reg 1(1).

4, 5

(Revoked by SI 2006/1294, reg 7, Schedule. Date in force: 1 June 2006: see SI 2006/1294, reg 1(1); for transitional provisions see reg 8 thereof.)

6 Revocation

The Allocation of Housing (England) Regulations 2000 are revoked.

GUARDIAN'S ALLOWANCE (GENERAL) REGULATIONS 2003

(SI 2003/495)

Notes

Made: 5 March 2003.

Authority: Social Security Contributions and Benefits Act 1992, s 77(3), (8), (9); Social Security Contributions and Benefits (Northern Ireland) Act 1992, s 77(3), (8), (9); Tax Credits Act 2002, s 54.

Commencement: 7 April 2003.

9 Residence condition

(1)   There shall be no entitlement to guardian's allowance in respect of a child [or qualifying young person] unless at least one of [the parents of that child or qualifying young person]—

    (a)   was born in the United Kingdom; or

    (b)   at the date of death of the parent whose death gives rise to the claim for guardian's allowance, has, in any two year period since the age of 16, spent at least 52 weeks of that period in Great Britain or Northern Ireland, as the case may require.

(2)   For the purposes of paragraph (1)(b) above, a person shall be treated as being present in Great Britain or Northern Ireland (as the case may require) where—

    (a)   his absence is by virtue of his employment—

        (i)   as a serving member of the forces within the meaning of regulation 140 of the Social Security (Contributions) Regulations 2001;

        (ii)   as an airman within the meaning of regulation 111 of those Regulations; or

        (iii)   as a mariner within the meaning of regulation 115 of those Regulations; or

    (b)   his absence is by virtue of his employment and that employment is prescribed employment within the meaning of regulation 114(1) of those Regulations (continental shelf operations).

[(3)   Where a child or qualifying young person has been adopted by two persons jointly references in paragraph (1) above to the parents of the child or qualifying young person are to be read as references to those two persons.

(3A)   Where a child or qualifying young person has been adopted by one person only, that person must satisfy the requirements of paragraph (1) above.]

(4)   Where regulation 5 applies, [the mother of the child or qualifying young person] must satisfy the requirement of paragraph (1) above.

Amendment

Para (1): words "or qualifying young person" in square brackets inserted by SI 2006/204, regs 2, 8(1), (2)(a).

Date in force: 10 April 2006: see SI 2006/204, reg 1.

Para (1): words "the parents of that child or qualifying young person" in square brackets substituted by SI 2006/204, regs 2, 8(1), (2)(b).

Date in force: 10 April 2006: see SI 2006/204, reg 1.

Paras (3), (3A): substituted, for para (3) as originally enacted, by SI 2006/204, regs 2, 8(1), (3).

Date in force: 10 April 2006: see SI 2006/204, reg 1.

Para (4): words "the mother of the child or qualifying young person" in square brackets substituted by SI 2006/204, regs 2, 8(1), (4).

Date in force: 10 April 2006: see SI 2006/204, reg 1.

IMMIGRATION APPEALS (FAMILY VISITOR) REGULATIONS 2003

(SI 2003/518)

Notes

Made: 5 March 2003.

Authority: Nationality, Immigration and Asylum Act 2002, ss 90(2), (3), 112(1), (2), (3).

Commencement: 1 April 2003.

1

These Regulations may be cited as the Immigration Appeals (Family Visitor) Regulations 2003 and shall come into force on 1st April 2003.

2

(1) For the purposes of section 90(1) of the Nationality, Immigration and Asylum Act 2002, a "member of the applicant's family" is any of the following persons—

- (a)   the applicant's spouse, father, mother, son, daughter, grandfather, grandmother, grandson, granddaughter, brother, sister, uncle, aunt, nephew, niece or first cousin;
- (b)   the father, mother, brother or sister of the applicant's spouse;
- (c)   the spouse of the applicant's son or daughter;
- (d)   the applicant's stepfather, stepmother, stepson, stepdaughter, stepbrother or stepsister; or
- (e)   a person with whom the applicant has lived as a member of an unmarried couple for at least two of the three years before the day on which his application for entry clearance was made.

(2) In these Regulations, "first cousin" means, in relation to a person, the son or daughter of his uncle or aunt.

TAX CREDITS (IMMIGRATION) REGULATIONS 2003

(SI 2003/653)

Notes

Made: 11 March 2003.

Authority: Tax Credits Act 2002, ss 42, 65(1), (3), (7), (9).

Commencement: 6 April 2003.

1 Citation and commencement

These Regulations may be cited as the Tax Credits (Immigration) Regulations 2003 and shall come into force on 6th April 2003.

2 Interpretation

In these Regulations—

"the Act" means the Tax Credits Act 2002;

"the Child Tax Credit Regulations" means the Child Tax Credit Regulations 2002;

["couple" has the meaning given by section 3(5A) of the Act;]

"immigration rules" has the meaning given by section 33 of the Immigration Act 1971;

"joint claim" has the meaning given by section 3(8) of the Act;

"limited leave" has the meaning given by section 33 of the Immigration Act 1971;

. . .

"person subject to immigration control" has the meaning in section 115(9) of the Immigration and Asylum Act 1999;

"refugee" means a person who has been recorded by the Secretary of State as a refugee within the definition in Article 1 of the Convention relating to the Status of Refugees done at Geneva on 28th July 1951 as extended by Article 1(2) of the Protocol relating to the Status of Refugees done at New York on 31st January 1967;

"tax credit" refers to either child tax credit or working tax credit and references to tax credits are to both of them;

"the Working Tax Credit Regulations" means the Working Tax Credit (Entitlement and Maximum Rate) Regulations 2002.

Amendment

Definition "couple" inserted by SI 2005/2919, art 7(1), (2)(a). Date in force: 5 December 2005: see SI 2005/2919, art 1.

Definition ""married couple" and "unmarried couple"" (omitted) revoked by SI 2005/2919, art 7(1), (2)(b). Date in force: 5 December 2005: see SI 2005/2919, art 1.

3 Exclusion of persons subject to immigration control from entitlement to tax credits
(1) No person is entitled to child tax credit or working tax credit while he is a person subject to immigration control, except in the following Cases, and subject to paragraphs (2) to (9).

Case 1

He is a person who—
- (a) has been given leave to enter, or remain in, the United Kingdom by the Secretary of State upon the undertaking of another person or persons, pursuant to the immigration rules, to be responsible for his maintenance and accommodation, and
- (b) has been resident in the United Kingdom for a period of at least 5 years commencing on or after the date of his entry into the United Kingdom, or the date on which the undertaking was given in respect of him, whichever is the later.

Case 2

He is a person who—
- (a) falls within the terms of paragraph (a) of Case 1, and
- (b) has been resident in the United Kingdom for less than the 5 years mentioned in paragraph (b) of Case 1,

but the person giving the undertaking has died or, where the undertaking was given by more than one person, they have all died.

. . .

Case 4

Where the claim is for working tax credit, he is—
- (a) a national of a state which has ratified the European Convention on Social and Medical Assistance (done in Paris on 11th December 1953) or of a state which has ratified the Council of Europe Social Charter (signed in Turin on 18th October 1961), and

    (b)   lawfully present in the United Kingdom.

The Case so described also applies where—

    (a)   the claim is for child tax credit,

    (b)   the award of child tax credit would be made on or after 6th April 2004, and

    (c)   immediately before the award is made (and as part of the transition of claimants entitled to elements of income support and income-based jobseeker's allowance, to child tax credit) the person is, or will on the making of a claim be, entitled to any of the amounts in relation to income support or income-based jobseeker's allowance which are described in section 1(3)(d) of the Act.

Case 5

Where the claim is for child tax credit, he is—

    (a)   a person who is lawfully working in the United Kingdom, and

    (b)   a national of a State with which the [European Union] has concluded an Agreement under [Article 217 of the Treaty on the Functioning of the European Union] providing, in the field of social security, for the equal treatment of workers who are nationals of the signatory State and their families.

(2)   Where one member of a . . . couple is a person subject to immigration control, and the other member is not or is within any of Cases 1 to 5 or regulation 5—

    (a)   the calculation of the amount of tax credit under the Act, the Child Tax Credit Regulations and the Working Tax Credit Regulations (including any second adult element or other element in respect of, or determined by reference to, that person),

    (b)   the method of making (or proceeding with) a joint claim by the couple, and

    (c)   the method of payment of the tax credit,

shall, subject to paragraph (3), be determined in the same way as if that person were not subject to such control.

(3)   Where the other member is within Case 4 or 5 or regulation 5, paragraph (2) shall only apply to the tax credit to which he (in accordance with those provisions) is entitled.

(4)   Where a person has submitted a claim for asylum as a refugee and in consequence is a person subject to immigration control, in the first instance he is not entitled to tax credits, subject to paragraphs (5) to (9).

(5)   If that person—

    (a)   is notified that he has been recorded by the Secretary of State as a refugee, and

    (b)   claims tax credit within [one month] of receiving that notification,

paragraphs (6) to (9) and regulation 4 shall apply to him.

(6)   He shall be treated as having claimed tax credits—

    (a)   on the date when he submitted his claim for asylum, and

    (b)   on every 6th April (if any) intervening between the date in sub-paragraph (a) and the date of the claim referred to in paragraph (5)(b),

rather than on the date on which he makes the claim referred to in paragraph (5)(b).

(7)   Regulations 7 and 8 of the Tax Credits (Claims and Notifications) Regulations 2002 shall not apply to claims treated as made by virtue of paragraph (6).

(8)   He shall have his claims for tax credits determined as if he had been recorded as a refugee on the date when he submitted his claim for asylum.

(9)   The amount of support provided under—

    (a)   section 95 or 98 of the Immigration and Asylum Act 1999,

(b)   regulations made under Schedule 9 to that Act, by the Secretary of State in respect of essential living needs of the claimant and his dependants (if any), or

(c)   regulations made under paragraph 3 of Schedule 8 to that Act,

(after allowing for any deduction for that amount under regulation 21ZB(3) of the Income Support (General) Regulations 1987) shall be deducted from any award of tax credits due to the claimant by virtue of paragraphs (6) and (8).

Amendment

Para (1): Case 3 (omitted) revoked by SI 2014/658, reg 3, as from 6 April 2014.

Para (1): in Case 5 para (b) words "European Union" in square brackets substituted by SI 2011/1043, art 4(1). Date in force: 22 April 2011: see SI 2011/1043, art 2; for transitional savings see art 3(3) thereof.

Para (1): in Case 5 in para (b) words "Article 217 of the Treaty on the Functioning of the European Union" in square brackets substituted by SI 2011/1043, art 5. Date in force: 22 April 2011: see SI 2011/1043, art 2; for transitional savings see art 3(3) thereof.

Para (2): words omitted revoked by SI 2005/2919, art 7(1), (3). Date in force: 5 December 2005: see SI 2005/2919, art 1.

Para (5): words in square brackets in sub-para (b) substituted by SI 2012/848, reg 7, as from 6 April 2012.

4 Modifications of Part 1 of the Act for refugees whose asylum claims have been accepted

(1)   For the purposes of claims falling within paragraph (2), Part 1 of the Act shall apply subject to the modifications set out in paragraphs (3) to (5).

(2)   A claim falls within this paragraph if it is a claim for tax credits which a person is treated as having made by virtue of regulation 3(6), other than a claim which he is treated as having made in the tax year in which he made his claim under regulation 3(5).

(3)   Omit sections 14 to 17 (initial decisions, revised decisions and final notices).

(4)   In section 18 (decisions after final notices)—

(a)   in subsection (1) for "After giving a notice under section 17" substitute "In relation to each claim for a tax credit made by a person or persons for the whole or part of a tax year";

(b)   omit subsections (2) to (9);

(c)   for subsection (10) substitute—

"(10)   Before making their decision the Board may by notice—

(a)   require the person, or either or both of the persons, by whom the claim is made to provide any information or evidence which the Board consider they may need for making their decision, or

(b)   require any person of a prescribed description to provide any information or evidence of a prescribed description which the Board consider they may need for that purpose,

by the date specified in the notice.";

(d)   in subsection (11) omit—

(i)   "any revision under subsection (5) or (9) and";

(ii)   paragraph (a);

(iii)   in paragraph (b), "in any other case,".

(5)   In section 19 (enquiries)—

(a)   in subsection (4), for paragraphs (a) and (b) substitute

"one year after that decision or, if—

(a)   the person, or either of the persons, to whom the enquiry relates is required by section 8 of the Taxes Management Act 1970 to make a return, and

(b)   the return becomes final on a day more than one year after that decision,

with that day (or, if both of the persons are so required and their returns become final on different days, with the later of those days).;"

(b)   in subsection (5) omit paragraph (a) and, in paragraph (b) "in any other case,";

(c)   omit subsection (6).

5 Transitional relief – claimants moving from income support and income-based jobseeker's allowance to child tax credit

In relation to child tax credit, a person is not treated for the purposes of these Regulations as subject to immigration control where—

(a)   the award of child tax credit would be made on or after 6th April 2004;

(b)   immediately before the award of child tax credit is made, he is, or will on the making of a claim be, entitled to any of the amounts in relation to income support or income-based jobseeker's allowance which are described in section 1(3)(d) of the Act; and

(c)   he is a person who, immediately before the award of child tax credit is made—

(i)   was receiving or entitled to income support by virtue of regulation 12(1) of the Social Security (Persons From Abroad) Miscellaneous Amendments Regulations 1996, and his claim for asylum has not been recorded by the Secretary of State as having been decided (other than on appeal) or abandoned; or

(ii)   was receiving or entitled to income support or income-based jobseeker's allowance by virtue of regulation 12(3) of the Social Security (Immigration and Asylum) Consequential Amendments Regulations 2000, and his claim for asylum has not been so recorded as having been decided (other than on appeal) or abandoned.

TAX CREDITS (RESIDENCE) REGULATIONS 2003

(SI 2003/654)

Notes

Made: 11 March 2003.

Authority: Tax Credits Act 2002, ss 3(7), 65(1), (7), (9).

Commencement: 6 April 2003.

1 Citation and commencement

These Regulations may be cited as the Tax Credits (Residence) Regulations 2003 and shall come into force on 6th April 2003.

2 Interpretation

(1)   In these Regulations—

"the Act" means the Tax Credits Act 2002;

"child" has the same meaning as it has in the Child Tax Credit Regulations 2002;

["couple" has the meaning given by section 3(5A) of the Act;]

"Crown servant posted overseas" has the meaning given in regulation 5(2);

"partner" means where a person is a member of a . . . couple, the other member of that couple;

"qualifying young person" has the meaning given in regulation 2, read with regulation 5, of the Child Tax Credit Regulations 2002;

"relative" means brother, sister, ancestor or lineal descendant.

(2)   In these Regulations a person is responsible for a child or qualifying young person if he is treated as being responsible for that child or qualifying young person in accordance with the rules contained in regulation 3 of the Child Tax Credit Regulations 2002.

Amendment

Para (1): definition "couple" inserted by SI 2005/2919, art 8(1), (2)(a). Date in force: 5 December 2005: see SI 2005/2919, art 1.

Para (1): in definition "partner" words omitted revoked by SI 2005/2919, art 8(1), (2)(b). Date in force: 5 December 2005: see SI 2005/2919, art 1.

3 Circumstances in which a person is treated as not being in the United Kingdom

(1)   A person shall be treated as not being in the United Kingdom for the purposes of Part 1 of the Act if he is not ordinarily resident in the United Kingdom.

(2)   [Paragraphs (1) and (6) do] not apply to a Crown servant posted overseas or his partner.

(3)   A person who is in the United Kingdom as a result of his deportation, expulsion or other removal by compulsion of law from another country to the United Kingdom shall be treated as being ordinarily resident in the United Kingdom [and paragraph (6) shall not apply]..

(4)   For the purposes of working tax credit, a person shall be treated as being ordinarily resident if he is exercising in the United Kingdom his rights as a worker pursuant to [Parliament and Council Regulation (EU) No 492/2011] or he is a person with a right to reside in the United Kingdom pursuant to [Council Directive No 2004/38/EC].

[(5)   A person shall be treated as not being in the United Kingdom for the purposes of Part 1 of the Act where he—

(a)   makes a claim for child tax credit (other than being treated as making a claim under regulation 11 or 12 of the Tax Credits (Claims and Notifications) Regulations 2002 or otherwise), on or after 1st May 2004; and

[(b)

(i)   does not have a right to reside in the United Kingdom; or

(i)   has a right to reside in the United Kingdom under:

–   regulation 15A(1) of the Immigration (European Economic Area) Regulations 2006, but only in a case where the right exists under that regulation because the person satisfies the criteria in regulation 15A(4A) of those Regulations; or

–   Article 20 of the Treaty on the Functioning of the European Union (in a case where the right to reside arises because a British citizen would otherwise be deprived of the genuine enjoyment of the substance of their rights as a European Union citizen)].]

(6)   Subject to paragraph (7), a person is to be treated as being in the United Kingdom for the purposes of Part 1 of the Act where he makes a claim for child tax credit only if that person has been living in the United Kingdom for 3 months before that claim plus any time taken into account by regulation 7 of the Tax Credits (Claims and Notifications) Regulations 2002 for determining for the purpose of that regulation when the claim is treated as having been made.

(7)   Paragraph (6) shall not apply where the person—

(a)   most recently entered the United Kingdom before 1st July 2014;

    (b)   is a worker or a self-employed person in the United Kingdom for the purposes of Council Directive 2004/38/EC (rights of citizens of the European Union and their family members to move and reside freely within the territory of the Member States);

    (c)   retains the status of a worker or self-employed person in the United Kingdom pursuant to Article 7(3) of Council Directive 2004/38/EC;

    (d)   is treated as a worker in the United Kingdom pursuant to regulation 5 of the Accession of Croatia (Immigration and Worker Authorisation) Regulations 2013 (right of residence of a Croatian who is an "accession State national subject to worker authorisation");

    (e)   is a family member of a person referred to in sub-paragraphs (b), (c), (d) or (i);

    (f)   is a person to whom regulation 4 applies (persons temporarily absent from the United Kingdom) and who returns to the United Kingdom within 52 weeks starting from the first day of the temporary absence;

    (g)   returns to the United Kingdom after a period abroad of less than 52 weeks where immediately before departing from the United Kingdom that person had been ordinarily resident in the United Kingdom for a continuous period of 3 months;

    (h)   returns to the United Kingdom otherwise as a worker or self-employed person after a period abroad and where, otherwise than for a period of up to 3 months ending on the day of returning, that person has paid either Class 1 or Class 2 contributions pursuant to regulation 114, 118, 146 or 147 of the Social Security (Contributions) Regulations 2001 or pursuant to an Order in Council having effect under section 179 of the Social Security Administration Act 1992;

    (i)   is not a national of an EEA State and would be a worker or self-employed person in the United Kingdom for the purposes of Council Directive 2004/38/EC if that person were a national of an EEA State;

    (j)   is a refugee as defined in Article 1 of the Convention relating to the Status of Refugees done at Geneva on 28th July 1951, as extended by Article 1(2) of the Protocol relating to the Status of Refugees done at New York on 31st January 1967;

    (k)   has been granted leave, or is deemed to have been granted leave, outside the rules made under section 3(2) of the Immigration Act 1971 where that leave is—

        (i)   granted by the Secretary of State with recourse to public funds, or

        (i)   deemed to have been granted by virtue of regulation 3 of the Displaced Persons (Temporary Protection) Regulations 2005;

    (l)   has been granted leave to remain in the United Kingdom by the Secretary of State pending an application for indefinite leave to remain as a victim of domestic violence;

    (m)   has been granted humanitarian protection by the Secretary of State under Rule 339C of Part 11 of the rules made under section 3(2) of the Immigration Act 1971.

(8)   In this regulation, a "family member" means a person who is defined as a family member of another person in Article 2 of Council Directive 2004/38/EC.

(9)   In this regulation, "EEA State", in relation to any time, means a state which at that time is a member State, or any other state which at that time is a party to the agreement on the European Economic Area signed at Oporto on 2nd May, together with the Protocol adjusting that Agreement signed at Brussels on 17th March 1993, as modified or supplemented from time to time.]

Amendment

Para (2): words "Paragraphs (1) and (6) do" in square brackets substituted by SI 2014/1511, regs 5, 6(1), (2). Date in force: 1 July 2014: see SI 2014/1511, reg 1.

Para (3): words "and paragraph (6) shall not apply" in square brackets inserted by SI 2014/1511, regs 5, 6(1), (3). Date in force: 1 July 2014: see SI 2014/1511, reg 1.

Para (4): words "Parliament and Council Regulation (EU) No 492/2011" in square brackets substituted by SI 2012/848, reg 8. Date in force: 6 April 2012: see SI 2012/848, reg 1(2).

Para (4): words "Council Directive No 2004/38/EC" in square brackets substituted by SI 2006/766, reg 4(1), (2)(ii). Date in force: 6 April 2006: see SI 2006/766, reg 1.

Para (5): inserted by SI 2004/1243, regs 2, 3. Date in force: 1 May 2004: see SI 2004/1243, reg 1(1).

Para (5): sub-para (b) substituted by SI 2012/2612, regs 5, 6. Date in force: 8 November 2012: see SI 2012/2612, reg 1.

Paras (6)–(9): inserted by SI 2014/1511, regs 5, 6(1), (4). Date in force: 1 July 2014: see SI 2014/1511, reg 1.

4 Persons temporarily absent from the United Kingdom

(1) A person who is ordinarily resident in the United Kingdom and is temporarily absent from the United Kingdom shall be treated as being in the United Kingdom during the first—

    (a)   8 weeks of any period of absence; or

    (b)   12 weeks of any period of absence where that period of absence, or any extension to that period of absence, is in connection with—

        (i)   the treatment of his illness or physical or mental disability;

        (ii)   the treatment of his partner's illness or physical or mental disability;

        (iii)   the death of a person who, immediately prior to the date of death, was his partner;

        (iv)   the death, or the treatment of the illness or physical or mental disability, of a child or qualifying young person for whom either he or his partner is, or both of them are, responsible; or

        (v)   the death, or the treatment of the illness or physical or mental disability, of his or his partner's relative.

(2) A person is temporarily absent from the United Kingdom if at the beginning of the period of absence his absence is unlikely to exceed 52 weeks.

5 Crown servants posted overseas

(1) A Crown servant posted overseas shall be treated as being in the United Kingdom.

(2) A Crown servant posted overseas is a person performing overseas the duties of any office or employment under the Crown in right of the United Kingdom—

    (a)   who is, or was, immediately prior to his posting or his first of consecutive postings, ordinarily resident in the United Kingdom; or

    (b)   who, immediately prior to his posting or his first of consecutive postings, was in the United Kingdom in connection with that posting.

6 Partners of Crown servants posted overseas

(1) The partner of a Crown servant posted overseas who is accompanying the Crown servant posted overseas shall be treated as being in the United Kingdom when he is either—

    (a)   in the country where the Crown servant is posted, or

    (b)   absent from that country in accordance with regulation 4 as modified by paragraphs (3) and (4).

(2) Regulation 4 applies to the partner of a Crown servant posted overseas with the modifications set out in paragraphs (3) and (4).

(3)   Omit the words "ordinarily resident in the United Kingdom and is".

(4)   In relation to a partner who is accompanying the Crown servant posted overseas the references to "United Kingdom" in the phrase "temporarily absent from the United Kingdom", in both places where it occurs, shall be construed as references to the country where the Crown servant is posted.

7 Transitional Provision—income support and income-based jobseeker's allowance

A person is exempt from the requirement to be ordinarily resident in the United Kingdom (which is set out in regulation 3(1)) in respect of child tax credit on and for three years after the date on which the award of child tax credit is made where—

(a)   the award of child tax credit would be made on or after 6th April 2004;

(b)   immediately before the award of child tax credit is made, he is, or will be on the making of a claim, entitled to any of the amounts in relation to income support and income-based jobseeker's allowance which are described in section 1(3)(d) of the Act; and

(c)   he is a person to which one or more of the following provisions applies—

(i)   paragraph (b) or (c) in the definition of "person from abroad" in regulation 21(3) of the Income Support (General) Regulations 1987;

(ii)   paragraph (b) or (c) in the definition of "person from abroad" in regulation 85(4) of the Jobseeker's Allowance Regulations 1996;

(iii)   paragraph (b) or (c) in the definition of "person from abroad" in regulation 21(3) of the Income Support (General) (Northern Ireland) Regulations 1987;

(iv)   paragraph (b) or (c) in the definition of "person from abroad" in regulation 85(4) of the Jobseeker's Allowance Regulations (Northern Ireland)1996.

IMMIGRATION (NOTICES) REGULATIONS 2003

(SI 2003/658)

Made: 11 March 2003.

Authority: Nationality, Immigration and Asylum Act 2002, ss 105, 112(1)–(3).

Commencement: 1 April 2003.

1 Citation and commencement

These Regulations may be cited as the Immigration (Notices) Regulations 2003 and shall come into force on the 1st April 2003.

2 Interpretation

In these Regulations—

"the 1971 Act" means the Immigration Act 1971;

"the 1997 Act" means the Special Immigration Appeals Commission Act 1997;

"the 1999 Act" means the Immigration and Asylum Act 1999;

"the 2002 Act" means the Nationality, Immigration and Asylum Act 2002;

"decision-maker" means—

(a)   the Secretary of State;

(b)   an immigration officer;

(c)   an entry clearance officer;

["EEA Decision" has the same meaning as in regulation 2(1) of the Immigration (European Economic Area) Regulations 2006];

"entry clearance officer" means a person responsible for the grant or refusal of entry clearance;

"immigration decision" has the same meaning as in section 82(2) [and (3A)] of the 2002 Act;

"minor" means a person who is under 18 years of age;

"notice of appeal" means a notice in the appropriate prescribed form in accordance with the rules for the time being in force under section 106(1) of the 2002 Act;

"Procedure Rules" means rules made under section 106(1) of the 2002 Act;

"representative" means a person who appears to the decision-maker—

(a)   to be the representative of a person referred to in regulation 4(1) below; and

(b)   not to be prohibited from acting as a representative by section 84 of the 1999 Act.

Amendment

Definition "EEA Decision" substituted by SI 2012/1547, reg 4, Sch 2, para 2. Date in force: 16 July 2012: see SI 2012/1547, reg 2(1).

In definition "immigration decision" words "and (3A)" in square brackets inserted by SI 2008/1819, reg 2(1), (2). Date in force: 1 August 2008: see SI 2008/1819, reg 1.

3 Transitional provision

These Regulations apply to a decision to make a deportation order which, by virtue of paragraph 12 of Schedule 15 to the 1999 Act,—

(a)   is appealable under section 15 of the 1971 Act (appeals in respect of deportation orders); or

(b)   would be appealable under section 15 of the 1971 Act, but for section 15(3) (deportation conducive to public good), and is appealable under section 2(1)(c) of the 1997 Act (appeal to Special Immigration Appeals Commission against a decision to make a deportation order).

4 Notice of decisions

(1)   Subject to regulation 6, the decision-maker must give written notice to a person of any immigration decision or EEA decision taken in respect of him which is appealable.

(2)   The decision-maker must give written notice to a person of the relevant grant of leave to enter or remain if, as a result of that grant, a right of appeal arises under section 83(2) of the 2002 Act.

[(2A)   The decision-maker must give written notice to a person of a decision that they are no longer a refugee if as a result of that decision a right of appeal arises under section 83A(2) of the 2002 Act.]

(3)   If the notice is given to the representative of the person, it is to be taken to have been given to the person.

Amendment

Para (2A): inserted by SI 2006/2168, regs 2, 3. Date in force: 31 August 2006: see SI 2006/2168, reg 1.

5 Contents of notice

[(1)   A notice given under regulation 4(1)—

(a)   is to include or be accompanied by a statement of the reasons for the decision to which it relates; and

(b)   if it relates to an immigration decision specified in section 82(2)(a), (g), (h), [(ha),] (i), (ia)[, (j) or (3A)] of the 2002 Act—

(i)   shall state the country or territory to which it is proposed to remove the person; or

(i)   may, if it appears to the decision-maker that the person to whom the notice is to be given may be removable to more than one country or territory, state any such countries or territories.]

(2)   A notice given under regulation 4(2) is to include or be accompanied by a statement of the reasons for the rejection of the claim for asylum.

[(2A)   A notice given under regulation 4(2A) is to include or be accompanied by a statement of the reasons for the decision that the person is no longer a refugee.]

(3)   Subject to paragraph (6), the notice given under regulation 4 shall also include, or be accompanied by, a statement which advises the person of—

(a)   his right of appeal and the statutory provision on which his right of appeal is based;

(b)   whether or not such an appeal may be brought while in the United Kingdom;

(c)   the grounds on which such an appeal may be brought; and

(d)   the facilities available for advice and assistance in connection with such an appeal.

(4)   Subject to paragraph (6), the notice given under regulation 4 shall be accompanied by a notice of appeal which indicates the time limit for bringing the appeal, the address to which it should be sent or may be taken by hand and a fax number for service by fax.

(5)   Subject to paragraph (6), where the exercise of the right is restricted by an exception or limitation by virtue of a provision of Part 5 of the 2002 Act, the notice given under regulation 4 shall include or be accompanied by a statement which refers to the provision limiting or restricting the right of appeal.

(6)   The notice given under regulation 4 need not comply with paragraphs (3), (4) and (5) where a right of appeal may only be exercised on the grounds referred to in section 84(1)(b), (c) or (g) of the 2002 Act by virtue of the operation of section 88(4), [88A(3),] [89(2)], 90(4), 91(2), 98(4) or (5) of that Act.

(7)   Where notice is given under regulation 4 and paragraph (6) applies, if the person claims in relation to the immigration decision or the EEA decision that—

(a)   the decision is unlawful by virtue of section 19B of the Race Relations Act 1976 (discrimination by public authorities);

(b)   the decision is unlawful under section 6 of the Human Rights Act 1998 (public authority not to act contrary to the Human Rights Convention) as being incompatible with the person's Convention rights; or

(c)   removal of the person from the United Kingdom in consequence of the immigration decision would breach the United Kingdom's obligations under the Refugee Convention or would be unlawful under section 6 of the Human Rights Act 1998 as being incompatible with the person's Convention rights,

the decision-maker must as soon as practicable re-serve the notice of decision under regulation 4 and paragraph (6) of this regulation shall not apply.

(8)   Where a notice is re-served under paragraph (7), the time limit for appeal under the Procedure Rules shall be calculated as if the notice of decision had been served on the date on which it was re-served.

Amendment

Para (1): substituted by SI 2006/2168, regs 2, 4. Date in force: 31 August 2006: see SI 2006/2168, reg 1.

Para (1): in sub-para (b) reference to "(ha)," in square brackets inserted by SI 2008/684, reg 2(1). Date in force: 1 April 2008: see SI 2008/684, reg 1.

Para (1): in sub-para (b) words ", (j) or (3A)" in square brackets substituted by SI 2008/1819, reg 2(1), (3). Date in force: 1 August 2008: see SI 2008/1819, reg 1.

Para (2A): inserted by SI 2007/3187, reg 6. Date in force: 1 December 2007: see SI 2007/3187, reg 1.

Para (6): reference to "88A(3)," in square brackets inserted by SI 2008/684, reg 2(2). Date in force: 1 April 2008: see SI 2008/684, reg 1.

Para (6): reference to "89(2)" in square brackets substituted by SI 2008/684, reg 2(2). Date in force: 1 April 2008: see SI 2008/684, reg 1.

6 Certain notices under the 1971 Act deemed to comply with the Regulations

(1)   This regulation applies where the power to—

    (a)   refuse leave to enter; or

    (b)   vary leave to enter or remain in the United Kingdom;

is exercised by notice in writing under section 4 of (administration of control), or paragraph 6(2) (notice of decisions of leave to enter or remain) of Schedule 2 to, the 1971 Act.

(2)   If—

    (a)   the statement required by regulation 5(3) is included in or accompanies that notice; and

    (b)   the notice is given in accordance with the provision of regulation 7;

the notice is to be taken to have been given under regulation 4(1) for the purposes of these Regulations.

7 Service of notice

(1)   A notice required to be given under regulation 4 may be—

    (a)   given by hand;

    (b)   sent by fax;

    (c)   sent by postal service in which delivery or receipt is recorded to:-

        (i)   an address provided for correspondence by the person or his representative; or

        (ii)   where no address for correspondence has been provided by the person, the last-known or usual place of abode or place of business of the person or his representative[;]

    [(c)   sent electronically;

    (d)   sent by document exchange to a document exchange number or address;

    (e)   sent by courier; or

    (f)   collected by the person who is the subject of the decision or their representative].

(2)   Where—

    (a)   a person's whereabouts are not known; and

    (b)

        (i)   no address has been provided for correspondence and the decision-maker does not know the last-known or usual place of abode or place of business of the person; or

        (ii)   the address provided to the decision-maker is defective, false or no longer in use by the person; and

    (c)   no representative appears to be acting for the person,

the notice shall be deemed to have been given when the decision-maker enters a record of the above circumstances and places the . . . notice on the relevant file.

(3)   Where a notice has been given in accordance with paragraph (2) and then subsequently the person is located, he shall be given a copy of the notice and details of when and how it was given as soon as is practicable.

(4)   Where a notice is sent by post in accordance with paragraph (1)(c) it shall be deemed to have been served, unless the contrary is proved,—

    (a)   on the second day after it was posted if it is sent to a place within the United Kingdom;

    (b)   on the twenty-eighth day after it was posted if it is sent to a place outside the United Kingdom.

(5) For the purposes of paragraph (4) the period is to be calculated—

  (a)   excluding the day on which the notice is posted; and

  (b)   in the case of paragraph (4)(a), excluding any day which is not a business day.

(6) In this regulation, "business day" means any day other than Saturday or Sunday, a day which is a bank holiday under the Banking and Financial Dealings Act 1971 in the part of the United Kingdom to which the notice is sent, Christmas Day or Good Friday.

(7) A notice given under regulation 4 may, in the case of a minor who does not have a representative, be given to the parent, guardian or another adult who for the time being takes responsibility for the child.

Amendment

  Para (1): in first sub-para (c)(ii) semi-colon inserted by virtue of SI 2008/684, reg 2(3)(a). Date in force: 1 April 2008: see SI 2008/684, reg 1.

  Para (1): second sub-para (c) and sub-paras (d)–(f) inserted by SI 2008/684, reg 2(3)(b). Date in force: 1 April 2008: see SI 2008/684, reg 1.

  Para (2): word omitted revoked by SI 2013/793, reg 2. Date in force: 28 April 2013: see SI 2013/793, reg 1.

NATIONALITY, IMMIGRATION AND ASYLUM ACT 2002 (COMMENCEMENT NO 4) ORDER 2003

(SI 2003/754)

Made: 14 March 2003.

Authority: Nationality, Immigration and Asylum Act 2002, s 162(1), (4), (6).

1 Citation and interpretation

(1) This Order may be cited as the Nationality, Immigration and Asylum Act 2002 (Commencement No 4) Order 2003.

(2) In this Order—

  "the 1971 Act" means the Immigration Act 1971;

  "the 1988 Act" means the Immigration Act 1988;

  "the 1993 Act" means the Asylum and Immigration Appeals Act 1993;

  "the 1997 Act" means the Special Immigration Appeals Commission Act 1997;

  "the 1999 Act" means the Immigration and Asylum Act 1999; and

  "the 2002 Act" means the Nationality, Immigration and Asylum Act 2002.

2 Commencement and appointed date provisions

(1) The provisions of the 2002 Act specified in column 1 of Schedule 1 to this Order shall come into force on the date specified in column 2 of that Schedule, but where a particular purpose is specified in relation to any such provision in column 3 of that Schedule, the provision concerned shall come into force on that date only for that purpose.

(2) The date appointed under section 162(4) of the 2002 Act for the purposes of section 8 of that Act is 1st April 2003.

3 Transitional provisions

(1) Subject to Schedule 2, the new appeals provisions are not to have effect in relation to events which took place before 1st April 2003 and, notwithstanding their

repeal by the provisions of the 2002 Act commenced by this Order, the old appeals provisions are to continue to have effect in relation to such events.

(2)   Schedule 2, which makes further transitional provisions, has effect.

4 Definitions for transitional provisions

(1)   In this Order—

    (a)   "the new appeals provisions" means sections 82 to 99 and sections 101 to 103 of the 2002 Act; together with any provision (including subordinate legislation) of—

        (i)   the 2002 Act;

        (ii)   the 1971 Act, the 1997 Act and the 1999 Act (all as amended by the 2002 Act);

which refer to those provisions;

    (b)   "the old appeals provisions" means—

        (i)   sections 13 to 17 of the 1971 Act;

        (ii)   subsections (1) to (4) of section 8 of the 1993 Act;

        (iii)   the 1997 Act (without the amendments made by the 2002 Act);

        (iv)   Part IV of, and Schedule 4 (except paragraphs 10 to 20 and 23) to, the 1999 Act;

        (v)   section 115 of the 2002 Act;

together with—

        (vi)   any subordinate legislation which applies to those provisions (unless specific provision is made to the contrary); and

        (vii)   any provision of the old Immigration Acts which refers to those provisions;

    (c)   "the old Immigration Acts" means the 1971 Act, the 1988 Act, the 1993 Act, the 1996 Act, the 1997 Act and the 1999 Act, all without the amendments made by the 2002 Act.

(3)   For the purposes of article 3 and Schedule 2, an event has taken place under the old Immigration Acts where—

    (a)   a notice was served;

    (b)   a decision was made or taken;

    (c)   directions were given; and

    (d)   a certificate was issued.

(4)   For the purposes of this Order—

    (a)   a notice was served;

    (b)   a decision was made or taken;

    (c)   directions were given; and

    (d)   a certificate was issued;

on the day on which it was or they were sent to the person concerned, if sent by post or by fax, or delivered to that person, if delivered by hand.

(5)   In this article—

    (a)   "the person concerned" means the person who is the subject of the notice, decision, directions or certificate or the person who appears to be his representative; and

    (b)   a reference to the issue of a certificate is a reference to the issue of a certificate under section 11, 12 or 72(2) of the 1999 Act or section 115 of the 2002 Act.

SCHEDULE 1

Article 2

Column 1	Column 2	Column 3
Section 4 (deprivation of citizenship).	1st April 2003	
Section 12 (British citizenship: registration of certain persons without other citizenship).	30th April 2003	
Section 13 (British citizenship: registration of certain persons born between 1961 and 1983).	30th April 2003	
Section 68 (1) to (5) (bail).	1st April 2003	
Section 72 (9) and (10) (serious criminal).	1st April 2003	
Section 77 (no removal while claim for asylum pending).	1st April 2003	
Section 78 (no removal while appeal pending).	1st April 2003	
Section 79 (deportation order: appeal).	1st April 2003	
Section 80 (removal of asylum-seeker to third country).	1st April 2003	So far as not already in force.
Section 81 (adjudicators).	1st April 2003	
Section 82 (right of appeal: general).	1st April 2003	
Section 83 (appeal: asylum claim).	1st April 2003	
Section 84 (grounds of appeal).	1st April 2003	
Section 85 (matters to be considered).	1st April 2003	
Section 86 (determination of appeal).	1st April 2003	
Section 87 (successful appeal: direction).	1st April 2003	
Section 88 (ineligibility).	1st April 2003	
Section 89 (visitor or student without entry clearance).	1st April 2003	
Section 90 (non-family visitor).	1st April 2003	
Section 91 (student).	1st April 2003	
Section 92 (appeal from within United Kingdom: general).	1st April 2003	
Section 93 (appeal from within United Kingdom: "third country" removal).	1st April 2003	
Section 94 (appeal from within United Kingdom: unfounded human rights or asylum claim).	1st April 2003	
Section 95 (appeal from outside United Kingdom: removal).	1st April 2003	
Section 96 (earlier right of appeal).	1st April 2003	
Section 97 (national security, &c.)	1st April 2003	
Section 98 (other grounds of public good).	1st April 2003	
Section 99 (sections 96 to 98: appeal in progress).	1st April 2003	
Section 100 (Immigration Appeal Tribunal).	1st April 2003	
Section 101 (appeal to Tribunal).	1st April 2003	
Section 102 (decision).	1st April 2003	
Section 103 (appeal from Tribunal).	1st April 2003	
Section 104 (pending appeal).	1st April 2003	

Column 1	Column 2	Column 3
Section 105 (notice of immigration decision).	1st April 2003	
Section 106 (rules).	1st April 2003	
Section 107 (practice directions).	1st April 2003	
Section 108 (forged document: proceedings in private).	1st April 2003	
Section 109 (European Union and European Economic Area).	1st April 2003	
Section 110 (grants).	1st April 2003	
Section 111 (monitor of certification of claims as unfounded).	1st April 2003	
Section 114 (1) and (2) (repeal).	1st April 2003	
Section 116 (Special Immigration Appeals Commission: Community Legal Service).	1st April 2003	
Section 117 (Northern Ireland appeals: legal aid).	1st April 2003	
Section 118 (leave pending decision on variation application).	1st April 2003	
Section 120 (requirement to state additional grounds for application).	1st April 2003	
Section 123 (advice about work permit, &c.).	[1st April 2004]	
Section 126 (physical data: compulsory provision).	1st April 2003	
Section 130 (Inland Revenue).	1st April 2003	
Section 142 (Advisory Panel on Country Information).	1st April 2003	
Section 147(1), (3) and (4) (employment).	1st April 2003	
Section 147(2) (employment).	1st April 2003	For the purpose of enabling subordinate legislation to be made under it.
Schedule 4 (Immigration and Asylum Appeals: Adjudicators).	1st April 2003	
Schedule 5 (The Immigration Appeal Tribunal).	1st April 2003	
Schedule 6 (Immigration and Asylum Appeals: Transitional Provision).	1st April 2003	
Schedule 7 (Immigration and Asylum Appeals: Consequential Amendments).	1st April 2003	So far as not already in force.

Column 1	Column 2	Column 3
Section 161 and Schedule 9 (repeals) (the entries relating to sections 3(9)(b), 29 and 31(d) of the Immigration Act 1971; to sections 19E(7) and 71A(1) of the Race Relations Act 1976; to sections 7 to 9, 10, 19 to 21, 22, 27(2), 28, 33, 44(2) and (3) of and Schedule 2 paragraph 3(1)(b) and Schedule 4 to the British Nationality Act 1981; to section 4(3)(b) of the British Nationality (Falkland Islands) Act 1983; to section 1(5) of the British Nationality (Hong Kong) Act 1990; to sections 2A, 4, 5(1)(a) and (b) and (2) and 7A of, and Schedule 2 to, the Special Immigration Appeals Commission Act 1997; to sections 15, and 56 to 81, of, and Schedules 2 to 4, and 14, to, the 1999 Act; and to Schedule 2 to the Race Relations Amendment Act 2000.	1st April 2003	

Amendment

In entry relating to the Nationality, Immigration and Asylum Act 2002, s 123, in column 2 words "1st April 2004" in square brackets substituted by SI 2003/2993, art 3. Date in force: 19 November 2003: see SI 2003/2993, art 2.

SCHEDULE 2

Article 3

1 Transitional provisions relating to the 2002 Act

(1) In this paragraph, a reference to a section or to a Schedule is to be read as a reference to a section of, or to a Schedule to, the 2002 Act, unless otherwise specified.

(2) Section 77 (no removal while claim for asylum pending) shall have effect in relation to a claim for asylum pending on 31st March 2003 as it has effect in relation to a claim for asylum pending under the 2002 Act.

(3) Section 78 (no removal while appeal pending) shall have effect in relation to an appeal pending under the old appeals provisions as it has effect in relation to an appeal pending under section 82(1) of the 2002 Act.

(4) Section 79 (deportation order: appeal) shall have effect in relation to an appeal pending under the old appeals provisions as it has effect in relation to an appeal pending under section 82(1) of the 2002 Act.

[(4A) Section 101(1) shall apply to a party to an appeal to an adjudicator under Part 4 of the 1999 Act which is determined on or after 9th June 2003, as it applies to a party to an appeal to an adjudicator under section 82 or 83.

(4B) Where section 101(1) applies by virtue of sub-paragraph (4A) above—

    (a)   sections 101(2) and (3), 102 and 103 shall apply in relation to any appeal or application for permission to appeal under section 101(1) subject to the modifications that—

        (i)   in section 102(1)(d), the reference to section 87 shall be treated as being a reference to paragraph 21 of Schedule 4 to the 1999 Act; and

        (ii)   in section 102(3), the reference to section 82 shall be treated as being a reference to Part 4 of the 1999 Act; and

    (b)   paragraphs 7, 22 and 23 of Schedule 4 to the 1999 Act shall not apply.]

(5) Section 115 (appeal from within the United Kingdom: unfounded human rights claim or asylum claim: transitional provision) shall continue to have effect in relation

to any person who made an asylum claim or human rights claim (as defined in subsection (10)) on or after 1st April 2003.

2 Transitional provisions relating to the appeals provisions of the 1971 Act

(1)   In this paragraph, a reference to a section or to a Schedule is to be read as a reference to a section of, or to a Schedule to, the 1971 Act, unless otherwise specified.

[(2)   Section 3C of the 1971 Act (continuation of leave pending variation decision), as substituted by section 118 of the 2002 Act, shall apply in relation to an application made before 1st April 2003, in respect of which no decision has been made on or before 1st April 2003, as it applies to such an application made after 1st April 2003.]

(3)   Section 5 (procedure for, and further provisions as to, deportation) is to continue to have effect in relation to—

    (a)   any person on whom the Secretary of State has, before 2nd October 2000, served a notice of his decision to make a deportation order; and

    (b)   any person—

        (i)   who applied during the regularisation period fixed by section 9 of the 1999 Act, in accordance with the Immigration (Regularisation Period for Overstayers) Regulations 2000, for leave to remain in the United Kingdom; and

        (ii)   on whom the Secretary of State has since served a notice of his decision to make a deportation order;

and, for the purposes of section 5, such a person is to be taken to be a person who is liable to deportation under section 3(5).

(4)   Section 13 (appeals against exclusions from the United Kingdom) is to continue to have effect where the decision to refuse leave to enter the United Kingdom, or to refuse a certificate of entitlement or an entry clearance, was made before 2nd October 2000.

(5)   Section 14 (appeals against conditions) is to continue to have effect where the decision to vary, or to refuse to vary, the limited leave to enter or remain was made before 2nd October 2000.

(6)   Section 15 (appeals in respect of deportation orders) is to continue to have effect in relation to—

    (a)   any person on whom the Secretary of State has, before 2nd October 2000, served a notice of his decision to make a deportation order; and

    (b)   any person—

        (i)   who applied during the regularisation period fixed by section 9 of the 1999 Act, in accordance with the Immigration (Regularisation Period for Overstayers) Regulations 2000, for leave to remain in the United Kingdom; and

        (ii)   on whom the Secretary of State has since served a notice of his decision to make a deportation order.

(7)   Section 16 (appeals against validity of directions for removal) is to continue to have effect where the directions for a person's removal from the United Kingdom were given before 2nd October 2000.

(8)   Section 17 (appeals against removal on objection to destination) is to continue to have effect—

    (a)   where the directions for a person's removal from the United Kingdom were given, or the notice specifying the destination of his removal was served, before 2nd October 2000; and

    (b)   in relation to any person—

        (i)   who applied during the regularisation period fixed by section 9 of the 1999 Act, in accordance with the Immigration (Regularisation Period for Overstayers) Regulations 2000, for leave to remain in the United Kingdom; and

(ii) on whom the Secretary of State has since served a notice of his decision to make a deportation order.

(9) Section 21 (references of cases by Secretary of State for further consideration) (including that section as applied by paragraph 4 of Schedule 2 to the 1993 Act) is to continue to have effect where the Secretary of State has referred a matter for consideration under that section before 2nd October 2000.

(10) Where an appeal is made under Part II (including that Part as it applies by virtue of Schedule 2 to the 1993 Act)—

    (a) paragraph 28 of Schedule 2 (stay on directions for removal) (including that paragraph as applied by paragraph 9 of Schedule 2 to the 1993 Act) is to continue to have effect;

    (b) the following provisions are not to have effect—

        (i) paragraph 29(1) of Schedule 2 (grant of bail pending appeal) (including that paragraph as applied by paragraph 9 of Schedule 2 to the 1993 Act and by section 3(6) of the 1996 Act), as amended by paragraph 66 of Schedule 14 to the 1999 Act;

        (ii) paragraph 3 of Schedule 3 (effect of appeals) including that paragraph as applied by paragraph 9 of Schedule 2 to the 1993 Act), as amended by paragraph 69 of Schedule 14 to the 1999 Act.

3 Transitional provision relating to the appeals provisions of the 1988 Act

Section 5 (restricted right of appeal against deportation in cases of breach of limited leave) is to continue to have effect—

    (a) where the directions for a person's removal from the United Kingdom were given, or the notice specifying the destination of his removal was served, before 2nd October 2000,

    (b) in relation to any person—

        (i) who applied during the regularisation period fixed by section 9 of the 1999 Act, in accordance with the Immigration (Regularisation Period for Overstayers) Regulations 2000, for leave to remain in the United Kingdom; and

        (ii) on whom the Secretary of State has since served a notice of his decision to make a deportation order.

4 Transitional provisions relating to the appeals provisions of the 1993 Act

(1) In this paragraph, a reference to a section or to a Schedule is to be read as a reference to a section of, or to a Schedule to, the 1993 Act, unless otherwise specified.

(2) In section 8 (asylum appeals)—

    (a) subsection (1) is to continue to have effect where the decision to refuse leave to enter was made before 2nd October 2000;

    (b) subsection (2) is to continue to have effect where the decision to vary, or to refuse to vary, the limited leave to enter or remain was made before 2nd October 2000;

    (c) subsection (3) is to continue to have effect where the decision to make a deportation order, or the decision to refuse to revoke a deportation order, was made before 2nd October 2000;

    (d) subsection (4) is to continue to have effect where the directions for a person's removal from the United Kingdom were given before 2nd October 2000.

(3) Where an appeal is made under Part II of the 1971 Act (including that Part as it applies by virtue of Schedule 2)—

    (a) section 9A (bail pending appeal from Immigration Appeal Tribunal), as amended by paragraphs 105 and 106 of Schedule 14 to the 1999 Act, is not to have effect;

(b) the reference in section 9A (without the amendments made by the 1999 Act) to section 9 (appeals from Immigration Appeal Tribunal) is to include a reference to paragraph 23 of Schedule 4 to the 1999 Act (appeals from Immigration Appeal Tribunal).

(4) Where an appeal is made under section 8, the section 8 appeals provisions are to continue to have effect.

(5) In this paragraph "the section 8 appeals provisions" means—

(a) paragraph 1 of Schedule 2 (asylum appeal rights to replace rights under the 1971 Act);

(b) paragraph 2 of Schedule 2 (scope of asylum rights of appeal);

(c) paragraph 3 of Schedule 2 (other grounds for appeal);

(d) paragraph 5 of Schedule 2 (special appeals procedures for claims without foundation);

(e) paragraph 6 of Schedule 2 (exception for national security);

(f) paragraph 7 of Schedule 2 (suspension of variation of limited leave pending appeal);

(g) paragraph 8 of Schedule 2 (deportation order not to be made while appeal pending);

(h) paragraph 9 of Schedule 2 (stay of removal directions pending appeal and bail).

(6) Where an appeal is made under section 8, the reference in paragraph 5 of Schedule 2 to section 20(1) of the 1971 Act (appeals to the Immigration Appeal Tribunal) is to include a reference to paragraph 22(1) of Schedule 4 to the 1999 Act (appeals to the Immigration Appeal Tribunal).

5 Transitional provision relating to the 1997 Act

(1) The amendments to the 1997 Act made by the provisions of the 2002 Act commenced by this Order are not to have effect in relation to an appeal which is pending, by virtue of section 7A of the 1997 Act, on 1st April 2003 and, notwithstanding their amendment by the provisions commenced by this Order, the old appeal provisions are to continue to have effect in relation to such an appeal.

6 Transitional provisions relating to the 1999 Act

(1) In this paragraph, a reference to a section or to a Schedule is to be read as a reference to a section of, or to a Schedule to, the 1999 Act, unless otherwise specified.

(2) Section 10 (removal of certain persons unlawfully in the United Kingdom) is not to have effect in relation to—

(a) any person on whom the Secretary of State has, before 2nd October 2000, served a notice of his intention to make a deportation order; and

(b) any person—

(i) who applied during the regularisation period fixed by section 9 of the 1999 Act, in accordance with the Immigration (Regularisation Period for Overstayers) Regulations 2000 for leave to remain in the United Kingdom; and

(ii) on whom the Secretary of State has since served a notice of his decision to make a deportation order;

and, for the purposes of section 5, such a person is to be taken to be a person who is liable to deportation under section 3(5).

(3) Where a certificate is issued under section 11 (removal of asylum-seeker to third country), as substituted by section 80 of the 2002 Act, before 1st April 2003 and an allegation is made after 1st April the allegation may be certified under section 72(2) of the 1999 Act, notwithstanding its repeal by the provisions of the 2002 Act commenced by this Order, and that certification shall have effect for the purposes of an appeal under the old appeal provisions.

(4) Subject to the provisions of the Order and any other enactment sections 59 to 78 and Schedules 2 to 4 shall continue to have effect in relation to events which took place before 1st April 2003.

(5) Where a decision has been taken under the Immigration Acts relating to a person's entitlement to enter or remain in the United Kingdom before 1st April 2003 there shall only be a right of appeal under section 65(1) where an allegation is made before 1st July 2003.

Amendment

Para 1: sub-paras (4A), (4B) inserted by SI 2003/1339, art 4. Date in force: 9 June 2003: see SI 2003/1339, art 2(2).

Para 2: sub-para (2) substituted by SI 2003/1040, art 2. Date in force: 8 April 2003: see SI 2003/1040, art 1.

NATIONALITY, IMMIGRATION AND ASYLUM ACT 2002 (SPECIFICATION OF PARTICULARLY SERIOUS CRIMES) ORDER 2004

(SI 2004/1910)

Made: 20 July 2004.

Authority: Nationality, Immigration and Asylum Act 2002, s 72(4)(a).

Commencement: 12 August 2004.

1

This Order may be cited as the Nationality, Immigration and Asylum Act 2002 (Specification of Particularly Serious Crimes) Order 2004 and shall come into force on 12th August 2004.

2

An offence of a description set out in any of Schedules 1 to 6 to this Order is hereby specified for the purposes of section 72(4)(a) of the Nationality, Immigration and Asylum Act 2002.

SCHEDULE 1

STATUTORY OFFENCES THAT APPLY THROUGHOUT THE UNITED KINGDOM

Offences under the Explosive Substances Act 1883

Section 2 (unlawfully and maliciously causing an explosion likely to endanger life or cause serious injury to property).

Section 3(1)(a) (unlawfully and maliciously doing an act, intending or conspiring to cause an explosion likely to endanger life or cause serious injury to property).

Section 3(1)(b) (unlawfully and maliciously making, possessing, or having under control, an explosive substance intending to endanger life or cause serious injury to property).

Section 4 (making, or knowingly possessing, an explosive substance in circumstances that lead to reasonable suspicion that such making or possession is for an unlawful object).

Offences under the Misuse of Drugs Act 1971

Section 4(3)(a) (supplying or offering to supply a controlled drug, where the offence in question is in respect of a Class A drug or Class B drug controlled by the Misuse of Drugs Act 1971).

Section 4(3)(b) (being concerned in the supply of a controlled drug, where the offence in question is in respect of a Class A drug or Class B drug controlled by the Misuse of Drugs Act 1971).

Section 4(3)(c) (being concerned in the making of an offer to supply a controlled drug, where the offence in question is in respect of a Class A drug or Class B drug controlled by the Misuse of Drugs Act 1971).

Section 5(3) (possessing a controlled drug intending to supply it to another, where the offence in question is in respect of a Class A drug or Class B drug controlled by the Misuse of Drugs Act 1971).

Section 8(a) (occupying or managing premises where the production or attempted production of a controlled drug is knowingly permitted on those premises).

Section 8(b) (occupying or managing premises where the supply, or attempted supply, of or the offer to supply a controlled drug is knowingly permitted on those premises).

Section 9(a) (smoking or otherwise using opium).

Section 9(b) (frequenting a place used for opium smoking).

Section 9(c)(i) (possessing pipes or utensils for use in connection with opium smoking which have been used, permitted or intended for use, for that purpose).

Section 9(c)(ii) (possessing utensils for use in connection with preparing opium for smoking which have been used, permitted or intended for use for that purpose).

Section 20 (assisting or inducing, while in the United Kingdom, the commission of an offence under a corresponding law outside the United Kingdom).

Offences under the Immigration Act 1971

Section 25(1)(a) (facilitating the breach of immigration law by a person who is not a citizen of the European Union).

Section 25A (facilitating, for gain, the arrival in the United Kingdom of an asylum seeker).

Section 25B (facilitating a breach of a deportation or exclusion order in force against a citizen of the European Union).

Offences under the Biological Weapons Act 1974

Section 1(1)(a) (developing, producing, stockpiling, acquiring or retaining a biological agent or toxin in a quantity that has no justification for peaceful purposes).

Section 1(1)(b) (developing, producing, stockpiling, acquiring or retaining a weapon, equipment or means of delivery designed to use a biological agent or toxin for hostile purposes or in an armed conflict).

Section 1(1A)(a) (transferring a biological agent or toxin for non-peaceful purposes or entering into an agreement to do so).

Section 1(1A)(b) (making arrangements for the transfer of a biological agent or toxin for non-peaceful purposes or entering into an agreement to do so).

Offences under the Customs and Excise Act 1979

Section 50(3) (importing or being concerned in importing goods contrary to any prohibition or restriction, intending to evade that prohibition or restriction, where the offence in question is in respect of a Class A drug or Class B drug controlled by the Misuse of Drugs Act 1971).

Section 68(1) (exporting or shipping as stores, or bringing to the United Kingdom for the purpose of exporting or shipping as stores, goods contrary to any prohibition or restriction, where the offence in question is in respect of a Class A drug or Class B drug controlled by the Misuse of Drugs Act 1971).

Section 68(2) (knowingly being concerned in exporting, or shipping as stores, any goods, intending to evade a prohibition or restriction, where the offence in question is in respect of a Class A or Class B drug controlled by the Misuse of Drugs Act 1971).

Section 170(2)(b) (knowingly being concerned in the fraudulent evasion of any prohibition or restriction in relation to goods, where the offence in question is in respect of a Class A or Class B drug controlled by the Misuse of Drugs Act 1971).

Offences under the Taking of Hostages Act 1982

Section 1(1) (detaining a person and threatening to kill, injure or continue to detain that person in order to compel a State, international governmental organisation or person to do, or abstain from doing, any act).

Offences under the Aviation Security Act 1982

Section 1(1) (unlawfully seizing, or exercising control of, an aircraft by using force or threats).

Section 2(1)(a) (unlawfully and intentionally destroying an aircraft in service or damaging such an aircraft so as to render it incapable of flight or endanger its safety in flight).

Section 2(1)(b) (unlawfully and intentionally committing an act of violence on board an aircraft in flight likely to endanger its safety).

Section 3(1) (unlawfully and intentionally destroying, damaging or interfering with any property used for the provision of air navigation facilities where such destruction, damage or interference is likely to endanger the safety of aircraft in flight).

Section 3(3) (intentionally communicating materially false, misleading or deceptive information which endangers, or is likely to endanger, the safety of an aircraft in flight).

Section 4(1)(a) (possessing, without lawful authority or reasonable excuse, a firearm or explosive, or article having the appearance of either, or any article made or adapted for injuring a person or destroying or damaging property, in any aircraft registered in the United Kingdom).

Section 4(1)(b) (possessing, without lawful authority or reasonable excuse, a firearm, explosive or article having the appearance of either or any article made or adapted for injuring a person or destroying or damaging property in any aircraft not registered in the United Kingdom when it is in, or flying over, the United Kingdom).

Section 4(1)(c) (possessing, without lawful authority or reasonable excuse, a firearm, explosive or article having the appearance of either or any article made or adapted for injuring a person or destroying or damaging property in an aerodrome in the United Kingdom).

Section 4(1)(d) (possessing, without lawful authority or reasonable excuse, a firearm, explosive or article having the appearance of either or any article made or adapted for injuring a person or destroying or damaging property in any air navigation installation in the United Kingdom).

Offences under the Nuclear Materials (Offences) Act 1983

Section 2(2)(a) (receiving, holding or dealing with nuclear material intending to do an act which is an offence referred to in section 1(1)(a) or (b) of the Nuclear Materials (Offences) Act 1983).

Section 2(2)(b) (receiving, holding or dealing with nuclear material being reckless as to whether another would do an act which is an offence referred to in section 1(1)(a) or (b) of the Nuclear Materials (Offences) Act 1983).

Section 2(3) (making a threat to do an act by means of nuclear material which is an offence referred to in section 1(1)(a) or (b) of the Nuclear Materials (Offences) Act 1983, intending that the person to whom the threat is made shall fear that it will be carried out).

Section 2(4) (threatening to obtain nuclear material by an act which is an offence referred to in section 1(1)(c) of the Nuclear Materials (Offences) Act 1983 in order to compel a state, international governmental organisation or person to do, or abstain from doing, an act).

Offences under the Criminal Justice Act 1988

Section 134(1) (intentionally inflicting severe pain or suffering on another, where the offender is a public official or person acting in an official capacity who does such acts in performance, or purported performance, of his official duties).

Section 134(2) (intentionally inflicting severe pain or suffering on another at the instigation, consent or acquiescence of a public official or person acting in an official capacity who at the time of such instigation, consent or acquiescence is acting in performance, or purported performance, of his official duties).

Offences under the Criminal Justice (International Co-operation) Act 1990

Section 12(1) (manufacturing or supplying a scheduled substance, knowing or suspecting that the substance is to be used for the unlawful production of a controlled drug).

Offences under the Aviation and Maritime Security Act 1990

Section 1(1) (intentionally committing an act of violence at an aerodrome serving international civil aviation with any device, substance or weapon which causes, or is likely to cause, serious personal injury or death and endangers the safe operation of that aerodrome or the safety of persons there).

Section 1(2)(a)(i) (unlawfully and intentionally destroying or seriously damaging property used for the provision of any facilities at an aerodrome serving international civil aviation with any device, substance or weapon in a way that endangers, or is likely to endanger, the safe operation of that aerodrome or the safety of persons there).

Section 1(2)(a)(ii) (unlawfully and intentionally destroying or seriously damaging an out of service aircraft at an aerodrome serving international civil aviation with any device, substance or weapon in a way that endangers, or is likely to endanger, the safe operation of that aerodrome or the safety of persons there).

Section 1(2)(b) (unlawfully and intentionally disrupting the services of an aerodrome serving international civil aviation with any device, substance or weapon in a way that endangers, or is likely to endanger, the safe operation of that aerodrome or the safety of persons there).

Section 9 (unlawfully seizing, or exercising of control, of a ship by force or with threats).

Section 13(1) (threatening to do an act to a ship or fixed platform which is an offence under section 11(1) of the Aviation and Maritime Security Act 1990).

Section 13(2) (threatening to do an act which is an offence under section 12(1) of the Aviation and Maritime Security Act 1990).

Offences under the Channel Tunnel (Security) Order 1994

Article 4(1) (unlawfully seizing, or exercising control, of a Channel Tunnel train by using force or threats).

Article 5(1) (unlawfully seizing, or exercising control, of the tunnel system by using force or threats).

Article 6(1)(a) (unlawfully and intentionally destroying a Channel Tunnel train or the tunnel system or any goods on a train or within the tunnel system so as to endanger, or to be likely to endanger, the safe operation of the train or the safety of the tunnel system).

Article 6(1)(b) (unlawfully and intentionally damaging a Channel Tunnel train or the tunnel system or any goods on a train or within the tunnel system so as to endanger, or to be likely to endanger, the safe operation of the train or the safety of the tunnel system).

Article 6(1)(c) (committing an act of violence on board a Channel Tunnel train or within the tunnel system likely to endanger the safe operation of the train or the safety of the tunnel system).

Article 6(2)(a) (unlawfully and intentionally placing a device or substance on a Channel Tunnel train likely to destroy or damage it, or goods on it, so as to endanger its safe operation).

Article 6(2)(b) (unlawfully and intentionally placing a device or substance in the tunnel system likely to destroy or damage it so as to endanger its safety).

Article 7(1) (unlawfully and intentionally destroying, damaging, or interfering with, the operation of property referred to in article 7(2) of the Channel Tunnel (Security) Order 1994 likely to endanger the safe operation of any Channel Tunnel train or the safety of the tunnel system).

Article 7(3) (intentionally communicating information, knowing it to be false in a material particular, which endangers the safe operation of any Channel Tunnel train or the safety of the tunnel system).

Article 8(1) (threatening to commit an offence under article 6(1) of the Channel Tunnel (Security) Order 1994 in order to compel a person to do, or abstain from doing, any act, where the making of such a threat is likely to endanger the safe operation of a train or the safety of the tunnel system).

Article 8(2) (threatening to commit an offence under article 7(1) of the Channel Tunnel (Security) Order 1994 in order to compel a person to do, or abstain from doing, any act, where the making of such a threat is likely to endanger the safe operation of a train or the safety of the tunnel system).

Offences under the Chemical Weapons Act 1996

Section 2(1)(a) (using a chemical weapon).

Section 2(1)(b) (developing or producing a chemical weapon).

Section 2(1)(c) (possessing a chemical weapon).

Section 2(1)(d) (participating in the transfer of a chemical weapon).

Section 2(1)(e) (engaging in military preparations, intending to use a chemical weapon).

Section 11(1)(a) (constructing premises, intending them to be used for producing a chemical weapon).

Section 11(1)(b) (altering premises, intending them to be used for producing a chemical weapon).

Section 11(1)(c) (installing or constructing equipment, intending it to be used for producing a chemical weapon).

Section 11(1)(d) (altering equipment, intending it to be used for producing a chemical weapon).

Section 11(1)(e) (occupying land and permitting construction of premises on it, intending those premises to be used for producing a chemical weapon).
Section 11(1)(f) (occupying land and permitting premises to be altered on it, intending those premises to be used for producing a chemical weapon).
Section 11(1)(g) (occupying land and permitting installation or construction on it of equipment, intending that equipment to be used for producing a chemical weapon).
Section 11(1)(h) (occupying land and permitting equipment to be altered on it, intending that equipment to be used for producing a chemical weapon).

Offences under the Terrorism Act 2000

Section 11(1) (belonging, or professing to belong, to a proscribed organisation).
Section 12(1) (inviting support for a proscribed organisation that is not restricted to the provision of money or property).
Section 12(2)(a) (arranging, managing or assisting in the arrangement or management of a meeting, knowing that it supports a proscribed organisation).
Section 12(2)(b) (arranging, managing or assisting in the arrangement or management of a meeting, knowing that it furthers the activities of a proscribed organisation).
Section 12(2)(c) (arranging, managing or assisting in the arrangement or management of a meeting, knowing that it is to be addressed by a member or professed member of a proscribed organisation).
Section 12(3) (addressing a meeting for the purpose of encouraging support or furthering the activities of a proscribed organisation).
Section 15(1) (inviting another to provide money or property, intending, or having reasonable cause to suspect, that it may be used for terrorist purposes).
Section 15(2) (receiving money or property, intending, or having reasonable cause to suspect, that it may be used for terrorist purposes).
Section 15(3) (providing money or property, intending, or having reasonable cause to suspect, that it may be used for terrorist purposes).
Section 16(1) (using money or property for terrorist purposes).
Section 16(2) (possessing money or property, intending, or having reasonable cause to suspect, that it may be used for terrorist purposes).
Section 17(1) (entering into, or becoming concerned in, an arrangement where money or other property is made available knowing, or having reasonable cause to suspect, that it may be used for terrorist purposes).
Section 18(1)(a) (entering into, or becoming concerned in, an arrangement facilitating the retention or control of terrorist property by concealment).
Section 18(1)(b) (entering into, or becoming concerned in, an arrangement facilitating the retention or control of terrorist property by removal from the jurisdiction).
Section 18(1)(c) (entering into, or becoming concerned in, an arrangement facilitating the retention or control of terrorist property by transfer to nominees).
Section 18(1)(d) (entering into, or becoming concerned in, an arrangement facilitating the retention or control of terrorist property in any other way).
Section 19(2) (not disclosing as soon as reasonably practicable a belief or suspicion, and the information on which the belief or suspicion is based, that an offence has been committed under sections 15 to 18 of the Terrorism Act 2000).
Section 38B(1)(a) (not disclosing information, knowing or believing it to be of material assistance in preventing an act of terrorism).
Section 38B(1)(b) (not disclosing information, knowing or believing it to be of material assistance in securing the apprehension, prosecution or conviction of a person for a terrorist offence).
Section 54(1)(a) (providing instruction or training in the making or use of a firearm).
Section 54(1)(aa) (providing instruction or training in the making or use of a radioactive material or weapon designed or adapted to discharge it).

Section 54(1)(b) (providing instruction or training in the making or use of an explosive).

Section 54(1)(c) (providing instruction or training in the making or use of a chemical, biological or nuclear weapon).

Section 54(2)(a) (receiving instruction or training in the making or use of a radioactive material or weapon designed or adapted to discharge it).

Section 54(2)(aa) (receiving instruction or training in the making or use of a radioactive material or weapon designed or adapted to discharge it).

Section 54(2)(b) (receiving instruction or training in the making or use of an explosive).

Section 54(2)(c) (receiving instruction or training in the making or use of a chemical, biological or nuclear weapon).

Section 54(3)(a) (inviting another to receive instruction or training where receipt would constitute an offence under section 54(2) of the Terrorism Act 2000).

Section 54(3)(b) (inviting another to receive instruction or training where receipt would constitute an offence under section 54(2) of the Terrorism Act 2000 but for the fact that it would take place outside the United Kingdom).

Section 56(1) (directing the activities of an organisation at any level which is concerned in the commission of a terrorist act).

Section 57(1) (possessing an article giving rise to a reasonable suspicion that possessing it is connected with the commission, preparation or instigation of a terrorist act).

Section 58(1)(a) (collecting or making a record of information of a kind likely to be useful to a person committing or preparing a terrorist act).

Section 58(1)(b) (possessing a record of information of a kind likely to be useful to a person committing or preparing a terrorist act).

Offences under the Anti-terrorism, Crime and Security Act 2001

Section 47(1)(a) (knowingly causing a nuclear weapon explosion).

Section 47(1)(b) (developing or producing a nuclear weapon, or participating in either activity).

Section 47(1)(c) (possessing a nuclear weapon).

Section 47(1)(d) (participating in the transfer of a nuclear weapon).

Section 47(1)(e) (engaging in military preparations intending, or threatening, to use a nuclear weapon).

Section 113(1) (using a noxious substance or thing in a way which causes serious violence or serious damage to property, endangers human life, creates a serious risk to health or safety or induces in the public a fear that such an act will endanger their lives or health or safety, and which is designed to influence the government or intimidate the public).

Section 114(1) (placing or sending a substance or thing, intending to induce a belief that it is a noxious substance or thing likely to endanger human life or create a serious risk to human health).

Section 114(2) (communicating information knowing or believing it to be false, intending to induce a belief that a noxious substance or thing is present in any place, thereby to endanger human life or create a serious risk to human health).

Offences under the Proceeds of Crime Act 2002

Section 327(1)(a) (concealing criminal property).

Section 327(1)(b) (disguising criminal property).

Section 327(1)(c) (converting criminal property).

Section 327(1)(d) (transferring criminal property).

Section 327(1)(e) (removing criminal property from England and Wales, Scotland or Northern Ireland).

Section 328(1) (entering into, or becoming concerned in, an arrangement, knowing or suspecting that it will facilitate the acquisition, retention, use, or control of criminal property).
Section 329(1)(a) (acquiring criminal property).
Section 329(1)(b) (using criminal property).
Section 329(1)(c) (possessing criminal property).
Section 332(1) (failing, as a nominated person, to disclose known or suspected money laundering as soon as reasonably practicable after the information on which that knowledge or suspicion is based is obtained in consequence of a disclosure under section 337 or 338 of the Proceeds of Crime Act 2002).
Section 333 (disclosing information likely to prejudice any investigation that might be conducted following the disclosure of information by a nominated person under section 337 or 338 of the Proceeds of Crime Act 2002).

SCHEDULE 2
OFFENCES UNDER THE COMMON LAW OF ENGLAND AND WALES AND STATUTORY OFFENCES THAT APPLY ONLY IN ENGLAND AND WALES

1
Offences under the Common Law of England and Wales.
   Manslaughter.

2
Statutory offences that apply only in England and Wales.

Offences under the Infant Life (Preservation) Act 1929)

Section 1 (doing a wilful act, intending to destroy the life of a child capable of being born alive that causes a child to die before it is born).

Offences under the Infanticide Act 1938

Section 1 (doing a wilful act causing the death of a child before it is over 12 months old, where that act is done by the mother of the child and her balance of mind is disturbed for reasons relating to lactation or the birth of the child).

Offences under the Theft Act 1968

Section 1(1) (dishonestly appropriating another's property, intending to permanently deprive him of it).
Section 8(1) (stealing, and before or at the time of doing so, using force or putting another in fear of being there and then subjected to force).
Section 9(1)(a) (entering a building as a trespasser, intending to steal, inflict or attempt to inflict grievous bodily harm or rape).
Section 9(1)(b) (having entered a building as a trespasser, stealing or attempting to steal or inflicting or attempting to inflict grievous bodily harm).
Section 10(1) (committing burglary with a firearm, imitation firearm, weapon of offence or explosive).
Section 12A (aggravated taking of a vehicle).

Offences under the Criminal Damage Act 1971

Section 1(1) (destroying or damaging, without lawful excuse, another's property intending to destroy or damage it or being reckless as to that).

Section 1(2) (destroying or damaging, without lawful excuse, property, intending, or being reckless as to whether, that destruction or damage would result and intending that damage or destruction to endanger the life of another or being reckless as to that).

Section 2 (threatening, without lawful excuse, to destroy or damage property, knowing that such a threat is likely to endanger another's life).

Section 3(a) (having in custody or under control anything intending, without lawful excuse, to use, or permit use of, it to destroy or damage another's property).

Section 3(b) (having in custody or under control anything, intending, without lawful excuse, to use, or permit use of, it to destroy or damage property knowing that such an act is likely to endanger another's life).

Offences under the Criminal Law Act 1977

Section 1 (agreeing to pursue a course of conduct which, if carried out as intended, necessarily amounts to the commission of an offence or would do so but for the fact that such commission is impossible, provided that the offence in question is an offence described either in Schedule 1 to this Order or this Schedule).

Section 51(1) (placing or dispatching an article, intending to induce a belief that it will explode or ignite and cause personal injury or property damage).

Section 51(2) (communicating information, knowing or believing it to be false intending to induce a belief that a bomb or other thing is liable to explode in a place).

Offences under the Magistrates Courts Act 1980

Section 44 (aiding, abetting, counselling or procuring the commission of a summary offence, provided that the offence in question is described in Schedule 1 to this Order or this Schedule).

Offences under the Criminal Attempts Act 1981

Section 1(1) (intending to commit an offence and doing an act that is more than merely preparatory to the commission of that offence, provided that the offence in question is described in Schedule 1 to this Order or this Schedule).

Offences under the Public Order Act 1986

Section 1(1) (being in a group of 12 or more people who use, or threaten, unlawful violence for a common purpose so as to cause a person of reasonable firmness present at the scene to fear for his safety).

Section 2(1) (being in a group of 3 or more people who use, or threaten, unlawful violence for a common purpose so as to cause a person of reasonable firmness present at the scene to fear for his safety).

Section 3(1) (using, or threatening, unlawful violence so as to cause a person of reasonable firmness present at the scene to fear for his safety).

Offences under the Protection from Harassment Act 1997

Section 4(1) (causing fear in another on at least two occasions that violence will be used against him, where the offender knows, or ought to know, that his course of conduct will cause such fear on each occasion).

Offences under the Crime and Disorder Act 1998

Section 29(1)(a) (maliciously wounding or causing grievous bodily harm so as to constitute an offence under section 20 of the Offences Against the Person Act 1861 that is racially or religiously aggravated).

Section 29(1)(b) (causing actual bodily harm so as to constitute an offence under section 47 of the Offences Against the Person Act 1861 that is racially or religiously aggravated).

Section 29(1)(c) (committing a common assault that is racially or religiously aggravated).

Section 31(1)(a) (committing an offence under section 4(1) of the Public Order Act 1986 that is racially or religiously aggravated).

Section 31(1)(b) (committing an offence under section 4A(1) of the Public Order Act 1986 that is racially or religiously aggravated).

Offences under the Sexual Offences Act 2003

Section 1(1) (intentionally penetrating the vagina, anus or mouth of another with a penis, where the victim does not consent and the offender does not reasonably believe that there is consent).

Section 2(1) (intentionally sexually penetrating the vagina or anus of another with a part of the body or anything else, where the victim does not consent and the offender does not reasonably believe that there is consent).

Section 3(1) (intentionally sexually touching another, where the victim does not consent and the offender does not reasonably believe that there is consent).

Section 4(1) (intentionally causing another to engage in sexual activity, where the victim does not consent and the offender does not reasonably believe that there is consent).

Section 5(1) (intentionally sexually penetrating the vagina, anus or mouth of another with a penis, where the victim is under 13).

Section 6(1) (intentionally sexually penetrating the vagina or anus of another who is under 13 with a part of the body or anything else).

Section 7(1) (intentionally sexually touching a person who is under 13).

Section 8(1) (intentionally causing or inciting another who is under 13 to engage in sexual activity).

Section 9(1) (intentionally sexually touching another who is 13 or under, or is 16 or under and the offender, who is 18 or over, does not believe that the victim is 16 or over).

Section 10(1) (intentionally causing or inciting another to engage in sexual activity, where the victim is 13 or under, or is 16 or under and the offender, who is 18 or over, does not believe that the victim is 16 or over).

Section 11(1) (intentionally engaging, for the purpose of sexual gratification, in sexual activity in a place where another is present or can observe and the offender, who is 18 or over, knows, believes or intends the victim to be there and the victim is 13 or under, or is under 16 and the offender does not reasonably believe that the victim is 16 or over).

Section 12(1) (intentionally causing, for the purpose of sexual gratification, another to watch or look at an image of a third person engaging in sexual activity, where the victim is 13 or under, or is under 16 and the offender does not reasonably believe that the victim is 16 or over).

Section 13(1) (committing an offence under section 9 to 12 of the Sexual Offences Act 2003 which would be an offence if the offender was 18).

Section 14(1) (intentionally arranging or facilitating something in any part of the world that, if done, would involve the commission of any offence under sections 9 to 13 of the Sexual Offences Act 2003).

Section 25 (intentionally sexually touching a family member, where the offender could reasonably be expected to know that the victim is a family member, and the victim is 13, or is under 18 and the offender does not reasonably believe that the victim is 18 or over).

Section 26 (intentionally inciting a family member to touch or allow himself to be touched sexually where the offender could reasonably be expected to know that the victim is a family member, and the victim is 13 or under, or is under 18 and the offender does not reasonably believe that the victim is 18 or over).

Section 30(1) (intentionally sexually touching another where the victim is unable to refuse by reason of a mental disorder and the offender could reasonably be expected to know that the victim has a mental disorder that is likely to render him unable to refuse).

Section 31(1) (intentionally inciting another to engage in sexual activity where the victim is unable to refuse by reason of a mental disorder and the offender could reasonably be expected to know that the victim has a mental disorder that is likely to render him unable to refuse).

Section 32(1) (intentionally engaging in sexual activity for sexual gratification in a place where a person who is unable to refuse by reason of a mental disorder observes it or the offender knows, believes or intends the victim to observe it and the offender knows or could reasonably be expected to know that the victim has a mental disorder that is likely to render him unable to refuse).

Section 33(1) (intentionally causing, for sexual gratification, another to watch, or look at an image of, a third person engaging in sexual activity, where the victim is unable to refuse by reason of mental disorder and the offender knows or could reasonably be expected to know that the victim has a mental disorder that is likely to render him unable to refuse).

Section 34(1) (intentionally sexually touching another with a mental disorder, where the victim agrees and such agreement is obtained by inducement, threat, or deception and the offender knows, or could reasonably be expected to know, about that mental disorder).

Section 35(1) (intentionally causing another with a mental disorder, by inducement, threat, or deception, to engage in sexual activity and the victim has a mental disorder which the offender knows, or could reasonably be expected to know, about).

Section 36(1) (intentionally engaging in sexual activity, for the purpose of sexual gratification, in a place where another with a mental disorder is present or observes it, or the offender knows, believes or intends the victim to observe it, because of inducement, threat or deception and the offender knows, or could reasonably be expected to know, that the victim has a mental disorder).

Section 37(1) (intentionally causing another with a mental disorder, by inducement, threat or deception, to watch or look, for the purposes of sexual gratification, at an image of a third person engaging in sexual activity, and the offender knows, or could reasonably be expected to know, that the victim has a mental disorder).

Section 38(1) (intentionally sexually touching another with a mental disorder which the offender knows, or could reasonably be expected to know, about, where the offender is involved in the victim's care).

Section 39(1) (intentionally causing or inciting another with a mental disorder to engage in sexual activity, where the offender knows or could reasonably be expected to know that the victim has a mental disorder and the offender is involved in the victim's care).

Section 61(1) (intentionally administering a substance to another knowing that the victim does not consent, with the intention of stupefying or overpowering the victim so that sexual activity can be engaged in with the victim).

Section 62(1) (committing an offence intending to commit a sexual offence under Part I of the Sexual Offences Act 2003).

Section 63(1) (trespassing on premises, knowing that, or being reckless as to whether, trespass is taking place and intending to commit a sexual offence under Part I of the Sexual Offences Act 2003).

SCHEDULE 3

OFFENCES UNDER THE COMMON LAW OF SCOTLAND AND STATUTORY OFFENCES THAT APPLY ONLY IN SCOTLAND

1

Offences under the Common Law of Scotland.

> Abduction.
>
> Abduction of women or girls with intent to rape.
>
> Aiding and abetting an offence under the Common Law of Scotland (provided that the offence in question is described in this paragraph of this Schedule).
>
> Assault with intent to rape or ravish.
>
> Assault and robbery.
>
> Attempted murder.
>
> Breach of the peace inferring personal violence.
>
> Clandestine injury to women.
>
> Conspiracy (in respect of an offence described in Schedule 1 to this Order or this Schedule).
>
> Culpable homicide.
>
> Culpable and reckless fire-raising.
>
> Indecent assault.
>
> Malicious mischief.
>
> Mobbing and rioting.
>
> Rape.
>
> Robbery.
>
> Theft by housebreaking.
>
> Threatening personal violence.
>
> Wilful fire-raising.
>
> Wrongful imprisonment.

2

Statutory offences that apply only in Scotland.

Offences under the Children and Young Persons (Scotland) Act 1937

Section 12 (ill-treating, neglecting, abandoning or exposing a child under 16, or causing such, where the offender is 16 and has parental responsibility for the victim or has charge or care of him).

Offences under the Civic Government (Scotland) Act 1982

Section 52 (taking and distributing indecent images of children).

Section 52A (possessing indecent images of children).

Offences under the Prohibition of Female Circumcision Act 1985

Section 1(1)(a) (excising, infibulating or otherwise mutilating the labia or clitoris of another).

Offences under the Criminal Law (Consolidation) (Scotland) Act 1995

Section 3(1) (having sexual intercourse with a member of the same household who is 16 or under where the offender is in a position of trust).

Section 5(1) (having sexual intercourse with a girl under 13).

Section 6 (engaging in lewd, indecent or libidinous behaviour towards a girl between 12 and 16, where that behaviour would have constituted a common law offence had that girl been under 12).

Section 50A(1)(a) (pursuing a racially aggravated course of conduct amounting to harassment that is intended to harass or which occurs in circumstances where it would appear to a reasonable person to constitute harassment).

Section 50A(1)(b) (acting in a racially aggravated manner which causes, or is intended to cause, alarm or distress).

Section 52(1) (wilfully or recklessly destroying or damaging property).

Offences under the Criminal Procedure (Scotland) Act 1995

Section 293(2) (aiding, abetting, counselling, procuring or inciting the commission of an offence against the provisions of any enactment, provided that the offence in question is described in Schedule 1 to this Order or in this paragraph of this Schedule).

Section 294 (attempting to commit an indictable offence, provided that the offence in question is described in Schedule 1 to this Order or this Schedule).

Offences under the Sexual Offences (Amendment) Act 2000

Section 3 (having sexual intercourse, or engaging in other sexual activity with, a person under 18, where the offender is 18 or over and is in a position of trust).

Offences under the International Criminal Court (Scotland) Act 2001

Section 1 (committing genocide, a crime against humanity or a war crime).

Offences under the Criminal Justice (Scotland) Act 2003

Section 22(1)(a)(i) (arranging or facilitating the arrival or travel in the United Kingdom of a person and intending to exercise control over prostitution of the victim or involving the victim in the production of obscene or indecent material).

Section 22(1)(a)(ii) (arranging or facilitating the arrival or travel in the United Kingdom of a person and believing that another will exercise control over prostitution of the victim or involving the victim in the production of obscene or indecent material).

Section 22(1)(b)(i) (arranging or facilitating the departure from the United Kingdom of a person and intending to exercise control over prostitution of the victim or involving the victim in the production of obscene or indecent material).

Section 22(1)(b)(ii) (arranging or facilitating the departure from the United Kingdom of a person and believing that another will exercise control over prostitution of the victim or involving the victim in the production of obscene or indecent material).

SCHEDULE 4

OFFENCES UNDER THE COMMON LAW OF NORTHERN IRELAND AND STATUTORY OFFENCES THAT APPLY ONLY IN NORTHERN IRELAND

1

Offences under the Common Law of Northern Ireland.

  Affray.
  Rape.
  Rioting.

2

Statutory offences that apply only in Northern Ireland.

Offences under the Offences Against the Person Act 1861

Section 52 (indecently assaulting a woman or a girl under 16).
Section 53 (abducting a woman by force, intending to have sexual intercourse with her).

Offences under the Criminal Law (Amendment) Act 1885

Section 4 (having unlawful sexual intercourse with a girl under 13).
Section 5 (having unlawful sexual intercourse with a girl under 16).

Offences under the Infanticide Act (Northern Ireland) 1939

Section 1(1) (doing a wilful act causing the death of a child before it is over 12 months old, where that act is done by the mother of the child and her balance of mind is disturbed for reasons relating to lactation or the birth of the child).

Offences under the Criminal Justice Act (Northern Ireland) 1945

Section 25(1) (doing a wilful act, intending to destroy the life of a child capable of being born alive that causes the child to die before it is born).

Offences under the Attempted Rape Act (Northern Ireland) 1960

Section 2 (committing assault intending to commit rape).

Offences under the Children and Young Persons Act (Northern Ireland) 1968

Section 20(1) (wilfully assaulting, ill-treating, neglecting, abandoning or exposing, or causing such, of a child of 16 where the offender has responsibility for the victim, in a manner likely to cause the victim unnecessary suffering or injury to health).
Section 22 (committing an act of gross indecency with or towards a child or inciting a child to perform such an act).

Offences under the Theft Act (Northern Ireland) 1969

Section 1(1) (dishonestly appropriating another's property, intending to permanently deprive him of it).
Section 8(1) (stealing, and before or at the time of doing so, using force or putting another in fear of being there and then subjected to force).
Section 9(1)(a) (entering a building as a trespasser, intending to steal, inflict or attempt to inflict grievous bodily harm or rape).
Section 9(1)(b) (having entered a building as a trespasser, stealing or attempting to steal or inflicting or attempting to inflict grievous bodily harm).
Section 10(1) (committing burglary with a firearm or imitation firearm, a weapon of offence or an explosive).

Offences under the Protection of the Person and Property Act (Northern Ireland) 1969

Section 3 (throwing, placing, attaching or using a petrol bomb, intending to destroy, or damage, the property of another, or to cause personal injury to another, or to give another reasonable cause to fear any destruction of property or personal injury or being reckless in regard to causing any such destruction, damage, injury or fear).

Offences under the Criminal Damage (Northern Ireland) Order 1977

Article 3(1) (destroying or damaging, without lawful excuse, another's property, intending to destroy or damage it or being reckless as to that).

Article 3(2) (destroying or damaging, without lawful excuse, property, intending, or being reckless as to whether, that destruction or damage would result and intending that damage or destruction to endanger the life of another or being reckless as to that).

Article 4 (threatening, without lawful excuse, to destroy or damage property, knowing that such a threat is likely to endanger another's life).

Section 5(a) (having in custody or under control anything, intending, without lawful excuse, to use, or permit use of, it to destroy or damage another's property).

Section 5(b) (having in custody or under control anything, intending, without lawful excuse, to use, or permit use of, it to destroy or damage property knowing that such an act is likely to endanger another's life).

Offences under the Criminal Law (Amendment) (Northern Ireland) Order 1977

Article 3(1) (placing or sending an article, intending to induce a belief that it is likely to explode or ignite and cause personal injury or damage to property).

Article 3(2) (communicating information, knowing or believing it to be false and intending to induce a false belief that a bomb or other explosive device is present).

Offences under the Firearms (Northern Ireland) Order 1981

Article 6(1) (possessing, purchasing, acquiring, manufacturing, selling or transferring any of the items referred to in Article 6(1) of the Firearms (Northern Ireland) Order 1981).

Article 6(1A) (possessing, purchasing, acquiring, manufacturing, selling or transferring any of the items referred to in article 6(1A) of the Firearms (Northern Ireland) Order 1981).

Article 17 (possessing a firearm or ammunition, intending to endanger life or cause serious injury to property or to enable another to do so).

Article 17A (possessing a firearm or imitation firearm, intending to cause, or enable another to cause, a person to believe that he will be the victim of unlawful violence).

Article 18(1) (making or attempting to make use of a firearm or imitation firearm, intending to resist or prevent the lawful arrest or detention of himself or any other person).

Article 18(2) (committing, or being arrested for, an offence specified in Schedule 1 of the Firearms (Northern Ireland) Order 1981 and possessing a firearm or imitation firearm without lawful object).

Article 19(1) (having a firearm or imitation firearm, intending to commit an indictable offence, or to resist arrest or to prevent the arrest of another).

Article 20(1) (having, without lawful authority or reasonable excuse, in public a loaded shot gun, loaded air weapon or any other firearm together with ammunition suitable for use in that firearm).

Article 21(1) (having a firearm, or imitation firearm when trespassing in a building without reasonable excuse).

Article 21(2) (having a firearm, or imitation firearm when trespassing on land without reasonable excuse).

Article 23 (possessing a firearm or ammunition giving rise to a reasonable suspicion that such possession is not for a lawful object).

Offences under the Magistrates Courts (Northern Ireland) Order 1981

Article 59 (aiding, abetting, counselling or procuring the commission of a summary offence, provided that the offence in question is described in Schedule 1 to this Order or this Schedule).

Offences under the Criminal Attempts and Conspiracy (Northern Ireland)
Order 1983

Article 3 (intending to commit an offence and doing an act that is more than merely preparatory to the commission of that offence, provided that the offence in question is described in Schedule 1 to this Order or this Schedule).

Article 9 (agreeing to pursue a course of conduct which, if carried out as intended, necessarily amounts to the commission of an offence to, or would do so but for the fact that such commission is impossible, provided that the offence in question is described in Schedule 1 to this Order or this Schedule).

Offences under the Public Order (Northern Ireland) Order 1987

Article 18 (using threatening, abusive, or insulting words or behaviour, displaying anything, doing any act or, being the owner or occupier of any land or premises, causing or permitting anything to be displayed or any act to be done, intending to provoke a breach of the peace or by which a breach of the peace or public disorder is likely to be occasioned).

Offences under the Road Traffic (Northern Ireland) Order 1995

Article 9 (causing the death of, or grievous bodily injury to, another by driving a mechanically propelled vehicle dangerously on a road or other public place).

Article 14(1)(a) (causing the death of, or grievous bodily injury to, another by driving without due care and attention, or without reasonable consideration, and being unfit to drive through drink or drugs).

Article 14(1)(b) (causing the death of, or grievous bodily injury to, another by driving without due care and attention, or without reasonable consideration, having consumed so much alcohol that the proportion of it in his breath, blood or urine exceeds the prescribed limit).

Article 14(1)(c) (causing the death of, or grievous bodily injury to, another by driving without due care and attention or without reasonable consideration and failing, without reasonable excuse, to provide a specimen in pursuance of Article 18 of the Road Traffic (Northern Ireland) Order 1995 within 18 hours of that incident).

Offences under the Protection from Harassment (Northern Ireland) Order 1997

Article 6 (causing fear in another on at least two occasions that violence will be used against him, where the offender knows or ought to know that his course of conduct will cause such fear on each of those occasions).

Offences under the Criminal Justice (Northern Ireland) Order 2003

Article 20 (committing assault, intending to commit buggery).
Article 21(1) (indecently assaulting a man).

SCHEDULE 5
STATUTORY OFFENCES THAT APPLY ONLY IN ENGLAND AND WALES AND SCOTLAND

Offences under the Firearms Act 1968

Section 5(1) (possessing, purchasing, acquiring, manufacturing, selling or transferring, without authorisation, any item listed in section 5(1) of the Firearms Act 1968).

Section 16 (possessing a firearm or ammunition, intending to endanger, or enable another to endanger, life).

Section 16A (possessing a firearm or imitation firearm, intending to cause, or to enable another to cause, a belief that unlawful violence will be used).

Section 17(1) (using, or attempting to use, a firearm, intending to prevent or resist lawful arrest or detention).

Section 17(2) (unlawfully possessing a firearm or imitation firearm while committing an offence listed in Schedule 1 to the Firearms Act 1968).

Section 18(1) (having a firearm or imitation forearm, intending to commit an indictable offence or to resist or prevent arrest).

Section 19 (unlawfully or unreasonably possessing, without lawful authority or reasonable excuse, a loaded shot gun or air weapon or any other firearm, whether loaded or not, together with ammunition suitable for use in that firearm).

Offences under the Road Traffic Act 1988

Section 1 (causing the death of another by driving a mechanically propelled vehicle dangerously on a road or other public place).

Section 3A(1)(a) (causing the death of another by driving without due care and attention, or without reasonable consideration, and being unfit to drive through drink or drugs).

Article 3A(1)(b) (causing the death of another by driving without due care and attention, or without reasonable consideration, having consumed so much alcohol that the proportion of it in his breath, blood or urine exceeds the prescribed limit).

Article 3A(1)(c) (causing the death of another by driving without due care and attention or without reasonable consideration and failing, without reasonable excuse, to provide a specimen in pursuance of section 7 of the Road Traffic Act 1988 within 18 hours of that incident).

SCHEDULE 6
OFFENCES UNDER THE COMMON LAW OF ENGLAND AND WALES AND NORTHERN IRELAND AND STATUTORY OFFENCES THAT APPLY ONLY IN ENGLAND AND WALES AND NORTHERN IRELAND

1

Offences under Common Law of England and Wales and Northern Ireland.
   False Imprisonment.
   Kidnapping.

2

Statutory offences that apply only in England and Wales and Northern Ireland.

Offences under the Accessories and Abettors Act 1861

Section 8 (aiding, abetting, counselling or procuring the commission of an indictable offence, provided that the offence in question is described in Schedule 1, Schedule 2 or Schedule 4 to this Order or this Schedule).

Offences under the Offences Against the Person Act 1861

Section 4 (soliciting, encouraging, persuading, endeavouring to persuade or proposing murder).

Section 16 (unlawfully threatening to kill, intending that the subject of the threat would fear that it would be carried out).

Section 18 (unlawfully and maliciously wounding or causing grievous bodily harm, intending to cause grievous bodily harm or to resist or prevent lawful apprehension or detention).

Section 20 (unlawfully and maliciously wounding or inflicting grievous bodily harm).

Section 21 (attempting to choke, suffocate or strangle another or attempting, by means calculated to choke, suffocate or strangle, to render that person insensible, unconscious or incapable of resistance and intending to commit an indictable offence).

Section 22 (applying or administering a stupefying or overpowering drug, matter or thing intending to commit an indictable offence).

Section 23 (unlawfully and maliciously administering a poison or destructive or noxious thing so as to endanger life or inflict grievous bodily harm).

Section 27 (unlawfully abandoning or exposing a child under 2 so as to endanger life or cause permanent injury).

Section 28 (unlawfully and maliciously exploding a substance causing burning, maiming, disfigurement, disablement or grievous bodily harm).

Section 29 (unlawfully and maliciously causing an explosion or sending or delivering an explosive substance, or placing or throwing a corrosive, destructive or explosive substance, intending to burn, maim, disfigure, disable or do grievous bodily harm).

Section 30 (unlawfully and maliciously placing or throwing an explosive substance on or near a building, ship or vessel intending to do bodily injury).

Section 32 (unlawfully and maliciously placing an obstruction on a railway or interfering with railway equipment intending to endanger safety).

Section 33 (unlawfully and maliciously throwing any object at a railway vehicle intending to injure or endanger the safety of any person in that vehicle).

Section 47 (committing assault occasioning actual bodily harm).

Offences under the International Criminal Court Act 2001

Section 51 (committing genocide, a crime against humanity or a war crime against the laws of England and Wales).

Section 58 (committing genocide, a crime against humanity or a war crime against the laws of Northern Ireland).

Offences under the Nationality, Immigration and Asylum Act 2002

Section 145(1) (arranging or facilitating the arrival or travel in the United Kingdom of a person, intending to exercise control over prostitution of the victim or involving the victim in the production of obscene or indecent material).

Section 145(2) (arranging or facilitating the travel within the United Kingdom by a passenger, believing an offence to have been committed under section 145(1) of the Nationality, Immigration and Asylum Act 2002 and intending to exercise control over prostitution of him or believing that another person will exercise such control).

Section 145(3) (arranging or facilitating the departure from the United Kingdom of a passenger, intending to exercise control over prostitution of him outside the United Kingdom or believing that another person will exercise such control outside the United Kingdom).

Offences under the Female Genital Mutilation Act 2003

Section 1(1) (excising, infibulating or otherwise mutilating the whole or part of a girl's labia majora, labia minora or clitoris).

Offences under the Sexual Offences Act 2003

Section 15(1) (meeting, or travelling, intending to meet a person under 16 who has been met or communicated with on two previous occasions, where the offender intends to do something that would constitute a relevant offence (as defined in section 15(2)(b) of the Sexual Offences Act 2003) and does not believe the victim to be over 16).

Section 16(1) (intentionally sexually touching a person under 13, or under 18, where the offender is in a position of trust in relation to the victim and does not reasonably believe that the victim is over 18).

Section 17(1) (intentionally causing or inciting another to engage in sexual activity, where the offender is a person who is 18 or over and is in a position of trust in relation to the victim, and the victim is under 13, or is under 18 and the offender does not reasonably believe that the victim is 18 or over).

Section 47(1) (intentionally obtaining the sexual services of a person under 13, or under 18 and the offender does not reasonably believe that the victim is 18 or over, where the offender has made or promised payment for those services or knows that another has made or promised payment).

Section 48(1) (intentionally causing or inciting another to become a prostitute or be involved in pornography, where the victim is under 13, or is under 18 and the offender does not reasonably believe that the victim is 18 or over).

Section 49(1) (intentionally controlling any activities of another relating to the latter's prostitution or involvement in pornography, where the victim is under 13, or is under 18 and the offender does not reasonably believe that the victim is 18 or over).

Section 50(1) (intentionally arranging or facilitating the prostitution or involvement in pornography of another, where the victim is under 13, or is under 18 and the offender does not reasonably believe that the victim is 18 or over).

Section 57(1)(a) (intentionally arranging or facilitating the arrival in the United Kingdom of another and intending to do something in respect of that person after arrival that would constitute an offence specified under section 60 of the Sexual Offences Act 2003).

Section 57(1)(b) (intentionally arranging or facilitating the arrival in the United Kingdom of another and believing that a third party is likely to do something in respect of that person after arrival that would constitute an offence specified under section 60 of the Sexual Offences Act 2003).

Section 58(1)(a) (intentionally arranging or facilitating travel within the United Kingdom by another and intending to do something in respect of that person during or after the journey that would constitute an offence specified under section 60 of the Sexual Offences Act 2003).

Section 58(1)(b) (intentionally arranging or facilitating travel within the United Kingdom by another and believing that a third party is likely to do something during or after the journey in respect of that person that would constitute an offence specified under section 60 of the Sexual Offences Act 2003).

ASYLUM AND IMMIGRATION (TREATMENT OF CLAIMANTS, ETC) ACT 2004 (COMMENCE-MENT NO 1) ORDER 2004

(SI 2004/2523)

Date made: 22 September 2004.

Authority: Asylum and Immigration (Treatment of Claimants, etc) Act 2004, s 48(3), (4).

1 Citation and interpretation

(1) This Order may be cited as the Asylum and Immigration (Treatment of Claimants, etc) Act 2004 (Commencement No 1) Order 2004.

(2) In this Order, "the 1999 Act" means the Immigration and Asylum Act 1999 and "the 2004 Act" means the Asylum and Immigration (Treatment of Claimants, etc) Act 2004.

2 Commencement

The provisions of the 2004 Act specified in column 1 of the Schedule to this Order shall come into force on 1st October 2004, but where a particular purpose is specified in relation to any such provision in column 2 of that Schedule, the provision concerned shall come into force on that date only for that purpose.

3 Transitional provision

Notwithstanding their repeal by section 33 of the 2004 Act (removing asylum-seeker to safe country), sections 11 (removal of asylum claimant under standing arrangement with member States) and 12 (removal of asylum claimants in other circumstances) of the 1999 Act and sections 80 (removal of asylum-seeker to third country) and 93 (appeal from within the United Kingdom: "third country" removal) of the Nationality, Immigration and Asylum Act 2002 shall continue to have effect in relation to a person who is subject to a certificate under section 11(2) or section 12(2) or (5) of the 1999 Act which was issued by the Secretary of State before 1st October 2004.

SCHEDULE

Article 2

Column 1	Column 2
Section 1 (assisting unlawful immigration)	
Section 3 (immigration documents: forgery)	
Section 6 (employment)	
Section 8(7), (10) and (11) (claimant's credibility)	For the purpose of enabling the Secretary of State to exercise the power to make subordinate legislation under section 8(7)
Section 15 (fingerprinting)	
Section 18 (control of entry)	
Section 27 (unfounded human rights or asylum claim)	
Section 28 (appeal from within the United Kingdom)	
Section 29 (entry clearance)	

Section 30 (earlier right of appeal)

Section 31 (seamen and aircrews: right of appeal)

Section 33 (removing asylum-seeker to safe country) and Schedule 3 (removal of asylum-seeker to safe country)

Section 34 (detention pending deportation)

Section 36 (electronic monitoring)

Section 37 (provision of immigration services)

Section 38 (Immigration Services Commissioner: power of entry)

Section 39 (offence of advertising services)

Section 40 (appeal to Immigration Services Tribunal)

Section 41 (professional bodies)

Section 42 (amount of fees)

Section 43 (transfer of leave stamps)

Section 44 (interpretation: "the Immigration Acts")

Section 45 (interpretation: immigration officer)

Section 46 (money)

Section 47 and Schedule 4 (repeals), the entries relating to section 8(9) of the Asylum and Immigration Act 1996, sections 11, 12, 85(1) and 87(3)(f) of the Immigration and Asylum Act 1999 and paragraph 1(1) of Schedule 6 to that Act and sections 80, 93 and 94(4)(a) to (j) of the Nationality, Immigration and Asylum Act 2002

IMMIGRATION (CLAIMANT'S CREDIBILITY) REGULATIONS 2004

(SI 2004/3263)

Made: 8 December 2004.

Asylum and Immigration (Treatment of Claimants, etc) Act 2004, s 8(7), (10), (11).

Commencement: 1 January 2005.

1 Citation and commencement

These Regulations may be cited as the Immigration (Claimant's Credibility) Regulations 2004 and shall come into force on the 1st January 2005.

2 Interpretation

In these Regulations —

"the 2004 Act" means the Asylum and Immigration (Treatment of Claimants, etc) Act 2004;

"representative" means a person who appears to the decision maker —

(a) to be the representative of a person; and

(b) not to be prohibited from acting as a representative by section 84 of the Immigration and Asylum 1999 Act.

3 Manner of notifying immigration decision

(1) For the purpose of section 8(5) of the 2004 Act a person may be notified of an immigration decision in any of the following ways —

(a) orally, including by means of a telecommunications system;

(b) in writing given by hand; or

(c) in writing

(i) sent by fax to a fax number;

(ii) sent by electronic mail to an electronic mail address; or

(iii) delivered or sent by postal service to an address,

provided for correspondence by the person or his representative.

(2) Where no fax number, electronic mail or postal address for correspondence has been provided by the person, notice of an immigration decision under paragraph (1)(c) may be delivered or sent by postal service to the last known or usual place of abode or place of business of the person or his representative.

(3) Notice given in accordance with paragraph (1) or (2) to the representative of the person, is to be taken to have been given to the person.

(4) In the case of a minor who does not have a representative, notice given in accordance with paragraph (1) or (2) to the parent, guardian or another adult who for the time being takes responsibility for the minor is taken to have been given to the minor.

4 Presumptions about receipt of notice

(1) For the purpose of section 8(5) of the 2004 Act notice of an immigration decision shall, unless the contrary is proved, be treated as received;

(a) where the notice is sent by postal service in which delivery or receipt is recorded to an address, on the recorded date of delivery or receipt, or on the second day after the day it was posted, whichever is the earlier;

(b) in any other case in which the notice is sent by postal service on the second day after the day it was posted; or

(c) in any other case, on the day and time that it was communicated orally, given by hand or sent by electronic mail or fax.

(2) For the purposes of determining the second day after a notice is posted under paragraph (1) (a) and (b) any day which is not a business day shall be excluded.

(3) In this regulation "business day" means any day other than Saturday or Sunday, a day which is a bank holiday under the Banking and Financial Dealings Act 1971 in the part of the United Kingdom from or to which the notice is sent, Christmas Day or Good Friday.

ASYLUM SEEKERS (RECEPTION CONDITIONS) REGULATIONS 2005

(SI 2005/7)

Made: 10 January 2005.

Authority: European Communities Act 1972, s 2(2).

Commencement: 5 February 2005 (applying only to a person whose claim for asylum is recorded on or after that date).

1 Citation and commencement

(1) These Regulations may be cited as the Asylum Seekers (Reception Conditions) Regulations 2005 and shall come into force on 5th February 2005.

(2) These Regulations shall only apply to a person whose claim for asylum is recorded on or after 5th February 2005.

2 Interpretation

(1) In these Regulations—

- (a) "the 1999 Act" means the Immigration and Asylum Act 1999;
- (b) "asylum seeker" means a person who is at least 18 years old who has made a claim for asylum which has been recorded by the Secretary of State but not yet determined;
- (c) "claim for asylum" means a claim made by a third country national or a stateless person that to remove him or require him to leave the United Kingdom would be contrary to the United Kingdom's obligations under the Convention relating to the Status of Refugees done at Geneva on 28th July 1951 and its Protocol;
- (d) "family members" means, in so far as the family already existed in the country of origin, the following members of the asylum seeker's family who are present in the United Kingdom and who are asylum seekers or dependants on the asylum seeker's claim for asylum:
  - (i) the spouse of the asylum seeker or his unmarried partner in a stable relationship;
  - (ii) the minor child of the couple referred to in paragraph (2)(d)(i) or of the asylum seeker as long as the child is unmarried and dependent on the asylum seeker;
- (e) "Immigration Acts" has the same meaning as in section 44 of the Asylum and Immigration (Treatment of Claimants, etc) Act 2004; and
- (f) "third country national" means a person who is not a national of a member State.

(2) For the purposes of these Regulations—

- (a) a claim is determined on the date on which the Secretary of State notifies the asylum seeker of his decision on his claim or, if the asylum seeker appeals against the Secretary of State's decision, the date on which that appeal is disposed of; and
- (b) an appeal is disposed of when it is no longer pending for the purposes of the Immigration Acts.

3 Families

(1) When the Secretary of State is providing or arranging for the provision of accommodation for an asylum seeker and his family members under section 95 or 98 of the 1999 Act, he shall have regard to family unity and ensure, in so far as it is reasonably practicable to do so, that family members are accommodated together.

(2) Paragraph (1) shall only apply to those family members who confirm to the Secretary of State that they agree to being accommodated together.

(3) This regulation shall not apply in respect of a child when the Secretary of State is providing or arranging for the provision of accommodation for that child under section 122 of the 1999 Act.

4 Provisions for persons with special needs

(1) This regulation applies to an asylum seeker or the family member of an asylum seeker who is a vulnerable person.

(2)   When the Secretary of State is providing support or considering whether to provide support under section 95 or 98 of the 1999 Act to an asylum seeker or his family member who is a vulnerable person, he shall take into account the special needs of that asylum seeker or his family member.

(3)   A vulnerable person is—

    (a)   a minor;

    (b)   a disabled person;

    (c)   an elderly person;

    (d)   a pregnant woman;

    (e)   a lone parent with a minor child; or

    (f)   a person who has been subjected to torture, rape or other serious forms of psychological, physical or sexual violence;

who has had an individual evaluation of his situation that confirms he has special needs.

(4)   Nothing in this regulation obliges the Secretary of State to carry out or arrange for the carrying out of an individual evaluation of a vulnerable person's situation to determine whether he has special needs.

5 Asylum support under section 95 or 98 of the 1999 Act

(1)   If an asylum seeker or his family member applies for support under section 95 of the 1999 Act and the Secretary of State thinks that the asylum seeker or his family member is eligible for support under that section he must offer the provision of support to the asylum seeker or his family member.

(2)   If the Secretary of State thinks that the asylum seeker or his family member is eligible for support under section 98 of the 1999 Act he must offer the provision of support to the asylum seeker or his family member.

6 Tracing family members of unaccompanied minors

(1)   So as to protect an unaccompanied minor's best interests, the Secretary of State shall endeavour to trace the members of the minor's family as soon as possible after the minor makes his claim for asylum.

(2)   In cases where there may be a threat to the life or integrity of the minor or the minor's close family, the Secretary of State shall take care to ensure that the collection, processing and circulation of information concerning the minor or his close family is undertaken on a confidential basis so as not to jeopardise his or their safety.

(3)   For the purposes of this regulation—

    (a)   an unaccompanied minor means a person below the age of eighteen who arrives in the United Kingdom unaccompanied by an adult responsible for him whether by law or custom and makes a claim for asylum;

    (b)   a person shall be an unaccompanied minor until he is taken into the care of such an adult or until he reaches the age of 18 whichever is the earlier;

    (c)   an unaccompanied minor also includes a minor who is left unaccompanied after he arrives in or enters the United Kingdom but before he makes his claim for asylum.

ADOPTIONS WITH A FOREIGN ELEMENT REGULATIONS 2005

(SI 2005/392)

Made: 24 February 2005.

Authority: Adoption and Children Act 2002, ss 83, 84; Adoption (Intercountry Aspects) Act 1999, s 1.

Commencement: 30 December 2005.

PART 1
GENERAL

1 Citation, commencement and application

(1) These Regulations may be cited as the Adoptions with a Foreign Element Regulations 2005 and shall come into force on 30th December 2005.

(2) These Regulations apply to England and Wales.

2 Interpretation

In these Regulations—

"the Act" means the Adoption and Children Act 2002;

"adoption support services" has the meaning given in section 2(6)(a) of the Act and any regulations made under section 2(6)(b) of the Act;

"adoptive family" has the same meaning as in regulation 31(2)(a) of the Agencies Regulations or corresponding Welsh provision;

"adoption panel" means a panel established in accordance with regulation 3 of the Agencies Regulations or corresponding Welsh provision;

"the Agencies Regulations" means the Adoption Agencies Regulations 2005;

"child's case record" has the same meaning as in regulation 12 of the Agencies Regulations or corresponding Welsh provision;

"CA of the receiving State" means, in relation to a Convention country other than the United Kingdom, the Central Authority of the receiving State;

"CA of the State of origin" means, in relation to a Convention country other than the United Kingdom, the Central Authority of the State of origin;

"Convention adoption" is given a meaning by virtue of section 66(1)(c) of the Act;

"Convention country" has the same meaning as in section 144(1) of the Act;

"Convention list" means—

    (a)   in relation to a relevant Central Authority, a list of children notified to that Authority in accordance with regulation 40; or

    (b)   in relation to any other Central Authority within the British Islands, a list of children notified to that Authority in accordance with provisions, which correspond to regulation 40.

"corresponding Welsh provision" in relation to a Part or a regulation of the Agencies Regulations means the provision of regulations made by the Assembly under section 9 of the Act which corresponds to that Part or regulation;

"prospective adopter's case record" has the same meaning as in [regulation 23(1)] of the Agencies Regulations or corresponding Welsh provision;

"prospective adopter's report" has the same meaning as in [regulation 30(2)] of the Agencies Regulations or corresponding Welsh provisions;

"receiving State" has the same meaning as in Article 2 of the Convention;

"relevant Central Authority" means—

    (a)   in Chapter 1 of Part 3, in relation to a prospective adopter who is habitually resident in—

        (i)   England, the Secretary of State; and

        (ii)   Wales, the National Assembly for Wales; and

    (b)   in Chapter 2 of Part 3 in relation to a local authority in—

        (i)   England, the Secretary of State; and

(ii)   Wales, the National Assembly for Wales;

"relevant local authority" means in relation to a prospective adopter—

(a)   the local authority within whose area he has his home; or

(b)   in the case where he no longer has a home in England or Wales, the local authority for the area in which he last had his home;

"relevant foreign authority" means a person, outside the British Islands performing functions in the country in which the child is, or in which the prospective adopter is, habitually resident which correspond to the functions of an adoption agency or to the functions of the Secretary of State in respect of adoptions with a foreign element;

"State of origin" has the same meaning as in Article 2 of the Convention.

Amendment

In definitions "prospective adopter's case record" and "prospective adopter's report" words in square brackets substituted by SI 2013/985, reg 10(1), Schedule, para 2(1), (2). Date in force: 1 July 2013: see SI 2013/985, reg 1.

PART 2
BRINGING CHILDREN INTO AND OUT OF THE UNITED KINGDOM

CHAPTER 1

BRINGING CHILDREN INTO THE UNITED KINGDOM

3 Requirements applicable in respect of bringing or causing a child to be brought into the United Kingdom

A person intending to bring, or to cause another to bring, a child into the United Kingdom in circumstances where section 83(1) of the Act applies must—

(a)   apply in writing to an adoption agency for an assessment of his suitability to adopt a child; and

(b)   give the adoption agency any information it may require for the purpose of the assessment.

4 Conditions applicable in respect of a child brought into the United Kingdom

(1)   This regulation prescribes the conditions for the purposes of section 83(5) of the Act in respect of a child brought into the United Kingdom in circumstances where section 83 applies.

(2)   Prior to the child's entry into the United Kingdom, the prospective adopter must—

(a)   receive in writing, notification from the Secretary of State that she has issued a certificate confirming to the relevant foreign authority—

(i)   that the person has been assessed and approved as eligible and suitable to be an adoptive parent in accordance with Part 4 of the Agencies Regulations or corresponding Welsh provision; and

(ii)   that if entry clearance and leave to enter and remain, as may be necessary, is granted and not revoked or curtailed, and an adoption order is made or an overseas adoption is effected, the child will be authorised to enter and reside permanently in the United Kingdom;

(b)   before visiting the child in the State of origin—

(i)   notify the adoption agency of the details of the child to be adopted;

(ii)   provide the adoption agency with any information and reports received from the relevant foreign authority; and

(iii)   [discuss with the adoption agency the] proposed adoption and information received from the relevant foreign authority;

    (c)   visit the child in the State of origin (and where the prospective adopters are a couple each of them); and

    (d)   after that visit—

        (i)   confirm in writing to the adoption agency that he has done so and wishes to proceed with the adoption;

        (ii)   provide the adoption agency with any additional reports and information received on or after that visit; and

        (iii)   notify the adoption agency of his expected date of entry into the United Kingdom with the child.

(3) The prospective adopter must accompany the child on entering the United Kingdom unless, in the case of a couple, the adoption agency and the relevant foreign authority have agreed that it is necessary for only one of them to do so.

(4) Except where an overseas adoption is or is to be effected, the prospective adopter must within the period of 14 days beginning with the date on which the child is brought into the United Kingdom give notice to the relevant local authority—

    (a)   of the child's arrival in the United Kingdom; and

    (b)   of his intention—

        (i)   to apply for an adoption order in accordance with section 44(2) of the Act; or

        (ii)   not to give the child a home.

(5) In a case where a prospective adopter has given notice in accordance with paragraph (4) and subsequently moves his home into the area of another local authority, he must within 14 days of that move confirm in writing to that authority, the child's entry into the United Kingdom and that notice of his intention—

    (a)   to apply for an adoption order in accordance with section 44(2) of the Act has been given to another local authority; or

    (b)   not to give the child a home,

has been given.

Amendment

Para (2): in sub-para (b)(iii) words in square brackets substituted by SI 2013/985, reg 10(1), Schedule, para 2(1), (3). Date in force: 1 July 2013: see SI 2013/985, reg 1.

5 Functions imposed on the local authority

(1) Where notice of intention to adopt has been given to the local authority, that authority must—

    (a)   if it has not already done so, set up a case record in respect of the child and place on it any information received from the—

        (i)   relevant foreign authority;

        (ii)   adoption agency, if it is not the local authority;

        (iii)   prospective adopter;

        (iv)   entry clearance officer; and

        (v)   Secretary of State, or as the case may be, the Assembly;

    (b)   send the prospective adopter's general practitioner written notification of the arrival in England or Wales of the child and send with that notification a written report of the child's health history and current state of health, so far as is known;

    (c)   send to the [clinical commissioning group] or Local Health Board (Wales), in whose area the prospective adopter has his home, [and to the National Health Service Commissioning Board if the prospective adopter's home is in England,] written notification of the arrival in England or Wales of the child;

    (d)   . . .

    (e)   ensure that the child and the prospective adopter are visited within one week of receipt of the notice of intention to adopt and thereafter not less than once a week until the review referred to in sub-paragraph (f) and thereafter at such frequency as the authority may decide;

(f)   carry out a review of the child's case not more than 4 weeks after receipt of the notice of intention to adopt and—

    (i)   visit and, if necessary, review not more than 3 months after that initial review; and

    (ii)   thereafter not more than 6 months after the date of the previous visit,

unless the child no longer has his home with the prospective adopter or an adoption order is made;

(g)   when carrying out a review consider—

    (i)   the child's needs, welfare and development, and whether any changes need to be made to meet his needs or assist his development;

    (ii)   the arrangements for the provision of adoption support services and whether there should be any re-assessment of the need for those services; and

    (iii)   the need for further visits and reviews; and

(h)   ensure that—

    (i)   advice is given as to the child's needs, welfare and development;

    (ii)   written reports are made of all visits and reviews of the case and placed on the child's case record; and

    (iii)   on such visits, where appropriate, advice is given as to the availability of adoption support services.

(2) Part 7 of the Agencies Regulations or corresponding Welsh provision (case records) shall apply to the case record set up in respect of the child as a consequence of this regulation as if that record had been set up under the Agencies Regulations or corresponding Welsh provision.

(3) In a case where the prospective adopter fails to make an application under section 50 or 51 of the Act within two years of the receipt by a local authority of the notice of intention to adopt the local authority must review the case.

(4) For the purposes of the review referred to in paragraph (3), the local authority must consider—

(a)   the child's needs, welfare and development, and whether any changes need to be made to meet his needs or assist his development;

(b)   the arrangements, if any, in relation to the exercise of parental responsibility for the child;

(c)   the terms upon which leave to enter the United Kingdom is granted and the immigration status of the child;

(d)   the arrangements for the provision of adoption support services for the adoptive family and whether there should be any re-assessment of the need for those services; and

(e)   in conjunction with the appropriate agencies, the arrangements for meeting the child's health care and educational needs.

(5) In a case where the local authority to which notice of intention to adopt is given ("the original authority") is notified by the prospective adopter that he intends to move or has moved his home into the area of another local authority, the original authority must notify the local authority into whose area the prospective adopter intends to move or has moved, within 14 days of receiving information in respect of that move, of—

(a)   the name, sex, date and place of birth of child;

(b)   the prospective adopter's name, sex and date of birth;

(c)   the date on which the child entered the United Kingdom;

> (d)   where the original authority received notification of intention to adopt, the date of receipt of such notification whether an application for an adoption order has been made and the stage of those proceedings; and
>
> (e)   any other relevant information.

Amendment

Para (1): in sub-para (c) words in first pair of square brackets substituted and words in second pair of square brackets inserted by SI 2013/235, art 11, Sch 2, Pt 1, para 80(1), (2). Date in force: 1 April 2013: see SI 2013/235, art 1(2).

Para (1): sub-para (d) revoked by SI 2010/1172, art 5, Sch 3, para 53(1), (2). Date in force: 5 May 2010: see SI 2010/1172, art 2(1).

6 Application of Chapter 3 of the Act

In the case of a child brought into the United Kingdom for adoption in circumstances where section 83 of the Act applies—

(a)   the modifications in regulations 7 to 9 apply;

(b)   section 36(2) and (5) (restrictions on removal) and section 39(3)(a) (partners of parents) of the Act shall not apply.

7 Change of name and removal from the United Kingdom

Section 28(2) of the Act (further consequences of placement) shall apply as if from the words "is placed" to "then", there is substituted "enters the United Kingdom in the circumstances where section 83(1)(a) of this Act applies".

8 Return of the child

(1) Section 35 of the Act (return of child) shall apply with the following modifications.

(2) Subsections (1), (2) and (3) shall apply as if in each place where—

(a)   the words "is placed for adoption by an adoption agency" occur there were substituted "enters the United Kingdom in circumstances where section 83(1) applies";

(b)   the words "the agency" occur there were substituted the words "the local authority"; and

(c)   the words "any parent or guardian of the child" occur there were substituted "the Secretary of State or, as the case may be, the Assembly".

(3) Subsection (5) shall apply as if for the words "an adoption agency" or "the agency" there were substituted the words "the local authority".

9 Child to live with adopters before application

(1) In a case where the requirements imposed by section 83(4) of the Act have been complied with and the conditions required by section 83(5) of the Act have been met, section 42 shall apply as if—

(a)   subsection (3) is omitted; and

(b)   in subsection (5) the words from "three years" to "preceding" there were substituted "six months".

(2) In a case where the requirements imposed by section 83(4) of the Act have not been complied with or the conditions required by section 83(5) have not been met, section 42 shall apply as if—

(a)   subsection (3) is omitted; and

(b)   in subsection (5) the words from "three years" to "preceding" there were substituted "twelve months".

CHAPTER 2

Taking Children out of the United Kingdom

10 Requirements applicable in respect of giving parental responsibility prior to adoption abroad

The prescribed requirements for the purposes of section 84(3) of the Act (requirements to be satisfied prior to the making of an order) are that—

    (a)   in the case of a child placed by an adoption agency, that agency has—

        (i)   confirmed to the court that it has complied with the requirements imposed in accordance with Part 3 of the Agencies Regulations or corresponding Welsh provision;

        (ii)   submitted to the court—

            (aa)   the reports and information referred to in regulation [17(2D) and (3), as appropriate] of the Agencies Regulations or corresponding Welsh provision;

            (bb)   the recommendations made by the adoption panel in accordance with regulations 18 (placing child for adoption)[, where applicable,] and 33 (proposed placement) of the Agencies Regulations or corresponding Welsh provision

            (cc)   the adoption placement report prepared in accordance with regulation 31(2)(d) of the Agencies Regulations or corresponding Welsh provision;

            (dd)   the reports of and information obtained in respect of the visits and reviews referred to in regulation 36 of the Agencies Regulations or corresponding Welsh provision; and

            (ee)   the report referred to in section 43 of the Act as modified by regulation 11;

    (b)   in the case of a child placed by an adoption agency the relevant foreign authority has—

        (i)   confirmed in writing to that agency that the prospective adopter has been counselled and the legal implications of adoption have been explained to him;

        (ii)   prepared a report on the suitability of the prospective adopter to be an adoptive parent;

        (iii)   determined and confirmed in writing to that agency that he is eligible and suitable to adopt in the country or territory in which the adoption is to be effected; and

        (iv)   confirmed in writing to that agency that the child is or will be authorised to enter and reside permanently in that foreign country or territory; and

    (c)   in the case of a child placed by an adoption agency the prospective adopter has confirmed in writing to the adoption agency that he will accompany the child on taking him out of the United Kingdom and entering the country or territory where the adoption is to be effected, or in the case of a couple, the agency and relevant foreign authority have confirmed that it is necessary for only one of them to do so.

Amendment

In para (a)(ii)(aa) words "17(2D) and (3), as appropriate" in square brackets substituted by SI 2012/1410, regs 8, 9(a). Date in force: 1 September 2012: see SI 2012/1410, reg 1.

In para (a)(ii)(bb) words ", where applicable," in square brackets inserted by SI 2012/1410, regs 8, 9(b). Date in force: 1 September 2012: see SI 2012/1410, reg 1.

11 Application of the Act in respect of orders under section 84

(1)   The following provisions of the Act which refer to adoption orders shall apply to orders under section 84 as if in each place where the words "adoption order" appear there were substituted "order under section 84"—

(a)   section 1(7)(a) (coming to a decision relating to adoption of a child);

(b)   section 18(4) (placement for adoption by agencies);

(c)   section 21(4)(b) (placement orders);

(d)   section 22(5)(a) and (b) (application for placement orders);

(e)   section 24(4) (revoking placement orders);

(f)   section 28(1) (further consequences of placement);

(g)   section 29(4)(a) and (5)(a) (further consequences of placement orders);

(h)   section 32(5) (recovery by parent etc where child placed and consent withdrawn);

(i)   section 42(7) (sufficient opportunity for adoption agency to see the child);

(j)   section 43 (reports where child placed by agency);

(k)   section 44(2) (notice of intention to adopt);

(l)   section 47(1) to (5), (8) and (9) (conditions for making orders);

(m)   section 48(1) (restrictions on making applications);

(n)   section 50(1) and (2) (adoption by a couple);

(o)   section 51(1) to (4) (adoption by one person);

(p)   section 52(1) to (4) (parental etc consent);

(q)   section 53(5) (contribution towards maintenance); and

(r)   section 141(3) and (4)(c) (rules of procedure).

(2)   Section 35(5) of the Act (return of child in other cases) shall apply to orders under section 84 of that Act as if in paragraph (b) of that subsection—

(a)   for the first reference to "adoption order" there were substituted "order under section 84(1)"; and

(b)   the words in brackets were omitted.

PART 3

ADOPTIONS UNDER THE CONVENTION

CHAPTER 1

REQUIREMENTS, PROCEDURE, RECOGNITION AND EFFECT OF ADOPTIONS WHERE THE UNITED KINGDOM IS THE RECEIVING STATE

12 Application of Chapter 1

The provisions in this Chapter shall apply where a couple or a person, habitually resident in the British Islands, wishes to adopt a child who is habitually resident in a Convention country outside the British Islands in accordance with the Convention.

13 Requirements applicable in respect of eligibility and suitability

(1)   A couple or a person who wishes to adopt a child habitually resident in a Convention country outside the British Islands shall—

[(a)   in the case of an adoption agency in Wales, apply in writing to the adoption agency for a determination of eligibility and an assessment of their suitability to adopt, and give the agency any information it may require for the purposes of the assessment, or

(b)   in the case of an adoption agency in England, notify the agency that they want to adopt a child, and give the agency any information it may require for the purposes of the pre-assessment process set out in Part 4 of the Agencies Regulations].

[(2) An adoption agency in Wales may not consider an application under paragraph (1)(a), and an adoption agency in England may not proceed with the pre-assessment process referred to in paragraph (1)(b), unless at the date of that application or notification (as the case may be)—]

    (a)   in the case of an application by a couple, they have both—
        (i)   attained the age of 21 years; and
        (ii)   been habitually resident in a part of the British Islands for a period of not less than one year ending with the date of application; and
    (b)   in the case of an application by one person, he has—
        (i)   attained the age of 21 years; and
        (ii)   been habitually resident in a part of the British Islands for a period of not less than one year ending with the date of application.

Amendment

Para (1): sub-paras (a), (b) substituted by SI 2013/985, reg 10(1), Schedule, para 2(1), (4)(a). Date in force: 1 July 2013: see SI 2013/985, reg 1.

Para (2): words in square brackets substituted by SI 2013/985, reg 10(1), Schedule, para 2(1), (4)(b). Date in force: 1 July 2013: see SI 2013/985, reg 1.

14 Counselling and information

(1) An adoption agency must provide a counselling service in accordance with [regulation 24(1)(a)] of the Agencies Regulations or corresponding Welsh provision and must—

    (a)   explain to the prospective adopter the procedure in relation to, and the legal implications of, adopting a child from the State of origin from which the prospective adopter wishes to adopt in accordance with the Convention; and
    (b)   provide him with written information about the matters referred to in sub-paragraph (a).

(2) Paragraph (1) does not apply if the adoption agency is satisfied that the requirements set out in that paragraph have been carried out in respect of the prospective adopter by another agency.

Amendment

Para (1): words in square brackets substituted by SI 2013/985, reg 10(1), Schedule, para 2(1), (5). Date in force: 1 July 2013: see SI 2013/985, reg 1.

15 Procedure in respect of carrying out an assessment

[(1) Where the adoption agency is satisfied that that the requirements in regulation 14 have been met the agency must consider the suitability of the prospective adopter in accordance with Part 4 of the Agencies Regulations.]

(3) The adoption agency must place on the prospective adopter's case record any information obtained as a consequence of this Chapter.

(4) The adoption agency must include in the prospective adopter's report—

    (a)   the State of origin from which the prospective adopter wishes to adopt a child;
    (b)   confirmation that the prospective adopter is eligible to adopt a child under the law of that State;
    (c)   any additional information obtained as a consequence of the requirements of that State; and
    (d)   the agency's assessment of the prospective adopter's suitability to adopt a child who is habitually resident in that State.

(5) The references to information in [regulations 30(2) and 30A(2)] of the Agencies Regulations or corresponding Welsh provisions shall include information obtained by the adoption agency or adoption panel as a consequence of this regulation.

Amendment

Para (1): substituted, in relation to England, for original paras (1), (2), by SI 2013/985, reg 10, Schedule, para 2(1), (6)(a). Date in force: 1 July 2013: see SI 2013/985, reg 1.

Para (5): words in square brackets substituted, in relation to England, by SI 2013/985, reg 10, Schedule, para 2(1), (6)(b). Date in force: 1 July 2013: see SI 2013/985, reg 1.

16 Adoption agency decision and notification

The adoption agency must make a decision about whether the prospective adopter is suitable to adopt a child in accordance with [regulation 30B] of the Agencies Regulations and regulations made under section 45 of the Act, or corresponding Welsh provisions.

Amendment

Words in square brackets substituted by SI 2013/985, reg 10(1), Schedule, para 2(1), (7). Date in force: 1 July 2013: see SI 2013/985, reg 1.

17 Review and termination of approval

The adoption agency must review the approval of each prospective adopter in accordance with [regulation 30D] of the Agencies Regulations or corresponding Welsh provision unless the agency has received written notification from the relevant Central Authority that the agreement under Article 17(c) of the Convention has been made.

Amendment

Words in square brackets substituted by SI 2013/985, reg 10(1), Schedule, para 2(1), (8). Date in force: 1 July 2013: see SI 2013/985, reg 1.

18 Procedure following decision as to suitability to adopt

(1) Where an adoption agency has made a decision that the prospective adopter is suitable to adopt a child in accordance with regulation 16, it must send to the relevant Central Authority—

- (a) written confirmation of the decision and any recommendation the agency may make in relation to the number of children the prospective adopter may be suitable to adopt, their age range, sex, likely needs and background;
- (b) the enhanced criminal record certificate obtained under [regulation 25] of the Agencies Regulations or corresponding Welsh provision;
- (c) all the documents and information which were passed to the adoption panel in accordance with [regulations 30(6) or (7)] of the Agencies Regulations or corresponding Welsh provision;
- (d) the record of the proceedings of the adoption panel, its recommendation and the reasons for its recommendation; and
- (e) any other information relating to the case as the relevant Central Authority or the CA of the State of origin may require.

(2) If the relevant Central Authority is satisfied that the adoption agency has complied with the duties and procedures imposed by the Agencies Regulations or corresponding Welsh provision, and that all the relevant information has been supplied by that agency, the Authority must send to the CA of the State of origin—

- (a) the prospective adopter's report prepared in accordance with [regulation 30] of the Agencies Regulations or corresponding Welsh provision;
- (b) . . .
- (c) a copy of the adoption agency's decision and the adoption panel's recommendation;
- (d) any other information that the CA of the State of origin may require;
- [(da) if the prospective adopter applied to the appropriate Minister for a review under section 12 of the Adoption and Children Act 2002, the

record of the proceedings of the panel, its recommendation and the reasons for its recommendation; and]

    (e)   a certificate in the form set out in Schedule 1 confirming that the—

        (i)   prospective adopter is eligible to adopt;

        (ii)   prospective adopter has been assessed in accordance with this Chapter;

        (iii)   prospective adopter has been approved as suitable to adopt a child; and

        (iv)   child will be authorised to enter and reside permanently in the United Kingdom if entry clearance, and leave to enter or remain as may be necessary, is granted and not revoked or curtailed and a Convention adoption order or Convention adoption is made.

(3)   The relevant Central Authority must notify the adoption agency and the prospective adopter in writing that the certificate and the documents referred to in paragraph (2) have been sent to the CA of the State of origin.

Amendment

Para (1): in sub-para (b) words in square brackets substituted by SI 2013/985, reg 10(1), Schedule, para 2(1), (9)(a). Date in force: 1 July 2013: see SI 2013/985, reg 1.

Para (1): in sub-para (c) words in square brackets substituted by SI 2013/985, reg 10(1), Schedule, para 2(1), (9)(b). Date in force: 1 July 2013: see SI 2013/985, reg 1.

Para (2): in sub-para (a) words in square brackets substituted by SI 2013/985, reg 10(1), Schedule, para 2(1), (9)(c).Date in force: 1 July 2013: see SI 2013/985, reg 1.

Para (2): sub-para (b) revoked by SI 2005/3482, reg 6(a)(i). Date in force: 30 December 2005: see SI 2005/3482, reg 1.

Para (2): in sub-para (d) word omitted revoked by SI 2005/3482, reg 6(a)(ii). Date in force: 30 December 2005: see SI 2005/3482, reg 1.

Para (2): sub-para (da) inserted by SI 2005/3482, reg 6(a)(iii). Date in force: 30 December 2005: see SI 2005/3482, reg 1.

19 Procedure following receipt of the Article 16 Information from the CA of the State of origin

(1)   Where the relevant Central Authority receives from the CA of the State of origin, the Article 16 Information relating to the child whom the CA of the State of origin considers should be placed for adoption with the prospective adopter, the relevant Central Authority must send that Information to the adoption agency.

(2)   The adoption agency must consider the Article 16 Information and—

    (a)   send that Information to the prospective adopter;

    (b)   [discuss with the prospective adopter]—

        (i)   that Information;

        (ii)   the proposed placement;

        (iii)   the availability of adoption support services; and

    (c)   if appropriate, offer a counselling service and further information as required.

[(3)   Where—

    (a)   the procedure in paragraph (2) has been followed;

    (b)   the prospective adopter has confirmed in writing to the adoption agency that he wishes to proceed to adopt the child,

the agency must notify the relevant Central Authority in writing that the requirements specified in sub-paragraphs (a) and (b) have been satisfied and at the same time it must confirm that it is content for the adoption to proceed.]

(4)   Where the relevant Central Authority has received notification from the adoption agency under paragraph (3), the relevant Central Authority shall—

    (a)   notify the CA of the State of origin that—

        (i)   the prospective adopter wishes to proceed to adopt the child;

    (ii)   it is prepared to agree with the CA of the State of origin that the adoption may proceed; and

  (b)   confirm to the CA of the State of origin that—

    (i)   in the case where the requirements specified in section 1(5A) of the British Nationality Act 1981 are met that the child will be authorised to enter and reside permanently in the United Kingdom; or

    (ii)   in any other case, if entry clearance and leave to enter and remain, as may be necessary, is granted and not revoked or curtailed and a Convention adoption order or a Convention adoption is made, the child will be authorised to enter and reside permanently in the United Kingdom.

(5) The relevant Central Authority must inform the adoption agency and the prospective adopter when the agreement under Article 17(c) of the Convention has been made.

(6) For the purposes of this regulation and regulation 20 "the Article 16 Information" means—

  (a)   the report referred to in Article 16(1) of the Convention including information about the child's identity, adoptability, background, social environment, family history, medical history including that of the child's family and any special needs of the child;

  (b)   proof of confirmation that the consents of the persons, institutions and authorities whose consents are necessary for adoption have been obtained in accordance with Article 4 of the Convention; and

  (c)   the reasons for the CA of the State of origin's determination on the placement.

Amendment

Para (2): in sub-para (b) words in square brackets substituted by SI 2013/985, reg 10(1), Schedule, para 2(1), (10). Date in force: 1 July 2013: see SI 2013/985, reg 1.

Para (3): substituted by SI 2009/2563, reg 2(1), (2). Date in force: 23 October 2009: see SI 2009/2563, reg 1.

20 Procedure where proposed adoption is not to proceed

(1) If, at any stage before the agreement under Article 17(c) of the Convention is made, the CA of the State of origin notifies the relevant Central Authority that it has decided the proposed placement should not proceed—

  (a)   the relevant Central Authority must inform the adoption agency of the CA of the State of origin's decision;

  (b)   the agency must then inform the prospective adopter and return the Article 16 Information to the relevant Central Authority; and

  (c)   the relevant Central Authority must then return those documents to the CA of the State of origin.

(2) Where at any stage before the adoption agency receives notification of the agreement under Article 17(c) of the Convention the approval of the prospective adopter is reviewed under [regulation 30D] of the Agencies Regulations or corresponding Welsh provision, and as a consequence, the agency determines that the prospective adopter is no longer suitable to adopt a child—

  (a)   the agency must inform the relevant Central Authority and return the documents referred to in regulation 19(1);

  (b)   the relevant Central Authority must notify the CA of the State of origin and return those documents.

(3) If, at any stage [before any Convention adoption is made and before the child's entry into the United Kingdom], the prospective adopter notifies the adoption agency that he does not wish to proceed with the adoption of the child—

(a) that agency must inform the relevant Central Authority and return the documents to that Authority; and

(b) the relevant Central Authority must notify the CA of the State of origin of the prospective adopter's decision and return the documents to the CA of the State of origin.

Amendment

Para (2): words in square brackets substituted by SI 2013/985, reg 10(1), Schedule, para 2(1), (11). Date in force: 1 July 2013: see SI 2013/985, reg

Para (3): words in square brackets substituted by SI 2009/2563, reg 2(1), (3). Date in force: 23 October 2009: see SI 2009/2563, reg 1.

21 Applicable requirements in respect of prospective adopter entering the United Kingdom with a child

Following any agreement under Article 17(c) of the Convention, the prospective adopter must—

(a) notify the adoption agency of his expected date of entry into the United Kingdom with the child;

(b) confirm to the adoption agency when the child is placed with him by the competent authority in the State of origin; and

(c) accompany the child on entering the United Kingdom unless, in the case of a couple, the adoption agency and the CA of the State of origin have agreed that it is necessary for only one of them to do so.

22 Applicable requirements in respect of an adoption agency before the child enters the United Kingdom

Where the adoption agency is informed by the relevant Central Authority that the agreement under Article 17(c) of the Convention has been made and the adoption may proceed, before the child enters the United Kingdom that agency must—

(a) send the prospective adopter's general practitioner written notification of the proposed placement and send with that notification a written report of the child's health history and current state of health, so far as it is known; [and]

(b) send the local authority (if that authority is not the adoption agency) and the [clinical commissioning group] or Local Health Board (Wales), in whose area the prospective adopter has his home, [and to the National Health Service Commissioning Board if the prospective adopter's home is in England,] written notification of the proposed arrival of the child into England or Wales [and, where the child is of compulsory school age, include in the notification to the local authority information about the child's educational history and whether the child has been or is likely to be assessed for special educational needs under the Education Act 1996]

(c) . . . .

Amendment

In para (a) word in square brackets inserted by SI 2010/1172, art 5, Sch 3, para 53(1), (3)(a). Date in force: 5 May 2010: see SI 2010/1172, art 2(1).

In para (b) words "clinical commissioning group" in square brackets substituted by SI 2013/235, art 11, Sch 2, Pt 1, para 80(1), (3)(a). Date in force: 1 April 2013: see SI 2013/235, art 1(2).

In para (b) words from "and to the" to "is in England," in square brackets inserted by SI 2013/235, art 11, Sch 2, Pt 1, para 80(1), (3)(b). Date in force: 1 April 2013: see SI 2013/235, art 1(2).

In para (b) words from "and, where the child" to "Education Act 1996" in square brackets substituted by SI 2010/1172, art 5, Sch 3, para 53(1), (3)(b). Date in force: 5 May 2010: see SI 2010/1172, art 2(1).

Para (c) revoked by SI 2010/1172, art 5, Sch 3, para 53(1), (3)(c). Date in force: 5 May 2010: see SI 2010/1172, art 2(1).

23 Applicable provisions following the child's entry into the United Kingdom where no Convention adoption is made

Regulations 24 to 27 apply where—

    (a)   following the agreement between the relevant Central Authority and the CA of the State of origin under Article 17(c) of the Convention that the adoption may proceed, no Convention adoption is made, or applied for, in the State of origin; and

    (b)   the child is placed with the prospective adopter in the State of origin who then returns to England or Wales with that child.

24 Applicable requirements in respect of prospective adopter following child's entry into the United Kingdom

(1)   A prospective adopter must within the period of 14 days beginning with the date on which the child enters the United Kingdom give notice to the relevant local authority—

    (a)   of the child's arrival in the United Kingdom; and

    (b)   of his intention—

        (i)   to apply for an adoption order in accordance with section 44(2) of the Act; or

        (ii)   not to give the child a home.

(2)   In a case where a prospective adopter has given notice in accordance with paragraph (1) and he subsequently moves his home into the area of another local authority, he must within 14 days of that move confirm to that authority in writing the child's entry into the United Kingdom and that notice of his intention—

    (a)   to apply for an adoption order in accordance with section 44(2) of the Act has been given to another local authority; or

    (b)   not to give the child a home,

has been given.

25 Functions imposed on the local authority following the child's entry into the United Kingdom

(1)   Where notice is given to a local authority in accordance with regulation 24, the functions imposed on the local authority by virtue of regulation 5 shall apply subject to the modifications in paragraph (2).

(2)   Paragraph (1) of regulation 5 shall apply as if—

    (a)   in sub-paragraph (a)—

        (i)   in head (i) for the words "relevant foreign authority" there is substituted "CA of the State of origin and competent foreign authority";

        (ii)   in head (v) there is substituted "the relevant Central Authority"; and

    (b)   sub-paragraphs (b) to (d) were omitted.

[26 Prospective adopter unable to proceed with adoption

(1)   Where the prospective adopter gives notice to the relevant local authority that he does not wish to proceed with the adoption and no longer wishes to give the child a home, he must return the child to that authority not later than the end of the period of seven days beginning with the date on which notice was given.

(2)   Where a relevant local authority have received a notice in accordance with paragraph (1), that authority must give notice to the relevant Central Authority of the decision of the prospective adopter not to proceed with the adoption.]

Amendment

Substituted by SI 2005/3482, reg 6 as from 30 December 2005.

27 Withdrawal of child from prospective adopter

(1) Where the relevant local authority are of the opinion that the continued placement of the child is not in the child's best interests—

    (a)   that authority must give notice to the prospective adopter of their opinion and request the return of the child to them; and

    (b)   subject to paragraph (3), the prospective adopter must, not later than the end of the period of seven days beginning with the date on which notice was given, return the child to that authority.

(2) Where the relevant local authority has given notice under paragraph (1), that authority must at the same time notify the relevant Central Authority that they have requested the return of the child.

(3) Where notice is given under paragraph (1) but—

    (a)   an application for a Convention adoption order was made prior to the giving of that notice; and

    (b)   the application has not been disposed of,

the prospective adopter is not required by virtue of paragraph (1) to return the child unless the court so orders.

(4) This regulation does not affect the exercise by any local authority or other person of any power conferred by any enactment or the exercise of any power of arrest.

28 Breakdown of placement

(1) This regulation applies where—

    (a)   notification is given by the prospective adopter under regulation 26 (unable to proceed with adoption);

    (b)   the child is withdrawn from the prospective adopter under regulation 27 (withdrawal of child from prospective adopter);

    (c)   an application for a Convention adoption order is refused;

    (d)   a Convention adoption which is subject to a probationary period cannot be made; or

    (e)   a Convention adoption order or a Convention adoption is annulled pursuant to section 89(1) of the Act.

(2) Where the relevant local authority are satisfied that it would be in the child's best interests to be placed for adoption with another prospective adopter habitually resident in the United Kingdom they must take the necessary measures to identify a suitable adoptive parent for that child.

(3) Where the relevant local authority have identified and approved another prospective adopter who is eligible, and has been assessed as suitable, to adopt in accordance with these Regulations—

    (a)   that authority must notify the relevant Central Authority in writing that—

        (i)   another prospective adopter has been identified; and

        (ii)   the provisions in regulations 14, 15 and 16 have been complied with; and

    (b)   the requirements specified in regulations 18 and 19 have been complied with.

(4) Where the relevant Central Authority has been notified in accordance with paragraph (3)(a)—

    (a)   it shall inform the CA of the State of origin of the proposed placement; and

    (b)   it shall agree the placement with the CA of the State of origin in accordance with the provisions in this Chapter.

(5) Subject to paragraph (2), where the relevant local authority is not satisfied it would be in the child's best interests to be placed for adoption with another

prospective adopter in England or Wales, it must liaise with the relevant Central Authority to arrange for the return of the child to his State of origin.

(6) Before coming to any decision under this regulation, the relevant local authority must have regard to the wishes and feelings of the child, having regard to his age and understanding, and where appropriate, obtain his consent in relation to measures to be taken under this regulation.

29 Convention adoptions subject to a probationary period

(1) This regulation applies where—

    (a)   the child has been placed with the prospective adopters by the competent authority in the State of origin and a Convention adoption has been applied for by the prospective adopters in the State of origin but the child's placement with the prospective adopter is subject to a probationary period before the Convention adoption is made; and

    (b)   the prospective adopter returns to England or Wales with the child before that probationary period is completed and the Convention adoption is made in the State of origin.

(2) The relevant local authority must, if requested by the competent authority of the State of origin, submit a report about the placement to that authority and such a report must be prepared within such timescales and contain such information as the competent authority may reasonably require.

30 Report of local authority investigation

The report of the investigation which a local authority must submit to the court in accordance with section 44(5) of the Act must include—

    (a)   confirmation that the Certificate of eligibility and approval has been sent to the CA of the State of origin in accordance with regulation 18;

    (b)   the date on which the agreement under Article 17(c) of the Convention was made; and

    (c)   details of the reports of the visits and reviews made in accordance with regulation 5 as modified by regulation 25.

31 Convention adoption order

An adoption order shall not be made as a Convention adoption order unless—

    (a)   in the case of—

        (i)   an application by a couple, both members of the couple have been habitually resident in any part of the British Islands for a period of not less than one year ending with the date of the application; or

        (ii)   an application by one person, the applicant has been habitually resident in any part of the British Islands for a period of not less than one year ending with the date of the application;

    (b)   the child to be adopted was, on the date on which the agreement under Article 17(c) of the Convention was made, habitually resident in a Convention country outside the British Islands; and

    (c)   in a case where one member of a couple (in the case of an application by a couple) or the applicant (in the case of an application by one person) is not a British citizen, the Home Office has confirmed that the child is authorised to enter and reside permanently in the United Kingdom.

32 Requirements following a Convention adoption order or Convention adoption

(1) Where the relevant Central Authority receives a copy of a Convention adoption order made by a court in England or Wales that Authority must issue a certificate in the form set out in Schedule 2 certifying that the adoption has been made in accordance with the Convention.

(2) A copy of the certificate issued under paragraph (1) must be sent to the—

    (a)   CA of the State of origin;

(b)   adoptive parent; and

(c)   adoption agency and, if different, the relevant local authority.

(3)   Where a Convention adoption is made and the relevant Central Authority receives a certificate under Article 23 of the Convention in respect of that Convention adoption, the relevant Central Authority must send a copy of that certificate to the—

(a)   adoptive parent; and

(b)   adoption agency and, if different, the relevant local authority.

33 Refusal of a court in England or Wales to make a Convention adoption order

Where an application for a Convention adoption order is refused by the court or is withdrawn, the prospective adopter must return the child to the relevant local authority within the period determined by the court.

34 Annulment of a Convention adoption order or a Convention adoption

Where a Convention adoption order or a Convention adoption is annulled under section 89(1) of the Act and the relevant Central Authority receives a copy of the order from the court, it must forward a copy of that order to the CA of the State of origin.

CHAPTER 2

REQUIREMENTS, PROCEDURE, RECOGNITION AND EFFECT OF ADOPTIONS IN
ENGLAND AND WALES WHERE THE UNITED KINGDOM IS THE STATE OF ORIGIN

35 Application of Chapter 2

The provisions in this Chapter shall apply where a couple or a person habitually resident in a Convention country outside the British Islands, wishes to adopt a child who is habitually resident in the British Islands in accordance with the Convention.

36 Counselling and information for the child

(1)   Where an adoption agency is considering whether a child is suitable for an adoption in accordance with the Convention, it must provide a counselling service for and information to that child in accordance with regulation 13 of the Agencies Regulations or corresponding Welsh provision and it must—

(a)   explain to the child in an appropriate manner the procedure in relation to, and the legal implications of, adoption under the Convention for that child by a prospective adopter habitually resident in the receiving State; and

(b)   provide him with written information about the matters referred to in sub-paragraph (a).

(2)   Paragraph (1) does not apply if the adoption agency is satisfied that the requirements set out in that paragraph have been carried out in respect of the prospective adopter by another agency.

37 Counselling and information for the parent or guardian of the child etc

(1)   An adoption agency must provide a counselling service and information in accordance with regulation 14 of the Agencies Regulations or corresponding Welsh provision for the parent or guardian of the child and, where regulation 14(4) of the Agencies Regulations or corresponding Welsh provision applies, for the father.

(2)   The adoption agency must also—

(a)   explain to the parent or guardian, and, where regulation 14(4) of the Agencies Regulations or corresponding Welsh provision applies, the father the procedure in relation to, and the legal implications of, adoption under the Convention by a prospective adopter in a receiving State; and

(b)   provide him with written information about the matters referred to in sub-paragraph (a).

(3) Paragraphs (1) and (2) do not apply if the adoption agency is satisfied that the requirements set out in that paragraph have been carried out in respect of the prospective adopter by another agency.

38 Requirements in respect of the child's permanence report and information for the adoption panel

(1) The child's permanence report which the adoption agency is required to prepare in accordance with regulation 17 of the Agencies Regulations or corresponding Welsh provision must include—

    (a)   a summary of the possibilities for placement of the child within the United Kingdom; and

    (b)   an assessment of whether an adoption by a person in a particular receiving State is in the child's best interests.

(2) [In a case falling within regulation 17(2C) of the Agencies Regulations or the corresponding Welsh provision,] the adoption agency must send—

    (a)   if received, the Article 15 Report; and

    (b)   their observations on that Report,

together with the reports and information referred to in regulation [17(2D)] of the Agencies Regulations or corresponding Welsh provision to the adoption panel.

(3) In a case falling within regulation 17(2) of the Agencies Regulations or the corresponding Welsh provision, the adoption agency must consider—

    (a)   if received, the Article 15 Report; and

    (b)   their observations on that Report together with the reports and information referred to in regulation 17(2D) of the Agencies Regulations or the corresponding Welsh provision

in deciding whether the child should be placed for adoption in accordance with the Convention.]

Amendment

Para (2): words from "In a case" to "corresponding Welsh provision," in square brackets inserted by SI 2012/1410, regs 8, 10(a). Date in force: 1 September 2012: see SI 2012/1410, reg 1.

Para (2): reference to "17(2D)" in square brackets substituted by SI 2012/1410, regs 8, 10(b). Date in force: 1 September 2012: see SI 2012/1410, reg 1.

Para (3): inserted by SI 2012/1410, regs 8, 10(c). Date in force: 1 September 2012: see SI 2012/1410, reg 1.

39 Recommendation of adoption panel

Where an adoption panel make a recommendation in accordance with regulation 18(1) of the Agencies Regulations or corresponding Welsh provision it must consider and take into account the Article 15 Report, if available, and the observations thereon together with the information passed to it as a consequence of regulation 38.

40 Adoption agency decision and notification

Where the adoption agency decides in accordance with regulation 19 of the Agencies Regulations or corresponding Welsh provision that the child should be placed for an adoption in accordance with the Convention it must notify the relevant Central Authority of—

    (a)   the name, sex and age of the child;

    (b)   the reasons why they consider that the child may be suitable for such an adoption;

    (c)   whether a prospective adopter has been identified and, if so, provide any relevant information; and

    (d)   any other information that Authority may require.

41 Convention list

(1) The relevant Central Authority is to maintain a Convention list of children who are notified to that Authority under regulation 40 and shall make the contents of that list available for consultation by other Authorities within the British Islands.

(2) Where an adoption agency—

    (a)   places for adoption a child whose details have been notified to the relevant Central Authority under regulation 40; or

    (b)   determines that an adoption in accordance with the Convention is no longer in the best interests of the child,

it must notify the relevant Central Authority accordingly and that Authority must remove the details relating to that child from the Convention list.

42 Receipt of the Article 15 Report from the CA of the receiving State

(1) This regulation applies where—

    (a)   the relevant Central Authority receives a report from the CA of the receiving State which has been prepared for the purposes of Article 15 of the Convention ("the Article 15 Report");

    (b)   the Article 15 Report relates to a prospective adopter who is habitually resident in that receiving State; and

    (c)   the prospective adopter named in the Article 15 Report wishes to adopt a child who is habitually resident in the British Islands.

(2) Subject to paragraph (3), if the relevant Central Authority is satisfied the prospective adopter meets the following requirements—

    (a)   the age requirements as specified in section 50 of the Act in the case of adoption by a couple, or section 51 of the Act in the case of adoption by one person; and

    (b)   in the case of a couple, both are, or in the case of adoption by one person, that person is habitually resident in a Convention country outside the British Islands,

that Authority must consult the Convention list and may, if the Authority considers it appropriate, consult any Convention list maintained by another Central Authority within the British Islands.

(3) Where a prospective adopter has already been identified in relation to a proposed adoption of a particular child and the relevant Central Authority is satisfied that prospective adopter meets the requirements referred to in paragraph (2)(a) and (b), that Authority—

    (a)   need not consult the Convention list; and

    (b)   must send the Article 15 Report to the local authority which referred the child's details to the Authority.

(4) The relevant Central Authority may pass a copy of the Article 15 Report to any other Central Authority within the British Islands for the purposes of enabling that Authority to consult its Convention list.

(5) Where the relevant Central Authority identifies a child on the Convention list who may be suitable for adoption by the prospective adopter, that Authority must send the Article 15 Report to the local authority which referred the child's details to that Authority.

43 Proposed placement and referral to adoption panel

(1) Where the adoption agency is considering whether a proposed placement should proceed in accordance with the procedure provided for in regulation 31 of the Agencies Regulations or corresponding Welsh provision it must take into account the Article 15 Report.

(2) Where the adoption agency refers the proposal to place the child with the particular prospective adopter to the adoption panel in accordance with regulation 31

of the Agencies Regulations or corresponding Welsh provision, it must also send the Article 15 Report to the panel.

44 Consideration by adoption panel

The adoption panel must take into account when considering what recommendation to make in accordance with regulation 32(1) of the Agencies Regulations or corresponding Welsh provision the Article 15 Report and any other information passed to it as a consequence of the provisions in this Chapter.

45 Adoption agency's decision in relation to the proposed placement

(1) Regulation 33 of the Agencies Regulations or corresponding Welsh provision shall apply as if paragraph (3) of that regulation or corresponding Welsh provision was omitted.

(2) As soon as possible after the agency makes its decision, it must notify the relevant Central Authority of its decision.

(3) If the proposed placement is not to proceed—

    (a)   the adoption agency must return the Article 15 Report and any other documents or information sent to it by the relevant Central Authority to that Authority; and

    (b)   the relevant Central Authority must then send that Report, any such documents or such information to the CA of the receiving State.

46 Preparation of the Article 16 Information

(1) If the adoption agency decides that the proposed placement should proceed, it must prepare a report for the purposes of Article 16(1) of the Convention which must include—

    (a)   the information about the child which is specified in Schedule 1 to the Agencies Regulations or corresponding Welsh provision; and

    (b)   the reasons for their decision.

(2) The adoption agency must send the following to the relevant Central Authority—

    (a)   the report referred to in paragraph (1);

    (b)   details of any placement order or other orders, if any, made by the courts; and

    (c)   confirmation that the parent or guardian consents to the proposed adoption.

(3) The relevant Central Authority must then send the documents referred to in paragraph (2) to the CA of the receiving State.

47 Requirements to be met before the child is placed for adoption with prospective adopter

(1) The relevant Central Authority may notify the CA of the receiving State that it is prepared to agree that the adoption may proceed provided that CA has confirmed that—

    (a)   the prospective adopter has agreed to adopt the child and has received such counselling as may be necessary;

    (b)   the prospective adopter has confirmed that he will accompany the child to the receiving State, unless in the case of a couple, the adoption agency and the CA of the receiving State have agreed that it is only necessary for one of them to do so;

    (c)   it is content for the adoption to proceed;

    (d)   in the case where a Convention adoption is to be effected, it has explained to the prospective adopter the need to make an application under section 84(1) of the Act; and

(e) the child is or will be authorised to enter and reside permanently in the Convention country if a Convention adoption is effected or a Convention adoption order is made.

(2) The relevant Central Authority may not make an agreement under Article 17(c) of the Convention with the CA of the receiving State unless—

    (a) confirmation has been received in respect of the matters referred to in paragraph (1); and

    (b) the adoption agency has confirmed to the relevant Central Authority that—

        (i) it has met the prospective adopter and explained the requirement to make an application for an order under section 84 of the Act before the child can be removed from the United Kingdom;

        (ii) the prospective adopter has visited the child; and

        (iii) the prospective adopter is content for the adoption to proceed.

(3) An adoption agency may not place a child for adoption unless the agreement under Article 17(c) of the Convention has been made and the relevant Central Authority must advise that agency when that agreement has been made.

(4) In this regulation, the reference to "prospective adopter" means in the case of a couple, both of them.

48 Requirements in respect of giving parental responsibility prior to a proposed Convention adoption

In the case of a proposed Convention adoption, the prescribed requirements for the purposes of section 84(3) of the Act (requirements to be satisfied prior to making an order) are—

    (a) the competent authorities of the receiving State have—

        (i) prepared a report for the purposes of Article 15 of the Convention;

        (ii) determined and confirmed in writing that the prospective adoptive parent is eligible and suitable to adopt;

        (iii) ensured and confirmed in writing that the prospective adoptive parent has been counselled as may be necessary; and

        (iv) determined and confirmed in writing that the child is or will be authorised to enter and reside permanently in that State;

    (b) the report required for the purposes of Article 16(1) of the Convention has been prepared by the adoption agency;

    (c) the adoption agency confirms in writing that it has complied with the requirements imposed upon it under Part 3 of the Agencies Regulations or corresponding Welsh provision and this Chapter;

    (d) the adoption agency has obtained and made available to the court—

        (i) the reports and information referred to in regulation [17(2D)] of the Agencies Regulations or corresponding Welsh provision;

        (ii) the recommendation made by the adoption panel in accordance with regulations 18[, where applicable,] and 33 of the Agencies Regulations or corresponding Welsh provisions; and

        (iii) the adoption placement report prepared in accordance with regulation 31(2) of the Agencies Regulations or corresponding Welsh provision;

    (e) the adoption agency includes in their report submitted to the court in accordance with section 43(a) or 44(5) of the Act as modified respectively by regulation 11, details of any reviews and visits carried out as consequence of Part 6 of the Agencies Regulations or corresponding Welsh provision; and

(f)   the prospective adopter has confirmed in writing that he will accompany the child on taking the child out of the United Kingdom to travel to the receiving State or in the case of a couple the agency and competent foreign authority have confirmed that it is necessary for only one of them to do so.

Amendment

In para (d), reference to "17(2D)" in square brackets substituted by SI 2012/1410, regs 8, 11(a) and words ", where applicable," in square brackets inserted by SI 2012/1410, regs 8, 11(b). Date in force: 1 September 2012: see SI 2012/1410, reg 1.

49 Local authority report

In the case of a proposed application for a Convention adoption order, the report which a local authority must submit to the court in accordance with section 43(a) or 44(5) of the Act must include a copy of the—

(a)   Article 15 Report;

(b)   report prepared for the purposes of Article 16(1); and

(c)   written confirmation of the agreement under Article 17(c) of the Convention.

50 Convention adoption order

An adoption order shall not be made as a Convention adoption order unless—

(a)   in the case of—

(i)   an application by a couple, both members of the couple have been habitually resident in a Convention country outside the British Islands for a period of not less than one year ending with the date of the application; or

(aa)   an application by one person, the applicant has been habitually resident in a Convention country outside the British Islands for a period of not less than one year ending with the date of the application;

(b)   the child to be adopted was, on the date on which the agreement under Article 17(c) of the Convention was made, habitually resident in any part of the British Islands; and

(c)   the competent authority has confirmed that the child is authorised to enter and remain permanently in the Convention country in which the applicant is habitually resident.

51 Requirements following a Convention adoption order or Convention adoption

(1) Where the relevant Central Authority receives a copy of a Convention adoption order made by a court in England or Wales, that Authority must issue a certificate in the form set out in Schedule 2 certifying that the adoption has been made in accordance with the Convention.

(2) A copy of the certificate must be sent to the—

(a)   CA of the receiving State; and

(b)   the relevant local authority.

(3) Where a Convention adoption is made and the Central Authority receives a certificate under Article 23 in respect of that Convention adoption, the relevant Central Authority must send a copy of that certificate to the relevant local authority.

CHAPTER 3

Miscellaneous Provisions

52 Application, with or without modifications, of the Act

(1) Subject to the modifications provided for in this Chapter, the provisions of the Act shall apply to adoptions within the scope of the Convention so far as the nature of the provision permits and unless the contrary intention is shown.

53 Change of name and removal from the United Kingdom

In a case falling within Chapter 1 of this Part, section 28(2) of the Act shall apply as if—

(a)   at the end of paragraph (a), "or" was omitted;

(b)   at the end of paragraph (b) there were inserted "or (c) a child is placed by a competent foreign authority for the purposes of an adoption under the Convention,"; and

(c)   at the end of subsection (2) there were inserted "or the competent foreign authority consents to a change of surname.".

54 Removal of children

(1) In a case falling within Chapter 1 of this Part, sections 36 to 40 of the Act shall not apply.

(2) In a case falling within Chapter 2 of this Part—

(a)   section 36 of the Act shall apply, as if—

    (i)   for the words "an adoption order" in paragraphs (a) and (c) in subsection (1) there were substituted "a Convention adoption order"; and

    (ii)   subsection (2) was omitted; and

(b)   section 39 of the Act shall apply as if subsection (3)(a) was omitted.

55 Modifications of the Act in respect of orders under section 84 where child is to be adopted under the Convention

The modifications set out in regulation 11 shall apply in the case where a couple or person habitually resident in a Convention country outside the British Islands intend to adopt a child who is habitually resident in England or Wales in accordance with the Convention.

56 Child to live with adopters before application for a Convention adoption order

Section 42 of the Act shall apply as if—

(a)   subsections (1)(b) and (3) to (6) were omitted; and

(b)   in subsection (2) from the word "If" to the end of paragraph (b) there were substituted "In the case of an adoption under the Convention,".

57 Notice of intention to adopt

Section 44 of the Act shall apply as if subsection (3) was omitted.

58 Application for Convention adoption order

Section 49 of the Act shall apply as if—

(a)   in subsection (1), the words from "but only" to the end were omitted;

(b)   subsections (2) and (3) were omitted.

59 Offences

Any person who contravenes or fails to comply with—

    [(a)   regulation 24 (requirements in respect of prospective adopter following child's entry into the United Kingdom);

(b)   regulation 26(1) (return of child to relevant local authority where prospective adopter does not wish to proceed);

(c)   regulation 27(1)(b) (return of child to relevant local authority on request of local authority or by order of court); or

(d)   regulation 33 (refusal of a court in England or Wales to make a Convention adoption order)]

is guilty of an offence and liable on summary conviction to imprisonment for a term not exceeding three months, or a fine not exceeding level 5 on the standard scale, or both.

Amendment

Paras (a)–(d) substituted, for paras (a)–(c) as originally enacted, by SI 2005/3482, reg 6(c). Date in force: 30 December 2005: see SI 2005/3482, reg 1.

SCHEDULE 1
CERTIFICATE OF ELIGIBILITY AND APPROVAL

Regulation 18

To the Central Authority of the State of origin

Re . . . [name of applicant]

In accordance with Article 5 of the Convention, I hereby certify on behalf of the Central Authority for [England] [Wales] that . . . [name of applicant] has been counselled, is eligible to adopt and has been assessed and approved as suitable to adopt a child from . . . [State of origin] by . . . [public authority or accredited body for the purposes of the Convention].

The attached report has been prepared in accordance with Article 15 of the Convention for presentation to the competent authority in . . . [State of origin].

This certificate of eligibility and approval and the report under Article 15 of the Convention are provided on the condition that a Convention adoption or Convention adoption order will not be made until the agreement under Article 17(c) of the Convention has been made.

I confirm on behalf of the Central Authority that if following the agreement under Article 17(c) of the Convention that—

[in the case, where the requirements specified in section 1(5A) of the British Nationality Act 1981 are met that the child . . . [name] will be authorised to enter and reside permanently in the United Kingdom]; or

[in any other case, if entry clearance and leave to enter and remain, as may be necessary, is granted and not revoked, or curtailed and a Convention adoption order or Convention adoption is made, the child . . . [name] will be authorised to enter and reside permanently in the United Kingdom.]

Name

[On behalf of the Secretary of State, the Central Authority for England]

Date

[the National Assembly for Wales, the Central Authority for Wales]

SCHEDULE 2
CERTIFICATE THAT THE CONVENTION ADOPTION ORDER HAS BEEN MADE IN ACCORDANCE WITH THE CONVENTION

Regulations 32 and 51

1

The Central Authority as the competent authority for [England] [Wales] being the country in which the Convention adoption order was made hereby certifies, in accordance with Article 23(1) of the Convention, that the child:

(a)   name . . . [name on birth certificate, also known as/now known as . . .]

sex: . . .
date and place of birth: . . .
habitual residence at the time of the adoption: . . .
State of origin: . . .

(b)   was adopted on: . . .
by order made by: . . . court in [England] [Wales]

(c)   by the following person(s):
(i)   family name and first name(s): . . .
sex: . . .
date and place of birth: . . .
Habitual residence at the time adoption order was made: . . .
(ii)   family name and first name(s): . . .
sex: . . .
date and place of birth: . . .
habitual residence at the time adoption order made: . . .

2

The competent authority for [England] [Wales] in pursuance of Article 23(1) of
the Convention hereby certifies that the adoption was made in accordance with
the Convention and that the agreement under Article 17(c) was given by:

(a)   name and address of the Central Authority in State of origin: . . .
date of the agreement: . . .
(b)   name and address of the Central Authority of receiving State: . . .
date of the agreement: . . .

Signed
Date

ASYLUM AND IMMIGRATION (TREATMENT OF CLAIMANTS, ETC) ACT 2004 (COMMENCEMENT NO 5 AND TRANSITIONAL PROVISIONS) ORDER 2005

(SI 2005/565)

Made: 7 March 2005.

Authority: Asylum and Immigration (Treatment of Claimants, etc) Act 2004, s 48(3)(a),
(4)–(6).

Transfer of Functions

Functions of the Asylum and Immigration Tribunal under this article transferred to the
First-tier Tribunal, by the Transfer of Functions of the Asylum and Immigration Tribunal Order
2010, SI 2010/21, art 2; for transitional provisions and savings see art 5(4), Sch 4, paras 14–18,
21 thereto.

1 Citation and interpretation

(1) This Order may be cited as the Asylum and Immigration (Treatment of
Claimants, etc) Act 2004 (Commencement No 5 and Transitional Provisions) Order
2005.

(2)   In this Order—
"the 2002 Act" means the Nationality, Immigration and Asylum Act 2002;
"the 2004 Act" means the Asylum and Immigration (Treatment of
Claimants, etc) Act 2004;

"adjudicator" means an adjudicator appointed, or treated as if appointed, under section 81 of the 2002 Act;

"appropriate appellate court" has the meaning given in section 103B(5) of the 2002 Act;

"appropriate court" has the meaning given in section 103A(9) of the 2002 Act;

"commencement" means the commencement date in article 2 of this Order;

"the old appeals provisions" means the following provisions, insofar as they continued to have effect immediately before commencement in relation to a pending appeal—

    (i)   Part IV of, and Schedule 4 to, the Immigration and Asylum Act 1999;

    (ii)   section 8(1) to (4) of the Asylum and Immigration Act 1993;

    (iii)   sections 13 to 17 of the Immigration Act 1971.

(3)   In this Order, references to a section by number alone are to the section so numbered in the 2002 Act.

2 Commencement provisions

The following provisions of the 2004 Act shall come into force on 4th April 2005—

    (a)   section 26(1) to (5) and (7) to (10),

    (b)   section 26(6), except that the insertion of section 103D into the 2002 Act shall not come into force in Northern Ireland;

    (c)   Schedule 1; and

    (d)   Schedule 2.

3 Transitional provisions: general

(1)   Where, immediately before commencement, an adjudicator or the Immigration Appeal Tribunal—

    (a)   has completed the hearing of an appeal, but has not produced his or its written determination; or

    (b)   has produced a written determination of an appeal but that determination has not been served on all the parties,

the appeal shall continue after commencement as an appeal to an adjudicator or the Immigration Appeal Tribunal, as the case may be, until the determination has been served on all the parties.

(2)   A member of the Asylum and Immigration Tribunal who, immediately before commencement was—

    (a)   an adjudicator; or

    (b)   a member of the Immigration Appeal Tribunal,

shall, notwithstanding section 26(1), (4) and (5) of the 2004 Act, be deemed to remain an adjudicator or member of the Immigration Appeal Tribunal after commencement, to the extent necessary for the purpose of completing the determination of an appeal in the circumstances specified in paragraph (1) of this article.

4

Subject to article 3—

    (a)   any appeal or application to an adjudicator which is pending immediately before commencement shall continue after commencement as an appeal or application to the Asylum and Immigration Tribunal; and

    (b)   any appeal to the Immigration Appeal Tribunal which is pending immediately before commencement shall continue after commencement as an appeal to the Asylum and Immigration Tribunal.

5

(1) This article applies, subject to article 3, in relation to any appeal which immediately before commencement is—

    (a)   pending before an adjudicator, having been remitted to an adjudicator by a court or the Immigration Appeal Tribunal; or

    (b)   pending before the Immigration Appeal Tribunal.

(2) The Asylum and Immigration Tribunal shall, after commencement, subject to rules under section 106 of the 2002 Act deal with the appeal in the same manner as if it had originally decided the appeal and it was reconsidering its decision.

(3) Following the determination of the appeal by the Asylum and Immigration Tribunal, a party—

    (a)   may not apply to the appropriate court under section 103A(1); but

    (b)   may, subject to section 103B(3), bring a further appeal on a point of law to the appropriate appellate court under section 103B(1).

6

(1) Where an application for permission to appeal to the Immigration Appeal Tribunal against an adjudicator's decision is pending immediately before commencement, it shall be treated after commencement as an application under section 103A(1) (subject to paragraph (4) and to article 9(4) below) for an order requiring the Asylum and Immigration Tribunal to reconsider the adjudicator's decision on the appeal.

(2) Where—

    (a)   an adjudicator has determined an appeal; and

    (b)   no application for permission to appeal to the Immigration Appeal Tribunal is pending immediately before commencement,

a party to the appeal may after commencement apply under section 103A(1) (as modified by paragraph (4) below) for an order requiring the Asylum and Immigration Tribunal to reconsider the adjudicator's decision on the appeal.

(3) Where, in a case to which paragraph (2) applies, a time period specified in rules under section 106 for applying for permission to appeal to the Immigration Appeal Tribunal has started to run before 4th April 2005, an application under section 103A(1) may, notwithstanding section 103A(3), be made at any time before the expiry of that time period.

(4) In relation to an application which, by virtue of this article, is made or treated as made under section 103A, that section shall apply with the modifications that—

    (a)   references to the Tribunal, except for the second such reference in section 103A(1), shall be interpreted as referring to the adjudicator who determined the appeal;

    (b)   references to the Tribunal's decision shall be interpreted as referring to the adjudicator's decision.

(5) Section 103D shall not apply in relation to a pending application which is treated as an application under section 103A by virtue of paragraph (1) of this article.

7

(1) An application to a court under section 101(2) (review of Immigration Appeal Tribunal's decision upon application for permission to appeal) which is pending immediately before commencement shall continue after commencement as if that section had not been repealed.

(2) A party who, immediately before commencement, was entitled to make an application to a court under section 101(2), may make such an application after commencement as if that section had not been repealed.

(3) Where, by virtue of this article, an application under section 101(2) is made or continues after commencement—

    (a)   paragraphs (a) and (c) of section 101(3) shall apply in relation to the application, as if they had not been repealed; and

    (b)   the judge determining the application may—

        (i)   affirm the Immigration Appeal Tribunal's decision to refuse permission to appeal;

        (ii)   reverse the Immigration Appeal Tribunal's decision to grant permission to appeal; or

        (iii)   order the Asylum and Immigration Tribunal to reconsider the adjudicator's decision on the appeal.

8

(1)   An appeal to the Court of Appeal or Court of Session under section 103 (appeal from Immigration Appeal Tribunal), or an application to the Court of Appeal or Court of Session for permission to appeal under section 103, which is pending immediately before commencement shall continue after commencement as if that section had not been repealed.

(2)   Where, immediately before commencement, an application to the Immigration Appeal Tribunal for permission to appeal under section 103 is pending—

    (a)   the application shall, following commencement, be determined by the Asylum and Immigration Tribunal; and

    (b)   section 103 shall continue to apply in relation to the application as if it had not been repealed, but with the modification in paragraph (5) below.

(3)   A party who—

    (a)   is granted permission to appeal under section 103; or

    (b)   immediately before commencement, was entitled to apply to the Court of Appeal or Court of Session for permission to appeal under section 103,

may, after commencement, appeal or apply for permission to appeal under section 103 (as the case may be) as if that section had not been repealed.

(4)   A party who, immediately before commencement, was entitled to apply to the Immigration Appeal Tribunal for permission to appeal under section 103, may apply to the Asylum and Immigration Tribunal for permission to appeal under that section; and section 103 shall continue to apply in relation to the application as if it had not been repealed, but with the modification in paragraph (5) below.

(5)   In relation to an application for permission to appeal under section 103 which is made to or determined by the Asylum and Immigration Tribunal pursuant to paragraph (2) or (4), section 103 shall apply with the modification that the references to the Tribunal in section 103(2) shall be interpreted as referring to the Asylum and Immigration Tribunal.

(6)   Where, after commencement, the Court of Appeal or Court of Session determines an appeal under section 103, section 103B(4) shall apply in relation to the appeal as it would in relation to an appeal under section 103B(1), but with the modification that the references to the Tribunal in paragraphs (a), (b) and (f) shall be interpreted as references to the Immigration Appeal Tribunal.

9 Further transitional provisions: appeals under the old appeals provisions

(1)   Where, immediately before commencement, an appeal to an adjudicator is pending to which any of the old appeals provisions apply, those provisions shall continue to apply to the appeal after commencement, subject (except where article 3 applies) to the modification that any reference in those provisions to an adjudicator shall be treated as a reference to the Asylum and Immigration Tribunal.

(2)   Subject to paragraphs (3) to (5), any provision in the old appeals provisions about appeals or applications to the Immigration Appeal Tribunal or to a court shall not have effect after commencement, and instead sections 103A to 103E shall have effect in relation to appeals decided under the old appeals provisions.

(3) Where sections 103A to 103E have effect by virtue of paragraph (2), they shall do so with the modification that references to section 82 or 83 shall be treated as including a reference to the old appeals provisions.

(4) Where an appeal or application for permission to appeal to the Immigration Appeal Tribunal under the old appeals provisions is pending immediately before commencement—

    (a) articles 4(b) and 5, or article 6(1), of this Order (as appropriate) shall apply; but

    (b) if, under the old appeals provisions, the appeal or application was not restricted to the ground that the adjudicator made an error of law, then it shall not be so restricted following commencement.

(5) In relation to an appeal which has been determined by the Immigration Appeal Tribunal under the old appeals provisions before commencement, article 8 of this Order shall apply with the references to section 103 being treated as including references to corresponding provisions in the old appeals provisions.

IMMIGRATION AND ASYLUM (PROVISION OF ACCOMMODATION TO FAILED ASYLUM-SEEKERS) REGULATIONS 2005

(SI 2005/930)

Made: 24 March 2005.
Authority: Immigration and Asylum Act 1999, ss 4(5), 166(3).
Commencement: 31 March 2005.

1 Citation and commencement

(1) These Regulations may be cited as the Immigration and Asylum (Provision of Accommodation to Failed Asylum-Seekers) Regulations 2005 and shall come into force on 31st March 2005.

(2) These Regulations apply to a person who is receiving accommodation when these Regulations come into force to the same extent as they apply to a person provided with accommodation after these Regulations come into force.

2 Interpretation

In these Regulations—

    "the 1999 Act" means the Immigration and Asylum Act 1999;

    "destitute" is to be construed in accordance with section 95(3) of the 1999 Act; and

    "reporting requirement" means a condition or restriction which requires a person to report to the police, an immigration officer or the Secretary of State, and is imposed under—

        (a) paragraph 21 of Schedule 2 to the Immigration Act 1971 (temporary admission or release from detention),

        (b) paragraph 22 of that Schedule, or

        (c) paragraph 2 or 5 of Schedule 3 to that Act (pending deportation).

3 Eligibility for and provision of accommodation to a failed asylum-seeker

(1) Subject to regulations 4 and 6, the criteria to be used in determining the matters referred to in paragraphs (a) and (b) of section 4(5) of the 1999 Act in respect of a person falling within section 4(2) or (3) of that Act are—

    (a) that he appears to the Secretary of State to be destitute, and

(b)   that one or more of the conditions set out in paragraph (2) are satisfied in relation to him.

(2)   Those conditions are that—

    (a)   he is taking all reasonable steps to leave the United Kingdom or place himself in a position in which he is able to leave the United Kingdom, which may include complying with attempts to obtain a travel document to facilitate his departure;

    (b)   he is unable to leave the United Kingdom by reason of a physical impediment to travel or for some other medical reason;

    (c)   he is unable to leave the United Kingdom because in the opinion of the Secretary of State there is currently no viable route of return available;

    (d)   he has made an application for judicial review of a decision in relation to his asylum claim—

       (i)   in England and Wales, and has been granted permission to proceed pursuant to Part 54 of the Civil Procedure Rules 1998,

       (ii)   in Scotland, pursuant to Chapter 58 of the Rules of the Court of Session 1994 or

       (iii)   in Northern Ireland, and has been granted leave pursuant to Order 53 of the Rules of Supreme Court (Northern Ireland) 1980; or

    (e)   the provision of accommodation is necessary for the purpose of avoiding a breach of a person's Convention rights, within the meaning of the Human Rights Act 1998.

4 Community activities: general

(1) Where the Secretary of State so determines, the continued provision of accommodation to a person falling within section 4(2) or (3) of the 1999 Act is to be conditional upon that person's performance of or participation in such community activity as is described in this regulation and is from time to time notified to the person in accordance with regulation 5.

(2)   In making the determination referred to in paragraph (1), regard will be had to the following matters—

    (a)   the length of time that he believes the person will continue to be eligible for accommodation,

    (b)   the arrangements that have been made for the performance of or participation in community activities in the area in which the person is being provided with accommodation,

    (c)   any relevant health and safety standards which are agreed between the Secretary of State and a person with whom he has made arrangements for the provision of community activities in the person's area,

    (d)   whether the person is in the Secretary of State's belief unable to perform or participate in community activities because of a physical or mental impairment or for some other medical reason,

    (e)   whether the person is in the Secretary of State's belief unable to perform or participate in community activities because of a responsibility for the care of a dependant child or of a dependant who because of a physical or mental impairment is unable to look after himself, and

    (f)   any relevant information provided to the Secretary of State, regarding the person's suitability to perform or participate in particular tasks, activities or a range of tasks or activities.

(3)   Paragraph (1) does not apply in relation to a person who is under the age of 18.

(4)   No condition on the continued provision of accommodation will require a person to perform or participate in community activities for more than 35 hours in any week, including the weekend.

5 Community activities: Relevant information

A notice under regulation 4(1) falls within this regulation if it contains the following information—

(a) the task, activity or range of tasks or activities in the area in which the person lives which are to be performed or participated in as community activities,

(b) the geographical location at which the community activities will be performed or participated in,

(c) the maximum number of hours per week that the person will be expected to perform or participate in community activities, where it is possible for the Secretary of State to so specify, and

(d) the date upon which the task, activity or range of tasks or activities to be performed or participated in as community activities will commence and, where it is possible for the Secretary of State to so specify, the length of time such community activities will last.

6 Other conditions on continued provision of accommodation

(1) The continued provision of accommodation to a person falling within section 4(2) or (3) of the 1999 Act is to be subject to such other conditions falling within paragraph (2) as—

(a) the Secretary of State may from time to time determine, and

(b) are set out in a notice to that person in writing.

(2) A condition falls within this paragraph to the extent that it relates to—

(a) complying with specified standards of behaviour,

(b) complying with a reporting requirement,

(c) complying with a requirement—

(i) to reside at an authorised address, or

(ii) if he is absent from an authorised address without the permission of the Secretary of State, to ensure that that absence is for no more than seven consecutive days and nights or for no more than a total of fourteen days and nights in any six month period, or

(d) complying with specified steps to facilitate his departure from the United Kingdom.

DISPLACED PERSONS (TEMPORARY PROTECTION) REGULATIONS 2005

(SI 2005/1379)

Made: 18 May 2005.

Authority: European Communities Act 1972, s 2(2).

Commencement: 15 June 2005.

1 Citation and commencement

These Regulations may be cited as the Displaced Persons (Temporary Protection) Regulations 2005 and shall come into force on 15th June 2005.

2 Interpretation

(1) In these Regulations—

(a) "the 2002 Act" means the Nationalizzty, Immigration and Asylum Act 2002;

(b)   "claim for asylum" has the same meaning as in section 18 of the 2002 Act;

(c)   "consular officer" has the same meaning as in article 2 of the Consular Fees (No2) Order 1999;

(d)   "entry clearance" has the same meaning as in article 2 of the Consular Fees (No2) Order 1999;

(e)   "local authority" means—

    (i)   in England and Wales, a district council, a county council, a county borough council, a London borough council, the Common Council of the City of London or the Council of the Isles of Scilly; and

    (ii)   in Scotland, a council constituted under section 2 of the Local Government etc (Scotland) Act 1994;

(f)   "registered social landlord"—

    (i)   in England and Wales, has the same meaning as in Part I of the Housing Act 1996; and

    (ii)   in Scotland, means a body in the register maintained under [section 20(1) of the Housing (Scotland) Act 2010];

(g)   "registered housing association" has the same meaning, in relation to Northern Ireland, as in Part II of the Housing (Northern Ireland) Order 1992;

(h)   "temporary protection" means limited leave to enter or remain granted pursuant to Part 11A of the Immigration Rules; and

(i)   "Temporary Protection Directive" means Council Directive 2001/55/EC of 20 July 2001 on minimum standards for giving temporary protection in the event of a mass influx of displaced persons and on measures promoting a balance of efforts between member States in receiving such persons and bearing the consequences thereof.

Amendment

Para (1): in sub-para (f) words in square brackets substituted by SI 2012/700, art 4, Schedule, Pt 2, para 14. Date in force: 1 April 2012: see SI 2012/700, art 1(3).

3 Means of subsistence

(1)   Any person granted temporary protection as a result of a decision of the Council of the European Union made pursuant to Article 5 of the Temporary Protection Directive shall be deemed for the purposes of the provision of means of subsistence to have been granted leave to enter or remain in the United Kingdom exceptionally, outside the Immigration Rules.

(2)   Subject to paragraph (3), paragraph (1) shall cease to apply on the date when the period of mass influx of displaced persons to which the grant of temporary protection relates ends in accordance with Chapter II of the Temporary Protection Directive.

(3)   Paragraph (1) shall continue to apply for a period not exceeding 28 days from the date referred to in paragraph (2) for as long as the conditions in paragraph (4) are satisfied and the person is in the United Kingdom.

(4)   Those conditions are—

    (a)   the person's grant of temporary protection has expired; and

    (b)   the person is taking all reasonable steps to leave the United Kingdom or place himself in a position in which he is able to leave the United Kingdom, which may include co-operating with a voluntary return programme.

4

"Means of subsistence" in regulation 3 means any means of subsistence governed by—

    (a)   Part VII of the Social Security Contributions and Benefits Act 1992;

(b) Part VII of the Social Security Contributions and Benefits (Northern Ireland) Act 1992;

(c) sections 1 and 3 of Part I of the Jobseekers Act 1995;

(d) articles 3 and 5 of Part II of the Jobseekers (Northern Ireland) Order 1995;

(e) the State Pension Credit Act 2002; or

(f) the State Pension Credit Act (Northern Ireland) 2002.

5 Housing: provision of accommodation

(1) The Secretary of State may provide, or arrange for the provision of, accommodation for any person granted temporary protection.

(2) Subject to paragraph (3), paragraph (1) shall cease to apply on the date when the period of mass influx of displaced persons to which the grant of temporary protection relates ends in accordance with Chapter II of the Temporary Protection Directive.

(3) Paragraph (1) shall continue to apply for a period not exceeding 28 days from the date referred to in paragraph (2) for as long as the conditions in paragraph (4) are satisfied and the person is in the United Kingdom.

(4) Those conditions are—

(a) the person's grant of temporary protection has expired; and

(b) the person is taking all reasonable steps to leave the United Kingdom or place himself in a position in which he is able to leave the United Kingdom, which may include co-operating with a voluntary return programme.

6

A local authority or the Northern Ireland Housing Executive may provide accommodation for those granted temporary protection in accordance with arrangements made by the Secretary of State under regulation 5.

7

When exercising his power under regulation 5 to provide, or arrange for the provision of, accommodation, the Secretary of State—

(a) shall have regard to the desirability, in general, of providing, or arranging for the provision of, accommodation in areas in which there is a ready supply of accommodation; and

(b) shall not have regard to any preference that those who have been granted temporary protection or their dependants may have as to the locality in which the accommodation is to be provided.

8 Housing: requests for assistance

(1) This regulation applies if the Secretary of State asks—

(a) a local authority;

(b) the Northern Ireland Housing Executive;

(c) a registered social landlord;

[(cc) a private registered provider of social housing;] or

(d) a registered housing association in Northern Ireland

to assist him in the exercise of his power under regulation 5 to provide, or arrange for the provision of, accommodation.

(2) The body to whom the request is made shall co-operate in giving the Secretary of State such assistance in the exercise of that power as is reasonable in the circumstances.

(3) This regulation does not require a registered social landlord [or a private registered provider of social housing] to act beyond his powers.

(4) The Secretary of State shall pay to a body listed in regulation 8(1) any costs reasonably incurred by that body in assisting the Secretary of State to provide, or arrange for the provision of, accommodation.

Amendment

Para (1): sub-para (cc) inserted by SI 2010/671, art 4, Sch 1, paras 39, 40. Date in force: 1 April 2010 : see SI 2010/671, art 1(2), and SI 2010/862, art 2.

Para (3): words "or a private registered provider of social housing" in square brackets inserted by SI 2010/671, art 4, Sch 1, paras 39, 41. Date in force: 1 April 2010: see SI 2010/671, art 1(2), and SI 2010/862, art 2.

9

A local authority or the Northern Ireland Housing Executive shall supply to the Secretary of State such information about its housing accommodation (whether or not occupied) as the Secretary of State may request.

10 Housing: direction by the Secretary of State

(1) If the Secretary of State considers that a local authority or the Northern Ireland Housing Executive has suitable housing accommodation, the Secretary of State may direct the authority or the Executive to make available such accommodation as may be specified in the direction for a period so specified to the Secretary of State for the purpose of providing accommodation under regulation 5.

(2) The Secretary of State shall pay to a body to which a direction is given costs reasonably incurred by the body in complying with the direction.

(3) Any such direction is enforceable, on an application made on behalf of the Secretary of State, by injunction or, in Scotland, by an order under section 45(b) of the Court of Session Act 1988.

11

Housing accommodation shall be suitable for the purposes of regulation 10 if it is—

- (a)   unoccupied;
- (b)   likely to remain unoccupied for the foreseeable future if not made available; and
- (c)   appropriate for the accommodation of persons with temporary protection or is capable of being made so with minor work.

12

(1) If the housing accommodation specified in a direction under regulation 10 is not appropriate for the accommodation of persons with temporary protection but is capable of being made so with minor work, the Secretary of State may require the directed body to secure that the work is carried out without delay.

(2) The Secretary of State shall meet the reasonable cost of carrying out the minor work.

13

Before giving a direction under regulation 10, the Secretary of State shall consult—

- (a)   such local authorities, local authority associations and other persons as he thinks appropriate in respect of a direction given to a local authority;
- (b)   the Northern Ireland Housing Executive in respect of a direction given to the Executive;
- (c)   the National Assembly of Wales in respect of a direction given to a local authority in Wales; and
- (d)   the Scottish Ministers in respect of a direction given to a local authority in Scotland.

14 Housing: rent liability

A person with temporary protection who is provided with accommodation under regulation 5 shall be liable to make periodical payments of, or by way of, rent in respect of the accommodation provided and [in relation to—

(a) any claim for housing benefit by virtue of regulation 3, such payments shall be regarded as rent for the purposes of regulation 14(1)(a) of the Housing Benefit Regulations 2006, regulation 12(1)(a) of the Housing Benefit (Persons who have attained the qualifying age for state pension credit) Regulations 2006 and regulation 10(1)(a) of the Housing Benefit (General) Regulations (Northern Ireland) 1987;

(b) any claim for universal credit by virtue of regulation 3, such payments shall be regarded as rent for the purposes of regulation 25(2) of, and paragraph 2 of Schedule 1 to, the Universal Credit Regulations 2013].

Amendment

Words in square brackets substituted by SI 2013/630, reg 60. Date in force: 29 April 2013: see SI 2013/630, reg 1(2).

15 Housing: notice to vacate

(1) A tenancy, licence or right of occupancy granted in order to provide accommodation under regulation 5 shall end on the date specified in a notice to vacate complying with paragraph (2) regardless of when the tenancy, licence or right of occupancy could otherwise be brought to an end.

(2) A notice to vacate complies with this paragraph if it is in writing and it specifies as the notice period a period of at least 7 days from the date of service by post of the notice to vacate.

16 Claims for asylum

(1) This regulation shall apply when a person granted temporary protection makes a claim for asylum which is recorded by the Secretary of State.

(2) When considering under section 55(1)(b) of the 2002 Act whether he is satisfied that the person has made his claim for asylum as soon as reasonably practicable after his arrival in the United Kingdom, the Secretary of State may disregard any time during which the person benefited from a grant of temporary protection.

17 Consular fees

Where a consular officer is satisfied that a person outside the United Kingdom will benefit from a grant of temporary protection on arrival at a port of entry in the United Kingdom, that person shall not be required to pay any fee prescribed by the Consular Fees (No 2) Order 1999 in connection with an application for entry clearance.

SCHEDULE

(The Schedule contains amendments to legislation outside the scope of this work.)

REPORTING OF SUSPICIOUS CIVIL PARTNERSHIPS REGULATIONS 2005

(SI 2005/3174)

Made: 15 November 2005.

Authority: Immigration and Asylum Act 1999, s 24A(3), (4)(a).

Commencement: 5 December 2005.

1 Citation, commencement and interpretation

(1) These Regulations may be cited as the Reporting of Suspicious Civil Partnerships Regulations 2005 and shall come into force on 5th December 2005.

(2) In these Regulations, unless the context otherwise requires "the 1999 Act" means the Immigration and Asylum Act 1999.

2 Reporting of suspicious civil partnerships

For the purpose of section 24A of the 1999 Act (duty to report suspicious civil partnerships) the person concerned shall—

(a) report his suspicions to the Secretary of State by making a report in writing or other permanent form giving the information specified in the Schedule to these Regulations [(to the extent that that information is available)], and

(b) forward that report to the Home Office, National Intelligence Unit, PO Box 1000, Hayes, Middlesex UB3 5WB or, where the Secretary of State has notified the Registrar General of another address to be used in relation to any particular registration authority, that address.

Amendment

Words in square brackets in para (a) inserted by SI 2014/1660, reg 3. Date in force 21 July 2014: see SI 2014/1660, reg 1.

SCHEDULE

Regulation 2

Information to be provided when reporting a suspicious civil partnership

Name and surname of each of the civil partners

Date of birth and/or age of each of the civil partners

Sex of each of the civil partners

Condition of each of the civil partners

Address (and registration authority of residence) of each of the civil partners

Nationality of each of the civil partners

Date of formation of civil partnership

Place of formation of civil partnership

Time of formation of civil partnership

Nature of evidence produced in respect of—

(i) name and age

(ii) condition

(iii) nationality

of the civil partners

Reasons for making the report

Full name of person making the report

Name of registration authority on whose behalf the report is being made

Date report made

HOUSING BENEFIT (PERSONS WHO HAVE ATTAINED THE QUALIFYING AGE FOR STATE PENSION CREDIT) REGULATIONS 2006

(SI 2006/214)

Made: 2 February 2006.

Authority: Social Security Act 1998, s 34; Social Security Administration Act 1992, ss 1, 5, 7,

7A, 75, 122E, 126A, 128A, 134; Social Security Contributions and Benefits Act 1992, ss 123, 130, 134–136, 136A, 137.

Commencement: 6 March 2006.

PART 2
PROVISIONS AFFECTING ENTITLEMENT TO HOUSING BENEFIT

10 Persons from abroad

(1) A person from abroad who is liable to make payments in respect of a dwelling shall be treated as if he were not so liable but this paragraph shall not have effect in respect of a person to whom and for a period to which regulation 10A (entitlement of a refugee to housing benefit) and Schedule A1 (treatment of claims for housing benefit by refugees) apply.

[(2) In paragraph (1), "person from abroad" means, subject to the following provisions of this regulation, a person who is not habitually resident in the United Kingdom, the Channel Islands, the Isle of Man or the Republic of Ireland.

(3) No person shall be treated as habitually resident in the United Kingdom, the Channel Islands, the Isle of Man or the Republic of Ireland unless he has a right to reside in (as the case may be) the United Kingdom, the Channel Islands, the Isle of Man or the Republic of Ireland other than a right to reside which falls within paragraph (4).

(4) A right to reside falls within this paragraph if it is one which exists by virtue of, or in accordance with, one or more of the following—

(a) regulation 13 of the Immigration (European Economic Area) Regulations 2006;

(b) regulation 14 of those Regulations, but only in a case where the right exists under that regulation because the person is—

 (i) a jobseeker for the purpose of the definition of "qualified person" in regulation 6(1) of those Regulations, or

 (ii) a family member (within the meaning of regulation 7 of those Regulations) of such a jobseeker;

[(bb) regulation 15A(1) of those Regulations, but only in a case where the right exists under that regulation because the claimant satisfies the criteria in regulation 15A(4A) of those Regulations;]

(c) Article 6 of Council Directive No 2004/38/EC; . . .

(d) [Article 45 of the Treaty on the Functioning of the European Union] (in a case where the person is seeking work in the United Kingdom, the Channel Islands, the Isle of Man or the Republic of Ireland)[; or

(e) Article 20 of the Treaty on the Functioning of the European Union (in a case where the right to reside arises because a British citizen would otherwise be deprived of the genuine enjoyment of the substance of their rights as a European Union citizen)].

(4A) A person is not a person from abroad if he is—

(za) a qualified person for the purposes of regulation 6 of the Immigration (European Economic Area) Regulations 2006 as a worker or a self-employed person;

(zb) a family member of a person referred to in sub-paragraph (za) within the meaning of regulation 7(1)(a), (b) or (c) of those Regulations;

(zc) a person who has a right to reside permanently in the United Kingdom by virtue of regulation 15(1)(c), (d) or (e) of those Regulations;]

(g) a refugee;

[[(h) a person who has been granted leave or who is deemed to have been granted leave outside the rules made under section 3(2) of the Immigration Act 1971 where that leave is—

> (i)   discretionary leave to enter or remain in the United Kingdom;
>
> (ii)   leave to remain under the Destitution Domestic Violence concession; or
>
> (iii)   leave deemed to have been granted by virtue of regulation 3 of the Displaced Persons (Temporary Protection) Regulations 2005;]

(hh)   a person who has humanitarian protection granted under those rules;]

(i)   a person who is not a person subject to immigration control within the meaning of section 115(9) of the Immigration and Asylum Act 1999 and who is in the United Kingdom as a result of his deportation, expulsion or other removal by compulsion of law from another country to the United Kingdom; [or]

(j)   . . .

[(jj)   . . .]

(k)   on state pension credit.]

(5) . . .

(6) In this regulation—

    . . .

"refugee" in this regulation means a person recorded by the Secretary of State as a refugee within the definition in Article 1 of the Convention relating to the Status of Refugees.

Amendment

Paras (2)–(4), (4A): substituted, for paras (2)–(4) as originally enacted, by SI 2006/1026, reg 5(1), (2)(a). Date in force: 30 April 2006: see SI 2006/1026, reg 1.

Para (4): sub-para (bb) inserted by SI 2012/2587, reg 6(1), (2). Date in force: 8 November 2012: see SI 2012/2587, reg 1.

Para (4): in sub-para (c) word omitted revoked by SI 2012/2587, reg 6(1), (3). Date in force: 8 November 2012: see SI 2012/2587, reg 1.

Para (4): in sub-para (d) words "Article 45 of the Treaty on the Functioning of the European Union" in square brackets substituted by SI 2012/1809, art 3(1), Schedule, Pt 2. Date in force: 1 August 2012 (except in its application to things done before 1 December 2009, being the date on which the Treaty of Lisbon came into force): see SI 2012/1809, art 2.

Para (4): sub-para (e) and word "; or" immediately preceding it inserted by SI 2012/2587, reg 6(1), (4). Date in force: 8 November 2012: see SI 2012/2587, reg 1

Para (4A): sub-paras (h), (hh) substituted for sub-para (h) as originally enacted, by SI 2006/2528, reg 6. Date in force: 9 October 2006: see SI 2006/2528, reg 1.

Para (4A): sub-para (h) further substituted by SI 2013/2536, reg 12(1), (3)(a). Date in force: 29 October 2013: see SI 2013/2536, reg 1(1).

Para (4A): in sub-para (i) word "or" in square brackets inserted by SI 2013/2536, reg 12(1), (3)(b). Date in force: 29 October 2013: see SI 2013/2536, reg 1(1).

Para (4A): sub-paras (j), (jj) revoked by SI 2013/2536, reg 12(1), (3)(c). Date in force: 29 October 2013: see SI 2013/2536, reg 1(1).

Para (5): revoked by SI 2013/2536, reg 12(1), (3)(c). Date in force: 29 October 2013: see SI 2013/2536, reg 1(1).

Para (6): definition "a European Economic Area State" (omitted) revoked by SI 2006/1026, reg 5(1), (2)(b). Date in force: 30 April 2006: see SI 2006/1026, reg 1.

[10A Entitlement of a refugee to Housing Benefit

(1) Where a person, who has made a claim for asylum, is notified that he has been recorded by the Secretary of State as a refugee, these Regulations shall have effect with respect to his entitlement to housing benefit for the relevant period which applies in his case in accordance with Schedule A1(treatment of claims for housing benefit by refugees), but that entitlement is—

(a)   subject to the provisions of Schedule A1; and

(b)   with respect to regulations 12 (rent) and 13 (maximum rent), subject to paragraph 4(8) of Schedule 3 to the Housing Benefit and Council Tax Benefit (Consequential Provisions) Regulations 2006 (saving).

(2) Any housing benefit which is payable in consequence of this regulation shall be in the form of a rent allowance.

(3) In this regulation and in Schedule A1, "refugee" means a person recorded by the Secretary of State as a refugee within the definition in Article 1 of the Convention relating to the Status of Refugees.]

Amendment

Inserted by SI 2006/217, reg 7, Sch 4, para 2(1).

Date in force: 6 March 2006 (this amendment has effect until the day on which the Asylum and Immigration (Treatment of Claimants, etc) Act 2004, s 12(2)(e) comes into force): see SI 2006/217, regs 1(1), 7, Sch 4, para 1.

COUNCIL TAX BENEFIT REGULATIONS 2006

(SI 2006/215)

Made: 2 February 2006.

Authority: Social Security Act 1998, s 34; Social Security Administration Act 1992, ss 1, 6, 7, 7A, 76, 77, 122E, 128A, 138, 139; Social Security Contributions and Benefits Act 1992, ss 123, 131–136, 137.

Commencement: 6 March 2006.

PART 1
GENERAL

7 Persons from abroad

(1) A person from abroad is a person of a prescribed class for the purposes of section 131(3)(b) of the Act but this paragraph shall not have effect in respect of a person to whom and for a period to which regulation 7A and Schedule A1 apply.

[(2) In paragraph (1), "person from abroad" means, subject to the following provisions of this regulation, a person who is not habitually resident in the United Kingdom, the Channel Islands, the Isle of Man or the Republic of Ireland.

(3) No person shall be treated as habitually resident in the United Kingdom, the Channel Islands, the Isle of Man or the Republic of Ireland unless he has a right to reside in (as the case may be) the United Kingdom, the Channel Islands, the Isle of Man or the Republic of Ireland other than a right to reside which falls within paragraph (4).

(4) A right to reside falls within this paragraph if it is one which exists by virtue of, or in accordance with, one or more of the following—

    (a)   regulation 13 of the Immigration (European Economic Area) Regulations 2006;

    (b)   regulation 14 of those Regulations, but only in a case where the right exists under that regulation because the person is—

        (i)   a jobseeker for the purpose of the definition of "qualified person" in regulation 6(1) of those Regulations, or

        (ii)   a family member (within the meaning of regulation 7 of those Regulations) of such a jobseeker;

    [(bb) regulation 15A(1) of those Regulations, but only in a case where the right exists under that regulation because the claimant satisfies the criteria in regulation 15A(4A) of those Regulations;]

    (c)   Article 6 of Council Directive No 2004/38/EC; . . .

    (d)   [Article 45 of the Treaty on the Functioning of the European Union] (in a case where the person is seeking work in the United Kingdom, the Channel Islands, the Isle of Man or the Republic of Ireland)[; or

    (e)   Article 20 of the Treaty on the Functioning of the European Union (in a case where the right to reside arises because a British citizen would otherwise be deprived of the genuine enjoyment of the substance of their rights as a European Union citizen)].

(4A)   A person is not a person from abroad if he is—

    (a)   a worker for the purposes of Council Directive No 2004/38/EC;

    (b)   a self-employed person for the purposes of that Directive;

    (c)   a person who retains a status referred to in sub-paragraph (a) or (b) pursuant to Article 7(3) of that Directive;

    (d)   a person who is a family member of a person referred to in sub-paragraph (a), (b) or (c) within the meaning of Article 2 of that Directive;

    (e)   a person who has a right to reside permanently in the United Kingdom by virtue of Article 17 of that Directive;

    [(f)   a person who is treated as a worker for the purpose of the definition of "qualified person" in regulation 6(1) of the Immigration (European Economic Area) Regulations 2006 pursuant to—

        (i)   . . . .

        (ii)   regulation 6 of the Accession (Immigration and Worker Authorisation) Regulations 2006 (right of residence of a Bulgarian or Romanian who is an "accession State national subject to worker authorisation");]

    (g)   a refugee;

    [(h)   a person who has exceptional leave to enter or remain in the United Kingdom granted outside the rules made under section 3(2) of the Immigration Act 1971;

    (hh)   a person who has humanitarian protection granted under those rules;]

    (i)   a person who is not a person subject to immigration control within the meaning of section 115(9) of the Immigration and Asylum Act and who is in the United Kingdom as a result of his deportation, expulsion or other removal by compulsion of law from another country to the United Kingdom;

    (j)   a person in Great Britain who left the territory of Montserrat after 1st November 1995 because of the effect on that territory of a volcanic eruption; . . .

    [(jj)   a person who—

        (i)   arrived in Great Britain on or after 28th February 2009 but before 18th March 2011;

        (ii)   immediately before arriving there had been resident in Zimbabwe; and

        (iii)   before leaving Zimbabwe, had accepted an offer, made by Her Majesty's Government, to assist that person to move to and settle in the United Kingdom; or]

    (k)   in receipt of income support[, an income-based jobseeker's allowance or on an income-related employment and support allowance].]

(5)   Paragraph 1 of Part 1 of the Schedule to, and regulation 2 as it applies to that paragraph of, the Social Security (Immigration and Asylum) Consequential Amendments Regulations 2000 shall not apply to a person who has been temporarily without funds for any period, or the aggregate of any periods, exceeding 42 days during any one period of limited leave (including any such period as extended).

(6)   In this regulation—

    . . .

"refugee" in this regulation, regulation 7A (entitlement of a refugee to council tax benefit) and Schedule A1 (treatment of claims for council tax benefit by refugees), means a person recorded by the Secretary of State as a refugee within the definition in Article 1 of the Convention relating to the Status of Refugees.

Amendment

Paras (2)–(4), (4A): substituted, for paras (2)–(4) as originally enacted, by SI 2006/1026, reg 2(1), (2)(a). Date in force: 30 April 2006: see SI 2006/1026, reg 1.

Para (4): sub-para (bb) inserted by SI 2012/2587, reg 7(1), (2). Date in force: 8 November 2012: see SI 2012/2587, reg 1.

Para (4): in sub-para (c) word omitted revoked by SI 2012/2587, reg 7(1), (3). Date in force: 8 November 2012: see SI 2012/2587, reg 1.

Para (4): in sub-para (d) words "Article 45 of the Treaty on the Functioning of the European Union" in square brackets substituted by SI 2012/1809, art 3(1), Schedule, Pt 2. Date in force: 1 August 2012 (except in its application to things done before 1 December 2009, being the date on which the Treaty of Lisbon came into force): see SI 2012/1809, art 2.

Para (4): sub-para (e) and word "; or" immediately preceding it inserted by SI 2012/2587, reg 7(1), (4). Date in force: 8 November 2012: see SI 2012/2587, reg 1.

Para (4A): sub-para (f) substituted by SI 2006/3341, reg 7.

Date in force: 1 January 2007: see SI 2006/3341, reg 1.

Para (4A): sub-para (f)(i) revoked by SI 2011/2425, reg 21(1), (3).

Date in force: 31 October 2011: see SI 2011/2425, reg 1(2).

Para (4A): sub-paras (h), (hh) substituted, for sub-para (h) as originally enacted, by SI 2006/2528, reg 7.

Date in force: 9 October 2006: see SI 2006/2528, reg 1.

Para (4A): sub-para (jj) inserted by SI 2009/362, reg 7(1), (3).

Date in force: 18 March 2009: see SI 2009/362, reg 1(2).

Para (4A): in sub-para (k) words ", an income-based jobseeker's allowance or on an income-related employment and support allowance" in square brackets substituted by SI 2008/1082, regs 42, 46.

Date in force: 27 October 2008: see SI 2008/1082, reg 1.

Para (6): definition "a European Economic Area State" (omitted) revoked by SI 2006/1026, reg 2(1), (2)(b).

Date in force: 30 April 2006: see SI 2006/1026, reg 1.

[7A Entitlement of a refugee to council tax benefit

Where a person, who has made a claim for asylum, is notified that he has been recorded by the Secretary of State as a refugee, these Regulations shall have effect with respect to his entitlement to council tax benefit for the relevant period which applies in his case in accordance with Schedule A1 (treatment of claims for council tax benefit by refugees) but subject to the provisions of that Schedule.]

Amendment

Inserted by SI 2006/217, reg 7, Sch 4, para 3(1).

Date in force: 6 March 2006 (this amendment has effect until the date on which the Asylum and Immigration (Treatment of Claimants, etc) Act 2004, s 12(2)(g) comes into force): see SI 2006/217, regs 1(1), 7, Sch 4, para 1.

COUNCIL TAX BENEFIT (PERSONS WHO HAVE ATTAINED THE QUALIFYING AGE FOR STATE PENSION CREDIT) REGULATIONS 2006

(SI 2006/216)

Made: 2 February 2006.

Authority: Social Security Act 1998, s 34; Social Security Administration Act 1992, ss 1, 6, 7,

7A, 76, 77, 122E, 128A, 138, 139; Social Security Contributions and Benefits Act 1992, ss 123, 131–136, 136A, 137.

Commencement: 6 March 2006.

PART 1
GENERAL

7 Persons from abroad

(1) A person from abroad is a person of a prescribed class for the purposes of section 131(3)(b) of the Act but this paragraph shall not have effect in respect of a person to whom and for a period to which regulation 7A and Schedule A1 apply.

[(2) In paragraph (1), "person from abroad" means, subject to the following provisions of this regulation, a person who is not habitually resident in the United Kingdom, the Channel Islands, the Isle of Man or the Republic of Ireland.

(3) No person shall be treated as habitually resident in the United Kingdom, the Channel Islands, the Isle of Man or the Republic of Ireland unless he has a right to reside in (as the case may be) the United Kingdom, the Channel Islands, the Isle of Man or the Republic of Ireland other than a right to reside which falls within paragraph (4).

(4) A right to reside falls within this paragraph if it is one which exists by virtue of, or in accordance with, one or more of the following—

    (a)   regulation 13 of the Immigration (European Economic Area) Regulations 2006;

    (b)   regulation 14 of those Regulations, but only in a case where the right exists under that regulation because the person is—

        (i)   a jobseeker for the purpose of the definition of "qualified person" in regulation 6(1) of those Regulations, or

        (ii)   a family member (within the meaning of regulation 7 of those Regulations) of such a jobseeker;

    [(bb)   regulation 15A(1) of those Regulations, but only in a case where the right exists under that regulation because the claimant satisfies the criteria in regulation 15A(4A) of those Regulations;]

    (c)   Article 6 of Council Directive No 2004/38/EC; . . .

    (d)   [Article 45 of the Treaty on the Functioning of the European Union] (in a case where the person is seeking work in the United Kingdom, the Channel Islands, the Isle of Man or the Republic of Ireland)[; or

    (e)   Article 20 of the Treaty on the Functioning of the European Union (in a case where the right to reside arises because a British citizen would otherwise be deprived of the genuine enjoyment of the substance of their rights as a European Union citizen)].

(4A) A person is not a person from abroad if he is—

    (a)   a worker for the purposes of Council Directive No 2004/38/EC;

    (b)   a self-employed person for the purposes of that Directive;

    (c)   a person who retains a status referred to in sub-paragraph (a) or (b) pursuant to Article 7(3) of that Directive;

    (d)   a person who is a family member of a person referred to in sub-paragraph (a), (b) or (c) within the meaning of Article 2 of that Directive;

    (e)   a person who has a right to reside permanently in the United Kingdom by virtue of Article 17 of that Directive;

    [(f)   a person who is treated as a worker for the purpose of the definition of "qualified person" in regulation 6(1) of the Immigration (European Economic Area) Regulations 2006 pursuant to—

        (i)   . . .

    (ii)   regulation 6 of the Accession (Immigration and Worker Authorisation) Regulations 2006 (right of residence of a Bulgarian or Romanian who is an "accession State national subject to worker authorisation");]

(g)   a refugee;

[(h)   a person who has exceptional leave to enter or remain in the United Kingdom granted outside the rules made under section 3(2) of the Immigration Act 1971;

(hh) a person who has humanitarian protection granted under those rules;]

(i)   a person who is not a person subject to immigration control within the meaning of section 115(9) of the Immigration and Asylum Act and who is in the United Kingdom as a result of his deportation, expulsion or other removal by compulsion of law from another country to the United Kingdom;

(j)   a person in Great Britain who left the territory of Montserrat after 1st November 1995 because of the effect on that territory of a volcanic eruption; . . .

[(jj)   a person who—

    (i)   arrived in Great Britain on or after 28th February 2009 but before 18th March 2011;

    (ii)   immediately before arriving there had been resident in Zimbabwe; and

    (iii) before leaving Zimbabwe, had accepted an offer, made by Her Majesty's Government, to assist that person to move to and settle in the United Kingdom; or]

(k)   on state pension credit.]

(5) Paragraph 1 of Part 1 of the Schedule to, and regulation 2 as it applies to that paragraph of, the Social Security (Immigration and Asylum) Consequential Amendments Regulations 2000 shall not apply to a person who has been temporarily without funds for any period, or the aggregate of any periods, exceeding 42 days during any one period of limited leave (including any such period as extended).

(6) In this regulation—

   . . .

"refugee" in this regulation, regulation 7A (entitlement of a refugee to council tax benefit) and Schedule A1 (treatment of claims for council tax benefit by refugees), means a person recorded by the Secretary of State as a refugee within the definition in Article 1 of the Convention relating to the Status of Refugees.

Amendment

Paras (2)–(4), (4A): substituted, for paras (2)–(4) as originally enacted, by SI 2006/1026, reg 3(1), (2)(a). Date in force: 30 April 2006: see SI 2006/1026, reg 1.

Para (4): sub-para (bb) inserted by SI 2012/2587, reg 8(1), (2). Date in force: 8 November 2012: see SI 2012/2587, reg 1.

Para (4): in sub-para (c) word omitted revoked by SI 2012/2587, reg 8(1), (3). Date in force: 8 November 2012: see SI 2012/2587, reg 1.

Para (4): in sub-para (d) words "Article 45 of the Treaty on the Functioning of the European Union" in square brackets substituted by SI 2012/1809, art 3(1), Schedule, Pt 2. Date in force: 1 August 2012 (except in its application to things done before 1 December 2009, being the date on which the Treaty of Lisbon came into force): see SI 2012/1809, art 2.

Para (4): sub-para (e) and word "; or" immediately preceding it inserted by SI 2012/2587, reg 8(1), (4). Date in force: 8 November 2012: see SI 2012/2587, reg 1.

Para (4A): sub-para (f) substituted by SI 2006/3341, reg 8.

Date in force: 1 January 2007: see SI 2006/3341, reg 1.

Para (4A): sub-para (f)(i) revoked by SI 2011/2425, reg 22(1), (3).

Date in force: 31 October 2011: see SI 2011/2425, reg 1(2).

Para (4A): sub-paras (h), (hh) substituted, for sub-para (h) as originally enacted, by SI 2006/2528, reg 8.

Date in force: 9 October 2006: see SI 2006/2528, reg 1.

Para (4A): in sub-para (j) word omitted revoked by SI 2009/362, reg 8(1), (2).

Date in force: 18 March 2009: see SI 2009/362, reg 1(2).

Para (4A): sub-para (jj) inserted by SI 2009/362, reg 8(1), (3).

Date in force: 18 March 2009: see SI 2009/362, reg 1(2).

Para (6): definition "a European Economic Area State" (omitted) revoked by SI 2006/1026, reg 3(1), (2)(b).

Date in force: 30 April 2006: see SI 2006/1026, reg 1.

[7A Entitlement of a refugee to council tax benefit

Where a person, who has made a claim for asylum, is notified that he has been recorded by the Secretary of State as a refugee, these Regulations shall have effect with respect to his entitlement to council tax benefit for the relevant period which applies in his case in accordance with Schedule A1 (treatment of claims for council tax benefit by refugees) but subject to the provisions of that Schedule.]

Amendment

Inserted by SI 2006/217, reg 7, Sch 4, para 3(1).

Date in force: 6 March 2006 (this amendment has effect until the date on which the Asylum and Immigration (Treatment of Claimants, etc) Act 2004, s 12(2)(g) comes into force): see SI 2006/217, regs 1(1), 7, Sch 4, para 1.

CHILD BENEFIT (GENERAL) REGULATIONS 2006

(SI 2006/223)

Made: 2 February 2006.

Authority: Finance Act 1999, s 133; Social Security Administration Act 1992, s 13; Social Security Contributions and Benefits Act 1992, ss 142–144, 145A, 146, 147, Schs 9, 10.

Commencement: 10 April 2006.

PART 6
RESIDENCE

21 Circumstances in which a child or qualifying young person treated as being in Great Britain

(1) For the purposes of section 146(1) of SSCBA, a child or qualifying young person who is temporarily absent from Great Britain shall be treated as being in Great Britain during—

    (a)   the first 12 weeks of any period of absence;

    (b)   any period during which that person is absent by reason only of—

        (i)   his receiving full-time education by attendance at a [school or college] in an EEA State or in Switzerland; or

        (ii)   his being engaged in an educational exchange or visit made with the written approval of the [school or college] which he normally attends;

    (c)   any period as is determined by the Commissioners during which the child or qualifying young person is absent for the specific purpose of being treated for an illness or physical or mental disability which commenced before his absence began; or

(d)   any period when he is in Northern Ireland.

(2)   For the purposes of section 146(1) of SSCBA, where a child is born while his mother is absent from Great Britain in accordance with regulation 24, he shall be treated as being in Great Britain during such period of absence after his birth as is within 12 weeks of the date on which his mother became absent from Great Britain.

Amendment
Para (1): in sub-para (b) words "school or college" in square brackets in both places they occur substituted by SI 2007/2150, regs 2, 7.

Date in force: 16 August 2007: see SI 2007/2150, reg 1.

23 Circumstances in which person treated as not being in Great Britain

(1)   A person shall be treated as not being in Great Britain for the purposes of section 146(2) of SSCBA if he is not ordinarily resident in the United Kingdom.

(2)   [Paragraphs (1) and (5) do] not apply to a Crown servant posted overseas or his partner.

(3)   A person who is in Great Britain as a result of his deportation, expulsion or other removal by compulsion of law from another country to Great Britain shall be treated as being ordinarily resident in the United Kingdom [and paragraph (5) shall not apply].

(4)   A person shall be treated as not being in Great Britain for the purposes of section 146(2) of SSCBA where he [makes a claim for child benefit on or after 1st May 2004] [and

(a)   does not have a right to reside in the United Kingdom; or

(b)   has a right to reside in the United Kingdom by virtue of—

(i)   regulation 15A(1) of the Immigration (European Economic Area) Regulations 2006, but only in a case where the right exists under that regulation because the person satisfies the criteria in regulation 15A(4A) of those Regulations; or

(ii)   Article 20 of the Treaty on the Functioning of the European Union (in a case where the right to reside arises because a British citizen would otherwise be deprived of the genuine enjoyment of the substance of their rights as a European Union citizen)].

[(5)   Subject to paragraph (6), a person is to be treated as being in Great Britain for the purposes of section 146(2) of SSCBA only if that person has been living in the United Kingdom for 3 months ending on the first day of the week referred to in that section.

(6)   Paragraph (5) does not apply where the person—

(a)   most recently entered the United Kingdom before 1st July 2014;

(b)   is a worker or a self-employed person in the United Kingdom for the purposes of Council Directive 2004/38/EC (rights of citizens of the European Union and their family members to move and reside freely within the territory of the Member States);

(c)   retains the status of a worker or self-employed person in the United Kingdom pursuant to Article 7(3) of Council Directive 2004/38/EC;

(d)   is treated as a worker in the United Kingdom pursuant to regulation 5 of the Accession of Croatia (Immigration and Worker Authorisation) Regulations 2013 (right of residence of a Croatian who is an "accession State national subject to worker authorisation");

(e)   is a family member of a person referred to in sub-paragraphs (b), (c), (d) or (i);

(f)   is a person to whom regulation 24 applies (persons temporarily absent from Great Britain) and who returns to Great Britain within 52 weeks starting from the first day of the temporary absence;

(g)   returns to the United Kingdom after a period abroad of less than 52 weeks where immediately before departing from the United Kingdom that person had been ordinarily resident in the United Kingdom for a continuous period of 3 months;

(h)   returns to Great Britain otherwise than as a worker or self-employed person after a period abroad and where, otherwise than for a period of up to 3 months ending on the day of returning, that person has paid either Class 1 or Class 2 contributions by virtue of regulation 114, 118, 146 or 147 of the Social Security (Contributions) Regulations 2001 or pursuant to an Order in Council having effect under section 179 of the Social Security Administration Act 1992;

(i)   is not a national of an EEA State and would be a worker or self-employed person in the United Kingdom for the purposes of Council Directive 2004/38/EC if that person were a national of an EEA State;

(j)   is a refugee as defined in Article 1 of the Convention relating to the Status of Refugees done at Geneva on 28th July 1951, as extended by Article 1(2) of the Protocol relating to the Status of Refugees done at New York on 31st January 1967;

(k)   has been granted leave, or is deemed to have been granted leave, outside the rules made under section 3(2) of the Immigration Act 1971 where the leave is—

     (i)   granted by the Secretary of State with recourse to public funds, or

     (ii)   deemed to have been granted by virtue of regulation 3 of the Displaced Persons (Temporary Protection) Regulations 2005;

(l)   has been granted leave to remain in the United Kingdom by the Secretary of State pending an application for indefinite leave to remain as a victim of domestic violence;

(m)   has been granted humanitarian protection by the Secretary of State under rule 339C of Part 11 of the rules made under section 3(2) of the Immigration Act 1971.

(7)   In this regulation, a "family member" means a person who is defined as a family member of another person in Article 2 of Council Directive 2004/38/EC.]

Amendment

Para (2): words in square brackets substituted by SI 2014/1511, regs 2, 3(1), (2). Date in force: 1 July 2014: see SI 2014/1511, reg 1.

Para (3): words in square brackets inserted by SI 2014/1511, regs 2, 3(1), (3). Date in force: 1 July 2014: see SI 2014/1511, reg 1.

Para (4): words in square brackets beginning with the words "makes a claim" inserted by SI 2007/2150, regs 2, 8. Date in force: 16 August 2007: see SI 2007/2150, reg 1.

Para (4): sub-paras (a), (b) and word "and" immediately preceding them substituted by SI 2012/2612, regs 2, 3. Date in force: 8 November 2012: see SI 2012/2612, reg 1.

Paras (5)–(7): inserted by SI 2014/1511, regs 2, 3(1), (4). Date in force: 1 July 2014: see SI 2014/1511, reg 1.

IMMIGRATION (EUROPEAN ECONOMIC AREA) REGULATIONS 2006

(SI 2006/1003)

Made: 30 March 2006.

Authority: European Communities Act 1972, s 2(2); Nationality, Immigration and Asylum Act 2002, s 109.

Commencement: 30 April 2006.

PART 1
INTERPRETATION ETC

1 Citation and commencement

These Regulations may be cited as the Immigration (European Economic Area) Regulations 2006 and shall come into force on 30th April 2006.

2 General interpretation

(1) In these Regulations—

"the 1971 Act" means the Immigration Act 1971;

"the 1999 Act" means the Immigration and Asylum Act 1999;

"the 2002 Act" means the Nationality, Immigration and Asylum Act 2002;

["the Accession Regulations" means the Accession (Immigration and Worker Registration) Regulations 2004;]

["civil partner" does not include—

    (a)   a party to a civil partnership of convenience; or

    (b)   the civil partner ("C") of a person ("P") where a spouse, civil partner or durable partner of C or P is already present in the United Kingdom;]

"decision maker" means the Secretary of State, an immigration officer or an entry clearance officer (as the case may be);

["deportation order" means an order made pursuant to regulation 24(3);]

["derivative residence card" means a card issued to a person, in accordance with regulation 18A, as proof of the holder's derivative right to reside in the United Kingdom as at the date of issue;]

"document certifying permanent residence" means a document issued to an EEA national, in accordance with regulation 18, as proof of the holder's permanent right of residence under regulation 15 as at the date of issue;

["durable partner" does not include the durable partner ("D") of a person ("P") where a spouse, civil partner or durable partner of D or P is already present in the United Kingdom and where that marriage, civil partnership or durable partnership is subsisting;]

["EEA decision" means a decision under these Regulations that concerns—

    (a)   a person's entitlement to be admitted to the United Kingdom;

    (b)   a person's entitlement to be issued with or have renewed, or not to have revoked, a registration certificate, residence card, derivative residence card, document certifying permanent residence or permanent residence card;

    (c)   a person's removal from the United Kingdom; or

    (d)   the cancellation, pursuant to regulation 20A, of a person's right to reside in the United Kingdom;

[but does not include decisions under regulations 24AA (human rights considerations and interim orders to suspend removal) or 29AA (temporary admission in order to submit case in person);]]

"EEA family permit" means a document issued to a person, in accordance with regulation 12, in connection with his admission to the United Kingdom;

"EEA national" means a national of an EEA State [who is not also a [British citizen]];

"EEA State" means—

    (a)   a member State, other than the United Kingdom;

    (b)   Norway, Iceland or Liechtenstein; or

    (c)   Switzerland;

"entry clearance" has the meaning given in section 33(1) of the 1971 Act;

"entry clearance officer" means a person responsible for the grant or refusal of entry clearance;

["exclusion order" means an order made under regulation 19(1B)";]

"immigration rules" has the meaning given in section 33(1) of the 1971 Act;

"military service" means service in the armed forces of an EEA State;

"permanent residence card" means a card issued to a person who is not an EEA national, in accordance with regulation 18, as proof of the holder's permanent right of residence under regulation 15 as at the date of issue;

[" . . . qualifying EEA State residence card" means—

    (a)   a document called a "Residence card of a family member of a Union Citizen" issued under Article 10 of Council Directive 2004/38/EC (as applied, where relevant, by the EEA Agreement) by an EEA State listed in sub-paragraph (b) to a non-EEA family member of an EEA national as proof of the holder's right of residence in that State;

    (b)   Germany and Estonia;]

"registration certificate" means a certificate issued to an EEA national, in accordance with regulation 16, as proof of the holder's right of residence in the United Kingdom as at the date of issue;

"relevant EEA national" in relation to an extended family member has the meaning given in regulation 8(6);

"residence card" means a card issued to a person who is not an EEA national, in accordance with regulation 17, as proof of the holder's right of residence in the United Kingdom as at the date of issue;

["spouse" does not include—

    (a)   a party to a marriage of convenience; or

    (b)   the spouse ("S") of a person ("P") where a spouse, civil partner or durable partner of S or P is already present in the United Kingdom;]

. . .

(2)   Paragraph (1) is subject to paragraph 1(a) of Schedule 4 (transitional provisions).

[(3)   Section 11 of the 1971 Act (construction of references to entry) shall apply for the purpose of determining whether a person has entered the United Kingdom for the purpose of these Regulations as it applies for the purpose of determining whether a person has entered the United Kingdom for the purpose of that Act.]

Amendment

Para (1): definition "the Accession Regulations" inserted by SI 2011/544, reg 5, Sch 2, para 1. Date in force: 1 May 2011: see SI 2011/544, reg 1(1).

Para (1): definition "civil partner" substituted by SI 2012/1547, reg 3, Sch 1, para 1(b). Date in force: 16 July 2012: see SI 2012/1547, reg 2(1).

Para (1): definition "deportation order" inserted by SI 2009/1117, reg 2, Sch 1, para 1(a)(i). Date in force: 1 June 2009: see SI 2009/1117, reg 1.

Para (1): definitions "derivative residence card" and "durable partner" inserted by SI 2012/1547, reg 3, Sch 1, para 1(a). Date in force: 16 July 2012: see SI 2012/1547, reg 2(1).

Para (1): definition "EEA decision" substituted by SI 2012/1547, reg 3, Sch 1, para 1(c). Date in force: 16 July 2012: see SI 2012/1547, regs 1, 4.

Para (1): in definition "EEA decision" words in square brackets inserted by SI 2014/1976, reg 3, Schedule, para 1(a). Date in force: 28 July 2014, subject to transitional provisions: see SI 2014/1976, reg 2(1).

Para (1): in definition "EEA national" words in square brackets beginning with the words "who is not also a" inserted by SI 2012/1547, reg 3, Sch 1, para 1(d). Date in force: 16 October 2012: see SI 2012/1547, reg 2(2); for transitional provisions see Sch 3 thereof.

Para (1): in definition "EEA national" words "British citizen" in square brackets substituted by SI 2012/2560, reg 2, Schedule, para 7(2). Date in force: 8 November 2012: see SI 2012/2560, reg 1.

Para (1): definition "exclusion order" inserted by SI 2009/1117, reg 2, Sch 1, para 1(a)(ii).

Date in force: 1 June 2009: see SI 2009/1117, reg 1.

Para (1): definition "qualifying EEA State residence card" inserted by SI 2013/3032, reg 4, Sch 1, para 1. Date in force: 7 April 2014: see SI 2013/3032, reg 2(2) and word omitted from that definition revoked by SI 2014/1976, reg 3, Schedule, para 1(b). Date in force: 28 July 2014, subject to transitional provisions: see SI 2014/1976, reg 2(1).

Para (1): definition "spouse" substituted by SI 2012/1547, reg 3, Sch 1, para 1(e). Date in force: 16 July 2012: see SI 2012/1547, reg 2(1).

Para (1): definition "United Kingdom national" (omitted) revoked by SI 2012/2560, reg 2, Schedule, para 7(1). Date in force: 8 November 2012: see SI 2012/2560, reg 1.

Para (3): inserted by SI 2009/1117, reg 2, Sch 1, para 1(b).

Date in force: 1 June 2009: see SI 2009/1117, reg 1.

3 Continuity of residence

(1) This regulation applies for the purpose of calculating periods of continuous residence in the United Kingdom under regulation 5(1) and regulation 15.

(2) Continuity of residence is not affected by—

    (a)   periods of absence from the United Kingdom which do not exceed six months in total in any year;

    (b)   periods of absence from the United Kingdom on military service; or

    (c)   any one absence from the United Kingdom not exceeding twelve months for an important reason such as pregnancy and childbirth, serious illness, study or vocational training or an overseas posting.

(3) But continuity of residence is broken if a person is removed from the United Kingdom under [these Regulations].

Amendment

Para (3): words "these Regulations" in square brackets substituted by SI 2009/1117, reg 2, Sch 1, para 2.

Date in force: 1 June 2009: see SI 2009/1117, reg 1.

4 "Worker", "self-employed person", "self-sufficient person" and "student"

(1) In these Regulations—

    (a)   "worker" means a worker within the meaning of [Article 45 of the Treaty on the Functioning of the European Union];

    (b)   "self-employed person" means a person who establishes himself in order to pursue activity as a self-employed person in accordance with [Article 49 of the Treaty on the Functioning of the European Union];

    (c)   "self-sufficient person" means a person who has—

        (i)   sufficient resources not to become a burden on the social assistance system of the United Kingdom during his period of residence; and

        (ii)   comprehensive sickness insurance cover in the United Kingdom;

    (d)   "student" means a person who—

        [(i)   is enrolled, for the principal purpose of following a course of study (including vocational training), at a public or private establishment which is—

            (aa)   financed from public funds; or

            (bb)   otherwise recognised by the Secretary of State as an establishment which has been accredited for the purpose of providing such courses or training within the law or administrative practice of the part of the United Kingdom in which the establishment is located;]

        (ii)   has comprehensive sickness insurance cover in the United Kingdom; and

(iii)   assures the Secretary of State, by means of a declaration, or by such equivalent means as the person may choose, that he has sufficient resources not to become a burden on the social assistance system of the United Kingdom during his period of residence.

(2)   For the purposes of paragraph (1)(c), where family members of the person concerned reside in the United Kingdom and their right to reside is dependent upon their being family members of that person—

(a)   the requirement for that person to have sufficient resources not to become a burden on the social assistance system of the United Kingdom during his period of residence shall only be satisfied if his resources and those of the family members are sufficient to avoid him and the family members becoming such a burden;

(b)   the requirement for that person to have comprehensive sickness insurance cover in the United Kingdom shall only be satisfied if he and his family members have such cover.

(3)   For the purposes of paragraph (1)(d), where family members of the person concerned reside in the United Kingdom and their right to reside is dependent upon their being family members of that person, the requirement for that person to assure the Secretary of State that he has sufficient resources not to become a burden on the social assistance system of the United Kingdom during his period of residence shall only be satisfied if he assures the Secretary of State that his resources and those of the family members are sufficient to avoid him and the family members becoming such a burden.

(4)   For the purposes of paragraphs (1)(c) and (d) and paragraphs (2) and (3), the resources of the person concerned and, where applicable, any family members, are to be regarded as sufficient if—

(a)   they exceed the maximum level of resources which a [British citizen] and his family members may possess if he is to become eligible for social assistance under the United Kingdom benefit system; or

(b)   paragraph (a) does not apply but, taking into account the personal situation of the person concerned and, where applicable, any family members, it appears to the decision maker that the resources of the person or persons concerned should be regarded as sufficient.]

[(5)   For the purpose of regulation 15A(2) references in this regulation to "family members" includes a "primary carer" as defined in regulation 15A(7).]

Amendment

Para (1): in sub-para (a) words "Article 45 of the Treaty on the Functioning of the European Union" in square brackets substituted by SI 2012/1809, art 3(1), Schedule, Pt 2. Date in force: 1 August 2012: see SI 2012/1809, art 2.

Para (1): in sub-para (b) words "Article 49 of the Treaty on the Functioning of the European Union" in square brackets substituted by SI 2012/1809, art 3(1), Schedule, Pt 2. Date in force: 1 August 2012: see SI 2012/1809, art 2.

Para (1): sub-para (d)(i) substituted by SI 2012/1547, reg 3, Sch 1, para 2(a). Date in force: 16 July 2012: see SI 2012/1547, reg 2(1).

Para (4): substituted by SI 2011/1247, reg 2(1), (2). Date in force: 2 June 2011: see SI 2011/1247, reg 1(1).

Para (4): in sub-para (a) words "British citizen" in square brackets substituted by SI 2012/2560, reg 2, Schedule, para 7(2). Date in force: 8 November 2012: see SI 2012/2560, reg 1.

Para (5): inserted by SI 2012/1547, reg 3, Sch 1, para 2(b). Date in force: 16 July 2012: see SI 2012/1547, reg 2(1).

5   "Worker or self-employed person who has ceased activity"

(1)   In these Regulations, "worker or self-employed person who has ceased activity" means an EEA national who satisfies the conditions in paragraph (2), (3), (4) or (5).

(2)   A person satisfies the conditions in this paragraph if he—

(a) terminates his activity as a worker or self-employed person and—
    (i) has reached the age at which he is entitled to a state pension on the date on which he terminates his activity; or
    (ii) in the case of a worker, ceases working to take early retirement;
(b) pursued his activity as a worker or self-employed person in the United Kingdom for at least twelve months prior to the termination; and
(c) resided in the United Kingdom continuously for more than three years prior to the termination.

(3) A person satisfies the conditions in this paragraph if—
(a) he terminates his activity in the United Kingdom as a worker or self-employed person as a result of a permanent incapacity to work; and
(b) either—
    (i) he resided in the United Kingdom continuously for more than two years prior to the termination; or
    (ii) the incapacity is the result of an accident at work or an occupational disease that entitles him to a pension payable in full or in part by an institution in the United Kingdom.

(4) A person satisfies the conditions in this paragraph if—
(a) he is active as a worker or self-employed person in an EEA State but retains his place of residence in the United Kingdom, to which he returns as a rule at least once a week; and
(b) prior to becoming so active in that EEA State, he had been continuously resident and continuously active as a worker or self-employed person in the United Kingdom for at least three years.

(5) A person who satisfies the condition in paragraph (4)(a) but not the condition in paragraph (4)(b) shall, for the purposes of paragraphs (2) and (3), be treated as being active and resident in the United Kingdom during any period in which he is working or self-employed in the EEA State.

(6) The conditions in paragraphs (2) and (3) as to length of residence and activity as a worker or self-employed person shall not apply in relation to a person whose spouse or civil partner is a [British citizen].

(7) [Subject to [regulations 6(2), 7A(3) or 7B(3)], for the purposes of this regulation—]
(a) periods of inactivity for reasons not of the person's own making;
(b) periods of inactivity due to illness or accident; and
(c) in the case of a worker, periods of involuntary unemployment duly recorded by the relevant employment office,
shall be treated as periods of activity as a worker or self-employed person, as the case may be.

Amendment

Para (6): words "British citizen" in square brackets substituted by SI 2012/2560, art 2, Schedule, para 7(2). Date in force: 8 November 2012: see SI 2012/2560, reg 1.

Para (7): words in first (outer) pair of square brackets substituted by SI 2011/544, reg 5, Sch 2, para 2. Date in force: 1 May 2011: see SI 2011/544, reg 1(1).

Para (7): words "regulations 6(2), 7A(3) or 7B(3)" in square brackets substituted by SI 2013/3032, reg 4, Sch 1, para 2. Date in force: 1 January 2014: see SI 2013/3032, reg 2(1).

6 "Qualified person"

(1) In these Regulations, "qualified person" means a person who is an EEA national and in the United Kingdom as—
(a) a jobseeker;
(b) a worker;
(c) a self-employed person;
(d) a self-sufficient person; or

    (e)   a student.

(2) [Subject to [regulations 7A(4) and 7B(4)], a person who is no longer working shall not cease to be treated as a worker for the purpose of paragraph (1)(b) if—]

    (a)   he is temporarily unable to work as the result of an illness or accident;

    [(b)   he is in duly recorded involuntary unemployment after having been employed in the United Kingdom for at least one year, provided that he—

        (i)   has registered as a jobseeker with the relevant employment office; and

        (ii)   satisfies conditions A and B;]

    [(ba)   he is in duly recorded involuntary unemployment after having been employed in the United Kingdom for less than one year, provided that he—

        (i)   has registered as a jobseeker with the relevant employment office; and

        (ii)   satisfies conditions A and B;]

    (c)   he is involuntarily unemployed and has embarked on vocational training; or

    (d)   he has voluntarily ceased working and embarked on vocational training that is related to his previous employment.

[(2A) A person to whom paragraph (2)(ba) applies may only retain worker status for a maximum of six months.]

(3) A person who is no longer in self-employment shall not cease to be treated as a self-employed person for the purpose of paragraph (1)(c) if he is temporarily unable to pursue his activity as a self-employed person as the result of an illness or accident.

[(4) For the purpose of paragraph (1)(a), a "jobseeker" is a person who satisfies conditions [A, B and, where relevant, C].

(5) Condition A is that the person—

    (a)   entered the United Kingdom in order to seek employment; or

    (b)   is present in the United Kingdom seeking employment, immediately after enjoying a right to reside pursuant to paragraph (1)(b) to (e) (disregarding any period during which worker status was retained pursuant to paragraph (2)(b) or (ba)).

(6) Condition B is that the person can provide evidence that he is seeking employment and has a genuine chance of being engaged.

(7) A person may not retain the status of a worker pursuant to paragraph (2)(b), or jobseeker pursuant to paragraph (1)(a), for longer than [the relevant period] unless he can provide compelling evidence that he is continuing to seek employment and has a genuine chance of being engaged.]

[(8) In paragraph (7), "the relevant period" means—

    (a)   in the case of a person retaining worker status pursuant to paragraph (2)(b), a continuous period of six months;

    (b)   in the case of a jobseeker, 182 days, minus the cumulative total of any days during which the person concerned previously enjoyed a right to reside as a jobseeker, not including any days prior to a continuous absence from the United Kingdom of at least 12 months.

(9) Condition C applies where the person concerned has, previously, enjoyed a right to reside under this regulation as a result of satisfying conditions A and B—

    (a)   in the case of a person to whom paragraph (2)(b) or (ba) applied, for at least six months; or

    (b)   in the case of a jobseeker, for at least 182 days in total,

unless the person concerned has, since enjoying the above right to reside, been continuously absent from the United Kingdom for at least 12 months.

(10) Condition C is that the person has had a period of absence from the United Kingdom.

(11) Where condition C applies—
- (a) paragraph (7) does not apply; and
- (b) condition B has effect as if "compelling" were inserted before "evidence".]

Amendment

Para (2): words from "Subject to" to "paragraph (1)(b) if—" in square brackets substituted by SI 2011/544, reg 5, Sch 2, para 3.

Date in force: 1 May 2011: see SI 2011/544, reg 1(1).

Para (2): words "regulations 7A(4) and 7B(4)" in square brackets substituted by SI 2013/3032, reg 4, Sch 1, para 3(a).

Date in force: 1 January 2014: see SI 2013/3032, reg 2(1).

Para (2): sub-para (b) substituted by SI 2013/3032, reg 4, Sch 1, para 3(b).

Date in force: 1 January 2014: see SI 2013/3032, reg 2(1); for transitional provisions see reg 6, Sch 3, para 1 thereto.

Para (2): sub-para (ba) inserted by SI 2013/3032, reg 4, Sch 1, para 3(c).

Date in force: 1 January 2014: see SI 2013/3032, reg 2(1); for transitional provisions see reg 6, Sch 3, para 1 thereto.

Para (2A): inserted by SI 2013/3032, reg 4, Sch 1, para 3(d).

Date in force: 1 January 2014: see SI 2013/3032, reg 2(1); for transitional provisions see reg 6, Sch 3, para 1 thereto.

Paras (4)–(7): substituted, for para (4) as originally enacted, by SI 2013/3032, reg 4, Sch 1, para 3(e).

Date in force: 1 January 2014: see SI 2013/3032, reg 2(1); for transitional provisions see reg 6, Sch 3, para 1 thereto.

Para (4): words "A, B and, where relevant, C" in square brackets substituted by SI 2014/1451, reg 3(1), (2); for transitional provisions see reg 4.

Date in force: 1 July 2014: see SI 2014/1451, reg 1.

Para (7): words "the relevant period" in square brackets substituted by SI 2014/1451, reg 3(1), (3); for transitional provisions see reg 4.

Date in force: 1 July 2014: see SI 2014/1451, reg 1.

Paras (8)–(11): inserted by SI 2014/1451, reg 3(1), (4); for transitional provisions see reg 4.

Date in force: 1 July 2014: see SI 2014/1451, reg 1.

7 Family member

(1) Subject to paragraph (2), for the purposes of these Regulations the following persons shall be treated as the family members of another person—
- (a) his spouse or his civil partner;
- (b) direct descendants of his, his spouse or his civil partner who are—
  - (i) under 21; or
  - (ii) dependants of his, his spouse or his civil partner;
- (c) dependent direct relatives in his ascending line or that of his spouse or his civil partner;
- (d) a person who is to be treated as the family member of that other person under paragraph (3).

(2) A person shall not be treated under paragraph (1)(b) or (c) as the family member of a student residing in the United Kingdom after the period of three months beginning on the date on which the student is admitted to the United Kingdom unless—
- (a) in the case of paragraph (b), the person is the dependent child of the student or of his spouse or civil partner; or
- (b) the student also falls within one of the other categories of qualified persons mentioned in regulation 6(1).

(3) Subject to paragraph (4), a person who is an extended family member and has been issued with an EEA family permit, a registration certificate or a residence card shall be treated as the family member of the relevant EEA national for as long as he

continues to satisfy the conditions in regulation 8(2), (3), (4) or (5) in relation to that EEA national and the permit, certificate or card has not ceased to be valid or been revoked.

(4)   Where the relevant EEA national is a student, the extended family member shall only be treated as the family member of that national under paragraph (3) if either the EEA family permit was issued under regulation 12(2), the registration certificate was issued under regulation 16(5) or the residence card was issued under regulation 17(4).

[7A Application of the Accession Regulations

(1)   This regulation applies to an EEA national who was an accession State worker requiring registration on 30th April 2011 ('an accession worker').

(2)   In this regulation—

"accession State worker requiring registration" has the same meaning as in regulation 1(2)(d) of the Accession Regulations;

"legally working" has the same meaning as in regulation 2(7) of the Accession Regulations.

(3)   In regulation 5(7)(c), where the worker is an accession worker, periods of involuntary unemployment duly recorded by the relevant employment office shall be treated only as periods of activity as a worker—

    (a)   during any period in which regulation 5(4) of the Accession Regulations applied to that person; or

    (b)   when the unemployment began on or after 1st May 2011.

(4)   Regulation 6(2) applies to an accession worker where he—

    (a)   was a person to whom regulation 5(4) of the Accession Regulations applied on 30th April 2011; or

    (b)   became unable to work, became unemployed or ceased to work, as the case maybe, on or after 1st May 2011.

(5)   For the purposes of regulation 15, an accession worker shall be treated as having resided in accordance with these Regulations during any period before 1st May 2011 in which the accession worker—

    (a)   was legally working in the United Kingdom; or

    (b)   was a person to whom regulation 5(4) of the Accession Regulations applied

(6)   Subject to paragraph (7), a registration certificate issued to an accession worker under regulation 8 of the Accession Regulations shall, from 1st May 2011, be treated as if it was a registration certificate issued under these Regulations where the accession worker was legally working in the United Kingdom for the employer specified in that certificate on—

    (a)   30th April 2011; or

    (b)   the date on which the certificate is issued where it is issued after 30th April 2011.

(7)   Paragraph (6) does not apply—

    (a)   if the Secretary of State issues a registration certificate in accordance with regulation 16 to an accession worker on or after 1st May 2011; and

    (b)   from the date of registration stated on that certificate.]

Amendment

Inserted by SI 2011/544, reg 5, Sch 2, para 4.

Date in force: 1 May 2011: see SI 2011/544, reg 1(1).

[7B Application of the EU2 Regulations

(1)   This regulation applies to an EEA national who was an accession State national subject to worker authorisation before 1st January 2014.

(2)   In this regulation—

"accession State national subject to worker authorisation" has the same meaning as in regulation 2 of the EU2 Regulations;

"the EU2 Regulations" means the Accession (Immigration and Worker Authorisation) Regulations 2006.

(3) Regulation 2(12) of the EU2 Regulations (accession State national subject to worker authorisation: legally working) has effect for the purposes of this regulation as it does for regulation 2(3) and (4) of the EU2 Regulations.

(4) In regulation 5(7)(c), where the worker is an accession State national subject to worker authorisation, periods of involuntary unemployment duly recorded by the relevant employment office must only be treated as periods of activity as a worker when the unemployment began on or after 1st January 2014.

(5) Regulation 6(2) applies to an accession State national subject to worker authorisation where the accession State national subject to worker authorisation became unable to work, became unemployed or ceased to work, as the case may be, on or after 1st January 2014.

(6) For the purposes of regulation 15, an accession State national subject to worker authorisation must be treated as having resided in accordance with these Regulations during any period before 1st January 2014 in which the accession State national subject to worker authorisation was legally working in the United Kingdom.

(7) An accession worker card issued to an accession State national subject to worker authorisation under regulation 11 of the EU2 Regulations before 1st January 2014 must be treated as if it were a registration certificate issued under these Regulations so long as it has not expired.]

Amendment

Inserted by SI 2013/3032, reg 4, Sch 1, para 4.
Date in force: 1 January 2014: see SI 2013/3032, reg 2(1).

8 "Extended family member"

(1) In these Regulations "extended family member" means a person who is not a family member of an EEA national under regulation 7(1)(a), (b) or (c) and who satisfies the conditions in paragraph (2), (3), (4) or (5).

(2) A person satisfies the condition in this paragraph if the person is a relative of an EEA national, his spouse or his civil partner and—

    (a)   the person is residing in [a country other than the United Kingdom] . . . and is dependent upon the EEA national or is a member of his household;

    (b)   the person satisfied the condition in paragraph (a) and is accompanying the EEA national to the United Kingdom or wishes to join him there; or

    (c)   the person satisfied the condition in paragraph (a), has joined the EEA national in the United Kingdom and continues to be dependent upon him or to be a member of his household.

(3) A person satisfies the condition in this paragraph if the person is a relative of an EEA national or his spouse or his civil partner and, on serious health grounds, strictly requires the personal care of the EEA national his spouse or his civil partner.

(4) A person satisfies the condition in this paragraph if the person is a relative of an EEA national and would meet the requirements in the immigration rules (other than those relating to entry clearance) for indefinite leave to enter or remain in the United Kingdom as a dependent relative of the EEA national were the EEA national a person present and settled in the United Kingdom.

(5) A person satisfies the condition in this paragraph if the person is the partner of an EEA national (other than a civil partner) and can prove to the decision maker that he is in a durable relationship with the EEA national.

(6) In these Regulations "relevant EEA national" means, in relation to an extended family member, the EEA national who is or whose spouse or civil partner is the relative

of the extended family member for the purpose of paragraph (2), (3) or (4) or the EEA national who is the partner of the extended family member for the purpose of paragraph (5).

Amendment

Para (2): in para (a) words "a country other than the United Kingdom" in square brackets substituted by SI 2011/1247, reg 2(1), (3).

Date in force: 2 June 2011: see SI 2011/1247, reg 1(1).

Para (2): in sub-para (a) words omitted revoked by SI 2012/2560, reg 2, Schedule, para 1. Date in force: 8 November 2012: see SI 2012/2560, reg 1.

[9 Family members of British citizens

(1) If the conditions in paragraph (2) are satisfied, these Regulations apply to a person who is the family member of a British citizen as if the British citizen ("P") were an EEA national.

(2) The conditions are that—

    (a)   P is residing in an EEA State as a worker or self-employed person or was so residing before returning to the United Kingdom;

    (b)   if the family member of P is P's spouse or civil partner, the parties are living together in the EEA State or had entered into the marriage or civil partnership and were living together in the EEA State before the British citizen returned to the United Kingdom; and

    (c)   the centre of P's life has transferred to the EEA State where P resided as a worker or self-employed person.

(3) Factors relevant to whether the centre of P's life has transferred to another EEA State include—

    (a)   the period of residence in the EEA State as a worker or self-employed person;

    (b)   the location of P's principal residence;

    (c)   the degree of integration of P in the EEA State.

(4) Where these Regulations apply to the family member of P, P is to be treated as holding a valid passport issued by an EEA State for the purpose of the application of regulation 13 to that family member.]

Amendment

Substituted by SI 2013/3032, reg 4, Sch 1, para 5.

Date in force: 1 January 2014: see SI 2013/3032, reg 2(1); for transitional provisions see reg 6, Sch 3, para 2 thereto.

10 "Family member who has retained the right of residence"

(1) In these Regulations, "family member who has retained the right of residence" means, subject to paragraph (8), a person who satisfies the conditions in paragraph (2), (3), (4) or (5).

(2) A person satisfies the conditions in this paragraph if—

    [(a)   he was a family member of a qualified person or of an EEA national with a permanent right residence when that person died;]

    (b)   he resided in the United Kingdom in accordance with these Regulations for at least the year immediately before the death of [the qualified person or the EEA national with a permanent right of residence]; and

    (c)   he satisfies the condition in paragraph (6).

(3) A person satisfies the conditions in this paragraph if—

    (a)   he is the direct descendant of—

        (i)   [a qualified person or an EEA national with a permanent right of residence] who has died;

        (ii)   a person who ceased to be a qualified person on ceasing to reside in the United Kingdom; or

    (iii)   the person who was the spouse or civil partner of [the qualified person or the EEA national with a permanent right of residence] mentioned in sub-paragraph (i) when he died or is the spouse or civil partner of the person mentioned in sub-paragraph (ii); and

  (b)   he was attending an educational course in the United Kingdom immediately before [he qualified person or the EEA national with a permanent right of residence] died or ceased to be a qualified person and continues to attend such a course.

(4) A person satisfies the conditions in this paragraph if the person is the parent with actual custody of a child who satisfies the condition in paragraph (3).

(5) A person satisfies the conditions in this paragraph if—

  [(a) he ceased to be a family member of a qualified person or of an EEA national with a permanent right of residence on the termination of the marriage or civil partnership of that person;]

  (b)   he was residing in the United Kingdom in accordance with these Regulations at the date of the termination;

  (c)   he satisfies the condition in paragraph (6); and

  (d)   either—

    (i)   prior to the initiation of the proceedings for the termination of the marriage or the civil partnership the marriage or civil partnership had lasted for at least three years and the parties to the marriage or civil partnership had resided in the United Kingdom for at least one year during its duration;

    (ii)   the former spouse or civil partner of [the qualified person or the EEA national with a permanent right of residence] has custody of a child of [the qualified person or the EEA national with a permanent right of residence];

    [(iii) the former spouse or civil partner of the qualified person or the EEA national with a permanent right of residence has the right of access to a child of the qualified person or the EEA national with a permanent right of residence, where the child is under the age of 18 and where a court has ordered that such access must take place in the United Kingdom; or]

    (iv) the continued right of residence in the United Kingdom of the person is warranted by particularly difficult circumstances, such as he or another family member having been a victim of domestic violence while the marriage or civil partnership was subsisting.

(6) The condition in this paragraph is that the person—

  (a)   is not an EEA national but would, if he were an EEA national, be a worker, a self-employed person or a self-sufficient person under regulation 6; or

  (b)   is the family member of a person who falls within paragraph (a).

(7) In this regulation, "educational course" means a course within the scope of Article 12 of Council Regulation (EEC) No 1612/68 on freedom of movement for workers.

(8) A person with a permanent right of residence under regulation 15 shall not become a family member who has retained the right of residence on the death or departure from the United Kingdom of [the qualified person or the EEA national with a permanent right of residence] or the termination of the marriage or civil partnership, as the case may be, and a family member who has retained the right of residence shall cease to have that status on acquiring a permanent right of residence under regulation 15.

Amendment

Para (2): sub-para (a) substituted by SI 2012/1547, reg 3, Sch 1, para 3(a).

Date in force: 16 July 2012: see SI 2012/1547, reg 2(1).

Para (2): in sub-para (b) words from "the qualified person" to "right of residence" in square brackets substituted by SI 2012/1547, reg 3, Sch 1, para 3(d).

Date in force: 16 July 2012: see SI 2012/1547, reg 2(1).

Para (3): in sub-para (a)(i) words from "a qualified person" to "right of residence" in square brackets substituted by SI 2012/1547, reg 3, Sch 1, para 3(e).

Date in force: 16 July 2012: see SI 2012/1547, reg 2(1).

Para (3): in sub-para (a)(iii) words from "the qualified person" to "right of residence" in square brackets substituted by SI 2012/1547, reg 3. Sch 1, para 3(d).

Date in force: 16 July 2012: see SI 2012/1547, reg 2(1).

Para (3): in sub-para (b) words from "the qualified person" to "right of residence" in square brackets substituted by SI 2012/1547, reg 3, Sch 1, para 3(d).

Date in force: 16 July 2012: see SI 2012/1547, reg 2(1).

Para (5): sub-para (a) substituted by SI 2012/1547, reg 3, Sch 1, para 3(b).

Date in force: 16 July 2012: see SI 2012/1547, reg 2(1).

Para (5): in sub-para (d)(ii) words from "the qualified person" to "right of residence" in square brackets substituted by SI 2012/1547, reg 3, Sch 1, para 3(d).

Date in force: 16 July 2012: see SI 2012/1547, reg 2(1).

Para (5): sub-para (d)(iii) substituted by SI 2012/1547, reg 3, Sch 1, para 3(c).

Date in force: 16 July 2012: see SI 2012/1547, reg 2(1).

Para (8): words from "the qualified person" to "right of residence" in square brackets substituted by SI 2012/1547, reg 3, Sch 1, para 3(d).

Date in force: 16 July 2012: see SI 2012/1547, reg 2(1).

PART 2
EEA RIGHTS

11 Right of admission to the United Kingdom

(1) An EEA national must be admitted to the United Kingdom if he produces on arrival a valid national identity card or passport issued by an EEA State.

[(2) A person who is not an EEA national must be admitted to the United Kingdom if he is—

    (a)   a family member of an EEA national and produces on arrival a valid passport and a qualifying EEA State residence card, provided the conditions in regulation 19(2)(a) (non-EEA family member to be accompanying or joining EEA national in the United Kingdom) and (b) (EEA national must have a right to reside in the United Kingdom under these Regulations) are met; or

    (b)   a family member of an EEA national, a family member who has retained the right of residence, a person who meets the criteria in paragraph (5) or a person with a permanent right of residence under regulation 15 and produces on arrival—

        (i)   a valid passport; and

        (ii)   an EEA family permit, a residence card, a derivative residence card or a permanent residence card.]

[(3) An immigration officer must not place a stamp in the passport of a person admitted to the United Kingdom under this regulation who is not an EEA national if the person produces a residence card, a derivative residence card, a permanent residence card or a qualifying EEA State residence card.]

(4) Before an immigration officer refuses admission to the United Kingdom to a person under this regulation because the person does not produce on arrival a document mentioned in paragraph (1) or (2), the immigration officer must give the person every reasonable opportunity to obtain the document or have it brought to him within a reasonable period of time or to prove by other means that he is—

(a)   an EEA national;

(b)   a family member of an EEA national with a right to accompany that national or join him in the United Kingdom; . . .

[(ba) a person who meets the criteria in paragraph (5); or]

(c)   a family member who has retained the right of residence or a person with a permanent right of residence under regulation 15.

[(5) A person ("P") meets the criteria in this paragraph where—

(a)   P previously resided in the United Kingdom pursuant to regulation 15A(3) and would be entitled to reside in the United Kingdom pursuant to that regulation were P in the country;

(b)   P is accompanying an EEA national to, or joining an EEA national in, the United Kingdom and P would be entitled to reside in the United Kingdom pursuant to regulation 15A(2) were P and the EEA national both in the United Kingdom;

(c)   P is accompanying a person ("the relevant person") to, or joining the relevant person in, the United Kingdom and—

    (i)   the relevant person is residing, or has resided, in the United Kingdom pursuant to regulation 15A(3); and

    (ii) P would be entitled to reside in the United Kingdom pursuant to regulation 15A(4) were P and the relevant person both in the [United Kingdom;]

(d)   P is accompanying a person who meets the criteria in (b) or (c) ("the relevant person") to the United Kingdom and—

    (i)   P and the relevant person are both—

       (aa) seeking admission to the United Kingdom in reliance on this paragraph for the first time; or

       (bb) returning to the United Kingdom having previously resided there pursuant to the same provisions of regulation 15A in reliance on which they now base their claim to admission; and

    (ii) P would be entitled to reside in the United Kingdom pursuant to regulation 15A(5) were P and the relevant [person there; or]

[(e)   P is accompanying a British citizen to, or joining a British citizen in, the United Kingdom and P would be entitled to reside in the United Kingdom pursuant to regulation 15A(4A) were P and the British citizen both in the United Kingdom.]

(6) Paragraph (7) applies where—

(a)   a person ("P") seeks admission to the United Kingdom in reliance on [paragraph (5)(b), (c) or (e)]; and

(b)   if P were in the United Kingdom, P would have a derived right of residence by virtue of regulation 15A(7)(b)(ii).

(7) Where this paragraph applies a person ("P") will only be regarded as meeting the criteria in [paragraph (5)(b), (c) or (e)] where P—

(a)   is accompanying the person with whom P would on admission to the United Kingdom jointly share care responsibility for the purpose of regulation 15A(7)(b)(ii); or

(b)   has previously resided in the United Kingdom pursuant to [regulation 15A(2), (4) or (4A)] as a joint primary carer and seeks admission to the United Kingdom in order to reside there again on the same basis.]

[(8)] But this regulation is subject to regulations 19(1)[, (1A)][, (1AB) and (2)].

Amendment

Para (2): substituted by SI 2013/3032, reg 4, Sch 1, para 6(a).
Date in force: 7 April 2014: see SI 2013/3032, reg 2(2).

Para (3): substituted by SI 2013/3032, reg 4, Sch 1, para 6(b).

Date in force: 7 April 2014: see SI 2013/3032, reg 2(2).

Para (4): in sub-para (b) word omitted revoked by SI 2012/1547, reg 3, Sch 1, para 4(c)(i).

Date in force: 16 July 2012: see SI 2012/1547, reg 2(1).

Para (4): sub-para (ba) inserted by SI 2012/1547, Sch 1, para 4(c)(ii).

Date in force: 16 July 2012: see SI 2012/1547, reg 2(1).

Para (5)–(7): inserted by SI 2012/1547, reg 3, Sch 1, para 4(d).

Date in force: 16 July 2012: see SI 2012/1547, reg 2(1).

Para (5): in sub-para (c)(ii) words "United Kingdom;" in square brackets substituted by SI 2012/2560, reg 2, Schedule, para 2(a).

Date in force: 8 November 2012: see SI 2012/2560, reg 1.

Para (5): in sub-para (d)(ii) words "person there; or" in square brackets substituted by SI 2012/2560, reg 2, Schedule, para 2(b).

Date in force: 8 November 2012: see SI 2012/2560, reg 1.

Para (5): sub-para (e) inserted by SI 2012/2560, reg 2, Schedule, para 2(b).

Date in force: 8 November 2012: see SI 2012/2560, reg 1.

Para (6): in sub-para (a) words "paragraph (5)(b), (c) or (e)" in square brackets substituted by SI 2012/2560, reg 2, Schedule, para 2(c).

Date in force: 8 November 2012: see SI 2012/2560, reg 1.

Para (7): words "paragraph (5)(b), (c) or (e)" in square brackets substituted by SI 2012/2560, reg 2, Schedule, para 2(c).

Date in force: 8 November 2012: see SI 2012/2560, reg 1.

Para (7): in sub-para (b) words "regulation 15A(2), (4) or (4A)" in square brackets substituted by SI 2012/2560, reg 2, Schedule, para 2(d).

Date in force: 8 November 2012: see SI 2012/2560, reg 1.

Para (8): renumbered as such by SI 2012/1547, reg 3, Sch 1, para 4(d).

Date in force: 16 July 2012: see SI 2012/1547, reg 2(1).

Para (8): words ", (1AB) and (2)" in square brackets substituted by SI 2013/3032, reg 4, Sch 1, para 6(c).

Date in force: 1 January 2014: see SI 2013/3032, reg 2(1).

Para (8): reference to ", (1A)" inserted by SI 2014/1976, reg 3, Schedule, para 2. Date in force: 28 July 2014, subject to transitional provisions: see SI 2014/1976, reg 2(1).

12 Issue of EEA family permit

(1) An entry clearance officer must issue an EEA family permit to a person who applies for one if the person is a family member of an EEA national and—

    (a)   the EEA national—

        (i)   is residing in the UK in accordance with these Regulations; or

        (ii)   will be travelling to the United Kingdom within six months of the date of the application and will be an EEA national residing in the United Kingdom in accordance with these Regulations on arrival in the United Kingdom; and

    [(b)   the family member will be accompanying the EEA national to the United Kingdom or joining the EEA national there.]

[(1A) An entry clearance officer must issue an EEA family permit to a person who applies and provides proof that, at the time at which he first intends to use the EEA family permit, he—

    (a)   would be entitled to be admitted to the United Kingdom by virtue of regulation 11(5); and

    (b)   will (save in the case of a person who would be entitled to be admitted to the United Kingdom by virtue of regulation 11(5)(a)) be accompanying to, or joining in, the United Kingdom any person from whom his right to be admitted to the United Kingdom under regulation 11(5) will be derived.

(1B) An entry clearance officer must issue an EEA family permit to a family member who has retained the right of residence.]

(2) An entry clearance officer may issue an EEA family permit to an extended family member of an EEA national who applies for one if—

(a)   the relevant EEA national satisfies the condition in paragraph (1)(a);

(b)   the extended family member wishes to accompany the relevant EEA national to the United Kingdom or to join him there; and

(c)   in all the circumstances, it appears to the entry clearance officer appropriate to issue the EEA family permit.

(3) Where an entry clearance officer receives an application under paragraph (2) he shall undertake an extensive examination of the personal circumstances of the applicant and if he refuses the application shall give reasons justifying the refusal unless this is contrary to the interests of national security.

(4) An EEA family permit issued under this regulation shall be issued free of charge and as soon as possible.

(5) But an EEA family permit shall not be issued under this regulation if the applicant or the EEA national concerned [is not entitled to be admitted to the United Kingdom as a result of regulation 19(1A) or [(1AB) or] falls to be excluded in accordance with regulation 19(1B)].

[(6) An EEA family permit will not be issued under this regulation to a person ("A") who is the spouse, civil partner or durable partner of a person ("B") where a spouse, civil partner or durable partner of A or B holds a valid EEA family permit.]

Amendment
Para (1): sub-para (b) substituted by SI 2011/1247, reg 2(1), (4).
Date in force: 2 June 2011: see SI 2011/1247, reg 1(1).
Paras (1A), (1B): inserted by SI 2012/1547, reg 3, Sch 1, para 5(a).
Date in force: 16 July 2012: see SI 2012/1547, reg 2(1).
Para (5): words from "is not entitled" to "with regulation 19(1B)" in square brackets substituted by SI 2012/1547, reg 3, Sch 1, para 5(b).
Date in force: 16 July 2012: see SI 2012/1547, reg 2(1).
Para (5): words "(1AB) or" in square brackets inserted by SI 2013/3032, reg 4, Sch 1, para 7.
Date in force: 1 January 2014: see SI 2013/3032, reg 2(1).
Para (6): inserted by SI 2012/1547, reg 3, Sch 1, para 5(c).
Date in force: 16 July 2012: see SI 2012/1547, reg 2(1).

13 Initial right of residence

(1) An EEA national is entitled to reside in the United Kingdom for a period not exceeding three months beginning on the date on which he is admitted to the United Kingdom provided that he holds a valid national identity card or passport issued by an EEA State.

(2) A family member of an EEA national [or a family member who has retained the right of residence who is] residing in the United Kingdom under paragraph (1) who is not himself an EEA national is entitled to reside in the United Kingdom provided that he holds a valid passport.

[(3) An EEA national or his family member who becomes an unreasonable burden on the social assistance system of the United Kingdom will cease to have a right to reside under this regulation.

(4) A person who otherwise satisfies the criteria in this regulation will not be entitled to reside in the United Kingdom under this regulation where the Secretary of State has made a decision under[—

(a)   regulation 19(3)(b), 20(1) or 20A(1); or

(b)   regulation 21B(2), where that decision was taken in the preceding twelve months].]

Amendment
Para (2): words "or a family member who has retained the right of residence who is" in square brackets inserted by SI 2012/1547, reg 3, Sch 1, para 6(a).

Date in force: 16 July 2012: see SI 2012/1547, reg 2(1).

Paras (3), (4): substituted, for para (3) as originally enacted, by SI 2012/1547, reg 3, Sch 1, para 6(b).

Date in force: 16 July 2012: see SI 2012/1547, reg 2(1).

Para (4): sub-paras (a), (b) substituted by SI 2013/3032, reg 4, Sch 1, para 8.

Date in force: 1 January 2014: see SI 2013/3032, reg 2(1).

14 Extended right of residence

(1) A qualified person is entitled to reside in the United Kingdom for so long as he remains a qualified person.

(2) A family member of a qualified person residing in the United Kingdom under paragraph (1) or of an EEA national with a permanent right of residence under regulation 15 is entitled to reside in the United Kingdom for so long as he remains the family member of the qualified person or EEA national.

(3) A family member who has retained the right of residence is entitled to reside in the United Kingdom for so long as he remains a family member who has retained the right of residence.

(4) A right to reside under this regulation is in addition to any right a person may have to reside in the United Kingdom under regulation 13 or 15.

[(5) A person who otherwise satisfies the criteria in this regulation will not be entitled to a right to reside in the United Kingdom under this regulation where the Secretary of State has made a decision under[—

    (a)   regulation 19(3)(b), 20(1) or 20A(1); or

    (b)   regulation 21B(2) (not including such a decision taken on the basis of regulation 21B(1)(a) or (b)), where that decision was taken in the preceding twelve months].]

Amendment

Para (5): substituted by SI 2012/1547, reg 3, Sch 1, para 7.

Date in force: 16 July 2012: see SI 2012/1547, reg 2(1).

Para (5): sub-paras (a), (b) substituted by SI 2013/3032, reg 4, Sch 1, para 9.

Date in force: 1 January 2014: see SI 2013/3032, reg 2(1).

15 Permanent right of residence

(1) The following persons shall acquire the right to reside in the United Kingdom permanently—

    (a)   an EEA national who has resided in the United Kingdom in accordance with these Regulations for a continuous period of five years;

    (b)   a family member of an EEA national who is not himself an EEA national but who has resided in the United Kingdom with the EEA national in accordance with these Regulations for a continuous period of five years;

    (c)   a worker or self-employed person who has ceased activity;

    (d)   the family member of a worker or self-employed person who has ceased activity;

    (e)   a person who was the family member of a worker or self-employed person where—

        (i)   the worker or self-employed person has died;

        (ii)   the family member resided with him immediately before his death; and

        (iii)   the worker or self-employed person had resided continuously in the United Kingdom for at least the two years immediately before his death or the death was the result of an accident at work or an occupational disease;

    (f)   a person who—

        (i)   has resided in the United Kingdom in accordance with these Regulations for a continuous period of five years; and

(ii)   was, at the end of that period, a family member who has retained the right of residence.

[(1A)   Residence in the United Kingdom as a result of a derivative right of residence does not constitute residence for the purpose of this regulation.]

(2)   [The] right of permanent residence under this regulation shall be lost only through absence from the United Kingdom for a period exceeding two consecutive years.

[(3)   A person who satisfies the criteria in this regulation will not be entitled to a permanent right to reside in the United Kingdom where the Secretary of State has made a decision under[—

(a)   regulation 19(3)(b), 20(1) or 20A(1); or

(b)   regulation 21B(2) (not including such a decision taken on the basis of regulation 21B(1)(a) or (b)), where that decision was taken in the preceding twelve months.]]

Amendment

Para (1A): inserted by SI 2012/1547, Sch 1, para 8(a).
Date in force: 16 July 2012: see SI 2012/1547, reg 2(1).
Para (2): word "The" in square brackets substituted by SI 2012/1547, reg 3, Sch 1, para 8(b).
Date in force: 16 July 2012: see SI 2012/1547, reg 2(1).
Para (3): substituted by SI 2012/1547, reg 3, Sch 1, para 8(c).
Date in force: 16 July 2012: see SI 2012/1547, reg 2(1).
Para (3): sub-paras (a), (b) substituted by SI 2013/3032, reg 4, Sch 1, para 10.
Date in force: 1 January 2014: see SI 2013/3032, reg 2(1).

[15A Derivative right of residence]

[(1)   A person ("P") who is not [an exempt person] and who satisfies the criteria in paragraph (2), (3), (4)[, (4A)] or (5) of this regulation is entitled to a derivative right to reside in the United Kingdom for as long as P satisfies the relevant criteria.

(2)   P satisfies the criteria in this paragraph if—

(a)   P is the primary carer of an EEA national ("the relevant EEA national"); and

(b)   the relevant EEA national—

(i)   is under the age of 18;

(ii)   is residing in the United Kingdom as a self-sufficient person; and

(iii)   would be unable to remain in the United Kingdom if P were required to leave.

(3)   P satisfies the criteria in this paragraph if—

(a)   P is the child of an EEA national ("the EEA national parent");

(b)   P resided in the United Kingdom at a time when the EEA national parent was residing in the United Kingdom as a worker; and

(c)   P is in education in the United Kingdom and was in education there at a time when the EEA national parent was in the United Kingdom.

(4)   P satisfies the criteria in this paragraph if—

(a)   P is the primary carer of a person meeting the criteria in paragraph (3) ("the relevant person"); and

(b)   the relevant person would be unable to continue to be educated in the United Kingdom if P were required to leave.

[(4A)   P satisfies the criteria in this paragraph if—

(a)   P is the primary carer of a British citizen ("the relevant British citizen");

(b)   the relevant British citizen is residing in the United Kingdom; and

(c)   the relevant British citizen would be unable to reside in the UK or in another EEA State if P were required to leave.]

(5)   P satisfies the criteria in this paragraph if—

(a)   P is under the age of 18;

(b)   P's primary carer is entitled to a derivative right to reside in the United Kingdom by virtue of paragraph (2) or (4);

(c)   P does not have leave to enter, or remain in, the United Kingdom; and

(d)   requiring P to leave the United Kingdom would prevent P's primary carer from residing in the United Kingdom.

(6)   For the purpose of this regulation—

   (a)   "education" excludes nursery education; . . .

   (b)   "worker" does not include a jobseeker or a person who falls to be regarded as a worker by virtue of [regulation 6(2); and]

   [(c)   "an exempt person" is a person—

      (i)   who has a right to reside in the United Kingdom as a result of any other provision of these Regulations;

      (ii)   who has a right of abode in the United Kingdom by virtue of section 2 of the 1971 Act;

      (iii)   to whom section 8 of the 1971 Act, or any order made under subsection (2) of that provision, applies; or

      (iv)   who has indefinite leave to enter or remain in the United Kingdom.]

(7)   P is to be regarded as a "primary carer" of another person if

   (a)   P is a direct relative or a legal guardian of that person; and

   (b)   P—

      (i)   is the person who has primary responsibility for that person's care; or

      [(ii)   shares equally the responsibility for that person's care with one other person who is not an exempt person].

[(7A)   Where P is to be regarded as a primary carer of another person by virtue of paragraph (7)(b)(ii) the criteria in paragraphs (2)(b)(iii), (4)(b) and (4A)(c) shall be considered on the basis that both P and the person with whom care responsibility is shared would be required to leave the United Kingdom.

(7B)   Paragraph (7A) does not apply if the person with whom care responsibility is shared acquired a derivative right to reside in the United Kingdom as a result of this regulation prior to P assuming equal care responsibility.]

(8)   P will not be regarded as having responsibility for a person's care for the purpose of paragraph (7) on the sole basis of a financial contribution towards that person's care.

(9)   A person who otherwise satisfies the criteria in paragraph (2), (3), (4)[, (4A)] or (5) will not be entitled to a derivative right to reside in the United Kingdom where the Secretary of State has made a decision under[—

   (a)   regulation 19(3)(b), 20(1) or 20A(1); or

   (b)   regulation 21B(2), where that decision was taken in the preceding twelve months].]

Amendment

Inserted by SI 2012/1547, reg 3, Sch 1, para 9.

Date in force: 16 July 2012: see SI 2012/1547, reg 2(1).

Para (1): words "an exempt person" in square brackets substituted by SI 2012/2560, reg 2, Schedule, para 3(a)(i).

Date in force: 8 November 2012: see SI 2012/2560, reg 1.

Para (1): reference to ", (4A)" in square brackets inserted by SI 2012/2560, reg 2, Schedule, para 3(a)(ii).

Date in force: 8 November 2012: see SI 2012/2560, reg 1.

Para (4A): inserted by SI 2012/2560, reg 2, Schedule, para 3(b).

Date in force: 8 November 2012: see SI 2012/2560, reg 1.

Para (6): in sub-para (a) word omitted revoked by SI 2012/2560, reg 2, Schedule, para 3(c)(i).

Date in force: 8 November 2012: see SI 2012/2560, reg 1.

Para (6): in sub-para (b) words "regulation 6(2); and" in square brackets substituted by SI 2012/2560, reg 2, Schedule, para 3(c)(ii).

Date in force: 8 November 2012: see SI 2012/2560, reg 1.

Para (6): sub-para (c) inserted by SI 2012/2560, reg 2, Schedule, para 3(c)(ii).

Date in force: 8 November 2012: see SI 2012/2560, reg 1.

Para (7): sub-para (b)(ii) substituted by SI 2012/2560, reg 2, Schedule, para 3(d).

Date in force: 8 November 2012: see SI 2012/2560, reg 1.

Paras (7A), (7B): inserted by SI 2012/2560, reg 2, Schedule, para 3(e).

Date in force: 8 November 2012: see SI 2012/2560, reg 1.

Para (9): reference to ", (4A)" in square brackets inserted by SI 2012/2560, reg 2, Schedule, para 3(f).

Date in force: 8 November 2012: see SI 2012/2560, reg 1.

Para (9): sub-paras (a), (b) substituted by SI 2013/3032, reg 4, Sch 1, para 11.

Date in force: 1 January 2014: see SI 2013/3032, reg 2(1).

[15B Continuation of a right of residence]

[(1) This regulation applies during any period in which, but for the effect of regulation 13(4), 14(5), 15(3) or 15A(9), a person ("P") who is in the United Kingdom would be entitled to reside here pursuant to these Regulations.

(2) Where this regulation applies, any right of residence will (notwithstanding the effect of regulation 13(4), 14(5), 15(3) or 15A(9)) be deemed to continue during any period in which—

    (a)   an appeal under regulation 26 could be brought, while P is in the United Kingdom, against a relevant decision (ignoring any possibility of an appeal out of time with permission); or

    (b)   an appeal under regulation 26 against a relevant decision, brought while P is in the United Kingdom, is pending . . .

(3) Periods during which residence pursuant to regulation 14 is deemed to continue as a result of paragraph (2) will not constitute residence for the purpose of regulation 15 unless and until—

    (a)   a relevant decision is withdrawn by the Secretary of State; or

    (b)   an appeal against a relevant decision is allowed and that appeal is finally determined . . .

(4) Periods during which residence is deemed to continue as a result of paragraph (2) will not constitute residence for the purpose of regulation 21(4)(a) unless and until—

    (a)   a relevant decision is withdrawn by the Secretary of State; or

    (b)   an appeal against a relevant decision is allowed and that appeal is finally determined . . .

(5) A "relevant decision" for the purpose of this regulation means a decision pursuant to regulation [19(3)(b) or (c)], 20(1) or 20A(1) which would, but for the effect of paragraph (2), prevent P from residing in the United Kingdom pursuant to these Regulations.

[(6) This regulation does not affect the ability of the Secretary of State to give directions for P's removal while an appeal is pending or before it is finally determined.

(7) In this regulation, "pending" and "finally determined" have the meanings given in section 104 of the 2002 Act.]]

Amendment

Inserted by SI 2012/1547, reg 3, Sch 1, para 10. Date in force: 16 July 2012: see SI 2012/1547, reg 2(1).

Paras (2)–(4): words omitted revoked by SI 2014/1976, reg 3, Schedule, para 3(a). Date in force: 28 July 2014, subject to transitional provisions: see SI 2014/1976, reg 2(1).

Para (5): words "19(3)(b) or (c)" in square brackets substituted by SI 2013/3032, reg 4, Sch 1, para 12. Date in force: 1 January 2014: see SI 2013/3032, reg 2(1).

Paras (6), (7): added by SI 2014/1976, reg 3, Schedule, para 3(b). Date in force: 28 July 2014, subject to transitional provisions: see SI 2014/1976, reg 2(1).

PART 3
RESIDENCE DOCUMENTATION

16 Issue of registration certificate

(1)   The Secretary of State must issue a registration certificate to a qualified person immediately on application and production of—

    (a)   a valid identity card or passport issued by an EEA State;

    (b)   proof that he is a qualified person.

(2)   In the case of a worker, confirmation of the worker's engagement from his employer or a certificate of employment is sufficient proof for the purposes of paragraph (1)(b).

(3)   The Secretary of State must issue a registration certificate to an EEA national who is the family member of a qualified person or of an EEA national with a permanent right of residence under regulation 15 immediately on application and production of—

    (a)   a valid identity card or passport issued by an EEA State; and

    (b)   proof that the applicant is such a family member.

(4)   The Secretary of State must issue a registration certificate to an EEA national who is a family member who has retained the right of residence on application and production of—

    (a)   a valid identity card or passport; and

    (b)   proof that the applicant is a family member who has retained the right of residence.

(5)   The Secretary of State may issue a registration certificate to an extended family member not falling within regulation 7(3) who is an EEA national on application if—

    (a)   the relevant EEA national in relation to the extended family member is a qualified person or an EEA national with a permanent right of residence under regulation 15; and

    (b)   in all the circumstances it appears to the Secretary of State appropriate to issue the registration certificate.

(6)   Where the Secretary of State receives an application under paragraph (5) he shall undertake an extensive examination of the personal circumstances of the applicant and if he refuses the application shall give reasons justifying the refusal unless this is contrary to the interests of national security.

(7)   A registration certificate issued under this regulation shall state the name and address of the person registering and the date of registration . . .

[(8)   But this regulation is subject to regulations 7A(6) and 20(1).]

Amendment

Para (7): words omitted revoked by SI 2013/1391, reg 2(a).

Date in force: 1 July 2013: see SI 2013/1391, reg 1.

Para (8): substituted by SI 2011/544, reg 5, Sch 2, para 5.

Date in force: 1 May 2011: see SI 2011/544, reg 1(1).

17 Issue of residence card

(1)   The Secretary of State must issue a residence card to a person who is not an EEA national and is the family member of a qualified person or of an EEA national with a permanent right of residence under regulation 15 on application and production of—

    (a)   a valid passport; and

    (b)   proof that the applicant is such a family member.

(2)   The Secretary of State must issue a residence card to a person who is not an EEA national but who is a family member who has retained the right of residence on application and production of—

    (a)   a valid passport; and

(b)   proof that the applicant is a family member who has retained the right of residence.

(3) On receipt of an application under paragraph (1) or (2) and the documents that are required to accompany the application the Secretary of State shall immediately issue the applicant with a certificate of application for the residence card and the residence card shall be issued no later than six months after the date on which the application and documents are received.

(4) The Secretary of State may issue a residence card to an extended family member not falling within regulation 7(3) who is not an EEA national on application if—

    (a)   the relevant EEA national in relation to the extended family member is a qualified person or an EEA national with a permanent right of residence under regulation 15; and

    (b)   in all the circumstances it appears to the Secretary of State appropriate to issue the residence card.

(5) Where the Secretary of State receives an application under paragraph (4) he shall undertake an extensive examination of the personal circumstances of the applicant and if he refuses the application shall give reasons justifying the refusal unless this is contrary to the interests of national security.

(6) A residence card issued under this regulation may take the form of a stamp in the applicant's passport and shall be . . . valid for—

    (a)   five years from the date of issue; or

    (b)   in the case of a residence card issued to the family member or extended family member of a qualified person, the envisaged period of residence in the United Kingdom of the qualified person,

whichever is the shorter.

[(6A) A residence card issued under this regulation shall be entitled "Residence card of a family member of an EEA national" or "Residence card of a family member who has retained the right of residence", as the case may be.]

(7) . . .

(8) But this regulation is subject to [regulations 20(1) and (1A)].

Amendment

Para (6): words omitted revoked by SI 2009/1117, reg 2, Sch 1, para 4(a).

Date in force: 1 June 2009: see SI 2009/1117, reg 1.

Para (6A): inserted by SI 2009/1117, reg 2, Sch 1, para 4(b).

Date in force: 1 June 2009: see SI 2009/1117, reg 1.

Para (7): revoked by SI 2013/1391, reg 2(b).

Date in force: 1 July 2013: see SI 2013/1391, reg 1.

Para (8): words "regulations 20(1) and (1A)" in square brackets substituted by SI 2009/1117, reg 2, Sch 1, para 4(c).

Date in force: 1 June 2009: see SI 2009/1117, reg 1.

18 Issue of a document certifying permanent residence and a permanent residence card

(1) The Secretary of State must issue an EEA national with a permanent right of residence under regulation 15 with a document certifying permanent residence as soon as possible after an application for such a document and proof that the EEA national has such a right is submitted to the Secretary of State.

(2) The Secretary of State must issue a person who is not an EEA national who has a permanent right of residence under regulation 15 with a permanent residence card no later than six months after the date on which an application for a permanent residence card and proof that the person has such a right is submitted to the Secretary of State.

(3) Subject to paragraph (5) . . ., a permanent residence card shall be valid for ten years from the date of issue and must be renewed on application.

(4) . . .

(5) A document certifying permanent residence and a permanent residence card shall cease to be valid if the holder ceases to have a right of permanent residence under regulation 15.

[(6) But this regulation is subject to regulation 20.]

Amendment

Para (3): words omitted revoked by SI 2009/1117, reg 2, Sch 1, para 5(a).

Date in force: 1 June 2009: see SI 2009/1117, reg 1.

Para (4): revoked by SI 2013/1391, reg 2(c).

Date in force: 1 July 2013: see SI 2013/1391, reg 1.

Para (6): inserted by SI 2009/1117, reg 2, Sch 1, para 5(b).

Date in force: 1 June 2009: see SI 2009/1117, reg 1.

[18A Issue of a derivative residence card]

[(1) The Secretary of State must issue a person with a derivative residence card on application and on production of—

(a)   a valid identity card issued by an EEA State or a valid passport; and

(b)   proof that the applicant has a derivative right of residence under regulation 15A.

(2) On receipt of an application under paragraph (1) the Secretary of State must issue the applicant with a certificate of application as soon as possible.

(3) A derivative residence card issued under paragraph (1) may take the form of a stamp in the applicant's passport and will be valid until—

(a)   a date five years from the date of issue; or

(b)   any other date specified by the Secretary of State when issuing the derivative residence card.

(4) A derivative residence card issued under paragraph (1) must be issued . . . as soon as practicable.

(5) But this regulation is subject to regulations 20(1) and 20(1A).]

Amendment

Inserted by SI 2012/1547, reg 3, Sch 1, para 11.

Date in force: 16 July 2012: see SI 2012/1547, reg 2(1).

Para (4): words omitted revoked by SI 2013/1391, reg 2(d).

Date in force: 1 July 2013: see SI 2013/1391, reg 1.

PART 4
REFUSAL OF ADMISSION AND REMOVAL ETC

19 Exclusion and removal from the United Kingdom

(1) A person is not entitled to be admitted to the United Kingdom by virtue of regulation 11 if his exclusion is justified on grounds of public policy, public security or public health in accordance with regulation 21.

[(1A) A person is not entitled to be admitted to the United Kingdom by virtue of regulation 11 if that person is subject to a deportation or exclusion order[, except where the person is temporarily admitted pursuant to regulation 29AA].

[(1AB) A person is not entitled to be admitted to the United Kingdom by virtue of regulation 11 if the Secretary of State considers there to be reasonable grounds to suspect that his admission would lead to the abuse of a right to reside in accordance with regulation 21B(1).]

(1B) If the Secretary of State considers that the exclusion of an EEA national or the family member of an EEA national is justified on the grounds of public policy, public security or public health in accordance with regulation 21 the Secretary of State may make an order for the purpose of these Regulations prohibiting that person from entering the United Kingdom.]

Para (2): in sub-para (b) words "or on grounds of abuse of rights in accordance with regulation 21B(2)" in square brackets inserted by SI 2013/3032, reg 4, Sch 1, para 15(a).

Date in force: 1 January 2014: see SI 2013/3032, reg 2(1).

Para (2): in sub-para (d) words "or (c)" in square brackets inserted by SI 2013/3032, reg 4, Sch 1, para 15(b).

Date in force: 1 January 2014: see SI 2013/3032, reg 2(1).

[20B Verification of a right of residence]

[(1) This regulation applies when the Secretary of State—

   (a)   has reasonable doubt as to whether a person ("A") has a right to reside under regulation 14(1) or (2); or

   (b)   wants to verify the eligibility of a person ("A") to apply for documentation issued under Part 3.

(2) The Secretary of State may invite A to—

   (a)   provide evidence to support the existence of a right to reside, or to support an application for documentation under Part 3; or

   (b)   attend an interview with the Secretary of State.

(3) If A purports to be entitled to a right to reside on the basis of a relationship with another person ("B"), the Secretary of State may invite B to—

   (a)   provide information about their relationship with A; or

   (b)   attend an interview with the Secretary of State.

(4) If, without good reason, A or B fail to provide the additional information requested or, on at least two occasions, fail to attend an interview if so invited, the Secretary of State may draw any factual inferences about A's entitlement to a right to reside as appear appropriate in the circumstances.

(5) The Secretary of State may decide following an inference under paragraph (4) that A does not have or ceases to have a right to reside.

(6) But the Secretary of State must not decide that A does not have or ceases to have a right to reside on the sole basis that A failed to comply with this regulation.

(7) This regulation may not be invoked systematically.

(8) In this regulation, "a right to reside" means a right to reside under these Regulations.]

Amendment
Inserted by SI 2013/3032, reg 4, Sch 1, para 16.
Date in force: 1 January 2014: see SI 2013/3032, reg 2(1).

21 Decisions taken on public policy, public security and public health grounds

(1) In this regulation a "relevant decision" means an EEA decision taken on the grounds of public policy, public security or public health.

(2) A relevant decision may not be taken to serve economic ends.

(3) A relevant decision may not be taken in respect of a person with a permanent right of residence under regulation 15 except on serious grounds of public policy or public security.

(4) A relevant decision may not be taken except on imperative grounds of public security in respect of an EEA national who—

   (a)   has resided in the United Kingdom for a continuous period of at least ten years prior to the relevant decision; or

   (b)   is under the age of 18, unless the relevant decision is necessary in his best interests, as provided for in the Convention on the Rights of the Child adopted by the General Assembly of the United Nations on 20th November 1989.

(5) Where a relevant decision is taken on grounds of public policy or public security it shall, in addition to complying with the preceding paragraphs of this regulation, be taken in accordance with the following principles—

    (a)   the decision must comply with the principle of proportionality;

    (b)   the decision must be based exclusively on the personal conduct of the person concerned;

    (c)   the personal conduct of the person concerned must represent a genuine, present and sufficiently serious threat affecting one of the fundamental interests of society;

    (d)   matters isolated from the particulars of the case or which relate to considerations of general prevention do not justify the decision;

    (e)   a person's previous criminal convictions do not in themselves justify the decision.

(6)   Before taking a relevant decision on the grounds of public policy or public security in relation to a person who is resident in the United Kingdom the decision maker must take account of considerations such as the age, state of health, family and economic situation of the person, the person's length of residence in the United Kingdom, the person's social and cultural integration into the United Kingdom and the extent of the person's links with his country of origin.

(7)   In the case of a relevant decision taken on grounds of public health—

    (a)   a disease that does not have epidemic potential as defined by the relevant instruments of the World Health Organisation or is not a disease [listed in Schedule 1 to the Health Protection (Notification) Regulations 2010] shall not constitute grounds for the decision; and

    (b)   if the person concerned is in the United Kingdom, diseases occurring after the three month period beginning on the date on which he arrived in the United Kingdom shall not constitute grounds for the decision.

Amendment

Para (7): words "listed in Schedule 1 to the Health Protection (Notification) Regulations 2010" in square brackets substituted in relation to England, Scotland and Northern Ireland by SI 2010/708, art 8, Sch 1, para 3 and in relation to Wales by SI 2010/1593, art 3, Schedule, para 4.

Date in force (in relation to England, Scotland and Northern Ireland): 6 April 2010: see SI 2010/708, art 1(1)(c).

Date in force (in relation to Wales): 26 July 2010: see SI 2010/1593, art 1(1).

[21A Application of Part 4 to persons with a derivative right of residence]

[(1)   Where this regulation applies Part 4 of these Regulations applies subject to the modifications listed in paragraph (3).

(2)   This regulation applies where a person—

    (a)   would, notwithstanding Part 4 of these Regulations, have a right to be admitted to, or reside in, the United Kingdom by virtue of a derivative right of residence arising under regulation 15A(2), (4)[, (4A)] or (5);

    (b)   holds a derivative residence card; or

    (c)   has applied for a derivative residence card.

(3)   Where this regulation applies Part 4 applies in relation to the matters listed in paragraph (2) as if—

    (a)   references to a matter being . . .justified on grounds of public policy, public security or public health in accordance with regulation 21. . . . referred instead to a matter being "conducive to the public good";

    (b)   the reference in regulation 20(5)(a) to a matter being "justified on grounds of public policy, public security or public health" referred instead to a matter being "conducive to the public good";

    (c)   references to "the family member of an EEA national" referred instead to "a person with a derivative right of residence";

    (d)   references to "a registration certificate, a residence card, a document certifying permanent residence or a permanent residence card" referred instead to "a derivative residence card";

(e)   the reference in regulation 19(1A) to a deportation or exclusion order referred also to a deportation or exclusion order made under any provision of the immigration Acts.

(f)   regulation 20(4) instead conferred on an immigration officer the power to revoke a derivative residence card where the holder is not at that time a person with a derivative right of residence; and

(g)   regulations 20(3), 20(6) and 21 were omitted.]

Amendment

Inserted by SI 2012/1547, reg 3, Sch 1, para 14.

Date in force: 16 July 2012: see SI 2012/1547, reg 2(1).

Para (2): in sub-para (a) reference to ", (4A)" in square brackets inserted by SI 2012/2560, reg 2, Schedule, para 4.

Date in force: 8 November 2012: see SI 2012/2560, reg 1.

Para (3): in sub-para (a) quotation marks omitted revoked by SI 2013/3032, reg 4, Sch 1, para 17.

Date in force: 1 January 2014: see SI 2013/3032, reg 2(1).

[21B Abuse of rights or fraud]

[(1)   The abuse of a right to reside includes—

(a)   engaging in conduct which appears to be intended to circumvent the requirement to be a qualified person;

(b)   attempting to enter the United Kingdom within 12 months of being removed pursuant to regulation 19(3)(a), where the person attempting to do so is unable to provide evidence that, upon re-entry to the United Kingdom, the conditions for any right to reside, other than the initial right of residence under regulation 13, will be met;

(c)   entering, attempting to enter or assisting another person to enter or attempt to enter, a marriage or civil partnership of convenience; or

(d)   fraudulently obtaining or attempting to obtain, or assisting another to obtain or attempt to obtain, a right to reside.

(2)   The Secretary of State may take an EEA decision on the grounds of abuse of rights where there are reasonable grounds to suspect the abuse of a right to reside and it is proportionate to do so.

(3)   Where these Regulations provide that an EEA decision taken on the grounds of abuse in the preceding twelve months affects a person's right to reside, the person who is the subject of that decision may apply to the Secretary of State to have the effect of that decision set aside on grounds that there has been a material change in the circumstances which justified that decision.

(4)   An application under paragraph (3) may only be made whilst the applicant is outside the United Kingdom.

(5)   This regulation may not be invoked systematically.

(6)   In this regulation, "a right to reside" means a right to reside under these Regulations.]

Amendment

Inserted by SI 2013/3032, reg 4, Sch 1, para 18.

Date in force: 1 January 2014: see SI 2013/3032, reg 2(1); for transitional provisions see reg 6, Sch 3, para 3 thereto.

PART 5
PROCEDURE IN RELATION TO EEA DECISIONS

22 Person claiming right of admission

(1)   This regulation applies to a person who claims a right of admission to the United Kingdom under regulation 11 as—

[(a)   a person, not being an EEA national, who—

(i)   is a family member of an EEA national;

(ii)   is a family member who has retained the right of residence;

(iii)   has a derivative right of residence;

(iv)   has a permanent right of residence under regulation 15; or

(v)   is in possession of a qualifying EEA State residence card; . . .]

[(b)   an EEA national, where there is reason to believe that he may fall to be excluded under regulation 19(1) [(1A) or (1AB)]][; or.

(c)   a person to whom regulation 29AA applies.]

(2)   A person to whom this regulation applies is to be treated as if he were a person seeking leave to enter the United Kingdom under the 1971 Act for the purposes of paragraphs 2, 3, 4, 7, 16 to 18 and 21 to 24 of Schedule 2 to the 1971 Act (administrative provisions as to control on entry etc), except that—

(a)   the reference in paragraph 2(1) to the purpose for which the immigration officer may examine any persons who have arrived in the United Kingdom is to be read as a reference to the purpose of determining whether he is a person who is to be granted admission under these Regulations;

(b)   the references in paragraphs 4(2A), 7 and 16(1) to a person who is, or may be, given leave to enter are to be read as references to a person who is, or may be, granted admission under these Regulations; and

(c)   a medical examination is not be carried out under paragraph 2 or paragraph 7 as a matter of routine and may only be carried out within three months of a person's arrival in the United Kingdom.

(3)   For so long as a person to whom this regulation applies is detained, or temporarily admitted or released while liable to detention, under the powers conferred by Schedule 2 to the 1971 Act, he is deemed not to have been admitted to the United Kingdom.

Amendment

Para (1): sub-para (a) substituted by SI 2013/3032, reg 4, Sch 1, para 19(a). Date in force: 7 April 2014: see SI 2013/3032, reg 2(2).

Para (1): sub-para (b) substituted by SI 2009/1117, reg 2, Sch 1, para 8. Date in force: 1 June 2009: see SI 2009/1117, reg 1.

Para (1): in sub-para (b) words "(1A) or (1AB)" in square brackets substituted by SI 2013/3032, reg 4, Sch 1, para 19(b). Date in force: 1 January 2014: see SI 2013/3032, reg 2(1).

Para (1): word omitted from sub-para (a) revoked and sub-para (b) inserted together with word preceding it, by SI 2014/1976, reg 3, Schedule, para 5. Date in force: 28 July 2014, subject to transitional provisions: see SI 2014/1976, reg 2(1).

23 Person refused admission

(1)   This regulation applies to a person who is in the United Kingdom and has been refused admission to the United Kingdom—

(a)   because he does not meet the requirement of regulation 11 (including where he does not meet those requirements because his EEA family permit, residence card[, derivative residence card] or permanent residence card has been revoked by an immigration officer in accordance with regulation 20); or

(b)   in accordance with regulation [19(1), (1A)[, (1AB)] or (2)].

(2)   A person to whom this regulation applies, is to be treated as if he were a person refused leave to enter under the 1971 Act for the purpose of paragraphs 8, 10, 10A, 11, 16 to 19 and 21 to 24 of Schedule 2 to the 1971 Act, except that the reference in paragraph 19 to a certificate of entitlement, entry clearance or work permit is to be read as a reference to an EEA family permit, residence card[, derivative residence card][, a qualifying EEA State residence card, or a permanent residence card].

Amendment

Para (1): in sub-para (a) words ", derivative residence card" in square brackets inserted by SI 2012/1547, Sch 1, para 16.

Date in force: 16 July 2012: see SI 2012/1547, reg 2(1).

Para (1): in sub-para (b) words "19(1), (1A) or (2)" in square brackets substituted by SI 2009/1117, reg 2, Sch 1, para 9.

Date in force: 1 June 2009: see SI 2009/1117, reg 1.

Para (1): in sub-para (b) reference to ", (1AB)" in square brackets inserted by SI 2013/3032, reg 4, Sch 1, para 20(a).

Date in force: 1 January 2014: see SI 2013/3032, reg 2(1).

Para (2): words ", derivative residence card" inserted by SI 2012/1547, reg 3, Sch 1, para 16.

Date in force: 16 July 2012: see SI 2012/1547, reg 2(1).

Para (2): words ", a qualifying EEA State residence card, or a permanent residence card" in square brackets substituted by SI 2013/3032, reg 4, Sch 1, para 20(b).

Date in force: 7 April 2014: see SI 2013/3032, reg 2(2).

24 Person subject to removal

[(1)   If there are reasonable grounds for suspecting that a person is someone who may be removed from the United Kingdom under [regulation 19(3)(b)], that person may be detained under the authority of [the Secretary of State] pending a decision whether or not to remove the person under that regulation, and paragraphs 17 and 18 of Schedule 2 to the 1971 Act shall apply in relation to the detention of such a person as those paragraphs apply in relation to a person who may be detained under paragraph 16 of that Schedule].

(2)   [Where a decision is taken to remove a person] under regulation 19(3)(a) [or (c)], the person is to be treated as if he were a person to whom section 10(1)(a) of the 1999 Act applied, and section 10 of that Act (removal of certain persons unlawfully in the United Kingdom) is to apply accordingly.

(3)   [Where a decision is taken to remove a person] under regulation 19(3)(b), the person is to be treated as if he were a person to whom section 3(5)(a) of the 1971 Act (liability to deportation) applied, and section 5 of that Act (procedure for deportation) and Schedule 3 to that Act (supplementary provision as to deportation) are to apply accordingly.

[(4)   A person who enters the United Kingdom in breach of a deportation or exclusion order shall be removable as an illegal entrant under Schedule 2 to the 1971 Act and the provisions of that Schedule shall apply accordingly].

(5)   Where such a deportation order is made against a person but he is not removed under the order during the two year period beginning on the date on which the order is made, the Secretary of State shall only take action to remove the person under the order after the end of that period if, having assessed whether there has been any material change in circumstances since the deportation order was made, he considers that the removal continues to be justified on the grounds of public policy, public security or public health.

(6)   A person to whom this regulation applies shall be allowed one month to leave the United Kingdom, beginning on the date on which he is notified of the decision to remove him, before being removed pursuant to that decision except—

(a)   in duly substantiated cases of urgency;

(b)   where the person is detained pursuant to the sentence or order of any court;

(c)   where a person is a person to whom regulation 24(4) applies.

[(7)   Paragraph (6) of this regulation does not apply where a decision has been taken under regulation 19(3) on the basis that the relevant person—

(a)   has ceased to have a derivative right of residence; or

(b)   is a person who would have had a derivative right of residence but for the effect of a decision to remove under regulation 19(3)(b).]

Amendment

Para (1): substituted by SI 2009/1117, reg 2, Sch 1, para 10(a).

Date in force: 1 June 2009: see SI 2009/1117, reg 1.

Para (1): words "regulation 19(3)(b)" in square brackets substituted by SI 2012/1547, reg 3, Sch 1, para 17(a).

Date in force: 16 July 2012: see SI 2012/1547, reg 2(1).

Para (1): words "an immigration officer" in italics revoked and subsequent words in square brackets substituted by SI 2012/1547, reg 3, Sch 1, para 17(a).

Date in force: 16 July 2012: see SI 2012/1547, reg 2(1).

Para (2): words "Where a decision is taken to remove a person" in square brackets substituted by SI 2009/1117, reg 2, Sch 1, para 10(b).

Date in force: 1 June 2009: see SI 2009/1117, reg 1.

Para (2): words "or (c)" in square brackets inserted by SI 2013/3032, reg 4, Sch 1, para 21.

Date in force: 1 January 2014: see SI 2013/3032, reg 2(1).

Para (3): words "Where a decision is taken to remove a person" in square brackets substituted by SI 2009/1117, reg 2, Sch 1, para 10(b).

Date in force: 1 June 2009: see SI 2009/1117, reg 1.

Para (4): substituted by SI 2009/1117, reg 2, Sch 1, para 10(c).

Date in force: 1 June 2009: see SI 2009/1117, reg 1.

Para (7): inserted by SI 2012/1547, Sch 1, para 17(b).

Date in force: 16 July 2012: see SI 2012/1547, reg 2(1).

[24AA Human rights considerations and interim orders to suspend removal

(1) This regulation applies where the Secretary of State intends to give directions for the removal of a person ("P") to whom regulation 24(3) applies, in circumstances where—

    (a)   P has not appealed against the EEA decision to which regulation 24(3) applies, but would be entitled, and remains within time, to do so from within the United Kingdom (ignoring any possibility of an appeal out of time with permission); or

    (b)   P has so appealed but the appeal has not been finally determined.

(2) The Secretary of State may only give directions for P's removal if the Secretary of State certifies that, despite the appeals process not having been begun or not having been finally determined, removal of P to the country or territory to which P is proposed to be removed, pending the outcome of P's appeal, would not be unlawful under section 6 of the Human Rights Act 1998 (public authority not to act contrary to Human Rights Convention).

(3) The grounds upon which the Secretary of State may certify a removal under paragraph (2) include (in particular) that P would not, before the appeal is finally determined, face a real risk of serious irreversible harm if removed to the country or territory to which P is proposed to be removed.

(4) If P applies to the appropriate court or tribunal (whether by means of judicial review or otherwise) for an interim order to suspend enforcement of the removal decision, P may not be removed from the United Kingdom until such time as the decision on the interim order has been taken, except—

    (a)   where the expulsion decision is based on a previous judicial decision;

    (b)   where P has had previous access to judicial review; or

    (c)   where the removal decision is based on imperative grounds of public security.

(5) In this regulation, "finally determined" has the same meaning as in Part 6.]

Amendment

Inserted by SI 2014/1976, reg 3, Schedule, para 6. Date in force: 28 July 2014, subject to transitional provisions: see SI 2014/1976, reg 2(1).

[24A Revocation of deportation and exclusion orders]

[(1)   A deportation or exclusion order shall remain in force unless it is revoked by the Secretary of State under this regulation.

(2)   A person who is subject to a deportation or exclusion order may apply to the Secretary of State to have it revoked if the person considers that there has been a material change in the circumstances that justified the making of the order.

(3)   An application under paragraph (2) shall set out the material change in circumstances relied upon by the applicant and may only be made whilst the applicant is outside the United Kingdom.

(4)   On receipt of an application under paragraph (2), the Secretary of State shall revoke the order if the Secretary of State considers that [the criteria for making such an order are no longer satisfied].

(5)   The Secretary of State shall take a decision on an application under paragraph (2) no later than six months after the date on which the application is received.]

Amendment

Inserted by SI 2009/1117, reg 2, Sch 1, para 11.

Date in force: 1 June 2009: see SI 2009/1117, reg 1.

Para (4): words "the criteria for making such an order are no longer satisfied" in square brackets substituted by SI 2012/1547, reg 3, Sch 1, para 18.

Date in force: 16 July 2012: see SI 2012/1547, reg 2(1).

PART 6
APPEALS UNDER THESE REGULATIONS

25 Interpretation of Part 6

(1)   In this Part—

. . .

["Asylum claim" has the meaning given in section 113(1) of the 2002 Act;]
"Commission" has the same meaning as in the Special Immigration Appeals Commission Act 1997;
["Human rights claim" has the meaning given in section 113(1) of the 2002 Act.]

. . .

. . .

(2)   For the purposes of this Part, and subject to paragraphs (3) and (4), an appeal is to be treated as pending during the period when notice of appeal is given and ending when the appeal is finally determined, withdrawn or abandoned.

(3)   An appeal is not to be treated as finally determined while a further appeal may be brought; and, if such a further appeal is brought, the original appeal is not to be treated as finally determined until the further appeal is determined, withdrawn or abandoned.

(4)   A pending appeal is not to be treated as abandoned solely because the appellant leaves the United Kingdom.

Amendment

Para (1): definition "Asylum and Immigration Tribunal" (omitted) revoked by SI 2010/21, art 5(2), Sch 2, paras 21, 22.

Date in force: 15 February 2010: see SI 2010/21, art 1; for transitional provisions and savings see art 5(4), Sch 4, paras 1, 14–18, 21 thereto.

Para (1): definition "Asylum claim" inserted by SI 2012/1547, reg 3, Sch 1, para 19(b).

Date in force: 16 July 2012: see SI 2012/1547, reg 2(1).

Para (1): definition "Human rights claim" inserted by SI 2012/1547, reg 3, Sch 1, para 19(b).

Date in force: 16 July 2012: see SI 2012/1547, reg 2(1).

Para (1): definition "the Human Rights Convention" (omitted) revoked by SI 2012/1547, reg 3, Sch 1, para 18(a).

Date in force: 16 July 2012: see SI 2012/1547, reg 2(1).

Para (1): definition "the Refugee Convention" (omitted) revoked by SI 2012/1547, reg 3, Sch 1, para 19(a).

Date in force: 16 July 2012: see SI 2012/1547, reg 2(1).

26 Appeal rights

(1)   Subject to the following paragraphs of this regulation, a person may appeal under these Regulations against an EEA decision.

(2)   If a person claims to be an EEA national, he may not appeal under these Regulations unless he produces a valid national identity card or passport issued by an EEA State.

[(2A)   If a person claims to be in a durable relationship with an EEA national he may not appeal under these Regulations unless he produces—

    (a)   a passport; and

    (b)   either—

        (i)   an EEA family permit; or

        (ii)   sufficient evidence to satisfy the Secretary of State that he is in a relationship with that EEA national.]

[(3)   If a person [to whom paragraph (2) does not apply] claims to be a family member who has retained the right of residence or the family member or relative of an EEA national he may not appeal under these Regulations unless he produces—

    (a)   . . . a passport; and

    (b)   either—

        (i)   an EEA family permit;

        [(ia)   a qualifying EEA State residence card;]

        (ii)   proof that he is the family member or relative of an EEA national; or

        (iii)   in the case of a person claiming to be a family member who has retained the right of residence, proof that he was a family member of the relevant person.]

[(3A)   If a person claims to be a person with a derivative right of [entry or] residence he may not appeal under these Regulations unless he produces a valid national identity card issued by an EEA State or a passport, and either—

    (a)   an EEA family permit; or

    (b)   proof that—

        (i)   where the person claims to have [a derivative right of entry or residence as a result of] regulation 15A(2), he is a direct relative or guardian of an EEA national who is under the age of 18;

        (ii)   where the person claims to have [a derivative right of entry or residence as a result of] regulation 15A(3), he is the child of an EEA national;

        (iii)   where the person claims to have [a derivative right of entry or residence as a result of] regulation 15A(4), he is a direct relative or guardian of the child of an EEA national;

        (iv)   where the person claims to have [a derivative right of entry or residence as a result of] regulation 15A(5), he is under the age of 18 and is a dependant of a person satisfying the criteria in [(i) or (iii);]

        [(v)   where the person claims to have a derivative right of entry or residence as a result of regulation 15A(4A), he is a direct relative or guardian of a British citizen.]]

(4)   A person may not bring an appeal under these Regulations on a ground certified under paragraph (5) or rely on such a ground in an appeal brought under these Regulations.

(5) The Secretary of State or an immigration officer may certify a ground for the purposes of paragraph (4) if it has been considered in a previous appeal brought under these Regulations or under section 82(1) of the 2002 Act.

(6) Except where an appeal lies to the Commission, an appeal under these Regulations lies to the [First-tier Tribunal].

(7) The provisions of or made under the 2002 Act referred to in Schedule 1 shall have effect for the purposes of an appeal under these Regulations to the [First-tier Tribunal] in accordance with that Schedule.

Amendment

Para (2A): inserted by SI 2012/2560, reg 2, Schedule, para 5(a).
Date in force: 8 November 2012: see SI 2012/2560, reg 1.
Para (3): substituted by SI 2012/1547, reg 3, Sch 1, para 20(a).
Date in force: 16 July 2012: see SI 2012/1547, reg 2(1).
Para (3): words "to whom paragraph (2) does not apply" in square brackets inserted by SI 2012/2560, reg 2, Schedule, para 5(b).
Date in force: 8 November 2012: see SI 2012/2560, reg 1.
Para (3): in sub-para (a) words omitted revoked by SI 2012/2560, reg 2, Schedule, para 5(c).
Date in force: 8 November 2012: see SI 2012/2560, reg 1.
Para (3): sub-para (b)(ia) inserted by SI 2013/3032, reg 4, Sch 1, para 22.
Date in force: 7 April 2014: see SI 2013/3032, reg 2(2).
Para (3A): inserted by SI 2012/1547, reg 3, Sch 1, para 20(b).
Date in force: 16 July 2012: see SI 2012/1547, reg 2(1).
Para (3A): words "entry or" in square brackets inserted by SI 2012/2560, reg 2, Schedule, para 5(d).
Date in force: 8 November 2012: see SI 2012/2560, reg 1.
Para (3A): in sub-para (b)(i)–(iv) words "a derivative right of entry or residence as a result of" in square brackets substituted by SI 2012/2560, reg 2, Schedule, para 5(e).
Date in force: 8 November 2012: see SI 2012/2560, reg 1.
Para (3A): in sub-para (b)(iv) words "(i) or (iii);" in square brackets substituted by SI 2012/2560, reg 2, Schedule, para 5(f).
Date in force: 8 November 2012: see SI 2012/2560, reg 1.
Para (3A): sub-para (b)(v) inserted by SI 2012/2560, reg 2, Schedule, para 5(f).
Date in force: 8 November 2012: see SI 2012/2560, reg 1.
Para (6): words "First-tier Tribunal" in square brackets substituted by SI 2010/21, art 5(2), Sch 2, paras 21, 23.
Date in force: 15 February 2010: see SI 2010/21, art 1; for transitional provisions and savings see art 5(4), Sch 4, paras 1, 14–18, 21 thereto.
Para (7): words "First-tier Tribunal" in square brackets substituted by SI 2010/21, art 5(2), Sch 2, paras 21, 23.
Date in force: 15 February 2010: see SI 2010/21, art 1; for transitional provisions and savings see art 5(4), Sch 4, paras 1, 14–18, 21 thereto.

27 Out of country appeals

(1) Subject to paragraphs (2) and (3), a person may not appeal under regulation 26 whilst he is in the United Kingdom against an EEA decision—

    (a) to refuse to admit him to the United Kingdom;

    [(aa) to make an exclusion order against him;]

    (b) to refuse to revoke a deportation [or exclusion] order made against him;

    (c) to refuse to issue him with an EEA family permit; . . .

    [(ca) to revoke, or to refuse to issue or renew any document under these Regulations where that decision is taken at a time when the relevant person is outside the United Kingdom; or]

    [(d) to remove him from the United Kingdom after he has entered the United Kingdom in breach of a deportation or exclusion order].

(2) [Paragraphs (1)(a) and (aa) do not apply where the person is in the United Kingdom and]—

(a)   the person held [a valid EEA family permit, registration certificate, residence card, [derivative residence card,] document certifying permanent residence][, permanent residence card or qualifying EEA State residence card] on his arrival in the United Kingdom or can otherwise prove that he is resident in the United Kingdom;

(b)   the person is deemed not to have been admitted to the United Kingdom under regulation 22(3) but at the date on which notice of the decision to refuse to admit him is given he has been in the United Kingdom for at least 3 months; [or]

[(c)   has made an asylum or human rights claim (or both), unless the Secretary of State has certified that the claim or claims is or are clearly unfounded.]

[(3)   Paragraph (1)(d) does not apply where the person has made an asylum or human rights claim (or both), unless the Secretary of State has certified that the claim or claims is or are clearly unfounded.]

Amendment

Para (1): sub-para (aa) inserted by SI 2009/1117, reg 2, Sch 1, para 12(a)(i).
Date in force: 1 June 2009: see SI 2009/1117, reg 1.
Para (1): in sub-para (b) words "or exclusion" in square brackets inserted by SI 2009/1117, reg 2, Sch 1, para 12(a)(ii).
Date in force: 1 June 2009: see SI 2009/1117, reg 1.
Para (1): in sub-para (c) word omitted revoked by SI 2012/1547, reg 3, Sch 1, para 21(a).
Date in force: 16 July 2012: see SI 2012/1547, reg 2(1).
Para (1): sub-para (ca) inserted by SI 2012/1547, reg 3, Sch 1, para 21(a).
Date in force: 16 July 2012: see SI 2012/1547, reg 2(1).
Para (1): sub-para (d) substituted by SI 2009/1117, reg 2, Sch 1, para 12(a)(iii).
Date in force: 1 June 2009: see SI 2009/1117, reg 1.
Para (2): words "Paragraphs (1)(a) and (aa) do not apply where the person is in the United Kingdom and" in square brackets substituted by SI 2009/1117, reg 2, Sch 1, para 12(b)(i).
Date in force: 1 June 2009: see SI 2009/1117, reg 1.
Para (2): in sub-para (a) words from "a valid EEA family permit" to "permanent residence" in square brackets substituted by SI 2009/1117, reg 2, Sch 1, para 12(b)(ii).
Date in force: 1 June 2009: see SI 2009/1117, reg 1.
Para (2): in sub-para (a) words "derivative residence card," in square brackets inserted by SI 2012/1547, reg 3, Sch 1, para 21(b).
Date in force: 16 July 2012: see SI 2012/1547, reg 2(1).
Para (2): in sub-para (a) words ", permanent residence card or qualifying EEA State residence card" in square brackets substituted by SI 2013/3032, reg 4, Sch 1, para 23.
Date in force: 7 April 2014: see SI 2013/3032, reg 2(2).
Para (2): in sub-para (c) word "or" in square brackets inserted by SI 2009/1117, reg 2, Sch 1, para 12(b)(iii).
Date in force: 1 June 2009: see SI 2009/1117, reg 1.
Para (2): sub-para (c) substituted by SI 2012/1547, reg 3, Sch 1, para 21(c).
Date in force: 16 July 2012: see SI 2012/1547, reg 2(1).
Para (3): substituted by SI 2012/1547, reg 3, Sch 1, para 21(d).
Date in force: 16 July 2012: see SI 2012/1547, reg 2(1).

28 Appeals to the Commission

(1) An appeal against an EEA decision lies to the Commission where paragraph (2) or (4) applies.

(2) This paragraph applies if the Secretary of State certifies that the EEA decision was taken—

(a)   by the Secretary of State wholly or partly on a ground listed in paragraph (3); or

(b)   in accordance with a direction of the Secretary of State which identifies the person to whom the decision relates and which is given wholly or partly on a ground listed in paragraph (3).

(3) The grounds mentioned in paragraph (2) are that the person's exclusion or removal from the United Kingdom is—

    (a)   in the interests of national security; or

    (b)   in the interests of the relationship between the United Kingdom and another country.

(4) This paragraph applies if the Secretary of State certifies that the EEA decision was taken wholly or partly in reliance on information which in his opinion should not be made public—

    (a)   in the interests of national security;

    (b)   in the interests of the relationship between the United Kingdom and another country; or

    (c)   otherwise in the public interest.

(5) In paragraphs (2) and (4) a reference to the Secretary of State is to the Secretary of State acting in person.

(6) Where a certificate is issued under paragraph (2) or (4) in respect of a pending appeal to the [First-tier Tribunal or Upper Tribunal] the appeal shall lapse.

(7) An appeal against an EEA decision lies to the Commission where an appeal lapses by virtue of paragraph (6).

(8) The Special Immigration Appeals Commission Act 1997 shall apply to an appeal to the Commission under these Regulations as it applies to an appeal under section 2 of that Act to which subsection (2) of that section applies (appeals against an immigration decision) but paragraph (i) of that subsection shall not apply in relation to such an appeal.

Amendment

    Para (6): words "First-tier Tribunal or Upper Tribunal" in square brackets substituted by SI 2010/21, art 5(2), Sch 2, paras 21, 24.

    Date in force: 15 February 2010: see SI 2010/21, art 1; for transitional provisions and savings see art 5(4), Sch 4, paras 14–18, 21 thereto.

[28A National security: EEA Decisions]

[(1) Section 97A of the 2002 Act applies to an appeal against an EEA decision where the Secretary of State has certified under regulation 28(2) or (4) that the EEA decision was taken in the interests of national security.

(2) Where section 97A so applies, it has effect as if—

    (a)   the references in that section to a deportation order were to an EEA decision;

    (b)   subsections (1), (1A), (2)(b) and (4) were omitted;

    (c)   the reference in subsection (2)(a) to section 79 were a reference to regulations 27(2) and (3) and 29 of these Regulations; and

    (d)   in subsection (2A), for sub-paragraphs (a) and (b), "against an EEA decision" were substituted.]

Amendment

    Inserted by SI 2013/3032, reg 4, Sch 1, para 24.

    Date in force: 1 January 2014: see SI 2013/3032, reg 2(1).

29 Effect of appeals to the [First-tier Tribunal or Upper Tribunal]

(1) This Regulation applies to appeals under these Regulations made to the [First-tier Tribunal or Upper Tribunal].

(2) If a person in the United Kingdom appeals against an EEA decision to refuse to admit him to the United Kingdom [(other than a decision under regulation 19(1), (1A) or (1B))], any directions for his removal from the United Kingdom previously given by virtue of the refusal cease to have effect, except in so far as they have already been carried out, and no directions may be so given while the appeal is pending.

(3) If a person in the United Kingdom appeals against an EEA decision to remove him from the United Kingdom [(other than a decision under regulation 19(3)(b)], any directions given under section 10 of the 1999 Act or Schedule 3 to the 1971 Act for his removal from the United Kingdom are to have no effect, except in so far as they have already been carried out, while the appeal is pending.

(4) But the provisions of Part I of Schedule 2, or as the case may be, Schedule 3 to the 1971 Act with respect to detention and persons liable to detention apply to a person appealing against a refusal to admit him or a decision to remove him as if there were in force directions for his removal from the United Kingdom, except that he may not be detained on board a ship or aircraft so as to compel him to leave the United Kingdom while the appeal is pending.

[(4A) In paragraph (4), the words "except that he" to the end do not apply to an EEA decision to which regulation 24AA applies.]

(5) In calculating the period of two months limited by paragraph 8(2) of Schedule 2 to the 1971 Act for—

  (a)   the giving of directions under that paragraph for the removal of a person from the United Kingdom; and

  (b)   the giving of a notice of intention to give such directions,

any period during which there is pending an appeal by him under is to be disregarded [(except in cases where the EEA decision was taken pursuant to regulation 19(1), (1A), (1B) or (3)(b)].

(6) If a person in the United Kingdom appeals against an EEA decision to remove him from the United Kingdom, a deportation order is not to be made against him under section 5 of the 1971 Act while the appeal is pending.

(7) Paragraph 29 of Schedule 2 to the 1971 Act (grant of bail pending appeal) applies to a person who has an appeal pending under these Regulations as it applies to a person who has an appeal pending under section 82(1) of the 2002 Act.

Amendment

Provision heading: words "First-tier Tribunal or Upper Tribunal" in square brackets substituted by SI 2010/21, art 5(2), Sch 2, paras 21, 25. Date in force: 15 February 2010: see SI 2010/21, art 1; for transitional provisions and savings see art 5(4), Sch 4, paras 14–18, 21 thereto.

Para (1): words "First-tier Tribunal or Upper Tribunal" in square brackets substituted by SI 2010/21, art 5(2), Sch 2, paras 21, 25. Date in force: 15 February 2010: see SI 2010/21, art 1; for transitional provisions and savings see art 5(4), Sch 4, paras 14–18, 21 thereto.

Para (2): words in square brackets inserted by SI 2014/1976, reg 3, Schedule, para 7(a). Date in force: 28 July 2014, subject to transitional provisions: see SI 2014/1976, reg 2(1).

Para (3): words in square brackets inserted by SI 2014/1976, reg 3, Schedule, para 7(b). Date in force: 28 July 2014, subject to transitional provisions: see SI 2014/1976, reg 2(1).

Para (4A): inserted by SI 2014/1976, reg 3, Schedule, para 7(c). Date in force: 28 July 2014, subject to transitional provisions: see SI 2014/1976, reg 2(1).

Para (5): words in square brackets inserted by SI 2014/1976, reg 3, Schedule, para 7(d). Date in force: 28 July 2014, subject to transitional provisions: see SI 2014/1976, reg 2(1).

[29AA Temporary admission in order to submit case in person

(1) This regulation applies where—

  (a)   a person ("P") was removed from the United Kingdom pursuant to regulation 19(3)(b);

  (b)   P has appealed against the decision referred to in sub-paragraph (a);

  (c)   a date for P's appeal has been set by the First Tier Tribunal or Upper Tribunal; and

  (d)   P wants to make submissions before the First Tier Tribunal or Upper Tribunal in person.

(2) P may apply to the Secretary of State for permission to be temporarily admitted (within the meaning of paragraphs 21 to 24 of Schedule 2 to the 1971 Act, as applied by this regulation) to the United Kingdom in order to make submissions in person.

(3)   The Secretary of State must grant P permission, except when P's appearance may cause serious troubles to public policy or public security.

(4)   When determining when P is entitled to be given permission, and the duration of P's temporary admission should permission be granted, the Secretary of State must have regard to the dates upon which P will be required to make submissions in person.

(5)   Where—

    (a)   P is temporarily admitted to the United Kingdom pursuant to this regulation;

    (b)   a hearing of P's appeal has taken place; and

    (c)   the appeal is not finally determined,

P may be removed from the United Kingdom pending the remaining stages of the redress procedure (but P may apply to return to the United Kingdom to make submissions in person during the remaining stages of the redress procedure in accordance with this regulation).

(6)   Where the Secretary of State grants P permission to be temporarily admitted to the United Kingdom under this regulation, upon such admission P is to be treated as if P were a person refused leave to enter under the 1971 Act for the purposes of paragraphs 8, 10, 10A, 11, 16 to 18 and 21 to 24 of Schedule 2 to the 1971 Act.

(7)   Where Schedule 2 to the 1971 Act so applies, it has effect as if—

    (a)   the reference in paragraph 8(1) to leave to enter were a reference to admission to the United Kingdom under these Regulations; and

    (b)   the reference in paragraph 16(1) to detention pending a decision regarding leave to enter or remain in the United Kingdom were to detention pending submission of P's case in person in accordance with this regulation.

(8)   P will be deemed not to have been admitted to the United Kingdom during any time during which P is temporarily admitted pursuant to this regulation.]

Amendment

  Inserted by SI 2014/1976, reg 3, Schedule, para 8. Date in force: 28 July 2014, subject to transitional provisions: see SI 2014/1976, reg 2(1).

[29A Alternative evidence of identity and nationality]

[(1)   Subject to paragraph (2), where a provision of these Regulations requires a person to hold or produce a valid identity card issued by an EEA State or a valid passport the Secretary of State may accept alternative evidence of identity and nationality where the person is unable to obtain or produce the required document due to circumstances beyond his or her control.

(2)   This regulation does not apply to regulation 11.]

Amendment

  Inserted by SI 2012/2560, reg 2, Schedule, para 6.

  Date in force: 8 November 2012: see SI 2012/2560, reg 1.

PART 7
GENERAL

30 Effect on other legislation

Schedule 2 (effect on other legislation) shall have effect.

31 Revocations, transitional provisions and consequential amendments

(1)   The Regulations listed in column 1 of the table in Part 1 of Schedule 3 are revoked to the extent set out in column 3 of that table, subject to Part 2 of that Schedule and to Schedule 4.

(2)   Schedule 4 (transitional provisions) and Schedule 5 (consequential amendments) shall have effect.

SCHEDULE 1
APPEALS TO THE [FIRST-TIER TRIBUNAL]

Amendment

Schedule heading: words "First-tier Tribunal" in square brackets substituted by SI 2010/21, art 5(2), Sch 2, paras 21, 26(b).

Date in force: 15 February 2010: see SI 2010/21, art 1; for transitional provisions and savings see art 5(4), Sch 4, paras 14–18, 21 thereto.

Regulation 26(7)

[1]

The following provisions of, or made under, the 2002 Act have effect in relation to an appeal under these Regulations to the [First-tier Tribunal] as if it were an appeal against an immigration decision under section 82(1) of that Act:

section 84(1), except paragraphs (a) and (f);

sections 85 to 87;

. . .

section 105 and any regulations made under that section; and

section 106 and any rules made under that section.

[2

Tribunal Procedure Rules have effect in relation to appeals under these Regulations.]

Amendment

Para 1: numbered as such by SI 2010/21, art 5(2), Sch 2, paras 21, 26(a).

Date in force: 15 February 2010: see SI 2010/21, art 1; for transitional provisions and savings see art 5(4), Sch 4, paras 14–18, 21 thereto.

Para 1: words "First-tier Tribunal" in square brackets substituted by SI 2010/21, art 5(2), Sch 2, paras 21, 26(b).

Date in force: 15 February 2010: see SI 2010/21, art 1; for transitional provisions and savings see art 5(4), Sch 4, paras 14–18, 21 thereto.

Para 1: words omitted revoked by SI 2010/21, art 5(2), Sch 2, paras 21, 26(c).

Date in force: 15 February 2010: see SI 2010/21, art 1; for transitional provisions and savings see art 5(4), Sch 4, paras 14–18, 21 thereto.

Para 2: inserted by SI 2010/21, art 5(2), Sch 2, paras 21, 26(d).

Date in force: 15 February 2010: see SI 2010/21, art 1; for transitional provisions and savings see art 5(4), Sch 4, paras 14–18, 21 thereto.

SCHEDULE 2
EFFECT ON OTHER LEGISLATION

Regulation 30

Leave under the 1971 Act

1

(1) In accordance with section 7 of the Immigration Act 1988, a person who is admitted to or acquires a right to reside in the United Kingdom under these Regulations shall not require leave to remain in the United Kingdom under the 1971 Act during any period in which he has a right to reside under these Regulations but such a person shall require leave to remain under the 1971 Act during any period in which he does not have such a right.

(2) [Subject to sub-paragraph (3),] where a person has leave to enter or remain under the 1971 Act which is subject to conditions and that person also has a right to reside under these Regulations, those conditions shall not have effect for as long as the person has that right to reside.

[(3) Where the person mentioned in sub-paragraph (2) is an accession State national subject to worker authorisation working in the United Kingdom during the accession period and the document endorsed to show that the person has leave is an accession worker authorisation document, any conditions to which that leave is subject restricting his employment shall continue to apply.

(4) In sub-paragraph (3)—

    (a)   "accession period" has the meaning [given in—

        (i)   regulation 1(2)(c) of the Accession (Immigration and Worker Authorisation) Regulations 2006, in relation to a person who is an accession State national subject to worker authorisation within the meaning of regulation 2 of those Regulations; and

        (ii)   regulation 1(2) of the Accession of Croatia (Immigration and Worker Authorisation) Regulations 2013, in relation to a person who is an accession State national subject to worker authorisation within the meaning of regulation 2 of those Regulations];

    (b)   "accession State national subject to worker authorisation" has the meaning [given in—

        (i)   regulation 2 of the Accession (Immigration and Worker Authorisation) Regulations 2006; and

        (ii)   regulation 2 of the Accession of Croatia (Immigration and Worker Authorisation) Regulations 2013; and]

    (c)   "accession worker authorisation document" has the meaning [given in—

        (i)   regulation 9(2) of the Accession (Immigration and Worker Authorisation) Regulations 2006, in relation to a person who is an accession State national subject to worker authorisation within the meaning of regulation 2 of those Regulations; and

        (ii)   regulation 1(2) of the Accession of Croatia (Immigration and Worker Authorisation) Regulations 2013, in relation to a person who is an accession State national subject to worker authorisation within the meaning of regulation 2 of those Regulations].]

Persons not subject to restriction on the period for which they may remain

2

(1) For the purposes of the 1971 Act and the British Nationality Act 1981, a person who has a permanent right of residence under regulation 15 shall be regarded as a person who is in the United Kingdom without being subject under the immigration laws to any restriction on the period for which he may remain.

(2) But a qualified person, the family member of a qualified person[, a person with a derivative right of residence] and a family member who has retained the right of residence shall not, by virtue of that status, be so regarded for those purposes.

Carriers' liability under the 1999 Act

3

For the purposes of satisfying a requirement to produce a visa under section 40(1)(b) of the 1999 Act (charges in respect of passenger without proper documents), "a visa of the required kind" includes an EEA family permit, a residence card[, a derivative residence card][, a qualifying EEA State residence card][, permission to be temporarily admitted under regulation 29AA] or a permanent residence card required for admission under regulation 11(2).

Appeals under the 2002 Act and previous immigration Acts

4

(1) The following EEA decisions shall not be treated as immigration decisions for the purpose of section 82(2) of the 2002 Act (right of appeal against an immigration decision)—

    (a)   a decision that a person is to be removed under regulation 19(3)(a) [or 19(3)(c)] by way of a direction under section 10(1)(a) of the 1999 Act (as provided for by regulation 24(2));

(b)   a decision to remove a person under regulation 19(3)(b) by making a deportation order under section 5(1) of the 1971 Act (as provided for by regulation 24(3));

(c)   a decision to remove a person mentioned in regulation 24(4) by way of directions under paragraphs 8 to 10 of Schedule 2 to the 1971 Act.

(2)   A person who has been issued with a registration certificate, residence card, [derivative residence card,] a document certifying permanent residence or a permanent residence card under these Regulations [(including a registration certificate under these Regulations as applied by regulation 7 of the Accession of Croatia (Immigration and Worker Authorisation) Regulations 2013)] or a registration certificate under the Accession (Immigration and Worker Registration) Regulations 2004, [or an accession worker card under the Accession (Immigration and Worker Authorisation) Regulations 2006,] [or a worker authorisation registration certificate under the Accession of Croatia (Immigration and Worker Authorisation) Regulations 2013,] or a person whose passport has been stamped with a family member residence stamp, shall have no right of appeal under section 2 of the Special Immigration Appeals Commission Act 1997 or section 82(1) of the 2002 Act. Any existing appeal under those sections of those Acts or under the Asylum and Immigration Appeals Act 1993, the Asylum and Immigration Act 1996 or the 1999 Act shall be treated as abandoned.

(3)   Subject to paragraph (4), a person may appeal to the [First-tier Tribunal] under section 83(2) of the 2002 Act against the rejection of his asylum claim where—

(a)   that claim has been rejected, but

(b)   he has a right to reside in the United Kingdom under these Regulations.

(4)   Paragraph (3) shall not apply if the person is an EEA national and the Secretary of State certifies that the asylum claim is clearly unfounded.

(5)   The Secretary of State shall certify the claim under paragraph (4) unless satisfied that it is not clearly unfounded.

(6)   In addition to the national of a State which is a contracting party to the Agreement referred to in section 84(2) of the 2002 Act, a Swiss national shall also be treated as an EEA national for the purposes of section 84(1)(d) of that Act.

(7)   An appeal under these Regulations against an EEA decision (including an appeal made on or after 1st April 2003 which is treated as an appeal under these Regulations under Schedule 4 but not an appeal made before that date) shall be treated as an appeal under section 82(1) of the 2002 Act against an immigration decision for the purposes of section 96(1)(a) of the 2002 Act.

(8)   Section 120 of the 2002 Act shall apply to a person if an EEA decision has been taken or may be taken in respect of him and, accordingly, the Secretary of State or an immigration officer may by notice require a statement from that person under subsection (2) of that section and that notice shall have effect for the purpose of section 96(2) of the 2002 Act.

(9)   In sub-paragraph [(2)], "family member residence stamp" means a stamp in the passport of a family member of an EEA national confirming that he is the family member of an accession State worker requiring registration [or an accession State national subject to worker authorisation working in the United Kingdom"] with a right of residence under these Regulations as the family member of that worker; and in this sub-paragraph "accession State worker requiring registration" has the same meaning as in regulation 2 of the Accession (Immigration and Worker Registration) Regulations 2004 [and "accession State national subject to worker authorisation" has the meaning given in regulation 2 of the Accession (Immigration and Worker Authorisation) Regulations 2006].

Amendment

Para 1: in sub-para (2) words "Subject to sub-paragraph (3)," in square brackets inserted by SI 2006/3317, reg 1(3), Sch 2, para 2(1), (2)(a)(i).

Date in force: 1 January 2007: see SI 2006/3317, reg 1(1).

Para 1: sub-paras (3), (4) inserted by SI 2006/3317, reg 1(3). Sch 2, para 2(1), (2)(a)(ii).

Date in force: 1 January 2007: see SI 2006/3317, reg 1(1).

Para 1: in sub-para (4)(a) words from "given in—" to the end in square brackets substituted by SI 2013/1460, reg 1(3), Schedule, paras 1, 2(a).

Date in force: 1 July 2013: see SI 2013/1460, reg 1(1).

Para 1: in sub-para (4)(b) words from "given in—" to the end in square brackets substituted by SI 2013/1460, art 1(3), Schedule, paras 1, 2(b).

Date in force: 1 July 2013: see SI 2013/1460, reg 1(1).

Para 1: in sub-para (4)(c) words from "given in—" to the end in square brackets substituted by SI 2013/1460, art 1(3), Schedule, paras 1, 2(c).

Date in force: 1 July 2013: see SI 2013/1460, reg 1(1).

Para 2: in sub-para (2) words ", a person with a derivative right of residence" in square brackets inserted by SI 2012/1547, reg 3, Sch 1, para 22.

Date in force: 16 July 2012: see SI 2012/1547, reg 2(1).

Para 3: words ", a derivative residence card" in square brackets inserted by SI 2012/1547, reg 3, Sch 1, para 23.

Date in force: 16 July 2012: see SI 2012/1547, reg 2(1).

Para 3: words ", a qualifying EEA State residence card" in square brackets inserted by SI 2013/3032, reg 4, Sch 1, para 25(a).

Date in force: 7 April 2014: see SI 2013/3032, reg 2(2).

Para 3: words ", permission to be temporarily admitted under regulation 29AA" inserted by SI 2014/1976, reg 3, Schedule, para 9. Date in force: 28 July 2014, subject to transitional provisions: see SI 2014/1976, reg 2(1).

Para 4: in sub-para (1)(a) words "or 19(3)(c)" in square brackets inserted by SI 2013/3032, reg 4, Sch 1, para 25(b).

Date in force: 1 January 2014: see SI 2013/3032, reg 2(1).

Para 4: in sub-para (2) words "derivative residence card," in square brackets inserted by SI 2012/1547, reg 3, Sch 1, para 24(a).

Date in force: 16 July 2012: see SI 2012/1547, reg 2(1).

Para 4: in sub-para (2) words from "(including a registration" to "Regulations 2013)" in square brackets inserted by SI 2013/1460, art 1(3), Schedule, paras 1, 3(a).

Date in force: 1 July 2013: see SI 2013/1460, reg 1(1).

Para 4: in sub-para (2) words "or an accession worker card under the Accession (Immigration and Worker Authorisation) Regulations 2006," in square brackets inserted by SI 2006/3317, reg 1(3), Sch 2, para 2(1), (2)(b).

Date in force: 1 January 2007: see SI 2006/3317, reg 1(1).

Para 4: in sub-para (2) words from "or a worker" to "Regulations 2013," in square brackets inserted by SI 2013/1460, art 1(3), Schedule, paras 1, 3(b).

Date in force: 1 July 2013: see SI 2013/1460, reg 1(1).

Para 4: in sub-para (3) words "First-tier Tribunal" in square brackets substituted by SI 2010/21, art 5(2), Sch 2, paras 21, 27.

Date in force: 15 February 2010: see SI 2010/21, art 1; for transitional provisions and savings see art 5(4), Sch 4, paras 14–18, 21 thereto.

Para 4: in sub-para (9) reference to "(2)" in square brackets substituted by SI 2012/1547, reg 3, Sch 1, para 24(b).

Date in force: 16 July 2012: see SI 2012/1547, reg 2(1).

Para 4: in sub-para (9) words "or an accession State national subject to worker authorisation working in the United Kingdom" and "and "accession State national subject to worker authorisation" has the meaning given in regulation 2 of the Accession (Immigration and Worker Authorisation) Regulations 2006" in square brackets inserted by SI 2006/3317, reg 1(3), Sch 2, para 2(1), (2)(c).

Date in force: 1 January 2007: see SI 2006/3317, reg 1(1).

SCHEDULE 3
REVOCATIONS AND SAVINGS
Regulation 31(2)

PART 1
TABLE OF REVOCATIONS

(1) *Regulations revoked*	(2) *References*	(3) *Extent of revocation*
The Immigration (European Economic Area) Regulations 2000	SI 2000/2326	The whole Regulations
The Immigration (European Economic Area) (Amendment) Regulations 2001	SI 2001/865	The whole Regulations
The Immigration (Swiss Free Movement of Persons) (No 3) Regulations 2002	SI 2002/1241	The whole Regulations
The Immigration (European Economic Area) (Amendment) Regulations 2003	SI 2003/549	The whole Regulations
The Immigration (European Economic Area) (Amendment No 2) Regulations 2003	SI 2003/3188	The whole Regulations
The Accession (Immigration and Worker Registration) Regulations 2004	SI 2004/1219	Regulations 3 and 6
The Immigration (European Economic Area) and Accession (Amendment) Regulations 2004	SI 2004/1236	Regulation 2
The Immigration (European Economic Area) (Amendment) Regulations 2005	SI 2005/47	The whole Regulations
The Immigration (European Economic Area)(Amendment) (No 2) Regulations 2005	SI 2005/671	The whole Regulations

PART 2
SAVINGS

1

The—

(a)   Immigration (Swiss Free Movement of Persons) (No 3) Regulations 2002 are not revoked insofar as they apply the 2000 Regulations to posted workers; and

(b)   the 2000 Regulations and the Regulations amending the 2000 Regulations are not revoked insofar as they are so applied to posted workers;

and, accordingly, the 2000 Regulations, as amended, shall continue to apply to posted workers in accordance with the Immigration (Swiss Free Movement of Persons) (No 3) Regulations 2002.

2

In paragraph 1, "the 2000 Regulations" means the Immigration (European Economic Area) Regulations 2000 and "posted worker" has the meaning given in regulation 2(4)(b) of the Immigration (Swiss Free Movement of Persons) (No 3) Regulations 2002.

SCHEDULE 4

TRANSITIONAL PROVISIONS

Regulation 31(2)

Interpretation

1

In this Schedule—

    (a)   the "2000 Regulations" means the Immigration (European Economic Area) Regulations 2000 and expressions used in relation to documents issued or applied for under those Regulations shall have the meaning given in regulation 2 of those Regulations;

    (b)   the "Accession Regulations" means the Accession (Immigration and Worker Registration) Regulations 2004.

Existing documents

2

(1) An EEA family permit issued under the 2000 Regulations shall, after 29th April 2006, be treated as if it were an EEA family permit issued under these Regulations.

(2) Subject to paragraph (4), a residence permit issued under the 2000 Regulations shall, after 29th April 2006, be treated as if it were a registration certificate issued under these Regulations.

(3) Subject to paragraph (5), a residence document issued under the 2000 Regulations shall, after 29th April 2006, be treated as if it were a residence card issued under these Regulations.

(4) Where a residence permit issued under the 2000 Regulations has been endorsed under the immigration rules to show permission to remain in the United Kingdom indefinitely it shall, after 29th April 2006, be treated as if it were a document certifying permanent residence issued under these Regulations and the holder of the permit shall be treated as a person with a permanent right of residence under regulation 15.

(5) Where a residence document issued under the 2000 Regulations has been endorsed under the immigration rules to show permission to remain in the United Kingdom indefinitely it shall, after 29th April 2006, be treated as if it were a permanent residence card issued under these Regulations and the holder of the permit shall be treated as a person with a permanent right of residence under regulation 15.

(6) Paragraphs (4) and (5) shall also apply to a residence permit or residence document which is endorsed under the immigration rules on or after 30th April 2006 to show permission to remain in the United Kingdom indefinitely pursuant to an application for such an endorsement made before that date.

Outstanding applications

3

(1) An application for an EEA family permit, a residence permit or a residence document made but not determined under the 2000 Regulations before 30 April 2006 shall be treated as an application under these Regulations for an EEA family permit, a registration certificate or a residence card, respectively.

(2) But the following provisions of these Regulations shall not apply to the determination of an application mentioned in sub-paragraph (1)—

    (a)   the requirement to issue a registration certificate immediately under regulation 16(1); and

    (b)   the requirement to issue a certificate of application for a residence card under regulation 17(3).

Decisions to remove under the 2000 Regulations

4

(1)   A decision to remove a person under regulation 21(3)(a) of the 2000 Regulations shall, after 29th April 2006, be treated as a decision to remove that person under regulation 19(3)(a) of these Regulations.

(2)   A decision to remove a person under regulation 21(3)(b) of the 2000 Regulations, including a decision which is treated as a decision to remove a person under that regulation by virtue of regulation 6(3)(a) of the Accession Regulations, shall, after 29th April 2006, be treated as a decision to remove that person under regulation 19(3)(b) of these Regulations.

(3)   A deportation order made under section 5 of the 1971 Act by virtue of regulation 26(3) of the 2000 Regulations shall, after 29th April 2006, be treated as a deportation made under section 5 of the 1971 Act by virtue of regulation 24(3) of these Regulations.

Appeals

5

(1)   Where an appeal against an EEA decision under the 2000 Regulations is pending immediately before 30th April 2006 that appeal shall be treated as a pending appeal against the corresponding EEA Decision under these Regulations.

(2)   Where an appeal against an EEA decision under the 2000 Regulations has been determined, withdrawn or abandoned it shall, on and after 30th April 2006, be treated as an appeal against the corresponding EEA decision under these Regulations which has been determined, withdrawn or abandoned, respectively.

(3)   For the purpose of this paragraph—

   (a)   a decision to refuse to admit a person under these Regulations corresponds to a decision to refuse to admit that person under the 2000 Regulations;

   (b)   a decision to remove a person under regulation 19(3)(a) of these Regulations corresponds to a decision to remove that person under regulation 21(3)(a) of the 2000 Regulations;

   (c)   a decision to remove a person under regulation 19(3)(b) of these Regulations corresponds to a decision to remove that person under regulation 21(3)(b) of the 2000 Regulations, including a decision which is treated as a decision to remove a person under regulation 21(3)(b) of the 2000 Regulations by virtue of regulation 6(3)(a) of the Accession Regulations;

   (d)   a decision to refuse to revoke a deportation order made against a person under these Regulations corresponds to a decision to refuse to revoke a deportation order made against that person under the 2000 Regulations, including a decision which is treated as a decision to refuse to revoke a deportation order under the 2000 Regulations by virtue of regulation 6(3)(b) of the Accession Regulations;

   (e)   a decision not to issue or renew or to revoke an EEA family permit, a registration certificate or a residence card under these Regulations corresponds to a decision not to issue or renew or to revoke an EEA family permit, a residence permit or a residence document under the 2000 Regulations, respectively.

[Periods of residence prior to the entry into force of these Regulations

6

(1)   Any period during which a person ("P"), who is an EEA national, carried out an activity or was resident in the United Kingdom in accordance with the conditions in subparagraph (2) or (3) is to be treated as a period during which the person carried out that activity or was resident in the United Kingdom in accordance with these

Regulations for the purpose of calculating periods of activity and residence there under.

(2) P carried out an activity, or was resident, in the United Kingdom in accordance with this subparagraph where such activity or residence was at that time in accordance with—

    (a)   the 2000 Regulations;

    (b)   the Immigration (European Economic Area) Order 1994 ("the 1994 Order"); or

    (c)   where such activity or residence preceded the entry into force of the 1994 Order, any of the following Directives which was at the relevant time in force in respect of the United Kingdom—

        (i)   Council Directive 64/221/EEC;

        (ii)   Council Directive 68/360/EEC;

        (iii)   Council Directive 72/194/EEC;

        (iv)   Council Directive 73/148/EEC;

        (v)   Council Directive 75/34/EEC;

        (vi)   Council Directive 75/35/EEC;

        (vii)   Council Directive 90/364/EEC;

        (viii)   Council Directive 90/365/EEC; and

        (ix)   Council Directive 93/96/EEC.

(3) P carried out an activity or was resident in the United Kingdom in accordance with this subparagraph where P—

    (a)   had leave to enter or remain in the United Kingdom; and

    (b)   would have been carrying out that activity or residing in the United Kingdom in accordance with these Regulations had the relevant state been an EEA State at that time and had these Regulations at that time been in force.

(4) Any period during which P carried out an activity or was resident in the United Kingdom in accordance with subparagraph (2) or (3) will not be regarded as a period during which P carried out that activity or was resident in the United Kingdom in accordance with these Regulations where it was followed by a period—

    (a)   which exceeded two consecutive years and for the duration of which P was absent from the United Kingdom; or

    (b)   which exceeded two consecutive years and for the duration of which P's residence in the United Kingdom—

        (i)   was not in accordance with subparagraph (2) or (3); or

        (ii)   was not otherwise in accordance with these Regulations.

(5) The relevant state for the purpose of subparagraph (3) is the state of which P is, and was at the relevant time, a national.]

Amendment

Para 6: substituted by SI 2012/1547, reg 3, Sch 1, para 25. Date in force: 16 July 2012: see SI 2012/1547, reg 2(1).

SCHEDULE 5

(Sch 5 contains amendments which, in so far as relevant to this work, have been incorporated at the appropriate place.)

BRITISH NATIONALITY (PROOF OF PATERNITY) REGULATIONS 2006

(SI 2006/1496)

Made: 5 June 2006.

Authority: British Nationality Act 1981, s 50(9A), (9B).

Commencement: 1 July 2006.

1

These Regulations may be cited as the British Nationality (Proof of Paternity) Regulations 2006 and shall come into force on 1st July 2006.

2

The following requirements are prescribed as to proof of paternity for the purposes of section 50(9A)(c) of the British Nationality Act 1981—

    (a)   the person must be named as the father of the child in a birth certificate issued within one year of the date of the child's birth; or

    (b)   the person must satisfy the Secretary of State that he is the father of the child.

3

The Secretary of State may determine whether a person is the father of a child for the purpose of regulation 2(b), and for this purpose the Secretary of State may have regard to any evidence which he considers to be relevant, including, but not limited to—

    (a)   DNA test reports; and

    (b)   court orders.

IMMIGRATION (PROVISION OF PHYSICAL DATA) REGULATIONS 2006

(SI 2006/1743)

Made: 3 July 2006.

Authority: Nationality, Immigration and Asylum Act 2002, s 126(1).

Commencement: 4 July 2006.

1 Citation, commencement and interpretation

These Regulations may be cited as the Immigration (Provision of Physical Data) Regulations 2006 and shall come into force on the day after they are made.

2

In these Regulations:

    "application" means:

        (a)   an application for entry clearance; or

        (b)   an application for leave to enter the United Kingdom where the person seeking leave to enter presents a Convention travel document endorsed with an entry clearance for that journey to the United Kingdom;

"Convention travel document" means a travel document issued pursuant to Article 28 of the Refugee Convention, except where that travel document was issued by the United Kingdom Government;

"Refugee Convention" means the Convention relating to the Status of Refugees done at Geneva on 28th July 1951 and its Protocol.

3 Power for an authorised person to require an individual to provide a record of his fingerprints and a photograph of his face

Subject to regulations 4 and 5, an authorised person may require an individual who makes an application to provide a record of his fingerprints and a photograph of his face.

4 Provision in relation to applicants under the age of sixteen

(1) An applicant under the age of sixteen shall not be required to provide a record of his fingerprints or a photograph of his face except where the authorised person is satisfied that the fingerprints or the photograph will be taken in the presence of a person aged eighteen or over who is—

    (a)   the child's parent or guardian; or

    (b)   a person who for the time being takes responsibility for the child.

(2) The person mentioned in paragraph (1)(b) may not be—

    (a)   an officer of the Secretary of State who is not an authorised person;

    (b)   an authorised person; or

    (c)   any other person acting on behalf of an authorised person as part of a process specified under regulation 6(2).

(3) An authorised person shall not require a person under the age of sixteen to provide a record of his fingerprints or a photograph of his face unless his decision to do so has been confirmed by a person designated for the purpose by the Secretary of State.

(4) This regulation shall not apply if the authorised person reasonably believes that the applicant is aged sixteen or over.

5 Provision in relation to section 141 of the Immigration and Asylum Act 1999

An applicant shall not be required to provide a record of his fingerprints or a photograph of his face under regulation 3 if he is a person to whom section 141 of the Immigration and Asylum Act 1999 applies, during the relevant period within the meaning of that section.

6 Process by which the applicant's fingerprints and photograph may be obtained and recorded

(1) An authorised person who requires an individual to provide a record of his fingerprints or a photograph of his face under regulation 3 may require that individual to submit to any process specified in paragraph (2).

(2) A process by which the individual who makes the application:

    (a)   attends a British Diplomatic mission or British Consular post where a record of his fingerprints or a photograph of his face is taken;

    (b)   attends a Diplomatic mission or Consular post of another State where a record of his fingerprints or a photograph of his face is taken by an official of that State on behalf of an authorised person; or

    (c)   attends other premises nominated by an authorised person where a record of his fingerprints or a photograph of his face is taken by a person on behalf of an authorised person.

7 Consequences of failure to comply with these Regulations

(1) Subject to paragraphs (2) and (3), where an individual does not provide a record of his fingerprints or a photograph of his face in accordance with a requirement imposed under these Regulations, his application may be treated as invalid.

(2) An application shall not be treated as invalid under paragraph (1) if it is for leave to enter the United Kingdom where the person seeking leave to enter presents a Convention travel document endorsed with an entry clearance for that journey to the United Kingdom.

(3) Where an application is of a type described in paragraph (2) and the applicant does not provide a record of his fingerprints or a photograph of his face in accordance with a requirement imposed under these Regulations, that application may be refused.

8 Destruction of information

Subject to regulation 9, any record of fingerprints, photograph, copy of fingerprints or copy of a photograph held by the Secretary of State pursuant to these Regulations must be destroyed by the Secretary of State at the end of ten years beginning with the date on which the original record or photograph was provided.

9

If an applicant proves that he is—

   (a)   a British citizen; or
   (b)   a Commonwealth citizen who has a right of abode in the United Kingdom as a result of section 2(1)(b) of the Immigration Act 1971,

any record of fingerprints, photograph, copy of fingerprints or copy of a photograph held by the Secretary of State pursuant to these Regulations must be destroyed as soon as reasonably practicable.

10

(1) The Secretary of State must take all reasonably practicable steps to secure:

   (a)   that data held in electronic form which relate to any record of fingerprints or photograph which have to be destroyed in accordance with regulation 8 or 9 are destroyed or erased; or
   (b)   that access to such data is blocked.

(2) The applicant to whom the data relates is entitled, on written request, to a certificate issued by the Secretary of State to the effect that he has taken the steps required by paragraph (1).

(3) A certificate issued under paragraph (2) must be issued within three months of the date on which the request was received by the Secretary of State.

11 Revocation and transitional provisions

(1) Subject to paragraphs (2) and (3), the Regulations specified in the Schedule are revoked.

(2) For the purposes of paragraph (3) only, "application" means an application within the meaning of regulation 2 of the Immigration (Provision of Physical Data) Regulations 2003 (the "2003 Regulations").

(3) Where a person made an application before these Regulations came into force, the 2003 Regulations will continue to apply for the purposes of that application as if they had not been revoked by paragraph (1).

SCHEDULE

Regulation 11

(1)	*(2)*
Orders revoked	*References*
The Immigration (Provision of Physical Data) Regulations 2003	SI 2003/1875
The Immigration (Provision of Physical Data) (Amendment) Regulations 2004	SI 2004/474

| The Immigration (Provision of Physical Data) (Amendment) (No 2) Regulations 2004 | SI 2004/1834 |
| The Immigration (Provision of Physical Data) (Amendment) Regulations 2005 | SI 2005/3127 |

IMMIGRATION (CONTINUATION OF LEAVE) (NOTICES) REGULATIONS 2006

(SI 2006/2170)

Made: 4 August 2006.

Authority: Immigration Act 1971, s 3C(6).

Commencement: 31 August 2006.

1 Citation and Commencement

These Regulations may be cited as the Immigration (Continuation of Leave) (Notices) Regulations 2006 and shall come into force on 31st August 2006.

2 Decision on an application for variation of leave

For the purpose of section 3C of the Immigration Act 1971 an application for variation of leave is decided—

(a) when notice of the decision has been given in accordance with regulations made under section 105 of the Nationality, Immigration and Asylum Act 2002; or where no such notice is required,

(b) when notice of the decision has been given in accordance with section 4(1) of the Immigration Act 1971.

REFUGEE OR PERSON IN NEED OF INTERNATIONAL PROTECTION (QUALIFICATION) REGULATIONS 2006

(SI 2006/2525)

Made: 11 September 2006.

Authority: European Communities Act 1972, s 2(2).

Commencement: 9 October 2006.

1 Citation and commencement

(1) These Regulations may be cited as The Refugee or Person in Need of International Protection (Qualification) Regulations 2006 and shall come into force on 9th October 2006.

(2) These Regulations apply to any application for asylum which has not been decided and any immigration appeal brought under the Immigration Acts (as defined in section 64(2) of the Immigration, Asylum and Nationality Act 2006) which has not been finally determined.

2 Interpretation

In these Regulations—

"application for asylum" means the request of a person to be recognised as a refugee under the Geneva Convention;

"Geneva Convention" means the Convention Relating to the Status of Refugees done at Geneva on 28 July 1951 and the New York Protocol of 31 January 1967;

"immigration rules" means rules made under section 3(2) of the Immigration Act 1971;

"persecution" means an act of persecution within the meaning of Article 1(A) of the Geneva Convention;

"person eligible for humanitarian protection" means a person who is eligible for a grant of humanitarian protection under the immigration rules;

"refugee" means a person who falls within Article 1(A) of the Geneva Convention and to whom regulation 7 does not apply;

"residence permit" means a document confirming that a person has leave to enter or remain in the United Kingdom whether limited or indefinite;

"serious harm" means serious harm as defined in the immigration rules;

"person" means any person who is not a British citizen.

3 Actors of persecution or serious harm

In deciding whether a person is a refugee or a person eligible for humanitarian protection, persecution or serious harm can be committed by:

    (a)   the State;

    (b)   any party or organisation controlling the State or a substantial part of the territory of the State;

    (c)   any non-State actor if it can be demonstrated that the actors mentioned in paragraphs (a) and (b), including any international organisation, are unable or unwilling to provide protection against persecution or serious harm.

4 Actors of protection

(1)   In deciding whether a person is a refugee or a person eligible for humanitarian protection, protection from persecution or serious harm can be provided by:

    (a)   the State; or

    (b)   any party or organisation, including any international organisation, controlling the State or a substantial part of the territory of the State.

(2)   Protection shall be regarded as generally provided when the actors mentioned in paragraph (1)(a) and (b) take reasonable steps to prevent the persecution or suffering of serious harm by operating an effective legal system for the detection, prosecution and punishment of acts constituting persecution or serious harm, and the person mentioned in paragraph (1) has access to such protection.

(3)   In deciding whether a person is a refugee or a person eligible for humanitarian protection the Secretary of State may assess whether an international organisation controls a State or a substantial part of its territory and provides protection as described in paragraph (2).

5 Act of persecution

(1)   In deciding whether a person is a refugee an act of persecution must be:

    (a)   sufficiently serious by its nature or repetition as to constitute a severe violation of a basic human right, in particular a right from which derogation cannot be made under Article 15 of the Convention for the Protection of Human Rights and Fundamental Freedoms; or

    (b)   an accumulation of various measures, including a violation of a human right which is sufficiently severe as to affect an individual in a similar manner as specified in (a).

(2)   An act of persecution may, for example, take the form of:

(a) an act of physical or mental violence, including an act of sexual violence;

(b) a legal, administrative, police, or judicial measure which in itself is discriminatory or which is implemented in a discriminatory manner;

(c) prosecution or punishment, which is disproportionate or discriminatory;

(d) denial of judicial redress resulting in a disproportionate or discriminatory punishment;

(e) prosecution or punishment for refusal to perform military service in a conflict, where performing military service would include crimes or acts falling under regulation 7.

(3) An act of persecution must be committed for at least one of the reasons in Article 1(A) of the Geneva Convention.

6 Reasons for persecution

(1) In deciding whether a person is a refugee:

(a) the concept of race shall include consideration of, for example, colour, descent, or membership of a particular ethnic group;

(b) the concept of religion shall include, for example, the holding of theistic, non-theistic and atheistic beliefs, the participation in, or abstention from, formal worship in private or in public, either alone or in community with others, other religious acts or expressions of view, or forms of personal or communal conduct based on or mandated by any religious belief;

(c) the concept of nationality shall not be confined to citizenship or lack thereof but shall include, for example, membership of a group determined by its cultural, ethnic, or linguistic identity, common geographical or political origins or its relationship with the population of another State;

(d) a group shall be considered to form a particular social group where, for example:

  (i) members of that group share an innate characteristic, or a common background that cannot be changed, or share a characteristic or belief that is so fundamental to identity or conscience that a person should not be forced to renounce it, and

  (ii) that group has a distinct identity in the relevant country, because it is perceived as being different by the surrounding society;

(e) a particular social group might include a group based on a common characteristic of sexual orientation but sexual orientation cannot be understood to include acts considered to be criminal in accordance with national law of the United Kingdom;

(f) the concept of political opinion shall include the holding of an opinion, thought or belief on a matter related to the potential actors of persecution mentioned in regulation 3 and to their policies or methods, whether or not that opinion, thought or belief has been acted upon by the person.

(2) In deciding whether a person has a well-founded fear of being persecuted, it is immaterial whether he actually possesses the racial, religious, national, social or political characteristic which attracts the persecution, provided that such a characteristic is attributed to him by the actor of persecution.

7 Exclusion

(1) A person is not a refugee, if he falls within the scope of Article 1 D, 1E or 1F of the Geneva Convention.

(2) In the construction and application of Article 1F(b) of the Geneva Convention:

(a) the reference to serious non-political crime includes a particularly cruel action, even if it is committed with an allegedly political objective;

    (b)   the reference to the crime being committed outside the country of refuge prior to his admission as a refugee shall be taken to mean the time up to and including the day on which a residence permit is issued.

(3) Article 1F(a) and (b) of the Geneva Convention shall apply to a person who instigates or otherwise participates in the commission of the crimes or acts specified in those provisions.

HOMELESSNESS (WALES) REGULATIONS 2006
(SI 2006/2646)

Made: 3 October 2006.

Authority: Housing Act 1996, s 185(2), (3).

Commencement: 9 October 2006.

1 Title, commencement and application

(1) The title of these Regulations is the Homelessness (Wales) Regulations 2006 and they come into force on 9 October 2006.

(2) These Regulations apply to Wales.

Initial Commencement

Specified date: 9 October 2006: see para (1) above.

2 Interpretation

(1) In these Regulations—

    "the 1971 Act" ("*Deddf 1971*") means the Immigration Act 1971;

    "the 1995 Act" ("*Deddf 1995*") means the Jobseekers Act 1995;

    "the 1996 Act" ("*Deddf 1996*") means the Housing Act 1996;

    ["the 2012 Act" ("*Deddf 2012*") means the Welfare Reform Act 2012 (2012 c 5);]

    "asylum-seeker" ("*ceisydd lloches*") means a person who is not under 18 and who made a claim for asylum which is recorded by the Secretary of State as having been made before 3 April 2000 but which has not been determined;

    "claim for asylum" ("*hawliad lloches*") means a claim that it would be contrary to the United Kingdom's obligations under the Refugee Convention for the claimant to be removed from, or required to leave, the United Kingdom;

    "the Common Travel Area" ("*Ardal Deithio Gyffredin*") means the United Kingdom, the Channel Islands, the Isle of Man and the Republic of Ireland collectively;

    "the immigration rules" ("*y rheolau mewnfudo*") means the rules laid down as mentioned in section 3(2) of the 1971 Act (general provisions for regulation and control);

    "limited leave" ("*caniatâd cyfyngedig*") means leave under the 1971 Act to enter or remain in the United Kingdom which is limited as to duration; and

    "the Refugee Convention" ("*y Confensiwn ynglyn â Ffoaduriaid*") means the Convention relating to the Status of Refugees done at Geneva on 28 July 1951, as extended by Article 1(2) of the Protocol relating to the Status of Refugees done at New York on 31 January 1967.

(2) For the purposes of the definition of "asylum-seeker", a claim for asylum is determined at the end of such period beginning—

    (a)   on the day on which the Secretary of State notifies the claimant of the decision on the claim; or

    (b)   if the claimant has appealed against the Secretary of State's decision, on the day on which the appeal is disposed of,

as may be prescribed under section 94(3) of the Immigration and Asylum Act 1999.

(3)   For the purposes of regulations 3(1)(i) (Class I)—

    (a)   "an income-based jobseeker's allowance" ("*lwfans ceisio gwaith ar sail incwm*")means a jobseeker's allowance, payable under the 1995 Act, entitlement to which is based on the claimant satisfying conditions which include those set out in section 3 of the 1995 Act (the income-based conditions);

    (b)   "income support" ("*cymhorthdal incwm*") has the same meaning as in section 124 of the Social Security Contributions and Benefits Act 1992 (income support); . . .

    (c)   a person is on an income-based jobseeker's allowance on any day in respect of which an income-based jobseeker's allowance is payable to that person and on any day—

        (i)   in respect of which that person satisfies the conditions for entitlement to an income-based jobseeker's allowance but where the allowance is not paid in accordance with section 19 of the 1995 Act (circumstances in which jobseeker's allowance is not payable); or

        (ii)   which is a waiting day for the purposes of paragraph 4 of Schedule 1 to the 1995 Act (waiting days) and which falls immediately before a day in respect of which an income-based jobseeker's allowance is payable to that person or would be payable to that person but for section 19 of the 1995 Act; [. . .

    (d)   "an income-related employment and support allowance" means an employment and support allowance payable under Part 1 of the Welfare Reform Act 2007 entitlement to which is based on the claimant satisfying conditions which include those set out in Part 2 of Schedule 1 to that Act][; and

    (e)   "employment and support allowance" ("lwfans cyflogaeth a chymorth") means employment and support allowance under Part 2 of the 2012 Act; and

    (f)   "universal credit" ("credyd cynhwysol") means universal credit under Part 1 of the 2012 Act].

Amendment

Para (1): definition "the 2012 Act" inserted by SI 2013/1788, reg 7(1), (2)(a). Date in force: 17 July 2013: see SI 2013/1788, reg 1(1).

Para (3): in sub-para (b) word omitted revoked by SI 2008/1879, reg 31(1), (2)(a). Date in force: 27 October 2008: see SI 2008/1879, reg 1(1).

Para (3): sub-para (d) and word "and" immediately preceding it inserted by SI 2008/1879, reg 31(1), (2)(b). Date in force: 27 October 2008: see SI 2008/1879, reg 1(1).

Para (3): in sub-para (c)(ii) word omitted revoked by SI 2013/1788, reg 7(1), (2)(b). Date in force: 17 July 2013: see SI 2013/1788, reg 1(1).

Para (3): sub-paras (e), (f) and word "; and" immediately preceding them inserted by SI 2013/1788, reg 7(1), (2)(c), (d). Date in force: 17 July 2013: see SI 2013/1788, reg 1(1).

3 Classes of persons subject to immigration control who are eligible for housing assistance

(1)   The following are classes of persons prescribed for the purposes of section 185(2) of the 1996 Act (persons subject to immigration control who are eligible for housing assistance)-

(a) Class A—a person recorded by the Secretary of State as a refugee within the definition in Article 1 of the Refugee Convention;

(b) Class B—a person—

  (i) who has been granted by the Secretary of State exceptional leave to enter or remain in the United Kingdom outside the provisions of the immigration rules; and

  (ii) whose leave is not subject to a condition requiring that person to maintain and accommodate themselves, and any person who is dependent on that person, without recourse to public funds;

(c) Class C—a person who has current leave to enter or remain in the United Kingdom which is not subject to any limitation or condition and who is habitually resident in the Common Travel Area other than a person—

  (i) who has been given leave to enter or remain in the United Kingdom upon an undertaking given by another person (that person's "sponsor") in writing in pursuance of the immigration rules to be responsible for that person's maintenance and accommodation;

  (ii) who has been resident in the United Kingdom for less than five years beginning on the date of entry or the date on which the undertaking was given in respect of that person, whichever date is the later; and

  (iii) whose sponsor or, where there more than one sponsor, at least one of whose sponsors, is still alive;

(d) Class D—a person who left the territory of Montserrat after 1 November 1995 because of the effect on that territory of a volcanic eruption;

(e) Class E—a person who is habitually resident in the Common Travel Area and who—

  (i) is a national of a state which has ratified the European Convention on Social and Medical Assistance done at Paris on 11 December 1953 or a state which has ratified the European Social Charter done at Turin on 18 October 1961 and is lawfully present in the United Kingdom; or

  (ii) before 3 April 2000 was owed a duty by a housing authority under Part III of the Housing Act 1985 (housing and homeless) or Part VII of the 1996 Act (homelessness) which is extant, and who is a national of a state which is a signatory to the European Convention on Social and Medical Assistance done at Paris on 11 December 1953 or a state which is a signatory to the European Social Charter done at Turin on 18 October 1961;

(f) Class F—a person who is an asylum-seeker and who made a claim for asylum—

  (i) which is recorded by the Secretary of State as having been made on his arrival (other than on his re-entry) in the United Kingdom from a country outside the Common Travel Area; and

  (ii) which has not been recorded by the Secretary of State as having been either decided (other than on appeal) or abandoned;

(g) Class G—a person who is an asylum-seeker and—

  (i) who was in Great Britain when the Secretary of State made a declaration to the effect that the country of which that person is a national is subject to such a fundamental change in circumstances that the Secretary of State would not normally order the return of a person to that country;

  (ii) who made a claim for asylum which is recorded by the Secretary of State as having been made within a period of three months from the day on which that declaration was made; and

  (iii) whose claim for asylum has not been recorded by the Secretary of State as having been either decided (other than on appeal) or abandoned;

 (h) Class H—a person who is an asylum-seeker and—

  (i) who made a relevant claim for asylum on or before 4 February 1996; and

  (ii) who was, on 4 February 1996, entitled to benefit under regulation 7A of the Housing Benefit (General) Regulations 1987 (persons from abroad);

 (i) Class I—a person who is on an income-based jobseeker's allowance[, an income-related employment and support allowance][, employment and support allowance,] or in receipt of [universal credit or] income support and is eligible for that benefit other than because—

  (i) that person has limited leave to enter or remain in the United Kingdom which was given in accordance with the relevant immigration rules and that person is temporarily without funds because remittances to that person from abroad have been disrupted; or

  (ii) that person has been deemed by regulation 3 of the Displaced Persons (Temporary Protection) Regulations 2005 to have been granted leave to enter or remain in the United Kingdom exceptionally for the purposes of the provision of means of subsistence; and

 (j) Class J—a person who has humanitarian protection granted under the Immigration Rules.

(2) In paragraph (1)(h)(i) (Class H), a relevant claim for asylum is a claim for asylum which—

 (a) has not been recorded by the Secretary of State as having been either decided (other than on appeal) or abandoned; or

 (b) has been recorded as having been decided (other than on appeal) on or before 4 February 1996 and in respect of which an appeal is pending which—

  (i) was pending on 5 February 1996; or

  (ii) was made within the time limits specified in the rules of procedure made under section 22 of the 1971 Act (procedure).

(3) In paragraph (1)(i)(i) (Class I), "relevant immigration rules" (*"rheolau mewnfudo perthnasol"*) means the immigration rules relating to—

 (a) there being or there needing to be no recourse

 (b) there being no charge on public funds.

(4) In paragraph (1)(i) (Class I), "means of subsistence" (*"moddion byw"*) has the same meaning as in regulation 4 of the Displaced Persons (Temporary Protection) Regulations 2005.

Amendment

Para (1): in sub-para (i) words ", an income-related employment and support allowance" in square brackets inserted by SI 2008/1879, reg 31(1), (3). Date in force: 27 October 2008: see SI 2008/1879, reg 1(1).

Para (1): in sub-para (i) words ", employment and support allowance," in square brackets inserted by SI 2013/1788, reg 7(1), (3)(a). Date in force: 17 July 2013: see SI 2013/1788, reg 1(1).

Para (1): in sub-para (i) words "universal credit or" in square brackets inserted by SI 2013/1788, reg 7(1), (3)(b). Date in force: 17 July 2013: see SI 2013/1788, reg 1(1).

4 Description of persons who are to be treated as persons from abroad ineligible for housing assistance.

(1) The following are descriptions of persons, other than persons who are subject to immigration control, who are to be treated for the purposes of Part VII of the 1996 Act (homelessness) as persons from abroad who are ineligible for housing assistance—

(a) subject to paragraphs (2) and (3), a person who is not habitually resident in the United Kingdom, the Channel Islands, the Isle of Man or the Republic of Ireland;

(b) a person whose right to reside in the United Kingdom, the Channel Islands, the Isle of Man or the Republic of Ireland is derived solely from Council Directive No 90/364/EEC or Council Directive No 90/365/EEC

(2) The following persons will not, however, be treated as persons from abroad who are ineligible pursuant to paragraph (1)(a)—

(a) a person who is a worker for the purposes of Council Regulation (EEC) No 1612/68 or (EEC) No 1251/70;

(b) a person who is an accession state worker requiring registration who is treated as a worker for the purpose of the definition of "qualified person" in regulation 6 of the Immigration (European Economic Area) Regulations 2006 pursuant to regulation 5 of the Accession (Immigration and Worker Registration) Regulations 2004;

(c) a person with a right to reside pursuant to the Immigration (European Economic Area) Regulations 2006, which is derived from Council Directive No 68/360/EEC, No 73/148/EEC or No 75/34/EEC;

(d) a person who left the territory of Montserrat after 1 November 1995 because of the effect on that territory of a volcanic eruption[;

(e) a person who—

(i) arrived in Great Britain on or after 28 February 2009 but before 18 March 2011;

(ii) immediately before arriving in Great Britain had been resident in Zimbabwe; and

(iii) before leaving Zimbabwe, had accepted an offer, made by Her Majesty's Government, to assist that person to settle in the United Kingdom].

(3) A person will not be treated as habitually resident in the United Kingdom, the Channel Islands, the Isle of Man or the Republic of Ireland for the purposes of paragraph (1)(a) if he does not have a right to reside in the United Kingdom, the Channel Islands, the Isle of Man or the Republic of Ireland.

Amendment

Para (2): sub-para (e) inserted by SI 2009/393, reg 3.

Date in force: 20 March 2009: see SI 2009/393, reg 1(1).

5 Transitional Provisions

The amendments made by these Regulations do not have effect in relation to an applicant whose application for housing assistance under Part VII of the 1996 Act was made before 9 October 2006.

6 Revocation

The Homelessness (Wales) Regulations 2000 are hereby revoked.

IMMIGRATION (CERTIFICATE OF ENTITLEMENT TO RIGHT OF ABODE IN THE UNITED KINGDOM) REGULATIONS 2006

(SI 2006/3145)

Made: 23 November 2006.

Authority: Nationality, Immigration and Asylum Act 2002, s 10(1).

Commencement: 21 December 2006.

Citation, commencement and interpretation

1

These Regulations may be cited as the Immigration (Certificate of Entitlement to Right of Abode in the United Kingdom) Regulations 2006 and shall come into force on 21st December 2006.

2

In these Regulations—

"the 1971 Act" means the Immigration Act 1971;

"the 1981 Act" means the British Nationality Act 1981;

"the 2002 Act" means the Nationality, Immigration and Asylum Act 2002;

["the 2008 Act" means the Human Fertilisation and Embryology Act 2008;]

"appropriate authority" means the authority to whom an application for a certificate of entitlement must be made, as determined in accordance with regulation 3;

"certificate of entitlement" means a certificate, issued in accordance with these Regulations, that a person has the right of abode in the United Kingdom;

"Governor", in relation to a territory, includes the officer for the time being administering the government of that territory;

"High Commissioner" means, in relation to a country mentioned in Schedule 3 to the 1981 Act, the High Commissioner for Her Majesty's Government in the United Kingdom appointed to that country, and includes the acting High Commissioner; and

"passport" includes a document which relates to a national of a country other than the United Kingdom and which is designed to serve the same purpose as a passport.

Amendment

Definition "the 2008 Act" inserted by SI 2009/1892, art 2, Sch 1, Pt 2, para 18(1), (2).

Date in force: 1 September 2009: see SI 2009/1892, art 1(1)(a).

Authority to whom an application must be made

3

An application for a certificate of entitlement must be made—

(a)   if the applicant is in the United Kingdom, to the Secretary of State for the Home Department;

[(b)   if the applicant is in any of the Channel Islands or the Isle of Man, to the Lieutenant-Governor or the Secretary of State for the Home Department;]

(c)   if the applicant is in a British overseas territory, to the Governor;

(d)   if the applicant is in a country mentioned in Schedule 3 to the 1981 Act, to the High Commissioner, or, if there is no High Commissioner, to the Secretary of State for the Home Department; and

(e)   if the applicant is elsewhere, to any consular officer, any established officer in the Diplomatic Service of Her Majesty's Government in the United Kingdom or any other person authorised by the Secretary of State in that behalf.

Amendment

Sub-para (b) substituted by SI 2011/2682, reg 2(1), (2). Date in force: In relation to an application for a certificate of entitlement received by the appropriate authority on or after 12 December 2011: see SI 2011/2682, reg 1(1).

Form of application

[4

(1)   Subject to paragraph (2), an application for a certificate of entitlement must be accompanied by—

(a)   the applicant's passport or travel document;

(b)   two photographs of the applicant taken no more than 6 months prior to making the application; and

(c)   the additional documents which are specified in the right-hand column of the Schedule in respect of an application of a description specified in the corresponding entry in the left hand column.

(2)   The requirement in paragraph (1)(c) may be waived in relation to a particular document if the appropriate authority—

(a)   is satisfied that it is appropriate to do so in light of the facts of the particular case; and

(b)   is otherwise satisfied that the applicant has a right of abode in the United Kingdom.

Amendment

Substituted by SI 2011/2682, reg 2(1), (3). Date in force: In relation to an application for a certificate of entitlement received by the appropriate authority on or after 12 December 2011: see SI 2011/2682, reg 1(1).

5

A passport produced by or on behalf of a person is valid for the purposes of regulation 4 if it—

(a)   relates to the person by whom or on whose behalf it is produced;

(b)   has not been altered otherwise than by or with the permission of the authority who issued it; and

(c)   was not obtained by deception.

Issue of certificate of entitlement

6

A certificate of entitlement will only be issued where the appropriate authority is satisfied that the applicant—

(a)   has a right of abode in the United Kingdom under section 2(1) of the 1971 Act;

[(b)   is not a person who holds:

(i)   a United Kingdom passport describing him as a British citizen,

(ii)   a United Kingdom passport describing him as a British subject with the right of abode in the United Kingdom, or

(iii)   a certificate of entitlement;]

(c)   is not a person whose exercise of his right of abode is restricted under
section 2 of the Immigration Act 1988 (restrictions on exercise of right of
abode in cases of polygamy); and

(d)   is not a person who is deprived of his right of abode by an order under
section 2A of the 1971 Act.

Amendment

Sub-para (b) substituted by SI 2011/2682, reg 2(1), (4). Date in force: In relation to an
application for a certificate of entitlement received by the appropriate authority on or after
12 December 2011: see SI 2011/2682, reg 1(1).

7

A certificate of entitlement is to be issued by means of being affixed to the passport or
travel document of the applicant.

Expiry and revocation of certificate of entitlement

8

A certificate of entitlement shall cease to have effect on the expiry of the passport or
travel document to which it is affixed.

9

A certificate of entitlement may be revoked by the Secretary of State for the Home
Department, an immigration officer, a consular officer or a person responsible for the
grant or refusal of entry clearance, where the person who revokes the certificate is
satisfied that the person in possession of the certificate (whether or not this is the
person to whom the certificate was issued)—

(a)   does not have the right of abode in the United Kingdom under
section 2(1) of the 1971 Act;

[(b)   is the holder of:

(i)   a United Kingdom passport describing him as a British citizen,

(ii)   a United Kingdom passport describing him as a British subject
with the right of abode in the United Kingdom,

(iii)   another certificate of entitlement;]

(c)   is a person whose exercise of his right of abode is restricted under
section 2 of the Immigration Act 1988; or

(d)   is a person who is deprived of his right of abode by an order under
section 2A of the 1971 Act.

Amendment

Sub-para (b) substituted by SI 2011/2682, reg 2(1), (5). Date in force: In relation to an
application for a certificate of entitlement received by the appropriate authority on or after
12 December 2011: see SI 2011/2682, reg 1(1).

Savings

10

The effect of a certificate described in section 10(6) of the 2002 Act is that it will cease
to have effect on the expiry of the passport or travel document to which it is affixed.

SCHEDULE
ADDITIONAL DOCUMENTS WHICH MUST ACCOMPANY AN APPLICATION
FOR A CERTIFICATE OF ENTITLEMENT

[Regulation 4(1)(c)]

Amendment

Enabling provision substituted by SI 2011/2682, reg 2(1), (6). Date in force: In relation to an
application for a certificate of entitlement received by the appropriate authority on or after

12 December 2011: see SI 2011/2682, reg 1(1).

Basis of application	Documents
Applicant was registered or naturalised as a British citizen on or after 1st January 1983	Applicant's registration or naturalisation certificate
Applicant was born in the United Kingdom before 1st January 1983	Applicant's full birth certificate, showing parents' details
Applicant was registered or naturalised as a citizen of the United Kingdom and Colonies in the United Kingdom before 1st January 1983	Applicant's registration or naturalisation certificate
Applicant is a Commonwealth (not British) citizen born before 1st January 1983 to a parent who was born in the United Kingdom	(i) Applicant's full birth certificate showing parents' details; and (ii) Parent's full UK birth certificate
Applicant is a female Commonwealth citizen who was married before 1st January 1983 to a man with right of abode in the United Kingdom	(i) Applicant's marriage certificate; and (ii) Evidence of applicant's husband's right of abode, eg passport or UK birth certificate
Applicant was born in the United Kingdom or the Falkland Islands on or after 1st January 1983, or in another qualifying British overseas territory on or after 21st May 2002	(i) Applicant's full birth certificate showing parents' details; (ii) Evidence of either parent's British citizenship or settled status at time of applicant's birth, eg a passport describing the relevant parent as a British citizen or indicating that he or she then had indefinite leave to remain; and [(iii) Parents' marriage or civil partnership certificate (if claiming through father or if claiming through woman who is a parent of the applicant by virtue of section 42 or 43 of the 2008 Act)]
Applicant was born outside the United Kingdom and the Falkland Islands on or after 1st January 1983, or outside the United Kingdom and any qualifying British overseas territory on or after 21st May 2002, to a parent born in the United Kingdom or the Falkland Islands (or, on/after 21 May 2002, any qualifying British overseas territory) or to a parent registered or naturalised in the United Kingdom prior to the applicant's birth	(i) Applicant's full birth certificate showing parents' details; [(ii) Parents' marriage or civil partnership certificate (if claiming through father or if claiming through woman who is a parent of the applicant by virtue of section 42 or 43 of the 2008 Act);] and (iii) Parents' full birth certificate, registration or naturalisation certificate
Applicant was born outside the United Kingdom and the Falkland Islands on or after 1st January 1983, or outside the United Kingdom and any qualifying British overseas territory on or after 21 May 2002, to a parent who, at the time of the birth, was a British citizen in service to which section 2(1)(b) of the British Nationality Act 1981 applies	(i) Applicant's full birth certificate; [(ii) Parents' marriage or civil partnership certificate (if claiming through father or if claiming through woman who is a parent of the applicant by virtue of section 42 or 43 of the 2008 Act);] and (iii) Evidence of parent's relevant employment at the time of the birth, eg a letter from the employer

Basis of application	Documents
Applicant was adopted in the United Kingdom, a qualifying British overseas territory, or otherwise under the terms of the Hague Convention on Intercountry Adoption	(i) Applicant's adoption certificate; and (ii) Evidence of adoptive parents' citizenship and, if a Convention adoption, of their place of habitual residence at the time of the adoption, eg in respect of citizenship, a passport, and in respect of habitual residence at the time of the Convention adoption, the adoption certificate
Applicant was a citizen of the United Kingdom and Colonies and was ordinarily resident in the United Kingdom for a continuous period of 5 years before 1st January 1983 and was settled in the United Kingdom at the end of that period	(i) Evidence of citizenship of the United Kingdom and Colonies, eg a passport or certificate of naturalisation or registration; and (ii) Evidence of settlement and 5 years' ordinary residence in the UK before 1983, eg, passport, P60s, details of National Insurance contributions, DSS claims, employers' letters
Applicant was a citizen of the United Kingdom and Colonies and had a parent who was born, adopted, registered or naturalised in the United Kingdom prior to the applicant's birth/adoption	(i) Applicant's full birth certificate or adoption certificate; [(ii) Parents' marriage or civil partnership certificate (if claiming through father or if claiming through woman who is a parent of the applicant by virtue of section 42 or 43 of the 2008 Act);] and (iii) Parent's full birth certificate, adoption, registration or naturalisation certificate
Applicant was a citizen of the United Kingdom and Colonies and had a grandparent born, adopted, registered or naturalised in the United Kingdom before the applicant's parent's birth/adoption	[(i) Parents' marriage or civil partnership certificate (if claiming through father or if claiming through woman who is a parent of the applicant by virtue of section 42 or 43 of the 2008 Act);] (ii) Parents' full birth certificate or adoption certificate; (iii) Applicant's full birth certificate or adoption certificate; (iv) Grandparents' marriage certificate (if claiming through grandfather); and (v) Grandparent's full birth certificate, adoption, registration or naturalisation certificate

Amendment

Words in square brackets substituted by SI 2009/1892, art 2, Sch 1, Pt 2, para 18(1), (3). Date in force: 1 September 2009: see SI 2009/1892, art 1(1)(a).

2006 No 3317

ACCESSION (IMMIGRATION AND WORKER AUTHORISATION) REGULATIONS 2006

Made 13th December 2006
Coming into force 1st January 2007

The Secretary of State, being a Minister designated for the purposes of section 2(2) of the European Communities Act 1972 in relation to measures relating to the right of entry into, and residence in, the United Kingdom and access to the labour market of the United Kingdom, in exercise of the powers conferred upon him by that section, and in exercise of the powers conferred upon him by section 2 of the European Union (Accessions) Act 2006, makes the following Regulations, a draft of which has been approved by resolution of each House of Parliament:

PART 1
GENERAL

1 Citation, commencement, interpretation and consequential amendments

(1) These Regulations may be cited as the Accession (Immigration and Worker Authorisation) Regulations 2006 and shall come into force on 1st January 2007.

(2) In these Regulations—

(a) "the 1971 Act" means the Immigration Act 1971;

(b) "the 2006 Regulations" means the Immigration (European Economic Area) Regulations 2006;

(c) "accession period" means the period beginning on 1st January 2007 and ending on [31st December 2013];

(d) "accession State national subject to worker authorisation" has the meaning given in regulation 2;

(e) "accession worker authorisation document" shall be interpreted in accordance with regulation 9(2);

(f) "authorised category of employment" means a category of employment listed in the first column of the table in Schedule 1;

(g) "authorised family member" has the meaning given in regulation 3;

(h) "civil partner" does not include a party to a civil partnership of convenience;

(i) "EEA State" means—

    (i) a member State, other than the United Kingdom;

    (ii) Norway, Iceland or Liechtenstein;

    (iii) Switzerland;

(j) "employer" means, in relation to a worker, the person who directly pays the wage or salary of that worker;

(k) "family member" shall be interpreted in accordance with regulation 7 of the 2006 Regulations;

(l) "highly skilled person" has the meaning given in regulation 4;

(m) "immigration rules" means the rules laid down as mentioned in section 3(2) of the 1971 Act applying on 1st January 2007;

(n) "letter of approval under the work permit arrangements" has the meaning given in paragraph 1(b) of Schedule 1;

(o) "registration certificate" means a certificate issued in accordance with regulation 16 of the 2006 Regulations;

(p) "relevant requirements" means, in relation to an authorised category of employment, the requirements set out in the second column of the table in Schedule 1 for that category;

(q) "Sectors Based Scheme" has the meaning given in paragraph 1(f) of Schedule 1;

(r) "spouse" does not include a party to a marriage of convenience;

(s) "student" has the meaning given in regulation 4(1)(d) of the 2006 Regulations;

(t)   "worker" means a worker within the meaning of Article 39 of the Treaty establishing the European Community, and "work" and "working" shall be construed accordingly.

(3)   Schedule 2 (consequential amendments) shall have effect.

Initial Commencement
Specified date: 1 January 2007: see para (1) above.

Amendment
Para (2)(c): the words '31 December 2013' in square brackets substituted by SI 2011/2816, reg 2. Date in force: 30 December 2011: see SI 2011/2816, reg 1.

2 "Accession State national subject to worker authorisation"

(1)   Subject to the following paragraphs of this regulation, in these Regulations "accession State national subject to worker authorisation" means a national of Bulgaria or Romania.

[(2)   A national of Bulgaria or Romania is not an accession State national subject to worker authorisation if on 31st December 2006 he had leave to enter or remain in the United Kingdom under the 1971 Act that was not subject to any condition restricting his employment or he is given such leave after that date.]

(3)   A national of Bulgaria or Romania is not an accession State national subject to worker authorisation if he was legally working in the United Kingdom on 31st December 2006 and had been legally working in the United Kingdom without interruption throughout the period of 12 months ending on that date.

(4)   A national of Bulgaria or Romania who legally works in the United Kingdom without interruption for a period of 12 months falling partly or wholly after 31st December 2006 shall cease to be an accession State national subject to worker authorisation at the end of that period of 12 months.

(5)   A national of Bulgaria or Romania is not an accession State national subject to worker authorisation during any period in which he is also a national of—

   (a)   the United Kingdom; or

   (b)   an EEA State, other than Bulgaria or Romania.

[(5A)   A national of Bulgaria or Romania is not an accession State national subject to worker authorisation during any period in which that national is the spouse, civil partner or child under 18 of a person who has leave to enter or remain in the United Kingdom under the 1971 Act that allows that person to work in the United Kingdom.]

(6)   A national of Bulgaria or Romania is not an accession State national subject to worker authorisation during any period in which he is the spouse or civil partner of a national of the United Kingdom or of a person settled in the United Kingdom.

[(6A)   A national of Bulgaria or Romania is not an accession State national subject to worker authorisation during any period in which he is a member of a mission or other person mentioned in section 8(3) of the 1971 Act (member of a diplomatic mission, the family member of such a person, or a person otherwise entitled to diplomatic immunity), other than a person who, under section 8(3A) of that Act, does not count as a member of a mission for the purposes of section 8(3).]

(7)   A national of Bulgaria or Romania is not an accession State national subject to worker authorisation during any period in which he has a permanent right of residence under regulation 15 of the 2006 Regulations.

[(8)   A national of Bulgaria or Romania is not an accession State national subject to worker authorisation during any period in which he is a family member of—

   (a)   an EEA national who has a right to reside in the United Kingdom under the 2006 Regulations, other than—

      (i)   an accession State national subject to worker authorisation; or

      (ii)   a person who is not an accession State national subject to worker authorisation solely by virtue of being the family member of a person mentioned in sub-paragraph (b) [or a worker mentioned in paragraph (8A)]; or

(b) an accession State national subject to worker authorisation who has a right to reside under regulation 14(1) of the 2006 Regulations by virtue of being a self-employed person, a self-sufficient person or a student falling within sub-paragraph (c), (d) or (e) of regulation 6(1) of those Regulations ("qualified person").]

[(8A) A national of Bulgaria or Romania is not an accession State national subject to worker authorisation during any period in which that national is the spouse, civil partner or descendant of an accession State national subject to worker authorisation who has a right to reside under regulation 14(1) of the 2006 Regulations by virtue of being a worker falling within sub-paragraph (b) of regulation 6(1) of those Regulations ("qualified person") provided that, in the case of a descendant, the descendant is under 21 or dependent on the accession State national subject to worker authorisation.]

(9) A national of Bulgaria or Romania is not an accession State national subject to worker authorisation during any period in which he is a highly skilled person and holds a registration certificate that includes a statement that he has unconditional access to the United Kingdom labour market.

[(10) A national of Bulgaria or Romania is not an accession State national subject to worker authorisation during any period in which he is in the United Kingdom as a student and—

(a) holds a registration certificate that includes a statement that he is a student who may work in the United Kingdom whilst a student in accordance with the condition set out in paragraph (10A); and

(b) complies with that condition.

(10A) The condition referred to in paragraph (10) is that the student shall not work for more than 20 hours a week unless—

(a) he is following a course of vocational training and is working as part of that training; or

(b) he is working during his vacation.

(10B) A national of Bulgaria or Romania who ceases to be a student at the end of his course of study is not an accession State national subject to worker authorisation during the period of four months beginning with the date on which his course ends provided he holds a registration certificate that was issued to him before the end of the course that includes a statement that he may work during that period.]

(11) A national of Bulgaria or Romania is not an accession State national subject to worker authorisation during any period in which he is a posted worker.

(12) For the purposes of paragraphs (3) and (4) of this regulation—

(a) a person working in the United Kingdom during a period falling before 1st January 2007 was working legally in the United Kingdom during that period if—

(i) he had leave to enter or remain in the United Kingdom under the 1971 Act for that period, that leave allowed him to work in the United Kingdom, and he was working in accordance with any condition on that leave restricting his employment; or

[(ia) he was exempt from the provisions of the 1971 Act by virtue of section 8(3) of that Act; or]

(ii) he was entitled to reside in the United Kingdom for that period under the Immigration (European Economic Area) Regulations 2000 or the 2006 Regulations without the requirement for such leave;

(b) a person working in the United Kingdom on or after 1st January 2007 is legally working during any period in which he—

(i)   falls within paragraphs (5) to [(10B)]; or

(ii)   holds an accession worker authorisation document and is working in accordance with the conditions set out in that document;

(c)   a person shall be treated as having worked in the United Kingdom without interruption for a period of 12 months if he was legally working in the United Kingdom at the beginning and end of that period and any intervening periods in which he was not legally working in the United Kingdom do not, in total, exceed 30 days.

(13)   In this regulation—

(a)   "posted worker" means a worker who is posted to the United Kingdom, within the meaning of Article 1(3) of Directive 96/71/EC concerning the posting of workers, by an undertaking established in an EEA State;

(b)   the reference to a person settled in the United Kingdom shall be interpreted in accordance with section 33(2A) of the 1971 Act.

Initial Commencement
Specified date: 1 January 2007: see reg 1(1).

Amendment
Para (2): substituted by SI 2007/475, reg 2(1), (2)(a).
Date in force: 16 March 2007: see SI 2007/475, reg 1(1).
Para (5A): inserted by SI 2009/2426, reg 2(1), (2)(a).
Date in force: 2 October 2009: see SI 2009/2426, reg 1.
Para (6A): inserted by SI 2007/3012, reg 2(1), (2)(a).
Date in force: 19 November 2007: see SI 2007/3012, reg 1(1).
Para (8): substituted by SI 2007/3012, reg 2(1), (2)(b).
Date in force: 19 November 2007: see SI 2007/3012, reg 1(1).
Para (8): in sub-para (a) para (ii) words "or a worker mentioned in paragraph (8A)" in square brackets inserted by SI 2009/2426, reg 2(1), (2)(b).
Date in force: 2 October 2009: see SI 2009/2426, reg 1.
Para (8A): inserted by SI 2009/2426, reg 2(1), (2)(c).
Date in force: 2 October 2009: see SI 2009/2426, reg 1.
Paras (10), (10A), (10B): substituted, for para (10) as originally enacted, by SI 2007/475, reg 2(1), (2)(c).
Date in force: 16 March 2007: see SI 2007/475, reg 1(1); for transitional provisions see reg 4 thereof.
Para (12): sub-para (a)(ia) inserted by SI 2007/3012, reg 2(1), (2)(c).
Date in force: 19 November 2007: see SI 2007/3012, reg 1(1).
Para (12): in sub-para (b)(i) reference to "(10B)" in square brackets substituted by SI 2007/475, reg 2(1), (2)(d).
Date in force: 16 March 2007: see SI 2007/475, reg 1(1).

[3 Authorised family member]
[A person is an authorised family member for the purpose of these Regulations if that person is the family member of an accession State national subject to worker authorisation who has a right to reside in the United Kingdom under regulation 14(1) of the 2006 Regulations as a worker, unless—

(a)   the worker is only authorised to work under these Regulations by virtue of holding an accession worker card issued in accordance with regulation 11 pursuant to an application as an authorised family member; or

(b)   the family member is the spouse or civil partner of the worker or a descendant of the worker who is under 21 or dependent on the worker.]

Amendment
Substituted by SI 2009/2426, reg 2(1), (3).
Date in force: 2 October 2009: see SI 2009/2426, reg 1.

4 "Highly skilled person"

(1) In these Regulations "highly skilled person" means a person who—

(a) meets the criteria specified by the Secretary of State for the purpose of paragraph 135A(i) of the immigration rules (entry to the United Kingdom under the Highly Skilled Migrant Programme) and applying on 1st January 2007, other than the criterion requiring a proficiency in the English language; or

(b) has been awarded one of the following qualifications and applies for a registration certificate or submits a registration certificate to the Secretary of State under regulation 7(4) within 12 months of being awarded the qualification—

[(i) a Higher National Diploma awarded by a relevant institution in Scotland; or

(ii) a degree, postgraduate certificate or postgraduate diploma awarded by a relevant institution in the United Kingdom].

(2) In paragraph (1)(b), "relevant institution" means an institution that is financed from public funds or included on the Department for Education and Skills' Register of Education and Training Providers on 1st January 2007.

Initial Commencement

Specified date: 1 January 2007: see reg 1(1).

Amendment

Para (1): sub-para (b)(i), (ii) substituted by SI 2007/3012, reg 2(1), (4).

Date in force: 19 November 2007: see SI 2007/3012, reg 1(1).

5 Derogation from provisions of Community law relating to workers

Regulations 6, 7 and 9 derogate during the accession period from Article 39 of the Treaty establishing the European Communities, Articles 1 to 6 of Regulation (EEC) No 1612/68 on freedom of movement for workers within the Community and Council Directive 2004/38/EC on the right of citizens of the Union and their family members to move and reside freely within the territory of the Member States.

Initial Commencement

Specified date: 1 January 2007: see reg 1(1).

PART 2

IMMIGRATION

6 Right of residence of an accession State national subject to worker authorisation

(1) An accession State national subject to worker authorisation shall, during the accession period, only be entitled to reside in the United Kingdom in accordance with the 2006 Regulations, as modified by this regulation.

(2) An accession State national subject to worker authorisation who is seeking employment in the United Kingdom shall not be treated as a jobseeker for the purpose of the definition of "qualified person" in regulation 6(1) of the 2006 Regulations and such a person shall be treated as a worker for the purpose of that definition only during a period in which he holds an accession worker authorisation document and is working in accordance with the conditions set out in that document.

(3) Regulation 6(2) of the 2006 Regulations shall not apply to an accession State national subject to worker authorisation who ceases to work.

Initial Commencement

Specified date: 1 January 2007: see reg 1(1).

7 Issuing registration certificates and residence cards to nationals of Bulgaria and Romania and their family members during the accession period

(1) Subject to paragraph (2), an accession State national subject to worker authorisation shall not be treated as a qualified person for the purposes of regulations 16 and 17 of the 2006 Regulations (issue of registration certificates and residence cards) during the accession period unless he falls within sub-paragraphs (c), (d) or (e) of regulation 6(1) of the 2006 Regulations.

(2) The Secretary of State shall issue a registration certificate to an accession State national subject to worker authorisation on application if he is satisfied that the applicant—

    (a)   is seeking employment in the United Kingdom; and

    (b)   is a highly skilled person.

(3) Where the Secretary of State issues a registration certificate during the accession period to a Bulgarian or Romanian national under paragraph (2) or in any case where he is satisfied that the Bulgarian or Romanian national is not an accession State national subject to worker authorisation [(other than solely by virtue of falling within paragraph (10) or (10B) of regulation 2)], the registration certificate shall include a statement that the holder of the certificate has unconditional access to the United Kingdom labour market.

(4) A Bulgarian or Romanian national who holds a registration certificate that does not include a statement that he has unconditional access to the United Kingdom labour market may, during the accession period, submit the certificate to the Secretary of State for the inclusion of such a statement.

(5) The Secretary of State shall re-issue a certificate submitted to him under paragraph (4) with the inclusion of a statement that the holder has unconditional access to the United Kingdom labour market if he is satisfied that the holder—

    (a)   is a highly skilled person; or

    (b)   has ceased to be an accession State national subject to worker authorisation other than solely by virtue of falling within [paragraph (10) or (10B) of regulation 2].

(6) A registration certificate issued to a Bulgarian or Romanian student during the accession period shall include a statement that the holder of the certificate is a student who [may work in the United Kingdom whilst a student in accordance with the condition set out in regulation 2(10A) and who, on ceasing to be a student, may work during the period referred to in regulation 2(10B)], unless it includes a statement under paragraph (3) or (5) that the holder has unconditional access to the United Kingdom labour market.

(7) But this regulation is subject to regulation 20 of the 2006 Regulations (power to refuse to issue and to revoke registration certificates).

Initial Commencement

Specified date: 1 January 2007: see reg 1(1).

Amendment

Para (3): words from "(other than solely" to "(10B) of regulation 2)" in square brackets inserted by SI 2007/475, reg 2(1), (4)(a).

Date in force: 16 March 2007: see SI 2007/475, reg 1(1).

Para (5): in sub-para (b) words "paragraph (10) or (10B) of regulation 2" in square brackets substituted by SI 2007/475, reg 2(1), (4)(b).

Date in force: 16 March 2007: see SI 2007/475, reg 1(1).

Para (6): words from "may work in" to "in regulation 2(10B)" in square brackets substituted by SI 2007/475, reg 2(1), (4)(c).

Date in force: 16 March 2007: see SI 2007/475, reg 1(1).

8 Transitional provisions to take account of the application of the 2006 Regulations to nationals of Bulgaria and Romania and their family members on 1st January 2007

(1) Where before 1st January 2007 directions have been given for the removal of a Bulgarian or Romanian national or the family member of such a national under paragraphs 8 to 10A of Schedule 2 to the 1971 Act or section 10 of the 1999 Act, those directions shall cease to have effect on and after that date.

(2) Where before 1st January 2007 the Secretary of State has made a decision to make a deportation order against a Bulgarian or Romanian national or the family member of such a national under section 5(1) of the 1971 Act—

    (a) that decision shall, on and after 1st January 2007, be treated as if it were a decision under regulation 19(3)(b) of the 2006 Regulations; and

    (b) any appeal against that decision, or against the refusal of the Secretary of State to revoke the deportation order, made under section 63 of the 1999 Act or section 82(2)(j) or (k) of the 2002 Act before 1st January 2007, shall, on or after that date, be treated as if it had been made under regulation 26 of the 2006 Regulations.

(3) In this regulation—

    (a) "the 1999 Act" means the Immigration and Asylum Act 1999;

    (b) "the 2002 Act" means the Nationality, Immigration and Asylum Act 2002;

    (c) any reference to the family member of a Bulgarian or Romanian national is a reference to a person who on 1st January 2007 acquires a right to reside in the United Kingdom under the 2006 Regulations as the family member of a Bulgarian or Romanian national.

Initial Commencement

Specified date: 1 January 2007: see reg 1(1).

PART 3
ACCESSION STATE WORKER AUTHORISATION

9 Requirement for an accession State national subject to worker authorisation to be authorised to work

(1) An accession State national subject to worker authorisation shall only be authorised to work in the United Kingdom during the accession period if he holds an accession worker authorisation document and is working in accordance with the conditions set out in that document.

(2) For the purpose of these Regulations, an accession worker authorisation document is—

    (a) a passport or other travel document endorsed before 1st January 2007 to show that the holder has leave to enter or remain in the United Kingdom under the 1971 Act, subject to a condition restricting his employment in the United Kingdom to a particular employer or category of employment;

    (b) a seasonal agricultural work card, except where the holder of the card has a document mentioned in sub-paragraph (a) giving him leave to enter the United Kingdom as a seasonal agricultural worker; or

    (c) an accession worker card issued in accordance with regulation 11.

(3) But a document shall cease to be treated as an accession worker authorisation document under paragraph (2)—

    (a) in the case of a document mentioned in paragraph (2)(a), at the end of the period for which leave to enter or remain is given;

    (b) in the case of a seasonal agricultural work card, at the end of the period of six months beginning with the date on which the holder of the card begins working for the agricultural employer specified in the card;

(c) in the case of an accession worker card, on the expiry of the card under regulation 11(7).

(4) For the purpose of this regulation—

    (a) "seasonal agricultural work card" means a Home Office work card issued by the operator of a seasonal agricultural workers scheme approved by the Secretary of State for the purpose of paragraph 104(ii) of the immigration rules;

    (b) the reference to a travel document other than a passport is a reference to a document which relates to a national of Bulgaria or Romania and which is designed to serve the same purpose as a passport.

Initial Commencement

Specified date: 1 January 2007: see reg 1(1).

10 Application for an accession worker card

(1) An application for an accession worker card may be made by an accession State national subject to worker authorisation who wishes to work for an employer in the United Kingdom if—

    (a) the employment concerned falls within an authorised category of employment; or

    (b) the applicant is an authorised family member.

(2) The application shall be in writing and shall be made to the Secretary of State.

(3) The application shall state—

    (a) the name, address, and date of birth of the applicant;

    (b) the name and address of the employer for whom the applicant wishes to work; and

    (c) unless the applicant is an authorised family member, the authorised category of employment covered by the application.

(4) The application shall be accompanied by—

    (a) the applicant's national identity card or passport; and

    (b) two passport size photographs of the applicant.

(5) Where the applicant is not an authorised family member, the application shall, in addition to the documents required by paragraph (4), be accompanied by—

    (a) where the relevant requirements for the authorised category of employment specified in the application require the applicant to hold a letter of approval under the work permit arrangements, that letter;

    (b) where sub-paragraph (a) does not apply, a letter from the employer specified in the application confirming that the applicant has an offer of employment with the employer; and

    (c) any other proof that the applicant wishes to provide to establish that he meets the relevant requirements.

(6) Where the applicant is an authorised family member, the application shall, in addition to the documents required by paragraph (4), be accompanied by—

    (a) a letter from the employer specified in the application confirming that the applicant has an offer of employment with the employer; and

    (b) proof that the applicant is an authorised family member.

(7) In this regulation "address" means, in relation to an employer which is a body corporate or partnership, the head or main office of that employer.

Initial Commencement

Specified date: 1 January 2007: see reg 1(1).

11 Issuing an accession worker card etc

(1) Subject to paragraph (2), the Secretary of State shall issue an accession worker card pursuant to an application made in accordance with regulation 10 if he is satisfied that the applicant is an accession State national subject to worker authorisation who—

(a)   is an authorised family member; or

(b)   meets the relevant requirements for the authorised category of employment covered by the application.

(2)   The Secretary of State shall not issue an accession worker card if he has decided to remove the applicant from the United Kingdom under regulation 19(3)(b) of the 2006 Regulations (removal on grounds of public policy, public security or public health).

(3)   An accession worker card issued under this regulation to an authorised family member shall include a condition restricting the applicant's employment to the employer specified in the application.

(4)   An accession worker card issued under this regulation pursuant to an application that was accompanied by a letter of approval under the work permit arrangements shall include the following conditions—

(a)   a condition restricting the applicant's employment to the employer specified in the application and any secondary employer; and

(b)   a condition restricting him to the type of employment specified in the letter of approval under the work permit arrangements.

(5)   In any other case, an accession worker card issued under this regulation shall include the following conditions—

(a)   a condition restricting the applicant's employment to the employer specified in the application; and

(b)   a condition restricting him to the authorised category of employment specified in the application.

(6)   An accession worker card issued under this regulation shall include a photograph of the applicant and shall set out—

(a)   the name, nationality and date of birth of the applicant;

(b)   the name and address of the employer specified in the application;

(c)   the conditions required by paragraph (3), (4) or (5), as the case may be; and

(d)   the date on which the card was issued.

(7)   An accession worker card shall expire if the holder of the card ceases working for the employer specified in the application.

(8)   Where the Secretary of State is not satisfied as mentioned in paragraph (1) or where paragraph (2) applies, he shall refuse the application and issue a notice of refusal setting out the reasons for the refusal.

(9)   An accession worker card or notice of refusal issued under this regulation shall be sent to the applicant by post together with the identity card or passport that accompanied the application.

(10)   In this regulation, "secondary employer" means, in relation to an applicant, an employer who is not specified in his application and who employs the applicant for no more than 20 hours a week when the applicant is not working for the employer who is specified in the application.

Initial Commencement

Specified date: 1 January 2007: see reg 1(1).

12 Unauthorised employment of accession State national—employer offence

(1)   Subject to paragraphs (2) and (3), an employer who employs an accession State national subject to worker authorisation during the accession period shall be guilty of an offence if—

(a)   the employee does not hold an accession worker authorisation document; or

(b)   the employee's accession worker authorisation document is subject to conditions that preclude him from taking up the employment.

(2) Subject to paragraph (4), in proceedings under this regulation it shall be a defence to prove that before the employment began there was produced to the employer a document that appeared to him to be a registration certificate issued to the worker and—

    (a)   the registration certificate contained a statement that the worker has unconditional access to the United Kingdom labour market; or

    [(b)   the registration certificate contained a statement that the worker is a student who may work in the United Kingdom whilst a student in accordance with the condition set out in regulation 2(10A) and who, on ceasing to be a student, may work during the period referred to in regulation 2(10B), and the employer has not employed that worker otherwise than in accordance with that condition or during that period].

(3) Subject to paragraph (4), in proceedings under this regulation it shall be a defence to prove that before the employment began there was produced to the employer a document that appeared to him to be an accession worker authorisation document that authorised the worker to take up the employment.

(4) The defence afforded by paragraph (2) and (3) shall not be available in any case where the employer—

    (a)   did not take and retain a copy of the relevant document; or

    (b)   knew that his employment of the worker constituted an offence under this regulation.

(5) A person guilty of an offence under this regulation shall be liable on summary conviction to a fine not exceeding level 5 on the standard scale.

(6) Where an offence under this regulation committed by a body corporate is proved to have been committed with the consent or connivance of, or to be attributable to any neglect on the part of—

    (a)   any director, manager, secretary or other similar officer of the body corporate; or

    (b)   any person purporting to act in such a capacity,

he, as well as the body corporate, shall be guilty of an offence and shall be liable to be proceeded against and punished accordingly.

(7) Where the affairs of a body corporate are managed by its members, paragraph (6) shall apply in relation to acts and defaults of a member in connection with his functions of management as if he were a director of the body corporate.

(8) Where an offence under this regulation is committed by a partnership (other than a limited partnership) each partner shall be guilty of an offence and shall be liable to be proceeded against and punished accordingly.

(9) Paragraph (6) shall have effect in relation to a limited partnership as if—

    (a)   a reference to a body corporate were a reference to a limited partnership; and

    (b)   a reference to an officer of the body corporate were a reference to a partner.

(10) An offence under this regulation shall be treated as—

    (a)   a relevant offence for the purpose of sections 28B and 28D of the 1971 Act (search, entry and arrest);

    (b)   an offence under Part III of that Act (criminal proceedings) for the purposes of sections 28E, 28G and 28H of that Act (search after arrest); and

    (c)   an offence referred to in section 28AA of that Act (arrest with warrant).

Initial Commencement

Specified date: 1 January 2007: see reg 1(1).

Amendment

Para (2): sub-para (b) substituted by SI 2007/475, reg 2(1), (5).

Date in force: 16 March 2007: see SI 2007/475, reg 1(1); for transitional provisions see reg 4 thereof.

13 Unauthorised working by accession State national—employee offence

(1) Subject to paragraph (2), an accession State national subject to worker authorisation who works in the United Kingdom during the accession period shall be guilty of an offence if—

(a) he does not hold an accession worker authorisation document; or

(b) he is working in breach of the conditions set out in his accession worker authorisation document.

(2) A person guilty of an offence under this regulation shall be liable on summary conviction to a fine not exceeding level 5 on the standard scale or imprisonment for not more than three months, or both.

(3) A constable or immigration officer who has reason to believe that a person has committed an offence under this regulation may give that person a notice offering him the opportunity of discharging any liability to conviction for that offence by payment of a penalty in accordance with the notice.

(4) The penalty payable in pursuance of a notice under paragraph (3) is £1000 and shall be payable to the Secretary of State.

(5) Where a person is given a notice under paragraph (3) in respect of an offence—

(a) no proceedings may be instituted for that offence before the expiration of the period of twenty one days following the date of the notice; and

(b) he may not be convicted of that offence if before the expiration of that period he pays the penalty in accordance with the notice.

(6) A notice under paragraph (3) must give such particulars of the circumstances alleged to constitute the offence as are necessary for giving reasonable information of the offence.

(7) A notice under paragraph (3) must also state—

(a) the period during which, by virtue of paragraph (5), proceedings will not be instituted for the offence;

(b) the amount of the penalty; and

(c) that the penalty is payable to the Secretary of State at the address specified in the notice.

(8) Without prejudice to payment by any other method, payment of a penalty in pursuance of a notice under paragraph (3) may be made by pre-paying and posting a letter containing the amount of the penalty (in cash or otherwise) to the Secretary of State at the address specified in the notice.

(9) Where a letter is sent in accordance with paragraph (8) payment is to be regarded as having been made at the time at which that letter would be delivered in the ordinary course of post.

Initial Commencement

Specified date: 1 January 2007: see reg 1(1).

14 Deception—employee offence

(1) A person is guilty of an offence if, by means which include deception by him, he obtains or seeks to obtain an accession worker card.

(2) A person guilty of an offence under this regulation shall be liable on summary conviction to a fine not exceeding level 5 on the standard scale or imprisonment for not more than three months, or both.

Initial Commencement

Specified date: 1 January 2007: see reg 1(1).

15 Offences under regulations 13 and 14—search, entry and arrest

An offence under regulation 13 or 14 shall be treated as—

(a) a relevant offence for the purpose of sections 28B and 28D of the 1971 Act (search, entry and arrest);

(b) an offence under Part III of that Act (criminal proceedings) for the purpose of sections 28E, 28G and 28H of that Act (search after arrest); and

(c) an offence under section 24(1)(b) of that Act for the purpose of sections 28A, 28CA and 28FA of that Act (arrest without warrant, entry of business premises to arrest and search for personal records).

Initial Commencement

Specified date: 1 January 2007: see reg 1(1).

SCHEDULE 1
AUTHORISED CATEGORIES OF EMPLOYMENT AND RELEVANT REQUIREMENTS

Regulation 1(2)

Authorised category of employment	Relevant requirements in relation to authorised category of employment
Authorised categories of employment requiring a letter of approval under the work permit arrangements	
Employment under the Sectors Based Scheme	The applicant—
	(1) holds a letter of approval under the work permit arrangements issued under the Sectors-Based Scheme; and
	(2) is capable of undertaking the employment specified in that letter.
Training or work experience	The applicant—
	(1) holds a letter of approval under the work permit arrangements issued under the Training and Work Experience Scheme; and
	(2) is capable of undertaking the training or work experience as specified in that letter.
Work permit employment	The applicant—
	(1) holds a letter of approval under the work permit arrangements issued in relation to work permit employment; and
	(2) is capable of undertaking the employment specified in that letter.
Other authorised categories of employment	
Airport based operational ground staff of an overseas air line	The applicant has been transferred to the United Kingdom by an overseas-owned airline operating services to and from the United Kingdom to take up duty at an international airport as station manager, security manager or technical manager.
Au pair placement	The applicant —
	(1) has and intends to take up an offer of an au pair placement;

Authorised category of employment	Relevant requirements in relation to authorised category of employment
	(2) is aged between 17 to 27 inclusive;
	(3) is unmarried and is not in a civil partnership; and
	(4) is without dependants.
Domestic worker in a private household	The applicant—
	(1) is over 18;
	(2) has been employed for at least a year outside the United Kingdom as a domestic worker under the same roof as his employer or in a household that the employer uses for himself on a regular basis; and
	(3) intends to be so employed by that employer in the United Kingdom.
Minister of religion, missionary or member of a religious order	The applicant—
	(1) if a minister of religion—
	(a) has either been working for at least one year as a minister of religion in any of the five years immediately prior to the date on which the application for the worker accession card is made or, where ordination is prescribed by a religious faith as the sole means of entering the ministry, has been ordained as a minister of religion following at least one year's full time or two years' part time training for the ministry; and
	(b) holds an International English Language Testing System Certificate issued to him to certify that he has achieved level 4 competence in spoken English, and the Certificate is dated not more than two years prior to the date on which the application for an accession worker card is made;
	(2) if a missionary, has been trained as a missionary or has worked as a missionary and is being sent or has been sent to the United Kingdom by an overseas organisation;
	(3) if a member of a religious order, is living or coming to live in a community maintained by the religious order of which he is a member and, if intending to teach, does not intend to do so save at an establishment maintained by his order; and
	(4) intends to work in the United Kingdom as a minister of religion, missionary or for the religious order of which he is a member.

Authorised category of employment	Relevant requirements in relation to authorised category of employment
Overseas government employment	The applicant intends to work in the United Kingdom for an overseas government or the United Nations or other international organisation of which the United Kingdom is a member.
Postgraduate doctors, dentists and trainee general practitioners	The applicant— (1) is a graduate from a medical or dental school who is eligible for provisional or limited registration with the General Medical Council or General Dental Council and intends to work in the United Kingdom as a doctor or dentist as part of his training; or (2) is a doctor, dentist or trainee general practitioner eligible for full or limited registration with the General Medical Council or the General Dental Council and intends to work in the United Kingdom as part of his postgraduate training or general practitioner training in a hospital or the Community Health Services.
Private servant in a diplomatic household	The applicant— (1) is over 18; and (2) intends to work in the United Kingdom as a private servant in the household of a member of staff of a diplomatic or consular mission who enjoys diplomatic privileges and immunity within the meaning of the Vienna Convention on Diplomatic Relations.
Representative of an overseas newspaper, news agency or broadcasting organisation	The applicant has been engaged by an overseas newspaper, news agency or broadcasting organisation outside the United Kingdom and is being posted to the United Kingdom by that newspaper, agency or organisation to act as its representative.
Sole representative	The applicant— (1) has been employed outside the United Kingdom as a representative of a firm that has its headquarters and principal place of business outside the United Kingdom and has no branch, subsidiary or other representative in the United Kingdom;

Authorised category of employment	Relevant requirements in relation to authorised category of employment
	(2) intends to work as a senior employee with full authority to take operational decisions on behalf of the overseas firm for the purpose of representing it in the United Kingdom by establishing and operating a registered branch or wholly owned subsidiary of that overseas firm; and (3) is not a majority shareholder in that overseas firm.
Teacher or language assistant	The applicant intends to work at an educational establishment in the United Kingdom under an exchange scheme approved by [the [Department for Education], [the Department for Business, Innovation and Skills]], the Scottish or Welsh Office of Education or the Department of Education, Northern Ireland, or administered by the British Council's Education and Training Group.
Overseas qualified nurses	The applicant— (1) has obtained confirmation from the Nursing and Midwifery Council that he is eligible for admission to the Overseas Nurses Programme; and (2) has been offered and intends to take up a supervised practice placement through an education provider that is recognised by the Nursing and Midwifery Council or a midwifery adaptation programme placement in a setting approved by that Council.

1

In this Schedule—

    (a)   "au pair placement" means an arrangement whereby a young person—

        (i)   comes to the United Kingdom for the purpose of learning English;

        (ii)   lives for a time as a member of an English speaking family with appropriate opportunities for study; and

        (iii)   helps in the home for a maximum of 5 hours per day in return for an allowance and with two free days per week;

    (b)   "letter of approval under the work permit arrangements" means a letter issued by the Secretary of State under the work permit arrangements stating that employment by the employer specified in the letter of the person so specified for the type of employment so specified satisfies the labour market criteria set out in those arrangements;

    (c)   "member of a religious order" means a person who lives in a community run by that order;

    (d)   "minister of religion" means a religious functionary whose main regular duties comprise the leading of a congregation in performing the rites and rituals of the faith and in preaching the essentials of the creed;

(e) "missionary" means a person who is directly engaged in spreading a religious doctrine and whose work is not in essence administrative or clerical;

(f) "Sectors Based Scheme" means the scheme established by the Secretary of State for the purpose of paragraph 135I(i) of the immigration rules (requirements for leave to enter the United Kingdom for the purpose of employment under the Sectors Based Scheme);

(g) "Training and Work Experience Scheme" means the scheme established by the Secretary of State for the purpose of paragraph 116(i) of the immigration rules (requirement for leave to enter the United Kingdom for approved training or work experience);

(h) "work permit arrangements" means the arrangements published by the Secretary of State setting out the labour market criteria to be applied for the purpose of issuing the work permits referred to in paragraphs 116(i) (Training and Work Experience Scheme) and 128(i) of the immigration rules and the immigration employment document referred to in paragraph 135I(i) (Sectors Based Scheme) of the immigration rules;

(i) "work permit employment" means a category of employment covered by the work permit arrangements, other than employment covered by the Sectors Based Scheme and the Training and Work Experience Scheme.

Initial Commencement

Specified date: 1 January 2007: see reg 1(1).

Amendment

In entry relating to "Teacher or language assistant" in column 2 words in square brackets beginning with the words "the Department for Children, Schools and Families," substituted by SI 2007/3224, art 15, Schedule, Pt 2, para 62.

Date in force: 12 December 2007: see SI 2007/3224, art 1(2).

In entry relating to "Teacher or language assistant" in column 2 words "Department for Education" in square brackets substituted by SI 2010/1836, art 6, Schedule, Pt 2, para 11(i).

Date in force: 18 August 2010: see SI 2010/1836, art 1(2).

In entry relating to "Teacher or language assistant" in column 2 words "the Department for Business, Innovation and Skills" in square brackets substituted by SI 2009/2748, art 8, Schedule, Pt 2, para 34.

Date in force: 13 November 2009: see SI 2009/2748, art 1(2).

SCHEDULE 2
CONSEQUENTIAL AMENDMENTS

Regulation 1(3)

1

The 2006 Regulations

2

(1) The 2006 Regulations are amended as follows.

(2) In Schedule 2 (effect on other legislation)—

    (a) in paragraph 1 (leave under the 1971 Act)—

        (i) at the beginning of sub-paragraph (2) there is inserted "Subject to sub-paragraph (3),";

        (ii) after sub-paragraph (2) there is inserted—

"(3)   Where the person mentioned in sub-paragraph (2) is an accession State national subject to worker authorisation working in the United Kingdom during the accession period and the document endorsed to show that the person has leave is an accession worker authorisation document, any conditions to which that leave is subject restricting his employment shall continue to apply.

(4)   In sub-paragraph (3)—

   (a)   "accession period" has the meaning given in regulation 1(2)(c) of the Accession (Immigration and Worker Authorisation) Regulations 2006;

   (b)   "accession State national subject to worker authorisation" has the meaning given in regulation 2 of those Regulations; and

   (c)   "accession worker authorisation document" has the meaning given in regulation 9(2) of those Regulations.";

   (b)   in paragraph 4 (appeals under the Nationality, Immigration and Asylum Act 2002 and previous immigration Acts)—

   (i)   in sub-paragraph (2), after "Accession (Immigration and Worker Registration) Regulations 2004," there is inserted "or an accession worker card under the Accession (Immigration and Worker Authorisation) Regulations 2006,";

   (c)   in sub-paragraph (9), after "accession State worker requiring registration" where it first occurs there is inserted "or an accession State national subject to worker authorisation working in the United Kingdom" and at the end of the sub-paragraph there is inserted "and "accession State national subject to worker authorisation" has the meaning given in regulation 2 of the Accession (Immigration and Worker Authorisation) Regulations 2006".

(3)   Paragraph 7(3)(a) of Schedule 5 (consequential amendments) is omitted.

Initial Commencement

Specified date: 1 January 2007: see reg 1(1).

Amendment

Para 1: revoked by SI 2011/544, reg 4, Sch 1. Date in force: 1 May 2011: see SI 2011/544, reg 1(1).

INTEGRATION LOANS FOR REFUGEES AND OTHERS REGULATIONS 2007

(SI 2007/1598)

Made: 4 June 2007.

Authority: Asylum and Immigration (Treatment of Claimants, etc) Act 2004, s 13.

Commencement: 11 June 2007.

1 Citation and commencement

These Regulations may be cited as the Integration Loans for Refugees and Others Regulations 2007 and shall come into force on the expiry of seven days beginning with the day on which they were made.

2 Interpretation

In these Regulations—

   "integration loan" means a loan granted in accordance with these Regulations;

   "applicant" means an applicant for an integration loan, and "application" is to be construed accordingly;

"decision" means a decision of the Secretary of State on an application;

"dependant" in relation to an applicant has the same meaning as dependant in relation to an asylum seeker under section 94(1) of the Immigration and Asylum Act 1999;

"immigration rules" means the rules made under section 3(2) of the Immigration Act 1971;

"financial position" means, in relation to an applicant, the following factors taken together—

    (a)   his income;

    (b)   his assets;

    (c)   his liabilities;

    (d)   his outgoings;

    (e)   the number of dependants he has.

3 Minimum and maximum amounts of integration loans

The Secretary of State may specify (and vary from time to time) a minimum and a maximum amount of an integration loan.

4 Eligibility to apply for an integration loan

(1) Subject to paragraph (3) the persons eligible to apply for an integration loan are persons who are refugees for the purpose of section 13(1) of the Asylum and Immigration (Treatment of Claimants, etc) Act 2004 and persons falling within one of the classes prescribed in paragraph (2).

(2) Those classes are—

    (a)   persons granted leave to enter or remain as a consequence of being granted humanitarian protection under the immigration rules;

    (b)   persons granted leave to enter or remain as a consequence of being a dependant of a refugee or a dependant of a person falling within sub-paragraph (a).

(3) An applicant for an integration loan—

    (a)   must be aged 18 or over;

    (b)   must not have already received a loan under these Regulations;

    (c)   must have been granted leave to enter or remain after the date of the coming into force of these Regulations;

    (d)   must not be insolvent.

(4) A person is insolvent for the purpose of this regulation if the Secretary of State is of the opinion that, having regard to his financial position, he would be incapable of making the repayments required under regulation 9.

5 Applications for integration loans

(1) To be valid an application for an integration loan—

    (a)   must be made in writing to the Secretary of State;

    (b)   must be made by an applicant who satisfies the criteria set out in regulation 4;

    (c)   must include the information set out in the Schedule and must stipulate the use to which the applicant intends to put an integration loan;

    (d)   must include a declaration by the applicant that the information given is correct to the best of his knowledge and belief.

(2) Where a valid application for an integration loan has been made the Secretary of State may make an integration loan.

6 Matters to be taken into account by the Secretary of State

(1) In determining whether or not to make an integration loan, the Secretary of State must, in addition to other matters appearing to him to be relevant, take into account—

(a) the length of time since the applicant was granted leave to enter or remain;

(b) the applicant's financial position;

(c) the applicant's likely ability to repay an integration loan;

(d) the information provided by the applicant as to his intended use of an integration loan;

(e) the available budget for integration loans.

(2) For these purposes "available budget" refers to the amount allocated by the Secretary of State for all integration loans in the financial year in which the application is being determined.

7 Conditions as to the use of an integration loan

(1) An integration loan may be subject to conditions, including a condition that it must be used in accordance with the intended use stipulated in the application.

(2) An integration loan may be subject to the condition that it will not be made until the applicant has signed a loan agreement which sets out—

(a) the amount of the loan;

(b) the conditions of the loan;

(c) the terms of repayment;

(d) the procedure by which the recipient of a loan may request a revision of the terms of repayment should his circumstances change.

8 Decision on an application

(1) The Secretary of State must issue a written decision on an application for an integration loan which sets out the following—

(a) whether the application is valid;

(b) if the application is valid, whether or not an integration loan will be made;

(c) if an integration loan is to be made, the amount of that loan, the conditions of that loan and the terms of repayment;

(d) the date by which the applicant must inform the Secretary of State that he would like the loan to be made.

(2) In making a decision the Secretary of State may take such steps, make such inquiries, and require from the applicant such further information as he considers necessary—

(a) to verify the information provided in the application;

(b) to satisfy himself that the applicant is eligible for an integration loan;

(c) to determine whether to make an integration loan, and if so the amount of the loan and the terms of repayment.

9 Repayment of an integration loan

(1) Where the recipient of an integration loan is in receipt of a specified benefit within the meaning of paragraph 1 of Schedule 9 to the Social Security (Claims and Payments) Regulations 1987, or of paragraph 1 of Schedule 8A to the Social Security (Claims and Payments) Regulations (Northern Ireland) 1987 [or is in receipt of universal credit as provided for in Part 1 of the Welfare Reform Act 2012], the terms of repayment may be set in accordance with paragraph (3).

(2) Where the terms of repayment are not set in accordance with paragraph (3) they must be set in accordance with paragraph (4).

(3) Terms of repayment set under this paragraph must specify—

(a) when recovery will commence;

(b) that recovery shall be made by way of deductions from benefit in accordance with Schedule 9 to the Social Security (Claims and Payments) Regulations 1987 or, as the case may be, Schedule 8A to the Social Security (Claims and Payments) Regulations (Northern Ireland) 1987 [or, as the case may be, by way of deductions from universal credit in accordance with Schedule 6 to the Universal Credit, Personal Independence Payment, Jobseeker's Allowance and Employment and Support Allowance (Claims and Payments) Regulations 2013].

(4)   Terms of repayment set under this paragraph must specify—

    (a)   when repayments shall commence;

    (b)   the intervals at which repayments must be made;

    (c)   the level of repayment;

    (d)   the methods by which repayment may be made.

Amendment

Para (1): words in square brackets inserted by SI 2013/380, reg 4, Sch 3, paras 4(1), (2). Date in force (for the purpose of personal independence payment): 8 April 2013: see SI 2013/380, reg 1(2). Date in force (for the purposes of universal credit, jobseeker's allowance and employment and support allowance): 29 April 2013: see SI 2013/380, reg 1(3).

Para (3): in sub-para (b) words in square brackets inserted by SI 2013/380, reg 4, Sch 3, para 4(1), (3). Date in force (for the purpose of personal independence payment): 8 April 2013: see SI 2013/380, reg 1(2). Date in force (for the purposes of universal credit, jobseeker's allowance and employment and support allowance): 29 April 2013: see SI 2013/380, reg 1(3).

10 Revision of the terms of repayment

(1)   Where the circumstances of the recipient of an integration loan change, the Secretary of State may revise the terms of repayment.

(2)   In determining whether or not to revise the terms of repayment, the Secretary of State must, in addition to other matters appearing to him to be relevant, take into account—

    (a)   any information provided by the recipient of an integration loan in support of a request for a revision of the terms of repayment;

    (b)   any information available to the Secretary of State as to the current financial position of the recipient of an integration loan;

    (c)   any information available to the Secretary of State as to a change of circumstances on the part of the recipient of an integration loan which might merit a revision of the terms of repayment of that loan.

(3)   The recipient of an integration loan must be informed in writing of a revision of the terms of repayment.

11 Joint applications for integration loans

(1)   Two people may make a joint application for an integration loan if—

    (a)   they are married to each other and are members of the same household;

    (b)   they are not married to each other but are living together as husband and wife;

    (c)   they are civil partners and members of the same household;

    (d)   they are two people of the same sex who are not civil partners but are living together as if they were.

(2)   Both parties to a joint application for an integration loan must satisfy the eligibility criteria set out in regulation 4 and must make a declaration in accordance with regulation 5(1)(d).

(3)   Joint recipients of an integration loan shall be jointly and severally liable for the repayments.

SCHEDULE

Regulation 5

Application Information

An applicant for an integration loan must provide the following information—

(a)   his full name;

(b)   other names by which he is or has been known;

(c)   his date of birth;

(d)   his address in the United Kingdom;

(e)   his telephone number (if any);

(f)   his email address (if any);

(g)   evidence that demonstrates the applicant satisfies regulation 4(1);

(h)   his national insurance number;

(i)   details of his income;

(j)   details of his assets;

(k)   details of his liabilities;

(l)   details of his outgoings;

(m)   confirmation as to whether any of his dependants or any member of his household has made an application for or received an integration loan;

(n)   the information in paragraphs (a) to (f) and (h) to (l) in relation to any dependants;

(o)   the amount he is seeking by way of an integration loan.

ASYLUM (PROCEDURES) REGULATIONS 2007

(SI 2007/3187)

Made: 8 November 2007.

Authority: European Communities Act 1972, s 2(2).

Commencement: 1 December 2007.

1 Citation and commencement

These Regulations may be cited as the Asylum (Procedures) Regulations 2007 and shall come into force on 1st December 2007.

2 Interpretation

In these Regulations—

"the 1997 Act" means the Special Immigration Appeals Commission Act 1997;

"the 2002 Act" means the Nationality, Immigration and Asylum Act 2002;

"asylum claim" and "human rights claim" have the meanings given to them in section 113 of the 2002 Act.

3, 4

(*Reg 3 amends the Nationality, Immigration and Asylum Act 2002, s 94; reg 4 inserts s 94A thereof.*)

---

5 Interpreters

(1)   Paragraph (2) applies where a person who has made an asylum or a human rights claim (or both)—

(a)   appeals under section 82, 83 or 83A of the 2002 Act or section 2 of the 1997 Act, and

(b)   by virtue of Rules made under section 106 of the 2002 Act or sections 5 and 8 of the 1997 Act is entitled to the services of an interpreter for the purposes of bringing his appeal.

(2)   The Secretary of State shall defray the costs of providing the interpreter.

(3)   Paragraph (5) applies where a person who has made an asylum claim or a human rights claim (or both) is party to—

    (a)   an appeal under section 103B, 103C or 103E of the 2002 Act, or

    (b)   an appeal under section 7 of the 1997 Act.

(4)   Paragraph (5) also applies where a person who has made an asylum or a human rights claim (or both) makes—

    (a)   an application to the supervisory jurisdiction of the Court of Session made by petition for judicial review,

    (b)   an application under section 31 of the Supreme Court Act 1981, or

    (c)   an application under section 18 of the Judicature (Northern Ireland) Act 1978.

(5)   The person mentioned in paragraphs (3) and (4) shall be entitled to the services of an interpreter for the purposes of the appeal or application—

    (a)   when giving evidence, and

    (b)   in such other circumstances as the court hearing the appeal or application considers it necessary.

(6)   Where a person is entitled to the services of an interpreter under paragraph (5), the Secretary of State shall defray the costs of providing such interpreter.

6

(Reg 6 amends the Immigration (Notices) Regulations 2003, SI 2003/658.).)

IMMIGRATION (RESTRICTIONS ON EMPLOYMENT) ORDER 2007

(SI 2007/3290)

Made: 15 November 2007.

Authority: Immigration, Asylum and Nationality Act 2006, ss 15(3), 15(7), 16(3), 16(5), 19(2), 23(3), 25(d).

Commencement: 29 February 2008.

1 Citation, commencement and interpretation

This order may be cited as the Immigration (Restrictions on Employment) Order 2007 and shall come into force on 29 February 2008.

2

In this order—

    "the 2006 Act" means the Immigration, Asylum and Nationality Act 2006; and

    "document" means an original document.

3 Excuse from paying civil penalty

(1)   To the extent provided for by paragraph (2) an employer is excused from paying a penalty under section 15 of the 2006 Act if—

    (a)   the employee or prospective employee produces to the employer any of the documents or combinations of documents described in list A in the Schedule to this Order; and

    (b)   the employer complies with the requirements set out in article 6 of this order.

(2) An employer will be excused under this article from paying a penalty under section 15 of the 2006 Act—

    (a)   for the duration of the employment, if the document or combination of documents is produced prior to the commencement of employment; or

    (b)   subject to article 5, for the remainder of the employment, if the document or combination of documents is produced after the employment has commenced.

[4

(1) To the extent provided for by paragraphs (2) and (3) an employer is excused from paying a penalty under section 15 of the 2006 Act if—

    (a)   the employee or prospective employee produces to the employer any of the documents or combination of documents described in part 1 of list B in the Schedule to this Order; and

    (b)   the employer complies with the requirements set out in article 6 of this Order.

(2) Subject to article 5 an employer will be excused under this article from paying a penalty under section 15 of the 2006 Act for the period for which a document produced under paragraph (1)(a) provides that the employment is permitted.

(3) If, on the date on which the period specified in paragraph (2) expires, the employer is reasonably satisfied that the employee has an outstanding application to vary his leave to enter or remain in the United Kingdom or the employee has an appeal pending against a decision on that application, the employer will be excused from paying that penalty for a further period beginning with the date on which the period specified in paragraph (2) expires and ending—

    (a)   after 28 days, or

    (b)   if earlier, on the date on which the Secretary of State gives the employer written notice that the employee does not have the right to undertake the employment in question.]

Amendment

Substituted, together with art 4A, for original art 4, by SI 2014/1183, arts 2, 3, as from 16 May 2014.

[4A

(1) To the extent provided for by paragraph (2) an employer is excused from paying a penalty under section 15 of the 2006 Act if—

    (a)   either—

        (i)   the employee or prospective employee produces to the employer a document described in paragraph 1 or 2 of part 2 of list B in the Schedule to this Order and the employer obtains a Positive Verification Notice issued by the Home Office Employer Checking Service which indicates that the person named in it is allowed to stay in the United Kingdom and is allowed to do the work in question; or

        (ii)   the employer obtains a Positive Verification Notice issued by the Home Office Employer Checking Service which indicates that the person named in it is allowed to stay in the United Kingdom and is allowed to do the work in question; and

    (b)   the employer complies with the requirements set out in article 6 of this Order.

(2) Subject to article 5 an employer will be excused under this article from paying a penalty under section 15 of the 2006 Act for a period of six months, beginning with the date of the Positive Verification Notice obtained under paragraph (1)(a).]

Amendment

Substituted, together with art 4, for original art 4, by SI 2014/1183, arts 2, 3, as from 16 May 2014.

5

An employer is excused from paying a penalty under section 15 of the 2006 Act by virtue of article 3(2)(b)[, article 4(2) or article 4A(2)] [only if the employee produces the relevant documents to the employer prior to the commencement of employment].

Amendment

Words in square brackets substituted by SI 2014/1183, arts 2, 4, as from 16 May 2014.

6

(1)   The requirements in relation to any documents or combinations of documents produced by an employee pursuant to [article 3, 4 or 4A] of this order are that—

(a)   the employer takes all reasonable steps to check the validity of the document [and retains a record of the date on which any check was made];

(b)   the copy or copies are retained securely by the employer for a period of not less than two years after the employment has come to an end;

(c)   if a document contains a photograph, the employer has satisfied himself that the photograph is of the prospective employee or employee;

(d)   if a document contains a date of birth, the employer has satisfied himself that the date of birth is consistent with the appearance of the prospective employee or employee;

(e)   the employer takes all other reasonable steps to check that the prospective employee or employee is the rightful owner of the document;

(f)   if the document is not a passport . . . the employer retains a copy of whole of the document in a format which cannot be subsequently altered;
    . . .

[(g)   if the document is a passport . . . , the employer retains a copy of the following pages of that document in a format which cannot be subsequently altered—

(i)   . . .

(ii)   any page containing the holder's personal details including nationality;

(iii)   any page containing the holder's photograph;

(iv)   any page containing the holder's signature;

(v)   any page containing the date of expiry; and

(vi)   any page containing information indicating the holder has an entitlement to enter or remain in the UK and undertake the work in question; and

(h)   . . .]

[(2)   A further requirement, if the employee or prospective employee is a student who has permission to work for a limited number of hours per week during term time whilst studying in the United Kingdom, is that the employer must obtain and retain details of the term and vacation dates of the course that the employee or prospective employee is undertaking.]

Amendment

Para (1) numbered as such and words in first pair of square brackets substituted by SI 2014/1183, arts 2, 5(1), (2)(a), as from 16 May 2014.

In sub-para (a) words in square brackets inserted by SI 2014/1183, arts 2, 5(2)(b), as from 16 May 2014.

In sub-para (f) words omitted in the first place revoked by SI 2014/1183, arts 2, 5(2)(c), as from 16 May 2014.

In sub-para (f) word omitted in the second place revoked by SI 2009/2908, arts 2, 3(a). Date in force: 24 November 2009: see SI 2009/2908, art 1(1).

Sub-paras (g), (h) substituted, for sub-para (g) as originally enacted, by SI 2009/2908, arts 2, 3(b). Date in force: 24 November 2009: see SI 2009/2908, art 1(1).

Words omitted from sub-para (g) revoked by SI 2014/1183, arts 2, 5(2)(d), (e), as from 16 May 2014.

Sub-para (h) revoked by SI 2014/1183, arts 2, 5(2)(f), as from 16 May 2014.

Para (2): added by SI 2014/1183, arts 2, 5(2)(g), as from 16 May 2014.

7

Nothing in this Order permits employers to retain documents produced by an employee for the purposes of [article 3, 4 or 4A] for any period longer than is necessary for the purposes of ensuring compliance with article 6.

Amendment

Words in square brackets substituted by SI 2014/1183, arts 2, 6, as from 16 May 2014.

8 Objections

The manner prescribed in which the notice of objection must be given is that it must contain—

    (a)   the reference number of the notice given under section 15(2) of the 2006 Act;

    (b)   the name and contact address of the employer;

    (c)   the name and contact address of the employee in respect of whom the penalty was issued;

    (d)   the full grounds of objection;

    (e)   where the employer requests permission to pay by instalments, full details of the employer's ability to pay the penalty;

    (f)   confirmation and details of any appeal made by the employer to a County Court or Sheriff Court on the basis that the employer is not liable to the penalty, he is excused payment by virtue of section 15(3) of the 2006 Act, or that the amount of the penalty is too high; and

    (g)   any documents to be relied upon in support of the objection.

9

The prescribed period within which a notice of objection must be given for the purposes of section 16(3)(d) of the 2006 Act is 28 days, beginning with the date specified in the penalty notice as the date upon which it is given.

10

The period prescribed for the purposes of section 16(5)(b) of the 2006 Act within which the Secretary of State must inform the objector of his decision is 28 days, beginning with the date on which the notice of objection was given to the Secretary of State.

11 Codes of Practice

The code of practice entitled "Civil Penalties for Employers", issued by the Secretary of State under section 19(1) of the 2006 Act shall come into force on 29 February 2008.

12

The code of practice entitled "Guidance for Employers on the Avoidance of Unlawful Discrimination in Employment Practice While Seeking to Prevent Illegal Working", issued by the Secretary of State under section 23(1) of the 2006 Act shall come into force on 29 February 2008.

SCHEDULE

Articles 3 and 4

List A

1

. . . A passport showing that the holder, or a person named in the passport as the child of the holder, is a British citizen or a citizen of the United Kingdom and Colonies having the right of abode in the United Kingdom.

[2

A passport or national identity card showing that the holder, or a person named in the passport as the child of the holder, is a national of a European Economic Area country or Switzerland.]

3

A . . . registration certificate or document certifying . . . permanent residence issued by the Home Office . . . to a national of a European Economic Area country or Switzerland.

4

A permanent residence card issued by the Home Office . . . to the family member of a national of a European Economic Area country or Switzerland.

5

[A current biometric immigration document issued by the Home Office] to the holder which indicates that the person named in it is allowed to stay indefinitely in the United Kingdom, or has no time limit on their stay in the United Kingdom.

6

[A current passport] endorsed to show that the holder is exempt from immigration control, is allowed to stay indefinitely in the United Kingdom, has the right of abode in the United Kingdom, or has no time limit on their stay in the United Kingdom.

7

[A current immigration status document] issued by the Home Office . . . to the holder with an endorsement indicating that the person named in it is allowed to stay indefinitely in the United Kingdom or has no time limit on their stay in the United Kingdom, when produced in combination with an official document giving the person's permanent National Insurance Number and their name issued by a Government agency or a previous employer.

8

A full birth certificate issued in the United Kingdom which includes the name(s) of at least one of the holder's parents, when produced in combination with an official document giving the person's permanent National Insurance Number and their name issued by a Government agency or a previous employer.

9

A full adoption certificate issued in the United Kingdom which includes the name(s) of at least one of the holder's adoptive parents when produced in combination with an official document giving the person's permanent National Insurance Number and their name issued by a Government agency or a previous employer.

10

A birth certificate issued in the Channel Islands, the Isle of Man or Ireland, when produced in combination with an official document giving the person's permanent National Insurance Number and their name issued by a Government agency or a previous employer.

11

An adoption certificate issued in the Channel Islands, the Isle of Man or Ireland, when produced in combination with an official document giving the person's permanent National Insurance Number and their name issued by a Government agency or a previous employer.

12

A certificate of registration or naturalisation as a British citizen, when produced in combination with an official document giving the person's permanent National Insurance Number and their name issued by a Government agency or a previous employer.

13

. . .

[List B—Part 1

1

A current passport endorsed to show that the holder is allowed to stay in the United Kingdom and is allowed to do the type of work in question.

2

A current biometric immigration document issued by the Home Office to the holder which indicates that the person named in it is allowed to stay in the United Kingdom and is allowed to do the work in question.

3

A current residence card (including an accession residence card or a derivative residence card) issued by the Home Office to a non-European Economic Area national who is a family member of a national of a European Economic Area country or Switzerland or who has a derivative right of residence.

4

A current immigration status document containing a photograph issued by the Home Office to the holder with an endorsement indicating that the person named in it is allowed to stay in the United Kingdom and is allowed to do the work in question, when produced in combination with an official document giving the person's permanent National Insurance Number and their name issued by a Government agency or previous employer.

List B—Part 2

1

A certificate of application issued by the Home Office under regulation 17(3) or 18A(2) of the Immigration (European Economic Area) Regulations 2006, to a family member of a national of a European Economic Area country or Switzerland stating that the holder is permitted to take employment which is less than 6 months old.

2

An application registration card issued by the Home Office stating that the holder is permitted to take the employment in question.]

Amendment

In List A, words omitted in each place revoked by SI 2014/1183, arts 2, 7, 8(a), (c), (g), as from 16 May 2014.

List A, Para 2: substituted by SI 2014/1183, arts 2, 8(b), as from 16 May 2014.

List A, Paras 5–7: words in square brackets substituted by SI 2014/1183, arts 2, 8(d)–(f), as from 16 May 2014.

List B substituted by SI 2014/1183, arts 2, 9, as from 16 May 2014.

IMMIGRATION AND ASYLUM (PROVISION OF SERVICES OR FACILITIES) REGULATIONS 2007

(SI 2007/3627)

Made: 20 December 2007.

Authority: Immigration and Asylum Act 1999, s 4(10), (11).

Commencement: 31 January 2008.

1 Citation and commencement

These Regulations may be cited as the Immigration and Asylum (Provision of Services or Facilities) Regulations 2007 and shall come into force on 31st January 2008.

2 Interpretation

In these Regulations—

"the 1999 Act" means the Immigration and Asylum Act 1999;

"ante-natal eligible period" means the period from eight weeks before the expected date of birth to the date of birth;

"child" means an individual who is less than 18 years old;

"destitute" is to be construed in accordance with section 95(3) of the 1999 Act;

"full birth certificate" means a birth certificate issued in the United Kingdom, which specifies the names of the child's parents;

"immigration officer" means a person appointed as an immigration officer under paragraph 1(1) of Schedule 2 to the Immigration Act 1971;

"maternity payment" means a payment of £250 made by the Secretary of State to a person supported under section 95 or section 98 of the 1999 Act to help with the costs arising from the birth of a child;

"mother" means a woman who is a supported person and who has provided evidence to satisfy the Secretary of State that she has given birth to a child;

"post-natal eligible period" means the period from the date of the birth to six weeks after the birth;

"pregnant woman" means a woman who is a supported person who has provided evidence to satisfy the Secretary of State that she is pregnant;

"provider" means a person providing facilities for the accommodation of persons by arrangement with the Secretary of State under section 4 of the 1999 Act;

"qualified person" has the same meaning as in section 84(2) of the 1999 Act;

"qualifying journey" means where—

    (a)   a single journey of a distance of not less than three miles; or

    (b)   where there is a specified need, a single journey of a distance of less than three miles;

"specified need" means where—

    (a)   the supported person is unable or virtually unable to walk a distance of up to three miles by reason of a physical impediment or for some other reason; or

    (b)   the supported person has one or more child dependants—

        (i)   aged under five; or

        (ii)   who are unable or virtually unable to walk a distance of up to three miles by reason of a physical impediment or for some other reason;

"supported person" means a person who is being provided with accommodation under section 4 of the 1999 Act and who is destitute; and "voluntary sector partner" means an organisation funded by the Secretary of State to deliver aspects of asylum support services.

3 Travel

(1) The Secretary of State may supply, or arrange for the supply of, facilities for travel for a qualifying journey to a supported person to—

    (a)   receive healthcare treatment, provided that the supported person has provided evidence that the qualifying journey is necessary; or

    (b)   register a birth.

(2) Subject to paragraph (3), if the Secretary of State supplies, or arranges for the supply of, facilities for travel for a qualifying journey to a supported person under paragraph (1) then, if necessary, the Secretary of State may also supply, or arrange for the supply of, facilities for travel for that qualifying journey to—

    (a)   one or more dependants of that supported person; and

    (b)   in the case of a supported person who is a child—

        (i)   a parent or guardian of that supported person or a person who for the time being takes parental responsibility for that supported person; and

        (ii)   if the parent, guardian or person who for the time being takes parental responsibility for that supported person himself has dependants then one or more of his dependants.

(3) The Secretary of State may only supply, or arrange for the supply of, facilities for travel under paragraph (2) to persons who are supported persons.

4 Birth certificates

The Secretary of State may arrange for the provision to a supported person of his child's full birth certificate.

5 Telephone calls and letters

(1) The Secretary of State may supply, or arrange for the supply of, facilities to make telephone calls—

    (a)   regarding medical treatment or care,

    (b)   to a qualified person,

    (c)   to a court or tribunal,

    (d)   to a voluntary sector partner,

    (e)   to a citizens advice bureau,

    (f)   to a local authority,

    (g)   to an immigration officer, or

    (h)   to the Secretary of State,

to a supported person aged 18 or over.

(2) The Secretary of State may supply, or arrange for the supply of, stationery and postage for correspondence—

    (a)   regarding medical treatment or care,

    (b)   to a qualified person,

    (c)   to a court or tribunal,

    (d)   to a voluntary sector partner,

    (e)   to a citizens advice bureau,

    (f)   to a local authority,

    (g)   to an immigration officer, or

    (h)   to the Secretary of State,

to a supported person aged 18 or over.

6 One-off supply of vouchers for pregnant women and new mothers

(1)   During the ante-natal eligible period, on application, the Secretary of State may supply, or arrange for the supply of, vouchers redeemable for goods to the value of £250 in respect of each expected child to a pregnant woman.

(2)   In a case where such support has not been provided under paragraph (1), during the post-natal eligible period, on application, the Secretary of State may supply, or arrange for the supply of, vouchers redeemable for goods to the value of £250 in respect of each new born child to a mother.

(3)   Paragraphs (1) and (2) shall not apply if a maternity payment has been made in respect of the child in question.

7 Additional weekly vouchers for pregnant women and children under three

(1)   For the duration of the pregnancy, on application, the Secretary of State may supply, or arrange for the supply of, vouchers redeemable for goods or services to the value of £3 per week to a pregnant woman.

(2)   Until the first birthday of a child who is a supported person, on application, the Secretary of State may supply, or arrange for the supply of, vouchers redeemable for goods or services to the value of £5 per week to him.

(3)   From the day after the first birthday of a child who is a supported person, until the third birthday, on application, the Secretary of State may supply, or arrange for the supply of, vouchers redeemable for goods or services to the value of £3 per week to him.

8 Additional weekly vouchers for clothing for children

Until the sixteenth birthday of a child who is a supported person, on application, the Secretary of State may supply, or arrange for the supply of, vouchers redeemable for clothing to the value of £5 per week to him.

9 Exceptional specific needs

(1)   If the Secretary of State is satisfied that a supported person has an exceptional need for:

    (a)   facilities for travel,

    (b)   facilities to make telephone calls,

    (c)   stationery and postage, or

    (d)   essential living needs,

she may provide for that need, notwithstanding that the conditions for the supply of those services or facilities referred to respectively in regulations 3, 5, and 6 are not satisfied.

(2)   In determining what are or are not to be treated as essential living needs, the Secretary of State shall have regard to regulations made under section 95(7) of the 1999 Act.

IMMIGRATION AND POLICE (PASSENGER, CREW AND SERVICE INFORMATION) ORDER 2008

(SI 2008/5)

Made: 3 January 2008.

Authority: Immigration Act 1971, Sch 2, paras 27, 27B; Immigration, Asylum and Nationality Act 2006, s 32.

Commencement: 1 March 2008.

PART 1
GENERAL

1 Citation and commencement

This Order may be cited as the Immigration and Police (Passenger, Crew and Service Information) Order 2008 and shall come into force on 1st March 2008.

2 Interpretation

(1) In this Order—

"the 1971 Act" means the Immigration Act 1971;

"the 2006 Act" means the Immigration, Asylum and Nationality Act 2006; and

"shuttle train", "through train", "train manager" and "international service" have the same meanings as in the Channel Tunnel (International Arrangements) Order 1993.

(2) For the purposes of this Order, information is known to the owner or agent of a ship or aircraft or a person operating an international service or his agent ("carrier") if it is held by that carrier and—

(a) if information of that nature is routinely held by the carrier on their carrier reservation system, departure control system or equivalent system; or

(b) if the information is obtained in the ordinary course of the carrier's business and is requested notwithstanding the fact that it is not held, or is not held routinely, on such a system.

PART 2
POWER OF IMMIGRATION OFFICER TO REQUIRE PASSENGER LIST AND PARTICULARS OF CREW

3 Power of immigration officer to require passenger list and particulars of crew

(1) This article applies to—

(a) a ship or aircraft arriving or expected to arrive in, or leaving or expected to leave, the United Kingdom; and

(b) a through train or shuttle train arriving or expected to arrive in, or leaving or expected to leave, the United Kingdom.

(2) Subject to paragraph (4), an immigration officer may require a responsible person in respect of a ship or aircraft to which this article applies to supply—

(a) a passenger list showing the names and nationality or citizenship of passengers arriving or leaving the United Kingdom on board the ship or aircraft; and

(b) the particulars of members of the crew of the ship or aircraft which are set out in paragraph 1 of Schedule 1.

(3) Subject to paragraph (4), an immigration officer may, in relation to a train to which this article applies, require a train manager or a person operating an international service or his agent to supply—

(a) a passenger list showing the names and nationality or citizenship of passengers arriving or leaving the United Kingdom on board the train; and

(b) the particulars of members of the crew of the train which are set out in paragraph 1 of Schedule 1.

(4) The information which may be requested under this article may only be requested to the extent to which it is known by the responsible person, train manager or person operating an international service or his agent in circumstances where the information is to be provided before a point in time at which passengers have boarded the ship or aircraft or through train or shuttle train in preparation for departure and it is no longer possible for further passengers or crew to do so.

(5) Where information has been requested in circumstances set out in paragraph (4), nothing in this article prevents that same information being requested from the responsible person, train manager or person operating an international service or his agent a second time where those same circumstances do not apply.

(6) For the purposes of paragraphs (2), (4) and (5) a responsible person is one of the persons specified in paragraph 27(4) of Schedule 2 to the 1971 Act.

4 Form and manner in which passenger list and particulars of crew to be provided: immigration officers

A passenger list and particulars of crew shall be provided under article 3 in an electronic form that is compatible with the technology used by the recipient of the data unless an alternative form and manner of information transmission is authorised by the recipient of the information.

PART 3
ACQUISITION OF PASSENGER AND SERVICE INFORMATION BY IMMIGRATION OFFICER

5 Passenger and service information: immigration officers

(1) Subject to paragraph (2), the passenger information and service information set out in paragraphs 2 (information which relates to passengers) and 3 (information which relates to a voyage or flight or international service) of Schedule 1 is specified for the purposes of paragraph 27B(9) and (9A) of Schedule 2 to the 1971 Act (passenger and service information).

(2) The information set out in paragraphs 2 and 3 of Schedule 1 is only specified for the purposes of paragraph 27B(9) and (9A) of Schedule 2 to the 1971 Act to the extent to which it is known by the owner or agent of a ship or aircraft or by the person operating an international service or his agent in circumstances where the information is to be provided before a point in time at which passengers have boarded the ship or aircraft or through train or shuttle train in preparation for departure and it is no longer possible for further passengers or crew to do so.

(3) Where information set out in paragraph 2 or 3 of Schedule 1 has been requested in circumstances set out in paragraph (2), nothing in this article prevents that same information being requested from the owner or agent of a ship or aircraft or from the person operating an international service or his agent a second time where those same circumstances do not apply.

(4) The passenger information and service information set out in Schedule 2 is specified for the purposes of paragraph 27B(9) and (9A) of Schedule 2 to the 1971 Act to the extent to which it is known to the owner or agent of a ship or aircraft or to the person operating an international service or his agent.

PART 4

POLICE ACQUISITION OF PASSENGER AND SERVICE INFORMATION

6 Passenger and service information: police

(1) Subject to paragraph (2), the passenger and service information set out in Schedule 3 is specified for the purposes of section 32(5)(a) of the 2006 Act (passenger and crew information: police powers) in respect of ships and aircraft and through trains and shuttle trains arriving or expected to arrive in, or leaving or expected to leave, the United Kingdom.

(2) The information set out in Schedule 3 is only specified for the purposes of section 32(5)(a) of the 2006 Act to the extent to which it is known by the owner or agent of a ship or aircraft or by the person operating an international service or his agent in circumstances where the information is to be provided before a point in time at which passengers have boarded the ship or aircraft or through train or shuttle train in preparation for departure and it is no longer possible for further passengers or crew to do so.

(3) Where information set out in Schedule 3 has been requested in circumstances set out in paragraph (2), nothing in this article prevents that same information being requested from the owner or agent of a ship or aircraft or from the person operating an international service or his agent a second time where those same circumstances do not apply.

(4) The passenger and service information set out in Schedule 4 is specified for the purposes of section 32(5)(a) of the 2006 Act to the extent to which it is known by the owner or agent of a ship or aircraft or by the person operating an international service or his agent.

7 Form and manner in which passenger and service information to be provided: police

Passenger and service information shall be provided under section 32 of the 2006 Act in an electronic form that is compatible with the technology used by the recipient of the data unless an alternative form and manner of information transmission is authorised by the recipient of the information.

8 Revocations

The following instruments are revoked—

    (a)   The Immigration (Particulars of Passengers and Crew) Order 1972;

    (b)   The Immigration (Particulars of Passengers and Crew) (Amendment) Order 1975; and

    (c)   The Immigration (Passenger Information) Order 2000.

SCHEDULE 1

INFORMATION SPECIFIED: IMMIGRATION

Articles 3(2)(b) and 5(1)

Particulars of crew

1

The information is—

    (a)   the following information as provided on the member of crew's travel document—

        (i)   full name;

        (ii)   gender;

        (iii)   date of birth;

        (iv)   nationality;

        (v)   type of travel document held;

        (vi)   number of travel document held;

        (vii)   expiry date of travel document held; and

(viii)   issuing State of travel document held;

(b)   where a travel document is not held, the type of identification relied upon together with the number, expiry date and issuing State of that identification;

(c)   the vehicle registration number of any vehicle in which the member of crew is travelling and which is being transported by ship or by aircraft or by through train or shuttle train and, if the vehicle has a trailer, the trailer registration number;

(d)   the number of crew on board the ship or aircraft or through train or shuttle train;

(e)   the fact that the person is a member of crew; and

(f)   in relation to crew on a ship—

(i)   the place of birth of the member of crew; and

(ii)   the rank, rating or equivalent of the member of crew.

Information which relates to passengers

2

The information is—

(a)   the following information as provided on the passenger's travel document—

(i)   full name;

(ii)   gender;

(iii)   date of birth;

(iv)   nationality;

(v)   type of travel document held;

(vi)   number of travel document held;

(vii)   expiry date of travel document held; and

(viii)   issuing State of travel document held;

(b)   where a travel document is not held, the type of identification relied upon together with the number, expiry date and issuing State of that identification; and

(c)   the vehicle registration number of any vehicle in which the passenger is travelling and which is being transported by ship or by aircraft or by through train or shuttle train and, if the vehicle has a trailer, the trailer registration number.

Information which relates to a voyage or flight or international service

3

The information is—

(a)   flight number, ship name, train service number or carrier running number;

(b)   name of carrier;

(c)   nationality of ship;

(d)   scheduled departure date;

(e)   scheduled departure time;

(f)   scheduled arrival date;

(g)   scheduled arrival time;

(h)   place and country from which the voyage or flight or international service departed immediately prior to arrival into the United Kingdom;

(i)   place in the United Kingdom into which the voyage or flight or international service first arrives from overseas;

(j)   any place in the United Kingdom to which a voyage or flight or international service which has arrived into the United Kingdom from overseas will subsequently go; and

(k)   number of passengers.

SCHEDULE 2
INFORMATION SPECIFIED TO EXTENT KNOWN BY CARRIER: IMMIGRATION

Article 5(4)

1

The passenger and service information is the following details in respect of a passenger—

(a)   name as it appears on the reservation;

(b)   place of birth;

(c)   issue date of travel document;

(d)   address;

(e)   sex;

(f)   any contact telephone number;

(g)   e-mail address;

(h)   travel status of passenger, which indicates whether reservation is confirmed or provisional and whether the passenger has checked in;

(i)   the number of pieces and description of any baggage carried;

(j)   any documentation provided to the passenger in respect of his baggage;

(k)   date of intended travel;

(l)   ticket number;

(m)   date and place of ticket issue;

(n)   seat number allocated;

(o)   seat number requested;

(p)   check-in time, regardless of method;

(q)   date on which reservation was made;

(r)   identity of any person who made the reservation;

(s)   any travel agent used;

(t)   any other name that appears on the passenger's reservation;

(u)   number of passengers on the same reservation;

(v)   complete travel itinerary for passengers on the same reservation;

(w)   the fact that a reservation in respect of more than one passenger has been divided due to a change in itinerary for one or more but not all of the passengers;

(x)   Code Share Details;

(y)   method of payment used to purchase ticket or make a reservation;

(z)   details of the method of payment used, including the number of any credit, debit or other card used;

(aa)   billing address;

(bb)   booking reference number, Passenger Name Record Locator and other data locator used by the carrier to locate the passenger within its information system;

(cc)   the class of transport reserved;

(dd)   the fact that the reservation is in respect of a one-way journey;

(ee)   all historical changes to the reservation;

(ff)   General Remarks;

(gg)   Other Service Information (OSI);

(hh)   System Service Information (SSI) and System Service Request information (SSR);

(ii) identity of the individual who checked the passenger in for the voyage or flight or international service;

(jj) Outbound Indicator, which identifies where a passenger is to travel on to from the United Kingdom;

(kk) Inbound Connection Indicator, which identifies where a passenger started his journey before he travels onto the United Kingdom;

(ll) the fact that the passenger is travelling as part of a group;

(mm) the expiry date of any entry clearance held in respect of the United Kingdom;

(nn) card number and type of any frequent flyer or similar scheme used;

(oo) Automated Ticket Fare Quote (ATFQ), which indicates the fare quoted and charged;

(pp) the fact that the passenger is under the age of eighteen and unaccompanied; and

(qq) where the passenger is a person under the age of eighteen and unaccompanied—

    (i) age;

    (ii) languages spoken;

    (iii) any special instructions provided;

    (iv) the name of any departure agent who will receive instructions regarding the care of the passenger;

    (v) the name of any transit agent who will receive instructions regarding the care of the passenger;

    (vi) the name of any arrival agent who will receive instructions regarding the care of the passenger;

    (vii) the following details in respect of the guardian on departure—

        (aa) name;

        (bb) address;

        (cc) any contact telephone number; and

        (dd) relationship to passenger; and

    (viii) the following details in respect of the guardian on arrival—

        (aa) name;

        (bb) address;

        (cc) any contact telephone number; and

        (dd) relationship to passenger.

SCHEDULE 3
INFORMATION SPECIFIED: POLICE

Article 6(1)

Information which relates to members of crew

1

The information is—

    (a) the following information as provided on the member of crew's travel document—

        (i) full name;

        (ii) gender;

        (iii) date of birth;

        (iv) nationality;

        (v) type of travel document held;

        (vi) number of travel document held;

        (vii) expiry date of travel document held; and

        (viii) issuing State of travel document held;

   (b)   where a travel document is not held, the type of identification relied upon together with the number, expiry date and issuing State of that identification; and

   (c)   the vehicle registration number of any vehicle in which the member of crew is travelling and which is being transported by ship or by aircraft or by through train or shuttle train and, if the vehicle has a trailer, the trailer registration number.

Information which relates to passengers

2

The information is—

   (a)   the following information as provided on the passenger's travel document—

       (i)   full name;

       (ii)   gender;

       (iii)   date of birth;

       (iv)   nationality;

       (v)   type of travel document held;

       (vi)   number of travel document held;

       (vii)   expiry date of travel document held; and

       (viii) issuing State of travel document held;

   (b)   where a travel document is not held, the type of identification relied upon together with the number, expiry date and issuing State of that identification; and

   (c)   the vehicle registration number of any vehicle in which the passenger is travelling and which is being transported by ship or by aircraft or by through train or shuttle train and, if the vehicle has a trailer, the trailer registration number.

Information which relates to a voyage or flight or international service

3

The information is—

   (a)   flight number, ship name, train service number or carrier running number;

   (b)   name of carrier;

   (c)   nationality of ship;

   (d)   scheduled departure date;

   (e)   scheduled departure time;

   (f)   scheduled arrival date;

   (g)   scheduled arrival time;

   (h)   place and country from which the voyage or flight or international service departed immediately prior to arrival into the United Kingdom;

   (i)   place in the United Kingdom into which the voyage or flight or international service first arrives from overseas;

   (j)   any place in the United Kingdom to which a voyage or flight or international service which has arrived into the United Kingdom from overseas will subsequently go; and

   (k)   number of passengers.

SCHEDULE 4

INFORMATION SPECIFIED TO EXTENT KNOWN BY CARRIER: POLICE

Article 6(4)

1

The passenger and service information is the following in respect of a passenger or, in so far as it applies (whether expressly or otherwise), in respect of a member of crew—

    (a)   name as it appears on the reservation;

    (b)   address;

    (c)   any contact telephone number;

    (d)   fax number;

    (e)   e-mail address;

    (f)   internet address;

    (g)   travel status of passenger or member of crew, which indicates whether reservation is confirmed or provisional and whether the passenger or member of crew has checked in;

    (h)   the number of pieces and description of any baggage carried;

    (i)   any documentation provided to the passenger or member of crew in respect of baggage;

    (j)   ticket number;

    (k)   date and place of ticket issue;

    (l)   seat number allocated;

    (m)   seat number requested;

    (n)   check-in time, regardless of method;

    (o)   date on which reservation was made;

    (p)   identity of any person who made the reservation;

    (q)   any other name that appears on the passenger's or member of crew's reservation;

    (r)   the fact that a reservation in respect of more than one passenger or member of crew has been divided due to a change in itinerary for one or more but not all of the passengers or members of crew;

    (s)   Code Share Details;

    (t)   method of payment used to purchase ticket or make reservation;

    (u)   details of the method of payment used, including the number of any credit, debit or other card used;

    (v)   Passenger Name Record Locator or other data locator used by the carrier to locate the passenger or member of crew within its information system;

    (w)   the name, address and contact details of the passenger's or member of crew's sponsor in the United Kingdom;

    (x)   the fact that the passenger is under the age of eighteen and unaccompanied;

    (y)   the fact that the passenger is under the age of eighteen and travelling with a person who has not declared himself to be a family member; and

    (z)   name and contact details of an adult dropping off an unaccompanied passenger under the age of eighteen at a port or station.

IMMIGRATION, ASYLUM AND NATIONALITY ACT 2006 (DATA SHARING CODE OF PRACTICE) ORDER 2008

(SI 2008/8)

Made: 8 January 2008.

Authority: Immigration, Asylum and Nationality Act 2006, s 37(2)..

Commencement: 1 March 2008.

1 Citation and commencement

This Order may be cited as the Immigration, Asylum and Nationality Act 2006 (Data Sharing Code of Practice) Order 2008 and shall come into force on 1st March 2008.

2 Entry into force of code of practice

The Code of Practice on the Management of Information Shared by the Border and Immigration Agency, Her Majesty's Revenue and Customs and the Police laid before Parliament on 10th January 2008 shall come into force on 1st March 2008.

IMMIGRATION (EMPLOYMENT OF ADULTS SUBJECT TO IMMIGRATION CONTROL) (MAXIMUM PENALTY) ORDER 2008

(SI 2008/132)

Made: 22 January 2008.

Authority: Immigration, Asylum and Nationality Act 2006, s 15(2).

Commencement: 29 February 2008.

1 Citation and Commencement

This Order may be cited as The Immigration (Employment of Adults Subject to Immigration Control) (Maximum Penalty) Order 2008 and shall come into force on 29th February 2008.

2 Maximum Penalty

For the purposes of section 15(2) of the Immigration, Asylum and Nationality Act 2006 (employment of adults subject to immigration control: penalty notice) the prescribed maximum is [£20,000].

Amendment

Sum in square brackets substituted (for original sum £10,000) by SI 2014/1262, art 2, except in respect of a penalty notice issued to an employer who has acted contrary to section 15(1) of the Immigration, Asylum and Nationality Act 2006 if, in respect of any employment to which the notice relates, the contravention occurred solely before 16 May 2014: see SI 2014/1262. art 1(2).

IMMIGRATION, ASYLUM AND NATIONALITY ACT 2006 (COMMENCEMENT NO 8 AND TRANSITIONAL AND SAVING PROVISIONS) ORDER 2008

(SI 2008/310)

Made: 8 February 2008.

Authority: Immigration, Asylum and Nationality Act 2006, s 62.

1 Citation and interpretation

(1) This Order may be cited at the Immigration, Asylum and Nationality Act 2006 (Commencement No 8 and Transitional and Saving Provisions) Order 2008.

(2) In this Order—

"the 2006 Act" means the Immigration, Asylum and Nationality Act 2006;

"the 2002 Act" means the Nationality, Immigration and Asylum Act 2002;

"the 1999 Act" means the Immigration and Asylum Act 1999;

"the 1996 Act" means the Asylum and Immigration Act 1996; and

"immigration rules" means rules made under section 3(2) of the Immigration Act 1971.

2 Commencement

(1) Subject to article 5 the following provisions of the 2006 Act shall come into force on 29th February 2008—

(a) sections 15 to 18 to the extent to which they are not already in force (penalty for employment of adult subject to immigration control);

(b) sections 21 and 22 (offence of employing adult subject to immigration control);

(c) section 24 (employment of adult subject to immigration control: temporary admission);

(d) section 26 (repeal); and

(e) in Schedule 3, the entries relating to the 1996 Act.

(2) The following provisions of the 2006 Act shall come into force on 29th February 2008—

(a) section 50(3)(a) (repeal); and

(b) in Schedule 3, the entries relating to section 31A of the Immigration Act 1971.

3

The following provisions of the 2006 Act shall come in to force on 1st April 2008—

(a) subject to article 4, section 4 (entry clearance);

(b) section 33 (freight information: police powers) for the purposes of making an order under subsection (5)(a); and

(c) section 47 (removal: person with statutorily extended leave).

4 Saving and Transitional Provision

Notwithstanding the commencement of section 4 of the 2006 Act and the substitution of section 88A of the 2002 Act and section 23 of the 1999 Act, section 4(1) (appeals: entry clearance) and section 4(2) of the 2006 Act (monitoring refusals of entry clearance) shall have effect only so far as they relate to applications of a kind identified in immigration rules as requiring to be considered under a "Points Based System" [and applications made for the purpose of entering the United Kingdom as a visitor, including applications made for the purpose of visiting a person of a class or description prescribed by regulations for the purpose of section 88A(1)(a) of the 2002 Act].

Amendment

Words in square brackets inserted by SI 2012/1531, art 2. Date in force: 9 July 2012: see SI 2012/1531, art 1.

5

(1) Notwithstanding the commencement of section 26 of the 2006 Act (repeal) the following provisions and instruments continue to have effect in relation to employment which commenced before 29th February 2008, including employment which continued on or after that date—

(a) sections 8 (restrictions on employment) and 8A (code of practice) of the 1996 Act;

(b) any Code of Practice in force immediately before 29th February 2008 under section 8A of the 1996 Act;

(c) the Immigration (Restrictions on Employment) Order 2004; and

(d) the Immigration (Restrictions on Employment) (Code of Practice) Order 2001.

(2) Sections 15 to 18, 21, 22, 24, 25 and 26 of the 2006 Act are of no effect in relation to employment of a kind mentioned in paragraph (1).

IMMIGRATION, ASYLUM AND NATIONALITY ACT 2006 (DUTY TO SHARE INFORMATION AND DISCLOSURE OF INFORMATION FOR SECURITY PURPOSES) ORDER 2008

(SI 2008/539)

Made: 28 February 2008.

Authority: Immigration, Asylum and Nationality Act 2006, ss 36(4), 38(4).

Commencement: 1 March 2008.

1 Citation, commencement and interpretation

(1) This Order may be cited as the Immigration, Asylum and Nationality Act 2006 (Duty to Share Information and Disclosure of Information for Security Purposes) Order 2008 and shall come into force on 1st March 2008.

(2) In this Order—

"the 2006 Act" means the Immigration, Asylum and Nationality Act 2006; and "shuttle train", "through train" and "international service" have the same meanings as in the Channel Tunnel (International Arrangements) Order 1993.

(3) Any power specified in this Order for the purposes of section 36(4)(a) or section 38(4)(a) of the 2006 Act should be read as including a reference to that power as modified under section 11 of the Channel Tunnel Act 1987 (regulation of the tunnel system: application and enforcement of law, etc).

2 Duty to share information obtained or held under specified powers

(1) Subject to paragraphs (2) and (3), the powers contained in the provisions set out in Schedule 1 to this Order are specified for the purposes of section 36(4)(a) of the 2006 Act (duty to share information).

(2) The powers are only specified to the extent to which they relate to—

(a)   passengers on a ship or aircraft or through train or shuttle train;

(b)   crew of a ship or aircraft or through train or shuttle train;

(c)   freight on a ship or aircraft or through train or shuttle train; or

(d)   flights or voyages or international services.

(3)   A power shall not be construed as being specified if or in so far as it relates to a matter to which section 7 of the Commissioners for Revenue and Customs Act 2005 (former Inland Revenue matters) applies.

3 Duty to share information relating to other matters specified in respect of travel or freight

(1)   Subject to paragraph (2), the matters in respect of travel and freight set out in Schedule 2 to this Order are specified for the purposes of section 36(4)(b) of the 2006 Act (duty to share information).

(2)   A matter shall not be construed as being specified if or in so far as—

(a)   disclosure of information relating to it may prejudice an investigation or prosecution whether in the United Kingdom or elsewhere;

(b)   the consent of a third party is required for disclosure of information relating to it and that consent has not been obtained;

(c)   disclosure of information relating to it is likely to cause loss of life or serious injury to any person;

(d)   non-disclosure of information relating to it is necessary for the purpose of safeguarding national security; or

(e)   disclosure of information relating to it would be in breach of an obligation of the United Kingdom or Her Majesty's Government under an international or other agreement.

4 Disclosure of information for security purposes: information obtained or held under specified powers

(1)   Subject to paragraphs (2) and (3), the powers contained in the provisions set out in Schedule 1 to this Order are specified for the purposes of section 38(4)(a) of the 2006 Act (disclosure of information for security purposes).

(2)   The powers are only specified to the extent to which they relate to—

(a)   passengers on a ship or aircraft or through train or shuttle train;

(b)   crew of a ship or aircraft or through train or shuttle train;

(c)   freight on a ship or aircraft or through train or shuttle train; or

(d)   flights or voyages or international services.

(3)   A power shall not be construed as being specified if or in so far as it relates to a matter to which section 7 of the Commissioner for Revenue and Customs Act 2005 (former Inland Revenue matters) applies.

5 Disclosure of information for security purposes: information relating to other matters specified in respect of travel or freight

The matters in respect of travel and freight set out in Schedule 2 to this Order are specified for the purposes of section 38(4)(b) of the 2006 Act (disclosure of information for security purposes).

SCHEDULE 1

POWERS SPECIFIED FOR THE PURPOSES OF SECTIONS 36(4)(A) AND 38(4)(A) OF THE 2006 ACT

Articles 2(1) and 4(1)

1

The provisions are—

(a) an order made under paragraph 27(2) of Schedule 2 to the Immigration Act 1971 (power to require provision of information in respect of a ship or an aircraft);

(b) paragraph 27B of Schedule 2 to the Immigration Act 1971 (passenger information);

(c) paragraph 27C of Schedule 2 to the Immigration Act 1971 (notification of non-EEA arrivals on a ship or aircraft);

(d) section 32 of the 2006 Act (passenger and crew information: police powers);

(e) section 35 of the Customs and Excise Management Act 1979 (report inwards) and any directions or regulations made under that provision;

(f) section 64 of the Customs and Excise Management Act 1979 (clearance outwards of ships and aircraft) and any directions made under that provision;

(g) section 77 of the Customs and Excise Management Act 1979 (information in relation to goods imported or exported);

(h) section 9 of the Commissioners for Revenue and Customs Act 2005 (ancillary powers); and

(i) Articles 181b (entry summary declaration) and 842a (exit summary declaration) and Annex 30A of Regulation (EEC) No 2454/93.

2

Until 1st July 2009 paragraph 1 shall have effect as if sub-paragraph (i) were omitted.

SCHEDULE 2
OTHER MATTERS IN RESPECT OF TRAVEL AND FREIGHT SPECIFIED FOR THE PURPOSES OF SECTIONS 36(4)(B) AND 38(4)(B) OF THE 2006 ACT
Articles 3(1) and 5

3

The matters are—

(a) the behaviour or suspected behaviour of a passenger, member of crew or person involved in the supply chain of a freight movement, whether already undertaken or anticipated, and including any possible connection with another person held by that passenger, member of crew or person;

(b) the behaviour or suspected behaviour of a person connected or possibly connected to a passenger, member of crew or person involved in the supply chain of a freight movement, whether already undertaken or anticipated, and including any possible connection with another person held by him;

(c) any action taken, considered or planned in relation to a passenger, member of crew, person involved in the supply chain of a freight movement or any person connected or possibly connected to any of those persons by—

   (i) the Secretary of State in so far as he has functions under the Immigration Acts;

   (ii) a chief officer of police; or

   (iii) Her Majesty's Revenue and Customs.

IMMIGRATION (DISPOSAL OF PROPERTY) REGULATIONS 2008

(SI 2008/786)

Made: 20 March 2008.

Authority: UK Borders Act 2007, s 26(5), (6).

Commencement: 17 April 2008.

1 Citation, commencement and interpretation

These Regulations may be cited as the Immigration (Disposal of Property) Regulations 2008 and shall come into force on 17th April 2008.

2

In these Regulations—

    (a)   "the 2007 Act" means the UK Borders Act 2007.

3 Property to which these Regulations apply

These Regulations apply to property where—

    (a)   the owner has not been ascertained,

    (b)   an order under section 26(2) of the 2007 Act (disposal of property: court order) cannot be made because of subsection (4)(a) of that section, or

    (c)   a court has declined to make an order under section 26(2) of the 2007 Act on the grounds that the court is not satisfied of the matters specified in subsection (4)(b) of that section.

4 Restrictions on disposal of property

(1) Subject to regulation 5(2), property to which these Regulations apply, other than money—

    (a)   which has been the subject of a forfeiture order under section 25C of the Immigration Act 1971 (forfeiture of vehicle, ship or aircraft) or section 25 of the 2007 Act (forfeiture of detained property) shall not be disposed of until it has remained in the possession of the Secretary of State for six months beginning with the date on which the forfeiture order was made; and

    (b)   which has not been the subject of a forfeiture order under section 25C of the Immigration Act 1971 or section 25 of the 2007 Act shall not be disposed of until it has remained in the possession of the Secretary of State for a year.

(2) Money which is property to which these Regulations apply shall be paid into the Consolidated Fund as soon as is reasonably practicable.

5 Sale of property

(1) Subject to paragraph (2), after the expiration of the relevant period referred to in regulation 4, property to which these Regulations apply other than money may be sold.

(2) Where the property is a perishable article or its custody involves unreasonable expense or inconvenience it may be sold at any time.

(3) Subject to paragraph (4), the proceeds of all sales under these Regulations shall be paid into the Consolidated Fund as soon as is reasonably practicable.

(4) The Secretary of State may apply the proceeds of all sales under these Regulations, and any money which is property to which these Regulations apply, to defray reasonable expenses incurred in the conveyance, storage, and safe custody of

the property and in connection with its sale and otherwise in acting pursuant to these Regulations.

6 Retention of property

After the expiration of the relevant period referred to in regulation 4, if, in the opinion of the Secretary of State, property to which these Regulations apply (other than money) can be used in the course of, or in connection with, a function under the Immigration Acts, the Secretary of State may determine that the property is to be retained by her and the property shall vest in the Secretary of State on the making of the determination.

7 Other disposal of property in the public interest

If the Secretary of State is satisfied that the nature of any property to which these Regulations apply is such that it is not in the public interest that it should be sold or retained, it shall, after the expiration of the relevant period referred to in regulation 4, be destroyed or otherwise disposed of in accordance with the direction of the Secretary of State.

EMPLOYMENT AND SUPPORT ALLOWANCE REGULATIONS 2008

(SI 2008/794)

Made: 25 March 2008.

Authority: Social Security Administration Act 1992, s 5(1); Social Security Act 1998, s 21(1)(a); Welfare Reform Act 2007, ss 2–5, 8, 9, 11, 12, 14, 16–18, 20, 23, 24, Sch 1, Pts 1, 2, Sch 2.

Commencement: 27 October 2008.

PART 3
CONDITIONS OF ENTITLEMENT—CONTRIBUTORY ALLOWANCE

11 Condition relating to youth—residence or presence

(1) The prescribed conditions for the purposes of paragraph 4(1)(c) of Schedule 1 to the Act as to residence or presence in Great Britain are that the claimant—

(a)   is ordinarily resident in Great Britain;

(b)   is not a person subject to immigration control within the meaning of section 115(9) of the Immigration and Asylum Act or is a person to whom paragraph (3) applies;

(c)   is present in Great Britain; and

(d)   has been present in Great Britain for a period of, or for periods amounting in aggregate to, not less than 26 weeks in the 52 weeks immediately preceding the relevant benefit week.

(2) For the purposes of paragraph (1), a claimant is to be treated as being resident and present in Great Britain where the claimant is absent from Great Britain by reason only of being—

(a)   the spouse, civil partner, son, daughter, father, father-in-law, mother or mother-in-law of, and living with, a member of Her Majesty's forces who is abroad in that capacity;

(b)   in employment prescribed for the purposes of paragraph 7(1)(c) of Schedule 2 to the Act in connection with continental shelf operations; or

(c)   abroad in the capacity of being an aircraft worker or mariner.

(3) This paragraph applies where a person is—

(a)   a member of a family of a national of an European Economic Area state;

(b)   a person who is lawfully working in Great Britain and is a national of a State with which the [European Union] has concluded an agreement under [Article 217 of the Treaty on the Functioning of the European Union] providing, in the field of social security, for the equal treatment of workers who are nationals of the signatory State and their families;

(c)   a person who is a member of a family of, and living with, a person specified in sub-paragraph (b); or

(d)   a person who has been given leave to enter, or remain in, the United Kingdom by the Secretary of State upon an undertaking by another person or persons pursuant to the immigration rules within the meaning of the Immigration Act 1971 to be responsible for that person's maintenance and accommodation.

(4)   A person is to be treated as having satisfied the residence or presence conditions in paragraph (1) throughout a period of limited capability for work where those conditions are satisfied on the first day of that period of limited capability for work.

Amendment

Para (3): in sub-para (b) words "European Union" in square brackets substituted by SI 2011/1043, art 4(1).

Date in force: 22 April 2011: see SI 2011/1043, art 2; for transitional savings see art 3(3) thereof. Para (3): in sub-para (b) words "Article 217 of the Treaty on the Functioning of the European Union" in square brackets substituted by SI 2011/1043, art 5.

Date in force: 22 April 2011: see SI 2011/1043, art 2; for transitional savings see art 3(3) thereof.

IMMIGRATION (BIOMETRIC REGISTRATION) (OBJECTION TO CIVIL PENALTY) ORDER 2008

(SI 2008/2830)

Made: 29 October 2008.

Authority: UK Borders Act 2007, ss 10, 14.

Commencement: 25 November 2008.

1 Citation, commencement and interpretation

This Order may be cited as the Immigration (Biometric Registration) (Objection to Civil Penalty) Order 2008 and shall come into force on 25th November 2008.

2

In this Order—

"the Act" means the UK Borders Act 2007;

"working days" means any day other than a Saturday, a Sunday, Christmas Day, Good Friday or a day which is a bank holiday under the Banking and Financial Dealings Act 1971 in the part of the United Kingdom where a person objecting to a penalty under section 10 of the Act resides.

3 Required form and contents of a notice of objection

Where a penalty notice is given under section 9(1) of the Act, a notice of objection to the penalty notice under section 10(1) of the Act must be given on the form set out in the Schedule to this Order.

4

The form must be completed in English or Welsh.

5

The notice of objection must include—

(a)   the penalty notice reference number;

(b)   the full name of the person issued with the penalty notice;

(c)   that person's date of birth;

(d)   that person's current residential address including postcode;

(e)   that person's signature;

(f)   the date on which the person signed the notice of objection; and

(g)   a list of any supporting evidence provided with the notice of objection.

6

Where an appeal has been brought under section 11(1) of the Act, the notice of objection must state—

(a)   the name and address of the county court or sheriff to which the grounds for appeal were submitted;

(b)   the date that the appeal was submitted; and

(c)   any court reference number.

7 Period of time for giving a notice of objection

A notice of objection under section 10(1) of the Act must be given to the Secretary of State before the expiry of thirty working days beginning with the date specified on the penalty notice.

8 Period of time for Secretary of State to notify response to notice of objection

The Secretary of State shall notify the response to a notice of objection under section 10(4) of the Act before the expiry of thirty-three working days beginning with the date that the Secretary of State received the notice of objection.

IMMIGRATION (BIOMETRIC REGISTRATION) REGULATIONS 2008

(SI 2008/3048)

Made: 24 November 2008.

Authority: UK Borders Act 2007, ss 5, 6(3), 6(6), 7, 8, 15(1)(g).

Commencement: 25 November 2008.

Citation, commencement and interpretation

1

These Regulations may be cited as the Immigration (Biometric Registration) Regulations 2008 and shall come into force on the day after the day on which they are made.

[2

In these Regulations—

"Certificate of Travel" means a travel document issued in the United Kingdom at the discretion of the Secretary of State to persons who have been formally and, in the view of the Secretary of State, unreasonably refused a passport by their own authorities and who have—

(a)   been refused recognition as a refugee or as a stateless person but have been granted discretionary leave to remain or humanitarian protection; or

(b)   been granted indefinite leave to enter or remain;

"Convention travel document" means a travel document issued pursuant to Article 28 of the Geneva Convention;

"dependant" means a spouse, a civil partner, an unmarried or same sex partner, or a child;

"Geneva Convention" means the Convention relating to the Status of Refugees done at Geneva on 28th July 1951 and the New York Protocol of 31st January 1967;

"humanitarian protection" means protection granted in accordance with paragraph 339C of the immigration rules;

"immigration rules" means the rules for the time being laid down as mentioned in section 3(2) of the Immigration Act 1971;

"leave to remain" means limited or indefinite leave to remain in the United Kingdom given in accordance with the provisions of the Immigration Act 1971 or the immigration rules;

"refugee" means a person who falls within Article 1(A) of the Geneva Convention and to whom regulation 7 of the Refugee or Person in Need of International Protection (Qualification) Regulations 2006 does not apply;

"Stateless Convention" means the Convention relating to the Status of Stateless Persons done at New York on 28th September 1954; and

"Stateless Person's Travel Document" means a travel document issued pursuant to Article 28 of the Stateless Convention.]

Amendment

Substituted by SI 2012/594, regs 2, 3. Date in force: 29 February 2012: see SI 2012/594, reg 1(2).

[3 Requirement to apply for a biometric immigration document

(1)   Subject to paragraph (6), a person subject to immigration control must apply for the issue of a biometric immigration document where he—

(a)   satisfies the condition in paragraph (2); or

(b)   is a person falling within paragraph (3).

(2)   The condition is that whilst in the United Kingdom the person makes an application—

(a)   for limited leave to remain for a period which, together with any preceding period of leave to enter or remain, exceeds a cumulative total of 6 months leave in the United Kingdom;

(b)   for indefinite leave to remain;

(c)   to replace a stamp, sticker or other attachment in a passport or other document which indicated that he had been granted limited or indefinite leave to enter or remain in the United Kingdom;

(d)   to replace a letter which indicated that he had been granted limited or indefinite leave to enter or remain in the United Kingdom;

(e)   to be recognised as a refugee or a person in need of humanitarian protection;

(f)   to be recognised as a stateless person in accordance with Article 1 of the Stateless Convention;

(g)   for a Convention Travel Document, Stateless Person's Travel Document or a Certificate of Travel and does not already hold a valid biometric immigration document; or

(h)   as the dependant of a person who is making an application in accordance with sub-paragraph (a), (b), (e) or (f).

(3)   Subject to paragraph (4), a person falls within this paragraph if he has been notified on or after 1st December 2012 that the Secretary of State has decided to grant him—

> (a)   limited leave to remain for a period which, together with any preceding period of leave to enter or remain, exceeds a cumulative total of 6 months leave in the United Kingdom; or
>
> (b)   indefinite leave to remain.

(4) A person does not fall within paragraph (3) if—

> (a)   he was required to apply for a biometric immigration document in respect of his application for that leave; or
>
> (b)   he was required to apply for a biometric immigration document in respect of any application mentioned in paragraph (2).

(5) Where a person is required to apply for a biometric immigration document, that application must be made on the form or in the manner specified for that purpose (if one is specified) in the immigration rules.

(6) These Regulations do not apply to a person who applies for or is granted leave to remain in accordance with paragraphs 56R and 56U of the immigration rules (Olympic or Paralympic Games Family Member Visitor or an Olympic or Paralympic Games Family Member Child Visitor).]

Amendment

Substituted by SI 2012/594, regs 2, 4. Date in force: 29 February 2012: see SI 2012/594, reg 1(2).

4

(*Revoked by SI 2012/594, regs 2, 5. Date in force: 29 February 2012: see SI 2012/594, reg 1(2).*)

Power for an authorised person to require a person to provide biometric information

5

(1) Subject to regulation 7, where a person makes an application for the issue of a biometric immigration document in accordance with regulation 3, an authorised person may require him to provide a record of his fingerprints and a photograph of his face.

(2) Where an authorised person requires a person to provide biometric information in accordance with paragraph (1), the person must provide it.

Power for the Secretary of State to use and retain existing biometric information

6

(1) This regulation applies where—

> (a)   a person makes an application for the issue of a biometric immigration document in accordance with regulation 3; and
>
> (b)   the Secretary of State already has a record of the person's fingerprints or a photograph of the person's face in his possession (for whatever reason).

(2) Where this regulation applies the Secretary of State may use or retain that information for the purposes of these Regulations.

Provision in relation to persons under the age of sixteen

7

(1) A person under the age of sixteen ("the child") must not be required to provide a record of his fingerprints or a photograph of his face in accordance with regulation 5 except where the authorised person is satisfied that the fingerprints or the photograph will be taken in the presence of a person aged eighteen or over who is—

> (a)   the child's parent or guardian; or
>
> (b)   a person who for the time being takes responsibility for the child.

(2) The person mentioned in paragraph (1)(b) may not be—

    (a)   an officer of the Secretary of State who is not an authorised person;

    (b)   an authorised person; or

    (c)   any other person acting on behalf of an authorised person under regulation 8(2)(d).

(3) This regulation does not apply if the authorised person reasonably believes that the person who is to be fingerprinted or photographed is aged sixteen or over.

Process by which a person's fingerprints and photograph may be obtained and recorded

8

(1) An authorised person who requires a person to provide a record of his fingerprints or a photograph of his face under regulation 5 may require the person to submit to any process, or any combination of processes, specified in paragraph (2).

(2) An authorised person may—

    (a)   require a person to make an appointment before a specified date, which the person must attend, to enable a record of his fingerprints or a photograph of his face to be taken;

    (b)   specify the date, time and place for the appointment;

    (c)   specify any documents which the person must bring to the appointment, or action which the person must take, to confirm his appointment and identity; . . .

    [(d)   require a person to attend premises before a specified date where a record of his fingerprints or a photograph of his face is taken by a person on behalf of an authorised person; and

    (e)   specify any documents which the person must bring to the premises, or action which the person must take to confirm his identity.]

(3) An authorised person may require a record of fingerprints or photograph to be of a particular specification.

(4) Where an authorised person requires a person to submit to any process, or any combination of processes, in accordance with paragraph (1), the person must submit to it.

Amendment

Para (2): word omitted from sub-para (c) revoked and paras (d), (e) substituted for original para (d), by SI 2012/594, regs 2, 6. Date in force: 29 February 2012: see SI 2012/594, reg 1(2).

Use and retention of biometric information

9

Subject to regulations 10 and 11, the Secretary of State may use a record of a person's fingerprints or a photograph of a person's face provided in accordance with these Regulations—

    (a)   in connection with the exercise of a function by virtue of the Immigration Acts;

    (b)   in connection with the control of the United Kingdom's borders;

    (c)   in connection with the exercise of a function related to nationality;

    (d)   in connection with the prevention, investigation, or prosecution of an offence;

    (e)   for a purpose which appears to the Secretary of State to be required in order to protect national security;

    (f)   in connection with identifying victims of an event or situation which has caused loss of human life or human illness or injury;

(g)   for the purpose of ascertaining whether any person has failed to comply with the law or has gained, or sought to gain, a benefit or service, or has asserted an entitlement, to which he is not by law entitled.

10

Subject to regulation 11, any record of a person's fingerprints or his photograph, or any copy of them, held by the Secretary of State pursuant to these Regulations must be destroyed if the Secretary of State thinks it is no longer likely to be of use in accordance with regulation 9.

11

If a person proves that he is—

(a)   a British citizen; or

(b)   a Commonwealth citizen who has a right of abode in the United Kingdom as a result of section 2(1)(b) of the Immigration Act 1971 (statement of right of abode in the United Kingdom),

any record of the person's fingerprints or his photograph, or any copy of them, held by the Secretary of State pursuant to these Regulations must be destroyed as soon as reasonably practicable.

12

(1)   The Secretary of State must take all reasonably practicable steps to secure—

(a)   that data held in an electronic form which relate to any record of fingerprints or photograph which has to be destroyed in accordance with regulation 10 or 11 are destroyed or erased; or

(b)   that access to such data is blocked.

(2)   The person to whom the data relate is entitled, on written request, to a certificate issued by the Secretary of State to the effect that he has taken the steps required by paragraph (1).

(3)   A certificate issued under paragraph (2) must be issued within three months of the date on which the request was received by the Secretary of State.

Issue of a biometric immigration document

13

(1)   The Secretary of State may issue a biometric immigration document to a person who has applied in accordance with regulation 3, provided the Secretary of State has decided to—

[(a)   grant limited leave to remain to the person for a period which, together with any preceding period of leave to enter or remain, exceeds a cumulative total of 6 months leave in the United Kingdom; or

(b)   grant indefinite leave to remain to the person; or

(c)   issue or replace a document to the person following an application mentioned in regulation 3(2)(c), (d) or (g).]

(2)   A biometric immigration document begins to have effect on the date of issue.

(3)   A biometric immigration document ceases to have effect on one of the dates specified in paragraph (4), whichever date occurs earliest.

(4)   The specified dates are—

(a)   the date that the person's leave to remain ceases to have effect, including where the leave to remain is varied, cancelled or invalidated, or is to lapse;

(b)   in the case of a biometric immigration document which was issued to a person aged [sixteen] or over, the date after the expiry of ten years beginning with the date of issue; or

(c)   in the case of a biometric immigration document which was issued to a person aged under [sixteen], the date after the expiry of five years beginning with the date of issue.

Amendment

Para (1): sub-paras (a)–(c) substituted by SI 2012/594, regs 2, 7. Date in force: 29 February 2012: see SI 2012/594, reg 1(2).

Para (4): in sub-para (b) word "sixteen" in square brackets substituted by SI 2009/819, regs 2, 5.

Date in force: 31 March 2009: see SI 2009/819, reg 1(1); for savings see reg 9 thereof.

Para (4): in sub-para (c) word "sixteen" in square brackets substituted by SI 2009/819, regs 2, 5.

Date in force: 31 March 2009: see SI 2009/819, reg 1(1); for savings see reg 9 thereof.

Requirement to surrender documents connected with immigration and nationality

14

(1) On issuing the biometric immigration document, the Secretary of State may require the surrender of other documents connected with immigration or nationality.

(2) Where the Secretary of State requires the surrender of other documents, the person must comply with the requirement.

Content of a biometric immigration document

15

(1) A biometric immigration document may contain some or all of the following information on the face of the document—

    (a)   the title of the document;

    (b)   the document number;

    (c)   the name of the holder;

    (d)   the holder's date of birth;

    (e)   the holder's place of birth;

    (f)   the holder's nationality;

    (g)   the sex of the holder;

    (h)   the period of leave to remain which the person is granted;

    (i)   the class of leave to remain which the person is granted;

    (j)   any conditions to which the limited leave to remain is subject or remarks relating to those conditions;

    (k)   the place and date of issue of the document;

    (l)   the period for which the document is valid;

    (m)   the holder's facial image;

    (n)   the signature of the holder;

    (o)   a machine readable code;

    (p)   a hologram;

    (q)   an emblem of the United Kingdom and the words "United Kingdom";

    (r)   the symbol of the International Civil Aviation Organization denoting a machine readable travel document which contains a contactless microchip; and

    (s)   any additional security features.

(2) A biometric immigration document may contain some or all of the following within a radio frequency electronic microchip embedded in the document—

    (a)   any of the information specified in paragraph (1)(a) to (m);

    (b)   information relating to a record of any two of the holder's fingerprints; and

    (c)   any additional security features.

Surrender of a biometric immigration document

16

(1) The Secretary of State may require the surrender of a biometric immigration document as soon as reasonably practicable if he thinks that—

(a) information provided in connection with the document was or has become false, misleading or incomplete;

(b) the document (including any information recorded in it) has been altered, damaged or destroyed (whether deliberately or not);

(c) an attempt has been made (whether successfully or not) to copy the document or to do anything to enable it to be copied;

(d) the document should be re-issued (whether because the information recorded in it requires alteration or for any other reason);

(e) the holder's leave to remain is to be varied, cancelled or invalidated, or is to lapse;

(f) a person has acquired the biometric immigration document without the consent of the holder or of the Secretary of State;

(g) the document has ceased to have effect under regulation 13(3) or has been cancelled under regulation 17; . . .

(h) the holder has died;

[(i) the holder has failed to produce a valid passport or travel document when required to do so by an immigration officer; or

(j) the holder has proved that he is a British citizen or a Commonwealth citizen who has a right of abode in the United Kingdom as a result of section 2(1)(b) of the Immigration Act 1971 (statement of right of abode in the United Kingdom)].

(2) Where a person is required to surrender the biometric immigration document under paragraph (1), the person must comply with the requirement.

Amendment

Para (1): in sub-para (g) word omitted revoked by SI 2009/819, regs 2, 6(a).

Date in force: 31 March 2009: see SI 2009/819, reg 1(1).

Para (1): sub-paras (i), (j) inserted by SI 2009/819, regs 2, 6(b).

Date in force: 31 March 2009: see SI 2009/819, reg 1(1).

Cancellation of a biometric immigration document

17

The Secretary of State may cancel a biometric immigration document if he thinks that—

(a) information provided in connection with the document was or has become false, misleading or incomplete;

(b) the document has been lost or stolen;

(c) the document (including any information recorded in it) has been altered, damaged or destroyed (whether deliberately or not);

(d) an attempt has been made (whether successfully or not) to copy the document or to do anything to enable it to be copied;

(e) a person has failed to surrender the document when required to do so under regulation [16(a) to (f), (h), (i) or (j)];

(f) the document should be re-issued (whether because the information recorded in it requires alteration or for any other reason);

(g) a person has acquired the biometric immigration document without the consent of the holder or of the Secretary of State; . . .

(h) the holder has died[; or

(i) the holder has proved that he is a British citizen or a Commonwealth citizen who has a right of abode in the United Kingdom as a result of section 2(1)(b) of the Immigration Act 1971 (statement of right of abode in the United Kingdom)].

Amendment

In para (e) words "16(a) to (f), (h), (i) or (j)" in square brackets substituted by SI 2009/819, regs 2, 7(a).

Date in force: 31 March 2009: see SI 2009/819, reg 1(1).

In para (g) word omitted revoked by SI 2009/819, regs 2, 7(b).

Date in force: 31 March 2009: see SI 2009/819, reg 1(1).

Para (i) and word "; or" immediately preceding it inserted by SI 2009/819, regs 2, 7(c).

Date in force: 31 March 2009: see SI 2009/819, reg 1(1).

Requirement for the holder of a document to notify the Secretary of State

18

The holder of a biometric immigration document must notify the Secretary of State as soon as reasonably practicable if he—

(a) knows or suspects that information provided in connection with the document was or has become false, misleading or incomplete;

(b) knows or suspects that the document has been lost or stolen;

(c) knows or suspects that the document (including any information recorded in it) has been altered or damaged (whether deliberately or not);

(d) was given leave to enter or remain in the United Kingdom in accordance with a provision of the immigration rules and knows or suspects that owing to a change of his circumstances he would no longer qualify for leave under that provision; or

(e) knows or suspects that another person has acquired the biometric immigration document without his consent or the consent of the Secretary of State.

Requirement to apply for a replacement biometric immigration document

19

(1) A person who has been issued with a biometric immigration document under regulation 13(1) is required to apply for a replacement biometric immigration document where his original document—

(a) has been cancelled under [paragraphs (a) to (g) of] regulation 17; or

(b) has ceased to have effect under regulation 13(4)(b) or (c).

(2) A person required to apply for a biometric immigration document under paragraph (1) must do so within 3 months beginning with the date that the original document was cancelled or ceased to have effect.

Amendment

Para (1): in sub-para (a) words "paragraphs (a) to (g) of" in square brackets inserted by SI 2009/819, regs 2, 8.

Date in force: 31 March 2009: see SI 2009/819, reg 1(1).

Application of these Regulations to a person who is required to apply for a replacement biometric immigration document

20

(1) These Regulations apply to a person who makes an application for a biometric immigration document in accordance with regulation 19 just as they apply to a person who makes an application for a document in accordance with regulation 3, with the modification in paragraph (2).

(2) The Secretary of State may issue a biometric immigration document to a person who has applied in accordance with regulation 19, provided the person has limited leave to remain.

Requirement to use a biometric immigration document

21

(1) The holder of a biometric immigration document must provide his document to an immigration officer or the Secretary of State, as applicable,—

- (a) where he is examined by an immigration officer under paragraph 2, 2A or 3 of Schedule 2 to the Immigration Act 1971;
- (b) where he is examined by an immigration officer under Article 7(2) of the Immigration (Leave to Enter and Remain) Order 2000;
- (c) where he is examined by the Secretary of State under Article 3 of the Immigration (Leave to Enter) Order 2001;
- [(d) where he makes an application for entry clearance, leave to enter or leave to remain;
- (da) where he makes an application to be recognised as a refugee, as a person in need of humanitarian protection, or as a stateless person in accordance with Article 1 of the Stateless Convention;
- (db) where he applies as a dependant of a person who makes an application mentioned in sub-paragraph (d) or (da);
- (dc) where he makes an application for a Convention Travel Document, Stateless Person's Travel Document or a Certificate of Travel;]
- [(e) when his dependant makes an application—
  - (i) for entry clearance, leave to enter, leave to remain; or
  - (ii) to be recognised as a refugee, as a person in need of humanitarian protection, or as a stateless person in accordance with Article 1 of the Stateless Convention;]
- (f) when he is the sponsor under the immigration rules of a person who seeks entry clearance, leave to enter or leave to remain in the United Kingdom.

(2) Where the holder of a biometric immigration document attends premises to take a test known under the immigration rules as the "Life in the UK Test", he must provide his document to the representative of the educational institution, or other person, who is administering the test.

(3) The holder of a biometric immigration document must provide his document to a prospective employer or employer—

- (a) prior to the commencement of his employment; and
- (b) [where he has limited leave to remain,] on the anniversary of the date that the document was first produced, provided he is still working for that employer on that date.

[(4) Where the holder of a biometric immigration document makes—

- (a) an application for a certificate of entitlement under section 10 of the Nationality, Immigration and Asylum Act 2002 that a person has the right of abode in the United Kingdom;
- (b) an application for a letter or other document confirming a person's immigration or nationality status or that a person is not a British citizen;
- (c) an application for naturalisation as a British citizen under section 6(1) or (2) of the British Nationality Act 1981, or as a British overseas territories citizen under section 18(1) or (2) of that Act; or
- (d) an application for registration under any provision of the British Nationality Act 1981,

he must provide his biometric immigration document to the Secretary of State or a person acting on behalf of the Secretary of State in connection with that application.]

Amendment

Para (1): sub-paras (d), (da)–(c), for sub-para (d) as originally enacted, by SI 2012/594, reg 8(1), (2)(a). Date in force: 29 February 2012: see SI 2012/594, reg 1(2).

Para (1): sub-para (e) substituted by SI 2012/594, regs 2, 8(1), (2)(b). Date in force: 29 February 2012: see SI 2012/594, reg 1(2).

Para (3): in sub-para (b) words "where he has limited leave to remain," in square brackets inserted by SI 2012/594, regs 2, 8(1), (3). Date in force: 29 February 2012: see SI 2012/594, reg 1(2).

Para (4): inserted by SI 2012/594, regs 2, 8(1), (4). Date in force: 29 February 2012: see SI 2012/594, reg 1(2).

Requirement to provide information for comparison

22

(1) A person who provides a biometric immigration document in accordance with [regulation 21] is required to provide biometric information for comparison with biometric information provided in connection with the application for the document.

(2) Where the document is provided to an authorised person, the authorised person may require the provision of the information in a specified form.

(3) Regulation 8 applies to a person required to provide information under paragraph (1) as it applies to a person who is required to provide biometric information under regulation 5.

Amendment

Para (1): words "regulation 21" in square brackets substituted by SI 2012/594, regs 2, 9. Date in force: 29 February 2012: see SI 2012/594, reg 1(2).

[23 Consequences of a failure to comply with a requirement of these Regulations

(1) Subject to paragraphs (3) and (4), where a person who is required to make an application for the issue of a biometric immigration document fails to comply with a requirement of these Regulations, the Secretary of State—

    (a)   may take any, or any combination, of the actions specified in paragraph (2); and

    (b)   must consider giving a notice under section 9 of the UK Borders Act 2007.

(2) The actions specified are to—

    (a)   refuse an application for a biometric immigration document;

    (b)   treat the person's application for leave to remain as invalid;

    (c)   refuse the person's application for leave to remain; and

    (d)   cancel or vary the person's leave to enter or remain.

(3) Where a person is required to apply for a biometric immigration document under regulation 3(2)(a) or (b) or as a dependant of a person who has made an application in accordance with regulation 3(2)(a) or (b) and fails to comply with a requirement of these Regulations, the Secretary of State—

    (a)   must refuse the person's application for a biometric immigration document;

    (b)   must treat the person's application for leave to remain as invalid; and

    (c)   may cancel or vary the person's leave to enter or remain.

(4) Where a person is required to apply for a biometric immigration document under regulation 3(2)(e), (f) or (g) or as the dependant of a person who has made an application in accordance with regulation 3(2)(e) or (f) and fails to comply with a requirement of these Regulations the Secretary of State—

    (a)   may refuse the application for a biometric immigration document; and

(b)   must consider giving a notice under section 9 of the UK Borders Act 2007.

(5)   Where any person apart from a person referred to in paragraph (1), (3) or (4) fails to comply with a requirement of these Regulations, the Secretary of State must consider giving a notice under section 9 of the UK Borders Act 2007.

(6)   The Secretary of State may designate an adult as the person responsible for ensuring that a child complies with the requirements of these Regulations.]

Amendment

Substituted by SI 2012/594, regs 2, 10. Date in force: 29 February 2012: see SI 2012/594, reg 1(2).

Revocation and transitional provisions

24

(1)   Subject to paragraph (2), the Immigration (Biometric Registration) (Pilot) Regulations 2008 are revoked.

(2)   The Immigration (Biometric Registration) (Pilot) Regulations 2008 continue to apply to a person who was required to apply for a biometric immigration document in accordance with regulation 3 of those Regulations before the coming into force of these Regulations, subject to paragraph (3).

(3)   These Regulations apply to any application for leave to remain falling within regulation 3 of these Regulations, which is made by a person referred to in paragraph (2) on or after the coming into force of these Regulations.

IMMIGRATION (BIOMETRIC REGISTRATION) (CIVIL PENALTY CODE OF PRACTICE) ORDER 2008

(SI 2008/3049)

Made: 24 November 2008.

Authority: UK Borders Act 2007, ss 13(6), 14.

Commencement: 25 November 2008.

1 Citation and commencement

This Order may be cited as the Immigration (Biometric Registration) (Civil Penalty Code of Practice) Order 2008 and shall come into force on the day after the day on which it is made.

2 Coming into force of the Code of Practice

The code of practice entitled "Code of practice about the sanctions for non-compliance with the biometric registration regulations", laid before Parliament in draft on 11th June 2008, relating to the imposition of a penalty under section 9(1) of the UK Borders Act 2007, shall come into force on the day that this Order comes into force.

HEALTH IN PREGNANCY GRANT (ENTITLE-MENT AND AMOUNT) REGULATIONS 2008

(SI 2008/3108)

Made: 9 December 2008.

Authority: Social Security Contributions and Benefits Act 1992, ss 140A(1), (2), (4)–(6), 140B(1), 175; Immigration and Asylum Act 1999, s 155(3), (5).

Commencement: 1 January 2009.

4 Circumstances in which a woman is to be treated as not being in Great Britain or Northern Ireland - general

(1) For the purposes of section 140A(3)(b) of SSCBA, a woman is to be treated as not being in Great Britain if—

    (a)   she is not ordinarily resident in the United Kingdom, or

    (b)   she does not have a right to reside in the United Kingdom.

(2) For the purposes of section 136A of SSCB(NI)A, a woman is to be treated as not being in Northern Ireland if—

    (a)   she is not ordinarily resident in the United Kingdom, or

    (b)   she does not have a right to reside in the United Kingdom.

(3) A woman who is in the United Kingdom as a result of deportation, expulsion or other removal by compulsion of law from another country to the United Kingdom shall be treated as being ordinarily resident in the United Kingdom.

APPEALS (EXCLUDED DECISIONS) ORDER 2009

(SI 2009/275)

Made: 5 February 2009.

Authority: Tribunals, Courts and Enforcement Act 2007, ss 11(5)(f), 13(8)(f).

Commencement: 1 April 2009.

1 Citation and commencement

This Order may be cited as the Appeals (Excluded Decisions) Order 2009 and comes into force on 1st April 2009.

[2 Excluded decisions

For the purposes of section 11(1) of the Tribunals, Courts and Enforcement Act 2007, the following decisions of the First-tier Tribunal are excluded decisions—

    (a)   a decision under section 103 of the Immigration and Asylum Act 1999 (appeals); and

    (b)   a decision under paragraphs 22, 23, 24, 29, 30, 31, 32 and 33 of Schedule 2 to the Immigration Act 1971.]

Amendment

Substituted by SI 2010/41, arts 2, 3.

Date in force: 15 February 2010: see SI 2010/41, art 1.

3

For the purposes of sections 11(1) and 13(1) of the Tribunals, Courts and Enforcement Act 2007, the following decisions of the First-tier Tribunal or the Upper Tribunal are excluded decisions—

(a) any decision under section 20(7), (8B) or (8G)(b) (power to call for documents of taxpayer and others), 20B(1B) or (6) (restrictions on powers under sections 20 and 20A) or 20BB(2)(a) (falsification etc of documents) of the Taxes Management Act 1970;

(b) any decision under section 35A(2) (variation of undertakings), 79A(2) (variation of undertakings) or 219(1A) (power to require information) of the Inheritance Tax Act 1984;

(c) any decision under section 152(5) (notification of taxable amount of certain benefits) or 215(7) (advance clearance by Board of distributions and payments) of the Income and Corporation Taxes Act 1988;

(d) any decision under section 138(4) of the Taxation of Chargeable Gains Act 1992 (procedure for clearance in advance);

(e) any decision under section 187(5) or (6) (returns and information) of, or paragraph 3(2) or 6(2) of Schedule 21 (restrictions on powers under section 187) to, the Finance Act 1993;

(f) any decision under paragraph 91(5) of Schedule 15 to the Finance Act 2000 (corporate venturing scheme: advance clearance);

(g) any decision under paragraph 88(5) of Schedule 29 to the Finance Act 2002 (gains and losses from intangible fixed assets: transfer of business or trade);

(h) any decision under paragraph 2, 4, 7, 9, 10, 11 or 24 of Schedule 13 to the Finance Act 2003 (stamp duty land tax: information powers);

(i) any decision under section 306A (doubt as to notifiability), 308A (supplemental information), 313B (reasons for non-disclosure: supporting information) or 314A (order to disclose) of the Finance Act 2004;

(j) any decision under section 697(4) of the Income Tax Act 2007 (opposed notifications: determinations by tribunal);

(k) any decision under regulation 10(3) of the Venture Capital Trust (Winding up and Mergers) (Tax) Regulations 2004 (procedure for Board's approval);

(l) any decision under regulation 5A (doubt as to notifiability), 7A (supplemental information), 12B (reasons for non-disclosure: supporting information) or 12C (order to disclose) of the National Insurance Contributions (Application of Part 7 of the Finance Act 2004) Regulations 2007;

[(m) any procedural, ancillary or preliminary decision made in relation to an appeal against a decision under section 40A of the British Nationality Act 1981, section 82, 83 or 83A of the Nationality, Immigration and Asylum Act 2002, or regulation 26 of the Immigration (European Economic Area) Regulations 2006].

Amendment

Para (m) inserted by SI 2010/41, arts 2, 4. Date in force: 15 February 2010: see SI 2010/41, art 1.

4 Revocations

The Appeals (Excluded Decisions) Order 2008 and the Appeals (Excluded Decisions) (Amendment) Order 2008 are revoked.

IMMIGRATION AND ASYLUM ACT 1999 (PART V EXEMPTION: LICENSED SPONSORS TIERS 2 AND 4) ORDER 2009

(SI 2009/506)

Made: 6 March 2009.
Authority: Immigration and Asylum Act 1999, ss 84(4)(d), 166.
Commencement: 31 March 2009.

1 Citation and Commencement

This Order may be cited as the Immigration and Asylum Act 1999 (Part V Exemption: Licensed Sponsors Tiers 2 and 4) Order 2009 and shall come into force on 31 March 2009.

2 Interpretation

In this Order—

"the Act" means the Immigration and Asylum Act 1999;

"immediate family" means a Tier 2 or Tier 4 migrant's spouse, civil partner, unmarried partner, same sex partner, dependant child under 18 or parent of a Tier 4 (Child) Student;

"immigration advice" and "immigration services" have the same meanings as in section 82 of the Act;

"immigration rules" means rules made under section 3(2) of the Immigration Act 1971;

"licensed sponsor" means a person who has been granted a sponsor licence;

"Points-based system" means the Points-based system under Part 6A of the immigration rules;

"sponsor licence" means a licence granted by the Secretary of State to a person who, by virtue of such a grant, is licensed as a Sponsor under Tiers 2, 4 or 5 of the Points-based System;

"Tier 2 migrant" means a migrant who (i) makes an application of a kind identified in the immigration rules as requiring to be considered under "Tier 2" of the immigration rules' Points-based system or (ii) has been granted leave under the relevant paragraphs of the immigration rules;

"Tier 4 migrant" means a migrant who (i) makes an application of a kind identified in the immigration rules as requiring to be considered under "Tier 4" of the immigration rules' Points-based system or (ii) has been granted leave under the relevant paragraphs of the immigration rules;

3 Exemption of licensed sponsors

(1) Subject to paragraphs (2) and (3) and for the purposes of section 84(4)(d) of the Act the following persons shall be specified, namely persons who are licensed sponsors of Tier 2 and Tier 4 migrants and who provide immigration advice or immigration services free of charge to those migrants or their immediate family.

(2) The immigration advice or services given must be restricted to matters relating to the migrant's application under Tier 2 or Tier 4 of the Points-based system or to an application for entry clearance, leave to enter or leave to remain made by that person's immediate family and which is dependent on the migrant's application under Tier 2 or Tier 4 of the Points-based system.

(3) For the purposes of paragraph (1), the person providing the immigration advice or immigration services must be the licensed sponsor.

UK BORDER AGENCY (COMPLAINTS AND MISCONDUCT) REGULATIONS 2010

(SI 2010/782)

Made: 15 March 2010.

Authority: Police and Justice Act 2006, ss 41, 49(3).

Commencement: 7 April 2010.

Citation and commencement

1

(1) These Regulations may be cited as the UK Border Agency (Complaints and Misconduct) Regulations 2010 and shall come into force on the 7th April 2010.

Interpretation

2

(1) In these Regulations—

"2002 Act" means the Police Reform Act 2002;

"2009 Act" means the Borders, Citizenship and Immigration Act 2009;

"2009 Regulations" means UK Border Agency (Complaints and Misconduct) Regulations 2009;

"chief officer" has the meaning given in section 29 (interpretation of Part 2) of the 2002 Act;

"complainant" shall be construed in accordance with paragraph (7);

"complaint" has the meaning given by regulation 8 (complaints, matters and persons to which these Regulations apply);

"conduct" includes acts, omissions and statements (whether actual, alleged or inferred);

"conduct matter" has the meaning given by regulation 8;

"customs revenue contractor" means a contractor exercising specified enforcement functions in relation to customs revenue functions within the meaning of section 7 (customs revenue functions of the Director) of the 2009 Act;

"customs revenue official" means a person designated as a customs revenue official under section 11 (designation of customs revenue officials) of the 2009 Act;

"DSI matter" means a "death or serious injury matter" and has the meaning given by regulation 8;

"Director of Border Revenue" has the meaning given by section 6 (the Director of Border Revenue) of the 2009 Act;

"disciplinary proceedings" means any proceedings or management process during which the conduct of a relevant officer, relevant official of the Secretary of State, relevant contractor, official exercising customs revenue functions or customs revenue contractor is considered in order to determine whether a sanction or punitive measure should be imposed against that person in relation to that conduct;

"document" means anything in which information of any description is recorded;

"immigration decision" has the meaning given in section 82(2) (right of appeal: general) of the Nationality, Immigration and Asylum Act 2002;

"IPCC" means the Independent Police Complaints Commission and has the meaning given by section 9(1) (the Independent Police Complaints Commission) of the 2002 Act;

"official exercising customs revenue functions" means a customs revenue official or an official of the Secretary of State otherwise exercising customs revenue functions within the meaning of section 7 (customs revenue functions of the Director) of the 2009 Act;

"the person complained against", in relation to a complaint, means the person whose conduct is the subject-matter of the complaint;

"the person investigating", in relation to a complaint, recordable conduct matter or DSI matter, means the person appointed or designated to investigate that complaint or matter or part of that complaint or matter;

"recordable conduct matter" means—

(a)   a conduct matter that is required to be recorded by the relevant appropriate authority under regulation 17 (conduct matters arising in civil proceedings) or 18 (recording etc of conduct matters in other cases), or has been so recorded; or

(b)   any matter brought to the attention of the relevant appropriate authority under regulation 13 (initial handling and recording of complaints);

"relevant appropriate authority"—

(c)   in relation to any complaint, conduct matter, DSI matter or investigation under Part 5 of these Regulations relating to the conduct of

(i)   a relevant officer;

(ii)   a relevant official of the Secretary of State; or

(iii)   a relevant contractor

means the Secretary of State; and

(d)   in relation to any complaint, conduct matter, DSI matter or investigation under Part 5 of these Regulations relating to the conduct of

(i)   an official exercising customs revenue functions; or

(ii)   a customs revenue contractor

(iii)   means the Director of Border Revenue.

"relevant contractor" means—

(a)   a contractor exercising specified enforcement functions in relation to immigration or asylum; or

(b)   a contractor exercising specified enforcement functions in relation to general customs functions within the meaning of Part 1 of the 2009 Act.

"relevant officer" means an immigration officer exercising specified enforcement functions;

"relevant official of the Secretary of State" means—

(i)   an official of the Secretary of State exercising specified enforcement functions in relation to immigration or asylum; or

(ii)   an official of the Secretary of State exercising general customs functions within the meaning of Part 1 of the 2009 Act.

"serious injury" means a fracture, a deep cut, a deep laceration or an injury causing damage to an internal organ or the impairment of any bodily function, or as defined in IPCC guidance; and

"UKBA" means the UK Border Agency.

(2) In these Regulations "specified enforcement functions" means subject to paragraph (3)—

(a)   powers of entry;

(b)   powers to search persons and property;

(c)   powers to seize or detain property;

(d) powers to arrest persons;

(e) powers to detain persons;

(f) powers to examine persons or otherwise obtain information (including powers to take fingerprints or to acquire other personal data); and

(g) powers in connection with the removal of persons from the United Kingdom;

(h) and include the exercise of such functions in connection with any authorisation granted under Part 2 (surveillance and covert human intelligence sources) of the Regulation of Investigatory Powers Act 2000..

(3) The following shall not be regarded as an enforcement function—

(i) the making of an immigration decision;

(ii) the making of any decision to grant or refuse asylum; or

(iii) the giving of any direction to remove persons from the United Kingdom.

(4) In these Regulations, references to "the relevant officer", "the relevant official of the Secretary of State", the "relevant contractor", the "official exercising customs revenue functions" and the "customs revenue contractor" in relation to a DSI matter, mean the relevant officer, relevant official of the Secretary of State, relevant contractor, official exercising customs revenue functions and the customs revenue contractor:

(a) who arrested the person who has died or suffered serious injury,

(b) in whose custody that person was at the time of the death or serious injury, or

(c) with whom that person had the contact in question;

and where there is more than one such officer it means, subject to paragraph (5), the one who so dealt with that person last before the death or serious injury occurred.

(5) Where it cannot be determined which of two or more officers dealt with a person last before a death or serious injury occurred, the relevant officer, relevant official of the Secretary of State, relevant contractor, official exercising customs revenue functions or customs revenue contractor will be the most senior of them.

(6) In these Regulations, references to "the complainant" in relation to anything which is or purports to be a complaint, are references to a person referred to in regulation 8(1), except in relation to complaints made by a person referred to in regulation 8(1)(d) where the complainant will be the person on whose behalf the complaint or purported complaint was made.

(7) For the purposes of these Regulations, a person is adversely affected if that person suffers any form of loss or damage, distress or inconvenience, if that person is put in danger or if that person is otherwise unduly put at risk of being adversely affected.

(8) References in these Regulations to the investigation of any complaint or matter by the relevant appropriate authority on its own behalf, under the supervision of the IPCC, under the management of the IPCC or by the IPCC itself shall be construed as references to its investigation in accordance with regulations 37 (investigations by the relevant appropriate authority on its own behalf), 39 (investigations supervised by the IPCC), 40 (investigations by a police force under the management or under the supervision of the IPCC), 41 (investigations managed by the IPCC) or, as the case may be, 42 (investigations by the IPCC itself).

Application: general

3

(1) Subject to regulations 6 (general functions of the IPCC) and 72 (revocation of the 2009 Regulations, saving and transitional provisions), the IPCC shall have functions in relation to relevant officers, relevant officials of the Secretary of State, relevant contractors, officials exercising customs revenue functions and customs revenue contractors in, or in relation to, England and Wales.

(2) The IPCC shall not have functions in relation to the exercise of a function conferred on a relevant officer, an official of the Secretary of State exercising specified

enforcement functions in relation to immigration or asylum, or a relevant contractor exercising specified enforcement functions in relation to immigration or asylum by or under Part 8 (detention centres and detained persons) of the Immigration and Asylum Act 1999.

PART 1
COMPLAINTS AND MISCONDUCT

Application of the Police Reform Act 2002

4

(1) Sections 9 (the Independent Police Complaints Commission), 19 (use of investigatory powers by or on behalf of the IPCC), 22 (power of the IPCC to issue guidance), 23 (regulations), 24 (consultation on regulations) and 27 (conduct of the IPCC's staff) of the 2002 Act shall apply in relation to the relevant appropriate authority with the following modifications.

(2) In section 22 of the 2002 Act—

  (a)   for subsection (1) substitute—
  "(1)   The Commission may issue guidance to the relevant appropriate authority and any person it sees fit concerning the exercise or performance, by the persons to whom the guidance is issued, of any of the powers or duties specified in subsection (2).".

  (b)   In subsection (2), in paragraph (b)(iii)—
    (b)
      (iii)   for "persons serving with the police" substitute "relevant officers, relevant officials of the Secretary of State, relevant contractors, officials exercising customs revenue functions or customs revenue contractors".

  (c)   for subsection (3) substitute—
  "(3)   Before issuing any guidance under this section, the Commission shall consult the relevant appropriate authority and any person it sees fit.".

(3) In section 23 of the 2002 Act—

  (a)   In subsection (2)(k), for "a person serving with the police" substitute "a relevant officer, relevant official of the Secretary of State, relevant contractor, official exercising customs revenue functions or customs revenue contractor".

  (b)   In subsection (2)(n), for "[local policing bodies] and chief officers" substitute "the Secretary of State".

  (c)   In subsection (2)(p)—
    (i)   for "chief officers" substitute "the relevant appropriate authority"; and
    (ii)   for "them" substitute "it".

(4) In section 24 of the 2002 Act—

  (a)   At the end of paragraph (a) insert "and";
  (b)   Omit paragraphs (b) and (c).

Amendment

  Para (3): in sub-para (b) words "local policing bodies" in square brackets substituted by SI 2011/3058, reg 25(1), (2). Date in force: 16 January 2012: see SI 2011/3058, reg 1(2).

5

(1) Paragraph 6 (staff) of Schedule 2 (the Independent Police Complaints Commission) to the 2002 Act shall apply in relation to the relevant appropriate authority and the IPCC may make arrangements with the relevant appropriate authority under which persons are engaged on temporary service with the IPCC.

General functions of the IPCC

6

(1) The functions of the IPCC in relation to the relevant appropriate authority, shall be—

(a) to secure the maintenance by the IPCC itself, and by the relevant appropriate authority, of suitable arrangements with respect to the matters mentioned in paragraph (2);

(b) to keep under review all arrangements maintained with respect to those matters;

(c) to secure that arrangements maintained with respect to those matters comply with the requirements of the provisions of this Part, are efficient and effective and contain and manifest an appropriate degree of independence;

(d) to secure that public confidence is established and maintained in the existence of suitable arrangements with respect to those matters and with the operation of the arrangements that are in fact maintained with respect to those matters;

(e) to make such recommendations, and to give such advice, for the modification of the arrangements maintained with respect to those matters, as appear, from the carrying out by the IPCC of its other functions, to be necessary or desirable.

(2) Those matters are—

(a) the handling of complaints made about the conduct of relevant officers, relevant officials of the Secretary of State, relevant contractors, officials exercising customs revenue functions and customs revenue contractors which the relevant appropriate authority—

(i) has a duty to refer to the IPCC under regulation 21(1) (reference of complaints to the IPCC) of these Regulations or,

(ii) may refer to the IPCC under regulation 21(5) or (6) (reference of complaints to the IPCC) of these Regulations;

(b) the recording of matters from which it appears that—

(i) there may have been conduct by such persons which constitutes or involves the commission of a criminal offence or behaviour justifying disciplinary proceedings, and

(ii) that conduct or behaviour is conduct or behaviour which the relevant appropriate authority has a duty to refer to the IPCC under regulation 23(1) (reference of conduct matters to the IPCC) or may refer to the IPCC under regulation 23(4) or (5) of these Regulations;

(c) the recording of matters from which it appears that a person has died or suffered serious injury during, or following, contact with a relevant officer, relevant official of the Secretary of State, relevant contractor, official exercising customs revenue functions or customs revenue contractor;

(d) the manner in which any such complaints or any such matters as are mentioned in paragraph (b) or (c) are investigated or otherwise handled and dealt with.

(3) It shall be the duty of the IPCC—

(a) to exercise the powers and perform the duties conferred on it by the following provisions of these Regulations in the manner that it considers best calculated for the purpose of securing the proper carrying out of its functions under paragraph (1); and

(b)   to secure that arrangements exist which are conducive to, and facilitate, the reporting of misconduct by persons in relation to whose conduct the IPCC has functions.

(4)   In carrying out its functions under paragraph (1)(d) and (e) the IPCC shall only have regard to the following matters—

    (a)   the handling of complaints which—

        (i)   fall within regulation 21(1) of these Regulations;

        (ii)   the IPCC has notified the relevant appropriate authority it requires to be referred to the IPCC for its consideration; or

        (iii) the relevant appropriate authority has referred to the Commission on the grounds that it would be appropriate to do so by reason of—

           (aa)   the gravity of the subject matter of the complaint; or

           (bb)   any exceptional circumstances;

    (b)   the recording of conduct matters which—

        (i)   fall within regulation 23(1) of these Regulations;

        (ii)   the IPCC has notified the relevant appropriate authority it requires to be referred to the IPCC for its consideration;

        (iii) the relevant appropriate authority has referred to the IPCC on the grounds that it would be appropriate to do so by reason of—

           (aa)   the gravity of the subject matter of the complaint; or

           (bb)   any exceptional circumstances;

    (c)   the recording of a DSI matter; and

    (d)   the manner in which any such complaints or any such matters mentioned in paragraph (b) or (c) are investigated or otherwise handled and dealt with.

(5)   It shall be the duty of the IPCC—

    (a)   to exercise the powers and perform the duties conferred on it by the provisions of these Regulations in the manner that it considers best calculated for the purpose of securing the proper carrying out of its functions under paragraph (1); and

    (b)   to secure that arrangements exist which are conducive to, and facilitate, the reporting of misconduct by persons in relation to whose conduct the IPCC has functions.

(6)   It shall also be the duty of the IPCC to carry out its functions under paragraph (1) in relation to the following:

    (a)   any DSI matter;

    (b)   those complaints falling within paragraph 4(a);

    (c)   those conduct matters falling within paragraph 4(b);

    (d)   those complaints or recordable conduct matters which the IPCC has notified the relevant appropriate authority that it requires to be referred to the IPCC for its consideration;

    (e)   those complaints or recordable conduct matters that the relevant appropriate authority has referred to the IPCC on the grounds that it would be appropriate to do so by reason of—

        (i)   the gravity of the subject-matter of the complaint; or

        (ii)   any exceptional circumstances; and

    (f)   any matter that is subject to any of the appeal rights set out in Part 8 (appeals) of these Regulations.

(7)   It shall also be the duty of the IPCC—

    (a)   to enter into arrangements with the Chief Inspector of the UKBA for the purpose of securing co-operation, in the carrying out of their respective functions, between the Chief Inspector of the UKBA, Her Majesty's Chief

Inspector of Prisons, and the Prison and Probation Ombudsman in relation to the exercise of functions by relevant officials, relevant officers of the Secretary of State, relevant contractors, officials exercising customs revenue functions and customs revenue contractors; and

(b) to provide those persons with all such assistance and co-operation as may be required by those arrangements, or as otherwise appears to the IPCC to be appropriate, for facilitating the carrying out by those persons of their functions.

(8) Subject to the other provisions of these Regulations, the IPCC may do anything which appears to it to be calculated to facilitate, or is incidental or conducive to, the carrying out of its functions under these Regulations.

(9) The IPCC may, in connection with the making of any recommendation or the giving of any advice to any person for the purpose of carrying out its functions under paragraph (1)(c), (d) or (e), impose any such charge on that person for anything done by the IPCC for the purposes of, or in connection with, the carrying out of that function as it thinks fit.

(10) Nothing in these Regulations shall confer any function on the IPCC in relation to so much of any complaint or conduct matter as relates to the direction and control of a relevant officer, relevant official of the Secretary of State, relevant contractor, official exercising customs revenue functions or customs revenue contractor.

Reports to the Secretary of State

7

(1) As soon as practicable after the end of each of its financial years, the IPCC shall make a report to the Secretary of State on the carrying out of its functions under these Regulations during that year.

(2) The IPCC shall also make such reports to the Secretary of State about matters relating generally to the carrying out of its functions under these Regulations as the Secretary of State may, from time to time, require.

(3) The IPCC may, from time to time, make such other reports to the Secretary of State as it considers appropriate for drawing the Secretary of State's attention to matters which—

(a) have come to the IPCC's notice; and

(b) are matters that it considers should be drawn to the Secretary of State's attention by reason of their gravity or of other exceptional circumstances.

(4) The IPCC shall prepare such reports containing advice and recommendations as it thinks appropriate for the purpose of carrying out its function under regulation 6(1)(e) (general functions of the IPCC).

(5) Where the Secretary of State receives any report under this regulation, the Secretary of State shall—

(a) in the case of every annual report under paragraph (1), and

(b) in the case of any other report, if and to the extent that the Secretary of State considers it appropriate to do so,

lay a copy of the report before Parliament and cause the report to be published.

(6) The IPCC shall send a copy of every report under paragraph (1), (3) and (4) to the Secretary of State and the relevant appropriate authority.

(7) The IPCC shall send a copy of every report made or prepared by it under paragraphs (3) or (4) to such of the persons (in addition to those specified in the preceding paragraphs) who—

(a) are referred to in the report, or

(b) appear to the IPCC otherwise to have a particular interest in its contents, as the IPCC thinks fit.

Complaints, matters and persons to which these Regulations apply

8

(1) In these Regulations references to a complaint are references (subject to the following provisions of this regulation) to any complaint about the conduct of a relevant officer, relevant official of the Secretary of State, relevant contractor, official exercising customs revenue functions or customs revenue contractor which is made (whether in writing or otherwise) by—

    (a)   a member of the public who claims to be the person in relation to whom the conduct took place;

    (b)   a member of the public not falling within sub-paragraph (a) who claims to have been adversely affected by the conduct;

    (c)   a member of the public who claims to have witnessed the conduct;

    (d)   a person acting on behalf of a person falling within any of sub-paragraphs (a) to (c).

(2) In these Regulations "conduct matter" means (subject to the following provisions of this regulation and regulation 13(2) (initial handling and recording of complaints)) any matter which is not and has not been the subject of a complaint but in the case of which there is an indication (whether from the circumstances or otherwise) that a relevant officer, relevant official of the Secretary of State, relevant contractor, official exercising customs revenue functions or customs revenue contractor may have—

    (a)   committed a criminal offence; or

    (b)   behaved in a manner which would justify the bringing of disciplinary proceedings.

(3) In these Regulations "DSI matter" means any circumstances (other than those which are or have been the subject of a complaint or which amount to a conduct matter)—

    (a)   in or in consequence of which a person has died or has sustained serious injury; and

    (b)   in relation to which the requirements of either paragraph (4) or (5) are satisfied.

(4) The requirements of this paragraph are that at the time of the death or serious injury the person—

    (a)   had been arrested by a relevant officer, relevant official of the Secretary of State, relevant contractor, official exercising customs revenue functions or customs revenue contractor and had not been released from that arrest; or

    (b)   was otherwise detained in the custody of a relevant officer, relevant official of the Secretary of State, relevant contractor, official exercising customs revenue functions or customs revenue contractor.

(5) The requirements of this paragraph are that—

    (a)   at or before the time of the death or serious injury the person had contact (of whatever kind, and whether direct or indirect) with a relevant officer, relevant official of the Secretary of State, relevant contractor, official exercising customs revenue functions or customs revenue contractor; and

    (b)   there is an indication that the contact may have caused (whether directly or indirectly) or contributed to the death or serious injury.

(6) The complaints that are complaints for the purposes of these Regulations by virtue of paragraph (1)(b) do not, except in a case falling within paragraph (8), include any made by or on behalf of a person who claims to have been adversely affected as a consequence only of having seen or heard the conduct, or any of the alleged effects of the conduct.

(7) A case falls within this paragraph if—

(a)   it was only because the person in question was physically present, or sufficiently nearby, when the conduct took place or the effects occurred that the person was able to see or hear the conduct or its effects; or

(b)   the adverse effect is attributable to, or was aggravated by, the fact that the person in relation to whom the conduct took place was already known to the person claiming to have suffered the adverse effect.

(8) For the purposes of this regulation a person shall be taken to have witnessed conduct if, and only if—

(a)   the person's knowledge of that conduct was acquired in a manner which would make that person a competent witness capable of giving admissible evidence of that conduct in criminal proceedings; or

(b)   the person had possession or control of anything which would in any such proceedings constitute admissible evidence of that conduct.

(9) For the purposes of these Regulations a person falling within paragraph 1(a) to (c) shall not be taken to have authorised another person to act on that person's behalf unless—

(a)   the person so acting is for the time being designated for the purposes of this regulation by the IPCC as a person through whom complaints may be made, or is of a description of persons so designated; or

(b)   the person so acting has been given, and is able to produce, the written consent of the person on whose behalf the person is taking action.

Direction and control matters

9

(1) Nothing in these Regulations shall have effect with respect to so much of any complaint as relates to the direction and control of a relevant officer, relevant official of the Secretary of State, relevant contractor, official exercising customs revenue functions or customs revenue contractor.

(2) The Secretary of State may issue guidance to any person he sees fits about the handling of so much of a complaint as relates to the direction and control of a relevant officer, relevant official of the Secretary of State, relevant contractor, official exercising customs revenue functions or customs revenue contractor.

Co-operation, assistance and information

10

(1) It shall be the duty of the relevant appropriate authority, the Chief Inspector of the UKBA, Her Majesty's Chief Inspector of Prisons and Her Majesty's Inspectorate of Constabulary to ensure that they are kept informed, in relation to relevant officers, relevant officials of the Secretary of State, relevant contractors, officials exercising customs revenue functions and customs revenue contractors, about all matters falling within paragraph (2).

(2) Those matters are—

(a)   matters with respect to which any provision of these Regulations has effect;

(b)   anything which is done under or for the purposes of any such provision; and

(c)   any obligations to act or refrain from acting that have arisen by or under these Regulations but have not yet been complied with, or have been contravened.

(3) Where the relevant appropriate authority requires a chief officer to provide a member of his force for appointment under regulation 38 (investigation by a police force at the request of the relevant appropriate authority) or where the IPCC requires the chief officer to provide a member of his force for appointment under regulation 40

(investigation by a police force under the management or under the supervision of the IPCC), it shall be the duty of the chief officer to whom the requirement is addressed to comply with it.

(4)   It shall be the duty of the Secretary of State, the relevant appropriate authority, a [local policing body] maintaining a police force within which a person is appointed under regulation 38 or 40 and the chief officer of a police force appointed under regulation 38 or 40 to provide—

(a)   the IPCC and every member of the IPCC's staff with all such assistance and co-operation as the IPCC or that member of staff may reasonably require for the purposes of, or in connection with, the carrying out of any investigation by the IPCC under these Regulations; and

(b)   the relevant appropriate authority and every member of the relevant appropriate authority's staff with all such assistance and co-operation as the relevant appropriate authority or those members of staff may reasonably require for the purposes of, or in connection with, the carrying out of any investigation by the relevant appropriate authority under these Regulations.

(5)   It shall be the duty of the relevant appropriate authority to ensure that a person appointed under regulations 38, 39 (investigations supervised by the IPCC), 40, 41 (investigations managed by the IPCC) and 42 (investigations by the IPCC itself) to carry out an investigation or part of an investigation is given all such assistance and co-operation in the carrying out of that investigation as that person may reasonably require.

Amendment

Para (4): words "local policing body" in square brackets substituted by SI 2011/3058, reg 25(1), (3). Date in force: 16 January 2012: see SI 2011/3058, reg 1(2).

Payment for assistance with investigations

11

(1)   This regulation applies where—

(a)   a police force is required to provide assistance in connection with an investigation under Part 5 of these Regulations (investigations);

(b)   a police force is required to provide the IPCC with assistance in connection with an investigation; or

(c)   a police force provides assistance by agreement under regulation 38(2) (investigation by a police force at the request of the relevant appropriate authority)or 40(2) (investigation by a police force under the management or under the supervision of the IPCC) of these Regulations.

(2)   For the purposes of this regulation assistance is required to be provided by a police force in connection with an investigation under Part 5 of these Regulations if the chief officer of that force complies with a requirement under regulation 10(4) (co-operation, assistance and information) that is made in connection with—

(i)   an investigation relating to the conduct of a person who, at the time of the conduct, was a relevant officer, relevant official of the Secretary of State, relevant contractor, official exercising customs revenue functions, or customs revenue contractor; or

(ii)   an investigation of a DSI matter in relation to which the person being investigated was, at the time of the death or serious injury, a relevant officer, relevant official of the Secretary of State, relevant contractor, official exercising customs revenue functions or customs revenue contractor.

(3)   Where the assistance is required to be provided by a police force to a relevant appropriate authority it shall pay to the [local policing body] maintaining that force such contribution towards the costs of the assistance—

- (a) as may be agreed between them; or
- (b) in the absence of an agreement, as may be determined in accordance with any arrangements which—
  - (i) have been agreed to by [local policing bodies] generally and the Secretary of State; and
  - (ii) are for the time being in force with respect to the making of contributions towards the costs of assistance provided, in connection with investigations under Part 5 of these Regulations; or
- (c) in the absence of any such arrangements, as may be determined by the Secretary of State.

(4) Paragraph (3) shall have effect in relation to assistance which a police force provides by agreement under regulation 38(2) or 40(2) as if the reference in that subsection to required to be provided were a reference to provided by agreement under regulation 38(2) or 40(2).

(5) Where the assistance is required to be provided by a police force to the IPCC, it shall pay to the [local policing body] maintaining that force such contribution (if any) towards the costs of the assistance—

- (a) as may be agreed between the IPCC and that authority; or
- (b) in the absence of an agreement, as may be determined in accordance with any arrangements which—
  - (i) have been agreed to by [local policing bodies] generally and by the IPCC; and
  - (ii) are for the time being in force with respect to the making of contributions towards the costs of assistance provided, in connection with investigations under this Part, to the IPCC; or
- (c) in the absence of any such arrangements, as may be determined by the Secretary of State.

Amendment

Paras (3), (5): words in square brackets substituted by SI 2011/3058, reg 25(1), (4). Date in force: 16 January 2012: see SI 2011/3058, reg 1(2).

PART 2
HANDLING OF COMPLAINTS AND CONDUCT MATTERS ETC

Duties to preserve evidence relating to complaints

12

(1) Where—

- (a) a complaint is made to the relevant appropriate authority about the conduct of a relevant officer, relevant official of the Secretary of State, relevant contractor, official exercising customs revenue functions or customs revenue contractor; or
- (b) the relevant appropriate authority becomes aware that a complaint about the conduct of a relevant officer, relevant official of the Secretary of State, relevant contractor, official exercising customs revenue functions or customs revenue contractor has been made to the IPCC,

the relevant appropriate authority shall take all such steps as appear to the relevant appropriate authority to be appropriate for the purposes of these Regulations for obtaining and preserving evidence relating to the conduct complained of.

(2) The duty of the relevant appropriate authority under paragraph (1) must be performed as soon as practicable after the complaint is made or, as the case may be, the relevant appropriate authority becomes aware of it.

(3) After that, the relevant appropriate authority shall be under a duty, until satisfied that it is no longer necessary to do so, to continue to take the steps which from time to

time appear to the relevant appropriate authority to be appropriate for the purposes of these Regulations for obtaining and preserving evidence relating to the conduct complained of.

(4)   It shall be the duty of the relevant appropriate authority to take all such specific steps for obtaining or preserving evidence relating to any conduct that is the subject-matter of a complaint as the relevant appropriate authority may be directed to take for the purposes of this regulation by the IPCC.

Initial handling and recording of complaints

13

(1)   Where a complaint is made to the IPCC—

    (a)   it shall ascertain whether the complainant is content for the relevant appropriate authority to be notified of the complaint; and

    (b)   it shall give notification of the complaint to the relevant appropriate authority if the complainant is so content.

(2)   Where the IPCC—

    (a)   is prevented by paragraph (1) from notifying any complaint to the relevant appropriate authority, and

    (b)   considers that it is in the public interest for the subject-matter of the complaint to be brought to the attention of the relevant appropriate authority and recorded under regulation 20 (recording and reference of conduct matters),

the IPCC may bring that matter to the relevant appropriate authority's attention under that regulation as if it were a recordable conduct matter, and (if it does so) the following provisions of these Regulations shall have effect accordingly as if it were such a matter.

(3)   Where the IPCC, or relevant appropriate authority gives notification of a complaint under paragraphs (1) or (2) or the IPCC brings any matter to the relevant appropriate authority's attention under paragraph (4), the person who gave the notification, or, as the case may be, the IPCC shall notify the complainant—

    (a)   that the notification has been given and of what it contained; or

    (b)   that the matter has been brought to the relevant appropriate authority's attention to be dealt with otherwise than as a complaint.

(4)   Where a matter is brought to the relevant appropriate authority's attention, the relevant appropriate authority shall record the complaint.

(5)   Nothing in this regulation shall require the notification or recording by any person of any complaint about any conduct if—

    (a)   that person is satisfied that the subject-matter of the complaint has been, or is already being, dealt with by means of criminal or disciplinary proceedings against the person whose conduct it was; or

    (b)   the complaint has been withdrawn.

Keeping of records

14

(1)   The relevant appropriate authority shall keep records, in such form as the IPCC shall determine, of—

    (a)   every complaint and purported complaint that is made to the relevant appropriate authority;

    (b)   every conduct matter recorded by the relevant appropriate authority under regulation 17(3) (conduct matters arising in civil proceedings); and

    (c)   every DSI matter recorded by the relevant appropriate authority under regulation 25 (duty to record DSI matters).

Failures to notify or record a complaint

15

(1)   This regulation applies where anything which is or purports to be a complaint has effect as being received by the relevant appropriate authority (whether in consequence of having been made directly to the relevant appropriate authority or by way of a notification under regulation 13(1) (initial handling and recording of complaints)).

(2)   If the relevant appropriate authority decides not to take action under regulation 13 for notifying or recording the whole or any part of what has been received, the relevant appropriate authority shall notify the complainant of the following matters—

    (a)   the decision to take no action and, if that decision relates to only part of what was received, the part in question;

    (b)   the grounds on which the decision was made; and

    (c)   whether the complainant has a right to appeal against that decision under this regulation.

(3)   The complainant shall have a right of appeal to the IPCC against any failure by the relevant appropriate authority to make a determination under regulation 13 or to notify or record anything under that regulation if the failure is in respect of conduct which the relevant appropriate authority is required to refer to the IPCC under regulation 21(1)(a) or (b) (reference of complaints to the IPCC).

(4)   On an appeal under this regulation, the IPCC shall—

    (a)   determine whether any action under regulation 13 should have been taken in the case in question; and

    (b)   if the IPCC finds in the complainant's favour, give such directions as the IPCC considers appropriate to the relevant appropriate authority as to the action to be taken for making a determination, or for notifying or recording what was received;

and it shall be for the relevant appropriate authority to comply with any directions given under sub paragraph (b).

(5)   Directions under paragraph (4)(b) may require action taken in pursuance of the directions to be treated as taken in accordance with any such provision of regulation 13 as may be specified in the direction.

(6)   The IPCC—

    (a)   shall give notification to the relevant appropriate authority and the complainant of any determination made by it under this regulation; and

    (b)   shall give notification to the complainant of any direction given by it under this regulation to the relevant appropriate authority.

Handling of complaints by the relevant appropriate authority

16

(1)   This regulation applies where a complaint has been recorded by the relevant appropriate authority unless the complaint—

    (a)   is one which has been, or must be, referred to the IPCC under regulation 21 (reference of complaints to the IPCC); and

    (b)   is not for the time being either referred back to the authority under regulation 22 (duties of the IPCC on references under regulation 21) or the subject of a determination under regulation 31 (power of the IPCC to determine the form of an investigation).

(2)   The relevant appropriate authority shall not be required by virtue of any provisions of this regulation to take any action in relation to the complaint but may handle the complaint in whatever manner it thinks fit or take no action in relation to the complaint.

Conduct matters arising in civil proceedings

17

(1) This regulation applies where—

    (a)   the relevant appropriate authority has received notification (whether or not under this regulation) that civil proceedings relating to any matter have been brought by a member of the public against the Secretary of State or the Director of Border Revenue, or it otherwise appears to the relevant appropriate authority that such proceedings are likely to be so brought; and

    (b)   it appears to the relevant appropriate authority (whether at the time of the notification or at any time subsequently) that those proceedings involve or would involve a conduct matter.

(2) Where the relevant appropriate authority becomes aware that those proceedings involve or would involve a conduct matter, the relevant appropriate authority shall record that matter.

(3) Where the relevant appropriate authority records any matter under this regulation it—

    (a)   shall first determine whether the matter is one which it is required to refer to the IPCC under regulation 23 (reference of conduct matters to the IPCC) or is one which it would be appropriate to so refer; and

    (b)   if it is not required so to refer the matter and does not do so, may deal with the matter in such other manner (if any) as it may determine.

(4) Nothing in paragraph (3) shall require the relevant appropriate authority to record any conduct matter if it is satisfied that the matter has been, or is already being, dealt with by means of criminal or disciplinary proceedings against the person to whose conduct the matter relates.

(5) For the purposes of this regulation civil proceedings involve a conduct matter if—

    (a)   they relate to such a matter; or

    (b)   they are proceedings that relate to a matter in relation to which a conduct matter, or evidence of a conduct matter, is or may be relevant.

Recording etc of conduct matters in other cases

18

(1) Where—

    (a)   a conduct matter comes (otherwise than as mentioned in regulation 17 (conduct matters arising in civil proceedings)) to the attention of the relevant appropriate authority; and

    (b)   it appears to the relevant appropriate authority that the conduct involved in that matter falls within paragraph (2)

it shall be the duty of the relevant appropriate authority to record that matter.

(2) Conduct falls within this paragraph if (assuming it to have taken place)—

    (a)   it appears to have resulted in the death of any person or in serious injury to any person; or

    (b)   it is of a description specified in paragraph (3).

(3) The following descriptions of conduct are specified for the purposes of paragraph (2)—

    (a)   a serious assault, as defined in guidance issued by the IPCC;

    (b)   a serious sexual offence, as defined in guidance issued by the IPCC;

    (c)   serious corruption, as defined in guidance issued by the IPCC;

    (d)   a criminal offence or behaviour aggravated by discriminatory behaviour on the grounds of a person's race, sex, religion, or other status identified in guidance by the IPCC;

(e)   a complaint which refers to an allegation of an infringement of Article 2 or 3 of the European Convention on Human Rights;

(f)   conduct whose gravity or other exceptional circumstances make it appropriate to record the matter in which the conduct is involved; or

(g)   conduct which is alleged to have taken place in the same incident as one in which conduct within sub-paragraph (a) to (e) is alleged.

(4)   Where the relevant appropriate authority records any matter under this regulation it—

(a)   shall first determine whether the matter is one which it is required to refer to the IPCC under regulation 23 (reference of conduct matters to the IPCC) or is one which it would be appropriate to so refer; and

(b)   if it is not required so to refer the matter and does not do so, may deal with the matter in such other manner (if any) as it may determine.

(5)   Nothing in paragraph (1) shall require the relevant appropriate authority to record any conduct matter if it is satisfied that the matter has been, or is already being, dealt with by means of criminal or disciplinary proceedings against the person to whose conduct the matter relates.

(6)   If it appears to the IPCC—

(a)   that any matter that has come to its attention is a recordable conduct matter, but

(b)   that that matter has not been recorded by the relevant appropriate authority,

the IPCC may direct the relevant appropriate authority to record that matter; and it shall be the duty of that authority to comply with the direction.

Duties to preserve evidence relating to conduct matters

19

(1)   Where the relevant appropriate authority becomes aware of any recordable matter relating to the conduct of a relevant officer, relevant official of the Secretary of State, relevant contractor, official exercising customs revenue functions or customs revenue contractor, it shall be its duty to take all such steps as appear to it to be appropriate for the purposes of these Regulations for obtaining and preserving evidence relating to that matter.

(2)   The duty of the relevant appropriate authority under paragraph (1) must be performed as soon as practicable after it becomes aware of the matter in question.

(3)   After that, the relevant appropriate authority shall be under a duty until it is satisfied that it is no longer necessary to do so, to continue to take the steps from time to time appearing to it to be appropriate for the purposes of these Regulations for obtaining and preserving evidence relating to the matter.

(4)   It shall be the duty of the relevant appropriate authority to take all such specific steps for obtaining or preserving evidence relating to any recordable conduct matter as they may be directed to take for the purposes of these Regulations by the IPCC.

PART 3
REFERRAL OF MATTERS TO THE IPCC

Recording and reference of conduct matters

20

(1)   Any conduct matter which is required to be referred to the IPCC shall be referred in such manner as the IPCC specifies and—

(a)   if the matter falls within paragraph (1)(a) or (b) of regulation 23 (reference of conduct matters to the IPCC), not later than the end of the day following the day on which it first becomes clear to the relevant appropriate authority that the conduct matter is one to which that paragraph applies, and

(b) if the matter falls within paragraph (1)(c) of regulation 23, not later than the end of the day following the day on which the IPCC notifies the relevant appropriate authority that the conduct matter is to be referred.

(2) Any DSI matter which is required to be referred to the IPCC shall be referred in such manner as the IPCC specifies and—

(a) in a case where the IPCC directs that the matter be referred to it, within time limits defined in guidance issued by the IPCC, but no later than the day on which the IPCC so directs;

(b) in any other case, within time limits defined in guidance issued by the IPCC, but no later than the day on which the matter first comes to the attention of the relevant appropriate authority.

Reference of complaints to the IPCC

21

(1) Where the complaint is—

(a) one alleging that the conduct complained of has resulted in death or serious injury;

(b) any complaint not falling within paragraph (a) but alleging conduct which constitutes—

(i) a serious assault, as defined in guidance issued by the IPCC;

(ii) a serious sexual offence, as defined in guidance issued by the IPCC;

(iii) serious corruption, as defined in guidance issued by the IPCC;

(iv) a criminal offence aggravated by discriminatory behaviour on the grounds of a person's race, sex, religion, or other status identified in guidance by the IPCC;

(v) a complaint which refers to an allegation of an infringement of Article 2 or 3 of the European Convention on Human Rights; or

(c) which arises from the same incident as one in which any conduct falling within paragraph (a) or (b) is alleged; or

(d) one in respect of which the IPCC notifies the relevant appropriate authority that it requires the complaint in question to be referred to the IPCC for its consideration,

it shall be the duty of the relevant appropriate authority to refer the complaint to the IPCC.

(2) In a case where there is no obligation under paragraph (1) to make a reference, the relevant appropriate authority may refer a complaint to the IPCC if that authority considers that it would be appropriate to do so by reason of—

(a) the gravity of the subject-matter of the complaint; or

(b) any exceptional circumstances.

(3) Where a complaint is required to be referred to the IPCC under paragraph (1)(a) or (b), notification of the complaint shall be given to the IPCC—

(a) not later than the end of the day following the day on which it first becomes clear to the relevant appropriate authority that the complaint is one to which that sub-paragraph applies, and

(b) in such manner as the IPCC specifies.

(4) Where a complaint is required to be referred to the IPCC under paragraph (1)(d), notification of the complaint shall be given to the IPCC—

    (a)   not later than the end of the day following the day on which the IPCC notifies the relevant appropriate authority that the complaint is to be referred, and

    (b)   in such manner as the IPCC specifies.

(5) Subject to paragraph (7), the following powers—

    (a)   the power of the IPCC by virtue of paragraph (1)(d) to require a complaint to be referred to it, and

    (b)   the power of the relevant appropriate authority to refer a complaint to the IPCC under paragraph (2),

shall each be exercisable at any time irrespective of whether the complaint is already being investigated by any person or has already been considered by the IPCC.

(6) Where the relevant appropriate authority refers a complaint to the IPCC under this regulation the relevant appropriate authority shall give a notification of the making of the reference—

    (a)   to the complainant, and

    (b)   except in a case where it appears to the relevant appropriate authority that to do so might prejudice a possible future investigation of the complaint, to the person complained against.

(7) A complaint that has already been referred to the IPCC under this regulation on a previous occasion—

    (a)   shall not be required to be referred again under this regulation unless the IPCC so directs; and

    (b)   shall not be referred in exercise of any power conferred by this regulation unless the IPCC consents.

(8) Where a complaint is required to be referred to the IPCC under paragraph (1)(d), notification of the complaint shall be given to the IPCC—

    (a)   not later than the end of the day following the day on which the IPCC notifies the relevant appropriate authority that the complaint is to be referred, and

    (b)   in such manner as the IPCC specifies.

Duties of the IPCC on references under regulation 21

22

(1) It shall be the duty of the IPCC in the case of every complaint referred to it by the relevant appropriate authority, to determine whether or not it is necessary for the complaint to be investigated.

(2) Where the IPCC determines under this regulation that it is not necessary for a complaint to be investigated, it may, if it thinks fit, refer the complaint back to the relevant appropriate authority in accordance with paragraph (3).

(3) In a case to which paragraph (2) applies the relevant appropriate authority shall not be required by virtue of any provisions of these Regulations to take any action in relation to the complaint but may handle the complaint in whatever manner it thinks fit, or take no action in relation to the complaint.

(4) Where the IPCC refers a complaint back under paragraph (2), it shall give a notification of the making of the reference back—

    (a)   to the complainant, and

    (b)   to the person complained against.

Reference of conduct matters to the IPCC

23

(1) It shall be the duty of the relevant appropriate authority to refer a recordable conduct matter to the IPCC if, (whether or not falling within regulation 18 (recording etc of conduct matters in other cases))—

(a)   that matter relates to any incident or circumstances in or in consequence of which any person has died or suffered serious injury which has not been previously reported as a DSI matter;

(b)   that matter is of a description specified in paragraph (2); or

(c)   the IPCC notifies the relevant appropriate authority that it requires that matter to be referred to the IPCC for its consideration.

(2)   Any matter which relates to conduct falling within the following descriptions is specified for the purposes of paragraph (1)(b)—

(a)   a serious assault, as defined in guidance issued by the IPCC;

(b)   a serious sexual offence, as defined in guidance issued by the IPCC;

(c)   serious corruption, as defined in guidance issued by the IPCC;

(d)   a criminal offence or behaviour which is liable to lead to a disciplinary sanction and which in either case was aggravated by discriminatory behaviour on the grounds of a person's race, sex, religion, or other status identified in guidance by the IPCC;

(e)   a complaint which refers to an allegation of an infringement of Article 2 or 3 of the European Convention on Human Rights;

(f)   conduct whose gravity or other exceptional circumstances make it appropriate to record the matter in which the conduct is involved; or

(g)   conduct which is alleged to have taken place in the same incident as one in which conduct with sub-paragraphs (a) to (e) is alleged.

(3)   The obligation on the relevant appropriate authority under paragraph (1)(a) or (1)(b) to refer a recordable conduct matter arises only if it is satisfied that the matter is one in respect of which there is an indication that the person may have—

(a)   committed a criminal offence; or

(b)   behaved in a manner which would justify the bringing of disciplinary proceedings and that such behaviour (if it had taken place) would be likely to lead to the termination of that person's office or employment.

(4)   In any case where there is no obligation under paragraph (1) to make a reference, the relevant appropriate authority may refer a recordable conduct matter to the IPCC if that authority considers that it would be appropriate to do so by reason of—

(a)   the gravity of the matter; or

(b)   any exceptional circumstances.

(5)   Where there is an obligation under this regulation to refer any matter to the IPCC, it must be so referred within such period as may be provided for in these Regulations.

(6)   The following powers—

(a)   the power of the IPCC by virtue of paragraph (1)(c) to require a matter to be referred to it, and

(b)   the power of the relevant appropriate authority to refer any matter to the IPCC under paragraph (3) or (4),

shall each be exercisable at any time irrespective of whether the matter is already being investigated by any person or has already been considered by the IPCC.

(7)   Where—

(a)   the relevant appropriate authority refers a matter to the IPCC under this regulation and

(b)   the relevant appropriate authority does not consider that to do so might prejudice a possible future investigation of that matter,

it shall give a notification of the making of the reference to the person to whose conduct that matter relates.

(8)   A matter that has already been referred to the IPCC under this regulation on a previous occasion—

(a) shall not be required to be referred again under this regulation unless the IPCC so directs; and

(b) shall not be referred in exercise of any power conferred by this regulation unless the IPCC consents.

Duties of the IPCC on references under regulation 23

24

(1) It shall be the duty of the IPCC, in the case of every recordable conduct matter referred to it by the relevant appropriate authority under regulation 23 (reference of conduct matters to the IPCC), to determine whether or not it is necessary for the matter to be investigated.

(2) Where the IPCC determines under this regulation that it is not necessary for a recordable conduct matter referred by the relevant appropriate authority to be investigated, it may if it thinks fit refer the matter back to the relevant appropriate authority to be dealt with by that person in such manner (if any) as that person or they may determine.

(3) Where—

(a) the IPCC refers a matter back to the relevant appropriate authority under this regulation, and

(b) the IPCC does not consider that to do so might prejudice a possible future investigation of that matter,

the IPCC shall give a notification of the making of the reference to the person to whose conduct that matter relates.

PART 4
HANDLING DSI MATTERS

Duty to record DSI matters

25

(1) Where a DSI matter comes to the attention of the relevant appropriate authority, it shall be its duty to record that matter.

(2) If it appears to the IPCC—

(a) that any matter that has come to its attention is a DSI matter, but

(b) that that matter has not been recorded by the relevant appropriate authority,

the IPCC may direct the relevant appropriate authority to record that matter; and it shall be the duty of that authority to comply with the direction.

Duty to preserve evidence relating to DSI matters

26

(1) Where a DSI matter comes to the attention of the relevant appropriate authority, it shall be its duty to take all such steps as appear to it to be appropriate for the purposes of these Regulations for obtaining and preserving evidence relating to that matter.

(2) The relevant appropriate authority's duty under paragraph (1) must be performed as soon as practicable after it becomes aware of the matter in question.

(3) After that, it shall be under a duty, until it is satisfied that it is no longer necessary to do so, to continue to take the steps from time to time appearing to it to be appropriate for the purposes of these Regulations for obtaining and preserving evidence relating to the matter.

(4) It shall be the duty of the relevant appropriate authority to take all such specific steps for obtaining or preserving evidence relating to any DSI matter as they may be directed to take for the purposes of this regulation by the IPCC.

Reference of DSI matters to the IPCC

27

(1) It shall be the duty of the relevant appropriate authority to refer a DSI matter to the IPCC.

(2) The relevant appropriate authority must do so within the period specified in regulation 21(3) (reference of complaints to the IPCC).

(3) A matter that has already been referred to the IPCC under this regulation on a previous occasion shall not be required to be referred again under this regulation unless the IPCC so directs.

Duties of IPCC on references under regulation 27

28

(1) It shall be the duty of the IPCC, in the case of every DSI matter referred to it by the relevant appropriate authority, to determine whether or not it is necessary for the matter to be investigated.

(2) Where the IPCC determines under this regulation that it is not necessary for a DSI matter to be investigated, it may if it thinks fit refer the matter back to the relevant appropriate authority to be dealt with by it in such manner (if any) as the relevant appropriate authority may determine.

Procedure where a conduct matter is revealed during investigation of a DSI matter

29

(1) If during the course of an investigation of a DSI matter it appears to a person appointed under regulation 39 (investigations supervised by the IPCC), 41 (investigations managed by the IPCC) or 42 (investigations by the IPCC itself) that there is an indication that a relevant officer, relevant official of the Secretary of State, relevant contractor, official exercising customs revenue functions or customs revenue contractor ("the person whose conduct is in question") may have—

    (a) committed a criminal offence, or

    (b) behaved in a manner which would justify the bringing of disciplinary proceedings,

the person so appointed shall make a notification to that effect to the IPCC.

(2) If, after considering a notification under paragraph (1), the IPCC determines that there is such an indication, it shall notify the relevant appropriate authority and send to it a copy of the submission under paragraph (1).

(3) If during the course of an investigation of a DSI matter it appears to a person appointed under regulation 38 (investigation by a police force at the request of the relevant appropriate authority), or 40 (investigation by a police force under the management or supervision of the IPCC) that there is an indication that a relevant officer, a relevant official of the Secretary of State, relevant contractor, official exercising customs revenue functions or customs revenue contractor ("the person whose conduct is in question") may have—

    (a) committed a criminal offence, or

    (b) behaved in a manner which would justify the bringing of disciplinary proceedings,

the person so appointed shall make a notification to that effect to the relevant appropriate authority and on completion of that investigation shall carry out the steps set out in regulation 61 (action by a police force on completion of an investigation report).

(4) Where the relevant appropriate authority—

    (a) is notified of a determination by the IPCC under paragraph (2), or

    (b) is notified of a determination by the person appointed under regulation 38 or 40 in accordance with regulation 61(2), it shall record the matter under regulation 18 (recording etc of conduct matters in other cases) as a conduct matter (and the other provisions of Part 5 of these Regulations (investigations) shall apply in relation to that matter accordingly).

(5) Where a DSI matter is recorded under regulation 18 as a conduct matter by virtue of paragraph (4)—

    (a) the person investigating the DSI matter shall (subject to any determination made by the IPCC under regulation 31(2) (power of the IPCC to determine the form of an investigation)) continue the investigation as if appointed to investigate the conduct matter, and

    (b) the other provisions of Part 5 of these Regulations shall apply in relation to that matter accordingly.

PART 5
INVESTIGATIONS

Inspections of the Secretary of State's premises on behalf of the IPCC

30

(1) Where—

    (a) the IPCC requires the relevant appropriate authority to allow a person nominated for the purpose by the IPCC to have access to any premises occupied by a relevant officer, relevant official of the Secretary of State, relevant contractor, official exercising customs revenue functions or customs revenue contractor and to documents and other things on those premises, and

    (b) the requirement is imposed for any of the purposes mentioned in paragraph (2),

it shall be the duty of the relevant appropriate authority to secure that the required access is allowed to the nominated person.

(2) Those purposes are—

    (a) the purposes of any examination by the IPCC of the efficiency and effectiveness of the arrangements made by the relevant appropriate authority for handling complaints or dealing with recordable conduct matters or DSI matters;

    (b) the purposes of any investigation by the IPCC under this Part or of any investigation carried out under its supervision or management.

(3) A requirement imposed under this regulation for the purposes mentioned in paragraph (2)(a) must be notified to the relevant appropriate authority at least 48 hours before the time at which access is required.

(4) Where—

    (a) a requirement imposed under this regulation for the purposes mentioned in paragraph (2)(a) requires access to any premises, document or thing to be allowed to any person, but

    (b) there are reasonable grounds for not allowing that person to have the required access at the time at which that person seeks to have it,

the obligation to secure that the required access is allowed shall have effect as an obligation to secure that the access is allowed to that person at the earliest practicable time after there cease to be any such grounds as that person may specify.

(5) The provisions of this regulation are in addition to, and without prejudice to—

    (a) the rights of entry, search and seizure that are or may be conferred on—

        (i) a person designated for the purposes of regulation 42 (investigations by the IPCC itself), or

        (ii) any person who otherwise acts on behalf of the IPCC,

    in that person's capacity as a constable or as a person with the powers and privileges of a constable; or

(b)   the obligations of the relevant appropriate authority under regulations 10 (co-operation, assistance and information) and 48 (provision of information to the IPCC).

Power of the IPCC to determine the form of an investigation

31

(1)   This regulation applies where—

    (a)   a complaint, recordable conduct matter or DSI matter is referred to the IPCC; and

    (b)   the IPCC determines that it is necessary for the complaint or matter to be investigated.

(2)   It shall be the duty of the IPCC to determine the form which the investigation should take.

(3)   In making a determination under paragraph (2) the IPCC shall have regard to the following factors—

    (a)   the seriousness of the case; and

    (b)   the public interest.

(4)   The only forms which the investigation may take in accordance with a determination made under this regulation are an investigation by—

    (a)   the relevant appropriate authority on its own behalf;

    (b)   a police force at the request of the relevant appropriate authority;

    (c)   the relevant appropriate authority under the supervision of the IPCC;

    (d)   a police force under the supervision of the IPCC;

    (e)   the relevant authority under the management of the IPCC;

    (f)   a police force under the management of the IPCC;

    (g)   the IPCC.

(5)   The IPCC may at any time make a further determination under this regulation to replace an earlier one.

(6)   Where a determination under this regulation replaces an earlier determination under this regulation, or relates to a complaint or matter in relation to which the relevant appropriate authority has already begun an investigation on its own behalf, the IPCC may give—

    (a)   the relevant appropriate authority, and

    (b)   any person previously appointed to carry out the investigation,

such directions as it considers appropriate for the purpose of giving effect to the new determination.

(7)   It shall be the duty of a person to whom a direction is given under paragraph (6) to comply with it.

(8)   The IPCC shall notify the relevant appropriate authority of any determination that it makes under this regulation in relation to a particular complaint, recordable conduct matter or DSI matter.

Appointment of persons to carry out investigations

32

(1)   No person shall be appointed to carry out an investigation under regulations 38 (investigation by a police force at the request of the relevant appropriate authority) to 41 (investigations managed by the IPCC)—

    (a)   unless that person has an appropriate level of knowledge, skills and experience to plan and conduct the investigation and to manage the resources that will be required during that process;

    (b)   if that person has any social, financial or other connection, whether or not within the work environment, with the person whose conduct is being investigated which could, on an objective appraisal of the material facts, give rise to a legitimate fear as to whether that investigation can be carried out impartially;

(c)   if that person works, directly or indirectly, under the management of the person whose conduct is being investigated.

Power of the IPCC to impose requirements in relation to an investigation which it is supervising

33

(1) For the purposes of regulation 39(6) (investigations supervised by the IPCC) the requirements which may be imposed by the IPCC on a person appointed to investigate a complaint, recordable conduct matter or DSI matter are, subject to paragraph (2), any reasonable requirements as to the conduct of the investigation as appear to it to be necessary.

(2) The IPCC shall not, under paragraph (1), impose any requirement relating to the resources to be made available by the relevant appropriate authority for the purposes of an investigation without first consulting that person and having regard to any representations that person makes.

Combining and splitting investigations

34

(1) A relevant appropriate authority which is carrying out an investigation on its own behalf may—

(a)   combine that investigation with another such investigation, or

(b)   split that investigation into two or more such separate investigations,

if it considers that it is more efficient and effective, or is otherwise in the public interest, to do so.

(2) Subject to paragraph (3), where the IPCC is supervising, managing or carrying out an investigation, it may—

(a)   combine that investigation with another investigation, or

(b)   split that investigation into two or more separate investigations,

if it considers that it is more efficient and effective, or is otherwise in the public interest, to do so.

(3) The IPCC shall not take any action under paragraph (2) in relation to a supervised or managed investigation except after consultation with the relevant appropriate authority.

Power of the IPCC to discontinue an investigation

35

(1) If, following a determination under regulations 22 (duties of the IPCC on references under regulation 21), 24 (duties of the IPCC on references under regulation 23) and 28 (duties of the IPCC on reference under regulation 27), it appears at any time to the IPCC (whether on an application by the relevant appropriate authority or otherwise) that a complaint or matter that is being investigated—

(a)   by the relevant appropriate authority on its own behalf, or

(b)   under the supervision or management of the IPCC,

is of a description of complaint or matter specified in paragraph (5), the IPCC may by order require the discontinuance of the investigation.

(2) Where the IPCC makes an order under this regulation or discontinues an investigation being carried out in accordance with regulation 42 (investigations by the IPCC itself), it shall give notification of the discontinuance—

(a)   to the relevant appropriate authority;

    (b)   to every person entitled to be kept properly informed in relation to the subject matter of the investigation under regulation 50 (duty to provide information for other persons); and

    (c)   in a case where the investigation that is discontinued is an investigation of a complaint, to the complainant.

(3) Subject to regulation 29 (procedure where conduct matter is revealed during investigation of DSI matter), where an investigation of a complaint or recordable conduct matter or DSI matter is discontinued in accordance with this regulation, neither the relevant appropriate authority nor the IPCC shall take any further action in accordance with the provisions of these Regulations in relation to that complaint or matter.

(4) The relevant appropriate authority shall comply with any order or notification given to it under this regulation.

(5) The descriptions of complaint or matter are—

    (a)   one in which the complainant refuses to co-operate to the extent that the IPCC considers that it is not reasonably practicable to continue the investigation;

    (b)   one which the IPCC considers is vexatious, oppressive or otherwise an abuse of the procedures for dealing with complaints, conduct matters or DSI matters;

    (c)   one which is repetitious, as defined in paragraph (6); or

    (d)   one which the IPCC otherwise considers is such as to make it not reasonably practicable to proceed with the investigation.

(6) A complaint is repetitious only if—

    (a)   it is substantially the same as a previous complaint (whether made by or on behalf of the same or a different complainant), or it concerns substantially the same conduct as previous conduct matter;

    (b)   it contains no fresh allegation which significantly affects the account of the conduct complained of;

    (c)   no fresh evidence, being evidence which was not reasonably available at the time the previous complaint was made, is tendered in support of it; and

    (d)   as respects the previous complaint or conduct matter, either—

        (i)   the requirements of regulation 63(2) (action by the IPCC in response to an investigation report under regulation 62) or 64(2) (determination by the relevant appropriate authority in response to an investigation report under regulation 62) were complied with;

        (ii)   the IPCC gave the relevant appropriate authority a direction under regulation 36(11)(b) (withdrawn and discontinued complaints); or

        (iii)   the complainant gave such notification that he withdrew the complaint as mentioned in regulation 36(1)(a) (complainant withdraws the complaint).

(7) The cases in which the IPCC is authorised to discontinue an investigation that is being carried out in accordance with regulation 42 are any cases where the complaint, conduct matter or DSI matter under investigation falls within paragraph (5).

(8) Any application by a relevant appropriate authority to the IPCC for an order that it discontinue an investigation shall be in writing and shall be accompanied by—

    (a)   a copy of the complaint, and

    (b)   a memorandum from the relevant appropriate authority containing a summary of the investigation undertaken so far and explaining the reasons for the application to discontinue the investigation.

(9) The relevant appropriate authority shall—

    (a)   send the complainant a copy of any such application on the same day as the day on which the application is sent to the IPCC, and

    (b)   supply any further information requested by the IPCC for the purpose of considering that application.

(10)   The IPCC shall not require the discontinuance of an investigation in a case where there has been no application to do so by the relevant appropriate authority unless it has consulted with that authority.

(11)   A determination given to a relevant appropriate authority by the IPCC under regulation 31(4)(a) (power of the IPCC to determine the form of an investigation) may—

    (a)   require the relevant appropriate authority to produce an investigation report on the discontinued investigation;

    (b)   where the investigation concerned a complaint, require the relevant appropriate authority to dispense with the requirements of these Regulations as respects that complaint;

    (c)   direct the relevant appropriate authority to handle the matter in whatever manner (if any) that authority thinks fit.

(12)   For the purposes of this regulation the steps that may be taken by the IPCC when an investigation is discontinued are—

    (a)   to produce an investigation report on the discontinued investigation and take any subsequent steps required under these Regulations;

    (b)   where the investigation concerned a complaint, to dispense with the requirements of these Regulations as respects that complaint;

    (c)   to handle the matter in whatever manner it thinks fit.

Withdrawn and discontinued complaints

36

(1)   If a relevant appropriate authority receives from a complainant notification in writing signed by the complainant or by a solicitor or other authorised agent on the complainant's behalf to the effect either—

    (a)   that the complainant withdraws the complaint, or

    (b)   that the complainant does not wish any further steps to be taken in consequence of the complaint,

then the relevant appropriate authority shall forthwith record the withdrawal or the fact that the complainant does not wish any further steps to be taken, as the case may be, and subject to the following provisions of this Regulation, these Regulations shall cease to apply in respect of that complaint.

(2)   Where a complainant gives such notification as is mentioned in paragraph (1) to the IPCC but, so far as is apparent to the IPCC, has not sent that notification to the relevant appropriate authority, then—

    (a)   the IPCC shall send a copy of the notification to the relevant appropriate authority;

    (b)   that relevant appropriate authority shall record the withdrawal or the fact that the complainant does not wish any further steps to be taken, as the case may be; and

    (c)   subject to the following provisions of this regulation, these Regulations shall cease to apply in respect of that complaint.

(3)   Where a complainant gives such notification as is mentioned in paragraph (1) to a relevant appropriate authority, or where the relevant appropriate authority receives a copy of a notification under paragraph (2), and it relates to a complaint—

    (a)   which was referred to the IPCC under regulation 21(1) (reference of complaints to the IPCC) and which has not been referred back to the relevant appropriate authority under regulation 22(2) (duties of the IPCC on references under regulation 21),

(b) which the relevant appropriate authority knows is currently the subject of an appeal to the IPCC under regulation 15 (failures to notify or record a complaint), or 70 (appeals to the IPCC with respect to an investigation), or

(c) which was notified to the relevant appropriate authority by the IPCC under regulation 13(1) (initial handling and recording of complaints),

then the relevant appropriate authority shall notify the IPCC that it has recorded the withdrawal of the complaint or the fact that the complainant does not wish any further steps to be taken, as the case may be.

(4) In a case falling within paragraph (3)(b) or (c), the relevant appropriate authority shall also—

(a) determine whether it is in the public interest for the complaint to be treated as a recordable conduct matter; and

(b) notify the IPCC of its determination and the reasons for the determination.

(5) In a case falling within paragraph (3)(a), the IPCC shall determine whether it is in the public interest for the complaint to be treated as a recordable conduct matter, and shall notify the relevant appropriate authority of its decision.

(6) Where a determination is made that a complaint is to be treated as a recordable conduct matter, then the provisions of these Regulations shall apply to that matter.

(7) Where a complainant gives such notification as is mentioned in paragraph (1) to a relevant appropriate authority, or where the relevant appropriate authority receives a copy of a notification under paragraph (2), and that notification relates to a complaint which does not fall within any of sub-paragraphs (a) to (c) of paragraph (3), then—

(a) the relevant appropriate authority shall determine whether it is in the public interest for the complaint to be treated as a recordable conduct matter;

(b) if the complaint is to be treated as a recordable conduct matter, the provisions of these Regulations shall apply to that matter;

(c) if the complaint is not to be treated as a recordable conduct matter, the provisions of these Regulations shall cease to apply in respect of that complaint.

(8) In a case where—

(a) a complaint has been subjected to an investigation by the relevant appropriate authority on its own behalf,

(b) the complaint is currently subject to an appeal to the IPCC under regulation 70, and

(c) the relevant appropriate authority has notified the IPCC under paragraph (4)(b) that it has determined that the complaint is not to be treated as a recordable conduct matter,

the IPCC shall consider whether it is in the public interest for that determination to be reversed, and if so it shall instruct the relevant appropriate authority to reverse the decision.

(9) Where a complainant indicates the wish to withdraw the complaint or the wish that no further steps are to be taken in consequence of the complaint, but the complainant fails to provide a notification to that effect in writing signed by or on behalf of the complainant, then—

(a) in the case of an indication received by the relevant appropriate authority, the authority shall take the steps set out in paragraph (10);

(b) in the case of an indication received by the IPCC, the IPCC shall refer the matter to the relevant appropriate authority which shall take the steps set out in paragraph (10).

(10) Those steps are—

(a) the relevant appropriate authority shall write to the complainant to ascertain whether the complainant wishes to withdraw the complaint or does not wish any further steps to be taken in consequence of the complaint;

(b) if the complainant indicates the wish to withdraw the complaint or does not wish any further steps to be taken in consequence of the complaint, or if the complainant fails to reply within 21 days, the relevant appropriate authority shall treat the indication as though it had been received in writing signed by the complainant;

(c) if the complainant indicates the wish not to withdraw the complaint, or the wish for further steps be taken to be taken in consequence of the complaint, the relevant appropriate authority shall start or resume the investigation as the case may be.

(11) The relevant appropriate authority shall notify the person complained against if—

(a) it records the withdrawal of a complaint or the fact that the complainant does not wish any further steps to be taken;

(b) it determines that a complaint shall be treated as a recordable conduct matter;

(c) the IPCC determines that a complaint shall be treated as a recordable conduct matter;

(d) the IPCC instructs it to reverse a decision not to treat a complaint as a recordable conduct matter;

(e) the provisions of these Regulations cease to apply in respect of a complaint.

(12) But nothing in paragraph (11) shall require the relevant appropriate authority to make a notification if it has previously decided under regulation 56(3) (notification of complaints etc) not to notify the person complained against of the complaint because it is of the opinion that that might prejudice any criminal investigation or pending proceedings or would be contrary to the public interest.

Investigations by the relevant appropriate authority on its own behalf

37

(1) This regulation applies if the relevant appropriate authority is required by virtue of any determination made by the IPCC under regulation 31 (power of the IPCC to determine the form of an investigation) to make arrangements for a complaint or recordable conduct matter or DSI matter to be investigated by the relevant appropriate authority on its own behalf.

(2) It shall be the duty of the relevant appropriate authority to appoint a person to investigate the complaint or matter.

Investigation by a police force at the request of the relevant appropriate authority

38

(1) This regulation applies where the relevant appropriate authority determines that there should be an investigation by a police force into an indication that a relevant officer, relevant official of the Secretary of State, relevant contractor, official exercising customs revenue functions or customs revenue contractor may have committed a criminal offence in connection with a complaint, recordable conduct matter or DSI matter.

(2) The relevant appropriate authority shall identify the police force whose force area includes the geographical area to which the subject matter of the complaint, recordable conduct matter or DSI matter most closely relates, and take steps to obtain the agreement of the chief officer of police of that force to the appointment of that force to carry out the investigation.

(3)   In the event that no agreement is reached under paragraph (2) the relevant appropriate authority may require the chief officer of police of any police force it considers appropriate to carry out the investigation.

(4)   A chief officer of police of a police force who agrees to or is required to carry out an investigation shall, if that person has not already done so, appoint a person serving with the police who is a member of that force to investigate that complaint.

(5)   Paragraphs (3) to (5) and (7) of regulation 40 (investigations supervised by the IPCC) shall apply as they apply to an investigation by the relevant appropriate authority which the IPCC has determined is one that it should supervise and the references to the relevant appropriate authority in those paragraphs shall be treated as references to the chief officer of police concerned.

(6)   An appointment of a person under paragraph (4) or (5) shall be notified by the chief of police concerned to the relevant appropriate authority. The IPCC may require that no appointment is made under paragraph (4) unless it has given notice to the chief officer that it approves the person serving with the police whom he proposes to appoint.

(7)   The person appointed to investigate the complaint or matter shall, in relation to an investigation under the management of the IPCC, be under the direction and control of the IPCC.

(8)   The person appointed to investigate the complaint or matter shall comply with all such requirements in relation to the carrying out of that investigation as may be imposed by these Regulations.

Investigations supervised by the IPCC

39

(1)   This regulation applies where the IPCC has determined that it should supervise the investigation by the relevant appropriate authority of any complaint or recordable conduct matter or DSI matter.

(2)   On being given notice of that determination, the relevant appropriate authority shall, if it has not already done so, appoint a person to investigate the complaint or matter.

(3)   The IPCC may require that no appointment is made under paragraph (2) unless it has given notice to the relevant appropriate authority that it approves the person whom that authority proposes to appoint.

(4)   Where a person has already been appointed to investigate the complaint or matter, or is selected under this paragraph for appointment, and the IPCC is not satisfied with that person, the IPCC may require the relevant appropriate authority, as soon as reasonably practicable after being required to do so—

(a)   to select another person falling within paragraph (2) to investigate the complaint or matter; and

(b)   to notify the IPCC of the person selected.

(5)   Where a selection made in pursuance of a requirement under paragraph (4) has been notified to the IPCC, the relevant appropriate authority shall appoint that person to investigate the complaint or matter if, but only if, the IPCC notifies the authority that it approves the appointment of that person.

(6)   The person appointed to investigate the complaint or matter shall comply with all such requirements in relation to the carrying out of that investigation as may be imposed by the IPCC in relation to that investigation.

Investigation by a police force under the management or under the supervision of the IPCC

40

(1)   This regulation applies where the IPCC determines that there should be an investigation by a police force under the management or supervision of the IPCC.

(2)   The IPCC shall—

    (a)   identify the police force whose force area includes the geographical area to which the subject matter of the complaint, recordable conduct matter or DSI matter most closely relates, and

    (b)   take steps to obtain the agreement of—

        (i)   the chief officer of police of that force, and

        (ii)   the relevant appropriate authority,

to the appointment by the IPCC of that force to carry out the investigation.

(3)   In the event that no agreement is reached under paragraph (2) the IPCC may require the chief officer of police of any police force it considers appropriate to carry out the investigation.

(4)   A chief officer of police of a police force who agrees to or is required to carry out an investigation shall, if that person has not already done so, appoint a person serving with the police who is a member of that force to investigate that complaint.

(5)   Paragraphs (3) to (6) of regulation 39 (investigations supervised by the IPCC) shall apply as they apply to an investigation by the relevant appropriate authority which the IPCC has determined is one that it should supervise and the references to the relevant appropriate authority in those paragraphs shall be treated as references to the chief officer of police concerned.

(6)   An appointment of a person under paragraph (4) shall be notified by the chief of police concerned to the relevant appropriate authority. The IPCC may require that no appointment is made under paragraph (4) unless it has given notice to the chief officer that it approves the person serving with the police who it is proposed to appoint.

(7)   The person appointed to investigate the complaint or matter shall, in relation to an investigation under the management of the IPCC, be under the direction and control of the IPCC.

(8)   The person appointed to investigate the complaint or matter shall comply with all such requirements in relation to the carrying out of that investigation as may be imposed by these Regulations.

Investigations managed by the IPCC

41

(1)   This regulation applies where the IPCC has determined that it should manage the investigation by the relevant appropriate authority of any complaint or recordable conduct matter or DSI matter.

(2)   Paragraphs (2) to (6) of regulation 39 (investigations supervised by the IPCC) shall apply as they apply in the case of an investigation which the IPCC has determined is one that it should supervise.

(3)   The person appointed to investigate the complaint or matter shall, in relation to that investigation, be under the direction and control of the IPCC.

Investigations by the IPCC itself

42

(1)   This regulation applies where the IPCC has determined that it should itself carry out the investigation of a complaint or recordable conduct matter or DSI matter.

(2)   The IPCC shall designate both—

    (a)   a member of the IPCC's staff to take charge of the investigation on behalf of the IPCC, and

    (b)   all such other members of the IPCC's staff as are required by the IPCC to assist that member.

(3)   A member of the IPCC's staff who—

    (a)   is designated under paragraph (2) in relation to any investigation, but

(b)   does not already, by virtue of section 97(8) (police officers engaged on service outside their force) of the Police Act 1996 have all the powers and privileges of a constable throughout England and Wales and the adjacent United Kingdom waters,

shall for the purposes of the carrying out of the investigation and all purposes connected with it, have all those powers and privileges throughout England and Wales and those waters.

(4) A member of the IPCC's staff who is not a constable shall not, as a result of paragraph (3), be treated as being in police service for the purposes of—

    (a)   section 280 (police service) of the Trade Union and Labour Relations (Consolidation) Act 1992; or

    (b)   section 200 (police officers) of the Employment Rights Act 1996.

(5) References in this regulation to the powers and privileges of a constable—

    (a)   are references to any power or privilege conferred by or under any enactment (including one passed after the making of these Regulations) on a constable; and

    (b)   shall have effect as if every such power were exercisable, and every such privilege existed, throughout England and Wales and the adjacent United Kingdom waters (whether or not that is the case apart from this paragraph).

(6) In this regulation "United Kingdom waters" means the sea and other waters within the seaward limits of the United Kingdom's territorial sea.

Relinquishing the IPCC's supervision or management of an investigation

43

(1) This regulation applies where the IPCC—

    (a)   relinquishes the management of an investigation in favour of a supervised investigation or an investigation by the relevant appropriate authority on its own behalf, or

    (b)   relinquishes the supervision of an investigation in favour of an investigation by the relevant appropriate authority on its own behalf.

(2) Where this regulation applies, the IPCC—

    (a)   shall notify the relevant appropriate authority, the complainant, any interested person within the meaning of regulation 50 (duty to provide information for other persons) and the person complained against of its decision, and the reasons for that decision; and

    (b)   shall send to the relevant appropriate authority any documentation and evidence gathered during its investigations as will assist the relevant appropriate authority to carry out its functions under these Regulations.

(3) Nothing in paragraph (2)(a) shall require the IPCC to make a notification to the person complained against if it is of the opinion that that might prejudice any criminal investigation or pending proceedings or would be contrary to the public interest.

Circumstances in which an investigation or other procedure may be suspended

44

(1) The IPCC may suspend any investigation or other procedure under these Regulations which would, if it were to continue, prejudice any criminal proceedings.

(2) A relevant appropriate authority may, subject to paragraph (3), suspend any investigation or other procedure under these Regulations which would, if it were to continue, prejudice any criminal investigation or proceedings.

(3) The IPCC may direct that any investigation or other procedure under these Regulations which is liable to be suspended under paragraph (2) shall continue if it is of the view that it is in the public interest to make such a direction.

(4) The IPCC shall consult the relevant appropriate authority before making such a direction.

Resumption of investigation after criminal proceedings

45

(1) Where the whole or part of the investigation of a complaint has been suspended until the conclusion of criminal proceedings, and after the conclusion of those proceedings the complainant has failed to express the wish for the investigation to start or be resumed, the IPCC or, as the case may be, the relevant appropriate authority shall take the steps set out in paragraph (2).

(2) The IPCC or relevant appropriate authority shall take all reasonable steps to contact the complainant to ascertain whether the complainant wants the investigation to start or be resumed as the case may be.

(3) If the complainant expresses the wish for the investigation to start or be resumed, the IPCC or the relevant appropriate authority shall start or resume the investigation as the case may be.

(4) The IPCC shall consult the relevant appropriate authority before starting or resuming the investigation.

(5) If the complainant indicates that the complainant does not want the investigation to start or be resumed, or if the complainant fails to reply within 21 days to a letter sent to the complainant by the IPCC or relevant appropriate authority, the IPCC or relevant appropriate authority as the case may be shall determine whether it is in the public interest for the complaint to be treated as a recordable conduct matter.

(6) If the IPCC or relevant appropriate authority determines that it is not in the public interest for the complaint to be treated as a recordable conduct matter, the provisions of these Regulations shall cease to apply to the complaint.

(7) If the IPCC or relevant appropriate authority determines that it is in the public interest for the complaint to be treated as a recordable conduct matter, regulations 17 (conduct matters arising in civil proceedings), 18 (recording etc of conduct matters in other cases), 19 (duties to preserve evidence relating to conduct matters), 23 (reference of conduct matters to IPCC), 24 (duties of the IPCC on references under regulation 23) and the provisions of Part 4 (handling DSI matters) of these Regulations shall apply to the matter.

(8) The IPCC or relevant appropriate authority shall notify the person complained against if paragraph (5) or (6) applies.

(9) Nothing in paragraph (8) shall require the IPCC or relevant appropriate authority to make a notification if it is of the opinion that that might prejudice any criminal investigation or pending proceedings or would be contrary to the public interest.

Restrictions on proceedings pending the conclusion of an investigation

46

(1) No criminal or disciplinary proceedings shall be brought in relation to any matter which falls to be determined under these Regulations until a report on that investigation has been submitted to the IPCC or to the relevant appropriate authority under regulation 62 (final reports on investigations: complaints, conduct matters and certain DSI matters) or 65 (final reports on investigations: other DSI matters).

(2) Nothing in this regulation shall prevent the bringing of criminal or disciplinary proceedings in respect of any conduct at any time after the discontinuance of the investigation in accordance with the provisions of these Regulations which relate to that conduct.

(3) The restrictions imposed by this regulation in relation to the bringing of criminal proceedings shall not apply to the bringing of criminal proceedings by the Director of

Public Prosecutions . . . in any case in which it appears to that person that there are exceptional circumstances which make it undesirable to delay the bringing of such proceedings.

(4) Where disciplinary proceedings are brought in relation to any matter which is the subject of an investigation under these Regulations, the relevant appropriate authority shall notify the IPCC of that fact before such proceedings are brought.

Amendment

Para (3): words omitted revoked by SI 2014/834, reg 3(3), Sch 3, paras 24, 25. Date in force: 27 March 2014: see SI 2014/834, art 1.

PART 6
PROVISION OF INFORMATION

Provision and use of information by the IPCC

47

(1) Where the IPCC, or any person acting on its behalf, obtains information in the course of performing a function conferred on it by regulation 6(1) they must not disclose it except as permitted by Part 6 (provision of information) of these Regulations.

(2) Where the IPCC, or any person acting on its behalf, obtains information in the course of performing a function conferred on it by regulation 6(1) they may not use it for any purpose other than the performance of a function under these Regulations.

Provision of information to the IPCC

48

(1) It shall be the duty of the relevant appropriate authority—

    (a)   to provide the IPCC with all such information and documents as may be specified or described in a notification given by the IPCC to the relevant appropriate authority, and

    (b)   to produce or deliver up to the IPCC all such evidence and other things so specified or described,

as appear to the IPCC to be required by it for the purposes of the carrying out of any of its functions.

(2) Anything falling to be provided, produced or delivered up by any person in pursuance of a requirement imposed under paragraph (1) must be provided, produced or delivered up in such form, in such manner and within such period as may be specified in—

    (a)   the notification imposing the requirement; or

    (b)   in any subsequent notification given by the IPCC to that person for the purposes of this paragraph.

(3) Nothing in this regulation shall require the relevant appropriate authority to provide the IPCC with any information or document, or to produce or deliver up any other thing, before the earliest time at which it is practicable for it do so.

Duty to keep the complainant informed

49

(1) In any case in which there is an investigation of a complaint in accordance with the provisions of these Regulations—

    (a)   by the IPCC, or

    (b)   under its management,

it shall be the duty of the IPCC to provide the complainant with all such information as will keep the complainant properly informed, while the investigation is being carried out and subsequently, of all the matters mentioned in paragraph (5).

(2)   In any case in which there is an investigation of a complaint in accordance with the provisions of these Regulations—

    (a)   by the relevant appropriate authority on its own behalf,

    (b)   under the supervision of the IPCC, or

    (c)   by the police under supervision of IPCC,

it shall be the duty of the person investigating to provide the complainant with all such information as will keep the complainant properly informed, while the investigation is being carried out and subsequently, of all the matters mentioned in paragraph (5).

(3)   Where paragraph (2) applies, it shall be the duty of the IPCC to give the relevant appropriate authority all such directions as it considers appropriate for securing that that authority complies with its duty under that subsection; and it shall be the duty of the relevant appropriate authority to comply with any direction given to it under this paragraph.

(4)   The IPCC shall consult the relevant appropriate authority before deciding whether or not to disclose information to the complainant in accordance with paragraph (1) or to give directions under paragraph (3), and shall have regard to any representations made to it by the relevant appropriate authority in taking that decision.

(5)   For the purposes of paragraphs (1) and (2) the matters of which the complainant must be kept properly informed are—

    (a)   the progress of the investigation;

    (b)   any provisional findings of the person carrying out the investigation;

    (c)   whether any report has been submitted under regulation 65 (final reports on investigations: DSI matters);

    (d)   the action (if any) that is taken in respect of the matters dealt with in any such report; and

    (e)   the outcome of any such action.

(6)   It shall be the duty of a person appointed to carry out an investigation under these Regulations to provide the IPCC or, as the case may be, the relevant appropriate authority with all such information as the IPCC or that authority may reasonably require for the purpose of performing its duty under this regulation.

Duty to provide information for other persons

50

(1)   A person has an interest in being kept properly informed about the handling of a complaint or recordable conduct matter or DSI matter which is the subject of an investigation in accordance with the provisions of these Regulations if—

    (a)   it appears to the IPCC or to a relevant appropriate authority that that person is a person falling within paragraph (2) or (3); and

    (b)   that person consented to the provision of information in accordance with this regulation and that consent has not been withdrawn.

(2)   A person falls within this paragraph if (in the case of a complaint or recordable conduct matter) that person—

    (a)   is a relative of a person whose death is the alleged result from the conduct complained of or to which the recordable conduct matter relates;

    (b)   is a relative of a person whose serious injury is the alleged result from that conduct and that person is incapable of making a complaint;

    (c)   has suffered serious injury as the alleged result of that conduct.

(3)   A person falls within this paragraph if (in the case of a DSI matter) that person—

    (a)   is a relative of the person who has died;

    (b)   is a relative of the person who has suffered serious injury and that person is incapable of making a complaint;

    (c)   is the person who has suffered serious injury.

(4) A person who does not fall within paragraph (2) or (3) has an interest in being kept properly informed about the handling of a complaint, recordable conduct matter or DSI matter if—

    (a)   the IPCC or a relevant appropriate authority considers that that person has an interest in the handling of the complaint, conduct matter or DSI matter which is sufficient to make it appropriate for information to be provided to that person in accordance with this regulation; and

    (b)   that person has consented to the provision of information in accordance with this regulation.

(5) In relation to a complaint, this regulation confers no rights on the complainant.

(6) A person who has an interest in being kept properly informed about the handling of a complaint, conduct matter or DSI matter is referred to in this regulation as an "interested person".

(7) In any case in which there is an investigation of the complaint, recordable conduct matter or DSI matter in accordance with the provisions of these Regulations—

    (a)   by the IPCC, or

    (b)   under its management,

it shall be the duty of the IPCC to provide the interested person with all such information as will keep the interested person properly informed, while the investigation is being carried out and subsequently, of all the matters mentioned in paragraph (11).

(8) In any case in which there is an investigation of the complaint, recordable conduct matter or DSI matter in accordance with the provisions of these Regulations—

    (a)   by the relevant appropriate authority on its own behalf, or

    (b)   under the supervision of the IPCC,

it shall be the duty of the relevant appropriate authority to provide the interested person with all such information as will keep him properly informed, while the investigation is being carried out and subsequently, of all the matters mentioned in paragraph (11).

(9) Where paragraph (8) applies, it shall be the duty of the IPCC to give the relevant appropriate authority all such directions as it considers appropriate for securing that that authority complies with its duty under that paragraph; and it shall be the duty of the relevant appropriate authority to comply with any direction given to it under this paragraph.

(10) The IPCC shall consult the relevant appropriate authority before deciding whether or not to disclose information to the interested person in accordance with paragraph (7) or to give directions under paragraph (9), and shall have regard to any representations made to it by the relevant appropriate authority in taking that decision.

(11) The matters of which the interested person must be kept properly informed are—

    (a)   the progress of the investigation;

    (b)   any provisional findings of the person carrying out the investigation;

    (c)   whether the IPCC or the relevant appropriate authority has made a determination under regulation 29 (procedure where conduct matter is revealed during investigation of a DSI matter);

    (d)   whether any report has been submitted under regulation 61 (action by a police force on completion of an investigation report), 63 (action by the IPCC in response to an investigation report under regulation 62) or 64 (action by the relevant appropriate authority in response to an investigation report under regulation 62);

    (e)   the action (if any) that is taken in respect of the matters dealt with in any such report; and

    (f)   the outcome of any such action.

(12) Paragraphs (5) and (6) of regulation 49 (duty to keep the complainant informed) apply for the purposes of this regulation as they apply for the purposes of that regulation.

(13) In this regulation "relative" means any spouse, partner, parent or adult child.

Duty to keep the relevant officer, relevant official of the Secretary of State, relevant contractor, official exercising customs revenue functions or customs revenue contractor informed

51

(1) If during the course of an investigation of a complaint which falls to be determined under these Regulations it appears to the person investigating that there is an indication that the relevant officer, relevant official of the Secretary of State, relevant contractor, official exercising customs revenue functions or customs revenue contractor ("the person whose conduct is in question") may have—

(a) committed a criminal offence; or

(b) behaved in a manner which would justify the bringing of disciplinary proceedings,

the person investigating the complaint or matter must give a notification that complies with paragraph (2) to the person whose conduct is in question..

(2) The notification will—

(a) provide sufficient details of the complaint or matter in question so that the person whose conduct is in question may make representations to the person investigating the complaint or matter;

(b) give the information about the effect of regulation 52 (duty to consider submissions from relevant officers, relevant officials of the Secretary of State, relevant contractors, officials exercising customs revenue functions and customs revenue contractors); and

(c) give such information that may be set out in guidance.

(3) Paragraphs (1) and (2) do not apply for so long as the person investigating the complaint or the matter considers that giving the notification might prejudice—

(a) the investigation, or

(b) any other investigation (including, in particular, a criminal investigation).

(4) In this regulation and regulations 53 (duty to provide certain information to the relevant appropriate authority) and 54 (manner in which duties to provide information to the complainant are to be performed), the person whose conduct is in question—

(a) in relation to an investigation of a complaint, means the person in respect of whom it appears to the person investigating that there is the indication mentioned in paragraph (1)

(b) in relation to an investigation of a recordable conduct matter, means the person to whose conduct the investigation relates.

(5) In this regulation "relevant document"—

(a) means a document relating to any complaint or matter under investigation; and

(b) includes such a document containing suggestions as to lines of inquiry to be pursued or witnesses to be interviewed.

(6) In this regulation "relevant statement" means an oral or written statement relating to any complaint or matter under investigation.

Duty to consider submissions from relevant officers, relevant officials of the Secretary of State, relevant contractors, officials exercising customs revenue functions and customs revenue contractors

52

(1) This regulation applies where a notification under regulation 51 (duty to keep the relevant officer, relevant official of the Secretary of State, relevant contractor, official exercising customs revenue functions or customs revenue contractor informed) has been issued to a relevant officer, relevant official of the Secretary of State, relevant contractor, official exercising customs revenue functions or customs revenue contractor ("the person whose conduct is in question").

(2) If—

    (a) the person whose conduct is in question provides the person investigating the complaint or matter with a relevant statement or a relevant document, or

    (b) any person provides the person investigating the complaint or matter with a relevant document,

the person investigating must consider the statement or document.

Duty to provide certain information to the relevant appropriate authority

53

(1) This regulation applies during the course of an investigation within regulation 51(1) (duty to keep the relevant officer, relevant official of the Secretary of State, relevant contractor, official exercising customs revenue functions or customs revenue contractor informed).

(2) The person investigating the complaint or matter must supply the relevant appropriate authority with such information in that person's possession as the relevant appropriate authority may reasonably request for the purpose of determining whether the person whose conduct is in question should be, or should remain, suspended from duty.

Manner in which duties to provide information to the complainant are to be performed

54

(1) For the purposes of regulations 49(4) (duty to keep the complainant informed) and 50(9) (duty to provide information for other persons), the manner in which the IPCC or, as the case may be, a relevant appropriate authority shall perform the duties imposed by those regulations is as follows.

(2) The IPCC, in a case falling within regulation 49(1) (duty to keep the complainant informed) or 50(7) (duty to provide information for other persons), shall inform the complainant or, as the case may be, the interested party—

    (a) of the progress of the investigation promptly and in any event-

        (i) if there has been no previous notification, within four weeks of the start of the investigation; and

        (ii) in any other case, within four weeks of the previous notification;

    (b) of any provisional finding of the person carrying out the investigation as frequently as the IPCC determines to be appropriate in order for the complainant to be kept properly informed.

(3) The relevant appropriate authority, in a case falling within regulation 49(2) or 50(8) shall inform the complainant or the interested party (as the case may be)—

    (a) of the progress of the investigation promptly and in any event-

        (i) if there has been no previous notification, within four weeks of the start of the investigation; and

        (ii) in any other case, within four weeks of the previous notification;

  (b)   of any provisional findings of the person carrying out the investigation as frequently as the relevant appropriate authority determine to be appropriate in order for the complainant to be kept properly informed.

(4) When an investigation has been completed, each complainant and interested person shall be notified—

  (a)   of the date on which the final report under regulation 62 (final reports on investigations: complaints, conduct matters and certain DSI matters) is likely to be submitted;

  (b)   of the date on which the notification under regulation 63(11) (action by the IPCC in response to an investigation report under regulation 62) is likely to be given.

(5) In performing the duties imposed by regulations 49(1) and (2), and 50(7) and (8), the IPCC or, as the case may be, the relevant appropriate authority shall determine whether it is appropriate for it to accept and take into account written representations from the complainant or, as the case may be, an interested person.

(6) As soon as practicable after those written representations have been taken into account, the IPCC or, as the case may be, the relevant appropriate authority shall send to the complainant or interested person a written account of how any concerns of that person will be addressed.

(7) Before notifying a complainant or interested person of how the IPCC has taken those written representations into account, the IPCC shall consult the relevant appropriate authority and shall have regard to any representations made to it in the notification.

(8) As soon as practicable after any disciplinary hearing or other action that is taken in respect of the matters dealt with in any report submitted under regulation 62, the IPCC or, as the case may be, a relevant appropriate authority shall notify any complainant and interested person of the outcome of that hearing or action, including the fact and outcome of any appeal against the findings of or sanctions imposed by such a hearing.

(9) Before notifying a complainant or interested person of the outcome of the disciplinary hearing and the outcome of any appeal against the findings of or sanctions imposed by such a hearing, the IPCC shall consult the relevant appropriate authority and shall have regard to any representations made to it.

(10) If the IPCC or, as the case may be, the relevant appropriate authority, considers that an investigation has made minimal or no progress since the previous notification, then the next notification may be made by any means that in the opinion of the IPCC or, as the case may be, the relevant appropriate authority is suitable.

Exceptions to the duty to keep the complainant informed and to provide information for other persons

55

(1) Subject to paragraph (2), the duties mentioned in regulation 49(1) and (2) (duty to keep the complainant informed) and regulation 50(7) and (8) (duty to provide information for other persons) shall not apply in circumstances where in the opinion of the IPCC, or, as the case may be, of the relevant appropriate authority, the non-disclosure of information is necessary for the purpose of—

  (a)   preventing the premature or inappropriate disclosure of information that is relevant to, or may be used in, any actual or prospective criminal proceedings;

  (b)   preventing the disclosure of information in any circumstances in which its non-disclosure—

    (i)   is in the interests of national security;

    (ii)   is for the purposes of the prevention or detection of crime, or the apprehension or prosecution of offenders;

(iii)   is required on proportionality grounds; or

(iv)   is otherwise necessary in the public interest.

(2) The IPCC or, as the case may be, the relevant appropriate authority shall not conclude that the non-disclosure of information is necessary under paragraph (1) unless it is satisfied that—

(a)   there is a real risk of the disclosure of that information causing an adverse effect; and

(b)   that adverse effect would be significant.

(3) The IPCC shall consult the relevant appropriate authority in any case under paragraph (1)(b) before deciding whether or not it is satisfied under paragraph (2).

(4) Notwithstanding paragraph (1), the IPCC, or as the case may be, the relevant appropriate authority shall consider whether the non-disclosure of information is justified under this regulation in circumstances where—

(a)   that information is relevant to, or may be used in, any actual or prospective disciplinary proceedings;

(b)   the disclosure of that information may lead to the contamination of the evidence of witnesses during such proceedings;

(c)   the disclosure of that information may prejudice the welfare or safety of any third party;

(d)   that information constitutes criminal intelligence.

Notification of complaints etc

56

(1) Where a complaint is recorded under regulation 13(4) (initial handling and recording of complaints), the relevant appropriate authority shall, subject to paragraphs (2) to (4), supply the complainant with a written notification setting out a record of that complaint.

(2) A notification supplied under this regulation may keep anonymous the identity of the complainant or of any other person.

(3) A relevant appropriate authority may decide not to supply the complainant with a notification under this regulation if it is of the opinion that to do so—

(a)   might prejudice any criminal investigation or pending proceedings, or

(b)   would otherwise be contrary to the public interest.

(4) Where a relevant appropriate authority decides not to supply such a notification, it shall keep that decision under regular review.

Notification of actions and decisions

57

(1) So far as not covered by regulation 63(11) and (12) (action by the IPCC in response to an investigation report under regulation 62) and regulation 70(6) and (7) (appeals to the IPCC with respect to an investigation), where the IPCC takes any action or decisions in consequence of it having received a memorandum under regulation 63(9) or regulation 70(3) of these Regulations, it shall notify such action or decisions, together with an explanation of its reasons for having taken them, to—

(a)   the relevant appropriate authority;

(b)   the complainant and any other interested person within the meaning of regulation 50(2) and (3);

(c)   subject to paragraph (3), the person complained against.

(2) Notwithstanding paragraph (1), the IPCC shall include in any notification under this regulation a statement as to whether it intends to bring and conduct, or otherwise participate or intervene in, any disciplinary proceedings.

(3) The IPCC may decide not to give such a notification and explanation to the person complained against if it is of the opinion that that notification might prejudice any criminal investigation, pending proceedings, or review of the complaint.

Information for complainant about disciplinary recommendations

58

(1) Where—

(a) the IPCC makes recommendations under regulation 67 (duties with respect to disciplinary proceedings) in the case of an investigation of a complaint, and

(b) the relevant appropriate authority notifies the IPCC that the recommendations have been accepted, the IPCC shall notify the complainant and every person entitled to be kept properly informed in relation to the complaint under regulation 50 (duty to provide information for other persons) of that fact and of the steps that have been, or are to be taken, by the relevant appropriate authority to give effect to it.

(2) Where in the case of an investigation of a complaint the relevant appropriate authority—

(a) notify the IPCC that it does not (either in whole or in part) accept recommendations made by the IPCC under regulation 67, or

(b) fails to take steps to give full effect to any such recommendations, it shall be the duty of the IPCC to determine what if any further steps to take under that regulation.

(3) It shall be the duty of the IPCC to notify the complainant and every person entitled to be kept properly informed in relation to the complaint under regulation 50—

(a) of any determination under paragraph (2) not to take further steps under regulation 67; and

(b) where they determine under that sub-paragraph to take further steps under that regulation, of the outcome of the taking of those steps.

Register to be kept by the IPCC

59

(1) The IPCC shall establish and maintain a register of all information supplied to it by a relevant appropriate authority under these Regulations.

(2) Subject to paragraph (3), the IPCC may publish or otherwise disclose to any person any information held on the register provided that the publication or disclosure is necessary for or conducive to the purpose of—

(a) learning lessons from the handling of, or demonstrating the thoroughness and effectiveness of local resolutions, of investigations by the IPCC or of managed or supervised investigations;

(b) raising public awareness of the complaints system; or

(c) improving the complaints system.

(3) Information may not be published or disclosed in circumstances where in the opinion of the IPCC the non-disclosure of information is necessary for the purposes mentioned in regulation 55(1)(a) and (b) (exceptions to the duty to keep the complainant informed and to provide information for other persons).

(4) The IPCC shall consult the relevant appropriate authority before disclosing information in accordance with paragraph (2) and shall have regard to any representations made to it by the relevant appropriate authority when deciding what to disclose.

Manner and time limits of notifications

60

(1) Any notification to be given under these Regulations shall—

(a) unless otherwise specified in these Regulations or determined in guidance issued by the IPCC, be given in writing;

(b) unless otherwise specified in these Regulations, be made within such period as the IPCC may determine in guidance.

(2) No time limit mentioned in these Regulations or determined by the IPCC shall apply in any case where exceptional circumstances prevent that time limit being complied with.

PART 7
REPORTS AND RECOMMENDATIONS

Action by a police force on completion of an investigation report

61

(1) This regulation applies on completion of an investigation by a person appointed in accordance with regulation 38 (investigation by a police force at the request of a relevant appropriate authority).

(2) On completion of that investigation the person appointed in accordance with regulation 38 shall determine whether the conditions set out in sub-paragraphs (4) and (5) are satisfied in respect of the report;

(3) If the person appointed in accordance with regulation 38 determines that those conditions are so satisfied, that person shall notify—

(a) the Director of Public Prosecutions . . . of the determination and send that person a copy of the report; and

(b) the relevant appropriate authority and the persons mentioned in paragraph (8) of its determination under paragraph (a).

(4) The first condition is that the report indicates that a criminal offence may have been committed by a person to whose conduct the investigation related.

(5) The second condition is that the circumstances are such that, in the opinion of the person appointed in accordance with regulation 38, it is appropriate for the matters dealt with in the report to be considered by the Director of Public Prosecutions . . .

(6) The Director of Public Prosecutions . . . shall notify the person appointed in accordance with regulation 38 of any decision of the Director to take, or not to take, action in respect of the matters dealt with in any report a copy of which has been sent to the Director under paragraph (3)(a).

(7) It shall be the duty of the person appointed in accordance with regulation 38 to notify the persons mentioned in paragraph (8) if criminal proceedings are brought against any person by the Director of Public Prosecutions . . . in respect of any matters dealt with in a report copied to the Director under paragraph (3)(a).

(8) Those persons are—

(a) in the case of a complaint, the complainant and every person entitled to be kept properly informed in relation to the complaint under regulation 50 (duty to provide information for other persons); and

(b) in the case of a recordable conduct matter, every person entitled to be kept properly informed in relation to that matter under that regulation.

Amendment

Paras (3), (5)–(7): words omitted revoked by SI 2014/834, reg 3(3), Sch 3, paras 24, 26. Date in force: 27 March 2014: see SI 2014/834, art 1.

Final reports on investigations: complaints, conduct matters and certain DSI matters

62

(1)   This regulation applies on the completion of an investigation of—

    (a)   a complaint, or

    (b)   a conduct matter.

(2)   A person appointed under regulation 37 (investigations by the relevant appropriate authority on its own behalf) shall submit a report on that person's investigation to the relevant appropriate authority.

(3)   A person appointed in accordance with regulation 38 (investigation by a police force at the request of the relevant appropriate authority) shall—

    (a)   submit a report on that person's investigation to the relevant appropriate authority; and

    (b)   send a copy of that report to the IPCC.

(4)   The report shall set out the determination of the person appointed in accordance with regulation 38 (investigation by a police force at the request of the relevant appropriate authority) as to whether the conditions set out in regulation 61(4) and (5) (action by a police force on completion of an investigation report) have been satisfied and whether the Director of Public Prosecutions . . . has been sent a copy of the investigation report in accordance with regulation 61(3)(a).

(5)   A person appointed under regulation 39 (investigations supervised by the IPCC), 40 (investigations by a police force under the management or under the supervision of the IPCC), or 41 (investigations managed by the IPCC) shall—

    (a)   submit a report on that investigation to the IPCC; and

    (b)   send a copy of that report to the relevant appropriate authority.

(6)   A person designated under regulation 42 (investigations by the IPCC itself) as the person in charge of an investigation by the IPCC itself shall submit a report on it to the IPCC.

(7)   A person submitting a report under this regulation shall not be prevented by any obligation of secrecy imposed by any rule of law or otherwise from including all such matters in that person's report as that person thinks fit.

(8)   A person who has submitted a report under this regulation on an investigation within regulation 52(1) (duty to consider submissions from relevant officers, relevant officials of the Secretary of State, relevant contractors, officials exercising customs revenue functions and customs revenue contractors) must supply the relevant appropriate authority with such copies of further documents or other items in that person's possession as the authority may request.

(9)   The relevant appropriate authority may only make a request in respect of a copy of a document or other item if the relevant appropriate authority—

    (a)   considers that the document or item is of relevance to the investigation, and

    (b)   requires a copy of the document or the item for either or both of the purposes mentioned in paragraph (10).

(10)   Those purposes are—

    (a)   complying with any obligation which the authority has under the disciplinary proceedings in relation to any person whose conduct is the subject-matter of the investigation;

    (b)   ensuring that any relevant officer, relevant official of the Secretary of State or official exercising customs revenue functions receives a fair hearing at any disciplinary proceedings in respect of any such conduct of that officer.

Amendment

Para (4): words omitted revoked by SI 2014/834, reg 3(3), Sch 3, paras 24, 27. Date in force: 27 March 2014: see SI 2014/834, art 1.

Action by the IPCC in response to an investigation report under regulation 62

63

(1) This regulation applies where—

(a) a report on an investigation carried out under the management of the IPCC is submitted to it under paragraph (3) of regulation 62 (final reports on investigations: complaints, conduct matters and certain DSI matters); or

(b) a report on an investigation carried out by a person designated by the IPCC is submitted to it under paragraph (5) of that regulation.

(2) On receipt of the report, the IPCC—

(a) if it appears that the relevant appropriate authority has not already been sent a copy of the report, shall send a copy of the report to that authority;

(b) shall determine whether the conditions set out in sub-paragraphs (3) and (4) are satisfied in respect of the report;

(c) if it determines that those conditions are so satisfied, shall notify the Director of Public Prosecutions . . . of the determination and send that person a copy of the report; and

(d) shall notify the relevant appropriate authority and the persons mentioned in paragraph (7) of its determination under paragraph (b) and of any action taken by it under paragraph (c).

(3) The first condition is that the report indicates that a criminal offence may have been committed by a person to whose conduct the investigation related.

(4) The second condition is that the circumstances are such that, in the opinion of the IPCC, it is appropriate for the matters dealt with in the report to be considered by the Director of Public Prosecutions . . .

(5) The Director of Public Prosecutions . . . shall notify the IPCC of any decision of the Director to take, or not to take, action in respect of the matters dealt with in any report a copy of which has been sent to the Director under paragraph (2)(c).

(6) It shall be the duty of the IPCC to notify the persons mentioned in paragraph (5) if criminal proceedings are brought against any person by the Director of Public Prosecutions . . . in respect of any matters dealt with in a report copied to the Director under paragraph (2)(c).

(7) Those persons are—

(a) in the case of a complaint, the complainant and every person entitled to be kept properly informed in relation to the complaint under regulation 50 (duty to provide information for other persons); and

(b) in the case of a recordable conduct matter, every person entitled to be kept properly informed in relation to that matter under that regulation.

(8) On receipt of the report, the IPCC shall also notify the relevant appropriate authority that it must determine—

(a) whether any relevant officer, relevant official of the Secretary of State, relevant contractor, official exercising customs revenue functions or customs revenue contractor (person whose conduct is in question) has a case to answer in respect of their conduct or has no case to answer; and

(b) what action (if any) the authority is required to, or will in its discretion, take in respect of the matters dealt with in the report; and

(c) what other action (if any) the authority will in its discretion take in respect of those matters.

(9) On receipt of a notification under paragraph (8) in relation to a relevant contractor or customs revenue contractor, the relevant appropriate authority shall make those determinations and submit a memorandum to the IPCC which sets out the determinations the authority has made.

(10)   On receipt of a notification under paragraph (8) in relation to a relevant officer, relevant official of the Secretary of State or official exercising customs revenue functions, the relevant appropriate authority shall make those determinations and submit a memorandum to the IPCC which—

    (a)   sets out the determinations the authority has made, and

    (b)   if the relevant appropriate authority has decided in relation to any person whose conduct is the subject-matter of the report that disciplinary proceedings should not be brought against that person, sets out its reasons for so deciding.

(11)   On receipt of a memorandum under paragraph (9) or (10), the IPCC shall—

    (a)   consider the memorandum and whether the relevant appropriate authority has made the determinations under paragraph (9) or (10)(a) that the IPCC considers appropriate in respect of the matters dealt with in the report;

    (b)   determine, in the light of its consideration of those matters, whether or not to make recommendations under regulation 67 (duties with respect to disciplinary proceedings); and

    (c)   make such recommendations (if any) under that regulation as it thinks fit.

(12)   On the making of a determination under paragraph (11)(b) the IPCC shall give a notification—

    (a)   in the case of a complaint, to the complainant and to every person entitled to be kept properly informed in relation to the complaint under regulation 49 (duty to keep the complainant informed); and

    (b)   in the case of a recordable conduct matter, to every person entitled to be kept properly informed in relation to that matter under regulation 50 (duty to provide information for other persons).

(13)   The notification required by paragraph (12) is one setting out—

    (a)   the findings of the report;

    (b)   the IPCC's determination under paragraph (11)(b); and

    (c)   the action which the relevant appropriate authority is to be recommended to take as a consequence of the determination.

(14)   Paragraphs (5) and (6) of regulation 49 (duty to keep the complainant informed) shall have effect in relation to the duties imposed on the IPCC by paragraph (12) of this regulation as they have effect in relation to the duties imposed on the IPCC by that regulation.

(15)   The IPCC shall be entitled (notwithstanding any obligation of secrecy imposed by any rule of law or otherwise) to discharge the duty to give a person mentioned in paragraph (12) notification of the findings of the report by sending that person a copy of the report.

Amendment

Paras (2), (4)–(6): words omitted revoked by SI 2014/834, reg 3(3), Sch 3, paras 24, 28. Date in force: 27 March 2014: see SI 2014/834, art 1.

Action by the relevant appropriate authority in response to an investigation report under regulation 62

64

(1)   This regulation applies where—

    (a)   a report of an investigation is submitted to the relevant appropriate authority in accordance with regulation 62(2) (final reports on investigations: complaints, conduct matters and certain DSI matters); or

    (b)   a report, or a copy of a report is sent to the relevant appropriate authority in accordance with regulation 62(3) or (4).

(2)   On receipt of the report or (as the case may be) of the copy, the relevant appropriate authority shall note the contents of the report and determine—

(a) whether any person to whose conduct the investigation related has a case to answer in respect of their conduct or has no case to answer;

(b) what action (if any) the authority is required to, or will in its discretion, take in respect of the matters dealt with in the report; and

(c) what other action (if any) the authority will in its discretion take in respect of those matters.

(3) On the making of the determinations under paragraph (2) the relevant appropriate authority shall give a notification—

(a) in the case of a complaint, to the complainant and to every person entitled to be kept properly informed in relation to the complaint under regulation 49 (duty to keep complainant informed); and

(b) in the case of a recordable conduct matter, to every person entitled to be kept properly informed in relation to that matter under regulation 50 (duty to provide information for other persons).

(4) The notification required by paragraph (3) is one setting out—

(a) the findings of the report;

(b) the determinations the authority has made under paragraph (2);

(c) the action (if any) which that authority has decided to take; and

(d) the complainant's right of appeal under regulation 70 (appeals to the IPCC with respect to an investigation).

(5) Paragraphs (5) and (6) of regulation 49 shall have effect in relation to the duties imposed on the relevant appropriate authority by paragraph (3) of this regulation as they have effect in relation to the duties imposed on the relevant appropriate authority by that section.

(6) Except so far as may be otherwise provided by paragraph (5), the relevant appropriate authority shall be entitled (notwithstanding any obligation of secrecy imposed by any rule of law or otherwise) to discharge the duty to give a person mentioned in paragraph (4) notification of the findings of the report by sending that person a copy of the report.

Final reports on investigations: DSI matters

65
(1) This regulation applies on the completion of an investigation of a DSI matter in respect of which neither the IPCC, nor the person appointed under regulation 38 (investigation by a police force at the request of the relevant appropriate authority) or 40 (investigation by a police force under the management or under the supervision of the IPCC) has made a determination that the person whose conduct is in question may have—

(a) committed a criminal offence; or

(b) behaved in a manner which would justify the bringing of disciplinary proceedings.

(2) The person investigating shall—

(a) submit a report on the investigation to the IPCC; and

(b) send a copy of that report to the relevant appropriate authority.

(3) A person submitting a report under this regulation shall not be prevented by any obligation of secrecy imposed by any rule of law or otherwise from including all such matters in his report as that person thinks fit.

(4) On receipt of the report, the IPCC shall determine whether the report indicates that a relevant officer, relevant official of the Secretary of State, relevant contractor, official exercising customs revenue functions or customs revenue contractor may have—

(a) committed a criminal offence, or

(b) behaved in a manner which would justify the bringing of disciplinary proceedings.

(5) If the IPCC determines under paragraph (4) that there is no indication in the report that an officer may have—

(a) committed a criminal offence, or

(b) behaved in a manner which would justify the bringing of disciplinary proceedings,

it shall make such recommendations or give such advice under regulation 6(1)(e) (general functions of the IPCC) (if any) as it considers necessary or desirable.

(6) Paragraph (5) does not affect any power of the IPCC to make recommendations or give advice under regulation 6(1)(e) in other cases (whether arising under these Regulations or otherwise).

Action by the IPCC in response to an investigation report under regulation 65

66

(1) If the IPCC determines under regulation 65(4) (final reports on investigations: other DSI matters) that the report indicates that a relevant officer, relevant official of the Secretary of State, relevant contractor, official exercising customs revenue functions or customs revenue contractor may have—

(a) committed a criminal offence, or

(b) behaved in a manner which would justify the bringing of disciplinary proceedings,

it shall notify the relevant appropriate authority in relation to the person whose conduct is in question of its determination and, if it appears that that authority has not already been sent a copy of the report, send a copy of the report to that authority.

(2) Where the relevant appropriate authority is notified of a determination by the IPCC under paragraph (1), it shall record the matter under regulation 18 (recording etc of conduct matters in other cases) as a conduct matter (and the other provisions of these Regulations shall apply in relation to that matter accordingly).

(3) Where a DSI matter is recorded under regulation 18 as a conduct matter by virtue of paragraph (2)—

(a) the person investigating the DSI matter shall (subject to any determination made by the IPCC under regulation 31(6) (power of the IPCC to determine the form of an investigation) investigate the conduct matter as if appointed or designated to do so, and

(b) the other provisions of these Regulations shall apply in relation to that matter accordingly.

Duties with respect to disciplinary proceedings

67

(1) This regulation applies where, in the case of any investigation, the relevant appropriate authority—

(a) has given, or is required to give, a notification under regulation 63(12) (action by the IPCC in response to an investigation report under regulation 62) of the action it is proposing to take in relation to the matters dealt with in any report of the investigation; or

(b) has submitted, or is required to submit, a memorandum to the IPCC under regulation 63 or 70 (appeals to the IPCC with respect to an investigation) setting out the action that it is proposing to take in relation to those matters.

(2) Subject to regulation 46 (restrictions on proceedings pending the conclusion of an investigation) and to any recommendations or directions under the following provisions of this regulation, it shall be the duty of the relevant appropriate authority—

(a) to take the action which has been or is required to be notified or, as the case may be, which is or is required to be set out in the memorandum; and

(b) in a case where that action consists of or includes the bringing of disciplinary proceedings, to secure that those proceedings, once brought, are proceeded with to a proper conclusion.

(3) Where this regulation applies to a relevant contractor or customs revenue contractor by virtue of paragraph (1)(b), the IPCC may make a recommendation to the relevant appropriate authority in respect of that person that the person has a case to answer in respect of their conduct or has no case to answer in relation to their conduct to which the investigation related and it shall be the duty of the relevant appropriate authority to notify the IPCC whether it accepts the recommendation and (if it does) to set out in the notification the steps that it is proposing to take to give effect to it.

(4) Where this regulation applies to a relevant officer, relevant official of the Secretary of State or official exercising customs revenue functions by virtue of paragraph (1)(b), the IPCC may make a recommendation to the relevant appropriate authority in respect of that person—

(a) that the person has a case to answer in respect of their conduct or has no case to answer in relation to their conduct to which the investigation related;

(b) that disciplinary proceedings are brought against that person in respect of the conduct to which the investigation related; or

(c) that any disciplinary proceedings brought against that person are modified so as to deal with such aspects of that conduct as may be so specified;

and it shall be the duty of the relevant appropriate authority to notify the IPCC whether it accepts the recommendation and (if it does) to set out in the notification the steps that it is proposing to take to give effect to it.

(5) If, after the IPCC has made a recommendation under this regulation, the relevant appropriate authority does not take steps to secure that full effect is given to the recommendation—

(a) the IPCC may direct the relevant appropriate authority to take steps for that purpose; and

(b) it shall be the duty of the relevant appropriate authority to comply with the direction.

(6) A direction under paragraph (5) may, to such extent as the IPCC thinks fit, set out the steps to be taken by the appropriate authority in order to give effect to the recommendation.

(7) Where the IPCC gives the relevant appropriate authority a direction under this regulation, it shall supply the relevant appropriate authority with a statement of its reasons for doing so.

(8) Where disciplinary proceedings have been brought in accordance with a recommendation or direction under this regulation, it shall be the duty of the authority to ensure that they are proceeded with to a proper conclusion.

(9) The IPCC may at any time withdraw a direction given under this regulation; and paragraph (8) shall not impose any obligation in relation to any time after the withdrawal of the direction.

(10) The relevant appropriate authority shall keep the IPCC informed—

(a) in a case in which this regulation applies by virtue of paragraph (1)(b), of whatever action it takes in pursuance of its duty under paragraph (2); and

(b) in every case of a recommendation or direction under this regulation, of whatever action it takes in response to that recommendation or direction.

Complaints against a person whose identity is not ascertained

68

(1) Where a complaint or conduct matter relates to the conduct of a person whose identity is not ascertained at the time at which the complaint is made or the conduct matter is recorded, or whose identity is not ascertained during or subsequent to, the investigation of the complaint or recordable conduct matter, then these Regulations shall apply in relation to such a person as if it did not include—

(a) any requirement for the person complained against to be given an opportunity to make representations;

(b) any requirement for the IPCC or the relevant appropriate authority to determine whether a criminal offence may have been committed by the person whose conduct has been the subject-matter of an investigation, or to take any action in relation to such a determination;

(c) any requirement for a relevant appropriate authority to determine whether disciplinary proceedings should be brought against a person whose conduct is the subject-matter of a report.

(2) Where the identity of such a person is subsequently ascertained, the IPCC and relevant appropriate authority shall take such action in accordance with these Regulations as they see fit.

PART 8
APPEALS

Appeals to the IPCC: failures to notify or record a complaint

69

(1) An appeal under regulation 15 against any failure referred to in regulation 15(3) (failures to notify or record a complaint) shall be made within 28 days of the date on which notification of that failure is made or sent to the complainant under regulation 15(2).

(2) Any such appeal shall be made in writing and shall state—

(a) details of the complaint;

(b) the date on which the complaint was made;

(c) the grounds for the appeal; and

(d) the date on which the complainant was notified of the determination or of the failure to record the complaint.

(3) Where the IPCC receives such an appeal it shall—

(a) notify the relevant appropriate authority of the appeal; and

(b) request any information from any person which it considers necessary to dispose of the appeal.

(4) Where the IPCC receives an appeal which fails to comply with one or more of the requirements mentioned in paragraph (2), it may decide to proceed as if those requirements had been complied with.

(5) The relevant appropriate authority shall supply to the IPCC any information reasonably requested under paragraph (3)(b).

(6) The IPCC shall determine the outcome of the appeal as soon as practicable.

(7) The IPCC shall notify the complainant and the relevant appropriate authority of the reasons for its determination.

(8) The IPCC may extend the time period mentioned in paragraph (1) in any case where it is satisfied that by reason of the special circumstances of the case it is just to do so.

Appeals to the IPCC with respect to an investigation

70

(1) This regulation applies where a complaint has been subjected to—

   (a) an investigation by the relevant appropriate authority on its own behalf; or

   (b) an investigation under the supervision of the IPCC following a determination under regulation 21 (reference of complaints to the IPCC), 23 (reference of conduct matters to the IPCC) or 27 (reference of DSI matters to the IPCC).

(2) The complainant shall have the following rights of appeal to the IPCC—

   (a) a right to appeal on the grounds that the complainant has not been provided with adequate information—

      (i) about the findings of the investigation; or

      (ii) about any determination of the relevant appropriate authority relating to the taking (or not taking) of action in respect of any matters dealt with in the report on the investigation;

   (b) a right to appeal against the findings of the investigation;

   (c) a right of appeal against any determination by the relevant appropriate authority that a person to whose conduct the investigation related has a case to answer in respect of their conduct or has no case to answer;

   (d) a right of appeal against any determination by a person appointed in accordance with regulation 38 (investigation by a police force at the request of the relevant appropriate authority) under regulation 63(2)(c) (action by the IPCC in response to an investigation report under regulation 62 or regulation 61(3) (action by police force on completion of an investigation report); and

   (e) where the complaint concerns the conduct of a relevant officer, relevant official of the Secretary of State or official exercising customs revenue functions, a right of appeal against any determination by the relevant appropriate authority relating to the taking (or not taking) of action in respect of any matters dealt with in the report, as a result of which it is not required to send the Director of Public Prosecutions . . . a copy of the report.

(3) On the bringing of an appeal under this regulation, the IPCC may require the person investigating to submit a memorandum to the IPCC which—

   (a) sets out whether the relevant appropriate authority has determined that a person to whose conduct the investigation related has a case to answer in respect of their conduct or has no case to answer;

   (b) sets out what action (if any) the relevant appropriate authority has determined that it is required to or will, in its discretion, take in respect of the matters dealt with in the report;

   (c) if the relevant appropriate authority is proposing to take any action, sets out what action it is proposing to take;

   (d) if the relevant appropriate authority has decided in relation to a person to whose conduct the investigation related; that disciplinary proceedings should not be brought against that person, sets out its reasons for so deciding and it shall be the duty of the relevant appropriate authority to comply with any requirement under this paragraph; and

   (e) if a person appointed in accordance with regulation 38 made a determination under regulation 63(2)(c) as a result of which it is not required to send the Director of Public Prosecutions . . . a copy of the report relating to the investigation, sets out the reasons for that determination.

(4) Where the IPCC so requires on the bringing of any appeal under this regulation in the case of an investigation by the relevant appropriate authority on its own behalf, the relevant appropriate authority shall provide the IPCC with a copy of the report of the investigation.

(5) On an appeal under this regulation, the IPCC shall determine such of the following as it considers appropriate in the circumstances—

    (a)   whether the complainant has been provided with adequate information about the matters mentioned in paragraph (2)(a);

    (b)   whether the findings of the investigation need to be reconsidered; and

    (c)   whether the relevant appropriate authority—

        (i)   has made such a determination as is mentioned in paragraph (3)(a) that the IPCC considers to be appropriate in respect of matters dealt with in the report, and

        (ii)   has determined that it is required to or will, in its discretion, take the action (if any) that the IPCC considers to be so appropriate; and

    (d)   whether the conditions set out in regulation 63(3) and (4) are satisfied in respect of the report on the investigation.

(6) If, on an appeal under this regulation, the IPCC determines that the complainant has not been provided with adequate information about any matter, the IPCC shall give the person investigating all such directions as the IPCC considers appropriate for securing that the complainant is properly informed.

(7) If, on an appeal under this regulation, the IPCC determines that the findings of the investigation need to be reconsidered, it shall either—

    (a)   review those findings without an immediate further investigation; or

    (b)   direct that the complaint be re-investigated.

(8) If, on an appeal under this regulation, the IPCC determines that the relevant appropriate authority has not made a determination as to whether there is a case for a person to whose conduct the investigation related to answer that the IPCC considers appropriate or has not determined that it is required to or will, in its discretion, take the action in respect of the matters dealt with in the report that the IPCC considers appropriate, the IPCC shall—

    (a)   determine, in the light of that determination, whether or not to make recommendations under regulation 67 (duties with respect to disciplinary proceedings); and

    (b)   make such recommendations (if any) under that regulation as it thinks fit.

(9) If, on an appeal under this regulation, the IPCC determines that the conditions set out in regulation 63(3) and (4) are satisfied in respect of the report, it shall direct the person appointed in accordance with regulation 38—

    (a)   to notify the Director of Public Prosecutions . . . of the IPCC's determination, and

    (b)   to send the Director a copy of the report.

(10) The IPCC shall give notification of any determination under this regulation—

    (a)   to the relevant appropriate authority;

    (b)   to the complainant;

    (c)   the person appointed in accordance with regulation 38 (if appropriate);

    (d)   to every person entitled to be kept properly informed in relation to the complaint under regulation 49 (duty to keep the complainant informed); and

    (e)   except in a case where it appears to the IPCC that to do so might prejudice any proposed review or re-investigation of the complaint, to the person complained against.

(11) The IPCC shall also give notification of any directions given to a person under this regulation—

(a)   to the complainant;

(b)   to every person entitled to be kept properly informed in relation to the complaint under regulation 50 (duty to provide information for other persons); and

(c)   except in a case where it appears to the IPCC that to do so might prejudice any proposed review or re-investigation of the complaint, to the person complained against.

(12)   The IPCC shall consult the relevant appropriate authority before giving it directions in accordance with paragraph (6), recommendations in accordance with paragraph (8), or a notification in accordance with paragraph (10) or (11) and shall have regard to any representations made to it by the relevant appropriate authority in giving those directions.

(13)   It shall be the duty of the person investigating to comply with any directions given to it under this regulation.

(14)   Any appeal made by a complainant under this regulation shall be made within 28 days of the date on which the person investigating sends a notification to the complainant of its determination under regulation 63(13) or 61(3) as to what action (if any) it will take in respect of the matters dealt with in the investigation report.

(15)   Any such appeal shall be in writing and shall state—

(a)   details of the complaint;

(b)   the date on which the complaint was made;

(c)   the grounds for the appeal; and

(d)   the date on which the complainant received notification under regulation 63(12) or 61(3).

(16)   Where the IPCC receives such an appeal it shall request any information from any person which it consider necessary to dispose of the appeal.

(17)   Where the IPCC receives an appeal which fails to comply with one or more of the requirements mentioned in paragraph (15), it may decide to proceed as if those requirements had been complied with.

(18)   The person investigating shall supply to the IPCC any further information requested of it under paragraph (16).

(19)   The IPCC shall determine the outcome of the appeal as soon as practicable.

(20)   The IPCC shall notify the complainant and the person investigating of the reasons for its determination.

(21)   The IPCC may extend the time period mentioned in paragraph (14) in any case where it is satisfied that by reason of the special circumstances of the case it is just to do so.

Amendment

Paras (2), (3), (9): words omitted revoked by SI 2014/834, reg 3(3), Sch 3, paras 24, 29. Date in force: 27 March 2014: see SI 2014/834, art 1.

Reviews and re-investigations following an appeal

71

(1)   On a review under regulation 70(7)(a) (appeals to the IPCC with respect to an investigation) of the findings of an investigation the powers of the IPCC shall be, according to its determination on that review, to do one or more of the following—

(a)   to uphold the findings in whole or in part;

(b)   to give the person investigating such directions—

(i)   as to the carrying out by the relevant appropriate authority of its own review of the findings,

(ii)   as to the information to be provided to the complainant, and

(iii)   generally as to the handling of the matter in future,

as the IPCC thinks fit;

(c)   to direct that the complaint be re-investigated.

(2) Where the IPCC directs under regulation 70 or paragraph (1) that a complaint be re-investigated, it shall make a determination of the form that the re-investigation should take.

(3) Paragraphs (3) to (8) of regulation 31 (power of the IPCC to determine the form of an investigation) shall apply in relation to a determination under paragraph (2) as they apply in the case of a determination under that regulation.

(4) The provisions of these Regulations shall apply in relation to any re-investigation in pursuance of a direction under regulation 70(9) or paragraph (1) of this regulation as they apply in relation to any investigation in pursuance of a determination under regulation 31.

(5) The IPCC shall give notification of any determination made by it under this regulation—

    (a)   to the relevant appropriate authority,

    (b)   the person appointed in accordance with regulation 38 (investigation by a police force at the request of the relevant appropriate authority) or regulation 40 (investigation by a police force under the management or under the supervision of the IPCC),

    (c)   to the complainant, and

    (d)   to every person entitled to be kept properly informed in relation to the complaint under regulation 49 (duty to keep the complainant informed),

except in a case where it appears to the IPCC that to do so might prejudice any proposed re-investigation of the complaint, to the person complained against.

(6) The IPCC shall also give notification of any directions given to the person investigating under this regulation—

    (a)   to the complainant, and

    (b)   to every person entitled to be kept properly informed in relation to the complaint under section

except in a case where it appears to the IPCC that to do so might prejudice any proposed review or re-investigation of the complaint, to the person complained against.

PART 9
REVOCATION, SAVING AND TRANSITIONAL PROVISIONS

Revocation of the 2009 Regulations, saving and transitional provisions

72

(1) The 2009 Regulations are revoked.

(2) Notwithstanding the revocation of the 2009 Regulations, regulation 72 of those Regulations shall continue to have effect in respect of those complaints, conduct matters or DSI matters to which it applies.

(3) These Regulations apply to a complaint, conduct matter or DSI matter relating to—

    (a)   a relevant officer, relevant official of the Secretary of State, relevant contractor, official exercising customs revenue functions or a customs revenue contractor where the conduct or matter is alleged to have occurred on or after 6th April 2010;

    (b)   a relevant officer, relevant official of the Secretary of State or an official exercising customs revenue functions where the conduct or matter is alleged to have occurred on or after 5th August 2009 and before 6th April 2010, but does not come to the attention of the relevant appropriate authority until on or after 6th April 2010; and

    (c)   an immigration officer exercising specified enforcement functions or an official of the Secretary of State exercising specified enforcement functions in relation to immigration or asylum where the conduct or matter is alleged to have occurred after 1st April 2007 and before 5th August 2009, but does not come to the attention of the relevant appropriate authority until on or after 6th April 2010.

(4) In this regulation the term "specified enforcement functions" has the same meaning as in the 2008 Regulations.

IMMIGRATION SERVICES COMMISSIONER (DESIGNATED PROFESSIONAL BODY) (FEES) ORDER 2010

(SI 2010/891)

Made: 22 March 2010.

Authority: Immigration and Asylum Act 1999, ss 86(10), (12), 166(3)(b).

Commencement: 21 April 2010.

1 Citation and commencement

This Order may be cited as the Immigration Services Commissioner (Designated Professional Body) (Fees) Order 2010 and shall come into force on 21st April 2010.

2 Fees

(1) The fee to be paid to the Commissioner by each designated professional body for the year 1st April 2009 to 31st March 2010 shall be the sum specified in the Schedule to this Order.

(2) The fee shall be paid on or before 30th April 2010.

SCHEDULE

Designated Professional Body	Fee to be paid
The Law Society	£87,640
The Law Society of Scotland	£10,240
The Law Society of Northern Ireland	£1,900
The Institute of Legal Executives	£9,040
The General Council of the Bar	£13,670
The Faculty of Advocates	£1,140
The General Council of the Bar of Northern Ireland	£1,760

IMMIGRATION AND NATIONALITY (FEES) ORDER 2011

(SI 2011/445)

Made: 17 February 2011.

Authority: Immigration, Asylum and Nationality Act 2006, s 51(1), (2).

Commencement: 18 February 2011.

Citation, commencement and interpretation

1

This Order may be cited as the Immigration and Nationality (Fees) Order 2011 and shall come into force on the day after the day on which it is made.

2

In this Order—

"the 1971 Act" means the Immigration Act 1971;

"the 1981 Act" means the British Nationality Act 1981;

"the 1982 Order" means the British Protectorates, Protected States and Protected Persons Order 1982;

"the 1997 Act" means the British Nationality (Hong Kong) Act 1997;

"the 1999 Act" means the Immigration and Asylum Act 1999;

"the 2006 Act" means the Immigration, Asylum and Nationality Act 2006;

["the 2007 Act" means the UK Borders Act 2007;]

"A-rated sponsor" means a sponsor who is recorded as being "A-rated" on the register of licensed sponsors maintained by the Secretary of State under the immigration rules;

"action plan" means an action plan issued under the immigration rules to a B-rated sponsor with which a B-rated sponsor must comply in order to become an A-rated sponsor;

["basic service" has the same meaning as provided in regulation 3 of the Immigration Control (Charges) (Basic Service) Regulations 2003;]

["biometric information" has the same meaning as provided in section 15 of the 2007 Act;]

"B-rated sponsor" means a sponsor who is recorded as being "B-rated" on the register of licensed sponsors maintained by the Secretary of State under the immigration rules;

"British protected person" has the same meaning as provided in section 50(1) of the 1981 Act;

"certificate of sponsorship" means an authorisation issued under the immigration rules by the Secretary of State to a sponsor in respect of one or more applications, or potential applications, for leave to remain in or enter the United Kingdom;

"consular functions" means any of the functions described in Article 5 of the Vienna Convention on Consular Relations set out in Schedule 1 to the Consular Relations Act 1968 or functions in the United Kingdom which correspond with those functions;

"consular premises" has the same meaning as provided in Article 1(1)(j) of the Vienna Convention on Consular Relations set out in Schedule 1 to the Consular Relations Act 1968;

["contractor" means a person with whom the Secretary of State has entered into a contract, by which the person agrees to provide certain services in connection with immigration and nationality to applicants outside the United Kingdom;]

["control port" means a port in which a control area is designated under paragraph 26(3) of Schedule 2 to the 1971 Act;]

"entry clearance" has the same meaning as provided in section 33(1) of the 1971 Act;

"the former nationality Acts" has the same meaning as provided in section 50(1) of the 1981 Act;

"the immigration rules" means rules made under section 3(2) of the 1971 Act;

"leave to enter the United Kingdom" means leave to enter the United Kingdom given in accordance with the provisions of the 1971 Act or the immigration rules;

"leave to remain in the United Kingdom" means leave to remain in the United Kingdom given in accordance with the provisions of the 1971 Act or the immigration rules;

"sponsor" means a sponsor under Part 6A of the immigration rules;

"sponsor licence" means a licence granted by the Secretary of State under the immigration rules allowing a person to act as a sponsor;

"student" means a person given leave to enter, or remain, in the United Kingdom under Tier 4 of the points-based system set out in the immigration rules.

Amendment

Definitions "the 2007 Act" and "biometric information" inserted by SI 2014/2038, art 2(1), (2).

Date in force: 1 September 2014: see SI 2014/2038, art 1.

Definitions "basic service", "contractor" and "control port" inserted by SI 2014/205, art 2(1), (2).

Date in force: 4 February 2014: see SI 2014/205, art 1.

Requirement to pay a fee for applications connected with immigration or nationality

3

(1) Applications to which this article applies must be accompanied by the fee specified in regulations made under section 51(3) of the 2006 Act.

(2) This article applies to applications for—

    (a)   leave to remain in the United Kingdom;

    (b)   entry clearance;

    (c)   variation of leave to enter, or remain in, the United Kingdom;

    (d)   permission for a student given leave to enter, or remain in, the United Kingdom to change their course of study or sponsor;

    (e)   the fixing of a stamp, sticker or other attachment which indicates that a person has been granted limited, or indefinite, leave to enter, or remain in, the United Kingdom on a passport or other document issued to the applicant;

    (f)   an immigration employment document, that is to say a work permit, or any other document which relates to employment and is issued for the purposes of the immigration rules or in connection with leave to enter or remain in the United Kingdom;

    (g)   a travel document not including a passport;

    (h)   naturalisation as a British citizen under the 1981 Act;

    (i)   the amendment of a certificate of registration or naturalisation as a British citizen issued under the 1981 Act;

    (j)   naturalisation as a British overseas territories citizen under section 18(1) or (2) of the 1981 Act;

    (k)   registration as a British citizen under section 1(3), (3A) or (4), 3(1), (2) or (5), 4(2) or (5), 4A, 4B, 4C, 4D, 10(1) or (2), or 13(1) or (3) of the 1981 Act, or paragraph 3, 4 or 5 of Schedule 2 to that Act;

    (l)   registration as a British overseas territories citizen under sections 24 and 13(1) or (3), or section 15(3) or (4), 17(1), (2) or (5), or 22(1) or (2) of the 1981 Act, or paragraph 3, 4 or 5 of Schedule 2 to that Act;

    (m)   registration as a British overseas citizen under section 27(1) of the 1981 Act, or paragraph 4 or 5 of Schedule 2 to that Act;

    (n)   registration as a British subject under section 32 of the 1981 Act, or paragraph 4 of Schedule 2 to that Act;

    (o)   registration as a British protected person under Article 7 of the 1982 Order;

    (p)   registration as a British citizen under section 1 of the 1997 Act;

(q)   a transit visa within the meaning of section 41(2) of the 1999 Act;

(r)   a certificate that a person has the right of abode in the United Kingdom, issued pursuant to section 10 of the Nationality, Immigration and Asylum Act 2002;

[(s)   a biometric immigration document within the meaning of section 5 of the 2007 Act;]

(t)   a sponsor licence, or the renewal of such a licence;

(u)   any change to a sponsor's status under the immigration rules; . . .

(v)   a letter or other document confirming—

    (i)   a person's immigration or nationality status; or

    (ii)   that a person is not a British citizen[; and

(w)   a registration certificate, a residence card, a document certifying permanent residence, a permanent residence card or a derivative residence card, issued pursuant to Part 3 of the Immigration (European Economic Area) Regulations 2006].

Amendment

Para (2): sub-para (s) substituted by SI 2014/2038, art 2(1), (3).

Date in force: 1 September 2014: see SI 2014/2038, art 1.

Para (2): in sub-para (u) word omitted revoked by SI 2014/205, art 2(1), (3)(a).

Date in force: 4 February 2014: see SI 2014/205, art 1.

Para (2): sub-para (w) and word "; and" immediately preceding it inserted by SI 2014/205, art 2(1), (3)(b).

Date in force: 4 February 2014: see SI 2014/205, art 1.

Requirement to pay a fee in respect of the provision on request of a service connected with immigration or nationality

4

[The Secretary of State, or a contractor, or any person appointed by, or acting on behalf of, the Secretary of State,] shall charge the fee specified in regulations made under section 51(3) of the 2006 Act in respect of the provision on request of any of the following services:

(a)   the registration of a declaration of a renunciation of British citizenship under section 12 of the 1981 Act;

(b)   the registration of a declaration of a renunciation of British overseas territories citizenship under sections 24 and 12 of the 1981 Act;

(c)   the registration of a declaration of a renunciation of British Overseas citizenship under sections 29 and 12 of the 1981 Act;

(d)   the registration of a declaration of a renunciation of the status of British subject under sections 34 and 12 of the 1981 Act;

(e)   the arrangement of a citizenship ceremony (the fee for the arrangement of the ceremony includes the administration of a citizenship oath and pledge at the ceremony);

(f)   the administration of a citizenship oath, or oath and pledge (where not administered at a citizenship ceremony);

(g)   the supply of a certified copy of a notice, certificate, order, declaration or entry given, granted or made under the 1981 Act, any of the former nationality Acts, or the 1997 Act;

(h)   the registration of a declaration of a renunciation of the status of British protected person under Article 11 of the 1982 Order;

[(i)   attendance by a representative of the Secretary of State, or a contractor, or any person appointed by the Secretary of State, at premises other than an office of the Home Office or consular premises for the purposes of any application, service or process referred to in this Order;]

(j)   the provision of any service by a representative of the Secretary of State[, or a contractor, or any person appointed by the Secretary of State] outside office hours relating to any application, process or service referred to in this Order;

[[(k)   arrangements for expediting the processing (or any element of the processing) of a claim or application in connection with immigration or nationality;

(l)   the arrangement of an appointment for the purposes of making a claim or application in connection with immigration or nationality in person, either at an office of the Home Office, at consular premises or at any other place;]

(m)   customer services for sponsors; . . .

(n)   the administration of any test a person is required to take for the purposes of the immigration rules];

[(o)   the acceptance or processing of a claim or application in connection with immigration or nationality at a place other than an office of the Home Office or consular premises;

(p)   the provision of a service or process in connection with immigration or nationality at a place other than an office of the Home Office or consular premises;

(q)   arrangements for expediting the entry of passengers into, or transit through, the United Kingdom; and

(r)   arrangements for the provision of immigration officers or facilities at a control port in addition to those (if any) required to provide a basic service].

Amendment

Words from "The Secretary of State," to "the Secretary of State," in square brackets substituted by SI 2014/205, art 2(1), (4)(a).

Date in force: 4 February 2014: see SI 2014/205, art 1.

Para (i) substituted by SI 2014/205, art 2(1), (4)(b).

Date in force: 4 February 2014: see SI 2014/205, art 1.

In para (j) words ", or a contractor, or any person appointed by the Secretary of State" in square brackets inserted by SI 2014/205, art 2(1), (4)(c).

Date in force: 4 February 2014: see SI 2014/205, art 1.

Paras (k)–(n) inserted by SI 2013/249, art 2(1), (2)(c).

Date in force: 8 February 2013: see SI 2013/249, art 1.

Paras (k), (l) substituted by SI 2014/205, art 2(1), (4)(d).

Date in force: 4 February 2014: see SI 2014/205, art 1.

In para (m) word omitted revoked by SI 2014/205, art 2(1), (4)(e).

Date in force: 4 February 2014: see SI 2014/205, art 1.

Paras (o)–(r) inserted by SI 2014/205, art 2(1), (4)(f).

Date in force: 4 February 2014: see SI 2014/205, art 1.

Requirement to pay a fee in respect of a process connected with immigration or nationality

5

[The Secretary of State, or a contractor, or any person appointed by, or acting on behalf of, the Secretary of State,] shall charge the fee specified in regulations made under section 51(3) of the 2006 Act in respect of the following processes:

(a)   the issuing of a certificate of sponsorship; . . .

  (b)   the issuing of an action plan; [. . .

  [(c)   taking a record of a person's biometric information where the person is required by regulations made under section 41 of the 1981 Act, section 126 of the Nationality, Immigration and Asylum Act 2002, or section 5 of the 2007 Act to provide such information for the purposes of an application or claim in connection with immigration or nationality;][; and

  (d)   the review on request of a decision to refuse an application or claim in connection with immigration or nationality].

Amendment

Words in first pair of square brackets substituted by SI 2014/2038, art 2(1), (4)(a).

Date in force: 1 September 2014: see SI 2014/2038, art 1.

In para (a) word omitted revoked by SI 2013/249, art 2(1), (3)(b).

Date in force: 8 February 2013: see SI 2013/249, art 1.

Para (c) and word (omitted) immediately preceding it inserted by SI 2013/249, art 2(1), (3)(c).

Date in force: 8 February 2013: see SI 2013/249, art 1.

Para (c): substituted by SI 2014/2038, art 2(1), (4)(b).

Date in force: 1 September 2014: see SI 2014/2038, art 1.

In para (b) word omitted revoked by SI 2014/205, art 2(1), (5)(a).

Date in force: 4 February 2014: see SI 2014/205, art 1.

Para (d) and word "; and" immediately preceding it inserted by SI 2014/205, art 2(1), (5)(b).

Date in force: 4 February 2014: see SI 2014/205, art 1.

Requirement to pay a fee in respect of applications, services and processes in connection with immigration or nationality involving the exercise of consular functions

6

Applications in connection with immigration or nationality (whether or not under an enactment) for anything to be done in the exercise of consular functions by any person authorised by the Secretary of State to exercise such functions must be accompanied by the fee specified in regulations made under section 51(3) of the 2006 Act.

7

The Secretary of State shall charge the fee specified in regulations made under section 51(3) of the 2006 Act in respect of:

  (a)   the provision on request of a service (whether or not under an enactment) in connection with immigration or nationality where the provision of that service requires anything to be done in the exercise of consular functions by any person authorised by the Secretary of State to exercise such functions; and

  (b)   a process (whether or not under an enactment) in connection with immigration or nationality where that process requires anything to be done in the exercise of consular functions by any person authorised by the Secretary of State to exercise such functions.

8

Articles 6 and 7 apply in relation to the exercise of consular functions whether or not those functions are exercised by consular officers or by persons who are not consular officers.

Revocation

9

The Immigration and Nationality (Fees) Order 2007, the Immigration and Nationality (Fees) (Amendment) Order 2008, and the Immigration and Nationality (Fees) (Amendment) Order 2009 shall cease to have effect on the coming into force of regulations made under section 51(3) of the 2006 Act in connection with this Order.

IMMIGRATION SERVICES COMMISSIONER (APPLICATION FEE) ORDER 2011

(SI 2011/1366)

Made: 29 May 2011.

Authority: Immigration and Asylum Act 1999, s 166(3), Sch 6, para 5(1).

Commencement: 8 July 2011.

1 Citation and commencement

This Order may be cited as the Immigration Services Commissioner (Application Fee) Order 2011 and shall come into force on 8th July 2011.

2 Interpretation

In this Order—

"the Act" means the Immigration and Asylum Act 1999;

"continued registration" means registration to be continued under paragraph 3(1) of Schedule 6 to the Act;

"immigration rules" means the rules made under section 3(2) of the Immigration Act 1971;

"level 1 adviser" means a person providing immigration advice or immigration services only in connection with—

(a) the matters set out in paragraphs (ba), (d), (e), (f) and (g) of the definition of "relevant matters" in section 82(1) of the Act; or

(b) the matter set out in paragraph (b) of the definition of "relevant matters" in section 82(1) of the Act, but only in so far as the advice or services is in connection with an application for, or for the variation of, entry clearance or leave to enter or remain in the United Kingdom for a purpose for which entry or remaining is permitted in accordance with the immigration rules;

"registration" means registration under section 84(2)(a) or (b) or (ba) of the Act;

"relevant advisers" is to be construed in accordance with article 3 of this Order.

3 Meaning of "relevant advisers"

"Relevant advisers" means, in respect of—

(a) an individual, that individual together with—

(i) the employees of that individual who provide immigration advice or immigration services, excluding such employees who are qualified under section 84(2)(c) to (e) of the Act, or who are persons to whom section 84(4) of the Act applies; and

(ii) the persons who provide immigration advice or immigration services who work under the supervision of that individual and his employees, excluding such persons who are qualified persons under section 84(2)(c) to (e) of the Act, or who are persons to whom section 84(4) of the Act applies; and

(b)   a body corporate or unincorporate—

  (i)   the members and employees of that body who provide immigration [advice] or immigration services, excluding such members and employees who are qualified persons under section 84(2)(c) to (e) of the Act, or who are persons to whom section 84(4) of the Act applies; and

  (ii)   the persons who provide immigration advice or immigration services who work under the supervision of such members and employees, excluding such persons who are qualified under sections 84(2)(c) to (e) of the Act, or who are persons to whom section 84(4) of the Act applies.

Amendment

Word in square brackets in para (b) inserted by SI 2014/2847, art 2(1), (2), as from 17 November 2014.

4 Fees payable for registration and continued registration

On an application for registration—

(a)   The fee payable by a level 1 adviser shall be £575;

(b)   The fee payable by any other person providing immigration advice or immigration services shall be the fee in column 2 of the Table of Fees set out in the Schedule to this Order ("the table") which applies in respect of that person's entry in column 1 of the table.

5

On an application for continued registration—

(a)   the fee payable by a level 1 adviser shall be £575;

(b)   the fee payable by any other person providing immigration [advice] or immigration services shall be the fee in column 3 of the table which applies in respect of that person's entry in column 1 of the table.

Amendment

Word in square brackets in para (b) inserted by SI 2014/2847, art 2(1), (3), as from 17 November 2014.

6

A person's entry in column 1 of the table shall be determined by reference to the number of relevant advisers in respect of that person at the date of the application for registration or, as the case may be, continued registration.

[6A Waiver of specified fee

On an application for registration or, as the case may be, continued registration, the Commissioner must waive all of the fee specified in this Order where the applicant is a person who—

(a)   provides immigration advice or immigration services in the course of a business that is not for profit; and

(b)   does not charge a fee, directly or indirectly, for the provision of that advice or those services.]

Amendment

Inserted by SI 2014/2847, art 2(1), (4), as from 17 November 2014.

7 Revocation

The Immigration Services Commissioner (Registration Fee) Order 2004 is hereby revoked.

SCHEDULE
TABLE OF FEES
Article 4

Column 1	Column 2	Column 3
Number of relevant advisers	Fee payable for registration	Fee payable for continued registration
1-4	£1,750	£1,290
5-9	£1,960	£1,600
10 and over	£2,370	£2,115

BORDERS, CITIZENSHIP AND IMMIGRATION ACT 2009 (COMMENCEMENT NO 2) ORDER 2011

(SI 2011/1741)

Made: 14 July 2011.

Authority: Borders, Citizenship and Immigration Act 2009, s 58(4)(a).

1 Citation

This Order may be cited as the Borders, Citizenship and Immigration Act 2009 (Commencement No 2) Order 2011.

2 Appointed date

The date appointed for the coming into force of section 53 (transfer of certain immigration judicial review applications) of the Borders, Citizenship and Immigration Act 2009 is 8th August 2011.

IMMIGRATION (PROCEDURE FOR MARRIAGE) REGULATIONS 2011

(SI 2011/2678)

Made: 7 November 2011.

Authority: Asylum and Immigration (Treatment of Claimants, etc) Act 2004, ss 19(2)(a), 21(2)(a), 23(2)(a).

Commencement: 1 December 2011.

1 Citation, commencement and interpretation

(1) These Regulations may be cited as the Immigration (Procedure for Marriage) Regulations 2011 and shall come into force on 1st December 2011.

(2) In these Regulations, "the 2004 Act" means the Asylum and Immigration (Treatment of Claimants, etc) Act 2004.

2 Specified registration districts in England and Wales

The registration districts in England and Wales listed in the Schedule are specified for the purposes of section 19(2)(a) of the 2004 Act.

3 Prescribed registration districts in Scotland

Every registration district in Scotland is prescribed for the purposes of section 21(2)(a) of the 2004 Act.

4 Prescribed registrars in Northern Ireland

The registrar of every register office in Northern Ireland is prescribed for the purposes of section 23(2)(a) of the 2004 Act.

5 Revocation

The Immigration (Procedure for Marriage) Regulations 2005 are revoked.

SCHEDULE
SPECIFIED REGISTRATION DISTRICTS IN ENGLAND AND WALES

Regulation 2

Barking and Dagenham
Barnet
Birmingham
Blackburn with Darwen
Brent
Brighton and Hove
Bristol
Cambridgeshire
Camden
Cardiff
[Ceredigion]
Conwy
Cornwall
Coventry
Croydon
Cumbria
Devon
Ealing
Enfield
Essex
Gloucestershire
Greenwich
Hackney
Hammersmith and Fulham
Hampshire
Haringey
Harrow
Havering
Hertfordshire
Hillingdon
Hounslow
Hull
Islington
Kensington and Chelsea
Kent

Specified registration authorities	Offices specified in relation to specified registration authorities
County of Ceredigion	[The register office for Ceredigion]
County Borough of Conwy	The register office for Conwy
County of Cornwall	The register office for Cornwall
City of Coventry	The register office for Coventry
London Borough of Croydon	The register office for Croydon
County of Cumbria	The register office for Cumbria
County of Devon	The register office for Devon
London Borough of Ealing	The register office for Ealing
London Borough of Enfield	The register office for Enfield
County of Essex	The register office for Essex
County of Gloucestershire	The register office for Gloucestershire
London Borough of Greenwich	The register office for Greenwich
London Borough of Hackney	The register office for Hackney
London Borough of Hammersmith and Fulham	The register office for Hammersmith and Fulham
County of Hampshire	The register office for Hampshire
London Borough of Haringey	The register office for Haringey
London Borough of Harrow	The register office for Harrow
London Borough of Havering	The register office for Havering
County of Hertfordshire	The register office for Hertfordshire
London Borough of Hillingdon	The register office for Hillingdon
London Borough of Hounslow	The register office for Hounslow
Royal Borough of Kensington and Chelsea	The register office for Kensington and Chelsea
County of Kent	The register office for Kent
City of Kingston upon Hull	The register office for Hull
Royal Borough of Kingston upon Thames	The register office for Kingston upon Thames
London Borough of Islington	The register office for Islington
London Borough of Lambeth	The register office for Lambeth
City of Leeds	The register office for Leeds
City of Leicester	The register office for Leicester
London Borough of Lewisham	The register office for Lewisham
County of Lincolnshire	The register office for Lincolnshire
City of Liverpool	The register office for Liverpool
Borough of Luton	The register office for Luton
City of Manchester	The register office for Manchester
London Borough of Merton	The register office for Merton
Borough of Middlesbrough	The register office for Middlesbrough
Borough of Milton Keynes	The register office for Milton Keynes
City of Newcastle upon Tyne	The register office for Newcastle upon Tyne
London Borough of Newham	The register office for Newham
County of Norfolk	The register office for Norfolk
County of Northamptonshire	The register office for Northamptonshire
City of Nottingham	The register office for Nottingham

Specified registration authorities	Offices specified in relation to specified registration authorities
County of Oxfordshire	The register office for Oxfordshire
County of Pembrokeshire	The register office for Pembrokeshire
City of Peterborough	The register office for Peterborough
City of Plymouth	The register office for Plymouth
County of Powys	The register office for Powys
Borough of Reading	The register office for Reading
London Borough of Redbridge	The register office for Redbridge
City of Sheffield	The register office for Sheffield
County of Shropshire	The register office for Shropshire
Borough of Slough	The register office for Slough
City of Southampton	The register office for Southampton
London Borough of Southwark	The register office for Southwark
City of Stoke on Trent	The register office for Stoke on Trent
County of Suffolk	The register office for Suffolk
County of Surrey	The register office for Surrey
City and County of Swansea	The register office for Swansea
Borough of Swindon	The register office for Swindon
London Borough of Tower Hamlets	The register office for Tower Hamlets
London Borough of Waltham Forest	The register office for Waltham Forest
London Borough of Wandsworth	The register office for Wandsworth
City of Westminster	The register office for Westminster
County of West Sussex	The register office for West Sussex
County Borough of Wrexham	The register office for Wrexham

Amendment

In column 2 entry "The register office for Ceredigion" substituted, for entry "The register office for Cardiganshire North" as originally enacted, by SI 2013/227, reg 2. Date in force: 7 March 2013: see SI 2013/227, reg 1.

CONSULAR FEES ORDER 2012

(SI 2012/798)

Made: 14 March 2012.

Authority: Consular Fees Act 1980, s 1(1).

Commencement: 6 April 2012.

1

This Order may be cited as the Consular Fees Order 2012 and comes into force on 6th April 2012.

2

In this Order—

"consular officer" means any person authorised by the Secretary of State to exercise consular functions, or functions in the United Kingdom which correspond with consular functions (including persons who are not, as well as persons who are, consular officers);

"consular employee" means any person in the administrative or technical service of the consular post or diplomatic mission;

"consular premises" means the building or parts of buildings used for the purposes of the consular post or diplomatic mission;

"direct costs" means expenses that are incidental to the performance of a service, such as the cost of posting documents to a customer's home address or travel costs;

"fast-track service" means an application made in person, either by the applicant or another person acting on behalf of the applicant, which is to be processed within seven days of that application having been made;

"fast-track collect service" means an application made in person, either by the applicant or by another person acting on behalf of the applicant, which is to be processed within seven days of that application having been made, and which permits the applicant or another person acting on behalf of the applicant to collect the passport in person;

"overseas service" in relation to legalisation means the service for the processing by consular officers at consular posts of applications made in person;

"premium service" in relation to legalisation means the same day service for the processing by a London legalisation office dedicated for companies, solicitors and notaries of applications made in person;

"premium service" in relation to passport applications means an application made in person, either by the applicant or another person acting on behalf of the applicant, which is to be processed within twenty-four hours of that application having been made;

"standard service" in relation to legalisation means the twenty-four hours service for the processing by the main legalisation office at Milton Keynes, of applications made in person at that office and the processing by that office of postal applications within a reasonable time period.

"the appropriate Registrar General" for the purpose of fee 13 means the Registrar General for England and Wales, the Registrar General of Births, Deaths and Marriages for Scotland, or the Registrar General in Northern Ireland, as the case may be, under the Foreign Marriage Order 1970 or the Civil Partnership (Registration Abroad and Certificates) Order 2005.

3

The fees set forth in the table in Parts 1 and 2 of Schedule 1 to this Order are prescribed to be levied by consular officers and by [registration officers under the Consular Marriages and Marriages under Foreign Law Order 2014] in the execution of each of their functions specified in those tables.

Amendment

Words in square brackets substituted by SI 2014/1110, arts 19, 20.

Date in force: 3 June 2014: see SI 2014/1110, art 1(1).

4

The statutory instruments listed in Schedule 2 to this Order are revoked by this Order.

SCHEDULE 1

Article 3

[PART 1
TABLE OF GENERAL CONSULAR FEES]

Amendment

Substituted by SI 2013/535, art 2.

Date in force: 6 April 2013: see SI 2013/535, art 1.

[Fee	I LEGALISATION	£
1	Legalising a signature or seal—	
	(i) Standard service (in addition to direct costs, if any)	30.00
	(ii) Premium service (in addition to direct costs, if any)	75.00
	(iii) Overseas service (in addition to direct costs, if any)	30.00
	II NOTARIAL AND RELATED MATTERS	£
2	Preparing any certificate, declaration or document not listed elsewhere in this table	
	(i) in English	45.00
	(ii) in any other language	70.00
3	Signing a declaration of existence (except if required by a department of Her Majesty's Government in the United Kingdom)	15.00
4	Administering an oath, marking of exhibits or making a declaration or affirmation	55.00
5	Witnessing a signature	20.00
6	Making or verifying a copy of a document (including certifying when necessary)	30.00
7	Uniting documents	20.00
8	Supplying certified copies of documents which form part of the records of a court which is, or was formerly, established under the Foreign Jurisdiction Acts 1890 and 1913, for each page	65.00

	III NATIONALITY	£
9	Administering an oath of British Citizenship under the British Nationality Act 1981	85.00
	IV BIRTHS, MARRIAGES, CIVIL PARTNERSHIPS AND DEATHS	£
10	Receiving notice of an intended marriage, civil partnership or overseas relationship	65.00
11	Issuing a certificate that no impediment to an intended marriage or civil partnership has been shown to exist, or issuing any local equivalent document for an intended marriage or overseas relationship in accordance with local law	
	(i) in English	65.00
	(ii) in any other language	65.00
12	Solemnising a marriage under the [Consular Marriages and Marriages under Foreign Law Order 2014] administering oaths to the parties and registering the marriage; or registering a civil partnership under the Civil Partnership (Registration Abroad and Certificates) Order 2005	140.00
13	Forwarding to the appropriate Registrar General a record of a marriage under the local law or an overseas relationship, together with any necessary certification	35.00
14	Administering an application for the registration of a birth or a death	105.00
15	Making an addition to or correction in the consular register as necessary	35.00
16	Issuing a certified copy of an entry in the consular register	65.00
17	Making a search (in addition to fee 2(i) or fee 16 where applicable)	
	(i) in the consular register of births, deaths, marriages or civil partnerships where the number or date of entry is not provided	65.00
	(ii) in the naturalisation, registration or renunciation records kept by a consular officer	80.00

	V LEGAL PROCEEDINGS	£
18	Forwarding a request to a local authority for the taking of evidence or the service of a document (including effecting service of a document in relation to proceedings in which State immunity is in issue), and returning any evidence received of service or attempted service of a document (provided by the Foreign and Commonwealth Office in proceedings where State immunity is in issue)	130.00
	VI MARITIME SERVICES	
19	Providing or administering a service not otherwise covered in this Schedule in relation to shipping, seamen and related matters, for each hour or part hour (to include travel time if performed away from the consular premises) and in addition to direct costs, if any	130.00
	VII EMERGENCY ASSISTANCE	£
20	Administering an application for, and if successful, providing, an Emergency Travel Document	95.00
21	Exceptionally, administering an application for, and, if successful, providing an Emergency Passport, on occasions when it is not possible to provide an Emergency Travel Document	75.00
22	Arranging, exceptionally, for currency to be made available against the deposit of funds	
	(i) £0.01–£99.99	10.00
	(ii) £100.00–£499.99	30.00
	(iii) £500.00 or more	80.00
	VIII OTHER SERVICES	£
23	Providing the services of a consular officer or a consular employee in relation to any other service which the consular post or diplomatic mission has agreed to undertake, for each hour or part hour (to include travel time if performed away from the consular premises) and in addition to direct costs, if any	130.00]

Amendment

Substituted by SI 2013/535, art 2.

Date in force: 6 April 2013: see SI 2013/535, art 1.

Fee 12: in column 2 words "Consular Marriages and Marriages under Foreign Law Order 2014" in square brackets substituted by SI 2014/1110, arts 19, 21.

Date in force: 3 June 2014: see SI 2014/1110, art 1(1).

[PART 2
TABLE OF CONSULAR FEES RELATING TO PASSPORT SERVICES]

Amendment

Substituted by SI 2013/1720, art 2(1), (2).

Date in force: 1 August 2013: see SI 2013/1720, art 1.

[Fee	I PASSPORT APPLICATION MADE OVERSEAS			£
A	Administering an application made abroad, including applications for replacing an expired passport, replacing a passport of restricted validity with a new passport of full validity, issuing a new passport with amended personal details and replacing a lost or stolen passport and, if the application is successful, providing a 32 page passport—			
	(a)		[unless (d) or (e)(i) applies,] where the applicant is aged 16 years or over, but born after 2nd September 1929 (in addition to direct costs if any, other than delivery costs to the extent that these fall within paragraphs C to F, and in addition to any fee relevant to the application set out in paragraphs C to F)	[83.00]
	(b)		where the applicant was born on or before 2nd September 1929 (in addition to direct costs if any, other than delivery costs to the extent that these fall within paragraphs C to F)	Nil
	(c)		[unless (e)(ii) applies,] where the applicant is under 16 years old (for a passport valid for 5 years) (in addition to direct costs if any, other than delivery costs to the extent that these fall within paragraphs C to F, and in addition to any fee relevant to the application set out in paragraphs C to F)	[53.00]
	(d)		where the applicant [is aged 16 years or over, but born after 2nd September 1929 and] is—	
		(i)	a member of or attached to Her Majesty's Diplomatic Service, and the passport is issued to the applicant in his or her official capacity,	72.50
		(ii)	an officer of Her Majesty's Government, and the passport is issued to the applicant in his or her official capacity	72.50
		(iii)	a member of or attached to Her Majesty's Armed Forces, and the application is made in accordance with the procedure whereby applications are checked and submitted to Her Majesty's Passport Office by Armed Forces personnel who are nominated for that purpose.	72.50

(e)		where a passport is issued to the applicant in his or her capacity as a dependant of a person falling within sub-paragraph (d) and the applicant is—	
	(i)	aged 16 years or over[, but born after 2nd September 1929]	72.50
	(ii)	under 16 years old (for a passport valid for 5 years)	46.00
B		Administering an application made abroad, including applications for replacing an expired passport, replacing a passport of restricted validity with a new passport of full validity, issuing a new passport with amended personal details and replacing a lost or stolen passport and, if the application is successful, providing a 48 page passport—	
	(a)	where the applicant does not fall within paragraph A(d)(iii) (Armed Forces passports) and is not a dependant of such a person (in addition to direct costs if any, other than delivery costs to the extent that these fall within paragraphs C to F, and in addition to any fee relevant to the application set out in paragraphs C to F)	[91.00]
	(b)	where the applicant falls within paragraph A(d)(iii) or is a dependant of such a person (in addition to direct costs if any, other than delivery costs to the extent that these fall within paragraphs C to F, and in addition to any fee relevant to the application set out in paragraphs C to F)	85.00

Fee		I PASSPORT APPLICATION MADE OVERSEAS	£
C		Arranging delivery of a passport for an application made abroad for a 32 or 48 page passport and if the application is successful, delivering the passport—	
	(a)	to a British Forces Post Office address where the applicant is a member of or attached to Her Majesty's Armed Forces or a dependant of such a person and the application is made in accordance with the procedure whereby applications are checked and submitted to Her Majesty's Passport Office by Armed Forces personnel who are nominated for that purpose.	Nil
	(b)	to a British Forces Post Office address or a United Kingdom address, where the applicant is a member of or attached to Her Majesty's Diplomatic Service, or a dependant of such a person, and the application has been made in that official capacity	Nil

			£
	(c)	to a British Forces Post Office address or a United Kingdom address, where the applicant is an officer of Her Majesty's Government, or a dependant of such a person, and the application has been made in that official capacity.	Nil
	(d)	to an overseas or United Kingdom address where the applicant was born on or before 2nd September 1929	Nil
	(e)	to a United Kingdom address (including a British Forces Post Office address where (a) to (d) do not apply)	3.00
	(f)	to a United Kingdom embassy, High Commission or consulate by diplomatic channels where (a) to (d) do not apply	11.41
	(g)	to an address specified by the applicant or the Secretary of State, where (a) to (f) do not apply	9.70
D	Arranging the return of supporting documents accompanying an application or applications (up to a maximum of four applications) made abroad for a 32 or 48 page passport—		
	(a)	to a United Kingdom address	Nil
	(b)	to an overseas address where the applicant (or all of the applicants) was born on or before 2nd September 1929	Nil
	(c)	to an overseas address specified by the applicant or the Secretary of State, where the applicant (or one of the applicants) was born after 2nd September 1929	10.16
E	Arranging for return of supporting documents accompanying an application made abroad for a 32 or 48 page passport to an address in the United Kingdom by secure delivery, at the applicant's request		3.00
F	Forwarding an application or applications (up to a maximum of four) made abroad for a 32 or 48 page passport to a Regional Passport Processing Centre or Application Processing Centre for consideration—		
	(a)	where the applicant (or one of the applicants) was born after 2nd September 1929	13.31
	(b)	where the applicant (or all of the applicants) was born on or before 2nd September 1929	Nil

Fee	II PASSPORT APPLICATION MADE IN THE UNITED KINGDOM	£
G	Administering an application made in the United Kingdom, including applications for replacing an expired passport, replacing a passport of restricted validity with a new passport of full validity, issuing a new passport with amended personal details and replacing a lost or stolen passport and, if the application is successful, issuing a 32 page passport—	

	(a)	for applications made by post—		
		(i)	where the applicant is aged 16 years and over but was born after 2nd September 1929	72.50
		(ii)	where the applicant is under 16 years old (for a passport valid for 5 years)	46.00
		(iii)	where the applicant was born on or before 2nd September 1929	Nil
	(b)	for applications made in person—		
		(i)	using the fast-track service	
			(aa) where the applicant is aged 16 years or over but was born after 2nd September 1929	103.00
			(bb) where the applicant is under 16 years old (for a passport valid for 5 years)	87.00
			(cc) where the applicant was born on or before 2nd September 1929	30.50
		(ii)	using the fast-track collect service—	
			(aa) where the applicant is aged 16 years or over but was born after 2nd September 1929	123.00
			(bb) where the applicant is under 16 years old (for a passport valid for 5 years)	103.50
			(cc) where the applicant was born on or before 2nd September 1929	50.50
		(iii)	using the premium service—	
			(aa) where the applicant is aged 16 years or over but was born after 2nd September 1929	128.00
			(bb) where the applicant is under 16 years old (for a passport valid for 5 years)	106.00
			(cc) where the applicant was born on or before 2nd September 1929	55.50
H	Administering an application made in the United Kingdom, including applications for replacing an expired passport, replacing a passport of restricted validity with a new passport of full validity, issuing a new passport with amended personal details and replacing a lost and stolen passport and, if the application is successful, issuing a 48 page passport—			
	(a)	for applications made by post		85.00
	(b)	for applications made in person—		
		(i)	using the fast-track service	111.00
		(ii)	using the fast-track collect service	123.00

	(iii)	using the premium service	137.00

Fee	II PASSPORT APPLICATION MADE IN THE UNITED KINGDOM	£
I	Administering an application made in the United Kingdom and, if the application is successful, issuing a collective passport—	
	(a) for applications made by post	39.00
	(b) for applications made in person	54.00
J	Arranging for return of supporting documents accompanying an application made in the United Kingdom for a 32 or 48 page passport to an address in the United Kingdom by secure delivery, at the applicant's request	3.00]

Amendment

Substituted by SI 2013/1720, art 2(1), (2).

Date in force: 1 August 2013: see SI 2013/1720, art 1.

Para A: in sub-para (a) words "unless (d) or (e)(i) applies," in square brackets inserted by SI 2014/509, art 2(1), (2)(a)(i).

Date in force: 7 April 2014: see SI 2014/509, art 1.

Para A: in sub-para (a) sum "83.00" in square brackets substituted by SI 2014/509, art 2(1), (2)(a)(ii).

Date in force: 7 April 2014: see SI 2014/509, art 1.

Para A: in sub-para (c) words "unless (e)(ii) applies," in square brackets inserted by SI 2014/509, art 2(1), (2)(b)(i).

Date in force: 7 April 2014: see SI 2014/509, art 1.

Para A: in sub-para (c) sum "53.00" in square brackets substituted by SI 2014/509, art 2(1), (2)(b)(ii).

Date in force: 7 April 2014: see SI 2014/509, art 1.

Para A: in sub-para (d) words from "is aged 16" to "September 1929 and" in square brackets inserted by SI 2014/509, art 2(1), (2)(c).

Date in force: 7 April 2014: see SI 2014/509, art 1.

Para A: in sub-para (e)(i) words ", but born after 2nd September 1929" in square brackets inserted by SI 2014/509, art 2(1), (2)(d).

Date in force: 7 April 2014: see SI 2014/509, art 1.

Para B: in sub-para (a) sum "91.00" in square brackets substituted by SI 2014/509, art 2(1), (3).

Date in force: 7 April 2014: see SI 2014/509, art 1.

SCHEDULE 2

Article 4

Statutory Instruments revoked	References
Consular Fees Order 2011	SI 2011/738
Consular Fees (Amendment) Order 2011	SI 2011/1691

IMMIGRATION APPEALS (FAMILY VISITOR) REGULATIONS 2012

(SI 2012/1532)

Made: 13 June 2012.

Authority: Nationality, Immigration and Asylum Act 2002, ss 88A(1)(a), 2(a), (c), 112(1), (3).

Commencement: 9 July 2012.

1 Citation and commencement

These Regulations may be cited as the Immigration Appeals (Family Visitor) Regulations 2012 and shall come into force on 9th July 2012.

2 Class or description of person to be visited

(1) A person ("P") is of a class or description prescribed for the purposes of section 88A(1)(a) of the Nationality, Immigration and Asylum Act 2002 (entry clearance), if—

    (a)   the applicant for entry clearance ("A") is a member of the family of P; and

    (b)   P's circumstances match those specified in regulation 3.

(2) For the purposes of paragraph (1), A is a member of the family of P if A is the—

    (a)   spouse, civil partner, father, mother, son, daughter, grandfather, grandmother, grandson, granddaughter, brother or sister;

    (b)   father-in-law, mother-in-law, brother-in-law or sister-in-law;

    (c)   son-in-law or daughter-in-law; or

    (d)   stepfather, stepmother, stepson, stepdaughter, stepbrother or stepsister;

of P.

(3) For the purposes of paragraph (1), A is also a member of the family of P if A is the partner of P.

(4) In this regulation, A is the partner of P if—

    (a)   A and P have been in a relationship that is akin to a marriage or civil partnership for at least the two years before the day on which A's application for entry clearance was made; and

    (b)   such relationship is genuine and subsisting.

(5) In this regulation—

    (a)   "father-in-law of P" includes the father of P's civil partner;

    (b)   "mother-in-law of P" includes the mother of P's civil partner;

    (c)   "brother-in-law of P" includes the brother of P's civil partner;

    (d)   "sister-in-law of P" includes the sister of P's civil partner;

    (e)   "son-in-law of P" includes the son of P's civil partner;

    (f)   "daughter-in-law of P" includes the daughter of P's civil partner;

    (g)   "stepfather of P" includes the person who is the civil partner of A's father (but is not A's parent);

    (h)   "stepmother of P" includes the person who is the civil partner of A's mother (but is not A's parent);

    (i)   "stepson of P" includes the person who is the son of A's civil partner (but is not A's son);

    (j)   "stepdaughter of P" includes the person who is the daughter of A's civil partner (but is not A's daughter);

    (k)   "stepbrother of P" includes the person who is the son of the civil parent of A's parent (but is not the son of either of A's parents); and

(l) "stepsister of P" includes the person who is the daughter of the civil partner of A's parent (but is not the daughter of either of A's parents).

3 Circumstances of the person to be visited

The circumstances of P mentioned in regulation 2(1)(b) are that P—

(a) is settled in the United Kingdom as defined in paragraph 6 of the immigration rules;

(b) has been granted asylum in the United Kingdom under paragraph 334 of the immigration rules; or

(c) has been granted humanitarian protection in the United Kingdom under paragraph 339C of the immigration rules.

4 Transitional provision

These Regulations apply only to an application for entry clearance made on or after the day on which they come into force.

ACCESSION OF CROATIA (IMMIGRATION AND WORKER AUTHORISATION) REGULATIONS 2013

(SI 2013/1460)

Made: 12 June 2013.
Authority: European Union (Croatian Accession and Irish Protocol) Act 2013, s 4.
Commencement: 1 July 2013.

PART 1
INTERPRETATION ETC

1 Citation, commencement, interpretation and consequential amendments

(1) These Regulations may be cited as the Accession of Croatia (Immigration and Worker Authorisation) Regulations 2013 and come into force on 1st July 2013.

(2) In these Regulations—

"the 1971 Act" means the Immigration Act 1971;

"the 2006 Act" means the Immigration, Asylum and Nationality Act 2006;

"accession period" means the period beginning with 1st July 2013 and ending with 30th June 2018;

"accession State national subject to worker authorisation" has the meaning given in regulation 2;

"accession worker authorisation document" has the meaning given in regulation8(2);

"authorised category of employment" means—

(a) employment for which the applicant has been issued by a sponsor with a valid certificate of sponsorship under Tier 2 or Tier 5 of the Points-Based System; or

(b) employment as—

(i) a representative of an overseas business;

(ii) a postgraduate doctor or dentist; or

(iii) a domestic worker in a private household;

"certificate of sponsorship" has the meaning given in paragraph 6 of the immigration rules, except that the reference to an application or potential application for entry clearance or leave to enter or remain as a Tier 2 migrant or a Tier 5 migrant is to be read as including a reference to an application or potential application for a worker authorisation registration certificate;

"certificate of sponsorship checking service" has the meaning given in paragraph 6 of the immigration rules, except that the reference to an application or potential application for entry clearance or leave to enter or remain as a Tier 2 migrant or a Tier 5 migrant is to be read as including a reference to an application or potential application for a worker authorisation registration certificate;

"civil partner" does not include a party to a civil partnership of convenience;

"EEA registration certificate" means a certificate issued in accordance with regulation 16 of the EEA Regulations;

"the EEA Regulations" means the Immigration (European Economic Area) Regulations 2006;

"EEA State" excludes the United Kingdom and includes Switzerland;

"employer" means, in relation to a worker, the person who directly pays the wage or salary of that worker, and "employ", "employment" and "employs" shall be construed accordingly;

"the EU2 Regulations" means the Accession (Immigration and Worker Authorisation) Regulations 2006;

"extended family member" has the meaning given in regulation 8 of the EEA Regulations;

"family member" has the meaning given in regulation 7 of the EEA Regulations;

"highly skilled person" has the meaning given in regulation3;

"immigration rules" means the rules laid down as mentioned in section 3(2) of the 1971 Act applying (except for in the definition of "relevant requirements") on 1stJuly 2013;

"Points-Based System" means the system established under Part 6A of the immigration rules;

"relevant requirements" means, in relation to an authorised category of employment, the requirements which, subject to any necessary modifications, a person in that category of employment was obliged to meet under the immigration rules in force on 9th December 2011 in order to obtain entry clearance or leave to enter or remain in the United Kingdom and which are set out in the relevant statement;

["relevant statement" means the statement entitled "the Statement of relevant requirements" dated April 2014 and published by the Secretary of State;]

"right to reside" shall be interpreted in accordance with the EEA Regulations and "entitled to reside" and "right of residence" shall be construed accordingly;

"sponsor" means the holder of a sponsor licence;

"sponsor licence" has the meaning given in paragraph 6 of the immigration rules;

"spouse" does not include a party to a marriage of convenience;

"student" has the meaning given in regulation 4(1)(d) of the EEA Regulations;

"Tier 2" and "Tier 5" shall be construed in accordance in paragraph 6 of the immigration rules, except that the reference to the grant of leave is to be read as including a reference to the issuing of a worker authorisation registration certificate;

"unmarried or same sex partner" means a person who is in a durable relationship with another person;

"work" and "working" shall be construed in accordance with the meaning of "worker"; and

"worker authorisation registration certificate" means a certificate issued in accordance with regulation 10 of these Regulations.

(3) The Schedule (consequential amendments) shall have effect.

Amendment

Para (2): definition "relevant statement" substituted by SI 2014/530, reg 2(1), (2).

Date in force: 6 April 2014: see SI 2014/530, reg 1(2).

2 "Accession State national subject to worker authorisation"

(1) Subject to the following paragraphs of this regulation, other than where these Regulations expressly refer to an accession State national subject to worker authorisation within the meaning of regulation 2 of the EU2 Regulations, in these Regulations "accession State national subject to worker authorisation" means a Croatian national.

(2) A Croatian national is not an accession State national subject to worker authorisation if, on 30th June 2013, he had leave to enter or remain in the United Kingdom under the 1971 Act that was not subject to any condition restricting his employment [(other than a condition restricting his employment as a doctor in training or as a dentist in training or as a professional sportsperson (including as a sports coach))], or he is given such leave after that date.

(3) A Croatian national is not an accession State national subject to worker authorisation if he was legally working in the United Kingdom on 30th June 2013 and had been legally working in the United Kingdom without interruption throughout the preceding period of 12 months ending on that date.

(4) A Croatian national who legally works in the United Kingdom without interruption for a period of 12 months falling partly or wholly after 30th June 2013 ceases to be an accession State national subject to worker authorisation at the end of that period of 12 months.

(5) For the purposes of paragraphs (3) and (4) of this regulation—

   (a)   a person working in the United Kingdom during a period falling before 1stJuly 2013 was legally working in the United Kingdom during that period if—

      (i)   he had leave to enter or remain in the United Kingdom under the 1971 Act for that period, that leave allowed him to work in the United Kingdom, and he was working in accordance with any condition of that leave restricting his employment;

      (ii)   he was exempt from the provisions of the 1971 Act by virtue of section 8(2) or (3) of that Act (persons exempted by order or membership of diplomatic mission); or

      (iii)   he was entitled to reside in the United Kingdom for that period under the EEA Regulations without the requirement for such leave;

   (b)   a person working in the United Kingdom on or after 1stJuly 2013 is legally working in the United Kingdom during any period in which he—

      (i)   falls within any of paragraphs (6) to (16) or (18); or

      (ii)   holds an accession worker authorisation document and is working in accordance with the conditions set out in that document; and

   (c)   a person shall be treated as having worked in the United Kingdom without interruption for a period of 12 months if—

      (i)   he was legally working in the United Kingdom at the beginning and end of that period; and

      (ii)   during that period of 12 months, if his work in the United Kingdom was interrupted, any intervening periods of interruption did not exceed 30 days in total.

(6) Other than during any period in which he is also an accession State national subject to worker authorisation within the meaning of regulation 2 of the EU2 Regulations, a Croatian national is not an accession State national subject to worker authorisation during any period in which he is also a national of—

   (a)   the United Kingdom; or

    (b)   an EEA State, other than Croatia.

(7) A Croatian national is not an accession State national subject to worker authorisation during any period in which he is also an accession State national subject to worker authorisation within the meaning of regulation 2 of the EU2 Regulations and is working in accordance with those Regulations.

(8) A Croatian national is not an accession State national subject to worker authorisation during any period in which he is the spouse, civil partner, unmarried or same sex partner, or child under 18 of a person who has leave to enter or remain in the United Kingdom under the 1971 Act and that leave allows him to work in the United Kingdom.

(9) A Croatian national is not an accession State national subject to worker authorisation during any period in which he is the spouse, civil partner, unmarried or same sex partner of—

    (a)   a national of the United Kingdom; or

    (b)   a person that is settled in the United Kingdom in accordance with the meaning given in section 33(2A) (interpretation—meaning of "settled") of the 1971 Act.

(10) A Croatian national is not an accession State national subject to worker authorisation during any period in which he is a member of a mission or other person mentioned in section 8(3) (member of a diplomatic mission, the family member of such a person, or a person otherwise entitled to diplomatic immunity) of the 1971 Act, other than a person who, under section 8(3A) (conditions of membership of a mission) of that Act, does not count as a member of a mission for the purposes of section 8(3).

(11) A Croatian national is not an accession State national subject to worker authorisation during any period in which he is a person who is exempt from all or any of the provisions of the 1971 Act by virtue of an order made under section 8(2) (exemption for persons specified by order) of that Act.

(12) A Croatian national is not an accession State national subject to worker authorisation during any period in which he has a permanent right of residence under regulation 15 of the EEA Regulations.

(13) Subject to paragraph (14), a Croatian national is not an accession State national subject to worker authorisation during any period in which he is a family member (X) of an EEA national (Y) who has a right to reside in the United Kingdom.

(14) Where Y is an accession State national subject to worker authorisation under these Regulations or an accession State national subject to worker authorisation within the meaning of regulation 2 of the EU2 Regulations, paragraph (13) only applies where X is the—

    (a)   spouse or civil partner of Y;

    (b)   unmarried or same sex partner of Y; or

    (c)   a direct descendant of Y, Y's spouse or Y's civil partner who is—

        (i)   under 21; or

        (ii)   dependant of Y, Y's spouse or Y's civil partner.

(15) A Croatian national is not an accession State national subject to worker authorisation during any period in which he is a highly skilled person and holds an EEA registration certificate issued in accordance with regulation 7 that includes a statement that he has unconditional access to the United Kingdom labour market.

(16) A Croatian national is not an accession State national subject to worker authorisation during any period in which he is in the United Kingdom as a student and either—

    (a)   holds an EEA registration certificate that includes a statement that he is a student who may work in the United Kingdom whilst a student in accordance with the condition set out in paragraph (17) and complies with that condition; or

(b)   has leave to enter or remain under the 1971 Act as a student and is working in accordance with any conditions attached to that leave.

(17)   The condition referred to in paragraph (16)(a) is that the student shall not work for more than 20 hours a week unless—

    (a)   he is following a course of vocational training and is working as part of that training; or

    (b)   he is working during his vacation.

(18)   A Croatian national who ceases to be a student at the end of his course of study is not an accession State national subject to worker authorisation during the period of four months beginning with the date on which his course ends provided he holds an EEA registration certificate that was issued to him before the end of the course that includes a statement that he may work during that period.

(19)   A Croatian national is not an accession State national subject to worker authorisation during any period in which he is a posted worker.

(20)   In paragraph (19), "posted worker" means a worker who is posted to the United Kingdom, within the meaning of Article 1(3) of the Council Directive 96/71/EC of the European Parliament and of the Council of 16 December 1996 concerning the posting of workers in the framework of the provision of services, by an undertaking established in an EEA State.

Amendment

Para (2): words from "(other than a" to "a sports coach))" in square brackets inserted by SI 2014/530, reg 2(1), (3).

Date in force: 6 April 2014: see SI 2014/530, reg 1(2).

3 "Highly skilled person"

(1)   In these Regulations "highly skilled person" means a person who—

    (a)   meets the requirements specified by the Secretary of State for the purpose of paragraph 245BB(c) (requirements for entry clearance as a Tier 1 (Exceptional Talent) migrant) of the immigration rules; or

    (b)   has been awarded one of the following qualifications and applies for an EEA registration certificate within 12 months of being awarded the qualification—

        (i)   a recognised bachelor, masters or doctoral degree;

        (ii)   a postgraduate certificate in education or professional graduate diploma of education; or

        (iii)   a higher national diploma awarded by a Scottish higher education institution.

(2)   For the purposes of paragraph (1)(b), the qualification must have been awarded by a higher education institution which, on the date of the award, is a UK recognised body or an institution that is not a UK recognised body but which provides full courses that lead to the award of a degree by a UK recognised body.

(3)   For the purposes of paragraph (1)(b)(iii), to qualify as a higher national diploma from a Scottish institution, a qualification must be at level 8 on the Scottish credit and qualifications framework.

(4)   In this regulation, a "UK recognised body" means an institution that has been granted degree awarding powers by a Royal Charter, an Act of Parliament or the Privy Council.

PART 2
APPLICATION OF THE EEA REGULATIONS AND OTHER INSTRUMENTS

4 Derogation from provisions of European Union law relating to workers

Pursuant to Annex V of the treaty concerning the accession of the Republic of Croatia to the European Union, signed at Brussels on 9 December 2011, Regulations 5 and 7 to 10 derogate during the accession period from Article 45 of the Treaty on the

Functioning of the European Union, Articles 1 to 6 of Regulation (EEC) No 1612/68 of the Council of 15 October 1968 on freedom of movement for workers within the Community and Directive 2004/38/EC of the European Parliament and of the Council of 29 April 2004 on the right of citizens of the Union and their family members to move and reside freely within the territory of the member States, amending Regulation (EEC) No 1612/68, and repealing Directives 64/221/EEC, 68/360/EEC, 72/194/EEC, 73/148/EEC, 75/34/EEC, 75/35/EEC, 90/364/EEC, 90/365/EEC and 93/96/EEC.

[5 Right of residence of an accession State national subject to worker authorisation]
[During the accession period, an accession State national subject to worker authorisation who is seeking employment in the United Kingdom shall not be treated as a jobseeker and shall be treated as a worker only in so far as it gives him a right to reside and only during a period in which he holds an accession worker authorisation document and is working in accordance with the conditions set out in that document.]

Amendment
Substituted by SI 2014/530, reg 2(1), (4).
Date in force: 6 April 2014: see SI 2014/530, reg 1(2).

6 Transitional provisions to take account of the application of the EEA Regulations to Croatian nationals and their family members on 1st July 2013
(1) Where, before 1st July 2013, any direction has been given for the removal of a Croatian national or the family member of such a national under paragraphs 8 to 10A of Schedule 2 (removal of persons refused leave to enter and illegal entrants) to the 1971 Act, section 10 (removal of certain persons unlawfully in the United Kingdom) of the 1999 Act or section 47 (removal: persons with statutorily extended leave) of the 2006 Act, that direction shall cease to have effect on that date.
(2) Where before 1st July 2013 the Secretary of State has made a deportation order against a Croatian national or the family member of such a national under section 5(1) (deportation orders) of the 1971 Act—
    (a)   that order shall, on and after 1st July 2013, be treated as if it were a decision under regulation 19(3)(b) of the EEA Regulations; and
    (b)   any appeal against that order, or against the refusal of the Secretary of State to revoke the deportation order, made before 1st July 2013 under section 63 (deportation orders) of the 1999 Act, or under section 82(2)(j) or (k) (right of appeal: general) of the 2002 Act shall, on or after that date, be treated as if it had been made under regulation 26 of the EEA Regulations.
(3) In this regulation—
    (a)   "the 1999 Act" means the Immigration and Asylum Act 1999;
    (b)   "the 2002 Act" means the Nationality, Immigration and Asylum Act 2002; and
    (c)   any reference to the family member of a Croatian national is, in addition to the definition set out in regulation 1(2), a reference to a person who on 1st July 2013 acquires a right to reside in the United Kingdom under the EEA Regulations as the family member of a Croatian national.

7 Issuing EEA registration certificates and residence cards
(1) During the accession period, regulation 6 of the EEA Regulations has effect as if, in paragraph (1), after "EEA national", there were inserted ", except an accession State national subject to worker authorisation within the meaning of regulation 2 of the Croatian Regulations," and after paragraph (1), there were inserted—
    "(1A) In these Regulations, a "qualified person" also means a person who is an accession State national subject to worker authorisation within the meaning of regulation 2 of the Croatian Regulations and in the United Kingdom as—

    (a)   a self-employed person;

    (b)   a self-sufficient person;

    (c)   a student; or

    (d)   a highly skilled person who is seeking employment or is employed in the United Kingdom.

[(1B) In regulation 14(2), regulation 16(3) and (5) and regulation 17(1) and (4) a "qualified person" includes an accession State national subject to worker authorisation within the meaning of regulation 2 of the Croatian Regulations where that accession State national subject to worker authorisation has a right to reside.]

(1C) In these Regulations—

    (a)   "the Croatian Regulations" means the Accession of Croatia (Immigration and Worker Authorisation) Regulations 2013; and

    (b)   "highly skilled worker" has the meaning given in regulation 1 of the Croatian Regulations."

(2) Subject to paragraph (6), an EEA registration certificate issued to a Croatian national during the accession period shall include a statement that the holder of the certificate has unconditional access to the United Kingdom labour market, unless that person is not an accession State national subject to worker authorisation solely by virtue of falling within paragraph (16) or (18) of regulation 2.

(3) A Croatian national who holds an EEA registration certificate that does not include a statement that he has unconditional access to the United Kingdom labour market may, during the accession period, submit the certificate to the Secretary of State for the inclusion of such a statement.

(4) The Secretary of State must re-issue a EEA certificate submitted to her under paragraph (3) with the inclusion of a statement that the holder has unconditional access to the United Kingdom labour market if she is satisfied that the holder—

    (a)   is a qualified person within the meaning of paragraph (1A) of regulation 6 of the EEA Regulations as applied by paragraph (1); or

    (b)   has ceased to be an accession State national subject to worker authorisation other than solely by virtue of falling within paragraph (16) or (18) of regulation 2.

(5) An EEA registration certificate issued to a Croatian national who is a student during the accession period shall include a statement that the holder of the certificate is a student who may work in the United Kingdom whilst a student in accordance with the condition set out in paragraph (17) of regulation 2 and who, on ceasing to be a student, may work during the period referred to in paragraph (18) of regulation 2, unless it includes a statement under paragraph (2) or (4) that the holder has unconditional access to the United Kingdom labour market.

(6) Where under paragraph (5) of regulation 16 of the EEA Regulations an EEA registration certificate is issued to a Croatian national extended family member[, with the exception of an extended family member who is an unmarried partner (including a same sex partner),] of an accession State national subject to worker authorisation, the certificate must include a statement that the certificate does not confer a permission to work.

[(7) Where under paragraph (1) or (4) of regulation 17 of the EEA Regulations a residence card is issued to a family member or an extended family member of an accession State national subject to worker authorisation—

    (a)   paragraph (6) of regulation 17 of the EEA Regulations shall not apply;

    (b)   the duration of that card shall be twelve months from the date of issue; and

    (c)   that card shall be entitled "Accession Residence Card".]

Amendment

Para (1): para (1B) (as set out) substituted by SI 2014/530, reg 2(1), (5)(a).

Date in force: 6 April 2014: see SI 2014/530, reg 1(2).

Para (6): words ", with the exception of an extended family member who is an unmarried partner (including a same sex partner)," in square brackets inserted by SI 2014/530, reg 2(1), (5)(b).

Date in force: 6 April 2014: see SI 2014/530, reg 1(2).

Para (7): inserted by SI 2014/530, reg 2(1), (5)(c).

Date in force: 6 April 2014: see SI 2014/530, reg 1(2).

PART 3
ACCESSION STATE WORKER AUTHORISATION AND ASSOCIATED DOCUMENTATION

8 Requirement for an accession State national subject to worker authorisation to be authorised to work

(1) An accession State national subject to worker authorisation shall only be authorised to work in the United Kingdom during the accession period if he holds an accession worker authorisation document and is working in accordance with the conditions set out in that document.

(2) For the purpose of these Regulations, an accession worker authorisation document means—

 (a) a passport or other travel document endorsed before 1st July 2013 to show that the holder has leave to enter or remain in the United Kingdom under the 1971 Act, subject to a condition restricting his employment in the United Kingdom to a particular employer or category of employment; or

 (b) a worker authorisation registration certificate endorsed with a condition restricting the holder's employment to a particular employer and authorised category of employment.

(3) In the case of a document mentioned in paragraph (2)(a), the document ceases to be a valid accession worker authorisation document at the point at which—

 (a) the period of leave to enter or remain expires; or

 (b) the document holder ceases working for the employer, or in the employment, specified in the document for a period of time that exceeds 30 days in total.

(4) In the case of a document mentioned in paragraph (2)(b), the document ceases to be a valid accession worker authorisation document at the point at which—

 (a) the document expires;

 (b) the document holder ceases working for the employer, or in the authorised category of employment, specified in the document for a period of time that exceeds 30 days in total; or

 (c) the document is revoked.

(5) For the purposes of this regulation, and regulations 9 and 11, the reference to a travel document other than a passport is a reference to a document which relates to a Croatian national and which can serve the same purpose as a passport.

9 Application for a worker authorisation registration certificate as an accession worker authorisation document

(1) An application for a worker authorisation registration certificate may be made by an accession State national subject to worker authorisation who wishes to work for an employer in the United Kingdom if the employment concerned falls within an authorised category of employment.

(2) The application shall be in writing and shall be made to the Secretary of State.

(3) The application shall state—

(a) the name, address in the United Kingdom or in Croatia, and date of birth, of the applicant;

(b) the name and address of the employer for whom the applicant wishes to work; and

(c) the authorised category of employment covered by the application.

(4) The application shall be accompanied by—

(a) proof of the applicant's identity in the form of—

  (i) a national identity card;

  (ii) a passport; or

  (iii) other travel document as defined by regulation 8(5);

(b) two passport size photographs of the applicant;

(c) where the relevant requirements require the applicant to hold a certificate of sponsorship, the certificate of sponsorship reference number;

(d) where sub-paragraph (c) does not apply, a letter from the employer specified in the application confirming that the applicant has an offer of employment with the employer; and

(e) a fee of £55.

(5) In this regulation "address" means, in relation to an employer which is a body corporate or partnership, the head or main office of that employer.

10 Issuing and revoking a worker authorisation registration certificate

(1) Subject to paragraph (3), the Secretary of State shall issue a worker authorisation registration certificate pursuant to an application made in accordance with the provisions of regulation 9 if the Secretary of State is satisfied that the applicant is an accession State national subject to worker authorisation who meets the relevant requirements.

(2) A worker authorisation registration certificate shall include—

(a) a condition restricting the employment of the document holder to the employer and the authorised category of employment specified in the application;

(b) a statement that the document holder has a right of residence in the United Kingdom as a worker whilst working in accordance with any conditions specified in the certificate;

(c) where the authorised category of employment specified in the application is one for which a certificate of sponsorship is required, a statement that the holder of the document has a right to engage in supplementary employment; and

(d) where the period of authorised employment is less than 12 months, a statement specifying the date on which the worker authorisation registration certificate expires.

(3) The Secretary of State may—

(a) refuse to issue, revoke or refuse to renew a worker authorisation registration certificate if the refusal or revocation is justified on grounds of public policy, public security or public health,

(b) refuse the application where the Secretary of State is not satisfied that regulation 9 or this regulation has been complied with or satisfied, or

(c) revoke a worker authorisation registration certificate where—

  (i) the document holder ceases working for the employer, or in the employment, specified in the document for a period of time that exceeds 30 days in total,

  (ii) deception was used in order to obtain the document, or

  (iii) the document was obtained on the basis of sponsorship by a sponsor whose licence has been withdrawn, and where the Secretary of State has refused to issue, revoked or refused to renew a worker authorisation registration certificate, she shall issue a notice setting out the reasons.

(4) A worker authorisation registration certificate or notice of refusal or revocation issued under this regulation shall be sent to the applicant by post together with the identity card or passport that accompanied the application.

(5) Subject to paragraph (6), in this regulation, "supplementary employment" means—

    (a)   employment in a job which appears on the shortage occupation list in Appendix K of the immigration rules; or

    (b)   employment in the same profession and at the same professional level as the employment for which the applicant has been issued with a certificate of sponsorship.

(6) "Supplementary employment" is subject to the condition that—

    (i)   the applicant remains working for the sponsor in the employment that the certificate of sponsorship checking service records that the applicant has been sponsored to do; and

    (ii)   the supplementary employment does not exceed 20 hours per week and takes place outside of the hours when the applicant is contracted to work for the sponsor in the employment the applicant is being sponsored to do.

(7) The Secretary of State shall ensure that the relevant statement is available to the public through her website and the library of the Home Office.

PART 4
PENALTIES AND OFFENCES

11 Unauthorised employment of accession State national—penalty for employer

(1) It is contrary to this regulation to employ an accession State national subject to worker authorisation during the accession period if that person is not the holder of a valid accession worker authorisation document or, where that person holds such a document, the person would be in breach of a condition of that document in undertaking the employment.

(2) The Secretary of State may give an employer who acts contrary to this regulation a notice requiring him to pay a penalty of a specified amount not exceeding £5,000.

(3) The Secretary of State may give a penalty notice without having established whether the employer is excused under paragraph (5).

(4) A penalty notice must—

    (a)   state why the Secretary of State thinks the employer is liable to the penalty;

    (b)   state the amount of the penalty;

    (c)   specify a date, at least 28 days after the date specified in the notice as the date on which it is given, before which the penalty must be paid;

    (d)   specify how the penalty must be paid;

    (e)   provide a reference number;

    (f)   explain how the employer may object to the penalty; and

    (g)   explain how the Secretary of State may enforce the penalty.

(5) Subject to paragraph (7), an employer is excused from paying a penalty under this regulation if—

    (a)   before the commencement of the employment, the employee or prospective employee produces to the employer any of the following documents—

(i)   an accession worker authorisation document that authorises the employee or prospective employee to take the employment in question;

(ii)   an EEA registration certificate which includes a statement that the holder has unconditional access to the United Kingdom labour market; or

(iii)   one of the following documents confirming that the document holder is not an accession State national subject to worker authorisation by virtue of regulation 2(6)—

(aa)   a passport;

(bb)   a national identity card; or

(cc)   other travel document as defined by regulation 8(5); and

(b)   the employer complies with the requirements set out in paragraph (6) of this regulation.

(6) The requirements are that—

(a)   the employer takes all reasonable steps to check the validity of the document;

(b)   the employer has satisfied himself that the photograph on the document is of the employee or prospective employee;

(c)   the employer has satisfied himself that the date of birth on the document is consistent with the appearance of the employee or prospective employee;

(d)   the employer takes all other reasonable steps to check that the employee or prospective employee is the rightful holder of the document; and

(e)   the employer securely retains a dated copy of the whole of the document in a format which cannot be subsequently altered for a period of not less than two years after the employment has come to an end.

(7) An employer is not excused from paying a penalty if the employer knew, at any time during the period of the employment, that the employment was contrary to this regulation.

(8) Nothing in these regulations permits an employer to retain documents produced by an employee or prospective employee for the purposes of paragraph (5) for any period longer than is necessary for the purposes of ensuring compliance with paragraph (6).

(9) The Secretary of State may issue a code of practice specifying factors to be considered by her in determining the amount of a penalty imposed under paragraph (2) of this regulation.

(10) The Secretary of State shall lay a code issued under paragraph (9) before Parliament and publish it.

(11) The Secretary of State may from time to time review the code and may revoke, or revise and re-issue it, following a review; and a reference in this section to the code includes a reference to the code as revised.

12 Unauthorised employment of accession State national—penalty for employer—objection

(1) This regulation applies where an employer to whom a penalty notice is given objects on the ground that—

(a)   he is not liable to the imposition of a penalty;

(b)   he is excused payment by virtue of regulation 11(5); or

(c)   the amount of the penalty is too high.

(2) The employer may give a notice of objection to the Secretary of State.

(3) A notice of objection shall—

(a)   be in writing;

(b)   give the full grounds of objection;

(c) give the reference number of the notice given under regulation 11(4);

(d) give the name and address of the head or main office of the employer;

(e) give the name and address of the employee in respect of whom the penalty was issued;

(f) contain details of any appeal made by the employer under regulation 13; and

(g) be given within 28 days, beginning with the date specified in the penalty notice as the date on which it was given.

(4) Where the Secretary of State receives a notice of objection to a penalty she shall consider it and—

(a) cancel the penalty;

(b) reduce the penalty;

(c) increase the penalty; or

(d) determine to take no action.

(5) Where the Secretary of State considers a notice of objection she shall—

(a) have regard to any code of practice issued under regulation 11(9) (in so far as the objection relates to the amount of the penalty);

(b) inform the objector in writing of her decision within 28 days, beginning with the date on which the notice of objection was given to the Secretary of State, or such longer period as she may agree with the objector;

(c) if she increases the penalty, issue a new penalty notice under regulation 11; and

(d) if she reduces the penalty, notify the objector of the reduced amount.

13 Unauthorised employment of accession State national—penalty for employer—appeal

(1) An employer to whom a penalty notice is given may appeal to the court on the ground that—

(a) he is not liable to the imposition of a penalty;

(b) he is excused payment by virtue of regulation 11(5); or

(c) the amount of the penalty is too high.

(2) The court may—

(a) allow the appeal and cancel the penalty;

(b) allow the appeal and reduce the penalty; or

(c) dismiss the appeal.

(3) An appeal shall be a re-hearing of the Secretary of State's decision to impose a penalty and shall be determined having regard to—

(a) any code of practice issued under regulation 11(9) that has effect at the time of the appeal (in so far as the appeal relates to the amount of the penalty), and

(b) any other matters which the court thinks relevant (which may include matters of which the Secretary of State was unaware),

and this paragraph has effect despite any provision of rules of Court.

(4) An appeal must be brought within the period of 28 days beginning with—

(a) the date specified in the penalty notice as the date upon which it is given; or

(b) if the employer gives a notice of objection and the Secretary of State reduces the penalty, the date specified in the notice of reduction as the date upon which it is given; or

(c) if the employer gives a notice of objection and the Secretary of State determines to take no action, the date specified in the notice of that determination as the date upon which it is given.

(5) An appeal may be brought by an employer whether or not—

(a)   he has given a notice of objection under regulation 12; or

(b)   the penalty has been increased or reduced under that regulation.

(6)   In this section "the court" means—

(a)   where the employer has his principal place of business in England and Wales, a county court;

(b)   where the employer has his principal place of business in Scotland, the sheriff and sheriff court; and

(c)   where the employer has his principal place of business in Northern Ireland, a county court.

14   Unauthorised employment of accession State national—penalty for employer—enforcement

(1)   A sum payable to the Secretary of State as a penalty under regulation 11 may be recoverable as if payable under a court order.

(2)   In proceedings for the enforcement of a penalty, no question may be raised as to—

(a)   liability to the imposition of the penalty;

(b)   the application of the excuse in regulation 11(5); or

(c)   the amount of the penalty.

(3)   Money paid to the Secretary of State by way of penalty shall be paid into the Consolidated Fund.

15 Unauthorised employment of accession State national—employer offence

(1)   A person commits an offence if he employs another ("the employee") knowing that the employee is an accession State national subject to worker authorisation and that—

(a)   the employee is not the holder of a valid accession worker authorisation document; or

(b)   the employee is prohibited from undertaking the employment because of a condition in his accession worker authorisation document.

(2)   A person guilty of an offence under this section shall be liable on summary conviction—

(a)   to imprisonment for a term not exceeding 51 weeks in England and Wales or 6 months in Scotland or Northern Ireland;

(b)   to a fine not exceeding level 5 on the standard scale; or

(c)   to both.

(3)   An offence under this regulation shall be treated as—

(a)   a relevant offence for the purpose of sections 28B (search and arrest by warrant) and 28D (entry and search of premises) of the 1971 Act; and

(b)   an offence under Part 3 of that Act (criminal proceedings) for the purposes of sections 28E (entry and search of premises following arrest), 28G (searching arrested persons) and 28H (searching persons in police custody).

(4)   In relation to an offence committed before the commencement of section 281(5) (alteration of penalties for other summary offences) of the Criminal Justice Act 2003, the reference to 51 weeks in paragraph (2)(a) shall be read as a reference to 6 months.

(5)   For the purposes of paragraph (1), a body (whether corporate or not) shall be treated as knowing a fact about an employee if a person who has responsibility within the body for an aspect of the employment knows the fact.

16 Unauthorised working by accession State national—employee offence and penalty

(1)   Subject to paragraph (2), an accession State national subject to worker authorisation who works in the United Kingdom during the accession period shall be guilty of an offence if he does not hold a valid accession worker authorisation document.

(2)   A person guilty of an offence under this regulation shall be liable on summary conviction—

    (a)   to imprisonment for a term not exceeding more than three months;

    (b)   to a fine not exceeding level 5 on the standard scale; or

    (c)   to both.

(3)   A constable or immigration officer who has reason to believe that a person has committed an offence under this regulation may give that person a notice offering him the opportunity of discharging any liability to conviction for that offence by payment of a penalty of £1000 in accordance with the notice.

(4)   Where a person is given a notice under paragraph (3) in respect of an offence under this regulation—

    (a)   no proceedings may be instituted for that offence before the expiration of the period of 21 days beginning with the day after the date of the notice; and

    (b)   he may not be convicted of that offence if, before the expiration of that period, he pays the penalty in accordance with the notice.

(5)   A notice under paragraph (3) must give such particulars of the circumstances alleged to constitute the offence as are necessary for giving reasonable information of the offence.

(6)   A notice under paragraph (3) must also state—

    (a)   the period during which, by virtue of paragraph (4), proceedings will not be instituted for the offence;

    (b)   the amount of the penalty; and

    (c)   that the penalty is payable to the Secretary of State at the address specified in the notice.

(7)   Without prejudice to payment by any other method, payment of a penalty in pursuance of a notice under paragraph (3) may be made by pre-paying and posting a letter by registered post or the recorded delivery service containing the amount of the penalty (in cash or otherwise) to the Secretary of State at the address specified in the notice.

(8)   Where a letter is sent in accordance with paragraph (7) payment is to be regarded as having been made at the time at which that letter would be delivered in the ordinary course of registered post or the recorded delivery service.

(9)   A constable or immigration officer may withdraw a penalty notice given under paragraph (3) if the constable or immigration officer decides that—

    (a)   the notice was issued in error;

    (b)   the notice contains material errors; or

    (c)   he has reasonable grounds to believe that the employee has committed an offence under regulation 17.

(10)   A penalty notice may be withdrawn—

    (a)   whether or not the period specified in paragraph (4)(a) has expired;

    (b)   under paragraph (9)(a) and (b), whether or not the penalty has been paid; and

    (c)   under paragraph (9)(c), only where the penalty has not yet been paid.

(11)   Where a penalty notice has been withdrawn under paragraph (9)—

    (a)   notice of the withdrawal must be given to the recipient; and

    (b)   any amount paid by way of penalty in pursuance of that notice must be repaid to the person who paid it.

(12)   Subject to paragraph (13), proceedings shall not be continued or instituted against an employee for an offence under paragraph (1) in connection with which a withdrawal notice was issued.

(13)   Proceedings may be continued or instituted for an offence in connection with which a withdrawal notice was issued if—

(a) where the withdrawal notice was withdrawn pursuant to paragraph (9)(b)—

   (i) a further penalty notice in respect of the offence was issued at the same time as the penalty notice was withdrawn; and

   (ii) the penalty has not been paid pursuant to that further penalty notice in accordance with paragraph (4)(a); or

(b) the withdrawal notice was withdrawn pursuant to paragraph (9)(c).

17 Deception—employee offence

(1) A person is guilty of an offence if, by means which include deception by him, he obtains or seeks to obtain a worker authorisation registration certificate.

(2) A person guilty of an offence under this regulation shall be liable on summary conviction—

(a) to imprisonment for a term not exceeding three months;

(b) to a fine not exceeding level 5 on the standard scale; or

(c) to both.

18 Offences under regulations 16 and 17—search, entry and arrest

An offence under regulation 16 or 17 shall be treated as—

(a) a relevant offence for the purposes of sections 28B (search and arrest by warrant) and 28D (entry and search of premises) of the 1971 Act;

(b) an offence under Part 3 of the 1971 Act (criminal proceedings) for the purposes of sections 28E (entry and search of premises following arrest), 28G (searching arrested persons) and 28H (searching persons in police custody) of that Act; and

(c) an offence under section 24(1)(b) of the 1971 Act for the purposes of sections 28A(1) (arrest without warrant), 28CA (business premises: entry to arrest) and 28FA (search for personnel records: warrant unnecessary) of that Act.

SCHEDULE

(The Schedule amends the Immigration (European Economic Area) Regulations 2006, SI 2006/1003 ante.)

IMMIGRATION AND NATIONALITY (COST RECOVERY FEES) REGULATIONS 2014

(SI 2014/581)

Made: 11 March 2014.

Authority: Immigration, Asylum and Nationality Act 2006, ss 51(3), 52(1), (3), (6).

Commencement: 6 April 2014.

Citation, commencement and interpretation

1

These Regulations may be cited as the Immigration and Nationality (Cost Recovery Fees) Regulations 2014 and come into force on 6th April 2014.

2

In these Regulations—

"the 1971 Act" means the Immigration Act 1971;

"the 1981 Act" means the British Nationality Act 1981;

"the 1999 Act" means the Immigration and Asylum Act 1999;

["the 2002 Act" means the Nationality, Immigration and Asylum Act 2002;]

["the 2007 Act" means the UK Borders Act 2007;]

"the 1982 Order" means the British Protectorates, Protected States and Protected Persons Order 1982;

"the 2008 Regulations" means the Immigration (Biometric Registration) Regulations 2008;

"the 2011 Order" means the Immigration and Nationality (Fees) Order 2011;

["administrative review" means the review on request of a decision in connection with immigration in the circumstances specified in the immigration rules;]

"biometric immigration document" has the same meaning as provided in section 5 of [the 2007 Act];

["biometric information" has the same meaning as provided in section 15 of the 2007 Act;]

"CESC national" means a person who is a national of a state which has ratified the European Social Charter, agreed by the Council of Europe at Turin on 18th October 1961;

"child" means a person under the age of 18;

"dependant" in respect of a person means—

    (a)   the spouse or civil partner of that person;

    (b)   someone who has been living with that person in a relationship akin to a marriage or civil partnership for at least two years; or

    (c)   a child of that person;

"Direct Airside Transit Visa" means a transit visa within the meaning of section 41(2) of the 1999 Act, authorising the holder to remain within an airport, without passing through immigration control, pending departure on another flight from the same airport;

"EC Association Agreement with Turkey" means the agreement establishing an Association between the European Community and Turkey signed at Ankara on 12th September 1963;

"entry clearance" has the same meaning as provided in section 33(1) of the 1971 Act;

"immigration employment document" means a work permit, or any other document which relates to employment and is issued for the purposes of the immigration rules or in connection with leave to enter or remain in the United Kingdom;

"immigration rules" means the rules for the time being laid down by the Secretary of State as mentioned in section 3(2) of the 1971 Act;

"indefinite leave" means leave to enter or remain (as the case may be) in the United Kingdom which is not limited as to duration;

"leave to enter the United Kingdom" means leave to enter the United Kingdom given in accordance with the provisions of the 1971 Act or the immigration rules, and any subsequent variation of that leave;

"leave to remain in the United Kingdom" means leave to remain in the United Kingdom given in accordance with the provisions of the 1971 Act or the immigration rules, and any subsequent variation of that leave;

"limited leave" means leave to enter or remain (as the case may be) in the United Kingdom which is limited as to duration;

["process used to take a record of a person's biometric information" means the process, or combination of processes to which a person may be required to submit in order to enable a record to be taken of that person's biometric information, where the person is required by regulations made under section 41 of the 1981 Act, section 126 of the 2002 Act or section 5 of the 2007 Act to provide such information for the purposes of an application or claim in connection with immigration or nationality;]

"sponsor" means a sponsor under Part 6A of the immigration rules;

"sponsor licence" means a licence granted by the Secretary of State to a person who, by virtue of such a grant, is licensed as a sponsor;

"Tier 2 Migrant", "Tier 4 Migrant", "Tier 5 Migrant" and "Tier 5 (Temporary Worker) Migrant" have the same meaning as provided in the immigration rules;

"transfer of conditions" means the fixing of a stamp, sticker or other attachment on a passport or other document issued to an applicant, which indicates that a person has been granted leave to enter or remain in the United Kingdom;

"travel document" means a document which is not a passport, allowing a person (or, if the person has died, the body of that person) to travel outside the United Kingdom, and is issued by the Home Office to persons who are stateless or cannot obtain or use a passport issued by their own country.

Amendment

Definitions "the 2002 Act", "the 2007 Act", "administrative review", "biometric information" inserted, words in square brackets in definition "biometric immigration document" substituted, and definition "process used" substituted by SI 2014/2398, reg 2(1), (2). Date in force: 1 October 2014, see SI 2014/2398, reg 1.

Fees for applications, services, and processes in connection with immigration and nationality

3

Schedule 1 (Fees for applications for entry clearance to enter the United Kingdom) has effect to specify the amount of the fees for the specified applications for entry clearance to enter the United Kingdom for the purposes of article 3(2)(b) of the 2011 Order, exceptions to the requirement to pay such fees, and circumstances in which such fees may be waived or reduced.

4

Schedule 2 (Fees for applications for sponsor licences, highly trusted sponsor status, and related applications and processes) has effect to specify the amount of the fees for—

(i) applications for the specified sponsor licences for the purposes of article 3(2)(t) of the 2011 Order;

(ii) applications for permission for a student given leave to enter, or remain in the United Kingdom to change their sponsor for the purposes of article 3(2)(d) of the 2011 Order;

(iii) applications for changes to a sponsor's status for the purposes of article 3(2)(u) of the 2011 Order; and

(iv) processes related to sponsors for the purposes of article 5(a) and (b) of the 2011 Order.

5

Schedule 3 (Fees for documents relating to immigration) has effect to specify—

(a) the amount of the fees for—

(i) the specified applications for a transfer of conditions for the purposes of article 3(2)(e) of the 2011 Order;

(ii) the specified application for an immigration employment document for the purposes of article 3(2)(f) of the 2011 Order;

    (iii)   the specified applications for travel documents for the purposes of article 3(2)(g) of the 2011 Order;

    (iv)   the specified application for a Direct Airside Transit Visa for the purposes of article 3(2)(q) of the 2011 Order;

    (v)   the specified applications for a registration certificate, a residence card, a document certifying permanent residence, a permanent residence card or a derivative residence card, for the purposes of article 3(2)(w) of the 2011 Order;

    (vi)   the specified applications for a biometric immigration document for the purposes of article 3(2)(s) of the 2011 Order;

    (vii)   the process used to take a record of a person's biometric information for the purposes of article 5(c) of the 2011 Order; . . .

(b)   exceptions to the requirement to pay the fees referred to in sub-paragraph (a)(iii), (vii) and (viii)[; and

(c)   circumstances in which the fee referred to in sub-paragraph (a)(vii) may be waived.]

Amendment

Word omitted from para (a) revoked and para (c) inserted together with word preceding it, by SI 2014/2398, reg 2(1), (3). Date in force: 1 October 2014, see SI 2014/2398, reg 1.

6

Schedule 4 (Fees for applications, processes and services in connection with nationality) has effect to specify—

(a)   the amount of the fees for the specified applications in connection with nationality for the purposes of article 3(2)(h), (i), (j), (k), (l), (m), (n), (o), (p), and (v) of the 2011 Order;

[(b)   the amount of the fees for the specified processes in connection with nationality for the purposes of article 5(c) and (d) of the 2011 Order; and]

(c)   the amount of the fees for the specified services in connection with nationality for the purposes of article 4(a), (b), (c), (d), (e), (f), (g) and (h) of the 2011 Order.

Amendment

Para (b) substituted by SI 2014/2398, reg 2(1), (4). Date in force: 1 October 2014, see SI 2014/2398, reg 1.

7

Schedule 5 (Fees for the exercise of consular functions in connection with immigration and nationality) has effect to specify the amount of the fees for the exercise of consular functions in connection with immigration and nationality for the purposes of articles 6 and 7 of the 2011 Order.

[**8**

Schedule 6 (Miscellaneous fees) has effect to specify—

(a)   the amount of the fee for the administration of the specified test for the purposes of article 4(n) of the 2011 Order; and

(b)   the amount of the fee for the process of conducting an administrative review for the purposes of article 5(d) of the 2011 Order.]

Amendment

Substituted by SI 2014/2398, reg 2(1), (5). Date in force: 1 October 2014, see SI 2014/2398, reg 1.

Number and description of the exception	Fees to which exception applies
2.1	**Officials of Her Majesty's Government**
No fee is payable in respect of an application made in connection with the official duty of any official of Her Majesty's Government.	All fees in Table 1
2.2	**Dependants of refugees or persons granted humanitarian protection**
No fee is payable in respect of an application made under paragraphs 352A to 352FI of the immigration rules.	All fees in Table 1
2.3	**Applications under the EC Association Agreement with Turkey**
No fee is payable in respect of an application made under the terms of the EC Association Agreement with Turkey.	All fees in Table 1

Table 3 (Waivers in respect of fees for applications for entry clearance to enter the United Kingdom)

Number and description of the waiver	Fees to which waiver applies
3.1	**General waiver**
No fee is payable in respect of an application where the Secretary of State determines that the fee should be waived.	All fees in Table 1
3.2	**Scholarships funded by Her Majesty's Government**
The official determining an application may decide to waive the payment of the fee or reduce the amount of the fee where the application is made by a candidate for, or holder of a scholarship funded by Her Majesty's Government and is in connection with such a scholarship.	All fees in Table 1
3.3	**International courtesy**
The official determining an application may decide to waive the payment of the fee or reduce the amount of the fee as a matter of international courtesy.	All fees in Table 1
3.4	**Visitors under a Foreign and Commonwealth Office Bilateral Programme**

The official determining an application may decide to waive the payment of the fee or reduce the amount of the fee where the applicant intends to visit the United Kingdom in connection with programmes operated by the Foreign and Commonwealth Office to give funds directly to Embassies and Missions outside the United Kingdom to support activities directly connected to the United Kingdom's international priorities.	All fees in Table 1
3.5	**Visitors under a Foreign and Commonwealth Office Strategic Programme**
The official determining an application may decide to waive the payment of the fee or reduce the amount of the fee where the applicant intends to visit the United Kingdom in connection with programmes of funding operated by the Foreign and Commonwealth Office to promote action on global issues in areas of strategic importance to the United Kingdom.	All fees in Table 1

SCHEDULE 2

FEES FOR APPLICATIONS FOR SPONSOR LICENCES, HIGHLY TRUSTED SPONSOR STATUS, AND RELATED APPLICATIONS AND PROCESSES

Regulation 4

Interpretation

1

In this Schedule—

"certificate of sponsorship" means an authorisation issued by the Secretary of State to a sponsor in respect of an application, or potential application, for leave to enter or leave to remain in the United Kingdom;

"Highly Trusted Sponsor Status" has the same meaning as provided in the immigration rules;

"register of licensed sponsors" means the register, maintained by the Secretary of State, of persons holding sponsor licences;

"small or charitable sponsor" means a sponsor that is—

    (a)   a company that is subject to the small companies regime under section 381 of the Companies Act 2006;

    (b)   in the case of a person who is not a company for the purposes of that section, a person who employs no more than 50 employees; or

    (c)   a charity within the meaning of section 1 of the Charities Act 2011, or section 1 of the Charities Act (Northern Ireland) 2008 or a body entered in the Scottish Charity Register;

"Tier" means the route, provided for in the immigration rules, by which a person seeking leave to enter or remain in the United Kingdom as a Tier 2 Migrant, a Tier 4 Migrant, a Tier 5 Migrant or a Tier 5 (Temporary Worker) Migrant applies for such leave to enter or remain.

Fees for applications for sponsor licences, highly trusted sponsor status and related applications and processes

2

(1)   Table 4 specifies the amount of the fees for the specified applications for sponsor licences.

(2)   Paragraph 3 makes provision for the amount of the fees (if any) to be paid in respect of—

    (a)   applications for sponsor licences in respect of more than one Tier;

    (b)   applications to add an additional Tier or additional Tiers to an existing valid sponsor licence; and

    (c)   applications for an additional licence or additional licences by a person holding an existing valid sponsor licence.

(3)   Table 5 specifies the amount of the fees for other specified applications and processes in connection with sponsorship.

Table 4 (Fees for applications for sponsor licences)

Number of fee	Type of application or process	Amount of fee
4.1	**Fees for applications for sponsor licences where the applicant is a small or charitable sponsor**	
4.1.1	Application for sponsor licence in respect of Tier 2 Migrants where the applicant is a small or charitable sponsor.	£536
4.1.2	Application for sponsor licence in respect of Tier 4 Migrants where the applicant is a small or charitable sponsor.	£536
4.1.3	Application for sponsor licence in respect of Tier 5 Migrants where the applicant is a small or charitable sponsor.	£536
4.2	**Fees for applications for sponsor licences where the applicant is not a small or charitable sponsor**	
4.2.1	Application for sponsor licence in respect of Tier 4 Migrants.	£536
4.2.2	Application for sponsor licence in respect of Tier 5 Migrants.	£536

Fees for other applications in connection with sponsorship

3

(1)   Where a person applies for a sponsor licence in respect of two or more Tiers, the fee payable is the highest fee chargeable in respect of a licence for any of the Tiers applied for.

(2)   Subject to sub-paragraph (3), where a person holding an existing valid sponsor licence applies to add an additional Tier or additional Tiers to that licence, the fee payable is the sum equivalent to the difference (if any) between the fee already paid for the licence, and the highest fee chargeable in respect of a licence for any of the additional Tiers applied for.

(3) If the fee already paid is equal to or greater than that chargeable in respect of a licence for each additional Tier applied for, no further fee is payable.

(4) Where a person holding an existing valid sponsor licence applies for a separate licence in respect of an additional Tier, the fee payable is the full fee chargeable in respect of a licence for that Tier.

Table 5 (Fees for other applications and processes in connection with sponsorship)

Number of fee	Type of application or process	Amount of fee
5.1	**Fee for Tier 4 Migrants changing to another sponsor**	
5.1.1	Application by a Tier 4 Migrant for permission to change to another sponsor for the purposes of paragraph 323A of the immigration rules, where the person's leave to enter or remain (as the case may be) in the United Kingdom as a Tier 4 Migrant results from an application for entry clearance or leave to remain in the United Kingdom made during the period beginning on 31st March 2009 and ending on 4th October 2009.	£160
5.2	**Fees for applications for Highly Trusted Sponsor Status**	
5.2.1	Application by a sponsor holding a sponsor licence in respect of Tier 4 Migrants to be awarded Highly Trusted Sponsor Status in respect of Tier 4 Migrants.	£536
5.3	**Fees for processes relating to sponsor licences**	
5.3.1	The issuing of a certificate of sponsorship in respect of an application or potential application for leave to enter or remain in the United Kingdom as a Tier 4 Migrant.	£14
5.3.2	The issuing of a certificate of sponsorship in respect of an application or potential application for leave to enter or remain in the United Kingdom as a Tier 5 Migrant other than where the application or potential application is for leave as a Tier 5 (Temporary Worker) Migrant and the applicant is a CESC national (in which case no fee is payable).	£14
5.3.3	The issuing of an action plan under the immigration rules to a sponsor who is recorded as being "B-rated" in the register of licensed sponsors, and with which that sponsor must comply in order to become a sponsor recorded as being "A-rated" in that register.	£1,476

SCHEDULE 3
FEES FOR DOCUMENTS RELATING TO IMMIGRATION

Regulation 5

Interpretation

1

(1) In this Schedule—

"the 2006 Regulations" means the Immigration (European Economic Area) Regulations 2006;

"assistance by a local authority" means assistance, accommodation or maintenance provided by a local authority (or, in Northern Ireland, an authority which has the same meaning as provided in article 2(2) of the Children (Northern Ireland) Order 1995) under—

    (a)   section 17, 20 or 23 of the Children Act 1989;

    (b)   section 22, 25 or 26 of the Children (Scotland) Act 1995; or

    (c)   article 18, 21 or 27 of the Children (Northern Ireland) Order 1995;

"certificate of travel" means a travel document issued in the United Kingdom at the discretion of the Secretary of State to persons who have been formally, and in the view of the Secretary of State, unreasonably refused a passport by the authorities in their own country and who have been—

    (a)   granted limited leave to remain in the United Kingdom or humanitarian protection under the immigration rules on rejection of a claim for asylum or for recognition as a stateless person; or

    (b)   granted indefinite leave to remain in the United Kingdom.

"claim for asylum" means a claim within the meaning of section 94(1) of the 1999 Act;

"convention travel document" means a travel document issued in accordance with Article 28 of the Convention relating to the Status of Refugees done at Geneva on 28th July 1951;

"document of identity" means a travel document issued in the United Kingdom to a person who is not a British citizen which enables the holder to make one journey out of the United Kingdom;

"stateless person's travel document" means a travel document issued in accordance with Article 28 of the Convention relating to the Status of Stateless Persons done at New York on 28th September 1954;

"work permit holder" means a person holding an extant work permit granted under the work permit provisions formerly contained in the immigration rules.

(2) For the purposes of this Schedule a claim for asylum is to be taken to be determined—

    (a)   on the date on which the Secretary of State notifies the claimant of the decision on the claim;

    (b)   if the claimant has appealed against the Secretary of State's decision, on the date on which the appeal is disposed of; or

    (c)   if the claimant has brought an appeal from within the United Kingdom against an immigration decision under section 82 of the Nationality, Immigration and Asylum Act 2002 or section 2 of the Special Immigration Appeals Commission Act 1997, on the day on which the appeal is disposed of.

Fees for documents relating to immigration

2

(1) Table 6 specifies the amount of the fees for the specified applications for documents relating to immigration.

(2) Table 7 provides for exceptions to the requirement to pay the fees specified in Table 6 for applications for travel documents.

(3) Table 8 specifies the amount of the fees for the specified applications for biometric immigration documents and the process used to take a record of a person's biometric information.

(4) Table 9 provides for exceptions to the requirement to pay the fees specified in Table 8.

[(5) Paragraph 3 confers a discretion on the Secretary of State to waive the specified fee.]

Table 6 (Fees for a transfer of conditions, immigration employment document, travel documents, Direct Airside Transit Visas, registration certificates and residence cards)

Number of fee	Type of application	Amount of fee
6.1	Fee for applications made in the United Kingdom for a transfer of conditions	
6.1.1	Application for a transfer of conditions where the application is made within the United Kingdom by post or courier or via the public website maintained by the Home Office, and the applicant has limited leave to enter or remain in the United Kingdom.	£107
6.1.2	Application for a transfer of conditions where the application is made within the United Kingdom by post or courier or via the public website maintained by the Home Office, and the applicant has indefinite leave to enter or remain in the United Kingdom.	£104
6.2	Fee for applications made overseas for a transfer of conditions (vignette transfer fee)	
6.2.1	Application for a transfer of conditions where the application is made outside the United Kingdom.	£109
6.3	Fee for applications for an immigration employment document	
6.3.1	Application for a letter to confirm an amendment to information held by the Home Office relating to employment as a work permit holder, which does not constitute a change requiring the applicant to make a new application for permission to work.	£22
6.4	Fees for applications for travel documents	
6.4.1	Application for a certificate of travel where the person in respect of whom the application is made is aged 16 or over when the application is received by the Secretary of State.	£246

6.4.2	Application for a certificate of travel where the person in respect of whom the application is made is under the age of 16 when the application is received by the Secretary of State.	£157
6.4.3	Application for a convention travel document, stateless person's travel document, or document of identity where the person in respect of whom the application is made is aged 16 or over when the application is received by the Secretary of State.	£69
6.4.4	Application for a convention travel document, stateless person's travel document, or document of identity where the person in respect of whom the application is made is under the age of 16 when the application is received by the Secretary of State.	£46
6.5	**Fee for an application for a Direct Airside Transit Visa**	
6.5.1	Application for a Direct Airside Transit Visa.	[£30]
6.6	**Fees for applications for documents referred to in the 2006 Regulations**	
6.6.1	Application for a registration certificate, a residence card, a document certifying permanent residence, a permanent residence card or a derivative residence card, issued pursuant to Part 3 of the 2006 Regulations.	£55

Table 7 (Exceptions to requirement to pay fees for applications for travel documents)

Number and description of the exception	Fees to which exception applies
7.1	**Travel documents for bodies being taken abroad for burial**
	No fee is payable in respect of an application for a travel document for a body that is being taken abroad for the purposes of burial or cremation.	Fees 6.4.1 to 6.4.4
7.2	**Travel documents for reconstruction or resettlement**

	No fee is payable in respect of an application for a travel document where the application is stated as being made in order to enable the applicant to participate in a project operated or approved by the Secretary of State for the purposes of enabling a person in the United Kingdom to make a single trip to a country outside the United Kingdom in order to assist the reconstruction of that country or to decide whether to resettle there.	Fees 6.4.1 to 6.4.4
7.3	**Travel documents for the purposes of the Assisted Voluntary Returns programme**	
	No fee is payable in respect of an application for a document of identity for the purposes of the Assisted Voluntary Returns programme operated by the Home Office.	Fees 6.4.3 and 6.4.4
7.4	**Travel documents for persons born on or before 2nd September 1929**	
	No fee is payable in respect of an application for a convention travel document or stateless person's travel document where the applicant was born on or before 2nd September 1929.	Fees 6.4.1 and 6.4.3

Table 8 (Fees for applications for biometric immigration documents and the process used to take a record of biometric information)

Number of fee	Type of application or process	Amount of fee
8.1	Fees for a mandatory application for a biometric immigration document following an application to replace a letter which indicated that the applicant had been granted leave to enter or remain in the United Kingdom	
8.1.1	Application for a biometric immigration document in accordance with regulation 3(1)(a) and (2)(d) of the 2008 Regulations where the applicant has limited leave to enter or remain in the United Kingdom, and fee 8.1.3 or 8.1.4 does not apply.	£107
8.1.2	Application for a biometric immigration document in accordance with regulation 3(1)(a) and 2(d) of the 2008 Regulations where the applicant has indefinite leave to enter or remain in the United Kingdom, and fee 8.1.3 or 8.1.4 does not apply.	£104

8.1.3	Application for a biometric immigration document in accordance with regulation 3(1)(a) and (2)(d) of the 2008 Regulations where the applicant has made a claim for asylum which has been granted, or has been granted humanitarian protection under the immigration rules.	£40
8.1.4	Application for a biometric immigration document in accordance with regulation 3(1)(a) and (2)(d) of the 2008 Regulations where the applicant has leave to remain in the United Kingdom under paragraphs 352A to 352FI of the immigration rules.	£40
8.2	**Fees for a mandatory application for a biometric immigration document following an application for a transfer of conditions**	
8.2.1	Application for a biometric immigration document in accordance with regulation 3(1)(a) and (2)(c) of the 2008 Regulations, where the applicant has limited leave to enter or remain in the United Kingdom.	£107
8.2.2	Application for a biometric immigration document in accordance with regulation 3(1)(a) and (2)(c) of the 2008 Regulations where the applicant has indefinite leave to enter or remain in the United Kingdom.	£104
8.3	**Fees for a mandatory application for a replacement biometric immigration document**	
8.3.1	Application for a biometric immigration document in accordance with regulation 19(1)(a) of the 2008 Regulations to replace a biometric immigration document which has been cancelled under regulation 17(a) or (d) to (i) of those Regulations, where the applicant has limited leave to enter or remain in the United Kingdom.	£107
8.3.2	Application for a biometric immigration document in accordance with regulation 19(1)(a) of the 2008 Regulations to replace a biometric immigration document which has been cancelled under regulation 17(a) or (d) to (i) of those Regulations, where the applicant has indefinite leave to enter or remain in the United Kingdom.	£104
8.3.3	Application for a biometric immigration document in accordance with regulation 19(1)(a) of the 2008 Regulations to replace a biometric immigration document which has been cancelled under regulation 17(b) or (c) of those Regulations.	£40

8.3.4	Application for a biometric immigration document in accordance with regulation 19(1)(b) of the 2008 Regulations to replace a biometric immigration document which has ceased to have effect under regulation 13(3) and (4)(b) or (c) of those Regulations.	£40
8.4	**Fee for taking a record of biometric information**	
8.4.1	The process used to take a record of a person's biometric information for the purposes of an application for a biometric immigration document referred to in fees 8.1.1 to 8.1.4, 8.2.1, 8.2.2, 8.3.1, 8.3.2 and 8.3.3.	£19.20
8.4.2	The process used to take a record of a person's biometric information for the purposes of an application for a biometric immigration document referred to in fee 8.3.4.	£19.20
8.4.3	The process used to take a record of a person's biometric information for the purposes of an application for a biometric immigration document in accordance with regulation 3(1)(a) and 2(a) and (b) of the 2008 Regulations.	£19.20
[8.4.4	The process used to take a record of a person's biometric information for the purposes of an application for a residence card, a permanent residence card or a derivative residence card, issued pursuant to Part 3 of the 2006 Regulations.	£19.20
8.4.5	The process used to take a record of a person's biometric information for the purposes of an application for a biometric immigration document where the fee is not specified elsewhere in these Regulations.	£19.20]

Table 9 (Exceptions to the requirement to pay fees for applications for biometric immigration documents and the process used to take a record of biometric information)

Number and description of the exception	Fees to which exception applies
9.1	Persons granted asylum or humanitarian protection, their dependants and stateless persons	

	No fee is payable for an application for a biometric immigration document if the applicant has been granted asylum, or has been granted humanitarian protection under the immigration rules, or has leave to remain in the United Kingdom under paragraphs 352A to 352FI of the immigration rules.	Fee 8.3.4
9.2	**Children born in the United Kingdom to persons granted asylum or humanitarian protection**	
	No fee is payable for an application for a biometric immigration document if the applicant is a child who was born in the United Kingdom to a person who had been granted asylum, or had been granted humanitarian protection under the immigration rules.	Fee 8.3.4
9.3	**Process used to take a record of a person's biometric information where exceptions 9.1 and 9.2 apply**	
	No fee is payable for the process used to take a record of a person's biometric information for the purposes of an application for a biometric immigration document to which exceptions 9.1 and 9.2 apply.	Fee 8.4.2
9.4	**Children being provided with assistance by a local authority**	
	[In relation to the specified fees,] no fee is payable for the process used to take a record of a person's biometric information if that person is a child who is being provided with assistance by a local authority.	Fees 8.4.1 to 8.4.3
9.5	**Applicants with leave to remain under the EC Association Agreement with Turkey**	
	[In relation to the specified fees,] no fee is payable for the process used to take a record of a person's biometric information if that person has leave to remain in the United Kingdom under the terms of the EC Association Agreement with Turkey.	Fees 8.4.1 to 8.4.3
9.6	**Process used to take a record of a person's biometric information where the person is exempt from paying the application fee for the connected application for leave to remain in the United Kingdom, or that application fee has been waived**	

No fee is payable for the process used to take a record of a person's biometric information where that record is taken for the purposes of an application for a biometric immigration document, made in accordance with regulation 3(1)(a) and (2)(a) of the 2008 Regulations, in connection with an application for leave to remain in the United Kingdom in relation to which the applicant is exempt from paying the application fee or the application fee has been waived.	Fee 8.4.3

[3 Waiver in respect of the fee listed at Table 8.4.5

The Secretary of State may waive the specified fee in respect of the process used to take a record of a person's biometric information.]

Amendment

Para 2(5) inserted; in Table 6 number in square brackets in fee 6.5.1 substituted; in Table 8, fees 8.4.4, 8.4.5 inserted; in Table 9, words in square brackets in points 9.4, 9.5 inserted; and para 3 inserted, by SI 2014/2398, reg 2(1), (6). Date in force: 1 October 2014, see SI 2014/2398, reg 1.

SCHEDULE 4

FEES FOR APPLICATIONS, PROCESSES AND SERVICES IN CONNECTION WITH NATIONALITY

Regulation 6

Interpretation

1

In this Schedule—

"application for registration or naturalisation" means—

(a) an application for naturalisation as a British citizen under section 6(1) or (2) of the 1981 Act;

(b) an application for naturalisation as a British overseas territories citizen under section 18(1) or (2) of the 1981 Act;

(c) an application for registration as a British citizen under section 1(3), (3A) or (4), 3(1), (2) or (5), 4(2) or (5), 4A, 4B, 4D, 10(1) or (2), or 13(1) or (3) of, or paragraph 3, 4 or 5 of Schedule 2 to, the 1981 Act;

(d) an application for registration as a British citizen under section 1 of the British Nationality (Hong Kong) Act 1997;

(e) an application for registration as a British overseas territories citizen under section 13(1) or (3) of the 1981 Act (as applied by section 24 of that Act), or sections 15(3) or (4), 17(1), (2) or (5), or 22(1) or (2) of, or paragraph 3, 4 or 5 of Schedule 2 to, that Act;

(f) an application for registration as a British overseas citizen under section 27(1) of, or paragraph 4 or 5 of Schedule 2 to, the 1981 Act;

(g) an application for registration as a British protected person under article 7 of the 1982 Order; or

(h) an application for registration as a British subject under section 32 of, or paragraph 4 of Schedule 2 to, the 1981 Act;

"certificate of registration or naturalisation" means a certificate of registration or naturalisation issued under the 1981 Act.

Fees for applications, processes and services in connection with nationality

2

(1) Table 10 specifies the amount of fees for the specified applications, processes and services in connection with nationality.

(2) The fees specified in Table 10 are subject to paragraph 3 (Multiple declarations of renunciation of British citizenship).

Table 10 (Fees for applications, processes and services in connection with nationality)

Number of fee	Type of application, process or service	Amount of fee
10.1	Fees for applications in connection with nationality	
10.1.1	Application for the amendment of a certificate of registration or naturalisation other than where the amendment is required to rectify an error made by the Secretary of State.	£85
10.1.2	Application for a certificate of entitlement within the meaning of section 33(1) of the 1971 Act where the application is made in respect of a person who is in the United Kingdom at the time that the application is made.	£144
10.1.3	Application for a certificate of entitlement within the meaning of section 33(1) of the 1971 Act where the application is made in respect of a person who is outside the United Kingdom at the time that the application is made.	£289
10.1.4	Application for a letter or other document confirming a person's nationality status or that a person is not a British citizen.	£85
10.2	Fees for processes in connection with nationality	
10.2.1	Application for the reconsideration of an application for a certificate of registration or naturalisation which has been refused by the Secretary of State.	£80
[10.2.2	The process used to take a record of a person's biometric information for the purposes of an application for registration or naturalisation.	£19.20]
10.3	Fees for services in connection with nationality	
10.3.1	Registration of a declaration of a renunciation of British citizenship under section 12 of the 1981 Act.	£144

10.3.2	Registration of a declaration of a renunciation of British overseas territories citizenship under sections 12 and 24 of the 1981 Act.	£144
10.3.3	Registration of a declaration of a renunciation of British overseas citizenship under sections 29 and 12 of the 1981 Act.	£144
10.3.4	Registration of a declaration of a renunciation of the status of British subject under sections 34 and 12 of the 1981 Act.	£144
10.3.5	Registration of a declaration of a renunciation of the status of British protected person under article 11 of the 1982 Order.	£144
10.3.6	The supply of a certified copy of a notice, certificate, order, declaration or entry given, granted or made under the 1981 Act, any of the former nationality Acts (within the meaning of section 50(1) of the 1981 Act), or the British Nationality (Hong Kong) Act 1997.	£85
10.4	**Fees for services in connection with citizenship ceremonies and citizenship oaths**	
10.4.1	The arrangement of a citizenship ceremony (including the administration of a citizenship oath and pledge at the ceremony).	£80
10.4.2	The administration of a citizenship oath, or oath and pledge where the oath, or oath and pledge, are not administered at a citizenship ceremony or by a justice of the peace.	£5

Multiple declarations of a renunciation of British citizenship

3

Where a person—

(a)   makes a declaration of a renunciation for which the fee is specified in Table 10; and

(b)   at the same time makes another such declaration;

the total fee payable in respect of those declarations is the same as that for registration of a single declaration.

Responsibility for paying the fee for the arrangement of a citizenship ceremony

4

(1) The fee specified in fee 10.4.1 in Table 10 for the arrangement of a citizenship ceremony is payable by the person who is required by section 42 of the 1981 Act to make a citizenship oath and pledge at a citizenship ceremony.

(2) Where the fee for the arrangement of a citizenship ceremony is not paid in accordance with sub-paragraph (1), the Secretary of State will not consider any related application for registration or naturalisation made by the person responsible for paying that fee.

Refunds of fees for the arrangement of a citizenship ceremony where an application is refused or the requirement to attend the ceremony is disapplied

5

Where the fee specified in fee 10.4.1 in Table 10 for the arrangement of a citizenship ceremony is paid in accordance with paragraph 4 it must be refunded where—

    (a)   the Secretary of State refuses to arrange the citizenship ceremony; or

    (b)   the Secretary of State decides that the registration should be effected or the certificate of naturalisation should be granted, but disapplies the requirement to make a citizenship oath and pledge at a citizenship ceremony because of the special circumstances of the case.

Amendment

In Table 10, fee 10.2.2 inserted by SI 2014/2398, reg 2(1), (7). Date in force: 1 October 2014, see SI 2014/2398, reg 1.

SCHEDULE 5

FEES FOR THE EXERCISE OF CONSULAR FUNCTIONS IN CONNECTION WITH IMMIGRATION AND NATIONALITY

Regulation 7

Interpretation

1

In this Schedule—

"the 1968 Act" means the Consular Relations Act 1968;

"consular employee" has the same meaning as provided in Article 1(1)(e) of the Vienna Convention on Consular Relations set out in Schedule 1 to the 1968 Act;

"consular officer" has the same meaning as provided in Article 1(1)(d) of the Vienna Convention on Consular Relations set out in Schedule 1 to the 1968 Act;

"consular post" has the same meaning as provided in Article 1(1)(a) of the Vienna Convention on Consular Relations set out in Schedule 1 to the 1968 Act;

"consular premises" has the same meaning as provided in Article 1(1)(j) of the Vienna Convention on Consular Relations set out in Schedule 1 to the 1968 Act;

"supporting documents" means any letter, certificate, declaration or other document which may be required by an authority in any country or territory in connection with an application;

"visa" includes an entry certificate, entry permit or other document which is to be taken as evidence of a person's eligibility for entry into a country or territory (other than a work permit).

Fees for the exercise of consular functions in connection with immigration and nationality

2

(1)   Table 11 specifies the amount of the fees for the exercise of the specified consular functions.

(2)   The fees in Table 11 are subject to paragraph 3 (charges for travel time where services are provided away from consular premises) and paragraph 4 (discretion to waive fees for the services of consular officers or employees).

Table 11 (Fees for the exercise of consular functions in connection with immigration and nationality)

Number of fee	Service provided	Amount of fee
11.1	General fee for the services of consular officers	

11.1.1	The provision of the services of a consular officer or consular employee in relation to any service which the consular post or diplomatic mission has agreed to undertake.	£130 per hour or part hour
11.2	**Fees for receiving, preparing and forwarding documents**	
11.2.1	Receiving, preparing or forwarding (or any one or more of these) supporting documents for an application for a visa where the consular officer does not have authority to issue that visa.	£115
11.2.2	Receiving, preparing or forwarding (or any one or more of these) supporting documents for an application for a residence permit or identity card issued by a country or territory other than the United Kingdom.	£115
11.2.3	Receiving, preparing or forwarding (or any one or more of these) any certificate or document except a travel document or an application for registration or naturalisation (within the meaning of Schedule 4 to these Regulations).	£115
11.3	**Fee for receiving applications for visas on behalf of Commonwealth countries or British Overseas Territories**	
11.3.1	Receiving, preparing or forwarding (or any one or more of these) supporting documents for an application for a visa for a country listed in Schedule 3 to the 1981 Act or a British Overseas Territory within the meaning of section 50(1) of the 1981 Act.	£115

Charges for travel time when services are provided away from consular premises.

3

For the purposes of calculation of the fee specified in fee 11.1.1 in Table 11, the hours or part hours during which the services of consular officers or employees are provided includes travel time where those services are provided away from the consular premises.

Discretion to waive fees for the services of consular officers or employees

4

The official responsible for determining whether the services of consular officers or employees should be provided may waive the payment of the fee specified for such services in Table 11 where the official considers it is appropriate to do so in the particular circumstances of the case.

[SCHEDULE 6

MISCELLANEOUS FEES

Regulation 8
Interpretation

1

In this Schedule—

"main applicant" means a person who has made an application or claim in connection with immigration, as distinct from a person applying as the dependant of such a person.

Fee for the administration of the Life in the UK Test

2

A fee of £50 is payable for the administration of the Life in the UK test, as provided for in Appendix KoLL (Knowledge of Language and Life) to the immigration rules.

Fee for the process of administrative review, together with provision for exemption from, and waiver or reduction of, that fee

3

(1) Subject to sub-paragraphs (2) to (5), a fee of £80 is payable by an applicant requesting administrative review of:

   (a)   a single decision; or

   (b)   two (or more) decisions relating to applications or claims made by a main applicant and a dependant (or dependants) of that person.

(2) No fee is payable for the administrative review of a decision if the applicant was exempt from payment of the fee for the application or claim to which that decision related (the "connected application"), or if the fee for the connected application was waived.

(3) If the outcome of the administrative review is that the decision in relation to the connected application is maintained, but for different or additional reasons to those specified in the decision under review, no fee is payable in respect of any request for administrative review of the revised decision, or of any subsequent decision made in relation to the connected application.

(4) The Secretary of State must refund the fee specified in sub-paragraph (1) if the outcome of the administrative review is that the decision in relation to the connected application is withdrawn.

(5) The Secretary of State may waive or reduce the fee specified in sub-paragraph (1).]

Amendment

Substituted by SI 2014/2398, reg 2(1), (8). Date in force: 1 October 2014, see SI 2014/2398, reg 1.

IMMIGRATION AND NATIONALITY (FEES) REGULATIONS 2014

(SI 2014/922)

Made: 2 April 2014.

Authority: Immigration, Asylum and Nationality Act 2006, ss 51(3), 52(1), (3), (6).

Commencement: 6 April 2014.

Citation and commencement

1

These Regulations may be cited as the Immigration and Nationality (Fees) Regulations 2014 and come into force on 6th April 2014.

Interpretation

2

(1) In these Regulations—

"the 1971 Act" means the Immigration Act 1971;

"the 2011 Order" means the Immigration and Nationality (Fees) Order 2011;

"approval letter from a designated competent body" means a letter from a designated competent body within the meaning of the immigration rules endorsing a proposed application for leave to remain in, or leave to enter the United Kingdom as a Tier 1 (Exceptional Talent) Migrant;

"certificate of sponsorship" means an authorisation issued by the Secretary of State to a sponsor in respect of one or more applications, or potential applications, for leave to remain in or leave to enter the United Kingdom;

"CESC national" means a person who is a national of a state which has ratified the European Social Charter, agreed by the Council of Europe at Turin on 18th October 1961;

"Channel Islands" means the Bailiwick of Guernsey and the Bailiwick of Jersey;

"child" means a person under the age of 18;

"contractor" means a person with whom the Secretary of State has entered into a contract, by which the person agrees to provide certain services in connection with immigration and nationality to applicants outside the United Kingdom;

"dependant" in respect of a person means—

    (a)   the spouse or civil partner of that person;

    (b)   someone who has been living with that person in a relationship akin to a marriage or civil partnership for at least two years; or

    (c)   a child of that person;

"EC Association Agreement with Turkey" means the agreement establishing an Association between the European Community and Turkey signed at Ankara on 12th September 1963;

"immigration and nationality fees regulations" means regulations made under sections 51(3) and 52(1) and (3) of the Immigration, Asylum and Nationality Act 2006;

"immigration or nationality application" means an application for which a fee is specified in these Regulations or other immigration and nationality fees regulations;

"immigration rules" means the rules for the time being laid down by the Secretary of State as mentioned in section 3(2) of the 1971 Act.

"leave to enter the United Kingdom" means leave to enter the United Kingdom given in accordance with the provisions of the 1971 Act or the immigration rules and any subsequent variation of that leave;

"leave to remain in the United Kingdom" means leave to remain in the United Kingdom given in accordance with the provisions of the 1971 Act or the immigration rules and any subsequent variation of that leave;

"main applicant" means a person who has made an application for leave to enter or remain in the United Kingdom, or has been granted leave to enter or remain in the United Kingdom, as distinct from a person applying as the dependant of such a person;

"Points-Based System" has the same meaning as provided in the immigration rules;

"shortage occupation certificate of sponsorship" means a certificate of sponsorship issued in respect of an applicant applying for leave to remain in the United Kingdom in order to take up employment in an occupation listed in the Shortage Occupation List set out in Appendix K to the immigration rules;

"sponsor" means a sponsor under Part 6A of the immigration rules;

"sponsor licence" means a licence granted by the Secretary of State to a person who, by virtue of such a grant, is licensed as a sponsor;

"Tier 1 (Entrepreneur) Migrant", "Tier 1 (Exceptional Talent) Migrant", "Tier 1 (General) Migrant", "Tier 1 (Graduate Entrepreneur) Migrant", "Tier 1 (Investor) Migrant", and "Tier 1 (Post-Study Work) Migrant" have the same meaning as provided in the immigration rules;

"Tier 2 Migrant", "Tier 2 (General) Migrant", "Tier 2 (Intra-Company Transfer) Long Term Staff Migrant", "Tier 2 (Intra-Company Transfer) Short Term Staff Migrant", "Tier 2 (Sportsperson) Migrant", "Tier 2 (Minister of Religion) Migrant", "Tier 2 (Graduate Trainee") Migrant" and "Tier 2 (Skills Transfer) Migrant" have the same meaning as provided in the immigration rules;

"Tier 4 Migrant" has the same meaning as provided in the immigration rules;

"Tier 5 Migrant", "Tier 5 (Temporary Worker) Migrant" and "Tier 5 (Youth Mobility) Temporary Migrant" have the same meaning as provided in the immigration rules;

"work permit holder" means a person holding an extant work permit granted under the work permit provisions formerly contained in the immigration rules.

(2)   In these Regulations, "entry clearance" has the same meaning as provided in section 33(1) of the 1971 Act, save that in regulation 7 and Schedule 5, it has the same meaning as provided in section 33(1) of the 1971 Act as extended to the Channel Islands.

Fees for applications, processes and services in connection with immigration and nationality

3

Schedule 1 (Fees for applications for leave to remain in the United Kingdom) has effect to specify—

    (a)   the amount of the fees for—

        (i)   specified applications for leave to remain in the United Kingdom and variation of such leave for the purposes of article 3(2)(a) and (c) of the 2011 Order;

        (ii)   an application for an approval letter from a designated competent body for the purposes of article 3(2)(f) of the 2011 Order; and

    (b)   exceptions to the requirement to pay the fees referred to in paragraph (a)(i).

4

Schedule 2 (Fees for applications for entry clearance to enter the United Kingdom) has effect to specify—

    (a)   the amount of the fees for—

        (i)   specified applications for entry clearance to enter the United Kingdom for the purposes of article 3(2)(b) of the 2011 Order;

        (ii)   an application for an approval letter from a designated competent body for the purposes of article 3(2)(f) of the 2011 Order; and

    (b)   exceptions to the requirement to pay the fees referred to in paragraph (a)(i) and circumstances in which such fees may be waived or reduced.

5

Schedule 3 (Fees in relation to Sponsor Licences) has effect to specify the amount of the fees for specified applications for sponsor licences, for premium customer services for sponsors, and for related processes for the purposes of articles 3(2)(t) and (u), 4(m), and 5 of the 2011 Order.

6

Schedule 4 (Fees for applications in connection with nationality) has effect to specify the amount of fees for specified applications in connection with nationality for the purposes of article 3(2)(h), (j), (k), (l), (m), (n), (o) and (p) of the 2011 Order.

7

Schedule 5 (Fees for entry clearance to enter the Channel Islands) has effect to specify the amount of fees for specified applications for entry clearance to enter either of the Channel Islands for the purposes of article 6 of the 2011 Order and exceptions to the requirement to pay such fees and circumstances in which such fees may be waived or reduced.

8

Schedule 6 (Fees for expediting applications, applications made in person, and optional services for applicants within the United Kingdom) has effect to specify—

(a)   the amount of the fees for—

      (i)   the attendance by a representative of the Secretary of State at a location of the applicant's choosing, for the purposes of article 4(i) of the 2011 Order;

      (ii)   the provision of services outside office hours for the purposes of article 4(j) of the 2011 Order;

      (iii)   the provision of arrangements for expediting the processing of immigration and nationality applications, made from within the United Kingdom, for the purposes of article 4(k) of the 2011 Order;

      (iv)   the provision of arrangements enabling immigration or nationality applications made from within the United Kingdom to be made in person, for the purposes of article 4(l) of the 2011 Order;

      (v)   optional services enabling expedited entry into the United Kingdom, for the purposes of article 4(q) of the 2011 Order; and

(b)   circumstances in which such fees may be waived or reduced.

9

Schedule 7 (Fees for expediting applications, applications made in person, and optional services for applicants outside the United Kingdom) has effect to specify—

(a)   the amount of the fees for—

      (i)   the acceptance or processing of an immigration or nationality application, or of information (including biometric information) in relation to such an application from outside the United Kingdom at a facility managed by a contractor or at any other place for the purposes of article 4(o) of the 2011 Order;

      (ii)   the provision of arrangements for expediting the processing (or an element of the processing) of immigration or nationality applications, made outside the United Kingdom, for the purposes of article 4(k) of the 2011 Order;

      (iii)   the provision by a contractor of services outside the United Kingdom outside office hours for the purposes of article 4(j) of the 2011 Order;

      (iv)   the provision of advice and assistance in relation to an immigration or nationality application to applicants outside the United Kingdom by way of the international contact centre service, for the purposes of article 7(a) of the 2011 Order; and

(b)   circumstances in which such fees may be waived or reduced.

Rate of Exchange

10

The rate of exchange for calculating the equivalents of fees set out in these Regulations but paid in a foreign currency must be based upon the rate of exchange which is generally prevailing on the date, and at the place of payment, but which may be adjusted by the Secretary of State (or a representative of the Secretary of State) in such a manner and to such an extent as that person considers expedient in the interests of administrative efficiency.

Consequences of failing to pay the specified fee

11

Where these Regulations specify a fee which must accompany an application for the purposes of the 2011 Order, the application is not validly made unless it is accompanied by the specified fee.

Revocation

12

The Immigration and Nationality (Fees) Regulations 2013 are revoked.

SCHEDULE 1

FEES FOR APPLICATIONS FOR LEAVE TO REMAIN IN THE UNITED KINGDOM AND FOR AN APPROVAL LETTER

Regulation 3
Interpretation

1

(1) In this Schedule—

"Article 3 or Refugee Convention application" means an application for leave to remain in the United Kingdom made on the basis that the applicant is—

 (a) a person making a claim for asylum which has either not been determined or has been granted;

 (b) a person who has been granted humanitarian protection under the immigration rules;

 (c) a person who has been granted limited leave to enter or remain in the United Kingdom outside the provisions of the immigration rules on the rejection of their claim for asylum;

 (d) a person who is a dependant of a person referred to in paragraph (a), (b) or (c) and is applying for leave to enter or remain in the United Kingdom under paragraphs 352A to 352FI of the immigration rules; or

 (e) a child who does not come within paragraph (d) who was born in the United Kingdom to a person referred to in paragraph (a), (b) or (c);

"assistance by a local authority" means assistance, accommodation or maintenance provided by a local authority (or in Northern Ireland, an authority, which has the same meaning as provided in Article 2(2) of the Children (Northern Ireland) Order 1995) under—

 (a) section 17, 20 or 23 of the Children Act 1989;

 (b) section 22, 25 or 26 of the Children (Scotland) Act 1995; or

 (c) article 18, 21 or 27 of the Children (Northern Ireland) Order 1995;

"claim for asylum" means a claim within the meaning of section 94(1) of the Immigration and Asylum Act 1999;

"Convention rights" means the rights identified as Convention rights by section 1 of the Human Rights Act 1998;

"indefinite leave to remain" means leave to remain in the United Kingdom for an indefinite period;

"limited leave to remain" means leave to remain in the United Kingdom for a limited period;

"qualifying work permit holder" means an applicant for limited leave to remain in the United Kingdom who—

    (a)   was granted leave to remain in the United Kingdom for 3 years as a Tier 2 Migrant on the basis that they were a Qualifying Work Permit Holder under Part 6A of the immigration rules;

    (b)   is applying to extend the duration of that leave to remain to 5 years; and

    (c)   is still working for the same employer and in the same role as they were when that leave to remain was granted;

"Specified Human Rights Application" means an application for limited leave to remain in the United Kingdom under—

    (a)   paragraph 276ADE of the immigration rules;

    (b)   section R-LTRP1.1 of Appendix FM to the immigration rules;

    (c)   section R-LTRPT.1.1 of Appendix FM to the immigration rules; or

    (d)   any other application which is not an Article 3 or Refugee Convention application and in which the applicant relies solely or primarily on a claim that to remove a person from the United Kingdom or to require a person to leave the United Kingdom would be unlawful under section 6 of the Human Rights Act 1998 (public authority not to act contrary to Convention rights).

(2) For the purposes of this Schedule a claim for asylum is to be taken to be determined on—

    (a)   the day on which the Secretary of State notifies the claimant of her decision on the claim;

    (b)   if the claimant has appealed against the Secretary of State's decision, the day on which the appeal is disposed of; or

    (c)   if the claimant has brought an appeal from within the United Kingdom, against an immigration decision under section 82 of the Nationality, Immigration and Asylum Act 2002 or section 2 of the Special Immigration Appeals Commission Act 1997 on the day on which the appeal is disposed of.

Fees for, and in connection with, applications for leave to remain in the United Kingdom

2

(1) Table 1 specifies the amount of the fees for the specified applications for limited leave to remain in the United Kingdom.

(2) Table 1.2.1 specifies the amount of the fee for an approval letter from a designated competent body.

(3) Table 2 specifies the amount of the fees for the specified applications for limited leave to remain in the United Kingdom by a dependent of a main applicant.

(4) Table 3 specifies the amount of the fees for the specified applications for indefinite leave to remain in the United Kingdom.

(5) Table 4 provides for exceptions to the requirement to pay the fees specified in Tables 1, 2 and 3.

(6) Paragraph 3 makes provision for the amount of the fees to be paid in respect of an application for limited leave to remain in the United Kingdom by a dependant of a main applicant, in cases where Table 2 does not apply.

(7) The fees specified in Tables 1 and 3 are subject to paragraph 4 (Applications by CESC nationals), and the fees specified in Tables 1, 2 and 3 are subject to paragraph 5 (Multiple applications for leave to remain in the United Kingdom).

Table 1 (Fees for applications for limited leave to remain in the United Kingdom and connected applications)

Number of fee	Type of application	Amount of fee
1.1	**General fees for applications for limited leave to remain in the United Kingdom**	
1.1.1	Application for limited leave to remain where the fee is not specified elsewhere in these Regulations or in other immigration and nationality fees regulations.	£601
1.2	**Fees for and in connection with applications for limited leave to remain in the United Kingdom under the Points-Based System**	
1.2.1	Application to the Home Office for an approval letter from a designated competent body in respect of a proposed application for limited leave to remain as a Tier 1 (Exceptional Talent) Migrant.	£437
1.2.2	Application for limited leave to remain as a Tier 1 (Exceptional Talent) Migrant where fee 1.2.1 applies.	£656
1.2.3	Application for limited leave to remain as a Tier 1 (Exceptional Talent) Migrant where fee 1.2.1 does not apply.	£1,093
1.2.4	Application for limited leave to remain as a Tier 1 (Entrepreneur) Migrant	£1,093
1.2.5	Application for limited leave to remain as a Tier 1 (General) Migrant.	£1,607
1.2.6	Application for limited leave to remain as a Tier 1 (Graduate Entrepreneur) Migrant.	£422
1.2.7	Application for limited leave to remain as a Tier 1 (Investor) Migrant.	£1,093
1.2.8	Application for limited leave to remain as a Tier 2 (General) Migrant, a Tier 2 (Intra-Company Transfer) Long Term Staff Migrant, a Tier 2 (Sportsperson) Migrant or a Tier 2 (Minister of Religion) Migrant where a certificate of sponsorship has been issued for a period of three years or less, and where fee 1.2.10 does not apply.	£601

1.2.9	Application for limited leave to remain as a Tier 2 (General) Migrant or Tier 2 (Intra-Company Transfer) Long Term Staff Migrant where a certificate of sponsorship has been issued for a period of more than three years, and where fee.1.2.11 does not apply.	£1,202
1.2.10	Application for limited leave to remain as a Tier 2 (General) Migrant where a shortage occupation certificate of sponsorship has been issued for a period of three years or less.	£428
1.2.11	Application for limited leave to remain as a Tier 2 (General) Migrant where a shortage occupation certificate of sponsorship has been issued for a period of more than three years.	£856
1.2.12	Application for limited leave to remain as a Tier 2 (Intra-Company Transfer) Short Term Staff Migrant, a Tier 2 (Graduate Trainee) Migrant or a Tier 2 (Skills Transfer) Migrant.	£428
1.2.13	Application for limited leave to remain as a Tier 4 Migrant.	£422
1.2.14	Application for limited leave to remain as a Tier 5 (Temporary Worker) Migrant.	£208
1.3	**Fees for other applications for limited leave to remain in the United Kingdom**	
1.3.1	Application for limited leave to remain as a representative of an overseas business under Part 5 of the immigration rules.	£1,093
1.3.2	Application for limited leave to remain as a retired person of independent means under Part 7 of the immigration rules.	£1,093

Table 2 (Fees for specified applications for limited leave to remain in the United Kingdom as a dependant)

Number of fee	Type of application for leave to remain	Amount of fee
2.1	**Specified fees for applications for leave to remain in the United Kingdom as the dependant of the main applicant**	
2.1.1	Application for limited leave to remain as the dependant of a Tier 1 (Exceptional Talent) Migrant.	£1,093
2.1.2	Application for limited leave to remain as the dependant of a Tier 1 (Post-Study) Work Migrant.	£324

Table 3 (Fees for applications for indefinite leave to remain in the United Kingdom)

Number of fee	Type of application for indefinite leave to remain	Amount of fee
3.1	General fees for applications for indefinite leave to remain in the United Kingdom	
3.1.1	Application for indefinite leave to remain where the fee is not specified in other immigration and nationality fees regulations.	£1,093

Table 4 (Exceptions in respect of fees for applications for, or in connection with, leave to remain in the United Kingdom)

Number and description of the exception	Fees to which exception applies
4.1	Article 3 or Refugee Convention applications
	No fee is payable in respect of an Article 3 or Refugee Convention application. — Fees 1.1.1, 3.1.1
4.2	Applications for leave to remain under the Destitution Domestic Violence concession
	No fee is payable in respect of an application made under the Destitution Domestic Violence concession operated outside the immigration rules by the Home Office. — Fee 1.1.1
4.3	Applications for leave to remain as a victim of domestic violence under paragraph 289A or Appendix FM or Appendix Armed Forces
	No fee is payable in respect of an application as a victim of domestic violence under paragraph 289A of, or Appendix FM or Appendix Armed Forces to the immigration rules, where at the time of making the application the applicant appears to the Secretary of State to be destitute. — Fee 3.1.1
4.4	Specified Human Rights Application where to require payment of the fee would be incompatible with the applicant's Convention rights

	No fee is payable in respect of a Specified Human Rights Application where to require payment of the fee would be incompatible with the applicant's Convention rights, because at the time of making the application the applicant appears to the Secretary of State to be destitute.	Fee 1.1.1
4.5	**Short term variation of leave to remain**	
	No fee is payable in respect of an application made to an immigration officer on arrival at a port of entry in the United Kingdom in respect of a person seeking variation of leave to remain in the United Kingdom for a period of up to 6 months.	Fees 1.2.13, 1.2.14, 1.3.1, 1.3.2
4.6	**Children being provided with assistance by a local authority**	
	No fee is payable in respect of an application made in respect of a person who, at the time of making the application is a child and is being provided with assistance by a local authority.	Fees 1.1.1, 1.2.13, 1.2.14, 3.1.1
4.7	**Applications under the EC Association Agreement with Turkey**	
	No fee is payable in respect of an application made under the terms of the EC Association Agreement with Turkey.	All fees in Tables 1, 2 and 3
4.8	**Applications from qualifying work permit holders**	
	No fee is payable in respect of an application from a qualifying work permit holder.	Fees 1.2.8 to 1.2.12
4.9	**Applications from stateless persons**	
	No fee is payable in respect of an application for an initial period of limited leave to remain as a stateless person or the family member of a stateless person under Part 14 of the immigration rules.	Fee 1.1.1
4.10	**Applications for variation of limited leave to remain in the United Kingdom to allow recourse to public funds in certain circumstances**	
	No fee is payable in respect of an application for variation of the conditions attached to a grant of limited leave to remain in the United Kingdom, in order to be permitted access to public funds, by a person who has been granted such leave under— (a) paragraph 276BE of the immigration rules; (b) paragraph D-LTRP1.2 of Appendix FM to the immigration rules; or (c) paragraph D-LTRPT.1.2 of Appendix FM to the immigration rules.	Fee 1.1.1

Applications by dependants

3

Except in respect of applications for which a fee is specified in Table 2, and subject to the exceptions set out in Table 4, the fee for an application for leave to remain made by a dependant of a main applicant (whether or not that application is made at the same time as that of the main applicant) is the fee specified in Table 1 or 3 (as the case may be) in respect of the main applicant's application.

Reduction in fees for certain applications made by CESC Nationals

4

(1)   Where an application for leave to remain in the United Kingdom of a kind set out in sub-paragraph (2) is made by a CESC national, and the applicant is the main applicant, the fee set out in Table 1 must be reduced by £55.

(2)   An application is of a kind mentioned in sub-paragraph (1) if it is an application for leave to remain in the United Kingdom as—

    (i)   a Tier 1 (Entrepreneur) Migrant;

    (ii)   a Tier 1 (Exceptional Talent) Migrant;

    (iii)   a Tier 1 (General) Migrant;

    (iv)   a Tier 1 (Graduate Entrepreneur) Migrant;

    (v)   a Tier 2 Migrant;

    (vi)   a Tier 5 (Temporary Worker) Migrant;

    (vii)   a work permit holder; or

    (viii)   a Highly Skilled Migrant within the meaning provided in the immigration rules.

Multiple applications for leave to remain in the United Kingdom

5

(1)   Where two or more applications for leave to remain in the United Kingdom in respect of the same person—

    (a)   are made at the same time; or

    (b)   are being considered at the same time by the Secretary of State,

a fee is payable only in respect of one of those applications.

(2)   The fee payable under sub-paragraph (1) must—

    (a)   be the higher, or the highest, of the fees specified in respect of those applications; or

    (b)   in any case where the fee specified for each application is the same, the fee for a single application.

SCHEDULE 2

FEES FOR APPLICATIONS FOR ENTRY CLEARANCE TO ENTER THE UNITED KINGDOM AND FOR AN APPROVAL LETTER

Regulation 4

Fees for, and in connection with, applications for entry clearance to enter the United Kingdom

1

(1)   Table 5 specifies the amount of the fees for the specified applications for entry clearance to enter the United Kingdom, and the amount of the fee for an application for an approval letter from a designated competent body.

(2)   Table 6 specifies the amount of the fee for specified applications for entry clearance to enter the United Kingdom by a dependant of the main applicant.

(3) Table 7 specifies the amount of the fee for an application for indefinite leave to enter the United Kingdom as the dependant of a member of HM forces.

(4) Table 8 provides for exceptions to the requirement to pay the fees specified in Tables 5, 6 and 7, and Table 9 confers a discretion on the Secretary of State to waive or reduce the fees specified in Tables 5, 6 and 7 in certain circumstances.

(5) Paragraph 2 makes provision for the amount of fees to be paid in respect of an application for entry clearance to enter the United Kingdom by a dependant of a main applicant in cases where Table 6 does not apply.

(6) The fees specified in Table 5 are subject to paragraph 3 (Applications by CESC nationals).

Table 5 (Fees for applications for entry clearance to enter the United Kingdom, and connected applications)

Number of fee	Type of application	Amount of fee
5.1	**General fee for applications for entry clearance to enter the United Kingdom**	
5.1.1	Application for entry clearance (other than an application by a person passing through the United Kingdom) where the fee is not specified elsewhere in these Regulations or other immigration and nationality regulations.	£289
5.2	**Fees for applications for entry clearance to enter the United Kingdom, and connected applications, under the Points-Based System**	
5.2.1	Application to the Home Office for an approval letter from a designated competent body in respect of a proposed application for entry clearance as a Tier 1 (Exceptional Talent) Migrant.	£437
5.2.2	Application for entry clearance as a Tier 1 (Exceptional Talent) Migrant where fee 5.2.1 applies.	£437
5.2.3	Application for entry clearance as a Tier 1 (Exceptional Talent) Migrant where fee 5.2.1 does not apply.	£874
5.2.4	Application for entry clearance as a Tier 1 (Entrepreneur) Migrant.	£874
5.2.5	Application for entry clearance as a Tier 1 (Graduate Entrepreneur) Migrant.	£310
5.2.6	Application for entry clearance as a Tier 1 (Investor) Migrant.	£874
5.2.7	Application for entry clearance as a Tier 2 (General) Migrant, a Tier 2 (Intra-Company Transfer) Long Term Staff Migrant, a Tier 2 (Sportsperson) Migrant or a Tier 2 (Minister of Religion) Migrant where a certificate of sponsorship has been issued for a period of three years or less, and fee 5.2.9 does not apply.	£514

5.2.8	Application for entry clearance as a Tier 2 (General) Migrant or Tier 2 (Intra-Company Transfer) Long Term Staff Migrant where a certificate of sponsorship has been issued for a period of more than three years, and fee 5.2.10 does not apply.	£1,028
5.2.9	Application for entry clearance as a Tier 2 (General) Migrant where a shortage occupation certificate of sponsorship has been issued for a period of three years or less.	£428
5.2.10	Application for entry clearance as a Tier 2 (General) Migrant where a shortage occupation certificate of sponsorship has been issued for a period of more than three years.	£856
5.2.11	Application for entry clearance as a Tier 2 (Intra-Company Transfer) Short Term Staff Migrant, a Tier 2 (Graduate Trainee) Migrant or a Tier 2 (Skills Transfer) Migrant.	£428
5.2.12	Application for entry clearance as a Tier 4 Migrant	£310
5.2.13	Application for entry clearance as a Tier 5 (Temporary Worker) Migrant	£208
5.2.14	Application for entry clearance as a Tier 5 (Youth Mobility) Temporary Migrant	£208
5.3	**Fees for applications for entry clearance to enter the United Kingdom as a visitor**	
5.3.1	Application for entry clearance as a visitor for a period of more than six months but not more than two years.	£300
5.3.2	Application for entry clearance as a visitor for a period of more than two years but not more than five years.	£544
5.3.3	Application for entry clearance as a visitor for a period of more than five years but not more than ten years.	£737
5.4	**Fees for other applications for entry clearance to enter the United Kingdom**	
5.4.1	Application for entry clearance for settlement in the United Kingdom.	£885
5.4.2	Application for entry clearance as a parent, grandparent, or other dependant relative of a person present and settled in the United Kingdom under Appendix FM of the immigration rules.	£1,982
5.4.3	Application for entry clearance as the senior employee of an overseas business under paragraph 144(ii)(a) of the immigration rules.	£514

5.4.4	Application for entry clearance as the employee of an overseas newspaper, news agency or broadcasting organisation under paragraph 144(ii)(b) of the immigration rules.	£514
5.4.5	Application for entry clearance as a short term student studying an English language course for a period of between six and eleven months.	£150
5.4.6	Application for entry clearance for a period of between six and eleven months under the English language concession operated outside the immigration rules.	£150

Table 6 (Specified fees for dependants)

Number of fee	Type of application for leave to remain	Amount of fee
6.1	**Specified fees for applications for entry clearance to enter the United Kingdom as the dependant of the main applicant**	
6.1.1	Application for entry clearance as the dependant of a Tier 1 (Exceptional Talent) Migrant.	£874
6.1.2	Application for entry clearance as the dependant of a Tier 1 (Post-Study) Work Migrant.	£518
6.1.3	Application for entry clearance as the dependant of a student under paragraphs 76 to 81 of the immigration rules.	£310

Table 7 (Fee for application for indefinite leave to enter the United Kingdom— dependants of Armed Forces Personnel)

Number of fee	Type of application	Amount of fee
7.1	**Fee for application for indefinite leave to enter the United Kingdom**	
7.1.1	Application for indefinite leave to enter the United Kingdom as the dependant of a member of the armed forces under Appendix Armed Forces to the immigration rules.	£1,093

Table 8 (Exceptions in respect of fees for applications for entry clearance to enter the United Kingdom)

Number and description of the exception		Fees to which exception applies
8.1	**Officials of Her Majesty's Government**	
	No fee is payable in respect of an application made in connection with the official duty of any official of Her Majesty's Government.	All fees in Tables 5, 6 and 7
8.2	**Dependants of refugees or persons granted humanitarian protection**	
	No fee is payable in respect of an application made under paragraphs 352A to 352FI of the immigration rules.	All fees in Tables 5, 6 and 7
8.3	**Applications under the EC Association Agreement with Turkey**	
	No fee is payable in respect of an application made under the terms of the EC Association Agreement with Turkey.	All fees in Tables 5, 6 and 7

Table 9 (Waivers in respect of fees for applications for entry clearance to enter the United Kingdom)

Number and description of the waiver		Fees to which waiver applies
9.1	**General waiver**	
	No fee is payable in respect of an application where the Secretary of State determines that the fee should be waived.	All fees in Tables 5, 6 and 7
9.2	**Scholarships funded by Her Majesty's government**	
	The official determining an application may decide to waive the payment of the fee or reduce the amount of the fee where the application is made by a candidate for or holder of a scholarship funded by Her Majesty's government and is in connection with such a scholarship.	All fees in Tables 5, 6 and 7
9.3	**International courtesy**	
	The official determining an application may decide to waive the payment of the fee or reduce the amount of the fee as a matter of international courtesy.	All fees in Tables 5, 6 and 7
9.4	**Visitors under a Foreign and Commonwealth Office Bilateral Programme**	

The official determining an application may decide to waive the payment of the fee or reduce the amount of the fee where the applicant intends to visit the United Kingdom in connection with programmes operated by the Foreign and Commonwealth Office to give funds directly to Embassies and Missions outside the United Kingdom to support activities directly connected to the United Kingdom's international priorities.	All fees in Tables 5, 6 and 7
9.5 **Visitors under a Foreign and Commonwealth Office Strategic Programme**	
The official determining an application may decide to waive the payment of the fee or reduce the amount of the fee where the applicant intends to visit the United Kingdom in connection with programmes of funding operated by the Foreign and Commonwealth Office to promote action on global issues in areas of strategic importance to the United Kingdom.	All fees in Tables 5, 6 and 7

Applications by dependants

2

Except in respect of applications for which a fee is specified in number 5.4.2 of Table 5, Table 6, or number 7.1.1 of Table 7, and subject to the exceptions and waivers set out in Tables 8 and 9, the fee for an application for entry clearance to enter the United Kingdom made by a dependant of a main applicant (whether or not that application is made at the same time as that of the main applicant) is the fee specified in Table 5 in respect of the main applicant's application.

Applications by CESC Nationals

3

(1)   Where an application for entry clearance to enter the United Kingdom of a kind set out in sub-paragraph (2) is made by a CESC national, and the applicant is the main applicant, the fee set out in Table 5 must be reduced by £55.

(2)   An application is of a kind mentioned in sub-paragraph (1) if it is an application for entry clearance to enter the United Kingdom as—

(i)   a Tier 1 (Entrepreneur) Migrant;

(ii)   a Tier 1 (Exceptional Talent) Migrant;

(iii)   a Tier 1 (General) Migrant;

(iv)   a Tier 1 (Graduate Entrepreneur) Migrant;

(v)   a Tier 2 Migrant;

(vi)   a Tier 5 (Temporary Worker) Migrant;

(vii) a work permit holder; or

(viii) a Highly Skilled Migrant within the meaning provided in the immigration rules.

SCHEDULE 3

FEES IN RELATION TO SPONSOR LICENCES

Regulation 5

Fees for applications for sponsor licences, for certificates of sponsorship or for premium customer services

1

(1)   In this Schedule—

"premium customer services" means the optional premium customer services offered by the Home Office to certain sponsors;

"small or charitable sponsor" means a sponsor that is—

(a)   a company that is subject to the small companies regime under section 381 of the Companies Act 2006;

(b)   in the case of a person who is not a company for the purposes of that section, a person who employs no more than 50 employees; or

(c)   a charity within the meaning of section 1 of the Charities Act 2011, or section 1 of the Charities Act (Northern Ireland) 2008 or a body entered in the Scottish Charity Register;

(2)   In this Schedule, reference to Tier 2, Tier 4 and Tier 5 premium customer services means the premium customer services offered to sponsors of persons applying for leave to remain in the United Kingdom under the stated Tier.

2

Table 10 specifies the amount of the fees for the specified applications for sponsor licences or the renewal of such a licence where the application is not in respect of a small or charitable sponsor, for the issuing of certificates of sponsorship, and for premium customer services for sponsors.

Table 10 (Fees in relation to sponsor licences)

Number of fee	Type of application, service, or process	Amount of fee
10.1	**Fees for applications for sponsor licences where applicant is not a small or charitable sponsor**	
10.1.1	Application for sponsor licence in respect of Tier 2 Migrants.	£1,476
10.1.2	Application for sponsor licence in respect of Tier 2 and Tier 4 Migrants.	£1,476
10.1.3	Application for sponsor licence in respect of Tier 2 and Tier 5 Migrants.	£1,476
10.1.4	Application for sponsor licence in respect of Tier 2, Tier 4 and Tier 5 Migrants.	£1,476
10.2	**Fees for premium customer services for sponsors**	
10.2.1	The provision of Tier 2 and Tier 5 premium customer services to a sponsor that is not a small or charitable sponsor for a period of 12 months.	£25,000
10.2.2	The provision of Tier 2 and Tier 5 premium customer services to a small or charitable sponsor for a period of 12 months.	£8,000

10.2.3	The provision of Tier 4 premium customer services to a sponsor for a period of 12 months.	£8,000
10.3	**Fees for the process of issuing certificates of sponsorship**	
10.3.1	The issuing of a certificate of sponsorship in respect of an application or potential application for leave to remain in or enter the United Kingdom as a Tier 2 Migrant where the application is not made in respect of a CESC national.	£184

SCHEDULE 4

FEES FOR APPLICATIONS IN CONNECTION WITH NATIONALITY

Regulation 6

Interpretation

1

(1) In this Schedule—

"the 1981 Act" means the British Nationality Act 1981;

"the 1982 Order" means the British Protectorates, Protected States and Protected Persons Order 1982;

"application for naturalisation as a British citizen" means an application for naturalisation as a British citizen under section 6(1) or (2) of the 1981 Act;

"application for naturalisation as a British overseas territories citizen" means an application for naturalisation as a British overseas territories citizen under section 18(1) or (2) of the 1981 Act;

"application for registration as a British citizen under the 1981 Act" means an application for registration as a British citizen under section 1(3), (3A) or (4), 3(1), (2) or (5), 4(2) or (5), 4A, 4B, 4D, 10(1) or (2), or 13(1) or (3) of the 1981 Act, or paragraph 3, 4 or 5 of Schedule 2 to that Act;

"application for registration as a British citizen under the 1997 Act" means an application for registration as a British citizen under section 1 of the British Nationality (Hong Kong) Act 1997;

"application for registration as a British overseas territories citizen" means an application for registration as a British overseas territories citizen under sections 13(1) or (3) of the 1981 Act (as applied by section 24 of that Act), or section 15(3) or (4), 17(1), (2) or (5), or 22(1) or (2) of, or paragraph 3, 4 or 5 of Schedule 2 to that Act;

"application for registration as a British overseas citizen" means an application for registration as a British overseas citizen under section 27(1) of, or paragraph 4 or 5 of Schedule 2 to, the 1981 Act;

"application for registration as a British protected person" means an application for registration as a British protected person under article 7 of the 1982 Order;

"application for registration as a British subject" means an application for registration as a British subject under section 32 of, or paragraph 4 of Schedule 2 to, the 1981 Act.

(2) In this Schedule, subject to regulation 11 of these Regulations, an application is 'made' on the date on which it is received by the Secretary of State or any person appointed to receive nationality applications.

Fees for applications relating to nationality

2

Table 11 specifies the amount of the fees for the specified applications relating to nationality.

Table 11 (Fees for applications relating to nationality)

Number of fee	Type of application	Amount of fee
11.1	**Fees for applications for naturalisation**	
11.1.1	Application for naturalisation as a British citizen.	£826
11.1.2	Application for naturalisation as a British overseas territories citizen.	£661
11.2	**Fees for applications for registration where the applicant is an adult**	
11.2.1	Application for registration as a British citizen under the 1981 Act, where the applicant is aged 18 or over at the time the application is made.	£743
11.2.2	Application for registration as a British citizen under the 1997 Act, where the applicant is aged 18 or over at the time the application is made.	£743
11.2.3	Application for registration as a British overseas territories citizen, where the applicant is aged 18 or over at the time the application is made.	£595
11.2.4	Application for registration as a British overseas citizen, where the applicant is aged 18 or over at the time the application is made.	£595
11.2.5	Application for registration as a British subject, where the applicant is aged 18 or over at the time the application is made.	£595
11.2.6	Application for registration as a British protected person where the applicant is aged 18 or over at the time the application is made.	£595
11.3	**Fees for applications for registration where the applicant is a child**	
11.3.1	Application for registration as a British citizen under the 1981 Act where the person in respect of whom the application is made is a child at the time the application is made.	£669
11.3.2	Application for registration as a British citizen under the 1997 Act, where the person in respect of whom the application is made is a child at the time the application is made.	£669
11.3.3	Application for registration as a British overseas territories citizen, where the person in respect of whom the application is made is a child at the time the application is made.	£536

11.3.4	Application for registration as a British overseas citizen, where the person in respect of whom the application is made is a child at the time the application is made.	£536
11.3.5	Application for registration as a British subject, where the person in respect of whom the application is made is a child at the time the application is made.	£536
11.3.6	Application for registration as a British protected person where the person in respect of whom the application is made is a child at the time the application is made.	£536

SCHEDULE 5
FEES FOR ENTRY CLEARANCE TO ENTER THE CHANNEL ISLANDS
Regulation 7

Interpretation

1

In this Schedule "work permit employment" means employment as a work permit holder under—

(a) rules made by the States of Guernsey Home Department in respect of the Bailiwick of Guernsey under section 3(2) of the 1971 Act.

(b) rules made by the Minister for Home Affairs in respect of the Bailiwick of Jersey under section 1(4) of the 1971 Act.

Fees for applications for entry clearance to enter the Channel Islands

2

(1) Table 12 specifies the amount of the fees for the specified applications for entry clearance to enter either of the Channel Islands where such applications are received outside the British Islands.

(2) Table 13 confers a discretion on the Secretary of State to waive the fees specified in Table 12.

(3) Paragraph 3 makes provision for the fees for applications for entry clearance to enter either of the Channel Islands by a dependant of a main applicant where such applications are received outside the British Islands.

Table 12 (Fees for applications for entry clearance to enter the Channel Islands)

Number of fee	Type of application for entry clearance to enter the Channel Islands	Amount of fee
12.1	**General fee for applications for entry clearance to enter either of the Channel Islands**	
12.1.1	Application for entry clearance where the fee is not specified elsewhere in this Schedule or in other immigration and nationality fees regulations.	£289

12.2	Fees for applications for entry clearance to enter either of the Channel Islands as a visitor	
12.2.1	Application for entry clearance as a visitor for a period of up to six months.	£83
12.2.2	Application for entry clearance as a visitor for a period of more than six months but not more than two years	£300
12.2.3	Application for entry clearance as a visitor for a period of more than two years but not more than five years.	£544
12.2.4	Application for entry clearance as a visitor for a period of more than five years but not more than ten years.	£737
12.3	Fees for applications for entry clearance to enter either of the Channel Islands for work permit employment or settlement	
12.3.1	Application for entry clearance to enter either of the Channel Islands for the purpose of undertaking work permit employment.	£514
12.3.2	Application for entry clearance to enter either of the Channel Islands for the purpose of settlement.	£885

Table 13 (Waivers in respect of fees for applications for entry clearance to enter the Channel Islands)

Number and description of the exception or waiver	Fees to which waiver applies
13.1	General waiver
	No fee is payable in respect of an application where the Secretary of State determines that the fee should be waived.	All fees in Table 12
13.2	Applications under the EC Association Agreement with Turkey
	No fee is payable in respect of an application made under the terms of the EC Association Agreement with Turkey.	All fees in Table 12

Applications by dependants

3

Subject to the Secretary of State's discretion to waive payment of a fee in accordance with the provision made in Table 13, the fee for an application for entry clearance to enter the Channel Islands as a dependant of a main applicant (whether or not that application is made at the same time as that of the main applicant) is the fee specified in Table 12 in respect of the main applicant's application.

SCHEDULE 6
FEES FOR EXPEDITING APPLICATIONS, APPLICATIONS MADE IN PERSON, AND OPTIONAL SERVICES FOR APPLICANTS (IN THE UNITED KINGDOM)

Regulation 8

Interpretation

1

In this Schedule—

"online application" means an application made via the public website maintained by the Home Office;

"Premium Services Centre" means a public office of the Home Office, at which applicants can access certain optional services in connection with immigration or nationality applications;

"registered travellers scheme" means the discretionary service offered by the Home Office enabling the expedited entry of persons registered on the scheme into the United Kingdom, or the transit of such persons through the United Kingdom;

"super premium service" means the super premium service for processing applications for leave to remain in the United Kingdom offered by the Home Office.

Fees for the provision of certain optional services in the United Kingdom, including the expedition of immigration or nationality applications

2

(1) Table 14 specifies the amount of the fees for the provision of the specified services.

(2) Paragraph 3 confers a discretion on the Secretary of State to waive or reduce the fees specified in Table 14.

Table 14

Number of fee	Description of application or service provided	Amount of fee
14.1	**Fee for expediting online and postal applications, and applications made by courier**	
14.1.1	The expedited processing of an immigration or nationality application made by post, courier or as an online application.	£300
14.2	**Fees for applications made in person (other than those made under the super premium service)**	
14.2.1	The arrangement of an appointment for the purposes of making an immigration or nationality application (or any part of such application) in person, where the application is made in the United Kingdom, and is not made under the super premium service.	£100
14.2.2	The expedited processing of an immigration or nationality application made in person, where the application is made in the United Kingdom, and is not made under the super premium service.	£300

14.3	Fees in relation to applications made under the super premium service	
14.3.1	The attendance by a representative of the Secretary of State at a location of the applicant's choosing, for the purposes of processing an immigration or nationality application (or any part of such an application) made under the super premium service.	£6,000
14.3.2	The expedited processing of an immigration or nationality application made under the super premium service.	£400
14.4	Fees for the provision of services outside office hours	
14.4.1	The acceptance of an immigration or nationality application made in person at a Premium Services Centre, outside office hours.	£300
14.5	Fees for the registered travellers scheme	
14.5.1	Administrative fee for the registration of additional identity documents in respect of persons registered on the registered travellers scheme.	£20
14.5.2	Annual subscription charge for membership of the registered travellers scheme.	£50

Waiver or reduction of fees specified in Table 14

3

The Secretary of State may waive or reduce any fee in respect of an application or service specified in Table 14.

SCHEDULE 7

FEES FOR EXPEDITING APPLICATIONS, APPLICATIONS MADE IN PERSON, AND OPTIONAL SERVICES FOR APPLICANTS (OUTSIDE THE UNITED KINGDOM)

Regulation 9

Interpretation

1

In this Schedule—

"biometric immigration document" has the same meaning as provided in section 5 of the UK Borders Act 2007

"biometric information" means any information about an applicant's external physical characteristics which an applicant must provide in order to obtain a biometric immigration document;

"international contact centre service" means the service by which advice and assistance in relation to immigration or nationality applications is provided to applicants outside the United Kingdom;

"priority settlement service" means the optional priority service offered to applicants outside the United Kingdom, by which applications for settlement are processed on an expedited basis;

"priority visa service" means the optional priority service offered to applicants outside the United Kingdom, by which applications for entry clearance to enter the United Kingdom are processed on an expedited basis;

"super priority visa service" means the optional priority service offered to applicants outside the United Kingdom, by which it is aimed to process applications for entry clearance to enter the United Kingdom within 24 hours of receipt of the application;

"User-Pays Visa Application Centre" means an office located outside the United Kingdom and managed by a contractor, at which applicants can access certain services in connection with immigration or nationality;

"web-chat facility" means the facility enabling applicants to communicate directly with an advisor at the international contact centre service, via the Internet.

Fees for the submission and processing of immigration and nationality applications outside the United Kingdom, together with fees for connected services

2

(1) Table 15 specifies the amount of fees for the provision of the specified services.

(2) Paragraph 3 confers a discretion on the Secretary of State to waive the fees specified in Table 15.

Table 15

Number of fee	Description of application or service provided	Amount of fee
15.1	Fee for submitting an immigration or nationality application, or documents or information in connection with such an application, outside the United Kingdom at a facility managed by a contractor	
15.1.1	The acceptance or processing by a contractor of an immigration or nationality application, or documents or information (including biometric information) in relation to such an application, at a User-Pays Visa Application Centre or at another facility managed by a contractor at any other location, either in person or by post or courier.	£59
15.2	Fees for expediting immigration or nationality applications	
15.2.1	The expedited processing, under the priority visa service, of an application for entry clearance to enter the United Kingdom.	£100
15.2.2	The expedited processing, under the super priority visa service, of an application for entry clearance to enter the United Kingdom.	£600
15.2.3	The expedited processing, under the priority settlement service, of an application for entry clearance to enter the United Kingdom.	£300

15.3	**Fee for the provision of services outside office hours by a contractor outside the United Kingdom**	
15.3.1	The acceptance or processing by a contractor, outside office hours, of an immigration or nationality application, or documents or information (including biometric information) in relation to such an application at a User-Pays Visa Application Centre, or at another facility managed by a contractor at any other location.	£50
15.4	**Fee for the provision of a 'passport pass-back' facility by a contractor outside the United Kingdom**	
15.4.1	The expedited return to the applicant of travel or identity documents, or both, where these have been provided by the applicant in the course of making an application for entry clearance to enter the United Kingdom.	£40
15.5	**Fees in connection with the international contact centre service**	
15.5.1	Fee for the provision of advice or assistance in relation to an immigration or nationality application to applicants outside the United Kingdom via a staffed telephone helpline.	£1.37 per minute
15.5.2	Fee for the provision of a single session of advice or assistance in relation to an immigration or nationality application to applicants outside the United Kingdom via the web-chat facility (such a session being no more than 10 minutes long).	£4

Waiver or reduction in respect of the fees listed in Table 15

3

The Secretary of State may waive or reduce any fee in respect of an application or service specified in Table 15.

IMMIGRATION ACT 2014 (SPECIFIED ANTI-FRAUD ORGANISATION) ORDER 2014

(SI 2014/1798)

Made: 8 July 2014.

Authority: Immigration Act 2014, s 40(4).

Commencement: 2 August 2014.

1 Citation and commencement

This Order may be cited as the Immigration Act 2014 (Specified Anti-fraud Organisation) Order 2014 and shall come into force on 2nd August 2014.

2 Specified anti-fraud organisation

For the purposes of section 40(3)(a) of the Immigration Act 2014, CIFAS, a company limited by guarantee with registered number 2584687, is specified as an anti-fraud organisation.

IMMIGRATION ACT 2014 (COMMENCEMENT NO 1, TRANSITORY AND SAVING PROVISIONS) ORDER 2014

(SI 2014/1820)

Made: 7 July 2014.

Authority: Immigration Act 2014, ss 73(1), 75(3).

Citation and interpretation

1

(1) This Order may be cited as the Immigration Act 2014 (Commencement No 1, Transitory and Saving Provisions) Order 2014.

(2) In this Order, "the Act" means the Immigration Act 2014.

Provisions coming into force on 14th July 2014

2

The day appointed for the coming into force of the following provisions of the Act is 14th July 2014—

  (a)   section 41 (regulation by Financial Conduct Authority);

  (b)   section 42 (meaning of bank and building society);

  (c)   section 43 (power to amend);

  (d)   section 46 (grant of driving licences: residence requirement);

  (e)   section 47 (revocation of driving licences on grounds of immigration status);

  (f)   section 73(6) (transitional and consequential provision) so far as it is necessary for the purpose of the provisions listed in sub-paragraph (g);

  (g)   Part 6 of Schedule 9.

Provisions coming into force on 28th July 2014

3

The day appointed for the coming into force of the following provisions of the Act is 28th July 2014—

  (a)   section 2 (restriction on removal of children and their parents etc);

  (b)   section 3 (Independent Family Returns Panel);

  (c)   section 4 (enforcement powers);

  (d)   section 5 (restrictions on detention of unaccompanied children);

  (e)   section 6 (pre-departure accommodation for families);

  (f)   section 7(1), (2) and (5) (immigration bail: repeat applications and effect of removal directions);

(g) section 8 (provision of biometric information with immigration applications);

(h) section 9 (identifying persons liable to detention);

(i) section 10 (provision of biometric information with citizenship applications);

(j) section 11 (biometric immigration documents);

(k) section 12 (meaning of "biometric information");

(l) section 13 (safeguards for children);

(m) section 14 (use and retention of biometric information);

(n) section 17(1) and (3) (certification of human rights claims made by persons liable to deportation);

(o) section 19 (Article 8 of the ECHR: public interest considerations);

(p) section 44 (appeals against penalty notices);

(q) section 45 (recovery of sums payable under penalty notices);

(r) section 63 (immigration advisers and immigration service providers) so far as it is necessary for the purpose of the provisions listed in sub-paragraph (aa);

(s) section 64 (Police Ombudsman for Northern Ireland);

(t) section 66 (deprivation if conduct seriously prejudicial to vital interests of the UK);

(u) section 67 (embarkation checks);

(v) section 70 (power to charge fees for attendance services in particular cases);

(w) section 71 (duty regarding the welfare of children);

(x) section 73(6) (transitional and consequential provision) so far as it is necessary for the purpose of the provisions listed in sub-paragraph (cc);

(y) Schedule 1 (enforcement powers);

(z) Schedule 2 (meaning of biometric information);

(aa) paragraph 6 of Schedule 7 (inspectors of registered persons);

(bb) Schedule 8 (embarkation checks); and

(cc) paragraphs 2, 8, 10(1) and (3), 11 to 16 and 32 and Parts 5 and 10 of Schedule 9.

Transitory and saving provision

4

. . .

Art 4 revoked by SI 2014/2771, art 14, as from 15 October 2014.

5

The commencement of section 44 does not have effect in relation to an appeal in respect of a penalty notice issued before 28th July 2014 (including a penalty notice issued before that date but withdrawn and, after that date, re-issued).

6

The commencement of section 45 does not have effect in relation to a sum payable to the Secretary of State as a penalty under section 15 of the Immigration, Asylum and Nationality Act 2006 if proceedings for the enforcement of the penalty were commenced before 28th July 2014.

7

(1) During the relevant period "chargeable function" in section 70 of the Act is to be read as a reference to an application, service or process in connection with immigration or nationality in respect of which a fee is chargeable pursuant to the Immigration and Nationality (Fees Order) 2011.

(2)   In paragraph (1), the relevant period means the period beginning on 28th July 2014 and ending on the date the first fees order made under section 68 of the Act comes into force.

IMMIGRATION ACT 2014 (COMMENCEMENT NO 2) ORDER 2014

(SI 2014/1943)

Made: 22 July 2014.

Authority: Immigration Act 2014, s 75(3).

1 Citation

This Order may be cited as the Immigration Act 2014 (Commencement No 2) Order 2014.

2 Commencement of provision

The date appointed for the coming into force of section 40 of the Immigration Act 2014 (prohibition on opening current accounts for disqualified persons) is 12th December 2014.

IMMIGRATION (PASSENGER TRANSIT VISA) ORDER 2014

(SI 2014/2702)

Made: 8 October 2014.

Authority: Immigration and Asylum Act 1999, s 41.

Commencement: 1 December 2014.

1 Citation and commencement

(1)   This Order may be cited as the Immigration (Passenger Transit Visa) Order 2014.

(2)   This Order comes into force on 1st December 2014.

2 Interpretation

(1)   Subject to paragraph (5), in this Order a "transit passenger" means a person to whom paragraph (2), (3) or (4) applies and who on arrival in the United Kingdom passes through to another country or territory without entering the United Kingdom.

(2)   This paragraph applies to a person who is a citizen or national of a country or territory listed in Schedule 1 to this Order.

(3)   This paragraph applies to a person holding a travel document issued by the purported "Turkish Republic of Northern Cyprus".

(4)   This paragraph applies to a person who holds a passport issued by the Republic of Venezuela that does not contain biometric information contained in an electronic chip.

(5)   A person to whom paragraph (2), (3) or (4) applies will not be a transit passenger if he—

    (a)   has the right of abode in the United Kingdom under the Immigration Act 1971;

    (b)   is a citizen or national of an EEA State; or

(c)   in the case of a citizen or national of the People's Republic of China, holds a passport issued by either the Hong Kong Special Administrative Region or the Macao Special Administrative Region.

(6) In this Order—

"Approved Destination Status Scheme" means a scheme for issuing visas to Chinese tour groups under—

(a)   the Memorandum of Understanding between the European Community and the National Tourism Administration of the People's Republic of China on visa and related issues concerning tourist groups from the People's Republic of China (ADS) signed at Beijing on 12th February 2004; or

(b)   a similar agreement between the People's Republic of China and a Schengen Acquis State;

"EEA State" means a country which is a contracting party to the Agreement on the European Economic Area signed at Oporto on 2nd May 1992 as adjusted by the Protocol signed at Brussels on 17th March 1993;

"Schengen Acquis State" means an EEA State (excluding the United Kingdom and Republic of Ireland) or Switzerland.

3 Requirement for a transit passenger to hold a transit visa

Subject to article 4, a transit passenger is required to hold a transit visa.

4 Exemption from the requirement for a transit passenger to hold a transit visa

A transit passenger is not required to hold a transit visa if he holds or a person with whom he arrives in the United Kingdom holds on his behalf—

(a)   a valid visa for entry to Australia, Canada, New Zealand or the United States of America;

(b)   a valid Australian Permanent Resident Visa;

(c)   a valid Canadian Permanent Resident Card issued on or after 28th June 2002;

(d)   a valid New Zealand Permanent Resident Visa;

(e)   a valid USA I-551 Permanent Resident Card issued on or after 21st April 1998;

(f)   an expired USA I-551 Permanent Resident Card provided it is accompanied by a valid I-797 letter authorising an extension of the period of permanent residency;

(g)   a valid USA I-551 Temporary Immigrant Visa;

(h)   a valid standalone US Immigration Form 155A/155B attached to a brown sealed envelope;

(i)   a valid common format Category D visa for entry to an EEA state or Switzerland;

(j)   a valid common format residence permit issued by an EEA State pursuant to Council Regulation (EC) No 1030/2002 or Switzerland;

(k)   a valid biometric visa issued by the Republic of Ireland;

(l)   a valid visa issued by a Schengen Acquis State under the Approved Destination Status Scheme where the transit passenger is undertaking a journey via the United Kingdom to a Schengen Acquis State;

(m)   a valid airline ticket for travel via the United Kingdom as part of a journey from a Schengen Acquis State to another country or territory, provided that the transit passenger does not seek to travel via the United Kingdom on a date more than 30 days from the date on which he last entered a Schengen Acquis State with a valid visa issued by a Schengen Acquis State under the Approved Destination Status Scheme;

(n)   a diplomatic or service passport issued by the People's Republic of China;

    (o)   a diplomatic or official passport issued by India; or
    (p)   a diplomatic or official passport issued by Vietnam.

5 Method of application for a transit visa

An application for a transit visa may be made to any British High Commission, Embassy or Consulate which accepts such applications.

6 Revocations

The Orders specified in Schedule 2 to this Order are revoked.

SCHEDULE 1
COUNTRIES OR TERRITORIES WHOSE NATIONALS OR CITIZENS NEED TRANSIT VISAS

Article 2(2)

Afghanistan
Albania
Algeria
Angola
Bangladesh
Belarus
Burma
Burundi
Cameroon
China
Congo
Democratic Republic of the Congo
Egypt
Eritrea
Ethiopia
Former Yugoslav Republic of Macedonia
Gambia
Ghana
Guinea
Guinea-Bissau
India
Iran
Iraq
Ivory Coast
Jamaica
Kenya
Kosovo
Lebanon
Lesotho
Liberia
Libya
Malawi
Moldova
Mongolia
Nepal
Nigeria
Pakistan
Palestinian Territories

Rwanda
Senegal
Serbia
Sierra Leone
Somalia
South Africa
South Sudan
Sri Lanka
Sudan
Swaziland
Syria
Tanzania
Turkey
Uganda
Vietnam
Yemen
Zimbabwe

SCHEDULE 2
REVOCATIONS

Article 6

Orders Revoked	References
The Immigration (Passenger Transit Visa) Order 2003	SI 2003/1185
The Immigration (Passenger Transit Visa) (Amendment) Order 2003	SI 2003/2628
The Immigration (Passenger Transit Visa) (Amendment) Order 2004	SI 2004/1304
The Immigration (Passenger Transit Visa) (Amendment) Order 2005	SI 2005/492
The Immigration (Passenger Transit Visa) (Amendment) Order 2006	SI 2006/493
The Immigration (Passenger Transit Visa) (Amendment) Order 2009	SI 2009/198
The Immigration (Passenger Transit Visa) (Amendment) (No 3) Order 2009	SI 2009/1229
The Immigration (Passenger Transit Visa) (Amendment) (No 4) Order 2009	SI 2009/1233
The Immigration (Passenger Transit Visa) (Amendment) Order 2011	SI 2011/1553
The Immigration (Passenger Transit Visa) (Amendment) Order 2012	SI 2012/116
The Immigration (Passenger Transit Visa) (Amendment) (No 2) Order 2012	SI 2012/771
The Immigration (Passenger Transit Visa) (Amendment) Order 2014	SI 2014/1513

IMMIGRATION ACT 2014 (COMMENCEMENT NO 3, TRANSITIONAL AND SAVING PROVISIONS) ORDER 2014

(SI 2014/2771)

Made: 15 October 2014.

Authority: Immigration Act 2014, ss 35(3), 73(1), 75(3).

PART 1
INTRODUCTION AND DAYS APPOINTED

Citation and interpretation

1

(1) This Order may be cited as the Immigration Act 2014 (Commencement No 3, Transitional and Saving Provisions) Order 2014.

(2) In this Order—

(a) "the 1971 Act" means the Immigration Act 1971;

(b) "the 2002 Act" means the Nationality, Immigration and Asylum Act 2002;

(c) "the Act" means the Immigration Act 2014;

(d) "the relevant provisions" means section 1 (removal of persons unlawfully in the UK), section 15 (right of appeal to First-tier Tribunal) and section 17(2) (place from which appeal may be brought or continued) of, and paragraphs 3, 4, 5, 6 and 7 and Part 4 of Schedule 9 (apart from paragraph 26(2), (3) and (5)) (transitional and consequential provision relating to appeals) to, the Act;

(e) "the saved provisions" means section 10 of the Immigration and Asylum Act 1999, sections 62, 72 and 76, and Part 5 of the 2002 Act, section 8(7) of the Asylum and Immigration (Treatment of Claimants, etc) Act 2004, section 47 of the Immigration, Asylum and Nationality Act 2006 and paragraph 19(10) of Schedule 1 to the Legal Aid, Sentencing and Punishment of Offenders Act 2012, as in force immediately prior to 20th October 2014.

Provisions coming into force on 20th October 2014 subject to saving provision

2

The day appointed for the coming into force of the following provisions of the Act, subject to the saving provision in articles 9, 10 and 11, is 20th October 2014—

(a) section 1;

(b) section 15;

(c) section 17(2);

(d) section 73(6) (transitional and consequential provision) so far as is necessary for the purpose of the provisions listed in sub-paragraph (e);

(e) paragraphs 1, 3, 4, 5, 6, 7, 9 and 10(2), and Part 4 of Schedule 9 to the extent not already commenced, apart from paragraph 26(2), (3) and (5).

Part 4 provisions coming into force on 20th October 2014

3

The day appointed for the coming into force of the following provisions of Part 4 of the Act (marriage and civil partnership), is 20th October 2014—

(a) section 49 (exempt persons) so far as is necessary for the purpose of making regulations;

(b) section 50 (conduct of investigation) so far as is necessary for the purpose of making regulations;

(c) section 51 (investigations: supplementary) so far as is necessary for the purpose of making regulations;

(d) section 52 (referral of proposed marriages and civil partnerships in England and Wales) so far as is necessary for the purpose of the provisions listed in sub-paragraph (e);

(e) paragraphs 1 (so far as it relates to the following provisions listed in this paragraph) and 4, 7, 8, 10, 15, 17, 18, 20, 21, 23, 24, 27 and 28 of Schedule 4 (referral of proposed marriages and civil partnerships in England and Wales) so far as is necessary for the purpose of making regulations;

(f) section 53 (extension of scheme to Scotland and Northern Ireland) so far as is necessary for the purpose of making orders;

(g) section 54 (supplementary provisions) so far as is necessary for the purpose of making regulations;

(h) Schedule 5 (sham marriage and civil partnerships: administrative regulations);

(i) section 60 (regulations about evidence);

(j) section 61 (notices).

Other provisions coming into force on 20th October 2014

4

The day appointed for the coming into force of the following provisions of the Act is 20th October 2014—

(a) section 7(3), (4) and (6) (immigration bail: repeat applications and effect of removal directions);

(b) section 16 (report by Chief Inspector on administrative review);

(c) section 38 (immigration health charge);

(d) section 63 (immigration advisers and immigration service providers) so far as is necessary for the purpose of the provisions listed in sub-paragraph (f);

(e) section 73(6) (transitional and consequential provision) so far as is necessary for the purpose of the provision listed in sub-paragraph (g);

(f) paragraphs 1 and 3 of Schedule 7;

(g) paragraph 1 of Schedule 9.

Provisions coming into force on 17th November 2014

5

The day appointed for the coming into force of the following provisions of the Act is 17th November 2014—

(a) section 63 (immigration advisers and immigration service providers) so far as is necessary for the purpose of the provisions listed in sub-paragraph (c);

(b) section 73(6) (transitional and consequential provision) so far as it is necessary for the purpose of the provisions listed in sub-paragraph (d);

(c) Schedule 7 (immigration advisers and immigration service providers) to the extent not already commenced;

(d) Part 8 of Schedule 9 (transitional and consequential provision relating to immigration advisers and immigration service providers).

Provisions coming into force on 1st December 2014 in certain areas only

6

(1)   The day appointed for the coming into force of the following provisions of the Act is 1st December 2014 in respect of premises located in the areas of the relevant local authorities specified in paragraph (2)—

  (a)   section 20 (residential tenancy agreement);

  (b)   section 21 (persons disqualified by immigration status or with limited right to rent);

  (c)   section 22 (persons disqualified by immigration status not to be leased premises);

  (d)   section 23 (penalty notices: landlords);

  (e)   section 24 (excuses available to landlords);

  (f)   section 25 (penalty notices: agents);

  (g)   section 26 (excuses available to agents);

  (h)   section 27 (eligibility period);

  (i)   section 28 (penalty notices: general);

  (j)   section 29 (objection);

  (k)   section 30 (appeals);

  (l)   section 31 (enforcement); and

  (m)   Schedule 3 (excluded residential tenancy agreements).

(2)   The relevant local authorities are—

  (a)   Birmingham City Council;

  (b)   Dudley Metropolitan Borough Council;

  (c)   Sandwell Metropolitan Borough Council;

  (d)   Walsall Metropolitan Borough Council; and

  (e)   Wolverhampton City Council.

Provisions coming into force on 1st December 2014

7

The day appointed for the coming into force of the following provisions of the Act is 1st December 2014—

  (a)   section 32 (general matters);

  (b)   section 33 (discrimination);

  (c)   section 34 (orders);

  (d)   section 35 (transitional provision);

  (e)   section 36 (Crown application); and

  (f)   section 37 (interpretation).

Provisions coming into force on 15th December 2014

8

The day appointed for the coming into force of the following provisions of the Act is 15th December 2014—

  (a)   section 68 (fees);

  (b)   section 69 (fees orders and fees regulations: supplemental);

  (c)   section 73(6) (transitional and consequential provision) so far as it is necessary for the purpose of the provisions listed in sub-paragraph (d);

  (d)   Part 11 of Schedule 9 (transitional and consequential provision relating to fees).

PART 2
TRANSITIONAL AND SAVING PROVISIONS AND REPEALS

Transitional and saving provision

9

Notwithstanding the commencement of the relevant provisions, the saved provisions continue to have effect, and the relevant provisions do not have effect, other than so far as they relate to the persons set out respectively in articles 10 and 11, unless article 11(2) or (3) applies.

10

The persons referred to in article 9 are—

- (a) a person ("P1") who becomes a foreign criminal within the definition in section 117D(2) of the 2002 Act on or after 20th October 2014; and
- (b) a person who is liable to deportation from the United Kingdom under section 3(5)(b) of the 1971 Act because they belong to the family of P1.

11

(1) The persons referred to in article 9 are a person ("P2") who makes an application on or after 20th October 2014 for leave to remain—

- (a) as a Tier 4 Migrant;
- (b) as the partner of a Tier 4 Migrant under paragraph 319C of the immigration rules; or
- (c) as the child of a Tier 4 Migrant under paragraph 319H of the immigration rules.

(2) The saved provisions have effect, and the relevant provisions do not have effect, where P2, having made an application of a kind mentioned in paragraph (1), at any time thereafter makes—

- (a) an application for leave to enter; or
- (b) any further application for leave to remain which is not of a kind that is mentioned in paragraph (1);

provided the subsequent application is not a protection claim or human rights claim, made while P2 is in the United Kingdom, other than at a port.

(3) Where paragraph (2) applies, the saved provisions also have effect, and the relevant provisions do not have effect, where a decision is taken in relation to P2—

- (a) which constitutes an immigration decision under section 82(2) of the 2002 Act as in force immediately prior to 20th October 2014; or
- (b) to which section 83 or 83A of the 2002 Act as in force immediately prior to 20th October 2014 applies.

(4) Where the relevant provisions apply, and an appeal has already been brought against an immigration decision under section 82(1) of the 2002 Act but before the relevant provisions applied, the reference to a "decision" in section 96(1)(a) of the 2002 Act is to be read as a reference to an "immigration decision".

(5) In this article—

- (a) "human rights claim" means—
  - (i) a claim made by a person to the Secretary of State that to remove the person from or require him to leave the United Kingdom would be unlawful under section 6 of the Human Rights Act 1998 (c 42) (public authority not to act contrary to Convention); or
  - (ii) an application for leave to remain made under paragraph 276ADE of, or Appendix FM to, the immigration rules;
- (b) "immigration decision" has the same meaning as in section 82(2) of the 2002 Act as in force immediately prior to 20th October 2014;

(c)   "immigration rules" means the rules for the time being laid down by the Secretary of State as mentioned in section 3(2) of the 1971 Act;

(d)   "Leave to enter the United Kingdom" means leave to enter the United Kingdom given in accordance with the provisions of, or made under, the 1971 Act;

(e)   "Leave to remain in the United Kingdom" means leave to remain in the United Kingdom given in accordance with the provisions of, or made under, the 1971 Act and any variation of leave to enter or remain by the Secretary of State;

(f)   "port" has the meaning in section 33(1) of the 1971 Act;

(g)   "protection claim" has the meaning given in section 82(2) of the 2002 Act;

(h)   "protection status" has the meaning given in section 82(2) of the 2002 Act;

(i)   "Tier 4 Migrant" has the same meaning as provided in the immigration rules.

12

For the purposes of section 35(3) of the Act, the day appointed as "the commencement day" is 1st December 2014.

13

Notwithstanding the commencement of Part 11 of Schedule 9 to the Act, the following statutory instruments remain in force—

(a)   the Immigration and Nationality (Fees) Regulations 2014;

(b)   the Immigration and Nationality (Cost Recovery Fees) Regulations 2014;

(c)   the Immigration and Nationality (Fees) Order 2011, so far as is necessary for the purposes of preserving the Regulations mentioned in sub-paragraphs (a) and (b).

Consequential revocation and saving

14

Article 4 of the Immigration Act 2014 (Commencement No 1, Transitory and Saving Provisions) Order 2014 is revoked.

15

But in any case in which a foreign criminal as defined in section 117D(2) of the 2002 Act has made a human rights claim which the Secretary of State certified under section 94B of that Act prior to 20th October 2014, section 92 of the 2002 Act (appeal from within the United Kingdom: general) continues to have effect as if the following provisions of that Act were omitted—

(a)   the reference in subsection (2) to an immigration decision of a kind specified in section 82(2)(j);

(b)   the reference in subsection (4)(a) to a human rights claim; and

(c)   subsection (4)(b).

IMMIGRATION (REMOVAL OF FAMILY MEMBERS) REGULATIONS 2014

(SI 2014/2816)

Made: 20 October 2014.

Authority: Immigration and Asylum Act 1999, s 10(10)(b).

Commencement: 14 November 2014.

Citation, commencement and interpretation

1

These Regulations may be cited as the Immigration (Removal of Family Members) Regulations 2014 and come into force on 14th November 2014.

2

In these Regulations—

"the Act" means the Immigration and Asylum Act 1999;

"family member" means a person who meets the conditions set out in section 10(3), (4) and (5) of the Act;

"P" means a person who is liable to be or has been removed from the United Kingdom under section 10(1) of the Act.

Giving of notice to a family member

3

A notice given to a family member in accordance with section 10(2) of the Act may be given—

    (a)   at any time prior to P's removal, or

    (b)   during the period of eight weeks beginning with the date on which P is removed.

Service of notice

4

(1)   A notice given to a family member in accordance with section 10(2) of the Act may be—

    (a)   given by hand,

    (b)   sent by fax,

    (c)   sent by postal service in which delivery or receipt is recorded to—

        (i)   an address provided for correspondence by the person or the person's representative, or

        (ii)   where no address for correspondence has been provided, the last-known or usual place of abode or place of business of the person or the person's representative,

    (d)   sent electronically,

    (e)   sent by document exchange to a document exchange number or address,

    (f)   sent by courier,

    (g)   collected by the person who is the subject of the decision or the person's representative.

(2)   Where—

    (a)   a person's whereabouts are not known, and

    (b)   no address is available for correspondence with either the person or the person's representative under paragraph (1)(c),

the notice shall be deemed to have been given when the Secretary of State or immigration officer enters a record of the above circumstances and places the signed notice on the relevant file.

(3)   Where notice is deemed to have been given in accordance with paragraph (2) and subsequently the person is located, the person is to be given a copy of the notice and details of when and how it was deemed to be served as soon as is practicable.

(4)   Where a notice is sent by post in accordance with paragraph (1)(c) it shall be deemed to have been served, unless the contrary is proved, on the second day after it was posted.

(5)   For the purposes of paragraph (4) the period is to be calculated—

(a)   excluding the day on which the notice is posted, and

(b)   excluding any day which is not a business day.

(6)   In this regulation, "business day" means any day other than Saturday or Sunday, a day which is a bank holiday under the Banking and Financial Dealings Act 1971 in the part of the United Kingdom to which the notice is sent, Christmas Day or Good Friday.

(7)   A notice to be given to a family member in accordance with section 10(2) of the Act may, in the case of a child below the age of 18 who does not have a representative, be given to P.

IMMIGRATION (RESIDENTIAL ACCOMMODATION) (PRESCRIBED CASES) ORDER 2014

(SI 2014/2873)

Made: 28 October 2014.

Authority: Immigration Act 2014, s 37(6)(a), (7).

Commencement: 1 December 2014.

Citation and commencement

1

This Order may be cited as the Immigration (Residential Accommodation) (Prescribed Cases) Order 2014 and comes into force on 1st December 2014.

Interpretation

2

In this Order—

"the Act" means the Immigration Act 2014;

"new joint tenancy" has the meaning given in article 3(1)(c);

"new occupier" means an adult occupying premises who did not have a right to occupy the premises under a residential tenancy agreement prior to the variation or assignment of that agreement or the grant of a further residential tenancy (as the case may be);

"original occupier" means an adult who had a right to occupy premises under a residential tenancy agreement prior to the variation or assignment of that agreement or the grant of a further residential tenancy (as the case may be);

"tenant assigned tenancy" has the meaning given in article 3(b);

"varied tenancy" has the meaning given in article 3(a).

Cases in which a residential tenancy agreement is to be treated as being entered into

3

A residential tenancy agreement is to be treated as being entered into for the purposes of Chapter 1 of Part 3 of the Act where a landlord—

(a)   consents to a variation of a residential tenancy agreement which grants the right to occupy the premises to one or more new occupiers ("a varied tenancy"),

(b)   consents to the assignment of a residential tenancy agreement by one or more tenants which results in the grant of the right to occupy the premises to one or more new occupiers ("a tenant assigned tenancy"), or

(c)   accepts a surrender of a residential tenancy agreement ("the surrendered tenancy") by the original occupier or by or on behalf of joint original occupiers and grants a further residential tenancy agreement starting from the time the surrendered tenancy ends to one or more of the original occupiers and one or more new occupiers ("a new joint tenancy").

4

A residential tenancy agreement granted by a landlord—

(a)   to a tenant who is outside the United Kingdom, or

(b)   to a tenant and one or more other adults who are outside the United Kingdom, whether or not they are named in the agreement,

on condition that the tenant will produce to the landlord documents confirming the tenant's, and where applicable, any adult's, right to rent residential premises following the tenant's, and where applicable the adult's, arrival in the United Kingdom, shall be treated as being entered into for the purposes of Chapter 1 of Part 3 of the Act on the day on which, under the terms of the residential tenancy agreement, the tenant is entitled to possession.

Cases in which a residential tenancy agreement is not to be treated as being entered into

5

A residential tenancy agreement is not to be treated as being entered into for the purposes of Chapter 1 of Part 3 of the Act where—

(a)   it arises—

(i)   by virtue of an order of a court,

(ii)   by or under any statutory provision,

(iii)   by operation of law, or

(b)   it arises between the same parties at the end of a term granted by a residential tenancy agreement as a result of a contractual right exercised by the tenant.

Modification of application of provisions

6

In relation to a residential tenancy agreement which is a varied tenancy, a tenant assigned tenancy, or a new joint tenancy, the provisions at sections 24 and section 26 of the Act have effect subject to the modifications set out in paragraphs 1 and 2 of the Schedule to this Order.

7

In relation to a residential tenancy agreement where the interest of a landlord is assigned to a new landlord, the provisions at section 24 and section 26 of the Act have effect subject to the modifications set out in paragraphs 3 and 4 of the Schedule to this Order.

SCHEDULE

MODIFICATION OF APPLICATION OF PROVISIONS

Articles 6 and 7

Excuses available for landlords

1

For the purposes of article 6, section 24 (excuses available to landlords) of the Act is modified as if for paragraph (4) there were substituted—

"(4)   But where compliance with the prescribed requirements discloses that a relevant occupier is a person with a limited right to rent, the landlord is excused under subsection (2)(a) only if—

(a)   in respect of an original occupier who had a right of occupation under a previous residential tenancy agreement, the requirements are complied with in relation to that occupier within such period as may be prescribed in relation to the entering into of that previous residential tenancy agreement, and

(b)   in respect of a new occupier, the requirements are complied with in relation to that occupier within such period as may be prescribed in relation to the entering into of the varied tenancy, tenant assigned tenancy or new joint tenancy agreement.".

Excuses available for agents

2

For the purposes of article 6, section 26 (excuses available to agents) of the Act is modified as if for paragraph (4) there were substituted—

"(4)   But where compliance with the prescribed requirements discloses that a relevant occupier is a person with a limited right to rent, the agent is excused under subsection (2) only if—

(a)   in respect of an original occupier who had a right of occupation under a previous residential tenancy agreement, the requirements are complied with in relation to that occupier within such period as may be prescribed in relation to the entering into of that previous residential tenancy agreement, and

(b)   in respect of a new occupier, the requirements are complied with in relation to that occupier within such period as may be prescribed in relation to the entering into of the varied tenancy, tenant assigned tenancy or new joint tenancy agreement.".

3

For the purposes of article 7, section 24 (excuses available to landlords) of the Act is modified as if for paragraph (6)(a) there were substituted—

"the landlord, or any previous landlord, has notified the Secretary of State of the contravention as soon as reasonably practicable;".

4

For the purposes of article 7, section 26 (excuses available to agents) of the Act is modified as if for paragraph (6)(a) there were substituted—

"the agent, or any previous landlord or agent, has notified the Secretary of State and if relevant, the landlord responsible for the contravention at the time of making the notification, as soon as reasonably practicable;".

IMMIGRATION (RESIDENTIAL ACCOMMODATION) (PRESCRIBED REQUIREMENTS AND CODES OF PRACTICE) ORDER 2014

(SI 2014/2874)

Made: 28 October 2014.

Authority: Immigration Act 2014, ss 24(2), (4), (7), (8), 26(2), (4), (7), (8), 29(3), (6), 32(6), 33(5), 34(1), 37(1).

Commencement: 1 December 2014.

Citation and commencement

1

This Order may be cited as the Immigration (Residential Accommodation) (Prescribed Requirements and Codes of Practice) Order 2014 and comes into force on 1st December 2014.

Interpretation

2

In this Order—

"the Act" means the Immigration Act 2014;

"asylum-seeker" has the meaning given in section 94(1) of the Immigration and Asylum Act 1999;

"biometric immigration document" has the meaning given in section 5 of the UK Borders Act 2007;

"claim for asylum" has the meaning given in section 94(1) of the Immigration and Asylum Act 1999;

"derivative residence card" means a card issued in accordance with regulation 18A of the Immigration (European Economic Area) Regulations 2006 to a person who is not an EEA or Swiss national;

"document" means an original document;

"Landlord Checking Service" means the enquiry and advice service for landlords and agents operated by the Home Office;

"occupier" means any adult who is authorised to occupy premises under a residential tenancy agreement;

"Positive Right to Rent Notice" means a document issued by the Landlord Checking Service which indicates that the person named in it is not disqualified from occupying premises under a residential tenancy agreement;

"prospective occupier" means an adult who, under a residential tenancy agreement, will be authorised to occupy premises;

"residence card" means—

    (a)   a residence card issued in accordance with regulation 17 of the Immigration (European Economic Area) Regulations 2006 or

    (b)   a document certifying permanent residence or a permanent residence card issued in accordance with regulation 18 of those Regulations,

and includes an "accession residence card" issued to a person who is not an EEA or Swiss national within the meaning of the Accession of Croatia (Immigration and Worker Authorisation) Regulations 2013.

The prescribed requirements

3

For the purposes of sections 24(2) and (7)(a) and 26(2) and (7)(a) of the Act, a landlord or agent complies with the prescribed requirements if the landlord or agent—

    (a)   obtains documents prescribed in article 4 from an occupier or prospective occupier; and

    (b)   in accordance with article 5, take steps to verify, retain, copy or record the contents of a document obtained under article 4.

4

The landlord or agent must—

    (a)   obtain from the occupier or prospective occupier—

        (i)   one document listed in List A in the Schedule to this Order; or

        (ii)   two documents listed in List B in the Schedule to this Order; or

    (b)   subject to article 6, obtain a Positive Right to Rent Notice in respect of the occupier or prospective occupier from the Landlord Checking Service where—

        (i)   the occupier or prospective occupier informs the landlord or agent that—

            (aa)   they have an outstanding application to vary their leave to enter or remain in the United Kingdom, or have an administrative review or appeal pending against a decision on that application, or

            (bb)   they are an asylum seeker or have an appeal pending against a determination made by the Secretary of State in respect of their claim for asylum, or

            (cc)   they have made an application for a residence card or derivative residence card within the last 6 months, or

            (dd)   they are a person to whom the Secretary of State has granted permission to occupy premises under section 21(3) of the Act, and

        (ii)   the occupier or prospective occupier provides the landlord or agent with their Home Office issued reference number in relation to that application, claim, administrative review, appeal or permission to occupy premises.

5

Where the landlord or agent obtains any document from an occupier or prospective occupier or the Landlord Checking Service pursuant to article 4, the landlord or agent must—

    (a)   take all reasonable steps to check the validity of the document;

    (b)   if a document contains a photograph, satisfy themselves that the photograph is of the occupier or prospective occupier;

    (c)   if a document contains a date of birth, satisfy himself that the date of birth is consistent with the appearance of the occupier or prospective occupier;

    (d)   take all other reasonable steps to check that the occupier or prospective occupier is the rightful owner of the document;

    (e)   if the document is not a passport or other travel document, retain a clear and legible copy of the whole of the document in a format which cannot be subsequently altered;

    (f)   if the document is a passport or other travel document (which is not in the form of a card), retain a clear and legible copy of the following pages of that document in a format which cannot be subsequently altered—

(i)   any page containing the holder's personal details including nationality;

(ii)   any page containing the holder's photograph;

(iii)   any page containing the holder's signature;

(iv)   any page containing the date of expiry; and

(v)   any page containing information indicating the holder has an entitlement to enter or remain in the UK;

(g)   if the document is a travel document in the form of a card, retain a clear and legible copy of the whole of that document in a format which cannot be subsequently altered;

(h)   record the date on which the copies were taken;

(i)   retain a clear and legible copy or copies securely for a period of not less than one year after the residential tenancy agreement has come to an end;

(j)   take all reasonable steps to identify any additional occupants of the property at the time the occupier or prospective occupier enters into the residential tenancy agreement.

6

If the Landlord Checking Service fails to respond to a request made by a landlord or agent under article 4(b) for confirmation of an occupier or prospective occupier's eligibility to occupy private residential accommodation within a period of 48 hours, not including Saturdays or Sundays, Christmas Day or Good Friday, or any day which is a bank holiday in England and Wales under the Banking and Financial Dealings Act 1971, then the landlord or agent may proceed as though the Landlord Checking Service had issued a Positive Right to Rent Notice.

7

Nothing in this Order permits landlords or agents to retain documents produced by an occupier or prospective occupier for the purpose of article 4 for any period longer than is necessary for the purposes of ensuring compliance with article 5.

Time for compliance with the prescribed requirements

8

The prescribed period within which the prescribed requirements must be complied with for the purposes of sections 24(4) and 26(4) of the Act is 28 days ending on the day before the day on which the residential tenancy agreement which authorises occupation is entered into.

Notification of contraventions to the Secretary of State

9

The prescribed form and manner of notification for the purposes of sections 24(8) and 26(8) of the Act is that it must be in writing and must—

(a)   contain—

(i)   the full name of the occupier who is believed to be a disqualified adult;

(ii)   the address of the premises in which the occupier has been granted a right of occupation;

(iii)   the name and contact address of the landlord;

(iv)   the name and contact address of any agent;

(v)   the date on which the occupier first became entitled to take up occupation; and

(b)   be accompanied by a copy of any documents relating to the occupier retained by the landlord or agent in accordance with article 5.

Objection

10

A notice of objection must contain—

(a)   the reference number of the notice given under section 23(1) or section 25(3) of the Act;

(b)   the name and contact address of the landlord;

(c)   the name and contact address of any agent;

(d)   the name and address of the occupier in respect of whom the penalty was issued;

(e)   the full grounds of objection; and

(f)   any documents to be relied upon in support of the objection.

11

The prescribed period within which a notice of objection must be given for the purposes of section 29(3)(d) of the Act is 28 days, beginning with the date specified in the penalty notice as the date upon which it is given.

12

The prescribed period for the purposes of section 29(6) of the Act within which the Secretary of State must inform the objector of the Secretary of State's decision is 28 days, beginning with the date on which the notice of objection was given to the Secretary of State.

Codes of Practice

13

The code of practice entitled "Code of practice on illegal immigrants and private rented accommodation: Civil penalty scheme for landlords and their agents", issued by the Secretary of State under section 32(1) of the Act comes into force on 1st December 2014.

14

The code of practice entitled "Code of practice for landlords: Avoiding unlawful discrimination when conducting 'right to rent' checks in the private rented residential sector", issued by the Secretary of State under section 33(1) of the Act comes into force on 1st December 2014.

SCHEDULE

Article 4

LIST A

1

A passport showing that the holder is a British citizen or a citizen of the United Kingdom and Colonies having the right of abode in the United Kingdom.

2

A passport or national identity card showing that the holder is a national of an EEA state or Switzerland.

3

A passport or travel document which has not expired endorsed to show that the holder is allowed to stay in the United Kingdom for a time limited period.

4

A registration certificate issued by the Home Office to a national of an EEA state or Switzerland under regulation 16 of the Immigration (European Economic Area) Regulations 2006.

5

A document certifying permanent residence issued by the Home Office to a national of an EEA state or Switzerland under regulation 18 of the Immigration (European Economic Area) Regulations 2006.

6

A permanent residence card issued by the Home Office to the family member of a national of an EEA state or Switzerland under regulation 18 of the Immigration (European Economic Area) Regulations 2006.

7

A residence card or derivative residence card which has not expired or been revoked.

8

A biometric immigration document which has not expired issued by the Home Office to the holder which indicates that the person named in it is allowed to stay indefinitely in the United Kingdom or has no time limit on their stay in the United Kingdom.

9

A biometric immigration document which has not expired issued by the Home Office to the holder which indicates that the person named is permitted to stay in the United Kingdom for a time limited period.

10

A passport or other travel document endorsed to show that the holder is exempt from immigration control, is allowed to stay indefinitely in the United Kingdom, has the right of abode in the United Kingdom, or has no time limit on their stay in the United Kingdom.

11

An immigration status document which has not expired containing a photograph issued by the Home Office to the holder with an endorsement indicating that the person named in it is allowed to stay in the United Kingdom indefinitely or has no time limit on their stay in the United Kingdom.

12

A certificate of registration or naturalisation as a British citizen.

LIST B

1

A full birth certificate issued in the United Kingdom which includes the name of at least one of the holder's parents.

2

A full adoption certificate issued in the United Kingdom which includes the name of at least one of the holder's adoptive parents.

3

A birth certificate issued in the Channel Islands, the Isle of Man or Ireland.

4

An adoption certificate issued in the Channel Islands, the Isle of Man or Ireland.

5

A letter issued by a government department or local authority no longer than 3 months before the date on which it is presented, confirming the holder's name and the earliest known contact between that government department or local authority and the holder and signed by a named official stating their name and professional address.

6

A letter, issued no longer than 3 months before the date on which it is presented, confirming the holder's name and signed by a British passport holder, stating how long the British passport holder has known the holder, the relationship between them, and giving the British passport holder's name, address and passport number.

7

A letter issued by a person who employs the holder issued no longer than 3 months before the date on which it is presented, which indicates the holder's name and confirming their status as an employee and employee reference number and states the employer's name and business address.

8

A letter issued by a police force in the United Kingdom no longer than 3 months before the date on which it is presented, confirming that the holder has been the victim of a crime and personal documents have been stolen, and stating the crime reference number.

9

A document issued by one of Her Majesty's forces or the Secretary of State confirming that the holder is or has been a serving member of that force.

10

An identity card issued by any of Her Majesty's forces.

11

A letter issued by Her Majesty's Prison Service, the Scottish Prison Service or the Northern Ireland Prison Service confirming that holder has been released from the custody of that service and confirming their name and date of birth .

12

A letter issued within 6 months of discharge by an officer of the National Offender Management Service in England and Wales, an officer of a local authority in Scotland who is a responsible officer for the purposes of the Criminal Procedure (Scotland) Act 1995 or an officer of the Probation Board for Northern Ireland confirming the holder's name and date of birth.

13

A current licence to drive a motor vehicle granted under Part 3 of the Road Traffic Act 1988 (to include the photocard licence in respect of licences issued on or after 1st July 1998) or Part 2 of the Road Traffic (Northern Ireland) Order 1981 (to include the photocard licence).

14

A current firearm or shot gun certificate granted by a chief officer of police under Part II of the Firearms Act 1968, a firearm certificate issued by the Chief Constable under article 5 of the Firearms (Northern Ireland) Order 2004 or a current authority issued by the Secretary of State or Scottish Ministers under section 5 of that Firearms Act 1968 or the Secretary of State under article 45 of the Firearms (Northern Ireland) Order 2004.

15

A certificate issued no longer than 3 months before the date on which it is presented, by the Disclosure and Barring Service under Part V of the Police Act 1997, the Scottish Ministers under Part 2 of the Protection of Vulnerable Groups (Scotland) Act 2007 or the Secretary of State under Part V of the Police Act 1997 in relation to the holder.

16

A document issued no longer than 3 months before the date on which it is presented, by Her Majesty's Revenue and Customs, the Department of Work and Pensions, the Northern Ireland Department for Social Development or a local authority confirming that the holder is in receipt of a benefit listed in section 115(1) or (2) of the Immigration and Asylum Act 1999.

IMMIGRATION ACT 2014 (TRANSITIONAL AND SAVING PROVISIONS) ORDER 2014

(SI 2014/2928)

Made: 6 November 2014.

Authority: Immigration Act 2014, s 73(1).

Commencement: 10 November 2014.

Citation, commencement and interpretation

1

(1)   This Order may be cited as the Immigration Act 2014 (Transitional and Saving Provisions) Order 2014 and comes into force on 10th November 2014.

(2)   In this Order—

(a)   "the 1971 Act" means the Immigration Act 1971;

(b)   "the 2002 Act" means the Nationality, Immigration and Asylum Act 2002;

(c)   "the Act" means the Immigration Act 2014;

(d)   "the Commencement Order" means the Immigration Act 2014 (Commencement No 3, Transitional and Saving Provisions) Order 2014;

(e)   "the relevant provisions" and "the saved provisions" have the meaning that they have in the Commencement Order.

Transitional and saving provisions

2

(1)   The saved provisions continue to have effect, and the relevant provisions do not have effect, other than—

(a)   in accordance with articles 9, 10 and 11 of the Commencement Order;

(b)   in relation to a deportation decision made by the Secretary of State on or after 10th November 2014 in respect of—

(i)   a person ("P") who is a foreign criminal within the definition in section 117D(2) of the 2002 Act;

(ii)   a person who is liable to deportation from the United Kingdom under section 3(5)(b) of the 1971 Act because they belong to the family of P.

(2)   In this article, "a deportation decision" means a decision to make a deportation order, a decision to refuse to revoke a deportation order, or a decision made under section 32(5) of the UK Borders Act 2007.

3

But paragraph 26(1) and (4) of Schedule 9 to the Act has effect generally.

Appendix 6

EUROPEAN LEGISLATION

Contents

CONSOLIDATED VERSION OF THE TREATY ON EUROPEAN UNION

HIS MAJESTY THE KING OF THE BELGIANS, HER MAJESTY THE QUEEN OF DENMARK, THE PRESIDENT OF THE FEDERAL REPUBLIC OF GERMANY, THE PRESIDENT OF IRELAND, THE PRESIDENT OF THE HELLENIC REPUBLIC, HIS MAJESTY THE KING OF SPAIN, THE PRESIDENT OF THE FRENCH REPUBLIC, THE PRESIDENT OF THE ITALIAN REPUBLIC, HIS ROYAL HIGHNESS THE GRAND DUKE OF LUXEMBOURG, HER MAJESTY THE QUEEN OF THE NETHERLANDS, THE PRESIDENT OF THE PORTUGUESE REPUBLIC, HER MAJESTY THE QUEEN OF THE UNITED KINGDOM OF GREAT BRITAIN AND NORTHERN IRELAND,

RESOLVED to mark a new stage in the process of European integration undertaken with the establishment of the European Communities,

DRAWING INSPIRATION from the cultural, religious and humanist inheritance of Europe, from which have developed the universal values of the inviolable and inalienable rights of the human person, freedom, democracy, equality and the rule of law,

RECALLING the historic importance of the ending of the division of the European continent and the need to create firm bases for the construction of the future Europe,

CONFIRMING their attachment to the principles of liberty, democracy and respect for human rights and fundamental freedoms and of the rule of law,

CONFIRMING their attachment to fundamental social rights as defined in the European Social Charter signed at Turin on 18 October 1961 and in the 1989 Community Charter of the Fundamental Social Rights of Workers,

DESIRING to deepen the solidarity between their peoples while respecting their history, their culture and their traditions,

DESIRING to enhance further the democratic and efficient functioning of the institutions so as to enable them better to carry out, within a single institutional framework, the tasks entrusted to them,

RESOLVED to achieve the strengthening and the convergence of their economies and to establish an economic and monetary union including, in accordance with the provisions of this Treaty and of the Treaty on the Functioning of the European Union, a single and stable currency,

DETERMINED to promote economic and social progress for their peoples, taking into account the principle of sustainable development and within the context of the accomplishment of the internal market and of reinforced cohesion and environmental protection, and to implement policies ensuring that advances in economic integration are accompanied by parallel progress in other fields,

RESOLVED to establish a citizenship common to nationals of their countries,

RESOLVED to implement a common foreign and security policy including the progressive framing of a common defence policy, which might lead to a common defence in accordance with the provisions of Article 42, thereby reinforcing the European identity and its independence in order to promote peace, security and progress in Europe and in the world,

RESOLVED to facilitate the free movement of persons, while ensuring the safety and security of their peoples, by establishing an area of freedom, security and justice, in accordance with the provisions of this Treaty and of the Treaty on the Functioning of the European Union,

RESOLVED to continue the process of creating an ever closer union among the peoples of Europe, in which decisions are taken as closely as possible to the citizen in accordance with the principle of subsidiarity,

IN VIEW of further steps to be taken in order to advance European integration,

HAVE DECIDED to establish a European Union and to this end have designated as their Plenipotentiaries:

(List of plenipotentiaries not reproduced)

WHO, having exchanged their full powers, found in good and due form, have agreed as follows:

TITLE I COMMON PROVISIONS

Article 1
(ex Article 1 TEU)

By this Treaty, the HIGH CONTRACTING PARTIES establish among themselves a EUROPEAN UNION, hereinafter called "the Union" on which the Member States confer competences to attain objectives they have in common.

This Treaty marks a new stage in the process of creating an ever closer union among the peoples of Europe, in which decisions are taken as openly as possible and as closely as possible to the citizen.

The Union shall be founded on the present Treaty and on the Treaty on the Functioning of the European Union (hereinafter referred to as "the Treaties"). Those two Treaties shall have the same legal value. The Union shall replace and succeed the European Community.

Article 2

The Union is founded on the values of respect for human dignity, freedom, democracy, equality, the rule of law and respect for human rights, including the rights of persons belonging to minorities. These values are common to the Member States in a society in which pluralism, non-discrimination, tolerance, justice, solidarity and equality between women and men prevail.

Article 2

(ex Article 2 TEU)

1. The Union's aim is to promote peace, its values and the well-being of its peoples.
2. The Union shall offer its citizens an area of freedom, security and justice without internal frontiers, in which the free movement of persons is ensured in conjunction with appropriate measures with respect to external border controls, asylum, immigration and the prevention and combating of crime.
3. The Union shall establish an internal market. It shall work for the sustainable development of Europe based on balanced economic growth and price stability, a highly competitive social market economy, aiming at full employment and social progress, and a high level of protection and improvement of the quality of the environment. It shall promote scientific and technological advance.
It shall combat social exclusion and discrimination, and shall promote social justice and protection, equality between women and men, solidarity between generations and protection of the rights of the child.
It shall promote economic, social and territorial cohesion, and solidarity among Member States.
It shall respect its rich cultural and linguistic diversity, and shall ensure that Europe's cultural heritage is safeguarded and enhanced.
4. The Union shall establish an economic and monetary union whose currency is the euro.
5. In its relations with the wider world, the Union shall uphold and promote its values and interests and contribute to the protection of its citizens. It shall contribute to peace, security, the sustainable development of the Earth, solidarity and mutual respect among peoples, free and fair trade, eradication of poverty and the protection of human rights, in particular the rights of the child, as well as to the strict observance and the development of international law, including respect for the principles of the United Nations Charter.
6. The Union shall pursue its objectives by appropriate means commensurate with the competences which are conferred upon it in the Treaties.

Article 4

1. In accordance with Article 5, competences not conferred upon the Union in the Treaties remain with the Member States.
2. The Union shall respect the equality of Member States before the Treaties as well as their national identities, inherent in their fundamental structures, political and constitutional, inclusive of regional and local self-government. It shall respect their essential State functions, including ensuring the territorial integrity of the State, maintaining law and order and safeguarding national security. In particular, national security remains the sole responsibility of each Member State.
3. Pursuant to the principle of sincere cooperation, the Union and the Member States shall, in full mutual respect, assist each other in carrying out tasks which flow from the Treaties.

The Member States shall take any appropriate measure, general or particular, to ensure fulfilment of the obligations arising out of the Treaties or resulting from the acts of the institutions of the Union.

The Member States shall facilitate the achievement of the Union's tasks and refrain from any measure which could jeopardise the attainment of the Union's objectives.

Article 5
(ex Article 5 TEC)

1. The limits of Union competences are governed by the principle of conferral. The use of Union competences is governed by the principles of subsidiarity and proportionality.

2. Under the principle of conferral, the Union shall act only within the limits of the competences conferred upon it by the Member States in the Treaties to attain the objectives set out therein. Competences not conferred upon the Union in the Treaties remain with the Member States.

3. Under the principle of subsidiarity, in areas which do not fall within its exclusive competence, the Union shall act only if and in so far as the objectives of the proposed action cannot be sufficiently achieved by the Member States, either at central level or at regional and local level, but can rather, by reason of the scale or effects of the proposed action, be better achieved at Union level.

The institutions of the Union shall apply the principle of subsidiarity as laid down in the Protocol on the application of the principles of subsidiarity and proportionality. National Parliaments ensure compliance with the principle of subsidiarity in accordance with the procedure set out in that Protocol.

4. Under the principle of proportionality, the content and form of Union action shall not exceed what is necessary to achieve the objectives of the Treaties.

The institutions of the Union shall apply the principle of proportionality as laid down in the Protocol on the application of the principles of subsidiarity and proportionality.

Article 6
(ex Article 6 TEU)

1. The Union recognises the rights, freedoms and principles set out in the Charter of Fundamental Rights of the European Union of 7 December 2000, as adapted at Strasbourg, on 12 December 2007, which shall have the same legal value as the Treaties.

The provisions of the Charter shall not extend in any way the competences of the Union as defined in the Treaties.

The rights, freedoms and principles in the Charter shall be interpreted in accordance with the general provisions in Title VII of the Charter governing its interpretation and application and with due regard to the explanations referred to in the Charter, that set out the sources of those provisions.

2. The Union shall accede to the European Convention for the Protection of Human Rights and Fundamental Freedoms. Such accession shall not affect the Union's competences as defined in the Treaties.

3. Fundamental rights, as guaranteed by the European Convention for the Protection of Human Rights and Fundamental Freedoms and as they result from the constitutional traditions common to the Member States, shall constitute general principles of the Union's law.

CONSOLIDATED VERSION OF THE TREATY ON THE FUNCTIONING OF THE EUROPEAN UNION

HIS MAJESTY THE KING OF THE BELGIANS, THE PRESIDENT OF THE FEDERAL REPUBLIC OF GERMANY, THE PRESIDENT OF THE FRENCH REPUBLIC, THE PRESIDENT OF THE ITALIAN REPUBLIC, HER ROYAL HIGHNESS THE GRAND DUCHESS OF LUXEMBOURG, HER MAJESTY THE QUEEN OF THE NETHERLANDS,

DETERMINED to lay the foundations of an ever closer union among the peoples of Europe,

RESOLVED to ensure the economic and social progress of their States by common action to eliminate the barriers which divide Europe,

AFFIRMING as the essential objective of their efforts the constant improvements of the living and working conditions of their peoples,

RECOGNISING that the removal of existing obstacles calls for concerted action in order to guarantee steady expansion, balanced trade and fair competition,

ANXIOUS to strengthen the unity of their economies and to ensure their harmonious development by reducing the differences existing between the various regions and the backwardness of the less favoured regions,

DESIRING to contribute, by means of a common commercial policy, to the progressive abolition of restrictions on international trade,

INTENDING to confirm the solidarity which binds Europe and the overseas countries and desiring to ensure the development of their prosperity, in accordance with the principles of the Charter of the United Nations,

RESOLVED by thus pooling their resources to preserve and strengthen peace and liberty, and calling upon the other peoples of Europe who share their ideal to join in their efforts,

DETERMINED to promote the development of the highest possible level of knowledge for their peoples through a wide access to education and through its continuous updating,

and to this end HAVE DESIGNATED as their Plenipotentiaries:

(List of plenipotentiaries not reproduced)

WHO, having exchanged their full powers, found in good and due form, have agreed as follows.

PART ONE PRINCIPLES

Article 1

1. This Treaty organises the functioning of the Union and determines the areas of, delimitation of, and arrangements for exercising its competences.

2. This Treaty and the Treaty on European Union constitute the Treaties on which the Union is founded. These two Treaties, which have the same legal value, shall be referred to as "the Treaties".

TITLE II PROVISIONS HAVING GENERAL APPLICATION

Article 7

The Union shall ensure consistency between its policies and activities, taking all of its objectives into account and in accordance with the principle of conferral of powers.

Article 8

(ex Article 3(2) TEC)

In all its activities, the Union shall aim to eliminate inequalities, and to promote equality, between men and women.

Article 9

In defining and implementing its policies and activities, the Union shall take into account requirements linked to the promotion of a high level of employment, the guarantee of adequate social protection, the fight against social exclusion, and a high level of education, training and protection of human health.

Article 10

In defining and implementing its policies and activities, the Union shall aim to combat discrimination based on sex, racial or ethnic origin, religion or belief, disability, age or sexual orientation.

PART TWO NON-DISCRIMINATION AND CITIZENSHIP OF THE UNION

Article 18

(ex Article 12 TEC)

Within the scope of application of the Treaties, and without prejudice to any special provisions contained therein, any discrimination on grounds of nationality shall be prohibited.

The European Parliament and the Council, acting in accordance with the ordinary legislative procedure, may adopt rules designed to prohibit such discrimination.

Article 19

(ex Article 13 TEC)

1. Without prejudice to the other provisions of the Treaties and within the limits of the powers conferred by them upon the Union, the Council, acting unanimously in accordance with a special legislative procedure and after obtaining the consent of the European Parliament, may take appropriate action to combat discrimination based on sex, racial or ethnic origin, religion or belief, disability, age or sexual orientation.

2. By way of derogation from paragraph 1, the European Parliament and the Council, acting in accordance with the ordinary legislative procedure, may adopt the basic principles of Union incentive measures, excluding any harmonisation of the laws and regulations of the Member States, to support action taken by the Member States in order to contribute to the achievement of the objectives referred to in paragraph 1.

Article 20

(ex Article 17 TEC)

1. Citizenship of the Union is hereby established. Every person holding the nationality of a Member State shall be a citizen of the Union. Citizenship of the Union shall be additional to and not replace national citizenship.

2. Citizens of the Union shall enjoy the rights and be subject to the duties provided for in the Treaties. They shall have, inter alia:

    (a)   the right to move and reside freely within the territory of the Member States;

    (b)   the right to vote and to stand as candidates in elections to the European Parliament and in municipal elections in their Member State of residence, under the same conditions as nationals of that State;

    (c)   the right to enjoy, in the territory of a third country in which the Member State of which they are nationals is not represented, the protection of the diplomatic and consular authorities of any Member State on the same conditions as the nationals of that State;

(d) the right to petition the European Parliament, to apply to the European Ombudsman, and to address the institutions and advisory bodies of the Union in any of the Treaty languages and to obtain a reply in the same language.

These rights shall be exercised in accordance with the conditions and limits defined by the Treaties and by the measures adopted thereunder.

Article 21
(ex Article 18 TEC)

1. Every citizen of the Union shall have the right to move and reside freely within the territory of the Member States, subject to the limitations and conditions laid down in the Treaties and by the measures adopted to give them effect.

2. If action by the Union should prove necessary to attain this objective and the Treaties have not provided the necessary powers, the European Parliament and the Council, acting in accordance with the ordinary legislative procedure, may adopt provisions with a view to facilitating the exercise of the rights referred to in paragraph 1.

3. For the same purposes as those referred to in paragraph 1 and if the Treaties have not provided the necessary powers, the Council, acting in accordance with a special legislative procedure, may adopt measures concerning social security or social protection. The Council shall act unanimously after consulting the European Parliament.

TITLE IV FREE MOVEMENT OF PERSONS, SERVICES AND CAPITAL

CHAPTER 1 WORKERS

Article 45
(ex Article 39 TEC)

1. Freedom of movement for workers shall be secured within the Union.

2. Such freedom of movement shall entail the abolition of any discrimination based on nationality between workers of the Member States as regards employment, remuneration and other conditions of work and employment.

3. It shall entail the right, subject to limitations justified on grounds of public policy, public security or public health:

(a) to accept offers of employment actually made;

(b) to move freely within the territory of Member States for this purpose;

(c) to stay in a Member State for the purpose of employment in accordance with the provisions governing the employment of nationals of that State laid down by law, regulation or administrative action;

(d) to remain in the territory of a Member State after having been employed in that State, subject to conditions which shall be embodied in regulations to be drawn up by the Commission.

4. The provisions of this Article shall not apply to employment in the public service.

Article 46
(ex Article 40 TEC)

The European Parliament and the Council shall, acting in accordance with the ordinary legislative procedure and after consulting the Economic and Social Committee, issue directives or make regulations setting out the measures required to bring about freedom of movement for workers, as defined in Article 45, in particular:

(a) by ensuring close cooperation between national employment services;

    (b)   by abolishing those administrative procedures and practices and those qualifying periods in respect of eligibility for available employment, whether resulting from national legislation or from agreements previously concluded between Member States, the maintenance of which would form an obstacle to liberalisation of the movement of workers;

    (c)   by abolishing all such qualifying periods and other restrictions provided for either under national legislation or under agreements previously concluded between Member States as imposed on workers of other Member States conditions regarding the free choice of employment other than those imposed on workers of the State concerned;

    (d)   by setting up appropriate machinery to bring offers of employment into touch with applications for employment and to facilitate the achievement of a balance between supply and demand in the employment market in such a way as to avoid serious threats to the standard of living and level of employment in the various regions and industries.

Article 47

(ex Article 41 TEC)

Member States shall, within the framework of a joint programme, encourage the exchange of young workers.

Article 48

(ex Article 42 TEC)

The European Parliament and the Council shall, acting in accordance with the ordinary legislative procedure, adopt such measures in the field of social security as are necessary to provide freedom of movement for workers; to this end, they shall make arrangements to secure for employed and self-employed migrant workers and their dependants:

    (a)   aggregation, for the purpose of acquiring and retaining the right to benefit and of calculating the amount of benefit, of all periods taken into account under the laws of the several countries;

    (b)   payment of benefits to persons resident in the territories of Member States.

Where a member of the Council declares that a draft legislative act referred to in the first subparagraph would affect important aspects of its social security system, including its scope, cost or financial structure, or would affect the financial balance of that system, it may request that the matter be referred to the European Council. In that case, the ordinary legislative procedure shall be suspended. After discussion, the European Council shall, within four months of this suspension, either:

    (a)   refer the draft back to the Council, which shall terminate the suspension of the ordinary legislative procedure; or

    (b)   take no action or request the Commission to submit a new proposal; in that case, the act originally proposed shall be deemed not to have been adopted.

CHAPTER 2 RIGHT OF ESTABLISHMENT

Article 49

(ex Article 43 TEC)

Within the framework of the provisions set out below, restrictions on the freedom of establishment of nationals of a Member State in the territory of another Member State shall be prohibited. Such prohibition shall also apply to restrictions on the setting-up of agencies, branches or subsidiaries by nationals of any Member State established in the territory of any Member State.

Freedom of establishment shall include the right to take up and pursue activities as self-employed persons and to set up and manage undertakings, in particular companies or firms within the meaning of the second paragraph of Article 54, under the conditions laid down for its own nationals by the law of the country where such establishment is effected, subject to the provisions of the Chapter relating to capital.

Article 50
(ex Article 44 TEC)

1. In order to attain freedom of establishment as regards a particular activity, the European Parliament and the Council, acting in accordance with the ordinary legislative procedure and after consulting the Economic and Social Committee, shall act by means of directives.

2. The European Parliament, the Council and the Commission shall carry out the duties devolving upon them under the preceding provisions, in particular:

(a) by according, as a general rule, priority treatment to activities where freedom of establishment makes a particularly valuable contribution to the development of production and trade;

(b) by ensuring close cooperation between the competent authorities in the Member States in order to ascertain the particular situation within the Union of the various activities concerned;

(c) by abolishing those administrative procedures and practices, whether resulting from national legislation or from agreements previously concluded between Member States, the maintenance of which would form an obstacle to freedom of establishment;

(d) by ensuring that workers of one Member State employed in the territory of another Member State may remain in that territory for the purpose of taking up activities therein as self-employed persons, where they satisfy the conditions which they would be required to satisfy if they were entering that State at the time when they intended to take up such activities;

(e) by enabling a national of one Member State to acquire and use land and buildings situated in the territory of another Member State, in so far as this does not conflict with the principles laid down in Article 39(2);

(f) by effecting the progressive abolition of restrictions on freedom of establishment in every branch of activity under consideration, both as regards the conditions for setting up agencies, branches or subsidiaries in the territory of a Member State and as regards the subsidiaries in the territory of a Member State and as regards the conditions governing the entry of personnel belonging to the main establishment into managerial or supervisory posts in such agencies, branches or subsidiaries;

(g) by coordinating to the necessary extent the safeguards which, for the protection of the interests of members and others, are required by Member States of companies or firms within the meaning of the second paragraph of Article 54 with a view to making such safeguards equivalent throughout the Union;

(h) by satisfying themselves that the conditions of establishment are not distorted by aids granted by Member States.

Article 51
(ex Article 45 TEC)

The provisions of this Chapter shall not apply, so far as any given Member State is concerned, to activities which in that State are connected, even occasionally, with the exercise of official authority.

The European Parliament and the Council, acting in accordance with the ordinary legislative procedure, may rule that the provisions of this Chapter shall not apply to certain activities.

Article 52

(ex Article 46 TEC)

1. The provisions of this Chapter and measures taken in pursuance thereof shall not prejudice the applicability of provisions laid down by law, regulation or administrative action providing for special treatment for foreign nationals on grounds of public policy, public security or public health.

2. The European Parliament and the Council shall, acting in accordance with the ordinary legislative procedure, issue directives for the coordination of the abovementioned provisions.

Article 53

(ex Article 47 TEC)

1. In order to make it easier for persons to take up and pursue activities as self-employed persons, the European Parliament and the Council shall, acting in accordance with the ordinary legislative procedure, issue directives for the mutual recognition of diplomas, certificates and other evidence of formal qualifications and for the coordination of the provisions laid down by law, regulation or administrative action in Member States concerning the taking-up and pursuit of activities as self-employed persons.

2. In the case of the medical and allied and pharmaceutical professions, the progressive abolition of restrictions shall be dependent upon coordination of the conditions for their exercise in the various Member States.

Article 54

(ex Article 48 TEC)

Companies or firms formed in accordance with the law of a Member State and having their registered office, central administration or principal place of business within the Union shall, for the purposes of this Chapter, be treated in the same way as natural persons who are nationals of Member States.

"Companies or firms" means companies or firms constituted under civil or commercial law, including cooperative societies, and other legal persons governed by public or private law, save for those which are non-profit-making.

Article 55

(ex Article 294 TEC)

Member States shall accord nationals of the other Member States the same treatment as their own nationals as regards participation in the capital of companies or firms within the meaning of Article 54, without prejudice to the application of the other provisions of the Treaties.

CHAPTER 3 SERVICES

Article 58

(ex Article 51 TEC)

1. Freedom to provide services in the field of transport shall be governed by the provisions of the Title relating to transport.

2. The liberalisation of banking and insurance services connected with movements of capital shall be effected in step with the liberalisation of movement of capital.

Article 59

(ex Article 52 TEC)

1.   In order to achieve the liberalisation of a specific service, the European Parliament and the Council, acting in accordance with the ordinary legislative procedure and after consulting the Economic and Social Committee, shall issue directives.

2.   As regards the directives referred to in paragraph 1, priority shall as a general rule be given to those services which directly affect production costs or the liberalisation of which helps to promote trade in goods.

Article 60

(ex Article 53 TEC)

The Member States shall endeavour to undertake the liberalisation of services beyond the extent required by the directives issued pursuant to Article 59(1), if their general economic situation and the situation of the economic sector concerned so permit.

To this end, the Commission shall make recommendations to the Member States concerned.

Article 61

(ex Article 54 TEC)

As long as restrictions on freedom to provide services have not been abolished, each Member State shall apply such restrictions without distinction on grounds of nationality or residence to all persons providing services within the meaning of the first paragraph of Article 56.

Article 62

(ex Article 55 TEC)

The provisions of Articles 51 to 54 shall apply to the matters covered by this Chapter.

CONSOLIDATED VERSION OF THE TREATY ON EUROPEAN UNION – PROTOCOL NO 30 ON THE APPLICATION OF THE CHARTER OF FUNDAMENTAL RIGHTS OF THE EUROPEAN UNION TO POLAND AND TO THE UNITED KINGDOM

(PROTOCOL No 30)

ON THE APPLICATION OF THE CHARTER OF FUNDAMENTAL RIGHTS OF THE EUROPEAN UNION TO POLAND AND TO THE UNITED KINGDOM

THE HIGH CONTRACTING PARTIES,

WHEREAS in Article 6 of the Treaty on European Union, the Union recognises the rights, freedoms and principles set out in the Charter of Fundamental Rights of the European Union,

WHEREAS the Charter is to be applied in strict accordance with the provisions of the aforementioned Article 6 and Title VII of the Charter itself,

WHEREAS the aforementioned Article 6 requires the Charter to be applied and interpreted by the courts of Poland and of the United Kingdom strictly in accordance with the explanations referred to in that Article,

WHEREAS the Charter contains both rights and principles,

WHEREAS the Charter contains both provisions which are civil and political in character and those which are economic and social in character,

WHEREAS the Charter reaffirms the rights, freedoms and principles recognised in the Union and makes those rights more visible, but does not create new rights or principles,

RECALLING the obligations devolving upon Poland and the United Kingdom under the Treaty on European Union, the Treaty on the Functioning of the European Union, and Union law generally,

NOTING the wish of Poland and the United Kingdom to clarify certain aspects of the application of the Charter,

DESIROUS therefore of clarifying the application of the Charter in relation to the laws and administrative action of Poland and of the United Kingdom and of its justiciability within Poland and within the United Kingdom,

REAFFIRMING that references in this Protocol to the operation of specific provisions of the Charter are strictly without prejudice to the operation of other provisions of the Charter,

REAFFIRMING that this Protocol is without prejudice to the application of the Charter to other Member States,

REAFFIRMING that this Protocol is without prejudice to other obligations devolving upon Poland and the United Kingdom under the Treaty on European Union, the Treaty on the Functioning of the European Union, and Union law generally,

HAVE AGREED UPON the following provisions, which shall be annexed to the Treaty on European Union and to the Treaty on the Functioning of the European Union:

Article 1

1. The Charter does not extend the ability of the Court of Justice of the European Union, or any court or tribunal of Poland or of the United Kingdom, to find that the laws, regulations or administrative provisions, practices or action of Poland or of the United Kingdom are inconsistent with the fundamental rights, freedoms and principles that it reaffirms.

2. In particular, and for the avoidance of doubt, nothing in Title IV of the Charter creates justiciable rights applicable to Poland or the United Kingdom except in so far as Poland or the United Kingdom has provided for such rights in its national law.

Article 2

To the extent that a provision of the Charter refers to national laws and practices, it shall only apply to Poland or the United Kingdom to the extent that the rights or principles that it contains are recognised in the law or practices of Poland or of the United Kingdom.

CHARTER OF FUNDAMENTAL RIGHTS OF THE EUROPEAN UNION

The peoples of Europe, in creating an ever closer union among them, are resolved to share a peaceful future based on common values.

Conscious of its spiritual and moral heritage, the Union is founded on the indivisible, universal values of human dignity, freedom, equality and solidarity; it is based on the principles of democracy and the rule of law. It places the individual at the heart of its activities, by establishing the citizenship of the Union and by creating an area of freedom, security and justice.

The Union contributes to the preservation and to the development of these common values while respecting the diversity of the cultures and traditions of the peoples of Europe as well as the national identities of the Member States and the organisation of their public authorities at national, regional and local levels; it seeks to promote balanced and sustainable development and ensures free movement of persons, services, goods and capital, and the freedom of establishment.

To this end, it is necessary to strengthen the protection of fundamental rights in the light of changes in society, social progress and scientific and technological developments by making those rights more visible in a Charter.

This Charter reaffirms, with due regard for the powers and tasks of the Union and for the principle of subsidiarity, the rights as they result, in particular, from the constitutional traditions and international obligations common to the Member States, the European Convention for the Protection of Human Rights and Fundamental Freedoms, the Social Charters adopted by the Union and by the Council of Europe and the case-law of the Court of Justice of the European Union and of the European Court of Human Rights. In this context the Charter will be interpreted by the courts of the Union and the Member States with due regard to the explanations prepared under the authority of the Praesidium of the Convention which drafted the Charter and updated under the responsibility of the Praesidium of the European Convention.

Enjoyment of these rights entails responsibilities and duties with regard to other persons, to the human community and to future generations.

The Union therefore recognises the rights, freedoms and principles set out hereafter.

TITLE I DIGNITY

Article 1   Human dignity
Human dignity is inviolable. It must be respected and protected.

Article 2   Right to life
1.   Everyone has the right to life.
2.   No one shall be condemned to the death penalty, or executed.

Article 3   Right to the integrity of the person
1.   Everyone has the right to respect for his or her physical and mental integrity.
2.   In the fields of medicine and biology, the following must be respected in particular:
    (a)   the free and informed consent of the person concerned, according to the procedures laid down by law;
    (b)   the prohibition of eugenic practices, in particular those aiming at the selection of persons;
    (c)   the prohibition on making the human body and its parts as such a source of financial gain;
    (d)   the prohibition of the reproductive cloning of human beings.

Article 4   Prohibition of torture and inhuman or degrading treatment or punishment
No one shall be subjected to torture or to inhuman or degrading treatment or punishment.

Article 5   Prohibition of slavery and forced labour
1.   No one shall be held in slavery or servitude.
2.   No one shall be required to perform forced or compulsory labour.
3.   Trafficking in human beings is prohibited.

TITLE II FREEDOMS

Article 6   Right to liberty and security
Everyone has the right to liberty and security of person.

Article 7 Respect for private and family life

Everyone has the right to respect for his or her private and family life, home and communications.

Article 8 Protection of personal data

1. Everyone has the right to the protection of personal data concerning him or her.
2. Such data must be processed fairly for specified purposes and on the basis of the consent of the person concerned or some other legitimate basis laid down by law. Everyone has the right of access to data which has been collected concerning him or her, and the right to have it rectified.
3. Compliance with these rules shall be subject to control by an independent authority.

Article 9 Right to marry and right to found a family

The right to marry and the right to found a family shall be guaranteed in accordance with the national laws governing the exercise of these rights.

Article 10 Freedom of thought, conscience and religion

1. Everyone has the right to freedom of thought, conscience and religion. This right includes freedom to change religion or belief and freedom, either alone or in community with others and in public or in private, to manifest religion or belief, in worship, teaching, practice and observance.
2. The right to conscientious objection is recognised, in accordance with the national laws governing the exercise of this right.

Article 11 Freedom of expression and information

1. Everyone has the right to freedom of expression. This right shall include freedom to hold opinions and to receive and impart information and ideas without interference by public authority and regardless of frontiers.
2. The freedom and pluralism of the media shall be respected.

Article 12 Freedom of assembly and of association

1. Everyone has the right to freedom of peaceful assembly and to freedom of association at all levels, in particular in political, trade union and civic matters, which implies the right of everyone to form and to join trade unions for the protection of his or her interests.
2. Political parties at Union level contribute to expressing the political will of the citizens of the Union.

Article 13 Freedom of the arts and sciences

The arts and scientific research shall be free of constraint. Academic freedom shall be respected.

Article 14 Right to education

1. Everyone has the right to education and to have access to vocational and continuing training.
2. This right includes the possibility to receive free compulsory education.
3. The freedom to found educational establishments with due respect for democratic principles and the right of parents to ensure the education and teaching of their children in conformity with their religious, philosophical and pedagogical convictions shall be respected, in accordance with the national laws governing the exercise of such freedom and right.

Article 15 Freedom to choose an occupation and right to engage in work

1. Everyone has the right to engage in work and to pursue a freely chosen or accepted occupation.

2. Every citizen of the Union has the freedom to seek employment, to work, to exercise the right of establishment and to provide services in any Member State.

3. Nationals of third countries who are authorised to work in the territories of the Member States are entitled to working conditions equivalent to those of citizens of the Union.

Article 16 Freedom to conduct a business

The freedom to conduct a business in accordance with Union law and national laws and practices is recognised.

Article 17 Right to property

1. Everyone has the right to own, use, dispose of and bequeath his or her lawfully acquired possessions. No one may be deprived of his or her possessions, except in the public interest and in the cases and under the conditions provided for by law, subject to fair compensation being paid in good time for their loss. The use of property may be regulated by law in so far as is necessary for the general interest.

2. Intellectual property shall be protected.

Article 18 Right to asylum

The right to asylum shall be guaranteed with due respect for the rules of the Geneva Convention of 28 July 1951 and the Protocol of 31 January 1967 relating to the status of refugees and in accordance with the Treaty on European Union and the Treaty on the Functioning of the European Union (hereinafter referred to as "the Treaties").

Article 19 Protection in the event of removal, expulsion or extradition

1. Collective expulsions are prohibited.

2. No one may be removed, expelled or extradited to a State where there is a serious risk that he or she would be subjected to the death penalty, torture or other inhuman or degrading treatment or punishment.

TITLE III EQUALITY

Article 20 Equality before the law

Everyone is equal before the law.

Article 21 Non-discrimination

1. Any discrimination based on any ground such as sex, race, colour, ethnic or social origin, genetic features, language, religion or belief, political or any other opinion, membership of a national minority, property, birth, disability, age or sexual orientation shall be prohibited.

2. Within the scope of application of the Treaties and without prejudice to any of their specific provisions, any discrimination on grounds of nationality shall be prohibited.

Article 22 Cultural, religious and linguistic diversity

The Union shall respect cultural, religious and linguistic diversity.

Article 23 Equality between women and men

Equality between women and men must be ensured in all areas, including employment, work and pay. The principle of equality shall not prevent the maintenance or adoption of measures providing for specific advantages in favour of the under-represented sex.

Article 24 The rights of the child

1. Children shall have the right to such protection and care as is necessary for their well-being. They may express their views freely. Such views shall be taken into consideration on matters which concern them in accordance with their age and maturity.

2. In all actions relating to children, whether taken by public authorities or private institutions, the child's best interests must be a primary consideration.

3. Every child shall have the right to maintain on a regular basis a personal relationship and direct contact with both his or her parents, unless that is contrary to his or her interests.

Article 25   The rights of the elderly

The Union recognises and respects the rights of the elderly to lead a life of dignity and independence and to participate in social and cultural life.

Article 26   Integration of persons with disabilities

The Union recognises and respects the right of persons with disabilities to benefit from measures designed to ensure their independence, social and occupational integration and participation in the life of the community.

TITLE IV SOLIDARITY

Article 27   Workers' right to information and consultation within the undertaking

Workers or their representatives must, at the appropriate levels, be guaranteed information and consultation in good time in the cases and under the conditions provided for by Union law and national laws and practices.

Article 28   Right of collective bargaining and action

Workers and employers, or their respective organisations, have, in accordance with Union law and national laws and practices, the right to negotiate and conclude collective agreements at the appropriate levels and, in cases of conflicts of interest, to take collective action to defend their interests, including strike action.

Article 29   Right of access to placement services

Everyone has the right of access to a free placement service.

Article 30   Protection in the event of unjustified dismissal

Every worker has the right to protection against unjustified dismissal, in accordance with Union law and national laws and practices.

Article 31   Fair and just working conditions

1. Every worker has the right to working conditions which respect his or her health, safety and dignity.

2. Every worker has the right to limitation of maximum working hours, to daily and weekly rest periods and to an annual period of paid leave.

Article 32   Prohibition of child labour and protection of young people at work

The employment of children is prohibited. The minimum age of admission to employment may not be lower than the minimum school-leaving age, without prejudice to such rules as may be more favourable to young people and except for limited derogations. Young people admitted to work must have working conditions appropriate to their age and be protected against economic exploitation and any work likely to harm their safety, health or physical, mental, moral or social development or to interfere with their education.

Article 33   Family and professional life

1. The family shall enjoy legal, economic and social protection.

2. To reconcile family and professional life, everyone shall have the right to protection from dismissal for a reason connected with maternity and the right to paid maternity leave and to parental leave following the birth or adoption of a child.

Article 34 Social security and social assistance

1. The Union recognises and respects the entitlement to social security benefits and social services providing protection in cases such as maternity, illness, industrial accidents, dependency or old age, and in the case of loss of employment, in accordance with the rules laid down by Union law and national laws and practices.

2. Everyone residing and moving legally within the European Union is entitled to social security benefits and social advantages in accordance with Union law and national laws and practices.

3. In order to combat social exclusion and poverty, the Union recognises and respects the right to social and housing assistance so as to ensure a decent existence for all those who lack sufficient resources, in accordance with the rules laid down by Union law and national laws and practices.

Article 35 Health care

Everyone has the right of access to preventive health care and the right to benefit from medical treatment under the conditions established by national laws and practices. A high level of human health protection shall be ensured in the definition and implementation of all the Union's policies and activities.

Article 36 Access to services of general economic interest

The Union recognises and respects access to services of general economic interest as provided for in national laws and practices, in accordance with the Treaties, in order to promote the social and territorial cohesion of the Union.

Article 37 Environmental protection

A high level of environmental protection and the improvement of the quality of the environment must be integrated into the policies of the Union and ensured in accordance with the principle of sustainable development.

Article 38 Consumer protection

Union policies shall ensure a high level of consumer protection.

TITLE V CITIZENS' RIGHTS

Article 39 Right to vote and to stand as a candidate at elections to the European Parliament

1. Every citizen of the Union has the right to vote and to stand as a candidate at elections to the European Parliament in the Member State in which he or she resides, under the same conditions as nationals of that State.

2. Members of the European Parliament shall be elected by direct universal suffrage in a free and secret ballot.

Article 40 Right to vote and to stand as a candidate at municipal elections

Every citizen of the Union has the right to vote and to stand as a candidate at municipal elections in the Member State in which he or she resides under the same conditions as nationals of that State.

Article 41 Right to good administration

1. Every person has the right to have his or her affairs handled impartially, fairly and within a reasonable time by the institutions, bodies, offices and agencies of the Union.

2. This right includes:

 (a) the right of every person to be heard, before any individual measure which would affect him or her adversely is taken;

 (b) the right of every person to have access to his or her file, while respecting the legitimate interests of confidentiality and of professional and business secrecy;

 (c) the obligation of the administration to give reasons for its decisions.

3. Every person has the right to have the Union make good any damage caused by its institutions or by its servants in the performance of their duties, in accordance with the general principles common to the laws of the Member States.

4. Every person may write to the institutions of the Union in one of the languages of the Treaties and must have an answer in the same language.

Article 42 Right of access to documents

Any citizen of the Union, and any natural or legal person residing or having its registered office in a Member State, has a right of access to documents of the institutions, bodies, offices and agencies of the Union, whatever their medium.

Article 43 European Ombudsman

Any citizen of the Union and any natural or legal person residing or having its registered office in a Member State has the right to refer to the European Ombudsman cases of maladministration in the activities of the institutions, bodies, offices or agencies of the Union, with the exception of the Court of Justice of the European Union acting in its judicial role.

Article 44 Right to petition

Any citizen of the Union and any natural or legal person residing or having its registered office in a Member State has the right to petition the European Parliament.

Article 45 Freedom of movement and of residence

1. Every citizen of the Union has the right to move and reside freely within the territory of the Member States.

2. Freedom of movement and residence may be granted, in accordance with the Treaties, to nationals of third countries legally resident in the territory of a Member State.

Article 46 Diplomatic and consular protection

Every citizen of the Union shall, in the territory of a third country in which the Member State of which he or she is a national is not represented, be entitled to protection by the diplomatic or consular authorities of any Member State, on the same conditions as the nationals of that Member State.

TITLE VI JUSTICE

Article 47 Right to an effective remedy and to a fair trial

Everyone whose rights and freedoms guaranteed by the law of the Union are violated has the right to an effective remedy before a tribunal in compliance with the conditions laid down in this Article. Everyone is entitled to a fair and public hearing within a reasonable time by an independent and impartial tribunal previously established by law. Everyone shall have the possibility of being advised, defended and represented. Legal aid shall be made available to those who lack sufficient resources in so far as such aid is necessary to ensure effective access to justice.

Article 48 Presumption of innocence and right of defence

1. Everyone who has been charged shall be presumed innocent until proved guilty according to law.

2. Respect for the rights of the defence of anyone who has been charged shall be guaranteed.

Article 49 Principles of legality and proportionality of criminal offences and penalties

1. No one shall be held guilty of any criminal offence on account of any act or omission which did not constitute a criminal offence under national law or international law at the time when it was committed. Nor shall a heavier penalty be imposed than the one that was applicable at the time the criminal offence was

committed. If, subsequent to the commission of a criminal offence, the law provides for a lighter penalty, that penalty shall be applicable.

2. This Article shall not prejudice the trial and punishment of any person for any act or omission which, at the time when it was committed, was criminal according to the general principles recognised by the community of nations.

3. The severity of penalties must not be disproportionate to the criminal offence.

Article 50 **Right not to be tried or punished twice in criminal proceedings for the same criminal offence**

No one shall be liable to be tried or punished again in criminal proceedings for an offence for which he or she has already been finally acquitted or convicted within the Union in accordance with the law.

TITLE VII GENERAL PROVISIONS GOVERNING THE INTERPRETATION AND APPLICATION OF THE CHARTER

Article 51 **Field of application**

1. The provisions of this Charter are addressed to the institutions, bodies, offices and agencies of the Union with due regard for the principle of subsidiarity and to the Member States only when they are implementing Union law. They shall therefore respect the rights, observe the principles and promote the application thereof in accordance with their respective powers and respecting the limits of the powers of the Union as conferred on it in the Treaties.

2. The Charter does not extend the field of application of Union law beyond the powers of the Union or establish any new power or task for the Union, or modify powers and tasks as defined in the Treaties.

Article 52 **Scope and interpretation of rights and principles**

1. Any limitation on the exercise of the rights and freedoms recognised by this Charter must be provided for by law and respect the essence of those rights and freedoms. Subject to the principle of proportionality, limitations may be made only if they are necessary and genuinely meet objectives of general interest recognised by the Union or the need to protect the rights and freedoms of others.

2. Rights recognised by this Charter for which provision is made in the Treaties shall be exercised under the conditions and within the limits defined by those Treaties.

3. In so far as this Charter contains rights which correspond to rights guaranteed by the Convention for the Protection of Human Rights and Fundamental Freedoms, the meaning and scope of those rights shall be the same as those laid down by the said Convention. This provision shall not prevent Union law providing more extensive protection.

4. In so far as this Charter recognises fundamental rights as they result from the constitutional traditions common to the Member States, those rights shall be interpreted in harmony with those traditions.

5. The provisions of this Charter which contain principles may be implemented by legislative and executive acts taken by institutions, bodies, offices and agencies of the Union, and by acts of Member States when they are implementing Union law, in the exercise of their respective powers. They shall be judicially cognisable only in the interpretation of such acts and in the ruling on their legality.

6. Full account shall be taken of national laws and practices as specified in this Charter.

7. The explanations drawn up as a way of providing guidance in the interpretation of this Charter shall be given due regard by the courts of the Union and of the Member States.

Article 53 Level of protection

Nothing in this Charter shall be interpreted as restricting or adversely affecting human rights and fundamental freedoms as recognised, in their respective fields of application, by Union law and international law and by international agreements to which the Union or all the Member States are party, including the European Convention for the Protection of Human Rights and Fundamental Freedoms, and by the Member States' constitutions.

Article 54 Prohibition of abuse of rights

Nothing in this Charter shall be interpreted as implying any right to engage in any activity or to perform any act aimed at the destruction of any of the rights and freedoms recognised in this Charter or at their limitation to a greater extent than is provided for herein.

COUNCIL DIRECTIVE 2001/55/EC

of 20 July 2001 on minimum standards for giving temporary protection in the event of a mass influx of displaced persons and on measures promoting a balance of efforts between Member States in receiving such persons and bearing the consequences thereof

Notes

Date of publication in Official Journal: OJ L212, 7.8.2001, p 12.

THE COUNCIL OF THE EUROPEAN UNION,

Having regard to the Treaty establishing the European Community, and in particular point 2(a) and (b) of Article 63 thereof,

Having regard to the proposal from the Commission[1],

Having regard to the opinion of the European Parliament[2],

Having regard to the opinion of the Economic and Social Committee[3],

Having regard to the opinion of the Committee of the Regions[4],

Whereas:

(1)   The preparation of a common policy on asylum, including common European arrangements for asylum, is a constituent part of the European Union's objective of establishing progressively an area of freedom, security and justice open to those who, forced by circumstances, legitimately seek protection in the European Union.

(2)   Cases of mass influx of displaced persons who cannot return to their country of origin have become more substantial in Europe in recent years. In these cases it may be necessary to set up exceptional schemes to offer them immediate temporary protection.

(3)   In the conclusions relating to persons displaced by the conflict in the former Yugoslavia adopted by the Ministers responsible for immigration at their meetings in London on 30 November and 1 December 1992 and Copenhagen on 1 and 2 June 1993, the Member States and the Community institutions expressed their concern at the situation of displaced persons.

(4)   On 25 September 1995 the Council adopted a Resolution on burden-sharing with regard to the admission and residence of displaced persons on a temporary basis[5], and, on 4 March 1996, adopted Decision 96/198/JHA on an alert and emergency procedure for burden-sharing with regard to the admission and residence of displaced persons on a temporary basis[6].

(5) The Action Plan of the Council and the Commission of 3 December 1998[7] provides for the rapid adoption, in accordance with the Treaty of Amsterdam, of minimum standards for giving temporary protection to displaced persons from third countries who cannot return to their country of origin and of measures promoting a balance of effort between Member States in receiving and bearing the consequences of receiving displaced persons.

(6) On 27 May 1999 the Council adopted conclusions on displaced persons from Kosovo. These conclusions call on the Commission and the Member States to learn the lessons of their response to the Kosovo crisis in order to establish the measures in accordance with the Treaty.

(7) The European Council, at its special meeting in Tampere on 15 and 16 October 1999, acknowledged the need to reach agreement on the issue of temporary protection for displaced persons on the basis of solidarity between Member States.

(8) It is therefore necessary to establish minimum standards for giving temporary protection in the event of a mass influx of displaced persons and to take measures to promote a balance of efforts between the Member States in receiving and bearing the consequences of receiving such persons.

(9) Those standards and measures are linked and interdependent for reasons of effectiveness, coherence and solidarity and in order, in particular, to avert the risk of secondary movements. They should therefore be enacted in a single legal instrument.

(10) This temporary protection should be compatible with the Member States' international obligations as regards refugees. In particular, it must not prejudice the recognition of refugee status pursuant to the Geneva Convention of 28 July 1951 on the status of refugees, as amended by the New York Protocol of 31 January 1967, ratified by all the Member States.

(11) The mandate of the United Nations High Commissioner for Refugees regarding refugees and other persons in need of international protection should be respected, and effect should be given to Declaration No 17, annexed to the Final Act to the Treaty of Amsterdam, on Article 63 of the Treaty establishing the European Community which provides that consultations are to be established with the United Nations High Commissioner for Refugees and other relevant international organisations on matters relating to asylum policy.

(12) It is in the very nature of minimum standards that Member States have the power to introduce or maintain more favourable provisions for persons enjoying temporary protection in the event of a mass influx of displaced persons.

(13) Given the exceptional character of the provisions established by this Directive in order to deal with a mass influx or imminent mass influx of displaced persons from third countries who are unable to return to their country of origin, the protection offered should be of limited duration.

(14) The existence of a mass influx of displaced persons should be established by a Council Decision, which should be binding in all Member States in relation to the displaced persons to whom the Decision applies. The conditions for the expiry of the Decision should also be established.

(15) The Member States' obligations as to the conditions of reception and residence of persons enjoying temporary protection in the event of a mass influx of displaced persons should be determined. These obligations should be fair and offer an adequate level of protection to those concerned.

(16) With respect to the treatment of persons enjoying temporary protection under this Directive, the Member States are bound by obligations under instruments of international law to which they are party and which prohibit discrimination.

(17) Member States should, in concert with the Commission, enforce adequate measures so that the processing of personal data respects the standard of protection of Directive 95/46/EC of the European Parliament and the Council of 24 October 1995 on the protection of individuals with regard to the processing of personal data and on the free movement of such data[8].

(18) Rules should be laid down to govern access to the asylum procedure in the context of temporary protection in the event of a mass influx of displaced persons, in conformity with the Member States' international obligations and with the Treaty.

(19) Provision should be made for principles and measures governing the return to the country of origin and the measures to be taken by Member States in respect of persons whose temporary protection has ended.

(20) Provision should be made for a solidarity mechanism intended to contribute to the attainment of a balance of effort between Member States in receiving and bearing the consequences of receiving displaced persons in the event of a mass influx. The mechanism should consist of two components. The first is financial and the second concerns the actual reception of persons in the Member States.

(21) The implementation of temporary protection should be accompanied by administrative cooperation between the Member States in liaison with the Commission.

(22) It is necessary to determine criteria for the exclusion of certain persons from temporary protection in the event of a mass influx of displaced persons.

(23) Since the objectives of the proposed action, namely to establish minimum standards for giving temporary protection in the event of a mass influx of displaced persons and measures promoting a balance of efforts between the Member States in receiving and bearing the consequences of receiving such persons, cannot be sufficiently attained by the Member States and can therefore, by reason of the scale or effects of the proposed action, be better achieved at Community level, the Community may adopt measures in accordance with the principle of subsidiarity as set out in Article 5 of the Treaty. In accordance with the principle of proportionality as set out in that Article, this Directive does not go beyond what is necessary in order to achieve those objectives.

(24) In accordance with Article 3 of the Protocol on the position of the United Kingdom and Ireland, annexed to the Treaty on European Union and to the Treaty establishing the European Community, the United Kingdom gave notice, by letter of 27 September 2000, of its wish to take part in the adoption and application of this Directive.

(25) Pursuant to Article 1 of the said Protocol, Ireland is not participating in the adoption of this Directive. Consequently and without prejudice to Article 4 of the aforementioned Protocol, the provisions of this Directive do not apply to Ireland.

(26) In accordance with Articles 1 and 2 of the Protocol on the position of Denmark, annexed to the Treaty on European Union and to the Treaty establishing the European Community, Denmark is not participating in the adoption of this Directive, and is therefore not bound by it nor subject to its application,

1 OJ C 311 E, 31.10.2000, p. 251.
2 Opinion delivered on 13 March 2001 (not yet published in the Official Journal).
3 OJ C 155, 29.5.2001, p. 21.
4 Opinion delivered on 13 June 2001 (not yet published in the Official Journal).
5 OJ C 262, 7.10.1995, p. 1.
6 OJ L 63, 13.3.1996, p. 10.
7 OJ C 19, 20.1.1999, p. 1.
8 OJ L 281, 23.11.1995, p. 31.

HAS ADOPTED THIS DIRECTIVE:

CHAPTER I
GENERAL PROVISIONS

Article 1

The purpose of this Directive is to establish minimum standards for giving temporary protection in the event of a mass influx of displaced persons from third countries who are unable to return to their country of origin and to promote a balance of effort between Member States in receiving and bearing the consequences of receiving such persons.

Article 2

For the purposes of this Directive:

(a) "temporary protection" means a procedure of exceptional character to provide, in the event of a mass influx or imminent mass influx of displaced persons from third countries who are unable to return to their country of origin, immediate and temporary protection to such persons, in particular if there is also a risk that the asylum system will be unable to process this influx without adverse effects for its efficient operation, in the interests of the persons concerned and other persons requesting protection;

(b) "Geneva Convention" means the Convention of 28 July 1951 relating to the status of refugees, as amended by the New York Protocol of 31 January 1967;

(c) "displaced persons" means third-country nationals or stateless persons who have had to leave their country or region of origin, or have been evacuated, in particular in response to an appeal by international organisations, and are unable to return in safe and durable conditions because of the situation prevailing in that country, who may fall within the scope of Article 1A of the Geneva Convention or other international or national instruments giving international protection, in particular:

(i) persons who have fled areas of armed conflict or endemic violence;

(ii) persons at serious risk of, or who have been the victims of, systematic or generalised violations of their human rights;

(d) "mass influx" means arrival in the Community of a large number of displaced persons, who come from a specific country or geographical area, whether their arrival in the Community was spontaneous or aided, for example through an evacuation programme;

(e) "refugees" means third-country nationals or stateless persons within the meaning of Article 1A of the Geneva Convention;

(f) "unaccompanied minors" means third-country nationals or stateless persons below the age of eighteen, who arrive on the territory of the

Member States unaccompanied by an adult responsible for them whether by law or custom, and for as long as they are not effectively taken into the care of such a person, or minors who are left unaccompanied after they have entered the territory of the Member States;

(g) "residence permit" means any permit or authorisation issued by the authorities of a Member State and taking the form provided for in that State's legislation, allowing a third country national or a stateless person to reside on its territory;

(h) "sponsor" means a third-country national enjoying temporary protection in a Member State in accordance with a decision taken under Article 5 and who wants to be joined by members of his or her family.

Article 3

1. Temporary protection shall not prejudge recognition of refugee status under the Geneva Convention.

2. Member States shall apply temporary protection with due respect for human rights and fundamental freedoms and their obligations regarding non-refoulement.

3. The establishment, implementation and termination of temporary protection shall be the subject of regular consultations with the Office of the United Nations High Commissioner for Refugees (UNHCR) and other relevant international organisations.

4. This Directive shall not apply to persons who have been accepted under temporary protection schemes prior to its entry into force.

5. This Directive shall not affect the prerogative of the Member States to adopt or retain more favourable conditions for persons covered by temporary protection.

CHAPTER II
DURATION AND IMPLEMENTATION OF TEMPORARY PROTECTION

Article 4

1. Without prejudice to Article 6, the duration of temporary protection shall be one year. Unless terminated under the terms of Article 6(1)(b), it may be extended automatically by six monthly periods for a maximum of one year.

2. Where reasons for temporary protection persist, the Council may decide by qualified majority, on a proposal from the Commission, which shall also examine any request by a Member State that it submit a proposal to the Council, to extend that temporary protection by up to one year.

Article 5

1. The existence of a mass influx of displaced persons shall be established by a Council Decision adopted by a qualified majority on a proposal from the Commission, which shall also examine any request by a Member State that it submit a proposal to the Council.

2. The Commission proposal shall include at least:

(a) a description of the specific groups of persons to whom the temporary protection will apply;

(b) the date on which the temporary protection will take effect;

(c) an estimation of the scale of the movements of displaced persons.

3. The Council Decision shall have the effect of introducing temporary protection for the displaced persons to which it refers, in all the Member States, in accordance with the provisions of this Directive. The Decision shall include at least:

(a) a description of the specific groups of persons to whom the temporary protection applies;

(b) the date on which the temporary protection will take effect;

(c) information received from Member States on their reception capacity;

(d) information from the Commission, UNHCR and other relevant international organisations.

4. The Council Decision shall be based on:

(a) an examination of the situation and the scale of the movements of displaced persons;

(b) an assessment of the advisability of establishing temporary protection, taking into account the potential for emergency aid and action on the ground or the inadequacy of such measures;

(c) information received from the Member States, the Commission, UNHCR and other relevant international organisations.

5. The European Parliament shall be informed of the Council Decision.

Article 6

1. Temporary protection shall come to an end:

(a) when the maximum duration has been reached; or

(b) at any time, by Council Decision adopted by a qualified majority on a proposal from the Commission, which shall also examine any request by a Member State that it submit a proposal to the Council.

2. The Council Decision shall be based on the establishment of the fact that the situation in the country of origin is such as to permit the safe and durable return of those granted temporary protection with due respect for human rights and fundamental freedoms and Member States' obligations regarding non-refoulement. The European Parliament shall be informed of the Council Decision.

Article 7

1. Member States may extend temporary protection as provided for in this Directive to additional categories of displaced persons over and above those to whom the Council Decision provided for in Article 5 applies, where they are displaced for the same reasons and from the same country or region of origin. They shall notify the Council and the Commission immediately.

2. The provisions of Articles 24, 25 and 26 shall not apply to the use of the possibility referred to in paragraph 1, with the exception of the structural support included in the European Refugee Fund set up by Decision 2000/596/EC[9], under the conditions laid down in that Decision.

9   OJ L 252, 6.10.2000, p. 12.

CHAPTER III
OBLIGATIONS OF THE MEMBER STATES TOWARDS PERSONS ENJOYING TEMPORARY PROTECTION

Article 8

1. The Member States shall adopt the necessary measures to provide persons enjoying temporary protection with residence permits for the entire duration of the protection. Documents or other equivalent evidence shall be issued for that purpose.

2. Whatever the period of validity of the residence permits referred to in paragraph 1, the treatment granted by the Member States to persons enjoying temporary protection may not be less favourable than that set out in Articles 9 to 16.

3. The Member States shall, if necessary, provide persons to be admitted to their territory for the purposes of temporary protection with every facility for obtaining the necessary visas, including transit visas. Formalities must be reduced to a minimum because of the urgency of the situation. Visas should be free of charge or their cost reduced to a minimum.

Article 9

The Member States shall provide persons enjoying temporary protection with a document, in a language likely to be understood by them, in which the provisions relating to temporary protection and which are relevant to them are clearly set out.

Article 10

To enable the effective application of the Council Decision referred to in Article 5, Member States shall register the personal data referred to in Annex II, point (a), with respect to the persons enjoying temporary protection on their territory.

Article 11

A Member State shall take back a person enjoying temporary protection on its territory, if the said person remains on, or, seeks to enter without authorisation onto, the territory of another Member State during the period covered by the Council Decision referred to in Article 5. Member States may, on the basis of a bilateral agreement, decide that this Article should not apply.

Article 12

The Member States shall authorise, for a period not exceeding that of temporary protection, persons enjoying temporary protection to engage in employed or self-employed activities, subject to rules applicable to the profession, as well as in activities such as educational opportunities for adults, vocational training and practical workplace experience. For reasons of labour market policies, Member States may give priority to EU citizens and citizens of States bound by the Agreement on the European Economic Area and also to legally resident third-country nationals who receive unemployment benefit. The general law in force in the Member States applicable to remuneration, access to social security systems relating to employed or self-employed activities and other conditions of employment shall apply.

Article 13

1. The Member States shall ensure that persons enjoying temporary protection have access to suitable accommodation or, if necessary, receive the means to obtain housing.
2. The Member States shall make provision for persons enjoying temporary protection to receive necessary assistance in terms of social welfare and means of subsistence, if they do not have sufficient resources, as well as for medical care. Without prejudice to paragraph 4, the assistance necessary for medical care shall include at least emergency care and essential treatment of illness.
3. Where persons enjoying temporary protection are engaged in employed or self-employed activities, account shall be taken, when fixing the proposed level of aid, of their ability to meet their own needs.
4. The Member States shall provide necessary medical or other assistance to persons enjoying temporary protection who have special needs, such as unaccompanied minors or persons who have undergone torture, rape or other serious forms of psychological, physical or sexual violence.

Article 14

1. The Member States shall grant to persons under 18 years of age enjoying temporary protection access to the education system under the same conditions as nationals of the host Member State The Member States may stipulate that such access must be confined to the state education system.
2. The Member States may allow adults enjoying temporary protection access to the general education system.

Article 15

1. For the purpose of this Article, in cases where families already existed in the country of origin and were separated due to circumstances surrounding the mass influx, the following persons shall be considered to be part of a family:

(a) the spouse of the sponsor or his/her unmarried partner in a stable relationship, where the legislation or practice of the Member State concerned treats unmarried couples in a way comparable to married couples under its law relating to aliens; the minor unmarried children of the sponsor or of his/her spouse, without distinction as to whether they were born in or out of wedlock or adopted;

(b) other close relatives who lived together as part of the family unit at the time of the events leading to the mass influx, and who were wholly or mainly dependent on the sponsor at the time.

2. In cases where the separate family members enjoy temporary protection in different Member States, Member States shall reunite family members where they are satisfied that the family members fall under the description of paragraph 1(a), taking into account the wish of the said family members. Member States may reunite family members where they are satisfied that the family members fall under the description of paragraph 1(b), taking into account on a case by case basis the extreme hardship they would face if the reunification did not take place.

3. Where the sponsor enjoys temporary protection in one Member State and one or some family members are not yet in a Member State, the Member State where the sponsor enjoys temporary protection shall reunite family members, who are in need of protection, with the sponsor in the case of family members where it is satisfied that they fall under the description of paragraph 1(a). The Member State may reunite family members, who are in need of protection, with the sponsor in the case of family members where it is satisfied that they fall under the description of paragraph 1(b), taking into account on a case by case basis the extreme hardship which they would face if the reunification did not take place.

4. When applying this Article, the Member States shall taken into consideration the best interests of the child.

5. The Member States concerned shall decide, taking account of Articles 25 and 26, in which Member State the reunification shall take place.

6. Reunited family members shall be granted residence permits under temporary protection. Documents or other equivalent evidence shall be issued for that purpose. Transfers of family members onto the territory of another Member State for the purposes of reunification under paragraph 2, shall result in the withdrawal of the residence permits issued, and the termination of the obligations towards the persons concerned relating to temporary protection, in the Member State of departure.

7. The practical implementation of this Article may involve cooperation with the international organisations concerned.

8. A Member State shall, at the request of another Member State, provide information, as set out in Annex II, on a person receiving temporary protection which is needed to process a matter under this Article.

Article 16

1. The Member States shall as soon as possible take measures to ensure the necessary representation of unaccompanied minors enjoying temporary protection by legal guardianship, or, where necessary, representation by an organisation which is responsible for the care and well-being of minors, or by any other appropriate representation.

2. During the period of temporary protection Member States shall provide for unaccompanied minors to be placed:

(a) with adult relatives;

(b) with a foster-family;

(c)   in reception centres with special provisions for minors, or in other accommodation suitable for minors;

(d)   with the person who looked after the child when fleeing.

The Member States shall take the necessary steps to enable the placement. Agreement by the adult person or persons concerned shall be established by the Member States. The views of the child shall be taken into account in accordance with the age and maturity of the child.

CHAPTER IV
ACCESS TO THE ASYLUM PROCEDURE IN THE CONTEXT OF TEMPORARY PROTECTION

Article 17

1.   Persons enjoying temporary protection must be able to lodge an application for asylum at any time.

2.   The examination of any asylum application not processed before the end of the period of temporary protection shall be completed after the end of that period.

Article 18

The criteria and mechanisms for deciding which Member State is responsible for considering an asylum application shall apply. In particular, the Member State responsible for examining an asylum application submitted by a person enjoying temporary protection pursuant to this Directive, shall be the Member State which has accepted his transfer onto its territory.

Article 19

1.   The Member States may provide that temporary protection may not be enjoyed concurrently with the status of asylum seeker while applications are under consideration.

2.   Where, after an asylum application has been examined, refugee status or, where applicable, other kind of protection is not granted to a person eligible for or enjoying temporary protection, the Member States shall, without prejudice to Article 28, provide for that person to enjoy or to continue to enjoy temporary protection for the remainder of the period of protection.

CHAPTER V
RETURN AND MEASURES AFTER TEMPORARY PROTECTION HAS ENDED

Article 20

When the temporary protection ends, the general laws on protection and on aliens in the Member States shall apply, without prejudice to Articles 21, 22 and 23.

Article 21

1.   The Member States shall take the measures necessary to make possible the voluntary return of persons enjoying temporary protection or whose temporary protection has ended. The Member States shall ensure that the provisions governing voluntary return of persons enjoying temporary protection facilitate their return with respect for human dignity.

The Member State shall ensure that the decision of those persons to return is taken in full knowledge of the facts. The Member States may provide for exploratory visits.

2.   For such time as the temporary protection has not ended, the Member States shall, on the basis of the circumstances prevailing in the country of origin, give favourable consideration to requests for return to the host Member State from persons who have enjoyed temporary protection and exercised their right to a voluntary return.

3.   At the end of the temporary protection, the Member States may provide for the obligations laid down in CHAPTER III to be extended individually to persons who

have been covered by temporary protection and are benefiting from a voluntary return programme. The extension shall have effect until the date of return.

Article 22

1. The Member States shall take the measures necessary to ensure that the enforced return of persons whose temporary protection has ended and who are not eligible for admission is conducted with due respect for human dignity.

2. In cases of enforced return, Member States shall consider any compelling humanitarian reasons which may make return impossible or unreasonable in specific cases.

Article 23

1. The Member States shall take the necessary measures concerning the conditions of residence of persons who have enjoyed temporary protection and who cannot, in view of their state of health, reasonably be expected to travel; where for example they would suffer serious negative effects if their treatment was interrupted. They shall not be expelled so long as that situation continues.

2. The Member States may allow families whose children are minors and attend school in a Member State to benefit from residence conditions allowing the children concerned to complete the current school period.

CHAPTER VI
SOLIDARITY

Article 24

The measures provided for in this Directive shall benefit from the European Refugee Fund set up by Decision 2000/596/EC, under the terms laid down in that Decision.

Article 25

1. The Member States shall receive persons who are eligible for temporary protection in a spirit of Community solidarity. They shall indicate — in figures or in general terms — their capacity to receive such persons. This information shall be set out in the Council Decision referred to in Article 5. After that Decision has been adopted, the Member States may indicate additional reception capacity by notifying the Council and the Commission. This information shall be passed on swiftly to UNHCR.

2. The Member States concerned, acting in cooperation with the competent international organisations, shall ensure that the eligible persons defined in the Council Decision referred to in Article 5, who have not yet arrived in the Community have expressed their will to be received onto their territory.

3. When the number of those who are eligible for temporary protection following a sudden and massive influx exceeds the reception capacity referred to in paragraph 1, the Council shall, as a matter of urgency, examine the situation and take appropriate action, including recommending additional support for Member States affected.

Article 26

1. For the duration of the temporary protection, the Member States shall cooperate with each other with regard to transferral of the residence of persons enjoying temporary protection from one Member State to another, subject to the consent of the persons concerned to such transferral.

2. A Member State shall communicate requests for transfers to the other Member States and notify the Commission and UNHCR. The Member States shall inform the requesting Member State of their capacity for receiving transferees.

3. A Member State shall, at the request of another Member State, provide information, as set out in Annex II, on a person enjoying temporary protection which is needed to process a matter under this Article.

4. Where a transfer is made from one Member State to another, the residence permit in the Member State of departure shall expire and the obligations towards the persons concerned relating to temporary protection in the Member State of departure shall come to an end. The new host Member State shall grant temporary protection to the persons concerned.

5. The Member States shall use the model pass set out in Annex I for transfers between Member States of persons enjoying temporary protection.

CHAPTER VII
ADMINISTRATIVE COOPERATION

Article 27

1. For the purposes of the administrative cooperation required to implement temporary protection, the Member States shall each appoint a national contact point, whose address they shall communicate to each other and to the Commission. The Member States shall, in liaison with the Commission, take all the appropriate measures to establish direct cooperation and an exchange of information between the competent authorities.

2. The Member States shall, regularly and as quickly as possible, communicate data concerning the number of persons enjoying temporary protection and full information on the national laws, regulations and administrative provisions relating to the implementation of temporary protection.

CHAPTER VIII
SPECIAL PROVISIONS

Article 28

1. The Member States may exclude a person from temporary protection if:
   (a) there are serious reasons for considering that:
      (i) he or she has committed a crime against peace, a war crime, or a crime against humanity, as defined in the international instruments drawn up to make provision in respect of such crimes;
      (ii) he or she has committed a serious non-political crime outside the Member State of reception prior to his or her admission to that Member State as a person enjoying temporary protection. The severity of the expected persecution is to be weighed against the nature of the criminal offence of which the person concerned is suspected. Particularly cruel actions, even if committed with an allegedly political objective, may be classified as serious non-political crimes. This applies both to the participants in the crime and to its instigators;
      (iii) he or she has been guilty of acts contrary to the purposes and principles of the United Nations;
   (b) there are reasonable grounds for regarding him or her as a danger to the security of the host Member State or, having been convicted by a final judgment of a particularly serious crime, he or she is a danger to the community of the host Member State.

2. The grounds for exclusion referred to in paragraph 1 shall be based solely on the personal conduct of the person concerned. Exclusion decisions or measures shall be based on the principle of proportionality.

CHAPTER IX
FINAL PROVISIONS

Article 29

Persons who have been excluded from the benefit of temporary protection or family reunification by a Member State shall be entitled to mount a legal challenge in the Member State concerned.

Article 30

The Member States shall lay down the rules on penalties applicable to infringements of the national provisions adopted pursuant to this Directive and shall take all measures necessary to ensure that they are implemented. The penalties provided for must be effective, proportionate and dissuasive.

Article 31

1. Not later than two years after the date specified in Article 32, the Commission shall report to the European Parliament and the Council on the application of this Directive in the Member States and shall propose any amendments that are necessary. The Member States shall send the Commission all the information that is appropriate for drawing up this report.

2. After presenting the report referred to at paragraph 1, the Commission shall report to the European Parliament and the Council on the application of this Directive in the Member States at least every five years.

Article 32

1. The Member States shall bring into force the laws, regulations and administrative provisions necessary to comply with this Directive by 31 December 2002 at the latest. They shall forthwith inform the Commission thereof.

2. When the Member States adopt these measures, they shall contain a reference to this Directive or shall be accompanied by such reference on the occasion of their official publication. The methods of making such a reference shall be laid down by the Member States.

Article 33

This Directive shall enter into force on the day of its publication in the Official Journal of the European Communities.

Article 34

This Directive is addressed to the Member States in accordance with the Treaty establishing the European Community.

ANNEX I

MODEL PASS FOR THE TRANSFER OF PERSONS ENJOYING TEMPORARY PROTECTION
[The full text of this form is currently unavailable – please refer to the original document]

ANNEX II

The information referred to in Articles 10, 15 and 26 of the Directive includes to the extent necessary one or more of the following documents or data:

(a)   personal data on the person concerned (name, nationality, date and place of birth, marital status, family relationship);

(b)   identity documents and travel documents of the person concerned;

(c)   documents concerning evidence of family ties (marriage certificate, birth certificate, certificate of adoption);

(d)   other information essential to establish the person's identity or family relationship;

(e)   residence permits, visas or residence permit refusal decisions issued to the person concerned by the Member State, and documents forming the basis of decisions;

(f)   residence permit and visa applications lodged by the person concerned and pending in the Member State, and the stage reached in the processing of these.

The providing Member State shall notify any corrected information to the requesting Member State.

COUNCIL DIRECTIVE 2003/9/EC (THE RECEPTION DIRECTIVE)

of 27 January 2003 laying down minimum standards for the reception of asylum seekers

Notes

Date of publication in Official Journal: OJ L31, 6.2.2003, p 18.

THE COUNCIL OF THE EUROPEAN UNION,

Having regard to the Treaty establishing the European Community, and in particular point (1)(b) of the first subparagraph of Article 63 thereof,

Having regard to the proposal from the Commission[1],

Having regard to the opinion of the European Parliament[2],

Having regard to the opinion of the Economic and Social Committee[3],

Having regard to the opinion of the Committee of the Regions[4]),

Whereas:

(1)   A common policy on asylum, including a Common European Asylum System, is a constituent part of the European Union's objective of progressively establishing an area of freedom, security and justice open to those who, forced by circumstances, legitimately seek protection in the Community.

(2)   At its special meeting in Tampere on 15 and 16 October 1999, the European Council agreed to work towards establishing a Common European Asylum System, based on the full and inclusive application of the Geneva Convention relating to the Status of Refugees of 28 July 1951, as supplemented by the New York Protocol of 31 January 1967, thus maintaining the principle of non-refoulement.

(3)   The Tampere Conclusions provide that a Common European Asylum System should include, in the short term, common minimum conditions of reception of asylum seekers.

(4)   The establishment of minimum standards for the reception of asylum seekers is a further step towards a European asylum policy.

(5)   This Directive respects the fundamental rights and observes the principles recognised in particular by the Charter of Fundamental Rights of the European Union. In particular, this Directive seeks to ensure full respect for human dignity and to promote the application of Articles 1 and 18 of the said Charter.

(6)   With respect to the treatment of persons falling within the scope of this Directive, Member States are bound by obligations under instruments of international law to which they are party and which prohibit discrimination.

(7) Minimum standards for the reception of asylum seekers that will normally suffice to ensure them a dignified standard of living and comparable living conditions in all Member States should be laid down.

(8) The harmonisation of conditions for the reception of asylum seekers should help to limit the secondary movements of asylum seekers influenced by the variety of conditions for their reception.

(9) Reception of groups with special needs should be specifically designed to meet those needs.

(10) Reception of applicants who are in detention should be specifically designed to meet their needs in that situation.

(11) In order to ensure compliance with the minimum procedural guarantees consisting in the opportunity to contact organisations or groups of persons that provide legal assistance, information should be provided on such organisations and groups of persons.

(12) The possibility of abuse of the reception system should be restricted by laying down cases for the reduction or withdrawal of reception conditions for asylum seekers.

(13) The efficiency of national reception systems and cooperation among Member States in the field of reception of asylum seekers should be secured.

(14) Appropriate coordination should be encouraged between the competent authorities as regards the reception of asylum seekers, and harmonious relationships between local communities and accommodation centres should therefore be promoted.

(15) It is in the very nature of minimum standards that Member States have the power to introduce or maintain more favourable provisions for third-country nationals and stateless persons who ask for international protection from a Member State.

(16) In this spirit, Member States are also invited to apply the provisions of this Directive in connection with procedures for deciding on applications for forms of protection other than that emanating from the Geneva Convention for third country nationals and stateless persons.

(17) The implementation of this Directive should be evaluated at regular intervals.

(18) Since the objectives of the proposed action, namely to establish minimum standards on the reception of asylum seekers in Member States, cannot be sufficiently achieved by the Member States and can therefore, by reason of the scale and effects of the proposed action, be better achieved by the Community, the Community may adopt measures in accordance with the principles of subsidiarity as set out in Article 5 of the Treaty. In accordance with the principle of proportionality, as set out in that Article, this Directive does not go beyond what is necessary in order to achieve those objectives.

(19) In accordance with Article 3 of the Protocol on the position of the United Kingdom and Ireland, annexed to the Treaty on European Union and to the Treaty establishing the European Community, the United Kingdom gave notice, by letter of 18 August 2001, of its wish to take part in the adoption and application of this Directive.

(20) In accordance with Article 1 of the said Protocol, Ireland is not participating in the adoption of this Directive. Consequently, and without prejudice to Article 4 of the aforementioned Protocol, the provisions of this Directive do not apply to Ireland.

(21) In accordance with Articles 1 and 2 of the Protocol on the position of Denmark, annexed to the Treaty on European Union and to the Treaty

establishing the European Community, Denmark is not participating in the adoption of this Directive and is therefore neither bound by it nor subject to its application,

[1] OJ C 213 E, 31.7.2001, p. 286.

[2] Opinion delivered on 25 April 2002 (not yet published in the Official Journal).

[3] OJ C 48, 21.2.2002, p. 63.

[4] OJ C 107, 3.5.2002, p. 85.

HAS ADOPTED THIS DIRECTIVE:

CHAPTER I
PURPOSE, DEFINITIONS AND SCOPE

Article 1 Purpose

The purpose of this Directive is to lay down minimum standards for the reception of asylum seekers in Member States.

Article 2 Definitions

For the purposes of this Directive:

(a) "Geneva Convention" shall mean the Convention of 28 July 1951 relating to the status of refugees, as amended by the New York Protocol of 31 January 1967;

(b) "application for asylum" shall mean the application made by a third-country national or a stateless person which can be understood as a request for international protection from a Member State, under the Geneva Convention. Any application for international protection is presumed to be an application for asylum unless a third-country national or a stateless person explicitly requests another kind of protection that can be applied for separately;

(c) "applicant" or "asylum seeker" shall mean a third country national or a stateless person who has made an application for asylum in respect of which a final decision has not yet been taken;

(d) "family members" shall mean, in so far as the family already existed in the country of origin, the following members of the applicant's family who are present in the same Member State in relation to the application for asylum:

(i) the spouse of the asylum seeker or his or her unmarried partner in a stable relationship, where the legislation or practice of the Member State concerned treats unmarried couples in a way comparable to married couples under its law relating to aliens;

(ii) the minor children of the couple referred to in point (i) or of the applicant, on condition that they are unmarried and dependent and regardless of whether they were born in or out of wedlock or adopted as defined under the national law;

(e) "refugee" shall mean a person who fulfils the requirements of Article 1(A) of the Geneva Convention;

(f) "refugee status" shall mean the status granted by a Member State to a person who is a refugee and is admitted as such to the territory of that Member State;

(g) "procedures" and "appeals", shall mean the procedures and appeals established by Member States in their national law;

(h) "unaccompanied minors" shall mean persons below the age of eighteen who arrive in the territory of the Member States unaccompanied by an adult responsible for them whether by law or by custom, and for as long as they are not effectively taken into the care of such a person; it shall include minors who are left unaccompanied after they have entered the territory of Member States;

(i) "reception conditions" shall mean the full set of measures that Member States grant to asylum seekers in accordance with this Directive;

(j) "material reception conditions" shall mean the reception conditions that include housing, food and clothing, provided in kind, or as financial allowances or in vouchers, and a daily expenses allowance;

(k) "detention" shall mean confinement of an asylum seeker by a Member State within a particular place, where the applicant is deprived of his or her freedom of movement;

(l) "accommodation centre" shall mean any place used for collective housing of asylum seekers.

Article 3 Scope

1. This Directive shall apply to all third country nationals and stateless persons who make an application for asylum at the border or in the territory of a Member State as long as they are allowed to remain on the territory as asylum seekers, as well as to family members, if they are covered by such application for asylum according to the national law.

2. This Directive shall not apply in cases of requests for diplomatic or territorial asylum submitted to representations of Member States.

3. This Directive shall not apply when the provisions of Council Directive 2001/55/EC of 20 July 2001 on minimum standards for giving temporary protection in the event of a mass influx of displaced persons and on measures promoting a balance of efforts between Member States in receiving such persons and bearing the consequences thereof[5] are applied.

4. Member States may decide to apply this Directive in connection with procedures for deciding on applications for kinds of protection other than that emanating from the Geneva Convention for third-country nationals or stateless persons who are found not to be refugees.

[5] OJ L 212, 7.8.2001, p. 12.

Article 4 More favourable provisions

Member States may introduce or retain more favourable provisions in the field of reception conditions for asylum seekers and other close relatives of the applicant who are present in the same Member State when they are dependent on him or for humanitarian reasons insofar as these provisions are compatible with this Directive.

CHAPTER II
GENERAL PROVISIONS ON RECEPTION CONDITIONS

Article 5 Information

1. Member States shall inform asylum seekers, within a reasonable time not exceeding fifteen days after they have lodged their application for asylum with the competent authority, of at least any established benefits and of the obligations with which they must comply relating to reception conditions.

Member States shall ensure that applicants are provided with information on organisations or groups of persons that provide specific legal assistance and organisations that might be able to help or inform them concerning the available reception conditions, including health care.

2. Member States shall ensure that the information referred to in paragraph 1 is in writing and, as far as possible, in a language that the applicants may reasonably be supposed to understand. Where appropriate, this information may also be supplied orally.

Article 6 Documentation

1. Member States shall ensure that, within three days after an application is lodged with the competent authority, the applicant is provided with a document issued in his or her own name certifying his or her status as an asylum seeker or testifying that he or she is allowed to stay in the territory of the Member State while his or her application is pending or being examined.

If the holder is not free to move within all or a part of the territory of the Member State, the document shall also certify this fact.

2. Member States may exclude application of this Article when the asylum seeker is in detention and during the examination of an application for asylum made at the border or within the context of a procedure to decide on the right of the applicant legally to enter the territory of a Member State. In specific cases, during the examination of an application for asylum, Member States may provide applicants with other evidence equivalent to the document referred to in paragraph 1.

3. The document referred to in paragraph 1 need not certify the identity of the asylum seeker.

4. Member States shall adopt the necessary measures to provide asylum seekers with the document referred to in paragraph 1, which must be valid for as long as they are authorised to remain in the territory of the Member State concerned or at the border thereof.

5. Member States may provide asylum seekers with a travel document when serious humanitarian reasons arise that require their presence in another State.

Article 7 Residence and freedom of movement

1. Asylum seekers may move freely within the territory of the host Member State or within an area assigned to them by that Member State. The assigned area shall not affect the unalienable sphere of private life and shall allow sufficient scope for guaranteeing access to all benefits under this Directive.

2. Member States may decide on the residence of the asylum seeker for reasons of public interest, public order or, when necessary, for the swift processing and effective monitoring of his or her application.

3. When it proves necessary, for example for legal reasons or reasons of public order, Member States may confine an applicant to a particular place in accordance with their national law.

4. Member States may make provision of the material reception conditions subject to actual residence by the applicants in a specific place, to be determined by the Member States. Such a decision, which may be of a general nature, shall be taken individually and established by national legislation.

5. Member States shall provide for the possibility of granting applicants temporary permission to leave the place of residence mentioned in paragraphs 2 and 4 and/or the assigned area mentioned in paragraph 1. Decisions shall be taken individually, objectively and impartially and reasons shall be given if they are negative.

The applicant shall not require permission to keep appointments with authorities and courts if his or her appearance is necessary.

6. Member States shall require applicants to inform the competent authorities of their current address and notify any change of address to such authorities as soon as possible.

Article 8 Families

Member States shall take appropriate measures to maintain as far as possible family unity as present within their territory, if applicants are provided with housing by the Member State concerned. Such measures shall be implemented with the asylum seeker's agreement.

Article 9 Medical screening

Member States may require medical screening for applicants on public health grounds.

Article 10 Schooling and education of minors

1. Member States shall grant to minor children of asylum seekers and to asylum seekers who are minors access to the education system under similar conditions as nationals of the host Member State for so long as an expulsion measure against them or their parents is not actually enforced. Such education may be provided in accommodation centres.

The Member State concerned may stipulate that such access must be confined to the State education system.

Minors shall be younger than the age of legal majority in the Member State in which the application for asylum was lodged or is being examined. Member States shall not withdraw secondary education for the sole reason that the minor has reached the age of majority.

2. Access to the education system shall not be postponed for more than three months from the date the application for asylum was lodged by the minor or the minor's parents. This period may be extended to one year where specific education is provided in order to facilitate access to the education system.

3. Where access to the education system as set out in paragraph 1 is not possible due to the specific situation of the minor, the Member State may offer other education arrangements.

Article 11 Employment

1. Member States shall determine a period of time, starting from the date on which an application for asylum was lodged, during which an applicant shall not have access to the labour market.

2. If a decision at first instance has not been taken within one year of the presentation of an application for asylum and this delay cannot be attributed to the applicant, Member States shall decide the conditions for granting access to the labour market for the applicant.

3. Access to the labour market shall not be withdrawn during appeals procedures, where an appeal against a negative decision in a regular procedure has suspensive effect, until such time as a negative decision on the appeal is notified.

4. For reasons of labour market policies, Member States may give priority to EU citizens and nationals of States parties to the Agreement on the European Economic Area and also to legally resident third-country nationals.

Article 12 Vocational training

Member States may allow asylum seekers access to vocational training irrespective of whether they have access to the labour market.

Access to vocational training relating to an employment contract shall depend on the extent to which the applicant has access to the labour market in accordance with Article 11.

Article 13 General rules on material reception conditions and health care

1. Member States shall ensure that material reception conditions are available to applicants when they make their application for asylum.

2. Member States shall make provisions on material reception conditions to ensure a standard of living adequate for the health of applicants and capable of ensuring their subsistence.

Member States shall ensure that that standard of living is met in the specific situation of persons who have special needs, in accordance with Article 17, as well as in relation to the situation of persons who are in detention.

3. Member States may make the provision of all or some of the material reception conditions and health care subject to the condition that applicants do not have sufficient means to have a standard of living adequate for their health and to enable their subsistence.

4. Member States may require applicants to cover or contribute to the cost of the material reception conditions and of the health care provided for in this Directive, pursuant to the provision of paragraph 3, if the applicants have sufficient resources, for example if they have been working for a reasonable period of time.

If it transpires that an applicant had sufficient means to cover material reception conditions and health care at the time when these basic needs were being covered, Member States may ask the asylum seeker for a refund.

5. Material reception conditions may be provided in kind, or in the form of financial allowances or vouchers or in a combination of these provisions.

Where Member States provide material reception conditions in the form of financial allowances or vouchers, the amount thereof shall be determined in accordance with the principles set out in this Article.

Article 14 Modalities for material reception conditions

1. Where housing is provided in kind, it should take one or a combination of the following forms:

    (a)   premises used for the purpose of housing applicants during the examination of an application for asylum lodged at the border;

    (b)   accommodation centres which guarantee an adequate standard of living;

    (c)   private houses, flats, hotels or other premises adapted for housing applicants.

2. Member States shall ensure that applicants provided with the housing referred to in paragraph 1(a), (b) and (c) are assured:

    (a)   protection of their family life;

    (b)   the possibility of communicating with relatives, legal advisers and representatives of the United Nations High Commissioner for Refugees (UNHCR) and non-governmental organisations (NGOs) recognised by Member States.

Member States shall pay particular attention to the prevention of assault within the premises and accommodation centres referred to in paragraph 1(a) and (b).

3. Member States shall ensure, if appropriate, that minor children of applicants or applicants who are minors are lodged with their parents or with the adult family member responsible for them whether by law or by custom.

4. Member States shall ensure that transfers of applicants from one housing facility to another take place only when necessary. Member States shall provide for the possibility for applicants to inform their legal advisers of the transfer and of their new address.

5. Persons working in accommodation centres shall be adequately trained and shall be bound by the confidentiality principle as defined in the national law in relation to any information they obtain in the course of their work.

6. Member States may involve applicants in managing the material resources and non-material aspects of life in the centre through an advisory board or council representing residents.

7. Legal advisors or counsellors of asylum seekers and representatives of the United Nations High Commissioner for Refugees or non-governmental organisations designated by the latter and recognised by the Member State concerned shall be granted access to accommodation centres and other housing facilities in order to assist the said asylum seekers. Limits on such access may be imposed only on grounds relating to the security of the centres and facilities and of the asylum seekers.

8. Member States may exceptionally set modalities for material reception conditions different from those provided for in this Article, for a reasonable period which shall be as short as possible, when:

    —   an initial assessment of the specific needs of the applicant is required,

    —   material reception conditions, as provided for in this Article, are not available in a certain geographical area,

— housing capacities normally available are temporarily exhausted,

— the asylum seeker is in detention or confined to border posts.

These different conditions shall cover in any case basic needs.

Article 15 Health care

1. Member States shall ensure that applicants receive the necessary health care which shall include, at least, emergency care and essential treatment of illness.

2. Member States shall provide necessary medical or other assistance to applicants who have special needs.

CHAPTER III
REDUCTION OR WITHDRAWAL OF RECEPTION CONDITIONS

Article 16 Reduction or withdrawal of reception conditions

1. Member States may reduce or withdraw reception conditions in the following cases:

    (a)   where an asylum seeker:

        — abandons the place of residence determined by the competent authority without informing it or, if requested, without permission, or

        — does not comply with reporting duties or with requests to provide information or to appear for personal interviews concerning the asylum procedure during a reasonable period laid down in national law, or

        — has already lodged an application in the same Member State.

When the applicant is traced or voluntarily reports to the competent authority, a duly motivated decision, based on the reasons for the disappearance, shall be taken on the reinstallation of the grant of some or all of the reception conditions;

    (b)   where an applicant has concealed financial resources and has therefore unduly benefited from material reception conditions.

If it transpires that an applicant had sufficient means to cover material reception conditions and health care at the time when these basic needs were being covered, Member States may ask the asylum seeker for a refund.

2. Member States may refuse conditions in cases where an asylum seeker has failed to demonstrate that the asylum claim was made as soon as reasonably practicable after arrival in that Member State.

3. Member States may determine sanctions applicable to serious breaching of the rules of the accommodation centres as well as to seriously violent behaviour.

4. Decisions for reduction, withdrawal or refusal of reception conditions or sanctions referred to in paragraphs 1, 2 and 3 shall be taken individually, objectively and impartially and reasons shall be given. Decisions shall be based on the particular situation of the person concerned, especially with regard to persons covered by Article 17, taking into account the principle of proportionality. Member States shall under all circumstances ensure access to emergency health care.

5. Member States shall ensure that material reception conditions are not withdrawn or reduced before a negative decision is taken.

CHAPTER IV
PROVISIONS FOR PERSONS WITH SPECIAL NEEDS

Article 17 General principle

1. Member States shall take into account the specific situation of vulnerable persons such as minors, unaccompanied minors, disabled people, elderly people, pregnant women, single parents with minor children and persons who have been subjected to

torture, rape or other serious forms of psychological, physical or sexual violence, in the national legislation implementing the provisions of Chapter II relating to material reception conditions and health care.

2. Paragraph 1 shall apply only to persons found to have special needs after an individual evaluation of their situation.

Article 18 Minors

1. The best interests of the child shall be a primary consideration for Member States when implementing the provisions of this Directive that involve minors.

2. Member States shall ensure access to rehabilitation services for minors who have been victims of any form of abuse, neglect, exploitation, torture or cruel, inhuman and degrading treatment, or who have suffered from armed conflicts, and ensure that appropriate mental health care is developed and qualified counselling is provided when needed.

Article 19 Unaccompanied minors

1. Member States shall as soon as possible take measures to ensure the necessary representation of unaccompanied minors by legal guardianship or, where necessary, representation by an organisation which is responsible for the care and well-being of minors, or by any other appropriate representation. Regular assessments shall be made by the appropriate authorities.

2. Unaccompanied minors who make an application for asylum shall, from the moment they are admitted to the territory to the moment they are obliged to leave the host Member State in which the application for asylum was made or is being examined, be placed:

  (a)   with adult relatives;
  (b)   with a foster-family;
  (c)   in accommodation centres with special provisions for minors;
  (d)   in other accommodation suitable for minors.

Member States may place unaccompanied minors aged 16 or over in accommodation centres for adult asylum seekers.

As far as possible, siblings shall be kept together, taking into account the best interests of the minor concerned and, in particular, his or her age and degree of maturity. Changes of residence of unaccompanied minors shall be limited to a minimum.

3. Member States, protecting the unaccompanied minor's best interests, shall endeavour to trace the members of his or her family as soon as possible. In cases where there may be a threat to the life or integrity of the minor or his or her close relatives, particularly if they have remained in the country of origin, care must be taken to ensure that the collection, processing and circulation of information concerning those persons is undertaken on a confidential basis, so as to avoid jeopardising their safety.

4. Those working with unaccompanied minors shall have had or receive appropriate training concerning their needs, and shall be bound by the confidentiality principle as defined in the national law, in relation to any information they obtain in the course of their work.

Article 20 Victims of torture and violence

Member States shall ensure that, if necessary, persons who have been subjected to torture, rape or other serious acts of violence receive the necessary treatment of damages caused by the aforementioned acts.

CHAPTER V
APPEALS

Article 21 Appeals

1. Member States shall ensure that negative decisions relating to the granting of benefits under this Directive or decisions taken under Article 7 which individually

affect asylum seekers may be the subject of an appeal within the procedures laid down in the national law. At least in the last instance the possibility of an appeal or a review before a judicial body shall be granted.

2. Procedures for access to legal assistance in such cases shall be laid down in national law.

CHAPTER VI
ACTIONS TO IMPROVE THE EFFICIENCY OF THE RECEPTION SYSTEM

Article 22 Cooperation

Member States shall regularly inform the Commission on the data concerning the number of persons, broken down by sex and age, covered by reception conditions and provide full information on the type, name and format of the documents provided for by Article 6.

Article 23 Guidance, monitoring and control system

Member States shall, with due respect to their constitutional structure, ensure that appropriate guidance, monitoring and control of the level of reception conditions are established.

Article 24 Staff and resources

1. Member States shall take appropriate measures to ensure that authorities and other organisations implementing this Directive have received the necessary basic training with respect to the needs of both male and female applicants.

2. Member States shall allocate the necessary resources in connection with the national provisions enacted to implement this Directive.

CHAPTER VII
FINAL PROVISIONS

Article 25 Reports

By 6 August 2006, the Commission shall report to the European Parliament and the Council on the application of this Directive and shall propose any amendments that are necessary.

Member States shall send the Commission all the information that is appropriate for drawing up the report, including the statistical data provided for by Article 22 by 6 February 2006.

After presenting the report, the Commission shall report to the European Parliament and the Council on the application of this Directive at least every five years.

Article 26 Transposition

1. Member States shall bring into force the laws, regulations and administrative provisions necessary to comply with this Directive by 6 February 2005. They shall forthwith inform the Commission thereof.

When the Member States adopt these measures, they shall contain a reference to this Directive or shall be accompanied by such a reference on the occasion of their official publication. Member States shall determine how such a reference is to be made.

2. Member States shall communicate to the Commission the text of the provisions of national law which they adopt in the field relating to the enforcement of this Directive.

Article 27 Entry into force

This Directive shall enter into force on the day of its publication in the Official Journal of the European Union.

Article 28 Addressees

This Directive is addressed to the Member States in accordance with the Treaty establishing the European Union.

EUROPEAN PARLIAMENT & COUNCIL DIRECTIVE 2004/38/EC (THE CITIZENS' DIRECTIVE)

of 29 April 2004 on the right of citizens of the Union and their family members to move and reside freely within the territory of the Member States amending Regulation (EEC) No 1612/68 and repealing Directives 64/221/EEC, 68/360/EEC, 72/194/EEC, 73/148/EEC, 75/34/EEC, 75/35/EEC, 90/364/EEC, 90/365/EEC and 93/96/EEC

Notes

Date of publication in Official Journal: OJ L158, 30.04.2004, p 77.

THE EUROPEAN PARLIAMENT AND THE COUNCIL OF THE EUROPEAN UNION,

Having regard to the Treaty establishing the European Community, and in particular Articles 12, 18, 40, 44 and 52 thereof,

Having regard to the proposal from the Commission[1],

Having regard to the Opinion of the European Economic and Social Committee[2],

Having regard to the Opinion of the Committee of the Regions[3],

Acting in accordance with the procedure laid down in Article 251 of the Treaty[4],

Whereas:

(1) Citizenship of the Union confers on every citizen of the Union a primary and individual right to move and reside freely within the territory of the Member States, subject to the limitations and conditions laid down in the Treaty and to the measures adopted to give it effect.

(2) The free movement of persons constitutes one of the fundamental freedoms of the internal market, which comprises an area without internal frontiers, in which freedom is ensured in accordance with the provisions of the Treaty.

(3) Union citizenship should be the fundamental status of nationals of the Member States when they exercise their right of free movement and residence. It is therefore necessary to codify and review the existing Community instruments dealing separately with workers, self-employed persons, as well as students and other inactive persons in order to simplify and strengthen the right of free movement and residence of all Union citizens.

(4) With a view to remedying this sector-by-sector, piecemeal approach to the right of free movement and residence and facilitating the exercise of this right, there needs to be a single legislative act to amend Council Regulation (EEC) No 1612/68 of 15 October 1968 on freedom of movement for workers within the Community[5], and to repeal the following acts: Council Directive 68/360/EEC of 15 October 1968 on the abolition of restrictions on movement and residence within the Community for workers of Member States and their families[6], Council Directive 73/148/EEC of 21 May 1973 on the abolition of restrictions on movement and residence within the Community for nationals of Member States with regard to establishment and the provision of services[7], Council Directive 90/364/EEC of 28 June 1990 on the right of residence[8], Council Directive 90/365/EEC of 28 June 1990 on the right of residence for employees and self-employed persons who have ceased their occupational activity[9] and Council Directive 93/96/EEC of 29 October 1993 on the right of residence for students[10].

(5) The right of all Union citizens to move and reside freely within the territory of the Member States should, if it is to be exercised under

objective conditions of freedom and dignity, be also granted to their family members, irrespective of nationality. For the purposes of this Directive, the definition of "family member" should also include the registered partner if the legislation of the host Member State treats registered partnership as equivalent to marriage.

(6)   In order to maintain the unity of the family in a broader sense and without prejudice to the prohibition of discrimination on grounds of nationality, the situation of those persons who are not included in the definition of family members under this Directive, and who therefore do not enjoy an automatic right of entry and residence in the host Member State, should be examined by the host Member State on the basis of its own national legislation, in order to decide whether entry and residence could be granted to such persons, taking into consideration their relationship with the Union citizen or any other circumstances, such as their financial or physical dependence on the Union citizen.

(7)   The formalities connected with the free movement of Union citizens within the territory of Member States should be clearly defined, without prejudice to the provisions applicable to national border controls.

(8)   With a view to facilitating the free movement of family members who are not nationals of a Member State, those who have already obtained a residence card should be exempted from the requirement to obtain an entry visa within the meaning of Council Regulation (EC) No 539/2001 of 15 March 2001 listing the third countries whose nationals must be in possession of visas when crossing the external borders and those whose nationals are exempt from that requirement[11] or, where appropriate, of the applicable national legislation.

(9)   Union citizens should have the right of residence in the host Member State for a period not exceeding three months without being subject to any conditions or any formalities other than the requirement to hold a valid identity card or passport, without prejudice to a more favourable treatment applicable to job-seekers as recognised by the case-law of the Court of Justice.

(10)   Persons exercising their right of residence should not, however, become an unreasonable burden on the social assistance system of the host Member State during an initial period of residence. Therefore, the right of residence for Union citizens and their family members for periods in excess of three months should be subject to conditions.

(11)   The fundamental and personal right of residence in another Member State is conferred directly on Union citizens by the Treaty and is not dependent upon their having fulfilled administrative procedures.

(12)   For periods of residence of longer than three months, Member States should have the possibility to require Union citizens to register with the competent authorities in the place of residence, attested by a registration certificate issued to that effect.

(13)   The residence card requirement should be restricted to family members of Union citizens who are not nationals of a Member State for periods of residence of longer than three months.

(14)   The supporting documents required by the competent authorities for the issuing of a registration certificate or of a residence card should be comprehensively specified in order to avoid divergent administrative practices or interpretations constituting an undue obstacle to the exercise of the right of residence by Union citizens and their family members.

(15)   Family members should be legally safeguarded in the event of the death of the Union citizen, divorce, annulment of marriage or termination of a registered partnership. With due regard for family life and human dignity,

and in certain conditions to guard against abuse, measures should therefore be taken to ensure that in such circumstances family members already residing within the territory of the host Member State retain their right of residence exclusively on a personal basis.

(16) As long as the beneficiaries of the right of residence do not become an unreasonable burden on the social assistance system of the host Member State they should not be expelled. Therefore, an expulsion measure should not be the automatic consequence of recourse to the social assistance system. The host Member State should examine whether it is a case of temporary difficulties and take into account the duration of residence, the personal circumstances and the amount of aid granted in order to consider whether the beneficiary has become an unreasonable burden on its social assistance system and to proceed to his expulsion. In no case should an expulsion measure be adopted against workers, self-employed persons or job-seekers as defined by the Court of Justice save on grounds of public policy or public security.

(17) Enjoyment of permanent residence by Union citizens who have chosen to settle long term in the host Member State would strengthen the feeling of Union citizenship and is a key element in promoting social cohesion, which is one of the fundamental objectives of the Union. A right of permanent residence should therefore be laid down for all Union citizens and their family members who have resided in the host Member State in compliance with the conditions laid down in this Directive during a continuous period of five years without becoming subject to an expulsion measure.

(18) In order to be a genuine vehicle for integration into the society of the host Member State in which the Union citizen resides, the right of permanent residence, once obtained, should not be subject to any conditions.

(19) Certain advantages specific to Union citizens who are workers or self-employed persons and to their family members, which may allow these persons to acquire a right of permanent residence before they have resided five years in the host Member State, should be maintained, as these constitute acquired rights, conferred by Commission Regulation (EEC) No 1251/70 of 29 June 1970 on the right of workers to remain in the territory of a Member State after having been employed in that State[12] and Council Directive 75/34/EEC of 17 December 1974 concerning the right of nationals of a Member State to remain in the territory of another Member State after having pursued therein an activity in a self-employed capacity[13].

(20) In accordance with the prohibition of discrimination on grounds of nationality, all Union citizens and their family members residing in a Member State on the basis of this Directive should enjoy, in that Member State, equal treatment with nationals in areas covered by the Treaty, subject to such specific provisions as are expressly provided for in the Treaty and secondary law.

(21) However, it should be left to the host Member State to decide whether it will grant social assistance during the first three months of residence, or for a longer period in the case of job-seekers, to Union citizens other than those who are workers or self-employed persons or who retain that status or their family members, or maintenance assistance for studies, including vocational training, prior to acquisition of the right of permanent residence, to these same persons.

(22) The Treaty allows restrictions to be placed on the right of free movement and residence on grounds of public policy, public security or public health. In order to ensure a tighter definition of the circumstances and

procedural safeguards subject to which Union citizens and their family members may be denied leave to enter or may be expelled, this Directive should replace Council Directive 64/221/EEC of 25 February 1964 on the coordination of special measures concerning the movement and residence of foreign nationals, which are justified on grounds of public policy, public security or public health[14].

(23) Expulsion of Union citizens and their family members on grounds of public policy or public security is a measure that can seriously harm persons who, having availed themselves of the rights and freedoms conferred on them by the Treaty, have become genuinely integrated into the host Member State. The scope for such measures should therefore be limited in accordance with the principle of proportionality to take account of the degree of integration of the persons concerned, the length of their residence in the host Member State, their age, state of health, family and economic situation and the links with their country of origin.

(24) Accordingly, the greater the degree of integration of Union citizens and their family members in the host Member State, the greater the degree of protection against expulsion should be. Only in exceptional circumstances, where there are imperative grounds of public security, should an expulsion measure be taken against Union citizens who have resided for many years in the territory of the host Member State, in particular when they were born and have resided there throughout their life. In addition, such exceptional circumstances should also apply to an expulsion measure taken against minors, in order to protect their links with their family, in accordance with the United Nations Convention on the Rights of the Child, of 20 November 1989.

(25) Procedural safeguards should also be specified in detail in order to ensure a high level of protection of the rights of Union citizens and their family members in the event of their being denied leave to enter or reside in another Member State, as well as to uphold the principle that any action taken by the authorities must be properly justified.

(26) In all events, judicial redress procedures should be available to Union citizens and their family members who have been refused leave to enter or reside in another Member State.

(27) In line with the case-law of the Court of Justice prohibiting Member States from issuing orders excluding for life persons covered by this Directive from their territory, the right of Union citizens and their family members who have been excluded from the territory of a Member State to submit a fresh application after a reasonable period, and in any event after a three year period from enforcement of the final exclusion order, should be confirmed.

(28) To guard against abuse of rights or fraud, notably marriages of convenience or any other form of relationships contracted for the sole purpose of enjoying the right of free movement and residence, Member States should have the possibility to adopt the necessary measures.

(29) This Directive should not affect more favourable national provisions.

(30) With a view to examining how further to facilitate the exercise of the right of free movement and residence, a report should be prepared by the Commission in order to evaluate the opportunity to present any necessary proposals to this effect, notably on the extension of the period of residence with no conditions.

(31) This Directive respects the fundamental rights and freedoms and observes the principles recognised in particular by the Charter of Fundamental Rights of the European Union. In accordance with the prohibition of

discrimination contained in the Charter, Member States should implement this Directive without discrimination between the beneficiaries of this Directive on grounds such as sex, race, colour, ethnic or social origin, genetic characteristics, language, religion or beliefs, political or other opinion, membership of an ethnic minority, property, birth, disability, age or sexual orientation,

[1] OJ C 270 E, 25.9.2001, p. 150.

[2] OJ C 149, 21.6.2002, p. 46.

[3] OJ C 192, 12.8.2002, p. 17.

[4] Opinion of the European Parliament of 11 February 2003 (OJ C 43 E, 19.2.2004, p.42), Council Common Position of 5 December 2003 (OJ C 54 E, 2.3.2004, p.12) and Position of the European Parliament of 10 March 2004 (not yet published in the Official Journal).

[5] OJ L 257, 19.10.1968, p. 2. Regulation as last amended by Regulation (EEC) No 2434/92 (OJ L 245, 26.8.1992, p. 1).

[6] OJ L 257, 19.10.1968, p. 13. Directive as last amended by the 2003 Act of Accession.

[7] OJ L 172, 28.6.1973, p. 14.

[8] OJ L 180, 13.7.1990, p. 26.

[9] OJ L 180, 13.7.1990, p. 28.

[10] OJ L 317, 18.12.1993, p. 59.

[11] OJ L 81, 21.3.2001, p. 1. Regulation as last amended by Regulation (EC) No 453/2003 (OJ L 69, 13.3.2003, p. 10).

[12] OJ L 142, 30.6.1970, p. 24.

[13] OJ L 14, 20.1.1975, p. 10.

[14] OJ 56, 4.4.1964, p. 850. Directive as last amended by Directive 75/35/EEC (OJ 14, 20.1.1975, p. 14).

HAVE ADOPTED THIS DIRECTIVE:

CHAPTER I
GENERAL PROVISIONS

Article 1 Subject
This Directive lays down:

(a)   the conditions governing the exercise of the right of free movement and residence within the territory of the Member States by Union citizens and their family members;

(b)   the right of permanent residence in the territory of the Member States for Union citizens and their family members;

(c)   the limits placed on the rights set out in (a) and (b) on grounds of public policy, public security or public health.

Article 2 Definitions
For the purposes of this Directive:

(1)   "Union citizen" means any person having the nationality of a Member State;

(2)   "Family member" means:

(a)   the spouse;

(b)   the partner with whom the Union citizen has contracted a registered partnership, on the basis of the legislation of a Member State, if the legislation of the host Member State treats registered partnerships as equivalent to marriage and in accordance with the conditions laid down in the relevant legislation of the host Member State;

(c) the direct descendants who are under the age of 21 or are dependants and those of the spouse or partner as defined in point (b);

(d) the dependent direct relatives in the ascending line and those of the spouse or partner as defined in point (b);

(3) "Host Member State" means the Member State to which a Union citizen moves in order to exercise his/her right of free movement and residence.

Article 3 Beneficiaries

1. This Directive shall apply to all Union citizens who move to or reside in a Member State other than that of which they are a national, and to their family members as defined in point 2 of Article 2 who accompany or join them.

2. Without prejudice to any right to free movement and residence the persons concerned may have in their own right, the host Member State shall, in accordance with its national legislation, facilitate entry and residence for the following persons:

(a) any other family members, irrespective of their nationality, not falling under the definition in point 2 of Article 2 who, in the country from which they have come, are dependants or members of the household of the Union citizen having the primary right of residence, or where serious health grounds strictly require the personal care of the family member by the Union citizen;

(b) the partner with whom the Union citizen has a durable relationship, duly attested.

The host Member State shall undertake an extensive examination of the personal circumstances and shall justify any denial of entry or residence to these people.

CHAPTER II
RIGHT OF EXIT AND ENTRY

Article 4 Right of exit

1. Without prejudice to the provisions on travel documents applicable to national border controls, all Union citizens with a valid identity card or passport and their family members who are not nationals of a Member State and who hold a valid passport shall have the right to leave the territory of a Member State to travel to another Member State.

2. No exit visa or equivalent formality may be imposed on the persons to whom paragraph 1 applies.

3. Member States shall, acting in accordance with their laws, issue to their own nationals, and renew, an identity card or passport stating their nationality.

4. The passport shall be valid at least for all Member States and for countries through which the holder must pass when travelling between Member States. Where the law of a Member State does not provide for identity cards to be issued, the period of validity of any passport on being issued or renewed shall be not less than five years.

Article 5 Right of entry

1. Without prejudice to the provisions on travel documents applicable to national border controls, Member States shall grant Union citizens leave to enter their territory with a valid identity card or passport and shall grant family members who are not nationals of a Member State leave to enter their territory with a valid passport. No entry visa or equivalent formality may be imposed on Union citizens.

2. Family members who are not nationals of a Member State shall only be required to have an entry visa in accordance with Regulation (EC) No 539/2001 or, where

appropriate, with national law. For the purposes of this Directive, possession of the valid residence card referred to in Article 10 shall exempt such family members from the visa requirement.

Member States shall grant such persons every facility to obtain the necessary visas. Such visas shall be issued free of charge as soon as possible and on the basis of an accelerated procedure.

3. The host Member State shall not place an entry or exit stamp in the passport of family members who are not nationals of a Member State provided that they present the residence card provided for in Article 10.

4. Where a Union citizen, or a family member who is not a national of a Member State, does not have the necessary travel documents or, if required, the necessary visas, the Member State concerned shall, before turning them back, give such persons every reasonable opportunity to obtain the necessary documents or have them brought to them within a reasonable period of time or to corroborate or prove by other means that they are covered by the right of free movement and residence.

5. The Member State may require the person concerned to report his/her presence within its territory within a reasonable and non-discriminatory period of time. Failure to comply with this requirement may make the person concerned liable to proportionate and non-discriminatory sanctions.

CHAPTER III
RIGHT OF RESIDENCE

Article 6 Right of residence for up to three months

1. Union citizens shall have the right of residence on the territory of another Member State for a period of up to three months without any conditions or any formalities other than the requirement to hold a valid identity card or passport.

2. The provisions of paragraph 1 shall also apply to family members in possession of a valid passport who are not nationals of a Member State, accompanying or joining the Union citizen.

Article 7 Right of residence for more than three months

1. All Union citizens shall have the right of residence on the territory of another Member State for a period of longer than three months if they:

    (a)   are workers or self-employed persons in the host Member State; or

    (b)   have sufficient resources for themselves and their family members not to become a burden on the social assistance system of the host Member State during their period of residence and have comprehensive sickness insurance cover in the host Member State; or

    (c)

        —   are enrolled at a private or public establishment, accredited or financed by the host Member State on the basis of its legislation or administrative practice, for the principal purpose of following a course of study, including vocational training; and

        —   have comprehensive sickness insurance cover in the host Member State and assure the relevant national authority, by means of a declaration or by such equivalent means as they may choose, that they have sufficient resources for themselves and their family members not to become a burden on the social assistance system of the host Member State during their period of residence; or

    (d)   are family members accompanying or joining a Union citizen who satisfies the conditions referred to in points (a), (b) or (c).

2. The right of residence provided for in paragraph 1 shall extend to family members who are not nationals of a Member State, accompanying or joining the Union citizen

in the host Member State, provided that such Union citizen satisfies the conditions referred to in paragraph 1(a), (b) or (c).

3. For the purposes of paragraph 1(a), a Union citizen who is no longer a worker or self-employed person shall retain the status of worker or self-employed person in the following circumstances:

(a) he/she is temporarily unable to work as the result of an illness or accident;

(b) he/she is in duly recorded involuntary unemployment after having been employed for more than one year and has registered as a job-seeker with the relevant employment office;

(c) he/she is in duly recorded involuntary unemployment after completing a fixed-term employment contract of less than a year or after having become involuntarily unemployed during the first twelve months and has registered as a job-seeker with the relevant employment office. In this case, the status of worker shall be retained for no less than six months;

(d) he/she embarks on vocational training. Unless he/she is involuntarily unemployed, the retention of the status of worker shall require the training to be related to the previous employment.

4. By way of derogation from paragraphs 1(d) and 2 above, only the spouse, the registered partner provided for in Article 2(2)(b) and dependent children shall have the right of residence as family members of a Union citizen meeting the conditions under 1(c) above. Article 3(2) shall apply to his/her dependent direct relatives in the ascending lines and those of his/her spouse or registered partner.

Article 8 Administrative formalities for Union citizens

1. Without prejudice to Article 5(5), for periods of residence longer than three months, the host Member State may require Union citizens to register with the relevant authorities.

2. The deadline for registration may not be less than three months from the date of arrival. A registration certificate shall be issued immediately, stating the name and address of the person registering and the date of the registration. Failure to comply with the registration requirement may render the person concerned liable to proportionate and non-discriminatory sanctions.

3. For the registration certificate to be issued, Member States may only require that:

– Union citizens to whom point (a) of Article 7(1) applies present a valid identity card or passport, a confirmation of engagement from the employer or a certificate of employment, or proof that they are self-employed persons;

– Union citizens to whom point (b) of Article 7(1) applies present a valid identity card or passport and provide proof that they satisfy the conditions laid down therein;

– Union citizens to whom point (c) of Article 7(1) applies present a valid identity card or passport, provide proof of enrolment at an accredited establishment and of comprehensive sickness insurance cover and the declaration or equivalent means referred to in point (c) of Article 7(1). Member States may not require this declaration to refer to any specific amount of resources.

4. Member States may not lay down a fixed amount which they regard as "sufficient resources" but they must take into account the personal situation of the person concerned. In all cases this amount shall not be higher than the threshold below which nationals of the host Member State become eligible for social assistance, or, where this criterion is not applicable, higher than the minimum social security pension paid by the host Member State.

5. For the registration certificate to be issued to family members of Union citizens, who are themselves Union citizens, Member States may require the following documents to be presented:

- (a) a valid identity card or passport;
- (b) a document attesting to the existence of a family relationship or of a registered partnership;
- (c) where appropriate, the registration certificate of the Union citizen whom they are accompanying or joining;
- (d) in cases falling under points (c) and (d) of Article 2(2), documentary evidence that the conditions laid down therein are met;
- (e) in cases falling under Article 3(2)(a), a document issued by the relevant authority in the country of origin or country from which they are arriving certifying that they are dependants or members of the household of the Union citizen, or proof of the existence of serious health grounds which strictly require the personal care of the family member by the Union citizen;
- (f) in cases falling under Article 3(2)(b), proof of the existence of a durable relationship with the Union citizen.

Article 9 Administrative formalities for family members who are not nationals of a Member State

1. Member States shall issue a residence card to family members of a Union citizen who are not nationals of a Member State, where the planned period of residence is for more than three months.

2. The deadline for submitting the residence card application may not be less than three months from the date of arrival.

3. Failure to comply with the requirement to apply for a residence card may make the person concerned liable to proportionate and non-discriminatory sanctions.

Article 10 Issue of residence cards

1. The right of residence of family members of a Union citizen who are not nationals of a Member State shall be evidenced by the issuing of a document called "Residence card of a family member of a Union citizen" no later than six months from the date on which they submit the application. A certificate of application for the residence card shall be issued immediately.

2. For the residence card to be issued, Member States shall require presentation of the following documents:

- (a) a valid passport;
- (b) a document attesting to the existence of a family relationship or of a registered partnership;
- (c) the registration certificate or, in the absence of a registration system, any other proof of residence in the host Member State of the Union citizen whom they are accompanying or joining;
- (d) in cases falling under points (c) and (d) of Article 2(2), documentary evidence that the conditions laid down therein are met;
- (e) in cases falling under Article 3(2)(a), a document issued by the relevant authority in the country of origin or country from which they are arriving certifying that they are dependants or members of the household of the Union citizen, or proof of the existence of serious health grounds which strictly require the personal care of the family member by the Union citizen;
- (f) in cases falling under Article 3(2)(b), proof of the existence of a durable relationship with the Union citizen.

Article 11 Validity of the residence card

1. The residence card provided for by Article 10(1) shall be valid for five years from the date of issue or for the envisaged period of residence of the Union citizen, if this period is less than five years.

2. The validity of the residence card shall not be affected by temporary absences not exceeding six months a year, or by absences of a longer duration for compulsory military service or by one absence of a maximum of twelve consecutive months for important reasons such as pregnancy and childbirth, serious illness, study or vocational training, or a posting in another Member State or a third country.

Article 12 Retention of the right of residence by family members in the event of death or departure of the Union citizen

1. Without prejudice to the second subparagraph, the Union citizen's death or departure from the host Member State shall not affect the right of residence of his/her family members who are nationals of a Member State.

Before acquiring the right of permanent residence, the persons concerned must meet the conditions laid down in points (a), (b), (c) or (d) of Article 7(1).

2. Without prejudice to the second subparagraph, the Union citizen's death shall not entail loss of the right of residence of his/her family members who are not nationals of a Member State and who have been residing in the host Member State as family members for at least one year before the Union citizen's death.

Before acquiring the right of permanent residence, the right of residence of the persons concerned shall remain subject to the requirement that they are able to show that they are workers or self-employed persons or that they have sufficient resources for themselves and their family members not to become a burden on the social assistance system of the host Member State during their period of residence and have comprehensive sickness insurance cover in the host Member State, or that they are members of the family, already constituted in the host Member State, of a person satisfying these requirements. "Sufficient resources" shall be as defined in Article 8(4). Such family members shall retain their right of residence exclusively on a personal basis.

3. The Union citizen's departure from the host Member State or his/her death shall not entail loss of the right of residence of his/her children or of the parent who has actual custody of the children, irrespective of nationality, if the children reside in the host Member State and are enrolled at an educational establishment, for the purpose of studying there, until the completion of their studies.

Article 13 Retention of the right of residence by family members in the event of divorce, annulment of marriage or termination of registered partnership

1. Without prejudice to the second subparagraph, divorce, annulment of the Union citizen's marriage or termination of his/her registered partnership, as referred to in point 2(b) of Article 2 shall not affect the right of residence of his/her family members who are nationals of a Member State.

Before acquiring the right of permanent residence, the persons concerned must meet the conditions laid down in points (a), (b), (c) or (d) of Article 7(1).

2. Without prejudice to the second subparagraph, divorce, annulment of marriage or termination of the registered partnership referred to in point 2(b) of Article 2 shall not entail loss of the right of residence of a Union citizen's family members who are not nationals of a Member State where:

    (a)   prior to initiation of the divorce or annulment proceedings or termination of the registered partnership referred to in point 2(b) of Article 2, the marriage or registered partnership has lasted at least three years, including one year in the host Member State; or (b)　by agreement between the spouses or the partners referred to in point 2(b) of Article 2 or by court order, the spouse or partner who is not a national of a Member State has custody of the Union citizen's children; or

(c)　this is warranted by particularly difficult circumstances, such as having been a victim of domestic violence while the marriage or registered partnership was subsisting; or

(d)　by agreement between the spouses or partners referred to in point 2(b) of Article 2 or by court order, the spouse or partner who is not a national of a Member State has the right of access to a minor child, provided that the court has ruled that such access must be in the host Member State, and for as long as is required.

Before acquiring the right of permanent residence, the right of residence of the persons concerned shall remain subject to the requirement that they are able to show that they are workers or self-employed persons or that they have sufficient resources for themselves and their family members not to become a burden on the social assistance system of the host Member State during their period of residence and have comprehensive sickness insurance cover in the host Member State, or that they are members of the family, already constituted in the host Member State, of a person satisfying these requirements. "Sufficient resources" shall be as defined in Article 8(4). Such family members shall retain their right of residence exclusively on personal basis.

Article 14 Retention of the right of residence

1. Union citizens and their family members shall have the right of residence provided for in Article 6, as long as they do not become an unreasonable burden on the social assistance system of the host Member State.

2. Union citizens and their family members shall have the right of residence provided for in Articles 7, 12 and 13 as long as they meet the conditions set out therein.

In specific cases where there is a reasonable doubt as to whether a Union citizen or his/her family members satisfies the conditions set out in Articles 7, 12 and 13, Member States may verify if these conditions are fulfilled. This verification shall not be carried out systematically.

3. An expulsion measure shall not be the automatic consequence of a Union citizen's or his or her family member's recourse to the social assistance system of the host Member State.

4. By way of derogation from paragraphs 1 and 2 and without prejudice to the provisions of Chapter VI, an expulsion measure may in no case be adopted against Union citizens or their family members if:

(a)　the Union citizens are workers or self-employed persons, or

(b)　the Union citizens entered the territory of the host Member State in order to seek employment. In this case, the Union citizens and their family members may not be expelled for as long as the Union citizens can provide evidence that they are continuing to seek employment and that they have a genuine chance of being engaged.

Article 15 Procedural safeguards

1. The procedures provided for by Articles 30 and 31 shall apply by analogy to all decisions restricting free movement of Union citizens and their family members on grounds other than public policy, public security or public health.

2. Expiry of the identity card or passport on the basis of which the person concerned entered the host Member State and was issued with a registration certificate or residence card shall not constitute a ground for expulsion from the host Member State.

3. The host Member State may not impose a ban on entry in the context of an expulsion decision to which paragraph 1 applies.

CHAPTER IV
RIGHT OF PERMANENT RESIDENCE

SECTION I

ELIGIBILITY

Article 16 General rule for Union citizens and their family members

1. Union citizens who have resided legally for a continuous period of five years in the host Member State shall have the right of permanent residence there. This right shall not be subject to the conditions provided for in Chapter III.

2. Paragraph 1 shall apply also to family members who are not nationals of a Member State and have legally resided with the Union citizen in the host Member State for a continuous period of five years.

3. Continuity of residence shall not be affected by temporary absences not exceeding a total of six months a year, or by absences of a longer duration for compulsory military service, or by one absence of a maximum of twelve consecutive months for important reasons such as pregnancy and childbirth, serious illness, study or vocational training, or a posting in another Member State or a third country.

4. Once acquired, the right of permanent residence shall be lost only through absence from the host Member State for a period exceeding two consecutive years.

Article 17 Exemptions for persons no longer working in the host Member State and their family members

1. By way of derogation from Article 16, the right of permanent residence in the host Member State shall be enjoyed before completion of a continuous period of five years of residence by:

    (a)   workers or self-employed persons who, at the time they stop working, have reached the age laid down by the law of that Member State for entitlement to an old age pension or workers who cease paid employment to take early retirement, provided that they have been working in that Member State for at least the preceding twelve months and have resided there continuously for more than three years.

If the law of the host Member State does not grant the right to an old age pension to certain categories of self-employed persons, the age condition shall be deemed to have been met once the person concerned has reached the age of 60;

    (b)   workers or self-employed persons who have resided continuously in the host Member State for more than two years and stop working there as a result of permanent incapacity to work.

If such incapacity is the result of an accident at work or an occupational disease entitling the person concerned to a benefit payable in full or in part by an institution in the host Member State, no condition shall be imposed as to length of residence;

    (c)   workers or self-employed persons who, after three years of continuous employment and residence in the host Member State, work in an employed or self-employed capacity in another Member State, while retaining their place of residence in the host Member State, to which they return, as a rule, each day or at least once a week.

For the purposes of entitlement to the rights referred to in points (a) and (b), periods of employment spent in the Member State in which the person concerned is working shall be regarded as having been spent in the host Member State.

Periods of involuntary unemployment duly recorded by the relevant employment office, periods not worked for reasons not of the person's own making and absences from work or cessation of work due to illness or accident shall be regarded as periods of employment.

2. The conditions as to length of residence and employment laid down in point (a) of paragraph 1 and the condition as to length of residence laid down in point (b) of paragraph 1 shall not apply if the worker's or the self-employed person's spouse or partner as referred to in point 2(b) of Article 2 is a national of the host Member State or has lost the nationality of that Member State by marriage to that worker or self-employed person.

3. Irrespective of nationality, the family members of a worker or a self-employed person who are residing with him in the territory of the host Member State shall have the right of permanent residence in that Member State, if the worker or self-employed person has acquired himself the right of permanent residence in that Member State on the basis of paragraph 1.

4. If, however, the worker or self-employed person dies while still working but before acquiring permanent residence status in the host Member State on the basis of paragraph 1, his family members who are residing with him in the host Member State shall acquire the right of permanent residence there, on condition that:

(a) the worker or self-employed person had, at the time of death, resided continuously on the territory of that Member State for two years; or

(b) the death resulted from an accident at work or an occupational disease; or

(c) the surviving spouse lost the nationality of that Member State following marriage to the worker or self-employed person.

Article 18 Acquisition of the right of permanent residence by certain family members who are not nationals of a Member State

Without prejudice to Article 17, the family members of a Union citizen to whom Articles 12(2) and 13(2) apply, who satisfy the conditions laid down therein, shall acquire the right of permanent residence after residing legally for a period of five consecutive years in the host Member State.

SECTION II

ADMINISTRATIVE FORMALITIES

Article 19 Document certifying permanent residence for Union citizens

1. Upon application Member States shall issue Union citizens entitled to permanent residence, after having verified duration of residence, with a document certifying permanent residence.

2. The document certifying permanent residence shall be issued as soon as possible.

Article 20 Permanent residence card for family members who are not nationals of a Member State

1. Member States shall issue family members who are not nationals of a Member State entitled to permanent residence with a permanent residence card within six months of the submission of the application. The permanent residence card shall be renewable automatically every ten years.

2. The application for a permanent residence card shall be submitted before the residence card expires. Failure to comply with the requirement to apply for a permanent residence card may render the person concerned liable to proportionate and non-discriminatory sanctions.

3. Interruption in residence not exceeding two consecutive years shall not affect the validity of the permanent residence card.

Article 21 Continuity of residence

For the purposes of this Directive, continuity of residence may be attested by any means of proof in use in the host Member State. Continuity of residence is broken by any expulsion decision duly enforced against the person concerned.

CHAPTER V
PROVISIONS COMMON TO THE RIGHT OF RESIDENCE AND THE RIGHT OF PERMANENT RESIDENCE

Article 22 Territorial scope
The right of residence and the right of permanent residence shall cover the whole territory of the host Member State. Member States may impose territorial restrictions on the right of residence and the right of permanent residence only where the same restrictions apply to their own nationals.

Article 23 Related rights
Irrespective of nationality, the family members of a Union citizen who have the right of residence or the right of permanent residence in a Member State shall be entitled to take up employment or self-employment there.

Article 24 Equal treatment
1. Subject to such specific provisions as are expressly provided for in the Treaty and secondary law, all Union citizens residing on the basis of this Directive in the territory of the host Member State shall enjoy equal treatment with the nationals of that Member State within the scope of the Treaty. The benefit of this right shall be extended to family members who are not nationals of a Member State and who have the right of residence or permanent residence.
2. By way of derogation from paragraph 1, the host Member State shall not be obliged to confer entitlement to social assistance during the first three months of residence or, where appropriate, the longer period provided for in Article 14(4)(b), nor shall it be obliged, prior to acquisition of the right of permanent residence, to grant maintenance aid for studies, including vocational training, consisting in student grants or student loans to persons other than workers, self-employed persons, persons who retain such status and members of their families.

Article 25 General provisions concerning residence documents
1. Possession of a registration certificate as referred to in Article 8, of a document certifying permanent residence, of a certificate attesting submission of an application for a family member residence card, of a residence card or of a permanent residence card, may under no circumstances be made a precondition for the exercise of a right or the completion of an administrative formality, as entitlement to rights may be attested by any other means of proof.
2. All documents mentioned in paragraph 1 shall be issued free of charge or for a charge not exceeding that imposed on nationals for the issuing of similar documents.

Article 26 Checks
Member States may carry out checks on compliance with any requirement deriving from their national legislation for non-nationals always to carry their registration certificate or residence card, provided that the same requirement applies to their own nationals as regards their identity card. In the event of failure to comply with this requirement, Member States may impose the same sanctions as those imposed on their own nationals for failure to carry their identity card.

CHAPTER VI
RESTRICTIONS ON THE RIGHT OF ENTRY AND THE RIGHT OF RESI-DENCE ON GROUNDS OF PUBLIC POLICY, PUBLIC SECURITY OR PUBLIC HEALTH

Article 27 General principles
1. Subject to the provisions of this Chapter, Member States may restrict the freedom of movement and residence of Union citizens and their family members, irrespective of

nationality, on grounds of public policy, public security or public health. These grounds shall not be invoked to serve economic ends.

2.   Measures taken on grounds of public policy or public security shall comply with the principle of proportionality and shall be based exclusively on the personal conduct of the individual concerned. Previous criminal convictions shall not in themselves constitute grounds for taking such measures.

The personal conduct of the individual concerned must represent a genuine, present and sufficiently serious threat affecting one of the fundamental interests of society. Justifications that are isolated from the particulars of the case or that rely on considerations of general prevention shall not be accepted.

3.   In order to ascertain whether the person concerned represents a danger for public policy or public security, when issuing the registration certificate or, in the absence of a registration system, not later than three months from the date of arrival of the person concerned on its territory or from the date of reporting his/her presence within the territory, as provided for in Article 5(5), or when issuing the residence card, the host Member State may, should it consider this essential, request the Member State of origin and, if need be, other Member States to provide information concerning any previous police record the person concerned may have. Such enquiries shall not be made as a matter of routine. The Member State consulted shall give its reply within two months.

4.   The Member State which issued the passport or identity card shall allow the holder of the document who has been expelled on grounds of public policy, public security, or public health from another Member State to re-enter its territory without any formality even if the document is no longer valid or the nationality of the holder is in dispute.

Article 28 Protection against expulsion

1.   Before taking an expulsion decision on grounds of public policy or public security, the host Member State shall take account of considerations such as how long the individual concerned has resided on its territory, his/her age, state of health, family and economic situation, social and cultural integration into the host Member State and the extent of his/her links with the country of origin.

2.   The host Member State may not take an expulsion decision against Union citizens or their family members, irrespective of nationality, who have the right of permanent residence on its territory, except on serious grounds of public policy or public security.

3.   An expulsion decision may not be taken against Union citizens, except if the decision is based on imperative grounds of public security, as defined by Member States, if they:

   (a)   have resided in the host Member State for the previous ten years; or
   (b)   are a minor, except if the expulsion is necessary for the best interests of the child, as provided for in the United Nations Convention on the Rights of the Child of 20 November 1989.

Article 29 Public health

1.   The only diseases justifying measures restricting freedom of movement shall be the diseases with epidemic potential as defined by the relevant instruments of the World Health Organisation and other infectious diseases or contagious parasitic diseases if they are the subject of protection provisions applying to nationals of the host Member State.

2.   Diseases occurring after a three-month period from the date of arrival shall not constitute grounds for expulsion from the territory.

3.   Where there are serious indications that it is necessary, Member States may, within three months of the date of arrival, require persons entitled to the right of residence to undergo, free of charge, a medical examination to certify that they are not suffering from any of the conditions referred to in paragraph 1. Such medical examinations may not be required as a matter of routine.

Article 30 Notification of decisions

1. The persons concerned shall be notified in writing of any decision taken under Article 27(1), in such a way that they are able to comprehend its content and the implications for them.

2. The persons concerned shall be informed, precisely and in full, of the public policy, public security or public health grounds on which the decision taken in their case is based, unless this is contrary to the interests of State security.

3. The notification shall specify the court or administrative authority with which the person concerned may lodge an appeal, the time limit for the appeal and, where applicable, the time allowed for the person to leave the territory of the Member State. Save in duly substantiated cases of urgency, the time allowed to leave the territory shall be not less than one month from the date of notification.

Article 31 Procedural safeguards

1. The persons concerned shall have access to judicial and, where appropriate, administrative redress procedures in the host Member State to appeal against or seek review of any decision taken against them on the grounds of public policy, public security or public health.

2. Where the application for appeal against or judicial review of the expulsion decision is accompanied by an application for an interim order to suspend enforcement of that decision, actual removal from the territory may not take place until such time as the decision on the interim order has been taken, except:

  − where the expulsion decision is based on a previous judicial decision; or

  − where the persons concerned have had previous access to judicial review; or

  − where the expulsion decision is based on imperative grounds of public security under Article 28(3).

3. The redress procedures shall allow for an examination of the legality of the decision, as well as of the facts and circumstances on which the proposed measure is based. They shall ensure that the decision is not disproportionate, particularly in view of the requirements laid down in Article 28.

4. Member States may exclude the individual concerned from their territory pending the redress procedure, but they may not prevent the individual from submitting his/her defence in person, except when his/her appearance may cause serious troubles to public policy or public security or when the appeal or judicial review concerns a denial of entry to the territory.

Article 32 Duration of exclusion orders

1. Persons excluded on grounds of public policy or public security may submit an application for lifting of the exclusion order after a reasonable period, depending on the circumstances, and in any event after three years from enforcement of the final exclusion order which has been validly adopted in accordance with Community law, by putting forward arguments to establish that there has been a material change in the circumstances which justified the decision ordering their exclusion.

The Member State concerned shall reach a decision on this application within six months of its submission.

2. The persons referred to in paragraph 1 shall have no right of entry to the territory of the Member State concerned while their application is being considered.

Article 33 Expulsion as a penalty or legal consequence

1. Expulsion orders may not be issued by the host Member State as a penalty or legal consequence of a custodial penalty, unless they conform to the requirements of Articles 27, 28 and 29.

2. If an expulsion order, as provided for in paragraph 1, is enforced more than two years after it was issued, the Member State shall check that the individual concerned is

currently and genuinely a threat to public policy or public security and shall assess whether there has been any material change in the circumstances since the expulsion order was issued.

CHAPTER VII
FINAL PROVISIONS

Article 34 Publicity

Member States shall disseminate information concerning the rights and obligations of Union citizens and their family members on the subjects covered by this Directive, particularly by means of awareness-raising campaigns conducted through national and local media and other means of communication.

Article 35 Abuse of rights

Member States may adopt the necessary measures to refuse, terminate or withdraw any right conferred by this Directive in the case of abuse of rights or fraud, such as marriages of convenience. Any such measure shall be proportionate and subject to the procedural safeguards provided for in Articles 30 and 31.

Article 36 Sanctions

Member States shall lay down provisions on the sanctions applicable to breaches of national rules adopted for the implementation of this Directive and shall take the measures required for their application. The sanctions laid down shall be effective and proportionate. Member States shall notify the Commission of these provisions not later than . . . * and as promptly as possible in the case of any subsequent changes.

* Two years from the date of entry into force of this Directive.

Article 37 More favourable national provisions

The provisions of this Directive shall not affect any laws, regulations or administrative provisions laid down by a Member State which would be more favourable to the persons covered by this Directive.

Article 38 Repeals

1. Articles 10 and 11 of Regulation (EEC) No 1612/68 shall be repealed with effect from . . . *

2. Directives 64/221/EEC, 68/360/EEC, 72/194/EEC, 73/148/EEC, 75/34/EEC, 75/35/EEC, 90/364/EEC, 90/365/EEC and 93/96/EEC shall be repealed with effect from . . . *

3. References made to the repealed provisions and Directives shall be construed as being made to this Directive.

* Two years from the date of entry into force of this Directive.

Article 39 Report

No later than . . . * the Commission shall submit a report on the application of this Directive to the European Parliament and the Council, together with any necessary proposals, notably on the opportunity to extend the period of time during which Union citizens and their family members may reside in the territory of the host Member State without any conditions. The Member States shall provide the Commission with the information needed to produce the report.

* Four years from the date of entry into force of this Directive.

Article 40 Transposition

1. Member States shall bring into force the laws, regulations and administrative provisions necessary to comply with this Directive by . . . *

When Member States adopt those measures, they shall contain a reference to this Directive or shall be accompanied by such a reference on the occasion of their official publication. The methods of making such reference shall be laid down by the Member States.

* Two years from the date of entry into force of this Directive.

2. Member States shall communicate to the Commission the text of the provisions of national law which they adopt in the field covered by this Directive together with a table showing how the provisions of this Directive correspond to the national provisions adopted.

Article 41 Entry into force

This Directive shall enter into force on the day of its publication in the Official Journal of the European Union.

Article 42 Addressees

This Directive is addressed to the Member States.

COUNCIL DIRECTIVE 2004/83/EC (THE QUALIFICATION DIRECTIVE)

of 29 April 2004 on minimum standards for the qualification and status of third country nationals or stateless persons as refugees or as persons who otherwise need international protection and the content of the protection granted

Notes

Date of publication in Official Journal: OJ L304, 30.09.2004, p 12.

THE COUNCIL OF THE EUROPEAN UNION,

Having regard to the Treaty establishing the European Community, and in particular points 1(*c*), 2(*a*) and 3(*a*) of Article 63 thereof,

Having regard to the proposal from the Commission[1],

Having regard to the opinion of the European Parliament[2],

Having regard to the opinion of the European Economic and Social Committee[3],

Having regard to the opinion of the Committee of the Regions[4],

Whereas:

(1) A common policy on asylum, including a Common European Asylum System, is a constituent part of the European Union's objective of progressively establishing an area of freedom, security and justice open to those who, forced by circumstances, legitimately seek protection in the Community.

(2) The European Council at its special meeting in Tampere on 15 and 16 October 1999 agreed to work towards establishing a Common European Asylum System, based on the full and inclusive application of the Geneva Convention relating to the Status of Refugees of 28 July 1951 (Geneva Convention), as supplemented by the New York Protocol of 31 January 1967 (Protocol), thus affirming the principle of non-refoulement and ensuring that nobody is sent back to persecution.

(3) The Geneva Convention and Protocol provide the cornerstone of the international legal regime for the protection of refugees.

(4) The Tampere conclusions provide that a Common European Asylum System should include, in the short term, the approximation of rules on the recognition of refugees and the content of refugee status.

(5)   The Tampere conclusions also provide that rules regarding refugee status should be complemented by measures on subsidiary forms of protection, offering an appropriate status to any person in need of such protection.

(6)   The main objective of this Directive is, on the one hand, to ensure that Member States apply common criteria for the identification of persons genuinely in need of international protection, and, on the other hand, to ensure that a minimum level of benefits is available for these persons in all Member States.

(7)   The approximation of rules on the recognition and content of refugee and subsidiary protection status should help to limit the secondary movements of applicants for asylum between Member States, where such movement is purely caused by differences in legal frameworks.

(8)   It is in the very nature of minimum standards that Member States should have the power to introduce or maintain more favourable provisions for third country nationals or stateless persons who request international protection from a Member State, where such a request is understood to be on the grounds that the person concerned is either a refugee within the meaning of Article 1(A) of the Geneva Convention, or a person who otherwise needs international protection.

(9)   Those third country nationals or stateless persons, who are allowed to remain in the territories of the Member States for reasons not due to a need for international protection but on a discretionary basis on compassionate or humanitarian grounds, fall outside the scope of this Directive.

(10) This Directive respects the fundamental rights and observes the principles recognised in particular by the Charter of Fundamental Rights of the European Union. In particular this Directive seeks to ensure full respect for human dignity and the right to asylum of applicants for asylum and their accompanying family members.

(11) With respect to the treatment of persons falling within the scope of this Directive, Member States are bound by obligations under instruments of international law to which they are party and which prohibit discrimination.

(12) The 'best interests of the child' should be a primary consideration of Member States when implementing this Directive.

(13) This Directive is without prejudice to the Protocol on asylum for nationals of Member States of the European Union as annexed to the Treaty Establishing the European Community.

(14) The recognition of refugee status is a declaratory act.

(15) Consultations with the United Nations High Commissioner for Refugees may provide valuable guidance for Member States when determining refugee status according to Article 1 of the Geneva Convention.

(16) Minimum standards for the definition and content of refugee status should be laid down to guide the competent national bodies of Member States in the application of the Geneva Convention.

(17) It is necessary to introduce common criteria for recognising applicants for asylum as refugees within the meaning of Article 1 of the Geneva Convention.

(18) In particular, it is necessary to introduce common concepts of protection needs arising sur place; sources of harm and protection; internal protection; and persecution, including the reasons for persecution.

(19) Protection can be provided not only by the State but also by parties or organisations, including international organisations, meeting the conditions of this Directive, which control a region or a larger area within the territory of the State.

(20) It is necessary, when assessing applications from minors for international protection, that Member States should have regard to child-specific forms of persecution.

(21) It is equally necessary to introduce a common concept of the persecution ground 'membership of a particular social group'.

(22) Acts contrary to the purposes and principles of the United Nations are set out in the Preamble and Articles 1 and 2 of the Charter of the United Nations and are, amongst others, embodied in the United Nations Resolutions relating to measures combating terrorism, which declare that 'acts, methods and practices of terrorism are contrary to the purposes and principles of the United Nations' and that 'knowingly financing, planning and inciting terrorist acts are also contrary to the purposes and principles of the United Nations'.

(23) As referred to in Article 14, 'status' can also include refugee status.

(24) Minimum standards for the definition and content of subsidiary protection status should also be laid down. Subsidiary protection should be complementary and additional to the refugee protection enshrined in the Geneva Convention.

(25) It is necessary to introduce criteria on the basis of which applicants for international protection are to be recognised as eligible for subsidiary protection. Those criteria should be drawn from international obligations under human rights instruments and practices existing in Member States.

(26) Risks to which a population of a country or a section of the population is generally exposed do normally not create in themselves an individual threat which would qualify as serious harm.

(27) Family members, merely due to their relation to the refugee, will normally be vulnerable to acts of persecution in such a manner that could be the basis for refugee status.

(28) The notion of national security and public order also covers cases in which a third country national belongs to an association which supports international terrorism or supports such an association.

(29) While the benefits provided to family members of beneficiaries of subsidiary protection status do not necessarily have to be the same as those provided to the qualifying beneficiary, they need to be fair in comparison to those enjoyed by beneficiaries of subsidiary protection status.

(30) Within the limits set out by international obligations, Member States may lay down that the granting of benefits with regard to access to employment, social welfare, health care and access to integration facilities requires the prior issue of a residence permit.

(31) This Directive does not apply to financial benefits from the Member States which are granted to promote education and training.

(32) The practical difficulties encountered by beneficiaries of refugee or subsidiary protection status concerning the authentication of their foreign diplomas, certificates or other evidence of formal qualification should be taken into account.

(33) Especially to avoid social hardship, it is appropriate, for beneficiaries of refugee or subsidiary protection status, to provide without discrimination in the context of social assistance the adequate social welfare and means of subsistence.

(34) With regard to social assistance and health care, the modalities and detail of the provision of core benefits to beneficiaries of subsidiary protection status should be determined by national law. The possibility of limiting the benefits for beneficiaries of subsidiary protection status to core benefits is to be understood in the sense that this notion covers at least

minimum income support, assistance in case of illness, pregnancy and parental assistance, in so far as they are granted to nationals according to the legislation of the Member State concerned.

(35) Access to health care, including both physical and mental health care, should be ensured to beneficiaries of refugee or subsidiary protection status.

(36) The implementation of this Directive should be evaluated at regular intervals, taking into consideration in particular the evolution of the international obligations of Member States regarding non-refoulement, the evolution of the labour markets in the Member States as well as the development of common basic principles for integration.

(37) Since the objectives of the proposed Directive, namely to establish minimum standards for the granting of international protection to third country nationals and stateless persons by Member States and the content of the protection granted, cannot be sufficiently achieved by the Member States and can therefore, by reason of the scale and effects of the Directive, be better achieved at Community level, the Community may adopt measures, in accordance with the principle of subsidiarity as set out in Article 5 of the Treaty. In accordance with the principle of proportionality, as set out in that Article, this Directive does not go beyond what is necessary in order to achieve those objectives.

(38) In accordance with Article 3 of the Protocol on the position of the United Kingdom and Ireland, annexed to the Treaty on European Union and to the Treaty establishing the European Community, the United Kingdom has notified, by letter of 28 January 2002, its wish to take part in the adoption and application of this Directive.

(39) In accordance with Article 3 of the Protocol on the position of the United Kingdom and Ireland, annexed to the Treaty on European Union and to the Treaty establishing the European Community, Ireland has notified, by letter of 13 February 2002, its wish to take part in the adoption and application of this Directive.

(40) In accordance with Articles 1 and 2 of the Protocol on the position of Denmark, annexed to the Treaty on European Union and to the Treaty establishing the European Community, Denmark is not taking part in the adoption of this Directive and is not bound by it or subject to its application,

[1] OJ C 51 E, 26.2.2002, p 325.
[2] OJ C 300 E, 11.12.2003, p 25.
[3] OJ C 221, 17.9.2002, p 43.
[4] OJ C 278, 14.11.2002, p 44.

HAS ADOPTED THIS DIRECTIVE:

CHAPTER I
GENERAL PROVISIONS

Article 1 Subject matter and scope

The purpose of this Directive is to lay down minimum standards for the qualification of third country nationals or stateless persons as refugees or as persons who otherwise need international protection and the content of the protection granted.

Article 2 Definitions

For the purposes of this Directive:

(a) 'international protection' means the refugee and subsidiary protection status as defined in (d) and (f);

(b) Geneva Convention' means the Convention relating to the status of refugees done at Geneva on 28 July 1951, as amended by the New York Protocol of 31 January 1967;

(c) 'refugee' means a third country national who, owing to a well-founded fear of being persecuted for reasons of race, religion, nationality, political opinion or membership of a particular social group, is outside the country of nationality and is unable or, owing to such fear, is unwilling to avail himself or herself of the protection of that country, or a stateless person, who, being outside of the country of former habitual residence for the same reasons as mentioned above, is unable or, owing to such fear, unwilling to return to it, and to whom Article 12 does not apply;

(d) 'refugee status' means the recognition by a Member State of a third country national or a stateless person as a refugee;

(e) 'person eligible for subsidiary protection' means a third country national or a stateless person who does not qualify as a refugee but in respect of whom substantial grounds have been shown for believing that the person concerned, if returned to his or her country of origin, or in the case of a stateless person, to his or her country of former habitual residence, would face a real risk of suffering serious harm as defined in Article 15, and to whom Article 17(1) and (2) do not apply, and is unable, or, owing to such risk, unwilling to avail himself or herself of the protection of that country;

(f) 'subsidiary protection status' means the recognition by a Member State of a third country national or a stateless person as a person eligible for subsidiary protection;

(g) 'application for international protection' means a request made by a third country national or a stateless person for protection from a Member State, who can be understood to seek refugee status or subsidiary protection status, and who does not explicitly request another kind of protection, outside the scope of this Directive, that can be applied for separately;

(h) 'family members' means, insofar as the family already existed in the country of origin, the following members of the family of the beneficiary of refugee or subsidiary protection status who are present in the same Member State in relation to the application for international protection:
— the spouse of the beneficiary of refugee or subsidiary protection status or his or her unmarried partner in a stable relationship, where the legislation or practice of the Member State concerned treats unmarried couples in a way comparable to married couples under its law relating to aliens,
— the minor children of the couple referred to in the first indent or of the beneficiary of refugee or subsidiary protection status, on condition that they are unmarried and dependent and regardless of whether they were born in or out of wedlock or adopted as defined under the national law;

(i) 'unaccompanied minors' means third-country nationals or stateless persons below the age of 18, who arrive on the territory of the Member States unaccompanied by an adult responsible for them whether by law or custom, and for as long as they are not effectively taken into the care of such a person; it includes minors who are left unaccompanied after they have entered the territory of the Member States;

(j) 'residence permit' means any permit or authorisation issued by the authorities of a Member State, in the form provided for under that State's legislation, allowing a third country national or stateless person to reside on its territory;

(k) 'country of origin' means the country or countries of nationality or, for stateless persons, of former habitual residence.

Article 3 More favourable standards

Member States may introduce or retain more favourable standards for determining who qualifies as a refugee or as a person eligible for subsidiary protection, and for determining the content of international protection, in so far as those standards are compatible with this Directive.

CHAPTER II
ASSESSMENT OF APPLICATIONS FOR INTERNATIONAL PROTECTION

Article 4 Assessment of facts and circumstances

1. Member States may consider it the duty of the applicant to submit as soon as possible all elements needed to substantiate the application for international protection. In cooperation with the applicant it is the duty of the Member State to assess the relevant elements of the application.

2. The elements referred to in of paragraph 1 consist of the applicant's statements and all documentation at the applicants disposal regarding the applicant's age, background, including that of relevant relatives, identity, nationality(ies), country(ies) and place(s) of previous residence, previous asylum applications, travel routes, identity and travel documents and the reasons for applying for international protection.

3. The assessment of an application for international protection is to be carried out on an individual basis and includes taking into account:

(a) all relevant facts as they relate to the country of origin at the time of taking a decision on the application; including laws and regulations of the country of origin and the manner in which they are applied;

(b) the relevant statements and documentation presented by the applicant including information on whether the applicant has been or may be subject to persecution or serious harm;

(c) the individual position and personal circumstances of the applicant, including factors such as background, gender and age, so as to assess whether, on the basis of the applicant's personal circumstances, the acts to which the applicant has been or could be exposed would amount to persecution or serious harm;

(d) whether the applicant's activities since leaving the country of origin were engaged in for the sole or main purpose of creating the necessary conditions for applying for international protection, so as to assess whether these activities will expose the applicant to persecution or serious harm if returned to that country;

(e) whether the applicant could reasonably be expected to avail himself of the protection of another country where he could assert citizenship.

4. The fact that an applicant has already been subject to persecution or serious harm or to direct threats of such persecution or such harm, is a serious indication of the applicant's well-founded fear of persecution or real risk of suffering serious harm, unless there are good reasons to consider that such persecution or serious harm will not be repeated.

5. Where Member States apply the principle according to which it is the duty of the applicant to substantiate the application for international protection and where aspects of the applicant's statements are not supported by documentary or other evidence, those aspects shall not need confirmation, when the following conditions are met:

(a) the applicant has made a genuine effort to substantiate his application;

(b) all relevant elements, at the applicant's disposal, have been submitted, and a satisfactory explanation regarding any lack of other relevant elements has been given;

(c) the applicant's statements are found to be coherent and plausible and do not run counter to available specific and general information relevant to the applicant's case;

(d) the applicant has applied for international protection at the earliest possible time, unless the applicant can demonstrate good reason for not having done so; and

(e) the general credibility of the applicant has been established.

Article 5 International protection needs arising sur place

1. A well-founded fear of being persecuted or a real risk of suffering serious harm may be based on events which have taken place since the applicant left the country of origin.

2. A well-founded fear of being persecuted or a real risk of suffering serious harm may be based on activities which have been engaged in by the applicant since he left the country of origin, in particular where it is established that the activities relied upon constitute the expression and continuation of convictions or orientations held in the country of origin.

3. Without prejudice to the Geneva Convention, Member States may determine that an applicant who files a subsequent application shall normally not be granted refugee status, if the risk of persecution is based on circumstances which the applicant has created by his own decision since leaving the country of origin.

Article 6 Actors of persecution or serious harm

Actors of persecution or serious harm include:

(a) the State;

(b) parties or organisations controlling the State or a substantial part of the territory of the State;

(c) non-State actors, if it can be demonstrated that the actors mentioned in (a) and (b), including international organisations, are unable or unwilling to provide protection against persecution or serious harm as defined in Article 7.

Article 7 Actors of protection

1. Protection can be provided by:

(a) the State; or

(b) parties or organisations, including international organisations, controlling the State or a substantial part of the territory of the State.

2. Protection is generally provided when the actors mentioned in paragraph 1 take reasonable steps to prevent the persecution or suffering of serious harm, inter alia, by operating an effective legal system for the detection, prosecution and punishment of acts constituting persecution or serious harm, and the applicant has access to such protection.

3. When assessing whether an international organisation controls a State or a substantial part of its territory and provides protection as described in paragraph 2, Member States shall take into account any guidance which may be provided in relevant Council acts.

Article 8 Internal protection

1. As part of the assessment of the application for international protection, Member States may determine that an applicant is not in need of international protection if in a part of the country of origin there is no well-founded fear of being persecuted or no real risk of suffering serious harm and the applicant can reasonably be expected to stay in that part of the country.

2. In examining whether a part of the country of origin is in accordance with paragraph 1, Member States shall at the time of taking the decision on the application have regard to the general circumstances prevailing in that part of the country and to the personal circumstances of the applicant.

3. Paragraph 1 may apply notwithstanding technical obstacles to return to the country of origin.

CHAPTER III
QUALIFICATION FOR BEING A REFUGEE

Article 9 Acts of persecution

1. Acts of persecution within the meaning of article 1 A of the Geneva Convention must:

    (a)   be sufficiently serious by their nature or repetition as to constitute a severe violation of basic human rights, in particular the rights from which derogation cannot be made under Article 15(2) of the European Convention for the Protection of Human Rights and Fundamental Freedoms; or

    (b)   be an accumulation of various measures, including violations of human rights which is sufficiently severe as to affect an individual in a similar manner as mentioned in (a).

2. Acts of persecution as qualified in paragraph 1, can, inter alia, take the form of:

    (a)   acts of physical or mental violence, including acts of sexual violence;

    (b)   legal, administrative, police, and/or judicial measures which are in themselves discriminatory or which are implemented in a discriminatory manner;

    (c)   prosecution or punishment, which is disproportionate or discriminatory;

    (d)   denial of judicial redress resulting in a disproportionate or discriminatory punishment;

    (e)   prosecution or punishment for refusal to perform military service in a conflict, where performing military service would include crimes or acts falling under the exclusion clauses as set out in Article 12(2);

    (f)   acts of a gender-specific or child-specific nature.

3. In accordance with Article 2(c), there must be a connection between the reasons mentioned in Article 10 and the acts of persecution as qualified in paragraph 1.

Article 10 Reasons for persecution

1. Member States shall take the following elements into account when assessing the reasons for persecution:

    (a)   the concept of race shall in particular include considerations of colour, descent, or membership of a particular ethnic group;

    (b)   the concept of religion shall in particular include the holding of theistic, non-theistic and atheistic beliefs, the participation in, or abstention from, formal worship in private or in public, either alone or in community with others, other religious acts or expressions of view, or forms of personal or communal conduct based on or mandated by any religious belief;

    (c)   the concept of nationality shall not be confined to citizenship or lack thereof but shall in particular include membership of a group determined by its cultural, ethnic, or linguistic identity, common geographical or political origins or its relationship with the population of another State;

    (d)   a group shall be considered to form a particular social group where in particular:

        —   members of that group share an innate characteristic, or a common background that cannot be changed, or share a characteristic or belief that is so fundamental to identity or conscience that a person should not be forced to renounce it, and

— that group has a distinct identity in the relevant country, because it is perceived as being different by the surrounding society;

— depending on the circumstances in the country of origin, a particular social group might include a group based on a common characteristic of sexual orientation. Sexual orientation cannot be understood to include acts considered to be criminal in accordance with national law of the Member States: Gender related aspects might be considered, without by themselves alone creating a presumption for the applicability of this Article;

(e) the concept of political opinion shall in particular include the holding of an opinion, thought or belief on a matter related to the potential actors of persecution mentioned in Article 6 and to their policies or methods, whether or not that opinion, thought or belief has been acted upon by the applicant.

2. When assessing if an applicant has a well-founded fear of being persecuted it is immaterial whether the applicant actually possesses the racial, religious, national, social or political characteristic which attracts the persecution, provided that such a characteristic is attributed to the applicant by the actor of persecution.

Article 11 Cessation

1. A third country national or a stateless person shall cease to be a refugee, if he or she:

(a) has voluntarily re-availed himself or herself of the protection of the country of nationality; or

(b) having lost his or her nationality, has voluntarily re-acquired it; or

(c) has acquired a new nationality, and enjoys the protection of the country of his or her new nationality; or

(d) has voluntarily re-established himself or herself in the country which he or she left or outside which he or she remained owing to fear of persecution; or

(e) can no longer, because the circumstances in connection with which he or she has been recognised as a refugee have ceased to exist, continue to refuse to avail himself or herself of the protection of the country of nationality;

(f) being a stateless person with no nationality, he or she is able, because the circumstances in connection with which he or she has been recognised as a refugee have ceased to exist, to return to the country of former habitual residence.

2. In considering points (e) and (f) of paragraph 1, Member States shall have regard to whether the change of circumstances is of such a significant and non-temporary nature that the refugee's fear of persecution can no longer be regarded as well-founded.

Article 12 Exclusion

1. A third country national or a stateless person is excluded from being a refugee, if:

(a) he or she falls within the scope of Article 1 D of the Geneva Convention, relating to protection or assistance from organs or agencies of the United Nations other than the United Nations High Commissioner for Refugees. When such protection or assistance has ceased for any reason, without the position of such persons being definitely settled in accordance with the relevant resolutions adopted by the General Assembly of the United Nations, these persons shall ipso facto be entitled to the benefits of this Directive;

    (b)   he or she is recognised by the competent authorities of the country in which he or she has taken residence as having the rights and obligations which are attached to the possession of the nationality of that country; or rights and obligations equivalent to those.

2.   A third country national or a stateless person is excluded from being a refugee where there are serious reasons for considering that:

    (a)   he or she has committed a crime against peace, a war crime, or a crime against humanity, as defined in the international instruments drawn up to make provision in respect of such crimes;

    (b)   he or she has committed a serious non-political crime outside the country of refuge prior to his or her admission as a refugee; which means the time of issuing a residence permit based on the granting of refugee status; particularly cruel actions, even if committed with an allegedly political objective, may be classified as serious non-political crimes;

    (c)   he or she has been guilty of acts contrary to the purposes and principles of the United Nations as set out in the Preamble and Articles 1 and 2 of the Charter of the United Nations.

3.   Paragraph 2 applies to persons who instigate or otherwise participate in the commission of the crimes or acts mentioned therein.

CHAPTER IV
REFUGEE STATUS

Article 13 Granting of refugee status

Member States shall grant refugee status to a third country national or a stateless person, who qualifies as a refugee in accordance with Chapters II and III.

Article 14 Revocation of, ending of or refusal to renew refugee status

1.   Concerning applications for international protection filed after the entry into force of this Directive, Member States shall revoke, end or refuse to renew the refugee status of a third country national or a stateless person granted by a governmental, administrative, judicial or quasi-judicial body, if he or she has ceased to be a refugee in accordance with Article 11.

2.   Without prejudice to the duty of the refugee in accordance with Article 4(1) to disclose all relevant facts and provide all relevant documentation at his/her disposal, the Member State, which has granted refugee status, shall on an individual basis demonstrate that the person concerned has ceased to be or has never been a refugee in accordance with paragraph 1 of this Article.

3.   Member States shall revoke, end or refuse to renew the refugee status of a third country national or a stateless person, if, after he or she has been granted refugee status, it is established by the Member State concerned that:

    (a)   he or she should have been or is excluded from being a refugee in accordance with Article 12;

    (b)   his or her misrepresentation or omission of facts, including the use of false documents, were decisive for the granting of refugee status.

4.   Member States may revoke, end or refuse to renew the status granted to a refugee by a governmental, administrative, judicial or quasi-judicial body, when:

    (a)   there are reasonable grounds for regarding him or her as a danger to the security of the Member State in which he or she is present;

    (b)   he or she, having been convicted by a final judgement of a particularly serious crime, constitutes a danger to the community of that Member State.

5. In situations described in paragraph 4, Member States may decide not to grant status to a refugee, where such a decision has not yet been taken.

6.   Persons to whom paragraphs 4 or 5 apply are entitled to rights set out in or similar to those set out in Articles 3, 4, 16, 22, 31 and 32 and 33 of the Geneva Convention in so far as they are present in the Member State.

CHAPTER V
QUALIFICATION FOR SUBSIDIARY PROTECTION

Article 15 Serious harm

Serious harm consists of:

(a)   death penalty or execution; or

(b)   torture or inhuman or degrading treatment or punishment of an applicant in the country of origin; or

(c)   serious and individual threat to a civilian's life or person by reason of indiscriminate violence in situations of international or internal armed conflict.

Article 16 Cessation

1.   A third country national or a stateless person shall cease to be eligible for subsidiary protection when the circumstances which led to the granting of subsidiary protection status have ceased to exist or have changed to such a degree that protection is no longer required.

2.   In applying paragraph 1, Member States shall have regard to whether the change of circumstances is of such a significant and non-temporary nature that the person eligible for subsidiary protection no longer faces a real risk of serious harm.

Article 17 Exclusion

1.   A third country national or a stateless person is excluded from being eligible for subsidiary protection where there are serious reasons for considering that:

(a)   he or she has committed a crime against peace, a war crime, or a crime against humanity, as defined in the international instruments drawn up to make provision in respect of such crimes;

(b)   he or she has committed a serious crime;

(c)   he or she has been guilty of acts contrary to the purposes and principles of the United Nations as set out in the Preamble and Articles 1 and 2 of the Charter of the United Nations;

(d)   he or she constitutes a danger to the community or to the security of the Member State in which he or she is present.

2.   Paragraph 1 applies to persons who instigate or otherwise participate in the commission of the crimes or acts mentioned therein.

3.   Member States may exclude a third country national or a stateless person from being eligible for subsidiary protection, if he or she prior to his or her admission to the Member State has committed one or more crimes, outside the scope of paragraph 1, which would be punishable by imprisonment, had they been committed in the Member State concerned, and if he or she left his or her country of origin solely in order to avoid sanctions resulting from these crimes.

CHAPTER VI
SUBSIDIARY PROTECTION STATUS

Article 18 Granting of subsidiary protection status

Member States shall grant subsidiary protection status to a third country national or a stateless person eligible for subsidiary protection in accordance with Chapters II and V.

Article 19 Revocation of, ending of or refusal to renew subsidiary protection status

1.   Concerning applications for international protection filed after the entry into force of this Directive, Member States shall revoke, end or refuse to renew the subsidiary

protection status of a third country national or a stateless person granted by a governmental, administrative, judicial or quasi-judicial body, if he or she has ceased to be eligible for subsidiary protection in accordance with Article 16.

2. Member States may revoke, end or refuse to renew the subsidiary protection status of a third country national or a stateless person granted by a governmental, administrative, judicial or quasi-judicial body, if after having been granted subsidiary protection status, he or she should have been excluded from being eligible for subsidiary protection in accordance with Article 17(3).

3. Member States shall revoke, end or refuse to renew the subsidiary protection status of a third country national or a stateless person, if:

(a) he or she, after having been granted subsidiary protection status, should have been or is excluded from being eligible for subsidiary protection in accordance with Article 17(1) and (2);

(b) his or her misrepresentation or omission of facts, including the use of false documents, were decisive for the granting of subsidiary protection status.

4. Without prejudice to the duty of the third country national or stateless person in accordance with Article 4(1) to disclose all relevant facts and provide all relevant documentation at his/her disposal, the Member State, which has granted the subsidiary protection status, shall on an individual basis demonstrate that the person concerned has ceased to be or is not eligible for subsidiary protection in accordance with paragraphs 1, 2 and 3 of this Article.

CHAPTER VII
CONTENT OF INTERNATIONAL PROTECTION

Article 20 General rules

1. This Chapter shall be without prejudice to the rights laid down in the Geneva Convention.

2. This Chapter shall apply both to refugees and persons eligible for subsidiary protection unless otherwise indicated.

3. When implementing this Chapter, Member States shall take into account the specific situation of vulnerable persons such as minors, unaccompanied minors, disabled people, elderly people, pregnant women, single parents with minor children and persons who have been subjected to torture, rape or other serious forms of psychological, physical or sexual violence.

4. Paragraph 3 shall apply only to persons found to have special needs after an individual evaluation of their situation.

5. The best interest of the child shall be a primary consideration for Member States when implementing the provisions of this Chapter that involve minors.

6. Within the limits set out by the Geneva Convention, Member States may reduce the benefits of this Chapter, granted to a refugee whose refugee status has been obtained on the basis of activities engaged in for the sole or main purpose of creating the necessary conditions for being recognised as a refugee.

7. Within the limits set out by international obligations of Member States, Member States may reduce the benefits of this Chapter, granted to a person eligible for subsidiary protection, whose subsidiary protection status has been obtained on the basis of activities engaged in for the sole or main purpose of creating the necessary conditions for being recognised as a person eligible for subsidiary protection.

Article 21 Protection from refoulement

1. Member States shall respect the principle of non-refoulement in accordance with their international obligations.

2. Where not prohibited by the international obligations mentioned in paragraph 1, Member States may refoule a refugee, whether formally recognised or not, when:

(a) there are reasonable grounds for considering him or her as a danger to the security of the Member State in which he or she is present; or

(b) he or she, having been convicted by a final judgement of a particularly serious crime, constitutes a danger to the community of that Member State.

3. Member States may revoke, end or refuse to renew or to grant the residence permit of (or to) a refugee to whom paragraph 2 applies.

Article 22 Information

Member States shall provide persons recognised as being in need of international protection, as soon as possible after the respective protection status has been granted, with access to information, in a language likely to be understood by them, on the rights and obligations relating to that status.

Article 23 Maintaining family unity

1. Member States shall ensure that family unity can be maintained.

2. Member States shall ensure that family members of the beneficiary of refugee or subsidiary protection status, who do not individually qualify for such status, are entitled to claim the benefits referred to in Articles 24 to 34, in accordance with national procedures and as far as it is compatible with the personal legal status of the family member.

In so far as the family members of beneficiaries of subsidiary protection status are concerned, Member States may define the conditions applicable to such benefits.

In these cases, Member States shall ensure that any benefits provided guarantee an adequate standard of living.

3. Paragraphs 1 and 2 are not applicable where the family member is or would be excluded from refugee or subsidiary protection status pursuant to Chapters III and V.

4. Notwithstanding paragraphs 1 and 2, Member States may refuse, reduce or withdraw the benefits referred therein for reasons of national security or public order.

5. Member States may decide that this Article also applies to other close relatives who lived together as part of the family at the time of leaving the country of origin, and who were wholly or mainly dependent on the beneficiary of refugee or subsidiary protection status at that time.

Article 24 Residence permits

1. As soon as possible after their status has been granted, Member States shall issue to beneficiaries of refugee status a residence permit which must be valid for at least three years and renewable unless compelling reasons of national security or public order otherwise require, and without prejudice to Article 21(3).

Without prejudice to Article 23(1), the residence permit to be issued to the family members of the beneficiaries of refugee status may be valid for less than three years and renewable.

2. As soon as possible after the status has been granted, Member States shall issue to beneficiaries of subsidiary protection status a residence permit which must be valid for at least one year and renewable, unless compelling reasons of national security or public order otherwise require.

Article 25 Travel document

1. Member States shall issue to beneficiaries of refugee status travel documents in the form set out in the Schedule to the Geneva Convention, for the purpose of travel outside their territory unless compelling reasons of national security or public order otherwise require.

2. Member States shall issue to beneficiaries of subsidiary protection status who are unable to obtain a national passport, documents which enable them to travel, at least when serious humanitarian reasons arise that require their presence in another State, unless compelling reasons of national security or public order otherwise require.

Article 26 Access to employment

1. Member States shall authorise beneficiaries of refugee status to engage in employed or self-employed activities subject to rules generally applicable to the profession and to the public service, immediately after the refugee status has been granted.

2. Member States shall ensure that activities such as employment-related education opportunities for adults, vocational training and practical workplace experience are offered to beneficiaries of refugee status, under equivalent conditions as nationals.

3. Member States shall authorise beneficiaries of subsidiary protection status to engage in employed or self-employed activities subject to rules generally applicable to the profession and to the public service immediately after the subsidiary protection status has been granted. The situation of the labour market in the Member States may be taken into account, including for possible prioritisation of access to employment for a limited period of time to be determined in accordance with national law. Member States shall ensure that the beneficiary of subsidiary protection status has access to a post for which the beneficiary has received an offer in accordance with national rules on prioritisation in the labour market.

4. Member States shall ensure that beneficiaries of subsidiary protection status have access to activities such as employment-related education opportunities for adults, vocational training and practical workplace experience, under conditions to be decided by the Member States.

5. The law in force in the Member States applicable to remuneration, access to social security systems relating to employed or self-employed activities and other conditions of employment shall apply.

Article 27 Access to education

1. Member States shall grant full access to the education system to all minors granted refugee or subsidiary protection status, under the same conditions as nationals.

2. Member States shall allow adults granted refugee or subsidiary protection status access to the general education system, further training or retraining, under the same conditions as third country nationals legally resident.

3. Member States shall ensure equal treatment between beneficiaries of refugee or subsidiary protection status and nationals in the context of the existing recognition procedures for foreign diplomas, certificates and other evidence of formal qualifications.

Article 28 Social welfare

1. Member States shall ensure that beneficiaries of refugee or subsidiary protection status receive, in the Member State that has granted such statuses, the necessary social assistance, as provided to nationals of that Member State.

2. By exception to the general rule laid down in paragraph 1, Member States may limit social assistance granted to beneficiaries of subsidiary protection status to core benefits which will then be provided at the same levels and under the same eligibility conditions as nationals.

Article 29 Health care

1. Member States shall ensure that beneficiaries of refugee or subsidiary protection status have access to health care under the same eligibility conditions as nationals of the Member State that has granted such statuses.

2. By exception to the general rule laid down in paragraph 1, Member States may limit health care granted to beneficiaries of subsidiary protection to core benefits which will then be provided at the same levels and under the same eligibility conditions as nationals.

3. Member States shall provide, under the same eligibility conditions as nationals of the Member State that has granted the status, adequate health care to beneficiaries of refugee or subsidiary protection status who have special needs, such as pregnant

women, disabled people, persons who have undergone torture, rape or other serious forms of psychological, physical or sexual violence or minors who have been victims of any form of abuse, neglect, exploitation, torture, cruel, inhuman and degrading treatment or who have suffered from armed conflict.

Article 30 Unaccompanied minors

1. As soon as possible after the granting of refugee or subsidiary protection status Member States shall take the necessary measures, to ensure the representation of unaccompanied minors by legal guardianship or, where necessary, by an organisation responsible for the care and well-being of minors, or by any other appropriate representation including that based on legislation or Court order.

2. Member States shall ensure that the minor's needs are duly met in the implementation of this Directive by the appointed guardian or representative. The appropriate authorities shall make regular assessments.

3. Member States shall ensure that unaccompanied minors are placed either:

  (a) with adult relatives; or
  (b) with a foster family; or
  (c) in centres specialised in accommodation for minors; or
  (d) in other accommodation suitable for minors.

In this context, the views of the child shall be taken into account in accordance with his or her age and degree of maturity.

4. As far as possible, siblings shall be kept together, taking into account the best interests of the minor concerned and, in particular, his or her age and degree of maturity. Changes of residence of unaccompanied minors shall be limited to a minimum.

5. Member States, protecting the unaccompanied minor's best interests, shall endeavour to trace the members of the minor's family as soon as possible. In cases where there may be a threat to the life or integrity of the minor or his or her close relatives, particularly if they have remained in the country of origin, care must be taken to ensure that the collection, processing and circulation of information concerning those persons is undertaken on a confidential basis.

6. Those working with unaccompanied minors shall have had or receive appropriate training concerning their needs.

Article 31 Access to accommodation

The Member States shall ensure that beneficiaries of refugee or subsidiary protection status have access to accommodation under equivalent conditions as other third country nationals legally resident in their territories.

Article 32 Freedom of movement within the Member State

Member States shall allow freedom of movement within their territory to beneficiaries of refugee or subsidiary protection status, under the same conditions and restrictions as those provided for other third country nationals legally resident in their territories.

Article 33 Access to integration facilities

1. In order to facilitate the integration of refugees into society, Member States shall make provision for integration programmes which they consider to be appropriate or create pre-conditions which guarantee access to such programmes.

2. Where it is considered appropriate by Member States, beneficiaries of subsidiary protection status shall be granted access to integration programmes.

Article 34 Repatriation

Member States may provide assistance to beneficiaries of refugee or subsidiary protection status who wish to repatriate.

CHAPTER VIII
ADMINISTRATIVE COOPERATION

Article 35 Cooperation

Member States shall each appoint a national contact point, whose address they shall communicate to the Commission, which shall communicate it to the other Member States.

Member States shall, in liaison with the Commission, take all appropriate measures to establish direct cooperation and an exchange of information between the competent authorities.

Article 36 Staff

Member States shall ensure that authorities and other organisations implementing this Directive have received the necessary training and shall be bound by the confidentiality principle, as defined in the national law, in relation to any information they obtain in the course of their work.

CHAPTER IX
FINAL PROVISIONS

Article 37 Reports

1. By 10 April 2008, the Commission shall report to the European Parliament and the Council on the application of this Directive and shall propose any amendments that are necessary. These proposals for amendments shall be made by way of priority in relation to Articles 15, 26 and 33. Member States shall send the Commission all the information that is appropriate for drawing up that report by 10 October 2007.

2. After presenting the report, the Commission shall report to the European Parliament and the Council on the application of this Directive at least every five years.

Article 38 Transposition

1. The Member States shall bring into force the laws, regulations and administrative provisions necessary to comply with this Directive before 10 October 2006. They shall forthwith inform the Commission thereof.

When the Member States adopt those measures, they shall contain a reference to this Directive or shall be accompanied by such a reference on the occasion of their official publication. The methods of making such reference shall be laid down by Member States.

2. Member States shall communicate to the Commission the text of the provisions of national law which they adopt in the field covered by this Directive.

Article 39 Entry into force

This Directive shall enter into force on the twentieth day following that of its publication in the Official Journal of the European Union.

Article 40 Addressees

This Directive is addressed to the Member States in accordance with the Treaty establishing the European Community.

COUNCIL DIRECTIVE 2005/85/EC (THE PROCEDURES DIRECTIVE)

of 1 December 2005 on minimum standards on procedures in Member States for granting and withdrawing refugee status

Notes

Date of publication in Official Journal: OJ L326, 13.12.2005, p 13.

THE COUNCIL OF THE EUROPEAN UNION,

Having regard to the Treaty establishing the European Community, and in particular point (1)(d) of the first paragraph of Article 63 thereof,

Having regard to the proposal from the Commission[1],

Having regard to the opinion of the European Parliament[2],

Having regard to the opinion of the European Economic and Social Committee[3],

Whereas:

(1) A common policy on asylum, including a Common European Asylum System, is a constituent part of the European Union's objective of establishing progressively an area of freedom, security and justice open to those who, forced by circumstances, legitimately seek protection in the Community.

(2) The European Council, at its special meeting in Tampere on 15 and 16 October 1999, agreed to work towards establishing a Common European Asylum System, based on the full and inclusive application of the Geneva Convention of 28 July 1951 relating to the status of refugees, as amended by the New York Protocol of 31 January 1967 (Geneva Convention), thus affirming the principle of non-refoulement and ensuring that nobody is sent back to persecution.

(3) The Tampere Conclusions provide that a Common European Asylum System should include, in the short term, common standards for fair and efficient asylum procedures in the Member States and, in the longer term, Community rules leading to a common asylum procedure in the European Community.

(4) The minimum standards laid down in this Directive on procedures in Member States for granting or withdrawing refugee status are therefore a first measure on asylum procedures.

(5) The main objective of this Directive is to introduce a minimum framework in the Community on procedures for granting and withdrawing refugee status.

(6) The approximation of rules on the procedures for granting and withdrawing refugee status should help to limit the secondary movements of applicants for asylum between Member States, where such movement would be caused by differences in legal frameworks.

(7) It is in the very nature of minimum standards that Member States should have the power to introduce or maintain more favourable provisions for third country nationals or stateless persons who ask for international protection from a Member State, where such a request is understood to be on the grounds that the person concerned is a refugee within the meaning of Article 1(A) of the Geneva Convention.

(8) This Directive respects the fundamental rights and observes the principles recognised in particular by the Charter of Fundamental Rights of the European Union.

(9)   With respect to the treatment of persons falling within the scope of this Directive, Member States are bound by obligations under instruments of international law to which they are party and which prohibit discrimination.

(10)   It is essential that decisions on all applications for asylum be taken on the basis of the facts and, in the first instance, by authorities whose personnel has the appropriate knowledge or receives the necessary training in the field of asylum and refugee matters.

(11)   It is in the interest of both Member States and applicants for asylum to decide as soon as possible on applications for asylum. The organisation of the processing of applications for asylum should be left to the discretion of Member States, so that they may, in accordance with their national needs, prioritise or accelerate the processing of any application, taking into account the standards in this Directive.

(12)   The notion of public order may cover a conviction for committing a serious crime.

(13)   In the interests of a correct recognition of those persons in need of protection as refugees within the meaning of Article 1 of the Geneva Convention, every applicant should, subject to certain exceptions, have an effective access to procedures, the opportunity to cooperate and properly communicate with the competent authorities so as to present the relevant facts of his/her case and sufficient procedural guarantees to pursue his/her case throughout all stages of the procedure. Moreover, the procedure in which an application for asylum is examined should normally provide an applicant at least with the right to stay pending a decision by the determining authority, access to the services of an interpreter for submitting his/her case if interviewed by the authorities, the opportunity to communicate with a representative of the United Nations High Commissioner for Refugees (UNHCR) or with any organisation working on its behalf, the right to appropriate notification of a decision, a motivation of that decision in fact and in law, the opportunity to consult a legal adviser or other counsellor, and the right to be informed of his/her legal position at decisive moments in the course of the procedure, in a language he/she can reasonably be supposed to understand.

(14)   In addition, specific procedural guarantees for unaccompanied minors should be laid down on account of their vulnerability. In this context, the best interests of the child should be a primary consideration of Member States.

(15)   Where an applicant makes a subsequent application without presenting new evidence or arguments, it would be disproportionate to oblige Member States to carry out a new full examination procedure. In these cases, Member States should have a choice of procedure involving exceptions to the guarantees normally enjoyed by the applicant.

(16)   Many asylum applications are made at the border or in a transit zone of a Member State prior to a decision on the entry of the applicant. Member States should be able to keep existing procedures adapted to the specific situation of these applicants at the border. Common rules should be defined on possible exceptions made in these circumstances to the guarantees normally enjoyed by applicants. Border procedures should mainly apply to those applicants who do not meet the conditions for entry into the territory of the Member States.

(17)   A key consideration for the well-foundedness of an asylum application is the safety of the applicant in his/her country of origin. Where a third country can be regarded as a safe country of origin, Member States

should be able to designate it as safe and presume its safety for a particular applicant, unless he/she presents serious counter-indications.

(18) Given the level of harmonisation achieved on the qualification of third country nationals and stateless persons as refugees, common criteria for designating third countries as safe countries of origin should be established.

(19) Where the Council has satisfied itself that those criteria are met in relation to a particular country of origin, and has consequently included it in the minimum common list of safe countries of origin to be adopted pursuant to this Directive, Member States should be obliged to consider applications of persons with the nationality of that country, or of stateless persons formerly habitually resident in that country, on the basis of the rebuttable presumption of the safety of that country. In the light of the political importance of the designation of safe countries of origin, in particular in view of the implications of an assessment of the human rights situation in a country of origin and its implications for the policies of the European Union in the field of external relations, the Council should take any decisions on the establishment or amendment of the list, after consultation of the European Parliament.

(20) It results from the status of Bulgaria and Romania as candidate countries for accession to the European Union and the progress made by these countries towards membership that they should be regarded as constituting safe countries of origin for the purposes of this Directive until the date of their accession to the European Union.

(21) The designation of a third country as a safe country of origin for the purposes of this Directive cannot establish an absolute guarantee of safety for nationals of that country. By its very nature, the assessment underlying the designation can only take into account the general civil, legal and political circumstances in that country and whether actors of persecution, torture or inhuman or degrading treatment or punishment are subject to sanction in practice when found liable in the country concerned. For this reason, it is important that, where an applicant shows that there are serious reasons to consider the country not to be safe in his/her particular circumstances, the designation of the country as safe can no longer be considered relevant for him/her.

(22) Member States should examine all applications on the substance, i.e. assess whether the applicant in question qualifies as a refugee in accordance with Council Directive 2004/83/EC of 29 April 2004 on minimum standards for the qualification and status of third country nationals or stateless persons as refugees or as persons who otherwise need international protection and the content of the protection granted[4], except where the present Directive provides otherwise, in particular where it can be reasonably assumed that another country would do the examination or provide sufficient protection. In particular, Member States should not be obliged to assess the substance of an asylum application where a first country of asylum has granted the applicant refugee status or otherwise sufficient protection and the applicant will be readmitted to this country.

(23) Member States should also not be obliged to assess the substance of an asylum application where the applicant, due to a connection to a third country as defined by national law, can reasonably be expected to seek protection in that third country. Member States should only proceed on this basis where this particular applicant would be safe in the third country concerned. In order to avoid secondary movements of applicants, common principles for the consideration or designation by Member States of third countries as safe should be established.

(24) Furthermore, with respect to certain European third countries, which observe particularly high human rights and refugee protection standards, Member States should be allowed to not carry out, or not to carry out full examination of asylum applications regarding applicants who enter their territory from such European third countries. Given the potential consequences for the applicant of a restricted or omitted examination, this application of the safe third country concept should be restricted to cases involving third countries with respect to which the Council has satisfied itself that the high standards for the safety of the third country concerned, as set out in this Directive, are fulfilled. The Council should take decisions in this matter after consultation of the European Parliament.

(25) It follows from the nature of the common standards concerning both safe third country concepts as set out in this Directive, that the practical effect of the concepts depends on whether the third country in question permits the applicant in question to enter its territory.

(26) With respect to the withdrawal of refugee status, Member States should ensure that persons benefiting from refugee status are duly informed of a possible reconsideration of their status and have the opportunity to submit their point of view before the authorities can take a motivated decision to withdraw their status. However, dispensing with these guarantees should be allowed where the reasons for the cessation of the refugee status is not related to a change of the conditions on which the recognition was based.

(27) It reflects a basic principle of Community law that the decisions taken on an application for asylum and on the withdrawal of refugee status are subject to an effective remedy before a court or tribunal within the meaning of Article 234 of the Treaty. The effectiveness of the remedy, also with regard to the examination of the relevant facts, depends on the administrative and judicial system of each Member State seen as a whole.

(28) In accordance with Article 64 of the Treaty, this Directive does not affect the exercise of the responsibilities incumbent upon Member States with regard to the maintenance of law and order and the safeguarding of internal security.

(29) This Directive does not deal with procedures governed by Council Regulation (EC) No 343/2003 of 18 February 2003 establishing the criteria and mechanisms for determining the Member State responsible for examining an asylum application lodged in one of the Member States by a third-country national[5].

(30) The implementation of this Directive should be evaluated at regular intervals not exceeding two years.

(31) Since the objective of this Directive, namely to establish minimum standards on procedures in Member States for granting and withdrawing refugee status cannot be sufficiently attained by the Member States and can therefore, by reason of the scale and effects of the action, be better achieved at Community level, the Community may adopt measures, in accordance with the principle of subsidiarity as set out in Article 5 of the Treaty. In accordance with the principle of proportionality, as set out in that Article, this Directive does not go beyond what is necessary in order to achieve this objective.

(32) In accordance with Article 3 of the Protocol on the position of the United Kingdom and Ireland, annexed to the Treaty on European Union and to the Treaty establishing the European Community, the United Kingdom has notified, by letter of 24 January 2001, its wish to take part in the adoption and application of this Directive.

(33)   In accordance with Article 3 of the Protocol on the position of the United Kingdom and Ireland, annexed to the Treaty on European Union and to the Treaty establishing the European Community, Ireland has notified, by letter of 14 February 2001, its wish to take part in the adoption and application of this Directive.

(34)   In accordance with Articles 1 and 2 of the Protocol on the position of Denmark, annexed to the Treaty on European Union and to the Treaty establishing the European Community, Denmark does not take part in the adoption of this Directive and is not bound by it or subject to its application,

¹   OJ C 62, 27.2.2001, p 231 and OJ C 291, 26.11.2002, p 143.

²   OJ C 77, 28.3.2002, p 94.

³   OJ C 193, 10.7.2001, p 77. Opinion delivered following non-compulsory consultation.

⁴   OJ L 304, 30.9.2004, p 12.

⁵   OJ L 50, 25.2.2003, p 1.

HAS ADOPTED THIS DIRECTIVE:

CHAPTER I
GENERAL PROVISIONS

Article 1 Purpose

The purpose of this Directive is to establish minimum standards on procedures in Member States for granting and withdrawing refugee status.

Article 2 Definitions

For the purposes of this Directive:

(a)   "Geneva Convention" means the Convention of 28 July 1951 relating to the status of refugees, as amended by the New York Protocol of 31 January 1967;

(b)   "application" or "application for asylum" means an application made by a third country national or stateless person which can be understood as a request for international protection from a Member State under the Geneva Convention. Any application for international protection is presumed to be an application for asylum, unless the person concerned explicitly requests another kind of protection that can be applied for separately;

(c)   "applicant" or "applicant for asylum" means a third country national or stateless person who has made an application for asylum in respect of which a final decision has not yet been taken;

(d)   "final decision" means a decision on whether the third country national or stateless person be granted refugee status by virtue of Directive 2004/83/EC and which is no longer subject to a remedy within the framework of Chapter V of this Directive irrespective of whether such remedy has the effect of allowing applicants to remain in the Member States concerned pending its outcome, subject to Annex III to this Directive;

(e)   "determining authority" means any quasi-judicial or administrative body in a Member State responsible for examining applications for asylum and competent to take decisions at first instance in such cases, subject to Annex I;

(f)   "refugee" means a third country national or a stateless person who fulfils the requirements of Article 1 of the Geneva Convention as set out in Directive 2004/83/EC;

(g)   "refugee status" means the recognition by a Member State of a third country national or stateless person as a refugee;

(h)   "unaccompanied minor" means a person below the age of 18 who arrives in the territory of the Member States unaccompanied by an adult responsible for him/her whether by law or by custom, and for as long as he/she is not effectively taken into the care of such a person; it includes a minor who is left unaccompanied after he/she has entered the territory of the Member States;

(i)   "representative" means a person acting on behalf of an organisation representing an unaccompanied minor as legal guardian, a person acting on behalf of a national organisation which is responsible for the care and well-being of minors, or any other appropriate representation appointed to ensure his/her best interests;

(j)   "withdrawal of refugee status" means the decision by a competent authority to revoke, end or refuse to renew the refugee status of a person in accordance with Directive 2004/83/EC;

(k)   "remain in the Member State" means to remain in the territory, including at the border or in transit zones, of the Member State in which the application for asylum has been made or is being examined.

Article 3 Scope

1. This Directive shall apply to all applications for asylum made in the territory, including at the border or in the transit zones of the Member States, and to the withdrawal of refugee status.

2. This Directive shall not apply in cases of requests for diplomatic or territorial asylum submitted to representations of Member States.

3. Where Member States employ or introduce a procedure in which asylum applications are examined both as applications on the basis of the Geneva Convention and as applications for other kinds of international protection given under the circumstances defined by Article 15 of Directive 2004/83/EC, they shall apply this Directive throughout their procedure.

4. Moreover, Member States may decide to apply this Directive in procedures for deciding on applications for any kind of international protection.

Article 4 Responsible authorities

1. Member States shall designate for all procedures a determining authority which will be responsible for an appropriate examination of the applications in accordance with this Directive, in particular Articles 8(2) and 9.

In accordance with Article 4(4) of Regulation (EC) No 343/2003, applications for asylum made in a Member State to the authorities of another Member State carrying out immigration controls there shall be dealt with by the Member State in whose territory the application is made.

2. However, Member States may provide that another authority is responsible for the purposes of:

(a)   processing cases in which it is considered to transfer the applicant to another State according to the rules establishing criteria and mechanisms for determining which State is responsible for considering an application for asylum, until the transfer takes place or the requested State has refused to take charge of or take back the applicant;

(b)   taking a decision on the application in the light of national security provisions, provided the determining authority is consulted prior to this decision as to whether the applicant qualifies as a refugee by virtue of Directive 2004/83/EC;

(c)   conducting a preliminary examination pursuant to Article 32, provided this authority has access to the applicant's file regarding the previous application;

(d)   processing cases in the framework of the procedures provided for in Article 35(1);

(e)   refusing permission to enter in the framework of the procedure provided for in Article 35(2) to (5), subject to the conditions and as set out therein;

(f)   establishing that an applicant is seeking to enter or has entered into the Member State from a safe third country pursuant to Article 36, subject to the conditions and as set out in that Article.

3.   Where authorities are designated in accordance with paragraph 2, Member States shall ensure that the personnel of such authorities have the appropriate knowledge or receive the necessary training to fulfil their obligations when implementing this Directive.

Article 5 More favourable provisions

Member States may introduce or maintain more favourable standards on procedures for granting and withdrawing refugee status, insofar as those standards are compatible with this Directive.

CHAPTER II
BASIC PRINCIPLES AND GUARANTEES

Article 6 Access to the procedure

1.   Member States may require that applications for asylum be made in person and/or at a designated place.

2.   Member States shall ensure that each adult having legal capacity has the right to make an application for asylum on his/her own behalf.

3.   Member States may provide that an application may be made by an applicant on behalf of his/her dependants. In such cases Member States shall ensure that dependant adults consent to the lodging of the application on their behalf, failing which they shall have an opportunity to make an application on their own behalf.

Consent shall be requested at the time the application is lodged or, at the latest, when the personal interview with the dependant adult is conducted.

4.   Member States may determine in national legislation:

(a)   the cases in which a minor can make an application on his/her own behalf;

(b)   the cases in which the application of an unaccompanied minor has to be lodged by a representative as provided for in Article 17(1)(a);

(c)   the cases in which the lodging of an application for asylum is deemed to constitute also the lodging of an application for asylum for any unmarried minor.

5.   Member States shall ensure that authorities likely to be addressed by someone who wishes to make an application for asylum are able to advise that person how and where he/she may make such an application and/or may require these authorities to forward the application to the competent authority.

Article 7 Right to remain in the Member State pending the examination of the application

1.   Applicants shall be allowed to remain in the Member State, for the sole purpose of the procedure, until the determining authority has made a decision in accordance with the procedures at first instance set out in Chapter III. This right to remain shall not constitute an entitlement to a residence permit.

2.   Member States can make an exception only where, in accordance with Articles 32 and 34, a subsequent application will not be further examined or where they will surrender or extradite, as appropriate, a person either to another Member State

pursuant to obligations in accordance with a European arrest warrant[6] or otherwise, or to a third country, or to international criminal courts or tribunals.

[6] Council Framework Decision 2002/584/JHA of 13 June 2002 on the European arrest warrant and the surrender procedures between Member States (OJ L 190, 18.7.2002, p 1).

Article 8 Requirements for the examination of applications

1. Without prejudice to Article 23(4)(i), Member States shall ensure that applications for asylum are neither rejected nor excluded from examination on the sole ground that they have not been made as soon as possible.

2. Member States shall ensure that decisions by the determining authority on applications for asylum are taken after an appropriate examination. To that end, Member States shall ensure that:

    (a)   applications are examined and decisions are taken individually, objectively and impartially;

    (b)   precise and up-to-date information is obtained from various sources, such as the United Nations High Commissioner for Refugees (UNHCR), as to the general situation prevailing in the countries of origin of applicants for asylum and, where necessary, in countries through which they have transited, and that such information is made available to the personnel responsible for examining applications and taking decisions;

    (c)   the personnel examining applications and taking decisions have the knowledge with respect to relevant standards applicable in the field of asylum and refugee law.

3. The authorities referred to in Chapter V shall, through the determining authority or the applicant or otherwise, have access to the general information referred to in paragraph 2(b), necessary for the fulfilment of their task.

4. Member States may provide for rules concerning the translation of documents relevant for the examination of applications.

Article 9 Requirements for a decision by the determining authority

1. Member States shall ensure that decisions on applications for asylum are given in writing.

2. Member States shall also ensure that, where an application is rejected, the reasons in fact and in law are stated in the decision and information on how to challenge a negative decision is given in writing.

Member States need not state the reasons for not granting refugee status in a decision where the applicant is granted a status which offers the same rights and benefits under national and Community law as the refugee status by virtue of Directive 2004/83/EC. In these cases, Member States shall ensure that the reasons for not granting refugee status are stated in the applicant's file and that the applicant has, upon request, access to his/her file.

Moreover, Member States need not provide information on how to challenge a negative decision in writing in conjunction with a decision where the applicant has been provided with this information at an earlier stage either in writing or by electronic means accessible to the applicant.

3. For the purposes of Article 6(3), and whenever the application is based on the same grounds, Member States may take one single decision, covering all dependants.

10 Guarantees for applicants for asylum

1. With respect to the procedures provided for in Chapter III, Member States shall ensure that all applicants for asylum enjoy the following guarantees:

    (a)   they shall be informed in a language which they may reasonably be supposed to understand of the procedure to be followed and of their rights and obligations during the procedure and the possible consequences of not complying with their obligations and not cooperating with the authorities. They shall be informed of the time-frame, as well as the means at their disposal for fulfilling the obligation to submit the elements as referred to in Article 4 of Directive 2004/83/EC. This information shall be given in time to enable them to exercise the rights guaranteed in this Directive and to comply with the obligations described in Article 11;

(b) they shall receive the services of an interpreter for submitting their case to the competent authorities whenever necessary. Member States shall consider it necessary to give these services at least when the determining authority calls upon the applicant to be interviewed as referred to in Articles 12 and 13 and appropriate communication cannot be ensured without such services. In this case and in other cases where the competent authorities call upon the applicant, these services shall be paid for out of public funds;

(c) they shall not be denied the opportunity to communicate with the UNHCR or with any other organisation working on behalf of the UNHCR in the territory of the Member State pursuant to an agreement with that Member State;

(d) they shall be given notice in reasonable time of the decision by the determining authority on their application for asylum. If a legal adviser or other counsellor is legally representing the applicant, Member States may choose to give notice of the decision to him/her instead of to the applicant for asylum;

(e) they shall be informed of the result of the decision by the determining authority in a language that they may reasonably be supposed to understand when they are not assisted or represented by a legal adviser or other counsellor and when free legal assistance is not available. The information provided shall include information on how to challenge a negative decision in accordance with the provisions of Article 9(2).

2.   With respect to the procedures provided for in Chapter V, Member States shall ensure that all applicants for asylum enjoy equivalent guarantees to the ones referred to in paragraph 1(b), (c) and (d) of this Article.

Article 11 Obligations of the applicants for asylum

1.   Member States may impose upon applicants for asylum obligations to cooperate with the competent authorities insofar as these obligations are necessary for the processing of the application.

2.   In particular, Member States may provide that:

(a) applicants for asylum are required to report to the competent authorities or to appear before them in person, either without delay or at a specified time;

(b) applicants for asylum have to hand over documents in their possession relevant to the examination of the application, such as their passports;

(c) applicants for asylum are required to inform the competent authorities of their current place of residence or address and of any changes thereof as soon as possible. Member States may provide that the applicant shall have to accept any communication at the most recent place of residence or address which he/she indicated accordingly;

(d) the competent authorities may search the applicant and the items he/she carries with him/her;

(e) the competent authorities may take a photograph of the applicant; and

(f) the competent authorities may record the applicant's oral statements, provided he/she has previously been informed thereof.

Article 12 Personal interview

1. Before a decision is taken by the determining authority, the applicant for asylum shall be given the opportunity of a personal interview on his/her application for asylum with a person competent under national law to conduct such an interview.

Member States may also give the opportunity of a personal interview to each dependant adult referred to in Article 6(3).

Member States may determine in national legislation the cases in which a minor shall be given the opportunity of a personal interview.

2. The personal interview may be omitted where:

(a) the determining authority is able to take a positive decision on the basis of evidence available; or

(b) the competent authority has already had a meeting with the applicant for the purpose of assisting him/her with completing his/her application and submitting the essential information regarding the application, in terms of Article 4(2) of Directive 2004/83/EC; or

(c) the determining authority, on the basis of a complete examination of information provided by the applicant, considers the application to be unfounded in cases where the circumstances mentioned in Article 23(4)(a), (c), (g), (h) and (j) apply.

3. The personal interview may also be omitted where it is not reasonably practicable, in particular where the competent authority is of the opinion that the applicant is unfit or unable to be interviewed owing to enduring circumstances beyond his/her control. When in doubt, Member States may require a medical or psychological certificate.

Where the Member State does not provide the applicant with the opportunity for a personal interview pursuant to this paragraph, or where applicable, to the dependant, reasonable efforts shall be made to allow the applicant or the dependant to submit further information.

4. The absence of a personal interview in accordance with this Article shall not prevent the determining authority from taking a decision on an application for asylum.

5. The absence of a personal interview pursuant to paragraph 2(b) and (c) and paragraph 3 shall not adversely affect the decision of the determining authority.

6. Irrespective of Article 20(1), Member States, when deciding on the application for asylum, may take into account the fact that the applicant failed to appear for the personal interview, unless he/she had good reasons for the failure to appear.

Article 13 Requirements for a personal interview

1. A personal interview shall normally take place without the presence of family members unless the determining authority considers it necessary for an appropriate examination to have other family members present.

2. A personal interview shall take place under conditions which ensure appropriate confidentiality.

3. Member States shall take appropriate steps to ensure that personal interviews are conducted under conditions which allow applicants to present the grounds for their applications in a comprehensive manner. To that end, Member States shall:

(a) ensure that the person who conducts the interview is sufficiently competent to take account of the personal or general circumstances surrounding the application, including the applicant's cultural origin or vulnerability, insofar as it is possible to do so; and

(b) select an interpreter who is able to ensure appropriate communication between the applicant and the person who conducts the interview. The communication need not necessarily take place in the language preferred by the applicant for asylum if there is another language which he/she may reasonably be supposed to understand and in which he/she is able to communicate.

4.   Member States may provide for rules concerning the presence of third parties at a personal interview.

5.   This Article is also applicable to the meeting referred to in Article 12(2)(b).

Article 14   Status of the report of a personal interview in the procedure

1.   Member States shall ensure that a written report is made of every personal interview, containing at least the essential information regarding the application, as presented by the applicant, in terms of Article 4(2) of Directive 2004/83/EC.

2.   Member States shall ensure that applicants have timely access to the report of the personal interview. Where access is only granted after the decision of the determining authority, Member States shall ensure that access is possible as soon as necessary for allowing an appeal to be prepared and lodged in due time.

3.   Member States may request the applicant's approval of the contents of the report of the personal interview.

Where an applicant refuses to approve the contents of the report, the reasons for this refusal shall be entered into the applicant's file.

The refusal of an applicant to approve the contents of the report shall not prevent the determining authority from taking a decision on his/her application.

4.   This Article is also applicable to the meeting referred to in Article 12(2)(b).

Article 15   Right to legal assistance and representation

1.   Member States shall allow applicants for asylum the opportunity, at their own cost, to consult in an effective manner a legal adviser or other counsellor, admitted or permitted as such under national law, on matters relating to their asylum applications.

2.   In the event of a negative decision by a determining authority, Member States shall ensure that free legal assistance and/or representation be granted on request, subject to the provisions of paragraph 3.

3.   Member States may provide in their national legislation that free legal assistance and/or representation is granted:

(a)   only for procedures before a court or tribunal in accordance with Chapter V and not for any onward appeals or reviews provided for under national law, including a rehearing of an appeal following an onward appeal or review; and/or

(b)   only to those who lack sufficient resources; and/or

(c)   only to legal advisers or other counsellors specifically designated by national law to assist and/or represent applicants for asylum; and/or

(d)   only if the appeal or review is likely to succeed.

Member States shall ensure that legal assistance and/or representation granted under point (d) is not arbitrarily restricted.

4.   Rules concerning the modalities for filing and processing requests for legal assistance and/or representation may be provided by Member States.

5.   Member States may also:

(a)   impose monetary and/or time-limits on the provision of free legal assistance and/or representation, provided that such limits do not arbitrarily restrict access to legal assistance and/or representation;

(b)   provide that, as regards fees and other costs, the treatment of applicants shall not be more favourable than the treatment generally accorded to their nationals in matters pertaining to legal assistance.

6.   Member States may demand to be reimbursed wholly or partially for any expenses granted if and when the applicant's financial situation has improved considerably or if the decision to grant such benefits was taken on the basis of false information supplied by the applicant.

Article 16 Scope of legal assistance and representation

1.   Member States shall ensure that a legal adviser or other counsellor admitted or permitted as such under national law, and who assists or represents an applicant for asylum under the terms of national law, shall enjoy access to such information in the applicant's file as is liable to be examined by the authorities referred to in Chapter V, insofar as the information is relevant to the examination of the application.

Member States may make an exception where disclosure of information or sources would jeopardise national security, the security of the organisations or person(s) providing the information or the security of the person(s) to whom the information relates or where the investigative interests relating to the examination of applications of asylum by the competent authorities of the Member States or the international relations of the Member States would be compromised. In these cases, access to the information or sources in question shall be available to the authorities referred to in Chapter V, except where such access is precluded in cases of national security.

2.   Member States shall ensure that the legal adviser or other counsellor who assists or represents an applicant for asylum has access to closed areas, such as detention facilities and transit zones, for the purpose of consulting that applicant. Member States may only limit the possibility of visiting applicants in closed areas where such limitation is, by virtue of national legislation, objectively necessary for the security, public order or administrative management of the area, or in order to ensure an efficient examination of the application, provided that access by the legal adviser or other counsellor is not thereby severely limited or rendered impossible.

3.   Member States may provide rules covering the presence of legal advisers or other counsellors at all interviews in the procedure, without prejudice to this Article or to Article 17(1)(b).

4.   Member States may provide that the applicant is allowed to bring with him/her to the personal interview a legal adviser or other counsellor admitted or permitted as such under national law.

Member States may require the presence of the applicant at the personal interview, even if he/she is represented under the terms of national law by such a legal adviser or counsellor, and may require the applicant to respond in person to the questions asked. The absence of a legal adviser or other counsellor shall not prevent the competent authority from conducting the personal interview with the applicant.

Article 17 Guarantees for unaccompanied minors

1.   With respect to all procedures provided for in this Directive and without prejudice to the provisions of Articles 12 and 14, Member States shall:

(a)   as soon as possible take measures to ensure that a representative represents and/or assists the unaccompanied minor with respect to the examination of the application. This representative can also be the representative referred to in Article 19 of Directive 2003/9/EC of 27 January 2003 laying down minimum standards for the reception of asylum seekers[7];

(b)   ensure that the representative is given the opportunity to inform the unaccompanied minor about the meaning and possible consequences of the personal interview and, where appropriate, how to prepare himself/herself for the personal interview. Member States shall allow the representative to be present at that interview and to ask questions or make comments, within the framework set by the person who conducts the interview.

Member States may require the presence of the unaccompanied minor at the personal interview, even if the representative is present.

2.   Member States may refrain from appointing a representative where the unaccompanied minor:

(a) will in all likelihood reach the age of maturity before a decision at first instance is taken; or

(b) can avail himself, free of charge, of a legal adviser or other counsellor, admitted as such under national law to fulfil the tasks assigned above to the representative; or

(c) is married or has been married.

3. Member States may, in accordance with the laws and regulations in force on 1 December 2005, also refrain from appointing a representative where the unaccompanied minor is 16 years old or older, unless he/she is unable to pursue his/her application without a representative.

4. Member States shall ensure that:

(a) if an unaccompanied minor has a personal interview on his/her application for asylum as referred to in Articles 12, 13 and 14, that interview is conducted by a person who has the necessary knowledge of the special needs of minors;

(b) an official with the necessary knowledge of the special needs of minors prepares the decision by the determining authority on the application of an unaccompanied minor.

5. Member States may use medical examinations to determine the age of unaccompanied minors within the framework of the examination of an application for asylum.

In cases where medical examinations are used, Member States shall ensure that:

(a) unaccompanied minors are informed prior to the examination of their application for asylum, and in a language which they may reasonably be supposed to understand, of the possibility that their age may be determined by medical examination. This shall include information on the method of examination and the possible consequences of the result of the medical examination for the examination of the application for asylum, as well as the consequences of refusal on the part of the unaccompanied minor to undergo the medical examination;

(b) unaccompanied minors and/or their representatives consent to carry out an examination to determine the age of the minors concerned; and

(c) the decision to reject an application for asylum from an unaccompanied minor who refused to undergo this medical examination shall not be based solely on that refusal.

The fact that an unaccompanied minor has refused to undergo such a medical examination shall not prevent the determining authority from taking a decision on the application for asylum.

6. The best interests of the child shall be a primary consideration for Member States when implementing this Article.

7   OJ L 31, 6.2.2003, p 18.

Article 18 Detention

1. Member States shall not hold a person in detention for the sole reason that he/she is an applicant for asylum.

2. Where an applicant for asylum is held in detention, Member States shall ensure that there is a possibility of speedy judicial review.

Article 19 Procedure in case of withdrawal of the application

1. Insofar as Member States provide for the possibility of explicit withdrawal of the application under national law, when an applicant for asylum explicitly withdraws his/her application for asylum, Member States shall ensure that the determining authority takes a decision to either discontinue the examination or reject the application.

2. Member States may also decide that the determining authority can decide to discontinue the examination without taking a decision. In this case, Member States shall ensure that the determining authority enters a notice in the applicant's file.

Article 20 Procedure in the case of implicit withdrawal or abandonment of the application

1. When there is reasonable cause to consider that an applicant for asylum has implicitly withdrawn or abandoned his/her application for asylum, Member States shall ensure that the determining authority takes a decision to either discontinue the examination or reject the application on the basis that the applicant has not established an entitlement to refugee status in accordance with Directive 2004/83/EC. Member States may assume that the applicant has implicitly withdrawn or abandoned his/her application for asylum in particular when it is ascertained that:

(a) he/she has failed to respond to requests to provide information essential to his/her application in terms of Article 4 of Directive 2004/83/EC or has not appeared for a personal interview as provided for in Articles 12, 13 and 14, unless the applicant demonstrates within a reasonable time that his/her failure was due to circumstances beyond his control;

(b) he/she has absconded or left without authorisation the place where he/she lived or was held, without contacting the competent authority within a reasonable time, or he/she has not within a reasonable time complied with reporting duties or other obligations to communicate.

For the purposes of implementing these provisions, Member States may lay down time-limits or guidelines.

2. Member States shall ensure that the applicant who reports again to the competent authority after a decision to discontinue as referred to in paragraph 1 of this Article is taken, is entitled to request that his/her case be reopened, unless the request is examined in accordance with Articles 32 and 34.

Member States may provide for a time-limit after which the applicant's case can no longer be re-opened.

Member States shall ensure that such a person is not removed contrary to the principle of non-refoulement.

Member States may allow the determining authority to take up the examination at the stage where it was discontinued.

Article 21 The role of UNHCR

1. Member States shall allow the UNHCR:

(a) to have access to applicants for asylum, including those in detention and in airport or port transit zones;

(b) to have access to information on individual applications for asylum, on the course of the procedure and on the decisions taken, provided that the applicant for asylum agrees thereto;

(c) to present its views, in the exercise of its supervisory responsibilities under Article 35 of the Geneva Convention, to any competent authorities regarding individual applications for asylum at any stage of the procedure.

2. Paragraph 1 shall also apply to an organisation which is working in the territory of the Member State concerned on behalf of the UNHCR pursuant to an agreement with that Member State.

Article 22 Collection of information on individual cases

For the purposes of examining individual cases, Member States shall not:

(a) directly disclose information regarding individual applications for asylum, or the fact that an application has been made, to the alleged actor(s) of persecution of the applicant for asylum;

(b)   obtain any information from the alleged actor(s) of persecution in a manner that would result in such actor(s) being directly informed of the fact that an application has been made by the applicant in question, and would jeopardise the physical integrity of the applicant and his/her dependants, or the liberty and security of his/her family members still living in the country of origin.

CHAPTER III
PROCEDURES AT FIRST INSTANCE

SECTION I

Article 23 Examination procedure

1.   Member States shall process applications for asylum in an examination procedure in accordance with the basic principles and guarantees of Chapter II.

2.   Member States shall ensure that such a procedure is concluded as soon as possible, without prejudice to an adequate and complete examination.

Member States shall ensure that, where a decision cannot be taken within six months, the applicant concerned shall either:

(a)   be informed of the delay; or

(b)   receive, upon his/her request, information on the time-frame within which the decision on his/her application is to be expected. Such information shall not constitute an obligation for the Member State towards the applicant concerned to take a decision within that time-frame.

3.   Member States may prioritise or accelerate any examination in accordance with the basic principles and guarantees of Chapter II, including where the application is likely to be well-founded or where the applicant has special needs.

4.   Member States may also provide that an examination procedure in accordance with the basic principles and guarantees of Chapter II be prioritised or accelerated if:

(a)   the applicant, in submitting his/her application and presenting the facts, has only raised issues that are not relevant or of minimal relevance to the examination of whether he/she qualifies as a refugee by virtue of Directive 2004/83/EC; or

(b)   the applicant clearly does not qualify as a refugee or for refugee status in a Member State under Directive 2004/83/EC; or

(c)   the application for asylum is considered to be unfounded:

      (i)   because the applicant is from a safe country of origin within the meaning of Articles 29, 30 and 31, or

      (ii)   because the country which is not a Member State, is considered to be a safe third country for the applicant, without prejudice to Article 28(1); or

(d)   the applicant has misled the authorities by presenting false information or documents or by withholding relevant information or documents with respect to his/her identity and/or nationality that could have had a negative impact on the decision; or

(e)   the applicant has filed another application for asylum stating other personal data; or

(f)   the applicant has not produced information establishing with a reasonable degree of certainty his/her identity or nationality, or it is likely that, in bad faith, he/she has destroyed or disposed of an identity or travel document that would have helped establish his/her identity or nationality; or

(g)   the applicant has made inconsistent, contradictory, improbable or insufficient representations which make his/her claim clearly unconvincing in relation to his/her having been the object of persecution referred to in Directive 2004/83/EC; or

(h) the applicant has submitted a subsequent application which does not raise any relevant new elements with respect to his/her particular circumstances or to the situation in his/her country of origin; or

(i) the applicant has failed without reasonable cause to make his/her application earlier, having had opportunity to do so; or

(j) the applicant is making an application merely in order to delay or frustrate the enforcement of an earlier or imminent decision which would result in his/her removal; or

(k) the applicant has failed without good reason to comply with obligations referred to in Article 4(1) and (2) of Directive 2004/83/EC or in Articles11(2)(a) and (b) and 20(1) of this Directive; or

(l) the applicant entered the territory of the Member State unlawfully or prolonged his/her stay unlawfully and, without good reason, has either not presented himself/herself to the authorities and/or filed an application for asylum as soon as possible, given the circumstances of his/her entry; or

(m) the applicant is a danger to the national security or public order of the Member State, or the applicant has been forcibly expelled for serious reasons of public security and public order under national law; or

(n) the applicant refuses to comply with an obligation to have his/her fingerprints taken in accordance with relevant Community and/or national legislation; or

(o) the application was made by an unmarried minor to whom Article 6(4)(c) applies, after the application of the parents or parent responsible for the minor has been rejected and no relevant new elements were raised with respect to his/her particular circumstances or to the situation in his/her country of origin.

Article 24 Specific procedures

1. Member States may provide for the following specific procedures derogating from the basic principles and guarantees of Chapter II:

(a) a preliminary examination for the purposes of processing cases considered within the framework set out in Section IV;

(b) procedures for the purposes of processing cases considered within the framework set out in Section V.

2. Member States may also provide a derogation in respect of Section VI.

SECTION II

Article 25 Inadmissible applications

1. In addition to cases in which an application is not examined in accordance with Regulation (EC) No 343/2003, Member States are not required to examine whether the applicant qualifies as a refugee in accordance with Directive 2004/83/EC where an application is considered inadmissible pursuant to this Article.

2. Member States may consider an application for asylum as inadmissible pursuant to this Article if:

(a) another Member State has granted refugee status;

(b) a country which is not a Member State is considered as a first country of asylum for the applicant, pursuant to Article 26;

(c) a country which is not a Member State is considered as a safe third country for the applicant, pursuant to Article 27;

(d) the applicant is allowed to remain in the Member State concerned on some other grounds and as result of this he/she has been granted a status equivalent to the rights and benefits of the refugee status by virtue of Directive 2004/83/EC;

(e) the applicant is allowed to remain in the territory of the Member State concerned on some other grounds which protect him/her against refoulement pending the outcome of a procedure for the determination of status pursuant to point (d);

(f) the applicant has lodged an identical application after a final decision;

(g) a dependant of the applicant lodges an application, after he/she has in accordance with Article 6(3) consented to have his/her case be part of an application made on his/her behalf, and there are no facts relating to the dependant's situation, which justify a separate application.

Article 26 The concept of first country of asylum

A country can be considered to be a first country of asylum for a particular applicant for asylum if:

(a) he/she has been recognised in that country as a refugee and he/she can still avail himself/herself of that protection; or

(b) he/she otherwise enjoys sufficient protection in that country, including benefiting from the principle of non-refoulement;

provided that he/she will be re-admitted to that country.

In applying the concept of first country of asylum to the particular circumstances of an applicant for asylum Member States may take into account Article 27(1).

Article 27 The safe third country concept

1. Member States may apply the safe third country concept only where the competent authorities are satisfied that a person seeking asylum will be treated in accordance with the following principles in the third country concerned:

(a) life and liberty are not threatened on account of race, religion, nationality, membership of a particular social group or political opinion;

(b) the principle of non-refoulement in accordance with the Geneva Convention is respected;

(c) the prohibition of removal, in violation of the right to freedom from torture and cruel, inhuman or degrading treatment as laid down in international law, is respected; and

(d) the possibility exists to request refugee status and, if found to be a refugee, to receive protection in accordance with the Geneva Convention.

2. The application of the safe third country concept shall be subject to rules laid down in national legislation, including:

(a) rules requiring a connection between the person seeking asylum and the third country concerned on the basis of which it would be reasonable for that person to go to that country;

(b) rules on the methodology by which the competent authorities satisfy themselves that the safe third country concept may be applied to a particular country or to a particular applicant. Such methodology shall include case-by-case consideration of the safety of the country for a particular applicant and/or national designation of countries considered to be generally safe;

(c) rules in accordance with international law, allowing an individual examination of whether the third country concerned is safe for a particular applicant which, as a minimum, shall permit the applicant to challenge the application of the safe third country concept on the grounds that he/she would be subjected to torture, cruel, inhuman or degrading treatment or punishment.

3. When implementing a decision solely based on this Article, Member States shall:

(a) inform the applicant accordingly; and

(b)   provide him/her with a document informing the authorities of the third country, in the language of that country, that the application has not been examined in substance.

4.   Where the third country does not permit the applicant for asylum to enter its territory, Member States shall ensure that access to a procedure is given in accordance with the basic principles and guarantees described in Chapter II.

5.   Member States shall inform the Commission periodically of the countries to which this concept is applied in accordance with the provisions of this Article.

SECTION III

Article 28 Unfounded applications

1.   Without prejudice to Articles 19 and 20, Member States may only consider an application for asylum as unfounded if the determining authority has established that the applicant does not qualify for refugee status pursuant to Directive 2004/83/EC.

2.   In the cases mentioned in Article 23(4)(b) and in cases of unfounded applications for asylum in which any of the circumstances listed in Article 23(4)(a) and (c) to (o) apply, Member States may also consider an application as manifestly unfounded, where it is defined as such in the national legislation.

Article 29 Minimum common list of third countries regarded as safe countries of origin

1.   The Council shall, acting by a qualified majority on a proposal from the Commission and after consultation of the European Parliament, adopt a minimum common list of third countries which shall be regarded by Member States as safe countries of origin in accordance with Annex II.

2.   The Council may, acting by a qualified majority on a proposal from the Commission and after consultation of the European Parliament, amend the minimum common list by adding or removing third countries, in accordance with Annex II. The Commission shall examine any request made by the Council or by a Member State to submit a proposal to amend the minimum common list.

3.   When making its proposal under paragraphs 1 or 2, the Commission shall make use of information from the Member States, its own information and, where necessary, information from UNHCR, the Council of Europe and other relevant international organisations.

4.   Where the Council requests the Commission to submit a proposal for removing a third country from the minimum common list, the obligation of Member States pursuant to Article 31(2) shall be suspended with regard to this third country as of the day following the Council decision requesting such a submission.

5.   Where a Member State requests the Commission to submit a proposal to the Council for removing a third country from the minimum common list, that Member State shall notify the Council in writing of the request made to the Commission. The obligation of this Member State pursuant to Article 31(2) shall be suspended with regard to the third country as of the day following the notification to the Council.

6.   The European Parliament shall be informed of the suspensions under paragraphs 4 and 5.

7.   The suspensions under paragraphs 4 and 5 shall end after three months, unless the Commission makes a proposal before the end of this period, to withdraw the third country from the minimum common list. The suspensions shall in any case end where the Council rejects a proposal by the Commission to withdraw the third country from the list.

8.   Upon request by the Council, the Commission shall report to the European Parliament and the Council on whether the situation of a country on the minimum

common list is still in conformity with Annex II. When presenting its report, the Commission may make such recommendations or proposals as it deems appropriate.

Article 30 National designation of third countries as safe countries of origin

1. Without prejudice to Article 29, Member States may retain or introduce legislation that allows, in accordance with Annex II, for the national designation of third countries other than those appearing on the minimum common list, as safe countries of origin for the purposes of examining applications for asylum. This may include designation of part of a country as safe where the conditions in Annex II are fulfilled in relation to that part.

2. By derogation from paragraph 1, Member States may retain legislation in force on 1 December 2005 that allows for the national designation of third countries, other than those appearing on the minimum common list, as safe countries of origin for the purposes of examining applications for asylum where they are satisfied that persons in the third countries concerned are generally neither subject to:

    (a)   persecution as defined in Article 9 of Directive 2004/83/EC; nor

    (b)   torture or inhuman or degrading treatment or punishment.

3. Member States may also retain legislation in force on 1 December 2005 that allows for the national designation of part of a country as safe, or a country or part of a country as safe for a specified group of persons in that country, where the conditions in paragraph 2 are fulfilled in relation to that part or group.

4. In assessing whether a country is a safe country of origin in accordance with paragraphs 2 and 3, Member States shall have regard to the legal situation, the application of the law and the general political circumstances in the third country concerned.

5. The assessment of whether a country is a safe country of origin in accordance with this Article shall be based on a range of sources of information, including in particular information from other Member States, the UNHCR, the Council of Europe and other relevant international organisations.

6. Member States shall notify to the Commission the countries that are designated as safe countries of origin in accordance with this Article.

Article 31 The safe country of origin concept

1. A third country designated as a safe country of origin in accordance with either Article 29 or 30 may, after an individual examination of the application, be considered as a safe country of origin for a particular applicant for asylum only if:

    (a)   he/she has the nationality of that country; or

    (b)   he/she is a stateless person and was formerly habitually resident in that country;

and he/she has not submitted any serious grounds for considering the country not to be a safe country of origin in his/her particular circumstances and in terms of his/her qualification as a refugee in accordance with Directive 2004/83/EC.

2. Member States shall, in accordance with paragraph 1, consider the application for asylum as unfounded where the third country is designated as safe pursuant to Article 29.

3. Member States shall lay down in national legislation further rules and modalities for the application of the safe country of origin concept.

SECTION IV

Article 32 Subsequent application

1. Where a person who has applied for asylum in a Member State makes further representations or a subsequent application in the same Member State, that Member State may examine these further representations or the elements of the subsequent application in the framework of the examination of the previous

application or in the framework of the examination of the decision under review or appeal, insofar as the competent authorities can take into account and consider all the elements underlying the further representations or subsequent application within this framework.

2. Moreover, Member States may apply a specific procedure as referred to in paragraph 3, where a person makes a subsequent application for asylum:

(a) after his/her previous application has been withdrawn or abandoned by virtue of Articles 19 or 20;

(b) after a decision has been taken on the previous application. Member States may also decide to apply this procedure only after a final decision has been taken.

3. A subsequent application for asylum shall be subject first to a preliminary examination as to whether, after the withdrawal of the previous application or after the decision referred to in paragraph 2(b) of this Article on this application has been reached, new elements or findings relating to the examination of whether he/she qualifies as a refugee by virtue of Directive 2004/83/EC have arisen or have been presented by the applicant.

4. If, following the preliminary examination referred to in paragraph 3 of this Article, new elements or findings arise or are presented by the applicant which significantly add to the likelihood of the applicant qualifying as a refugee by virtue of Directive 2004/83/EC, the application shall be further examined in conformity with Chapter II.

5. Member States may, in accordance with national legislation, further examine a subsequent application where there are other reasons why a procedure has to be re-opened.

6. Member States may decide to further examine the application only if the applicant concerned was, through no fault of his/her own, incapable of asserting the situations set forth in paragraphs 3, 4 and 5 of this Article in the previous procedure, in particular by exercising his/her right to an effective remedy pursuant to Article 39.

7. The procedure referred to in this Article may also be applicable in the case of a dependant who lodges an application after he/she has, in accordance with Article 6(3), consented to have his/her case be part of an application made on his/her behalf. In this case the preliminary examination referred to in paragraph 3 of this Article will consist of examining whether there are facts relating to the dependant's situation which justify a separate application.

Article 33 Failure to appear

Member States may retain or adopt the procedure provided for in Article 32 in the case of an application for asylum filed at a later date by an applicant who, either intentionally or owing to gross negligence, fails to go to a reception centre or appear before the competent authorities at a specified time.

Article 34 Procedural rules

1. Member States shall ensure that applicants for asylum whose application is subject to a preliminary examination pursuant to Article 32 enjoy the guarantees provided for in Article 10(1).

2. Member States may lay down in national law rules on the preliminary examination pursuant to Article 32. Those rules may, inter alia:

(a) oblige the applicant concerned to indicate facts and substantiate evidence which justify a new procedure;

(b) require submission of the new information by the applicant concerned within a time-limit after he/she obtained such information;

(c) permit the preliminary examination to be conducted on the sole basis of written submissions without a personal interview.

The conditions shall not render impossible the access of applicants for asylum to a new procedure or result in the effective annulment or severe curtailment of such access.

3. Member States shall ensure that:

(a) the applicant is informed in an appropriate manner of the outcome of the preliminary examination and, in case the application will not be further examined, of the reasons for this and the possibilities for seeking an appeal or review of the decision;

(b) if one of the situations referred to in Article 32(2) applies, the determining authority shall further examine the subsequent application in conformity with the provisions of Chapter II as soon as possible.

SECTION V

Article 35 Border procedures

1. Member States may provide for procedures, in accordance with the basic principles and guarantees of Chapter II, in order to decide at the border or transit zones of the Member State on applications made at such locations.

2. However, when procedures as set out in paragraph 1 do not exist, Member States may maintain, subject to the provisions of this Article and in accordance with the laws or regulations in force on 1 December 2005, procedures derogating from the basic principles and guarantees described in Chapter II, in order to decide at the border or in transit zones as to whether applicants for asylum who have arrived and made an application for asylum at such locations, may enter their territory.

3. The procedures referred to in paragraph 2 shall ensure in particular that the persons concerned:

(a) are allowed to remain at the border or transit zones of the Member State, without prejudice to Article 7;

(b) are be immediately informed of their rights and obligations, as described in Article 10(1) (a);

(c) have access, if necessary, to the services of an interpreter, as described in Article 10(1)(b);

(d) are interviewed, before the competent authority takes a decision in such procedures, in relation to their application for asylum by persons with appropriate knowledge of the relevant standards applicable in the field of asylum and refugee law, as described in Articles 12, 13 and 14;

(e) can consult a legal adviser or counsellor admitted or permitted as such under national law, as described in Article 15(1); and

(f) have a representative appointed in the case of unaccompanied minors, as described in Article 17(1), unless Article 17(2) or (3) applies.

Moreover, in case permission to enter is refused by a competent authority, this competent authority shall state the reasons in fact and in law why the application for asylum is considered as unfounded or as inadmissible.

4. Member States shall ensure that a decision in the framework of the procedures provided for in paragraph 2 is taken within a reasonable time. When a decision has not been taken within four weeks, the applicant for asylum shall be granted entry to the territory of the Member State in order for his/her application to be processed in accordance with the other provisions of this Directive.

5. In the event of particular types of arrivals, or arrivals involving a large number of third country nationals or stateless persons lodging applications for asylum at the border or in a transit zone, which makes it practically impossible to apply there the provisions of paragraph 1 or the specific procedure set out in paragraphs 2 and 3, those procedures may also be applied where and for as long as these third country nationals or stateless persons are accommodated normally at locations in proximity to the border or transit zone.

SECTION VI

Article 36 The European safe third countries concept

1. Member States may provide that no, or no full, examination of the asylum application and of the safety of the applicant in his/her particular circumstances as described in Chapter II, shall take place in cases where a competent authority has established, on the basis of the facts, that the applicant for asylum is seeking to enter or has entered illegally into its territory from a safe third country according to paragraph 2.

2. A third country can only be considered as a safe third country for the purposes of paragraph 1 where:

(a)   it has ratified and observes the provisions of the Geneva Convention without any geographical limitations;

(b)   it has in place an asylum procedure prescribed by law;

(c)   it has ratified the European Convention for the Protection of Human Rights and Fundamental Freedoms and observes its provisions, including the standards relating to effective remedies; and

(d)   it has been so designated by the Council in accordance with paragraph 3.

3. The Council shall, acting by qualified majority on a proposal from the Commission and after consultation of the European Parliament, adopt or amend a common list of third countries that shall be regarded as safe third countries for the purposes of paragraph 1.

4. The Member States concerned shall lay down in national law the modalities for implementing the provisions of paragraph 1 and the consequences of decisions pursuant to those provisions in accordance with the principle of non-refoulement under the Geneva Convention, including providing for exceptions from the application of this Article for humanitarian or political reasons or for reasons of public international law.

5. When implementing a decision solely based on this Article, the Member States concerned shall:

(a)   inform the applicant accordingly; and

(b)   provide him/her with a document informing the authorities of the third country, in the language of that country, that the application has not been examined in substance.

6. Where the safe third country does not re-admit the applicant for asylum, Member States shall ensure that access to a procedure is given in accordance with the basic principles and guarantees described in Chapter II.

7. Member States which have designated third countries as safe countries in accordance with national legislation in force on 1 December 2005 and on the basis of the criteria in paragraph 2(a), (b) and (c), may apply paragraph 1 to these third countries until the Council has adopted the common list pursuant to paragraph 3.

CHAPTER IV
PROCEDURES FOR THE WITHDRAWAL OF REFUGEE STATUS

Article 37 Withdrawal of refugee status

Member States shall ensure that an examination to withdraw the refugee status of a particular person may commence when new elements or findings arise indicating that there are reasons to reconsider the validity of his/her refugee status.

Article 38 Procedural rules

1. Member States shall ensure that, where the competent authority is considering withdrawing the refugee status of a third country national or stateless person in accordance with Article 14 of Directive 2004/83/EC, the person concerned shall enjoy the following guarantees:

(a) to be informed in writing that the competent authority is reconsidering his or her qualification for refugee status and the reasons for such a reconsideration; and

(b) to be given the opportunity to submit, in a personal interview in accordance with Article 10(1)(b) and Articles 12, 13 and 14 or in a written statement, reasons as to why his/her refugee status should not be withdrawn.

In addition, Member States shall ensure that within the framework of such a procedure:

(c) the competent authority is able to obtain precise and up-to-date information from various sources, such as, where appropriate, from the UNHCR, as to the general situation prevailing in the countries of origin of the persons concerned; and

(d) where information on an individual case is collected for the purposes of reconsidering the refugee status, it is not obtained from the actor(s) of persecution in a manner that would result in such actor(s) being directly informed of the fact that the person concerned is a refugee whose status is under reconsideration, nor jeopardise the physical integrity of the person and his/her dependants, or the liberty and security of his/her family members still living in the country of origin.

2. Member States shall ensure that the decision of the competent authority to withdraw the refugee status is given in writing. The reasons in fact and in law shall be stated in the decision and information on how to challenge the decision shall be given in writing.

3. Once the competent authority has taken the decision to withdraw the refugee status, Article 15, paragraph 2, Article 16, paragraph 1 and Article 21 are equally applicable.

4. By derogation to paragraphs 1, 2 and 3 of this Article, Member States may decide that the refugee status shall lapse by law in case of cessation in accordance with Article 11(1)(a) to (d) of Directive 2004/83/EC or if the refugee has unequivocally renounced his/her recognition as a refugee.

CHAPTER V
APPEALS PROCEDURES

Article 39 The right to an effective remedy

1. Member States shall ensure that applicants for asylum have the right to an effective remedy before a court or tribunal, against the following:

(a) a decision taken on their application for asylum, including a decision:

  (i) to consider an application inadmissible pursuant to Article 25(2),

  (ii) taken at the border or in the transit zones of a Member State as described in Article 35(1),

  (iii) not to conduct an examination pursuant to Article 36;

(b) a refusal to re-open the examination of an application after its discontinuation pursuant to Articles 19 and 20;

(c) a decision not to further examine the subsequent application pursuant to Articles 32 and 34;

(d) a decision refusing entry within the framework of the procedures provided for under Article 35(2);

(e) a decision to withdraw of refugee status pursuant to Article 38.

2. Member States shall provide for time-limits and other necessary rules for the applicant to exercise his/her right to an effective remedy pursuant to paragraph 1.

3. Member States shall, where appropriate, provide for rules in accordance with their international obligations dealing with:

(a) the question of whether the remedy pursuant to paragraph 1 shall have the effect of allowing applicants to remain in the Member State concerned pending its outcome;

(b) the possibility of legal remedy or protective measures where the remedy pursuant to paragraph 1 does not have the effect of allowing applicants to remain in the Member State concerned pending its outcome. Member States may also provide for an ex officio remedy; and

(c) the grounds for challenging a decision under Article 25(2)(c) in accordance with the methodology applied under Article 27(2)(b) and (c).

4. Member States may lay down time-limits for the court or tribunal pursuant to paragraph 1 to examine the decision of the determining authority.

5. Where an applicant has been granted a status which offers the same rights and benefits under national and Community law as the refugee status by virtue of Directive 2004/83/EC, the applicant may be considered as having an effective remedy where a court or tribunal decides that the remedy pursuant to paragraph 1 is inadmissible or unlikely to succeed on the basis of insufficient interest on the part of the applicant in maintaining the proceedings.

6. Member States may also lay down in national legislation the conditions under which it can be assumed that an applicant has implicitly withdrawn or abandoned his/her remedy pursuant to paragraph 1, together with the rules on the procedure to be followed.

CHAPTER VI
GENERAL AND FINAL PROVISIONS

Article 40 Challenge by public authorities

This Directive does not affect the possibility for public authorities of challenging the administrative and/or judicial decisions as provided for in national legislation.

Article 41 Confidentiality

Member States shall ensure that authorities implementing this Directive are bound by the confidentiality principle as defined in national law, in relation to any information they obtain in the course of their work.

Article 42 Report

No later than 1 December 2009, the Commission shall report to the European Parliament and the Council on the application of this Directive in the Member States and shall propose any amendments that are necessary. Member States shall send the Commission all the information that is appropriate for drawing up this report. After presenting the report, the Commission shall report to the European Parliament and the Council on the application of this Directive in the Member States at least every two years.

Article 43 Transposition

Member States shall bring into force the laws, regulations and administrative provisions necessary to comply with this Directive by 1 December 2007. Concerning Article 15, Member States shall bring into force the laws, regulations and administrative provisions necessary to comply with this Directive by 1 December 2008. They shall forthwith inform the Commission thereof.

When Member States adopt those provisions, they shall contain a reference to this Directive or shall be accompanied by such a reference on the occasion of their official publication. The methods of making such reference shall be laid down by Member States.

Member States shall communicate to the Commission the text of the provisions of national law which they adopt in the field covered by this Directive.

Article 44 Transition

Member States shall apply the laws, regulations and administrative provisions set out in Article 43 to applications for asylum lodged after 1 December 2007 and to procedures for the withdrawal of refugee status started after 1 December 2007.

Article 45 Entry into force

This Directive shall enter into force on the 20th day following its publication in the Official Journal of the European Union.

Article 46 Addressees

This Directive is addressed to the Member States in conformity with the Treaty establishing the European Community.

ANNEX I

DEFINITION OF "DETERMINING AUTHORITY"

When implementing the provision of this Directive, Ireland may, insofar as the provisions of section 17(1) of the Refugee Act 1996 (as amended) continue to apply, consider that:

– "determining authority" provided for in Article 2(e) of this Directive shall, insofar as the examination of whether an applicant should or, as the case may be, should not be declared to be a refugee is concerned, mean the Office of the Refugee Applications Commissioner; and

– "decisions at first instance" provided for in Article 2(e) of this Directive shall include recommendations of the Refugee Applications Commissioner as to whether an applicant should or, as the case may be, should not be declared to be a refugee.

Ireland will notify the Commission of any amendments to the provisions of section 17(1) of the Refugee Act 1996 (as amended).

ANNEX II

DESIGNATION OF SAFE COUNTRIES OF ORIGIN FOR THE PURPOSES OF ARTICLES 29 AND 30(1)

A country is considered as a safe country of origin where, on the basis of the legal situation, the application of the law within a democratic system and the general political circumstances, it can be shown that there is generally and consistently no persecution as defined in Article 9 of Directive 2004/83/EC, no torture or inhuman or degrading treatment or punishment and no threat by reason of indiscriminate violence in situations of international or internal armed conflict.

In making this assessment, account shall be taken, inter alia, of the extent to which protection is provided against persecution or mistreatment by:

(a) the relevant laws and regulations of the country and the manner in which they are applied;

(b) observance of the rights and freedoms laid down in the European Convention for the Protection of Human Rights and Fundamental Freedoms and/or the International Covenant for Civil and Political Rights and/or the Convention against Torture, in particular the rights from which derogation cannot be made under Article 15(2) of the said European Convention;

(c) respect of the non-refoulement principle according to the Geneva Convention;

(d) provision for a system of effective remedies against violations of these rights and freedoms.

ANNEX III

DEFINITION OF "APPLICANT" OR "APPLICANT FOR ASYLUM"

When implementing the provisions of this Directive Spain may, insofar as the provisions of "Ley 30/1992 de Régimen jurídico de las Administraciones Públicas y del Procedimiento Administrativo Común" of 26 November 1992 and "Ley 29/1998 reguladora de la Jurisdicción Contencioso-Administrativa" of 13 July 1998 continue to apply, consider that, for the purposes of Chapter V, the definition of "applicant" or "applicant for asylum" in Article 2(c) of this Directive shall include "recurrente" as established in the abovementioned Acts.

A "recurrente" shall be entitled to the same guarantees as an "applicant" or an "applicant for asylum" as set out in this Directive for the purposes of exercising his/her right to an effective remedy in Chapter V.

Spain will notify the Commission of any relevant amendments to the abovementioned Act.

EUROPEAN PARLIAMENT AND COUNCIL DIRECTIVE 2011/36/EU

of 5 April 2011

on preventing and combating trafficking in human beings and protecting its victims, and replacing Council Framework Decision 2002/629/JHA

Notes

Date of publication in Official Journal: OJ L101, 15.4.2011, p 1.

THE EUROPEAN PARLIAMENT AND THE COUNCIL OF THE EUROPEAN UNION,

Having regard to the Treaty on the Functioning of the European Union, and in particular Article 82(2) and Article 83(1) thereof,

Having regard to the proposal from the European Commission,

Having regard to the opinion of the European Economic and Social Committee,[1]

After consulting the Committee of the Regions,

After transmission of the draft legislative act to the national parliaments,

Acting in accordance with the ordinary legislative procedure,[2]

Whereas:

(1)   Trafficking in human beings is a serious crime, often committed within the framework of organised crime, a gross violation of fundamental rights and explicitly prohibited by the Charter of Fundamental Rights of the European Union. Preventing and combating trafficking in human beings is a priority for the Union and the Member States.

(2)   This Directive is part of global action against trafficking in human beings, which includes action involving third countries as stated in the 'Action-oriented Paper on strengthening the Union external dimension on action against trafficking in human beings; Towards global EU action against trafficking in human beings' approved by the Council on 30 November 2009. In this context, action should be pursued in third countries of origin and transfer of victims, with a view to raising awareness, reducing vulnerability, supporting and assisting victims, fighting the root causes of trafficking and supporting those third countries in developing appropriate anti-trafficking legislation.

(3)   This Directive recognises the gender-specific phenomenon of trafficking and that women and men are often trafficked for different purposes. For this reason, assistance and support measures should also be gender-specific where appropriate. The 'push' and 'pull' factors may be different depending on the sectors concerned, such as trafficking in human beings into the sex industry or for labour exploitation in, for example, construction work, the agricultural sector or domestic servitude.

(4)   The Union is committed to the prevention of and fight against trafficking in human beings, and to the protection of the rights of trafficked persons. For this purpose, Council Framework Decision 2002/629/JHA of 19 July 2002 on combating trafficking in human beings[3], and an EU Plan on best practices, standards and procedures for combating and preventing trafficking in human beings[4] were adopted. Moreover, the Stockholm Programme — An open and secure Europe serving and protecting citizens[5], adopted by the European Council, gives a clear priority to the fight against trafficking in human beings. Other measures should be envisaged, such as support for the development of general common indicators of the Union for the identification of victims of trafficking, through the exchange of best practices between all the relevant actors, particularly public and private social services.

(5)   The law enforcement authorities of the Member States should continue to cooperate in order to strengthen the fight against trafficking in human beings. In this regard, close cross-border cooperation, including the sharing of information and the sharing of best practices, as well as a continued open dialogue between the police, judicial and financial authorities of the Member States, is essential. The coordination of investigations and prosecutions of cases of trafficking in human beings should be facilitated by enhanced cooperation with Europol and Eurojust, the setting-up of joint investigation teams, as well as by the implementation of Council Framework Decision 2009/948/JHA of 30 November 2009 on prevention and settlement of conflict of jurisdiction in criminal proceedings[6].

(6)   Member States should encourage and work closely with civil society organisations, including recognised and active non-governmental organisations in this field working with trafficked persons, in particular in policy- making initiatives, information and awareness-raising campaigns, research and education programmes and in training, as well as in monitoring and evaluating the impact of anti-trafficking measures.

(7)   This Directive adopts an integrated, holistic, and human rights approach to the fight against trafficking in human beings and when implementing it, Council Directive 2004/81/EC of 29 April 2004 on the residence permit issued to third-country nationals who are victims of trafficking in human beings or who have been the subject of an action to facilitate illegal immigration, who cooperate with the competent authorities[7] and Directive 2009/52/EC of the European Parliament and of the Council of 18 June 2009 providing for minimum standards on sanctions and measures against employers of illegally staying third-country nationals[8] should be taken into consideration. More rigorous prevention, prosecution and protection of victims' rights, are major objectives of this Directive. This Directive also adopts contextual understandings of the different forms of trafficking and aims at ensuring that each form is tackled by means of the most efficient measures.

(8)   Children are more vulnerable than adults and therefore at greater risk of becoming victims of trafficking in human beings. In the application of this Directive, the child's best interests must be a primary consideration,

in accordance with the Charter of Fundamental Rights of the European Union and the 1989 United Nations Convention on the Rights of the Child.

(9) The 2000 United Nations Protocol to Prevent, Suppress and Punish Trafficking in Persons, Especially Women and Children, supplementing the United Nations Convention against Transnational Organised Crime and the 2005 Council of Europe Convention on Action against Trafficking in Human Beings are crucial steps in the process of enhancing international cooperation against trafficking in human beings. It should be noted that the Council of Europe Convention contains an evaluation mechanism, composed of the Group of experts on action against trafficking in human beings (GRETA) and the Committee of the Parties. Coordination between international organisations with competence with regard to action against trafficking in human beings should be supported in order to avoid duplication of effort.

(10) This Directive is without prejudice to the principle of non-refoulement in accordance with the 1951 Convention relating to the Status of Refugees (Geneva Convention), and is in accordance with Article 4 and Article 19(2) of the Charter of Fundamental Rights of the European Union.

(11) In order to tackle recent developments in the phenomenon of trafficking in human beings, this Directive adopts a broader concept of what should be considered trafficking in human beings than under Framework Decision 2002/629/JHA and therefore includes additional forms of exploitation. Within the context of this Directive, forced begging should be understood as a form of forced labour or services as defined in the 1930 ILO Convention No 29 concerning Forced or Compulsory Labour. Therefore, the exploitation of begging, including the use of a trafficked dependent person for begging, falls within the scope of the definition of trafficking in human beings only when all the elements of forced labour or services occur. In the light of the relevant case-law, the validity of any possible consent to perform such labour or services should be evaluated on a case-by-case basis. However, when a child is concerned, no possible consent should ever be considered valid. The expression 'exploitation of criminal activities' should be understood as the exploitation of a person to commit, inter alia, pick-pocketing, shop-lifting, drug trafficking and other similar activities which are subject to penalties and imply financial gain. The definition also covers trafficking in human beings for the purpose of the removal of organs, which constitutes a serious violation of human dignity and physical integrity, as well as, for instance, other behaviour such as illegal adoption or forced marriage in so far as they fulfil the constitutive elements of trafficking in human beings.

(12) The levels of penalties in this Directive reflect the growing concern among Member States regarding the development of the phenomenon of trafficking in human beings. For this reason this Directive uses as a basis levels 3 and 4 of the Council conclusions of 24- 25 April 2002 on the approach to apply regarding approximation of penalties. When the offence is committed in certain circumstances, for example against a particularly vulnerable victim, the penalty should be more severe. In the context of this Directive, particularly vulnerable persons should include at least all children. Other factors that could be taken into account when assessing the vulnerability of a victim include, for example, gender, pregnancy, state of health and disability. When the offence is particularly grave, for example when the life of the victim has been endangered or the offence has involved serious violence such as torture, forced drug/medication usage, rape or other serious forms of psychological, physical or sexual violence, or has otherwise caused particularly serious

harm to the victim, this should also be reflected in a more severe penalty. When, under this Directive, a reference is made to surrender, such reference should be interpreted in accordance with Council Framework Decision 2002/584/JHA of 13 June 2002 on the European arrest warrant and the surrender procedures between Member States[9]. The gravity of the offence committed could be taken into account within the framework of the execution of the sentence.

(13) In combating trafficking in human beings, full use should be made of existing instruments on the seizure and confiscation of the proceeds of crime, such as the United Nations Convention against Transnational Organised Crime and the Protocols thereto, the 1990 Council of Europe Convention on Laundering, Search, Seizure and Confiscation of the Proceeds from Crime, Council Framework Decision 2001/500/JHA of 26 June 2001 on money laundering, the identification, tracing, freezing, seizing and confiscation of instrumentalities and the proceeds of crime[10], and Council Framework Decision 2005/212/JHA of 24 February 2005 on Confiscation of Crime-Related Proceeds, Instrumentalities and Property[11]. The use of seized and confiscated instrumentalities and the proceeds from the offences referred to in this Directive to support victims' assistance and protection, including compensation of victims and Union trans-border law enforcement counter-trafficking activities, should be encouraged.

(14) Victims of trafficking in human beings should, in accordance with the basic principles of the legal systems of the relevant Member States, be protected from prosecution or punishment for criminal activities such as the use of false documents, or offences under legislation on prostitution or immigration, that they have been compelled to commit as a direct consequence of being subject to trafficking. The aim of such protection is to safeguard the human rights of victims, to avoid further victimisation and to encourage them to act as witnesses in criminal proceedings against the perpetrators. This safeguard should not exclude prosecution or punishment for offences that a person has voluntarily committed or participated in.

(15) To ensure the success of investigations and prosecutions of human trafficking offences, their initiation should not depend, in principle, on reporting or accusation by the victim. Where the nature of the act calls for it, prosecution should be allowed for a sufficient period of time after the victim has reached the age of majority. The length of the sufficient period of time for prosecution should be determined in accordance with respective national law. Law enforcement officials and prosecutors should be adequately trained, in particular with a view to enhancing international law enforcement and judicial cooperation. Those responsible for investigating and prosecuting such offences should also have access to the investigative tools used in organised crime or other serious crime cases. Such tools could include the interception of communications, covert surveillance including electronic surveillance, the monitoring of bank accounts and other financial investigations.

(16) In order to ensure effective prosecution of international criminal groups whose centre of activity is in a Member State and which carry out trafficking in human beings in third countries, jurisdiction should be established over the offence of trafficking in human beings where the offender is a national of that Member State, and the offence is committed outside the territory of that Member State. Similarly, jurisdiction could also be established where the offender is an habitual resident of a Member State, the victim is a national or an habitual resident of a Member State, or the offence is committed for the benefit of a legal

person established in the territory of a Member State, and the offence is committed outside the territory of that Member State.

(17) While Directive 2004/81/EC provides for the issue of a residence permit to victims of trafficking in human beings who are third-country nationals, and Directive 2004/38/EC of the European Parliament and of the Council of 29 April 2004 on the rights of the citizens of the Union and their family members to move and reside freely within the territory of the Member States[12] regulates the exercise of the right to move and reside freely in the territory of the Member States by citizens of the Union and their families, including protection from expulsion, this Directive establishes specific protective measures for any victim of trafficking in human beings. Consequently, this Directive does not deal with the conditions of the residence of the victims of trafficking in human beings in the territory of the Member States.

(18) It is necessary for victims of trafficking in human beings to be able to exercise their rights effectively. Therefore assistance and support should be available to them before, during and for an appropriate time after criminal proceedings. Member States should provide for resources to support victim assistance, support and protection. The assistance and support provided should include at least a minimum set of measures that are necessary to enable the victim to recover and escape from their traffickers. The practical implementation of such measures should, on the basis of an individual assessment carried out in accordance with national procedures, take into account the circumstances, cultural context and needs of the person concerned. A person should be provided with assistance and support as soon as there is a reasonable-grounds indication for believing that he or she might have been trafficked and irrespective of his or her willingness to act as a witness. In cases where the victim does not reside lawfully in the Member State concerned, assistance and support should be provided unconditionally at least during the reflection period. If, after completion of the identification process or expiry of the reflection period, the victim is not considered eligible for a residence permit or does not otherwise have lawful residence in that Member State, or if the victim has left the territory of that Member State, the Member State concerned is not obliged to continue providing assistance and support to that person on the basis of this Directive. Where necessary, assistance and support should continue for an appropriate period after the criminal proceedings have ended, for example if medical treatment is ongoing due to the severe physical or psychological consequences of the crime, or if the victim's safety is at risk due to the victim's statements in those criminal proceedings.

(19) Council Framework Decision 2001/220/JHA of 15 March 2001 on the standing of victims in criminal proceedings[13] establishes a set of victims' rights in criminal proceedings, including the right to protection and compensation. In addition, victims of trafficking in human beings should be given access without delay to legal counselling and, in accordance with the role of victims in the relevant justice systems, to legal representation, including for the purpose of claiming compensation. Such legal counselling and representation could also be provided by the competent authorities for the purpose of claiming compensation from the State. The purpose of legal counselling is to enable victims to be informed and receive advice about the various possibilities open to them. Legal counselling should be provided by a person having received appropriate legal training without necessarily being a lawyer. Legal counselling and, in accordance with the role of victims in the relevant justice systems, legal representation should be provided free of charge, at least when the victim

does not have sufficient financial resources, in a manner consistent with the internal procedures of Member States. As child victims in particular are unlikely to have such resources, legal counselling and legal representation would in practice be free of charge for them. Furthermore, on the basis of an individual risk assessment carried out in accordance with national procedures, victims should be protected from retaliation, from intimidation, and from the risk of being re-trafficked.

(20) Victims of trafficking who have already suffered the abuse and degrading treatment which trafficking commonly entails, such as sexual exploitation, sexual abuse, rape, slavery-like practices or the removal of organs, should be protected from secondary victimisation and further trauma during the criminal proceedings. Unnecessary repetition of interviews during investigation, prosecution and trial should be avoided, for instance, where appropriate, through the production, as soon as possible in the proceedings, of video recordings of those interviews. To this end victims of trafficking should during criminal investigations and proceedings receive treatment that is appropriate to their individual needs. The assessment of their individual needs should take into consideration circumstances such as their age, whether they are pregnant, their health, a disability they may have and other personal circumstances, as well as the physical and psychological consequences of the criminal activity to which the victim was subjected. Whether and how the treatment is applied is to be decided in accordance with grounds defined by national law, rules of judicial discretion, practice and guidance, on a case-by-case basis.

(21) Assistance and support measures should be provided to victims on a consensual and informed basis. Victims should therefore be informed of the important aspects of those measures and they should not be imposed on the victims. A victim's refusal of assistance or support measures should not entail obligations for the competent authorities of the Member State concerned to provide the victim with alternative measures.

(22) In addition to measures available to all victims of trafficking in human beings, Member States should ensure that specific assistance, support and protective measures are available to child victims. Those measures should be provided in the best interests of the child and in accordance with the 1989 United Nations Convention on the Rights of the Child. Where the age of a person subject to trafficking is uncertain, and there are reasons to believe it is less than 18 years, that person should be presumed to be a child and receive immediate assistance, support and protection. Assistance and support measures for child victims should focus on their physical and psycho-social recovery and on a durable solution for the person in question. Access to education would help children to be reintegrated into society. Given that child victims of trafficking are particularly vulnerable, additional protective measures should be available to protect them during interviews forming part of criminal investigations and proceedings.

(23) Particular attention should be paid to unaccompanied child victims of trafficking in human beings, as they need specific assistance and support due to their situation of particular vulnerability. From the moment an unaccompanied child victim of trafficking in human beings is identified and until a durable solution is found, Member States should apply reception measures appropriate to the needs of the child and should ensure that relevant procedural safeguards apply. The necessary measures should be taken to ensure that, where appropriate, a guardian and/or a representative are appointed in order to safeguard the minor's best interests. A decision on the future of each unaccompanied child victim

should be taken within the shortest possible period of time with a view to finding durable solutions based on an individual assessment of the best interests of the child, which should be a primary consideration. A durable solution could be return and reintegration into the country of origin or the country of return, integration into the host society, granting of international protection status or granting of other status in accordance with national law of the Member States.

(24) When, in accordance with this Directive, a guardian and/or a representative are to be appointed for a child, those roles may be performed by the same person or by a legal person, an institution or an authority.

(25) Member States should establish and/or strengthen policies to prevent trafficking in human beings, including measures to discourage and reduce the demand that fosters all forms of exploitation, and measures to reduce the risk of people becoming victims of trafficking in human beings, by means of research, including research into new forms of trafficking in human beings, information, awareness-raising, and education. In such initiatives, Member States should adopt a gender perspective and a child-rights approach. Officials likely to come into contact with victims or potential victims of trafficking in human beings should be adequately trained to identify and deal with such victims. That training obligation should be promoted for members of the following categories when they are likely to come into contact with victims: police officers, border guards, immigration officials, public prosecutors, lawyers, members of the judiciary and court officials, labour inspectors, social, child and health care personnel and consular staff, but could, depending on local circumstances, also involve other groups of public officials who are likely to encounter trafficking victims in their work.

(26) Directive 2009/52/EC provides for sanctions for employers of illegally staying third-country nationals who, while not having been charged with or convicted of trafficking in human beings, use work or services exacted from a person with the knowledge that that person is a victim of such trafficking. In addition, Member States should take into consideration the possibility of imposing sanctions on the users of any service exacted from a victim, with the knowledge that the person has been trafficked. Such further criminalisation could cover the behaviour of employers of legally staying third-country nationals and Union citizens, as well as buyers of sexual services from any trafficked person, irrespective of their nationality.

(27) National monitoring systems such as national rapporteurs or equivalent mechanisms should be established by Member States, in the way in which they consider appropriate according to their internal organisation, and taking into account the need for a minimum structure with identified tasks, in order to carry out assessments of trends in trafficking in human beings, gather statistics, measure the results of anti-trafficking actions, and regularly report. Such national rapporteurs or equivalent mechanisms are already constituted in an informal Union Network established by the Council Conclusions on establishing an informal EU Network of National Rapporteurs or Equivalent Mechanisms on Trafficking in Human Beings of 4 June 2009. An anti-trafficking coordinator would take part in the work of that Network, which provides the Union and the Member States with objective, reliable, comparable and up-to-date strategic information in the field of trafficking in human beings and exchanges experience and best practices in the field of preventing and combating trafficking in human beings at Union level.

The European Parliament should be entitled to participate in the joint activities of the national rapporteurs or equivalent mechanisms.

(28) In order to evaluate the results of anti-trafficking action, the Union should continue to develop its work on methodologies and data collection methods to produce comparable statistics.

(29) In the light of the Stockholm Programme and with a view to developing a consolidated Union strategy against trafficking in human beings aimed at further strengthening the commitment of, and efforts made, by the Union and the Member States to prevent and combat such trafficking, Member States should facilitate the tasks of an anti-trafficking coordinator, which may include for example improving coordination and coherence, avoiding duplication of effort, between Union institutions and agencies as well as between Member States and international actors, contributing to the development of existing or new Union policies and strategies relevant to the fight against trafficking in human beings or reporting to the Union institutions.

(30) This Directive aims to amend and expand the provisions of Framework Decision 2002/629/JHA. Since the amendments to be made are of substantial number and nature, the Framework Decision should in the interests of clarity be replaced in its entirety in relation to Member States participating in the adoption of this Directive.

(31) In accordance with point 34 of the Interinstitutional Agreement on better law-making[14], Member States are encouraged to draw up, for themselves and in the interest of the Union, their own tables which will, as far as possible, illustrate the correlation between this Directive and the transposition measures, and to make them public.

(32) Since the objective of this Directive, namely to fight against trafficking in human beings, cannot be sufficiently achieved by the Member States and can therefore, by reason of the scale and effects of the action be better achieved at Union level, the Union may adopt measures in accordance with the principle of subsidiarity as set out in Article 5 of the Treaty on European Union. In accordance with the principle of proportionality, as set out in that Article, this Directive does not go beyond what is necessary to achieve that objective.

(33) This Directive respects fundamental rights and observes the principles recognised in particular by the Charter of Fundamental Rights of the European Union and notably human dignity, the prohibition of slavery, forced labour and trafficking in human beings, the prohibition of torture and inhuman or degrading treatment or punishment, the rights of the child, the right to liberty and security, freedom of expression and information, the protection of personal data, the right to an effective remedy and to a fair trial and the principles of the legality and proportionality of criminal offences and penalties. In particular, this Directive seeks to ensure full respect for those rights and principles and must be implemented accordingly.

(34) In accordance with Article 3 of the Protocol on the position of the United Kingdom and Ireland in respect of the area of freedom, security and justice, annexed to the Treaty on European Union and the Treaty on the Functioning of the European Union, Ireland has notified its wish to take part in the adoption and application of this Directive.

(35) In accordance with Articles 1 and 2 of the Protocol on the position of the United Kingdom and Ireland in respect of the area of freedom, security and justice, annexed to the Treaty on European Union and to the Treaty on the Functioning of the European Union, and without prejudice to

Article 4 of that Protocol, the United Kingdom is not taking part in the adoption of this Directive and is not bound by it or subject to its application.

(36) In accordance with Articles 1 and 2 of the Protocol on the position of Denmark annexed to the Treaty on European Union and to the Treaty on the Functioning of the European Union, Denmark is not taking part in the adoption of this Directive and is not bound by it or subject to its application,

[1] Opinion of 21 October 2010 (not yet published in the Official Journal).

[2] Position of the European Parliament of 14 December 2010 (not yet published in the Official Journal) and decision of the Council of 21 March 2011.

[3] OJ L 203, 1.8.2002, p. 1.

[4] OJ C 311, 9.12.2005, p. 1.

[5] OJ C 115, 4.5.2010, p. 1.

[6] OJ L 328, 15.12.2009, p. 42.

[7] OJ L 261, 6.8.2004, p. 19.

[8] OJ L 168, 30.6.2009, p. 24.

[9] OJ L 190, 18.7.2002, p. 1.

[10] OJ L 182, 5.7.2001, p. 1.

[11] OJ L 68, 15.3.2005, p. 49.

[12] OJ L 158, 30.4.2004, p. 77.

[13] OJ L 82, 22.3.2001, p. 1.

[14] OJ C 321, 31.12.2003, p. 1.

HAVE ADOPTED THIS DIRECTIVE:

Article 1 Subject matter

This Directive establishes minimum rules concerning the definition of criminal offences and sanctions in the area of trafficking in human beings. It also introduces common provisions, taking into account the gender perspective, to strengthen the prevention of this crime and the protection of the victims thereof.

Article 2 Offences concerning trafficking in human beings

1. Member States shall take the necessary measures to ensure that the following intentional acts are punishable:

The recruitment, transportation, transfer, harbouring or reception of persons, including the exchange or transfer of control over those persons, by means of the threat or use of force or other forms of coercion, of abduction, of fraud, of deception, of the abuse of power or of a position of vulnerability or of the giving or receiving of payments or benefits to achieve the consent of a person having control over another person, for the purpose of exploitation.

2. A position of vulnerability means a situation in which the person concerned has no real or acceptable alternative but to submit to the abuse involved.

3. Exploitation shall include, as a minimum, the exploitation of the prostitution of others or other forms of sexual exploitation, forced labour or services, including begging, slavery or practices similar to slavery, servitude, or the exploitation of criminal activities, or the removal of organs.

4. The consent of a victim of trafficking in human beings to the exploitation, whether intended or actual, shall be irrelevant where any of the means set forth in paragraph 1 has been used.

5. When the conduct referred to in paragraph 1 involves a child, it shall be a punishable offence of trafficking in human beings even if none of the means set forth in paragraph 1 has been used.

6. For the purpose of this Directive, 'child' shall mean any person below 18 years of age.

Article 3 Incitement, aiding and abetting, and attempt

Member States shall take the necessary measures to ensure that inciting, aiding and abetting or attempting to commit an offence referred to in Article 2 is punishable.

Article 4 Penalties

1. Member States shall take the necessary measures to ensure that an offence referred to in Article 2 is punishable by a maximum penalty of at least five years of imprisonment.

2. Member States shall take the necessary measures to ensure that an offence referred to in Article 2 is punishable by a maximum penalty of at least 10 years of imprisonment where that offence:

  (a)   was committed against a victim who was particularly vulnerable, which, in the context of this Directive, shall include at least child victims;

  (b)   was committed within the framework of a criminal organisation within the meaning of Council Framework Decision 2008/841/JHA of 24 October 2008 on the fight against organised crime,[1]

  (c)   deliberately or by gross negligence endangered the life of the victim; or

  (d)   was committed by use of serious violence or has caused particularly serious harm to the victim.

3. Member States shall take the necessary measures to ensure that the fact that an offence referred to in Article 2 was committed by public officials in the performance of their duties is regarded as an aggravating circumstance.

4. Member States shall take the necessary measures to ensure that an offence referred to in Article 3 is punishable by effective, proportionate and dissuasive penalties, which may entail surrender.

---

[1]   OJ L 300, 11.11.2008, p. 42.

Article 5 Liability of legal persons

1. Member States shall take the necessary measures to ensure that legal persons can be held liable for the offences referred to in Articles 2 and 3 committed for their benefit by any person, acting either individually or as part of an organ of the legal person, who has a leading position within the legal person, based on:

  (a)   a power of representation of the legal person;

  (b)   an authority to take decisions on behalf of the legal person; or

  (c)   an authority to exercise control within the legal person.

2. Member States shall also ensure that a legal person can be held liable where the lack of supervision or control, by a person referred to in paragraph 1, has made possible the commission of the offences referred to in Articles 2 and 3 for the benefit of that legal person by a person under its authority.

3. Liability of a legal person under paragraphs 1 and 2 shall not exclude criminal proceedings against natural persons who are perpetrators, inciters or accessories in the offences referred to in Articles 2 and 3.

4. For the purpose of this Directive, 'legal person' shall mean any entity having legal personality under the applicable law, except for States or public bodies in the exercise of State authority and for public international organisations.

Article 6 Sanctions on legal persons

Member States shall take the necessary measures to ensure that a legal person held liable pursuant to Article 5(1) or (2) is subject to effective, proportionate and dissuasive sanctions, which shall include criminal or non-criminal fines and may include other sanctions, such as:

- (a) exclusion from entitlement to public benefits or aid;
- (b) temporary or permanent disqualification from the practice of commercial activities;
- (c) placing under judicial supervision;
- (d) judicial winding-up;
- (e) temporary or permanent closure of establishments which have been used for committing the offence.

Article 7 Seizure and confiscation

Member States shall take the necessary measures to ensure that their competent authorities are entitled to seize and confiscate instrumentalities and proceeds from the offences referred to in Articles 2 and 3.

Article 8 Non-prosecution or non-application of penalties to the victim

Member States shall, in accordance with the basic principles of their legal systems, take the necessary measures to ensure that competent national authorities are entitled not to prosecute or impose penalties on victims of trafficking in human beings for their involvement in criminal activities which they have been compelled to commit as a direct consequence of being subjected to any of the acts referred to in Article 2.

Article 9 Investigation and prosecution

1. Member States shall ensure that investigation into or prosecution of offences referred to in Articles 2 and 3 is not dependent on reporting or accusation by a victim and that criminal proceedings may continue even if the victim has withdrawn his or her statement.

2. Member States shall take the necessary measures to enable, where the nature of the act calls for it, the prosecution of an offence referred to in Articles 2 and 3 for a sufficient period of time after the victim has reached the age of majority.

3. Member States shall take the necessary measures to ensure that persons, units or services responsible for investigating or prosecuting the offences referred to in Articles 2 and 3 are trained accordingly.

4. Member States shall take the necessary measures to ensure that effective investigative tools, such as those which are used in organised crime or other serious crime cases are available to persons, units or services responsible for investigating or prosecuting the offences referred to in Articles 2 and 3.

Article 10 Jurisdiction

1. Member States shall take the necessary measures to establish their jurisdiction over the offences referred to in Articles 2 and 3 where:

- (a) the offence is committed in whole or in part within their territory; or
- (b) the offender is one of their nationals.

2. A Member State shall inform the Commission where it decides to establish further jurisdiction over the offences referred to in Articles 2 and 3 committed outside its territory, inter alia, where:

- (a) the offence is committed against one of its nationals or a person who is an habitual resident in its territory;
- (b) the offence is committed for the benefit of a legal person established in its territory; or
- (c) the offender is an habitual resident in its territory.

3. For the prosecution of the offences referred to in Articles 2 and 3 committed outside the territory of the Member State concerned, each Member State shall, in those cases referred to in point (b) of paragraph 1, and may, in those cases referred to in paragraph 2, take the necessary measures to ensure that its jurisdiction is not subject to either of the following conditions:

    (a)   the acts are a criminal offence at the place where they were performed; or

    (b)   the prosecution can be initiated only following a report made by the victim in the place where the offence was committed, or a denunciation from the State of the place where the offence was committed.

Article 11 Assistance and support for victims of trafficking in human beings

1. Member States shall take the necessary measures to ensure that assistance and support are provided to victims before, during and for an appropriate period of time after the conclusion of criminal proceedings in order to enable them to exercise the rights set out in Framework Decision 2001/220/JHA, and in this Directive.

2. Member States shall take the necessary measures to ensure that a person is provided with assistance and support as soon as the competent authorities have a reasonable-grounds indication for believing that the person might have been subjected to any of the offences referred to in Articles 2 and 3.

3. Member States shall take the necessary measures to ensure that assistance and support for a victim are not made conditional on the victim's willingness to cooperate in the criminal investigation, prosecution or trial, without prejudice to Directive 2004/81/EC or similar national rules.

4. Member States shall take the necessary measures to establish appropriate mechanisms aimed at the early identification of, assistance to and support for victims, in cooperation with relevant support organisations.

5. The assistance and support measures referred to in paragraphs 1 and 2 shall be provided on a consensual and informed basis, and shall include at least standards of living capable of ensuring victims' subsistence through measures such as the provision of appropriate and safe accommodation and material assistance, as well as necessary medical treatment including psychological assistance, counselling and information, and translation and interpretation services where appropriate.

6. The information referred to in paragraph 5 shall cover, where relevant, information on a reflection and recovery period pursuant to Directive 2004/81/EC, and information on the possibility of granting international protection pursuant to Council Directive 2004/83/EC of 29 April 2004 on minimum standards for the qualification and status of third country nationals or stateless persons as refugees or as persons who otherwise need international protection and the content of the protection granted[1] and Council Directive 2005/85/EC of 1 December 2005 on minimum standards on procedures in Member States for granting and withdrawing refugee status[2] or pursuant to other international instruments or other similar national rules.

7. Member States shall attend to victims with special needs, where those needs derive, in particular, from whether they are pregnant, their health, a disability, a mental or psychological disorder they have, or a serious form of psychological, physical or sexual violence they have suffered.

[1]   OJ L 304, 30.9.2004, p. 12.

[2]   OJ L 326, 13.12.2005, p. 13.

Article 12 Protection of victims of trafficking in human beings in criminal investigation and proceedings

1. The protection measures referred to in this Article shall apply in addition to the rights set out in Framework Decision 2001/220/JHA.

2. Member States shall ensure that victims of trafficking in human beings have access without delay to legal counselling, and, in accordance with the role of victims in the

relevant justice system, to legal representation, including for the purpose of claiming compensation. Legal counselling and legal representation shall be free of charge where the victim does not have sufficient financial resources.

3. Member States shall ensure that victims of trafficking in human beings receive appropriate protection on the basis of an individual risk assessment, inter alia, by having access to witness protection programmes or other similar measures, if appropriate and in accordance with the grounds defined by national law or procedures.

4. Without prejudice to the rights of the defence, and according to an individual assessment by the competent authorities of the personal circumstances of the victim, Member States shall ensure that victims of trafficking in human beings receive specific treatment aimed at preventing secondary victimisation by avoiding, as far as possible and in accordance with the grounds defined by national law as well as with rules of judicial discretion, practice or guidance, the following:

(a) unnecessary repetition of interviews during investigation, prosecution or trial;

(b) visual contact between victims and defendants including during the giving of evidence such as interviews and cross-examination, by appropriate means including the use of appropriate communication technologies;

(c) the giving of evidence in open court; and

(d) unnecessary questioning concerning the victim's private life.

Article 13 General provisions on assistance, support and protection measures for child victims of trafficking in human beings

1. Child victims of trafficking in human beings shall be provided with assistance, support and protection. In the application of this Directive the child's best interests shall be a primary consideration.

2. Member States shall ensure that, where the age of a person subject to trafficking in human beings is uncertain and there are reasons to believe that the person is a child, that person is presumed to be a child in order to receive immediate access to assistance, support and protection in accordance with Articles 14 and 15.

Article 14 Assistance and support to child victims

1. Member States shall take the necessary measures to ensure that the specific actions to assist and support child victims of trafficking in human beings, in the short and long term, in their physical and psycho-social recovery, are undertaken following an individual assessment of the special circumstances of each particular child victim, taking due account of the child's views, needs and concerns with a view to finding a durable solution for the child. Within a reasonable time, Member States shall provide access to education for child victims and the children of victims who are given assistance and support in accordance with Article 11, in accordance with their national law.

2. Members States shall appoint a guardian or a representative for a child victim of trafficking in human beings from the moment the child is identified by the authorities where, by national law, the holders of parental responsibility are, as a result of a conflict of interest between them and the child victim, precluded from ensuring the child's best interest and/or from representing the child.

3. Member States shall take measures, where appropriate and possible, to provide assistance and support to the family of a child victim of trafficking in human beings when the family is in the territory of the Member States. In particular, Member States shall, where appropriate and possible, apply Article 4 of Framework Decision 2001/220/JHA to the family.

4. This Article shall apply without prejudice to Article 11.

Article 15 Protection of child victims of trafficking in human beings in criminal investigations and proceedings

1. Member States shall take the necessary measures to ensure that in criminal investigations and proceedings, in accordance with the role of victims in the relevant justice system, competent authorities appoint a representative for a child victim of trafficking in human beings where, by national law, the holders of parental responsibility are precluded from representing the child as a result of a conflict of interest between them and the child victim.

2. Member States shall, in accordance with the role of victims in the relevant justice system, ensure that child victims have access without delay to free legal counselling and to free legal representation, including for the purpose of claiming compensation, unless they have sufficient financial resources.

3. Without prejudice to the rights of the defence, Member States shall take the necessary measures to ensure that in criminal investigations and proceedings in respect of any of the offences referred to in Articles 2 and 3:

  (a) interviews with the child victim take place without unjustified delay after the facts have been reported to the competent authorities;
  (b) interviews with the child victim take place, where necessary, in premises designed or adapted for that purpose;
  (c) interviews with the child victim are carried out, where necessary, by or through professionals trained for that purpose;
  (d) the same persons, if possible and where appropriate, conduct all the interviews with the child victim;
  (e) the number of interviews is as limited as possible and interviews are carried out only where strictly necessary for the purposes of criminal investigations and proceedings;
  (f) the child victim may be accompanied by a representative or, where appropriate, an adult of the child's choice, unless a reasoned decision has been made to the contrary in respect of that person.

4. Member States shall take the necessary measures to ensure that in criminal investigations of any of the offences referred to in Articles 2 and 3 all interviews with a child victim or, where appropriate, with a child witness, may be video recorded and that such video recorded interviews may be used as evidence in criminal court proceedings, in accordance with the rules under their national law.

5. Member States shall take the necessary measures to ensure that in criminal court proceedings relating to any of the offences referred to in Articles 2 and 3, it may be ordered that:

  (a) the hearing take place without the presence of the public; and
  (b) the child victim be heard in the courtroom without being present, in particular, through the use of appropriate communication technologies.

6. This Article shall apply without prejudice to Article 12.

Article 16 Assistance, support and protection for unaccompanied child victims of trafficking in human beings

1. Member States shall take the necessary measures to ensure that the specific actions to assist and support child victims of trafficking in human beings, as referred to in Article 14(1), take due account of the personal and special circumstances of the unaccompanied child victim.

2. Member States shall take the necessary measures with a view to finding a durable solution based on an individual assessment of the best interests of the child.

3. Member States shall take the necessary measures to ensure that, where appropriate, a guardian is appointed to unaccompanied child victims of trafficking in human beings.

4. Member States shall take the necessary measures to ensure that, in criminal investigations and proceedings, in accordance with the role of victims in the relevant

justice system, competent authorities appoint a representative where the child is unaccompanied or separated from its family.

5. This Article shall apply without prejudice to Articles 14 and 15.

Article 17 Compensation to victims

Member States shall ensure that victims of trafficking in human beings have access to existing schemes of compensation to victims of violent crimes of intent.

Article 18 Prevention

1. Member States shall take appropriate measures, such as education and training, to discourage and reduce the demand that fosters all forms of exploitation related to trafficking in human beings.

2. Member States shall take appropriate action, including through the Internet, such as information and awareness- raising campaigns, research and education programmes, where appropriate in cooperation with relevant civil society organisations and other stakeholders, aimed at raising awareness and reducing the risk of people, especially children, becoming victims of trafficking in human beings.

3. Member States shall promote regular training for officials likely to come into contact with victims or potential victims of trafficking in human beings, including front-line police officers, aimed at enabling them to identify and deal with victims and potential victims of trafficking in human beings.

4. In order to make the preventing and combating of trafficking in human beings more effective by discouraging demand, Member States shall consider taking measures to establish as a criminal offence the use of services which are the objects of exploitation as referred to in Article 2, with the knowledge that the person is a victim of an offence referred to in Article 2.

Article 19 National rapporteurs or equivalent mechanisms

Member States shall take the necessary measures to establish national rapporteurs or equivalent mechanisms. The tasks of such mechanisms shall include the carrying out of assessments of trends in trafficking in human beings, the measuring of results of anti-trafficking actions, including the gathering of statistics in close cooperation with relevant civil society organisations active in this field, and reporting.

Article 20 Coordination of the Union strategy against trafficking in human beings

In order to contribute to a coordinated and consolidated Union strategy against trafficking in human beings, Member States shall facilitate the tasks of an anti-trafficking coordinator (ATC). In particular, Member States shall transmit to the ATC the information referred to in Article 19, on the basis of which the ATC shall contribute to reporting carried out by the Commission every two years on the progress made in the fight against trafficking in human beings.

Article 21 Replacement of Framework Decision 2002/629/JHA

Framework Decision 2002/629/JHA on combating trafficking in human beings is hereby replaced in relation to Member States participating in the adoption of this Directive, without prejudice to the obligations of the Member States relating to the time limit for transposition of the Framework Decision into national law.

In relation to Member States participating in the adoption of this Directive, references to the Framework Decision 2002/629/JHA shall be construed as references to this Directive.

Article 22 Transposition

1. Member States shall bring into force the laws, regulations and administrative provisions necessary to comply with this Directive by 6 April 2013.

2. Member States shall transmit to the Commission the text of the provisions transposing into their national law the obligations imposed on them under this Directive.

3. When Member States adopt these measures, they shall contain a reference to this Directive or shall be accompanied by such a reference on the occasion of their official publication. The methods of making such reference shall be laid down by the Member States.

Article 23 Reporting

1. The Commission shall, by 6 April 2015, submit a report to the European Parliament and the Council, assessing the extent to which the Member States have taken the necessary measures in order to comply with this Directive, including a description of action taken under Article 18(4), accompanied, if necessary, by legislative proposals.

2. The Commission shall, by 6 April 2016, submit a report to the European Parliament and the Council, assessing the impact of existing national law, establishing as a criminal offence the use of services which are the objects of exploitation of trafficking in human beings, on the prevention of trafficking in human beings, accompanied, if necessary, by adequate proposals.

Article 24 Entry into force

This Directive shall enter into force on the day of its publication in the *Official Journal of the European Union*.

Article 25 Addressees

This Directive is addressed to the Member States in accordance with the Treaties.

EUROPEAN PARLIAMENT AND COUNCIL REGULATION 492/2011/EU

of 5 April 2011

on freedom of movement for workers within the Union

Notes

Date of publication in Official Journal: OJ L141, 27.5.2011, p 1.

(codification)

(Text with EEA relevance)

THE EUROPEAN PARLIAMENT AND THE COUNCIL OF THE EUROPEAN UNION,

Having regard to the Treaty on the Functioning of the European Union, and in particular Article 46 thereof,

Having regard to the proposal from the European Commission,

After transmission of the draft legislative act to the national parliaments,

Having regard to the opinion of the European Economic and Social Committee[1],

Acting in accordance with the ordinary legislative procedure[2],

Whereas:

(1) Regulation (EEC) No 1612/68 of the Council of 15 October 1968 on freedom of movement for workers within the Community[3] has been substantially amended several times[4]. In the interests of clarity and rationality the said Regulation should be codified.

(2) Freedom of movement for workers should be secured within the Union. The attainment of this objective entails the abolition of any discrimination based on nationality between workers of the Member States as regards employment, remuneration and other conditions of work and employment, as well as the right of such workers

to move freely within the Union in order to pursue activities as employed persons subject to any limitations justified on grounds of public policy, public security or public health.

(3)   Provisions should be laid down to enable the objectives laid down in Articles 45 and 46 of the Treaty on the Functioning of the European Union in the field of freedom of movement to be achieved.

(4)   Freedom of movement constitutes a fundamental right of workers and their families. Mobility of labour within the Union must be one of the means by which workers are guaranteed the possibility of improving their living and working conditions and promoting their social advancement, while helping to satisfy the requirements of the economies of the Member States. The right of all workers in the Member States to pursue the activity of their choice within the Union should be affirmed.

(5)   Such right should be enjoyed without discrimination by permanent, seasonal and frontier workers and by those who pursue their activities for the purpose of providing services.

(6)   The right of freedom of movement, in order that it may be exercised, by objective standards, in freedom and dignity, requires that equality of treatment be ensured in fact and in law in respect of all matters relating to the actual pursuit of activities as employed persons and to eligibility for housing, and also that obstacles to the mobility of workers be eliminated, in particular as regards the conditions for the integration of the worker's family into the host country.

(7)   The principle of non-discrimination between workers in the Union means that all nationals of Member States have the same priority as regards employment as is enjoyed by national workers.

(8)   The machinery for vacancy clearance, in particular by means of direct cooperation between the central employment services and also between the regional services, as well as by coordination of the exchange of information, ensures in a general way a clearer picture of the labour market. Workers wishing to move should also be regularly informed of living and working conditions.

(9)   Close links exist between freedom of movement for workers, employment and vocational training, particularly where the latter aims at putting workers in a position to take up concrete offers of employment from other regions of the Union. Such links make it necessary that the problems arising in this connection should no longer be studied in isolation but viewed as interdependent, account also being taken of the problems of employment at the regional level. It is therefore necessary to direct the efforts of Member States toward coordinating their employment policies,

---

[1]   OJ C 44, 11.2.2011, p. 170.

[2]   Position of the European Parliament of 7 September 2010 (not yet published in the Official Journal) and decision of the Council of 21 March 2011.

[3]   OJ L 257, 19.10.1968, p. 2.

[4]   See Annex I.

HAVE ADOPTED THIS REGULATION:

CHAPTER I
EMPLOYMENT, EQUAL TREATMENT AND WORKERS' FAMILIES

SECTION 1

ELIGIBILITY FOR EMPLOYMENT

Article 1

1. Any national of a Member State shall, irrespective of his place of residence, have the right to take up an activity as an employed person, and to pursue such activity, within the territory of another Member State in accordance with the provisions laid down by law, regulation or administrative action governing the employment of nationals of that State.

2. He shall, in particular, have the right to take up available employment in the territory of another Member State with the same priority as nationals of that State.

Article 2

Any national of a Member State and any employer pursuing an activity in the territory of a Member State may exchange their applications for and offers of employment, and may conclude and perform contracts of employment in accordance with the provisions in force laid down by law, regulation or administrative action, without any discrimination resulting therefrom.

Article 3

1. Under this Regulation, provisions laid down by law, regulation or administrative action or administrative practices of a Member State shall not apply:

  (a)   where they limit application for and offers of employment, or the right of foreign nationals to take up and pursue employment or subject these to conditions not applicable in respect of their own nationals; or

  (b)   where, though applicable irrespective of nationality, their exclusive or principal aim or effect is to keep nationals of other Member States away from the employment offered.

The first subparagraph shall not apply to conditions relating to linguistic knowledge required by reason of the nature of the post to be filled.

2. There shall be included in particular among the provisions or practices of a Member State referred to in the first subparagraph of paragraph 1 those which:

  (a)   prescribe a special recruitment procedure for foreign nationals;

  (b)   limit or restrict the advertising of vacancies in the press or through any other medium or subject it to conditions other than those applicable in respect of employers pursuing their activities in the territory of that Member State;

  (c)   subject eligibility for employment to conditions of registration with employment offices or impede recruitment of individual workers, where persons who do not reside in the territory of that State are concerned.

Article 4

1. Provisions laid down by law, regulation or administrative action of the Member States which restrict by number or percentage the employment of foreign nationals in any undertaking, branch of activity or region, or at a national level, shall not apply to nationals of the other Member States.

2. When in a Member State the granting of any benefit to undertakings is subject to a minimum percentage of national workers being employed, nationals of the other Member States shall be counted as national workers, subject to Directive 2005/36/EC of the European Parliament and of the Council of 7 September 2005 on the recognition of professional qualifications[1].

[1]   OJ L 255, 30.9.2005, p. 22.

Article 5

A national of a Member State who seeks employment in the territory of another Member State shall receive the same assistance there as that afforded by the employment offices in that State to their own nationals seeking employment.

Article 6

1.   The engagement and recruitment of a national of one Member State for a post in another Member State shall not depend on medical, vocational or other criteria which are discriminatory on grounds of nationality by comparison with those applied to nationals of the other Member State who wish to pursue the same activity.

2.   A national who holds an offer in his name from an employer in a Member State other than that of which he is a national may have to undergo a vocational test, if the employer expressly requests this when making his offer of employment.

SECTION 2

EMPLOYMENT AND EQUALITY OF TREATMENT

Article 7

1.   A worker who is a national of a Member State may not, in the territory of another Member State, be treated differently from national workers by reason of his nationality in respect of any conditions of employment and work, in particular as regards remuneration, dismissal, and, should he become unemployed, reinstatement or re-employment.

2.   He shall enjoy the same social and tax advantages as national workers.

3.   He shall also, by virtue of the same right and under the same conditions as national workers, have access to training in vocational schools and retraining centres.

4.   Any clause of a collective or individual agreement or of any other collective regulation concerning eligibility for employment, remuneration and other conditions of work or dismissal shall be null and void in so far as it lays down or authorises discriminatory conditions in respect of workers who are nationals of the other Member States.

Article 8

A worker who is a national of a Member State and who is employed in the territory of another Member State shall enjoy equality of treatment as regards membership of trade unions and the exercise of rights attaching thereto, including the right to vote and to be eligible for the administration or management posts of a trade union. He may be excluded from taking part in the management of bodies governed by public law and from holding an office governed by public law. Furthermore, he shall have the right of eligibility for workers' representative bodies in the undertaking.

The first paragraph of this Article shall not affect laws or regulations in certain Member States which grant more extensive rights to workers coming from the other Member States.

Article 9

1.   A worker who is a national of a Member State and who is employed in the territory of another Member State shall enjoy all the rights and benefits accorded to national workers in matters of housing, including ownership of the housing he needs.

2.   A worker referred to in paragraph 1 may, with the same right as nationals, put his name down on the housing lists in the region in which he is employed, where such lists exist, and shall enjoy the resultant benefits and priorities.

If his family has remained in the country whence he came, they shall be considered for this purpose as residing in the said region, where national workers benefit from a similar presumption.

SECTION 3

WORKERS' FAMILIES

Article 10
The children of a national of a Member State who is or has been employed in the territory of another Member State shall be admitted to that State's general educational, apprenticeship and vocational training courses under the same conditions as the nationals of that State, if such children are residing in its territory.
Member States shall encourage all efforts to enable such children to attend these courses under the best possible conditions.

CHAPTER II
CLEARANCE OF VACANCIES AND APPLICATIONS FOR EMPLOYMENT

SECTION 1

COOPERATION BETWEEN THE MEMBER STATES AND WITH THE COMMISSION

Article 11
1.   The Member States or the Commission shall instigate or together undertake any study of employment or unemployment which they consider necessary for freedom of movement for workers within the Union.
The central employment services of the Member States shall cooperate closely with each other and with the Commission with a view to acting jointly as regards the clearing of vacancies and applications for employment within the Union and the resultant placing of workers in employment.
2.   To this end the Member States shall designate specialist services which shall be entrusted with organising work in the fields referred to in the second subparagraph of paragraph 1 and cooperating with each other and with the departments of the Commission.
The Member States shall notify the Commission of any change in the designation of such services and the Commission shall publish details thereof for information in the *Official Journal of the European Union*.

Article 12
1.   The Member States shall send to the Commission information on problems arising in connection with the freedom of movement and employment of workers and particulars of the state and development of employment.
2.   The Commission, taking the utmost account of the opinion of the Technical Committee referred to in Article 29 ('the Technical Committee'), shall determine the manner in which the information referred to in paragraph 1 of this Article is to be drawn up.
3.   In accordance with the procedure laid down by the Commission taking the utmost account of the opinion of the Technical Committee, the specialist service of each Member State shall send to the specialist services of the other Member States and to the European Coordination Office referred to in Article 18 such information concerning living and working conditions and the state of the labour market as is likely to be of guidance to workers from the other Member States. Such information shall be brought up to date regularly.
The specialist services of the other Member States shall ensure that wide publicity is given to such information, in particular by circulating it among the appropriate

employment services and by all suitable means of communication for informing the workers concerned.

SECTION 2

Machinery for vacancy clearance

Article 13

1. The specialist service of each Member State shall regularly send to the specialist services of the other Member States and to the European Coordination Office referred to in Article 18:

(a) details of vacancies which could be filled by nationals of other Member States;

(b) details of vacancies addressed to third countries;

(c) details of applications for employment by those who have formally expressed a wish to work in another Member State;

(d) information, by region and by branch of activity, on applicants who have declared themselves actually willing to accept employment in another country.

The specialist service of each Member State shall forward this information to the appropriate employment services and agencies as soon as possible.

2. The details of vacancies and applications referred to in paragraph 1 shall be circulated according to a uniform system to be established by the European Coordination Office referred to in Article 18 in collaboration with the Technical Committee.

This system may be adapted if necessary.

Article 14

1. Any vacancy within the meaning of Article 13 communicated to the employment services of a Member State shall be notified to and processed by the competent employment services of the other Member States concerned.

Such services shall forward to the services of the first Member State the details of suitable applications.

2. The applications for employment referred to in point (c) of the first subparagraph of Article 13(1) shall be responded to by the relevant services of the Member States within a reasonable period, not exceeding 1 month.

3. The employment services shall grant workers who are nationals of the Member States the same priority as the relevant measures grant to nationals vis-à-vis workers from third countries.

Article 15

1. The provisions of Article 14 shall be implemented by the specialist services. However, in so far as they have been au- thorised by the central services and in so far as the organisation of the employment services of a Member State and the placing techniques employed make it possible:

(a) the regional employment services of the Member States shall:

(i) on the basis of the information referred to in Article 13, on which appropriate action will be taken, directly bring together and clear vacancies and applications for employment;

(ii) establish direct relations for clearance:

— of vacancies offered to a named worker,

— of individual applications for employment sent either to a specific employment service or to an employer pursuing his activity within the area covered by such a service,

      —   where the clearing operations concern seasonal workers who must be recruited as quickly as possible;

(b)   the services territorially responsible for the border regions of two or more Member States shall regularly exchange data relating to vacancies and applications for employment in their area and, acting in accordance with their arrangements with the other employment services of their countries, shall directly bring together and clear vacancies and applications for employment.

If necessary, the services territorially responsible for border regions shall also set up cooperation and service structures to provide:

      —   users with as much practical information as possible on the various aspects of mobility, and

      —   management and labour, social services (in particular public, private or those of public interest) and all institutions concerned, with a framework of coordinated measures relating to mobility,

(c)   official employment services which specialise in certain occupations or specific categories of persons shall cooperate directly with each other.

2.   The Member States concerned shall forward to the Commission the list, drawn up by common accord, of services referred to in paragraph 1 and the Commission shall publish such list for information, and any amendment thereto, in the *Official Journal of the European Union.*

Article 16

Adoption of recruiting procedures as applied by the implementing bodies provided for under agreements concluded between two or more Member States shall not be obligatory.

SECTION 3

MEASURES FOR CONTROLLING THE BALANCE OF THE LABOUR MARKET

Article 17

1.   On the basis of a report from the Commission drawn up from information supplied by the Member States, the latter and the Commission shall at least once a year analyse jointly the results of Union arrangements regarding vacancies and applications.

2.   The Member States shall examine with the Commission all the possibilities of giving priority to nationals of Member States when filling employment vacancies in order to achieve a balance between vacancies and applications for employment within the Union. They shall adopt all measures necessary for this purpose.

3.   Every 2 years the Commission shall submit a report to the European Parliament, the Council and the European Economic and Social Committee on the implementation of Chapter II, summarising the information required and the data obtained from the studies and research carried out and highlighting any useful points with regard to developments on the Union's labour market.

SECTION 4

EUROPEAN COORDINATION OFFICE

Article 18

The European Office for Coordinating the Clearance of Vacancies and Applications for Employment ('the European Coordination Office'), established within the Commission, shall have the general task of promoting vacancy clearance at Union level. It shall be responsible in particular for all the technical duties in this field which, under the provisions of this Regulation, are assigned to the Commission, and especially for assisting the national employment services.

It shall summarise the information referred to in Articles 12 and 13 and the data arising out of the studies and research carried out pursuant to Article 11, so as to bring to light any useful facts about foreseeable developments on the Union labour market; such facts shall be communicated to the specialist services of the Member States and to the Advisory Committee referred to in Article 21 and the Technical Committee.

Article 19

1. The European Coordination Office shall be responsible, in particular, for:

   (a)   coordinating the practical measures necessary for vacancy clearance at Union level and for analysing the resulting movements of workers;

   (b)   contributing to such objectives by implementing, in cooperation with the Technical Committee, joint methods of action at administrative and technical levels;

   (c)   carrying out, where a special need arises, and in agreement with the specialist services, the bringing together of vacancies and applications for employment for clearance by those specialist services.

2. It shall communicate to the specialist services vacancies and applications for employment sent directly to the Commission, and shall be informed of the action taken thereon.

Article 20

The Commission may, in agreement with the competent authority of each Member State, and in accordance with the conditions and procedures which it shall determine on the basis of the opinion of the Technical Committee, organise visits and assignments for officials of other Member States, and also advanced programmes for specialist personnel.

CHAPTER III
COMMITTEES FOR ENSURING CLOSE COOPERATION BETWEEN THE MEMBER STATES IN MATTERS CONCERNING THE FREEDOM OF MOVEMENT OF WORKERS AND THEIR EMPLOYMENT

SECTION 1

THE ADVISORY COMMITTEE

Article 21

The Advisory Committee shall be responsible for assisting the Commission in the examination of any questions arising from the application of the Treaty on the Functioning of the European Union and measures taken in pursuance thereof, in matters concerning the freedom of movement of workers and their employment.

Article 22

The Advisory Committee shall be responsible in particular for:

   (a)   examining problems concerning freedom of movement and employment within the framework of national manpower policies, with a view to coordinating the employment policies of the Member States at Union level, thus contributing to the development of the economies and to an improved balance of the labour market;

   (b)   making a general study of the effects of implementing this Regulation and any supplementary measures;

   (c)   submitting to the Commission any reasoned proposals for revising this Regulation;

(d)   delivering, either at the request of the Commission or on its own initiative, reasoned opinions on general questions or on questions of principle, in particular on exchange of information concerning developments in the labour market, on the movement of workers between Member States, on programmes or measures to develop vocational guidance and vocational training which are likely to increase the possibilities of freedom of movement and employment, and on all forms of assistance to workers and their families, including social assistance and the housing of workers.

Article 23

1. The Advisory Committee shall be composed of six members for each Member State, two of whom shall represent the Government, two the trade unions and two the employers' associations.

2. For each of the categories referred to in paragraph 1, one alternate member shall be appointed by each Member State.

3. The term of office of the members and their alternates shall be 2 years. Their appointments shall be renewable.

On expiry of their term of office, the members and their alternates shall remain in office until replaced or until their appointments are renewed.

Article 24

The members of the Advisory Committee and their alternates shall be appointed by the Council, which shall endeavour, when selecting representatives of trade unions and employers' associations, to achieve adequate representation on the Committee of the various economic sectors concerned.

The list of members and their alternates shall be published by the Council for information in the *Official Journal of the European Union*.

Article 25

The Advisory Committee shall be chaired by a member of the Commission or his representative. The Chairman shall not vote. The Committee shall meet at least twice a year. It shall be convened by its Chairman, either on his own initiative, or at the request of at least one third of the members.

Secretarial services shall be provided for the Committee by the Commission.

Article 26

The Chairman may invite individuals or representatives of bodies with wide experience in the field of employment or movement of workers to take part in meetings as observers or as experts. The Chairman may be assisted by expert advisers.

Article 27

1. An opinion delivered by the Advisory Committee shall not be valid unless two thirds of the members are present.

2. Opinions shall state the reasons on which they are based; they shall be delivered by an absolute majority of the votes validly cast; they shall be accompanied by a written statement of the views expressed by the minority, when the latter so requests.

Article 28

The Advisory Committee shall establish its working methods by rules of procedure which shall enter into force after the Council, having received an opinion from the Commission, has given its approval. The entry into force of any amendment that the Committee decides to make thereto shall be subject to the same procedure.

SECTION 2
THE TECHNICAL COMMITTEE

Article 29

The Technical Committee shall be responsible for assisting the Commission in the preparation, promotion and follow-up of all technical work and measures for giving effect to this Regulation and any supplementary measures.

Article 30

The Technical Committee shall be responsible in particular for:

(a)   promoting and advancing cooperation between the public authorities concerned in the Member States on all technical questions relating to freedom of movement of workers and their employment;

(b)   formulating procedures for the organisation of the joint activities of the public authorities concerned;

(c)   facilitating the gathering of information likely to be of use to the Commission and the undertaking of the studies and research provided for in this Regulation, and encouraging exchange of information and experience between the administrative bodies concerned;

(d)   investigating at a technical level the harmonisation of the criteria by which Member States assess the state of their labour markets.

Article 31

1.   The Technical Committee shall be composed of representatives of the Governments of the Member States. Each Government shall appoint as member of the Technical Committee one of the members who represent it on the Advisory Committee.

2.   Each Government shall appoint an alternate from among its other representatives — members or alternates — on the Advisory Committee.

Article 32

The Technical Committee shall be chaired by a member of the Commission or his representative. The Chairman shall not vote. The Chairman and the members of the Committee may be assisted by expert advisers.

Secretarial services shall be provided for the Committee by the Commission.

Article 33

The proposals and opinions formulated by the Technical Committee shall be submitted to the Commission, and the Advisory Committee shall be informed thereof. Any such proposals and opinions shall be accompanied by a written statement of the views expressed by the various members of the Technical Committee, when the latter so request.

Article 34

The Technical Committee shall establish its working methods by rules of procedure which shall enter into force after the Council, having received an opinion from the Commission, has given its approval. The entry into force of any amendment which the Committee decides to make thereto shall be subject to the same procedure.

CHAPTER IV
FINAL PROVISIONS

Article 35

The rules of procedure of the Advisory Committee and of the Technical Committee in force on 8 November 1968 shall continue to apply.

Article 36

1. This Regulation shall not affect the provisions of the Treaty establishing the European Atomic Energy Community which deal with eligibility for skilled employment in the field of nuclear energy, nor any measures taken in pursuance of that Treaty.

Nevertheless, this Regulation shall apply to the category of workers referred to in the first subparagraph and to members of their families in so far as their legal position is not governed by the above-mentioned Treaty or measures.

2. This Regulation shall not affect measures taken in accordance with Article 48 of the Treaty on the Functioning of the European Union.

3. This Regulation shall not affect the obligations of Member States arising out of special relations or future agreements with certain non-European countries or territories, based on institutional ties existing on 8 November 1968, or agreements in existence on 8 November 1968 with certain non-European countries or territories, based on institutional ties between them.

Workers from such countries or territories who, in accordance with this provision, are pursuing activities as employed persons in the territory of one of those Member States may not invoke the benefit of the provisions of this Regulation in the territory of the other Member States.

Article 37

Member States shall, for information purposes, communicate to the Commission the texts of agreements, conventions or arrangements concluded between them in the manpower field between the date of their being signed and that of their entry into force.

Article 38

The Commission shall adopt measures pursuant to this Regulation for its implementation. To this end it shall act in close cooperation with the central public authorities of the Member States.

Article 39

The administrative expenditure of the Advisory Committee and of the Technical Committee shall be included in the general budget of the European Union in the section relating to the Commission.

Article 40

This Regulation shall apply to the Member States and to their nationals, without prejudice to Articles 2 and 3.

Article 41

Regulation (EEC) No 1612/68 is hereby repealed.

References to the repealed Regulation shall be construed as references to this Regulation and shall be read in accordance with the correlation table in Annex II.

Article 42

This Regulation shall enter into force on the 20th day following its publication in the *Official Journal of the European Union*.

This Regulation shall be binding in its entirety and directly applicable in all Member States.

ANNEX I
REPEALED REGULATION WITH LIST OF ITS SUCCESSIVE AMENDMENTS

Council Regulation (EEC) No 1612/68
(OJ L 257, 19.10.1968, p. 2)

    Council Regulation (EEC) No 312/76
    (OJ L 39, 14.2.1976, p. 2)

    Council Regulation (EEC) No 2434/92
    (OJ L 245, 26.8.1992, p. 1)

    Directive 2004/38/EC of the European Parliament and of
    the Council
    (OJ L 158, 30.4.2004, p. 77)

Only Article
38(1)

ANNEX II
CORRELATION TABLE

Regulation (EEC) No 1612/68	This Regulation
Part I	Chapter I
Title I	Section 1
Article 1	Article 1
Article 2	Article 2
Article 3(1), first subparagraph	Article 3(1), first subparagraph
Article 3(1), first subparagraph, first indent	Article 3(1), first subparagraph, point (a)
Article 3(1), first subparagraph, second indent	Article 3(1), first subparagraph, point (b)
Article 3(1), second subparagraph	Article 3(1), second subparagraph
Article 3(2)	Article 3(2)
Article 4	Article 4
Article 5	Article 5
Article 6	Article 6
Title II	Section 2
Article 7	Article 7
Article 8(1)	Article 8
Article 9	Article 9
Title III	Section 3
Article 12	Article 10
Part II	Chapter II
Title I	Section 1
Article 13	Article 11
Article 14	Article 12
Title II	Section 2
Article 15	Article 13
Article 16	Article 14
Article 17	Article 15
Article 18	Article 16

Regulation (EEC) No 1612/68	This Regulation
Title III	Section 3
Article 19	Article 17
Title IV	Section 4
Article 21	Article 18
Article 22	Article 19
Article 23	Article 20
Part III	Chapter III
Title I	Section 1
Article 24	Article 21
Article 25	Article 22
Article 26	Article 23
Article 27	Article 24
Article 28	Article 25
Article 29	Article 26
Article 30	Article 27
Article 31	Article 28
Title II	Section 2
Article 32	Article 29
Article 33	Article 30
Article 34	Article 31
Article 35	Article 32
Article 36	Article 33
Article 37	Article 34
Part IV	Chapter IV
Title I	—
Article 38	—
Article 39	Article 35
Article 40	—
Article 41	—
Title II	—
Article 42(1)	Article 36(1)
Article 42(2)	Article 36(2)
Article 42(3), first subparagraph, first and second indents	Article 36(3), first subparagraph
Article 42(3), second subparagraph	Article 36(3), second subparagraph
Article 43	Article 37
Article 44	Article 38
Article 45	—
Article 46	Article 39
Article 47	Article 40
—	Article 41
Article 48	Article 42
—	Annex I
—	Annex II

EUROPEAN PARLIAMENT AND COUNCIL REGULATION 604/2013/EU

of 26 June 2013

establishing the criteria and mechanisms for determining the Member State responsible for examining an application for international protection lodged in one of the Member States by a third-country national or a stateless person (recast)

Notes

Date of publication in Official Journal: OJ L180, 29.6.2013, p 31.

THE EUROPEAN PARLIAMENT AND THE COUNCIL OF THE EUROPEAN UNION,

Having regard to the Treaty on the Functioning of the European Union, and in particular Article 78(2)(e) thereof,

Having regard to the proposal from the European Commission,

Having regard to the opinion of the European Economic and Social Committee[1],

Having regard to the opinion of the Committee of the Regions[2],

Acting in accordance with the ordinary legislative procedure[3],

Whereas:

(1) A number of substantive changes are to be made to Council Regulation (EC) No 343/2003 of 18 February 2003 establishing the criteria and mechanisms for determining the Member State responsible for examining an asylum application lodged in one of the Member States by a third-country national[4]. In the interests of clarity, that Regulation should be recast.

(2) A common policy on asylum, including a Common European Asylum System (CEAS), is a constituent part of the European Union's objective of progressively establishing an area of freedom, security and justice open to those who, forced by circumstances, legitimately seek protection in the Union.

(3) The European Council, at its special meeting in Tampere on 15 and 16 October 1999, agreed to work towards establishing the CEAS, based on the full and inclusive application of the Geneva Convention Relating to the Status of Refugees of 28 July 1951, as supplemented by the New York Protocol of 31 January 1967 ('the Geneva Convention'), thus ensuring that nobody is sent back to persecution, i.e. maintaining the principle of *non- refoulement*. In this respect, and without the responsibility criteria laid down in this Regulation being affected, Member States, all respecting the principle of *non- refoulement*, are considered as safe countries for third- country nationals.

(4) The Tampere conclusions also stated that the CEAS should include, in the short-term, a clear and workable method for determining the Member State responsible for the examination of an asylum application.

(5) Such a method should be based on objective, fair criteria both for the Member States and for the persons concerned. It should, in particular, make it possible to determine rapidly the Member State responsible, so as to guarantee effective access to the procedures for granting international protection and not to compromise the objective of the rapid processing of applications for international protection.

(6) The first phase in the creation of a CEAS that should lead, in the longer term, to a common procedure and a uniform status, valid throughout the Union, for those granted international protection, has now been

completed. The European Council of 4 November 2004 adopted The Hague Programme which set the objectives to be implemented in the area of freedom, security and justice in the period 2005-2010. In this respect, The Hague Programme invited the European Commission to conclude the evaluation of the first- phase legal instruments and to submit the second-phase instruments and measures to the European Parliament and to the Council with a view to their adoption before 2010.

(7) In the Stockholm Programme, the European Council reiterated its commitment to the objective of establishing a common area of protection and solidarity in accordance with Article 78 of the Treaty on the Functioning of the European Union (TFEU), for those granted international protection, by 2012 at the latest. Furthermore it emphasised that the Dublin system remains a cornerstone in building the CEAS, as it clearly allocates responsibility among Member States for the examination of applications for international protection.

(8) The resources of the European Asylum Support Office (EASO), established by Regulation (EU) No 439/2010 of the European Parliament and of the Council[5], should be available to provide adequate support to the relevant services of the Member States responsible for implementing this Regulation. In particular, EASO should provide solidarity measures, such as the Asylum Intervention Pool with asylum support teams, to assist those Member States which are faced with particular pressure and where applicants for international protection ('applicants') cannot benefit from adequate standards, in particular as regards reception and protection.

(9) In the light of the results of the evaluations undertaken of the implementation of the first-phase instruments, it is appropriate, at this stage, to confirm the principles underlying Regulation (EC) No 343/2003, while making the necessary improvements, in the light of experience, to the effectiveness of the Dublin system and the protection granted to applicants under that system. Given that a well-functioning Dublin system is essential for the CEAS, its principles and functioning should be reviewed as other components of the CEAS and Union solidarity tools are built up. A comprehensive 'fitness check' should be foreseen by conducting an evidence-based review covering the legal, economic and social effects of the Dublin system, including its effects on fundamental rights.

(10) In order to ensure equal treatment for all applicants and beneficiaries of international protection, and consistency with the current Union asylum *acquis*, in particular with Directive 2011/95/EU of the European Parliament and of the Council of 13 December 2011 on standards for the qualification of third-country nationals or stateless persons as beneficiaries of international protection, for a uniform status for refugees or for persons eligible for subsidiary protection, and for the content of the protection granted[6], the scope of this Regulation encompasses applicants for subsidiary protection and persons eligible for subsidiary protection.

(11) Directive 2013/33/EU of the European Parliament and of the Council of 26 June 2013 laying down standards for the reception of applicants for international protection[7] should apply to the procedure for the determination of the Member State responsible as regulated under this Regulation, subject to the limitations in the application of that Directive.

(12) Directive 2013/32/EU of the European Parliament and of the Council of 26 June 2013 on common procedures for granting and withdrawing international protection[8] should apply in addition and without prejudice

to the provisions concerning the procedural safeguards regulated under this Regulation, subject to the limitations in the application of that Directive.

(13) In accordance with the 1989 United Nations Convention on the Rights of the Child and with the Charter of Fundamental Rights of the European Union, the best interests of the child should be a primary consideration of Member States when applying this Regulation. In assessing the best interests of the child, Member States should, in particular, take due account of the minor's well-being and social development, safety and security considerations and the views of the minor in accordance with his or her age and maturity, including his or her background. In addition, specific procedural guarantees for unaccompanied minors should be laid down on account of their particular vulnerability.

(14) In accordance with the European Convention for the Protection of Human Rights and Fundamental Freedoms and with the Charter of Fundamental Rights of the European Union, respect for family life should be a primary consideration of Member States when applying this Regulation.

(15) The processing together of the applications for international protection of the members of one family by a single Member State makes it possible to ensure that the applications are examined thoroughly, the decisions taken in respect of them are consistent and the members of one family are not separated.

(16) In order to ensure full respect for the principle of family unity and for the best interests of the child, the existence of a relationship of dependency between an applicant and his or her child, sibling or parent on account of the applicant's pregnancy or maternity, state of health or old age, should become a binding responsibility criterion. When the applicant is an unaccompanied minor, the presence of a family member or relative on the territory of another Member State who can take care of him or her should also become a binding responsibility criterion.

(17) Any Member State should be able to derogate from the responsibility criteria, in particular on humanitarian and compassionate grounds, in order to bring together family members, relatives or any other family relations and examine an application for international protection lodged with it or with another Member State, even if such examination is not its responsibility under the binding criteria laid down in this Regulation.

(18) A personal interview with the applicant should be organised in order to facilitate the determination of the Member State responsible for examining an application for international protection. As soon as the application for international protection is lodged, the applicant should be informed of the application of this Regulation and of the possibility, during the interview, of providing information regarding the presence of family members, relatives or any other family relations in the Member States, in order to facilitate the procedure for determining the Member State responsible.

(19) In order to guarantee effective protection of the rights of the persons concerned, legal safeguards and the right to an effective remedy in respect of decisions regarding transfers to the Member State responsible should be established, in accordance, in particular, with Article 47 of the Charter of Fundamental Rights of the European Union. In order to ensure that international law is respected, an effective remedy against such decisions should cover both the examination of the application of this Regulation and of the legal and factual situation in the Member State to which the applicant is transferred.

(20) The detention of applicants should be applied in accordance with the underlying principle that a person should not be held in detention for the sole reason that he or she is seeking international protection. Detention should be for as short a period as possible and subject to the principles of necessity and proportionality. In particular, the detention of applicants must be in accordance with Article 31 of the Geneva Convention. The procedures provided for under this Regulation in respect of a detained person should be applied as a matter of priority, within the shortest possible deadlines. As regards the general guarantees governing detention, as well as detention conditions, where appropriate, Member States should apply the provisions of Directive 2013/33/EU also to persons detained on the basis of this Regulation.

(21) Deficiencies in, or the collapse of, asylum systems, often aggravated or contributed to by particular pressures on them, can jeopardise the smooth functioning of the system put in place under this Regulation, which could lead to a risk of a violation of the rights of applicants as set out in the Union asylum *acquis* and the Charter of Fundamental Rights of the European Union, other international human rights and refugee rights.

(22) A process for early warning, preparedness and management of asylum crises serving to prevent a deterioration in, or the collapse of, asylum systems, with EASO playing a key role using its powers under Regulation (EU) No 439/2010, should be established in order to ensure robust cooperation within the framework of this Regulation and to develop mutual trust among Member States with respect to asylum policy. Such a process should ensure that the Union is alerted as soon as possible when there is a concern that the smooth functioning of the system set up by this Regulation is being jeopardised as a result of particular pressure on, and/or deficiencies in, the asylum systems of one or more Member States. Such a process would allow the Union to promote preventive measures at an early stage and pay the appropriate political attention to such situations. Solidarity, which is a pivotal element in the CEAS, goes hand in hand with mutual trust. By enhancing such trust, the process for early warning, preparedness and management of asylum crises could improve the steering of concrete measures of genuine and practical solidarity towards Member States, in order to assist the affected Member States in general and the applicants in particular. In accordance with Article 80 TFEU, Union acts should, whenever necessary, contain appropriate measures to give effect to the principle of solidarity, and the process should be accompanied by such measures. The conclusions on a Common Framework for genuine and practical solidarity towards Member States facing particular pressures on their asylum systems, including through mixed migration flows, adopted by the Council on 8 March 2012, provide for a 'tool box' of existing and potential new measures, which should be taken into account in the context of a mechanism for early warning, preparedness and crisis management.

(23) Member States should collaborate with EASO in the gathering of information concerning their ability to manage particular pressure on their asylum and reception systems, in particular within the framework of the application of this Regulation. EASO should regularly report on the information gathered in accordance with Regulation (EU) No 439/2010.

(24) In accordance with Commission Regulation (EC) No 1560/2003[9], transfers to the Member State responsible for examining an application for international protection may be carried out on a voluntary basis, by supervised departure or under escort. Member States should promote voluntary transfers by providing adequate information to the applicant and should ensure that supervised or escorted transfers are undertaken in

a humane manner, in full compliance with fundamental rights and respect for human dignity, as well as the best interests of the child and taking utmost account of developments in the relevant case law, in particular as regards transfers on humanitarian grounds.

(25) The progressive creation of an area without internal frontiers in which free movement of persons is guaranteed in accordance with the TFEU and the establishment of Union policies regarding the conditions of entry and stay of third-country nationals, including common efforts towards the management of external borders, makes it necessary to strike a balance between responsibility criteria in a spirit of solidarity.

(26) Directive 95/46/EC of the European Parliament and of the Council of 24 October 1995 on the protection of individuals with regard to the processing of personal data and on the free movement of such data[10] applies to the processing of personal data by the Member States under this Regulation.

(27) The exchange of an applicant's personal data, including sensitive data on his or her health, prior to a transfer, will ensure that the competent asylum authorities are in a position to provide applicants with adequate assistance and to ensure continuity in the protection and rights afforded to them. Special provisions should be made to ensure the protection of data relating to applicants involved in that situation, in accordance with Directive 95/46/EC.

(28) The application of this Regulation can be facilitated, and its effectiveness increased, by bilateral arrangements between Member States for improving communication between competent departments, reducing time limits for procedures or simplifying the processing of requests to take charge or take back, or establishing procedures for the performance of transfers.

(29) Continuity between the system for determining the Member State responsible established by Regulation (EC) No 343/2003 and the system established by this Regulation should be ensured. Similarly, consistency should be ensured between this Regulation and Regulation (EU) No 603/2013 of the European Parliament and of the Council of 26 June 2013 on the establishment of 'Eurodac' for the comparison of fingerprints for the effective application of Regulation (EU) No 604/2013 establishing the criteria and mechanisms for determining the Member State responsible for examining an application for international protection lodged in one of the Member States by a third-country national or a stateless person and on requests for the comparisons with Eurodac data by Member States' law enforcement authorities and Europol for law enforcement purposes[11].

(30) The operation of the Eurodac system, as established by Regulation (EU) No 603/2013, should facilitate the application of this Regulation.

(31) The operation of the Visa Information System, as established by Regulation (EC) No 767/2008 of the European Parliament and of the Council of 9 July 2008 concerning the Visa Information System (VIS) and the exchange of data between Member States on short-stay visas[12], and in particular the implementation of Articles 21 and 22 thereof, should facilitate the application of this Regulation.

(32) With respect to the treatment of persons falling within the scope of this Regulation, Member States are bound by their obligations under instruments of international law, including the relevant case-law of the European Court of Human Rights.

(33) In order to ensure uniform conditions for the implementation of this Regulation, implementing powers should be conferred on

the Commission. Those powers should be exercised in accordance with Regulation (EU) No 182/2011 of the European Parliament and of the Council of 16 February 2011 laying down the rules and general principles concerning mechanisms for control by the Member States of the Commission's exercise of implementing powers[13].

(34) The examination procedure should be used for the adoption of a common leaflet on Dublin/Eurodac, as well as a specific leaflet for unaccompanied minors; of a standard form for the exchange of relevant information on unaccompanied minors; of uniform conditions for the consultation and exchange of information on minors and dependent persons; of uniform conditions on the preparation and submission of take charge and take back requests; of two lists of relevant elements of proof and circumstantial evidence, and the periodical revision thereof; of a *laissez passer*; of uniform conditions for the consultation and exchange of information regarding transfers; of a standard form for the exchange of data before a transfer; of a common health certificate; of uniform conditions and practical arrangements for the exchange of information on a person's health data before a transfer, and of secure electronic transmission channels for the transmission of requests.

(35) In order to provide for supplementary rules, the power to adopt acts in accordance with Article 290 TFEU should be delegated to the Commission in respect of the identification of family members, siblings or relatives of an unaccompanied minor; the criteria for establishing the existence of proven family links; the criteria for assessing the capacity of a relative to take care of an unaccompanied minor, including where family members, siblings or relatives of the unaccompanied minor stay in more than one Member State; the elements for assessing a dependency link; the criteria for assessing the capacity of a person to take care of a dependent person and the elements to be taken into account in order to assess the inability to travel for a significant period of time. In exercising its powers to adopt delegated acts, the Commission shall not exceed the scope of the best interests of the child as provided for under Article 6(3) of this Regulation. It is of particular importance that the Commission carry out appropriate consultations during its preparatory work, including at expert level. The Commission, when preparing and drawing up delegated acts, should ensure a simultaneous, timely and appropriate transmission of relevant documents to the European Parliament and to the Council.

(36) In the application of this Regulation, including the preparation of delegated acts, the Commission should consult experts from, among others, all relevant national authorities.

(37) Detailed rules for the application of Regulation (EC) No 343/2003 have been laid down by Regulation (EC) No 1560/2003. Certain provisions of Regulation (EC) No 1560/2003 should be incorporated into this Regulation, either for reasons of clarity or because they can serve a general objective. In particular, it is important, both for the Member States and the applicants concerned, that there should be a general mechanism for finding a solution in cases where Member States differ over the application of a provision of this Regulation. It is therefore justified to incorporate the mechanism provided for in Regulation (EC) No 1560/2003 for the settling of disputes on the humanitarian clause into this Regulation and to extend its scope to the entirety of this Regulation.

(38) The effective monitoring of the application of this Regulation requires that it be evaluated at regular intervals.

(39) This Regulation respects the fundamental rights and observes the principles which are acknowledged, in particular, in the Charter of Fundamental Rights of the European Union. In particular, this Regulation seeks to ensure full observance of the right to asylum guaranteed by Article 18 of the Charter as well as the rights recognised under Articles 1, 4, 7, 24 and 47 thereof. This Regulation should therefore be applied accordingly.

(40) Since the objective of this Regulation, namely the establishment of criteria and mechanisms for determining the Member State responsible for examining an application for international protection lodged in one of the Member States by a third-country national or a stateless person, cannot be sufficiently achieved by the Member States and can therefore, by reason of the scale and effects of this Regulation, be better achieved at Union level, the Union may adopt measures in accordance with the principle of subsidiarity as set out in Article 5 of the Treaty on European Union (TEU). In accordance with the principle of proportionality, as set out in that Article, this Regulation does not go beyond what is necessary in order to achieve that objective.

(41) In accordance with Article 3 and Article 4a(1) of Protocol No 21 on the position of the United Kingdom and Ireland in respect of the Area of Freedom, Security and Justice, annexed to the TEU and to the TFEU, those Member States have notified their wish to take part in the adoption and application of this Regulation.

(42) In accordance with Articles 1 and 2 of Protocol No 22 on the position of Denmark, annexed to the TEU and to the TFEU, Denmark is not taking part in the adoption of this Regulation and is not bound by it or subject to its application,

---

[1]   OJ C 317, 23.12.2009, p. 115.

[2]   OJ C 79, 27.3.2010, p. 58.

[3]   Position of the European Parliament of 7 May 2009 (OJ C 212 E, 5.8.2010, p. 370) and position of the Council at first reading of 6 June 2013 (not yet published in the Official Journal). Position of the European Parliament of 10 June 2013 (not yet published in the Official Journal).

[4]   OJ L 50, 25.2.2003, p. 1.

[5]   OJ L 132, 29.5.2010, p. 11.

[6]   OJ L 337, 20.12.2011, p. 9.

[7]   See page 96 of this Official Journal.

[8]   See page 60 of this Official Journal.

[9]   OJ L 222, 5.9.2003, p. 3.

[10] OJ L 281, 23.11.1995, p. 31.

[11] See page 1 of this Official Journal.

[12] OJ L 218, 13.8.2008, p. 60.

[13] OJ L 55, 28.2.2011, p. 13.

HAVE ADOPTED THIS REGULATION:

CHAPTER I
SUBJECT MATTER AND DEFINITIONS

Article 1 Subject matter

This Regulation lays down the criteria and mechanisms for determining the Member State responsible for examining an application for international protection lodged in one of the Member States by a third-country national or a stateless person ('the Member State responsible').

Article 2 Definitions

For the purposes of this Regulation:

(a) 'third-country national' means any person who is not a citizen of the Union within the meaning of Article 20(1) TFEU and who is not national of a State which participates in this Regulation by virtue of an agreement with the European Union;

(b) 'application for international protection' means an application for international protection as defined in Article 2(h) of Directive 2011/95/EU;

(c) 'applicant' means a third-country national or a stateless person who has made an application for international protection in respect of which a final decision has not yet been taken;

(d) 'examination of an application for international protection' means any examination of, or decision or ruling concerning, an application for international protection by the competent authorities in accordance with Directive 2013/32/EU and Directive 2011/95/EU, except for procedures for determining the Member State responsible in accordance with this Regulation;

(e) 'withdrawal of an application for international protection' means the actions by which the applicant terminates the procedures initiated by the submission of his or her application for international protection, in accordance with Directive 2013/32/EU, either explicitly or tacitly;

(f) 'beneficiary of international protection' means a third-country national or a stateless person who has been granted international protection as defined in Article 2(a) of Directive 2011/95/EU;

(g) 'family members' means, insofar as the family already existed in the country of origin, the following members of the applicant's family who are present on the territory of the Member States:

— the spouse of the applicant or his or her unmarried partner in a stable relationship, where the law or practice of the Member State concerned treats unmarried couples in a way comparable to married couples under its law relating to third-country nationals,

— the minor children of couples referred to in the first indent or of the applicant, on condition that they are unmarried and regardless of whether they were born in or out of wedlock or adopted as defined under national law,

— when the applicant is a minor and unmarried, the father, mother or another adult responsible for the applicant, whether by law or by the practice of the Member State where the adult is present,

— when the beneficiary of international protection is a minor and unmarried, the father, mother or another adult responsible for him or her whether by law or by the practice of the Member State where the beneficiary is present;

(h) 'relative' means the applicant's adult aunt or uncle or grandparent who is present in the territory of a Member State, regardless of whether the applicant was born in or out of wedlock or adopted as defined under national law;

(i) 'minor' means a third-country national or a stateless person below the age of 18 years;

(j) 'unaccompanied minor' means a minor who arrives on the territory of the Member States unaccompanied by an adult responsible for him or her, whether by law or by the practice of the Member State concerned, and for as long as he or she is not effectively taken into the care of such an adult; it includes a minor who is left unaccompanied after he or she has entered the territory of Member States;

(k) 'representative' means a person or an organisation appointed by the competent bodies in order to assist and represent an unaccompanied minor in procedures provided for in this Regulation with a view to ensuring the best interests of the child and exercising legal capacity for the minor where necessary. Where an organisation is appointed as a representative, it shall designate a person responsible for carrying out its duties in respect of the minor, in accordance with this Regulation;

(l) 'residence document' means any authorisation issued by the authorities of a Member State authorising a third-country national or a stateless person to stay on its territory, including the documents substantiating the authorisation to remain on the territory under temporary protection arrangements or until the circumstances preventing a removal order from being carried out no longer apply, with the exception of visas and residence authorisations issued during the period required to determine the Member State responsible as established in this Regulation or during the examination of an application for international protection or an application for a residence permit;

(m) 'visa' means the authorisation or decision of a Member State required for transit or entry for an intended stay in that Member State or in several Member States. The nature of the visa shall be determined in accordance with the following definitions:

— 'long-stay visa' means an authorisation or decision issued by one of the Member States in accordance with its national law or Union law required for entry for an intended stay in that Member State of more than three months,

— 'short-stay visa' means an authorisation or decision of a Member State with a view to transit through or an intended stay on the territory of one or more or all the Member States of a duration of no more than three months in any six-month period beginning on the date of first entry on the territory of the Member States,

— 'airport transit visa' means a visa valid for transit through the international transit areas of one or more airports of the Member States;

(n) 'risk of absconding' means the existence of reasons in an individual case, which are based on objective criteria defined by law, to believe that an applicant or a third- country national or a stateless person who is subject to a transfer procedure may abscond.

CHAPTER II
GENERAL PRINCIPLES AND SAFEGUARDS

Article 3 Access to the procedure for examining an application for international protection

1. Member States shall examine any application for international protection by a third-country national or a stateless person who applies on the territory of any one of them, including at the border or in the transit zones. The application shall be examined by a single Member State, which shall be the one which the criteria set out in Chapter III indicate is responsible.

2. Where no Member State responsible can be designated on the basis of the criteria listed in this Regulation, the first Member State in which the application for international protection was lodged shall be responsible for examining it.

Where it is impossible to transfer an applicant to the Member State primarily designated as responsible because there are substantial grounds for believing that there are systemic flaws in the asylum procedure and in the reception conditions for applicants in that Member State, resulting in a risk of inhuman or degrading treatment within the meaning of Article 4 of the Charter of Fundamental Rights of the European Union, the determining Member State shall continue to examine the criteria set out in Chapter III in order to establish whether another Member State can be designated as responsible.

Where the transfer cannot be made pursuant to this paragraph to any Member State designated on the basis of the criteria set out in Chapter III or to the first Member State with which the application was lodged, the determining Member State shall become the Member State responsible.

3. Any Member State shall retain the right to send an applicant to a safe third country, subject to the rules and safeguards laid down in Directive 2013/32/EU.

Article 4 Right to information

1. As soon as an application for international protection is lodged within the meaning of Article 20(2) in a Member State, its competent authorities shall inform the applicant of the application of this Regulation, and in particular of:

(a) the objectives of this Regulation and the consequences of making another application in a different Member State as well as the consequences of moving from one Member State to another during the phases in which the Member State responsible under this Regulation is being determined and the application for international protection is being examined;

(b) the criteria for determining the Member State responsible, the hierarchy of such criteria in the different steps of the procedure and their duration, including the fact that an application for international protection lodged in one Member State can result in that Member State becoming responsible under this Regulation even if such responsibility is not based on those criteria;

(c) the personal interview pursuant to Article 5 and the possibility of submitting information regarding the presence of family members, relatives or any other family relations in the Member States, including the means by which the applicant can submit such information;

(d) the possibility to challenge a transfer decision and, where applicable, to apply for a suspension of the transfer;

(e) the fact that the competent authorities of Member States can exchange data on him or her for the sole purpose of implementing their obligations arising under this Regulation;

(f) the right of access to data relating to him or her and the right to request that such data be corrected if inaccurate or be deleted if unlawfully processed, as well as the procedures for exercising those rights, including the contact details of the authorities referred to in Article 35 and of the national data protection authorities responsible for hearing claims concerning the protection of personal data.

2. The information referred to in paragraph 1 shall be provided in writing in a language that the applicant understands or is reasonably supposed to understand. Member States shall use the common leaflet drawn up pursuant to paragraph 3 for that purpose.

Where necessary for the proper understanding of the applicant, the information shall also be supplied orally, for example in connection with the personal interview as referred to in Article 5.

3.   The Commission shall, by means of implementing acts, draw up a common leaflet, as well as a specific leaflet for unaccompanied minors, containing at least the information referred to in paragraph 1 of this Article. This common leaflet shall also include information regarding the application of Regulation (EU) No 603/2013 and, in particular, the purpose for which the data of an applicant may be processed within Eurodac. The common leaflet shall be established in such a manner as to enable Member States to complete it with additional Member State-specific information. Those implementing acts shall be adopted in accordance with the examination procedure referred to in Article 44(2) of this Regulation.

Article 5 Personal interview

1.   In order to facilitate the process of determining the Member State responsible, the determining Member State shall conduct a personal interview with the applicant. The interview shall also allow the proper understanding of the information supplied to the applicant in accordance with Article 4.

2.   The personal interview may be omitted if:

(a)   the applicant has absconded; or

(b)   after having received the information referred to in Article 4, the applicant has already provided the information relevant to determine the Member State responsible by other means. The Member State omitting the interview shall give the applicant the opportunity to present all further information which is relevant to correctly determine the Member State responsible before a decision is taken to transfer the applicant to the Member State responsible pursuant to Article 26(1).

3.   The personal interview shall take place in a timely manner and, in any event, before any decision is taken to transfer the applicant to the Member State responsible pursuant to Article 26(1).

4.   The personal interview shall be conducted in a language that the applicant understands or is reasonably supposed to understand and in which he or she is able to communicate. Where necessary, Member States shall have recourse to an interpreter who is able to ensure appropriate communication between the applicant and the person conducting the personal interview.

5.   The personal interview shall take place under conditions which ensure appropriate confidentiality. It shall be conducted by a qualified person under national law.

6.   The Member State conducting the personal interview shall make a written summary thereof which shall contain at least the main information supplied by the applicant at the interview. This summary may either take the form of a report or a standard form. The Member State shall ensure that the applicant and/or the legal advisor or other counsellor who is representing the applicant have timely access to the summary.

Article 6 Guarantees for minors

1.   The best interests of the child shall be a primary consideration for Member States with respect to all procedures provided for in this Regulation.

2.   Member States shall ensure that a representative represents and/or assists an unaccompanied minor with respect to all procedures provided for in this Regulation. The representative shall have the qualifications and expertise to ensure that the best interests of the minor are taken into consideration during the procedures carried out under this Regulation. Such representative shall have access to the content of the relevant documents in the applicant's file including the specific leaflet for unaccompanied minors.

This paragraph shall be without prejudice to the relevant provisions in Article 25 of Directive 2013/32/EU.

3.   In assessing the best interests of the child, Member States shall closely cooperate with each other and shall, in particular, take due account of the following factors:

(a)   family reunification possibilities;

(b)   the minor's well-being and social development;

(c)   safety and security considerations, in particular where there is a risk of the minor being a victim of human trafficking;

(d)   the views of the minor, in accordance with his or her age and maturity.

4.   For the purpose of applying Article 8, the Member State where the unaccompanied minor lodged an application for international protection shall, as soon as possible, take appropriate action to identify the family members, siblings or relatives of the unaccompanied minor on the territory of Member States, whilst protecting the best interests of the child.

To that end, that Member State may call for the assistance of international or other relevant organisations, and may facilitate the minor's access to the tracing services of such organisations.

The staff of the competent authorities referred to in Article 35 who deal with requests concerning unaccompanied minors shall have received, and shall continue to receive, appropriate training concerning the specific needs of minors.

5.   With a view to facilitating the appropriate action to identify the family members, siblings or relatives of the unaccompanied minor living in the territory of another Member State pursuant to paragraph 4 of this Article, the Commission shall adopt implementing acts including a standard form for the exchange of relevant information between Member States. Those implementing acts shall be adopted in accordance with the examination procedure referred to in Article 44(2).

CHAPTER III
CRITERIA FOR DETERMINING THE MEMBER STATE RESPONSIBLE

Article 7 Hierarchy of criteria

1.   The criteria for determining the Member State responsible shall be applied in the order in which they are set out in this Chapter.

2.   The Member State responsible in accordance with the criteria set out in this Chapter shall be determined on the basis of the situation obtaining when the applicant first lodged his or her application for international protection with a Member State.

3.   In view of the application of the criteria referred to in Articles 8, 10 and 16, Member States shall take into consideration any available evidence regarding the presence, on the territory of a Member State, of family members, relatives or any other family relations of the applicant, on condition that such evidence is produced before another Member State accepts the request to take charge or take back the person concerned, pursuant to Articles 22 and 25 respectively, and that the previous applications for international protection of the applicant have not yet been the subject of a first decision regarding the substance.

Article 8 Minors

1.   Where the applicant is an unaccompanied minor, the Member State responsible shall be that where a family member or a sibling of the unaccompanied minor is legally present, provided that it is in the best interests of the minor. Where the applicant is a married minor whose spouse is not legally present on the territory of the Member States, the Member State responsible shall be the Member State where the father, mother or other adult responsible for the minor, whether by law or by the practice of that Member State, or sibling is legally present.

2.   Where the applicant is an unaccompanied minor who has a relative who is legally present in another Member State and where it is established, based on an individual examination, that the relative can take care of him or her, that Member State shall unite the minor with his or her relative and shall be the Member State responsible, provided that it is in the best interests of the minor.

3. Where family members, siblings or relatives as referred to in paragraphs 1 and 2, stay in more than one Member State, the Member State responsible shall be decided on the basis of what is in the best interests of the unaccompanied minor.

4. In the absence of a family member, a sibling or a relative as referred to in paragraphs 1 and 2, the Member State responsible shall be that where the unaccompanied minor has lodged his or her application for international protection, provided that it is in the best interests of the minor.

5. The Commission shall be empowered to adopt delegated acts in accordance with Article 45 concerning the identification of family members, siblings or relatives of the unaccompanied minor; the criteria for establishing the existence of proven family links; the criteria for assessing the capacity of a relative to take care of the unaccompanied minor, including where family members, siblings or relatives of the unaccompanied minor stay in more than one Member State. In exercising its powers to adopt delegated acts, the Commission shall not exceed the scope of the best interests of the child as provided for under Article 6(3).

6. The Commission shall, by means of implementing acts, establish uniform conditions for the consultation and the exchange of information between Member States. Those implementing acts shall be adopted in accordance with the examination procedure referred to in Article 44(2).

Article 9 Family members who are beneficiaries of international protection

Where the applicant has a family member, regardless of whether the family was previously formed in the country of origin, who has been allowed to reside as a beneficiary of international protection in a Member State, that Member State shall be responsible for examining the application for international protection, provided that the persons concerned expressed their desire in writing.

Article 10 Family members who are applicants for international protection

If the applicant has a family member in a Member State whose application for international protection in that Member State has not yet been the subject of a first decision regarding the substance, that Member State shall be responsible for examining the application for international protection, provided that the persons concerned expressed their desire in writing.

Article 11 Family procedure

Where several family members and/or minor unmarried siblings submit applications for international protection in the same Member State simultaneously, or on dates close enough for the procedures for determining the Member State responsible to be conducted together, and where the application of the criteria set out in this Regulation would lead to their being separated, the Member State responsible shall be determined on the basis of the following provisions:

(a) responsibility for examining the applications for international protection of all the family members and/or minor unmarried siblings shall lie with the Member State which the criteria indicate is responsible for taking charge of the largest number of them;

(b) failing this, responsibility shall lie with the Member State which the criteria indicate is responsible for examining the application of the oldest of them.

Article 12 Issue of residence documents or visas

1. Where the applicant is in possession of a valid residence document, the Member State which issued the document shall be responsible for examining the application for international protection.

2. Where the applicant is in possession of a valid visa, the Member State which issued the visa shall be responsible for examining the application for international protection, unless the visa was issued on behalf of another Member State under a

representation arrangement as provided for in Article 8 of Regulation (EC) No 810/2009 of the European Parliament and of the Council, of 13 July 2009, establishing a Community Code on Visas[1]. In such a case, the represented Member State shall be responsible for examining the application for international protection.

3. Where the applicant is in possession of more than one valid residence document or visa issued by different Member States, the responsibility for examining the application for international protection shall be assumed by the Member States in the following order:

(a) the Member State which issued the residence document conferring the right to the longest period of residency or, where the periods of validity are identical, the Member State which issued the residence document having the latest expiry date;

(b) the Member State which issued the visa having the latest expiry date where the various visas are of the same type;

(c) where visas are of different kinds, the Member State which issued the visa having the longest period of validity or, where the periods of validity are identical, the Member State which issued the visa having the latest expiry date.

4. Where the applicant is in possession only of one or more residence documents which have expired less than two years previously or one or more visas which have expired less than six months previously and which enabled him or her actually to enter the territory of a Member State, paragraphs 1, 2 and 3 shall apply for such time as the applicant has not left the territories of the Member States.

Where the applicant is in possession of one or more residence documents which have expired more than two years previously or one or more visas which have expired more than six months previously and enabled him or her actually to enter the territory of a Member State and where he has not left the territories of the Member States, the Member State in which the application for international protection is lodged shall be responsible.

5. The fact that the residence document or visa was issued on the basis of a false or assumed identity or on submission of forged, counterfeit or invalid documents shall not prevent responsibility being allocated to the Member State which issued it. However, the Member State issuing the residence document or visa shall not be responsible if it can establish that a fraud was committed after the document or visa had been issued.

Article 13 Entry and/or stay

1. Where it is established, on the basis of proof or circumstantial evidence as described in the two lists mentioned in Article 22(3) of this Regulation, including the data referred to in Regulation (EU) No 603/2013, that an applicant has irregularly crossed the border into a Member State by land, sea or air having come from a third country, the Member State thus entered shall be responsible for examining the application for international protection. That responsibility shall cease 12 months after the date on which the irregular border crossing took place.

2. When a Member State cannot or can no longer be held responsible in accordance with paragraph 1 of this Article and where it is established, on the basis of proof or circumstantial evidence as described in the two lists mentioned in Article 22(3), that the applicant — who has entered the territories of the Member States irregularly or whose circumstances of entry cannot be established — has been living for a continuous period of at least five months in a Member State before lodging the application for international protection, that Member State shall be responsible for examining the application for international protection.

If the applicant has been living for periods of time of at least five months in several Member States, the Member State where he or she has been living most recently shall be responsible for examining the application for international protection.

[1]   OJ L 243, 15.9.2009, p. 1.

Article 14 Visa waived entry

1. If a third-country national or a stateless person enters into the territory of a Member State in which the need for him or her to have a visa is waived, that Member State shall be responsible for examining his or her application for international protection.

2. The principle set out in paragraph 1 shall not apply if the third-country national or the stateless person lodges his or her application for international protection in another Member State in which the need for him or her to have a visa for entry into the territory is also waived. In that case, that other Member State shall be responsible for examining the application for international protection.

Article 15 Application in an international transit area of an airport

Where the application for international protection is made in the international transit area of an airport of a Member State by a third-country national or a stateless person, that Member State shall be responsible for examining the application.

CHAPTER IV
DEPENDENT PERSONS AND DISCRETIONARY CLAUSES

Article 16 Dependent persons

1. Where, on account of pregnancy, a new-born child, serious illness, severe disability or old age, an applicant is dependent on the assistance of his or her child, sibling or parent legally resident in one of the Member States, or his or her child, sibling or parent legally resident in one of the Member States is dependent on the assistance of the applicant, Member States shall normally keep or bring together the applicant with that child, sibling or parent, provided that family ties existed in the country of origin, that the child, sibling or parent or the applicant is able to take care of the dependent person and that the persons concerned expressed their desire in writing.

2. Where the child, sibling or parent referred to in paragraph 1 is legally resident in a Member State other than the one where the applicant is present, the Member State responsible shall be the one where the child, sibling or parent is legally resident unless the applicant's health prevents him or her from travelling to that Member State for a significant period of time. In such a case, the Member State responsible shall be the one where the applicant is present. Such Member State shall not be subject to the obligation to bring the child, sibling or parent of the applicant to its territory.

3. The Commission shall be empowered to adopt delegated acts in accordance with Article 45 concerning the elements to be taken into account in order to assess the dependency link, the criteria for establishing the existence of proven family links, the criteria for assessing the capacity of the person concerned to take care of the dependent person and the elements to be taken into account in order to assess the inability to travel for a significant period of time.

4. The Commission shall, by means of implementing acts, establish uniform conditions for the consultation and exchange of information between Member States. Those implementing acts shall be adopted in accordance with the examination procedure referred to in Article 44(2).

Article 17 Discretionary clauses

1. By way of derogation from Article 3(1), each Member State may decide to examine an application for international protection lodged with it by a third-country

national or a stateless person, even if such examination is not its responsibility under the criteria laid down in this Regulation.

The Member State which decides to examine an application for international protection pursuant to this paragraph shall become the Member State responsible and shall assume the obligations associated with that responsibility. Where applicable, it shall inform, using the 'DubliNet' electronic communication network set up under Article 18 of Regulation (EC) No 1560/2003, the Member State previously responsible, the Member State conducting a procedure for determining the Member State responsible or the Member State which has been requested to take charge of, or to take back, the applicant.

The Member State which becomes responsible pursuant to this paragraph shall forthwith indicate it in Eurodac in accordance with Regulation (EU) No 603/2013 by adding the date when the decision to examine the application was taken.

2. The Member State in which an application for international protection is made and which is carrying out the process of determining the Member State responsible, or the Member State responsible, may, at any time before a first decision regarding the substance is taken, request another Member State to take charge of an applicant in order to bring together any family relations, on humanitarian grounds based in particular on family or cultural considerations, even where that other Member State is not responsible under the criteria laid down in Articles 8 to 11 and 16. The persons concerned must express their consent in writing.

The request to take charge shall contain all the material in the possession of the requesting Member State to allow the requested Member State to assess the situation.

The requested Member State shall carry out any necessary checks to examine the humanitarian grounds cited, and shall reply to the requesting Member State within two months of receipt of the request using the 'DubliNet' electronic communication network set up under Article 18 of Regulation (EC) No 1560/2003. A reply refusing the request shall state the reasons on which the refusal is based.

Where the requested Member State accepts the request, responsibility for examining the application shall be transferred to it.

CHAPTER V
OBLIGATIONS OF THE MEMBER STATE RESPONSIBLE

Article 18 Obligations of the Member State responsible

1. The Member State responsible under this Regulation shall be obliged to:

   (a) take charge, under the conditions laid down in Articles 21, 22 and 29, of an applicant who has lodged an application in a different Member State;

   (b) take back, under the conditions laid down in Articles 23, 24, 25 and 29, an applicant whose application is under examination and who made an application in another Member State or who is on the territory of another Member State without a residence document;

   (c) take back, under the conditions laid down in Articles 23, 24, 25 and 29, a third-country national or a stateless person who has withdrawn the application under examination and made an application in another Member State or who is on the territory of another Member State without a residence document;

   (d) take back, under the conditions laid down in Articles 23, 24, 25 and 29, a third-country national or a stateless person whose application has been rejected and who made an application in another Member State or who is on the territory of another Member State without a residence document.

2. In the cases falling within the scope of paragraph 1(a) and (b), the Member State responsible shall examine or complete the examination of the application for international protection made by the applicant.

In the cases falling within the scope of paragraph 1(c), when the Member State responsible had discontinued the examination of an application following its withdrawal by the applicant before a decision on the substance has been taken at first instance, that Member State shall ensure that the applicant is entitled to request that the examination of his or her application be completed or to lodge a new application for international protection, which shall not be treated as a subsequent application as provided for in Directive 2013/32/EU. In such cases, Member States shall ensure that the examination of the application is completed.

In the cases falling within the scope of paragraph 1(d), where the application has been rejected at first instance only, the Member State responsible shall ensure that the person concerned has or has had the opportunity to seek an effective remedy pursuant to Article 46 of Directive 2013/32/EU.

Article 19 Cessation of responsibilities

1. Where a Member State issues a residence document to the applicant, the obligations specified in Article 18(1) shall be transferred to that Member State.

2. The obligations specified in Article 18(1) shall cease where the Member State responsible can establish, when requested to take charge or take back an applicant or another person as referred to in Article 18(1)(c) or (d), that the person concerned has left the territory of the Member States for at least three months, unless the person concerned is in possession of a valid residence document issued by the Member State responsible.

An application lodged after the period of absence referred to in the first subparagraph shall be regarded as a new application giving rise to a new procedure for determining the Member State responsible.

3. The obligations specified in Article 18(1)(c) and (d) shall cease where the Member State responsible can establish, when requested to take back an applicant or another person as referred to in Article 18(1)(c) or (d), that the person concerned has left the territory of the Member States in compliance with a return decision or removal order issued following the withdrawal or rejection of the application.

An application lodged after an effective removal has taken place shall be regarded as a new application giving rise to a new procedure for determining the Member State responsible.

CHAPTER VI
PROCEDURES FOR TAKING CHARGE AND TAKING BACK

SECTION I

START OF THE PROCEDURE

Article 20 Start of the procedure

1. The process of determining the Member State responsible shall start as soon as an application for international protection is first lodged with a Member State.

2. An application for international protection shall be deemed to have been lodged once a form submitted by the applicant or a report prepared by the authorities has reached the competent authorities of the Member State concerned. Where an application is not made in writing, the time elapsing between the statement of intention and the preparation of a report should be as short as possible.

3. For the purposes of this Regulation, the situation of a minor who is accompanying the applicant and meets the definition of family member shall be indissociable from that of his or her family member and shall be a matter for the Member State responsible for examining the application for international protection of that family member, even if the minor is not individually an applicant, provided that it is in the minor's best interests. The same treatment shall be applied to children born after the

applicant arrives on the territory of the Member States, without the need to initiate a new procedure for taking charge of them.

4. Where an application for international protection is lodged with the competent authorities of a Member State by an applicant who is on the territory of another Member State, the determination of the Member State responsible shall be made by the Member State in whose territory the applicant is present. The latter Member State shall be informed without delay by the Member State which received the application and shall then, for the purposes of this Regulation, be regarded as the Member State with which the application for international protection was lodged.

The applicant shall be informed in writing of this change in the determining Member State and of the date on which it took place.

5. An applicant who is present in another Member State without a residence document or who there lodges an application for international protection after withdrawing his or her first application made in a different Member State during the process of determining the Member State responsible shall be taken back, under the conditions laid down in Articles 23, 24, 25 and 29, by the Member State with which that application for international protection was first lodged, with a view to completing the process of determining the Member State responsible.

That obligation shall cease where the Member State requested to complete the process of determining the Member State responsible can establish that the applicant has in the meantime left the territory of the Member States for a period of at least three months or has obtained a residence document from another Member State.

An application lodged after the period of absence referred to in the second subparagraph shall be regarded as a new application giving rise to a new procedure for determining the Member State responsible.

SECTION II

PROCEDURES FOR TAKE CHARGE REQUESTS

Article 21 Submitting a take charge request

1. Where a Member State with which an application for international protection has been lodged considers that another Member State is responsible for examining the application, it may, as quickly as possible and in any event within three months of the date on which the application was lodged within the meaning of Article 20(2), request that other Member State to take charge of the applicant.

Notwithstanding the first subparagraph, in the case of a Eurodac hit with data recorded pursuant to Article 14 of Regulation (EU) No 603/2013, the request shall be sent within two months of receiving that hit pursuant to Article 15(2) of that Regulation.

Where the request to take charge of an applicant is not made within the periods laid down in the first and second subparagraphs, responsibility for examining the application for international protection shall lie with the Member State in which the application was lodged.

2. The requesting Member State may ask for an urgent reply in cases where the application for international protection was lodged after leave to enter or remain was refused, after an arrest for an unlawful stay or after the service or execution of a removal order.

The request shall state the reasons warranting an urgent reply and the period within which a reply is expected. That period shall be at least one week.

3. In the cases referred to in paragraphs 1 and 2, the request that charge be taken by another Member State shall be made using a standard form and including proof or circumstantial evidence as described in the two lists mentioned in Article 22(3) and/or relevant elements from the applicant's statement, enabling the authorities of the requested Member State to check whether it is responsible on the basis of the criteria laid down in this Regulation.

The Commission shall, by means of implementing acts, adopt uniform conditions on the preparation and submission of take charge requests. Those implementing acts shall be adopted in accordance with the examination procedure referred to in Article 44(2).

Article 22 Replying to a take charge request

1. The requested Member State shall make the necessary checks, and shall give a decision on the request to take charge of an applicant within two months of receipt of the request.

2. In the procedure for determining the Member State responsible elements of proof and circumstantial evidence shall be used.

3. The Commission shall, by means of implementing acts, establish, and review periodically, two lists, indicating the relevant elements of proof and circumstantial evidence in accordance with the criteria set out in points (a) and (b) of this paragraph. Those implementing acts shall be adopted in accordance with the examination procedure referred to in Article 44(2).

(a) Proof:

(i) this refers to formal proof which determines responsibility pursuant to this Regulation, as long as it is not refuted by proof to the contrary;

(ii) the Member States shall provide the Committee provided for in Article 44 with models of the different types of administrative documents, in accordance with the typology established in the list of formal proofs;

(b) Circumstantial evidence:

(i) this refers to indicative elements which while being refutable may be sufficient, in certain cases, according to the evidentiary value attributed to them;

(ii) their evidentiary value, in relation to the responsibility for examining the application for international protection shall be assessed on a case-by-case basis.

4. The requirement of proof should not exceed what is necessary for the proper application of this Regulation.

5. If there is no formal proof, the requested Member State shall acknowledge its responsibility if the circumstantial evidence is coherent, verifiable and sufficiently detailed to establish responsibility.

6. Where the requesting Member State has pleaded urgency in accordance with the provisions of Article 21(2), the requested Member State shall make every effort to comply with the time limit requested. In exceptional cases, where it can be demonstrated that the examination of a request for taking charge of an applicant is particularly complex, the requested Member State may give its reply after the time limit requested, but in any event within one month. In such situations the requested Member State must communicate its decision to postpone a reply to the requesting Member State within the time limit originally requested.

7. Failure to act within the two-month period mentioned in paragraph 1 and the one-month period mentioned in paragraph 6 shall be tantamount to accepting the request, and entail the obligation to take charge of the person, including the obligation to provide for proper arrangements for arrival.

SECTION III

PROCEDURES FOR TAKE BACK REQUESTS

Article 23 Submitting a take back request when a new application has been lodged in the requesting Member State

1. Where a Member State with which a person as referred to in Article 18(1)(b), (c) or (d) has lodged a new application for international protection considers that another

Member State is responsible in accordance with Article 20(5) and Article 18(1)(b), (c) or (d), it may request that other Member State to take back that person.

2. A take back request shall be made as quickly as possible and in any event within two months of receiving the Eurodac hit, pursuant to Article 9(5) of Regulation (EU) No 603/2013.

If the take back request is based on evidence other than data obtained from the Eurodac system, it shall be sent to the requested Member State within three months of the date on which the application for international protection was lodged within the meaning of Article 20(2).

3. Where the take back request is not made within the periods laid down in paragraph 2, responsibility for examining the application for international protection shall lie with the Member State in which the new application was lodged.

4. A take back request shall be made using a standard form and shall include proof or circumstantial evidence as described in the two lists mentioned in Article 22(3) and/ or relevant elements from the statements of the person concerned, enabling the authorities of the requested Member State to check whether it is responsible on the basis of the criteria laid down in this Regulation.

The Commission shall, by means of implementing acts, adopt uniform conditions for the preparation and submission of take back requests. Those implementing acts shall be adopted in accordance with the examination procedure referred to in Article 44(2).

Article 24 Submitting a take back request when no new application has been lodged in the requesting Member State

1. Where a Member State on whose territory a person as referred to in Article 18(1)(b), (c) or (d) is staying without a residence document and with which no new application for international protection has been lodged considers that another Member State is responsible in accordance with Article 20(5) and Article 18(1)(b), (c) or (d), it may request that other Member State to take back that person.

2. By way of derogation from Article 6(2) of Directive 2008/115/EC of the European Parliament and of the Council of 16 December 2008 on common standards and procedures in Member States for returning illegally staying third-country nationals[1], where a Member State on whose territory a person is staying without a residence document decides to search the Eurodac system in accordance with Article 17 of Regulation (EU) No 603/2013, the request to take back a person as referred to in Article 18(1)(b) or (c) of this Regulation, or a person as referred to in its Article 18(1)(d) whose application for international protection has not been rejected by a final decision, shall be made as quickly as possible and in any event within two months of receipt of the Eurodac hit, pursuant to Article 17(5) of Regulation (EU) No 603/2013.

If the take back request is based on evidence other than data obtained from the Eurodac system, it shall be sent to the requested Member State within three months of the date on which the requesting Member State becomes aware that another Member State may be responsible for the person concerned.

3. Where the take back request is not made within the periods laid down in paragraph 2, the Member State on whose territory the person concerned is staying without a residence document shall give that person the opportunity to lodge a new application.

4. Where a person as referred to in Article 18(1)(d) of this Regulation whose application for international protection has been rejected by a final decision in one Member State is on the territory of another Member State without a residence document, the latter Member State may either request the former Member State to take back the person concerned or carry out a return procedure in accordance with Directive 2008/115/EC.

When the latter Member State decides to request the former Member State to take back the person concerned, the rules laid down in Directive 2008/115/EC shall not apply.

5. The request for the person referred to in Article 18(1)(b), (c) or (d) to be taken back shall be made using a standard form and shall include proof or circumstantial evidence as described in the two lists mentioned in Article 22(3) and/or relevant elements from the person's statements, enabling the authorities of the requested Member State to check whether it is responsible on the basis of the criteria laid down in this Regulation.

The Commission shall, by means of implementing acts, establish and review periodically two lists indicating the relevant elements of proof and circumstantial evidence in accordance with the criteria set out in Article 22(3)(a) and (b), and shall adopt uniform conditions for the preparation and submission of take back requests. Those implementing acts shall be adopted in accordance with the examination procedure referred to in Article 44(2).

Article 25 Replying to a take back request

1. The requested Member State shall make the necessary checks and shall give a decision on the request to take back the person concerned as quickly as possible and in any event no later than one month from the date on which the request was received. When the request is based on data obtained from the Eurodac system, that time limit shall be reduced to two weeks.

2. Failure to act within the one month period or the two weeks period mentioned in paragraph 1 shall be tantamount to accepting the request, and shall entail the obligation to take back the person concerned, including the obligation to provide for proper arrangements for arrival.

SECTION IV

PROCEDURAL SAFEGUARDS

Article 26 Notification of a transfer decision

1. Where the requested Member State accepts to take charge of or to take back an applicant or other person as referred to in Article 18(1)(c) or (d), the requesting Member State shall notify the person concerned of the decision to transfer him or her to the Member State responsible and, where applicable, of not examining his or her application for international protection. If a legal advisor or other counsellor is representing the person concerned, Member States may choose to notify the decision to such legal advisor or counsellor instead of to the person concerned and, where applicable, communicate the decision to the person concerned.

2. The decision referred to in paragraph 1 shall contain information on the legal remedies available, including on the right to apply for suspensive effect, where applicable, and on the time limits applicable for seeking such remedies and for carrying out the transfer, and shall, if necessary, contain information on the place where, and the date on which, the person concerned should appear, if that person is travelling to the Member State responsible by his or her own means.

Member States shall ensure that information on persons or entities that may provide legal assistance to the person concerned is communicated to the person concerned together with the decision referred to in paragraph 1, when that information has not been already communicated.

3. When the person concerned is not assisted or represented by a legal advisor or other counsellor, Member States shall inform him or her of the main elements of the decision, which shall always include information on the legal remedies available and the time limits applicable for seeking such remedies, in a language that the person concerned understands or is reasonably supposed to understand.

Article 27 Remedies

1. The applicant or another person as referred to in Article 18(1)(c) or (d) shall have the right to an effective remedy, in the form of an appeal or a review, in fact and in law, against a transfer decision, before a court or tribunal.

2. Member States shall provide for a reasonable period of time within which the person concerned may exercise his or her right to an effective remedy pursuant to paragraph 1.

3. For the purposes of appeals against, or reviews of, transfer decisions, Member States shall provide in their national law that:

    (a)   the appeal or review confers upon the person concerned the right to remain in the Member State concerned pending the outcome of the appeal or review; or

    (b)   the transfer is automatically suspended and such suspension lapses after a certain reasonable period of time, during which a court or a tribunal, after a close and rigorous scrutiny, shall have taken a decision whether to grant suspensive effect to an appeal or review; or

    (c)   the person concerned has the opportunity to request within a reasonable period of time a court or tribunal to suspend the implementation of the transfer decision pending the outcome of his or her appeal or review. Member States shall ensure that an effective remedy is in place by suspending the transfer until the decision on the first suspension request is taken. Any decision on whether to suspend the implementation of the transfer decision shall be taken within a reasonable period of time, while permitting a close and rigorous scrutiny of the suspension request. A decision not to suspend the implementation of the transfer decision shall state the reasons on which it is based.

4. Member States may provide that the competent authorities may decide, acting *ex officio*, to suspend the implementation of the transfer decision pending the outcome of the appeal or review.

5. Member States shall ensure that the person concerned has access to legal assistance and, where necessary, to linguistic assistance.

6. Member States shall ensure that legal assistance is granted on request free of charge where the person concerned cannot afford the costs involved. Member States may provide that, as regards fees and other costs, the treatment of applicants shall not be more favourable than the treatment generally accorded to their nationals in matters pertaining to legal assistance.

Without arbitrarily restricting access to legal assistance, Member States may provide that free legal assistance and representation not be granted where the appeal or review is considered by the competent authority or a court or tribunal to have no tangible prospect of success.

Where a decision not to grant free legal assistance and representation pursuant to this paragraph is taken by an authority other than a court or tribunal, Member States shall provide the right to an effective remedy before a court or tribunal to challenge that decision.

In complying with the requirements set out in this paragraph, Member States shall ensure that legal assistance and representation is not arbitrarily restricted and that the applicant's effective access to justice is not hindered.

Legal assistance shall include at least the preparation of the required procedural documents and representation before a court or tribunal and may be restricted to legal advisors or counsellors specifically designated by national law to provide assistance and representation.

Procedures for access to legal assistance shall be laid down in national law.

---

1   OJ L 348, 24.12.2008, p. 98.

SECTION V

DETENTION FOR THE PURPOSE OF TRANSFER

Article 28 Detention

1. Member States shall not hold a person in detention for the sole reason that he or she is subject to the procedure established by this Regulation.

2. When there is a significant risk of absconding, Member States may detain the person concerned in order to secure transfer procedures in accordance with this Regulation, on the basis of an individual assessment and only in so far as detention is proportional and other less coercive alternative measures cannot be applied effectively.

3. Detention shall be for as short a period as possible and shall be for no longer than the time reasonably necessary to fulfil the required administrative procedures with due diligence until the transfer under this Regulation is carried out.

Where a person is detained pursuant to this Article, the period for submitting a take charge or take back request shall not exceed one month from the lodging of the application. The Member State carrying out the procedure in accordance with this Regulation shall ask for an urgent reply in such cases. Such reply shall be given within two weeks of receipt of the request. Failure to reply within the two-week period shall be tantamount to accepting the request and shall entail the obligation to take charge or take back the person, including the obligation to provide for proper arrangements for arrival.

Where a person is detained pursuant to this Article, the transfer of that person from the requesting Member State to the Member State responsible shall be carried out as soon as practically possible, and at the latest within six weeks of the implicit or explicit acceptance of the request by another Member State to take charge or to take back the person concerned or of the moment when the appeal or review no longer has a suspensive effect in accordance with Article 27(3).

When the requesting Member State fails to comply with the deadlines for submitting a take charge or take back request or where the transfer does not take place within the period of six weeks referred to in the third subparagraph, the person shall no longer be detained. Articles 21, 23, 24 and 29 shall continue to apply accordingly.

4. As regards the detention conditions and the guarantees applicable to persons detained, in order to secure the transfer procedures to the Member State responsible, Articles 9, 10 and 11 of Directive 2013/33/EU shall apply.

SECTION VI

TRANSFERS

Article 29 Modalities and time limits

1. The transfer of the applicant or of another person as referred to in Article 18(1)(c) or (d) from the requesting Member State to the Member State responsible shall be carried out in accordance with the national law of the requesting Member State, after consultation between the Member States concerned, as soon as practically possible, and at the latest within six months of acceptance of the request by another Member State to take charge or to take back the person concerned or of the final decision on an appeal or review where there is a suspensive effect in accordance with Article 27(3).

If transfers to the Member State responsible are carried out by supervised departure or under escort, Member States shall ensure that they are carried out in a humane manner and with full respect for fundamental rights and human dignity.

If necessary, the applicant shall be supplied by the requesting Member State with a *laissez passer*. The Commission shall, by means of implementing acts, establish the design of the *laissez passer*. Those implementing acts shall be adopted in accordance with the examination procedure referred to in Article 44(2).

The Member State responsible shall inform the requesting Member State, as appropriate, of the safe arrival of the person concerned or of the fact that he or she did not appear within the set time limit.

2. Where the transfer does not take place within the six months' time limit, the Member State responsible shall be relieved of its obligations to take charge or to take back the person concerned and responsibility shall then be transferred to the requesting Member State. This time limit may be extended up to a maximum of one year if the transfer could not be carried out due to imprisonment of the person concerned or up to a maximum of eighteen months if the person concerned absconds.

3. If a person has been transferred erroneously or a decision to transfer is overturned on appeal or review after the transfer has been carried out, the Member State which carried out the transfer shall promptly accept that person back.

4. The Commission shall, by means of implementing acts, establish uniform conditions for the consultation and exchange of information between Member States, in particular in the event of postponed or delayed transfers, transfers following acceptance by default, transfers of minors or dependent persons, and supervised transfers. Those implementing acts shall be adopted in accordance with the examination procedure referred to in Article 44(2).

Article 30 Costs of transfer

1. The costs necessary to transfer an applicant or another person as referred to in Article 18(1)(c) or (d) to the Member State responsible shall be met by the transferring Member State.

2. Where the person concerned has to be transferred back to a Member State as a result of an erroneous transfer or of a transfer decision that has been overturned on appeal or review after the transfer has been carried out, the Member State which initially carried out the transfer shall be responsible for the costs of transferring the person concerned back to its territory.

3. Persons to be transferred pursuant to this Regulation shall not be required to meet the costs of such transfers.

Article 31 Exchange of relevant information before a transfer is carried out

1. The Member State carrying out the transfer of an applicant or of another person as referred to in Article 18(1)(c) or (d) shall communicate to the Member State responsible such personal data concerning the person to be transferred as is appropriate, relevant and non-excessive for the sole purposes of ensuring that the competent authorities, in accordance with national law in the Member State responsible, are in a position to provide that person with adequate assistance, including the provision of immediate health care required in order to protect his or her vital interests, and to ensure continuity in the protection and rights afforded by this Regulation and by other relevant asylum legal instruments. Those data shall be communicated to the Member State responsible within a reasonable period of time before a transfer is carried out, in order to ensure that its competent authorities in accordance with national law have sufficient time to take the necessary measures.

2. The transferring Member State shall, in so far as such information is available to the competent authority in accordance with national law, transmit to the Member State responsible any information that is essential in order to safeguard the rights and immediate special needs of the person to be transferred, and in particular:

(a) any immediate measures which the Member State responsible is required to take in order to ensure that the special needs of the person to be transferred are adequately addressed, including any immediate health care that may be required;

(b) contact details of family members, relatives or any other family relations in the receiving Member State, where applicable;

(c) in the case of minors, information on their education;

(d) an assessment of the age of an applicant.

3. The exchange of information under this Article shall only take place between the authorities notified to the Commission in accordance with Article 35 of this Regulation using the 'DubliNet' electronic communication network set-up under Article 18 of Regulation (EC) No 1560/2003. The information exchanged shall only be used for the purposes set out in paragraph 1 of this Article and shall not be further processed.

4. With a view to facilitating the exchange of information between Member States, the Commission shall, by means of implementing acts, draw up a standard form for the transfer of the data required pursuant to this Article. Those implementing acts shall be adopted in accordance with the examination procedure laid down in Article 44(2).

5. The rules laid down in Article 34(8) to (12) shall apply to the exchange of information pursuant to this Article.

Article 32 Exchange of health data before a transfer is carried out

1. For the sole purpose of the provision of medical care or treatment, in particular concerning disabled persons, elderly people, pregnant women, minors and persons who have been subject to torture, rape or other serious forms of psychological, physical and sexual violence, the transferring Member State shall, in so far as it is available to the competent authority in accordance with national law, transmit to the Member State responsible information on any special needs of the person to be transferred, which in specific cases may include information on that person's physical or mental health. That information shall be transferred in a common health certificate with the necessary documents attached. The Member State responsible shall ensure that those special needs are adequately addressed, including in particular any essential medical care that may be required.

The Commission shall, by means of implementing acts, draw up the common health certificate. Those implementing acts shall be adopted in accordance with the examination procedure laid down in Article 44(2).

2. The transferring Member State shall only transmit the information referred to in paragraph 1 to the Member State responsible after having obtained the explicit consent of the applicant and/or of his or her representative or, if the applicant is physically or legally incapable of giving his or her consent, when such transmission is necessary to protect the vital interests of the applicant or of another person. The lack of consent, including a refusal to consent, shall not constitute an obstacle to the transfer.

3. The processing of personal health data referred to in paragraph 1 shall only be carried out by a health professional who is subject, under national law or rules established by national competent bodies, to the obligation of professional secrecy or by another person subject to an equivalent obligation of professional secrecy.

4. The exchange of information under this Article shall only take place between the health professionals or other persons referred to in paragraph 3. The information exchanged shall only be used for the purposes set out in paragraph 1 and shall not be further processed.

5. The Commission shall, by means of implementing acts, adopt uniform conditions and practical arrangements for exchanging the information referred to in paragraph 1 of this Article. Those implementing acts shall be adopted in accordance with the examination procedure laid down in Article 44(2).

6. The rules laid down in Article 34(8) to (12) shall apply to the exchange of information pursuant to this Article.

Article 33 A mechanism for early warning, preparedness and crisis management

1. Where, on the basis of, in particular, the information gathered by EASO pursuant to Regulation (EU) No 439/2010, the Commission establishes that the application of this Regulation may be jeopardised due either to a substantiated risk of particular pressure being placed on a Member State's asylum system and/or to problems in the

functioning of the asylum system of a Member State, it shall, in cooperation with EASO, make recommendations to that Member State, inviting it to draw up a preventive action plan.

The Member State concerned shall inform the Council and the Commission whether it intends to present a preventive action plan in order to overcome the pressure and/or problems in the functioning of its asylum system whilst ensuring the protection of the fundamental rights of applicants for international protection.

A Member State may, at its own discretion and initiative, draw up a preventive action plan and subsequent revisions thereof. When drawing up a preventive action plan, the Member State may call for the assistance of the Commission, other Member States, EASO and other relevant Union agencies.

2. Where a preventive action plan is drawn up, the Member State concerned shall submit it and shall regularly report on its implementation to the Council and to the Commission. The Commission shall subsequently inform the European Parliament of the key elements of the preventive action plan. The Commission shall submit reports on its implementation to the Council and transmit reports on its implementation to the European Parliament.

The Member State concerned shall take all appropriate measures to deal with the situation of particular pressure on its asylum system or to ensure that the deficiencies identified are addressed before the situation deteriorates. Where the preventive action plan includes measures aimed at addressing particular pressure on a Member State's asylum system which may jeopardise the application of this Regulation, the Commission shall seek the advice of EASO before reporting to the European Parliament and to the Council.

3. Where the Commission establishes, on the basis of EASO's analysis, that the implementation of the preventive action plan has not remedied the deficiencies identified or where there is a serious risk that the asylum situation in the Member State concerned develops into a crisis which is unlikely to be remedied by a preventive action plan, the Commission, in cooperation with EASO as applicable, may request the Member State concerned to draw up a crisis management action plan and, where necessary, revisions thereof. The crisis management action plan shall ensure, throughout the entire process, compliance with the asylum *acquis* of the Union, in particular with the fundamental rights of applicants for international protection.

Following the request to draw up a crisis management action plan, the Member State concerned shall, in cooperation with the Commission and EASO, do so promptly, and at the latest within three months of the request.

The Member State concerned shall submit its crisis management action plan and shall report, at least every three months, on its implementation to the Commission and other relevant stakeholders, such as EASO, as appropriate.

The Commission shall inform the European Parliament and the Council of the crisis management action plan, possible revisions and the implementation thereof. In those reports, the Member State concerned shall report on data to monitor compliance with the crisis management action plan, such as the length of the procedure, the detention conditions and the reception capacity in relation to the inflow of applicants.

4. Throughout the entire process for early warning, preparedness and crisis management established in this Article, the Council shall closely monitor the situation and may request further information and provide political guidance, in particular as regards the urgency and severity of the situation and thus the need for a Member State to draw up either a preventive action plan or, if necessary, a crisis management action plan. The European Parliament and the Council may, throughout the entire process, discuss and provide guidance on any solidarity measures as they deem appropriate.

CHAPTER VII
ADMINISTRATIVE COOPERATION

Article 34 Information sharing

1.   Each Member State shall communicate to any Member State that so requests such personal data concerning the applicant as is appropriate, relevant and non-excessive for:

(a)   determining the Member State responsible;

(b)   examining the application for international protection;

(c)   implementing any obligation arising under this Regulation.

2.   The information referred to in paragraph 1 may only cover:

(a)   personal details of the applicant, and, where appropriate, his or her family members, relatives or any other family relations (full name and where appropriate, former name; nicknames or pseudonyms; nationality, present and former; date and place of birth);

(b)   identity and travel papers (references, validity, date of issue, issuing authority, place of issue, etc.);

(c)   other information necessary for establishing the identity of the applicant, including fingerprints processed in accordance with Regulation (EU) No 603/2013;

(d)   places of residence and routes travelled;

(e)   residence documents or visas issued by a Member State;

(f)   the place where the application was lodged;

(g)   the date on which any previous application for international protection was lodged, the date on which the present application was lodged, the stage reached in the proceedings and the decision taken, if any.

3.   Furthermore, provided it is necessary for the examination of the application for international protection, the Member State responsible may request another Member State to let it know on what grounds the applicant bases his or her application and, where applicable, the grounds for any decisions taken concerning the applicant. The other Member State may refuse to respond to the request submitted to it, if the communication of such information is likely to harm its essential interests or the protection of the liberties and fundamental rights of the person concerned or of others. In any event, communication of the information requested shall be subject to the written approval of the applicant for international protection, obtained by the requesting Member State. In that case, the applicant must know for what specific information he or she is giving his or her approval.

4.   Any request for information shall only be sent in the context of an individual application for international protection. It shall set out the grounds on which it is based and, where its purpose is to check whether there is a criterion that is likely to entail the responsibility of the requested Member State, shall state on what evidence, including relevant information from reliable sources on the ways and means by which applicants enter the territories of the Member States, or on what specific and verifiable part of the applicant's statements it is based. It is understood that such relevant information from reliable sources is not in itself sufficient to determine the responsibility and the competence of a Member State under this Regulation, but it may contribute to the evaluation of other indications relating to an individual applicant.

5.   The requested Member State shall be obliged to reply within five weeks. Any delays in the reply shall be duly justified. Non-compliance with the five week time limit shall not relieve the requested Member State of the obligation to reply. If the research carried out by the requested Member State which did not respect the maximum time limit withholds information which shows that it is responsible, that Member State may not invoke the expiry of the time limits provided for in Articles 21, 23 and 24 as a reason for refusing to comply with a request to take charge or take back. In that case, the time limits provided for in Articles 21, 23 and 24 for submitting a request to take

charge or take back shall be extended by a period of time which shall be equivalent to the delay in the reply by the requested Member State.

6. The exchange of information shall be effected at the request of a Member State and may only take place between authorities whose designation by each Member State has been communicated to the Commission in accordance with Article 35(1).

7. The information exchanged may only be used for the purposes set out in paragraph 1. In each Member State such information may, depending on its type and the powers of the recipient authority, only be communicated to the authorities and courts and tribunals entrusted with:

   (a)   determining the Member State responsible;

   (b)   examining the application for international protection;

   (c)   implementing any obligation arising under this Regulation.

8. The Member State which forwards the information shall ensure that it is accurate and up-to-date. If it transpires that it has forwarded information which is inaccurate or which should not have been forwarded, the recipient Member States shall be informed thereof immediately. They shall be obliged to correct such information or to have it erased.

9. The applicant shall have the right to be informed, on request, of any data that is processed concerning him or her.

If the applicant finds that the data have been processed in breach of this Regulation or of Directive 95/46/EC, in particular because they are incomplete or inaccurate, he or she shall be entitled to have them corrected or erased.

The authority correcting or erasing the data shall inform, as appropriate, the Member State transmitting or receiving the information.

The applicant shall have the right to bring an action or a complaint before the competent authorities or courts or tribunals of the Member State which refused the right of access to or the right of correction or erasure of data relating to him or her.

10. In each Member State concerned, a record shall be kept, in the individual file for the person concerned and/or in a register, of the transmission and receipt of information exchanged.

11. The data exchanged shall be kept for a period not exceeding that which is necessary for the purposes for which they are exchanged.

12. Where the data are not processed automatically or are not contained, or intended to be entered, in a file, each Member State shall take appropriate measures to ensure compliance with this Article through effective checks.

Article 35 Competent authorities and resources

1. Each Member State shall notify the Commission without delay of the specific authorities responsible for fulfilling the obligations arising under this Regulation, and any amendments thereto. The Member States shall ensure that those authorities have the necessary resources for carrying out their tasks and in particular for replying within the prescribed time limits to requests for information, requests to take charge of and requests to take back applicants.

2. The Commission shall publish a consolidated list of the authorities referred to in paragraph 1 in the *Official Journal of the European Union*. Where there are amendments thereto, the Commission shall publish once a year an updated consolidated list.

3. The authorities referred to in paragraph 1 shall receive the necessary training with respect to the application of this Regulation.

4. The Commission shall, by means of implementing acts, establish secure electronic transmission channels between the authorities referred to in paragraph 1 for transmitting requests, replies and all written correspondence and for ensuring that senders automatically receive an electronic proof of delivery. Those implementing acts shall be adopted in accordance with the examination procedure referred to in Article 44(2).

Article 36 Administrative arrangements

1. Member States may, on a bilateral basis, establish administrative arrangements between themselves concerning the practical details of the implementation of this Regulation, in order to facilitate its application and increase its effectiveness. Such arrangements may relate to:

(a)   exchanges of liaison officers;

(b)   simplification of the procedures and shortening of the time limits relating to transmission and the examination of requests to take charge of or take back applicants.

2. Member States may also maintain the administrative arrangements concluded under Regulation (EC) No 343/2003. To the extent that such arrangements are not compatible with this Regulation, the Member States concerned shall amend the arrangements in such a way as to eliminate any incompatibilities observed.

3. Before concluding or amending any arrangement referred to in paragraph 1(b), the Member States concerned shall consult the Commission as to the compatibility of the arrangement with this Regulation.

4. If the Commission considers the arrangements referred to in paragraph 1(b) to be incompatible with this Regulation, it shall, within a reasonable period, notify the Member States concerned. The Member States shall take all appropriate steps to amend the arrangement concerned within a reasonable time in such a way as to eliminate any incompatibilities observed.

5. Member States shall notify the Commission of all arrangements referred to in paragraph 1, and of any denunciation thereof, or amendment thereto.

CHAPTER VIII

CONCILIATION

Article 37 Conciliation

1. Where the Member States cannot resolve a dispute on any matter related to the application of this Regulation, they may have recourse to the conciliation procedure provided for in paragraph 2.

2. The conciliation procedure shall be initiated by a request from one of the Member States in dispute to the Chairman of the Committee set up by Article 44. By agreeing to use the conciliation procedure, the Member States concerned undertake to take the utmost account of the solution proposed.

The Chairman of the Committee shall appoint three members of the Committee representing three Member States not connected with the matter. They shall receive the arguments of the parties either in writing or orally and, after deliberation, shall propose a solution within one month, where necessary after a vote.

The Chairman of the Committee, or his or her deputy, shall chair the discussion. He or she may put forward his or her point of view but may not vote.

Whether it is adopted or rejected by the parties, the solution proposed shall be final and irrevocable.

CHAPTER IX

TRANSITIONAL PROVISIONS AND FINAL PROVISIONS

Article 38 Data security and data protection

Member States shall take all appropriate measures to ensure the security of transmitted personal data and in particular to avoid unlawful or unauthorised access or disclosure, alteration or loss of personal data processed.

Each Member State shall provide that the national supervisory authority or authorities designated pursuant to Article 28(1) of Directive 95/46/EC shall monitor independently, in accordance with its respective national law, the lawfulness of the processing, in accordance with this Regulation, of personal data by the Member State in question.

Article 39 Confidentiality

Member States shall ensure that the authorities referred to in Article 35 are bound by the confidentiality rules provided for in national law, in relation to any information they obtain in the course of their work.

Article 40 Penalties

Member States shall take the necessary measures to ensure that any misuse of data processed in accordance with this Regulation is punishable by penalties, including administrative and/or criminal penalties in accordance with national law, that are effective, proportionate and dissuasive.

Article 41 Transitional measures

Where an application has been lodged after the date mentioned in the second paragraph of Article 49, the events that are likely to entail the responsibility of a Member State under this Regulation shall be taken into consideration, even if they precede that date, with the exception of the events mentioned in Article 13(2).

Article 42 Calculation of time limits

Any period of time prescribed in this Regulation shall be calculated as follows:

(a)   where a period expressed in days, weeks or months is to be calculated from the moment at which an event occurs or an action takes place, the day during which that event occurs or that action takes place shall not be counted as falling within the period in question;

(b)   a period expressed in weeks or months shall end with the expiry of whichever day in the last week or month is the same day of the week or falls on the same date as the day during which the event or action from which the period is to be calculated occurred or took place. If, in a period expressed in months, the day on which it should expire does not occur in the last month, the period shall end with the expiry of the last day of that month;

(c)   time limits shall include Saturdays, Sundays and official holidays in any of the Member States concerned.

Article 43 Territorial scope

As far as the French Republic is concerned, this Regulation shall apply only to its European territory.

Article 44 Committee

1.   The Commission shall be assisted by a committee. That committee shall be a committee within the meaning of Regulation (EU) No 182/2011.

2.   Where reference is made to this paragraph, Article 5 of Regulation (EU) No 182/2011 shall apply.

Where the committee delivers no opinion, the Commission shall not adopt the draft implementing act and the third subparagraph of Article 5(4) of Regulation (EU) No 182/2011 shall apply.

Article 45 Exercise of the delegation

1.   The power to adopt delegated acts is conferred on the Commission subject to the conditions laid down in this Article.

2.   The power to adopt delegated acts referred to in Articles 8(5) and 16(3) shall be conferred on the Commission for a period of 5 years from the date of entry into force of this Regulation. The Commission shall draw up a report in respect of the delegation of power not later than nine months before the end of the 5-year period. The delegation of power shall be tacitly extended for periods of an identical duration, unless the European Parliament or the Council opposes such extension not later than three months before the end of each period.

3. The delegation of power referred to in Articles 8(5) and 16(3) may be revoked at any time by the European Parliament or by the Council. A decision to revoke shall put an end to the delegation of the power specified in that decision. It shall take effect the day following the publication of the decision in the *Official Journal of the European Union* or at a later date specified therein. It shall not affect the validity of any delegated acts already in force.

4. As soon as it adopts a delegated act, the Commission shall notify it simultaneously to the European Parliament and to the Council.

5. A delegated act adopted pursuant to Articles 8(5) and 16(3) shall enter into force only if no objection has been expressed either by the European Parliament or the Council within a period of four months of notification of that act to the European Parliament and to the Council or if, before the expiry of that period, the European Parliament and the Council have both informed the Commission that they will not object. That period shall be extended by two months at the initiative of the European Parliament or of the Council.

Article 46 Monitoring and evaluation

By 21 July 2016, the Commission shall report to the European Parliament and to the Council on the application of this Regulation and, where appropriate, shall propose the necessary amendments. Member States shall forward to the Commission all information appropriate for the preparation of that report, at the latest six months before that time limit expires.

After having submitted that report, the Commission shall report to the European Parliament and to the Council on the application of this Regulation at the same time as it submits reports on the implementation of the Eurodac system provided for by Article 40 of Regulation (EU) No 603/2013.

Article 47 Statistics

In accordance with Article 4(4) of Regulation (EC) No 862/2007 of the European Parliament and of the Council of 11 July 2007 on Community statistics on migration and international protection[1], Member States shall communicate to the Commission (Eurostat), statistics concerning the application of this Regulation and of Regulation (EC) No 1560/2003.

[1]   OJ L 199, 31.7.2007, p. 23.

Article 48 Repeal

Regulation (EC) No 343/2003 is repealed.

Articles 11(1), 13, 14 and 17 of Regulation (EC) No 1560/2003 are repealed.

References to the repealed Regulation or Articles shall be construed as references to this Regulation and shall be read in accordance with the correlation table in Annex II.

Article 49 Entry into force and applicability

This Regulation shall enter into force on the twentieth day following that of its publication in the *Official Journal of the European Union*.

It shall apply to applications for international protection lodged as from the first day of the sixth month following its entry into force and, from that date, it will apply to any request to take charge of or take back applicants, irrespective of the date on which the application was made. The Member State responsible for the examination of an application for international protection submitted before that date shall be determined in accordance with the criteria set out in Regulation (EC) No 343/2003.

References in this Regulation to Regulation (EU) No 603/2013, Directive 2013/32/EU and Directive 2013/33/EU shall be construed, until the dates of their application, as references to Regulation (EC) No 2725/2000[2], Directive 2003/9/EC[3] and Directive 2005/85/EC[4] respectively.

This Regulation shall be binding in its entirety and directly applicable in the Member States in accordance with the Treaties.

2   Council Regulation (EC) No 2725/2000 of 11 December 2000 concerning the establishment of 'Eurodac' for the comparison of fingerprints for the effective application of the Dublin Convention (OJ L 316, 15.12.2000, p. 1).

3   Council Directive 2003/9/EC of 27 January 2003 laying down minimum standards for the reception of asylum seekers (OJ L 31, 6.2.2003, p. 18).

4   Council Directive 2005/85/EC of 1 December 2005 on minimum standards on procedures for granting and withdrawing refugee status (OJ L 326, 13.12.2005, p. 13).

ANNEX I

REPEALED REGULATIONS (REFERRED TO IN ARTICLE 48)

Council Regulation (EC) No 343/2003
(OJ L 50, 25.2.2003, p. 1)
Commission Regulation (EC) No 1560/2003 only Articles 11(1), 13, 14 and 17
(OJ L 222, 5.9.2003, p. 3)

ANNEX II

CORRELATION TABLE

Regulation (EC) No 343/2003	This Regulation
Article 1	Article 1
Article 2(a)	Article 2(a)
Article 2(b)	—
Article 2(c)	Article 2(b)
Article 2(d)	Article 2(c)
Article 2(e)	Article 2(d)
Article 2(f)	Article 2(e)
Article 2(g)	Article 2(f)
—	Article 2(h)
—	Article 2(i)
Article 2(h)	Article 2(j)
Article 2(i)	Article 2(g)
—	Article 2(k)
Article 2(j) and (k)	Article 2(l) and (m)
—	Article 2(n)
Article 3(1)	Article 3(1)
Article 3(2)	Article 17(1)
Article 3(3)	Article 3(3)
Article 3(4)	Article 4(1), introductory wording
—	Article 4(1)(a) to (f)
—	Article 4(2) and (3)
Article 4(1) to (5)	Article 20(1) to (5)
—	Article 20(5), third subparagraph
—	Article 5
—	Article 6
Article 5(1)	Article 7(1)

Regulation (EC) No 343/2003	This Regulation
Article 5(2)	Article 7(2)
—	Article 7(3)
Article 6, first paragraph	Article 8(1)
—	Article 8(3)
Article 6, second paragraph	Article 8(4)
Article 7	Article 9
Article 8	Article 10
Article 9	Article 12
Article 10	Article 13
Article 11	Article 14
Article 12	Article 15
—	Article 16
Article 13	Article 3(2)
Article 14	Article 11
Article 15(1)	Article 17(2), first subparagraph
Article 15(2)	Article 16(1)
Article 15(3)	Article 8(2)
Article 15(4)	Article 17(2), fourth subparagraph
Article 15(5)	Articles 8(5) and (6) and Article 16(2)
Article 16(1)(a)	Article 18(1)(a)
Article 16(1)(b)	Article 18(2)
Article 16(1)(c)	Article 18(1)(b)
Article 16(1)(d)	Article 18(1)(c)
Article 16(1)(e)	Article 18(1)(d)
Article 16(2)	Article 19(1)
Article 16(3)	Article 19(2), first subparagraph
—	Article 19(2), second subparagraph
Article 16(4)	Article 19(3)
—	Article 19(3), second subparagraph
Article 17	Article 21
Article 18	Article 22
Article 19(1)	Article 26(1)
Article 19(2)	Article 26(2) and Article 27(1)
—	Article 27(2) to (6)
Article 19(3)	Article 29(1)
Article 19(4)	Article 29(2)
—	Article 29(3)
Article 19(5)	Article 29(4)
Article 20(1), introductory wording	Article 23(1)
—	Article 23(2)
—	Article 23(3)
—	Article 23(4)
Article 20(1)(a)	Article 23(5), first subparagraph
—	Article 24
Article 20(1)(b)	Article 25(1)

Regulation (EC) No 343/2003	This Regulation
Article 20(1)(c)	Article 25(2)
Article 20(1)(d)	Article 29(1), first subparagraph
Article 20(1)(e)	Article 26(1), (2), Article 27(1), Article 29(1), second and third subparagraphs
Article 20(2)	Article 29(2)
Article 20(3)	Article 23(5), second subparagraph
Article 20(4)	Article 29(4)
—	Article 28
—	Article 30
—	Article 31
—	Article 32
—	Article 33
Article 21(1) to (9)	Article 34(1) to (9), first to third subparagraphs
—	Article 34(9), fourth subparagraph
Article 21(10) to (12)	Article 34(10) to (12)
Article 22(1)	Article 35(1)
—	Article 35(2)
—	Article 35(3)
Article 22(2)	Article 35(4)
Article 23	Article 36
—	Article 37
—	Article 40
Article 24(1)	—
Article 24(2)	Article 41
Article 24(3)	—
Article 25(1)	Article 42
Article 25(2)	—
Article 26	Article 43
Article 27(1), (2)	Article 44(1), (2)
Article 27(3)	—
—	Article 45
Article 28	Article 46
—	Article 47
—	Article 48
Article 29	Article 49

Regulation (EC) No 1560/2003	This Regulation
Article 11(1)	—
Article 13(1)	Article 17(2), first subparagraph
Article 13(2)	Article 17(2), second subparagraph
Article 13(3)	Article 17(2), third subparagraph
Article 13(4)	Article 17(2), first subparagraph
Article 14	Article 37
Article 17(1)	Articles 9, 10, 17(2), first subparagraph

Regulation (EC) No 1560/2003	This Regulation
Article 17(2)	Article 34(3)

STATEMENT BY THE COUNCIL, THE EUROPEAN PARLIAMENT AND THE COMMISSION

The Council and the European Parliament invite the Commission to consider, without prejudice to its right of initiative, a revision of Article 8(4) of the Recast of the Dublin Regulation once the Court of Justice rules on case C-648/11 MA and Others vs. Secretary of State for the Home Department and at the latest by the time limits set in Article 46 of the Dublin Regulation. The European Parliament and the Council will then both exercise their legislative competences, taking into account the best interests of the child.

The Commission, in a spirit of compromise and in order to ensure the immediate adoption of the proposal, accepts to consider this invitation, which it understands as being limited to these specific circumstances and not creating a precedent.

Appendix 7

INTERNATIONAL MATERIALS

Contents

UN CONVENTION RELATING TO THE STATUS OF REFUGEES

Done at Geneva on 28 July 1951

Entry into force 22 April 1954, in accordance with Article 43

Text United Nations Treaty Series No 2545, Vol 189, p 137

Preamble
The High Contracting Parties
Considering that the Charter of the United Nations and the Universal Declaration of Human Rights approved on 10 December 1948 by the General Assembly have affirmed the principle that human beings shall enjoy fundamental rights and freedoms without discrimination,
Considering that the United Nations has, on various occasions, manifested its profound concern for refugees and endeavoured to assure refugees the widest possible exercise of these fundamental rights and freedoms,
Considering that it is desirable to revise and consolidate previous international agreements relating to the status of refugees and to extend the scope of and the protection accorded by such instruments by means of a new agreement.
Considering that the grant of asylum may place unduly heavy burdens on certain countries, and that a satisfactory solution of a problem of which the United Nations has recognised the international scope and nature cannot therefore be achieved without international co-operation,
Expressing the wish that all states, recognizing the social and humanitarian nature of the problem of refugees, will do everything within their power to prevent this problem from becoming a cause of tension between states,
Noting that the United Nations High Commissioner for Refugees is charged with the task of supervising international conventions providing for the protection of refugees, and recognising that the effective co-ordination of measures taken to deal with this problem will depend upon the co-operation of states with the High Commissioner,

Have agreed as follows:

Note

The Convention was adopted by the United Nations Conference of Plenipotentiaries on the Status of Refugees and Stateless Persons, held at Geneva from 2 to 25 July 1951. The Conference was convened pursuant to resolution 429(V), adopted by the General Assembly of the United Nations on 14 December 1950. For the text of this resolution, see Official Records of the General Assembly, Fifth Session, Supplement No 20(A/1775), p 48, The Text of the Final Act of the Conference is reproduced in the Appendix.

CHAPTER 1
GENERAL PROVISIONS

Article 1 Definition of the term 'Refugee'

A For the purposes of the present Convention, the term 'refugee' shall apply to any person who:

(1) Has been considered a refugee under the Arrangements of 12 May 1926 and 30 June 1928 or under the Conventions of 28 October 1933 and 10 February 1938, the Protocol of 14 September 1939 or the Constitution of the International Refugee Organization;

Decisions of non-eligibility taken by the International Refugee Organization during the period of its activities shall not prevent the status of refugee being accorded to persons who fulfil the conditions of paragraph 2 of this section;

(2) As a result of events occurring before 1 January 1951 and owing to well-founded fear of being persecuted for reasons of race, religion, nationality, membership of a particular social group or political opinion, is outside the country of his nationality and is unable or, owing to such fear, is unwilling to avail himself of the protection of that country; or who, not having a nationality and being outside the country of his former habitual residence as a result of such events, is unable or, owing to such fear, is unwilling to return to it.

In the case of a person who has more than one nationality, the term 'the country of his nationality' shall mean each of the countries of which he is a national, and a person shall not be deemed to be lacking the protection of the country of his nationality if, without any valid reason based on well-founded fear, he has not availed himself of the protection of one of the countries of which he is a national.

B

(1) For the purposes of this Convention, the words 'events occurring before 1 January 1951' in Article 1, Section A, shall be understood to mean either

(a) 'events occurring in Europe before 1 January 1951'; or

(b) 'events occurring in Europe or elsewhere before 1 January 1951', and each contracting state shall make a declaration at the time of signature, ratification or accession, specifying which of these meanings it applies for the purpose of its obligations under this Convention.

(2) Any contracting state which has adopted alternative (a) may at any time extend its obligations by adopting alternative (b) by means of a notification addressed to the Secretary-General of the United Nations.

C This Convention shall cease to apply to any person falling under the terms of section A if:

(1) He has voluntarily re-availed himself of the protection of the country of his nationality; or

(2) Having lost his nationality, he has voluntarily re-acquired it, or

(3) He has acquired a new nationality, and enjoys the protection of the country of his new nationality; or

(4) He has voluntarily re-established himself in the country which he left or outside which he remained owing to fear of persecution; or

(5) He can no longer, because the circumstances in connection with which he has been recognized as a refugee have ceased to exist, continue to refuse to avail himself of the protection of the country of his nationality;

Provided that this paragraph shall not apply to a refugee falling under section A(1) of this Article who is able to invoke compelling reasons arising out of previous persecution for refusing to avail himself of the protection of the country of nationality;

(6) Being a person who has no nationality he is, because the circumstances in connection with which he has been recognized as a refugee have ceased to exist, able to return to the country of his former habitual residence;

Provided that this paragraph shall not apply to a refugee falling under section A(1) of this Article who is able to invoke compelling reasons arising out of previous persecution for refusing to return to the country of his former habitual residence.

D This Convention shall not apply to persons who are at present receiving from organs or agencies of the United Nations other than the United Nations High Commissioner for Refugees protection or assistance.

When such protection or assistance has ceased for any reason, without the position of such persons being definitely settled in accordance with the relevant resolutions adopted by the General Assembly of the United Nations, these persons shall *ipso facto* be entitled to the benefits of this Convention.

E This Convention shall not apply to a person who is recognized by the competent authorities of the country in which he has taken residence as having the rights and obligations which are attached to the possession of the nationality of that country.

F The provisions of this Convention shall not apply to any person with respect to whom there are serious reasons for considering that:

(a) he has committed a crime against peace, a war crime, or a crime against humanity, as defined in the international instruments drawn up to make provision in respect of such crimes;

(b) he has committed a serious non-political crime outside the country of refuge prior to his admission to that country as a refugee;

(c) he has been guilty of acts contrary to the purposes and principles of the United Nations.

Article 2 General obligations
Every refugee has duties to the country in which he finds himself, which require in particular that he conform to its laws and regulations as well as to measures taken for the maintenance of public order.

Article 3 Non-discrimination
The contracting states shall apply the provisions of this Convention to refugees without discrimination as to race, religion or country of origin.

Article 4 Religion
The contracting states shall accord to refugees within their territories treatment at least as favourable as that accorded to their nationals with respect to freedom to practise their religion and freedom as regards the religious education of their children.

Article 5 Rights granted apart from this Convention
Nothing in this Convention shall be deemed to impair any rights and benefits granted by a contracting state to refugees apart from this Convention.

Article 6 The term 'in the same circumstances'
For the purpose of this Convention, the term 'in the same circumstances' implies that any requirements (including requirements as to length and conditions of sojourn or residence) which the particular individual would have to fulfil for the enjoyment of the right in question, if he were not a refugee, must be fulfilled by him, with the exception of requirements which by their nature a refugee is incapable of fulfilling.

Article 7 Exemption from reciprocity

1 Except where this Convention contains more favourable provisions, a contracting state shall accord to refugees the same treatment as is accorded to aliens generally.

2 After a period of three years' residence, all refugees shall enjoy exemption from legislative reciprocity in the territory of the contracting states.

3 Each contracting state shall continue to accord to refugees the rights and benefits to which they were already entitled, in the absence of reciprocity, at the date of entry into force of this Convention for that state.

4 The contracting states shall consider favourably the possibility of according to refugees, in the absence of reciprocity, rights and benefits beyond those to which they are entitled according to paragraphs 2 and 3, and to extending exemption from reciprocity to refugees who do not fulfil the conditions provided for in paragraphs 2 and 3.

5 The provisions of paragraphs 2 and 3 apply both to the rights and benefits referred to in Articles 13, 18, 19, 21 and 22 of this Convention and to rights and benefits for which this Convention does not provide.

Article 8 Exemption from exceptional measures

With regard to exceptional measures which may be taken against the person, property or interests of nationals of a foreign state, the contracting states shall not apply such measures to a refugee who is formally a national of the said state solely on account of such nationality. Contracting states which, under their legislation, are prevented from applying the general principle expressed in this Article, shall, in appropriate cases, grant exemptions in favour of such refugees.

Article 9 Provisional measures

Nothing in this Convention shall prevent a contracting state, in time of war or other grave and exceptional circumstances, from taking provisionally measures which it considers to be essential to the national security in the case of a particular person, pending a determination by the contracting state that that person is in fact a refugee and that the continuance of such measures is necessary in his case in the interests of national security.

Article 10 Continuity of residence

1 Where a refugee has been forcibly displaced during the Second World War and removed to the territory of a contracting state, and is resident there, the period of such enforced sojourn shall be considered to have been lawful residence within that territory.

2 Where a refugee has been forcibly displaced during the Second World War from the territory of a contracting state and has, prior to the date of entry into force of this Convention, returned there for the purpose of taking up residence, the period of residence before and after such enforced displacement shall be regarded as one uninterrupted period for any purposes for which uninterrupted residence is required.

Article 11 Refugee seamen

In the case of refugees regularly serving as crew members on board a ship flying the flag of a contracting state, that state shall give sympathetic consideration to their establishment on its territory and the issue of travel documents to them or their temporary admission to its territory particularly with a view to facilitating their establishment in another country.

CHAPTER II
JURIDICAL STATUS

Article 12 Personal status

1   The personal status of a refugee shall be governed by the law of the country of his domicile or, if he has no domicile, by the law of the country of his residence.

2   Rights previously acquired by a refugee and dependent on personal status, more particularly rights attaching to marriage, shall be respected by a contracting state, subject to compliance, if this be necessary, with the formalities required by the law of that state, provided that the right in question is one which would have been recognized by the law of that state had he not become a refugee.

Article 13 Movable and immovable property

The contracting states shall accord to a refugee treatment as favourable as possible and, in any event, not less favourable than that accorded to aliens generally in the same circumstances, as regards the acquisition of movable and immovable property and other rights pertaining thereto, and to leases and other contracts relating to movable and immovable property.

Article 14 Artistic rights and industrial property

In respect of the protection of industrial property, such as inventions, designs or models, trade marks, trade names, and of rights in literary, artistic and scientific works, a refugee shall be accorded in the country in which he has his habitual residence the same protection as is accorded to nationals of that country. In the territory of any other contracting state, he shall be accorded the same protection as is accorded in that territory to nationals of the country in which he has his habitual residence.

Article 15 Right of association

As regards non-political and non-profit-making associations and trade unions the contracting states shall accord to refugees lawfully staying in their territory the most favourable treatment accorded to nationals of a foreign country, in the same circumstances.

Article 16 Access to courts

1   A refugee shall have free access to the courts of law on the territory of all contracting states.

2   A refugee shall enjoy in the contracting state in which he has his habitual residence the same treatment as a national in matters pertaining to access to the Courts, including legal assistance and exemption from *cautio judicatum solvi*.

3   A refugee shall be accorded in the matters referred to in paragraph 2 in countries other than that in which he has his habitual residence the treatment granted to a national of the country of his habitual residence.

CHAPTER III
GAINFUL EMPLOYMENT

Article 17 Wage-earning employment

1   The contracting state shall accord to refugees lawfully staying in their territory the most favourable treatment accorded to nationals of a foreign country in the same circumstances, as regards the right to engage in wage-earning employment.

2   In any case, restrictive measures imposed on aliens or the employment of aliens for the protection of the national labour market shall not be applied to a refugee who was already exempt from them at the date of entry into force of this Convention for the contracting state concerned, or who fulfils one of the following conditions:

    (a)   He has completed three years' residence in the country,

(b)   He has a spouse possessing the nationality of the country of residence. A refugee may not invoke the benefits of this provision if he has abandoned his spouse,

(c)   He has one or more children possessing the nationality of the country of residence.

3 The contracting states shall give sympathetic consideration to assimilating the rights of all refugees with regard to wage-earning employment to those of nationals, and in particular of those refugees who have entered their territory pursuant to programmes of labour recruitment or under immigration schemes.

Article 18 Self-employment

The contracting states shall accord to a refugee lawfully in their territory treatment as favourable as possible and, in any event, not less favourable than that accorded to aliens generally in the same circumstances, as regards the right to engage on his own account in agriculture, industry, handicrafts and commerce and to establish commercial and industrial companies.

Article 19 Liberal professions

1 Each contracting state shall accord to refugees lawfully staying in their territory who hold diplomas recognized by the competent authorities of that state, and who are desirous of practising a liberal profession, treatment as favourable as possible and, in any event, not less favourable than that accorded to aliens generally in the same circumstances.

2 The contracting states shall use their best endeavours consistently with their laws and constitutions to secure the settlement of such refugees in the territories, other than the metropolitan territory, for whose international relations they are responsible.

CHAPTER IV
WELFARE

Article 20 Rationing

Where a rationing system exists, which applies to the population at large and regulates the general distribution of products in short supply, refugees shall be accorded the same treatment as nationals.

Article 21 Housing

As regards housing, the contracting states, in so far as the matter is regulated by laws or regulations or is subject to the control of public authorities, shall accord to refugees lawfully staying in their territory treatment as favourable as possible and, in any event, not less favourable than that accorded to aliens generally in the same circumstances.

Article 22 Public education

1 The contracting states shall accord to refugees the same treatment as is accorded to nationals with respect to elementary education.

2 The contracting states shall accord to refugees treatment as favourable as possible, and, in any event, not less favourable than that accorded to aliens generally in the same circumstances, with respect to education other than elementary education and, in particular, as regards access to studies, the recognition of foreign school certificates, diplomas and degrees, the remission of fees and charges and the award of scholarships.

Article 23 Public relief

The contracting states shall accord to refugees lawfully staying in their territory the same treatment with respect to public relief and assistance as is accorded to their nationals.

Article 24 Labour legislation and social security

1 The contracting states shall accord to refugees lawfully staying in their territory the same treatment as is accorded to nationals in respect of the following matters:

(a)   In so far as such matters are governed by laws or regulations or are subject to the control of administrative authorities: remuneration, including family allowances where these form part of remuneration, hours of work, overtime arrangements, holidays with pay, restrictions on home work, minimum age of employment, apprenticeship and training, women's work and the work of young persons, and the enjoyment of the benefits of collective bargaining;

(b)   Social security (legal provisions in respect of employment injury, occupational diseases, maternity, sickness, disability, old age, death, unemployment, family responsibilities and any other contingency which, according to national laws or regulations, is covered by a social security scheme), subject to the following limitations:

(i)   There may be appropriate arrangements for the maintenance of acquired rights and rights in course of acquisition;

(ii)   National laws or regulations of the country of residence may prescribe special arrangements concerning benefits or portions of benefits which are payable wholly out of public funds, and concerning allowances paid to persons who do not fulfil the contribution conditions prescribed for the award of a normal pension.

2 The right to compensation for the death of a refugee resulting from employment injury or from occupational disease shall not be affected by the fact that the residence of the beneficiary is outside the territory of the contracting state.

3 The contracting states shall extend to refugees the benefits of agreements concluded between them, or which may be concluded between them in the future, concerning the maintenance of acquired rights and rights in the process of acquisition in regard to social security, subject only to the conditions which apply to nationals of the states signatory to the agreements in question.

4 The contracting states will give sympathetic consideration to extending to refugees so far as possible the benefits of similar agreements which may at any time be in force between such contracting states and non-contracting states.

CHAPTER V
ADMINISTRATIVE MEASURES

Article 25 Administrative assistance

1 When the exercise of a right by a refugee would normally require the assistance of authorities of a foreign country to whom he cannot have recourse, the contracting states in whose territory he is residing shall arrange that such assistance be afforded to him by their own authorities or by an international authority.

2 The authority or authorities mentioned in paragraph 1 shall deliver or cause to be delivered under their supervision to refugees such documents or certifications as would normally be delivered to aliens by or through their national authorities.

3 Documents or certifications so delivered shall stand in the stead or the official instruments delivered to aliens by or through their national authorities, and shall be given credence in the absence of proof to the contrary.

4 Subject to such exceptional treatment as may be granted to indigent persons, fees may be charged for the services mentioned herein, but such fees shall be moderate and commensurate with those charged to nationals for similar services.

5 The provisions of this Article shall be without prejudice to Articles 27 and 28.

Article 26 Freedom of movement

Each contracting state shall accord to refugees lawfully in its territory the right to choose their place of residence and to move freely within its territory, subject to any regulations applicable to aliens generally in the same circumstances.

Article 27 Identity papers

The contracting states shall issue identity papers to any refugee in their territory who does not possess a valid travel document.

Article 28 Travel documents

1 The contracting states shall issue to refugees lawfully staying in their territory travel documents for the purpose of travel outside their territory unless compelling reasons of national security or public order otherwise require, and the provisions of the Schedule to this Convention shall apply with respect to such documents. The contracting states may issue such a travel document to any other refugee in their territory, they shall in particular give sympathetic consideration to the issue of such a travel document to refugees in their territory who are unable to obtain a travel document from the country of their lawful residence.

2 Travel documents issued to refugees under previous international agreements by parties thereto shall be recognized and treated by the contracting states in the same way as if they had been issued pursuant to this article.

Article 29 Fiscal charges

1 The contracting states shall not impose upon refugees duties, charges or taxes, of any description whatsoever, other or higher than those which are or may be levied on their nationals in similar situations.

2 Nothing in the above paragraph shall prevent the application to refugees of the laws and regulations concerning charges in respect of the issue to aliens of administrative documents including identity papers.

Article 30 Transfer of assets

1 A contracting state shall, in conformity with its laws and regulations, permit refugees to transfer assets which they have brought into its territory, to another country where they have been admitted for the purposes of resettlement.

2 A contracting state shall give sympathetic consideration to the application of refugees for permission to transfer assets wherever they may be and which are necessary for their resettlement in another country to which they have been admitted.

Article 31 Refugees unlawfully in the country of refuge

1 The contracting states shall not impose penalties, on account of their illegal entry or presence, on refugees who, coming directly from a territory where their life or freedom was threatened in the sense of Article 1, enter or are present in their territory without authorisation, provided they present themselves without delay to the authorities and show good cause for their illegal entry or presence.

2 The contracting states shall not apply to the movements of such refugees restrictions other than those which are necessary and such restrictions shall only be applied until their status in the country is regularised or they obtain admission into another country. The contracting states shall allow such refugees a reasonable period and all the necessary facilities to obtain admission into another country.

Article 32 Expulsion

1 The contracting states shall not expel a refugee lawfully in their territory save on grounds of national security or public order.

2 The expulsion of such a refugee shall be only in pursuance of a decision reached in accordance with due process of law. Except where compelling reasons of national security otherwise require, the refugee shall be allowed to submit evidence to clear

himself, and to appeal to and be represented for the purpose before competent authority or a person or persons specially designated by the competent authority.

3   The contracting states shall allow such a refugee a reasonable period within which to seek legal admission into another country. The contracting states reserve the right to apply during that period such internal measures as they may deem necessary.

Article 33 Prohibition of expulsion or return ('refoulement')

1   No contracting state shall expel or return ('refouler') a refugee in any manner whatsoever to the frontiers of territories where his life or freedom would be threatened on account of his race, religion, nationality, membership of a particular social group or political opinion.

2   The benefit of the present provision may not, however, be claimed by a refugee whom there are reasonable grounds for regarding as a danger to the security of the country in which he is, or who, having been convicted by a final judgment of a particularly serious crime, constitutes a danger to the community of that country.

Article 34 Naturalisation

The contracting states shall as far as possible facilitate the assimilation and naturalisation of refugees. They shall in particular make every effort to expedite naturalisation proceedings and to reduce as far as possible the charges and costs of such proceedings.

CHAPTER VI
EXECUTORY AND TRANSITORY PROVISIONS

Article 35 Co-operation of the national authorities with the United Nations

1   The contracting states undertake to co-operate with the Office of the United Nations High Commissioner for Refugees, or any other agency of the United Nations which may succeed it, in the exercise of its functions, and shall in particular facilitate its duty of supervising the application of the provisions of this Convention.

2   In order to enable the Office of the High Commissioner or any other agency of the United Nations which may succeed it, to make reports to the competent organs of the United Nations, the contracting states undertake to provide them in the appropriate form with information and statistical data requested concerning:

    (a)   the condition of refugees,

    (b)   the implementation of this Convention, and

    (c)   laws, regulations and decrees which are, or may hereafter be, in force relating to refugees.

Article 36 Information on national legislation

The contracting states shall communicate to the Secretary-General of the United Nations the laws and regulations which they may adopt to ensure the application of this Convention.

Article 37 Relation to previous Conventions

Without prejudice to Article 28, paragraph 2, of this Convention, this Convention replaces, as between parties to it, the Arrangements of 5 July 1922, 31 May 1924, 12 May 1926, 30 June 1928 and 30 July 1935, the Conventions of 28 October 1933 and 10 February 1938, the Protocol of 14 September 1939 and the Agreement of 15 October 1946.

CHAPTER VII
FINAL CLAUSES

Article 38 Settlement of disputes

Any dispute between parties to this Convention relating to its interpretation or application, which cannot be settled by other means, shall be referred to the International Court of Justice at the request of any one of the parties to the dispute.

Article 39 Signature, ratification and accession

1   This Convention shall be opened for signature at Geneva on 28 July 1951 and shall thereafter be deposited with the Secretary-General of the United Nations. It shall be open for signature at the European Office of the United Nations from 28 July to 31 August 1951 and shall be re-opened for signature at the Headquarters of the United Nations from 17 September 1951 to 31 December 1952.

2   This Convention shall be open for signature on behalf of all states members of the United Nations, and also on behalf of any other state invited to attend the Conference of Plenipotentiaries on the Status of Refugees and Stateless Persons or to which an invitation to sign will have been addressed by the General Assembly. It shall be ratified and the instruments of ratification shall be deposited with the Secretary-General of the United Nations.

3   This Convention shall be open from 28 July 1951 for accession by the states referred to in paragraph 2 of this Article. Accession shall be effected by the deposit of an instrument of accession with the Secretary-General of the United Nations.

Article 40 Territorial application clause

1   Any state may, at the time of signature, ratification or accession, declare that this Convention shall extend to all or any of the territories for the international relations of which it is responsible. Such a declaration shall take effect when the Convention enters into force for the state concerned.

2   At any time thereafter any such extension shall be made by notification addressed to the Secretary-General of the United Nations and shall take effect as from the ninetieth day after the day of receipt by the Secretary-General of the United Nations of this notification, or as from the date of entry into force of the Convention for the state concerned, whichever is the later.

3   With respect to those territories to which this Convention is not extended at the time of signature, ratification or accession, each state concerned shall consider the possibility of taking the necessary steps in order to extend the application of this Convention to such territories, subject, where necessary for constitutional reasons, to the consent of the governments of such territories.

Article 41 Federal clause

In the case of a federal or non-unitary state, the following provisions shall apply:

(a)   With respect to those Articles of this Convention that come within the legislative jurisdiction of the federal legislative authority, the obligations of the Federal Government shall to this extent be the same as those of Parties which are not federal states,

(b)   With respect to those Articles of this Convention that come within the legislative jurisdiction of constituent states, provinces or cantons which are not, under the constitutional system of the federation, bound to take legislative action, the Federal Government shall bring such Articles with a favourable recommendation to the notice of the appropriate authorities of states, provinces or cantons at the earliest possible moment.

(c)   A federal state party to this Convention shall, at the request of any other contracting state transmitted through the Secretary-General of the United Nations, supply a statement of the law and practice of the Federation and its constituent units in regard to any particular provision of the Convention showing the extent to which effect has been given to that provision by legislative or other action.

Article 42 Reservations

1 At the time of signature, ratification or accession, any state may make reservations to articles of the Convention other than to Articles 1, 3, 4, 16(1), 33, 36–46 inclusive.

2 Any state making a reservation in accordance with paragraph 1 of this article may at any time withdraw the reservation by a communication to that effect addressed to the Secretary-General of the United Nations.

Article 43 Entry into force

1 This Convention shall come into force on the ninetieth day following the day of deposit of the sixth instrument of ratification or accession.

2 For each state ratifying or acceding to the Convention after the deposit of the sixth instrument of ratification or accession, the Convention shall enter into force on the ninetieth day following the date of deposit by such state of its instrument of ratification or accession.

Article 44 Denunciation

1 Any contracting state may denounce this Convention at any time by a notification addressed to the Secretary-General of the United Nations.

2 Such denunciation shall take effect for the contracting state concerned one year from the date upon which it is received by the Secretary-General of the United Nations.

3 Any state which has made a declaration or notification under Article 40 may, at any time thereafter, by a notification to the Secretary-General of the United Nations, declare that the Convention shall cease to extend to such territory one year after the date of receipt of the notification by the Secretary-General.

Article 45 Revision

1 Any contracting state may request revision of this Convention at any time by a notification addressed to the Secretary-General of the United Nations.

2 The General Assembly of the United Nations shall recommend the steps, if any, to be taken in respect of such request.

Article 46 Notifications by the Secretary-General of the United Nations

The Secretary-General of the United Nations shall inform all Members of the United Nations and non-member states referred to in Article 39:

    (a)   of declarations and notifications in accordance with Section B of Article 1;

    (b)   of signatures, ratifications and accessions in accordance with Article 39;

    (c)   of declarations and notifications in accordance with Article 40;

    (d)   of reservations and withdrawals in accordance with Article 42;

    (e)   of the date on which this Convention will come into force in accordance with Article 43;

    (f)   of denunciations and notifications in accordance with Article 44;

    (g)   of requests for revision in accordance with Article 45.

In Faith Whereof the undersigned, duly authorized, have signed this Convention on behalf of their respective Governments,

DONE at Geneva, this twenty-eighth day of July, one thousand nine hundred and fifty-one, in a single copy, of which the English and French texts are equally authentic and which shall remain deposited in the archives of the United Nations, and certified true copies of which shall be delivered to all Members of the United Nations and to the non-member states referred to in Article 39.

SCHEDULE

Paragraph 1

1 The travel document referred to in Article 28 of this Convention shall be similar to the specimen annexed hereto.

2 The document shall be made out in at least two languages, one of which shall be English or French.

Paragraph 2

Subject to the regulations obtaining in the country of issue, children may be included in the travel document of a parent or, in exceptional circumstances, of another adult refugee.

Paragraph 3

The fees charged for issue of the document shall not exceed the lowest scale of charges for national passports.

Paragraph 4

Save in special or exceptional cases, the document shall be made valid for the largest possible number of countries.

Paragraph 5

The document shall have a validity of either one or two years, at the discretion of the issuing authority.

Paragraph 6

1 The renewal or extension of the validity of the document is a matter for the authority which issued it, so long as the holder has not established lawful residence in another territory and resides lawfully in the territory of the said authority. The issue of a new document is, under the same conditions, a matter for the authority which issued the former document.

2 Diplomatic or consular authorities, specially authorised for the purpose, shall be empowered to extend, for a period not exceeding six months, the validity of travel documents issued by their Governments.

3 The contracting states shall give sympathetic consideration to renewing or extending the validity of travel documents or issuing new documents to refugees no longer lawfully resident in their territory who are unable to obtain a travel document from the country of their lawful residence.

Paragraph 7

The contracting states shall recognise the validity of the documents issued in accordance with the provisions of Article 28 of this Convention.

Paragraph 8

The competent authorities of the country to which the refugee desires to proceed shall, if they are prepared to admit him and if a visa is required, affix a visa on the document of which he is the holder.

Paragraph 9

1 The contracting states undertake to issue transit visas to refugees who have obtained visas for a territory of final destination.

2 The issue of such visas may be refused on grounds which would justify refusal of a visa to any alien.

Paragraph 10

The fees for the issue of exit, entry or transit visas shall not exceed the lowest scale of charges for visas on foreign passports.

Paragraph 11

When a refugee has lawfully taken up residence in the territory of another contracting state, the responsibility for the issue of a new document, under the terms and conditions of Article 28, shall be that of the competent authority of that territory, to which the refugee shall be entitled to apply.

Paragraph 12

The authority issuing a new document shall withdraw the old document and shall return it to the country of issue, if it is stated in the document that it should be so returned; otherwise it shall withdraw and cancel the document.

Paragraph 13

1   Each contracting state undertakes that the holder of a travel document issued by it in accordance with Article 28 of this Convention shall be re-admitted to its territory at any time during the period of its validity.

2   Subject to the provisions of the preceding sub-paragraph, a contracting state may require the holder of the document to comply with such formalities as may be prescribed in regard to exit from or return to its territory.

3   The contracting states reserve the right, in exceptional cases, or in cases where the refugee's stay is authorised for a specific period, when issuing the document, to limit the period during which the refugee may return to a period of not less than three months.

Paragraph 14

Subject only to the terms of paragraph 13, the provisions of this Schedule in no way affect the laws and regulations governing the conditions of admission to, transit through, residence and establishment in, and departure from, the territories of the contracting states.

Paragraph 15

Neither the issue of the document nor the entries made thereon determine or affect the status of the holder, particularly as regards nationality.

Paragraph 16

The issue of the document does not in any way entitle the holder to the protection of the diplomatic or consular authorities of the country of issue, and does not confer on these authorities a right of protection.

ANNEX

Specimen Travel Document

The document will be in booklet form (approximately 15 x 10 centimetres). It is recommended that it be so printed that any erasure or alteration by chemical or other means can be readily detected, and that the words 'Convention of 28 July 1951' be printed in continuous repetition on each page, in the language of the issuing country.

(Cover of booklet)
TRAVEL DOCUMENT
(Convention of 28 July 1951)
No. . . .

(1)

TRAVEL DOCUMENT

(Convention of 28 July 1951)

This document expires on . . . unless its validity is extended or renewed.

Name . . .

Forename(s) . . .

Accompanied by . . . child (children)

1. This document is issued solely with a view to providing the holder with a travel document which can serve in lieu of a national passport. It is without prejudice to and in no way affects the holder's nationality.

2. The holder is authorized to return to . . . [state here the country whose authorities are issuing the document] on or before . . . unless some later date is hereafter specified.

[The period during which the holder is allowed to return must not be less than three months]

3. Should the holder take up residence in a country other than that which issued the present document, he must, if he wishes to travel again, apply to the competent authorities of his country of residence for a new document. [The old travel document shall be withdrawn by the authority issuing the new document and returned to the authority which issued it.][1]

(This document contains . . . pages, exclusive of cover.)

[1]   The sentence in brackets to be inserted by Governments which so desire.

(2)

Place and date of birth . . .

Occupation . . .

Present residence . . .

* Maiden name and forename(s) of wife . . .

* Name of forename(s) of husband . . .

Description

Height . . .

Hair . . .

Colour of eyes . . .

Nose . . .

Shape of face . . .

Complexion . . .

Special peculiarities . . .

Children accompanying holder

Name	Forename(s)	Place and date of birth	Sex
. . .	. . .	. . .	
. . .	. . .	. . .	. . .
. . .	. . .	. . .	. . .
. . .	. . .	. . .	. . .

* Strike out whichever does not apply.

(This document contains . . . pages, exclusive of cover.)

(3)

Photograph of holder and stamp of issuing authority
Finger-prints of holder (if required)
Signature of holder . . .
(This document contains . . . pages, exclusive of cover.)

(4)

1. This document is valid for the following countries:

. . .

. . .

. . .

. . .

2. Document or documents on the basis of which the present document is issues:

. . .

. . .

. . .

. . .

Issued at . . .
Date . . .
Signature and stamp of authority issuing the document
Fee paid:
(This document contains . . . pages, exclusive of cover.)

(5)

Extension or renewal of validity
Fee paid: From . . .
                                   To . . .
Done at: Date . . .
Signature and stamp of authority extending or renewing the validity of the document:

Extension or renewal of validity
Fee paid: From . . .
                                   To . . .
Done at: Date . . .
Signature and stamp of authority extending or renewing the validity of the document:
(This document contains . . . pages, exclusive of cover.)

(6)

Extension or renewal of validity

Fee paid:

From . . .
To . . .

Done at:

Date . . .

Signature and stamp of authority extending or renewing the validity of the document:

Extension or renewal of validity
Fee paid:

From . . .
To . . .

Done at:

Date . . .

Signature and stamp of authority extending or renewing the validity of the document:

(This document contains . . . pages, exclusive of cover.)

(7–32)

Visas

The name of the holder of the document must be repeated in each visa.

(This document contains . . . pages, exclusive of cover.)

APPENDIX

FINAL ACT OF THE 1951 UNITED NATIONS CONFERENCE OF PLENIPO-
TENTIARIES ON THE STATUS OF REFUGEES AND STATELESS PERSONS

I The General Assembly of the United Nations, by Resolution 429(V) of 14 December 1950, decided to convene in Geneva a Conference of Plenipotentiaries to complete the drafting of, and to sign, a Convention relating to the Status of Refugees and a Protocol relating to the Status of Stateless Persons.

The Conference met at the European Office of the United Nations in Geneva from 2 to 25 July 1951.

The Governments of the following twenty-six states were represented by delegates who all submitted satisfactory credentials or other communications of appointment authorizing them to participate in the Conference:

Australia	Israel
Austria	Italy
Belgium	Luxembourg
Brazil	Monaco
Canada	Netherlands
Colombia	Norway
Denmark	Sweden
Egypt	Switzerland (the Swiss delegation also represented Liechtenstein)
France	Turkey
Germany, Federal Republic of	United Kingdom of Great Britain and Northern Ireland
Greece	United States of America
Holy See	Venezuela

Iraq   Yugoslavia

The Governments of the following two states were represented by observers:

Cuba   Iran

Pursuant to the request of the General Assembly, the United Nations High Commissioner for Refugees participated, without the right to vote, in the deliberations of the Conference.

The International Labour Organisation and the International Refugee Organization were represented at the Conference without the right to vote.

The Conference invited a representative of the Council of Europe to be represented at the Conference without the right to vote.

Representatives of the following Non-Governmental Organizations in consultative relationship with the Economic and Social Council were also present as observers:

Category A
International Confederation of Free Trade Unions
International Federation of Christian Trade Unions
Inter-Parliamentary Union

Category B
Agudas Israel World Organization
Caritas Internationalis
Catholic International Union for Social Service
Commission of the Churches on International Affairs
Consultative Council of Jewish Organizations
Co-ordinating Board of Jewish Organizations
Friends' World Committee for Consultation
International Association of Penal Law
International Bureau for the Unification of Penal Law
International Committee of the Red Cross
International Council of Women
International Federation of Friends of Young Women
International League for the Rights of Man
International Social Service
International Union for Child Welfare
International Union of Catholic Women's Leagues
Pax Romana
Women's International League for Peace and Freedom
World Jewish Congress
World Union for Progressive Judaism
World Young Women's Christian Association

Register
International Relief Committee for Intellectual Workers
League of Red Cross Societies
Standing Conference of Voluntary Agencies
World Association of Girl Guides and Girl Scouts
World University Service

Representatives of Non-Governmental Organizations which have been granted consultative status by the Economic and Social Council as well as those entered by the Secretary-General on the Register referred to in Resolution 288 B(X) of the Economic and Social Council, paragraph 17, had under the rules of procedure adopted by the Conference the right to submit written or oral statements to the Conference.

The Conference elected Mr. Knud Larsen, of Denmark, as President, and Mr A Herment, of Belgium, and Mr Talat Miras, of Turkey, as Vice-Presidents.

At its second meeting, the Conference, acting on a proposal of the representative of Egypt, unanimously decided to address an invitation to the Holy See to designate a plenipotentiary representative to participate in its work. A representative of the Holy See took his place at the Conference on 10 July 1951.

The Conference adopted as its agenda the Provisional Agenda drawn up by the Secretary-General (A/CONF 2/2/Rev 1). It also adopted the Provisional Rules of Procedure drawn up by the Secretary-General, with the addition of a provision which authorized a representative of the Council of Europe to be present at the Conference without the right to vote and to submit proposals (A/CONF 2/3/Rev 1).

In accordance with the Rules of Procedure of the Conference, the President and Vice-Presidents examined the credentials of representatives and on 17 July 1951 reported to the Conference the results of such examination, the Conference adopting the report.

The Conference used as the basis of its discussions the draft Convention relating to the Status of Refugees and the draft Protocol relating to the Status of Stateless Persons prepared by the *ad hoc* Committee on Refugees and Stateless Persons at its second session held in Geneva from 14 to 25 August 1950, with the exception of the preamble and Article 1 (Definition of the term 'refugee') of the draft Convention. The text of the preamble before the Conference was that which was adopted by the Economic and Social Council on 11 August 1950 in Resolution 319 B II(XI). The text of Article 1 before the Conference was that recommended by the General Assembly on 14 December 1950 and contained in the Annex to Resolution 429(V). The latter was a modification of the text as it had been adopted by the Economic and Social Council in Resolution 319 B II(XI)[1].

The Conference adopted the Convention relating to the Status of Refugees in two readings. Prior to its second reading it established a Style Committee composed of the President and the representatives of Belgium, France, Israel, Italy, the United Kingdom of Great Britain and Northern Ireland and the United States of America, together with the High Commissioner for Refugees, which elected as its Chairman Mr. G. Warren, of the United States of America. The Style Committee re-drafted the text which had been adopted by the Conference on first reading, particularly from the point of view of language and of concordance between the English and French texts.

The Convention was adopted on 25 July by 24 votes to none with no abstentions and opened for signature at the European Office of the United Nations from 28 July to 31 August 1951. It will be re-opened for signature at the permanent headquarters of the United Nations in New York from 17 September 1951 to 31 December 1952.

The English and French texts of the Convention, which are equally authentic, are appended to this Final Act.

---

[1] The texts referred to in the paragraph above are contained in document A/CONF 2/1.

II The Conference decided, by 17 votes to 3 with 3 abstentions, that the titles of the chapters and of the articles of the Convention are included for practical purposes and do not constitute an element of interpretation.

III With respect to the draft Protocol relating to the Status of Stateless Persons, the Conference adopted the following resolution:

The Conference,

Having considered the draft Protocol relating to the Status of Stateless Persons,

Considering that the subject still requires more detailed study,

Decides not to take a decision on the subject at the present Conference and refers the draft Protocol back to the appropriate organs of the United Nations for further study.

IV The Conference adopted unanimously the following recommendations:

A
(Facilitation of refugee travels)[1]

The Conference,

Considering that the issue and recognition of travel documents is necessary to facilitate the movement of refugees, and in particular their resettlement,

Urges Governments which are parties to the Inter-Governmental Agreement on Refugee Travel Documents signed in London on 15 October 1946, or which recognize travel documents issued in accordance with the Agreement, to continue to issue or to recognize such travel documents, and to extend the issue of such documents to refugees as defined in Article 1 of the Convention relating to the Status of Refugees or to recognize the travel documents so issued to such persons, until they shall have undertaken obligations under Article 28 of the said Convention.

[1] Headline added.

B
(Principle of unity of the family)[1]

The Conference,

Considering that the unity of the family, the natural and fundamental group unit of society, is an essential right of the refugee, and that such unity is constantly threatened, and

Noting with satisfaction that, according to the official commentary of the *ad hoc* Committee on Statelessness and Related Problems (E/1618, p. 40) the rights granted to a refugee are extended to members of his family,

Recommends Governments to take the necessary measures for the protection of the refugee's family, especially with a view to:

(1) Ensuring that the unity of the refugee's family is maintained particularly in cases where the head of the family has fulfilled the necessary conditions for admission to a particular country,

(2) The protection of refugees who are minors, in particular unaccompanied children and girls, with special reference to guardianship and adoption.

[1] Headline added.

C
(Welfare services)[1]

The Conference,

Considering that, in the moral, legal and material spheres, refugees need the help of suitable welfare services, especially that of appropriate non-governmental organizations,

Recommends Governments and inter-governmental bodies to facilitate, encourage and sustain the efforts of properly qualified organizations.

[1] Headline added.

D
(International co-operation in the field of asylum and resettlement)

The Conference,

Considering that many persons still leave their country of origin for reasons of persecution and are entitled to special protection on account of their position,

Recommends that Governments continue to receive refugees in their territories and that they act in concert in a true spirit of international co-operation in order that these refugees may find asylum and the possibility of resettlement.

E

(Extension of treatment provided by the Convention)

The Conference,

Expresses the hope that the Convention relating to the Status of Refugees will have value as an example exceeding its contractual scope and that all nations will be guided by it in granting so far as possible to persons in their territory as refugees and who would not be covered by the terms of the Convention, the treatment for which it provides.

In Witness Whereof the President, Vice-Presidents and the Executive Secretary of the Conference have signed this Final Act.

Done at Geneva this twenty-eighth day of July one thousand nine hundred and fifty-one in a single copy in the English and French languages, each text being equally authentic. Translations of this Final Act into Chinese, Russian and Spanish will be prepared by the Secretary-General of the United Nations, who will, on request, send copies thereof to each of the Governments invited to attend the Conference.

The President of the Conference:	Knud Larsen
The Vice-Presidents of the Conference:	A Herment
	Talat Miras
The Executive Secretary of the Conference:	John P Humphrey

UN CONVENTION RELATING TO THE STATUS OF STATELESS PERSONS

New York, 28 September 1954

ENTRY INTO FORCE: 6 June 1960, in accordance with article 39.

REGISTRATION: 6 June 1960, No. 5158.

STATUS: Signatories: 23. Parties: 84.

TEXT: United Nations, *Treaty Series*, vol. 360, p.117.

Note: The Convention was adopted by the United Nations Conference on the Status of Stateless Persons, held at the Headquarters of the United Nations in New York from 13 to 23 September 1954. The Conference was convened pursuant to resolution 526A (XVII)[1] of 26 April 1954 of the Economic and Social Council of the United Nations. For the Final Act, recommendation and resolution adopted by the Conference, see United Nations, *Treaty Series*, vol. 360, p. 117.

Participant	Signature		Accession(a), Succession(d), Ratification
Albania			23 Jun 2003 a
Algeria			15 Jul 1964 a
Antigua and Barbuda			25 Oct 1988 d
Argentina			1 Jun 1972 a
Armenia			18 May 1994 a
Australia			13 Dec 1973 a
Austria			8 Feb 2008 a
Azerbaijan			16 Aug 1996 a
Barbados			6 Mar 1972 d
Belgium	28 Sep	1954	27 May 1960
Belize			14 Sep 2006 a
Benin			8 Dec 2011 a
Bolivia (Plurinational State of)			6 Oct 1983 a
Bosnia and Herzegovina[2]			1 Sep 1993 d
Botswana			25 Feb 1969 d
Brazil	28 Sep	1954	13 Aug 1996
Bulgaria			22 Mar 2012 a
Burkina Faso			1 May 2012 a
Chad			12 Aug 1999 a
China[3]			
Colombia	30 Dec	1954	
Costa Rica	28 Sep	1954	2 Nov 1977
Côte d'Ivoire			3 Oct 2013 a
Croatia[2]			12 Oct 1992 d
Czech Republic			19 Jul 2004 a
Denmark	28 Sep	1954	17 Jan 1956
Ecuador	28 Sep	1954	2 Oct 1970
El Salvador	28 Sep	1954	
Fiji			12 Jun 1972 d
Finland			10 Oct 1968 a
France	12 Jan	1955	8 Mar 1960
Gambia			1 Jul 2014 a
Georgia			23 Dec 2011 a
Germany[4,5]	28 Sep	1954	26 Oct 1976
Greece			4 Nov 1975 a
Guatemala	28 Sep	1954	28 Nov 2000
Guinea			21 Mar 1962 a
Holy See	28 Sep	1954	
Honduras	28 Sep	1954	1 Oct 2012
Hungary			21 Nov 2001 a
Ireland			17 Dec 1962 a
Israel	1 Oct	1954	23 Dec 1958
Italy	20 Oct	1954	3 Dec 1962
Kiribati			29 Nov 1983 d

Latvia			5 Nov 1999 a
Lesotho			4 Nov 1974 d
Liberia			11 Sep 1964 a
Libya			16 May 1989 a
Liechtenstein	28 Sep	1954	25 Sep 2009
Lithuania			7 Feb 2000 a
Luxembourg	28 Oct	1955	27 Jun 1960
Madagascar[6]			[20 Feb 1962 a]
Malawi			7 Oct 2009 a
Mexico			7 Jun 2000 a
Montenegro[7]			23 Oct 2006 d
Mozambique			1 Oct 2014 a
Netherlands	28 Sep	1954	12 Apr 1962
Nicaragua			15 Jul 2013 a
Niger			7 Nov 2014 a
Nigeria			20 Sep 2011 a
Norway	28 Sep	1954	19 Nov 1956
Panama			2 Jun 2011 a
Paraguay			1 Jul 2014 a
Peru			23 Jan 2014 a
Philippines	22 Jun	1955	22 Sep 2011
Portugal			1 Oct 2012 a
Republic of Korea			22 Aug 1962 a
Republic of Moldova			19 Apr 2012 a
Romania			27 Jan 2006 a
Rwanda			4 Oct 2006 a
Senegal			21 Sep 2005 a
Serbia[2]			12 Mar 2001 d
Slovakia			3 Apr 2000 a
Slovenia[2]			6 Jul 1992 d
Spain			12 May 1997 a
St. Vincent and the Grenadines			27 Apr 1999 d
Swaziland			16 Nov 1999 a
Sweden	28 Sep	1954	2 Apr 1965
Switzerland	28 Sep	1954	3 Jul 1972
The former Yugoslav Republic of Macedonia[2]			18 Jan 1994 d
Trinidad and Tobago			11 Apr 1966 d
Tunisia			29 Jul 1969 a
Turkmenistan			7 Dec 2011 a
Uganda			15 Apr 1965 a
Ukraine			25 Mar 2013 a
United Kingdom of Great Britain and Northern Ireland[3]	28 Sep	1954	16 Apr 1959
Uruguay			2 Apr 2004 a
Zambia			1 Nov 1974 d
Zimbabwe			1 Dec 1998 d

DECLARATIONS AND RESERVATIONS
(UNLESS OTHERWISE INDICATED, THE DECLARATIONS AND RESERVATIONS WERE MADE UPON RATIFICATION, ACCESSION OR SUCCESSION.)

ANTIGUA AND BARBUDA

"The Government of Antigua and Barbuda can only undertake that the provisions of articles 23, 24, 25 and 31 will be applied in Antigua and Barbuda so far as the law allows."

ARGENTINA

The application of this Convention in territories whose sovereignty is the subject of discussion between two or more States, irrespective of whether they are parties to the Convention, cannot be construed as an alteration, renunciation or relinquishment of the position previously maintained by each of them.

AUSTRIA

Reservation:

The Republic of Austria shall only be bound by Article 27 insofar as it applies to stateless persons lawfully in the territory of the Republic of Austria.

Declaration:

The Republic of Austria will fulfil its obligation under Article 28 by issuing alien passports to stateless persons lawfully staying in its territory.

BARBADOS

"The Government of Barbados . . . declares with regard to the reservations made by the United Kingdom on notification of the territorial application of the Convention to the West Indies (including Barbados) on the 19th March, 1962 that it can only undertake that the provisions of Articles 23, 24, 25 and 31 will be applied in Barbados so far as the law allows.

"The application of the Convention to Barbados was also made subject to reservations to Articles 8, 9 and 26 which are hereby withdrawn."

BOTSWANA[8]

"(a)   Article 31 of the said Convention shall not oblige Botswana to grant to a stateless person a status more favourable than that accorded to aliens in general;

"(b)   Articles 12 1) and 7 2) of the Convention shall be recognized as recommendations only."

BULGARIA

"1.   Reservation to Article 7, paragraph 2:

'In accordance with Article 38, paragraph 1 of the Convention, the Republic of Bulgaria reserves the right not to apply the provision of Article 7, paragraph 2.'

2.   Reservation to Article 21:

'The Republic of Bulgaria shall apply Article 21 according to the conditions and the order provided for by the national legislation of the Republic of Bulgaria.'

3.   Reservation to Article 23:

'The Republic of Bulgaria shall apply Article 23 according to the conditions and the order provided for by the national legislation of the Republic of Bulgaria.'

4.   Reservation to Article 24, paragraph 1, subparagraph (b) and Article 24, paragraph 2:

'The Republic of Bulgaria shall apply Article 24, paragraph 1, subparagraph (b) and Article 24, paragraph 2 according to the conditions and the order provided for by the national legislation of the Republic of Bulgaria.'

5. Reservation to Article 24, paragraph 3:

'The Republic of Bulgaria shall apply Article 24, paragraph 3 only concerning agreements which will be concluded in the future.'

6. Reservation to Article 27:

'Pursuant to Article 27 of the Convention, the identity document ('Stateless person foreign-travel certificate') shall be issued to stateless persons, who have been granted this status on the territory of the Republic of Bulgaria and having permanent or long-term residence permit in accordance with the national legislation of the Republic of Bulgaria. In accordance with the national legislation, the person who has been granted the status of stateless person will be granted right to residence and a document 'Residence permit', which is not an identity document, will be issued.'

7. Reservation to Article 28:

'Pursuant to Article 28 of the Convention, the document 'Stateless person foreign-travel certificate', which is both an identity document and a travel document, will be issued to persons to whom the Republic of Bulgaria has granted status of stateless person and having permanent or long-term residence permit on the territory of the Republic of Bulgaria. The abovementioned document will not be issued to persons who have been granted status of stateless person in another country, unless they have permanent or long-term residence in the Republic of Bulgaria and because of insurmountable reasons, duly proven by respective documents, can not renew their travel document from the state which initially issued it.'

8. Reservation to Article 31:

'Article 31 shall not oblige the Republic of Bulgaria to grant to stateless persons a status more favourable than that accorded to aliens in general.' "

Costa Rica[9]

Czech Republic

" . . . Acceding to the Convention we declare the following:

1. Pursuant to Article 27 of the Convention, identity papers shall be issued only to stateless persons having permanent residence permits in the territory of the Czech Republic in accordance with the country's national legislation.

2. Article 23 of the Convention shall be applied to the extent provided by the national legislation of the Czech Republic.

3. Article 24, paragraph 1(b) shall be applied to the extent provided by the national legislation of the Czech Republic.

4. Pursuant to Article 28 of the Convention, travel documents shall be issued to stateless persons having permanent residence permits in the territory of the Czech Republic in accordance with the country's national legislation. Such persons shall be issued "aliens' passports" stating that their holders are stateless persons under the Convention of 28th September 1954."

Denmark[10]

Denmark is not bound by article 24, paragraph 3.

The provisions of article 24, paragraph 1, under which stateless persons are in certain cases placed on the same footing as nationals, shall not oblige Denmark to grant stateless persons in every case exactly the same remuneration as that provided by law for nationals, but only to grant them what is required for their support.

Article 31 shall not oblige Denmark to grant to stateless persons a status more favourable than that accorded to aliens in general.

El Salvador

El Salvador signs the present Convention with the reservation that the expression "treatment as favourable as possible", referred to in those of its provisions to which reservations may be made, must not be understood to include the special treatment which has been or may be granted to the nationals of Spain, the Latin American countries in general, and in particular to the countries which constituted the United Provinces of Central America and now form the Organization of Central American States.

Fiji

The Government of Fiji stated that the first and third reservations made by the United Kingdom are affirmed but have been redrafted as more suitable to the application of Fiji in the following terms:

"1.   The Government of Fiji understands articles 8 and 9 as not preventing them from taking in time of war or other grave and exceptional circumstances measures in the interests of national security in the case of a stateless person on the ground of his former nationality. The provisions of article 8 shall not prevent the Government of Fiji from exercising any rights over property or interests which they may acquire or have acquired as an Allied or Associated Power under a Treaty of Peace or other agreement or arrangement for the restoration of peace which has been or may be completed as a result of the Second World War. Furthermore the provisions of article 8 shall not affect the treatment to be accorded to any property or interests which at the date of entry into force of this Convention in respect of Fiji were under the control of the Government of the United Kingdom of Great Britain and Northern Ireland or of the Government of Fiji respectively by reason of a state of war which existed between them and any other State.

"2.   The Government of Fiji cannot undertake to give effect to the obligations contained in paragraphs 1 and 2 of article 25 and can only undertake to apply the provisions of paragraph 3 so far as the law allows.

"Commentary: No arrangements exist in Fiji for the administrative assistance for which provision is made in article 25 nor have any such arrangements been found necessary in the case of stateless persons. Any need for the documents or certificates mentioned in paragraph 2 of that article would be met by affidavit.

"All other reservation made by the United Kingdom to the above-mentioned Convention is withdrawn."

Finland[11]

"(1)   A general reservation to the effect that the application of those provisions of the Convention which grant to stateless persons the most favourable treatment accorded to nationals of a foreign country shall not be affected by the fact that special rights and privileges are now or may in future be accorded by Finland to the nationals of Denmark, Iceland, Norway and Sweden or to the nationals of any one of those Countries;

"(2)   A reservation to article 7, paragraph 2, to the effect that Finland is not prepared, as a general measure, to grant stateless persons who fulfil the conditions of three years residence in Finland an exemption from any legislative reciprocity which Finnish law may have stipulated as a condition governing an alien's eligibility for same right or privilege;

"(3)   A reservation to article 8 to the effect that that article shall not be binding on Finland;

"(4) . . .

"(5)   A reservation to article 24, paragraph 1 (b) and paragraph 3 to the effect that they shall not be binding on Finland;

"(6)   A reservation to article 25, to the effect that Finland does not consider itself bound to cause a certificate to be delivered by a Finnish authority, in the place of the authorities of a foreign country, if the documentary records necessary for the delivery of such certificate do not exist in Finland;

"(7)   A reservation with respect to the provisions contained in article 28. Finland does not accept the obligations stipulated in the said article, but is prepared to recognize travel documents issued by other Contracting States pursuant to this article."

FRANCE

The provisions of article 10, paragraph 2, are regarded by the French Government as applying only to stateless persons who were forcibly displaced from French territory, and who have, prior to the date of entry into force of this Convention, returned there direct from the country to which they were forced to proceed, without in the meantime having received authorization to reside in the territory of any other State.

GERMANY[4,5]

1.   Article 23 will be applied without restriction only to stateless persons who are also refugees within the meaning of the Convention of 28 July 1951 relating to the Status of Refugees and the Protocol of 31 January 1967 relating to the Status of Refugees, but otherwise only to the extent provided for under national legislation;

2.   Article 27 will not be applied.

GUATEMALA

Guatemala signs the present Convention with the reservation that the expression "treatment as favourable as possible", referred to in those of its provisions to which reservations may be made, must not be understood to include the special treatment which has been or may be granted to the nationals of, Spain, the Latin American countries in general, and in particular to the countries which constituted the United Provinces of Central America and now form the Organization of Central American States.

Guatemala ratifies the present Convention with the reservation that the expression "treatment as favourable as possible", referred to in those of its provisions to which reservations may be made, shall not be understood to include the special treatment which Guatemala has granted or may grant to nationals of Spain, the Latin American countries in general, and in particular the countries which constitute the Central American Integration System (SICA), which are those countries which constituted the United Provinces of Central America, plus the Republic of Panama.

HOLY SEE

"The Convention will be applied in the form compatible with the special nature of the State of the Vatican City and without prejudice to the norms that grant access thereunto and sojourn therein."

HONDURAS

Honduras signs the present Convention with the reservation that the expression "treatment as favourable as possible", referred to in those of its provisions to which reservations may be made, must not be understood to include the special treatment which has been or may be granted to the nationals of Spain, the Latin American countries in general, and in particular to the countries which constituted the United Provinces of Central America and now form the Organization of Central American States.

HUNGARY[12]

Reservation to Article 28 of the Convention:

"The Republic of Hungary shall apply the provisions contained in Article 28 by issuing a travel document in both Hungarian and English languages, entitled 'Utazási Igazolvány hontalan személy részére / Travel Document for Stateless Person' and supplied with the indication set out in Paragraph 1, Subparagraph 1 of the Schedule to the Convention."

IRELAND

"The Government of Ireland understand the words 'public order' and 'in accordance with due process of law', as they appear in article 31 of the Convention, to mean respectively, 'public policy' and 'in accordance with the procedure provided by law'."

"With regard to article 29 (1), the Government of Ireland do not undertake to accord to stateless persons treatment more favourable than that accorded to aliens generally with respect to

(a)   The stamp duty chargeable in Ireland in connection with conveyances, transfers and leases of lands, tenements and hereditaments, and

(b)   Income tax (including sur-tax)."

ITALY[13]

The provisions of articles 17 and 18 are recognized as recommendations only.

KIRIBATI

[The following reservations originally made by the United Kingdom were reformulated as follows in terms suited to their direct application to Kiribati]:

"1.   The Government of Kiribati understands articles 8 and 9 as not preventing them from taking in time of war or other grave and exceptional circumstances measures in the interests of national security in the case of a stateless person on the ground of his former nationality. The provisions of article 8 shall not prevent the Government of Kiribati from exercising any rights over property or interests which they may acquire or have acquired as an Allied or Associated Power under a Treaty of Peace or other agreement or arrangement for the restoration of peace which has been or may be completed as a result of the Second World War. Furthermore, the provisions of article 8 shall not affect the treatment to be accorded to any property or interest which at the date of entry into force of this Convention in respect of the Gilbert Islands were under the control of the Government of the United Kingdom of Great Britain and Northern Ireland by reason of a state of war which exists or existed between them and any other State.

"2.   The Government of Kiribati can only undertake to apply the provisions of sub-paragraph (b) of paragraph 1 of article 24 so far as the law allows.

"3.   The Government of Kiribati cannot undertake to give effect to the obligations contained in paragraphs 1 and 2 of article 25 and can only undertake to apply the provisions of paragraph 3 so far as the law allows."

LATVIA

"In accordance with article 38 of the [Convention] the Republic of Latvia reserves the right to apply the provisions of paragraph 1 (b) of Article 24 subject to limitations provided for by the national legislation."

"In accordance with article 38 of the [Convention] the Republic of Latvia reserves the right to apply the provisions of Article 27 subject to limitations provided for by the national legislation."

LESOTHO[14]

"1. In accordance with article 38 of the Convention, the Government of the Kingdom of Lesotho declares that it understands articles 8 and 9 as not preventing it from taking in time of war or other grave and exceptional circumstances measures in the interest of national security in the case of a stateless person on the ground of his former nationality. The provisions of article 8 shall not prevent the Government of the Kingdom of Lesotho from exercising any rights over property or interests which they may acquire or have acquired as an Allied or Associated Power under a Treaty of Peace or other agreement or arrangement for the restoration of peace which has been or may be completed as a result of the Second World War. Furthermore the provisions of article 8 shall not affect the treatment to be accorded to any property or interests which at the date of entry into force of this Convention in respect of Lesotho were under the control of the Government of the United Kingdom of Great Britain and Northern Ireland or of the Government of Lesotho by reason of a state of war which existed between them and any other State.

"2. The Government of the Kingdom of Lesotho cannot undertake to give effect to the obligations contained in paragraphs 1 and 2 of article 25 and can only undertake to apply the provisions of paragraph 3 so far as the laws of Lesotho allow.

"3. The Government of the Kingdom of Lesotho shall not be bound under article 31 to grant to a stateless person a status more favourable than that accorded to aliens generally."

MEXICO[15]

The Government of Mexico is convinced of the importance of ensuring that all stateless persons can obtain wage-earning employment as a means of subsistence and affirms that stateless persons will be treated, in accordance with the law, under the same conditions as aliens in general, without prejudice to the application of article 7 of the Federal Labour Act, which establishes the proportion of alien workers that employers are authorized to employ in Mexico, as well as other legal principles relating to work by aliens in the country, for which reason the Government of Mexico lodges an express reservation to article 17 of this Convention.

The Government of Mexico does not consider itself obliged to guarantee stateless persons greater facilities for their naturalization than those accorded to aliens in general, for which reason it lodges an express reservation to the contents of article 32 of the Convention.

NETHERLANDS

The Government of the Kingdom reserves the right not to apply the provisions of article 8 of the Convention to stateless persons who previously possessed enemy nationality or the equivalent thereof with respect to the Kingdom of Netherlands;

With reference to article 26 of the Convention, the Government of the Kingdom reserves the right to designate a place of principal residence for certain stateless persons or groups of stateless persons in the public interest.

NICARAGUA

The Republic of Nicaragua declares that the expression "treatment as favourable as possible", referred to in those of its provisions to which reservations may be made, shall not be understood to include the special treatment which Nicaragua has granted or may grant to nationals of Spain, the Latin American countries in general, and in particular the countries which constitute the Central American Integration System (SICA), which are those countries which constituted the United Provinces of Central America, plus the Republic of Panama.

PHILIPPINES

"(a) As regards Article 17, paragraph 1, granting stateless persons the right to engage in wage-earning employment, [the Government of the Philippines] finds that this provision conflicts with the Philippine Immigration Act of 1940, as amended, which classifies as excludable aliens under Section 29 those coming to the Philippines to perform unskilled labour, and permits the admission of pre-arranged employees under Section 9 (g) only when there are no persons in the Philippines willing and competent to perform the labour or service for which the admission of aliens is desired.

"(b) As regards Article 31, paragraph 1, to the effect that 'the Contracting States shall not expel a stateless person lawfully in their territory, save on grounds of national security or public order', this provision would unduly restrict the power of the Philippine Government to deport undesirable aliens under Section 37 of the same Immigration Act which states the various grounds upon which aliens may be deported.

"Upon signing the Convention [the Philippine Government], therefore hereby [registers] its nonconformity to the provisions of Article 17, paragraph 1, and Article 31, paragraph 1, thereof, for the reasons stated in (a) and (b) above."

PORTUGAL

"Under paragraph 1 of Article 38 of the Convention, the Portuguese Republic declares that in all cases where the stateless persons are accorded the most favourable treatment accorded to nationals of a foreign country, this clause shall not be interpreted as covering the regime applicable to nationals of Brazil, nationals from the European Union countries or nationals from other countries with which Portugal has established or may establish community relations, namely the Portuguese speaking States."

REPUBLIC OF MOLDOVA

"According to article 38 part 1 from the Convention, [the] Republic of Moldova reserves the right to apply [the] provisions of articles 23, 24, 25 and 31 from the Convention according to the national legislation.

According to article 38 part 1 from the Convention, [the] Republic of Moldova reserves the right to apply the provisions of article 27 from the Convention only in regards with stateless which statute has being recognized by the Republic of Moldova, and for that who have permission to stay on the territory of [the] Republic of Moldova."

ROMANIA

"1. With reference to the application of Article 23 of the Convention, Romania reserves its right to accord public relief only to stateless persons which are also refugees, under the provisions of the Convention of 28 July 1951 relating to the Status of Refugees and of the Protocol of 31 January 1967 relating to the Status of Refugees or, as the case may be, subject to the provisions of the domestic law;

2. With reference to the application of Article 27 of the Convention, Romania reserves its right to issue identity papers only to stateless persons to whom the competent authorities accorded the right to stay on the territory of Romania permanently or, as the case may be, for a determined period, subject to the provisions of the domestic law;

3. With reference to the application of Article 31 of the Convention, Romania reserves its right to expel a stateless person staying lawfully on its territory whenever the stateless person committed an offence, subject to the provisions of the legislation in force."

SLOVAKIA

"The Slovak Republic shall not be bound by article 27 to that effect it shall issue identity papers to any stateless person that is not in possession of a valid travel document. The Slovak Republic shall issue identity papers only to the stateless person present on the territory of the Slovak Republic who have been granted long-term or permanent residence permit."

SPAIN

"[The Government of the Kingdom of Spain] makes a reservation to article 29, paragraph 1, and considers itself bound by the provisions of that paragraph only in the case of stateless persons residing in the territory of any of the Contracting States."

ST. VINCENT AND THE GRENADINES

"The Government of St. Vincent and the Grenadines can only undertake that the provisions of articles 23, 24, 25 and 31 will be applied in St. Vincent and the Grenadines so far as the law allows."

SWEDEN[16]

(1) . . . .

(2) To article 8. This article will not be binding on Sweden.

(3) To article 12, paragraph 1. This paragraph will not be binding on Sweden.

(4) To article 24, paragraph 1 (b). Notwithstanding the rule concerning the treatment of stateless persons as nationals, Sweden will not be bound to accord to stateless persons the same treatment as is accorded to nationals in respect of the possibility of entitlement to a national pension under the provisions of the National Insurance Act; and likewise to the effect that, in so far as the right to a supplementary pension under the said Act and the computation of such pension in certain respects are concerned, the rules applicable to Swedish nationals shall be more favourable than those applied to other insured persons.

(5) To article 24, paragraph 3. The provisions of this paragraph will not be binding on Sweden.

(6) To article 25, paragraph 2. Sweden does not consider itself obliged to cause a Swedish authority, in lieu of a foreign authority, to deliver certificates for the issuance of which there is insufficient documentation in Sweden.

UNITED KINGDOM OF GREAT BRITAIN AND NORTHERN IRELAND

"I have the honour further to state that the Government of the United Kingdom deposit the present instrument of ratification on the understanding that the combined effects of articles 36 and 38 permit them to include in any declaration or notification made under paragraph 1 of article 36 or paragraph 2 of article 36 respectively any reservation consistent with article 38 which the Government of the territory concerned might desire to make."

"When ratifying the Convention relating to the Status of Stateless Persons which was opened for signature at New York on September 28, 1954, the Government of the United Kingdom have deemed it necessary to make certain reservations in accordance with paragraph 1 of Article 38 thereof the text of which is reproduced below:

(1) The Government of the United Kingdom of Great Britain and Northern Ireland understand Articles 8 and 9 as not preventing them from taking in time of war or other grave and exceptional circumstances measures in the interests of national security in the case of a stateless person on the ground of his former nationality. The provisions of Article 8 shall not prevent the Government of the United Kingdom of Great Britain and Northern Ireland from exercising any rights over property or interests which they may acquire or have acquired as an Allied or Associated Power under a Treaty of Peace or other agreement or arrangement for the restoration of peace which has been or may be completed as a result of the Second World War. Furthermore, the provisions of Article 8 shall not affect the treatment to be accorded to any property or interests which at the date of entry into force of this Convention for the United Kingdom of

Great Britain and Northern Ireland are under the control of the Government of the United Kingdom of Great Britain and Northern Ireland by reason of a state of war which exists or existed between them and any other State.

(2) The Government of the United Kingdom of Great Britain and Northern Ireland, in respect of such of the matters referred to in sub-paragraph (b) of paragraph 1 of Article 24 as fall within the scope of the National Health Service, can only undertake to apply the provisions of that paragraph so far as the law allows.

(3) The Government of the United Kingdom of Great Britain and Northern Ireland cannot undertake to give effect to the obligations contained in paragraphs 1 and 2 of Article 25 and can only undertake to apply the provisions of paragraph 3 so far as the law allows."

Commentary: "In connexion with sub-paragraph (b) of paragraph 1 of Article 24 which relates to certain matters within the scope of the National Health Service, the National Health Service (Amendment) Act 1949 contains powers for charges to be made to persons not ordinarily resident in Great Britain (which category would include some stateless persons) who receive treatment under the Service. These powers have not yet been exercised but it may be necessary to exercise them at some future date. In Northern Ireland the Health Services are restricted to persons ordinarily resident in the country except where regulations are made to extend the Services to others. For these reasons, the Government of the United Kingdom, while prepared in the future, as in the past, to give the most sympathetic consideration to the situation of stateless persons, find it necessary to make reservation to sub-paragraph (b) of Article 24.

"No arrangements exist in the United Kingdom for the administrative assistance for which provision is made in Article 25 nor have any such arrangements been found necessary in the case of stateless persons. Any need for the documents or certifications mentioned in paragraph 2 of that Article would be met by affidavit."

ZAMBIA[17]

The Government of the Republic of Zambia considers paragraph 1 of article 22 to be a recommendation only, and not a binding obligation to accord to stateless persons national treatment with respect to elementary education;

The Government of the Republic of Zambia reserves the right under article 26 to designate a place or places of residence for stateless persons;

The Government of the Republic of Zambia does not consider itself bound under article 28 to issue a travel document with a return clause in cases where a country of second asylum has accepted or indicated its willingness to accept a stateless person from Zambia;

"The Government of the Republic of Zambia shall not undertake under article 31 to grant treatment more favourable than that accorded to aliens generally with respect to expulsion."

TERRITORIAL APPLICATION

Participant	Date of receipt of the notification	Territories
France	8 Mar 1960	Departments of Algeria, of the Oases and of Saoura, Guadeloupe, Martinique and Guiana and the five Overseas Territories (New Caledonia and Dependencies, French Polynesia, French Somaliland, the Comoro Archipelago and the Islands of St. Pierre and Miquelon)

Participant	Date of receipt of the notification	Territories
Netherlands[18]	12 Apr 1962	Netherlands New Guinea and Suriname
United Kingdom of Great Britain and Northern Ireland[3,14,19,20,21,22,23]	14 Apr 1959	Channel Islands and Isle of Man
	7 Dec 1959	High Commission Territories of Basutoland, Bechuanaland Protectorate and Swaziland
	9 Dec 1959	Federation of Rhodesia and Nyasaland
	19 Mar 1962	Bermuda, British Guiana, British Honduras, British Solomon Islands Protectorate, British Virgin Islands, Colony of Aden, Falkland Islands (Malvinas), Fiji, Gambia, Gilbert and Ellice Islands, Hong Kong, Kenya, Malta, Mauritius, North Borneo, North Borneo, St. Helena, Sarawak, Seychelles, State of Singapore, Uganda, West Indies and Zanzibar

DECLARATIONS AND RESERVATIONS
(UNLESS OTHERWISE INDICATED THE DECLARATIONS AND RESERVATIONS WERE MADE UPON NOTIFICATION OF TERRITORIAL APPLICATION.)

UNITED KINGDOM OF GREAT BRITAIN AND NORTHERN IRELAND[3,14,19,20,21,22,23]

CHANNEL ISLANDS AND ISLE OF MAN

"(i)   The Government of the United Kingdom of Great Britain and Northern Ireland understand Articles 8 and 9 as not preventing the taking in the Isle of Man and in the Channel Islands, in time of war or other grave and exceptional circumstances, of measures in the interests of national security in the case of a stateless person on the ground of his former nationality. The provisions of Article 8 shall not prevent the Government of the United Kingdom of Great Britain and Northern Ireland from exercising any rights over property or interests which they may acquire or have acquired as an Allied or Associated Power under a Treaty of Peace or other agreement or arrangement for the restoration of peace which has been or may be completed as a result of the Second World War. Furthermore, the provisions of Article 8 shall not affect the treatment to be accorded to any property or interests which, at the date of entry into force of this Convention for the Isle of Man and the Channel Islands, are under the control of the Government of the United Kingdom of Great Britain and Northern Ireland by reason of a state of war which exists or existed between them and any other State.

"(ii)   The Government of the United Kingdom of Great Britain and Northern Ireland can only undertake that the provisions of sub-paragraph (b) of paragraph 1 of Article 24 and of paragraph 2 of that Article will be applied in the Channel Islands so far as the law allows, and that the provisions of that sub-paragraph, in respect of such matters referred to therein as fall within the scope of the Isle of Man Health Service, will be applied in the Isle of Man so far as the law allows.

"(iii)   The Government of the United Kingdom of Great Britain and Northern Ireland cannot undertake that effect will be given in the Isle of Man and the Channel Islands to paragraphs 1 and 2 of Article 25 and can only undertake that the provisions of paragraph 3 will be applied in the Isle of Man and the Channel Islands so far as the law allows."

HIGH COMMISSION TERRITORIES OF BASUTOLAND, BECHUANALAND PROTECTORATE AND SOUAZILAND

[Same reservations, in essence, as those made for the Channel Islands and the Isle of Man, under Nos. (i) and (iii).]

FEDERATION OF RHODESIA AND NYASALAND

[Same reservations, in essence, as those made for the Channel Islands and the Isle of Man, under No. (iii).]

BRITISH GUIANA, BRITISH SOLOMON ISLANDS PROTECTORATE, FALKLAND ISLANDS, GAMBIA, GILBERT AND ELLICE ISLANDS, KENYA, MAURITIUS

[Same reservations, in essence, as those made for the Channel Islands and the Isle of Man, under Nos. (i) and (iii)].

BRITISH HONDURAS, HONG KONG

[Same reservations, in essence, as those made for the Channel Islands and the Isle of Man, under Nos. (i) and (iii).]

NORTH BORNEO

[Same reservations, in essence, as those made for the Channel Islands and the Isle of Man.]

FIJI

(i)   The Government of the United Kingdom of Great Britain and Northern Ireland understand articles 8 and 9 as not preventing the taking in Fiji, in time of war or other grave and exceptional circumstances, of measures in the interests of national security in the case of a stateless person on the ground of his former nationality.

(ii)   The Government of the United Kingdom of Great Britain and Northern Ireland, in respect of the provisions of sub-paragraph (b) of paragraph 1 of article 24, can only undertake that effect will be given in Fiji to the provisions of that paragraph so far as the law allows.

(iii)   The Government of the United Kingdom of Great Britain and Northern Ireland cannot undertake that effect will be given in Fiji to paragraphs 1 and 2 of article 25 and can only undertake that the provisions of paragraph 3 will be applied in Fiji so far as the law allows.

THE STATE OF SINGAPORE

(i)   The Government of the United Kingdom of Great Britain and Northern Ireland cannot undertake that effect will be given in the State of Singapore to article 23.

THE WEST INDIES

(i)   The Government of the United Kingdom of Great Britain and Northern Ireland cannot undertake that effect will be given in the West Indies to articles 8, 9, 23, 24, 25, 26 and 31.

Notes:

1   *Official Records of the Economic and Social Council, Seventeenth Session, Supplement, No. 1* (E/2596), p. 12.

2   The former Yugoslavia had acceded to the Convention on 9 April 1959. See also note 1 under "Bosnia and Herzegovina", "Croatia", "former Yugoslavia", "Slovenia", "The Former Yugoslav Republic of Macedonia" and "Yugoslavia" in the "Historical Information" section in the front matter of this volume.

3   On 10 June 1997, the Secretary-General received communications concerning the status of Hong Kong from the Governments of the the United Kingdom and China (see also note 2 under "China" and note 2 under "United Kingdom of Great Britain and Northern Ireland"

regarding Hong Kong in the "Historical Information" section in the front matter of this volume). Upon resuming the exercise of sovereignty over Hong Kong, China notified the Secretary-General that the Convention will also apply to the Hong Kong Special Administrative Region.

In addition, the notification made by the Government of China contained the following declaration:

The Government of the People's Republic of China cannot undertake that effect will be given in the Hong Kong Special Administrative Region to article 25, paragraphs 1 and 2 of the Convention, and can only undertake that the provisions of paragraph 3 of the said article will be applied in the Hong Kong Special Administrative Region so far as the law there allows.

Within the above ambit, responsibility for the international rights and obligations of a Party to the [said Convention] will be assumed by the Government of the People's Republic of China.

4   Instrument of ratification received by the Secretary-General on 2 August 1976 and supplemented by notification of reservation received on 26 October 1976, the date on which the instrument is deemed to have been deposited. See also note 1 under "Germany" regarding Berlin (West) in the "Historical Information" section in the front matter of this volume.

5   See note 2 under "Germany" in the "Historical Information" section in the front matter of this volume.

6   By a notification received by the Secretary-General on 2 April 1965, the Government of Madagascar denounced the Convention; the denunciation took effect on 2 April 1966.

7   See note 1 under "Montenegro" in the "Historical Information" section in the front matter of this volume.

8   In the notification of succession, the Government of Botswana also maintained the reservations made by the Government of the United Kingdom of Great Britain and Northern Ireland on extension of the Convention to the Bechuanaland Protectorate. For the text of the reservations, see *"Declarations and reservations made upon notification of territorial application"*, under United Kingdom.

9   The reservation made upon signature was not maintained upon ratification. For the text of the reservation, see United Nations, *Treaty Series*, vol. 360, p. 196.

10   In a communication received on 23 August 1962, the Government of Denmark informed the Secretary-General of its decision to withdraw as from 1 October 1961 the reservation to article 14 of the Convention.

In a communication received on 25 March 1968, the Government of Denmark informed the Secretary-General of its decision to withdraw as from that date, the reservation to article 24, paragraph 2, of the Convention. For the text of the reservations withdrawn by the above communications, see United Nations, *Treaty Series*, vol. 360, p. 132.

11   In a communication received on 30 September 1970, the Government of Finland notified the Secretary-General of its decision to withdraw the reservation formulated in its instrument of accession to article 12, paragraph 1, of the Convention. For the text of the said reservation, see United Nations, *Treaty Series*, vol. 648, p. 368.

12   On 3 July 2012, the Government of Hungary notified the Secretary-General of a partial withdrawal of its reservation to articles 23 and 24 made upon accession. The reservation made upon accession read as follows:

"The Republic of Hungary shall apply the provisions contained in Articles 23 and 24 in such a way that it ensures to stateless persons having permanent domestic residence equal treatment with its own citizens."

13   In a communication received on 25 January 1968, the Government of Italy notified the Secretary-General of the withdrawal of the reservations made at the time of signature to articles 6, 7 (2), 8, 19, 22 (2), 23, 25 and 32 (see United Nations, *Treaty Series*, vol. 189, p. 192).

14   Reservations 1 and 2 had been formulated by the Government of the United Kingdom in respect of the territory of Basutoland. Reservation 3 constitutes a new reservation, which was made subject to the provisions of article 39 (2) of the Convention.

15   On 11 July 2014, the Government of Mexico notified the Secretary-General of the partial

withdrawal of the reservation made upon accession. The portion of the reservation which has been withdrawn read as follows:

The Government of Mexico lodges an express reservation to article 31 of the Convention, and, therefore, refers to the application of article 33 of the Political Constitution of the United Mexican States.

16   In a communication received on 25 November1966, the Government of Sweden has notified the Secretary-General that it has decided, in accordance with paragraph 2 of article 38 of the Convention, to withdraw some of its reservations to article 24, paragraph 1 (b), and the reservation to article 24, paragraph 2 of the Convention. In a communication received on 5 March 1970, the Government of Sweden notified the Secretary-General of the withdrawal of its reservation to article 7, paragraph 2, of the Convention. For the text of the reservations to article 24, paragraph 1 (b), as originally formulated by the Government of Sweden in its instrument of ratification, and of the reservation to article 7, paragraph 2, see United Nations, *Treaty Series*, vol. 529, p. 362.

17   In its notification of succession, the Government of Zambia declared that it withdrew the reservations made by the Government of the United Kingdom upon extension of the Convention by the latter to the former Federation of Rhodesia and Nyasaland. The reservations reproduced herein are new reservations, which were made subject to the provisions of article 39 (2) of the Convention.

18   In the note accompanying the instrument of ratification, the Government of the Netherlands stated, with reference to article 36, paragraph 3 of the Convention, that "if at any time the Government of the Netherlands Antilles agrees to the extension of the Convention to its territory, the Secretary-General shall be notified thereof without delay. Such notification will contain the reservations, if any, which the Government of the Netherlands Antilles might wish to make with respect to local requirements in accordance with article 38 of the Convention." See also note 1 under "Netherlands" regarding Aruba/Netherlands Antilles in the "Historical Information" section in the front matter of this volume.

19   See note 1 under "United Kingdom of Great Britain and Northern Ireland" in the "Historical Information" section in the front matter of this volume.

20   See accession by Uganda.

21   See succession by Lesotho.

22   See succession by Fiji.

23   In a letter addressed to the Secretary-General on 22 March 1968, the President of the Republic of Malawi, referring to the Convention relating to the Status of Stateless Persons, done at New York on 28 September 1954, stated the following:

"In my letter to you of the 24th November 1964, concerning the disposition of Malawi's inherited treaty obligations, my Government declared that with respect to multilateral treaties which had been applied or extended to the former Nyasaland Protectorate, any Party to such a treaty could on the basis of reciprocity rely as against Malawi on the terms of that treaty until Malawi notified its depositary of what action it wished to take by way of confirmation of termination, confirmation of succession, or accession.

"I am to inform you as depositary of this Convention that the Government of Malawi now wishes to terminate any connection with this Convention which it might have inherited. The Government of Malawi considers that any legal relationship with the afore-mentioned Convention relating to the Status of Stateless Persons, New York, 1954 which might have devolved upon it by way of succession from the ratification of the United Kingdom, is terminated as of this date."

PROTOCOL RELATING TO THE STATUS OF REFUGEES OF 31 JANUARY 1967

Entry into force 4 October 1967, in accordance with Article VIII

Text United Nations Treaty Series No 8791, Vol 606, p 267

The States Parties to the present Protocol,

Considering that the Convention relating to the Status of Refugees done at Geneva on 28 July 1951 (hereinafter referred to as the Convention) covers only those persons who have become refugees as a result of events occurring before 1 January, 1951,

Considering that new refugee situations have arisen since the Convention was adopted and that the refugees concerned may therefore not fall within the scope of the Convention,

Considering that it is desirable that equal status should be enjoyed by all refugees covered by the definition in the Convention irrespective of the dateline 1 January 1951,

Have agreed as follows:

Article I General provision

1   The states parties to the present Protocol undertake to apply Articles 2 to 34 inclusive of the Convention to refugees as hereinafter defined.

2   For the purpose of the present Protocol, the term 'refugee' shall, except as regards the application of paragraph 3 of this Article, mean any person within the definition of Article 1 of the Convention as if the words 'As a result of events occurring before 1 January 1951 and . . . ' and the words ' . . . as a result of such events', in Article 1 A (2) were omitted.

3   The present Protocol shall be applied by the states parties hereto without any geographic limitation, save that existing declarations made by states already Parties to the Convention in accordance with Article 1 B (1)(a) of the Convention, shall, unless extended under Article 1 B (2) thereof, apply also under the present Protocol.

Notes

The Protocol was signed by the President of the General Assembly and by the Secretary-General on 31 January 1967. The text of the General Assembly Resolution 2198 (XXI) of 16 December 1966 concerning the accession to the 1967 Protocol relating to the Status of Refugees is reproduced in Appendix.

Article II Co-operation of the national authorities with the United Nations

1   The states parties to the present Protocol undertake to co-operate with the Office of the United Nations High Commissioner for Refugees, or any other agency of the United Nations which may succeed it, in the exercise of its functions, and shall in particular facilitate its duty of supervising the application of the provisions of the present Protocol.

2   In order to enable the Office of the High Commissioner, or any other agency of the United Nations which may succeed it, to make reports to the competent organs of the United Nations, the states parties to the present Protocol undertake to provide them with the information and statistical data requested, in the appropriate form, concerning:

- (a)   The condition of refugees;
- (b)   The implementation of the present Protocol;
- (c)   Laws, regulations and decrees which are, or may hereafter be, in force relating to refugees.

Article III Information on national legislation

The states parties to the present Protocol shall communicate to the Secretary-General of the United Nations the laws and regulations which they may adopt to ensure the application of the present Protocol.

Article IV Settlement of disputes

Any dispute between states parties to the present Protocol which relates to its interpretation or application and which cannot be settled by other means shall be referred to the International Court of Justice at the request of any one of the parties to the dispute.

Article V Accession

The present Protocol shall be open for accession on behalf of all states parties to the Convention and of any other State Member of the United Nations or member of any of the specialized agencies or to which an invitation to accede may have been addressed by the General Assembly of the United Nations. Accession shall be effected by the deposit of an instrument of accession with the Secretary-General of the United Nations.

Article VI Federal clause

In the case of a federal or non-unitary state, the following provisions shall apply:

(a) With respect to those articles of the Convention to be applied in accordance with Article 1, paragraph 1, of the present Protocol that come within the legislative jurisdiction of the federal legislative authority, the obligations of the Federal Government shall to this extent be the same as those of states parties which are not federal states;

(b) With respect to those articles of the Convention to be applied in accordance with Article I, paragraph 1, of the present Protocol that come within the legislative jurisdiction of constituent states, provinces or cantons which are not, under the constitutional system of the federation, bound to take legislative action, the Federal Government shall bring such articles with a favourable recommendation to the notice of the appropriate authorities of states, provinces or cantons at the earliest possible moment;

(c) A Federal State Party to the present Protocol shall, at the request of any other state party hereto transmitted through the Secretary-General of the United Nations, supply a statement of the law and practice of the Federation and its constituent units in regard to any particular provision of the Convention to be applied in accordance with Article I, paragraph 1, of the present Protocol, showing the extent to which effect has been given to that provision by legislative or other action.

Article VII Reservations and declarations

1   At the time of accession, any state may make reservations in respect of Article IV of the present Protocol and in respect of the application in accordance with Article I of the present Protocol of any provisions of the Convention other than those contained in Articles 1, 3, 4, 16(1) and 33 thereof, provided that in the case of a state party to the Convention reservations made under this Article shall not extend to refugees in respect of whom the Convention applies.

2   Reservations made by states parties to the Convention in accordance with Article 42 thereof shall, unless withdrawn, be applicable in relation to their obligations under the present Protocol.

3   Any state making a reservation in accordance with paragraph 1 of this Article may at any time withdraw such reservation by a communication to that effect addressed to the Secretary-General of the United Nations.

4   Declarations made under Article 40, paragraphs 1 and 2, of the Convention by a state party thereto which accedes to the present Protocol shall be deemed to apply in respect of the present Protocol, unless upon accession a notification to the contrary is addressed by the state party concerned to the Secretary-General of the United Nations. The provisions of Article 40, paragraphs 2 and 3, and of Article 44, paragraph 3, of the Convention shall be deemed to apply *mutatis mutandis* to the present Protocol.

Article VIII Entry into force

1 The present Protocol shall come into force on the day of deposit of the sixth instrument of accession.

2 For each state acceding to the Protocol after the deposit of the sixth instrument of accession, the Protocol shall come into force on the date of deposit by such state of its instrument of accession.

Article IX Denunciation

1 Any state party hereto may denounce this Protocol at any time by a notification addressed to the Secretary-General of the United Nations.

2 Such denunciation shall take effect for the state party concerned one year from the date on which it is received by the Secretary-General of the United Nations.

Article X Notifications by the Secretary-General of the United Nations

The Secretary-General of the United Nations shall inform the states referred to in Article V above of the date of entry into force, accessions, reservations and withdrawals of reservations to and denunciations of the present Protocol, and of declarations and notifications relating hereto.

Article XI Deposit in the archives of the Secretariat of the United Nations

A copy of the present Protocol, of which the Chinese, English, French, Russian and Spanish texts are equally authentic, signed by the President of the General Assembly and by the Secretary-General of the United Nations, shall be deposited in the archives of the Secretariat of the United Nations. The Secretary-General will transmit certified copies thereof to all states members of the United Nations and to the other states referred to in Article V above.

APPENDIX

GENERAL ASSEMBLY RESOLUTION 2198 (XXI)

Protocol relating to the Status of Refugees

The General Assembly,

Considering that the Convention relating to the Status of Refugees, signed at Geneva on 28 July 1951[1], covers only those persons who have become refugees as a result of events occurring before 1 January 1951,

Considering that new refugee situations have arisen since the Convention was adopted and that the refugees concerned may therefore not fall within the scope of the Convention,

Considering that it is desirable that equal status should be enjoyed by all refugees covered by the definition in the Convention, irrespective of the date-line of 1 January 1951,

Taking note of the recommendation of the Executive Committee of the Programme of the United Nations High Commissioner for Refugees[2] that the draft Protocol relating to the Status of Refugees should be submitted to the General Assembly after consideration by the Economic and Social Council, in order that the Secretary-General might be authorised to open the Protocol for accession by Governments within the shortest possible time,

Considering that the Economic and Social Council, in its resolution 1186 (XLI) of 18 November 1966, took note with approval of the draft Protocol contained in the addendum to the report of the United Nations High Commissioner for Refugees and concerning measures to extend the personal scope of the Convention[3] and transmitted the addendum to the General Assembly,

1 *Takes note* of the Protocol relating to the Status of Refugees, the text of which is contained in the addendum to the report of the United Nations High Commissioner for Refugees;

2 *Requests* the Secretary-General to transmit the text of the Protocol to the States mentioned in article V thereof, with a view to enabling them to accede to the Protocol[4].

1495th plenary meeting,

16 December 1966.

Notes

[1]   United Nations, *Treaty Series*, vol 189 (1954), No 2545.

[2]   See A/6311/Rev 1/Add 1, part two, para 38.

[3]   *Ibid*, part one, para 2.

[4]   The Protocol was signed by the President of the General Assembly and by the Secretary-General on 31 January 1967.

Convention relating to the status of refugees, 28 July 1951 (UNTS, vol 189, p 137); entry into force: 22 April 1954.

UK GOVERNMENT RESERVATION TO THE 1951 CONVENTION RELATING TO THE STATUS OF REFUGEES

(i)   The Government of the United Kingdom of Great Britain and Northern Ireland understand articles 8 and 9 as not preventing them from taking in time of war or other grave and exceptional circumstances measures in the interests of national security in the case of a refugee on the ground of his nationality. The provision of article 8 shall not prevent the Government of the United Kingdom of Great Britain and Northern Ireland from exercising any rights over property or interests which they may acquire or have acquired as an Allied or Associated Power under a Treaty of Peace or other agreement or arrangement for the restoration of peace which has been or may be completed as a result of the Second World War. Furthermore, the provision of article 8 shall not affect the treatment to be accorded to any property or interests which, at the date of entry into force of this Convention for the United Kingdom of Great Britain and Northern Ireland, are under the control of the Government of the United Kingdom of Great Britain and Northern Ireland by reason of a state of war which exists or existed between them and any other state.

(ii)   The Government of the United Kingdom of Great Britain and Northern Ireland accept article 17, paragraph 2, with the substitution of 'four years' for 'three years' in subparagraph (a) and with the omission of subparagraph (c).

(iii)   The Government of the United Kingdom of Great Britain and Northern Ireland cannot undertake to give effect to the obligations contained in article 25, paragraphs 1 and 2, and can only undertake to apply the provision of paragraph 3 so far as the law allows.

UK GOVERNMENT COMMENTARY:

In connection with article 24, paragraph 1, subparagraph (b) relating to certain matters within the scope of the National Health Service, the National Health Service (Amendment) Act, 1949, contains powers for charges to be made to persons not ordinarily resident in Great Britain (which category would include refugees) who receive treatment under the Service. While these powers have not yet been exercised it is possible that this might have to be done at some future date. In Northern Ireland the Health Services are restricted to persons ordinarily resident in the country except where regulations are made to extend the Service to others. It is for these reasons that the Government of the United Kingdom while they are prepared in the future, as in the past, to give the most sympathetic consideration to the situation of refugees, find it necessary to make a reservation to article 24, paragraph 1, subparagraph (b), of the Convention.

The scheme of Industrial Injuries Insurance in Great Britain does not meet the requirements of article 24, paragraph 2, of the Convention. Where an insured person has died as the result of an industrial accident or a disease due to the nature of his employment, benefit cannot generally be paid to his dependants who are abroad unless they are in any part of the British Commonwealth, in the Irish Republic or in a country with which the United Kingdom has made a reciprocal agreement concerning the payment of industrial injury benefits. There is an exception to this rule in favour of the dependants of certain seamen who die as a result of industrial accidents happening to them while they are in the service of British ships. In this matter refugees are treated in the same way as citizens of the United Kingdom and Colonies and by reason of article 24, paragraphs 3 and 4, of the Convention, the dependants of refugees will be able to take advantage of reciprocal agreements which provide for the payment of United Kingdom industrial injury benefits in other countries. By reason of article 24, paragraphs 3 and 4, refugees will enjoy under the scheme of National Insurance and Industrial Injuries Insurance certain rights which are withheld from British subjects who are not citizens of the United Kingdom and Colonies.

No arrangements exist in the United Kingdom for the administrative assistance for which provision is made in article 25 nor have any such arrangements been found necessary in the case of refugees. Any need for the documents or certifications mentioned in paragraph 2 of that article would be met by affidavits.

UNITED NATIONS CONVENTION ON THE RIGHTS OF THE CHILD

Adopted and opened for signature, ratification and accession by General Assembly Resolution 44/25 of 20 November 1989

Entry into force: 2 September 1990, in accordance with Article 49.

Preamble

THE STATES PARTIES TO THE PRESENT CONVENTION,

Considering that, in accordance with the principles proclaimed in the Charter of the United Nations, recognition of the inherent dignity and of the equal and inalienable rights of all members of the human family is the foundation of freedom, justice and peace in the world,

Bearing in mind that the peoples of the United Nations have, in the Charter, reaffirmed their faith in fundamental human rights and in the dignity and worth of the human person, and have determined to promote social progress and better standards of life in larger freedom,

Recognizing that the United Nations has, in the Universal Declaration of Human Rights and in the International Covenants on Human Rights, proclaimed and agreed that everyone is entitled to all the rights and freedoms set forth therein, without distinction of any kind, such as race, colour, sex, language, religion, political or other opinion, national or social origin, property, birth or other status,

Recalling that, in the Universal Declaration of Human Rights, the United Nations has proclaimed that childhood is entitled to special care and assistance,

Convinced that the family, as the fundamental group of society and the natural environment for the growth and well-being of all its members and particularly children, should be afforded the necessary protection and assistance so that it can fully assume its responsibilities within the community,

Recognizing that the child, for the full and harmonious development of his or her personality, should grow up in a family environment, in an atmosphere of happiness, love and understanding,

Considering that the child should be fully prepared to live an individual life in society, and brought up in the spirit of the ideals proclaimed in the Charter of the United Nations, and in particular in the spirit of peace, dignity, tolerance, freedom, equality and solidarity,

Bearing in mind that the need to extend particular care to the child has been stated in the Geneva Declaration of the Rights of the Child of 1924 and in the Declaration of the Rights of the Child adopted by the General Assembly on 20 November 1959 and recognized in the Universal Declaration of Human Rights, in the International Covenant on Civil and Political Rights (in particular in Articles 23 and 24), in the International Covenant on Economic, Social and Cultural Rights (in particular in Article 10) and in the statutes and relevant instruments of specialized agencies and international organizations concerned with the welfare of children,

Bearing in mind that, as indicated in the Declaration of the Rights of the Child, "the child, by reason of his physical and mental immaturity, needs special safeguards and care, including appropriate legal protection, before as well as after birth",

Recalling the provisions of the Declaration on Social and Legal Principles relating to the Protection and Welfare of Children, with Special Reference to Foster Placement and Adoption Nationally and Internationally; the United Nations Standard Minimum Rules for the Administration of Juvenile Justice (The Beijing Rules); and the Declaration on the Protection of Women and Children in Emergency and Armed Conflict, Recognizing that, in all countries in the world, there are children living in exceptionally difficult conditions, and that such children need special consideration,

Taking due account of the importance of the traditions and cultural values of each people for the protection and harmonious development of the child, Recognizing the importance of international cooperation for improving the living conditions of children in every country, in particular in the developing countries,

HAVE AGREED AS FOLLOWS:

PART I

Article 1
For the purposes of the present Convention, a child means every human being below the age of 18 years unless under the law applicable to the child, majority is attained earlier.

Article 2
1. States Parties shall respect and ensure the rights set forth in the present Convention to each child within their jurisdiction without discrimination of any kind, irrespective of the child's or his or her parent's or legal guardian's race, colour, sex, language, religion, political or other opinion, national, ethnic or social origin, property, disability, birth or other status.
2. States Parties shall take all appropriate measures to ensure that the child is protected against all forms of discrimination or punishment on the basis of the status, activities, expressed opinions, or beliefs of the child's parents, legal guardians, or family members.

Article 3
1. In all actions concerning children, whether undertaken by public or private social welfare institutions, courts of law, administrative authorities or legislative bodies, the best interests of the child shall be a primary consideration.
2. States Parties undertake to ensure the child such protection and care as is necessary for his or her well-being, taking into account the rights and duties of his or her parents, legal guardians, or other individuals legally responsible for him or her, and, to this end, shall take all appropriate legislative and administrative measures.
3. States Parties shall ensure that the institutions, services and facilities responsible for the care or protection of children shall conform with the standards established by

competent authorities, particularly in the areas of safety, health, in the number and suitability of their staff, as well as competent supervision.

Article 4

States Parties shall undertake all appropriate legislative, administrative, and other measures for the implementation of the rights recognized in the present Convention. With regard to economic, social and cultural rights, States Parties shall undertake such measures to the maximum extent of their available resources and, where needed, within the framework of international co-operation.

Article 5

States Parties shall respect the responsibilities, rights and duties of parents or, where applicable, the members of the extended family or community as provided for by local custom, legal guardians or other persons legally responsible for the child, to provide, in a manner consistent with the evolving capacities of the child, appropriate direction and guidance in the exercise by the child of the rights recognized in the present Convention.

Article 6

1. States Parties recognize that every child has the inherent right to life.
2. States Parties shall ensure to the maximum extent possible the survival and development of the child.

Article 7

1. The child shall be registered immediately after birth and shall have the right from birth to a name, the right to acquire a nationality and. as far as possible, the right to know and be cared for by his or her parents.
2. States Parties shall ensure the implementation of these rights in accordance with their national law and their obligations under the relevant international instruments in this field, in particular where the child would otherwise be stateless.

Article 8

1. States Parties undertake to respect the right of the child to preserve his or her identity, including nationality, name and family relations as recognized by law without unlawful interference.
2. Where a child is illegally deprived of some or all of the elements of his or her identity, States Parties shall provide appropriate assistance and protection, with a view to re-establishing speedily his or her identity.

Article 9

1. States Parties shall ensure that a child shall not be separated from his or her parents against their will, except when competent authorities subject to judicial review determine, in accordance with applicable law and procedures, that such separation is necessary for the best interests of the child. Such determination may be necessary in a particular case such as one involving abuse or neglect of the child by the parents, or one where the parents are living separately and a decision must be made as to the child's place of residence.
2. In any proceedings pursuant to paragraph 1 of the present article, all interested parties shall be given an opportunity to participate in the proceedings and make their views known.
3. States Parties shall respect the right of the child who is separated from one or both parents to maintain personal relations and direct contact with both parents on a regular basis, except if it is contrary to the child's best interests.
4. Where such separation results from any action initiated by a State Party, such as the detention, imprisonment, exile, deportation or death (including death arising from any cause while the person is in the custody of the State) of one or both parents or of

the child, that State Party shall, upon request, provide the parents, the child or, if appropriate, another member of the family with the essential information concerning the whereabouts of the absent member(s) of the family unless the provision of the information would be detrimental to the well-being of the child. States Parties shall further ensure that the submission of such a request shall of itself entail no adverse consequences for the person(s) concerned.

Article 10

1. In accordance with the obligation of States Parties under Article 9, paragraph 1, applications by a child or his or her parents to enter or leave a State Party for the purpose of family reunification shall be dealt with by States Parties in a positive, humane and expeditious manner. States Parties shall further ensure that the submission of such a request shall entail no adverse consequences for the applicants and for the members of their family.

2. A child whose parents reside in different States shall have the right to maintain on a regular basis, save in exceptional circumstances personal relations and direct contacts with both parents. Towards that end and in accordance with the obligation of States Parties under Article 9, paragraph 1, States Parties shall respect the right of the child and his or her parents to leave any country, including their own, and to enter their own country. The right to leave any country shall be subject only to such restrictions as are prescribed by law and which are necessary to protect the national security, public order (*ordre public*), public health or morals or the rights and freedoms of others and are consistent with the other rights recognized in the present Convention.

Article 11

1. States Parties shall take measures to combat the illicit transfer and non-return of children abroad.

2. To this end, States Parties shall promote the conclusion of bilateral or multilateral agreements or accession to existing agreements.

Article 12

1. States Parties shall assure to the child who is capable of forming his or her own views the right to express those views freely in all matters affecting the child, the views of the child being given due weight in accordance with the age and maturity of the child.

2. For this purpose, the child shall in particular be provided the opportunity to be heard in any judicial and administrative proceedings affecting the child, either directly, or through a representative or an appropriate body, in a manner consistent with the procedural rules of national law.

Article 13

1. The child shall have the right to freedom of expression; this right shall include freedom to seek, receive and impart information and ideas of all kinds, regardless of frontiers, either orally, in writing or in print, in the form of art, or through any other media of the child's choice.

2. The exercise of this right may be subject to certain restrictions, but these shall only be such as are provided by law and are necessary:

  (a) For respect of the rights or reputations of others; or
  (b) For the protection of national security or of public order (*ordre public*), or of public health or morals.

Article 14

1. States Parties shall respect the right of the child to freedom of thought, conscience and religion.

2. States Parties shall respect the rights and duties of the parents and, when applicable, legal guardians, to provide direction to the child in the exercise of his or her right in a manner consistent with the evolving capacities of the child.

3. Freedom to manifest one's religion or beliefs may be subject only to such limitations as are prescribed by law and are necessary to protect public safety, order, health or morals, or the fundamental rights and freedoms of others.

Article 15

1. States Parties recognize the rights of the child to freedom of association and to freedom of peaceful assembly.

2. No restrictions may be placed on the exercise of these rights other than those imposed in conformity with the law and which are necessary in a democratic society in the interests of national security or public safety, public order (*ordre public*), the protection of public health or morals or the protection of the rights and freedoms of others.

Article 16

1. No child shall be subjected to arbitrary or unlawful interference with his or her privacy, family, home or correspondence, nor to unlawful attacks on his or her honour and reputation.

2. The child has the right to the protection of the law against such interference or attacks.

Article 17

States Parties recognize the important function performed by the mass media and shall ensure that the child has access to information and material from a diversity of national and international sources, especially those aimed at the promotion of his or her social, spiritual and moral well-being and physical and mental health.

To this end, States Parties shall:

   (a)   Encourage the mass media to disseminate information and material of social and cultural benefit to the child and in accordance with the spirit of Article 29;

   (b)   Encourage international co-operation in the production, exchange and dissemination of such information and material from a diversity of cultural, national and international sources;

   (c)   Encourage the production and dissemination of children's books;

   (d)   Encourage the mass media to have particular regard to the linguistic needs of the child who belongs to a minority group or who is indigenous;

   (e)   Encourage the development of appropriate guidelines for the protection of the child from information and material injurious to his or her well-being, bearing in mind the provisions of Articles 13 and 18.

Article 18

1. States Parties shall use their best efforts to ensure recognition of the principle that both parents have common responsibilities for the upbringing and development of the child. Parents or, as the case may be, legal guardians, have the primary responsibility for the upbringing and development of the child. The best interests of the child will be their basic concern.

2. For the purpose of guaranteeing and promoting the rights set forth in the present Convention, States Parties shall render appropriate assistance to parents and legal guardians in the performance of their child-rearing responsibilities and shall ensure the development of institutions, facilities and services for the care of children.

3. States Parties shall take all appropriate measures to ensure that children of working parents have the right to benefit from child-care services and facilities for which they are eligible.

Article 19

1. States Parties shall take all appropriate legislative, administrative, social and educational measures to protect the child from all forms of physical or mental violence, injury or abuse, neglect or negligent treatment, maltreatment or exploitation, including sexual abuse, while in the care of parent(s), legal guardian(s) or any other person who has the care of the child.

2. Such protective measures should, as appropriate, include effective procedures for the establishment of social programmes to provide necessary support for the child and for those who have the care of the child, as well as for other forms of prevention and for identification, reporting, referral, investigation, treatment and follow-up of instances of child maltreatment described heretofore, and, as appropriate, for judicial involvement.

Article 20

1. A child temporarily or permanently deprived of his or her family environment, or in whose own best interests cannot be allowed to remain in that environment, shall be entitled to special protection and assistance provided by the State.

2. States Parties shall in accordance with their national laws ensure alternative care for such a child.

3. Such care could include, inter alia, foster placement, *kafalah* of Islamic law, adoption or if necessary placement in suitable institutions for the care of children. When considering solutions, due regard shall be paid to the desirability of continuity in a child's upbringing and to the child's ethnic, religious, cultural and linguistic background.

Article 21

States Parties that recognize and/or permit the system of adoption shall ensure that the best interests of the child shall be the paramount consideration and they shall:

(a) Ensure that the adoption of a child is authorized only by competent authorities who determine, in accordance with applicable law and procedures and on the basis of all pertinent and reliable information, that the adoption is permissible in view of the child's status concerning parents, relatives and legal guardians and that, if required, the persons concerned have given their informed consent to the adoption on the basis of such counselling as may be necessary;

(b) Recognize that inter-country adoption may be considered as an alternative means of child's care, if the child cannot be placed in a foster or an adoptive family or cannot in any suitable manner be cared for in the child's country of origin;

(c) Ensure that the child concerned by inter-country adoption enjoys safeguards and standards equivalent to those existing in the case of national adoption;

(d) Take all appropriate measures to ensure that, in inter-country adoption, the placement does not result in improper financial gain for those involved in it;

(e) Promote, where appropriate, the objectives of the present article by concluding bilateral or multilateral arrangements or agreements, and endeavour, within this framework, to ensure that the placement of the child in another country is carried out by competent authorities or organs.

Article 22

1. States Parties shall take appropriate measures to ensure that a child who is seeking refugee status or who is considered a refugee in accordance with applicable international or domestic law and procedures shall, whether unaccompanied or

accompanied by his or her parents or by any other person, receive appropriate protection and humanitarian assistance in the enjoyment of applicable rights set forth in the present Convention and in other international human rights or humanitarian instruments to which the said States are Parties.

2. For this purpose, States Parties shall provide, as they consider appropriate, co-operation in any efforts by the United Nations and other competent intergovernmental organisations or nongovernmental organisations co-operating with the United Nations to protect and assist such a child and to trace the parents or other members of the family of any refugee child in order to obtain information necessary for reunification with his or her family. In cases where no parents or other members of the family can be found, the child shall be accorded the same protection as any other child permanently or temporarily deprived of his or her family environment for any reason, as set forth in the present Convention.

Article 23

1. States Parties recognize that a mentally or physically disabled child should enjoy a full and decent life, in conditions which ensure dignity, promote self-reliance and facilitate the child's active participation in the community.

2. States Parties recognize the right of the disabled child to special care and shall encourage and ensure the extension, subject to available resources, to the eligible child and those responsible for his or her care, of assistance for which application is made and which is appropriate to the child's condition and to the circumstances of the parents or others caring for the child.

3. Recognizing the special needs of a disabled child, assistance extended in accordance with paragraph 2 of the present article shall be provided free of charge, whenever possible, taking into account the financial resources of the parents or others caring for the child, and shall be designed to ensure that the disabled child has effective access to and receives education, training, health care services, rehabilitation services, preparation for employment and recreation opportunities in a manner conducive to the child's achieving the fullest possible social integration and individual development, including his or her cultural and spiritual development.

4. States Parties shall promote, in the spirit of international cooperation, the exchange of appropriate information in the field of preventive health care and of medical, psychological and functional treatment of disabled children, including dissemination of and access to information concerning methods of rehabilitation, education and vocational services, with the aim of enabling States Parties to improve their capabilities and skills and to widen their experience in these areas. In this regard, particular account shall be taken of the needs of developing countries.

Article 24

1. States Parties recognize the right of the child to the enjoyment of the highest attainable standard of health and to facilities for the treatment of illness and rehabilitation of health. States Parties shall strive to ensure that no child is deprived of his or her right of access to such health care services.

2. States Parties shall pursue full implementation of this right and, in particular, shall take appropriate measures:

(a) To diminish infant and child mortality;

(b) To ensure the provision of necessary medical assistance and health care to all children with emphasis on the development of primary health care;

(c) To combat disease and malnutrition, including within the framework of primary health care, through, *inter alia*, the application of readily available technology and through the provision of adequate nutritious foods and clean drinking-water, taking into consideration the dangers and risks of environmental pollution;

(d) To ensure appropriate pre-natal and post-natal health care for mothers;

(e)   To ensure that all segments of society, in particular parents and children, are informed, have access to education and are supported in the use of basic knowledge of child health and nutrition, the advantages of breastfeeding, hygiene and environmental sanitation and the prevention of accidents;

(f)   To develop preventive health care, guidance for parents and family planning education and services.

3. States Parties shall take all effective and appropriate measures with a view to abolishing traditional practices prejudicial to the health of children.

4. States Parties undertake to promote and encourage international co-operation with a view to achieving progressively the full realization of the right recognized in the present article. In this regard, particular account shall be taken of the needs of developing countries.

Article 25

States Parties recognize the right of a child who has been placed by the competent authorities for the purposes of care, protection or treatment of his or her physical or mental health, to a periodic review of the treatment provided to the child and all other circumstances relevant to his or her placement.

Article 26

1. States Parties shall recognize for every child the right to benefit from social security, including social insurance, and shall take the necessary measures to achieve the full realization of this right in accordance with their national law.

2. The benefits should, where appropriate, be granted, taking into account the resources and the circumstances of the child and persons having responsibility for the maintenance of the child, as well as any other consideration relevant to an application for benefits made by or on behalf of the child.

Article 27

1. States Parties recognize the right of every child to a standard of living adequate for the child's physical, mental, spiritual, moral and social development.

2. The parent(s) or others responsible for the child have the primary responsibility to secure, within their abilities and financial capacities, the conditions of living necessary for the child's development.

3. States Parties, in accordance with national conditions and within their means, shall take appropriate measures to assist parents and others responsible for the child to implement this right and shall in case of need provide material assistance and support programmes, particularly with regard to nutrition, clothing and housing.

4. States Parties shall take all appropriate measures to secure the recovery of maintenance for the child from the parents or other persons having financial responsibility for the child, both within the State Party and from abroad. In particular, where the person having financial responsibility for the child lives in a State different from that of the child, States Parties shall promote the accession to international agreements or the conclusion of such agreements, as well as the making of other appropriate arrangements.

Article 28

1. States Parties recognize the right of the child to education, and with a view to achieving this right progressively and on the basis of equal opportunity, they shall, in particular:

(a)   Make primary education compulsory and available free to all;

(b)   Encourage the development of different forms of secondary education, including general and vocational education, make them available and accessible to every child, and take appropriate measures such as the introduction of free education and offering financial assistance in case of need;

(c)   Make higher education accessible to all on the basis of capacity by every appropriate means;

(d)   Make educational and vocational information and guidance available and accessible to all children;

(e)   Take measures to encourage regular attendance at schools and the reduction of drop-out rates.

2.   States Parties shall take all appropriate measures to ensure that school discipline is administered in a manner consistent with the child's human dignity and in conformity with the present Convention.

3.   States Parties shall promote and encourage international cooperation in matters relating to education, in particular with a view to contributing to the elimination of ignorance and illiteracy throughout the world and facilitating access to scientific and technical knowledge and modern teaching methods. In this regard, particular account shall be taken of the needs of developing countries.

Article 29

1.   States Parties agree that the education of the child shall be directed to:

(a)   The development of the child's personality, talents and mental and physical abilities to their fullest potential;

(b)   The development of respect for human rights and fundamental freedoms, and for the principles enshrined in the Charter of the United Nations;

(c)   The development of respect for the child's parents, his or her own cultural identity, language and values, for the national values of the country in which the child is living, the country from which he or she may originate, and for civilizations different from his or her own;

(d)   The preparation of the child for responsible life in a free society, in the spirit of understanding, peace, tolerance, equality of sexes, and friendship among all peoples, ethnic, national and religious groups and persons of indigenous origin;

(e)   The development of respect for the natural environment.

2.   No part of the present article or Article 28 shall be construed so as to interfere with the liberty of individuals and bodies to establish and direct educational institutions, subject always to the observance of the principle set forth in paragraph 1 of the present article and to the requirements that the education given in such institutions shall conform to such minimum standards as may be laid down by the State.

Article 30

In those States in which ethnic, religious or linguistic minorities or persons of indigenous origin exist, a child belonging to such a minority or who is indigenous shall not be denied the right, in community with other members of his or her group, to enjoy his or her own culture, to profess and practise his or her own religion, or to use his or her own language.

Article 31

1.   States Parties recognize the right of the child to rest and leisure, to engage in play and recreational activities appropriate to the age of the child and to participate freely in cultural life and the arts.

2.   States Parties shall respect and promote the right of the child to participate fully in cultural and artistic life and shall encourage the provision of appropriate and equal opportunities for cultural, artistic, recreational and leisure activity.

Article 32

1. States Parties recognize the right of the child to be protected from economic exploitation and from performing any work that is likely to be hazardous or to interfere with the child's education, or to be harmful to the child's health or physical, mental, spiritual, moral or social development.

2. States Parties shall take legislative, administrative, social and educational measures to ensure the implementation of the present article. To this end, and having regard to the relevant provisions of other international instruments, States Parties shall in particular:

(a) Provide for a minimum age or minimum ages for admission to employment;

(b) Provide for appropriate regulation of the hours and conditions of employment;

(c) Provide for appropriate penalties or other sanctions to ensure the effective enforcement of the present article.

Article 33

States Parties shall take all appropriate measures, including legislative, administrative, social and educational measures, to protect children from the illicit use of narcotic drugs and psychotropic substances as defined in the relevant international treaties, and to prevent the use of children in the illicit production and trafficking of such substances.

Article 34

States Parties undertake to protect the child from all forms of sexual exploitation and sexual abuse. For these purposes, States Parties shall in particular take all appropriate national, bilateral and multilateral measures to prevent:

(a) The inducement or coercion of a child to engage in any unlawful sexual activity;

(b) The exploitative use of children in prostitution or other unlawful sexual practices;

(c) The exploitative use of children in pornographic performances and materials.

Article 35

States Parties shall take all appropriate national, bilateral and multilateral measures to prevent the abduction of, the sale of or traffic in children for any purpose or in any form.

Article 36

States Parties shall protect the child against all other forms of exploitation prejudicial to any aspects of the child's welfare.

Article 37

States Parties shall ensure that:

(a) No child shall be subjected to torture or other cruel, inhuman or degrading treatment or punishment. Neither capital punishment nor life imprisonment without possibility of release shall be imposed for offences committed by persons below eighteen years of age;

(b) No child shall be deprived of his or her liberty unlawfully or arbitrarily. The arrest, detention or imprisonment of a child shall be in conformity with the law and shall be used only as a measure of last resort and for the shortest appropriate period of time;

(c)   Every child deprived of liberty shall be treated with humanity and respect for the inherent dignity of the human person, and in a manner which takes into account the needs of persons of his or her age.

In particular, every child deprived of liberty shall be separated from adults unless it is considered in the child's best interest not to do so and shall have the right to maintain contact with his or her family through correspondence and visits, save in exceptional circumstances;

(d)   Every child deprived of his or her liberty shall have the right to prompt access to legal and other appropriate assistance, as well as the right to challenge the legality of the deprivation of his or her liberty before a court or other competent, independent and impartial authority, and to a prompt decision on any such action.

Article 38

1.   States Parties undertake to respect and to ensure respect for rules of international humanitarian law applicable to them in armed conflicts which are relevant to the child.

2.   States Parties shall take all feasible measures to ensure that persons who have not attained the age of 15 years do not take a direct part in hostilities.

3.   States Parties shall refrain from recruiting any person who has not attained the age of 15 years into their armed forces. In recruiting among those persons who have attained the age of 15 years but who have not attained the age of eighteen years, States Parties shall endeavour to give priority to those who are oldest.

4.   In accordance with their obligations under international humanitarian law to protect the civilian population in armed conflicts, States Parties shall take all feasible measures to ensure protection and care of children who are affected by an armed conflict.

Article 39

States Parties shall take all appropriate measures to promote physical and psychological recovery and social reintegration of a child victim of: any form of neglect, exploitation, or abuse; torture or any other form of cruel, inhuman or degrading treatment or punishment; or armed conflicts. Such recovery and reintegration shall take place in an environment which fosters the health, self-respect and dignity of the child.

Article 40

1.   States Parties recognize the right of every child alleged as, accused of, or recognized as having infringed the penal law to be treated in a manner consistent with the promotion of the child's sense of dignity and worth, which reinforces the child's respect for the human rights and fundamental freedoms of others and which takes into account the child's age and the desirability of promoting the child's reintegration and the child's assuming a constructive role in society.

2.   To this end, and having regard to the relevant provisions of international instruments, States Parties shall, in particular, ensure that:

(a)   No child shall be alleged as, be accused of, or recognized as having infringed the penal law by reason of acts or omissions that were not prohibited by national or international law at the time they were committed;

(b)   Every child alleged as or accused of having infringed the penal law has at least the following guarantees:

(i)   To be presumed innocent until proven guilty according to law;

(ii)   To be informed promptly and directly of the charges against him or her, and, if appropriate, through his or her parents or legal guardians, and to have legal or other appropriate assistance in the preparation and presentation of his or her defence;

3. A State Party which has submitted a comprehensive initial report to the Committee need not, in its subsequent reports submitted in accordance with paragraph 1 (b) of the present article, repeat basic information previously provided.

4. The Committee may request from States Parties further information relevant to the implementation of the Convention.

5. The Committee shall submit to the General Assembly, through the Economic and Social Council, every two years, reports on its activities.

6. States Parties shall make their reports widely available to the public in their own countries.

Article 45

In order to foster the effective implementation of the Convention and to encourage international cooperation in the field covered by the Convention:

(a) The specialized agencies, the United Nations Children's Fund, and other United Nations organs shall be entitled to be represented at the consideration of the implementation of such provisions of the present Convention as fall within the scope of their mandate. The Committee may invite the specialized agencies, the United Nations Children's Fund and other competent bodies as it may consider appropriate to provide expert advice on the implementation of the Convention in areas falling within the scope of their respective mandates. The Committee may invite the specialized agencies, the United Nations Children's Fund, and other United Nations organs to submit reports on the implementation of the Convention in areas falling within the scope of their activities;

(b) The Committee shall transmit, as it may consider appropriate, to the specialized agencies, the United Nations Children's Fund and other competent bodies, any reports from States Parties that contain a request, or indicate a need, for technical advice or assistance, along with the Committee's observations and suggestions, if any, on these requests or indications;

(c) The Committee may recommend to the General Assembly to request the Secretary-General to undertake on its behalf studies on specific issues relating to the rights of the child;

(d) The Committee may make suggestions and general recommendations based on information received pursuant to Articles 44 and 45 of the present Convention. Such suggestions and general recommendations shall be transmitted to any State Party concerned and reported to the General Assembly, together with comments, if any, from States Parties.

PART III

Article 46

The present Convention shall be open for signature by all States.

Article 47

The present Convention is subject to ratification. Instruments of ratification shall be deposited with the Secretary-General of the United Nations.

Article 48

The present Convention shall remain open for accession by any State. The instruments of accession shall be deposited with the Secretary-General of the United Nations.

Article 49

1. The present Convention shall enter into force on the thirtieth day following the date of deposit with the Secretary-General of the United Nations of the twentieth instrument of ratification or accession.

2. For each State ratifying or acceding to the Convention after the deposit of the twentieth instrument of ratification or accession, the Convention shall enter into force on the thirtieth day after the deposit by such State of its instrument of ratification or accession.

Article 50

1. Any State Party may propose an amendment and file it with the Secretary-General of the United Nations. The Secretary-General shall thereupon communicate the proposed amendment to States Parties, with a request that they indicate whether they favour a conference of States Parties for the purpose of considering and voting upon the proposals. In the event that, within four months from the date of such communication, at least one third of the States Parties favour such a conference, the Secretary-General shall convene the conference under the auspices of the United Nations. Any amendment adopted by a majority of States Parties present and voting at the conference shall be submitted to the General Assembly for approval.

2. An amendment adopted in accordance with paragraph 1 of the present article shall enter into force when it has been approved by the General Assembly of the United Nations and accepted by a two-thirds majority of States Parties.

3. When an amendment enters into force, it shall be binding on those States Parties which have accepted it, other States Parties still being bound by the provisions of the present Convention and any earlier amendments which they have accepted.

Article 51

1. The Secretary-General of the United Nations shall receive and circulate to all States the text of reservations made by States at the time of ratification or accession.

2. A reservation incompatible with the object and purpose of the present Convention shall not be permitted.

3. Reservations may be withdrawn at any time by notification to that effect addressed to the Secretary-General of the United Nations, who shall then inform all States. Such notification shall take effect on the date on which it is received by the Secretary-General

Article 52

A State Party may denounce the present Convention by written notification to the Secretary-General of the United Nations. Denunciation becomes effective one year after the date of receipt of the notification by the Secretary-General.

Article 53

The Secretary-General of the United Nations is designated as the depositary of the present Convention.

Article 54

The original of the present Convention, of which the Arabic, Chinese, English, French, Russian and Spanish texts are equally authentic, shall be deposited with the Secretary-General of the United Nations. IN WITNESS THEREOF the undersigned plenipotentiaries, being duly authorized thereto by their respective governments, have signed the present Convention.

COUNCIL OF EUROPE CONVENTION ON ACTION AGAINST TRAFFICKING IN HUMAN BEINGS

Warsaw 16 May 2005

Council of Europe Treaty Series – No. 197

Preamble

The member States of the Council of Europe and the other Signatories hereto,

Considering that the aim of the Council of Europe is to achieve a greater unity between its members;

Considering that trafficking in human beings constitutes a violation of human rights and an offence to the dignity and the integrity of the human being;

Considering that trafficking in human beings may result in slavery for victims;

Considering that respect for victims' rights, protection of victims and action to combat trafficking in human beings must be the paramount objectives;

Considering that all actions or initiatives against trafficking in human beings must be non-discriminatory, take gender equality into account as well as a child-rights approach;

Recalling the declarations by the Ministers for Foreign Affairs of the Member States at the 112th (14–15 May 2003) and the 114th (12–13 May 2004) Sessions of the Committee of Ministers calling for reinforced action by the Council of Europe on trafficking in human beings;

Bearing in mind the Convention for the Protection of Human Rights and Fundamental Freedoms (1950) and its protocols;

Bearing in mind the following recommendations of the Committee of Ministers to member states of the Council of Europe: Recommendation No. R (91) 11 on sexual exploitation, pornography and prostitution of, and trafficking in, children and young adults; Recommendation No. R (97) 13 concerning intimidation of witnesses and the rights of the defence; Recommendation No. R (2000) 11 on action against trafficking in human beings for the purpose of sexual exploitation and Recommendation Rec (2001) 16 on the protection of children against sexual exploitation; Recommendation Rec (2002) 5 on the protection of women against violence;

Bearing in mind the following recommendations of the Parliamentary Assembly of the Council of Europe: Recommendation 1325 (1997) on traffic in women and forced prostitution in Council of Europe member states; Recommendation 1450 (2000) on violence against women in Europe; Recommendation 1545 (2002) on a campaign against trafficking in women; Recommendation 1610 (2003) on migration connected with trafficking in women and prostitution; Recommendation 1611 (2003) on trafficking in organs in Europe; Recommendation 1663 (2004) Domestic slavery: servitude, au pairs and mail-order brides;

Bearing in mind the European Union Council Framework Decision of 19 July 2002 on combating trafficking in human beings, the European Union Council Framework Decision of 15 March 2001 on the standing of victims in criminal proceedings and the European Union Council Directive of 29 April 2004 on the residence permit issued to third-country nationals who are victims of trafficking in human beings or who have been the subject of an action to facilitate illegal immigration, who cooperate with the competent authorities;

Taking due account of the United Nations Convention against Transnational Organized Crime and the Protocol thereto to Prevent, Suppress and Punish Trafficking in Persons, Especially Women and Children with a view to improving the protection which they afford and developing the standards established by them;

Taking due account of the other international legal instruments relevant in the field of action against trafficking in human beings;

Taking into account the need to prepare a comprehensive international legal instrument focusing on the human rights of victims of trafficking and setting up a specific monitoring mechanism,

Have agreed as follows:

CHAPTER 1
PURPOSES, SCOPE, NON-DISCRIMINATION PRINCIPLE AND DEFINITIONS

Article (1) Purposes of the Convention

(1) The purposes of this Convention are:

(a) to prevent and combat trafficking in human beings, while guaranteeing gender equality;

(b) to protect the human rights of the victims of trafficking, design a comprehensive framework for the protection and assistance of victims and witnesses, while guaranteeing gender equality, as well as to ensure effective investigation and prosecution;

(c) to promote international cooperation on action against trafficking in human beings.

(2) In order to ensure effective implementation of its provisions by the Parties, this Convention sets up a specific monitoring mechanism.

Article 2 – Scope

This Convention shall apply to all forms of trafficking in human beings, whether national or transnational, whether or not connected with organised crime.

Article 3 – Non-discrimination principle

The implementation of the provisions of this Convention by Parties, in particular the enjoyment of measures to protect and promote the rights of victims, shall be secured without discrimination on any ground such as sex, race, colour, language, religion, political or other opinion, national or social origin, association with a national minority, property, birth or other status.

Article 4 – Definitions

For the purposes of this Convention:

(a) 'Trafficking in human beings' shall mean the recruitment, transportation, transfer, harbouring or receipt of persons, by means of the threat or use of force or other forms of coercion, of abduction, of fraud, of deception, of the abuse of power or of a position of vulnerability or of the giving or receiving of payments or benefits to achieve the consent of a person having control over another person, for the purpose of exploitation. Exploitation shall include, at a minimum, the exploitation of the prostitution of others or other forms of sexual exploitation, forced labour or services, slavery or practices similar to slavery, servitude or the removal of organs;

(b) The consent of a victim of 'trafficking in human beings' to the intended exploitation set forth in subparagraph (a) of this article shall be irrelevant where any of the means set forth in subparagraph (a) have been used;

(c) The recruitment, transportation, transfer, harbouring or receipt of a child for the purpose of exploitation shall be considered 'trafficking in human beings' even if this does not involve any of the means set forth in subparagraph (a) of this article;

(d) 'Child' shall mean any person under eighteen years of age;

(e) 'Victim' shall mean any natural person who is subject to trafficking in human beings as defined in this article.

CHAPTER II
PREVENTION, CO-OPERATION AND OTHER MEASURES

Article 5 – Prevention of trafficking in human beings

(1) Each Party shall take measures to establish or strengthen national co-ordination between the various bodies responsible for preventing and combating trafficking in human beings.

(2) Each Party shall establish and/or strengthen effective policies and programmes to prevent trafficking in human beings, by such means as: research, information, awareness raising and education campaigns, social and economic initiatives and training programmes, in particular for persons vulnerable to trafficking and for professionals concerned with trafficking in human beings.

(3) Each Party shall promote a Human Rights-based approach and shall use gender mainstreaming and a child-sensitive approach in the development, implementation and assessment of all the policies and programmes referred to in paragraph 2.

(4) Each Party shall take appropriate measures, as may be necessary, to enable migration to take place legally, in particular through dissemination of accurate information by relevant offices, on the conditions enabling the legal entry in and stay on its territory.

(5) Each Party shall take specific measures to reduce children's vulnerability to trafficking, notably by creating a protective environment for them.

(6) Measures established in accordance with this article shall involve, where appropriate, non-governmental organisations, other relevant organisations and other elements of civil society committed to the prevention of trafficking in human beings and victim protection or assistance.

Article 6 – Measures to discourage the demand

To discourage the demand that fosters all forms of exploitation of persons, especially women and children, that leads to trafficking, each Party shall adopt or strengthen legislative, administrative, educational, social, cultural or other measures including:

    (a)   research on best practices, methods and strategies;

    (b)   raising awareness of the responsibility and important role of media and civil society in identifying the demand as one of the root causes of trafficking in human beings;

    (c)   target information campaigns involving, as appropriate, inter alia, public authorities and policy makers;

    (d)   preventive measures, including educational programmes for boys and girls during their schooling, which stress the unacceptable nature of discrimination based on sex, and its disastrous consequences, the importance of gender equality and the dignity and integrity of every human being.

Article 7 – Border measures

(1) Without prejudice to international commitments in relation to the free movement of persons, Parties shall strengthen, to the extent possible, such border controls as may be necessary to prevent and detect trafficking in human beings.

(2) Each Party shall adopt legislative or other appropriate measures to prevent, to the extent possible, means of transport operated by commercial carriers from being used in the commission of offences established in accordance with this Convention.

(3) Where appropriate, and without prejudice to applicable international conventions, such measures shall include establishing the obligation of commercial

carriers, including any transportation company or the owner or operator of any means of transport, to ascertain that all passengers are in possession of the travel documents required for entry into the receiving State.

(4)   Each Party shall take the necessary measures, in accordance with its internal law, to provide for sanctions in cases of violation of the obligation set forth in paragraph 3 of this article.

(5)   Each Party shall adopt such legislative or other measures as may be necessary to permit, in accordance with its internal law, the denial of entry or revocation of visas of persons implicated in the commission of offences established in accordance with this Convention.

(6)   Parties shall strengthen co-operation among border control agencies by, *inter alia*, establishing and maintaining direct channels of communication.

Article 8 – Security and control of documents

Each Party shall adopt such measures as may be necessary:

(a)   To ensure that travel or identity documents issued by it are of such quality that they cannot easily be misused and cannot readily be falsified or unlawfully altered, replicated or issued; and

(b)   To ensure the integrity and security of travel or identity documents issued by or on behalf of the Party and to prevent their unlawful creation and issuance.

Article 9 – Legitimacy and validity of documents

At the request of another Party, a Party shall, in accordance with its internal law, verify within a reasonable time the legitimacy and validity of travel or identity documents issued or purported to have been issued in its name and suspected of being used for trafficking in human beings.

CHAPTER III
MEASURES TO PROTECT AND PROMOTE THE RIGHTS OF VICTIMS, GUARANTEEING GENDER EQUALITY

Article 10 – Identification of the victims

(1)   Each Party shall provide its competent authorities with persons who are trained and qualified in preventing and combating trafficking in human beings, in identifying and helping victims, including children, and shall ensure that the different authorities collaborate with each other as well as with relevant support organisations, so that victims can be identified in a procedure duly taking into account the special situation of women and child victims and, in appropriate cases, issued with residence permits under the conditions provided for in Article 14 of the present Convention.

(2)   Each Party shall adopt such legislative or other measures as may be necessary to identify victims as appropriate in collaboration with other Parties and relevant support organisations. Each Party shall ensure that, if the competent authorities have reasonable grounds to believe that a person has been victim of trafficking in human beings, that person shall not be removed from its territory until the identification process as victim of an offence provided for in Article 18 of this Convention has been completed by the competent authorities and shall likewise ensure that that person receives the assistance provided for in Article 12, paragraphs 1 and 2.

(3)   When the age of the victim is uncertain and there are reasons to believe that the victim is a child, he or she shall be presumed to be a child and shall be accorded special protection measures pending verification of his/her age.

(4)   As soon as an unaccompanied child is identified as a victim, each Party shall:

(a)   provide for representation of the child by a legal guardian, organisation or authority which shall act in the best interests of that child;

(b)   take the necessary steps to establish his/her identity and nationality;

(c)   make every effort to locate his/her family when this is in the best interests of the child.

Article 11 – Protection of private life

(1) Each Party shall protect the private life and identity of victims. Personal data regarding them shall be stored and used in conformity with the conditions provided for by the Convention for the Protection of Individuals with regard to Automatic Processing of Personal Data (ETS No. 108).

(2) Each Party shall adopt measures to ensure, in particular, that the identity, or details allowing the identification, of a child victim of trafficking are not made publicly known, through the media or by any other means, except, in exceptional circumstances, in order to facilitate the tracing of family members or otherwise secure the well-being and protection of the child.

(3) Each Party shall consider adopting, in accordance with Article 10 of the Convention for the Protection of Human Rights and Fundamental Freedoms as interpreted by the European Court of Human Rights, measures aimed at encouraging the media to protect the private life and identity of victims through self-regulation or through regulatory or co-regulatory measures.

Article 12 – Assistance to victims

Each Party shall adopt such legislative or other measures as may be necessary to assist victims in their physical, psychological and social recovery. Such assistance shall include at least:

(a)   standards of living capable of ensuring their subsistence, through such measures as: appropriate and secure accommodation, psychological and material assistance;

(b)   access to emergency medical treatment;

(c)   translation and interpretation services, when appropriate;

(d)   counselling and information, in particular as regards their legal rights and the services available to them, in a language that they can understand;

(e)   assistance to enable their rights and interests to be presented and considered at appropriate stages of criminal proceedings against offenders;

(f)   access to education for children.

(2) Each Party shall take due account of the victim's safety and protection needs.

(3) In addition, each Party shall provide necessary medical or other assistance to victims lawfully resident within its territory who do not have adequate resources and need such help.

(4) Each Party shall adopt the rules under which victims lawfully resident within its territory shall be authorised to have access to the labour market, to vocational training and education.

(5) Each Party shall take measures, where appropriate and under the conditions provided for by its internal law, to co-operate with non-governmental organisations, other relevant organisations or other elements of civil society engaged in assistance to victims.

(6) Each Party shall adopt such legislative or other measures as may be necessary to ensure that assistance to a victim is not made conditional on his or her willingness to act as a witness.

(7) For the implementation of the provisions set out in this article, each Party shall ensure that services are provided on a consensual and informed basis, taking due account of the special needs of persons in a vulnerable position and the rights of children in terms of accommodation, education and appropriate health care.

Article 13 – Recovery and reflection period

(1)   Each Party shall provide in its internal law a recovery and reflection period of at least 30 days, when there are reasonable grounds to believe that the person concerned is a victim. Such a period shall be sufficient for the person concerned to recover and escape the influence of traffickers and/or to take an informed decision on cooperating with the competent authorities. During this period it shall not be possible to enforce any expulsion order against him or her. This provision is without prejudice to the activities carried out by the competent authorities in all phases of the relevant national proceedings, and in particular when investigating and prosecuting the offences concerned. During this period, the Parties shall authorise the persons concerned to stay in their territory.

(2)   During this period, the persons referred to in paragraph 1 of this Article shall be entitled to the measures contained in Article 12, paragraphs 1 and 2.

(3)   The Parties are not bound to observe this period if grounds of public order prevent it or if it is found that victim status is being claimed improperly.

Article 14 – Residence permit

(1)   Each Party shall issue a renewable residence permit to victims, in one or other of the two following situations or in both:

    (a)   the competent authority considers that their stay is necessary owing to their personal situation;

    (b)   the competent authority considers that their stay is necessary for the purpose of their co-operation with the competent authorities in investigation or criminal proceedings.

(2)   The residence permit for child victims, when legally necessary, shall be issued in accordance with the best interests of the child and, where appropriate, renewed under the same conditions.

(3)   The non-renewal or withdrawal of a residence permit is subject to the conditions provided for by the internal law of the Party.

(4)   If a victim submits an application for another kind of residence permit, the Party concerned shall take into account that he or she holds, or has held, a residence permit in conformity with paragraph 1.

(5)   Having regard to the obligations of Parties to which Article 40 of this Convention refers, each Party shall ensure that granting of a permit according to this provision shall be without prejudice to the right to seek and enjoy asylum.

Article 15 – Compensation and legal redress

(1)   Each Party shall ensure that victims have access, as from their first contact with the competent authorities, to information on relevant judicial and administrative proceedings in a language which they can understand.

(2)   Each Party shall provide, in its internal law, for the right to legal assistance and to free legal aid for victims under the conditions provided by its internal law.

(3)   Each Party shall provide, in its internal law, for the right of victims to compensation from the perpetrators.

(4)   Each Party shall adopt such legislative or other measures as may be necessary to guarantee compensation for victims in accordance with the conditions under its internal law, for instance through the establishment of a fund for victim compensation or measures or programmes aimed at social assistance and social integration of victims, which could be funded by the assets resulting from the application of measures provided in Article 23.

Article 16 – Repatriation and return of victims

(1)   The Party of which a victim is a national or in which that person had the right of permanent residence at the time of entry into the territory of the receiving Party shall, with due regard for his or her rights, safety and dignity, facilitate and accept, his or her return without undue or unreasonable delay.

(2)   When a Party returns a victim to another State, such return shall be with due regard for the rights, safety and dignity of that person and for the status of any legal proceedings related to the fact that the person is a victim, and shall preferably be voluntary.

(3)   At the request of a receiving Party, a requested Party shall verify whether a person is its national or had the right of permanent residence in its territory at the time of entry into the territory of the receiving Party.

(4)   In order to facilitate the return of a victim who is without proper documentation, the Party of which that person is a national or in which he or she had the right of permanent residence at the time of entry into the territory of the receiving Party shall agree to issue, at the request of the receiving Party, such travel documents or other authorisation as may be necessary to enable the person to travel to and re-enter its territory.

(5)   Each Party shall adopt such legislative or other measures as may be necessary to establish repatriation programmes, involving relevant national or international institutions and non governmental organisations. These programmes aim at avoiding re-victimisation. Each Party should make its best effort to favour the reintegration of victims into the society of the State of return, including reintegration into the education system and the labour market, in particular through the acquisition and improvement of their professional skills. With regard to children, these programmes should include enjoyment of the right to education and measures to secure adequate care or receipt by the family or appropriate care structures.

(6)   Each Party shall adopt such legislative or other measures as may be necessary to make available to victims, where appropriate in co-operation with any other Party concerned, contact information of structures that can assist them in the country where they are returned or repatriated, such as law enforcement offices, non-governmental organisations, legal professions able to provide counselling and social welfare agencies.

(7)   Child victims shall not be returned to a State, if there is indication, following a risk and security assessment, that such return would not be in the best interests of the child.

Article 17 – Gender equality

Each Party shall, in applying measures referred to in this chapter, aim to promote gender equality and use gender mainstreaming in the development, implementation and assessment of the measures.

CHAPTER IV
SUBSTANTIVE CRIMINAL LAW

Article 18 – Criminalisation of trafficking in human beings

Each Party shall adopt such legislative and other measures as may be necessary to establish as criminal offences the conduct contained in article 4 of this Convention, when committed intentionally.

Article 19 – Criminalisation of the use of services of a victim

Each Party shall consider adopting such legislative and other measures as may be necessary to establish as criminal offences under its internal law, the use of services which are the object of exploitation as referred to in Article 4 paragraph a of this Convention, with the knowledge that the person is a victim of trafficking in human beings.

Article 20 – Criminalisation of acts relating to travel or identity documents

Each Party shall adopt such legislative and other measures as may be necessary to establish as criminal offences the following conducts, when committed intentionally and for the purpose of enabling the trafficking in human beings:

  (a)   forging a travel or identity document;

(b) procuring or providing such a document;

(c) retaining, removing, concealing, damaging or destroying a travel or identity document of another person.

Article 21 – Attempt and aiding or abetting

(1) Each Party shall adopt such legislative and other measures as may be necessary to establish as criminal offences when committed intentionally, aiding or abetting the commission of any of the offences established in accordance with Articles 18 and 20 of the present Convention.

(2) Each Party shall adopt such legislative and other measures as may be necessary to establish as criminal offences when committed intentionally, an attempt to commit the offences established in accordance with Articles 18 and 20, paragraph a, of this Convention.

Article 22 – Corporate liability

(1) Each Party shall adopt such legislative and other measures as may be necessary to ensure that a legal person can be held liable for a criminal offence established in accordance with this Convention, committed for its benefit by any natural person, acting either individually or as part of an organ of the legal person, who has a leading position within the legal person, based on:

(a) a power of representation of the legal person;

(b) an authority to take decisions on behalf of the legal person;

(c) an authority to exercise control within the legal person.

(2) Apart from the cases already provided for in paragraph 1, each Party shall take the measures necessary to ensure that a legal person can be held liable where the lack of supervision or control by a natural person referred to in paragraph 1 has made possible the commission of a criminal offence established in accordance with this Convention for the benefit of that legal person by a natural person acting under its authority.

(3) Subject to the legal principles of the Party, the liability of a legal person may be criminal, civil or administrative.

(4) Such liability shall be without prejudice to the criminal liability of the natural persons who have committed the offence.

Article 23 – Sanctions and measures

(1) Each Party shall adopt such legislative and other measures as may be necessary to ensure that the criminal offences established in accordance with Articles 18 to 21 are punishable by effective, proportionate and dissuasive sanctions. These sanctions shall include, for criminal offences established in accordance with Article 18 when committed by natural persons, penalties involving deprivation of liberty which can give rise to extradition.

(2) Each Party shall ensure that legal persons held liable in accordance with Article 22 shall be subject to effective, proportionate and dissuasive criminal or non-criminal sanctions or measures, including monetary sanctions.

(3) Each Party shall adopt such legislative and other measures as may be necessary to enable it to confiscate or otherwise deprive the instrumentalities and proceeds of criminal offences established in accordance with Articles 18 and 20, paragraph a, of this Convention, or property the value of which corresponds to such proceeds.

(4) Each Party shall adopt such legislative or other measures as may be necessary to enable the temporary or permanent closure of any establishment which was used to carry out trafficking in human beings, without prejudice to the rights of *bona fide* third parties or to deny the perpetrator, temporary or permanently, the exercise of the activity in the course of which this offence was committed.

Article 24 – Aggravating circumstances

Each Party shall ensure that the following circumstances are regarded as aggravating circumstances in the determination of the penalty for offences established in accordance with Article 18 of this Convention:

- (a) the offence deliberately or by gross negligence endangered the life of the victim;
- (b) the offence was committed against a child;
- (c) the offence was committed by a public official in the performance of her/his duties;
- (d) the offence was committed within the framework of a criminal organisation.

Article 25 – Previous convictions

Each Party shall adopt such legislative and other measures providing for the possibility to take into account final sentences passed by another Party in relation to offences established in accordance with this Convention when determining the penalty.

Article 26 – Non-punishment provision

Each Party shall, in accordance with the basic principles of its legal system, provide for the possibility of not imposing penalties on victims for their involvement in unlawful activities, to the extent that they have been compelled to do so.

CHAPTER V
INVESTIGATION, PROSECUTION AND PROCEDURAL LAW

Article 27 – Ex parte and ex officio applications

(1) Each Party shall ensure that investigations into or prosecution of offences established in accordance with this Convention shall not be dependent upon the report or accusation made by a victim, at least when the offence was committed in whole or in part on its territory.

(2) Each Party shall ensure that victims of an offence in the territory of a Party other than the one where they reside may make a complaint before the competent authorities of their State of residence. The competent authority to which the complaint is made, insofar as it does not itself have competence in this respect, shall transmit it without delay to the competent authority of the Party in the territory in which the offence was committed. The complaint shall be dealt with in accordance with the internal law of the Party in which the offence was committed.

(3) Each Party shall ensure, by means of legislative or other measures, in accordance with the conditions provided for by its internal law, to any group, foundation, association or non-governmental organisations which aims at fighting trafficking in human beings or protection of human rights, the possibility to assist and/or support the victim with his or her consent during criminal proceedings concerning the offence established in accordance with Article 18 of this Convention.

Article 28 – Protection of victims, witnesses and collaborators with the judicial authorities

(1) Each Party shall adopt such legislative or other measures as may be necessary to provide effective and appropriate protection from potential retaliation or intimidation in particular during and after investigation and prosecution of perpetrators, for:

- (a) Victims;
- (b) As appropriate, those who report the criminal offences established in accordance with Article 18 of this Convention or otherwise co-operate with the investigating or prosecuting authorities;
- (c) witnesses who give testimony concerning criminal offences established in accordance with Article 18 of this Convention;

(d)   when necessary, members of the family of persons referred to in subparagraphs a and c.

(2)   Each Party shall adopt such legislative or other measures as may be necessary to ensure and to offer various kinds of protection. This may include physical protection, relocation, identity change and assistance in obtaining jobs.

(3)   A child victim shall be afforded special protection measures taking into account the best interests of the child.

(4)   Each Party shall adopt such legislative or other measures as may be necessary to provide, when necessary, appropriate protection from potential retaliation or intimidation in particular during and after investigation and prosecution of perpetrators, for members of groups, foundations, associations or non-governmental organisations which carry out the activities set out in Article 27, paragraph 3.

(5)   Each Party shall consider entering into agreements or arrangements with other States for the implementation of this article.

Article 29 – Specialised authorities and co-ordinating bodies

(1)   Each Party shall adopt such measures as may be necessary to ensure that persons or entities are specialised in the fight against trafficking and the protection of victims. Such persons or entities shall have the necessary independence in accordance with the fundamental principles of the legal system of the Party, in order for them to be able to carry out their functions effectively and free from any undue pressure. Such persons or the staffs of such entities shall have adequate training and financial resources for their tasks.

(2)   Each Party shall adopt such measures as may be necessary to ensure co-ordination of the policies and actions of their governments' departments and other public agencies against trafficking in human beings, where appropriate, through setting up co-ordinating bodies.

(3)   Each Party shall provide or strengthen training for relevant officials in the prevention of and fight against trafficking in human beings, including Human Rights training. The training may be agency-specific and shall, as appropriate, focus on: methods used in preventing such trafficking, prosecuting the traffickers and protecting the rights of the victims, including protecting the victims from the traffickers.

(4)   Each Party shall consider appointing National Rapporteurs or other mechanisms for monitoring the anti-trafficking activities of State institutions and the implementation of national legislation requirements.

Article 30 – Court proceedings

In accordance with the Convention for the Protection of Human Rights and Fundamental Freedoms, in particular Article 6, each Party shall adopt such legislative or other measures as may be necessary to ensure in the course of judicial proceedings:

(a)   the protection of victims' private life and, where appropriate, identity;

(b)   victims' safety and protection from intimidation,

in accordance with the conditions under its internal law and, in the case of child victims, by taking special care of children's needs and ensuring their right to special protection measures.

Article 31 – Jurisdiction

(1)   Each Party shall adopt such legislative and other measures as may be necessary to establish jurisdiction over any offence established in accordance with this Convention, when the offence is committed:

(a)   in its territory; or

(b)   on board a ship flying the flag of that Party; or

(c)   on board an aircraft registered under the laws of that Party; or

(d)   by one of its nationals or by a stateless person who has his or her habitual residence in its territory, if the offence is punishable under criminal law where it was committed or if the offence is committed outside the territorial jurisdiction of any State;

(e)   against one of its nationals.

(2)   Each Party may, at the time of signature or when depositing its instrument of ratification, acceptance, approval or accession, by a declaration addressed to the Secretary General of the Council of Europe, declare that it reserves the right not to apply or to apply only in specific cases or conditions the jurisdiction rules laid down in paragraphs 1 (d) and (e) of this article or any part thereof.

(3)   Each Party shall adopt such measures as may be necessary to establish jurisdiction over the offences referred to in this Convention, in cases where an alleged offender is present in its territory and it does not extradite him/her to another Party, solely on the basis of his/her nationality, after a request for extradition.

(4)   When more than one Party claims jurisdiction over an alleged offence established in accordance with this Convention, the Parties involved shall, where appropriate, consult with a view to determining the most appropriate jurisdiction for prosecution.

(5)   Without prejudice to the general norms of international law, this Convention does not exclude any criminal jurisdiction exercised by a Party in accordance with internal law.

CHAPTER VI
INTERNATIONAL CO-OPERATION AND CO-OPERATION WITH CIVIL SOCIETY

Article 32 – General principles and measures for international co-operation

The Parties shall co-operate with each other, in accordance with the provisions of this Convention, and through application of relevant applicable international and regional instruments, arrangements agreed on the basis of uniform or reciprocal legislation and internal laws, to the widest extent possible, for the purpose of:

–   preventing and combating trafficking in human beings;
–   protecting and providing assistance to victims;
–   investigations or proceedings concerning criminal offences established in accordance with this Convention.

Article 33 – Measures relating to endangered or missing persons

(1)   When a Party, on the basis of the information at its disposal has reasonable grounds to believe that the life, the freedom or the physical integrity of a person referred to in Article 28, paragraph 1, is in immediate danger on the territory of another Party, the Party that has the information shall, in such a case of emergency, transmit it without delay to the latter so as to take the appropriate protection measures.

(2)   The Parties to this Convention may consider reinforcing their co-operation in the search for missing people, in particular for missing children, if the information available leads them to believe that she/he is a victim of trafficking in human beings. To this end, the Parties may conclude bilateral or multilateral treaties with each other.

Article 34 – Information

(1)   The requested Party shall promptly inform the requesting Party of the final result of the action taken under this chapter. The requested Party shall also promptly inform the requesting Party of any circumstances which render impossible the carrying out of the action sought or are likely to delay it significantly.

(2)   A Party may, within the limits of its internal law, without prior request, forward to another Party information obtained within the framework of its own investigations when it considers that the disclosure of such information might assist the receiving Party in initiating or carrying out investigations or proceedings concerning criminal offences established in accordance with this Convention or might lead to a request for co-operation by that Party under this chapter.

(3) Prior to providing such information, the providing Party may request that it be kept confidential or used subject to conditions. If the receiving Party cannot comply with such request, it shall notify the providing Party, which shall then determine whether the information should nevertheless be provided. If the receiving Party accepts the information subject to the conditions, it shall be bound by them.

(4) All information requested concerning Articles 13, 14 and 16, necessary to provide the rights conferred by these Articles, shall be transmitted at the request of the Party concerned without delay with due respect to Article 11 of the present Convention.

Article 35 – Co-operation with civil society

Each Party shall encourage state authorities and public officials, to co-operate with non-governmental organisations, other relevant organisations and members of civil society, in establishing strategic partnerships with the aim of achieving the purpose of this Convention.

CHAPTER VII
MONITORING MECHANISM

Article 36 – Group of experts on action against trafficking in human beings

(1) The Group of experts on action against trafficking in human beings (hereinafter referred to as 'GRETA'), shall monitor the implementation of this Convention by the Parties.

(2) GRETA shall be composed of a minimum of 10 members and a maximum of 15 members, taking into account a gender and geographical balance, as well as a multidisciplinary expertise. They shall be elected by the Committee of the Parties for a term of office of 4 years, renewable once, chosen from amongst nationals of the States Parties to this Convention.

(3) The election of the members of GRETA shall be based on the following principles:

(a) they shall be chosen from among persons of high moral character, known for their recognised competence in the fields of Human Rights, assistance and protection of victims and of action against trafficking in human beings or having professional experience in the areas covered by this Convention;

(b) they shall sit in their individual capacity and shall be independent and impartial in the exercise of their functions and shall be available to carry out their duties in an effective manner;

(c) no two members of GRETA may be nationals of the same State;

(d) they should represent the main legal systems.

(4) The election procedure of the members of GRETA shall be determined by the Committee of Ministers, after consulting with and obtaining the unanimous consent of the Parties to the Convention, within a period of one year following the entry into force of this Convention. GRETA shall adopt its own rules of procedure.

Article 37 – Committee of the Parties

(1) The Committee of the Parties shall be composed of the representatives on the Committee of Ministers of the Council of Europe of the member States Parties to the Convention and representatives of the Parties to the Convention, which are not members of the Council of Europe.

(2) The Committee of the Parties shall be convened by the Secretary General of the Council of Europe. Its first meeting shall be held within a period of one year following the entry into force of this Convention in order to elect the members of GRETA. It shall subsequently meet whenever one-third of the Parties, the President of GRETA or the Secretary General so requests.

(3) The Committee of the Parties shall adopt its own rules of procedure.

Article 38 – Procedure

(1) The evaluation procedure shall concern the Parties to the Convention and be divided in rounds, the length of which is determined by GRETA. At the beginning of each round GRETA shall select the specific provisions on which the evaluation procedure shall be based.

(2) GRETA shall define the most appropriate means to carry out this evaluation. GRETA may in particular adopt a questionnaire for each evaluation round, which may serve as a basis for the evaluation of the implementation by the Parties of the present Convention. Such a questionnaire shall be addressed to all Parties. Parties shall respond to this questionnaire, as well as to any other request of information from GRETA.

(3) GRETA may request information from civil society.

(4) GRETA may subsidiarily organise, in co-operation with the national authorities and the 'contact person' appointed by the latter, and, if necessary, with the assistance of independent national experts, country visits. During these visits, GRETA may be assisted by specialists in specific fields.

(5) GRETA shall prepare a draft report containing its analysis concerning the implementation of the provisions on which the evaluation is based, as well as its suggestions and proposals concerning the way in which the Party concerned may deal with the problems which have been identified. The draft report shall be transmitted for comments to the Party which undergoes the evaluation. Its comments are taken into account by GRETA when establishing its report.

(6) On this basis, GRETA shall adopt its report and conclusions concerning the measures taken by the Party concerned to implement the provisions of the present Convention. This report and conclusions shall be sent to the Party concerned and to the Committee of the Parties. The report and conclusions of GRETA shall be made public as from their adoption, together with eventual comments by the Party concerned.

(7) Without prejudice to the procedure of paragraphs 1 to 6 of this article, the Committee of the Parties may adopt, on the basis of the report and conclusions of GRETA, recommendations addressed to this Party (a) concerning the measures to be taken to implement the conclusions of GRETA, if necessary setting a date for submitting information on their implementation, and (b) aiming at promoting co-operation with that Party for the proper implementation of the present Convention.

CHAPTER VIII
RELATIONSHIP WITH OTHER INTERNATIONAL INSTRUMENTS

Article 39 – Relationship with the Protocol to prevent, suppress and punish trafficking in persons, especially women and children, supplementing the United Nations Convention against transnational organised crime

This Convention shall not affect the rights and obligations derived from the provisions of the Protocol to prevent, suppress and punish trafficking in persons, especially women and children, supplementing the United Nations Convention against transnational organised crime, and is intended to enhance the protection afforded by it and develop the standards contained therein.

Article 40 – Relationship with other international instruments

(1) This Convention shall not affect the rights and obligations derived from other international instruments to which Parties to the present Convention are Parties or shall become Parties and which contain provisions on matters governed by this Convention and which ensure greater protection and assistance for victims of trafficking.

(2) The Parties to the Convention may conclude bilateral or multilateral agreements with one another on the matters dealt with in this Convention, for purposes of

supplementing or strengthening its provisions or facilitating the application of the principles embodied in it.

(3)   Parties which are members of the European Union shall, in their mutual relations, apply Community and European Union rules in so far as there are Community or European Union rules governing the particular subject concerned and applicable to the specific case, without prejudice to the object and purpose of the present Convention and without prejudice to its full application with other Parties.

(4)   Nothing in this Convention shall affect the rights, obligations and responsibilities of States and individuals under international law, including international humanitarian law and international human rights law and, in particular, where applicable, the 1951 Convention and the 1967 Protocol relating to the Status of Refugees and the principle of *non-refoulement* as contained therein.

CHAPTER IX
AMENDMENTS TO THE CONVENTION

Article 41 – Amendments

(1)   Any proposal for an amendment to this Convention presented by a Party shall be communicated to the Secretary General of the Council of Europe and forwarded by him or her to the member States of the Council of Europe, any signatory, any State Party, the European Community, to any State invited to sign this Convention in accordance with the provisions of Article 42 and to any State invited to accede to this Convention in accordance with the provisions of Article 43.

(2)   Any amendment proposed by a Party shall be communicated to GRETA, which shall submit to the Committee of Ministers its opinion on that proposed amendment.

(3)   The Committee of Ministers shall consider the proposed amendment and the opinion submitted by GRETA and, following consultation of the Parties to this Convention and after obtaining their unanimous consent, may adopt the amendment.

(4)   The text of any amendment adopted by the Committee of Ministers in accordance with paragraph 3 of this article shall be forwarded to the Parties for acceptance.

(5)   Any amendment adopted in accordance with paragraph 3 of this article shall enter into force on the first day of the month following the expiration of a period of one month after the date on which all Parties have informed the Secretary General that they have accepted it.

CHAPTER X
FINAL CLAUSES

Article 42 – Signature and entry into force

(1)   This Convention shall be open for signature by the member States of the Council of Europe, the non member States which have participated in its elaboration and the European Community.

(2)   This Convention is subject to ratification, acceptance or approval. Instruments of ratification, acceptance or approval shall be deposited with the Secretary General of the Council of Europe.

(3)   This Convention shall enter into force on the first day of the month following the expiration of a period of three months after the date on which 10 Signatories, including at least 8 member States of the Council of Europe, have expressed their consent to be bound by the Convention in accordance with the provisions of the preceding paragraph.

(4)   In respect of any State mentioned in paragraph 1 or the European Community, which subsequently expresses its consent to be bound by it, the Convention shall enter

into force on the first day of the month following the expiration of a period of three months after the date of the deposit of its instrument of ratification, acceptance or approval.

Article 43 – Accession to the Convention

(1) After the entry into force of this Convention, the Committee of Ministers of the Council of Europe may, after consultation of the Parties to this Convention and obtaining their unanimous consent, invite any non-member State of the Council of Europe, which has not participated in the elaboration of the Convention, to accede to this Convention by a decision taken by the majority provided for in Article 20 *d.* of the Statute of the Council of Europe, and by unanimous vote of the representatives of the Contracting States entitled to sit on the Committee of Ministers.

(2) In respect of any acceding State, the Convention shall enter into force on the first day of the month following the expiration of a period of three months after the date of deposit of the instrument of accession with the Secretary General of the Council of Europe.

Article 44 – Territorial application

(1) Any State or the European Community may, at the time of signature or when depositing its instrument of ratification, acceptance, approval or accession, specify the territory or territories to which this Convention shall apply.

(2) Any Party may, at any later date, by a declaration addressed to the Secretary General of the Council of Europe, extend the application of this Convention to any other territory specified in the declaration and for whose international relations it is responsible or on whose behalf it is authorised to give undertakings. In respect of such territory, the Convention shall enter into force on the first day of the month following the expiration of a period of three months after the date of receipt of such declaration by the Secretary General.

(3) Any declaration made under the two preceding paragraphs may, in respect of any territory specified in such declaration, be withdrawn by a notification addressed to the Secretary General of the Council of Europe. The withdrawal shall become effective on the first day of the month following the expiration of a period of three months after the date of receipt of such notification by the Secretary General.

Article 45 – Reservations

No reservation may be made in respect of any provision of this Convention, with the exception of the reservation of Article 31, paragraph 2.

Article 46 – Denunciation

(1) Any Party may, at any time, denounce this Convention by means of a notification addressed to the Secretary General of the Council of Europe.

(2) Such denunciation shall become effective on the first day of the month following the expiration of a period of three months after the date of receipt of the notification by the Secretary General.

Article 47 – Notification

The Secretary General of the Council of Europe shall notify the member States of the Council of Europe, any State signatory, any State Party, the European Community, to any State invited to sign this Convention in accordance with the provisions of Article 42 and to any State invited to accede to this Convention in accordance with the provisions of Article 43 of:

    (a)   any signature;

    (b)   the deposit of any instrument of ratification, acceptance, approval or accession;

    (c)   any date of entry into force of this Convention in accordance with Articles 42 and 43;

(d) any amendment adopted in accordance with Article 41 and the date on which such an amendment enters into force;

(e) any denunciation made in pursuance of the provisions of Article 46;

(f) any other act, notification or communication relating to this Convention

(g) any reservation made under Article 45.

In witness whereof the undersigned, being duly authorised thereto, have signed this Convention.

Done at Warsaw, this 16th day of May 2005, in English and in French, both texts being equally authentic, in a single copy which shall be deposited in the archives of the Council of Europe. The Secretary General of the Council of Europe shall transmit certified copies to each member State of the Council of Europe, to the non-member States which have participated in the elaboration of this Convention, to the European Community and to any State invited to accede to this Convention.

GLOSSARY

AAPD	Asylum and Appeals Procedures Unit
AC	Administrative Court
AC	Appeal Cases (Law Reports)
ACD	Asylum Casework Directorate
ACU	Asylum Coordination Unit
ACPI	Advisory Panel on Country Information
ADSU	Asylum Decision Service Unit
AFIS	Automated Fingerprint Identification System
AI	Amnesty International
AIT	Asylum and Immigration Tribunal
AJRU	Appeal and Judicial Review Unit
All ER	All England Law Reports
AN	Application form for naturalisation as a British citizen
AO	Adjudication Officer
APC	Appeals Processing Centre
API	Asylum Policy Instructions
APIS	Advance Passenger Information System
APU	Asylum Policy Unit
APPU	Asylum Processes and Procedures Unit
ARC	Asylum/Application Registration Card
ASA	Asylum Support Adjudicator
ASU	Asylum Screening Unit
BC	British citizen
BCU	Business Cases Unit
BDTC	British Dependent Territories citizen (now BOTC)
BID	Bail for Immigration Detainees
BOC	British Overseas citizen
BOTC	British Overseas Territories citizen
BPP	British Protected Person
BS	British subject
BUS	Application form for leave to remain as business person, sole representative, retired person of independent means, investor or innovator
CA	Court of Appeal
CAC	Complaints Audit Committee (Home Office)
CAC	House of Commons Constitutional Affairs Committee
CAST	Complete Action Service Team (Home Office)
CD	Communications Directorate (Home Office)

CE/CoE	Council of Europe
CEDAW	UN Convention for the Elimination of Discrimination against Women
CEHR	Commission for Equality and Human Rights
CERA	Certificate of Entitlement to the Right of Abode
CERD	UN Convention for the Elimination of All Forms of Racial Discrimination
CFAPT	Children and Fairness Asylum Policy Team (Home Office)
CIO	Chief Immigration Officer
CIPU	Country Information and Policy Unit (Home Office)
CIREA	Centre for Information, Discussion and Exchange on Asylum
CLR	Controlled Legal Representation
CLS	Community Legal Service
CLT	Central Law Training
Cm	House of Commons Command Paper
Cmnd	House of Commons Command Paper
CMOPU	Contact Management Operational Policy Unit (Home Office)
CMT	Case Management Team (Home Office)
CMT+	Case Management Team Plus (Home Office)
COA (Marriage)	Certificate of Authorisation for Marriage, and application form for obtaining it
COROC/CRC	UN Convention on the Rights of the Child
CTA	Common Travel Area
CW4BO	Close Working for Better Outcomes (Home Office)
DCA	Department for Constitutional Affairs
DEPMU	Detention Escorting and Population Management Unit (Home Office)
DIJ	Designated Immigration Judge
DL	Discretionary leave
DO	Deportation Order
DSP	Diplomatic Service Procedures
DSPU	Detention Services Policy Unit (Home Office)
E&E	Evidence and Enquiry
EC	European Community
EC	Entry clearance
ECAA	EC Association Agreement
ECCA Main	Application form for FLR/ILR as a self-employed person under the EC Association Agreement with Bulgaria or Romania
ECHR	European Convention on Human Rights
ECSMA	European Convention on Social and Medical Assistance
ECtHR	European Court of Human Rights
ECIP	Entry clearance Issuing Post

ECO	Entry clearance officer
ECJ	European Court of Justice
EDI	European Directorate Instructions
EEA	European Economic Area
EEC	European Economic Community
EEC1	Application form for residence permit for EEA national
EEC2	Application form for indefinite leave to remain for EEA national or family member
EEC3	Application form for residence stamp for non-EEA family member of accession worker
EFTA	European Free Trade Area
ELR	Exceptional leave to remain; application form for ILR for person granted ELR
EO	Enforcement Officer
EPU	Enforcement Policy Unit (Home Office)
ERCU	Enforcement and Removals Coordination Unit (Home Office)
ERD	Enforcement and Removals Directorate (Home Office)
EU	European Union
Eurodac	European Central Database System for Fingerprinting Asylum seekers and other aliens
EWCA Civ	England and Wales Court of Appeal Civil Division (case citation)
EWHC (Admin)	England and Wales High Court (Administrative Court) (case citation)
EWS	Early Warning system (EC)
FLR	Further leave to remain
FLR(M)	Application form for further leave to remain based on marriage
FLR(O)	Application form for further leave to remain for other purposes
FLR(S)	Application form for further leave to remain as a student
FLR(SEGS)	Application form for further leave to remain under the Science and Engineering Graduate Scheme
FCO	Foreign and Commonwealth Office
FOI	Freedom of Information
FSJ	Freedom, Security and Justice
HC	House of Commons Paper
HMRC	Her Majesty's Revenue & Customs
HOPO	Home Office Presenting Officer
HP	Humanitarian protection
HRW	Human Rights Watch
HSMP	Highly Skilled Migrant Programme, and application form to remain in programme
ICCPR	International Covenant on Civil and Political Rights

ICESCR	International Covenant on Economic, Social and Cultural Rights
IDI	Immigration Directorates' Instructions
IED	Immigration employment document
IFB	Immigration Fingerprint Bureau (Home Office)
IJ	Immigration Judge
ILR	Indefinite leave to remain
IM2	Application form for entry clearance
Imm AR	Immigration Appeal Reports
IND	Immigration and Nationality Department (Home Office)
INDIS	IND Intelligence Section (Home Office)
INLR	Immigration and Nationality Law Reports
INDP	IND Policy Unit (Home Office)
INEB	Immigration and Nationality Enquiry Bureau
IAC	Immigration Appeal Chamber
IO	Immigration Officer
IOM	International Organisation for Migration
IRIS	Iris Recognition Information System
IS	Immigration Service (Home Office)
IS96	Immigration Service Form 96 (temporary admission)
IS151	Immigration Service Form 151 (continued detention)
ISTDU	Immigration Service Training and Development Unit
JCHR	Parliamentary Joint Committee on Human Rights
JECU	Joint Entry Clearance Unit (Home and Foreign Office)
JHA	Justice and Home Affairs (European Council)
JIC	Joint Intelligence Cell
LAB	Legal Advisers' Branch (Home Office)
LEO	Local Enforcement Office (Home Office)
LSC	Legal Services Commission
LTE	Leave to enter
LTR	Leave to remain
MAU	Multiple Applications Unit (Home Office)
MCU	Ministerial Correspondence Unit (Home Office)
MMD	Managed Migration Directorate
MMSR	Managed Migration Strategy and Review (Home Office)
MODCU	Management of Detained Cases Unit (Home Office)
NASS	National Asylum Support Service (Home Office)
NEAT	NASS Eligibility and Assessment Team (Home Office)
NI	Nationality Instructions
NIU	National Intelligence Unit
NSA	Non-suspensive appeal
NTL	Endorsement of 'no time limit' in passport; application form for transfer of stamp to new passport
NWCIS	North West Consortia Induction Service (Home Office)

NWP	North West Project (asylum process) (Home Office)
OASIS	Operational Advisory Service for Immigration Service
OEM	Operational Enforcement Manual
OISC	Office of the Immigration Service Commissioner
PBS	Points Based System
PEO	Public Enquiry Office (Home Office)
PNC	Police National Computer
PNR	Passenger Name Record
POU	Presenting Officers' Unit (Home Office)
QBD	Queens Bench Division (Divisional Court)
RANS	Restricted Access to NASS Support (Home Office)
RCU	Residual Casework Unit (Home Office)
RESCU	Removals Strategy/Resettlement and Coordination Unit (Home Office)
RFRL	Reasons for refusal letter
RLE	Refusal of leave to enter
ROA	Right of abode
RRU	Residual Registry Unit (Home Office)
SAB	Subject Access Bureau
SEF	Statement of Evidence Form
SEGS	Science and Engineering Graduates Scheme
SET(M)	Application form for settlement on the basis of marriage
SET(O)	Application form for settlement in all other cases
SI	Statutory Instrument
SIJ	Senior Immigration Judge
SSHD	Secretary of State for the Home Department
STANA	Superfast Track and Non-suspensive Appeal (Home Office)
TEU	Treaty on the European Union
TFEU	Treaty on the Functioning of the European Union
TOC	Transfer of conditions of leave into new passport; application form for transfer
TP	Temporary Protection
UASC	Unaccompanied asylum seeking child
UDHR	Universal Declaration of Human Rights
UFV	Uniform Format Visa (EC)
UKHL	United Kingdom House of Lords (case citation)
UKRP	United Kingdom Residence Permit
UNCAT	United Nations Convention Against Torture
UNCHR	United Nations Commission for Human Rights
UNHCR	United Nations High Commission(er) for Refugees
VARP	Voluntary Assisted Returns Programme
VWL	Visa Warnings List
WICU	Warnings Index Computerised Unit (reports on overstayers etc) (Home Office)

WLR   Weekly Law Reports
WP   Work permit
WSU   Workflow Support Unit (Home Office)